Dictionary
of the
Hausa Language

R. C. ABRAHAM
M.A., D.LITT.

1956 Exchange Visiting Professor to Atlanta University, Georgia. 1956 U.S. Government Fulbright Award. 1953–1958 Bursary Holder, University College of Ibadan, Nigeria. Late Lecturer in the Languages of Ethiopia, Somali and Hamitic Philology, School of Oriental and African Studies. Formerly Anthropological Officer and Government Linguist, Government of Nigeria

HODDER AND STOUGHTON
LONDON   SYDNEY   AUCKLAND   TORONTO

ISBN 0 340 17657 1

First published 1958
Fourth impression 1978

Printed in Great Britain for
Hodder and Stoughton Educational,
a division of Hodder and Stoughton Ltd, London,
by Biddles Ltd, Guildford, Surrey

Dictionary
of the
Hausa Language

This book is the result of many years research into the Hausa language. In it, Dr Abraham demonstrates very clearly the tonal nature of Hausa, and with the aid of innumerable sentence examples, every shade of meaning is taken into account and illustrated. Idioms, sayings and proverbs are also included, so that anyone using the dictionary will be entirely conversant with all aspects of one of the most widely spoken languages of West Africa.

PREFACE TO THE SECOND EDITION

The older generation of Administrative Officers who served in the Northern Provinces of Nigeria were introduced to Robinson's *Hausa Dictionary* at an early stage of their career and were told that Hausa is spoken over a wide range, including Algeria and Morocco. This was a slight exaggeration, as during residence and travels in various parts of Algeria I have never met anybody who understood Hausa, and it is certainly not current among the Berber-Arab population of the northern seaboard between the Canaries and Asyut.

Nevertheless, it is understood over an extensive area: apart from the millions who speak it as their mother-tongue in Northern Nigeria and Ghana, it is becoming more and more understood every day by the Yoruba, Ibo and other Southern Nigerians. A movement is gaining impetus very rapidly to adopt Hausa as the official tongue for central and regional parliamentary debates in place of English which, as a non-African language, is not welcomed for Government use in a country now independent. The people feel that they should use an indigenous, national speech.

Hausa is spoken as far north as Agades, and Hausa-speakers are met with even at Tamanrasset in the Hoggar. In the east it is well known to the Kanuri of Bornú and in Fort Lamy. Hausa is spoken in the north-west of Nigeria and beyond: in fact, many speak it in Timbuktu. While *en route* to Eritrea via the Sudan, I was amazed to see a young girl selling bean-cakes and calling out 'Waina! Waina!' She told me that she was of Kano origin and that there were many hundreds of Hausas living in Wadi Medani like herself. These people of Wadi Medani and many other towns of the Sudan were Hausa pilgrims to Mecca who ran short of money on their return journey and were unable to make their way back to their home-towns in Nigeria. They have retained Hausa and taught it to their children born in the Sudan. At Marseilles I met a contingent of French Colonial Troops travelling from Timbuktu to the Officers' Training School at Fréjus, these being Tou-couleurs, many of whom spoke quite adequate Hausa.

Enough has been said to show how easily speakers of other languages learn to converse in Hausa. Does this mean that Hausa is an easy language? Yes and no. To learn sufficient to carry on a conversation is obviously very simple as seen from the fact that so many non-Hausas can easily do so by picking it up without the help of explanatory grammars. But Hausa is a language in which correct speech is dependent on tone and stress, the interplay of which constitute the essential rhythm. Once this rhythm is neglected, the language bears little resemblance to the speech of those Hausa-born, whether of high or low degree, for the labourer speaks as accurately and rhythmically as the high official. The unrhythmic Hausa spoken by the foreigner, whether an African or a European, deeply offends the Hausa who hears it, and this certainly does not help in fostering brotherly relations. The non-Hausa must therefore study the tones and the formal grammar if he wishes to be respected by the Hausa people who take such pride in their language that they call it 'The Language' (Hausā derived from Arabic al-lisān, Hebrew hallāshōn).

What is the reason that the tones of Hausa were for so many years unsuspected, when the tones distinguishing one tense from another are so vital? It is because in Europe we have sentence-tone, whereas African languages have an inherent tone for every word said in isolation, such tone being obligatory without alternative tone being allowed except in a trifling number of instances. In various contexts, depending on the surrounding words, these inherent tones are changed in accordance with the principles I have discovered. Examples of English sentence-tone are (a) 'If I'd known you were there, I shouldn't have gone' (where I did not go, the sentence meaning 'even if . . .') and (b) the same sentence with different intonation meaning that I did go, but I should not have gone had I known you to be there. In (a), 'known' has a much higher tone than in (b).

English intonation is dealt with in Chapter XV, p. 247, of Dr. Ida Ward's Phonetics of English (1944); also in Chapter XIV of Professor Daniel Jones's The Pronunciation of English (1950). French intonation is briefly treated in Chapter XVII of The Phonetics of French (1932) by Dr. Lilias Armstrong. This subject has also been elaborated by Miss H. Coustenoble.

Our being habituated to this sentence-tone blunts our hearing of isolated words in African languages so that we are unaware of their existence and consider every sentence merely as a composite whole, having, like English, a sentence-tone. I myself contested the existence of tones in Hausa for this very reason, but when I pronounced baba, not knowing as I did later that it has six tones varying with the meaning, I was reproved by a meeting of ten Hausas who said that my versions of this

iv

word were unintelligible. That I did not hear the distinction of tone from tone was more than remarkable, as I had come to Nigeria from Burma with its tonic language. Years after this I was asked by the Lieutenant-Governor of the Northern Provinces: 'Surely you don't *really* believe Hausa has tones?'

In the first edition of my dictionary, published in 1949, I was thus able to throw much new light on the nature of Hausa. After the dictionary had been in use for several years, Professor Lukas, Director of the African Institute at Hamburg University, wrote an article in the journal *West Africa* (November 1959). He said: 'Those who think Hausa a simple language are now few: and if there was any justification for this view, it is only that other Nigerian languages are even more difficult and certainly less well adapted for students interested in acquiring an African vernacular. Among Dr. R. C. Abraham's numerous publications, the most important is undoubtedly his Hausa-English Dictionary . . . which shows the language to be an almost unparalleled medium of African thought. It was there that he showed his unique skill in analysing an African language. His publications are, from a practical and scientific angle, of the greatest importance and should be in the hands of all concerned with West Africa who want to have a deeper insight into African peoples and their minds.'

The student is referred to an article by Mr. F. W. Parsons 'An Introduction to Gender in Hausa' (*African Language Studies* I, 1960) and a valuable study of 'The Verbal System in Hausa' (*Afrika und Uebersee* Band XLIV).

For further information on the phonetics of Hausa, the student should read three articles by J. Carnochan: 1. The article discussed on page 135 (Section 217b) of my *Hausa Sound System*; 2. 'A Study of Quantity in Hausa' (*BSOAS* XIII, 4, 1951, 1032); 3. 'Glottalization In Hausa' (*Transactions of the Philological Society*, 1952). These are contributions of the highest value and often correct backslidings on my part. They should be read by all who are interested in Hausa.

'Some Problems in Hausa Phonology', a brief but interesting article by Professor J. Greenberg, appeared in the journal *Language* No. 17–4, 1941. Dr. Carleton T. Hodge published a five-page article entitled 'Morpheme Alternants and the Noun Phrase in Hausa' in *Language* No. 21–2, 1945, and a sixty-page dissertation 'An Outline of Hausa Grammar' forming a Supplement to Volume 23–4 in 1957.

Where in the original Preface (see below) I refer to my *Introduction to Spoken Hausa* and to *Modern Grammar of Spoken Hausa*, the names of these books should be changed to *The*

Language of the Hausa People*Part I and Part II respectively, as the two books *Introduction* and *Modern Grammar* sold out rapidly and have now been replaced in one volume by *The Language of the Hausa People*, published by University of London Press Ltd in 1959. This grammar should be in the hands of every user of this *Hausa Dictionary*, as should its sister volume, *Hausa Literature and the Hausa Sound System*,*also published in 1959 by University of London Press Ltd.

1961   R. C. ABRAHAM

*These books are now out of print.

vi

PLAN OF THE DICTIONARY

1. Uncommon words or usages are marked with a star (e.g. *mufuradī) and should not be used by Europeans, as either they are of limited usage or employed only by persons who know Arabic, etc. Any words marked *Sk.* (i.e. Sokoto), *Zar.* (i.e. Zaria), *Kt.* (i.e. Katsina), etc., should be used only with caution and knowledge of the person whom one is addressing.

2. The conjugation of the verbs is indicated thus, e.g.

girmamā *Vb.* 1C

means that this verb is conjugated according to Type 1C shown in the Verb Table at the head of the dictionary.

N.B.—If from the English sense shown, one is doubtful whether a verb is transitive or intransitive, the reference-number given will clear up such doubt, for verbs of Type 3 are intransitive and all other Types are transitive.

3. Some acquaintance with my *Introduction to Spoken Hausa* and *Modern Grammar* is assumed, hence the following forms which are regularly formed from every verb, are omitted unless some deviation in sense or construction renders their insertion necessary :—

(*a*) Forms in -ē or -i from Changing Verbs. But if the final consonant also changes, such changed forms are shown both under the root-form and separately alphabetically, so that under **fansā**, we find **fanshē** and **fanshi**, and we also find **fanshē** and **fanshi** listed alphabetically and referred back to **fansā**.

(*b*) Passive forms in -u (Gram. 113).

(*c*) Forms in -ō denoting " motion towards speaker " (Gram. 129).

(*d*) Past participle passive (Gram. 79*e*).

(*e*) -e forms denoting result (Gram. 80*d*).

(*f*) Intensive verbs (Gram. 179).

(*g*) Forms of repeated action (Mod. Gram. (*c*) on page 141), e.g. **gi'ne-ginē"**.

4. Where a number preceded by " Gram." or " Gr." is quoted (as e.g. in Paragraph 3 above), this refers to the relevant Section in both of my grammars, but where the matter in question is only to be found in my *Modern Grammar of Spoken Hausa*, then the reference-number is preceded by an abbreviation, i.e. Mod. Gram. 9 or M.G. 8.

5. (*a*) Where the sign = appears between two Hausa words and no English translation follows (e.g. **mikitsīyā** = **makitsīyā**), then explanation must be sought under the second word.

(*b*) Where the sign = appears after an English meaning, this is merely for information, and no further action is necessarily called for e.g. (= **tsumbē** 2, at the end of **alhūtsa**). But if the abbreviation *q.v.* is added, then the second word must be looked up (e.g. **ganzāki** morning-star = **gamzāki**, *q.v.*).

(*c*) Where a Hausa word appears in brackets inside the English translation, this indicates the Hausa equivalent for the word standing immediately before and does not mean, even if such Hausa word is the last word in the translation, that it is a synonym for the whole of the translation—to indicate the latter, the sign = should appear as in 5(*b*) above. Thus, in **alhūtsa**, we find " having two compartments (**gidā**) (*it is used for charms* (**lāya**), *galena*

vii

(tōzại̦ī), etc.) = tsụmbē ". This indicates that the equivalent of this kind of " compartment " is ̣gidā, that " galena " is tōzại̦ī, and that the whole word ại̦hūtsạ is synonymous with the word tsụmbē.

6. When *x* (meaning " for example ") stands in an entry, this as a general rule means that the example given is illustrative of the sort of use to which the word is put, and that other examples can be formed on the same plan. But where I employ the words " used in ", these indicate that this is a set expression, allowing of no variation, or at least none known to me.

7. Phrases in inverted commas indicate that the English meaning is metaphorical, colloquial, or slangy, e.g. " he bit off more than he could chew ".

8. Sometimes a word appears in brackets in the Hausa text and has its counterpart in the English text, e.g. " yā (tā) ị̣sa mụtụm he (she) has become adult " means " yā ị̣sa mụtụm he has become adult. tā ị̣sa mụtụm she has become adult ".

9. *Long* vowel has line *above* it, e.g. mātā, so any vowel unmarked, is short, e.g. matạ.

10. ŋ indicates ng as in English " sing ". ằ indicates vowel heard in English " cut ", e.g. rằi.

11. Tones are marked as in my grammars, i.e. (1) *high* tone is unmạrked, e.g. kai. (2) *low* tone is marked by a line *below* the vowel to which it applies, e.g. shị. (3) *falling* tone has arrow *below*, e.g. kại. (4) interrogative tones are marked ∧ and ⊥? as explained in Section 163 of the grammars, e.g. yā bā kạ dộkị?

12. Unlike in my grammars, stress is marked *after* the stressed syllable, e.g. gị'ne-gịne" (first and fourth syllables stressed).

13. (*a*) Homophones (i.e. words of the same sound except for differences of tone and vowel-length) are separated from one another thus :—

gindi A. (gịndī) . . .

B. (gindī) . . .

(*b*) In some cases (especially where there is much matter to be entered), even words quite identical in sound are sub-divided when their senses differ, e.g.

sa A.1 (sạ̄) put . . .

A.2 (sạ̄) ox . . .

B. (sạ) his . . .

(*c*) Sometimes the *same* word is sub-divided. Thus where we find for example " *Vd.* ganī A2.5 " this refers to the fact that ganī is divided into A1 which is in column 2 of page 298, and A2 which is in column 2 of page 299, so that " ganī A2.5 is a subdivision to be found on page 300. This classification is indicated by the fact that the number following A, B, etc., is in thin type, while the final number (which indicates the sub-paragraph of A1, etc.) is in thick type.

14. No distinction has been made between the two types of " r " (" Modern Grammar " 5) except in the rare cases where this distinction affects the meaning, e.g. barạ.

15. The sign ∼ indicates that the word at the head of the paragraph is to be repeated, e.g. in the paragraph dạ̄rīyā, " (1) yā shā ∼ " means " (1) yā shā dạ̄rīyā ". When an English word is written, e.g " coat(s) ", this means that the corresponding Hausa word has both singular and plural senses.

16. Abbreviations.

A.	indicates	" anything ".
adv.	,,	" adverb ".
Ar.	,,	" derived from Arabic ".
Asb.	,,	" Asbin Tuareg word ".
conj.	,,	" conjunction ".
d.f.	,,	" derived from ".
Eng.	,,	" English word ".
f.	,,	" feminine ".
Fil.	,,	" Filani word ".
Had.	,,	" Hadejiya Hausa ".
imp.	,,	" imperative ".
intens. or *int.*	,,	" intensive form of verb ".
Kr.	,,	" Kanuri word ".
Kt.	,,	" Katsina Hausa ".
lit.	,,	" literally ".
m.	,,	" masculine ".
n.o.	,,	" the verb takes the following form before noun object ".
Nor.	,,	" Northern Hausa, " i.e. Damagaram, Gobir, etc.
Nu.	,,	" Nupe word ".
P.	,,	" person ".
pl.	,,	" plural ".
p.o.	,,	" the verb takes the following form before objective pronoun ".
S.	,,	" something ".
Sec. v.n.	,,	" secondary verbal noun ".
sg.	,,	" singular ".
Sk.	,,	" Sokoto Hausa ".
T.	,,	" thing ".
Vb.	,,	" verb ".
Vd.	,,	" vide ".
v.n.	,,	" verbal noun ".
x	,,	" e.g.," " for example ".
Yor.	,,	" Yoruba word ".
Zar.	,,	" Zaria Hausa ".

VERB TABLE REFERRED TO BY INDEX NUMBERS
IN THE DICTIONARY

Note 1.—All verbs are shown in 3rd singular ' he ', but the other subject-pronouns are given for each tense.

Note 2.—Where the verb has the same form before both a noun object and a pronoun object, this is indicated by, e.g. **yā kāmạ shi/dōkị**, meaning that before a pronoun object like **shi** we say **yā kāmạ shi**, and before a noun object, we also use the form **kāmạ** and say **yā kāmạ dōkị**.

Note 3.—The verbs are arranged as follows :—

1. Unchanging Verbs (first syllable high tone).

    A. 2-syllable verbs, e.g. **kāmạ, kātsẹ, sạ.**
    B. 1-syllable in diphthong, e.g. **kai, hau.**
    C. 3-syllable verbs, e.g. **daŋƙạrā, daddạɓē, ɗaụkā, ɗaụkē.**
    D. 4-syllable verbs, e.g. **ragargazā, dabaibạyē.**
    E. Verbs of ' motion towards ' in -o, e.g. **kāwō, kakkāwō, dabaibayō.**

2. Changing Verbs (first syllable low).

    2-syllables, e.g. **hạrbā ;** 3-syllables, **tạmbayạ ;** 4-syllables, **tạntạmbayạ.** Also the slightly irregular **ɗaukạ** and **ɗība.**

3. Intransitive Verbs.

    (*a*) Those having same tones as *unchanging verbs* and modelled on them, e.g. **wucẹ, gilmạ, fandạrē, zurạrā, kwạntā, ɗaụkē, kakkantạrā, dābilbịlē, shigō, gaŋgarō, kakkantarō.**

    (*b*) Those having the same tones as *changing verbs* and modelled on them, e.g. **fịta, dạnnu, tsūfā, hạƙurạ, fạskạru, bịbbịrkiɗạ.**

4. Causal Verbs.

    E.g. **tarar dạ** *or* **tad dạ ;** **fitar dạ** *or* **fid dạ ;** **zubar dạ** *or* **zub dạ ;** **ɓatar dạ** *or* **ɓad dạ,** *etc.*

5. Mixed Verbs, e.g. **shā, jī, sō, bīyā.**

1. UNCHANGING VERBS

(First syllable high tone)

A. Two-syllable verbs, e.g. kāmạ̄ ' seized ', kātsẹ ' scraped out ', sā̧ ' put ' (cf. 28*).

	With Object Understood	With Object Expressẹd
Past . . .	yā kāmạ. yā kātsẹ. yā sā̧.	yā kāmạ shi/dōkị. yā kātsẹ shi/battạ. yā sā̧ shi/rānā.
	The other subject-pronouns are nā, kā, kin, tā, mun, kun, sun, an (12). The Relative forms (133*) are na, ka, kikạ, ya (*or* yi *or* i), ta, mukạ, kukạ, sukạ, akạ.	
Future . . .	zaị kāmạ *or* yā̧ kāmạ. zaị kātsẹ *or* yā̧ kātsẹ. zaị sā̧ *or* yā̧ sā̧.	zaị kāmạ shi/dōkị. yā̧ kāmạ shi/dōkị. zaị kātsẹ shi/battạ. yā̧ kātsẹ shi/battạ. zaị sā̧ shi/rānā. yā̧ sā̧ shi/rānā.
	The other subject-pronouns are (14) zan, zā kạ, zā kị, zā tạ, zā mụ, zā kụ, zā sụ, zā ạ ; and (118) nā̧, kā̧, kyā̧, tā̧, mā̧, kwā̧, sā̧, ā̧.	
Habitual . .	ya kạŋ kāmạ. ya kạŋ kātsẹ. ya kạn sā̧.	ya kạŋ kāmạ shi/dōkị. ya kạŋ kātsẹ shi/battạ. ya kạn sā̧ shi/rānā.
	The other subject-pronouns are na kạn, ka kạn, ki kạn, ta kạn, mu kạn, ku kạn, su kạn, a kạn.	
Subjunctive . .	yạ kāmạ. yạ kātsẹ. yạ sā̧.	yạ kāmạ shi/dōkị. yạ kātsẹ shi/battạ. yạ sā̧ shi/rānā.
	The other subject-pronouns are ṇ, kạ, kị, tạ, mụ, kụ, sụ, ạ.	
Imperative Negative and Subjunctive Negative.	This is kadạ *or* kạr prefixed to *subjunctive*, e.g. kadạ yạ kāmạ ; kadạ kạ sā̧ rānā.	

	With Object Understood	With Object Expressed
Imperative with Subject before it.	kạ kāmạ (*masc.*). kị kātsẹ (*fem.*). kụ sạ̄ (*plural*).	kạ kāmạ shi/dōkị. kị kātsẹ shi/battạ. kụ sạ̄ shi/rānā.
Imperative without Subject before it.	kạ̄ma. kạ̄tse. sā.	kạ̄mā shi ; kạ̄mạ dōkị. {kạ̄tsē shi [1] {kạ̄tse battạ.[1] {kạ̄tsẹ shi [1] {kạ̄tsẹ battạ.[1] sạ̄ shi ; sā rānā.
Verbal Noun . .		kāmạ shi/dōkị. kātsẹ shi/battạ. sạ̄ shi/rānā.
Progressive . .	yanạ̄ kāmạ̄wā. yanạ̄ kātsẹ̄wā. yanạ̄ sạ̄wā.	yanạ̄ kāmạ shi/dōkị. yanạ̄ kātsẹ shi/battạ. yanạ̄ sạ̄ shi/rānā.
	The other subject-pronouns are (16) n nạ̄, kanạ̄, kinạ̄, tanạ̄, munạ̄, kunạ̄, sunạ̄, anạ̄. The Relative forms (133*) are nikẹ̄ (*or* nakẹ̄), kakẹ̄, kikẹ̄, yakẹ̄ (*or* yikẹ̄ *or* ikẹ̄), takẹ̄, mukẹ̄, kukẹ̄, sukẹ̄, akẹ̄.	

B. One-syllable verbs ending in diphthong, e.g. **kai** ' brought ', **hau** ' mounted '.

	With Object Understood	With Object Expressed
Past . . .	yā kai. yā hau.	yā kai shị/dōkị. yā hau shị/dōkị.
	The other subject-pronouns are nā, kā, kin, tā, mun, kun, sun, an (12). The Relative forms (133*) are na, ka, kikạ, ya (*or* yi *or* i), ta, mukạ, kukạ, sukạ, akạ.	
Future . . .	zại kai *or* yạ̄ kai. zại hau *or* yạ̄ hau.	zại kai shị/dōkị. yạ̄ kai shị/dōkị. zại hau shị/dōkị. yạ̄ hau shị/dōkị.

[1] Two-syllable verbs in -e allow these alternatives.

	With Object Understood	With Object Expressed
	The other subject-pronouns are (14) zạn, zā kạ, zā kị, zā tạ, zā mụ, zā kụ, zā sụ, zā ạ ; and (118) nạ̄, kạ̄, kyạ̄, tạ̄, mạ̄, kwạ̄, sạ̄, ạ̄.	
Habitual . .	Substitute ya kạn for zại of *future !*	
	The other subject-pronouns are na kạn, ka kạn, ki kạn, ta kạn, mu kạn, ku kạn, su kạn, a kạn.	
Subjunctive . .	Substitute yạ for zại of *future !*	
	The other subject-pronouns are ṇ, kạ, kị, tạ, mụ, kụ, sụ, ạ.	
Imperative Negative and Subjunctive Negative.	This is kadạ or kạr prefixed to *subjunctive*, e.g. kadạ yạ kai ; kadạ kạ hau shị.	
Imperative with Subject before it.	Substitute kạ (*masc.*), kị (*fem.*), kụ (*plural*) for zại of *future !*	
Imperative without Subject before it.	kai. hau.	kại shi ; kai dōkị. hạu shi ; hau dōkị.
Verbal Noun . .		kai shị/dōkị. hawansạ. hawan dōkị *or* hawā dōkị.
Progressive . .	yanạ̄ kạiwā. yanạ̄ hawā.	yanạ̄ kai shị/dōkị. yanạ̄ hawansạ. yanạ̄ hawan dōkị *or* yanạ̄ hawā dōkị.
	The other subject-pronouns are (16) n nạ̄, kanạ̄, kinạ̄, tanạ̄, munạ̄, kunạ̄, sunạ̄, anạ̄. The Relative forms (133*) are nikẹ̄ (*or* nakẹ̄), kakẹ̄, kikẹ̄, yakẹ̄ (*or* yikẹ̄ *or* ikẹ̄), takẹ̄, mukẹ̄, kukẹ̄, sukẹ̄, akẹ̄.	

C. Three-syllable verbs daŋƙạrā ' compressed ', daddạɓē ' kept on beating an earth-floor ', ɗaukā ' postponed ', ɗaukē ' removed all of '. *N.B.*—Where daddạɓē is not shown below, it is because it has the same forms as daŋƙạrā but with final -e ; similarly, where ɗaukē is not shown below, it is because it has the same forms as ɗaukā but with final -e.

	With Object Understood	With Object Expressed
Past . . .	yā daŋḵg̣rā.	yā daŋḵg̣rā shi. yā daŋḵg̣ṛa tāḇa.
	yā ḍaụkā.	yā ḍaụkā shi. yā ḍaụkạ rānā.
	yā ḍaụkē.	yā ḍaụkē su. ⎰yā ḍaụkē kāyā. ⎱yā ḍaụkẹ kāyā.
	The other subject-pronouns are **nā, kā, kin, tā, mun, kun, sun, an** (12). The Relative forms (133*) are **na, ka, kikạ, ya** (*or* **yi** *or* **i**), **ta, mukạ, kukạ, sukạ, akạ.**	
Future . . .	Substitute **zại** (14) *or* **yā̱** (118) for **yā** of *past!*	
	The other subject-pronouns are (14) **zạn, zā kạ, zā kị, zā tạ, zā mụ, zā kụ, zā sụ, zā ạ ;** ˙ and (118) **nā̱, kā̱, kyā̱, tā̱, mā̱, kwā̱, sā̱, ā̱.**	
Habitual . .	Substitute **ya kạn** for **yā** of *past!*	
	The other subject-pronouns are **na kạn, ka kạn, ki kạn, ta kạn, mu kạn, ku kạn, su kạn, a kạn.**	
Subjunctive . .	Substitute **yạ** for **yā** of *past!*	
	The other subject-pronouns are **ṇ, kạ, kị, tạ, mụ, kụ, sụ, ạ.**	
Imperative negative and Subjunctive Negative.	This is **kadạ** *or* **kạr** preffixed to *subjunctive*, e.g. **kadạ kạ daŋḵg̣rā ; kạr kạ ḍaụkạ rānā.**	
Imperative with Subject before it.	Substitute **kạ** (*masc.*), **kị** (*fem.*), **kụ** (*plural*) for **yā** of *past!*	
Imperative without Subject before it.	daŋḵg̣rā. dạddạ6ē.	daŋḵg̣rā shi. daŋḵg̣ṛa tāḇa. dạddạ6ē shi. ⎰dạddạ6ẹ ḍākị. ⎱dạddạ6e ḍākị.

	With Object Understood	With Object Expressed
	d̯aukā.	d̯aukā shi. d̯auk̯a rānā.
	d̯aukē.	d̯aukē su. ⎰d̯auk̯e kāyā. ⎱d̯auke kāyā.
Verbal Noun . .		daŋk̯arā shi. daŋk̯ar̯a tāb̯a. d̯aukā shi. d̯auk̯a rānā. d̯aukē shi. ⎰d̯auk̯e kāyā. ⎱d̯auke kāyā.
Progressive . .	yaŋā daŋk̯ar̯āwā.	Prefix **yaŋā** to *verbal noun !*
	yaŋā d̯auk̯āwā.	Prefix **yaŋā** to *verbal noun !*
	The other subject-pronouns are (16) n nā, kanā, kinā, tanā, munā, kunā, sunā, anā. The Relative forms (133*) are nikē (*or* nakē), kakē, kikē, yakē (*or* yikē *or* ikē), takē, mukē, kukē, sukē, akē.	

D. Four-syllable verbs, e.g. **ragargazā** ' shattered ', **dabaibayē** ' hobbled a horse by the forefeet '. *N.B.*—Where **dabaibayē** is not shown below, it is because it has the same forms as **ragargazā** but with final -e.

	With Object Understood	With Object Expressed
Past . . .	yā ragargazā.	yā ragargazā shi. yā ragargaz̯a tukunyā.
	The other subject-pronouns are nā, kā, kin, tā, mun, kun, sun, an (12). The Relative forms (133*) are na, ka, kik̯a, ya (*or* yi *or* i), ta, muk̯a, kuk̯a, suk̯a, ak̯a.	
Future . . .	Substitute z̯ai (14) *or* yā̯ (118) for yā of *past !*	

	With Object Understood	With Object Expressed
	The other subject-pronouns are (14) zą̄n, zā ką̄, zā ki̱, zā tą̄, zā mu̱, zā ku̱, zā su̱, zā ą̱ ; and (118) ną̄, ką̄, kyą̄, tą̄, mą̄, kwą̄, są̄, ą̄.	
Habitual . .	Substitute **ya ką̄n** for **yā** of *past !*	
	The other subject-pronouns are **na ką̄n, ka ką̄n, ki̱ ką̄n, ta ką̄n, mu ką̄n, ku ką̄n, su ką̄n, a ką̄n.**	
Subjunctive . .	Substitute **ya̱** for **yā** of *past !*	
	The other subject-pronouns are **n̠, ka̱, ki̱, ta̱, mu̱, ku̱, su̱, a̱.**	
Imperative Negative and Subjunctive Negative.	This is **kadą̱** or **ka̱r** prefixed to *subjunctive*, e.g. **kadą̱ ka̱ ragargą̱zā.**	
Imperative with Subject before it.	Substitute **ka̱** (*masc.*), **ki̱** (*fem.*), **ku̱** (*plural*) for **yā** of *past !*	
Imperative without Subject before it.	rą̱gą̱rgą̱zā.	rą̱gą̱rgą̱zā shi. rą̱gą̱rgą̱za̱ tukunyā.
	dą̱bą̱ibą̱yē.	dą̱bą̱ibą̱yē shi. ⎰dą̱bą̱ibą̱ye̱ dōki̱. ⎱dą̱bą̱ibą̱ye dōki̱.
Verbal Noun . .		ragargą̱zā shi. ragargą̱za̱ tukunyā.
Progressive . .	**yaną̱ ragargą̱zą̄wā.**	Prefix **yaną̱** to *verbal noun.*
	The other subject-pronouns are (16) n **ną̄, kaną̄, kiną̄, taną̄, muną̄, kuną̄, suną̄, aną̄.** The Relative forms (133*) are **nikē̱ (or nakē̱), kakē̱, kikē̱, yakē̱ (or yikē̱ or ikē̱), takē̱, mukē̱, kukē̱, sukē̱, akē̱.**	

E. Verbs of ' motion towards ' ending in **-o** (129), e.g. **kāwō** ' brought ', **kakkāwō** ' kept on bringing ', **dabaibayō** ' hobbled the horse and came '.

	With Object Understood	With Object Expressed
Past . . .	yǎ kāwō. yǎ kakkāwō. yǎ dabaibayō.	yǎ kāwō shị/kāyǎ. yǎ kakkāwō shị/kāyǎ. yǎ dabaibayō shị/dōkị.
	The other subject-pronouns are nǎ, kǎ, kin, tǎ, mun, kun, sun, an (12). The Relative forms (133*) are na, ka, kikạ, ya (*or* yi *or* i), ta, mukạ, kukạ, sukạ, akạ.	
Future . . .	Substitute zạị (14) *or* yạ̌ (118) for yǎ of *past!*	
	The other subject-pronouns are (14) zạn, zā kạ, zā kị, zā tạ, zā mụ, zā kụ, zā sụ, zā ạ ; and (118) nạ̌, kạ̌, kyạ̌, tạ̌, mạ̌, kwạ̌, sạ̌, ạ̌.	
Habitual . .	Substitute ya kạn for yǎ of *past!*	
	The other subject-pronouns are na kạn, ka kạn, ki kạn, ta kạn, mu kạn, ku kạn, su kạn, a kạn.	
Subjunctive . .	Substitute yạ for yǎ of *past!*	
	The other subject-pronouns are ṇ, kạ, kị, tạ, mụ, kụ, sụ, ạ.	
Imperative Negative and Subjunctive Negative.	This is kadạ *or* kạr prefixed to *subjunctive*, e.g. kadạ kạ kāwō.	
Imperative with Subject before it.	Substitute kạ (*masc.*), kị (*fem.*), kụ (*plural*) for yǎ of *past!*	
Imperative without Subject before it.	kạ̌wō. kạkkạ̌wō. dạbạibạyō.	kạ̌wō shị/kāyǎ. kạkkạ̌wō shị/kāyǎ. dạbạibạyō shị/dōkị.
Verbal Noun . .		kāwō shị/kāyǎ. kakkāwō shị/kāyǎ. dabaibayō shị/dōkị.
Progressive . .	yanạ̌ kāwǫwā. yanạ̌ kakkāwǫwā. yanạ̌ dabaibayǫwā.	yanạ̌ kāwō shị/kāyǎ. yanạ̌ kakkāwō shị/kāyǎ. yanạ̌ dabaibayō shị/dōkị.

2. CHANGING VERBS
(First syllable low tone)

Two-syllable verbs, e.g. **harbā** 'shot person'; three-syllable verbs, e.g.
tambaya 'asked'; four-syllable verbs, e.g. **tantambaya** 'kept on asking'.
Also the slightly irregular verbs **dauka** 'lifted, carried'; **dība** 'drew water'.

	With Object Understood	With Object Expressed
Past . . .	yā harbā.	yā harbē shi. yā harbi Daudā.
	yā tambaya.	yā tambayē shi. yā tambayi Daudā.
	yā tantambaya.	yā tantambayē shi. yā tantambayi Daudā.
	yā dauka.	yā daukē shi. yā dauki kāyā.
	yā dība.	yā dēbē shi. yā dēbi rūwā.
	The other subject-pronouns are **nā, kā, kin, tā, mun, kun, sun, an** (12). The Relative forms (133*) are **na, ka, kikā, ya** (*or* **yi** *or* **i**), **ta, mukā, kukā, sukā, akā.**	
Future . . .	Substitute **zai** (14) *or* **yā** (118) for **yā** of *past !*	
	The other subject-pronouns are (14) **zan, zā ka, zā ki, zā ta, zā mu, zā ku, zā su, zā a** ; and (118) **nā, kā, kyā, tā, mā, kwā, sā, ā.**	
Habitual . .	Substitute **ya kan** for **yā** of *past !*	
	The other subject-pronouns are **na kan, ka kan, ki kan, ta kan, mu kan, ku kan, su kan, a kan.**	
Subjunctive . .	Substitute **ya** for **yā** of *past !*	
	The other subject-pronouns are **n, ka, ki, ta, mu, ku, su, a.**	
Imperative Negative and Subjunctive Negative.	This is **kada** *or* **kar** prefixed to *subjunctive*, e.g. **kada ka tambaya ; kar ka harbē shi.**	

	With Object Understood	With Object Expressed
Imperative with Subject before it.	Substitute **kạ** (*masc.*), **kị** (*fem.*), **kụ** (*plural*) for **yā** of *past !*	
Imperative without Subject before it.	hạrbi.	hạrbẹ (*or* hạrbạ) shi. hạrbi Daudạ.
	tạmbạyi.	tạmbạyẹ (*or* tạmbạyạ) shi. tạmbạyi Daudạ.
	dạukā.	dạukẹ (*or* dạukạ) shi. dạuki kāyā.
	dẹ̄bi.	dẹ̄bẹ (*or* dẹ̄bạ) shi. dẹ̄bi rūwā.
	tạntạmbạyi.	tạntạmbạyẹ (*or* tạntạm- bạyạ) shi. tạntạmbạyi Daudạ.
Verbal Noun . .		hạrbarsạ *or* hạrbassạ *or* hạrbā tasạ. hạrbar Daudạ. tạmbạyạrsạ, *etc.*/Daudạ. tạntạmbạyạrsạ, *etc.*/ Daudạ. dạukạn (*or* dạukạr) sạ. dạukạn (*or* dạukạr) kāyā. dībạnsạ : dībạn rūwā.
Progressive . .	yanạ̄ hạrbā. yanạ̄ dạukạ. yanạ̄ dība.	Prefix **yanạ̄** to *verbal noun !*
	The other subject-pronouns are (16) n nạ̄, kanạ̄, kinạ̄, tanạ̄, munạ̄, kunạ̄, sunạ̄, anạ̄. The Relative forms (133*) are nikẹ̄ (*or* nakẹ̄), kakẹ̄, kikẹ̄, yakẹ̄ (*or* yikẹ̄ *or* ikẹ̄), takẹ̄, mukẹ̄, kukẹ̄, sukẹ̄, akẹ̄.	

3. INTRANSITIVE VERBS

Allowing for the fact that intransitives are not used before an object, the remaining parts are modelled on transitive verbs having the same tones.

A. Examples of treatment of intransitive verbs modelled on Unchanging Verbs : two-syllable verbs, e.g. **wucę** ' passed by ', **gilmạ** ' passed by '. Three-syllable verbs, e.g. **fandạrē** ' deviated ', **zurạ̄rā** ' thing fell into well ', **kwạntā** ' lay down ', **dʼaukē** ' rain ceased '. Four-syllable verbs, **kakkantạrā** ' keep on swerving towards ', **dābilbịlē** ' place is in wet, trampled state '. Verbs of ' motion towards ' in -o (129) ; two-syllables, e.g. **shigō** ' entered here ' ; three-syllables, e.g. **gaŋgarō** ' rolled this way ' ; four-syllables, e.g. **kakkantarō** ' kept swerving in this direction '.

Past . . .	yā wucę. yā gilmạ.	yā kakkantạrā. yā dābilbịlē.
	yā fandạrē. yā zurạ̄rā. yā kwạntā. yā dʼaukē.	yā shigō. yā gaŋgarō. yā kakkantarō.
	For the other subject-pronouns, *vide past* of 2 above.	
Future . . .	Substitute **zaị** (14) *or* **yạ̄** (118) for **yā** of *past!* For the other subject-pronouns, *vide future* of 2 above.	
Habitual . .	Substitute **ya kạn** for **yā** of *past!* For the other subject-pronouns, *vide habitual* of 2 above.	
Subjunctive . .	Substitute **yạ** for **yā** of *past!* For the other subject-pronouns, *vide subjunctive* of 2 above.	
Imperative Negative and Subjunctive Negative.	This is **kadạ** *or* **kạr** prefixed to *subjunctive*, e.g. **kadạ kạ wucę ; kạr kị shigō.**	
Imperative with Subject before it.	Substitute **kạ** (*masc.*), **kị** (*fem.*), **kụ** (*plural*) for **yā** of *past!*	
Imperative without Subject before it.	wụcē. gịlmā. fandạrē. zụrạ̄rā. kwạntā.	kạkkạntạrā. shịgō. gạŋgạrō. kạkkạntạrō.

Verbal Noun Referring to Subject.	wucēwarsạ. gilmāwarsạ. fandạrēwā tasạ. zurārāwā tasạ. kwạntāwā tasạ. ḍaụkēwā tasạ.	kakkantạrāwā tasạ.[1] dābilbịlēwā tasạ.[1] shigǭwarsạ. gaŋgarǭwarsạ.[1] kakkantarǭwarsạ.[1]
Progressive . .	yanā wucēwā. yanā gilmāwā. yanā fandạrēwā. yanā zurārāwā. yanā kwạntāwā. yanā ḍaụkēwā. For the other subject-pronouns, *vide progressive* of 2 above.	yanā kakkantạrāwā. yanā dābilbịlēwā. yanā shigǭwā. yanā gaŋgarǭwā. yanā kakkantarǭwā.

B. Examples of intransitive verbs modelled on Changing Verbs : the fịta type (112 (c)) and tsūfā type (112 (b)) show certain differences from Changing Verbs.

Two syllables fịta ' went out ' (low, high ; *vide* note above) ; dạnnu ' was well pressed down ' (-u verbs 113) ; tsūfā ' became old ' (high, high (112 (b)). Three-syllable verbs, e.g. hạƙurạ ' was patient ' ; fạskạru ' wood was well chopped ' (-u verb 113). Four-syllables, e.g. bịbbịrkiḍạ ' horse, *etc.*, kept rolling on the ground '.

Past . . .	yā fịta. yā dạnnu. yā hạƙurạ. yā tsūfā. yā fạskạru. yā bịbbịrkiḍạ. For the other subject-pronouns, *vide past* of 2 above.
Future . . .	Substitute zại (14) *or* yā̰ (118) for yā or *past !* For the other subject-pronouns, *vide future* of 2 above.
Habitual . .	Substitute ya kạn for yā of *past !* For the other subject-pronouns, *vide habitual* of 2 above.
Subjunctive . .	Substitute yạ for yā of *past !* For the other subject-pronouns, *vide subjunctive* of 2 above.

[1] Not much used.

Imperative Negative and Subjunctive Negative.	This is **kadạ** or **kạr** prefixed to *subjunctive*, e.g. **kadạ kạ fịta** (of course, many· intransitives would not have any sense in imperative).
Imperative with Subject before it.	Substitute **kạ** (*masc.*), **kị** (*fem.*), **kụ** (*plural*) for **yā** of *past!* (of course, many intransitives would not have any sense in imperative).
Imperative without Subject before it.	**fịta tsụ̄fā hạ̣kụri** (many intransitives would not have any sense in imperative).
Verbal Noun Referring to Subject.	**fịtā tasạ.** **tsūfansạ.** **hạ̣kurạ tasạ.** The -**u** verbs are not so used (**113** (*a*)³.)
Progressive . .	**yanạ̄ fịtā.** **yanạ̄ dạnnūwā.** **yanạ̄ hạ̣kurạ.** **yanạ̄ tsūfā.** **yanạ̄ fạskạrūwā.** **yanạ̄ bịbbịrkidạ.** For the other subject-pronouns, *vide progressive* of 2 above.

4. CAUSAL VERBS (167)

These consist of (*a*) two-syllable forms ending in consonant, diphthong, or long vowel and having three-syllable alternatives, e.g. **tad dạ** or **tarar dạ** 'overtook'; **fịd dạ** or **fịtar dạ** 'removed', **zub dạ** or **zubar dạ** 'threw things away'; **ɓad dạ** or **ɓatar dạ** 'spent'; **hau dạ** or **hawar dạ** 'mounted person on'; **mai dạ** or **mayar dạ** 'restored thing to'; **sai dạ** or **sayar dạ** 'sold'; **shā dạ** or **shāyar dạ** 'gave drink to'; **cī dạ** or **cīyar dạ** 'gave food to'.

(*b*) Three-syllable forms without two-syllable alternative, e.g. **hūtad dạ** 'gave rest to'; four-syllable forms, e.g. **shagalad dạ** (one consonant before -**ad**) 'diverted person from', **karantad dạ** (two consonants before -**ad**) 'educated'. Also five-syllable forms, e.g. **ɗawainīyad dạ** 'provided for the needs of guests'.

	With Object Understood	With Object Expressed
Past . . .	**yā tarar** or **taras.** **yā fịtar** or **fịtas.**	⎧ **yā tad dạ shī.** ⎨ **yā tarar** (or **taras** or **tarad**) **dạ shī.** ⎩ **yā tarshē shị.**
	yā zubar, *etc.* **yā ɓatar,** *etc.*	
	yā hawar, *etc.* **yā mayar,** *etc.*	⎧ **yā tad dạ Daudạ.** ⎨ **yā tarar** (or **taras** or ⎩ **tarad**) **dạ Daudạ.**

	With Object Understood	With Object Expressed
	yā sayar, *etc.* yā shāyar, *etc.* yā cīyar, *etc.* yā hūtar, *etc.* yā shagalar, *etc.* yā karantar, *etc.* yā ďawainīyar, *etc.*	⎰yā fid dạ ita. ⎱yā fitar dạ ita. ⎱yā fisshē tạ. ⎰yā fid da kāyā. ⎱yā fitar da kāyā. (With similar alternatives for the remainder, i.e. yā zub dạ shī *or* zubshē shị ; ɓad dạ shī *or* ɓasshē shị ; hau dạ shī *or* haushē shi ; mai dạ shī *or* maishē shị ; sai dạ shī *or* saishē shị ; shā dạ shī *or* shāshē shị ; cī dạ shī *or* cīshē shị ; as to the rest, the -shē forms are used in Sokoto, but not much in Kano, i.e. yā hūtasshē shị ; yā shagalshē shị ; yā karantasshē shị ; yā ďawainīyasshē shị).

The other subject-pronouns are **nā, kā, kin, tā, mun, kun, sun, an (12).** The Relative forms **(133*)** are **na, ka, kikạ, ya** (*or* yi *or* i), **ta, mukạ, kukạ, sukạ, akạ.**

Future . . .	Substitute **zại (14)** or **yā̦ (118)** for **yā** of *past !* The other subject-pronouns are **(14) zạn, zā kạ, zā kị, zā tạ, zā mụ, zā kụ, zā sụ, zā ạ** ; and **(118) nā̦, kā̦, kyā̦, tā̦, mā̦, kwā̦, sā̦, ā̦.**
Habitual . .	Substitute **ya kạn** for **yā** of *past !*
	The other subject-pronouns are **na kạn, ka kạn, ki kạn, ta kạn, mu kạn, ku kạn, su kạn, a kạn.**
Subjunctive . .	Substitute **yạ** for **yā** of *past !*
	The other subject-pronouns are **ṇ, kạ, kị, tạ, mụ, kụ, sụ, ạ.**

	With Object Understood	With Object Expressed
Imperative Negative and Subjunctive Negative.	This is kadǎ or kǎr prefixed to *subjunctive*, e.g. kadǎ kǎ sayar ; kǎr kụ mayar.	
Imperative with Subject before it.	Substitute kǎ (*masc.*), kị (*fem.*), kụ (*plural*) for yǎ of *past !*	
Imperative without Subject before it.	fịtar *or* fịtas. ⎧fịtar (*or* fịtad *or* fịtas) dǎ shī/kāyā. ⎨fịd dǎ shī/kāyā. ⎩fịsshē shị.	
	ɓȃtar *or* ɓǎtas.	ɓǎtad (*or* ɓǎtas *or* ɓǎtar) dǎ shī/kudī. ɓǎd dǎ shī/kudī. ɓǎsshē shị.
	mǎyar *or* mǎyas.	mǎyar (*or* mǎyas *or* mǎyad) dǎ shī/kudī. mại dǎ shī/kudī. mạishē sụ.
	kǎrǎntar *or* kǎrǎntas. *etc.*	kǎrantar (*or* kǎrǎntad *or* kǎrǎntas) dǎ shī/Daudǎ. kǎrǎntasshē shị. *etc.*
Verbal Noun		fịd dǎ shī/kāyā. fịtar (*or* fịtas *or* fịtad) dǎ shī/kāyā. fịsshē shị. karantar, *etc.*, dǎ shī/Daudǎ. karantasshē shị. *etc.*
	etc.	
Progressive	yanǎ tarǎrwā *or* tarǎswā. yanǎ fịtǎrwa *or* fịtǎswā. yanǎ sayǎrwā, *etc.* yanǎ karantǎrwā, *etc.*	Prefix yanǎ to *verbal noun !*
	The other subject-pronouns are (16) n nǎ, kanǎ, kinǎ, tanǎ, munǎ, kunǎ, sunǎ, anǎ. The Relative forms (133*) are nikę̄ (*or* nakę̄), kakę̄, kikę̄, yakę̄ (*or* yikę̄ *or* ikę̄), takę̄, mukę̄, kukę̄, sukę̄, akę̄).	

5. MIXED VERBS

These are partially of *changing* and partially of *unchanging* type and consist of one-syllable verbs in long vowel (e.g. shā ' drank ', jī ' heard ', sō ' wanted '), and two-syllable verbs in long final vowel, e.g. bīyā ' paid ' (84–8).

	With Object Understood	With Object Expressed
Past . . .	**yā shā. yā jī. yā sō. yā bīyā.**	**yā shā shi̱/rūwā.** **yā jī shi̱. yā ji ma̱gana̱ tasa̱.** **yā bīyā shi̱/Dauda̱.**
	The other subject-pronouns are **nā, kā, kin, tā, mun, kun, sun, an (12)**. The Relative forms **(133*)** are **na, ka, kika̱, ya (*or* yi *or* i), ta, muka̱, kuka̱, suka̱, aka̱.**	
Future . . .	Substitute **za̱i (14)** *or* **yā̱ (18)** for **yā** of *past !*	
	The other subject-pronouns are **(14) za̱n, zā ka̱, zā ki̱, zā ta̱, zā mu̱, zā ku̱, zā su̱, zā a̱ ;** and **(118) nā̱, kā̱, kyā̱, tā̱, mā̱, kwā̱, sā̱, ā̱.**	
Habitual . .	Substitute **ya ka̱n** for **yā** of *past !*	
	The other subject-pronouns are **na ka̱n, ka ka̱n, ki ka̱n, ta ka̱n, mu ka̱n, ku ka̱n, su ka̱n, a ka̱n.**	
Subjunctive . .	Substitute **ya̱** for **yā** of *past !*	
	The other subject-pronouns are **n̠, ka̱, ki̱, ta̱, mu̱, ku̱, su̱, a̱.**	
Imperative Negative and Subjunctive Negative.	This is **kada̱** *or* **ka̱r** prefixed to *subjunctive*, e.g. **kada̱ ka̱ shā ; ka̱r ki̱ bīyā.**	
Imperative with Subject before it.	Substitute **ka̱** (*masc.*), **ki̱** (*fem.*), **ku̱** (*plural*) for **yā** of *past !*	
Imperative without Subject before it.	**shā.** **jī.** **bīyā.**	**shā̱ shi. shā rūwā.** **jī shi. ji ma̱gana̱ tasa̱.** **bīyā shi̱** *or* **bi̱yā̱ shi.** **bīyā Dauda̱.**

	With Object Understood	With Object Expressed
Verbal Noun . .		shạnsạ/shạn rūwā.
		jịnsạ/jịm mạganạ.
		{ sạnsa (**10** (*a*) (iii)).
		{ sạn Daudạ (**10** (*a*) (iii)).*
		bīyạnsạ/bīyạn Daudạ.
Progressive . .	yanā̰ shā̰. yanā̰ jị̄. yanā̰ sọ̄. yanā̰ bīyạ.	Prefix **yanā̰** to *verbal noun !*

The other subject-pronouns are (**16**) n nā̰, kanā̰, kinā̰, tanā̰, munā̰, kunā̰, sunā̰, anā̰. The Relative forms (**133***) are nikḛ̄ (*or* nakḛ̄), kakḛ̄, kikḛ̄, yakḛ̄ (*or* yikḛ̄ *or* ikḛ̄), takḛ̄, mukḛ̄, kukḛ̄, sukḛ̄, akḛ̄.

* ' the loving David.'

DICTIONARY
OF THE HAUSA LANGUAGE

A

(ạ) (1) (*impersonal pronoun denoting subjunctive.* Gr. 13a,13b, 122)(a) yanạ̃ sọ̃ ạ zō he wants people to come. ạ zō let someone come ! kadạ ạ zō = kạr ạ zō nobody is to come ! (b) ạ yī yau, ạ yī gọ̃be, shī nẹ̃ aikị perseverance wins ! (c) in Ạ zaunạ tā cẹ̃ manạ ạ zaunạ, sǎi mụ zaunạ if we're forced to stay, then we must stay (*here,* Ạ zaunạ *is treated as proper name*). in Ạ fịta tā cẹ̃ musụ ạ fịta, sǎi ạ fịta if they're forced to quit, then they must quit (*here,* Ạ fịta *is treated as proper name*). (d) Vd. compounds of ạ. (e) ạ bā mụ, ạ fī mụ Vd. bā 4b. (f) ạ bar mạ Allạ̃ sanị Vd. sanị 2b.viii. (g) ạ gashẹ bạ̃ mǎi Vd. rōmō 1ç. (h) ạ gạmu ạ Lāhirạ Vd. marịkịcī. (j) ạ aiki kạrē Vd. aikā 1d. (k) ạ kau dạ kǎi Vd. tōfā 2. (l) ạ barị ạ hūcẹ Vd. rạbō 7c. (m) ạ dụbi rūwā Vd. tsạkī 1b. (n) ạ taunạ Vd. tsakūwạ 3. (o) ạ yi waccẹ zā ạ yi Vd. wạndạ 2b. (p) ạ cī yau Vd. yau 1f. (q) ạ zaunạ lāfīyạ Vd.zaunạ 1e. (r) ạ zō gạrēnị Vd. zō 1e. (s) (i) ạ k̃ārạ dawākị ? Vd. B̃arnō 2. (ii) ạ k̃ārạ dạmisạ kāyạ̄ ? Vd. dạmisạ 4. (iii) ạ k̃ārạ wạ gạ̃rī rūwạ̄ ? Vd. gạ̃rī 1c. (iv) ạ k̃ārạ gudumạ Vd. gụdumạ 1b. (t) ạ cī, ạ ragẹ Vd. cī 26e. (u) ạ sam mụtụm Vd. cịnikị 4. (v) ạ cụ̃di gunạ Vd. cụ̃dā 2. (w) ạ kai dambē Vd. dambē 6. (x) ạ hanạ ka gụdu ? Vd. dọ̃kā 2a.iii. (y) ạ kai karā Vd. gạban 4a. (z) ạ kọ̃ri mụtụm Vd. gụdu 2d.vii. (z) (i) ạ tạ̃ru Vd. kạrē 11. (z) (ii) ạ sai dạ k̃ụ̃rụ Vd. k̃ụ̃rụ 1a.ii. (2) (*denoting subjunctive but replacing* sụ) x mutạ̃nam Masạr dạ sū, sǎi (= sụ) kāmạ hannun jūnā the Egyptians and they are shaking hands together. (3) (*impersonal pronoun after* zā Gr. 14) x zā ạ tạfi people will go.

(4) (*impersonal pronoun used in negative past and future.* Gr. 20) x bạ ạ zō ba people have not come. bạ zā ạ zō ba people will not come. (5) *Prep.* at, in (a) x mun sạyē shị ạ Kanọ we bought it at Kano. gạ̃ ni ạ dʼākị here I am in the house ! tarkō yā kāmạ shi ạ wuyạ the trap closed on his neck. (b) (*this preposition vanishes in the progressive.* Gr. 58) x nā gan shị ạ k̃asạ I saw it on the ground, *but* yanạ̃ k̃asạ it is on the ground. ạ sararī yakẹ̃ = yanạ̃ sararī it is manifest. ạ irịn halinsụ in view of the nature of their character. (c) Vd. ạ jūjī. (6) to (a) (*this preposition may replace* wạ, mạ *before noun, but observe order of the sentence!*) x sun kai harị ạ Masạr = sun kai wạ Masạr harị they raided Egypt. ạbin dạ kẹ̃ dạ̃mūwar Hausạ̃wā, shī nẹ̃ kai harị ạ Arnā = shī nẹ̃ kai wạ Arnā harị what was troubling the Hausas, was how to raid the pagans (Vd. gạ 7b). (b) Sk. = zūwạ̃ 2 x tā aikẹ dạ zanẹ ạ gidam bịkī she sent the cloth to the compound where the feast was to be held. tā bīyō shị ạ k̃ōfạ̃ she followed him to the doorway. (7) (*in senses* 5 *or* 6 *above, the prep. can be omitted*) x yā mutụ k̃ōfạ̃r gidāna he died at the doorway of my home. yā sạuka wani gidā he lodged at a certain compound. sun kai harị Masạr they raided Egypt. (8) (*prefixed to verbal noun* = participation) x bābụ laifī ạ sham bạ̃rạ̃sā ? is it no crime to drink liquor ? dud dạ kai ạ yịn aikin nạn ? were *you* then a party to that ? dud dạ nī ạ yinsa yes, *I* was concerned in it. (9) (*usually precedes noun of state* (Gr. 80d) *unless progressive is used,* cf. 5b *above*) x yā tad dạ ạkwīyạ ạ

fẹ̄ɗe = yā tad da akwīya tanā fẹ̄ɗe he found the goat already flayed. gā māshi kafe (= a kafe) a jikinsa there is the spear sticking into his body !

(10) (*precedes* -ce. Gr. 97) *x* a Lārabce in Arabic. a Tūrance in English, French, etc.

(11) from in, from off *x* yā fāɗi a dōki he fell off the horse. yā fīgē mini a hannūna he snatched it out of my hand. ki ɗaukō mini nāma a gidā bring me the meat from inside the house. kasarsu tā tāshi a kasar amāna kē nan their country has ceased to be neutral.

(12) a tō well then . . . (= a'a).

a (a) **(1)** (*impersonal pronoun used after* zā. Gr. 17) *x* zā a Kano people will go to Kano. **(2)** (*impersonal pronoun used to transmit orders of a superior.* Gr. 18) *x* a faɗa maka I have been instructed to inform you that . . . **(3)** (*impersonal pronoun used after* bā. Gr. 22) *x* bā a da rūwā one has no water. **(4)** *cf.* ad. **(5)** (*impersonal pronoun used in negative habitual.* Gr. 20) *x* ba a kan zō ba people do not come.

a (ā) (*impersonal negative pronoun of progressive.* Gr. 19) *x* bā ā zūwa people are not coming.

a (ā) (*impersonal pronoun denoting probable future.* Gr. 118–121) *x* **(1)** ā tafi people will probably go. **(2)** ā ci māsa *Vd.* māsa 3. **(3)** ā cē fa ? *Vd.* cē 8. **(4)** ā ɗauki karē *Vd.* karē 2. **(5)** ā tambayi lābārin kitso ? *Vd.* kundumī. **(6)** ā rina *Vd.* mahaukacī 1*a*.viii.

a (ā) fancy ! (= a'a).

a'a A. (a'a) **(1)** fancy ! (= ā). **(2)** well then . . . (= a tō, *q.v. in* a 12).

    B. (ā'ā) **(1)** no ! **(2)** ā'ā, Masar banda fāɗūwā there is not the slightest fear of Egypt being captured.

    C. (ā'a) *Sk.* how ? (= kāka *q.v.*).

a''afā *Vb.* 1C *intens. from* afa.

a'ahā = ā'ahā = kash 1 *q.v.*

a''aika A. (a''aika) *Vb.* 2 *intens. from* aika.

    B. (a''aikā) *Vb.* 1C *intens. from* aika.

abā *Vd.* abu 1*b*.

abābā *Vd.* abu.

abadā *Ar.* **(1)** (*a*) will for ever *x* har ∽ zan yi salla I'll always remain a Muslim. (*b*) unceasingly *x* har ∽ kanā salla you do nothing but pray all the time. (*c*) (*negatively*) will never *x* har ∽ ba zam bar salla ba I shall never cease to be a Muslim. in sun kuskurē, har ∽ if they make a mistake, they will never get another chance. (*d*) *Vd.* ābādin. **(2)** *f.* any strong European cloth, black or white (*cf.* atamfā).

abadan = abadan = abadā 1 ∽*q.v.* (*Vd. also* ābādin).

abadin A. (ābādin) *Ar.* har abadā ābādin = har abadan ābādin = abadā 1 *q.v.*

    B. (abadin) *Kt.* bā gaira bā abadin = bā gaira abadin without rhyme or reason.

abadul ābādi *Ar.* *x* har abadul ābādi = abadā 1 *q.v.*

abaibai, abaibaɗai *Vd.* abu.

abăicī *m.*, *f.* **(1)** posthumous child *x* ābaicin Audu yā zō the boy born after his father Audu's death has come. **(2)** Abăicī *name for any* posthumous child (= Mayau = Maida = Maimakō 4), *cf.* Ā jēfas, băitō.

***abājē** *used in* 'yar abājē = agōfatā *q.v.*

abākuru *m.* (*sg.*, *pl.*) small cake made from groundnuts, Bambarra ground nuts (gujīyā) or bean-flour.

abakwā *m.*, *f.* (*sg.*, *pl.*). **(1)** novice. **(2)** Abakwan rīgā descendant(s) of mixed marriages between Hausa men and Tiv, etc., women (*cf.* tābūshe 2).

abalalu = afalalu.

a bamban **(1)** *m.*, *f.* = gōyō 1*a*. **(2)** *Cf.* bamban.

a bā mu *m.* **(1)** projecting beard (= *Kt.* mun hana. *cf.* a kai cikī). **(2)** *Vd.* bā B.1 4*b*.

***abantakū** *m.* type of guineacorn.

abara A. (Ā bara) = Ā bar shī, Ā bar ta.

    B. (abārā) *f.* **(1)** A. ponderous. **(2)** type of heavy canoe.

abarbā *Yor.* *f.* pineapple(s) (*its epithet is* ∽ a bar banzā) (= hantsa 5*b* = faināfur).

a bar banzā *Vd.* abarbā.

Ā bar shī *m.* *name for any boy* (*means* " may he be spared ! " *and is intended* to ward off the evil eye. *It is one of the names given a* ɗaŋ wābị *q.v.*), *cf.* **Ạ jēfas ; Ạ bar tạ ; barạ** A.2 2c, d; **Bạrau.**

Ạ bar tạ *name for any girl (corresponding to* **Ạ** bar shị *for boy*) = **Bạraukạ 1.**

abạsạ̄ (1) (*said by carrier*) up with the load ! (2) *Vd.* **hōɓẹ̄sạ.**

abạsạ̄rạ̄ = **abạsạ̄.**

ạbạshĩyạ *Eng. m.* overseer.

ạbassamạ (1) *f.* loud thunderclap(s). (2) (*a*) I swear I did not do it ! (*b*) I swear I won't do it ! (*cf.* **ạrādụ 2**).

***abạtạ** *f.* stomatitis of the tongue (= *Kt.* hartạtandẹ).

ạbạtayạ *f.* (1) *Eng.* overtime. (2) gambling (cācā) with two dice per player.

Ạ bat tạ = **Ạ bar tạ.**

abạucē *Vb.* 3A *x* (1) yā ∼ he's got out of hand (= **ạbautạ**). (2) yā ∼ minị he's too much for me.

ạbautạ *Vb.* 3B yā ∼ = **abạucē 1.**

abạutaccē *m.* (*f.* **ạbautaccīyā** *pl.* **ạbạutattū** P. out of control.

abạ̄wā *f.* (1) coarse thread (= **abụrdugạ** 2a). (2) girmā dạ azzịkī waddạ ta sā jan sā dạ ∼ persuasion is better than force (*Vd.* azzịkī 4b). (3) *Vd.* ƙīrị 2, andị ā.

Abbạ (1) (*preceding name in case of Arab man*) Mister. (2) *Vd.* **Tūrancī 1c,** yạ̄yā 2h, iŋkallạ.

abbani A. (abbạnī) *Kr. m.* (1) father. (2) paternal uncle.

B. (ạbbạnī) *Kr. m. used in* ∼ kurạ father's elder brother.

abbạ̄sạ̄ = abbạ̄sạ̄rạ̄ = abạ̄sạ̄ *q.v.*

Abdụ = **Audụ.**

abdugā *Sk.* = **audụgā.**

Abdullāhị *man's name* (*Vd.* bindigạ 11).

ạbēlạ *f.* European candle(s) = **kyandịr.**

***ạbidạ** *f.* type of woman's collarette.

ābịdī *Ar. m.* (*f.* **ābidịyā**) *pl.* **ạbịdai** worshipper, member of religious congregation.

***ạbịdō** *Yor. m.* kolanut(s) of the type called **hannun rūwā.**

ạbin *Vd.* **ạbụ.**

ạbincī *m.* food *x* (1) sunā cịŋ ∼ they're having a meal. **sun dẹ̄bi daŋgā, sun yi** ∼ dạ shī they used bits of fence as fuel to cook their food. **sunā ∼ dạ mạ̄i** they cook their food in oil. (2)

(ạbincī *is often treated as plural*) *x* **ạbincin dabbạ sū nẹ̄ cịyāwạ dạ** . . . the foodstuffs of cattle are grass and . . . **waɗansu** ∼ certain foods. **manyaŋ ạbincinsụ** their staple food. (3) (*a*) sāmụŋ ạbincī earning one's living. (*b*) sāmụŋ ạbincin ɗan tsạ̄kō *Vd.* sāmụle. (4) ạbin cị *Vd.* ạbụ 1a.iii.

ạbīyạ *Kt.* (*pl.* **ạbīyai**) = **ạbōkīyā.**

abkạ = **aukạ.**

ạbkē *Kt. m.* (1) type of girls' game. (2) yā yi minị ∼ he entered my house unceremoniously. (3) sun yi masạ ∼ unasked, they helped him (owner of large farm) by going unknown to him and doing collective-farmwork (gayyā) on his farm.

ạbōkā *Zar. m.* = **ạbōkī.**

ạ ɓōƙarạ *m.* (*sg. and pl.*) (1) (*a*) railway pump-trolley (*its epithet is* ∼ kā fl ƙarē gudụ). *cf.* bọ̄ƙarạ. (*b*) *Vd.* ƙanẹ 5b. (2) type of woman's blouse of the tagụ̄wā type.

ạbōkī *m.* (*f.* **ạbōkīyā** = **ạbụ̄ya**) *pl.* **ạbōkai** = ***ạbọ̄ƙanai** (1) (*a*) friend. (*b*) babbaŋ ạbōkiŋ aŋgọ bridegroom's best man. (*c*) Gḗrō ạbōkin Sarkī *Vd.* ạlkālī. (*d*) Mại dạ ạbōkī barạ *Vd.* barạ A.2 1e. (2) (*preceding in genitive*) sharer in *x* (*a*) ạbōkiŋ aikị fellow-worker (*for similar cases, Vd.* bautā, fadā, gạ̄bā, tạfīyạ, tạrayyạ, tārū, wạ̄sā, gaisụ̄wā 4, zạncē 1a). (*b*) *Vd.* gādā 1e. (*c*) ạbōkiŋ kīwọ *Vd.* burtū 5. (3) *Vd.* ạbōkīyā.

ạbōkīyā *f.* (*pl.* **ạbọ̄kai**) female friend of man or woman (*Vd.* **ạbōkī**).

Abōrạ, Abōrāwā *Vd.* **Abōrẹ.**

abọrcē *Vb.* 3A flew into a rage (*cf.* **Abōrẹ 3,** bọ̄rē) = **bōracē.**

Abōrẹ *m.* (*f.* **Abōrạ**) *pl.* **Abōrāwā** (1) member of the Filani Clan so named. (2) vicious cow, ox, cattle of that Clan. (3) cantankerous P.

ạbụ *m.* (*genitive* **ạbin**) *pl.* **abụ̄būwạ** = **abubbạ** = **ạbaibai** (*cf.* 11, 12 *below*) = ***abạ̄bā** = ***ạbaibạɗai** (1) (*a*) thing. (*aa*) (*in genitive*) thing of, thing for *x* (i) ạbiŋ adō article of adornment, jewelry (*Vd.* adō). (ii) ạbim fạdā *Vd.* fạdā 2b (*cf.* 5h *below*). (iii) yā bā nị ạbin cịn nāmạ = yā bā nị ạbin cịŋ gōrọ he gave me a little money. (iv) ạbin

sa̱wā a̱ ba̱kinsu̱ their food.   (v) ba̱i
sa̱mi wani a̱bin cȩ̄wā ba a̱ wanna̱ŋ
za̱ncē he could find no fault with this
proposal. (Vd. cȩ̄wā 2b.) (vi) a̱bin sha̱
rānī Vd. sha̱ rānī. (vii) a̱bin jȩ̄fa̱wā =
a̱bin jīfa̱ missile (Mod. Gram. 90c),
but a̱bin jȩ̄fā = a̱bin jīfa̱ thing shot at
(x animal hunted, target). (viii) a̱bin
jīfa̱n yuŋwa̱ Vd. wākē 5b. (ix) a̱biŋ
haushī Vd. haushī.   (x) a̱bin diŋki̱n
dūnīya̱ Vd. Wazīri̱. (xi) a̱biŋ wutā
fuel (Vd. wutā 1b.i,ii). (xii) abūbūwa̱n
ciki̱ Vd. ciki̱ 1c. (xiii) a̱bin da̱rīyā,
a̱bin ta̱usa̱yī Vd. da̱rīyā 7. (xiv) a̱bin
lallē Vd. fa̱rkā 2b. (b) (when following
fem. noun in the sense " is a thing ",
a̱bā may replace a̱bu̱, Mod. Gram. 8c)
x ƙīra̱ a̱bar a̱mfa̱nī cȩ̄ = ƙīra̱ a̱biŋ
a̱mfa̱nī nȩ̄ (Gram. 23a.iii) smithing is a
useful thing.   nōmā a̱biŋ a̱mfa̱nī nȩ̄
farming (masculine noun) is a useful
thing. (c) (singular a̱bu̱ often follows
plural adj. such as wadansu̱, in plural
sense, Mod. Gram. 176d) x ka̱ sa̱mi
tōzō kō hanta̱ kō wadansu̱ a̱bu̱ buy
hump, liver or some other similar
things ! sū nȩ̄ ma̱nya̱ŋ a̱bin da̱ akȩ̄
sa̱yē they are the main things which
they buy.   (d) a̱biŋ the thing in
question x (i) da̱ yakȩ̄ a̱biŋ, na ka̱'she-
ka̱shē" nȩ̄, bā na̱ cikī seeing the affair
is a question of murder, I wish to have
nothing to do with it.   a̱biŋ, sǎi
wanda̱ ya ganī it must be seen to be
believed (a̱biŋ may be replaced by a̱bu̱,
Vd. 5 below).   (ii) a̱biŋ da̱ ka̱mar
wu̱yā, gurgūwā da̱ auran nēsa̱ what a
difficult thing ! (iii) Vd. 5. (e) wani
a̱bu̱ (i) anything of importance x ba a̱
tafa̱ ganiŋ a̱lāma̱ za̱i zamā wani a̱bu̱ a̱
dūnīya̱ ba it did not look as if it would
come to anything.   ra̱ƙumī wani a̱bu̱
nȩ̄ ? who cares a straw for a camel !
(cf. 4 below, don 2a, b). (ii) Vd. wani
1a, 5a.
   (2) property x (a) ma̱i ~ pl. ma̱sū ~
prosperous.   (b) ma̱sū ~ da̱ a̱binsu̱,
kūrā da̱ kalla̱biŋ kitsȩ = kūrā tā ga
sānīya̱ tana̱ lāshȩ dīyā tata̱, tā cȩ̄
" ma̱sū ~ su ka̱n cī da̱ rānā, mara̱s ~
sǎi da̱ darē (or . . . mara̱s ~ sǎi ya̱
da̱ŋgana̱) " some people have all the

luck ! (c) yā ka̱māta̱ ka̱ lūrā da̱ a̱biŋka̱
keep an eye on your property ! (d) suna̱
nēma̱ŋ a̱biŋ ka̱nsu̱ they're seeking to
earn their livelihood.   bā su da̱ a̱biŋ
ka̱nsu̱ they've no property of their
own.   (e) a̱bin sa̱na'a̱rsu̱ the implements of their trade.   (f) ma̱i ~ shī
nȩ̄ da̱ bara̱ no rich man without
cadgers !   (g) a̱bim mutu̱m, a̱biŋ
wa̱sansa̱ training makes perfect. (h) in
da̱ a̱biŋka̱, ana̱ ƙaunarka̱ ; im bābu̱
a̱biŋka̱, ka̱rē yā fī ka̱ only the rich are
courted.   (j) ma̱i a̱bin ru̱fā, shī kȩ̄
kūkan dārī, huntū yā ba̱ ga̱skīyā ga̱
ita̱cē often it is the rich man who fusses
over a trifling loss. (k) a̱bu̱ da̱ yawa̱ yā
sāba̱ bacȩ̄wā a̱ fāda̱, ba̱ Ta̱ka̱lmī ba
you're lucky to have got off so lightly !
(Vd. fāda̱ 4.) (l) ma̱i da̱ a̱biŋ wani
nāka̱ Vd. wa̱jiri̱. (m) ma̱i sa̱ŋ a̱biŋka̱
Vd. ba̱rāwo̱ 1a. (n) a̱biŋ arō bā ya̱
rufȩ katara̱ one cannot make free with
a borrowed thing : a guest cannot
behave as he would at home.
   (3) a̱bin da̱ that which x (a) (i) a̱bin
da̱ muka̱ ganī in our opinion. (ii) Vd.
wani 5a. (b) a̱bin da̱ ya sa̱ sukȩ̄ yi̱,
dōmin sun sani̱ . . . the reason they
do it is because they know that . . .
(c) a̱bin da̱ suka̱ yi, sǎi suka̱ fāda̱ masa̱
what they did was to attack him. (d)
a̱bin da̱ ya taba̱ hanci̱, ido̱ sǎi ya̱ yi
rūwā what affects one, also affects the
other. (e) a̱bin da̱ ka shūka̱, shī zā
ka̱ girbȩ as you sow, so shall you reap
(Vd. shūka̱ 1a.ii). (f) a̱bin da̱ aka̱
gasa̱ shi, yā ga wutā Vd. dafa̱ 1e. (g) a̱bin
da̱ bāƙī ya daura̱ Vd. bāƙī 1b.xvi.
(h) a̱bin da̱ babba ya ganī yana̱ ƙasa̱,
yāro̱ kō yā hau rīmī, ba̱ za̱i gan shi
ba young P. has not the mature judgment of his seniors. (j) a̱bin da̱ rūwan
zāfī ya dafa̱ Vd. rūwā C.10. (k) a̱bin
da̱ ya zō, shī akȩ̄ ya̱yī at Rome do as
Rome does ! (l) a̱bin da̱ ma̱i dōki̱ kȩ̄ so̱
Vd. bāwa̱ 1g. (m) a̱bin da̱ ya kōrō
bērā Vd. bērā 1k. (n) (i) a̱bin da̱ dāma
ta jūrȩ Vd. dāma 1g.   (ii) a̱bin da̱
zūcīya̱ ta dauka̱ Vd. dauka̱ 1e.i. (o) a̱bin
da̱ ya ci Dōma̱ Vd. Dōma̱. (p) a̱bin da̱
ba̱i isa a̱ jā Vd. ƙīri̱ 2.
   (4) da̱ wani a̱bu̱ x uku̱ da̱ wani a̱bu̱

three and a bit (= kăi 7a.v. = 'yā'yā 1f = ragī 1), cf. 1e above. shękara uku da wani abu three years and a bit.

(5) the affair (cf. 1d above) x (a) abu yā yī all is O.K. : things went well. (b) abin yā zō kammu " now we're in the soup ! " (c) dā ⁓ kamar wāsā har ya zamā aminci it began as a joke and ended in real friendship. (d) mutānē bā sa san yin ⁓ săi in sun ga kā yi ⁓ su zō su yi maka people lack the guts to steal, but they bide their time and rob a thief. (e) yā yi ta mur'de-murdē abinsa then he became convulsed with pain. (f) babban ⁓ shī nē, macē tā rigā mijinta bawali (said by labourers) what a serious affair ! (g) abin yā zō dăidăi, mai ido daya yā lēka būta what unexpected luck ! (h) abim fadā na mai bāki nē, bēbe săi ya dangana what cannot be cured, must be endured (cf. 1aa.ii above). (j) abu yā zamā na Audu Audu became top dog. (k) abu yā zame masa bīyu, gaba wutā, bāya wutā he was between the devil and the deep sea. (l) ⁓ a sararī Vd. gaba-gaba.

(6) abim bā īyāka immensely x Allā yā nufē shi da kiba, abim bā īyāka God caused him to become immensely fat.

(7) abinka x (a) tafi abinka clear out ! jē ka gida abinka be off home ! (b) sun wuce abinsu they went about their affairs. (c) yā zauna abinsa can he stayed where he was. (d) zai zauna abinsa he'll remain independent. (e) abinka da macē you know what kittle-cattle women are ! abinka da jāhilī a dolt remains a dolt !

(8) abin shanya bā a hana rānā take the chance when it offers !

(9) abim banzā, hanci bā kafā it's handsome but useless (Vd. banzā 1a).

(10) abin kan īyāka the plants gamba, yākuwā.

(11) abaibai garēshi he's possessed by the spirits mabīyā.

(12) abaibam bāki teeth. yā yi mini abaibam bāki he abused me (cf. bāki 2h).

(13) For compounds of abin, Vd.

abincī, adō, ciki 1c, kallō, kasa 1g, murna, shā, sō, wutā 1b.
Abū = Habū.
Abū Bakar man's name (originally the friend of The Prophet) (he is called Sadaukī = Wan dawa = Siddīku = gāgara 3c = Gāgarau = Garba = Habū).
abubba, abūbūwa Vd. abu.
abucē = abaucē.
Abūjā f. the place Abuja.
abukkīya Kt. = abōkīya.
aburduga (1) what a lot of spinning has been done ! (2) f. (a) = abāwā 1a. (b) Vd. ayanyana.
abūrinka (1) (a) I challenge you (one male) to a fight ! (= tamānīya 2). (b) if several persons are challenged, we say abūrinku. (2) The reply accepting the challenge is tāwāyę.
abūtā = abūtaka f. (sg., pl.). (1) (a) friendship. (b) nā daura ⁓ da shī I made him my friend. (c) wadannan ⁓ these friendships. (2) bā nā ⁓ da biri, sandāna ya kwam bisa = kōwā ya yi ⁓ da biri sandansa bā ya makēwā a bisa it's no good having a friend at court if one cannot get one's desires fulfilled. (3) Vd. fāra 2d.
abūya = abōkīya.
acahaku (said by women) well cheerio, you women, good luck ! (reply is āmin, Allā ya sā).
acakau = akacau.
acakwā m., f. = Kt. acakō m. (sg., pl.) raffia (gwangwalā) tray for carrying load (cf. sēmā).
acamo m. type of Yoruba pastry.
acca f. the cereal grass Digitaria exilis (much grown on Jos Plateau) = Zar. intāya, cf. guzgus.
a cē fa ? Vd. cē 8.
acīci = cīcīyau.
acicincin m. (sg., pl.) small rectangular type of mat.
a cī da măi m. (sg., pl.). (1) balls of rice or millet (or of beans at Kt.) served with oil (= sharaf 2d = cancangā 2 = shasshakā). (2) type of cloth. (3) kōwā ya cī da măi, kudinsa P. can do as he likes with his own property ; it's well worth the large outlay.

ạ cĭ kạ ạ fẹ̀re epithet of the fruit of the trees gundurū, gọ̄rubạ.
acịkōkō = cikōkō.
ạcịyau = cịcịyau.
acūrạkĭ m. branding-iron for donkey, to mark ownership or cure sickness (= madōshĭ 2a), cf. kằmā 2, lalạs.
ad Sk. (the -d assimilates to the next consonant) is, are x (1) nĭ ab bạbba I'm the senior. shĭ as Sarkĭ he is the chief. shĭ an na huɗū he is the fourth. (2) (with shĭ omitted) nĭ ad dạ = nĭ ad dạ shĭ I have it. sū ad dạ they are the ones in favour (with the chief, etc.). bạ̀ kạu kū ad dạ bạ ? well, you're rich aren't you ?
*ādạ = ạl'ādạ.
ạdạ'ā̀ f. (1) (a) nā yi masạ ∼ I thanked him. (b) Vd. kurmusū 2. (2) (a) mun jē ạdạ'ar Kạnde (Audụ) we went to the marriage-service of Kạnde (woman) or Audụ (man). (b) Vd. aurē 6c.
*ạdạ'āmị = *ạddạ'āmị.
adabạlĭ Kt. m. (sg., pl.). (1) patch riveted on damaged sword. (2) any scar (= tabọ 1a). (3) hannūna ∼ nẹ̀ my arm has never been the same since I broke it.
*ạdạbir m. a poor type of mạŋgul salt.
ạdạdā̀ m. (pl. ạdạdai) rectangular thatched house.
adad dạ = adar dạ.
adạdĭ m. (pl. ạdạdai) Ar. (1) (a) total x ạdạdinsụ gōmạ nē they total ten. (b) sunạ̀ naŋ bạ̀ ∼ they're in great profusion. (2) written representation of any numeral. (3) ạdạdinsạ yā cịka his prison-sentence has expired.
*ạdagwarjẹ m. = ɗaŋ kyarkọ.
adạjjō Sk. (Yor.) used in ɗaŋ ∼ m. halfpenny.
ạdakạ f. (pl. adakōkĭ = ạdạkū = ạdạkai) (1) wooden or metal case, trunk, etc. (2) any large load. (3) type of short gun.
ạdạkō Nu. m. small waistcloth worn by women over their other clothing.
adakōkĭ Vd. ạdakạ.
adala A. (ạdālạ) f. yā yi minị ∼ he did me a good turn (cf. ādalcị).
B. (ādạlā) Vd. ādạlĭ.
ạɗalạshĭ Ar. m. satin, velvet (= mạlallạs).

ādalcị Ar. m. (1) justice, fairness. (2) acting justly, honestly (cf. ạdālạ).
ādạlĭ m. (f. ādạlā) pl. ạdạlai Ar. just, honest, righteous.
Adạm = Adạŋ.
Adamạ f. (1) woman's name. (2) epithet for any cat.
Adamāwā f. Adamawa Emirate. (2) Vd. banzā, Baadamẹ.
ādamụ = ạ̄dạmū m. Adam (name for boy born Friday, cf. Hawạ) (his epithet is ∼ mại sūnan Jumma'ạ = Mạnzo), Vd. Adạŋ.
Adạŋ Ar. m. (1) Adam (Vd. ạ̄dạmū). (2) ɗaŋ ∼ m. (f. 'yar ∼) pl. 'yaŋ ∼ person, human being (= bāwạ 3). (3) yā zamā ɗaŋ ∼ he behaved rudely. yā yi minị ta ɗaŋ ∼ he treated me shabbily. (4) Bạnī ∼ Ar. mankind.
adana A. (ạdạnā) (f. of ạdạnĭ). (1) A. inferior. (2) adv. nā sạ̄mē shị ∼ I got it cheaply, easily.
B. (ādạnā) Vb. 1C looked carefully after T. (Vd. ādạnĭ) = kirkịntā = Kt. tānadạ 2.
ạdạnạsā Sk. f. nā sạ̄mi ∼ I got a bargain (cf. ạdạnā 2).
ạdandẹ = ạdandị m. type of European cotton fabric (= wāgạmbạrī).
adani A. (ạdạnĭ) m. (f. ạdạnā) Ar. (1) destitute. (2) Vd. ạdạnā.
B. (ādạnĭ) m. (Sec. v.n. from ādạnā) x yanạ̀ ādạninsạ = yanạ̀ ādạnā shi he's looking after it carefully.
adaŋkịyā (Eng. " I don't care "). (1) I don't care (= ạnōbịsī). (2) f. (a) inferior thing(s). (b) ∼ dạ sallạ English cap. (c) ∼ m. being on remand. (3) zamaŋ ∼ m. being on remand.
ạdaŋkwalō m. (1) = adaŋkịyā 2a,b. (2) zamaŋ ∼ = adaŋkịyā 3.
ādạntā = ādạnā.
adar A. (ādạr) f. The Tuareg area of Adrar (Vd. banzā).
B. (adar dạ) Vb. 4B x nā ∼ sạ̀kō I delivered the message. nā ∼ lābārịn dạ na ji I repeated the news I'd heard.
ạdarạshĭ m. (pl. ạdạrạsai) meal accompanied by rich gravy.
adas dạ = adar dạ.
ạdā̀shē = ạ̄dā̀shĭ m. (1) (a) (i) sun shiga ∼ they're contributing to a pool, each

taking the money in the pool in turn.
(ii) *Vd.* hannū 1*k.* (*b*) yā zubạ ~ he
paid his contribution to the pool
(*cf.* zubị 4). (2) yā kwạshi ~ (*a*) he
won the money in the pool. (*b*) he got
a bargain, had a stroke of luck.
aḍāshima *f.* (*Eng.* " dash me ") present,
tip (= kyautā).
adawa A. (aḍāwạ) *Ar. f.* hostility, enmity.
*B. (aḍawạ) = taḍawạ.
aḍāyā *f.* = aḍalạshī.
adda A. (aḍḍā) *f.* (*pl.* addunạ). (1) matchet.
(2) leper's fingerless handstump. (3)
rịgan naŋ kaŋ ~ cệ this gown has its
lower part reinforced both in front and
behind (*cf.* ƙaƙō 8).
    B. (ad dạ) *Vd.* aḍ.
*aḍḍạ'āmị *Ar. m.* food.
addabạ *Vb.* 2 *Ar.* pestered, perplexed.
addạbabbē *m.* (*f.* addạbabbīyā) *pl.*
addạbabbū nagger, pesterer.
addabạrī *m.* (*pl.* addạbạrai) pad for pack-
animal.
aḍḍạbībị = hatsạbībị.
aḍḍā'ịrā *f.* (*pl.* aḍḍā'irōrī) (*Ar.* " circle ").
(1) shortsleeved gown such as worn by
N.A. police (= dā'irạ = *Sk.* bậ ni māsū).
(2) (*no pl.*) a place and its environs
x aḍḍā'ịrar Kanọ Kano and there-
abouts. aḍḍā'ịran naŋ, bậ indạ bai tākạ
ba he's travelled all over this district.
addakạ. (1) (*Ar.* 'ahdaka) *used in* ~ wa ~
I conjure you by your oath to me !
(2) *f.* = aḍakạ.
*addakạrī *m.* (1) miserly. (2) useless
P. or T.
*aḍḍakīkị = ḍakīkị.
aḍḍalạshī = aḍalạshī.
addạnā = āḍạnā.
addarạs = aḍarạshī.
addau *used in* tuŋ ~ from the earliest
times.
*aḍḍawạ = taḍawạ.
aḍḍẹ *Sk. m.* = izgịlī.
aḍḍibịrī *m.* (*pl.* aḍḍịbịrai) (*Ar.* " anus "
cf. dubura) = jậ kutụr.
aḍḍīlạ = aḍīlạ.
aḍḍīnị (*Ar.-Hebrew*) *m.* (*pl.* aḍḍīnai).
(1) any religion (= bautā 3*b*). (2) (*sometimes used as pl.*) *x* manya-manyaŋ
aḍḍīnịŋ ƙasạr the main religions of the
country.

aḍḍu'ạ *f.* (*pl.* addu'ō'ī). (1) (*a*) the invocations succeeding the laudatory
prayers (sallạ *q.v.*) in the five daily
prayer-times. (*b*) ~ tạ gạmu dạ ịjābạ
Vd. sadakạ. (*c*) iŋ Allậ yā ƙi aḍḍu'ạr
birị, săi yạ mutụ ạ gōnar arnẹ
one cannot fight against ill fortune.
(2) expressing good wishes *x* yā
yi musụ ~ he expressed his goodwill towards them (*by a formula such
as* kạ saụka lāfīyạ may you arrive
safely ! *or* Allậ yạ kai mụ may we
live to do it as you wish !). (3) expressing the hope that *x* yā yi masạ ~
Allậ yạ rāyạ shi he expressed to him the
hope he might enjoy long life.
aḍḍubụrī = aḍḍibịrī.
aḍḍunạ *Vd.* aḍḍā.
aḍḍūrū *m.* (*sg., pl.*) piece reinforcing tip
of sword-scabbard.
adibidị *m.* the giving of food to their
sweethearts by girls, one of whose
friends has just been married.
adīdīsainị *m.* white metal sheets imported
from North Africa.
aḍīkọ *m.* (*pl.* adīkunạ ⇒ aḍīkai =
aḍīkwai). (1) handkerchief (= mashāfī
2). (2) headkerchief (1, 2 = mayānī).
aḍīlạ *f.* (*pl.* adīlōlī = aḍīlū). (1) any
large load. (2) (*formerly*) load of
20,000 or 50,000 cowries.
āḍịlī, āḍilcị = āḍạlī, āḍalcị *respectively.*
aḍindimā *f.* type of wingless grasshopper.
aḍịrē *m.* (*sg., pl.*) Yoruba black and white
cloth.
ado A. (adō) *m.* (1) adornment *x* (*a*) sun
ci (= sun yi) ~ they togged themselves up. (*b*) kāyaŋ ~ = ạbiŋ adō
m. articles for adornment, jewellery,
etc. (*c*) ạmfānịŋ ạbiŋ ~ ḍaurậwā if
one has a thing, one should make use
of it. (*d*) yā zō bậ ~, bậ lậbārị he
turned up unexpectedly. (*e*) *Vd.*
ạrahā 5. (2) smallpox marks.
    B. (ậdō) = ậḍamū.
aḍuḍụ *m.* (*pl.* aḍuḍai) large lidded-basket.
aḍullū *m.* (*pl.* aḍullai) = ƙundạ 1.
aḍundumā = aḍindimā.
aḍungurē *m.* somersaulting in sitting
position (= tụntsụrạ gudunyạ = *Kt.*
tụkụbyelbyel. *cf.* ạlkāfụrā).
aḍūrū *Vd.* aḍḍūrū.

ądųrūkų *m.* (*sg., pl.*) (1) (*a*) tree (*New-bouldia laevis*) from which strong fences can be made. (*b*) ~ māgąnim mąi kwāriŋ kąi the obdurate need a strong hand. (2) simpleton(s).

adūwą *f.* (*pl.* adūwōyī) (1) Desert Date-tree (*Balanites aegyptiaca*), *cf.* kwąikwąyē, agǫ 3, dąbāgirā, hąŋgūgų. (2) tūwaŋ ~ = birī-birī. (3) sąmāriŋ ~ *m.* ragged clothing. (4) daŋ ~ *m.* female pudenda.

*ądūwwi *Ar. m.* enemy.

af (1) = ąp. (2) *Vd.* afat.

afą *Vb.* 1A (*cf.* afę, ąfē, afį). (1) threw into one's mouth (powder or a number of groundnuts, etc.) = yāfą 2*b* = hąmfudą = *Kt.* gumą 2*a, cf.* gumbųdā. (2) tā ~ (*a*) she after doing rų́dē, threw finely-ground flour into the pot when the coarser-flour (tsąkī) was nearly cooked. (*b*) she made cheap tūwō without any tsąkī. (3) *cf.* afat, afį 4.

afąjājaŋ = afųjājaŋ.

afalalu A. (ąfąlalų) *m.* (*Ar.* afzalu " superior ") *x* shī nę̄ ~ dą nī (1) he excels me. (2) he is senior to me.

B. (afąlalų) *used in* ~ kąn dabbōbī ! kōwā ya sau ką, yā̧ nēmō ką (*lit.* Camel thou precious beast ! Whoever lets you loose will have to fetch you) what a time he's been away on this errand ! (= ąikā 1.*a.*ii).

afaną *f.* (1) (*corruption of Ar.* anfa'a) = ąmfą̄nī. (2) *x* bą̄ ka dą afąną ? kąŋ barcī har yąnzu ? have you so little sense of propriety that you drowse on like this ? (*cf.* dā'ą).

*afaŋgąlī *m.* (1) clay door of pigeon-cot. (2) clay-lid of rųfēwā.

*afarąmī = afarą̄rī.

afarą̄rī *Zar. m.* cream.

ąfari *m.* ornamental increase to thickness of doorway.

afat *used in* afat ta fārį = af ta fārį = afą̄war fārį first of all *x* afat ta fārį aką kashę shi the prime cause of the matter was his being killed.

ąfątā *m.* (*pl.* afatōcī). (1) pale type of the kola nuts called hannun rūwā. (2) *cf.* ąbątā.

ąfątą̄tū *m.* (1) mercerized cotton, artificial silk thread. (2) *Vd.* silikį 3.

afą̄wā *Vd.* afat.

afe A. (afę) *totality form* (Gram. 44c) *from* afą.

B. (ąfē) *m.* (1) acting as in afą 2 *x* tā yi ~ . (2) being occupied in the act of afą 2 *x* tang ~ she's occupied in throwing finely-ground flour, etc.

affąfadąraŋ = affąfąi = affąfairaŋ (1) bother ! (2) *m.* sleeveless gown reaching to knees (*so called, as if P. stretches himself, his buttocks become exposed and he says " bother ! "*) (= *Kt.* ąllambąram 2).

afį *m.* (1) (*Sec. v.n. of* afą 1) *x* yang afiŋ gyądā = yang afą g. he is throwing handfuls of groundnuts into his mouth. (2) courage-endowing medicine for hunter, warrior, hunting-dog. (3) pagans' putting ashes on heads in obeisance. (4) afịm fārị = afat.

Afīrē = Afīrį = Afīrųwā *name for girl born tiny* (*cf.* Agwīdų, Fīrī, Fịrō, mącē 26).

Afīrką *f.* (1) Africa. (2) (*minefields Hausa*) any major mining-machinery (*x* steam-shovel).

afka = auka.

ąfnō *m., f.* Kanuri term for a Hausa(s).

afo A. (afǫ) (1) = afūwā. (2) = ahǫ.

B. (ā̧fǫ) *Vd.* ā̧fų.

C. (ąfǫ) *Vd.* cịttā 6.

*afǫdą *m.* big, gelded (fịdīyayyē) male camel.

afǫlą̄ = afōląkī *Vd.* ahǫlą̄, ahōląkī.

Afrịl *Eng. m.* April.

af ta fārị = afat.

afu A. (afų) *m.* = afūwā.

B. (ā̧fų) *Eng. m.* (1) penny-half-penny. (2) *Vd.* kōrą 1*e*.

C. (ąfu) *Vb.* 3B is eager to *x* yā ~ cikin sāmųn sąrautą = afūwar sāmųn sąrautą ya yi he is (was) eager to get office.

afųjājaŋ *adv.* (1) fast *x* yang tąfīyą ~ he's walking fast. (2) with difficulty (*x* P. struggling to support household, etc.).

ąfumbą = ąhumbą.

afųrgugų *m.* dearth-period between gērō and dāwą harvests.

afųrgumą *f.* yang ~ he's 'devoting his full attention to it (*x* trader in many branches, big eater, P. carrying big load).

afurī *Vd.* **ahurī.**

afutū *m.* (*sg.*, *pl.*) type of mat made from **kalanga** (= na afutū).

afuwa A. (afūwā) *f.* *Ar.* (1) **yā yi minị** ~ he showed me leniency. **yā sāmi** ~ he was leniently treated. (2) **nā sāmi** ~ I am now recovered from illness.
B. (afūwā) *Vd.* **afu.**

afūwō (1) greeting ! (*said by Kano woman-visitor to women of household visited.* N.B.—*Woman greeting persons of both sexes, says* **salāmā alēkuŋ** ! *A man meeting a respectable woman whom he knows, in the street, does not greet her for she averts her face. A woman meeting a female acquaintance in the street, says* x **Kandē** *or* **Wancē,** *the reply being* **ị**) = **Alā** 3, *cf.* gāfarā 3c, **salam** nagō. (2) *m.* slacker (*for male using greeting* **afūwō** *instead of male's greeting* **salāmu alēkuŋ** *is thought slack*). (3) **daŋ** ~ *m.* (*f.* 'yar ~) *pl.* 'yaŋ ~ P. thieving from house whose occupants are out (*i.e., visitor receiving no reply to his* **ahūwō** ! 1, *concludes nobody is at home*).

Afzịŋ *f.* = **Asbịŋ.**

Afzināwā *Vd.* **Baafzinę.**

agā (1) *f.* (*a*) possessing much of x **yanā agar kudī** he has plenty of money. **sunā agar rigunā** they have many gowns. (*b*) **yā kāwō** ~ he's a swanker. (2) **Agā, ųbaŋ 'yaŋ aikị** what a fine gang-headman ! (**hēlumā**).

agadā x (1) **marǫkā suŋ hūrā minị** ~ beggars (**marǫkā** *q.v.*) blew their horns before my house. (2) **nā shā** ~ I received visit from hornblowing-beggars.

Agaddabū x ~ **tākā shibā** epithet of any woman named **Zạinabụ.**

agadǫdā = **agadụdā** *Sk.* *f.* waterskin (= salkā).

***agāgū** *m.* (1) type of yellow bead. (2) type of cloth.

agajarī = **agazarī.**

āgajē *Vd.* **āgazā.**

agaji A. (āgaji) *Vd.* **āgazā.**
B. (āgajī) *m.* help x yi minị ~ help me ! (= taịmakō).

C. (agajī) *Zar.* *m.* long matchet of South Zaria pagans.

agalamī *m.* (*pl.* **agalummā**) *Sk.* = būzū 1a.

agalanda *f.* (1) panegyric by professional beggars (*Vd.* **marǫkī**) known as 'yan ~ . (2) (at **shādị**) egging on boxer, combatant (*cf.* **gumbirị**).

agalandāyę *m.* being occupied in doing **agalandā.**

Agalāwā *Vd.* **darangamị.**

agalummā *Vd.* **agalamī.**

***agammū** *m.*, *f.* (*sg.*, *pl.*) low-browed P.

agānā *f.* (1) smallpox (= rānī 5 = mashassharā 1b *q.v.*). (2) kā mai dā ~ cīwǫ you are a fusser. (3) **agānar kashī** equine rheumatism. (4) **agānar fātā** suppurative horse-yaws. (5) **fake dā** ~ *Vd.* **hanzarī** 1d.

a gangarō *m.* (1) deserter from the enemy. (2) = banzaŋ garī 1.

aganīyā *f.* (*pl.* **aganīyōyī**) type of **tagūwā.**

agar *m.* **yā yi** ~ (1) he's full-grown and strong. (2) he has much authority.

agarā *f.* (*pl.* **agarai** = agarōrī). (1) Achilles tendon of man or beast. (2) rear knee-tendons of man or beast.

agarcē *Vb.* 3A = **agartā** *Vb.* 3B became powerful (in strength or authority).

agartaccē *m.* (*f.* **agartaccīyā**) *pl.* **agartattū** powerful in strength or authority.

agāwagi *m.* (*sg.*, *pl.*) type of purgative-seed.

***agayau-gayaụ** *m.* = riŋkyū.

āgazā *Vb.* 2 (*p.o.* **āgajē,** *n.o.* **āgaji**). (1) helped. (2) shored up (1, 2 = tāgazā).

agazarī *m.* hot period at end of rains (*its epithet is* **Agazarī, makās dawākin Sarkī**).

agēdụ *m.* (1) (*a*) narrowness. (*b*) **mai** ~ narrow. (2) **mai 'yaŋ** ~ (*adj. added to name of any native cloth woven in narrow strips for the wealthy*) x **farī mai 'yan** ~ , **sākị** m. 'y. ~ , kudī m. 'y. ~ , barāgē m. 'y. ~ , etc. (N.B.—*Usually 12 such strips are joined to make a fatalā, and 60 for woman's bodycloth* (**zanę**)), *cf.* **tayā ragō, albadā.**

Agēgę *f.* (1) *place-name.* (2) **daŋ** ~ *m.* (*pl.* 'yaŋ ~) type of Nigerian kolanut.

aggā *Yor.* *m.* leader(s) of a band of persons.

***aggaị** *m.* (1) **yā yi** ~ he set out. (2) ~

gạrēshị he's touchy. (3) tā yi ~ she left her husband's home in a huff.

agịdị (1) *f.* = kụyaŋgạ. (2) *m.* (*a*) type of blancmange made from guineacorn (*cf.* mādīdī). (*b*) *Zar. m.* = kwarạmī.

agīgị *m.* (1) any load carried by animal on one side of the body (*there being a corresponding one to balance on the other side*). (2) nā yi agīgị " I had to sweat blood ".

ạ gijị gīwā *m.* trivial P. got up to look important.

ago A. (ạgō) *m.* (*pl.* ạgwạnnī) faked gambling-cowrie (= gọ̄dọ̄gō), *cf.* tụlū 4, nịkē, laffạ 3.

    B. (agọ) *m.* (1) yā yi ~ he's strong. (2) kọ̄gī yā yi ~ river is in flood. *(3) a fish-poison made from the trees gạmạ fadạ and adūwạ.

agōfạtạ *m.* (*pl.* agọ̄fạtai) big calabash for transport of loads.

ạ gōgẹ *m.* = kimbā 1*a*, 3 (*Vd. also* kimbā 4).

agōgō = agōgō *m.* (*pl.* agọ̄gai = agōgunạ). (1) watch, clock. (2) ~ mai bugā̄wā (*a*) alarm-clock. (*b*) clock striking the hours, etc.

agọ̄lạ̈ *m.*, *f.* (*pl.* agōlōlī = agọ̄lai = agōlunạ) stepchild (*epithet is* Agọ̄lạ̈ mai wụyar ban nāmạ Stepchild, to whom the giving of meat is so thankless a task !).

agụdī *m.* (*pl.* agụdʼai) hip-joint (= ịngwallọ = *Kt.* kụtōlọ).

agudīmạ *m.* = shạ̈maki 2*a*.

agụdū = agụdī.

agūfạtā = agōfạtā.

agufi A. (agufī = agụfī) *m.* (*sg.*, *pl.*) capon(s).

    B. (agufị̈-agufị) = ạ kạ̈i ạ kạ̈i.

agụgụ *m.* plant (Malefern ?) used as remedy for tapeworm.

agụlū *Sk. f.* = ụngụlū.

agumō *m.* type of bark used as cure for fever.

agushī *m.* melon-seeds for making soup.

Agustạ *Eng. f.* month of August.

agūwạ *Sk. f.* = ayyā̄rā.

ạgwā = ịgwā.

agwadā *f.* (*pl.* agwadōjī) = rēmā.

agwagō = agōgō.

ạgwā̄gwā *f.* (*pl.* ạgwā̄gī). (1) (*a*) duck

(= kạ̈zā 6). (*b*) tọ̄raŋ ~ drake. (2) wani tsuntsū yanā̄ gudụn rūwā, ~ cikin rūwa takẹ̄ nēmā one man's meat is another's poison.

Agwai *m.* (1) the Filani (*Vd.* Bạfilācẹ). (2) Agwan rūwā Europeans. (*Vd.* Bạtūrẹ).

agwajā *f.* (*sg.*, *pl.*) launch, tender.

ạgwālā *Nor. f.* = ịgwā.

agwalē *Nor. m.* = fēlēḳē.

Agwandō *Vd.* lạkā.

ạgwạnnī *Vd.* ạgō.

Agwīdụ = Agwīdụmā *f.* *name for short girl* (*cf.* Ạfīrē).

*agyā̄gū = ạgā̄gū.

agyamā *Kt. f.* stealing a fowl by means of a bone tied to string.

ạhạ̈ = a'a 1.

ạhaf = ạp.

ạhaihẹ̄ (*said by banteringly laughing woman*) that's the stuff to give the troops !

ahạlī (1) (*Ar.* ahli people) = īyālị̈. (2) Ahạlilkịtābị *Ar.* People having a religious book (Christians, Jews, Parsis, etc.).

ạhap = ạp.

aharạs = aharạshī *m.* (*sg.*, *pl.*) brown or bay horse.

ạhayyē = ạhaihẹ̄.

ạhiŋ *Sk. m.* am bugạ wạ ɓarāwọ ~ block of wood has been attached to thief's arm to prevent his escape.

ạhir (1) shut up ! (2) stop it !

aho A. (ahọ) *Nor. m.* miscarriage.

    B. *Vd.* afo.

*ahọ̄dạ̈ *Vd.* *afọ̄dạ̈.

ahọ̄lạ̈ = ahōlạkī *m.* (*f.* ahōlạkā) *pl.* ạhọ̄lạkai foal of donkey or camel.

ahu *Vd.* afu.

ạhumbạ *Sk. f.* numerousness *x* sun yi ~ they're numerous.

ahụrī *Kt. m.* (1) = ạlfarmā. (2) fractiousness.

ạhūwō = ạfūwō.

ai A. (ai) (1) well ! (2) fancy ! (3) what ! (4) *Vd.* ai kitịfī.

    B. (ai) ~ tọ̄ oh, I see !

    C. (ā'ị) *abbreviation of* ā'ịshạtụ.

aibạtā *Vb.* 1C blamed, found fault with.

aibị = aibụ.

Aịbō mazan dawạ, ạlhērịŋkụ gyāraŋ hanyạ, kụ ci gạrī, kụ kwānā ạ hanyạ *epithet of* Eụropean.

aibu *m.* (*pl.* **aibōbī = aibe-aibē**) *Ar.*
(1) fault, blemish (= **naƙasu** = **makūsā**). (2) **masōyiŋka bā ya ganiŋ aibunka** everyone is perfect in the eyes of a person who loves him.

aika A. (**aikā**) *Vb.* 2 (*Vd.* **aiki** 2). (1) (*a*) sent *person* x (i) **nā aikē shi kasūwā** I sent him to market. **munā ~ tasu** we're sending them (*cf.* **aike da, aike, aikē**). (ii) **aŋ aiki bāwa garinsu** what a time he is in returning! (= **afalalu**). (*b*) **mai kamaz zūwa kaŋ ~** what a hard worker! (*c*) **aiki yāro inda ya sō, ka fi ganiŋ hanzarinsa** the willing horse is the best worker (*Vd.* **saurī** 1*c*). (*d*) **a aiki karē ya aiki wutsīya?** what right have you to depute work given you to do, to another? (2) (*sarcastic use of indefinite future in sense of* " doing ") x **ya saŋ haliŋ irim mutānan nāsa " sā ~ "** he knew what equivocal behaviour to expect from his folk. **" ya ~ " shaidar manyam bana** that's the sort of behaviour we expect to-day! **in dăi ɓerā nē, ya ~ halinsa nē** what else is to be expected of a rat! (*cf.* **aikata**). (3) Sk. God ordained x **iŋ Allā ya ~ ka yi haji** if God ordains that you make the pilgrimage. . . .
    B. (**aika**) *Vb.* 1A (1) (*a*) = **aikata** 1. (*b*) **amfānin sani aikāwā** *Vd.* **sani** 2*b*.vi. (2) = **aike, aike da** 3, 4.
    C. (**aika da**) = **aike da**.

aika-aika *f.* act of carelessness.
aikacayya = **aikatayya**.

aikace A. (**aikacē**) *Vb.* 1C. (1) (*a*) did completely. (*b*) finished work on T. (*cf.* **aikata, aikatā**). (2) **ya aikace abincī** he devoured the food. (3) **tā ~ ni** she bewitched me (= **sāmā** 1*a*.iii). (4) **nā ~ ta** I had sexual relations with her (= **cī** 16*a*).
    B. (**aikacē**) *Vd.* **aikata**.

aikace-aikacē *m.* various tasks (*d.f.* **aikatā**).
aikaci *Vd.* **aikata**.
aikakkēnīyā *f.* = **aikayya**.

aikata A. (**aikatā**) *Vb.* 1C (*cf.* **aiki** 1*b*).
(1) did, acted x **yā ~ haka = yā aikata haka** (Mod. Gram. 88*a*³) he acted thus. **yā ~ mini alhēri** he treated me kindly, liberally. **yā aikata sharri**

he did evil (*cf.* **aikā** 2). (2) worked at, on x **nā aikata rīgā** I worked on sewing of the gown (*cf.* **aikata, aikacē**). (3) *Vd.* **ƙyēya** 2.
    B. (**aikata**) *Vb.* 2 (*p.o.* **aikacē**, *n.o.* **aikaci**) partially finished work on T. x **nā aikaci rīgā** (*cf.* **aikatā, aikacē**).

aikatau (1) *m.* working for wages x **mun zō ~** we've come to get a job with you (*cf.* **niƙau, ƙōdagō**). (2) *m., f.* worker for wages.

aikatayya *f.* mutual work.

aikayya *f.* (*cf.* **aikā**) mutually sending messages x **shēkara uku ba mu gāna ba săi ~** for 3 years we've sent messages, not met.

aike A. (**aikē**) *m.* (*cf.* **aikā**) x **nā yi masa ~** I sent P. to him specially, with message (*cf.* **sautu, sāƙō, sallahu, aike**). **kulluŋ yanā ~ gunsu** he's always sending P. expressly to them with messages.
    B. (**aike**) *Vb.* 1A x **nā aike wurinsa** I sent P. expressly to give him a message (*cf.* **aikē**). **nā ~ masa** (= **nā ~ masa wai**) **bā nā zūwa** I sent telling him I'd not be coming. **yā aikō " gā ni naŋ tafe ! "** he sent a message to say he was already on his way. **nā ~ Kano = nā ~ wa Kano** I sent a message to Kano (*cf.* **aike da** 1 3rd example).

aike da *Vb.* 1A (1) sent *thing* (*cf.* **aikā**) x **nā ~ kājī wurinsa** I sent him chickens. **munā aikēwā da takarda gunsa** we're sending him a letter. **yā aike musu da cēwā yanā zūwa** he sent them a message that he was coming (*cf.* **aike**). **kāyan da akē aikēwā** the goods which are being sent. (2) sent P. in another's custody (*cf.* **aikā**) **Sarkī yā ~ shī tāre da dōgari** the chief sent him in the charge of an N.A. policeman. (3) sent one's junior officially (*cf.* **aikā**) x **sun ~ sōja** they ordered soldiers to go there. (4) sent as one's representative (*cf.* **aikā**) x **suŋ ~ waƙīlinsu zūwa Masar** they sent their envoy to Egypt.

ai'ke-aikē *m.* = **aikace-aikacē**.
aikēkēnīyā *f.* = **aikayya**.

aiki *m.* (*pl.* **ayyuka** = *Sk.* **ayyukka**).
(1) (*a*) deed, act (*cf.* **aikatā**) x (i) **Jāmus nē da wannaŋ ~** the Germans were the

perpetrators of this deed. **yā yi fushī sabo dạ wannạŋ** ~ he was angry at this act. **sun sā̧mi aikįn yį** they've found work "to do. (ii) **yanā̧ aikįm banzā** he's acting disgracefully. (iii) **aikįm banzā, mạkā̧fo dạ wạịwayạ** *epithet of* **banzā**. (*b*) work *x* (i) **yā yi** ~ he worked. **yanā̧** ~ he's at work. (ii) **yā fịta** ~ he has given up his job, he has been dismissed. (iii) **yā ci** ~ he worked hard. (iv) **yā jā** ~ sạnnū-sạnnū he worked at a snail's pace. (v) **gidaŋ aikį** *m*. (*pl*. **gidā̧jaŋ** ~) factory. **birā̧naŋ ayyukạ** industrial towns. (vi) *Vd*. **barkạ** 1*b*. (vii) **yanā̧ aikįn rịgā** he's working on the gown (= **ɗiŋkị** 3). (viii) **aikįn sụrụkai** *Vd*. **jirƙō**. (ix) **tsō̧fạffiŋ kudī nȩ̄, bā sā̧** ~ they are old coins out of circulation. (x) **māgạniŋ** ~ **yį** well begun is half done. (xi) **yi ta** ~ set to work ! (xii) **ạbōkiŋ** ~ fellow-worker, classmate, colleague. (xiii) **injį bā yā̧** ~ the machine is out of order. (xiv) **yā ajịyẹ** ~ he resigned from his job, office. (xv) **yinị yā įsa** ~ *Vd*. **sạmmakō** 1*c*. (xvi) **shī nȩ̄ aikį** *Vd*. **ạ** 1*b*. (xvii) **hạnạ aikį** *Vd*. **mụsayyạ, mạrkā** 2*a*.ii. (xviii) **ụban 'yaŋ** ~ *Vd*. **agā** 2. (xix) **kā fi aikįm mālạmī** *Vd*. **mālạmī** 1*c*.iv ; **gaịkau** ; **gwạụrau**. (xx) **aikįm bā̧baŋ gīwā** *Vd*. **bā̧ba** 3. (xxi) **hạkīkạr** ~ *Vd*. **baŋ gạskīyā**. (xxii) **gandụŋ** ~ *Vd*. **bāwạ** 10. (xxiii) **ɓarnar** ~ *Vd*. **fāsạ** 1*e*. (xxiv) **ƙā̧rẹ** ~ *Vd*. **gạrmā** 1*a*.ii. (*c*) **yi** ~ **dạ** made use of *x* **tambayōyįn dạ zā ạ yi** ~ **dạ sū** the form of questions to be employed. **bạ sụ yi** ~ **dạ shāwạrwarịn nam ba** they did not act on that advice. (*d*) effect *x* **yạudarạd dạ Jāmụs sukạ yi musụ tā yi** ~ **wandạ dukạn lallāshimmụ har ạbạdā bạ zaị īyạ ba** the deceitfulness of the Germans to them has had an effect which our persuasiveness could never have had. **dạbārạ tasụ, săi** ~ **takȩ̄ yį sō̧săi** their plan is most successful. (*e*) **suŋ kāmạ** ~ (i) they've set to work. (ii) they've begun quarrelling. (*f*) **am bā̧ agōgō** ~ the clock (watch) has been wound up. (*g*) **sāmụnsạ** ~ **nȩ̄** it's difficult to get it. **lallȩ̄, aikįn naŋ**

yā yi ~ this is truly, a tough job. (*h*) magic *x* **an yi masạ** ~ (i) he's been taught the use of charms (**sammụ**). (ii) he's been given medicine at hospital. **wannạŋ cīwọ** ~ **nē** this illness is due to magic. ~ **akạ yi musụ, bạ ạ banzā sukạ zō ba** they came from *sorcery*, not voluntarily. (2) (*Sec. .v.n. of* **ạikā**) *x* **yanā̧ aikįnsạ** = **yanā̧ ạikā tasạ** he is sending him.

ai kitịfī = **kitịfī**.

aikō *Vd*. **aikẹ**.

aikō dạ *Vd*. **aikẹ dạ**.

aimakạ *f*. small harmless centipede.

ạimē *m*. **nā yi masạ** ~ I looked carefully after it.

ainī (1) = **ainihī**. (2) *Vd*. **farlụ**.

ainihī (*Ar*. itself). (1) *m*. realness *x* **aihinim mạganạ** the real facts of the case. **ainihim mutā̧naŋ ƙasạr** the real inhabitants of the land. **ainihiŋ įndạ sukȩ̄** exactly where they are. (2) **na** ~ (*f*. **ta** ~) *pl*. **na** ~ real, fine *x* **maƙȩ̄rī nȩ̄ na** ~ he is a fine smith. **yārinyạ cē ta** ~ she's a splendid girl (*cf*. **ainụ**).

ainịŋ = **ainụ**.

*aini**yā** *Ar*. *f*. lower grinding-stone with upper stone on it.

ainụ (*Ar*. eye, self) *adv*. (1) thoroughly *x* **yā īyạ Hausā** ~ he knows Hausa really well. **sunā̧ aikị** ~ they're working hard. (2) very much *x* **yā fi sauƙiŋ kudī** ~ it's very much cheaper. (3) (*negatively*) not at all *x* **baị san shị** ~ **ba** he doesn't know anything about it (*cf*. **ainihī**).

ainụŋ = **ainụ**.

ā'ishā = **a'ịshatụ** *woman's name* Ayesha (*Vd*. **Shatụ**, **ā'ị**, **dāki** 9).

ai tō *Vd*. **ai**.

aiy- *Vd*. **ayy-**.

ajab *m*. = **ajạbạ** *f*. *Vd*. **ạl'ajạbī** *in same sense*.

ạjabaŋ *Ar*. how wonderful !

ajabō *m*. (1) a scalp-disease of women due to wearing dōkạ-pad or overtight piaiting. (2) **yā yō** ~ **ạ kạnsạ** he brought trouble on himself.

ajagalgalī (1) what a muddy place ! *(2) *m*. donkey with long mane and tail.

ajala A. (**Ajạlạ**) *x* ~ **rā̧gwaŋ arnā** Emir's messenger, thou prey for pagans !

B. (ajala) *Nor. f.* trouble *x* nā shā ~ I suffered trouble.

ajalī *Ar. m.* (*pl.* ajula = *Sk.* ajulla).
(1) period allowed *x* (*a*) an yi mini ~ I've received definite time to pay the debt, etc. (= ikaya 2). mun yi ~ da shī kaŋ aiki we've laid down the time wherein he must complete the task. (*b*) aŋ kāra masa ~ he's been granted an extension of the time-limit (= daga 1*d* = wakafī 2 = ōda 3). (2) the allotted span of life *x* (*a*) ajalinsa yā kāre his life is over. (*b*) ɓaunā cẹ ajalinsa he met his fate from a bush-cow. (*c*) ajalinsa yā yi kira he was fated to die far from home (= kasā 1*f*). (*d*) *Vd.* dade 4*a*.ii. (*e*) iŋ kā ga aŋ kāma zōmō yanā gudu, ajalinsa yā zō everybody has his allotted span of life. (3) credit *x* nā saya kaŋ ~ I bought on credit (= lāmunī 1*b*, cf. lakadaŋ). (4) ajalim mai dākī *Vd.* rāgaya 3.

ajaltā *Vb.* 1C fixed time-limit (ajalī *q.v.*) for *x* aŋ ~ mini kwānā uku I've received 3 days' grace to complete it, etc.

ajamī (*Ar.* " Persian, foreign ") *m.* written matter in any script provided the language is nor Arabic.

ajaŋabai *Vd.* baajanabe.

ajaŋakū *m.* type of velvet.

Ajauru *x* ~ attakabāru Kolanut, thou eminent one !

aje A. (aje) *Vb.* 1A = ajīyē.
B. (ajē) *Sk. m.* ambush, ambushing.

aje bīcinka *f.* an early-ripening type of guineacorn.

A jēfas *name given* daŋ wābi *q.v.* (boy) or 'yar wābi (girl) (*lit.* " let it be thrown away ! " *i.e. to avert evil eye*) = Kyauta, *cf.* A bar shi, A mantā, Mantai, Mantau, Audī, A jūjī, Abaicī, Akwarē 2, amfāna 4, baiwā 2, darē 4*k*, Bartō, daŋgana 2*c*, Gwārī 2*c*, Wā ka sō.

ajī *m.* (*sg., pl.*) (1) school-class. (2) heap. (3) loading up a pack-animal *x* zō ka taya ni ~ come and help me load the animal ! (4) *Sk.* times *x* ~ uku three times (= sau). (5) *Kt.* Sarkī yā yi masa ~ the Emir imposed a task on him (*x* on District-head).

ajijjiɓā = alilliɓā.

---

ajijjiyē *Vb.* 1D *intens. from* ajiyē.

ajīlō *m.* (*sg., pl.*) iron-band at end of spearshaft.

ajiŋgi *m.* head of the local ɓōrī and usually followed by many women and a pimp (*his epithet is* Jiŋgim = ~ babam ɓōrī) = kaurā 3 = ubam mutānē = uban saidu.

ajiŋgirī *m.* = gantamau 1.

ajirwā *Sk. f.* = ajīwā.

ajīwā *Sk. f.* (1) carrying a small load on a larger. (2) carrying vessel of water on head and another on one's palm.

ajīya *f.* (1) (*sec. v.n. of* ajīyē) *x* yanā ~ tasa = yanā ajīyē shi he's putting it' down. dākin ajīyar abincī larder.
(2) T. deposited *x* (*a*) yā bā ni ~ he deposited money, etc., with me. (*b*) dākin ~ store. (*c*) (i) ba ka saŋ ajīyad da Allā ya yi masa ba don't judge him too hastily ! (ii) ajīyar Allā *Vd.* ɓōyōtō. (*d*) takardar ~ savings-certificate. (*e*) bā ā ba kūrā ajīyar nāma one does not set a wolf to guard a lamb. (*f*) ajīya māganiŋ wata rānā put a bit by for a rainy day !
(3) A. put down, put away, hidden.
(4) Treasurer = ma'aji (*his epithet is* Kawāta).
(5) yā saka ~ he has leucoma.
(6) (*a*) an yi masa ~ he has bone-necrosis ascribed to spirits putting bone-fragment in his ulcer (= nāma 1*d* = kashī 6). (*b*) da ~ a dākinsa an evil-charm (sammu) is said to be buried in his home (= biso 2 = binnē 3 (*cf.* 8*a*)).
(7) *Vd.* ajīyē 13.
(8) *Kt.* yanā da ~ (*a*) he has magic powers (*cf.* 6 *above;* rauhānai). (*b*) he has swollen testicles (= kāyā 4*a*).

ajiye A. (ajīyē) *Sk. m.* = ajē.
B. (ajīyē) *Vb.* 1C (*Vd.* ajīya 1). (1) (*a*) put *x* ka ~ shi naŋ put it here ! (= sa shi naŋ, *Vd.* sa D. ; mai da 6). (*b*) stationed *x* suŋ ajīye sōja 'yan gādi they stationed soldiers as police. (2) put down *x* yā ajīye kāyā he (carrier) put down his load (= yā sa kāyā, *Vd.* sa E). (3) (*with dative*) nā ~ masa abincī I set food before him. (4) (*a*) put *thing* on *x* nā ~ shi a tēɓur I put it on

the table (= nā ɗōrạ shi, *etc.* = nā aza shi, *etc.* = nā sạ̈ shi, *etc.*), *Vd.* sạ̈ C.2. (*b*) *But* put *person* on donkey, etc., is ɗōrạ = azạ, *not* ajīyē, *cf.* gwāmạ. (5) (*a*) (i) set aside as surplus, saved (money, etc.), set apart (food, etc.) for later use *x* ạ bankị yanạ̈ dạ fạm 500 ạ ajīye he has £500 in the bank = ɓōyę 1*d*, (*Vd.* dunkụlā 2). (ii) kōwā ya ∼, yā ɗaukạ lay something by for a rainy day ! (iii) bạ sụ ajīyę kōmē ba sǎi amajā they showed nothing but slackness. (iv) *Vd.* girkę 1. (*b*) allotted *x* lōkacịn dạ akạ ∼ don kạrạtū the period allotted to study. kōwā ya ajīyę ɗākị don kạrụwai anyone who reserves a room for whores . . . (6) suspended (an official), *cf.* 14 *below.* (7) (*a*) put thing or things in receptacle *x* nā ∼ shi cikin ạkwātị I put it away in the box (*cf.* zubạ 2, sạ̈ A.). (*b*) kept *x* (i) yā ajīyę mōtạ (ɗōkị, kạrē, *etc.*) he kept a motorcar, horse, dog, *etc.* (*for animals* = kīwǫ). bā sạ̈ ajīyę sōjạ they maintain no standing army. (ii) ajīyę kạrankạ don kạran gidan wani meet a person with his own weapons ! (*c*) reserved *x* sun ajīyę Yạrīmạ ; wannạn sạrautạ cē ta 'yā'yan Sarkī the post of Yarima is not open to all, but is reserved for chiefs' sons. (8) deposited *x* (*a*) nā ajīyę fạm ukụ gạrēshị I deposited £3 with him. (*b*) anạ̈ ∼ masạ fạm ukụ kōwạnę watạ £3 are placed to his credit monthly. (9) accepted as deposit *x* bā nạ̈ ajīyę kuɗin kōwā I accept no deposits. (10) postponed continuance of remaining work *x* mụ ajīyę aikị sǎi gōbe let us postpone the rest of our work till to-morrow ! (= hūtạ 2), *cf.* fāsạ. yā rōƙi Allạ̈, akạ ∼ he besought God, but no favourable reply was forthcoming. (11) kept P. waiting. (12) yā ajīyę ɓarāwǫ he harboured a thief. (13) yā ajīyę zūcīyā he sighed. ạjīyạr zūcīyā *f.* sighing, a sigh (*cf.* sạ̈ B.12). (14) (*a*) yā ajīyę sạrautạ he resigned office (*cf.* 6) = yā ajīyę rawạnī. (*b*) yā ajīyę wạ Sarki rawạnī he submitted his resignation to the chief. (*c*) yā ajīyę aikị he resigned from his post. (15) *Sk., Kt.*

kāzā tā ajīyę ƙwǎi the hen's about to lay (= ɗaukạ *q.v. under* ƙwǎi 1*a*). ạjīzạ *Ar. f.* (*pl.* ạjīzai) = ạjūzā. ājīzī *m.* (*f.* ājīzā) *pl.* ạjīzai mortal, not divine. Ạ jūjī = Ạ jēfas. ajulạ *Vd.* ajạlī. ạjūzā *f.* (*pl.* ạjūzai) *Ar.* crone (*cf.* ạzūjī) (*epithet is* ∼ kạryar dangị). ajūzancị *m.* (1) woman's being advanced in age. (2) trickery. (3) scandalmongering. ạjūzī = ạzūjī. aka A. (akạ) (1) (*impersonal prefix for relative past*, Gram., 133*) *x* ∼ zō then people came. (2) (*sometimes replaces* sukạ) *x* jạma'ạ akạ ɗaukı hạyānīyạ then the people shouted. B. (akạ̈) *Vd.* Mod. Gram. 140*c*. ạkạbar = akbar. ạkạbisạ *Sk. f.* stalks for screening bride's bed. akacau = akayau. a kǎi, ạ kǎi *adv.* continually *x* yanạ̈ zūwạ ∼ he keeps on coming (= ạgufị *q.v.*). ạ kai cikī *m.* beard turning in towards neck (*cf.* ạ bā mụ). akaifā *f.* (*pl.* ạkaifū). (1) claw, talon, fingernail (*cf.* farcę). (2) dermatoid cyst under horse's eyelid (= farcę 1*c*). (3) yanạ̈ gasạ ∼ he's eating tūwō (= farcę 1*d*). (4) *Vd.* ɓarin ∼ . akala A. (akạlā) *f.* (*sg., pl.*) leading-rope of camel. B. (ạkala) (1) *used in* ∼ mụ ga tsawam bāyankạ be off ! (*Vd.* kalạ). *(2) *f.* (*a*) = akụshī. (*b*) cattle-trough. akạlī *x* ɗan ∼ *Sk. m.* an official title. ạ̈kạllạ (*Ar.* least) (1) *m.* but few *x* ạ cikim mutānē ∼ nē wạndạ zai yī but few would attempt it. (2) at least *x* ∼ mạ̈ gamạ warkạ 2 we'll complete at least 2 pages. (3) *conj.* it is at least that *x* ∼ yạ bā sạbạ'im bāyā he must be at least 70 years of age. ạ kạn *Vd.* kạn. ạkanda *m.* type of children's game. *akanna = ạkannę = ạkandạ *q.v.* akanzạ *f.* tattooing below the temples. ạkạrạ̈ *Yor. m.* (*sg., pl.*) (1) beanflour-cake. (2) European biscuit. (3) ∼ kōƙī type of European cloth.

akarambānạ = karambānạ.

akarārā m.,f. (sg.,pl.) dark-brown horse or donkey.

akarạs m. an yi masạ ∼ (a) sword (or matchet) has been scraped with curved tool to sharpen it (cf. kōdạ). (b) P. has been reinstated. (b) he's been praised by his superior (cf. kōdạ 2).

akạrdā m. a food of uncooked flour with ramạ-leaves and water (= rūmācē = rambọ 1).

akạsā m. type of European cloth.

akạsī m. (1) = nạƙasụ. *(2) (Ar. reflection in water) antithesis x (a) ƙarī akạsim baƙī nē white is the reverse of black. (b) ạbin dạ mukē sọ ∼ nē gạ na Jāmụs what we want is the reverse of what the Germans wish. (c) ạbin yā zō dạ ∼ things turned out the reverse of what was expected.

akaskạs Nor. m. (sg., pl.) small datefruit.

*akạstā Ar. (1) Vb. 1C inverted (x said RAGO for GORA), cf. akạsī 2. (2) Vb. 3A (a) acted contrary to duty, etiquette, etc. (b) became completely changed.

akạtā f. (pl. akạtai) Zar. = malạfā.

*akatạs m. jāƙī yā yi ∼ load has galled donkey's shoulder.

Akạtūbạr Eng. m. October.

akawạl = akawạlī m. (f. akawạlā) pl. akạwạlai black horse (= ciccirọ = Kt. kīyārạ).

akāwū m. (pl. akāwunạ = akāwū-akāwū = Sk. akāwunnị). (1) clerk. (2) ∼ gā nākạ = akāwū gā shi m. type of coiffure (cf. gā nākạ).

ạ ƙawwạmā shi Kt. let it be shared out !

akayau m. (sg., pl.) jingling anklet of dancer (= ƙọrọsō q.v.).

akạzā m. (sg., pl.) cream-coloured donkey.

akazaudā f. (1) Sk. (a) irịŋ ∼ nē they're Filani. (b) sun yi ∼ the Filani have migrated. (2) Zar. type of Filani drumming.

akbar Ar., used in Allāhụ ∼ (1) God is the Greatest ! (prayer-formula) cf. kabarạ. (2) good heavens ! (3) how sad !

akē (used for impersonal in present relative with positive sense, Gram. 133*) x lōkạcin dạ ∼ zūwạ when one comes. yạushē ∼ yị when is it done ? (cf. kē 1).

*aƙibạ Ar. f. good result x (1) Allā yạ bā dạ kyạkkyāwar ∼ God prosper the venture ! (2) bā shi dạ ∼ it doesn't look hopeful.

aƙīƙạ = haƙīƙạ.

akkạrā ƙọfī = ạkạrā 3.

*akkạsā = *akạstā.

*akkirō m. = akụshī 1.

akōgārū = akūgwạrū.

akọkari m. (sg., pl.) type of tree prevalent south of the Benue. (2) yā bugạ ∼ he carried out a type of divination.

ạkōkīyā = ạkọtīyā.

ạkōkō m. grey baft = maltị (its epithet is namūzụ, bā sayanịạ akē ba).

ạ kọri kadạ m. a children's water-game.

ạkọtīyā f. (sg., pl.) short blunderbuss.

ạkū m., f. (sg., pl.) parrot (epithet is Akū kuturū = Akū bā kyā rufị).

akūbạ = ụkūbạ.

ạkụbar = ạkbar.

ạ kufị, ạ kufị = ạ kǎi, ạ kǎi.

akūgwạrū m. check-matting cloth.

ạkul (1) stop it ! (2) (followed by relative forms (Gram. 133a*) when positive verb follows) I warn you that if you ... x (a) ∼ kukạ tabạ, kwā ƙōnẹ I warn you that if you touch it you'll get burnt ! mum fargā kul Jāmụs sukạ ci wannạŋ yāƙị, mū kụwā mun lālạcē we realize only too clearly that we are done for if the Germans win this war. (b) ∼ ka cī nị, kā mutụ don't eat me lest you die ! (this is epithet of old cassava, considered poisonous, hence: (c) ạkul m. = gạntạmau). (3) (followed by negative verb) x ∼ bạ kạ barị ba ... I warn you that if you don't cease ..., then ... (4) Vd. kul.

akumārī m. (pl. ạkụmārai) pad for pack-animal (Vd. lafērū, manadạrī).

akụrī m. a food of kurnạ and magaryā berries.

akurkī m. (pl. ạkụrkai) (1) fowl-pen. (2) ƙwāi ạ bakạ yā fi kāzā ạ ∼ a bird in the hand is worth two in the bush. (3) im mūgụwar kāzā tā shigạ ∼, kōwạcce ta zō, sǎi tạ sārē tạ no kīshīyā is welcomed by the others. (4) akurkin dundū, wāwā kā sakạ hannū don't put your head in a noose !

akurū (1) *used in* **Na** ⁓ a Gwari
(= **Bagwārī**). (2) **Na** ⁓ **kaŋka a dame**
epithet of any Gwari.

akushī *m.* (*pl.* **akusa**) (1) (*a*) wooden food-
bowl (= **bakī dan danyā** = **bukurū** 2).
(*b*) **kwaryā ta bi kwaryā, in tā bi** ⁓,
tā wātse let everyone act according to
his abilities and not aim too high !
(2) **akushiŋ Allā** (*a*) market.   (*b*)
weighing-scales. (3) *Vd.* **babba bọkọkọ**
under **babba** 5*a.*

*akutī *m.* (*sg., pl.*) small, lidless box.

*akūya = akwīya.

*akwā *Zar. f.* (1) ladder (= **tsāni** 1).
(2) = **gōje** 1.

akwai (1) (*a*) there is, are, was, were
x ⁓ **kudī** there is some money (= **da**
13). ⁓ **shī** it is to be had (*Vd.* **wanda**
2*a*, **wani** 5*a*). (*b*) **akwai = da akwai**
yes there is some (*reply to* is there
any ?), Gram. 21. (2) **mai** ⁓ *m., f.* (*pl.*
māsū ⁓) prosperous P. (3) *Vd.* **kọkwai.**

*akwākū *m.* (*sg., pl.*) shop-counter.

akwalā *f.* (*sg., pl.*) charm to prevent
opponent's gun firing.

akwārā *f.* (*sg., pl.*) (1) repeating-rifle.
(2) repeating-pistol.

akwarā waje *f.* = **mēdī.**

Akwarē (1) *name of a notorious Zaria
thief.* (2) *m., f.* = **A jēfas.**

akwashā = *Sk.* **akwasā** *f.* (*sg., pl.*) pointed
rod used in weaving.

akwashī = akushī.

a kwata *f.* type of gambling (*cf.* **kwata** 2).

akwāti *m.* (*pl.* **akwātuna** = **akwātai** =
akwātuttuka = **akwātōcī**) box (*cf.*
gidā 2).

akwatō *m.* (1) small calabash used as
soap-dish. (2) (*a*) type of embroidery.
(*b*) *Vd.* **gindiŋ** ⁓ . (3) **mai** ⁓ *m.* type of
zayyana.

akwātu = akwāti.

akwīya *f.* (*pl.* **awākī = awākai =
awākuna = akwīyōyī**). (1) (*a*) she-
goat (*cf.* **bunsurū**). (*b*) **daŋ** ⁓ **nē**
(*vulgar*) " he's a regular ram ". (*c*)
**wannaŋ lābāri yā sa akwīyar cikiŋka
tā yi kūkā** this news terrified you.
(*d*) **inā** ⁓ **zā ta da kāyan tāki** don't
attempt the impossible ! (*e*) ⁓ **tā
mutu, tā bara fāta wuyā** P. has been
left in the lurch. (*f*) **in zā ka daure**

akwīyarka, ka daure ta a magaryā
when you speak, speak the truth !
(*g*) **mai** ⁓ **yā bi darē ballē mai kūrā** ? if
a rich man feels apprehension, how
much more a poor man ?   (*h*) ⁓ **a
daure in tā sāmi saki, bābu zamā** put a
beggar on horseback and he'll ride to
the devil.   (*j*) **karambāniŋ** ⁓ **gai da
kūrā** it's attempting the impossible.
(*k*) ⁓ **tā ji wukā** " he's been touched in
a tender spot ".   (*l*) **tākwaŋ** ⁓
(*vulgarly*) = **farji.**   (*m*) **bā a bā kūrā
jiraŋ akwīya = kūrā** 36. (*n*) **da ganiŋ
kūrā, an san tā ci** ⁓ appearance is an
index to character. (*o*) **da kūkaŋ
kūrā da bacēwar** ⁓ **duka daya nē** they
are cause and effect. (*p*) **an yi mana
" taya, Kūrā, mu ci** ⁓ ! " an attempt
was made to trick us. (*q*) **da dāmā nē,
gudu da awākī** act in good time !
(*r*) **rānar kāyā,** ⁓ **bā bisā ba ce** don't
attempt the impossible ! (*s*) **ana raba
ka da kīwaŋ awākī, kanā fadi kyalla tā
haifu** don't keep on talking about a P.
whom nobody wants to hear about !
(*t*) **kōwā da kīwaŋ da ya karbe shi,
makwabciŋ** ⁓ **yā sayi kūrā** everyone
for himself ! (*u*) **tātsattsīyar akwīya** *Vd.*
tātsā 1*d.*   (*v*) **kọshiŋ akwīya** *Vd.*
barēwā 1*b.*   (*w*) **daŋ akwīyana** *Vd.*
dāmushērē. (*x*) **kuntar** ⁓ *Vd.* **janyayyē.**

(2) *Zar.* (*a*) sheep.   (*b*) headstrong
girl.

(3) type of yellow guineacorn.

(4) **kan** ⁓ *m.* = **kwantai** 1.

(5) **wutsīyar** ⁓ *f.* blabber.

(6) **kāshiŋ awākī** *Vd.* **samna** ; **kāshiŋ
awākī.**

akwīyanci *m.* headstrongness of girls
(*cf.* **akwīya** 2*b*).

akyamanī *m.* flesh round animal's ribs.

akyarā *Zar. f.* plant giving bad tobacco,
but good **furē** 1*a.*ii.

ala A. (**ālā**) *f.* (1) (*a*) **tā yi** ⁓ she tittivated
herself (including lip-staining with kola,
etc.). (*b*) *Vd.* **dauri** 5*b.* (2) **yā yi** ⁓
= **salēba** 1.

B. (**Alā**) (*used in following for* **Allā**).
(1) ⁓ **kai mu gọbe = Alā kai mu**
God spare us till to-morrow ! (2) ⁓ **shī
maka albarka** God bless you ! (3) ⁓ **bā
mu = afuwō** 1.   (4) (*a*) ⁓ **cīshē mu**

sorry, I've nothing to give you to-day, beggar ! (= ci gạba). (b) Vd. cī dạ 1a.ii, 3 ; hạ̧kurī 4. (5) ~ gammanạ m. (a) wrinkles from old age. (b) au revoir ! ((b) = Alạ̄ gamma mụ.) (c) yā zamā ~ gammanạ he's a bad payer. (6) mun yi ~ ịshē mụ = mun yi ~ maimạitā manạ we've tasted the new season's crop. (7) (a) ~ kōrō = Alạ̄ kōrō rībạ give me a bit of the food you're carrying, please ! (if she gives, she does so, saying gạ̄ shi ! If she refuses, she says ~ ạ̄miŋ or iŋ aŋ kōrō kạ, kạ zō gidammụ) = ɗanɗanō. (b) tā bā nị ~ kōrō = nā kạrɓi ~ kōrō she gave me some food as in 7a (receiver says Allạ̄ yạ bā dạ kạ̧sūwā !). (8) ~ rụfi ạsīrimmụ greeting used by old women. (Vd. rufạ 1d). (9) cf. Alạ bạ̧i, Alạbạshī, Alạsūwāmụ. (10) (a) ~ tsīnẹ m. the treadle-peg called kai ka zō q.v. (b) Vd. tsīnẹ 2. (11) ~ sēnị long life to you ! (= rạŋkạ yạ daɗẹ). (12) Alạ̄ sabbinanị Vd. sabbinanị. (13) Alạ̄ yạ fisshē kạ farị Vd. yabanyạ.

alạ'andị Vd. ɓataŋ ~ .

alabai A. (alabại) = alabẹ.

B. (Alạ bạ̧i) name for slave or slave-girl (cf. Alạ̄, Alạbạshī).

Alạ̄ bā mụ Vd. Alạ̄ 3.

Alạbạshī (lit. God give it ! cf. Alạ bạ̧i) ~ kạ bā nī please give it to me !

alabẹ m. (sg., pl.) double leather-purse (= ƙumārọ 2).

Alạ̄ cīshē mụ Vd. Alạ̄ 4.

ạl'ādạ f. (pl. ạl'ādū = ạl'ạ̄dai = al'ādōdī) Ar. (1) (a) custom. (b) na ~ m. (f. ta ~) pl. na ~ customary x bịkiŋ ~ the usual marriage-feast. (2) (a) tanạ̄ ạl'ādạr mātā she is undergoing her menstruation. (= haila). (b) Vd. kasaŋkī 2. (3) medicine x anạ̄ ~ dạ shī it's used as medicine. yā īyạ ~ he knows the use of drugs. yanạ̄ dạ ạl'ādạr cīwaŋ kạ̧i he has headache-cures.

aladẹ m. (pl. alạdai) pig, boar (cf. gạdū).

alạ̄fā f. thrush-disease of horses.

alạ̄fāfarā f. = alạ̄fāfarō m. = affạfai 2, q.v.

Alạ̄ gamma mụ au revoir ! (cf Alạ̄ 5b).

Alạ̄ gamma nạ Vd. Alạ̄ 5.

alagidigō m. beads, cowries, etc., round

women's hips (now replaced by jịgịdā) (= guŋgunturī = Sk. kwatanā).

alagullē m. type of patterned white calico.

alạgwaidạ x ~ mại nāmạŋ ƙyẹ̄yạ derisory epithet of Gwari.

alạgwaidọ = alạgwaidạ.

alagwạmī m. (1) = lagwạnī. (2) = alabẹ. (3) = ƙwạ̄rō 5b.

Alại Vd. ạlbarkạ 1.

ạlaikạ = ạlēkạ.

Alạ̄ ịshē mụ Vd. Alạ̄ 6.

ạl'ajạbī = ạl'ajịbī = al'ajạfī m.' (pl. ạl'ạjạbai = al'ajubạ) Ar. (1) (a) surprise. (b) yā yi ~ he was surprised. yā yi ạl'ạjạbinsạ it surprised him. (2) ạbiŋ ~ anything wonderful, strange.

al'ạjē Vb. 1C Sk. intens. from ajẹ.

alakạ Vd. tūwaŋ alakạ.

ạlạ̧ƙaƙại Vd. ạlƙaƙại.

ạl'akạrī m. (1) material (usually scarlet) for ạlkyabbạ (if not scarlet, we mention the colour as adj. x fariŋ ~ white burnous fabric). (2) = mulụfi 2.

alakạs Nor. m. (sg., pl.) large date.

alakō Vd. ta alakō.

Alạ̄ kōrō Vd. Alạ̄ 7.

alakwạyī m. (sg., pl.). (1) reins. (2) tassel on reins (epithet is bạ̄ ki gạskīyā = bạ̄ ki maganạ = bạ̄ ki mutuncị).

alala A. (ạlạlā) m. type of bean-food.

B. (ạlạlā). (1) nā tạfi wurinsạ, ya cẹ̄ ~ I went to him, but he made a fuss and refused. (2) ~ , bạn yi ba I swear I didn't do it (= lā lā q.v.).

al'ala A. (ạl'alạ) Vb. 2 pestered x ~ gạrēshị he makes a nuisance of himself.

B. (ạl'ạlā) f. pestering x ~ gạrēshị he makes a nuisance of himself.

alale A. (ạlālẹ) m. the tree called Akee apple (Blighia sapida), Vd. Gwạnjā 3.

B. (ạlạlē) m. = ạlạlā.

*alalimbọ Nor. m. a children's game.

*alallạfā Sk. f. martingale (= malallạfī).

alallạmī m. (pl. ạlạllạmai). (1) plant used as substitute for henna. (2) ~ dạ kạmar lallẹ, bạ zā kạ kōmạ lallẹ ba epithet of any pretence or makeshift. (3) re-using henna on body (cf. bạzawạrā 2).

ạlāmạ = hạlāmạ.

*ạlāmāfī m. blemish, fault.

Alạ̄ maimạitā Vd. Alạ̄ 6.

ạl'amạrī *m.* (*pl.* al'amurạ = *Sk.* al'a-murrạ) *Ar.* (1) (*a*) affair. (*b*) ạl'amạrin dūnīyạ *Vd.* sạnnū 2*b*.ii. (2) wụyar ~ gạrēshị he's hard to get on with.

*ạlambakē *m.* type of game.

alạmmusurụ = alạmusurụ.

alamta A. (ạlamtạ) *Vb.* 3B is marked *x* Kanọ tā ~ ạ tạswīrạ Kano is marked on the map.
    B. (alạmtā) *Vb.* 1C. (1) put mark on T. (2) showed a sign *x* bạ mụ ~ mung kạrai bạ we gave no sign that we were exhausted.

ạl'ạmūdị *m.* (*pl.* ạl'ạmūdai) *Ar.* pillar (= dōgarị 3 = ginshịkị 1*a*), *cf.* cībịyā 3*c*.

al'amurạ *Vd.* ạl'amạrī.

alạmusurụ (*Ar.* anā 'ālimus sirri am I aware of the unknown ?) *x* ~ nē nị ? am I omniscient ? (= lummạkaifạ 2).

alạndayạ *f.* groundnuts after pounding and extraction of oil.

alạŋkọ̄sạ̄ *m.*, *f.* (*sg.*, *pl.*) idler (*epithet is* ~ gạ̄ kwăi).

*ạlạŋkwạ̄ *f.* (*sg.*, *pl.*) brick (= tūbạlī).

*alantarạkup (*said by children*) God preserve us from it !

alārọ *m.*   (1) carrying loads for hire. (2) ɗaŋ ~ (*pl.* 'yaŋ ~) carrier, labourer (*also called* alārọ *which is both sg. and pl.*).

*ạl'arshị *Ar. m.* (1) sky, heavens. (2) God's throne.

Allạ̄ rụfi ạsīrimmụ *Vd.* Allạ̄ 8.

alạrụm *m.* (*Eng.* guard-room) lock-up, guard-room.

alạshī = alạbạshī.

Allạ suwā mụ (*corruption of* Allạ̄ yạ sō mụ) = ạfūwō 1.

ạlā tīlạs (*hybrid Arabic and Hausa*) by force (*Vd.* tīlạs).

Allạ̄ tsīnẹ *Vd.* Allạ̄ 10.

ālātụ *Ar. m.* tools, clothing, furniture.

ạl'aurạ *Ar. f.* the private parts of the body (*cf.* aurē).

ạlāwạ (*Ar.* halwā sweet) = ạlēwạ.

alawāyụ = alawayyọ.

alawayyọ *m.* unpatterned white European material, especially a type of calico (= lēlē = zạwwātị), *cf.* sạndā 3.

alạwusại = alạwusẹ *m.* a good type of Nigerian salt (= bạ̄kin jạ̄kī 2).

ālāyạ *f.* = ālāyẹ *m.* skin-bottle for oil or honey (= tandū 4).

alayyạdī *m.* oil from palm-kernels, *cf.* mạn jā.

alayyạfō *m.* spinach.

albada A. (ạlbadạ) *f.* (*pl.* ạlbạdū = ạlbạdạnū = ạlbạdạnai (*d.f. Ar.* al batnu "inside") (1) (*a*) each of the *narrow* strips composing body of a gown of native farī woven by *males* (ạlbadạ *is also called* cikị, *but only the term* cikị 11 *is applied to the* broad *strips* (i) *composing a gown of European cloth made from* sạndā, (ii) *of native cloths woven by* females. *To make a* girkē-*gown, the European cloth is cut into strips* (cikị) *for sewing by hand*). (*b*) cūnạ dạ ~ *Vd.* cūnạ 2*c*. (2) *cf.* agēdụ, sayar dạ 3, cikị 11, kwaryā 2, 3, fashị 5.
    B. (ạlbạdā) (1) (*Ar.* al badawiyya " Beduin ") what a simpleton ! = ~ minạl jạfā. (2) *Sk.* = sautụ.

ạlbadạŋ *m.* = ạlbadạ.

*albại *m.* = alabẹ.

ạlbạjajjạrī = ạlmụbazzạrī.

*ạlbạ̄kī *m.* = ạlbāshī.

ạlbarạs *Ar. m.* (1) leprosy (= kuturtạ). (2) *Vd.* ɗauriŋ ạlbarạs.

ạlbarkạ *Ar. f.* (*pl.* ạlbạrkạtai). (1) blessing *x* Allạ̄ yi makạ ~ = Allạ̄ yạ yi makạ ~ = Alại makạ ~ = Allạ̄ shī makạ ~ God bless you ! ụbansạ yā shī (= ụbansạ yā sạ) masạ ~ his father said to him " May God bless you ! " (*cf.* Allạ̄ 2, barkạ, ạlbarkạcī) (2) (*a*) No thanks ! (*said by seller refusing* tayị), *cf.* sallạmā. (*b*) ịdam mūgụn tayị yā shịga lifịdī, ~ tạ fisshē shị (*lit.* if a deceitful bid disguises itself, refusal to sell will checkmate it) cunning must be met with cunning. (*c*) bā yạ̄ kārẹ̄wā yạu kō gōbe, jībi mā ~ it will not come to an end now or even in the near future. (3) (*a*) yā yi ~ he's prosperous. yārọ yā yi ~ the lad is thriving. gōnā tā yi ~ the farm is productive. mạ̄tạ tasạ tā yi ~ his wife is prolific. (*b*) Allạ̄ yạ sạ ~ ạ nōnạŋ ūwạr may the baby thrive ! (*c*) *Vd.* dạ̄munā. (4) nā sạmi ~ tasạ I received benefits from him (*cf.* ạlbarkạcī). (5) *Nor.* = rại dọ̄rẹ. (6) rashịŋ ~ *Vd.* rashị 1*e.* (7) *Vd.* tsīnẹ 2*a* ; ɗēbẹ 5.

ạlbarkạcī (*hybrid Ar.-Hausa*) *m.*   (1) kindness at the hands of, benefits received from *x* ạ cikiŋ ạlbarkạciŋkạ mukạ sāmụ it was through your kindness that we got it (*cf.* ạlbarkạ 4). nā ci ạlbarkạciŋkạ I received a favour from you. (2) kōwā, sắi fad̦iŋ ạlbarkạcim bạ̄kinsạ yakẹ̄ yị̄ everyone is putting his own construction on the matter. (3) ạlbarkạcin *prep.* thanks to *x* (*a*) ạlbarkạcin rūwā tsịre-tsịrē su kạn rạ̄yu plants sprout thanks to rain. (*b*) kōmē d̄āki ya sāmụ, ạlbarkạciŋ k̄ōfạ a child owes all to its parents. (*c*) ạlbarkạciŋ kạ̄zā, k̄adạŋgarẹ ya shā rūwaŋ kaskō (*lit.* it was owing to kindness shown the *chicken* by its owner, that the lizard drank water) benefiting by another's advantages.

ạlbạrụs = ạlbạrūshị *Ar. m.* (1) gunpowder. (2) mildew used as ingredient of gunpowder.

ạlbạrūsạ *f.* yā bā tạ ~ he gave her (his sweetheart) a nasty shock when she caught him red-handed in a liaison with another.

ạlbạrūshị *Vd.* ạlbạrụs.

*ạlbas *Nor. m.* (1) do not be alarmed ! (2) harm *x* sāran d̄aŋ gidā bạ̄ shi ~ the bite of the snake d̄aŋ gidā is harmless.

ạlbasạ *f.* (*pl.* albasōshị) *Ar.* (1) onion = k̄ōgị 2*b* (*Vd.* jāɓā 4). (2) (*a*) ~ bạ̄ ta halin rūwā he's " not a good chip of the old block ". (*b*) kōwā ya ci ~ , bạ̄kinsạ zại yi wārī as you sow so shall you reap. (*c*) bā ạ̄ aram bạ̄kim mụtụm ạ ci masạ ~ don't put words in a person's mouth ! (*d*) nā tōyạ mại, nā mạncē dạ ~ the details were attended to, but the important part was neglected. (*e*) kạ ci minị ~ *Vd.* ạ̄rā. (3) = gwāzā 2. (4) ~ tā yi karā type of game. (5) ạlbasạr kūrā = ạlbasạr kwạ̄dī type of malodorous wild lily. (6) ạlbasạr gizọ (*a*) = 5 *above*. (*b*) trader's making his broker return unsold articles at night, to check remainder (*epithets are* Ạlbasạr gizọ, yinị dạ dạshē, kwānā gidā = yinị dạshē, kwānā birgāmị). (*c*) baŋ ạɓīna, ạlbasạr gizọ, yinị dạshē, kwānā gidā (*said by disgruntled cadger*) return me my gift and

I'll be off ! (7) ạlbasạr kạram ɓikī *Kt.* = 6*b* above. (8) ạlbasạ mại ganyē = sāfā 1*b*.

albạsharā *f.* type of children's game.

ạlbāshī (*Ar.* alma'āshi) *m.* (1) monthly salary (*cf.* lādā, gaɓạ 3, sātī 2*a*). (2) d̄aŋ ~ *m.* (*f.* 'yar ~) *pl.* 'yaŋ ~ P. on monthly salary.

albasōshī *Vd.* ạlbasạ.

*ạlbattụ *Ar. m.* extravagance.

*albīk̄i *Nor. f.* midwife (= ụŋgōzọ̄mạ).

ạlbishịr = ạlbishịrī *Ar. m.* (1) good news. (2) ạlbishịriŋkạ ! I've brought you some good news ! (*B., the recipient of the news, replies* gōrọ I'll give you some kolas ! *A. then says* bạ̄ ni gōraŋ give me the kolas then ! *B. answers* ā'ạ̄, fạdā minị no, tell me first ! *After A. has told B., then A. says* bạ̄ ni gōrọna mạnạ. *If a prostitute brought the news to B., she might reply* gōrọ bāwạ nē *when B. said* gōrọ *to her. B. would then reply* fạtẹ̄-fatē).

*ạlbujajjạrī = ạlmụbazzạrī.

ale A. (ạlē) mun yi ~ we're quits !

B. (alē-ạlē) *Nor. m.* sitting carelessly so that privies are visible.

*alēfạtā = d̄aŋ gōshī *q.v. under* gōshī 2.

ạlēkạ *x* (1) sạlāmạ ~ greeting (*said to one P., cf.* ạlēkụŋ) (*reply is* ạssạlāmụ !). (2) *Vd.* sạlāmạ, sạlāmụŋ.

ạlēkụŋ (1) sạlāmụ ~ greeting ! (*said to several persons, cf.* ạlēkạ) (*reply is* ạssạlāmụ), *Vd.* sạlāmạ, sạlāmụŋ. (2) *If A. and B. are begging and A. calls out* d̄aŋūwạ !, *B. knows that A. has managed to cadge some food and replies to A.* ạlēkụŋ ! (3) bạ̄kī ~ *adv.* silently. (4) *Vd.* tạ̄ɓī 2.

ạlẹ̄lẹ̄ = ạlạ̄lẹ̄.

ạlẹ̄nā *Kt.* you bloody blind person there !

ạlẹ̄nīyạ = ạlẹ̄nīyạ raŋkại *Kr.* be off !

ạlēwạ (*Ar.* halwā sweet) *f.* (1) type of sweet made from honey, sugar or tạkandā plus fruit of d̄ọrawạ, d̄inyā or kanyā (*its epithet is* Ạlēwạ shā jạ̄yayyạ Thou sweet pulled hither and thither in the making ! = cạrkwai 4). tanạ̄ shaŋ ~ she's eating ~ (= arambad̄ī). (2) (*hawkers' cry*) ạlēwā ạnīnī buy my sweets ! (*note changed tone of* ạlēwạ). (3) (*a*) anạ̄ ~ dạ shī they're noisily

badgering him (x to pay debt, go somewhere, etc.). (b) Vd. ciŋ ~ . (4) Vd. zāk̃ī 1a.v. (5) ạlēwạr wuri̧ Vd. dādī 5.
ạlfadarī m. (f. ạlfadarā) pl. ạlfạdạrai = ạlfạdạrū. (1) (a) mule = jạk̃i̧n dōki̧ (for epithet Vd. gạidā 3). (b) (in computations, used optionally for plural) x ~ yā yi 300 there were a total of 300 mules (cf. jạk̃ī, dōki̧). *(2) ạlfadariŋ kạ̄zā black and white chicken.
ạlfahạrī Ar. m. ostentatiousness, boastfulness, showing off (= tạ̃k̃amā 2, q.v.).
ạlfā'idạ f. = fā'idạ.
alfālu̧ Ar. m. (1) bringing luck x gidạŋ yā yi mini̧ ~ the compound was auspicious to me (= bặicī 2). bar tạfīyạn nạŋ, bạ̄ ta dạ ~ abandon this journey, it's ill-omened ! (2) yā yi mini̧ kyạkkyāwaŋ ~ he expressed his good wishes to me (cf. kyạu̧ 2b, ạlkạbā'i̧, shu'u̧mī, nạhīsā).
alfan A. (ạlfaŋ) = ạlfyaŋ.
B. (ạlfaŋ) (Ar. alfahmu) m. sagacity.
ạlfandā x zāk̃i̧ ~ epithet of any chief.
alfānu̧ = alfālu̧.
ạltạ̄ri = ạlfahạrī.
alfarmā (Ar. al hurmatu) f. (1) arrogance x yā nūnạ mini̧ ~ he behaved arrogantly to me (= mulki̧ 3). (2) (a) Audu̧, ~ gạrēshi̧ Audu is of high rank, noble origin, is in great favour. (b) an yi masạ ~ he's been leniently treated because of rank, origin, or popularity.
ạlfạ̄shā (Ar. alfahsha) f. abuse, scurrility (= mūgu̧n bạ̄ki̧), cf. bātsā.
ạlfātihạ = fātīyạ.
*ạlfạtīkạ f. = ạlwạtīkạ.
ạlīātīyạ f. = fātīyạ.
ạlfạwāmī = ạlhạwāmī.
alfeŋ = ạlfyaŋ.
ạlfēri̧ Kt. = ạlhēri̧.
ạlfici̧ Nor. m. mischiefmaking.
ạlfijir = ạlfijirī Ar. m. (1) ~ yā k̃ētō = ~ yā yī it's the early morning time, half darkness half light. (2) dạ ~ at the time described above.
ạlfīmī Kt. = ạlhīnī.
ạlfiŋ Sk. = ạlfyaŋ.
ạlfīnī = ạlhīnī.
*ạlfi̧ntar = *ạlfi̧ntạs = *ạlfi̧nti̧s, q.v.

ạlfinti̧ m. white drill.
*ạlfi̧nti̧s Ar. m. type of wheaten food.
ạlfōwạ = ạlhōwạ.
ạlfūtạ = ạlhūtạ.
ạlfu̧tu̧wā f. ạbiŋ ~ anything amazing.
ạlfyaŋ Ar. f. 2,000. ~ dạ bi̧yar 2,005 ; 2,500. ~ dạ shidạ 2,006 ; 2,600.
ạlgabbạ f. (pl. ạlgạbbū) (Ar. aljubba). (1) the lateral (ạ gi̧ci̧ye) lining of certain gowns (as tagu̧wā) (cf. ku̧rūru̧, shāfi̧). (2) ~ k̃ark̃wantạ gambạ epithet of anything worn out.
ạlgaitạ (pl. ạlgaitai) Ar. (1) f. type of reed-instrument. (2) m. player of 1.
Ạlgạ̄jē name for any magāji̧yā 3 or woman named Fātsumạ.
algajējȩ = aŋgajējȩ.
ạlgạrāgī Kt. m. = fu̧ŋkạsō.
*ạlgạragi̧s m. an oil-less wheaten food.
ạlgạrārạ Ar. f. Hessian material.
ạlgargi̧ Kt. m. = k̃ēlēk̃ē.
ạlgari̧f = ạlgaru̧f m. seeds of common cress (Lepidium sativum) (= lạfsu̧r), cf. zạmạntarōri̧.
ạlgarwạ = ạlgarwai m. = ạlēwạ.
algasa A. (algạsā) Vd. algạshī.
B. (ạlgasạ) Sk. f. (1) = gārā 2a. (2) the white cloth given husband by bride's parents for return to them blood-stained to show she was virgin when married.
algạshī m. (f. algạsā) pl. ạlgạsai. (1) adj. (a) grass-green, emerald-green (= k̃ōrȩ = tsaŋwā), cf. bak̃ī. (b) algạshi-algạshi light greenish. (2) m. greenness as in 1a.
ạlgāyạ (Ar. alghāyatu). (1) f. limit, utmost extent, maximum. (2) adv. anyhow x ~ dặi m̱ bīyā at all events I'll pay.
ạlgazaru̧ (Ar. aljazīru) m., f. spendthrift, slapdash P. (his epithet is Gamzạrā = ạlgazaru̧ māgạni̧ŋ ku̧din zạmāni̧).
algu̧ŋgumanci̧ m. mischief making.
algu̧ŋgumī m. (f. ạlgu̧ŋgu̧mā) pl. ạlgu̧ŋgumai mischief maker.
algu̧ŋgunci̧ Sk. m. mischief making.
algu̧s = algushi̧ = algushu̧ Ar. m. fraud.
algwaramanci̧ Sk. m. = algu̧ŋgumanci̧.
algwarạmī m. (f. ạlgwarạmā) pl. ạlgwarạmai Sk. mischief maker.
ạlhā'inī m. (f. ạlhā'i̧nā) pl. ạlhạ̄'i̧nai.

(1) dishonest. (2) treacherous (*cf.* hā'incị).

ạlhajị *m.* (*f.* **ạlhajịyā**) *pl.* **ạlhạjai = ạlhạzai** *Ar.* (1) P. who has done the pilgrimage to Mecca (*cf.* **hajị, fạnzạ, baitụ**). (2) name for P. born (*a*) on day start made for or return begun from Mecca, (*b*) on Great Festival. (*c*) name given to P. in memory of ancestor who made the pilgrimage. (*d*) *Vd.* **Baitụllāhị**. (3) a white ram or cock, etc. (4) name of a **bọrī** spirit supposed to be dressed in white gown *x* **Mālạm ∼ yā hau kạntạ** she is possessed by the **Ạlhajị**-spirit. (5) type of plant. (6) **ạlhajịyar ƙafạ** whiteness of soles of the feet (*considered unlucky*) = **farar ƙafạ**.

ạlhakī *m.* (*pl.* **alhukạ** = *Sk.* **alhukkạ**) (*Ar.* **alhaqqi** rights). (1) (*in the weighing of sins in the scales at the Resurrection, the sins of another against whom one has offended, are heaped into one's own scales*, hence :—) (*a*) **yā ɗauki ∼** he committed a crime. **doŋ ɗaukạr ∼ sukạ yi hakạ** they did so from criminality. (*b*) **mū dǎi bạ mu dạ ạlhakiŋ kōwā** we at least, are not to blame. (*c*) **in yārọ yā ƙi mạganạr iyāyansạ, yā ɗauki ạlhakinsụ** a disobedient lad sins against his parents. (*d*) **ạlhakīna yā kāmạ ka** retribution for your offence against me has fallen on you. (*e*) **∼ kwīkẃīyọ nē, ụbaŋgijinsạ yakẹ bị** retribution is inescapable (N.B.—**lādā** 2 *first example, is antithesis to* **ạlhakī**). (*f*) **∼ dạ rōmō, ạ shiga iyākar wuyạ** people sin if it helps them (*Vd.* **wuyạ** 1*g*). (2) **yā fid dạ ạlhakiŋ ūwā = yā fita ạlhakiŋ iyāyansạ** (*a*) it (child) burned a patch on its arm (or rubbed centre of brow) with idea of paying debt to mother (or parents) for mother's birth-pangs and to avoid having to pay in the next world. (*b*) child behaved dutifully to mother (or parents). (3) **ɗaŋ ƙạramiŋ ∼ man** who is nincompoop. (4) (*a*) wages (= **hakkị**). (*b*) **n nạ bā kạ kudī dubū ɗarī ạlhakiŋ hannun dạ na yaŋkẹ** I'm offering you 100,000 cowries as compensation for your hand which I

cut off. (5) **ạlhakiŋ idọ** small amount (of food, etc.) given P. seeing T. he likes (*x* that food) in another's possession. (6) *Vd.* **bạlagạ** 2.

ạlhālī *Ar.* *adv.* (1) as a matter of fact (*cf.* **hālị**). (2) at the moment in question *x* **sạn dạ ka tafō, ∼ munạ zạụne** we were seated at the moment you came : **iŋ kā zō gọbe wạr hakạ, ∼ kạ gan nị** if you come at this time tomorrow, you'll see me : **∼ munạ kạrạtū** at the moment we're reading. (3) (*followed by subjunctive*) it would be best to *x* **∼ kụ tạfi tạre** why not go together ?

Alhamdụ *Ar.* *m.* (1) = **fātīyạ** 1. (2) **Ạlhamdụm mụtụm ita cẹ sịttīnīyạssạ** it's a poor thing but mine own (= **gạtari** 1*c*). (3) **∼ lịllāhị** ! God be praised (*said after meal, hearing good news, etc.*), *cf.* **darạs, hamdalạ**. (4) **Ạlhamdụ = Ạlhamdụ lịllāhị** (*a*) *reply to greeting like* **yāyạ akạ jī dạ sanyī** (*q.v. under* **sanyī**) ; **ịnā gạjīyạ,** *etc.* (*b*) *Vd.* **barkạ** 3. (5) **ạlhamdụ lịllāhị ạlā kulli hāliŋ** praise to God for whatever he has done ! (6) **am maishē shi Ạlhamdụŋ ƙasạ** he's been demoted.

Ạlhạmis = Ạlhạmīshịyạ *Ar.* *f.* (1) **Ạlhạmīshin dạ ta wucẹ** last Thursday (Mod. Gram. 10*d*). **ạlhạmīshin dạ ya zō** on the Thursday when he came. (2) **Ạlhạmis = ran Ạlhạmis** *adv.* on Thursday. (3) **kōwā ya cikạ bịkiŋ ∼ bạ yạ yi na Jumma'ạ ba** you can't have a cake and eat it too. (4) *Vd.* **Lạmī**.

***alhanạ** (1) *f.* preventing P. carrying out project. (2) *m.*, *f.* P. preventing another carrying out project.

ạlhantạnā = tạlhātạnā.

ạlhạnzịr *m.* (*pl.* **ạlhạnzīrai**) *Ar.* (1) boar (= **mūgụn dawạ = gạdū**). (2) pig. (3) *Vd.* **lālạcē** 3.

ạlhargạ, *Ar. f.* door-hasp.

ạlhạrīnị (*Ar.* **alharīrī**) *m.* (1) various silky fabrics such as **rūmị, warwạr,** etc. (*cf.* **asilịkī**). (2) **gīwar ∼** *f.* packet of *such fabric* (*cf.* **war-wạr** 2).

ạlhāsạlī = hāsạlī.

Alhasạŋ man's name (*twin boys are named* **Ạlhasạŋ** *and* **Ḥusainị**).

ạlhạwāmī *m.* (1) tinder made from

rīmī. (2) yā sā̰ mini ~ he slandered me and got me into trouble. (3) ɗaŋ Kano ~ nḛ̄ Kano children are pert and destructive.

alhazai *Vd.* alhaji.

alhēri *Ar. m.* (1) (*a*) (i) kindness. (ii) yā yi mini ~ he did me a kindness. (iii) alhēriŋ Allā̰ ya̰ gai da̰ mū God give us good fortune ! (iv) alhēriŋ Allā̰ ya̰ gaishē sṵ good luck to them ! (*b*) ~ gadam barcī nḛ̄ doing a favour is a good investment. (*c*) ya̰s da̰ ~ bāya, ka̰ ɗaukē shḭ a̰ ga̰ba a kindness is never without profit. (2) (*a*) inā lā̰bārḭ what's the news ? (*reply* sǎi ~ fine, thanks !) (*b*) Allā̰ ya̰ sā̰ mṵ ji ~ may we hear good news ! (3) liberality *x* (*a*) bābṵ ~ garēshi he's stingy. (*b*) mṵtṵm ma̰i ~ liberal P. (*c*) kṵ bḭdi ~ ga̰ ma̰i sakḭm fuska̰, look for gifts from a smiling face ! (*cf.* sa̰ke 2). (4) ~ bā̰ shi ka̰ɗaŋ don't look a gift horse in the mouth ! (5) mun ra̰bu da̰ ~ we parted on good terms. (6) *Vd.* kwal 2*b*, tsa̰mmānḭ 4. (7) alhēriŋkṵ gyāraŋ hanya̰ *Vd.* A̰ibō.

alhīmī = alhīnī *Ar. m.* sad meditation *x* ka̰ka̰ aka̰ ji da̰ alhīmī (*formula of condolence*) I hope you are not feeling quite so grief-stricken as previously !

alhinti = alfinti.

alhinzir = alhanzir.

alhōwa̰ *f.* (1) strips of red leather. (2) = kṵlūdṵ.

alhudahuda̰ (*Ar.* hudhud) *f.* (*sg., pl.*) Senegal hoopoe (*epithet is* mahaddacī) = makarantā 3*b*.ii.

alhuka̰ *Vd.* alhaki.

alhūta̰ *Ar. f.* (*sg., pl.*) woman's headkerchief (= kallabī = fa̰tala̰).

alhūtsa̰ (*Ar.* alkhaita thread) *f.* small, narrow bag or purse made of gwandā or sākḭ and having two compartments (gidā) (*it is used for charms* (lāya̰), galena (tōza̰lī), *etc.*) = tsṵmbē 2 = *Kt.* mayānī 2.

ali A. (A̰lī) *m.* (1) (*a*) *man's name* (*originally name of son-in-law of the Prophet*), *cf.* A̰līyya̰. (*b*) *epithet of* 1*a is* Gadaŋgā = Garga̰ = Ma̰i saŋgō = Gargāmḭ. (2) *Vd.* zākḭ 2.
B. (alḭ) (1) alḭ = ɗaŋ alḭ *m.* the index-

finger (= sa̰bāba̰). (2) ɗaŋ ~ yā hau ka̰nta̰ she is possessed by the bōrī-spirit ɗaŋ alḭ, which is said to be spirit of orphan seeking her pity. (3) *cf.* gwaida̰.

Alibāwā *pl.* a Filani tribe in Sokoto and Katsina (*sg. is* Ba̰alibḭ).

alibidḭ *m.* = adibidḭ.

alibō *m.* (1) yam-flour. (2) slices of dried yam.

alif A. (alḭf = alīfḭ) *m.* (*pl.* alīfai) *Ar.* (1) the letter aleph. (2) ~ jā the small superimposed aleph such as stands over the m in the word rahmānu when its aleph is omitted (*called in Arabic* alif khanjarī) *cf.* imāla̰.
B. (alḭf) *Ar. f.* thousand. ~ tā fi ɗarī a thousand is greater than a hundred. alīfin da̰ ka bā shi the 1,000 you gave him. alīfin naŋ that 1,000. ~ da̰ ɗarī = ~ wa̰ minya̰ 1,100 (*cf.* alṵ). ~ wa̰ mētaŋ 1,200. ~ da̰ ɗarī ukṵ 1,300 ; ~ da̰ ukṵ 1,003 ; 1,300. ~ wa̰ arba̰minya̰ 1,400. ~ wa̰ ha̰msa̰minya̰ 1,500. ~ da̰ shida̰ 1,600 ; 1,006. ~ da̰ bakwa̰i 1,700 ; 1,007. ~ da̰ ɗarī takwa̰s 1,800. ~ da̰ ɗarī tara̰ 1,900.

alikwī = lukwī.

alillibā *f.* the tree *Cordia abyssinica.*

al'ilmṵ indahū *Vd.* dara̰s.

alimbīkī *m.* = kasankī.

al'ishā *Sk.* = lishā.

*alītafā *f.* = ɗaŋ gōshī *q.v. under* gōshī 2.

Alīyya̰ *f.* the present Islamic cycle, a period of strife (*as was that of* A̰lī *q.v.* : *the succeeding cycle is* Maha̰dīyya̰).

aljamā (*Ar.* aljam'a gathering) *f.* (1) yā taŋka̰ ~ (*a*) he gave a party (= da̰'awā 3). (*b*) he vied with others to gain reputation for giving alms (*cf.* kō tā kwānā̰ ?). (2) ~ tā ci shūnī (*a*) they are competing in alms-giving, liberality. (*b*) the party is in full swing (*Vd.* shūnī 1*d*). (3) ~ da̰ masōyiŋ wani kōshiŋ wa̰hala̰ it's a case of love's labour lost (*Vd.* sō̰ 1*d*).

aljan = aljanī *m.* (*f.* aljana̰) *pl.* aljanū = aljannū *q.v.* = aljannī = aljanai = aljannai *Ar.* (1) evil spirit (*cf.* aljannū) = ka̰sa̰ 12*c* = dōdō 1 = fatalwā 1. (2) ~ yā bṵgē shi he's mad. (3)

uncontrollable P. (**4**) very skilled P. (*cf.* ịblīshị, janjancị, shạitsạŋ 2*b*). (**5**) ạljanad darē *Vd*. Burụŋgū.

aljancį *m.* (**1**) being uncontrollable. (**2**) being very skilful (*cf.* ạljaŋ **4**).

ạljanī *Vd*. ạljaŋ.

ạljanjạnī *m.* (*f.* ạljanjạnā) *pl.* ạljạnjạnai = ạljaŋ.

ạljannạ *Ar. f.* (**1**) (*a*) Paradise (= dārạs sạlāmụ 1). (*b*) sun ji kạmar zā ạ sā su ∼ they were delirious with joy. (*c*) *Vd*. tsạkạ-tsakạ, ŋgō 1. (**2**) ạljannạr dūnīyạ delightful place (N.B.—ạljannạ *and* gōnā *are both derived from Arabic* " garden "). (**3**) rạ̄irạyiŋ ∼ = rāɓā 3.

ạljạnnū (**1**) *Vd*. ạljaŋ. (**2**) evil spirit.

ạljīfū *m.* (*pl.* ạljīfai = aljīfunạ) *Ar. m.* (**1**) (*a*) pocket. (*b*) Wazīrịnsạ na cikiŋ ∼ the Waziri, his intimate friend. (*c*) ɗan cikiŋ ạljīfunsạ one who is a mere toady to him. (**2**) ạljīfum bāya mại wụyar sā hannū what a touchy person ! (**3**) zanẹ dạ ∼ *Vd*. shịrīrịtā. (**4**) tarō ạ ∼ *Vd*. tarō 1*b*. (**5**) gạbaŋ ∼ *Vd*. nikạ 2*e*.ii. (**6**) tạ nụna ạ ∼ *Vd*. ɗinyā 4.

ạljịmā *Kt. f.* = ạljạmā.

Ạljimma'ạ = Ạljumma'ạ *Ar. f.* (**1**) Friday. (**2**) bā kulluŋ sāfīyā takē ∼ ba you cannot expect an unbroken spell of good luck (*Vd*. Jumma'ạ 1*c*). (**3**) *Vd*. Jumma'ạ, ạ̄dạmū, Hawạ.

ạlkabā'į *Ar. m.* yā yi minị ∼ he spoke ill of me, he wished me ill (*Vd*. alfālụ).

ạlkabbạ *Vd*. ạlkyabbạ.

ạlkadạrī *Ar. m.* value *x* zīnārīyā tā fī azụrfā ∼ gold is more valuable than silver.

ạlkạdạrīyyạ = ạlkịdịrīyyạ.

ạlkāfụrā *f.* somersaulting standing (= mại gidantạ = *Kt.* kutubyalbyạl), *cf.* adụŋgurē, kafạ 2*p*.

Ạlkāhirạ *f.* Cairo.

alkājīyā *Kt. f.* = tsirgāgịyā.

ạlkakại *x* yā zamā ∼ gạrēshị it's a " thòrn in the flesh to him " *i.e.* he can't get rid of T. or P. (= kaŋkạ 1 = baraŋkam-baraŋkạm) ; *its epithet is* ∼ auram mại dạ wutā (*cf.* wutā 1*n* ; gāwā 3*b*).

ạlkākị *m.* type of wheaten food.

ạlkạ̄lā *f.* (**1**) the quarter where the ạlkālī lives. (**2**) *Vd*. alkālāwā.

ạlkalạmī *m.* (*pl.* alkalumạ (*Vd*. **4**) = alkalamạ = *Sk.* alkalummạ) *Ar.-Greek.* (**1**) (*a*) pen, pencil (*epithet is* Tsạntsạndō bā̄kịŋkạ dạ kudī). (*b*) bạkiŋ ∼ *m.* nib. (*c*) sun sā bā̄kiŋ ạlkalạmī they signed the document. (*d*) *cf.* gāgarō 2 : kafiŋ ∼ . (**2**) penis (=azakạrī). (**3**) figure, letter. (**4**) alkalumạ *pl.* arithmetic.

alkālancị = *alkālancị *m.* (**1**) judgeship. (**2**) chatter.

alkālāwā *pl.* persons in service of an ạlkālī (*their epithet is* na ạlkạ̄lā mạsū kōfatạŋ kudī).

alkalcị *m.* = alkālancị.

ạlkālī = *ạlkālī *m.* (*pl.* ạlkạ̄lai) *Ar.* (**1**) (*a*) judge (*epithets are* Gērō ạbōkin Sarkī = Kụlīyạ mạntạ sạbō (*Vd*. sạbō **3**) = Mūsạ gēran tākị = gā gōran zumạ, gā na madācī = tạdawạr karkashī, būwāyạ mạlạmai (*cf.* mālạmī 1*c*.iv). (*b*) ạlkāliŋ ạlkạ̄lai Chief Judge. (**2**) chatterbox. (**3**) (*a*) scales. (*b*) A. used as standard of measurement. (**4**) ạlkālim mīyạ salt (= gishirī). (**5**) ạlkālin tūwō = mārā 1. (**6**) ạlkālim bābā part of garment to be re-dyed screwed into knot, to be compared with results. (**7**) ạlkāliŋ hanyạ *Sk.* any way of indicating to P. following one, which road to choose at crossroads. (**8**) yạ̄raŋ ∼ hunger : aŋ kōri yạ̄raŋ ∼ hunger has been appeased.

alkạltā *Vb.* 1C to appoint P. ạlkālī.

alkalumạ *Vd*. ạlkalạmī.

alkamạ (*Ar.* alqamhu) *f.* (**1**) (*a*) wheat. (*b*) alkamạ bisạ dūtsẹ, Allā ya kạm bā kị rūwā he's fortune's favourite (= dạshē 4*c*). (**2**) yā yi wạ hakōrā ∼ he lightly stained his teeth with kola or tobacco-flowers. (**3**) alkamạr tụrurūwā type of weed.

ạlkāmurạ *f.* (**1**) type of turban-muslin. (**2**) dạbaibạyiŋ ∼ gā taushi, gā cin sau *epithet of* P. deceptively looking mild. *(**2**) type of grass.

ạlkaŋgādọ *Fil. m.* (*used in songs in sense of* zakạmī *which is considered to render mad*).

ạlkarfạ (**1**) I swear that not *x* ∼

baŋ gan shi ba on my word, I've never seen him ! : ~ ba zaŋ yi ba I swear I'll never do it ! (2) yā tsaya ~ sǎi yā dauka he insisted on taking it (1, 2 = bal).

alkarif = algarif.

alkarya Ar. f. (pl. alkaryai = alkaryū = alkaryōyī). (1) any unwalled town (cf. birnī) = marāyā 2. (2) ~ sǎi aŋ karya town-life costs dear. (3) abin naŋ yā yi ~ this is a fine article.

alkashāfa Ar. f. any flimsy cheap gown or saddlecover.

alkashī = algashī.

alkataf = alkatap m. dyeing beard blue with kudujī.

alkatakar = alkatakarfa = alkarfa.

Alkausarā Ar. f. one of the rivers of Paradise.

alkāwarī ≒ Sk. alkāwalī m. (pl. alkāwarai = alkāwura) (Ar. al kauli speech). (1) (a) (i) promise. (ii) alkāwarinsu na zā su zō their promise to come. (b) (i) yā yi (= yā dauki) ~ he made a promise. (ii) sun yi ~ wanda bā yā tāshi, suka cē : . . they made an inflexible promise that . . . (iii) yā yi alkāwarī kaŋ a bar su he promised to release them. (iv) alkāwarinsu yanā naŋ tsaye their promise has been kept. (c) (i) yā daukam mini ~ = yā daura ~ da nī cēwā . . . he promised me to . . . (ii) yā yi ~ da mū := yā yi ~ garēmu he made us a promise. (iii) sun yi ~ sun cē zā su yī = sun yi alkāwarin su yī = sun yi alkāwarin zā su yī they promised to do it. (d) (i) yā cika ~ he kept his promise. (ii) jirāgyansa ba su cika masa ~ ba his ships did not come up to his expectations. (iii) mun yi ~ kada mu yī = mun yi alkāwarim bā mā yī = mun yi alkāwarim ba zā mu yi ba we've promised not to do it. (iv) ~ yā cika the promise has been kept : the courtship has ended in marriage. (e) ba su dauki ~ a bākiŋ kōmē ba they set no store by promises. (f) takardar ~ I.O.U. (g) yā tā da ~ = yā karya ~ = yā warware ~ = yā warware igiyar ~ = yā kwance ~ = sāba 4b. (i) he broke his promise. (ii) Vd. alwāshī, talālābūwā 2. (2) Tsōfaŋ ~ Old Testament. Sābaŋ ~ New

Testament. (3) mai ~ m., f. (pl. māsū ~) reliable P. or T. (4) = tsattsāgī.

alkāwartā Vd. 1D promised.

alkāwura Vd. alkāwarī.

alkazib = alkazub = alkazubu Ar. m. telling a lie.

alkebba = alkyabba.

*alkibiri (Ar. alkibrīt) = farar wutā.

alkidirī m. (pl. alkidirai) Ar. iron pot.

*alkidirīyya Ar. f. muzzle-loading pistol.

alkilla Vd. arkilla.

alkintā Vb. 1C. (1) did carefully. (2) looked carefully after.

*alkīya f. zigzag-stitch.

alkīyāma = alkīyāma Ar. f. (1) raŋ ~ f. Resurrection-day. (2) har ~ ta tsaya till the Day of Judgment.

*alkō m. (1) = ta alakō. (2) weak P.

alkōtīyā f. = akōtīyā.

alkōmī = arkōmī.

alkubus (Ar. alkhubzu) m. type of wheaten food.

alkūki (Ar. alkūkhi) m. (pl. alkūkai). (1) niche in wall for lamp ; lamp-stand. (2) part of a jalāla. (3) mālamiŋ ~ scholar who takes notes which he never consults.

alkunya (Ar. alkināya) f. (pl. alkun-yōyī). (1) using a euphemism or what is known to anthropologists as " avoidance " x saying Wānę instead of mentioning name of P. who has done wrong or parent referring to first-born son as yāraŋ naŋ "that boy" from superstition, etc.: tā yi wa mijinta ~ she referred to her husband as shī instead of calling his name (on the whole question Vd. " Mod. Gram.", Appendix III) = bōyō 3, cf. kārā 2a.iii, lē, kināya. *(2) the -n sign (tanwīn) of Arabic writing when the tail is written backwards before succeeding " f " or " b " to show that it is pronounced " m ".

Alkur'aŋ = Alkur'āni m. (pl. Alkur'ānai). (1) The Koran (= lāya 2, Allā 6n). (2) I swear by the Holy Koran ! (3) makarantar ~ Koranic school, on leaving which pupil can proceed to ilimī 2, q.v. (4) yā sauki Alkur'aŋ Vd. saukā 1d.

alkusūsanci m. = kinibībi.

alkusūsu m. hypocrite : mischief maker.

alkwararô *m.*, *f.* (*pl.* ạlkwạrạrai) P. selling by measure.

alkwatō *Sk. m.* = kạtantaŋwạ.

ạlkyabbạ *f.* (*pl.* ạlkyạbbū) *Ar.* (1) burnous. (2) yā yāfạ (= jitạ) ~ he draped burnous over his shoulders (*cf.* k̄ōk̄wā 1*d*). (3) *Vd.* yāfạ 1*c*.

Allā *m.* (*Ar.* Ạllāhụ). (1) (*a*) God (*epithet is* Būwāyi, gāgạrạ mịsālị). (*b*) iŋ ~ yā yạrdā = dạ īkwạŋ ~ (*cf.* 4*j*) = bisạ īkwạŋ ~ God willing . . . (*c*) gamạ da ~ *Vd.* gamạ 1*e*.iii. (*d*) ~ yā ịsa *Vd.* ịsa 2. (*e*) bābụ gạ ~ bābụ gạ kōwā it is (was) of no use to anyone (*f*) *x* anā naŋ, rạn naŋ, ịnā yạ ~ bābụ yạ ~ sāi ya sāmi dạbārạ he suddenly bethought himself of a plan. (*g*) ~ yā sō kạ you had a lucky escape ! (*h*) kō kai na ~ you'll be wise to take the advice given you ! (*j*) *cf.* Alā, allā-allā, Ạllāhụ, Alā sūwā mụ, sitilaŋ, sụbhānạllāhị, wạllāhị, Tạ'ālā, tụbarkallā, lā ịlāhạ, mādạllā, summat Ạllāhị, ilallạ, yā 2*b*, bārakallā, kuntụ bịllāhị. (*k*) (i) munā tāmụ, ~ nā tāsạ = k̄ạddarạ 2. (ii) ta ~ bā tāsụ ba they are miscreants. (*l*) yanā naŋ dạ rạnsạ na ~ he is safe and sound. (*m*) rāyukạd dạ sukạ hạlakạ, wannạŋ sāi ạ bar wạ ~ sanị God alone knows how many perished ! (*n*) tsạkānī dạ ~ *Vd.* tsạkānī 3*c*. (*o*) rāi gạ ~ *Vd.* rāi 1*a*.vii. (*p*) *Vd.* cikạ 1*f*. (2) *invocations to God*. (*a*) Allā Tạ'ālā God almighty ! (*b*) (i) ~ Sarkin sākayyạ O God the requiter ! (ii) *Vd.* wutā 1*v*. (*c*) iŋ wadạnnạn sun shā wuyā, su kạn cẹ " Allā ! ", ạmmā Jāmụs, ạ'ūzụ bịllāhị ! if these people are hard pressed, they say " God help us ! ", but the Germans are outside the pale entirely. (*d*) ~ mại girmā = Allā Sarkī = Sarkin sạrautạ good heavens ! (*e*) *Vd.* yā 2. (3) *precatory expressions*. (*a*) Allā yạ būɗạ dājị *Vd.* būɗạ 4. (*b*) ~ yạ būɗẹ masạ God prosper him ! (*cf.* būɗẹ 1*e*). (*c*) *Vd.* wadai. (*d*) ~ yạ amf̄ānā good luck ! (*said on being informed of a birth*). (*e*) ~ yạ bā dạ lādā God reward you ! (*Vd.* gaisūwā 5). (*f*) ~ yạ tạimạki mại tạimakō good luck to the helpful ! (*g*) ~ yạ jā zạmānịŋkạ long life to you ! (*h*) ~ yạ bā kạ nasarạ

(*said to a senior*) if I might venture to make a suggestion . . . (*cf.* tạrā 2*a*). (*j*) (i) ~ yạ sā *Vd.* sā A1. G2. (ii) ~ yạ sạ yạ sam mụ *Vd.* sanị 1*a*.ii. (*k*) ạlhērịŋ ~ yạ gai dạ mū God give us good fortune ! (*l*) ~ yạ kai mụ *Vd.* ạddu'ạ 2. (*m*) ~ yạ fisshē kạ tsakạ mại wuyā, bā farkō ba, k̄arkō may you remain ever virtuous ! (*n*) ~ yạ sanasshē mụ *Vd.* mālạmī 1*c*.v, tạmbayạ. (*o*) *Vd. below* 4*c*, *f*, *g*, *h* ; 7*q*. (*p*) ~ yạ bā dạ kạsūwā *Vd.* Allā 7*b*. (*q*) ~ yạ ɓōyẹ shi *Vd.* madāci. (*r*) *Vd.* cī dạ 1*a*.ii. (*s*) ~ yạ tsarẹ *Vd.* dā 1*b*. (*t*) *Vd.* dạdā ; dadẹ 2. (*u*) ~ yạ yāyẹ masạ *Vd.* duhụ 1*b*. (*v*) ~ yạ bā kạ hạkurī *Vd.* hạkurī 2,3. (*w*) ~ yạ bā mụ jịŋkirī *Vd.* jịŋkirī. (4) *exclamations*. (*a*) doŋ ~ for goodness sake *x* doŋ ~ kạ yi saurī = iŋ kanā wạ ~ kạ yi saurī for goodness sake, hurry up ! (*b*) (i) mun rōk̄ē kụ ~ dạ Ạnnabi kụ zō we conjure you to come ! (ii) *Vd.* baŋgō 2. (*c*) ~ yạ bā kạ hạkurī *Vd.* hạkurī. (*d*) ạllā ? really ? (*reply* Allā yes, truly !). (*e*) ~ shī nẹ Sarkī God's will be done ! (*f*) ~ yạ gāfạttạ Mālạm *Vd.* gāfạrtā, nạ'am. (*g*) ~ yạ kyautā *Vd.* kyạutā 2, 3. (*h*) (i) ~ yạ tsīnẹ makạ ạlbarkạ *Vd.* tsīnẹ. (ii) *Vd.* lạ'anạ. (*j*) īkwạŋ ~ fancy ! ; how wonderful ! (*cf.* 1*b above*). (*k*) ~ nārị gōdẹ *Vd.* mạkāf̄ọ 5. (*l*) Wạllāhị ~ *Vd.* Wạllāhị. (5) *compounds with* Allā *as first word :* (*a*) Allạŋ k̄wāyā *Vd.* tsīrukụ. (*b*) Allạn nāsạ *Vd.* 7*m below*. (6) *compounds with* Allā *as second word :* (*a*) ạjīyạr ~ *Vd.* ạjīyạ 2*c*. (*b*) cụtar ~ *Vd.* ba'ạ. (*c*) bāi na ~ *Vd.* bāinā. (*d*) tārịŋ ~ *Vd.* tārị 1*b*. (*e*) bạfādạŋ ~ *Vd.* mālạmī 1*d*. (*f*) f̄ōraŋ ~ *Vd.* rāk̄umī 1*d*. (*g*) yaŋkaŋ ~ *Vd.* yaŋkā 2*c*. (*h*) ɗākịŋ ~ the Kạ'abạ at Mecca. (*j*) (i) mụtumịŋ ~ honest P. (ii) wandạ ya ga ~ pious P. (*k*) diŋkịŋ ~ *m.* suture of genitals or anus. (*l*) dōkịŋ ~ (*said by children*) the mantis k̄ōk̄ị-k̄ōk̄ị. (*m*) dabbạr ~ *Vd.* kūrā 1*a*. (*n*) Littāfịŋ ~ *m.* the Koran (= Alkụr'ạŋ). (*o*) bāwạŋ ~ *Vd.* bāwạ 3. (*p*) tākịŋ ~ *Vd.* dạɓạrō. (*q*) dādịŋ ~ *Vd.* dādī 1*c*.vii. (*r*) tsōraŋ Allā *Vd.* tsōrō 1*bb*. (*s*) rūwạŋ ~ *Vd.* gāwō.

(t) Vd. ƙayạr ~ . (7) proverbs with Allā̰ : (a) ~ yā yi dā̰munā Vd. zạ̄tō 3. (b) ~ yā ƙī shi Vd. yawạ 5. (c) bābu nēsạ gạ ~ to God all is possible. (d) ~ kạŋ kāwō ki gidā Vd. tạntabạrā. (e) ~ yạ kai damō gạ harāwạ, kō bai ci ba, yā̰ yi birgimā may the wish be fulfilled ! (f) ~ nā̰ mutā̰nē, jā̰ɓā tā ga bā̰kim mijintạ (said by women) it is a case of the pot calling the kettle black ! (g) ~ yā yi matạ māgạnī, Sarkiŋ Kanọ dạ ganim fā̰rā only·God can lighten our troubles. (h) ~ shī ya hōrẹ wạ rā̰ƙumī ƙayạ it (difficult T.) has become second nature to him (= hūwā̰cē 1). (j) ~ shī kẹ̄ bā̰ kūrā gishirī, nāmạ kō ạ kā̰sūwā tā̰ sāmu epithet of warrior or dogged worker. (k) ~ yā gyārạ rīmī, cēdīyā tạ bar fushī one must take things as one finds them. (l) ~ yạ ƙārạ wạ kōgī rūwā, ḳududdufī yạ sāmu may you prosper and we share in your prosperity ! (m) ~ ˈyā yi Allạn nāsạ, wai Bạmāgujẹ yā iskẹ biri yā mutụ ạ gōnā tasạ what unexpected good luck ! (n) iŋ ~ yā ƙi ạddu'ạr biri, săi yạ mutụ ạ gōnar arnẹ one cannot fight against ill luck. (o) bạkaŋ gizọ shī bā̰ ~ ba Vd. bạkā 8d.ii. (p) " ~ sụtụri buƙwī ! " n̩ ji kīshīyar mai dōrō (said by woman) God forbid I should do such a thing ! (q) (i) ~ yạ tsạri gā̰tarī Vd. tsạrā 2. (ii) ~ yạ tsạrē mu dạ " dā̰ nā sani ! " Vd. dā̰ 1b. (r) Vd. 3m ; 1k. i.

allā̰-allā̰ f. (1) eagerness x yanā̰ ~ yạ yī he's all agog to do it (cf. bạndīri). (2) God ! God ! (Vd. hạllā̰-hallā).

ạllagazọ Kt. m. stomach.

Allāh Vd. Allā̰, Ạllāhu.

*allạhē Vb. 3A. (1) resigned oneself. (2) yā ~ mini he kept on at me, gave me no peace.

Ạllāhu (1) Ạllāhu ạkbar. (a) prayer-formula, God is the Greatest ! (cf. kabarạ). (b) my word ! (c) how sad ! (2) in shā ~ if God wills (Vd. in 4). (3) Vd. Allā̰, sallạllāhu. (4) (a) Ạllāhu wạ'ạlamu we're in God's hands ! (b) kōmē yakẹ̄ yī, ~ wạ'ạlamu God alone knows what he's up to ! (5 Ạllāhummạ Vd. salāti.

allaka A. (ạllakạ) = tạ'ạllakạ. *B. (allakā = ạllakạ) f. (1) = ɓaɓɓarkīyā. (2) sediment of flour in preparation of kōko.

Alla koro Vd. Alā̰ 7.

allam bā kụ = shạllū.

ạllambạram (1) = ạlkarfạ. (2) Kt. = affạfai 2. (3) leather-worker's board (= ạllō 4).

allạmusuru Vd. alạmusuru.

ạllạn ci kōrō m. (1) being very poor, being inured to indignities. (2) yā kōmạ ~ he's reduced to begging.

*ạllạŋkā f. act of watering plants.

allantakạ f. x yā yi mini ~ he treated me honestly.

allan yā halạkuŋ x yā tạfī ~ he died, disappeared.

Allạn Yā̰kūbạ (in ɓōrī jargon) God.

Allạ sūwā mụ Vd. Alā̰sūwāmụ.

ạllātu my word !

Allā̰ yạ ishē mụ Vd. Alā̰ 6.

allạzī (Ar. "which") used in kōwạnẹ allạzī dạ nāsạ āmā̰nū everyone has his niche in the world.

*allērā f. = andīrā.

ạllī m. (1) chalk from lime or burnt bones (= mataɓī), cf. kōsạ. (2) bạn cẹ̄ dạ shī ~ gawạyī ba I didn't say a word to him (= uffạŋ). (3) yā taɓạ (= taɓō) ~ he asked permission : tạɓō mini ~ mụ tạfi garī ask leave for me and we'll go to town together ! (4) gajẹrē nẹ̄ kạmar inūwạr ~ he's very short.

*allikị Vd. *allukị.

*allīrā = andīrā.

ạllō (Ar. allauhu) m. (pl. allunạ). (1) school-slate (= makaranta 3b.i). (2) wooden board with Koranic text on it. (3) ạllaŋ kā̰fadạ (a) shoulder-blade (= Sk. kạmfallī). (b) Vd. ɓallẹ 1d. (4) yā fitar dạ sābaŋ ~ he came out with a new idea (= ficē). (5) ạllan dụ̄kā̰wā = ạllambạram 3.

ạllōbā Sk. f. = ạnnōbā.

*allụhē = allạhē.

*allukị = allukkị m. type of big-thorned tree.

ạllụmbur = ạlkarfạ.

allunạ Vd. ạllō.

allūra (Ar. alibratu) f. (pl. allūrai).

(1) needle (*epithet is* hana arō) = madiŋkīyā = tamfasūwā (*cf.* asirkā 2). (2) yā yi masa ∼ he (doctor) gave him an injection. (3) ∼ mai kai pin. (4) ∼ tā tōnō garmā investigation of small matter often reveals a larger. (5) ku bar ganiŋ kaŋkanta, ∼ karfe cē " good things are wrapped up in small parcels ", " don't look a gift horse in the mouth ! " (6) ∼ bā tā kōkarī cikiŋ gidan takōbī don't attempt the impossible ! (7) *Vd.* harbiŋ allūra ; asirkā 2 ; dauriŋ allūra. (8) bā ni da kafā kō i ta ∼ I've not a moment to spare (*Vd.* i). (9) kamar an jēfa ∼ rījīyā it is like looking for a needle in a haystack.

almājirci *m.* discipleship.

almajiri (almājiri) *m.* (*f.* almājirā) *pl.* almājirai (*Ar.* almuhājiri) (1) disciple of P. : pupil of P. (*epithet of* 1, 2 *is* Ta mājira dōdan tsaki). (2) almājirī = ∼ mai rōkō *euphemism for* beggar. (*Vd.* bara A.1, marōkī). (3) *when scholar is addressed* Allā ya gāfatta Mālam ! *he often modestly replies* almājirī not a scholar, a mere learner ! (4) *Vd.* dōkiŋ almājirai.

almājirtad da *Vb.* 4B took P. as one's pupil.

almakashī (*Ar.* almiqassu) *m.* (*pl.* almakasai). (1) scissors. (2) Dōgō, almakashin dāji *epithet of* train.

almanāni *Ar. m.* (1) hinge. (2) door-pivot on which it swings.

almanzūrīyā *f.* telling a lie.

almārā (*Ar.* almar'a vision). (1) fable (= tātsūnīyā). (2) a mere fiction.

Almasīhu (*Ar.* anointed). (1) the Messiah. (2) daŋ ∼ *m.* (*f.* 'yar ∼) *pl.* 'yā'yaŋ ∼ an apostate to Christianity from Islam. (3) Īsā ∼ Jesus Christ.

almauru *m.* = almūru.

alminjar *m.* European rat-trap.

almiski *m.* = miski.

almōru *m.* = almūru.

almōsa (*Ar. word*) *Sk. f.* any knife.

Almū *m.* (1) name for man called Almusdafā or P. born on a Monday. (2) yā gamu da ∼ he got syphilis (= tunjērē).

almubazzaranci *Ar. m.* extravagance.

almubazzarī *m.* (*f.* almubazzarā) *pl.* almubazzarai *Ar.* spendthrift.

*almūdā *Ar. f.* small knife.

almūdu = almudda *Sk.* = alkwararō.

Almuharram *Ar. m.* = Muharram.

almukwīda *x* ∼ kwārō mai kai *epithet of* hypocrite.

*almulku = haŋkatīlō.

almunāni = almanāni.

almundahana (*Ar.* almudāhanatu) *f.* fraud.

almunjar *m.* = alminjar.

almūru (*Ar.* almaghrïbu) *m.* late dusk.

Almusdafā Mustapha (*Vd.* Almū).

almuski *m.* = miski.

almutsutsai *m.* (1) evil spirit(s) causing madness (*epithet is* ∼ kāzā kaŋki da mōtsī = ∼ mai 'yaŋ gabas = ∼ bagabashī) = tambōdai. (2) yā cika ∼ he is mad.

almuzazzarī *m.* = almubazzarī.

alo hallo !

alōbā *f.* = annōbā.

*alōlami *Nor. m.* = bakwalī.

Na alōlō = Banufē.

Altine name for girl born on a Monday (= Tani), *cf.* Tine.

alu *used in* :—alu wa minya 1,100 ∼ wa mētaŋ 1,200. ∼ wa arbaminya 1,400. ∼ wa hamsaminya 1,500 (*Vd.* alif).

alubō = alibō.

*aluku *x* na ∼ *m.* (*f.* ta ∼) *pl.* na ∼ bumpkin.

alukwī *m.* = lukwī.

al'ul (*Ar.* al'ūdu) *m.* incense (= turārē 2 = gumāri).

al'uma = al'umma.

*alumbukī = alumbucī *m.* = kasankī.

al'umma *Ar. f.* (*pl.* al'ummai). (1) nation *x* sauraŋ al'umma the other nations (*Vd.* saurā 1e.ii). (2) the public.

alūtuttukī *Sk. m.* the sparrow *Fringellaria septemstriata*.

alwalā (*Ar.* alwudū'a) *f.* (1) (*a*) ceremonial ablutions (*cf.* malallautā). (*b*) in rūwaŋka bai isa alwalā ba, sai ka yi taimama ka tāshi if you're not rich, practice ecomony ! (*c*) *Vd.* taimama. (2) rāgō yanā da ∼ the ram has black feet and patches round eye. (3) *Vd.* kāfircim māgē ; alwallā.

alwali *m.* (1) = walī 2 (*but in some places where women live away from their homes (cf.* aurē 4) *and so have no*

walį, *the word* ąlwalį = shūgąbaŋ aurē).
*(2) *Nor.* ring on sword on spear.
ąlwąllā (1) *f.* = ąlwąlā. (2) *m.* ąlwąllansą
yā kąrai (*a*) the crisis of his illness is
over. (*b*) his prosperity has declined
(*both* = lallę 1*g*).
alwaŋkā *Kt. f.* woman who washes the
bride.
alwąnząŋ *Kt. m.* = kudundurįŋ īyą.
alwąrā *f.* = inyāwarā.
ąlwąrdī *m.* = wąrdī.
ąlwasą *Ar. f.* breadth.
ąlwāshī (*Ar.* alwus'a breadth) *m.* (1)
boastfulness. (2) yā shā ~ = yā ci ~
= yā yi ~ he boasted. (3) ~ bą yākį
ba nę boasting is easy. (4) kyąŋ ~
(= kyąŋ ąlkāwąrī) cikąwā a promise
is crowned by its fulfilment. (5) shą ~
m., f. (*sg., pl.*) braggart.
ąlwątīką *f.* triangle.
alyąrā = ayyąrā.
āmadā *Ar. f.* various types of solo or
chorus singing containing the word
āmadā " I praise God ".
ąmadįŋ *Vd.* gairą 2*c.*
Āmadų *man's name* (*nickname is* Gųrūzą),
Vd. Madō, ząbųrą dawāki.
ąmagį *m.* a native cloth of same colouring
as bųnū.
amāgūwą *f.* doing abundantly *x* yaną ~
dą kāyā he has an immense load.
yaną ~ dą cīwǫ he's seriously ill.
kōgī yā yi ~ the river is in spate.
amai *m.* (1) (*a*) vomiting (= zōbā =
cēdą), *cf.* mai dą 8, kumallō 4, haras dą.
(*b*) kōwā ya ciką cį dą yawą, yą yi ~
kō kumburī the pot goes to the well
once too often. (*c*) amaŋ hąrsāshį
aką yi musų a volley was fired at them.
(2) being forced to disgorge ill-gotten
gains. (3) amam mussą = bulbulī.
(4) kā fl ~ *Vd.* dōkį 1*d.*
ąmajā *f.* slackness, indolence.
ąmakąlī *f.* = kawā.
ąmālai *Vd.* amālę.
amālālą *m., f.* (*sg., pl.*) P. wetting his
bed (= fltsārī 4).
amālę (1) *m.* (*f.* amālįyā) *pl.* ąmālai.
(*a*) monstrous ram, horse, donkey, or
camel. (*b*) (i) amālam mutąnē influential
P. amāląn Sarākuną mighty Chief.
(ii) wani kāyā sǎi ~ abilities differ.

(*c*) longest string of mōlō (= gīwā 3).
(*d*) woman's plaits falling to her
shoulders. (2) formula in boys' or
girls' singing.
ąmaltą *Vb.* 3B became fully-developed,
over-developed.
ąmąmē *Nu. m.* (*sg., pl.*) mat of tukurwā
used by canoe-men camping on river-
banks.
amamēgi (*Yor.* twins) the epidemics of
1914 and 1920.
amam mussą = bulbulī.
ąmāną *Ar. f.* (1) (*a*) friendliness *x* (i) dą ~
tsąkāninsų there is a feeling of friendly
trust between them. an yi ~ matters
were settled on a friendly basis. ~ tā
shiga tsąkāninsų they became reconciled. (ii) *Vd.* fuską 8. (*b*) alliance *x*
mun yi ~ dą sū we came to a friendly
understanding with them. yā kullą ~
dą sū he made an alliance with them.
(2) reliability of P. or T. *x* (*a*) Audų ~
gąrēshį Audu is honest. (*b*) ~ tā
yi ~ P. in whom reliance was put has
justified the trust. (3) entrusting *x* nā
bā ką ąmāną tasą I entrusted it to you.
jirągyąn dą aką bą d'an rąkīyą ~ the
ships entrusted to the care of the vessel
escorting the convoy. (4) T. entrusted
to *x* (*a*) yā ci ~ tasą = yā tabą ~ tasą
(i) he embezzled the T. entrusted to
him. (ii) he behaved treacherously to
him. (*b*) kōwā ya ci ąmānąr wani,
Allą yą ci tāsą = kōwā ya ci ąmāną,
ąmāną tą cī shį treachery begets
treachery. (*c*) bą sų ci ąmānąrmų ba
they were not false to us. (*d*) d'aŋ ~
m. (*f.* 'yar ~) *pl.* 'yam ~ adopted
child (= talląfī 3). (5) Audų ąmānątā
nę Audu is my confidant. (6) (*a*) am
bā sų ~ they've been given quarter
(in war) (= amincį 3). (*b*) sun cę
" Amāną ! " they (enemy) surrendered.
sun cę dą Jāmus " Amāną ! " they
surrendered to the Germans. (*c*) yā
yi ~ dą sū he surrendered to them.
(7) kasar ~ a neutral country. (8) (*a*)
nā bā shį ~ I trusted him. nā bā shį
īyąkar ~ I trusted him implicitly.
(*b*) ąbim bą ~ a trustworthy T. (*c*) dą
dōkį, dą kōgī, dą mącē, bā ą bā sų ~
don't trust a horse, a river or a woman !

(9) yā tā dạ ~ (i) he behaved dishonestly. (ii) he rebelled. (10) Vd.
fuskạr ạmānạ, jālisạŋ, warwạrē,
yāwon 1.
ạmạŋgā m. type of black and white
cloth.
amaŋkwarō f. slavegirl (= kụyaŋgạ).
aman mussạ Vd. amō.
Ạ mạntā = Ạ jēfas (but only applied to
female).
āmạ̄nū used in kōwạnẹ allạzī dạ nāsạ
āmạ̄nū everyone has his niche in the
world.
amara A. (ạmārạ) f. = sạ̄fīfạ.
    B. (ạmarạ) Vb. 3B. (1) became
married. (2) dōkị yā ~ the horse is full-
grown.
amarcị m. (1) tanạ̄ zamaŋ ~ she's
a bride. (2) yā yi ~ (a) he (husband)
has returned from his journey. (b)
he has washed his gown.
ạmạrdạgwai Sk. m. rope round donkey's
neck.
ạmạr dạ kạ̈i f. woman previously married
who can thus marry husband of her
choice without reference to parents'
wishes.
amạ̄rē Vd. amaryā.
*amạrī Ar. m. imperative mood of any
verb.
ạmạrmarī Vd. amaryā.
amạrōd̄od̄ọ = na mạrōd̄od̄ọ.
ạmartạ Vb. 3B = ạmarạ.
amaryā f. (pl. amạ̄rē = *amạrmarī (derived from same origin as the word aurē).
(1) bride. (2) anything new (such as early
stage of bụrtuntụnā) x amaryar ƙasā
new pot, new native oven. amaryar
yāƙị new Chief going to war for the
first time. amaryar watạ new moon (=
haskē 1c). (3) amaryar dōkị = zạ̄gē.
(4) bạ kạ īyạ d̄aukạr amaryassạ ba it
is far beyond your powers. (5) amaryar
bụzūzụ dung-ball made by young
bụzūzụ. (6) (a) amaryar bōkọ virgin
taken to husband's house as mock
bride to distract guests' attention from
real bride (amaryar gạskīyā). (b) Vd.
bōkōnị. (7) amaryar jēgọ = amaryar
ƙannī nursing-mother (Vd. aŋgọ 2).
(8) Vd. gēzạ. (9) sunạ̄ amaryar sukụ̄wā
they're galloping with their arms round

each other's necks. (10) kōmē wạ̈yaŋ ~
ạ shā mạntạ even Homer nods. (11) sun
shịga yịm bāya-bāya, tākị d̄ăi-d̄ăi,
tạ̄īyạr amạ̄rē they began to retreat
unobtrusively. (12) Vd. waŋkaŋ
amaryā, būlālạ 3, kā fi amaryā.
amasa A. (ạmasạ) Vb. 3B Kt. = gạ̈wurtạ.
    B. (Amạ̄sạ) Kt. epithet of Sarkim
pāwạ.
amasạnī = amōsạnī.
amasāyẹ = amasāyị m. (1) haversack.
(2) piston-rod of locomotive.
āmatạ x lāyuŋ ~ fruit of d̄ọrawạ (this
word is used in fable).
amāwạlī m. (pl. amāwulạ). (1) the long
part of turban used by Chiefs to cover
the mouth x yā yi ~ = yā jā ~ = yā
zubạ ~ he covered his mouth as above.
(2) cf. fūnị, fēcẹ 2, gabcẹ 2d, bọ̄lọ̄lō 5,
tạ̈kuŋkụmī 1, kạrbū 4.
amāyad dạ Vb. 4B = amạ̄yē Vb. 3C.
(1) vomited T. up (= gyātsẹ 2b =
kōmō 1c). (2) gạrī yā cịka har yā
amạ̄yē the town is over-full.
ạ māzạyā Vd. māzạyā.
ạmbạci (1) Vd. ạmbạtạ. (2) ~ bạ̈ yị̄ ba
m. empty boasting.
ambālīyạ f. congestion x gạrī yā yi ~
town is congested : rūwạ̄ yā yi ~ ạ
d̄akị water poured into the house.
ambata A. (ạmbạtạ) Vb. 2 (cf. ambatō)
(n.o. ạmbạci, p.o. ạmbạcē) (Ar. anba'a)
mentioned.
    B. (ambạtạ) Vb. 1C. (1) = ạmbatạ.
(2) (with dative) mentioned T. to P.
x nā ~ masạ mạganạn naŋ I mentioned
that to him.
ambato (ambatō). (1) Secondary v.n. of
ạmbatạ x yanạ̄ ambatansạ = yanạ̄
ạmbatạ tasạ he's mentioning it. (2)
kāyā ạbiŋ ~ the aforementioned property. (3) d̄aŋ hạlak, kā ƙi ~ (said by
women) " talk of the devil . . . "
ạmbēcī Sk. m. = gwambạzā 1.
ambō Sk. m. anything stinking.
ambola A. (ạmbōlạ) f. stretching out
hand with extended fingers as graphic
expression of the insult ūwāƙạ !
(cf. daƙūwạ 2, gundụŋ-gundụŋ).
    B. (ambōlạ) Eng. f. envelope.
ambụlā Vb. 1C (1) = ambụtā. (2) is (was)
in strength x kọ̄gī yā ~ the river is

(was) in spate. yāḵi yā ambulō manạ the army swooped on us.
ambŭlī x ∼ jạ dōkị *epithet of* kūrẹ 1.
ambụtā (1) (*a*) *Vb.* 1C x yā ∼ manạ ḵūrā he smothered us in dust. (*b*) *cf.* ambụlā.
(2) *Kt. f.* (*pl.* ạmbụttai). (*a*) (*obsolescent word*) type of bin. (*b*) damịm bāḵin rụmbū ḍaukạ kō yau kō gọbe *epithet of* P. about to obtain some office (= damị 2).
ambụ̄wā *Sk. f.* threadworm (= ayạmbā).
ạmdīyyạ (*Ar.* premeditation) *used in* an yi kisạn kặi ∼ premeditated murder has been committed.
Amḗrīkạ *f.* America.
amfana A. (ạmfānạ). (1) *Vb.* 3B (*Ar.* anfa'a). (*a*) became serviceable (x cassava through ripening, pupil through progress, etc.). (*b*) nā ∼ thank you for asking me to join you, but I've already had my meal ! (*c*) benefited by x yā ∼ dạ zamansạ he benefited by his stay. (2) *Vb.* 3 (*a*) derived benefit from x yārọ, yā ạmfāni mālạminsạ the pupil benefited from his master's tuition. (*b*) benefited P. x yārọ yā ạmfāni mālạminsạ the pupil did benefit to his master. bạ sụ ∼ kōmē ba ạ dūnīyạ they have done nothing beneficial in the world. (3) *name for* female slave. (4) = A jḗfas *but only applied to a* female.
B. (amfānā) *Vb.* 1C (1) did benefit to x yā ∼ ni = yā ∼ minị it was of benefit to me. (2) Allā̲ yạ ∼ (*said on being informed of a birth*) good luck ! (3) Allā̲ yạ amfānạ shaurạn (*said by recipient of alms, present*) thank you ! (4) *Vd.* ạmfānannē 2.
ạmfānannē *m.* (*f.* ạmfānannīyā) *pl.* ạmfānạnnū. (1) of proved utility. (2) Allā̲ yạ mai dạ ∼ (*said to* P. *who has had misfortune or to woman bereft of child*) better luck next time ! (*cf.* amfānā).
ạmfānī (*Ar.* annaf'i) *m.* (1) (*a*) advantage. (*b*) gēmụ bā yā̲ biṇ gēmụ sǎi dạ ∼ nobody consorts with another except for some good reason. (*c*) ạmfānịṇ ạbiṇ adō ḍaurā̲wā it's no use possessing fine things if one makes no use of them. (2) (*a*) (i) usefulness x yanā̲ dạ ∼ = yā

yi ∼ it is useful. bā̲ shi dạ ∼ it's useless. yā yi minị ∼ it is (was) of use to me. (ii) ạmfānin zụnubị rōmō one only sins for profit. (iii) ạmfānin nōnọ farī it is utility one requires, not mere beauty. (iv) yā wucẹ ạmfānī it is overripe. (*b*) making use of x anā̲ ∼ dạ shī wajạṇ ạbincī it is used as food. an yi ∼ dạ shī wajạṇ ạbin shā̲ it was used as a beverage. Jāmus sunā̲ sọ̣ sụ sā̲mi ḵasā̲ ịndạ zā ạ riḵạ ∼ dạ iriṇ kuḍinsụ kad̆ăi the Germans want to get a country where only their currency is valid. anā̲ ragẹ ∼ dạ shī yạnzu it is less used nowadays. bā ā̲ ạmfānī dạ kōgin nạṇ this river is not used. (*c*) benefiting x sạrautạ tasạ tā yi ạmfānịṇ ḵasạr his reign was of benefit to the country. (3) (*a*) ạmfānī = ạmfānịṇ gōnā crops x Kanāwā sun yi ạmfānī bana the Kano people had good crops this year. gyạdā dạ saurạṇ ∼ groundnuts and other produce. (*b*) (*often treated as plural*) x waḍansu ∼ certain crops. mạnyaṇ ạmfāninsụ their chief crops. (4) ạmfānin sanị aikā̲wā *Vd.* sanị 2*b*.vi. (5) ịnā̲ ạmfānin ḵibạ *Vd.* tạlōlō.
ạmfānu *Vb.* 3B is (was) usable, serviceable.
ā̲miṇ *Ar.* (1) Amen ! (*cf.* Alā̲ 7). (2) 'yaṇ ∼ claqueurs of an Emir, " yes "-men. (3) 'yaṇ ∼ sụ amsạ (*said by* P. *hearing another uttering good wish such as* Allā̲ yạ sā̲ " may God grant it ! ") May the Angels grant it !
amina A. (Amīnạ = *Amịnā) *f.* (1) (*a*) woman's name (*epithet is* Gwạrjē), *Vd.* Takō. (*b*) the Prophet's foster-mother, *hence* ḍaṇ ∼ *is title of any man named* Muhammadụ. (2) yā dadẹ kạmar gānŭwar ∼ it's as old as the hills (*cf.* Mạndawạrī 2). (3) ∼ mại darē *epithet of* hyena or Amịnạ 1*a* (*she is called* Kūrā).
B. (āminạ) = ā̲miṇ 1.
ạmīnai *Vd.* ạmīnị.
amịncē *Vb.* 1C (*Ar.*) (1) nā ∼ dạ shī = nā ∼ masạ I trust (trusted) him. suṇ ∼ dạ hanyạ they feel safe about the method. sun sā̲ zukā̲tạṇ amịncēwā gạrēshị they trusted him implicitly.

(2) (*negatively*) did not dare to *x* bā tā ∼ tā fid dā tāsar ba she had not the courage to exhibit the plate.

aminci *Ar. m.* (1) (*a*) reliability of P. or T. (*b*) mai ∼ *m., f.* (*pl.* māsū ∼) reliable. (2) friendship, friendliness *x* (*a*) yā sā musu ∼ he pacified them. (*b*) bāyan gaisūwā dā sō dā yardā dā ∼ after friendly greetings (*opening phrase of letters to superiors, cf.* gaisūwā 3). (*c*) ∼ ya tābbatā garēku dā jin kan Ubangiji God have you in his keeping ! (*ending of letter*). (3) am bā su ∼ they were granted quarter in war (= āmānā 6).

aminī *Ar. m.* (*f.* amīnīyā) *pl.* amīnai. (1) friend on whose honesty one can rely. (2) bā yā ∼ sǎi amīnīyā he's interested only in women. (3) ally.

aminta A. (amintā) *Vb.* 3B. (1) nā ∼ dā shī I trust (trusted) him. (2) (*only in past form*) nā ∼ I consent (consented). B. (amintā) *Vb.* 1C. (1) did work well *x* an amintā ginin nan this building has been reliably done, strongly made. (2) an amintā wurin the place has been fortified.

amintaccē *m.* (*f.* amintaccīyā) *pl.* amintattū reliable.

*aminya = amya.

Amīru *m.* (*pl.* Amīrai) *Ar.* Emir.

āmmā *Ar.* (1) (*a*) but. (*b*) (āmmā is often omitted) *x* dā sū dā Tūrāwā, sun yi dǎidǎi in dǎi wajan ilimī, bā farar fātā ba they are the equal of Europeans in knowledge but are not white-skinned. bā sū kadǎi sukē kōkarī ba, duk mutānan dā kē kaunar 'yanci not *they* alone are striving, but also all who love freedom. bā ā Tūrai kadǎi ba, duk dūnīyā not in Europe alone, but in the whole world. (*c*) ∼ duk dā wannam fa nevertheless. (*d*) ∼ habā wannam bai hanā shi ba nevertheless this did not prevent him. (2) ∼ bāyan hakā as regards my reason for writing (*used in letters, after greetings*). (3) *Sk.* as for *x* ∼ halinsu as regards their character. . . .

āmman = āmmā.

āmmānā = āmmānin but.

amō *m.* (1) voice of bell, drum,

gun, etc. (2) ∼ bā nāmā ba ne don't mistake the shadow for the substance ! (3) karfē dǎyā bā yā amō it takes two to make a quarrel ; remove the mote from your own eye ! (4) *Vd.* gwarjē 1*b*, 2. (5) amam mussā = bulbulī.

amōdarī *m.* (1) blepharitis (= *Kt.* murtsukū). (2) amōdarin kā = amōsanī 2.

Amōre *x* 'yan ∼ Northern Filani bowmen-highwaymen.

amōsanī *m.* (1) rheumatism. (2) amōsanin kā dandruff (= kwarkwashī 1 = amōdarī 2).

amrē *Sk. m.* = aurē.

amsa A. (amsā). (1) *Vb.* 1A (*a*) replied to call, greeting, question *x* (i) bā tā ∼ masā dā kōmē ba she made him no reply. tā ∼ tanā sōna she answered that she loves me. yā yi sallamā, akā ∼ masā he uttered a greeting and it was acknowledged. (ii) n nā amsāwā thank him for his greetings ! (*said when person says,* e.g. Audu yanā gaishē kā Audu sends you his compliments). (iii) wannan sōjā yā ∼ sūnansā this soldier replied to his name ; this man is a real soldier. (iv) yā jē, yā ∼ he appeared when sent for by the Court. (*b*) consented *x* tā ∼ dā'awā tasā she admitted the truth of his claim. nā ∼ masā zancansā I agreed with what ʻhe said ; I agreed to his proposal. nā ∼ zam bā shi auran Zainabu I agreed to give him Zainabu to wife. (*c*) echoed gārun gidansā yā fādi, nāwa ya ∼ the wall of his compound fell and mine echoed in sympathy. kōgī yā ∼ muryar zākī the river echoed the lion's roar. (*d*) joined in chorus of song (*Vd.* wākā 1*a*.iii). (*e*) nāmā yanā amsāwā the meat has gone bad. (2) *f.* (*a*) a reply (= jawābi 2). (*b*) an echo *x* kōgī yā yi amsar muryā tasā the river echoed back his voice. B. (amsā) *Vb.* 2 (*p.o.* amshē, *n.o.* amshi). (1) received *x* nā amshi kudī ā hannunsā I received money from him. (2) *Vd.* shēhu 3*c*.

Amsa gayyā *x* ∼ kī zūwā *epithet of* P. failing to perform what he promised.

ạmsạ kūwwạ *f.* echo.

amshe A. (amshẹ) *Vb.* 1A. (1) took by force *x* nā ∼ matạ kuɗī I took money from her by force. (2) yā ∼ he acknowledged the greeting on behalf of his superior by saying a gaishē kạ when not his business to reply. (3) accommodated *x* ƙasan nan tanạ̄ īyạ ∼ bīyum mutạ̄nạn dạ kẹ̄ cikintạ that country can accommodate twice its present population.

B. (ạmshē) *m.* *x* bā nạ̄ cịŋ ∼ *Vd.* lāyạ 7.

amshi A. (amshị) *m.* (1) joining in refrain. (2) *cf.* mạkāfọ 5.

B. (ạmshi) *Vd.* ạmsā.

ạmshi, gạsō *Sk. m.* agent, servant.

amsūwā *f.* = amsạ 2.

ạmūmụ = ạtụmurmụr 1.

ạmuni *Vd.* ạyū.

amyạ (1) *f.* (*pl.* amyōyī) beehive (= zumạ 2*a*.ii = gidā 2*a*.ii). (2) *Vd.* anyạ ; hanyạ 6.

an (*past impersonal,* Gram. 12*a*). (1) (*a*) an zō people have come. (*b*) = sun *x* burgū an shā wụyā these " rats " (i.e. beleaguered garrison) are in difficulties. (*c*) (*negative*) *x* bạ̄ an zō ba people have not come (*not so common as* bạ ạ zō ba, *Vd.* bạ̄ C.1 2). (2) aŋ saŋ halin ƙarē, ƙan ɗaukō shị if one needs a P., one must put up with his defects. (3) an cẹ̄ dạ ƙarē " tūwō yā yi yawạ'ạ gidam bịkī ", yā cẹ̄ " mụ ganī ạ ƙas ! " seeing is believing ! (4) an cẹ̄ dạ ƙarē yạ ɗauki damị *Vd.* ƙarē 32. (5) aŋ ƙi cịŋ ƙarē, aŋ kōmō an ci kwiƙwīyọ straining at a gnat and swallowing a camel. (6) am bar jạ̄ƙī *Vd.* tēƙị 1*b*. (7) an yi gudụŋ gạrā *Vd.* gudụŋ gạrā. (8) aŋ ạiki bāwạ *Vd.* ạikā 1*a*.ii. (9) an ci gīwā *Vd.* cī 26*h*. (10) am fāɗō dạgạ ƙan dabīnọ *Vd.* dabīnọ. (11) an dadẹ anạ̄ rūwa *Vd.* dadẹ 1*c*. (12) aŋ harbi ƙarē *Vd.* ƙarē 12. (13) an cẹ̄ dạ mạkāfọ *Vd.* mạkāfọ 1*e*.

ana A. (anạ̄). (1) (*impersonal Progressive,* Gram. 16*a*) *x* ∼ zūwạ people are coming. ∼ ƙamar jībi zại tāshị at the time of writing, he plans to start in two days or so. (2) *x* ∼ naŋ, ∼ naŋ, sǎi sukạ zō = anạ̄ naŋ, rạn naŋ sǎi

sukạ zō then suddenly they came. (3) bạ̄ ∼ zūwạ ba = *the much commoner* bā ạ zūwạ people are not coming (Gram. 19*a*), *Vd.* bạ̄ . . . ba C1. 2. (4) ∼ sọ *Vd.* sọ 1*c*. (5) ∼ yạban kūrā *Vd.* kūrā 30. (6) anạ̄ gạ yāƙị *Vd.* yāƙị 1*l*. (7) anạ̄ barịn na zaune *Vd.* zaune 2*b*. (8) anạ̄ rabạ ka dạ kīwọ *Vd.* rabạ 1*f*. (9) anạ̄ wata *Vd.* wani 4*b*. (10) anạ̄ ganiŋ wuyạm birị *Vd.* wuyạ 1*l*. (11) anạ̄ zạ̄ɓē *Vd.* zạ̄ɓē 5. (12) anạ̄ tūwō *Vd.* barẹkatạ. (12) anạ̄ fushī dạ gạurākạ *Vd.* ɓērū. (14) anạ̄ darạ *Vd.* darạ 1*c*. (15) anạ̄ dạrīyā *Vd.* tạunā 2*a*.iv. (16) anạ̄ lahīyā *Vd.* dōkị 1*m*. (17) anạ̄ kūkan targaɗẹ *Vd.* kūkā 1*b*.v. (18) anạ̄ tsāwā *Vd.* kurman 1.

B. (ạnā) (1) where ? (*Vd.* ịnā). (2) ∼ dạ manạ̄nị *Vd.* nānẹ 1*d*.

C. (ạnạ̄) (1) how on earth can I ! (2) where on earth could I get it ! (3) how can that be !

*anạb *Ar. m.* (*sg., pl.*) grape.

ạnagọ *Sk. m.* yanạ̄ ∼ he's suffering hunger as he cannot enjoy furā without milk and there is no milk to be had.

aŋ'ạunā *Vb.* 1C *intens. from* aunạ.

anạwātịr *Eng. m.* lavender-water.

ancanī *Kt. m.* = hancinī.

andīrā *f.* (*pl.* ạndịrai) heddle of loom separating warp (zạrē) from woof (abạ̄wā) = *Kt.* zargagā.

ạnfạnī *Vd.* ạmfạnī.

anga A. (aŋgạ) *Eng. f.* anchor.

B. (aŋgạ) *Zar.* where ? *x* zạ̄ ka ∼ nẹ̄ where are you off to ?

angaje A. (aŋgạjē) *Vb.* 1C pushed over (*cf.* ạŋgazạ).

B. (aŋgạjē). (1) *Vd.* ạŋgazạ. (2) *m.* (*a*) = bạ̄ƙạcē. (*b*) *Sk.* nodding from drowsiness.

aŋgajējẹ *m.* (*f.* aŋgajējịyā) *pl.* aŋgajē-ạŋgajē abundant (*of liquid or granular*) *x* yā bā nị gishirī ∼ he gave me much salt. yā bā nị dāwạ aŋgajējịyā he gave me much guineacorn (*in both cases, we could say* aŋgajē-ạŋgajē ; *cf.* aŋgazā).

angaji A. (ạŋgạji) *Vd.* ạŋgazạ.

B. (aŋgạjī) *m.* (*secondary v.n. of* ạŋgazạ) *x* sunạ̄ aŋgạjinsạ = sunạ̄ ạŋgazạ tasạ they are pushing him.

angalala *f.* (1) cotton-fluff. (2) nap of material.

angalē *m.* (1) type of cheap tobacco (= būḳị 2). (2) yāyiŋ ∼ *m.* = bana bā kwabọ.

angarā *f.* (1) bag of plaited grass in which young Gwaris keep money. (2) yārọ bābụ ∼ marāyạ a boy without a money-bag is no better than an orphan.

Angas *m.* the Angass people.

angaya *Sk. f.* (1) = rūdūwā 1. (2) *Nor.* dạŋ kạŋ ∼ *m.* (*f.* 'yar kạŋ ∼) *pl.* 'yaŋ kạŋ ∼ a favourite (= gabā 9a).

angāyē *Vd.* angọ.

angaza A. (angazạ). (1) *Vb.* 2 (*Vd.* angaji) (*p.o.* angajē, *n.o.* angaji) pushed. (2) *m.*, *f.* attack *x* suŋ kai ∼ ạ Masạr they attacked Egypt. sum fārạ sābaŋ ∼ they have opened a new attack.

B. (angazā) *Vb.* 1C. (1) pushed onto, into. (2) gave much liquid or granular matter *x* nā ∼ masạ gyadā (hatsī) (kudī) I gave him abundant groundnuts (corn) (money), *cf.* angajējẹ. (3) suŋ angazạ dukạŋ ḳarfinsụ they used all their strength. yā angazạ dukạŋ ḳarfinsạ yạ cī mụ he applied all his strength to conquering us.

angizạ = angazạ.

angọ *m.* (*pl.* angāyē = angwāyē = angwunạ). (1) (*a*) bridegroom (*epithet is* Angọ, watạ sābaŋ ganī = ∼ bā gūdạ = Jēsạ = Sarkiŋ watạ dạ kwānā gōmạ = Angọ, hanạ gādā = ḳịgō = ạrūsị = āwạl). (*b*) samāriŋ ∼ bridegroom's friend-attendants. (*c*) babbaŋ abōkiŋ ∼ best man. (2) angwaŋ ḳannī = *Sk.* angwaŋ jēgọ man whose wife is a nursing-mother (*Vd.* amaryā 7). (3) Angọ *name for* boy. (4) *Kt.* gudụŋ ∼ *m.* mock flight of bridegroom and his friends before wedding. (5) hawaŋ angwāyē *m.* parading of bridegroom and friends after wedding (= *Kt.* tāka angọ). (6) angwaŋ kūrā kanā dakạ, a kạŋ daurạ aurē, iŋ kā ฉ̄tō wajẹ, aurē yā mutụ when the cat's away, the mice play. (7) *Vd.* wankaŋ angọ. (8) bọriŋ ∼ *Vd.* bọrī 4.

angulū = ungulū.

angunci = angwanci.

anguryā *f.* (1) cottonseed (*cf.* guryā).

(2) tā gamu dạ ∼ , ta washē tạ *woman* got hæmorrhoids.

Angustạ = Angushạt *m.* August.

angūwā = angwā = ungūwā *q.v.*

angwanci *m.* (1) marriage-feast (= walīmạ = bịkī). (2) being a bridegroom *x* yanā zamaŋ ∼ he is a bridegroom.

angwāyē *Vd.* angọ.

anhū *Nor.* = ungō.

*anīdị *Ar. m.* stubborn P.

anini A. (anīnī) *m.* (*pl.* anīnai). (1) tenth of a penny. (2) button (= matsạ 1*h*). (3) military officer's star of rank. (4) tsakāninsụ, bā shirị kō na ∼ they hate the sight of one another.

*B. anīnị *m.* (*pl.* anīnai) *Ar.* man with undersized penis.

anītā *Vb.* 3A exerted one's best efforts (*cf.* anīyạ).

anīyạ *Ar. f.* (1) (*a*) yā yi ∼ he exerted himself to the utmost. (*b*) yā daurạ ∼ (= yā dauri ∼ = yā yi ∼ = yā dauḳi ∼) zaị yī he decided, determined to do it. yā daurạ anīyạr fādạ musụ he decided to attack them. sun yi nīyyạ bā sā fāsāwā they're determined not to give up. nīyyạrsa wai yạ sāmi fādạ his object was to get into favour. nīyyạ tasụ, bạ zā sụ zāmẹ ba sǎi . . . their intention was not to halt till . . . (*c*) yanā anīyạr zūwạ he's eager to come. (*d*) *Vd.* ḳwaryā 1*g*. (2) (*a*) buck up ! (*b*) gee up ! (3) sạnnū dạ ∼ greeting ! (*reply is* sạnnū kadăi). (4) yā yi ∼makōmīyā he's hoist with his own petard. (5) *Vd.* bịsmillā 2. (6) (*a*) anīyạrkạ tạ bī kạ evil recoils on the doer. (*b*) baḳar ∼ evil character. maị baḳar ∼ evilly disposed P. kyạk-kyāwar ∼ gạrēshi he has a good character. (7) dạ ∼ on purpose (= takạnas *q.v.*). (8) ḳwarai dạ ∼ extremely.

ankạ *Sk.* = akạ.

ankallạ = inkallạ.

ankara A. (ankarạ) *Vb.* 3B *x* (1) yā wucẹ, baŋ ∼ ba he passed, but I did not notice. bạ sụ ∼ ba, sǎi gā su suŋ kinsạ kǎi cikiŋ hatsạrī they did not notice that they were in danger. (2) Audụ, ∼ gạrēshi Audu is observant.

B. (Ankarạ) *f.* Accra.

anku = ankwạf = ankwạ *Eng. f.* (*sg.*,

pl.) handcuff. **an sā masạ** ~ he has been handcuffed.

aŋkuntạs *Kt. m.* type of thick-headed bulrush-millet.

aŋkwạ *Vd.* **aŋku.**

aŋkyarō *x* **ƙashiŋ** ~ *m.* persistent ill-luck. **maɩ ƙashiŋ** ~ *m.*, *f.* persistently unlucky P.

annā *Vd.* **arnẹ.**

anna'ạshī *Ar. m.* bier (= **mạƙạrā** 1*a*).

annabci *Ar. m.* (1) prophesying. (2) prophecy.

annabị *m.* (*pl.* **annabāwā** (*Hebrew-Ar.*)). (1) any prophet. (2) (*a*) the Prophet Muhammad. (*b*) **Ạnnabị Mụhammadụ sall Ạllāhụ ạlaɩhị wa sạllamạ** the Prophet Muhammad, on whom be peace! (*Vd.* **Mụhammadụ**). (*c*) (i) **Shūƙạbaŋ Annabāwā** the prophet. Muhammad. (ii) *Vd.* **cɩƙạmakị.** (*d*) (i) **mun rọ̄ƙēkụ Ạllā dạ Ạnnabị kụ** zō we conjure you to come! (ii) *Vd.* **baŋgō** 2. (*e*) *Vd.* **mūdạnabị.** (3) sun zamā kạmaŋ ~ dạ kāfirī they're like "oil and water" (= shiɓạ 3). (4) *Vd.* **bạmmī.**

*****annafaƙạ** *Ar. f.* food, provisions.

annākɩyā *f.* sweatiness of face, neck, and shoulders and its effect on clothing (= **maiƙọ** 3).

annakō *Sk. m.* type of small hare.

annạkwạshā *f.* = **dạrmạsōsụ̄wā.**

annamīmanci *Ar. m.* mischief making.

annạmīmị *m.* (*f.* **annạmīmɩyā**) *pl.* **annạmɩmai** *Ar.* mischief maker.

annasarạ *f.* = **nasarạ.**

annạshụ̄wā *Ar. f.* (1) feeling happy about something (= **nịshātsị** *q.v.*). (*cf.* **fạra'ạ**). (2) **annạshụ̄war kụrēgē** false air of benevolence in P. who gives nothing to anyone.

annẹ = **arnẹ.**

annishụ̄wā *f.* = **annạshụ̄wā.**

annɩtā = **anɩtā.**

anniya A. (**annīyạ**) *f.* = **aniyạ.**
    B. (**annīyā**) *Vd.* **arnẹ.**

annukurạ *Ar. f.* hostility.

annō̄bā *f.* (*Ar.* **alwabā'**). (1) (*a*) widespread epidemic : plague. (*b*) **māgạniŋ ạllō̄bā** *Vd.* **yawạ** 6. (2) *Vd.* **sạŋƙạrau, rậi** 1*q*.

annumụr = **annumụrī** *m.* fistula of withers of donkẹy, camel.

annūrị *Ar. m.* (1) afterglow of sun. (2) aureole emanating from saint's grave. (3) (*a*) **yanā dạ** ~ he has a cheerful expression. (*b*) **annūrɩm fuskạ, kaurɩŋ hanjī** bright faces shows full stomachs !

anọ *m.* (1) **sunā** ~ = **raushị** 2. (2) **yā yi** ~ it looks good, it is of good quality. (3) wedding-festivities. (4) *Kt.* an yi musụ ~ the bride's parents have given presents to her and the bridegroom during the wedding-feast (**bɩkī**) = *Kt.* **bāyē** 2.

anōbịsī (*Eng.* it's not my business) = **adaŋkɩyā** 1.

*****ansa** = **amsa.**

antạ *Sk.* = **hantạ.**

antạyā *Vb.* 1C *Kt. x* **yā** ~ **mini rūwā** he threw water over me and drenched me.

anukurạ *Sk. f.* = **annukurạ.**

anya A. (**anyạ**) (1) *f.* (*pl.* **anyōyī**) = **amyạ.** (2) well I never ! (3) ~ **haƙạ zā kạ yi mịnị** ? is *that* how you treat me ! (*reply* har dạ zumạ).
    B. (**ạnya** ?) (1) yes, I suppose it's as you say ! (2) My word ! (3) Bother !

anza (**ạnzā**) *Sk. f.* the tree **hạnzā** *q.v.*

ạp (1) bother it all ! (2) by the way . . . (3) ~ **doŋ wannạŋ kaɗai, mẹ̣ zaɩ sā** well, what does *that* matter ! '(4) *Vd.* **afat.**

ar (1) ~ **dạ kai** damn you ! ~ **dạ shī** blast him ! (2) ~ **naŋ, kụ** look, there he is ! (*i.e. escaped prisoner, hunted quarry, etc.*).

ara A. (**ạrā**) (*Ar.* **a'āra**). *Vb.* 2. (1) borrowed T. *itself* to be handed back (*cf.* **rạntā, arō, rạncē, bāshi**) *x* nā **ạri rɩgā ạ wurinsạ** I borrowed a gown from him. (2) *Vd.* **arō.** (3) **kadạ kạ ạri bākīnā, kạ ci mini ạlbasạ** don't put words in my mouth ! (4) *Vd.* **yāfạ** 1*c.* (5) = **arạ** 2*b.*
    B. (**arạ**) (1) *Vb.* 1A. (*a*) lent T. *itself* to be handed back (*cf.* **rạntā rạncē, arō, bāshi**) *x* nā ~ **masạ rɩgā** I lent him a gown. **ạbiŋ wani wụyar arāwā gạrēshi** how can one lend another's property ! (*b*) *Vd.* **arō.** (*c*) nā ~ **masạ rɩgā·** I borrowed a gown for him. (2) *f.* (*a*) = **tụbau.** (*b*) **arạ** = **ạrā.** (i) basketry fishtrap. (ii) **im bạ**

a gamu a arą ba, a gamu a kōmā I'll get even with you *somehow* !

C. (arā) *Yor. m., f.* novice(s), greenhorn(s) (*pl. also* arārē).

arą-arą *m., f.* (*sg., pl.*) type of long-legged ram, goat, sheep (= *Zar.* gambąrī 2).

arąbī *Sk. m.* yā ci ∼ = yā karɓi ∼ he accepted a bribe.

Ạrąbīyyạ Arabic language ; Arabic sciences, makarantar ∼ school where Arabic subjects are taught.

arādụ *Ar. f.* (1) (*a*) thunder. (*b*) dūtsąŋ ∼ = gątariŋ ∼ . (2) (*a*) *For oaths formed with* arādụ, *Vd.* famfatsā, kuɓēwā, gājimąrē 4, kwaŋkwatsī, shaushau, tarnatsā. (*b*) *Vd.* 5 *below.* (3) arādụ caŋ = ạbassamạ 2 (*but the former is only said jokingly*). (4) tarar dạ arādụ dạ kā ya yi = tarar dạ arādụ dom fādiŋ kậi ya yi he interfered in matters above his head. (5) *Sk.* (*a*) yā shā arādụ, ta kāmạ he was false to his oath. (*b*) nā shā ∼ bạ zaŋ yi ba I swear not to do it. (*c*) *Vd.* 2 *above.*

araŋcī = araŋcī *m.* (*Ar.* arraŋ'). (1) thread's being of fine gauge. (2) araŋcīŋ kyaụ = araŋīyạ 4.

araŋīyạ *f.* (1) (*a*) finely-spun thread = ayạnyanạ (*cf.* araŋcī). (*b*) finely-woven fabric. (2) araŋīyạr diŋkī fine (*i.e.* tiny) sewing. (3) araŋīyạr rụɓụtū good tiny writing. (4) Kạnde, araŋīyạr kyaụ garētạ Kande has good, small features, is small and neatly-built. zanạn naŋ araŋīyạr kyaụ garēshi this cloth is of superior thinnish texture (*cf.* nāmạ 2*c*).

araŋīyancī *m.* = araŋcī.

arafō *m., f.,* weak (*re person(s), pot(s), calabash(es)*).

aragullē *Vd.* alagullē.

arahā *f.* (*Ar.* arrukhsā). (1) (*a*) cheapness *x* yanạ dạ ∼ = yā yi ∼ it is cheap. (*b*) ∼ tā fādī there's a slump. arahā tā fādī, maị sayē baị zō ba bargains were lost as there were no buyers. (*c*) suŋ karyar masạ arahā they sold it to him cheaply (*Vd.* karyạ 1*e*). (*d*) rashịn tayị, a kạm bar arahā any port in a storm. (2) A. in general use, easily got. (3) the

psychological moment for *x* yā sạmi arahar Sarkī he seized on just the right moment to address the chief. (4) arahar tsạdā garēshi = arahar ƙafạr birnī garēshi it's cheap but requires expense to put it in order. (5) arahar kunū garēshi = arahar kunū bā tạ adō it's cheap and nasty. (6) *adv. x* nā sạmē shi ∼ I got it easily, cheaply.

arahō *Vd.* arafō.

araı *m.* = ƙōsäi.

arairayạ *f.* = arērēyạ.

arakatā *f.* = arkatā.

arạkē *Sk. m.* = rạkē.

arakkạs *Sk. m.* squabbling.

aralạ *Vb.* 3B *Ar.* (1) happened *x* cīwọ yā ∼ illness arose. cīwọ yā aralam masạ illness befell him. yāƙi yā ∼ war broke out. ạddīnị yā ∼ a new religion has arrived. (2) is abundant *x* dāwạ tā ∼ ạ kạsūwā guineacorn is (was) abundant in the market.

arallē *m.* play where girls make a noise by gripping the little finger of the left hand with the index-finger of the right hand and then release it with a snapping sound.

*arālō *Vb.* 1E = aralạ 1.

arambadī *m.* (1) = ạlēwạ. (2) = ɗaɗau.

araŋgama *f.* (1) coming to grips in wrestling. (2) accidentally colliding. (3) yā shā ∼ he suffered trouble.

araŋgyadạ *x* araŋgyadạ ƙyāɗạ taŋīyạ bā tākạ ba what a senseless thing to do !

araptaki *Vd.* arautaki.

arạrē *Vd.* arā.

*ạ rarrạbē *m.* type of small loincloth(s).

ararraɓī *m.* the tree hanū.

ararraŋī *m.* yanạ ararraŋim faɗạ = ɓaɓɓaƙī.

ararrafō *Skt. m.* type of locust.

aras A. (ārạs = ārạshī) *m.* (1) ṅā ji ∼ I heard a chance remark apposite to what I was saying or thinking. (2) ārạshī na bāyan daŋgā, maị kashę aurē chance apposite words heard behind a wall often lead to divorce ! (3) (*with pl.* ārạsai) *Sk.* = aharạs. (4) *cf.* ārạshī.

B. (aras) *m.* (1) brittleness *x* kāyaŋ ∼ breakables. (2) ∼ dạ kai = ar 1. (3) nā ga kaitō, nā ga ∼ I've had my good and my bad times (= tsalam 1*b*).

āraṣhī *m.* (1) *Vd.* āraṣ. (2) *Ar.* compensation laid down in Mahommedan law for wounding.

a rausa *f.* game where participants collide heavily with one another (= bāṣhā = rauṣhē = jēmau), *epithet is* ḳarfī da ḳarfī.

arautaki *m.* pincers ; pliers.

arauyē *m.* (1) ∼ nānāyē song sung by women whilst grinding (*Vd.* nānāyē). (2) gāriṇ arauyē flour for making into the gruel called ḳunuṇ arauyē.

arayē *m.* = arauyē.

arba *Ar. f.* (1) 4,000. ∼ da bīyar 4,005 ; 4,500. (2) *in gambling, if cowries fall two with the slit underneath* (kifē), *and four with slit on top, we say* sun yi arba. (3) mun yi arba da shī we met him unexpectedly (= kaciɓiṣ). (4) mutum yā yi ∼ *Vd.* wuyā 1*h*.

arba'iṇ *Ar. f.* (1) 40. (2) daṇ ∼ *m.* early-ripening variety of beans, maize, sweet-potatoes, etc. (= dāmunā 2).

arbaminya = arbamīya *Ar. f.* 400.

arbu *Ar. m.* (*used in counting dollars, hides*) *x* rīyal 5 da ∼ five and a quarter Maria Theresa dollars.

are A. (arē) *Vb.* 1A. (1) borrowed all of (*cf.* arā). (2) (*with dative*) lent all of *x* nā ∼ masa sū duka (*cf.* arā).
     B. (arē) *f.* the letter " r ".

are-are (1) come sheep ! (2) *m.* = ara-ara.

Arēmī *Yor. m., f.* contemptuous name for Yoruba(s), *Vd.* Bayarabe.

arērēwa = arērēya *Sk. Kt. f.* conversation of women aimed at attracting the attention of males, when talking either to men or women.

arēwā (1) *adv.* northwards *x* (*a*) yā tafi (= yā yi) ∼ he went north. (*b*) ∼ sak due northwards. (2) yā hauri ∼ he died. (3) *prep. x* ∼ da (= ∼ ga) Kano = daga ∼ da Kano to the north of Kano. karaṇ da aka yi wajaṇ ∼ da Masar the battles in the countries north of Egypt. (4) *f.* regions north of *x* ∼ duka tā zo all the northerners came. yā tafi arēwar Kano = yā tafi arēwaciṇ Kano he went to north of Kano.

arēwacī *Vd.* arēwā 4.

arewanci (arēwancī) *m.* (1) Northerners' language or customs. (2) area lying north of (*Vd.* arēwā 4).

arēwatancī *m.* = arēwancī.

arēwātāwā = arēwāwā *pl. m.* Northerners.

arfīyanci *m.* = arafīci.

arfū *x* daṇ ∼ *m.* type of pepper.

ar gida *Kt. f.* senior wife (= ūwar gidā).

argini *Sk. m.* = rabbī.

argiṣ = argishiṇka *Kt.* = ar 1.

Arguṇgu = Arguṇguṇ (1) place so called in Sokoto (*Vd.* Hausā). (2) *m.* type of large gautā.

Ari *x* gadaṇ ∼ sâi Fanna nobody but me (you, *etc.*) would put up with such a thing !

arigidī *m.* (*sg., pl.*) black and white Yoruba cloth.

arigiza *Vd.* ayā.

*āriḷī *Ar. m.* event (*cf.* arala).

ariṇgizō *m.* (1) *x* (*a*) ma'aunī yā yi ∼ the scales registered short. (*b*) kā yi mini ariṇgizam pam 2 you paid me two pounds too little. (2) cowries (*Vd.* wuri).

arīrīta *Vb.* 2. (*p.o.* arīrīcō, *n.o.* arīrīci) urged P. to do T. (= zalzala).

ārīya *f.* = arō.

arjā *f.* trouble *x* nā shā ∼ da shī it gave me trouble.

arkanē *m.* yā shā ∼ he had a bad time.

arkatā *f.* garrulity.

arkillā *f.* (*pl.* arkillū). (1) native black and white cloth. *(2) python. (3) arkillā-arkillā *adj.* variegated.

arkōmī *m., f.* (*f. also* arkōmīyā) *pl.* arkōmai = alkwararō.

arkwanci *m.* work of arkōmī.

arkwararō = alkwararō.

armasa *Vb.* 1C made T. well, did T. well (*x* gown, building, etc.).

armashī *m.* (1) (*secondary v.n. of* armasā) *x* sunā armashiṇ gini = sunā armasa gini they're building well. (2) excellence, pleasantness *x* (*a*) ∼ gareshi it is excellent. Kano tanā da ∼ Kano is a pleasant place. (*b*) sunā ∼ da jūnā they're on good terms (= āsā *q.v.*).

arnā (1) *Vd.* arne. (2) *Kt. m.* (*a*) = gwani 4. (*b*) *epithet of* wooden mazari.

arnākīyā = annākīyā.

ar naŋ, ḳụ̆ *Vd.* ar 2.

arnẹ *m.* (*f.* arnị̆yā) *pl.* arnā. (1) any pagan (*epithet is* bā̤ ka gidā̤ birnī să̆i ƙauyẹ). (2) *Vd.* kurcīyā 1*k*, shā dạ 2*b*. (3) arnā̤ sun tam mạ ƙajị, să̆i mīyau (*literally* pagans attacked reed-buck but all they got was spittle) in spite of their machinations, I ousted them all. (4) arnạn rāmị *Vd.* gafīyạ. (5) yạrdā dạ ~ *Vd.* yạrdā 2*b*. (6) rā̤gwaŋ arnā *Vd.* Ajạlạ. (7) arnā nẹ, gụmā̤gụman Jạhannamạ they are scoundrels destined for hell-fire. (8) gōnar ~ *Vd.* ạddu'ạ 1*c*. (9) bụgi asnẹ *Vd.* bụgā̤ 8. (10) madarar arnā *Vd.* gīyạ.

arō *m.* (1) (*secondary v.n. of* ạrā̤) *x* nā̤ yi aran rị̆gā = nā̤ ạri rị̆gā I borrowed a gown. (2) loan of T. *itself to be returned* (*Vd.* rạncē, bāshị) *x* (*a*) yā̤ bā̤ dạ aran rị̆gā he lent a gown. yā̤ bā̤ nị aran rị̆gā he lent me a gown. (*b*) kāyaŋ ~ *m.* borrowed property (*cf.* arạ). (*c*) haƙɔ̆raŋ ~ false teeth. (*d*) *Vd.* mai dạ 2*h*. (*e*) ƙafạr wani mại wụyar ~, im bạ tạ yi tsawō ba, tā̤ yi gạjērē borrowed plumes are hard to wear. (*f*) kō̤inā̤ mại ~ zā̤ shi, dạ sanị̆m mại rị̆gā he who pays the piper, calls the tune. (*g*) ạbiŋ ~ bā̤ yā̤ rufẹ katarā̤ one cannot make free with a borrowed thing, a guest cannot behave as he would at home. (*h*) bā̤ ā̤ aram bā̤kim mụtụm ạ ci masạ ạlbasạ don't put words in a person's mouth ! (*j*) hạnạ ~ *Vd.* ạllūrạ. (*k*) zanạŋ ~ *Vd.* kạtạmbirị. (3) *adv.* on loan *x* yā̤ bā̤ nị rị̆gā ~ he gave me a gown on loan.

arọ-arọ = arẹ-arẹ 1.

arɔ̆taki *Vd.* ạrautaki

arrạhē *Vd.* allạhē.

ạrrạkē *Sk.* *m.* = rạkē.

arshị *Vd.* yā̤.

artābụ *Vd.* attābụ.

artai *m.* (1) excrement (= kāshī). (2) yā̤ shā̤ ~ he suffered trouble. am bā̤ shị ~ he was given trouble, pain, punishment (*cf.* kāshī).

ạ'ru-ạrū‖ *x* tuŋ ~ since long long ago.

arugumạ *f.* load of pots or calabashes (*epithet is* ~ rībạ kim fi ūwā).

Arugụŋgụŋ = Argụŋgụŋ.

ạrūsị *Ar.* ~ bā̤ gū̆dạ *epithet of* bridegroom.

arūtạŋ-arūtạŋ *Kt.* = ạru-ạrū.

arwā (*Ar.* arrau'a) *f.* (1) inspiring feeling of helpless fear *x* kūrā̤ tā̤ yi (= tā̤ zubạ) masạ ~ seeing the hyena petrified him with fear (= waibụ̄wā̤ = gizọ 2*d*). (2) yā̤ yi (= zubạ) minị ~ he cast spell on me by *incantation* (1, 2 = ƙōfī = gizọ 2*d* = ƙwārī 5), *cf.* sammụ, lāyạ. (3) *Kt.* = dūbā̤ 2.

ạryạŋ = ụryạŋ.

arzikī = azzikī.

ạrzuk = bā̤but.

arzuta A. (ạrzutạ) *Vb.* 3B is (was) prosperous.

  B. (arzụtā = *Sk.* arzụttā) *Vb.* 1C rendered prosperous.

as *Vd.* cas, as-as; kā̤zā 1*a*.x.

asa A. (āsā) (*Ar.* assā'atu) *f.* = armashī *x* (1) rị̆gan nạŋ ~ gạrētạ this gown is nice. (2) zamā̤ yā̤ yi musụ ~ they're on pleasant terms. (3) wannạŋ cinikī yā yiwō shị dạ ~ he got this cheaply. (4) shẹkaraŋ nạŋ tā̤ zō̤ dạ ~ this year has been prosperous.

  B. (asā) *East Hausa f.* = ƙasā.

asa-asa A. (ạsā̤-asā̤) *m.* restlessness.

  B. (asạ-asạ) = as-as.

Ạsabạr *Ar.* *f.* (1) Saturday (= sātī = subdụ). Ạsabạcin naŋ = Ạsabạrin naŋ this Saturday. Ạsabạcin (= Ạsabạrin) dạ ya zō the Saturday he came. (2) mại zūcīyar ~ thief ; dishonest P.

Asabari A. (Ạsabạrī) *Vd.* Ạsabạr.

  B. (asabạrī) (*Ar.* assābūriyya) *m.* (*pl.* ạsạbạrai) mat of tsaurē.

Asabe (Ạsạbē) name given girl born on Saturday.

asabẹrī *m.* = asabạrī.

asabēru *m.* = dīdībāko.

asā̤bụ *m.* balls of pounded leaves added by Tuareg to the food tụkudī.

asā̤kē *Vd.* askā̤.

ạ sakō *m.* (1) tending flocks for payment. (2) kạraŋ ~ sheep-dog (*cf.* sạkā̤ 1*a*). (3) zāmạniŋ ~, wā̤tạu sạn dạ Ballọ ya yi wạ bāyī ~ the time of ạ sakō, i.e. when the Emir Bello of Kano ordered dissolution of marriages between slaves and free Muslims (*cf.* sạkā̤ 1*b*). (4) *kā zamā̤ ~ you're a good-for-nothing !

asala A. (asā̤lā̤) *Sk.* *f.* = tasā̤lā̤ 1, 2.

B. (ạsạlā) = ạssạlā.

C. (ạsạlā) (*abbreviation of* ạssạlāmu)
x ~ bāk̃ō bạ yā̃ rasạ sallamạr gidā
ba = ~ bāk̃ō bạ yā̃ rasạ tạmbayạr hālị
ba Bride, welcome to your husband's
home ! (*formula used in song*).

ạsạlai *Vd.* asalī.

*asalạkī *Ar. m.* (*pl.* ạsạlạkai = asulukạ)
small bag for broken saltpetre.

asalạŋ *Ar. adv.* (1) originally (*Vd.*
ạsālatạŋ). (2) (*plus negative*) not in the
least x ~ bại īyạ ba he cannot do it at all.

ạsālatạŋ x tuŋ asalạŋ ~ originally.

ạsạlātụ *Ar. m., f.* (1) the Daylight call to
prayer. (2) tuŋ ~ yanā̃ naŋ he's been
waiting since dawn (*cf.* ạssạlā, sạlātị,
sallạ).

asalī *Ar. m.* (*pl.* ạsạlai). (1) origin.
(2) pedigree x asalin Sarkim Bạrnō,
Shạm the Shehu of Bornu traces
his pedigree to Syria. asalinsạ
Bạbarbarẹ nē he's of Kanuri stock.
(3) principle. (4) reason, cause x inā
asalịn dạ ka yi'hakạ why did you do so ?
asalim mạganạ yanā̃ dạgạ Tūrai the
real cause lies in Europe. asalin cịm
mạdugū, munāfuncị nē akạ yi the
real reason for the defeat of the
caravan-leader was intrigue (= dạlīlị 1).
(5) ạ asalī originally.

asalwạyī *m.* horse's leading-rope(s)
(= mazāgī 3).

Asạma'ụ *woman's name.*

asamụ *Nor.* = sammụ.

asancị *Kt. m.* = babbaucị.

ạsạndūk̃ị *Kt. m.* = sạndūk̃ị.

ạsānī *m.* (1) tuŋ ~ from the earliest times.
(2) (*only negative sense*) x bā̃ shi dạ ~
it's unlimited. bā̃ su dạ ạsānin yawạ
they're numberless. inā ạsānin yawạŋ
kuɗinsạ what limit is there to his
wealth !

Asạntē Ashanti (*Vd.* dārạ 2*b* ; gạŋgamī
2*d*).

asara A. (ạsārạ) *f.* = hạsārạ.

B. (ạsạrā) *m., f.* nincompoop(s).

asarancị *m.* being a nincompoop.

ạsạrarrē *Vd.* hạsạrarrē.

ạsạrāru *Vd.* ạsīrī 5.

ạsārịkī = asāruk̃ụ *Ar. m.* (*f.* ạsārịkā)
thief ; rogue.

as-as (1) away fowls ! ; away animals !

(*cf.* has). (2) k̃ā̃zā mại jịmiriŋ as
epithet of headstrong P.

asasạshī *Kt. m.* = kaitạraŋ.

*ạsāsị *Ar. m.* foundations of house.

ạsawāk̃ị = asawā̃k̃ī *Ar. m.* (1) toothbrush
(*cf.* shịwākā). (2) red donkey.

Asbịn (1) Azben (*cf.* Hausā). (2)
dōk̃iŋ Asbịn *Vd.* sạntịlō. (3) mịnuŋ
Asbịn *Vd.* mịnū 2. (4) *Vd.* rāk̃umī 1*f*,
zạkaŋkạu, gyārā 1*f*. (5) *Vd.* Bạafzinẹ.

asfạraŋ *Ar. m.* saffron.

ash = kash.

Ash'abụ x Mālạm Ash'abụ yā̃ wạhalạ,
yā̃ wahalas *epithet of* troublesome P.

ashạccī *Nor.* used in ɗaŋ ashạcciŋ ūwā
blast you !

ạ shā dạ manạ̄nī *Kt.* = inā dạ manạ̄nī *Vd.*
nānẹ.

ạ shā lā̃fīyạ *m.* (1) root of a certain
tree for aperient. (2) (*Abuja Hausa*)
ạ shā lā̃fīyạ = ạ shā dạ lā̃fīyạ
tạllaŋ kōko ạ Hạbūjā *epithet of* gruel
(*because they say gruel was called
kōko but was changed to kōko from
respect for Chief's son Kōkọ*).

ashā̃līyạ *f.* half a segment of kolanut
(*Vd.* azā̃rā).

asham *Ar. m.* special evening devotions
during Ramadan.

ashạma'ạ *Ar. f.* candle (= ạbēlạ).

ạshānā *f.* (1) (*a*) match(es). (*b*) (i) gidaŋ ~
m. matchbox. (ii) *Vd.* fạŋkō 2. (2)
type of red and white European
cloth.

ashar A. (ạshạr) *Ar. m.* (1) abusive
language. (2) *Vd.* farin cik̃ị 2.

B. (ashạr) (1) = kurī 1. (2) *Vd.*
mạrhạbā 2.

ashara A. (asharā) *f.* (1) type of tobacco
(*epithet is* ~ bā̃ mā̃gā̃gī). (2) *Zar.*
miscarriage.

B. (ạshạrā) *f.* = ạshạr.

ashạrāru *m.* (*f.* ạshạrārịyā) *pl.* ạshạrā̃rai
Ar. (1) foulmouthed P. (2) evil-living P.
(3) scum of humanity.

ashā̃re-ạshā̃rē *m.* repeated abusiveness.

*ashạrgạ *f.* indecisive struggle exhausting
both sides.

ạsharīyạ *f.* = ạshạr.

ạsharkwatōtạ = ạsharkwatōtọ *m.* unseemly talk before seniors (*cf.* sharkwạtā).

ạ shā rūwạn tsuntsāyē *m.* game of children.

ạshāshā *m.* plaited grass bag(s).

ashe A. (ạshē). (1) (*standing first in clause*) well !, oh ! *x* ~ yā zō jịyạ ? oh, he came yesterday, did he ? tun dạ mātā sukẹ yịŋ hakạ, ~ sum fi kōmē ƙarfī as women do that, then they are stronger than anything else ! (2) (*following a verb*) *x* suŋ gānẹ ạshē dǎi gạskīyar mạganạ tasạ well, now they realize the truth of what he said. wạtọ kā ga ạshē yā ɓad dạ kai for in fact he has betrayed you. tā ga ~ mạƙāfọ nē well, she saw he was blind.

B. (ạshē ?) really ? ; fancy !

ashịbtā *Vd.* ashụtā.

ạshịrịŋ *Ar. f.* 20.

ashō = ashū *Yor. m.* wool-embroidered perforated canvas uppers of carpet-slippers ready for making-up.

āshūrā *Ar. f.* devotions done on 19th Muharram.

ashụtā (*Ar.* asshabaka) *f.* bird snare or fish net made of mẹdī.

āsibcị *m.* the relationship denoted by āsibī.

asibi A. (āsịbī) *Ar. m.* (*pl.* āsịbai) the type of male blood-relation who in Muslim inheritance receives only part of the estate.

B. (Asibị) *Sk.* = Asạbē.

Asibịcī *Vd.* Asabạcī.

Asibịt *Vd.* Asabạr.

asịbitị *Eng. m.* hospital.

asigịrī *m.* metal-shafted spear.

asilịkī *Ar. m.* tinsel-thread (*cf.* ạlhạrīnị).

ạsịrce *used in* ạ ~ in secret.

ạsīrī *Ar. m.* (*pl.* ạsīrai = ạsīrū = asīrirrukạ. *Vd. also* 5). (1) (*a*) a secret. (*b*) yā tōnẹ ạsīrinsụ he blabbed their secrets (= bạŋkạdā 2), *cf.* tōnạ. (*c*) dạgạ ~ secretly. (*d*) nā gayạ masạ cikiŋ ~ I told him secretly. (*e*) suŋ ƙullạ ~ tạre they have a secret in common. (*f*) (i) mạtar mụtụm marufar ạsīrinsạ *Vd.* marufā 3. (ii) *Vd.* darē 1*a.*ii. (2) *Vd.* rufạ 1*d.* (3) ạsīrimmụ

dạ mikitsịyā the secret is between us two (*for* mikitsịyā *is the only one knowing amount of padding put into woman's coiffure*). (4) *cf.* būɗẹ 1*k*. (5) asạrārụ *pl.* magic charm or remedy (*epithet is* ~ bạ mạmāki).

asirkā *f.* (1) hole (*a*) bored in nose of pack-ox (*cf.* zạrī), (*b*) in vessel where warp is woven. (2) ạllūrạ mại ~ any darning needle (*cf.* ạllūrạ, bạsillā, bạ Jạkarā, sāran tūrụ).

asịrtā *Vb.* 1C *x* yā ~ minị he told me in secret.

ạsịrū *Vd.* ạsīrī.

asīsītā *f.* (*pl.* ạsīsịtai) the bird Ruby-cheeked Cordon Blue (*Uraeginthus bengalus*).

askā *f.* (*pl.* asạ̄ƙē). (1) (*a*) razor. (*b*) askar dubū dạ ta wurị (*lit.* one razor costs 1,000 and another costs one cowry, but it is a razor all the same) one must cut one's coat according to one's cloth. (*c*) *Vd.* lādaŋ ~, tsaurī 1. (2) (*a*) penknife (*cf.* wuƙā). (*b*) scalpel (*often used for making round hide-boxes*). (3) (*a*) type of pattern in plaited mats. (*b*) 'yaŋ asạ̄ƙē the elongated and pointed " tongues " embroidered on gowns (six on left shoulder, two on right chest) = lāyạ 3*b*, *cf.* mạlụm-mālum. (4) (*a*) sunạ̄ dạ ~ they have hereditary facial tribal-marks (= shạsshāwạ = tsāgā 2 = wutā 3*c*), *cf.* jạrfā, zụbē, zānạ 3, kurmā 2. (*b*) ~ ɗayā, mạganạ ɗayā *Vd.* ŋgas. (5) tanạ̄ dạ ~ she has a certain vaginal disease (*thought to cause razor-like edge giving soft chancre to man sleeping with her*) = miŋgyaŋ = yaŋkā 2*d*. (6) short pieces joining upright bars of gạrmā to centre-bar. (7) kạ yi ~ hurry up ! (8) mạtaccīyar ~ deposed P. who is a nuisance to his successor. (9) jirgịŋ ~ *m.* cantankerous P. (*Vd.* jirgī 6.). (10) ~ tā ɓacẹ *Vd.* birinciŋ kulạ. (11) ƙarfạŋ ~ *Vd.* tsaurī 1. (12) *Vd.* shāshẹ 1*b*.

askalāyẹ *Sk. m.* type of edible grasshopper(s).

askạr *m.* = bạaskarẹ.

askẹ *Vb.* 1A. (1) shaved *x* nā ~ kạ̌i I shaved my head. yā ~ minị kạ̌i he shaved my head. **nā ∼ gēmu** I shaved off my long beard (*cf.* **gyāram fuska**). (2) (*a*) **nā ∼** I've given up that habit (= **saukę 4**). (*b*) *Vd.* **sąmartaka**. (3) **yā ∼ ni** he abused me. (4) *Sk.* **dōkina yā ∼ su sarai** my horse outpaced them all. (5) *Vd.* **askį**.

askį *m.* (1) ·act of shaving head (*this is regularly done monthly to men and all infants, cf.* **kundumē 2b**). (*a*) **nā yi ∼** I shaved my head. **yā yi minį ∼** he shaved my head (*cf.* **gyāram fuska**). (*b*) **yā̧ yi masa ∼** *Vd.* **kuturū 1b**. (2) (*secondary v.n. of* **askę**) *x* **yana̧ askę ka̧i = yana̧ askin ka̧i** he's shaving his head. (3) **zā̧ mu ∼** (*said by women*) we're going to where first shaving of infant's head was done this morning, seventh day after birth. (4) **∼ yā zō gaba̧n gōshī** it's within an ace of completion (*Vd.* **ga̧bā 9**). (5) *Vd.* **sāmu 2c**.

askunnīyā *Sk. f.* (1) = **tufānīyā**. (2) **∼ d̶a̶i tā sam fitā tai** nobody knows where he's gone to.

asnę *Sk.* (1) = **arnę**. (2) *Vd.* **buga 8**.

Assabar = Asabar.

Assabat = Assabit *Sk. f.* Saturday = **Asabar** *q.v.*

assābu̧ = asābu̧.

assafā *Vb.* 1C = **alkintā**.

assa̧kā *Vb.* 1C *x* **mu assa̧ka kāyansa̧ ga̧ba** let us push forwards load on donkey or pack-ox which has slipped backwards (*cf.* **zunku̧d̶ā 1b**).

assa̧lā̧ *f.* (1) Come to prayer ! (*said in some places by the* **lādan** *after saying* **hayya̧ ala̧s salā** *q.v.*), *cf.* **a̧sa̧lātu, sa̧lāti, salla̧**. (2) **·yana̧ ∼** he's shouting, screaming.

assa̧lāmu *Vd.* **a̧lēka, a̧lēkun, asa̧lā**.

asshā how distressing !

asshāhi *Ar. m.* (1) tea (= **shāhi = shāyi 2**). (2) **yā buga̧ ∼** he made tea.

Assibicī = Assubu̧cī = *Sk.* **Assibit**. *Vd.* **Asabar**.

astagfiru̧llāha̧ (1) may God pardon me ! (*for unintentional perjury, etc.*). (2) *expression indicating* regret, surprise, fear (*cf.* **sāfiru̧lla̧**).

a̧sū *m.* (1) type of cloth-destroying moth (= *Sk.* **su̧sūwa̧**). (2) *m., f.*

wastrel (*epithet is ∼* **b̶āta̧ kudī**) *x* **kai ka̧man ∼ nȩ̄** you waste everything.

asu̧ba̧ *f.* = **asu̧bāhi** *m.* (1) time just before sunrise *x* **asu̧bāhi· yā yī** it's already just before sunrise. **asu̧bā̧ tana̧ yī** it's getting on for pre-sunrise time. (2) *Vd.* **kwal 2b**. (3) *Vd.* **tāshin ∼**. (4) **dōdan ∼** *Vd.* **la̧dan**.

asubancī *m.* = **sa̧mmakō 1a**.

asulku̧mī *Ar. m.* (*pl.* **asulkuma̧**) small-mouthed dressed skin bag.

asuluka̧ *Vd.* **asala̧kī**.

asurkā *Vd.* **asirkā**.

asurku̧mī *Vd.* **asulku̧mī**.

asussu̧bā̧ *f.* = **asu̧ssu̧bāhi** *m.* earliest stage of **asu̧bā̧**.

asūsu *m.* (1) moneybox of child or woman (= **banki 5b**). (2) **tā yi asūsun sulę uku̧ a̧ banki** she put away 3s. in the moneybox. (3) **yā yi ∼** he has made a good investment (*e.g. said where marriage does not materialize and dower is returned to suitor : where P., by fattening animal, sells at good price and recoups himself fully for cost and upkeep, etc.*).

asūtā *Vd.* **ashu̧tā**.

asūwa *m.* (*sg., pl.*) grey donkey.

asu̧wāki *Vd.* **a̧sa̧wāki**.

aswa̧ *m.* = **asūwa̧**.

Aswad *used in* **Bahar ∼ = Baharu̧l Aswad** *Ar. m.* the Black Sea.

a̧t *Sk.* = **a̧p**.

ata'āmi *Vd.* **a̧d̶d̶a'āmi**.

atafā *f.* (1) ginned-cotton. (2) **shiga atafā Māla̧m** (*said jokingly for* **gāfa̧rtā 2a**).

a̧ tāga̧ji gwīwa̧ (1) the cry of (*a*) cooked-meat hawkers. (*b*) beggars. (2) *m.* any cooked meat for sale.

atakāku̧m staff of **tu̧mfāfīyā**-wood used by Asbin traders for securing loads on their camels.

atakē *adv.* in large quantities.

a̧tā̧kwī *m.* *x* **yā daura̧ minį ∼** he swindled me.

atalā *Sk. m.* red monkey.

atala̧shī *Vd.* **a̧dala̧shī**.

a̧tamfā *f.* any strong-patterned European cloth = **cākiri 2b** (*cf.* **a̧ba̧dā**).

atannu̧tī (rustic) = **ta̧'annu̧tī**.

ataras = atarashī *m.* type of red kolanut from the Gold Coast.

atasāshī *Sk.* = kaitạraŋ.

atasāyẹ *Vd.* atisāyẹ.

ātātā *Sk.* yā kai nị ∼ he reduced me to desperation.

atạtau *Kt.* yā ƙī ∼ he refused point-blank.

ạtē *Yor. m.* (*sg., pl.*) small basket, many of which superimposed, are used by retailers of kolas, soap, tobacco (= tẹrẹrē).

ạtikẹ = ạtiki *m.* talc-powder.

Atīƙu = Atīƙu man's name.

ạtilẹ = ạtilis *m.* (*sg., pl.*) name of oil-producing tree (*Canarium schweinfurthii*).

atisāyẹ *Eng. m.* exercising a horse.

atishāwạ *f.* (1) sneezing. (2) sun yō minị ∼ = sun yi minị ∼ dạ faɗạ = sun yi minị atishāwạr damō = sun yi minị atishāwạr dilā they suddenly " went for " me.

ạ tọ well then . . .

*ạtsạ'āmị *Vd.* ạdɗạ'āmị.

atsabībancị *Vd.* hatsabībancị.

ạtsalạshī *Vd.* ạdalạshī.

ạtsāyā *f.* = ạdalạshī.

Attā (1) = Attāhiru. (2) Attā īgbịrạ the Attah of Igbirra. (3) *Vd.* garạ 3 ; ạttā garạ.

*ạtṭạ'āmị *Vd.* ạdɗạ'āmị.

attābu *Ar. m.* trouble, difficulty.

ạttā garạ *f.* (*sg., pl.*) (1) coconut. (2) coconut-tree. (3) *Vd.* garạ 3 ; kwā- kwạ 4.

Attāhiru man's name (= Attā 1).

attājircị *m.* = tajircị.

ạttājịrī *m.* (*f.* ạttājịrā) *pl.* ạttājịrai wealthy trader (= tājịrī).

attakā (*Ar.* attāqatu power) *only negatively* *x* bạ shi dạ ∼ he's a listless P.

ạttakạbāru *Vd.* Ajauru.

ạttalạshī *Vd.* ạdalạshī.

Attaniŋ *Sk. f.* = Littiniŋ.

attạtai, attạtairaŋ *Vd.* affạfai, affạfairaŋ.

Attaurā (*Hebrew-Ar.*) *f.* Old Testament.

ạttē *m.* = ạtē.

*ạttsạ'āmị *Vd.* ạdɗạ'āmị.

atubau = atạtau.

atụmātụr *Eng. m.* (*sg., pl.*) tomato.

ạtụmurmur. (1) what terrific buttocks ! (= ạmūmụ). (2) naɗị kạmaŋ ∼ what a man he is for wearing turbans night and day !

atụnī *m.* dysentery (= *Sk.* dịɗɗirạ 1).

atụrābị (*Ar.* sand). (1) scattering *x* yā yi minị ∼ dạ kāyā he scattered my goods (= ạwātsīmạ 2). (2) aikị yā yi minị ∼ the work is (was) beyond me.

ạturẹ *m.* (1) throwing handful of earth at P. in play or mockery. (2) ạturẹ bā yạ rabạ kạrē dạ kūrā desperate affairs need desperate remedies.

ạturfāŋ *m.* (*sg., pl.*) type of large drum.

*ạturkụmāmī *m.* (*f.* ạturkụmāmā) *pl.* ạturkụmạmai. (1) any squat camel or P. (2) what a brave fellow !

atụshāwạ *Vd.* atịshāwạ.

au A. (au) *Ar.* (1) whether . . . or ∼ kạ zō (= au kā zō), ∼ bạ kạ zō ba, ōhō I don't care whether you come or not. (2) (*with subjunctive*) must either . . . or *x* au ạ ɗaukē nị sōjạ, au m mutụ either I must be enlisted as a soldier or I must die !

    B. (au) = ạp.

Aụdī = A jēfas.

audigā *Vd.* audugā.

Audụ man's name (*Vd.* Dūmā).

audugā *f.* (1) cotton (*cf.* atạfā, aŋgụryā). (2) ciŋ ∼ = taɓiŋ ∼ gathering cotton. (3) zạ ni ṇ yi ∼ I'm off to buy or spin cotton. (4) hatsī yā yi ∼ corn's become mildewed. (5) audụgar rĭmī *Vd.* rĭmī 1*b*. (6) audụgar ɗaŋuwā tā fạsu (*a*) his faults are being bandied about. (*b*) " he's been taken down a peg ".

aụfāku (*Ar.*) *Sk. m.* mālạmiŋ ∼ = mālạmī maị bugụŋ hātịmī *q.v.* *under* hātịmī.

aujīyā *Sk. f.* game of hitting one another with forearm or elbow. (2) game of kicking one another sideways ((2) = tādīyā 2).

aukạ (1) *Vb.* 3A (*Ar.* waqa'a). (*a*) (well, house) collapsed. (*b*) (trap) closed. (*c*) attacked *x* (i) ạbōkaŋ gābā suŋ ∼ manạ the enemy attacked us. yā ∼ ạ gōnammụ it attacked our farm. (ii) yā ∼ minị dạ faɗạ he " went for me ". (iii) wani tsautsạyī yā ∼ some obstacle prevented its success. (iv) ƙaddarạ tā aukō minị misfortune befell me. (v) yā aukō minị he entered my house without permission. (*d*) ∼ dạ encountered *x* yā ∼ dạ wani mutụm he encountered somebody.

(e) **rānā taṇā aukāwā** the sun is obscured by haze. (*f*) *Vd.* **aukam, aukō, auku.** (2) *Vb.* 1A. (a) poured out. (b) threw things away.

aukam (*only before dative*) befell P. *x* **wahalad da ta aukar mini = wahalad da ta aukam mini** the calamity which befell me. **wahalad da ta aukar wa Audu** the calamity which befell Audu (*Vd.* **auka, auku**).

aukāwā (1) *Vd.* **auka** 1*e*. (2) *f.* valley.

aukē = abkē.

auki *m.* (1) (a) expansion. (b) progress *x* (i) **tafīya yā ki yi musu** ~ they could make no progress. (ii) **dōmin ~ akē yiŋ kunū, ya kōmō ya rasa** ~ the expectations were not realized. (2) lasting long *x* **kudīna sun yi** ~ my money lasted a long time.

aukō *Vd.* **auka, auku**.

auku *Vb.* 3B (*Ar.* **auqa'a**) happened *x* **wahala tā** ~ trouble arose (*cf.* **auka, aukam**). **abin da ya** ~ what occurred. **abin da ya ~ garēsu** what happened to them (= aukam). **hamayya tā ~ tsakāninsu** rivalry arose between them.

*aulu *Ar. m.* dividing out estate of deceased by Muslim Law.

auna A. (**auna**) *Vb.* 1A (*Vd.* **awo**). (1) weighed, measured. (2) tested, examined P. or T. (3) **yā ~ masa zāgi** he abused him. (4) **nā ~ azziki** I had a stroke of luck (*Vd.* **azziki** 2). (5) straightened (*road, wall*). (6) aimed *x* (a) (i) **yā ~ bindiga** he aimed the gun (= **gwada** 6*a*). (ii) **da ya ~ sau daya kō sau bīyū, sǎi ya wuce shi** after a trial leap or two, it passed him. (b) pondered on, planned T. (= **sāka** 1*b*.i). (7) *Vd.* **aunē**.

B. (**aunā**) *Vb.* 2. (1) measured part of. (2) measured from one's supplies the amount needed for the day's use (*cf.* **awo** ; **aunāka**). (3) bought by measure (*cf.* **awo**). (4) measured and removed. (5) aimed at *x* **yā auni barēwā** he aimed at the gazelle (= **dūba** 2*b* = **bārata** = **kyārā** = **dāidāita**). (6) faced towards (= **fuskanta**).

aunāka *f.* (1) **yā yi mata** ~ bridegroom gave her (his bride) corn and money prior to her moving to his home.

(2) **mai dumbula ūwar** ~ *epithet of* liberal woman corn-seller. (3) *Sk.* giving out the day's household supplies (*cf.* **aunā** 2).

aune A. (**aune**). (1) *Vb.* 1A (a) measured completely ; weighed completely. (b) tested all of ; examined all of. (2) *Vb.* 3A *x* **kafa tā** ~ foot is swollen. **kōgī yā** ~ river is in flood.

B. (**aunē**) *m.* **nā yi ~ da shī = nā yi ku auna da shī** I unexpectedly met him.

C. (**aunē**) *m.* = **daŋkarē**.

aura A. (**aurā**) (*Ar.* **'aurat** "pudenda") *Vb.* 3. (1) married (the P. who becomes one's wife or husband) *x* **Audu yā auri Kande** Audu married Kande. **Kande tā auri Audu** Kande married Audu (*cf.* **auru**). (2) suited *x* **māganin yā aurē ni** that medicine suited me. **kāsūwā tā aurē shi** his business is thriving. (3) (*before dative*) married P. to another *x* **nā auram masa 'yāta** I married my daughter to him. **nā aurar wa dāna Hadīja** I married my son to Hadija (*Vd.* **aura : aurar**).

B. (**aura**) *Vb.* 1A. (1) (*with dative*) *x* **nā ~ masa 'yāta** I married my daughter to him. **nā ~ wa dāna Hadīja** I married my son to Hadija (= **aurā** 3 = aurar). (2) *Kt.* = **haura**. (3) *m.* = **auraki**.

aurad da = aurar da.

auraki *m.* (*f.* **auraka**) light-coloured donkey.

auran *Vd.* **aurē**.

aurar da *Vb.* 4B. (1) **nā ~ 'yāta garēshi** I married my daughter to him. **nā ~ Hadīja ga dāna** I married my son to Hadija (*Vd.* **aurā** 3, **aura**). (2) **aurar da kǎi = amar da kǎi**.

aurarrē (1) *m.* (*pl.* **aurarrū**) hen-pecked husband (*cf.* **ma'auri**). (2) **aurarrīyā** *f.* (*pl.* **aurarrū**) married (*re* woman ; *for* man, *Vd.* **aurē** 1*a*, **gidā** 1*l*, **giji**); *cf.* **ma'aurīya**.

auratayya = **aurayya** *f.* intermarriage *x* **Bararō bā sā ~ da Hābe** nomad Filani do not intermarry with the indigenous population.

aure A. (**aurē**) (*Ar.* **'aurat** pudenda) *m.* (1) marriage *x* (a) **an yi masa** ~ he is

married. **an yi matạ** ~ she is married
(*cf*. **ạurarrē** 2). (*b*) **yanạ̄ nēmantạ
dạ** ~ = **yanạ̄ nēmaɳ aurantạ** he's sueing for her hand. (*c*) **nēmaɳ aurē** *m*.
courting (*Vd*. **tashị**). (*d*) *Vd*. **mạcẹ̄** 4,
dūkạ 2*b*. (*e*) **yārọ yā sō** ~ **gidansụ
bābụ gōdīyā** one must exercise patience.
(*f*) *for the stages of marriage, Vd*.
aurē 6. (2) (*a*) **auran jịn dādī** = **auran
sạn zūcīyā** (i) marriage of two persons
of disparate age or different class, etc.
(ii) temporary marriage (*called in Ar*.
tamattu' *and forbidden*). (*b*) *Vd*.
ɗūrạ 1*g*. (3) **sãi tā yi auraɳ kisạɳ wutā
kānạ tạ kōmạ gidam mijịntạ** now that
her husband has given her a triple
divorce (**sakịm battạ**) she cannot
resume the marriage till she has in
between married another man. (4) (*a*)
auran Dạndī a marriage where the
couple meet away from parents' homes
and so marry without the ordinary
formalities of **wạlīyyị** (*Vd*. **6** *below* :
ạlwalị). (*b*) *Vd*. **ɗauki sạndaɳkạ**.
(5) *x* **tạttạbạrai aurē ukụ** three pairs of
of pigeons. (6) *Stages of marriage* :
(*a*) I, the prospective bridegroom who is
courting or sueing for a girl (**yanạ̄
nēmantạ dạ aurē = yanạ̄ tashịntạ**)
send my marriage-intermediary
(**shụ̄gạbaɳ aurē**) who may be man or
woman, to the P. having authority to
give her in marriage (**wạlīyyịntạ = mại
bā dạ aurē**), this being whoever is most
nearly related to her (her grown son,
her father, etc.) with presents (**kudịɳ
aurē**) amounting to several pounds.
(*b*) Then if my advances are favourably
received by her **wạlị**, after a short
time, my **shụ̄gạbaɳ aurē** will take about
5*s*. to him (**kudịn tunị**) saying " We
are mindful : we want the marriage-
ceremony performed " (**munạ̄ tunị,
munạ̄ sọ ạ ɗaurạ aurē**) ; if her guardian
agrees, he says " Come in two days ! "
(*c*) On the second, etc., day I go with
my **shụ̄gạba** and say " We've come
seeking prosperity " (**mun zō nēmaɳ
arzịkī**) to which her guardian replies
mum bā kạ (*Vd*. **ạzzimmạ** 2). I reply
" Here is the gift for courting and
gratitude " (**gạ̄ nēmā dạ ạdạ'ā**), this

being about 4*s*. : " Here is the present
for the Father and Mother : here is 1*s*.
for the dignitary performing the ceremony " (**gạ̄ kumā kyạutar ụbā dạ ūwā :
gạ̄ sulẹ na Mālạmī**), *Vd*. **kudī** 1n. Next
they will fix the bride price I must pay
(**zā sụ yaɳkẹ minị sạdākị**), i.e. minimum
6*d*. (the quarter of a dinar *Vd*. **sạdākị**),
but usually 8*s*. are given : then the
marriage-service will be read for us (**zā
ạ ɗaurạ manạ aurē**), *cf*. **9**. (*d*) This
ɗaurịɳ aurē is usually done on Thursday
morning and she may go to her
husband's house that night, but in
Filani households, this is often delayed
for 1–12 months after the marriage-
ceremony (**ạdạ'ā**) in the case of a
virgin. When the time comes, I send
the bride's-present (**sạdākị**) and many
cloths to the bride, together with
kolas for fixing the day (**gōrạn sạ̄ rānā**)
and presents for the bridesmaids
(**kuɗin 'yam mātā**), this being accompanied by a request to her father that
on the 7th of the month I mention, he
may permit the marriage-feast to take
place (**yạ bā dạ izịnim bịkī**). His leave
having been given, on the due date,
the bridegroom gives the banquet (**zại
yi bịkī = aɳgwancị = wạlīmạ**), the
bride by then having moved to her
husband's house (**tā rigā tā tārẹ
gidam mijịntạ**) but not appearing
during the banquet (*Vd*. **būɗar
kãi**). (7) **igīyạr** ~ *Vd*. **igīyạ** 7.
(8) *Vd*. **shịgar 'yam mātaɳ amạ̄rē**.
(9) **aɳgwaɳ kūrā kanạ̄ ɗakạ, a kạn
ɗaurạ aurē, iɳ kā fitō wạje, aurē yạ̄
mutụ** when the cat is away, the mice
play (*cf*. **6***c*). (10) **auran Sarkin nōmā**
Vd. **nōmā** 1*b*.ii. (11) **auram mại dạ
wutā** *Vd*. **ạlƙaƙai**. (12) **auram mụzūrū**
Vd. **mụzūrū** 1*e*. (13) **gurgụ̄wā dạ
auran nēsạ** *Vd*. **ạbụ** 1*d*.ii. (14) **auran
rufi** *Vd*. **rufị** 6. (15) **raɳ** ~ *Vd*. **budịrī**.
(16) **dạ̄kạtā, ạ yi ma** ~ *Vd*. **dạ̄kạtā**.
(17) **auraɳ kulụmā** *Vd*. **dirịndāsọ**.
(18) **auram mutạ̄nan yạnzu** *Vd*. **dūkạ**
2*b*. (19) **auran ɗūrạ rūwā** *Vd*. **ɗūrạ** 1*g*.
(20) *Vd*. **kwānaɳ** ~ .
B. (**aurẹ**) *Vb*. 1A *x* **yā** ~ **minị mạ̄tāta**
he married my ex-wife.

a̠urō *m.* (*sg., pl.*) tsetse-fly (= **tsandō**).

a̠uru *Vb.* 3Ḃ *x* tā̠ ∼ she's not yet too old to marry (*cf.* i̠sa 3*b*, a̠urā).

ausa̠gī *m.* (1) yard of cloth (*i.e.* half du̠ngū 4). (2) yā yi mini̠ turku̠dī da̠ ∼ he was very generous to me. (3) *Nor.* = wāwā 2.

ausigi̠r *m.* = asigi̠rī.

a̠utā *m., f.* (1) the youngest of several brothers or sisters *x* Audu shī nē̠ ∼ Audu is the youngest. Ka̠nde ita cē̠ ∼ Kande is the youngest. nī au̠tan haifu̠wā nē̠ I'm the "baby" (= dangware̠). (2) au̠tan daudā̠ = ƙulī-ƙulī (*so called because rolled between the hands and dirtied*). (3) au̠tan yātsa̠ little-finger (= ƙurī 2*a*). (4) kada̠ ka̠ zame̠ mini au̠tam fikā̠fikī lā̠lā̠ta̠ a̠bōkin tāshi̠ = don't act the dog in the manger !. (5) *Vd.* masō̠yī 2.

auyatar *Vd.* ayautar.

Auyo̠ *Vd.* Hausā.

Auzi̠ṇ = Afzi̠n.

a̠'ūzu̠ bi̠llāhi̠ (*Ar.* "I take refuge in God") *formula used* (*a*) *before lying down or relieving oneself or beginning study.* (*b*) *after yawning.* (*c*) (i) *after hearing something unpleasant.* (ii) i̠ṇ wada̠nnaṇ sun shā wu̠yā, su ka̠n cē̠ "Allā̠ !", a̠mmā Jāmu̠s, a̠'ūzu̠ bi̠llāhi̠ if these people are hard-pressed they say "God help us !", but the Germans are outside the pale entirely.

Auzunāwā *Vd.* Ba̠auzu̠nī.

awa A. (a̠wā) *Kt.* = i̠wā.

B. (awa̠) *Eng. f.* hour (= awo̠).

A̠wai (1) *Vd.* Dōma̠. (2) ɗaṇ ∼ *m.* type of salt (*Vd.* baura̠ 2).

awai da̠ = ayautar da̠.

a̠waiki̠ *m.* (*pl.* a̠wa̠ikai) type of wooden or stone armlet (*cf.* awākī).

awaitar da̠ = ayautar da̠.

awaki A. (awākī) *Vd.* a̠kwīya̠ ; ɗauri̠ṇ ∼ .

B. (a̠waki̠) *m.* = a̠waiki̠.

awal *x* āwa̠l hana̠ gāɗā *epithet of* bridegroom (*for girl while playing is taken away to be hennaed for wedding*).

awalaja̠ *Yor. x* (1) am mīƙa̠ (= aṇ kasa̠ = an zuba̠) mini̠ ∼ cash was proffered me (seller) with implication "take it or leave it !" sun zuba̠

awalaja̠r rä̠i da̠ yawa̠ they (army) staked all and suffered heavy casualties.

āwar *m.* a poor type of salt (= ɗi̠gau).

a̠wargajī string of gō̠ruba̠ nuts used as lepers' weapon.

awa̠rtaki̠ *m.* = a̠rautaki̠.

awarwarō *m.* (*sg., pl.*). (1) convolvulus. (2) type of thin, metal bracelet.

a̠wātsīma̠ (*d.f.* wātse̠) *f.* (1) desertion by one's staff *x* yā̠rā sun yi masa̠ ∼ retainers or servants have deserted a deposed or dismissed P. lēbura̠ sun yi mini̠ ∼ my carriers threw down their loads and deserted me (*cf.* wātse̠). (2) = atu̠rābi̠ 1.

awāye̠ = awāyo̠ *x* ∼ kā̠jim birnī *epithet of* cute P. (*cf.* wā̠yō).

a̠waza̠ *f.* (*pl.* a̠wa̠zai = a̠wa̠zū). (1) rib. (2) rūwaṇ ∼ *m.* thin layer of meat on breast of animal. (3) *cīwaṇ a̠wa̠zai = haƙa̠rƙarī 2.

awo A. (awo̠) *m.* (*Ar.* waznu). (1) (*secondary v.n. of* auna̠ 1, 2 *and* a̠unā 2, 3, 5) *x* yana̠ auna̠ shi = yana̠ awa̠nsa̠ he's weighing it. awa̠ṇ ga̠ba nikē̠ sō̠, ba̠ awa̠m bāya ba I want the luggage, merchandise, etc., to accompany me by passenger-train, not follow by goods-train. yana̠ a̠unar hatsī = yana̠ awa̠ṇ hatsī he's buying corn by measure. (2) purchasing one's daily food-supply instead of having stored corn to draw on *x* ya̠nzu muna̠ ∼ (*hence, epithet is* Awo̠, naƙā̠ce̠ mai gidā " how harassing it is for the head of the family to have to depend on buying corn from day to day !"). (3) (*a*) corn bought by measure (= *Sk.* cē̠ƙanē 3). (*b*) da̠ rānā akē̠ ∼ , in darē yā yī, sä̠i a̠ ci tūwō don't buy a pig in a poke ! (*c*) standard measure *x* awa̠ṇ gya̠ɗā the amount of ground nuts equivalent to the standard measure. (*d*) mai ∼ ya̠ bar gā̠sā da̠ mai hatsi̠ṇ gōnā don't attempt what is beyond you ! (4) fortune-telling (= dūbā 2). (5) *Eng.* hour *x* yā yi aiki̠ ∼ uku̠ he worked for 3 hours. (6) pound in weight (*cf.* dūtse̠ 5). (7) weight *x* awa̠nsa̠ yā yi nawa̠ what does it weigh ? *(8) (*a*) metre of poem. (*b*) musical tone in speech (8*b* = murya̠). (9) aiming a gun (*cf.* a̠unā 5).

B. (ạwō) *Zar.* there is *x* kudī, ∼ sū there is money. ∼ shī tụkụnā ạ dāki he's as yet still at home.

C. (āwō) *Sk.* quite so ! (= *Sk.* ō 3). awolajạ *Vd.* awalajạ.

awụ *Vd.* awọ.

awulajạ *Vd.* awalajạ.

ạwụrū = ạwurū *m.* (*sg.*, *pl.*) tsetse-fly (= tsandō).

ạwuskī *m.* (*sg.*, *pl.*) short-tailed horse.

awwalī *Ar. m.* (1) beginning. (2) tuŋ awwalim fārị from the very beginning.

aya Λ. (āyạ) *Ar. f.* (*pl.* āyōyī). (1) (*a*) any sign of punctuation. (*b*) wannạŋ kalmạ tā zō bāyaŋ ∼ this word begins a new sentence. (*c*) yā kai ∼ cikin jạwābịnsạ he paused in his speech. (2) verse of Koran. (3) proof, sign of T. *x* suŋ ga ∼ they've seen something confirmatory. jạwābịnsạ yā zamẹ manạ ∼ bạbba his speech is a portent to us. (4) āyạr kạrē = āyạr   dilā = āyạr   gizọ = lāyạ 8 *q.v.* (5) *Sk.* nether grinding-stone (= dūtsạn nikạ).

B. (ayā) *f.* (1) (*a*) (i) fruit or grass of tigernut (*Cyperus esculentus*). (ii) *epithet is* arigizạ = *Kt.* Ayā rigizạ. (*b*) *Vd.* dạkū, gụndurạ 2. (*c*) yā kai ∼ matsukā he " put his head into the lion's mouth ". (*d*) *Vd.* azzịkī 1*h.* (*e*) doŋ ∼ tạ ji tsọrō *Vd.* taunạ 1*b.* (*f*) rụmbuŋ ∼ *Vd.* rụmbū 3. (2) *Vd.* aya wạjẹ, dūbam mashẹkā ∼, ganim mashẹkā ∼.

C. *Vd.* ạyē.

ạyạ-ayạ *f.* wild variety of tigernut-grass and fruit (*Cyperus rotundus*) = *Sk.* girāgirī.

ạyạbạ *f.* (1) (*a*) banana, bananas, plantain(s). (*b*) *Vd.* cī 1*c*, shā A. 1*e*. (2) gụngumaŋ ∼ tsōfwā nạ ganịŋkạ kẹ kwānā dạ dārī what a useless thing !

ạyāgạ = dạŋ ạyāgạ *m.* petty village-headman.

ayagi A. (Ạyāgī) *m.* (1) Yoruba(s) (*Vd.* Bạyarabẹ). (2) quarrelsome P. (3) *Vd.* Bạnufē.

B. (ạyagi) *m.* the coarse part filtered off kōko.

āyạlā *Yor. f.* (*sg.*, *pl.*) type of short-sleeved gown.

ayạmbā *f.* *x* yā gạmu dạ ∼ he has threadworm (= kwarbā = jalbị = *Sk.* ambụ̄wā) *Vd.*, tsīlā.

āyạŋ *Eng. m.* the ironing of washed clothes *x* kạ yi masạ ∼ iron it (garment) ! = waŋkị 2*b*.

ayaŋgō = ạyaŋgwā *f.* a red type of guineacorn.

ayạnyanạ *f.* = ạrạfīyạ 1*a* (*epithet is* ∼ kim fi abụrdugạ).

āyạrī *Ar. m.* (*pl.* āyarōrī). (1) trading-caravan. su kạn tạfi dạ ∼ they start out as a caravan. (2) members of caravan *x* ∼ sun rikạ fitọwā the members of the caravan kept on going out of the town.

ayau dạ = ayautad dạ *Vb.* 4B used, made use of.

aya wạjẹ (1) *Sk.* *formula used by panegyrist* (marọkī) *at wedding.* (2) *Kt. m.* champion challenging P. to race, wrestle, etc.

ayayā *f.* small-sized groundnuts, beans, guineacorn.

ạ yāyẹ lāfīyạ *m.* infants' coloured patch-work cap.

ạyē *Kt. used in* bā ạyansạ ba nẹ that's in keeping with his character (good or bad).

āyōyī *Vd.* āyạ.

ạyū *m.* (*sg.*, *pl.*) manatee (*epithet is* ạmunị, kākam mãi ; tūrū nāmaŋ wākạ " Festival of rich food ! Drum, this is food to eulogize ! ").

ayya A. (ayyạ) (1) = anyạ. (2) *Vd.* ī 2*b*.

B. (ạyyā ?) = ạnyā ?

ayyạhahạ *x* ∼ mai gyạmbō yā ci karọ dạ turmī what a peck of trouble !

ayyana A. (ayyạnā) *Vb.* 1C *Ar.* (1) = bayyạnā. (2) appointed (*date, etc.*).

B. (ạyyanạ) *Vb.* 3B. (1) is plain, obvious. (2) yā ∼ ạ kạmmu, mụ yī it is incumbent on us to do it.

ayyara A. (ayyạrā) *f.* type of purgative shrub (= tạyā ni gōyō 3 = *Sk.* agūwạ.

B. (ạyyạrā) *Vd.* shaftarē.

Ayyūbạ *the name* Job.

ayyukạ *Vd.* aikị.

ayyururwị *f.* the yelling of women rejoicing.

azạ *Vb.* 1A. (1) put *thing* on another (*cf.* ajīyē, gwāmạ). (2) put *person* on animal, etc. *x* nā ∼ yārọ ạ kạn tạkarkạrī I put the boy·on back of pack-ox (= dõrạ) (cf. ajịyē, gwāmạ). (3) ạzā ni put my load on my head for me ! (= dʼaukạ 1g). (4) yā ∼ takọ̃bī bisạ ạl'ummạ he put the people to the sword. (5) (with dative) imposed task on P. x (a) yā ∼ musụ bāwạ dʼạrī he imposed on them delivery of 100 slaves. (b) ạŋ azạ dõkõkī laws were imposed, passed.

ạzābạ Ar. f. (pl. ạzạ̃bū = azābõbī). (1) anguish, trouble, annoyance. (2) torturing P. physically x aŋ gwadạ musụ azābạ anguish, physical torture was inflicted on them (= nũnạ). sun shā ∼ they suffered anguish, etc.

ạzạ̃babbē m. (f. ạzạ̃babbīyā) pl. ạzạ̃bạbbū P. making a nuisance of himself.

azabọrạ̃ Sk. f. part of the sheath of the adũwạ fruit.

ạzabtạ Vb. 2 (p.o. ạzạbcē, n.o. ạzạbci). (1) worried. (2) inflicted physical torture on.

ạzafạr Kt. = ạzahạr.

ạzạfạrīyyạ Vd. ạzahạr.

Azagandị used in ∼ mugunyạr kīshīyā epithet of bad co-wife.

ạzahạr f. = ạzạhạrīyyạ Ar. f. (1) (a) the time between 2 and 3 p.m. (b) ∼ tā yī it is between 2 and 3 p.m. (2) ạzahạrim fārị the time just prior to 2 p.m.

azaizạitā Vb. 1D exaggerated.

azakạrī Ar. m. (pl. ạzạkạrai). (1) penis (Kt. epithet is Gọ̃dī), cf. gạbā 2a, dịdī, bụrā, ịŋgạtũtạ, wutsīyā 2, kũsụ 2, ạlkạlạmī 2. *(2) peg securing pole of irrigation-apparatus (lạmbū) to supports.

ạzal Ar. (1) tum fil ∼ from time immemorial. (2) f. misfortune x (a) ∼ tā ạuku a misfortune has occurred. (b) ∼ bā ta dạ makawā you cannot fight Fate !

ạzạlīyạ f. = ạzal 2.

azamạ Ar. f. being about to do x yanạ̃ azamạr sallạ (tạfīyạ) he is about to pray (set out), etc. (Vd. azạntā).

azancī m. (pl. ạzạntai). (1) meaning. (2) being sensible x (a) dạ azancim mạganạ kakẹ̃ you talk sense. Audụ ∼ gạrēshi Audu has plenty of sense. (b) Vd. kwānāŋ ∼ . (3) topic x azancin nẽmaŋ aurē the topic of courting.

azạntā Vb. 1C is (was) about to x muŋ azạntạ tạfīyạ we are (were) about to set out (Vd. azamạ).

ạzạntai Vd. azancī.

azạ̃rā f. (pl. ạzạ̃rū = azārõrī). (1) section of split tree used for roofing (usually giginyạ is employed, in which case azạ̃rā = ḳyamị). (2) half a two-segmented kolanut, i.e. one segment (= ɓārị 1), cf. ashạ̃līyạ, ḳwạr, tsallị.

Azạ̃rē f. place-name.

azargaɠ m. (pl. ạzạrgạgai) rag for tying up limbs encased in henna (cf. azazzargī).

azargī m. = azargīyā f. = azargagī q.v.

ạzazzā Kt. f. enmity.

ạzạzzalạ Vb. 2. = ạrịrītạ.

azazzargī Sk. m. (pl. ạzạzzạrgai) slipknot (cf. azargagī).

Azbịŋ = Asbịŋ.

ạzīmụŋ-azīmụŋ = allạ-allạ.

azịnā Ar .f. (1) yā cikạ = he makes a nuisance of himself. (2) yā zubạ ∼ tasạ ạ kạ̃ina he nagged me.

ạzīzĩtạ Vb. 2 (p.o. ạzịzịcē, n.o. ạzịzịci) = ạrịrītạ.

azkunnịyā Vd. askunnịyā.

aznā Vd. arnā.

ạzuhụr Vd. ạzahạr.

ạzũjī m. (f. ạzũzā) pl. ạzụ̃zai (Ar. 'ajũz). (1) Sk. old man. (2) gossip, scandalmonger (cf. ạjũzā).

azụkụkụ m. a food made of leaves plus flour or roasted bulrush millet.

ạzụmcē Vd. ạzumtạ.

azụmĩ (Ar. assaumi cf. French pain d'azime) m. (1) The Great Fast of Ramadan (Vd. mũdạnabị, ḳishirwā 1b, sāmụ 1b, tạdʼawwa'ạ). (a) yanạ̃ ∼ (i) he's Fasting. (ii) yā karyạ ∼ . Vd. karyạ 1d. (b) Vd. shā E.2a. (c) gīwā tā shā rũwā dạ yawạ, bạllē tā yi ∼ Vd. rũwā C.9f. (2) kadạ kạ yi azụmiŋ shẹ̃karạ, kạ kurkụrē dạ bakin ruwā (or . . . kạ kurkụrē dạ tạfannũwā) don't undo all your previous good ! (3) azụmin jẽmāgẹ̃ = azụmim mõdā merely pretending to fast. (4) azụmiŋ kạffārạ Vd. kạfārạ 1a. (5) wataŋ azụmin tsọ̃fạffī m. the month of Rajab q.v. (6) azụmin dũ gạrị month of Rạmạlaŋ. (7) dõdaŋ ∼ Vd. dọ̃dõ ɓ.

ạzumtạ *Vb.* 2. (*p.o.* ạzụmcē, *n.o.* ạzụmci) *x* yā ạzụmci watạn naŋ he fasted throughout that month (*Vd.* azụmī).

azurārē *m.* = zurārē.

azụrfā (*Ar.* assarīfa) *f.* silver.

azurmụƙī *m.* intestinal worm(s) in horses.

ạzururū *Kt. m.* = ịndararō.

ạzūzā *Vd.* ạzūjī.

azūzancị acting as in ạzūjī 2.

ạzzakạrī *Vd.* ạzakạrī.

ạzzālụmī *m.* (*f.* ạzzālụmā) *pl.* ạzzālụmai *Ar.* oppressor.

azzạmā *Vb.* 1C *Ar.* paid honour to.

azzịƙī (*Ar.* arrizqi) *m.* (*pl.* azzukạ). (1) prosperity *x* (*a*) yā yi ～ = yanā cikiŋ ～ he's prosperous. (*b*) yā ƙārạ musụ ～ it made them wealthier. (*c*) nēmaŋ ～ *Vd.* aurē 6*c.* (*d*) tākarā dạ mai ～ hạlakạ don't emulate those better off than yourself ! (*e*) ～ rịgar ƙayạ, kanā jā, yanā jạŋkạ prosperity brings responsibilities (= rịgā 1*q*). (*f*) dạ ～ dạ hasadạ, tạre sukẹ kwānā (*said by* marōƙā) prosperity is often accompanied by niggardliness. (*g*) ～ bā rịgā ba, bạllē 'yạŋūwā sụ tūɓẹ = 1*e above*. (*h*) ƙaryar ～ shịgar rụmbuŋ ayā dạ igīyạ it's beyond him but he doesn't realize so. (*j*) ƙanshiŋ ～ *Vd.* ƙan-shī. (2) good luck *x* (*a*) yā yi (= yā aunạ) ～ he had a stroke of good luck (= gạmō 2*d*). (*b*) barkạ dạ ～ (i) congratulations on your lucky escape (good luck, etc.) ! (ii) (*said by woman*) congratulations on your safe accouchement ! (iii) *reply to* 2*b*.i, ii *is* barkạ kạdǎi. (3) (*a*) (i) yanā cikiŋ ～ he has an assured position. (ii) yanā cikiŋ azzịkiŋ Audụ he's in Audu's employ. (iii) yā ci azzịkiŋ Audụ he's benefiting by the patronage of Audu ; he's being leniently treated because of his ties with Audu. (*b*) wạndạ bại ci azzịkiŋ wani ba, bā ā ciŋ azzịkinsạ one good turn deserves another. (*c*) *Vd.* ạlbarkạcī 3. (*d*) *Vd.* gōmạ 3. (4) favourableness *x* (*a*) ạbịm bā na ～ ba nẹ it was profitless. suŋ ga ạbịm bā ～ they saw things were going badly. (*b*) girmā dạ ～ peacefully *x* gạya masạ girmā dạ ～ yạ bīyā nị tell him to pay me before any un-pleasantness occurs ! girmā dạ ～

wạddạ ta sā jạn sā dạ abāwā (*lit.* which leads to (sā) a bull (sā) being pulled along with thick thread) persuasion is better than force (*Vd.* girma-girma). suŋā zamaŋ girmā dạ ～ they're living on terms of mutual respect. nā barō gidāna bā girmā, bā ～ I left home willy-nilly. im bạ sụ bā shị ba dạ girmā dạ azzịƙī if they do not give him it peace-fully. (*c*) yā rōƙi azzịƙī, yạ bā shị hanyạ, yạ wucẹ he asked him as a favour to allow him to pass through his territory. (*d*) *Vd.* girmā 1*c.* (5) rashiŋ ～ *m.* (*a*) ill luck. (*b*) shamelessness. (6) azzịkin dọmin dọmin *Vd.* dọmin-dọmin ; dạlīlị 4*b.* (7) azzịkim Maryamạ = azzịkim mụzūrū prosperity accompanied by niggardliness. (8) ịnā rūwaŋ ～ dạ mūgụŋ gāshị nothing succeeds like success (*Vd.* mūgụŋ gāshị).

ạzzimmạ *Ar. f.* (1) accepting responsi-bility for T. *x* (*a*) mun tsayạ ～ tasạ we make (made) ourselves responsible for his debt, etc. (*b*) nā kạrɓi fam bīyar ～ tasạ I made myself responsible for the £5 owed by him. n nā nēmam fam bīyar ～ tasạ he owes me the £5 for which I went guarantee. (2) nā kạrɓi ～ tasạ I vouch for him ! (*said by my* shūgạba *after the words* mum bā kạ (*Vd.* aurē 6*c*). (3) *cf.* zimmạ.

azzukạ *Vd.* azzịƙī.

azzịrtā *Vb.* 1C enriched *x* aikịmmụ yanā azzịrtạ tājịrai our work is enriching the wealthy classes.

B

ba A. (bā) (1) there is not, are not, was not, were not (Mod. Gram. 21). *x* (*a*) ～ mǎi there is no oil (*Vd.* bābụ). ạbịŋ, ～ kyaŋ ganī it is (was) an ugly sight. (*b*) (*if* bā *is followed by pronoun, this has form as in* Mod. Gram. 46) *x* ～ sū ạ naŋ there are none of them here. (*c*) (Mod. Gram. 175) ～ wạndạ ya zō nobody has come. ～ wạndạ yakẹ zūwạ nobody is coming. ～ ạbịŋ dạ ya fạru nothing has happened. ～ wạndạ mukạ ganī we saw nobody.

(d) *(denoting* decease) *x* **bāyam ~ shī** after his death. **am bā da lābāri ~ sū** it has been announced that they are dead. *(e)* **wani wanda im ~ Audu săi shī** a colleague of Audu's. *(2)* *(as second clause)* without *x* **kōwā suka ganī ~ fitila** whoever is seen without a lamp. *(3)* (Mod. Gram. 22). *(a)* **~ ni da kudī = bā ni kudī** I have no money. **bā su da haŋkalī** they have (had) no sense. *(b)* **~ aikin da sukē, irin yi muku hari** they devote all their attention to raiding you. *(4)* *Vd.* **bābu, ban, gaira,** cas. *(5)* *Vd.* **bā** B.1 *first line,* **bā** B.2 *(6)* **bā wanda, bā wani, bā kōwā, bā abin da** *Vd.* **wani** 5*a.* *(7)* **bā rūwā** *Vd.* **rūwā** G. *(8)* **bā īyākā** *Vd.* **abu** 6. *(9)* **bā zatō** *Vd.* **tsammāni** 7. *(10)* *(a)* **bā m** *Vd.* **mm.** *(b)* **bā tsalam** *Vd.* tsalam. *(c)* **bā balak** *Vd.* balak. *(d)* **bā zarētā** *Vd.* **zarētā.** *(e)* **bā ki gaskīyā = bā ki magana = bā ki mutunci** *Vd.* alakwayi. *(f)* **bā girmā** *Vd.* **girmā** 1*c.*ii. *(g)* *Vd.* **bā haya, bā tāka.** *(11)* *proverbs with* **bā :**—*(a)* **bā măi, bā rōmō** *Vd.* **rōmō** 1*c.* *(b)* **bā ka gidā** *Vd.* arne. *(c)* (i) **bā darē** *Vd.* shiŋkāfā 1*c.* (ii) **bā irin darē** *Vd.* **jēmāge** 1*c.* *(d)* **bā kōmē a tsulīyā** *Vd.* **tsulīyā** 4. *(e)* **bā bākī** *Vd.* mutūwa 1*a.*iv. *(f)* **bā shi ga tsuntsū** *Vd.* tsuntsū 3. *(g)* an yi masa " shigō, shigō, bā zurfī ! " they " led him on ". *(h)* **bā lāfiya** *Vd.* tāba 2. *(j)* **bā kūkā** *Vd.* bōkōni. *(k)* **bā ka cē** *Vd.* **cē** 9. *(l)* **bā ki ƙaya** *Vd.* cēdīyā. *(m)* **bā cūu** *Vd.* cuu 2. *(n)* **Bā dādī** *Vd.* **dādī** 1*d.* *(o)* *Vd.* kukuru kuku. *(12)* **bā = bā** *f.* *(a)* the *letter* " b ". *(b)* *the letter* " b " *(though the letters* " d " *and* " **d'u** " *have the separate names* dal *and* dā'u *respectively).* *(c)* **kamar digwam bā nē kawai aka sā** it is a mere beginning.

B. 1 (bā) *Vb.* *(becomes* **bā** *before noun.* *Vd.* Mod. Gram. 87 *for conjugation).* *(1)* gave to *x* **yā ~ ni** he gave (it) to me. **yā ~ ni shī** he gave it to me. **yanā bā Audu rīgā** he's giving Audu a gown. **bā shi ita da wuyā** it'd be hard to give her to him *(cf.* bāi, **bā da,** ban). *(2)* **zūcīyāta tā ~ ni n rūga** instinct warned me to flee. *(3)* **bā ni haŋkalinka** pay attention to

what I am saying ! *(4)* *(a)* **ram ~ ku, ran yabō** people soon forget favours. *(b)* (i) **a ~ mu, a fī mu ; in aŋ hana mu, dăidăi da mū akē** *(said* by **maroƙā**) if you give us charity, you will excel us, but if you refuse, you will remain people of no account, just as we are. (ii) *Vd.* **a bā mu.** *(5)* caused emotion to P. *x* **yā ~ ni haushī** it annoyed me *(Vd. similarly* māmāki, dārīyā). *(6)* outdistanced by *x* **anā naŋ, săi ƙarāwaŋ ya bā dōgarai gōnā bīyŭ** then the thief outdistanced the N.A. police by two fields. *(7)* **~ shi bāyā** *Vd.* **bāyā** 1*b.* *(8)* **bā shi hanya** *Vd.* **hanya** 1*b.* *(9)* **bā shi iska** *Vd.* **iska** 3. *(10)* **bā shi sā'a** *Vd.* **sā'a** 4*d.* *(11)* **bā shi wurī** *Vd.* **wurī** 1*c.* *(12)* **bā shi rūwā** *Vd.* **rūwā** A.13. *(13)* **Alā bā mu** *Vd.* **afūwō** 1. *(14)* *Vd.* **bā hawā sama, bā hā, bā mayāƙā, a bā mu, bā ni kăi, bā ni ƙafa, bā ni māsū, bā ni ƙwaryā, bā kūkan, bā sājē, bā sūsa, bā ta kāshī, bā ta kulkī, bā zata, bā kāshī.** *(15)* *proverbs with* **bā :**—*(a)* **bā a bā kūrā** *Vd.* **kūrā** 36. *(b)* **zai bā ka rīgā** *Vd.* **rīgā** 1*o.* *(c)* **bā kau da halī** *Vd.* yunwa 1*a.* *(d)* **a kam bā dōki rūwā** *Vd.* **rūwā** C.18. *(e)* **bā bareyī rūwā** *Vd.* **rūwā** A.20. *(f)* **bā mātāka** *Vd.* baunī. *(g)* **a bā ki, a hūta** *Vd.* **yunwa** 1*h.* *(h)* **bā su, ka hūta** *Vd.* **bāshi** 2*a.* *(j)* **bā lāsar bākī** *Vd.* **carkwai** 4. *(k)* **bā cācā ; bā rikica** *Vd.* cirin. *(l)* **bā māyē** *Vd.* dagara. *(m)* **bā fāshiŋ gayyā** *Vd.* Dumau 2. *(n)* **bā gincira** *Vd.* gincira. *(o)* **bā jan sau** *Vd.* Girga. *(p)* **bā dāwaya** *Vd.* karo 2. *(q)* **bā rufan ciki** *Vd.* kibīya. *(r)* **bā yā da gātarī** *Vd.* ƙwaŋƙwambishī. *(16)* *Vd.* **bā** 12.

B. 2 (bā) *(negatives the progressive,* Mod. Gram. 19) *x* **(1) bā nā zūwa = bā ni zūwa** I am not coming *(Vd.* C1. 2). **bā yā aiki** he's not working *(cf.* **bāi** 3). *(2) cf.* C.1, C.2, D *below.* *(3)* *proverbs with* **bā :** *(a)* **bā a bā kūrā** *Vd.* kūrā 36). *(b)* **bā a wa ido** *Va.* shāmaki 3*b.* *(c)* **bā a hawā sama** *Vd.* tsāni 2*b* *(cf.* **bā hawā sama).** *(cc)* **bā a hawā itācē** *Vd.* hawā 1*a.*vii. *(d)* **bā a gama wutā** *Vd.* shiba 3. *(e)* **bā a cē ya shā rūwā** *Vd.* wākē 4. *(f)* **bā a gaya wa kare** *Vd.* kare 27. *(g)* **bā a tsayāwā** *Vd.* tsaya

1d. (h) bā ā̱ dafa̱ dafi̱ Vd. tu̱ŋkū 1d.
(j) bā ā̱ aram bā̱kī Vd. a̱lbasa̱ 1c. (k) bā̱
ā̱ sakē̱wā Vd. wa̱rkī 3. (l) bā ā̱ mūgu̱n
Sarkī Vd. mūgu̱ 1d. (m) bā ā̱ sani̱m
murna̱r ka̱rē Vd. murna̱ 2b. (n) bā
ā̱ kō̱ya̱ŋ ka̱rā̱tū Vd. tuku̱rī 2. (o) bā
ā̱ gama̱ gudu̱ Vd. sūsa̱ 2b. (p) bā ā̱
ƙwācē̱ Vd. yāro̱ 1n. (q) wa̱nda̱ bā ā̱
yaba̱ ka să̱i tā ɓāci̱ nē it is a case of
nobody being a prophet in his own
country. (r) bā ā̱ wāwa̱ Vd. būshīyā.
(s) bā nā̱ yi̱ŋ ƙwă̱ina Vd. za̱kara̱ 1d.
(t) bā nā̱ a̱bū̱tā da̱ biri̱ Vd. a̱bū̱tā 2. (u)
bā kyā̱ rufi̱ Vd. a̱kū. (v) bā ā̱ bō̱rī Vd.
bō̱rī 2a. (w) bā ā̱ wa̱ biri̱ Vd. burtū 3.
(x) bā ā̱ dabo̱ Vd. dabo̱ 2. (y) bā ā̱
shan zuma̱ sai an shā harbi̱ per aspera
ad astra. (z) bā ā̱ darē Vd. darē 4m.
(z) (i) bā ā̱ fā̱fa̱ Vd. fā̱fa̱ 3. (z) (ii) bā
ā̱ nēma̱ŋ kī̱fī Vd. faƙo̱ 5. (z) (iii) bā
nā̱ fasa̱ ra̱ndā Vd. fasa̱ 1f. (z) (iv) bā ā̱
gī̱yā Vd. gī̱ya̱ 1b. (z) (v) bā ā̱ hū̱da̱ ciki̱
Vd. hū̱da̱ 1h. (z) (vi) bā ā̱ rawā Vd.
jū̱yi̱ 1d. (z) (vii) bā ā̱ nēmar wa̱ kida̱ŋ
girbi̱ Vd. kida̱ 1c. (z) (viii) bā ā̱ sā̱
miki̱ lōkō Vd. kwā-kwā̱.

C. 1 (bā̱ . . . ba) (negatives noun or
phrase) x (1) (a) (i) bā̱ Audu̱ ba not
Audu. wanna̱ŋ a̱jīya̱ bā̱ iri̱ŋ wa̱dda̱
da̱ kā sō, să̱i ka̱ dī̱ba̱ ba nē̱ this deposit
of money is not of the kind that you
can cash whenever the mood takes you.
(ii) x laifi̱n da̱ bā̱ tsā̱fi̱ ba any crime
short of idolatry. (iii) x bā̱ dom mā
arzi̱kinsu̱ ba kadă̱i, să̱i dō̱min sū . . .
not only because of their wealth, but
also because they . . . (iv) (Kt. can
repeat final ba) x bā̱ Audu̱ ba nē̱ ba it
is not Audu. (2) (bā̱ . . . ba with past
tense especially after bā̱ da̱ or " if ",
sometimes replaces D below and B.2.1
above) x im bā̱ yā yi ba = im ba̱i yi ba
if he does not do so (cf. 3, 4 below).
bā̱ yanā̱ zūwa̱ ba = bā yā̱ zūwa̱ he is
not coming. (3) im bā̱ . . . ba (a)
(followed by noun) with the exception of
x (i) Ta̱rābu̱lus, im bā̱ wada̱nsu wurā̱rē
ba, duka̱nta̱ ha̱mādā̱ cē all Tripolitania
except certain places is desert. ka̱
gaya̱ mini̱ im bā̱ ƙaryā ba tell me provided it is not a lie ! im bā̱ ja̱kā da̱yā
ba, bā nā̱ saya̱swā I won't sell unless I

get £100 for it. sa̱na'a̱, im bā̱ gādo̱ ba,
tanā̱ da̱ wu̱yā a craft is hard to practise
unless hereditarily acquired. bā̱ su
da̱ wurin zamā im bā̱ na̱m ba they have
nowhere to live except here. (ii) Vd. in
7. (b) (followed by construction of 2 above)
if . . . without x im bā̱ a̱ŋ kula̱ da̱ shī
ba if one acts without due attention to
this. (4) bā̱ da̱ . . . ba (followed by
construction of 2 above) conj. without
x bā̱ da̱ wani Ba̱lārabe̱ yā ma̱tsu ba
without any Arab being pressed for
space. za̱i sāmam musu̱ shī bā̱ da̱
sun yi yā̱ƙi̱ ba he'll obtain it for them
without the necessity of their making
war. yā yi̱wu im bā̱ da̱ mun yā̱ƙē su̱
ba ? would it be possible without
going to war with them ? bā̱ da̱ yā
sani̱ ba without his knowledge. tā
yi haka̱ bā̱ da̱ kō tā taɓa̱ ji̱nsa̱ ba she
did this without even having heard
of it (cf. kō 7a.iii). sun ta̱fi bā̱ da̱ su̱ŋ
kula̱ ba they went away thoughtlessly.
(5) bā̱ să̱i . . . ba Vd. să̱i C.4, and J.1.
(6) x bā̱ māla̱mī ba, kō jāhi̱lī ba̱ yā
fa̱di haka̱ ba apart from a scholar,
not even an illiterate would speak this.
(7) da̱ga bā̱ . . . ba Vd. da̱ga 4a. (8) bā̱
ka̱man . . . ba especially x kōwā yanā̱
da̱ kudī, bā̱ ka̱ma̱ŋ Audu̱ ba all have
money especially Audu. yanā̱ sa̱nsu
duka̱ bā̱ ka̱ma̱ŋ Audu̱ ba he loves all
of them, especially Audu (= tun 2).
(9) bā̱ dō̱min . . . ba Vd. don 6, 1c ;
dō̱min 6, 2b. (10) cf. B.2 above, C.2,
D below. (11) proverbs with bā̱ . . .
ba :—(a) bā̱ shi̱gar rāmi̱n kūrā kē̱
da̱ wu̱yā ba Vd. kūrā 25a. (b) bā̱
kisa̱ŋ ka̱rē ba Vd. ka̱rē 43. (c) bā̱ kā
da̱ gīwā ba Vd. gīwā 1j. (d) bā̱ dūka̱n
rūwan sama̱ ba Vd. sama̱ 1e. (e) bā̱
riki̱da̱ kē̱ da̱ wu̱yā ba Vd. ri̱kida̱. (f)
bā̱ sā̱bam ba Vd. sā̱bō 4. (g) bā̱ shanyē
ba Vd. shanyē 1b. (h) (i) bā̱ kullu̱ŋ
sāfīyā Vd. A̱ljumma'a̱. (ii) bā̱ kullu̱ŋ
akē̱ kwānā ba Vd. gadō 1a.ii. (j) bā̱ jā
ba nē̱ Vd. Tūrancī 1c. (k) bā̱ don
tsawō Vd. tsawō 1e. (l) bā̱ dū karā
ba Vd. tsaiko̱ 1c. (m) bā̱ ra̱bō ba Vd.
ra̱bō 6d. (n) bā̱ farkō ba Vd. Alla̱ 3m.
(o) bā̱ tāsu̱ ba Vd. Alla̱ 1k.ii. (p) bā̱
gō̱ban dada̱ Vd. gō̱be 3. (q) bā̱ dawa̱

ba *Vd.* cādī. (*r*) bā̆ fīgyan yārǫ ba *Vd.* dinyā. (*s*) bā̆ ganim mātā ba *Vd.* fạtaụcī. (*t*) bā̆ naŋ gizǫ kē sāk̯ar ba *Vd.* gizǫ 2*a*.iv. (*u*) bā̆ sāraŋkạ ba *Vd.* gwad̯ayī. (*v*) bā̆ kūkāna ba *Vd.* kūkā 1*b*.iv.

C. 2 (bā̆) *used in* bā̆ kạn (*contraction of* bạ ya kạn he is not in the habit of ... (*Vd.* halī 3), *cf.* A, B.2, C.1 *above* ; D *below*.

D (bạ ... ba). (1) (*negatives all tenses but progressive and subjunctive,* Mod. Gram. 20) *x* bạ kạ zō ba you did not come. im baị yi ba if he does not do so (*cf.* C.1, section 2). bạ zạn zō ba I shall not come. bạ na kạn zō ba I am not in the habit of coming. (2) *cf.* baị; bạn; bụ; bị; A ; B2 ; C.1.2; C2. (3) *proverbs with* bạ ... ba :—(*a*) bạ ạ fịta rūwa ba *Vd.* mātsạ 1*c*. (*b*) bạ ạ san shịgarkạ ba *Vd.* sạndī. (*c*) bạ ạ sam maị cịn tūwō ba *Vd.* tūwō 14. (*d*) bạ nā̆ ĩyạ saurạŋ wutā ba *Vd.* saurā 1*f*. (*e*) bạ kạ ĩyạ nōmā ba = mīyạ 10. (*f*) bạ kạ.sạyā ba *Vd.* sạyā 2. (*g*) bạ kạ ci k̯afạ ba *Vd.* cūrị 4. (*h*) bạ kạ ci jịkī ba *Vd.* dụnjī. (*j*) bị kị rufẹ cībịyā ba *Vd.* falmạrạŋ. (**4**) (*the second of two successive negatived verbs may stand in either past tense or past relative tense,* M.G. 139*a*) *x* im bạ kụ zō, kun yi (= kukạ yi) aikị ba if you don't come and work ....

E (bạ) (1) (*prefix indicating* inhabitant *or* trade) *x* Bạkanǫ *m.* (*f.* Bạkanūwā) *pl.* Kanāwā P. of Kano (*Vd. these alphabetically*). bạdūkụ *m.* (*pl.* dụkạ̄wā) leather-worker (*Vd. these alphabetically*). (2) = fạ (*cf.* F.3 *below also*).

F (bạ ?) (1) (*sarcastic interrogative final particle used thus*) kā zō~so you've come, have you ! yā jē ~ oh, he went there, did he ! kā ji ~ surely you understood what I said ! nā cē ~ oh, I say ! jạwābịŋ k̯aryā ~ naturally it's a lie, isn't it ? (2) (*interrogative form of* G.1 *below*) *x* dăidăi dạ wannạm ~ one just like this ? (3) (*mainly used after personal pronoun in following type of sentence*). A. says, " I hear C. has committed a crime." B. replies yā̆ yi hakạ kụ̄wā̆ ? " Surely not ? " A. replies

babbansạ dạ shī bạ ? " It's not in keeping with his known good conduct ". *Similarly :*—A. says, " I hear you've acted wrongly thus." B. replies nā̆ yi hakạ kụ̄wā̆ ? " Is it *likely* I'd do such a thing ! " A. says mālạminkạ dạ kaị bạ ? " No, it's surely *not* the way a scholaṛ like you would act ! " (*cf.* haụkā 4).

G (ba) (1) = fa. (2) *Vd.* baba-baba.

ba'ạ *Ar. f.* mockery *x* (1) yā yi minị ~ he derided me. (2) d̯am ~ scoffer; teaser. (3) bā̆ ~ ba ta kashẹ ūwar gizǫ ba, cụ̄tar Allā̆ cē I know you are only " pulling my leg ".

Bạabōrẹ *m.* (*f.* Bạabōrịyā) *pl.* Abōrāwā = Abōrẹ.

Bạadamẹ *m.* (*f.* Bạadamịyā) *pl.* Adamāwā P. of Adamawa.

Bạādarẹ *m.* (*f.* Bạādarịyā) *pl.* ādarāwā P. of ādar.

bạ'ạdīyyạ *Ar. f.* (1) yā saŋ k̯ablīyyạ dạ bạ'ạdīyyạ he knows the world inside out. (2) nā kāwō matạ k̯ablīyyạ dạ bạ'ạdīyyạ, ta k̯ī I tried hard to persuade her but without success. **(3) an addition to end of devotions to balance previous involuntary omission (*cf.* k̯ablīyyạ).

Bạafzinẹ = Bạafzịnī *m.* (*f.* Bạafzinịyā = Bạafzịnā) *pl.* Afzināwā P. of Asben. Bạafzịnin dōkị Asben horse.

*Bạajanabẹ = Bạajạnạbī *m.* (*f.* Bạajanabịyā = *Kt.* Bạajanabạ) *pl.* Ạjạnạbai *Ar.* alien, stranger.

Bạalibị *m.* (*f.* Bạalibịyā) *pl.* Alibāwā a member of this Filani tribe of *Kt.* and *Sk.*

bạ'ạncē *Vd.* bạ'antạ.

*Bạannạbī *m.* descendant of the Prophet Muhammad (*Vd.* ạnnabị).

bạ'antạ *Vb.* 2 (*p.o.* bạ'ạncē, *n.o.* bạ'ạnci) derided (*cf.* ba'ạ).

ba'asạ *Vd.* wạlā.

ba'ạsī *Ar. m.* nā bi (= nā nẹmi) ba'ạsinsạ I investigated it.

bạaskarẹ *m.* (*pl.* askarāwā) *Ar.* (1) soldier. (2) Govt. or N.A. policeman.

Bạauzụnī *m.* (*f.* Bạauzunịyā) *pl.* Auzunāwā = Bạafzinẹ.

baba A. (bā̆ba) *m.* (1) (*a*) father. (*b*) namesake of one's father. (*c*) P. of one's father's generation who is one's

equal or inferior. (d) ~ yā ịsa Vd.
Gwārī 1c. (e) ~ yā takarkạrē Vd. īyạ 1d.
(2) Vd. cẹ 7. (3) aikịm bậbaŋ gīwā
idling about. (4) tā yi ~ ạ zaurẹ = tā
yi ~ nậ zaurẹ she pulled her cloth
over her face to hide that side. (5) ~
baŋ gaŋ kạ ba pulling headcloth over
eyes by woman giving the " glad eye ".
(6) ~ bạn ji ba large cap whose flaps
cover the ears. (7) ~ dạ būzū corn not
fully denuded of bran. (8) (a) ~ rọdō
type of plant (cf. lọdā). (b) yā cī nị
dạ ~ rọdō he intimidated me (= bụrgā).
(9) ~ hụm type of plant. (10) ~
zụrundụm = tubụrā. (11) Bậba (a)
avoidance-name (ạlkunyạ) for one's
son named after one's father (Vd.
ạlkunyạ). (b) Vd. yậyā A.1, section 2h.
(12) Vd. wậ ya zậgi bậbạ. (13) bậbam
bọrī Vd. ajịŋgi.
  A.1 (bậ . . . ba) Vd. ba C.1.
  A.2 (bạ . . . ba) Vd. ba D.
  B. (bậbā) m. (pl. bậbạnī = bậbạnnī =
Sk. bậbai). (1) bậbā = bậban Sarkī
Emir's eunuch. (2) sexually impotent
man (= lạ'īfị q.v.).
  C. (bābạ) f. paternal aunt.
  D. (bābā) (1) (a) indigo (cf. lallẹ
1a.ii, tsāmī 3, shūnī, cābọ, dagwalọ,
dạmbilāgọ). (b) an yaŋkẹ ~ the
indigo-crop has been gathered. (c)
cūrịm ~ round pat of indigo
(= kuntukurū). (d) gōnar ~ dạ ita
dạ biri sǎi ganī you cannot get blood
from a stone ! (2) sǎi dạ ~ ạ rugā
taking coals to Newcastle. (3) Vd.
gaŋgau, cī 6, jậtau 2b. (4) bābam
fạdamạ ; bāban takō ; bāban tạlakị ;
bāban tāmu various types of plants.
(5) sậ hannū ạ ~ Vd. sậ B.1c. (6)
ạlkālim bābā Vd. ạlkālī 6. (7) bābaŋ
kậkā Vd. cābọ 4. (8) bābaŋ kōwā Vd.
dagwalọ. (9) kậwō ~ Vd. hōrẹ.
baba-baba A. (bậbạ-bậbạ) m. type of
wild indigo (cf. bābā).
  B. (ba-ba-ba-ba) x wutā tā kāmạ ~
the fire burned and crackled.
babacī Sk. m. type of grass growing in
wet places.
ɓāɓāgī = ɓậɓāgumī m. (f. ɓậɓāgumā)
= ɓāgumēmẹ.
bậba hụm Vd. bậba 9.

bậbai Vd. bậbā.
bābājị Sk. m. (sg., pl.) Filani panegyrist
(marọkī).
bậbậkērē m. (1) kyaurē yā yi ~ the
door does not fit (as too long or too
broad). (2) yā yi minị ~ he blocked
my way with outstretched arms. (3)
yanậ ~ he (young actor, young actress)
is imitating hyena at tậshē games
(= kūrā 1e). (4) making false
promises.
bậ ɓalak, bậ zaɓak uselessly.
Bạbambadẹ = Bạbambādẹ m. (f. Bạbam-
badịyā, etc.) pl. Bambadāwā, etc. (1)
one of the tribe so called, who is professional cadging-beggar (Vd. marọkī).
(2) wide-mouthed pot made by that
tribe.
bābạncē Vb. 3A (male) became impotent.
Bậbando = Bậbandi = bậba 4.
bạbanẹ m. (f. bạbanạ) pl. banāwā P.
between 15 and 40 years old (cf. bana ;
bạbạra).
bậbaŋ gīwā Vd. bậba 3.
babani A. (bābạnī) f. = bābạ.
  B. (bậbānī) m. = bậba.
  C. (bậbạnī) Vd. bậbā.
bạbanjẹ. (1) m. man who has not done
the pilgrimage = fạnzạ (cf. ạlhajị).
*(2) bạbanjīyā f. = hạrāmīyạ 1.
babara A. (bạbậra) m., f. old-fashioned
P. (cf. bạbanẹ ; bậra).
  B. (bābarā) m. = barbarā.
Bạbarbarẹ m. (f. Bạbarbarīyā) pl. Barẹ-
barī. (1) P. of the tribe so called
(Vd. Fannạ 2 ; barẹkatạ). (2) Bạbarbarẹ
m. = Bạbarbarạ f. type of fine sword.
(3) Bạbarbarīyar gyạdā = Bạgwārī 4d.
ɓaɓarē gambolling from joy, etc.
bābarẹ-bābarẹ piebald ; multicoloured.
bạbậri Kt. m. = bạbậra.
bạbarkwanẹ m. (pl. barkwanāwā). (1)
joker. (2) Sk. strong, resolute P.
Bạbarnẹ m. (f. Bạbarnịyā) pl. Barnāwā
P. of Bornu.
babarniya A. (bạbạrnīyā = ɓaɓạrnīyā) f.
(1) cracking of dumaŋ kāshī. (2) =
ɓaɓarē.
  B. Vd. Bạbarnẹ.
bậba rọdō Vd. bậba 8.
ɓāɓātū m. quarrelsome talking.
bậba zụrundụm Vd. bậba 10.

babba A. (b̦abba) *m.*, *f.* (*pl.* mänyā =
mä'nya-mänyā" = *Sk.* mäy'ya-
mäyyā" = *Kt.* *b̦abbunāna = *rustic*
*b̦abbuna). (1) (*a*) big *x* (i) b̦abban
dōki = dōki b̦abba big horse. b̦abbar
gōdīyā = gōdīyā b̦abba big mare. (ii)
mänyaŋ äbincinsu their staple food
(*Vd.* äbincī 2 *for reason for pl.*). (*b*)
b̦abbar sallä *Vd.* sallä 1*c*. (*c*) d̦am
b̦abbaŋ gidā son of a rich family (*cf.*
b̦abbar gidā). (*d*) kalmä tā fārä dä
b̦abbam bak̦ī the word begins with a
capital letter. (*e*) b̦abban d̦an yātsä
thumb. (*f*) b̦abban shūkä *Vd.* shūkä
2*c*.iii. (*g*) b̦abbaŋ äbōkiŋ aŋgo *Vd.*
äbōkī 1*b*. (*h*) ～ dä dādī, ämmā dä
wuyä a strong servant is useful, but
consumes much food. (*j*) mä'nya-
mänyā" *pl.* the rich, the upper classes,
influential people. (*k*) (i) mäi
mänya-mänyaŋ kyäu nē = mänyaŋ
kyäu gäreshi he has big but good
features. (ii) *Vd.* k̦ashi 4, burūdu 2.
(2) important *x* (*a*) sū nē mänyā they're
the most important ones. mäganär
gōnā ita cē b̦abba farming is the most
important thing. (*b*) b̦abbaŋ äbin dä
ya rabä mu dä sū, shī nē an zäb̦ē mu
the main difference between us is that
we are the ones chosen. (*c*) b̦abbaŋ äbu
shī nē, mäcē tā rigä mijintä bāwälī
(*said by labourers*) what a serious
affair ! (*d*) (*in genitive before pl.*) *x*
b̦abbam mutänē an important P. (*lit.*
a big one of the people). b̦abban
sarākunä a mighty chief. dukä mäi
sänä'ä yanä dä k̦aryā, ämmā mak̦ērī
shī nē b̦abbansu all craftsmen lie, but
the smith is the biggest liar of them all
Vd. b̦abbar gidā. (3) (*a*) adult *x* b̦abbam
mutum adult male. b̦abbar mäcē a
grown woman. (*b*) ～ dä yārö ya kän
cē people great and small say that . . .
(*c*) äbin dä ～ ya ganī yanä k̦asä,
yārö kō yā hau rīmī, bä zäi gan shi
ba a young P. has not the judgment of
an older P. (4) (*a*) elder, eldest. (*b*)
senior *x* (i) shī nē b̦abbansu he is the
senior of them. b̦abban d̦ansä his
eldest son (*cf.* k̦aramī). b̦abbarsu the
senior wife among them, the eldest
girl of the brothers and sisters. (ii) ～

jūjī nē, kōwā ya zō dä shärā, yä zubä
the P. matured by years must be long-
suffering (*Vd.* b̦abba jūjī). (iii) b̦abbaŋkä
dä kai ? kä rik̦ä shaŋ azumī ? should
a man of your standing go on breaking
the Fast ! (Mod. Gram. 164*a*). b̦abbark̦i
dä k̦ē ? kinä lälätä ? is it fitting that a
woman like you. should go about
prostituting yourself ! (*c*) P. of mature
age (*cf.* mänyantä). (5) (*a*) ～ bōk̦ōk̦ō =
b̦abba gōhōhō P. entitled to seniority
but who is mere puppet (*epithet is*
Yäyā, käwō akushiŋkä). (*b*)
Vd. kiŋkimbōd̦i. (*c*) mūgum ～ *Vd.*
gäraŋhōtsämī. (6) bigness *x* yārö ～
dä shī a big boy. ～ gäreshi it is big.
～ gärēkä knowing you as I do, I
cannot but believe you. (7) mänyā
(*pl. of majesty*) *x* (*a*) Wänë mänyā nē
So-and-so is a P. of rank. (*b*) Mänyā,
gātaŋ wäsā hail, thou owner of the
thing which others lack ! (*c*) mänyan
dawä (i) lion. (ii) Noble Sir ! (*Vd.*
dawä 1*b*). (*d*) Mänyam birnī *Vd.*
bäsarākë. (8) *Vd.* b̦abba-*compounds* ;
b̦abban-*compounds* ; b̦abbar-*compounds*.

B. (b̦abbā) *Vd.* bābë.

C. (babbā) *Vb.* kept on giving (*intensive from* bā).

b̦abba bōk̦ōk̦ō *Vd.* b̦abba 5.

б̦aбб̦aci *Vb.* (*intensive from* б̦aci).

b̦abba dä jäkä *m.* Saddle-bill = African
Jabiru (*Ephippiorhynchus senegalensis*).

b̦abba gōhōhō *Vd.* b̦abba 5.

*б̦aбб̦agumī *Kt. m.* = б̦agumēmë.

b̦abba jūjī *m.* (1) = zak̦amī. (2) (*a*) long-
suffering P. (*b*) *Vd.* b̦abba 4*b*.ii.

babbaka A. (b̦abbākä) *m.* mat-wall or
cornstalk-wall inside tsäŋgaya to ensure
privacy (*cf.* gägarä Bädau ; räkä mäi
giji ; sāб̦i ; gūramī).

B. (babbäkä) *Vb.* 1C. (1) tā babbäkä
nämä she grilled or toasted meat
(*either for eating next day, in which
case the meat is briefly hung on a stake
held in the hand over the fire ; or for
immediate eating, in which case the
meat is kept hanging long over the fire—
in this sense = gasä*), *cf.* k̦yāfë, k̦aurärā.
(2) tā babbäkä käzā she singed the
plucked fowl to give it consistency.
(3) yā babbaka wutä (*a*) he used up

much firewood. (*b*) he made a large fire. (4) yā babbàkà itàcē he heated pole (*e.g. of* gamfū *tree*) in fire to straighten or lengthen it.

C. (babbàkà) *f.* (*secondary v.n. of* babbàkà) *x* (1) tanà babbakàr kàzā = tanà babbàkà kàzā she's singeing fowl *as in* B.2 *above.* (2) anà babbakàr gīwā ; à ji ƙamshin zōmò ? can a busy P. stop for a thing of no importance ? (3) wurin dà akè babbakàr gīwā, wà zai kulà dà ƙaurim ɓērà who will heed a boy when elders are talking ?

ɓaɓɓakà *Vb.* 2 = ɓaɓɓakē 1.

babba kà rakà mai giji = sāɓi 2.

babbake A. (babbàkē) *Vb.* 1C = babbàkā.
   B. (babbàkē) *Vb.* 3A. (1) (*a*) blocked up place with one's body ; took up a lot of room. (*b*) monopolized conversation or task. (2) *Vb.* 1C Ingila tā ∼ wà Jāmus hanyàr cin dūnīyà England has stood in the way of the Germans subjugating the world.

ɓaɓɓakē (1) *Vb.* 1C. (*a*) uprooted. (*b*) ƙurjī yā ɓaɓɓakè ƙafàrsà the ulcer spread over his foot. (*c*) yā ɓaɓɓakè ƙafàrsà he knocked a bit of skin off his foot. (*d*) drank much of. (*e*) *Vd.* ɓaɓɓakō. (2) *Vb.* 3A *x* ƙurjinsà yā ∼ his ulcer spread.

ɓaɓɓakì *m.* yanà ɓaɓɓakim faɗà he's talking angrily.

ɓaɓɓakō *Vb.* 3A *x* hadirì yā ∼ storm's gathered (*cf.* ɓaɓɓakē 2).

babbaƙu *Vd.* baƙī B.2, section 4.

babbakwalī *m.* = bakwalī.

ɓaɓɓalcē = ɓakyalcē.

babbalnīyā = balbalnīyā.

babban baƙo (babbam bàƙō) *Vd.* jabgarò.

babban bango (babbam bangò) *Vd.* bangō 2.

babban bara (babbam bàra) *m.* any unpleasant T. thought finally scotched, but in fact merely dormant.

babban barci (babbam barcī) *Vd.* barcī 2.

babban bunsuru (babbam bunsurū) *Vd.* bunsurū 5.

babban dūtsè *Vd.* Fallau.

babbaŋ gumì *Vd.* gumì 1*c*.

babbaŋ gwāzā *m.* (1) prosperous but touchy P. (2) = babbar gwāzā.

babbaŋ ƙanè *Vd.* ƙanè 7.

babban nadì *Vd.* sō sō banzā.

babbar dafūwā *Vd.* dafūwā 1*d*.

babbar gīdā *f.* second wife of Chief (*cf.* babba 1*c*).

babbar gwāzā *f.* (1) type of European cloth. (2) *Vd.* babbaŋ gwāzā.

babbar inūwà *Vd.* inūwà 6.

babbar jàkā *Vd.* būrumā 2.

babbar laya (babbal lāyà) *Vd.* bagàjigì.

babba rigingìne *Sk. m.* new bulrush-millet heads split and laid to dry.

ɓaɓɓarkīyā *f.* = dalàkì 1.

babbar sallà *Vd.* sallà 1*c*.

babbar sānīyā *Vd.* maraƙī 1*b*.

babbartā *Fil. f.* (1) = ƙadandè. (2) root of sàbara.

babba tōmō *Vd.* Galàdīma.

babbaucē *Vb.* 3A behaved in the silly way pagans do.

babbaucì *m.* (1) the language or ways of pagans (= *Kt.* asancì). (2) tukunyā tanà ∼ the pot is full of delicious food.

babbāwà *m.* (*f.* babbaunīyā) *pl.* bàibàyī = *Sk.* bàibài. (1) pagan. (2) (*a*) babbāwaŋ watà European month (30–31 days). (*b*) babbaunīyar shèkarà European year of 365 days (*cf.* Balàrabè). (3) ƙaràtum baubāwà, ya cē " faɗi, m faɗi mù kàrè sururu ! " rushing at work " like a bull at a gate " (*as pagan cannot say* ɗ *or* ƙ *and so says* faɗi *for* faɗi *and* kàrè *for* ƙàrè).

babbunānà *Vd.* babba.

bābè *m.* (*pl.* bābuna = *babbā). (1) large type of non-gregarious locust. (2) bari nēman jinī wurim ∼ you can't get blood from a ·stone ! (3) ∼ mai ƙarfiŋ gàbā what a generous person ! (4) *Vd.* gāfarà 3*e*. (5) ƙyaurī nè mūgum ∼ the boy (girl) is undergrown.

ɓāɓè *Vb.* 3A *x* sum ∼ = àbūtā tasù tā ∼ they've quarrelled and separated (= wātsè 2).

bābì *Ar. m.* (1) (*a*) chapter. (*b*) category *x* à wànè ∼ zā mù ajìyē shì how shall we classify him ? (2) bà à sam bābin dà yakè cikì ba it's not clear what he is driving at, it's not clear what he is up to. (3) inà bābinsà what underlies the matter ?

bābù = bà there is not *q.v.* (2) (*replaces* bà *in reply to question*) *x* dà nàmà ?

is there any meat ? (*reply* bābu no, there is none). (3) bạ ạbin dạ bābu nothing is lacking. (4) jinjirī, bạ kạ sam "bābu" ba *epithet of* persistent P. (5) minus *x* ạshirim bīyū bābu 18. aɳ kafạ gạriɳ shękarạ 12 kę nam bābu watạ 3 the town was founded 12 years ago all but 3 months. (*cf.* gairạ 1). (6) bābu nēsạ *Vd.* Allą 7*c* (7) bābu gạ Allą *Vd.* Allą 1*e*. (8) im bābu ạbiɳkạ *Vd.* ạbu 2*h*. (9) bābu wāwā *Vd.* wāwā 1*b*, 3. (10) bābu gạ tsuntsū *Vd.* ɓạkạtantạɳ. (11) jirạ̄ci ∼ *Vd.* ɓatar dạ 5.

bạbūdę *m.* (*pl.* būdāwā) fortune-teller (*epithet is* ∼ bū dạ gārā).

ɓābulkā = **ɓāburkā**.

bābunạ *Vd.* **bābę**.

bạ̄bur *m.* (*pl.* bạ̄buṛai) (*Ar. from Ital.* vapore) motor-cycle (= butu-butu 2).

bạ̄buṛạ *Vb.* 2 *x* yā bạ̄buṛi dōki dạ sukūwā he galloped the horse at a furious pace.

bạ̄buṛci *Vd.* **bạ̄buṛtạ**.

ɓābuṛkā *f.* (1) big hole in wall or ground. (2) gap from loss of teeth.

bạ̄buṛtạ *Vb.* 2 (*p.o.* bạ̄buṛcē, *n.o.* bạ̄buṛci) *x* yā bạ̄buṛcē ni dạ fadạ he ranted at me.

Bạbūshę *m.* (*f.* Bạbūsạ) *pl.* Būsāwā P. of Būsa.

bạ̄but *adv.* profusely (*re pustules, ants, grass, people, etc.*).

bācạ *Eng. f.* voucher.

bạ cācā *Vd.* cirin.

ɓācaccē = **ɓātaccē**.

ɓācal *Kt. m.* = **ɓācē**.

baccạ *Kt. f.* charm hung round neck by Filani for producing fecundity of cows.

baccī *m.* = **barcī**.

bācę *Kt.* = **bātsę**.

ɓace A. (ɓācē) *m.* yā yi mini ∼ he "queered my pitch".

B. (ɓācę) *Vd.* ɓāci A.1, section **4**.

C. (ɓạcē) *Vd.* ɓạtā.

D. (ɓacē) *Vd.* ɓạtā.

E. (ɓacę). (1) *Vd.* ɓatạ. (2) *Vb.* 3A (*a*) vanished *x* watạ yanạ ɓacēwā the moon's disappearing. asalinsạ har yā ∼ so that his origin is shrouded in the mists of the past. (*b*) *Sk. Kt.* (i) became lost *x* yā ɓacę garkę = yā ɓacę ạ garkę it has wandered from the herd. (ii) made a mistake. (*c*) *Sk.*

yā ∼ hanyạ he mistook the road. (*d*) *Vd.* kūrā 39. (*e*) yā sābạ ɓacēwā ạ fādạ *Vd.* ạbu 2*k*.

bạcēwạ *Sk.* = **mạgạntayyạ**.

ɓacēwā *Vd.* ɓacę 2, ɓatạ.

ɓācī = **baicī**.

ɓaci A.1 (ɓāci) *Vb.* (1) became spoiled. yanạ ɓāci it is becoming spoiled. (2) (*a*) zūcīyā tatạ tā ∼ = rạntạ yā ∼ she became vexed, sad. (*b*) ạbiɳ yā ∼ = rānā tā ∼ things went wrong. (*c*) kō dājī yā ∼, gīwā tā fi gudu nil desperandum ! (*d*) wạndạ bā ạ̄ yabạ ka sāi tā ∼ nē it is a case of nobody being a prophet in his own country. (*e*) sā'ạrsu tā ∼ their luck was out. (3) *Vd.* ɓātạ 8. (4) (*before dative*, ɓācę *is used*) *x* (*a*) aiki yā ɓācę masạ his work did not succeed. (*b*) rānā tā ɓācę mini I had bad luck. (*c*) dawạ yā ɓācę masạ evil befell him in the bush (*x* robbery, death while hunting, loss of direction, etc.).

A.2 (ɓāci) *m.* (1) *x* kōmē ɓācim mutum however evil a P. may be. (2) (*a*) ɓācin zūcīyā vexation, sadness. (*b*) ɓācin zūcīyā yā shiga tsạkāninsu they became mutually embittered (*cf.* ɓāci A.1 2 *above*). (3) ɓācin rānā bad luck, disappointment (*cf.* ɓāci A.1 *above*). (4) *Sk.* insults. (5) *Sk.* (*secondary v.n. of* ɓạtā) *x* munạ ɓācinsạ = munạ ɓạtā tasạ we're insulting him.

B. (ɓạ̄ci) *Vd.* ɓạtā.

C. (ɓạci) *Vd.* ɓạtā.

bạcūcanę = *Sk.* **bạcūcanạ** *m.* (*f.* bạcūcanīyā) *pl.* cūcanāwā. (1) P. born in slavery of slave-parents (*so called, as knowing the secrets of the family, he thinks to himself* "cụcę ni ɳ cụcē kạ" "you blab about me and I'll blab about you !") (= dīmājọ = ƙinnī). (2) bạcūcanạɳ aiki attempting too many things at once. (3) bạcūcanạm bāshi adding to one's many debts which are already beyond one. (4) *Vd.* **bạgarīyę ; bullạm ; cūcananci**.

ba da A. (bā dạ) *Vb.* 4A (*Vd.* Mod. Gram. 87). (1) gave *x* yā ∼ rīgā he gave a gown. yā ∼ rīgā gạrēni he gave me a gown. yā ∼ ita he gave it (gown). yanạ̄ bāyạrwā he's giving (it).

(2) **sum ⁓ garī** (*a*) they surrendered the
town. (*b*) they gave in (*in argument,
etc.*). (3) betrayed *x* **yā ⁓ Audu** he
betrayed Audu. **dąmunā tā ⁓ mū**
we had a bad rainy-season. **fatauci yā
bāshē shi** his trading-venture was
a failure. (4) outwitted *x* **yā ⁓ ni** he
outwitted me. **yāķi yā ⁓ mū** the fight
went against us. **nā ⁓ sānīyā** I dodged
the oncoming cow. (5) **nā ⁓ haŋkąlī
gąrēshi** I paid attention to him. **yanā ⁓
ķarfī gą cinikiŋ gyądā** he specializes in
the groundnut-trade. **yā ⁓ ķarfī gą
itącē** he leaned against a tree. (6)
yanā ⁓ ķōķarī he is doing his best.
(7) **yā ⁓ bāyā** (*a*) he turned his back. (*b*)
he retreated *x* **dārī yā ⁓ bāyā** the cold
weather is over. **fatauci yā ⁓ bāyā**
there's a slump in itinerant-trading.
ąkallą yā ⁓ sabą'im bāyā he's at least
70 years old (*Vd.* **bāyā** 1*b*). (8) **rūwā
yā ⁓ iską kwānan naŋ** there's been a
lull in the rains lately (*Vd.* **iską** 3*a*).
(9) **ąbōkaŋ gābā sum bā dą ķąi** the
enemy surrendered (*Vd.* **bā ni ķąi**).
(10) **bā dą bāķī** *Vd.* **bāķī** 4*d*, 2*r*. (11)
Allā yą bā dą ķąsūwā *Vd.* **Alą** 7*b*. (12)
Vd. **bā ; bąi ; sā'ą ; wāką.**
    B. (**bāda**) *Vb.* 1A *Sk. x* **yā ⁓ ta** he
gave it (gown) (*cf.* A.1 *above*). **bā yā
bądūwā** it cannot be given.
    C. (**bą dą**) *conj.* without *Vd.* **bą** C.1
section **4**.

bada *Vb.*, 1A sprinkled *x* **nā ⁓ masą yāji**
I sprinkled condiments over it (*cf.*
barbądā).
badā-badā *f.* indistinct-speaking.
bą dādą *f.* empty promises.
badądą *adv.* (1) **kadą yą tąfi ⁓** don't let
it rove at large ! (2) **Audu ⁓ yakē**
Audu's daft. (3) **badim ⁓** many years
hence.
badādąntaką *f.* friendship.
bą dadę *Vd.* **dadę.**
Bą dādī *Vd.* **dādī** 1*d*.
badādī *m.* (*f.* **badādīyā**) bosom-friend.
badagēlą *Kt. f.* any knife.
badāgulā *Kt.* = **mąjāgulā.**
bādąkkā *Vb.* 1C *Nor.* = **bā dą.**
Badakkarę *m.* (*f.* **Badakkarīyā**) *pl.*
    Dakąrkarī P. of the **Dakąrkarī** *q.v.*
Bądākǫ *m.* = **Bądākūwā** *f. x* **Bądākǫ yā**

hau kąntą the **bǫrī**-spirit called **Bądākǫ**
has possessed her.
badala A. (**bādalā**) *f.* (1) = **gwalalō.**
(2) ledge inside town walls where
defenders stand (= **dąkąlī** 2). (3)
mound of refuse from dyepits. (4)
dam ⁓ m. (*pl.* **'yam ⁓**). (*a*) = **dāgirą.**
(*b*) bastard.
    B. (**bądalą**) *Vb.* 3B. *Sk.* = **shągalą 1.**
badalad dą *Vb.* 4B. *Sk.* distracted attention of P.
badąlī *Ar. m.* (1) exchange *x* (*a*) **an yi
badąlinsą dągą Kanǫ zūwą Baucī** he's
been transferred from Kano to Bauchi
(= **canji** 2*a*). (*b*) **yā yi badąlin rīgā** (i)
he changed his gowṇ, putting on another.
(ii) he exchanged his gown. (2) *Kt.*
an ci badąlinsą he's been humiliated.
badąltā *Vb.* 1C = **baddąlā.**
Bądamāgarę *m.* (*f.* **Bądamāgarīyā**) *pl.*
    Damāgarāwā P. of **Dąmāgąram.**
bądam-badam *m.* = **bądam-badąmā** *f.*
(1) floundering about in A. (*x swimming,
reading, writing, etc.*) = **funjum-
funjum.** (2) **bądam-badam ą rūwa yā fi
⁓ ą wuta** choose the lesser evil !
bądāmę *m.* (*f.* **bądāmīyā**) right-handed P.
badandąmā *Vb.* 3A floundered (*as in*
bądam-badam).
badandąmē *Vb.* 3A became disordered.
badaŋgarci *m.* delight.
badaŋkamā *f.* type of sugar-cane, rice,
guineacorn, or broad-leafed tobacco.
badannīyā *f.* = **bądam-badam.**
*bądarai *m.* (1) living-things. (2) *Vd.*
badarę.
badarę *m.* (*f.* **badarīyā**) *pl.* **bądarai** (*Ar.*
badri new moon). (1) young man
(*epithet is* **⁓ sābaŋ ķarfī**). (2) **badaraŋ
watą** moon 4–7 days old (*Vd.* **watą** 1*e*.ii).
(3) **badaraŋ jāķī** donkey of age and
strength to carry loads.
badarę *m.* halfpenny (= **sīsi** 1*b*).
badashārē *m.* useless, idle fellow.
Bādau (1) **kūrąm ⁓** *epithet of* any **Sarkim
pāwą** (*cf.* **kūrę** 1*b* ; **fāwą** 1*c*). (2) *cf.*
gągarą Bādau. (3) *cf.* **shāwąrāķi.**
badaudī *m.* = **sulkē.**
Badaurī *m.* (*f.* **Bądaura**) *pl.* **Dąurāwā.**
(1) P. of **Daurā.** (2) **yaną dą ciki
kaman na Bądauriŋ ķąrē** he's painfully
thin.

badayĭ *Sk. m.* type of grass.

6ad da A. (6ad dạ) *Vb.* 4A. (1) = 6atar
dạ. (2) 6ad dạ bāḵō *Vd.* turbạ.
B. (6addạ) 1A *Sk.* = 6atar dạ.

baddạlạ *Vb.* 1C changed *x* (1) Ạljumma'ạ,
anạ baddạlạ tufạ on Fridays people
change their clothes. (2) mụ ~ let's
return by a different route ! (3)
neglected P. or T. in one's care.

6addallā *f.* = 6ardallā.

ba6darẹ-ba6darẹ *Kt.* = dabbarẹ-dabbarẹ.

baddē *m.* = bardē.

ba6dọ *Sk. f.* girl born after several
males.

Badẹ *f.* Bedde.

badẹ (1) *Vb.* 1A *x* am ~ masạ yājị =
badạ. (2) *Kt.* bạbbam ~ = bạbambadẹ
2.

bạdi (1) *adv.* (*a*) next year. (*b*) *Vd.*
ba6dadạ 3. (*c*) banzā ~ bạ rạ̈i do not
make castles in the air ! (2) *f. x*
(*a*) bạdi waccạn the year after next.
(*b*) gyāram ~ *Vd.* hūrạ 2*a*.

bādị *Kt. m.* = silly chatter.

Badigẹ *m.* (*f.* Bạdigĭyā) *pl.* Digāwā P.
practising customs called Digancī.

bado A. (badọ) *m.* (1) water lily, water
lilies (*cf.* ḵwạlā). (2) *cf.* tạ̈ka ạ ~ .
B. (bādō) *Vb.* 1E *Sk. x* yā ~ mini shĭ
he gave me it (= bādạ).

bạdō *m. or adv.* (1) yā zaunạ ~ he
sat exposing his person. yā rufẹ
ḵōfạ ~ he didn't close the door properly. sunạ̈ rawar ~ young people
are doing an obscene type of dance.
wannạn rufị ~ nẹ it's not properly
closed. (2) ~ ginịn (or darā) gadō ạ
bāyan dāḵị *epithet of* badly-done work.
(3) mun yi ~ ; munạ̈ zạncansạ, ạshē
yanạ̈ naŋ we " spoke of the devil "
(= kạnḵị 2*b.*i). (4) *Vd.* bọdō.

bạdōdarā *f.* big-buttocked slut.

bạdōkọ *m.* expert rider.

bādu *Vd.* bā dạ.

bạ duhụ *m.* (1) charm conferring invisibility. (2) bạ duhụn sūrị magical
substance found in termites' nest.

bạdūjalā *f.* (1) English drum. (2) cotton
from American seed.

bạdūkụ = *bạdūḵụ *m.* (*pl.* dụ̈ḵạ̈wā =
bạdūḵai). (1) leather-worker. (2) ūwar
~ *Vd.* bōrin tiŋkẹ.

Bādụm *f.* (1) Ibadan. (2) *x* dam Bādụm
m. type of Nigerian kolanut.

Bạduŋgurẹ *m.* (*f.* Bạduŋgurĭyā) *pl.*
Duŋgurāwā P. of Zunguru (Dụŋgurụm).

bạdūnạyĭ = bạdūnịyĭ = *Zar.* bạdūnī =
budūnịyĭ.

bạdūsā = bạdussā *f.* (1) A. of poor
quality. (2) ugly woman.

bạdūsayā *f.* (1) type of poor matt writing-
paper. (2) = bạdūsā 2.

bạfāda = *Kt.* bạfādẹ = *Sk.* bạfādị *m.*
(*pl.* fādāwā = *Sk.* fạ̈dạ̈wā). (1) (*a*)
courtier. (*b*) bā ạ mūgụn Sarkī sȧi
mūgụm bạfādẹ the chief is not evil
but he has evil counsellors. (2) any
N.A. employee. (3) cajoler. (4) *Vd.*
mālạmĭ 1*d.* (5) *Vd. next entry.*

bạfādịyā *f.* (*pl.* fādāwā = *Sk.* fạ̈dạ̈wā).
(1) woman attached to the palace.
(2) woman full of blandishment.

bạfājẹ *m.* = bạfādạ.

Bạfạransị *m.* (*f.* Bạfạransịyā *pl.* Fạrạnsại
q.v. Frenchman (*cf.* Fạrạnsại).

bạfatạkẹ *m.* (*f.* bạfatāḵịyā) *pl.* fatạ̈kē
= farkē.

baffạ *m.* = bappạ.

Bạfilācẹ = Bạfillācẹ *m.* (*f.* Bạfilātạ =
Bạfillātạ *Vd. next entry*) *pl.* Filạ̈nĭ
= Fillạ̈nĭ. (1) one of the Filani
people (*epithet is* tạ̈ dạ gạ̈bā, rịgạ gudụ ;
Vd. nāmạ 1*f*, gandū 2*e*, Ạgwại,
Akạzaudạ, Jạudā). (2) *Vd.* Filạ̈nĭ ;
Bạfilātạnā ; kādọ ; Bạrạrō.

Bạfilātạnā = Bạfillātạnā *f.* (1) Filani
woman (*Vd. last entry*). (2) weed
for increasing milk of nursing-mother.
(3) ~ tā ta6ạ shi he's paralysed (*cf.*
Innạ 3*b*). (4) type of reddish biting-
ant. (5) type of reddish tobacco.
(6) type of red Bambarra groundnut.

Bạfilātạnĭ = Bạfillātạnĭ *m.* = Bạfilācẹ (*f.*
and pl. as in last two entries).

Bạfillācẹ, Bạfillātạ *Vd.* Bạfilācẹ.

bāfọ *m.* (1) dam ~ fluteplayer. rawar
bāfọ dancing to the strains of a
flute. (2) *Eng.* metal, etc., bath.

Bạfulātạnĭ *m.* Bạfulātạnā *f.* *Vd.* Bạfilācẹ,
Bạfilātạnā.

bāfụnā *f. x* yā zubạ masạ ~ he " led
him on " with wild talk.

bāfụr *Ar. m.* taurā-tree gum used as
incense.

bāfūrẹ *Sk. m.* type of weed.

baga A. (bāgā) *f.* breadth *x* yā fi wancạŋ ~ it's broader than that one.
  B. (bāgạ) *f. Vd.* būshīyā 4.

ɓāgā *m., f.* any P. laughing senselessly at everything.

baga-baga A. (bạgā-bạgā = bạgā-bạgā) *f.* = bạdạm-badam.
  B. (bagā-bagā) *Kt. m.* = bụrgā.

ɓagā-ɓạgā *Vd.* ɓaŋgarērẹ.

Bạgabạshī *m.* (*f.* Bạgabashīyā) *pl.* Gabasāwā. (1) Easterner. (2) *Vd.* ạlmụtsụtsai.

Bạgạdāzạ *f.* Bagdad.

bāgadẹ = bāgadē *Kt. m.* earth-oven inside house with metal bars on which meat is grilled.

bạgai *Kt.* = bạgāyī.

bagajā *m.* = rūwam ~ *m.* impure water lying stagnant in borrowpits, holes, etc.

bagajī *Kt. m.* = bạgajā.

bạgạjigī, bạbbal lāyạ what a wealthy, generous P. !

bạgạlāḍīmẹ *m.* type of black and white cloth.

bāgalājē *x* ḍam bāgalājē *m.* = wạinā 5.

bạgandẹ *Sk. m.* type of big fãifãi-mat.

bāgarā *f.* (1) joking *x* yạ yi minị ~ he joked with me. (2) na ~ *epithet of any* dōgarị.

bạgarẹ *Vd.* Jạtau.

bagari A. (bạgạrī) *Sk.* = ḍaŋ gạrī (*Vd.* gạrī).
  B. (bạgạrī) *Vd.* bạgạrūwā.

bạgạrīyē *m.* curved-pommelled Bornu saddle (an inferior type is bạcūcanạm ~).

Bạgạrmī *m., f.* Bagarmi person(s) (= bạ ta kulkī).

bạgạrūwā *f.* (*pl.* bạgạrī) = gạbạrūwā.

ɓagas (1) ạ ~ easily ; cheaply ; without trouble. (2) *Sk. m.* tūwō without gravy (= gāyā 2*b*.i).

bagas-bagas *x* rīgā tā yi bagas-bagas gown has just a nice tinge of indigo-dye.

bạgạudayā *f.* = bạgōdayā.

bạgauji *Nor. m.* = bạgōdayā.

bāgāyā *Vb.* 1C *Kt.* made circuit of, went round (= gēwạyā).

bạgayẹ *Kt. m.* substitute (= mạimakō).

bạgāyī *m.* the shrub *Cadaba farinosa,*

whose leaves are mixed with flour of bulrush millet to make bạlạmbō.

bagazạm *x* ḍam bagazạm *m.* fast breed of horse.

bạgạzụŋ *Eng. m.* magazine-rifle.

bạgạzunzụmī *Vd.* bụgụzunzụmī.

bage A. (bāgẹ) *m.* (1) great warrior (*epithet is* ~ mại aikịm mutūwạ). (2) stubborn P. (3) stubbornness. (4) *Vd.* duhụ 6. (5) bāgẹ-bāgẹ *adj.* piebald, variegated (= dabbarẹ-dabbarẹ).
  B. (bagẹ) *Vb.* 3A lurked in hiding.

ɓāgẹ = gāwurtạ.

baggạ *x* nā cī, nā yi baggạ I ate to repletion.

bạgidājẹ *m.* (*f.* bạgidājīyā) *pl.* gịdāḍāwā. (1) simpleton ; bumpkin ; uncouth rustic (= mūzī 1 = kaŋkị 4 = tāshịŋ ƙauyẹ), *Vd.* futuk. (2) ~, ~ nē once a rustic, always a rustic !

bạgīmī *m.* = bịgīmī.

bā gincirạ *Vd.* gincirạ.

bạgindẹ *Kt. m.* (*pl.* gịndāwā). (1) cottonseller. (2) salt-seller.

bāgirị. (1) *m.* bāgirị = bāgirịn yạnyawạ half-caste. (2) *adj.* bāgirị-bāgirị variegated, piebald (= bāgẹ 5).

bā girmā *Vd.* girmā 1*c*.ii.

Bāgirmī = Bāgạrmī.

bạgirō *m.* fetichism (*epithet is* ~ kạkan tsāfị).

bạgō = ɓạgō *m.* (1) (*a*) hunter's lying in wait for prey. (*b*) yā tạfi ~ (i) he's gone to the dākịm ~ (*i.e.* hut for awaiting prey). (ii) he's gone to hunter's tree-platform (*cf. Kt.* sagị 3*c*). (2) ɓaunā tā fi ~ you won't catch such a one napping ! (3) bushdrive enveloping the game in the centre. (4) *cf.* ḍagōgō 2*b*.i.

bā gōban daɗạ *Vd.* gōbe 3.

bạgōbiri *m.* (1) a certain bọrī-spirit (*epithet is* ~ bāwạ). (2) Bạgōbirī *m.* (*f.* Bạgōbirā) *pl.* Gōbirāwā P. of Gōbir.

bạgōdā = bạgōdayā *Kt. f.* hoe with metal haft given bride among the Maguzāwā by her parents.

bạgōzagī *m.* = ɓaɓɓakī.

bāgū *m.* deception *x* yā yi minị ~ he lied to me.

bā gūḍạ *Vd.* aŋgọ.

bạ gudālẹ *m.* (*f.* bạ gudālạ) *Nor.* short-legged, shorthorned ox (= gudālẹ).

bạgullīyā *f.* *used in* nā kaɗạ wạ Audu ~ I spun my top clockwise to make the game harder for my opponent Audu.

Bạgūmạlī *m.* (*f.* Bạgūmạlā = Bạgūmạliyā) *pl.* Gūmalāwā P. of Gūmạl.

ɓāgumē *Vb.* 3A = gāwurtạ.

ɓāgumēmẹ *m.* (*f.* ɓāgumēmīyā) huge.

ɓagura A. (ɓāgụrā) *Vb.* 1C chipped piece off T.

 B. (ɓāgurạ). (1) *Vb.* 3B became chipped (= ɓalgạcẹ). (2) *f. x* yanạ dạ ~ it (pot, etc.) is chipped, it (wall) is abraded.

ɓagure A. (ɓāgụrē) *Vb.* 3A = ɓāgurạ.

 B. (ɓāgurẹ) *m.* (*sg., pl.*) chip (ɓalgạcẹ).

ɓagusa A. (ɓāgụsā) *Vb.* 1C = ɓāgụrā.

 B. (ɓāgusạ) = ɓāgurạ.

bạgwạndarā *f.* (1) variety of cotton (= gwandai 2). (2) variety of guineacorn.

bạgwạnjā *f.* brass basin from the Gold Coast (= dīyā 5c), *Vd.* Gwạnjā.

Bạgwārī = Bạgwārẹ *m.* (*f.* Bạgwārīyā) *pl.* Gwārạwā. (1) (*a*) Gwari P. (*b*) P. as ignorant as a Gwari. (*c*) *Vd.* futuk, alạgwaidạ, Na akurū. (2) yā gạmu dạ ~ he got severe primary syphilis (*Vd.* tụnjērē). (3) *Vd.* Gwārī. (4) Bạgwārīyā *f.* (*a*) (i) Gwari woman. (ii) *Vd.* jạkin 3. (*b*) variety of guineacorn. (*c*) a quick ripening maize. (*d*) = gyạdā 1b.

bạ hạ (*lit.* that which causes one to exclaim " ha ! ") *m.* (*sg., pl.*). (1) expert boxer. (2) gwạurau ~ *m.* (*sg., pl.*). (*a*) European doctor. (*b*) syphilis (*epithet is* Gwạurau bạ hạ, kịskō kā fi aikịm mālạm). yā gạmu dạ gwạurau bạ hạ he got syphilis (*cf.* mālạmī 1c.iv).

Bạhabashẹ *m.* (*f.* Bạhabashīyā) *pl.* Habashāwā an Abyssinian.

Bạhaɗējẹ *m.* (*f.* Bạhaɗējīyā) *pl.* Haɗējāwā P. of Hadeija.

bạhago *m.* (*f.* bạhagụwā) *pl.* bạhagwai. (1) lefthanded P. (2) contrary P. (3) ~ tausạ dāma *epithet of* clumsy P. or clumsy work. (4) (*a*) bạhagụwar tụkā string with left-handed twist. (*b*) *Vd.* tụkā 2d. (5) ạbụ yā zamā bạhagwạn tạrnaƙī the matter is full of contradictions.

bahạr = bahạrī (*Ar.* sea, Mediterranean).

(1) *(a)* sea, large river. *(b)* learned man. (2) ɗam ~ *m.* (*f.* 'yar ~) *pl.* 'yam ~ riding-donkey (*cf.* bakari). (3) Bạhar mālīyạ = Bạharụl mālīyạ (*Ar.* salty sea) The Red Sea. *(4) Bạharụl Aswạd = Bahạr Aswạd The Black Sea. (5) Bahạr Rụm The Mediterranean Sea. (6) *Vd.* bahạrī.

bahạrī *m.* (*f.* bahạrā). (1) *x* baƙim ~ yā zō that damned outsider has come. baƙar bahạrā tā cẹ̄ . . . that slut said . . . (2) *Vd.* bahạr.

bahạsī *m.* = ba'ạsī.

Bạhaushẹ *m.* (*f.* Bạhaushīyā) *pl.* Hausạwā. (1) P. whose mother-tongue is Hausa (*Vd.* hausā). (2) *epithet is* ~ mai baŋ haushī.

bạ hawā samạ = *Sk.* bạ hawā bisạ. (1) epithet of buffalo (ɓaunā). (2) *cf.* bā ạ hawā samạ *under* tsānị, kwạdō 1a.iv, ƙarƙārạ, rạbō 7e.

bạ hayạ *x* gidam ~ *m.* public latrine.

bạ̄hẹ cry uttered by boys jumping into water (= lạlẹ).

bahīlancị = bahilcị *m.* miserliness.

bạhīlī *m.* (*f.* bạhīlīyā) *pl.* bạhīlai *Ar.* miser.

bāhọ = bāfọ.

bāhụnā = bāfụnā.

bāhụr = bāfụr.

bai A. (bại). (1) (*a*) gave T. to P. *x* yā ~ Sarkī dōkị he gave the Chief a horse. yanạ ~ Sarkī shī he's giving it to the Chief (Mod. Gram. 87), *cf.* bā, bā dạ. (*b*) *Sk.* yanạ ~ he's giving it (= bāyarwā *q.v. under* bā dạ 1). (*c*) *Vd.* Alạ bại, bại ƙanạŋkạ, bại mayạ̄ƙā. (2) (*same sense as* bāyā *but limited to use in the following expressions*). (*a*) (noun) (i) dōkị yā yi ~ the horse's back is galled. (ii) yā fitạ ta ƙōfạr ~ he went out by the backdoor (= maduddukịyā = kụrdē 4). (*b*) (adv.) (i) cikī dạ ~ inside and out. (ii) wurī yā tāshị ~ ɗayā the place is level. abūbūwạn nạŋ sun tāshị ~ ɗayā these things are very similar. (*c*) *Kt.* zạ ni ~ I'm going to the latrine (= bāyaŋ gidā). (3) *Sk. x* im ~ saƙị if he doesn't let him go (= bā yạ̄ *q.v. under* bā).

 B. (bại) (Mod. Gram. 20) *x* ~ zō ba he has not come (*Sk. also uses* bạ yạ *e.g.* bạ yạ zō ba).

C. (băi) *Sk.* (1) *m.* watering horses *x* yă tạfî, yanạ ban dōkị he has gone to water the horse. (2) = bāyī *q.v. under* bāwạ. (3) *Vd.* băinā.

ɓai *Vd.* yallạ.

baibai A. (băibăi) *adv.* (1) (*a*) inside-out. (*b*) back to front. (2) an ɗaurẹ shi ~ his hands are (were) tied behind his back. (3) an ɗaurẹ dōkị ~ horse is (was) tied to post by off-legs. (4) yă fādị ~ he fell on his back.

B. (băibăi) *Vd.* bạbbāwạ.

C. (băibăi) *x* gishirin nạŋ ~ yakẹ the salt in this is insufficient. haŋkạlinsạ ~ yakẹ his intelligence is low (*cf.* băibạyē 5).

băibăicē (1) *Kt. Vb.* 1C *x* am băibăicẹ ɗākị the thatching of the house is complete. (2) *Vb.* 3A *x* ạl'amạrinsạ yă ~ his affairs have gone askew.

băibăitā (1) *Kt. x* yă ~ minị = băibạyā 5. (2) *Sk.* yă ~ he made himself scarce ; he kept out of sight.

ɓaiɓāyā *Sk.* = 'yạ'yyāwạ 1.

baibaya A. (băibạyạ) *Kt.* (1) *Vb.* 2 (*a*) = băibạyē 1. (*b*) thatched T. partly ; thatched some of the houses. (*c*) kā băibạyi kōwā *Vd.* shūcị 2. (2) *f.* (*a*) the thatch. (*b*) ɓātạ ~ *Vd.* būnū.

B. (băibạyā) *Kt. Vb.* 1C (1) yă băibạyạ shūcị ạ kạn ɗākị = yă ~ wạ ɗākị shūcị he thatched the house with grass (= băibạyē 1). (2) yă băibạyạ rawạnī he wound on. his turban hurriedly and badly. (3) am ~ masạ he (*district-head or village-head*) has been invested with office. (4) adulterated *x* shūnịŋ (tụrặrạŋ) (zanạŋ) bā shi dạ kyạu, am ~ masạ mại kyạu this indigo (scent) (cloth) is poor, so has been adulterated with some of good quality. am ~ wạ tūwō mīyạ insufficient gravy has been poured over the food. (5) yă ~ minị he came to assistance of me (*x poorer P.* ; *P. not skilled in setting out his case in law court*) (*cf.* băibạyē 3).

C.~ (băibāya) *f.* (1) yă tạfî dạ ~ he went backwards. (2) *Kt.* an yi minị ~ = băibạyā 5.

baibaye A. (băibạyē) *Vb.* 1C (1) *Kt.* thatched *x* am băibạyẹ ɗākị the house

has been thatched (= băibạyā 1 = jiŋkẹ *q.v.*). (2) *Kt.* thatched all of (*cf.* băibaya). (3) *Kt.* yă ~ shi dạ kāyā he gave him gifts (*cf.* băibạyā 5). (4) nā ~ shi- I backed him ; I chose him as my candidate for chieftainship, etc. (5) ƙasā tā băibạyẹ samạ the earth only just covers it (*cf.* băibăi).

B. (băibạyē) *Kt. m.* (1) the act of thatching (= jiŋkā *q.v.*). (2) (*secondary v.n. of* băibạyạ 1) *x* anạ băibạyạr ɗākị = anạ băibạyan ɗākị the house is being thatched.

băibạyī *Vd.* bạbbāwạ.

băicī = băicị *m.* (1) meaning, reason *x* inā băicinsạ what is the reason (meaning) of this ? (2) bringing luck *x* dōkịna yanạ dạ ~ my horse is lucky to me (= alfālụ). (3) daŋgi sun yi masạ ~ = daŋgi sun rufẹ masạ ~ his family've fulfilled their duty in bringing him gifts on festive occasions such as births, etc. (4) behind (*used as follows*) (*a*) yanạ dạ ~ he has many younger brothers, sisters, children, subjects, etc. (*b*) ƙanạm ~ P. very much younger than P. referred to (= ƙanẹ 4). (*c*) dạgạ ~ *adv.* afterwards. (*d*) *Sk.* cịm ~ *m.* backbiting. (*e*) *Vd.* băicin ; ạbăicī.

băicin (1) *conj.* after *x* ~ an yi hakạ akạ kōmō they returned after doing this. (2) *prep.* except *x* băicim mahạuƙạcī wạ̄ zại yī who but a madman would do so ! (= bạndạ).

'Baidụ *Vd.* gafîyạ 4 ; hǫri ~ ; bạr ni dạ ~.

*băiƙā *Vb.* 1C (*Zamfara Hausa*) gave to. băi ƙanạŋkạ dạ girmā *m.* = tuɓụrā 1.

băikō *m.* = băiwā 1, 2.

băi mayăƙā *m.* = tuɓụrā 1.

baina A. (băinā = băi na Allạ) *f.* = tsạ̄da 1*a*.

B. (bainạ) *f.* = bayā.

bainạl malạ'i *Ar.* publicly.

bainī = bainū *f.* = tsạ̄da 1*a*.

baita A. (baitạ) *m., f.* = baitụ.

B. (băitā) *Kt. Vb.* 1C (1) passed beyond (= wucẹ). (2) went to latrine.

băitakin *prep. x* ~ hakạ săi . . . = băitakin naŋ săi . . . after that, they . . .

Ba̱ i̱tālīye̱ *m.* (*f.* Ba̱ i̱tālīyā) *pl.* i̱tālīyāwā an Italian.

*baiti̱ *m.* (*pl.* baitōcī = baitōtī) *Ar.* verse ; distich.

Baiti̱l mu̱k̬addas *m.* Jerusalem.

bäitō = bäitō *x* d̬am ⁓ = a̱baicī 1, 2.

baitu̱ *m., f.* P. who has made the pilgrimage to Mecca (= a̱lhaji̱).

Baitu̱llāhi̱ name given P. called A̱lhaji̱.

baitu̱lmal = baitu̱lmāli̱ *Ar. m.* Native treasury (*cf.* ku̬dī 1*d* ; kēbi̱ ; ma'aji 2).

bai'u̱ *Vd.* wa̱lā ⁓.

baiwa A.(bäiwā)*f.* (*pl.* ba̱'ye-ba̱ye̱ⁱⁱ) (1) gift, giving *x* yā yi masa̱ bäiwā da̱ yawa̱ he treated him liberally. kā yi mana̱ bäiwā da̱ shī you presented us with it. (2) betrothal *x* an yi bäiwar Ka̱nde da̱ Audu̱ Kande has been betrothed to Audu. an yi masa̱ ⁓ da̱ kē you've been betrothed to him. (3) generosity *x* Audu̱ ⁓ ga̱rēshi̱ Audu is liberal.

   B. (bäiwā) *f.* (*pl.* bāyī) (1) female slave (*Vd.* · bāwa̱ ; ku̱yanga̱). (2) = A̱ jēfas (*but only applies to female*). (3) bäiwar Alla̱ (*a*) = 2 *above.* (*b*) = tsa̱da 1*a.* (*c*) girl given to husband without dower being asked from him (= 'yar sadaka̱).

ba̱ iyākā *Vd.* a̱bu̱ 6.

ba̱ izo̱ *m.* = kwantai 3.

bajā-bajā = ti̱njim.

bajāgu̱lā *f.* = ma̱jāgu̱lā.

bajajā = ti̱njim.

bajajja̱gā *Kt.* = wajajja̱gā.

ba̱ Jākarā *f.* (*lit.* give to River Jakara !) darning needle (= yanka̱ 2*f*), *cf.* asirkā 2.

bajallē *m.* type of dance.

bajamfa̱rī *m.* = ra̱i d̬ōrē.

Bajāmushe̱ *m.* (*f.* Ba̱jāmushīyā) *pl.* Jāmu̱s = Jāmusāwā a German (*for sg.* Jāmu̱s *q.v. is also used*).

Bajāri̱ *m.* (*f.* Ba̱jā̱rā) *pl.* Jārāwā (1) P. of Jarawa tribe. (2) baja̱rā*f.* = ba̱gwārī 4*d.*

bajau *m.* (1) gishirī yā yi ⁓ food is well flavoured with salt. (2) an d̬aure̱ shi ⁓ he's been securely tied. (3) bāki̱nsa̱ yā yi ⁓ da̱ gōro̱ his mouth is red with kola.

bajawa̱rī, bajawa̱rā *Vd.* ba̱zawa̱rī, ba̱zawa̱rā *respectively.*

baje A. (ba̱je̱) *m.* (1) an yi ⁓ cornstalks have been spread out to serve as a bed. (2) farming without ridges and furrows (*as done in the North*).

   B. (ba̱je̱) (1) *Vb.* 1A (*a*) demolished (*house, mound, etc.*). (*b*) am ⁓ gidansa̱ his family has been removed from office. (2) *Vb.* 3A (*a*) (i) became demolished. (ii) became scattered, dispersed *x* sum ⁓ ciki̱n ga̱rī they became dispersed in the town (= ba̱zu). ta haka̱, cīyāwa̱ kē baje̱wā this is how grass spreads. (*b*) hadiri̱ yā ⁓ storm dispersed (= hadiri̱ 1*b*). (*c*) bāshi̱ yā ⁓ the debt outstanding is lost. (3) *m.* (*a*) = far-ji̱. (*b*) *Sk.* ⁓ ga̱rēta̱ she is broad-hipped.

ba̱ ji̱dā *Vd.* ji̱dā.

bajimba̱ *f.* (*sg., pl.*) small red bead.

*bajirō = ba̱girō.

Ba̱juku̱nī *m.* (*f.* Ba̱jukunīyā) *pl.* Jukunāwā Jukun person.

baka A. (baka̱) (*locative of* bāki̱, M.G. 24) (1) a̱ ⁓ in the mouth *x* (*a*) yā sa̱ a̱ ⁓ he put it in his mouth. (*b*) kaī nē ka sā masa̱ a̱ ⁓ *you* put him up to doing it. (*c*) (i) kā sā masa̱ a̱ ⁓ ba̱ ka̱ bā shi̱ ba you did not give it to him as promised. (ii) *Vd.* sa̱ A. 4, bāki̱ 1*b*.vi. (*d*) duk maganan na̱n, iyāka̱cinta̱ baka̱, ba̱ ta̱ jē zūcī ba all this talk was mere " eyewash ". (*e*) an d̬aukē shi̱ a̱ ⁓ he is being unfavourably spoken of.   yā d̬aukē ni̱ a̱ ⁓ he backbit me. (*f*) kuna̱ ⁓, muna̱ kunnē we're all agog to hear what you've got to say. (2) (M.G. 24*d*) (*a*) (i) yana̱ aiki̱ ⁓ da̱ hancī he's working might and main (*cf.* bāki̱ da̱ hanci̱). (ii) hannū ⁓, hannū k̬waryā greedy eating, tireless working. (iii) yā hau musu̱ hannū baka̱, hannū k̬waryā he attacked them forthwith. (*b*) yā cī da̱ ⁓ he fell on his face. (3) ⁓ bīyū = bāki̱ bīyū. (4) ta ⁓ tana̱ ⁓, ta zūcī tana̱ zūcī it is a smiling face cloaking pain or anger. (5) yā kai aiki̱nsa̱ da̱ ⁓ he exaggerated. kada̱ ka̱ kai ni̱ da̱ ⁓ don't exaggerate about me ! (6) (*a*) *Kt.* 'yar ⁓ *f.* = 'yar bāki̱ *f.* = 'yam baka̱ *pl. m.* tribal-marks (za̱nē) cut at corners of mouth. (*b*) *Kt.* d̬am ⁓ *m.* (*pl.* 'yam ⁓) (i) eulogizing-beggar (= mak̬ērim baka̱). (ii) garrulous P.

(*Vd.* kunāmạ 1*b*).   (iii) = 6*a above.*
(7) dạgạ ~ furē yā fi tābạ *epithet of*
furē 1*a*.ii.   (8) na ~ nā zubā *Vd.*
taunā 2*a*.iii.   (9) ạ ~ zumai nẹ *Vd.*
zumụ 3.   (10) *Vd.* malmal ; dakạn ~ ;
daram ~ *under* darē 11.

B. (baƙā) *m.* (*pl.* bakkunạ = bakuŋ-
kunạ = *Kt.* bakaŋkunạ, bakkunnạ) (1)
(*a*) bow.   (*b*) yā jā ~ he distended his
bow.   (*c*) 'yam ~ *pl. m.* archers.
(2) yā yi ~ it is bent in a curve.   (3) an
jūyạ masạ gịndim baƙā friend has
turned against him (= jūyạ 1*d*.ii).
(4) gạjērē mai ~ spirit credited with
causing diseases of unknown origin
x gạjērē mai ~ yā harbē shi he has a
disease of unknown origin (*Vd.* gạjērē 2).
(5) yanā cikiŋ hammạr ~ = hannum
~ bai sạkē shi ba he's in a tight corner
(*cf.* 9).   (6) yā nūnạ kurcīyā ~ he gave
P. a hint of the inner state of affairs.
(7) catch of lock ;   trigger of Dane-
gun.   (8) baƙaŋ gizọ *m.* (*a*) rainbow
(= gājịmạrē 1*b* = kyạŋkyēnau = sagō
2 = mashā 3*b*).   (*b*) ceiling-arch (*cf.*
ɗauriŋ gūgā).   (*c*)   *Sk.* = haƙōrī
5*a*.   (*d*) (i) dog-in-the-manger :   acting
as dog-in-the-manger.   (ii) baƙaŋ gizọ
shī bā Allā ba, ya kạŋ hanạ wạ
Allā rūwā skinflint often prevents the
liberal giving.   (*e*) type of spirit
(gājịmạrē 2) living in wells.   (9) (*a*)
hannum baƙansạ nē that's just in his
line !   (*b*) *Vd.* 5 *above* ;   hannun 1.
(9a) n nā kạm ~ I've decided irrevocably.   (10) baƙan shiɓạ *m.* small
bow for preparing cotton for spinning
(= *Kt.* masaɓī 2).   (11) *Vd.* Sarkim ~.
C. (bāƙā) *m.* tray for displaying
sweets, kolas, kiḷishī by 'yam ~.
baƙā *Vd.* baƙī.
ɓāƙạ *f.* small hole where potters store
clay to keep moist.
Bạkabẹ *m.* (*f.* Bạkabīyā) *pl.* Kabāwā
(1) P. of Kabi.   (2) *Vd.* bạkim Baƙabạ.
bakace A. (bākạcē) *Vb.* 1C winnowed
corn with tray (fāiƙāi) to remove bran
= būsā   2 = *Sk.* bēcẹ 4 = fētanē 2
(*cf.* cāsạ, taŋkạɗē, bāƙạcē).
B. (bāƙạcē) *m.* (1) being occupied
in winnowing as in A *above x* tanā ~
(= fētsā 2 = aŋgạjē 2*a*).   (2) (*secondary*

v.n. of bākạcē) *x* tanā bākạcẹ hatsī
= tanā bāƙạcaŋ hatsī she's winnowing
corn.
bạkadānīyā *f.* (1) type of guineacorn.
(2) the leprosy ƙurzunā.
bākad dạ *Nor. Vb.* 4B = bā dạ.
Bạkādirẹ *m.* (*f.* Baƙādirīyā) *pl.* Kādirāwā
P. of the Kadiriyya sect (*Vd.* hallā-
hallā ;   bạndīri).
baƙāƙē *Vb.* baƙī.
bakale A. (bakālẹ) *Kt.* = bakkālẹ.
B. (bākālẹ) *x* ɗam ~ *m.* song of
women at dances or while grinding.
bạkaŋ *m.* (1) lying unable to sleep.   (2)
pretending to be asleep (*epithet is* ~
wandạ ya fi barcī dādī).
bakance A. (bāƙạncē) (1) *m.* (*pl.* bāƙạntai)
vowing by God to do specific T. in
a given contingency (*cf.* rantsẹ, rantsūwā).   (2) *Vd.* bāƙạntạ 2.
B. (bāƙạncē) *Vb.* 1C = bāƙạntạ 1, 2.
bāƙạnci *Vd.* bāƙạntạ.
Bạkanẹ *m.* = Baƙanọ.
ɓaƙānē *Vd.* ɓaunā.
bạkaŋ gizọ *Vd.* bạkā 8.
bakaŋkunạ *Vd.* baƙā.
Bạkanọ *m.* (*f.* Baƙanūwā) *pl.* Kanāwā
(1) P. of Kano.   (2) *Vd.* Baƙanūwā,
yāƙi 1*k.*
bạkan shiɓạ *Vd.* bạkā 10.
bāƙạntạ *Vb.* 2 (*p.o.* bāƙạncē, *n.o.* bāƙạnci)
x yā bāƙạnci ạbụ kạzā he vowed to
do so and so in a given contingency.
(2) *Sk. Vb.* 3B deteriorated in character.
(3) *m.* (*pl.* bāƙạntai) = bāƙạncē 1.
baƙāntā *Vb.* 1C (1) (*a*) blackened.   (*b*) yā
~ ni he slandered me.   (2) yā ~ mini
cikị he rendered me despondent (*Vd.*
baƙin cikị).
bāƙạntai *Vd.* bāƙạncē.
baƙạntakạ *f.* blackness.
Baƙanūwā *f.* (1) *Vd.* Baƙanọ.   (2) type of
(*a*) gạrmā, (*b*) cotton, (*c*) marrow.
bā ƙārạ *Vd.* ƙārạ.
baƙạrārā = baƙạrārīyā *f.* sterile woman
or female animal (= jūyạ 3).
bakari *used in* ɗam ~ *m.* (1) any donkey
(*cf.* bahạr 2).   (2) ɗam ~ bā hawam
magạbātā ba if you act in a way out
of keeping with your status, you'll rue
it, he who touches pitch, becomes defiled.
baƙarƙashīyā = mạƙarƙashīyā.

*bākas dạ *Vb.* 4B *Nor.* gave to (= **bāyar dạ** *q.v.*).

bạ kāshī *Vd.* **bē'ẹ, bō'ẹ.**

bạƙashī *x* **yanạ dạ azzịkī** ~ he's fortune's favourite.

bākạtā *Vb.* 3B (1) dodged, swerved. (2) **hanyạ tā** ~ **tā yi kudụ** the road veers southwards.

bākatad dạ *Vb.* 3C (1) turned diagonally, placed diagonally (= **gizgạyā**) *x* **yā** ~ **hanyạ** he built the road deviatingly. (2) misled P. (*literally or figuratively*). (3) **yā** ~ **zạncē** he changed the conversation. (4) *Vd.* **bākatar.**

Bạƙātāgumī *m.* (*f.* **Bạƙātāgumịyā**) *pl.* **Kātāgumāwā** P. of Katagum.

bạkạtaạ *x* **yanạ zạune** ~ he's sitting idly.

bạkạtantạŋ *x* **bat̥ạm** ~, **bābụ gạ tsuntsū, bābụ gạ tarkō** " falling between two stools " (= **zạbạrī** 2), *Vd.* **bat̥ạn.**

bākatar (*dative form of obsolete verb* **bạkatạ,** M.G. 114) (1) turned diagonally *x* **watạ yā** ~ **kudụ** horns of the crescent moon now point south (= **zubar** 2 = **harbar** 3 = **māzạyā** = **shūrạ** 2*b* = **gizgạyā** 2 = **gōcẹ** 1*a.*ii = **kēsạ** 1*b*). (2) *Vd.* **bākatad dạ.**

bạkạtatạŋ = **bạttatạŋ** 2.

Bạkatsinẹ *m.* (*f.* **Bạkatsinịyā**) *pl.* **Katsināwā** P. of Katsina.

bạƙauyẹ *m.* (*f.* **bạƙauyịyā**) *pl.* **ƙauyạ̄wā** villager.

Bạkāzaurẹ *m.* (*f.* **Bạkāzaurịyā**) *pl.* **Kāzaurāwā** P. of Kazaure.

baƙē-baƙē *m.* (1) **cikị yā yi masạ** ~ he was replete. (2) **yā yi** ~ he's getting on in the world.

bạ kēsạ̄wā *Vd.* **bardē.**

bạkī *m.* (*pl.* **bākunạ** = **bākuŋkunạ**) (1) (*a*) *Vd. separately* (i) **bạkin** *in sense of* all of, in exchange for, as the equivalent of, on the verge of, when. (ii) **bạkin**-compounds. (iii) **bạkī dạ hancị.** (iv) **bạkī ƙanạŋ ƙafạ.** (v) **bạkin dūnịyạ.** (vi) **bakạ.** (*b*) mouth, opening, entrance *x* (i) **bạkiŋ ƙwaryā** mouth of calabash (*cf.* **wuyạ). tukunyā tanạ dạ fādim** ~ the pot is wide-mouthed. (ii) **tsạya dagạ** ~ stand near the entrance ! (iii) **bạkiŋ ạlkalạmī** *Vd.* **ạlkalạmī.** (iv) **yā riƙẹ** ~ he showed surprise (*cf.* 2*b below*). (v) **munạ naŋ** ~ **sạke**

we stood open-mouthed in wonder. (vi) **ạbin sạ̄wā ạ bạkinsụ** their food (*Vd.* **bakạ** 1). (vii) **mum bubbugē musụ** ~ we gave them a bad time. (viii) **yā tāsam musụ** ~ **būɗe** he attacked them full-tilt (*cf.* **būɗẹ** 1*a.*i). (ix) ~ **yạ bōkā sǎi sukạ zō** then they suddenly appeared. (x) **sum bar mụ** ~ **wōfī** they left us hungry. (xi) **bạkinsạ zại yi wārī** *Vd.* **ạlbasạ** 2*b.* (xii) **aram** ~ *Vd.* **ạlbasạ** 2*c.* (xiii) **sǎi** ~ **yā cī, idọ kẹ̄ kunyạ** P. who has accepted a bribe reveals the fact by the shifts he is driven to adopt. (xiv) **kōwā ya ɗēbō dạ zāfī, bạkinsạ** as you sow, so shall you reap. (xv) **bạkin dạ Allạ̄ ya tsāgạ, bā yạ̄ hanạ shi ạbincī** God provides for all his creatures. (xvi) **ạbin dạ** ~ **ya ɗaurạ, hannū bā yạ̄ kwancēwā** a promise is not a knot to be untied by the hands (*cf.* **ɗaurịm** ~). (xvii) **bạkin dạ ya cī, yạ gōdẹ** ! **bạkin dạ ya cī, bại gōdẹ ba, bạkiŋ wutā yā fi shị** nothing is so despicable as ingratitude (*Vd.* **bạkiŋ wutā**). (*c*) *Kt.* 'yar ~ *f.* = **bakạ** 6*a.* (*d*) *Vd.* **bakạ.** (*e*) *Vd.* **mạ̄rạ bạkiŋkạ** *Vd.* **yạ̄fạcē.** (*f*) **yi kirạ dạ bạkiŋkạ** *Vd.* **yạ̄fạcē.** (*g*) **zāƙim bạkī** *Vd.* **zāƙī** 2. (*h*) **bạ bạkī** *Vd.* **mutūwạ** 1*a.*iv. (*j*) **tsōmạ bạkī** *Vd.* **tsōmạ.** (*k*) **kadạ kạ ạri bạkīna** *Vd.* **ạrā** 3. (*l*) **barịm bạkī** *Vd.* **yuŋwạ** 1*f.* (*m*) **dūbam bạkiŋ gạ̄tarī** *Vd.* **sārā** 5. (*n*) **bạkiŋkạ dạ kuɗī** *Vd.* **ạlkalạmī** 1*a.* (*o*) **bạkim mijịntạ** *Vd.* **Allạ̄** 7*f.* (*p*) **bạkin jạkā** = **bạkim burgāmị** *Vd.* **burgāmị** 2. (*q*) **sạ̄ bạkī maiƙọ** *Vd.* **farī** 2*d.*

(2) (*in the following expressions*) speaking, speech *x* (*a*) **bạn yi** ~ **dạ kōwā ba** = **bạkīna dǎi, bạn yi dạ kōwā ba** I did not address a word to a soul. (*b*) **yā kāmạ** ~ he kept silence (*cf.* 1*b.*iv *above*). (*c*) **sum fi kōwā** ~ they are the most vocal of people. (*d*) **yā fitō** ~ **dạ haƙọ̄rā, ya cẹ** . . . he then openly said . . . (*e*) **dādim** ~ **gạrēshị** (i) he's all things to all men. (ii) he eggs on people to quarrel. (iii) *Vd.* **ban maganạ** 4. (*f*) ~ **bīyū gạrēshị** he's two-faced. (*g*) **bạkinsụ dạban-dạban** their versions do not tally. (*h*) (i) **ạbạibam** ~ *Vd.* **ạbụ** 12. (ii) **cīwạm** ~

offensive words. (j) ~ **ạlēkuŋ** Vd.
ạlēkuŋ 3. (k) **yā cikạ** ~ he blustered.
(l) **ƙāƙạ har yakẹ dạ bākim musu dạ
sụ** how can he possibly stand out
against them? (m) Vd. **jịm bāƙī.**
(n) ~ **yā īyạ ɗaurẹ ƙafạ, yạ yaŋkạ
wuyạ** guard your tongue, it can lay
you low! (o) **yạnzu** ~ **yā mutụ** words
fail. (p) **yā yi mūgụm** ~ he spoke
indecently, abusively (= **ạlfāshā**), cf.
bātsā. (q) Vd. **gamạ** 1c. (r) **yā bā dạ** ~
he gave his consent (cf. **4**d below).
(s) **dạ kạ ci ạbim maị** ~, **gāra kạ ci
na ƙazāmī** if you give charity, don't
pretend you gave more than was the
case! (t) x **bạ zā sụ shiryạ ba sǎi kā
sā̀** ~ they will not make up their
quarrel till you intervene. **kadạ kạ
sā̀** ~ (i) don't interfere! (ii) don't
speak! **mẹ ya sā̀ bākiŋkạ cikī** what
business is it of yours! (cf. **sā̀** B.7).
(u) **ụbansạ yā yi masạ** ~ he doesn't
prosper as his father, etc., cursed him
by saying "**Allạ̄ yạ tsīnẹ makạ ạlbarkạ**"
(similarly, **an yi masạ** ~ he's been
warned that if he doesn't mend his
ways, he'll come to a bad end). (v)
bākiŋkạ yā kāmạ ni = **bākin dūnīyạ
yā kāmạ ni** = **bākin mutā̀nẹ yā kāmạ
ni** Vd. **bākin dūnīyạ.** (w) **jā** ~ shut
up! (cf. x). (x) **nēmam** ~ = **jịm** ~
= **jạm** ~ (cf. w) = **kālam** ~ m.
quarrelsomeness. (y) **sạyam** ~ custom
whereby bride remains silent till she
is paid the price of speech by her
husband or his best man (cf. **furā** 5).
(z) Vd. **ɗaurịm** ~ (cf. **1**b.xvi above).
(z) (i) ~ **dạ tsawō na maị musụ nē**
rather than reply angrily and bring
trouble on yourself, keep silent!
(z) (ii) **ạbim fạɗā na maị** ~ **nẹ, bēbē
sǎi yạ dạnganạ** what cannot be cured
must be endured. (z) (iii) **kashẹ** ~
Vd. **kashẹ** 5. (z) (iv) **sāmụm** ~ Vd.
sāmụ 2b. (z) (v) Vd. **sāram** ~. (z) (vi)
Vd. **yaŋkạ** 1a.ii. (z) (vii) Vd. **bakạ.**

(3) edge x (a) **yanā̀ bākiŋ ƙōfạ** he's
near the doorway. **yanā̀ bākiŋ wannạŋ
dāgā** he's on this war-front. **bākiŋ
kạsūwā** on the edge of the market, near
the market (cf. **gēfẹ, gaŋgā**). (b) **kạ sōmạ
dạgạ bākin naŋ** begin from here! (c) **zā̀**

ni **bākin jējị** I'm going to the bush
to relieve myself. (d) **bākin jirgī**
railway station. (e) **tā gamạ bākin
zanẹ** she cut an old cloth and joined it
in the middle for further use (cf.
gamạ 1c). (f) **turmin naŋ yā yi
bākin cikī** this roll of cloth is joined
in the middle, not made in one piece
(= **yaŋkā** 1d.i). (g) **yanā̀ bākiŋ gwạfī**
Vd. **gwạfī.** (h) **bākin zạrē** (i) the
beginning of a reel of thread. (ii) x in
**yā sạyi littāfịŋ don yạ sā̀mi bākin
zạrē dạgạ cikī, tọ̄ ạlbarkạ** if he buys
the book in order to find there a
solution to the problem, then he won't
succeed in finding it. (j) **bākiŋ kọ̄gī** Vd.
kọ̄gī 2. (k) **bākin rā̀fī** Vd. **kọ̄gī** 2.
(l) cf. **bākin 4.**

(4) conclusion, limit x (a) Vd. **kashẹ**
5. (b) **mạganạ tā̀ yi** ~ **yạu** the matter
will be settled to-day. (c) **kụrkunū
yā yi** ~ the guineaworm has extruded.
(d) **nū̀na mini bākiŋ indạ zan yi** show
me the extent of what I'm to do!
bākiŋ īkọna kẹ̄ naŋ that is the limit
of my authority! (e) **yā bā dạ** ~, **yā
cẹ̄ iŋ an sallạmā kwabọ ukụ, yạ sạyā** he
limited his buying-price to threepence
(cf. **2**r above). (f) cf. **bākin** 1, 4.

(5) (a) ~ **ɗayā** simultaneously. (b) x
sụ yi ta yịn yāƙin naŋ har yạ ƙārẹ ~
ɗayā let them proceed with that war
till it is completely finished!

(6) (a) **ɗam** ~ m. small amount of
thread wound on spindle and ready
for transfer to larger spindle (= **mazarī**
1b). (b) large grains of gunpowder
substituted for cap in dane-guns.
(c) good perfume on cork of bottle to
trick scent-customer.

baƙi A. (bā̀ƙī) Vd. **bā̀ƙō.**

B. 1 (baƙī) m. (f. baƙā) pl. **baƙāƙē**
adj. (1) (a) black, very dark blue, very
dark green. (b) **Baƙī, tạkarkạrim
Fir'aunạ** epithet of railway-train. (c) **maị
baƙar fātạ** Vd. **fātạ** 1a. (d) ~ **kirin**
Vd. **kirin, sidiƙ, sil, sit, suɓul.** (e) **kōwā
ya ga birị, dạ baƙiŋ hannunsạ ya gan
shi** everyone is as God made him, good
or bad. (f) **cikim baƙar tukunyā
a kạm fitar dạ farin tūwō** don't despise
a thing because of its lack of beauty!

Allā yā sā baƙar tukunyā tā fitar manạ dạ farin tūwō God changed our bad luck to good luck. (g) baƙiŋ ƙarfẹ Vd. ƙarfẹ. (h) (i) sum bincịkē shi baƙinsạ dạ farinsạ they investigated it fully. (ii) Vd. farī 2f, g. (iii) iŋ kā ga farī, kā ga baƙī Vd. birgimā 4. (j) baƙim bạntē Vd. tsịrārạ 1b. (k) baƙim 6ērā Vd. 6ērā 3. (l) baƙat tāsạ Vd. fādụ̄wā 3b. (m) im ～ zā kạ yi Vd. fafat. (2) baƙin dāji dense bush (cf. duhūwạ, duhụ). (3) unpleasant x (a) baƙin shēgẹ a rogue. (b) Kt. baƙin rạ̈i evil character. (c) yā yi minị ～ it was unpleasant to me. (d) baƙin lạ̄bāri bad news (cf. farī 2c.iii). (e) baƙiŋ kīshị bitter jealousy. gạ̈dajjīyar ƙịyayyạ irim baƙar kụ̄wā hereditary hatred of the bitterest kind. baƙạ̈ƙyam maƙịyaŋkụ your bitter enemies. (f) (i) baƙar magạnạ angry words. yā yi minị baƙar magạnạ he spoke angrily to me. (ii) Vd. farī 2f. (g) baƙar zūcịyā (= baƙar ạnīyạ) gạrēshị he's bad tempered. (h) baƙar gạskīyā an unpalatable truth. (j) munā cikim baƙar wụyā we're in terrible trouble. (k) baƙin jinī Vd. jinī 4. (l) Baƙī na Sarkī, dạgạ cị, săi tụ̄6ā epithet of dagacị q.v. (m) baƙar hājạ unsaleable goods. (n) baƙiŋ harshẹ gạrēshị = yanā dạ baƙiŋ harshẹ kạmar na tuŋkīyā he casts the evil eye. (o) baƙar inūwạ, gwamma rānā dạ kē better an honest stranger than a false friend. (4) mại baƙiŋ kạ̈i m.,f. ignorant P. (cf. fariŋ kạ̈i). (5) ɗam ～ m. (a) white-billed weaverbird (Textor albirostris). (b) black bush-robin (Cercotrichas podobe). (c) type of snake. (d) ɗam ～ m. (f. 'yar baƙā) (i) P. of very dark colour. (ii) evil P. (6) baƙin rūwā (a) clear water, drinking-water (= B2, section 5 below). (b) madūbī mại baƙin rūwā clear mirror. (c) being of a dark shade x yā fī sụ baƙin rūwā it is of a darker shade than they are. (d) Vd. azụmī 2. (7) Vd. baƙī-compounds, baƙin-compounds, baƙi-baƙi, bạ̈ƙƙai, bunū, būnū, tsụmmā 3, bạntē.

B. 2 (baƙī) noun m. (pl. baƙạ̈ƙē = babbaƙū) (1) (a) blackness. (b) the

black part of T. (2) any speech-sound. (3) (a) any letter of the Latin alphabet. (b) any consonant of the Arabic alphabet (cf. farfarū, karyạ 2, karyẹ 4). (c) yārọ yanā babbaƙū the boy has reached the stage of writing the alphabet (cf. hạjjạtū). (d) yā ɗaurạ baƙī he formed a letter. (e) (i) yā jā ～ he read out passage of text for another to interpret or comment on. (ii) Vd. fasạ 1n. (f) kalmạ tā fārạ dạ bạbbam baƙī the word begins with a capital letter. (4) maƙẹ̄rim babbaƙū smith making farm-tools (cf. maƙẹ̄rī 1b). (5) Kt. babbaƙun rūwā = B.1 6a. (6) the cloth farī 1e q.v. dyed indigo.
6aƙī Vd. 6atạn.

bāƙī ạlēkụŋ Vd. ạlēkụŋ.

baƙi-baƙi (1) adj. m. (f. baƙa-baƙa) (a) blackish, dark blueish, dark greenish (Vd. baƙī). (b) shẹ̄karạ gụdā munā tāre dạ shī, baŋ ga ～ tāre dạ shī ba after a year's acquaintance, I've never fallen out with him. (2) m. blackish, etc., thing x yā ga～he saw a blackish T.

bāƙī dạ hancị x tsạkāniŋ Kanọ dạ Cālāwā ～ nē it is a mere stone's throw from Kano to Challawa. gā su ～ kạmar yādị 400 they were quite near at hand, some 400 yards away from each other only (cf. bakạ 2).

baƙịdāhụmī = ƙịdāhụmī.
baƙī ɗan danyā m. = akụshī.
bā ki gạskīyā Vd. alakwạyī 2.
bāƙī ƙanạŋ ƙafạ adv. in silence.
bā ki ƙayạ Vd. cēdīyā.
bāƙim Vd. bāƙin.
bā ki magạnạ = bā ki mutuncị Vd. alakwạyī 2.

bāƙin (genitive of bāƙī) (1) all of (cf. bāƙī 4) x an tārạ bāƙiŋ kārụ̄wạd dạ takẹ cikiŋ Ikkō all the prostitutes in Lagos have been collected. (2) prep. in exchange for x (a) nā bā dạ zanẹ ạ ～ gōrọ I exchanged my cloth for kolanuts. (b) (bāƙin is sometimes omitted) x yā sạyi dōkịm bāwạ 12 he bought a horse in exchange for 12 slaves. (3) prep. as the equivalent of x (a) bā ạ̈ kạr6aŋ kudī ～ zạkkā money is not receivable as the equivalent of the tithe on livestock. yā bā nị rị̃gā kạrɓā ạ ~ sulę bịyar he gave me a gown as the equivalent of the five shillings owed me. (b) yā mai dạ shī bạ̃ ạ ~ kōmē ba he considered it trivial. bạ sụ ɗaụki rạm muṭụm ạ ~ kōmē ba they set no store on human life. (4) prep. on the verge of x yanạ̃ ~ nụnā it's almost ripe. yanạ̃ ~ zūwạ he's just about to arrive (Vd. bạ̃kī 4). (5) conj. when x bạ̃kịn dạ mukạ gan sụ, mukạ kirā sụ when we saw them, we called them. (6) Vd. bạ̃kin-compounds.

bakin Bakaba (bạ̃kim Bạkabạ) m. (1) smearing lips with indigo after rubbing with tobacco-flowers (= bạ̃kim burtū 1). (2) black mark at junctions of segments of kolas when split. (3) stain on neck of gown from wearing black turban.

bakin bango (bạ̃kim bạŋgō) Vd. wạndō.

bakim bạntē Vd. tsịrārạ 1b.

bakim ɓērā Vd. ɓērā 3.

bakin biri (bakim birị) m. (1) Vd. bụnū. (2) Sk. dark camel. (3) Kt. a charm used by professional thief to enable him to vanish.

bakin bunu (bakim būnū) Vd. būnū 2.

bakin burtu (bạ̃kim burtū) m. (1) = bạ̃kim bạkabạ 1. (2) Sk. type of dōkạ.

bakin buta (bạ̃kim būtạ) m. stem of gourd.

bạ̃kin cạrkī (1) red-petalled tobacco-flowers (fụrē). (2) staining the teeth except near gums (= sāraŋ kọ̃fatọ 2), cf. shiŋkāfā 2. (3) metal leather-patterner.

ɓakịncē Vb. 3A = ɓakintạ.

bakin cikị m. sadness x yā sạ̃mi ~ = yā yi ~ he's sad. munạ̃ bakin cikị kaŋ wannạŋ we're sad about that. Vd. rụmbū 4. yawạm bạkkan cikị gạrēshị he's oppressed with sorrow (Vd. bakạntā).

bạ̃kin cikī Vd. bạ̃kī 3f.

bạ̃kin darạ m. an opening move in the game darạ.

bạ̃kin dūnīyạ m. (1) ~ (= bạkim mutạ̃nē) yā kāmạ ni people's prediction of my misfortune has thereby resulted in my misfortune (= hau). bạ̃kiŋkạ yā kāmạ ni your ill-wishes about me have thereby resulted in my misfortune, etc. ; your praising me has thereby offended God and led to my misfortune (so it is said bạ̃kim mutạ̃nē bā shi dạ kyaụ it's

dangerous to be too much praised !). (2) running of line of sparks or fire over sooty outside of vessel, this being eaten with tūwō to ward off effects of 1 above. (3) white marks on the nails.

bakin fara (bạ̃kim fạ̃rā) m. (1) turban with red edge. (2) type of edge-finish of caps mạrạ̃fīyạ and tạ̃gīyạ.

bạ̃kiŋ gadō m. (1) front of bed. (2) Vd. kuryạ 1b, 2.

bạ̃kiŋ gạŋgā x ~ gạrēshị he's two-faced.

bạ̃kiŋ gātarī Vd. sārā 5.

bạ̃kiŋ gwạfī Vd. gwạfī.

bạ̃kin jāɓā x ~ gạrēshị he is uncircumcised.

bạ̃kin jạ̃kī m. (1) white border of the gwandā cloth. (2) = alạwusaị.

bakiŋ jinī Vd. jinī 4.

bạ̃kiŋ jirgī Vd. bạ̃kī 3d.

bạ̃kiŋ kaɓau = bạ̃kiŋ kadạ.

bạ̃kiŋ kadạ m. (1) x an jēfạ minị kāyā ạ ~ = an jēfạ minị kāyā ạ bạ̃kiŋ kaɓau my property has been commandeered for a Chief. (2) type of long guineacorn.

bakiŋ kạ̈i Vd. bakī 4.

bakiŋ kạrē x kā shạ̃fi ~ ạ rị̃garkạ you've dirtied your gown on a cooking-pot.

bakiŋ kạrfẹ Vd. kạrfẹ.

bakiŋ kārụ̃wạ m. thief.

bạ̃kiŋkạ yā jā ma Kt. m. tree whose top only is dead.

bạ̃kiŋ kạ̈zā m. (1) ~ nẹ̃ he's an ingrate ; he's unreliable (for fowl eats, rubs mouth, and forgets). (2) ~ gạrēshị he's a breaker of promises. (3) Vd. linzāmị 1a.ii.

bakiŋ kụmallō Vd. kụmallō 4.

bạ̃kiŋ kwaryā Vd. kwaryā

bakin maciji (bạ̃kim macị̃jī) m. = hakōrim macị̃jī 1.

bakin mai (bakim mạ̈i = mạ̈i bakī) m. (1) type of groundnut-oil (= mạn rụ̃rūwạ q.v. under mạŋ gyạɗā 2). (2) oil for sump or gearbox of cars.

bakin maiki (bạ̃kim maikị) Kt. m. type of broad arrow.

bakin marạɗi (bạ̃kim marạɗī) Vd. marạɗī.

bakin musu (bạ̃kim musụ) Vd. musụ 2c.

bakin mutane (bạ̃kim mutạ̃nē) = bạ̃kin dūnīyạ.

bakin mutum (bā̀kim mútùm) (1) *m.* stone
used for necklaces, it being white round
the rim of the perforations. (2) *Vd.*
bā̀kin dūnîyā̀.

bā̀kin rā̀ƙumī *m.* (1) head of bulrush-
millet which has become split. (2) ∼
gàrēshì he's harelipped. (3) shī ∼ nḕ,
yanā̀ dà kàmar fâdûwā he's pleasant-
spoken but stingy (= lēɓḕ 2). (4) type
of guinea-corn.

bā̀kin rùmbū *Vd.* damì 2.

baƙin rūwā *Vd.* baƙī 6.

bā̀kin shīƙā̀ *m.* poor grains, perquisite of
winnower (= gàban 12), *cf.* zubò 2,
bā̀kiŋ wuƙā̀.

bā̀kin sūdā *m.* the herb *Polycarpaea
corymbosa.*

baƙintā̀ *Vb.* 3B (1) made a mistake.
(2) became flummoxed.

baƙintad dà *Vb.* 4B flummoxed P.

bā̀kin tēkì *Vd.* tēkì 3.

bā̀kin tsūdū *m.* small spindle of thread.

bā̀kin tùmbī *m.* fee given skinner of an
animal.

bā̀kin turmī shā̀ kwàrannīyā *epithet of*
quarrelsome P.

bā̀kiŋ wuƙā̀ *m.* broken cornheads, perquisite of cutter (*cf.* bā̀kin shīƙā̀,
zubò 2).

bā̀kiŋ wutā *m.* (1) (*a*) (i) firebrand (*i.e.
torch of* sīyāyè) = *Kt.* mūshē. (ii)
kōwànę bā̀kiŋ wutā dà nāsà hayāƙī
everyone has his niche in the world. (*b*)
shī ∼ nḕ he's a " firebrand ".
(2) *Vd.* bā̀kī 1*b*.xvii. macḕ 2.

bā̀kin zàrē *Vd.* bā̀kī 3*h*.

bākīrḕ grass-roof of cornbin (rùfēwā,
rùmbū) : (bākīrḕ = bōtò 2*a* = rùmbū
1*f* = *Kt.* bisà 2*d* = *Sk.* majicī), *cf.*
kùtuɓì 2.

bākìtā̀ *Vb.* 3A = bākàtā̀.

ɓakītà *Vb.* 3B *Kt.* = ɓakintà.

ɓakkā *Sk. Vb.* 1C gave to (= bā̀ dà)

baƙƙai *Vd.* baƙin cikì.

bakkàlḕ *m.* ossification of pedal-bones or
of lateral cartilages of horse's foot.

ɓakkàtā̀ *Sk. f.* bargain.

ɓakkò *m.* baobob (= kūkà).

bakkunà *Vd.* bàkā.

baƙo A. (bā̀ƙō) *m.* (*f.* bā̀ƙwā) *pl.* bā̀ƙī
(1) guest *x* (*a*) nā̀ yi ∼ I have a guest
(*cf.* bāƙuncì 1*b*). (*b*) bā ā̀ gayà wà kàrē

gidam bā̀ƙī = bìkī 1*g.* idònà yā̀ yi ∼ dirt,
etc., has got into my eye (*hence, epithet of*
eye *is* Idò, bā kā̀ sàm ∼ = Idò, kā
ƙi jinim ∼ Eye, how you hate a guest !
*N.B.—These epithets are also applied
to* inhospitable P.). (*d*) kàrambā̀nim
∼ yà cūdi mā̀tar mā̀sū gidā what
impertinence ! (*e*) *Vd.* gayà 5. (*f*)
bā̀ƙwan tīlàs *Vd.* ƙardā. (*g*) mīyā̀gum
bā̀ƙī *Vd.* ̣barḕkatà. (*h*) bàbbam ∼
Vd. jàbgarò. (*j*) kaŋwar bā̀ƙī *Vd.*
kaŋwā 1*b.* (2) (*a*) stranger. (*b*) ∼
rūwaŋ gùjè nḕ a stranger soon passes
on. (*c*) ∼ rābā̀ nḕ, ɗaŋ gàrī kabà
a stranger is a mere bird of passage.
(*d*) ìdam bà kà ga ∼ ba, bà kā̀ yi masà
màrhabā ba don't meet trouble half-
way ! (*e*) nauyī bā̀ƙwam mài dōkì
shī yà cī, dōkìnsà yà cī this is beyond
one ! (*f*) ∼ màkāfò nḕ, kō yanā̀
dà idò a talented novice is still a
novice (*Vd.* dìndimī 2). (*g*) ∼ nā̀ dà
idò, bà na ganiŋ gàrī ba a novice is
far from being expert (*Vd.* ganiŋ
gàrī). (*h*) ɓàd dà ∼ *Vd.* turbà. (*j*)
bā̀ƙwam mīkì *Vd.* mīkì 1*a.*ii. (*k*) *Vd.*
asàlā. (3) strange *x* àbin naŋ ∼ nḕ
this is unusual. (4) *Vd.* bā̀ƙon daurō.
B. (Bā̀ƙo) (1) man's name (*Vd.*
Dārārī ; Bā̀ƙwandi; karò 6). (2) dà
∼ dà Tùkurà duk Umbutāwā nḕ it's
six of one and half a dozen of the
other.

baƙò-bakō *Kt. m. used in* yā yi minì ∼
rumfar ganyē he deceived me.

ɓakò-ɓàkò *m.* tukunyā tā yi ∼ pot is all
cracked.

baƙon dauro (bā̀ƙwan daurō) *m.* measles.

Baƙōnḕ *m.* (*f.* Baƙōnīyā̀) *pl.* Kōnāwā
aborigine of Zaria (*Vd.* Kōnà 2).

baƙòsanī *m.* (1) yawā̀m ∼ gàrēshì he's
bad-tempered. (2) Gubrī shā̀ ∼ *epithet of
any* Galādīmà.

Bākudā̀i = Bākudàyī *name for slave (lit.*
you've no power to work evil to me,
only God can do so).

bā̀ kūkaŋ hàntsī *m.* = ìnjihàu.

bàkūkīyā *f.* type of hoe.

bākunà *Vd.* bā̀kī.

bakunāshę *Kt. m.* = kudī.

bā̀ƙuncē *Vd.* bā̀ƙuntà.

baƙunci A. (bā̀ƙuncì) *m.* (1) (*a*) being guest,

stranger, unusual (*Vd.* bặƙŏ). (*b*) nä yi masạ ~ I was his guest (= bặƙuntạ), *cf.* bặƙŏ 1*a*. (2) ịnä ~ are you feeling more at home now ? (*reply* dạ gŏdẹ Allặ = da sauƙĩ).

B. (bặƙụnci) *Vd.* bặƙuntạ.

bakunkuna *Vd.* bặƙĩ, bạƙä.

baƙunta A. (bặƙuntạ) *Vb.* 2 (*p.o.* bặƙụncē, *n.o.* bặƙụnci) was guest of *x* nä bặƙụncē shị kwänä gŏmạ I was his guest for 10 days (= bäƙunci 1*b*). mum bäƙuntŏ kạ we've come to stay with you.

B. (bặƙụntä) *f.* = bäƙunci.

C. (bäƙụntä) *Vb.* 1C (*with dative*) behaved unusually towards P. *x* yặ ~ minị hälị he showed me a new aspect of his character.

bäƙuntad dạ *Vb.* 4B (1) am ~ shĩ dạgạ gạrinsụ (*a*) he has been exiled. (*b*) he's been transferred to place where he is a stranger. (2) mạganạn nạṇ tä ~ nĩ this word's new to me. (3) *Vd.* bäƙuntar.

bặƙuntakạ *f.* = bäƙunci.

bäƙuntar *x* mạganạn nạṇ tä ~ this word sounds unfamiliar (= bäƙuntad dạ 2).

bakurɗẹ *m.* black and blue cloth joined to säƙị cloth.

bạkurmẹ *m.* (*pl.* ƙụrmặwä) servant of Saṇ kurmị.

bäkụrü *m.* = ặbäkụrü.

ɓäkutü (1) *m.* neckless gourd-bottle. (2) *m., f.* big-buttocked (*used as name for boy or girl*).

ɓặƙüwạ *f.* a light-coloured earth for glazing pottery.

bặƙwä *Vd.* bặƙŏ.

bakwại *f.* (1) seven. (2) week. (3) *Vd.* Hausä ; banzä. (4) ɗam ~ *m.* (*f.* 'yar ~) = bạkwạinĩ. (5) na ~ *m.* (*f.* ta ~) *pl.* na ~ *adj.* (*a*) seventh. (*b*) kŏmē ya sặmi shặmüwä, watạm bakwại nē ya jäwŏ matạ whatever has happened to him is through unfamiliar milieu. (*c*) (i) watạm bakwại maƙärar ränĩ ; im bäbụ dặmunä (= im bặ rüwä), dạ ạlặmuntạ patience is always rewarded. (ii) *Vd.* shặmüwä 4. (6) *Vd.* bana 2*c*.

bạkwạinĩ = *Kt.* bạkwạimĩ *m., f.* child born after 7 months.

bạkwalä *f.* high round cap.

bạkwạlĩ *m.* (1) dewlap(s) (= lēɓẹ 4*b*). *(2) Adam's apple.

bäƙwanci *m.* = bäƙunci.

bạƙwan dạurŏ *Vd.* bặƙon dạurŏ.

Bặƙwandi = Bặƙwando name for man called Bặƙo.

ɓakwänē *Vd.* ɓaunä.

bạkwanĩkẹ *m.* (*f.* bạkwanĩkĩyä) *pl.* kwanĩkäwä (1) joker. (2) untrustworthy P.

Bạkwạntagŏrẹ *m.* (*f.* Bạkwạntagŏrĩyä) *pl.* Kwantagŏräwä P. of Kontagora (Kwạntạgŏrä).

ɓakwatŏ *m.* vagina (= farjị).

Bạkwäyạmĩ = Bạkwäyạmē *m.* (*pl.* Kwäyamäwä) member of the small-statured Katagum Barebari Clan so named.

bạkyä *Sk. x* yanặ tsạye ~ he's standing motionless.

ɓakyạlallē = ɓakyạltaccē.

ɓakyạlcē *Vb.* 3A (1) was (is) slacker, lounger. (2) yä ~ ƙạmar mạṇ wurị ạ tandü he roved idly.

ɓakyạltaccē *m.* (*f.* ɓakyạltaccĩyä) *pl.* ɓakyạltạttü idler, lounger.

ɓakyalụ (1) *m.* being an idler. (2) *m., f.* idler (*epithet is* mạṇ wurị ạ tandü).

bal A. (bal) (1) = ạlkarfạ 1, 2. (2) nä fạdä, ka cẹ ~ you contradicted me.

B. (bạl) *x* wutä tä yi ~ fire burned up : rạunĩ yä yi ~ wound is inflamed.

ɓal *indicates* suddenness *x* munặ wucẹwä, säi mukạ ji ~ ya harbē mụ we were passing when suddenly we felt a sting.

bala A. (bälä) *Kt. f.* disturbance of surface of water by a fish.

B. (Bạlä) name for boy born on a Wednesday (*cf.* Bạlärabẹ ; lặrặbä).

bala-bala *f. x* mun yi ~ we roasted unshelled groundnuts under burning grass.

balaga A. (bạlagạ) *Ar. Vb.* 3B (1) reached puberty (*cf.* mafarkĩ 2). (2) bä ki ạlhakim ~ säi yä yi ƙyüyar bặƙĩ *epithet of* nympho-maniac (*cf.* tạbarmä 4). (3) *Vd.* täshịm ~.

B. (bạlägạ) *Ar. f.* being possessed of lively intelligence.

balạgandē = balạgandä *Sk. m.* kabạ dyed greenish for making straw-hat (mạlạfä), mat (fặifặi), etc.

balạgandi *Sk. m.* tüwŏ made from adüwạ (*cf.* barbaɗēɗẹ).

bạlägirŏ (1) = bạlägurŏ. (2) = rạṇgazạ.

bạlạgĩ tsindir = bạlạgĩ tsiṇgir *m., f.* precocious child.

balāgurō m. (1) going for a walk (= yāwǫ). (2) any journey of about a year. (3) cf. balāgirō.

balāhirā x tsǫkāninsu da gāɓā ⌢ there's undying enmity between them (Vd. lāhira).

balā'i Ar. m. calamity.

ɓalak A. (ɓalak) x ɓā ⌢, ɓā zaɓak it's a useless thing (= sīdīdī).
    B. (ɓalak-ɓalak) adv. yanā ɓararrakǫ ⌢ = yanā zaɓaɓɓakǫ ⌢ it's boiling with a sizzling sound (cf. ɓal-ɓal).

ɓalākuce Vb. 3A = ɓakyǫlce.

balallakǫ m. = balōkōkǫ.

balam-balam. (1) wuʂā tā yi kaifī ⌢ the knife is very sharp. (2) mai bākī ⌢ m., f. eloquent P.

balama A. (balamā) f. = falamā.
    B. (balamā) Vd. balamī.

ɓalamɓantanī. (1) m. man roving idly. (2) ɓalamɓantanā f. (a) woman roving idly. (b) idle roving.

bā lam, bā tsam useless thing (= sīdīdī).

balambō m. name of a food (= farsa) (Vd. bagāyī).

balamī m. (f. balamā) pl. balamai type of large-eared sheep usually hornless.

ɓalangandi m. (1) idle roving. (2) witlessness. (3) what an indecent cloth she's wearing !

balangazǫ m. striving hard.

balangē Vd. shagali 2.

balangu Sk. m. type of roasted meat.

balanshi m. = balas.

balar m. any trousers with ample ankles and crutch (cf. tēki 3).

Balārabe m. (f. Balāraba = Balārabīyā) pl. Lārabāwā. (1) Arab (Vd. gandū 2f). (2) Balārabe m. (Balāraba f.) name respectively for boy, girl born Wednesday (cf. Lāraba ; Balā ; Nārai). (3) Balārabīyar shēkara year of 354 days (cf. babbāwa). (4) Balārabaŋ wata month of 29 or 30 days.

balas A. (balas) m. = balar.
    B. (balas = balashī) Eng. m. (1) unsold balance of goods. (2) striking a balance in book-keeping.

balāsā Nor. f. = balāsanā.

balāsanā f. (1) long, thin needle. (2) the fodder weed kunungurū q.v. (3) Vd. bindiga 4.

bā lāsar bākī Vd. carkwai 4.

balāsayā f. = balāsanā 2.

ɓālāshā m., f. P. often laughing.

balashī Vd. balas.

balaskīyā f. A. adulterated (x inferior fatala : coin damaged during conversion into ornament, etc.).

balau = falau.

ɓalau emphasizes gapingness of hole x (1) yā ɓarke ⌢ it is badly torn. (2) yā būɗe bākī ⌢ he opened his mouth wide.

balau-balau A. (balau-balau) = falau.
    B. (balau-balau) Zar. m. = gīlo.

ɓalaulauce Vb. 3A = ɓalaulauta Vb. 3B Zar. = ɓakyǫlce q.v.

balāwure m. = lāwur.

balāye m. (1) an extinct dance like taƙai. (2) ɗam ⌢ (f. 'yar ⌢) = bakwanīke.

balāyī Sk. m. = tōyī.

balbaɗa Kt. = barbaɗa.

bal-bal = bal.

ɓal-ɓal A. (ɓal-ɓal) (1) = ɓalak. (2) zūcīyā tasa tanā ⌢ his heart is palpitating (cf. ɓalak-ɓalak).
    B. (ɓal-ɓal) = ɓel-ɓel.
    C. (ɓal-ɓal) m. idle roving.

balbala Vb. 1C x yā balbala wutā he made bright fire.

ɓalɓalce Vb. 3A. = ɓakyǫlce.

balbalnīyā f. x wutā tanā ⌢ fire's burning brightly.

ɓalɓalnīyā f. the sound of boiling (cf. ɓalak-ɓalak).

ɓalɓalta Vb. 3B = ɓakyǫlce.

ɓalɓashī Kt. m. = ɓarɓashī.

balbatē m. = fatē-fatē.

balbēla f. (pl. balbēlū). (1) (a) buff-backed heron, i.e. cattle-egret (Bubulcus ibis). (b) epithet is ⌢ cī da mǫtsiŋ wani Cattle-egret you sponger ! (also applied to P. who is sponger). (3) yā yi ⌢ he's dressed all in white. (4) Vd. sāba 2 ; biki 1e.

balbēta f. scalpel used by tandū-makers.

ɓalce = ɓallē.

ɓale-ɓale A. (ɓalē-ɓalē) = ɓalau 1.
    B. (ɓalē-ɓalē) m. idle roving.

*balērī m. = ɗan Lērī.

ɓalērī m. (f. ɓalērīyā) Fil. very black-skinned P.

ɓalgace A. (ɓalgace) Vb. 3A is (was) chipped (= ɓāgura).

B. (ɓalgacẹ) *m.* (*sg., pl.*) a chip (= ɓagurẹ).

ɓalgata A. (ɓalgatạ). (1) *Vb.* 3B = ɓalgạcē. (2) yanā dạ ∼ it has a piece chipped out.

   B. (ɓalgạtā) *Vb.* 1C. (1) chipped a pot, etc. (2) broke a piece off kola, cassava, tooth, etc.

balgē *m.* = balạgandē.

ɓ̣alī *Vd.* jan ∼ .

*balīdancị *Ar. m.* being backward in study.

balīdị *Ar. m.* (*pl.* balị̄dai) backward in study.

bālịgī *m.* (*f.* bālịgā) *pl.* bālịgai pubert, adult.

balịƙọtō = balịƙụnjī *Sk. m.* = bạrōrọ 1.

balkạram worthless.

balkarancị *m.* worthlessness.

ɓalkẹ *Kt.* = ɓarkẹ.

balkwatōjị *Sk. m., f.* scatterbrained P.

ɓalla A. (ɓallạ) *Vb.* 1A. (1) (*a*) hooked up. (*b*) secured T. by pulling knotted end through loop *x* yā ∼ gịndī he tied hobbling-rope on horse. yā ∼ tạ̄kạlmī he pulled his sandal thong up over his heel (*cf.* ɓallẹ, ɓạllu). (2) yā ∼ yātsạ he made flipping-sound with his fingers. (3) (*with dative*) (*a*) yā ∼ minị harbị it (*hornet, etc.*) stung me ; it (*horse, etc.*) kicked me. (*b*) yā ∼ minị yātsạ he flicked his finger towards me (*e.g. to let approacher know I'm praying, etc.*).

   B. (ɓạllā) *Vb.* 2 = ɓallẹ 1.

ballạƙē. (1) *Vb.* 1C. (*a*) put T. out of alignment *x* yā ballaƙō idọ he everted his eyelid (*to frighten child*). (*b*) kā ballaƙō wụyā you're asking for the impossible. (2) *Vb.* 3A became out of alignment *x* fātạr idọ tā ballaƙō eyelid has become everted through illness.

bạllantā = bạllantạnā = bạllē.

ballạrā *Vb.* 1C = ballạƙē 1.

ballạrē *Vb.* 3A = ballạƙē 2.

bạllē. (1) (*preceding a noun or pronoun, after negative sentence*). (*a*) how much less *x* nī bạn īyạ ba ∼ kai I'm unable, so how much less are you ! bạn īyạ hawan jạ̄kī ba ∼ dōkị I can't ride a donkey, far less a horse ! (*b*) ∼

har (*followed by subjunctive*) far less that *x* bạ sụ īyạ wannạm ba, ɓallē har sụ cẹ̄ they can't do this far less can they say that . . . bạ̄ su dạ ƙarī̄ sụ tarẹ su, ɓallē har sụ ƙọrē su they are not strong enough to resist them, far less to repel them. (2) (*after affirmative sentence*) how much more kai kā īyạ ∼ nī seeing you're able, how much more am I ! (3) *Vd.* bạrē 2, rūwā C. 9*f.*

ɓalle A. (ɓallẹ). (1) *Vb.* 1A (*a*) (i) un-hooked. (ii) released knotted end of rope from loop *x* nā ∼ gịndī I undid the hobbling-rope (*cf.* ɓallạ, ɓạllu). (iii) sum ɓallẹ dōgwaŋ ƙarƙẹ they tore up the railway-line. (*b*) snapped T. across. (*c*) yā ∼ ni dạ harbi = ɓallạ 3*a*. (*d*) am ∼ ta = *am ∼ matạ ạllaŋ kạ̄fadạ she should be a virgin, but is not (= budurcị 3). (2) *Vb.* 3A (*a*) T. snapped across. (*b*) yā ∼ dạ sụrūtụ He's garrulous. (*c*) *cf.* ɓạllu.

   B. (ɓạllē) *m.* = fadẹ.

   C. (ɓallē). (1) wạ̄san ɗam ∼ = yāƙin ɗam ∼ a game of children where I aim with a big datestone (kibīyạ) at my opponent's datestones which are arranged in piles representing a chief with his zagị, Gạlạdīmạ, Cirọ̄mạ, etc. ; each pile contains superimposed date-stones. (2) ɗam ∼ (*a*) datestone (*cf.* ƙwallō). (*b*) clitoris.

ballị *m.* (1) leading a devil-may-care life. (2) = bargị 2. (3) the behaviour of drunken P. (4) disturbance of water by fish, frog (= ɓụllā 2).

ɓạl'li-ɓạllī'' *m.* ƙịrjī yanā ∼ (*a*) heart is palpitating from running. (*b*) baby's heart has severe palpitations.

ɓallīyā *f.* (1) an yi wạ lạmbū ∼ the channels of the irrigated farm have been opened to let in water (= būdị 5). (2) type of jạlālạ. (3) = ƙunshi ạ ɓarakạ.

ballo A. (ballō) *m.* = sạ̄cē 2.

   B. (ballọ). (1) *Sk. m.* torch of grass (*cf.* bạ̄kiŋ wutā). (2) *Vd.* Bello.

ballōdẹ *m.* type of wạrkī.

ballū *Zar. m.* = sạ̄cē 2.

ɓạllu *Vb.* 3B *x* yā ∼ he's got on in the world (*cf.* ɓallạ, ɓallẹ).

balmạ *f.* (1) Bilma salt. (2) balmạb

bakạ flattery, blarney (= malmal dạ bakạ).

ɓalō *Sk. m.* = ɓugạ 1*a.*

ɓaloɓalo A. (ɓalō-ɓạlō) *adj. pl.* large and round.

B. (ɓạlō-ɓalō) *m.* = ɓạlē-ɓalē.

bạlōƙōƙọ *m.* (1) roaring of camel. (2) gobbling of turkey. (3) yanạ bạlōƙōƙwạm fadạ he's raging.

balōtạ *Eng. f.* blotting-paper.

bālụ *Fil. x* ɗam ⁓ *m.* ram (= rạ̄gō).

ɓalwai = ɓakyalụ 1, 2.

bạ m *Vd.* bạ 10*a.*

bạm *m.* the sound of the slamming of a door.

ɓam *m.* sound of popping.

ɓamā (1) *f.* (*a*) vibrating-tongue of bāɗọ, sīrīƙi (*cf.* bḙ̄lī 2). (*b*) yā cikạ ⁓ he looks well-developed or prosperous. (2) *Vb.* (*only used as follows*) an tsạttsōkạnē shi, ya'⁓ after constantly being irritated, he could contain himself no longer (= ɓụga 4 = ƙārā 1*b*).

bạ mạgạ̄gī *Vd.* asharā.

Bạmāgujḙ *m.* (*f.* Bạmāgujīyā) *pl.* Māguzāwā (*Ar.* fireworshipper). (1) member of the pagan Maguzawa tribe of Kano and Katsina. (2) (*a*) Allạ yā yi Allạn nāsạ, wai ⁓ yā iskḙ biri yā mutụ ạ gōnā tasạ what unexpected good luck! (*cf.* Allạ 7*n*). (*b*) *Vd.* biri 1*b.* (3) *Vd.* kạ̄yō, daudạ 3*b*, gaidā.

bamai *Sk. m.* (1) = bammōmī. (2) im bạ ka dạ makạdī, yi ⁓ if one has no powerful friends, one must stand up for oneself.

Bạmāḷiḳi *m.* (*pl.* Mālikāwā) follower of the Maliki sect.

bạmạllā *f.* type of guinea-corn.

bāmancī *m.* being a novice (bāmī).

Bạmangḙ *m.* (*f.* Bạmangīyā) *pl.* Mangāwā member of this despised Barebari Clan.

Bạmarādḙ *m.* (*f.* Bạmarādīyā) *pl.* Marādāwā P. of Marādī.

Bạmasạrī *m.* (*f.* Bạmasạrā) *pl.* Masarāwā. (1) an Egyptian (*cf.* Masạr). (2) *adj.* of good quality. (3) ḳiḷī ⁓ cream-coloured horse (= ḳiḷī 3).

bạ mạtāka *Vd.* baunī.

bạ mayạ̄ƙā *m.* = tuburā 1.

bāmạyē *Vd.* bāmī.

bạ mạyē *Vd.* dạgarạ.

bambaɗancī *m.* (1) cadging done·by a Bạbambaɗḙ. (2) an yi masạ ⁓ he has been praised.

bambaɗāwā *Vd.* bạbambaɗḙ.

Bambāɗọ *m.* = Bạbambaɗḙ 1, 2.

bambakwạlī *m.* = bakwạlī.

ɓambạlạn *x* yā zō ɓamɓạlạn dạ bakạ he came staring like a gaby.

bambam = bamban.

ɓam-ɓam. (1) yā cịka ⁓ it's full to the brim. (2) = gam-gam.

bambami A. (bambamī) *m.* (1) the climbing plant *Alchornea cordata.* (2) the Sunbird (*Hedydipna platura*); *it lines nest with cotton, hence chaffing of P. with leaky roof by saying* Kurcīyā, anạ̄ rūwā? Dove, is it raining? (*reply is :* Kai bambamī, bạri tọnam fadạ !).

B. (bạmbạmī) *m.* raising the voice in anger.

C. (bambạ̄mī) *m.* upper part of giginyạ (*this always being broader but weaker than lower part called* kwangi); *it is often used for* indararō.

bamban A. (bambaŋ). (1) *adj. m., f.* (*sg., pl.*) different *x* (*a*) mạsū kạmạnnū ⁓ those differing in appearance. (*b*) *Vd.* sāƙi 1*b* ; bạmmī 1. (2) *m.* (*a*) difference *x* sun yi ⁓ dạ jūnā they differ from each other. yā shā bambaŋ dạ shī it differs from it. (*b*) mun shā ⁓ we missed each other on the road. (3) *adv.* differently *x* mun zō ⁓ we came at different times.

B. (bạmban) (1) bạmbaŋ = ạ bạmbaŋ *m., f.* = gōyō 1. (2) *adv.* tạfi ⁓ = hau ⁓ get on my back !

bambancē *Vb.* 3A = bạmbantạ.

bambancị *m.* (1) (*a*) difference *x* yā yi ⁓ it differed. sun yi ⁓ they differ from each other. (2) bā ạ̄ nūnạ wani bambancị no discrimination is made.

bambạnkā *Vb.* 1C. (1) kept on patching (*Vd.* bạnkạ). (2) yā ⁓ mini he concealed the truth from me or about me (= bạnkạ 2).

bạmbạnƙarạ *f.* = ạlfaharī.

bambạnkīyā *Kt. f.* = bumbunƙīyā.

bambanta A. (bạmbantạ) *Vb.* 3B. (1) differed *x* sum ⁓ dạ jūnā they differ (differed) from each other. **(2)** *Vd.* **tābạ** 1*a*.

B. (bambạntā) *Vb.* 1C distinguished, differentiated.

ɓamɓar *x* am bar **shị** ⁓ he's now penniless.

ɓamɓarạ *Vb.* 2. **(1)** broke off (*maize grains, bark, plaster*). **(2)** separated T. sticking to another. **(3) dạ kyar na ɓambạrē shị** with *difficulty* I got a little from that miser.

bambạrākwaị. **(1)** *m.* abnormal state of affairs *x* (*a*) **idọna yā yi minị** ⁓ my eye seems queer. **anạ ganinsạ** ⁓ it seems unusual. (*b*) ⁓ **namijị dạ sūnā Hājạrā** what a peculiar thing ! (= *Kt.* **wạ̄baị,** *q.v.*). **(2) yā sạki dōkịnsạ** ⁓ he left his horse to roam uncared for. **yā bar gidansạ** ⁓ he left his family uncared for. **(3) = tạntạrwaị.**

bambaram A. (bambaram) *Vd.* **bambarmēmẹ.**

B. (bạmbạram) = bambạrākwaị.

ɓambạrē. **(1)** *Vb.* 1C broke off (*as in* **ɓambạrạ**) *all of.* **(2)** *Vb.* 3A T. peeled off.

bambarmēmẹ *m.* (*f.* **bambarmēmịyā**) *pl.* **bambaram-bambạrạm** of huge capacity (*room, vessel*).

bambarō *m.* **(1)** puffiness ; swelling (*of corpse, dead fish, etc.*) *x* **cikịnsạ yā yi** ⁓ his stomach became puffed up. **gạ̄rī yā yi** ⁓ flour swelled up. **(2)** the floating up and down in water of the puffy body of dead T. *x* **gāwā tanạ̄** ⁓ **ạ rūwa** (= **ɓōkọ̄kọ̄** 2). **(3)** (*or* **maị** ⁓) metal jew's harp (*cf.* **zạgạdū**). **(4)** ⁓ **maị gōnā** (*a*) *exclamation* used to warn farmer that cattle have maliciously been allowed into his farm, the delinquent's loincloth (**wạrkī**) being taken off as proof of guilt. (*b*) *x* **Audụ yā yi wạ maị gōnā bạmbarō** Audu warned the farmer *as above.*

ɓamɓarōkị *m.* **(1)** bark. **(2)** shell of (*a*) egg (= **kamɓōrī** 1*b*) or (*b*) groundnut (= **kamɓōrī** 1*a*). **(3)** scurf of scalp-disease ; scab ; bits of skin from desquamation.

ɓamɓarwạ *f.* = **durwā** 4.

ɓamɓas = ɓagas 1.

bạmbū = bạmbaŋ.

bạmburụŋ *m.*, *f.* (*sg.*, *pl.*) gluttonous (*P. or animal*) = **tārū** 3.

bạmbus = bạmbūshị *m.* (*sg.*, *pl.*) melon.

ɓamẹ. **(1)** *Vb.* 1A closed (*door ; mouth of gourd, etc., with a stopper*) *x* am ⁓ **ɓuk** its mouth has been tightly closed (*N.B.—sometimes* **ɓamẹ** *means* " opened "). **(2)** *Vb.* 3A is closed *x* **bạ̄kiŋ gọ̄rā yā** ⁓ the mouth of the gourd-bottle is (was) closed (*N.B.—sometimes* **ɓamẹ** *means* " is (was) open ").

bam farī *Vd.* **ban farī.**

bāmī *m.* (*pl.* **bāmạ̄yē**). **(1)** (*a*) novice *x* **sākạr** ⁓ weaving done by novice. (*b*) *epithet of novice is* ⁓ **sạndaŋ kanyạ.** (*c*) *Vd.* **gạ̄gạrạ** 2. **(2)** embroidered leather apron of hunters.

bam mạganạ *Vd.* **ban mạganạ.**

bạmmī *m.* **(1)** palm wine (*epithet is* ⁓ **bambaŋ dạ ganiŋ Ạnnabị** = ⁓ **haukạtạ yārọ**). **(2)** ⁓ **dạ maŋ jā, ɗan lịmaŋ dạ nā'ịbī** they're practically identical with each other.

bammōmī *m.* white metal ornaments for harness.

bāmōtạ *f.* **(1)** an insect noted for constant sleeping. **(2) yā shā ˈfurā** ⁓ he ate **ˈfurā** made of **maịwā** affected by the blight called **dandọ̄nā,** and fell into a deep sleep.

ban A. (bạn) *x* **(1) bạn ci ba** I've not eaten (*Vd.* **bạ . . . ba**). **(2) bạn sạ̄ ạ kā ba** *Vd.* **tạgīyạ** 3. **(3) bạn ci bịkī ba** *Vd.* **bịkī** 1*f*.

B. (bạn). **(1)** (Mod. Gram. 19*b*) ⁓ **ni zūwạ = ⁓ zūwạ** I'm not coming. **(2)** (Mod. Gram. 22*b*) ⁓ **dạ kudī = ⁓ ni dạ kudī** I've no money. **(3)** *Sk.* (*contraction of* **bāyan** " back of ") *x* (*a*) ⁓ **dāki = bāyaŋ gidā** (*q.v. under* **bāyạ** 2*d*), *cf.* **baŋ garkā.** (*b*) ⁓ **damō = baŋ guzạ** thing dry on surface, but wet below (*Vd.* **baŋ gyạ̄rē : baŋ gīwā**).

C. (ban) **(1)** (Mod. Gram. 87*c*) *x* **ạbin naŋ dạ** ⁓ **tsọ̄rō yakẹ** this is alarming (*Vd. alphabetically compounds of* **ban** *plus following word*). **(2)** (*contraction of* **bạ** ni) *x* **baŋ ạbīna** give me my property ! (*cf.* **bịyaŋ dạddawā**).

bana A. (bana). **(1)** *adv.* this year. **(2)** *f.* (*a*) the current year *x* **bana-banan naŋ** this very year. (*b*) year of age of cattle

x sā̰   maị ∼ bīyū = sā̰ ∼ bīyū = sā̰ ɗam ∼ bīyū ox or bull two years of age (we can also say sā̰ maị shḕkarạ bīyū ox or bull two years of age). sānīyā maị shḕkarạ bīyū cow two years of age). bijimī ∼ bīyū big bull two years old. rā̰ƙumī ∼ huɗū camel four years old (cf. ɗākị 8).   (c) ∼ bakwaị maị wụyar karọ what a tough customer! (d) ɗam ∼ maị gā̰rī fine new season's cassava. (e) ɗam ∼ m. (f. 'yar ∼) pl. 'yam ∼ = bạzāmanẹ.   (3) dāɗim ∼ Vd. tunạ 1a.ii.   (4) ∼ nā yi harāwạ Vd. bā̰ra 1d. (5) ∼ bā̰ harkạ = bana bā̰ kwabọ f. short tagūwā (= aŋgalē 2).

     B. (bāṇā̰) f. (sg., pl.) type of fish.

banancī m. (1) = zāmanancī. (2) **banancim** bana akạ yī it was done this very year.

Bạnasārẹ m. (f. **Bạnasārīyā**) pl. **Nạsārā** = **Nasārāwā** (Ar. "Nazarene").   (1) Christian (= **Kiristạ**). (2) European. (3) P. in employ of European (cf. **Nasārāwā, Nạsārā**).   (4) kā fi **Nạsārā** Vd. ƙarkē.

banatị Eng. m. (sg., pl.) bayonet. (2) **sun** lāshi banatị they swore fealty.

banāwā Vd. bạbanẹ.

banda A. (bandạ) f. drying meat or fish over a fire.

     B. (ban dạ = bạn dạ). (1) apart from x (a) ∼ shī wā̰ zaị yạrdạ apart from him who would agree! (= barẹ = bāicin 2). (b) there's no likelihood x ā̰'ā̰, Masạr, ∼ fāɗūwā there is no fear that Egypt will be captured. (2) (substitute for kadạ in imperative negative) x ∼ yawạm magana don't jaw such a lot! sun tāshi wai ∼ mụ shigō they departed saying "let us not enter!" = kadạ mụ shigō.   (3) (followed by subjunctive) it is far from being the case that x yā nūnạ manạ ∼ dāi yạ yi bāya he pretended to us that he did not intend to retreat.   (4) ∼ mụtụm Vd. shūkạ 1a.iii.

     C. (bandā) Vd. bạndar ƙasạ.

bandạ Vb. 3A used as follows yā ∼ , yā bas sụ he went on ahead of his companions. yā ∼ ūwā dūnīyạ he vanished abroad (Vd. dūnīyạ 1b.ii).

***bandạcē** Vb. 1C dried meat or fish over a fire (cf. bạndạ).

bạn dākị Vd. bạn 3.

bandal x yā cịka ∼ it is chock full.

bandạm-bandam = fụnjụm-funjum.

bạn damō Vd. bạn 3.

bạndar ƙasạ f.   (1) an yi masạ ∼ (i) he's been betrayed. (ii) he's been tricked into "giving himself away" (= mạkarƙashīyā 1).   (2) ạkwai wata ∼ wạddạ kḕ nēman hụrūwā tạ rabạ shi dạ Sạrā̰kan yāƙịnsạ there is a straw showing which way the wind of his policy blows and which is liable to separate him from his generals.

***bandata** A. (bandạtā) Vb. 1C = *bandạcē.

     *B. (bạndatạ) Vb. 3B (meat, fish) was dried over the fire.

bandīrị m. vessel beaten by Bạkādirẹ q.v. chanting Allā̰, Allā̰ !

bandō m. = tūwan rūwā.

bạn fari (bam farī) m. = cā̰sar farī.

bạngā̰ f. (pl. bạnguna) small drum kept in bag (it is tapped with the fingers, not with drumstick).

bạnga-bạngā̰ f.   (1) (a) an yi wạ Sarkī ∼ travelling chief has group of horsemen on either side (= fāifāi 3). (b) an yi wạ jirā̰gyan rūwā ∼ the ships travelled in an escorted convoy.   (2) yụŋwạ tā (cīwọ yā) yi minị ∼ hunger (illness) troubled me. (3) crowded round x shānū sun yi musụ ∼ cattle crowded round them. kurā̰mē sun yi manạ ∼ we're enclosed by ravines.

bangaje A. (baŋgajē) Vb. 1C. (1) pushed away. (2) pushed over.

     B. (bạŋgajē). (1) m. making ridges for guinea-corn, millet, beans, cotton, maịwā (it is done with gạrmā̰-hoe at beginning of rains where soil poor and no manure (tākị) available. After sowing dāwạ or gērō, 3 weeks later, fasạ hụdā (= fasạ baŋgajē), Vd. hụdā 2b) is done with fartaŋạ-hoe : 30 days later, maimai-hoeing is done, then possibly later, sassaryā or further hụdā (for ordinary hoeing, Vd. nōmā)) (baŋgajē = wọrā 2), Vd. ƙụfurtū, hụdā. (2) Vd. bạŋgazạ.

baŋgaji Vd. bạŋgazạ.

baŋ gajīyạ m. x zā̰ mu ∼ we're off to congratulate P. who's finished some tiring task such as journey, giving banquet, etc.

ɓangalē Vb. 3A. (1) x zánę yā ~ matạ her cloth flapped open. (2) cf. waŋgalē.

baŋgam = baŋɓam.

ɓangara A. (ɓaŋgarạ) = ɓāgurạ.
B. (ɓaŋgarā) = ɓāgurā.

baŋgarạ bạndau m. irrelevant talk.

ɓangarērẹ m. (f. ɓaŋgarērīyā) pl. ɓaŋgar-ɓaŋgar = ɓagāɓagā adj. consisting of huge chunks.

ɓaŋgarī m. Agalawa feasting at weddings.

ban garkā x ɗam baŋ garkā = Sk. ɗam bāyaŋ gidā = Sk. 'dam bāyaŋ garkā m. the son of a slave girl who on death of her master, marries, she previously having been freed on bearing her master a child (cf. ban 3).

baŋgārọ Fil. m., f. (sg., pl.) = mahaucī 1.

ɓangashā = ɓaŋgasā f. great bargain, e.g. nā sạmi ~.

ban gaskīyā m. (1) (a) reliability of P. x Audu ~ gạrēshị Audu is a reliable P. (b) ~ hạkīkạr aikị dogged wins ! (2) trusting in P. x nā yi masạ ~ I placed reliance in him. Audu ~ gạrēshị Audu is a trustful P.

ɓangatatā Sk. f. great bargain.

baŋgāyē Vd. baŋgō.

bangaza A. (baŋgazạ) Vb. 2 (p.o. baŋgajē, n.o. baŋgaji) pushed.
B. (baŋgazā) Vb. 1C = dumbulā 1.

baŋgazạrumī m. (f. baŋgazạrumā) feckless P.

baŋgazau what a lot ! x wannaŋ dāwạ ~ what a lot of guineacorn !

ɓangel = ɓaŋgyel.

baŋgī m. (1) ignorant P. (2) masterless man (without supporter). (3) unripe groundnuts. (4) bạntam ~ loincloth made of the cloth called baŋgī.

baŋ girmā m. (1) yā yi minị ~ he showed me respect. (2) baŋ girman rūdị lip-service.

baŋ gīwā m. spoiled appearance of kolas unaffecting taste.

bango A. (baŋgō) m. (pl. baŋgāyē = baŋgwāyē). (1) wall of hut or house (cf. kataŋgā ; gārū). (2) (a) wall round compound (both 1, 2a = kataŋgā). (b) (replying to doŋ Allạ dạ Annabi ! " for God's sake help me ! "), P. says (i) kā gamạ ni dạ babbam (or dạ mạnyam) baŋgō very well, I'll help you. (ii)

ā'ạ, bar gamạ ni dạ babbam baŋgō sorry, I can't help you. (c) nā ƙyālẹ ka sabọ dạ babbam ~ I'll overlook your offence from pity. (3) cover of book. (4) piece of cloth for reinforcing garment over outside of shoulders. (5) baŋgō = baŋgwan zākị epithet of dọgarị. (6) Cf. tạkạ ~ ; wutar ~ ; bị ~. (7) 'yar ~ f. (a) A children's game of standing on the hands with the feet against a wall. (b) coitus in upright position. (8) tūrā tā kai baŋgō Vd. tūrā 2b. (9) kạ dạ baŋgō Vd. rimā 2. (10) dọdam ~ Vd. dọdō 6.
B. (baŋgō) m. (pl. baŋgunạ). (1) = Dịje. (2) bạkim ~ Vd. dōmạ 2. (3) Sk. any large neckless gourd. (4) Sk. yā shiga baŋgwan dạ bạ fạfā he has got into a scrape (= gọrā 1d.i).

ɓangōrī m. (pl. ɓaŋgōrai). (1) big lump or chip. (2) big potsherd.

baŋ guzạ Vd. ban 3b.

baŋgunạ Vd. bạŋgā ; baŋgō.

baŋgwalā Vd. ta ~ .

ɓaŋgwalēlẹ m. (f. ɓaŋgwalēlīyā) pl. ɓaŋgwal-ɓaŋgwạl = ɓaŋgwạlgwạl large and round x gōrọ ɓaŋgwạlgwạl dạ shī large kolas.

ɓaŋgwalī m. (f. ɓaŋgwalā) pl. ɓaŋgwal-ɓaŋgwạl = ɓaŋgwalēlẹ.

baŋgwạlī Sk. m. x tā tafĩ ~ she (Filani) went to her parents' home for her first confinement.

Bạgwandẹ m. (f. Bạgwandịyā) pl. Gwandāwā P. of Gwandu.

baŋgwāyē Vd. baŋgō.

baŋ gwīwạ m. throwing P. off the scent (lit. or figuratively) (= Kt. walaŋkēdūwā 2).

baŋ gyārē m. (1) being cooked or ripe only on the outside. (2) being only superficially healed. (3) mạganạ tasạ ~ his words are half true, half lies.

baŋgyel m. type of short gown.

ɓaŋgyel x tā ɗaurạ ɗan zanẹ ɓaŋgyel she wore a very small insufficient cloth.

baŋ hannū m. (1) nā yi ~ dạ shī I shook hands with him (= mụsāfaha = sun-nạtā). (2) stretching out hand to help P. over stream, etc.

baŋ haushī m. annoyance x (1) yā yi

minị ∽ he annoyed me. (2) dạ ∽ ya kẹ he's very aggravating (2 = tūrịn zūcịya). (3) *Vd.* Bạhaushẹ ; guzạ 2.

bạni *Fil.* = bạnu.

Bạnī Adạm *pl.* mankind.

bạ̈ ni ƙafạ. (1) give me a leg-up the wall ! (2) give me leg-room! (3) (*said by penniless* cācā-*player*) give me a loan! (4) *Vd.* baŋ ƙafạ.

bạ̈ ni kạ̈i *Kt. m. used in* gōnan naŋ sǎi ∽ ⁱthe crops in this farm are only good here and there (*cf.* bā dạ 9).

bạ̈ ni ƙwaryā *m. x* sun yi ∽ they've had an altercation. sun sākẹ ∽ they had another quarrel.

bạ̈ ni māsū *Sk. m.* = ạddā'ịrā 1.

Bạningẹ *m.* (*f.* Bạningịyā) *pl.* Niŋgāwā P. of Niŋgī.

baŋ iskạ *m. Vd.* iskạ 4.

banjạgarạ = manjạgarạ.

bạnjama *Vb.* 3B. (1) ạl'amạrī yā ∽ the matter's become serious (= buŋƙāsạ). (2) lạ̈bārị yā ∽ news spread far and wide. (3) yā ∽ he lost his head. (4) kōmẹ zā tạ ∽ , bạnjam what's going to happen to me, let it happen !

banka A. (baŋkā) *Vb.* 2. (1) urgẹd (horse) on. (2) drove P. away angrily. (3) = baŋkadạ 3. (4) drank much of. (5) yā baŋki rūwā he swum through *or* passed through much water *or* rain. yā baŋki rāɓa he went through heavy dew. yā baŋkō ɗārī he's come through very cold weather. (6) (*a*) nā baŋki rịgā dạ mahọ I patched the gown (*Vd.* mahọ). (*b*) sum baŋki wannạm bạbbar kītạr ƙịyayyạ wạddạ kẹ tsạkāninsu they've patched up the bitter hostility between them. (*c*) *cf.* baŋke-baŋkē. (7) yā baŋki kudī he squandered *or* embezzled money.

B. (baŋkạ) *Vb.* 1A (*plus dative*). (1) added to *x* nā ∽ wạ rịgā mahọ = baŋkā 6*a*. am ∽ wạ kạrkarā yāƙị countryside's been invaded. am ∽ wạ jẹ̈jị wutā bush has been set fire to. (2) yā ∽ minị tādị = bambạŋkā 2. (3) yā ∽ ạ gujẹ he took to his heels.

bankadạ A. (baŋkạdā) *Vb.* 1C. (1) lifted up edge of mat, cloth, etc. (2) yā baŋkạdạ ạsīrīna he revealed my

secret (= sịlīlị 2 = fạllasạ = ạsīrī 1*b*), *Vd.* tōnạ. (3) yā ∽ ƙōfạ he put the door ajar (*cf.* baŋkạɗē 2). (4) = baŋkadạ 3. (5) *Vd.* haŋkạdā 2.

B. (baŋkadạ) *Vb.* 2. (1) = baŋkạdā. (2) nā shā ∽ my secret's been revealed. (3) jostled, pushed *x* yā baŋkạɗē nị dạ kạ̈fadạ he jostled me (= baŋkā 3), *cf.* baŋkạɗē 3. (4) ɓạrāwạn dōkị dagạ baŋkadạr taskirar ūwā yakẹ sōmạ̈wā nip it in the bud ! (*Vd.* ɓạrāwọ 1*c*).

baŋkạɗē *Vb.* 1C. (1) = baŋkạdā 1. (2) ˙yā ∽ ƙōfạ he opened the door wide (*cf.* baŋkạdā 3). (3) jostled and knocked over *x* yā ∽ ni dạ kạ̈fadạ (*cf.* baŋkadạ 3).

baŋ ƙafạ *m.* giving P. leg-up a wall, etc. (*as in* bạ̈ ni ƙafạ).

baŋƙam *x* yā cịka ∽ it's full to the brim.

baŋkamā *f.* insolence to a superior.

baŋkamēmẹ = baŋkamī *m.* (*f.* baŋkamē-mịyā = baŋkamā) *pl.* baŋkaŋ-baŋkaŋ broad.

baŋƙarā *Vb.* 1C = baŋƙarạ *Vb.* 2. (1) (*a*) trussed a fowl. (*b*) tied hands of P. behind his back. (2) warped T. (3) yā baŋƙarạ ƙịrjī he protruded his chest. (4) tā baŋƙarɔ̌ cikịn kwānọ she slyly pushed up bottom of measure to make it hold less.

baŋƙarạ tạ̈fī *m.* being a cadger of tobacco.

baŋƙarē (1) *Vb.* 1C = baŋƙarā 1, 2, 3. (2) *Vb.* 3A. (*a*) became warped. (*b*) bottom of vessel is fraudulently pushed up to hold less.

baŋkārī. (1) = buŋkārī. (2) *adj. m.* (*f.* baŋkārā) broad (*place*).

baŋƙari *interjection of surprise at* T. *denoted by* baŋƙarā, baŋƙarē.

baŋ kāshī (1) punishment *Vd.* kāshī. (2) *Vd.* tirɗẹ.

baŋkẹ *Vb.* 1A. (1) jostled and knocked over (*cf.* baŋkā 3). (2) drunk up all the large quantity available (*cf.* baŋkā 4). (3) nā ∽ rịgā dạ mahọ = baŋkā 6. (4) yā ∽ kudī he squandered *or* embezzled all the money (*cf.* baŋkā 7).

baŋ'ke-baŋkē‖ *m.* continual patching *x* anạ baŋke-baŋkē makeshift plans are being adopted (*Vd.* baŋkā 6).

baŋkị *m.* (1) = mahọ. (2) = datsīyā 1. (3) cloth used as compound-wall of chief when travelling. (4) *Kt.* riɓị

dạ ~ = niŋkịm bạ niŋkịn. (5) *Eng.*
(*a*) (i) bank (for money). (ii) bank (of
road or cutting). (*b*) = asūsụ 1.
baŋkiɗa = baŋkaɗa.
baŋ kụŋkurū. (1) type of cap-pattern.
(2) type of native cloth with dark and
light blue basketry patterns.
baŋkwai *Sk. m.* (1) selling fish or cassava.
(2) 'yar ~ (*a*) female fish-seller. (*b*)
name for daughter of fish-seller.
baŋƙwalēlẹ = baŋƙwalī *m.* (*f.* baŋƙwalēlịyā
= baŋƙwalā) *pl.* baŋƙwal-baŋƙwạl
huge.
baŋƙwạlƙwạl *m.* hugeness *x* yanạ dạ kại ~
he has a huge head.
baŋ kwānā *m. x* nā yi ~ dạ shī I took
leave of him (= salamạ 2). dina ta
baŋ kwānā farewell-dinner.
ban magana (bam mạganạ) *m.* (1) coaxing,
soothing. (2) ~ bā yạ kai tsōfō gōnā you
can take a horse to the water, but you
cannot make him drink. (3) ~ bā
yạ̈ kai tsōfō zaŋgọ sǎi furā ạ būtạ
the labourer is worthy of his hire.
(4) ~ (= dāɗim bạƙī) shī kạ̈ sạ̈
ɓạrāwọ dạrīyā ạ rụmbū cajoling a
malefactor to get the better of him.
ban mamaki (bam mạ̈mākị) *m. x*
yanạ̈ dạ ~ it's wonderful, surprising.
ɓạnnā = ɓạrnā.
ban nāmạ *Vd.* agọ̄lạ̈.
bạn ni dạ mūgụ = *Sk.* bạn ni *m.* (1) acne
in pubert boys (*cf.* yayyafā 3). (2)
mạị ~ *m.* large kolas with excrescences.
ban rūwā *m.* (1) (*a*) watering horses.
(*b*) (i) watering an irrigated farm. (ii)
tạimakwam ~ *m.* irrigational measures.
(2) tempering metal in water. (4) *Vd.*
rūwā A.13.
ban sāmụ *Vd.* dạ̈munā 1*f.*
ban sanyī *m.* cooling iron in sand.
ban shạ̈'awạ̈ *m. x* ~ gạrēshị he is handsome.
ban shunī *m.* (1) giving garment indigo
tint by rubbing indigo (shūnī) on the
body *or* by wearing the garment touching a dyed one *or* by sleeping in it on
indigoed mat (= *Kt.* tọ̄ɓē), *cf.* shūnī 3,
bụrsụnē, dafạ̈ 2*c*, dakạ̈ 1*g*, jiƙẹ, lēlā 4. (2)
sprinkling mixture of indigo (shūnī)
and dụsar gērō or sand on garment,

and then beating it to tinge it with
indigo (*Vd.* shūnī 3*b*, bụrsụnē, bụgē 1).
*ɓantā *f.* (*sg., pl.*) sparrow (= gwarā).
ban tạ̈fī *Vd.* tạ̈fī 1*e*.
ɓantạ̈lā *Vb.* 1C. (1) *Kt.* = ɓạntarạ̈. (2)
Sk. = ɓạllạ̈ 1.
ɓantale A. (ɓạntạ̈lē) *m.* = fadẹ.
    B. (ɓantalẹ) *m.* = ɓantarẹ.
ɓạntarạ̈ *Vb.* 2 broke piece off hard T.
ɓantare A. (ɓạntạ̈rē) *Vb.* 3A. (1) piece
became broken off hard T. (2) =
ɓạ̈ŋgạ̈lē.
    B. (ɓantarẹ) *m.* piece broken off
hard T.
    C. (ɓạntạ̈rē) *m.* (1) yā (tā) yi ~
he (she) wore loincloth without pulling
it through the legs. (2) zanẹ yā yi
matạ̈ ~ cloth too small for her flapped
open (= kwạ̈dō 7 = wạlƙiyā 3).
*bạntarmạ̈ *Sk. f.* firebrand (= bạ̈kiŋ
wutā *q.v.*).
ɓantashā *f.* = ɓạŋgashā.
ban tausạyī *m. x* ạbụ mạị ~ a thing
inspiring sympathy.
bante A. (bạntē) *m.* (*pl.* bantunạ̈). (1) (*a*)
loincloth (*Vd.* wutsīyạ̈ 1*a*). (*b*) dạ
tsịrārạ̈ gāra baƙim bạntē half a loaf
is better than no bread. (2) an sạ̈
masạ̈ ~ he's now 7–9 years old and
ready to wear loincloth. (3) baby's
napkin. (4) cloth put for adornment
over hindquarters of horse. (5) ornamental edge of thatch roof. (5) anything put at bottom of cooking-
steamer to prevent food falling through
or blocking holes. (7) = bạraŋkaɓạ̈.
(8) dōkịnsạ̈ ~ gạrēshị his horse tucks
in its tail. (9) bạ tạ̈ kai ~ ba = bạ tạ̈
kai ba she was no virgin at marriage
(*said because previously village-girls
kept on bạntē till marriage and then
changed it for a mụkurū*) = budurcị 3.
(10) lāfīyạ̈ gạrēshị kạmam ~ = shī
~ nẹ̈ he has no will of his own. (11)
ganim bạntam Wạmbai anything impossible. (12) *Vd.* bạntan dạ̈rạ̈zau,
barkạ̈ 7. (13) bạntan lifịdī quilted
armour for loins of cavalry.
    B. (bantẹ) *m.* (1) cheating in trading.
(2) yā yi minị ~ he disputed with me
about total owing (= harambē).
*ɓantẹ *Vb.* 1A *x* bạ ạ̈ ~ ta ba tụkụnā

she (Filani wife gone to parents' home for first confinement) has not yet been brought back to husband's house after receiving present of the ɓantī cloth from him.
ɓantī *m. x* aŋ kai matạ ∼ her husband has sent her the ɓantī cloth as present (*Vd.* ɓantẹ).
*ɓantīyọ *m.* sun tạfi gạrim ɓantīyạŋ Kạnde they've gone to ceremony of husband giving wife Kande the ɓantī cloth *q.v.*
bạn tọ̄nō *Nor. m.* searching over market-ground for odds and ends after market has dispersed.
ban tsọ̄rō *m. x* ạbụ maị ∼ a terrifying thing.
bantunạ *Vd.* bạntē.
bạnu *Fil. x* yā ∼ he's at his wits' ends.
bạnụs = bạnūshị *m.* poor red serge, flannel, etc.
Bạnufē *m.* (*f.* Bạnufīyā) *pl.* Nufāwā. (1) Nupe P. (= Na ạlōlō = Takwạ). (2) wani kāyā sǎi Bạnufē, wạccẹ Ạyāg̣ī maị d̃an dōrọ (*said by woman*) who am I to be able to do it ? (3) rǎi kạŋ ga rǎi, Bạnufē yā ga kōko that is just in his line.
bạŋwaị *Zar. m.* = bammōmī.
banyẹ *Vb.* 1A *Sk.* = fanyẹ.
banzā *f.* (1) (*a*) uselessness *x* (i) mụtumịm, ∼ useless P. ạbim ∼ useless T. (*their epithets are* Banzā girman shūcị, bạ yantā = Banzā girmam mahạukạcī, k̃aramim maị lāfīyạ yā fī shị (*cf.* 1*j below*) = kyạm ∼ , kyạm macịjī = ạbim ∼ hancị bạ kafā = aikịm ∼ mạkāfọ dạ waịwayạ). (ii) banzā bā tạ̈ sạ yạ yī he has some good reason for doing it. (iii) dạ mukạ yī, banzā ta fādị we had no difficulty in doing it. (iv) kā ga mutạ̈nam banzā you bloody fools ! (*b*) yanạ̈ cịmmụ da ∼ he's tricking us. (*c*) anạ̈ ta nịshādị, fạdi ∼ fạdi wọ̄fī lighthearted chatter is going on. (*d*) ∼ gudụŋ k̃urụ, bạ zaị k̃etạrẹ hụ̃dā ba he thinks himself cleverer than he is. (*e*) ∼ tā kọ̄ri wọ̄fī = banzā tā kas wọ̄fī, d̃aŋ kōlị yā kashẹ dịllālị Greek met Greek, two villains queered each other's pitch. (*f*) ∼ bā tạ̈ kai zōmō kạ̈sūwā = hannū, ∼ bā

yạ̈ d̃aukạŋ wutā im bạ̈ mâgạnī dạ shạrịftakạ nobody acts without good reason, there's more than meets the eye ! (*g*) ∼ kisạm macịjim mātā, aŋ kashẹ, bạ ạ sārẹ kạm ba half measures are no good. (*h*) ∼ farịŋ idọ bābụ ganī *epithet of* P., T. belying its good exterior = faŋkạm fayạu. (*j*) banzā girmam mahạukạcī, k̃aramī maị wạ̈yō yā fī shị better a sensible boy than a foolish adult (*cf.* 1*a*). (*k*) bạ karọ ∼ = bạ shạ̈rā ∼ *Vd.* tạ̈rō 3. (*l*) tsōfam banzā *Vd.* zaunạ 1*e.* (*m*) ạ bar banzā *Vd.* ạbạrbā. (*n*) banzā bạd̃ī *Vd.* bạd̃i 1*c.* (*o*) maị rạm ∼ *Vd.* dạ̈kārẹ. (*p*) cịŋkị ∼ *Vd.* gafīyạ. (2) *adj.* useless *x* yā zamā ∼ gạ shūkạ it's useless for sowing. ∼ nẹ̈ ạ yi hakạ it's useless to do so. (3) Banzā bakwaị the States of Zạmfạrạ, Nufē, Kabị, Yāwụrī, Yarạbā, Bạrgū, Gurmạ. *But according to Katsina, the States are :*—Gūmạl, Misạu, Kạzaurē, Kạ̈tāgum, Jama'ārẹ, Gwạmbē, Adamāwā. *The Sokoto version is :*—Zạmfạrạr Filạ̈nī, Kabị Ta Keɓe, ādạr, Birnịŋ Gwārī, Kạcinạ Lākā, Kụyambana, Kwạtaŋkwarō. *cf.* Hausā bakwaị. (4) (*a*) d̃am ∼ *m.* (*pl.* 'yam ∼) whitlow. (*b*) d̃am ∼ *m.* (*f.* 'yar ∼) *pl.* 'yam ∼ useless P. (*c*) d̃am banzā yạ̈shī nẹ̈ ; kō an duŋk̃ụlā shi, bā yạ̈ duŋk̃ụlūwā a useless P. is worse than useless. (5) *adv.* (*a*) in vain *x* (i) nā tạfi ∼ I went in vain. (ii) ạ banzā, yawạ bạ̈ dādī abundant but inferior (*Vd.* dādī 1*f*). (iii) wannạŋ taịmakō yā tạfi ạ banzā this help is wasted (*cf.* zō 4). (iv) kặi bā yạ̈ fashẹ̈wā ạ banzā *Vd.* fashẹ 1*a*.iii. (*b*) cheaply ; gratis *x* nā sạ̈mē shị ạ ∼ I got it cheaply *or* free. gạ̈ rūwā ∼ ạ naŋ there's water here for the mere asking. (6) banza-banza *adv. x* (*a*) nā sạ̈mē shị banza-banza I got it fairly cheaply. (*b*) kadạ kạ dụɓē nị banza-banza do not look at me in that contemptuous way ! (*c*) kanạ̈ ganīna banza-banza you despise me. (7) gwarzō ∼ *m.* making farm-ridges after rains, for spring sowing (= fạrạ-fạrạ). (8) bạtum ∼ *Vd.* bạtū 4. (9) *Vd.* banzan *plus following word.*

ban zaṇẹ *m.* cock's drooping one wing with anticipation prior to copulation with hen.

banzaŋ gạrī *m.* (1) valueless citizen who has no senior, nor fixed abode (= ạ gaŋgarō 2). (2) *Vd.* banzar birnī.

banzạntā *Vb.* 1C. (1) despised (= wōfịntā = wāsạntā). (2) failed to look after P. or T. (3) squandered.

banzantad dạ *Vb.* 4B = banzạntā.

banzar birnī *f.* (1) = banzaŋ gạrī. (2) the fact of one of two mutually complementary events or articles being absent (*e.g.* P. with money going to station after train gone ; gown not arrived from tailor in time for Festival) *x* zạran naŋ yā zamā banzar birnī this thread isn't worth putting in a decent needle (*epithet is* banzar birnī, yāḳị yā ci d'aŋ Kanọ ạ Gōgau).

banzar gạrī *f.* = banzaŋ gạrī.

bạō *Katagum Hausa* = bāḳō.

bappạ = bappanyọ *m.* (1) paternal uncle. (2) *Vd.* yạyā A.2*h.*

bar *Vd.* barị.

bara A.1 (barạ) (*rolled* -r- *Mod. Gram.* 5).*f.* (1) (*a*) (i) begging for alms *x* yanạ ~ he is begging (*Vd.* ạlmājịrī 2, kumbạlī). yanạ barạd dōkị he is begging to be given a horse. (ii) yā kai musụ ~ he went to them begging. (iii) rashịn ta maị ~ *Vd.* rashị 1*m.* (iv) *Vd.* masussukā. (v) hatsim ~ *Vd.* gạuraị-gauraị. (2) jāḳī yā (maçẹ tā) yi ~ the donkey (woman) pushed its (her) way out of the crowd and moved forward along the edge. (3) *Sk. x* nā yi ~ tai ạ ḳōfạr gạrī I caught up with him at the town-gate and passed him.

A.2 (barạ) (*flapped* -r- *Mod. Gram.* 5). (1) *m.* (*f.* baranyạ) *pl.* barōrī = *Sk.* barwā, barwai, *bạrrai, *barūrūwạ. (*a*) (i) servant. (ii) baraŋ ụbaŋkị *Vd.* Burụŋgū. (iii) *Vd.* dịyā 4. (iv) yā yi barōrī bīyū he has two servants. (*b*) barạm barạ yā fi ụbandāḳị ạlfarmā a servant is often more arrogant than his master. (*c*) barạm maị tsāmī the servant of a rich man. (*d*) kōwā ya sāmụ, yạ yi ~ = maị ạbụ shī nẹ dạ ~ no rich man without spongers ! (*cf.* darị 3). (*e*) Maị dạ ạbōkī ~ what a

rich, liberal man ! (*f*) Na dụḳe bạ ka ~ *Vd.* dụḳe. (*g*) baransạ nẹ he can't hold a candle to him. (*h*) baraŋ gashị *Vd.* tsịrē 2. (2) *Vb.* 1A (*a*) = barị. (*b*) *Vd.* barạ-*compounds* ; barị 5*b.* (*c*) *Vd.* ạ barạ ; dụḳe. (*d*) Nā barạ = A bar shi, A bar tạ. (*e*) tā ~ fātạ wụyā *Vd.* mutụ 1*a.*vii.

B. (barā) *Zar.* = barạ A.2 section 2*a.*

C. *(bạrā) *Ar.* is (was) acquitted, declared innocent.

E. (bạra). (1) *f.* (*a*) last year. (*b*) ~ waccaŋ the year before last. (*c*) mụtumịm ~ an out-of-date person. (*d*) dẹnạ zạncam " bạra nā yi wāḳe, bana nā yi hạrāwạ " don't harp on the " good old days " ! (*e*) yā wuçẹ kạmaŋ gụmāgụmam ~ it's a thing of the past (*Vd.* dārī 2). (*f*) kōwā ya tunạ ~ *Vd.* tunạ 1*a.*ii. (*g*) *Vd.* bạbbam bạra. (2) bạra = ạ bạra *adv.* last year.

F. (bạrā) *f.* (1) aiming at *x* (*a*) yā yi ~ baị sāmụ ba he aimed but missed. (*b*) ạbim ~ *m.* target. nā kafạ ạbim ~ I erected a target. (2) bạrar makōdī *Vd.* shirwạ 1*c.* (3) ~ dạ kā (*a*) firing wildly. (*b*) acting or replying without consideration. (4) *Vd.* shạ ~ , kạu dạ ~ , karam ~ .

G. (barā) *Sk. f.* loud wrangling.

ɓara A. (ɓarạ) *Vb.* 1A. (1) shelled, peeled (groundnuts, gujīyā, cassava, banana, potato, etc.). (2) (*a*) yā ~ ɓāwō he stripped off bark. (*b*) mum ɓārạ kạmmụ dagạ cikịŋ wannaŋ kwạsfā ta " wai munạ zamaŋ ạmānạ " we swept from our minds the false assumption of being at peace. (3) yā ~ gōrọ he split a kolanut into segments. (4) yā ~ bāḳī he shouted. (5) baị ~ ba not a word did he reply.

B. (ɓạrā) *Vb.* 3 = ɓārạ 1, 2, 3.

bạ rāɓa *Bauchi Hausa* ~ fur *m.* swift horse.

bạ'ra-bạrāᵘ *Zar.* (1) *adv.* sporadically *x* hatsī yā tsirō ~ corn's sprouted here and there. (2) *f.* inūwạn naŋ ~ cẹ there are alternate patches of sun and shade under tree.

bạ rabẹ *x* bạ ~ tsạkāninsụ there's no difference between them.

ɓarāɓụsai *Vd.* ɓarɓashī.

barabuskǫ = burabuskǫ.

barācē Vd. barātạ.

barādā Vd. bardē.

barādạ = burādạ.

barad dạ Vb. 4A. (1) led to acquittal x bā abin dạ ya ∼ shī (= bā abin dạ ya barāshē shị) sǎi wannạṇ it was this alone that led to his acquittal (cf. barā). (2) Allā yā barāshē shị he had a stroke of luck. Allā yā barāshē nị, nā sāmụ I got it by luck (cf. barātạ).

barad dạ Vb. 4B. (1) dropped T. which became scattered. (2) tā ∼ dā she had miscarriage, abortion. (3) ∼ bakạ = bar dạ bakạ.

baraddai = barādē = barādinnị Vd. bardē.

baradị Eng. m. (1) bread. (2) loaf.

baragadạ f. (1) senseless talk. (2) " pidgin " Hausa, English, etc. (3) any haphazard adornment of cap or gown. (4) large drum beaten with two sticks. (5) Zar. = sǭyē 1.

barạ gadō gāshị epithet of man slow to ejaculate when copulating.

barạ gadō shūnī epithet of prostitute (and hence of wife considered sterile through loose ways).

barāgazạ = burāguzạ.

barāgē m. (1) type of native cloth, red, white, and black (cf. agēdū, tayạ ragō). (2) mai manyam ∼ big-boned young P. yā fī shị manyam ∼ he (young P., animal) is bigger-boned than the other (cf. ƙashī 4). (3) Vd. bargō.

barạ gurbị m. (1) P. or T. left behind after others have gone. (2) eggs left unhatched, addled egg. (2 = rubau = Kt. dakwayẹ = dungẹ 2 = gunyạ 1).

barāgusai = barāguzai = burābusai q.v. under barbashī.

Barahājẹ m. (f. Barahājịyā = Barahāzạ) pl. Rahāzāwā. (1) P. of the Filani Clan so called. (2) Barahāzạ f. type of bǫrī spirit.

barai Vd. barāwǫ.

baraicē Vb. 3A Kt. = barạncē.

baraitad dạ Vb. 4B Kt. = barad dạ.

barā'izai m. x yā cikạ ∼ he acts un-accountably because possessed by evil spirits.

baraje A. (barājē) Vd. bardē.

B. (barajẹ) m. type of strong white European cloth.

barakạ (1) Vb. 3B = barkẹ 1. (2) f. (a) (i) place where stitching has come undone. (ii) barakar zanẹ Vd. bikī 1h. (b) blemish. (c) dōkị yā yi ∼ horse became thin over its quarters (= daurạ warkī). (d) yā yi minị ∼ he betrayed my secret. (e) sun yi wạ kạnsụ ∼ friends became estranged. (f) Vd. ƙunshị 6.

barākādī Kt. m. idle roaming.

bārakallā Ar. (1) jolly good ! ; how fine it is ! (2) reply to a greeting (both = tubarkallā 1).

barākugumā Nor. f. disrespectful talk.

barāƙumā f. (1) = tāƙamā 1a. (2) woman who has no periods while suckling child (epithet is barāƙumā, tā gǫyi mijị, tā gǫyi dā). (3) woman bearing after 12 months instead of 9.

barāƙuntạ Sk. Vb. 3B = fargā.

barạ magādā m. work well done ; reliable T.

barambajau m. (sg., pl.) metal anklet of children (cf. ƙǫrǫsō).

barambaƙamī m. hefty man.

baram-barạm m. sun yi ∼ friends have become estranged.

barambaramā f. = baŋkamā.

barambōdī m. (f. barambōdịyā). (1) scatterbrained P. (2) f. (a) barambōdịyā intractable mare or cow. (b) Audụ barambōdịyā garēshị Audu is in-tractable.

barambōtsạmī Sk. m. = barambōdī 1, 2b.

barāmū (1) (a) any mineral. (b) māsū ginam barāmū miners. (2) any ex-cavation from which ore, salt, potter's-clay is taken.

barancakī Kt. m. = baraŋkacī.

barạncē m. = barạntakạ.

barạncē Vb. 3A. (1) became spilled. (2) cikịntạ yā ∼ she had a miscarriage (cf. barad dạ 2).

bārancī m. being uncouth.

barandạ f. speculative buying without weighing, for sale or return (cf. bịlkārạ), hence the saying ∼ bā kāyā ba : im bạ tạ ci ba, tạ gyarẹ.

barandamī m. (pl. barandạmai) type of hatchet.

baraŋ dawọ *m.* T. put at bottom of cooking-pot to prevent contents sticking or burning.

baraŋgwajẹ *m.* food of mixed groundnuts, ḳaɓēwạ and yākūwā (= *Kt.* raɓī).

baraŋkaɓạ = baraŋkaɓīyā *f.* bed-valance (= lẹ̄lẹ̄gaji 2 = ɓantē 7).

baraŋkacī *m.* beanlike plant used as rattle.

baraŋ̀kam *Kt.* = ɓaŋ̀kam.

baraŋ̀kam-baraŋ̀kam (1) *m.* (*a*) yā yi ~ it's too large to enter the doorway. (*b*) = ạlḳaḳai. (*c*) curling up *x* tạ̄barmā tā yi ~ mat has curled up. (2) *adv.* (*a*) nā ḳọ̄shi ~ I'm quite replete. (*b*) sạ̄ yanạ̄ dạ ḳaɓō ~ = ḳafan sạ̄ yā yi ~ bull has widely-curving horns. (*c*) jạ̄kī (zōmō) (mutum) yanạ̄ dạ kunnūwạ ~ donkey (hare) (person) has large protruding ears.

ɓarantad dạ *Vb.* 4B = ɓarad dạ.

baṛantakạ *f.* being a servant.

ɓaṛantinni *Sk. m.* = gwạfā 1.

baranyạ *f.* (1) *Vd.* barạ A2. (2) *Sk.* junior rival-wife (kīshīyā).

ɓārārā = *Kt.* ɓạ̄rạ̄rā. (1) *f.* (*a*) loud talking. (*b*) blabbing. (2) *m.*, *f.* blabber.

ɓarar da = ɓarad dạ.

Bạraṛō = Bararōji *m.*, *f.* (*sg.*, *pl.*) nomad Filani (*epithet is* fata-fata ḳạt tākalmạ), *Vd.* Bạfīlācẹ.

bararrajẹ *Vb.* 3A = ishisshirē.

ɓararraka A. (ɓạrạrrakạ) *Vb.* 3B. (1) boiled on continuously (= wạtsạttsakạ). (2) (seam) split. (3) yanạ̄ ɓạrạrrakạr kūkā he's crying noisily, howling. (4) *Vb.* 2 *x* yā ɓạrạrrakē ni dạ zāgi he roundly abused me.

B. (ɓararrakā) *Vb.* 1D boiled T. continuously (= wạtsạttsạkā).

ɓararrakė A. (ɓararrakē) *Vb.* 3A is (was) in tatters, shreds (*cf.* ɓarkẹ).

B. (ɓạrạrrakē) *m.* herbal drink continuously boiled.

ɓạrạrrạki-ɓạrạrrạkī *used in* ~ bạ̄ cin yau ba nẹ̄, bạ̄ cin gọ̄be ba, jībi mā ạlbarkạ *epithet of* T. which benefits nobody *i.e.* greedy man can't wait for food to be taken off the fire, while miser says the food is not for to-day or even tomorrow).

ɓạrạrrazạ *Vb.* 3B = ishisshirē.

bararrē *m.* (*f.* bạrarrīyā) *pl.* ɓạrạrrū freed-slave (*cf.* bari).

ɓaras A. (ɓaras dạ) = ɓarad dạ.

B. (ɓạrạs). (1) itạ̄cē yā karyẹ ~ wood snapped snap ! (2) *Vd.* ɓạrạs-ɓạrạs.

baras *m.* = ạlbaras.

bạ̄rạ̄sā *f.* (*derived from reversing Ar.* sharāba) European intoxicating drinks (*cf.* gīyạ).

ɓạrạs-ɓạrạs (1) an niḳạ ~ it's coarsely-ground. (2) *Vd.* ɓạrạs.

barāshē *Vd.* barad dạ.

barata A. (bạrātạ). (1) *Vb.* 3B is (was) lucky. (2) *Vb.* 2 (*p.o.* bạrạ̄ci, *n.o.* bạrạ̄cē) obtained by begging *x* nā bạrạ̄ci dōḳi I got a horse by begging (*Vd.* barạ A.1).

B. (bạ̄ratạ) *Vb.* 2 (*p.o.* bạ̄rạ̄cē, *n.o.* bạ̄rạ̄ci) took aim at (= ạunā 5).

barātad dạ *Vb.* 4B = barad dạ.

bạratuŋkusạ = buruntuŋkusạ.

Bạrau = Ạ bar shi.

ɓạrau *x* ɓạrau-ɓạrau sạssạ̄tau why, you're offering below cost price !

Bạraukạ (1) = Ạ bar tạ. (2) name for any woman called Ḳande.

bạraukī *Vd.* kunnē 1*d.*

ɓạraunīyā *f.* (1) *Vd.* ɓạrāwọ. (2) ɓạraunīyar hanyạ (*a*) side-track. (*b*) temporary track. (*c*) railway-deviation. (*d*) line for bringing up railway-ballast. (3) ɓạraunīyar ḳōfạ low doorway at back of village-house. (4) ɓạraunīyar tạ̄gūwạ first travellers of the season bringing salt from the far north. (5) ɓạraunīyar takạrdā letter containing news secretly obtained.

ɓạrāwọ *m.* (*f.* ɓạraunīyā) *pl.* ɓạrạ̄yī = *Sk.* ɓarai. (1) (*a*) thief. (*b*) *his epithet is* mai sạn ạbinḳạ wandạ ya fī ḳạ dạbāra. (*c*) ɓạrāwạn dōḳi dạgạ ḳạ̄zā ya fārạ = ɓạrāwạn dōḳi dạgạ taskirar ūwā ya fārạ *Vd.* taskirā. (*d*) mai rēnạ ḳạdam ~ nē an ungrateful P. is no better than a thief. (*e*) kūrā tā cinyẹ ~ the biter bit ! (= burum 3). (2) *Vd.* ɓạrauniyā, dawākī 2*b.* (3) ɓạrāwạm bisạ = ɓạrāwạn rāgā overhanging branch catching in loads carried on the head. (4)

ɓarāwạn tsạye broker (= dịllālị). (5)
(a) ɓạrāwạn zạune receiver of stolen
goods who has fixed abode (cf. tugụ,
garāzuŋ).　(b) ƙanạm ~ Vd. tugụ.
(6) ɓạrāwạŋ waŋkā woman's bathing
earlier than usual (about 5 a.m.)
because bathing-place will later be
thronged. (7) ɓạrāwạŋ hụ̄lā = ɓạrāwạn
tāgīyạ Vd. sạ̄ C.1b. (8) bā yạ̄ hanạ ~
Vd. sakẹ 1d.
baraya A. (bạrāyā) m.　(1) stable
(= shạ̄makị 1a).　(2) Kt. (a) place
reserved for householder to eat food
(= tụrākā 1). (b) 'yam ~ = tụrākā 2.
(3) title in Sokoto, Bauchi, and Argungu.
(4) 'yar ~ f. = sōrō 3.
　B. (bārayạ) f. Maguzawa funeral-
games.
ɓạrāyī Vd. ɓạrāwọ.
barbạ x ɗam ~ m. type of small, Bauchi
pony.
ɓarɓacē Vb. 3B intensive from ɓacẹ.
barbaɗa A. (barbạdā) Vb. 1C scattered,
sprinkled x yā barbạdạ tākị ạ gōnā he
scattered manure on the farm (cf.
badạ, warwạdā).　(2) yā barbạdạ
lạ̄bārị he spread the news.
　B. (bạrbadạ). (1) Vb. 2 = barbạdā.
(2) f. yawạm ~ gạrēshị (a) he is a
chatterbox. (b) he roves about.
bạrbạdaɗɗē m. (f. bạrbạdaɗɗīyā) pl.
bạrbạdạɗɗū a rover.
barbaɗe A. (barbạdē).　(1) Vb. 1C
scattered or sprinkled all of (cf.
barbạdā).　(2) Vb. 3A led a roving,
idle life.
　B. (bạrbạdē) m. being occupied in
scattering manure.
barbaɗēdẹ m. ƙulī-ƙulī crumbled up for
bạlạgandị.
bạrbạdī m. (1) (a) crumb. (b) bạrbạdī =
'yam ~ pl. m. (i) crumbs. (ii) remnants. (iii) few survivors. (c) bạrbạdin
tọkar sịgārị cigarette-ash.　(2) act of
sprinkling x sun yi wạ Masạr ~ dạ
bọm they bombed Egypt.　(3) cf.
ɓarɓashī.　(4) anạ̄ ~ dạ shī he is the
subject of talk.
barbaje A. (barbajẹ) m.　(1) = bōbwā.
(2) type of biting-fly.　(3) Vd. bāyā
1a.ii ; gīwā 1l.
　B. (barbạjē) int. from bajẹ.

bạrbạr Vd. bọrbọr.
barbara A. (barbarā) m., f. (1) copulation
by animals.　(2) bụnsurū yanạ̄ ~ the
billygoat is making the burbling noise
preliminary to copulation.　(3) eagerness to do, get T.　(4) yanạ̄ ~ tasạ
he's in his usual fractious mood.　(5)
maị barbaram mạganạ P. bubbling
with excited chatter.　(6) barbaran
yạnyāwạ = barbarạn yạnyāwạ m., f.
(sg., pl.) half-caste ; hybrid = jạ̄kin
5b (cf. gamạ̄ 3).
　B. (bạrbarạ) Vb. 2 (animal) copulated with (another).
ɓarɓarkīyā f. = dạḷạkī.
barbarō m. = bāsụmạ.
bạrbartā m. (1) sạ̄barạ-root (Vd. sạ̄barạ).
(2) sour milk (cf. barcī 3).
ɓarɓarwạ f. trembling.
ɓarɓạshī m. (pl. ɓạrạ̄ɓụsai). (1) crumb ;
small fragment of T. (as of burning
stick, etc.) (= bạrbạdī 1a).　(2) flake
x ɓạrɓạshiŋ ƙazwā flakes of skin
peeled off through scabies ; ɓạrɓạshin
tụnjērē ditto through syphilis (= kwạrkwashī 2).　(3) ɓạrɓạshim mạganạ
false accusation.　(4) yā sạ̄ minị ~ he
caused me to be falsely accused.
ɓạrɓat Kt. = bạ̄but.
ɓạrɓạ̄tā Vb. 1C int. from ɓātạ.
barbazā Vb. 1C int. from bazạ.
barci A. (barcī) m.　(1) sleep x (a) yā yi ~
he went to sleep. yanạ̄ ~ he is asleep
(= kwānā A.2, section 3a). daran nạm
bạn yi ~ ba I couldn't sleep last night.
mụ jē, mụ yi ~ (= mụ kwạntā) let's have
a sleep ! (cf. kwạntā ; kwānā A.1 ; kwānā
A.2, section 3a). (b) ~ yā kwāshẹ shi =
~ yā dạukē shị he fell asleep.　(c) yā
yi ~ kại ɗayā he slept through the
night with only one change of position.
(d) yam ~ m. dribbling by sleeper
(= yau 1b = Kt. sạlēɓạ 2).　(dd)
wāwam ~ m. deep sleep.　(e) mūgụn
yārọ kā yi barcī ? are you going to
cease your evil ways ? (he is supposed
to reply threateningly n nạ̄ jị, ka zāgi
Sarkī).　(f) gadam ~ Vd. ạlhērị 1b.
(g) maị gadō yā sō ~ , " Maị tạbarmā
sāi kạ naɗẹ ! " the day of reckoning
comes.　(h) yā fi ~ dādī Vd. bạkaŋ.
(j) wurim ~ Vd. tīlạs 1c. (k) (i) hạnạ ~

Vd. zaƙarnaƙo.   (ii) hana ∼ *Vd.* tunkwīyau 1*b*.   (*l*) kōwā ya ɗauki bāshim ∼ *Vd.* bāshi 5.   (*m*) mai dōkar ∼ *Vd.* ɓuge 2.   (2) death *x* babbam ∼ death.   tā haifu, ammā ɗanta yanā ∼ her child is stillborn.   (3) (*a*) nōno yanā ∼ the milk is curdled (*cf.* barbartā, tsāmī 1*f, g*).   (*b*) mai yanā ∼ the oil is solidified.   (*c*) Audu man rūrūwa nē, bā yā ∼ Audu is very cute.   (4) (*a*) astringent taste of green dates, kolas, potash, etc.   (= baurī = daurī 2 = *Sk.* ɗabrī = *Sk.* kalcī), *cf.* gancī, gāīī 3.   (*b*) kōme ɗacī, kōmē baurī, bā mā dangana sǎi mun ga ƙwado we shall stick it out to the bitter end.   (5) *Vd.* ˙zōmō 3, cīwon 2.

B. (barci) (*d.f. unused verb* bartā) *x* nā ∼ ƙafa I saw my chance.   in yā ∼ ƙafa, yā zō he'll come if he gets the chance.   muka yi bartaƙ ƙafa muka zō so we seized our chance and came.

C. *cf.* borcī.

ɓar da (1) *Vb.* 4A = ɓarad da.   (2) ∼ baka *m.* blurting out what one ought not to have said.

ɓardallā *f.* swelling which sometimes occurs when P. receives a cut or when face-markings are cut on P. (*its cure requires incision*).

bardē *m.* (*pl.* barādē = barājē = *Sk.* barādā, baraddai, barādinni).   (1) bardan Sarkī mounted attendant of chief (*epithet is* Bardē, bā kēsāwā = Sumba = Kēsau).   (2) bardan yāƙi cavalryman (*epithet is* Bardē Sarkin yāƙi), *cf.* 9 *below*.   (3) Bardē (*a*) *an official title* (*epithet is* Garāza).   (*b*) *Vd.* wutā 1*v*.   (4) *Sk.* Barādē *title of* an important councillor of the Emir.   (5) *Kt.* harama, barādē *Vd.* harama 2.   (6) the first dates of the season.   (7) yā hau ∼ he is riding without a saddle (*cf.* wāgā 4, hawam ∼).   (8) a ∼ nakē (*a*) I (a male) am wearing neither trousers nor loincloth, but only one big cloth.   (*b*) I (a female) am wearing no mukurū.   (9) ∼ yā hau kanta she is possessed by the bōrī-spirit called bardē (*epithet is* Bardē Sarkin yāƙi), *cf.* 2 *above*.   (10) bardan gōyō child about 18 months old and nearly ready for weaning.   (11) yā yi ɗitar bardan

guza he absconded.   (12) bardan Jaudī busybody.

bardi *Kt. m.* pus (= mugunya).

bardō *m.* (*sg., pl.*).   (1) Cape dove, i.e. Longtailed-dove   (*Oena capensis*), *epithet is* Bardō, mai kīwan tsabta.   (2) stingy P.

bare A. (bārē) *m., f.* (*sg., pl.*).   (1) (*a*) stranger.   (*b*) = shigēge.   (*c*) ba zā mu maishē su ∼ ba cikin al'amuran ƙasāshan Tūrai we shan't leave them without a say in European affairs.   (*d*) mūgun nāka ₍ yā fi ∼ na wani better my own than a borrowed thing ! (= mūgun gātarī).   (2) wanda ya yi kōkawa a ∼ , kō yā yi kāye, ā jūye shi it's hard to be popular abroad.

B. (barē) (1) = ballē.   (2) sun yi ∼ dūniya they've quarrelled irretrievably.   (3) *Vd.* barē bana.

C. (bare) (1) = banda *x* ∼ nī wā zai yardā who but me would agree ! (2) Bare (*a*) *name for* dogs.   (*b*) da wani ƙarē bā Bare ba ? it is six of one and half a dozen of the other.   (*c*) yā ranta a gōnar Bare = yā nōma gōnar Bare = yā yi nōmam Bare = *Kt.* yā ci nōmam Bare he fled hotfoot (= dība 1ee = *Kt.* durwā 3).   (*d*) yā ranta a na Bare = yā ranta a na ƙarē = *Kt.* yā dība cikin na ƙarē = *c above.*

D. (bārē = bārē-bārē) *m.* = bārēma.

ɓare (1) *Vb.* 1A = ɓāra 1, 2, 3.   (2) *Vb.* 3A *x* ƙurarrajī sum ∼ pimples have burst (= ƙyanƙyashē 2*b*).   (3) *Sk. m.* = ɓāri.

barē bana *Kt. epithet of* baɽewā.

bare-bare A.   (bare-bare) = bābare-bābare.

B. (barē-barē) = baram-baram.

C. (bārē-bārē) *m.* = bārēma.

bārē bārēma = bārēma.

Barēbarī *Vd.* Babarbare.

barēganī *Vd.* bargō.

barēkata *f.*   (1) petals of yākūwa (= sōɓarōdo).   (2) Barēkata, miyāgum bāƙī.   anā tūwō, kuna dafa wākē what disobliging individualists the Kanuri are !

bārēma (1) *f.* farming for hire.   (2) *m.* (*sg., pl.*) man farming for hire.

baɽewā *f.* (*pl.* barēyī).   (1) (*a*) gazelle

(*epithet is* barē bana), *Vd.* gammō 4. (*b*)
kuŋ gwammące ƙōshim ∼ dạ na ạkwīyạ
= giginyạ 2. (*c*) kōmē gudụm ∼ ạ hannum maị dawạ zā tạ kwaŋ =kōmē gudụm
∼ tạ bar dāji (i) there's no escaping Fate.
(ii) no subject can be fully mastered.
(*d*) ∼ tạ yi gudụ ? ɗantạ yạ yi rạrrạfẹ̄ ?
like breeds like. (*e*) barēwạ̄, yi tsallaŋkị
lāfīyạ life can now be enjoyed as that
particular anxiety is over. (*f*) bạ̄
bargēyī rūwā gạrēshị he's a great liar.
(2) gazelle-coloured horse. (3) barēwar
kūsā field-rat (= *Sk.* guɗɗū).

bargēyī (1) *Vd.* barēwā. (2) yanạ̄ bạ̄ ∼
rūwā he's telling lies.

bargā *f.* (*pl.* bargunạ). (1) stable ;
tethering-place in compound for horses
(= shạ̄makị = mōrị = barāyā 1). (2)
kō bargar wạnẹ dattījọ tạ̄ zaunạ (*lit.*
she'd grace the home of *any* respected
P.) (*a*) what a fine woman ! (*b*) what
a fine mare ! (3) ∼ Sarkin dōkị
epithet of shạ̄makị 2. (4) ɗam ∼
(*a*) stableboy. (*b*) = zạ̄gē.

bargajā (1) = tịnjim. (2) how badly this
work is done !

ɓargaję = ɓargajī *m.* hefty man.

bargi *m.* (1) large cornbin of double
grass-mats. (2) ∼ kētạ kōmā barbel,
thou breaker of nets ! (= ɓallị 2).

bạr'gi-bạrgī" *m.*, *f.* (*sg.*, *pl.*). (1)
quick-tempered P. who soon cools
down and regrets his anger (*epithet is* ∼
tukunyar Gwārī : sǎi ạ nēmam mikị
gurbị ; *Vd.* birgimā 4.). (2) scatter-
brained P. (*epithet is* ∼ sallạr kūrā).

bargo A. (bạrgō) *m.* (*pl.* bargunạ = barēganī) (*d.f. Ar.* burqu'). (1) any blanket
(*cf.* kụntū). (2) yā yāfạ bạrgwaŋ gīwā the
upper part of his body having no covering, he kept himself warṃ by folding his
arms across his chest. (3) pounding the
hands and arms of prisoners of war.
B. (bargọ) *Sk. m.* a red earth used in
making mīyạ.

ɓargō (1) marrow. (2) ɓargwaŋ
kạ̈i brain-substance. (3) ɓargwan dōkị
type of guineacorn, cloth, or bead.
(4) ∼ tsayę *Kt. m.* strapping youth.
(5) ɓargō *pl.* ɓarạ̄gē marrow-bone (*Vd.*
ɓarạ̄gē).

Bạrgū *f. Vd.* banzā.

bargunạ *Vd.* bargā ; bargō.

Bạrhāzạ name of a ɓōrī-spirit.

bạrhō *m.* (1) (*a*) knife like gārīyọ (*epithet
is* ∼ ƙīrạr sanyī). (*b*) *Vd.* sāram
bạrhō. (2) strong youth.

bari A.1 (barị) (*for conjugation Vd.*7 *below*).
(1) (*a*) left *x* yā bar shị nạŋ he left it
here. yā bar dūnīyạ he died. (*b*) (*with
dative*). (i) yā bar minị shī he left it for
me. nā bar makạ kuɗịŋ, kạ jūyạ I give
you a free hand to trade in the money.
duk sǎi ạ bar minị let it all be handed
over to me ! rāyukạd dạ sukạ hạlakạ,
wannan sǎi ạ bar wạ Allạ̄ sanị God
alone knows how many perished. (ii)
nā bar makạ *Vd.* bāshị 4. (iii) ạ bara
darị *Vd.* darị. (*c*) kạ bar shị gạ Allạ̄
yạ sākạ makạ leave it to God to avenge
you ! (*d*) *x* barị ta hatsī, kōwạnẹ irịn
tsirọ yanạ̄ ɓācị apart from corn, every
kind of crop is perishing (*cf.* bar ta
kallaŋ kai). (*e*) kōmē gudụm barēwā, tạ̄
bar dāji *Vd.* barēwā 1*c.* (*f*) *Vd.* 7*b below.*
(*g*) ạ bar wạ ɗam maị gidā kạrē *Vd.* tạ̄rā
2*b.* (*h*) anạ̄ barịn na zạune *Vd.* zạune 2*b.*
(*j*) turɓạ bā tạ̄ barịŋ gidā *Vd.* turɓạ 2.
(*k*) bạr shị ịndạ ka gan shị *Vd.* mụtụm
9*h.* (*l*) am bar fạ̈kī *Vd.* tēkị 1*b.* (*m*) ạ
bar banzā *Vd.* ạbạrbā. (*n*) bā yạ̄
barịŋ ƙātọ *Vd.* bugụ 1*c.*

(2) (*a*) allowed (*the construction is the
same as that stated for* sạ̄ *in* Gram.
159A *i.e. verb with* future *sense is
followed by* subjunctive. *With* past
sense, barị *in the* past tense *requires
the following verb to be in the* past
tense *or* subjunctive (*cf.* 2*c below.*
If barị *is in the* relative past, *then so is
the verb following* barị) *x* Allạ̄ yạ bar
mu, mu sāmụ may God allow us to get
it ! yanạ̄ barịmmụ mụ yī he's allowing
us to do it. yā bar dōkị yā (= yạ)
gudụ he let the horse run away.
lōkạcịn dạ akạ bar sụ sukạ yī when they
were allowed to do it. (*b*) *x* barị mụ
tạfi let's start out ! barị ŋ zō ŋ taịmakē
kạ let me come and help you ! barị
dǎi ŋ hūtạ I think I'll have a rest.
(*c*) *x* bạ sụ kō barị garī yạ wāyẹ ba sǎi
sukạ haŋgo ạɓōkaŋ gạɓā they caught
sight of the enemy afar even before
dawn.

(3) (soldier, place) surrendered *x* gạrī yā ~ the town surrendered.

(4) (*a*) ceased *x* (i) bạri kūkā stop crying ! (ii) nā bar tạfīyạ sǎi gọbe I've postponed going till to-morrow (= fāsạ). (iii) nā bar tạfīyạ I've cancelled the journey (= fāsạ). (iv) " ạ barị, ạ hūcẹ ! " shī ya kāwō rạbaŋ wani procrastination gives your adversary his chance. (v) kụ bar zamā stand up ! (vi) kại barị, hakạ sukạ yi in short, this is how they acted. (vii) bạri murnạ doŋ kạraŋkạ yā kāmạ zākị don't count your chickens before they're hatched ! (*Vd.* giriŋgidịshī). (*b*) mại bāwạ shī kẹ dạ bari the one who pays the piper, calls the tune. (*c*) bā sạ jịm " bạri ! " they won't listen to advice. (*d*) wạndạ bại ji " bạri ! " ba, yạ ji " hōhọ ! " once bitten, twice shy. (*e*) bạri tsọraŋ kirạ ạ fādạ, ji tsọran lạịfịn dạ ka yi it is the fact of *sinning* you should take to heart, not merely the fact that the Emir has sent for you. (*f*) bar fạdā (i) don't say it ! (ii) naturally !, of course ! (*g*) bạri taụnā, na bakạ nạ zụbā don't be in too much of a hurry ! (*h*) kụ bar ganiŋ ƙaŋƙantạ *Vd.* ạllūrạ 5. (*j*) bạri murnạ *Vd.* murnạ 2*c*. (*k*) mại gōnā bạri tsạ̄kī *Vd.* tsạ̄kī 2*b*. (*l*) bạri nēman jinī *Vd.* bābẹ 2. (*m*) kụ bar kisạn jēmāgẹ *Vd.* jēmāgẹ 1*d*. (*n*) bat tọnan cikịnsạ *Vd.* ɓaurē 3. (*o*) bạri gaịgayē *Vd.* gaịgayē. (*p*) bạri wallē, bạri wargī *Vd.* ƙạshim bạri wallē.

(5) (*a*) yā bar kạnsạ. (i) he is unmanageable. (ii) the thing is useless. (*b*) Allạ yạ barạ kạnsạ ạ sāmụ long life to the baby ! (*said by women visitors to a woman after her confinement*).

(6) *Vd.* Ạ bar shị, Ạ bar tạ, barạ, bạri tsụ̄kī, bạr mạ kại, bạr ni dạ ɓaidụ, bạn ni, bạr ni dạ mūgụ, dā 2*f*, birạ, shakkạ 3, tantamā.

(7) (*conjugation*) (*a*) past, future, subjunctive (*when object is understood*) barị. (*when object is stated*) bar. (*b*) (i) progressive (*without object*) barị. (*with object*) barịn *x* yanạ̄ barị he's leaving (it). yanạ̄ barịŋ Audụ he's leaving Audu. yanạ̄ barịnsạ he's leaving it. (ii) *Vd.* **4***a above*. (iii) barịŋ

kurcīyar gidā ƙọshin nāmạ he has better fish to fry. (iv) barịŋ kāshī ạ cikị, bā yạ̄ māganin yuŋwạ speak out when the time comes ! (v) barịm ɓākī kurụm shī ya kāwō jịn yuŋwạ cause and effect ! (*c*) imperative (*without object*) bạri. (*with pronoun object*) bạr *x* bạr shi leave it ! (*with noun object*) bar = bạri *x* bar kūkā = bạri kūkā stop crying !

A.2 (barị) *m.* (1) *Zar.* = bạbbākạ. (2) *Vd.* barị 7*b*.

B. (ɓạrī) *Sk.* = bạ̄ra *x* bạ̄rī yạccaŋ the year before last.

ɓari A. (ɓạ̄rī) *m.* (1) an yi ~ lawcourts are in recess because of festival. (2) mun yi ~ = an yi manạ̄ ~ we (schoolboys) are now on holiday because of festival (*cf.* tạshē : hūtū). (3) = tạshē 2.

B. (ɓạrị) *m.* shivering ; trembling.

C. (ɓạrī) *m.* (1) letting fall, dropping T. (*cf.* ɓarad dạ) *x* (*a*) jạ̄kī yā yi ~ dạ kāyā the donkey dropped its load. (*b*) nā yi ~ dạ shī I'm no longer friendly with him. (*c*) yā yi ~ dạ aikịŋ he's given up that work. (*d*) bā ạ̄ ~ ạ tsīnẹ dū if a transaction falls through you're bound to suffer some loss. (*e*) yanạ̄ ~ dạ kudī he's squandering money. (*f*) yā yi ~ he's been deposed. (*g*) tā yi ~ she's had a miscarriage or abortion (= zubar dạ 2*a*). (*h*) yā yi ~ *Vd.* tsīrạ 1*a*.ii. (2) gyạttạ ~ mender of calabashes (*Vd.* gyạttā). (3) *Vd.* ɓarin-*compounds.*

D. (ɓạrị) *m.* (1) (*a*) = azạ̄rā 2. (*b*) wạndạ ya bā kạ ɓạrịŋ gōrọ, in yā saŋ gụdā, yā bā kạ even a small gift shows goodwill (saŋ *is d.f.* sam *q.v.* " got "). (2) = ɓārīyạ *x* ɓarịŋ arẹ̄wā northern regions. (3) *Vd.* ɓarịn-*compounds.*

bạrigizạ *Kt. f.* extravagance.

bārikancī *m.* the undesirable ways of P. mentioned in bāriki 2.

bārī kạtsugụ *Kr.* = tsụ̄gē 3.

bārikāwā *pl. m.* servants of Europeans or persons regularly living with Europeans (*cf.* bāriki 2).

bāriki *Eng. m.* (*pl.* bārikōkī = bạrikai). (1) rest-house, European station, barracks, camp. (2) ɗam ~ *m.* (*f.* 'yar ~)

pl. 'yam ∼ soldier, messenger, malam and others who, though in European employ, do not live with Europeans (*cf.* bārikāwā).

bą rįkicą *Vd.* cirin.

barīmą *Ar. f.* (1) corkscrew. (2) ƙūsą mai ∼ screw.

ɓarįŋ akaifā *m.* tiny bit of kolanut.

ɓarim bąkī *m.* = ɓar dą 2.

barindą *Sk. m.* = barinję.

bārįŋgō *Sk. m.* = gargarī.

ɓārįŋ gurārą *used in* tsąkāninsu ∼ nē there's no difference between them.

barinję *m.* (*f.* barinjīyā) *pl.* rindāwā = rinji. (1) (*a*) Filani slave living near his master's village. (*b*) sǎi rugā tā kwānā lāfīyą rinji kę̄ kwānā lāfīyą one's master's misfortune is one's own. (2) meat seller (= mahaucī). (3) rinji *pl.* slave-village (*Vd.* 1).

ɓarįŋ kwą̄kyārą = *Sk.* ɓarįŋ kuŋkyārą (1) = ɓar dą 2. (2) extravagance.

barin makauniya (ɓarim mąkaunīyā) *m.* (*lit.* blind woman dropping various grains and being unable then to sort them out). (1) anything mixed up (*e.g.* variegated cloth ; bracelet of various colours). (2) yā yi minį ∼ he slapped me over the eyes.

bari shakką *Vd.* shakką 3.

bari tantamā *Vd.* tantamā.

bari tsūkī *Sk. m.* epithet of bulrush-millet sproutéd in poor soil, but regarded as better than no crop at all.

ɓariya A. (ɓārīyą) *f.* region *x* ɓārīyar arę̄wā northern regions. ɓārīyar hannun dāma on the right (= ɓari 2).

B. (ɓarīyą) *f.* (1) the Nile-perch. (2) *Vd.* ɓaryą.

ɓarjajje (ɓąrjajjē) = ɓąrzajjē.

barjak (barjak) = farjak.

ɓarje A. (ɓarję) *Vb.* 1A ground all of (*Vd.* ɓarzą).

B. (ɓąrjē). (1) *Vd.* ɓąrzā. (2) *m.* (*a*) = ɓąrzā 1*b.* (*b*) *Kt.* = ƙufurtū. (*c*) *Sk.* = fīri. (*d*) *Sk.* first signs of hair on the chin.

ɓarji A. (ɓarji) *Vd.* ɓąrzā 2.

B. (ɓarji) *m.* = ɓąrzā 1*b.*

barka A.1 (barką) *Ar. m.* (1) (*a*) (i) ∼ dą rānā good day ! (*cf.* 5). (ii) ∼ dą zūwą = ∼ dą isǭwā glad to see you !,

---

glad you are back safely ! (iii) ∼ dą azzįkī *Vd.* azzįkī 2*b.* (*b*) ∼ dą aikį = barkąŋką dą aikį I hope the work I see you at may proceed well ! (*reply is* hǫhǫ jūnā *if the greeter is also at work*). (*c*) ∼ dą shigǭwā welcome ! (*reply,* ∼ kądǎi). (*d*) barkąntą your best course is to say no more, otherwise you'll involve yourself in contradictions ! (*e*) *Vd.* wutā 1*p.* (*f*) barkąmmu dą sāmum bąkī *Vd.* sāmu 2*b.* (2) yā yi minį ∼ he used valedictory wish to me (*using expression such as in* 1) : *cf.* ąlbarką. (3) barką *is replied to sneezer saying* ąlhamdu lįllāhį (barką *is said by both sexes, but male should rightly say* yarhąmullāhu). (4) zą̄ mu gidam ∼ we (women, hāji, men returned from journey) are off to congratulate woman on her confinement. (5) ∼ dą rānā (*a*) *Vd.* 1*a.* (*b*) *m.* cadger. (6) nā įsa ∼ (*a*) I've realized my wish. (*b*) an yi ta ∼ one's wishes have been fulfilled. (*c*) yā yi ∼ he had a stroke of luck. (*d*) barkąmmu we're in luck's way ! (7) ∼ bąntę̄, 'yā tā haifu ram būɗar kąi all's not gold that glitters ! (8) jēji bai ƙārę ciŋ wutā ba, fąrā bā tą̄ yi wą 'yarūwā tatą ∼ don't count your chickens before they're hatched !

A.2 (Barką) man's name *x* (1) gą̄ kushēwar ∼ , gą̄ ta ką̄ransą the two are inseparable like David and Jonathan. (2) nōmam ∼ wurin jīyą *m.* constantly harping on one's past statements or deeds.

ɓarka A. (ɓarką) *Vb.* 1A (*Ar.* faraqa). (1) ripped open. (2) forced one's way through *x* (*a*) nā ∼ daŋgā I forced my way thro' the fence. sum ɓarkō cikiŋ ƙasarmu they invaded our country. (*b*) ɓarką wurin naŋ don rūwā yą wucę make a hole here whereby the water may flow away ! (*c*) yā ∼ ta he deflowered her (virgin). (3) unsewed.

B. (ɓarkā) *Vb.* 2. (1) ripped off. (2) pulled up plants (dāwą ; maiwā) for transplanting.

barkace A. (barkącē) *Vd.* barkątą.

B. (barkącē) *Vb.* 3A deteriorated.

barkącēwą *f.* = barkątayyą.

barkaci *Vd.* barkątą.

barkallā = bārakallā.

barkatạ *Vb.* 2 (*p.o.* barkạcē, *n.o.* barkạci) congratulated P. by using formula as in barkạ 1.

ɓarkạtā *Vb. negatively used.* (1) tun sāɓē bạm ɓarkạtạ kōmē ba I've not done a stroke of work to-day. (2) baị ∼ minị kōmē ba he hasn't done the slightest T. for me. (3) bā shaurā yạ ɓarkạtạ kōmē he's a useless kind of P.

bạrkạtaị *adv.* (1) (*a*) in disorder. (*b*) *Vd.* cī 14. (2) gạrī yā yi ∼ these are hard times.

bạrkạtayyạ *f.* mutual congratulation (*as in* barkạ 1).

ɓarkẹ (1) *Vb.* 3A. (*a*) (seam, wall) split. (*b*) (i) yā ∼ dạ dārīyā he burst out laughing. (ii) yā ∼ dạ kūkā he burst out crying (i, ii = fashẹ). (iii) yā ∼ dạ zāwọ he had diarrhœa. (iv) kūrā tā ∼ dạ zāwọ *Vd.* kūrā 30. (*c*) crowd or water streamed out of place. (*d*) yā ɓarkō it (crowd or water) streamed into place. (2) *Vb.* 1A = ɓarkạ.

ɓar'ke-ɓarkē '' *m.* shreds of cotton material.

ɓarkị *m.* (1) strips of native cloth tacked together (kaŋgẹ) for dyeing. (2) small piece of cloth (= ƙyallē). (3) yā yi ∼ (*a*) he's cadged T. (*b*) he's got some advantage. (*c*) thief got good haul.

barkọ *x* ∼ dạ yājị, itācam Baucī *cry of pepper-hawkers.*

bạrkọnō *m.* (1) (*a*) (i) generic name of pepper. (ii) nā ci ∼ I picked peppers. (iii) *Vd.* barkọ, barkwạdạsō. (*b*) kụduddụɓim ∼ īyāƙacim mạcẹ gwīwạ women are very cautious. (*c*) namijị ∼ nẹ, sǎi an taunạ zā ạ san yājịnsạ it takes time to know a person. (2) Audu ∼ nē = Audụ bạrkọnam mutānē nẹ Audụ is irascible (= yājị 2*a* = wutā 2). (3) bạrkọnan tsōfwā insect making one's eyes smart. (4) bạrkọnaŋ hạmsiŋ *Vd.* dādī 5. (5) *Vd.* gwāgwạdā. (6) bạrkọnaŋ wurị *Vd.* hanzarī 2*b*.

ɓarkūwā *Sk. f.* place where stitch is undone or wall is cracked.

bạrkwạdạsō *m.* joking name for pepper by women.

barkwanānāwā *Vd.* bạbarkwanẹ.

barkwancị *m.* (1) joking (*cf.* bạbarkwanẹ). (2) cikị yā yi matạ ∼ she found she wasn't pregnant after all.

bạr mạ kāị *m.* T. one made well, as it is for oneself, not for sale.

bạrmịt = barmụs *Eng. m.* vermouth.

bạrmūshị *m.* pall (= *Kt.* marạkī 2).

bạrmụt *m.* = bạrmịt.

bạrmụtālị *m.* any French silver coin.

barnạ *f.* wearing white and black turbans together.

ɓarnā *f.* (1) damage *x* (*a*) yā yi ∼ he did damage. (*b*) kā fayẹ ɓarnā kạmaŋ gātam birị boy, you're as destructive as a monkey ! (*c*) wurim ɓarnar gīwā bā ā kulāwā dạ ɓarnar birị in face of serious disaster small woes pass unnoticed. (*d*) abịŋ zaị kai gạ ɓarnā it will lead to trouble. (*e*) tsīgī yakẹ ɓarnā *Vd.* tsīgī 4, ɓērū. (*f*) birị yā yi ∼ *Vd.* birị 1*c*. (*g*) fāshị ɓarnar aikị *Vd.* fāsạ 1*e*. (*h*) ūwar ∼ *Vd.* gāgạ. (2) any undesirable act or conduct (*x* brawling, extravagance, mistakes, etc.*) (3) tūwam ∼ feast on day after bride goes to husband's house. (4) ɓarnar cikị violent diarrhœa.

ɓarnạcē *Vb.* 1C = ɓarnạtā *Vb.* 1C = ɓarnạtạ *Vb.* 2 (*p.o.* ɓarnạcē, *n.o.* ɓarnạci) damaged.

ɓarnatad dạ *Vb.* 4B squandered.

Barnāwā *Vd.* Bạbarnẹ.

bạr ni dạ 'Baidu *Kt. m.* type of large leather bag (= hōri 'Baidụ).

bạr ni dạ mūgụ = bạn ni dạ mūgụ.

Bạrnō (1) Bornu. (2) ạ ƙārạ ∼ dawākị ? debt on top of debt ! (= dāmisạ 4). (3) *Vd.* tākutạhā.

bạrnus = bạrnūsị *Ar. m.* burnous.

barọ *m.* (1) dried fruit of kanyạ. (2) quid of chewed tobacco. (3) *Sk.* hay (= iŋgirịcī 1).

ɓarọ *m.* (1) fool. (2) = fạnzạ.

barōdō *m.* barōdan jiminā = jam bạrōdō. (1) (*a*) full grown cock ostrich. (*cf.* jiminā; bịcịlmī). (*b*) suŋ haƙẹ, idạnsụ idạn jam bạrōdō sǎi iccẹ they stood aloof, glaring. (2) bạrōdan tạlotạlō full grown cock-turkey. (3) *Vd.* jan ∼ .

barōgī *Kt. m.* = ƙaŋgū 2.

barōrī *Vd.* barạ A.2.

baroro A. (barōrọ = bārōrọ) *m.* (1) (*a*) crop of bird (*cf.* tantānī) = *Sk.* balikọtō = *Sk.* balikunjī = kurūru 1 = kundū = *Sk.* kunjī. (2) blister.
  B. (Barọrō) = Bararō.

barōshi *Eng. m.* brush. ka yi masa ~ brush it !

barrādi *Ar. m.* teapot.

barrai *Vd.* bara A.2.

barsā *Vb.* 2 *Nor.* = bazgā.

barshē *Kt.* = ballē.

barta A. (barta) = batta.
  B. (bartā) *Vb.* 2 *Vd.* barci.

bar ta kallaŋ kai apart from you *x* ~ ; kō wanda ya fī ka ba zai yi mini haka ŋ kyālẹ ba I'd not suffer such treatment from your superior, far less from you (*cf.* bari 1*d*).

bartakē *m.* = abāwā 1.

bartak kafa *Vd.* barci.

bartī *Kt. m.* (1) returning to school after barī. (2) Filani migration from wet-season grounds to dry-season grazing (*Vd.* rānī 3).

bartīla *f.* white topee such as worn ceremonially by administrative officers.

Bartō = A jēfas (but only applied to girl).

baru A. (bārū) *f.* hyena.
  B. (barū) *x* ~ dūkīyas sama *epithet of* pigeon.

baru = barọ 1.

*barūda *Ar. f.* mai ~ P. liable to chills. sanyinsa ~ nē he's liable to chills (*cf.* harāra 4*b*).

barugāgẹ *m., f.* (barugāgīyā). (1) P. living in rugā. (2) retiring kind of P.

barugumzā = būrumā 2.

baruma *m. Hadejiya Hausa* village-headman.

Barūmayī *m.* (*f.* Barūmayā) *pl.* Rūmāwā (1) Filani tribe of Birnin Rūmā in *Kt.* (2) *cf.* tāshin jākin 'yan Rūmā.

barunjẹ = barinjẹ.

barūrūwa *Vd.* bara A.2.

barūshi = barōshi.

bā rūwāna *m.* any fragile plant on riverbank giving way when clutched for support (*cf.* rūwā G).

barwā, barwai *Vd.* bara A.2.

barya *f.* (1) *Vd.* bārīya, barīya. (2) dam ~ any rat.

barza (1) lower part of outside of town wall

(hence, if wall falls, whole wall becomes barza). (2) *Kt.* lower part of outside or inside of town wall. (3) *Jos Mining Hausa* barzar kūrā limestone (= farsar kūrā).

barza A. (barza) *Vb.* 1A (*cf.* barzā 1) (1) ground flour coarsely for burabuskọ (*cf.* fantsarā). (2) tā ~ tūwō she made barzọ-food (*cf.* tsakī, *Kt.* tantadī, lilis, fantsarā).
  B. (barzā). (1) *f.* (*a*) being occupied in coarse grinding to make burabuskọ. (*b*) *Secondary v.n. of* barza. (2) *Vb.* 2 (*p.o.* barjē, *n.o.* barji). (*a*) yā barjē ni = yā barjē ni da zāgi he roundly abused me. (*b*) yā barji dōkinsa he spurred on his horse full gallop. (*c*) yā barji nōmā he kept on hoeing with all his might (*Vd.* garzā 2).

Barzahu *Ar. m.* place of waiting of departed spirits three days before Judgment-day.

barzānīyā *f.* aimless roving.

barzọ *m.* (1) tūwam ~ the food tūwō made of coarsely-ground flour (*cf.* barza). (2) *Sk.* one speaking without thought.

bas *Ar.* only *x* sulẹ gōma ~ only 10*s.* ka kira shi ~ merely call him !

bas (1) yā karyẹ ~ it snapped snap ! (2) yā yi ~ da kūkā he burst out crying.

basa A. (bāsā) *Sk.* = bā da *x* yā ~ he gave (it).
  B. (Bāsa) (1) *m., f.* (*sg., pl.*) P. of the Bassa Tribe of Kabba and Niger Provinces. (2) gīwar ~ cloth with alternate strips of farī and sākị.

bāsā *Vb.* 2 (*p.o.* bāshē, *n.o.* bāshi) broke off branch or fruit.

basa-basa = bāibāi.

bāsad da *Sk.* = bāsā.

basafalẹ *m.* (*f.* basafalīyā) *adj.* unusual.

bāsaisai *Vd.* bāshi.

bā sājẹ *m.* slyly benefiting by a coincidence (*x thief shouting " stop thief ! " ; P. sent with letter using chance to state his own case, etc.) : its epithet is* fitsārim mai jēgọ " urinating of a nursing-mother " (*for she blames her child*) = *Kt.* wā kā rabẹ (*Vd.* jēgọ 3).

basake ciki *m.* (*sg., pl.*) intimate friend (*cf.* sake 2).

bạsakkarę *m. pl.* sakkarāwā *Sk.* carpenter.

Bạsakkwacę *m.* (*f.* Bạsakkwacịyā = *Sk.* Bạsakkwatạ) *pl.* Sakkwatāwā. (1) Sokoto P. (2) *Vd.* Shēhụ 3c ; jạllō 3.

bạsạko cikị *Kt.* = bạsạke cikị.

bạsambānę *m.* (*pl.* sambanāwā) P. with Arab father and Hausa, etc., mother.

bāsancē *Vd.* bāsantạ.

bạsaŋgalā *f.* type of horse's gait (= jijjigę 2).

bāsantạ *Vb.* 2 (*p.o.* bāsancē, *n.o.* bāsanci) *x* nā bāsanci sulę uḳụ I incurred a debt of 3s.

bāsanyạ *Sk. f.* ~ tamạtar bāshị borrowing to pay a debt.

bạsarākę = *Sk.* bạsaraucę *m.* (*pl.* sarākuna *which is also pl. of* Sarkī). (1) officeholder under Emir (= sạrạ̄kī *q.v.* = rawạni 2 = sạrạ̄kai = masạrạuci). (2) *his epithet is* Tụŋgumạ, mạnyam birnī = jan dọ̄rinī, matạ̄kạ yārọ rụmā). (3) *wife of* 1 *is* bạsarākịyā. (4) *Vd.* matsạ sạrạ̄kī.

Bạsarkę *m.* (*f.* Bạsarkịyā) *pl.* Sarkāwā one of the Sarka people in Argungu who are fishermen.

bāsāsạ *f.* (1) the depredations of the war between Yūsufụ and Tukụr in Kano in 1893. (2) (*a*) any destructive war. (*b*) yā haddạsạ ~ he started civil war. (*c*) zā kạ yi minị bāsāsạ ? do you expect me to sell to you at a loss ?

basgō *Vd.* bazgō.

bāshā *f.* (1) the game ạ rausạ. (2) tanạ ~ dạ mazā she's a " tomboy ".

bāshādạ *Kt. f.* = binjimā.

bāshākālạ *Sk.* tā yi ~ her mouth is stained with kolanut.

bāshāḳọ *m.* = mạshāḳọ.

ɓashar *used in* yā yi ~ dạ mụrmụshī he smiled broadly.

ɓashar-ɓashạr = fashā-fạshạ.

Basharī *man's name.*

bāshāshạ = wāshāshạ.

bāshē *Vd.* bā dạ.

ɓāshē *Vd.* ɓạsā.

bạ̄'she-bạ̄shē‖ *m.* constant incurring of debts.

bashi A. (bāshī) *m.* (*pl.* bāsūsūwạ = bāsūsukạ = bāsōshī = *Sk.* bāsaisai). (1) loan of money *x* yā bā nị bāshim pạm bịyar he lent me five pounds (bāshị =

sum not repayable for some time, *cf.* rạncē, rạntā, rạntā). (2) (*a*) debt (*epithet is* ~ bạ̄ su, kạ hūtạ = Ḳutuŋkū, ɗan tsịyā na fārị). (*b*) (i) yā ci ~ = yā ɗauki ~ = yā kạrɓi ~ he incurred a debt. (ii) yā ɗauki bāshin dōkị he bought a horse on credit. (iii) dạ gọ̄be kạn ɗau ~ *Vd.* gọ̄be 1e. (*c*) kạn ɗau ~ *Vd.* lallamī. (*d*) yā cinyę ~ he borrowed and failed to pay. (*e*) *Vd.* bī 8. (*f*) yā bā nị bāshin rīgā he sold me a gown on credit. (*g*) ~ hanjī nē, yanạ̄ cikiŋ kōwā debt is common to everybody. (*h*) *cf.* tūwam ~ . (3) kadạ rạncē yạ zamā ~ pay your debt when it is due ! (*cf.* 1). (4) nā bar makạ ~ I'll get even with you yet ! (5) kōwā ya ɗauki bāshim barcī, yạ̄ bīyā you cannot burn the candle at both ends. (6) yā ci bāshim fariŋ watạ he's got syphilis (*said to cause splitting of head*), *Vd.* watạ 1e. (7) zạn-cansạ wani kudī, wani ~ his statement is half true, half false. (8) tamạtar ~ *Vd.* bāsanyạ. (9) tā zamā ~ *Vd.* ŋgō 2b. (10) tsōfam ~ *Vd.* fatarā 2.

B. (bāshī) *m.* stench (= wārī).

ɓạ̄shi *Vd.* ɓạsā.

bashinō *m.* (1) = shūnim battạ, *q.v. under* shūnī 3. (2) sharp practice. (3) false statement.

bāshirkinī *m.* rubbing oil into skins to add to their weight.

*bạ̄ shirwạ *Sk.* ɗam ~ = mazạ̄wọ̄yiŋ kạsūwā.

basīdạ *f.* = bạsītsạ.

bạsillā *f.* (*pl.* bạsillū = bạsillai = basillōlī) (1) large needle for sewing leather, etc. (= *Kt.* tạsūɓalā), *cf.* asirkā 2. (2) ~ ạbin diŋkin dūnịyạ Waziri, thou peacemaker !

bāsịmạ *Kt. f.* = bāsụmạ.

Bạsīnī *m.* (*f.* Bạsīnịyā) *pl.* Sīnāwā Chinaman.

bạsīrạ *Ar. f.* insight.

bạsītsạ *f.* type of stitching (= ciŋ wuyạ).

ɓaskatạ *f. used in* ɓaskatạ tā fāɗị the thing is " in the bag ".

bāsōshī *Vd.* bāshi.

ɓasshē *Vd.* ɓatar dạ.

bạ̄ su, kạ hūtạ *Vd.* bāshị 2a.

bāsụḳur *Eng. m.* bicycle (= dōkiŋ ḳarfę = *Sk.* lạulāwạ).

bāsuֱmֱa *f.* (*pl.* bāsumōmī) any coloured
or patterned European cloth (*Vd.*
sֱandā 3) = barbarō.
bāsur = bāsūri = bāsūrֱe *Ar. m.* piles
(haemorrhoids), *cf.* rānā 4*j*.
bֱa sūsֱa *f.* (1) = ֱkazwā 1. (2) = daudֱar
Maguzāwā. (3) yā jֱēֱfē ni dֱa ~ placing
his fingers in sling-shape, he flicked
gravel at me.
bāsūsūwֱa = bāsūsukֱa *Vd.* bāshi.
bata A. (batֱa) *Vb.* 3A *Sk. x* nā ~ dֱa
shī I chatted with him (*cf.* bֱatū).
  B. (bātֱa) *f.* sun jā ~ they (soldiers,
spectators, etc.) formed a line (= dāgā).
  C. (bātā) *Sk. f.* bundle of thatching-
grass.
ɓata A. (ɓātֱa) *Vb.* 1A. (1) (*a*) (i) spoiled.
(ii) yanֱā ~ ֱkasā he is stirring up revolt.
(*b*) (i) gֱa indֱa zā ֱa ~ haŋkֱalin darֱe,
ֱa yi sūnā it is a matter requiring consideration.   (ii) ɓātֱa haŋkֱalin darē
kֱa yi sūnā here are some puzzles,
quizzes for you to solve ! (*c*) Kֱāzā,
ɓātֱa wuriŋ kwānaŋki you spoil your
chances.   (2) (*a*) yā ~ yārinyֱa he
seduced a girl. (*b*) yā ~ ֱkaŋwֱa *Vd.*
ɓērā 1*h*. (3) yā ~ fuskֱa he scowled.
(4) (*a*) mum ~ = ɓātֱāwā tā shigֱa
tsֱakānimmu we have quarrelled.   (*b*)
yā ~ tsֱakānimmu it caused us to
quarrel.   (*c*) yֱanzu mun sֱami ~
wֱāsansu now we can foil them. (5) (*a*)
(i) yā ~ rֱǎi he became despondent,
offended.   (ii) yā ~ mini rֱǎi = yā ~
mini zūciֱyā he saddened me, offended
me. (iii) ~ ukֱu *Vd.* tuntuɓֱe 3, kֱunū
1*a*.   (*b*) ~ kֱǎi to worry oneself *x*
kadֱa kֱa ~ kֱaŋkֱa ֱa wurintֱa do not
feel worried about her ! (6) (*a*) tukunyā
tā ~ wuyֱansֱa the pot boiled over
(= hֱaukā 2*b* = bֱorī 3).   (*b*) ~ bֱākī
Vd. bֱorī 3*b*. (7) yā ~ sūnāna he brought
me into disrepute.   mֱai ~ sūnaŋ Allֱa
blasphemer.   (8) (*a*) ֱa ~ zūciֱyas sֱa,
san naŋ mīyֱa tֱa yi dādī = sǎi zūciֱyas
sֱa tā ɓāci, mīyֱa kֱaŋ yi zāֱkī everyone
acts on the principle of " devil take the
hindmost ! " ; desperate causes need
desperate remedies.   (*b*) ~ mīyֱa *Vd.*
mīyֱa 9*g*.   (9) ~ kīwֱo *m., f.* constitu-
tionally thin P. or animal who resists
all efforts at fattening. (10) squandered

(money, etc.) *x* (*a*) bֱa zֱai ~ lōkֱacinsֱa
gֱa jiŋ lֱābārinsֱa ba he won't waste his
time in listening to an account of it
(= ɓatar dֱa).   (*b*) ɓātֱa nākֱa *Vd.*
kֱatalֱa.   (10A) spent *x* ֱabiŋ dֱa akֱa ~
the amount spent (= ɓatar dֱa).   (11)
yā ~ jī he did not hear it properly.
yā ~ ganī he did not see it clearly.
(12) ~ mֱa gizֱo yānā *Vd.* yānā 3*b*.
(13) (*a*) ~ gֱārī *Vd.* wākē 9.   (*b*) ~
bֱaibayֱa *Vd.* būnū.   (14) ~ farī *Vd.*
mֱākubֱa 2.   (15) ɓātֱa mֱōrīyֱa *Vd.*
Giֱndau.   (16) ɓātֱa ragō gōnā *Vd.*
ֱkuduֱjī.   (17) *Vd.* ɓātֱa-*compounds.*
(18) *f. name for* girl whose marriage-
expenses cost her husband much
money.
  B. (ɓātā) *Vb.* 2 (*p.o.* ɓֱacē, *n.o.* ɓֱaci)
Sk. abused P. (= zֱāgā), *Vd.* ɓāci 5.
  C. (ɓatֱa) (1) *Vb.* (*progressive* yanֱā
ɓatֱa = yanֱā ɓacēwā, *cf.* ɓacֱe) (*before
dative, we use* ɓacֱe) (*a*) (i) became lost *x*
jֱākīna yā ~ = jֱākīna yā ɓacֱe mini
I lost my donkey. (ii) *Vd.* matֱambayī.
(iii) watֱa yā ɓacֱe matֱa her periods
have not come, showing she is pregnant
(*cf.* ɓatֱaŋ watֱa).   (iv) ɓace mini dֱa
ganī get out of my sight ! (v) hֱājֱar
mֱāsū gֱarī yā ~ *Vd.* rānā 7*a*.   (vi) yā
dadֱe dֱa ~ *Vd.* fādֱa 4. (vii) askā tā ~
mֱai kōrā *Vd.* biֱrinciŋ kulֱa. (*b*) made
a mistake. (*c*) vanished. (*d*) lost one's
way *x* (i) yā ~ = yā ~ hanyֱa = hanyֱa
tā ɓacֱe masֱa he lost his way (=
hanyֱa 1*h* = yā dֱa 4*a*). (ii) iŋ idֱo
zֱai ~, yֱa ~ ֱa tsakֱar kā if you *must*
make ducks and drakes of your money,
do it *yourself* rather than give it to
some rogue to squander ! (iii) wֱandֱa
bֱai ~ dֱa darֱe ba, bֱa yֱa ~ dֱa rānā ba
if P. is able to do difficult T., then how
much more a T. which is easy ! (*e*) *Vd.*
bֱautā 4. (2) *m.* mistake *x* (*a*) ~ mukֱa
yi we made a mistake. (*b*) dֱa ɓatֱaŋ
rֱigā, gāra kֱarantsֱayī a slight loss is
better than a big one. (*c*) *Vd.* ɓֱakatan-
taŋ.   (*d*) kīwֱam ~ *Vd.* tantabֱarā.
(*e*) *Vd.* ɓatan-*compounds.*
  D. (ɓātā) *Vb.* 2 (*p.o.* ɓֱacē, *n.o.* ɓֱacī)
x watֱa yā ɓֱacē tֱa = ɓatֱa 1*a* iii..
bֱa tֱākā *f.* (1) haunted or forbidden place.
(2) cemetery.

bặ ta kāshī *m.* sun yi ⁓ they came to blows.

bặtặ̄kashī *m.* herb used as substitute for karkashī.

bặtakệrī *m.* = bặzāḳīyā.

bặ ta kulkī *m., f. (sg., pl.)* Bagirmi.

ɓātal *Kt. m.* = ɓācē.

bātặlā *Vb.* 1C *Sk.* = ɓātặ.

bātalad dặ *Vb.* 4B *Sk.* squandered.

bātặl gwaŋgặ *m.* type of thin bặsillā-needle for sewing mashimfidī, kặtīfặ or lifịdī.

batali A. (bātặlī) *Sk. m. (Ar.)* spoiling ; squandering *x* yanặ̄ bātặlinsặ he's spoiling it, squandering it.

B. (bặtặlī) *Kt. m.* spoiling ; squandering *x* yanặ̄ ⁓ dặ shī he's spoiling it, squandering it.

bặtālīyặ *Eng. f.* battalion. fặs bặtālīyặ the First Battalion.

Bặtặmbūtụ *m. (f.* Bặtặmbūtịyā) *pl.* Tambūtāwā (1) P. of Timbuctoo. (2) *Vd.* hặmīlặ.

ɓatặŋ alặ'andị = ɓatặm ɓặkặtantặŋ = ɓatặm ɓặkī = ɓatặm biriŋkụlā *(cf.* birinciŋ kulặ) = *ɓatặŋ kặtặgặŋgặnā *m.* = ɓặkặtantặŋ *q.v.*

ɓātanci *Zar.* (1) slandering. (2) quarrel *(cf.* ɓātā).

ɓatặŋ gautā *x* bar ṇ sam ɓatặŋ gautāna I'm going on the spree, let to-morrow go hang !

ɓatặŋ kặi *m.* losing one's way. yā yi tānặdī kō dặ zại yi ɓatặŋ kặi he took steps in case he should lose his way.

bặtaŋkōlệ *Kt. m.* = mặtaŋkōlệ.

ɓatặŋ nōnọ ặ ḳirjim bụdurwā sudden disappearance.

ɓatặŋ wặlāwặlā = ɓatặŋ warkặ *m.* = ɓặkặtantặŋ.

ɓatặŋ watặ *m.* ceasing of menstruation (hailặ) through pregnancy *(cf.* ɓatặ 1*a.*iii).

bātanyặ *Sk. f.* = bātā.

ɓātặ ragō gōnā *Vd.* ḳudụjī.

ɓatar dặ *Vb.* 4A. *(p.o. also* ɓasshē) (1) spent *x* nā ⁓ kudī I spent money. kadặ kặ ɓasshē sụ don't spend *or* squander it (money) ! (= shāfệ 1 *b.vi* = ɓātặ 10, 10A = kashệ 3*h*). (2) disposed of *x* ɓatar minị dặ dōḳịna dispose of my horse for me ! (3) *(a)* yā ⁓ sauna he misled me (*literally* or *figuratively*). *(b)* gudụm

ɓad dặ san dōḳị *m.* playful flight of bride to parents' home after wedding. *(c)* ɓặd dặ bặ̄ḳō *Vd.* turbặ. *(d)* ɓad dặ ặbiŋkặ *Vd.* gāwụrzặ ; kặtalặ. (4) yā ⁓ kặmā he disguised himself. (5) ɓặd dặ kọ̄kwai, jịrặci bābụ *epithet of* wastrel.

bặtặrnặ̄ḳā *f.* (1) ambling gait of horse *(cf.* tặrnặḳī). (2) unintelligible statement.

Bặtặsặyī *m. (f.* Bặtặsặyā) *pl.* Tāsāwā P. of Tāsāwā.

bātặyā *Vb.* 3A *Sk.* went for a stroll.

ɓặtayyặ *f. Sk.* mutual abuse.

bặtē *Zar.* = batē-bặtệ *Kt. m.* = fatē-fặtệ.

Bặtōraŋkệ *m. (f.* Bặtōraŋkịyā = Bặtōraŋkặ) *pl.* Tōraŋkāwā member of the ruling Filani family at Sokoto.

bātsā *Ar. f.* lewd conversation *(cf.* ặlfặshā).

batsa-batsa A. (bātsa-bātsa) variegated *x* yā sặ rawặnī ⁓ he put on variegated turban.

B. (batsa-batsa) = tịnjim.

bặ tsalam *Vd.* bặ 10*b.*

bặtsai *Vd.* batsīyặ.

bặtsặl-bặtsặl = bặtsặr-bặtsặr *m.* poor quality of work *x* ặbincin nặŋ ⁓ ya-kệ this food's been badly prepared.

bặtsallē *Vd.* dặddawā 1*b.*

batsatsa A. (bātsātsa) *x* gāshịnsặ yā tsayặ ⁓ his hair stood on end.

B. (bặtsātsặ) what ruffled hair ! : what ruffled feathers !

C. (batsatsa) = tịnjim.

D. (bặtsātsặ) *Sk. f.* the move in darặ preventing opponent putting down his last piece (= kụllālēnịyā 1 = kụndumbặ).

batsặtsē *Vb.* 1C *Sk.* set out pieces as in bặtsātsặ.

bātsệ (1) *Vb.* 1A filled T. to the brim. (2) *Vb.* 3A *(a)* is (was) full to the brim. *(b)* is (was) enraged. *(c)* garin nặŋ, cịkarsặ dặ bātsệwā tasặ in the whole of this town.

batsīyặ *f. (pl.* batsīyōyī = *Sk.* bặtsai) Gambian oribi.

batso A. (bặtsō) = bặdō.

B. (batsọ) *Vd.* dặddawā 1*b.*

batsō-bặtsō = bặtsặl-bặtsặl.

battặ (1) *f. (pl.* battōcī). *(a)* small receptacle of hide, metal, or wood for

snuff, tobacco, etc. (b) yaŋkam ～ m.
evenly slicing through meat, fish,
sugarcane, etc. (c) battạr ạgụlū Kt. =
tābạr ụŋgụlū. (2) m., f. very short P.
(3) Vd. karọ for karạm battạr k̃arfẹ.
(4) Vd. shikạm battạ. (5) shūnim
battạ Vd. shūnī 3.

battạl x d̃am ～ Sk. m. spendthrift.

battạlā Vb. 1C Sk. (1) squandered.
(2) spoiled.

battalad dạ Vb. 4B Sk. squandered.

battạrī m. (pl. bạttạrai) = gafakạ.

bạttatạŋ Ar. (1) yā bar sụ ～ he left them
uncared for. (2) suddenly x ～
sāi mukạ gan shị we suddenly saw him.

battị = battạ 3.

battōcī Vd. battạ.

bạtū m. (pl. batūtūwạ = batuttukạ) Sk.
(1) conversation x sunạ̄ ～ they're conversing. (2) matter, affair (1, 2 =
mạganạ). (3) bạtun dūnīyạ small talk.
(4) bạtum banzā rein-tassel held by
rider. (5) bạtun regarding x lạ̄bārịn dạ
zā ạ yi bạtunsạ the news which will be
given about it.

Bạtūrẹ m. (f. Bạtūrịyā) pl. Tūrāwā =
Tụ̄rạ̄wā (1) (a) white man, European
(including Arab or Syrian), Vd. jā
A.3b. (b) for epithet, Vd. tsūlịyā 7 ;
Aibō, Ạgwại 2. (2) sạnnū ～ (a)
greeting, White man ! (b) greeting,
you Croesus ! (3) name for boy born
on Tuesday, implying he will be rich
like a European (a girl born on Tuesday
is called Bạtūrịyā), cf. gandū 2f, kudī
1q, Tūrancī, Tạlātạ, Tūrai, bāwạ 8a. ii.
(4) ạbin nạm ～ nē = hājạn nạm
Bạtūrịyā cẹ this article brings in a large
profit. (5) Bạtūrẹ = mại hancịm ～
two-holed cowry. (6) bạtūrạn cācā P.
financing gambler (cf. Tūrancī 3, gạ̄gū).
(7) kai nẹ Bạtūrạn tudụ (said mockingly)
you albino, you ! (cf. zạbīyā). (8)
bạtūrịyā f. (a) red chicken. (b) type of
grasshopper.

Bạturkị m. (f. Bạturkịyā) pl. Tụrkạ̄wā
a Turk.

bạturūtụrụ Sk. m. disease causing P. to
stare open-mouthed.

batuttukạ, batūtūwạ Vd. bạtū.

bau A. (bau) (1) = bal 2. (2) = ạlkarfạ
1, 2.

B. (bau) (1) = bạl. (2) k̃ilū tā
jāwō ～ it's the thin edge of the wedge !

ɓau A. (ɓau) x mĩkịnsạ yā yi ～ his sore
place has spread.

B. (ɓau) x yanạ̄ da k̃arfī kạmam ～
he's immensely strong.

bā'ū m. the bird tsạ̄da.

baubạucē, baubāwạ etc. Vd. babbạucē,
bạbbāwạ etc.

Baucī f. (1) Bauchi. (2) Vd. banzā ;
barkọ.

baud̃ạ (1) Vb. 3A x yā ～ ūwā dūnīyạ
he vanished into the great world.
(2) Baud̃ạ name of town in Kano x yā
jē ～ he dodged missile, obstacle, or
question.

baud̃ad dạ Vb. 4A caused to deviate or
swerve.

baud̃ad̃d̃ē m. (f. bạud̃ad̃d̃īyā) pl. bạud̃ạd̃d̃ū
(1) crooked. (2) strayed animal. (3)
apostate.

baud̃arī = bọ̄d̃arī.

baud̃ẹ (1) swerved, dodged aside, stepped
aside x (a) hanyạ tā ～ the road bends (=
kaucẹ 1a.i = waskẹ = gōcẹ = wandạrā 1). (b) behaved or spoke evasively.
(c) k̃afạ tasạ tā ～ his foot turns outwards from disease (= būd̃ẹ 2c). (2)
Vb. 3A swerved from, dodged T. x
yā ～ hanyạ (a) he left the road and
went into the bush. (b) he is a lax
Muslim.

baud̃ị what swerving ! : what a dodger !

baud̃īyā f. swervingness : being a dodger :
evasiveness (= waskīyā).

baujē = jan baujē.

baujị m. Sk. (1) saddlegirth. (2) =
būlālạ 2.

ɓaunā f. (pl. ɓakwạ̄nē = ɓakạ̄nē = Sk.
ɓaunōnī). (1) dwarf buffalo (= sạ̄ A.2
1m page 753) (epithet is: ～ mahạrbiŋkị
yanạ̄ samạ = Maŋgạ ūwar shānū =
Kt. shạ̄ bạ̄rā = Tụkurạ = bạ̄ hawā
samạ). (2) Vd. gọ̄shī 3 ; bạgō 2.
(3) tọ̄ram ɓaunā = kụtuŋkū 1. (4) Vd.
kāshim ～.

baunī m. sternum with attached meat
(epithet is gạ̄tsi, bạ̄ mạ̄tākạ = sạ̄ri, bạ̄
mạ̄tākạ), Vd. cịji.

ɓaunōnī Vd. ɓaunā.

baurạ f. (1) (a) sharp-edged iron armlet
used in shancī (cf. kụmantakā). (b) the

contest shancī in which (1) is used by Māguzāwā. (2) load of Ạwai salt. , (3) ~ dạ jā yakẹ how red it is !

bā'ūrā *used in* dam ~ *epithet of* jackal (dilā).

ɓaurạyẹ *Vd.* ɓaurẹ.

ɓaurẹ *m.* (*pl.* ɓaurạyẹ) (1) (*a*) fig-tree (*Ficus gnaphalocarpa* and other varieties). (*b*) farim ~ *Ficus capensis.* (2) ɓaurạŋ kīyāshī = dạmagị. (3) fig-fruit, figs. (4) iŋ kanạ cịm ~ bạt tọnan cikịnsạ leave well alone ! (5) *cf.* tūwam ~ .

baurērẹ *m.* (1) the climbing lily *Gloriosa superba* (= gạtarī 9). (2) tūwam ~ mīyạr gạdạŋkūkạ (*said by eulogizing beggar*) Great Chief ! (*cf.* gạdạkūkạ).

bauri A. (baurị) = baurạ 3.
B. (baurī) = barcī 4.

baurụ *m.* (1) foot and mouth disease. (2) rinderpest (2 = būshīyā 3).

baushẹ *m.* (1) (*a*) a tree of the terminalia species used for bows and staffs. (*b*) ~ tun yanạ ɗanyẹ a kạn tausạ shi yạ mīkẹ to train a man, catch him young ! (2) kadạ kạ yi minị ~ don't beat about the bush with me ! (3) maị ~ *m.* epidemics of 1914 and 1920 (= tuŋkwīyau 2). (4) *Kt.* greeting to Sarkim bạkā.

baushị (1) *Sk. m.*= baushẹ. (2) *Kt. epithet of* fearless leader.

bauta A. (baụtā) *f.* (1) (*a*) slavery. (*b*) ạɓōkam ~ tasạ his fellow-slaves. (*c*) gudụ dạ mạrī bā yạ māganim ~ one must face realities. (*d*) igīyạr ~ *Vd.* yaŋkẹ 1*c*.iii. (*e*) *Vd.* gamị 3*c*. (2) looking after *x* yanạ yi matạ ~ he's looking after her, providing for her. (3) serving *x* sun yi masạ ~ they became his (ruler's) subjects. yanạ ta baụtar Allạ he serves God. (4) sǎi am ɓatạ akẹ ~ per aspera ad astra ! (5) *Vd.* baụtu.
B. (baụtā *Vb.* 1C (*with dative*) *x* (1) yā ~ masạ (*a*) he concentrated all his efforts on it. (*b*) he served him faithfully. (*c*) he looked after him, provided for him. (2) yā ~ masạ kǎi dạ ƙafạ he obeyed him implicitly. (3) ạɓim baụtāwā. (*a*) deity. (*b*) religion (3*b* = ạddīnị).

ɓautạ *f.* (1) noise of flapping upper arm against one's side (= tạs). (2) ~ yakẹ yī he's overjoyed.

bautad dạ *Vb.* 4B enslaved.

baụtu *Vb.* 3B (1) is (was) well-disciplined. (2) is (was) reliable (*cf.* baụtā, baụtā).

bauyā *Vd.* bāwạ.

bāwạ *m.* (*f.* bạiwā = *Sk.* bauyā) *pl.* bāyī = *Sk.* bǎi (1) (*a*) (i) slave. (ii) suŋ kāmạ bāyī they took prisoners in war (*Vd.* bursụnạ). (iii) *Vd.* ạlbishịr. (iv) *Vd.* Bạgọbirī. (v) *Vd.* kaŋwā 1*g*. (*b*) ɗaŋ hạlạs akẹ zạrgī, ~ sǎi sandạ a word to the worthy suffices, but beating must be used for the worthless. (*c*) bāwạŋ gīwā *Vd.* gīwā 1*n*. (*d*) bāwạŋ kāyā *Vd.* kāyā 1*a*.vii. (*e*) bāwạŋ gandū = bāwạŋ gọnā *Vd.* 10 *below,* shạ 1*b*. (*f*) hannū bāwạm bạkī the hand carries food to the mouth. (*g*) ạbịn dạ maị dōkị kẹ sọ bạ shī nẹ maị ~ kẹ sọ ba tastes differ. (*h*) yā yi masạ dạki ~ yạ mạntạ gạtarī he threw him off the scent. (*j*) hasadạ bā tạ hānạ ~ rạbō envy cannot stop the good man succeeding. (2) Bāwạ *name for any* ɗaŋ wābị (*is abbreviation for* Bāwạŋ Allạ *Vd.* 3 *below,* Gạzamạ). (3) (*a*) bāwạŋ Allạ *m.* (*f.* bạiwar Allạ) *pl.* bāyiŋ Allạ person, human being (= ɗaŋ Adạŋ). wani bāwạŋ Allạ someone. (*b*) Audụ bāwạŋ Allạ nē Audu is an upright P. (4) Bāwạ mạkau *name of* a bọrī-spirit (= wạnzāmị 2), *cf.* Innạ 3*a*. (5) bāwạm bụnū striped black and blue cloth. (6) bāwạŋ tụrurūwā = shạ dụndū. (7) watạm ~ = Zụlƙīdạ. (8) (*a*) ta ~ rānar sāmụ (i) how lucky Wednesdays are ! (ii) *Kt.* how lucky Tuesdays are ! (*b*) Ta ~ (= 'Yar ~) kim fi kwānā ạ dājị *epithet of* motor-car. (9) aŋ ạiki ~ gạrinsụ what a time he is in returning ! (10) Bāwạ, ganduŋ aiki what a hard worker ! (*cf.* 1*e*). (11) bāwạŋ cikị glutton. (12) (*a*) bāwạŋ yạrdā yā fi " nawạ ka sạyạ " a willing, unpaid worker is preferable to an unwilling hireling. (*b*) *Vd.* Cizgārī 7. (13) *Vd.* bǎiwā, barị 4*b*. (14) kạm bāyī *Vd.* shạmakị 2*a*. (15) gạŋgar jịkī ~ nē *Vd.* zūcīyā 1*k*. (16) rạkạ ~ *Vd.* rakạ 1*c*. (17) bāwạŋ gādọ *Vd.* sạnsạŋ gạrī. (18) ~ dạ gwaiwā *Vd.*

ciriŋgizạ.   (19) bāwạn Sarkī Vd.
daskārī.   (20) bāwạn kīshịyā Vd.
fạrkā 2b.   (21) na ∼ Vd. farkē.   (22)
bāwạm masụntā Vd. fatsā 1b.   (23)
bāwạn yākị Vd. Gizgạ̄rạ.   (24) dam ∼
mại kwạrin tạ̄barmā Vd. kwạrī 3.

*ɓāwā f. = ɓāwō.

bạ̄wại = bạmbạrākwại.

bawạlcē Vb. 1C urinated T. out.

bawạlī Ar. m. (1) (a) urine (= sanyī 12a).
(b) yā yi ∼ he urinated (polite term) =
fitsārī = Sk. sai.   (2) mạcē̦ tā rigā
mijịntạ ∼ Vd. ạbụ 5f.

bawạltā Vb. 1C = bawạlcē.

ɓāwō m. (1) (a) bark. (b) shell ; rind
(= kwạsfā q.v.).   (c) ɓāwan 'yā'yaŋ
itạ̄cē empty pod.   (2) (a) ∼ adv.
cheaply ; gratis.   (3) yanạ̄ dạ ɓāwō-
ɓāwo it has a sort of rind.

bāwụl Eng. m. 'yam ∼ ball-bearings.

baya A. (bāyā) m. (1) (a) (i) the back.
(ii) bāyaŋ gīwā s̆ai bạrbajẹ s̆ai cạrkī
epithet of certain great men.   (iii) yā
yi ∼ bạ̄ zanẹ he acted witlessly and
landed in trouble (cf. 2g.ii below).
(b) (i) nā bā shị ∼ I turned my back
on him (Vd. bā dạ 7), cf. bāya 1a.
(ii) x yā bạ̄ Kano ∼ kạdaŋ s̆ai ya mutụ
hardly had he travelled a short way
from Kano before he died. (c) nā ga
bāyaŋ aikị I've finished the work.
(d) Allạ̄ yạ sạ̄ mụ ga bāyam makī-
yammụ God confound our enemies !
(e) (i) Vd. jūyạ 1d. (ii) yā būdẹ̦ bāyansạ
he exposed himself to attack. (f) yā
gọyi bāyāna = yā kōmạ bāyāna (i) he
helped me. (ii) he concurred with me.
(Vd. mārạ 1 ; baya 1a.i ; dāfạ 6a).
(g) dōkị yanạ̄ dạ ∼ the horse has a sore
back. (h) dōkị nē ∼ wạje it's a horse
whose hindquarters fall away (cf.
gantsarwā). (j) (i) sun rufẹ̦ bāyansạ
they followed him as escort. (ii) sun
rufẹ̦ masạ ∼ they protected, helped
him. (k) yā ci bāyammụ he backbit us.
(l) dạga bāyan cf. bāya 3b. (m) Vd.
fādim bāyā. (n) fịtar ∼ piles, prolapse.

  (2) compounds of bāyan. (a) bāyam
birnī rural districts outside birnī.
(b) bāyan dākị (i) = 2d.i.ii.   (ii) Vd.
bạḍō 2. (c) bāyaŋ gạrī (i) rural districts
(contrasted with urban) x ạlkālim bāyaŋ

gạrī district judge.   (ii) = 2d.i.ii.
(d) bāyaŋ gidā (i) lavatory x yā tạfi
bāyaŋ gidā he's gone to the lavatory
(= Sk. ban 3a), Vd. baŋ garkā.
yā gamạ bāyaŋ gidā he's finished
attending to calls of nature.   yā yi
bāyaŋ gidā he attended to a call of
nature. (ii) excrement x nā tākạ bāyaŋ
gidā I trod on excrement (Vd. nạjasạ).
(iii) Sk. dam bāyaŋ gidā (f. 'yar b.g.)
pl. 'yan b.g. Vd. baŋ garkā.   (iv) Vd.
hụda 7c.   (v) kọ̄ma baŋ dākị Vd.
kyạutā. (e) nāmạ yā sọyu, yā yi bāyaŋ
k̆ōsǎi the meat is just nicely fried. (f)
bāyam mārạyā Zar. type of thatching
grass. (g) bāyan tukunyā (i) outside of
pot.   (ii) bāyan tukunyā bạ̄ zanẹ nē this
is a witless procedure (cf. 1a.iii above).

  (3) Vd. bāya, bāyan, bặi 2, ban 3.

  B. (bāya) (1) adv. backwards x
(a) (i) yā kōmạ ∼ = yā kōmạ dạ ∼
= yā jūyạ dạ ∼ = yā jā dạ ∼ = yā
yi ∼ (cf. bāyā 1b, f) = yā bi ta ∼ (cf.
1d) he went backwards, retreated ; it
(speed, progress, payments, illness,
etc.,) has lessened. bạ sụ jā ba = bạ
sụ jā dạ bāya ba they did not retreat.
sun jā dạ ∼ dạ tạk̆amā they retreated
in good order.   jạ̄ dạ ∼ irịn ta
Mụhạmmạdīyạ = gyāran dagā. sirdị
yā yi ∼ the saddle is too far back.
(ii) suŋ k̆i gạba, suŋ k̆i ∼, suŋ k̆i kặi,
suŋ k̆i gịndī they behaved mulishly.
(b) aikị yā jā dạ ∼ (i) speed of the
work has slowed down.   (ii) little of
the work remains still to be done.
(c) jạ̄ dạ ∼ gạ rạ̄gō bạ̄ gudu ba nē̦
reculer pour mieux sauter (Vd. dagā 4).
(d) kōmē ya yi yạ̄ bi ta ∼ whatever he
does, he'll be the loser. (e) mụ waiwạyā
∼, mụ haŋgạ gạba one should provide
for the future in the light of the past.
(2) adv. at the back, behind x (i) am
bar shị ạ ∼ it's been left behind.
yanạ̄ ∼ = ạ bāya yakē̦ he is at the
back. (ii) lạ̄bārị nạ̄ ∼ news is still to
come. ạshē maganạ nạ̄ ∼ the real
affair is (was) still to come. (iii) wannạŋ
karo dạ akạ yi, bạ̄ ∼ yakē̦ ba this
battle was no trifle. (iv) yạddạ mukē̦
dạ jạrụntakạ, sū mā bạ̄ ∼ ba nē̦ they
are just as brave as ourselves. (v) ạbụ

yā zamę masą bīyū, gąba wutā, bāya wutā it was a matter of his being between the devil and the deep sea. (vi) ∼ dāmisą Vd. kūrā 34. (vii) ∼ mąi tąkąicī Vd. gąba 1.a.iii. (3) (a) dągą ∼ adv. afterwards x dągą ∼ săi suką ƙī later on they refused. (b) dągą bāyan (d.f. bāyā) prep. after x dągą bāyąn nąŋ then after that. (4) (a) ą ∼ adv. in the past x (i) ąbin dą muką fądā ą ∼ what we've already mentioned. (ii) cf. ƙyēyą 3, gąba 1a. vii. (iii) tuną bāya Vd. tuną 1a.iv. (b) na ∼ m. (f. ta ∼) pl. na ∼ adj. (i) past x ą wątąnnim ∼ during the past few months, a few months ago. kwānam ∼ the other day. shēkarum ∼ some years ago. jąrąbum ∼ past calamities. (ii) the rear x mun yi musu na ∼ kąrē ką cīzọ we reduced them to a state of feeling " devil take the hindmost ! " (ii) sakin na bāya Vd. saƙi 2f. (5) yā mutu, bąi bar ∼ ba he died without offspring. (6) ∼ tā haifu there have been further developments (cf. gąba 4, 3h). (7) ∼ gą prep. x ∼ gą Audu (a) after Audu's departure. (b) behind Audu (= bāyan). (8) Vd. bāyā, bāyan.

C. (bāyā) f. a wild grass with edible grain (= baina).

baya-baya A. (bāya-bāya) m. (1) ąbin nąm ∼ yakē this is becoming less. (2) gishirin nąm ∼ yakē = bāibāi. (3) sun shiga yim ∼ tāƙi dăi-dăi tąfīyąr amąrē they began to retire unobtrusively. (4) mum bī su ∼ kąmar yādi ukụ we followed hard on their traces at a distance of about three yards.

B. (bāyā-bąyā) x yanā da gēmu (sąjē) ∼ he has long, thick beard (sidewhiskers).

ƃaya-ƃąyą x yaną dą askā ∼ he has long, broad, tribal-markings (= tayā-tąyā).

bāyad dą = bāyar dą.

Bąyahūdi = Bąyahūde m. (f. Bąyahūdiyā) pl. ˙Yahūdāwā Jew.

bąyālą Ar. f. (1) margin of page. (2) unsown margin of farm. (3) constellation referred to by fortune-tellers. (4) dūkiyā tā yi masą ∼ he has ample means. (5) Vb. 3B Sk. sufficed.

bąyamā f. the tree Swartzia madagascarensis.

bąyammā f. (1) pernicious anæmia (= farā 3 = shāwarą 5 = mayaŋƙwanīyā = maƙēƙashīyā = malālącī 2). (2) jaundice. (3) infantile diarrhœa (= kurgā = samą 1h = rānā 4j). (4) Vd. bąyammī.

bąyammī m. (f. bąyammā) pl. yammāwā (1) westerner. (2) Vd. bąyammā.

bāyan (1) prep. (a) behind x (i) suną bāyansą they are behind him. (ii) Vd. bāyā 1f. (b) on person's side x ą zūcīyā suną bāyammu in their hearts, they are our supporters, on our side. sun shiga yāƙi bāyanmu they entered the war on our side. muną bāyansą ą kąn yą yī we support his opinion that he should do it. (2) prep. after x (a) ∼ wannąŋ after this. (b) (i) ∼ dubuŋ gaisūwā after cordial greetings, I am writing to say that . . . (ii) ∼ gaisūwā Vd. amincį 2b. (c) ∼ haƙą Vd. ąmmā 2. (d) tum bāyan Vd. tun 1c.ii. (3) prep. after the departure of x bāyansą (= dągą bāyansą) aką yī shi it was done after his departure. (4) if person at place A is separated from place C by a hill B, he says dūtsąm B yaną bāyan C. Similarly, if river B separates place A from place C, person on the bank nearer A is bāyaŋ kōgī from the point of view of a person at A (cf. gąban 3). (5) conj. after x ∼ kun tąfi, aką nęmē ku = bāyan dą kuką tąfi, aką nęmē ku they looked for you after you had left. (6) for compounds of bāyan (genitive of bāyā), Vd. bāyā 2.

bąyāni Ar. m. explanation.

Bąyarabę m. (f. Bąyarabīyā) pl. Yarabāwā = Yarbāwā (1) Yoruba P. (cf. Ąyāgī, Ąrēmī, Bąyaruƃę). (2) Vd. Yarąbā. (3) cinikin Yarabāwā Vd. kwąlō-kwalō.

Bąyarīmę m. (f. Bąyarīmiyā) pl. Yarīmāwā (1) member of the Filani Clan of that name. (2) bąyarīmiyā f. type of furā. (3) cf. Yarīmancī.

bāyar dą = bā dą.

Bąyaruƃę m. (f. Bąyaruƃīyā) pl. Yaruƃāwā a Filani tribe in Kt. (cf. Bąyarabę).

bąyaushē (preceded by kō) x kō ∼ aką tąmbąyē ką, săi ką ƙī whenever you are asked, you refuse (*cf.* yąushę, kōyąushē).

bǎyǎyǎ *x* yanā dā gēmu ∼ he has a long, thick beard.

bǎyayyą = bāyayyēnīyā *f.* (1) bickering. (2) = kąrɓēɓēnīyā.

baye A. (bǎyē) *m.* (1) copulation of mare and horse (*cf.* haikę*ʼ*2, nūnī) = *Kt.* ɗaukī 3. (2) *Kt.* = anǫ 4. B. (bāyę) *Nor. m.* = tūrē 1.

bāye-bǎyē *Vd.* bǎiwā.

bāyī (1) *Vd.* bāwą, bǎiwā. *(2) = ban rūwā 1*a*.

bāyu *x* ząi ∼ zūwą faɗą it'll lead to a quarrel.

bayyana A. (bayyąnā) *Vb.* 1C (1) explained *x* (*a*) yā ∼ minī shī he explained it to me (*cf.* zayyąnā 2). (*b*) explained that *x* am ∼ musu yā fi kyąu su yī it was explained to them that it would be better to do so. mum ∼ mukų cēwā yanā yī = mum ∼ mukų yanā yī = mum ∼ mukų kamar yanā yī we've explained to you that he's doing it. (*c*) yā ∼ cēwā . . . he said that . . . (*d*) ąbin dā muką ∼ ą kan lābārinsą our description of it. (2) disclosed *x* sum ∼, sū makīyansą nē they've shown clearly that they're his enemies. (3) exposed P. *x* am ∼ shi, yā bąyyąnu his reputation has been torn to shreds. B. (bąyyąnā) (1) *Vb.* 2 = bayyąnā 2, 3. (2) *Vb.* 3B (matter, meaning) is (was) clear, was revealed *x* ƙurājē sum ∼ ą jikinsą pimples appeared on him.

bayyanad dā *Vb.* 4B = bayyąnā.

bąyyąnannē *m.* (*f.* bąyyąnannīyā) *pl.* bąyyąnannū clear, manifest.

bąyyąne *x* ą ∼ obviously.

baza A. (bazą) (1) *Vb.* 1A (*a*) = baję 1*a*. (*b*) spread out to dry. (*c*) spread (rumours, etc.) *x* sunā ∼ ƙarąirai ą kan mąganąr sąyąŋ gyaɗā they're spreading lies about the buying of groundnuts. sum ∼ jī ta jī ta they spread rumours. (2) *Vb.* 3A yā ∼ cikiŋ gąrī he's gone prowling in the town. B. (bązā) *f.* (1) fringed leather apron of dancers. (2) yanā rawā dā bązar wani he lives on reflected glory (= rawā 1*f*).

C. (bazā) *f* (*pl.* bazōjī) ring on saddle or girth for tightening.

Bązabarmę *m.* (*f.* Bązabarmīyā) *pl.* Zabarmāwā (1) P. of Zabarma. (2) bązabarmę *m.* fringed honeycomb-cloth.

bązāƙą *f. Kt.* (1) = bązāƙīyā. (2) type of bean (= zāƙǫ).

bā zāƙę *x* karā ∼ *the cry* of those exposing for sale (tąllą) sugarcane (rąkē *or* tąkanɗā).

bązāƙīyā *f.* pulled cassava which after 2–3 months becomes very sweet (= zāƙǫ = zāƙī 7).

bązākumą *Kt. f.* variegated fowl.

baząmā *Vb.* 3A = bązamą *Vb.* 3B bolted, ran away.

bązāmanę = bązāmanī *m.* (*f.* bązāmąnā = bązāmanīyā) *pl.* zāmanāwā. (1) one of the modern " bright young things " who in the opinion of their elders have no sense of dignity, who " swim with the tide ", etc. (= bana 2*e*). (2) up-to-date P. (*cf.* zāmanancī).

Bązamfąrī = Bązamfąrę *m.* (*f.* Bązamfąrā) *pl.* Zamfarāwā. (1) P. of Zamfara. *(2) bązamfąrī = rǎi ɗǫrē.

bā zānā *m.* the tree *Commiphora kerstingii* (used for fences).

bazarā *f.* (1) ∼ tā yī hot season just before the rains has come. (2) rūwam ∼ mąi tā dā mazā ą tsąye what an energetic P ! (3) umbrella (= laimą). (4) (*a*) sun yi minī bazarar damō = atishāwą 2. (*b*) yā yi bazarar damō, yā yi wąje he leaped outside as if possessed. (5) gąrī yā yi masą bazarar māgē he's having a struggle to support himself. (6) ąlāmum bazarā ą ƙofąr ɗāki ākę ganī coming events cast their shadows before them. (7) kąram ∼ *Vd.* karen 2.

bazar-bazar A. (bąząr-bąząr) *x* yanā tąfīyą ∼ he's in rags. B. (bazar-bąząr) *x* rīgarsą tā zamā ∼ his gown's ragged. C. (bąząr-bąząr) *x* gā māsū ganyē ∼ here are some of these leafclad pagans !

bā ząrētā *Vd.* bā 10*d*.

bązarnīyā *f.* = bąrzānīyā.

bā zątā *f.* *x* yā yi minī ∼ he surprised me.

bā zątō *Vd.* bā 9.

bązaurę *Zar. m.* lower grinding-stone (= dūtsąn niƙą).

bazawarā f. (pl. zawarāwā). (1) (a) woman no longer married (= zawara = mātar mazā 1). (b) ~ tasu the husbandless woman whom they are courting (cf. zawarcı 2). (c) Vd. ungulū 2, rakīyar ~ . (2) T. to be re-used as in alallamī 3.

bazawarī m. suitor of a bazawara.

bazayyanā f. type of bead.

Bazazzagī m. (f. Bazazzagā = Bazazzagīyā) pl. Zazzagāwā = Zagēzagī. (1) P. of Zaria (cf. Turunkū). (2) Vd. hūtsū ~ .

bazazzarī m. (f. bazazzarā) spendthrift.

ɓazgā Vb. 2. (1) pulled off branch, maize-cob, etc. (2) yā ɓazgō mini rēshe he stole or damaged my property ; he caused me loss (= rēshe 3).

ɓazge Vb. 3A became severed : rēshe yā ~ da shī branch gave way and he fell.

ɓazgēge m. (f. ɓazgēgīyā) huge.

bazgo Sk. m. type of bean.

bazo-bazo A. (bazō-bazo) m., f. (sg., pl.) wastrel.
    B. (bazō-bazo) Kt. shūka tā fitō ~ the crops sprouted prolifically.

bazōjī Vd. bazā.

bazu Vd. baje.

bēbancē Vd. 3A. (1) is (was) deaf. (2) pretended to be deaf and dumb.

bēbancı m. = bēbantaka f.) being deaf and dumb.

bēbē m. (f. bēbīyā) pl. bēbāyē. (1) (a) deaf-mute. (b) Vd. fada 2b.v. (c) ~ săi ya dangana Vd. abu 5h. (2) yana ta bēbē he's making noises indicative of enjoying food.

Bēbı Vd. mālamī 2.

bēce Vb. 1A. (1) (farmer) scraped (ground). (2) (fowl) scrabbled. (3) ~ gāshı to undo and comb woman's hair. (4) Sk. Kt. = bākace. (5) cf. fēce.

bēcī = baicī.

bēcīyā f. doing any act denoted by bēce.

bē'e. (1) x ~ ba kāshī = dēwa yā'e. (2) Vd. bē'ē'ē, bō'e.

bē'ē'ē. (1) used in ōhō'ō'ō, karim ~ (said by women) what is it to do with me ? (= ōhō 1). (2) Vd. bē'e.

bēganta Vb. 2 (p.o. bēgance, n.o. bēganci) longed for.

ɓēgē m. (pl. bēgannī) (Ar. baghay). (1) longing x munā ɓēgyansa we're longing for him. dādin zamā shī ya kāwō ~ happy association makes one long for the absent (= mangartū). (2) dinki yā yi ~ the stitches went in the wrong direction. (3) bēgyam bunū type of cloth like bunū.

bēgila (pl. bēgilōlī). (1) f. bugle x yanā busa ~ he's blowing the bugle. ~ tana tāshi the bugle is sounding. (2) m. bugler.

bēgwā f. (pl. bēgwōyī) porcupine (epithet Dāɓu gajērā).

bējē m. (1) fringed leather-loincloth. (2) yanā nāsa ~ = yanā ta bējansa he's having a good time (Vd. ishisshirē). (3) Nor. yā kaɗa masa ~ he overthrew him in wrestling.

bējī Sk. m. = bēza-salt.

bēkē m. surprise x nā ga bēkyansa it surprised me. bar bēkēna don't be surprised at me !

ɓel-ɓel m. (1) butter " doctored " by churning with hot water (cf. bugaggē 2). (2) butter churned by movement of kīgaga when cattle migrate. (3) yāwam ~ idle roving (cf. yāwo).

belbēla Kt. f. = balbēla.

bēlī = bēlū m. (1) uvula (= haki 3). (2) = ɓamā 1 or its lining. (3) any small excrescence. (4) zam fitam maka da ~ I'll give you a share of what I've been given.

Bello (1) man's name (Vd. dibgau). (2) Vd. ballo.

bēna f. (1) hide with adherent hair. (2) dōrawa producing only poor fruit.

bēnāyē Vd. bēnē.

bēnē m. (pl. bēnāyē) Vd. sōrō 1c, 1d, 1e, jākin 2, kwatashi, matākī.

bēnī m. the bird tsāda.

ɓērā m. (pl. ɓērāyē = ɓērarrakī) (Ar. fa'ra) (1) (a) rat, mouse (Vd. dōrōgō) = Sk. kūsu. (b) ~ yā kētara ni I went to bed supperless (Vd. dētara 2). (c) in kā ga ~ yanā kaiwā yanā kāwōwa, kyānwā bā tā gidā = in kā ga ~ yanā saki, kyānwā bā tā gidā = im māgē bā tā nan, ~ săi ya sake when the cat is away, the mice play. (d) a yi waccē zā a yi, ~ yā shanye gārin kyānwā the harm is done now so I'll have to take the consequences. (*e*) **yanā dạ wāyō kạmam** ~ he's very cute. (*f*) ~ **nā** ganin **rāmịnsạ, bā yā yạrdā wutā tạ cī shị** everyone looks after himself. (*g*) in **dăi** ~ **dạ sātạ, dạddawā mā dạ dộyī** it takes two to make a quarrel ; take the mote out of your own eye ! (*h*) ~ **yā 6ātạ kạŋwạ tasạ, yā cę̄ har jịkīna yā yi sanyī** getting small gift instead of the large gift expected. (*j*) **kaurim** ~ *Vd.* **bạbbakạ** 3. (*k*) **ạbịn dạ ya kōrō** ~ **har yā sā yā fādạ wuta, tō, yā kūwā fi wutạr zāfī** desperate causes need desperate remedies. (*l*) ~ **dạ kufkụmī** *Vd.* **dūnīyạ** 1*l*. (*m*) **gạigạyam** ~ *Vd.* **gạigạyē**. (*n*) **gọbarar** ~ *Vd.* **kāmạ hannū** 2. (*o*) **6ēran taŋkā** *Vd.* **kịrị kọrē**. (2) **tsịyā gạrēshị kạmam 6ēram masallācī** he's as poor as a church mouse. (3) **farim** ~ = **bakim** ~ scandalmonger, traitor, informer. (4) **6ēram bisạ** tree squirrel. (5) **6ēram Masạr** guinea-pig. (6) **6ēraŋ kyaurō = gyạzbī**. (7) *cf.* **sam 6ērā, wutsīyạr 6ērā, dạkū ;** *Vd.* **kụrũcīyar 6ērā**. (8) **kụnnam 6ērā** *Vd.* **kụnnē** 3. (9) (*no plural*) the tree *Ficus capensis* (= **6aurē** 1*b*).

bērạ *f.* (*pl.* **bērōrī**) (1) (*a*) girl whose breasts are not yet formed (younger than **bụdurwā**). (*b*) *Vd.* **gwaidạ**. (2) small tattooing razor (= **jạrfā** 3 = **6intilā** 3 = **dīdīwạlā**). (3) *Kt.* Sarkim ~ = **Sarkin 'yam mātā**.

6ērạrrakī, 6ērạyē *Vd.* **6ērā**.

bērē *x* **takạrdar** ~ *f.* forged letter, letter with false news.

bērōrī *Vd.* **bērạ**.

6ērū = 6ērī *m.* (*sg.*, *pl.*) (1) Tawny-flanked wren warbler (*Prinia mistacea*) = **tsīgī** 3*b*. (2) **anā fushī dạ gạurākạ,** ~ **yanā 6arnā** blaming P. who has acted on false information given him by subordinates (*Vd.* **tsīgī** 4).

betę *m.* = **fạtę̄-fatē**.

bētsọ *Sk.* *m.* (*Ar.* **būzạ**) beer.

bēzạ = *6ēzạ *f.* (1) yellowish salt from Azben, Taudeni etc. (*cf.* **gạllō**). (2) **yā zubạ manạ** ~ he told us pleasant news which was deliberately false.

bi A. (**bī**) *Vb.* 5 (*for progressive, Vd.* **bị** *below*) (1) (*a*) followed *x* **nā** ~ **shị**

= **nā bi masạ** I followed him. **yanā bịnsụ = yanā bi musụ** he's following them. **yā bi mịsālịnsụ** he followed their example. **nā bi shāwarạ tasạ** I followed his advice. **nā bi mạganạrtạ** I gave in to her. (*b*) *for sense* investigated, *Vd.* **ussị, sīsị,** diddigī, **hakkị, kādī, kwakkwafī**. (*c*) *Vd.* **bị bại, bị baŋgō, bị bị san dōkị, bị dạ bị, bī dạ gwarzō, bị daŋgị, bị dạ sartsę, bị ta dạ, bị ni dạ, bị ta zạizại, bị tsāmī, bị tsatsō**. (*d*) **yā bi zūwạ Kanọ** he came to Kano. (*e*) **kọgin naŋ yā bi zūwạ Kanọ** this river flows towards Kano. (*f*) **wannaŋ yanā bịŋ wannạŋ** all this is in the right sequence. (*g*) **gēmụ bā yā bịŋ gēmụ sǎi dạ ạmfānī** nobody consorts with another except for some good reason. (2) obeyed *x* (*a*) **sunā bịŋ Kanọ** they are under the jurisdiction of Kano. (*b*) **sum bịyu** they're submissive. (*c*) **bạ zā sụ bi ba** they (enemy) will not surrender. **sun cę̄ sum bī** they agreed to surrender. (*d*) **in dā zā ạ bi shāwarạ tasạ nē, dā har gidā zā mụ rikạ bịn Jāmụs** if we were to listen to him, we should comply with all the demands of the Germans. (*e*) **yanā bịŋ Allā** he's Godfearing. **yā yī shị na bịŋ Allā** he did that in the service of God. (*f*) **kōwā ya bī, ạ bī shị** the obedient will be obeyed. (*g*) **nā tūbā, nā bi Allā, nā bī kạ** please forgive me this one lapse ! (3) (*a*) **dạ A, dạ B, wānēnę̄ ạ cikinsụ yakę̄ bịŋkạ** who was born next after you, A or B ? (*b*) **tanā bịm mazā** (i) she was the first female child born after successive males. (ii) she's a loose woman (*in sense* (ii), *we can also say* **bịm mazā gạrētạ**). (*c*) **yanā bịm mātā** (i) he was the first male child born after successive females. (ii) he's a regular rake (*in sense* (ii), *we can also say* **bịm mātā gạrēshị**), *cf.* **nē̄mā** 1*a*.iv. (5) bet on *x* **nā bi kilị** I back the grey horse. **mē̄ ka bị, dạmarạ ?** kō kạn Sarkị heads or tails ? **cịkā ?** kō **mārā, mē̄ ka bị** do you bet on odds or evens ? (6) **ạnnīyạrkạ tạ bī kạ** may your evil recoil on you ! (7) (*a*) **watạ yā bi rānā** there's no moon to-day. (*b*) **tanā bịŋ watạ** she is menstruating (= **hailạ**). (8) tried to enforce payment *x* (*a*) **yā tạfi bịm bāshị** he's gone to collect a debt. **zạ̄ ni m̥ bi bāshị** I'm off to collect a debt. **yanạ̄ bịntạ bāshị** he is owed money by her. (*b*) **bi bāshịŋ kạ̣kā** *Vd.* **kạrạmbạ̄nī.** (*c*) **nā bi jinịŋ Audụ** I sought compensation for Audu, my murdered kinsman (*Vd.* **bị jinī**). (9) travelled via *x* (*a*) **nā bi ta kạ̄sūwā** I went via the market. **yanạ̄ ta bị ta kạn tụrurūwā** he is treading on black ants. **ịnā sukạ bị** which way did they go ? **gạ̄ ịndạ sukạ bi** *this* is the way they went. **hanyạn naŋ, ta ịnā ta bị** where does this road lead ? **hanyạr tā bi ta gịndin dūtsẹ** the road skirts the hill. (*b*) **yā bi ḳasā** he went by land. (*c*) **mūgụn lạ̣bārị yạ bi ḳasā** may bad news pass on its way ! (*d*) **nā bi darē = nā bi duhụn darē** I travelled there by night. **yā bīyō darē** he travelled here by night (*cf.* **yạŋkā 5, yī 1***n*). (*e*) *Vd.* **kūrā 37.** (*f*) **kadạ kạ bi ta kạnsạ = kadạ kạ bi tāsạ** don't follow his example ! (*g*) **nā bi ta kạnsạ = nā bi ta wurinsạ** I called at his house. **mụ bī, mụ gai dạ shī** let's go and pay our respects to him ! **duk yā bi sụ** he visited them all. **sunạ̄ bịŋ ḳauyukạ, sunạ̄ rūshẹ̄wā** they're making their way into the villages and devastating them. **ạ bi daŋgi dukạ, ạ gaggaishē sụ** one must pay a round of complimentary calls on all the family ! (*Vd.* **bị daŋgi**). (*h*) (i) **yā bi hanyạr Kano** he took the Kano road. (ii) **hanyạr lāfīyạ, bị ta dạ shẹkarạ** the longest way round is the shortest way home. (iii) **hanya ạbar bị** *Vd.* **wạzīrị.** (iv) **hanyạr bā tạ̄ bịyūwā** the road is not traversable. (v) **wannạn dọkā bā tạ̄ bịyūwā gạ Jāmụs** this principle is not applicable in the case of the Germans. (vi) went in certain direction of the compass *x* **yā bi yạmmā** (*Vd.* **yạmmā**). (vii) **bi ta bāya** *Vd.* **bāya 1***a, d.* (10) **bi shānū** *Vd.* **sā A.2, 1***f.* (10A) **bi sau** *Vd.* **sau 1***a.* (11) **yā bi rūwā** it is lost, it has all come to nothing. (12) *Vd.* compounds of **bī.** *Vd.* **bī dạ, bịye.**

B. (**bị**) (1) (*progressive of* **bī**) *x* **nī nẹ̄ babba, shī yakẹ̄ bịna** I'm the oldest and he was born next (*cf.* **bī 3**). **yanạ̄ bị, yanạ̄ bị har yā jē gạ dūtsạŋ** he went on and on till he reached the mountain (*cf.* **bī 9**). **hanyạr bạ̄ ta dạ dādim bị** the road is not easily traversable (*cf.* **bī 9**). **bịm mazā** *Vd.* **bī 3***b.* **bịn dạ sukẹ̄ yi masạ** their pursuit of him. *Vd.* **bī 9***h.*iii. (2) **wani ~** sometimes.

C. (**bị**) *x* (1) **bị kị zō ba** you (*feminine*) did not come (*d.f.* **bạ kị zō ba**). (2) *Vd.* compounds of **bị.**

bị bại *m.* anything supplementary (*x* bringing 2nd load to complete delivery ; sending message after message ; giving present after present ; " flogging dead horse ") *x* **an yi minị ~** I have been called on for further unexpected effort or contribution. **cīwọ yā yi masạ ~** illness unexpectedly returned to him.

bị baŋgō *m.* leak in roof letting water trickle down (= **jịrwạ̄yē 2**).

ɓiɓɓikēkẹ = ɓuɓɓukēkẹ.

bībīkọ *m.* dogging P.'s footsteps.

bị bị san dōkị *m.* (1) amusing a child by running one's fingers up its arm and tickling it. (2) = **bị bại.** (3) closely watching P. to " catch him out ".

bibiya A. (**bībịyā**) *Vb.* 1C (*int. from* **bịyạ 1** *especially as follows*) (1) related in sequence. (2) read again and again to memorize. (3) **iŋ kā ~** on further consideration, perhaps you will . . .

B. (**bībịyā**) *Vb.* 2 (*int. from* **bị**) *x* **kōịnā, yanạ̄ ~ tasạ** he follows him everywhere.

C. (**bībịyā**) *Vb.* 5 *int. from* **bīyā.**

bicẹ (1) *Vb.* 3A. (*a*) (*lamp, fire*) went out. (*b*) **haskyansạ yā ~** he's not up to his former standard. **haskyaŋ kạ̄sūwā yā ~** trade isn't what it was. (2) *Vb.* 1A (*a*) extinguished. (*b*) **yā ~ su dạ shī** he covered them with it (*chaff, smoke, dust*). **yā bitō mụ dạ ḳūrā** he covered us with dust. (*c*) **yā ~ ɗākị dạ ḳanshī** he filled the room with a sweet odour.

bici A. (**bīcī**) *m.* (1) *Sk.* grainless bulrush-millet. (2) *Kt.* **cịm ~** *m.* backbiting.

(3) *Vd.* aje bīcinkạ.

B. (bicī) *Kt.* cịm ~ *m.* humiliating a P.

bicikkidạ *Sk. f.* (1) ~ cē she's a dirty, ugly woman. (2) an yi wạ nāmạ ~ meat has been roasted in embers.

bịcilmī *m., f.* (*pl.* bịcịlmai). (1) black ostrich *or* its feathers (*cf.* jịminā ; bạrōdō). (2) ~ gāshịn kudī *epithet of* rich P.

bicit-bicit *Nor. m.* = hututu.

bī dạ *Vb.* 4A. (1) yā bī dạ sū = yā bīshē sụ (*a*) he led them. (*b*) he disciplined them. (*c*) he subjugated them. (2) yā bī dạ hanyạ he made the road serviceable ; he made the road widely used. (3) yā bīyō dạ kāyā he imported goods. yā ~ kāyā he exported goods.

bidạ *m.* (*pl.* bidōdī). (1) (*a*) thatchingneedle. (*b*) yā mai dạ ~ he repaid loan. (2) bidạ = dam bidạ (*a*) iron rod for pressing out cottonseed. (*b*) dark viper considered two-headed (*a, b* = mugurjī 2). (3) ~ ƙī tạnƙwasạ (*a*) thou inflexible ruler ! (*b*) what a miser ! (4) adult of the fish 'yan cịnī. (5) *Kt.* gạrdam ~ the game gạrdō.

bịdā *Vb.* 2. (1) looked for (*Vd.* bịdīyạ) (= nēmā). (2) kụ bịdi ạlhēri gạ mai sakịm fuskạ look for gifts from a smiling face !

bī dạ bī continuously ; successively.

bịdạ-bidạ *m.* (1) the viper bidạ. (2) strong, well-built P.

bī dạ gwarzō *m.* secondary parotitis.

bị dangi *m.* (1) tanạ ~ she's roving about. (2) = bịyē 1. (3) yā yi minị ~ he abused me. (4) *Kt.* cadging funds from relatives to buy way to official position *or* to refund sum embezzled *or* to pay dīyyạ, etc. (5) *Vd.* bī 9*g last example.*

bị dạ sartsẹ *m.* = fī dạ sartsẹ.

Biddạ *f. the place* Bida.

bidi A. (bīdị) *m.* type of thick cloak.

B. (bịdī) *m.* (1) dark-grey roan horse. jam ~ red roan horse. ~ baƙī roan horse. (2) brownish gujīyā. (3) Audụ yā yi ~ = yā sakạ ~ Audu is going grey (= furfurtạ). (4) kạdam farā tā cī, tā fī ~ (lit. if white nut wins in

game cācar kincē, it's better than the brown) half a loaf's better than no bread. (5) sǎi am fasạ, a kạn sam ~ (*a*) all is not gold that glitters. (*b*) it takec time to know a P. (*Vd.* namijị 7).

bidi'ạ *f.* (*pl.* bịdị'ū = bidi'ō'ī) *Ar.* heresy against one's religion or sect (*includes all* drumming).

bidi-bidi A. (bịdī-bidī) *m.* groping.

B. (bidi-bidi) (1) *x* ganinsạ ~ nē his sight is poor. (2) *Vd.* biji-biji.

bịdiddigī *m.* (*pl.* bịdịddịgai) variety of edible frog.

bidịddịkē = budụddụkē.

bịdīdị *Sk. m.* aimless roving.

bịdịdịyau *m.* = sansạn.

bidigā-bịdịgā *x* yanạ dạ shī ~ he has plenty of it.

bịdịgējẹ *x* anạ bịdịgējạn nēmansạ it's being sought eagerly.

bịdịgis *Kt.* yā ƙī ~ he refused pointblank.

bidik *Kt.* yā ga ~ he was " fed up ".

bịdịngau *Kt. m.* = bụrdịngau.

bịdinnīyā *f.* = bạdạm-badam.

bidirī *m.* = budịrī.

bịdīyạ *f.* (*secondary v.n. of* bịdā) *x* yanạ ~ tasạ = yanạ bịdā tasạ he's seeking it.

bidīyē *Vb.* 1C sought (= bịdā).

bidōdī *Vd.* bidạ.

bịf *x* yā kāshē shị ~ he (wrestler) threw him (opponent) down with a thud (*cf.* dịm ; bụk).

bịgā *f.* (*pl.* bīgōgī) *Sk.* cave ; lair.

bịgairạ *Vd.* gairạ 2*c.*

bīgālẹ *Sk.* ~ dūkịyar bisạ dākị *epithet of* pigeon.

bige *Vd.* buge.

bigidājẹ *Kt.* = bạgidājẹ.

bīgịlạ = bēgịlạ.

bigịmī *m.* (*pl.* bigịmai) woven vesselcover (fǎifǎi).

bigirẹ *Sk. m.* place (= bụgē 3).

bigirō *m.* = bịjirō.

bigizụrā = bụgizụrā.

bīgōgī *Vd.* bịgā.

bịhī *Ar.* kō ~ bạn sani ba I don't know in the least. tun sāfē kō ~ bạ kụ yi ba you've not done a stroke of work to-day.

bịjā-bijā (1) *m., f.* = bịjī-bijī 1. (2) *f.* = bịjī-bijī 2.

bijāgī = būjāgī.

bijājẹ = bijāyẹ.

*bijājị Fil. m. = taurā 1 (cf. bijāyẹ ; daurị 2).

bijārā f. big type of groundnut with streaky shell.

bijāyẹ Fil. m. (1) ox with drooping horns (= kūrā 9a ; cf. bijājị ; daurị 3). (2) wannąŋ izgar dōkị ~ nē this horse-tail-switch is very hairy.

biji-biji A. (bijị-bijī) (1) m., f. (sg., pl.) scatterbrained P. (2) m. feckless work.

   B. (biji-biji) (1) adj. (a) = bidi-bidi. (b) adv. in disorder. (2) Sk. m. faint light of earliest dawn x gąrī yaną ~, muką tāshị we set out at earliest dawn.

bijigā-bijigā x yaną dą shī ~ he has plenty of it.

bijijjigā Kt. = wujijjigā.

bijima Vd. bijimī.

bijimī m. (pl. bijịmai). (1) (a) big bull. (b) kaską bā tą kōmē dą bijimī, săi tą shā jinī tą tāshị what a parasite ! (c) wuyąm bąjinī Vd. wuyą 8. (d) ƙirgịm bijimī Vd. sąnnū 2b.iii. (2) man outstanding for size, character, etc. (such woman is bijimā) x bijimin Sarkī mighty chief. (3) yā yi fuskạr ~ he looked enraged (Vd. fuskạ 1c). (4) fitsārim ~ m. type of zigzag stitch. (5) Vd. māƙarą.

bị jinī m. seeking compensation for murdered kinsman (cf. bī 8).

bijintą f. possessing or showing qualities of bijimī 2 x mąi hālịm ~ nē he's outstanding. yā yi ~ he did outstanding act.

bijirą Vb. 3B. (1) bccame out of control (cf. bijịrē ; bijirō). (2) sum bijiram masą ą jējị they suddenly attacked him in the bush. (3) ąbịn dą ya bijiram musụ jīyą what befell them yesterday. (4) bąsīrą tā bijiram minị an idea struck me.

bijịrē Vb. 3A x yā ~ minị he refused to follow my orders (cf. bijirą).

bijịrērēnịyā f. mutual recriminations.

bijiro A. (bijịrō) m. ~ kąkan tsāfị epithet of fetichism.

   B. (bijirō) (1) = bijirą 2, 3, 4. (2) came in large numbers x sum ~ dą

dōyą they brought much cassava.

rūwą yā ~ it has rained heavily (cf. bijira).

bịk = bịf.

bika A. (bịkā) Vb. 2 x yā bịki mątā tasą he tried to conciliate his runaway wife into returning (cf. bīkọ).

   B. (bịkā) Sk. m. (pl. bikąkē) baboon (= gwaggọ).

   C. (bịkā) Vb. 1C Kt. travelled via, etc. (= bī 9).

bịkatą = bịkantą Vb. 2 x yā bịkąci mątā tasą = bịkā.

bīkē = bēkē.

biki A. (bịkī) m. (pl. bukūkūwą) (1) (a) (i) feast (especially for wedding, Vd. aurē 6d, aŋgwancị). (ii) yā yi ~ he gave a feast. (iii) mụ jē ~ let us go to the banquet ! (Vd. gąndọkī). (b) hūtum ~, 'yar matsịyącī tā mutụ raŋ gārā getting relief from one's troubles. (c) lą'she-lāshē" dą tąrō shī nę ~ plenty ,tb eat and good company is as good as a banquet. (d) mụ ci ~ let's go on the spree ! (e) bịkim farar kāzā, bąlbēlą bą gąyyā ba cę that goes without saying. (f) bąn ci ~ ba, ~ yą cị nị? where there's no profit, why risk loss ? (g) hąukatạr ~ gayą mijịm bāya tārę̄wā stupidly doing pointless act = bąƙō 1b (Vd. gąrmā 1a.iii). (h) (i) ūwar ~ hostess at feast. (ii) ūwar ~ bą rūwąŋkị dą ɓarakạr zanẹ what a slovenly woman ! (j) bịkin są bą kyąutā ba nę he's thrown a sprat to catch a whale. (k) ram ~ akę̄ ƙiŋ huntū, raŋ kwąɓar ƙasā ą nēmō shị everything has its own time and place. (l) ~ dăi bą sąrautą ba nę all is not gold that glitters. (m) gayą mąi zūcịyā ~ bą mąi dūkịyā ba court the resolute, not the rich ! (n) bịkiŋ wani Vd. kundumī. (o) mai dą ƙwaryā ~ Vd. ƙwaryā 1k. (2) ~ gąrēshị he's spending lavishly. (3) bịkiŋ kansą yakę̄ yị " he can stand on his own feet ". (4) bịkiŋ kulą what do I care !, what does it matter to me ? (5) contribution to feast x ąbōkīna yā kāwō minị ~ my friend brought me a contribution for my feast. (6) needing x (a) bā ną bịkinsą I don't need it inā bikīna dạ shī how does it concern me ? (*b*) bikim magāji bā yā hanạ na magājīyā the needs of the borrower are subservient to those of the owner. (7) gōbe dạ ∼ *m.* makeshift trousers (= gōbe 7 *q.v.*). (8) *Vd.* hanạ ∼. (9) bā ∼ *Vd.* zaune 3*c.* (10) gidam ∼ *Vd.* tūwō 21. (11) zaman dūnīyạ ∼ *Vd.* zamā 2*a.x.* (12) bikin ƙawar ƙawā *Vd.* ɗọri ihirī. (13) bikin Aḷhamis *Vd.* Aḷhamis 3. (14) gāgarạ ∼ *Vd.* gāgarạ.

B. (bikī) please ! *x* ∼ kạ bā ni rīgā please give me a gown !

ɓiki A. (ɓīki) *Kt. m.* nincompoop.

B. (ɓikī) *Vd.* kạram ɓikī.

bīki *m.* (1) period of .breast-feeding a child. (2) inā rūwam mazā dạ ∼ don't be a busybody ! (3) devoting attention to *x* sǎi kạ yi wạ ƙasan nạm ∼ you must work up this clay well. sǎi dạ na shā ∼ tukunā na sāmu I only got it after much effort. yā yi wạ kạrātunsạ ∼ he brushed up his reading.

bikiki *x* yanā tạfīyạ ∼ his clothes are trailing on the ground.

bīkilī *m.* (*f.* bīkilā) *pl.* bikilai. (1) bay horse (*also called* jam ∼ *or* ∼ ƙwārạ). (2) baƙim ∼ brown horse.

ɓikincē *Kt. Vb.* 3A became flummoxed, etc. (= ɓạkintạ).

*bikirā *Ar. f.* virgin.

ɓikītạ *Kt. Vb.* 3B became flummoxed, etc. (= ɓạkintạ).

bīkọ *m.* (1) (*a*) trying to conciliate runaway wife or enemy *x* yā yi bīkwạm mātā tasạ. (*b*) yāji bạ bīkọ *Vd* santarantan 2. (2) bīkwan sạndā = bīkwạn sōjạ bringing home runaway-wife by force. (3) mun sạmi ∼ rain fell after we'd sown our crops. (4) yā yi mini ∼ he coached me in reading Koran (*cf.* darạsū ; bīyạ 1*c* ; bītạ). (5) an hadạ ƙafạ, sǎi ∼ the two half-arches of ɗaurin gūgā *or* bạkan gizọ (*Vd.* ƙafạ 8*a.*ii) have been joined (*Vd.* hadi 4) and it now remains to add beam which reinforces the lintel-beam. (6) *Zar.* sun tạfi ∼ they've gone to a wedding. (7) bīkwan ƙwaryā present for bringers of cooked food sent as contribution to

feast (= *Kt.* maiƙọ 4). (8) bīkwạm māshi a conquered area and its inhabitants.

bila A. (bilạ) *Vb.* 1A = billạ 2.

B. (bilā) *Ar.* without *x* mutānē ∼ haddin innumerable persons.

bilākạ *x* haunī ∼, dāma ∼ Chief, look out for holes on the right and left ! (*cf.* faram).

bilākiman *Eng.* " blackman " *m.* native tobacco.

bilāyī *m.* behaving as if still young *x* bilāyin tsūfā takē yī though old, she still powders her face, etc., like girl.

bilbice A. (bilbicē) *Kt. int. from* bicẹ.

B. (bilbilcē) *Vd.* bilbiltạ.

bilbidạ *Sk. int. from* bidā.

bilbila = bulbula.

bilbilō (1) *m.* swallow (*Hirundo aethiopica*) = *Sk.* ciccīyā. (2) bilbilō = bilbilọ *Kt. m.* butterfly.

bilbis *Vd.* gạl-gal.

bilbishe *Kt. int. from* bishẹ.

bilbiltạ *Vb.* 2 (*p.o.* bilbilcē, *n.o.* bilbilci) surpassed.

bilbītā *Vb.* 1C *Kt. int. from* bītạ.

bilhụ *m. x* yā zubạ mini bilhụ he told me a lie, an impossible story.

bililliƙī *Sk. m.* larger intestine.

bilimbītūwā *f.* fruitless search.

bilkārạ *f.* (1) speculative buying without weighing, for resale (*cf.* barạndạ). (2) magana tasạ ∼ cē his statement is unreliable.

bilkạran worthless.

Bilƙisụ woman's name (*epithet is* Gado).

billạ *Vb.* 1A (1) yā ∼ fụlā he extended his hands sharply inside a cap to shape it or flick off dust. (2) am ∼ shūnī ạ cikin karōfī prepared-indigo (shūnī) has been deceitfully added to poor dye in dyepit. am ∼ ƙasar mabugā ạ cikin karōfī earth impregnated with prepared-indigo (shūnī) from place where indigo is beaten into gowns, has been deceitfully added to poor dye in dyepit. (3) *Vd.* fillạ.

ɓilla = ɓulla.

billāhi *Vd.* kuntụ ∼.

billạrē *Kt.* = ballạƙē.

ɓiḷḷau *x* ɗam ∼ *Sk. m.* palpitations of the heart.

bille A. (billē) *m.* (1) tribal mark consisting of cut from nose outwards to jaw, as done by **Sulluɓāwā** *or* **Bambadāwā** (= **shą̄tųnē** = *Kt.* **fētąlī** (*cf.* **zųbē**) (*generic term is* **shąsshāwą** = **askā**). (*N.B.—two cuts each side are made by* **Nufāwā**). (2) *Kt.* tribal mark consisting of 5 cuts on one side of face and 6–7 on the other (2 = **yarīmancī** = **durɓancī** 2).

    B. (billę) *Vb.* 1A = **billą**.

*ɓillę = **ɓallę**.

billi *m.* the act denoted by **billą** 2.

billō *m.* black patch on farm from burning of leaves.

bįlų *Bauchi Hausa m.* large beerpot.

bįlumbītųwā *f.* fruitless search.

bima A. (bimą) *Vd.* **bumą**.﹅

    B. (**Bįmą**) *f.* (1) Bima Hill near New Gombe. (2) *Vd.* **kā ƙi** ~.

bįmbįnī *m.* (1) = **bį̄ bąi**. (2) constantly thinking of *x* **taną̄ bįmbįnim mutūwąr mijįntą** she always dwells on the memory of her late husband. (3) **yaną̄ bįmbįnim mąganąr** he's making exhaustive inquiry into the matter.

bin A. (bįn) (1) *Vd.* **bī**. (2) *Nor.* = **ban** 1.

    B. (bin) = **bį̄ ni** follow me ! (*cf.* **bin dą zugū**).

bį̄ ną̄sō *m.* type of guinea-corn or cassava thriving in damp soil.

bincikā *Vb.* 1C = **binciką** *Vb.* 2 (*Vd.* bincikē) investigated T. *x* **sum bincikā shi baƙinsą dą farinsą** they investigated it fully. **yā bincikō wą dūnīyą wannąŋ** he discovered this and revealed it to the world.

bincike A. (bincikē) *Vb.* 1C = **bincikā**.

    B. (bincikē) *m.* (*Secondary v.n. of* bincikā) *x* **yaną̄ bincikyansą** = **yaną̄ bincikā shi** = **yaną̄ binciką tasą** = **yaną̄ bincikē shi** he's investigating it.

bincililī *Sk. m.* = **mącililī**.

bincilmī *Kt. m.* = **bįcilmī**.

ɓincinā *Vb.* 1C = **ɓinciną** *Vb.* 2 (1) pinched off fragment *x* **nā ɓincini gōrǫ** I pinched off a bit of kolanut. (2) **nā ɓincinē shi dą ƙyar** I just managed to squeeze a trifle out of him ; **bā yą̄ ɓincinūwā** he's an utter skinflint.

bincirā *Vb.* 1C **tā bincirą bąkī** she pursed up her lips.

bindą *f.* (1) **yā tāshi tsąye** ~ **as he** got up, he flapped his gown backwards with his arm (from lightheartedness or to get rid of dust). (2) **mąganąr tā yi** ~ the matter's common knowledge. (3) hitting water with hands or feet when swimming.

bin dą zugū *Kt.* = **bį̄ ni dą zugū**.

bindi A. (bindį) *Sk. m.* (1) tail of animal (= **wutsīyą**). (2) **yā yā dą** ~ he died. (3) **sulę mąi** ~ a shilling with figure of a lion.

    B. (bindī) *m.* (1) the horn **kǫbirą** 1 *q.v.* (2) = **zillī**.

bindigą *f.* (*pl.* bindigōgī) *Ar.* (1) (*a*) firearm (*epithet is* **gidigō ūwar fadą**). (*b*) (artillery) gun (= **įgwā**). (*c*) **bindigą mąi harbi nēsą** long-range gun. (*d*) ~ **mąi rūwā** machine-gun. (2) **jirgī yā yi bindigą** the ship exploded. **ƙafąr kēkē tā yi bindigą** the cycle-tyre burst. (3) (*a*) ~ **cikįŋ dą mųguntą** thou evil one ! (*b*) ~ **bą tą saŋ wāsā ba** don't play with fire ! (4) **bindigąr bąlāsanā** form of popgun. (5) **bindigąr karā** = **bindigąr sąkainā** child's toy-gun made of shards and cornstalks. (6) **bindigąr tąkandā** = **bindigąr sillē** pieces of sugarcane heated by child and struck against hard object to emit report. (7) **bindigąr ƙasā** = **bindigąr tąɓō** clay toy-gun (*cf.* **nānę** 1*d*). (8) **bindigąr ƙashī** toy-gun made of rear legbone of ram. (9) **bindigąr tąlo-tąlō** (*a*) the groaning noise **bus** made by turkey after spreading plumage (*cf.* **tūsą** 2). (*b*) **kadą ką cī ni dą bindigąr tąlo-tąlō** don't try to intimidate me ! (10) **bindigąr ƙųrā** flit-gun. (11) **Mąi** ~ *nickname for man called* **Ąbdųllāhi**. (12) **dam** ~ *m.* (*pl.* 'yam ~) gunman (*cf.* **kącallą**). (13) **bindigą ą rūwa** *Vd.* **saɓą** 3*b*.

bindǫ *Sk. m.* sling.

bindų *m.* = **bundų**.

ɓįŋ'ge–ɓįŋgē" *m.* petty cadging.

bingel *Vd.* **bįŋgyąl**.

bingi A. (bįŋgī) *Sk. m.* pond ; borrowpit.

    B. (bįŋgi) fowl with ruffled feathers = **fįŋgi** *q.v.*

    C. (bįŋgī) *m.* (*f.* bįŋgīyā) (1) any large donkey. *(2) *m.* = **bąŋgī**.

ɓiŋgil = ɓiŋgilī.

biŋgilē *Kt.* = buŋgụlē.

ɓiŋgilgil *x* tā ɗaurạ ɗan zanẹ ~ dạ shī she wore a tiny insufficient cloth.

ɓiŋgilī *m.* (*f.* ɓiŋgilā) *pl.* ɓiŋgil-ɓiŋgil tiny (*re* garment).

biŋgillạ *Sk. f.* = biŋgyallạ.

ɓiŋgirā (1) *Vb.* 3A toppled over and rolled into or on to T. *x* yā ~ cikin rāmị. (2) *Sk. Vb.* 1C to roll T. along (= mirginā 1*a*).

ɓiŋgirad dạ *Vb.* 4B caused to topple over.

ɓiŋgirē *Vb.* 3A (1) toppled over. (2) *Sk.* rolled along. (3) (*a*) yā ~ he died. (*b*) he is asleep.

ɓiŋgirērēnịyā *f.* acting *as in* ɓiŋgirē 1, 2.

ɓiŋgirī *m.* (1) fowl-disease (= fuffuk *q.v.*). (2) cirrhosis of liver in cattle due to liver-fluke. (3) yā yi ~ he died suddenly.

biŋgyal *m.* = biŋgyallạ *f.* = ɓiŋgyallạ *f.* = 'yar biŋgyallạ *f.* sleeveless shirt (*cf.* binjimā).

bịnī-bịnī = binị-binị constantly *x* ~ sǎi yạ zō yạ nẹmē shị he constantly comes in search of it. ~ bạ ka dạ wurin zụ̄wạ? sǎi gidānạ? is my home the *only* place you frequent?

bị ni dạ zugū *m.* physic-nut (= cị ni dạ zugū).

bị ni kạ lālạ̄cē *m.* (1) fragile part of branch (= rẹɗūwā). (2) tassels (= gọrụbai 2). (3) *epithet of bird* yautǎi.

bị ni kạ tsịntā *m.* tā yi ~ she has a coin suspended from her neck by a cord hanging down her back.

binịnī *m.* pollen (= bunụnī *q.v.*).

bịŋ īyā̀yē *m.* ~ gạrēshị he's a good son.

binjimā *f.* (*pl.* binjimōmī) sleeveless, wide-skirted shirt (*previously much in vogue*) = shāyạ 1*a* = *Kt.* bạ̄shādạ (*cf.* bịŋgyal).

biŋkịcē *Vb.* 1C = bincịkē.

binne A. (binnạ = binnẹ) *Vb.* 1A (1) buried P., T. (*cf.* shūkạ 1*c*; kai 3*a*.vii). (2) mạ̄ jī, mạ̄ ganī, am binnẹ tsōfwā dạ rạ̌i it seems impossible, but let's wait and see what'll happen. (3) ~ rāmị to fill in a hole (= cikẹ 1).
    B. (bịnnē) *m.* (1) sowing just before the rains. (2) " throwing a sprat to catch a whale." (3) buried charm (= ajīyạ 6*b q.v.*).

binnī *m.* walled town (= birnī *q.v.*).

bịnọ̄ what do I care?

Bīnōnọ extinct official position at Katsina.

bị nōnọ (1) *f.* type of guineacorn giving very white flour. (2) *m., f.* (*sg., pl.*) suckling bought with its dam.

ɓintạ *Vb.* 1A *Nor.* = ɓincinạ.

ɓintilā *f.* (1) short woman. (2) short gown. (3) scalpel (= bērạ 2, *q.v.*). (4) small white mat used by women.

bintsịrā *Vb.* 1C (1) pursed lips. (2) joggled buttocks, etc. (= buntsụrā *q.v.*).

Bīnūwại *m.* (1) River Benue. (2) hannum ~ " posh " looking harlot (= kịlākị).

bira A. (birạ) (1) *used in following*: nā faɗạ makạ kạ barị !, *reply,* nā ~ I told you to leave off ! : (reply) well, I *have* left off. (2) *f.* (*a*) *x* anạ̄ birạ = anạ̄ barị people are ceasing to do it. (*b*) *Sk.* ash borne on the wind.
    B. (bịra) *Vb.* 3B is (was) practically ripe (*re* dates, bananas, pawpaws, ɗọrawạ, ɗinyā, sheanut and a few other trees) = kōyạ 2*b* = harbạ, *cf.* nụna ; ƙōsạ 2*c* ; gōgẹ 2*a*, katsẹ 2*e*.
    C. *cf.* bụ̄ru.

ɓịrā *Vb.* 3B (1) jumped. (2) (lamb) gambolled.

bira-bira *f.* = bura-bura.

bịrạ̄birai *Vd.* birbirī.

birai *Vd.* birị.

bị rānā *m.* = bīyạ rānā.

birạ̄nē *Vd.* birnī.

birārị *m.* (1) jumping. (2) surging forward to get at T. (= haŋƙōrō *q.v.*).

birbịcē *Vb.* 1C *int. from* bicẹ.

birbijẹ = birbizọ.

birbirī *m.* (*pl.* bịrạ̄birai) (1) Bruce's fruit pigeon (*Vinago waalia*). (2) type of insectivorous bat.

birbiro A. (bịrbirọ) *m.* any adornment.
    B. (birbirō) *Nor. m.* = birbirī 2.

bịrbis *x* yanạ̄ cạŋ ~ he's up there.

bịrbiscэ̄ *Vd.* bịrbistạ.

bịrbishī *Sk.* (1) *m.* summit. (2) bịrbishin in excess of *x* sunạ̄ bịrbishiŋ gōmạ they're in excess of 10.

ɓịrɓishī *m.* = ɓarɓashī.

bịrbistạ *Vb.* 2 (*p.o.* bịrbịscē, *n.o.* bịrbịsci) *Sk.* surpassed.

birbịtā *Vb.* 1C *int. from* bitạ.

birbizọ *m.* refuse-pit (= bizọ).

bircici *m.* unkemptness (= burcici *q.v.*).

birdidi *x* an yi masa bŭlāla har wurin ya
yi ∼ he has wheals from his whipping
(*Vd.* rudŭ-rudŭ).

birdimēme, etc., huge (= firdimēme *q.v.*).

birdinnŭwa *Kt. f.* type of edible locust
(= burdŭdŭwa *q.v.*).

birga A. (birga) = burga.
   B. (birgā) = burgā.
   C. (birgā) *Kt. f.* anā birgar gwāzā
koko-yam is being cooked with potash or
ashes to remove acrid flavour.

bir'ga-birgā" *Sk.* quick-tempered =
bar'gi-bargī" 1 *q.v.*

birgāmi *m.* goatskin-bag (= burgāmi *q.v.*).

birge *Vb.* 1A whisked milk (= burga *q.v.*).

birgī *Sk. m.* (1) manuring ground by
tethering oxen there. (2) any trampled
place.

*bir'gi-birgī" quick-tempered (= bargi-
bargī *q.v.*).

*birgijē = birkicē.

birgijēje *m.* (*f.* birgijējīyā) hefty.

Birgiji an extinct official position at Kano.

birgimā *f.* (1) (*a*) animal's (*x* horse,
donkey) rolling on the ground
(= mabugā 2 *q.v.*). (*b*) *Vd.* 'damō 13.
(2) in jākī yā ga tōkā, sǎi ∼ that's in
your (his, etc.) line! (= jākī 1*d*).
(3) *Sk.* freshness of horse. (4) birgimar
hankāka, fikāfikim burtū = birgimar
hankāka, in ka ga farī, kā ga bakī
epithet of quick-tempered P. (= bargi-
bargī *q.v.*) or of P. who is Jekyll and
Hyde. (5) birgimar kaskō *Kt.* lightly
frying meat (= gashin kaskō *q.v.*).

biri A. (biri) *m.* (*f.* birinya) *pl.* birōrī =
birai (1) (*a*) (i) any monkey (*epithet is*
Wandu). (ii) *Vd.* bakim biri. (*b*) (i)
sǎi ∼ yā zō hannum Mālam ya kan
yi gŭda, in yā zo hannum Māguzāwā,
sǎi ya yi kŭkā when the cat's away,
the mice play (*as* Māguzāwā eat
monkeys, but Muslims not). (ii)
māganim ∼ karam Māguzāwā that is
the only way of getting the better of
him. (iii) ∼ yā mutu a gōnar arne
Vd. addu'a 1*c*. (*c*) (i) kō an kashe
∼, yā rigā yā yi barnā shutting the
stable-door after the horse is stolen.
(ii) kā faye barnā kaman gātam ∼
you're as destructive as a monkey.

(*d*) (i) rūwan rūwā wanda ∼ bā yā sō
humiliation can be borne from
superiors, but not from their servitors.
(ii) rūwan rūwā n ji ∼ *Vd.* rūwā
B. 17. (*e*) "Allā wadai!" bā ta
kōmē da dam ∼ he's utterly brazen.
(*f*) ∼ bai ki murŭcī ba, sǎi dǎi wuyar
haka all seek success, but it's hard to
attain. (*g*) kō ∼ yā karye, ya hau
rumfū = lālāce 3. (*h*) kō ∼ yā san
gōnar gwāzā, sǎi ya gēwaye ta do not
attack P. stronger than yourself!
(*j*) barnar ∼ *Vd.* barnā. (*k*) anā ganin
wuyam ∼, a kan daure shi a wutsī
from respect one uses a pseudonym.
(*l*) ∼ yā san jibad da yake wa kāshī
everyone knows his own limitations.
(*m*) kōwā ya ga ∼, da bakin hannunsa
ya gan shi everyone is as God made
him, good or bad. (*n*) tsugune ba ta
kāre ba (*the person to whom this is said,*
replies an sai da ∼ an sayi kare the
matter's far from finished!). (*o*) zā
mu fēde maka ∼ har wutsīya we shall
reveal all the details to you. (*p*) ∼ sǎi
ganī *Vd.* bābā 1*d*. (*q*) ∼ bōko *Vd.*
bōko 1*c*. (*r*) bā a yi wa ∼ burtū *Vd.*
burtū. (*s*) būzum ∼ *Vd.* mālami 1*c.*xi.
(*t*) bā nā abuta da ∼ *Vd.* abuta 2. (*u*)
Vd. kan ∼. (2) ∼ kanā ganin garī.
kāfin ka gan shi, yā rigā yā gan ka
never underrate your opponent! (*Vd.*
ganin garī). (3) ∼ da gishirī *epithet of*
"the man in the street" (talaka).
(4) an yi wa barāwo daurim ∼ thief
has been tied round the waist. (5) ∼
yā hau kanta she's possessed by the
bōrī spirit called biri, this enabling
her to climb high. (6) flour in which
furā is rolled (= burburko). (7) dattijam
∼ *Vd.* dattijo 1*b*. (8) tākim ∼ *Vd.*
tāki 2*c.*iv. (9) tarnakim ∼ *Vd.* tarnakī.
(10) dukum ∼ *Vd.* duku 2. (11) *Vd.*
wutsīyar biri, tūwam biri, gāgara biri,
ta'adim biri, gudum biri.
   B. (birī) *m.* dried, pounded fruit of
dum-palm (gōruba).

biri-biri A. (biri-biri) *m.* (1) ganinsa ∼
ne his sight is poor. (2) faint light of
early dawn *x* garī yā yi ∼ it was the
time of the faint light of early dawn
(*Sk.* biji-biji 2).

B. (birī-birī) x yā yi minị $\sim$ he " threw dust in my eyes ".

C. (birī-birī) m. a food of flour flavoured with desert-datetree (adūwạ) juice (= adūwạ 2).

Birigēdīyạ *Eng. m.* Brigadier.

birīji m. groundnuts (*cf.* kwalcị).

birik *Sk.* = biris.

birincin kulạ x (1) $\sim$ askā tā bacẹ maị kōrā what do I care! ; what does it matter ? (2) *cf.* birinkulā ; biris 2.

biringan *Eng. m.* Bren-gun.

biringizau m. cowries.

birinkādūwā f. gadding about.

birinkinsạ = birinkintạ *Vb.* 3B assumed serious proportions (= gāwurtạ *q.v.*).

birinkulā *Vd.* batạn.

birinkyādūwā f. = birinkādūwā.

birinyạ *Vd.* birị.

biris m. (1) ignoring P. (*its epithet is* ungulū tā tākạ shūnī, ta cẹ " kō biris ! "); mun yi $\sim$ dạ shī we ignored him. (2) (*said by women*) kō $\sim = \sim$ kullē $= \sim$ kutukullē (*Vd.* birincin kulạ) what do I care ! (3) *adv.* in abundance.

birishin kulạ *Kt.* = biris 2.

birītītị m. silly chatter.

birji m. gravel (= burjị *q.v.*).

birjik *adv.* abundantly.

birkēkẹ m. (*f.* birkēkīyā) huge.

birki *Eng. m.* (*pl.* birkōkī) (1) brick. (2) = burkị.

birkicē (1) *Vb.* 3A is (was) in disorder x gidansạ yā $\sim$ (*a*) his home is in disorder. (*b*) his home is rent by quarrels. hankạlinsạ yā $\sim$ he's not right in his mind. (2) *Vb.* 1C (*a*) muddled together. (*b*) disorganized. (*c*) (current) swept P. away. (*d*) (i) rolled T. over. (ii) (wrestler) threw opponent. (iii) bạ kā dạ gīwā kẹ dạ wuyā ba, kāfin ạ birkicē ta, ạ yankạ ta it's easy to begin anything, but hard to see it through to the end. (*e*) (i) stripped off (garment) by turning inside out. (*f*) threw out (contents of wide vessel).

birkicī exclamation of surprise at act denoted by birkicē.

birkiɗa A. (birkiɗā) *Vb.* 1C (1) yā birkiɗạ rigā ạ ƙas he soiled his gown

by sitting or letting it trail. (2) yā birkiɗạ gōnā dạ tākị he manured the farm. (3) tā birkiɗạ nāmạ ạ gishirī she rolled meat in salt to flavour it. (4) kept on turning (dambū *or* māsạ for all surfaces to be evenly cooked). (5) mixed things together. (6) muddled up. (7) *Sk.* = rikiɗā.

B. (birkiɗạ) *Vb.* 3B (1) (animal x horse, donkey) rolled on the ground (*cf.* birgimā). (2) rigā tā $\sim$ ạ ƙas gown became soiled from sitting or trailing on ground. (3) lēmạ tā $\sim$ the lēmạ gown lost its indigo gloss. (4) sum $\sim$ they're mixed up, muddled together. (5) *Sk.* = rikiɗạ.

birkiɗaɗɗēnīyā rolling over and over on ground.

birkiɗē (1) *Vb.* 1C = birkiɗā 1-6. (2) *Vb.* 3A = birkiɗạ 2-5.

birkiɗēɗẹ m. (*f.* birkiɗēɗīyā) huge.

birkiɗēɗēnīyā f. rolling over and over on the ground.

birkilạ m. (*pl.* birkilōlī) *Eng.* bricklayer.

birkita A. (birkitạ) *Vb.* 3B = birkicē 1. B. (birkitā) *Vb.* 1C = birkicē 2.

birkitad dạ *Vb.* 4B = birkicē 2.

birnancī m. the pertness and cocksureness of sophisticated townsmen (= marāyancī), *cf.* zāmanancī, birnī.

birnē m. sowing before rains fully set in when they are late (= bursunē 2).

birnī m. (*pl.* birānē) (1) (*a*) walled town (*cf.* alkaryạ, garī). (*b*) birnin kūrā *Vd.* kūrā 53. (*c*) zūcīyar mutum birninsạ your mind is your best counsellor. (2) (*a*) capital x birnim Fạransī the capital of France, Paris. (*b*) town (*as contrasted with country*) x dawākī dạ na $\sim$ dạ na ƙauyẹ horses both from the capital and from the " bush ". bạ maị zūwạ $\sim$ dạga ƙauyẹ nobody comes into " Town " from the " country " (= kwatạ 1*c*). (3) Birnin Gwārī *Vd.* banzā. (4) (*a*) yā shigạ birninsạ = yā shigẹ birninsạ he is in congenial company. (*b*) *Vd.* Dālā 2*c*. (*c*) dūwaiwai yā ƙi shigā $\sim$ *Vd.* gaddamạ. (5) *Sk.* = gārū, *i.e.* townwall. (6) birnin (= gārun) ƙauyẹ yā sōmạ fādūwā reaping has begun. (7) birnin rāirayī (*a*) spendthrift. (*b*) anything (*x* money, knowledge, etc.) hard to amass but easy to lose (*epithet is* Birnin ràirayī, dạ wuyar tāyạrwā, dạ saurin rūshẹ̄wā). (*c*) *Vd.* talạkạ 2*b.* (8) cīwạm birnī *m.* syphilis (= tunjērē). (9) mạnyam ~ *Vd.* bạsarākẹ. (10) bāyam ~ *Vd.* bāyā 2*a.* (11) kạjim ~ *Vd.* awāyẹ. (12) ƙafạr ~ *Vd.* ạrạhā 4. (13) bạ̄ ka gidā ~ *Vd.* arnẹ. (14) jạkim ~ *Vd.* jạkin 3.

birōrī *Vd.* biri̦.

bi̦rtuntu̦nā *f.* smut-fungus (= bu̦rtuntu̦nā *q.v.*).

bi̦s *Sk.* = bisạ.

bisa A. (bisạ) (1) bisạ = bisạ kạn *prep.* (*a*) (i) on, on to.   (ii) sunạ̄ ~ kạnsạ they are attacking him. (iii) kōmē ta ~ ƙārẹ̄wā tạ̄ yi ƙasạ no smoke without fire ! (iv) sāram ~ bā yā kisạ̦ itạ̄cē small loss is not ruin. (*b*) dạgạ ~ kạn from on *x* yā fāɗō dạgạ ~ kạn ɗāki̦ he fell off the roof. (*c*) dạgạ ~ dạ above *x* dạgạ ~ dạ kọ̄gwaŋ itạ̄cē above the cavity in the tree. (*d*) re *x* (i) ~ zạncan nạŋ re this matter. (ii) *Sk.* ~ gạ kyau, yā fī tạ he's better than she is. (*e*) in accordance with *x* ~ ạl'ādạ tasạ in accordance with his custom. ~ īkwạŋ Allạ̄ in accordance with God's will. (*f*) *conj.* according to how *x* ~ gạ yạddạ sukạ sābạ according to their habit (*cf.* 5 *below*). (2) (*a*) *adv.* up above *x* (i) ~ dạ ƙasạ above and below. (ii) sạndāna yạ kwam ~ *Vd* ạbū̀tā 2. (iii) yā yi sārā dạ mu̦tu̦m ạ ~ *Vd.* sārā 3. (*b*) ạ ~ = dạgạ ~ up above *x* yanạ̄ ~ = yanạ̄ dạgạ bisạ he's up above. (*c*) tafīyạ ~ *f.* journeying on horseback (*cf.* samạ 2*c,* ƙasạ 3). (*d*) *Kt.* ɗam ~ *m.* grass roof of cornbin (= bākīrẹ). (3) *Sk. m.* (*a*) the top. (*b*) bisạn *prep.* above. (4) *cf.* samạ. (5) = bi̦sạ = 1*f above.* (6) *Vb.* 1A *Kt.* buried (= binnẹ).

  B. (bi̦sạ) *Sk.* (1) *conj.* according as *x* ~ yā sani̦, ya aikạ he did it fully realizing its import (= bisạ 1*f*). (2) *prep.* against *x* Allạ̄ yạ tayạ mu ~ maƙiyammu̦ God help us against our foes !

  C. (bisā) *f.* (*pl.* bisạ̄shē = bisạ̈isạ̈i)

(1) (*a*) domestic quadruped (= dabbạr gidā). (*b*) ƙanānạm bisạ̄shē goats, sheep. (*c*) rānar kāyā ạkwīyạ bạ̄ ~ ba cẹ̄ don't attempt the impossible !   (2) height *x* yā fī tạ ~ he's taller than she is. (3) = bishīyạ.

  D. (bi̦sā) *Kt. f.* an tạfi wurim ~ tasạ people have gone to where he is to be buried.

  E. (bisạ̄) (*said by ushers*) disperse, for the Emir's audience is over !

bi̦ sạbcē = bi̦ saucē.

bisa-bisạ (1) *adj.* superficial (= garma-garma). (2) *adv.* superficially.

bisạ̈isạ̈i *Vd.* bisā.

bi̦sạlạ̄mī *m.* (1) (*a*) scimitar (= haŋkạti̦lō = hi̦ndī). (*b*) *epithet is* ~ dạ kūɗạ = gạyạ jinī "nā wucẹ". (2) in rūwā yā ci mu̦tu̦m, kō am bā shi̦ ~ sại yạ kāmạ a drowning man clutches at a straw.

Bi̦ sallạ *name for* child born the day after a festival.

bisạn *Vd.* bisạ 3*b.*

bisānī *x* dạgạ ~ (= ạ ~ = sại dạgạ bi̦sānin naŋ) sukạ tāshi̦ then they finally set out.

bi̦ sartsẹ *m. Euphorbia lateriflora* (= fī̦ dạ sartsẹ *q.v.*).

bisạ̄shē *Vd.* bisā.

bi̦ saucē *m., f.* (*sg., pl.*) P. with no will of his own.

bi̦sbistạ *Vb.* 2 (*p.o.* bi̦sbiscē, *n.o.* bi̦sbisci) surpassed.

bish dạ ƙayạ *epithet of* hedgehog (būshīyā).

bishaishai *Vd.* būshīyā.

bi̦shakki̦l ạnfusi̦ *Ar.* only by a fluke *x* ~ mukạ ku̦butạ only by a fluke did we escape (= dạ kyar).

bi̦ shānū *Zar. m.* type of sandals (= faɗẹ).

bi̦shārạ *Ar. f.* good tidings.

bishe A. (bishẹ) *Kt. Vb.* 1A buried (= binnẹ).

  B. (bīshē) *Vd.* bī̦ dạ.

bishi *m.* (1) rump of meat. (2) *Kt.* type of drum.

bishi̦nō *m.* = bạshi̦nō.

bishi̦r = bishi̦rī *m.* type of red and white saddlecover.

bishi̦rāɗi̦ *m.* big bishi̦r.

bishiya A. (bishīyạ) *f.* (*pl.* bishīyōyī) (1) any tree. (2) *Vd.* daƙwạ̄lẹ.

B. (bishīyā) *f.* hedgehog (= būshiyā *q.v.*).

bisimillẹ̃ = bismillẹ̃.

biskiti *Eng. m.* (*pl.* biskitōcī) biscuit.

bismillẹ̃ *Ar.* (1) (*a*) please stand up! (*b*) please sit down! (*c*) pray approach! (*d*) pray enter! (*e*) (i) please start work! (ii) bismillẹ̃ cē kawai it is a mere beginning. (iii) dẹgẹ nẹn nē zā mụ fārẹ rubũtẹ bismillẹrmụ this is where we begin to act. (iv) sĀi sukẹ hau musụ bẹ̃ salamẹ, bẹ̃ bismillẹ̃ then they attacked them forthwith. (v) ẹ wẹnnẹŋ karọ, mum fārẹ sẹ̃ bismillẹ̃ dẹ wurī we've made a good beginning with this attack. (2) join us in our meal! (*reply*, ẹ dau ẹnīyẹ no thanks, I'm replete). (3) an yi masẹ ~ he's been given leave to enter, etc. (4) yā yi ~ ukụ he said bismillāhi *q.v.* three times. (5) ~ dẹ nī dẹ kai you'll regret your treatment of me! (6) *Vd.* bismillāhi ; kibtẹ 3.

bismillāhi *Ar.* (1) *formula said on* standing up, sitting down, starting work, beginning meal, etc. (*cf.* bismillẹ̃). (2) good heavens! (3) Bismillāhirrẹhmāni-rrẹhim in the name of God the Merciful! (*Vd.* lāyẹ 1*a*.i).

bisnẹ *Vb.* 1A *Sk.* buried (= binnẹ).

bisọ *m.* (1) (*a*) act of burying. (*b*) haifũwā tatẹ gōmẹ, bẹ tẹ tabẹ̃ ~ ba none of her 10 children have died. (2) an yi masẹ ~ = am fitar masẹ dẹ ~ evil charm has been buried in his house (= ajīyẹ 6*b*). (3) ẹ bā nị farim ~ give me a present to celebrate your luck! (*said to lucky suitor of girl by unlucky suitor or by grandfather to lucky suitor*). (4) nā īyẹ bisẹm mai dōrō har kẹzāzẹ tasẹ I wasn't born yesterday!

bistẹ *f.* mail, post (= bustẹ *q.v.*).

bita A. (bītẹ = *Kt.* bịtā) *f.* (1) nā yi masẹ ~ I (a more skilled fellow pupil of his) went through a non-Koranic text with him (*cf.* bīkọ 4 ; bīyẹ 1*c*). (2) mai ~ assistant Arabic-teacher.

B. (bitẹ) (1) *f.* (*Eng.* beater) repairing the permanent way of the railway, the workers being called 'yam ~ *or* 'yan digẹ. (2) *Vb.* 1A (*with dative*) *x* yā

bitẹ musụ kụrā he covered them in dust (*cf.* bicẹ).

bị ta dẹ kallō *m.* type of woman's striped cloth.

bị ta dẹ kụllī *m.* constant nagging or punishment.

bị ta daudau = bị ta zaizai.

bị ta dẹ zugū *m.* physic-nut (= bị ni dẹ zugū).

bị ta dwandwaŋ *m.* = bị ta zaizai.

bịtẹlmaŋ *m.* treasury (= baitụlmāli, *q.v.*).

bitẹ wutā *m.* convolvulus (= yaryẹdī 1).

bị ta zaizai *m.* (1) type of ant seen in pairs, one urging on the other (= gẹmẹdīdī). (2) (*a*) P. dogging one. (*b*) dogging a P. (3) tā bā shi ~ = tā cīshē shi ~ = yā gẹmu dẹ ~ she put a drug in her vagina to cause her husband to love her.

bịtịlmī *Sk. m.* = bịcịlmī.

bitirī poor quality bulrushmillet-heads (= kụftirī).

bitittịkē *Vb.* 3A is (was) in a bad temper (= bututtụkē, *q.v.*).

bitō *Vd.* bicẹ 2*b*.

bị tsāmī *m.* (*sg.*, *pl.*) type of small fly infesting fruit, etc.

bị tsatsō *m.* worn-out cloth repaired by cutting in half where worn and turning those edges to become new outer edges (*epithet is* ~ matukar wụyā), *cf.* gami 3*a*.

bituk = butuk.

bịtụlmāli *m.* treasury.

biya A. (bīyẹ) (1) *Vb.* 1A (*a*) *x* nā ~ ta kansẹ = nā ~ ta wurinsẹ I called at his house (= bī 9 *q.v.*). (*b*) (i) read with audible movement of the lips (*cf.* dūbẹ 6). (ii) read (passage) aloud. (*c*) nā ~ masẹ kẹrātū I (teacher) went over passage in Koran or other book with him (pupil), *cf.* bītẹ; gayẹ 4 ; bīkọ ; darẹsū. (*d*) added T. to T. *x* kẹ ~ wata igīyẹ kẹŋ wannẹŋ join another rope to this! jīyẹ am bā shi rịgā, yau akẹ ~ dẹ wẹndō yesterday he was given a gown and to-day trousers. (*e*) Allẹ̃ yẹ ~ bẹ̃kiŋkẹ may God grant your wish, bring your statement to pass! (*f*) *Vd.* bīyẹ compounds (g) *cf.* tikā. (2) *m.* (v.n. of bīyā 1) *x* (*a*) munẹ̃ bīyẹnsẹ we're paying it (him). (*b*) **bīyam bukātā yā fi cin rība** fulfilment of desires is better than profit (*Vd.* **bīyā** 1*b*). (*c*) *Vd.* **bīyan**-*compounds.* (*d*) *Vd.* **farim** ~. (3) *m.* (*Sk. f.*) wages, salary, purchase-price. (4) *Eng. f.* beer.

B. (**bīyā**) (1) *Vb.* 5 (*Vd.* **bīyā** 2) (*a*) paid *x* **yā** ~ **shi** he paid him ; he paid for it. **yā** ~ **ni bāshina** he paid me the debt owing. **yā** ~ **mini bāshina gun Audu** he paid for me the debt I owed Audu. (*b*) **yā** ~ **mini bukātā** (*or* **murādina**) (i) he granted my wish. (ii) it met my requirements (*Vd.* **bīyā** 2*b*). (iii) *Vd.* **ungulū 7**. (*c*) **himmarsu tā** ~ **su** their courage was all that could be required. (2) *Vb.* 3A *x* **murādina yā** ~ = **bukātata tā** ~ my wishes have been fulfilled.

C. (**bīyā**) *Sk. f.* (1) (*a*) **hanyar bā ta dā dādim** ~ the road is not pleasant to traverse (= **bi** *q.v.*) (*b*) **abim** ~ *Vd.* **Wazīri**. (2) **sunā bīyar Allā** they obey God (= **bin**).

bīyad dā *Vb.* 4A subjugated (= **bī dā**, *q.v.*).

bīyā gāwā *Kt. m.* pounded bulrush-millet flour given those who attended a funeral (= **jingir**).

bīyā kōrā *Vd.* **dakakī**.

bīyal *Sk.* = **bīyar** *q.v.*

bīyan daddawar mutānan ƙauye *m.* paying for T. previously bought and at same time taking another on credit (*epithet is* **gā na jīyā, ban na yau** !).

bīyantā *Vb.* 1C *Sk.* (1) = **bīyā** 1*d*. (2) = **bīyā** 1*a x* **bāshin nan bā shi bīyantūwā** this debt cannot be paid.

bīyar *f.* (1) (*a*) five *x* **bīyar tā fi uku** 5 exceeds 3. (*b*) (*after* the thousands beginning from 2,000, *we can use* **bīyar** *for* five hundred) *x* **alfyan dā** ~ 2,500 ; 2,005. **talātā dā** ~ 3,005 ; 3,500. **arbā dā** ~ 4,500 ; 4,005. etc. (*b*) *Vd.* **bīyū** 3*b*. (2) **wōkacī** ~ *m.* the 5 daily Muslim prayer times. **yāro nē ; wōkacī** ~, **ɗayā bā yā wuce shi** though only a boy, he's already a devout Muslim. (3) **bīyar dn su** = **bīyārinsu** = *Kt.* **bīyardāninsu** five of them. (4) **gidam** ~ *m.* five-square pattern on gown.

bīyā rānā *m.* the undershrub *Crotalaria obovata*.

bīyar dā *Vb.* 4A subjugated (= **bī dā** *q.v.*).

bīyat *Sk.* = **bīyar**, *q.v.*

bīyatā *Vb.* 1C *Sk.* (1) = **bīyā** 1*d*. (2) = **bīyantā** 2.

bīyau *m.* child or animal which follows P. it knows.

bīyayyā *f.* obedience ; loyalty. *x* **bā wadfandā sukā fī su** ~ **gā Sarkī** the chief has no more faithful followers than they. **kaifim bīyayyarku garēni** your zealous obedience to me.

bīyayyē *m.* (**bīyayyīyā** *f.*) *pl.* **bīyayyū** (1) disciplined. (*d.f.* **bī dā**). (2) **hanyā bīyayyīyā** traversed road (*d.f.* **bī**).

biye A. (**bīye**) *Vb.* 1A (*with dative*) (1) **kadā kā** ~ **masa** don't follow his example ! (2) **nā** ~ **masa abu** I went over the whole passage with him (*as in* **bīyā** 1*c q.v.*). (3) **nā** ~ **masa san zūcīyā tasā** I granted his request : **kadā a** ~ **wā zūcīyā santā** don't follow evil instincts !

B. (**bīyē**) *m.* (1) following persons permanently migrated, wrongly to collect their tax as if still resident in former place *x* **an yi musu** ~ they've been followed *as above* : **yanzu an hana** ~ *the practice mentioned above* has been made illegal (= **bī dangi** 2). (2) **yā saukē Alkur'an, ammā dā** ~ he's been right through Koran from text, not from writing-board (**allō**) = **gayē** 2.

C. (**bīye**) *x* **yanā bīye dā bāyan wutar dawā** he is following the path of a bush-fire (*Vd.* **bī**). **sunā** ~ **dā Kano** they're under jurisdiction of Kano.

biyu A. (**bīyu**) *Vb.* 3B *x* (1) **hanyar bā tā bīyūwā** the road is not traversable (*Vd.* **bī** 9). (2) **sum** ~ they're disciplined, tractable (*Vd.* **bī** 2).

B. (**Bīyu**) *f.* Biyu District.

C. (**bīyū**) *f.* (1) (*a*) (i) two. (ii) **wannan yā rabā musu hankali bīyū** this made them hesitate (*Vd.* **5** *below*). (*b*) **na** ~ *m.* (*f.* **ta** ~) *pl.* **na** ~ (i) the second. (ii) **a gidā bā shi dā na** ~ he has no equal so long as nobody else competes with him. (*c*) **na** ~ *adv.* secondly. (*d*) *x* **ashirim** ~ **bābu** 18. **talātin** ~

bābu 28. ạrbạ'im ~ bābu 38 *etc.* (2) ɗam ~ *m.* (*a*) one of twins (*Vd.* tagwāyē). (*b*) 'yam ~ *pl.* twins. (*c*) 'Yam ~ *name given* one of two twins (either sex) *x* yāka 'Yam bīyụ come here, Twin! (3) (*a*) of two kinds *x* dạbāra tā zamā ~ two kinds of plan are possible. (*b*) bīyun the double of *x* sun yi bīyummụ yawạ they outnumber us by two to one (*cf.* ukụ). sun yi ~ ɗŋ ạbin dạ mukạ ƙērạ bạra they are double what we manufactured last year (*Vd.* amshẹ 3). (4) idansạ ~ nẹ he's awake. (5) haŋkạlinsạ yā rạbu ~ his thoughts are elsewhere, he's distrait (*Vd.* 1*a*.ii *above*). (6) tā yi jūnā ~ she's pregnant. (7) bākī ~ garēshi (*a*) he's a " twister ". (*b*) he never sticks to the same story. (8) zūcīyā ~ garēshi he's a thief, dishonest. (9) magana ~ garēshi he is two-faced (*cf.* 14). (10) gidā ~ māganiŋ gōbarā don't put all your eggs in one basket ! (11) gidā ~ lālāta kạrē don't fall between two stools ! (12) gidạm ~ nẹ there's this world and the next. (13) idan nī ɗam mutụm ~ nẹ, sǎi nā rāmạ I'll be revenged as sure as I'm trueborn ! (14) (*a*) zạn yi magana bīyụ ? shall I give you a word of advice ? (*cf.* 9). (*b*) fuskạ ~ *f.* hypocrisy. (15) Dāmishi, kā ƙi ganī ~ he's one who insists on his orders being obeyed at once (*Vd.* dāmisạ 2). (16) ạbu yā zamẹ masạ ~, gạba wutā, bāya wutā it was a matter of his being between the devil and the deep sea. (17) masō ~ *Vd.* masō 3. (18) mīyạ ~ *Vd.* mīyạ 13. (19) yā rabạ ɗayā ~ *Vd.* rabạ 1*m*. (20) darē ~ *Vd.* darē 5. (21) *Vd.* dūbam ~ shā bīyar, bīyụ byụ, dūban bīyū, cikị 6, zakkạ, kwānā A.1 5.

bīyụ byụ (1) sun yi minị ~ the two events occurred to me simultaneously. (2) ~ kāmuŋ gafīyạr ɓaidụ " falling between two stools " (*Vd.* gafīyạ 4).

bị zāƙi *m.* the tree cị zāƙi *q.v.*

bīzarō *used in* ūwar ~ *f.* slut (= ta bīzarō).

bizbistạ = bisbistạ.

biznạ *Vb.* 1A *Sk.* buried (= binnẹ *q.v.*).

bizọ *Sk. m.* rubbish-heap, refuse-pit (= birbizọ).

bōbạ (1) *Sk. m.* redhaired goat with black stripe along back. (2) *Vd.* būbụ 3.

bōbāwạ = bạbbāwạ.

bobo A. (bōbọ) *m.* = būbụ. B. (bōbō) *Sk. m.* type of. insect (= shā darē).

bōbụ *m.* = būbụ.

bōbūwā = bōbwā *f.* (*sg., pl.*) (1) spiderfly infesting horses (= bạrbajẹ). (2) gadfly. (3) bōbwar tạttabạrā a pigeon parasite.

ɓōɓūwā = ɓōɓwā *Sk. f.* brain (= ƙwaƙwalwā).

bōcạ *Eng. f.* voucher.

bōdạ *f.* (1) the cry of horse or ox roused by proximity of rival, etc. (2) cry of animal on heat (*cf.* ɓōlōlō). (3) prancing and excitement of spirited horse. (4) living in comfortable circumstances. (5) type of children's water-game (*cf.* 'yā).

bōɗaɗɗạr (1) yanạ dạ hancị ~ he is large-nosed. (2) tanạ tạfīyạ ~ she's walking with quivering buttocks.

bōɗaɗɗạrī *m.* (*f.* bōɗaɗɗạrā) (1) large-nosed. (2) big-buttocked.

bōdạmī *m.* wrapping for broken potash (= burɗụmī, *q.v.*).

bōɗar-bọ̄ɗạr = bōɗaɗɗạr.

bōɗạrī *m.* (*pl.* bōɗạrai). (1) the small, furry mammal zorilla (*epithet is* Na rārạ). (2) mai tūsạ kạmar ~ P. always farting. (3) tūsạ tā ƙārẹ ạ bōɗạrī sǎi shēwạ evil P. is at end of his tether. (4) bạ ạ yi kōmē ba, an dannẹ kạm bōɗạrī, am bar shākịrā the mischief is scotched, not killed.

bōɗạrī *m.* (*f.* bōɗạrā) = bōɗaɗɗạrī.

bōdẹ *m.* (*sg., pl.*) *Sk.* (1) gift by merchant on his return. (2) wharf. (3) customs-duty. (4) cost of freight by rail or water. (5) a former levy on travellers.

boɗo A. (boɗō) (1) yā zaunạ ~ he sat exposing his person (= bạɗō *q.v.*). (2) ɗam = you rogue ! B. (bọ̄ɗọ̄) *x* yanạ dạ hancị ~ (= bōɗaɗɗạr 1).

bōɗọ̄ɗọ̄ (1) ~ bọ̄ɗaɗɗạr. (2) = boɗō 1.

bō'ẹ bạ kāshī oh ! (*cry of pain*), *cf.* bē'ẹ.

bōgazā *f.* (1) large hen. (2) big slut.
bọjantạ *Vb.* 3B acted *as in* **bōjwā**.
bọjō *m.* (1) **yanā̤ ~ a̤ kā̤sūwā** it's cheap. (2) *Zar.* stunted goat.
bōjwā *f.* (1) rapid travelling by trader (*called* **ɗam ~**) unencumbered by women or heavy baggage (epithet *is* **~ sa̤mā̤riŋ kwānọ**) = **fijigạ** = **gụrumfạ** (*cf.* **kirī**). (2) **mụ yi bōjwa bōjwa** let's travel fast and far!
bōkā *m., f.* (*pl.* **bōkā̤yē**). (1) (*a*) native doctor (*Vd.* **gwa̤urau**). (*b*) **gwa̤urau bōkan Tūrai** *epithet of* European doctor (*Vd.* **likitạ**). (*c*) **bōkaŋ giji̤ bā yā̤ cī̤** = **bōkaŋ giji̤ bā yā̤ ci̤ŋ kā̤zā** = **bōkar giji̤ bā tā̤ ci̤** (*lit.* one's family doctor gets no fee) nobody is a prophet at home! (2) (*a*) wizard. (*b*) **yā zamā ƙa̤rya̤tạ bōkā** he is one who falsifies predictions. (*c*) **bā̤kī ya̤ bōkā, sā̤i suka̤ zō** then they suddenly appeared. (*d*) **yā gā̤ga̤ri ~** *Vd.* **mālạmī** 1*c*.iv. (*e*) *Vd.* **kā fi ~**. (3) mirror. (4) **bōkaŋ Allā̤** the scarlet insect **dā̤munā 9**. (5) **bōkaŋ gidā** *Sk.* the weed **na̤nnafō** *q.v.* (6) **bōkaŋ gijẹ** *Sk.* = **bōkaŋ giji̤** (*in* 1 *above*).
bōkanci̤ *m.* (1) acting as **bōkā 1, 2**. (2) **bōkanci̤n zūcī ga̤rēshi̤** he is distressed in mind.
bọƙarạ *Vb.* 3B = **bōƙa̤rā** *Vb.* 3A. (1) used every ounce of one's strength. (2) **yanā̤ bọƙarạ** he's swanking. (3) *Vd.* **a̤ bọƙarạ**.
bōƙa̤rē *Vb.* 3A refused to listen to reason.
bōƙasā *f.* = **bōgazā**.
bōkā̤yē *Vd.* **bōkā**.
bōkiti̤ *Eng. m.* (*pl.* **bōkitōcī**) bucket.
bōkọ *m.* (1) deceit, fraud, *e.g.* (*a*) (i) **yā yi masạ ~** he "doctored" the article (*cf.* **cụụ**): (ii) he deceived him. (*b*) T. treated as in **1** *x* **wanna̤ŋ tụrā̤rē ~ nē** this is adulterated perfume. (*c*) (i) **biri̤ ~ takẹ yi̤** she's girded herself with ropes to look like rich woman wearing many **jigi̤dā**. (ii) **biri̤ ~ yakẹ yi̤** = **1***a above*. (*d*) **rufi̤ŋ ƙōfa̤n naŋ ~ nē** this door's not properly closed: **ƙwaryar ~** calabash falsely looking full. (*e*) **yāƙim ~** mock-warfare; manœuvres. (*f*) *Vd.* **amaryā 6**; **karfasā**. (2) *Eng.* book *x* **ka̤rā̤tum ~** secular education: **makarantar ~** Govt.-controlled school.
bọkọ-bōkọ *m.* deception, fraud (*Vd.* **bōkọ 1**).
bọkọ̄kọ̄ *m.* (1) **an rufẹ ƙōfạ ~** = **an yi wạ ƙōfạ ~** = **bōkọ** 1*d*. (2) **gāwā tā tāsō, tanā̤ ~** = **gāwā tā tāsō a̤ ka̤n rūwā ~** corpse is bobbing up and down in the water (= **ba̤mbarō 2**). (3) *Vd.* **ba̤bba 5**; **ki̤ŋki̤mbōɗi̤**. (4) *Zamfara Hausa* cockroach.
bọkōkụ̄wā *f.* = **bōkọ 1***b*.
bōkōni̤ *x* **amaryar ~ bā̤ kūkā, bā̤ gūɗa̤** *epithet of* middling T. (*cf.* **amaryā 6**).
bola A. (**bọlạ**) *m., f.* (*sg., pl.*) white-faced horse or camel with white-ringed eyes (*cf.* **būlẹ**; **da̤nda 1***b*).
B. (**bōlạ**) *f. Zar.* refuse-pit.
ɓōlōlō *m.* cry of male camel on heat (*cf.* **bōdạ 2**).
bọlọ̄lō *m.* (1) drink made from **ɗọrawa̤**-pods (*cf.* **da̤gwada̤gō 2**). (2) flesh hanging from gullet of turkey or pelican. (3) any food made with water where milk is generally used (*cf.* **gā̤hūhụ**). (4) pounded bulrush-millet mixed with water (= **gụmbā**). (5) *Sk.* long part of turban (= **amāwa̤lī**).
bọm *Eng. m* (*sg., pl.*) bomb *x* (1) **sum bụgē mụ dạ ~** they bombed us. (2) **ɗam bọm** *m.* (*pl.* **'yam ~**) = **majē̤fī bọm** *m.* (*pl.* **majē̤fā bọm**) bomber-plane.
ɓọngyal *x* **tā ɗaurạ ɗan zanẹ ɓọŋgyal** she wore tiny, insufficient cloth (*cf.* **ba̤ngyel**).
Bọ̄nọ̄ *Vd.* **wa̤nzāmi̤** 1*c*.
bọ̄nọ̄nọ (1) **yanā̤ naŋ ~** he's idling about. (2) **yanā̤ naŋ ~ dạ bakạ** (= **~ dạ bā̤kī** = **~ dạ hanci̤**) he's being robbed without his knowledge.
bōrạ (*f.*) (*pl.* **bōrōrī**). (1) a disliked wife (*cf.* **mōwạ**). (2) **fushim ~** ineffectual anger. (3) **kụmburī a̤ mōwa̤, sakīya̤ a̤ bōrạ** "kissing goes by favour". (4) *Vd.* **mōwạ** 1*c*.
bōrạcē *Vb.* 3A flew into a rage (= **abọrcē**, *q.v.*).
bōrạcī *m.* (*a word used by women*) = **bōranci̤**.
bōramā *f.* (1) type of big sheep from the east. (2) **bōramar kā̤zā** big hen. (3) **bōramar būtạ** big gourd-bottle. (4)

bōramar haifūwā woman not conceiving till previous child about 5 years old.

bōrąncē = **bōrącē** *q.v.*

bōrancį *m.* (*a word used by women*) being a **bōrą** *x* **tanā̰ fāmā dą** ~ she's struggling against her husband's dislike.

bọrbọr *m.* gambolling of an animal.

bọrcī *m.* = **bōrancį**.

bǭrē *m.* (1) rebelliousness, intractability (*cf.* **abọrcē**). (2) sun yi masą **bǭrē** they rebelled against him. (3) yā tā dą **bǭrē** he revolted. (4) 'dam ~ *m.* (*f.* 'yar ~) *pl.* 'yam ~ rebel.

ɓōrē *Sk. m.* fig (= **ɓaurē** *q.v.*).

bọ̄rī *m.* (1) (*a*) the cult of being spirit-possessed. (*b*) yā hau ~ he's in state of **bọ̄rī** ecstasy. (*c*) ~ yā hau shį (i) = 1*b*. (ii) he's expert in **bọ̄rī**. (*d*) dam ~ *m.* (*f.* 'yar ~) *pl.* 'yam ~ devotee of **bọ̄rī** rites (= **kā̰rā** 5). (*e*) *Vd.* **jąngarai**. (2) (*a*) bā ā̰ ~ dą san jįkī = bā ā̰ ~ dą sanyin jįkī for P. really eager, no sacrifice can be too great. (*b*) halįn **gōdīyā**, halim **bọ̄rī** there's not a pin to choose between the two persons. (3) (*a*) tukunyā tanā̰ ~ pot's boiling over (= **wuyą** 1*h* = **zų̄ba** 2). (*b*) tukunyā įdan tā yi **bọ̄rī**, sai tą **ɓātą** **bā̰kįntą** cutting off one's nose to spite one's face. (*c*) taląką **bọ̄rin** tukunyā **gąrēshį** the poor are fleeced by those in power. (4) **bọ̄rįn ąngǫ** food-purchases by bridegroom's friends for giving to bridesmaids ('yam mātan aurē) on day after feast (**bįkī**). (5) **bọ̄rim bundųn** = **bọ̄rįn kunyą** feeling confused by ill-advised statement made by oneself or by another about oneself. (6) **bọ̄rin dankį** (*a*) tiny calabash. (*b*) **wāwā bọ̄rin dankį** *epithet of* fool. (7) **bọ̄rįn gyądā** (*a*) disease blackening groundnuts and making them bitter. (*b*) useless P. (*c*) *Vd.* **burum-burum**. (8) **bọ̄rįn kųrkunū** fleeting, irritating rash before guineaworm extrudes (= **gyąrgyąrtū** = **sā̰mīyyą** 2). (9) *Sk.* **bọ̄rįn kūką** rash said to be due to baobob-juice. (10) **bọ̄rin jā̰kī** infantile convulsions (= **tąfīyą** 7). (11) sandan 'yam ~ *Vd.* **sąndā** 1*n*. (12) **bā̰bam bọ̄rī** *Vd.* **ajįngį**.

bọ̄rin tįnkę *m.* (*sg., pl.*). (1) Marabou

stork. (2) tum bą ą haifį ūwar bądūkų ba, ~ yakę dą jąkā "teaching one's grandmother to suck eggs".

bōrōrī disliked wives (*Vd.* **bōrą**).

bororo A. (**bọrōrọ**) *m.* (1) crop of bird. (2) blister.
     B. (**Bọrōrō**) = **Bąrą̄rō**.

bōrų *m.* (1) rinderpest. (2) foot-and-mouth disease.

bọsarā *f.* big-buttocked woman (*epithet is* ~ karyą gadō).

bọsōrų̄wā *f.* (1) = **bọsarā**. (2) pointless or evasive talk. (3) a poor quality cf (*a*) tobacco; (*b*) saddle-cover (**jąlālą**); (*c*) gown; (*d*) cap (**tągīyą**).

ɓōtą *f.* (1) noise of flapping upper arm against side (= **ɓautą** *q.v.*). (2) (*a*) **ɓōtą** *Sk. f.* (*pl.* **ɓōtōcī**) haft (= **ƙōtą** *q.v.*). (*b*) *cf.* **tąllar ɓōtōcī** *under* **tąllą** 3.

bōtįran *Eng. m.* boat-train.

bōtọ *m.* (*pl.* **bōtōcī**). (1) roof-mat along centre of top of rectangular thatch-roof. (2) **bōtọ** = dam ~ (*a*) (= **bākįrę**) conical grass roof of corn bin (**rųmbū** *or* **rųfēwā**) or dyepit (**karōfī**). (*b*) grass-roof of grass-shelter (**rųmfā**), there being no mud wall (= **sarkę** 1). (3) funnel made from neck of bottle-gourd (**būtą**) = **mazurārī** 2.

ɓōtōcī *Vd.* **ɓōtą**.

bōtōcī *Vd.* **bōtọ**.

bọ̄tọ̄ramī *m.* (1) scarecrow made of bul-rush-millet stalks, with ragged gown, and pot (**tukunyā**) as hat. (2) an zubą ~ kąn zānā the stems of tobacco-plants have been put between split-beams (**azā̰rā**) and grass mats (**zānā**) of roof, to prevent depredations of white-ants to roof. (3) (*a*) mythical creature with large nostrils. (*b*) hancįm ~ gąrēshį he has huge nostrils.

ɓōtsąrē *Vb.* 3A *Nor.* yā ~ minį he defied me.

bōtsō (1) *m.* muddled state, *e.g.* dākį yā yi ~ the house is muddled up with furniture, loads, etc. **bōtsam mąganą** gąrēshį he's incoherent. (2) *m., f.* (*sg., pl.*) incoherent or untidy P.

bōtsọ̄tsọ confusedly *x* yanā̰ mąganą ~ he talks incoherently.

bōwąlī = **bawąlī**.

bǭyā *Sk. f.* slave girl (*Vd.* **bauyā, bāwą**).

ɓoye A. (**ɓōye̩**). (1) *Vb.* 1A (*Vd.* **ɓōyō**). (*a*) (i) hid T. (ii) **yā ~ mini̩ shī** he hid it (knowledge) from me. (*b*) (i) **yā ~ ra̩nsa̩** he made himself scarce. (ii) **ɓōye̩ ra̩ŋka̩**! im ba̩ haka̩ ba, a̩ yī ba̩nda̩ kai go while the going is good! (*c*) **Alla̩ ya̩ ~ shi a̩ kō̩gwam maɗa̩cī** *Vd.* **maɗa̩cī** 2. (*d*) **yanā ~ kudī** he's saving money (= **aji̩ye̩** 5*a*.i). (2) *Vb.* 3A is (was) hidden.

B. (**ɓō̩ye**) *x* **a̩ ~** *adv.* hidden; secretly.

bō̩yī *Eng. m.* (*pl.* **bō̩yī-bō̩yī**) steward-boy.

Ɓoyi̩ = Ɓō̩yi̩ (1) child born long after previous one (*considered hidden for years in womb*). (2) name for *such child* (*Vd.* **ɓō̩yō̩tō**).

ɓōyō *m.* (1) *Secondary v.n.* of **ɓōye̩** *x* (*a*) **muna̩ ɓōyansa̩ = muna̩ ɓōye̩ shi** we're hiding it. (*b*) **ɓōyan cībi̩yā** *Vd.* **cībi̩yā** 2. (*c*) **ɓōyam maganạ** *Vd.* **ciki̩** 4*a*.v. (2) **wa̩sam ~** *m.* (*a*) hide-and-seek. (*b*) surreptitious sexual intercourse of boys and girls. (3) **ɓōyan sūnā** superstitiously avoiding mention of name of P. (= **a̩lkunya̩** *q.v.*). (4) **ɓōya̩ŋ ha̩ŋkāka̩** forgetting where one hid T. (5) (*a*) **ɓōya̩ŋ ka̩i** leaving first page of book blank. (*b*) **ɓōya̩ŋ ka̩rā** leaving last page of book blank. (6) **ɓōya̩ŋ wāwā** (*a*) hiding T. but leaving clues. (*b*) supposed delay in rising of moon night a̩fter full-moon.

ɓō̩yō̩tō *x* **~ a̩jīya̩r Alla̩** *epithet of* **Ɓōyi̩** 2.

bōza̩ *f.* drumming and playing before chief on Friday night.

bō̩zō *x* **yana̩ ~ a̩ ka̩sūwā** it's cheap (= **bō̩jō** 1).

brōdi̩ *Eng. m.* bread; loaf; roll.

bu A. (**bu̩u̩**) *adv.* (1) (*a*) abundantly. (*b*) **yā tā da̩ inji̩m ~** he revved up the engine. (2) in disorder *x* **ga̩ gāshi̩nta̩ ~** her hair is untidy.

B. (**bu̩**) *x* **yā ce̩ ~** , **yā ce̩ me̩** he kept changing his mind.

C. (**bu̩**) *x* **bu̩ mu̩ zō ba** we didn't come. **bu̩ ku̩ zō ba** you didn't come. **bu̩ su̩ zō ba** they didn't come (*d.f.* **ba̩ . . . ba**).

ɓuɓa̩ *f.* (1) bargain *x* **nā sa̩mi ~ = nā sa̩mē shi̩ ~** I got it dirt-cheap.

(2) nymphomaniac (= **ta̩barmā wu̩yā**).

bubbu̩cī *Sk. m.* the grass *Panicum interruptum*.

ɓuɓɓuga̩ *Vb.* 3B (water of spring, sweat, etc.) welled up (= **tsattsafō**).

bubbu̩gē *Vd.* **ba̩kī** 1*b*.vii.

ɓuɓɓukēke̩ *m.* (*f.* **ɓuɓɓukēkīyā**) *pl.* **ɓuɓ-ɓukai-ɓuɓɓu̩ka̩i** hefty.

ɓuɓɓukī *m.* (*f.* **ɓuɓɓukā**) = **ɓuɓɓukēke̩**.

ɓuɓɓul *x* **Audu̩ yā yi ~** Audu's corpulent (= **ɓulɓul** *q.v.*).

ɓuɓɓu̩rjī *m.* type of bird.

bubbu̩rnīyā = ɓuɓɓu̩rnīyā *f.* (1) gambolling from joy, etc. (2) cracking of **duma̩ŋ kāshī**.

ɓuɓɓu̩tai *Kt. m.* **yana̩ ɓubbu̩tam faɗa̩** he's talking angrily (= **ɓa̩ɓɓa̩kī**).

būbu̩ *m.* (1) small twigs for firewood (= **būyāgī = mara̩bā** 5 = **ki̩ra̩rē** 1 = *Kt.* **ya̩ŋgā**). (2) pyorrhœa or ulceration of mouth in children (*cf.* **nōwa̩, ci̩zal, gu̩ɓa̩r ka̩rē, candi̩**). (3) **na ~** (= **na bōba̩ = na bōbo̩ = na bōbu̩) ne̩ma̩ ka̩ŋka̩ ka̩ne̩ = na būbu̩ na̩ŋ wa̩ ka̩ŋka̩ ka̩ne̩** (*a*) *epithet of* billygoat (*as it burbles before copulation and does so with its mother*). (*b*) *epithet of any* Don Juan.

būbu̩ku̩wā *f.* (1) the earliest type of grass springing up in dry season (*Tripogon minimus*). (2) **kaɗa̩ ka̩ yi sa̩mmakwan ~** don't make a good start and then tail off! (= **ku̩ru̩** 1*b*). (3) *Sk.* pelican (= **kwa̩sā-kwa̩sā**).

bu̩bu̩rnīyā = bubbu̩rnīyā.

būbwā = bōbwā.

bu̩cārā = ma̩cārā.

buce̩ = bice̩.

būɗa̩ *f.* d:y, windy harmattan haze (*cf.* **hu̩ntūru̩**).

buɗa A. (**būɗa̩**) *Vb.* 1A. (1) **yā ~ ba̩kī** he broke his fast at night in **azu̩mī** (*cf.* **būɗe̩** 1*a*; **būɗō**). (2) **ku̩ ~ masa̩ wurī ya̩ zauna̩** give him room to sit down! (3) **am ~ masa̩ kafā = am ~ masa̩ ka̩fa̩** he's been given a chance. (4) (*a*) **Alla̩ ya̩ ~ dāji̩** God prosper your hunting! (*said to hunter giving P. meat*) (*cf.* **bu̩ɗad dawa̩** : **būɗe̩** 1*e*). (*b*) (i) **yā ~ mini̩** he acquainted me fully with the matter. (ii) **am ~ maganạ = būɗā** 2. (*c*) **yā shāre̩ ka̩sā**, yā ∼ he (soothsayer) made a clear patch on the ground with his hand, to draw symbols. (5) *for other senses Vd.* būɗę. (6) *Vd.* būɗạ littāfị ; būɗạ rumbū.

B. (būɗā) *Vb.* 2. (1) took off cover and removed it *x* tā būɗi tukunyā she lifted cover off cooking pot and removed it (*cf.* būɗe 1*a*.iv). (2) yā būɗi ạsīrīna he revealed my secret (= būɗạ 4 *b*.ii = būɗę 1*a*.xii). (3) *Vd.* būɗad dawạ ; būɗar kầi ; būɗar kunnē.

C. (būɗạ) *f.* yā yi ∼ = būɗạ bāḳī ya yi = būɗạ 1.

D. (buɗạ) *Vb.* 1A *Sk.* sprinkled T. over *x* nā ∼masạ yājị I sprinkled condiments over it (= baɗạ).

būɗad dawạ *f.*.' (1) (*a*) the opening hunt of the season. (*b*) *cf.* būɗạ 4*a*. (2) sowing various cereals as prognostication among Maguzawa (= dāmunā 7, *q.v.*).

bū dạ gārā *Vd.* bạbūɗę.

bū dạ gwarzō *m.* secondary parotitis (= bī dạ gwarzō).

bū dạ kāyā *m.* cheap fringed quilt used as bodycloth.

būɗạ littāfị *m.* = būɗe littāfị.

būdancī *m.* fortune-telling.

būɗar *m.* Maria Theresa dollar (= līyạr).

buɗārē *Sk.* virgins (*Vd.* buɗurwā).

būɗar kầi *f.* (1) removing henna-wrappings from head of bride *or* bridegroom when the ḳunshị period is over, just before the feast (bịkī). (2) *Vd.* barkạ 7, aurē 6*d*, lallę 1*d*, karị 6*c*.

būɗar kunnē *Kt. f.* drumming by bōrī on eve of infant's naming-day (*thought that if not done, child will be dolt*), *Vd.* sūnā 5*c*.

būɗạ rumbū *m.* forcible confiscation of corn during famine.

būɗau *m.* butterfly.

būdāwā fortune-tellers (*Vd.* bạbūɗę).

buddarī *Kt. m.* (1) large-nosed. (2) big-buttocked.

buɗe A. (būɗę). (1) *Vb.* 1A (*in* 1*a–f below, we can substitute* būɗạ *for* būɗę). (*a*) opened *x* (i) yā ∼ bāḳī he opened his mouth (*cf.* būɗe, būɗō, būɗạ 1). (ii) yā ∼ idọ he opened his eyes (*cf.* 1*g*, 2*b below*). (iii) yā ∼ takạrdā he opened the letter. (iv) tā ∼ tukunyā = tā ∼ fầifāi

dagạ kạn tukunyā = tā ∼ ạbincī she lifted the cover from cooking pot to examine contents (*cf.* būɗā) ; *Vd.* fầifāi 1*b*.iv ; būɗe fầifaŋkị. (v) yā ∼ al'amạriŋ tsịrārạrsạ he explained the matter fully. (vi) yā ∼ bāyansạ he exposed himself to attack. (vii) yā ∼ haḳōrā he snarled. (viii) yā ∼ ḳōfạ he removed the screen from the doorway ; he opened the door. (ix) yā ∼ littāfị he opened the book. (x) yā ∼ wayạr iskạ he turned on the radio. (xi) yā ∼ yāḳị he declared war. sum būɗę fagyē they have opened a front (in war). (xii) yā ∼ ạsīrīna = būɗā 2. (*b*) yā ∼ kansạ he revealed his identity. (*c*) yā ∼ dōkị he reined in his horse too abruptly, straining its chest (*cf.* zāmę 1*a*.ii). (*d*) yā ∼ mini kārā he put me to shame. (*e*) (i) Allā yạ ∼ masạ God prosper him ! yā ∼ cịnikī it caused trade to thrive (*cf.* būɗạ 4). (*f*) nā ∼ masạ jinī I bled it (horse, donkey). (*g*) (i) yā ∼ idọ dạ ḳīrạ he learned smithing as a small child. (ii) kuɗī har ∼ masạ idọ sukę yị sabọ dạ yawạ wealth has unbalanced him (*cf.* 1*a above*). (iii) sum fārạ ∼ idọ gạ ạmfāninsạ they've begun to realize its value. (iv) yā ∼ musụ idọ hè brought them to their senses. (*h*) yā ∼ ni he acted in a way (by skilful work, being well-dressed, etc.) which roused my admiration. (*j*) sum ∼ wạ gạriŋ wutā they opened fire on the town. sum ∼ bindigōgī they opened fire with their guns. (*k*) wạ kạ ∼ *the name by which woman previously poor calls to slave girl whom she can now afford to keep. The latter when summoned by her mistress calling out these words, replies* Ạsīrịŋ dạ Allā ya rufę. (*l*) (2) būɗạ, būɗā, būɗe fầifaŋkị, būɗe littāfị. (2) *Vb.* 3A (*a*) (i) is (was) open. (ii) rānā tā ∼ ḳwaiŋ the sun is blazing. (iii) yāḳị yā ∼ war broke out. (iv) wannạŋ ḳōfạ tā ∼ manạ this avenue is open to us. (v) ḳarạïransụ sum ∼ they stand revealed as liars. (*b*) idānunsạ yā ∼ he's no novice (*cf.* 1*a*, *g above*). (*c*) ḳafạssā tā ∼ his foot turns outwards from disease (= bauɗę 1*c*). (*d*) absconded. (*e*) dōkị yā ∼

horse is strained *as in* 1c *above.* (*f*) (i) cinikī yā bũɗu trade has progressed. (ii) da wannan yāḳi ya bũɗu tsakānimmụ when that war broke out between us. (*g*) *Vd.* bũɗō ; ḳạrā 2*b*.ii.

B. (bũɗe). (1) *adj.* open *x* idạnsạ yanạ̃ ~ his eye is open. yā tāsam musụ bạ̄kī bũɗe he attacked them full tilt (*cf.* bũɗẹ 1*a*.i). (2) yanạ̃ ~ dạ bạ̄kī he has his mouth open.

C. (bũɗē) *m.* (1) an yi matạ ~ women tested her (bride's) virginity at wedding-festival (= gānē = *Kt.* shan rũmạ̄cē), *cf.* ci̇kā 2*f.* (2) *Kt.* action of ɗam būɗi̇ (*Vd.* būɗi̇ 8).

bũɗe fại̇fanḳi (1) *m.* the tūwō received by casual guest. (2) *Vd.* bũɗẹ 1*a*.iv.

būɗējị *m.* (*sg.*, *pl.*) fortune-teller (= bạbūɗẹ).

bũɗe littāfi̇ *m.* butterfly (*Vd.* mālạmī 2).

būɗi̇ *m.* (1) yā sạ̄mi ~ he made progress (*in trade, knowledge, etc.*). (2) (*a*) yā yi ~ he did outstanding act. (*b*) Allạ̄ yạ bā ni̇ ~ God grant me great skill ! (3) an sạ̄mi ~ we've got a dry spell in the rains (= būshi̇). (4) breast-stroke in swimming. (5) an yi wạ lạmbū ~ channels of irrigated farm have been opened to let in water (= ɓalliyā). (6) būɗi̇m bạ̄kī *Sk.* = bũɗạ. (7) būɗi̇n dāji̇ *Sk.* = bũɗad dawạ. (8) ɗam ~ *Kt. m.* beggar threatening to defecate in public in market unless given charity (= mazạ̄wọ̄yiη ḳạsũwā).

būɗi̇kkē *Vb.* 1C *Sk.* = būɗẹ.

budi̇rī *m.* (1) feeling of restlessness (*epithet by women is* ~ sham mai̇ gidā raη aurē) *x* an yi masạ ~ he feels unsettled. dabbạ tā tsinkẹ, tanạ̃ ~ domestic animal has broken loose and is wandering uneasily. yau nā kwānā ~ I couldn't sleep through uneasiness, pain, etc. (2) noise of drumming, etc. (*epithet is* ~ tūsạ tsạye) *x* suη kwānā sunạ̃ ~ they spent the night making a disturbing noise of drumming, singing, etc. anạ̃ ~ ạ gidansạ play, etc., is going on at his house (= *Sk.* bụrēɗē).

būɗō *Vb.* 1E *x* aiki̇ yā ~ bạ̄kī there's much work to do (*cf.* būɗạ). nasarạ tā

būɗō manạ = tā būɗō manạ bạ̄kī we have prospects of victory.

bũɗu *Vb.* 3B *Vd.* būɗẹ 2.

būdū *m.* fodder-grass dried standing (= yạ̄yē 3).

budu-bụdũ thick and coarse (= guzur-gụzụr *q.v.*).

buɗu-buɗu (1) ganinsạ ~ nẹ̃ he has poor sight. (2) yā yi ~ dạ ḳụrā he's covered in dust.

bụduddụgī *m.* (*pl.* bụdụddụgai) type of edible frog.

buɗuɗɗụkē (1) *Vb.* 3A. (*a*) idạnsạ yā ~ (i) he has sore eyes. (ii) he has poor sight. (*b*) (cloth) is faded ; (cloth) is '' on its last legs ''. (2) *Vb.* 1C crumpled, spoiled appearance of (clothing). (3) *Vd.* bututtụkē.

buɗụmā *f.* overgrown slut. kē buɗụmạ̄ ho, you big slut !

bụdụm-budum *m.* = bụdụnnīyā *f.* floundering about in work (= bạdạm-badam *q.v.*).

bụdũnīyī *m.* uppish and pushful man.

bụdụnnīyā *f.* = bụdụm-budum.

budurci̇ *m.* (1) virginity. (2) yā ɗạuki buduɾci̇ntạ he took her as a virgin (= bụdurwā 1*b*). (3) bạ tạ kai ~ ba she was not virgin at marriage (= kai 1*a*.iii = ɓallẹ 1*d*. = bụdụrūḳụ), *Vd.* bụdurwā 2. (4) *Vd.* masassạḳī 2.

bụdūrī = bụdūrī *m.* girl's first husband.

bụdurụ *x* ta ~, ji̇kī dū dādī *epithet of* bụdurwā (*said by* marọ̄ḳā).

bụdụrūḳụ cē = bụdurwā 2.

bụdurwā *f.* (*m. is* saurạyī) *pl.* 'yam mātā *q.v.* = budurwọ̄yī = *Kt.* bụdụr-wai = *Sk.* budạ̄rē (*Ar.* bātūl *from Hebrew* bethūlā). (1) (*a*) unmarried girl of marriageable age (*lit.* virgin) = *Sk.* ḳur-ḳi̇yā (*cf.* gwaidạ). (*b*) yā ɗạukē tạ ~ he married her as a virgin (= budurci̇ 2). (*c*) yā iskẹ ta ~ on marriage, he found her still a virgin (*cf.* bụdurụ). (*d*) *Vd.* dātsạ 2*b*, *c*. (*e*) sạ̄ ~ ciki̇ *Vd.* gajaη hạḳurī. (2) bụdurwar dawākī = bụdur-war gōdi̇yā unmarried girl no longer virgin = bụdụrūḳụ =.kwabọ = sạrēwạ 2 = tsuntsũ 2*a* (*epithet is* ḳụsumburwạ), *cf.* kai 1*a*.iii. (3) *in* tsạ̄rancē *we say e.g.* Ḳạnde bụdurwā tasạ cē Kande is his masturbation-partner (*cf.* saurạyī ; dạ̄ḳū).

bufū *m.* sack (= buhū *q.v.*).

buga A. (bugā) *Vb.* 2 (*progressive uses* bugu *q.v.*). (1) (*a*) (i) thrashed (with stick, etc.) = dōkā 2*a*.i. (ii) rūwā yā bugē ni rain beat down on me. (iii) zazzaɓī yā bugē ni I had fever. jante yā bugē ni I had feverish cold. (iv) threshed on threshing floor (*i.e.* when quantity is large) (*cf.* tuma, sussukā, cāsa). (*b*) struck (with hand, etc.) *x* (i) yā bugi zane (rīgā) he beat the body-cloth (gown) in lieu of ironing. (ii) yā bugi hātimī a cikin (a jikin) takardā he affixed seal or postmark to the letter, paper (= bugā 1*g*). (iii) yā bugi dōki he spurred up the horse. (iv) sirdi yā·bugi dōki saddle chafed the horse. (v) tā bugi nōno (shūnī) she churned milk (indigo). (2) yā bugi ƙirjī (= yā bugi lāya = *Kt.* yā bugi gaɓā), yā cē he firmly maintained, swore that. ... yā bugi ƙirjī, yā cē sǎi yā yī he said come what may he would do it. (3) (*a*) in kā bugi uku cikin gōma, su zamā talātin if you multiply 3 by 10, you get 30. (*b*) nā bugi lissāfi I totted up the figures. (4) (*a*) (i) nā bugi cikim magana I investigated the affair. (ii) yā bugi cikina he "pumped me". (*b*) nā bugi ƙasā I drew horoscope (*Vd.* ƙasā 3), I told fortunes by sand-divining, *Vd.* akōkari. (5) = buga 1*b*, *f*. (6) watan nan, sau bīyū na bugi Kano I went to Kano twice this month. (7) yā bugi sammakō he made an early start. (8) nā bugi asne *Sk.* she stained my gown with indigo (shūnī) when sleeping with me on it. (9) (*a*) mum bugi cāɓī we went through much mud. (*b*) nā bugi sanyī I suffered from cold. (*c*) mum bugō rūwā we had much rain (*cf.* buga 2). (10) yā bugi tambarī (*a*) he beat the drum. (*b*) = 1*b*.ii *above.* (11) yā bugi tūwō he devoured the tūwō. (12) *Vd.* buga 1*c*.v.

B. (buga) (1) *Vb.* 1A (*progressive often uses* bugu *q.v.*). (*a*) = bugā 1–4, 7, *x* yā buga zane = bugā 1*b*.i. (*b*) sunā ~ jarīda they're printing the newspaper (= dāɓa). am ~ shi da nā'ūra ⇒ am ~ shi bugun dūtse it's been printed.

am ~ shi da kekyan rubūtū it has been typed (*cf.* bugu 2). (*c*) (i) yā ~ bindiga he fired the gun. sum buga wutā they opened fire. yā ~ masa bindiga he fired the gun at him. (ii) yā ~ yāƙi he made war. (iii) sum ~ (= sun kada) gangar yāƙi sabo da mū they declared war on us. (iii) munā ta bugāwā da sū we're fighting with them. (iv) sun yi " buga m buga ! " they were fighting. (v) sunā nan tsaye ta " buga, a bugē su ! " they're offering stubborn resistance. (*d*) tā ~ gurāsa (i) she threw dough to make it rise. (ii) she made good profit. (*e*) *Vd.* gwanjō ; tsāwā 2*b*. (*f*) yā ~ waya (i) he sent telegram. (ii) he spread news. (iii) kōwā ya ~ waya zā a yi lōko let the carriers pass the message on from man to man, to halt ! (iv) yā ~ waya he lied. (*g*) (*with dative*) imposed T. on P. *x* am ~ masa marī he's been hand-cuffed *or* shackled. yā ~ mata mundāyē he put bracelets on her. am ~ haraji tax has been imposed. am ~ musu haraji taxes have been imposed on them. yā ~ musu hari he raided them. nā ~ musu sīsi sīsi I estimated them at 6*d.* each. yā ~ masa hātimī (tambarī) he affixed seal or postmark to it (= bugā 1*b*.ii). (*h*) nā ~ masa jinī (i) I gave him a thrashing. (ii) I bled him, it (horse, etc.). (iii) I " bled him white ". yā ~ mini jinī a ciki he hurt my feelings. (2) *Vb.* 3A (*a*) iska tā buga wind blew (= būsa 2*a*). iska tā bugō mana daga kudu the wind blew on us from the south. (2) (*a*) tun asuba, ya ~ ya tafi he set out at dawn. (*b*) nā ~ nan, nā ~ nan, ɓan sāmu ba = nā ~ gaɓas, nā ~ yamma, ɓan sāmu ba I've vainly looked everywhere (*cf.* buga 6).

ɓuga A. (ɓuga). (1) *f.* (*a*) supplementary exit from rodent's burrow (= *Sk.* ɓalō). (*b*) magana tā yi ~ " the cat's out of the bag ". (2) *Vb.* 3A. (*a*) = ɓuga 1, 3. (*b*) gafīya tā ~ sōrō bandicoot burrowed into sōrō.

B. (ɓuga) *Vb.* 3B (*progressive* yanā ɓugā). (1) gafīya tā ~ bandicoot burrowed its way through wall, etc. (2) magana tā ~ = ɓuga 1*b*. (3) yā ~ a Kano he suddenly turned up at Kano. (4) = ɓamā 2.

buga-buga = baga-baga *q.v.*.

bugad dạ *Vd.* bugar dạ.

bugaggē *m.* (*f.* bugaggīyā) *pl.* bugaggū *adj.* (1) beaten. (2) mạn shānū ~ butter "doctored" by churning with hot water (= ɓelɓel). (3) intoxicated. (4) bugaggīyā = hanyạ bugaggīyā *f.* highroad.

bugaggēnīyā *f.* = bugayyạ.

Bugājē *Vd.* būzū 2.

bụgājī *m.* yanạ bụgājim faɗạ he's talking angrily (= ɓaɓɓakī).

bugar dạ *Vb.* 4B. (1) yā ~ nī it (moving animal) knocked me over (= būsad da). (2) yā bugar = yā bugar dạ izgā (i) he's dead. (ii) (*said jokingly*) he's asleep.

bugau *m.* (1) beating a gown for fee. (2) black-quarter disease. (3) *Kt.* gyạɗā tā yi ~ groundnut-crop has white skin but no kernels (= kilākị 3). (4) ~ na gabạs, tambạrin wạdā *epithet of* rainy-season (dạmunā). (5) ~ matat-tarā *epithet of* Tụrākī.

bugayyạ *f.* hitting each other (= buge-bụgē).

bugạ zāɓī *m.* (*sg., pl.*) short-toed eagle (*Circaetus gallicus*).

buge A. (bugẹ) *Vb.* 1A. (1) (*a*) (i) beat and knocked over. (ii) knocked out (boxer, opponent, war-tank, etc.). (iii) cīwọ yā ~ ni illness incapacitated me. (*b*) defeated in war. (*c*) mum bubbugē musụ bākī we gave them a bad time. (2) haunī yā ~ kạnsạ (= yā sạrē shi (*Vd.* sạrā 1*b*.iii) = yā kashẹ shi) (*cf.* yạnkạ 1*a*.iv) the executioner beheaded him. (3) (*totality-form of* bugā, bugạ) *x* yā ~ zannūwạ dukạ he has beaten all the clothes in lieu of ironing. (4) sum ~ gạrī they razed the town to the ground. (5) = bụgē 3.

B. (bụgē) *m.* (1) giving garment indigo-tint (= ban shūnī 2 *q.v.*). (2) garment treated *as in* 1. (3) *Sk.* bụgē = bugẹ (*pl.* bugūgūwạ) (*a*) place (= wurī = ɓigirẹ). (*b*) *Vd.* sūsạ 2*c*.

ɓugẹ *Vb.* 3A. (1) idled about *x* yā ~ dạ zamā ạ kạsūwā he idled about in the market. (2) maị dōkar barcī yā ~ dạ gyạngyạɗī he doesn't practise what he preaches.

bụ'ge-bụgē" *m.* (1) = bugayyạ. (2) in kā ji mạkāfọ yā cẹ ạ yi wạsam ~, yā kāmạ sạndā nẹ there's more than meets the eye (= duffạ 2).

bugizụrā *Kt. f.* type of children's game.

bugu A. (bụgu) *Vb.* 3B. (1) was (is) intoxicated (*cf.* mạyē). (2) is (was) replete. (3) gōrọ yā ~ the kolas have become overheated in transit.

B. (bugụ) *m.* (1) (*a*) (*v.n. of* bugā, bugạ) *x* anạ bugụnsạ he's being beaten. (*b*) bugụn cikị, sạ dōrō attack a P. in his weak spot ! (*c*) ~ dạ fārị bā yạ barin fātọ tsạye persistence wins. (*d*) ~ shī kẹ sạ fātạ taushī constant dripping wears the rock. (*e*) an yi wạ rịgā ~ the gown has been beaten *as in* bugā 1*b*.i (*but dative of person is not allowed, for we cannot say* an yi wạ Audụ bugụ *in the sense of* Audu has been beaten). (*f*) volley *x* an kashẹ su ~ ɗayā one volley killed them all. (*g*) attack *x* sun kai ~ they attacked. an kai musụ ~ they were attacked. (*h*) threshing *as in* bugā 1*a*.iv. (*j*) a blow (*Vd.* wāwā 1*e*). (2) (*a*) an yi masạ bugụn dūtsẹ it has been printed. wannạn Ạlƙur'ạn, na bugụn dūtsẹ nẹ this is a printed Koran (*cf.* rụbūtū 3, bugạ 1*b*). (*b*) Audu bugụn dūtsẹ nẹ Audu is daft. (3) bạ ạbin dạ ya sạmi dōkịnsạ sại bugụn hanyạ his horse is merely suffering from hard travelling. (4) *Sk.* bugụ ! take care you don't fall ! (*said to those behind one on road*), *cf.* faram. (5) bugụn ạljan madness. (6) tạdawạn nạn ~ takẹ this ink comes off on next page. (7) *Kt.* bugụm magaryab bisạ punishing superiors for inferiors to beware. (8) ɗam ~ *m.* (*a*) mallet of cloth-beaters. (*b*) block of wood on neck of vicious bull (= kulkī 1*b*, *q.v.*). (9) bugụn laimạ *m.* dull black gown (= dōmōsō 3), *Vd.* laimạ 4. (10) wạsam bugụn wuyạ *Vd.* yārọ 1z.iv.

bugūgūwạ *Vd.* bụgē 3.

ɓugus *x* yā yi ~ it's easier or nearer than expected.

buguzụn (1) *m., f.*, ungainly, untidy P. (2) yā cī sụ dạ ~ he intimidated them (= bụrgā). (3) yanạ zạune ~ dạ shī he's sitting in untidy, ungainly fashion (*pl.* sunā̀ zaune buguzum-buguzuŋ dà sū). (4) tanā̀ tàfīyà buguzuŋ-buguzuŋ she's walking in ungainly way. (5) *Vd.* buguzunzumī.

buguzunzumī (1) *m.* (*f.* buguzunzumā̀) *pl.* buguzum-buguzuŋ big, fat, untidy, *or* ungainly P. (2) *Vd.* buguzuŋ.

buhā̀ *m.* kṑ ∼ baì fī shi shàn tā́bà ba he's an inveterate smoker.

buhū *m.* (*pl.* buhunà = buhuŋhuna = buhūhūwà). (1) (*a*) sack. (*b*) fā̀tàr ∼ empty sack. (2) buhun tudù = buhuŋ Kanǫ any native cloth. (3) (*a*) baƙim ∼ police-uniform. (*b*) maì baƙim ∼ Government policeman (= sàndā 2*a*).

bujā̀-bujā (1) *m.*, *f.* (*sg.*, *pl.*) scatter-brained P. (2) *m.* feckless work.

būjāgī *m.*, *f.* untidy-looking P.

būjāyè *m.* (1) bullseye on target (= būzāyè *q.v.*). (2) ox with drooping horns (= bijāyè *q.v.*).

būjè *m.* type of trousers with large crutch (= tunguza = dàrbāki = *Sk.* dumburum,) *cf.* gōnā 2*c*. (2) *epithet is* ∼ shā̀rà ƙazāmā dāki.

buji A. (būjī) *m.* dry, windy harmattan haze (= būdà).
   B. (buji) (1) what a wind ! (2) what a large hyena !
   C. buji-buji = biji-biji.

bujirà *Vb.* 3B became out of control (= bijirà *q.v.*).

buk *x* yā kāshē shi ∼ he (wrestler) threw him (opponent) down with a thud (*cf.* b:ȋ).

būƙà *Vb.* 1A *x* yā ∼ shi dà ƙasā he flung him (it) to the ground.

buƙàcē *Vb.* buƙātà.

būƙad dà *Vb.* 4B = būƙà *q.v.*

būƙādī *m.* (1) *epithet of* big P. *or* big cloth *x* ∼ bàbban zanè what a big cloth ! (2) *Kt.* light behaviour of married woman.

būƙàlē *Sk. m.* = tōsarō 2.

*****buƙārī** *Ar. m.* compasses.

būƙā̀sa = buƙā̀sa *m.*, *f.*, big fat P.

buƙātà (1) *Vb.* 2 (*p.o.* buƙàcē, *n.o.* buƙàci) needed *x* yā buƙàci gyàdā he needed groundnuts (= 2*a*.ii). yanā̀ buƙātàr kudī = yanā̀ dà buƙātàr kudī he needs money. yā ∼ yà zūwà

gyārā it needs mending. (2) *f.* (*a*) (i) a need, requirement. (ii) *x* yā yi buƙā̀tàr gyàdā he needed groundnuts (= 1). (*b*) one's daily needs *x* (i) ∼ tasà tā fì sāmunsà his expenditure exceeds his income. (ii) ∼ bā tà̀ kisàm mutum, àbinsà takè cì̀ (*a* beggar's cry). (iii) yanā̀ dà ∼ dà yawà he has big expenses. (iv) n nā̀ dà ∼ I have a favour to ask of you ! (*c*) (i) thing needed (*pl.* buƙātū). (ii) bīyàm ∼ yā fì cin rībà fulfilment of wishes is better than profit. (iii) *Vd.* bīyā 1*b*, 2, bīyà 2*b*, uŋgulū 7.

bukātad dà *Vb.* 4B necessitated *x* yā ∼ ni shigar mōtà it necessitated my going by car.

buƙātū *Vd.* buƙātà 2*c*.

būkè *m.* chain-mail helmet.

būkè *x* ∼ nē, dà gā̀riŋka akè tūwō, à bā kà̀ hannū what a simpleton !

buki A. (buƙī) *m.* = biƙī.
   B. (būki) = būkè.

būƙi *m.* (1) showing off *x* yanā̀ ∼ dà kudī he's showing off owing to his wealth. (2) poor type of tobacco (= aŋgalē).

būƙi *Kt. m.* nincompoop.

bukkà *f.* (*pl.* bukkōkī). (1) hut of grass or stalks (= gàban 14*a*). (2) kwānā ∼ yā fì kwānā sōran dà bā̀ kudī better a modest competence than making a big show when one has not the means !

buku A. (buƙū = bukkū = *Kt.* bukkū) *m.* guineacorn which has grown black and poor and is given to donkeys (*epithet is* ∼ dāwàr jā̀kai).
   B. (būkǫ) *Sk. m.* type of perch (= karfasā *q.v.*).

buƙū *m.* (1) convexity. (2) ā̀ yi ∼ bā̀ dōrǫ ? can one " make bricks without straw " ? (3) *cf.* buƙū-buƙū.

buƙu-buƙu A. (buƙū-buƙū) = buƙwī-buƙwī. (1) yanā̀ tàfīyà ∼ (*a*) he (hunchback) is walking stoopingly. (*b*) he (criminal disguised as in burtū) is walking along stealthily. (2) yā kwāshi rawā buƙwī-buƙwī he (hunchback) began to dance. (3) Allā suturi buƙwī ! n ji kīshīyar maì dōrō = Allā sitiri buƙwī ! 'yā tā ga dōraŋ ūwā tatà (*said by women*) God forbid I should do it ! God preserve *me* from shame ! **(4)** *cf.* **buƙū.**

    B. (buƙū-buƙū̧) *adj.* **(1)** large-buttocked. **(2)** *pl.* large and round.

bukudu̧ *Jos mining Hausa m.* black sand containing but little tin.

bukūkūwa̧ *Vd.* **bi̧kī.**

buƙulu̧ = **buƙu̧lū** *m.* playing " dirty trick " on P. (= **gayya̧**), *epithet is* ∼ **gadō bāyan dāki̧.**

bu̧kunāshi̧ *m.* a native black and red cloth.

bukurū (1) ∼ **mūgu̧n sirdi̧** what a cantankerous person ! **(2)** *m.* (*pl.* **bukwā̧rē**) wooden food bowl (= **aku̧shī**).

buƙus *m.* method of fowl-stealing.

bukut *x* **ya fītō** ∼ he came out " like a streak of lightning ".

bukwā̧rē *Vd.* **bukurū 2.**

bu̧ƙwī-buƙwī = **bu̧ƙū-bu̧ƙū.**

ɓul = **bukut.**

bula̧ = **bulu̧.**

ɓula A. (ɓūla̧). (1) *Vb.* 1A stove hole in T. **(2)** *Vb.* 3A *Sk.* (inside of thighs) is skinned from riding.

    B. (ɓula̧) *x* **tūwam** ∼ *m.* kind of dumpling (= **tūwan rūwā**).

ɓūlā-ɓū̧la̧ *Vd.* **ɓūlēlę.**

ɓula̧ɓulākę = **ɓula̧ɓullākę** *Kt. m.* suppurative neck glands.

bu̧lāgurō = **ba̧lāgurō.**

bu̧lākạ *used in* **hauni** ∼, **dāma** ∼ look out for holes ! (*said by attendants of travelling ruler*), *cf.* **fa̧ram.**

bu̧lā̧ƙai *adv.* contemptuously.

būlāla̧ *f.* (*sg., pl.*). **(1)** hippo-hide whip (*cf.* **kurfō ; ƙwa̧ra̧ŋgwamā**). **an yi masa̧** ∼ he's been flogged. **an yi masa̧** ∼ **gōma̧** he's been given 10 lashes. **(2) yā ga̧mu da̧** ∼ he has herpes across the chest (= **tamaulā 2** = *Sk.* **ba̧uji 2**). **(3) būlāla̧r amaryā** the extra nights which legally husband may spend with bride (*epithet is* **būlāla̧r amaryā tā dōki ūwar gidā**).

būlāli̧yā *f.* **(1)** = **būlāla̧.** **(2)** formula eulogizing the Prophet.

bula̧ma̧ *m. Hadejiya Hausa* village-headman.

bu̧lāyī *x* **bu̧lāyin tsūfā takę yi̧** though old, she dresses like a girl (= **gīgī 2**b.ii).

bu̧lbu̧dī *m.* crumb(s) = **ba̧rba̧dī** *q.v.*

bul-bul *x* **yā ci̧ka** ∼ it's chock-full.

ɓul-ɓul *x* **Audu̧ yā yi** ∼ = **Audu̧** ∼ **da̧ shī** Audu's fat.   **muta̧nan na̧ŋ sun yi** ∼ = **muta̧nan na̧m** ∼ **da̧ sū** = **muta̧nan na̧m ɓuɓɓul-ɓuɓɓul da̧ sū** these people are fat. **shānunsa̧ sun yi** ∼ his cows are sleek.

bulbula A. (bulbu̧lā) *Vb.* 1A. **(1)** (*a*) filled narrow-mouthed vessel with gurgling sound, by immersing in stream *x* **nā bulbu̧la̧ būta̧ a̧ rūwa.** (*b*) **yā bulbu̧la̧** he poured water in a thin stream (= **tuttu̧lā** = **duldu̧lā** = **tsīyā̧yā** = **bulbu̧la̧** *q.v.*), *cf.* **zuba̧, ɗūra̧. yā bulbu̧la̧ rūwā a̧ būta̧** he poured water in thin stream into the gourd-bottle (*cf.* **bulbu̧lē**) = **ɗūra̧. (2) yā bulbu̧la̧ rawa̧nī** (*a*) he pulled **amāwa̧li** of turban over his chest. (*b*) he wound a large turban round his head. **(3)** persevered at work *x* **tana̧ bulbu̧la̧ kaɗi̧** she's spinning away. **ana̧ bulbu̧la̧ ɗārī ya̧u** there's an icy wind to-day.

    B. (bu̧lbu̧la̧) **(1)** (*a*) *Vb.* 2 **nā bu̧lbu̧li būta̧ a̧ rūwa** = **nā bu̧lbu̧li rūwā a̧ būta̧** = **bulbu̧lā 1**a, b. (*b*) *cf.* **tsīyā̧ya̧.** **(2)** *f.* garrulity *x* **Audu̧** = **ga̧rēshi̧** (= **tsīyā̧ya̧ 3**).

bulbulad da̧ *Vb.* 4B poured away fluid from narrow-mouthed vessel, with gurgling sound (= **tsīyā̧yē 1**), *Vd.* **bulbu̧lē.**

bulbu̧lē (1) *Vb.* 1C **nā bulbu̧lē rūwā a̧ būta̧** I poured the water with gurgling sound out of the gourd-bottle (*cf.* **bulbu̧lā**) = **bulbulad da̧.** **(2)** *Vb.* 3A **rūwā yā** ∼ **a̧ būta̧** water gurgled out of narrow-mouthed vessel (= **tsīyā̧ya̧ 2**a).

bulbuli A. (bulbu̧lī). (1) *exclamation of surprise at act of* **bulbu̧lā, bu̧lbu̧la̧, bulbu̧lē.** **(2)** *m.* regurgitation of a suckling (= **tu̧mbu̧dī 1**).

    B. (bu̧lbu̧lī) *Sk. m.* **bu̧lbu̧lim mussa̧** type of stinking grass (= **amam mussa̧**).

bulbulō *m.* **(1)** butterfly. **(2)** swallow (= **bilbilō** *q.v.*).

bulcę *Vb.* 3A *Kt.* remained unpacified (= **burtsę** *q.v.*).

ɓulcę *Vb.* 1A *Sk.* abraded.

būlę *m.* ox or dog with white face and feet (*cf.* **ɓōla̧**).

ɓūlę *Vb.* 3A. **(1)** is (was) stove in. **(2) yā** ∼ **da̧ zāwa̧yī** he had an attack of diarrhœa.

ɓūlēlẹ *m.* (*f.* ɓūlēlị̄yā) *pl.* ɓūlā-ɓū̃lã̄ fat.

ɓulgụcē = gutsụrē 1, 2.

ɓulgụtā *Vb.* 1C. (1) broke bit off (= gutsụrē 1). (2) bại ~ minị kōmē ba he did not do me the slightest service.

bulkạram worthless.

bulkarancị *m.* worthlessness.

bulkụmī *m.* (*f.* bulkụmā) *pl.* bụlkụmai ignorant P.

bullạ *Vb.* 1A = billạ.

ɓulla A. (ɓụllā) (1) *Vb.* 2. (*a*) appeared *x* cīwọ (yāƙị) yā ~ = cīwọ (yāƙị) yā ɓullō illness (war) appeared. cīwọ yā ɓullam masạ = cīwọ yā ɓullō masạ illness suddenly attacked him. yā ~ cikī he suddenly appeared inside there. (*b*) mum ɓullō dạ sābwar hanyạ we found a new method. (2) *f.* jumping of fish or frog in water (= ballị 4 = bụrmā).

B. (ɓullạ) *Vb.* 1A stove T. in (= ɓūlạ).

bullạm *m.* = bullạmā *f.*, *pl.* bullamōmī. (1) gown of narrow strips of native weave. (2) bạcūcanạm bullạm *m.* *ditto* of poor quality.

bullạshē *Vb.* 1C *Sk.* (1) turned T. inside out. (2) revealed.

ɓullẹ (1) *Vb.* 1A stove T. in. (2) *Vb.* 3A is (was) stove in.

bullō *m.* black patch on farm from burning of leaves.

ɓullō *Vd.* ɓụllā.

ɓullukēkẹ = ɓullukī *m.* (*f.* ɓullukēkị̄yā = ɓullukā) *pl.* ɓullukai-bụllụkại huge.

bụlluŋ ƙōƙị *m.* an aquatic game.

bụlmā *Kt.* *f.* jumping of fish or frog in water (= bụrmā *q.v.*).

bulọ *Eng.* *m.* cubes of blue (= bulụ *q.v.*).

bultsẹ *Vb.* 3A *Kt.* remained unpacified (= burtsẹ *q.v.*).

bulụ *Eng.* *m.* cubes of washing-blue (= shūnī 5) *x* rịgan nạŋ, aŋ kaɗạ matạ ~ water has been blued for washing this gown.

bụlūdī *m.* (*pl.* bụlụ̄dai) type of catfish (ƙụruŋgụ).

ɓulu-ɓulu *Vd.* ɓalo-ɓalo.

būlūgạrī *Fil.* *m.* (1) swizzle-stick. (2) hanyạ tā yi ~ the road forks. (3) shaving of weaned girl's head (= ɗaurị̄ŋ gū̃gā 3 *q.v.*).

ɓulụk-ɓụlụk *x* yaŋã ɓạrạrrakạ ~ it's boiling with a sizzling sound.

bulụ̄ƙụnjī *Kt.* *m.* crop of bird.

bụlullụƙī *Sk.* *m.* greater intestine.

bụlụm (1) *adv.* for a long time *x* yā zaunạ ~ he stayed a long time. Audụ, ~ bạ ạ gan shị ba Audu's been a deuce of a time away on that errand ! (2) *m.* yā yi ~ cikin dūnịyạ he's disappeared into the great world. (3) *Vd.* bụlum-bụlum.

bụlụmbītū̃wā *f.* fruitless search.

bulumbuƙwi *x* yā zaunạ ~ he stayed a long time (= bụlụm *q.v.*).

bụlum-bụlum *m.* (1) the sound heard when stirring (kaɗị) indigo (shūnī). (2) act of stirring indigo. (3) *cf.* bụlum.

bụlụm-bulumī *m.* = bụlum-bụlum.

bū̃lụŋƙwīyạ *f.* scrotal affection causing enormous testicles (*Vd.* gwaiwā 1*b*).

bulus (1) an niƙạ shi ~ it's finely-ground (= lilis). (2) dạ zūwạ sãi gã kudī ~ immediately on arrival, there was the money cash down.

bụm *x* yā fāɗị ~ it fell with hollow sound (*x* full sack into truck), *cf.* bịf.

bumạ (1) *f.* (*a*) tarkwam ~ *m.* hole for trapping rodents or birds. (*b*) yā fāɗạ ~ he " fell into a trap ". (*c*) type of game played. (*d*) *Kt.* harpoon (= sạŋgō *q.v.*). (2) *Vb.* 1A reinforced with grass-matting *x* (*a*) ɗāƙị yā fāɗị, akạ ~ zānā the hut fell and was then reinforced with grass-matting. (*b*) am ~ zānā ạ daŋgā the fence has been strengthened with grass-mats. zānā tā fāɗị, akạ ~ wata the grass-matting collapsed and was repaired with a new one (*cf.* mahọ 2).

bụmbū *m.* (*pl.* bumbunạ). (1) whole gourd (gụdan dumā) from which pulp (tōtū̃wā) not yet removed (= ƙundụmāsạ = *Sk.* gụndumbulī 1). (2) cowry with no hole in it.

bumbuŋkīyā *f.* (1) repeated patching. (2) deceitful talk.

bụmbuntạ *Vb.* 3B (1) is (was) conceited. (2) bụmbuntạ = bumbuntō appeared profusely (*seed, rash, crowd, etc.*). (3) bumbụntạ kại *m.*, *f.* conceit.

bụmburụŋ *m.*, *f.* (*sg.*, *pl.*) gluttonous P. or animal.

bumị reinforcement as in **bumạ 2** x **an yi wạ dākị** ~.

būnā = **būnārẹ**.

ɓụnā (1) *m.* farm already worked where soil is therefore fertile. (2) *adv.* **yā sạ̄mē shị** ~ he got it easily or cheaply.

būnārẹ *Fil. m., f. (sg., pl.)*. (1) cantankerous P. (2) vicious ox.

ɓụnāsai (1) *m.* smiling. (2) *adv.* **yā sạ̄mē shị** ~ = **ɓụnā 2**.

ɓuncụnā = **ɓincịnā**.

bundạ *f.* flapping one's gown with arm (= **bindạ** *q.v.*).

bundi *Vd.* **bindi**.

bundụ *m.* (1) dado on inside wall. (2) flowering spikes of **gyāranyạ**.

bụndukụlī *Sk. m.* gizzard.

bụndum (1) x **yā cịka** ~ it's brimful (*pl.* **sun cịka bundum-bụndụṇ**). **dabbạ tā yi kibạ** ~ the animal's very plump. (2) *cf.* **bụndụṇ**.

bundụmā *Vb.* 1C poured out much of.

bundum-bundun A. (**bụndụm-bundụṇ**) *m.* floundering about in a task (= **bạdạm-badam**).

    B. (**bundum-bụndụṇ**) *Vd.* **bụndum** ; **bundumēmẹ**.

bundumēmẹ = **bundumī** *adj., m. (f.* **bundumēmịyā** = **bundumā**) *pl.* **bundum-bụndụṇ** fat-bellied (*pot, P., pit*).

bụndụṇ *Vd.* **bọ̄rī 5** ; **bụndum**.

bụndụndụṇ *m.* x **yā yi** ~ he's fat-bellied *as in* **bundumēmẹ** *q.v.*

bunga A. (**bụɲgā**) *f.* (1) T. or woman of poor appearance or little value. (2) *Zar.* = **bụɲgā**. (3) *Sk.* (*a*) **nāmạn nạṇ** ~ **nẹ̄** this animal died of its own accord and is thus not legally eatable (= **mūshẹ**). (*b*) **yā yi** ~ he died. (*c*) **yā jā** ~ he got a bargain. (4) **hạrạ̄ri** ~ *Kt. m.* type of facial tattooing.

    B. (**bụɲgā**) *f.* (*pl.* **bunguṇạ**) yam-heap.

buɲgāro *m., f. (sg., pl.) Fil.* meatseller (= **mahaụcī**).

ɓụɲgāsā *Sk. f.* **yā sạ̄mi** ~ he got a bargain.

ɓụṇ'ge-ɓụɲgē‖ *m.* petty cadging.

buɲgū *m.* (*pl.* **buɲgwạ̄yē**) ignorant lout.

ɓuɲgū *Sk. m.* old brick fallen down or disintegrated.

buɲgū-buɲgū *Sk. m.* palm-wood canoe (= *Sk.* **dūkūmạ**).

buɲgulạ *Vb.* 3B *Kt.* became overturned, upset.

buɲgulad dạ *Vb.* 4B *Kt.* upset, overturned.

buɲgụlē *Vb.* 3A *Kt.* became overturned, upset.

buɲgunạ *Vd.* **buɲgā**.

ɓụɲgurạ *Vb.* 3B *Kt.* became chipped (= **ɓạ̄gurạ**).

buɲgwạ̄yē *Vd.* **buɲgū**.

buɲgyal = **biɲgyal**.

būnịyā *Sk. f.* pọllen (= **bunụnī** *q.v.*).

bunjum A. (**bụnjum**) x **nā ga rūwā** ~ **ạ rịjịyā** I saw the well was full of water.

    B. (**bunjụm**) x **yā fādạ rūwa** ~ he fell headlong intọ the water.

    C. (**bụnjụm - bunjum** = **fụnjụm - funjum**.

buɲkā = **bạɲkā**.

buɲkārī *m.* (1) name of a mythical book x **kō̄ kā kạrạnci** ~ even if you were to study this mythical book. .... (2) **wannạṇ luɲgạ** ~ **cẹ̄** this expression is worthless. (3) *cf.* **baɲkārī**.

buɲkasa A. (**bụɲkāsạ**) *Vb.* 3B. (1) (matter) became serious (= **gạ̄wurtạ** = **haɲgulạ** = **mūlihạ 1** = **tạɓarạ** = **mātan lifidạ**), *cf.* **būwāyạ**. (2) became full-grown. (3) P. became wealthy or important.

    B. (**buɲkạ̄sā**) *Vb.* 1C x **yā buɲkạ̄sạ rundunōnī** he sent armies in large numbers.

buɲkạ̄shē *Vb.* 3A = **buɲkạ̄sạ 1**.

buɲkẹ = **baɲkẹ**.

buɲkū *m.* **shūkạ tā yō̄** ~ germinating seed pushed up ground.

buɲkụcē *Vb.* 1C. *Kt.* (1) = **bincịkā**. (2) muddled up (= **birkịcē**).

buɲkuɗo *Vb.* 3A **sum** ~ they (*ants, pimples, etc.*) appeared profusely.

buɲkumēmẹ = **buɲkumī** *adj. m. (f.* **buɲkumēmịyā** = **buɲkumā**) *pl.* **buɲkum-buɲkụṇ** huge and round.

buɲkusa A. (**bụɲkusạ**) *Vb.* 3B. (1) **shūkạ tā** ~ = **shūkạ tā buɲkusō̄** = **buɲkū** *q.v.* (2) **mạ̄mam bụdurwā yā** ~ girl's breasts have begun forming (*cf.* **kabarạ**).

    B. (**buɲkụsā**) *Vb.* 1C germinating plant pushed up soil (*cf.* **bụɲkū**).

bụnsurū *m. (f.* **ạkwīyạ** *q.v.*) *pl.* **bụnsụrai** = **bunsurạ** = **bunsurōrī** = *Kt.* **bunsurrạ**. (1) billygoat. (2) **bụnsurum bạrkọ̄nō**

small type of pepper. **(3) bunsurun
dāji** types of oat-like grasses (especially
Heteropogon contortus). **(4) bunsurum
fadama = bunsurum fage** malodorous
plant used to cure colds. **(5) babbam
bunsurū yā shā tsāri** ? has the important
guest been given refreshment ? (*reply,
ī, sǎi da ya shā tukunā, san nan ya bā
kanāna* yes, and after him, his servants).
(6) *cf.* **rēmā.**

buntsura A. (buntsurā) *Vb.* **1A. (1) tā
buntsura bākī** she pursed her lips.
(2) tā buntsura gindī she walked with
joggling buttocks. **(3) akwīya tā
buntsura wutsīya** the goat kept its tail
in normal vertical position. **dōki
(rākumī) yā buntsura wutsīya** horse
(camel) erected tail vertically prior to
running. **(4) tā buntsura furā** she
hastily made **furā** by stirring the cooked
furā in the water **(shēgē)** in which it
was cooked (*cf.* **buntsurē, nashē).**

B. (buntsura) *Vb.* 2 = **buntsurā** 2, 3, 4.

buntsura wutsī *m., f.* goat (*in bōrī
jargon*).

buntsur-buntsur = buntsur-buntsur *x*
tana tafīya ～ she's walking with
joggling buttocks.

buntsure A. (buntsurē) *Vb.* 1C = **buntsurā.**

B. (buntsurē) *m.* **(1)** preparing
furā as in **buntsurā 4. (2) furā** *so
prepared* (*cf.* **shēgē).**

buntu *m.* rice-husks (*cf.* **shēfe).**

buntuna *Kt.* = **bincinā.**

buntur A. (buntur = buntur-buntur) *x* **nā
gan ta (shi)** ～ I saw her (his) big
naked buttocks (= **tumbur**).

B. (buntur) *x* **yā fādi** ～ he (*short P.
or small T.*) fell over.

bunturāwā *f.* an official position at Daura.

buntur-buntur = buntsur buntsur *q.v.*

buntur-buntur *Vd.* **buntur.**

bunture *Vb.* 3A fell over *as in* **buntur.**

bunturun = buntur.

buntusū *m.* **yā sāmi** ～ he got a bargain.

bunu A. (bunū) *m.* (*pl.* **bunūnūwa).
(1)** woman's black and blue cloth
resembling **gwado** (*it is also called* ～
bakim biri). (2) bāwam ～ *Vd.* **bāwa 5.
(3) bēgyam bunū** *Vd.* **bēgē 3.**

B. (būnū) *m.* **(1)** decayed thatch-

grass. **(2) bakim** ～ (*a*) = **1.** (*epithet
is* **bakim** ～ **bāta baibaya). (b)** P. who
is " black sheep ". **(3) mai** ～ **a gindī
bā yā kai gudummōwar gōbara** those
who live in glass houses shouldn't
throw stones ! **(4) magana zārar** ～ **cē**
a word once spoken cannot be recalled !
(5) sululū na ～ *epithet of* snakes or
lizards. **(6) na** ～ (*a*) = **5** *above.* **(b)**
the Kano official who used to cut off
the hands of thieves in accordance with
Muslim law.

C. (bunu) *Ar.* son of (= **ibinu**) *x*
Bunul Haddābi the Caliph Umar.

bunū-bunū = bunū-bunū *m.* **(1)** deceit.
(2) slapdash work.

bununī *m.* pollen of guineacorn, maize,
bulrush-millet.

bununuwa A. (bunūnūwā) *Sk. f.* stye
(= **hazbīyā 2).**

B. (bunūnūwa) *Vd.* **bunū.**

bura A. (būrā) *f.* (*pl.* **būrōrī = būruna). (1)**
penis (= **azakari). (2) burag gallā**
wax entry to nest of the bee **gallā.
(3) būrar jākī** (i) type of fungus. (ii) the
Aroid plant *Amorphophallus dracon-
toides.* **(4) būrar karē** the Aroid plant
Amorphophallus Barteri. **(5) hana** ～
Vd. **tsātsa.**

B. (būra) *f.* **(1)** flank of horse or
donkey near hind legs, where spur is
applied. **(2)** *Hadejiya Hausa* **yā sāmu** ～
he was lucky. **(3)** *Vd.* **būra** ～ *compounds.*

C. (bura) *f.* **(1)** (*rolled -r-*) type of
white Bauchi cloth. **(2)** (*cerebral -r-*)
ceasing (= **bira** *q.v.*).

D. (bura) *Vb.* 3B = **bira.**

E. *Vd.* **būru.**

F. (Bura) *f.* **(1)** Bura district in
Gombe. **(2) 'yar** ～ *f.* gown of loosely-
woven thick thread.

bura *Vb.* 3B **(1)** jumped. **(2)** (*lamb*)
gambolled.

būrābāyā *f.* type of creeper.

bura-bura *f.* **(1)** many selling **simultaneously** and so knocking bottom
out of market (*epithet is* ～ **kashe
kāsūwā). (2)** hasty slapdash work
(*also called* **burāburancī).**

burābusai crumbs (*Vd.* **barbashī).**

burabusko *m.* the food **tūwō** when made

from coarse flour of bulrush-millet (*cf.* ɓarza, saisainō) = ciracī.

buɽāɗạ *Vb.* 3B (1) sped away. (2) lost one's wits.

ɓuɽāgusai crumbs (*Vd.* ɓurgushẹ).

buɽāguzạ *f.* yanạ̄ ~ he's living lavishly.

ɓuɽāguzai crumbs (*Vd.* ɓurgujẹ).

bụ̄ɽạ hancī *m.* large green caterpillar with two silver stripes on head (*it is believed to enter nose of P.*).

bụ̄ɽạ kạ̄i *epithet of* the white ant zagō.

bụ̄ɽạ kọ̄gō *m.* hawk, etc. (= hụ̄ɽạ kọ̄gō = shāhọ *q.v.*).

bụ̄rag gallā *f. Vd.* bụ̄rā 2.

buɽaŋ *x* Dam buɽaŋ an official position at Kano, etc.

burạ̄rā *Vb.* 1C *x* am burạ̄rạ hayāƙī there is dense smoke (= tunnuƙā).

burạ̄rē *m.* the causing of dense smoke.

ɓūrāri *m.* (1) conceit. (2) *Sk.* (*a*) hopping, gambolling. (*b*) struggling to get free.

burar jaki ; burar kare *Vd.* bụ̄rā.

buɽātsai *Kt.* gāshị yā yi ~ hair's ruffled (= buɽwāтsai *q.v.*).

bụ̄rau *m.* ~ yā kāmạ ƙafạrsạ larvae of digger-wasp have attacked his feet (= rụ̄rau).

burāzā gravels (*Vd.* burjị).

bụ̄rbat *Kt.* abundantly.

burbucē *Vb.* 1C *int. from* bicẹ.

burbụ̄dā *Vb.* 1C *int. from* būɗạ.

burbụdī *m.* crumb(s) (= ɓarɓadī *q.v.*).

burbụ̄rā *Vb.* 1C *x* am ~ masạ shūnī indigo's been lightly sprinkled on it (*head, cloth*).

burbụ̄rē *m.* (1) act of sprinkling indigo *as in* burbụ̄rā). (2) *Vd.* fụ̄rē 2c.

burburī *Sk. m.* type of (*a*) pigeon ; (*b*) bat (= birbirī *q.v.*).

burburkọ *m.* flour in which furā is rolled (= biri 6).

bụ̄rbụrnīyā *f.* (1) cracking of dumaŋ kāshī. (2) gambolling with joy.

burburo A. (bụ̄rburọ) *m.* any adornment. B. (burburō) *m.* = burburī.

burbụrtā *Vb.* 1C yā burbụrtạ ƙasā he lightly hoed round crops.

burburwa A. (bụrbụrwā) *f.* mild scabies ; mild crawcraw. B. (burburwạ) *Sk. f.* (1) (*a*) the fodder-grass kọ̄mayyạ (*Eragrostis tremula*). (*b*) burburwạr fạdamạ the grass

Eragrostis biformis. (2) ~ haŋgyan nēsạ (*a*) *epithet of* P. not coming up to expectations. (*b*) *epithet of* Katsina.

ɓurɓushī *m.* crumb, flake (= ɓarɓashī *q.v.*).

burbụtā *Vb.* 1C *int. from* bitạ.

bụrci *Vd.* bụrtā.

bụrcịcị *m.* (1) gāshị yā yi ~ hair's dishevelled or standing on end (= bụrtsai = bụrtsātsạ). (2) fātạ tāsạ tā yi ~ his skin's rough. (3) yā yi ~ it is of uneven texture.

burdā-burdạ̄ *adj.* (1) of coarse texture (= guzur-guzur). (2) *Vd.* burɗumēmẹ.

burdī-burɗī = burdā-burɗā.

burdē *Kt. m.* = burdūdūwạ.

burdịdị *m.* weals from whipping (= birdịdị *q.v.*).

burdiŋgau *m.* (*sg., pl.*) sausage-fly.

bụrdū *m.* = bụrdūdūwạ.

burduddụgī *m.* (*pl.* bụrdụddụgai) type of edible frog.

bụrdūdūwạ *f.* (*sg., pl.*) type of big edible locust.

burduk *adv.* abundantly.

burdumạ = bụrtumạ.

burɗumēmẹ *m.* (*f.* burɗumēmīyā) *pl.* burɗā-burɗạ̄ huge.

burdumi A. (burdumī) *m.* (*pl.* burdumạ = burdumōmī) dumpalm (kabạ) wrapping for packing broken potash (= fardạ) (*it is after such use made into the ink dạkē*). B. (burdumī) *Sk. m.* jumping about.

bụrdunnụ̄wā *Zar. f.* = bụrdūdūwạ.

būrẹ *Sk. m.* large penis.

bụrēdē *Sk. m.* noise of drumming, etc. (= budịrī *q.v.*).

burga A. (burgạ) *Vb.* 1A. (1) whisked (milk, etc.) with swizzle-stick. (2) emasculated man with swizzling motion to render him eunuch. (3) yā ~ wutā he made fire by friction of maiwā, etc. stalks on each other igniting mixture of pith (tāshīyạ) and horse-dung. (4) yā ~ mōtạ he drove the car at lightning speed. (5) ~ makọ̄riŋkạ wāwā *epithet of* fearless P. or touchy P. B. (bụrgā). (1) *Vb.* 2 blustered at P. ; upbraided. (2) *f.* (*a*) bluster *x* yā cī nị dạ ~ he intimidated me with bluster (= rūbạ = kūrī = kụrārī), *cf.* gọ̄dọ̄gō 1*b*, dọ̄dō 6. (*b*) presenting arms by soldiers.

C. (burgā) *f.* administering remedy to exorcise devils causing hysteria in hunter or girl (*cf.* girkã 2).

burgãgạ *Vb.* 2. (1) pursued. (2) drove away (= kǭrā).

bûrgãgau *m.* hero.

burgāmị *m.* (*pl.* burgạngāmai = bûrgāmai = burgạngamī). (1) (*a*) goatskin bag. (*b*) bạ sụ yạrdā sun shịga burgãmịṇ kūrā bạ they refused to surrender. (*c*) *Vd.* ạlbasạ 6*b*. (2) yā kwancẹ bạkim ∿ (= y.k. bạkin jạkā) he's chattering away. (3) burgãmịṇ ạbōkī yā hūjẹ his faults are being bandied about : he's been "taken down a peg ".

burgancị *m.* staying of female companion ('yar ∿ = 'yar zaman dãkị) with bride to keep her company for a time (*this period is called* zaman dãkị).

burgạngāmai *Vd.* burgãmị.

burgẹ *Vb.* 1A = burgạ 1, 2, 3.

bụrgī *m.* (1) manuring ground by tethering oxen there. (2) trampled place.

burgū *m.* (1) (*a*) bandicoot. (*b*) burgū an shā wụyā, anạ bā sụ wutā these " rats " (i.e. beleaguered army) are in difficulties and are being hounded out. (2) *cf.* tsallē 1*d.*

ɓurgujẹ *m.* (*pl.* ɓụrãgụzai) crumb : fragment.

bụrgumā *f.* (*pl.* burgumōmī). (1) virgin-goat. (2) ∿ kitsạnkị shī ya jā mikị yạnkā (*a*) *epithet of* virgin-goat. (*b*) *epithet of* popular girl. (3) ạ kashẹ ta ∿ nip it in the bud ! (= wutā 1z.iii). (4) *Sk.* type of striped cloth.

ɓụrgụngụṇ = ɓụrgwị.

ɓụrgushẹ *m.* (*pl.* ɓụrãgụsai) crumb : fragment.

ɓụrgwị = ɓụrgwịgwị (1) *adv.* immensely fat and round *x* yanạ dạ kại ∿ he has a huge head. (2) ụbaṇ ɓụrgwị *m.* (*f.* ūwar ɓụrgwị) you thief, you'd like me to *give* the thing away, not sell it to you !

bụrhānā *Ar. f.* yā zubạ musụ ∿ what he told them was all poppycock or unintelligible.

buri A. (būrị) *m.* cravings *x* mutūwạ yạnkẹ ∿ Death, severer of cravings !

B. (burị) *Kt. m.* (1) = burgā. (2) = burburkọ.

ɓurị *Vd.* ginị 8.

buri-buri = biri-biri *q.v.*

burījị *Fil. m.* groundnuts (*cf.* kwalcị).

bụrjakkatā *Nor.* it was only with difficulty that . . . (= kyar).

burjị *m.* (*pl.* burãzā). (1) kind of gravel. (2) gravelly hillock. (3) yā tụnkwịyi ∿ he's dead.

burji-burji *x* ganinsạ ∿ nẹ he has poor sight.

bụrjik *adv.* abundantly.

burka A. (burkạ) *Kt.* (1) *Vb.* 1A = burgạ. (2) *Vb.* 3A mạtā tasạ tā ∿ his wife has left him through temper (= yājị 2*b*).

B. (bụrkā) *Kt.* = bụrgā.

bụrkākạ = burkạkē.

bụrkạkau *m.* hero ; great worker ; big eater.

burkạkē *Vb.* 1C *Kt.* yā burkạkẹ aikịṇ he's " broken the back of " the work. sum burkạkẹ ƙasā they've to all intents and purposes gained possession of the country.

burkị (1) (*a*) brake *x* yā yi ∿ he put on the brakes. (*b*) yā jā ∿ he halted (= linzāmị). (*c*) yā jā burkị ƙụụ he (walker, attacker, etc.) came to a dead stop. (2) go carefully ! (3) *Vd.* birkị.

burkụcē = birkịcē.

burkụdā *x* tā burkụdạ nāmạ ạ gishirī she rolled meat in salt to flavour it (*for other meanings Vd.* birkịdā).

burkullẹ *Kt. m.* 4-leaved Senna (*Cassia absus*) = fīdilī.

burƙụmē *Vb.* 1C (wrestler) downed (opponent).

burkuta A. (burkụtā) *Vb.* 1C muddled up (= birkịcē 2 *q.v.*).

B. (bụrkutạ) is (was) muddled up (= birkịcē 1 *q.v.*).

burkutū *m.* (1) type of beer. (2) burkutū = burkutū-burkutū T. badly done ; scamped work.

burma A. (burmạ). (1) *Vb.* 1A (*a*) tā ∿ rūwā she inverted small ƙǭƙō calabash on larger one full of water to prevent it spilling (= dạddạkā 1 = *Sk.* gụnkạ). (*b*) deceived, tricked P. (*c*) kạ ∿ bạkin shāfị cikī, kạ dịnkẹ turn in the edge-threads when hemming!   (d) (with dative) pierced x **yā ~ masā wuƙā** he stabbed him.   **yā ~ ƙafā ā rāmị** he plunged his foot through into a hole. **yā ~ ƙafā ā sōrō** he put his foot through the flat mud roof.   (e) **tā ~ rūwā ā tukunyā** she poured much water in the pot. (f) **yā ~ kansā cikiŋ gidā** he entered unceremoniously (= **kūtsā** 1b). (2) Vb. 3A (a) (earth, roof, toothless-mouth) caved in.   (b) **fātạr idọ tā ~** eyelid has become everted by illness (= **gantsạrē** 2b). (c) **yā ~ dā gudụ** he took to his heels.

B. (**bụrmā**). (1) Vb. 2 (a) **tā bụrmi rūwā** = **burmā** 1a. (b) **tā bụrmi tūwō** she golloped up much **tūwō**. (c) **tanā bụrmar zanē** her big cloth resounds as she walks. **yanā bụrmar rịgā** his ample gown resounds as he walks (cf. **tambạrī** 10).   (2) f. disturbance of water by fish or frog (= **balḷị** 4 = **ɓụllā** 2).

Ç. (**bụrmā**) f. (pl. **burmuna**) grass-bag for storing clothing, etc.

burma A. (**ɓurmā**).   (1) Vb. 1A (a) stove in (pot).   (b) **yā ~ sōrō** = **burmā** 1d last example. (2) Vb. 3A = **burmā** 2a.

B. (**ɓurmā**) f. (pl. **ɓurmōmī**) type of rat-trap.

burmad dā Vb. 4B tricked, deceived (= **burmā** 1b).

ɓụrmā hancī m. type of caterpillar (= **bụr̄ā hancī** q.v.).

burmę Vb. 3A caved in (= **burmā** 2a).

ɓurme A. (**ɓurmę**) Vb. 3A. (1) caved in (= **burmā** 2a). (2) is (was) stove in.

B. (**ɓurmē**) Sk. m. = **ɓụruntū**.

burmēmę adj. m. (f. **burmēmịyā**) pl. **burum-bụrụm** huge.

burmị m. (1) inverting calabash (itself called ɗam **burmị**) as in **burmā** 1a (Vd. **maburmī** 2). (2) (a) **burmị** = ɗam **burmị** the smaller of two halves of kolanut (Vd. **hụ̄lā** 5). (b) Vd. 1 above. (3) **kōwā ya yi gụri'ā dā shī, ~ zaị ɗaukā** he's the prince of rogues. (4) **wārịm masakī ɓā ka ạbōkim ~** Thou Peerless One ! (5) **dōkị yanā dā ~** horse has malformed mouth. **tāgīyạn naŋ tanā dā ~** lining of the cap does not cover whole of interior.

burmị x ɗam **burmị** m. type of bit for horses.

ɓurmōmī Vd. **ɓurmā**.

burmuƙa A. (**burmụƙā**). (1) Vb. 1C **yā ~ masā wuƙā** he stabbed him with knife. (2) Vb. 3A **yā ~ ā gụje** he took to his heels.

B. (**bụrmuƙā**) Vb. 2 Sk. drove away.

burmuna Vd. **bụrma**.

ɓurnā Vd. **sạkā ~**.

burọ m. type of fish.

burōdị Eng. m. (1) bread ; loaf. (2) **yā sạmi kuɗim ~** he earned his livelihood.

burōgī m. band round drum to keep the skin taut.

būrōrī Vd. **būrā**.

burshụnā Vb. 1C = **bursụnā**.

bursū Sk. m. type of spear.

bursuna A. (**bursụnā**) Vb. 1C.   (1) smeared T. with (salt, gravy, indigo) x **tā ~ wā nāmā gishirī = tā bursụnā gishirī ā nāmā** she added salt to the meat. (2) **yā bursụnā rịgā ā ƙasā** (or **ā ƙasā**) he dirtied his gown by sitting on ground.

B. (**bursụnā**) Eng. m. (pl. **bursunōnī** = **bursụnā**). (1) (a) prisoner in custody (= **kāmammę** 1b). (b) **yanā ~** he's in jail, in custody (whether Government or N.A.), cf. **jārum**. (c) **gidam ~** m. prison. (2) prisoner of war x **yā kāmā su bursụnā** he took them prisoner (= **kāmammę** 1a).

bursune A. (**bursụnē**) Vb. 1C = **bursụnā** 1 x **tā bursụnę gishirī ā nāmā**.

B. (**bụrsụnē**) m. (1) indigo rubbed in or rubbing indigo in as in **ban shūnī** (q.v.) x **~ ta yi ā kā** she rubbed indigo into her hair. (2) sowing before rains fully set in, when they're late (= **bịrnē**).

bursụsụ x **jịkinsā yā yi ~** his skin looks rough, feels rough, is covered with dust.

bụrtā Vb. 2 (p.o. **burcē**, n.o. **bụrci**) craved for.

burtạlī Fil. m. hedged in cattle-track (= **lāwạlī**).

burtāyē ground hornbills Vd. **burtū**.

bụrtsā f. (Ar. **birāzā**). (1) cattle or human excrement covered with soil by beetles. (2) **mạganā tā yi ~** the matter has cropped up again.

burtsai *Kt. m.* gāshi yā yi ⁓ hair's ruffled (= burwātsai *q.v.*).

burtsatsa A. (burtsātsa) *f.* gāshi yā yi ⁓ hair's ruffled (= burcici *q.v.*).

  B. (burtsātsa) *Vb.* 2 *Sk.* drove away.

burtse *Vb.* 3A (1) remained unpacified. (2) (*a*) exuded in one place when pressed down elsewhere. (*b*) acted evasively *x* in nā tabō ka naŋ, ka ⁓ naŋ you " wriggle like an eel ".

burtsīyā *f.* yā yi ⁓ he's indecently dressed.

burtsūtsu *Kt.* = burtsai.

burtū *m.* (*pl.* burtāyē). (1) Abyssinian ground hornbill (*Bucorus abyssinicus*). (2) yā shiga ⁓ (*a*) he's disguised. (*b*) he used stratagem. (3) bā ā yi wa biri ⁓ he's too fly to be caught thus. (4) (*a*) yā yi mini kūkam ⁓ he gave me a present. kūkam ⁓ gareshi he's liberal. (*b*) *Vd.* kāzā 1*g* ; tsāda 2. (5) deceitful P. (*epithet is* ⁓ makas abōkiŋ kīwo). (6) fikāfikim ⁓ *Vd.* birgimā 4. (7) *Vd.* bākim burtū.

burtukēke = burtukī *adj. m.* (*f.* burtukēkiyā = burtukā) *pl.* burtukai-burtukai very plump).

burtuma *Vb.* 2 drove away.

burtumau *m., f.* fearless P.

burtumī *Zar. m.* beehive (= amya).

burtuntunā *f.* (1) smut-fungus affecting guineacorn (*cf.* dōmanā). (2) guineacorn *so affected* (*cf.* turbūshi).

burtūtu *m.* = burtsātsa.

burtuttukī *Sk. m.* (*pl.* burtuttukai) type of edible frog.

buru A. (būru) *Vb.* 3B *x* im masīfar yāki tā būru garēmu if the calamity of war comes on us.

  B. (būru) (1) būru aljanar darē *epithet of* hyena. (2) *cf.* bauru.

buru-buru *x* ganinsa ⁓ nē he has poor sight.

*buru̱ūda *Ar. f.* (1) mai ⁓ P. liable to chills. (2) sanyinsa ⁓ nē he is very liable to chills (*Vd.* sanyī 7, harāra).

burūde *Fil. m. Kt.* masarā tā yi ⁓ maize has terminal inflorescence (= *Sk.* maburkākī 2).

burudu A. (burūdu) *m.* (1) T. of coarse texture, especially cheap abāwā thread *x* takardan naŋ (rīgan naŋ) ⁓ cē this paper (gown) is of coarse texture.

(2) burūduŋ kyau garēta she has big but good features (*Vd.* babba 1*k*).

  B. (burūdu) *m.* (1) = burūdu. *(2) gunpowder (= albarus *q.v.*).

būrūgali *Fil. m.* swizzle-stick (= būlūgari *q.v.*).

būrūgu = burugu *Sk. m.* the fodder-grass *Panicum stagninum*.

buruji *Ar. m.* (*pl.* buruzai). (1) yā sāmi ⁓ (*a*) he found out an auspicious day by divination (dūbā), etc. (*Vd.* fitar da 4*b*, sā'a 4). (*b*) he was lucky. (2) yā zō a ⁓ he came at lucky moment. (3) type of furā made with juice of madi. (4) kulikulī cakes made from new groundnuts (*child born at that season* (kwāzārī) *is called* mai buruji).

būrūku *m.* (1) nincompoop. (2) type of small shrub (*epithet is* Wāwā ka jē magōrī).

būrūkuku *m.* (1) type of bean food (= tūwaŋ wākē). (2) children's game.

burum *m.* (1) (*a*) hugeness (of stomach, house, clothing) *x* zane nē ⁓ da shī it's a huge cloth (*pl.* zannūwa nē burum-burum da sū). (*b*) *cf.* būrumā. (2) nā ji ⁓ I heard an explosion. (3) ⁓ tā ci ⁓ ; kūrā tā ci barāwo tit for tat (= kūrā 26). (4) *Vd.* burum da.

burum *x* mai bāki ⁓ *m., f.* toothless P. rāmi yā burme ⁓ earth caved in with a rush.

būrumā (1) (*a*) būrumar jakā huge bag. būrumar būta huge gourd-bottle. (*b*) *Vd.* burum. (2) ⁓ babbar jakā *epithet of* big bag, glutton, pot-bellied P.

burum-burum A. (burum-burum). (1) *Vd.* burmēme. (2) *Vd.* burum.

  B. (burum-burum) *used in* ⁓ kanki da bōriŋ gyada *formula used in blindman's buff* (mādindimī).

burum da (1) *Vb.* 4B *Kt.* tricked, entrapped. (2) *epithet of* bog (*Vd.* damba).

būruna *Vd.* būrā.

burundumī *adj. m.* (*f.* ⁓ burundumā) huge (*bag, ewer, gourd, granary*).

Buruŋgū aljanad darē ; kōwā ya yi darē, baraŋ ubanki nē *epithet of* hyena (*Vd.* kūrā).

buruŋguzā *f.* (1) inferior (*re tobacco*, daddawā). (2) big woman, sheep, goat, donkey. (3) face-ornament for horse (= tinjimā). (4) type of drum used by 'yam fǫtō or at wrestling-matches.

burŋntā *Vb.* 1C *Kt.* rolled cotton between the hands to make into thread (= murzą).

burŋntū *Kt. m.* act of rolling the strands *or* the thread-strands rolled *as in* **burŋntā.**

ɓuruntū *m.* (1) fidgeting hither and thither. (2) pilfering ; looting. ɗam ∼ pilferer ; looter.

burŋntumau *m.* fearless P.

burŋntuŋkusą *f.* inferior woman, tobacco, fruit, etc. (*epithet is* ∼ **kaɗanyąm mēlę**).

burŋrŋ *m.* a gruel of coarse flour.

burus *m.* ignoring P. (= biris *q.v.*).

burūshi (1) *Eng. m.* brush (= barōshi). (2) *Ar. m.* gunpowder (= ąlbarųs *q.v.*).

burūtsū *Kt. m.* (1) poorly-done work. (2) pointless chatter (*cf.* sǫki burūtsū).

burŋzai *Vd.* burŋjī.

burwątsai (1) **gāshi yā yi** ∼ hair is ruffled (= burcici). **furā tā yi** ∼ this furā food is lumpy. (2) **yaną dūbansų** ∼ he's looking contemptuously at them.

burzū *m.* type of weed in farms (*Vernonia Perrottetii*).

bų́s (1) *m.* (*a*) any pungent smell. (*b*) bang ! *x* **nā ji harbi** ∼ I heard the report of a gun. (*c*) groaning of turkey (*Vd.* bindigą 9). (2) *adv.* **yaną dą ɗǫyī** ∼ it has a pungent stench.

ɓus *Vd.* ɓusą.

busa A. (būsą). (1) *Vb.* 1 A (*a*) blew (horn, etc.). (*b*) **yą** ∼ **ąbincī** he blew on bit of food to cool it before putting it into his mouth (*for cooling food in bulk, cf.* fīfįtā). (*c*) **Allą yā** ∼ **masą rąi** God breathed life into him. (*d*) (i) caused to swell *x* **nā** ∼ **masą iską** I pumped it up. (ii) **yā** ∼ **ąkwīyą** = **sąlkā** 1*c*. (*e*) **bąr shi dăi săi yā** ∼ **dą făifăi** let him gang his gley, he'll soon regret it ! (2) *Vb.* 3A (*a*) **iską tā** ∼ wind blew (=bugą 2*a*). (*b*) (clothing, earth) became dry. (*c*) **yąu gąrī yā** ∼ we've had a few rainless days (*Vd.* būshį). (3) *f.* (*a*) act of blowing with mouth *x* **yaną** ∼ he is blowing trumpet, horn. (*b*) idle chatter. (*c*) **yaną būsąr tŋlū** he's trying to cadge from miser. (*d*) good

day Trumpetblower ! (*e*) **Sarkim** ∼ ; **Gąlądīmąm** ∼ *Vd.* marǫkī. (4) **kąfō săi** ∼ *Vd.* kąfō 4*a*.

B. (būsā) *Vb.* 2 (*p.o.* **būshē**, *n.o.* **bŋshi**). (1) = būsą 1*a, b.* (˙) winnowed (= bākącē *q.v.*). (3) (*a*) **yā bŋshi iską** he lived " like a lord " (= ishisshirē 3). (*b*) **yā būsar mini iską** (i) he gave me a share of his good luck. (ii) he put on airs with me.

C. (būsą) *f.* chunks of boiled yam (dōyą).

D. (Būsa) *f.* the place Busa.

ɓusą *Vb.* 1A *x* **am** ∼ **kōtą** haft's been pierced for blade. **yā** ∼ **tāgą** he pierced hole in wall as window. **am** ∼ **ɓus** haft or wall has been pierced clean through (*cf.* sǫkā).

būsad dą *Vb.* 4B (moving animal, cycle) knocked P. over (*does not apply to car knocking P. over, Vd.* kā dą 2) = **bugar dą.**

būsą gwaggǫ *Kt.· m.* stomatitis of the tongue.

būsakī *m.* (*f.* būsakā) big, fat P.

bŋsasshē *m.* (*f.* bŋsasshīya) *pl.* bŋsąssū *adj.* (1) dry (*cf.* būshę). (2) **aiki bŋsasshē** poorly-paid employment (*cf.* maikǫ). (3) **bą sų yī shi ba hakąnaŋ bŋsasshē** it was not uselessly that they did it.

būsau *m.* (1) ∼ **yā kāmą kafąrsą** = ∼ **yakę yī** larvae of digger-wasp attacked his foot (= fŋrau = mąkaifų = mąkarfǫ 3 = rŋrau 2). (2) *Kt.* drying up of corn before grains formed (*cf.* shirą).

Būsāwā *Vd.* Bąbūshę.

būshākę *m.* (*f.* būshākįyā) big, unkempt P.

būshākī (1) *m.* (*f.* būshākįyā) big, unkempt P. (2) **aikį yā yi** ∼ the work to be done is limitless.

bushara A. (bushārą) *Ar. f.* good tidings. B. (bushārā) *Kt. f.* **karam** ∼ *m.* hollow reed used as rattle (= mącārā).

būshāshą *f.* having a jolly good time ; luxurious living.

bushe A. (būshę). (1) *Vb.* 3A (*a*) became dry. (*b*) P. became thin. (*c*) **gąrī yā** ∼ town's become impoverished. (*d*) **yā** ∼ he drew himself up erect to salute, etc. (= kamę 3*a*). (*e*) **yā** ∼ **dą dąrīyā** he burst out laughing (= fashẹ 1*b* = shē̃ka 1*d*.ii). (*f*) yārọ yā ∼ boy has cut first tooth. (2) *Vb.* 1A (*a*) blew out (lamp etc.) (= hūrẹ 1*e*). (*b*) blew T. away *x* ka ∼ miṇi cīyāwa a idọ blow this bit of grass out of my eye ! (= hūrẹ 1*e*). yā ∼ miṇi kīyāshī a hanci he blew small ants out of my nose. (*c*) winnowed (= bākacē *q.v.*). (*d*) yā ∼ mata ḳunnē he put her up to leaving her husband.

B. (ɓushē) (1) *m.* yā ci ∼ he slept on the bare ground. (2) *Vd.* bụ̄sā.

ɓushẹ *Vb.* 1A. (1) = ɓusa. (2) *Sk.* deflowered (a virgin).

bū̠'she-bū̠shē‖ *m.* continual trumpeting.

bū̠she gāshi *m.* (1) ∼ ya yi wa barēwā, ammā yā kuskụrē though he got right up to the gazelle, his shot missed. (2) ba mai īya fitọ̄wā ∼ ya gaya masa nobody would dare to tell him openly.

bushi A. (būshi) *m.* (1) yau, an yi mana ∼ to-day we had a short dry spell in the rains (= būdi 3 = ban iska *q.v. under* iska 3*a*). (2) what a wind ! (3) what fine winnowing ! (*cf.* bū̠shẹ 2*c*).

B. bū̠shī *m.* (1) hatsī yā yi ∼ the corn has grown grainless. (2) *Sk.* = bū̠sau 2.

C. (bū̠shi) *Vd.* bū̠sā.

bushinō *m.* (1) = shūnin batta. (2) sharp practice. (3) false statement.

bushirī *m.* type of red and white saddle-cover.

bū̠shīyā *f.* (*pl.* bū̠shīyōyī = bishā̠ishā̠i). (1) (*a*) hedgehog (*epithet is* bish da ḳaya). (*b*) yā yi ∼ he curled himself up to keep warm. (*c*) mā ga tsīram (= mā ga tsīrar) ∼ a fariŋ wata we must devise a plan. (*d*) bā a wāwar ḍam ∼ don't waste your breath on a person who thinks he can do the impossible ! (*e*) *Vd.* darē 9, gādā 1*e*, kutụrī. (2) bū̠shīyā = bū̠shīyar kitsọ hairbrush of hedgehog skin. (3) rinderpest (= baurụ 2 = *Sk.* zā̠gau). (4) (*a*) bū̠shīyar karā pile of cornstalks made on farm in early January (= bāga = daba). (*b*) bū̠shīyar gērō pile of millet made on farm in late August (*Vd.* zọ̄garī) = bāga = daba = ḳiriga *q.v.* (*c*) bū̠shīyar dāwa pile of guineacorn

on farm made in December after the guineacorn has been reaped (sāraŋ giṇdī) ; it is left seven days on the ground (saŋkacẹ) and then the heads are cut off (yaŋkaŋ kā̠i) ; the corn is placed on a bed of cornstalks (karā), then covered with cornstalks and surrounded with cornstalks (= bāga = daba = ḳiriga *q.v.*). (*d*) *Vd.* ḳiriga. (5) small string of wool or cowries suspended from girl's neck (= dọ̄daŋ azụmī). (6) 'yan shīla sun yi ∼ young pigeons have begun to become fledged.

būsiḳī *adj. m.* (*f.* būsiḳā = būsiḳē̠ḳīyā) big, fat P.

buskuḍa A. (buskuḍa) *Vb.* 3B sat or lay on bare ground and so risked spoiling good clothing.

B. (buskụḍā) *Vb.* 3A fidgeted (= muskụḍā *q.v.*).

busọ *m.* act of burying (= bisọ *q.v.*).

busshīyā *Kt. f.* = būshīyā.

busta *f.* (1) post, mail *x* an saka shi a ∼ it's been posted : yā zō a ∼ it came by post. (2) bustar gōrọ load of kolas (= kataku).

busur-busur = busụsur-busụsur *x* tana tafīya ∼ she's walking with her fat legs rubbing together.

but A. (but) *x* ∼ sā̠i ya fitō he suddenly appeared. yā yi ∼ he made sudden leap. yā yi ∼, ya fita waje he suddenly leaped out.

B. (bụt) any pungent smell (= bus 1*a*, 2).

buta A. (būta) *f.* (*pl.* būtōcī). (1) (*a*) gourd-bottle (= mātar ḍaŋ kō i = gọ̄rā 1*b*.i). (*b*) bā̠kim ∼ stem of gourd. (*c*) bottle of clay or metal. (2) ∼ im ba ta yi tsīraŋ kōmē ba, ta yi na igīya he lives on reflected glory. (3) yā lē̠ka būta *Vd.* abụ 5*g*. (4) ɓurā a būta *Vd.* bam magana 3. (5) *Vd.* ḍaurim būta.

B. (buta) (1) *f.* repairing the permanent way (= bita). (2) *Vd.* bita 2.

būtā̠cī wisps floating on surface of liquid (= firkā̠kī 1).

būtanci *m.* tyrannizing over P. (= wulā-kanci).

butar A. (bụtar = bụ̄lārī) *m.* Maria Theresa dollar (= lịyar).

B. (butārī) (1) spitted intestines (=
lifidī 2*b*).   (2) what dust !   (3) what
wind !

butạ wutā *m*. convolvulus (= yaryạ̄dī).

ɓutẹ *Vd*. kwạrkwatạ 2.

būtẹr *m*. = būtạr.

ɓūti *Vd*. jạ̈ nạ̈ ~.

ɓūtịyā *Sk*. *f*. (1) anus (= tsūlịyā).   (2)
ɗam ɓūtịyar ūwā you bloody fool !

būtōcī *Vd*. būtạ.

butsā-butsạ̈ *Vd*. būtsụ̄sụ.

butsai (1) *Vd*. tsaf 5.   (2) am bazạ̈ lạ̈ɓạ̈rai
butsai they spread baseless rumours.

būtsạrē *Vb*. 3A.   (1) (donkey) bucked.
(2) P. behaved rebelliously.   (3) refused point-blank.

būtsạrī *m*. (1) (*a*) bucking of donkey.
(*b*) rebelliousness of P. ;   (*c*)
refusing point-blank ;   intractability
(1 = tūtsū). (2) kāyā bā yạ̈ rạ̈ɓar jạ̈kī,
~ yạ̈ rabạ̈ su (*a*) " murder will out ".
(*b*) it's no use kicking against the
pricks. (3) bad tempered P. (*epithet is*
~ gạ̈riŋ wākẹ̄). (4) *cf*. tūtsū 2.

butsatsa A. (būtsātsạ̈) *m*., *f*. pugnacious
P. (*epithet is* ~ kāyaŋ kabạ̈, kōịnā
sūkạ̈, gạba tsịnī, bāya tsịnī).
B. (būtsātsạ̈) *x* gāshi yā yi ~ hair's
dishevelled (= bụrcịcī *q.v.*).

butsil *x* ɗam butsil *m*. part of a loom.

būtsụ̄tsụ untidy *x* tanạ̈ dạ̈ kạ̈i ~
= tanạ̈ dạ̈ kạ̈i butsū-būtsụ̄ = tanạ̈
dạ̈ kạ̈i butsā-būtsạ̈ her hair's
dishevelled.   wannạŋ aikị ~ yakẹ̄ =
butsū-būtsụ̄ yakẹ̄ = butsā-būtsạ̈ yakẹ̄
this work's done " all anyhow "

buttamī *Zamfara Hausa m*. beehive (=
amyạ̈).

buttuntunā *f*. smut fungus (= bụrtuntụnā *q.v.*).

būtu *m*. nā sạ̈mi ~ I got a bargain.

butu-butu A. (butū-būtụ̄) abundantly
(= dạ̈ɓāɓạ̈ *q.v.*).
B. (butu-butu) (1) yā yi ƙụrā ~ he's
smothered in dust.   (2) *m*. (*sg., pl.*)
motor-cycle (= bạ̈bur).

ɓutuk stark naked *x* yā fitō ~ he came
out naked (= tsịrārạ̈).

bụ̄tụ̄kū *m*. (1) sā rịgan naŋ, kạ̈ ɗe̱ɓe̱
minị ~ put on this gown for me
and work off the surplus indigo
(shūnī) !   (2) *Sk*. = shūnī.

butulci *m*. ingratitude.

bụtụlū *m*., *f*. (*pl*. bụtụlai).   (1) ungrateful
P.   (2) *Vd*. kufai 4.

bụtum-bụtumī *Kt*. *m*. effigy (= mụtum-
mụtumī *q.v.*).

*bụtuntụnā *f*. = bụrtuntụnā.

bụtur-bụtur with joggling buttocks (=
bụntsur-bụntsur *q.v.*).

buturī = bụturī *m*. (1) poor quality
bulrush-millet-heads (= kụ̈ftirī). (2) ~
hụ̈tā a poor type of guineacorn (= cī
dạ̈ gērō 1).

būtụrūkụ *m*. being very cheap or of poor
quality.

bututtụkẹ̄ *Vb*. 3A.   (1) is (was) out of
temper.   (2) yā ~ fuskạ̈ he frowned.
(3) (cloth) is faded, etc.   (4) *Vd*.
buɗuɗɗụkẹ̄.

bututu A. (būtūtū) *m*. (*sg., pl.*).   (1)
hollow stem of pumpkin or pawpaw-
leaf used as trumpet by children.
(2) gourd-funnel (= mazurārī 2). (3)
(*a*) hose-nozzle.   (*b*) būtūtum famfọ
pipe-line. *(4) the bird ragwam mazā.
B. (bụ̄tụ̄tụ) *x* kạntạ̈ yā yi ~ =
būtsụ̄tsụ.

būtụ̄wā *f*. (1) poor tobacco.   (2) stable-
bedding and refuse (= tạttakā).

bụ̄ụ̄ *Vd*. bụ.

būwạ̈ *Sk*. *f*. weaverbird (= jịrā).

bụ̄wāyạ̈ (1) *Vb*. 3B (*a*) is (was) impossible.
(*b*) shiri yā bụ̄wāyạ̈ tsạ̈kānimmụ
relations became very strained between
us. (2) *Vb*. 2 (*a*) is (was) beyond P. (=
gạ̈garạ̈), *cf*. buŋkāsạ̈. (*b*) overcame P. (=
rịnjāyạ̈). (3) bụ̄wāyạ̈ mạ̈lamai *Vd*. ạlkālī.

bụ̄wạ̈yayyẹ̄ *m*. (*f*. bụ̄wạ̈yayyīyā) *pl*. bụ̄-
wạ̈yạyyụ uncontrollable P.

būwāyẹ̈ (1) *m*. (*a*) work beyond P. (*b*) =
būwāyī 1. (2) *m*., *f*. = bụ̄wạ̈yayyẹ̄.

būwạ̈yi (1) *epithet of a* shạ̈makị (= Ḳōrau).
(2) ~ gạ̈garạ̈ mịsāli (*a*) *epithet of* God.
(*b*) *epithet of* A. amazing.

būyạ̈ *f*. (1) metal-ore.   (2) = būyāgī. (3)
būyạr mutạ̈nẹ̄ crowd.

ɓūyā = ɓuyā (1) *Vb*. 3B hid one-
self. (2) *m*. (*verbal noun of* 1) (*a*) yanạ̈
~ he's hiding. (*b*) ɓūyan rānā (watạ̈)
eclipse of sun (moon), *Vd*. kụsūfị.
(*c*) bạ̈ wurim ~ *Vd*. fagẹ̄ 2*b*, gandū 2*g*.

būyāgī (1) *m*. small twigs for firewood
(= būbụ). (2) *m*., *f*. contentious P.

(3) (*a*) what a trailing gown ! (*b*) what a hairy face !

būyāyạ *adv.* untidily. (2) yanậ dạ gēmụ ~ he has long, thick beard.

būyāyī *m.* = būyāgī 2.

*buzạ *Ar. f.* type of beer.

buzai A. (bụzai̲). (1) *m.*, *f.* ground-squirrel (= kụrēgē). (2) yanậ dạ gēmụ ~ he has a fluffy beard. (3) zạncē yā yi ~ news spread.

B. (buzai̲) *Sk. m.* (1) zạncē yā yi ~ nothing came of the matter. (2) *cf.* būzāyẹ.

būzārạ *m.*, *f.* (*sg.*, *pl.*). (1) irascible P. (2) opprobrious term for Būzū people.

buzạrē *Vd.* buzurwā.

buzaye A. (būzāyẹ) *Eng. m.* (*sg.*, *pl.*). (1) bullseye on target. (2) tā yi masạ ~ she infected him with venereal disease. (3) *cf.* buzai.

B. (būzāyē) *Vd.* būzū.

ɓuzgụcē *Vb.* 1C snapped off piece of.

ɓuzgụtā *Vb.* 1C = ɓuzgutạ *Vb.* 2 (*p.o.* ɓuzgụcē, *n.o.* ɓuzgụci) snapped off piece of.

būzū (1) *m.* (*pl.* būzā̰yē = būzunậ) (*a*) (i) undressed skin-mat or loin-cloth (= *Sk.* agalạmī). (ii) iŋ kā ƙi mạrāyạ dạ rīgar ~, wata rānā ậ gan shi dạ ta ƙarfẹ poor to-day, rich to-morrow. (*b*) sun rufẹ (= sun naɗẹ) kại dạ ~ sǎi sukạ . . . . they screwed up their courage and . . . (*c*) būzum biri̲ nēsạ gạ mālạm how does such a thing concern me ! (*d*) bậba da ~ *Vd.* bậba 7. (2) *m.* (*f.* Būzwā = Būzūwā) *pl.* Būzāyē = Bugậjē (*a*) Tuareg serf (*epithet is* Būzū, ƙanạŋ ḳạrē, aŋ ḳọrē ḳạ, kanậ kūwwạ, bạrē iŋ kai nẹ ka yi ḳọrā = Wailạ mại kāmạ ɗayā). (*b*) *Vd.* būzārạ. (*c*) bạ zā sụ yạrdā ba sǎi suŋ ga ạbi̲n dạ ya tūrẹ ~ naɗi̲ they will only be induced to agree, with difficulty. (*d*) *Vd.* gạmbạrī.

buzū-bụzū *x* yanậ dạ gāshi̲ ~ he's very hairy (= muzū-mụzū).

bụzumạ *Vb.* 3B *Kt.* took to one's heels.

būzunạ *Vd.* būzū.

buzurwā *f.* (*pl.* buzurwōyī = buzārē). (1) long-haired goat or sheep. (2) ~ nē he's hirsute. (3) how hairy ! (4) ɗam buzurwar ạkwīyạ, kō bại yī gāshi̲

kōi̲nā ba, yậ yi ạ katạttarī heredity is inescapable.

būzūwā *Vd.* būzū 2.

buzuzu A. (bụzūzụ) *m.* (*pl.* bụzụ̄zai). (1) (*a*) dung-beetle, stag-beetle (*cf.* kurkụrwātạ) = mazan dụŋƙulạ. (*b*) in darē yā yi darē, ~ nāmạ nē at night all cats are grey. (*c*) mại tūwan darē kē ḳậ cī, dạ ~ don't lock the stable after the horse has gone ! (2) ~ bậ ka dāɗin tạunā (*a*) what a cantankerous person ! (*b*) what a tenacious person ! (3) *Zar.* (*a*) type of hairy caterpillar. (*b*) ~ dạ gāshi̲ yakē how hairy he is ! (4) the part of native bit pressing ˙on horse's tongue (*now legally forbidden*). (5) ornamental end of pin or swordhilt. (6) bụzūzụŋ ƙasạ *epithet of* energetic ɗam fọ̄tō. (7) amaryar ~ dung-ball made by young bụzūzụ. (8) *Zar.* bụzūzụŋ tābạ large quid of chewed tobacco (*cf.* ƙamailā). (9) *Nor.* bụzūzụŋ dawākī horned stag-beetle.

B. (bụzūzụ) *x* yanậ dạ gēmụ ~ he has a thick beard.

būzwā *Vd.* būzū 2.

ɓwạlạmɓwantạnī *Kt.* idle roving (= ɓạlạmɓantạnī *q.v.*).

bwanẹ *Fil. m.* trouble.

bwạni = bwạnu = suffered trouble.

bwạrcī *m.* being a disliked wife (= bōranci̲ *q.v.*).

bwīyyạ *Kt. f.* metal-ore (= būyạ *q.v.*).

ɓyel-ɓyẹl *m.* " doctored " butter (= ɓel-ɓẹl *q.v.*).

byallō *m.* double-thickness in gown (= sạ̄cē *q.v.*).

ɓyamɓyarwạ *f.* lark-quail (= durwā 4).

ɓyậsā *Vb.* 2 (*p.o.* ɓyāshē, *n.o.* ɓyậshi) broke off branch or fruit.

byṵ̄ = bīyū *q.v.*

C

ca A. (cậ) *f.* (1) thinking (*used as follows*) ~ nikē yanậ naŋ I thought he was present. (2) ~ nikē kwī mutậnē fancy that ! (3) letter " ch " (*with sound in Arabic like* " th " *in Eng.* think).

B. (cậ) *f.* nā ji ~ I heard sputtering of boiling fat.

C. (ca) *f.* **sun** yi **masạ** ～ they thronged round him.

caɓa A. (cāɓạ) *Vb.* 1C. (1) made knife notchy by use. (2) *x* rendered sloppy, slushy *x* **shānū sun** ～ **hanyạ** cattle've made the road slushy. (3) (*a*) **yā** ～ **aiki̱** he worked fecklessly. (*b*) **yā** ～ **magana** he talked drivel. (4) **tā** ～ **adō** she togged herself up. (5) **yā** ～ **kāshī** he trod on excrement (*cf.* **cāɓu̱lā** 3). (6) **yā** ～ **mini̱** **magana** he spoke to me sarcastically or angrily. (7) **yā** ～ **matạ wuƙā** (**takōɓī**) he slashed her with knife (sword).

B. (cạɓā) *Vb.* 2 *Kt.* = **cafẹ** 1, 2.

cạɓạɓạ = **cāɓạ̄ɓạ** (1) in profusion (= **dạ̄ɓāɓạ** *q.v.*). (2) = **cạɓạl**.

caɓa-caɓa in profusion = **dạ̄ɓāɓạ** *q.v.*

cạɓạl (1) *m.* messiness *x* **hanyạ tā yi** ～ road's miry. (2) *adv.* messily *x* **tā zub dạ mīyạ** ～ she spattered soup about when throwing it away. **wurī** ～ **hạkạ** fancy there being such a messy place ! **yā fạḍi magana** ～ he spoke at random. (3) *Sk. m.* the game **carabkē**.

cạɓạlɓạl = **cạɓạl**.

caɓalɓalē *Vb.* 3A = **cāɓẹ** 1.

cạɓạlɓạlī = **cạɓạlɓạlō** *m.* (1) mud. (2) **hanyạ tā yi** ～ road's muddy.

caɓalo A. (cạ̄ɓālọ). (1) *m.*, *f.* driveller (= **kwāɓọ**), *cf.* **kyạsfī** 2. (2) *m.* (*a*) drivel. (*b*) poor **tūwō**.

B. (caɓalọ) *m.* = **cạɓạlɓạlī**.

caɓe A. (cāɓẹ). (1) *Vb.* 3A (*a*) **hanyạ tā** ～ road's slushy. (*b*) **gyạmbō** (**idọ**) **yā** ～ ulcer (eye) is purulent (*for further examples*, *Vd.* **kwāɓẹ** 2). (2) *Vb.* 1*a* = **cāɓạ** 1-5.

B. (cāɓē) *m*, (1) boys' game of striking sickle (**lau̱jē**) edges together. (2) what drivelling talk !

C. (caɓẹ) *Vb.* 1C *Kt.* = **cafẹ** 1, 2.

caɓī A. (cạ̄ɓī) *m.* (1) (*a*) slush. (*b*) **hanyạ tā yi** ～ road's slushy. (2) **tạkạ cạ̄ɓī** *m.* = **cāɓu̱lā** 3.

B. (cāɓi̱). (1) ～ **yā cāɓạ adō** how he's togged up ! (2) ～ **hanyạ tā yi cạ̄ɓī** how muddy the road is !

caɓiya A. (cāɓīyā) *f.*: (1) = **cāɓē** 1. (2) **ƙarfạn nạ̱ŋ** ～ **gạrēshi̱** this metal chips quickly.

B. (caɓīyā) *Kt. f.* = **cafīyā**.

cabkạcaɓẹ *used in* ～ **cācar mạkāfọ** what rich food !

caɓo A. (cāɓọ) *m.* (1) indigo gathered just before end of rains. (2) drivel. (3) what drivel ! (4) driveller (*epithet is* **cāɓọ**, **bābaŋ kạ̀kā**).

B. (cạɓō) *Sk.*, *Kt. m.* mud (= **tạɓō** *q.v.*).

caɓu̱ *Sk.*, *Kt. m.* bits of meat and rice from ox killed for naming of child.

cāɓu̱lā (1) *Vb.* 1C = **cāɓạ** 1-5. (2) **cạɓu̱lạ gēmu̱** *m.* a food of groundnuts plus cassava or sweet potatoes or dried sorrel (= **cạ̀ku̱ɓē** = *Kt.* **tsạmōdagī**). (3) **cạ̀ɓu̱lạ kāshī** *m.* clogs (= **dạŋgạrạfai** = **tạ̀kạ cạ̀ɓī**) (*cf.* **cāɓạ** 5).

cāɓu̱lē *Vb.* 3A = **cāɓẹ** 1.

cācā *f.* (1) (*a*) gambling (*epithet is* **Gaṇgạ ūwar tsi̱yā** = **Gwaskā haṇạ kyau̱**). (*b*) ～ **māganim mai̱ daṇgi̱** ; **kō sun yi dubū dạri̱**, **sạ̀ ƙī shi̱** gambling soon estranges P. from his relatives. (2) *Vd.* **cī** 11*j*, *k*, *l* ; **di̱kkạṇ**. (3) **dan** ～ *m.* (*pl.* **'yan** ～) (*a*) gambler (= **gujīyā** 9). (*b*) dice (*3b* = **dōki̱n cācā**). (4) **cācar bakạ** = **cācar bạ̀kī** = **cācar kuṇcē** = **cācar kuṇci̱** (*a*) garrulity. (*b*) harping on T. (*c*) *Vd.* **bi̱dī** 4. (5) **shạrī̱fi̱n cācā** skilful gambler. (6) **bạ̀** ～ *Vd.* **ci̱rin**.

cạcạ̀ɓau = **cạcạ̀ɓō** = **cācāɓulā** *m.*, *f.* driveller.

cācāku̱cē *Zar. m.* (1) garrulity. (2) harping on T.

cạcạ̄nīyā *f.* hubbub of voices.

caccaɓā *Sk. f.* (1) big-made girl. (2) big laying-hen.

caccafā *f.* = **caccafī** *m. Sk.* drizzle (= **tsattsafī**).

caccaga *Kt.* **tsattsaga**.

caccạ̄gī *Kt. m.* the shrub **matsattsāgī**.

cạccakạ *Vb.* 2. (1) rammed (earth, etc.) *x* **nā cạccạki̱ ạddakạ** I rammed the charge into the dane-gun (= **tsattsạgā** 1). (2) pester P. by cadging.

cạccạ̀kai *m.* the rattle **ƙōṛōsō** *q.v.*

cạ̀ci̱m in profusion (= **ti̱njim** *q.v.*).

cạ̀ci̱ri̱ndọ = **cạ̀ci̱ri̱ndọ** *Kt. m.* **sun** yi ～ crowd gathered.

cācukwī *m.* **nā** yi **masạ** ～ I seized him (thief, etc.) by the neck of his gown.

cạ̀dā *Kt.* = **tsạ̀dā**.

cadi A. (cādī) *m.*, *f.* (*sg.*, *pl.*) miser (*epithet is* ~ bā dawā ba).

B. (Cādi) *m.* Lake Chad.

caf (1) ~ yā cafę he caught it adroitly when thrown. (2) yā yi ~ dā shī it (garment) suits him.

cafa A. (cafā) *Vb.* 2 = cafę 1, 2, 3, 5.

B. (cafā) *Vb.* 1C = cafę 6.

C. (cafā) *Kt.* *f.* the bird ƙyafā.

caf-caf A. (caf-caf) *used in* ~ dā māi tā fi ~ dā rūwā = ~ dā māi bā tā ɓātāwā it's better to have surplus than cut things too fine.

B. (caf-caf) *adv.* (1) yanā sayūwā ~ it's very saleable. (2) yā yi adō ~ he's smartly dressed.

cafalā *f.* young chicken.

cafe A. (cafę) *Vb.* 1A. (1) caught T. thrown. (2) clutched at moving T. (= ribcę 1*b*). (3) (crocodile, dog, etc.) snapped at. (4) kā ~ mini you took the words out of my mouth. (5) " snapped up " T. on sale. (6) ornamented the outside of house *as in* cafē.

B. (cafē) *m.* a compound (made of black earth mixed with wet solution of bagārūwā seeds) which is plastered on walls or around door of rich persons ; pebbles are pushed into this plaster and beaten to fix, ornamental patterns then being drawn with stick (tsiŋkē) ; is then left for a day to harden and on successive days is wetted twice with bagārūwā fluid and twice with mākubā solution.

caffā = cappā *f.* (1) yā kai masā ~ (*a*) he recognized him as overlord. (*b*) he (servant, etc.) entered his service. (2) yā yi ~ gārēshi he swore fealty to him (= mabāyi'ā).

caffata = cappata *Vb.* 2 (*p.o.* caffacē, *n.o.* caffaci) served *etc.* P. *as in* caffā.

cafīyā *f.* acting as in cafę 1-3.

cafka *Vb.* 2 = cafę 1, 2, 3, 5.

cafkacē *Vb.* 3A. (1) is (was) abundant. (2) magana tā ~ matter became serious.

cafkata A. (cafkatā) *Vb.* 3B = cafkacē.

B. (cafkatā) *x* an cafkatā rūwā ā ābincī food has been made too watery.

cafkę *Vb.* 1A = cafę 1, 2, 3, 5.

cafkīyā *f.* = cafīyā.

cāga *Vb.* 1A *Kt.* = tsāga.

cagadē *Sk.* *m.* = cagwadē.

cāgar kāi *Sk.* *f.* loud crying of infant.

caggu-caggu *m.* buying odds and ends.

cāginaginī *Kt.* *m.* finickiness (= ƙyāmā).

cagīya *f.* searching : investigation (= cigiya *q.v.*).

cagwadē *m.* = cagwadā *f.* (1) loquacity. (2) harping on T.

cai = cai-cai *adv.* (1) yanā dā wāyō ~ he's very cunning. (2) yanā dā zāƙī ~ it's very sweet.

cāję *Vb.* 1A *Eng.* (1) charged P. criminally. (2) mun ~ we've totted up the balance in the transactions between us.

cāji *Eng.* *m.* (1) (*a*) charging P. criminally. (*b*) ~ ofis *m.* police charge-office. (2) type of drum beaten by marōƙā.

cak completely *x* rūwā yā ɗaukē ~ rain's completely ceased. yā tāshi dagā garī ~ he's left the town for good. yanā kamā dā shī ~ they're alike as two peas.

caka A. (cakā) *Vb.* 2. (1) stabbed *x* nā cakē shi dā māshi I stabbed him with a spear. yā caki kwībin dōki dā ƙā'imī he spurred up the horse. (2) yā caki ɗaŋ wākē dā tsiŋkē he ate ɗaŋ wākē *q.v.* by impaling on sticks.

B. (cakā) *Vb.* 1A (*with dative*) yā cakā masā māshi *etc.* = cakā.

C. (cākā) *used in* 'yan ~ over-cute person(s).

caka-caka A. (caka-caka) in profusion = dāɓāɓā *q.v.*

B. (cakā-cakā) *f.* = cakaɗīdī.

cakadī = cakaɗīdī *m.* (1) silly chatter. (2) anā mini ~ I'm being disparaged (*whether present or not*).

cakaftū *m.* (1) unceasing chatter. (2) yanā ta cakaftunsā he's managed to get hold of plenty of money.

cakaikai *m.*, *f.* (*sg.*, *pl.*) loquacious P.

cakalkalē *Vb.* 3A = cāɓę 1.

cākānīyā *f.* noisy chatter.

cākansamī *m.* (*pl.* cākansamai). (1) rattle worn on dancers' ankles = cika saurā (*cf.* ƙōrōsō *q.v.*). (2) tinkling metal ornaments of horse.

cakara A. (cakarā) *f.* an edible Aroid tuber (*Anchomanes Dalzielli*).

B. (cạkarạ) *Vd.* gạnyau.

cạkarkạrī *m.* = cạkarkạrā *f.* (1) well-pulley. (2) part of loom made from kernel of dum-palm. (3) *Sk.* device for scaring birds off date-palms.

cạkasam *x* yanạ̄ dạ gāshị ~ he is very hairy. yāyị yanạ̄ naŋ ~ there are masses of grass.

cakau *Sk. m.* = cạkansamī.

cạkaurạ (1) *f.* (*a*) protuberant teeth. (*b*) the rattle lālājọ. (2) *m., f.* (*sg., pl.*) P. with protuberant teeth.

cakẹ *Vb.* 1A. (1) stabbed *x* nā ~ shi da māshị = cạkā *q.v.* nā ~ māshị ạ ƙas I stuck a spear in the ground. (2) dōkị yạ̄ ~ ƙafạssạ horse is standing on tip of one foot. (3) kạzā tā zūrạ tā ~ chicken pecked at it.

caki A. (cakī) *m.* (*sg., pl.*). (1) (*a*) gourd (būtạ) filled with stones for rattling. (*b*) gwaiwā dạ kudī cakī cẹ people sin if it is advantageous to them. (2) a dishonest method of throwing gambling-cowries ('yan cācā). (3) kạ̄ kai ~ you'll be forced to tell the truth. (4) dōkị yā yi ~ = dōkị yā kaɗạ ~ horse flicked its tail (= yāfạ 3).

    B. (cạkī) *Kt. m.* pepper-seedlings (= tsạ̄kī *q.v.*).

    C. (cakị) *Eng. m.* (*sg., pl.*) cheque.

cạkinạ *used in songs :* ~ cạ̄kiŋkiŋ ~ leper's diseased foot.

cākịnē *Vb.* 3A *Sk.* = cā6ẹ 1.

Cạ̄kiri (1) *m., f.* (*pl.* Cạ̄kịrai) *properly a* Jekri, *but also applied to* Ibo, Yoruba, etc. (= kụŋkuruŋ kudụ). (2) *m.* (*pl.* cạ̄kịrai) (*a*) type of bird. (*b*) any strong, patterned European cloth (= ạtạmfā). (*c*) circular mat (= cībịyar kūrā *q.v.*).

cạ̄kiryạ *f.* type of gambling.

cakkyacẹ *Kt. m.* the rattle lālājọ.

cạ̄kō *Kt. m.* chicken (= tsạ̄kō *q.v.*).

cạ̄kọnī *m.* = cạkwạlī 1.

cākụ6ā *Vb.* 1C. (1) an cākụ6ạ mặi cikiŋ ạbincin naŋ this food has been made nice and oily. (2) sun cākụ6ạ mạganạ they've warmed up to an argument. (3) yārọ yā cakụ6ạ ạbincī the boy messed the food about by fingering it.

cakuɓe A. (cākụ6ē). (1) *Vb.* 3A (*a*) yā ~

it (rice, beans, tūwō) is sloppy. (*b*) gwandạ tā ~ pawpaw is over-ripe. (*c*) is (was) slushy. (2) *Vb.* 1C *x* an ~ wākē (shiŋkāfā) dạ mặi the beans (rice) are cooked nice and oily.

    B. (cạ̄kụ6ē) *m.* the food cạ̄6ụlạ gēmụ *q.v.*

cākụɗā *Vb.* 1C. (1) mixed (rice with oil, etc.) round and round with spoon (*cf.* dāmạ). (2) = cākụ6ā 2. (3) = cākụɗē 2. (4) yā cākụɗạ aikị he did but little work.

cākụɗē *Vb.* 3A. (1) (*a*) became mixed (*as in* cākụɗā). (*b*) ạl'amạrī yā ~ matters have gone from bad to worse. (2) sun ~ they've quarrelled.

cākụlā *Vb.* 1C = cākụɗā.

cākụle = cākụɗē.

cākụlẹ̄tị *m.* (1) chocolate. (2) 'yan ~ *pl. m.* chocolates.

cạ̄kulkul = cạ̄kulkulī = *Kt.* cạ̄kulkulō (1) tickling armpits of children (*cf.* tsịkarạ). (2) anạ̄ cạ̄kulkulim mạganạ they started and then deferred discussion again and again.

cạ̄kunạ *Vb.* 2 provoked ; teased P. (= tsọ̄kanạ *q.v.*).

cākur-cākur *Vd.* cākurkur.

cakuri A. (cākurī) *adj. m.* (*f.* cākurā) short, slight P.

    B. (cākụrī) *Kt. m.* provoking a P. (= tsạ̄kụrī *q.v.*).

cakurkur A. (cākurkur) *x* mụtumin naŋ ~ dạ shī this man's short and slight (*pl.* mutạ̄nan naŋ cākur-cākur dạ sū).

    B. (cākurkụr) *used in* ɗan ~ *m.* (*f.* 'yar ~) *pl.* 'yan ~ short, slight P.

cạ̄kurkụrī *x* ɗan ~ *m.* (*f.* 'yar cạ̄kur-kụrā) short, slight P.

*cākụtā = cākụɗā.

cakwā *Zar. f.* leech (= mạtsạttsạkū).

cạkwaikwaiwạ *f.* (*sg., pl.*). (1) starling. (2) chatterbox.

cạkwạl = cakwal-cạkwạl = cạkwạlī *q.v.*

cakwạlē *Vb.* 3A = cā6ẹ 1.

cakwali A. (cakwālī) *m.* = cakadī.

    B. (cạkwạlī) *m.* (1) hanyạ tā yi ~ road's slushy. (2) idọ yā yi ~ eye is purulent. mại cạkwạliŋ idọ P. with purulent eyes.

cakwalkwạlē *Vb.* 3A is (was) slushy.

cąkwąlkwąlī = cąkwąlkwąlō *m.* = cąkwąlī 2.

cakwalǫ *m.* (1) measure holding 4 handfuls of corn (= mūdanabị *q.v.*). (2) type of bag made of dum-palm (kabạ) leaves.

cākwarkwar = cākurkur.

cakwat small *x* dan yārǫ nē ~ dạ shī he's a tiny lad (*pl.* 'yan yąrā nę̄ cakwatcakwat dạ sū).

cālī *m.* (*sg., pl.*). (1) network-bag (*epithet is* ~ mại yawạŋ k͂ōf͂ōfī). (2) P. full of threadbare excuses.

cąlị-cālī *Kt. x* an yi masạ ~ 2-4 persons lifted it each holding one side of it (= d̄aukạn 'yam makarantā).

cạlillindǫ *Kt. m.* throwing T. up into air (= tsạlạllę̄kū).

calịndō *said in boys' game* (= cilạndō *q.v.*).

callạ = cillạ.

camai (1) yanạ̄ dạ tsāmī ~ it's very acid. (2) mụtụ̄m nē ~ dạ shī he's small-built.

cạmāyǫ *m., f.* (*sg., pl.*) short, slight P.

camб̃ala A. (camб̃alā) *Vb.* 1C = cāб̃ạ 1-5.

B. (camб̃alā) *f.* fine-figured girl.

camб̃alēlīyā *x* yārinyạ cē ~ dạ ita she's a fine-figured girl.

cambas-cambas in profusion.

camfạ *Vb.* 1A = cạmfā *Vb.* 2 regarded T. as portent (*cf.* camfị).

camfạcē *Vb.* 1C = cạmfatạ *Vb.* 2 (*p.o.* cạmfạcē) = camfạ.

camfị *m.* yawạn camfị gạrēshị he's superstitious.

cạmfō *Nor. m.* muzzle (= tạ̄kụŋkụmī 2).

cạmōlạ *Zar. f.* West African genet (= inyāwarā).

campa = camfa.

camuka *Kt.* = tsamuka.

can A. (cạŋ). (1) there (*visible.* M.G., Chapter 25) *x* yanạ̄ ~ it is over there (=naŋ). (2) that (*visible*) *used after preceding low tone : x* dōkịn ~ that horse over there (*cf.* cạŋ).

B. (cạŋ) (1) there (*invisible.* M.G., Chapter 25) *x* nā gan shị ~ I saw him there. nā bi ta ~ I passed through there (=naŋ). (2) (=naŋ) the one in question *x* ạ cikin shēkarạr ~ in the year in question. Ạsabạrcịn ~ on the Saturday

in question (N.B. caŋ *is often omitted x* dōkịŋ = dōkịn caŋ the horse under reference). (3) then (=naŋ) *x* ~ sǎi sukạ farkạ then they revived. dạgạ ~ sǎi dōkị ya abạucē after that the horse became out of hand. sukạ k͂ī sǎi ~ ạsụb̃ạ they refused till later at dawn. tun caŋ dạ̄ mā, dạttịjam banzā nę̄ even in those days, they were evil leaders.

C. (cạŋ) that (*visible.* M.G. Chapter 25) *used after preceding high tone : x* gạrin ~ that town over there. gōdīyar ~ that mare there (*cf.* cạŋ).

*cānā = caŋ.

cạncak completely *x* sun tāshị ~ they've gone away for good.

cạncạkwatǫ *m.* = *Kt.* cancạkwatạ *f.* (1) loquacity. (2) harping on T. (3) = cạ̄kulkulī 2.

cạncamnō *Kt. m.* = jụ̄cē 1.

cancạnā *Vb.* 1C. (1) eked out (*Vd.* cạncạnē). (2) yā cancạnạ mạganạr he harped on the matter.

cancạnạ kwanīkạ *m.* type of creeper.

cancạncē *Vb.* 1C = cạncantạ.

cạncạndō *Kt. m.* pencil, pen (*Vd.* ạlkalạmī).

cạncạnē *m.* (1) eking out (= tsantsanī 3 = tsimī 1*a* = rēf͂ạtā 2). (2) harping on T.

cạncạŋgā *f.* (1) = tsịrē 1. (2) the food ạ cī dạ mǎi.

cancanī *Kt. m.* finickiness (= tsantsanī *q.v.*).

cạncaŋ kwanīkạ = cạncạnạ kwanīkạ.

cạncantạ *Vb.* 2 (*p.o.* cạncạncē, *n.o.* cạncạnci). (1) suited, befitted P. (2) deserved *x* sun cạncạnci ạ yạb̃ē sụ they deserve praise. (3) bạ zā sụ cạncạnci ịndạ k͂ārịn naŋ ya nụf͂ā ba they will not benefit in the way this increase of pay was intended to benefit them.

cạncarambę *x* dan ~ *m.* (*f.* 'yar ~) *pl.* 'yan ~ small but good P. or T.

cancēnī *Kt. m.* = cancanī.

candal *x* yā cịka ~ it's brimful.

candị *Sk. m.* pyorrhœa (*cf.* bũbụ).

cane A. (canę) *Vb.* 1A. (1) said (= cę̄). (2) thought *x* n nạ̄ canę̄wā zại zō I think he'll come (= cę̄).

B. (canę) *imperative of* canę̄). (1) ~ dạ shī yạ zō tell him to come ! (2) bãbụ wani ∼ nā canę there's nothing more to be said ! (3) *Vd.* turmĭ 8, ƙwā̰ 3, sā̰ A.2 2.

caŋga-caŋga *f.* = caŋkącakārę.

caŋgal (1) *m.* contracted Achilles-tendon *x* ƙafąssą tā yi ∼ he has contracted Achilles-tendon (= cōbę). (2) *m.*, *f.* *such* P.

canja *Vb.* 1A = caṇjā *Vb.* 2 = canjad dą *Vb.* 4B *Eng.* (1) changed (money). (2) transferred P. to another place of duty.

canjąras *m.* (1) an equal exchange (*epithet is* ∼ gwaiwas sā̰). (2) mun yi ∼ dą shĭ he and I are equally matched (= tindindim). (3) sun tāshi ∼ they're equally matched.

canję A. (canję) *Vb.* 1A = canją.
  B. (caṇję) *Vd.* cąnzā.

canji *Eng. m.* (1) change for money (= musāyā 3*a*). (2) (*a*) an yi canjinsą he's been transferred elsewhere (= badąlĭ 1*a* = musāyā 3*b*). (*b*) canjin gādi *m.* changing of the guard. (3) canjinsą yā zō his relief's come (= musāyā 3*c* = mąimakō 1*b*). (4) cąnji *Vd.* cąnzā.

caŋkącakārę *m.* (1) running short. (2) falling between two stools.

caŋkaf = cąŋkas *x* tā yi adō ∼ she's all togged up.

caŋkō *m.* (*sg.*, *pl.*). (1) type of snare or fishtrap. (2) thread-winding apparatus (= yārǫ 4*b*).

caŋkwaną *Vb.* 2 *Kt.* provoked, teased P. (= tsōkaną).

caŋwā *Kt.* = tsaŋwā.

caŋyē *Kt.* = ciŋyē.

cąnzā *Vb.* 2 (*p.o.* canję, *n.o.* cąnji) = canją.

cappącē = caffącē.

car A. (car). (1) *x* yā mĭƙę tsąye ∼ it's vertical (= cir *q.v.*). (2) *Vd.* car dą.
  B. (car). (1) away with you ! (*said to chicken, beggar, trickster*). (2) yā cillą masą rūwā ∼ he squirted stream of water over him.

cara A. (cārā). (1) *f.* (*a*) crowing of cock. (*b*) ząkarą ą rątąye bā yā ∼ the underdog has to eat humble pie. (*c*) ɗan ząkarą wąndą ząi yi cārā, shirwą bā tā̰ ɗauką let the cobbler stick to his last ! (*d*) shĭ kaɗăi kę cārā ą wurinsu

he behaves autocratically to them. (*e*) ząkaran dą Allā̰ ya nufē shi dą cārā, anā̰ muzūrū, anā̰ shāhǫ, săi yā yĭ nothing can prevent the person destined to succeed. (*f*) crying out. (*g*) type of playing and singing. (2) *Vb.* 3B (*a*) (cock) crew. (*b*) P. cried out. (*c*) (beggar) burst into song. (*d*) lā̰dan yā ∼ muezzin sounded call to prayer. (*e*) P. began type of playing and dancing *so called.*
  B. (carą) *Vb.* 1A yā ∼ mini māshi he threw a spear at me.
  C. (cąrā) *Vb.* 2 yā cąrēni dą māshi he threw spear at me.

carabkē *m.* (1) game of catching on back of hand, stones thrown into air (= *Sk.* cąɓąl 3). (2) anā̰ ∼ dą ita she has many suitors.

caraf suddenly *x* ∼ ya kāmą ni he suddenly clutched me. dą sōmą mąganąta ∼ săi ya cafę he interrupted me as soon as I began to speak.

cąrainĭyā *Kt. f.* (1) loquacity. (2) harping on T.

carambaɗakwallē *m.* = caraŋgwaɗas.

carambē *x* ɗan ∼ *m.* (*f.* 'yar ∼) small but good T. or P.

caraŋgwaɗaɗas = caraŋgwaɗas becomingly *x* wannąn rawąni yā kąrɓē shi ∼ this turban suits him well.

cararras *x* yārǫ ɗan ∼ dą shĭ small but good-looking lad.

cararrąshĭ *adj. m.* (*f.* cąrarrąsā) *pl.* carascąrąs small but good-looking.

caras (1) *m.* yā yi ∼ he's small but good-looking. (2) *Vd.* cąrarrąshĭ.

car-car = cir 2 *q.v.* yā cika ∼ it's brimful. yā bĭyā ni ∼ he paid me in full. uku ∼ 3 exactly. gōmą ∼ 10 exactly, etc. yā yi ∼ it's complete, brimful.

car dą *Vb.* 4B *Kt.* spat out (= tsar dą).

carę (1) *Vb.* 3A is (was) expert. (2) *Vb.* 1A yā ∼ ni dą māshi he launched a spear at me.

cąrĭ *m.* an yi masą ∼ = an yi masą cąrim mąƙąƙĭ they gave him no peace.

cąrkĭ *m.* (*pl.* cąrkĭ = carkuną). (1) (*a*) rhinoceros-bird (*it pecks at wounds on donkey with galled back*). (*b*) bāyan gĭwā săi ∼ *Vd.* bāyā 1*a*.ii. (2) type of black bird seen on cattle.

(3) carkiŋ gīwā *another type.* (4) Cąrkī,
hayą manyā = Cąrkī hayę manyā
epithet of foolhardy P. or child. (5) *Vd.*
bąkin cąrkī ; tsagē 3.
carkō-cąrkǭ *m.* deadlock (= jagō-jągǭ *q.v.*).
carkōkō *x* yā zauną ~ he sat mewed up
(= cōkōkō *q.v.*).
carkuną *Vd.* cąrkī.
carkwaďa A. (cąrkwaďą) *Vb.* 2 *x* nā
cąrkwąďē shi dą būlālą I flogged him.
  B. (carkwąďā) *Vb.* 1C (*with dative*)
nā ~ masą būlālą = cąrkwaďą.
carkwąďē *Vb.* 1C *x* nā ~ shi dą būlālą =
cąrkwaďą.
carkwąďi what a whipping !
cąrkwai (1) yaną̄ dą zāƙī ~ it's
very sweet (= ząrƙwai). (2) yaną̄
dą zāfī ~ it's very painful. (3) an yi
masą būlālą ~ he's been severely
flogged. (4) ~ bą̄ lą̄sar bą̄kī (*a*)
epithet of ąlēwą *or* honey. (*b*) the cry
of those exposing for sale (tąllą) honey
or ąlēwą.
carną *Vb.* 1A shot T. a long way (=
cillą *q.v.*).
cartą *Vb.* 1A *Kt.* spat out (= tsartą *q.v.*).
cas A. (cas) A. tidily *x* an shiryą kāyā ~
the things have been neatly arranged.
(2) bą̄ ~, bą̄ as uselessly *x* yā zō bą̄ ~
bą̄ as he came without the slightest
gift (= sīdīdī).
  B. (cąs) *m.* (1) the rattling-sound
of metal on metal. (2) the sound arising
during work as in cą̄sā. (3) *Vd.* tąɓą
kuru.
  C. (cąs) *a reply in the game* kulę.
casa A. (cāsą) *Vb.* 1A. (1) ~ hatsī to
thresh grain from chaff (ƙaiƙayī) in a
mortar, *i.e.* when quantity is small (*cf.*
bugā 1*a*.iv ; bākącē; zurcę; tąŋkąďē) =
sussuƙā = tsāɓącē. (2) beat P. (3)
yā ~ ƙaryā he told a lie.
  B. (cą̄sā) *Vb.* 2 (*p.o.* cą̄shē, *n.o.*
cąshi). (1) = cāsą 1. (2) taną̄ cą̄sar
farī she's bleaching the rice (= bam
farī). (3) ciki gąrēshi kąman yā cī
bą̄ ~ = c.g. kąman yā cī bą̄ sussuƙą
he's very stout.
cą̄sa'iŋ *f.* 90 (= tisa'iŋ *q.v.*).
cą̄sau *m.* (1) for payment, working as in
cāsą 1. (2) Cą̄sau ną̄ rawā, Sarą ną̄
kallō he's been " seen through ".

cashe A. (cāshę) *Vb.* 1A. (1) threshed
(*as in* cāsą) *all* the grain. (2) sun
cāshę mąganą they thrashed out their
differences. (3) sun ~ they speeded
up tempo of their dancing.
  B. (cāshē) *Vd.* cą̄sā.
cąshi *Vd.* cą̄sā.
cashiya (cāshīyā) *f.* acting as in cāshę 3.
cąskuru *Vd.* dąɓąkuru.
cąskwakwąyą *f.* bead-band round women's
hips.
cąssā *f.* bow-leggedness *x* ~ gąrēshi he's
bow-legged (= *Sk.* tarkōshī).
cau A. (cau). (1) (*a*) up camel ! (*b*)
down camel ! (*c*) kō bą̄ ka rą̄ƙumī, kā
san ~ wilfully or stupidly misunder-
standing order given one. (2) at it, dog !
  B. (cąu) sound of whipping or caning.
caucawą = cąucāwą *Kt.* *f.* the swift
tsąttsēwą.
cauďą *Vb.* 1A = carkwąďā.
cauďi what a whipping !
caulą *Vb.* 1A *Kt.* = carkwąďā.
cāwąrākī *Sk.* *m.* crocodile (= kado).
cāwaryą *Kt.* *f.* leucoma = tsāwuryą.
cazbī *m.* (*pl.* cazbuną) (*Ar.* tasbīh).
(1) (*a*) rosary (= tąsbahą), *cf.* kąrambą.
(*b*) yā jā ~ he told his beads. (2) cązbiŋ
kurēgē = cązbim mą̄gē the cakes ƙulī-
ƙulī.
ce A. (cē, cę) *Vd.* nē.
  B. (cę̄) (1) (1) (*a*) said, told *x* (i) ką ~ dą shī
yą zō = cę̄ dą shī yą zō tell him to come !
yā ~ zai zō = yā ~ cę̄wā zai zō he said
he would come. yā ~ haką he spoke
thus. yaną̄ cę̄wā haką he's speaking
thus, he is saying this. nā ~ dą sū
haką =nā ~ musu haką I said this to
them. yaną̄ ~ wani ąbu = yaną̄ cę̄wā
wani ąbu he's saying something. (ii) săi
ąbin dą ka cę̄ (*Vd.* M.G. 139*b*[3]) it's for
you to give orders, it's for *you* to decide.
(iii) bą̄ wandą zai ~ masą kōmē wajan
wą̄sanni he has no equal as an athlete.
(iv) bā ą̄ cę̄ yą shā rūwā *Vd.* wākē 4.
(v) wandą ya cę̄ kā cę̄ *Vd.* damō 4*b*.
(*b*) an ~ dą mąkāfo " gą̄ ido ! ", ya
cę̄ " dą ďǫyī " it's sour grapes. (*c*) an ~
dą kąrē " tūwō yā yi yawą " *Vd.*
kąrē 29. (2) (*a*) aną̄ ~ (= aną̄ cę̄wā)
dą shī Daudą (= aną̄ ~ masą Daudą)
his name is David. ƙą̄ƙą akę̄ cę̄wā dą

shị what is it called ? (b) an cẹ̆ dạ kạrē Muhammạŋ Vd. wai 3a.ii. (3) săi kạ cẹ̆ like x jặkin naŋ yanặ tạfīyạ săi kạ ∼ dōkị nẽ this donkey has a gait like a horse. ƙarfī gạrēshị săi kạ ∼ zāki = ƙarfī gạrēshị kặ ∼ zāki = ƙarfī gạrēshị kặ cẽ zāki = ƙarfī gạrēshị kai kặ cẹ̆ zāki he's as strong as a lion. (4) (a) considered that x an ∼ dạ shĩ maƙạryạcĩ he's considered a liar. nā ∼ zại zō gọ̄be I thought he'd come to-morrow. n nặ cẹ̆wā wani nẹ̆ I took him (you, etc.) for someone else. nā ∼ dạ shĩ mūgụm mutụm I consider him a rogue. n nặ cẹ̆wā zan zō nẹ̆ I thought to myself " let me come ! ". (b) cẹ̆ mā munặ īyặwā well supposing for the sake of argument that we could do it.... (c) kặfịn ạ ∼ = kặfịn x kặfịŋ ạ ∼ muŋ isō, sū kụ̄wā suŋ gudụ they had fled before we even arrived. kặfịŋ ạ ∼ suŋ gamạ shiri, ɗārī yặ shigō winter will have come before they've even finished their preparations. (d) maintained x (i) sunặ nūnặ cẹ̆wā they maintain that . . . yịŋ hakạ yā nūnặ cẹ̆wā the fact of this having been done proves that . . . (ii) bặ wạndạ ya cẹ̆ yā ga ƙạrƙashinsạ it was so deep that it was impossible to see its bottom. (iii) in dặ ặ ∼ mun yi hakạ, dặ . . . if it were the case that we had done so, then . . . (iv) dạ cẹ̆wā ɗārī yā wucẹ̆, ya tāshị he set out as soon as the winter was over. (e) decided x sun ∼ dạ jirặgē zā sụ zō, zā sụ kōmạ gidā they decided they'd go home when the ships arrived. (5) kạmar ạ ∼ it is as if one were to say . . . ; the word in question is used as follows . . . (6) " sukạ ∼ " kẹ̆ naŋ it's mere rumour. (7) Wānẹ̆, cẹ̆ dạ mutụm " Bặba ! " kạ kash nị epithet of polite hypocrite. (8) ặ ∼ = ặ ∼ fạ ? yes, of course, it is as you say. (9) bặ " ka cẹ̆, na cẹ̆ " there's nothing more to be said ! (10) na cẹ̆ (= n cẹ̆) kō = na cẹ̆ (= n cẹ̆) kọ̄ ? dăi = na cẹ̆ kō in dăi = n cẹ̆ dăi (expresses query by 1st pers. singular) na cẹ̆ kō kuŋ gạmu dạ shị ? I wonder whether you met him ? (11) Vd. cẹ̆wā below and

its uses in 1, 2, 4 above. (12) For tone of this verb in relative sentence, Vd. 1a.ii above. (13) Vd. dặ kạ cẽ, canẹ̆.
cēbēbē Kt. m. the bird tsēbēbe q.v.
cēbur Eng. m. shovel (= shēbur).
cẹ̄cē Vd. cẹ̄tā.
cēcēkụcē m. (1) loquacity. (2) harping on T.
cẹ̄ci Vd. cẹ̄tā.
cēdạ f. vomiting (= amai).
cēdīyā f. (pl. cēdīyōyī = Sk. cẹ̄dạkū) (1) (a) the fig-tree Ficus Thonningii (Vd. gulụbā). (b) ∼ bặ ki ƙayạ epithet of easygoing P. (c) ∼ tạ bar fushī Vd. rīmī 1d. (3) ganyan ∼ m. mediumly blue colour.
cēfạnā Vb. 1C took handful of flour or corn, etc., from one's stock, for use.
cēfanad dạ Vb. 4B sold off one's property bit by bit for purchase of daily supplies.
cẹ̄fạnē m. (1) buying ingredients for soup (cf. mạsạrūfị). (2) kinặ san cẹ̄fạnẹ̆ ? would you like corn in exchange for the milk you're selling me rather than cash ? (reply, Ī, kặwō, mụ ganī yes !). (3) Sk. corn bought by measure (= awọ 3a).
cēgumī Kt. = tsēgumī.
cēkạɗē Vb. 3A Sk. dodged aside (= baudẹ̆).
cēmạ Kt. f. type of arrow (= tsaimạ q.v.).
cēnạ = caŋ (cf. cēnī).
cendị Sk. m. small butter-calabash (= kātā q.v.).
cēnẹ̆ = canẹ̆.
cēnī Kt. = caŋ 2, caŋ x dōkịn ∼ that horse there. mạcạn ∼ that woman there (cf. cēnīyā, cēnạ).
cēnīyā Sk. = cēnī x dōkịn ∼ that horse there. mạcạn ∼ that woman there.
cera A. (cērā) Kt. f. = cārā.
  B. (cẹ̄rā) Sk. f. fennec (= yạnyawạ).
cērērīyā = tsararrīyā.
cērị m. hole made in ground for skinning ox (= tērị).
cẹ̄rū m. the knife wuƙar gịndī.
cẹ̄tā Vb. 2 (p.o. cẹ̄cē, n.o. cẹ̄ci) (Vd. cẹ̄tō) rescued, liberated.
cẹ̄tō m. (1) (secondary v.n. of cẹ̄tā) x munặ cẹ̄tansạ = munặ cẹ̄tā tasạ we're rescuing him. (b) gudụn cẹ̄tan rặi m. fleeing in panic, stampeding. (c) Vd.

cī dạ ~. (2) cackling of alarmed poultry (= kwạrmatọ 3).

cẹ̃wā *f.* (1) (*progressive and v.n. of* cẹ̃) (1) *Vd.* cẹ̃ 11. (2) (*a*) statement *x* ~ mukạ yi " kụ kāwō shị ! " what we said was to bring it. yā aikẹ musụ dạ ~ yanā̃ zūwạ he sent to tell them he was coming. (*b*) bā̤ ka dạ ta ~ you've " not a leg to stand on ". baị sāmi ta ~ ba he seemed to have lost his power of speech. kanā̃ dạ ta cẹ̃wā̤ ? have you any excuse to offer ? have you any answer to the allegation ? baị sāmi wani ạbin ~ ba ạ wannạŋ zạncē he could find no fault with this proposal. saurā nī, bā̤ ni dạ ta ~ cikiŋ ạl'amạriŋ I've no say in the matter, it is outside my sphere (*Vd.* fặdā 1*d*). (3) that (*after verbs of* saying, *etc.*) *x* (*a*) yā bayyạnā̃ ~ he said, explained that . . . (*b*) *Vd.* cẹ̃ 1*a*.i. (*c*) nā sāmi lā̤bāṛị ~ I've heard that . . . (*d*) mụ tunạ mukụ ~ let us remind you that . . . (*e*) *cf.* kạman 5, wai.

ci A. (cī) *Vb.* 5 (1) (*a*) ate. (*b*) ạbiŋ yā tsạnantạ, yā̤ḳi yā ḳi cị, yā ḳi ciŋyẹ̃wā matters became so serious that the war has come to a standstill. (*c*) (i) ate certain fruits (dabīnọ, ɗinyā, maŋgwạrọ, tāɓọ *q.v.*, gọrubạ *q.v.*, ạyạbạ), *but cf.* shā A.1*e*. (ii) yā ci tābạ *Vd.* tābạ 1*b*, 1*c*. (iii) *cf.* tūwō 1*b*. (iv) ci na marạc cị *Vd.* kudā̤sạ. (*d*) *for* proverbs, *Vd.* 26. (*e*) *for* cī *used with the following words, Vd. that word, i.e.* adō, ạmānạ 4*a*, azziḳī 3, badặlī 2, bāshị 2*b*, biḳī 1*d*, *f*, bāyā 1*k*, ɗācī 2, dādī 5, dāgụmī 2, ɗamarạ 1*e*, dạndặkē, ɗarọ, diddigā, diddigẹ, dubū 3, dundūnīyā 2, dụŋgumī, dūnīyạ 1*k*, dūnū, farā 2, firtsī 2, furē 1*b*, fuskạ 3, gạba 1*b*.v, gaɓạ 3, gāɗọ 1*a*, gạjīyạ, gam 1*b*, gidā 1*g*, giṇdī 1*g*, hancị 1*g*, hazbīyā 3, irlị, īyā̤kā 1*c*, jējị 4, ḳafạ 15, karị 3*a*, kārimī, karnī 2, karọ 1*a*, ḳasā 1*b*, kāshī 1*e*, kā̤sūwā 1*b*, 1*c*, kudā 1*f*, ḳundū, kunyạ 2*a*.i, kūrā 5, 6 (*cf. below* 11*e*, 26 *w, x, y, z*), kurnạ, kwā-kwā̤ 3, lādā, lagọ, lallẹ 1*b*, laŋḳō, lāyạ 2*b*, lifịdī 7, mọrīyạ 1*b*, mọrō 2, mutuncị, nāmạ 1*a*.ii, 1*b*, rạɓō 6, rā̤i 1*h*, rānī 3, rība̤ 1*c*, *d*, rashawạ, shūnī 1*d*, sọ̆kē 2, tạrā 2,

tạrī, turạ, tūshīyā 2, wāk̆ẽ (*q.v. under* 26*o below*), yā̤jị 1*b*.ii, yuŋwạ 2*d*, zālī, zarạ̤fī, zūcịyā 1*f*. (*f*) *Vd.* mị kā̤ cī nị, ạ cī dạ mā̤i, ạ cī kạ ạ fẹ̃re, zạuna kạ ci dōyạ, kā̤ cī kā̤ rātạyā. (*g*) cī tamā *Vd.* tamā 1*b*. (*h*) ci sau *Vd.* ạlkāmurạ. (*j*) ci tsõfwā *Vd.* nānẹ 1*d*.

(2) (*a*) kọ̆gī (rūwā) yā ~ shị he was drowned. (*b*) in rūwā yā ci mụtụm, kō am bā shị kaifin takọ̆bī (= kō am bā shị bịsạlā̤mī), sǎi yạ kāmạ drowning man clutches at a straw. (*c*) *Vd.* cị̆ 1*c*.

(3) ci kạŋkạ (*said by woman*) be silent, flatterer ! you will bring the evil eye on me (*cf.* 11).

(4) abraded *x* (*a*) igīyạ tā ci ḳafạssạ the cord abraded his foot (*Vd.* 23*d*) = zāgẹ. (*b*) *cf.* igīyạ 2. (*c*) kā̤ ci kāyaŋ kōwā *Vd.* dawạ 7. (*d*) cīwọ yanā̃ cịna pain is gnawing at me. (*e*) mạganạr tanā̃ cịna I'm eating out my heart over it. (*f*) yā ci mịl ukụ he covered a distance of 3 miles. (*g*) rūwā yā ci gōnā water flooded the farm. (*h*) bạ kạ ci ḳafạ ba *Vd.* cūrị 4.

(5) (*a*) yā ci kudī he embezzled money. (*b*) yā ci kuɗiŋ he spent the money. (*c*) ụbantạ yā ci kuɗim mazā ukụ her father accepted bride-price from three different suitors. (*d*) an ci kuɗintạ bride-price has been paid for her. (*e*) tā ci zannūwạ she (divorcee) took the cloths given her by her late husband as she was legally entitled thereto having been married to him over three months.

(6) zanẹ yā ci bāɓā the cloth took the indigo-dye well.

(7) Kā̤zā, cī kị gōgẹ what an ungrateful person ! (*cf.* bā̤kiŋ kā̤zā).

(8) yā ci ḳasā he did obeisance by throwing dust over his shoulder (= hụrwā).

(9) (*a*) fịtilạ tanā̃ cị̆ the lamp is alight. fịtilạ tā kwānā tanā̃ cị̆ the lamp burned all night. wutā tā· ci gidā = gidā yā ci wutā *Vd.* wutā 1*o*, *p*, *s*. rịgā tā ci wutā the gown became burned or scorched. itā̤caŋ, bā yạ ciŋ wutā this wood won't " catch ". itā̤caŋ, ciŋ wutā gạrēshị this wood is inflammable (*Vd.* cị̆ 3).

(10) yā ci sạrautạ he became ruler.

shĭ yakē cĭ yąnzu he is the present ruler. Sarkinsų mąi cĭ the reigning Emir.

(11) won x (a) bąi cīwō kąnsų ba he was unable to persuade them over (cf. 3, 23). (b) yā cīwō kąnsų (i) he managed to get ahead of them. (ii) he outwitted them (cf. 23 below). (bb) Vd. kąi 1A. (c) yā cī sų he conquered them. (d) sun ci gąrĭ Vd. gąrĭ 1f. (e) kō an ci birniŋ kūrā, bā ą bą kąrē dillancį there are always seniors and juniors. (f) yā ci nasarą he was victorious. (g) yaną cįmmų dą banzā he is tricking us. (h) nā ci shį gyārā I found him out in a mistake. (j) cācā tā cī shį he lost at gambling. (k) yā cī shį cācā he won against him at gambling. (l) yā ci cācā (i) he won at gambling. (ii) " he came out on top ". (m) an cī shį kudĭ fąm bĭyū = an ci masą kudĭ fąm bĭyū two pounds were won from him. (n) yā ci (= yā cīwō) dōkį he got a horse as loot. (o) yā ci dōkįnsą he made his horse prance. (p) dą gįndĭ kąn ci nāmąn dōkį go the right way to work ! (q) yā cī nį darą he huffed me at draughts. (r) yā ci jarrąbąwā he passed the examination (cf. 11v). (s) yā ci mazā cikį = yā ci mazā ą cikį he's redoubtable (cf. 17a). (t) yāƙį yā cī shį he was captured in war. (u) sun ci yāƙiŋ they won the war. mun ci yāƙin naŋ we won that war. an ci masą ĭyąkar ƙasā his frontier has been filched away. (v) dą aką jarrąbā shi, bąi ci kōmē ba he failed to get any marks in his examination (cf. 11r). (w) yā ci kwąf he won (football, etc.) cup. (x) ųban cįŋ āyąrĭ the leader of those who attacked and destroyed the caravan. (y) ƙadam farā tā cĭ Vd. bĭdĭ 4. (z) Vd. igĭyą 2.

(12) (a) lallę yā ci kāshĭ the henna failed to give the required effect, i.e. failed to " set ". (b) cįŋ kāshĭ gąrēshį he has foolish ways.

(13) (a) gathered the crops bąrkōnō, dąnƙo, ƙārō, tābợ, tsintsīyā, audugā q.v. (b) (i) yā ci (= yā shā) zumą he ate honey, he gathered honey. (ii) Vd. jĭnĭyā, zumą 1c, d.

(14) wannąŋ aikį yā ci bąrkątąi this work is slapdash.

(15) (followed by v.n., etc.) underwent severely x yā ci dūkạ he was severely beaten (= shā B.10b), Vd. shā B, gudų 2d.i, tąfīyą 2a.iii, zamā 2a.iii, wąhalą 1b, aikį 1b.iii, wųyā 2, dūnīyą 1k.

(16) (a) yā cĭ tą he slept with her (= tąkā 1d = tārą 2 = aikącē 4 =_ dįkā = kwānā A.1.3 = kwalę 1a = Sk. gwąɓā), cf. jįmā'į, turmĭ 7a, lōƙą, dōɓąnē, dōdąnā 3. (b) taną cįm mātā she indulges in lesbianism. (c) cf. 17.

(17) (a) cįm mazā gąrētą (i) she's a whore. (ii) all her husbands die because she is ill-omened (cf. 11s). (b) rĭjįyan nąŋ cįm mutąnē gąrētą this well causes people to become dizzy and fall inside. (c) Ƙande, cįm mutąnē gąrētą Kande is a sorceress. (d) cf. 16.

(18) contained x gidan nąŋ ząi ci bąƙimmų duką this compound will accommodate all our guests (cf. cĭ 2) = cinyē 1d.

(19) is efficacious x (a) māgąnĭ (lallę) (bābā) yā cĭ dą kyąu the medicine (henna) (indigo) is efficacious (cf. cĭ 3, māgąntā). (b) askā tā cĭ dą kyąu the razor shaves well. (c) kąu dą bąran nąm bā tą tạ cĭ this charm against being wounded is valueless.

(20) (a) yā cĭ dą bakạ he fell forwards on to the ground (= kifą 3). (b) yā cĭ dą kā he fell hitting his head (= sallą 3). (c) yā cĭ dą zūcĭ he was all agog.

(21) yąrā nē cĭ mą ząune they're very young children.

(22) (a) Vd. compounds where 1st word is cĭ or cįn. (b) Vd. cĭ dą. (c) Vd. compounds where 1st word is cĭ dą. (d) Vd. cim.

(23) (a) kāyan yąrdā (= kāyan rā'į) bā yą cįŋ kąi a voluntary act does not irk one (cf. 3, 11). (b) yā ci kansą he hemmed it (= kalmąsā), cf. dājĭyā. (bb) Vd. rōrĭyą 2, ganĭ A.2 2d. (c) suną cįŋ kansų they're squabbling. (d) kāyā yā ci minį kąi the load made my (labourer's) head sore (cf. 4). (e) cf. 11.

(24) yā ci zaraẹ̃na he abused me (*cf.* cịnyē 1*b*).

(25) 'yaŋ ku̧-cī-ku̧-bā-nị *pl.* rag, tag and bobtail.

(26) proverbs (*a*) su ka̧n cī da̧ rānā *Vd.* a̧bu̧ 2*b*. (*b*) yā cī har yā kai masa6ar gātarī *Vd.* masa6ā. (*c*) kā ci damị *Vd.* tsīruku̧, damị 5. (*d*) ci ya̧ŋkā *Vd.* ya̧ŋkā 1*e.* (*e*) a̧ cī, a̧ rage dǫmiŋ gǫbe = a̧ cī ya̧u, a̧ cī gǫbe, shī nẹ̃ cị put a bit away for a rainy day ! (*f*) kōwā ya ci kā̧zā, shī kẹ̃ da̧ ita possession is nine points of the law. (*g*) in doŋ a̧ cī, ba̧ a̧ sayar ba, kā̧zā tā ẹ̃ dōkị the value of a thing depends for what it is to be used. (*h*) an ci gīwā mā, tā ƙārẹ, ba̧llẹ̃ ga̧dā he gave me no share in his great good luck, so how much less in his small windfall. (*j*) cị da̧ yawa̧ shī ya ka̧n sā̧ ga̧mbā = da̧ n ci dādī n yi wa̧hala̧, gāra n ci mara̧d dādī a̧ hu̧ce (*cf.* dādī 5, 6) murder will out ! (*k*) kōwā ya cika̧ cị da̧ yawa̧, yā̧ yi amai kō ku̧mburī the pot goes to the well once too often. (*l*) da̧ ka̧ ci a̧bim ma̧i bā̧kī, gāra ka̧ ci na ƙazāmī when giving charity, don't pretend you gave more than you did ! (*m*) sǎi bā̧kī yā cī, idǫ ka̧n ji kunya̧ taking bribes brings disgrace. (*n*) cī da̧ mǫtsiŋ wani *epithet of bird* ba̧lbēla̧. (*o*) (i) bā ā̧ cẹ̃ da̧ ma̧i ciŋ wākẹ ya̧ shā rūwā, shī mā yā̧ shā teaching one's grandmother to suck eggs. (ii) *Vd.* wākẹ̃ 2, 4, 8. (*p*) ba̧ a̧ sam ma̧i ciŋ tūwō ba sǎi mīya̧ tā ƙārẹ you don't know your real friends till trouble comes. (*q*) " ci nāka̧, n ci ŋ̄wa ! " bā̧ rōwa̧ ba nẹ̃, mūgu̧n zamā nẹ̃ let us each go our own way ! (*Vd.* ci nāka̧). (*r*) dam mẹ̃ suka̧ hau masa̧ da̧ ba̧i ci musu̧ ba, ba̧i shā musu̧ ba̧ why did they attack him who had never harmed them ? (*cf.* cim). (*s*) wā̧ya̧ŋ a̧ cī nẹ̃, aŋ kōri ƙarẹ̃ da̧ga̧ gindin ɗinyā it's a mere pretext, in order to get it for oneself. (*t*) sun cẹ̃ a̧ cī they said " go to the devil ! " (= sun cẹ̃ a̧ dafa̧ = sun cẹ̃ a̧ ya̧ŋka̧ = sun cẹ̃ a̧ kashẹ). (*u*) kōwā ya ci hatsin ra̧ncē, nāsa̧ ya ci borrowing is only putting off the evil day. (*v*) an

ƙi ciŋ ka̧rē, aŋ kōmō an ci kwīkwīyǫ = *Sk.* kā ƙi cịn damō, ka ci kiskī straining at a gnat and swallowing a camel. (*w*) an yi mana̧ " ta̧ya, Kūrā, mu̧ ci a̧kwīya̧ ! " an attempt was made to trick us. (*x*) da̧ ganiŋ kūrā, an san tā ci a̧kwīya̧ appearance is an index to character. (*y*) tā̧ ci a̧binta̧ *Vd.* kūrā 38. (*z*) yā ci kūrā *Vd.* kūrā 5, 6. (*z*) (i) ci birniŋ kūrā *Vd.* (xiv) *below.* (*z*) (iA) kā̧ cī, kā̧ rāta̧yā you'll have your bellyful of it (work, etc.) ! = guma̧ 1 (*Vd.* rāta̧yā 2*f*). (*z*) (ii) kōwā ya ci zōmō, yā ci gudu̧ no reward without effort. (*z*) (iii) yā ci ra̧bansa̧ his luck was shortlived (*Vd.* cịn ra̧bō). (*z*) (iv) cī bā̧ cā̧sā = cī bā̧ su̧ssuka̧ *Vd.* cā̧sā 3. (*z*) (v) ci 6aurē *Vd.* 6aurē 4. (*z*) (vi) bā̧ sāmu̧ŋ kẹ̃ da̧ wu̧yā ba, wurin cị *Vd.* sāmu̧ 2*e*.ii. (*z*) (vii) bā̧kin da̧ ya cī *Vd.* bā̧kī 1*b*.xvii. (*z*) (viii) a̧ cī ka̧ da̧ lu̧rā *Vd.* tu̧bānī 3. (*z*) (ix) ci bịkī *Vd.* bịkī 1*d*, *f.* (*z*) (x) yā ci shiŋkāfar ra̧ncē *Vd.* shiŋkāfā 1*b*. (*z*) (xi) ā̧ ci māsa̧ *Vd.* māsa̧ 3. (*z*) (xii) ganī bā̧ cị ba, dā̧ ka̧rē ba̧i kwānā da̧ yu̧ŋwa̧ ba there's many a slip 'twixt cup and lip. (*z*) (xiii) kōwā ya ci da̧ ma̧i *Vd.* a̧ cī da̧ ma̧i 3. (*z*) (xiv) an ci birniŋ kūrā *Vd.* 11*e above*, kūrā 5, 6. (*z*)(xv) a̧ ci mǫrō *Vd.* mǫrō 2, mǫrīyā 1*b*. (*z*)(xvi) ci wutā *Vd.* 9 *above*, wutāl *o*, *p*, *s*. (*z*) (xvii) in rūwā yā ci mu̧tu̧m *Vd.* 2*b above.* (*z*) (xviii) da̧ gindī ka̧n cī *Vd.* 11*p above.* (*z*) (xix) ka̧dam farā tā cī *Vd.* 11*y above.* (*z*) (xx) ci a̧lbasa̧ *Vd.* a̧lbasa̧ 1*b*, *c*, *e.* (*z*) (xxi) kāyan ya̧rdā *Vd.* 23*a above.* (*z*) (xxii) yā ci wuƙā *Vd.* dǫrǫgō.

B. (cị̄) (1) (*progressive and v.n. of* cī) *x* (*a*) yana̧ da̧ wu̧yar ∼ it is hard to eat. suna̧ ciŋ nāma̧ they're eating meat. ka̧ shirya̧ wurin ∼ dom mu̧tu̧m uku̧ lay 3 places at table ! ba̧ mu̧ ya̧rdā da̧ ciŋ da̧ suka̧ wa̧ ƙasan nam ba we do not approve of their conquering that country (*Vd. sense* 11 of cī). (*b*) *Vd.* cī 1*b*, 4, 10, 11, 12, 16, 17, 19, 23, 26*j*, 26*z*.vi. (*c*) gōnar ciŋ rūwā cẹ̃ the farm is flooded (*cf.* cī 2). (*d*) *Vd.* wāwan cị̄. (*e*) da̧ga̧ ∼ *Vd.* dagacị. (*f*) cịŋkị banzā *Vd.* gaẹ̃ya̧. (*g*) sā̧ rặi gạ cị, shī kẹ̃ kāwō yuŋwạ thinking of food makes one hungry. (h) yā hau musu dạ cị he attacked them fiercely. (j) ~ dạ yawạ Vd. gambā. (k) ganī bạ̃ ~ ba Vd. ganī A.2 3b.

(2) appetite, being of big capacity x cị gạrēshị he has a big appetite. rụmbun naŋ cị gạrēshị this bin is capacious (cf. cī 18).

(3) itặcan naŋ, cị gạrēshị this wood burns well (cf. cī 9). māgạnin naŋ, cị gạrēshị this medicine is efficacious (cf. cī 19).

(4) food for x (a) nāmạ dọ̃min cin 'yan sarkạ food for the convicts. (b) bạ̃ shi dạ cin yạu, bạ̃ shi dạ na gọ̃be he has food neither for to-day nor for to-morrow.

cibājirā Kt. f. big-built girl.
cībanyạ Kt. f. umbilical hernia (= cībị 1).
cibdʼạ̄wā Kt. fancy!
cibdʼị fancy!
cịɓe Kt. adv. in profusion.
cibi A. (cībị) m. (1) umbilical hernia. (2) n̥ yi maganạ, ~ yạ zamā kạrị? why should I make matters worse by making a fuss? iŋ kā yi hakạ, sǎi ~ yạ zamā kạrị if you do so, there's no end to the hullaboo that'll be raised.

B. (cībị) adv. (locative form of cībịyā, Mod Gr. 24a) x yā sọ̃kē shị ạ ~ he pierced him through the navel. rūwā yā kai īyạ̃kā ~ the water reached up to one's navel.

C. (cibī) m. small metal spoon.
D. (cibị) Kt. m. pile (= tsibị q.v.).
cibcị Kt. m. thatching-grass (= shūcị q.v.).
cịɓị-cịɓị (1) sun dʼaukạ ~ they struggled along with the heavy load. (2) tanạ̃ tạfe ~ dạ dʼūwạiwai she's joggling her buttocks as she walks.
cịbilbilọ m. (sg., pl.) kingfisher (= cị na wụyā q.v.).
cibịrbirạ Kt. f. type of bat.
cịbirī Kt. m. island (= tsibirī q.v.).
ciɓis = ciɓus.
cībịyā f. (1) navel (cf. cībī). (2) (a) rānar waŋkā bā ạ̃ ɓōyan ~ one must know when to speak out frankly! (b) bị kị rufẹ ~ ba Vd. falmạraŋ. (3) (a) centre of circular T. (b) central pillar

of ceiling (cf. ạl'ạmūdị). (c) Kanọ cībịyar cịnikī cẹ̃ Kano's a trade-centre. sun yi cībịyā ạ̃ Kanọ they made Kano their place of assembly. (4) ~ tasạ Kanọ he was born at Kano.
(5) circular spread of hair at back of head of some persons (= kawanyạ 2).
(6) cībịyar kūrā (a) type of circular mat (= cạkirị 2c). (b) type of cushion. (c) embroidery-pattern. (d) type of embroidered anklet on trousers. (e) shell of snail (= kạtantaŋwạ).
cibrạ Vb. 1A Sk. kneaded into balls (= cūra q.v.).
cibus = cibus-cịbus x sum fitō ~ they appeared profusely (= dạ̃ɓāɓạ q.v.).
ciɓus = ciɓus m. (1) mun yi ~ dạ shī we met him unexpectedly. (2) dạ wannaŋ dạ wancaŋ, ~ dạ ruɓus there's little to choose between them, for none are good ((2) = raŋ dạ kwaŋ = sạkwaf = sịttiŋ 2 = zạ̃ɓē 3).
cicci A. (ciccị) Kt. m. thatching-grass (= shūcị q.v.).
B. (ciccī) Vb. int. from cī ate again and again.
cicciɓa A. (cicciɓā) f. (1) big-made girl. (2) big laying-hen.
B. (cicciɓạ) Vb. 2 lifted heavy load x yā cicciɓi kāyā.
C. (cicciɓā) Vb. 1C yā ~ mini kāyā he helped me lift heavy load.
cicciḍā Vb. 1C gave climber a push upwards (= tittịḍā q.v.).
ciccifī m. drizzle = tsattsafī q.v.
cicciję Vb. 3A exerted all one's strength.
cịccikạ f. (1) ~ gạrēshị he's conceited. (2) yanạ̃ ~ = yanạ̃ ~, yanạ̃ kụmburī he's angry.
cịccindō Sk. m. throwing T. up into the air (= tsạlạllẹ̃kū).
cicciro m. (1) black horse (= akawạlī). (2) dạndan ~ m. black horse with five white points.
cicciya A. (cịccịyạ) Vb. 2 int. from cī ate again and again.
B. (cicciyā) Sk. f. swallow (= bilbilō 1).
cịcē Vd. cịtā.
cici A. (cīcị) used in ~ tā kashẹ said playfully by one woman to another woman friend in reply to dạ wutạ̃? could

you let me have some embers?; for explanation Vd. **wutā** 1*v.*ii.

B. (**cịcị**) (1) ~ **mẹ kẹ cikiŋ hannūnạ** = ~ **cịciŋkạ** = **kạ** ~ **kạ** ~ guess what I have in my hand ! (*Vd.* **cịtā** ; **kạ saŋ, kạ saŋ**). (2) *Sk.* ~ **yā kāmạ ka** the bogeyman'll catch you if you don't watch out, naughty child !

C. (**cịcị**) *used in* **sunạ** ~ **kibau** they're engaged in archery contest.

cīcītạ *Kt. f.* children's game (= **tsītsītạ**).

cịciwā *Kt. f.* type of tree (*Maerua angolensis*) = **mạndēwā**.

cịcīyạ *Vb.* 2 *int. from* **cī** ate again and again.

cī cịyāwạ *m.* type of fish.

cịcīyau *m., f.* (*sg., pl.*) glutton (= **cịyau** = **acīcị**).

cī dạ *Vb.* 4A (1) (*a*) fed *x* (1) **nā cīshē shị** I fed him. (ii) **Allạ** (= **Alạ̄**) **cīshē mụ, mụ sāmụ** God grant that we get it ! (iii) *Vd.* **Alạ̄** 4*a.* (*b*) **an** ~ **shī gạba** he's been promoted. (2) **yā** ~ **Mụsụlmī gubạ** (*a*) he caused Muslims to eat what is forbidden them. (*b*) *Vd.* **gubạ** 3. (3) **Alạ̄ cīshē mụ** *a cry of beggars.* (4) *cf.* **cī dạ cẹtō ; cī dạ gērō ; cī dạ dāwạ.**

cida A. (**cidạ**) *f.* (1) rumbling of thunder. (2) **sun yi manạ** ~ they all thronged round us.

B. (**Cịdā**) (1) (*abbreviation of* **Cị dāwạ** *q.v.*) name given to child of **Bạmāgujẹ** born at time of **dāwạ**-harvest (*cf.* **Cịgē**). (2) *m.* a **bọrī** spirit supposed to be a **Bạmāgujẹ.**

cī dạ cẹtō *used in* **yā** ~ he took a bribe to use his influence to get P. off punishment of his crime.

cī dạ gērō *m.* (1) a poor type of guineacorn (= **buturī hụ̄tā**). (2) a sweet type of **tạkạndā** sugarcane (= **ƙundu-ƙundu**). (3) *cf.* **Cịgē.**

cī dạ karā *m.* type of **tạkạndā** sugarcane.

cī dạ mọ̄tsiŋ wani *Vd.* **bạlbēlạ.**

Cị dāwạ (**Cị gērō**) (**Cị ramạ**) (**Cị wākē**) (1) name bestowed on child of meat-sellers (**mahautā**) or **Māguzāwā** by parent or grandparent of child when latter is born at time of harvest of the *crops* mentioned. (2) **Cị dāwạ yā ɗaukō Cị kạ̄jī** (*lit.* if P. named **Cị dāwạ** comes to your house, he becomes Eater of Chickens) guests entail expense. (3) *cf.* **Cịdā ; Cịgē.**

cīdọ *m.* = **sārā** 2*a.*i.

cif A. (**cif** = **cịf** = **cif dạ cif**) (1) fully *x* **shẹkạrunsạ ạrbạ'iŋ** ~ he's fully 40 years old. **gọrọ ƙwaryā gụdā** ~ a full 100 kolanuts. **an shiryạ** ~ all is arranged. (2) **yā ɗauru** ~ it's tied tightly. (3) **yā tsayạ** ~ *Kt.* he came to a dead stop. (4) **sōjạ cif** soldiers all complete.

B. (**cịf**) all of them, of it, etc. **sun tạru** ~ they've all collected. **yā yā dạ cịyāwạ** ~ he threw away all the grass.

cị fạ̄rā *m.* Lesser kestrel (*Falco neumanni*).

cifcị *Kt. m.* thatching-grass (= **shūcị** *q.v.*).

cifdị fancy !

ciffạlī *Fil. m.* hawking of milk by Filani women to barter for corn.

cịfīrị *Kt. m.* = **fēlēƙē.**

cifit *Kt. m.* a little.

cifjōjị (1) European judge. (2) Chief judge (*cf.* **jōjị**).

cīgạ *Sk.* **ɗan** ~ *m.* (*f.* **'yar** ~) rebellious, tempestuous P.

ci gaba A. (**cị gạba**) *m.* progress *x* **aikinsụ yā ƙi** ~ their work made no progress (*Vd.* **gạba** 1*b.v.*).

B. (**ci gạba**) ' sorry, I've nothing to give you ' (*said to beggar, i.e.* **ạlmājịrī**) = **Alạ̄** 4*a.*

Cịgē = **Cị gērō** *q.v. under* **Cị dāwạ.**

ciggạl *Sk. m.* wrestler's getting opponent's head under his arm.

cigịtā *Vb.* 1C searched for (*Vd.* **cigīyạ**).

cigīyạ *f.* searching for.

cị gọrọ *m.* (1) the bird waxbill (*Estrelda sp.*). (2) name given child born with red mouth. (3) *epithet of* insect **sạŋkạrā**. (4) the **bọrī**-spirit called **Daŋ gạlạ̄dīmạ.**

cigul *Sk. m.* shortness (= **tsugul** *q.v.*).

cije A. (**cịjẹ**) (1) *Vb.* 1A (*a*) bit. (*b*) held, gripped with the teeth (*cf.* **cịnyē** 1*h*). (*c*) **yā** ~ **bạ̄kī** (**hannū**) (**yātsạ**) he bit his mouth (hand) (finger) in anger, remorse, or determination. (*d*) **dōkị yā** ~ **bạ̄kī** horse has white underlip. (2) *Vb.* 3A (*a*) became jammed. (*b*) (i) is (was) obstinate. (ii) is (was) resolute.

B. (**cịjē**) (1) *Vd.* **cịzā.** (2) *m. x* **ạ kwancẹ** ~ undo the leather-and-cowry fastener of neck of the waterskin !

C. (**cịje**) *x* **yanạ̄** ~ = **yanạ̄** ~ **dạ shī** he's gripping it between his teeth.

cịji = *Vd.* **cịzā.**

cịji bā mātarkạ *Kt. epithet of* baunī.
cik *x* yā tsayạ ~ he stopped dead.
cika A. (cikạ) (1) *Vb.* 1A (*a*) filled *x* (i)
nā ~ shi dạ rūwā I filled it with water.
an ~ gishirī ạ mīyạ the soup's been
oversalted. (ii) yā ~ ƙundunsạ he's
had a good meal. (iii) kā cịkạ ? *Vd.*
kwạndo. (*b*) (i) yā ~ mini cikị I'm
" fed up " with him. (ii) *Vd.* cịkạ cikị.
(*c*) yā ~ musụ igīyōyī he tied them
(prisoners) up securely. (*d*) fulfilled *x*
iŋ kā ~ ạbin naŋ if you perform this.
yā ~ mạganạ tasạ he kept his word.
sun ~ ụmụrnịn dạ ya ạikē shị they
carried out the command on account of
which he had been sent. yā ~ ạlkāwạrī
he fulfilled his promise (*Vd.* ạlkāwạrī
1*d*). (*e*) completed *x* (i) yā ~ shēkarạ
gōmạ he's ten years old. anạ̄ ~
ƙidāyạ dạ sū they're included in the
total. bạ tạ ~ iddạ ba tụkụnā she hasn't
yet completed the statutory period
legally required before remarriage. yā
~ he died. (ii) (*with dative*) *x* an ~
masạ sulẹ bịyar he's been paid the remaining five shillings owing him (*Vd.*
cikọ). (iii) added money to increase pay
of P. to nearest round number (usually
10, 20, etc., and occasionally 5) *x* an ~
(= an dadạ) masạ sulẹ takwạs his pay
of *e.g.* 32 shillings has been increased to
40. (iv) kai kạ̄ cikạ *m.* part of stolen
goods, finding of which renders P. at
whose house found, liable for total
goods stolen. (*v*) *x* kadạ ạ ~ musụ
harāji they are not to be heavily
taxed ! (*f*) yā ~ Allạ̄ ạ zūcī he is
honest. (*g*) (i) yā ~ bākī he's presumptuous, he blusters. (ii) *Vd.* cịkạ
bākin. (*h*) (i) yā ~ fuskạ = yā ~ idọ
he looks impressive. (ii) yā ~ minị
fuskạ (= yā ~ mīnị idọ), bạ zaŋ īyạ
faɗạ masạ ba he's too important a P. for
me to dare to tell it. (iii) kyautạ tā ~
masạ idọ the present pleased him. (*j*)
(i) yā ~ kāi rūwā = cikạ rūwā garēshị
he's conceited (*epithet is* kōwā ya cikạ
kāi rūwā, yạ̄ ragẹ). (ii) cikạ rūwā *Vd.*
rūwā A17. (*k*) *Kt.* cịkā ni, ạzā ni,
taụlalin 'yan rāfī what a spineless
person ! (*l*) *x* aikị yā ~ gabā there's
much work. (*m*) yā ~ minị gabā " it

took my breath away " (*Vd.* gabā
1*f.* iii). (*n*) kụ ~ *Kt. m.* back-door
(= maduddukā). (*o*) *Vd.* cikạ compounds. (2) cikạ *Vb.* 3A = cikạ dạ is
(was) characterized by *x* yā cikạ
haukā = yā cikạ dạ haukā he has an
ungovernable temper. yā ~ fushī he's
bad-tempered. yā ~ muryạ he's loud-
voiced. tā ~ kyaụ she's good,
pretty.
• B. (cikạ) *Vb.* 3B (1) (*a*) is (was) full
(*progressive* cịkā *q.v., Vd.* cikō). (*b*)
cikịŋkạ yā ~ taf (i) your stomach is
overfull. (ii) you're quite " fed up ".
(*c*) kōgī kạn ~ *Vd.* yayyafī 2. (2) (*a*)
became complete *x* shēkarạ tā ~ the
year came to an end. adạdinsạ yā ~
his sentence in prison has expired.
kwạ̄nạkinsạ sun ~ he's dead. yā ~
ɗaŋ kirkị he's a real good son. (*b*) is
(was) fulfilled *x* (i) gūrinsạ yā ~ his
desire has been fulfilled. (ii) *Vd.*
ạlkāwạrī 1*d.* (3) yā ~ (i) he's angry.
(ii) he is " fed up ".
C. (cịkā) (1) *Vb.* 2 cornered (a commodity) *x* yā cịki bạrkōnō he cornered
pepper (*cf.* cikọ 3, sārā 2*a.*i). (2) *f.* (*a*)
(*progressive and v.n. of* cịka) *x* wụyar
~ gạrēshị it's hard to fill. cịkar shēkarạ
the end of the year. ạ rānar cịkar
shēkarạ on the last day of the year.
(*b*) tā yi cịkaɗ ɗākī she's filled out since
her marriage. (*c*) yanạ̄ ~ = yanā ~,
yanā bātsēwā he's angry. (*d*) yanạ̄ ~
he's swanking. (*e*) ~ dạ mārā even and
odd. (*f*) tanạ̄ dạ ~ she was tested at
būɗē and found to be a virgin (*said by
one girl to another*). (*g*) cịkar *prep.* in
the whole of *x* cịkar gạrin naŋ in all
this town.
D. cīkạ *Kt. f.* point of a grain of
bulrush-millet (= fịrtsī).
cikạ bākiŋ guzumā *f.* stunted corn (*cf.*
cikạ 1*g*).
Cịkạ cikị *m.* (1) the month of Ạlmụharrạm (*cf.* cikạ 1*b*). (2) Sallạr ~ *f.*
New Year's festival on 9-10th of
Ạlmụharrạm (*cf.* Wọwwō).
cī ƙadaŋgarū *m.* (*sg., pl.*) (1) North
African chanting goshawk (*Melierax
metabates*). (2) Little goshawk
(*Micronius gabar*).

cī ka̱ ɗau ga̱rmarka̱ Vd. shā ga̱rī.

cika̱ fagē m. type of small shrub.

cika̱ gidā Sk. m. castor-oil plant (= zu̱r-
ma̱n).

cika̱kkē m. (f. cika̱kkīyā) pl. cika̱kkū
adj. (1) full. (2) fat. (3) P. of even
temper.

cīkāle̱ Sk. m. (said by women) bed of
cornstalks.

cīka̱lī Zar. m. = cīka̱s.

cika̱maki̱ m. Cika̱maki̱ɲ Annabāwā Muhammad Seal of the Prophets !

cika̱ masaki̱ɲka̱ expression used to infant
being bathed.

cikansamī = ca̱kansamī.

cikanya̱ Kt. f. stomach (= ciki̱ q.v.).

cikāra̱ Had. f. wallet with two compartments (= za̱bīra̱).

cī ka̱ rage̱ m. children's game with fire.

cīka̱s m. (1) fault, blemish.   (2) yā sa̱
masa̱ ~ he disparaged him (= tsirra̱).
(3) da̱ba̱runsu̱ sum fāra̱ ~ their schemes
are beginning to go wrong.

cika̱sā Vb. 1C = cika̱ 1e.ii, iii.

cika̱ sa̱urā m.   (1) type of plant with
rattling seeds.   (2) rattle worn on
dancers' ankles (= ca̱kansamī).   (3)
ga̱rī yā yi cika̱ sa̱urar mu̱zūrū these are
hard times.

cika̱ te̱kū Vd. fa̱m 2.

cike A. (cike̱) (1) Vb. 1A filled in x yā ~
rāmi̱ he filled in the hole (= binne̱ 3). (2)
Vb. 3A (a) (i) dōki̱ yā ~ horse is tired
out, horse is replete. (ii) yā ~ sabo̱ da̱
a̱bin na̱ɲ he's " fed up " about this. (b)
wuƙā tā ~ the knife is blunt (=
dāku̱shē 1). (c) ƙurjī yā ~ the ulcer has
begun to heal.

    B. (cike̱) (1) x (a) yana̱ ~ da̱ rūwā
it is full of water. (b) (the logical thing
with which anything is filled can
alternatively be reversed in order) x
ga̱ sōja̱ ~ da̱ jirāge̱ = ga̱ jirāge̱ ~ da̱
sōja̱ we have ships filled with soldiers.
jirāgyan rūwā suna̱ naɲ ~ da̱ te̱kū the
sea was full of ships. (2) muna̱ ~ da̱
shī we're " fed up " with it.

ciki A. (cikī) adv. (1) inside x (a) nā gan
ta̱ a̱ ~ I saw her inside there. tana̱ ~
= tana̱ da̱ga ~ = a̱ cikī take̱ she's
inside. (b) ~ da̱ ba̱i inside and out.
(2) inclusive x sule̱ gōma̱ da̱ kuɗiɲ

a̱bincī a̱ ~ ten shillings pay inclusive of
food-allowance. (3) murna̱ sa̱i ta kōma̱
~ that was an end of the rejoicing.
(4) n̩ saɲ a̱bi̱n da̱ nake̱ ~ that I may
know just where I stand. (5) a̱bi̱n da̱
taka̱rdar ke̱ ~ the contents of the
letter. (6) ba̱ mu̱ saɲ a̱bi̱n da̱ yake̱ ~ ba
we don't know what he's up to. shi̱m,
me̱ Jāmu̱s ke̱ ~ ne̱ ya̱nzu̱ I wonder
what the Germans are up to now ? (7)
(a) ɗan ~ m. (pl. 'yan ~) soft shoe
worn with sandals. (b) 'yar ~ f. type
of tagu̱wā (cf. ciki̱ 4b). (8) ba̱kin ~ Vd.
ba̱kī 3 f. (9) cf. ciki̱, cikin. (10) ɗā da̱ga
~ Vd. za̱llim.   (11) yaɲkan ~ Vd.
yaɲkā 1d.

    B. (ciki̱) m. (pl. cikkuna̱) (1) (a) (i)
stomach. (ii) Vd. cikin 1a.iv, v. (b) tun
tana̱ ~ while she was still in her
mother's womb. (c) kāyan ~ =
abūbūwa̱n ~ = Sk. ~ m. entrails.
(d) maci̱jī yā jā ~ the snake crawled
along (Vd. ja̱n ~). (e) ~ da̱ ga̱skīyā,
wuƙā bā ta̱ yaɲka̱ shi an honest P.
cannot be harmed by slander. (f) ~
ba̱i saɲ kya̱utar jīya̱ ba ingratitude is
common to Man. (g) da rūwan ~ a ka̱n
jā na rījīyā nothing succeeds like
success. (h) (i) yā shā, tā fi ciki̱nsa̱
" he bit off more than he could chew ".
(ii) da̱idāi da̱ cikiɲka̱ Vd. rūwā C9b.
(j) bāwa̱n ~ glutton. (k) a̱bin ta̱imak-
wan ciki̱nsa̱ his livelihood. (1) wutar ~
f. energy. (2) (a) yana̱ da̱ zurfin ~ he's
" a dark horse " (= mu̱ƙu-mu̱ƙū). (b)
ba̱ a̱ sa̱n cikiɲka̱ ba Vd. tādạlī. (3) (a)
yā cika̱ mi̱niɲ ~ I am " fed up with
him " (Vd. cika̱ ciki̱). (b) n̩ na̱ da̱ cikiɲsa̱
(= n̩ na̱ ~ da̱ shī), ba̱ɲ haife̱ ba tu̱ku̱nā
I've had all I can stand of him, but I'm
biding my time. (c) cikiɲka̱ yā cika taf
(i) your stomach is over-full.   (ii)
you're quite " fed up ". (4) pregnancy
x (a) (i) tā sa̱mi ~ she's recently
pregnant (N.B. tana̱ da̱ ~ = tā yi
ciki̱ she's pregnant, but if stage of
pregnancy is stressed, tana̱ da̱ ~ means
she's advanced in pregnancy (= tāsa̱
4d), while tā yi ~ means she's recently
pregnant). (ii) tana̱ da̱ ~ tsōfō she's
advanced in pregnancy (= tāsa̱ 4d).
(iii) yā yi mata̱ ~ he made her pregnant.

(iiiA) *cf.* **barkwancị**. (iv) **tā yi cikịn shēgẹ** she (unmarried girl) is (was) pregnant. (v) **bạ ạ yi ∼ dọmịŋ hatsī** (= **dọmin tūwō**) **ba, săi dom ɓōyam mạganạ** what a blabber ! (vi) **sā bụdurwā ∼** *Vd.* **gajaŋ hạkurī**. (b) **dan cikịnā nẹ** he's my son (cf. **cikī** 7, **cikị** 13 *below*). (5) **jạkā tanā dạ ∼** the bag is capacious (*cf.* 6). (6) (a) **jạkā tanā dạ ∼ bīyū** the bag has two compartments. (b) **yanā dạ ∼ bīyū** (i) he's two-faced. (ii) he's a wizard. (c) **cikịn tubụrā** *Vd.* **tubụrā** 3. (7) **n nā sạnsạ ∼ bā hatsī ba** I want it desperately. (8) **an rabạ ∼** they have shared the loss. (9) **yā bụgi cikịna** he "pumped" me (*Vd.* **bụgā** 4). (10) **rặịrạyin ∼ gạrētạ** she bears lovely children. (11) (a) each of the units which go to make up the breadth of a turban *x* **rawạnī ∼ takwạs** a turban consisting of eight units (N.B. *good turban should contain* 30 **cikị** ; *length of turban is measured in* **kāmụ**, *e.g.* **rawạnī cikị takwas, kāmụ takwạs**), (b) *Vd.* **ạlbadạ**. (12) *Vd.* **baƙin ∼**, **farin ∼**. (13) **dan cikịŋ ūwā** bother you ! (*cf.* 4b *above*), *Vd.* **ūwā** 1c. (14) **rūwan ∼** *Vd.* **rūwā** B. 2. (15) *cf.* **cikī, cikin, cikịŋ gidā, cikịŋ kīshīyā, daurẹ** 1d, **rụb dạ ∼, kadạ** 1m. (16) **bugụn ∼** *Vd.* **bugụ** 1b. (17) **∼ dawạ nē** *Vd.* **jējị** 5. (18) **∼ lāfīyạ** *Vd.* **lāfīyạ** 2b.

cikilkịshē *Vb.* 3A **yā ∼** it (work, etc.) is beyond one.

cikin (*genitive of* **cikī**) *prep.* (1) (a) (i) in *x* **yanā ∼ dākị** he's in the house. **yanā ∼ aikịm bạtūrẹ** he works for a European. (ii) **fartanyạ tanā ∼ ƙōtạ** the hoe-blade is fixed in its haft (*cf.* **jịkin**). **dalmạ tanā ∼ pensụr** the lead is in the pencil (*cf.* **jịkin**). **saiwā tanā ∼ƙasā** the root is in the ground (*cf.* **jịkin**). (iii) **ƙasan naŋ, cikintạ dạ wạjantạ duk gạnimạr Jāmụs cē** this entire country has fallen a prey to the Germans. (iv) **kuŋ ga cikim mafarkinsạ** this is his real ambition. (v) **don ∼ kị** *Vd.* **nōmā** 1b.ii. (b) within *x* **zai tāshị ∼ kwānā bīyū** he'll depart within two days. (2) from in *x* (a) **yā dạuki ạlkalạmī ạ ∼ ạkwạtị** he took a pen out of the box. **anā sāmụŋ wutā ∼ kạŋkarā** fire is got from flint (*cf.* **jịkin**). **anā dībạm mặị ạ ∼**

gyạdā oil is extracted from groundnuts (*cf.* **jịkin**). **mun sōkẹ sūnansạ ∼ Sarākunạ** we have deleted him from among the chiefs (*Vd.* **tumɓụkē**). (b) **tun ∼ watạn Yūlị sukạ zō** they've been here since as early as July. (c) **a ∼ baƙar tukunyā a kạm fitar dạ farin tūwō** don't despise a thing because of its lack of beauty ! (3) among *x* **dayā dạgạ cikinsụ** one of them (*cf.* 7 *below*). **ạ cikinsụ** (= **dạgạ cikinsụ**) **ạkwai Audu** among them is Audu. **wani dạgạ cikinsụ** = **wani ạ cikinsụ** one of them. **wandạ ya ƙī cikinsụ** whoever of them refuses. **mạcē cikimmụ wạddạ ta yi zịnā** any of our women who commits adultery. **kadạ kōwā cikinsụ yạ yi jặyayyạ** let none of them bicker ! **tsēgụmī yanā dạgạ ∼ ạbin dạ ya tā dạ hụsūmạ** malice is one of those things which lead to strife. (4) **ạshịriŋ dạ Sha'ạbaŋ ∼ hudū dạ Fạbạrā'ịr** the 20th of the month of S. corresponding to 4th February. (5) **wạkīlị ạ ∼ kạrɓar rạbaŋkụ** an attorney authorized to receive your share. (6) through *x* **yā dịga ∼ rāmịn naŋ** it dripped through this hole. (7) **dayā ạ cikiŋkạ** (a) now you've done me a bad turn, but I'll get my own back ! (*cf.* 3 *above, first example*). (b) that's one point to me ! (*in games* '**yā, lạŋgạ, gạrdō, shạllū**). (8) *Vd.* **cikin**-*compounds*.

cikịŋ gidā = **cikịŋ gidā** *m.* the part of the compound where bulk of the residents live (= **ƙundū** 2, *cf.* **tụrākā**).

cikiŋkịnē = **cikirkịshē** *Kt.* = **cikilkịshē** *q.v.*

cikịŋ kīshīyā *m.* (1) hobbling right foreleg of horse to left hind-leg *or* viceversa (= **tạrnaƙim birị**). (2) **yā yi mịnị ∼** he deceived me. (3) (a) **dạfūwā tā yi ∼** bits of this food are properly cooked and other bits are raw. (b) badly-done work for another. (4) type of black and white cloth.

cikirkịshē = **cikiŋkịnē**.

cikirkitạ *Sk.* *f.* fowl with permanently ruffled feathers (= **fịŋgi**).

cikīyạ *f.* = **cigīyạ**.

cikkunạ stomachs *Vd.* **cikị**.

ciko A. (**cikō**) *m.* (1) balance outstanding *x* **yā kạrɓi cikwạŋ hakkịnsạ** he received what was owing him'. **nā ga lēburạ**

tarạ, ịnā na cikwạŋ gōmạ I see 9 carriers, where's the 10th ? am bā shị cikwạn sulẹ bịyar he's been paid the remaining 5s. owing him (cf. cikạ 1e). cikwạŋ ukụ yā biyō kạ there's balance of 3 outstanding against you. (2) ∼ baị bīyō mụ bạ ? will we " get away with it " without punishment ? (3) cornering commodity (Vd. cịkā). (4) buying large quantity of food which friend of opposite sex was seen eating in public (considered impropriety) and sending it to him or her to shame. (4a) type of embroidery-stitch. (5) yā yi wạ kwōtạ ∼ he inserted wedge between loose blade and haft to steady it. (6) cikwạŋ gạrī valueless citizen (= banzaŋ gạrī q.v.) (7) cikwạm mạganạ tautology for embellishment of speech.
B. (cikō) Vb. 3A (1) (pot, well, river) is (was) full. (2) Vd. cịka. (3) ƙurjī yā ∼ ulcer has started to heal as pus is ready to issue (cf. rārạkē 2b).
cikōkō m. (1) type of rattle. (2) = cilạkōwạ 1. (3) Kt. late kernel-less fruit of fan-palm (giginyạ).
cị kōrō Vd. ạllạn ∼.
cịkōwạ f. kọ̄gī yā yi ∼ river's in spate (= kāwō 1b = hạuhawạ), cf. hạɗamī. hatsī yā yi ∼ there's a glut of corn.
cikū m. cheese (= cukū).
cikụrfā f. long, narrow corn-bag made of palm-leaves.
cịkurī Vd. cilạkōwạ.
cikwạn Vd. cikọ.
cikwī m. (1) poor variety of cotton. (2) = cikū.
cikwīkwịyā Vb. 1D (1) tangled T. (2) yā ∼ rawạnī he wound on his head ragged turban. (3) yā ∼ tsụmmā he tied ragged garment round his loins.
cikwīkwịyē (1) Vb. 3A. (a) become tangled. (b) became crumpled (cloth). (2) Vb. 1D. (a) seized P. by his garments to force him to pay debt. (b) tangled T. (c) tsụmmā yā ∼ masạ = tsụmmā yā ∼ shi he's in tatters.
cila A. (cilạ) (1) ɗan ∼ m. (pl. 'yan ∼) pigeon (= shilạ). (2) ɗan ∼ maị gīgī epithet of (i) pigeon, (ii) timid P.
B. (cīlā) Kt. f. tapeworm (= tsīlā q.v.).

cilạkōwạ f. (sg., pl.). (1) (a) various types of hornbill (Lophoceos nasutus ; L: semifasciatus ; L. erythrorhynchus) (= cikōkō 2). (b) epithet is mẹ zā ạ yi dạ nāmạn cịkurī : naŋ ƙashī, naŋ jījịyā. (2) small metal instrument for marking lines on leather.
cilạndō used in ∼ bạ̄kiŋ kọ̄gī said by boys at play wanting storm to break on them (= Kt. shạrindọ 2).
cīlạstā Vb. 1C Kt. = tīlạstā, q.v.
cịlē m. (1) fag-end (of cassava, cigarette, sugarcane). (2) ∼ yakẹ cị he lives on the leavings of others. (3) mashạ̄ ∼ m., f. (pl. mashạ̄yā ∼) cadger of odds and ends.
cilgạ Vb. 3A Kt. jumped down (= tsirgạ, q.v.).
cilịkōwạ Kt. f. = cilịkkō Sk. m. = cilạkōwạ q.v.
cililligā f. (1) ear-lobe (= rāfạ̄nī 2 = lēɓẹ 4c). (2) any ear-ring (= lạllagạ kunnē).
cilịndō = cilạndō.
cilịndugụŋ m. (1) gạrī yā yi ∼ it rained from morn till night. (2) gạrī yā yi minị ∼ I am " broke ".
cilịŋgọ̄rọ m. clay-pillars for bed (= tuntụŋgọ̄rọ.
cillạ (1) Vb. 1A. (a) (i) shot (arrow) far. (ii) yā īyạ ∼ jīfạ he can throw far. (b) ∼ fitsārī to shoot out long stream of urine (= shillạ). (c) = cinnạ. (d) Kt. yā ∼ īhụ he yelled. (e) yā ∼ tsallē he jumped. (2) Vb. 3A yā ∼ ạ gụje he took to his heels (= shillạ).
cillạ̄lō dạ gụdaŋ waịnā m. a children's game.
*cịllī m. boy's uncircumcised penis.
cilmī Sk. x ɗan ∼ m. stopper for gourd-bottle (gyạndamā).
cilụndugụŋ Vd. cilịndugụŋ.
cilụŋkō m. = cilạkōwạ.
cim (1) (d.f. cī) Vb. (used before dative) met x nā ∼ masạ I encountered him. mun ∼ mạ Audụ we came upon Audu (= haikẹ 2b). nā ∼ mạ bụkātạta I got my desire. Vd. dōlẹ 2, cī 26r. (2) Zar. yā bā nị ∼ he gave me a trifle.
cīmā f. (1) food. (2) tạfō, gạ̄ irịn cịmarkạ this is in your line ! (3) Vd. yāƙị 1a.ii, nāmạ 1a.i.

cį maɗaukī $x \sim$ gąrēshį he makes a nuisance of himself (x by . dogging creditors).

cįmaką *f.* = cįmā.

cį mą ząune *Vd.* cī 21.

cįm b . . . *Vd.* cįn b . . .

cimbįrē *Vb.* 3A *Kt.* is (was) stunted.

cįmbųlum = cįmbųrum *m.* any insect-pest damaging pumpkins and root-crops.

cimbus-cimbus in profusion (= dąɓāɓą, *q.v.*).

cįmfą *Vd.* cirin.

cįm fuską *Vd.* cįn fuską.

cįmmantą *Vb.* 3B *Kt.* became less.

cįmōlą *f.* West African genet (= in-yāwarā).

cimrą *Kt.* = cūrą.

cįn-compounds, *Vd. alphabetically.*

cina A. (cįnā) *Vb.* 2 *Kt.* selected (= tsįnā, *q.v.*).

B. (ciną) *f.* (*pl.* cinikką) *Sk.* wooden skewer for dried meat (tsįrē) = tsiŋkē.

cįnācī *Kt. m.* finickiness (= tsāginąginī).

cinai *Vd.* cinyą.

ci nāką *used in* $\sim$, ņ ci nąwa, bą rōwą ba cę̄, mūgųn zamā nę̄ this skinflint has met his match ! (*Vd.* cī 26*q*).

cįn ąlēwą *used in* cįn ąlēwąr mągē yakę̄ yį he's in trouble.

cinana *Kt.* = tsinana.

cī na wųyā *m.* (*sg., pl.*) various types of kingfisher (*Alcedo quadribrachys ; Ispidina picta*) = macį 3 = cįbilbilǫ.

cin ɓaure (cįm ɓaurē) *Vd.* ɓaurē 4.

cin baya (cįm bāyā = *Sk.* cįm bǎicī) *m.* backbiting.

cin bici *Vd.* bīcī, bicī.

cincę̄ *Vb.* 1A *Kt.* = tsincę̄.

cįncī *Kt.* = cįcī.

cįncim in profusion (= tįnjim, *q.v.*).

cįncindǫ *Kt. m.* = tsąntsąndō, *q.v. under* ąlkaląmī.

cįncįrindǫ *Kt. m.* sun yi $\sim$ crowd gathered.

cincīyā *Kt.* = tsintsīyā.

cįn dādī *Vd.* dādī 5.

cįn damō *Vd.* damō 2.

cįn dawǫ *Kt.* contest between girl-friends of bride and those of bridegroom.

cindǫ (1) *m.* sixth digit (= shįdąnīyā). (2) *m., f.* P. with sixth finger.

cįn dufų *m.* type of children's game.

cindufųrī *m.* donkey-crupper (= ją̄ kutųr *q.v.*), *cf.* rągazą.

cįn dūnīyą *m.* enjoying life (*Vd.* dūnīyą 1*k*).

cin fuska (cįm fuską) *m.* $\sim$ gąrēshį he humiliates people.

cįŋ gaɓą *Vd.* gaɓą 3.

cįŋgālumī *Kt. m.* destitute (= tsąŋgālumī, *q.v.*).

cingami A. (cįŋgāmī) *m.* struggling to do a task.

B. (cįŋgami) *Nor. m.* digging-stick.

cįŋ gąrā *m.* (1) an yi wą sakīyą $\sim$ abscess has been punctured twice or more to let out pus. (2) being punctured in several places x wąndaŋką $\sim$ gąrēshį your trousers have several holes. (3) lengthening the warp-threads. (4) gyądā mai $\sim f.$ good groundnuts.

cįŋgiriŋgātā *Kt. f.* seriousness of a matter.

cįn gōrǫ *Vd.* ąbu 1*aa*.iii.

cįŋ gulūlu *Vd.* gulūlu.

cįŋ hazbīyā *Vd.* hazbīyā 3.

cįnī (1) *Kt. m.* point (= tsįnī) *q.v.* (2) 'yan $\sim$ *Vd.* bidą 4.

cī ni dą zugū *m.* physic-nut (= bį̄ ni da zugū).

cįnikantą *Vb.* 2 (*p.o.* cįnikąncē, *n.o.* cįnikąnci) = cįnūtą.

cįnikī *m.* (*pl.* cįnikai = cinike-cįnikē = *Sk.* cinukką = *Kt.* cįnikkai). (1) (*a*) trading x yaną cįnikiŋ gōrǫ he trades in kolanuts. bā ną̄ barinsą ą yi masą $\sim$ I'm not agreeable to people trading in it. (*b*) ąbōkin $\sim m.$ P. with whom one trades. (2) yā yi $\sim$ he made an offer for the article. (3) bą shi dą wani $\sim$ sǎi shan tāɓą he smokes ceaselessly. (4) ą sam mutųm ą kąn cįnikinsą, kō dą shaŋ gīyą yakę̄ morals make the man. (5) cįnikin dūnīyą dīɓąn nōnǫ nē as you act to others, so they will act to you. (6) cįnikin Yarabāwa *Vd.* kwąlǭ-kwalō.

cinikką *Vd.* ciną, ciŋkę̄.

cinjima *Vd.* tinjima.

ciŋkā *Vd.* ciŋkę̄.

cįŋ kaɗanyą *Vd.* dįmbalą.

cįŋ ƙafąr ką̄zā *Vd.* ƙafąr ką̄zā.

cįŋkąl = cįŋkāli *m.* type of white alloy (= ƙyaurē 2).

cinjimēmę = tinjimēmę.

cịŋ kạrē *Vd.* kạrē 30.

cịŋ kāshi *Vd.* cī 12.

ciŋkau-cịŋkau *Sk. m.* a horse-disease (= rịŋkyū, *q.v.*).

cịŋkẹ *Sk., Kt. m.* (*pl.* cịŋkunạ = cịŋkā = cinikkạ). (1) skewer, etc. (= tsịŋkē, *q.v.*). (2) iron nail for puncturing abscesses (= kibīyạr sakīyạ). (3) metal or bone hairpin for scratching woman's head (= masōshī). (4) destitute P. (5) yā yi mạ wurịn caŋ ∼ he made straight for there (= dọ̄sā). kai na wō mạ ∼ I've come straight to you.

cịŋ k̃ẹtā *Vd.* rụ̄zū 1*a.*

cịŋkị banzā *Vd.* gafīyạ.

cịŋkis *x* kạsūwā tā cịka ∼ market is thronged.

cinkisa A. (cịŋkịsā) *Vb.* 1C. (1) yā cịŋkịsạ matāshịŋ k̃ại he stuffed the cushion. (2) yā ∼ manạ he pestered us so much that we couldn't shake him off (= *Kt.* zạnzamạ). (3) yā ∼ minị aikịn naŋ he imposed on me that unwelcome task,
    B. (cịŋkisạ) *f.* (1) yā yi minị ∼ he importuned me (= zạnzọ̄mā). ∼ gạrēshị he's importunate. (2) rags used for stuffing pads, etc.

cịŋkịshē (1) *Vb.* 1C *x* yā ∼ minị it (food) satiated me (= gịnsā). (2) *Vb.* 3A. (*a*) wurī yā ∼ place is overcrowded. (*b*) kạsūwā tā ∼ market is full of sellers, but no buyers.

cịŋkọ = cịŋkụ *m.* five-franc piece (= shuŋkụ).

cịŋkōsō *noun or adv.* (1) superabundance *x* hatsī yā yi ∼ ạ kạsūwā = hatsī yanạ̄ kạsūwā ∼ market's flooded with corn. tụnjērē yā yi masạ ∼ he's racked with syphilis. (2) *m.* syphilis (= tụnjērē).

cịŋ kūkạr rēmā *m.* fortitude under stress.

cinkuna A. (cịŋkunạ) *Vb.* 2 *Kt.* provoked, irritated (= tsọ̄kanạ).
    B. (cịŋkunạ) *Vd.* cịŋkẹ.

cịŋ kụnāmạr k̃adạŋgarẹ *m.* = cịŋ kūkạr rēmā.

cịŋkūrị̄tā *f.* aik̃ị yā yi minị ∼ I'm " fed up " with work.

cịŋkụshē = cịŋkịshē.

cịŋ k̃wam makaunịyā *used in* iŋ kā kāmạ mạganạ, kā kāmạ k̃ẹ naŋ kạmar ∼ once you speak, you never stop.

cin magaga (cịm mạ̄gāgạ) *Vd.* mạ̄gāgạ.

cin mummuk̃e (cịm mụmmụk̃ē) *x* an yi musụ ∼ = an yi musụ kisạm mụmmụk̃ē they've been oppressed.

cin mutunci (cịm mutuncị) *m.* humiliating a person (*Vd.* mutuncị).

cinnạ *Vb.* 1A yā ∼ masạ wutā he set fire to it (grass, house).

cịnnākạ *m.* (*pl.* cịnnạ̄kū = cịnnạ̄kī). (1) type of biting ant (*cf.* tụmạ dạ gayyạ). (2) cịnnākạn tsakạr gidā, hanạ mātā tạgạŋganē what a quarrelsome person ! (3) cịnnākạn tsakạr gidā type of game. (4) yā kashẹ ∼ = yā kashẹ cịnnạ̄kī he broke off indigo (shūnī) and sprinkled it here and there on his gown. (5) ∼ bạ kạ san na gidā bạ " all are fish that come to his net ", he's no respecter of persons.

cịn nāmạ *Vd.* nāmạ 1*a*.ii, 1*b*.

cinōtạ *f.* a soup-stuff made from fish (= dạddawā 1*e*).

cịn rạbō *m.* (1) azzịkinsạ ∼ nẹ̄ his career or life was short. (2) *Vd.* rạbō 6*b*.

cịn rạ̃i *m.* (1) ∼ gạrēshị he's importunate. (2) *Vd.* rạ̃i 1*h*.

cịn rānī *Vd.* rānī 3.

cịn rūwā *x* wurin naŋ ∼ nẹ̄ this place is covered with water.

cịn sạ *Vd.* gajạ ganī.

cịn sau *Vd.* ạlkāmurạ.

cintạ *Vb.* 1A selected (= tsintạ *q.v.*).

cịn tāb̃ọ *Vd.* tāb̃ọ.

cịn tānā *Kt. m.* = k̃ạcīyạ.

cịn tsạ̄tsē *Vd.* tsạ̄tsē.

cịn tsuntsạ̄yē *m.* (1) yārinyạn naŋ ∼ cẹ̄ this girl is no longer a virgin (= b̃udurwā 2). (2) yārā sunạ̄ yịn ∼ the boys are defiling little girls.

cịn tūjī *m.* = sāran tūjī.

cịn tūshị̄yā *Vd.* tūshị̄yā 2.

cintūwā *Kt.* = tsintūwā.

cịn tūwō *Vd.* shā 1*g*.iii, iv.

cịnụ̄cē *Vd.* cịnūtạ.

cinukkạ *Vd.* cịnik̃ī.

cịnūtạ *Vb.* 2 (*p.o.* cịnụ̄cē, *n.o.* cịnụ̄ci) got by trading *x* yạu nā cịnụ̄ci sulẹ gōmạ I did ten shillings' worth of trade to-day.

cịnūwụyā = cī na wụyā.

cịn wutsīyạ *Vd.* jūyạ 4, wutsīyạ 1*c, d*.

cịn wuyạ *m.* the stitching called bạsītsạ.

cinyạ *f.* (*pl.* cinyōyī = *Sk.* cinai, cunai,

cunnai). (1) thigh (*epithet is* Cinya, gaŋgar mātā *because women laugh and slap their thighs*). (2) gā ∼ *Vd.* mįƙā 2*b*. (3) ƙamar ∼ *Vd.* cōƙạlī 2.

cinyar *m.* (1) cry·of kite. (2) cry to terrify children.

cin yau *Vd.* ɓararraƙi.

cinyē (1) *Vb.* 1C. (*a*) (i) ate up. (ii) yā ∼ fat he devoured it all. (iii) spent all *x* nā cinye kudīna I spent all my money. (iv) cī'ye-cįyē" yā fi cinyēwā gently and steadily does it ! (v) kō yā yį, zai ∼ nę *Vd.* rēna 5. (*b*) yā ∼ minį zarạfī he wasted my time (*Vd.* cī 24). (*c*) stole *x* yā cinye sạ he stole the bull. yā ∼ minį kudīna (i) he embezzled my money. (ii) he won all my money from me. (*cc*) cinye bāshi *Vd.* bāshi 2*d*. (*d*) contained (= cī 18 *q.v.*). (*e*) *Kt.* yā ∼ su he was even better dressed than they were. (*f*) yā cinye wutā ƙurmus it was burnt " to a frazzle ". (*g*) abbreviated (a word) *x in explaining that* ayau dạ *is abbreviated form of* ayautar, dạ, *we say* an cinye " tar ". (*h*) bit T. through (*x* horse *re* reins), *cf.* cįję. (2) *Vb.* 3A. (*a*) ƙafạssa tā ∼ his leg is eaten away by an ulcer. (*b*) itạcē yā ∼ all the firewood is consumed.

cinyōyī *Vd.* cinya.

cin zanzanā *m. Vd.* zanzanā.

cin zārī *Vd.* zārī.

cin zuma *Vd.* zuma 1*d*.

cip = cip completely (= cif *q.v.*).

cipci *Kt. m.* thatching-grass (= shūci *q.v.*).

cippạlī *m.* hawking of milk by Filani women to barter for corn.

cir A. (cįr) (*said to chicken, beggar, trickster*) clear out !

B. (cir) (1) yā mīƙẹ tsaye ∼ it is vertical. (2) yā cika ∼ it is brimful. watạ ∼ a full month. shękara 20 ∼ a full 20 years. rānā tā yi tsaka ∼ the sun's reached the zenith (= carcar *q.v.*). (3) tēbur yā tsaya ∼ the table stands firmly.

cira A. (cira) (1) *Vb.* 1A. (*a*) raised, lifted up (= dạga) *x* (i) yā ∼ hannūwa he raised his arms. (ii) yā ∼ hannū he waved at me, him, etc. (iii) jįgįdā ta ƙan ∼ kutyrinta the bẹad-belt makes

her hips stand out. (iv) yā ∼ murya he spoke loudly. (v) *Vd.* 1*d below*. (vi) ∼ gindī *Vd.* gindī 2. (*b*) an ∼ shi he has been promoted or honoured. (*c*) postponed *x* an ∼ tạfiya the journey has been postponed (= fāsa 1*a*). kanạ aikį, bā ƙạ ∼ rānā you work every day without exception. (*d*) raised one's head *x* kạ yi ruƙū'u, kạ ∼ do obeisance in prayer, then raise your head ! (*cf. a, g*). (*e*) yā ∼ ƙafạ = yā ∼ sāwu (i) he puts his best foot foremost (= dạga 1*e*.i). (ii) muka ∼ ƙafạ we got the upper hand. (*f*) *Kt.* exceeded slightly (= dara). (*g*) yanạ ∼ kại he's arrogant, *cf.* 1*d* (= dạga 1*d*). bạ wanda ya įsa ∼ kại garēshį he's too powerful to resist. (*h*) yā yi cira kalma he divided word into two parts, half on each line of writing. (*j*) yā cirō dạga bạkim Mālạm M. he studied under Malam M. (*k*) *Vd.* hamạtā : cirā : cire. (2) *Vb.* 3A. (*a*) relieved P. of one's presence *x* kạ ∼ mana kạdaŋ leave us for a while ! (*b*) became high (*cf.* dạga) *x* rānā tā ∼ sun is fairly high (8–9 a.m.). dāwa tā ∼ guinea-corn is fairly high. yāro yā ∼ lad's well grown. (*c*) is (was) postponed *x* tạfiya tā ∼. (*d*) North Kano Hausa (*cord, thread, etc.*) snapped.

B. (cįrā) (1) *Vb.* 2. (*a*) pulled out *x* nā ciri ƙūsa I pulled out the nail. nā ciri maganar dạga bạkinsa I got the news out of him. (*b*) thinned out crops *x* yā ciri rōgo he thinned out cassava (*the stem* (itạcansa) *being replanted* (dasa) *and the root eaten*) = zabgẹ 1*e*, *cf.* 2*b below*. (*c*) = cire 1*b*, *e*. (2) *f*. (*a*) yā yi ∼ he's skinned inside of thighs from overwalking, etc. (*b*) an yi wạ dāwa (gērō) ∼ guinea-corn (millet) has been thinned out at nōmam firį, the pulled out stems (gindī) being thrown away (*cf.* 1*b above ;* ƙwạcē). (3) *Vd.* cirar- and cįri-*compounds.*

C. (cīra) *f.* keloid on upper eyelid, etc.

D. (cīrā) *Vb.* 3B *Kt.* escaped (= tsīrā *q.v.*).

ciraci *m.* the food tūwō when made from coarse flour of bulrush millet (= byrabuskọ).

cirak kaya Kt. used in ~ kudim mararrabā money thrown down at crossroads for enemy to pick up and fall ill by magic.

cī rama Vd. cī dāwa.

ciranci (1) duties of Cirōma. (2) townquarter where Cirōma lives.

cī rānī m. = cin rānī m. (Vb. rānī 3) x sun zō cī rānī.

cirāra Kt. naked (= tsirāra q.v.).

cirar dangā f. yā yi wa mātassa ~ he installed new wife, divorcing and turning out previous one.

cirar kaya Vd. cirak kaya.

cirar kōdago f. (1) Kt. attaining a higher status. (2) Sk. = cirar kwallō 1.

cirar kwallō f. (1) seizing foot of wrestling opponent, throwing him up, then dashing him down (= Sk. cirar kōdago). (2) suddenly dismissing P. and reducing to destitution.

cirar shisshinīyā Sk., Kt. f. (1) rearing up of horse (= tabaryā). (2) lifting P. high in the air as warning.

cirbe A. (cirbe) Vb. 1A Sk. weeded at nōmam firi time with the small hoe called kalme.

B. (cirbē) m. weeding as in cirbe.

cirbī Kt. m. excrescence on " parson's nose " of fowl (= tsirbī).

cirbi what a large quantity !

cire A. (cire) (1) Vb. 1A. (a) (i) pulled T. out of, pulled T. off x sun cire masauki they struck camp. yā cire musu fūlā he saluted, congratulated them (by taking off his cap). (ii) dismissed P. (iii) = tūbe 2a. (b) yā ~ mātar Audu he eloped with Audu's wife. (c) = cira 1c. (d) deducted x an ~ ushirā the tenth due to the Treasury has been deducted from the estate. (e) (with dative) (i) pulled T. away from. (ii) Vd. cire mini kaya, m fī ka gudu. (iii) dā, an cire musu al'amuram baitulmal previously, they were debarred from handling Treasury affairs. (iv) ~ gindi Vd. cira 1a.vi. (f) Kt. snapped T. ; snapped off T. (= tsinke). (g) cf. cirā. (h) Vd. cire-compounds. (2) Vb. 3A. (a) is (was) torn off ; came off x anīnī yā ~ button came off. wuyan tūlū (tukunyā) yā ~ the neck of the

ewer (cooking pot) is broken off (cf. karye, tsinke). (b) Kt. yā ~ he ran off with another's wife ; he eloped with a girl.

B. (cirē) m. (1) grass pulled up by hand for fodder (cf. yanke ; kade). (2) an yi wa maiwā ~ the bulrushmillet maiwā has been pulled up for transplanting. (3) yā yi cire he eloped with another's wife.

cire mn kaya (1) m. type of children's game in water. (2) yā yi mini ~, m fī ka gudu that pupil of mine has now surpassed me.

cirfā Kt. f. plan (= tsirfā q.v.).

ciri A. (ciri) m. (1) sun yi ~ = sun dauki ~ people rushed en masse to see T., do T., catch thief, etc. (2) nā ji ~ I heard noise of crowd rushing along as in 1.

B. Kt. = tsiri q.v.

ciribi m. (1) profusion x ciribim mutānē many people. (2) (a) deep mire (x from horse trampling the ground at hobbling-post turke). (b) slushy cowdung (as in cow-pen). (3) al'amari yā yi ~ the matter is much protracted.

ciri daidai m. an yi musu ~ the two of them have been shackled together by the feet.

cirimbici Vd. cirin.

cirin used in the type of gambling where P. closes both fists saying cirin kō cimfā " right or left hand ? " ; if his partner chooses right hand, the P. replies cirimbici bā cācā ; but if his partner chooses left hand, the P. replies bā rikica.

ciringiza (ciringiza) used in ~ bāwa da gwaiwā epithet of P. whose performance falls short of his reputation.

ciriniya (cirinīyā) Nor f. the petty worries of daily life.

ciriri A. (cīrīri) m. Sk. the gum-bearing tree Combretum Kerstingii (= dagēra).

B. (cīrīrī) Kt. x yā yi ciki ~ he's pot-bellied (= tsīrīrī q.v.).

cirie Kt. = tirie.

cirkaka f. sun yi ~ two combatants are hesitating about their next move. yā yi ~ he's at a loss to know how to act.

cirkau *Kt.* how thin he is ! (= tsirkau *q.v.*).

cirkō-cirkō = cirkāka.

cirkōko = cōkōko.

cirmā-cirmā *Kt.* confusedly (= tsirma-tsirma *q.v.*).

cirnāka *Sk.* = cinnāka.

cirō *Vd.* cira 1*j* ; cirā ; cire.

cirōkī *m.* (1) cock's comb. (2) abscesses of the scalp. (3) abscesses on animal's back. (4) yanā da gāshi a kā cirōki-cirōki he has tufts of hair dotted about his head. (5) yanā da kurarrajī cirōki-cirōki he's covered in pustules.

cirōko (1) what badly-fitting thatch ! (2) his cap's far too small for his head !

cirōkōkō *Kt. m.* careless weeding (= tsambarē 2).

Cirōma (1) name of an official position (*epithet is* Gimba). (2) tūɓaɓɓan Sarkī yā fi 'yan Sarkī gōma duk da ubansu Cirōma " it's better to have loved and lost . . ." (3) *Vd.* Kacalla 2.

ciryā *Kt. f.* parakeet (= tsiryā *q.v.*).

cirza (1) *Kt.* kicked up the ground (= turza *q.v.*). (2) *Sk. f.* the feline called dagē.

cīsad da *Vb.* 4A *Sk.* fed (= cī da *q.v.*).

cīshē (1) *Vd.* cī da. (2) *Vd.* Alā 4. (3) *m.* name given southern entrance to compound, this being considered lucky.

cīshī *Kt. m.* good quality (= kīshī).

cissāwa *Sk. f.* chinks in roof through which light penetrates.

cītā *Vb.* 2 (*p.o.* cīcē, *n.o.* cīci). (1) made a guess *x* ban sani ba, ammā zan ~ I don't know but I'll make a guess (= tītā). (2) *Vd.* cīci.

cītalī *m.* am fid da ~ sign of omission has been inserted in the writing (= karā 4 = gyārā 3 = shītalī = tatalī).

cī tamā *m.* (*sg., pl.*) smith (*Vd.* tamā).

citta A. (cittā) *f.* (1) Melegueta pepper (*Amomum melegueta*) = *Sk.* gyandamā 2. (2) the pepper filfil. (3) tā shā ~ she separated from her husband in a huff (*cf.* yāji 2*b*). (4) jikinsa yā yi ~ he (old P.) became wrinkled. (5) gindin ~ *m.* cantankerous P. yā ci gindin ~ = yā taɓō gindin ~ he came in contact with a cantankerous P. (6) cittar aho ginger.

B. (cittā) (1) on the 4th day ahead. (2) shēkaran ~ on the 5th day ahead.

cīwa *Kt. f.* impertinence (= tsīwa *q.v.*).

cīwace *Vd.* cīwo.

Cī wākē *Vd.* Cī dāwa.

ciwō A. (cīwo) *m.* (*pl.* cīwace-cīwacē = cī'we-cīwē" = cūrūtā = ciwirwitā = cuwurwutā). (1) (*a*) illness, disease. (*b*) yā yi ~ he fell ill. yanā ~ = yā sāmi ~ he's ill. (*c*) yā tāshi daga ~ he rose from a sickbed. (*d*) yā kwanta ~ he lay sick. (*e*) mai da agānā ~ *Vd.* agānā 2. (2) pain *x* (*a*) yā ji ~ (i) he felt pain. (ii) he suffered injury. (*b*) yā ji mini ~ it (thorn, etc.) caused me sudden pain (*cf.* jī 4C). (*c*) dōki yā tsēre, yā bar shi cikin ~ the horse bolted leaving him with his body smarting. (*d*) *Vd.* kule. (*e*) (i) cīwan ido sāi hakurī what cannot be cured must be endured. (ii) *Vd.* tamfā. (*f*) fāmi yā fi jin ~ zāfī reopening a matter is bitterer than the original matter. (*g*) kōwā ya san cīwan kansa, yā san na wani suffering makes a P. more humane. (3) being offended *x* (*a*) nā ji cīwam maganassa I was offended at what he said. (*b*) yā ji mini ~ he offended me (*Vd.* jī 4C, cūtā 1*b*). (*c*) bā dūkan rūwan sama kē da ~ ba *Vd.* sama 1*e*. (*d*) " sannū ! " bā tā warke ~ fine words butter no parsnips. (4) drawback *x* (*a*) cīwan abin, bā ni da dōki my drawback is in lacking a horse. (*b*) yā san cīwan kansa he knows his own failings. (*c*) bai san inda kansa yakē ~ ba he doesn't know what is best for him. (5) *Vd.* dadi 4, cūtā, *compounds of* cīwon. (6) type of owl.

B. (cīwō) *m.* (1) types of climber yielding rubber (*Landolphia owariensis, Landolphia florida*). (2) ~ kā nūna, kā ki fādūwā what a stingy person !

C. (cīwō) *Vd.* cī 11*a*, 23.

ciwan (cīwan) (*genitive of* cīwo). (1) cīwam bākī *m.* offensive words (*Vd.* abu 12). (2) cīwam barcī *m.* sleeping sickness (= kirmun = dudduru 2), *cf.* sammōre. (3) cīwam birnī *m.* syphilis (= tunjērē). (4) cīwan sanyī *m.* gonorrhœa (= gumbā 2 = *Kt.* gōlōɓō), *cf.* fyauka, daude. (5) cīwan Gwārī *Vd.* dangwalōlo.

ciwunną *Vd.* cūną 2.
ciwurwutā *Vd.* cīwǫ.
cīyad dą = cī dą.
cīyau *m., f. (sg., pl.)* glutton (= acīcį).
cįyāwą *f. (pl.* cįyąyī). (1) (*a*) grass
(= hakį). (*b*) blade of grass *x* yā
tsīgę ~ ukų he plucked three blades of
grass. (*c*) *Vd.* dōkį 1*g.* (*d*) cikin ~
Vd. sukųŋ-sukųŋ. (*e*) ɗanyar ~ *Vd.*
ɗanyē 2*b.* (2) (*a*) ɗan ~ *m.* (*pl.*
'yan ~) boy bringing grass for horses.
(*b*) *Vd.* mutų 1*a.*vi. (*c*) yaną yi masą ~
he cuts grass for him. (3) cįyāwąr idǫ
leucoma (= hakīyą). (4) *Kt.* may your
new horse thrive !
cįyayyą *f.* eating a meal together by
several persons whose food was cooked
separately.
cį'ye-cįyē‖ *m.* (1) constant eating. (2) ~
yā fi cįnyęwā gently and steadily does it !
ciyo A. (cīyǫ) *m.* illness (= cīwǫ *q.v.*).
    B. (cīyō) *Sk.* = cīwō.
ciza A. (cįzā) *Vb.* 2 (*p.o.* cįjē, *n.o.* cįji),
Vd. cīzǫ. (1) bit (*Vd.* sąrā 1*c*, hąrbā 3).
(2) yā cįji hųlā he bit pattern into cap
(*cf.* sąmazādawą). (3) yā cįji bąkī he
bit his lips from anger or remorse
(= cīję 1*c q.v.*). (4) mąganą tā cįjē
nį I'm burning to tell what I know.
(5) wąndą ya cįji hancįŋką *Vd.* hancį
1*f.*
    B. (cīzą) (1) *Vb.* 1A (*a*) = cįzā
1–4. (*b*) tun sāfē bąn ~ ɓa I've had no
kolanut to-day. (2) *Vb.* 3A (*a*) bābā
(jā) yā ~ the indigo (red dye) is of good,
dark colour. (*b*) yaną cīząwā it is
rather dear. (*c*) gishirī yā ~ ą mīyą
the soup's a bit over-salted. (*d*) an ~
profit was obtained. (3) yaną cīząwā
he is a favourite.
cįzākā *Kt. f.* hairy caterpillar (= gįzākā
q.v.).
cį zākī *m.* a tree with sweet berries (*root
used as aphrodisiac*).
cįzal = cįzar *m.* pyorrhœa ; various
diseases of the gums (*cf.* būbų 2).
cįząrą *f.* (1) blepharitis ; ectropion. (2)
Kt. = cįzar.
cįzgā *Vb.* 2 wrenched out (= fįzgā *q.v.*).
cizgārī *m.* (1) big, strong P. (2) expert ;
industrious P. (3) difficult task.
(4) tough meat. (5) cumbersome horse.

(6) tool become blurted. (7) (*a*) ~
bāwąn yąrdā *Vd.* shąmakį. (*b*) *cf.*
bāwą 12.
cīzǫ *m.* (1) (*secondary v.n. of* cįzā) *x*
aną cīząnsą = aną cįzā tasą it's being
bitten. (2) act of biting *x* (*a*) fųlan
nąŋ, an yi matą ~ a pattern's been
bitten into this cap. (*b*) kōwā yā
yi ~ wurim faɗą, yā ji zāfin dąnnā
nobody acts without a motive. (*c*)
ąbǫkąŋ gąbā suŋ kāwō musų ~ the
enemy attacked them. sun ji ~ dągą
dāma they were attacked on the right.
(*d*) na bāya kąrē kę ~ *Vd.* kąrē 5*e.* (*e*)
kō dą cīzǫ dą yāgų zā sų cī they'll
gain the victory cost what it may.
(*f*) cīzǫ bą haushį *Vd.* mūmįnī 1*b.* (*g*)
cīząm bąkī *Vd.* ragō 1*b.* (3) cīząŋ
kųrēgē = cīząn na rēgą a " softy ".
cōbę contracted Achilles tendon *x* fafąssą
tā yi ~ (= cąŋgąl 1, 2 *q.v.* = dāgį 5 =
sāran shūką 2).
cōcę *Vd.* Nā cōcę.
coge A. (cōgę) *Vb.* 1A excepted (= tōgę
q.v.).
    B. (cōgē) *m.* in game ląŋgą, stooping
to hold left big-toe with right hand.
cōgumī *Kt. m.* scandalmongering (= tsēgumī *q.v.*).
cōiŋ *x* yā jī shį ~ he found it sweet-
tasting.
coka A. (cōkā) (1) (*d.f.* sǫkā) *Vb.* 2 (*in the
game* 'yā 5*b, rag is buried and boys say
cǫki* ! " prod the earth and transfix the
rag ! " ; *if he succeeds, they say* yā
cǫki 'yā). (2) *f.* a previous fetich-place
in Kano City for Māguzāwā.
    B. (cōką) *Vb.* 1A. (1) yaną ~ fafą
he walks on ball of foot owing to contracted Achilles tendon. (2) yā ~ wą
fasā sąndā he prodded earth with stick
as in cǫkā 1.
cōkąlī *m. (pl.* cōkulą). (1) spoon (= *Sk.*
kųyāfą). (2) itącąn dą a kąn yi cōkąlī
dą shī kąmar cinyą yakę, dą sąssafą
yą fārę slow but sure.
cǫkaną *Vb.* 2 *Kt.* provoked, irritated
(= tsǫkaną *q.v.*).
coke A. (cōkē) *m.* play *as in* cǫkā 1.
    B. (cōkę) *Vb.* an cōkę sąndā ą fasā
stick has been prodded into ground *as
in* cǫkā 1.

cōkō *x* ɗan cōkō *m.* woman's fringed handkerchief.

cōkōkō = cǭkǭkǭ *used in* yā zaunạ ∼ (1) he sat mewed up from cold or grief. (2) it (thatch, cap) fits badly. (3) T. sits insecurely on base. (4) *Kt.* he sat idly.

cōkulạ *Vd.* cōkạlī.

cololo A. (cōlōlō) *Nor. m.* standing on tiptoe of both feet to reach T. high up (= ɗagē).

    B. (cǭlōlǫ) *Kt.* tall P. (= tsǭlōlǫ *q.v.*).

cụ *Vd.* cụụ.

cụbụs = cubus-cụbụs *x* sum fitō ∼ they appeared profusely (= dạ̄ɓāɓạ *q.v.*).

cuɓụs *m.* mun yi ∼ dạ shī we met him unexpectedly (= ciɓụs *q.v.*).

cụcan *Vd.* cụcē.

cūcanạ *f.* inferior type of bạgạrīyẹ saddle.

cūcanancī *m.* (1) effrontery (*cf.* bạcūcanẹ). (2) three small lines cut at both corners of slaves' lips.

cūcanāwā slaves born in slavery of slaveparents (*Vd.* bạcūcanẹ).

cụcē (1) *Vd.* cụtā. (2) ɗan cụcaɲ ūwā = cụcū.

cụci *Vd.* cụtā.

cụcū *x* ɗan cụcuɲ ūwā = ɗan cụcùɲ ụbā bother you ! (*cf.* ụbākạ ; ūwā 1c).

cuɗa A. (cūɗạ) *Vb.* 1A. (1) kneaded (*cf.* cūrạ). (2) massaged. (3) kō an cūɗạ, an jūyạ, mạ̄ ci nasarạ whatever vicissitudes we suffer, yet we'll win. (4) an cūɗạ, an cūɗạ battle was hotly joined.
    B. (cụ̄ɗā) *Vb.* 2. (1) = cūɗạ. (2) ạ cụ̄ɗi gunạ dạ mạntạ giving P. a present from proceeds of transaction with him. (3) Sarkī yā cụ̄ɗē sụ the Emir showed them he wasn't to be trifled with. (4) cụ̄ɗar rūwā mại tāshi *epithet of* cantankerous P. (5) *cf.* bạ̄kō 1d ; cūɗẹ ; cụ̄ɗu. (6) shạ̄ cụ̄ɗā *Vd.* wạrkī. (7) cụ̄ɗē ni *Vd.* zamā 2a.*x.*

cuɗanya A. (cụ̄ɗanyạ) *Vb.* 3B sun ∼ (1) things became mixed together. (2) persons became intimate.
    B. (cūɗạnyā) *Vb.* 1C mixed things together.

cụ̄ɗayyạ *f.* intimacy.

cūɗẹ (1) *Vb.* 1A. (*a*) yā ∼ wannạɲ dạ wancạɲ he mixed this thing with that. (*b*) Sarkī yā ∼ su = cụ̄ɗā 3. (2) *Vb.* 3A. (*a*) became muddled *x* mạganạ

tā cūɗẹ, har mā bạ mạ̄ cẹ̄ " gạ̄ iriɲ wainad dạ akẹ̄ tōyạ̄wā " ba the matter is so involved that we cannot explain what is going on. (*b*) zanẹ yā ∼ cloth is crumpled (*cf.* cūɗạ ; cụ̄ɗā ; cụ̄ɗu). (*c*) ạbiɲ yā ∼ manạ things are (were) not going well with us.

cụ̄ɗu *Vb.* 3B sun ∼ dạ jūnā they're intimate (*cf.* cūɗẹ).

cukkụ *Sk. m.* phthisis.

cukọ *Kt. m.* balance outstanding (= cikọ *q.v.*).

cukū *m.* cheese.

cuku-cuku A. (cukū-cụkụ̄) *m.* (1) being tangled. (2) being ragged *x* tsụmmā yā yi masạ ∼ he's in tatters. (3) ƙurạrrajī sun yi masạ he's covered in pustules. (4) talaucį yā yi masạ ∼ destitution has reduced him to dire straits. (5) an ɗaurẹ shi ∼ prisoner's securely bound.
    B. (cụkụ̄-cukū) *m.* kadạ kạ yi minį ∼ don't gabble so !

cukuf = cukup.

cụkumạ *Vb.* 2 = cukụmē.

cukumạ̄rạ *f.* cheese (= cukū).

cukụmē *Vb.* 1C seized P. by neck of gown.

cụkūmụrdī *x* sunạ̄ cụkūmụrɗim faɗạ they're quarrelling fiercely.

cụkụmụrɗụɲ = sụkụkụ.

cukuɲ-cụkụɲ = cukū-cụkụ̄.

cụkụɲkunạ *Vb.* 2 provoked, irritated (= tsǭkanạ *q.v.*).

cụkụɲkụnē (1) *Vb.* 1D *x* talaucį (= gạrī) yā ∼ shi (= yā ∼ masạ) = cukū-cụkụ̄ 4. (2) *Vb.* 3A mạganạ tā ∼ the matter's in muddle. rīgā tā ∼ the gown's tattered (= cukū-cụkụ̄).

cukup *used in* tsōfō ∼ very old man (= kutup 1).

cukụrfā *f.* (*pl.* cukurfōfī = cụkụrfai) long narrow corn-bag made of palm-leaves.

cukurkụɗē = cukurkụshē *x* yā ∼ minį it's beyond me.

cukurrụfā = *cukurụfā = cukụrfā *q.v.*

cukus-cụkụs = cukū-cụkụ̄.

cukwī *m.* (1) poor type of cotton. (2) cheese (= cukū).

cukwī-cụkwī = cukū-cụkụ̄.

cukwīkwiyā *Vb.* 1D tangled up T. (= cikwīkwịyā *q.v.*).

cukwĩmạ *Kt. f.* torch (= jĩnĩyā 2 *q.v.*).

cul *m.* (1) yā yi ⁓ horse (donkey) has abscesses on back (= kwānaryạ 2). (2) suŋ harbạ kibĩyạ cul cul they fired a hail of arrows.

culundụguŋ *m.* (1) gạrĩ yā yi ⁓ it rained from morn till night. (2) gạrĩ yā yi minị ⁓ I'm " broke ".

cumbus-cumbus in profusion (= dạ̃bạ̃bạ̃ *q.v.*).

cũnạ (1) *Vb.* 1A. (*a*) egged on *x* yā ⁓ kạrē he egged the dog on. yā ⁓ minị kạrē he egged on the dog against me. (*b*) yā ⁓ musụ bạ̃kõ (ạlmājịrĩ) he foisted unwanted guest (beggar) on them. (1 = *Kt.* shĩshịtā = *Kt.* sunnạ 1*c* = dõdạnā). (2) *f.* (*pl.* cũnõnĩ = *Kt.* ciwunnạ). (*a*) gusset joining sleeve to rĩgā (= *Kt.* tattũ), *cf.* jēmāgẹ 3. (*b*) gusset under armpit of tagũwā. (*c*) yā kāmạ ni ạ ⁓ = yā kāmạ ni ⁓ dạ ạlbadạ I see no way of avoiding it.

cunai *Sk.* thighs (*Vd.* cinyạ).

cũnē *m.* an yi masạ ⁓ he's been egged on (*cf.* cũnạ).

cuŋgulạ *Vb.* 2 *Kt.* pinched (= tsuŋgulạ).

cuŋko = cuŋku *m.* five-franc piece (= shuŋku).

cuŋkulạ *Vb.* 2 = tsuŋgulạ *q.v.*

cuŋkum = cuskurụrụŋ.

cuŋkunạ *Vb.* 2 *Kt.* provoked, irritated (= tsõkanạ).

cuŋkus in profusion (= ciŋkis *q.v.*).

cuŋkushē *Kt.* = ciŋkishē.

cunnạ *Vb.* 1A *Kt.* = cũnạ 1.

cunnai *Sk.* thighs (*Vd.* cinyạ).

cũnõnĩ *Vd.* cũnạ 2.

cunõtạ *f.* a soup-stuff made of fish (= dạddawā 1*e*).

cup completely (= cif *q.v.*).

cur = cir.

cura A. (cũrạ) *Vb.* 1A (*Vd.* cũrị). (1) kneaded into balls (*cf.* cũdạ). (2) collected many things together. (3) *Kt.* pierced (= tsũrạ).

B. (cũrā) *Vb.* 2 (1) = cũrạ. (2) nā cũri furā ta kwabọ uku I bought 3*d.* worth of furā (*only applied to things amalgamated into one mass x* nạ̃kĩyạ).

cũrạkĩ *m.* = acũrạkĩ.

cũrẹ *Vb.* 1A (*totality form of* cũrạ, cũrā) *x* kneaded all of.

cũrị *m.* (1) (*secondary v.n. of* cũrạ) *x* tanạ cũrịnsạ = tanạ cũrạ shi she's kneading it. (2) kneaded ball (= duŋkulĩ 1 = mulmulẹ) *x* cũrịm bābā round pat of indigo (= kuntukurũ). cũrịm furā ball of furā = lailayẹ (*Vd.* cũsā 2, mārā 2, hõcẹ 2). (3) an duŋkulē shi cũrị-cũrị it was kneaded into balls. (4) cũrịn tsummā bạ kạ ci kafạ ba, kā ci zũcĩyā *epithet of* ragged gown preventing P. appearing in public (= mạrin tsummā), *Vd.* dụnjĩ, mạrĩ 2.

cũrũtā *Vd.* cĩwọ.

cus A. (cus) *used in* kudĩ ⁓ cash down.

B. (cus) *f.* kazwā tā fitõ ⁓ scabies appeared abundantly.

cusa A. (cũsạ) *Vb.* 1A. (1) stuffed T. into *x* nā ⁓ tsummā ạ rāmị I stuffed rags into the hole (= kimsạ 3*a*). (2) yā ⁓ kại, ya shigõ he entered without a " by your leave " (= kimsạ 3*d*). (3) an ⁓ magana kam magana one blessed thing after another ! (= wani 4*b*). (4) (*with dative*) forced T. on P. *x* an ⁓ masạ rĩgā he's been forced to take the gown.

B. (cũsā) *f.* (1) an yi wạ dõkị ⁓ the horse has been forcibly fed (*cf.* tsịndụmē). (2) cake of kũkạ, bran (dụsā) and potash (kaŋwā) for forcibly feeding horse (*in Kt. this is made from* gubdũ).

cũsai = *Sk.* cũsāyĩ *m.* syphilis (= tụnjērē *q.v.*).

cushe A. (cũshẹ). (1) *Vb.* 1A stuffed completely (*cf.* cũsạ). (2) *Vb.* 3A. (*a*) kõfạ tā ⁓ the doorway is blocked by crowd, etc. (*b*) kạsũwā tā ⁓ there's a slump.

B. (cũshē) *m.* (1) yanạ ⁓ he's occupied in packing corn into granary. (2) yā matsạ hannũ, yā yi ⁓ through shortage of paper, he wrote tiny, fine characters (*cf.* kạrmạtsē).

cuskurụrụŋ = cuskurụrụŋ *m.* (1) putting on several gowns and huge turban. (2) yā yi ⁓ he's at his wits' ends what to do.

cũtā (1) *f.* (*a*) (i) illness, disease (*cf.* cĩwọ). (ii) kudim mại ⁓ na mại māganĩ nẽ P. wanting T. will go to any lengths. (*b*) offensive act, oppression *x* yā yi minị ⁓ he did an act offensive to me

(*cf.* cīwǫ 3). (*c*) cụtar Allǎ *Vd.* ba'ǎ.
(*d*) jǎ wǎ daŋgị ∼ *Vd.* tụŋkŭ 1*b*. (2)
Vb. 2 (*p.o.* cụ̆cĕ, *n.o.* cụ̆ci). (*a*) deceived.
(*b*) (i) injured. (ii) oppressed. (iii) yǎ
cụ̆ci kạnsạ "he cut off his nose to
spite his face". (iv) *Vd.* bạcŭcanẹ.
(*c*) iŋ kǎ yĭ, kǎ cụtu if you do it, you'll
be sorry! (*d*) yǎ cụtu he is very ill.

cụụ (1) sun yi naŋ ∼, sun yi caŋ ∼ they
bustled about. (2) (*a*) *adv. and m.*
sound of sputtering oil. (*b*) bǎ ∼, bǎ
bōkǫ, bǎ gudụŋ wutǎ, ɗaŋ k̆ārǎyĕ here
is the best Karaye shea-oil for lamps,
buy, buy! (*said by girls exhibiting it at*
tạllạ).

cụ̆wǎ-cụ̆wǎ *Sk. f.* mutǎnĕ sunǎ ∼ people
are busily astir.

cụwŏ *m.* the plant cịwŏ *q.v.*

cuwunnạ *Kt.* gussets (*Vd.* cŭnạ).

cuwurwutā illnesses (*Vd.* cīwǫ).

cūyẹ *Sk. m.* testicle (= gwaiwǎ).

cwai *x* yanǎ dạ wǎyŏ ∼ he's very cunning
(= cai *q.v.*).

D

da A. (dạ) (1) (*a*) (i) together with *x*
darajạ ∼ martabạ prestige and rank.
yǎ zŏ dạ (= yǎ zŏ tǎre dạ) Daudạ he
came with David. yǎ bǎ nị cị dạ shǎ he
gave me food and drink. (ii) *Vd.* 13*b below*.
(iii) dạ jinĭ ạ bakạ *Vd.* yau 1*a.*ii. (iv)
Vd. dạ īyạ. (*b*) (*after* yanǎ, *etc.,* Gram.
22, 23*b*) is, was, were, etc., possessed of
x (i) yanǎ dạ kyạu it is good. yanǎ
dạ f̆ādĭ it is broad. tanǎ dạ kudĭ she
has money. bǎ ka dạ rŭwǎ you've no
water. sạn naŋ, bǎ ni dạ shĭ at that
time, I had none of it. Hijirǎ tanǎ dạ
shĕkarạ 1278 akạ yĭ it occurred in the
Mahommedan year 1278 (*cf.* 5 *below*).
Jǎmụs nĕ dạ wannạŋ aikị it was the
Germans who did this (Gram. 137).
(ii) (dạ *sometimes stands at end*) *x*
wata dạbārạ nak̆ẹ dạ it is a different
plan I am occupied with. (iii) bǎ dạ . . .
ba without (*Vd.* bǎ . . . ba). (2)
(*repeated*) both . . . and *x* (*a*) dạ
rānǎ dạ watạ both the sun and
the moon. yanǎ dạ 'yǎ'yǎ ukụ, dạ
Audụ, dạ Ali dạ Bǎba he had three
children, Audu, Ali, and Baba. (*b*)

dạ kŭkaŋ kūrā, dạ б̆acĕwar ạkwīyạ
dukạ ɗayā nǎ they are cause and
effect. (*c*) dạ nĭ, dạ kai, kōwǎ ya fāsạ,
shĕgẹ nĕ = shĕgẹ kǎ fāsạ *q.v.* (*d*) dạ
kǎị dạ kāyā *Vd.* mạllakạ 2*a*. (3) (*a*) by
means of *x* yǎ sǫ̆kĕ nị dạ wuk̆ā he
stabbed me with a knife. (*b*) on account
of *x* tǎ fashẹ dạ kŭkā she burst out
crying. sum fịrgitạ dạ wannạŋ they are
terrified by this. yǎ yi wạhalạ dạ mŭ he
took trouble on our account. (*c*) regarding
k̆asạd dạ ta yi kyạu dạ ginị earth which
is good for building purposes. yǎyạ zā
mụ yi dạ shị what shall we do regarding
him? mẹ̆ ka ganĭ dạ yārạn naŋ what
is your opinion about this boy? (4) (*a*)
in relation to *x* ịnǎ yak̆ẹ dạ dākịŋkạ
where is it situated in relation to your
house? (= dạgạ 6). Audụ shĭ nǎ̆
na ukụ dạ mayǎ̆wā Audu ruled third in
the succession. (*b*) (*exceeded, fell short*
of, etc.) by *x* yǎ fĭ sụ dạ bĭyŭ he exceeds
them by two. yǎ ragẹ garịŋ dạ kwānā
ɗayā sǎi dōkịŋ ya mutụ when short of
his destination by one day, the horse
died. bāyaŋ Hijirar Ạnnabị dạ shĕkarạ
2, sukạ karб̆ẹ k̆asạr they overran the
country two years after the flight of the
Prophet. (*c*) yǎ rantsẹ dạ Allǎ he
swore by God. (5) (*indicating date in*
month) *x* huɗū dạ Fạbạrā'ịr 1929 on
the 4th of February, 1929 (*cf.* 1*b*
above). ạ cikịŋ watạn Zụlhajị ạshịrịŋ
dạ shĭ on the 20th of the month of Z.
takạrdarkụ ạbar yị wạ tārihạ 23 dạ
Sha'ạbaŋ your letter dated 23rd of S.
(= gạ 8). (6) (*prefixed to noun, forms*
adverb) *x* (*a*) dạ sāfĕ in the morning.
mutǎnĕ dạ yawạ many persons. kudĭ
dạ yawạ much money. (*b*) dạ darĕ = dạ
dạddarĕ *Vd.* darĕ 1*b, e.* (7) (Gram.
177*d, idiomatically replacing* dạgạ).
(*a*) from *x* yǎ hūtạ dạ wạhalạ he had no
further trouble. nā rạbu dạ shĭ I
separated from him. nā hạkurạ dạ
shĭ I've resigned myself to doing without it. nā mạntā dạ shĭ I've forgotten
it. nā gạji dạ sū I'm tired of them.
kulluŋ б̆atạ dạ hanyạ nik̆ẹ yị I keep on
losing the way. (*b*) since *x* yǎ yi shĕkarạ
ɗarĭ dạ ginǎ̆wā it has been built 100
years. shĕkarạ ta gōmạ dạ yịnsạ the

10th year since it was done. **shēkarạrsạ 20 dạ yiŋ aurē** it was 20 years since he had married. **zạmāninsạ yanā dạ shēkarạ 20 dạ sạrautạ, sǎi** . . . when he had ruled 20 years, then . . . **yạu shēkarạr Sābam Birnī dạ kafāwā, yạu shēkarạ 88** it is now 88 years since the foundation of S.B. town. **iŋ aŋ kwānā bīyū dạ haifūwạr, sǎi ạ yī** it must be done two days after she gives birth (*cf.* **18** *below*). (*c*) than *x* (i) **gāra dōkị dạ jạkī** a horse is better than a donkey. **gwạmmạ jīyạ dạ yạu** yesterday was better than to-day. **nā fi sạntạ dạ Kạnde** I liked her better than Kande. **mum fi jị anā ambatan jīrāgyan samạ dạ na rūwā** we hear more mention of aeroplanes than of ships (*cf.* **19** *below*). (ii) **dạ bābụ wāwā** *Vd.* **wāwā 1***b*. (iii) **dạ sābaŋ ginị** *Vd.* **yạbē 2***b*. (iv) **dạ tsịrārạ** *Vd.* **tsịrārạ 1***b*. (v) *Vd.* **19** *below*. (vi) **dạ batạn rịgā** *Vd.* **batạ 2***b*. (*d*) *Sk.* from *x* **yā fịta dạ Sīfāwạ zūwạ Kano** he set out from S. for Kano. (8) (*preceding v.n.*) as soon as *x* (*a*) **dạ jinsạ sǎi ya yi fushī** on hearing it he became angry. **dạ shịgā tasạ sǎi** . . . as soon as he entered, then . . . **dạ ajịyẹ kāyā, sǎi ya gan sụ** as soon as he had put down his load he caught sight of them. (*b*) **dạ ganiŋ kūrā an san tā ci ạkwīyạ** appearance is an index to character. (9) (*elliptically used* M.G. 54*c*) *x* **muŋ gaisạ dạ shī** he and I passed the time of day. **muŋ gānạ dạ Daudạ** David and I had a chat. **mụ tạfi dạ kai** let's go together ! **sunā tạfịyạ dạ kạrē** the dog and he (jackal) were travelling together. **zạn rabạ kū, dạ mātarkạ** I'll divorce you from your wife. **n nā sạm mụ yi zịnā dạ kē** I want to commit adultery with you.

(10) who, which (*the preceding noun usually takes genitival form* (*but cf.* **10***b below*) *and final syllable, if high, takes falling tone, cf.* **wạndạ**) (*a*) (i) (*in nominative*) **dōkịn dạ ya zō** = **dōkịn naŋ dạ ya zō** the horse which came. **mātad dạ bā tạ zūwạ** the woman who is not coming (*cf.* M.G. 133*b*. i). (ii) (*in accusative*) **mụtumịn dạ**

mukạ ganī the person whom we saw. (*iii*) (*plus preposition*) **mụtumịn dạ mukẹ zūwạ dạgạ wurinsạ** the person from whose house we are coming. **wuḳad dạ na kashẹ shi dạ ita** the knife with which I killed him (*cf.* **11** *below*). **mụtānạn dạ akạ yi musụ rạunī** the persons on whom wounds were inflicted. **mụtumịn dạ kukạ ga mạganạssạ tā fi azancī** he whose words seem to you the wisest. (*b*) (*sometimes the noun retains its original form before* **dạ,** *this, however, being the rule when* **dạ** *refers not to the previous word, but to a sentence*) *x* **nā gōdẹ wạ Allā dạ ya nụfā sukạ zō** I thank God who destined them to come. **dōkị dạ ya mutụ** the horse which died. **hawan dawākī, dạ bạ zại yiwu ba** mounting horses, a thing which is impossible. (*c*) (*Sk.*) **ạbin dạ nag ganī** = **ạbịn dạ na ganī** what I saw. **ạbịn dạ yag ganī** = **ạbịn dạ ya ganī** what he saw. **ạbịn dạ tag ganī** = **ạbịn dạ ta ganī** what she saw. **ạbịn dạ mug ganī** = **ạbịn dạ mukạ ganī** what we saw. **ạbịn dạ ag ganī** = **ạbịn dạ akạ ganī** what one saw, *etc.* (*similarly for words beginning in other consonants x* **ạbịn dạ naḍ ḍaukạ**).

(11) (*cf.* **wạndạ 3**) (*a*) wherein *x* **gạrịn dạ akạ sōkē shi ya mutụ** the town wherein he was stabbed and died. **kịndạn dạ yakẹ tārạ gārī** the basket in which he keeps flour. (*b*) wherefore *x* **sun cikạ ụmụrnịn dạ akạ ạikē sụ** they fulfilled the command on account of which they had been sent. **dạlīlị kẹ naŋ dạ akạ yī** *that* is why it was done. (*c*) whereto *x* **turkyạn dạ akạ ḍaurẹ dōkịnsạ** the peg to which his horse was tethered. **ḳasạd dạ sukạ kōmạ** the country to where they went. **gạrịn dạ akạ ạikē shi** the town whither he was sent. **bạ sụ sāmi ạbịn dạ sukẹ bārā ba** they did not get what they were aiming at. (*d*) whence *x* **dạgạ ḳauyukạn dạ sukẹ zūwạ** in the villages whence they come (*Vd.* **dạgạ 1***a*.iii). (*e*) whereof *x* **Sarākunạn dạ mukạ bā kụ lạbārị** the Emirs of whom we gave you news. **mụtumịn dạ akẹ tsōrō** a man of whom one is afraid. (12) whereby *x* **bā**

ni dạ ƙarfin dạ zạn ɗaukē shi I have not
enough strength to lift it (*cf.* indạ 2*a*).
(13) there is, are, was, were *x* (*a*) dạ
takạrdā? is there any paper? i, dạ
ita (= dạ ạkwai) yes, there is some
(paper) (= ạkwai). (*b*) *x* kō sū suŋ
ƙarai = kō dạ sū suŋ ƙarai even they
lost heart. bạ mu sā dạ sū (= bạ mu
sā su) cikin lissāfi ba we've not included them in the total. rubūta dạ nī
cikim masōyaŋkạ include me also
among your wellwishers! (*c*) (dạ *is
sometimes omitted*) *x* ạ wani wurī, mil
ɗạrī tsạkāninsu dạ mū in some places
there are 100 miles between them and
us. (*d*) dạ rānar ƙin dillancị Vd.
rānā 7*a*. (*e*) in dạ ạbiŋkạ Vd. ạbu 2*h*.
(*f*) tun dạ while there still is Vd. tun
3*a*.iv, v.
(14) (*a*) when (*past sense*, M.G. 181)
x dạ mukạ gạbācē su, sǎi sukạ gudu =
dạ mukạ gạbācē su, sǎi dạ sukạ gudu
when we approached them they fled (*cf.*
sǎi dạ *under* sǎi H, J). (*b*) when (*future
sense*, M.G. 186) *x* dạ sun zō, sǎi n tạfi
kạsūwā when they come, I'll go to
market (*Vd.* in 1). (*c*) (*habitual sense*)
x dạ yārọ yā yi shẹkarạ gōmạ, ạ gamạ
shi cikin jạma'ạr sạmārī when a boy
reaches the age of ten, it is advisable
to put him among young men.
(15) (*a*) because *x* dạ bā sā iyāwā,
su ƙyālẹ seeing that they are not up to
it, let them leave the matter! dạ yakẹ
kanā naŋ in view of the fact that you're
available. lạifinsạ nē dạ yā bar shi yạ
tạfi it is his fault for allowing him to go.
(*b*) it is because *x* ạbin dạ ya sā akạ
yaudạrē shi ɗayā nē, dạ shī yā ɗaukạ
kōwā dattījọ nē kamansạ what led him
astray was one thing — it was because
he thought all to be men of honour
like himself. dạ sun tāsạ bạ ạ kōyạ
musu kōmē ba sǎi muguntạ it is due
to the fact that they grew up with no
training but the incitement to evil.
(16) (*a*) with the result that *x* mẹ
na yi dạ zā ạ rabạ ni dạ mātātạ what
have I done that I should be separated
from my wife? wā ya tạmbạyē shi dạ
ya sā bāƙinsạ nobody inquired of him
so why should he have put in his word?

kā maishē mu ƙarūwại nẹ? dạ zā kạ
zō manạ dạ darē hạkạ? do you take
us for whores that you come thus at
night? (*b*) that *x* (i) nā shiryạ dạ zạn ci
ạbincī ạ wani gidā I've arranged to dine
out. nā yi māmāki dạ bu ku tạfi ba
I'm surprised that you did not go.
yā yi azzikī dạ bạ ạ kāmạ shi ba he
was lucky not to have been arrested.
nā gōdẹ muku dạ kukạ kashẹ kūrā I'm
grateful that you killed the hyena.
bā shī nẹ ɓarkō ba dạ ya yī it is not
the first time that he has done it. (ii)
Vd. dạlīli 1*b*.
(17) dạ . . . dạ whether or not *x* dạ
kā yī, dạ kā barị ōhō = dạ kā yī, dạ
kadạ kạ yī, ōhō I don't care whether
you do it or not (*cf.* ūwā 1*e*).
(18) *conj.* since (*cf.* 7*b above*) *x* yạu
shẹkarạ hạmsiŋ kẹ naŋ dạ ya zō it is
50 years since he came. rạbammu
(= rạba) dạ mu jē caŋ, kwānā ɗayā
it is one day since we went there.
(19) *conj.* than that (*cf.* 7*c above*) *x*
(*a*) sum fi sō su zaunạ dạ su kōmạ
wurinsạ they prefer remaining where
they are rather than to go to him.
yā fi ạrahā ạ sạyē shi nạŋ dạ ạ tạfi
Kano it is cheaper to buy it here than
to go to Kano. (*b*) dạ bābu wāwā,
gwạmmạ dạ wāwā half a loaf is better
than no bread. (*c*) dạ n ci dādī n yi
wạhalạ, gāra n ci marạd dādī, ạ hụcè
murder will out. (*d*) dạ dūban rēni,
gāra gābā tạ tsayạ (*said by* marōƙī)
rather enmity than being scorned!
(*e*) dạ kạ ci ạbim mai bāƙī gāra kạ ci
na ƙazāmī if you give charity, don't
pretend you gave more than you did.
(*f*) dạ ạ ƙwācẹ yārọ rịgā Vd. rịgā 1*t*.
(*g*) Vd. 7*c above*.
(20) *cf.* bāyạn dạ; kō dạ (*under* kō 6);
lōkạcin dạ.
B. (dā) *adv.* (1) (*a*) dā = ạ dā =
zāmạnin dā = cikin zāmạnin dā formerly, of old. (*b*) dā mā, tun tuni long,
long ago. (*c*) dā mā, yāyạ lāfīyạr kūrā,
ballē tạ yi haukā things were bad
enough before, so what about now!
(*cf.* 2*a*.ii *below*, dā 5*a*.ii). (2) in the first
place, originally (*a*) (*used in first clause*)
(i) dā zā tạ cẹ masạ . . . sǎi ūwā tatạ

ta hanạ ta her first instinct was to say to him that . . . but her mother prevented her. dạ̄, ạbụ kạmar wạ̄sā har ya zamā aminci̱ na gạskīyā what started as a joke turned into real friendship. dạ̄, yạu, zā ạ yi bi̱kī the original intention was to hold the feast to-day. (ii) dạ̄ mā it is well known that x dạ̄ mā, tūbạlin zālunci̱ bā yạ̄ gini̱m mulki̱ it is a universal truth that rule founded on oppression cannot succeed. dạ̄ mā, sǎi an shā wụyā, a kạn tunạ Allạ̄ it's always the case that one only remembers God when in trouble. (iii) dạ̄ mā (introduces proverb) dạ̄ mā an cẹ̄ " fāshi̱ 6ạrnar aiki̱ " it is a trusty proverb which says " don't put off till to-morrow what you can do to-day ! ". (b) (used in second clause) (i) already (with kạ̄fi̱n in first clause) x kạ̄fi̱n sụ isō, dạ̄ mā aŋ aikō dạ mạnzaŋ the messenger had been already dispatched before they even arrived. kạ̄fi̱ŋ kạ fārạ shaŋ ạlwāshī, dạ̄ mā yā kạmātạ kạ . . . before boasting, you should first . . . (ii) originally x im bạ̄ rashi̱ŋ haŋkạlī ba, dạ̄ mā mẹ̄ zại sạ̄ yạ̄ yi hakạ but for his lack of sense, how could he have acted so in the first place ? (c) Vd. 1b, c above. (3) just now x dạ̄ ạbi̱n dạ nakẹ̄ shiri̱ ŋ gayạ mukụ kẹ̄ naŋ that's what I was on the point of saying. (4) then (after sǎi " only when ") x sǎi an shā fāmā dạ shī, dạ̄ yạ fi̱ta it cannot be got outside without great exertion. sǎi dạ akạ shā fāmā dạ shī, dạ̄ ya fi̱ta it was only got outside after much exertion (M.G. 181d). (5) f. Arabic letter " d " (=dạl).

C. (dạ̄) (1) if (past unrealized condition) (a) (i) dạ̄ an tạmbạyē ni̱, dạ̄ nā yạrdā (or second clause dạ̄ nạ̄ yạrdā or sǎi ṇ yạrdā etc. Vd. M.G. 187a) had I been asked, I'd have agreed. dạ̄ an tạmbạyē ni̱, dạ̄ ban yạrdā ba (or 2nd clause dạ̄ bạ nạ̄ yạrdā ba) had I been asked, I wouldn't have agreed. dạ̄ mun sani̱ kanạ̄ naŋ, dạ̄ bạ mụ jē ba had we known you were there, we shouldn't have gone (cf. kō 8c). (ii) dạ̄ kụnnē yā jī, dạ̄ ji̱kī yā tsīrā forewarned is forearmed. (iiа) dạ̄ kā ganī Vd.

dạ̄kārẹ. (iii) (in dạ̄ can also be used before 1st clause) in dạ̄ 'yaŋ gādi̱ nē na sōsǎi, dạ̄ suŋ kāmạ 6ạrạ̄yi̱n naŋ had they been police worth the name, they'd have caught those thieves. (iv) (negative 1st clause) dạ̄ ban yi ba, dạ̄ nā tafō dạ saurī hạkạ ? had I not done it, is it likely I'd have come so soon ? (= in 8). (b) (i) Allạ̄ yạ̄ tsarẹ mu dạ̄ " dạ̄ nā sani̱ " = Kt. " dạ̄ nā sani̱ " dōrō cẹ̄ may we never have to indulge in vain regrets ! ; look before you leap ! ; it's no good crying over spilt milk (= ƙyēyạ 3). (ii) wandạ ya hau dōki̱n " dạ̄ nā sani̱ ", yạ̄ wạhalạ regrets after the event are useless. (iii) Vd. dạ̄ kạ cẹ̄. (c) (sometimes 1st clause is omitted) gạ̄ ạbi̱n dạ nakẹ̄ fạɗạ makạ ; dạ̄ yạnzu mun ji lạ̄bāri̱ sarai I wish you'd listened to me : (if you had), by now we'd know fully. (d) (sometimes both dạ̄ or 1st dạ̄ is omitted) bại saŋ ki̱ ba, zại bā ni̱ tụrạ̄rẹ̄ ŋ kāwō mi̱ki̱ ? if he did not know you, would he have sent me to you with perfume ? (dạ̄ omitted before both clauses). kanạ̄ naŋ zạune, sǎi kạ ga jạ̄kai sun tafō had you been there, you'd have seen the donkeys coming (dạ̄ omitted before first clause). (2) if (remote possibility) (a) dạ̄ ạ tạmbạyē ni̱, dạ̄ nạ̄ yạrdā (or 2nd clause dạ̄ nā yạrdā, etc., Mod. Gr., 188) were I to be asked, I'd agree. dạ̄ (or in dạ̄) zạn sāmụ, sǎi ṃ bīyā if I were to get it, I'd pay. (b) dạ̄ dūnīyạ dạ gạskīyā Vd. dūnīyạ 2h. (3) otherwise x saurā kạɗaŋ, dạ̄ aŋ kāmạ shi he was within an ace of being caught. sā6ạ̄wā sukạ yi, dạ̄ suŋ gạmu dạ shī they took different routes, otherwise they'd have met. kā kụskurạ yạu, dạ̄ kā hạlakạ you had a narrow escape from death to-day. (4) dạ̄ bạ̄ dōmin . . . ba had it not been for the fact that x dạ̄ bạ̄ dōmi̱ŋ gwạnī nẹ̄ ba, dạ̄ bạm bā shi aiki̱ ba but for his skill, I'd not've given him work. bạ̄ doŋ gwạnī nẹ̄ ba, dạ̄ mun sạllạmē shi̱ it was only owing to his skill that we did not dismiss him. im bạ̄ doŋ hakạ ba, dạ̄ nā yạrdā but for this I'd have agreed (Vd. don 6, dōmin 6, in 7). (5) dạ̄ mā (a) (i) would that x dạ̄ mā nạ̄ yī would that I'd done it ! **dą mā bạn yi ba** would that I had not done it ! (ii) **dą mā nā yĩ, dą nā sāmų** (*epithet of* **dąmunā,** *there being play on words* **dą-mā-nā** *and* **dąmunā** *and the words being put in mouth of a slacker*). (b) **dą mā kạ bā nị sulę bĩyar** might I suggest you give me 5s. for it ? **dą mā 5s.** I respectfully suggest you change your price to 5s. (*cf.* **dā** 1b, c ; 2). (6) *Vd.* **dą dạ gōrāna : dą̃ nā shā, kō 5 ; dą kạ cē.**

ɗa A. (**ɗā**) m. (f. **'yā** = Sk., Kt. **ɗĩyā**) pl. **'yā'yā** = **'yā'yąyē** = Sk., Kt. **ɗĩyā** (1) (a) **ɗā** = **ɗā namijị** son. (b) **kyạn ∼ yạ gāji ụbansạ** a son should emulate his father's virtues. (c) **ɗam bạbbaŋ gidā** the son of a rich family. (d) **ɗā ną ganĩ** Vd. **tĩlạs 1e.** (e) **kązā mại 'yā'yā** Vd. **shirwạ 1d.** (f) **ɗā dạ haƙōrĩ** Vd. **ɗĩyaŋ 2.** (g) **fushĩ bā yą̃ haifụ̃war ∼** Vd. **fushĩ 1a.ii.** (h) **∼ kwạnce** Vd. **guzumā 4.** (2) freeman (not slave) (a) **yaną ∼** he is a freeman. (b) **'yā'yā na Fạransai** the Free French. (c) **yā cikạ ∼** he's a fine fellow. (d) **sun cikạ 'yā'yā** they're real men. (e) **Mālạm, kā ji aikịn 'yā'yā** what prowess ! (f) **nā bar shị ∼** (i) I manumitted him (slave), *cf.* **'yancị.** (ii) I remitted his debt to me. (iii) I dismissed him. (3) honest man x (a) **∼ bā yą̃ mạganạ bĩyū** an honest man is not two-faced. (b) **tĩlạshin ɗā** Vd. **tĩlạshĩ.** (c) **ɗā dạgạ cikĩ** Vd. **zạllim.** (d) Vd. **mūgụn ɗā.** (4) **ɗā** = **ɗan rinị** cassava or potato blackened in mud and lines cut in it by girls for play. (5) (a) upper grinding-stone (= **marēdĩ 2**), *cf.* **dūtsę 7, magạntsạrĩ 2b.** (b) **dūtsạn naŋ ɗansạ yā fịta** = **ɗansạ yā ficę** this lower-grindingstone is worn out. (6) (a) **ɗā** = **ɗaŋ itącē** pl. **'yā'yā** = **'yā'yaŋ itącē** fruit. **gyạɗā tā yi ɗā** the groundnuts have fruited. **lęmū yā yi ɗā** = **yā yi 'yā'yā** the lime-tree fruited. **ɗaŋ giginyạ** fruit of deleb. **ɗaŋ gōrubạ** fruit of dum-palm (*cf.* **ƙwallō**). (b) **∼ na cikĩ** son ; kernel, pip x **ɗan lęmū na cikĩ** pl. **'yā'yan lęmū na cikĩ** lime-pip *cf.* **ƙwallō**). (7) *for diminutives* Vd. **ɗan.** (8) Vd. **ɗan, 'yā'yā, ɗaŋubā, ɗaŋũwā, 'yarũwā, 'yā.** (8) = **tạɓạ kunnē.**

ɗā'ạ Ar. f. **yā san ∼** = **yaną dạ ∼** he's well bred. **yārọ (yārinyạ) mại ∼** boy (girl) observing proper etiquette (= **ladạbĩ 2** = **yạkạnā 2** = **kĩmạ 2c**), *cf.* **afanạ 2.**

dạ'ạwā Ar. f. (1) one's case legally x **mun ji ∼ tasạ** ; **yạnzu, mụ ji tākạ** we've heard his side of the case, let's hear yours ! **mại dạ dạ'ạwarkạ** plead your case ! (= **mai dạ 2a.iii**). **nā gyārạ masạ ∼ tasạ** I showed him how to set out his case to best advantage. **tā amsạ ∼ tasạ** she admitted the truth of his case. (2) baseless claim x **yaną dạ'ạwar harbị** he pretends he can shoot, boasts about his shooting. **kuɗinsạ ∼ nę** his wealth's a myth (= **rĩyạ 3**), *cf.* **kākalē.** (3) **yā taŋkạ ∼** he gave a party, etc. (= **ạljạmā 1,** q.v.).

dab (1) close up to x (a) **gidansạ yaną̃ dab dạ hanyạ** his compound is close to the road. **dab dạ kōgĩ** close up to the river. (b) **∼ dạ ∼ sukę** they're close together. (2) **gạjērē nę ∼ dạ ƙasạ** it is of low stature.

dabạ f. (1) Vd. **būshĩyā 4.** (2) collecting by hunters at rendezvous. (3) surrounding of bush by spearmen and sitting in trees awaiting game. (4) collecting by women to prepare indigo (**shūnĩ**).

daɓa A. (**daɓạ**) (1) Vb. 1A. (a) **tā ∼ ɗākị** she hardened earth floor by beating (Vd. **dạɓē**). (b) (*with dative*) applied profusely x **tā ∼ kạtạmbirị** she plastered her face with black cosmetic. **an ∼ wạ ją̃kĩ kāyā** donkey's heavily laden. **an ∼ masạ tsạ̃dā** its price is extortionate. **an ∼ hatsĩ ạ gōnạr bana** the farm has a fine corn-crop this year. (c) **an ∼ masạ mārị** he's been well slapped. **an ∼ masạ būlālạ** he's been well whipped. **an ∼ masạ kibĩyạ** he's received deep arrow-wound. **yā ∼ musụ wuƙā** he stabbed them deeply. (d) **∼ bāshị kạm bāshị** to pile debt on debt. **∼ laifĩ kạn laifĩ** to commit one crime on top of another. (e) **yā ∼ ạ ƙas** he acted without provocation. (f) *cf.* **dafkạ.** (2) Vb. 3A journeyed on and on x **tun dạ ạlfijir ya hūdō mukạ daɓō** we've been plodding along since dawn.

B. (dāɓą) f. Lesbianism without artificial penis (cf. mādigō).

dāɓą Vb. 1A Ar. printed (= bugą 1b).

dąba'ą f. Ar. doubled leaf of paper (= tsąbaką = ƙursą), cf. tūshę 5.

dą̄ɓāɓą = daɓa-daɓa x sum ﬁtō ~ = sun yi ~ they (pustules, ants, etc.) appeared in dense mass.

dąbagi̱ Sk. m. (pl. dąbuggą) hill.

dąbāgirā f. flowers and leaves of young desert-date (adūwą).

dabaibąicē Kt. = dabaibąyē.

dabaibaya A. (dabaibąyā) Vb. 1D. (1) an ~ igīyą ą dōki̱ horse's forefeet have been hobbled (Vd. tąrnaƙi̱). (2) tangled T. up.

B. (dabaibąyą) Vd. dąbaibąyī 2.

dabaibąyē (1) Vb. 1D. (a) an ~ dōki̱ = dabaibąyā 1. (b) yā ~ ni he wasted my time. (c) tangled T. (d) entangled (P.'s feet, etc.). (2) Vb. 3A. (a) is (was) tangled. (b) is (was) tongue-tied. (c) spoke or behaved like a pagan (= gwārąncē).

dąbaibąyī m. (1) hobbling forefeet of horse, etc. x an yi wą dōki̱ ~ (Vd. dabaibąyā). (2) dąbaibąyī m. (pl. dabaibaya = dąbaibąyū = Kt. dabaibwīyą). (a) rope for hobbling forefeet of horse, etc. (b) Vd. ąlkāmurą. (3) ƙulli̱n ~ slight umbilical hernia (cf. mąjaƙwar).

daɓakuru A. (daɓą̄kurų = dąɓą̄kurau) m., f. (sg., pl.) ugly P.

B. (dąɓą̄kurų) used in ~ cąskurų what poorly done work !

dą̄ɓą̄lō m., f. (sg., pl.). (1) witless P. (2) slatternly, unpleasant looking P.

dąbaŋ (1) (a) different x wurī na dąbaŋ a different place. ką̄wō wani ~ bring a different one ! sun zamā dąbaŋ dąban nę̄ they differ entirely. ~ dą wannąŋ different from this one. sha'ąninsų ~, nāmų ~ our circumstances differ from theirs. (b) wata ~, māląmī dą kudi̱ŋ kidą how incongruous they are with one another ! (2) separate x suną̄ hąɗe, bą̄ dąbaŋ dąbam ba they're joined, not separate. (3) ta są̄ ~ Vd. są̄ A2, 1e.

daɓąnā Vb. 1C Sk. = daɓą 1b, d.

dąbanniyā f. = dąbę̄nīyā.

dąɓanniyā f. constant going to and fro.

dąɓanǫ m. a sweet juice in dǭrawą blossom (= darɓā).

dąbanyą f. plaited-mat for outside apex of conical thatch.

dąbārą f. (pl. dąbąrū = dabąrbarī = dabārōrī = dąbąrce-dąbąrcē) Ar. (1) plan x (a) yā yi ~ he made a plan. (b) yā yi mini̱ ~ (i) he made a plan for me. (ii) he planned to get the better of me. (bb) wąndą ya ﬁ ką ~ Vd. sǭ 1e. (c) yā ƙullą musų ~ he plotted against them. (d) ~ tasų, sǎi aiki̱ takę̄ yi̱ sǫsǎi their plan is most successful. (e) sun dąuki̱ dąbārąŋ nąŋ they adopted this plan. (f) wannąŋ ~ tā ﬁta this plan succeeded. (g) wannąŋ ~ bą tą fisshē shi̱ ba this plan did not effect his purpose. (2) i̱nā ~ what's to be done ? i̱nā dąbārąmmų dą sų what's our best way of coping with them ? bą̄ ni dą ~ I'm at my wits' ends. sǎi yą sąmi dąbārąr kąnsą he must make his own arrangements ! (3) ~ bā tą̄ dąurą kāyā sǎi dą igīyą wild-cat schemes benefit nobody. (5) Vd. dōki̱ 1s.

dąɓąrɓąr x yaną̄ dą kaurī ~ it's very solid.

dabarbarī Vd. dąbārą.

dąɓarɓashī = daɓarɓas adj. m. (f. dąɓarɓąsā = daɓarɓąs) pl. dąɓąrɓąsai = daɓas-daɓas squat x yārinyą cē dąɓarɓąsā she's a squat girl (Vd. daɓas).

dabąrcē Vb. 1C. (1) bewitched (= mā̄gąncē q.v.). (2) cheated P.

dąbąrce-dąbąrcē Vd. dąbārą.

dabar-dabar A. (dabar-dąbąr). (1) m. (a) altercation. (b) sun yi ~ they're hostilely facing each other (cf. dābur). (2) adv. sun tāshi̱ ~ they stood up from respect for superior (not applied to one person standing up).

B. (dąbar-dabar) m. yaną̄ ~ he's floundering about in the work (= bądąm-badam).

dąɓarō m. moist, black, loamy soil (epithet is ~ tāki̱ŋ Allą̄).

dabārōrī Vd. dąbārą.

dabą̄rtā Vb. 1C mų ~, mų ganī let's see what we can devise ! (cf. dąbārą). bā yą̄ dąbąrtūwā (a) nothing can be devised for it. (*b*) he's not one who'll accept advice.

daɓas = dạɓạs (1) *m.* squatness *x* **yārinyạ cē ~ dạ ita** she's a squat girl (*pl.* **'yam mātā nē daɓas-daɓas dạ sū**). (2) *adv.* **yā zaunạ ~** he (horseman, pot, etc.) sits (sat) firmly (*pl.* **sun zaunạ daɓas-daɓas**), *cf.* **lage-lage 2, tạkwạs 1, dạɓarɓạshī, dafa'ạŋ, dạgōgō**.

daɓasɓas = daɓas.

daɓas-daɓas *Vd.* **daɓas, dạɓarɓạshī**.

dạɓāshirī *adj. m.* (*f.* **dạɓāshirā**) *pl.* **dạɓāshịrai** squat P.

dabạyē *Vb. Kt.* = **dabaibạyē**.

dạɓāzạ *f.* (1) coarse-ground flour. (2) coarse grinding (*cf.* **fantsạrā, dạŋgartsọ, lilis**).

dabbạ *Ar. f.* (*but is masculine if referring to previously mentioned masculine as in* **1c** *below*) *pl.* **dabbōbī = daɓōbī**. (1) any animal, reptile, insect, fish *x* (*a*) **dabbạr gidā** domestic animal. (*b*) **dabbạr jējị** wild animal. (*c*) **dạ ganim macījī, ya ji tsọran bạbban dabbạn naŋ** on seeing the snake, he felt afraid of that big creature. (2) (*collective*) cattle, animals, etc., **garkyạn dạ ~ ta gamẹ** a herd where the cattle of two owners are amalgamated. (3) **mutānē akē kīwọ, bạ ~ ba** though animal can be left alone to graze, be on your guard against men! (4) **kạn dabbōbī** *Vd.* **afạlalụ**. (5) **dabbạr Allạ** *Vd.* **kūrā 1a**. (6) **~ nạ gạ mại hawaŋ kūrā** *Vd.* **kūrā 35**.

dabbarẹ-dabbarẹ *adj. m., f.* (*sg., pl.*) spotted (*cf.* **rōdị-rōdị**).

dabbōbī *Vd.* **dabbạ**.

dạbdalạ *f.* (*pl.* **dabdalōlī**). (1) long rope on neck of grazing colt for tethering (*cf.* **tālālā**). (2) **nā sạyē shị tun yanạ ~ I** bought it as a colt. (3) going repeatedly to and fro (= **kạiwā dạ kāwọwā**).

dab darē *Kt.* **yanạ aikị tun sāfē har ~ he** works from morn till night.

daɓe A. (**dạɓē**) *m.* (1) (*a*) **an yi wạ dākị ~** floor of house was beaten to harden it (*cf.* **daddạlē, duɓạkē**). (*b*) beaten-floor (= *Sk.* **faɓọ 3**). (2) being occupied as in **1** *x* **tanạ ~** she's beating the floor. (3) (*secondary v.n. of* **daɓẹ**) *x* **tanạ dạɓan d̃ākị = tanạ daɓẹ d̃āki** she is beating

floor, etc. (4) **~ kaurin d̃ākị** what a blockhead! (5) **dạɓansạ yā ji mākubạ** what deserved good luck! (6) **ūwar ~** *f.* motor road-roller (= **jirgī 7a**). (7) **zamaŋ kisạŋ ~** *m.* overstaying one's welcome (*Vd.* **kisạ 3**). (8) **tạshi ƙasạ, kọma dạɓē** the two are identical. (9) **tsakūwạ d̃ayā bā tạ ~** *Vd.* **tsakūwạ**. (10) **kọkawạ dạ dạɓē** *Vd.* **tirịjī**. (11) **zaŋgwạn dạɓē** *Vd.* **zạŋgọ 4**. (12) *Vd.* **dạɓaŋ kufai ; dạŋgwạrạ ~**.
     B. (**daɓẹ**) *Vb.* 1A = **daɓạ 1a**.

dạɓēnīyā *f.* **aikị yā yi minị ~** the work's beyond me.

dạɓaŋ kufai *m.* fruitless occupation (*d.f.* **dạɓē**).

dạɓgai *Vd.* **dạbgī**.

dabgajā *f.* (1) **~ mūgụŋ gōrọ** *epithet of* damaged kolanuts. (2) *epithet of* messy T. *x* **Audụ ~ dạ shī** how messy Audu's mouth is! **wannạŋ tsụmmā ~** what a foul rag!

dạbgē *m.* (1) broth in which meat's been boiled up. (2) **shạn ~** *m.* luxurious living.

dạbgī *m.* (*pl.* **dạbgai**). (1) ant-eater (= *Sk.* **dābụgī**). (2) industrious P.

dabị *m.* (1) grass-shelter (= **rụmfā**). (2) hunter's roofed-shelter. (3) cleared space before house-door or compound of chief, for people to gather in (*cf.* **fạfạrandạ 2, fagē 1b**). (4) tethering-place (**turkẹ**) for colt when back from grazing.

dāɓị *m.* = **dāɓạ**.

dāɓị = daɓ'ị *Ar. m.* act of printing.

dạbī'ạ = tsạbī'ạ.

dabilbila A. (**dạ̄bilbilā**) *f.* = **dạbdalạ 3**.
     B. (**dạ̄bilbịlā**) *Vb.* 1D. (1) trampled up ground. (2) messed up (work, etc.).

dạ̄bilbịlē *Vb.* 3A. (1) (place) is trampled up. (2) **aikị yā ~** work has been messed up.

dạ̄bil-dābil = dạ̄bịlē-dābilē = dạ̄bụl-dābul, *q.v.*

dạ̄bilwā *f.* = **dạbdalạ 3**.

dabīnọ (1) *m.* date ; dates (*cf.* **zạrbā, sịkkī, gọdā, kililī, cī 1c, nōnọ 3, bardē 6**). (2) *m.* (*f.* **dabīnụwā = dabīnịyā**) *pl.* **dạbīnai** date palm. (3) **am fādō dạgạ kạn dabīnọ, an zarcẹ rījịyā** out of the frying-pan into the fire.

dabka = dafka.

dabo A. (dabọ) *m.* (1) (*a*) conjuring (= tsątsubą 1 = sịddabaru). (*b*) 'yā'yan ~ marionettes. (2) (*a*) bā ą̄ ~, bą rịgā " you can't make bricks without straw ". (*b*) rịgar dabąnsą tā kēcę he has been " rumbled ". (3) yārọ yaną̄ ~ the boy's making first efforts at standing erect. (4) taną̄ ƙasą, taną̄ ~ the matter is still undecided. (5) mą̄ ga dabąn tsútsą ą̀ rānā we must devise a plan.
B. (Dābọ) (1) name for 4th son (= Yerọ), *cf.* Dikkọ. (2) name for any Ibịrāhīmu.

dabōbī animals (*Vd.* dabbą).

daɓōsą *f.* squat woman.

dabrą *Kt.* close to = daurą.

ɗabrī *Sk. m.* astringent taste (= barcī 4, *q.v.*).

dabri = dauri.

dabsa A. (dąbsā) *Vb.* 2 (*p.o.* dąbshē, *n.o.* dąbshi) *Kano Village Hausa* collided with.
B. (dabsā) *Kano Village Hausa f.* act of colliding with.

dabshe A. (dabshẹ) *Vb.* grazed ; became grazed (= daujẹ).
B. (dąbshē) *Vd.* dąbsā.

dąbtī *m.* warmed up tūwō (= ɗumąmē).

dabtū *m.* yaną̄ shąn ~ dą shī he's toiling away at it.

Dā̀ɓu *Vd.* bēgwā.

dą̀būbū *Sk. m.* profusion *x* sun yi ~ they're profuse.

dą̀bugą *Sk. Vb.* 2 pestered P. by following him or her about everywhere.

Dą̄ɓu gąjērā *epithet of* porcupine (bēgwā).

dąbuggą *Sk.* hills (*Vd.* dąbagị).

dābugī *Sk. m.* ant-eater (= dąbgī, *q.v.*).

dabulbula = dabilbila.

dą̀bul-dābul = dą̀bulḕ-dābulē *m.* (1) trampling up ground. (2) being in muddled state. (3) badly done task. (4) a dance of blind people.

dā̀bur *m.* (1) yā yi ~ he's ready to pick a quarrel (*cf.* dabar-dąbąr). (2) sōją sun yi ~ soldiers are drawn up on parade or for attack. (3) *Vd.* dābur-dą̀bur.

dā̀ɓurā̀ *f.* = dā̀ɓurī 3.

dā̀ɓurcḕ (1) *Vb.* 1A dumbfounded. (2) *Vb.* 3A is (was) dumbfounded.

dābur-dą̀bur *m.* (1) = dabar-dąbąr. (2) *Vd.* dābur.

dā̀ɓurī *m.* (1) the gums (= dāsąshī). (2) whole of cow's mouth as sold by butchers (*cf.* gąndā). (3) lymphangiectasis of upper lip (= nā̀ɓūwā). (4) dā̀ɓurịn sānīyā horse purslane (*Trianthema monogyna* ; *T. pentandra*).

dā̀būwą = dą̀būwą *f.* the food tūwō dried, broken up and cooked with oil (= tịkirą).

dąbzā *Sk. f. T.* whose goodness has been extracted (= fąŋkō 1, *q.v.*).

dąbzō *Sk. m.* = dąbzā.

dace A. (dācẹ) *Vb.* 3A. (1) (*a*) is (was) fitting *x* yā ~ ką yī you ought to do it. yā ~ dą kai it befits you. sun ~ dą jūnā they suit each other. (*b*) *Vd.* fątḕ-fātḕ 2. (2) nā ~ dą shī I met him unexpectedly.
B. (dą̀cē) *used in* yā yi kāmun ~ he " hit the nail on the head " (= tsiŋkẹ 2*a*.iii).

dācī *m.* bitterness *x* (1) (*a*) yā yi ~ = yaną̄ da ~ it is bitter (*cf.* gancī). (*b*) lą̀bārị mąi ~ unpleasant news. (*c*) yāƙị tā fārą ~ the fortune of war turned in favour of the enemy. (*d*) kōmē ~ *Vd.* kōmē 4*d*.i. (2) yā ji ~ = yā ci ~ = yā shā ~ he laughed jeeringly. (3) yā ji dācim mągąnąr he was upset or vexed by that. (4) gąskīyā ~ gąrētą nobody likes to hear an unpalatable truth. (5) ɗācịn halī = dācin rą̀i unpleasant disposition. (6)Allą̄ yą̀ ɓōyẹ shi ą̀ kọ̀gwan ~ (*said by women to mother of new-born baby*) God preserve the child (ɗācī here = madą̀cī, *q.v.*).

Dą̄dā *Vd.* yą̀yī 6.

daɗa A. (daɗą) (1) *Vb.* 1A (*Ar.* zāda). (*a*) (i) did more *x* ƙarfimmụ yaną̄ ~ rągūwā ą̀ hankąlī, ą̀ hankąlī our strength is gradually decreasing. yā ~ bayyąnā musụ shī he explained it to them more fully. (ii) (*with dative*) gave more of (= ƙārą 1*a*) *x* ką ~ minị nōnọ give me some more milk ! an ~ minị kudī my salary has been increased. an ~ masą sulẹ takwąs his pay of *e.g.* thirty-two shillings has been increased to forty (= ciką 1*e*.iii). (*b*) did again *x* nā ~ ganinsą I saw him again (= ƙáɽạ 2). (c) dạɗu Vb. 3B. (i) became more x ạbịn dạ yạ dạɗu dạ ạbịn dạ ya ɽạgu what increased and what decreased. yā ƙāɽạ dạɗūwā it increased still more. (ii) mun ∼ m., f. bastard (= shēgẹ 1a). (d) yā yi ɗam bạ gọban dáɗạ he did an act he later regretted. (e) Vd. dáɗa-compounds. (f) ∼ daŋgi = dáɗạ dūnīyạ Vd. dạɗǎi 4. (g) dáɗịn dáɗạ̄wā Vd. dáɗị 7. (2) Sk. adv. indeed x yā ji kunyạ ∼ he felt ashamed indeed. ∼ yạnzu now indeed. (b) ∼ kumā sǎi ya tạfi then after that he went away. (c) ∼ fā hakạnan nạ̄ quite so ! (d) ∼ dǎi that's just like you !

B. (dạɗā) Vb. 2 used in Allạ̄ dạɗē mụ dạ lāfīyạ God increase our wellbeing ! kụ dạɗē mụ, mụ dạɗē kụ let us mutually benefit one another ! munạ̄ dạɗar jūnā dạ shāwaɽạ we are profiting by each other's advice.

C. (dāɗā) Sk. f. (secondary v.n. of dāɗẹ) x munạ̄ dāɗarsạ = munạ̄ dāɗẹ shi we're stopping it up.

ɗáɗa A. (dạɗā) used in dạ̄ɗar bạ̄kī f. smacking the lips.

B. (dāɗạ) Vb. 1A. (1) sharpened edge of tool (= wāsạ). (2) yā ∼ ƙaryā he told a " whopping " lie. (3) yā ∼ shi dạ ƙasā (i) he violently threw him down. (ii) it reduced him to desperation. (4) (plus dative) applied T. to T. x yā ∼ wạ dawạ wutā he set fire to the " bush ". yā ∼ kwạllī ạ idọ he applied antimony to his eyes. yā ∼ masạ wuƙā he slashed him. yā ∼ masạ ƙaryā he lied to or against him. yā∼ masạ māɽị he slapped him.

dáɗaɗa A. (dāɗạɗā) Vb. 1C rendered pleasant.

B. (dạ̄ɗaɗạ) Vb. 3B is (was) pleasant.

C. (dāɗạ̄ɗā) pleasant (pl. of dạɗɗāɗā, q.v.).

dạ̄ɗạɗạ nōmā m. useful drizzle during farming season.

dạ dạd darē at night (Vd. darē).

dạɗaɗɗe m. (f. dạɗaɗɗīyā) pl. dạɗạɗɗū ancient.

dạ̄ dạ gọ̄rāna m. the bird, Black-winged stilt (Himanotopus).

dạ̄ɗạ̄hōrō Nor. m. wastrel.

dạɗǎi (1) always x (a) ∼ hakạ halinsạ yakẹ so he always behaves. (b) kōwā ya daɗẹ, yạ̄ ga dạɗai live and learn ! (2) (negatively) never x ∼ bạn saŋ wannạm ba I never got to know of this. (3) (emphatic negative reply) oh, no ! (4) ∼ dūnīyạ = ∼ dáɗạ daŋgi (followed by negative verb) never x ∼ dūnīyạ bạn saŋ wannạm ba = 2.

dáɗạ kyạu m. (1) type of mica for adorning interior of rooms (epithet is ∼, kyạm mazā, kyạm mātā). (2) epithet of lạ'asạr, q.v.

dadala A. (dādạlā) Vb. 1C Sk. = dādạrā.

B. (dādạlạ) Vd. Shạ̄ ∼.

ɗaɗạlī m. an affection of the testicles (= ƙābā 2b).

dādạrā Vb. 1C nā ∼ masạ wuƙā I ran blunt knife over it = gāgạrā (cf. dāɗạrā).

dāɗạrā Vb. 1C = dāɗạ 1, 4 x yā ∼ masạ wuƙā he slashed him (cf. dāɗạrā).

dādāɽẹ m. Filani leather-apron (=dīɗạmī).

dāɗạrē Vb. 1C yā ∼ shi dạ wuƙā he slashed him (= dāɗạrā).

ɗaɗas x an niƙạ shi ∼ it's finely-ground (= lilis).

dāḍạshī Kt. m. the gums (= dāsạshī).

dạ̄ɗạshinā Kt. f. rich gravy (= dạrmạsōsụ̄wā).

ɗaɗau adv. emphasizing heat of sun, good patterning of calabash, sweetness, sufficiency of salt, etc., x rānā tā yi ƙūnā ∼ sun is blazing hot.

daɗāwạ f. type of guineacorn.

dạɗạ zạŋgū m. part of embroidery of gownneck.

dạɗɗāɗā adj. m., f. (pl. dāɗạ̄ɗā) nice.

daddaga A. (dạddāgạ) f. (1) iron-band or pointed ferrule at end of spear-shaft (= dāgạ-dāgạ). (2) tool for removing hair from hides.

B. (daddạgā) Vb. 1C (with dative). (1) tā ∼ wạ tūwō mīyạ = tā daddạgạ tūwō ạ mīyạ she poured too little soup over the tūwō. (2) tā daddạgạ fuɽē ạ haƙọ̄rā she applied tobacco-flowers to her teeth with tapping movement (cf. gōgạ 1b). (3) yā ∼ wạ dōkịnsạ ƙā'imī he spurred his horse on. (4) nā ∼ masạ ạbincī I broke up food for him (toothless P. or colt).

daddage A. (daddạgē) Vb. 1C. (1) poured

out all the small amount of liquid available (*cf.* **daddagā**). (2) = **diddigē**.

B. (**daddagē**) *m. secondary v.n. of* **daddagā** *x* **yanā daddagyan dōki da ƙā'imī** = **yanā daddagā wa dōki ƙā'imī** he's spurring on his horse.

ɗaɗɗaka A. (**ɗaɗɗaka**) *Vb.* 2. (1) drank much of. (2) uprooted. (3) took P. with one against his will.

B. (**ɗaɗɗakā**) *Vb.* 1C. (1) **tā ~** **rūwā** she inverted small **ƙōƙō** calabash on larger one full of water to prevent it spilling (= **burma** 1*a*). (2) (*with dative*) (*a*) **nā ~ masa rūwā** I gave him much water to drink. (*b*) **nā ~ masa bāshi** I lent him large sums. **A yā ɗaɗɗakō wa B bāshi** A (son or agent) involved B (his father or principal) in heavy debts. (*c*) infected with disease *x* **yā ~ mata tunjērē** he infected her with syphilis. (*d*) **yā ~ masa magana** he incited him (= **zuga**). (*e*) **yā ~ mata ciki** he made her (immature young wife or his mistress) pregnant. (*f*) **yā ~ mata baƙin ciki** he grieved her. (*g*) **yā ~ mini karātu** he taught me much.

ɗaɗɗakē *Sk. m.* (*secondary v.n. of* **ɗaɗɗakā** 1) *x* **tanā ɗaɗɗakyan rūwā** = **tanā ɗaɗɗaka rūwā** she's inverting, etc.

daddaƙī *m.* investigation (= **diddigī**, *q.v.*).

daddala *Sk., Kt. f.* = **dabdala**.

daddale *Vb.* 1C. (1) smoothed **furā** by tapping with wet pestle in mortar. (2) settled point at issue. (3) smoothened floor with **madaɓī** after hardening by beating (**daɓē**).

daddali *m.* = **dadali**.

daddara *used in* **bā yā ~** he doesn't mend his ways. **yanā da wuyar ~** he's practically incorrigible.

ɗaɗɗātā (1) *adj. m., f.* (*pl.* **ɗātātā**) bitter. (2) *f.* = **dātanniyā**.

daddauka *Vb.* 2 kept on lifting (*int. from* **dauka**).

daddaunā *adj. m., f.* (*pl.* **daunānā**) greasy with perspiration (*cf.* **daunī**).

daddawā *f.* (1) (*a*) black cakes made from fermented seeds of locust-bean tree (**dōrawa**) used for flavouring soup (*epithet is* **ūwar tūwō**) *Vd.* **miji** 2 ; **raddawā ; kan ƙudā 1, nī da ūwā ;**

kunnē 3 ; **fito** 3. (*b*) **daddawar batso** *similar* cakes made from fermented seeds of hemp (**rama**) or Red sorrel (**yākūwā**), *Vd.* **miji** 2 (*epithet is* ta **batsallē, mai gidā a haƙōrī**). (*c*) **daddawar gurjī** = **daddawar gullī** *similar* cakes from fermented seeds of **gurjī**. (*d*) **daddawar kā tsāme** *similar* cakes from seeds of baobab (**kūka**), *cf.* **kā tsāme**. (*e*) **daddawar kīfī** = **cinōta**. (2) sun yi **daddawā** they've come to blows. (3) **yi mini daddawā** (*said by one woman to another*) give me my corn for grinding bit by bit so that I'll finish sooner than I expect ! (4) **anā ~ da shī** it's a " drug in the market " (*cf.* **māsa** 2). (5) type of girls' game. (6) **daddawā gaya mandā baƙī** the pot is calling the kettle black. (7) **an shā ~ da shī** it gave much trouble. (8) **jirgin ~** slow train (not express). (9) in **dăi ɓērā da sāta, daddawā mā da dōyī** it takes two to make a quarrel ; take the mote out of your own eye ! (10) *Vd.* **bīyan daddawā, lātun**.

daddōfā *Kt. f.* sycophancy ; flattery.

daddōka *f.* Western waterbuck (*Kobus defassa*) = **gwambaza**.

ɗaɗɗōrī *m.* (1) a creeper used in tannery (*Vitis quadrangularis*) = **gēwaya tsāmīyā**. (2) piling things on each other. (3) building with clay not made up into bricks (= **gōgā**).

ɗaɗɗoya A. **daɗɗōya**) *f.* (1) a fragrant herb like Basil (*Ocimum ; Aeolanthus Buettneri*) (= **saraƙūwā** 5 = **kā fi amaryā**). (2) **daddōyar gōnā** = **dad-dōyar fadama** = **daddōyar karē** type of weed (*Hyptis spicigera ; Leucas martinicensis*).

B. (**daddōyā**) *adj. m., f. sg.* stinking (*Vd.* **dōyī**).

daɗe A. (**daɗe**) *Vb.* 3A. (1) remained long *x* (*a*) **yā ~** (i) he is old. (ii) *Vd.* **Amīna** 2. (iii) he has been away a long time, is late in returning. **nā ~ n nā ganinsa** I've been seeing him since long ago. **yā ~ yanā aiki** he's been at work a long time. (*b*) *x* **yā yi zugum, aka ~, kāna ya cē** he reflected, then after a while, he said . . . (*c*) (i) **an ~ anā rūwa, ƙasā nā shanyēwā** let sleeping dogs lie ! (ii) *Vd.* **rūwā** C.24*a*.

(d) **kōwā ya daɗe̞, ya̞ ga da̞ɗǎi** live and learn !　(e) **kōmē ta daɗe̞, haka̞ zā a̞ yi** this'll be done in the end.　**kōmē ta daɗe̞, ma̞ ci nasara̞** in the long run we'll be victorious.　(2) (a) **ra̞ŋkai ~** (for **ra̞ŋka̞ ya̞ ~**) = **Allā̞ shi̞ ~ da̞ ra̞ŋka̞** long life to you !　**ran Sarkī ya̞ daɗe̞** God give you long life, Chief !　(Vd. **jima̞** 5b).　(b) Vd. **na̞'am**.　(3) (a) **ba̞ŋ gan shi̞ tun da̞ daɗe̞wā ba** it is long since I saw him.　**da̞ daɗe̞wā aka̞ sōma̞** it was begun long ago.　**yana̞ aiki̞ tun da̞ daɗe̞wā** he's been at work long.　(b) **ba̞ daɗe̞wā su̞ zō** they'll soon come now.　**naŋ ga̞ba, ba̞ da̞ daɗe̞wā ba, zā mu̞ zō** very soon we'll come.　(4) (a) (i) **kō ba̞ ~ = kul ba̞ ~ = kō ba̞, ~ kō ba̞ jima̞** sooner or later x **kō ba̞ ~ zā a̞ yī** it is bound to be done sooner or later.　(ii) **kō ba̞ ~ mu̞tu̞n nē aja̞linsa̞** if you don't mend your ways, you'll come to a bad end.　(b) **kō ba̞ ~ fa̞karā ita ka̞n zamā za̞būwā** (used in song) sooner or later a prince becomes a king ; from acorns mighty oaks arise.　(5) **yā ~ da̞ ɓata̞** Vd. **fāɗa̞** 4 ; **ta̞ka̞lmī** 4.

　B. (dāɗe̞) (1) Vb. 1A (= **tōshe̞**) stopped up (mouth of jar, etc.) ; cf. **dāɗā**.　(2) Vb. 3A became stopped up x **ba̞sīra̞ tā dāɗe̞** power of judgment became dimmed.　(3) m. rope for tethering two oxen together or for securing calf to dam whilst being milked (cf. **ta̞ŋgē** 2).

ɗaɗe A. (dāɗe̞) (1) Vb. 1A. (a) (sandal) chafed (foot) ; (saddle) chafed bottom (of rider doing **hawam bardē**), etc. (cf. **la̞sau**).　(b) (pepper, etc.) burned (mouth).　(c) **~ ha̞nnū** to flick one's fingers to get rid of T. or in gambling.　(d) **wutā tā ~ dawa̞** fire consumed the " bush ".　(e) **yā ~ shi da̞ māri̞** he slapped him (= **dāɗa̞** 4).　**yā ~ shi da̞ wuƙā** he slashed him (= **dāɗa̞** 4).　(2) Vb. 3A.　(a) is (was) chafed, etc., as in 1a, b (= **zāge̞** 2d).　(b) ran away.

　B. (ɗa̞ɗē) m. **mu̞ ta̞fi gōnā, mu̞ yi ~** let's go and make fire-belt round the farm.

ɗaɗi A. (dāɗī) m. pleasantness x (1) (a) **nā ji ~ = nā shā ~** I feel (felt) happy.

suna̞ zaman ji̞n ~ da̞ jūnā they're on the best of terms (cf. 1c ; 4).　(b) (i) **kōmē dāɗin tūwō, bā ya̞ ƙim ma̞i** nobody (nothing) is perfect.　(ii) **kōmē dāɗin tālālā, saki̞ yā fi̞ shi̞** freedom is better than the lightest bonds.　(c) (i) **yā ji dāɗin** he liked x **ban ji dāɗin ma̞gana̞rka̞ ba** I don't like what you said.　**su̞ ji dāɗin shi̞gā bāƙi̞n ka̞sa̞shē** that they may enjoy entering foreign countries.　**sum fi̞ ji̞n dāɗin jīma̞r jājāyam fātū** they prefer tanning red skins.　**don su̞ ji dāɗim fāɗa̞wā Masa̞r** that they might with ease attack Egypt.　(ii) cf. 1a ; 4.　(iii) **iŋ kā taɓa̞ ji̞kim ma̞ce̞ da̞ nufi̞n ji̞n ~** if you touch a woman to obtain sexual excitation.　(iv) **auran ji̞n ~** Vd. **aurē** 2.　(v) **ya̞u ban ji ~ ba** I feel out of sorts to-day.　(vi) **kā ji dāɗiŋka̞** you're in luck's way !　(vii) **ƙa̞ƙa̞ aka̞ ji da̞ dāɗiŋ Allā** condolences on your bereavement ! (reply is **da̞ gōɗīya̞**).　(d) " **Ba̞ ~** " **tana̞ gidan** " **Nā ƙōshi** " it is the rich man who grumbles at loss, not the poor man.　(e) **ga̞rin ~ ba̞ kusa ba ne̞** one's ambition is always just beyond one's reach.　(f) (i) **ba̞bba da̞ ~ a̞mmā da̞ wu̞yā** a strong servant is useful but eats much food.　(ii) **a̞ banzā, yawa̞ ba̞ dāɗī** Vd. **yawa̞** 8.　(g) **yāƙi̞ yā murɗō mana̞ wajan dāɗin** the war turned in our favour.　(h) **bā ka dāɗin ta̞unā** Vd. **bu̞zūzu̞** 2.　(j) **dāɗīna da̞ shī bā ya̞ nēmam faɗa̞** what I like about him is that he is not quarrelsome.　(k) **ba̞bban rashi̞n dāɗiŋ a̞bi̞n kumā** but the worst of the matter is that . . . (2) (a) **ra̞nsa̞ yā yi masa̞ ~** he felt happy.　(b) **duk lōka̞ci̞n da̞ ra̞mmu̞ ya yi mana̞ ~ sǎi mu̞ ta̞fi** we go whenever we feel inclined.　(c) **da̞ dāɗin zūcīya̞** peacefully.　(3) (a) **mai dāɗim bāƙī ne̞ = dāɗim bāƙī ga̞rēshi̞** (i) he's all things to all men.　(ii) he eggs on people to quarrel.　(b) Vd. **ban ma̞gana̞** 4.　(4) (a) (i) **bā ma̞ ~ da̞ shī** we don't get on with him.　(ii) **shiri̞ yā ƙi dāɗī tsa̞kāninsu̞** they did not get on well with one another (cf. 1a above).　(b) **dūnīya̞ tā yi ~** the world has become peaceful ; everything is fine in the best of all possible

worlds. (5) (a) ci̱n ~ ga̱rēshi̱ (i)
he's used to every luxury. (ii) he leads
a carefree life.   (b) ci̱n ~ sa̱bō my
word, I enjoyed that food ! (said by
P. belching to show his appreciation of
food provided. Host replies ci̱n ~ sa̱bō,
a̱lēwa̱r wuri̱, ba̱rkōna̱ŋ ha̱msi̱ŋ).   (c)
da̱ ṇ ci ~ ṇ yi wa̱hala̱ Vd. da̱ 19c.
(6) (a) Audu̱ yana̱ da̱ ~ = Audu̱ dādin
sha'anī ga̱rēshi̱ = Audu̱ dādi̱ŋ ka̱i
ga̱rēshi̱ Audu is a reasonable P.   (b)
ba̱ shi da̱ ~ don't underrate him, he's
one to be reckoned with ! (Vd. k̲yal 2a).
(7) dādin dōya̱ da̱ ma̱n jā what superficial friendship ! (8) (a) rūwan ~ good
drinking-water. (b) Vd. rūwā B.3. (9)
x bā sa̱ īya̱ sāmu̱ŋ kudī a̱ ta dādī they
cannot get money easily.   (10) zar
dādī = dādī zar happily.   (11) bā a̱
k̲in dādī Vd. wu̱yā 1g.   (12) ji̱kī dū
dādī Vd. bu̱duru̱. (13) dādim bana Vd.
tuṇa̱ 1a.ii.   (14) a̱ far maka̱ ba̱ ~ Vd.
dūtse̱ 1g.
    B. kā maishē ni̱ da̱di̱ŋ kwa̱sā you
take me for a fool (= gārā 4).
    C. (dadi̱) m. (1) increase. (2) extra
amount   " thrown   in "   by seller
(= gyārā). (3) exaggeration x Kanāwā
bā sa̱ k̲aryā sa̱i ~ Kano people don't
lie, they only exaggerate. (4) tuntube̱
dadi̱ŋ gushi̱ŋ ga̱ba, im ba̱ ka̱ ji cīwo̱
ba what an unexpected bargain ! ;
we got off lightly ! (5) dadi̱, ūwar miji̱
tā k̲i ci̱n tūwō ; da̱ sāfē a̱ dafa̱ wa̱
jīkō'ki̱ŋki̱ opprobrious exclamation about
P. who is bastard. (6) ka̱man ~ exclamation by P. withdrawing T. refused
by another when offered. (7) dadin
dadāwā adv. and into the bargain.
(8) dadi̱n daka̱n rakō = daka̱n rakō
foolishly landing oneself in an even
worse plight. (9) ka̱n dadi̱ ; ka̱ŋ ūwar
dadi̱ Vd. rufi̱ 7.
dādi̱ m. (1) an yi wa̱ wuk̲ā ~ the knife-
edge was sharpened (= wāshi̱). (2)
(secondary v.n. of dāda̱ 1) x (a) yana̱
dādi̱ŋ wuk̲ā = yana̱ dāda̱ wuk̲ā he's
sharpening the knife-edge. (b) dādi̱ŋ
wuk̲ā bā ya̱ fad da̱ ga̱ban dōk̲i̱ what
affair is it of mine ! (3) what a slap !
(cf. dāda̱ 4).
da̱īdīdi̱dō used in ~ barcim ma̱i ido̱ dayā

that one-eyed P. has shut his only eye
in sleep !
da̱di̱ŋ kwa̱sā Vd. da̱di̱.
dādirā = dāda̱rā.
dādīya̱ = Sk. da̱dīyā f. cat (= kya̱ŋwā).
dādīyā Sk. f. stopping up mouth of jar,
etc. (cf. dāde̱).
dadu Vd. dada̱ 1c.
dādubū m. (1) surprise attack.   (2) by
surprise going to where one's debtor is
being paid and demanding settlement.
da̱dugu̱mājī m. (1) hopeless rags.   (2)
type of trousers.
da̱duma̱ Vb. 2. (1) clutched with both
hands (cf. k̲āk̲umē).   (2) ~ mūgu̱m
māla̱mī yā yi ya̱ŋkā, yā yi fīda̱ epithet
of rapacious P.
da̱duma̱ Vb. 2 drove away (= kōrā).
da̱dumāsa̱ (1) m., f. (sg., pl.) rapacious
P. or animal. (2) kai ~ you loutish
slacker ! ; you grubby-looking lout !
da̱dume̱ Vb. 1C = da̱duma̱.
dādu̱rā = dāda̱rā.
daf close up to (= dab q.v.).
da̱f x yā hau ~ he mounted (horse)
nimbly.   yā da̱fe̱ ~ he leaped on it
nimbly.
dafa A. (dafa̱) (Ar. tabakha). (1) (a)
cooked. (b) bā a̱ ~ dafi̱ dōmin tu̱ŋkū
don't go on a wild-goose chase ! (c)
a̱bin da̱ rūwan zāfī ya ~ i̱ŋ a̱ŋ ha̱kura̱,
sa̱i rūwan sanyī ya̱ ~ time remedies all
things. (cc) ma̱i hak̲urī shī ya ka̱n ~
dūtse̱ patience wins. (d) sun ce̱ " a̱
dafa̱ ! " = sun ce̱ " a̱ cī ! " = sun ce̱
" a̱ ya̱ŋka̱ " ! = sun ce̱ " a̱ kashe̱ ! "
they said " go to the devil ! "   (e)
a̱bin da̱ aka̱ ~ da̱ wa̱nda aka̱ sōya̱,
duk lābāri̱n wutā suka̱ ji, a̱bin da̱ aka̱
gasa̱ shi, yā ga wutā fīlī da̱ fīlī what
went before was nothing, but now, this
is a titanic battle (for in dafa̱ or sōya̱,
the pot is interposed between food and
fire, whereas in gasa̱, the meat is in
contact with the fire). (2) darkened x
(a) rānā tā ~ shi he's sunburnt. (b)
yā ~ ba̱kinsa̱ he stained his mouth with
kolanut. (c) yā ~ rīgā tasa̱ da̱ shūnī,
tā da̱fu he blued his gown by wearing
it in contact with a dyed one (Vd. ban
shūnī). (3) treated cruelly, tyrannically
x yā ~ māta̱ tasa̱ he ill-treated his

wife (= gasą 1*d*). (4) yā ～ kuɗinsą he spent much on food. (5) *Vd.* dąfā ni. (6) ～ wą jĭkōkiŋki *Vd.* dadį 5. (7) yą ～ ₣ąfō *Vd.* mutum 9*c.* (8) ～ wākē *Vd.* barękatą.

B. (dąfā) *Zar. f.* boiled rice.

C. (dāfą) *Vb.* 1A. (1) pressed on with one's palm *x* (*a*) (i) nā ～ tēbur I pressed on the table.   nā ～ masą tsānį I pressed on the ladder to steady it for him to mount or descend. yā ～ takąrdā he pressed his palm on the paper to conceal it.   yā ～ kunnē he (singer) pressed on his ears to make his voice well heard. (ii) mąkāfo bai saŋ aną ganinsą ba săi an ～ kansą it's no good playing the ostrich ! (*cf.* 4 *below*). (*b*) *x* 'yan dǫkā sun ～ ɓąrāwo the N.A. police drove the thief to bay (= matsą 1*c.*v), *cf.* dąfā 3. (*c*) *Vd.* dāfę. (2) yā ～ he levered himself up from sitting position. (3) iŋ kā kasą masą sulę gōmą, yā ～ (*said by broker*) if you offer my principal ten shillings, he'll probably accept it. (4) yā ～ kansą he went off at full speed (*cf.* 1*a.*ii). (5) kept on doing *x* yā ～ zāginsu he kept on abusing them.   idona yā ～ cīwo my eye is continually sore (= diŋgą). (6) (*a*) Sarkī yā ～ Audu = yā ～ kaŋ Audu the Chief favoured Audu.   sū nę suką ～ bāyansą they were the ones who were his partisans. (*b*) yā sąmu tudun dāfąwā he's found a supporter (*Vd.* tudu 4*b*). (7) yā ～ minį laifī he falsely accused me (= lifką 1*b* = dafą 2).

D. (dąfā) *Vb.* 2 (1) = dāfą 1, 6, *x* nā dąfi tēbur.   nā dāfar masą tsānį. Sarkī yā dąfi Audu. (2) nā dāfar muku Audu I calmed down Audu for you. (3) (*a*) yā dąfi bāyansu he followed hard on their heels.   sun dāfō bāyam mōtąrsą they followed his motor-car closely. (*b*) mun dąfi bāyansu we pressed hard on them (enemy) *cf.* dāfą 1*b*. (*c*) yā dąfi bāyāna he favoured me.

dafa A. (dafą) *Vb.* 1A. (1) yā ～ hannū ą rįgā he (tailor) joined sleeves to body of gown. (2) (*with dative*) accused falsely *x* yā ～ masą sātą he falsely accused him of theft (= dāfą 7 = dafą 1*c*).

B. (dąfā) *f.* refusal of child to be separated from its mother.

C. (dāfą) (1) *Vb.* 1A (*a*) stuck T. on to *x* nā ～ shi jikim baŋgō I stuck it on to the wall. (*b*) stuck T. into (*x* slip of wood into damaged table ; slip of paper into book) *x* nā ～ takąrdā cikin littāfi. (*c*) accused falsely *x* yā ～ masą sātą (= dafą 2). (2) *Vb.* 3A crouched in sitting position.

dafa'aŋ (1) yā zauna ～ it sits firmly (= daɓas 2 *q.v.*). (2) yā zauną ～ he has an established status without a care in world.

dąfāfą (1) profusely (= dąɓāɓą *q.v.*). (2) *Vb.* 3B (*a*) travelled on steadily, *etc.* (= dikāką *q.v.*). (*b*) P. made rude denial.

dafal *Kt. m.* children's gambling game.

dafalē *m.* any white-necked dog.

dąfā ni *m.* (1) unscrupulous debtor. (2) yā shiga rįgad ～ that debtor says " Do your worst, you can't get blood from a stone " (= *Kt.* mį ką cī nį).

dāfārā *f.* (1) a vine (*Vitis pallida*) from whose root a gum is obtained forming an ingredient of the cement lāso (= *Kt.* mąlędūwā), *cf.* lǫdā. (2) yā zubar dą ～ sick P. emitted saliva which is last sign of approaching death.

dafardu *m.* (1) Elk's-horn fern (*Platy-cerium aethiopicum*) which is rubbed on hands to attract opposite sex. (2) yā zamę minį ～ he sticks to me like a limpet.

dafau *m.* (1) (*a*) very poor quality meat cooked and sold in small pieces. (*b*) aną shąn ～ = aną cin ～ people are eating stew of meat *as in* (*a*) plus old straps, pepper, groundnuts, etc. (= ragadādą = ruguduɱą 2 = gandā 2 = kąkuɱā), *cf. Kt.* laŋgaɓū. (2) boiled dried-groundnuts (= dąmunā kusa).

dafdala *Kt.* = dabdalą.

dafe A. (dafę) (1) *Vb.* 1A. (*a*) cooked all of (*cf.* dafą). (*b*) = dafą 2. (*c*) yā dafę kuɗinsą he spent all his money on food (*cf.* dafą 4). (2) *Vb.* 3A (*a*) is (was) damaged by heat *x* gōro yā ～ dą hayāₖī the kolanuts are damaged by smoke.   furā tā ～ the food furā has been overcooked (*but* tūwō yā ∼ the food tūwō is nicely cooked). (*b*) is (was) sunburned. (*c*) bǎkinsǎ yā ∼ his mouth is stained with kola-nut.

B. (dāfẹ) *Vb*. 1A. (1) = dāfạ 1*a*.i ; 1*b* ; 3 ; 4 ; 6*a*. (2) (*a*) yā ∼ ƙyēyạ he fled. (b) *Vd*. sạki nā dāfẹ. (3) kept on doing *x* yā ∼ kạn zāgịnsạ he kept on abusing him (= dāfạ 5). (4) *Vd*. dōkịn dāfẹ.

C. (dǎfē) *m*. (1) yā yi ∼ he pressed his hand on the ground. (2) *Kt*. catching fish by boys (= lālubē *q.v.*).

D. (dǎfe) (1) yanǎ ∼ dạ mū he's favouring us (*cf*. dāfạ 6*a*). (2) 'yad ∼ *f*. woman bọ̄rī devotee on whom another woman relies (= ƙwaryā 1*d*).

ɗafe A. (ɗafẹ) *Vb*. 3A. (1) (*a*) stuck to *x* (i) yā ∼ gạ bangō it stuck to the wall. (ii) ∼ gạ Filǎnī *Vd*. kāɗọ. (iii) yā ∼ minị he stuck to me like a leech (= nānẹ 2*a*). (*b*) is (was) stuck in *x* takạrdā tā ∼ cikin littāfị the slip of paper's stuck into the book. (2) leaped up on to *x* yā ∼ kạn dōkị he leapt on to the horse. yā ∼ dạ rēshẹ he jumped on to branch (*cf*. ɗaf).

B. (ɗafē) *m*. (1) wannạm bǎ ∼ ba nẹ garēnị this is not incumbent on me. *(2) exclamation used in game ɗafal.

dạffā *Vd*. dāfị.

dafi A. (dafị) *m*. (1) poison. (*cf*. gubạ ; maɗas). (2) bā ǎ dafạ dafị dọ̄min tụnkū don't go on wild goose chase ! (3) zạkarạn ganin ∼ *Vd*. zạkarạ 7. (4) ɗọyin ∼ *Vd*. ɗọyī 4. (5) *Vd*. kạd ∼.

B. (dāfị) *m*. (1) patches of leprosy (= ɗimī 2 = tambạrī 4). (2) pattern embroidered in tinsel. (3) pressing on with palm of hand (*cf*. dāfạ). (4) wutā hanạ ∼ = gǎgạrạ ∼ *epithet of* cantankerous P. (*Vd*. wutā 2).

dǎfīfī profusely (= dǎɓāɓạ *q.v.*).

dāfịlā *Sk*. *f*. = dāhịlā.

dafka A. (dafkạ) *Vb*. 1A (*with dative*). (1) applied profusely *x* an ∼ wạ jǎkī kāyā the donkey's heavily laden (= daɓạ 1*b*, *c*, *d*). (2) an ∼ masạ kibīyạ (*a*) he's deeply wounded by arrow. (*b*) he's been heavily over-charged by seller. (*c*) he has been given

venereal disease by woman. (3) yā dạfku dạ kāyā (*a*) he's heavily laden. (*b*) he has heavy calls on his purse.

B. (dạfkā) (1) *Vb*. 2 devoured greedily. (2) Dạfkā gidan jīyǎ *epithet of* stick-in-the-mud P. *or* P. very inapt at task.

dạfkakạ *Vb*. 2. (1) (P. ; misfortune) harassed P. (2) *Vd*. hạsārạ.

dafkau *used in* ∼ dạfkạki maị ạkwai toy-snake.

dafke A. (dafkẹ) *Vb*. 1A ∼ = dafkạ *x* an dafkẹ jǎkī dạ kāyā the donkey is heavily laden.

B. (dạfkē) *m*. (1) joining two loads as one (= gwǎmē). (2) the red type of the trousers called kāmụn ƙafạ (= gạmē 1 *q.v.*).

dafkị *m*. patch put over worn material (= mahọ).

dafkō *m*. the snake called ɗan gidā.

dạfsạssạr *x* yanǎ dạ bǎkī dạfsạssạr he's thick-lipped.

dafshẹ *Vb*. grazed (skin) = daujẹ.

daftạrī *m*. (*pl*. dạftạrai). (1) register ; ledger (= zumāmị = dīwānị). (2) daftạriŋ harājị tax-register. (3) daf-tạriŋ ạlkālī court-records.

dạftī *m*. warmed-up tuwō (= ɗụmạmē).

dạfūwā *f*. (1) (*a*) act of cooking *x* tanǎ ∼ she's cooking the food. (*b*) dākịn ∼ *m*. kitchen = girkị 3 (*cf*. sūyạ). (*c*) yụnwạ māgạnim mugunyạr dạfūwā any port in a storm ! (*d*) bạbbar dạfūwā maị ƙārẹ jārịn yārọ what a well-grown woman ! (*e*) kǎmịn yạ sǎmi na dạfūwā, nī mā nǎ sǎmu na gashị I'll outdo him yet. (2) (*a*) beans cooked with flour. (*b*) boiled macaroni, rice, or guinea-corn. (3) dạfūwar ƙaf = *Sk*. dạfūwar daƙaf = *Sk*. dạfūwar ƙadaf *used in* nāmạn naŋ, an yi masạ ∼ this meat was cooked for so long that all the gravy became richly soaked into it. (4) dạfūwar ƙas roasting of undried ground-nuts, beans, etc., in trench (= kǎmā). (5) dạfūwar rịgā well-dyed blue gown.

daga A. (dạgạ) (1) (*a*) from place (*cf*. 1*b*) *x* (i) ∼ inǎ from where ? ∼ Kano sukạ zō it was from Kano they came. (ii) yā jāwō sụ ∼ duhụ he educated, enlightened them. (iii) dạgạ . . . dạ

from which x bạ sụ gānẹ ～ bậkịn
dạ wannạm muryạ kẹ fịtā ba they did
not understand from whose mouth this
voice is issuing. ～ ƙauyụkạn dạ sukẹ
zūwạ in the villages from which they
come (*Vd.* dạ 11*d*). (*b*) ～ wurin from
person (*cf.* 1*a*) x mun zō ～ wurinsạ
we've come from him. mun zō ～ wurin
Audụ we've come from Audu. (*c*) ～
gạ (*followed by possessive pronoun*)
from x (i) ～ gạrēnị from me. ～ gạrēsụ
from them. (ii) ～ gạrēmụ har
'yā'yammụ from now on till the time
of our children. (*d*) (i) ～ bậra zūwạ
bana between last year and this year.
～ nạŋ zūwạ watạŋ gọbe between now
and next month. ～ yạu kậmịŋ kwānā
gōmạ kạ sāmụ you'll get it in the next
ten days. (ii) *Vd.* tun 1*f*.ii. (2) at
x (*a*) (i) yanạ̄ wạje = yanạ̄ dạgạ wạje
it's outside (*cf.* nạŋ, cikī). yā sạ̄
tsōkạr ～ bậkin tēkị he put the joint
of meat just inside the mouth of the
bag. yā tsayạ ～ wani gạrī he halted at
a certain town. Allạ̄ yā yi dạgạ
wajạŋkạ God is on your side. (ii)
～ bisạ *Vd.* bisạ 1*c* ; 2*b*. (iii) ～ ƙasạ
down below. (*b*) arẹ̄wā (= dạgạ
arẹ̄wā) dạ birnī on the north of the
town. ～ kudụ yakẹ it is to the south.
(3) after x (*a*) (i) ～ bāya afterwards.
(ii) ～ yạu from now onwards. (*b*)
(dạgạ *followed by noun or pronoun* . . .
sǎi *followed by noun or pronoun*). (i)
dạgạ nī sǎi kai nobody can do it except
you or I (*this is exception to* 1*b, c
above, as* wurin, gạ *are not here used
before personal pronoun*). ～ cācā sǎi
bọ̄rī when tired of gambling he turned
to bọ̄rī-practices. ～ azụrfā sǎi zīnārịyā
both silver and gold. ～ shī sǎi rịgā
ɗayā he has only one gown (*cf.* 4*a*). ～
shī sǎi kạransạ he has nothing but a
dog. ya kōmạ duk dạgạ azụrfā sǎi
zīnārịyā it became filled with gold and
silver. ～ Bạrạrō sǎi arnā after the
nomad Filani there remain the pagans
to be mentioned. ～ A sǎi B, ～ B
sǎi C after A came the reign of B, and
then C. succeeded B. (ii) dạgạ " Mạr-
habā Sarkin Pāwạ ! " sǎi zāƙim mịyạ ?
how can such a course of action lead

to the desired result ? (iii) dạgạ fakẹ
rūwā *Vd.* ramạ 1*b*. (iv) ～ cị *Vd.*
dagacị. (*c*) (dạgạ *followed by noun or pronoun* . . . sǎi *with verb*). (i) dạgạ naŋ sǎi =
Sk. dạgạ shī kọ̄ sǎi = *Sk.* dạgạ (*adverbial
usage*), sǎi then x dạgạ naŋ sǎi sukạ mutụ
after that, they died. (ii) sun sạukạ
Kanọ, ～ Kanọ sukạ sạukạ Cālāwā, ～
Cālāwā, sǎi Gabasāwā they lodged
first at Kano, then at C., and finally
at G. ～ zagī, sǎi akạ bā shi dōkị he
was promoted from runner-by-a-horse
to mounted rank. ～ gudụnsụ sǎi mukạ
jī . . . after their flight we heard
that . . . dạgạ gudụŋ gyāran lāyū, sum
mīƙe after a strategic retreat, they
broke into a run. (*e*) (dạgạ *followed by
verb*) dạgạ kā ji ɗayā yā 6atạ, sǎi
bīyū kọ̄ ukụ first you hear one is lost,
then two or three. dạgạ am fārạ kọ̄yạ
musụ, har suŋ kai gạ īyạ yị after being
novices, they became experts. dạgạ
sun ji " kạyyā ! ", sukạ yạrdā as
soon as they heard the remark " come
to your senses ! " they concurred. (*e*)
Vd. tun 1*f*.i. (4) (*a*) dạgạ bậ . . . ba
failing x (i) dạgạ bậ Sarkī ba, sǎi
bạtūrẹ failing the chief, recourse must
be had to the European (*Vd.* 3*b*.i
above ; sǎi A.2*b, c*). (ii) dạgạ bậ haƙō
ba *Vd.* Gaikau. (*b*) *Sk.* when x dạgạ yā
zō, sǎi mukạ gan shi we saw him
when he came (= san dạ). (5) *cf.* dạ 7.
(6) in reference to x indạ ƙasạr takẹ
dạgạ gạrinsụ where the country is
situated relatively to their own town
(= dạ 4*a*).

B. (dagā) *f.* (*pl.* dagāgē) bangle-
charm worn on forearm (= kạmbū =
dāgumī 3). (2) maị dagar hannū *m., f.*
(*pl.* mạsū d.h.) lucky P. (3) yā murɗạ ～
he cast a spell on P. (4) yā yi gudụŋ
gyāran ～ he made a strategic retreat
(*Vd.* rạ̄gō 5) = Muhạmmạdịyyạ 1*d* =
gyārā 1*d q.v.* (5) *Vd.* dagacị.

C. (dāgā) *f.* (1) (*a*) sun jā (= sun
girkạ = sun shāyạ = sun shātạ = sun
shā) dāgā they're drawn up in line of
battle, they joined battle (= bātạ).
(*b*) sunạ̄ bậkin ～ they're on the battlefield, at the front. yanạ̄ bậkin
wannạŋ ～ he is on this war-front.

(2) yā yi ∼ dą shī, ya ƙi yąrdā he tried hard but was unable to get his consent. (3) ɗāgar wąsā playground for dancing, drumming (= fagē 1d.i).

ɗaga A. (ɗagą) (1) Vb. 1A. (a) (i) lifted up x yā ∼ kąi samą he looked upwards (= cirą 1a). yā ∼ tūtąr ąmāną gąrēsu he waved a flag of surrender to them. (ii) removed. (b) exceeded slightly (= ɗarą). (c) yā ∼ minį ająlī he extended my time for paying the debt (= ająlī 1b). (d) yaną̄ ∼ kąi = yaną̄ ∼ hancį he's putting on airs (= cirą 1g). (e) (i) yaną̄ ∼ ƙafą he is putting his best foot forward (= mīƙą 1d = cirą 1e). (ii) suną̄ ∼ ƙafą gąba ɗayā, aną̄ tąfīyąr ąbūtā they are on the best of terms together. (iii) săi jirą mukę̄ mutum yą ∼ ƙafą, mu są̄ ą yi Kirsimētį bą̄ dą shī ba if we see anyone move, we'll " bump him off ". (f) ∼ hannū rangwamąn dūką nē (i) what an unexpected bargain ! (ii) we got off lightly. (2) Vb. 3A. (a) (i) (moon, star, price, sun, crops) became higher (= tąskā = cirą 2b). (ii) projected upwards x ƙirjin dōkį yā ∼ the horse's chest projects upwards. (i, ii = mīƙą 2a.ii q.v.) (iii) = tąskā 2. (b) (i) went away x bą̄ zā ką ∼ ba săi ką bīyā you don't budge from here unless you pay ! (ii) retreated (in war).

B. (ɗagā) f. arrogance (cf. ɗagą 1d).

ɗagąbi-ɗagąbi m. the game gąrdō q.v.

dagacį = Sk. dagacę̄ m. (pl. dągątai). (1) village-headman (epithets are Dagacįn ƙauyę̄ macį ąwąkai Headman, taker of goats as bribes ! = Dagacį dagar wutā, dagą cī săi tūƙā Headman, thou bangle of fire, after peculation, deposition ! (Vd. baƙi 3l). (1A) Vd. Sarkī 2. (2) cf. tāshin dagacįn ƙauyę̄.

dą̄gą-dā̄gą f. iron band at end of spear (= daddā̄gą q.v.).

ɗagad dą̄ Vb. 4B = ɗagą 1a.

dagą̄gē Vd. dagā.

dagai-dagai = dagwai-dagwai.

dągainīyā f. gait of tired P.

dagą̄jambą (1) m., f. P. with messy lips or body. (2) what a messy P. or T. !

dą̄gąjē Vd. dą̄gazą.

ɗagąjinā f. stone for putting under cooking pot (= ɗan sąƙō q.v.).

dągąjįrau m. grubby lout.

dą̄galą Kt. (1) scraped out (ointment, etc.) from jar (= lą̄katą). (2) yaną̄ dą̄galąr fadą he's stirring up a quarrel.

dagale A. (dā̄galē) Vb. 1C Kt. = dą̄galą 1.

B. (dā̄galē) Kt. m. a drink made from pods of locust bean (dōrawą) and water of tamarind (tsāmīyā) = gwaggǫ 1b.

dagalgajē Kt. = dagargąjē.

dągallabǫ Sk. m. fine sediment (= dą̄laƙī 2 q.v.).

dagalǫ Sk. m. = dagwalǫ.

dągannīyā f. = dągainīyā.

dagara A. (dą̄garą) Kt. ∼ bą̄ mą̄yē, shą̄ye-shą̄yam mąi mātā gōmą epithet of the millet dąurō.

B. (dā̄gą̄rā) Vb. 3A limped from tiredness, illness.

C. dā̄gą̄rą m., f. (sg., pl.) (impolitely) leper (= na ∼), Vd. kuturū.

ɗagar dą̄ = ɗagad dą̄.

dagargąja A. (dagargąjē) (1) Vb. 3A disintegrated. (2) Vb. 1D devoured all the large amount available.

B. (dągargąjē) Vd. dągargazą.

dągargazą Vb. 2 (p.o. dągargąjē, n.o. dągargąji) ate large amount of.

dągarnīyā f. = dągainīyā.

dagaryā used in dagaryar idǫ upper or lower margin of eyelids (i.e. place where they meet when eye closed and where galena (tōząlī) is applied).

dagątai village-headmen (Vd. dagacį).

ɗagā̄wą = ɗagā.

dą̄gazą Vb. 2 (p.o. dą̄gąjē, n.o. dą̄gąji) Sk. = dągargazą.

dą̄gą̄zau m. = dągąjįrau.

dage A. (dagē) m. (1) type of wild feline (= Sk. cirzą). (2) cantankerous P.

B. (dāgę̄) Vb. 3A. (1) behaved mulishly. (2) took a firm stand (= tākę̄ 2d = tirję̄ 1a).

ɗage A. (ɗagę̄) (1) Vb. 1A yā ∼ ƙafą he (P. with sore foot ; horse, etc.) tip-toed one foot (cf. ɗagē). (2) Vb. 3A (a) (washed garment, leg, arm) shrunk (cf. dangąlē 2 ; ƙagę̄). (b) sat apart alone.

B. (ɗagē) m. standing on tiptoe of

both feet to reach high T. *x* yā yi ∼ yā ɗaukō shi he stood on tiptoe and reached it down (*cf.* ɗage) = Kt. tantaɗō.

C. (ɗage) *Kt.* sunā dūbammu ∼ they're looking contemptuously at us (= shēkēkē).

dageji *Sk. m.* = dagē.

ɗagēra *f.* the gum-bearing tree *Combretum Kerstingii* (= *Sk.* cīrīri).

dagi A. (dāgi) *m.* (*pl.* dāguna) (1) digging-rod (= matōnī = maginī = mahakī). (2) shameless P. (*epithet of* 1, 2 *is* ∼ māganin kasā mai taurī). (3) fingerless or toeless leper. (4) narrow beard on glabrous man. (5) kafassa tā yi ∼ he has contracted Achilles tendon (= cōbe).

B. (dāgī) *m.* (*pl.* dāguna) (1) feline's paw (= duŋgū 6). (2) metal tool for stamping design on leather, etc. (3) the intertwined ovals forming pattern called durkusan tāgūwa.

dāgilgiji *m.* (*f.* dāgilgizā) *pl.* dāgilgizai *Kt.* short P.

dāgira *m., f.* (*pl.* dāgirāwā = dāgirōrī) seasonal immigrant from French territory doing odd-jobs and water-carrying (= ɗaŋ gā rūwā = bādalā 4*a* = ēha = *Kt.* gānūwā 5*b*).

dagōdagō *m.* = dagwadagō.

ɗagō-ɗagō = ɗagōgō 1.

ɗagōgō (1) *adv.* yā zauna ∼ it sits shakily on its base (*cf.* daɓas). (2) (*a*) aŋ kai shi ∼ he's been put in the stocks (= tūru 1). (*b*) (i) any fierce animal wounded during hunt. (ii) *Kt.* tō ∼, tō ∼ ; sǎi muŋ kōmō so this is as far as you're coming hunting with us and now you're going back to hunt for women !

dāgū *used in* dāgu, cimar zākī Meat, thou food of the lion !

ɗagu *Fil. m.* (*sg., pl.*) shelf made of cornstalks.

ɗagū-ɗagū = ɗagōgō 1.

dagula A. (dāgulā) *Vb.* 1C spoiled (= ɓāta).

B. (dāgula) *Vb.* 3B. (1) is (was) spoiled (= ɓāci). (2) hankalinsa (= ransa) yā ∼ he's disturbed in mind (= ɓāci 2*a*).

dāgulau *m., f.* (*sg., pl.*) cantankerous P.

dāgulē *Vb.* 3A is (was) spoiled (= ɓāci).

dāgulgulā = dāgwalgwalā.

daguma A. (dāguma) *Vb.* 2 = dāgumē.

B. (dāguma) *Vd.* dāgumī.

dāgumē *Vb.* 1C (1) seized front of neck of person's gown with both hands (= dāgumī 2). (2) arrested P.

dāgumī *m.* (*pl.* dāguma) (1) (*a*) plaited-leather dog-collar (= gāgara biri). (*b*) kūrā tā fi dāgumī sǎi sarka he's utterly brazen. (2) yā ci dāguminsa he caught hold of the neck-front of that person's gown with both hands (= dāgumē 1). (3) bangle-charm worn on forearm (= dagā). (4) yā karya ∼ he tied his gown-sleeves behind his neck (= *Sk.* gudūgu), *Vd.* gwarlōɓa.

dāguna *Vd.* dāgi ; dāgī.

dāgura *Vb.* 2 (1) gnawed at. (2) made an attempt at.

dāguri gurzau *m.* P. claiming invulnerability (= taurī 2*c*).

dagurji *Kt. m.* large amount (= dugurji *q.v.*).

dagwāɓa *Kt. f.* rich gravy (= darma-sōsūwā).

dagwadagō *m.* (1) (*a*) sedimentary liquid (*such as of* tsakim furā *or* tsakin kunū) (= durguɓī = *Kt.* gwaɓe 2). (*b*) = dalakī 1. (*c*) *Vd.* maŋ gyaɗā 3. (2) drink made from pulp of pod of locustbean (ɗōrawa) and water of tamarind (tsāmīyā) = gwaggo 1*b* = daŋgwamī 1 (*cf.* ɓōlōlō 1). (3) hankalinsa yā yi ∼ he's disturbed in mind.

dagwai-dagwai *used in* (1) yāː? (yārinya) ∼ plump boy (girl) aged about two and beginning to walk. (2) yāro yā yi ∼ the boy is plump, aged about two, and beginning to walk.

dagwājirī *m.* (*f.* dagwājirā) grubby lout.

dagwalan *m. x* yā yi dagwalan he's stupid.

dagwalāyī *m.* a herbal gruel.

dagwalgwalā *Vb.* 1D soiled ; made a mess of.

dagwalgwalē *Vb.* 3A is (was) soiled ; is (was) in a mess.

dagwalgwalō *m.* food or water in soiled state.

dagwallatsī *m.* yā yi ∼ he (it) is in messy state.

dagwalo A. (dagwalǫ) *m.* (1) used-up indigo-dye. (2) ～ bābaŋ kōwā *epithet of* generous P.
B. (dǫgwǫlō) *m.* = dǫgwǫlaŋ.
dǫgwǫlǫ̣lǫ = dǫgwǫlaŋ.
dagwaŋ-dagwaŋ *Kt.* in profusion (= dǭ-6ā6ǫ *q.v.*).
ɗagwaŋ-ɗagwaŋ without intermission *x* yanā bīye dǫ nī ～ he follows me about everywhere. yā kāsǫ zamā, ～ yǫ kai naŋ, yǫ kāwō naŋ he fidgets to and fro.
ɗagwarwā *f.* large stone resting on smaller one.
ɗagwargwar *x* ɗan ɗagwargwar = ɗag-wargwǫshī.
ɗagwargwǫshī *m.* (*f.* ɗagwargwǫsā) *pl.* ɗagwǫrgwǫsai small but symmetrical *x* yārinyǫ cē ɗagwargwǫsā (*cf.* dagwas).
ɗagwas = ɗagwargwǫshī *x* yārinyǫ cē ɗagwas dǫ ita she's a small, well-formed girl (*pl.* 'yam mātā nē ɗagwas-ɗagwas dǫ sū).
dāgwīyǫ *Vb.* 2 (1) gnawed at. (2) ate very much (*meat*).
dāgwīyau *epithet of* hyena (*Vd.* kūrā).
ɗahę *Vb.* 3A *Kt.* = ɗafę.
dāhịlā *Ar. f.* woman not highly sexed (*cf.* hārịjā).
dāhịr (1) undoubtedly. (2) wannaŋ ～ nē this is definitely so. (3) suŋ ga ～ they've seen the true state of affairs. (4) yā tǫki ～ he knows it for sure (= dǫlīlị 1g = tǫkǫmaimai).
Dāhịru man's name.
dāhụmǫ *m.* type of European black and red cloth.
dǫhūwā = dǫfuwā.
dǎi (1) (*a*) indeed *x* hakǫ ～ nę that's how matters stand. (*b*) (*like* kụ̄wā, kumā, mā 2 *q.v.*, *it is inserted without affecting the construction which would stand if dǎi were not there*) *x* kǫmar mịsālịn dǎi yǫddǫ mukę̄, hakǫ sū mā they are just like ourselves. (2) in ～ = ịdan ～ (*a*) *x* ịdan ～ bụkātǫssǫ tā bīyā provided his wish is fulfilled. (*b*) *x* in ～ fịtinǫ tanǭ aụkūwā if dissension *must* occur. (3) kadǫ ～ apart from *x* sukǫ kāmǫ mazā, kadǫ ～ ǫ yi zǫncam mātā then they captured males, not to mention women ! (4) (*added to name*

of P. called) **Audụ dǎi** ! (5) *Vd.* **sǎi dǎi** *under* sǎi B.2.
dǎi (1) one (= ɗayā). (2) *cf.* dǎi-dǎi.
dǎidǎi = *Sk.* daidai (1) *adj.* (*a*) correct *x* (i) ǫbịn dǫ ka yi ～ nē what you did was correct. (ii) tǭ, ～ righto ! (iii) bǭ ～ ba nē ǫ yī it is not permissible to do so. (iv) ɓarfī yā zō ～ they are evenly matched (*cf.* 4.*a* ii). (*b*) straight *x* kǫ tā dǫ shī ～ straighten it ! (*c*) (i) don yǫ zō ～ dǫ sū that it may correspond with them. zā mụ tsayǫ ～ dǫ kōwā we shall enjoy equal status with everyone. (ii) don sụ kōmǫ ～ dǫ ～ that they all become of equal status. (iii) *cf.* 4*a*.ii, 4*b*.ii, iii *below*. (iv) wǫrkī dǎidǎi gịndī *Vd.* wǫrkī 4. (v) dǎidǎi dǫ mū akę̄ *Vd.* bā B.1, 4*b*. (2) *m.* (*a*) (i) correctness *x* yā yi ～ it's correct. (ii) rịgarkǫ tā yi ～ dǫ kai the gown suits, fits you. in rịgā tā yi makǫ dǎidǎi *Vd.* rịgā 1*n.* wannǫm bai yi ～ dǫ wancǫm ba this does not correspond with that. (iii) wannǫm bai yi masǫ ～ ba this plan does (did) not suit him. (*b*) one equal to *x* kǫ nē̦mi ～ dǫ kai seek one (girl, etc.) of your own status ! (3) *Vd.* 'yan ～. (4) *adv.* (*a*) correctly, exactly *x* (i) sulę̄ gōmǫ ～ exactly ten shillings. (ii) ǫbịn yā zō ～, mai idǫ ɗayā yā lēɓǫ būtǫ what unexpected luck ! (*cf.* 1*a.* iv). (iii) *Vd.* cịri dǎidǎi. (iv) yaŋkǫ dǎidǎi *Vd.* yaŋkǫ 1*c.*ii. yǫ cikǫ fadịn ～ yǫddǫ sukę̄ yị̄ he must describe fully how they act. sụ kǭyi ～ yǫddǫ hālịn ɓasā yakę̄ they should learn fully about the country. (*b*) straight *x* yā zaunǫ ～ he sat up straight. tsǫya ～ stand up straight ! (4) *prep.* (*a*) corresponding with *x* (i) ～ wurịn dǫ mukǫ gǫmu dǫ at the very place where we met before. ǫ ～ lōkǫcin nan nē sukǫ zō it was at exactly *this* time that they came. (ii) lādā ～ aikịnsǫ = lādā ～ dǫ aikịnsǫ wages commensurate with his work. ～ kǫnsǫ = dǎidǎi dǫ kǫnsǫ exactly over his head. wani ǫbụ ～ (= wani ǫbụ ～ dǫ) bǭkịn ɓōfǫ a thing of just the same size as the door-way (*cf.* 1*c above*). (*b*) (i) ～ rūwā, ɓurjī = dǎidǎi ɓurjī, ～ rūwā = ～ cị, ～ ɓarfī all act according to their

abilities. (ii) **ɗăidăi dạ cikiŋkạ** *Vd.*
rūwā C.9*b*. (iii) ~ **dạ kạŋ kōwā** *Vd.*
daŋkwarā.

ɗăi-ɗăi (1) *adv.* (*a*) (i) one by one *x* **kāyan**
naŋ, ajīyē su ~ = **kāyan naŋ, ajīyē**
su ~ **dạ** ~ put these loads down singly !
magaŋganū ~ = **magaŋganū** ~ **dạ** ~
words one by one. (ii) **mun yi karọ dạ**
sū, mun yi ɗăi-ɗăi dạ sū we attacked
and decimated them. (iii) **ạkwai**
jirăgyan rūwā ~ **kạmar yạddạ jirăgyaŋ**
ƙasā sukẹ̄ there are various types of
ships just as there are various methods
of land-transport. (*b*) **yană kwạnce** ~
he's lying sprawled out. (*c*) (i) **yană**
tākạ̄wā ~ he's mincing along with
swaggering gait. (ii) **săi tạƙā** ~ **sukẹ̄**
they're advancing only step by step.
(2) (*a*) only a few *x* **cikin dabbōbiŋ** ~
nẹ̄ sukạ fi gīwā fạsāhạ among the
animals, only few are more intelligent
than the elephant. ~ **sukạ zō** = sun
sō ~ **dạ** ~ only a few came. **bă ni**
dạ sū săi ~ I've only a few. (*b*) only
one or so *x* ~ **nẹ̄ wạndạ bai nẹ̄mē**
nị ba I was courted by all but one or
two. (3) it is only rarely *x* **ɗăi-ɗăi**
rănạd dạ zā tạ fitō, bạ ạ yi rūwā ba it
is only rarely that the sun rises without
there being rain.

daidaice A. (**dăidăicē**) (1) *Vb.* 1C. =
dăidăitạ. (2) *Vb.* 3A = **dăidăitạ 2.**
   B. (**dăidăicē**) *Vd.* **dăidăitạ 1.**

dăiɗăicē *Vb.* 3A. (1) = **ɗăidăitạ.** (2)
deteriorated.

daidaita A. (**dăidăitā**) *Vb.* 1C. (1) straightened ; equalized ; arranged sym-
metrically. (2) **yā kạmātạ mijị yạ**
dăidăitạ kwānā by Muslim law, a husband must sleep same number of nights
(1 or 2) with each wife in turn. (3)
sun ~ they've made friends again.
(4) **yā** ~ **shi gạ bukātạrsạ** he adapted
it to his requirements. (5) **yā dăidăitạ**
Masạr dạ sauraŋ ƙasạ̄shan dūnīyā
he brought Egypt into line with other
countries. (6) **akạ** ~ **ạ bari** so they
arranged to abandon it. (7) **yā dăi-**
dăitā tsạkāniŋ ƙasạ̄shē he kept peace
between the nations.
   B. (**dăidăitạ**) (1) *Vb.* 2 (*p.o.* **dăidăicē**,
n.o. **dăidăici**). (*a*) aimed at *x* **nā**

dăidăici bạrēwā I aimed at the gazelle
(= **ạunā 5**). (*b*) **yā dăidăici Kanọ** he
went straight to Kano (= **dọ̄sā**).
(*c*) corresponded with *x* **kạ dăidăici**
lōkạcin zūwạna your arrival must
coincide with mine ! (2) *Vb.* 3B (*a*)
became level, even, symmetrical. (*b*)
hanyạd dạ zā tạ kai sụ gạ ~ **dạ wannạŋ**
zạmānị the way in which they can keep
up with the times.

ɗaiɗaita A. (**dăidăitạ**) *Vb.* 3B became
scattered ; dispersed.
   B. (**dăidăitā**) *Vb.* 1C. (1) arranged
one by one. (2) scattered, dispersed.
(3) **Allā yạ dăidăitạ ạnīyạ tasạ** God confound him !

dăidăitō *m.* levelness ; straightness ;
equality ; correctness ; symmetry.

dăidăitōnị *m.* **yā yi** ~ he arrived at the
right moment. **yā yi** ~ **dạ jirgī** he
arrived in time for the train.

dăidăiwā *Nor.* one by one (= **ɗăi-ɗăi**).

dăidăi wạ dăidạ = **dăi-dăi 1-3.**

ɗăiɗăwā one by one = **ɗăi-ɗăi.**

daidayā *Sk. f.* (1) the millipede **ƙadan-**
dōnīyā. (2) **daidayar ƙọ̄rē** display of
calabashes in wife's house (= **daŋkị**
q.v.).

ɗaiɗaya A. (**dăiɗaya**) *Vb.* 2. (1) stripped
off epidermis with knife (*cf.* **dăkā**).
(2) **yā dăiɗayi nāmạ** he cut meat into
small pieces. (3) pared edge of leather
to even it.
   B. (**dăiɗayā**) *Vb.* 1C (*derived from*
ɗăi-ɗăi) poured insufficient liquid over
x **tā dăiɗayạ mīyạ kạn tūwō.**
   C. (**ɗăi ɗayā**) *Kt.* one by one
(= **ɗăi-ɗăi**).

ɗaiɗaye A. (**dăiɗayē**) (1) *Vb.* 1C = **dăi-**
ɗayạ. (2) *Vb.* 3A **hannū yā** ~ skin
peeled off the hand.
   B. (**dăiɗayē**) *m.* (1) (*secondary v.n.*
of **dăiɗayā**) *x* **tană dăiɗayam mīyạ** =
tană dăiɗayạ mīyạ she's pouring too
little soup over the tūwō. (2) **mīyạŋ**
naŋ ~ **cẹ̄** the soup on this tuwō is
insufficient.

ɗăi dạ zakkạ *Sk. m.* measure holding 4
handfuls of corn (= **mūdạnabi**
q.v.).

ɗaiɗōyạ *f.* = **dạddōyạ.**

dā'imī *Ar. m.* (*f.* **dā'imā**) everlasting *x*

Allā yą yi maną suturą dā'ịmā God forgive our sins in the next world !

dainą *Vb.* 1A ceased doing (= **dēną** *q.v.*).

dā'irą *Ar. f. (pl.* **dā'irōrī**). (1) circle *x* mun yi ∼ = muŋ girką ∼ we ranged ourselves in a circle. (2) type of gown (= **ąddā'ịrā** 1).

daitą *f.* (1) being uncooked, unripe, *etc.* (*as in* danyē *q.v.*). (2) puerperal fever.

daiwą yā'ę *Sk.* fancy ! (= **dēwą** *q.v.*), *cf.* yā'ę.

dą iyą *used in* ∼ muką jē giji, sǎi wata rānā, iyą *formula used* in a children's game (= **jąŋ gundą**).

daje A. (**dāję**) *Vb.* 1A. (1) made reinforcing-edge to mat (**tąbarmā, zānā**) *or* gwądǫ cloth (= **tantsę** = **kitsę** 2*b*), *cf.* **dājīyā, gwīwą** (5). an ∼ tąbarmā dą jā the mat has been edged in red (*Vd.* **dāzą**). (2) sun ∼ shi dą sąndā they hit him with a stick.

B. (**daję**) *m.* (*f.* **dajịyā**) *pl.* **dązzā** handsome.

dāji *m.* (*pl.* **dāzuzzuką** = **dāzūzūwą**). (1) the "bush", jungle. (2) *Vd.* daurịn dāji, **būdą** 4. (3) harbịn∼*m.* (*a*) blackquarter *x* harbịn ∼ yā sąmi shānummu our cattle have blackquarter disease (= māshi 2 = **mahąrbī** 3*b* = **hąrbau**). (*b*) *Vd.* harbịn dawą, dawą 5. (4) *Vd.* dawą, jēji. (5) kō ∼ yā ɓāci, gīwā tā fi gudu nil desperandum. (6) sǎi ∼ yā yi yawą, zāki kąn zauną ą cikinsą the poor get nothing unless the rich have a surplus. (7) kōmē gudụm bąrēwā, tą bar ∼ no subject can be fully mastered (*Vd.* bąrēwā 1*c*). (8) ∼ bai gamą cịŋ wutā ba, fąrā bā tą yi wą 'yarūwā tatą barką don't rejoice till you are out of the wood ! (9) kwānā ą ∼ *Vd.* bāwą 8*b*.

dājịnē *Kt. m.* wiping one's nose on back of one's hand (= **shąɓunē** 1).

dajiya A. (**dajịyā**) *Vd.* daję.

B. (**dājịyā**) *f.* (1) (*secondary v.n. of* dāję) *x* yaną dājịyar tąbarmā = yaną dāję tąbarmā. (2) (*a*) the reinforced edge of a mat (= **tantsi**). (*b*) reinforced edge of *x* wąrkī-loincloth (= kalaŋkūwā 5*c*) or of top of thatched corridor (shịrąyī), *Vd.* dāję. (*c*) *Vd.* cịŋ kǎi 2 *in* cī 23*b*.

---

daka A. (**daką**) (1) *Vb.* 1A (*Ar.* daqqa). (*a*) (i) did *final* pounding *x* tā ∼ hatsī she pounded corn (*cf.* surfē, ribdi, turzą 1*b*, dandąkā, zurcę). (ii) an ∼ tābą leaf-tobacco was treated by pounding saŋkā very fine, then mixing into it powdered potash (gąrịŋ kaŋwā) and shea-oil (mąŋ kadanyą) : *it is used for* snuff (gąrin tābą) or quid (kamailā) for sucking. (*b*) kadą ką ∼ tąwa (*lit.* don't pound *my* corn !) don't imitate me ! kōwā ya ∼ ta wani, yą rasą turmin ∼ tāsą mind your own business ! (*c*) a ∼ masą gōrǫ ą turmī may he live to a ripe age ! (*d*) (i) beat P. or T. (= **dǫkā**). (ii) rūwā yā ∼ shi rain pelted on him. (iii) rūwąn dą ya dakē ką, shī nę rūwā devote all your consideration to those who do good to you ! (*Vd.* dąkā 3). (iv) *Vd.* kāshī 2*b*. (v) = kwaŋkwąsā 1*a*, *e.g.* yā ∼ kōfą he knocked at the door. (*e*) *x* ą ∼ buhun nąŋ thump this sack on the ground to level its contents ! (*f*) kāyā yā ∼ shi heavy load has exhausted him. (*g*) *Sk.* yā ∼ mą rịgā shūnī he blued his gown by wearing it next to a dyed one (= ban shūnī). (*h*) *Vd.* surā, dąką mū, tsallē, tsāwā 2*b*, hąrārā 3. (2) *m.* (*a*) being occupied in *final* pounding of corn *x* taną ∼ she's pounding. (*b*) (*secondary v.n. of* daką) *x* taną dakąn hatsī = taną daką hatsī she's pounding the corn. (*c*) an yi matą ∼ feast celebrating consummation of her (virgin's) marriage has been held (*this is 7-30 days after wedding and bloodstained cloth is exhibited*). (*d*) sākąn nąŋ taną dą ∼ this is a close weave. (*e*) dōkịŋ kąrfę yaną ∼ rim of unpumped cycle is bumping. (*f*) zūcịyassą taną ∼, taną tąŋkadē, he's all of a flutter. zūcịyāta taną dakąn ukụ ukụ "my heart is in my mouth". (*g*) gąrī, ąbin ∼ dą hakōrī cry of hawkers of spitted meat (tsịrē). (*h*) namijịn ∼ = daŋkarō 1. (*j*) *Vd.* tsaiwā 2, dakąn-compounds, daka 4, daki duką, dąką-compounds.

B. (**dąkā**) *Vb.* 2. (1) = daką 1*a*, *d*.i, *d*ii, *e*, *f*. (2) *Vd.* daką 1*d*.iii. (3) yā yi masą dạki bāwạ yạ mạntā gātarī he threw him off the scent. (4) *Vd.* dạki dukạ.

C. (dạkạ) = dạgạ.

ɗaka A. (ɗakạ) (*locative of* ɗāki, Mod. Gram. 24). (1) in the house *x* (*a*) yanā ∼ he's in the house or room. (*b*) yā shiga ∼ he entered the house. shigō ∼ come in ! (*c*) yā sā ta ạ ∼ he took her as his concubine (*cf.* sạ̄ɗakạ). (*d*) aŋ kai shi ∼ best-man and two other youths pushed bridegroom into bride's room at end of feast (biki). (2) bā yā ∼ he's sexually impotent (*cf.* lạ'īfi). (3) ∼ ciluŋ, wạje ciluŋ poverty at home, pouring rain outside ! (4) dakạn ∼, shīkạd ∼, tạŋkạɗam bạkiŋ gadō (i) it's purely the concern of the family circle. (ii) it's a marriage between relations. (5) 'yan ∼ *Sk. m. pl.* one of the sạrautạ. (6) rạndar ∼ *Vd.* rạndā 1*c,d*, (7) dūnīyạɗ ∼ *Vd.* dūnīyạ 1*l.*

B. (dā̱kā) *Vb.* 2 (1) stripped epidermis from skins or bark from tree (*cf.* ɗạ̄iɗayạ). (2) ɗạkar bạ̄kī smacking the lips with zest (*cf.* ɗākẹ).

C. (ɗākạ) *Zar.* = ɗaukạ.

dakace A. (dākạcē) *Vb.* 3A. (1) waited. (2) ∼ har waited till (= dākạtā 1, 2).

B. (dạ̄kạcē) *Vd.* dạ̄katạ.

C. (dạ̄ kạ cē) regrets *x* nā yi ∼ bạn yi ba I regretted having done it (= yạ kạ cē), *cf.* dạ̄ 1*b.*

dakaci A. (dākạcī) *m.* (*secondary v.n. of* dạ̄katạ) *x* munā dākạcinsạ = munā dạ̄katạssạ we're waiting for him.

B. (dạ̄kạci) *Vd.* dạ̄katạ.

C. (dakaci) *Sk. m.* village-head (= dagaci *q.v.*).

ɗā̱kạ-ɗākạ *m.* hut for guests ; shack on farm or for watching cows.

dạkạ dukạ = dạki dukạ.

daƙaf (1) being devoid of liquid *x* rạndan naŋ ∼ takẹ this waterpot is empty. (2) dạfūwar ∼ *Vd.* dạfūwā 3.

dạƙaiƙaya *Vb.* 2 (1) ate much of. (2) *Sk.* (*intensive of* dịka *said by women*) yā dạƙaiƙayē tạ he had connection with her unceasingly.

daƙaiƙayē *Vb.* 1D devoured all the large amount available.

dakaka A. (dạkakạ = dạkakạkạkạ) *m.*

(1) (*a*) rushing-sound (of river, storm, hastening crowd, heavy vehicle). (*b*) *adv. x* suŋ ga ạbu tạfe ∼ they saw something come rumbling up. (2) silent, indecisive P.

B. dạkākạ ; dakạ̄kā *Vd.* dịkākạ ; dịkākā.

ɗakaka exceedingly *x* kạ̄sūwā tā cịka ∼ market's packed.

dakakī *used in* ∼ bīyạ kọrā *epithet of* Emir, warrior, strong P.

dakạ̄kiri *m., f.* dolt.

dạkā̱kisau (1) mighty P. (2) strong P. (*cf.* dạkākạ).

ɗakale A. (ɗākạlē) *Vb.* 3A cikịnsạ yā ∼ his stomach became thin (*cf.* lakap).

B. (ɗākālẹ) (1) *m.* tanā dạ ∼ she (woman or domestic animal after giving birth) has no milk in breast. (2) *f.* woman, etc., having n̈o milk *as in* 1. (3) yā shā ∼ mūgụm mā̱mā what a stingy person ! (4) what a thin tummy ! (*cf.* ɗākạlē).

dạkạlī *m.* (1) low, mud platform at door of prosperous person's house or compound, or in his house. (2) ledge inside town walls where defenders stand (= bādalā 2). (3) *Vd.* tukụbā.

dạkamạ *used in* na ∼, mạnzaŋkạ hōgẹ, bā kā jiŋ kirạ sāi jīfạ deaf man,, strong measures are needed with you ! (*epithet of* kurmā).

dạkạ mū *m.* (*expression used by beggar*) remnants of children's food given to beggar (*lit.* beat us for rejecting it !).

dakạ na ummạ *Vd.* Dakạrkarī.

dakan baka (dakạm bakạ) *m.* eating unground grain.

dākạncē *Vb.* 3A = dākạcē.

dakạn ɗaka *Vd.* ɗakạ 4.

daƙaŋ-daƙaŋ *Kt.* (1) greasy appearance. (2) slowly (= diƙiŋ-diƙiŋ *q.v.*).

dakan danshī *used in* hanci kạmar ∼ flat nose.

dakan jīyạ *used in* ∼ kā ƙi tsāmī *epithet of* thin, weak P., looking always the same age (= *Kt.* dawọ 5).

dakạŋ kūkạ *used in* yā yi mini ∼ he (P. whom I asked to help me up with load) angrily banged it down on my head.

dakạn rakō *m.* foolishly landing oneself in an even worse plight (= daɗi 8).

dākanta = dākata.

dakaŋ Wambai *m.* = waskanē.

dākarci *m.* shamelessness (*cf.* dākārę 2).

dākārę (1) *m.* (*pl.* dākārū = dākārai). (*a*) (i) infantryman in pre-Administration days (= karmā), *cf.* sātī. (ii) *epithet is* ~ mai ram banzā, dā kā ganī, dā kā ɗaukạ. (iii) (*collectively*) *x* dōki yā fi 2,000 bandā ~ the cavalry exceeded 2,000 apart from the infantry. (*b*) any unmounted traveller (1*b* = marātayī 3) (1*a*, *b* = ɗaŋ ƙasạ *q.v. under* ƙasạ 12*b*). (2) dākārę *m.* (*f.* dākārīyā) *pl.* dākārū = dākārai shameless P. (3) dākāraŋ Habība the insect tsanyạr fatauci *q.v.*

dakāridọ *m.* type of children's game.

Dakạrkarī *m.* (1) the tribe so called (*Vd.* Bạdakkarę). (2) *epithet is* ~ dakạ na ummạ.

daƙāsari *Sk. m.* (1) fingerless and toeless leper. (2) strong P.

daƙashī *m.* first milk from camel, goat, or sheep after giving birth (*considered harmful to offspring, so fried* (tōyạ) *and eaten salted*) = kandi.

dakasō *Kt. m.* type of large, strong gown.

dakata A. (dākatā) *Vb.* 1C. (1) (*with dative*) waited for *x* nā ~ masạ I waited for him (= jirā). (2) waited *x* (*a*) nā ~ har yā zō I waited till he came. kō dākatāwar manti ɗayā bạ zā mu yi ba we won't delay a moment. kō wata dākatāwā bạ su yi ba they didn't delay a moment. (*b*) yā kamātạ ạ ~ dạ wannaŋ shāwarạ it would be better to postpone putting this plan into action. (*c*) *Vd.* dākatā, dākacē, dākatạ. (3) rūwā yā ~ there's a lull in the rains.

B. (dākatạ) *Vb.* 2 (*p.o.* dākacē, *n.o.* dākaci) waited for *x* nā dākacē shi I waited for him (*Vd.* dākacī, dākọ).

C. (dākatā) *m.* (*sg., pl.*) early type of sweet-potato (daŋkali); *its epithet is* Yārọ, ~ ạ yi ma aurē Boy, wait for your wedding !

dạkau *m.* pounding corn for pay.

daƙau *adv. Kt.* (1) wurī yā yi ~ the soil is dried and hard (*cf.* faƙọ). (2) yanā dạ ƙarfī ~ it's very strong.

ɗake A. (ɗakę) (1) *Vb.* 1A. (*a*) pounded all of (*Vd.* dakạ). (*b*) = dakạ 1*f*. (*c*)

destroyed spermatic cords of bull or goat to fatten = dạndaƙạ 2 (*cf.* fiɗīyē), *Vd.* 3 *below.* (*d*) devoured (much food). (*e*) concealed *x* tā ~ ạɓincī she concealed the food. (*e*) misappropriated *x* am bā shi sulę bīyū yạ kai wạ Audu, ya ~ he was given 2*s.* to take to Audu but he misappropriated it. (*f*) an ~ (= an tōshę) bākin tsanyạ dạ taɓaryā the matter's concluded. (*g*) mun dakę kalmōmī we've distorted the pronunciation. (2) *Vb.* 3A is (was) old hand at *x* yā ~ dạ ɗaukaŋ kāyā he's an old hand at carrying loads (*Vd.* hannū 2*g*). (3) dakę *m.* (*pl.* dạkkā) bullock (*cf.* 1*c above*).

B. (dạkē) *m.* (1) ink made from burdumī (= zugē 2). (2) condiments added to food of nursing mother or circumcized boy.

C. (dākę) *m.* (1) jumping into water in sitting position (= dīyạm). (2) *m., f.* ox or cow with red or black head and light-coloured body.

D. (dākē) silence !

ɗake A. (ɗākę) (1) *Vb.* 1A. (*a*) yā ~ bākī he smacked his lips with zest (*cf.* dạkā 2). (*b*) yā ~ mini harshę it (*e.g.* tamarind) made my tongue sore. (*c*) stripped off all epidermis from skin or bark from tree (*cf.* dākạ). (2) *Vb.* 3A harshęnā yā ~ my tongue is sore (*cf.* 1*b*).

B. (ɗākē) *m.* epidermis (= fuskā).

dạƙęƙę *Zar. m.* pretending not to hear when called.

dakęnō *m.* = sārā 2*a*.i.

ɗāki *m.* (*pl.* dākunạ). (1) (*a*) house (*usually refers to round, thatched house* (kagọ)), *cf.* gidā, sōrō, kagọ, kudandaŋ, hayi, jiŋkā. (*b*) (i) gindin ~ *m.* floor of house. (ii) wuyạn ~ *Vd.* wuyạ 1*c*. (iii) bāyan ~ *Vd.* bāyā 2*b*, ban 3. (*c*) ~ yā tāshi ? rāgaya tā zaunạ ? does a servant remain after his master's departure ? (*d*) kōmē ~ ya sāmu, ạlbarkạciŋ ƙōfạ a child owes all to its parents. (*e*) tā sāmi ~ *Vd.* sōrō 3. (*f*) 'yar zaman ~ *Vd.* burganci. (*g*) (i) dākiŋ kūrā, sǎi 'yā'yantạ it is a dangerous place, it is a dangerous T. to do (*Vd.* kūrā 18). (2) (*a*) room in house.

(b) dākin dạfūwā kitchen. (c) dākin ạbincī dining-room. (d) dākin kwānā bedroom. (e) dākin ạjīyạr ạbincī larder, pantry. (3) dākin Allā Mecca, the Kaba (Kạ'abạ) at Mecca. (4)~yā kēwạyē dạ rạhōnīyā said when P. is helped or leniently treated because of his connection with another P. whom one likes or honours. (5) dan ~ lad helping woman in cooking in return for his keep (= rānā 3a), cf. gidā 1k, ūwar dāki 1b. (6) (a) dan ~ dayā dạ mạkạnī poor P. (b) Vd. dayā 1d.i. (7) Kt. nā nēmē shi ạ dākin zumuncị, yā ƙī I tried to persuade him but to no purpose (= fuskạ 8). (8) a year in reckoning horse's age (cf. bana 2b). (9) Mai ~ (a) f. name for any woman called ā'ịshā. (b) f. Mai dākina tā cē . . . my wife said that . . . Mai dākinkạ tā zō your wife has come (= gidā 1n). (c) m. occupier of house x mai ~ shī ya sạn ịndạ rūwā yakē zum masạ (or zubam masạ) the wearer knows "where the shoe pinches". (10) 'yar ~ maidservant (her mistress is her ūwar dāki). (11) kaurin ~ Vd. dạɓē 4. (12) ~ yā fādạ Vd. zō 1e. (13) daukạr ~ Vd. shāwarạ 1j. (14) kim fi ~ Vd. rugā 1a. (15) ~ dạ rumfā Vd. rumfā 3. (16) cịkad ~ Vd. cịkā 2b. (17) ~ dạ duhụ Vd. dambē 2. (18) Vd. dakạ, ụban dāki, ūwar dāki.

dạki bạri m. strong and reliable (P., T., or animal).

dạki bāwạ Vd. dạkā 3.

daki-daki adv. group by group, one by one.

dạki dukạ m. reducing corn to flour without pounding-for-removal-of-bran (surfē) = duk dạ duk.

*dạƙīƙạ Ar. f. minute of time (= manti).

dakikancị m. stupidity.

dạkīkị m. (f. dạƙīkīyā) pl. dạƙīkai stupid P.

dạ̄ƙilạ (1) = dā̄ƙirạ. (2) Kt. na ~ = dāgārạ

dā̄ƙilē Vb. 3A. (1) failed to reply when called or addressed. (2) idạnsạ yā ~ his eye is purulent. (3) wuyạnsạ yā ~ he's short necked.

daƙin-daƙin Kt. = daƙan-dakan.

dā̄ƙirạ (1) Vb. 2 devoured much of. (2) Vb. 3B = dā̄ƙilē 1.

dā̄ƙirē = dā̄ƙilē.

dạki rif = dạki dukạ.

dā̄ƙirin dạƙū = dāƙiriṇ ƙōƙī adv. to repletion x yā ci nāmạ ~ he ate meat to repletion.

*dạki tsai = dạki dukạ.

dạkkā bullocks (Vd. dakẹ 3).

dakkyarẹ Sk. m. (1) balls of cooked flour pounded in mortar prior to being made into furā. (2) furā made from guineacorn flour.

dako A. (dākọ) m. (1) (secondary v.n. of dạ̄kata) x munā dākwansạ = munā dạ̄katạ tasạ we're waiting for him. (2) ambush x an sạ sōjạ dākwạn ịndạ zại ɓullō soldiers have been stationed to ambush him when he appears. (3) outpost duty. (4) epithet of the position Dan rīmī at Kano (cf. Ƙạcallạ 2). (5) Vd. sạ hạṇkạ̄kī dākọ.

B. (dakō) (1) m. (a) carrying load short distance for payment x within town-limits. dan ~ such carrier. (b) Dakō (or Ạ dakō) macịjim mātā epithet of the harmless snake dạṇ gidā (=gidā 1k.ii = farim macịjī = mūdī). (2) Vb. 1E Vd. sụrā ; tsallē.

dakō = daƙọ m. dark, rich, dry clay-soil.

dako-dako A. (dākō-dākọ) m. altercation (= dabar-dạbar q.v.).

B. (dakō-daƙọ) Kt. m. altercation (= dabar-dạbar q.v.).

daƙōƙī Sk. m. nape of the neck (= dōkin wuyạ).

dạƙọ̄kisạ Kt. m. (1) man professing to be invulnerable (= shā dā̄dalạ). (2) (a) blunt knife. (b) slow P. or animal.

dạƙū = Kt. dakụ m. game of girls and boys where beginning with little-toe, each toe is held and dạƙū said, reply being fạrā or ayā (cf. daƙūwạ) : when big-toe is reached, girl is asked ịnā sūnan saurạyiṇkị "what's the name of your tsạ̄rạncē partner ? " and she replies e.g. Gạmbō naming the actual person (or if she has no such partner, she replies ɓērā or mụzūrū). When big toe is reached, boy is asked ịnā sūnam bụdurwarkạ "what's the name of your **tsạrạncē** partner ? '' and he replies *x* **Ƙạnde** (or if he has no partner, he replies **sānīyā** or **shirwạ**). (2) **dạƙū-dạƙū** *Vd.* **daƙūwạ**. (3) *Vd.* **dāƙịrin ~.**

dāƙumạ = dāduma̤.

daƙuna A. (**dāƙụnā**) *Vb.* 1C messed up (clean T.).

B. (**dāƙunạ**) *Vb.* 3B it (clean T.) became soiled.

C. (**dāƙụnạ kāyā**) *m.*, *f.* (*sg.*, *pl.*) P. fingering goods without intention of buying.

dʹākunạ houses (*Vd.* **dāƙị**).

dāƙụndā *f.* dilatoriness.

dakuŋ-dạƙụŋ *x* **yanā̤ aikị** ~ he's making no progress.

dāƙuŋ-dāƙụŋ (1) **aŋ kāmạ shi** ~ he's securely tied up. (2) **yanā̤** ~ he's suffering trouble.

dāƙụnē *Vb.* 3A = **dāƙunạ**.

dakụŋkụ (1) *m.* type of children's game. (2) what strong weave !

dạƙuŋkuŋ dạƙusā̤rā *epithet of* (1) invincible warrior. (2) leper. (3) *Vd.* **dāƙusā̤rī**.

dakusa A. (**dāƙusạ**) *Vb.* 3B = **dākụshē**.

B. (**dākụsā**) *Vb.* 1C blunted (*cf.* **daŋkwafạ** 1*a*).

dākusad dạ *Vb.* 4B blunted.

dāƙusā̤rī *m.* (*f.* **dāƙusā̤rā**) (1) invulnerable P. (2) ugly P. (3) *Vd.* **dāƙuŋkuŋ**.

dāƙụsau *m.*, *f.* invulnerable P. (= **shā̤ dādalạ**).

dākụshārị = dākushārī *m.* (*f.* **dākụshārạ = dākushārā**) ugly P.

dāƙụshē *Vb.* 3A (1) is (was) blunt (= **cikẹ** 2*b* = *Kt.* **dāsạshē**). (2) (*luck, intelligence, etc.*) waned *x* **kyạnsạ yā** ~ he's lost his good looks. **sūnansạ yā** ~ he's lost his reputation. **rānā̤ tā** ~ sun's bedimmed.

dāƙụshi (1) how blunt ! (2) what invulnerability !

daƙūwạ *f.* (1) type of sweets made from tigernuts (**ayā**) or groundnuts (*epithet* is **Dạƙū dạƙū 'yar ayā**) (*cf.* **dạƙū**). (2) **yā yi minị** ~ he has made the insulting gesture **ạmbōlạ** to me (*epithet is* **daƙūwạ masōmim faɗạ**). (3) fawn-coloured horse or goat (= **sāri** 2). (4) **yā shā** ~ **dạ shī** it caused him much trouble.

dạkwacī *m.* the whole *x* **dạkwacinsụ** all of them (= **yạkwacī** = **dukkạcī**).

daƙwā-dạƙwā̤ *pl.* large and round *x* **rūwā yā sakō** ~ the rain (*e.g.* harvest-rain) fell in large drops (= **kwaɗā-kwạɗạ**), *Vd.* **daŋƙwalēlẹ**.

daƙwale A. (**daƙwā̤lē**) *Vd.* **daƙwalwā**.

B. (**daƙwā̤lẹ**) *used in* **hawam bishīyạd daƙwā̤lẹ** *m.* (i) climbing tree but being unable to descend. (ii) " biting off more than one can chew ".

dạkwai there is (= **ạkwai**).

daƙwal-dạƙwạl = daƙwā-dạƙwā̤.

daƙwalwā *f.* (*pl.* **daƙwā̤lē**). (1) big laying-hen. (2) big-made girl. (3) **dạƙwalwar ụŋgụlū** ugly big-made girl. (4) **gịndin** ~ *m.* type of cloth (*Vd.* **gịndin ~**).

dakwạŋkụ-dakwạŋkụ *m.* = **dakụŋkụ** 1.

dạkwạnnīyā *Sk. f.* slow walking.

dʹakwạrā *f.* (1) *Acacia senegal* (*from which is got gum arabic*). (2) *Acacia Dudgeoni*.

dʹakwạrī dʹakwambạ *used in* ~ **namijị dạ mārạ** epithet of man with big chest and small stomach.

daƙwarƙwar *m.* hale old man.

dakwayẹ *Kt.* *m.* addled egg (= **bạrạ gurbị**).

dā̤ƙwīyạ *Vb.* 2. (1) gnawed at. (2) ate much (*meat*) (all = **dā̤gwīyạ**).

dal *f.* the Arabic letter " d " (= **dā̤** 5).

dʹal *Vd.* **dʹallạ, dʹạl-dʹạl**.

dala A. (**dā̤lā**) *m.* (1) Cardinal bird (*Pyromelana flammiceps*) (= **dā̤lō** *q.v.* = **mulụfī**). (2) (*a*) Dala Hill in Kano City (*cf.* **dā̤la-dā̤lā**) (*b*) **Dā̤lā ƙyā̤shin tūbạlī** one can never have too much of a good thing. (*c*) **ganin Dā̤lā bā̤ shigā birnī ba nē** don't count your chickens before they're hatched ! (*Vd.* **shigẹ** 2*e*).

B. (**dalạ**) *f.* (*pl.* **dalōlī**) *Eng.* (1) two-shilling piece (= **fạtakạ**). (2) French 5-franc piece (= **shuŋkụ**). (3) Maria Theresa dollar (= **līyạr**). (4) soldier's medal (= **mindạ**). (5) girl's name (*epithet is* ~ **ūwar kudī**). (6) (*a*) **shā̤makin** ~ *m.* penny (= **kwabọ**). (*b*) (*said by women*) **mẹ akạ sāmụ** what sex was the child ? (*reply*) **dalạ** a girl ! (*cf.* **kwabọ**).

dalābū *Sk. m.* poor drinking-water.

dǎ'la-dạ̄lā" **ya yi** it's ochre-coloured (*cf.* dạ̄lā 2).

dạ̄lāgọ (1) what a dribbler ! (2) how slimy ! (3) *m.* form of madness where P. dribbles and laughs. (4) *m., f.* dribbler.

Dạlā'ilụ *m.* name of a book of prayers (*full name in Arabic is* Dalā'ilu'l khairāti).

dạlạkī *m.* (1) precipitate of dyepit or of lime (= dạgwadạgō 1*b* = ɓaɓɓarkīyā), *cf.* gwīɓạ. (2) fine sediment of gruel (kōko) (*obtained by passing through sieve or filtering* (tạ̄tā) *through cloth* : *it is used for making* gāyaŋ kōko, *Vd.* gāyā 1*c*) = *Sk.* dạgallaɓọ. (3) *Vd.* maŋ gyạdā 3.

dalala A. (dạlạlạ) *x* yanạ̄ dạ yaukī ~ it's very viscous.

B. (dạ̄lālạ) = dạ̄lāgọ 1, 2, 4.

dạlạlī *m.* mucosity ; sliminess.

ɗạlạlī *m.* roving about.

dạlạmɓạyā *Sk. f.* one strand of skein being longer than the rest.

dalam-dalam *m.* insufficiency of salt or condiments in food *x* ạbincī yā yi ~ (= galmi-galmi).

ɗạlāmụsai (*Ar.* from same root as English "talisman") *m.* type of written charm.

dalaŋ-dalaŋ = dalam-dalam.

ɗạlaŋgashị *adv.* easily, without trouble.

dalas *f.* poor-quality furā.

dạlau = dạlạlạ.

dạ̄layạ (1) *Vb.* 2 pared. (2) *Vd.* dālạ̄yẹ.

dālạ̄yẹ (1) *Vb.* 1C. (*a*) = dạ̄layạ. (*b*) plated with silver, etc. (2) *Vb.* 3A ạbinsụ yā ~ they are in keeping (*x.* bride with bridegroom ; naming of child and feast given).

ɗạl-ɗạl *m.* palpitation of heart or pulse *x* gạbāna yanạ̄ ~ my heart's going pit-a-pat (*cf.* zọ̄gī).

dale A. (dālẹ) *m.* (1) lavish living. (2) migration. (3) *Sk.* an yi wạ sōjạ ~ the soldier has been transferred elsewhere.

B. (dạ̄lẹ) *Kt. m.* = dạ̄lī.

ɗạlẹ̄-ɗạlē *m.* = ɗạlọ̄-ɗạlō.

dālẹ̄jị *Kt. m.* = dạ̄lī.

dalgẹ *m. Zar.* blot of ink (= dạ̄ŋgwạlē).

dali A. (dālị) *Ar. f.* the Arabic letter " d " (= dạl).

B. (dạ̄lī) *m.* (1) the soft-wooded tree *Commiphora Kerstingii* (*much used for*

compound-fences) (*Kt. epithet is* hanạ gọbarā). (2) = dạ̄lō 4.

dạlīkī *m.* game of children.

dạlīlị *m.* (*pl.* dạlīlai) *Ar. m.* (1) cause, reason (= hujjạ 1*a* = asalī 4 sharạdī 2) *x* (*a*) ịnā dạlīlin dạ ka zọ what's your reason for coming ? bạ̄ ni dạlīlin dạ ka cẹ̄ hakạ tell me why you said so ! (*b*) dạlīlin zūwạnsụ kẹ̄ naŋ = shī nẹ̄ dạlīlin dạ sukạ zō *that's* why they came (*or* dạlīlị kẹ̄ naŋ sukạ (= dạ sukạ) zō. (*c*) sun nēmō dạlīlai, sum bā mụ they adduced reasons to justify themselves to us. (*d*) in yā yi hakạ, dạlīlịŋ yā ịsa dạlīlị if this is what he did then he had good reason. (*dd*) dạlīlin dạ ya sạ̄ sukạ zō (= dạlīlin sụ zō), Filạ̄nī sum ɓātạ masarautạr (*or insert* dọ̄min *after comma*) the reason why they came was because the Filani had despoiled the capital. (*e*) mīkịyā bạ̄ ki sạukā banzā sǎi dạ dạlīlị nobody acts without cause. (*f*) *Vd.* gairạ 2*c*. (*g*) *Kt.* yā tạ̄ki ~ he knows for sure (= dāhịr 4). (2) (*a*) through *x* dạlīlị dạ kai (= dạlīliŋkạ) nẹ̄ mukạ sāmụ it was through *you* that we got it. (*b*) is because ạbin dạ ya sạ̄ mukạ ji tsọ̄rō, dạlīlịm (= dạlīlị kụ̄wā) mun ji rūrị the reason why we were afraid is due to the fact that we heard a roaring. (*c*) it is because dạlīlị dǎi yanạ̄ san dā nẹ̄ it's because he wants a son. dạlīlị kụ̄wā, sun zāgē mụ the reason why is because they've insulted us. (3) means of getting (= sanạdī 1*a* = silạ) *x* bạ̄ shi dạ dạlīlin sāmụnsạ he has no means of getting it. (4) intermediary (= sanạdī 1*b* = silạ) *x* (*a*) wạ̄nēnẹ̄ dạlīlịŋ aurạŋ who was the marriage-intermediary ? (*b*) Audụ nẹ̄ ya yi minị dạlīlị har na sạ̄mi dōkị wurin Sarkī it was through the medium of *Audu* that I got a horse from the chief (*in this example, for* dạlīlị *we can substitute* dạlīlịŋ wạ dạlīlạ = dạlīlin dạlīlatạŋ = dạlīlịŋ wa ạlā zālikạ = azzịkin dọ̄min dọ̄min (*Vd.* dọ̄min-dọ̄min) = *Sk.* dạlīlịŋ wadạlā). (*c*) dạlīlị yā fi dūkịyā influence is better than riches. (5) origin *x* (*a*) dạlīlịn Sarākunạ dukạ, wani mụtụm sūnansạ

Daŋ abdullāhi all the Emirs trace their origin to a man named Dan Abdullahi. garin naŋ, dalīlinsa su Filānī nē na mutānan Sakkwatō that town was founded by Sokoto Filanis. (b) an ɗēbę sarai, bā shī, bā dalīlinsa it's been removed and there isn't a trace of it. (7) nēman ~ m. picking a quarrel.

dalla (1) f. (a) jirgin ~ m. line made by child down forehead (Vd. jirgī 3b). (b) Zar. children's game with earth. (2) Vb. 1A Vd. dallō 1.

ɗalla Vb. 1A (1) projected missile by springy act (arrow from bow ; crooked first finger against thumb, etc.). yā ~ ɗal he projected it flip ! (2) kunāma tā ~ masa harbi scorpion stung him. (3) yā ɗallō minī tsakūwa he threw gravel at me.

dalla-dalla A. (dalla-dalla) adv. separately ; group by group.
　　B. (dalla-dallā) adj. (m., f. ; sg., pl.) spotted ; spotty (= dabbarę-dabbarę).

dallafa Vb. 3B = dallafē Vb. 3A Kt. yā ~ garēnī he stuck to me like a limpet.

dallaja = dallaza.

dallakī Sk. m. fine sediment (= dalakī q.v.).

dallamayē m. x sunā ~ da shī they keep lifting it up and putting it down.

dallarā (1) Vb. 1C yā ~ minī wutā he happened to touch me with a lighted brand. (2) cf. dallarō.

dallarē Vb. 1C yā ~ ni da wutā = dallarā.

dallarō Vb. 1E (1) yā ~ wutā he lighted a brand at the fire. (2) rāḱumī yā ~ wutā male camel protruded red gland when on heat. (3) yā ~ harshę he put out his tongue (= dallō 1b). (4) Vd. dallarā.

dallasa = dallaza.

dallashē (1) Vb. 1C = dallazā. (2) Vb. 3A = dallaza.

dallaza A. (dallazā) Vb. 1C (1) blunted edge of (= dākusā). (2) (a) maltreated P. (b) left T. where likely to spoil (through weather, etc.). (3) adulterated T.
　　B. (dallaza) Vb. 3B (1) edge of T. became blunt. (2) fell into disgrace. (3) went to the bad.

ɗalle A. (ɗallę) Vb. 1A yā ~ ni da tsakūwa, etc. (= ɗalla 3).
　　B. (ɗallē) m. boys' gambling-game.

dallō (1) Vb. 1E. (a) = dallarō 2. (b) yā dallō (= dallō da) harshę he showed his tongue between his lips (= dallarō 3). (2) Vb. 3A T. protruded. (3) Sk. m. carrying child or animal on one's shoulder.

dalma lead ; tin (= darma q.v.).

dalmi-dalmi m. = dalam-dalam.

ɗālō m. (1) calf (= marakī). (2) dribbler. (3) Sk. the tree ɗālī q.v. (4) (a) Cardinal bird (= mulufī = ɗālā). (b) Kt. ḱwan ~ type of blue alkyabba (= ḱwan mulufī).

ɗalō-ɗalō m. idle roving.

dalōlī two shilling-pieces, etc. (Vd. dala).

dālumā f. = daḱwalwā.

ɗam Sk. used in ɗam min give me ! (= sam).

ɗam x yā fāɗī ~ it fell with hollow sound (x full sack into iron truck, cf. bif).

dama A. (dāma) (1) f. (a) hannun ~ m. (i) right hand. (ii) right hand side. (b) a hannun ~ tasa yakē (i) it is on the right of it. (ii) he is his right-hand man. (c) hanyar ~ = hanya wajan ~ the road to the right. (d) har ŋ kwantā ~ ba zan yi ba never should I act so. (e) hannun ~ māganim makalāmā largess silences slander. (f) mai hannū dukạ ~ m., f. liberal P. (g) abin dạ ~ ta jūrę, hagum ba tā jūrę ba everyone's patience differs. (2) prep. on the right of x (a) dāma (= a ~) garēshi on his right. ~ da hanya on the right of the road. (b) sū nē ~ da Sarkī they're the chief's favourites. (3) ~ kākyau, hauni kākyau may you always prosper ! (Vd. kākyau). (b) Vd. bilāka. (4) tausa ~ Vd. bahāgo 3.
　　B. (dāmā) f. (1) chance. (a) (i) bā ni da ~ ŋ yī yau I can't manage to do it to-day (= sararī 2). bā shi da dāmar musu he has no chance to refuse. (ii) ku yī tun da ~ do it while you have the chance ! (iii) da dāmā nē, gudu da awākī act in good time ! (b) (i) bā ~ it's impossible ; it's out of the question. yā ga bā ~ = yā ji bā ~ he

had to own himself beaten, outwitted. suŋ ganī bạ ∼ they saw the matter was hopeless. yā ga bạ dāmar yạ cī sụ yạnzu he saw no chance of conquering them at present. (ii) doŋ kadạ sụ ga dāmarsụ lest they " try their hand " ! (iii) bạ dāmar ukụ sụ yi ạmfạnī sǎi an dadẹ three of them are out of action for a long time. (iv) ạbim bạ ∼ an indescribably wonderful thing. (c) yanạ ganin ∼ yạ īyạ he thinks himself up to it. (d) nā bā kị dāmar kwānā ukụ I give you three days to think it over. (2) x in nā ga ∼ nạ yī I'll do it if I choose to. ganin ∼ mukạ yī we did it because it suited us to do it. (3) mụ kirā shị yạ zō, kō mạ ji ∼ let's send for him and perhaps we'll enjoy ourselves ! (4) an equal x munạ ganin dāmassạ we feel equal to doing it. bạ shi dạ ∼ he has no equal. kanạ ganin dāmātạ ? nẹ ? do you really think yourself of the same calibre as myself ? (5) dạ dāmā (a) quite a few x (i) adj. mutạnē dạ ∼ sunạ yị quite a few people do so. (ii) noun pl. da ∼ cikinsụ sukạ shigō kasarmụ a largish number of them immigrated into our country. cikinsụ ạkwai dạ dāma wadạndạ bā sạ sọ there are quite a few persons among them who do not wish to do so. (iii) sạu dạ ∼ often. (iv) abūbūwạ mạsū ∼ a good few things. (b) (i) dạ ∼ dǎi yes, fairly well (reply to x does he sew well ?), cf. dāma-dāma. (ii) dạ ∼ Sarkī ạ kạn jạkī better half a loaf than no bread. (6) improvement x lạbạrai sum fārạ ∼ the news has begun to improve. dạ ạbịn ya yi ∼ when matters improved somewhat. yā ji (= yā yi) ∼ he's feeling better.

C. (dạmā) Vb. 2 (progressive is usually dāmụ) worried x yā dạmē nị he worried me. yanạ dāmụnsụ it's worrying them.

D. (dạ mā) Vd. dạ 5.

E. (dāmạ) Vb. 1A (1) wet-mixed x (a) tā ∼ furā she mixed flour to make furā. an ∼ kụnū paste has been mixed for gruel. an ∼ salạlạ Vd. salạlạ. yā ∼ kasā he mixed clay for building (Vd. kwāɓạ, cākụdā, tūkạ, gaurạyā,

hautsụnā). (b) tạ ∼ tūwō she made bad tūwō (= kwāɓạ, cf. tūkạ). (c) kōwā ya ∼ dạ gwīɓī, shī zại shā ạbinsạ as you sow, so shall you reap. (2) (a) muddled up T. (b) bewildered P. (a, b = kwāɓạ = rūdạ 1a). (bb) yā ∼ kạnsạ he's at sixes and sevens. (c) nā dạmu I'm perplexed. ạbin dạ kẹ dạmūwā tasụ shī nẹ kai mukụ harị the cause of their perplexity is how to raid you. (d) Vd. dạmạ compounds. (3) yanạ dāmạwā he's living lavishly (= kwāɓạ). tanạ dāmạwā ạ gidam mijịntạ she's living with her husband in prosperity. (4) yā ∼ hannun rūwā = kwāɓạ 1d.

dama A. (dạmā) Vb. 2 tautened x yā dạmi bạkā he tautened bow into a curve. yā dạmi zanẹ he pulled out cloth to rid it of creases.

B. (dāmạ) Vb. 1A (with dative). (1) nā ∼ masạ būlālạ I flogged him. (2) Sk. attached T. to another x an ∼ masạ itạcē.

dama-dama A. (dāma-dāma) (1) slightly x yā īyạ dịŋkị ? can he sew ? ; reply, dạ dāma-dāma dǎi only slightly (cf. dāmā 5): epithet is ∼ wạddạ bā tạ cikin yạbō " slightly " which isn't much use. (2) yanạ ∼ dạ shī (i) he's keen on it. (ii) he's keen to get it.

B. (dạma-dạma) x jịkīna ∼ nakẹ jịnsạ I feel out of sorts. munạ ganinsạ ∼ he seems out of form (= hakạ-hakạ = mạshạr-mạshạr).

dạmạdạnyē = Kt. dạmạdạnyū m. firewood proving to be not properly dry (= tsạntsāmā 2b).

dāmad dạ Vb. 4B confused, perplexed P. (= dāmạ 2b).

dạmạ fịce = dạma-fịta f. unprepossessing young wife.

Dạmāgạram f. the place so called.

Damāgarāwā Vd. Bạdamāgarẹ.

damagẹrẹ m. type of wild feline (= dagē).

dạmagi m. (= ɓaurē 2) the red-flowered weed Chrozophora senegalensis.

dạmāgirā f. flowers and leaves of young desert date (adūwạ).

damạimai Vd. damō.

dạmạ kạsūwā Vd. hadirị.

dạmạ kōnō used in kadạ kạ yi ∼ take

care you don't let your clothing get
burned by match or tobacco falling
on it !
dāmāƙullē *m., f.* shortnecked P. (= mādā-
ƙullē).
damāƙwi-dạmāƙwi *x* aŋ kāmạ shi ~
he's securely tied up.
ɗamạl gwạrājī *m. Sk.* type of climbing
plant which is apt to trip people.
dạmāmạ *Kt.* = dạmạ-dạmạ.
damāmē monitors (*Vd.* damō).
Dạmāmusau *epithet of* Emir, brave
warrior, gobbling animal.
damāmushē *Vb.* 1D (1) ate up quickly.
(2) captured completely.
dạmanā *Vd.* dạmunā.
ɗamānīyā *Kt. f.* (1) wrangling. (2)
struggling with P. or task.
damar *Kt.* yanạ̃ zaune ~ he's prosperous.
ɗamarạ *f.* (*pl.* ɗamạrū = ɗamarōrī). (1)
(*a*) (i) belt. (ii) yā shiga ~ = yā
ɗaurạ ~ = yā ɗaurẹ ~ he put on belt.
(*b*) yā yi ~ (*pl.* sun yi ɗamạrū) he
girded up his loins (*literally and figuratively*). (*c*) yā ƙārạ ~ he screwed up
his courage still more. (*d*) ɗamarạr
zūcī tā fi ta jikī a good character is
better than wealth. (*e*) (i) sun ci ~
they got ready for boxing. (ii) yā ci
(= yā cīwō = yā yi) ɗamarạ he made
his preparations. (iii) sunạ̃ jan ɗamạ-
runsụ they're making their preparations. (iv) sun sākẹ sạbabbin ɗamạrū
sụ ci mụ they made fresh efforts to
conquer us. (v) aŋ ƙārạ musụ ɗamạrū
they have received further munitions.
(2) (*a*) the interlaced triangles (Shield of
David) *e.g.* on penny. (*b*) mē ka bi :
ɗamarạ ? kō kạn Sarkī heads or tails ?
ɗamạr cikị *f.* breakfast before setting out.
dāmar dạ *Vb.* 4A confused, perplexed P.
(= dāmạ 2*b*).
*ɗamarmarā *f.* spiteful, false accusation.
ɗamạrū belts (*Vd.* ɗamarạ).
dāma rufe = dāma fịce.
dāmạ rūwā *Vd.* kwạsā-kwạsā.
ɗamāsā *Vb.* 3B *Kt.* (P. or animal) grew
up quickly.
dạmāshērē *m.* (1) slow worker. (2) *cf.*
dạmushērē.
dāmạ shirị *m., f.* (*sg., pl.*) cantankerous P.
damạ̃tsā forearms (*Vd.* dantsẹ).

dạmātsīrī *m.* type of harmless, green
snake (= ɗanyē 2*b*).
Dạmau *Sk.* = Dụmau.
dạmbā *f.* (1) (*a*) bog. (*b*) weeds masking
presence of underlying water (*epithet
is* ~ bụrụm dạ wāwā = ~ shịgar mại
gāgā) = rūwā A.16*c*. (2) deception,
tricking.
dambạcē *Vb.* 1C knocked P. over in
boxing.
dambạɗā *f.* (1) *Kt.* dampness seeping
through floor (= laimạ 1). (2) *Sk.*
soiled state of clothing.
ɗambambạm *Vd.* ɗanbambạm.
dambạrā *Vb.* 1C daubed on much of T.
x tā dambạrạ shūnī ạ kạntạ she be-
smothered her hair with indigo. tā ~
tạ̃barmā dạ tạɓō she bespattered the
mat with mud.
dambạrɓạr *x* yanạ̃ dạ kaurī ~ it's very
solid.
dambạrɓạrī *m.* (*f.* dạmɓarɓạrā) *pl.* damɓar-dạmɓạr solid.
dạmɓarɓạsā *f.* squat girl.
damɓar-dạmɓạr *Vd.* dạmɓarɓạrī.
damɓare A. (damɓarē) *Vb.* 3A is (was)
bespattered with *x* tạ̃barmā tā ~
dạ tạɓō = tạɓō yā ~ ạ tạ̃barmā the
mat's bespattered with mud.
B. (dạmɓarē) *m.* solid, round embroidery on gown (*cf.* tambạrī 2).
dambạrgo = dạmɓarko *m.* ill-made (*P.
or article*).
dambạrwā *f.* quarrelling.
dambas = dạmbạsɓạs in profusion (= dạ-
ɓāɓạ *q.v.*).
dambạsā *f.* pleasant-looking, squat
girl.
dambạzā *Vb.* 1C (*with dative*) applied T.
profusely to *x* an ~ wạ dōkị adō much
adornment has been hung on horse.
an ~ matạ niƙạ she's been given much
grinding to do. nā ~ masạ hatsī
I gave him much corn.
dambazō *Vb.* 3A (ants, pimples, etc.)
appeared profusely *x* ƙurạrrajī sun ~
masạ many pimples appeared on him.
dambē *m.* (1) (*a*) boxing. (*b*) ɗan ~ *m.*
boxer. (2) ~ ɗākị dạ duhụ ; na wạje
shi kẹ̃ ganin sararī let the cobbler stick
to his last ! (3) yā yi ~ yā yi kwạrāyạ
he knows the ways of the world.

(4) kuŋkūrū yanā san dambē, damtsansa yā gaza don't attempt the impossible. (5) mē ya raba ~ da fada the two are identical. (6) a kai ~ Katsina ? " taking coals to Newcastle " (Vd. kai 3f).

dambī m. beginning of pods of locustbean (dōrawa) to ripen. (2) dambidambī m. beginning of sores or madness to improve.

dambilāgo m. indigo-plants (bābā) after shūnī extracted.

dambilam (pl. dambilōlī). (1) m. (a) rich P. (b) large town. (c) expensive T. (2) f. prostitute with large clientele.

dambilo m. (pl. dambilōlī) (Eng. downbelow) hold of vessel.

dambilōlī Vd. dambilo ; dambilam.

dambū m. (1) (a) (i) various foods including flour steamed with onion or hemp (rama) leaves. (ii) ~ yā hau the dambū is fully cooked. (iii) ~ mai sauriŋ hawā epithet of quick-tempered P. (c) an jūya shi ~ tālīya, ya ki all efforts to persuade him failed. (2) dambun tukunyā bean-flour and leaves boiled together.

dambūbu m. (1) calf of leg (= Sk. maturzai). (2) shin (both = shā rābā q.v.).

damci Sk. m. (1) forearm (= damtse q.v.). (2) dan damciŋ ūwā bother you !

dame A. (dame) Sk. m. = dami.
  B. (dāme) (1) Vb. 1A. (a) mixed all of T. into paste (Vd. dāma). (b) confused, puzzled (= dāma). (c) yā ~ su, yā shanyē he surpasses them. (2) Vb. 3A (a) became muddled, confused (= kwābe 2 q.v. for examples). (b) bai ki ta dāme ba Vd. masudī. (c) kanka a dāme Vd. akurū.
  C. (dāmē) m. (1) the way rūdē is prepared. (2) mixture of bran and water given to animals (both = kwābē).

dāme (1) Vb. 1A (a) = dāmā. (b) overcharged P. (2) Vb. 3A ciki yā ~ the stomach has sunken in.

dame-dame A. (damē-damē) (1) yanā ~ da kudinsa (kāyansa) he won't let his money (property) out of his sight (= sanke-sankē). (2) yā cika ciki, yanā ~ he has stomach-ache from

over-eating or over-drinking. (3) yanā ~ da kāshī he urgently wants to go to latrine but sees no chance (all = makēmakē).
  B. (damē-damē) hungrily x yā dāwō ~ he returned hungry.

damfa-damfa in profusion (= dābābā q.v.).

damfamē Vb. 1C an ~ gidā compound's been fenced with a damfamī.

damfamī m. (pl. damfuma) temporary fence of grass, stalks, etc.

damfara A. (damfarā) Vb. 1C. (1) compressed (= danna 1b). (2) collected. (3) (with dative) applied profusely x an ~ wa bangō farar kasā whitewash has been slapped on the wall. an ~ masa māshi he's been deeply pierced with spear. an ~ masa sātā he's been seriously robbed.
  B. (damfara) Vb. 3A sun ~ they're gathered in a large crowd.

damfara A. (damfarā) Vb. 1C (1) caused T. to adhere to x an ~ shi jikim bangō it's been stuck on to the wall. (2) = dāfa 1.
  B. (damfara) Vb. 3B stuck to ; clung to.

damfare A. (damfarē) (1) Vb. 1C. (a) = damfarā 1, 2. (b) an ~ shi da māshi he's been deeply pierced with spear (= damfarā 3). (c) kept P. waiting. (2) Vb. 3A kasā tā ~ wet soil began to dry.
  B. (damfarē) m. compressed butter.

damfare Vb. 3A stuck to ; clung to x yā ~ mini = yā ~ garēni.

damfari what a collection ! ; what compression ! etc. (as damfarā).

damfarkamī m. (f. damfarkamā) (1) big strong P. (2) Sk. the weed Monechma hispida.

damfuma Vd. damfamī.

damgērē m. the plant dankadafī q.v.

dami m. (pl. dammuna = damma =dammai). (1) (a) bundle of corn. (b) damin cīyāwa bundle of grass (Vd. kundumāsa 2). (2) damim bākin rumbu, dauka kō yau kō gōbe = damim bākin rumbu, zai fāda kō yau kō gōbe he is (you are, etc.) about to become a Chief (= Kt. ambutā 2). (3) damin shūci

bundle of thatching-grass. **(4) damiŋ
itātūwạ** bundle of sticks. **(5) kā ci ~,
kā kāsạ ɗaukạr ƙwāyā** what an idle
lout ! (*Vd.* **tsīrukụ**). **(6) ~ yā tsiŋkẹ
ạ giŋdiŋ kargō = tsiŋkẹ** 2*a*.iii. **(7)
tā fāru, tā ƙārẹ,** an yi wạ mại ~ ɗayā
sātạ (*a*) a clean sweep has been made
of it. (*b*) what staggering news ! (*cf.*
ƙudugum). **(8) damịm mạīwā** *Vd.*
zōɓīyā. **(9)** an cẹ dạ kạrē yạ ɗaụki ~
Vd. **kạrē** 32. **(10) damịŋ gujīyā** *Vd.*
namiji 7. **(11) gā̀ ~** *Vd.* **gạrāje** 2.
(12) damịn dāwạ *Vd.* **gūgūwạ.**
dāminā = dāmunā.
dāmisạ *m., f.* (*pl.* **dāmisōshī**). **(1)** leopard
(*cf.* **tuŋkīyā** 2, **wạnzāmị** 3). **(2) ~
ƙị sạbō = ~ kā ƙi ganī bīyū** what a
cantankerous person ! (*Vd.* **dāmishị** 4).
(3) dāmisạr rūwā type of fish. **(4) ạ
ƙārạ ~ kāyā̀ ?** debt on debt ! (*Vd.*
Bạrnō 2). **(5) gā̀ ~** *laudatory drum-
rhythm for* Chief's son (*Vd.* **gufƙụŋ**).
(6) ~ wuriŋ wani kyạŋwā some people
are fearless. **(7) bāya ~** *Vd.* **kūrā** 34.
(8) kōwā ya ga ~ yā sam bā̀ kạrē
ba nẹ̀ it is obvious. **(9) mạƙīyiŋkạ bā
yā̀ yạbaŋkạ, kō kā kāmạ ~ kạ bā
shị** a bitter enemy is implacable.
dāmishērē *words used in the* game **dāmụs-
hērē** *q.v.*
dāmishị *Kt. m.* **(1) = dāmisạ. (2)
dāmishịŋ ƙasā** hard worker. **(3)
dāmishịm mazā** (*only used in songs*)
pugnacious man. **(4) Dāmishị, kā
ƙi ganī ɓiyū** he's one who insists on his
orders being obeyed at once (*Vd.*
dāmisạ 2).
dāmisōshī *Vd.* **dāmisạ.**
damƙạ = daŋƙạ.
dammā *Vd.* **damị.**
dammai *Vd.* **damị.**
dammacī *Kt. m.* **~ gạrại** he's a reserved P.
dammānị *Sk. m.* **= tsạmmānị.**
dam mẹ̀ why ? (*Vd.* **doŋ**).
dammi A. (**dammị**) *Sk. m.* **= damị.**
  B. (**dam mị**) *Sk.* **= dam mẹ̀.**
dammunạ *Vd.* **damị.**
damō *m.* (*pl.* **damā̀mē = damạīmai**). **(1)**
land-monitor. **(2)** *Sk.* **kā ƙi ciŋ ~,
ka ci kiskī** refusing T. and then per-
force having recourse to T. still inferior
(= **cī** 26*v*). **(3) ~ ɗaŋ gạrāyā yạrī**

yạrī type of girls' game. **(4)** (*a*) **~
sarkiŋ hạƙurī** what patience ! (*b*)
**~ sarkiŋ hạƙurī, kurụm tā gamshē
kạ dạ kōwā, wạndạ ya cẹ̀ kā cẹ̀, shī
ya cẹ̀ = 4***a***. (5) kunā̀ bariŋ ~, yanā̀**
zamā guzạ check him while there's
yet time ! **(6) ịnā tukunyar damṑ,
ịnā ta guzạ** the two are identical. **(7)
yā̀ yi bazarar ~, ya yi wạjẹ** he leaped
outside as if possessed. **(8) sun yi minị
atịshāwạr ~** they suddenly " went for
me " (*Vd.* **atịshāwạ** 2). **(9) bạn ~** *m.*
T. dry on surface but wet below. **(10)**
(*a*) **yā̀ shịga girman ~** he's in prison.
(*b*) **yā̀ daŋƙẹ damansạ, yā̀ kai shị gidā**
he took him prisoner. **(11)** (*a*) **gōgyan ~**
m. (i) the gum-tree *Combretum sp.*
(ii) *Kt.* type of ear-ring. (*b*) **wuyạn ~**
m. the tree *Combretum leonense.* **(12)
harshạn ~ gạrēshị** (*a*) it (whip,
double-headed bulrush millet, etc.) is
forked. (*b*) he's two-faced. **(13) Allā̀
yạ kai ~ gạ hạrāwạ, kō bại ci ba, yā̀
yi birgimā** may the wish be fulfilled !
(14) kisạn ~ haŋkạlī nẹ̀, īyā̀wā nẹ̀
act cautiously ! **(15)** *Vd.* **garkẹ̀** 1*b*.
damō-damṑ *m. used in* **hannunsạ (bā̀kinsạ)
yā̀ yi ~** his hands (mouth) are messy
from soup, blood, filth, etc.
ɗamo-ɗamo = ɗame-ɗame.
ɗamra *Sk.* **= ɗaura.**
ɗamriŋ kirū *Kt. m.* the torture **kạŋgạrē** 1.
ɗamrin rījịyā *Vd.* **rījịyā.**
ɗamrin samjị *Sk. m.* woman's making up
her long load.
ɗamrō *Sk.* **= dạurō.**
damsạkūkạ = gạnsạkūkạ.
damsạsā *Vb.* 1C **= dansạsā.**
damshī *Kt. m.* **= danshī.**
damtsẹ *Kt. m.* forearm (**= dantsẹ** *q.v.*).
damu A. (**dāmụ**) *m.* (*secondary v.n. of*
dā̀mā) *x* **yanā̀ dāmụnsụ =** *less commonly* **yanā̀ dāmassụ** he's worrying
them.
  B. (**dā̀mu**) *Vd.* **dāmạ** 2*c*.
dāmuƙạ *Vb.* 2 clutched with both hands.
dāmuƙā̀sạ (1) *m., f.* dirty-looking P.
(2) what a hard worker !
dāmụlā *Vb.* 1C **= dāgụlā.**
dāmunā *f., m.* **(1)** (*a*) the rainy-season.
(*b*) (i) *epithet is* **~ mại ạlbarkạ = ~ darē.**
Vd. also **bụgau** 4. (ii) **dā̀ mā nā̀ yī, dā̀**

nā sāmu *is epithet of* dāmunā *there
being play on words* dā mā nā *and*
dāmunā *and the words being put in
mouth of a slacker.* (c) ~ tā fādi
sōsǎi the wet-season's well set in
(= tāgūwą 3*b*). (d) ~ tā yi zurfī
wet-season's well advanced. (e) dāmunā tā yi shigar zōmō, tā yi fitar
gīwā wet season set in scantily but
later was abundant. (f) dāmunā
mai ban sāmu *epithet of* liberal P. (g)
Vd. wahalą 1*e*.ii. (h) Zątanku *is name
given male or female slave by mistress
who has unexpectedly become prosperous.
Such female-slave when called by her
name* Zątanku *being uttered, replies*
Allą yā yi dāmunā. (k) im bābu
dāmunā *Vd.* watą 2*o*. (l) ~ tā bāshē
shi *Vd.* fąllē 1*b*. (2) ~ bīyū early-
ripening variety of beans, maize,
sweet-potatoes, etc. (= arbą'in 2). (3)
am masą dāmunan nikę iri he's had
nothing but calamities. (4) ~ kusa
boiled dried-groundnuts (= dąfau 2).
(5) ~ tā kāmą yārǫ the baby lad has
infantile convulsions (= tąfīyą 7). (6)
~ tā yi kyau the rainy-season is good ;
young cereals (yabanyą) are good. (7)
sowing cereals by Maguzawa to prog-
nosticate luck at wedding or prog-
nosticate luck of crops (= būdad
dawą 2). (8) ďan ~ a finger-disease.
(9) a scarlet insect (= kąrammuski *q.v.*).

dāmushērē (1) *in the game where boys form
circle and one tries to break through,*
ďan ąkwīyąna *is said, and reply is*
dāmushērē. (2) *cf.* dāmāshērē.

damutse A. dāmutsā = dāmutsē *Vb.* 1C
mixed food with the hand.

B. (dāmutsē) *m.* act of mixing food
with hand.

damuttsā forearms (*Vd.* dantsę).

dāmuzgū *m.* masticating by animal whose
mouth is full.

ďan (*lit.* son of ; *Vd.* dā) (1) (*pl. formed
with* 'yan) *forms many sobriquets x*
ďan sąndā *pl.* 'yan sąndā policeman.
ďan Adąn human being (*Vd. these
compounds under second word*). (2)
(*with f.* 'yar ; *pl.* 'yan) *indicates place
of origin or profession x* ďan Kano *m.*
(*f.* 'yar Kano) *pl.* 'yan Kano P. of

Kano. ďan kąsūwā, *etc.*, market-trader.
(3) (*with fem.* 'yar, *pl.* 'yā'yan *prefixed to
noun in plural*) *indicates the young of
animals x* ďan tinkīyā *m.* (*f.* 'yar tinkīyā)
pl. 'yā'yan tumākī lamb. (4) (ďan *before
masc. noun,* 'yar *before fem. noun,* 'yan
before plural). (*a*) *forms diminutive x* ďan
yārǫ *pl.* 'yan yārā little boy. 'yar
tinkīyā *pl.* 'yan tumākī small ewe.
ďan wannąn this little one. wadąn-
nąn 'yan gudā uku these three
small ones. don ďan wannąn ąbu
kadą . . . for so small a matter,
do not . . . ąbu mai ďan nawyī
a slightly heavy thing. ąbu mai
ďan kauri-kauri (*i*) thickish T. (*ii*)
stiffish amount of money. cikin ďan
wannąn lōkącī in so short a time.
(*b*) ('yan *is also used before
collectives*) *x* nā yi 'yan wahąle-wahąlē
I gave some small presents. don 'yan
ƙwanki uku nę ? all this fuss about
your three trifling eggs ? 'yan kāyā
small belongings. wadansu 'yan tąrkącē some odds and ends. (*c*) (ďan *is
also prefixed to verbs*) *x* gāra dǎi mu
ďan dākątā kadąn we'd better wait a
bit ! yaną ďan karkącēwā it twists
about a bit (*x* road). mu ƙārą ďan
waiwąyāwā kąn yākin let us cast
another glance on this war ! ďan
jūrę kadąn wait a bit ! (*d*) (ďan *prefixed to word already indicating a
diminutive, leaves sense unchanged*)
x ďam mąrakī = mąrakī calf. 'yam
maruƙą = maruƙą calves. (5) (ďan
before fem. animal denotes the male) *x*
ďan tinkīyā ram (= rāgō). ďan
ąkwīyą billy goat (= bunsurū). 'yan
tumākī rams (= rāguną). 'yan awākī
billy goats (= bunsurai). (6) ďan
shēkarą sittin man sixty years old
(*Vd.* shēkarą). (7) *Vd.* ďanubā, ďanūwā.
(8) *for* ďan-*compounds, Vd.* second word.
(9) ďan gā rūwā *Vd.* dāgirą.

ďana A. (ďaną) *Vb.* 1A (1) (*a*) an ~
kibīyą ą bąkā arrow's been fitted on to
bowstring (= hadą 1*l*). (*b*) an ~ bąkā
marriageable girl (article for sale) has
been tricked out to enhance value.
(2) ~ tarkō to set spring of trap.
~ bindigą to cock trigger of gun.

kunāmạ tā ⁓ harbi scorpion raised tail to sting. (3) (a) tā ⁓ sulę ạ hancī she fixed shilling to hole in her nose (= dasạ 6). (b) mak̞ĕrī yā ⁓ tarō smith fixed spindle to threepenny bit (for use as in 3a) (= dōsạ 1e = turkę 1d), cf. d̞ōnạ. (4) Sk. ⁓ kāyā to balance load on one's head without holding it. (5) nī, nā ⁓ ; kai kumā, d̞ạna (said in game lạŋgạ) I'm hopping holding one foot, you do the same ! (6) Vd. d̞ōnạ. B. (d̞ānạ) Vb. 1A (1) (a) measured T. out in units equal to distance of thumb to middle finger (= tak̞ạ). (b) measured land with tape or chain. (2) (a) fried in oil (k̞ōsǎi, fuŋkạsō, fạŋkē) = gasạ 1b.ii. (b) ⁓ brōdi gạ tạnd̞ĕrū to bake bread by contact with side of oven. (3) went for a short ride x sam mini k̞ĕkyạŋkạ, n̩ ⁓ lend me your bike to use for a moment ! (4) (with dative) applied T. to x (a) yā ⁓ mini wutā he burned me with lighted brand. yā ⁓ wutā ạ d̞āki he set fire to the house. yā ⁓ wutā ạ tukunyar tābạ he lit his pipe. (b) yā ⁓ mini tsạ̄dā he overcharged me. yā ⁓ mini kibīyạ he wounded me with arrow. kunāmạ tā ⁓ masạ harbi the scorpion stung him. yā d̞ānạ masạ hạrsāshi he (rifleman, gunner) fired at him

danana x an zubạ masạ mǎi ⁓ very much butter has been added to it (tūwō). nāmạn nạn̩ yanā dạ mǎi ⁓ this meat is very rich (= shanana).

dạ̄ nā shā f. rich gravy (= dạrmạsōsụwā).

danạyā f. freshly-mixed furā with sour milk.

d̞anbambam (d̞ambambạm) m. Sk. kā d̞aukō ⁓ you brought trouble on yourself.

dancę Kt. m. forearm (= dantsę q.v.).

danda A. (dandā) bare x dandar k̞asā bare ground. dandar gadō bed without coverings.

B. (d̞ạnda) (1) m., f. (sg., pl.). (a) (i) horse white on at least 4 out of 5 places (legs and head). (b) ⁓ bōlạ ditto where both eyes and forehead white (Vd. bōlạ). (c) Vd. cicciro. (2) dạnda = dạn'da-dạndā" m. (a) depigmentation from syphilis, etc. (b) T.

with patches of lighter colour than the rest.

C. (dạndā) f. leakiness x sōrō yā yi ⁓ the flat-topped house is leaking.

dandaɓa A. (dandạɓā) Vb. 1C patted T. to compress it.

B. (dandạɓā) f. pleasant-looking, squat girl.

dandabạlī Sk. m. = dandamạlī.

dandaɓas squat = daɓas q.v.

dạndaɓạsā squat girl.

dandạɓē Vb. 1C = dandạɓā.

dandagaryā = dandā

dạndajai Kt. (1) m. T. left about carelessly. (2) adv. left about carelessly.

d̞anḍak x an d̞aukē ⁓ it's been completely removed.

dandak̞a A. (dandạk̞ā) Vb. 1C (1) (a) pounded (salt, pepper) on stone or log instead of dakạ, i.e. instead of pounding in mortar. (b) pounded cotton on mugurjī. (2) maltreated ; beat P. (Vd. dandạk̞ạ 3).

B. (dandạk̞ạ) Vb. 2 (1) = dandạk̞ā. (2) destroyed spermatic cords of bull or goat to fatten (= dakę 1c) cf. fidīyē. (3) what a drubbing ! x yā dandạk̞ā ta ⁓ what a drubbing he gave her !

dandak̞e A. (dandạk̞ē) Vb. 1C. (1) = dandạk̞ā 1a, dandạk̞ạ 2. (3) ⁓ yātsạ to knock one's finger accidentally.

B. (dandạk̞ē) m. (1) T. pounded. (2) Allā yạ sạ̄ kạ tsūfā har kạ ci ⁓ may you live to a hoary old age !

dạndakwạryạ (1) f. the sweet nạ̄kīyạ. (2) how solid and good ! (re furniture, etc.).

dandạlī m. open-space for recreation (Vd. dātsạ 2a).

dandamạlī m. raised doorstep (= dōkin̩ k̞ōfạ).

dạndambillē Sk. m. crowd (= tạ̄rō).

dandan A. (dandạn̩) (1) firmly x k̞ōfạr tā dạnnu ⁓ door's firmly closed. (2) m. kạn sōrō ⁓ yak̞ę roof of flat-topped house is solid. cik̞i yā yi ⁓ stomach is firm.

B. (dạndạn̩) in profusion (= dạ̄ɓạ̄ɓạ q.v.).

dạndānạ f. (1) the herb Schwenkia americana. (2) hạrshạnsạ yā ji ⁓ he enunciates clearly.

d̞and̞ana A. (d̞and̞ạnā) Vb. 1C (1) tasted.

(2) (a) experienced x yā ~ talaucį he suffered poverty. yā ~ kūɗạrsạ he suffered trouble. (b) (with dative) caused P. to experience x yā ~ musụ dādī he made them glad. yā ~ matạ mutūwạ he was the cause of her death. sun sạ Jāmụs ɗanɗạnạ irįn dafįn dạ sukạ shāyad dạ waɗansu they've " paid the Germans back in their own coin ".   B. (ɗanɗanạ) Vb. 2 (1) = ɗanɗạnā 1, 2a.   (2) = ɗanɗạnē 1.   (3) int. of ɗanạ.

dan dạ naŋ Sk. at once (= naŋ dạ naŋ).

ɗanɗạm bạ haukạ m. = ɗanɗạni haukạci.

ɗanɗane A. (ɗanɗạnē) Vb. 1C (1) ~ ƙōsǎi ạ yājị to dip cakes in condiments. (2) yā ~ yājị he used up the condiments by dipping cakes into them.   B. (ɗanɗanẹ) m. (1) a mere taste. (2) trifling task.

dạndạŋginā f. (1) Sk. walking with short steps.   (2) Sk. sowing seeds closely : epithet is ~ shūkạn yạ̄rā.   (3) Kt. boggling.

dandagurzā f. x rịgan naŋ tā shā ~ = anạ̄ ~ dạ rịgạr this gown's (1) had hard wear, (2) has passed from owner to owner.

ɗanɗạni haukạci m. (1) mere taste of pleasant T,   (2) only finding trivial amount of work to do.

dạndạŋkirįn m. boggling.

ɗanɗanō give me bit of the food you're carrying ! (= Alạ̄ 7 q.v.).

dandạntā Vb. 1C evened up loads on pack-animal.

dạndarạ Zar. used in bā yạ̄ ~ he doesn't mend his ways (= dạddarạ q.v.).

dạndạrai Kt. = dạndajai.

dandari A. (dạndarį) m. coccyx (cf. gịndigịrī ; ƙịrīrị).   B. (dandarī) m. (f. dandaryā) bare (= dandā) x yā kwạntā ạ gadō dandarinsạ he lay down on a bare bed. yā zaunạ ạ dandaryar ƙasā he sat on the bare floor.

dạndạrīrīyạ used in dạndạrīrīyạ = dạndạrīrīyạ dạndo hush-a-bye baby !

dandarmēmẹ = dandarmī m. (f. dandarmēmịyā = dandarmā) huge !

dandaryā Vd. dandarī.

dạndas = dạndak.

ɗanɗasa A. (ɗanɗạsā) Vb. 1C (1) did (task, work) well.   (2) applied T. to x kụnāmạ tā ~ masạ harbị scorpion stung him (= ɗānạ 4).   B. (ɗạnɗasạ) Vb. 2 x kụnāmạ tā ɗanɗạshē shị dạ harbị the scorpion stung him = (ɗānạ 4).

ɗanɗạshē Vd. ɗạnɗasạ.

ɗanɗashēshẹ adj. m. (f. ɗanɗashēshīyā) well-done (work).

ɗanɗashi A. (ɗanɗạshi) what good work !   B. (ɗạnɗashi) Vd. ɗạnɗasạ.

dandatsa A. (dạndatsạ) Vb. 2 (1) mocked P. (2) int. from dạtsā.   B. (dandạtsā) Vb. 1C int. from datsạ.

dandatse A. (dạndạtsē) m. grass chopped for fodder, etc. (= dạtsē 1), cf. ƙurshẹ 2.   B. (dandạ̄tsē) = dātsẹ.

dạndazại = dạndajai.

dạndazō (1) adv. in profusion.   (2) x yā maishē nị ~ he thought me an easy prey.

Dạndī m. (1) (a) generic term for places south of Zaria, the latter being called zaurạn ~.   (b) ɗan ~ m. (f. 'yar ~) pl. 'yan ~ (i) P. migrating to such area with object of leading loose life x working on Plateau minefield, prostitution, etc. (term is applied even to P. leading profligate life in Kano or other Hausa town) ; cf. kurmị 2. (ii) scoundrel.   (c) gūrạ̄yan ~ Vd. gūrū 8.   (d) ƙạfan ~ Vd. ƙạfō 7.   (2) auran ~ Vd. aurē.

dạndīkwạlọ m. chunks of yam or sweet-potato fried in oil.

ɗaṇḍọ (1) how sweet !   (2) how salty !   (3) what a burning pain !

dandōnā f. a blight affecting maịwā (cf. bamōtạ).

dạndōrīyạ dạndo hush-a-bye baby !

dạndọsạ f. axe resembling dundụrūsụ (epithet is Dōsạ gạ̄tarįn Gwārī : ạ yi sārā, ạ yi shūkạ), Vd. Gūgạrạ.

dạndumī Hadejiya Hausa m. night-blindness (= dịndimī q.v.).

ɗanɗūwā (1) f. type of sugarcane.   (2) = ɗanɗọ.

ɗane A. (ɗanẹ) Vb. 3A leaped on to (= ɗarẹ).

B. (ɗanē) Vd. sạkā 2b.

C. (ɗānẹ) Vb. 1A (1) measured all ; fried all (as in ɗānạ). (2) kunāmạ tā ~ shi dạ harbị scorpion stung him (= ɗānạ 4 q.v.).

daŋgā f. (pl. daŋgōgī) (1) (a) fence of compound or cotton-plot, etc. (= Kt. tsạŋgayā), cf. dạrnī ; gạ̄rū. (b) yā hakạ ~ he dug holes for uprights of fence. (2) yā yi wạ mạ̄tā tasạ cịrar daŋgā he installed new wife, divorcing and turning out previous one. (3) yanạ̄ ~ (a) he (loser in gambling i.e. cācā) is refusing to pay. (b) P. is refusing T. from shyness. (4) gạman ~ dạ gạrạ̄funī ya gamạ mu we're not related, but are fortuitously together (x through common task, etc.), (Vd. gạmō 1d). (5) cf. tạ̄kạ ~. (6) sạmạ̄rin daŋgā Vd. zōgalagandị.

dangace A. (daŋgạcē) Vb. 1C surrounded with fence (daŋgā).

B (daŋgạcē) Vd. daŋgatạ.

ɗangace A. (ɗaŋgạcē) Vb. 3A withdrew and remained aloof.

B. (ɗaŋgace) x bạ̄ rūwāna, n nạ̄ dạgạ ~ I'm not affected by that affair.

daŋgaci Vd. daŋgatạ.

daŋga-ɗaŋgạ adj. too short to fit (clothing ; door).

daŋgạlē Vb. 1C yā ~ ƙafạ he (P. with sore foot ; horse, etc.) tiptoed one foot (= ɗagẹ 1). (2) Vb. 3A it shrunk (re washed garment or leg: but not arm ; cf. ƙagẹ ; ɗagẹ 2a).

ɗaŋgalfai Sk. = ɗạŋgạrạfai.

daŋgalgal Sk. (1) yā zaunạ ~ he sat long idly. (2) sunạ̄ naŋ ~ they're alive and well.

ɗangalgal x zanẹ yā yi ~ washed cloth has shrunk (cf. ɗaŋgạlē).

daṅgana A. (daŋgạnā) f. meat prepared with condiments.

B. (daŋganạ) (1) Vb. 3B. (a) sǎi kạ ~ you must resign yourself to it ! (b) nā ~ dạ Audụ I resigned myself to putting up with Audu. nā ~ dạ hạsārạ I steeled myself to the loss. (c) yā ~ gạ Allạ̄ he resigned himself to God's will (cf. hạƙurạ 2, 3), (d) bēbē sǎi yạ ~ Vd. ạbụ 5h. (e) marạs ạbụ sǎi yạ ~ Vd. ạbụ 2b. (2) f. (a) resignation x yā

ɗauki ~ he resigned himself. (b) pledge x (i) yā bā dạ shī ~ he gave it as a pledge, pawned it (= jịŋginạ 2). (ii) kā kaɓẹ ~ " you've given yourself away ". (iii) yā kaɗạ ~ tasạ he squandered his substance ; he spoiled his chances. (c) name given child whose predecessors died young (cf. ɗaŋ wābị).

C (daŋgạnā) Vb. 3C. (1) (a) pawned x nā ~ shi wuriŋ Audụ, nā kạrɓi sulẹ gōmạ I pawned it with Audu for 10s. (= jịŋginā 1b). (b) propped T. against x nā ~ shi dạ baŋgō I leaned it against wall (= jịŋginā 1a). (2) Vb. 3A. (a) leaned against x nā ~ dạ baŋgō I leaned against wall. (b) reached x har kạ ~ dạ kạ̄sūwā till you reach the market. sun daŋganō dạ Masạr they have reached Egypt. (c) extended to x gōnā tā ~ dạ bạ̄kiŋ kōgī the farm extends to the river. Masạr tā daŋganō dạ Tūnạs Egypt extends as far as Tunis (= ɗaukạ 1p).

daŋganad dạ Vb. 4B = daŋganā 1a.

daŋgananne m. (f. daŋganannīyā) pl. daŋganannū P. of resigned mind. ~ yā fi ƙōsasshē it's better to be contented than wealthy.

daŋgancē Vd. daŋgantạ.

dangane A. (daŋganē) Vb. 3A = daŋgạnā 2a.

B. (daŋganẹ) regarding x ~ dạ kudī regarding money.

daŋgaŋgaŋ = daŋga-ɗaŋgạ.

daŋganō Vd. daŋganā 2b.

danganta A. (daŋgantạ) (1) Vb. 2 (a) (i) is (was) related to x yā daŋgạnci Audụ = yā ~ dạ Audụ = yā ~ gạ Audụ he's related to Audu. (ii) kusan tạ daŋgạnci ƙasammụ wajan yanạyī it nearly corresponds with our country in climate. (b) suited x magạnaŋ naŋ tā daŋgạncē shi this description suits him. (2) Vb. 3B is (was) dependent on x azzịkimmụ yā ~ gạ cịnikī dạ waɗansu ƙasạ̄shē our prosperity is dependent on foreign trade.

B. (daŋgạntā) Vb. 1C (1) affiliated P. or T. to x yā ~ kansạ gạ Filạ̄nī he claims Filani descent. nā ~ shi dạ ɓạrnā I consider him evil. (2)

entrusted x nā ～ Audu kan kīwan dōki = nā ～ kīwan dōki ga Audu I entrusted Audu with care of the horse.

dangantad da *Vb.* 4B = dangantā 1.

dangantaka *f.* relationship.

dangaṛafai = *Kt.* dangaṛfai *m.* (*pl.* dangaruḟa). (1) clog-shoe (= cāɓulā 3). (2) arch of the instep.

dangarama *f.* (1) raised step at doorway (= dōkin ḟōfa). (2) raised ground in compound for directing flow of water. (3) *Kt. epithet of* Chief.

dangarezā *f.* blossom of tamarind (tsāmīyā) = *Kt.* yatū-yatū.

dangarfai *Vd.* dangarafai.

dangarīrīya *f.* (1) eking T. out (= janjānī). (2) continued hawking; exhibiting goods vainly x anā ～ da abin nan.

dangartso *m.* (1) coarse-ground flour. (2) coarse grinding (= dābāza *q.v.*).

dangaruḟa *Vd.* dangaṛafai.

dangashē *Vb.* = dangacē.

dangashī *m.* = dingishī.

dangata *Vb.* 2 (*p.o.* dangacē, *n.o.* dangaci) surrounded with fence (= dangacē).

dangazā *Vb.* 3C (*with dative*) applied profusely (= dambaza *q.v.*).

dangerā *f.* = dangirā *q.v.*

dangēre *m.* the plant daŋkadafi *q.v.*

dangi A. (dangi) *m.* (1) (*a*) (i) relative; relatives (*pl. also* danguna = dangōgī). (ii) bā rūwāna, bā rūwan dangina what is it to do with me ? (iii) *Vd.* rāḟumi 4. (*b*) (i) yā ḟi ～ he brooks no rival. (ii) *cf.* darangami 2. (*c*) yā tāra ～ da nī he's related to me. (*d*) tanā ḟirgad ～ her breasts have begun to develop (= ḟusāshi). (2) type x (*a*) danginsa Filānī nē he's of Filani race. duka a cikin dangim barāmū yā fi su it's pre-eminent among things of a mineral type. yā yāfe mini dukan irin dangin abin da na yi masa he pardoned me every type of thing I did to him. barēwā tanā cikin dangin akwīya the gazelle is of the goat type. ḟāwō danginsa bring one like it! ḟāwō danginsu = ḟāwō dangōginsu bring others like them ! yā bā ta dangōgin abūbuwa tāri he brought her all kinds of fine things. (*b*) hauḟā

dangi dangī nē, kōwā da irin nāsa everyone has his own particular failing. (*c*) *Vd.* darma 4. (3) dan ～ *m.* (*f.* 'yar ～) *pl.* 'yan ～ (*a*) P. with many relatives. (*b*) tūwan dan ～ bā yā cika rūwā = tūwan dan ～ bā yā rūwā P. with many relatives never lacks a helper ; blood is thicker than water. (4) tanā bī ～ she's roving about, etc. = bī dangi *q.v.* (5) dangin dangirā = dangin dangyarērē (*a*) useless relatives. (*b*) (i) kada ka yi mini tāran ～ = kada ka yi mini tāran dangin dangirā don't interfere in my affairs ! (ii) *Vd.* tāra 1*c.* (6) dangin ōhō = dangin dangirā. (7) dangin na ūwāki (*a*) sycophant(s), toady, toadies. (*b*) *Vd.* gayyā 4*a.* (7) nēman ～ *m.* = kākalē 1*a.* (8) māganim mai dangi *Vd.* cācā 1*b.* (9) dada dangi *Vd.* dadai 4. (10) dangin shirwa *m.* tyrant. (11) karyar dangi *Vd.* ajūzā. (12) dangin zuma *Vd.* zuma 1*c.*iii. (13) jā wa dangi cūtā *Vd.* tunkū 1*b.* (14) dangin gōro *Vd.* gōro 1*a.*v.

B. (dangī) *m.* ～ shā mai *epithet of* old shield of white oryx or giraffe-hide.

dangida *f.* beaded leather-bangle.

dangirā *f.* (1) head of hemp (rama) = *Kt.* garnūwā. (2) type of itch. (3) *Vd.* dangi 5.

dango *m.* = dangōlīya.

dangō *m.* (1) = dangōlī. (2) newly-hatched locust (fāra). *(3) apocopated line in certain Arabic metres (*Vd.* Palmer's *Arabic Gram.* ; Wright's *Arabic Gram.*).

dangōgī *Vd.* dangi ; dangā.

dangōlī *m.* sixth finger or toe (= shidānīyā).

dangōlī *m.* = dangōlīya *f.* x yā yi mini ～ da shī he proffered it to me but then withdrew it (= dōdo 3 *q.v.* ; lēḟū 2), *cf.* ḟwala 1.

dangula *Vd.* dangwalī.

danguna *Vd.* dangi.

dangwala *Vb.* 1C (1) dipped T. into x yā dangwala lōma a mīya he dipped a pinch of food into the gravy (*cf.* tsōma). (2) yā ～ tawada a takardā he dropped a blot on the paper.

daŋgwalē m. blot in writing (= kwambalē).

daŋgwalī m. (pl. daŋgulạ = Kt. daŋgullạ). (1) looped rope for tethering calves (= taŋgē q.v.), cf. ɗauriṇ 'yam maruƙạ. (2) Kt. an yi manạ ⁓ = maraƙī 3. (3) Sk. 'yan daŋgullạ pl. calves (= 'yam maruƙạ).

ɗaŋgwalōlọ m. (1) fragile T. (2) fussing about trifles (epithet is ⁓ cīwaṇ Gwārī).

ɗangwama A. (ɗaŋgwamā) f. type of short-handled hoe.

B. (ɗaŋgwạmā) Vb. 3A (tired P.) struggled along.

daŋgwamī (1) m. the drink dạgwadạgō 2 (epithet is ⁓ kạs gwīwạ). (2) adv. yā zaunạ ⁓ he outstayed his welcome (= kisạ 3).

dangwara A. (dạŋgwarạ) Vb. 2 (1) (a) tā daŋgwari kạn yārọ she rapped child on the head with her knuckles (done by women) = daŋƙwasạ q.v., cf. daŋgwarī; daŋgwarad dạ 2. (b) yā daŋgwari kantạ he rapped her head when itching from lice, etc. (= daŋƙwafạ 2). (2) persecuted. (3) cf. duŋgurạ.

B. (daŋgwạrā) Vb. 1C (1) (with dative). (a) handed T. to P. secretly x nā ⁓ masạ gōrọ I handed him the kolanut secretly (cf. hannạntā). (b) nā ⁓ masạ tūwō I slapped the tuwō down unceremoniously before him. (2) tā ⁓ mīyạ ạ tūwō she poured insufficient gravy over the tuwō. (3) yā ⁓ sallạ = yā ⁓ gōshī he touched ground with forehead in prayer. (4) cf. daŋgwarad dạ ; duŋgurā.

C. (daŋgwarā) Kt. f. small, tight cap (= daŋkwarā q.v.).

daŋgwarạ dạɓē m. (1) hernia. (2) excessive development of clitoris = kakērẹ (this is said to cause nymphomania ; cf. hārijā, mazaunī 2).

daŋgwarad dạ Vb. 4B (1) put T. down unceremoniously (cf. daŋgwạrā 1b). (2) bumped down peevish child (cf. daŋgwarạ 1). (3) dismissed a servant. (4) left relatives behind one when going on journey. (5) nā yī, nā yī har na daŋgwarar after trying, I gave it up as a bad job. (6) Vd. daŋgwarar ; cf. daŋgwạrā.

daŋgwarar (1) became tired. (2) Vd. daŋgwarad dạ.

dangware A. (daŋgwạrē) Vb. 1C = daŋgwarạ.

B. (daŋgwạrē) m. rider's leaving reins loosely on horse's neck.

C. (daŋgwarẹ) m., f. (sg., pl.) youngest of several brothers or sisters (= ạutā).

daŋgwargwar = daŋgaŋgal 2.

daŋgwạrī m. (secondary v.n. of daŋgwarạ) x tanạ̄ daŋgwarin yārọ = tanạ̄ daŋgwarạr yārọ she's rapping child on head with knuckles. (2) (a) tanạ̄ yi masạ daŋgwariṇ ƙwaryā one wife is denying son of rival wife proper share of food. (b) anạ̄ yi matạ daŋgwariṇ ƙwaryā one wife is denying rival wife proper share of food (= ƙwaryā 1e).

daŋgyarērē Vd. daŋgi 5.

ɗaŋgyashī Kt. m. limping (= ɗiŋgishī q.v.).

ɗaŋgyisā Vb. 3A Kt. limped.

ɗani A. (ɗaṇi) m. (1) male knob-billed goose = dinyā 2 (Sarkidiornis melanotus), cf. kwarwạ. (2) deceitfully giving sample of salt; scent, etc., superior to T. it represents. (3) (secondary v.n. of ɗanạ 1, 2) x yanạ̄ ɗaniṇ (= yanạ̄ ɗanạ) kibīyạ ạ bạkā he's fitting arrow to bow. (4) hanciṇ ⁓ the vaulting called ƙafạr kạzā q.v. under ƙafạ 8b.

B. (ɗāṇi) m. (1) unit of measurement from thumb to middle finger (= taƙi). (2) (secondary v.n. of ɗanạ 1, 2) x yanạ̄ ɗaniṇ gōnā = yanạ̄ ɗanạ gōnā he's chaining out farm, etc. (3) being occupied in act of ɗanạ 2 x tanạ̄ ⁓ she's frying cakes in oil.

C. (ɗāni) suffix x gōmạɗāninsụ 10 of them. ụkụɗāninsụ 3 of them. bịyạrɗāninsụ 5 of them (cf. dīnī).

dạ̄nīnīyạ f. (1) dilly-dallying ; shilly-shallying. (2) eddying of dust-storm or water. (2) ⁓ tafarkiṇ shānū place where many cow-tracks are inextricably mixed.

daniya A. (danīyā) Vd. danyā.

B. (dānīyā) (Kt. zạurancē) = tānīyā.

danja (Eng. danger) an shā ⁓ they quarrelled bitterly (= hatsạrī 3) (epithet is ⁓ wutar bāya).

dạnjam abundantly (= ṭịnjim).

danjini *Zar. m.* fried blood (= hạntạ wuyạ).

daŋ̣kạ *f.* bale of 4,000 gịndī of paper (*cf.* rizmạ).

danƙa A. (daŋ̣ƙạ) *Vb.* 1A. (1) *x* nā ~ masạ shī I gave him a handful of it. (2) nā ~ musụ shī = nā ~ shi ạ hannunsụ = nā ~ shi gạrēsụ I entrusted them with it.
B. (dạŋ̣ƙā) *Vb.* 2 (1) (*a*) gripped hold of (*Vd.* daŋ̣ƙẹ 1*b*). (*b*) pulled out handful of. (*c*) yā dạŋ̣ƙi hanyạ he set out (= kāmạ). yā dạŋ̣ƙi hanyạn naŋ he followed that road. (*d*) *Vd.* dạŋ̣ƙi dubū. (2) *f.* cikịnsạ yanạ̄ ~ he has a spasm of stomach-ache.

dạŋ̣kạdafī = dạŋ̣kạdạfī *m.* (1) the burry plant crablouse (= kwạrkwatạ 2*b*). (2) (= damgērẹ) the burry plants *Desmodium lasiocarpum* or *Triumfetta pentandra*.

daŋ̣kạfē *Vb.* 3A *x* yā ~ gạrēshị it stuck to him.

dạŋ̣kai *Nor. m.* clay feeding-trough; clay manger.

dạŋ̣kalị *m.* (*sg.*, *pl.*) sweet-potato = kūdạkū = lāwur (*epithet is* shạ̄ kụshē).

dạŋ̣kam silence; silently *x* yā yi ~ he remained silent. sun tsayạ ~ they remained motionless. Audụ ~ nẹ̄ Audu's taciturn: rūwā yanạ̄ naŋ ~ this expanse of water is stagnant (*cf.* dịŋkiŋ).

danƙara A. (daŋ̣ƙạrā) *Vb.* 1C. (1) pressed down compressible T (*x* flour, earth, wet concrete, cotton), *cf.* dannạ. (2) pierced deeply *x* nā ~ masạ māshị I pierced him deeply with spear. nā ~ masạ naushị I gave him a mighty punch. (3) yā ~ mini mạganạ he offended me.
B. (dạŋ̣ƙarạ) *Vb.* 2 ate much of (*but not applied to* furā).

danƙare A. (daŋ̣ƙarē) (1) *Vb.* 3A (*a*) is (was) compressed *as in* daŋ̣ƙạrā 1. (*b*) stuck to; clung to *x* yā ~ mini = yā ~ gạrēnị it stuck to me. (2) kāyā yā ~ ni load made my neck stiff. (3) nā ~ shi dạ māshị = daŋ̣ƙạrā 2. (4) *Vd.* ƙạbạrạ.
B. (daŋ̣ƙarē) *m.* measuring of cotton

for girls' spinning-bee (dīdībākọ) = aunē.

daŋ̣ƙari what a lot *x* daŋ̣ƙari, anạ̄ bạbban yāƙị what a vast war!

daŋ̣ƙarō *m.* (1) pounding wetted, bruised, bulrush-millet (gērō) without separation of bran (= namijị 11). (2) *such* flour or *such* flour mixed with honey or sour milk. (3) jirgin ~ *m.* (*a*) motor road-roller (= ūwar dạβē). (*b*) dilatory P.

daŋ̣ƙē *m.* method of setting out draughtsmen in darạ

danƙe A. (daŋ̣ƙẹ) (1) *Vb.* 1A. (*a*) *x* ƙārō yā ~ mini rīgā the gum caused my gown to stick together. (*b*) = dạŋ̣ƙā 1*a*, *b*, *c* *x* yā daŋ̣ƙẹ damansạ, yā kai shị gidā he took him prisoner (*Vd.* damō 10). (2) *Vb.* 3A various portions of article stuck together.
B. (dạŋ̣ƙē) *m.* (1) making long stitches. (2) (*a*) simultaneously putting into one's mouth any two different foods. (*b*) yā iyạ ~ he knows how to eke out *such food.*

daŋ̣kērīyā *f.* " making compliments "; bashfulness (= fịlāƙọ).

daŋ̣kị *m.* (1) display of whitened calabashes in wife's house (*each calabash stands on dish* (tāsạ): *previously, used to stand on* tardẹ) (= *Sk.* daidayā 2). (2) cornstalk-bed on which 1 stands. (3) *Vd.* bọ̄rī 6.

dạŋ̣ƙi *m.* handful.

dạŋ̣ƙi dubū grip its mane to steady yourself!

Dạŋ̣kō *m.* spirit supposed to take snakeform and talk with bọ̄rī devotees (*epithet is* ~ ɗam Mūsạ = Samamī cịkạ saụrā).

daŋ̣ƙọ *m.* (1) (*a*) rubber. (*b*) yā ci ~ he gathered rubber. (*c*) ɗan ~ *m.* (*pl.* 'yan ~) man buying shea-butter for re-sale. (2) (*a*) stickiness. (*b*) yā yi ~ it lasted long (= yauƙī 4) *x* kudī bā sạ̄ ~ ạ hannunsạ money " burns a hole in his pocket ". zamansụ yā yi ~ their friendship is enduring. (3) tyre. (4) ~ bā yạ̄ ƙādụ̄wā ƙasạ, yạ tāshị banzā blackmailer is sure to find *some* luck. (6) dud dạ ƙạlō ạ cin daŋ̣ƙọ? you busybody! (7) daŋ̣ƙwạn riƙọ *m.*

(a) stingy P. (b) what a stingy P. !

daŋkwafạ Vb. 2 (1) (a) blunted a pointed T. (cf. dākụsā). (b) = daŋƙwasạ. (2) reduced P. to silence. (3) (a) turned P. from unwise course of action. (b) wannạŋ, sǎi an daŋkwạfē nị ạ kạn? sạ do you think I need telling not to do it !

daŋkwafạ Vb. 2 (1) = daŋƙwasạ. (2) = daŋgwarạ 1b.

daŋkwạfau epithet of Emir.

daŋkwạfē Vb. 1C = daŋkwafạ.

Dạŋkwaị f. (1) place in Kano Province. (2) zạmanạ rūwan ~ (a) what long companionship, marriage, etc. ! (b) how this visitor stays on and on !

daŋƙwalēlẹ = daŋƙwalī m. (f. daŋƙwalēlīyā = daŋƙwalā) pl. daŋƙwaldaŋƙwal = daƙwal-daƙwal = daƙwādaƙwā large and round = ƙwādalēlẹ.

daŋkwarā f. small, tight cap (epithet ~ dǎidǎi dạ kạŋ kōwā).

dạŋkwarạ Vb. 3B (1) cikị yā ~ stomach is sunken in. (2) ƙafạfunsạ sun ~ (a) he has high insteps. (b) he's bandy.

daŋkwararē m. used in daŋkwararaŋ ƙafạ instep.

daŋkwạrē m. temporary coiffure without using dōkạ.

dankware A. (daŋkwạrē) (1) Vb. 3A = daŋkwarạ. (2) Vb. 1C yā dạŋkwạrẹ cikịnsạ he has contracted his stomach to show his hunger.

B. (daŋkwarẹ) m. used in daŋkwaraŋ ƙafạ instep.

dạŋkwarō Sk. m. stilts (= kwạrā-kwạrā).

dankƙwasa A. (daŋƙwasạ) Vb. 2 (p.o. daŋƙwashē, n.o. daŋƙwạshi). (1) tā daŋƙwạshi kạn yārọ she rapped boy with her knuckles, palm downwards (done by women to child) = daŋgwarạ 1a = daŋƙwafạ 1 = daŋkwafạ 1c = ƙwạŋgwarạ (cf. daŋƙwạsā).

B. (daŋƙwạsā) Vb. 1C x Ƙande tā ~ matạ kǎi Kande deloused her head for her (= daŋgwarạ 1b).

dankƙwashe A. (daŋƙwạshē) Vb. 1C = daŋkwasạ.

B. (daŋƙwạshē) Vd. daŋkwasạ.

daŋƙwạshī m. (secondary v.n. of daŋƙwasạ) x tanạ̄ daŋƙwạshin yārọ =

tanạ̄ daŋƙwasạr yārọ she's rapping boy, etc.

danna A. (dannạ) (1) Vb. 1A. (a) pressed on T. (cf. dirtsẹ). (b) compressed (a, b = tausạ) (b = damfạrā 1), cf. daŋƙạrā. (c) pressed T. on to x nā ~ fācị kạn rōbạ I pressed the patch on to the tyre. (d) forced P. to x nā ~ shi, ya sạyā I forced him to buy it (= tausạ), cf. dạnnā 3. (2) dannō Vb. 3A (majestic P. ; awe-inspiring T.) came, drew near (x Emir ; storm ; Ramadan ; crowd).

B. (dạnnā) Vb. 2. (1) = dannạ 1 x (a) yā ji zāfin ~ P. downed in wrestling felt himself quite beaten. (b) Vd. cīzọ 2b. (2) snubbed, reduced P. to silence. (3) persuaded P. (= tạusā), cf. dannạ 1d. (4) dạnnar gịndī by drumming at house of senior wife (ūwar gidā), diverting her notice from introduction of new bride x anạ̄ yi wạ ūwar gidā dạnnar gịndī = dạnnar ƙịrjī (= tsạrō 2).

dannẹ Vb. 1A (1) ~ ƙōfạ to close door tightly (= garƙẹ). (2) bore patiently x yā ~ zāgi he disregarded the insult. tā ~ zūcịyā she resigned herself. (3) excelled. (4) (" entirely " form of dannạ 1a, b, d and dạnnā 2, 3) x (a) nā ~ shi (i) I (wrestler) held down opponent from rising. (ii) I made him subservient to my will (cf. dirtsẹ 3). (b) yā ~ takạrdā he weighted down the paper (cf. dirtsẹ 4). (c) yā ~ kudī he misappropriated or hid the money. (d) Vd. bōdạrī 4.

danni A. (dạnnī) m. fence oï cornstalks (= dạrnī q.v.).

B. (dannị m. = dannīyā f.) felling-stitch.

Danọ epithet of Magạji.

dansạkūkạ f. alga on water ; moss (= gạnsạkūkạ).

dansạsā Vb. 1C. (1) moistened. (2) x nā ~ masạ I helped him.

danshī m. (1) moisture. (2) dampness of ground or house (= laimạ). (3) ~ yā kāmạ yārọ the baby lad has infantile convulsions (= tạfīyạr rūwā). (4) Allạ̄ yạ sạ̄ ni ạ danshiŋkạ God grant me your good luck ! (5) hancị kạmar

dakạn ∼ flat nose. (6) **danshi-danshi**
fair amount of moisture . *x* **indạ
kḙ dạ** ∼ where the ground's fairly
moist.

dạntsā *Vb.* 2 *Kt.* = **dạŋƙā.**

dantsḙ (1) *Vb.* 1A *Kt.* = **dirtsḙ.** (2) *m.*
(*pl.* **damạtsā** = *Sk.* **damụttsā**). (*a*)
(i) arm just above or below elbow. (ii)
Vd. **zāgḙ** 1*e*. (iii) **yā wārḙ** ∼ he opened
his arms. (iv) **wārḙ dantsạŋkạ, kạ
ɗaukạ** take it by force if you can !
(v) ∼ **yā gazạ** *Vd.* **dambē 4.** (*b*) **yanạ̄
dạ** ∼ he's a bringer of luck. (*c*) **lāyạr**
∼ **nē** he's a nincompoop (*cf.* **lāyun** ∼).
(*d*) type of arrangement of beams in
flat roof.

ɗaŋụbā (*d.f.* **dā, ụbā**) *m.* (*f.* **'yarụbā**) *pl.*
'yaŋụbā. (1) half-brother by same father
(*usually mutually hostile, so* **'yaŋubancị**
m. hostility, *cf.* **daŋūwā 4**) = **lị'abbị,** *Vd.*
tụrākā 2. (2) hangnail (= *Zar.*
fiffizgīyā).

ɗaŋūwā (*d.f.* **dā, ūwā**) *m.* (*f.* **'yarūwā**) *pl.*
'yaŋūwā (1) (*a*) brother (*strictly* full brother, *but commonly used for* any brother,
relative, fellow-countryman). **ɗaŋūwansạ** his brother, etc. (Mod. Gram.
8*e*.i). (*b*) **'yaŋūwammụ Mụsụlmī** our
fellow Muslims. (*c*) ∼ **rabịn jịkī** what
affects your family affects you. (*d*)
in **ɗaŋūwaŋkạ nạ̄ tụnjērḙ, kai kọ̄ kạ
shā rịgạ kafī** when trouble befalls your
neighbour, look out for yourself ! (*e*)
ɗaŋūwạ̄ *Vd.* **ạlēkụ̄ŋ 2.** (2) **'yaŋū-
wantạ** (*a*) her brothers and sisters.
(*b*) her fellow-wives *x* **kadạ kị faɗạ wạ
'yaŋūwaŋkị** don't tell your fellow-
wives ! (3) one of a pair *x* **ạ cikinsụ,
wạ̄ ya fi ɗaŋūwansạ** which of the two is
better ? **ạ cikinsụ, wạ̄cēcḙ ta fi 'yarūwā
tatạ** which of the two women is the
better ? (4) **'yaŋūwancị** *m.* = **'yạŋūwạntakạ** *f.* being on friendly terms
(*cf.* **ɗaŋụbā, lị'abbị**).

ɗaŋwā *Sk. f.* = **ɗanị.**

danyā *f.* (1) (*a*) the tree *Spondias sp.*
(*it has plum-like fruit*), *cf.* **ku'ḙ, luddḙ.**
(*b*) *cf.* **baƙī ɗan** ∼. (2) warty growths on
child's face. (3) *Vd.* **turmī 10.**

ɗanyā (1) *Vd.* **ɗanyē.** (2) ill-considered
act. (3) anæmia, jaundice, etc. (= **shāwarạ 5** *q.v.*).

ɗanyạcē *Vb.* 3A (1) became moist. (2)
(sore, quarrel) broke out again.

ɗanyạtā *Vb.* 1C (1) moistened. (2) revoked (arrangement).

ɗanyē *adj. m.* (*f.* **ɗanyā**) *pl.* **ɗanyū** =
ɗanyū. (1) (*a*) raw, uncooked. (*b*)
kạmar zā ạ cịnyē su ɗanyē as if they
were to be eaten alive. (*c*) (i) **ɗanyaŋ
kaskō** unbaked pot. (ii) **ɗanyaŋ kaskō
bā yạ̄ kai rūwā bạn ɗākị** *epithet of* one
of the Sarkim **Mụsụlmī.** (2) (*a*) unripe.
(*b*) **ɗanyar cịyāwạ** = **ɗanyaŋ haƙị**
(i) green grass. (ii) the snake **dạ̄mạtsīrī.**
(iii) *cf.* **fụrē** 1*a*.ii. (*c*) **ạl'amạrī yā
kōmạ** ∼ the pact, arrangement has
been revoked. (3) (*a*) inexperienced.
(*b*) **iskōkinsạ ɗanyū nḙ** evil spirits have
only just begun taking possession of
him. (4) ill-considered *x* (*a*) **yā yi
ɗanyar magạnạ** he spoke in an ill-
considered way, talked nonsense
(= **sarɓā** = **shaftarē 3,** *cf.* **shataf**). (*b*) **yā
yi minị ɗanyaŋ hukumcị** he played me
a dirty trick (= **gayyạ**). (*c*) **mai ɗanyaŋ
ƙại** *m., f.* P. of ill-considered ways. (5)
(*a*) moist (*re* crops, fruit, soil, washed
clothing, untanned leather, etc.). (*b*)
wutā tā ci ∼ **bạllē ƙēƙạsasshē** if a
penalty affects an influential P., how
much more so a poor man ! (*c*) **baushḙ
tun yanạ̄** ∼ a **ƙạn tausạ shi yạ mīƙḙ**
to train a P., catch him young ! (*d*)
ɗanyar fātạ bā tạ̄ fạsūwā go on, child,
eat some more, you won't burst ! (5Λ)
ɗanyaŋ ƙirgị *Vd.* **shimfịdā 4.** (6)
kāyan naŋ ∼ **nḙ** this is stolen property.
(7) **baƙar rịgā laimạ ɗanyā** well-dyed
new black gown. (8) **yārinyạ cē ɗanyā**
she is a big-made girl. (9) **wannaŋ
sạ̄** ∼ **nḙ** this ox is vicious. (10) **ɗanye-
ɗanye** rawish. (11) *Kt.* **sunạ̄ ɗanyaŋ
ganyē** they're close friends.

dap = **dab.**

dapka = **dafka.**

dapshḙ = **daujḙ.**

dạptī = **dạftī.**

dạr (1) *Vd.* **darạ** 1*d*. (2) **yā kētạ rịgā** ∼
he tore the gown rip !

ɗar A. (**ɗar**) (1) *Vd.* **ɗarḙ.** (2) *x* **nā** ∼
masạ shḙƙarū I'm slightly older than
he is (*Vd.* **ɗarạ**).

  B. (dạr) *m. or adv.* fear ; in fear *x*

(1) gabāna yā yi ～ I felt terrified. gabāna ɗar-ɗar, tsūlīyāta ɗar-ɗar I was in a cold sweat. ɗar-ɗar sunā jin tsōraŋ kadạ ạ tōnạ lạifinsụ they were terrified lest they be found out. kō ɗar bại yi ba he showed no fear. (2) zūcīyāta tanā ɗar-ɗar my heart's beating like a drum. (3) ɗar dạ gạbā = ɗar dạ zūcī m. terror.

dara A. (darạ) (1) ʄ. (a) (i) game like draughts played on board (kōmī), each player having 6 rows of 6 holes (gurbị) and 12 draughtsmen ('yā'yā), those of one player being of stone (dūtsẹ) and those of his opponent being of stalk (karā). (ii) For hurhuɗū ; darạr shānū ; darạr kūrā ; darạr kāshiŋ awākī Vd. ƙwadọ 2. (iii) Vd. bākin ～ ; dilā 2 ; jạbar ; gwaisạ. (b) (i) gidan darạ m. type of embroidery-pattern. (ii) mại gidan darạ m. type of European cotton material. (c) (i) anā darạ, gā darē ya yī one blessed thing after another ! (Vd. darị 5). (ii) anā darạ dōmiŋ ạ kasạ nē people act to gain advantage. (d) frisking of sheep or goat. yanā darạ ɗar-ɗar it's frisking gaily. (2) granted T. to P. for rest of his life x nā darạ makạ gidan naŋ muddin raŋkạ.

    B. (darā) ʄ. (sg., pl.). (1) fez (= hūlad darā). (2) jad ～ red fez. farad ～ white fez.

    C. (dārạ) (1) (cerebral " r ") used in (a) kadạ kạ ～ sǎi tā ƃācị he who laughs last, laughs best. (b) kun sō kụ ～, Allā yā hanạ laughter turned into tears. (c) kuturū ～ makāfọ Vd. dārīyā 3. (2) (rolled " r ", Mod. Gram. 5) Ar. ʄ. the world used in (a) ～ bā gidā ba the world is transitory. (b) ～ haushin ragō epithet of Ashanti.

darạ (1) Vb. 1A = darā Vb. 2 exceeded slightly (= cirạ 1ʄ = ɗagạ 1b = saʄạ 2) x kạɗaŋ sukạ ～ ạ cẹ musụ hākimai they are but little superior in status to District Heads. (2) Vb. 3A took oneself off. (3) ɗarā gaɗō Vd. baɗō.

dara'ạ Ar. ʄ. (1) Kano Hausa breadth x ～ tasạ tā yi kāmụ gụdā kō fīye dạ hakạ its breadth is 18 inches or more. (2) Kt. 18 inches (= kāmụ 5a). (3) Sk. third of

a yard (when applied・to plain white cotton fabric) = kwatạ 1b. (4) x nā yi ～ dạ shī I happened to meet him.

ɗarạbba-ɗarạbbā Kt. adj. m., ʄ. (sg., pl.) spotted.

darā-darā adj. m., ʄ. (sg., pl.) fine and big (re writing, eyes, stripes) x tanā dạ idọ ～ she has fine, big eyes.

daraja A. (darajạ) Ar. ʄ. (pl. darajū = darajōjī). (1) rank x (a) ～ tasụ dạbaŋ they differ in rank, value. (b) darajạrsụ tā hau they have been promoted. (c) bạ sụ san darajạr rǎi ba they set no store by human life. (2) high value x (a) mụtụm (ạbụ) mại ～ valuable P. (thing). (b) ạbụ wandạ ～ tasạ tā īyạ bīyạŋ ạbin dạ akẹ ƃātāwā a sum large enough to recoup them for the expenditure. (c) gōran rūwā yā sō yạ kashẹ darajạr azụrfā aluminium bids fair to oust silver. (d) fātun jājāyạŋ awākī sum fi ～ wurin Tụ̄rāwā the skins of red goats command the highest price with Europeans. (e) darajạr gōrọ Vd. gōrọ 1a.iv. (3) respecting x yā bā sụ ～ he showed them the respect due. (4) Nor. rung, step, stair.

    B. (darajā) Vb. 1C showed due respect to.

darajạntā = Sk. darajjīyā Vb. 1D showed due respect to.

darakancị Ar. m. blustering cuteness.

darạkī m. (ʄ. darạkā) pl. darạkai cute blusterer.

daram in perfect condition x ɗākị yanā naŋ ～.

daram bakạ Vd. darē.

darạmbūwā ʄ. (pl. darạmbī). (1) children's plaited-grass armlet (cf. jēmạ 2a ; mundūwā). (2) audụgā tā yi ～ thread became twisted. (3) game where aim is to encircle cowries with grass-rings (Vd. gēgẹ). (4) worn-out cycle.

darạŋ-daraŋ m. being of roving disposition.

darạŋgamị used in (1) darạŋgamị = darạŋgamina dạ shī = inā darạŋgamina dạ shī = Kt. middarạŋgamina dạ shī what has it to do with me ? (2) ～ ạ galā dạ ƙin daŋgi epithet of the

Agalawa (who hate each other), *cf.* daŋgị 1*b*.

daranyạ (1) *Vd.* darị (2) *Kt. f.* duststorm (= hōlōƙō).

dặrarạ *Vb.* 3B (1) felt urgent need for immediate eating, drinking, departure (= ƙagautạ). (2) dōkị yā ∼ = yā yi ∼ thirsty horse sulkily refused to assuage its thirst when kept waiting for further water to be brought.

dặrārạ *Vd.* dặrīyā 3.

dặrặrặkŭ *Vd.* dặrīyā.

darặrē nights (*Vd.* darē).

dặrạrē *Vb.* 3A withdrew to remain alone (= dangạcē).

Darari A. (Dārārī) *used in* Karọ ∼ name for any P. called Bặƙo (*Vd.* karọ 6).
   B. (dặrặrī) *m.* (1) track of snake. (2) gặ macịjī kwạnce, anặ bugụn ∼ blaming the innocent and acquitting the guilty (= tēkị 1*b*).

dạrạrrasạ *Vb.* 3B (1) *int. from* dạrsā *x* rūwā yanặ ∼ water's dripping. (2) rūwā yanặ ∼ it's drizzling.

dararrạshē *Vb.* 3A (1) sat in relaxed posture. (2) led carefree life.

daras (1) *Vd.* darē. (2) = das 1.

darạs = darạsī *Ar. m. this word written in margin, means* here ends 1st, 2nd, etc., eighth of Koran; *when reader reaches* darạs, *he says* ạlhamdụ lịllāhị, *his tutor* (muhaddạsī) *replying* ạl'ilmụ indạllāhị = ạl'ilmụ indạhū (*Vd.* kwānā A.1, 4 ; darạsū).

Dārạs salāmụ *Ar. f.* (1) Paradise (= ạljannạ). (2) nā zạci bạ zạŋ ƙārạ ganinsạ ba sǎi ∼ I never thought to see him again in this life. (3) Daresalaam town.

darạsū *Ar. m.* (*pl.* darạsai). (1) (*a*) correction by muhaddạsī of portions of Koran written on pupils' slates *x* yanặ yi musụ ∼. (*b*) yā karantad dạ mū darạsai he showed us how to act. (2) mālạmin ∼ scholar whose profession is *as in* (1) (*cf.* bīƙọ 4). (3) *cf.* darạsī.

darạtā saws (*Vd.* dartọ).

darạttā *Vb.* 1C *Kt.* paid due respect to.

darặyē nights (*Vd.* darē).

dặrāzau *used in* bạntan ∼ embroidered apron of females.

darƃā *f.* (1) sticky juice in blossom of

locust-bean tree (= dạbanọ). (2) sticky blight on guinea-corn or beans = madị 2 (*cf.* mandō).

dạrbākị *m.* the trousers called būjẹ.

darƃẹ *Vb.* 3A *Sk.* is (was) indolent.

dạrbẹdā *f.* flitting from task to task without completing any.

dạrbūkạ *f.* camel-howdah (= haudạjī).

dạr-dạr *Vd.* darạ 1*d* ; dạr.

dạr-dạr terror *Vd.* dạr.

dạrdūmạ *f.* coarse-wool blanket.

dare A. (darē) *m.* (*pl.* darặyē = darặrē). (1) (*a*) (i) night. yā yi ∼ night's fallen. ∼ yanặ yị night's falling. ∼ yā yi musụ night caught them on the road, etc. (ii) *its epithet is* Darē, rịgar mūgụ = Darē marufar ạsīrī = Darē matuƙar yāwạm bặƙō. (iii) ạbincin ∼ *m.* supper, dinner. (*b*) dạ ∼ = dạd ∼ = dạ dạ darē = dạ dạd darē at night *x* (i) Lahạdị dạ darē on Sunday night. Jumma'ạ dạ darē on Friday night (*cf.* 1*c*). dạ daran naŋ on that night. (ii) marạs ạbu sǎi dạ darē *Vd.* ạbu 2*b*. (*c*) (*for Muslims, night precedes day*) *thus,* daran Jumma'ạ Thursday night. daran Lahạdị Saturday night (*cf.* 1*b*.i). daran sallạ eve of the Festival. raŋ Ạlhamịs, daran Jumma'ạ on Thursday night. (*d*) haƙạ dǎi, bặ ∼, bặ rānā har sukạ gamạ ƙặi this (discussion) went on uninterruptedly till they reached agreement. sun sạki injị, bặ ∼, bặ rānā they sped along incessantly. (*e*) dạ dạ ∼ baƙī *m.* (i) dyeing cloth fairly dark. (ii) *such* cloth. (iii) colour of *such* cloth. (iv) treacherous persons living on border of enemy country and attacking at night. (2) (*a*) yā yi ∼ he arrived after dark. (*b*) shūkạ tā yi ∼ the crops were sown late. (3) yā bi ∼ *Vd.* bī 9*d*. (4) (*a*) in nā yi makạ rānā, kadạ kạ yi minị ∼ don't repay my good with evil ! (= inūwạ 3). (*b*) inūwạr ∼ *Vd.* gạrmā 2*b*. (*c*) girman ∼ dayā *Vd.* gambạ. (*d*) mạrhabar ∼ *Vd.* gạmzākị. (*e*) ạ yi ∼ dǎi *Vd.* mụtum 9*m*. (*f*) dọmin ∼ akẹ sạndā, dạ rānā kō dạ karā nặ dōgarạ in difficulties one needs held, but at other times, one can stand alone. (*g*) yạushẹ ∼ ya yị har shạsshāwạ zā tạ ƃatạ (i) how can a P. be

deceived by so threadbare an excuse !
(ii) prosperity should not lead you to
despise your friends. (*h*) in ∼ yā
yi ∼ būzūzu nāmạ nē at night, all
cats are grey. (*j*) dạ rānā akẹ awọ,
dạ ∼ sǎi ạ ci tūwō (*labourers' talk*)
don't buy a pig in a poke ! (*k*) (i)
daran tūwō bặ kwānā dạ yunwạ ba
nẹ̆ better late than never ! (*epithet of
child born late in mother's life*). (ii)
tūwan darē *Vd.* tūwō 20. (*l*) bặ ∼ gạ
mai shinkāfā, sǎi dǎi rashin ạbin
wutā if one has means, other difficulties
are trivial. (*m*) bā ặ ∼ ạ gidā = 4*l.*
(*n*) ∼ gạ mai rạbō hạntsī nẹ̆ all that
some people touch turns to gold. (*o*)
wạndạ bai ɓatạ dạ ∼ ba, bạ yặ ɓatạ
dạ rānā ba if a P. can do a hard T., how
much more so an easy thing ! (*p*) (i)
rūwan ∼ gạmạ dūnīyạ what a liberal
person ! (ii) *Vd.* rūwā B.3A. (*q*) (i)
kōmē nīsan ∼ garī yặ wāyẹ = kōmē
tsananin darē, garī zai wāyẹ every cloud
has a silver lining. (ii) kōwā ya yi
ƙaryar ∼ garī yặ wāyẹ murder will
out. (*r*) bābu irin daran dạ jēmāgẹ
bai ganī ba fortune's wheel revolves.
(*s*) hankalin ∼ *Vd.* ɓatạ 1*b.* (*t*) mai ∼
Vd. Amīnạ 3. (*u*) ạljanad ∼ *Vd.*
Burungū. (*v*) tumun ∼ *Vd.* zặɓē 4.
(*w*) wạnzāmin ∼ *Vd.* ma'ạskī 2. (*x*)
su kạn cī dạ ∼ *Vd.* ạbu 2*b.* (*y*) im
bạ ạ rạgi ∼ ba *Vd.* rạgā 2. (*z*) yā fi ∼
duhu *Vd.* sani 2*b.* vii. (*z*) (i) san indạ ∼
ya yi makạ *Vd.* sani 1*a.*ix. (*z*) (ii) kōwā
ya yi ∼ *Vd.* Burungū. z (iii) gặ ∼ yā yī
Vd. darạ 1*c*, dari 5. (5) an yi ∼ bīyū
there was eclipse of the sun (*Vd.*
kusūfi). (6) Allặ yạ jā darặyē long life
to you ! (7) yā yi masạ ∼ ạ idọ he
slapped him over the face. (8) Sarkin ∼
Kt. an obsolete sạrautạ (= Sarkin
sạurī). (9) daram būshīyā = daran
taurẹ sleepless night (especially from
hunger). (10) daran kūrẹ (*a*) = 9. (*b*)
ạbin yā yi daran kūrẹ the affair is
difficult. (11) daram bakạ " making
compliments " (= fīlākọ.) (12) *Vd.* sāran
darē, shặ darē, wutar darē, dab darē.
B. (dārẹ) *Vb.* 3A. (1) became
scattered. (2) cracked. (3) it (water)
ran off sloping surface (= darjẹ 1*b*).

ɗare A. (ɗarẹ) *Vb.* 1A leaped up on to *x*
yā ∼ kạn dōki he leapt on to the horse.
ɗar sukạ ∼ they leapt nimbly on to
it (*cf.* ɗạrē).
B. (ɗạrē) *m.* (1) yā yi hawan ∼ he
rode with his feet crossed on one side
of horse (*cf.* ɗarẹ). (2) zaman ∼ *m.* the
rigid sitting of chief indicating he is in
strictly official mood.
C. (ɗarē) *used in* tum bạ ạ yi ɗárē
(*or* ɗaras) ba, akạ yi kwandi you're
trying to " teach your grandmother to
suck eggs ".
darēbạ *Eng. m.* (*f.* darēbīyā) *pl.* darē-
bōbī. (1) motor-driver. (2) engine-
driver. (3) = durōbạ.
dạrẹ-darē *m.* evening meal prepared late
x tūwan nan ∼ nẹ̆.
ɗặrẹrẹ *x* kanặ dūbansạ ∼ you're looking
at him contemptuously (= shẹ̆ƙẹ̆ƙẹ).
dạrēshi *m.* = dạrīshi.
Dạrfọ̆t *f.* Darfur.
dargajī *m.* = dargazặ *f.* the shrub *Grewia
mollis.*
dạrgēzọ *m.* refrain sung by girls at ablutions of bride (= *Kt.* turgēzạ).
dạrgōzō *m.* grubby lout.
darhạmī (Arabic coin) *m.* (1) bặ ni dạ
kō ∼ I'm " broke ". (2) callous above
knee of horse, donkey, or mule.
dari A. (dari) *m.* (*f.* daranyạ). (1) Senegal
hartebeeste. (2) sǎi ạ barạ ∼ ƙwansạ
he's the only one who'd put up with
such a thing ; he's the only one suited
to the task. (3) ∼ shặ bặrā *epithet of*
rich P. with enemies (*cf.* gwankī ;
barạ A.2, 1*d*). (4) children's game
where each tries to draw out longest
straw. (5) gặ darạ, gặ ∼, gặ darē
yā yī one blessed thing after another !
(*cf.* darạ 1*c*).
B. (dāri) *m.* dimension *x* (1) ɗākin
nan yā fi wancạn ∼ this house is
bigger, longer or broader than that one.
dabbạn nan ∼ gạrētạ this animal is
long-bodied. yā fi wancạn dōki ∼
it's better-proportioned than that
horse. (2) murabbạ'ī mai ∼ *m.* an
oblong.
ɗari A. (ɗarī) *f.* hundred *x* (1) pạm ∼
a hundred pounds sterling (*cf.* jạkā).
∼ tā fi hạmsin 100 is greater than 50.

ɗarūrūwạn naŋ mẹ̄nēnẹ̄ ya rabạ sụ how many hundreds lie between them ? (*as in comparing Muslim Year* 1100 *with* 700). (2) *cf.* ɗạrīnīyạ, zạŋgū. (3) (*a*) *x* ∼ ukụ ta kudī 300,000 cowries. (*b*) *x* ∼ ukụ ta wuri̠-wuri̠ = ɗạrī ukụ ta 'yạŋ hannū 300 cowries.

B. (dārī) *m.* (1) (*a*) coldness due to wind (sanyī *q.v. has same sense but* damp-cold *is translated by* sanyī *not by* dārī) *x* (i) mun shā ∼ yạu it's been chilly, cold and windy to-day. (ii) n nạ̄ ji̠n ∼ = ɗārī yā kāmạ ni = nạ̄ ɗạuki (= ɗaukō) ∼ I'm feeling cold (*Vd.* 4 *below,* sanyī 1*c*.ii). (iii) dāki̠n naŋ dạ ∼ yakẹ̄ this house is airy and cold. (iv) an yi ∼ there was cold, windy weather. anạ̄ ∼ it's cold and windy. (v) *Vd.* mụkū-mụkū. (*b*) yạ̄yạ ka ji dạ ɗāri̠ how's the cold weather treating you ? (*reply,* dạ gọ̄dīyā = kwānạkinsạ nē fine, thanks !). (*c*) shiri̠n shi̠gā ∼ preparations for wintering. (*d*) ∼ yā sạuka the cold season has come. (*e*) shī kẹ̄ kūkan ∼ *Vd.* ạbụ 2*j.* (*f*) rānā tsakạ māgạnin ∼ a friend in need is a friend indeed. (*g*) *Vd.* zạ̄gā 1*b*.iii. (*h*) mafarkin ∼ *Vd.* sūtai. (2) ɗarim bạ̄ra yā wucẹ dạ gụmạ̄gụmansạ it's no good harping on the days of yore (*Vd.* bạ̄ra 1*e*). (3) ɗāriŋ wākẹ̄ 1st part of cold season (*followed by* dāriŋ kạ̄kā, *then by* hụntūrụ, *i.e.* harmattan). (4) (*a*) ∼ yā kāmạ shi he's feeling shy or ashamed. yanạ̄ ji̠n ɗārinsụ he is shy of them. (*b*) *Vd.* 1*a*.ii. (*c*) *Vd.* shạ̄ ∼. (5) dāri-dāri *m.* moderate cold due to wind. (*b*) dāri-dāri yakẹ̄ yi̠ dạ nī he's becoming less friendly to me. (*c*) yanạ̄ dāri-dāri he's timid.

dạ̄rịgō *m.* the cattle-plague of 1891 (= sạnnū 5).

ɗạrīnī *m.* = ɗạrīnīyạ *f. e.g.* ɗạrīninsụ 11 of them.

dạ̄rīrīko *Vd.* dạ̄rīyā 9.

dạrīshi̠ (*Eng.* dress) *m.* yā yi ∼ he togged himself up.

dạ̄rīyā *f.* (*pl.* dạ̄rạ̄rạ̄kū) (1) laughter *x* (*a*) yā yi ∼ he laughed. (*b*) yā shā ∼ he split his sides with laughing. (*c*) yā bā ni̠ ∼ he made me laugh, he amused me. (*d*) yā yi mini̠ ∼ he laughed at me.

(*e*) jad ∼ laughter covering mortification or anger. (*f*) sâi mạganạ ta yi ta ∼ the matter finally became a farce. (*g*) anạ̄ ∼, mai tạunā ya kạ̠n ƙōshi slow and steady wins. (*h*) sun sạ̄mi haƙōran ∼ they became happy. (*j*) dạ̄ mun yạrdā, dạ̄ yạnzu i̠nā mukạ̄ ga haƙōran dạ̄rīyạ̄ had we agreed, what a sorry position would be ours to-day ! (*k*) sạ̄ ɓạrāwọ ∼ *Vd.* bam mạgạnạ 4. (2) indạ akạ kạrɓi dạ̄rīyar mạkāfọ, naŋ ka kạm fasạ ƙwaryā if you like a person, he can do no wrong in your eyes. (3) dạ̄rī-yar dạ̄rạ̄rạ, huntū dạ̄rīyar mai tsụmmā, kuturū dārạ mạkāfọ it's a case of the pot calling the kettle black. (4) dạ̄rīyar kạrē (*a*) display of fierceness. (*b*) kōwā yai dạ̄rīyar kạrē, ạ̄ bar shi̠ show firmness and people will not pester you ! (5) dạ̄rīyar ƙudā laugh of infant, showing first sign of sense. (6) zanạntạ yanạ̄ ∼ her cloth is gaping open. (7) ạbin ∼, ạbin tạusạyī pride comes before a fall. (8) ∼ bạ̄ lōtọ (*a*) cutting off lips of criminal. (*b*) ∼ bạ̄ lōtọ gạrēshi̠ he laughs without cause, he's always open-mouthed. (9) dạ̄rīrīkwạm mạgạutā joy of several persons at an enemy's misfortune.

darje A. (darjẹ) (1) *Vb.* 3A (*a*) = tirjẹ 1*b*. (*b*) water ran off sloping surface (= dārẹ 3). (*c*) *Sk.* yārọ yā ∼ dạga kạn dūtsẹ boy slid down rock in play. (*d*) behaved obstinately. (*e*) mạganạ tā ∼ affair is settled. (*f*) *Sk.* became grazed. (2) *Vb.* 1A (*a*) squashed T. with slithering motion (= tirjẹ 2*a*). (*b*) ∼ dōki̠ to pull horse up dead (= tūjẹ 1*c* = tirjẹ 2*a*). (*c*) ∼ mạgana to settle affair. (*d*) ∼ yạ̄ɓē to fill up holes in lower part of wall with plaster. (*e*) *Sk.* ∼ zạrē to twist strands to form ply. (*f*) *Sk.* grazed (skin). (*g*) did profusely *x* tā ∼ ji̠kintạ dạ waŋkā she thoroughly washed herself by rubbing. yā ∼ ni̠ dạ zāgi̠ (dūkạ) he abused (beat) me severely. tā ∼ niƙạ she did a lot of grinding. (*h*) *Vd.* tirjẹ.

B. (darjē) (1) *m.* twisted thread (*as for necklace, etc.*) = mụrjē 1*b*. (2) *Vd.* dạrzā.

darji *Vd.* dạrzā.

darjīyā *f.* poor type of silken cord (**sallīyā**).

darkaka *Kt.* = dirkaka.

darkancī *Ar. m.* blustering cuteness.

ɗarkwai *x* ~ **nē** it is straight (= **sōsǎi** 2*a* = **tōtar**).

darmā *f.* (1) tin (= **kuzā**). (2) lead. (3) gērō yā yi ~ grain in bulrush-millet heads has set. (4) *x* **Musulmī daŋgin** ~ **nē** a Muslim is one who follows God's precepts.

ɗarmā *Nor.* = ɗaurā.

darmāsōsūwā *f.* = **darmōsō** *m.* rich gravy ; rich soup.

darnācē *Vb.* 1C surrounded place with cornstalk-fence (**darnī**).

darnākwashā *f.* rich gravy ; rich soup.

darni A. (**darnī**) *m.* (*pl.* **darnukā**) (1) cornstalk-fence (*cf.* **dangā**). (2) *cf.* **rābā** ~. B. (**darnī**) *Hadejiya Hausa m. used in* **ɗan** ~ native doctor (= **bōkā**).

dārō *m.* (*pl.* **dāruna** = **dārōrī**) large brass basin.

ɗarō *x* **nā ci darānsā** I just missed meeting him.

dārōba *Eng. m.* warder = duröba *q.v.*

darōba *Vd.* durōba.

dārōrī *Vd.* dārō.

darrahē *Vb.* 1C *Kt.* **kā darrahē raŋkā** resign yourself ! (= **dangana**).

ɗarsa A. (**ɗarsā**) (1) *Vb.* 1A (*a*) poured out in drops (= **ɗigā** 1). (*b*) sprinkled. (2) *Vb.* 3A. (*a*) dripped. (*b*) yā **ɗarsu ā** zūcīyāta (i) it's now clear to me. (ii) now I remember ! (iii) *cf.* **ɗarsa** 2. B. (**ɗarsa**) *Vb.* 3B (*progressive* **ɗarsā**). (1) = **ɗarsā** 2*a*. (2) **bā tā tabā ɗarsam masā a rāi zai bā su ko kwabo ba** it never entered his mind to give them even a sou (= **ɗarsa** 2*b*).

darsāshē *Vb.* 3A *Kt.* (1) sat in relaxed posture. (2) led carefree life.

darshē (1) *m., f.* (*sg., pl.*) witless P. (2) what a messy mouth !

ɗarshi *m.* (*pl.* **ɗar'she-ɗarshē"**) drip ; drop.

ɗarsō *Vb.* 3A dripped (= **ɗarsa** 2*a*).

ɗarsu *Vd.* **ɗarsa** 2*b*.

dartō *m.* (*pl.* **darātā**). (1) saw. (2) file. (3) ~ **magāgarim mazā** what a fearless P. ! (4) *Vd.* **zartō**.

dartsā *f.* sores at corners of mouth.

dārumā *Kt. f.* binding used on inside apex of beehive-roof (= **murɗakā** *q.v.*).

dāruna large brass basins (*Vd.* dārō).

darūrā *f.* anxiety *x* **munā darūrar wuriŋ kwānā** we're anxious about where to lodge overnight. **n nā darūrar mātata** I'm anxious about my wife.

darūrūwā *Vd.* darī.

darūsā *m., f.* (1) glutton. (2) strong energetic P.

darwayā *Vb.* 2 *Kt.* plated (= **dauraya** *q.v.*).

darza A. (**darzā**) (1) *Vb.* 2. (*a*) = darjē 2*b*, *d*, *e*, *f*, *g*. (*b*) dōkī yā darji hatsī horse ate much corn. B. (**darza**) (1) **waŋkan darzā** *m.* African of lightish colour (= **waŋkan tarwadā**). (2) *Vb.* 1A = darjē 2*g*.

darzājē (1) *Sk. m.* a method of fish-catching (2) *Vd.* darzāzā.

darzāzā (1) *Vb.* 2 (*p.o.* **darzājē**, *n.o.* **darzāji**) = darzāzā *Vb.* 1C drove (motor or cycle) rapidly. (2) darzāzā *Vb.* 3A (motor or cycle) travelled rapidly. (3) **Darzāzā** *epithet of* Emir.

darzo *Vd.* darjē ; darzā.

das A. (**das**) evenly *x* **an yaŋkē shi** ~ it's evenly cut. B. (**dās**) (1) *x* **tanā tafīyā das-das** she's walking with heavy tread. (2) = **das** 1. (3) (*said by woman*) you bad child, belching so !

ɗas A. (**ɗas**) *x* yā zaunā ~ it sits firmly (= **dabas** *q.v.*). B. (**ɗas**) (1) *x* yā ɗigō ɗas ɗas it dripped slowly. (2) *m. or adv.* fear ; in fear (= **ɗar** *q.v.*).

dasa A. (**dasā**) *Vb.* 1A. (1) (*a*) transplanted (dāwā ; maiwā ; rakē ; daŋkali ; rōgo), *Vd.* **dasasshē**. (*b*) gave P. a "leg-up" in life. (2) inoculated *in native style x* **an** ~ **masā mashassharar Audu** he's been inoculated with lymph from Audu's smallpox (*cf.* lambā). (3) ~ **fure** to put flowers in moist pot to prevent from fading. (4) **an** ~ **masā zanē** another piece of cloth's been added to it to increase its size. **zanē yā ƙōne, an** ~ a piece was added to replace the burnt place in the material. (5) **an** ~ **hannun rīgā** sleeves have been sewn on to the gown. (6) **tā** ~ **sule ā hancī** she affixed shilling to her nose (= ɗanẹ̄ 3). (7) yā ∼ masẹ̄ kibīyẹ̄ he fired and hit him with arrow.   (8) yā ∼ gēmụ he's let his beard grow.

B. (dasā) *f.* type of gourd (dumā) with short neck.

ɗasa A. (ɗasẹ̄) *Vb.* (1) = ɗarsẹ̄. (2) = dasẹ̄ 6.

B. (ɗạsa) *Vb.* 3B = dạrsa.

C. (ɗasā) well *x* ɗāki yā yi kyau̥ ∼ the house is fine.

D. (ɗā̱sā) *Vb.* 2 (*p.o.* dạ̄shē, *n.o.* dạ̄shi). (1) broke off (branch; leaf; fruit). (2) yā ∼ dạgạ bā̱kiŋ Audụ he studied under Audu.

dāsạshē *Vb.* 3A *Kt.* is (was) blunt (= dākụshē *q.v.*).

dāsạshī *m.* (1) the gums (= dāɓụrī 1). (2) *Kt.* whole of cow's mouth as sold by butchers (= dāɓụrī 2).   (3) mại ∼ toothless P.

ɗạsạshī *Sk. m.* putting on airs (= ạlfahạrī).

dạsasshē *m. used in* ∼ kā fi tsịrarrē he's prospered more than his former equals; stranger has become more at home than the townspeople (*Vd.* dasẹ̄).

dashare A. (dāshạrē) *Vb.* 3A lingered.

B. (dāsharẹ̄) *used in* ∼ ma'aunin Tsakūwạ̄ *epithet of* (1) dirty P. (2) P. always laughing.

dashe A. (dạshē) *m.* (1) (*secondary v.n. of* dasẹ̄ 1, 3, 4) *x* yanā̱ dạshan iṛị = yanā̱ dasẹ̄ iṛị he's transplanting seedlings. (2) being occupied in transplanting *x* (*a*) yanā̱ ∼ he's out transplanting.   (*b*) yini dạshē *Vd.* ạlbasẹ̄ 6.   (3) *m., f.* P. prospered through receiving "leg-up" (*cf.* dasẹ̄ 1*b*) *x* Audụ dạsham Bạtūrẹ̄ nē Audu's got on through being backed by the European. (4) *m.* (*a*) planted-out seedling (*cf.* yā̱yē 2, yā̱mushị 2). (*b*) bā̱ ∼ ba nẹ̄, shūkạ nē he's not a newcomer, but of local birth. (*c*) dạshan dạ Allā̱ kē̱ sọ̄, kō bā̱ rūwā, yā̱ kāmạ he's "Fortune's" favourite (= alkamạ 1*b*). (5) ∼ akạ yi masạ na mạshassharar Audụ = dasẹ̄ 2. (6) dạsham mạkaunīyā̱ (*a*) planting slips of cassava, etc., head downwards. (*b*) wrestler's lifting opponent and banging head on ground.

B. (dashẹ̄) (1) *Vb.* 1A *totality-form of*

dasạ *x* an ∼ iṛị all the seedlings have been transplanted. (2) *Vb.* 3A muryạssạ̄ tā ∼ his voice is hoarse (= dushẹ̄).

dạ̄shē *Vd.* dạ̄sā.

dashi A. (dashị) *m.* (*secondary v.n. of* dasạ *except* 3) *x* yanā̱ dashịŋ iṛị = yanā̱ dasạ iṛị he's transplanting seedlings.

B. (dā̱shī) *m.* (1) (*a*) the resin-yielding shrub African myrrh (*Balsamodendron africanum*). (*b*) *Vd.* sạyā̱ 2. (2) (*a*) ∼ mại yawạn rā̱i *epithet of* P. surviving much illness. (*b*) *Vd.* rā̱i 1*q.* (3) Taɓaryad ∼ (*a*) *f.* string puzzle. (*b*) *epithet for any man called* Mụhammadụ.

C. (dāshị) (*Eng.* dash) *m.* tip, present *x* yā yi minị ∼ dạ gōrọ he gave me some kolanut.

dā̱shi *Vd.* dạ̄sā.

dạ'shi-dạ̄shī‖ (1) *adj. m., f.* (*sg., pl.*) spotted (= dabbarẹ̄-dabbarẹ̄). (2) *Zar. m.* embroidery-pattern of dots between lines.

dāshimạ *f.* = dāshị.

dāshirạ *m., f.* strong P.

dā̱shīshị *m.* (1) ornamentation of numnah (lạbbāṭị). (2) ground wheat cooked in broth.

dạ̄shīyạ *f.* (*pl.* dạ̄shīyū). (1) any new unused calabash or other vessel. (2) child which has never had smallpox.

daskarad dạ *Vb.* 4B caused to coagulate.

daskarẹ̄ *Vb.* 3A. (1) became coagulated. (2) (steam) condensed (1, 2 = sandạrẹ̄).

daskārī *m.* strong, fearless P. (*epithet is* ∼ bāwạn Sarkī).

dạskin dạ rīdī the bogeyman.

ɗaskwạnā *Vb.* 1C. (1) poured out T. in drops (= ɗarsạ 1). (2) yā ɗaskwạnạ kibīyạ he punctured sore with arrow to let out pus.

dạskwạnē *m.* = ạlhakiŋ ūwā q.v. *under* ạlhakī 2.

dạskwạnē *m.* act of pouring T. out in drips.

dāsōrī *m.* mại ∼ *m., f.* (1) toothless P. (2) *Vd.* hakōrī 1*a*.iii.

dassi *Sk. m.* evil ways.

dāsụnā *Vb.* 1C *Sk.* felled, knocked down (= kā dạ).

dạ̄sūsū *m.* (1) mange in domestic animals. (2) indigo-dye with little dyeing-power left.

dāta *Vb.* 3A (*no progressive*). (1) **yāro
yā** ∼ boy is between 7 and 10 years
old (= **taskā** 2). (2) **hatsī yā** ∼ corn is
some 4 feet high.

dāta *f.* (1) the tomato-like **gautā** *q.v.*
(2) **dāta** *f.* = **dan** ∼ *m.* type of fish.

dāta-dāta *f.* = **dātarnīyā** 1.

dātannīyā = **dātarnīyā** *f.* (1) the bitter
grass *Thelepogon elegans.* (2) = **dāta** 2.
(3) gall-bladder (= **matsarmamā**). (4)
type of small white frog poisonous to
cattle (= **sēsē**).

dato *Sk. m.* the gravy called **kwado**.

datsa A. (**dātsa**) (1) *Vb.* 1A. (*a*) (i) cut
off bit of. (ii) bit off piece of. (*b*) ∼
cīyāwa to chop up grass for fodder.
(*c*) (i) ∼ **zane** to perforate cloth (rat ;
careless cloth-beater ; **tsanyar fataucī**,
etc.). (ii) **yā** ∼ **gārū** it (battering-ram)
breached the town wall. (*d*) to divide
into groups *x* **a** ∼ **su bīyū, rabi su zō
nan, rabi su kōma gidā** let them be
detailed into two parties, one to come
here and the rest to return home !
(2) *f.* (*a*) playground (= **fagyan wāsā**),
Vd. **fagē, dandalī.** (*b*) **yanā da budurwā
a** ∼ he has a fiancée. (*c*) **tanā** ∼ she's
not yet married. **tun tanā** ∼ ever since
she was young . . . (*d*) *Vd.* **tsalam** 3.
(*e*) *Kt.* = **dātsā.**

B. (**dātsā**) *f.* = **tūwan dātsā** *m.* guinea-
corn or millet which is ground, but
without **surfē** being done, this being
destined for poor **kunū, fatē-fatē,
dambū**, *etc.*

C. (**dātsā**) (1) *Vb.* 2 = **dātsa** 1. (2) =
datsā 2.

D. (**datsā**) *Vb.* 2. (1) (*a*) **yā datsi
māsū wucēwā** = **yā datsi hanya** he
intercepted the passers-by. (*b*) **yā datsi
rūwā** he dammed up water. (2) **yā datsi
kwari da kadādā** he made transverse
ridges across the ends of the furrows.

E. (**datsa**) *Vb.* 1A inserted distinctive-
coloured bead into necklace *x* **an** ∼
kyalkyalī cikim murjānī (*cf.* **datsi**).

dātsa-dātsa in fragments *x* **Jāmus sun
rurrūshe garin nan** ∼ the Germans
destroyed that town by bombing.

datse A. (**dātse**) (1) *Vb.* 1A. (*a*) = **dātsa** 1.
(*b*) *x* **yā** ∼ **mini magana** he interrupted
what I was saying. (*c*) **yā** ∼ **magana**

he left his sentence unfinished. (2) *Vb.*
3A. (*a*) **zane yā** ∼ cloth's in holes *as in*
dātsa 1*c*.i. (*b*) **furē yā** ∼ tobacco-
flower-staining has worn off from teeth-
edges. (*c*) (commodity) has come to
an end.

B. (**dātsē**) *m.* (1) chopped grass for
fodder (*cf.* **kurshe** 2). (2) fermented
indigo not made into blocks. (3) *Kt.* =
dātsī.

C. (**datse**) *Vb.* 1A = **datsā.**

datsi A. (**dātsī**) *m.* (1) the grass *Aristida
Sieberiana* (*used for mixing into building-
clay or for thatching*). (2) **yā kad** ∼ he
took to his heels (N.B. **kad** *is derived
from* **kas** killed).

B. (**datsi**) *m.* (1) **datsi** = **dan datsi** *m.*
distinctive-coloured stone inserted into
necklace (*cf.* **datsa**). (2) = **datsīyā.**

datsīyā *f.* (1) (*a*) damming up water.
(*b*) making crevices watertight (1 =
banki 2). (2) type of dog-trap. (3) part
of weavers' " comb ".

dattāko *m.* (1) being respectable and of
sound judgment *x* **yā nūna** ∼ he
behaved with dignity. (2) *Vd.* **dattījantaka, dattijo.**

dattāwā *Vd.* **dattijo.**

dattī A. (**dattī**) (*Eng.* dirty) *m.* (1) **yā
yi** ∼ it (place, thing) is dirty. (2) refuse,
excrement, etc. (*Vd.* **daufa**).' (3) **mai
dūban** ∼ *m.* scavenger, sanitary-
labourer, sanitary-inspector.

B. (**Dattī**) *term of address to* P. named
after one's grandfather.

dattībai *Vd.* **dattijo.**

dattījantaka *f.* (1) = **dattāko.** (2) being
of age or dignity of a **dattijo.** (3) **nā
rantse da girman dattījantakata** (*said
by labourers*) I swear it is true !

dattijo *m.* (*f.* **dattījūwā**) *pl.* **dattāwā** =
dattījāwā = **dattijai** = **dattībai** =
dattībe). (1) (*a*) a true gentleman, i.e.
respectable P. of sound judgment
whether of late middle age (as strictly
denoted by the word) or not (*epithet
is* **kurum tā gamshē ka** = **kurum tā
raba ka da kōwā**). (*b*) **dattijam biri**
late middle-aged P. comporting himself
unsuitably. (*c*) **Dattijo, an ji kunya** what
a disgrace ! (*d*) **dattijam majalisa** the
President of the Council. (*e*) *Vd.* **bargā**

2. (2) ɗan ∼ *m. epithet of* indigo (shūnī).

dạttsā *Kt.* = dạrtsā.

dạtū *Sk. m.* the gravy called kwaɗǫ *q.v.*

dau *emphasizes* deepness of hue *x* rānā tā yiwō ∼ the sun rose redly. rānā tā yi ∼ the sun set redly. nā ga rānā ∼ I saw the sun was scarlet (*cf.* ɗau). jinī yā fitō ∼ stream of blood gushed out. wutā tā yi ∼ the fire blazed. rawạnī yā yi ∼ the turban is darkly dyed. rạunī yā yi ∼ the wound is inflamed.

ɗau A. (ɗau) (1) (*a*) = ɗaukạ. (2) gishirī yā ji ∼ it (food) is very salty ! (3) yanā dạ zākī ∼ it is very sweet. (4) kwạllī yā ji ạ idō ∼ antimony has been applied abundantly to the eyes.

B. (ɗau) *x* wutā tā yi zāfī ∼ the fire's blazing-hot (*cf.* dau). rạunī yā ɗauki zāfī ∼ the wound is inflamed. bạrkǫnō yanā dạ yāji ∼ the pepper's very hot. kụnāmạ tā hạrbē ni ∼ the scorpion stung me fiercely.

C. (ɗau) *x* wutā tā yi zāfī ∼ = ɗau.

ɗā'ụ *f.* the letter " ɗ ".

Daudạ (1) David. (2) *Vd.* daudīyyạ.

daudạ *f.* (1) (*a*) dirt (= dạttī). (*b*) kō yạnzu rūwā nā māganin ∼ essentials do not change. (*c*) gōbe ∼ *Vd.* farī 2*g.*iii. (2) emaciation of baby (*ascribed to mother having sexual intercourse during suckling period*). (3) daudạr bāyī type of grass with sharp seeds adhering to clothing. (*b*) daudạr Māguzāwā prickly plant used by circumcised boys to keep other children away (= bā sūsạ 2). (4) daudạr ciki = macījī 13. (5) daudạr dūnīyạ pelf. (6) daudạr gǫrā, ạ cikī a kạn shā tạ one must take the rough with the smooth. (7) daudạr kại dandruff. (8) daudạr kụnnē wax in the ear. (9) ạutan daudạ = kulī-kulī.

ɗau-ɗau without intermission (= dagwạn-dagwạn *q.v.*).

daudawā *f.* the black cakes called dạddawā *q.v.*

ɗaudaуạ *Vb.* 2 = ɗaiɗayạ.

daudẹ *m.* gonorrheal rheumatism (*cf.* cīwǫn 4).

daudīyyạ *f.* = daudīyyi *m.* chain-armour (*Vd.* Daudạ).

Daudụ (1) *epithet of any* Galādīmạ.

(2) yes, sir ! (*reply made when any clerk calls for P.*). (3) ɗan ∼ yā hau kạnsạ he's possessed by the bǫrī-spirit so-called which takes form of man dressed as woman. (4) *Vd.* daudụn kụndī.

ɗau dukạ (1) *m.*, *f.* fine P. (2) *Vd.* mạkạrā.

daudụn kụndī *m.* type of calico.

ɗau galmā *Vd.* shā gārī.

daugī *m.* ant-eater (= dạbgī *q.v.*).

dauje (1) *Vb.* 1A grazed (skin). (2) *Vb.* 3A (skin, etc.) is grazed.

dauji *m.* (*pl.* dāzuzzukạ) the " bush " (= dāji *q.v.*).

ɗauka A. (ɗaukạ) *Vb.* (*past* yā ɗaukē shi. yā ɗauki kāyā. *progressive* yanā ɗaukạr kāyā = yanā ɗaukạn kāyā. yanā ɗaukạ. *imperative* ɗaukā = kạ ɗaukạ. ɗaukẹ shi = kạ ɗaukē shi. ɗauki sandā = kạ ɗauki sandā). (1) (*a*) took up *x* (i) yā ɗauki kāyā he took up the load. (ii) shāwarạ ɗaukạr dākị where there's a will there's a way. (iii) cikinsạ yā ∼ he's replete. (iv) santsī yā ɗaukē ni I slipped. (v) barcī yā ɗaukē shi he fell asleep. (vi) fitilạ tā ɗauki idǫna the lamp dazzled me. (vii) jirgī yā ɗauki rūwā the boat's leaking, water swirled into the boat. (viii) jirginsạ yā ɗauki rūwā he's been found out. (ix) jēji yā ɗauki wutā the bush caught fire. tukunyā tā ɗauki wutā the pot has become hot. (x) yā ɗauki kafạ tasụ = yā ɗauki sansụ he misrepresented what they said (*Vd.* ɗaukạr kafạ), *cf.* ɗaukē 1*d.* (xi) yā ɗaukam masạ kafạ = ɗaukē 1*d.*iii. (xii) yā ɗauki kạnsạ dạ kafāfūwạnsạ, yā cẹ bai san kōwā ba sāi Sarkin Kanọ he stated categorically that he follows no overlord but the Emir of Kano. (xiii) yā ɗauki hạnkạ-lintạ, yanā yāwǫ dạ shī he told her a pack of lies (*cf.* ɗaukē 1*b.*ii). (xiv) took it upon oneself *x* sun ɗauki aikin kashẹ gōbarā they have assumed responsibility for putting out conflagrations. yā ɗauki shūgabancị = yā ɗauki gạba he took the lead. yā ɗauki gạban yākịn he assumed leadership in that war (*Vd.* gạba 3*b*). nā ɗauki zạrgī I take the blame. yā ɗauki wạhalạ = yā ɗaukar wạ kạnsạ wạhalạ he voluntarily undertook the troublesome task.

bǎ ạbin dạ zại ɗaukạ ạ jikinsạ he will get no advantage. (xv) yā ɗạuki hanyạr Kano he took the road to Kano. yā tĭlạstā mu, mụ ɗạuki hanyạn naŋ he forced us to adopt this plan (= kāmạ 10a). (xvi) yā ɗạukē nị ạ bakạ he backbit me. (xvii) began to x yā ɗạuki zugạ su he set about egging them on (cf. ɗaukō). (xviii) yā ɗạuki farĭ Vd. farĭ 2a.iv. (xix) yạ ɗaukạ Vd. ajĭyē 5a.ii. (xx) kā kāsạ ɗaukạr ƙwǎyā Vd. damị 5 ; tsĭrukụ. (xxi) ụbā kạ ɗaukạ Vd. tĭlạs 2e. (xxii) ɗaukạ kō yạu Vd. ambụtā 2 ; damị 2. (xxiii) ɗạuki amaryā Vd. amaryā 4. (xxiv) Vd. kaŋwā 1b.

(b) carried, transported, took x (i) yā ɗạuki kāyā zūwạ Kano he carried the load to Kano. (ii) yā ɗaukam minị ạlbạshĭ he received my pay for me. (iii) yā ɗaukam masạ kāyā he carried his load for him ; he stole the load from him. (iv) Allạ̄ yā ɗạuki rạnsụ they died. (v) nā ɗạuki kạrē doŋ haushị, yā kōmō yaŋạ tuŋkwụyĭ it was unsuitable for its purpose (Vd. kạrē 31).

(c) deceived x (i) hanyạ tā ɗạukē nị I went astray. hanyạ tā ɗạukē mụ zūwạ Kano we took the Kano road by mistake. (ii) kạmā tā ɗạukē nị I was misled by the resemblance. (iii) zūcĭyā tā ɗạukē shị he made a mistake through absentmindedness (= shạgalạ).

(cc) assumed as being x (i) yā ɗaukạ kōwā dattĭjo nē kạmansạ he took it for granted that everybody is a gentleman like he is. kadạ kạ ɗaukạ do not assume that . . . ! (ii) mun ɗaukạ ạ rāyukạmmụ ạ kạn zā ạ shēkạrạ bĭyar we assume that 5 years will be required. (iii) sun ɗạuki ạbin ạ hạgunce they misunderstood the matter. (iv) wannạm bụkātạr gyạdā, an ɗaukē tạ gạban dukạn taịmakwan yāƙị the need for groundnuts must be given first place in priority for war supplies. (v) bạ sụ ɗạuki ạlkāwạrĭ ạ bạ̄kiŋ kōmē ba they set no store by the promise. (vi) kadạ kạ ɗạuki wannạm mạganạ kạmar ba'ạ don't take these words in the sense of ridicule !

(d) contracted contagious disease x yā ɗạuki (= yā ɗaukō) tụnjērē he contracted syphilis.

(e) (i) accepted proposal x ạbin dạ ya ~, nĭ bạn ~ ba I won't put up with what he does. aŋ azạ musụ bāwạ ɗạrĭ, sukạ ~ a levy of 100 slaves was imposed on them and they agreed to supply them. bạ zại ɗạuku ba the proposal's not acceptable. ạbịn dạ zūcĭyā ta ~ gạŋgar jịkĭ bāwạ nē where there's a will, there's a way. (ii) accepted x sun ɗạuki dạbārạn naŋ they accepted that plan. au ạ ɗạukē nị sōjạ, au m mutụ either let me be accepted as a soldier or let me die !

(f) replied in unison x sukạ ~ gạba ɗayā then they replied agreeing unanimously. sukạ ~ " gạ̄ gạdā ! " then they all shouted out together " There's a duiker ! ".

(g) helped P. put load on head x ɗạukẹ ni put my load on my head for me ! (= ɗōrạ 3 = azạ 3).

(h) applied word in sense of x an ɗạuki " ɗaŋ Adạŋ " ạ kạm " mụtum " the word " ɗaŋ Adạŋ " is used in the sense of " person ".

(j) became pregnant (only cow ; mare ; camel) x sānĭyā tā ~ = sānĭyā tā ɗạuki cikị (cf. ɗạukē 2a).

(k) kạ̄zā tā ɗau ƙwǎi hen's about to start laying (= Sk. Kt. ajĭyē).

(l) nā ɗạuki muryạrkạ I recognize your voice.

(m) yā ɗạuki rānā (i) he fixed a date for doing T. (cf. ɗạukā 1c). (ii) he travelled in heat of the sun.

(n) yā ɗạuki sā'ạ Vd. sā'ạ 4a.

(o) Vd. ạlkāwạrĭ 1b.i, c, e ; bāshị 2b ; bụdurwā 1b ; daŋganạ 2 ; ɗārĭ 1a.ii fagē 4 ; fansā 2 ; farĭ 2a.iv ; fọtō ;

gạba 3*b* ; gabārạ ; gāgū ; kạrātū 2*c* ; murnạ 1*c* ; numfāshī 2 ; saŋgalī 2*c* ; saŋhọ 3 ; zāfī 3 ; zōbẹ 1*c*.

(*p*) *x* ạbịn dạ ya ~ dạgạ Kanọ har kudụ (= fyādạ 2 = dạŋganạ 2*c* = kāmạ 10*b*) the area extending south of Kano (*cf.* gamạ 2*d*.ii, dịra 5).

(*q*) *cf.* daukā ; daukē ; daukō : dauku ; daukạ wuyạ ; dau ; dau ni ; *compounds of* dauki.

(2) *m.*, *f.* (*a*) (*v.n.* ; *progressive of* 1) *x* (i) yanạ daukạnsạ = yanạ daukạrsạ he's lifting it up, carrying it, etc. (ii) *Vd.* compounds of daukạn *and* daukạr *and* dauki *alphabetically.* (*b*) paramour *x* Kạnde ~ tasạ cē Kande is his paramour. Audụ daukạntạ nē Audu is her paramour (= fạrkā 3). (*c*) dan daukạ *m.* shallow circular basket.

B. (daukā) (1) *Vb.* 1C. (*a*) raised T. with intention of looking underneath and replacing (*as* fāifāi cover of dish). (*b*) yā ~ ƙafạ he put his best foot foremost (*cf.* daukē 1*d* ; daukạ 1*a*.x). (*c*) yā ~ rānā he postponed date (*cf.* daukạ 1*m*). (*d*) (*with dative*) removed *x* ūwā tasạ tā ~ masạ nōnọ (*lit.* his mother withdrew her breast from him) he's a rank outsider (*cf.* daukē 1*a*). (2) *Vb.* 3A. (*a*) withdrew for a time *x* kụ ~ manạ please leave me for a while ! (*b*) rānā tā ~ it's about 10 a.m. by the height of the sun. (*c*) rūwā yā ~ rain's begun to stop (*cf.* daukē). (3) *cf.* daukạ : daukē ; daukō ; dauku.

daukacī *m.* the whole *x* daukacinsụ all of them.

daukạd dā *Vd.* daukạr dā.

daukakạ *Vb.* 2. (1) (P. ; misfortune) harassed P. (2) *Vd.* hạsārạ.

daukaka A. (daukạkā) *Vb.* 1C. (1) lifted up (= daukạ 1). (2) honoured. (3) promoted P. (4) helped.

B. (daukạkạ) (1) *Vb.* 2 = daukạkā. (2) *Vb.* 3B (*a*) became raised up. (*b*) became higher than before. (*c*) became honoured. (*d*) became promoted. (3) *f.* being honoured, enjoying respect.

daukakkeniyā *f.* (1) severe fracas. (2) wordy battle.

daukakkīyā *f.* yā yi minị ~ he falsely accused me.

daukạn-compounds, *Vd. also* daukạr.

daukạn dumam magājī dạ nīshị *m.* irrelevant anger.

daukạm furā ạ rāgayạ *m.* children's game of lifting one another up by the chin.

daukạn rūwā *Vd.* daukạr rūwā.

daukạn 'yam makarantā *m.* an yi masạ ~ (1) he (boy) has been lifted up to be caned (= ịnā 4*d*). (2) 2–4 persons lifted it, each holding one side of it (2 = tạtạkōrō = daukạr rūwā 2 = *Kt.* sạlkā 3 = *Kt.* cạlị-cālī).

daukạn yārọ *Vd.* yārọ 1*f*.

daukar A. (daukạr) *Vd.* daukạ 2.

B. (daukar) *the form of* daukạ *used before dative, cf.* daukạ 1*a*.xi.

daukạr-compounds, *Vd. also* daukạn.

daukạr dā *f.* type of cheating in gambling (cācā).

daukạr dākị *Vd.* shāwarạ 1*j*.

daukạr dawạm marātayī *Sk. f.* = daukạm furā ạ rāgayạ.

daukạr duhụ *Vd.* gundurū.

daukạr dụŋgū *Vd.* dụŋgū 4.

daukạr idọ *f.* being dazzled by light (*Vd.* idọ 1*k*).

daukạr ƙafạ *f. x* an yi manạ ~ they misrepresented what we said (*Vd.* daukạ 1*a*.x).

daukạr mạrī *m.* (1) jerking rope which is round ox's hind leg to lassoo other leg also. (2) type of operation in weaving.

daukạr rūwā *f.* (1) = tạfīyạ 7. (2) an yi masạ daukạn rūwā = daukạn 'yam makarantā 2.

daukạ wuyạ *m.*, *f.* (1) (*a*) child carried on shoulders, as slow in learning to walk. (*b*) ~ baị san " nā gaji " ba one half of the world doesn't know how the other half lives.

daukayyạ *f.* = daukakkēnịyā.

dauke A. (daukē) (1) *Vb.* 1C. (*a*) removed *x* yā ~ minị gāwā he removed the corpse for me (*cf.* daukā 1*d*). fịtịlạ tā ~ minị idọ the lamp dazzled me. yā ~ hụlā he took off his cap (*cf.* tūɓẹ 2). an ~ rūwā the rain's ceased. (*b*) stole *x*

(i) yā ~ minı̣ kāyā he stole my goods.
(ii) yā ~ haŋkalinsụ he hoodwinked
them (cf. ɗaukạ 1a.xiii). (c) tā ɗaukẹ
ɗā she (mother) weaned her boy;
she (grandmother) took home newly-
weaned boy to accustom him to cessation of suckling. (d) (i) yā ɗaukẹ ƙafạ
it (animal) is lame. (ii) yā ɗaukẹ
ƙafạ dagạ . . . he's ceased doing . . .
(iii) yā ~ masạ ƙafạ he cheated him or
brought false charge against him (cf.
ɗaukā 1b; ƙafạ 7b; ɗaukạ 1a.x.
(e) yā ɗaukẹ kại dagạ . . . (i) he gave up
hope of getting . . . ; pretended not to
want . . . (ii) he turned blind eye
to . . . (f) yā ~ ta caŋ he went that way.
(g) abịn dạ na kạn yi, sǎi yạ ~ he
imitates all I do (cf. ɗaukạ 1e). (h)
(with dative) relieved P. of x yā ~ masạ
kāyā he relieved him of his load
(= both senses of ɗaukạ 1b.iii). nā ~
masạ wạhalạ I relieved him of trouble.
yā ~ minı̣ he acted as my representative. (j) Vd. numfāshı̄ 2. (2) Vb.
3A (a) dried up x rūwā yā ~ it is not
raining any longer; rainy-season is
over. yā ~ it (sugar-cane, i.e. rạkē
or tạkandā) is juiceless. sānı̣yā tā ~
udder of cow has dried (cf. ɗaukạ 1j).
(b) (clothing) shrunk. (c) Vd. ƙafạ
7b; numfāshı̄ : sau 1a.v. (d) wuyạn
tụ̄lū (tukunyā) yā ~ neck of ewer
(pot) is broken off. (e) sun ɗaukē
they bore it (attack) patiently; they
stood firm. (f) cf. ɗaukạ : ɗaukā :
ɗaukō : ɗaụku.
    B. (ɗaukē) (1) Vd. ɗaukạ 1. (2)
m. (a) suppository for rectal complaints
in children (= matsı̣ 3). (b) yā bā
nı̣ ~ he sold me cotton or corn on
credit. nā ɗaukō ~ I got cotton or
corn on credit (i) applied to cotton put
away at cotton-harvest in September
and sold about July on credit. (ii)
applied to corn sold about July and to
be repaid at harvest time in cash, or
one bundle for one, or two for one
((ii) = hạnsakō q.v.). (c) an yi minı̣ ~
I (vendor) have been forced to hand
over part of my wares to market
official as levy.
    C. (ɗaüke) (1) x yanậ ~ he's being

carried. (2) yanậ ~ dạ shı̄ he's carrying
it.
ɗaụ'ke-ɗaukēⁱⁱ m. habitual pilfering,
especially from master or parent (cf.
sānē, ƙwaŋgē).
ɗauke fāifaŋkı̣ m. tūwō given to casual
guest.
ɗaukēkēnı̣yā f. = ɗaukakkēnı̣yā.
ɗauki A. (ɗaukı̄) m. (1) help. (2) (a) yā
yi ~ he did an act of prowess. (b)
sum būɗẹ wani ɗaukı̄ they opened a
campaign, began military operations.
sun sāmi hanyạr yịn ɗaukı̄ zūwạ
Masạr they managed to fight their way
into Egypt. yā kai ɗaukı̄ he made a
strong attack (c) (sometimes treated as
pl.). sun yi mạnyan ɗaukı̄ kạm Masạr
they made powerful attacks on Egypt.
(3) Kt. mounting of mare (or she-
camel) by stallion x gōɗı̣yā bạ tạ
kāmạ ɗaukịn nam ba the mare didn't
get pregnant during that mounting
(= bạyē 1).
    B. (ɗauki) (1) m. issuing the share
due to each member of the household
x tā yi musụ ~ she issued out their
rations. kụ zō, gậ ɗaukiŋkụ come and
get your rations ! (refers to dainties
x fruit, meat, wạinā, but not corn,
for wives are free to help themselves to
this. But Kt. applies also to corn. In
case of Chief issuing weekly supplies to
dependents, includes corn and money)
(= Kt. ɗaụ ni 2). (2) Vd. ~ bậ daɗı̣.
(3) Vd. ɗaukạ.
    C. (ɗaukı̄) Kt. m. keen desire (= ɗōkı̄
q.v.).
ɗauki bậ daɗı̣ m. (1) serious struggle or
dispute. (2) sunậ ~ they're enemies.
ɗauki kaŋwā Vd. kaŋwā 1b.
ɗauki kwạriŋkạ m. = ɗauki sandaŋkạ.
ɗauki, sạkā f. type of quilted saddle-
cover.
ɗauki sandaŋkạ used in auran ɗauki
sandaŋkạ m. marriage where husband
lives in wife's home, sometimes returning to own home for farming, etc.
(= jẹ ka dạ kwạriŋkạ = Kt. surkutẹ),
cf. aurē 4.
ɗaukō Vb. 1E (1) began (in the following
usages) yā ~ mutūwạ it's dying (referring only to animals, trees, plants,

cf. nēmā 2). waṇdō yā ∼ mutūwa
trousers are worn out. yā ∼ kyau he
(it) has begun to improve (*cf.* ɗauka
1*a*.xvii). yā ∼ lālācēwā he (it) has
begun to deteriorate. yā ∼ tsūfā
–he (it) has begun to age. (2) tā ∼
wajan ūwā she takes after her mother.
(3) *cf.* ɗauka; ɗaukā ; ɗaukē.

ɗauku *Vb.* 3B (1) ɗaukūwā muka yi
we misunderstood. yā ∼ he became
confused, this preventing him understanding or expressing himself in-
telligibly on that occasion. (2) kāyan
naṇ bā yā ɗaukūwā this load is too
heavy to lift or to carry.

daula A. (daula) *Ar. f.* (1) (*a*) power.
(*b*) yā yi ∼ he ruled. (2) (*a*) wealth. (*b*)
ɗan ∼ *m.* son of rich parents. (*c*) kāyan
∼ *m.* luxury articles (jewellery, etc.).
B. (daulā) *f.* best quality antimony
(tōzalī) = gallō 1*b* = hanta 2*c*.

ɗaumāɗatal *m.* nincompoop (*epithet is* ∼
zagin zagāgē).

ɗaumāshī *m.* the shrub *Vernonia
Kotschyana.*

daunānā *Vd.* ɗaddaunā.

ɗauna *Vb.* 1A *Kt.* issued out rations *as
in* ɗau ni 2.

daunī *m.* greasiness of neck or head such
as dirties hat or neck of gown.

ɗau ni (1) " ∼, kada ka tam mini " gareshi
he's vacillating, fickle. (2) *Kt.* tā yi
musu ∼ she issued their rations
(= ɗauki 2 *q.v.*).

daura A. (daura) (1) close up to *x* gidansu
yanā ∼ da hanya their compound is
near the road (= dab *q.v.*). (2) *Vd.*
∼ da ∼.
B. (Daurā) *f.* (1) (*a*) Daura Emirate
(*cf.* Baɗaurī). (*b*) *epithet of* Daura City
is Gābi kaṇ ƙasā. (3) *Vd.* dauranci.

ɗaura A. (ɗaura) (1) *Vb.* 1A. (*a*) tied T.
on to *x* (i) an ∼ masa sirdi it (horse)
has been saddled. nā ∼ littāfi ga
kāyā I tied the book on to the load.
(ii) yā ∼ mini magana he accused me
falsely (*Vd.* ɗaurarrīyar magana, *Vd.*
1*d below*). (iii) an ∼ mata aurē her
marriage-ceremony has been performed
(*Vd.* aurē 6*c*, 9). (iv) kada a ∼ mini
jakar tsāba, kājī su riƙa bī ni don't
falsely accuse me ! (v) abin da bāƙī

ya ∼, hannū bā yā kwancēwā a
promise is not a knot to be untied by the
hands (*Vd.* ɗaurim bāƙī). (vi) amfānin
abiṇ aɗō, ɗaurāwā it is no use possessing
fine things if one makes no use of them.
(*b*) put on *x* nā ∼ tufa I put on clothes.
tā ∼ zane she put on her cloth (*cf.* ɗaure
1*c*, gindī 1*b*.iii). yā ∼ damara he put
on a belt. yā ∼ warkī he put on a skin-
loincloth (*Vd.* ɗaura warkī). tā ∼
fatala she put on a headkerchief. tā ∼
dūwātsū a wuya she put on a necklace.
(*c*) (i) tied up (load, animal, etc.).
(ii) ∼ kāyā *Vd.* dabāra 3. (iii) ∼ gindī
Vd. ɗaure 1*e*. (iv) imprisoned P. = ɗaure
1*a*.ii (*cf.* ɗaurā). (*d*) settled *x* mun ∼
magana we've settled the transaction
(*Vd.* 1*a*.ii *above*, ɗaurarrīyar magana). an
∼ ciniki the affair has been clinched.
an ∼ aurē the marriage-ceremony has
been performed (*Vd.* aurē 6*c*, 9).
(*e*) yā ∼ tafīya he made preparations
for journey. yā ∼ yāƙi *Vd.* yāƙi
1*bb*.iii. (*f*) yā ∼ magana da nī he
made me a promise. (*g*) *Vd.* ɗauriṇ
allūra. (*h*) *for compounds of* ɗaura,
Vd. second word. (*j*) *cf.* ɗaure. (*k*) ∼
ɗaure 1*d*.i, ii. (2) *Vb.* 3A *x* hadiri yā ∼
= hadiri yā ɗauru (= yā ɗaurō =
yanā ɗaure) a storm threatens.
B. (ɗaurā) *Vb.* 2 (1) tied and removed. (2) tied P. or T. now no longer
tied *x* an ɗaurē shi he was once in
prison. nā ɗauri dōki uku I used to
keep three horses. (3) yā ɗauri yāƙi
he made preparations for war (= ɗaura
1*e*). (4) yā ɗauri kansa (i) he " made
compliments ". (ii) he perjured himself before the court. (5) *cf.*
ɗaure.

ɗaurace *Vd.* ɗaurata.

daura da daura *x* suna ∼ they (towns,
etc.) are side by side ; they're quite
close together (*cf.* daura).

dauranci *m.* (*derived from* Daurā) =
giciye.

ɗauranta *Vb.* 2 = ɗaurata.

ɗaurāra *Vb.* 2 *Kt.* looked at T. or P.
afar (= hanga), *Vd.* ɗaurārō.

ɗaurārō *Kt. m.* (*secondary v.n. of* ɗaurāra)
x yanā ɗaurārō he's looking afar.
yanā ɗaurāransa = yanā ɗaurāra tasa

he's looking into the distance to try and catch sight of him.

daurarrē *m.* (*f.* daurarrīyā) *pl.* daurarrū patient P.

daurarrē *m.* (*f.* daurarrīyā) *pl.* daurarrū. (1) bound, tied. (2) daurarrīyar magana (*a*) affair long since settled (*Vd.* daura 1*d*). (*b*) a " frame-up " (*epithet is* daurarrīyar magana wadda ta fi sūkam māshi cīwo), *Vd.* daura 1*a.*ii.

daurata *Vb.* 2 (*p.o.* dauracē, *n.o.* dauraci) is (was) close to, side by side with (*cf.* daura) *x* gidāna yā dauraci nāsa daga arēwā my compound's quite near his, looking north.

dauratayya *f.* being side by side, close to each other (*Vd.* daura).

Daurāwā *Vd.* Badaurī.

daura warkī (1) mun yi masa daura warkī we've done the bulk of it. (2) *Sk.* daura warkinka *f.* the hoeing called gā nāka *q.v.* (3) dōki yā sōma daura warkī horse is thin in hindquarters (= baraka 2*c*). (4) *Vd.* daura 1*b.*

dauraya A. (dauraya) (1) *Vb.* 2 (*a*) rinsed vessel or clothing. (*b*) plated *x* nā daurayē shi da azurfā I plated it with silver. (2) *f.* coat of plating.

B. (daurayā) *Vb.* 1C plated *x* nā dauraya azurfā a jikinsa = nā ~ masa azurfā I plated it with silver.

dauraye A. (daurayē) *Vb.* 1C. (1) = dauraya. (2) washed (body, vessel, clothes, etc.).

B. (daurayē) *m.* (1) coat of plating. (2) tā haifi daurayan shēgē she bore legitimate child after illegitimate one.

daure *Vb.* 3A bowed to the inevitable, exercised self-control, patience (= jūre 1 = tankwashē 1*c*) *x* yā ~ wahala he bore trouble bravely. nā ~ masa I was long-suffering with him.

daure A. (daure) (1) *Vb.* 1A. (*a*) (i) tied up (load, animal, etc.) = daura 1*c.* (ii) imprisoned P. (= daura 1*c.*iv), *cf.* daurā, rāi 1*j.* (iii) makadī yā ~ ta drummer captured girl in play for her to be ransomed by her sweetheart. (iv) Alla ya ~ God prosper your new horse ! (v) kōwā ya ~ kūrā yā san yadda zai yi ya kwance ta look before you leap ! (vi) bāki yā iya ~ kafa

Vd. bāki 2*n.* (vii) ~ akwīya *Vd.* akwīya 1*f*, daure 2. (viii) da wurī a kan ~ *Vd.* sammakō 1*b.* (*b*) yā ~ damara he put on a belt. (*c*) tā ~ zanē she's taken her best cloth into everyday use (*cf.* daura 1*b*). (*d*) (i) yā ~ ciki he refrained from food though hungry ; he worked earnestly. (ii) hatsī yā ~ ciki corn is about to produce ears (= kunshi 5 = daura 1*k*). (iii) yā ~ mata ciki he gave her medicine for abortion or delay in development of foetus. (*e*) yā ~ mini gindī he helped me. (*f*) yā ~ kansa = daurā 4. (*g*) *Vd.* fuska 1*c*, girā 1*b*, jijiyā 2, daurin albaras, daurin dawa, daurin hannū, daurin kasā, daurin kirjī. (2) *Vb.* 3A. (*a*) cikina yā ~ I'm constipated. (*b*) fuskassa tā ~ he's frowning.

B. (daure) *x* (1) yanā ~ it is tied up (Mod. Gram. 80*d*). (2) akwīya a ~ in tā sāmi saki, bābu zamā put a beggar on horseback and he'll ride to the devil (*cf.* akwīya 1*f*). (3) *Vd.* daura 2. (4) zāki a ~ *Vd.* zāki 1*g.*

dauri A. (dauri) *m.* (1) circular band round drum to keep skin taut (= kangū 1). (2) = taurā 1. (3) ox with drooping horns (= bijāye).

B. (daurī) *m.* (1) (*a*) an infant's tonic. (*b*) sāran ~ bā dā " counting one's chickens before they're hatched " (= giringidishī). (*c*) bari ŋ ga irin daurin da ūwā tasa ta bā shi (*said by P. about to beat naughty boy*) let's see if he's got any courage ! (2) astringent taste (as of green dates, kolas, potash, etc.) = barcī 4 = *Sk.* kalcī. (3) dishonestly dyeing with gamji, fārū or flour of dōrawa (= ganda 1*b*). (4) daurin dabē decoction of locust beans (dōrawa) or Egyptian mimosa (gabārūwā) for floor making or strengthening water-skins.

C. (daurī) *Sk. adv.* of old *x* zāmanin ~ olden times. 'yam mātan ~ bā na yanzu ba the girls of old, not the modern ones.

dauri A. (daurī) *m.* (1) (*a*) (*secondary v.n. of* daure) *x* anā daurin kāyā = anā daure kāyā the load's being tied up. (b) act of tying x yā shā ∼ he was imprisoned. (c) Vd. rǎi 1j. (2) sheets of paper tied into form of book. (3) an yi wạ baƙịŋ ∼ circle's been written over Arabic consonant to show it is unvowelled (called in Ar. jazma = sukūn). (4) short marginal notes (= ɗurrị). (5) (a) coating T. with ash, or flour of ɗōrawa as undercoat for dye. (b) ɗaurịŋ ālạ coating teeth with lime-juice or tamarind (tsāmīyā) as undercoat for tobacco-flour juice to stick to. (6) firm hold in wrestling. (7) an yi wạ kụnū ∼ a little tamarind (tsāmīyā) juice's been added to gruel to give acid taste. (8) an yi wạ mīyạ ∼ (a) guineacorn-flour has been added to make up for paucity of baobob (kūkạ) flour in the soup. (b) potash has been added to lessen acidity (tsāmī) of soup left standing overnight. (9) charm consisting of the Arabic word liyastakhlifannahum ! to prevent fall of cracked wall. (10) ɗaurịŋ kạdādā ridge across ends of furrows (= kạdādā). (11) Vd. Compounds of ɗaurị below.

　B. (ɗaurī) = daurī 2.

ɗaurịŋ ạlbarạs x an ɗaurẹ masạ ạlbarạs = an yi masạ ɗaurịŋ ạlbarạs he's been given remedy to prevent spread of leprosy on him.

ɗaurịŋ ạllūrạ m. an yi masạ ∼ = an ɗaurạ masạ ạllūrạ needle's been tied across his fingernail as torture.

ɗaurịŋ awākim mạkạ̄fī = Kt. ɗaurịŋ awākim mạkạ̄fọ m. type of string-puzzle.

ɗaurin baki (ɗaurịm bǎkī) m. (1) nā yi masạ ∼ = nā ɗaurẹ masạ bǎkī I used on him a charm to soften terms of his reply (x to prevent P. refusing loan ; to prevent severe sentence) (cf. bǎkī 1b.xvi). (2) an yi wạ rījịyā ∼ well-mouth has been built up with wood and stone. (3) part of the embroidery (sụrfānị) on cap.

ɗaurin biri (ɗaurịm birị) Vd. birị 4.

ɗaurin butar makafi (ɗaurịm būtạr mạkạ̄fī) m. suffering x yụŋwạ tā yi masạ ∼ hunger troubled him.

ɗaurịŋ cikị m. Vd. ɗaurẹ 1d.

ɗaurịn dājị m. = ɗaurịn dawạ.

ɗaurịn ɗaŋgwạlī Kt. m. = ɗaurịn 'yam maruƙạ 2.

ɗaurịn dawạ = ɗaurịn jējị = ɗaurịn dājị m. an yi masạ ∼ = an ɗaurẹ masạ dawạ, etc., he was given charm enabling him to pass safely through dangerous " bush ".

ɗaurịn girā m. (1) pulling out P.'s eyebrows with tweezers (matsēfatā) to cure blepharitis. (2) frowning.

ɗaurịn gụ̄gā m. (1) calabash for drawing water, this having several sticks (ƙafạ) placed in it in form like umbrella-ribs : lower ends are tied to inside circumference by piercing holes and passing string through : rope for letting into well is secured to apex of the sticks : if sticks are not used, but ropes passed below the calabash in similar umbrella-rib form, this is called ɗaurịn kate-kate. (2) vaulting of ceiling shaped as in 1 x sōrō ∼ mai ƙafạ 10 nē it's mud-topped building with vaulting containing 10 half-arches (cf. ƙafạ 8, bạkā 8b) = hayị 4. (3) method of shaving girl's head just after weaning (= kundụmē 2b = būlūgạrī 3 q.v.), cf. sạfē 2.

ɗaurịn gwarmai m. (1) yā yi minị ∼ = yā ɗaurạ minị gwarmai he brought cleverly-concocted false charge against me. (2) tying twine, thread, etc., into puzzle difficult to undo.

ɗaurịn hadirị m. charm to stop rain which is preventing work.

ɗaurịn hannū m. nā yi masạ ∼ = nā ɗaurẹ masạ hannū I applied charm to child to cure it of pilfering.

ɗaurịn jējị m. = ɗaurịn dawạ.

ɗaurịn kǎi Vd. ɗaurā 4.

ɗaurịŋ kạlaŋgū m. (1) gạrī yā yi masạ ∼ he's having a hard time. (2) yārinyạ cē mai ∼ = yārinyạ cē mai ƙịrạr kạlaŋgū she's a slender girl with good hips (Vd. ƙịrạ 1e).

ɗaurịŋ kanjaụ m. = ɗaurịŋ kạlaŋgū 1.

ɗaurịŋ kanzagī m. = ɗaurịŋ kạlaŋgū 1.

ɗaurịŋ ƙasā m. an yi masạ ∼ = an ɗaurẹ masạ ƙasā he has been given charm with effect of " seven-league boots ".

ɗaurin̳ kate-kate *m.* (1) *Vd.* **ɗaurin̳ gūgā** 1. (2) = **ɗaurin̳ kalan̳gū** 1.

ɗaurin̳ ƙirjī *m.* **tā yi ~ = tā ɗaurę ƙirjī** she for first time secured cloth above her breasts (*done by Filani at age of seven, but others give feast 3 months after marriage when bride first secures cloth above breasts*).

ɗaurin̳ kuntukurū = **ɗaurin̳ kurkutū** *m.* = **ɗaurin̳ kalan̳gū** 1.

ɗaurin rǎi *Vd.* **rǎi** 1*j*.

ɗaurin rīdim Mǎda *m.* = **ɗaurin̳ kǎlan̳gū** 1.

ɗaurin̳ rījịya *Vd.* **rījịyā** 3.

ɗaurin rūwā *m.* (1) charm used by 'yam fǫtō or pagans to cause storm to pass. (2) charm used to bring luck in fishing.

ɗaurin tākurī *m.* = **ɗaurin̳ kalan̳gū** 1.

ɗaurin 'yam maruƙa (1) tethering cows back to back (*cf.* **dan̳gwalī** ; **tan̳gē**). (2) **an yi mana ~** we have been given T. to divide with another P. (= *Kt.* **ɗaurin dan̳gwalī**).

ɗaurīyā *f.* endurance ; being long-suffering.

ɗaurō *m.* (1) the millet *Pennisetum spicatum* (= **maiwā**), *Vd.* **ɗagara**. (2) **in an ƙi ~, inā wani hatsin̳** " don't throw away dirty water before you've got clean ! ". (3) *Bauchi Hausa* self-seeded groundnuts (= **gyaurō**). (4) *Vd.* **bǎƙon ~**.

ɗaurō *Vd.* **ɗaura** 2.

ɗaurų *m.* = **dauri** 2.

ɗauru *Vd.* **ɗaura** 2 ; **dawa** 6.

ɗausā *Vb.* 2 (*p.o.* **ɗaushē**, *n.o.* **ɗaushi**) *x* **yā ɗaushē ni** it saved me trouble ; it relieved me of the necessity of doing it.

dausashē *Vb.* 3A (sore, ulcer, etc.) is (was) nearly healed.

dausassar *x* **yanā da bǎkī dausassar** he's thick-lipped.

dausayī *m.* (1) well-watered pastureland. (2) prosperity.

ɗaushā = **ɗaushan̳** *Kt.* = **ɗaushē** 2.

daushassar = **dausassar**.

daushe A. (**daushē**) *m.* (1) previous year's kolanuts after new crop is available. (2) **hawan ~** *m.* short ride by chief and followers on second day of any festival.
    B. (**daushę**) (1) *Vb.* 1A grazed

(skin). (2) *Vb.* 3A (skin) is (was) grazed.

ɗaushe (1) *Vd.* **ɗausā**. (2) (*a*) **a ~** easily ; gratis *x* **nā sāmē shi a ɗaushe** I got it easily, etc. (*b*) **daga ɗaushe gārar kishīyā** it's an ill wind that blows nobody any good.

ɗaushi *Vd.* **ɗausā**.

dausǫ *m.* (1) flying chips from woodchopping. (2) **nā yi ~** I've got an abrasion.

dautū *m.* **yanā shan ~ da shī** he's toiling away at it.

dauwama A. (**dauwama**) *Ar.* (1) *Vb.* 3B. (*a*) endured for ever ; is (was) permanent. (*b*) **ka ~ a kansa** persevere at it ! (2) *f.* permanence *x* **aikị mai ~** permanent work. **gidan ~** *m.* Paradise. (3) *Vb.* 2 **ka dauwamē shi** = 1*b*.
    B. (**dauwamā**) *Vb.* 1C rendered permanent *x* (1) **Allā ya ~ Jāmus cikim baƙim cikị** may God cause the Germans perpetual grief ! (2) **yā ~ ni a kansa** he put me in permanent charge of it.

dauwamammē *m.* (*f.* **dauwamammīyā**) *pl.* **dauwamammū** permanent.

dauwamē *Vb.* 3A = **dauwama** 1.

dauza *Vb.* 1A *x* **yā ~ kǎi a ban̳gō** he ran full-tilt against the wall.

dawa A. (**dāwa**) *f.* (*pl.* **dāwōyī** = **dāwawakī**). (1) (*a*) guinea-corn (*Sorghum vulgare*). (*b*) (*used as pl.*) *x* **~ iri iri waɗanda lōkacin nūnarsu daban daban nę** various types of guinea-corn which ripen at different seasons. (*c*) **hancin ~** *m.* guineacorn-chaff. (*d*) **jikin ~ duk gǎrī nę** an inferior has no choice but to obey orders (*Vd.* **talǎka** 2). (*e*) **tūwan ~, mīyar kūka bā wadā ba nę, kuturū mā yanā yī** (*said by husband in reply to wife taunting him with ingratitude*). (2) seeds of waterlily (**baɗǫ**) = **ƙwǎlā** 2. (3) large swelling on back of hand from hit with top as forfeit in game **katantan̳wa** (= **ƙaura** 4), *cf.* **jǎtau** 1*b*, **ƙwǎyā** 3, **kan̳gar** 2. (4) (*a*) **dāwar masarā** maize (= **masarā** 1*a*). (*b*) **~ da mūdu** maize-cobs (= **gōyō** 1*c*). (5) **dāwar haƙǫ, mai gīgī ka tabą** *epithet of* Chief's son. (6) **yanā nēman dāwar kunū** " he's looking for pickings ". (7) **furad ~** *Vd.* **Shan̳gai**. (8) *Vd.* **cị ~**.

(9) dāwar jặkai *Vd.* bũkũ. (10) dōdan ∼ *Vd.* dōdō 7.

B. (dawa) *m.*, *f.* (*pl.* dawuzzā = dāzuzzukạ = dawai). (1) (*a*) the " bush ", jungle. (*b*) manyan ∼ (i) *epithet of* lion (= wan ∼). (ii) Noble Sir ! (iii) wan ∼ *Vd.* wā 3*c*. (2) ∼ nē he's full of intrigue. (3) yā jā ∼ he got it cheap. (4) dawaŋ wani karkarar wani abilities, experiences differ. (5) (*a*) ∼ yā tabạ shi = dawạ yā harbē shi he has disease of unknown origin attributed to the spirit gajērē mai bakā. (*b*) *Vd.* ūwar dawạ, son 7, Innạ 3*b*, harbin dawạ. (6) ∼ yā dauru (i) I'm replete. (ii) preliminaries of journey, etc., have all been completed (*cf.* 9). (7) ∼ kā ci kāyaŋ kōwā *epithet of* dishonest P. (8) būdạ ∼ *Vd.* būdạ 4. (9) (*a*) an yi masạ daurin dawạ = an daurẹ masạ ∼ he was given charm enabling him to pass safely through dangerous " bush " (*cf.* 6). (*b*) *Vd.* baci 4*c*. (10) gudun ∼ *m.* diarrhœa. (11) *Kt.* Sarkin ∼ the official who collects tax from rural traders (*x* from honey-gatherers). (12) *Vd.* dāji, jēji. (13) mālamin ∼ *Vd.* dilā. (14) *Vd.* mūgun dawạ, marin ∼, wā kẹ ∼. (15) tạ sā kạ ∼ *Vd.* son 7. (16) bā ∼ ba *Vd.* cādī. (17) ∼ sukạ tārạ *Vd.* zōmō 8. (18) mazan ∼ *Vd.* Aibō. (19) *Vd.* karyar ∼.

dawa-dāwạ *f.* the grass *Rottbœllia exaltata*.

dawāfi *Ar.* *m.* making circuit of the Kābạ during Pilgrimage.

dawai A. (Dāwai) *name for* child of divorcee who becomes remarried to husband because found pregnant after divorce.
B. (dawai) *Vd.* dawạ.

dawai A. (dāwai) *Sk.* *x* kanā dūbansạ ∼ you're looking contemptuously at him.
B. (dawai) *Sk.* *m.* = dawainīyā.

dawai-dawai only with the greatest difficulty *x* ∼ mukạ sāmu only with the greatest difficulty did we get it.

dawainīyā *f.* (1) struggling with task *x* munā dawainiyar aikin naŋ we're struggling with this work. yanā dawainiyar nēmaŋ abincī he's having a

struggle to live. (2) kặkạ akạ ji dạ dawainiyā how are you ? ; *reply*, dạ gōdīyā (*cf.* tantaŋgā 3). (3) yā yi mini ∼ he helped me on. (4) n nā ∼ dạ gidāna (bậkī) I'm doing my best to support my family (entertain guests) properly.

dawainīyad dạ *Vb.* 4A *Kt.* (1) worried P. (2) ∼ bậkō to provide for a guest.

dāwaiwai *Sk.* = dāwai.

dāwaiwainīyā *f.* (1) constant going to and fro. (2) beating about the bush.

dawajẹwā *x* mun yi ∼ dạ shī we arranged with him.

dawaki A. (dawākī) (*pl. of* dōki *q.v.*). (1) unground grains of corn or rice put in furā *or* kunū to give something to bite on. (2) (*a*) main rafters reaching up to top of thatch-roof ; main beams of roof-frame (tsaiko) ; *cf.* kạrā-kạrā 3. (*b*) baraÿin ∼ smaller rafters. (3) dawākin cācā gambling-cowries. (4) dawākin sarki *Vd.* agazari. (5) Sarkin ∼ an official title (*cf.* Sarkin dōki).
B. (Dawākī) (1) *name of town in Kano*. (2) dan ∼ best prepared indigo.

Dạwānau *Vd.* kaunā 2.

dawaŋ-dawaŋ *x* rigassạ tā yi ∼ his gown's filthy.

dạwarā *f.* (1) circling-dance. (2) = dānīnīyạ.

dāwawaki *Vd.* dāwạ.

dawaya A. (dāwạyā) *Kt.* (1) *Vb.* 1C returned thither (= kōmạ). (2) dāwayō = dāwō.
B. (dạwaya) *Vb.* 2 *Kt.* (1) returned to *x* zạzzặbī yā dạwayē ni fever returned to me. (2) *Vd.* karọ 2.

dāwayad dạ *Vb.* 4B *Kt.* caused to return.

dawaye A. (dạwạyē) *m.* pen cut on the slant (= jirgē).
B. (Dāwạyẹ) = Dāwai.

dāwayō *Vb.* 3A *Kt.* = dāwō.

dawayyā *Vd.* dawọ.

dawo A. (dawọ) *Sk.*, *Kt.* *m.* (*pl.* dawayyā). (1) (*a*) ball of furā without milk (= gāyā 2*d*). (*b*) idam bạ kạ shā gudan ∼ ba kadạ kạ shā gudan rānā don't tempt the heat on an empty stomach ! (2) ready mixed furā. (3) dawaŋ watạ full orb of the moon (= gāyaŋ watạ). (4) dan ∼ *m.* the sweet **nǎkīyǎ**. (5) dawǎn jīyǎ kā ƙi **tsāmī** *epithet of* thin, weak P. always looking the same age (= **dakǎn jīyǎ**). (6) **cin** ∼ *Kt. m.* contest between girlfriends of bride and those of bridegroom. (7) **ƙŏshīyǎ tasǎ tanǎ ƙan** ∼ he's popular with his superior ; he's wealthy and liberal. (8) *Vd.* **barǎn dawǫ.**

B. (dāwō) *Vb.* 3A (1) returned hither *x* **dǎgǎ nǎŋ zūwǎ Masǎr fǎm 26 duk dǎ dāwǫwǎ** it (fare) from here to Egypt is £26 return (= **kōmō**), *cf.* **dāwǎyā.** (2) **dāwō dǎ** (*a*) caused to return *x* **Allǎ yǎ dāwō dǎ kai lāfīyǎ** may you return safely ! (*b*) restored *x* **sun dāwō dǎ 'yanci gǎ dūnīyǎ** they've restored freedom to the world.

dāwôyī *Vd.* **dāwǎ.**

dǎwurā = **dǎwarā.**

dǎwurwuri *m.* circling-dance.

dawǔzzā *Vd.* **dawǎ.**

dǎwwamǎ *Vd.* **dǎuwamǎ.**

ɗaya A. (dayā) *m.* (1) (*a*) (i) one. (ii) **mū dǎi, gūrǐmmu** ∼ **nǎ, shī ƙǎ naŋ ƙǔwā,** ∼ **tak ǎ zukǎtammu, mu kashǎ shi** we have one desire and one alone and that is to kill him. (iii) **kō** ∼ **bai kai lǎbāri ba** they perished to the last man. (iv) **bǎ ɗayan dǎ ka aikǎ** you've not done *one* of them. (v) ∼ **nǎ dǎ Sarkī** he is intimate with the Chief. (vi) **dǎ mū, dǎ sū duk, kǎi yā zō** ∼ they and we are unanimous. **kǎnsu** ∼**nǎ gǎ yinsǎ** they are unanimous that it should be done. (vii) **gami** ∼ *Vd.* **kūrā 46.** (viii) **yā rabǎ** ∼ **bīyū** he treated one of his relations unfairly. (*b*) **ɗayansu** one of them (males). **ɗayarsu** one of them (females). (*c*) **watǎn** ∼ *m.* January. (*d*) (i) **mutum** ∼ **bā yǎ ɗaukǎr ɗāki** many hands make light work. (ii) **ɗan ɗāki** ∼ *Vd.* **ɗāki 6***a.* (*e*) **karǫ** ∼ **kō dǎ tǫraŋ gīwā ǎ bugǎ** = ∼ **ta mai gǎyyā mǎ yi** there's no harm in trying everything once. (*f*) (i) **sārā** ∼ **bā yǎ kā dǎ itǎcē** Rome wasn't built in a day. (ii) **mai sārā** ∼ *Vd.* **injihau.** (*g*) (i) **idǫ** ∼ **yā lēƙǎ būtǎ** *Vd.* **ǎbu 5***g.* (ii) **mai idǫ** ∼ *Vd.* **gǎrārǎ 2***b.*ii. (*h*) **ƙarfǎ** ∼ *Vd.* **amō.** (*j*) **dōki** ∼ **ǎ fagē** *Vd.* **dōki 1***c.* (*k*)

rānarkǎ ∼ *Vd.* **suŋgumī.** (1) **wāƙǎ** ∼ *Vd.* **niƙǎ 2***f.* (*m*) **wākē** ∼ *Vd.* **wākē 9.** (*n*) **tsintsīyā** ∼ *Vd.* **tsintsīyā 1***d.* (*o*) **yā yi kirǎŋki sau** ∼ *Vd.* **ta alakō.** (*p*) **iskǎ** ∼ *Vd.* **iskǎ 7.** (*q*) ∼ **nǎ nāsǎ** *Vd.* **masǫ 3.** (*r*) **rǐgarki** ∼ *Vd.* **rǐgā 1***m.* (*s*) **askā** ∼ *Vd.* **ŋgas.** (*t*) **mai gidā** ∼ **wāwā** *Vd.* **Dōzǎ.** (*u*) **girman darē** ∼ *Vd.* **gambǎ.** (*v*) **kǎsūwarkǎ** ∼ *Vd.* **gǎskamī.** (*w*) **laifī** ∼ *Vd.* **gwarzō 1***b.* (*x*) **itǎcē** ∼ *Vd.* **itǎcē 1***d.* (2) the same *x* (*a*) **dū** ∼ **nǎ** = **dukǎ** ∼ **nǎ** it's all the same. **duɗ** ∼ **nǎ** it doesn't matter, never mind. **aikinsu** ∼ **nǎ** their function or work is identical. (*b*) **wurī yā tāshi bǎi** ∼ the place is level (*Vd.* **bǎi 2***b.*ii). (*c*) **bǎkī** ∼ = **gǎba** ∼ simultaneously (*Vd.* **gǎba 1***a.*viii, **bǎkī 5**). (*d*) **kǎnsu** ∼ **nǎ** they're of the same age, stature, status, intelligence. (*e*) **farinsu** ∼ *Vd.* **nōnǫ 1***b.* (3) ɗaya-ɗaya one by one (= **ɗǎi-ɗǎi**). (4) ∼ **dǎ** (*a*) corresponding with *x* **sun cī** ∼ **dǎ cikinsu** they are replete. **nā shā māgani** ∼ **dǎ ciki** I've filled my stomach with medicine. **makarantarsu** ∼ **dǎ ta Jāmus** their methods are identical with those of the Germans. (*b*) corresponding with that which *x* **ǎ bi hanyǎ** ∼ **dǎ akǎ bi** follow the same road as before ! (5) (*a*) the one *x* ∼ **mai shaidǎ ya cǎ** . . . then the one who was his witness said that . . . **kai kumā ɗayǎ, tǎsō** now you the other one, stand up ! ∼ **mǎtā tasǎ** the particular wife of his of whom we're speaking. (*b*) (i) **ɗayā** . . . **ɗayaŋ** one . . . the other *x* ∼ **yā zō, ɗayǎm bai zō ba** one came but the other did not. (ii) ∼ **yā halǎkǎ** ∼ the one killed the other, they killed one another. (*c*) the only one *x* **ita** ∼ she only, she alone. **tǎfi kai** ∼ only you go ! (6) one of *x* ∼ **zǎkaraŋ** one of those cocks. ∼ **ɗaŋ** = **ɗayan 'yā'yansǎ** one of his children. (7) **wannǎn nē fā** ∼ = **nam fā** ∼ no, I can't agree to your suggestion. (8) ∼ **dǎ** ∼ = **farat** ∼ = **maza** ∼ = **faɗ** ∼ suddenly *x* **farat** ∼ **sǎi ya gudu** he suddenly fled. (9) ∼ **ǎ cikiŋkǎ** *Vd.* **cikin 7.** (10) **fǎɗaɗ** ∼ *Vd.* **fǎɗā 2***c.*

B. (**ɗǎyā**) *Vb.* 2 an **ɗǎyi yāwā** they

stripped off the fibre called **yāwā** *q.v.*
yā ɗāyi ɓāwō he stripped bark (off
ramą ; kargō ; kūką) ; *cf.* **sīyāye̩.**
 C. (**ɗāyā**) *f.* (*secondary v.n. of* **ɗāyā**)
x **yanā ɗāyar ɓāwō** = **yanā ɗāyar
ɓāwō** he's stripping off bark *as in*
ɗāyā.
ɗayānī = **dīyan.**
ɗayąntā *Vb.* 1C **yā ɗayąntą Allā** he
believes in the unity of God.
Dāye̩ *used in* **na** ~ *term used for* **tūgandē-**
peppers in **tallą.**
dāye̩ *Vb.* 1A = **ɗāyā.**
dąyī *m.* (1) the thistle *Centaurea cal-
citrapa.* (2) **ąlēwąr** ~ *Vd.* **zāk̓ī** 1*a.*v.
daza A. (**dāzą**) *Vb.* 1A. (1) arranged
things in groups. (2) (*with dative*) (*a*)
an ~ **masą sąndā** he's been hit with a
stick. (*b*) made reinforcing edge to *x*
tābarman nąŋ, an ~ **matą jā** this mat
has been edged in red (*Vd.* **dājīyā**).
 B. (**dāzā**) *f.* reinforced-edge of mat
(= **dājīyā** *q.v.*).
dāzą wą dāzai *x* **dāzą wą dāzai ni** he
(she, it) is good in himself and enhanced
by concomitants (*x* position *plus*
the means to maintain it ; bravery
plus weapons, *etc.*).
dāzązą *x* **yanā dą gēmu** ~ he has fluffy
beard : **yanā da wutsīyą** ~ it has
bushy tail (*Vd.* **Fątu** 2).
dązgā *Vb.* 2 *Sk.* ate much of.
dązu (1) just now. (2) *Vd.* **Sarkī** 1*b.*
dązunē *Sk. m.* smearing T. on to another
(= **shāɓunē**).
dāzuzzuką *Vd.* **dāji̩.**
dazzā *Vd.* **daje̩.**
ɗēbą *Vd.* **dībą.**
ɗēbabbē *m.* (*f.* **ɗēbabbīyā**) *pl.* **ɗēbąbbū**
P. on whom curse has been laid (*Vd.*
ɗēbe̩ 5 ; tsīne̩ 2*a*).
ɗēbar *Vd.* **dībą.**
ɗebe A. (**ɗēbe̩**) *Vb.* 1A. (*a*) removed. (*b*)
set aside (portion of money, etc.) *x* **ku**
~ **wani abu dągą cikiŋ ąlbāshiŋku** set
aside a portion of your salary ! (*c*)
made an exception in the case of
(= **tōge̩**). (*d*) took all the things out of.
(*e*) plucked all of. (*f*) drew all (the
water), etc. (*cf.* **dībą**). (2) **yā** ~
k̓aunā dągą abiŋ naŋ he's ceased to
hanker after it ; he gave up all hope of

getting it (= **tsąmmāni̩** 5), *Vd.* **k̓aunā.**
(3) *Sk., Kt.* **ką** ~ **hannū dągą gąrēshi̩**
have nothing to do with it ! (4) *x* **nā** ~
kēwar Audu = **nā** ~ **wą Audu kēwā**
I went to stay three days with Audu
to comfort him for loss of dearly-
loved one ; I went to chat with him to
relieve his loneliness (*cf.* **jēje̩to̩**). (5)
yā ~ **masą ąlbarką** he laid curse on
him (*Vd.* **dēbabbē**). (6) ~ **dōki̩** to
pull up horse sharply (*cf.* **dībą** 1*e*) =
zāme̩ 1*a.*i. (7) **nā** ~ **masą rabiŋ kunnē**
I sliced off a bit of his ear. (8) *Sk.*
yā ~ **k̓afārą** he atoned for breach of
religion (*Vd.* **k̓afārą**). (9) *Sk.* (*a*) ~
kānsą to behead him (= **sārā** 1*b.*iii).
(*b*) **nā** ~ **kāina dągą gąrēshi̩** I gave it
up. (10) *cf.* **dībą ; dēbō ; yānā** 3*b.*
 B. (**dēbē**) *Vd.* **dībą.**
dēbi *Vd.* **dībą.**
dēbō *Vd.* **dībą ; dēbe̩.**
dēbō *x* **tā dēbō ruwā** she drew water and
brought it (*from* **dībą** *q.v.*).
dēdąmī *m.* = **dīdąmī.**
dēfąnā *Vb.* 1C took out small amount of.
deffo̩ *Eng. m.* depot.
dēfī *m.* (1) edge. (2) tip.
dēgīyā (1) *Sk.* exchange of food by women
(= **kāwō** 5). (2) *Kt.* sending present of
food to neighbour to vaunt over him.
deidei *Vd.* **dăidăi.**
dēlą *f.* (1) **Dēlą** name given any woman
called **Kande** (= **Dēlū**). (2) white-
and-red goat.
dēli̩ *f.* the Arabic " d " (= **dal**).
Dēlū name given any woman called
Kande (= **Dēlą**).
dēną *Vb.* 1A (1) ceased doing T. (2)
dęną ząncam " bāra " *Vd.* **bāra** 1*d.*
dengidą *f.* (*sg., pl.*) leather-bangle ornamented with beads.
dērē *x* **n nā dągą dērē** it's not my affair.
ɗerere A. (**dērēre̩**) *x* **sunā dūbammu** ~
they're looking at us contemptuously.
 B. (**dērērē**) *x* **yā zauną** ~ it sits
shakily on base.
dēshī *m.* (1) edge. (2) tip.
ɗētarā *Vb.* 1C (1) crossed over (= **k̓ētarā**
q.v.). (2) **kadą ɓērā yą** ~ **ni** may I get a
little food ! (*it being believed that rat
will not pass over body of P. who has
eaten food*), *Vd.* **k̓ētarā 4.**

dēwạ yā'ẹ *Sk.* fancy ! (= wạ̄ 1*c* = wad-
darẹ 1), *cf.* yā'ẹ.
dị *Sk. m. (pl.* dị̄yai) long, thin bamboo
canoe-pole.
dị̄ *x* mutạ̄nē ⁓ large number of people.
dībạ *Sk.* looked at (= dūbạ).
dībạ (1) *Vb. (past* yā dẹ̄bi rūwā. yā dẹ̄bē
shị. *progressive* yanạ̄ dībạn rūwā. yanạ̄
dībạnsạ. yanạ̄ dībạ. *imperative* dẹ̄bi =
kạ dībạ. dẹ̄bẹ shi = kạ dẹ̄bē shị.
dẹ̄bi rūwā. *before dative* nā dībạ
masạ rūwā = nā dēbạ masạ rūwā =
nā dībar masạ rūwā = nā dēbar masạ
rūwā). (*a*) extracted a substance *x*
(i) yā dẹ̄bi mạ̄i he extracted oil (from
groundnuts, palm-kernels, etc.). (ii)
in wannạn nē sukạ rọ̄ƙā, lallē nẹ̄
sukạ ⁓ dạ yawạ if this is their request
then their demands were excessive.
(iii) kōwā ya-dēbo dạ zāfī, bạ̄kinsạ as
you sow, so shall you reap. (iv) tā
dẹ̄bi rūwā she drew water (from well,
etc.) (= zạ̄gā 1*e* = jā A.1, 1*b*.i). (v)
yā dẹ̄bi wutā he took some burning wood
to make a fire. (vi) kyạutar " dẹ̄bi ! "
bạ̄ kyạutạ ba when P. says " help yourself to it ! ", it means going short.
yā yi minị kyạutar " dẹ̄bi ŋ ga hannuŋkạ ! " he gave me only a small present.
" dẹ̄bi dạ kạŋkạ ! " māgạnim mại
zạ̄rī " help yourself ! " is the test of
the greedy P. (vii) dạ girmā, bạ̄ ⁓
Vd. fạŋkō 4. (*b*) gathered, plucked.
(*c*) (i) scooped up (*Vd.* kaɓạncē 1*c*). (ii)
wạndansạ yanạ̄ dībạn ƙasā his trousers
are picking up dust. (iii) cikiŋ wannạŋ
yāƙi bạ̄ ạbin dạ sukạ ⁓ they made no
gains in this war. bạ̄ ạbin dạ zā sụ ⁓
gạrēmụ they would be no match for
us. (iv) injin nạ̄ dībạrsụ the motor is
hurrying them along. (v) zā ạ ⁓
cikiŋ kudin naŋ ạ tạimạki mayạ̄ƙā
one must dip into these funds to help
the fighting men. (*d*) (i) utilized *x*
mālạmī yạ dẹ̄bi wōkạcin dạ akạ ajịyē
doŋ kạṛạ̄tū the teacher should utilize
for it the time allotted for reading.
(ii) nā ⁓ masạ lōkạcī dạ yawạ I
devoted much time to it. (*e*) yā dẹ̄bi
dōki he started the horse off at a gallop
(*cf.* dēbẹ 6). (*ee*) yā ⁓ ạ gụje = *Kt.*
yā ⁓ cikin na kạṛē he took to his

heels (*cf.* rạntā ; barẹ 2*c*.). (*f*) Sarkī
yā ƙasạ dōkị, sukạ wạtsu cikiŋ ƙasā,
sunạ̄ dībạn shānū the Emir deployed
his cavalry who spread and took cattle
as booty. ỉyạ̄kar mutạ̄nạn dạ ya
yạ̄ƙā ya ⁓, dukạ ạ maishē sụ let them
restore all the prisoners whom he took !
yā dẹ̄bi mutạ̄nē dạ yawạ he took many
prisoners of war. (*g*) led astray *x*
ƙụrụcīyā tā dẹ̄bē nị my youthfulness led
me astray (= ɓad dạ). (*h*) *Vd.* dēbẹ.
(*j*) Jāmụs sun dẹ̄bi ƙasā, sun rifẹ ạ
hannū, sunạ̄ cẹwā " duk dūnīyạn naŋ,
ban zāɓẹ ba " the Germans have challenged the whole world to fight (person
takes handful of earth plus some of his
spittle, turns, and with his hand behind
his back, says tạŋkwạɓē ! If the other
knocks it out of his hand, he says
ƙạ̄ƙa ban shā nōnaŋ ūwāta, nā ƙōshi
bạ ? zā kạ zubar minị ? The other
replies insultingly dạ kai dạ ūwạr
tākạ, kạzaŋ ūwākụ) ; *Vd.* taŋkwạɓē.
(*k*) bā yạ̄ dẹ̄bar wạ wani *Vd.* mīyạ 9*c*.
(*l*) dẹ̄bi wạ̄rẹ̄ *Vd.* wạ̄rẹ̄. (*m*) kụ dẹ̄bi
gịndin zubọ *Vd.* zubọ. (2) *m., f. (v.n.* of
1) *x* (*a*) tanạ̄ dībạn rūwā = tanạ̄
dībạr rūwā she is drawing water (from
well, etc.). (*b*) yā tạfi dībạr iskạ he
has gone for a stroll. (*c*) cinikin dūnīyạ
dībạn nōnọ nē do as you will be done
by ! (*d*) sōjạmmụ dībạm farkō suŋ
isō the first instalment of our soldiers
has arrived. (*e*) dībạr gēzạ Agalawa
dancing at weddings. (*f*) dībạn tūjī
Maguzawa harvest-dancing. (*g*) dībạŋ
gōnā *Vd.* gōnā 1*b*. (*h*) dībạŋ gwīwạ
Vd. gwīwạ 3.
dibārạ *Sk. f.* plan, stratagem (= dạbārạ
q.v.).
dibbu = dibbị *Kt. m.* magic, sorcery
(= tsubbụ).
dībẹ *Sk.* looked completely (through book,
etc.) = dūbẹ.
dibga A. (dibgạ) *Vb.* 1A. (1) poured much
x tā ⁓ gạ̄rī ạ tukunyā she poured much
flour into the pot. (2) did abundantly
x an ⁓ masạ sātạ he was severely
robbed. an ⁓ musụ wutā they suffered
from serious fire. gōnā tā ⁓ hatsī
the farm had fine corn-crop. an ⁓
rūwā there's been heavy rain. yā ⁓

bindigạ he fired a gun loudly. an ∽ musụ harị they were severely raided. an ∽ masạ kudī he's been heavily taxed. an ∽ masạ kibīyạ (māshị) he's been badly wounded with arrow (spear). an ∽ masạ sạndā he's been severely thrashed. (3) yā ∽ kạnsạ dawạ he's disappeared.
B. (dịbgā) Vb. 2 (1) drove away. (2) an dịbgē shị dạ sạndā he's been seriously thrashed (= dịbgạ 2).

Dịbgau (1) name for any P. called Ballọ. (2) Kt. Storm, thou terrible one!

dịbge A. (dịbgẹ) (1) Vb. 1A x an ∽ shi dạ sạndā = dịbgā 2. (2) Vb. 3A Kt. is (was) beside oneself.
B. (dịbgē) Kt. m. burying pauper without shroud (= kạrɓi ạ jikạ q.v.).

dịbgēgẹ adj. m. (f. dịbgēgịyā) very big, broad, or abundant.

dịbgị what a lot!

dịbgibarạ x dịbgibarạ bạ jạllō f. showing concern at T. not one's affair.

dībị Sk. m. fortune-telling (= dūbā).

dịbị Zar. m. (1) T. placed on another. (2) surplus (= dọ̄rīyā).

diɓi-diɓi A. (dịɓi-dịɓī) (1) near x ∽ ya jē, ya kōmō he only went short way and returned. (2) constantly (= bịnī-bịnī q.v.).
B. (diɓi-diɓi) x yạrā ∽ plump little children.
C. (diɓi-diɓị) x yanạ̄ tạfīyạ ∽ he's walking slowly and cumbrously.

dībịyā Vb. 1C Zar. put T. on another T. (= dọ̄rạ).

dibtū m. (1) early start (= sạmmakō q.v.). (2) yanạ̄ shạn ∽ dạ shī he's toiling away at it.

dībụ Kt. m. worn-out hide-bag (= Sk. jēbū).

dīdạmī = dīdārẹ m. Filani leather-apron.

dīdạu (1) yanạ̄ yāwọ ∽ he's roving aimlessly. (2) anạ̄ ganinsạ ∽ he's being looked at contemptuously; he is regarded as a fool.

diddiɓā f. big-made girl.

dịddifạ f. Sacred ibis (= jinjimī).

dịddigā f. (1) remainder consisting of crumbs, wisps, grains (= rūwā B4 = Kt. tarkẹ = tạttakā 2). (2) yanạ̄ cịn ∽

he's living on the wreck of his resources. (3) Vd. kurcīyā 1l.

diddige A. (diddịgē) Vb. 3A. (1) became ragged. (2) hatsī yā ∽ only wisps of the corn are left (1, 2 = sussụkē 2).
B. (diddigẹ) m. (pl. dịgạ̄digai = dụgạ̄dụgai). (1) heel (Vd. digạ̄digī; dundūnīyā). (2) yanạ̄ cịn diddigẹna (a) he's treading on my heels. (b) he's junior to me. (c) he's worrying me to pay my debt to him. (d) Vd. dundūnīyā.

diddigī m. (1) nā bi diddigim mạganạr I investigated the matter. (2) Sk. yā cikạ ∽ he's a mischief-maker.

diddịkā Vb. 3A crouched down. yanạ̄ diddịkẹ he's crouching.

diddịkī Sk. m. = diddigī 2.

dịdɗirạ Sk. f. yanạ̄ ∽ (1) he has dysentery (= atụnī). (2) he's dripping oil from anus from eating too oily food (1, 2 = dịgā 2).

dịddirnā m., f. short, thickset P.

dịdī m. (1) penis (word used by boys for ạzakạrī). (2) Vd. gạmạ ∽.

dīdībạ̄kọ m. girls' spinning-bee contest (= asabērụ), cf. daŋkạrē, kashē.

dịdịbnīyā f. = dịdimnīyā.

dīdịdī m. (1) anạ̄ ∽ dạ shī he's being disparaged. (2) anạ̄ dīdịdim mạganạr the rumour's being discussed on the sly.

dīdīfīrī m. affectation.

didịm x (1) yā yi duhụ didịm (a) it's pitch-dark. (b) he's stone-blind. (2) Vd. fafat.

didịmạ Sk. f. = dịdimnīyā.

dịdimnīyā f. = dịdim-dịdim m. (1) noise of beating on calabashes or of feet on hollow roof, etc. (2) place being frequented.

dīdīrī = didirīcī m. affectation.

dịdịrnīyā f. = dịdimnīyā.

dịdis x an nikạ shi ∽ it's finely ground (= lilis).

dīdịtā Vb. 1C sunạ̄ ∽ shi they're discussing the rumour on the sly (Vd. dīdịdī).

dīdīwạlā f. tattooing-scalpel (= bērạ 2).

dīdọ adv. (1) gratis. (2) uselessly (= banzā q.v.).

didụm = didịm.

dīfạnā Vb. 1C = dẹfạnā.

dīfar-dīfar x yanā numfāshī ∼ (P. ; fire ; lamp) is about to expire.

difil-difil = dīfar-dīfar.

diga (*Eng.* digger) *f.* (*pl.* digōgī). (1) pick-axe (= masārī 1). (2) (*a*) track prepared for laying railway. (*b*) *Sk.* motor-road. (3) dan ∼ *m.* workman who repairs the permanent way (= dam bita). (4) *Sk.* 'yar ∼ *f.* type of short gown.

diga A. (diga) *Vb.* 1A (1) poured out in drops (= darsa 1*a*). (2) squeezed out *x* (*a*) anā ∼ rūwan lēmū juice's being squeezed from lime-fruit (= mātsa 1*a*.i). (*b*) anā ∼ madi a tukunyā juice's being squeezed into pot to make the drink madi. tanā ∼ madi daga madambacī zūwa tukunyā she's pouring the madi in drops from steamer into pot. (3) filtered *x* yā ∼ rūwā ta cikin tōkā he filtered water through ashes (= tācē). (4) yā ∼ tōkā he filtered liquid through ashes for flavouring (1–4 = tarārā).

    B. (diga) *Vb.* 3B (*progressive* digā). (1) dripped (= tarāra). (2) yā ∼ cikin tōkā = yā ∼ ta cikin tōkā it percolated (was filtered) through ashes. (3) yā digu he's got on in the world.

    C. (digā) *f.* (1) *Vd.* diga. (2) yanā ∼ = diddira.

digaci *m.* village-head (= dagaci *q.v.*).

digādigī *m.* (*pl.* digādigai) (1) heel. (2) *Vd.* wali 5 ; diddige.

digal *x* 'yan digal *m.* robber-bands intercepting people on roads to sell them into slavery.

Digancī *m.* puritanical customs of certain Filani Muslims (*e.g.* rigid purdah), *cf.* Badige.

digau *Kt. m.* the salt called āwar.

Digāwā those practising Digancī (*sg. is* Badige).

dige A. (dige) (1) *Vb.* 1A = diga. (2) *Vb.* 3A = diga

    B. (digē) *m.* (1) liquid filtered *as in* diga 3, 4. (2) any filtered liquid. (3) yā yi ∼ = yā yi diddira.

    C. (digē) *m.* standing on tiptoe of both feet to reach high T. (*cf.* dage).

di'ge-digē" (1) *Vd.* digō. (2) = idon 9A.

digi *m.* (1) first stages *x* yanā digin aiki he's preparing his tools or materials to

start work. kāzā daya ita cē digin dūkiyā tasa one hen was the foundation of his wealth. nā yi masa digin sarauta (aurē) I paved the way for his chieftain-ship (marriage) = diri 3. (2) trading-capital (= kudī 5*a*).

digil (1) *m.* shortness *x* wandō nē ∼ da shī they're a short pair of trousers (*pl.* wanduna nē digil-digil da sū). (2) *adv.* dan gajērē nē ∼ he's a very short man.

digilgil = digil.

digimī ,*m.* = digimnīyā *f.* (1) making preparations for *x* munā digimin tafīya we're preparing for our journey. (2) noise and bustle of festive occasion. (3) munā digimin zancan we're making extensive enquiries into the matter.

digin-digin *x* tun ∼ from of old (= gādin-gādin *q.v.*).

digir *x* dan ∼ *m.* (*f.* 'yar ∼) *pl.* 'yan ∼ short P.

digirā *x* dan ∼ *m.* = dan digir.

digira *Vb.* 3B (*pustules, etc.*) became large.

digirgir = digil.

digirgirā *Vd.* digirgirī.

digirgirē *m.* (1) balancing load on head without holding it. (2) walking on tiptoe owing to damaged tendons. (cōbe). (3) yanā ∼ ya yi kaman Audu he's emulating Audu's superior position.

digirgirī *m.* (*f.* digirgirā) *pl.* digirgirai (1) short. (2) handle (hanci) of itinerant scribe's ink-bottle.

digirgishī *x* dan ∼ *m.* (*f.* 'yar digirgisā) short P.

digirgizā *f.* short T. of *f.* gender (*especially* short, ugly woman).

digiyyamā *Hadejiya Hausa* fancy !

digō *m.* (*pl.* di'ge-digē"). (1) drip, drop. (2) (*a*) dot placed above or below Arabic consonants (*x* Arabic " b ", " n "). (*b*) kamar digwam bā nē kawai aka sā it is a mere beginning (*Vd.* bā 12). (3) (*secondary v.n. of* diga) *x* yanā digwan tōkā = yanā diga tōkā he's filtering liquid through ashes for flavouring.

digōgī *Vd.* diga.

digu *Vd.* diga 3.

dīho *m.* (1) dampness. (2) *x* yanā da dan ∼ he is prosperous.

Dijambar *m.* December.

Dịje name for any woman called **Hạdĳạ** *q.v.*

dik *m.* (1) drop of T. (2) sound of dripping.

*dikạ all (= **dukạ** *q.v.*).

dịkā *Vb.* 2 (*in coarse talk*) had sexual intercourse with woman (*cf.* **dạƙaiƙayạ** 2) = **cī 16a** *q.v.*

dikaka A. (**dịkākạ**) (1) *Vb.* 3B. (*a*) travelled on doggedly. (*b*) **yā dikākō** he (Emir, important P.) drew near. (2) *Vb.* 2 (*a*) acted resolutely on *x* (i) **yā dịkāki aikị** he set to work with a will. (ii) **mụ dịkāki ạbōkaŋ gạbā** let's make resolute attack on the enemy ! **sun dịkākē shi rịdịdị-dịdịdị** they attacked him resolutely. (*b*) **nā dikākō Kanọ** I travelled doggedly on till I reached Kano. (*c*) **yā dịkāki mōtạ** he drove the car at lightning speed. (*d*) **yā ~ cikin rūwa** he struggled through water beyond his depth. B. (**dikạkā**) *Vb.* = **dịkākạ**.

Dịkạkau *epithet of* Emir.

dịkạkē *m.* (*secondary v.n. of* **dịkākạ**) *x* **yā yi ~ ạ rūwa** he struggled through water beyond his depth. **Sarkī yā yi ~** Emir drew near. **sunạ dịkạkyaŋ aikị** they're working doggedly.

dịkīkị stupid (= **dạkīkị** *q.v.*).

dịkīkị *Kt.* exceedingly *x* **kạsūwā tā cịka ~** market's thronged.

diƙil = **digil**.

diƙiŋ-diƙiŋ = **dịƙiŋ-dịƙiŋ** (1) filthy *x* **rịgassạ tā yi ~** his gown's filthy. (2) *adv.* (*a*) **yanạ tạfīyạ ~** he's walking slowly. (*b*) **diƙiŋ-diƙiŋ tạfīyạ cē, laịfin jāƙī kwạncīyā = diƙis-diƙis tạfīyạ cē, laịfin jāƙī kāyẹ** slight progress is better than none.

diƙir = **diƙirƙir** *Kt.* **yanạ dạ taurī ~** it (fruit, swelling) is very hard.

diƙirƙirī = **digirgirī 1**.

diƙis-diƙis = **diƙiŋ-diƙiŋ**.

dịkkạŋ *m.* (1) **nā yi ~** (*a*) I won at gambling. (*b*) I got a bargain. (2) the type of gambling called **gōbarā 3**.

Dikkọ *name for* eldest son of same mother (*cf.* **Dābọ** ; **Yerọ** ; **Sambọ**).

dikọ *m. used in* **dikwạm birị** climbing the trunk of **gōrubạ** *or* **giginyạ** tree by folding one's arms round the tree.

Dịkwā *f.* Dikwa.

dịkyakkyarị *Kt.* *m.* the drum called **kyạkkyarẹ**.

dịl (1) **nā jī ~** I heard the truth. (2) **nā ga ~** I saw the true state of affairs.

dilā *m.* (*pl.* **dilōlī = dilạlē**) (1) (*a*) jackal (*epithet is* **mashancīyā = shācị gandạyau**, **mashạ rūwā dạ na gōbe, kō dawạ kạ ɓācị = shēhụ**, **mālạmin dawạ = ɗam bā'ūrā**). (*b*) *Vd.* **shēwạ 3**. (2) *Sk.* form of game **darạ**. (3) **āyạr dilā** *Vd.* **āyạ 4**. (4) **sun yō minị atịshāwạr ~** they suddenly "went for" me (*Vd.* **atịshāwạ**).

dilạlē *Vd.* **dilā**.

dilẹ (1) dauntless. (2) **~ shạ cụdā** *epithet of* loincloth **warƙī**.

diliŋ = **diluŋ**.

dịllālị *Ar.* *m.* (*f.* **dịllālīvā**) *pl.* **dịllạlai**. (1) broker (= **tsạye 13**). (2) **jạkin ~** *m.* broker's assistant. (3) **ɓanzā tā kas wōƒī, ɗaŋ kōlị yā kashẹ dịllālị** Greek met Greek. (4) **dịllālim ƙarẹtanī** *Vd.* **kyaŋkyạŋ-kyaŋ**.

dillancị *m.* (1) trade of brokerage. (2) **ạkwai rānar ƙin dillancị, ran dạ hājạr mai gạrī ta ɓatạ** the day of reckoning comes. (3) *Vd.* **kūrā 53**.

dillẹ *m.* type of gambling with groundnuts.

dilōlī *Vd.* **dilā**.

diluŋ (1) *m.* (*a*) originally a rhythm for butchers' dance, but now a dance by loose girls *x* **sun tạfi wurin ~** they have gone to *such dance* (*epithet is* **~ gạŋgar 'yaŋ wutā**). (*b*) immersion *x* **yā yi ~ cikin rūwa** he sank into the water (= **dụlmuyạ 1**). **yā yi ~ cikin dūnīyạ** he vanished. **yā yi ~ cikin shūnī** he became covered in dye. (2) *adv.* (*a*) **yā nutsẹ ~** he sank into water completely. (*b*) **yā yi duhụ ~** (i) it's pitch-dark. (ii) he's stone-blind.

ɗim A. (**ɗịm**) (1) **yā ƙāɗị ~** it fell with a thud (*cf.* **ɓuk**). (2) *m.* **ɛn jī ~** a thud was heard. **anạ jin ɗim diɗịm** a bang was heard. B. (**ɗịm**) (1) *adv.* hugely *x* **yanạ dạ cikị ~** he has huge paunch. (2) *Vd.* **~ balạ**.

dimạ *Vb.* 1A plunged weapon into P. (= **dumạ** *q.v.*).

ɗima A. (**ɗīmạ = ɗimạ**) *Vb.* 1A an **~ masạ sạndā** he's been thrashed (= **ɗumạ** *q.v.*)

B. (dīmā = dịmā) *Vb.* 2 thrashed (= dụmā *q.v.*).

dīmājọ *m., f.* P. born in slavery of slave-parents (= bạcūcanẹ 1).

ɗimạmā *Vb.* 1C warmed up (food) (= ɗumạmā *q.v.*).

dịmantạ *Vb.* 2 (*p.o.* dịmạncē, *n.o.* dịmạnci) yā dịmạnci gōnā he went constantly to his farm. nā ~ kạŋ kạrạtū I persevered in my studies (= dịŋgạ 1*a*).

dīmạntā *Sk. Vb.* 3A = dīmạụcē.

ɗimāsārẹ *m.* (*f.* dimāsāriyā) huge.

Dịmau (1) Storm, thou mighty one ! (2) *epithet of* Emir, *etc.* (= dakakī *q.v.*).

ɗīmạụcē *Vb.* 3A = dịmautạ *Vb.* 3B. (1) became nonplussed. (2) *Vd.* zōmō 2*a*.

dīmautad dạ *Vb.* 4A nonplussed.

ɗịmautu *Vb.* 3B is (was) nonplussed.

dịm balạ dịm balạ cịn kaɗanyạr Fulạnī *f.* pretending to dislike work or food, etc., but persevering to the bitter end (*Vd.* ɗum bēlạ).

ɗimbī *Kt. m.* superabundance (= ɗumbū *q.v.*).

dimbịjē *Vb.* 1C took much of (= dumbụjē *q.v.*).

dimd . . . *Vd.* dind . . .

ɗimɗimta A. (dịmɗimtạ) *Vb.* 3B *Kt.* became of greater magnitude (= gạwurtạ).

B. (dimdịmtā) *Vb.* 1C *Kt.* increased magnitude of.

dimẹ *Vb.* 1A surpassed (= dumẹ).

dimẹ = dīmẹ *Vb.* 1A thrashed (= ɗumẹ *q.v.*).

ɗimi A. (dịmī) *m.* (1) warmth *x* (*a*) rūwā yā yi ~ the water's warm. (*b*) (i) yanạ jịn dịmiŋ wutā he's warming himself by fire. (ii) ạ ji dịmintạ *Vd.* wutā 1*m.* (*c*) kạ mayar dạ kīfịŋ dākịn dạfūwā, kạ ajịyē shi dạ dịminsạ put the fish back in the kitchen and keep it warm ! (2) (*a*) kwạɗō yā fāɗạ ạ rūwan ~ *Vd.* dūnịyạ 1*m.* (*b*) rūwan ~ *m.* leprosy-patch. yā gạmu dạ rūwan ~ he's got leprosy (= rūwan zāfī = dāfị 1 = tambạrī 4 = zāfī 1*c.*iii). (3) dịmim mutạnē hubbub. (4) *Sk.* garrulity. (5) anạ jịn ~ dạ shī it's unsaleable (*cf.* māsạ 2).

B. (dịmị) (1) *adv.* abundantly. (2) (*a*) what a lot ! (*b*) what a thrashing !

dimilmilọ *m.* Longtailed cormorant (*Phalacrocorax afr.*).

dimir = dimir-dimir *m.* (1) hardness of fruit or swellings. (2) strength *x* yārọ ~ dạ shī a strong lad.

dịmịr *x* nā gan shị ~ = nā tad dạ shī fuskạ ~ I found him sullen, frowning. gạrī yā yi ~ the weather is threatening.

dịmịs = dụmụs.

Dimishḳu *f.* Damascus.

dịmtsā *Vb.* 2 took out handful of (= dịntsā *q.v.*).

dīmụŋ (1) undoubtedly. (2) wannạŋ dīmụŋ nē it is certainly so.

dimunta A. (dīmụntā) *Vb.* 1C established as true.

B. (dịmuntạ) *Vb.* 3B is (was) proved true.

dīmūwā *f.* nā yi ~ (1) I lost my way. (2) I was nonplussed.

din (dŋ) *x* injịn na mōtạ yanạ kiɗị dŋ dŋ dŋ the engine of the car was drumming.

ɗin A. (ɗŋ-ŋ) (1) (*a*) the one in question *x* baḳī ~ the black one. shī ~ yes, *he* is the one I mean. wannạŋ ~ bạn san shị ba I don't know *that* one. Audụ ~ yes, *that* Audu. kai ~ you ! (*b*) mụtụm ~ nạŋ *Kt.* this very person. (*c*) (*with suffixed pronoun*) *x* dōḳị ɗịmmụ this horse of ours. (*d*) (*any numeral may add* ɗŋ-ŋ, *but those ending in a consonant preferably add it, in order to indicate* " the one in question ") *x* ukụŋ = ukụ ~ the three in question. bịyar ~ the five in question. (2) haḳạ ~ exactly thus.

B. (ɗŋ) (1) (*particle suffixed to form genitive of numerals*) *x* (*a*) bịyar ɗnsụ = bịyārinsụ five of them. ukụ ɗịmmụ = ukụmmụ three of us. gōmạ ɗnsụ = gōmạnsụ ten of them (male or female). (*b*) sun yi bịyū ɗŋ ạbịn dạ mukạ ḳērạ bạra they are double what we manufactured last year (*cf.* bịyū 3*b*). (*c*) (*similarly used with ordinals*) *x* na ukụ ɗnsụ the third of them. (2) *Vd.* dīnī, dānī.

dinạ = dīnạ *f.* (1) (*Eng.* dinner) *x* yā kirā sụ ~ he invited them to dinner. ~ ta bạŋ kwānā farewell dinner. (2) *Vd.* igīyạ 7.

dinana A. (dịnānạ) *Vb.* 3B become dis-coloured, tarnished, mildewed.

B. (din**ā**nā) *Vb.* 1C to discolour, tarnish, mildew.

dinane A. (din**ā**nē) *Vb.* 3A = din**ā**n**a̤**.

B. (din**ā**nē) *Sk. m.* walking through water beyond one's depth *x* yā yi ~ **a̤** rūwa.

dīnārị (*Latin-Ar. m.* gold). (1) = zīnārịyā. (2) *Vd.* s**a̤**dākị.

dindi**6**ā *f.* (1) type of grasshopper. (2) big made girl.

dịndīkwa̤lọ *m.* chunks of yam or sweet-potato cooked in oil (= gịndīkwa̤lọ).

ɗinɗimēm**ẹ** = ɗinɗimī *adj. m.* (*f.* ɗin-ɗimēmịyā = ɗinɗimā) *pl.* ɗinɗim-ɗinɗim huge.

dịndimī (1) (*a*) night-blindness. (*b*) mut**ā̤**nē su k**a̤**m mai da dịndimī cīwọ some people fuss over a trifle. (2) *x* b**ā̤**ɓō yan**ā̤** d**a̤** ~ a stranger feels at sea anywhere. (3) dịndimịŋk**a̤** d**a̤** gātā ; makant**a̤**rk**a̤** **a̤**biŋ kallō you've resources which I'm not so lucky to have.

ɗinɗimta *Vd.* ɗimɗimta.

dịndịn *Vd.* s**a̤**kw**a̤**f 3.

dịndịndiŋ (1) perpetually. (2) tun ~ since of old. (3) *Vd.* dŋ.

dịndịŋgē *m.*, *f.* inexperienced thief or prostitute.

ɗinɗinta *Vd.* ɗimɗimta.

dịndịris *x* rānā tā yi dịndịris = tā fāɗị dịndịris sun's quite set.

dindirmēm**ẹ** *m.* (*f.* dindirmēmịyā) huge.

dindishẹ *Kt. m.* the gum-tree dīshẹ.

dinga A. (dịŋg**a̤**) (1) *Vb.* 1A. (*a*) kept on doing *x* yā ~ k**a̤**r**ā̤**tū he kept on read-ing. mun dịŋga yā̤ḳị kḕ naŋ we intend to keep on fighting ; we kept on fight-ing. yā ~ t**a̤**fịy**a̤** he travelled on. ta k**a̤**n ~ murn**a̤** she keeps on rejoicing (= rik**a̤** = dịmant**a̤** = kōshi 3 = dōs**a̤** 1*c* = dāf**a̤** 5), *cf.* k**a̤**n. (*b*) mụ ~, mụ ganī well, we'll see ! (2) *f.* (*a*) beaten ground before doorway. (*b*) doorstep (= dōkịŋ ḳōf**a̤**). (*c*) ~ d**a̤** gāshịm b**ā̤**kī (*said by women*) vagina (= farjị).

B. (dịŋgā) *Vb.* 2 (1) = dịŋg**a̤** 1*a*. (2) *Kt.* went straight to *x* k**a̤** dịŋgi Kanọ go straight to Kano ! (= dōs**a̤**).

dinga-dinga = dịŋgaŋ-dịŋgaŋ *adv.* straight *x* ~ s**ā̤**i ya zō gidā he came straight home. yan**ā̤** t**a̤**fịy**a̤** ~ he's

hurrying along without turning to right or left.

dịŋgarfai = ɗaŋgar**a̤**fai.

dịŋgāzumī *m.* (*f.* dịŋgāzumā = dịŋ-gāz**a̤**) (1) grubby P. (2) brave warrior.

dịŋgiɗ**a̤** *f.* = deŋgiɗ**a̤**.

dịŋgi-dịŋgi *Sk. m.* (1) affair of long standing. (2) delaying interminably.

ɗịŋgilgil *m.* shortness (= ɗigil *q.v.*).

dịŋgim**a̤** (1) *Vb.* 3B (several persons) collected and started out. (2) *Vb.* 2 drove away several persons.

dịŋgimēm**ẹ** = dịŋgịŋgimī *m.* (*f.* dịŋ-gimēmịyā = dịŋgịŋgịmā) *pl.* dịŋgịŋ-dịŋgịŋ huge.

dịŋgịŋgịŋ *m.* hugeness *x* yārọ nē ~ d**a̤** shī he's a huge lad.

dịŋgirisā *Sk. f.* limping.

dịŋgịsā *Vb.* 3A (1) limped. (2) *cf.* ɗuŋ-gusā.

dịŋgishī *m.* (1) (*a*) limping. (*b*) lameness (1 = gurguntā). (2) im maw**a̤**dācī yan**ā̤** ~, matsịyā̤cī ya kary**a̤** shi he's become impoverished by cadgers.

dịŋgizā *Vb.* 1C applied T. profusely to (= damb**a̤**zā *q.v.*).

dīnī *Kt.* = ɗin *q.v.* ; *x* gōm**a̤** dīninsụ ten of them. ukụ dīnimmụ three of us (*note changed tone of* ukụ ; gōm**a̤**. *cf.* ɗānī).

dininī *m.* small party of people *x* s**ā̤**i mun yi ~ zā mụ t**a̤**fi we'll start when there are a few of us.

dịŋjī *m.* rags (= tsụmmā).

ɗinka A. (ɗịŋk**a̤**) *Vb.* 1A (1) made T. by sewing *x* yā ~ minị rīgā he (tailor) has made me a gown (= ɗịŋkẹ 1*a*) (*cf.* ɗịŋkā ; ɗịŋkẹ). (2) yā ~ zụmunt**a̤** (*a*) he contracted relationship by giving him his daughter in marriage. (*b*) he reconciled disputants or enemies. (3) (*a*) yā ~ dūnịya = 2*b*. (*b*) *Vd.* ɗịŋkị 2*b*. (*c*) **a̤**bin ɗịŋkịn dūnịya *Vd.* W**a̤**zīrị. (4) in z**a̤**mānị yā ~ rīgā, lallē yā k**a̤**māt**a̤** **a̤** sak**a̤** one must bow to Fate.

B. (ɗịŋkā) *Vb.* 2 sewed T. partially (*cf.* ɗịŋk**a̤** ; ɗịŋkẹ ; ɗịŋku).

ɗịŋkau *m.* sewing for pay.

ɗịŋkẹ · (1) *Vb.* 1A. (*a*) = ɗịŋk**a̤** 1 *x* k**a̤** s**a̤**mi fāt**a̤**, k**a̤** ~ āy**a̤** d**a̤** shī get some leather and make the text into an amulet! (b) sewed together (torn place, etc.) x (i) an ∼ rĭgā the rent in the gown has been sewn up. an ∼ bạkin jạkā the mouth of the bag has been sewn up. (ii) muŋ gēwạyē, dom mụ diŋkẹ su we made a detour to outflank them. (c) kibĭyạ tā ∼ su the arrow transfixed two adjacent parts. (2) Vb. 3A (a) mụtụm (dōkị) yā ∼ P. (horse) is plump. (b) gạrĭ yā ∼ town is thronged. (3) cf. diŋkạ; diŋku.

diŋkị m. (1) being occupied in sewing x yanạ ∼. (2) (secondary v.n. of diŋkẹ 1a, b, c) x (a) yanạ diŋkin rĭgā = yanạ diŋkẹ rĭgā he's making a gown. (b) (i) sun yi shāwarạr diŋkin dūnĭyạ they're consulting how to reform the world. (ii) Vd. diŋkạ 3a. (iii) ạbin diŋkin dūnĭyạ Vd. Wạzĭrị. (3) embroidering x rĭgā duk dạ wạndō, an yi musụ ∼ both gown and trousers are embroidered (= aikị 1b.vii). (4) Vd. compounds of diŋkị alphabetically. (5) māyan diŋkị Vd. māyē 2b.

diŋkiŋ m. (1) silence (= dạŋkam q.v.). (2) gạrĭ yā yi ∼ it's sultry. (3) young leaves of cēdĭyā, diŋyā, etc., eaten as food.

diŋkiŋ Allạ m. seam of genitals and anus.

diŋkin sarkạ m. type of embroidered pattern.

diŋkin tsābạ Vd. tsābạ 3b.

diŋkin yaryar Sk. m. seam of the perineum (= diŋkiŋ Allạ).

diŋku Vb. 3B (1) kadạ kạ yi kạryā wạddạ bā tạ diŋkūwa don't tell a barefaced lie! (lit. which cannot be sewn). (2) dōkị yā ∼ = diŋkẹ 2a.

dinnikā Vb. 1C (1) an dinnikạ hayākĭ ạ dākị house is full of smoke. (2) yā dinnikạ kạtantaŋwạ player unfairly overturned spinning-top.

dinnikẹ A. (dinnikē) Vb. 3A. (1) (a) dākị yā ∼ dạ hayākĭ house is full of smoke (= muskẹ = murtụkē). (b) tụrạrē yā ∼ ạ dākị the house was impregnated with perfume. (c) kụrā tā ∼ dust rose in clouds. (2) fadạ yā ∼ serious quarrel arose. (3) cf. tunnụkẹ.

B. (dinnikē) m. unfairly overturning spinning-top (kạtantaŋwạ).

dinshẹ m. (1) type of acacia (= jūshị). (2) Kt. bunch (of bananas, dates, dọrawạ pods, etc.).

dintsa A. (dịntsā) Vb. 2 took out handful of. B. (dintsạ) Vb. 1C gave P. handful of x nā ∼ masạ kudĭ I gave him handful of money.

dintsẹ Vb. 1A = dịntsā.

dintsị m. handful.

dinyā f. (sg., pl.) (1) spur-winged goose (Plectropterus gambensis). (2) Knob-billed goose = dạnị (Sarkidiornis melanotus). (3) epithet of 1, 2 is dinyā bạ fīgyan yārọ ba.

dinyā f. (sg., pl.) (1) (a) the tree Vitex Cienkowskii whose black plum-like fruit are used for making madị: epithet is hanạ mātā zạrē. (b) Vd. cĭ 1c; shā A.1e. (2) dinyar birị the shrub Vitex diversifolia. (3) (a) wearing two black gowns simultaneously. (b) wearing all black clothing. (4) dinyar mạkāfọ tạ nụna ạ ạljĭfunsạ he won't let his property out of his sight. (5) yārọ dạ fụlā, babba dạ fụlā, girman 'yan ∼ why do persons so different imitate one another! (6) wạyaŋ ạ cĭ nẹ, aŋ kọri kạrē dạgạ gindin dinyā it's a mere pretext in order to get it for himself (cf. kanyạ 3).

dĭ ọ (Eng. D.O.) District Officer; Divisional Officer.

dir Vd. dịra 1b.

dira A. (dịra) Vb. 3B (1) (a) P. leapt down; (bird) swooped down (= tsirgạ 1). (b) (with dative) x zākị yā diram masạ lion pounced on him. yā diram (= yā dir) minị dạ fadạ he ranted at me. (2) (a) alighted (from horse; ladder). (b) landed at (from boat, ship) (2 = sạuka). (3) x yā ∼ cikin shiŋgē he leapt over fence. (4) yā ∼ gạ aikị he's well on with his work. (5) x hanyạ tā ∼ dạ Kanọ road extends to Kano (cf. daukạ 1p).

B. (dirạ) Vb. 1A (1) banged down (load in taking it off one's head or to even up protruding sticks, etc.) = kwakkwạfē. (2) ∼ ginị to build reliably. (3) nā ∼ masạ māshị I pierced him with spear. (4) -Kt. yā ∼ minị tsāwā he scolded me.

dirad dạ Vb. 4B (1) = dirạ 1 ; cf. dịra 2b.
(2) x an ∼ hanyạ har Kanọ road's
been extended to Kano.

dirbai m. cadging by the professional
beggars 'yan ∼ (Vd. marọ̄kī).

dir dạ Vb. 3A = dirad dạ.

dirdir m. (f. dirdirā) short but strong.

dire A. (dirẹ) (1) Vd. 3A (a) = dịra 1a, 2, 5.
(b) rịgā tā ∼ gown reaches the ground.
(2) lallẹ yā ∼ henna-stain has worn off.
(2) Vb. 1A = dirạ 1. (3) x yā sạ̄mi kudī,
yā ∼ he jumped for joy at getting the
money.
B. (dịrē) m. (1) the type of gown
called gịrkē. (2) Vd. dirē.
C. (dịre) nā gan shị ạ ∼ yạ kantụ
I found it done ; I found him grown-up
(cf. dirị).
D. (dịrē) m. game like turning
" cartwheels " (cf. raunin dịrē) = tsirgē.

dirēbạ = darēbạ.

dirhạmī (Arabic coin) m. (1) bạ ni dạ
kō ∼ I'm " broke ". (2) callus above
knee of horse, donkey, mule.

diri A. (dirị) m. (1) unit for counting salt-
blocks (kantụ) x yā kāwō kantụ ∼
gụdā he brought one kantụ (cf. dịre).
(2) yanạ̄ dạ kyạn ∼ he (it) has shapely
buttocks ; (P. ; house ; animal) is well-
proportioned. tanạ̄ dạ kyạn ∼ she has
shapely buttocks ; she is well-propor-
tioned. (3) first stages (= digị).
(4) exclamation of surprise at act
denoted by dirạ ; dịra.
B. (dịrī) m. any vague noise (buzz
of voices, of distant car, etc.) =
jīzạ.

dirị-dirī m. = dirịndāsọ.

dirịn dạ rānī m. type of hemp (ramạ)
maturing in hot season.

dirịndas x nā gayạ masạ ∼ I told him
point-blank.

dirịndāsọ m. dilly-dallying (epithet is ∼
auraṇ Kulụmā).

dirịnīyā f. = dirịndāsọ.

dīrirī Kt. m. anạ̄ ∼ dạ shị he's being disparaged (= dīdịdī q.v.).

dịris (1) x rūwā yā zubō ∼ a few drops of
water were spilled. (2) ∼ tā dịgạ, tā
tāshị type of song and game.

dịrishị (Eng. dress) m. yā yi ∼ he togged
himself up.

dirje A. (dirjẹ) Vb. slithered, squashed,
etc. (= darjẹ q.v.).
B. (dịrjē) Vd. dạrzā.

dirkạ f. (pl. dirkōkī) (1) forked-stick
(= gwạfā). (2) (a) type of (i) gambling.
(ii) children's game. (b) trick in
hopping-wrestle.

dịrka A. (dịrkā) Vb. 2 (1) x nā dịrkē shị
dạ sạndā = dịrka 1a. (2) drank much
of.
B. (dịrkạ) (1) Vb. 1A (with dative) x
(a) nā ∼ masạ sạndā I thoroughly
thrashed him. nā ∼ masạ wukā
(māshị) I deeply plunged knife (spear)
in him. (b) an dịrkạ musụ ịgwā a
mass of artillery-fire was let loose on
them (b = wātsạ 1a). (c) x tā ∼ hannū
cikin rāmị she poked her hand in hole.
yā ∼ kạnsạ cikin dūnīyạ he vanished.
(2) Vb. 3A entered unexpectedly x
yā ∼ cikin dākị he entered house unexpectedly. yā ∼ dūnīyạ he vanished.

dịrkạ-dịrkạ x taskōkī dịrkạ-dịrkạ numberless storehouses.

dirkạ̄kā = dikạ̄kā.

dịrkākạ = dikākạ 1 ; 2a, b, c.

Dịrkạ̄kau epithet of Emir (= sukuku
makạkạ).

dịrkẹ Vb. 1A (1) nā ∼ shi dạ sạndā =
dịrka 1a. (2) drunk up all the large
amount available (cf. dịrkā 2).

*dịrkif = kịrtif.

dịrkōkī Vd. dịrkạ.

dịrkōkōnīyā Kt. f. lads' game of jumping
from height or from hole to hole
(= tsirgē).

dịrku Vb. 3B entered suddenly x ạbọ̄kaṇ
gạ̄bā sun ∼ cikiṇ gạrī the enemy
suddenly penetrated into town
(= dịrkạ 2).

dirnịkā Vb. 1C = dinnịkā.

dirshạṇ x yā zaunạ ∼ he sat for long
idly.

dirshē Vd. dirad dạ.

dirtsạ Vb. 1A (1) = dirtsẹ. (2) (with
dative) kā ∼ minị kwaryā ạ hannū
you squeezed the calabash on to my
hand. yā ∼ masạ hakọ̄rā he gripped
it with his teeth.

dirtsẹ Vb. 1A (1) pressed T. down with
edge or tip of T. (as with stick, finger,
etc. ; cf. dannạ) x kā ∼ hannūna dạ

ƙwaryā you squeezed the calabash on to my hand. (2) yā ~ shi dạ haƙọrā = dirtsạ 2. (3) bent P. to one's will (= dannẹ 4a.ii). (4) overloaded x an ~ jāƙī dạ kāyā = kāyā yā ~ jāƙī (cf. dannẹ 4b). (5) yā ~ ni it overstrained my resources (as visit of guests, etc.).

dirza A. (dirzạ) Vb. 1A tā ~ jịkintạ dạ waŋkā she scrubbed herself (= darjẹ 2g q.v.).

B. (dịrzā) Vb. 2 squashed, etc. (= dạrzā q.v.).

dis m. (1) drip ; drop. (2) sound of dripping.

disa = dasa.

Dịsambạ f. December.

dīsạnā Vb. 1C took out little of (= dēfạnā).

dīsạrā = dīsạnā.

dis-dis = idọn 9A.

disfensạ Eng. m. (pl. disfensōshī) dispenser.

dishe A. (dishẹ) Vb. 3A became dim (= dushẹ).

B. (dīshẹ) m. type of gum-tree.

disịndisịnō Kt. m. mixture of cassava and groundnuts.

diskārī m. strong, fearless P. (= daskārī q.v.).

dịssā Nor. f. bran (= dụsā).

dīwạ f. (1) pus (= mūgụ 3). (2) the grass Rhytachne congœnsis used for making the mats tufānịyā or asabạrī. (3) Sk. anus (= tsūlịyā).

dīwānị Ar. m. register (= daftạrī).

dịyā Sk., Kt. f. (pl. dīyā children = 'yā'yā). (1) daughter. (2) free-woman. nā bar tạ ~ I manumitted her (cf. 'yā ; dā). (3) ~ ạ rūwa the game 'yā ạ rūwa q.v. under 'yā 5a. (4) dịyar rānā female servant (= rānā 3b = baranyạ), cf. ūwar dākị 1b. (5) Kt. dịyar rūwan sanyī (a) woman's young female pal (ƙawā). (b) daughter of 5a. (c) type of brass-basin called bạgwạnjā. (d) Vd. rūwā A.24. (6) tanạ lāshẹ dīyā Vd. ạbụ 2b.

Dīyạdī Kt. official responsible for safeconduct of travellers or Chiefs.

dịyai long, thin bamboo canoe-poles (Vd. dị).

dịyạm m. jumping into water sitting (cf. hāzā, zụlumbụ, jūyị 4) = dākẹ 1.

dịyaŋ = dīyānī = dan dạyānī (1) completely (epithet is ~ zūwạŋ kại dạ kāshī) x aŋ gamạ ~ it's completely finished. yā dạukē su ~ he removed them all. (2) dīyānī, haifūwar dā dạ haƙōrī it's mere child's-play ! (3) well, what did I tell you ! (= kalmạ'iŋ). (4) (negatively) not in the least x ~ bạ zam bā kạ ba I'll certainly not give it to you !

dịyaucị Sk. m. (1) being freeman or freewoman (= 'yancị q.v.). (2) honesty, self-respect.

dịyauta A. (dīyạutā) Sk. Vb. 1C manumitted a slave (= 'yạntā).

B. (dīyautạ = dīyạutakạ) Sk. f. = dīyaucị.

dịyyạ (1) Ar. f. (a) compensation payable for accidental homicide or wounding. (b) war-indemnity. (2) m., f. contemporary ; P. of equal status with (= sa'ạ). (3) dīyyạr adv. about x dīyyạr dạrī approximately 100.

Dīzạ = Dīzọ.

Dịzambạ f. December.

Dīzọ name for any woman called Hạdījạ q.v.

dn Vd. din.

dōɓạ Vb. 1A (1) x yā ~ ƙwaryā ạ bạ̄kī = yā ~ bạ̄kī ạ ƙwaryā he put his lips deep into the calabash to drink. yā ~ bạ̄kī ạ rūwa he put his lips deep in the water to drink (cf. kafạ 2g). (2) yā ~ bạ̄kī he interfered.

dōɓạnā Vb. 1C. (1) = dōɓạ. (2) = dōdạnā.

dọ̄ɓạnē m. yā yi matạ ~ he (uncircumcized lad) had sexual intercourse with her.

dọ̄ɓarọ m., f. P. of ill-considered speech.

dọ̄dan Vd. dọ̄dō.

dōdạnā Vb. 1C (1) applied (fire) to (= dānạ 4a q.v.). (2) shot at close range x nā ~ masạ kibịyạ. (3) yā ~ matạ bụ̄rā he had sexual intercourse with her. (4) yā ~ madōshī ạ ƙōtạ he applied hot boring-tool to burn hole in haft. (5) yā ~ musụ bạ̄ƙō (ɓạrāwọ) he gave quiet hint to stranger (thief) of their premises as being a place likely

to suit him as lodging (house to rob) =
kunnạ 3 = dōnạ 2 = ijē = cūnạ 1*b*.
ɗōɗanā *Vb*. 1C (1) tā ɗōɗanạ mại (mīyạ)
ạ ạbincī she added slight amount of
fried-butter (gravy) to food.   tā
ɗōɗanạ nōnọ ạ furā she was niggardly
in adding milk to the furā.   (2) yā
ɗōɗanạ barkọnō ạ idansạ he made his
eye smart by touching with peppery
finger. (3) = dōdạnā.
dọ̄dạnē *m*. being occupied in act denoted
by dōdạnā *x* maharbī yā yi masạ ~
hunter shot it at close range.
dọ̄dạnī ; dọ̄danniȳā *Vd*. dọ̄dō.
ɗọ̄ɗar straight *x* hancinsạ ~ nẹ̄ he has a
straight nose.   hanyạ ~ straight road.
hanyạ tā mīkẹ̄ ~ the road runs straight.
dọ̄darā *f*. = tụ̄darā.
ɗōɗarōkọ *m*. affectation.
dọ̄daya = dạiɗayạ.
dōdẹ *Vb*. 1A to stop up (mouth of jar,
etc.) (= dāɗẹ *q.v.*).
dōdīyā *f*. stopping up (= dāɗā *q.v.*).
dodo A. (dōdọ) *m*. (1) *x* sun yi ~ they
(soldiers, ants, etc.) form (formed)
long line.   (2) kwạrkwatạ tā yi ~
lice collected all over person's head.
(3) yā yi mini ~ dạ shī he proffered
it to me but then withdrew it (= dạn-
gọ̄līyā), *cf*. ƙwạlēlē ; ƙwạlā.   (4) (*a*)
spitting fish (kanyā-fruit) on stick for
transporting *x* an yi wạ kīfī ~ fish has
been spitted.   (*b*) yā bā nị kīfī ~ gụdā
he gave me one stick of spitted fish.
     B. (dọ̄dō) *m*. (*f*. dọ̄danniȳā) *pl*.
dọ̄dạnī = *Sk*. dọ̄dạnnī. (1) (*a*) goblin,
evil spirit (= fatalwā = ạljan). (*b*) ~
gụdā mukẹ̄ yi wạ tsāfī we all have the
same aim.   (*c*) munāfuncị ~, ụbạn-
gijinsạ ya ƙạn ci evil recoils on the
doer.   (2) T. inspiring fear (*x* Emir,
European, etc.).   (3) rings painted
round eyes as magic to ward off smallpox.   (4) *name given* P. born hairy-
headed. (5) dọ̄dan azụmī small string
of wool or cowries suspended from
girl's neck (= būshīyā 5).   (6) yā yi
mini dọ̄dan gōnā = yā yi mini dọ̄dam
bangō he intimidated me (= burgā).
(7) dọ̄dan dāwạ = ƙudujī.   (8) dọ̄dan
gẹ̄rē a famous tsāfī of the Gerawa in
Bauchi. (9) dọ̄dan ƙwaryā = 6 *above*.

(10) in akạ sạ̄mi lāmụnī gạ ~ shigā
rūwa wani ạbụ nẹ̄ ? if you get a chance,
take it !   (11) (*a*) n nạ̄ jịn dọ̄dan
kụnnē my ears are buzzing.   (*b*) yā
kashẹ mini dọ̄dan kụnnē he gave me a
hard slap. (12) shellfish separated from
its shell *x* dọ̄dan ƙatantanwạ snail
severed from its shell. (13) Dọ̄dan
ạsụbā *epithet of* lādạn.   (14) dọ̄dan
tsakī *Vd*. ạlmājịrī 1.
ɗōɗọ *m*. = ɗōɗarōkọ.
dōdōnīyā *f*. variety of mantis.
dọ̄dọ̄rịdō = dọ̄dọ̄rịdọ *m*. (1) = dọ̄dō 6.
     (2) = dōdọ 3. (3) showing off *x* yanạ̄ ~
dạ kudī he's swanking with his wealth.
ɗōɗoya *Kt*. = ɗạɗɗōyạ 1.
ɗōfạ *Vb*. 1A = ɗōfanā *Vb*. 1C stuck T.
on to (= ɗāfạ 1 *q.v.*).
ɗōfane A. (ɗọ̄fạnē) *m*. act of sticking T.
on to.
     B. (ɗọ̄fạne) *x* ạ ~ takẹ̄ she's likely
to part from her husband at any time.
ɗōfị *m*. arrow filed so as to break off in
wound.
dōfụlō = dōhụlō.
dōgạcē *Vb*. 3A withdrew and sat alone
(= dangạcē).
dogara A. (dōgạrā) *Vb*. 1C.   (1) (*a*) yā
dōgạrạ sandā (i) he levered himself
up from sitting-position with a stick.
(ii) he (old man, cripple) leaned on
stick (*cf*. dōgạrē).   (*b*) yā ~ yā tāshị
he (tired man) levered himself up from
sitting position (1*a*, *b* = tōkạrā 2).
(2) (*a*) har n dōgạrạ karā bạ zan yi
ba never shall I do so. (*b*) dạ karā ạ̄ ~
Vd. sandā 1*e*. (3) yanạ̄ dōgạrạ tukurwā
cikin kọ̄gī he's poling the boat along
(*cf*. tūƙạ 1*c*).
     B. (dọ̄garạ) (1) *Vb*. 3B.   (*a*) yā ~
dạ (= yā ~ gạ) sandā he (old man,
cripple) leaned on a stick (*cf*. dōgạrē).
(*b*) yā ~ dạ (= yā ~ gạ) Audu he
relied on Audu. yā ~ gạ Allạ̄ he put
his trust in God. (2) ạbin ~ T. or P.
relied on.
dōgarāwā *Vd*. dōgarị.
dōgarcị *m*. being a dōgarị.
dōgarē (1) *Vb*. 1C *x* yā dōgarẹ sandā he
leaned lightly on a stick (*cf*. dōgạrā
1*a*.ii, dọ̄garạ, tōkạrā, tōkạrē).   (2)
relied on *x* yā ~ gạrēshị he relied on

him, it (= dọ̄garạ 1b). (3) propped up (= tōkạrē 1).

dōgari m. (pl. dọ̄garai = dōgarāwā = Sk. dọ̄garrai). (1) (a) Native Administration policeman (epithet is Na bāgarā = Na kīgo, bạ̄ ku tạ̄rar madakā). (b) yā yi fuskạr dọ̄garai he frowned, scowled (Vd. fuskạ 1c). (c) armed ship escorting convoy. (d) Vd. wạ̄ ya zạ̄gi ∼. (2) buttress. (3) pillar (= gimshikị).

dōgạ̄yē Vd. dōgō.

dōgazā f. (1) big hen. (2) big slut.

dōgẹ Vb. 3A Kt. behaved mulishly (= dāgẹ).

dōgō m. (f. dōgūwā = dōgwā) pl. dōgạ̄yē = dōgwạ̄yē. (1) (a) adj. tall, long x (i) dōgwan yārọ = yārọ dōgō tall lad. (ii) dōgwaŋ ḳạshĪ upper bone of hind leg of cattle. (iii) Dōgō, ạlmakạshin dāji epithet of train. (iv) gūrịn naŋ ∼ nẹ̄ this wish is far-fetched. (b) tall P. (cf. zạŋgwarmạdi). (2) (a) x yārọ nē ∼ dạ shĪ he is a tall lad. yārinyạ cē dōgwā dạ ita she's a tall girl. yạ̄rā nẹ̄ dōgạ̄yē dạ sū they're tall lads. (b) yārọ mại ∼ lad sprung up quickly. (c) Mālạm ∼ polite term of address to dwarf (wạ̄dā). (3) Vd. dōgwā.

ɗọ̄gōgọ = ɗọ̄gōgō x aŋ ajị̄yē shi ∼ it has been placed unsteadily.

dōgontakạ Vd. dọ̄gwạntakạ.

ɗọ̄gōzọ m. = dọ̄kĪ.

dōgūwā = dōgwā f. (1) Vd. dōgō. (2) type of kerchief (fạtalạ). (3) the spirit Innạ 3a.

dọ̄gwạntakạ f. tallness, length.

dōgwạ̄yē Vd. dōgō.

dōhịlō = dōhụlō m. (1) antennæ of grasshopper. (2) (a) fool. (b) ∼ ḳạfam fạ̄rā dạ tsịnĪ, bạ̄ sūkạ what a fool !

doka A. (dọ̄kā) (1) f. (pl. dōkōkĪ). (a) order x aŋ azạ dōkōkĪ laws were imposed, passed. an yi ∼ ạ bĪyā gandū dạ saurĪ an order has been issued to pay tax promptly. an yi ∼ kadạ ạ yĪ this has been forbidden (= ụmạrnĪ). (b) dọ̄rawạ a ḳạn yi wạ ∼, tsāmĪyā kōwā yạ dĪbạ, tāsạ cē the law only occupies itself with important matters. (c) ɗan ∼ x (i) ɗan dọ̄kaŋ Kanọ a Kano

N.A. city-policeman. (ii) ɗan dọ̄kam ɓọ̄ye = ɗan taurĪ member of the Zaria secret police. (d) dọ̄kar jējị dense bush (= ḳwaŋḳōlĪ 2). (e) mại dọ̄kar barcĪ Vd. ɓugẹ 2. (2) Vb. 2 (progressive is generally formed with dūkạ). (a) thrashed x (i) yā dọ̄kē nị dạ sạndā he beat me with a stick (= bụgā 1a = dakạ 1 d.i). (ii) gurgụ yanạ̄ ganĪ, a ḳạn sạ̄ri sạndā ạ dọ̄kē shị he is in no position to retaliate against his oppressive superior (Vd. gurgụ 1c). (iii) ạ dọ̄kē kạ ạ hanạ kạ gụdụ ? why should a double wrong be inflicted on a person ? (iv) tā dọ̄ki ūwar gidā Vd. būlālạ 3. (b) shāfọ yā dọ̄ki kurcĪyā the hawk hit the pigeon with its wing.

B. (dōkạ) (1) f. (a) (i) pad used for puffing out women's hair x tā kafạ ∼ she did her coiffure with a dōkạ. (ii) cf. zagĪ 2, gōrạ 1g. (b) the tree Isoberlinia doka (cf. fakālẹ). (c) fattiness of back of horse's neck. (d) horse's being goose-rumped. (e) bịkiŋ wani ∼, bịkiŋ wani kwạmbē tastes differ (cf. ḳạrḳarā 3). (2) Vb. 1A (with dative). (a) yā ∼ minị sạndā = dọ̄kā 2. (b) bā ạ dōkạ̄wā Vd. sạndā 1m.ii.

dọ̄kạcạkam Sk. completely (= kạcọ̄kam q.v.).

dọ̄kạcē Vd. dọ̄katạ.

dọ̄kacĪ all (= ɗạkwacĪ q.v.).

dọ̄kạci Vd. dọ̄katạ.

dọ̄kad dājị = dọ̄kā 1d.

dọ̄kakkē x dọ̄kakkĪyar hanyạ f. frequented road.

dọ̄kakkēnịyā f. severe fracas ; wordy battle (= ɗạukakkēnịyā).

ɗọ̄kantạ Vb. 3B x nā ∼ dạ zūwạntạ = nā ∼ tạ zō I'm eager for her to arrive.

dọ̄kar dājị Vd. dọ̄kad dājị.

ɗọ̄kạrin dōkōkọ (1) top-heavy ; unsteady. (2) = ɗạkwạrĪ

dọ̄katạ Vb. 2 Kt. ordered that x an dọ̄kạcē sụ, sụ bĪyā gandū dạ saurĪ they've been ordered to pay tax promptly. an dọ̄kạci Audụ kadạ yạ yĪ Audu has been forbidden to do it.

dōkẹ Vb. 1A (1) yā ∼ ni dạ sạndā = dọ̄kā 2. (2) surpassed x yā ∼ ni ạ kudĪ (kạrạ̄tū) he has more money (learning) than I have. (3) (a) yā kai, yā ∼ he's big-made. (b) yā ka̱i sama̱, yā ∼ he's tall and broad. (4) ∼ aiki̱ to make short work of task x aiki̱ŋ kwānā uku̱ nē, rānā dayā ya ∼.

dōki̱ m. (pl. dawākī = da̱wa̱̱kai). (1) (a) (i) horse (f. gō̱dī̱yā). (ii) (collective) horses, cavalry x yā fasa̱ dōki̱ he deployed his cavalry. dōki̱ yā yi 50 the cavalry totalled 50. dōki̱ yā yi 2,000 ba̱nda̱ da̱kāra̱ the cavalry amounted to 2,000, apart from the infantry. dōki̱ŋ gidansa̱ 100 ne̱ he has 100 horses at home. (iii) ma̱i ∼ Vd. ma̱i 1a, Vd. below 1g, k, r, v, z.viii. (b) Vd. dōki̱n-compounds separately. (c) ∼ ɗayā a̱ fagē, gudu̱ ga̱rēshi̱ P. whose statements cannot be checked, talks big. (d) ∼ kā fi amai epithet of glutton. (e) ∼ kā fi kisa̱m ma̱i gōnā (lit. Horse, you're too powerful to be killed by the farmer whose crops you damage !) epithet of physically strong or influential P. (f) (i) wa̱nda̱ ya hau dōki̱n "dā̱ nā sani̱" yā̱ wa̱hala̱ don't do what you'll later regret ! (ii) Vd. dā̱ 1b, dōki̱n zūcī̱yā. (g) ma̱i ∼ ya̱ ce̱ ya̱ mutu̱ ba̱rē ɗan cī̱ya̱̱wa̱ ? if you refuse good advice, don't afterwards blame your adviser ! (h) ɓa̱rāwa̱n ∼ da̱ga̱ kā̱zā ya fāra̱ ∼ ɓa̱rāwa̱n ∼ da̱ga̱ taskirar ūwā ya fāra̱ Vd. taskirā. (j) dōki̱ŋ hari̱ tun yanā̱ turke̱ a ka̱ŋ guje̱ masa̱ = dōki̱ŋ hari̱ a̱ guje̱ shi̱ tun da̱ga̱ shā̱maki̱ don't leave things till the last minute !, forewarned is forearmed. (k) a̱bi̱n da̱ ma̱i ∼ke̱ sō̱, ba̱ shī nē̱ ma̱i bāwa̱ ke̱ sō̱ ba tastes differ. (l) dōki̱ŋ kūrā im ba̱i sa̱wu ba, ta̱ ci a̱binta̱ unsold food is no loss as vendor will eat it himself. (m) anā̱ lahīyā da̱ ∼ nē̱ ? it's impossible. (n) gwa̱nin ∼ wa̱nda̱ ke̱ ka̱nsa̱ possession is nine points of the law. (o) gwa̱nin ∼ wa̱nda̱ ya hau = 1n. (p) ∼ yā sam maha̱yinsa̱ everyone knows his own business best. (q) ha̱sāra̱d ∼ sǎi Sarkī a big loss is trivial to the rich. (r) (i) ma̱i ∼ yā kōma̱ kutu̱r he's gone down in the world. (ii) Vd. kutu̱r 3. (s) ∼ in yā ga̱ji, tīla̱s kū̱wā ba̱ ta sauran sa̱ shi sǎi dǎi da̱bāra̱ when matters become difficult, compulsion

must be replaced by guile. (t) da̱ ∼ da̱ kō̱gī Vd. a̱māna̱ 8c. (u) (i) tsō̱fan ∼ Vd. sa̱nē 2, tsōfō 1g. (ii) kōmē tsūfan ∼ Vd. tsūfā 2. (v) tsūlī̱yar ma̱i ∼ Vd. tsūlī̱yā 4. (w) jā̱ ∼ Vd. ambu̱lī. (x) fāɗad da̱ ga̱ban ∼ Vd. wukā 1f. (y) in sun sa̱mi ∼ da̱ sukū̱wā Vd. sukū̱wā 1d. (z) kā̱zā tā fi ∼ Vd. sayar da̱ 4. (z) (i) a ka̱m ba̱ ∼ Vd. saurā 1c. (z) (ii) ∼ da̱ jā̱kī ba̱ su̱ mutu̱ ba Vd. mīki̱ 2c. (z) (iii) bu̱durwar dawākī Vd. bu̱durwā 2. (z) (iv) ci nāma̱n ∼ Vd. cī 11p. (z) (v) a̱ kāra̱ dawāki̱ ? Vd. Ba̱rnō. (z) (vi) dawākin Sarkī Vd. agaza̱rī. (z) (vii) gāwar ∼ Vd. gāwā 1a.iii. (z) (viii) ba̱kwam ma̱i ∼ Vd. nauyī 1d. (1A) Vd. san dōki̱, tāshi̱n dōki̱, tsabta̱ 1d, u̱ban dawākī, dōki̱n rūwā. (1B) Sarkin ∼ Vd. ma̱rōdōɗo̱, ba̱rgā 3. (1C) ga̱ban ∼ Vd. ga̱bā 1e. (2) trading capital (jāri̱). (3) (a) rafter (Vd. dawākī 2). (b) dōki̱ŋ ga̱rmā centre of 3 strips of metal joining blade of ga̱rmā to haft (= gōje̱ 1). (4) a move in the game of dara̱. (5) warp-threads in weaving.

dō̱kī m. (1) eagerness. (2) throbbing pain (= zō̱gī). (3) Vd. gōma̱ 2c.

dōki̱ŋ Alla̱ (said by children) the mantis ƙōƙi̱-ƙōƙi̱.

dōki̱ŋ a̱lmā̱ji̱rai = dōki̱n dāfe̱ = dōki̱n ɗam madāfī game where 3 boys put their hands on each other's shoulders imitating body of horse, first boy holding the feet of the third boy.

dōki̱ŋ Asbi̱n Vd. sa̱ntī̱lō.

dōki̱n cācā m. (pl. dawākin cācā) gambling-cowrie (= cācā 3b).

dōki̱n dāfe̱ = dōki̱ŋ a̱lmā̱ji̱rai.

dōki̱n ɗam madāfī = dōki̱ŋ a̱lmā̱ji̱rai.

dōki̱n da̱ nā sani̱ Vd. dōki̱ 1f.

dōki̱ŋ ga̱rmā Vd. dōki̱ 3b.

dōki̱ŋ hari̱ Vd. dōki̱ 1j.

dōki̱ŋ karā m. child's hobby-horse (cf. ta̱cūcū ; dōki̱ŋ ƙasā).

dōki̱ŋ ƙarfe̱ m. bicycle (= bāsu̱ku̱r).

dōki̱ŋ kargō slow-moving little boy is asked kanā̱ sō̱ ka̱ hau doki̱ŋ kargō ? and if he agrees, he is playfully flicked along with a twig (= Kt. dōki̱ŋ wuya̱).

dōkịŋ ƙasā *m.* child's clay-horse (*cf.* **dōkịŋ karā**).

dōkịŋ ƙōfạ *m.* raised doorstep (= **gụdụŋkā** = **dandamạlī** = *Kt.* **tụdụŋkā** = **daŋgạramạ 1** = **diŋgạ** 2*b*), *cf.* **tạyā ni shịgā.**

dōkịŋ ƙōƙō *m.* piece of calabash used in children's game (= **tāƙō 1**).

dōkịŋ kōwā (1) ~ **zaŋ hau** I'll go on Shanks' pony. (2) **ƙasā** ~ *epithet of* helpful P.

dōkịŋ kūrā *Vd.* **kūrā 38.**

dokin maciji (dōkịm macịjī) *used in* **hawan dōkịm macịjī** being expert in use of article unfortunately owned by another, i.e. possession is nine points of the law (*Vd.* **sāmụ 3***a*)

dōkịŋ rūwā *m.* channel carrying water from **jīgọ** or **cạkarkarạ** to beds of irrigated-farm (**lạmbū**).

dǫkintạ = **dǫkantạ.**

dōkịŋ tāƙō = **dōkịŋ ƙōƙō.**

dōkịŋ tsuntsāyē *m.* the bird Longtailed Flycatcher.

dōkịŋ tụrurūwā *m.* the spider **mạƙạrā.**

dōkịŋ wuyạ *m.* (1) nape of neck (= *Sk.* **daƙōƙī**). (2) *Kt.* = **dōkịŋ kargō.**

dōkịŋ zāgē *m.* led horse for use of travelling chief (= **zāgē** = **amaryar dōkị**).

dōkịŋ zūcịyā *used in* **yā hau** ~ he did an act he regretted (= **gōdịyā 3**), *cf.* **dōkị 1***f.*

dōkōkī *Vd.* **dōƙā.**

dǫƙōƙọ *m.* bending oneself down slightly.

dǫƙōƙọ = **dǫkōkō** *x* **dǫƙōƙọ nē** it's top-heavy, unsteady. **aŋ ajịyē shi** ~ it's been placed unsteadily.

dǫƙwarōƙwạrǫ = **dǫƙōƙọ.**

dōlanci *m.* foolishness.

dōlạshī *m.* compulsion *x* **dōlạshinsạ yạ kạrɓā** he must accept it willy-nilly (*Vd.* **dōlẹ**).

dōlẹ (1) (*with subjunctive*) there is per-force the necessity that *x* **dạ yā cẹ yanạ zūwạ,** ~ **yạ zō** since he said he would come, he must come. **yā zamā** ~ **nē gạ mātā sụ yī** women have no choice but to do so. ~ **mụ zāɓi ɗayā** we're forced to choose one of them. (2) *f.* compulsion *x* (*a*) **anạ naŋ,** ~ **ta cim masạ** then in course of time he found himself forced to bow to fate. (*b*) **sun sạ mu** ~ **sǎi mun rǫƙē sụ in zā**

mụ fịta they've forced us to ask their leave before we go out. (3) **na** ~ *m.* (*f.* **ta** ~) *pl.* **na** ~ compulsory, obligatory. (4) ~ **yā'ẹ** fancy! (= **dēwạ yā'ẹ**).

dōlẹ-dōlẹ *m.* white grub of dungheaps (= **gwāzarmạ**).

dōlịndōsọ *m.* = **dǫrī ịhirī.**

dōlō *m.* (*f.* **dōlūwā** = **dōlwā**) *pl.* **dōlạyē** fool.

dom *Vd.* **ɗum.**

doma A. (**dōmạ**) *Vb.* 1A. (1) = **dōɓạ.** (2) *x* **sun** ~ **shi cikim mạganạ** they urged him to an evil course (= **tsōmạ 2**).

    B. (**Dōmạ**) *f.* (1) (*a*) New Gombe. (*b*) **ạbin dạ ya ci** ~ **bạ zại bar Ạwai ba** we'll sink or swim together! (2) **wạndan** ~ trousers with embroidered legs (= **wạndō bạkim bạŋgō** = **kāmụŋ ƙafạ 1***b* = **lāwur 3**), *cf.* **gạmē.**

dōmạnā *f.* a black blight on **daụrō** (*cf.* **bụrtuntụnā**).

dǫmạshī *m.* the shrub *Vernonia kotschyana.*

dǫmin = **don** (1) on behalf of, for the sake of *x* **dǫmīna** for my sake. **dǫmintạ** on her account. **dǫmī Allā** = **dǫmiŋ Allạ** for God's sake! **dǫmī Annabị** = **dǫmiŋ Annabị** for the Prophet's sake! (2) on account of *x* (*a*) ~ **haƙạ mukạ zō** *this* is why we came (*Vd.* **don 1**). (*b*) **bạ kụwā** ~ **kōmē ba sǎi sabọ dạ nīsā** from the very fact of its remoteness (*cf.* 6 *below*, **kōmē 3***a.*iii). **sun yi wannạŋ jạwābị bạ** ~ **kōmē ba sǎi** ~ **sụ bayyanạ nīyyạrsụ** they did it with the express purpose of showing their intentions (= **don 1***c*). (*c*) **bạ** ~ **hatsī** (= **bạ** ~ **tūwō**) **akạ yi cikị ba** one's inside is for concealing secrets, not only for filling with food (*Vd.* **tūwō 10**). (*d*) ~ **darē akē sạndā, dạ rānā kō dạ karā ạ dōgạrā** desperate causes need desperate remedies. (*e*) ~ **ƙại akē hūlā, har ƙyēyạ tạ sāmụ** your dependents share in your good luck. (*f*) ~ **kạrē, ạ yi gōɓarā** the fullest investigation will be welcome to me, for I'm not involved (= **jēmagẹ 1***b*). (*g*) ~ **kā rātsạ rūwā** *Vd.* **rātsạ 1***b.* (*h*) ~ **munāfụkī** *Vd.* **munāfụkī 1***c.* (*j*) *Vd.* **don 1***c, d, e, f, g.* (*k*) ~ **ganiŋ hadirị** *Vd.* **ganī**

A.2.1g. (3) ~ ɗaŋ wannaŋ abu, kada ka cẹ . . . for such a trifling cause do not say that . . . (Vd. 2b above, don 2). (4) (a) in order that x ~ ya gānẹ that he may understand. abin da ya sạ na kirā ka, ~ ka taimakẹ ni my reason for sending for you was the wish that you might help me (= don 4). (b) ~ kada Vd. don 4b. (5) (a) because x (i) nā tafi ~ nā san shi I went because I knew him. ~ mun sāmi hanya muka zō it's because we found a way that we have come. abin da ya sạ muka yi ~ muka ji an cẹ the reason why we did so was because we heard it said that . . . (ii) dǫmiŋ gā shi suŋ ga . . . for they considered that . . . (= don 5). (b) (same sense but dǫmin omitted) abin da ya sạ muka yi, n nā cẹwā . . . we did so because I thought that . . . abin da ya sạ na bar gidāna, kōwanẹ gēmu yā bar gidansa I left my home for the same reason as would induce every P. of sense to do so. (6) dā bā ~ had it not been for fact that (= don 6 q.v.) x dā bā ~ suka kuskurē shi ba, dạ suŋ kā dạ shī had it not been for the fact that they missed him, they'd have felled him (Vd. dā 4). (7) Vd. don 3, 7. (8) Vd. dǫmin-dǫmin.

dǫmin-dǫmin (1) used in kōwā bai sā rigar ~ ba, yā tafi tsirāra = wanda bai ci azzikin ~ ba, yā mutu matsiyācī nobody can successfully do without help from others. (2) Vd. dalīli 4b.

dǫmōsō m. (1) being dirty-bodied. (2) rich oiliness of soup. (3) rīgā tā yi ~ it's a dull-black gown (= bugun laima). (4) yā yi ~ cikin kōrẹ his body's stained from dark-dyed gown worn next his skin. (5) boorish P.

don (1) = dǫmin 1, 2 x (a) (i) don nī for my sake. danka for your sake. dansa muka zō it was through him that we came. (ii) bā mā yin sanyī wai don tsōraŋ hasāra we do not shrink from it merely from fear of losses. (iii) doŋ wai Vd. wai 3f. (iv) kō wai = wai doŋ kō Vd. wai 3d. (b) dam mẹ = Sk. dom mī why ? (c) sun yī, bā doŋ kōmē ba nẹ sǎi su yaudarē mu they did it with the express purpose of deceiving

us (= dǫmin 2b). (d) don tūwaŋ gǫbe Vd. tukunyā 1e. (e) don cikiŋki = doŋ kaŋki Vd. nōmā 1b.ii. (f) doŋ Allā Vd. Allā 4. (g) doŋ wuyā bā ā ƙi Vd. wuyā 1g. (h) Vd. dǫmin 2c to 2h. (2) (a) conj. owing to the mere fact that x doŋ kā gan shi, kada ka yi tsammāni do not think merely because you see it, that . . . ammā doŋ a yi haka, wannam bā kōmē ba nẹ sōsǎi ga nasara but the mere fact of doing so is not in itself enough to ensure victory (= dǫmin 3), cf. abu 1e. (b) prep. for a mere trifle like x af, doŋ wannaŋ kaɗǎi, mẹ zai sā well, what does that matter ! ~ ɗaŋ wannaŋ abu, kada for such a trifle, do not . . . ! ~ 'yaŋ ƙwaŋki uku nẹ ? is all this fuss over your wretched three eggs ? ~ wannaŋ = in ~ wannaŋ that is nothing to worry about ! ~ wannaŋ, da saukī it's mere child's play ! ~ wannaŋ, wani abu nẹ ? it's not of the slightest importance ! ~ dǎi Audu don't let the matter of Audu exercise you, for . . . ! don cikinsa as far as his tummy is concerned, don't worry ! (= dǫmin 3), cf. dǫmin 2b ; inā 1a.iv ; abu 1e ; kacal ; kalīlaŋ. (3) conj. (with subj.) if it is necessary to do, if it means doing x doŋ ka dẹbi jakuŋa, ka yi makāmai, ƙuɗiŋka sum bata kẹ naŋ in a case where you spend money on armaments your money is spent uselessly. in dǎi ~ a ɗaukē shi nẹ, ban yardā ba if it is a case of taking him away, then I don't agree. (4) conj. (with subj.) (a) in order that x ~ ya gānẹ that he may understand. in ~ su bā mu tsōrō suka faɗi haka, tō hausar ba ta fita ba if they said this to frighten us, then their plan failed (= dǫmin 4). (b) ~ kada ya zō lest he come ! (= dǫmin 4). (5) because x dom mun sāmi hanya muka zō it's because we found a way that we have come. abin da ya sā suka īya, ~ sun isō da wurī what enabled them to do it was because they arrived early (Vd. dǫmin 5 for other examples). (6) bā don (= dǫmin 6) (a) had it not been for the fact that (as 1st clause) x bā doŋ gwani nẹ ba, dā mun sallamē shi it was only on account of his being *skilful* that we did not dismiss him. im bạ̄ doŋ hakạ ba, dạ̄ nā yạrdā but for this, I would have agreed. bạ̄ doŋ kun (= bạ̄ doŋ kukạ) zō ba . . . but for the fact of your coming . . . (*Vd.* dạ̄ 4). (*b*) (*as 2nd clause*) *x* saurā kạdaŋ yuŋwạ tạ ƙārạsā ni, bạ̄ don nā tsịnci wani mūshạm mạraƙī ba I was on the point of dying of hunger had I not chanced on the carcass of a calf. (7) after *x* dom mun tạfi tạ̄re bīkwạm mạcē, kạ̄ bar nị hạkạ ? would you thus leave me in the lurch after we've gone together to persuade the runaway wife to return ? dạ ya kạrɓi kāyā, dom mun shịga gạrī, ya zamā bēbē he took the load and after we'd entered the town he became deaf and dumb.

dōnạ *Vb.* 1A *Kt.* (1) yā ∼ ƙwaryā ạ bạ̄kī = dōɓạ 1. (2) yā ∼ musụ bạ̄ƙō (ɓạrāwọ) he gave quiet hint to stranger (thief) of their premises as being a place likely to suit him as lodging (house to rob) (= dōdạnā 5).

dōnạ *Vb.* 1A (1) tā ∼ sulẹ ạ hancī she fixed shilling to hole in her nose (= d<i>ạnạ</i> 3 *q.v.*). (2) yā ∼ fụlar tsịrē he stuck tiny bit of fat on to end of stick of spitted meat.

dōnại = dōnạinại *x* yaṇạ̄ dūbammụ ∼ he's looking at us contemptuously.

done A. (dōnẹ) *Vb.* 1A (1) *Kt.* stopped up (= tōshẹ). (2) *Vd.* sạ̄ri kạ ∼.

B. (dōnē) *m.* (1) act of purifying shea-butter. (2) = dōnō 1.

dōnị *m.* (1) being occupied in act of dōnạ *x* maƙẹrī yaṇạ̄ ∼ the smith's affixing spindles to coins (*Vd.* dạnạ 3*b*). (2) dan ∼ " stem " on fez or saucepan-lid, etc., for lifting.

dōnō *m.* (1) fertilizing a rice-farm by pulling up the crop and leaving it there to ferment. (2) *such* rice-farm.

dōnọnọ *x* yaṇạ̄ dūbantạ ∼ he's looking contemptuously at her.

dōrạ *Vb.* 1A (1) (*a*) put T. *or* P. on *x* nā ∼ littāfị ạ kạnsạ I put the book on it (= *Sk.* rabkạ). nā ∼ yārọ ạ kan tạkarkạrī I put the boy on the back of the pack-ox (= azạ 2), *cf.* ajịyē 4, gwāmạ. (*b*) tukunyā tạ dōrạ *Vd.*

murfụ 2*e*.ii. (2) set (broken limb). (3) helped P. put load on his head (= daukạ 1*g*). (4) kụ ∼ samạ now that you've completed one kạ̈i of farm-ridges, start on another kạ̈i (*Vd.* kunyā) = hayạ 1*e*. (5) yā ∼ he went away. (6) (*before dative*) added T. to *x* (*a*) an ∼ masạ bīyạm fạm 30 payment of £30 has been imposed on him. hạrājin dạ akạ ∼ masạ the tax at which he has been assessed. tā ∼ masạ zanẹ she added a bit of cloth to it. (*b*) yā yi shẹkarạ 50 har ya ∼ he's 50 years of age and more. (*c*) an ∼ masạ kirạ the call was passed on to him. (*d*) an ∼ masạ laifī he's been falsely accused. (*e*) *Sk.* yā ∼ fadị he kept on talking. (7) *Vd.* sāƙạ 2*c*.iii ; rạ̈i dọ̄re.

dōrad dạ *Vb.* 4B (1) ∼ dạ lạ̄bārị disseminated news. (2) bạ nạ̄ dōrar ba I feel far from sure about it (*both* = ƙārad dạ).

dōran *Vd.* dōrō.

dọ̄rawạ *f.* (*pl.* dọ̄rạyī). (1) (*a*) locustbean-tree (*Parkia filicoidea*) (*pulp in pods if eaten before the rains, causes vomiting. so tree's epithet is* ∼ makashịyā deadly locust bean). (*b*) *cf.* kāshiŋ awākī, gardạ̄, gạskamī, kalwā, dạddawā, bēnạ, tụ̄tū, saŋkẹ̄dā 3, sạbadạ, nōnọ 3, darɓā, dạmbī, bọ̄lọ̄lō. (2) ∼ mại hannun sạke *epithet of* liberal P. (3) type of harmless yellow snake. (4) dọ̄rawạ-dọ̄rawạ *adj.* *m.*, *f.* (*sg.*, *pl.*) light-yellow. (5) dọ̄rōwạ ạ kạn yi wạ dọ̄kā ; tsāmīyā, kōwā yạ dībạ, tāsạ cē the law only occupies itself with important things. (6) *Vd.* sạukar ∼.

dōrạye *Vd.* dōrō 7.

dọ̄rạyī *Vd.* dọ̄rawạ.

dore A. (dōrẹ) *Vb.* 3A (1) is (was) permanent ; lasted long. (2) *cf.* rạ̈i dọ̄re.

B. (dọ̄rē) *m.* (1) woman's artificial switch of hair. (2) being unable to eat customary meal before dawn in Ramadan (*cf.* sạɓi zạrce). (3) putting burnous (ạlkyabbạ) over head instead of on shoulders. (4) (*a*) joining two short bundles of bulrush-millet to form long one. (*b*) *such* bundle. (5) building with clay but not bricks (= gọ̄gạ̄).

dọ̄rērẹ *m.* = dọ̄rē 2.

dōrị *m.* (1) (*secondary v.n. of* dōrạ) *x* an

yi masạ ∼ an addition has been made
to it. (2) setting broken limb *x* maị ∼
bone-setter.   an sạ masạ karan ∼
splint's been applied to it.   yā yi wạ
hannūna ∼ he set my broken arm.
kạryā tasạ bạ ta ∼ ba cē his·fracture's
not settable.

dǫri ịhirī = dǫriṇ dǫsō *m.*, *f.* (1) (*a*)
friend's friend. (*b*) dependent's dependent. ' (*c*) servant's servant (*epithet*
is ∼ bịkiṇ ƙawar ƙawā). (2) yā zamā ∼
ạ gụna I regard him as unimportant.

dǫrinā *f.* (*sg.*, *pl.*) hippopotamus (*epithet*
is Dōjị (= Dōzạ) ūwar rūwā).   (2)
Sk. whip of hippo-hide *x* an yi masạ ∼
he's been flogged.   (3) ∼ gạ nākị = ∼
ŋgō swimmer's pushing across river
non-swimmer holding on ͺto calabash
(*cf.* gạ nākạ). (4) *cf.* dǫrinī.

dǫriṇ dǫgazō *Sk.* *m.* (1) adding further
details to actual news or message. (2)
T. done through several intermediaries.
(3) carrying a pot on another.

dǫriṇ-dǫriṇ *m.* passing on message received (*cf.* sạƙō).

dǫrinī *Vd.* basarākẹ.

dǫrīyā *f.* (1) T. placed on or added to
another.   (2) surplus *x* kudin naŋ
sunạ dạ ∼ this sum contains a surplus.

doro A. (dōrō) *m.* *sg.*, *pl.* (1) (*a*) convexity ;
hump   on   back·;   being   round-
shouldered.   (*b*) yā yi ∼ he hunched
his shoulders. (*c*) ạ yi bụƙū bạ dōrǫ ?
can one make " bricks without straw ?"
(*d*) *Vd.* bụƙū-bụƙū. (*e*) *Vd.* Bạnufē.
(*f*) " dạ nā sanị " ∼ cē *Vd.* dạ 1*b.*i.
(*g*) bugụn cikị, sạ dōrō kicking P. in
the stomach makes him bend ; attack
a person at his weak point ! (*h*) yā
hau dōraŋ ạbǫkaŋ gạbā he attacked the
enemy. (*j*) dōraŋ ūwā *Vd.* bụƙū-
bụƙū. (*k*) bisạm maị dōrō *Vd.* bisǫ 4.
(2) *x* (*a*) adansạ ∼ nē he's wearing
"͘ borrowed plumes ". (*b*) mạganạssạ ∼
cē he's telling a lie. (3) body of saddle-
cloth jạlālạ. (4) (*a*) yā hau dōraŋ ƙasā
he set out. (*b*) *Vd.* hau 1A. (5) dōram
mạgē failing to reply. (6) dōran zạbō =
dōran zạbūwā convexity.   (7) dōrō
pl. dōrạyē single thickness of a numnah
(lạbbātị).

B. (dōrǫ) *Sk.* *m.* the kicking-game
mạngạrē.

Dǫrǫgō *Kt.* *used in* na ∼ (1) rat (*epithet*
is Na ∼ īyālịn tīlạs, yā ci wuƙā, yā
bar kụbē). (2) what a rogue !

dǫrōwạ = *Sk.* dǫrūwạ *f.* (*pl.* dǫrǫyī) =
dǫrawạ.

dos A. (dǫs) *x* yā zaunạ ∼ it sits firmly
(= dạ6as *q.v.*).

B. (dǫs) (1) yā digō dǫs dǫs it
dripped slowly. (2) *m.* or *adv.* fear, in
fear (= dạr *q.v.*).

dosa A. (dǫsā) *Vb.* 2 (*p.o.* dǫshē, *n.o.*
dǫshi). (1) set out for *x* hanyạn naŋ,
inā ta dǫsā where does this road lead
to ? yā dǫshi Kanǫ he set out for Kano.
(2) (*a*) went to place by direct route *x*
yā dǫshi Kanǫ he made a bee-line for
Kano. sun dōsō naŋ they've come here
direct (= dạidạitạ 1*b* = kịntatạ 1 =
Kt dịŋgā 2).   sanyī yā dōsō the cold
season is near. (*b*) tsawam fagyam
fāmā yā dǫshi miḷ 400 the war-front
extends to 400 miles. (*c*) wuriṇ naŋ
yā dǫshi mil 200 dạgạ Kanǫ that
place is 200 miles from Kano.

B. (dōsạ) (1) *Vb.* 1A (*a*) hafted (a
tool) *x* yā ∼ gạtarī ạ ƙōtạ he hafted the
axe (= gwa6ạ = kwa6ạ), *cf.* kwa6ẹ.
(*b*) set P. at task *x* ạ kai mụ, ạ ∼ take
us and set us to work ! (*c*) kept on
doing *x* yā ∼ tạfīyạ he kept on
travelling (= diŋgạ). (*d*) yā ∼ ƙwaryā
ạ bạkī = dō6ạ 1. (*e*) maƙẹrī yā ∼
tarō the smith fixed a spindle to the
threepenny bit (= dạnạ 3 *q.v.*). (*f*)
Vd. sạri dōsa. (2) *f.* (*a*) type of girls'
dance. (*b*) type of cloth. (*c*) ∼ gạtariŋ
Gwārī *epithet of* the axe dandǫsa.

dosana A. (dōsạna) *Vb.* 2 (1) obtained.
(2) yā ∼ gạ mālạminsạ he obtained his
knowledge from his teacher.   (3) yā
dǫsạni ạlfarmā wurinsụ he's related to
those important persons.

B. (dōsạnā) *Vb.* 1C (1) applied fire to
x yā dǫsạnạ wutā ạ dākị, *etc.*, he set
fire to house (= dạnạ 4*a* *q.v.*).   (2)
an dǫsạnạ sakīyạ abscess has been
punctured with hot arrow-head to let
out pus. (3) an dǫsạnạ hancintạ her
nostril's been pierced to insert stone
for adornment.

doshe A. (dōshē) (1) *m.* short-cut, direct-road *x* hanyan naŋ ∽ cẹ̃ = yaŋkẽ 2 = sōkẽ 3 = tōtar = fẽtsē (*cf.* gẽwayē). (2) *Vd.* dōsā.

　B. (dōshẹ) *Vb.* 1A = dōsā 2.

doshi A. (dōshi) *Vd.* dōsā.

　B. (dōshị) *m.* acting *as in* dōsạ.

dōshirọ *m., f.* (*sg., pl.*) simpleton.

doso A. (dōsō) *m., f.* (*sg., pl.*). (1) fool. (2) grubby P. (3) name of a town in Zabarma.

　B. (dōsō) *Vd.* dōsā.

dososo A. (dōsōsọ) *m.* (*f.* dōsōsūwā) = dōsō 1, 2.

　B. (dōsōsọ) *x* yanā dạ bạ̄kī ∽ he's thicklipped (= dạfsạssạr).

dōyạ *f.* (*sg., pl.*). (1) (*a*) (i) yam (*epithet is* ∽ cịmar mutānaŋ kudụ), *Vd.* būsạ. (ii) cassava (= rōgọ). (2) *Zar.* tuber, bulb *x* ganyan naŋ ya kạn yi ∽ ạ ƙasạ this plant has a tuber. (3) dādin ∽ dạ mạn jā superficial friendship which covers enmity. irịn zamansụ, irịn zamā nẹ̃ na ∽ dạ mạn jā, bisạ-bisạ they are merely outwardly on friendly terms. (4) dōyạr bisạ certain edible bulbs of yam family (*Dioscorea*). (5) dōyạr dājị wild cassava. (6) dōyạr kudụ = 1*a.*i. *(7) = barạ gurbị. (8) *Vd.* zạuna (= tsugụna) kạ ci dōyạ.

dọ̄yī *m.* (1) (*a*) stench (= wārī). (*b*) odour of musk. (*c*) lạ̄bārịn naŋ yā fārạ ∽ this news is becoming wearisome (= wārī). (2) yanā jịn dọ̄yim mutānē = yanā jịn dọ̄yin dūnīyạ he's haughty. (3) mun ji dọ̄yim maganạ we've heard rumours of it. (4) yā shā dọ̄yin dafị he's heard of his impending arrest. (5) yā cẹ̃ " dạ dọ̄yī " *Vd.* cẹ̃ 1*b.* (6) dạddawā dạ dọ̄yī *Vd.* 6ērā 1*g.*

Dōzạ *Kt.* (1) *epithet of* dōrinā *q.v.* (2) ∽ (= Na rēgạ) maị gidā ɗayā wāwā *epithet of* ƙurēgē.

dōzuŋ *Eng. m.* (*used in trading*) dozen.

drọ = drọk *Eng. m.* (*sg., pl.*) drawer in table, etc.

dū (1) all (= dukạ *q.v.*). (2) azụmin ∽ garī *m.* month of Ramalaŋ.

ɗụ̄ *adv.* moving in large numbers *x* sun zō ∽ many have come.

dụ'ā'ị = ạddu'ạ.

dub *Vd.* dub dub dub.

duba A. (dūbạ) *Vb.* 1A (*progressive generally uses* dūbā *q.v.*). (1) looked *x* dạ sukạ ji hakạ, sukạ ∽ sukạ gan shị on hearing this, they looked and saw him. yanā dūbạ̄wā he's having a look round, he's looking about him. (2) (*a*) (i) looked at P. or T. (ii) *Vd.* dụ̄bā. (*b*) took aim at (= ạunā 5). (*c*) paid careful attention to (work). (3) inspected *x* (*a*) nā ∽ ɗākunạ dukạ, baŋ gan shị ba I examined all the houses, but didn't see him. (*b*) dụ̄bạ ta wuyạnsạ *Vd.* rịgā 1*o.* (4) divined with sand *x* kạ kumạ dūbạ̄wā make another horoscope with sand ! (*Vd.* dūbā 2). (5) (*a*) yā ∽ hanyạ tasụ he awaited them. (*b*) (i) dụ̄bạ mini hanyạ you'll be wise to accept my advice ! (ii) dụ̄ba mini hanyạ, makāfọ yā sō tsēgụmī take care you don't speak against a P. in his hearing ! (*cf.* kaŋkị 2*b*). (6) read to oneself silently (*cf.* bịya 1*b*, karạntā, nazạrī 2). (7) visited sick P. *x* zā ni ṇ ∽ shi = zā ni ṇ ∽ lāfịyạ tasạ I'll go and see how he is.

　B. (dụ̄bā) *Vb.* 2 (*progressive generally uses* dūbā). (1) = dūbạ *except* 7. (2) ạ dụ̄bi rūwā, ạ dụ̄bi tsạkī look before you leap !, all is not gold that glitters. (3) wạ̄ ta dụ̄bā = dūbal.

　C. (dūbā) *m.* (1) (*forms progressive of* dūbạ, dụ̄bā) *x* tanā dūbansạ she's looking at him. n nā̄ masạ dūbam mụtụm nẹ̃ wạndạ . . . I regard him as a person who . . . iŋ kā bī shị dạ ∽ if you glance at it. mạ̄sū dūbaŋ gạba far-seeing people. (2) fortune-telling with sand *x* yā yi minị ∽ he cast my horoscope. yanā ∽ he's a fortune-teller (= tsịŋkāyā 3 = tụhumạ 2*b* = haɗɗị = awọ 4 = hịsābị = ƙasā 3 = *Kt.* arwā), *Vd.* farī 2*d*, bugā 4. (3) *Vd.* dūban-*compounds.*

dubāgirā *f.* flowers or leaves of young desert-date (adūwạ).

dubāƙē *m.* those employed in beating (dạ6ē) floor of house.

dūbal *used in* 'yar ∽ *Sk.* spinning-top game (= wạ̄ ta dụ̄bā).

dubalaŋ *m.* type of thick, white calico.

dūbạlī (*French* double) *m.* 2-franc piece.

duban bakin gatari (dūbam bạ̄kịŋ gạtarī) *Vd.* sārā 5.

duban biyu (dūbam bīyŭ shā bīyar) *m.* looking contemptuously at P.

dūbaŋ gaba *Vd.* dūbā.

dūbā garī *m.* (*sg.*, *pl.*) sanitary inspector.

dūbaŋ garkę *m.* squinting, cast in eye (= farallī = dūbaŋ gōrā 1).

dūbaŋ gōrā *m.* (1) = dūbaŋ garkę. (2) closing one eye (= kannē).

dūbaŋ hadiriŋ kājī *m.* = dūbam mashēƙā ayā.

dūbaŋ ƙudā *Vd.* kudā 1*e.*

duban mashɛka aya (dūbam mashēƙā ayā) *m.* (1) looking contemptuously at P. (2) *Vd.* dūban rēni.

dūban rēni *m.* (1) = dūban mashēƙā ayā. (2) da ∼ gāra gābā ta tsaya (*said by* marōƙā) rather enmity than being scorned !

dūban rūdūwā *m.* = dūbaŋ garkę.

dubārą *Nor.* = dabārą.

dubāta *Vd.* dubū 2*a.ii.*

dūbayyą *f.* (1) mutual esteem. (2) foresight (= tsiŋkāyā).

dubbai *Vd.* dubū.

dub dub dub *m.* noise of rat's step.

dūbę *Vb.* 1A looked thoroughly, looked at all of (*cf.* dūba).

ɗubga A. (ɗubgā) = ɗibgā.

B. (ɗubgą) = ɗibgą.

dūbi *m.* (1) dūbin zumą collecting honey (*Vd.* zumą 1d.i). (2) *Kt.* = dūbā.

dubtū *m.* (1) early start on journey (= sammakō). (2) yaŋ shan ∼ da shī he's toiling away at it.

dubū *f.* (*pl.* dubbai) (1) (*a*) (i) thousand *x* ∼ tā fi ɗarī a thousand exceeds a hundred. dōki ∼ 1,000 cavalry. ∼ ukų 3,000 (*Vd.* Mod. Gram. 108*f*). suŋā naŋ dubū a kaŋ wata dubū they are innumerable. (ii) *Vd.* zambar. (*b*) million *x* ∼ ukų 3 million (*Vd.* Mod. Gram. 108 *f*). (2) (*a*) dubun thousands of *x* (i) da dubunsą there are thousands like him. munā da dubunsu we have thousands of them. bāyan dubuŋ gaisūwā after best greetings, I'm writing to say that … (ii) dubun dubāta myriads and myriads. (*b*) (dubbai *is sometimes used with noun in singular*) *x* sōją dubbai countless soldiers. jama'a dubbai a huge crowd.

dubban sōjąn da aką kāmą the thousands of troops who were captured.

mutānē dubbai countless numbers of people. suŋā naŋ dubbai they're innumerable. (3) yā ci ∼ he gripped mane to avoid falling off horse. (4) yā san ∼, dubū tā san shi he's renowned. (5) a rabą dą ∼ (*said by women*) may your bereavement sit lightly on you ! (6) gaskīyā wuyar fadā garētą ; iŋ kā fadi, sāi ką hau ɗan dubū don't expect popularity if you tell people the truth ! (7) *Kt.* former forced levy when a chief returned from war or visit to Sarkim Musulmī at Sokoto. (8) sūką dubū *Vd.* sūką 7. (9) tākalmī dubū *Vd.* tākalmī 5. (10) dubū ɗarī *Vd.* cācā 1b. (11) askar dubū *Vd.* askā 1b. (12) tā fi dubū *Vd.* mariƙicī. (13) *Vd.* daŋki dubū.

dubū (1) yaŋ ∼ dą ∼ it's a mere stone's throw away (= *Kt.* tubū). (2) *m.* gleet, etc. (3) dubū-dubū immediately *x* ∼ ya jē, ya kōmō kę naŋ.

dubulaŋ *m.* type of thick, white calico.

dubura *Ar. f.* (1) anus (= tsūlīyā *q.v.*). (2) *cf.* addibirī.

dubūraŋ *m.* (1) large well-stocked market. (2) populous town. (3) *Kt.* renowned P.

dubūrī *Sk. m.* = dubūrā.

dubus *adj. m., f.* (*sg., pl.*) quite near.

dubus-dubus *Kt.* = shifit-shifit.

dūci *Sk.*, *Kt. m.* stone (= dūtsę *q.v.*).

duɗalī = duɗɗalī.

dud dą in spite of (*Vd.* duką).

duɗɗalī *m.* (1) the contest called sharo *q.v.* (2) arena for *such* contest. (3) smoky-fire made of sābarą or yāyi, lit to keep flies away from cows.

dudduɓā *f.* big-made girl.

dudduƙa *f.* (*sg., pl.*) Sacred (White) Ibis (*Threskiornis œthiopicus*) = jinjimī.

duddugā = diddigā.

dudduge A. (duddugē) *Vb.* 3A = diddigē.

B. (dudduge) *m.* = diddige.

duddugī *m.* (1) nā bi duddugim magana I investigated it. (2) *Sk.* yā ciką ∼ he's mischief-maker.

dudduƙā *Vb.* 3A crouched. yaŋ dudduƙe he's crouching down (*cf.* madudduƙā). dudduƙe yakę tafīyą he's riding bent over his saddle.

duddu̱lā = d̶udd̶u̱lā *Vb.* 1C nā̱ duddu̱la̱
bu̱ta̱ a̱ rūwa I filled the narrow-
mouthed gourd-bottle by immersion
(= bulbu̱lā *q.v.*).

duddūnīyā *Kt. f.* heel (= dundūnīyā
q.v.).

du̱ddu̱ru̱ *m.* (1) any stream. du̱ddu̱ru̱ŋ
Gayā the marshy area between Kano
and dūtsa̱ŋ Ga̱dā̱wur. (2) yā ga̱mu
da̱ ~ he got sleeping sickness (= cī-
wo̱n 2). (3) *Vd.* kurcīyā 1*h.*

du̱ddūsā *m., f. (pl.* dūsā̱sā) corpulent (*cf.*
dūshī).

d̶ud̶d̶uskā *Sk.* an nika̱ shi ~ it's finely-
ground (= lilis).

Dūdu̱ name for any woman called Ka̱nde
q.v. (= Dūdūwā).

dūdūdū *adv.* at the moment *x* dōki̱n na̱ŋ ~
ba̱i fi d̶a̱rī ba at the moment, the horses
are not above a hundred. ~ na̱ŋ ga̱ba,
ba̱ za̱i wuce̱ kwānā 10 ba as far as I
can see, it won't take more than ten
days from now to do.

dūdūwā *f.* (1) type of children's song.
(2) = Dūdu̱.

dufa̱ffā *Vd.* duhūwa̱.

duffa̱ *f.* (1) game where children pelt each
other with clods. (2) kōwā ya ce̱
" a̱ yi ~ ", yā tāka̱ dūtse̱ nē there's more
than meets the eye ! (= ma̱kāfo̱ 1*k*).

duftū = dubtū.

dufu̱ *m.* = duhu̱.

dugā̱dugī *m. (pl.* du̱gā̱du̱gai) heel (*Vd.*
diddige̱).

dūgāji *m., f. (sg., pl*). (1) grubby lout.
(2) Dūgāji name for any man called
Īsā.

d̶ugō *m.* = d̶igō.

du̱gu-du̱gu = du̱'gu-du̱gū " *m.* (1) yā yi ~
= ga̱rī yā yi masa̱ ~ he's in difficulties,
nonplussed. (2) du̱'gu-du̱gū" = du̱r'gu-
du̱rgū".

d̶ugul *m.* shortness (= d̶igil *q.v.*).

dugulō = du̱gu̱lō *m., f. (sg., pl*). fool.

du̱gum *adv.* silently and pensively
(= ju̱gum *q.v.*).

du̱gu̱mājī = du̱gu̱zu̱ŋ.

dugumi A. (dugumī) *m.* persevering at *x*
yanā̱ dugumi̱n aiki̱.
   B. (du̱gumī) *Kt.* = du̱gum.

dugunzuma A. (du̱gu̱nzuma̱) (1) *Vb.*
3B (*a*) became serious *x* fad̶a̱ŋ yā ~

the quarrel's got beyond control (*cf.*
dugunzumī). (*b*) ra̱nsa̱ yā ~ he felt
desperate. (2) *Vb.* 2 is (was) beyond
one's power to deal with *x* fad̶a̱ŋ yā
du̱gu̱nzu̱mē ni̱.
   B. (dugunzu̱mā) *Vb.* 1D *x* sun
du̱gu̱nzu̱ma̱ ja̱ma'a̱ they incited, stirred
up the public.

dugunzumī *m.* excess of *x* yanā̱ da̱ du̱gun-
zumi̱n gāshi̱ (gēmu̱) he has shaggy
hair (beard). dugunzumi̱n aiki̱ too
much work.

dugurguje A. (dugurgu̱jē) disintegrated,
etc. (= dagarga̱jē *q.v.*).
   B. (du̱gu̱rgu̱jē) *Vd.* du̱gu̱rguza̱.

dugurguji A. (du̱gu̱rgu̱jī) *x* d̶an du̱gurgu̱jī
m. (*f.* 'yar du̱gu̱rgu̱zā) *pl.* du̱gu̱rgu̱zai
short P.
   B. (du̱gu̱rgu̱ji) *Vd.* du̱gu̱rguza̱.

dugurgur *m.* shortness (= d̶igil *q.v.*).

dugurguza A. (du̱gu̱rguza̱) *Vb.* 2 (*p.o.*
du̱gu̱rgu̱jē, *n.o.* du̱gu̱rgu̱ji) ate much of
(= da̱ga̱rgaza̱ *q.v.*).
   B. (du̱gurgu̱zā) *Vd.* du̱gurgu̱jī.

du̱gurji̱ *m.* large amount *x* tanā̱ du̱gurji̱n
nika̱ she's doing much grinding. yanā̱
du̱gurji̱n kūkā he's very sad.

du̱guru̱ *m.* (1) tireless manual worker.
(2) *Kt.* name of famous evil spirit.

du̱gu̱zu̱ŋ *x* (1) yā yi su̱mā ~ he's shaggy-
haired. (2) yā zō da̱ tsu̱mmā ~ he
came clad in rags.

du̱gu̱zunzu̱mī *m.* (*f.* du̱gu̱zunzu̱mā) *pl.*
du̱gu̱zu̱nzu̱mai shaggy-haired.

duhu̱ *m.* (1) (*a*) darkness *x* (i) yā yi ~ =
an yi ~ = anā̱ ~ = ga̱rī yā yi ~ =
duhu̱ yā yī night's fallen. (ii) yā yi ~
k̶irin it's pitch-dark. dāki̱n na̱ŋ yā
yi ~ this is a dark room. (ii) kada̱ ka̱
yi mini̱ ~ don't stand there blocking
out my light ! (iii) rashi̱n sani̱ yā fi
darē ~ nothing is worse than
ignorance. (iv) ignorance *x* su̱nā̱
cikin duhu̱ they are uneducated, ignorant. yā jāwō su̱ da̱ga duhu̱ he
educated, enlightened them. a̱bi̱ŋ
yā shige̱ mana̱ duhu̱ the affair mystifies
us. (v) ba̱ zā a̱ k̶āra̱ ganin duhu̱nsa̱ a̱
ma̱jalisa̱ ba his presence will never be
again seen in the council-chamber.
(vi) wanna̱ŋ ra̱ban duhu̱ nē this is an
unfair sharing-out (*Vd.* jibgā 2). (vii)

jĩfan ∼ *Vd.* jĩfa̧ 6. (*b*) (i) Allā ya̧
yāyȩ masa̧ duhu̧ŋ kaba̧rī God lighten
for him the darkness of the grave !
(*Vd.* ta̧'azīyya̧ ; gaisūwā 5). (ii)
Allā ya̧ ƙāra̧ maka̧ duhu̧ŋ kaba̧rī
may you rot in a gloomy grave ! (*c*)
Audu̧ yā yi ∼ Audu's blind. (2) dark
colour *x* yā yi ∼ it's a dark colour
(*when contrasted ; cf.* farī). shūdi̧
yā yi ∼ it's a dark blue. (3) denseness
x (*a*) (i) ƙasā tā yi ∼ the land is thickly
wooded (*cf.* duhūwa̧, baƙī 2). (ii) ∼
ba̧ wurim 6uyā *Vd.* fagē 2*b*. (iii) sāƙan
na̧m ba̧ ta da̧ ∼ this is not a close
weave. (iv) gōna̧r tā yi ∼ the farm has
a dense crop. (5) duhu̧ŋ kä̧i ga̧rēshi
he is a blockhead. (6) duhu̧n rōgo̧ =
duhu̧ŋ ƙyāra̧ = duhu̧m bāgȩ *Kt* " a
broken reed " (= wālā 2). (7) waḑa̧rī
cikin ∼ *Vd.* waḑa̧rī 1*d*. (8) jāwō da̧ga̧
∼ *Vd.* da̧ga̧ 1*a*.ii. (9) dāƙi da̧ ∼ *Vd.*
dambē 2. (10) *Vd.* ba̧ duhu̧. (11) daukar
∼ *Vd.* gundurū.
duhuli̧ *Ar. m.* (*polite term*) sexual intercourse (= ji̧mā'i̧ *q.v.*).
duhunta̧ (1) *Vb.* 2 (*p.o.* du̧hu̧ncē, *n.o.*
du̧hu̧nci) dumbfounded. (2) *Vb.* 3B
is (was) dark *x* darē yā ∼ ya̧u to-
night it is very dark.
duhūwa̧ *f.* (*pl.* duhūwōyī = *Kt.* dufa̧ffā
= *Kt.* duhwa̧hwā). (1) thickly-wooded
place in otherwise open country (*cf.*
duhu̧ 3, kurmi, sarƙaƙƙīyā, baƙī 2) =
Kt. ƙuncī 4. (2) yā shiga ∼ he's in rage.
Dūjal (*Ar.* Addajjālu) Antichrist.
Dujamba̧r *m.* December.
duje A. (dūjȩ) *Vb.* 1A *x* yā ∼ mini̧ gwīwa̧
it grazed my knee.
    B. (dūjȩ) *Vd.* dūzā.
dūji *Vd.* dūzā.
duka A. (duka̧) (1) (*a*) every *x* dū mu̧tu̧m =
duk mu̧tu̧m = duka̧ mu̧tu̧m = duka̧m
mu̧tu̧m = mu̧tu̧m duka̧ everyone. (*b*)
duka̧ rāƙumi ha̧msiŋ (= rāƙumī ha̧msiŋ
duka̧), a̧ bā da̧ bana hudū on every
50 camels, one must pay tithe of a
four-year-old one. (*c*) duk kōwā yā
sani̧ everyone knows. (*d*) duk kōi̧nā
everywhere (*cf.* 3 *below*). (*e*) duka̧ ma̧i
sana'a̧ *Vd.* ba̧bba 2*d*. (2) (*a*) all *pl.*
x mutā̧nē dū = mutā̧nē duk = mutā̧nē
duka̧ = dū mutā̧nē = duk mutā̧nē =

duka̧ mutā̧nē = dukam mutā̧nē all
people, all the people. a̧shē duk kŭ,
tsa̧mmāni̧ kukȩ̄ yā ba̧ su̧ ? well, do
you all think that he gave it them ?
(*b*) duka̧ bīyū both. duka̧ uku̧ all three
of them, us, etc. (*c*) (i) entirely *x*
duk am bā shi̧ 'yan Ja̧bū they paid him
entirely in counterfeit. duk ba̧ ka̧
sani̧ ba̧ ? do you know nothing at all
about it ? duk kā 6āta̧ mini̧ lōka̧cī
a̧ banzā you've entirely wasted my
time. a̧shē, dā̧ duk haka̧ a̧l'ama̧ri̧ŋ
ya̧kȩ̄ ? is this all the whole matter
amounts to ? (ii) in . . . entirely
(cikin *often omitted*) *x* duk cikin yāƙi̧n
naŋ throughout that war. duk dūnīya̧
in the whole world. duk ga̧ri̧ŋ in the
whole town. duk tsawan dā̧muna̧n
naŋ throughout that wet season (*cf.*
4 *below*). (3) (*imparts indefinite sense*) *x*
i̧nda̧ muka̧ jē duka̧, sǎi mu̧ŋ gan shi̧
wherever we went (go), we saw (see) him
(= kōi̧nā : *for alternative constructions,*
Vd. Mod. Gram. 185). duk i̧nda̧ na nȩmā,
ba̧n sā̧mē shi̧ ba wherever I sought I
didn't find him. lōka̧ci̧n da̧ na zō duka̧
(= duk lōka̧ci̧n da̧ na zō), sǎi nā gan
shi̧ whenever I came (come), I saw
(see) him (= kōya̧ushē *Vd.* Mod. Gram.
185). a̧bin da̧ ya bā mu̧ duka̧, sǎi mu̧ŋ ƙi
whatever he offered (offers) us, we
refused (refuse) (= kōmē, *Vd.* Mod.
Gram. 185). wa̧nda̧ ya zō duka̧
(= duka̧ŋ wa̧nda̧ ya zō, *Vd.* wa̧nda̧ 4),
ba̧m bā shi̧ ba no matter who came, I
gave nothing (= kōwā). hanya̧d da̧
muka̧ bi duka̧ (= kōwa̧cȩ hanya̧ muka̧
bi), sǎi mu̧ŋ ga̧ji whatever road we
follow, we tire. san da̧ ya zō duka̧,
sunā̧ (= sukȩ̄) ƙara̧tū whenever he
came, they were reading. duk kōwā
ya bā mu̧, sǎi mun yi murna̧ whoever
gave (gives) us, we were (are) pleased
(= kōwā, *Vd.* 185). duk wani aiki̧
mu̧tu̧m ya yi whatever act a man does.
duk kōi̧nā muka̧ ta̧fi wherever we went
(go), *cf.* 1*d*. duk ran ra̧nsa̧ ya sō, sǎi
ya̧ yī he can do it whatever time he
feels inclined. duk kō nawa̧ suka̧
bīyā whatever sum they paid. duk
sa̧d da̧ wani ya ta6a̧ ni any time that
anybody attacks me . . . (4) (*a*) whole

of *x* dukạŋ ƙayạ the whole of the thorns. dukạm mụgụntā the whole wickedness. yā cịnyẹ nāmạ dukạnsạ he ate up all the meat. (*b*) *cf.* 2*c*.ii *above.* (*c*) dū gạrī *Vd.* azụmī 6. (5) dū dạ hakạ = duk dạ hakạ = dud dạ hakạ nevertheless *x* kō dạ ya cẹ hakạ, duk dạ wannạŋ, haŋkạlinsạ nạ̄ wajan d̃ansạ though he spoke so, his thoughts were on his son. sụŋ kēwạyē mu, ạmmā duk dạ hakạ mukạ yi ta yāƙị they surrounded us but nevertheless we put up a fight. duk dạ wannạŋ, sǎi sukạ ƙī nevertheless they refused. ạmmā duk wannạn nīsā, bạ sụ gạji ba in spite of this distance they did not tire. duk yawạnsụ bạ su dạ ƙarfī in spite of their numbers, they have no strength. (6) duk (= dud̃) d̃ayā nẹ̄ = dū d̃ayā nẹ̄ = dukạ d̃ayā nẹ̄ it's all the same, it doesn't matter. (7) mại hannū dukạ dāma *m., f.* liberal P. (8) *Vd.* mū dukạ. (9) *cf.* dukkạ, duk dạ duk. (10) dud dạ kạ̄lō *Vd.* kạ̄lō.

B. (dūkạ) *m.* (1) (*secondary v.n. of* dōkā) *x* (*a*) yanạ̄ dūkạntạ he's beating her. (*b*) dūkạn rūwā bạ yā hanạ gwạrjē amō ba envy cannot cause fate to deviate. (*c*) bạ dūkạn rūwan samạ kẹ dạ cīwọ ba, rūwạŋ ganyē it is the humiliation put on one by an underling that irks one, not that done by a superior. (*d*) dūkạŋ kạ̄wō wuƙā *Vd.* wuƙā 1*e*. (*e*) anạ̄ dūkạn tēkị *Vd.* tēkị 1*b*. (*f*) duhụ yanạ̄ dūkạn duhụ tit for tat ! (*g*) dạ shī akẹ̄ ∼ *Vd.* sạndā 1*j*. (2) a thrashing, punch, blow *x* (*a*) yā yi minị ∼ = yā sạ̄mē nị dạ ∼ he struck me. (*b*) ∼ dạ gūrụ, ∼ dạ lāyạ, auram mutạ̄nan yạnzu marriage these days is nothing but bitter strife. (*c*) dūkạn ƙwaryā akẹ̄ yi matạ one wife is denying rival wife or latter's child proper share of food (= daŋgwạrī 2 = ƙwaryā 9*a*). (*d*) *Vd.* gānin ∼. (*e*) harārạ bạ̄ ∼ ba cẹ̄ hard words break no bones. (3) rạ̄gwan naŋ ∼ gạrēshị this ram butts. (4) zạzzạɓī yanạ̄ dūkạnsụ they have fever. (5) yā ci (= yā shā) ∼ he was beaten.

C. (dūkā) *Vb.* (*must have object*) *x*

yā ∼ nị he beat me, he struck me (= dōkā).

duƙa A. (dūƙạ) *Vb.* 3A. (1) (*a*) stooped, bent down. (*b*) *Vd.* gạbạ-gạbạ. (2) bạ zā kạ sayar ba sǎi kạ ∼ you won't find a buyer unless you reduce the price. (3) set to with a will *x* yā ∼ har shī mā ya zamā mālạmī he worked on and on till he became a scholar. sun ∼ cikin shāwarạ they considered deeply. sun ∼ hīrā they settled down to a good chat. (4) set out. (5) yā ∼ ạ gụje he fled.

B. (dụƙā) *Vb.* 2 (*in coarse talk*) had intercourse with woman (= cī 16*a q.v.*). dūƙad dạ *Vb.* 4B *Kt.* yā ∼ kǎị he bent his head (= suŋkwīyad dạ).

duƙạ̄kē *m.* (*secondary v.n. of* dịkākạ *q.v.*) *x* sunạ̄ dụƙạ̄kyan aikị they're working doggedly, *etc.*

dūkanci *m.* being a leather-worker. dụ̄ƙạ̄wā leather-workers (*Vd.* bạdūkụ).

duk dạ duk *m.* reducing corn to flour without doing pounding for removal of bran (sụrfē) = dạki dukạ.

duƙe A. (dụ̄ƙe) *m.* (1) *x* (*a*) yanạ̄ ∼ he's stooping. (*b*) act of stooping *x* yā kōmạ dụ̄ƙyansạ he resumed his stooping. (2) na ∼, bạ ka barạ sǎi wạndạ ya bar kạ *epithet of* farm ŋg (nōmā). *N.B.—There is here pun on the two senses* barạ A.2 1 *and* 2.

B. (dūƙẹ) *Vb.* 3B slumped *x* kạsūwā tā ∼ this market has lost its trade. kạsūwar ạbin naŋ tā ∼ this commodity's slumped. dūnīyạ tā ∼ masạ his prosperity's declined.

dūkịyā *f.* (*pl.* dūkōkī = dūkīyōyī). (1) (*a*) wealth. (*b*) ∼ gāshịŋ hancị it's painful to lose one's property ! (*c*) kwānā lāfịyạ ∼ it's a great asset to pass a peaceful night. (*d*) zūcịyā tā fị ∼ it's better to be wise than wealthy. (*e*) rǎị yā fị dūkịyā health is better than wealth. (*f*) gạyạ mại zūcịyā bịkī, bạ mại dūkịyā ba court the resolute, not the rich ! (*g*) dūkịyar gādọ *Vd.* sạna'ạ. (2) abundant property. (3) kan ∼ *m.* trading-capital (= jārị). (4) dūkịyar samạ *Vd.* tạntabạrā.

dukkạ emphatic form of dukạ *x* dukkạnsụ *all* of them.

dukkạcī *m.* the whole *x* dukkạcinsụ all of them (= ɗakwacī = dukkạnī).

dukkani A. (dukkạnī) *m.* = dukkạcī.

*B. (dukkānị) *Ar. m.* shop (= kạntī).

dụkkī *Sk. m.* (*pl.* dukkōkī) the nettle-tree (*Celtis integrifolia*) = zụ̄wō.

dukkōkī *Vd.* dụkkī.

dūkōkī *Vd.* dūkị̄yā.

ɗukụ *m.* (1) (*in coarse talk*) having sexual intercourse with *x* yā sạ̄mi yārinyạ, yanạ̄ ɗukụntạ (*cf.* dịkā). (2) ɗukụm birị dragging oneself up a tree.

duku-duku (1) *x* mum fịta tun ⌒ we started at earliest dawn. (2) *Vd.* duru-duru ; dukū-dụkū.

dukū-dụkū A. (dukū-dụkū) (1) mum fịta tuŋ kạ̄jī ⌒ = duku-duku. (2) sunạ̄ yịŋ kạ̄jī ⌒ villagers are eating dawn-meal of Ramadan (sạhụr). (3) large and round (*pl.*) *x* rūwā yā sakō ⌒ rain (*e.g.* harvest-rain) fell in large drops.

B. (dụkū-dụkū) *x* tạfi ⌒ kadạ sụ gaŋ kạ go stealthily or crouchingly lest you be seen !

dụkuf *Sk. m.* shortness *x* (1) gạjērē nẹ̄ ⌒ dạ shī he (it) is short. (2) ɗan ⌒ (*f.* 'yar ⌒) *pl.* 'yan ⌒ short P.

dukufạ = dụkufạ *Vb.* 3B *x* yā ⌒ kaŋ aikịŋ he devoted all his energy to the work.

dukuku A. (dụkūkụ) *m., f.* glumly hesitant P.

B. (dụkụkụ) *x* nā ga fuskạssạ ⌒ I noticed he was glumly hesitant.

dụkulkụshī *x* ɗan dụkulkụshī = dụkur-kụshī.

dūkūmạ *Sk. f.* palmwood-canoe (= bụŋgū-buŋgū).

dụkụmcē *Sk. m.* an cī shị ⌒ he was swindled,

dụkum-dụkum *adv.* travelling in dark (= fụgum-fụgum *q.v.*).

dụkumī *m.* (*f.* dụkumā) hornless ox, ram, or goat.

dukuŋ-dukuŋ filthy (= dikiŋ-dikiŋ *q.v.*).

dụkuŋkụnē *Vb.* 3A (1) is (was) filthy. (2) is (was) crumpled.

dụkurkụrī = dụkurkụr = dụkurkụs *m.* (*f.* dụkurkụrā = dụkurkụsā) *pl.* dụkur-kụrai = dụkurkụsai *used in* ɗan dụkur-kụrī *m.* (*f.* 'yar dụkurkụrā) *pl.* 'yan dụkurkụrai short P.

---

dukụrṁushị *x* ɗan dukụrmushị short P.

dukus (1) *x* gạjērē nẹ̄ ⌒ dạ shī he (it) is short. (2) dukus *f.* = gujīyā ⌒ *q.v.* (3) *m.* type of fowl-stealing.

dụkushī = dụkushī *m.* (*pl.* dụkụsai = dụkụsai). (1) (*a*) colt. (*b*) dụkushin rạ̄kụmī camel-foal. (*c*) dụkushin sạ̄ bull-calf. (2) dụkụsā = dukusā = dụkusar gōdị̄yā filly. (*b*) dụkusar rạ̄kụmā female camel-foal. (*c*) dụku-sar sānị̄yā young virgin cow. (*d*) *Kt.* dụkusā *f.* = dukus 2. (3) dụkushim fariŋ watạ young moon. (4) dụkushiŋ gēmụ newly-sprouted beard. (5) dụkushiŋ kurjī newly-appeared pustule. (6) ɗan dụkushī (*a*) = 1 *above.* (*b*) leapfrog.

dukụsūrụ *x* ɗan dukụsūrụ *m.* short man.

dụkuskus *m.* (*f.* dụkuskụsā) *pl.* dụkụs-kụsai short P.

dukwī *m.* (1) children's trick of lighting cotton-rag on toe of sleeper. (2) magic medicine of fowl-thieves to silence fowls.

ɗul *adv. x* gạ̄ shi caŋ ⌒ there it is, far over there !

dulaskē *Kt. m.* fool.

dūlāyē *Vd.* dūlū.

ɗul-ɗul *m.* = tul-tul *q.v.*

duldụlā *Vb.* 1C *Sk.* nā duldụlạ rūwā ạ būtạ I filled the gourd-bottle by immersion (= bulbụlā *q.v.*).

dūlẹ-dūlẹ *m.* gạrī yā yi ⌒ sky's a bit overcast.

dullu A. (dullū) *Sk. m.* boy's arrow of tamarind (tsāmị̄yā) = kundạ 1.

B. (dụllū) *m.* (*sg., pl.*) the fig-tree *Ficus sp.*

du mạyā *Sk.* = dulmụyā.

dulmuya A. (dụlmụyạ = dụlmīyạ) *Vb.* 3B sank far into *x* (1) yā ⌒ cikin rūwa he sank in the water (= diluŋ 1*b*). (2) yā ⌒ cikim mạganạ (*a*) he studied it deeply. (*b*) he became involved in it.

B. (dulmụyā) *Vb.* 1C immersed T. in.

dulmuyad dạ *Vb.* 4A. (1) engulfed *x* kōgī yā ⌒ shī. (2) was cause of downfall of P.

dulmụyē *Vb.* 3A = dụlmuyạ.

dūlū *m.* (*pl.* dūlāyē) type of deep basket.

dụlụlụ *x* yanạ̄ dạ yaukī ⌒ it's very viscous.

dulunta
232
dumbū

duluntạ *Vb.* 2 (*p.o.* **dulunçē**, *n.o.* **dulunci**) *Sk.* treat P. tyrannically (= **zạluntạ**).

dum A. (**dum**) *x* **yā shigō** ⁓ he entered unceremoniously.

B. (**dum**) *x* **kạnsạ yā yi** ⁓ his hair stood on end.

dum A. (**dum**) (1) **an dạukē** ⁓ they've been completely removed. (2) **ajịyē shi** ⁓ put it down carefully!

B. (**dum**) (1) *x* **yanạ dạ dọyī** ⁓ it has a frightful stench. (2) *Vd.* **dumdum**.

duma A. (**dumā**) *m.* (*pl.* **dumạmē**) (1) (*a*) *generic name for the* gourds and pumpkins (*cucurbitaceae*) ; *the various types are named differently according to their shapes, i.e.* **ƙwaryā** ; **lūdạyī** ; **zụnġurū** ; **būtạ** ; **shạntū**. (*b*) *Vd.* **dạukạn dumā** ; **bumbū**. (*c*) *Vd. compounds of* **duman**. (*d*) **madạ̃cī yanạ radạn dumā** = **dumā yanạ radạm madạ̃cī** the pot is calling the kettle black. (*e*) **fid dạ jạkī dạgạ** ⁓ *Vd.* **jạkī** 1*j*. (*f*) **bạbban** ⁓ **nē** *Vd.* **fạ̃fā** 1*c*. (2) **yā yi** ⁓ he failed to reply (3) ⁓ **mại kai dā nēsạ** *epithet of* Hausa travellers. (4) **tạ̃kạlmin** ⁓ *Vd.* **tạ̃kạlmī** 5.

B. (**dumạ**) *f.* type of beer.

C. (**dumạ**) *Vb.* 1A (1) *x* **nā** ⁓ **masạ wuƙā** I plunged knife into him. (2) **yā** ⁓ **bạ̃kī ạ ƙwaryā** he put his mouth deep into the food-vessel (= **dōbạ** *q.v.*).

D. (**Dūmā**) *rustic Hausa* name for man called Audu.

duma A. (**dumā**) (1) *Vb.* 2 (*a*) beat *x* **an dụmē ni dạ sạndā** I've been beaten with a stick. (*b*) **yā dụmi hankạlīna** it worried me. (*c*) piled up much of T. (2) *f.* (*v.n. and progressive of* **dụma**).

B. (**dụma**) *Vb.* 3B = **dumẹ** 2.

C. (**dumạ**) *Vb.* 1A. (1) **an** ⁓ **mini sạndā** = **dụmā** 1*a*. (2) **yā** ⁓ **mini hankạlī** = **dụmā** 1*b*. (3) (*a*) heated (= **dumạmā**). (*b*) (smell, etc.) permeated *x* **zạzzạɓī yā** ⁓ **jikinsạ** he is feverish.

dụmạ-dumā *m., f.* short, thickset P.

dumama A. (**dumạmā**) *Vb.* 1C. (1) heated *x* **tā dumạmạ tūwō (mīyạ)** she warmed up the **tūwō (mīyạ)**. (2) *cf.* **dụmā** 1*b*.

B. (**dụmamạ**) *Vb.* 3B became warm *x* **yạu gạrī yā** ⁓ (1) it's a bit warmer to-day. (2) the town's alarmed to-day.

dumạmē *Vd.* **dumā**.

dụmạmē *m.* warmed-up **tuwō** (= *Sk.* **zạ̃fạfē** = **dạbtī**), *cf.* **dunġurẹ**.

duman dūtsẹ *m.* the plant **gạdạkūkạ** *q.v.*

dumạŋ ġirkē *m.* three gourd-drums beaten simultaneously.

dumạŋ kadạ *m.* (1) the convolvulus *Ipomoea repens*. (2) ⁓ **yanạ yạdō**, **yanạ hụdā** : har **yā mutụ, bại sakạ gundạ ba** *epithet of* (*a*) P. belying his good appearance. (*b*) evil P. well-dressed.

dumạŋ kāshī *m.* gourd which at once cracks (*cf.* **bạbạrnīyā**).

duman rạ̃fī *m.* = **dumạŋ kadạ** 1.

dūmarạ *f.* disease affecting fowls or mouth-edge of goats.

dumari A. (**dūmāri**) *used in* ⁓ **tambạriŋ wạdā** Storm (**hadiri**) thou drum of prosperity !

B. (**dụmarī**) *m.* (1) **aikịn nạŋ** ⁓ **nē** this work's slovenly. (2) reselling horse after fattening it up.

dụm'atạŋ unexpectedly.

Dụmau (1) *Vd.* **Sintạli**. (2) ⁓ **na gabạs** = ⁓ **bạ fāshịŋ gạyyā** *epithets of* storm (**hadiri**).

dụmbā *x* **dụmbā ūwar safarạ** ; **dạgạ gạrēki sǎi barcī** getting office is like trading, for one lacks for nought !

dumɓaɓa *Vd.* **ƙīrạ** 1*g*.

dụmɓạrī = **dụmɓạrū**.

dumɓārō *Vb.* 3A sprouted.

dụmɓạrū *m.* (*sg., pl.*). (1) (*a*) sprouting. (*b*) sprouts. (2) lip.

dụmɓārumạ *f.* (1) unseemly speech. (2) *Vd.* **dụmɓārumī**.

dụmɓārumī *m.* (*f.* **dụmɓārumā**) P. of unseemly speech.

dumɓạyē *Vd.* **dumbū**.

dụm bēlạ (*Fil.* it is not nice) **dụm bēlạ, dụm bēlạ, çiŋ kadanyạr Filānī** you accept the gift but then decry it (*Vd.* **dịm balạ**).

dumbū *m.* (*pl.* **dumɓạyē**). (1) any worn-out tool. (2) type of bird. (3) **'yan dumɓạyē** *m.* odds and ends sold to purchase other T.

dumbū = **dumbī** *m.* (1) much *x* **dumbuŋ**

itặcē = itặcē ∽ much wood. yā kāwǫ hatsī ∽ gụdā = yā kāwō hatsī mai ɗumbun yawą he brought much corn. (2) huge x yāƙi ɗumbū = ɗumbun yāƙi a huge war.

dumbuje A. (dumbụjē) Vb. 1C took much of T. composed of units (x grain, money, kolas), Vd. dumbụlā.
B. (dumbuję) m. (1) pile. (2) dumbuję-dumbuję in piles.
C. (dụmbụjē) (1) Vd. dụmbuzą. (2) m. (a) band of plaited leather (= ƙwặrō 5). (b) necklace of small red beads. (3) sowing thickly in holes (as by inexperienced children).

dumbụjī (1) m. (a) large amount. (b) = dụngụjī. (2) Vd. dụmbuzą.

dumbula A. (dụmbulą) Vb. 2 = dumbụjē q.v. x (1) nā dụmbụli hatsī I took out much corn. (2) ąkwīyą tā dumbulam mini hatsī the goat ate much of my corn. (3) nā dumbulam masą kudī I gave him much money. (4) Vd. aunāką 2.
B. (dumbụlā) Vb. 1C. (1) nā ∽ masą kudī = dụmbulą 3. (2) Kt. dumbụ'ą gūgā to bang bucket into well to fill it (= tamfątsā).
C. (dumbulā) f. (in songs) bigbosomed girl.

dumbulad ą Vb. 4A threw away much of or knocked over much of T. composed of units (grain, money, kolas).

dụmbụlē Kt. acting as in dumbụlā 2 (= tạmfątsē 1).

Dụmbụlum f. (1) town in Kano. (2) ɗan ∽ m. saddle with high backpiece.

dumɓurō = dumɓārō.

dụmburụm Sk. m. (sg., pl.) the trousers called būję.

dụmbus = dumbus-dụmbụs in profusion (= dạɓāɓą q.v.).

dumɓusō = dumɓārō.

dumbuza A. (dumbụzā) (1) = dumbụlā 1. (2) sowed as in dụmbụjē 3.
B. (dụmbuzą) Vb. 2 (p.o. dụmbụjē, n.o. dụmbụji) = dumbụjē.

dumbuzga Sk. = dumbuza.

dụmcī Sk. = dụmtsī.

ɗụm-ɗụm m. being lukewarm x rūwan nąŋ yā yi ∽.

ɗumɗuma = ɗumama.

dumę (1) Vb. 1A surpassed. (2) Sk. m. (a) gourd (= dumā). (b) rānā tā yi ∽ ; un is setting.

ɗumę (1) Vb. 1A (a) an ∽ ni dą sąndā = ɗumą 1. (b) = ɗumą 2, 3. (2) Vb. 3A. a) is (was) hot x jikinsą yā ∽ he has fever. (b) hąŋkạlinsą yā ∽ he's distracted. (c) is (was) permeated with x ɗāƙi yā ∽ dą ƙanshī house is permeated with nice smell (= gumę). jiƙī yā ∽ dą cīwǫ the body's racked with pain. gạrī yā ∽ dą tsǭrō the town's alarmed.

dụmfāmą (1) f. type of kerchief. (2) m., f. energetic P.

dụmfārą Vb. 2 x yā dụmfāri birnimmụ he came direct to our town.

dumfaro (dumfārō) Sk. = dumɓārō.

ɗumi A. (ɗụmī) m. warmth, etc. (= ɗịmī q.v.).
B. (ɗumi) abundantly (= ɗimi q.v.).

*ɗumką = ɗiŋką.

dummi A. (dummī) Sk. m. type of fish.
B. (dum mi) Zar. why ?

dumshę m. the tree dinshę q.v.

dumtsę took out handful of (= dintsę).

dụmtsī Sk. m. upper part of calf of leg (= dạmbūbụ).

dumū-dụmū̧ (1) m. being messy (= damō̧-dąmō̧ q.v.). (b) tussle. (2) adv. aŋ kāmą shi ∽ he was caught red-handed.

dumulmulǫ m. Longtailed Cormorant (Phalacrocorax afr.).

dumur m. strength (= dimir q.v.).

dụmụrmusą Vb. 2 (p.o. dụmụrmụshē, n.o. dụmụrmụshi) ate large amount of (= dạgargazą).

dụmụs = dụmụs-dụmụs abundantly.

dumwī-dụmwī̧ Sk. dumū-dụmū̧.

dụmwịnīyā Nor. f. dilly-dallying.

duna A. (dūna) m. very slack P. or T. (cf. dụŋhū).
B. (dūną) Vd. taushę 3.

dunana A. (dụnāną) Vb. 3B is (was) discoloured (= dịnāną q.v.).
B. (dunạnā) = dinạnā q.v.

dundę Vb. 3A (1) gạrī yā ∽ (a) it's overcast. (b) P.'s sight has failed. (2) idǫ yā ∽ eyelids are glued together.

dundū m. (1) fist. (2) tā yi masą ∽ = tā kai masą ∽ she gave him a punch (generally on the back) (cf. nąusā). (3) Sk. type of yam. (4) cīwǫ mai ∽

the influenza epidemic of 1918 (= **Mārī-sūwā**). (5) *Vd.* **shā** ~.

ɗundū *m.* (*sg.*, *pl.*) (1) the acacia-like shrub *Dichrostachys nutans.* (2) **akurkin ɗunɗū, wāwā kā sakā hannū** don't put your head in a noose !

dunduɓā *f.* (1) type of grasshopper. (2) big-made girl.

dunduɓus very near *x* **dagā naŋ zūwā caŋ,** ~ **nē.**

dundufā *f.* = **tūdarā.**

dunɗum *m.* (1) **garī yā yi** ~ = **dunɗē 1.** (2) **idọ yā yi** ~ = **dunɗē** (2).

ɗunɗumā *Vb.* 1C = **ɗumamā.**

ɗunɗumēmẹ = **ɗunɗumī** *m.* huge (= **ɗin-ɗimēmẹ** *q.v.*).

dundumī *m.* night-blindness (= **dindimī** *q.v.*).

dundungē *m.*, *f.* inexperienced thief or prostitute.

dundūnīyā = *Kt.* **dundunnīyā** *f.* (*pl.* **dundūnīyōyī**). (1) heel. (2) **yanā cin** ~ **tasụ** (*a*) he's treading on their heels (= **sārā** 1*k* = *Kt.* **sāɓar tākalmī**). *b*) he's dogging them to get them to pay debt owing him. (*c*) he's hoping to succeed them in office. (*d*) *Vd.* **diddigẹ.**

dundurus A. (**dundurus**) *x* **rānā tā fāɗi** ~ = **tā yi** ~ sun's quite set.

    B. (**dundurus**) *m.* (1) numbness of limb. (2) **gōshī** ~ protruding brow.

dundushẹ *Kt.* *m.* the tree **dīshẹ.**

dundurūsụ *m.* (*pl.* **dundurūsai**). (1) type of large adze. (2) **yā yi dundurūsụn tsōfwā** he wetted hard soil to soften it for digging.

dunga A. (**dungā**) *Vb.* 1A *Kt.* kept on doing (= **diŋga** *q.v.*).

    B. (**dungā**) *Sk.* *f.* the hoe **hauyā.**

dungāzumī *m.* (*f.* **dungāzumā**). (1) hairy-faced ; shaggy ; grubby P. (2) brave warrior.

dungẹ (1) *m.*, *f.* short P. (2) *m.* addled egg (= **barā gurbi**).

dungī *m.* (1) giraffe-hide shield. (2) adult giraffe (**rākumin dawā**).

dungi-dungi = **diŋgi-diŋgı.**

dungū *m.* (*pl.* **dunguna**). (1) (*a*) stump of maimed arm. (*b*) **dungū mūgụŋ hannū, iŋ aŋ ƙī kā, bā wani** make the best of a bad bargain ! (2) **tā yi** ~ she wrapped her hand in henna (*cf.* **ƙunshi**). (3)

(*added to* **kāmụ**) *x* **zanāntā kāmụ bīyū dā** ~ her cloth is twice 18 inches long plus length from elbow to end of closed fist (*cf.* **durƙusō** 3). (4) **dungū** *m.* = **ɗaukar dungū** *f.* 2 yards of European (**sandā**) or native cotton-material *x* **ā sayō mini farī** ~ **bīyū** I want 4 yards of **farī** bought me ! (*cf.* **ausāgī**). (5) deception *x* **sun nūnā masā** ~ = **dungū akā bā shi** deception was practised on him. (6) feline's paw (= **dāgī**). (7) exterior wall-corner *x* **dungun naŋ na gabās** this eastern wall-corner. (8) *Sk.* **tā yi dungum mashēru** her hands are coveᵣed with honey or oil, lucky rich woman ! (9) **dungum mussā** the pattern called **durƙusan tāgūwā.**

dungu-dungu *x* **mum fita tun dungu-dungu** *Kt.* we started at earliest dawn (= **duku-duku**).

dụŋ'gu-dụŋgū" *f.* short-legged chicken (*cf.* **mụgudūwā**).

dunguji *m.* raw cotton as brought from plantation (= **kādā**).

dungule *Kr.* *m.* oil ; grease ; butter.

dungulmī *m.* stump of maimed arm (= **dungū** 1).

dungulūlụ *Sk.* *m.* broken-pointed knife.

dungum completely *x* **zam bā kā shi** ~ I'll give you all of it. **yā ƙārẹ** ~ it's quite finished. **sum bar ƙasarsụ** ~ they completely migrated. **an ɗaukē** ~ it's been completely removed. (2) **an yi masā** ~ he's been stripped of his possessions (*Vd.* **dụŋgumī** 2). (3) *Vd.* **kāɓakī** 1*d*.

dungum *Vd.* **dungun.**

ɗunguma A. (**ɗunguma**) (1) *Vb* 2 drove away (body of persons). (2) *Vb.* 3B. (*a*) (party of persons) started out. (*b*) **mun** ~ **kaŋ Kanọ** we arrived at Kano. (*c*) **sukā** ~, **sukā āɗa wā sōjammụ** they (the troops) then proceeded to attack our soldiers.

    B. (**dungumā**) *Vb.* 1C = **dunguma** 2.

ɗungumī *m.* removing completely *x* **an ci dunguminsā** (1) he was beggared. (2) he was left " without a leg to stand on " (= **dungum** 2). **mēsā tā hadīyē shi dunguminsā** the python swallowed him whole.

dungun *Vd.* **dungum.**

duŋguŋ *m.* (1) extreme closeness *x* **sāi dà mukà yi ∼ dà shī, sạn naŋ mukà gan shi** we didn't see him till we were right on top of him. (2) **∼ dà mai kilī** (*a*) thick harmattan-haze (*cf.* **huntūru**). (*b*) **nā yi ∼ dà mai kilī dà sū** I encountered them all of a sudden (= **kạcibis** 1).

dunguna *Vd.* **duŋgū**.

duŋguŋguŋ *x* **yā hau dōki ∼** heavily-clothed horseman was mounted on big horse.

ɗuŋguŋgurum = **ɗuŋgum**.

dungura A. (**duŋgurā**) *f.* = **aduŋgurē**.

B. (**duŋgura**) *Vb.* 2 (1) brushed against. (2) (hornless *or* blunt-horned animal) butted (*cf.* **tuŋkwīyà** 1*a*). (3) = **daŋgwara**.

C. (**duŋgurā**) (1) *Vb.* 1C = **daŋgwarā** 1. (2) *Vb.* 3A reached *x* **har kà ∼ dà kàsūwā** till you reach the market.

duŋgura dàbē = **daŋgwara dàbē**.

Duŋgurāwā *Vd.* **Bàduŋgure**.

dungure A. (**duŋgurē**) *m.* = **aduŋgurē**.

B. (**duŋgure**) *m.* lump of warmed-up tūwō (**ɗumàmē**) (= **kari** 5).

C. (**duŋgurē**) *Vb.* 3A = **duŋgurā** 2.

duŋgurgur *m.* shortness (= **ɗigil** *q.v.*).

dunguri A. (**duŋgurī**) *m.* (*f.* **duŋgurā**) short.

B. (**duŋgurī**) = **daŋgwarī**.

duŋgurmā *Sk.* *f.* the **tururūwā** ant in winged stage.

dungurmi A. (**duŋgurmī**) *m.* stump of maimed arm (= **duŋgū** 1).

B. (**duŋgurmī**) *x* **yanà dà duŋgurmiŋ gōshī** = **yanà dà gōshī ∼** he has protuberant forehead.

ɗuŋgurum = **ɗuŋguruŋgum** = **ɗuŋgum**.

Duŋgurum Zungeru.

ɗuŋgusā *Vb.* 3A. (1) moved away a short distance. (2) *cf.* **ɗingisā**.

ɗuŋgushē *m.* (1) scamping work. (2) cheating in gambling, etc.

dunguza A. (**duŋguzā**) *Vb.* 1C applied T. profusely to (= **dambazā** *q.v.*).

B. (**duŋguza**) *f.* the trousers **būje**.

dungwī (1) *f.* short woman. (2) *m.* embroidered ankleband of trousers.

duŋhū *m.* (*pl.* **duŋhuna**). (1) calabash with pokerwork pattern. (2) (*a*) very black P. (*cf.* **dūna**). (*b*) entirely black

horse. (*c*) sword devoid of markings. (3) **duŋhun sāki** a cloth solely **sāki**.

dūnìyà (*Ar.* the lower place) *f.* (*pl.* **dūnìyōyī**). (1) (*a*) the world (*antithesis is* **lāhira**). **∼ à fāɗin nan nātà, bà mu dà mataimakī** we have not a friend in the world. (*b*) (i) **yā shiga ∼** he went abroad. (ii) **yā fyāɗa kầi** (= **yā bandà) ūwā ∼ kàkā tafarki** he vanished into the great world. (iii) **kàkan ∼** *Vd.* **kàkā** 2*c*. (*c*) **∼ bā tà tàbbata** life is transitory. (*d*) **∼ matākim bēnē, wani gàba dà wani** there's always someone sen'or and someone junior. (*e*) **Audu ∼ nē** Audu is a law unto himself. (*f*) **∼ tā yi sararī** the sky has cleared. (*g*) **ɗan ∼** *m.* (*f.* **'yar ∼**) *pl.* **'yan ∼** (i) profligate P. (ii) *Vd.* **sạnnū** 2*a*.iv. (*h*) **kōwā ya cē ∼ ūwā tasà cē, yà sōma kūkā** look before you leap ! (*j*) **yā shā ∼** = **∼ tā san shi** (i) he's much travelled. (ii) T. is much used. (*k*) **yanà cin ∼** he's enjoying life. (*l*) **dūnìyaɗ ɗakà, bērā dà ƙuƙumī** *some* people have all the luck. (*m*) **∼ jūyi-jūyi, kwàɗō yā fāɗa à rūwan dimī** what an unlucky period ! (*n*) (i) **mutànan ∼ in sun sàmi dōki dà sukūwā, sāi su ƙurè shi** don't overwork the willing horse ! (ii) **mutànan ∼ iŋ kà sakè** *Vd.* **sakè** 2*b*. (*o*) **mai kyau nē na idan ∼** it is excellent. (*p*) **yā bar ∼** he died. (*q*) **zaman ∼ bìkī nè, cūɗē ni, ŋ cūɗē kà** the world necessitates people helping each other. (*r*) *Vd.* **bàkin dūnìyà**. (2) affairs of the world, people of the world *x* (*a*) **yā sàmi ∼** he got in the world, he conquered far and wide. (*b*) **∼ tā yi dāɗī** the world has become peaceful, everything is fine in the best of all possible worlds. (*c*) **yanà ∼** he has prospered. (*e*) **∼ bà su ƙarɓā ba** the world did not accept it (Mod. Gram. 9*d*). (*f*) **yanà sò duk ∼ kōwā yà sàki jikī** he wishes everyone to feel at home. (*g*) **an tārà masà ∼** all his misdeeds are being bandied about. (*h*) **dā ∼ dà gàskīyā, sāi à yi wà mazarī rìgā dà wandō** (*lit.* if the world were just, the spindle (as it is the cause of wealth to women) should be clothed in gown and trousers) those who share your poverty deserve also a share when you become prosperous. (3) ~ ịnā gabaŋkị type of fringed kerchief. (4) barē ~ Vd. barē 2. (5) daɗạ ~ Vd. dadai 4. (6) ạl'amạrin ~ Vd. sạnnū 2b.ii. (7) ạbin ɗiŋkịn ~ Vd. Wazīrị. (8) Vd. tsan-tsan ~. (9) gamạ ~ Vd. gamạ 1m.

dunję Kt. m. bunch of bananas, dates, ɗọrawạ-pods (= dinshę).

dụnjī m. ragged clothing (epithet is ~ kạs kạ̃faɗạ, bạ kạ ci jịkī ba, kā ci zūcịyā), cf. cūrị 4.

ɗuŋkạ = diŋkạ.

ɗuŋkị = ɗịŋkị.

dụŋkū m. (1) Kt. pounded seeds of baobob (kūkạ). (2) flour of baobob (= gạ̃riŋ kūkạ), Vd. kūkạ.

ɗụŋku = ɗịŋku.

dunƙula A. (duŋƙulā) Vb. 1C. (1) (a) x an ~ shi cūrị-cūrị it has been kneaded into balls. (b) ɗam banzā yạ̃shī nẹ̃, kō an duŋƙulā shi, bā yạ̃ duŋƙulūwā a useless P. is worse than useless. (2) yạ̃ duŋƙulạ kudī he saved up his money (= ajīyē 5a.i). (3) dunƙulạ kāyā to collect many goods or articles.

    B. (dụŋƙulạ) (1) Vb. 2 = duŋƙulā. (2) Vb. 3B. (a) (i) huddled oneself up. (ii) (hedgehog) rolled itself up. (b) (horse) gathered itself for leap. (3) Vd. mazan duŋƙulạ.

duŋƙulallē m. (f. duŋƙulallīyā) pl. dụŋ-ƙulạllū short-necked P.

dunƙule A. (duŋƙulē) (1) Vb. 1C. (a) = dụŋƙulā. (b) ~ hannū to clench the fist (= ƙullẹ 1b). (2) Vb. 3A = dụŋ-ƙulạ 2.

    B. (duŋƙulẹ-duŋƙulẹ) adv. in balls, lumps.

duŋƙulī m. (sg., pl.). (1) kneaded-ball (= cūrị 2). (2) clenched fist. (3) dụŋƙulī m. (f. duŋƙulā) short-necked P.

dụŋkurkị m., f. (1) grubby P. (2) sullen P. (3) doltish P.

dụŋkurkụɗā f. (sg., pl.) type of small, black grasshopper.

dụŋkụrumạ (1) m., f. (a) hornless cow, ox, or goat. (b) shy child. (2) f. (a) worn-out tool. (b) woman without dōkạ head-dress.

dunshẹ m. (1) type of acacia. (2) bunch of bananas (= dinshẹ q.v.).

dụntsī Sk. m. calf of leg (= dạmbūbụ).

dunsumī m. (f. dunsumā). (1) hairy P. (2) Kt. = daƙwalwā.

dụnsurmạ m., f. grubby, unkempt P. (= mụdụƙūƙị = wātsạbirịtā).

duntsa A. (dụntsā) Vb. 2 took out handful of.

    B. (duntsạ) Vb. 1A gave handful of x nā ~ masạ kudī.

dūnū x nā ci dūnunsạ (1) I seized him round waist, imprisoning his arms. (2) I left him " without a leg to stand on ".

dụnūnụ = dununū m., f. grubby, unkempt P.

dunyā f. spur-winged goose (= dinyā q.v.).

ɗunyā f. the tree ɗinyā q.v.

ɗura A. (ɗūrạ) (1) Vb. 1A. (a) (i) poured liquid through narrow orifice x yā ~ rūwā ạ būtạ he poured water into bottle (= bulbụlā 1b). nā ~ mặi ạ mōtạ I poured petrol into the car-tank (cf. zubạ, tsīyậyā). (ii) an ~ sōjạ cikiŋ ƙạŋƙanaŋ kōmī the soldiers were disgorged into a small boat (from hold of steamer). (b) yanạ̃ ~ rịgā he's packing seams of a gown with the thread abạ̃wā, using bạsillā-needle. (c) yā ~ kudī ạ littāfị he entered money in his cashbook. (d) yā ~ minị zāgị he abused me. (e) mạ̃rūrụ yā ɗūru pus collected in abscess. mutạ̃nē sun ɗūru ạ ƙasạn naŋ people poured into that country. (f) dōkị yā ɗūru horse's fattened out. (g) auran ~ rūwā marriage of an old man. (2) Kt. f. = ɗūrā 2b.

    B. (ɗūrā) Vb. 2 (1) (a) = ɗūrạ 1a. (b) poured T. through narrow orifice and removed the container. (c) tsūlịyassạ tā ɗūri rūwā he was in a funk. (2) f. (a) yā yi wạ yārọ ~ he poured medicine down the lad's throat. (b) tạttabarā tā yi wạ ɗantạ ~ pigeon fed its young with its bill. (c) an yi masạ ɗụ̃rar ɗam mạkaunīyā he was flustered by being given 2nd task before 1st completed.

ɗurg̃rē Vb. 3A trickled out (= zurg̃rē q v.).

durbai *m.* cadging by the professional beggars 'yan ~ (*Vd.* marǭƙī).

durɓancī *Kt. m.* (1) leather loincloth (= warkī). (2) the tribal marks called billē 2.

durbāwā *Vd.* durōbạ.

dūrbōbī *Vd.* durōbạ.

durɓuna A. (durɓunā) *Vb.* 1C. (1) yā durɓunạ fuskạ he frowned, grimaced (= yātsịnā), *cf.* gātsịnā. (2) *x* yā ~ wạ fuskạ tǭkā (shūnī) he rubbed ashes (indigo), etc., on his face.

    B. (durɓunạ) *Vb.* 3A fuskạ tasạ tā ~ he's scowling. garī yā ~ sky's overcast.

durɓunē (1) *Vb.* 1C *Kt.* yā durɓunẹ fuskạ ~ = durɓunā 1. (2) *Vb.* 3A fuskạ tasa tā ~ = durɓunạ.

durɓuni what a scowl !

ɗure A. (ɗurẹ) *Vb.* 1A poured (*as in* ɗurạ) all of.

    B. (ɗūrẹ̄) *m.* (1) food poured into gourd-bottle (būtạ) by young cowherds who will be away all day (2) = ɗūrā 2*a.*

durgū *m.* (*f.* durgwā) short-legged P., animal or bird.

durguɓī *m.* sedimentary liquid (= dagwadạgō *q.v.*).

dur'gu-durgūǁ *m.* sedimentary liquid (= dagwadạgō *q.v.*).

durgwīyạ *East Kano f.* the food furā.

durhulli how black !

dūri *m.* (*in coarse talk*). (1) vagina (*Vd.* farji). (2) *Vd.* dūru.

ɗūri *m.* (1) (*secondary v.n. of* ɗūrạ) *x* yanạ ɗūrim mại ạ mōtạ = yanạ ɗūrạ mại ạ mōtạ. (2) the part of a gown packed *as in* ɗūrạ 1*b.*

dūrīyạ *f.* = tsīgī 1.

ɗūrīyạ *x* kō ~ bạ ạ ji ba not a scrap of news has been heard.

durjạ *Kt. f.* rung, step, stair (= darajạ) *x* durjạr bēnē stairway to upper storey.

durkuf = durkup = durkum = kirtif *q.v.*

durkumullạ *Sk. f.* contradicting a P.

durƙusa A. (durƙusā) *Vb.* 3A. (1) knelt down. (2) durƙusạ wạdā bạ gajī-yạ̄wā ba nẹ needs must when the devil drives.

    B. (durƙusạ) *Vb.* 3B persevered *x* dạmunā tā ~ rains have really set in (= tạ̄gūwạ 3*b*). sạrautạ tā ~ ạ gidansạ

his family have permanently got chiefship. yā ~ zại yi zạncē he's settled down to a good talk.

durƙusad dạ *Vb.* 4B caused P. or animal to kneel.

durƙusan tāgūwạ *m.* pattern used in embroidery and building (*consists of two interlaced loops*), *Vd.* dāgī 3 ; duṇgū 9.

durƙushē *Vb.* 3A (1) fell on the knees through weakness. (2) (*a*) (price) fell. (*b*) (resources) diminished.

durƙusō = *Kt.* durƙushī *m.* (1) (*a*) kneeling. (*b*) *Vd.* kwạ̄ɗō 1*a*.ii. (2) durƙusantạ nawạ how many times has she given birth ? (3) *Sk.* (*added to* kāmu) *x* zanạntạ kāmu bīyū dạ ~ her cloth is twice 18 inches long, plus length of middle finger's tip to middle joint (*cf.* duṇgū 3) = tạƙōƙō 2.

durmīyạ *Vb.* 3B sank far into (= dulmuyạ *q.v.*).

durmuƙē *m.* unfairly overturning spinning-top (katantaṇwạ).

durmusā *Vb.* 1C *Kt.* dirtied one's garment on the ground (= turmusā).

durǭ *Eng. m.* drawer in table, etc.

durōbạ *Eng. m.* (*f.* durōbịyā) *pl.* durōbōbī = durbōbī = durbāwā. (1) prison-warder. (2) = dirēbạ.

ɗurri *Ar. m.* short explanatory notes in book (= ɗauri 4).

dūru (*coarse*) used in ɗan dūruṇ ūwā what a bastard you are ! (*cf.* dūri).

ɗūru *Vd.* ɗūrạ 1*e, f.*

duru-duru A. (duru-duru) *m.* (1) mum fitạ tun ~ we started at earliest dawn (= duku-duku). yā zō naṇ dạ ~ he came here at earliest dawn. (2) idạnsạ yā yi ~ he can only see dimly (*because of faint light of dawn or of* ạlmūru). (3)· haṇkalinsạ yā yi ~ he's perplexed.

    B. (duru-duru) *m., f.* (1) dim-sighted P. (2) feckless P.

durum = ɗurum *m. or. adv.* (1) garī yā yi ~ (*a*) it's oppressive (*as in* bazarā *season*). (*b*) sky's overcast (through mist (hazō) or clouds (gizạ̄-gizai)). (2) garī yā yi masạ ~ he's blind. (3) yau ~ yakẹ he feels liverish to-day. (4) kansa yā yi ~ he is all of a dither.

duruma A. (**dụrumạ**) *m.*, *f.* (**1**) blind P. (**2**) deaf and dumb P. (*cf.* **dụrụm**).

    B. (**Durūmạ**) *used in* '**yan** ⁓ the traditional Katsina place of execution (*cf.* **Mallērị**).

    C. (**durumạ**) *Vd.* **durụmī**.

durụmī *m.* (*pl.* **durumạ** = *Kt.* **durummạ**) the fig-tree *Ficus syringifolia* (= *Sk.* **ɗaŋ kumāsạ**).

dụrụmnīyā *f.* looking hither and thither (= **fạfụtụkā** *q.v.*).

durūnạ *f.* sewing or spinning, etc., done by artificial light.

duruŋgū *m.* (*sg.*, *pl.*) wart-hog (= **gạdū**)·

ɗurus in drips (= **ɗiris** *q.v.*).

durwa A. (**durwā**) *f.* (**1**) tucking end of loincloth into waistband, after drawing it between legs (*said that when done by girls, it is to prevent rape* (**fạɗē**)) ; *Vd.* **saŋƙę**. (**2**) hem of the gown **kōrę**. (**3**) leather bands on underside of saddle. (**4**) lark-quail (*Ortyxelos meiffrenii*) = **ɓamɓarwạ**. (**5**) *Kt.* helping P.

    B. (**dụrwā**) *m.* (**1**) black-and-white dog. (**2**) sword with black blade. (**3**) *Kt.* **yā ci nōman** ⁓ = **barę 2***c*.

durwạcē *Vb.* 1C tucked in loincloth *as in* **durwā 1** (= **saŋƙę**).

dụrwatạ *Vb.* 2 (*p.o.* **dụrwạcē**, *n.o.* **dụrwạci**). (**1**) = **durwạcē**. (**2**) **wutā tā** (= **yāƙị yā**) **durwatō gạrī** fire (war) has overwhelmed the town.

ɗus A. (**ɗus**) firmly (= **ɗas** *q.v.*).

    B. (**ɗụs**) in drips (= **ɗạs** *q.v.*).

dụsā = **dụsā** *f.* (**1**) (*a*) (i) bran. (ii) *Vd.* **fạdamạ**. (*b*) metal-filings.   **dụsar zīnārīyā** gold-tinsel (= **kumfan 5**). (**2**) syphilitic affections of the vulva. (**3**) **dụsar kwarnō** scrapings of inside of skins, dyed light-blue and used as eye-remedy.

ɗūsạ *f.* the thatching-grass *Setaria aurea*.

dusad dạ *Vb.* 4A tarnished, dimmed.

dūsạrạ *m.*, *f.* energetic P. (*epithet is* ⁓ **gātariŋ Gwārī**).

dūsạsā *pl.* of **dụddūsā** corpulent.

dusāsad dạ *Vb.* 4A *Sk.* tarnished, dimmed.

dusạshē *Vb.* 3A became dim, tarnished (= **dushę** *q.v.*).

dūshāƙị *m.*, *f.* grubby, unkempt P.

dushạshē = **dusạshē**.

dushe A. (**dushę**) *Vb.* 3A became dim, tarnished *x* **rānā tā** ⁓ sun's over-clouded.   **rīgā tā** ⁓ gown's faded. **muryạssạ tā** ⁓ his voice's become faint. **tạurārạnsạ yā** ⁓ = **rānarsạ tā** ⁓ his luck's waned.

    B. (**dūshę**) the acacia **dinshę**.

dūshī *m.* bulkiness.

dushi-dushi *x* **idạnunsạ** ⁓ **sukę** he is nearly blind (= **muci-muci**).

duskura A. (**duskụrā**) *Vb.* 1C blunted (= **dākụsā**).

    B. (**dụskurạ**) *Vb.* 3B is (was) blunt (= **dākụshē**).

duskụrē *Vb.* 3A = **dụskurạ**.

ɗuskwi A. (**ɗụskwī**) (**1**) *m.* (*sg.*, *pl.*) horned-owl. (**2**) **tanạ dạ cikị** ⁓ = **ɗụskwị**.

    B. (**ɗụskwị** = **ɗụskwịkwị**) *used in* **cikịntạ yā yi** ⁓ her stomach is distended (*by dropsy or advanced pregnancy*).

dụssā *Kt.* *f.* = **dụsā**.

dususu A. (**dụsūsụ**) *m.* bran from unwetted, ground corn (= **sūrūrụ**).

    B. (**dụsụsụ**) *m.* being of nondescript colour.

dut *Sk.* all (= **dukạ** *q.v.*).

dūtsę = *Sk.* **dūtsị** *m.* (*pl.* **dūwạtsū** = **dūtsunạ** = **dụwạrwạtsai** = **dūwạrwatsū** = **dūwạrwatsī**). (**1**) (*a*) stone. (*b*) **dūtsạm bindigạ** flint of gun. (*c*) **dūtsạŋ ạrādụ** stone celt (= **gātariŋ ạrādụ**). (*d*) **dūtsạŋ wāshị** grindstone. (*e*) **alkamạ bisạ** ⁓, **Allạ ya kạm bā kị rūwā** = **dạshē 4***c*. (*f*) ⁓ **bā yạ zamā rūwā** you can't make a silk purse out of a sow's ear. (*g*) ⁓ **ạ far makạ bā dādī, kạ far wạ mụtụm, bā dādī** an energetic P. is energetic whatever befalls him. (*h*) **dūtsạŋ niƙạ, kā fi gạbaŋ ạljīfū** *epithet of* important P. (*Vd.* **7**). (*j*) (i) **ƙwăi dạ** ⁓ **bā sạ hạɗūwā** oil and water won't mix. (ii) *Vd.* **haɗạ 1***c*. (*k*) **halī zạnan** ⁓ **nē** character is immutable. (*l*) **dūtsạŋ dạ kę cikin rūwā, bai saŋ anạ rānā ba** = **dūtsạŋ dạ kę cikin rūwā, bai san zaman dạ rānā ba** one half of the world doesn't know how the other half lives (*Vd.* **sanị 1***a*.xvii, **gạji 1***d*). (*m*) **karạn** ⁓ *Vd.* **karọ 2**. (**2**) (*a*) rock. (*b*) **mại**

haƙurī ya kạn dafạ ⁓ patience conquers ! (c) ⁓ bạ ka fạrgạbā what a dauntless warrior ! (3) hill, mountain (cf. tudụ). (4) bead x dūwạ̄tsum mātā jewellery. (5) one cwt. (cf. awọ 6). (6) one of the pieces used by one of the two players of darạ q.v. (cf. karā 3). (7) (a) dūtsẹ = dūtsạn nikạ (i) lower grinding-stone for corn (= marēdī = Sk. āyạ 5). (ii) seller's tạllạ is hạnạ gōrị. (iii) Vd. 1h above. (8) bugụn ⁓ Vd. bugụ 2. (9) tākạ ⁓ Vd. duffạ. (10) bạbban ⁓ Vd. Fạllau 2.

dūtsunạ Vd. dūtsẹ.

dụ̄wā Zar. f. black, loamy soil.

ɗúwai Vd. dūwạ̄wū.

ɗúwainịyā Kt. = ɗūwạ̄wū.

dūwạrwatsū, dūwạ̄tsū Vd. dūtsẹ.

ɗūwạ̄wū m. = Sk. ɗúwai m. = ɗūwạiwai m. = ɗūwaiwayạ f. = Sk. dūwạyyā f. = Kt. ɗūwainịyā f. (1) buttocks. (2) gaddamạr gudụ, ɗūwạiwai yā ƙi shịgā Vd. gaddamạ. (3) gạskīyā ɗúwạiwai nẹ̄, dạ kạntạ yakẹ̄ zạune truth needs no puffing. (4) sūsạr ⁓ Vd. gudụ 2d.v.

dụ̄wū m. (sg., pl.) type of large, black scorpion.

dụ̄zā Vb. 2 (p.o. dụ̄jē, n.o. dụ̄ji). (1) did profusely (= darjẹ 2g q.v.). (2) yā dụ̄ji dōkị he pulled up his horse dead (= darjẹ 2b). (3) grazed (person's skin). (4) tore out handfuls (of feathers or hair).

duzuzu A. (dụ̄zūzụ) m. hairy man.
    B. (dụ̄zūzụ) x yanạ̄ dạ gāshị ⁓ he's very hairy.

dw, ɗw (if not found below) Vd. d, ɗ, e.g. ɗwācī Sk. = ɗācī : dwaɗẹ Sk. = daɗẹ, etc.

dwạ̄dwārịsā Kt. f. (1) big laying hen. (2) big-made girl.

dwạ̄gā Vb. 2 Sk. stripped off, etc. (= zạ̄gā q.v.).

ɗwai Sk. m. stench, etc. (= ɗọyī q.v.).

ɗwaiɗwāyạ Sk. f. ɗaɗɗōyạ.

dwālaƙēƙẹ m. (f. dwālaƙēƙịyā) Kt. huge.

dwālaƙī m. (f. dwālaƙā) huge.

dwaljẹ Kt. = darjẹ.

ɗwam Vd. ɗum.

dwạndwạŋ Kt. in profusion (= dạ̄ɓā ɓạ).

dwạs x tanạ̄ tạfīyạ dwạs-dwạs she's walking heavily (= dạs q.v.).

ɗwātạ Kt. = ɗātạ.

dwạ̄tạnnā Sk. f. type of bitter grass, etc. (= dạ̄tạnniyā q.v.).

dwāyạ Kt. f. yam, etc. (= dōyạ q.v.).

E

ē (1) yes (= ī). (2) well . . .

'ẹ̄bē Kano rustic Hausa = ɗẹ̄bē x tā ⁓ shị she drew it (water), Vd. dībạ.

ēfanẹ = ēfịnẹ Eng. m. halfpenny.

ẹ̄fau Sk. m. dark-grey donkey (cf. ịdabạr ; gōhō ; jạŋ gọ̄rā).

ēgọ Fil. m. dropsy (= ūwa 2).

ēgịr Eng. m. egret-feathers.

ēhạ Zar. m. (sg., pl.) seasonal immigrant (= dāgịrạ q.v.).

ēhọ-ēhọ m. screaming x sunạ̄ ⁓ they're screaming. sun cẹ̄ " ēhọ-ēhọ " they screamed (cf. īhụ).

ēkạ Eng. f. acre.

ēkịs (Eng. " x ") m. an sạ̄ ⁓ cross was written against it to mark it as wrong (cf. rāyạt).

ēlạ̄wạ Nor. m. rope, string (= igīyạ).

elẹmẹntarẹ Eng. f. Elementary School.

en'ẹ̄ m. Native Administration (cf. Sarkī 1m).

ēnī m. (sg., pl.) type of Yoruba mat much used by Hausas.

'ētạrē Katagum Hausa crossed (= ƙḗtạrē q.v.).

F

fa A. (fā) f. (pl. fạnnai) rock-outcrop (= fạlalẹ).
    B. (fa) indeed x (i) nī fa . . . I indeed . . . nā ⁓ gayạ makạ = nā gayạ makạ ⁓ why, I told you ! dạ̄ ⁓ nī nẹ̄ na jē Kanọ had it been I indeed who went to Kano. (ii) ạ̄ cẹ̄ fa ? Vd. cẹ̄ 8.
    C. (fạ) what about ? x nī ⁓ well, what about me ? Audụ ⁓ well, what about Audu ?
    D. (fạ̄ạ̄) (1) wutā tā kāmạ ⁓ fire blazed up. bọm yā fashẹ ⁓ the bomb burst with a bang. (2) rūwā yā zubō ⁓ water burst its way out.

Fạbạrā'ịr = Fạbrairụ m. February.

faca-faca A. (faca-faca) *f.* scattering *x* **kājī sun yi ∼ dạ hatsī** fowls scattered the corn.

B. (facā-fạcā) abundantly *x* **hatsī yanā kāsūwā ∼** there's much corn in the market. **yau kāsūwā ∼** to-day's market is full of commodities.

C. (fạcā-facā = fạcā-fạcā) *f.* (1) squandering *x* **yanā ∼ da kuɗī.** (2) **mun yi tạfīyạ ∼** we had to splash our way through much water. (3) **yārā sunā ∼ ạ rūwa** children are playing in water.

fạcạkā *f.* squandering *x* **yanā ∼ da kuɗī.**

facal A. (facạl) *m.* sound of falling into shallow water *x* **yā fāɗạ ạ rūwa ∼** he fell plop into the water.

B. (facal-fạcal) = **fạcā-fạcā** 2, 3.

facạr-facạr *Kt.* = **fatsạr-fatsạr.**

face A. (fācẹ) *Vb.* 1A. (1) **nā ∼ mājinā** I blew my nose. **yā fyātō** he blew it (mucus) out of his nose. (2) (*with dative*) *Vd.* **fạtā** 2.

B. (fạcē) (1) except *x* **dukạ sun shigō ∼ shī** they've all entered with the exception of him. (2) *conj.* except that *x* **sun yi shiri dukạ ∼ Audu bai ɗaurạ sirdi ba** they're all ready except that Audu hasn't saddled up yet. (3) *Kt.* = **bạllē** *x* **kai kā īyạ ∼ nī** you're able to do it so how much the more am I ! (4) *Kt.* like (= **kạman**) *x* **shī ∼ ubansạ** he's like his father. (5) *Vd.* **fạtā.**

faci A. (fācị) (*Eng.* patch) *m.* (*sg., pl.*) (1) patch to repair tyre. (2) blaze down length of horse's face.

B. (fạci) *Vd.* **fạtā.**

faɗ *Vd.* **faɗ ɗayā.**

fāɗạ *f.* (1) (*a*) Chief's residence. (*b*) Chief's audience-chamber (*cf.* **fādancī, fagạcī**). (*c*) **am mayar dạ shī ∼** he's been made a member of the cabinet. (*d*) **fādạr fịtinạ tā kōmạ Masạr** the scene of war has shifted to Egypt. (*e*) **caŋ kudu fādạr mại takẹ** the southern region is rich in petroleum. (2) **yā sāmi ∼** he's become one of the Chief's retinue (= **sō** 2*b*). (3) **yā fī nị ∼** he's more in favour than I am. (4) **ạbu yā daɗẹ dạ ɓatạ ạ ∼ bạrē Tākạlmī** (*lit.* a certain thing was long since lost from

the palace, so far more so will this man **Tākạlmī** vanish) you're lucky to have got off so lightly ! (*Vd.* **ạbu** 2*k*). (5) **∼ kāsūwạ cẹ ?** what presumptuousness in entering thus without a by-your-leave ! (6) *Vd.* **Sarkim ∼, tūwam ∼, mạtar ∼, mātam ∼.** (7) **kwaryar ∼** *Vd.* **Sintạlī.** (8) **kirạ ạ ∼** *Vd.* **barị** 4*e*. (9) **bar tsōram ∼** *Vd.* **tsōrō** 3.

faɗa A. (faɗạ) (1) *m.* (i) quarrel. (ii) **suŋ kāmạ ∼ = faɗạ yā mōtsu tsạkāninsu** (*cf.* 1*f. below*) a quarrel arose between them. (iii) **∼ bā nākạ bạ ? kā ɗaukạ kā yāfạ ?** do not interfere in other people's business ! (*cf.* **yāfạ** 1*c*). (iv) **jirgin samạ mại ∼** fighter plane (= 1*a*.x*ib*). (v) **ạbōkim ∼** enemy. (vi) **farkwam ∼, nūnạ hannū** coming events cast their shadows before them. (vii) *Vd.* **girmā** 1*a*.xvi. (viii) *Vd.* **rabạ** 3. (ix) **yā tākalō ∼** he brought trouble on himself. (*x*) **sunā faɗạŋ zạkạrū** they're hostilely staring at one another. (xi) **ɗam ∼** *m.* (*pl.* **'yam ∼**). (*a*) quarrelsome P. (*b*) fighter plane (*b* = 1*a*.iv *above*). (xii) **ūwar ∼** *Vd.* **bindigạ.** (xiii) **∼ dạ māsū īyāyē** *Vd.* **mạrāyạ** 3. (xiv) **masōmim ∼** *Vd.* **daƙūwạ** 2. (xv) **faɗạŋ iblīsai** *Vd.* **murtukū.** (xvi) **faɗạŋ gwaggọ** *Vd.* **gwaggọ** 2*e*. (xvii) **shā ∼** *Vd.* **shā** B.16*a*. (xviiⁿ) **sābam ∼** *Vd.* **sābō** 2. (xix) *Vd.* **tsạŋkī.** (xx) *Vd.* **gạmạ ∼.** (xxi) **masọ ∼** *Vd.* **habaicī.** (*b*) (i) **yā yi ∼ dạ nī** he quarrelled with me. (ii) **yā yi minị ∼** he scolded me = **yā fāɗạ minị dạ faɗạ.** (*c*) **yanā nēmam ∼ = yanā jạm ∼ = yanā kālam ∼** he is picking a quarrel. (*d*) **tūwan nạm ∼ gạrēshi** this tūwō is scalding hot. (*e*) **munā faɗạŋ Kanọ** we're hurrying on to Kano. (*f*) battlefield *x* (i) **wurim ∼** *m.* battlefield. (ii) **muŋ kāmạ ∼ dạ sū** we opened hostilities with them (*cf.* 1*a*.ii). (iii) **kāyam ∼** *m.* armaments, weapons. (iv) **kōwā ya kwānā wurim ∼ shī ya yi kōrā** the early bird catches the worm. (v) *Sk.* **yā kāwō musu ∼** he attacked the enemy. (*g*) *cf.* **tạyā ni ∼.** (2) (*the form of* **fạɗā** *used before dative*) *x* (*a*) **yā ∼ musu hakạ** he told them this, he spoke thus to them. (*b*) **a ∼ makạ**

I have been instructed to inform you that . . . (Gram. 18). (c) yau kā ~ mākwī = kā ~ musu yau = yau kā ~ ƙawāyaŋka to-day you'll rue the very day you were born ! (d) Vd. faɗō.

B. (faɗā) (1) Vb. 2 (v.n. is also faɗi 1c q.v.). (a) said x (i) yā faɗi maganan naŋ he said this. faɗi tāka maganar mu ji let's hear your version ! faɗinsa da wuyā = faɗā tasa da wuyā it's hard to say it. (ii) faɗi m ~ = sā n sā. (iii) Vd. faɗa 2. (b) (i) " faɗi ! ba a tambayē ka ba " garēshi he's a busy-body. (ii) Vd. sūdā 1b. (c) anā ta nishāɗi, faɗi banzā, faɗi wōfī light-hearted chatter is going on. (d) bā shi da ta ~ " he hasn't a leg to stand on " (cf. cēwā 2b). (e) wannaŋ, ai bā sǎi am ~ ba this is obvious. (f) Vd. faɗō. (g) faɗi da " kūwā ", ƙāre da " Wallāhi ! " speak clearly and swear to the truth of what you say ! (2) f. (a) thing said (= magana 2b) x faɗar Allā bā tā tāshi the decrees of God are inescapable. bā a karɓar ~ tata no-body believes what she says. (b) abim ~ m. (i) things to be discussed. (ii) spoken words, conversation. (iii) act causing P. to be talked about. (iv) the power of speech. (v) abim ~ na mai bāki nē, bēbe sǎi ya daŋgana what cannot be cured must be endured. (vi) Vd. raba 4, faɗi 1c.iii. (c) yanā faɗaɗ (= yanā mai faɗaɗ) ɗayā a wurinsu he's their favourite. nāma yanā faɗaɗ ɗayā a kāsūwā meat is in great demand (cf. faɗi 1c.iv).

C. (fāɗa) Vb. 3A. (1) (a) (i) fell into, fell on (Vd. fāɗi). yā ~ a rūwa he fell into the water (cf. 2) (= fāɗi 3). (ii) yā ~ faƙo he got into trouble. (iii) fiting tā ~ dissension arose. (b) (i) yā ~ cikiŋ garī he went into the town. (ii) yā ~ sōja he entered the army. (iii) nā ~ yāki I waged war. (iv) sum ~ wutar igwar Jāmus they came under the German artillery-fire. (c) inda hanyaŋ naŋ ta ~ kārauka where this road debouches on to the highway. (d) yā ~ hannunsu he fell into their clutches. (e) bai ~ masa sōsǎi ba it does not correspond with it exactly.

(f) wani abu yā fāɗō mini a rāi an idea has occurred to me. yā fāɗō mini da kyar I can only vaguely remember it. (g) kō kaŋ wā ya ~ Vd. wuce 2a.ii. (h) ɓērā yā ~ wuta Vd. ɓērā 1k. (j) zai ~ yau Vd. dami 2. (k) ~ rījiyā Vd. rījiyā 1b, e, f. (1) ɗāki yā ~ Vd. zō 1e. (m) ~ a rūwan ɗimī Vd. dūnīya 1m. (2) threw oneself into, on to x (a) yā ~ a rūwa he jumped into the water (cf. 1a.i) = nitsa 2. (b) yā ~ su = yā ~ musu = yā ~ garēsu he attacked them. (c) yā ~ mini da faɗa he ranted at me (= hau 1c.i). (cc) Vd. far. (d) ~ manyā garēshi he has no respect for his superiors. (e) ɓarāwo yā ~ a ɗaka a thief attacked the house. (f) yā ~ mini da dūka he belaboured me with blows. (g) yā ~ mata he raped her (= fāɗē). (3) set about x yā ~ nēmaŋ Kande he started courting Kande. yā ~ makarantā he began his schooling. (4) mum ~ naŋ, mum ~ caŋ we wandered about. (5) became reduced in bulk or quantity. (6) Vd. fāɗa wutā.

faɗāci Vd. faɗāta.

faɗaɗa A. (fāɗaɗa) Vb. 3B became broad.
  B. (fāɗaɗā) Vb. 1C broadened.
  C. (fāɗāɗā) broad (pl. of faffāɗā).
  D. (faɗaɗa) Vb. 3 Sk. stalked (= sa-ɗāɗa q.v.).

fāɗad da Vb. 4A. (1) dropped T. (2) (a) caused T. to fall. (b) yā fēɗam mini da gabā it disheartened me. (c) fāɗad da gaban dōki Vd. wuƙā 1f.

fā'ɗa-fāɗē∥ m. seeking hither and thither (cf. fāɗa 3).

faɗaka Vb. 3B. (1) awoke. (2) yā ~ da shī he's " alive " to it ; he realized it.

faɗakad da Vb. 4A. (1) awakened. (2) yā ~ nī it's made me alert ; caused me to realize the facts.

faɗa ƙawāyanka Vd. māƙwi.

faɗama f. (pl. faɗamōmī = faɗamū). (1) marshy ground x faɗamar shiŋkāfā paddy-field. (2) cattle disease rendering carcasses watery. (3) irin tafīyarsa ~ kusa nē the sound of its gallop shows it to be a slow, thin horse (epithet is ~ kusa dūsā nā giji). (4) wutar ~ f. = wutar 'yōla.

faɗa mãkwį *Vd.* mãkwį.

faɗamfaɗamā *f.* floundering about in work.

fādancī *m.* (1) (*a*) anā ∼ audience is being held by chief (*cf.* fāɗa). (*b*) yā tafi wajam ∼ he went to the audience-chamber. (*c*) ∼ yā cika audience-chamber is full. (*d*) ∼ yā wātsę = ∼ yā fashę = aŋ gama ∼ the audience is over. (2) obsequiousness ; flattery. (3) insincerity.

faɗandę *Fil. m.* sour milk with its full curd and cream (= kindirmō = sãrē 2 = tsāmī 1*g* = tsantsāmā 2*a* = babbartā), *cf.* nōnǫ.

fāɗar da = fāɗad da.

faɗātạ *Vb.* 2 (*p.o.* faɗãcē, *n.o.* faɗãci) to scold P.

fādāwā *Sk.* fāɗāwā courtiers (*pl. of* bafāɗa).

fāɗa wuta *m.* (*sg., pl.*). (1) moth. (2) epilepsy.

fāɗayyạ *f.* (1) = fāɗa-fāɗē. (2) straining every nerve.

fad da = fāɗad da.

faɗɗai *Vd.* faɗį 1*b.*

fad ɗayā instantly (= farat *q.v.*).

faɗe A. (fāɗē) *m.* yā yi matạ ∼ he raped her (= fāɗạ 2*g*), *cf.* shigē 2.
B. (faɗę) *Fil. m.* type of sandal (= ɓallē = ɓantalē = kad digãdigī = *Zar.* bį shānū).
C. (fāɗę) (*the form of* fāɗį *with dative*) *Vb.* 3A *x* rānā tā ∼ musu a jēji the sun set while they were in the " bush ".

fã'ɗe-fāɗē" = fã'ɗa-fāɗē".

Fādī abbreviation of woman's name Fātsuma.

faɗi A. (fāɗį) *Vb.* (*progressive* yanā fāɗūwā) (*Vd.* fāɗę). (1) (*a*) (i) fell down. (ii) garī yā ∼ the town was captured. (iii) birniŋ (= gãruŋ) ƙauyę yā sōmạ fāɗūwā *Vd.* birnī 6. (iv) muŋ gayạ muku iriŋ rāyukaŋ da kę fāɗūwā we have told you of the great number of casualties. (*b*) prostrated himself *x* yā ∼ yā gai da Sarkī he prostrated himself in salutation of the chief. (2) (*a*) fell over. (*b*) gwanin rawā yā fāɗi *Vd.* yau 2*g.* (3) fell on to, into (= fāɗạ 1*a.*i) *x* (*a*) yā ∼ a hanyạ it fell on to the road. yā ∼ cikin taskạr harsāshį it fell into the explosives-magazine. (*b*)

(i) yā ∼ a ƙasạ it fell on the ground. (ii) maganạ tasạ bā tạ fāɗūwā ƙasạ banzā his words have weight. (4) fell off *x* yā ∼ a dōkį = yā ∼ dagạ kaŋ dōkį he fell off the horse (= fāɗō). (5) (*a*) fell out *x* haƙōrī yā ∼ a tooth fell out (= famfạrē 1*b*) (*cf.* zubę 2*f*). (*b*) lapsed *x* azumī yā ∼ a kansạ he is beyond the age of obligatory fasting. shēkarạ ta bīyar tā ∼ there is no liability for tax in the 5th year. shēkarạ bā tạ fāɗūwā a jikạ *Vd.* jikī 2*d.* (*c*) = saukạ 4*a.* (6) became cheap *x* gōrǫ yā ∼ kolas are now cheaper. kãsūwā tā ∼ = arạhā tā ∼ there's a slump. (7) yā ∼ (*a*) he's dead. (*b*) his luck is out. (8) tā ∼ she (virgin) has begun to menstruate (*cf.* hailạ). (9) (*a*) rānā tā ∼ the sun has set (*cf.* gọrā 5). (*b*) taurārạnsạ yā ∼ his luck is out. (10) dạmunā tā ∼ the wet season has begun. (11) gabansạ yā ∼ he lost heart (= *Kt.* zubę 2*h*). (12) *Vd.* fāɗūwā, fāɗō, fāɗę, fāɗi tāshi, fāɗi ka mutu.
B. (fāɗī) *m.* (1) (*a*) breadth. (*b*) dūnīyạ, a fāɗin nan nātạ, bā mu da mataimakī we have not a friend in the world. (*c*) mu ga ta fāɗī, tsūtsạ tā kā da kuɗī it has happened though regarded as impossible. (*d*) fāɗin rūwā *Vd.* faŋkạm fayau. (2) *Vd.* fāɗin-*compounds.* (3) zamam ∼ = harɗē 4.
C. (faɗi) (1) *m.* (*a*) an yi masạ ∼ he's been warned he'll come to a bad end. (*b*) prediction (*pl.* faɗɗai) *x* an yi masạ ∼ zai yi sarautạ it has been foretold that he'll rule. (*c*) (*v.n. of* faɗā) *x* (i) a tẽkū kūwā mukę ∼ a jī it is on the sea that we are undisputed masters. sū nẽ kẽ faɗi a jī they are the ones in authority. (ii) kōwā, sǎi faɗiŋ albarkạcim bãkinsạ yakę yį everyone is putting his own construction on the matter. (iii) an yi masạ abim ∼, a cẽ kamar Annabi yā riŋjãyi kãfirai something memorable was done, as for example, a defeat inflicted on the pagans by the Prophet (*cf.* faɗā 2*b*). (iv) yā yi musu ∼ ɗayā he mentioned it to them casually (*cf.* faɗā 2*c*). (2) *Vb. Kt.* (= faɗā 1) *x* abin da ya ∼ what he said.

fǎɗi banzā *Vd.* fǎɗā 1c.

fǎɗi kạ mutu *m.* crockery (= taŋgaram), *cf.* tāsạ 2b ; farantị.

Fādimatạŋ = Fātsumạ.

fāɗim bāyā *Kt. m.* farming for wages (= ƙōdagō).

fǎɗi m fǎɗā *m.* = sā ṇ sạ̄.

fāɗiŋ kǎi *m.* (1) over-rating one's abilities. (2) dọmim fāɗiŋ kǎi bā ạ̄ tạrbaŋ ạrādu dạ kā = māyē 2b.

fāɗin rǎi = fāɗin zūciyā *m.* conceit.

fǎɗi tǎshi *m.* looking after *x* yanạ̄ yi wạ iyālịnsạ (bạ̄ƙō) ~ he's attending to the wants of his household (guest).

faɗo A. (fāɗō) *Vb.* 4A (1) (a) fell down, off *x* (a) yā ~ dạgạ kạn dōkị he fell off the horse. 'yā'yā sum ~ dạgạ kạŋ itạ̄cē fruit fell off the tree (= fāɗị 4). (b) am fāɗō dạgạ kạn dabīnọ, an zarcẹ rījịyā out of the frying-pan into the fire. (2) *Vd.* fāɗạ 1f.

B. (faɗō) *Vb.* 1E said and came *x* kạ faɗō kuɗiŋ hājạrkạ you'll have to sell off cheap ! (*cf.* fạɗā).

fǎɗum-fāɗum *m.* looking hither and thither (= fạ̄fụtụkā *q.v.*).

fāɗụwā *East Hausa f.* chief's residence (= fāɗạ *q.v.*).

fāɗụwā *f.* (1) *Vd.* fāɗị. (2) fāɗụwar gạbā losing heart (*Vd.* fāɗị 11). (3) (a) failure of transaction ; loss of profit *x* rībạ tasạ tā kōmạ fāɗụwā his profit became loss. (b) fāɗụwar baƙat tāsạ getting the worst of deal. (4) fāɗụwar gạrī sound of falling meteorite. (5) fāɗụwar mạganạ slip of the tongue. (6) (a) wạ̄ ya ƙi fāɗụwar mại rụmbū : mại kāzā̀ ? kō mại ạkwīyạ it's an ill wind which blows nobody any good. (b) kā ƙi fāɗụwā *Vd.* cịwō. (7) tā yi fāɗụwar murhụ her cooking somehow turned out wrong. *(8) (a) fāɗụwar rufu'ạ Arabic tanwīn, *i.e.* nominative -un (as in " kalbun "). (b) fāɗụwar fatahạ Arabic accusative -an (as in " kalban "). (c) fāɗụwar kisirạ Arabic genitive -in (as in " kalbin "). (9) fāɗụwar mại wạrkī *Vd.* tạkwạs 2a. (10) ƙasạ yakē ~ *Vd.* tsananī 1b.

fafa A. (fāfạ) *Vb.* 1A. (1) yā ~ ƙwaryā he split open gourd, etc. (*Vd.* fāfẹ). (2) yā ~ gyạɗā he shelled groundnuts.

(3) bā ạ̄ ~ gọrā rānar tạfīyạ don't leave things till last minute ! (= fāfẹ 1b), *Vd.* fạ̄fā 2b. (4) nā ~ masạ gōnā I gave him large part of my ground for his farm.

B. (fạ̄fā) (1) *Vb.* 2. (a) cleared large area for farm. (b) (*with dative*) nā fāfar masạ gōnā (i) I encroached on his farm. (ii) = fāfạ 4. (c) Wānẹ babban dumā nẹ ; indạ akạ tad dạ shī sǎi ~ he is most liberal. (2) fạ̄fā = fāfā *f.* (a) being occupied in splitting open gourds *x* yanạ̄ ~ he's splitting gourds (*cf.* fāfạ 1). (b) bạ̄ fạ̄fā *Vd.* baŋgō 4, gọrā 1d.

fạfạ-fạfạ quickly *x* bindigōgī mạsū harbị fạfạ-fạfạ quick-firing guns.

fafaka A. (fāfạkā) (1) groped in *x* nā fāfạkạ dākị I groped about in the house. nā fāfạkạ ạljīfūna I groped in my pocket (= lālụbā). (2) *Vb.* 1C yā fāfạkạ hannū cikin rāmị he groped in hole with his hand.

B. (fạ̄fakạ) *Vb.* 2 (1) groped for *x* yanạ̄ fạ̄fakạr fịtilạ he is groping for lamp (= lālubạ). (2) (fire) severely damaged (garment, house, etc.) *x* wutā tā fạ̄fạki rīgā tasạ.

fafake A. (fāfạkē) (1) *Vb.* 1C (fire) completely destroyed T. (2) *Vb.* 3A (well-mouth) crumbled.

B. (fạ̄fakē) *m.* (*secondary v.n. of* fāfạkā *or* fạ̄fakạ) *x* yanạ̄ ~ he's groping (= māmarē). yanạ̄ fạ̄fạkyam fịtilạ he's groping for the lamp.

fạ̄fạkī *m.* (*used after* mūdụ) *x* hatsī mūdụ 5 dạ ~ five measures of corn and an extra bit (*cf.* rạgī).

fạfạnnīyā *Kt. f.* looking hither and thither (= fạ̄fụtụkā), (*cf.* fạffannīyā).

fạ̄farạ *Vb.* 2 pursued ; drove away ; rounded up.

fạ̄farandạ (Eng. veranda) *f.* (1) veranda. (2) cleared space before house-door or compound of chief or wealthy P. for people to gather in (*cf.* dabị 3).

fạ̄farạtaŋ = fạ̄firạtaŋ = fạ̄furạtaŋ (1) entirely ; completely. (2) yā ƙi ~ he refused point-blank.

fạfạrnīyā *f.* = fạfạnnīyā.

fạfạs-fạfạs immediately.

fafat A. (fafat) *used in* (1) yā wạŋku ~

it's been spotlessly washed (= **fat**).
(2) **im bakī zā kạ yi, kạ yi didim** : **im farī zā kạ yi, kạ yi** ⌢ whatever your hand finds to do, do with all your might! (3) **yā kārẹ** ⌢ it's quite finished. B. (**fạfạt**) *m.* **kạzā tanạ̄** ⌢ chicken's fluttering. **gạbāna yanạ̄** ⌢ my heart's fluttering.

fāfātā *Vb.* 3A (1) **mum** ⌢ we've had serious quarrel. (2) failed to get one's way. (3) **yā fāfātō nị** he kept on at me.

fạfạyā-fạfạyā *f.* sound of quick walking.

faf dạ jiɓā *m.* horse of medium height and age (= **māgumẹ** 2).

fāfẹ (1) *Vb.* 1A. (*a*) = **fāfạ** 1, 2 *x* **yā** ⌢ **baŋgō** he made hole in wall. **yā** ⌢ **minị kậi** (**cikị**) he wounded me in head (stomach), *etc.* (*b*) **bā ạ̄** ⌢ **gyạndamā ran tạfīyạ** = **fāfạ** 3. (*c*) cleared whole of large area for farm (*cf.* **fạ̄fā** 1*a*). (*d*) **wutā tā** ⌢ **masạ rịgā** = **fạ̄fakạ** 2. (*e*) = **fạ̄fā** 1*b*.i. (2) *Vb.* 3A. (*a*) (garment) faded. (*b*) (well-mouth) crumbled (= **fāfạkē** 2). (*c*) (sore-place) spread *x* **kafạssạ tā** ⌢ sore-place on his leg spread (2 = **wāgẹ**).

fạffādā *adj. m.*, *f.* (*pl.* **fādạ̄dā**) very broad.

faffagọ *m.* (1) container only partially full. (2) **faffagwạŋ kātọ** burly fellow.

fạffakā *Kt. f.* flapping the wings (= **fụffụkā** *q.v.*).

fạffannīyā = **fạffạrnīyā** *f.* (1) fluttering of bird. (2) trembling; quivering (*cf.* **fạfạnnīyā**).

faffat = **fafat**.

fạ̄fil *Sk.* **yā cịka** ⌢ it's quite full (= **fal**).

fāfir = **fāfịr** = **fāfịratạŋ** = **fāfạratạŋ** *q.v.*

fāfịtịkā *Kt. f.* = **fāfụtụkā**.

fāfuŋgạ *f.* (1) big hole. (2) wide-mouthed well, hole, or pot. (3) toothless mouth.

fāfur = **fāfụr** = **fāfụratạŋ** = **fāfạratạŋ** *q.v.*

fāfụtụkā *f.* (1) looking hither and thither. (2) " straining every nerve " *x* **munạ̄** ⌢ **mụ gamạ aikịmmụ dạ saurī**.

fagaci A. (**fagạcī**) *m.* inner council-chamber where chief tries cases, holds audience with counsellors and receives friends (*cf.* **fādạ**). B. (**Fagạci**) *Zar.* an official position.

fagāgē *Vd.* **fagē**.

fagam-fagam = **fạgam-fạgamtū** *m.* = **fạgạmnīyā** *f.* = **fāfụtụkā** *q.v.*

Fagaŋ *Vd.* **kạ̄kạ̄kī** 3.

fạganẹ *Sk. m.* clay-lid of **rụfēwā** bin (= **afaŋgạlī** 2).

fạgānīyā *f.* = **fāfụtụkā**.

fagat *Sk.* suddenly (= **farat** *q.v.*).

fagē *m.* (*pl.* **fagāgē**). (1) (*a*) (i) any cleared open space (= **fīlī** 2*a* = **farzạyī**). (ii) **fagē** *sometimes has pl. adj.*) *x* **mạnyam fagyan yākị** the main theatres of war (*Vd.* 5 *below*). (iii) **yā shārẹ** ⌢ " he started the ball rolling ". (iv) **shạrar** ⌢ *Vd.* **shạrā** 2*e*. (*b*) space at entrance to compound (= **faŋgalī** = *Sk.* **garkā** 2), *cf.* **dabị**. (*c*) **fagē** = **fagyan sukūwā** (i) galloping-ground. (ii) lap on race-course *x* **dōkị bạ zai kai wannạm** ⌢ **ba** the horse will not last out this lap. (*d*) (i) **fagyaŋ wạ̄sā** playground (= **fịtinạ** 2*c* = **dātsạ** 2 = **dāgā** 3). (ii) **wannạm bạ fagyaŋkạ ba nẹ** this is not " in your line ". (iii) **gwạnin dạ kẹ fagē, shī makạdī kạm bi** beggars can't be choosers ! (*e*) **dōkị dayā ạ** ⌢ *Vd.* **dōkị** 1*c*. (2) (*a*) farm for **ayā** ; **ạlkamạ** ; **audụgā** ; **bābā** ; **dạŋkalị** ; **barkōnō** ; **gujīyā** ; **gyạdā** ; **rạkē** ; **rōgọ** ; **shịŋkāfā** (*cf.* **gōnā**). (*b*) **fagyaŋ gujīyā duhụ bạ wurim ɓuyā** *epithet of* " whited sepulchre". (3) (*a*) **har yạnzu yā kai nị fagyaŋ** I'm even *now* in possession of it. (*b*) **anạ̄ naŋ dăi, har ya kai gạ fagyaŋ yanạ̄ cị, hannū yanạ̄ rawā** things got to such a pitch that he could not eat without his hand trembling. **ta kai dăi fagyạm bā yạ̄ jiŋ kaŋ ụbaŋ** things went so far that he forgot his filial duty. (4) (*a*) **fagyaŋ wadạrī** place where thread is made into weaving-lengths. (*aa*) **Zạinabụ tā dauki fagyaŋ Kạnde** (i) Zainabu spaced out **wadạrī** pegs same distance apart (between **mạrī** and **gwaurō**) as those of Kande. (ii) Zainabu became marriageable just as Kande was married. (*b*) **fagyantạ** (= **rūwam fagyantạ**) **kwaryā shidạ nē** *Vd.* **rūwā** B.4*b*. (*c*) **rūwam** ⌢ = **dịddigā**. (5) (*a*) **fagyam fāmā** = **fagyan yākị** battlefield (*Vd.* 1*a*.ii). (*b*) **sun jā fagē** they fought a battle. (*c*) **sum būdẹ fagē** they have opened a front (of war). (6) **fagyam fyādị** (*a*) threshing-place. (*b*) place of **sharọ** contest. (7) **yā**

ga fagyaŋ gazạ̄wā he fell short. (8)
fagyam mutūwạ age of 60 upwards.
(9) sātạr ∼ ta yi she (woman in purdah)
went out of doors without husband's
permission.

faggọ *Fil. m.* (1) woman's load ready for
transport (= rūdwā). (2) yā yā dạ ∼
he's gone " sponging " on P.

fạhamạ *used in* nā fạhamạ now I understand! ; now I remember ! (*cf.* fạhimtạ).

fahạmī *Ar. m.* (1) intelligence. (2) drug
to produce intelligence.

fahamō = fạhamạ.

fahạrī *Ar. m.* = fạhạrīyạ *f.* ostentation ;
boastfulness ; showing-off (= ạlfahạrī *q.v.*).

*fạhartạ *Vb.* 3B behaved boastfully (*cf.*
fahạrī).

fạhimtạ *Ar.* (1) *Vb.* 2, 3B understood *x* nā
∼ dạ shī = nā fạhimcē shị I understand
(understood) it (= gānẹ = jī 2*a* =
hạŋkaltạ). yā ∼ yạddạ ya zamā asalim
mạganạ yanạ̄ dạgạ Tūrai he understood
why it is the real cause lies in Europe
(*cf.* fahimtō, fạhamạ). (2) *f.* intelligence.

fạhimtaccē *m.* (*f.* fạhimtaccīyạ) *pl.*
fạhimtạttū intelligent.

fahimtad dạ *Vb.* 4A caused P. to understand T.

fahimtō *Vb.* 1E. (1) understood one T.
on analogy of another (*cf.* fạhimtạ).
(2) understood T. by recollecting T.
previously forgotten.

fại openly *x* ∼ dạ 6ọye openly and
secretly.

fā'idạ *Ar. f.* (1) benefit. (2) profit. (3)
small present *x* nā sạmi ∼.

fạ̄'idantạ *Vb.* 2, 3B benefited by *x* mum
∼ dạ zamaŋkạ = mum fạ̄'idạnci
zamaŋkạ we benefited by your stay.
ạbin dạ zā kạ ∼ a thing whereby you'll
benefit.

fā'idantad dạ *Vb.* 4B caused P. to benefit
by T.

fạ̄'idạntu *Vb.* 3B *x* nā ∼ dạ shī I benefited
by it.

fạ̄ifạ (*Eng.* paper) *f.* currency-note.

faifai A. (fāifāi) *m.* (*pl.* fạyạ̄fạyǎi = Kt.
fayạ̄fǎi). (1) (*a*) (i) circular mat used
for covering vessels (= tǎitǎi). (ii)
yanạ̄ diŋkịm ∼ he's making such mat,
(iii) talạkạ ∼ nẹ ; kōịnā akạ jūyạ.

taŋkadẹ zại yi the people are mere
clay in hands of the rulers. (*b*) (i)
gramophone record. (ii) yā sauyạ
fǎifǎi he changed his tone. (iii) sunạ̄
kallō, sụ ga ịndạ fǎifǎi zại kạrkatạ
they're " sitting on the fence ". (iv)
lōkạcī yā yī dạ zā ạ būdạ sābam fǎifǎi
the time has come for a change of
fortune (*lit.* to put on a new disc). (ivA).
Vd. būdẹ 1*a*.iv. (v) yā jūyạ fǎifǎi
zūwạ gạ wannạŋ he turned his topic to
this. (*c*) (*mining term*) circular steel-
plate on gamjigo *q.v.* (*d*) part of snares
(= taskirā 3*a*). (2) gạmshẹ̄kā tā yi ∼
cobra expanded its hood. (3) dōkị yā
yi ∼ travelling chief has group of
horsemen on either side (= bạŋgạ-
baŋgạ). (4) kụnū yā yi ∼ gruel has
film on surface (*cf.* fạ̄ifǎi). (5) tā yi
mini ∼ she lifted her opened legs to
facilitate my copulating with her.
(6) *Vd.* dạuke fǎifạŋki ; būdẹ fǎifạŋki.
(7) būsạ dạ fǎifǎi *Vd.* būsạ 1*e*.

B. (fǎifǎi) *adv.* (1) in thin layer *x*
∼ akạ zubạ maŋ ạ tūwō the oil only
lightly covers the tūwō. (2) gạrī yā
yiwō ∼ dawn appeared faintly.

fǎifǎitā *Vb.* 3A ran away.

failū = fẹlū.

fạināfụr *Eng. m.* (*sg.*, *pl.*) pineapple
(= ạbạrbā *q.v.*).

Fạ̄jị name for any woman called Fātsumạ.

*fājircị *Ar. m.* depravity.

*fājịrī *m.* (*f.* fājịrā) *pl.* fājịrai depraved.

faka A. (fakạ) *Vb.* 3A. (1) took shelter ;
concealed oneself *x* n nạ̄ sọ̄ ṇ sạmi
wurī m̱ ∼ I'm looking for a refuge
(from rain ; pursuit, etc.) (= laɓẹ =
rāɓạkā 2). (2) fakạ dạ sheltered
behind *x* (*a*) nā fakạ dạ Audụ don ṇ
sạmē shị I used Audu's good offices to
get it. (*b*) fakạ̄wā ya yi dạ Audụ he
talked at someone else using Audu as
a mere blind. (*c*) yā ∼ dạ cīwọ he
malingered (= laɓẹ). (*d*) *Vd.* fakẹ.

B. (fạkā) *Vb.* 2 (1) lay in wait for.
(2) eavesdropped on P. (3) nā fạki
idansạ I waited to catch him off his
guard. (4) nā fạki numfāshinsạ, na
bā shị mạganạ I waited for the right
moment and then put forward my
request to him.

C. (fā̱kā) *Vb.* 2. (1) slapped (with sleeve of gown or with sandal). (2) hit down (fruit with stick). (3) (bird of prey) struck (another) with its wing.

fakad da̱ *Vb.* 4B concealed.

faka-faka A. (fakā-fa̱kā̱) *adj. m., f.* (*sg., pl.*) broad and thin.

B. (fa̱kā̱-fakā) *f.* looking hither and thither (= fā̱fu̱tu̱kā *q.v.*).

faka̱icē *Vb.* 3A = faka̱.

faḵai̱kai *Vd.* fa̱ḵo.

faḵā̱ḵē̱ *Vd.* fa̱ḵo.

fakāle̱ *m.* variety of silk got from dōka̱ tree (*cf.* tsāmīyā 2).

fa̱ka̱m-fakam *m.* looking hither and thither (= fā̱fu̱tu̱kā *q.v.*).

fa̱kānī *m.* 2,000 kolanuts.

fa̱kā̱nīyā̱ *f.* looking hither and thither (= fā̱fu̱tu̱kā *q.v.*).

fa̱karā *f.* (*pl.* fa̱ka̱rū = fa̱ka̱rai =faka-rōrī). (1) bush-fowl, francolin (= makwarwā *q.v.*). (2) kō ba̱ da̱ɗe̱ fa̱karā ita ka̱n zamā zā̱būwā (*said in song*) sooner or later prince becomes king. (3) *Vd.* fayau.

*faḵaru̱ *Ar. m.* poverty.

fakat A. (fa̱kat) *Ar.* that's all I wanted, thank you ! (= shī kē̱ na̱ŋ).

B. (fakat) *Kt. m.* the fowl-disease fuffuk.

fa̱kā̱tau *m., f.* (*sg., pl.*) P. with poor sight who thus jostles others.

fake A. (fake̱) *Vb.* 1A. (1) = faka̱ 1. (2) fake̱ da̱ = faka̱ 2 *x* (*a*) am ∼ da̱ guzumā, a̱ŋ ha̱rbi ka̱rsanā̱ an allusion to P. was made (*as in* faka̱ 2*b*). (*b*) fake̱ da̱ agā̱nā *Vd.* hanzarī 1*d*. (3) sheltered from *x* nā ∼ rūwā I sheltered from rain. (4) da̱ga̱ ∼ rūwā, ku̱mfa̱ shūka̱ ra̱ma̱ ? why make matters worse ? ; give him an inch and he takes an ell.

B. (fa̱kē) *Kt. m.* = fa̱kō.

fake-fake *Zar.* thin and flimsy.

fā̱ḵil *x* yā ci̱ka ∼ it's chock-full (= fal).

fa̱ḵīri̱ *Ar. m.* (*f.* fa̱ḵīri̱yā̱) *pl.* fa̱ḵīrai destitute (= matsi̱yā̱cī).

fa̱ḵkai *Vd.* fa̱ḵo.

fa̱kō *m.* ambushing *x* yanā̱ fa̱kwansa̱ he's lying in wait for it (= kwantō 2*a*).

fa̱ḵo = *Kt.* fa̱ḵō *m.* (*pl.* fa̱ḵā̱ḵē = fa̱kū-ḵūwa̱ = fa̱ka̱i̱kai = *Sk.* fa̱ḵḵai). (1)

hard, barren place (= ḵēḵūwā = *Sk.* fa̱ndaḵō = tsandaurī 1) *cf.* daḵau, tsa̱darī ; shā̱ɓūwā. (2) yā yi shūka̱ a̱ ∼ he acted uselessly. (3) *Sk.* fa̱ḵwa̱n d̄ā̱ki̱ beaten floor of room (= da̱ɓē 1*b*). (4) fitsārim ∼ evil recoiling on doer (*cf.* mu̱gu̱ntā 2). (5) bā ā̱ nēma̱ŋ kīfī a̱ ∼ he's a skinflint. (6) yā fā̱ɗa̱ ∼ he got into trouble. (7) *Vd.* tsira̱ fa̱ḵō.

fa̱ku *used in* (1) yā fa̱ku he's passed away, God rest his soul ! (2) fa̱kūwar A̱nnabi̱ the Prophet's demise.

fa̱ḵūḵūwa̱ *Vd.* fa̱ḵo.

fal A. (fal) (1) yā ci̱ka ∼ it's chock-full. (2) *Kt.* fa̱rī ∼ snow-white (= fat *q.v.*). (3) *Sk.* yā ∼ mini̱ he ranted at me (= far).

B. (fa̱l) (1) shining brightly *x* nā̱ ga haskyam fi̱tila̱ ∼ I saw lamp shining brightly. nā ga takō̱bī ∼ I saw a sword gleaming. wutā tā kāma̱ ∼ fire burnt up brightly. (2) yā bu̱ɗe̱ bā̱kinsa̱ ∼ he opened his mouth wide. (3) *Vd.* fa̱l-fa̱l.

fā̱lā *f.* bargain *x* yā sā̱mi ∼ he got a bargain.

falā-fa̱lā̱ *adj. pl.* broad and thin (= lafā-la̱fā̱).

falalā *Ar.f.* (1) prosperity. (2) abundance *x* gōnā cē̱ ∼ da̱ ita it's a spacious farm. (3) falalar zūcī̱yā contentment (= wa̱dar zūcī).

fa̱lale̱ = fa̱lali̱ *m.* (1) rock outcrop (= fā). (2) cement slaughter-slab.

falāmā *f.* (1) unpalatable mīya̱. (2) fu̱rā unpalatable, as too little milk.

fala̱ŋ (1) *m.* (*a*) single thickness of cloth, etc. (*cf.* ni̱ŋki̱ bīyū *two* thicknesses). (*b*) lōka̱ci̱n da̱ mulki̱ yanā̱ ∼ ɗayā in the days when the Emirs were arbiters of life and death. (2) *adv.* fala̱ŋ-fala̱ŋ separately. (3) *Vd.* fa̱llē ; fela̱ŋ.

fala̱sī *m.* (1) *Ar.* tenth of penny (= a̱nīnī). (2) interior ridge of cowrie.

falaskīyā *f.* T. adulterated, *etc.* (= balas-kīyā *q.v.*).

Fa̱la̱sdīnu̱ *f.* Palestine.

fa̱lau *adv.* (1) shining brightly (= fa̱l *q.v.*). (2) flutteringly (*garment in wind, etc.*).

fale-fale *adj. m., f.* (*sg., pl.*) thin and flimsy.

falfādā = falfādīyā = falfāɗuwā *Sk. f.* epilepsy.

faḷ-faḷ (1) flutteringly (*garment in wind, etc.*). (2) *cf.* faṛ-faṛ.

falfala A. (faḷfaḷā) the basket ḷēfē.

  B. (faḷfaḷā) *Vb.* 3A yā ~ ɗa gudu he fled.

faḷfaḷnīyā *Sk. f.* (1) brightness of lamp. (2) sheen, gloss.

faḷgabā *Kt. f.* terror (= faṛgabā *q.v.*).

fāḷi *Sk. m.* = faḷḷē 3.

faḷīshaŋ (*Eng.* pleasure) *m.* touring car (*contrasted with* lorry).

fāḷīya *f.* (*sg., pl.*) type of fish.

falka *Vb.* 3A *Kt.* (1) awoke (= farka). (2) *Vb.* 1A ripped (= farka). (3) falkāwar kāsā *f.* being wise *after* the event.

falke A. (falkē) *m.* (1) itinerant trader (= farkē *q.v.*). (2) type of fish.

  B. (falke) *Vb.* 3A *Kt.* is (was) ripped (= farke *q.v.*).

falkin darē *Kt. adv.* in the middle of the night (*cf.* talātaini).

falla A. (faḷḷa) *Vb.* 1A yā ~ ɗa gudu he fled.

  B. (faḷḷā) *Vb.* 2 lopped off (*Vd.* faḷḷē).

faḷḷāku = *Kt.* faḷḷāko *m.* food brought by mistress to lover (*Vd.* Faḷḷau 2).

faḷlaḷā (*Ar.* to broaden) *Vb.* 1C (*with dative*). (1) increased opportunities of P. *x* am ~ masa he's been specially favoured. (2) ka ~ mini give me more room to move !

fallaŋ = falaŋ.

fallasa A. (faḷḷasa) *Vb.* 2 (*p.o.* faḷḷashē, *n.o.* faḷḷashi) shamed P. by revealing his secrets (= taḷḷa 2 = tambarī 11 = tērērē 3 = tsīrī = rārē 1e = *Kt.* tayyace = *Kt.* tarwātū 2).

  B. (faḷḷasā) *Vb.* 1C squandered.

fallasad da *Vb.* 4A squandered.

faḷḷasasshē *m.* (*f.* faḷḷasasshīyā) *pl.* faḷḷasassū blabber.

faḷḷashē *Vd.* faḷḷasa.

Faḷḷau *m.* (1) name of a flat-topped hill at Gano. (2) *if mistress is seen taking food to her lover and asked what it is, she replies* ~ nē babban dūtsē, *i.e.* mind your own business ! (*Vd.* faḷḷāku).

falle A. (falle) (1) *Vb.* 3A yā ~ ɗa gudu he fled. (2) *Vb.* 1A (*a*) completely lopped off, severed (*cf.* faḷḷā). (*b*) am ~ masa kāi he's been beheaded (= sārā 1*b.*iii = ƙille).

  B. (falle) *m.* one unit *x* takarɗā ~ ɗayā single sheet of paper. kāyā ~ ɗayā only one load (*cf.* gudā 1*d*, falaŋ).

  C. (faḷḷē) *m.* (1) (*a*) (*secondary v.n. of* faḷḷā) *x* anā faḷḷansa = anā faḷḷassa it's being lopped off. (*b*) anā faḷḷaŋ hatsī (= kāwō 4*a*) heads of standing corn are being lopped off (*because only sparse crop due to poor rain, and not worth reaping* (girbi): *epithet is* Faḷḷē, mūguŋ girbi : kōwā ya yi ka, ɗamunā tā bāshē shi). (3) dagaci yā yi musu ~ village-head got in tax early by using duress.

faḷḷō *Hadejiya Hausa m.* grass roof of corn-bin (rumbū).

faḷmaki *Kt. m.* sudden attack *x* an yi musu ~.

falmaraŋ *f.* (*sg., pl.*) waistcoat (*epithet is* ~ bi ki rufe cībīyā ba : kuɗiŋki sum fi na gārē).

Falmataŋ name for any woman called Fātsuma.

fam A. (fam) *adv.* (1) securely *x* yā ɗauru ~ it's securely tied. (2) dōki yā ƙētare rāmi ~ horse leapt clear across the hole. (3) *cf.* fam-fam.

  B. (fam) *Eng. m.* (*pl.* fammai = famfamai). (1) pound sterling. (2) ~ cika tēkū zam bā ka = tantalaminya.

fama A. (fāmā) *m.* (1) struggling *x* yanā ~ ɗa aiki = yanā fāmaŋ aiki he's striving to finish the work. sai ɗa muka shā ~, muka sāmu we only got it after utmost effort. sunā ~ they're quarrelling. n nā ~ da cīwo I'm afflicted with illness. (2) mazājam ~ *Vd.* namiji 1*c*.

  B. (fāma) *Vb.* 1A. (1) *x* am ~ Audu (= an yi masa fāmi) matter of Audu's crime, etc., considered closed, has been reopened ; " he has been touched on a sore spot." (2) (*a*) hurt in place already sore *x* yā ~ kansa = yā yi wa kansa fāmi he hurt his already sore head. (*b*) *Vd.* tabo 2*b*.

fam-fam A. (fam-fam) *adv.* (1) = fam 1. (2) *emphasizes* swelling or fullness.

B. (fam-fạm) m. small tin (= gwaŋ-gwaŋ 1, q.v.).

C. (fạm-fam) (1) adv. completely x yā ƙārę ~. (2) m. gruel of pounded rice or of pounded corn.

D. (fạm-fạm) Vd. fạm-fạm-fạm.

famfamā Sk. f. cranium.

fạmfạmai Vd. fạm.

fam-fam-fam A. (fam-fạm-fam) completely x yā ƙārę ~ (= fạm-fam 1).

B. (fạm-fạm-fạm) x yanā tạfīyạ ~ he's treading clumsily.

famfamī m. (1) wooden trumpet blown for Chief = fārai (cf. kākākī). (2) dōkị yanā ~ horse's fidgeting and jerking its head up.

fạmfạmnīyā Sk. f. looking hither and thither (= fāfutụkā).

fạmfạŋgārị m. (f. fạmfạŋgārīyā) dull-witted lout.

famfara A. (famfạrā) (1) Vb. 3A yā ~ dạ gudụ he fled. yā ~ dạ sukūwā he galloped quickly. yā famfarō gidā he hastened home. (2) Vb. 1C used in (a) yā famfạrạ dōkị he galloped his horse quickly. (b) yā famfạrạ tuntubę he had a bad stumble. (3) cf. famfạrē.

B. (fạmfarạ) f. (1) shedding milk-teeth (= kạrāyạ 2g). (2) cf. ţamfaryā.

fạmfạrạfạm adv. empty-handed.

fạmfạrarrē m. (f. fạmfạrarrīyā) pl. fạm-fạrạrrū shameless.

fạmfạrạtạŋ adv. entirely (= fāfạrạtạŋ q.v.).

famfạrē (1) Vb. 3A. (a) yā ~ ạ guję he fled (= famfạrā 1). (b) (tooth) fell out (as milk tooth or by accident) (= fādị 5a), cf. zubę 2f. (c) Kt. (tool) became unhafted (= kwaɓę 2a). (2) Vb. 1C. (a) Kt. unhafted (tool) (= kwaɓę). (b) yā famfạrę ƙafạ he stumbled and hurt his foot. (c) yā ~ mini haƙōrī he knocked out my tooth.

famfarērę m. (f. famfarērīyā) = fam-farmēmę.

famfarīyā = famfaryā Kt. f. (1) x fartanyạr tanā ~ the hoe constantly becomes unhafted. (2) ƙūsạ māgạnim ~ epithet of small, strong P. or animal.

famfarmēmę m. (f. famfarmēmīyā) huge (re hole or house).

famfarmī m. (f. famfarmā) = famfar-mēmę.

famfarō (1) Sk. m., f. (sg., pl.) destitute (= matsīyācī). (2) Vd. famfạrā.

famfaryā Vd. famfarīyā.

famfatsa A. (famfạtsā) Vb. 1C = ţạm-fatsạ Vb. 2 shattered.

B. (famfatsā) Kt. ạrādụ tạ yi minị ~ I swear I didn't ! ; I swear I won't !

famfạtsē (1) Vb. 1C shattered. (2) Vb. 3A is (was) shattered.

famfatsī Kt. m. = famfatsā.

famfọ Eng. m. (pl. famfunā) pump.

fāmị = fāmụ m. (1) Vd. fāmạ. (2) fāmịŋ gyạmbō yā fi gyạmbō zāfī = fāmị yā fi jịn cīwọ zāfī reopening a matter is bitterer than the original matter.

fạmmai Vd. fạm.

fạŋ = fạm.

fancạ Eng. f. (sg., pl.) puncture in tyre.

fandạƙā Vb. 1C x yā fandạƙạ kwānọ hę (seller) pushed up bottom of tin fraudulently to decrease holding-capacity.

fạndạƙai = fạndạƙaiƙai m. shallowness x rūwā (kwānọ) yā yi ~ water (tin) is shallow.

fạndạƙaiƙayī m. (f. fạndạƙaiƙayā) shallow.

fandạƙē Vb. 3A Sk. (place) is hard and barren.

fandạƙō m. (1) hard, barren place (= faƙọ). (2) waterless well. (3) miserly P. (= marọwạcī). (4) kạntạ ~, mę zā ạ kitsạ how plait such scanty tresses !

fạndal = fạndam used in yā cịka ~ it's chock-full.

fandamēmę = fandamī m. (f. fanda-mēmīyā = fandamā) huge.

fanɗarad dạ Vb. 4A caused to swerve ; caused to become apostate.

fạnɗạrarrē m. (f. fạnɗạrarrīyā) pl. fạn-ɗạrạrrū apostate.

fanɗạrē Vb. 3A (1) yā ~ dạgạ hanyạ he swerved off, strayed from the road (= rātsę 1a). (2) yā ~ dạgạ ạddīnị he apostasized (= rātsę 1b). (3) yā ~ dạgạ mạgạnạr sauransụ he differed from the rest in opinion. (4) (road, branch) is (was) crooked. (5) x kō tarŏ bai ~ ba not even a threepenny-bit is missing.

fanę *Eng. m.* (*sg., pl.*) penny.

fangalī *m.* (*pl.* **fangullą = fangalai = fangalŏlī** = *Sk.* **fangallai**). (1) space at entrance to compound (= **fagē** 1*b*). (2) broad plain. (3) beds of irrigated-farm (**lambū**) = **kŏmī** 1*d*. (4) woman's plot of **murūcī**. (5) **mai fangaliŋ kąi** *m., f.* big-headed P.

fangamī *m.* straight, flat, iron stirrup (= **zįrnąwį**).

fangarą *Vb.* 2 *Kt.* kicked *as in* **mąŋgarą** *q.v.*

fangīmą *f.* (1) looking hither and thither (= **fąfutųkā**). (2) making wild guesses.

fangullą *Vd.* **fangalī**.

fanjāmą *Eng. f.* pyjamas.

fanką *Eng. f.* punkah.

fankacēcę *m.* (*f.* **fankacēcįyā**) very broad.

fankamā (1) *f.* insolence to a superior. (2) *Vd.* **fankamī**.

fankamēmę *m.* (*f.* **fankamēmįyā**), *pl.* **fankam-fankąm** = **fankam-fankąŋ** very broad.

fankąm fayąu *m.* (1) broad, shallow expanse of water. (2) P., T. belying good exterior or whose qualities are disappointing (*epithet is* ~, **fādin rūwā, bą̄ zurfī**) = sululū **kąsau** = **fankŏ** 2 = **farī** 2*e* = **hūhų** 3 = **karąrrawą**.

fankamī (1) (*with fem.* **fankamā**). (*a*) very broad. (*b*) very big (*re* horse). (*c*) fool. (2) *m.* = **fangamī**.

fankankąmī *m.* (*f.* **fankankąmā**) *pl.* **fankam-fankąm** = **fankami** 1.

fankankąŋ *used in* **fādī gąrēshį** ~ it is very broad.

fankashalcį = **fankashālancį** *m.* (1) senselessness. (2) extravagance, prodigality.

fankąshālį *m.* (*f.* **fankąshālįyā**) *pl.* **fankąshālai**. (1) senseless P. (2) extravagant P.

fankąsŏ *Sk.* = **fankąsū** *Kt.* the cake **funkąsŏ** *q.v.*

fankē (*Eng.* pancake) *m.* (*sg., pl.*) fried cake of English flour.

fankŏ *m.* (1) T. deprived of its essence (*x* used tea-leaves; empty match-box; impotent male; impoverished P.) = **tįkā** 1 = *Sk.* **dąbzā**), *cf.* **sānę**. (2) (*a*) P. belying good appearance (*x* weak

P. looking strong; mean P. of rich exterior) = **fankąm fayąu**. (*b*) *epithet is* **Fąŋkŏ** gidan **ąshānā**. (3) counterfeit money (= **dan Jąbū**). (4) ~ **lūdayiŋ kŏko : dą** girmā, **bą̄ dībą** *epithet of* (*a*) miser. (*b*) the ladle **makamfacī**.

fanną (1) *Vd.* **Arị** ; **hawą̄yē** 2 ; **gąrmā** 1*c*. (2) **Na** ~ **fą̄rā irįn yawą** ; **kŏįnā ka jē, dą dubunsų** *epithet of* **Bąbarbarę**.

fąnnai (1) rocky outcrops (*pl. of* **fā**). (2) *Vd.* **fannị** 1.

fannị *Ar.* (1) *m.* (*pl.* **fannŏnī** = **fąnnai**). (*a*) type, category *x* **ą wąnę** ~ **ka dąukē shị** in what category of P. do you put him ? **ą fannim mųtumịŋ kirkį muką dąukē shị** we consider him upright. *(b)* science *x* **fannįn tąurą̄rī** astronomy ; astrology. *(c)* **shą̄ fannŏnī** *m., f.* highly learned P. (2) **fannị-fannị** *adv.* of many kinds *x* **yaną̄ dą sanị fannị-fannị** he has a knowledge of many subjects.

fąnnū rocky outcrops (*pl. of* **fā**).

fansa A. (**fąnsā**) *Vb.* 2 (*p.o.* **fąnshē**, *n.o.* **fąnshi**). (1) redeemed (slave) (= **kąrbā** 1*d*). (2) ransomed (prisoner of war). (3) (*a*) bought (Koran). (*b*) bought T. which one *asks* P. to sell one, he not having put it on sale (*Vd.* **sąyā** ; **fansad dą**).

B. (**fąnsā**) *f.* (1) (*a*) (*secondary v.n.* of **fąnsā**) *x* **yaną̄ fansar bāwą** = **yaną̄ fansar bāwą** he's redeeming the slave. (*b*) ransom-price *x* **bāwą yā karyą** ~ the slave has arranged price of his ransom with his master. **ųbangijịm bāwą yā karyą masą** ~ the master has fixed ransom-price of his slave. (2) **yā dąukŏ** (= **yā dąu**) **fansā** (*a*) he retaliated, revenged himself. (*b*) he rewarded P., made requital of good with good. (*c*) **nā dąukŏ fansar Audų** I took revenge (retaliated) for the injury done Audu. (*d*) **ną̄ dąukŏ fansā ą kąnsų** I'll be revenged on them (*cf.* **fanshę, sāką**).

fansad dą *Vb.* 4A sold *under same conditions as* **fąnsā** 3.

fanshe A. (**fanshę**) *Vb.* 1A retaliated for *x* **yā** ~ **tąkaicin dą aką yi masą** he revenged himself for the annoyance he'd suffered (*cf.* **fansā** 2) = **farkę** 2*b*.

B. (**fąnshē**) *Vd.* **fąnsā**.

fanshi *Vd.* fansā.

fantamạ *f.* saddlecover (jạlālạ) having tinsel edges (= kā ƙi Bīmạ).

fantamēmẹ, *etc.* = faŋkamēmẹ.

fantạntaŋ = faŋkạŋkaŋ.

fantaryạ *Nor. f.* the hoe fartanyạ *q.v.*

fantsạ *Vb.* 1A = *Kt.* fantsạlā *Vb.* 1C = fantsạmā.

fantsama A. (fantsạmā) *Vb.* 1C. (1) yā fantsạmạ tạrō he scattered the crowd. (2) yā fantsạmạ lạ̄bārị he spread the news. (3) itạ̣cē yā fantsạmạ 'yā'yā tree has abundant fruit. (4) yā fantsạmạ dawākī he sent out cavalry. (5) yā ~ minị rūwā he splashed me with water.
B. (fạntsamạ) *Vb.* 3B. (1) (crowd) scattered. (2) (news) spread.

fantsamad dạ *Vb.* 4B = fantsạmā 1, 2.

fạntsạmạ idō (*lit.* what spurts into the eye) *m.* (1) boiled meat exposed for sale. (2) driveller.

fantsạmē *Vb.* 3A = fạntsama.

fantsạmi what a prolific tree ! (*cf.* fantsạmā 3).

fantsara A., (fantsạrā) *Vb.* 1C. (1) tā fantsạrạ niƙạ she ground corn coarsely. tā fantsạrạ tūwō she ground corn coarsely for tūwō (= ganjạrā = gantsạrā 1*b* = yaŋgạrā), *cf.* ɓarzạ ; dạ̄bāzạ. (2) am fantsạrạ rānā yạu sun was scorching to-day (= ganjạrā). (3) itạ̣cē yā fantsạrạ 'yā'yā tree has abundant fruit.
B. (fạntsarạ) what coarse grinding !

fantsare A. (fantsạrē) (1) *Vb.* 3A rānā tā ~ yạu = fantsạrā 2. (2) *Vb.* 1C ƙạrē yā ~ (= fantsarō) minị haƙọrā the dog snarled at me.
B. (fạntsarẹ) *m.* coarsely-ground flour.

fantsar-fantsar = fạntsạrtsạr.

fạntsạrtsạr *adv.* an niƙạ shi ~ it (flour) is coarsely-ground (*cf.* lilis).

fanyā *f.* (1) cleared piece of ground. (2) yā shā ~ (*a*) he went roundabout way. (*b*) he went round to head P. or animal off (= kạ̈i 1A.*b.*ii). (*c*) *Kt.* he went along road-edge to get ahead of others. (3) *Kt.* yā yi ~ while eating in company, he made some ordinary remark which through their enjoyment of their

food, sent the others into fits of laughter (= *Sk.* sịntī).

fanyạcē *Vb.* 1C revealed, explained.

fanyar *adv.* clearly visible *x* gạ̄ tạurạ̄rī ~.

fanyạtu *Vb.* 3B (1) is (was) clearly visible. (2) is (was) easy to understand.

fanyẹ *Vb.* 1A (1) = fanyạcē. (2) scraped ground to clear weeds.

fạnzạ *m.* yanạ̄ ~ he's never done Mecca pilgrimage = ɓarọ 2 = bạbanjẹ (*cf.* ạl-hajị).

far A. (far) *used in* (*a*) yā ~ minị (i) he attacked me. (ii) he ranted at me (*derived from* fādạ 2). (*b*) dūtsẹ ạ far makạ bạ̄ dādī, kạ far wạ mụtụm bạ̄ dādī energetic P. is energetic whatever befall him.
B. (fạr) (1) abundantly *x* mutạ̄nē sunạ̄ naŋ ~. tạurạ̄rī sum fitō ~. (2) *cf.* far-fạr.
C. (fạr) *East Hausa m.* ostentatiousness, boastfulness (= fạ̄rīyạ).

fara A. (fārạ) *Vb.* 1A (= sōmạ = kāmạ 4) (*it is followed by v.n. or noun with verbal sense*). (1) began to *x* (*a*) (*followed by v.n.*) yā ~ sāmụn saukī he has begun to recover. hadirị yā ~ tāsọ̄wā a storm has begun to blow up. yā ~ bā tạ he paid her the first instalment. wutā tā ~ hụrūwā the fire began to burn up well. (*b*) (*followed by noun with verbal sense*) yā ~ girmā it has begun to become big. sum ~ ƙọ̄ƙarī they've begun to exert themselves. lạ̄bārai sum ~ dāmā the news has begun to improve. yā ~ ɗaŋ halī he's up to his tricks again. (*c*) zā mụ ~ ta kạm farin lạ̄bārị we'll begin with relating the good news. (*d*) *for intransitive sense, Vd.* 5 *below.* (*e*) dạgạ kạ̄zā (= dạgạ taskirā) ya fārạ *Vd.* taskirā. (*f*) ta kạm fārạ haƙạ *Vd.* tsanyạ 1*c.* (2) began by *x* (*a*) yā ~ zūwạ gidam mijịn 'yā tasạ he went first to his son-in-law's house. kạ ~ kạrạ̄tū (= kạ ~ yiŋ kạrạ̄tū), kānạ kạ yi rụbụ̄tū first read, then write ! (*b*) bạ̄ ạbin dạ sukạ ~ yị̄ sǎi sukạ kwāshẹ ạbincimmụ their first act was to remove our food. (*c*) bại ~ wata mạganạ ba sǎi ya cẹ̈ . . . his first act was to declare that . . . (3) did for the first time x **ạ wurīna ta** ∼ **haifụ̄wā** it was as *my* wife that she first conceived. (4) was the first to do x (a) **wg̣ ya** ∼ **ginịn sumuntị ạ Kanọ** who initiated concrete-building at Kano ? (= **firtsạ** = **tā dạ** 1c *q.v.* = **fg̣rā** 1 = **fārad dạ** = **tsịrā** 1a). (b) **wg̣ ya** ∼ **zūwạ ạ cikiŋkụ** which of you arrived first ? **shī ng̣ ya** ∼ **minị zạncạŋ** *he* broached it to me. (5) (*intransitive*) x (a) **kalmạ tā** ∼ **dạ bạbbam bakī** the word begins with a capital letter (= **fg̣ru** 2a). (b) **yg̣yạ akạ** ∼ **har ka yi rg̣i** how does it come about that you're alive ? (c) "**dạ hakạ mukạ fārạ**", **kuturū yā ga maị kyạsfī** learn from what has befallen me !

B. (**fg̣rā**) (1) *Vb.* 2 = **fārạ** 4 *q.v.* x **wg̣ ya fg̣ri ginịn sumuntị ạ Kanọ** who initiated concrete-building at Kano ? (= **fārạ** 4a = **fārad dạ**). **shī ng̣ ya fg̣rē nị dạ zạncạŋ** *he* broached it to me (*all* = **sọ̄mā**). (2) *f.* (*sg.*, *pl.*) *pl.* **fg̣rī** = **fārōrī** (a) (i) locust, grasshopper (*cf.* **d̶aŋgō** 2 ; **wutar fg̣rā**). (ii) **dạ sāfē a kạŋ kāmạ** ∼. **in rānā tā yī, sǎi sụ tāshị** the early bird catches the worm. (b) **zūwg̣m** ∼ **dạ rānī** = **zūwạm fg̣rar Garkọ** *m.* " a wild goose chase ". (c) *Vd.* **fg̣rar tụmfāfīyā**. (d) **sū** ∼ **kg̣ rabạ nē** they're pals. **g̣būtā ram** (= **g̣būtā ramau**) **tsạkāninsụ kạmar sg̣ rabạ** ∼ there is the closest friendship between them. (e) **bg̣kim** ∼ *m.* (i) turban with red edge. (ii) type of edge-finish of caps **mạrạfīyạ, tg̣gīyạ**. (f) *Vd.* the game **dạkū**. (g) **ganim fg̣rā** *Vd.* **Allg̣** 7g. (h) ∼ **irịn yawạ** *Vd.* **fannạ**. (j) *Vd.* **barkạ** 8 ; **cị fg̣rā**. (k) **kạfam fg̣rā** *Vd.* **dōhịlō**.

C. (**farā**) *f.* (1) white (*Vd.* **farī**). (2) **yā ci** ∼ = **yā cī dạ** ∼ he's in luck. (3) (a) **farā** = **farar mạshassharā** anæmia. (b) ∼ **makēkashīyā** anæmia with cadaverousness (a, b = **bạyammā** 1). (c) *Vd.* **sạndā** 2. (4) *Vd.* **farar-**compounds.

fạra'ạ *Ar. f.* permanently cheerful disposition (= **wạlwạlā**), *cf.* **nịshātsị ; g̣nnạshụ̄wā**.

farābịtị *Eng. m.* private soldier.

farg̣cē *Vb.* 3A became anæmic (*cf.* **farā** 3).

fārad dạ *Vb.* 4A initiated x **wg̣ ya** ∼

ginịn sumuntị who initiated cement-buildings ? (= **fg̣rā**).

farad dạ farad suddenly, unexpectedly (= **farat** *q.v.*).

farad dạ laụjē *m.* (*sg.*, *pl.*) tireless servant-lad.

fg̣rạ-farạ *f.* after rains, making ridges for spring-sowing (= **hūrạ** 2b = **gwarzō** 3 = **wọ̄rā**).

fg̣rāgạ *Ar. f.* (1) leisure. (2) opportunity. (3) bargain.

farag gēzạ *f.* the shrub *Combretum aculeatum.*

farai A. (**fārai**) *m.* the wooden trumpet **famfamī** *q.v.*
B. (**farai**) used in **darē** ∼ all night long (= *Kt.* **farat** 3).

***farạlī** *Ar. m.* = **fạrillạ** 1.

fạrạllī *m.* cast in the eye (= **dūbaŋ garkẹ** = *Kt.* **hạrg̣rạ garkẹ**).

farạltā *Ar. Vb.* 1C imposed as religious duty (*cf.* **fạrillạ**).

faram (1) **yanạ̄ dạ hūdạ** ∼ it has a gaping hole (*pl.* **yanạ̄ dạ hūdōjī faram-fg̣ram**). (2) ∼ **bisạ** you behind me, beware of overhanging branch ! (*cf.* **bụlākạ ; bugụ** 4 ; **lif** 3).

farạm-farạm = **faram-fg̣ram** *m.* or *adv.* (1) **yanạ̄ tạfīyạ** ∼ I hear him walking quickly. (2) *Vd.* **faram**.

fg̣ramfataŋ = **faramfataŋ** entirely (= **fg̣-fạratạŋ** *q.v.*).

fg̣randạ *Eng. f.* veranda, *etc.* (= **fg̣fg̣randạ** *q.v.*).

faraŋgaịtā (1) *Vb.* 3A travelled slowly from illness, fatigue, etc. (2) **faraŋgaitō** *Vb.* 1E. (a) limped to (place) through illness, etc., x **yā faraŋgaitō gidāna**. (b) (*opprobriously used*) x **yā faraŋgaitō gạrēkạ** he went to cadge from you or to collect debt from you with whom he was on bad terms. (c) *Vd.* **fạraŋgaitaccē**.

faraŋgaitaccē *m.* (*f.* **fạraŋgaitaccīyā**) *pl.* **fạraŋgaitattū**. (1) P. or animal straying into place through not knowing where to go. (2) P. tired out from journey. (3) P. sheltering behind influential P.

fạraŋgaitū *m.* looking hither and thither (= **fg̣fụtụkā** *q.v.*).

farạnjī *Sk. m.* bride's white cloth (= **tsg̣lālạ**).

farₐŋkamā *f.* smallpox with only few isolated pustules.

Farₐnsₐ = Farₐnsₐ̦i.

Farₐnsₐ̦i (1) *m.* (*a*) (i) Frenchman ; Frenchmen (*Vd.* Bₐfₐransi̦). (ii) 'yā'yā na ⁓ the Free French. (iii) ⁓ Mafₐḑātā the Fighting French. (*b*) ₐshānar ⁓ red-headed, highly-inflammable safety-matches. (2) *f.* (*a*) France. (*b*) Frenchwoman ; Frenchwomen.

Farₐnsi̦ *f.* = Farₐnsₐ̦i 2*a.*

farₐntā *Vb.* 1C (1) whitened. (2) yā ⁓ mini̦ ciki̦ = yā ⁓ mini̦ zūci̦yā = yā ⁓ mini̦ rₐ̦i (*cf.* farin ciki̦). he made me happy.

fₐrₐntam entirely (= fₐ̄fₐratₐŋ *q.v.*).

faranti̦ (*Eng.* plate) *m.* (*pl.* fₐrₐntai). (1) plate(s) (*cf.* fₐ̦ḑi kₐ mutu̦ ; haƙōrī 6*b*). (2) shallow metal or wooden tray.

farₐntū *Kt. m.* looking hither and thither (= fₐ̄futukā *q.v.*).

fₐrₐrₐ *adv.* (1) boundlessly *x* dubū ⁓ countless thousands. shₑ̄kₐrū ⁓ year after year. gₐrī ⁓ numberless towns. kudī ⁓ unlimited money. gōnā cₑ̄ ⁓ it's an immense farm. (2) *Vd.* fₐrₐuci. (3) sukₐ zaunₐ fₐrₐrₐ ₐbinsu̦ then they stood staring like gabies.

farārₐ̄cē *Vb.* 3*a* is (was) anæmic (*Vd.* fₐrā).

farₐ̄rē white (*pl. of* farī).

farar gēzₐ = farag gēzₐ.

farar gwₐnā *f.* foresight ; thrift (= tānₐḑī).

farar ƙafₐ *f.* ⁓ gₐrēshi̦. (1) his feet have very white soles (considered unlucky) = ₐlhaji̦ 6. (2) he's very unlucky (= farin sau).

farar ƙasā *f.* whitewash *x* yā shāfₐ ⁓ ji̦kim baŋgō he whitewashed the wall.

farar ƙayₐ *f.* the gum-yielding *Acacia sieberiana.*

farar kₐ̄zā *Vd.* bi̦kī 1*e.*

farar maganₐ *Vd.* farī 2*f.*

farar mₐshasshₐrā *Vd.* mₐshasshₐrā 2.

fararrₐutā *Vb.* 1D = faraurₐutā.

fₐ̄rₐrrē *adj. m.* (*f.* fₐ̄rarrīyā) *pl.* fₐ̄rₐrrū (1). having been begun (*Vd.* fārₐ). (2) ⁓ ƙārₐrrē no sooner said than done !

farar ri̦gā *Vd.* ri̦gā 1*r.*

farar sa'ₐ *Kt. f.* the white bead gu̦mbā 4*a.*

farar tsūtsₐ *f.* tapeworm (= tsīlā *q.v.*).

fₐ̄rar tu̦mfāfi̦yā *f.* malodorous green locust, said to be poisonous to eat (= gam).

farar wutā *f.* sulphur (= ₐlkibi̦rī = *kalmuntakō).

farar zūci̦yā *f.* (1) equability. (2) happiness (*cf.* farī 1*c.*ii).

farₐ̄shē damaged kolas (*Vd.* farsā).

farāshi̦ (*Eng.* price) *m.* (1) price (of articles such as hides, ground-nuts, etc., in transactions with European firms). (2) fee paid to prostitute.

farat (1) *adv. or m.* instantly *x* ⁓ (= farat ḑayā) sₐ̈i ya amsₐ he answered immediately. ya yi ⁓, ya tāshi̦ then he at once set out (= maza 2). (2) *x* ₐkwiyₐ kudī farat ḑayā cₑ̄ goats command a ready sale. (3) *Kt.* darₑ̄ ⁓ all night long (= farai). (4) (*a*) yā yi farat-farat dₐ mū he received us kindly. (*b*) farat-farat *m.*, *f.* (*sg.*, *pl.*) cordial P.

fₐ̄ratₐ *Vb.* 3B behaved boastfully (*cf.* fₐ̄rīyₐ).

fₐ̄rau (1) *m.* (*negatively*) *x* bₐ̄ ⁓ nₑ̄ gₐrēkₐ ba *you* did not institute it. bₐ̄ ₐ zₐmānimmu̦ nē ⁓ ba ₐ ga ₐbōkī yā kōmₐ maƙi̦yī to-day is not the first time that a friend has become an enemy. (2) *Vd.* farau-farau.

farauce A. (farₐucē) *Vb.* 1C. (1) = fₐrautₐ 1. (2) am ⁓ shi, yā fₐrautu it (area) has been thoroughly hunted over. (3) am ⁓ shi all his belongings have been confiscated (= wāshₑ 1), *cf.* fₐrautₐ 1*b.*
   B. (fₐrₐucē) *Vd.* fₐrautₐ.

fₐrₐuci (1) *Vd.* fₐrautₐ. (2) ⁓ fₐrₐrₐ *epithet of* hunting (*because of uncertainty of obtaining game, cf.* fₐrₐrₐ).

farau-farau (1) *m.* (*a*) water containing a little flour or furā (= iḑon 9), *cf.* ƙunārī. (*b*) gₐ̄rim mai rōwₐ ₐ ⁓ ya kₐŋ ƙārₑ the miser always stints himself. (2) *adv.* only in small numbers *x* mutₐ̄nē sunₐ̄ nam ⁓ there are but few people here (*cf.* faraurₐucē).

faraurₐucē *Vb.* 3A is (was) few *x* gₐrī yā ⁓ the town is denuded of people (*cf.* farau-farau).

faraurauta A. (faraurₐutā) *Vb.* 1D mixed (flour or furā) to make farau-farau.

B. (farȧurautȧ) *Vb.* 2 int. from farautȧ.

farauta A. (farautȧ). (1) *Vb.*: 2 (*p.o.* farȧucē, *n.o.* farȧuci). (*a*) hunted (an animal) *x* am farȧuci zōmō a hare was hunted. (*b*) farautō *Vb.* 1E. (i) captured *x* mum farautō bāwȧ we've captured a slave. (ii) got by cadging *x* nā farautō rȧgā I cadged a gown. (2) *f.* (*a*) hunting. (*b*) *Vd.* farȧuci 2. (*c*) kidȧm ∼ *Vd.* zōmō 2. (*d*) ram ∼ *Vd.* karē 2. B. (farautā) *Vd.* farcȩ.

farcak *used in* yā gudu ∼ he fled " at the double ".

farce A. (farcȩ) (1) *m.* (*pl.* farautā = *Kt.* faruttȧ). (*a*) (i) fingernail, toenail (= *Sk.* kumbā), *cf.* akaifā. (*b*) *Sk.* finger (= yātsȧ). (*c*) cyst under upper eyelid of horse (= akaifā). (*d*) yanȧ kōnȧ ∼ he's eating tūwō (= tūwō 1*b* = akaifā ɜ). (*e*) aŋ gōgȩ masȧ ∼ " he's been taken down a peg ". (2) *Vb.* 3A yā ∼ ȧ gujȩ he fled. (3) *Vb.* 1A. (*a*) yā ∼ kasā he hoed hard ground lightly (= kankarē 1), *cf.* kaftȧ. (*b*) scraped T. (to remove dirt ; weeds ; bark ; writing ; fish-scales, etc.) (= kankarē 2). (*c*) abraded, causing slit in material or skin of P. (*cf.* zāgȩ) = karcȩ 1*b*. (*d*) *Kt.* yā ∼ gyȧdā he hoed up groundnuts (= fardā). B. (farcē) *Vd.* fartā.

farci *Vd.* fartā.

farda A. (fardȧ) *f.* wrapping for broken potash (= burdumī *q.v.*). B. (fardā) (1) *Ar. m.*, *f.* outstanding P. (2) *Kt.* ∼ dȧ ∼ openly.

farda A. (fardā) (1) *Vb.* 2 yā fardi gyȧdā he hoed up groundnuts (= *Kt.* farcȩ 3*d*). (2) *f.* yanȧ ∼ he's occupied in hoeing up ground-nuts. B. (fardȧ) *Vb.* 1A slit open front of animal, etc.

fardȩ *Vb.* 1A slit up completely : hoed up all of (*cf.* fardā ; fardȧ).

farēkani paramours (*pl. of* farkā 3).

farēsani damaged kolas (*pl. of* farsā).

farētani hoes (*pl. of* fartanyȧ).

farfada A. (farfādā) *m.*, *f.* (*pl.* fādȧdā) broad. B. (farfādā) *f.* = farfādīyā. C. (farfȧdā) *Vb.* 3A *intensive from* fȧdȧ.

farfȧdē *Vb.* 3A recovered completely (*cf.* farfādō).

farfādīyā = farfȧdyā *f.* epilepsy.

farfādō *Vb.* 3A recovered from illness, fainting, fatigue, or poverty. yā ∼ sarai he's completely recovered (= gyāzȧjē *q.v.*), *cf.* farkō.

*farfājīyā *f.* ▽pen space before compound (= faŋgalī).

far-far *m.* (1) = farfarnīyā. (2) *cf.* fal-fal. '

farfarā *f.* = *Rustic* farfarī *m.* (1) early type of guineacorn. (2) farfarā *f.* cheap writing-paper sold by Arabs.

farfarnīyā *f.* quivering, trembling (= ɓarį).

farfarū (*pl. of* farī 2). (1) Arabic consonants plus vowel-signs (*cf.* bakī B.2, 3*b* ; hajjȧtū). (2) makērim ∼ smith of white metals (*cf.* bakī B.2, 4).

farfarwȧ *f.* trembling.

farfasā *Vb.* 1C : (*int. from* fasȧ) kept on shattering.

farfētsī *m.* shrub *Schwenkia americana* (medicine for children).

fargā (1) *Vb.* 3B. (*a*) realized *x* yā ∼ dȧ shī he realized it (*progressive* yanȧ ∼ dȧ shī). (*b*) realized that *x* sȧi sukȧ ∼ yāki yā nufō su kȩ naŋ then they realized that war had come upon them. (2) *Vd.* farga-farga ; fargar Jāji ; kȧn tȧ ∼.

fargabā *f.* (1) dread. (2) *Vd.* dūtsȩ 2*c*.

fargadā *Sk. f.* simultaneous falling of both wrestlers (= zubar gadō).

farga-farga *adv.* occasionally.

fargar jāji *f.* being wise after the event.

fari A. (fārį) (1) (*a*) beginning *x* fārįn aiki the beginning of the work. (*b*) fārįn shįgā, uŋgōzōmar Wāsȧi *epithet of* novice. (2) (*a*) na ∼ *m.* (*f.* ta ∼) *pl.* na ∼ first *x* dōki na fārį = dōkįm fārį the first horse. (*b*) (i) dam ∼ one's eldest son. dam fārįna = dāna na fārį my eldest son. 'yar fārį eldest daughter. 'yar fārįna = 'yāta ta fārį my eldest daughter (*Vd.* ita; Mod. Gram. Appendix 3, Section D.) (ii) masōyin dam fārį bȧ na autā ba nȩ tastes differ. (*c*) dan tsįyā na fārį *Vd.* bāshį 2*a*. (3) (*a*) dȧ ∼ *adv.* first of all. (*b*) fārįm fārȧwā at the very outset. (4) fārįn *prep.* at the beginning of *x* **fārin** zūwammu when we first came.

B. (**farī**) (1) *m.* (*a*) (i) whiteness *x* yanā dā ∼ kal it's snow-white. **wannan** yā fi wancan ∼ this one's whiter than that. (ii) the white part of T. *x* **farinsa** its white part. (*b*) fairness of hue *x* yā yi ∼ it's of lightish colour. yā fi ni ∼ he's fairer than I am (*contrast is* duhu). (*c*) (*Vd.* Mod. Gram. 80*c*) *x* (i) **fuskassa** tā yi ∼ he turned pale. (ii) **ransa** yā yi ∼ = zūcīyassa tā yi ∼ he rejoiced (*cf.* 2*c* ; zūcīyā 9). (iii) gērō yā yi ∼ bulrush-millet grains have set in head. (iv) **magana** tā yi ∼ the affair has turned out well. (*d*) **bam** ∼ *m.* act of bleaching rice (= cāsar **farī**). (*e*) (i) strip(s) of native white cloth (*when dyed with indigo, it is called* bakī), *cf.* agēdu ; taya ragō ; tsābā 3 ; fīrī ; lagab. (ii) **bamban da na farī** *Vd.* sāki 1*b.* (*f*) **dam** ∼ *m.* the harmless snake dan gidā (*Vd.* dakō 1*b*). (*g*) *Vd.* **farfarū**. (*h*) *Vd.* **farā** ; **firī, wata** 1*e.*

(2) *adj. m.*
(*f.* **farā**) *pl.* **farārē** (*Vd.* **farfarū**). (*a*) (i) white *x* **farin tsuntsū** white bird. **farar rīgā** white gown. rīgā cē **farā da ita** it's a very white gown. (ii) **rīgā farā bā tā bā** 'yarūwā **tata** shūnī don't lord it over your equals ! (iii) **nā san shi farin sani** I know him well. (iv) **almājirī** yā dauki ∼ the pupil took back his pen unused, as he wrote out Koran from memory without corrections being needed by his teacher (those who have memorized Koran (**mahardatā**) are graded into *firstly* P. able to write texts on slate without being word-perfect, these being called **'yan sātū** ; *secondly* **mai daukam farī** = **likārī** P. who are word-perfect ; *thirdly* **gangaram** who teach those who are professional writers of Koran on slates (**allō**) ; *fourthly* **gwanī** who is past-master). (*b*) (i) fair-skinned (*re* African. *For* European, *Vd.* jā A3.*b*). (ii) **'yar farā** fair-skinned African woman (= sillīya 2). (*c*) (i) **farin ciki** *Vd. alphabetically* (*cf.* 1*c*.ii *above*). (ii) **farar zūcīyā** *Vd.* zūcīyā 9. (iii)

farin lābāri good news (*cf.* bakī 3*d*). (iv) **Allā yā sā bakar tukunyā tā fitar mana da farin tūwō** God changed our bad luck to good luck. (*d*) **farin hannū** (= furin hannū) sā bākī maiko *epithet of* divination (dūbā). (*e*) **banzā, farin ido, bābu ganī** fair without, foul within ! (= fankam fayau). (*f*) **ban gaya masa farar magana ba, ban gaya masa bakar magana ba** I didn't address a word to him (= uffan). (*g*) (i) **sum bincikē shi bakinsa da farinsa** they investigated it fully. (ii) **in kā ga** ∼ kā ga bakī *Vd.* birgimā 4. (iii) **halinsa** ∼ da bakī nē, yau shūnī, gōbe dauda *epithet of* (i) Chief (*for he can act arbitrarily*). (ii) the world. (*h*) **farar hūlā** African civilian (*contrasted with military*). (*j*) *Vd.* **farin-** *and* **farar**-*compounds.* *Vd.* **farā ; fat ; likkāfa** 5. (*k*) im farī zā ka yi *Vd.* **fafat.** (*l*) **kadam farā tā cī** *Vd.* bīdī 4. (*m*) **rīgā farā** *Vd.* shūnī 1*e*.iii. (*n*) **amfānin nōno farī** *Vd.* nōno 1*e.* (*o*) **farinsu daya** *Vd.* nōno 1*b.* (*p*) **farin ido** *Vd.*banzā 1*h.*

C. (**fārī**) locusts (*Vd.* **fārā**).

D. (**fārī**) conceit (= fahari *q.v.*).

E. (**fari**) *m.* (1) long, unwelcome, dry spell in the rains (*cf.* iska 3*a*). (2) **sunā zatam** ∼ *Vd.* mahassadī. (3) **Allā ya fisshē ka** ∼ *Vd.* yabanya.

F. (**fārī**) (1) *m.* tā yi mini ∼ she ogled me, gave me the glad eye (= **kada** 1*k* = kashē 10*a*.ii = kākalē 2*a*.ii = kyar-kyarā 2 = marmadī). (2) *f.* Paris.

farilla *f.* (*pl.* **farillai**) (*Ar.* farīza). (1) (*a*) any observance made obligatory religiously (*x* fasting *i.e.* azumi; Friday-prayers, etc.), *cf.* farlu, sunna, nāfila. (*b*) any obligatory amount in Muslim Law *x* **abin da kē tsakānin wannam** ∼ **da wannam** ∼ amounts intermediate between the two standard totals. (2) (*a*) certainty *x* **gōbe farillar zūwansa** he's sure to come to-morrow. (*b*) **watan nam** ∼ **nē** this is a 30-day month (*for if moon not seen on 29th, it is sure to be seen on 30th*), *cf.* nūsan. (3) indispensable P. or T. *x* **Audu nē cikin abin nan** Audu is indispensable in this matter.

faril lagai = **farin lagai** *m.* type of salt.

farin ɓērā *Vd.* ɓērā 3.

farin biso (farim bisọ) *m.* ạ̀ bā nị̀ ~ give me a present to celebrate your luck ! (*said to lucky suitor of girl by unlucky suitor or by grandfather to lucky suitor*).

farin biya (farim bīyạ) *m.* payment in coin (*or previously* in cowries) contrasted with payment in kind (*cf.* fariṇ kudī, kạrɓā 2*f*, tsābạ 2*a*, Gwārī 10).

farin cikị̣ *m.* (1) happiness. yā yi ~ dạ shī he is (was) pleased with it. (2) farin cikịṇ ạshar short-lived joy. (3) *Vd.* farī 1*c*.ii, Jumma'ạ̀ 1*c*.

farin fasum (farim fạsụm) *m.* short-lived joy.

farin feto (farim fētọ) *m.* yā farạ̀cē, yā zamā ~ he's anæmic and sickly looking. hannuntạ̀ yā zamā ~ henna has worn off her hand.

fariṇ gạmō *m.* good luck.

fạ̀rị̀ṇ gēzā *Vd.* sāri 2.

fariṇ hannū *Vd.* farī 2*d*.

fariṇ idọ *Vd.* farī 2*e*.

farin jinī *m.* popularity *x* Audụ ~ gạrēshị Audu is popular (= mụhibbạ̀ 1 = tagōmạshī), *Vd.* jinī 4.

fariṇ kạ̀i *m.* (1) *Vd.* kaṇwā 1*c*. (2) mại ~ *m., f. (pl.* mạ̄sū ~) educated P. (*cf.* bạฟ̄ī 4).

fariṇ ฟ̣arfẹ *m.* any white metal (brass; zinc, tin, etc.).

fariṇ kāyā *m.* white clothes *x* ɗan sạndā yā sạ̀ ~ the policeman disguised himself in mufti (*Vd.* rị̀gā 1*k*).

fariṇ kōmō *m.* weak P.

fariṇ kudī *m.* (1) coined money (*or previously* cowries). (2) payment in coined money (*or previously* in cowries) contrasted with payment in kind (= tsābạr kudī), *cf.* tsābạr ฟarfẹ, farim bīyạ, kạrɓā 2*f*, kudī 1*p*).

fariṇ kụmallō *Vd.* kụmallō 3.

fariṇ kūrẹ *used in* ~ mại rērọ *m.* type of children's game.

farin lagai = faril lagai.

farin maciji (farim macị̀jī) *m.* the harmless snake *whose epithet is* dakō.

farin sanị̣ *Vd.* farī 2*a*.iii.

farin sāwū *m.* = farar ฟafạ̀.

farin shāhọ *Vd.* shāhọ.

fạ̀rị̀n shigā *Vd.* fārị̣ 1*b*.

farin tūwō *Vd.* tukunyā 1*f*.

fariṇ watạ *Vd.* watạ 1*e*.

farin yau *Vd.* yau 1*a*.ii.

Fārisạ̀ *Ar. f.* Persia.

fạ̄rīyạ̀ *Ar. f.* ostentatiousness, boastfulness, showing off (= ạ̀lfahạrī).

fạrjak abundantly.

fạrjị̣ *Ar.* (*polite term*) vagina (*cf.* mātūcị̣ = diṇgạ 2*c* = dūrị̣ = gạbā 2*a* = gạịdō = gatọ 1 = gēshē 2).

farka A. (farkạ) (1) *Vb.* 3A. (*a*) (i) awakened. (ii) yā ~ barcī = yā ~ dạgạ barcī he awoke from sleep. (*b*) P. revived from faint. (*c*) (drooping flower) revived. (*d*) *Vd.* farkō, falkạ 3.

    B. (fạrkā) (1) (*rolled* -r-, Mod. Gram. 5) *Vb.* 2 ripped and removed (*x* cloth-rags). (2) (*cerebral* -r-) *f.* (*a*) fornication, adultery (= zịnā). (*b*) ạ̀bin lallē, ~ dạ bāwạṇ kīshị̣yā what a desperate remedy ! (*epithet is* kā yī dạ kunyạ̀, kā barị gạ̄ kudī). (*c*) (*abusively*) ɗam ~ yọu fellow, you're a bastard ! (= shⁱgẹ̀ 3*a*). 'yam fạrkam matsị̣yātạn nạṇ these blasted paupers ! (3) fạrkā *m., f.* (*pl.* farẹ̄kanī = farkunạ̀ = farkōkī) paramour (= dạukā 2*b*).

farkad dạ *Vb.* 4B awakened P.

farke A. (farkẹ) (1) *Vb.* became ripped. (2) *Vb.* 1A. (*a*) ripped up. (*b*) = fanshẹ. (*c*) yā ~ bāshị̣ he paid his debt. sum ~ there is no longer debt outstanding between them.

    B. (farkē) *m.* (*f.* farkyā = farkīyā) *pl.* fatạ̄kē. (1) (*a*) itinerant trader (= masạfạrcī), *cf.* fataucị̣. (*b*) *Vd.* falkē. (*c*) ~ mại fạrkakkīyar mạganạ how dishonest traders are ! (*with same meaning :* farkē na bāwạ, ฟanạṇ kạ̣rē = farkē kā yi wutā, mạ̄tarkạ hayā฿ī = farkē kā fi Nạsārā sallạ̀ dạ sāfē, Nạsārā yā fi kạ bīyạṇ ạ̀lbāshī = farkē ɗaṇ gidaṇkạ̀ ạ̀bōkiṇ gạ̄barkạ = farkē ɗaṇ gidaṇ wani ạ̀bōkiṇ zạṇcaṇkạ). (2) *Kt.* fatạ̄kē quickly-moving clouds (= jị̣dā).

    C. (Farke) boy's name.

farki what a lot of work *or* travel !

*farฟ̣ị̣ *Ar. m.* difference *x* bạ̄ ~ tsạ̀kāninsụ there's no difference between them.

farkīyā *Vd.* farkē.

farkō (1) *Vb.* 3A recovered from illness, etc. (= farฟādō *q.v.*). (2) *m.* (*a*) (i) beginning x a farkwaŋ (= da farkwaŋ) wannaŋ al'amari suŋ (= suka) ga alāmar ba zai zō ba they saw signs at the outset of the matter that he was unlikely to come. da farkwan zūwansa when he first arrived. (ii) Allā ya fisshē ka tsaka mai wuyā, bā farkō ba, karkō may you always remain virtuous ! (b) da ~ first of all. (c) (i) na ~ adv. firstly. (ii) adj. na ~ m. (f. ta ~) pl. na ~ 1st. (d) farkwam fada, nūna hannū coming events cast their shadows before them. (e) the first time x (i) bā shī nē farkō ba da ya yī this is not the first time he has done so. (ii) wannaŋ shī nē farkwaŋ a ga yā yi haka this is the first time he has done so. wannaŋ zīyāra, ita cē farkwam muka gan shi this visit was the first time we ever saw him.

farkōki paramours (pl. of farkā 3).

*farku m. = farki.

farkuna paramours (pl. of farkā 3).

farkyā Vd. farkē.

farlī m. cast in the eye (= faralli q.v.)

Far lōmi f. Fort Lomy.

*farlu m. (Ar. farzu). (1) T. made obligatory religiously (= farilla q.v.). (2) ~ ainī such obligation if it must be done personally. (3) ~ kifāya such obligation if it may be deputed (N.B.—2, 3 may be used metaphorically; thus, if I expect five persons and only Audu comes, I can say kifāya (or farlu kifāya) nē well, you must be their representative !).

farmaki m. sudden attack x mutūwa tā yi masa ~ death suddenly assailed him.

farmalaŋ Sk.f. waistcoat (= falmaraŋ q.v.).

farō-farō m. = farau-farau.

fārōrī locusts (pl. of fārā 2).

*farraka A. (farrakā) Vb. 1C Ar. (1) severed. (2) distinguished.
    *B. (farraka) Vb. 3B. Ar. (friends, etc.) became estranged.

farsa A. (farsā = Zar. farsā) f. poultice.
    B. (farsa) (1) f. (a) the food balambō. (b) farsar kūrā limestone. (2) Vb. 3A rejoiced over gift.
    C. (farsā) f. (1) Vd. farsā. (2) farsā (pl. farāshē = farēsanī) kola-nuts accidentally split into sections.

farta A. (farta) (1) Vb. 3A yā ~ a guje he fled. (2) Vb. 1A yā ~ kasā = farce 3a.
    B. (fartā) Vb. 2 Kt. (1) yā farci gyada he hoed up ground-nuts (= fardā). (2) fartak kasā = kartak kasā.

fartak used in yā gudu fartak he fled " at the double ".

fartakē Vb. 3A (cloth) faded.

fartak kasā = kartak kasā.

fartanya f. (pl. farētanī = fartanyōyī). (1) small hoe with triangular blade (Vd. firi ; maimai ; sassaryā ; baŋgajē ; kufurtū) = hauyā. (2) fartanyar dūke short-handled hoe used stooping. (3) fartanyar tsaye long-handled hoe used standing. (4) dillālim farētanī Vd. kyaŋ-kyaŋ-kyaŋ.

fartētę m. shallowness x kōgin ŋam ~ yakē this river's shallow.

fartīla f. white topee (= bartīla q.v.).

farto A. (farto) m. strong, fearless man.
    B. (fartō) Vd. farce 2, farta, fartā.

fartū m. sun yi ~ they annulled bargain, marriage, friendship, etc.

faru A. (fāru) Vb. 3B (Ar. afra'a). (1) ·happened, occurred (= wanzu 2). (2) (a) began (intransitive, cf. fāra 1, 5). (b) tā ~, tā kare, an yi wa mai dami dayā sāta (a) a clean sweep was made of it. (b) what staggering news ! (cf. kudugum).
    B. (fārū) m. (1) (a) the resin-bearing tree Odina Barteri. (b) fārum makīyāyā type of wild vine (= Kt. yayo). (2) Fārū Vd. kākā 1A.

Fāruku = Fāruku name for any man called Umaru.

farutta Vd. farce.

fas A. (fas) Vd. fashe 1a, fāsa 1a.
    B. (fas) (1) (Eng. pass) yā yi ~ cikin jarrabāwā he passed the examination. (2) (Eng. first). (a) wannaŋ dōki yā yi ~ this horse came in first, won the race. (b) yā yi kōwane gishirī ~ it is the premier salt. (c) Fas Batālīya The 1st Battalion.

fasa A. (fasa) (Ar. fazza). (1) Vb. 1A. (a) (i) ground roughly as in fashi 4a (cf. nika). (ii) iŋ am ~ yā kare Vd. wuyā 1j. (b) shattered x (i) yā ~ kwāi he broke the egg(s) (cf. karya). (ii) sum ~ mana kwăi a kā they foiled us. (iii) săi am fasa Vd. bidi 5. (iv)

fasǎ ƙwaryā *Vd.* dǎrīyā 2.   (v) bā ǎ
fasǎ ƙwaryā *Vd.* mǎyē 2*b*.   (*c*) yā ~
minį kǎi he wounded me in the head.
(*d*) am ~ tǎrō the crowd has been dispersed.   (*e*) tā ~ ƙunduntǎ she's been
delivered of a child.   (*f*) bā nǎ ~
rǎndad dakǎ, na wǎje bai shigō ba
don't throw away dirty water before
you've got clean !   (*g*) am ~ mǎŋgul
piece has been broken off block
(kantų) of Asbin salt with kurfū-
stone (*cf.* yaŋkę 1*c*.ii).   (*h*) *Vd.* fǎsu ;
tandū 2*b*.   (*j*) yā ~ dōkį he deployed
his cavalry (*cf.* 1*m*).   (*jj*) am ~ hǎrājį
tax has been announced, imposed.
am ~ musų hǎrājį tax has been imposed on them.   (*k*) (i) ya ~ fushinsǎ =
yā ~ kųmburinsǎ he got the chance to
vent his rage (*cf.* 1*k*.v).   (ii) yanǎ ~
fushinsǎ he's having a fine time, enjoying himself to his heart's content.   (iii)
~ fushī, kashę kudī *epithet of* train.   (iv)
fasǎ fushī *noun m.* children's game of
throwing white-earth balls at wall.   (v)
fǎsǎ kųmburī *noun m.* purslane (*cf.* 1*k*.i ;
3*b*.ii).   (*l*) am ~ mūdų ǎ kǎsūwā price of
corn has fallen.   (*m*) jīyǎ dōkįna bai ~ ba
yesterday my horse got no corn (*cf.* 1*j*).
(*n*) A yanǎ jam baƙī, B yanǎ fasǎwā
A's reading and B's explaining what's
read.   (*o*) yā ~, yǎnzu yanǎ tishį he's
now going through Koran for second
time.   (*p*) (i) gǎmshęƙā tā ~ kǎi
cobra's erected hood = (ƙōshīyǎ 5).
(ii) yanǎ ~ kǎi he's arrogant.   (iii)
yanǎ ~ kǎi kwānan naŋ it (commodity)
has become dear.   (*q*) *Vd.* hųdā 2*b* ;
baŋgajē ; ƙufurtū.   (*r*) he perforated
(garment).   (*s*) ~ gǎrāmǎ *Vd.* gǎrāmǎ.
(2) *Vb.* 3A.   (*a*) yā ~ kūkā he burst out
crying (= fashę 1*b*).   (*b*) = fashe 1.
(3) *Compounds* :   (*a*) fǎsǎ gǎyyā *m.*
epithet of warrior.   (*b*) fǎsa, gįna *m.*
= ragę 1*a*.iii.   (*c*) fasǎ ƙābā *m.*   (i) the
creeper yǎdǎ ƙwaryā.   (ii) *Kt.* purslane
(*Vd.* fǎsǎ kųmburī *in* 1*k*.v *above*).   (*d*)
fǎsǎ kǎnnau *epithet of* large monkey
("router of dogs ")*ı*.   (*e*) fǎsǎ kwǎrī *m.*
the spice-bark tree *Zanthoxylum senegalense.*   (*f*) fǎsǎ manǎmā *m.* first grey
hairs on woman's temples.

   B. (fāsǎ) (1) *Vb.* 1A.   (*a*) postponed

beginning T.   *x* nā ~ tǎfīyǎ (i) I've
postponed the journey (= cirǎ 1*c*).
(ii) nā ~ tǎfīyǎ (*or* nā ~ tǎfīyǎ fas) I've
postponed the journey indefinitely.   (*b*)
nā ~ tǎfīyǎ sǎi gōbe I've postponed my
journey till to-morrow (*cf.* barį 4*a*.ii, iii ;
ajįyē 10).   (*c*) mų sōmǎ aikį bǎ fāsǎwā
let's get to work without delay !
(*cf.* fāshį).   (*d*) kǎ bǎ dōkįna rūwā
rānā dayā, kǎ ~ rānā dayā water my
horse every other day !   (*e*) doŋ ƙim
fāsǎwā akę tsōram mahaukǎcī : fāshį
bǎrnar aikį don't procrastinate ! (*lit.*
one fears a madman because he whips
out and uses a weapon, etc.).   (*f*)
shēgę kǎ ~ *Vd.* shēgę 4.   (2) *Vb.* 3A
is (was) postponed *or* postponed indefinitely *x* tǎfīyǎ tā ~ the journey
has been postponed (= rūwā A.2*c* =
shā A.1*l*).

fǎsādį *Ar. m.* profligacy.

fǎsāhǎ (*Ar.* eloquence) *f.*   (1) skill.   (2) ~
nǎ gabǎs no, you flatter me ! (*deprecatingly said*).

fasǎlī *Ar. m.*   (1) (*a*) orderliness, symmetry
x yanǎ dǎ kyam ~ it is well con-
structed,   well-arranged   (= labdį =
mǎ'anǎ 2).   (*b*) bǎ shi dǎ dādim ~ he's
difficult to get any sense out of, hard
to deal with.   (2) fasǎlī *m.* (*pl.* fǎsǎlai =
fasalōlī).   (*a*) dividing out *x* (i) an
sǎ ni fasǎlįŋ gōrǒ I've been told to
divide out the kolas.   (ii) an rabǎ aikį ~
fasǎlī the work's been shared out task
by task.   *(b*) chapter.   *(c*) season.

fasǎltā *Vb.* 1C   (1) yā fasǎltǎ dākį he
marked out the house (= shātǎ).   (2)
did T. methodically *x* am fasǎltǎ
rįgā the gown has been properly cut
out.   (3) divided T. into sections.

fasǎrā *Vb.* 1C *Ar.* explained passage in
book (= fassǎrā *q.v.*).

fǎsasshē *m.* (*f.* fǎsasshīyā) *pl.* fǎsǎssū
adj.   (1) shattered.   (2) fǎsasshīyar
ƙōtǎ deposed P. who is thorn in the
side of his successor (= tsųmmā 2).

fǎsau *m.* chapping (= fǎsō *q.v.*).

fashā-fǎshǎ *f.*   splitting   lengthwise   *x*
hųdā tā yi ~ the bloom is fully out.
rōgǒ yā dafu, yā yi ~ the cassava is
cooked nice and soft.   yā shā dūkǎ,
jįkinsǎ yā yi ~ he has been beaten to

tatters. **bằkinsą yằ yi** ⌣ his mouth is stained with kolanut (= **tashā-tạshā**).
fashar = **fashā-fạshā**.
fashạr-fashạr *Kt.* an **niɓạ shi** ⌣ it is coarsely ground (*cf.* **lilis**).
iashe A. (**fashẹ**) (**1**) *Vb.* 3A. (*a*) is (was) shattered *x* (i) **ɓwǎi yā** ⌣ the egg is broken. **yā** ⌣ **fus** it burst with a cracking sound (*cf.* **karyẹ**). (ii) **tặrō yā** ⌣ = **mutặnē sum** ⌣ **fas** = **sun yi fas** the crowd dispersed. (iii) **kặi bā yặ fashẹwā ạ banzā, im bặ ɓạbbā ba, sǎi an yi rōtsị** nobody acts without an object. (*b*) **yā** ⌣ **dạ kūkā (dặrīyā)** he burst out crying (laughing) (= **kēcẹ** 1*b* = **shā** B. 2*a* = **ɓāɓặtā** = **6arkẹ** 1*b*.i,ii = **fasạ** 2*a* = **būshẹ** 1*e* = **tuntsụrē** 2*c*), *cf.* **ribcẹ** 2*f.* (*c*) became threadbare *x* **rịgā tā** ⌣. (*d*) (i) **rānā tā** ⌣ the sun is well up. (ii) **rānā tā fasō** the sun is just risen above the horizon. (iii) **tum fasọwar ạlfijịr mukạ tāsō** we started at dawn. (*e*) **kansạ yā** ⌣ (i) he has been wounded in the head. (ii) he has cranial disease causing hollows in his head. (**2**) *Vb.* 1A = **fasạ** 1*b*, *k*.i, *l*.
   B. (**fạshē**) *m.* Bambarra-groundnuts (**gujīyā**) soaked, roasted, and then broken up.
   C. (**fashē**) *m.* children's gambling-game of hitting egg on egg (*cf.* **ɓyạŋɓyạsā**).
fashi A. (**fashị**) *m.* (**1**) (*secondary v.n. of* **fasạ** 1) *x* **yanặ fashịm mạŋgul** = **yanặ fasạ mạŋgul** he's breaking up the **mạŋgul** salt. (**2**) (*a*) highway robbery *x* **an yi minị** ⌣. (*b*) **maị** ⌣ = **dam** ⌣ (*pl.* **mặsū** ⌣ = 'yam ⌣) footpad. (*c*) **jirặgyan samạ 'yam** ⌣ raiding aeroplanes. (**3**) **fashịŋ gōshī** the cut down centre of brow (i) of Barebari people. (ii) to cure convulsions of baby. (**4**) (*a*) rough grinding (*cf.* **niɓạ**). (*b*) **wụyar niɓạ** ⌣ *Vd.* **wụyā** 1*j*. (**5**) **fashịŋ ukụ** (**fashịŋ hudū**) one third (one fourth) part of a **ciɓị**-strip (*q.v. under* **ạlbadạ**) of European material (**sandā**).
   B. (**fāshi**) *m.* (**1**) (*a*) postponement, delay *x* **mụ sōmạ aikị bābụ** ⌣ let us set to work forthwith! (*cf.* **fāsạ** 1*a*). (*b*) ⌣ **6ạrnar aikị** *Vd.* **fāsạ** 1*e*. (*c*) **fāshịn sallạ** menstruation *x* **tanặ fāshịn**

sallạ she is now menstruating (= **hailạ**). (**2**) (*secondary v.n. of* **fāsạ** 1, **2**) *x* **munặ fāshịŋ aikị yạu** = **munặ fāsạ aikị yạu** we're not working to-day. **kặsūwan nạŋ kōwạcẹ rānā takẹ cị, bā tặ fāshị** = **bā tặ fāsặwā** this market is held every day without exception. (**3**) a poor type of **balmạ** or **kantụ** salt. (**4**) **fāshịŋ gạyyā** *Vd.* **Dụmau** 2.
fāsikancị = **fāsikcị** *Ar.* *m.* profligacy (= **zịnā**).
fāsịkī *m.* (*f.* **fāsịkā**) *pl.* **fạsịkai** profligate P.
*****fasikta** A. (**fāsịktạ**) is profligate.
*****B. (**fāsịktā**) accused of profligacy.
fāsinjạ *Eng.* (**1**) *m., f.* (*sg., pl.*) third-class passenger (*cf.* **faskilạŋ**). (**2**) *m.* (*sg., pl.*) one of the unemployed. (*b*) passenger-train. (**3**) *f.* prostitute.
faskạ *Vb. Sk.* (**1**) ripped. (**2**) **yā** ⌣ **minị mārị** he slapped me.
faskace A. (**faskạcē**) *Vb.* 1C. (**1**) = **faskạrē** *x* **yā faskạcẹ ɓafạ** he split his foot with hoe, etc. **yā** ⌣ **minị kặi** he wounded me in the head. (**2**) *Sk.* **tā** ⌣ she quitted her husband.
   B. (**fạskạcē**) *Vd.* **fạskatạ**.
faskara A. (**fạskarạ**) (**1**) *Vb.* 3B. (*a*) is (was) unruly. (*b*) is (was) impossible *x* **yā** ⌣ **ạ kāmạ shi** = **kāmụnsạ yā** ⌣ it's impossible to catch it (animal). (**2**) *Vb.* 2. (*a*) is beyond P. *x* **daukạnsạ yā fạskạrē nị** it's too heavy for me to lift it. (*b*) **yā fạskạri itặcē** he split firewood. (**3**) *f.* unruliness *x* ⌣ **gạrēshị** he's unruly.
   B. (**fạskạrā**) *Vb.* 1C = **fạskarạ** 2*b*.
   C. (**faskarā**) = **fạskạrē** 3*a*.
fạskạrạ kọyō *m.* P. or T. hard to deal with.
fạskạrarrē *m.* (*f.* **fạskạrarrīyā**) *pl.* **fạskạrạrrū** unruly P.
fạskạrạ tọyī *m.* the prickly herb *Blepharis linearifolia.*
faskare A. (**fạskạrē**) *Vb.* 1C = **fạskarạ** 2*b*.
   B. (**fạskạrē**) *m.* (**1**) (*secondary v.n. of* **fạskarạ** 2*b*) *x* **yanặ fạskạraŋ itặcē** = **yanặ fạskạrạr itặcē** he's splitting wood. (*b*) being occupied in act of splitting firewood *x* **yanặ** ⌣ he's splitting wood. (*c*) split-firewood. (**2**) (*a*) shaving only one side of head of meatsellers (**mafautā**), boxer *or* **dạŋ wābị** child (= **sārīyā** 2). (*b*) *Sk.* coiffure of (i)

bride for 14 days. (ii) nursing-mother (mai jego) for 40 days. (3) (a) weaving with white woof and black and white warp. (b) staining two upper and lower centre-teeth of boys or women.

faskata Vb. 2 (p.o. **faskace**, n.o. **faskaci**) = **faskace**.

faske (1) Vb. 1A **yā ~ ni da māri** he slapped me. (2) Vb. 3A Sk. is split.

faski m. (1) breadth of T. (2) being very broad.

faskilan Eng. (1) m. first-class (on train or boat). (2) m., f. (sg., pl.) first-class passenger (cf. **fāsinja, taskilan**).

faso A. (**fasō**) m. (1) chapping of hands, etc. (= **tūkā** 2c.i = **nankarwā** 1). (2) splitting of perineum in childbirth. (3) splitting of new calabash.

B. (**fasō**) Vd. **fashe** 1d.

fas ōfis Eng. m. post-office.

fassara A. (**fassarā**) Vb. 1C Ar. explained passage in book.

B. (**fassara**) f. explaining of, explanation of passage of book.

fasu Vb. 3B (cf. **fasa**). (1) (a) burst x **audugā tā ~** cotton bolls have burst. **dōrawa tā ~** locust-bean tree is budding (Vd. **hūda** 1). (b) **audugar danūwā tā fasu** (i) his faults are being bandied about. (ii) " he's been taken down a peg ". (c) **danyar fātā bā tā fasūwā** Vd. **danyē** 5d. (d) ~ **kōwā ya sāmu** Vd. **rīmī** 1b.ii. (2) **fasūwar katanga** dispersing, each P. going his own way. (3) **fasūwar kwaryā** f. (a) = (2). (b) **sāi muka ji lābārin kamar fasūwar kwaryā** the news " struck us all of a heap ".

fāsum Vd. farin ~.

fat A. (**fat**) adv. (1) used in (a) **farī ~** snow-white. (b) (in f. **farī** is optionally used for **farā**) x **kankarā tā rufe tsaunuka farī fat** (= **farā fat**) snow covered the hills with a white layer. **yārinya cē farī fat** (= **farā fat**) she's a very fair-skinned girl. **yā sā rīgā farī fat** he put on a snow-white gown (cf. **jā** A2.f.ii ; **kirin**). (2) completely (when following the verbs **cinyē; shanyē; kāre ; tsinke ; yanke** q.v.).

B. (**fat**) used in **yā māre shi ~** he slapped him hard.

fata A. (**fātā**) Vb. 2 (p.o. **fāce**, n.o. **fāci**). (1) hoped that x **mum fāci mu kai Kano lāfīya** we hope(d) to reach Kano safely. **mum fāci ka dāwō lāfīya** we hope you may return safely. (2) hoped for x **fāci lāfīyar wani don tāka** = **fāce wa wani lāfīya don tāka** do as you will be done by ! (Vd. **fātā**).

B. (**fātā**) m. (Kt. f.). (1) hoping that ; hoping for x (a) **munā ~ ka kōmō** we're hoping you'll return. **yanā ~ zai** (= **yanā ~ ya**) **aurē ta** he's hoping to marry her. (b) **yā yi mini fātan alhēri** he wished me well. (c) **fātansa bai sāmi karɓā ba** his wish was not realized (Vd. **fātā**). (2) ~ **nagarī lamīri** (lit. a pious formula uttered at random is often stored up for the future) this is used when x P. says automatically **Allā ya taimakē mu** " God be our helper ! " and then later he alone escapes from calamity, etc. (Vd. **lamīri** 2b). (3) **kaddara tā rigā ~** Man proposes, God disposes.

C. (**fātā**) (1) f., m. (pl. **fātū** = **fātōcī**). (a) (i) skin (of P. or animal, cf. **rigā** 2) x **mai bakar ~** m.,f. (pl. **māsū bakar ~**) negro. '**yanūwammu nē bakar ~** they are our negro relations. **tsakānin Tūrāwā da bakar ~** between Europeans and negroes. **sū bakar fātā nē** they are negroes. (ii) leather x **~ maram māi** stiff leather. (iii) **an ga nan fātā tā yi taushi** they saw there was a " weak spot " here. **bugu shī kē sā fātā taushi** constant dripping wears the rock (Vd. 1h). (b) **fātar kīfī** scales of fish. (c) (i) **fātar bākī** lip. (ii) **zancē irin na fātar bākī** = **maganar fātar bākī** insincere protestations ; lies. (d) **fātar ido** eyelid. (e) **fātar lēmō** peel of lime-fruit. (f) **fātun kunnūwa** ears. (g) **wannan rīgā tā fi waccan ~** this gown's of stouter material than that one. (h) Sk. **inda ~ ta hi tabshī, nan akē mai da jīma** one takes the line of least resistance (Vd. 1a.iii). (j) **ido yā rēna ~** he's landed himself in trouble. (k) **zā mu sā hannū a ~** we'll begin work. (l) **danyar fātā bā tā fasūwā** go on child, eat some more, you won't burst ! (m) **fātar buhū** Vd. **buhū** 1b.

(n) im fātạ akẹ sọ Vd. tarạ 2. (o) Vd.
agānar fātạ. (p) tā barạ fātạ wụyā Vd.
mutụ 1a.vii. (2) Vb. 1A x yā ∼ mājinā
jikim baŋgō he blew out mucus from
his nose on to the wall (cf. fācẹ).

fata-fata A. (fata-fata). (1) used in aŋ
kǭrē sụ ∼ = an yi musụ ∼ = an yi
musụ kǭrar kạrē ∼ they've been driven
away ; they've been routed helter-
skelter. (2) ∼ kạt tākalmạ epithet of
Barạrō Filani.
   B. (fatạ-fatạ) f. an dafạ ạbincī, yā
yi ∼ food's overcooked and so, sloppy.
   C. (fatā-fatạ) (only pl. sense) broad
x an yi rụbụ̄tū ∼ it has been written
in broad script. ƙafạ̄fū ∼ broad feet.

*fatahạ Ar. f. Arabic vowel-sign for
" a " (= rafa'ạ), Vd. fādụ̄wā 8 :
jạ̄kin 5A.

fatai adv. snow-white x yā wạŋku ∼
it's washed specklessly (cf. fat).

fạtakạ (Eng. florin) f. (pl. fạtạkū =
fatakōkī = Sk. fạtạttạkū) 2s. piece
(= dalạ 1).

fạtạ̄kē itinerant-traders (pl. of farkē,
bạfatākẹ).

fatạkkạ Sk. m. the plant Pergularia
tomentosa.

fatakōkī ; fạtạkū Vd. fạtakạ.

fạtalạ = fatalạ (Ar. plaited) f. (pl. fạtạlū = fatalōlī) woman's headkerchief
(= ạlhūtạ = tā kai tā kōmō = Kt. tā
kai tā kāwō), cf. agēdụ̄, fịtinạ 2e.

fạtalī m. scattering x tā yi ∼ dạ kāyansạ
she scattered his property about.

fatalōlī ; fạtạlū Vd. fạtalạ.

fatalwā ⅟= Sk. fạtalwā f. (1) goblin,
ghost (= dōdō 1 = ạljaŋ). (2) Kt.
ạllō yanạ̄ ∼ the wooden slate habitually
retains traces of former writing even
after being washed. (3) having thoughts
inconsolably fixed on lost T. x tanạ̄
fatalwar dā she imagines she sees her
dead son everywhere.

fataŋ-fataŋ completely (= fạ̄fạrataŋ q.v.).

fatantạnā Vb. 1D cut into small portions.

fatanyạ f. the hoe fartanyạ q.v.

fatarā Ar. f. (1) cessation x mun yi
fatarar ganiŋkạ we've not seen you
for some time. yā yi fatarar zūwạ
makarantā he's absented himself from
school. (2) ∼ tā sạ̄mē shị = ∼ tā

rufẹ shi he's become impoverished
(epithet is Fatarā mai tā dạ tsōfam
bāshị). (3) mai fatarar zūcī m., f.
(a) an ingrate. (b) irreconcilable P.

fạ̄tạrī m. (sg., pl.). (1) woman's loin-
cloth (= mụkurū = Sarkim fādạ 2 =
tǭbī = gāgarạ 15). (2) Vd. wutsīyạ 1h.

fatạrkawạ f. looking hither and hither
(= fạ̄fụtụkā q.v.).

fatattạkā Vb. 1D = fạtạttaka Vb. 2.
(1) lacerated. (2) subdivided country
into areas. (3) routed x mum fạtạttạkẹ
sụ dạgạ caŋ we scattered them and
ejected them from there. (4) ranted at
P. (5) fạtạttạkạ rīrịrī (a) m. leaving P.
in the lurch. (b) m., f. (sg., pl.) P.
acting as in (a). (6) fạtạttạkạ tạ̄rō
epithet of chief or European.

fatattạkē Vb. 3A is (was) lacerated.

fạtạttạkū Vd. fạtaka.

fatau used in kōrẹ ∼ adj. very dark
green.

fatauci A. (fatauci) m. (1) (a) itinerant-
trading (cf. farkē) = tạjāwạlī = safarạ. (b) bạ ạ tabạ ganim fatauci dạ
rība iriŋ wannạm ba no such success
has ever before been seen. fataucimmụ
zai yi rība we'll be successful. (2)
striving to reach x (a) munạ̄ fatauciŋ
Kanọ yau. (b) yā sạmi bạbbar rība, iriŋ
waddạ yakẹ fataucin nēmā he obtained
a signal advantage, such as he aimed at
getting. (3) cf. tsanyạ 3.
   B. (fatạuci) Zar. m. bull-roarer of
pagans (epithet is ∼ bạ̄ ganim mātā ba).

fạtawā (Ar. fatwā) f. (1) (a) ạlkālī yanạ̄
nēmam ∼ the judge is consulting
assessors (mụfụtai) on legal point.
(b) n nạ̄ dạ ∼ I've come to you for
information. (2) request x yanạ̄
fạtawar rạncē he's seeking a loan
(= shạkạwā).

fate-fate A. (fạtẹ̄-fatē = Zar. fatẹ) m. (1)
(a) a mushy food of flour and onions or
garạ̄funī, etc. (= gaddamạ 5 = Sk.
mạ̄ye-mạ̄yē). (b) Vd. laŋgạ. (2) ∼
yā dācẹ dạ maŋ kadaŋyạ they suit one
another. (3) yanạ̄ shaŋ ƙauyạm ∼
m. he's beating about the bush. (4)
Vd. ạlbishịr. (5) broad-bladed sword.
   B. (fate-fate) adj. m., f. (sg., pl.) thin
and flimsy (= fale-fale).

Fātī = **Fātsuma**.

fątigi = **fųtukį**.

Fātihą = **Fātīyą** *Ar. f.* (1) (*a*) prayer consisting of 1st verse of Koran. **yā jā Fātihą** he read the first verse of the Koran (= **Alhamdu** 1). (2) **yā shāfą** ~ **on** finishing saying *this prayer*, worshipper said **Fātihą āmįŋ** and passed his hands down his face. (3) **ą yi** ~ *said by the parties* who have settled terms of sale, marriage, etc. (4) **ą yi** ~, **ą tāshį** nothing more can be done, for the matter's too serious!

fatkę *Vb.* 1A *Sk.* (1) snapped T. (= **tsiŋkę**). (2) **yā** ~ **bāshį** he paid the debt.

fātō *Vd.* **fācę** blow one's nose.

fātōcī skins (*pl. of* **fātą**).

fątǫmā *Kr. m.* (*pl.* **fątǫmai** = **fātōmōmī**) one who lodges travellers (= **zaŋgōmą**).

fatsā *f.* (1) (*a*) fishing with hook and line. (*b*) fish-hook (*epithet is* ~ **bāwąm masųntā** : **Allą ną bā ką, kaną bąi bāyā** " God gives you fish, and when you're drawn out, you catch in people's backs ! ''). (*c*) **yā są** (= **saką**) ~ **ą rūwa** he lowered his fishing-line into the water. (*d*) **dam** ~ *m.* fisherman who uses hook. (*d*) *Vd.* **fatsī**. (2) eking out resources *x* **yaŋ** ~ **tasą** he's eking it out.

fątsąl-fątsąl poor quality work (= **bątsąl-bątsąl** *q.v.*).

fątsąm *used in* **sąiwā tā yi fątsąm** roots spread far and wide.

fatsąr-fatsąr *noun or adv.* **rānā tā yi** ~ noonday heat is intense. **įnā zą mu cikin wannąŋ rānā** ~ where can we go in this blazing noonday-heat ?

fatsątsē *Vd.* **fatsī**.

fatsę *Vb.* 1A ceased T. suddenly *x* **suką** ~ **mągana** they suddenly relapsed into silence.

fatsī *m.* (*f.* **fatsā**) *pl.* **fatsątsē** light 'red-skinned P. (= **waŋkan darzą**).

Fātsumą woman's name (*she is also called* **Zārā** = **Fątu** = **Fādī** = **Falmataŋ** = **Fātī** = **Algājē** = **Gąjī** = **Fājį**).

fattanyą *f.* the hoe **fartanyą**.

fatu A. (**fātū**) skins (*pl. of* **fātą**).
B. (**Fątu**) (1) *abbreviation of* **Fātsumą**. (2) ~ (= **Fątu kulę**) **wutsīyą dązązą** *epithet of* cat. (3) *Vd.* **fątumą** 3.

fątumą *f.* (*pl.* **fātumōmī**). (1) the cap **habąr kadą**. (2) ~ **furfur** *epithet of* (*a*) firefly, (*b*) quick-spinning woman. (3) **dūnīyą ta kąn yi fątu, ta kąn yi** ~ fortune is fickle !

fau A. (**fau**) *noun or adv.* (1) **rānā tā yi** ~ sun's blazing. (2) **yā kāmą wutā** ~ it suddenly caught fire. (3) **zāɓī** ~ very sweet ; nicely salted. (4) **yā tsērę** ~ (*a*) he got clean away (*cf.* **tsilak** 2). (*b*) he's far superior.
B. (**fau**) *used in* **yā mąrē nį** ~ he gave me hard slap (= **fat** = **tau**).
C. (**fau**) (1) *emphasizes* clear expanse *x* **rānā tā fitō** ~ sun shone from clear, open sky. **fīlī** ~ extensive open country. (2) **wurī yā haskę** ~ the place was brilliantly lit up. (3) **sāi aką ji fau** then news suddenly came that . . .

fauce A. (**faucę**) *Vb.* 1A. (1) (bird) swooped on, to seize T. (= **sųrā** = **wałcę**). (2) (thief, etc.) snatched up T. (1, 2 = **ząrā** 2*b*.i). (3) *x* **wąlɓīyā tā** ~ **minį ganī** lightning dazzled me.
B. (**faucē**) *Vd.* **fautā**.

faudą *Vb.* 3A travelled far.

faufau (1) completely (= **fąfąrątaŋ** *q.v.*). (2) (*negatively*) never *x* ~ **bą ząm bā ką ba** I'll certainly never give you it ! (= **mąsau**).

faulą *Vb.* 3A *used in* **yā** ~ **dą gudu** he fled.

faumą *f.* boastfulness, showing-off (= **hōmą** *q.v.*).

fauru *used in* **fauru dągwīyau dabbąr Allą** *epithet of* hyena.

fauta A. (**fautā**) *Vb.* 1C cut up meat for sale (*cf.* **fāwą**).
B. (**fautā**) *Vb.* 2 (*p.o.* **faucē**, *n.o.* **fauci**) = **faucę** 1, 2.

fautį *Ar. m.* **yā yi minį** ~ (1) I failed to get it. (2) I no longer have it.

fāwą = **pāwą** (1) (*a*) being cutter-up and seller of meat. (*b*) *Vd.* **fincē**. (*c*) (i) **Sarkim pāwą** Head of the meat-sellers (*epithet is* **Sarkim** ~ **kūrąm Bądau** = **Amāsą** =**kūrąn shānū**, *Vd.* **kūrę**). (ii) **gōdīyar Sarkim pāwą** *Vd.* **wutā** 1*a*. (*d*) **wątandā tā jūyę** ~ *Vd.* **wątandā**. (*e*) **dągą marąbar Sarkim pāwą ?** *Vd.* **marąbā** 3. (*f*) *Vd.* **mahaucī**. (*g*) **wuɓar** ~ *Vd.*

gąbā 1*d*. (2) cutting of horse's mouth by bit. (3) bleeding of anus from piles.

*fawwalą *Ar. Vb.* 1C *x* nā ∽ masą shī I entrusted him with it.

fāyą *f.* (1) amniotic flow (*Vd.* zāƙī 6). (2) **fāyąr baką** loss of teeth (*mainly in case of pregnant woman*).

fayā-fąyą *used in* yaną dą gēmų (sąjē) ∽ he has bushy beard (side-whiskers).

fąyąfąyāi *Vd.* fäifäi.

fayąŋ-fąyąŋ *m.* sound of quick walking.

fayau A. (fayau) (1) *epithet of* francolin (fąkarā) = mīyą 13. (2) *used in* wuƙā tā yi kaifī ∽ knife's sharp. gishirī yā ji ∽ food's nicely salted. yaną mąganą ∽ he's of pleasant address.
    B. (fąyau) (1) = fąu ; fayā-fąyą. (2) *used in* yaną dą fuską ∽ he has pleasant, healthy face.
    C. *Vd.* fąŋkąm fayau.

faye *Vb.* 3A is (was) characterized by *x* (1) yā ∽ nīsā it's far. yā ∽ girmaŋ ƙąi he's an arrogant P. bąi ∽ ąmfąnī ba it's not useful. (2) *Vd.* ƙąrnā 1*b*. (3) (*with dative*) wurī yā faye musų sanyī the place is too cold for them.

fayil *Eng. m.* file (of papers).

fąyų *used in* ą ∽ *adv.* (1) gratis. (2) uselessly.

fayyące *Vb.* 1C *Kt.* explained, revealed (= fanyące).

farząyī = faząyī *m.* cleared open space (= fągē).

fązbūtų (*Eng.* postboat) *m.* (*sg., pl.*) mailboat.

fēce *Vb.* 1A. (1) (farmer) scraped up (ground) to make farm (= bēcę *q.v.*). (2) yā ∽ amāwąlī he left long piece of turban hanging below his chin (*cf.* amāwąlī). (3) (*a*) tā ∽ zanę she's put on her cloth to the best advantage. (*b*) yā ∽ adō he togged himself up. (4) yā ∽ ƙaryā he told a "whopper". (5) yā ∽ dą gudų he fled.

fēci (1) *expression of surprise at act as in* fēcę. (2) *Kt.* = fāci 2.

fēdą *Eng. f.* (*pl.* fēdōdī) bicycle-pedal.

fedą A. (fēdą) *Vb.* 1A (*Vd.* fīɗą). (1) flayed. (2) drew (a fowl for cooking). (3) ∽ gōnā to begin ridging a farm, etc. (= sąftā *q.v.*), *Vd.* fędē.
    B. (fędā) *Vb.* 2 = fēdą 1, 2.

---

fēdalī *Sk. m.* = fīdilī.

fede A. (fēdę) *Vb.* 1A. (1) = fēdą. (2) zā mų fēdę maką biri har wutsīyą we shall reveal it to you without reserve.
    B. (fędē) *m.* (1) *secondary v.n. of* fēdą 3 (*q.v.*) *x* yaną fędaŋ gōnā = yaną fēdą gōnā (= shērį = tsągē 1), *cf.* rufị 5. (2) type of tribal-mark with a cut from brow to mouth (*such as done by Angass*).

fēdōdī *Vd.* fēdą.

fēdūwā = fēdwā *f.* act of whistling (= fītọ).

fēfę *Vb.* 3A (colour or cloth) faded.

fēgị *Eng. m.* (*pl.* fēgōgī). (1) peg. (2) yā kafą ∽ (*a*) he pegged out the ground. (*b*) he threw out a hint.

fēƙe *Sk.* = fīƙe.

fēƙųwā *f.* (1) barren place. (2) stingy P., etc. (= ƙēƙųwā *q.v.*).

felan-felaŋ *m.* (1) yā yi minị ∽ he flattered me. (2) *Vd.* falaŋ.

fēlēƙē *m.* (1) affectation. (2) ogling ; coquetry ; simpering. (1, 2 = kwąrkwasą).

fęlų *m.* peppermint (= mintị = nạ'ąnạ'ą).

fēlūwā = fēlwā *f.* (1) curved brass ornament for horse's face. (2) ƙafąssą tā yi ∽ his tibia is curved by congenital syphilis. (3) soughing sound •of whip, etc., cutting through air.

fēnị *Eng. m.* (*sg., pl.*) penny.

fenshọ (1) pension (*cf.* tąusąyī 4). (2) yā yi ∽ he is on pension. (3) jirgịŋ yā yi ∽ tųnī the ship had long been out of commission.

fensil = fensịr *Eng. m.* (*pl.* fensirōrī) pencil.

fentị *Eng. m.* paint *x* an shāfę shi dą baƙim fentị it is painted black.

fērą (1) *Vb.* 1A. (*a*) pared T. into or on to (*cf.* fērę). (*b*) iską tā ∽ ƙasā cikin rījịyā wind blew dust into well. (*c*) yā ∽ ƙaryā he told a "whopper". (2) *Vb.* 3A yā ∽ dą gudų he fled.

feraya A. (fērąyā) *Vb.* 1C = fērą.
    B. (fęrayą) *f.* (1) (*secondary v.n. of* fērę) *x* yaną fęrayąr ƙwaryā = yaną fērę ƙwarya he's paring calabash. (2) being occupied in paring calabashes *x* yaną ∽.

fĕrayĕ *Vb.* 1C = fĕrę.

fere A. (fĕrę) (*Ar.* barā). (1) *Vb.* 1A. (*a*) pared. (*b*) yā ~ ₭aryā he told a "whopper". (*c*) sharpened to a point. (2) *Vb.* 3A. (*a*) to swerve off. (*b*) yā ~ dạ gudụ he fled.

B. (fĕre) (1) yanạ̄ ~ it's been pared. (2) *cf.* ạ cī kạ ạ ~.

fĕrę dạ fĕrę *used in* (1) nā san shị ~ I know it thoroughly. (2) nā fītō ~, nā gayạ masạ I told him straight out.

fĕrĕrę = fĕrę dạ fĕrę.

fĕrị what a lie ! (*cf.* fĕrę 1*b*).

feriya A. (fĕrīyā = fĕryā) *f.* (1) paring. (2) swerving.

B. (fĕrīyạ) *Kt.* = fĕrayạ.

fĕsạ *Vb.* 1A (1) spurted water from one's mouth (*Vd.* fĕsasshē). (2) yā ~ he blabbed. (3) (*a*) ~ ₭aryā to tell a lie. (*b*) spread (false report, etc.) *x* yanạ̄ fĕsạ musụ lạ̄bārị he is spreading false news among them. am fĕsạ musụ wata ₭aryạr another lying report was spread among them. (4) fĕsō *Vb.* 3A burst forth abundantly *x* tụrurūwā sum fĕsō black ants have appeared in swarms. cịyāwạ tā fĕsō grass has sprouted abundantly. ₭urạrrajī sum fĕsō masạ he's very pimply.

fĕsar dạ *Vb.* 4B = fĕsạ 1.

fĕsasshē *m.* (*f.* fĕsasshīyā) *pl.* fĕsạssū. (1) T. upon which water has been spurted from the mouth to soften. (2) worn out (garment).

feshe A. (fĕshę) *Vb.* 1A = fĕsạ 1-3.

B. (fĕshē) *m.* innuendo (= shạ̄gụ̄ɓē).

fĕshī *m.* (1) splashing of rain into house. (2) nā ji fĕshim maganạ I heard rumour about it. (3) *Kt.* = fĕshē.

fĕsō *Vd.* fĕsạ 4.

fĕsū *m.* lie *x* yā zubạ minị ~ he told me a lie (*Vd.* fĕsạ 3*a*).

fĕtai = fĕtal *adv. emphasizes* clear expanse (= fạu *q.v.*) *x* hanyạ tā sạ̄mu fĕtai there was a clear road to their desires.

fĕtạlī *Kt. m.* the tribal-mark billē 1 *q.v.*

fetana A. (fĕtạnā) *Vb.* 1C. (1) took out small amount of. (2) (*with dative*) *x* yā ~ masạ dāwạ he took out and gave him a little guinea-corn.

B. (fĕtanạ) *Vb.* 2 inflicted glancing wound on *x* yā fĕtạnē nị dạ wu₭ā he gave me glancing wound with the knife. fartanyạ tā fĕtạnē shị hoe gave him a glancing wound.

fĕtạnē *Vb.* 1C. (1) = fĕtạnā. (2) winnowed (corn) = bākạcē *q.v.*

fetete A. (fĕtētę) = fĕtai.

B. (fĕtētę) *m.* shallowness *x* kōgin nạm ~ yakę this river's shallow.

feto A. (fĕtō) *m.* very abbreviated shorttrousers (*cf.* gajĕrē 1*c*).

B. (farim fĕtọ) *m.* anæmia (*Vd.* farin fĕtọ).

fetsa A. (fĕtsạ) (1) *Vb.* 1A. (*a*) passed through (place) without deviating (= rātsạ 1*a*.i), *cf.* fĕtsā 1*a*. (*b*) yā ~ minị kāshī it (baby) defecated on me. (2) *Vb.* 3A *x* mum ~ mun yi kudụ we travelled dead south. hanyạ tā ~ tā yi kudụ the road goes due south (= fĕtsā 1*d* = fĕtsę 2). (3) *f.* infant's fæces.

B. (fĕtsā) (1) *Vb.* 2. (*a*) (road or P.) encroached on (place), *cf.* fĕtsạ 1*a*. (*b*) wounded superficially (= fĕtanạ). (*c*) yā fĕtsi cịyāwạ he removed fronds from grass for mat-making (= sarcę 1*b*). (*d*) = fĕtsạ 2 *x* yā ~ yạ zō dăidăi dạ mahayī he (boatman) went diagonally in order to float back with the current to the required place on the opposite bank. (2) *f.* winnowing (= bạ̄kạcē).

fetse A. (fĕtsę) (1) *Vb.* 1A = fĕtsā 1*b*. (2) *Vb.* 3A mum ~ mun yi kudụ = fĕtsạ 2.

B. (fĕtsē) *m.* short cut (= dọshē).

fĕtụr *Eng. m.* petrol.

fi A. (fī) *Vb.* 5 exceeded. (1) (*a*) (i) sum fi gōmạ there are more than ten of them. ginin dạ ya shękarạ dạrī har yā fī mā buildings 100 years old or more. (ii) is better than *Vd.* 3 *below.* (*b*) (*followed by word denoting a quality in sense* " as to ", *indicates* " more ", " most ") *x* (i) yā fī nị ₭arfī he is stronger than I am (*lit.* he exceeds me as to strength). yā fī ʂụ dukạ ₭arfī he is the strongest of them all. sum fī mụ yawạ sạu wajan nawạ they greatly outnumber us. (ii) wạndạ ya fī kạ dạbārạ *Vd.* sọ 1*e.* (iii) kā fi kūkā cīwọ *Vd.* yạ₭ē. (iv) kā fi karĕ

gudu *Vd.* ạ bōƙarạ. (v) yā fī kạ
dạbārạ *Vd.* ɓạrāwọ 1*b.* (vi) yā fī darē
duhu *Vd.* sanị 2*b.*vii. (vii) kā fī Nạsārā
sallạ *Vd.* farkē. (viii) baị fī kạ tsụmmā
ba *Vd.* mụtụm 9*f.* (ix) kā fī ƙayạ tsīnī
Vd. fīƙē. (*x*) kā fī zanạŋ arō *Vd.*
kạtạmbirị. (*c*) (*as* 1*b but without object,
here* fī and *v.n.* or *noun of quality produce
sense of* " more " *in conjunction with
verbal sense*) *x* nā fī saŋ wannạŋ = nā fī
jịn dādiŋ wannạŋ I prefer this one (*lit.*
I exceed as to the liking this one).
wannạŋ yā fī kyạụ this one is better.
yā yi shāwarạ yā fī kyạu kadạ ạ yī
he decided it would be better not to do
it. sum fī sọ sụ zaunạ dạ sụ kōmạ
wurinsạ they prefer remaining where
they are, to going to him. gạskīyā
cē bạ fịn sọ ba it is the truth, not mere
partiality. mum fī jī anạ̄ ambatan
jirạ̄gyan samạ dạ na rūwā we hear more
mention of aeroplanes than of ships.
zaị fī taịmakō wajaŋ gyārạ al'amurạŋ
ƙasā he will be more helpful in the
administration of the country. (*d*)
yā fī gạbam mạmākị it's most extraordinary (*Vd.* gạban 3*c*). (*e*) has the
usual habit of *x* iskạ tā fī zūwạ dạgạ
yammā the wind usually blows from
the west. sum fī ƙērạ kāyaŋ aikịŋ
gōnā they mostly make farm-
implements. (2) (*with object* " all
others " *understood*) *x* itātūwạŋ Kanọ
sum fī girmā Kano has the biggest
trees. (3) is beyond one (= gạ̄garạ 2*b*)
x (*a*) aikịn naŋ yā fī ƙarfīna this work
is too much for me (*Vd.* fịŋ ƙarfī).
(*b*) kūrā tā fī dāgụmī sǎi sarƙạ he is
utterly brazen. (*c*) (*object* " one's
abilities " *understood*) *x* yā kai harị,
yā fī ạ ƙirgạ he made innumerable
raids (*lit.* he raided, it is beyond one's
powers to count). wannạŋ ạl'amạrī baị
fī ạ shiryạ shi dạ shāwarạ ba this affair
is not beyond settling by consultation.
(*d*) tā fī cikịnsạ *Vd.* shā A.1*p.* (*e*) kā
fī kisạm maị gōnā *Vd.* dōkị 1*e.* (*f*)
tā fī cikịnsạ *Vd.* cikị 1*h.* (*g*) kā fī
amai *Vd.* dōkị 1*d.* (*h*) kā fī aikịm
mālạm *Vd.* mālạmī 1*c.*iv, ivA. (*j*)
yā fī gạba rạ̄tse *Vd.* gạba 1*a.*iv. (*k*)
kā fī sautụ *Vd.* gạidā 3. (*l*) kim fī

ƙarfin yārọ *Vd.* gabạrạ. (4) is better,
best *x* bạ ạbịn dạ ya fī sǎi mụ hūtạ
we had better rest. dạbārạd dạ ta fī
sǎi sụ tạ̄ru the best thing would be for
them to gather together. (*b*) bạ wani
mụhimmịn ạbụ dạ ya fī ạ taịmạkē
sụ nothing is more important than to
help them. wannạŋ yā fī dạ ạ bayyạnạ
dukạ it is better to do this than to
explain it all. (*c*) (*plus subjunctive*) is
better than that *x* yā fī ạ rātạyā *Vd.*
sạ̄ A.4. (*d*) is better than *x* (i) dōkị yā
fī jạ̄kī a horse is better than a donkey.
(ii) kim fī ūwā *Vd.* arụgumạ. (iii) yā
fī " nawạ ka sạyạ̄ " *Vd.* bāwạ 12. (iv)
kim fī dākị *Vd.* rugā 1*a.* (v) kạ̄zā tā
fī dōkị *Vd.* sayar dạ 4. (vi) sạna'ạ
tā fī dūkịyar gādọ *Vd.* sạna'ạ. (vii) yā
fī kạ̄zā ạ sạke *Vd.* tallē 1*b.* (viii) yā
fī bạrē *Vd.* mūgụ 1*f.* (ix) gyāraŋ
hancị yā fī gyāraŋ gōnā *Vd.* gyārā 1*l.*
(x) gạskīyā tā fī Tūrancī truth is better
than wealth. (xi) ạ fī mụ *Vd.* bā
B1.4*b.* (xii) kạrē yā fī kạ *Vd.* ạbụ 2*h.*
(xiii) kim fī ƙurmusū *Vd.* gạndā.
   B. (fī) (1) *v.n. and progressive of*
fī. (2) *x* zọbbā bịyar kō ~ five rings or
even more (= fīye *q.v.*). (3) iskạ tā
tāsō ~ a strong wind is blowing.

fice A. (ficẹ) *Vb.* 3A. (1) passed by
(= wucẹ) *x* shāwarạssạ bạ tạ̄ ~ haƙạ
ba his advice will be just this. (2) (*a*)
= fịta *except* 5, 7, 8. (*b*) *Vd.* dạ̄ma
ficẹ.
   B. (ficē) *m.* (1) innovation *x* sābam ~
nẹ̄ it's a new fashion. yā fītad dạ
wani sābam ~ he introduced an in-
novation (= salō 1 = launị = fịrtsị =
tsirị = sauyị). (2) standing out in
relief (*tattooing, sewing-pattern, etc.*) *x*
dịŋkị yā yi ~.
   C. (fịcē) *m.* protruding beyond his
(its) fellows.

fici A. (fịci) *m. used in* shịgi dạ ~
(1) restlessness. (2) being mischievous
tattler.
   B. (ficị) *m.* (1) wani ~ = ficị-ficị
sometimes. (2) *Zar.* sạm ~ togging
self up.
   C. (ficī) *Kt. m.* = ficē.

fici-fici A. (ficị-ficị) sometimes.
   B. (fici-fici) *pl. adj.* small and flat.

fici̱kō *m.* looking hither and thither (= fā̱fu̱tu̱kā *q.v.*).

ficil *Kt. m.* garment's being very small (= figil *q.v.*).

fída̱ *f.* (1) (*secondary v.n. of* fēḍa̱) *x* yana̱ fīḍar a̱kwīya̱ = yana̱ fēḍa̱ a̱kwīya̱ he's flaying the goat. (2) being occupied in flaying *x* yana̱ ∼. (3) *Vd.* fincē 2 ; dā̱duma̱.

fídabu̱rdi̱ = fídabu̱ldi̱ *Eng. m.* P.W.D.

fi̱ da̱ sartse̱ *m. Euphorbia lateriflora* (remedy for syphilis and lice on women).

fida̱'u̱ *Ar. m.* prayers for the dead said by Malam for fee.

fid da̱ (1) *Vb.* 4A = fitar da̱. (2) fid da̱ ka̱fāra̱ *Vd.* ka̱fāra̱.

fidda̱ *Sk. Vb.* 1A = fid da̱.

fi̱d da̱ hakūkūwa̱ *m.* waterside-plant *Dyschoriste Perrottetii* (= sansa̱ŋ = bi̱dīdīyau).

fi̱d da̱ kä̱i *m.* (1) custom incumbent on Muslims to give certain persons four measures of corn at end of Fast (azu̱mī), *Vd.* mūda̱nabi̱ ; mūdu̱ 1*b* (= *Sk.* kōnō 1). (2) the measuring vessel used for *such corn* (= mūda̱nabi̱). (3) *Vd.* fitar da̱ 2.

fi̱d da̱ sartse̱ = *Kt.* fi̱d da̱ saruttsa̱ = fi̱ da̱ sartse̱ *q.v.*

fi̱ddau *Kt. m.* piece of paper spoilt while writing.

fiddā'u̱ *m.* = fi̱dā'u̱.

fi̱ddiŋ always *x* ∼ haka̱ yake̱ yi̱ so he always acts ! ∼ ji̱ddiŋ tu̱tur ilalla̱ absolutely *always* (*cf.* ilalla̱ ; ji̱ddiŋ).

fi̱ddō *Kt. m.* ∼ fi̱ddau.

fidi̱ *Kt.* said (= fa̱dā) *x* a̱bi̱n da̱ ya fi̱di̱ what he said.

fīdilī *m.* the Senna *Cassia absus* (*for eye-diseases*) = *Kt.* ḵu̱rī-ḵu̱rī = *Kt.* burkulle̱.

fi̱dīya̱ *f.* (*secondary v.n. of* fidīye̱) *x* yana̱ fi̱dīya̱r bu̱nsurū = yana̱ fidīye̱ bu̱nsurū he is castrating the billy-goat.

fidīye̱ *Vb.* 1C castrated (billy-goat ; *less often* ram or stallion), *cf.* dake̱ 1*c*.

fiffi̱ge̱ *Vb.* 3A is destitute.

fi̱ffi̱kā *f.* flapping the wings, *etc.* (= fu̱ffu̱kā *q.v.*).

fiffike̱ *m.* (*pl.* fi̱kā̱fi̱kai). (1) (*a*) wing. (*b*) zā su̱ yi ∼ su̱ tāshi̱ bisa̱ they were

about to fly away. (*c*) fi̱kā̱fi̱kammu̱ sum fāra̱ gāshi̱ we've begun to become strong. (*d*) *Vd.* fikā̱fikī. (2) hair-twists on neck or back of horse (*said to show speed*).

fiffi̱ḵē *Vb.* 3A acted in a way showing one is determined to be "top dog" (= kyaŋkye̱nē *q.v.*), *cf.* fi̱ḵi̱nīya̱, ha̱ḵī-ḵi̱cē.

fiffita A. (fi̱ffi̱ta̱) *Vd.* firfita C, D.
   B. (fiffi̱tā) *Vb.* 1C = fi̱fi̱tā.
   C. (fi̱ffi̱tā) = fi̱fi̱tā.

fiffizgīyā *Zar. f.* hangnail (= ḍa̱ŋu̱bā).

fifike̱ *Sk. m.* = fiffike̱.

fifīko̱ *m.* (1) superiority, precedence over. (2) excess (1, 2 = fīko̱).

fi̱fi̱rnīyā *f.* (1) affectation. (2) officiousness.

fifita A. (fi̱fi̱ta̱) *Vb.* 2 (*p.o.* fi̱fi̱cē, *n.o.* fi̱fi̱ci) surpassed.
   B. (fi̱fi̱tā) *Vb.* 1C. (1) promoted *x* am ∼ shi a̱ ka̱nsu̱ he's been promoted over them. (2) tā fi̱fi̱ta̱ a̱bincī she fanned the food to cool it (= fi̱fi̱tā 3*b* = hurhūtā 1 = saisa̱itā 2*a*), *cf.* būsa̱ 1*b*.
   C. (fi̱fi̱tā) *f.* (1) (*secondary v.n. of* fi̱fi̱tā) *x* tana̱ fi̱fi̱tar a̱bincī = tana̱ fi̱fi̱ta̱ a̱bincī she's fanning the food to cool it. (2) being occupied in fanning food *x* tana̱ fi̱fi̱tā. (3) (*a*) tā yi masa̱ ∼ she fanned him. (*b*) tā yi wa̱ a̱bincī ∼ she fanned the food to cool it (2*b* = fi̱fi̱tā 2).

figa A. (fi̱gā) *Vb.* 2. (1) (*a*) plucked out *x* (i) tā fi̱gi gāshi̱ŋ kä̱zā she plucked the (dead) chicken. (ii) yā fi̱gi jiminā he plucked (live) ostrich (1*a*.ii = tūje̱ 1*b* = fi̱gā 2*b*). (iii) fi̱ge̱ kä̱zā *Vd.* i̱yar da̱ 2. (iv) *cf.* fi̱zgā, fincikā. (*b*) snatched away *x* yā fi̱gi taka̱rdā a̱ hannūna he snatched the paper out of my hand (= fi̱zgā 1*b*). (*c*) made rent in *x* ḵaya̱ tā fi̱gi ri̱gā the thorn made a rent in the gown. (*d*) yā fi̱gi dōki̱nsa̱ he made his horse take a sudden leap forward. (*e*) rapidly unsheathed *x* yā fi̱gi takọ̄bī he unsheathed his sword like lightning. (2) *f.* (*a*) (i) being occupied in plucking (dead) chicken *x* tana̱ fi̱gā = (1*a*.i). (ii) *Kt.* fi̱gar kūrā *Vd.* kūrā 7. (*b*) (*with dative*) plucking (live) ostrich *x* yā yi wa̱ jiminā ∼ (= 1*a*.ii).

B. (fîgạ) *Vb.* 1A. (1) yā ∼ dāwạ he stripped guinea-corn heads for fodder (= zāgā 1*c*.ii). (2) dạ ∼ dạ yāgạ mukạ kai we only reached there with the utmost difficulty (= dạ kyar). (3) *Vd.* fịtar fîgạ.

C. (fîgā) *f.* yā yi ∼ it (bird) moulted.

fige A. (fîgẹ) *Vb.* 1A. (1) (*a*) = fîgā 1*a*, *b*, *c* (*x* tā ∼ gāshị̀ŋ kāzā. yā ∼ minị̀ takạrdā). (*b*) kadạ kạ ∼ kāzā săi tā īyar dạ mutūwạ await the psychological moment ! (2) stripped all heads of dāwạ for fodder (*cf.* fîgạ).

B. (fîgẹ̄) *m.* (1) guinea-corn stripped from stalks for fodder (= yāgẹ̄). (2) bạ̄ fîgyan yārọ̄ ba *Vd.* dinyā. (3) thieving by snatching. (4) a poor type of tūwō food.

figil *m.* smallness of garment *x* rīgā cḕ ∼ dạ ita it's a small gown (*pl.* rīgunạ nē figil-figil dạ sū).

figini A. (fîginị) *m.* (1) ostrich-feather fan. (2) fanning with *such fan.*

B. (fîginî) *m.* twenty-five centime piece.

fîgi, rūtsa *m.* slapdash work.

*fihirisạ *Ar.f.* (1) index of book. (2) table of contents.

fi'ilî *Ar. m.* (1) affectation. (2) being meddlesome. (3) contrariety. *(4) (*with pl.* fị'ilai) any verb.

fij'atạŋ *Ar.* unexpectedly.

fijigạ (1) *f.* rapid travelling by trader (= bōjwā *q.v.*). (2) fijigā-fịjigā̀ *x* yā zō nạm fijigā-fịjigā̀ he only got here with the utmost difficulty.

fijil *Ar. m.* (1) radish. (2) turnip.

fijịnnîyā *Kt. f.* (1) swinging the arms in walking. (2) animal's jerking itself to shake off flies.

Fīkạ *f.* the Bolewa town of this name famed for dates.

fîkạ (1) *f.* (*pl.* fîkōkī). (*a*) canine-tooth (= fîrạ = zagạ). (*b*) dōkị̀ jar ∼ big horse. sạmārí jar ∼ strapping youth. mạcẹ̄ jar ∼ robust woman. (*c*) *cf.* zagạ. (2) *Vb.* 1A = fîkẹ.

fikāfīkī *m.* (*pl.* fịkāfịkai). (1) (*a*) wing. (*b*) *Vd.* fiffīkẹ. (2) fikāfīkim burtū nẹ̄ *Vd.* birgimā 4. (3) *Vd.* ạutā ; lālācẹ̄.

fîkẹ A. (fîkẹ) *Vb.* 1A sharpened T. to a point.

B. (fîkẹ̄) *m.* (1) filing one's teeth to a point *x* an yi masạ ∼. (2) (*a*) T. artificially sharpened to a point. (*b*) ∼ kā fi kayạ tsịnī *epithet of* P. " too big for his boots ".

fikī-fîkī *m.* striving with task foolishly thought within one's powers.

*fikihụ *Ar. m.* science of Muslim religious law.

fikịnîyā *f.* (1) = fîkī-fîkī. (2) striving to be ". top-dog " (*cf.* fiffīkẹ̄). (3) affectation ; ogling.

fîkọ *m.* superiority : precedence over (= fîfīkọ).

fil A. (fil) *adv.* (1) *emphasizes* having become red *x* idạnsạ yā yi jā ∼ his eyes are swollen and red. zanẹ̄ yā ci bābā ∼ cloth is dyed good, deep colour. (2) sābō ∼ brand-new (= ful).

B. (fịl) *adv.* (1) kumfā yā tāshị ∼ froth rose bubblingly. kūrā tā tāshị ∼ dust rose in clouds. (2) yā yi kibạ ∼ he's corpulent.

fîlạcẹ̄ *Vb.* 1C *Kt.* tricked P. (= hîlạcẹ̄).

fîlāfīlī *m.* (*pl.* fịlāfịlai = fụlāfụlai *but pl. generally used with sense of sg. or pl.*). (1) canoe-paddle (= matūkī 1). (2) " horn " of chief's turban (*Vd.* kụnnẹ̄ 2*b*).

fîlai *m.* yāwạm ∼ takẹ̄ yị̄ = kārūwạr ∼ cẹ̄ she's a wandering whore.

fîlākọ (*derived from* Filānī) *m.* (1) bashfulness. (2) " making compliments " (= Fillancī = kusfā 3 = kūrā 6 = kunyạ 2*e* = kārā 4 = daŋkērīyā = taushị 1), *cf.* rāfạsạ 2, kērē 2*b*.ii, darē 11. (3) bearing pain without wincing. (4) deceit.

Filani A. (Filānī). (1) the Filani race (*pl. of* Bạfilācẹ *q.v.*). (2) hālịm ∼ = fîlākọ. (3) *Vd.* gandū 2*e*. (4) cịŋ kadanyạr Fulānī *Vd.* dịmbalạ.

B. (Filāni) (1) *girl's name.* (2) *in royal household, 2nd and other wives call and refer to senior wife as* Filāni (*Vd.* Mod. Gram, Appendix 3, D.vi), *Vd.* yāyā 2.

fîlānịyā *used in* fịlānịyarkạ = dam fîlānịyar ūwā blast you ! (*to male*) (*Vd.* ūwā). fịlānịyarkī = 'yar fîlānịyar ūwā blast you ! (to female).

filaskō *m.* (1) the Senna *Cassia obovata* (*leaves must be washed before use, as* snakes are said to eat it). **(2) fi̇laskwam Makậ** = **Filaskwam Masậr** type of large senna.

Filậsū playful term for **Filậnī** by others (pun on -**nī** " me " and -**sū** " them "). **fi̇latậ** Ar. Vb. 2 Kt. (p.o. **fi̇lậcē**, n.o. **fi̇lậci**) tricked P. (= **hi̇latậ**).

Filātancī m. = **Fillancī**.

filau m. (1) = **filai**. (2) Eng. (sg., pl.) pillow.

filậyē Vd. **fi̇lī**.

fil ậzal Ar. used in **tum fil ậzal** from time immemorial.

filẹ = **filai**.

filfil A. (**filfi̇l**) Ar. m. type of capsicum (= **ci̇ttā 2**).

B. (**fil-fil** = **fil-fil-fil**). (1) flutteringly x **tsuntsū yā tāshi̇** ~ small bird rose with whirring of wings. **iskậ tā kwāshẹ takậrdā** ~ wind sent the paper fluttering away (cf. **filfilwậ**). **tūtậrmu tanậ tāshi̇ fil-fil-fil** our flag is waving. (2) cf. **fir**.

filfilọ m. (1) butterfly. (2) (a) child's kite. (b) windmill-toy.

filfilwậ f. (1) fluttering x **takậrdā tanậ** ~ **ậ samậ** paper is fluttering through air (cf. **fil-fil**). (2) Sk. = **filậfilī**.

filfi̇ta Sk. = **firfita**.

fi̇lī m. (pl. **filậyē**). (1) open country. (2) (a) cleared place, open space (= **sararī** = **fagē** 1a.i). (b) **filin jirgin samậ** aerodrome. (3) (a) **ậ** ~ **yakẹ** it's clear, obvious. (b) (i) **yā fitō ậ** ~ he spoke un-equivocally. (ii) **yậnzu ậbu yā fitō fi̇lī** now " the cat's out of the bag ". (c) ~ **dậ** ~ adv. (i) frankly ; openly ; publicly. (ii) **yā tāshi̇ tsậye, fi̇lī dậ fi̇lī** he " came out into the open ". (iii) **yā ga wutā fi̇lī dậ fi̇lī** Vd. **dafậ** 1e. (3) chance x (a) **zậi sậmi** ~ **yậ zō** he'll get a chance to come. (b) **sun sậmi fi̇lin sukựwā** they " got a clear field ". (c) **aŋ kậrậ būdẹ fi̇lī garēsu** they have been given more scope.

fi̇lillịkī m. (f. **fi̇lillịkā**) pl. **fi̇lillịkai** baby (= **jinjịrī**).

filkad dậ Nor. took out (= **fitad dậ** q.v.).

fillậ Vb. 1A. (1) = **billậ**. (2) **yā** ~ **kwaryā** he told a " whopper ".

filla-fi̇lla adv. (1) one by one. (2) **yā fậdi magana** ~ he enunciated clearly.

Fillancī m. (1) the Filani language (= **Filātancī**). (2) = **fi̇lākọ**.

Fillậnī = **Filậnī**.

Fillậsū = **Filậsū**.

fi̇llē Kt. m. **dagaci̇ yā yi musu̇** ~ village head got in tax early by using duress (= **fậllē 3**).

fi̇lō Kt. m. a climber with edible tubers.

fi̇mfiŋ Sk. m. lampblack (= **fumfuŋ** q.v.).

fimfirim x **nī, kō** ~ I've none at all.

fimfiris m. **yā yi** ~ he ignored call (= **fumfurus** q.v.).

fi̇n Vd. **fi̇**.

fi̇nāfu̇r Eng. m. (sg., pl.) pineapple.

fince A. (**fi̇ncē**) Vd. **fi̇ntā**.

B. (**fincē** = **fi̇ncē**) m. (1) (a) per-quisites of assistants of meat-cutters (**mafậutā**). (b) any " perks ". (2) **kōwā ya bā kậ pāwậ** (= **fi̇dậ**), **yā sō kậ yi** ~ if P. gives you a chance, it's for you to take it ! (3) **ậbu yā gậgậri 'yam pāwậ bậrē 'yam** ~ can tyro out-strip expert !

fi̇nci Vd. **fi̇ntā**.

fincikā Vb. 1C = **fi̇ncikậ** Vb. 2. (1) dragged at T. to detach handful (feathers, hairs, meat, etc.). (2) dragged and managed to detach handful (cf. **fi̇gā**).

fi̇ncikē Vb. 1C = **fincikậ**.

fi̇ndī Kt. m. curved, one-edged sword (= **hi̇ndī**).

fiŋgi (1) m. fowl with permanently ruffled feathers = Kt. **kudugu** = Sk. **cikirkitậ** (epithet is ~ **kậzar tsāfi̇**). (2) epithet of too-short bodycloth or gown.

fiŋgilgil m. shortness = **figil** q.v.

fiŋgilī m. (f. **fiŋgilā**) pl. **figil-figil** x **ri̇gā cẹ** ~ **dậ ita** it's a small gown (pl. **ri̇gunậ nē figil-figil dậ sū**).

fiŋgīmậ f. (1) looking hither and thither (= **fậfu̇tu̇kā** q.v.). (2) making wild guesses.

fiŋgyallậ f. the sleeveless shirt **biŋgyallậ** q.v.

fi̇nī Sk. m. lampblack (= **fumfuŋ** q.v.).

***fi̇njālī** Ar. m. (pl. **fi̇njậlai**). (1) cup. (2) tumbler.

fi̇njim = **fu̇njum**.

fi̇njirậ Vb. 3B Sk. became out of control (= **bi̇jirậ** q.v.).

finjịrē Vb. 3A **yā** ~ **mini̇** he behaved insubordinately to me.

fiŋ ƙarfī *m. x* an yi manạ fiŋ ƙarfī. (i) we are out-matched. (ii) we were oppressed. mun yi musụ fiŋ ƙarfī we overcame them (*Vd.* fī 3).

fiŋƙāsō = fuŋƙāsō.

*finnạr *Ar. m.* hurricane-lamp (*word almost obsolete*).

fintā *Vb.* 2 (*p.o.* fincẹ, *n.o.* finci). (1) (assistant of mahaucī) cut off meat as perquisite. (2) P. got " perks " (*cf.* fincẹ).

fintiƙīrị *m.* (*f.* fintiƙīrīyā) *pl.* fintiƙīrai destitute.

fintiŋkau = fintiŋkyū *Kt.* yā tsērẹ ~ he was easily first.

fir (1) = fil-fil. (2) yā ƙī ~ he refused pointblank. (3) yā fita ~ he went away, never to return.

fira A. (firạ) (1) *f.* (*pl.* firōrī) canine-tooth (= fīƙạ *q.v.*). (2) (*secondary v.n.* of fērẹ) *x* yanạ fīrạr ƙwaryā = yanạ fērẹ ƙwaryā he's paring the calabash. (3) *Sk.* yā yi ~ it (child) lost milk-teeth (= ƙarāyạ).

    B. (fira) *Vb.* 3B *Sk.* (bird) whirred into air (*cf.* fil-fil).

    C. (fīrā) *Kt. f.* chatting (= hīrā *q.v.*).

firātaŋ completely (= fāfarataŋ *q.v.*).

Fir'aunạ *Ar. m.* (1) Pharaoh. (2) Baƙī, tạkarkạrim ~ *epithet of* train.

fircẹ *Vb.* 1A (1) eluded one's grasp *x* ƙāzā tā ~ mini. (2) extricated oneself from a " jam ".

firci *Sk. m.* = firtsi.

firdā *Vb.* 2 hoed up ground-nuts (= fardā *q.v.*).

firɗēɗẹ *m.* (*f.* firɗēɗīyā) *pl.* firɗā-firɗā huge (*re* P. or domestic animal).

firdị what a large domestic animal or P. !

firɗimēmẹ *m.* (*f.* firɗimēmīyā) *pl.* firɗā-firɗā = firɗēɗẹ.

firɗimī *m.* (*f.* firɗimā) *pl.* firɗim-firɗim = firɗēɗẹ.

firẹ *Vb.* 1A yā ~ gōnā he completed 1st weeding of farm (*Vd.* firị).

firfircẹ *Vb.* 3A (P.'s hair) went quite grey.

fir-fịr-fir *x* yā ƙī ~ ; yā fita ~ = fir 2, 3.

firfirtạ *f.* affectation : finickiness.

firfita A. (firfītā) fanned food (= fīfītā 2 *q.v.*).

    B. (firfītā) *f.* fanning (= fīfītā *q.v.*).

    C. (firfita *Vb.* 3B = firfīta) kept going out (*int. from* fita).

    D. (firfītā) *f. used in* iŋ kā īyạ shisshigā, kā īyạ ~ *you* got yourself into the scrape, now it's for *you* to get yourself out of it (*cf.* fītā 1c).

firgāgạ *Vb.* 2 pursued ; drove away ; rounded up (= fāfarạ).

firgicẹ (1) *Vb.* 3A is (was) terrified. (2) *Vb.* 1C terrified.

firgigit = *Kt.* firgigī. (1) *m.* sudden affrighted movement *x* yā yi ~. (2) *adv. x* yā tāshị ~ he got up in sudden fright.

firgita A. (firgitā) *Vb.* 1C terrified.

    B. (firgita) *Vb.* 3B is (was) terrified *x* sum firgitā dạ wannaŋ they're terrified on account of this.

firgitad dạ *Vb.* 4B terrified.

firi A. (firị) *m.* (1) *used in* nōmam ~ *m.* first-weeding of corn crop (fartanyạ *is used*), *Vd.* nōmā, cirbē ; hurạncē ; cirā 2b ; ɓarjē 2c. (2) ~ dạ mai-mai yakẹ yị he's uselessly imposing extra work on himself. (3) yā yi mini ~ dạ maimai he gave me a small present following big one.

    B. (Fīrī) (1) name for girl (*occasionally* boy) born tiny (*cf.* Afīrē). (2) *m.* narrow strips of farī 1e material.

    C. (firī) *m.* (1) whiteness of body from cold, dust, or bathing in muddy water *x* jikinsạ yā yi ~ (= furu-furu = furī *q.v.*). (2) *Vd.* tandū.

firicī *m.* speaking *x* yā yi ~ he spoke (*cf.* furtạ).

fīri-fīri *Vd.* fīrīrī.

firinkyū *used in* yanạ dạ kunnūwạ firiŋkyū firiŋkyū he has protruding ears.

fīrīrī *m.* (*f.* fīrīrīyā) *pl.* fīri-fīri long, narrow, and thin.

firit (1) *m.* being long, narrow, and thin *x* ạbin naŋ ~ dạ shī. (2) yā fita ~ he went away suddenly.

firita *Vb.* 3B escaped *x* sā yā ~ ạ garkẹ cow escaped from the fold.

fīrītsị *Zar. m.* cornstalk-flute (= sīrīƙi).

fīriwụl = frīwụl.

firjẹ *Vb.* 3A = *Kt.* firjanyē 3A to " kick over the traces " *x* tā firjẹ masạ she rebelled against his (husband's) authority (= tumbę 2). dōkį yā firję lįnzāmį horse refused to obey the bit.

firjī m. (1) *being occupied in act of* furzą *x* yaną firjī he's spitting out bits of kolanut ; horse is snorting. (2) yā yi minį ~ he ranted at me. (3) *cf.* shą ~.

firkąkī m. (1) wisps floating on surface of liquid (= būtącī). (2) germinating-part of beans (or locust beans) separated out after pounding.

firmitsa A. (firmįtsā) (1) *Vb.* 1C. (*a*) yā firmįtsą dōkį cikin tąrō he urged his horse through the crowd. (*b*) *Vd.* tirmųtsā. (2) *Vb.* 3A. (*a*) forced one's way through crowd *x* yā ~ cikin tąrō (= tōtsą 2 = tirmųtsā). (*b*) *x* yā ~ cikin cįnikī he traded as part-time occupation.

　B. (firmitsą) *Vb.* 2 unexpected event flummoxed unprepared P. (= mą-mayą 2) *x* zūwąm bąkī yā firmįtsē nį unexpected arrival of guests flummoxed me.

irmitsī m. (1) dense crowd. (2) being flummoxed (as firmitsą) *x* an yi masą haifųwā cikįm ~ a child was born to him at a most inconvenient moment (= kųtsē 2 = tįtsē 1).

Fįrō (1) name for girl born tiny = Ąfīrē. (2) 'Dam ~ name for boy born tiny.

"irōrī *Vd.* firą.

irtą (1) *Vb.* 1A spoke (= furtą *q.v.*). (2) *Vb.* 3A escaped *x* kązā tā ~ hen eluded P.

irtsą *Vb.* 1A inaugurated (custom) = tsįrā = fārą 4, *cf.* firtsį.

firtsą fakō *Sk.* m. the weed *Tribulus terristris* (= tsīdau).

firtsę *Vb.* 3A = firję.

firtsi A. (firtsį) m. custom which is in-novation = ficē 1 *q.v.* (*cf.* firtsą).

　B. (firtsī) m. (1) (*a*) point of bulrush-millet grain (= *Kt.* cīką). (*b*) gērō yā dąukį ~ bulrush-millet has " set ". (2) yā ci ~ he's lusty fellow.

Firu A. (Fįrū) = Fįrō.

　B. (firū) *adv.* in tiny fashion *x* watą yā tsayą ~ new moon's tiny (*after pl. noun, we use* firu-firu).

　C. (firū-firų) *used in* yaną dą kun-nūwą ~ he has small, protuberant ears.

firwątā (1) *Sk. Vb.* 3A yā ~ there's now a dry spell in the rains. (2) firwątąwā *Sk. f.* leisure.

firyā *f.* small-headed drumstick (*cf.* gulą).

firzą *Vb.* 1A to spit out (bits of kola), etc. (= furzą *q.v.*).

fisā *f.* cashew-tree ; its fruit or nuts.

fisādį *Ar. m.* profligacy.

fisąkā *Vd.* fuską face.

fishi A. (fishī) m. anger (= fushī *q.v.*).

　B. (fīshī) m. (1) dressing woman's hair (= rōrīyā 1). (2) ɗam fīshiŋ ūwā blast you ! (*to male*). 'yar fīshiŋ uwā blast you ! (*to female*), *Vd.* ūwā 1c.

fiska A. (fiską) face (= fuską *q.v.*).

　B. (fiskā) *f.* epidermis (= fuskā).

fiskį = fiskų *Ar. m.* profligacy.

fisshē *Vd.* fitar dą.

fita A. (fįta) *Vb.* 3B (*Vd.* fįtā). (1) went out. (2) (*a*) went out from *x* (i) yā ~ gąrī = yā ~ cikiŋ gąrī = ya ~ dągą gąrī = yā ~ dągą cikiŋ gąrī he went out of the town. yā ~ kōfą = yā ~ dągą kōfą = yā ficę kōfa = yā ficę dągą kōfą he went out of the door. (ii) yā ~ aikį he's lost his job ; he has resigned. (iii) yā ~ ą takąrdā it (stamp, etc.) came unstuck from the letter. (iv) nā ~ (= nā ~ dągą) sha'ąninsą I've lost interest in it. (iv) yā ~ dągą zūcīyāta I no longer like it. (*b*) is (was) appeased *x* yuŋwą bą tą ~ ba hunger was not appeased. gąjīyą tā ~ fatigue vanished. (*c*) mun san yaddą zai ~ we know how it will turn out. (*d*) iŋ Ą ~ ta cę musu ą ~, sǎi ą ~ if they are forced to quit, then they must quit (*Vd.* ą 1c). (*e*) *Vd.* ąlhakī 2. (*f*) bą ą ~ rūwa ba, bā ą mātsą warkī don't be in too much of a hurry !, don't count your chickens before they're hatched ! (*g*) sǎi yą fitō dą firī *Vd.* matsīyącī 2. (*h*) ɗansą yā ficę *Vd.* ɗā 5b. (3) went out to *x* yā ~ yākį he went out to war. mų ~ bāyam birnī let's go out into the country ! yā ~ sararī he reached open country. (4) (*a*) (crop) germinated, (tooth) appeared (= fitō). (*b*) (i) (sun, moon) came out (*cf.* tsayą 1f). (ii) *Vd.* rānā 1d. (*c*) *Sk.* watą yā ~ new moon has appeared. wataŋ azųmī

yā ~ new moon of Ramadan has appeared (= tsayą). (5) (a) succeeded x wannąŋ dąbārą tā ~ this plan succeeded (cf. fitar dą 1g). nā ~ I made a profit. shāwarą (wąhalą) tasą tā ~ his plan (efforts) were successful. (b) aŋ waŋkę rīgā, tā ~ the gown is well washed (cf. suɓul). (c) an surfę hatsī, yā ~ the corn has been winnowed. (6) (cement, mąkubą-juice) lost adhesiveness. (7) gōdīyā tā ~ the mare is on heat (= hūda 3). (8) iŋ kā fądā, kā ~ if you admit it, that will be the end of the matter. (9) gishirī yā ~ kaŋ kązā the " guilt is off the gingerbread ". (10) Vd. fitō. (11) mum ~ kōgī we forded the river (= rātsą 1a.ii), Vd. fitō 4. (12) fita dą = fitō 4.
B. (fitā) (v.n. of fita) f. x (1) (a) fitar rānā sunrise. (b) shūką tā yi kyąm ~ the crop has come up well. (c) ąbin shigā dą ~ yakę yī he's living from hand to mouth (cf. firfitā). (d) mai ~ Vd. mąshassharā. (2) profit x hājąn naŋ tanā dą ~ there is profit to be made on these goods. (3) Vd. fitar-compounds.
C. (fitā) f. large leaves used for packing kolanuts.
D. (fitą) Vb. 1A Zar. fanned (food to cool it) = fifītā 2.
E. (fitā) Zar. f. fanning food to cool it (= fifītā).
fitaccĕ m. (f. fitaccīyā) pl. fitąttū. (1) renowned. (2) ex- x fitaccan sōjā an ex-soldier. fitaccan Sarkī an ex-Chief.
fitad dą = fitar dą.
fitaną = fĕtaną.
fitar bardaŋ guzą used in yā yi ~ he decamped through fear, hunger, etc.
fitar bāyā f. (1) piles. (2) prolapse.
fitar dą Vb. 4B (p.o. also fisshĕ). (1) (a) took out T. or P. (= fitō 4). (b) deposed, dismissed x am fisshē shi he's been dismissed. yā fisshē tą he got rid of her (concubine), cf. sōrō 3. (c) removed (one's clothes). (d) am ~ hanyą dągą naŋ zūwą Kano road has been made from here to Kano. (e) yā fid dą zūcīyā (= tsąmmāni) dągą gąrēshi he gave up hope of getting it (Vd. tsąmmāni 5, dēbę 2). sum fid dą kaunā gą

zūwą they have given up all idea of coming. (f) yā ~ targadę it cured the sprain. (g) (i) yā ~ kansą dągą laifī he was able to prove himself innocent. (ii) yanā īyą fid dą hannunsą he can stand aloof. (iii) dąbārąssą tā fisshē shi his cunning got him out of his fix. (iv) Allą yą fisshē ką God see you safely through ! (cf. fita 5). (v) Allą yą fisshē ką tsaką mai wuyā, bą farkō ba, karkō may you ever remain virtuous ! (vi) wannąŋ dąbārą bą tą fisshē shi ba this plan did not effect his purpose. (vii) hanyąd dą zā tą fisshē sų a method which will suit them. (2) displayed x (a) (i) yā ~ kąi it (corn) has developed a head. (ii) Vd. fid dą kąi, kąfārą, mūdąnabi. (iii) ~ mūdu Vd. mūdu 1b. (b) macijī yā ~ kansą the snake showed its head at mouth of hole, etc. (c) rąkumī yā ~ wutā the camel protruded red-gland from its mouth. (d) yā ~ hīlą he used cunning. (e) yā ~ muryą he spoke clearly, he raised his voice. (g) tā ~ halintą she showed herself " in her true colours ". (h) yā ~ launiŋ wāką he intoned a different song. (3) recognized P., identified T. (= shaidā 3 = rabę 2). (4) (a) ~ rānā to miss out one day (in working, etc.). (b) (i) yā ~ rānā (= yā ~ sā'ą = yā ~ zaŋgo) on day fixed as propitious (burujī), he set out a short way (on journey or when going to make war) and halted there for a while (re war, we can also say yā fid dą tūtą). (ii) yā fid dą zaŋgo cikin taurārūwar nasarą he set out as in 4b.i under the best auspices. (iii) yā ~ sā'ąr fadą he fixed a propitious time for the attack. (iv) sum fid dą ran dą zā sų ci nasarą they've fixed the date when they'll be victorious. (5) nā fitar masą dą idɔ I glared at him. (6) yā ~ mū kōgī he ferried us across the river (= kētarad dą 1a), cf. fitō 4, fitɔ. (7) (a) har yanā ~ Jumma'ą he is reckoning out the Muslim calendar. (b) yā ~ jumlą he added up the total. (8) Vd. kąfārą, fid dą kąi, fid dą hakūkūwą, fid dą sartsę, ąlhakī 2, karā 4.

fîtar fîga *f.* decamping through hunger, fear, etc.

fîtar ginā *f.* leaving place for ever.

fîtar gīwā *Vd.* zōmō 10.

fîtar ƙafa *f.* involving self in trouble through ill-considered act or words.

fîtar kucīcī *f.* = fîtar kutsu = fîtar Isufāwā = fîtar fîga.

fîtas da = fîtar da.

fîtas sirā *f.* = fîtar fîga.

fîti-fîti A. (fîti-fîti) *m.* (*sg., pl.*) red type of ƙumā-flea (= tsando).

　　B. (fîti-fîti) *Vd.* fîtītī ; fîtītī.·

fîtik *x* bagidājē ～ ignorant rustic (= futuk).

fîtiki *Eng. m.* fatigue-duty by police, etc. (= futuki, *q.v.*).

fîtila *f.* (*pl.* fîtilū = fîtilōlī) (*Ar.* twisted). (1) lamp. (2) skein of the thread takwalā or of the silky-fabrics alharīnī.

fîtina (1) *Vb.* 2 annoyed, pestered. (2) *f.* (*a*) troublesomeness of P., etc. (*b*) (i) cause of trouble *x* yuŋwa ～ cē garēmu famine is a cause of trouble to us. (ii) fîtina (*pl.* fîtinōnī) dissension *x* ～ tā auku = ～ tā mōtsu dissension, revolution arose. (*c*) yārā sun tafi wurim ～ the boys have gone off to play (= fagē 1*d*). (*d*) *x* da ～ yakē he's a skilled worker (*cf.* shaitsaŋ 2*b*). (*e*) woman's red-and-black fatala (kerchief) = guntūwā 2 = yaŋkā 2*h*.

fîtinannē *m.* (*f.* fîtinannīyā) *pl.* fîtinannū. (1) troublesome P. (2) P. very skilled at his work (*cf.* fîtina 2*d*).

fîtinta *Vb.* 2 (*p.o.* fîtincē, *n.o.* fîtinci) = fîtina 1.

fîtiti A. (fîtītī) *m.* (*f.* fîtītīyā) *pl.* fîti-fîti small (*re* child) *x* dan yārọ ～ a little lad.

　　B. (fîtītī) *m.* (*f.* fîtītīyā = fîtītīyā) *pl.* fîti-fîti narrow (*re* mat, blanket, etc.) *x* tābarmā fîtītīyā a narrow mat.

fîto A. (fîtō) *Vb.* 3A (*Vd.* fîta). (1) (*a*) came out *x* (i) inā (= daga inā) suka fîtọ where have they come from ? wani sābaŋ ƙarfẹ yā ～ 'yan shēƙarun naŋ a new metal has been put on the market in the last few years. (ii) yanzu abu yā ～ a fîlī now " the cat is out of the bag ". (iii) fîtō masa ta inda ka ga dāmā stick at nothing so long as you get the better of him ! (iv) fîtō zancan nēmaŋ aurē raise the subject of suing for the girl's hand ! (v) in dā abiŋ a yi " fîtō m fîtō ! " nē had it been a case of open battle. (vi) nā rasa inda zam ～ masa he's too much for me. (*b*) = fîta 4*a*, *b*. (2) yā ～ he (suitor) declared his intentions. (3) muryassa tā ～ his voice has lost its hoarseness. (4) fîtō da (*a*) brought out *x* yā ～ da gārī he produced some flour (from his bag, etc.) (= fîtar da 1*a*). am ～ da sābabbiŋ kudī new money has been issued. (*b*) am ～ da sū kōgī they've been ferried to this bank of the river (*cf.* fîta 11, fîtar da 6, fîtọ). (5) *Vd.* fîta.

　　B. (fîtọ) *m.* (1) (*a*) ferrying *x* yā yi mana ～ he ferried us across (*cf.* fîtō 4*b*, fîtar da 6, fîta 11). (*b*) mai ～ (i) ferry-man. (ii) sāba mai ～ *Vd.* sāba 3. (*c*) (i) gīwar ～ *f.* raft of tanned oxhide (ƙilābọ). (ii) *Vd.* gadō 1*e*. (*d*) conducting or guiding through unfamiliar country *x* an yi musu ～. (2) an yi masa ～ (*a*) they've repaired it (mud-roof or fallen mud-wall). (*b*) it (garment) has been patched after damaged part removed (*cf.* mahọ). (3) act of drying locust-bean seeds during preparation of daddawā (*this being followed by* shanya). (4) an yi masa ～ he's been deposed. (5) an yi masa ～ it's been dyed a dark colour. (6) *Kt.* sūnam ～ = yaŋkā 1*b*. (7) an yi wa shiŋkāfā ～ the rice has been husked. (8) kudim ～ (*a*) ferry-fee. (*b*) levy on caravans. (*c*) customs-duty *x* an ƙara wa kāyaŋ naŋ kudim ～ the duty on it has been increased. (9) *Vd.* fîtō. (10) *East Hausa* serving out tūwō (= kwāsā).

　　C. (fîtō = fîtọ) *m.* guinea-corn beer.

　　D. (fîtọ) *m.* whistling *x* yana ～ (1) he's whistling (= fēdwa = *Kt.* shēwa 2). (2) " he's putting on side ".

fîtsa *Kt.* = fētsa.

fîtsara A. (fîtsara). (1) *Vb.* 2 sum fîtsari mutum they publicly disgraced a person with abuse. (2) *f.* an yi masa ～ = 1.

　　B. (fîtsara) (1) *Vb.* 3B ·is (was)

shameless. (2) *f.* shamelessness, abandoned behaviour.

fitsд̈rarre *m.* (*f.* fitsд̈rarrīyā) *pl.* fitsд̈rд̣rrū shameless.

fitsд̈rē *Vb.* 1C. (1) urinated out (T. drunk). (2) yā fitsд̈rę ƙafд̣ƙunsд̣ = yā fitsд̈rē he's quite shameless (= zāwд̣yē 1*b.*ii).

fitsārī *m.* (1) (*a*) urine (= bawд̣lī). (*b*) *Vd.* gōyō 1*a.*iii. (2) fitsārim bûtд̣ (*or* fitsārin tūlū) bд̣ na mātā nę̄ ba it's not "in your line". (3) *Vd.* bд̣ sāję. (4) mд̣i fitsāriɲ kwд̣nce *m.*, *f.* bedwetter (= amд̣lālд̣). (5) fitsārim bijimī type of zigzag stitch. (6) fitsārim ƙaƙǫ = fitsāriɲ ƙēƙųwā (*a*) evil recoiling on doer. (*b*) *cf.* mų̄gų̄ntā 2. (7) fitsāriɲ ƙudā (*a*) fly-marks. (*b*) honey (*Vd.* zumд̣). (8) *Kt.* fitsāriɲ kwд̣ɗō reddish, slimy growth on water-surface (= gansд̣kūkд̣ = lanyar kwд̣ɗī). (9) fitsārin sд̣nɗōkǫ fried butter. (10) fitsāriɲ gwaurō boil on the knee (= ƙų̄runzūzūwд̣).

fittā = fitā.

fiyд̣-fīyд̣ *f.* heavy treading.

fiyākд̣ *Sk.* *abbreviation of* fīye dд̣ hakд̣ more than this.

fiyāyд̣ (1) *Vb.* 3B is (was) mildewed. (2) *f.* mildew (= fų̄mfų̄nā), *cf.* kд̣ɗā 2*b.*

fiyд̣yē *Vb.* 3A is (was) mildewed.

fiyayyд̣ *f.* superiority; precedence over (= fīfīkǫ).

fiyayyē *m.* (*f.* fiyayyīyā) *pl.* fiyд̣yyū superior.

fiye A. (fīye) exceeding *x* (1) ∼ dд̣ hakд̣ more than this (*cf.* fiyākд̣). uku tanā̄ ∼ dд̣ bīyū three is more than two. wani ∼ dд̣ wannаɲ one better than this. (2) fīye dд̣ kōyд̣ushe more than ever. (3) sunā̄ sд̣n su yi hakд̣ fīye dд̣ kîmд̣ they're very keen to do so. gā̄ zāfin rānā ∼ dд̣ kîmд̣ the sun was unusually hot.

B. (fīyę) *Vb.* 1A. (1) is (was) characterized by (= fayę *q.v.*). (2) (*with dative*) is (was) preferable *x* Kanǫ tā ∼ minī I find Kano preferable.

Fizаɲ the firm of Patterson, Zochonis.

fizga A. (fizgā) *Vb.* 2. (1) (*a*) wrenched out (hair, etc.), *cf.* fizgę, fīgā. (*b*) wrenched away *x* yā fizgi takд̣rdā д̣

hannūna he snatched paper out of my hand (= fīgā 1*b*). igīyд̣r rūwā tā fizgē shī current swept him away. yā fizgi haɲkд̣linsд̣ = yā fizgar masд̣ haɲkд̣lī it bereft him of presence of mind. gīyд̣r kudī tā fizgē shī glamour of wealth has unsteadied him. (*c*) yā fizgi kд̣nsд̣ = ƙwācę 1*b*. (2) *f.* *x* kōgin nд̣m ∼ gд̣rēshī this river has a dangerous current.

B. (fizgд̣) *Vb.* 1A = fizgā 1.

fizgau *Vd.* mд̣rim fizgau.

fizge A. (fizgę) *Vb.* 1A = fizgā 1 *x* mun fizgę mulkim fagyаɲ dд̣gд̣ hannunsд̣ we've wrested the victory from him.

B. (fizgē) *m.* (1) branch wrenched off kargō *or* sд̣barд̣ trees. (2) plundering property *x* an yi minī ∼ (= ƙwācē).

fo- *if not found below, Vd.* ho-.

fōcę = hōcę.

fōdд̣ *Eng.* *f.* (1) talc-powder. (2) *Vd.* sукōlд̣.

fōfau completely (= fд̣ufau *q.v.*).

fōfę *Vb.* 3A (colour, cloth) faded.

frīwul *Eng.* *m.* freewheel.

fu- *if not found below, Vd.* hu-.

fuffūdā = huhhų̄dā.

fuffūjē *Vb.* 3A is thoroughly pierced (*int. from* hūję).

fuffuk *m.* type of fowl-disease (= бiɲgirī 1).

fuffuкā *f.* (1) flapping the wings. (2) anā̄ hanд̣ shi, yanā̄ ∼ he's being held back in his struggles to get at opponent (= *Kt.* tūƙē 4). (3) boastfulness.

fuffuke *m.* wing (= fiffikę *q.v.*).

fufus *used in* gyд̣dā tā yi fufus groundnuts are kernel-less.

fugumд̣ *f.* heavy load *x* yā yiwō ∼ he brought heavy load.

fugum-fugum *used in* yanā̄ tд̣fīyд̣ ∼ (1) he's travelling silently *or* in dark. (2) blind man is feeling his way along.

fu- *if not found here, Vd.* hu-.

fuj'д̣ = fuja'д̣ *f.* ya yi ∼ = mutūwд̣r ∼ ya yi he died suddenly.

fuj'atаɲ *Ar.* suddenly.

fuji'д̣ = fuju'д̣ *f.* = fuj'д̣.

fuкāfukī *m.* wing (= fiкāfikī *q.v.*).

ful A. (ful) *adv.* (1) *emphasizes* redness (= fil *q.v.*). (2) sābō ∼ brand new (= saɲkā 3).

B. (ful) *adv.* ƙūrā tā tāshi ∼ dust rose in clouds, *etc.* (= fil *q.v.*). ·

fūlā *Vd.* hūlā.

fulāfulī *m.* canoe-paddle (= filāfilī *q.v.*).

fulāko *m.* bashfulness, etc. (= filāko *q.v.*).

Fulānī = Filānī.

fu- *if not found here, Vd.* hu-.

fulāwa *Eng. f.* wheaten flour.

fulla A. (fulla) *Vb.* 1A = billa.

B. (fullā) *f.* fezz (= hulā *q.v.*).

fulōti *Eng. m.* township-plot, etc.

fulus *x* an niƙa shi ∼ it's finely ground (= bulus *q.v.*).

fumfun A. (fumfuŋ) *m.* (1) soot on lamp (*cf.* kuŋkunnīyā). (2) tā shā ∼ she blackened her teeth with lampblack.

B. (fumfuŋ) *used in* cikinsa yā kumbura ∼ his tummy's distended.

fumfunā = fumfūnā *f.* mildew (= fīyāya).

fumfurus *m. or adv.* yā yi ∼ he ignored call or request. yanā zamansa ∼ (i) he's sitting ignoring call, etc. (ii) he's brazening out his conduct.

fu- *if not found here, Vd.* hu-.

funi A. (funi) *Vd.* man funi.

B. (fūni) *m.* (1) covering mouth and nose with amāwalī of turban (*cf.* tākuŋkumī). (2) *Sk.* any turban.

funjum A. (funjum) *adv.* in plenty (*re* water) *x* nā ga rūwā ∼ a rijiyā I saw the well was full of water.

B. (funjum) *used in* yā fāɗa rūwa ∼ he fell plop into the water.

funjumā *Vb.* 3A yā ∼ cikin rūwa he fell plop into the water.

funjum-funjum *m.* (1) floundering about in T. (swimming, reading, writing, etc.) = budum-budum. (2) type of swimming. (3) (*a*) sound of shaking of fluid in bottle. (*b*) iŋ kā ji gōrā nā ∼, bai cika ba "empty vessels make the most noise".

funƙāsō *m.* wheaten cake fried in oil (= tarmō-tarmō).

Funtūwa *f.* the place so called.

fur A. (fur) (1) flutteringly *x* tsuntsū yā tāshi ∼ (= fil-fil *q.v.*). (2) *Vd.* bā rābā. (3) completely (= fāfaratan *q.v.*).

B. (fur) *used in* murjānim ∼ fine red coral.

fu- *if not found here, Vd.* hu-.

fura A. (furā) *f.* (1) (*a*) balls (cūri) of cooked flour (*preferably* gērō, *cf.* markaɗā) for mixing up in milk. (*b*) yanā sham ∼ he is eating furā (*cf.* tūwō 1*b*). (*c*) *cf.* shēgē 1 ; danayā ; gāhūhu, surki. (*d*) furad dāwa *Vd.* Shangai. (*e*) furā a būta *Vd.* bam magana 3. (*f*) *Vd.* bāmōta 2. (*g*) furar Naito *Vd.* kū kā. (2) dom furar wani mai nōno, sā ƙāsariŋka gōrā independence is best, on no matter how modest a scale. (3) mē ya kai furā zane why did you act so? (*reply*, ƙazantar dāmu from lack of ability). (4) furad da zā ta zube bā tā tārar gurbi there's no fighting Fate. (5) sayam ∼ bridesmaid's bringing stone hidden by cloth in calabash, for bridegroom to buy on pretence he is giving 7*s.* or 8*s.* for furā (*cf.* bākī 2*y*). (6) furā-furā = furar madi *balls as in* 1*a* made for sale.

B. (fūra) *Vb.* 1A = hūra.

furanni *Vd.* furē.

fūrau *m.* larvae of digger-wasp (= būsau *q.v*).

furce *Vb.* 3A eluded one's grasp (= firce).

furcici *x* gāshi yā yi ∼ hair's dishevelled (= burcici *q.v.*).

furɗā *Vb.* 2 yā furɗi gyaɗā he hoed up groundnuts (= firɗā *q.v.*).

fu- *if not found above Vd.* hu-.

fure A. (furē) *m.* (*pl.* furanni). (1) (*a*) (i) blossom(*Vd.* hūdā 2). (iA)tāba tā yi∼the tobacco (has) blossomed. (ii) tobacco-blossom (*epithet is* sharafī ɗanyaŋ haki = baka 7), *cf.* tsattsagē, tsīgī 2, māƙilā 2*b*. tūta 3. (iii) *Vd.* haƙōrī 1*a.iii*. (*b*) tā ci ∼ (i) she gathered tobacco-flowers. (ii) she stained her teeth with tobacco-flowers. (2) (*a*) hīrā tā ci ∼ conversation became animated(*Vd.* hīrā 2). (*b*) yanzu kibīya tā ci ∼ you'll get an arrow in you in a moment ! (*said by robber, etc., to intimidate*). (*c*) tā ci ∼ = tā ci furfurē = tā ci burburē *m.* type of children's game. (3) wata nā ∼, wata nā 'yā'yā things keep cropping up (= kutsē 3). (4) furan jūjī Datura plant (= zaƙamī). (5) furan 'yan Sarkī the tree *Lonchocarpus.* (6) *Vd.* ƙaryā 3*b*.

B. (furę) *Fil. m., f.* (*sg., pl.*) whitish ox or cow.

C. (fūrẹ) *Vb.* 1A blew T. away, *etc.*
(= hūrẹ *q.v.*).
fu- *if not found here, Vd.* hu-.
fur-fur (1) *Kt. m.* (*sg.*, *pl.*) tawny pipit
(*Anthus campestris*). (2) *Vd.* fątumạ 2.
furfura A. (furfurā) *f.* (1) grey hairs.
(2) furfurar gyątumī = furfurar tsōfwā
the grass *Aerua tomentosa.* (3) kō kā
yi ~ i̧ ta k̠aji̧, sǎi kā biyā you *shall*
pay, come what may !
B. (furfurạ) *Vb.* 2 = furfụrā *Vb.* 1C.
(1) bartered (*cf.* raŋgamad dạ). (2)
exchanged *x* nā furfụri dōki̧ dạ jąkī
I exchanged donkey and got horse.
furfurad dạ *Vb.* 3A = fụrfurạ.
furfụrcē *Vb.* 3A (person's hair) went quite
white (*Vd.* furfurtạ).
furfure A. (furfụrē) *m.* (1) (*secondary v.n.
of* furfurạ) *x* yanā furfuransạ = yanā
fụrfurạrsạ he's bartering it (*cf.* raŋ-
gamā). (2) *Vd.* fụrē 2*c.*
B. (furfụrē) *Vb.* 1C bartered all ;
exchanged all (*cf.* furfurạ).
fụrfurtạ *Vb.* 3B (person's hair) went
grey (= bi̧dī 3).
fụrgāḍạ = fụrgāgạ.
fụrgāgạ *Vb.* 2 pursued ; drove away ;
rounded up.
furi A. (furi̧) = firi̧.
B. (furī) *Kt.* (1) = firī. (2) furiŋ
hannū *Vd.* farī 2*d.*
furi-furi = furu-furu.
fu- *if not found here, Vd.* hu-.
fụrjạ-fụrjạ *x* sǎi gā shi fụrjạ-fụrjạ there
he was hurrying along.
furje = firjẹ.
fụrk̠ąkī *m.* wisps floating on surface,
etc. (= fi̧rk̠ąkī *q.v.*).
furmutsa = firmitsa.
fursụnạ = bursụnạ.
furtạ *Vb.* 1A. (1) mentioned *x* nā ~ masạ
shī I mentioned it to him. kadạ kạ ~
shi = kadạ kạ ~ dạ shī don't make
mention of it ! sum furtạ yāk̠i̧ dạ mū
they declared war on us. (2) *Vd.* firtạ.
fụrtumạ *Vb.* 2 drove away.
furtụmī *m.* (*pl.* furtumạ) bullock.
fụrtụtụ (1) *adv. emphasizes* bursting out
abundantly *x* k̠urạrrajī sum fitō masạ ~
pimples have appeared on him (= dā-
ɓāɓạ). (2) ji̧kinsạ yā yi ~ his body's
itching. (3) unevenness of spun thread.

fu- *if not found here, Vd.* hu-.
furụcī *m.* speaking *x* yā yi ~ he spoke
(*cf.* furtạ).
furu-furu *m.* ji̧kinsạ yā yi ~ his body's
white from dust, cold, bathing in
muddy water (*Vd.* firī).
fụrụmfujụmā *f.* = fụnjụm-funjum.
furumfurmā *f.* = furumfurmī *m.* hole
thinly covered by crust of earth.
fururu A. (fụrụrụ) boundlessly *x* dubū ~
countless thousands (= fạrạrạ *q.v.*).
B. (fururu) = furu-furu.
fụryā *f.* small-headed drumstick (*cf.* gulạ).
furzạ *Vb.* 1A. (1) yā ~ gōrọ he spat out
bits of kola. (2) yā ~ rūwā he (toothless P. ; elephant) sprayed water from
mouth.
fu- *if not found here, Vd.* hu-.
furzad dạ *Vb.* 4B = furzạ.
fus A. (fus) *adv. emphasizes* noise of
shattering (*Vd.* fashẹ). (2) *m.* fluff
which collects in one's pockets. (*b*) (i)
bā shi dạ kō ~ he has no means, he
has no strength. (ii) *Vd.* hạntsī 4.
B. (fụs) *m.* gyạḍā tā yi ~ the ground-
nuts are kernel-less (= huhụs = kụmfalalō).
fụsā-fusā *m., f.* (*sg., pl.*) quick-tempered.
fusākā *Vd.* fuskạ.
fusata A. (fusātā) *Vb.* 1C angered P.
B. (fụsātạ) *Vb.* 3B is (was) angry.
fushī *m.* (1) (*a*) anger. (i) yanā ~ = yanā
ta ~ = yā yi ~ he's angry. (ii) ~
bā yā haifūwar ḍā sǎi makāfọ to lose
one's temper " cuts no ice ". (iii) mai ~
m., f. (*pl.* mạsū ~) angry P. (*epithet is
damim maiwā mai zōɓīyā*). (iv) mai ~
bā yā rāmạ gayyạ revenge is effected
by quiet pondering, not by rage. (v)
fasạ ~ *Vd.* fasạ 1*k.* (vi) cēdīyā tạ
bar ~ *Vd.* rīmī 1*d.* (vii) anā ~ dạ
gaurākạ *Vd.* tsīgī 4. (viii) *Vd.* zōmō 5.
(*b*) gạrī yā tāshi̧ dạ ~ the sky was
sullen at dawn. (2) kafạssạ tā yi ~
his foot is swollen. (3) fushim bōrạ
ineffectual anger. (4) fushim Mājị-
ɓạri̧ = fushiŋ Hạmau " cutting off
one's nose to spite one's face " (= kụm-
fan 4).
fu- *if not found here, Vd.* hu-.
fuska A. (fuskạ) *f.* (*pl.* fuskōkī = fusākā =
fisākā). (1) (*a*) (i) face. (ii) ~ bīyū

hypocrisy (*cf.* bīyū 8, 9). (iii) sun sā ∼ wajam Masạr they aim at taking Egypt. (iv) sakịm ∼ *Vd.* sakị 2*b.*iv. (v) inḍạ bạ kạ ga ∼ ba *Vd.* tsạmmānị 4. (vi) shimfịḍạ ∼ *Vd.* shimfịḍā 1*b.* (vii) ạ tạmbạyi ∼ *Vd.* sararī 1*e.*iii. (viii) duk wannạŋ gạjīyạ bạ sụ sauyạ ∼ ba in spite of all their fatigue, they did not give up. (ix) lạ̄bārịm ∼ *Vd.* lạ̄bārị 1*a.*viii. (x) ạnnūrịm ∼ *Vd.* ạnnūrị 3*b.* (xi) *Vd.* sạ̄re-sạ̄rē. (xii) ɓātạ fuskạ *Vd.* ɓātạ 3. (xiii) cikạ fuskạ *Vd.* cikạ 1*h.* (xiv) ∼ gōnā cệ *Vd.* gệwayạ 1*b.* (*b*) (i) broad part of T. (*x* face of coin *as contrasted with* gẹ̄fẹ its edge). (ii) fuskạr rūwā surface of the water. (*c*) yā yi fuskạr bịjimī = yā yi fuskạr shānū = yā yi fuskạr dōgạrai = yā ɗaurẹ fuskạ = yā ɗaurẹ girā he scowled, frowned (= girā 1*b*). (*d*) fuskạr tạ̄kạlmī shoe-uppers. (*e*) sun yi ∼ dạ ∼ dạ sụ they confronted them. (*f*) gamạ ∼ *Vd.* gamạ 1*j.* (*g*) Allạ̄ yạ haɗạ fuskōkimmụ may we meet again soon! (*reply* ạ̄miŋ). (2) mụtụm mại ∼ nē = mụtụm mại fuskạr mutạ̄nē nệ = fuskạ gạrēshị he's a popular man, pleasant man. (3) cịm ∼ gạrēshị he humiliates people before others. yā ci ∼ tasụ he publicly humiliated them. (4) ∼ yakệ yị he is troubled with his eyes. (5) (*a*) embroidery on front of gown. (*b*) (i) tanạ̄ dạ ∼ mại sai dạ rịgā she's beautiful. (ii) ∼ mại sai dạ rịgā, ạlbadạ kāyā cệ what a handsome person or gown!, quality counts! (6) cheapness of foodstuffs *x* wannạŋ gōrọ yanạ̄ dạ ∼ these kolanuts are cheap. (7) direction *x* (*a*) fuskạr gabạs *adv.* eastwards. fuskạr arệwā northwards. ạ fuskạr naŋ in that direction. (*b*) ta wạcẹ ∼ sukạ fī mụ in what way are they superior to us? (*c*) sunạ̄ fuskạr Sarkī (i) they are in the employ of the Chief. (ii) they are on the side of the Chief. (8) nā nệmē shị ạ fuskạr ạmānạ̄ = nā nệmē shị ạ fuskạr zumuncị = nā nệmē shị ạ fuskạr jịyayyạ I tried to settle my dispute with him in a friendly way (*cf.* ɗākị 7).

B. (fuskā) *f.* epidermis (= ɗạ̄kē), *cf.* karnī.

fuskanta A. (fụskantạ) *Vb.* 2 faced *x* yā fụskạnci gabạs it faces east (= ạụnā 6).

B. (fuskạntā) *Vb.* 1C turned T. facing *x* nā ∼ shi gabạs I turned it to face eastwards.

fuskantad dạ *Vb.* 4B = fuskạntā.

fuskōkī *Vd.* fuskạ.

fut = fus.

fuskụ *Ar. m.* profligacy.

fu- *if not found here, Vd.* hu-.

futō = fitō.

futu-futu = furu-furu.

futuk *used in* bạgidājẹ ∼ = Bạgwārī ∼ clodhopper.

fụtukị *Eng. m.* (1) fatigue-duty. (2) cutting grass short with matchet (*done by police, soldiers, prisoners, labourers*).

futụshī *Kt. m.* upper part of calf of leg (= dạmbūbụ).

fwạttā salt-slabs (*pl. of* hōcẹ *q.v.*).

fyācẹ (1) *Vb.* 1A nā ∼ mājinā I blew my nose (= fācẹ *q.v.*). (2) *Sk. Vb.* 3A. (*a*) is (was) tired out. (*b*) is (was) "fed up".

fyācị *m.* blaze down length of horse's face (= fācị *q.v.*).

fyaɗa A. (fyạ̄ɗā *Vb.* 2 hit with flexible T. *x* nā fyạ̄ɗē shi dạ būlālạ I flogged him. sunạ̄ fyạ̄ɗar fạrī they're hitting down flying locusts.

B. (fyạ̄ɗạ) (1) *Vb.* 1A. (*a*) nā ∼ masạ būlālạ = fyạ̄ɗā. (*b*) slapped T. down on ground *x* nā ∼ ƙwaryā dạ ƙasā I slapped down calabash on the ground. (*c*) yā ∼ kại ūwā dūnīyạ he's gone abroad. (*d*) nā ∼ nịasạ idọ I stared at him silently. (*e*) poured T. into another to mix *x* tā ∼ dāwạ cikiŋ gērō she mixed guinea-corn with millet. nā ∼ rūwā ạ nōnọ I poured water into the milk (*cf.* zubạ). (*f*) did much of *x* yā ∼ aikị he did much work. am ∼ sātạ big theft's been done. am ∼ rūwā there's been heavy rain. am ∼ masạ kuɗī its price has been greatly raised. (2) *Vb.* 3A extended *x* yā ∼ tun dạgạ naŋ har Kano it extends from here to Kano (= ɗaukạ 1*p*).

fyāɗad dạ *Vb.* 4B nā ∼ ƙwaryā dạ ƙasā = fyạ̄ɗạ 1*b.*

fyaɗɗạ *Sk. f.* screen for bride's bed.

fyaɗe A. (fyāɗe) *Vb.* 1A. **(1)** hit with
flexible T. and knocked over *x* **nā** ~
shi da̱ būlāla̱ I whipped him so that he
fell (*cf.* **fyāɗā**). **mum fyādō jirāgyan
sama̱nsu̱ ƙas** we shot down their aeroplanes. **(2)** beat to shreds *x* **ƙa̱ŋƙarā
tā** ~ **ganyē** hail tore leaves to shreds.
(3) emaciated *x* **ta̱fīya̱n naŋ tā** ~ **dōki̱**
that journey emaciated the horse.
(4) yā sa̱ sa̱ndā, yā ~ **kuɗī** he squandered his money. **(5) yā** ~ **he** (P.,
animal) has become thin.
    B. (fya̱ɗē) *m.* rape *x* **yā yi mata̱** ~
he raped her (= **fa̱ɗē**).

fyādī *Kano m.* canteen, shop (= **shāgo̱** 1).

fyāɗi̱ *m.* **(1)** (*a*) (*secondary v.n. of* **fya̱ɗā**) *x*
suna̱ fyāɗi̱nsa̱ da̱ būlāla̱ = **suna̱ fya̱ɗas-
sa̱ da̱ būlāla̱** they're flogging him.
(*b*) the threshing called **bugu̱** (*Vd.*
bu̱gā 1*a*.iv). **(2)** pious exhortation by
begging-scholar (**ma̱i ha̱dīsi̱**). **(3)** the
sharo̱ contest. **(4)** (*a*) **dū** ~ **ɗayā nē**
they're much the same. (*b*) **a̱ bar su̱
duka̱** ~ **ɗayā** - (i) leave them all in
the same place ! (ii) sell them all at
same price ! (*c*) **yana̱ yi mana̱ fyāɗi̱n
'yaŋ kaɗanya̱** he treats us all the same.
(5) fagyam ~ *Vd.* **fagē 6.**

fyalfyācī *Kt.* = **fyarfya̱cī.**

fyalla A. (fyalla̱) yā ~ **da̱ gudu̱** he fled.
    B. (fya̱llā) *Vb.* 2 = **fa̱llā.**

fyarfya̱cī *m.* sore on foot of P. (or on
hoof of horse) from travelling.

fyarfyādīyā *f.* epilepsy.

fyat (1) farī ~ snow-white. **(2)** completely (*Vd.* **fat**).

fyau = **fyu̱** 1.

fyauce̱ *Vb.* 1A (bird) swooped on
(= **fauce̱** *q.v.*).

fyātō *Vb.* 3A **yā** ~ he blew it out of his
nose (*Vd.* **fāce̱**).

fyauka̱ *Fil. f.* **(1)** gonorrhœa (**ciwon 4**)
with bleeding. **(2)** bilharzia.

fyautᶐlī *Sk.* the tribal-marking **billē 1.**

fyu̱ = **fyu̱** **(1)** *adv. emphasizes* whizzing *x*
nā ji būlāla̱ ~ I heard whistling of
whip through air. **shāho̱ yā kāwō
su̱rā** ~ hawk swooped down whizz !
(2) *m.* **yā yi** ~ he looks haggard.

ga A. (ga̱) *prep.* (*becomes* **ga̱rē** *before
possessive pronoun*). **(1)** (*a*) in the
presence of *x* **suna̱ ga̱rēshi̱** they're

at his house ; they're in his company.
(*b*) **nā ta̱fi ga̱rēku̱** I went to you. **(2)**
in the opinion of *x* **ga̱ Dauda̱ ba̱i
ka̱māta̱ a̱ yi haka̱ ba** in David's
opinion it is not right to do so (*cf.* **ganī**
A.2, **5**). **(3)** (*a*) regarding, in reference
to *x* **ga̱ gudu̱ yā fī ni̱** he excels me in
speed. **la̱ifī ga̱ maha̱ifī** a crime against a
father. **yā ka̱māta̱ ga̱ Sarkī ya̱ yi haka̱,
in yā yi, ba̱ kōmē ga̱rēshi̱** a chief's duty is
to act so, and if he does, he is guilty of
no offence. **muŋ ga misāli̱nsa̱ ga̱ Audu**
we saw the same thing in the case of
Audu. **wanna̱ŋ dōkā bā ta̱ bi̱yūwā ga̱
Jāmu̱s** this principle is not applicable
in the case of the Germans. **ƙasā tā
zamā ka̱ɗaŋ ga̱rēshi̱** the district is too
small for him. (*b*) against *x* **Allā yana̱
taimakwansa̱ ga̱ maƙīyā** God is helping
him against his enemies. **bā a̱ zāre̱
takōbī ga̱ a̱l'umma̱** it is not lawful for
a ruler to draw his sword against his
subjects. **(4)** on the side of *x* **muna̱ ga̱
Sarkī** we're partisans of, dependants
of the chief. **(5)** (*a*) in, on, near *x*
yana̱ ri̱ƙe da̱ māshi̱ ga̱ hannunsa̱ he's
holding a spear in his hand. **yā sa̱
fu̱lā ga̱ kᶐi** he put on his fezz. **yā
kafa̱ tsi̱rē ga̱ wutā** he planted spitted
meat by the fire. (*b*) from in, from on
x **tā kwance̱ lāyu̱ ga̱ ka̱nta̱** she undid the
charm from her head. **(6)** (*a*) in the
possession of *x* **da̱ sule̱ gōma̱ ga̱rēni̱** I
have 10 shillings. **kyau ga̱rēshi̱** it is
good. **kudī ga̱rēsu̱** they're dear. (*b*)
from the possession of *x* **nā ka̱rɓi
sule̱ ga̱rēta̱** I received a shilling from
her (= **da̱ga ga̱rēta̱**). **yā sa̱yā ga̱
ma̱rāyū** he bought it from the orphans
(= **da̱ga wurin**), *Vd.* **7bb below, sa̱yā 1e.**
(7) (*a*) (*alternative to* " of ", " with ",
" to ", *in some cases*) *x* **yana̱ kusa da̱** (=
yana̱ kusa ga̱) **Kano** it is near Kano.
yana̱ bāya ga̱rēsu̱ = **yana̱ bāyansu̱** it is
behind them. **yana̱ ga̱ba ga̱rēsu̱** = **yana̱
ga̱bansu̱** it is in front of them. **bāya
ga̱rēni̱** = **bāyāna** after my departure. **yā
kai Kano̱** = **yā kai ga̱ Kano̱** he reached
Kano. **yana̱ gabas da̱ shī** = **yana̱ gabas
ga̱rēshi̱** it lies to the east of it. **yā ha̱ngā
gabas ga̱rēshi̱** he looked to his east. (*b*)
(*alternative to* **masa̱, musu̱,** etc.) *x*

yā kai musu b̧ārā = yā kai b̧ārā
ģarēsu he aimed (a gun, etc.) at them
(*for corresponding process before noun,*
Vd. ạ 6*a*). (*bb*) *Vd.* 6*b above last example,*
sạyā 1*e.* (*c*) (*used after* dạgạ, kusa, nēsạ,
nīsā, arẽwā, yạmmā *q.v.*). (8) (*indicates
date in month*) *x* hudū gạ Fạbạrā'ịr 1929
on the 4th February, 1929. dạgạ ran ukụ
gạ watạm Fạbạrā'ịr zūwạ ran ạshịrịŋ
ģarēshị from the 3rd to 20th of February
(= dạ 5). (9) by (*after passive verb*) *x*
Masạr bā tạ̧ cịwūwā gạ Jāmus Egypt
cannot be conquered by the Germans.
bindigạn nạŋ bā tạ̧ harbūwā gạ mụtụm
ɗayā this gun cannot be fired by one
man. (10) *conj.* in a case where *x* ịnā gạ
ķarɛ̄ yā zō dặidặi well then, what would
happen in the case where they were
evenly matched ? (*Vd.* ịnā 3*a*).
   B. (ģā) (1) (*a*) (i) here is ! *x* ∼ kudɛ̄
here's some money for you ! ∼ macịjɛ̄
look, there's a snake ! (*Vd.* 1*b below*).
∼ shi = *Kt.* ∼ a = *Kt.* ģā ya here
it is ! (ii) ∼ ģōran zumạ, ∼ na ma-
ɗặcɛ̄ *epithet of* ạlkālɛ̄. (iii) there is
x ∼ ạlāmạ dūnịyạ tā yi dādɛ̄ it looks as
if the world has settled down. (iv)
is situated *x* ģarịŋ naŋ ∼ shi caŋ
dạgạ gāb̧ạr tȩ̣kū that town lies on the
coast. (v) *cf.* ganɛ̄ A1.7*g.* (vi) ∼ dạmisạ
Vd. dạmisạ 5. (*b*) (i) tsạkānịnsụ bā
" ģā macịjɛ̄ ! " there's bitter enmity
between them. (ii) ∼ macịjɛ̄ kwạnce
Vd. dārạ̧rɛ̄ 2. (*c*) *x* bạ nạ̧ cȩ̣ " ģā shi "
ba I'm not in a position to describe it.
(*d*) ∼ darạ *Vd.* darị 5. (*e*) ∼ hannūna
Vd. marạbɛ̄ 3. (*f*) ∼ idọ *Vd.* cȩ̣ 1*b*,
idọ 1*o.* (*g*) ∼ ķwặi *Vd.* alaŋķọ̧sạ̧.
(*h*) ∼ na jɛ̄yạ *Vd.* bɛ̄yạn dạddawā.
(*j*) ∼ rạddē *Vd.* rạddawā. (*k*) ∼ taushɛ̄
Vd. ạlkāmurạ. (*l*) ∼ cinyạ *Vd.* mɛ̄ķā
2*b.* (*m*) ∼ bābā *Vd.* ģaŋgau. (*n*) ∼
damị *Vd.* ģarạ̧jē 2. (*o*) *Vd.* ạķạwū ģā
shi, ģā ķātọ, ģā nākạ, ģā nōmā, ģā
rūwā, ģā tạ̧wa. (2) ģā shi well, for *x*
ģā shi kụ̄wā (= ģā shi kumā har)
kōwā yā sanị well, everyone knows
that . . . yạ̧yạ akạ yi bạn ji bạ, ģā shi
bạn rintsạ ba how is it I didn't hear,
seeing that I didn't shut an eye ?
dọ̃miŋ ģā shi suŋ ga . . . for they considered that. . . . (3) (*a*) ģā ta naŋ see

if my words don't come true ! (*b*)
ģā̧ ta, ģā̧ ta naŋ *introductory words of*
fable (*cf.* ģātanā).
   C. (ga) (1) *f.* good appearance *x*
Audu yā fɛ̄ sụ ∼ Audu is handsomer
than they are. Kạnde, ∼ ģarẹ̄tạ Kande
is good-looking. (2) (*the form of* ganɛ̄
used before noun-object) *Vd.* ganɛ̄ 7*c.*
(3) *Sk.* (*if last syllable of preceding noun
is high, such syllable takes falling tone*)
this *x* dōkịŋ ga this horse. jāķịŋ ga
this donkey (= naŋ).
   D. (gā) *Vd.* ganɛ̄ 7*e.*
gab (1) near *x* ∼ dạ ķō̧gɛ̄ near the river
(= dab *q.v.*). (2) *cf.* gaf. (3) yanā̧ ∼
nẹ̄ dạ yạ yɛ̄ he's on the point of doing it.
gaba A. (ģabā) *m.* (1) (*a*) front of the
body (*cf.* ģaba). (*b*) (i) ģabansạ yā
fādị he lost heart. (ii) yā fāɗam minị
dạ ∼ it disheartened me. (iii) fāɗad
dạ ģaban dōkị *Vd.* wuķā 1*f.* (*c*) (i)
sun sạ̧ ∼ ģabạs they turned eastwards.
(ii) Mụsụlmɛ̄ duk na dūnịyạ̧ mại mai
dạ ∼ ģabạs all the Muslims who pray
towards Mecca. (*d*) bā shi dạ ∼ yạ
wuķar pāwạ he's senseless. (*e*) hatsɛ̄
yā yi ģaban dōkị the corn is about
3 feet high. (*f*) (i) yā ciķạ minị ∼ it
" took my breath away ". (ii) aiķị yā
ciķạ ∼ there's too much work. (iii)
bạ zai ciķạ musụ ∼ ba it won't be
beyond their powers. (*g*) ģabāna ģabạs
God forbid ! (*h*) mụtụm mại ∼ tsạye
reckless P. (*his epithet is* ķạwarɛ̄). (*j*)
Vd. ģaba, ģaban. (2) (*a*) (*euphemism*)
male or female genital organs (*cf.* ģindɛ̄
1*c.*; farjị ; ạzaķarɛ̄). (*b*) dạ mutūwạr ∼
ģāra gwaiwā a slight misfortune is
better than a serious one. (3) (*a*)
fathom *x* rɛ̄jịyan naŋ ∼ ukụ cẹ̄ this
well is 3 fathoms deep. (*b*) height of
P. measured by arms outstretched
horizontally. (4) (*with pl.* gabbunạ)
one foreleg plus ribs of slaughtered cow,
goat, or sheep. (5) (*a*) ģabaŋ gishirɛ̄
middle part of kạntụ of salt. (*b*)
ģabaŋ gishirɛ̄ yā fi kwaɗọ what a great
man ! (6) *prep.* towards *x* yā yi ∼
arẽwā he went north. (7) *adv.* yā
ạmbạcē shị ∼ dạ ∼ he mentioned it
completely. (8) ɗaŋ ∼ (*pl.* 'yaŋ ∼).
(*a*) breastband of horse. (*b*) woman's

metal pendant. (c) fringed wạrkī-
apron. (9) (a) ɗaŋ gạbaŋ gɵ̄shī =
ɗaŋ gạbaŋ gabā̀rạ m. (f. 'yar g.g.) pl.
'yaŋ g.g. a favourite, Vd. gabā̀rạ
(= lḛ̄lē 2 = mɵ̄rị 2a = mɵ̄wạ 2 =
Nor. ạŋgayā 2). (b) Vd. askị 4. (10)
Vd. gạbā gaɗị, sāraŋ gạbā. (11) tɵ̄taŋ
gạbā Vd. tɵ̄tɵ 2. (12) bụgi gạbā Vd.
bụgā 2. (13) ƙarfiŋ gạbā Vd. bābẹ 3.
(14) bạ ạ saŋ gạbaŋkạ ba Vd. mazarī
1a.ii.

B. (gạba) (1) adv. (a) in front x
(i) yanā̀ ∼ = ạ ∼ yakḛ he's in front.
(ii) kɵ̄ wani yanā̀ dạ ạbin zạrgī, 'yaŋūwammụ sū kḛ ∼ those mainly to blame
are our own people. (iii) ∼ maị wụyā,
bāya maị tạkaịcī to be a senior is hard,
to be a junior, vexatious. (iv) kɵ̄gī yā
fi " gạba rā̀tse ! " the river is un-
fordable. (v) sun zamā ∼ kūrā, bāya
dạ̄misạ they're between the devil and
the deep sea. (vi) ∼ wutā, bāya wutā
Vd. ạbụ 5k. (vii) naŋ gạba = dạgạ ∼
in future (cf. gạban 3b, bāya 4). naŋ ∼
bā̀ dạ daɗḛwā ba, zā mụ zɵ̄ very soon
we'll come. (viii) ∼ ɗayā at once,
simultaneously. ạl'amạrī yā tāsɵ̄
masạ ∼ ɗayā the affair struck him all
of a heap. ạl'amạriŋ ∼ ɗayā the
whole affair. (ix) gạba tsị̄nī Vd.
būtsātsạ. (x) kāmụn na gạba Vd.
sakị 2f. (b) forwards, to the front x
(i) yā yi ∼ = yā wucẹ ∼ he went in
front, forward. (ii) kụ ƙārạ ∼ go
forward ! (iii) sirdị yā yi ∼ the saddle
slipped forward. (iv) yā yi ∼ he has
made progress. likkāfạr kāfircị tā
yi gạba heathenism is on the increase.
sun yi gạba ƙamar tạfīyạr mị̄l ukụ
they advanced a distance of about three
miles. (v) yā ci ∼ he's made progress
(cf. gạba-gạba). (vi) ci ∼ continued
x muŋ ga yā fi kyau tụkụnā mụ ƙārạ
ciŋ ∼ dạ rubū̀tā su ƙamar dā̀ it seems
to us best to continue writing them in
the same way as before for the present.
sukạ ci ∼ dạ shāwarạ tasụ then they
continued with their deliberations. mụ
ci ∼ dạ tạfīyạ let us move on ! (cf. cị̄
gạba). mukạ ci ∼ dạ yāwọ so we continued our stroll. (vii) wannaŋ ạjīyạ
bā tā̀ jā̀ dạ bāya : dạgạ ∼ dǎi, sǎi ∼

this contribution does'not become less,
but as you're promoted (1b.v above),
it increases proportionately. (viii)
suŋ ƙi ∼, suŋ ƙi bāya Vd. bāya 1a.ii.
(ix) majḛ gạba Vd. majḛ ; safẹ. (x)
daɗiŋ gushiŋ gạba Vd. tuntubẹ 2. (2)
gạba dạ prep. x (a) yanā̀ ∼ dạ nī
he's in front of me ; he's senior to me ;
he's abler than I am. (b) tanā̀ sɵ̄na ∼
dạ kīmạ she loves me boundlessly (cf.
gạban 3c). bụkātạ tasạ kḛ naŋ ∼ dạ
kɵ̄mē it's his dearest wish. (3) m. what
is in front x (a) (i) kɵ̄wā yā kāmạ
gạbansạ each went his own way. (ii)
sɵ̄ yakḛ yạ kāmạ gạbansạ he wants to
follow his own course. (iii) suŋ kāmạ
gạbansụ, im bā kā̀ yị̄, bā̀ ni wurī they
fled helter-skelter. (iv) Vd. wurī 1c.v.
(b) (i) yā ɗaụki ∼ he took the lead.
yā ɗaụki gạban yā̀ƙị he took charge of
military operations (Vd. 3c). yā ɗaụki ∼,
yā fārạ kai musụ bugụ he forestalled
them in attacking. (ii) cf. (c) below,
jā̀gạba, shū̀gạba. (c) yā jāwɵ̄ gạban
wannaŋ yā̀ƙị he is in command in
this war (Vd. gạba 3b, gạban 1b,
jā̀gạba). (d) mā̀sū dūbaŋ ∼ far-
seeing people. (e) (i) kɵ̄wā yā yi
ta zarạfiŋ gạbansạ everyone followed
his bent. (ii) am bar sụ, sụ yi ta sha'ạniŋ
gạbansụ they've been left to manage
their own affairs. (f) sun tsarẹ gạban
Jāmụs they resisted the Germans.
(g) (i) ạbin dạ ya sā̀ ∼ his intention,
aim. ạbin dạ ya sā̀ gạba, wannạn nē
this was his aim. sun sā̀ Birnị̄n Kanọ ∼
they aimed at taking Kano. bā mā̀
yin sanyī gạ ạbin dạ mukạ sā̀ ∼ we're
not slow in putting our intentions into
effect. (ii) inda̧ ka sā̀ ∼, nan nḛ
hanyạ if you don't succeed the first
time, try, try again ! (h) ∼ dạ gạbantạ
even the greatest finds someone greater
than himself (cf. bāya 6). (j) yanā̀
kasạfiŋ gạbansạ = yanā̀ sha'ạniŋ gạbansạ he's occupied in his own affairs,
he's minding his own business. (k) (i)
yā ƙwācẹ gạbaŋkạ he outdid you. (ii)
yā ƙạrɓi (= yā ƙwācı̧) gạbaŋ kạnsạ
he took the lead. (l) yā shā gạbansụ =
yā shā musụ gạba he got ahead of them
(= kā̀ị 1A). (4) f., used in ∼ tā fi bāya

yawą = gąba n̨ą naŋ there's always the future ! (5) Vd. gąbā, gąban, gudųŋ gąba.

C. (gāɓā) f. (1) (a) (i) enmity. (ii) gāɓad dą ̨kę̨ tsąkāninsu dą jūnā their mutual hatred. (iii) yaną̨ zamaŋ ∼ dą sū he's on bad terms with them. (b) (i) yā bā su ∼ he made war on them. (ii) yā rubųtā masą takąrdar ∼ he sent him a written declaration of war. (c) tą dą gāɓā, rigą gudu Filani thou P. quarrelsome and then quick to run away ! (d) gāra gāɓā tą tsayą Vd. dūban rēni. (e) mai dą māshi̧ raŋ gāɓā Vd. māshi̧ 1c. (2) (a) ąbōki̧ŋ ∼ m. enemy. ąbōki̧ŋ gāɓā tasą = ąbōki̧ŋ gāɓansą his enemy (Vd. Mod. Gram. 8e.ii). (b) ąbōki̧ŋ gāɓarką Vd. ꝑarḳe.

D. (gāɓā) f. Bateleur eagle (= gag-gāfā).

gaɓa A. (gaɓą) f. (pl. gaɓōɓī = gaɓāɓūwą = gaɓuɓɓą = gąɓɓai = gaɓɓună = Sk. gąggąɓū). (1) (a) (i) joint, limb. (ii) yā kāmę gaɓuɓɓąnsą he has no vices. (b) hatsī yā fid dą ∼ cornplant's begun developing nodules. (2) (a) right moment for x gaɓąr tāshi̧mmu tā yī it's time for us to set out. ḍăiḍăi ḳaŋ ∼ just at the right moment. kā kāmą ḳaŋ ∼ you've done just the right thing. bąn san gaɓąr ąbi̧m ba I don't know its proper price. (b) acme x yaną̨ gaɓąr ꝑarfinsą he's at height of his strength (= gāyą 2a). (3) wages x am bīyā shi̧ ∼ tasą he's been paid his wages (= lādā 1 q.v.). ci̧ŋ ∼ gąrēshi̧ he doesn't pay fair wages. gaɓąta niḳę̨ cī I live by manual labour. (4) (negatively) unmethodical x aiki̧n naŋ bābu ∼ this work's unmethodical.

B. (gāɓą) f. (1) (a) steep river bank (= gaŋgāmā = gaggāfā 2). (b) gări̧n naŋ, gą̨ shi caŋ dąga gāɓąr tęku that town lies on the coast. (2) yā kāwō ∼ he's about to see his wishes realized.

gaɓąɓą = gąɓā-gąɓā.

gaɓāɓūwą Vd. gaɓą.

gabaci A. (gąɓāci) Vd. gąɓāta.

B. (gabacī m. = gabacīyā f.) = gabashī.

C. (gabāci̧) m. (1) promotion x yā sąmi ∼ he's been promoted. (2) i̧nā ∼

how are you ? (greeting by villager to petty chief).

gaba-gaba A. (ga'ba-gąba"). (1) m. progress (epithet is ∼ yi̧ ꝑwaryar rōrọ). ∼ yakę yī he's making progress (Vd. gąba 1b.v). (2) adv. slowly but surely.

B. (gąbą-gąbą) f. (1) leather-apron. (2) ąbu ą̨ sararī, mąi ∼ yā dūḳą "the cat's out of the bag now ! ".

gaɓa-gaɓa A. (gaɓā-gaɓā) adv. like a gaby x săi ką tafō ∼ bą̨ haŋkąli̧ ? ką tsayą ḳam mutą̨nę̨ ? you would come and stare like a gaby.

B. (gaɓā-gąɓā) (1) adv. in large chunks x an sārą shi ∼ it (salt, firewood, etc.) is cut in large chunks. (2) f. used in dāwą tā yi ∼ guinea-corn's produced stout stalks.

gąbā gadi̧ (1) fearlessly x yā tą̨fi ∼ = yā tą̨fi gąbansą gadi̧ he went fearlessly. (2) cheap, strong type of alakwąyī.

gaban (genitive of gąba). (1) prep. in front of x (a) yaną̨ gąbansu he's in front of them. (b) yā shi̧ga gąbam mutą̨nē he assumed the leadership (Vd. gąba 3b, c). (2) prep. in the presence of x ą̨ gąbammu suka yī it was in our presence that it was done. (3) prep. (a) on the further side of x yaną̨ ∼ kōgī (dūtsę) it's on the further side of the river (hill), cf. bāyan 4. (b) after x bą ą̨ saŋ ąbi̧n dą ya fą̨ru ą̨ ∼ raŋ nam ba it is not known what happened after that day (cf. gąba 1a.vii). (c) beyond x yā fi ∼ li̧ssāfi̧ it is uncountable. yā fi ∼ mą̨māki̧ it is more than wonderful (cf. gąba 2b). (d) conj. beyond the possibility that x yawą̨nsu yā fi ∼ ą̨ ꝑidą̨yā they are countless. (4) note that gaban is also genitive of gąba and gąbā q.v. (4a) tuŋ ∼ conj. before x ą̨ kai karā maꝑaurací tuŋ ∼ ꝑaurā bą tą̨ zō ba (said by beggars, i.e. marọ̄ꝑa) give me alms and so lay up treasure in Heaven ! (5) gąbaŋ ąljīfū Vd. niꝑą 2e.ii. (5a) ∼ gąbą̨rą Vd. gąbą̨rą. (6) ∼ gadō the side of the bed farther from the wall (epithet is ∼ gadō maꝑaukar zāfī, this also being epithet of certain Chiefs), Vd. bą̨ki̧ŋ gadō. (7) ∼ gārā Vd. gārā. (8) ∼ gąyyā Vd. gąyyā. (9) ∼ gishirī Vd. gąɓā 5. (9a) gabaŋ gǭshī *Vd*. gạbā 9. (10) ∼ hạntsī *Vd*. rawar hạntsī. (10*a*) ∼ kābarē a food of bruised bulrush-millet with potash and water. (11) ∼ kǎi becoming independent *x* yā yi ∼ kạnsạ he followed his own counsel. yā sǎmi ∼ kạnsạ he has started his own household. tā sǎmi ∼ kạntạ (i) she's now married. (ii) she's living on her own. (12) ∼ shīkạ poor grains which are the perquisite of the winnowers (= bạ̄kin shīkạ), *cf*. zubọ 2, bạ̄kiŋ wukā. (13) ∼ wukā metal binding securing blade to knife (= *Kt*. matsɪ̱ 4). (14) (*a*) ∼ zākɪ̱ temporary grass-shelter (= bukkạ). (*b*) yā yi minɪ ∼ zākɪ̱ he failed to pay me the balance owing. (*c*) dōkɪ̱ maɪ ∼ zākɪ̱ horse considered good because its chest projects (kɪ̱rjī yā dạgạ) and hindquarters are slender (gɪndī yā zāmẹ̄).

gáɓancɪ̱ *m*. being a simpleton.

gạbānī = gạbạnnī *x* (1) gạbạnniŋ Azụmī on the eve of the Fast. yanạ̄ gạbạnnin zūwạ he's just about to arrive. (2) gạbạnninsụ yakẹ̄ it is in front of them (= gạban 1).

gabanyạ *f*. (1) (*a*) wasting disease in the young. (*b*) shūkạ yā yi ∼ the seeds have not thriven. (2) *Sk*. flatulent distension.

gabạr = gabạs.

gabạ̄rạ *f*. (1) exertion, striving (*epithet is* ∼ kim fi karfin yārọ) *x* shī nẹ̄ ya dau ∼ = shī ya dau gạbaŋ ∼ it was *he* who took all the trouble over it. munạ̄ ∼ dạ shī we're striving with it. (2) daŋ gạbaŋ ∼ *m*. (*f*. 'yar gạbaŋ ∼) a favourite (*Vd*. gạbā 9).

gaɓar-gaɓar in large chunks (= gaɓā-gaɓạ̄).

gạɓạ̄rūwā *f*. (*pl*. gạɓạ̄rī). (1) (*a*) Egyptian mimosa (*Acacia arabica, the original source of gum arabic : also used in tanning and dyeing*). (*b*) *Vd*. karkō, kanshī 5. (*c*) in dạ̄ ∼ ạbar kirkɪ̱ cē, bạ ạ̄ bạ̄ majẹ̄mā ita ba there's more than meets the eye. (*d*) *Vd*. inūwạ 1*a*.iii. (*e*) *epithet of* gạɓạ̄rūwā *is* Ta majẹ̄mā. (*f*) ∼ tā fi kūkạ *Vd*. rēnạ 7. (2) gạɓạ̄rūwar kasạ *Cassis mimosoides* (*used in potion for invulnerability*). (3) gạɓạ̄rūwar Makạ an edible type of

mimosa. (4) gạɓạ̄rūwar Masạr Jerusalem thorn (*Parkinsonia aculeata*) = sạssạbānī. (5) sạndaŋ ∼ *Vd*. sạndā 1*k*.

gabạs (1) *prep*. east of *x* yanạ̄ ∼ dạ Kanọ it's east of Kano. yā hanga ∼ garēshɪ̱ he looked to his east. yanạ̄ ∼ garēshɪ̱ it is to the east of it. (2) *adv*. (*a*) eastwards *x* yanạ̄ ∼ it is eastwards. (*b*) gạbāna ∼ God forbid ! (*c*) fạsahạ nạ̄ ∼ (*said deprecatingly*) no, you flatter me ! (3) *f*. the east *x* ∼ dukạ tā zō all the easterners came (*cf*. gabashī). (4) (*a*) yā yi ∼ he went eastwards. (*b*) an yi ∼, shī yā yi yạmmā he's a devious or deceitful P. (5) 'yaŋ ∼ (*said by devotee of* bǫrī) evil spirits (*Vd*. ạlmụtsụtsai). (6) na ∼ *Vd*. Dụmau 2. (7) bụgau na ∼ *Vd*. bụgau 4. (8) jīfạ ∼ *Vd*. jīfạ 5.

gạɓāsā *f*. *x* nā sǎmi ∼ I got it cheap.

Gabasancī *m*. ways or speech of Easterners.

Gabasāwā Easterners (*Vd*. Bạgabạshī).

gabashī = *Kt*. gabascī *m*. = gabashīyạ *f*. = *Kt*. gabascīyạ *f*. region eastwards *x* gabashiŋ Kanọ region east of Kano.

gạbātạ (1) *Vb*. 3B, 2. (*a*) is (was) leader *x* yā ∼ cikiŋ aikɪn naŋ he's the senior in this work. yā gạbācē mụ he's our leader. (*b*) approached *x* yā gạbāci Kanọ he approached Kano. Sallạ tā gạbātō the Festival is near. (*c*) passed beyond *x* yā gạbāci Baucī he passed beyond Bauchi. (*d*) *person* died. (2) *f*. (*a*) promotion *x* yā sǎmi ∼ he's been promoted. (*b*) ɪnā ∼ (*greeting by villagers to petty chief*) how are you ?

gabātad dạ *Vb*. 4B promoted P. ; elected P. leader.

Gạbātau *epithet of* paramount Chief.

gabātō *Vd*. gạbātạ.

gạɓazgạ *Sk*. *f*. extortion by chiefs (= yāwọn 1), *cf*. rạ̄ciŋ gɪ̄gamạ.

gabba A. (gabbạ) *f*. type of the gạbā 8*a* breastplate for horses.
　　B. (gabbā) *Vd*. gēbẹ.

gaɓɓai limbs (*pl. of* gaɓạ).

gabbunạ forelegs plus ribs of slaughtered cow, goat, or sheep (*pl. of* gạbā 4).

gaɓɓụnạ̄ limbs, joints (*pl. of* gaɓạ).

gabce A. (gabcẹ̄) (1) *Vb*. 3A. (*a*) (wall, riverbank) collapsed. (*b*) (clothing) became threadbare. (*c*) ran short *x*

zạrē yā ⌒ minį my thread ran out. (d)
rūwā yā ⌒ = hadirị yā ⌒ dạ rūwā it
rained in torrents. yā ⌒ da mạganạ
he chattered away. (2) Vb. 1A (a)
caused to collapse x rūwā yā ⌒ shi
water demolished it (wall, riverbank).
(b) bit off, broke off much of x nā ⌒
tūwō. (c) deducted much x nā ⌒
kuḍinsạ = nā ⌒ masạ kuḍī I deducted
much of his money. (d) yā ⌒ amāwạlī
he respectfully uncovered folds of
turban from mouth (Vd. amāwạlī).
B. (gạbcē) Vd. gạbtā.

gabdā f. = ḍaŋ gabdā m. Sk. the bean-
food ḍaŋ gaudā.

gabḍạ Vb. 1A Sk. used in nā ⌒ masạ
mārị I slapped him.

gābē m. vicious top-playing (kạtantaŋwạ).

gabi A. (gābī) Kt. m. Bateleur eagle
(= gaggāfā).
B. (Gābị) (1) epithet of the official
position Makạmā. (2) ⌒ kạŋ ḵasā
epithet of city of Daura.

gabje A. (gabjẹ) Vb. 1A. (1) hit hard x
yā ⌒ ni dạ sạndā. (2) collided with and
knocked over. (3) heaped up one's
total supply of T. on x yā ⌒ itạcē ạ
wuta he heaped all his wood on the fire
(cf. gạbzā).
B. (gạbjē) Vd. gạbzā.

gabjējẹ m. (f. gabjējịyā) pl. gabzai-
gạbzạị huge : plentiful.

gabji A. (gabjị) what a slap !, stumble !,
collision !, prodigality !
B. (gạbji) Vd. gạbzā.

gạbjiŋ (1) m. large-grained type of guinea-
corn. (2) adv. abundantly x hatsī yanạ
naŋ ⌒ there's plenty of corn (gạbjiŋ
is only applied to guinea-corn, bulrush-
millet (gērō) or ground-nuts).

gablā Sk. f. huge chunk of butcher's-meat.

gābọ (1) m. (f. gābụwā) simpleton. (2)
Gābọ ḍaŋ uŋgụlū, kā girmā, kanạ ciŋ
kāshī you naughty boy !

gabọ m. (pl. gubbā = gabōbā). (1) tooth
(= haḵōrī). (2) kadạ kị yākō minị ⌒
(said by females to each other) don't
squabble with me !

gabōbā Vd. gabọ.

gaḃōḃī limbs (pl. of gaḃạ).

gaḃōtarị = gaḃōtarī m. (f. gaḃōtarā)
senseless P. or T.

gabta A. (gạbtā) Vb. 2 (p.o. gạbcē,
n.o. gạbci). (1) = gabcẹ 2a, b. (2)
" peached " on P.
B. (gạbtạ) Vb. 1A (with dative). (1)
(wall, riverbank) collapsed into or on to
x gạrū yā ⌒ kạn dạḃē house wall collapsed on to the floor. (2) x nā ⌒ masạ
haḵọrā I dug my teeth into it. nā ⌒
masạ gạtarī I wounded him deeply with
axe.

gabtara A. (gạbtarạ) Vb. 2 = gabcẹ 2a, b.
B. (gạbtarā) Vb. 1C. (1) broke off
much and gave P. x nā ⌒ māsạ tūwō.
(2) = gabtạ 2.

gabtạrē (1) Vb. 1C. (a) = gabcẹ 2a, b. (b)
nā gabtạrē shi dạ haḵọrā = gabtạ 2.
(2) Vb. 3A = gabcẹ 1.

gabtarō m., f. a " softy ".

gabū Sk. m. cakes of pounded dried onion-
leaves (cf. lawạshī).

gaḃū used in 'yar ⌒ f. rags, tatters
(= tsụmmā).

gaḃuḃḃạ joints, limbs (pl. of gaḃạ).

gāḃuḃụ m. senseless man.

gāḃụwā f. senseless woman (f. of gāḃọ).

gabza A. (gabzạ) Vb. 1A. (1) hit hard x
yā ⌒ ni dạ sạndā he hit me hard with
stick (= gabjẹ 1). (2) (a) suŋ ⌒ (i)
they collided. (ii) they came to blows.
(b) collided with x dōkị yā ⌒ karọ dạ
shī horse collided with it. yā ⌒ ḵafạ ạ
sạiwā he knocked his foot against a
root. ya ⌒ tuntuḃẹ he had a bad
stumble (cf. gabjẹ). (3) heaped up
much of one's supply x yā ⌒ itạcē ạ
wuta he heaped much of his wood on the
fire (= razgạ). (4) yā ⌒ ni dạ shī he
embroiled me with him (my superior).
B. (gạbzā) (1) Vb. 2. (a) dōkị yā
gạbjē shi dạ karọ. yā gạbji sạiwā dạ
ḵafạ. yā gạbjē nị dạ sạndā = gabzạ 1, 2.
(b) did much of x tā gạbji aikị (nifạ) she
did much work (grinding), cf. gabzạ 3.
(c) kansạ yā gạbzu his head suffered
serious impact. (2) f. suffering impact
x yanạ shaŋ ⌒ (a) it (animal) is
being butted. (b) he's being blamed for
everything.

gabzai-gạbzạị huge ; plentiful (pl. of
gabjējẹ).

gạbzayyạ f. struggling.

gạbzu Vd. gạbzā 1c.

gące *Kt. m.* sarcasm (= gạtsē *q.v.*).

gaci A. (gạcī) *or* jaŋ gạcī *m.* copper = (tagụllā).

B. (gacī) *m.* (1) riverbank (= kōgī 2*a*). (2) (*a*) yā kai ⌒ = yā tākạ ⌒ (i) swimmer has touched ground on further side. (ii) his difficulties are over. (*b*) yā kai nị ⌒ (i) he took me across stream. (ii) he got me out of my difficulties. (3) ạbiŋ yā kai ⌒ things have gone too far !

gada A. (gạdā) *Vb.* 2 (*p.o.* gạjē, *n.o.* gạji) (*Vd.* gādọ) inherited *x* (1) yā gạji ụbansạ = yā gạji dūkīyar ụbansạ = yā gādō ụbansạ he inherited his father's property. (2) hakạ sukạ ⌒ such is their custom (*Vd.* gājẹ). (3) Audụ zại gạji hạlīfạ Audu will succeed him as leader. (4) yanạ̄ sọ̄ yạ gạji ụbansạ *Vd.* matsīyạcī 3.

B. (gạdā) *f.* (1) (*a*) crested duiker (*Cephalophus grimmi*). (*b*) *Vd.* cī 26*h*. (2) gạdar dūtsẹ Klipspringer (*Nanotragus oreotragus. Oreotragus saltatrix*). (3) gạdar kurmị red-flanked duiker (*Cephalophus rufilatus*). (4) boasting *x* (*a*) yanạ̄ gạdar dūkīyā he's swanking because of his wealth. (*b*) dạ kụrū gạdā tā yi sūnā fancy his being able to do that ! (5) lūdạyī ⌒; iŋ kā kāmạ, kạ bạ̄ dạŋuwaŋkạ, yạ kāmạ take heart, for luck comes to all in turn !

C. (gadạ) (*Eng.* girder) *f.* (1) permanent bridge (*contrasted with makeshift bridge*), *Vd.* kạdarkọ. (2) ⌒ bạ̄ kōwā type of woman's blouse of tagụ̄wā type.

D. (gạdạ) *Sk.* from = dạgạ *q.v.*

gādā *f.* (1) (*a*) girls' singing and clapping. (*b*) gambolling of horse. (*c*) harshạnsạ yanạ̄ ⌒ he's smacking his lips. (*d*) yā kwānā yanạ̄ ⌒ happiness kept him awake. (*e*) ạbōkiŋ gādar būshīyā, kụŋkurū the two persons cannot clash, their wants being self-exclusive. (*f*) Aŋgọ, hanạ ⌒ *epithet of* bridegroom. (2) gādar dōkị dạ dōkị single combat on horseback. (3) gādar lēlā type of female dance (*Vd.* lēlā). (4) sāmụŋ gạrī, kuturū ⌒ cikin ramạ *epithet of* parvenu (= sāmụ 6).

gạdạbi-gạdạbi *Sk., Kt. m.* the game gạrdō.

gādad dạ = gādar dạ.

gadā-gạdạ *pl. adj.* beautiful (*re* eyes ; writing) = marā-mạrā.

gadagi A. (gạdagī) *m.* the fodder grasses *Alysicarpus vaginalis* and *Alysicarpus rugosus*.

B. (gạ̄dāgị) *m.* (1) bulrush-millet (gērō) dried over fire (babbạkā). (2) flour of *such*.

gạ̄dagọ = gạ̄dạ̄gurjī *Kt. m.* lusty and fearless P.

gạ̄dājē beds (*pl. of* gadō).

gạ̄dajje *m.* (*f.* gạ̄dajjīyā) *pl.* gạ̄dạddū *adj.* (1) inherited (*Vd.* gạdā). (2) gạ̄dajjīyar kīyayyạ irịm bakạr kụ̄wā hereditary hatred of the bitterest kind.

gạdạkūkạ *f.* the creeper *Aristolochia albida* (*remedy for* guinea-worm (= dụman dūtsẹ). (2) *Vd.* baurērẹ.

gạdambō *Sk. m.* deep hole ; old well.

gạ̄ dạ̄misạ *Vd.* dạ̄misạ 5.

Gạdạŋgā *epithet of* man called Ạlī (*derived from* gạdaŋgamī).

gạdaŋ-gadaŋ with all one's might.

Gạdaŋgamā (1) *epithet of* any woman called Hạdījạ. (2) musical instrument of calabash with strings.

gạdaŋgamī *m.* burly fellow (*cf.* Gạdạŋgā).

gạdạ̄nīyā *Kt. f.* officiousness.

gạ̄dạntā *Vb.* 3A sung and clapped, *etc.*, as in gạ̄dā *q.v.*

gạdārạ (*Ar.* treachery) *f.* (1) *x* kadạ kạ yi (= kadạ kạ kāwō) minị ⌒ (*a*) don't double-cross me ! (*b*) don't cheek me ! (2) *cf.* gadẹ ; gādirçị.

gādar dạ *Vb.* 4B (1) bequeathed *x* yā gādar masạ sạrautạ he bequeathed the rule to him (*Vd.* Mod. Gram. 170b). (2) caused *x* gaddamạ tanạ̄ ⌒ gạ̄bā quarrelling causes enmity.

gadar-gạdar *pl. adj.* (1) long and broad *x* wākē ⌒ long and broad beans. rụbūtun naŋ ⌒ yakẹ this writing's very bold.

gadạrī *Nor. m.* trouble (= garạrī *q.v.*).

Gạdas *Vd.* kāwạrā.

gạdạshạrē *m.* (1) man who is a " rake ". (2) behaving " rakishly ".

gạdạsumī *m.* (*f.* gạdạsumā) senseless P.

gạdau-gạdau *used in* yanạ̄ tạfīyạ ⌒ he's swaying along.

gạdạ̄ŋkūkạ *Vd.* baurērẹ ; gạdạkūkạ.

gadauniyā *f.* officiousness.

gadawa *f.* booth (rumfā) with flat stalk-roof.

gadẵwa *f.* whitish type of guinea-corn.

gadẵyē wart-hogs (*pl. cf.* gadū).

gaddama *f.* (*pl.* gaddandamī). (1) wrangle, dispute *x* (*a*) suna ~ they're quarrelling. (*b*) abu yā zo da gaddama the affairs became in a muddle. (2) an yi masa ~ the truth of his statement was disputed. (3) turning out adversely *x* dãmunā tā yi mini ~ wet-season was unfavourable to my crops. (4) gaddamar gudu, d̃uwaiwai yā ƙi shigā birnī beginning T. is easy, but it's hard to stick at it till it's finished : baulked at the last minute ! (= kūrā 25*a*). (5) gaddamar darē the food fatē-fatē.

gaddantā *Vb.* 3A disputed, wrangled.

gade A. (gade) *m.* (1) kada ka yi (= kada ka kāwō) mini ~ = gadāra. (2) refusing to pay gambling-debt.
B. (gāde) = gāje.
C. (gāde) *Kt.* = gāje (*Vd. under* gādā inherited).

gade *Vb.* 1A toasted meat or fish (= ƙyāfe *q.v.*).

gade-gade *used in* bari ~ da ranka don't excite yourself so !

gadi A. (gādī) *m.* wart-hog (= gadū).
B. (gādi) (*Eng.* guard) *m.* (1) nightwatch. mai ~ *m.* night-watchman. (2) canjin gādi *m.* changing of the guard. (3) *Vd.* wucin gādi.
C. (gādi) *Kt.* = gāji (*Vd. under* gādā inherited).

gadi *Vd.* gabā ~.

gādin-gādin *used in* tun ~ from time immemorial.

gādirci *Ar. m.* (1) deceit ; treachery. (2) *cf.* gadāra.

gādirgā *used in* yā tsaya ~ ba zai yi ba he refused point-blank to do it.

gādiri *m.* (*f.* gādirā) *pl.* gādirai deceitful : treacherous (*cf.* gādirci).

gado A. (gādō) *Vb.* 1E inherited (*Vd.* gādā).
B. (gādo) *m.* (1) (*a*) (i) property inherited *x* nā ci gādansa I inherited his property. (ii) bāwan gādo *Vd.* sansan gari. (iii) dūkiyar gādo *Vd.* sana'a. (iv) raban gādo *Vd.* rabō 1*c*. (*b*)

inherited quality *x* harbi ga d̃an jāki ~ nē what's bred in the bone comes out in the flesh. (2) (*secondary v.n. of* gādā) *x* ana gādan halī = ana gādar halī character is inherited, hereditary. (3) nā yi ~ I got a bargain. (4) wane irin gādan ubāna nē ban yi ba have I failed to carry out any of the precepts enjoined on me by my father before he left me in charge ? (5) Gādo *epithet of any* Magāji. (6) na ~ *m.* (*f.* ta ~) *pl.* na ~ (*a*) hereditary. (*b*) maƙiyanku na gādan gado your hereditary enemies of long standing.
C. (gādō) *m.* (*pl.* gāduna). (1) spotted weaverbird (*Plesiosittagra cucculatus*) = jirā = *Kt.* mārai. (2) ~ ba ka san tarkō ba what a foolhardy person !
D. (gado) *m.* (*pl.* gādāje). (1) (*a*) (i) bed. (ii) bã kullun akē kwānā a ~ ba nobody can expect an unbroken run of good luck. (*b*) (i) alhēri gadam barcī nē one good turn deserves another. (ii) mai ~ yā sō barcī, " Mai tābarmā sãi ka nade ! " the day of reckoning has come. (*c*) (i) gaban ~ *m.* the side of the bed farther from wall (*epithet is* Gaban ~ mad̃aukar zāfī, this also being the epithet of some chiefs). (ii) *Vd.* bākin gado. (iii) ginin gado *Vd.* bad̃o 2. (iv) *Vd.* shāfa gadanka. (v) gadan Ari *Vd.* Ari. (vi) *Vd.* bara gado gāshi ; bara gado shūnī. (vii) karya gado *Vd.* bōsara. (viii) gado bāyan d̃aki *Vd.* buƙulu. (ix) *Vd.* zubar gado. (*d*) (i) gadan sarauta throne. (ii) mai jiran ~ heir apparent, second in command. (*e*) gadam fito raft (*Vd.* fito 1*c*.i). (*f*) gadam masassaƙā carpenter's bench. (*g*) kan ~ *Vd.* kan gado. (*h*) gadan kāji fowl-crate. (*j*) (*rustic*) gadan rījiyā *Vd.* rījiyā 3. (*k*) gadan jīgo place where jīgo is fixed. (2) gadam bāyā (*a*) part of body from small of back to between shoulders (*considered especially good meat*). (*b*) wa zai gasa wa karē gado who troubles about a poverty stricken person ! (3) ingarma ~ powerful stallion.
E. (Gado) (1) *name for child* born after twins (= Gambo). (2) Gado =

Mai gado *name for any woman called* Bilƙīsu.

gado-gado *adv.* in rows.

gadū *m.* (*pl.* gaduna = gadāyē = gadōjī) wart-hog (*Phacochœros œthiopicus*) (= durungū = mūgun dawa = alhinzir), *cf.* aladē, gunzū, gursunū.

ga'du-gadu" (1) *m.* sun yi ~, sum fādā masā they attacked him " ball-headed ". (2) *adv.* sunā aiki ~ they're working " all out " (= shajara majara 1).

gaduna A. (gaduna) wart-hogs (*pl. of* gadū).
B. (gāduna) *pl. of* gādō.

gadūnīyā = gidūnīyā.

gaf (1) close to *x* yanā ~ dā kōgī it's near the river (= gab). (2) *x* rāgō yanā dara gaf gaf gaf ram's leaping about.

gafaka *f.* (*pl.* gafakōkī) (1) satchel (= battarī), *cf.* jaƙā. (2) yā rātaya gafakarsā, yā gudu he's taken to his heels.

gāfara (1) *f.* (*a*) pardoning *x* yā yi mini ~ he forgave me. (*b*) nā rōkē shi ~ I begged him to pardon me. (*c*) ~ Risāla yakē yī the Malam with satchel (gafaka) is cadging at the naming-ceremony (*at Kt. he is called* gāfara kaɓakī). (*d*) Allā ya yi masā gāfara R.I.P. ! (2) (*a*) sun cē musu " gāfara sā ! " they put them on their guard. (*b*) mun gaji dā " gāfara sā ! " bā mu ga ƙafō ba we're tired of hearing idle threats. (3) gāfara = gāfara dăi (*a*) (i) excuse me ! (ii) make way please ! (iii) may I come in ? (*b*) not so much noise please ! (*c*) gāfara = ~ yē = gāfaranku *salutation by woman entering house* (*cf.* afūwō). (*d*) ~ dagā nan please move away ! (*e*) gāfara bābē = *Zar.* gāfara bāhē *m.* sowing in unweeded soil.

gafarta A. (gāfarta) *Vb.* 2 (*p.o.* gāfarcē, *n.o.* gāfarci) pardoned P. *x* nā gāfarcē shi I pardoned him.
B. (gāfarta) *Vb.* 1C. (1) (*with dative*) pardoned P. *x* nā ~ masā I forgave him. (2) (*a*) gāfatta Mālam = Allā ya gāfatta Mālam salutation Malam ! (*cf.* almājīrī 3 ; na'am ; shiga 3). (*b*) *the word* gāfattā *alone, is* rude greeting. (*c*) gāfatta karātum Mālam *is* joking greeting to scholar.

gaf gaf gaf *Vd.* gaf.

gāfī *m.* (1) prosperity, abundance *x* (*a*) gāfim māmā garēta she has rich milk in her breasts (= rūwā B.15), *Vd.* gōrā 2. (*b*) gāfim māmā garēshi he's prosperous. (*c*) gōnā mai gāfin shūka rich farm. ƙasar tanā dā ~ it's rich land. (*d*) yanā dā gāfin cinikī he's a rich trader. (2) yanā kan ~ it (wealth, fever, anger, gallop, *etc.*) is at its peak (= gāya 2*a*). (3) mai ~ *m.*,*f.* irascible P. (3) the taste of raw beans (*cf.* barcī 4).

gafiya A. (gafīya) *f.* (*pl.* gafīyōyī). (1) bandicoot (*epithet is* Zirga, arnan rāmi = karāhīya, cinki banzā, barinki banzā). (2) 'yan ~ hunters of bandicoots. (3) ~ makashinki yinā gindinki (*lit.* your tail is your ruin) " murder will out ". (4) an jēfi ~ dā ~ = bīyū byu kāmun gafīyar 'Baidu " falling between two stools ". (5) kanā haƙō masā ~, yanā haƙō maka macījī he repays good with evil. (6) ƙashin ~ garēshi he's persistently unlucky. (7) musun ~ pointless contradictions. (8) tāgumin ~ *Vd.* tāgumī 4. (9) *Vd.* rīmī 6*a*.
B. (gāfīyā) *f.* (*pl.* gāfīyōyī). (1) pattern on left shoulder of gown (= gātarī 2). (2) *Sk.* axe (*Vd.* gātarī 6).

gafō = gahō.

gaftara A. (gaftara) *Vd.* 2. (1) caused to collapse. (2) bit off, broke off much of (= gabcē 2*a*, *b q.v.*).
B. (gaftarā) *Vb.* 1C. (1) broke off much and gave P. *x* nā ~ masā tūwō. (2) nā ~ masā gātarī I gave him deep-hatchet-wound. nā ~ masā haƙōrā I dug my teeth into it.

gaftarō *m.*, *f.* a " softy ".

gaga A. (gāgā) *f.* (1) (*a*) being all of a dither ; being light-headed *cf.* gīgīcē. (*b*) *cf.* dambā ; rūwā A.16*c*. (*c*) kā girmā dā gāgā *Vd.* Turunkū. (2) = fiƙīnīyā. (3) gāgam barcī heaviness on waking from sleep (*cf.* wāwam barcī).
B. (Gāga) (1) *epithet of* brave warrior. (2) ~ ūwar ɓarnā *epithet of* spend-thrift.

gagab A. (gagab) *x* yanā dā ƙwārī ~ he's very strong (= gagau *q.v.*).
B. (gagab) = gagal.

gāgā̀cē *Vb.* 3A became all of a dither (= gīgī̀cē).

gagai *m.* any aphrodisiac (farin ∼ *being best-known*).

gạgạl *used in* gā̀ rānā ∼ it's already round 7 a.m.

gạgānīyā *f.* struggling with task or P.

gagar = gagar-gagar *adv.* x yanā̀ dạ farfī ∼ it's tough. ∼ yakḕ he's very strong (*Vd.* gar-gar).

gagara A. (gā̀gara) (1) *Vb.* 3B. (*a*) behaved rebelliously x dōkị yā ∼. (*b*) is impossible x yā ∼ kāmu it's impossible to catch it. (2) *Vb.* 2 (*a*) behaved rebelliously to x dōkị yā gā̀garē nị. (*b*) is (was) beyond one x (i) yā gā̀gari Audu cị it's impossible for Audu to eat it (= bū̀wāyạ). (ii) sanịnsạ yā gā̀gari mālạm, yā gā̀gari bōkā̀ it is unknown to all (*Vd.* mālạmī 1c.iv) = fī 3. (iii) gā̀gari Mālạm *Vd.* mālạmī 1c.iv,iva. (iv) tūwō bā yā̀ gā̀garạrkạ *Vd.* tūwō 4b. (v) yā gā̀gari 'yam pāwạ *Vd.* fincḕ 3. (3) *f.* (*a*) rebelliousness x Audụ ∼ gạrēshị Audu's stubborn. (*b*) being skilled at work x maginịn nan ∼ gạrēshị that builder is expert (*cf.* shạitsạn 2b). (*c*) Garbạ, Gā̀garạ name for any man called Ạbūbakạr.

B. (gā̀garā) *Vb.* 1C (1) rendered rebellious. (2) yā ∼ shi he (wrestler) tested him (another, for strength). (3) yā ∼ masạ wukā̀ (zartọ) he applied blunt knife (file) to it (= dādạrā).

C. (gā̀garạ) (1) ∼ Bạ̀dau *m.* (*sg., pl.*) (*a*) beam across entrance to stockade (*cf.* 10 *below* ; sạkatạ 2). (*b*) *epithet of* chief. (*c*) earth-wall inside round-hut (fagọ) for privacy (= gūrạmī 2), *cf.* bạbbākạ. (2) ∼ bāmī T. offering difficulty. (3) ∼ birị *m.* plaited-leather dog-collar (=dāgumī 1). (*b*) guinea-corn when head droops (= *Kt.* zāgō). (4) ∼ birnī *m.* (*sg., pl.*) worn-out, small, black gown. (5) ∼ bịkī *m.* (*sg., pl.*) T. not in demand. (6) ∼ dāfị *epithet of* fire. (7) ∼ gā̀sā *epithet of* Chief. (8) ∼ kọ̄yọ̄ *epithet of* difficult P. or T. (9) ∼ kuntā = *Kt.* gā̀gạrạ kwantā *m.* (*a*) knotted type of hobbling-rope. (*b*) ạbụ yā zamā gā̀gạrạ kwantā the whole matter is a puzzle. (10) ∼ kūrẹ *m.*

(*a*) junction of spine and head. (*b*) kneecap. (*c*) door-bar fitting into holes on both sides. (*d*) beam to keep door shut (one end buttressed against big stone, the other against middle of door) = matōkarī 3 = madannī = jijigẹ 1b (*cf.* 1a *above* ; sạkatạ 2 ; kūbạ). (*e*) bone-peg in ground keeping door shut. (11) ∼ kuturtạ *used in* yā kai ∼ kuturtạ (i) he (leper) has fingerless hand. (ii) he is destitute. (12) ∼ kwantā *Kt.* = 9. (13) ∼ mịsālị *Vd.* būwạ̄yī 2. (14) gā̀gạrạ shāfọ *Vd.* tsā̀kō 1c. (15) ∼ shạrī'ạ *m.* woman's loin-cloth (= fạ̄tạ̄rī). (16) ∼ Yạ̄sin *m. epithet of* hated superior who is impossible to eject.

gā̀gạrarrē *m.* (*f.* gā̀gạrarrīyā) *pl.* gā̀gạrạrrū. (1) rebellious P. (= tū̀kā 2c.ii) (2) skilled worker (*Vd.* gā̀gạrạ 3b). (3) *Vd.* rā̀gạyạ 1b.

Gā̀gạrau *epithet of* any Ạbūbakạr *or of* warrior or difficult P. or T.

Gā̀garẹ *used in* Garbạ, Gā̀garẹ name for any man called Ạbūbakạr.

gā̀gārịmī = gā̀gārụmī.

gā̀garō *m.* (*sg., pl.*). (1) central stem of palm branch. (2) pen (ạlkalạmī) made from 1 or from bamboo or reed, *etc.*

gā̀gārụmī *m.* (*f.* gā̀gārụmā) *pl.* gā̀gārụmai. (1) loutish. (2) important (*re* affair, news).

gā̀garwạ *Sk. f.* children's game of rolling vessel-covers (fạifại) along ground.

gā̀gātạ *Vb.* 3B is (was) flabbergasted (*cf.* gā̀gā).

gagau A. (gagau) *used in* yanā̀ dạ farfī ∼ he (it) is strong.

B. (gạgạu) *used in* gā̀ rānā ∼ it's already round 7 a.m.

C. (gạgạu) *Sk. m.* any aphrodisiac (= gagai *q.v.*).

gagga A. (gaggạ) *epithet of* strong horse.

B. (gaggā) *Vd.* gāgọ.

gaggạbē *Vb.* 2 dislodged firmly-embedded T.

gaggạbē (1) *Vb.* 1C = gaggạbạ. (2) *Vb.* 3A. (*a*) (T. firmly embedded) has become shaky. (*b*) (wall) split preparatory to falling.

gaggạbū *Vd.* gabạ.

gaggādạ *Vb.* 2 *int. from* gādā.

gaggaɓa A. (gaggāɓā) *f.* (1) Bateleur eagle (*Terathopius ecaudatus*) = gāɓā = shāhọ 3. (2) = gāɓạ 1.

B. (gaggāɓạ) *f.* type of axe.

C. (gạggāɓā) *adj. m., f.* prosperous, abundant *x* gạggāɓar ƙasā rich land. (2) tanạ dạ gạggāɓan nōnọ her breasts have rich milk (*cf.* gāɓī).

gaggạƙē *Vd.* gaƙẹ.

gạggausā *adj. m., f.* (*pl.* gausạ̄sā). (1) big and strong. (2) tall and strong.

gaggauta A. (gạggautạ) *Vb.* 3B. (1) hurried. (2) is (was) over-eager. (3) is (was) tired of waiting. (4) Allā yạ gaggautō manạ dạ nasarạ God bring us speedy victory !

B. (gaggautā) *Vb.* 1C speeded T. up.

gạggautsā *adj. m., f.* (*pl.* gautsạ̄tsā). (1) brittle (*cf.* gautsī). (2) blurter out. (3) gautsạ̄tsā *pl.* persons dying in early middle age as did their forbears (*cf.* gautsī 2).

gaggāwā *f.* (1) (*a*) hastening *x* kạ yi ~ make haste ! (*b*) bạ mā yi gaggāwar cēwā muŋ gamạ ba we will not prematurely say we have finished. (*c*) kadạ mụ yi gaggāwar dạrīyā tụkụnā we must not count our chickens before they're hatched ! (*cf.* giriŋgiɗishī). (*d*) kōwā ya hau ~ yanā yiŋ tuntuɓẹ the more haste, the less speed. (*e*) maị ~ *m., f.* (*pl.* māsū ~) quick *x* nasarạ maị ~ speedy victory. (2) gaggāwar gạtsāɓū making haste without benefit.

gāgọ *m.* (*pl.* gạggā). (1) pagan villagehead. (2) (*a*) prostitute's *amant de cœur.* (*b*) girl's masturbation-partner in tsạ̣rạncē (= saurạyī 1*b*). (3) (*a*) energetic P. (*b*) anā karạŋ gạggā dạ gạggā a mighty struggle is in progress. (4) (*a*) large gourd-spoon. (*b*) ~ lūdạyiŋ ƙẹ̄tā, kōwā ya shā ɗayā, yā ƙọshi *epithet of* P. taking " lion's share ".

gāgū (1) *m.* bạtūrẹ dạ ~ P. both financing gambler and himself playing. yā ɗau gāgunsạ *such person* threw dice (saɓạ cācā), *cf.* Bạtūrẹ 6. (2) *epithet of* any Mādākī.

gāguŋ *m.* type of very viscous rubber.

gāgurmạ *m., f.* energetic or brave P.

gahawạ *Ar. f.* coffee.

gạhō *m.* exposing the private-parts in stooping.

Gahọ̄tạ *used in* kadạ kạ yi gyārạŋ ~ don't be penny-wise and poundfoolish.

gahọ̄tarị = gahōtarī *m.* (*f.* gahōtarā) senseless P. or T.

gāhūhụ *m.* (1) (*a*) flour or furā mixed with water instead of with milk (*cf.* ƙạsarī 2*a* ; bọ̄lọ̄lō 3 ; gāyā 2*d* ; mākārụ). (*b*) *Vd.* 3*b below.* (2) irascibly tactless man. (3) gāhūhụ̄wā *f.* (*a*) savourless mīyạ. (*b*) furā with water instead of with milk (*Vd.* 1 *above*).

gaibạ (*Ar.* hidden). (1) an yi matạ ~ she's been granted divorce as husband long disappeared. (2) takạrdar ~ *such* bill of divorce (*cf.* gaibị).

gaiɓạlī *Kt. m.* the food garɓạlī.

gaibị = gaibụ *Ar. m.* (1) T. invisible *x* bạ zạn sạyi ~ ba I'll not buy a " pig in a poke ". (2) kā shiga dạ ~ you believe any nonsense. (3) saniŋ ~ gạ (= saniŋ ~ sǎi) Allā only God knows many a thing mysterious to Man. (4) *cf.* gaibạ.

gai da A. (gai dạ) *Vb.* 4A (*p.o. also* gaishē). (1) (*a*) yā ~ shī = yā gaishē shị = yā yi masạ gaisūwā he (inferior) saluted, greeted him (*for superior, senior waits for inferior to initiate recognition*). (*b*) *progressive of* 1*a is* yanā ~ shī = yanā gaishē shị = yanā yi masạ gaisūwā. (*c*) ~ kūrā *cf.* kạrạmbānī 4. (*d*) anā ta yāƙi, bạ maị ~ wani bitter war is going on. (2) (*contrary to* 1 *above, in the following expressions, action does not lie from inferior towards superior*). (*a*) (i) Jạma'ạ, Sarkī yā gaishē kụ Assembled People, the Emir presents his compliments to you ! (ii) nā gaishē kụ greetings to you, Assembly of Chiefs ! (*x* said by Governor in opening his address). (*b*) (i) a gaishē kạ I am ordered to acknowledge your greeting ! (*said by attendant of Chief or European when inferiors greet them,* Mod. Gram. 18). (ii) *Vd.* amshẹ 2. (*c*) (i) Audụ yanā gaishē kạ = Audụ yā cẹ̄ ạ gaishē kạ Audu sends you his compliments (*used when bearer of compliments* *is person or letter, or if greeter is waiting to see you and sends you his compliments by servant or messenger, cf.* gaisūwā). (ii) gayar minį dą Audų please remember me to Audu ! (iii) nā gayar maką dą Audų I remembered you to Audu. *N.B.— the expressions in 2c* i–iii *may be used between* equals). (iv) *Vd.* gaisūwā 2. (v) *Vd.* amsą 1*a.*ii. (*d*) ką gai dą gidā (i) remember me to your folks at home ! (ii) adieu ! (*e*) (i) ąlhērįn Allā yą gaishē sų bravo !, best of luck to them ! (ii) ąlhērįn Allā yą gai dą mū God give us good fortune ! (3) *cf.* gaisūwā, gaisą, gąi dą yąyā. (4) ⁓ saurąyī *Vd.* gwalaŋgwasō.

B. (gaidą) *Sk. Vb.* 1A = gai dą.

C. (gąidā) (1) *m., f.* (*a*) a Bąmāguję-pagan (*epithet* ⁓ mąi nīsaŋ gōnā). (2) *Kt. f.* measles (= ƙyąndā). (3) ⁓ kā fi sautų ; săi dam mąsū gidā *epithet of* mule.

gąi dą yąyā *m.* (*sg., pl.*) small, covered, brass basin or basket used by woman sending present to friends.

gaidō *used in* dan gaįdō *m.* vagina (*term used by children*).

gaigąi *adv.* in full view ; openly.

gaigaya A. (gaigayą) *Vb.* 2 gnawed ; nibbled.

B. (gaigāyą) *Kt. f.* rice or tūwō with oil and condiments but gravyless (= gāyą-gāyą).

C. (gaigayā) *Vb.* 1C kept on telling (*int. from* gayą).

gaigaye A. (gaigayē) *Vb.* 1C = gaigayą.

B. (gaigayē) *m.* (1) (*secondary v.n. of* gaigayą) *x* yanā gaigayansą = yanā gaigayą tasą he's nibbling it. (2) act of nibbling, gnawing. (*a*) dōkįn naŋ ⁓ gąrēshį this horse nips one's hand. (*b*) kadą ką yi minį gaigayam ɓērā (*lit.* don't nibble at me like a rat !) don't beat about bush ! (*c*) bąri ⁓, yąnzu kā ci tumų all in good time !

gaiką *Vb.* 1A = gaikad dą *Vb.* 4B *Nor.* = gai dą.

gaikau *m.* (1) P. or T. certain to have desired effect. (2) *Vd.* tųnjērē 1*d.*

gairą *Ar.* (1) *prep.* minus (*used with any multiple of* 10 *starting with* 20, *to deduct* 1 *or* 2) *x* ąshirįn ⁓ bīyū 18. dąrī ⁓ dayā 99. ąlfyaŋ ⁓ mētaŋ 1,800.

ąlfyaŋ ⁓ minyą 1,900 (*cf.* bābų 5). (2) *f.* (*a*) deficit *x* dayā yā yi ⁓ there's one short. yā kāwō kudī dăidăi bā ⁓ he brought the exact sum without shortage. (*b*) blemish *x* rashįn gąskīyā yā yi masą ⁓ untruthfulness mars him. (*c*) bā ⁓, bā dąlīlį = bā ⁓, bā sababī = bā ⁓, bā sabąk = bā ⁓, bā ąbadįn = bā ⁓ ąbadįn = bį ⁓ ąmadįn = bįgairį bįshai'įn = *Kt.* bį ⁓ bį dąlīlį without rhyme or reason (= hujją 1*b*).

gairahųm *Vd.* gayyā.

gaisą *Vb.* 1A. (1) nā ⁓ dą shī he and I (equals) greeted one another. yanā gaisāwā dą Audų he and Audu (equals) are exchanging greetings. sunā gaisāwā they're exchanging greetings = gaisū-wā 4 (*cf.* gai dą ; gaisūwā). (2) *Vd.* sudę 1*c.*

gaisad dą *Vb.* 4B *Sk., Kt.* = gai dą.

gaishē *Vd.* gai dą.

gaisūwā *f.* (1) yā yi masą ⁓ = yā yi ⁓ ą wurinsą (*progressive* yanā yi masą ⁓) he saluted him (a superior) on meeting him (= gai dą 1*a*),‚ *cf.* sąlāmųŋ. (2) Audų yā cę ą yi masą ⁓ Audu (your inferior) sends you his compliments (*used when bearer of compliments is person or letter, or if greeter is waiting to see you and sends you his compliments by servant or messenger ; cf.* gai dą 2*c.*i *and N.B. to* 2*c.*iii). ką yi minį ⁓ wurim Bątųrę give the European my compliments ! (*Vd.* gai dą 2*c.*ii *and N.B. to* 2*c.*iii). (3) .(*in letters to superior*) *x* (*a*) dągą Hākįmin A, Garbą, ⁓ dą amincį zūwą Sarkįn Kano, Audų dam Mąmūdų. Bāyaŋ haką . . . most profound and respectful salutations from the District-head of A, Garba, to the Emir of Kano, Audu Son of Mamudu. I write to say that . . . (*b*) *cf.* amincį 2 ; sąlāmųŋ 2. (4) mutual salutations (*between two persons no matter what their respective status*) sunā ⁓ = sunā gaisāwā they're exchanging mutual greetings (*x* barką dą ąsubā greeting on the early morning ! *plus reply* barką kądăi), *Vd.* gaisą. wōkącįŋ ⁓ a kąn cę " įnā gajīyą " when exchanging salutations, people say " I hope you are not tired ! ". kō ⁓ mā bąbų ? (*jokingly*) don't you now even greet me when we meet ? **ạbōkiŋ gaisūwạr ya kạn cẹ** " **Ạlhamdụ lịllāhị** " the P. greeted replies " Thank you, I'm well " (*cf.* **Ạlhamdụ 3**). (5) **gaisūwar mutūwạ** condolence on a death *x* **Audụ yanạ̃** yi **masạ gaisūwā** Audu's expressing his condolences to him, *saying* **sạnummụ dạ rashị** *and receiving reply* **sạnnū kạdǎi, Allạ̄ yạ bā dạ lādā** (*cf.* **duhụ** 1*b* ; **tạ'azīyyạ** ; **jẹjẹtọ** ; **makōkī**). (6) yā yi **masạ** ~ (*a*) he gave him (superior) (i) customary offering sanctioned by usage. (ii) bribe to secure position or some advantage. (*b*) he gave him (guest) present of food on arrival (*b* = **sạukā 2c**). (7) **nāmạ yanạ̃** ~ the meat's going bad (= **kōrẹ 1b.ii**).

gạiwā *f.* (*pl.* **gaiwōyī**). (1) lunged-mudfish (*Protopterus annectens*). (2) **ḳạshin** ~ **gạrēshị** he's persistently unlucky.

gajabā *Kt. f.* muddy-surroundings of well (*cf.* **bagajā**).

gaja-gaja A. (**gaja-gaja**) *m.* (*sg., pl.*) type of fish.

B. (**gajā-gạjạ̃**) *Vd.* **gạ̄jạ̃jạ.**

gạjạgạl = **gạjạl.**

gạjạganī *m.* (1) meddlesomeness (*epithet is* ~ **wạndạ ya hanạ cịn sạ̄**) = **kāsạ ganī**. (2) **daŋ** ~ *m.* (*f.* '**yar** ~) *pl.* '**yaŋ** ~ busybody.

gạ̄jạ̃jạ *m., f.* (*pl.* **gajā-gạjạ̃**) dirty (= **ḳạ̄- cạ̄cạ** *q.v.*).

gạjạjjē = **gạdajjē.**

gạjạjjẹrū short (*pl. of* **gạjērē**).

gạjạl *m.* messiness (= **cạ̣bạl 1, 2** *q.v.*).

gạjānīyā *f.* trouble.

gajaŋ hạḳurī (*d.f.* **gajē**) *m.* (1) impetuousness (*cf.* **kāshị 3**). (2) ~ **shī ya sạ̄ bụdurwā cikị** impetuousness lands one in trouble. (3) ~ **shī ya sạ̄** " **Wānẹ, mẹ ka shūkạ** " don't ask ridiculous questions !

gajạrcẹ *Vb.* 3A. (1) (*a*) became short. (*b*) yā ~ he (P. who previously looked thin) has now through nourishment lost his tall, thin appearance. (2) = **ga- jạrtā**.

gajarta A. (**gajạrtā**) *Vb.* 1C shortened.

B. (**gajartạ**) *f.* shortness.

gajartad dạ *Vb.* 4B shortened.

gạjạwur *m.* (*sg., pl.*) P. owning horse

available for war service, but without trappings.

gajạ zamā *m.* fidgetiness (= **mụtsụnīyā** = *Kt.* **tsạutsạunīyā**).

gaje A. (**gājẹ**) *Vb.* 1A. (1) (*a*) inherited property of P. (*cf.* **gạ̄dā**). (*b*) took complete possession of *x* **cịyāwạ tā** ~ **wurịŋ** the place is overgrown with grass. **suŋ** ~ **gạrịŋ** they captured the town. (2) succeeded to rule or trade without hereditary right *x* **yā** ~ **maḳērạr, ạmmā shī bại gạji ḳīrạ ba** he inherited the smithy, but his forbears were not smiths.

B. (**gạ̄jē**) *Vd.* **gạ̄dā.**

C. (**gajē**) *m.* (1) small amount of thread on spindle. (2) *Kt.* impetuousness (= **gajaŋ hạḳurī**).

gajē-gạjẹ *m. used in* yā yi ~ **dạ ạbincī** he wasn't hungry enough to finish up the food.

gạjẹganī = **gajạganī.**

gạjẹjēnīyā *f.* several persons alternately inheriting.

gajeŋ hạḳurī *Vd.* **gajaŋ hạḳurī.**

gajere A. (**gạjērē**) (*d.f. Ar.* **qasīri**) *m.* (*f.* **gạjērịyā** = **gạjērụ̄wā** = **gạjērā**) *pl.* **gạjẹrū** = **gạjạjjẹrū** = *Sk.* **gạjẹjẹrū**). (1) (*a*) short. (*b*) (i) short P. (ii) **kōwā ya rēnạ** ~ **bại tākạ kụnāmạ ba nẹ̃** one learns from experience. (*c*) **gạjẹraŋ wạndō** short trousers (*Vd.* **fētō**). (*d*) **gạjẹraŋ hanzarī** *Vd.* **hanzarī 1d**. (2) ~ **mại bạkā** (= ~ **dạ bạkā** = **Gạjērē**) yā **hạrbẹ shị** he has disease of unknown origin believed due to the spirit ~ **mại bạkā** (*whose epithet is* **Mại gạrājē**, *cf.* **dawạ 5a, maharbī 3**. *N.B. this spirit is thought to appear if a woman drops a plate* (*Vd.* **sạ̄barạ 3, tsārā 2**). (3) **gạjērā** *f.* any viper (= **kụbūbūwạ**). (4) **gạjẹraŋ ḳạshī** upper bone of foreleg of cattle.

B. (**Gạjēre**) *man's name.*

gajẹ zamā = **gajạ zamā.**

gaji A. (**gạji**) *Vb.* (*has only this one form*). (1) (*a*) is (was) tired (*cf.* **gạjīyạ**). (*b*) **muŋ** ~ **dạ** " **gāḳarạ sạ̄ !** ", **bạ mụ ga ḳạḳō ba** we're tired of hearing idle threats. (*c*) **iŋ aŋ** ~ **kō ạ rānā, sǎi ạ hūtạ** beggars cannot be choosers. (*d*) " **Dạukạ wuyạ** " **bại saŋ** " **Nā gaji** "

ba one half of the world does not know how the other half lives (cf. dauka wuya, dūtse 1l). (e) Gaji tā aikō " a hūta ! " (lit. Miss Tired sent to say " have a rest ! ") resting gives one fresh energy. (f) dōki in yā gaji, tīlas kūwā bǎ ta sauran sǎ shi sǎi dǎi dabāra when circumstances become difficult, compulsion must be replaced by guile. (2) wuƙā tā ～the knife is (was) worn-out. rīgarka tā ～ your gown is (was) worn-out.
    B. (gaji) used in bai kāmō kōmē ba sǎi ～ he got nothing for his pains.
    C. (gaji) Vd. gajīyad.
    D. (gǎjī) (1) m. the grass gǎjirī. (2) Gǎjī name for any woman called Fātsuma.
    E. (gǎji) Vd. gǎdā.
gǎjimǎrē = gǎjimǎrē = gǎjimǎrai = gǎjimǎrī m. (1) (a) fleecy cloud(s), cf. girgije. (b) rainbow (= baƙā 8a). (2) yā gamu da ～ he is ill, due to the spirit bakaŋ gizo which lives in wells (Vd. baƙā 8e). (3) cuttlefish (used as remedy for leucoma, i.e. hakīya) = kumfan 2. (4) da ～ I swear I didn't or won't do it ! (abassama).
gǎjiŋ-gǎjiŋ used in tuŋ ～ from time immemorial.
gajiŋ haƙurī Vd. gajaŋ haƙurī.
gǎjiramī m. = gǎjirā f. large pot for storing corn, etc.
gǎjirī m. (1) abundant but poor tūwō (= tūwam fāda). (2) the reed-grass Cymbopogon hirtus (used for zānā-mats). (3) gǎjirin namiji energetic man.
gǎjirmī m. large pot for storing corn, etc.
gajiya A. (gajīya) f. (1) fatigue x (a) yā sōma ～ he's becoming tired. nā yi ～ I'm tired. ～ tā fīta fatigue has vanished (from me, him, etc.). (b) inā rūwaŋ ganī da ～ Vd. ganī A.2.3a. (2) zā mu baŋ ～ we're off to congratulate P. on having finished some tiring task (e.g. giving banquet, journey, etc.). (3) (a) inā ～ I hope you're feeling rested ? (reply, bǎ ～ = sǎi ta yau = alhamdu = alhamdu lillāhi). (b) gajīya ! greeting to bōrī devotee on returning to earth from leap.
    B. (gajīya) Vb. 3A. (1) fell short (= gaza). (2) durƙusa wǎdā bǎ gaji-

yǎwā ba nē needs must when the devil drives. (3) wata isā kaŋ wata isā gajīyǎwā cē too many cooks spoil the broth ! (4) cf. gajīyō.
    C. (gǎjīya) used in nā ci ～ tasa it was of use to me.
gajīyad da Vb. 4B = gajī da 4A tired a P.
gajīyayyē m. (f. gajīyayyīyā) pl. gajīyayyū (1) adj. tired (cf. gaji). (2) P. unequal to task (cf. gajīyā) = gazajjē.
gajīye x a ～ suka zō they arrived tired.
gajīyō Vb. 3A. (1) became poor. (2) is (was) rendered desperate. (3) cf. gajīyā.
gǎkaiwa f. beans cooked alone (= ƙūlū 1).
gǎ ƙāto (1) m. sitting in pool whilst one's clothes are being washed and dried. (2) what offers for my services ?
gaƙe (1) Vb. 1A. (a) prevented P. leaving place x yā ～ ni caŋ. (b) aŋ gaggaƙe wuriŋ the place's crowded. (2) Vb. 3A. (a) wurī yā ～ (a) place's crowded. (b) it's impossible to do it. (b) Sk. gulbī yā ～ river's in spate.
gaƙi (1) how strong ! ; how big ! (2) an sǎ shi a kōgwaŋ ～ he is unable to get out of place or difficulty.
gāko Kt. m. pagan village head, etc. (= gāgo q.v.).
gǎ ƙwǎi Vd. alaŋƙōsǎ.
gal used in gǎ rānā ～ it's already round 7 a.m.
gālā = gala used in (1) nā sǎmē shi a ～ I got it cheaply or easily. (2) Vd. daraŋgami.
*galaba Ar. f. winning.
galabaita A. (galǎbaita) Vb. 3B is (was) beside oneself.
    B. (galǎbaitā) Vb. 1D rendered P. beside himself.
Galādanci = Kt. Galādunci m. (1) position of Galādīma. (2) the town-quarter where Galādīma lives.
*galadī Ar. m. mistake.
Galādīma m. (pl. Galādīmōmī). (1) (a) an official position (epithet is Gardāye = Ƙashiŋ garī = Babba tōmō ƙashiŋ garī = Gwauraŋ gīwā = Gubrī shǎ baƙōsanī = Daudu). (b) Galādīmam būsa Vd. marōƙī. (c) Vd. Sarki 1b ; tāshiŋ Galādīmaŋ ƙauye. (2) daŋ ～ yā hau kanta the bōrī-spirit so called possesses her (= cī gōrọ 4).

Galādunci = Galādanci.

gala-gala = *gala-gala m., f. (sg., pl).
(1) simpleton x ka bar ganinsa ~ ;
da wayansa yakē he's no fool. (2) ~
da wayō P. who looks like simpleton,
but is far from being so.

galahē = galantōyī.

gālāla (1) f. bargain x nā ga ~ I got it
cheap. zai kāma ta da yaudara ; yā
ga ~ he decided to seize her by guile,
for he saw he'd made a find. (b) yā
yi ~ he behaved like a simpleton. (2)
adv. yā ajīyē shi ~ he left it about
carelessly.

galallawa (1) = galantōyī. (2) f. an
daura ~ plate or basin has been hung
on room-wall for ornament.

galamadi m., f. simpleton (epithet is ~
sautum madī, bā ƙōƙō).

galambī m. ɲliable rope used for tying
prisoners.

galaŋ (Eng. gallon) m. (sg., pl.) small tin
for spare petrol (cf. garwā).

galantōyī (1) m. (a) being simpleton. (b)
wandering aimlessly. (2) m.,f. (sg., pl.)
(a) simpleton. (b) idle roamer.

*galatsī Ar. m. mistake.

galau A. (galau) m. wandering aimlessly.
     B. (galau) used in yanā kallō ~
he's staring vacantly.
     C. (galau-galau) used in yanā yāwo ~
he's wandering aimlessly.

galaulawa = galallawa.

galauniyā f. wandering aimlessly.

galɓaƙlī Kt. m. the food garɓalī.

galbarō m. wandering aimlessly.

galbi Fil. m. wet-season pasturage of
cattle (= mashēkarī).

galēji Nor. m. type of playing and dancing.

galgadī Kt. m. = gargadī.

gal-gal m. (1) aimless wandering. (2)
nī makadin na ~ : daga bāya nakā
tsaya (said to competitors, disputants,
etc.) go it ! (= Kt. na bilbis).

Galgālīya f. (1) Shuwa Arabic. (2) aimless
wandering.

galgasā Kt. = gargasa.

galhanga (1) m., f. (sg., pl.) simpleton =
gala-gala. (2) m. gum from copaiba
balsam tree (cf. mājē 1b).

gālibaŋ Ar. usually.

gālibī Ar. (1) m. majority x gālibinsu the

majority. of them. (b) (followed by
sing. noun) the bulk of x gālibin yāƙinsu
wajan tēkū yakē the bulk of their war-
effort is naval. gālibin duk sābwar
kalma the bulk of new words. (2) adv.
(a) usually. (b) for the most part.
(3) m. last for boots (= magwajī 2).

galigaɓāsā f. bargain x nā ga ~ = nā
sāmi ~ I got it cheap.

gālīhu used in bā shi da ~ he's without
means.

galla A. (galla) (Ar. corn) f. (1) money
paid by slave to owner in lieu of
rendering service (= murgu). (2) (a)
hire. (b) rent. (3) gallar ƙasā (a)
presents (considered compulsory)
brought to District Head on his
return from journey or when he sends
for Village Heads to announce tax, etc.
(b) presents to Emir by District
Heads at Salla.
     B. (gallā) f. (sg., pl.). (1) (a) small
type of stingless bee (= zanyā =
rakūwā = mazanyā). (b) (i) the sweetness in the body of this bee, eaten by
children. (ii) shāye-shāyaŋ da akē
wa ~, bā ā wa zuma don't reckon without your host ! (c) Vd. būrā 2. (2)
stinging insect like dauber-wasp, nesting
in cornstalks.

gallaba A. (gallaba) Vb. 2 worried P.
     B. (gallabā) Vb. 1C forced ʃ. on P.
x yā ~ mini aikiŋ he forced me to do
the unwelcome task.

gallababbē m. (f. gallababbīyā) pl. gal-
lababbū pesterer.

gallāfīrī m. wandering aimlessly.

gallagaɓāsā f. bargain x nā ga ~ = nā
sāmi ~ I got it cheap.

gallaƙanci Kt. m. being a country
bumpkin.

gallaƙī m. (f. gallaƙā) Kt. country
bumpkin.

gallaŋ m. (1) (a) ceremonial galloping of
horsemen in line. (b) yanā ~ da
dōkinsa he's making his horse rear and
prance (= taɓi 1). (c) dōki yanā ~
horse's rearing and jibbing. (c) =
taɓaryā 2. (2) jumping for joy.

gallazā Vb. 1C = gallabā.

gallō m. (1) (a) any Asbin salt (cf. bēza).
(b) gallan tōzalī best quality antimony

(tōzạlī) = dạulā. (2) (a) dōkị yā yi ⁓ horse reared up (= gallạŋ 1c). (b) wurị yā yi ⁓ gambling-cowrie turned half over.

galmā *Sk. f.* hoe (= gạrmā *q.v.*).

galmī *Sk. m.* tastiness of food x ạbincī yā yi ⁓.

galmi-galmi *m.* ạbincī yā yi ⁓ food is insufficiently salted (= dalam-dalam).

gālūdayạ = *Kt.* gālūdīyạ *f.* aimless wandering (*epithet is* ⁓ tạllạm mutạnaŋ ƙārạ̄yē).

gālūlū *m.* yā yi minị ⁓ dạ shī he proffered it to me but then withdraw it (= dạŋgọ̄lī).

galūrạ *f.* the dye gạrūrạ *q.v.*

galwaŋgạ *m., f.* simpleton (= gạlhaŋgạ).

gam A. (gạm) *Eng. m.* gum.

B. (gam) (1) *m.* (a) malodorous, green locust said to be poisonous to eat (= fạ̄rar tụmfāfīyā). (b) yā ci ⁓ he brought trouble on himself. (c) an sạ̄ masạ ⁓ he (prisoner) has been secured to log with staple (= garam 1). (2) *adv.* firmly (= gam-gam *q.v.*). (3) (*abbreviation of* gamạ) *used in* nā ⁓ makạ dạ Allạ̄ I conjure you in God's name ! (= gamạ 1e.iii).

C. *Vd.* gam dạ.

gama A. (gamạ) (*Ar.* jama'a). (1) *Vb.* 1A. (a) (i) finished doing x aŋ ⁓ ạbincī they have finished cooking the food : they have finished eating the food. (ii) yā ⁓ shāwarạ he decided on his course of action. (iii) sukạ cẹ̄ " aŋ gamạ " they replied " it is as good as done ". kạmar aŋ gamạ I'll do it forthwith. (iv) yā ⁓ musụ he exterminated them, made a clean sweep of them. (v) *Vd.* gạmu. (b) (c–o *below, have sense* joined). (c) suŋ ⁓ bạ̄kī (i) they colluded. (ii) they happened to say the same T. simultaneously. (iii) *Vd.* gamị 3. (d) combined x (i) nā ⁓ shi dạ wancạŋ I've combined it with that one. (ii) gạmā shi cikinsạ put it inside that thing ! (iii) suŋ ⁓ mazaunī they share the same quarters. suŋ ⁓ zamā wurī daƴā they went to live together. (iv) dạ kūrā dạ kạrē bā sạ̄ ⁓ mazaunī = bā ạ̄ ⁓ wutā dạ shiƀạ oil and water won't mix. (v) bā ạ̄ ⁓ gudụ dạ sūsạr

katarā *Vd.* gudụ 2d.v. (vi) suŋ ⁓ ƙasạn naŋ cikin tāsụ they amalgamated that land with their own. (vii) yā ⁓ mu yāƙị dạ ạbọ̄kammụ he involved us in war with our friends. (viii) muŋ ⁓ kalmōmin naŋ cikiŋ harshạmmụ we've incorporated those words in our language. (ix) suŋ ⁓ gwīwạ they pooled their resources. (e) put persons in mutual relationship x (i) Sarkī yā ⁓ muftī dạ ạlkālī the Emir put the judge in consultation with an assessor. (ii) Sarkī yā ⁓ ni dạ dọgarī the chief sent me in company with a N.A. policeman. (iii) nā ⁓ ka dạ Allạ̄ I adjure you by God ! (= gam 3), *Vd.* baŋgō 2b. (iv) mutạ̄nan dạ bā sạ̄ saŋ ạ ⁓ su dạ Allạ̄ pitiless folk. (v) ịnā ạbin dạ ya ⁓ ni dạ kại what have I to do with your affairs ! mẹ̄ ya ⁓ ka dạ itạ what brings you into association with her ? ; what have you in common with her ? ; what caused you to quarrel with her ? (g) aŋ ⁓ jịkī they've come to blows. yā ⁓ jịkī dạ sū he came to hostilities with them. (h) (i) muŋ ⁓ idọ our glances met. (ii) nā ⁓ idọ dạ shī his glance and mine chanced to meet. (iii) suŋ ⁓ ⁓ idọ dạ kū they caught sight of you. (j) (i) yā ⁓ fuskạ he frowned. (ii) muŋ ⁓ fuskạ we met face to face. bại yạrdā suŋ (= bại yạrdā sụ) ⁓ fuskạ ba he was afraid to meet him face to face. (k) (i) suŋ ⁓ kại they allied themselves ; they consulted together (*cf.* gamẹ 1b). (ii) suŋ ⁓ kạnsụ dạ sauran dūnīyạ they've allied themselves with other nations. (iii) suŋ ⁓ kại ạ kaŋ kadạ ạ būdạ mạganạr they've agreed together not to reveal the matter. (iv) bā nạ̄ ⁓ kạina dạ shī I am not " in the same street with him ". (v) *Vd.* kại 1a.xii. (l) (i) yā ⁓ girā he frowned. (ii) hadirị (= garī) yā ⁓ girā the sky is lowering. (m) lạbārin naŋ yā ⁓ dūnīyạ = yā ⁓ garī that news is widely known (*Vd.* gamạ garī). (n) duk gamạ̄wā, bạ mụ fi shẹ̄karạ gụdā ba dạ saninsạ from first to last we've only known him one year. (o) (*with dative*) provided P. with x tā ⁓ masạ kāyaŋ girmā she provided him with the appurtenances of a respectable P. yā ~ wa̱ dōki̱ kāyā he fully caparisoned the horse. (p) cf. gamma̱. (q) Vd. ga̱ma̱-compounds. (2) Vb. 3A. (a) is (was) ready. (b) is (was) used up. (c) is (was) dead. (d) is (was) joined to (= game̱ 2a) x (i) yā ~ da̱ sū ciki̱ŋ wanna̱ŋ si̱yāsa̱ he co-operated with them in this concession. (ii) za̱i mi̱ḵe̱ tun da̱ga̱ Masa̱r har ya̱ gama̱ da̱ Tūna̱s it will extend from Egypt to Tunis (cf. ɗauka̱ 1p). (iii) suŋ gama̱ da̱ Masa̱r they went as far as Egypt. (iv) a̱bu in yā gama̱ da̱ datti̱jo̱ if a matter is entrusted to a reliable person. (3) Gama̱ name for child whose parents are of different stock (cf. barbarā 6). (4) cf. ga̱mu.

B. (ga̱mā) (1) Vb. 2. (a) pleased x yā ga̱mē ni̱ it pleased me. (b) (clothing) suited P. (c) abused P. (2) (a) because x ~ nā san shi̱ because I know him. (b) as for x ~ halinsu̱ as regards their temperament . . . (3) = gā x ga̱mā ni here I am ! ga̱mā lalle̱ henna, buy, buy ! (cf. lalle̱). •

C. (gāma̱) f. showing off, boastfulness (= hōma̱).

ga̱maɗa̱ f. (1) milking cows early, then grazing them near by, to allow one to eat one's food before taking them to real pasturage. (2) Kt. grazing cattle early and returning later for milking.

gamaɗē m. (1) alternately pooling services or resources (= gu̱ri'a̱ 1). (2) making communal use of same place x ḵāji̱ sunā̱ ~ various hens are using the same laying-place (= ga̱mayya̱), cf. ta̱rayya̱.

ga̱ma̱ di̱di̱ m. (sg., pl.) insect, male and female of which travel joined together (= jā na kūka̱ = bi̱ ta za̱iza̱i 1).

ga̱ma̱ faɗa̱ m. (sg., pl.). (1) the ma̱rgā-tree or its pods (said to cause dissension). (2) Vd. ago̱ 3.

ga̱mā-ga̱mā f. vacillation.

gama gari A. (ga̱ma̱ ga̱ri̱). (1) (a) (i) T. prevalent, T. in common use. (ii) poor type of kola-nut. (b) cf. ga̱ma̱ 1m ; rūwā C.15.

B. (gama̱ ga̱ri̱) m. roving x ~ ga̱rēshi̱ he roams.

ga̱ma̱ gōnā Vd. sa̱ŋkace̱.

ga̱ma̱ji̱gō m. (sg., pl.) instrument used by European miners when boring for tin.

ga̱maka̱ = ga̱maki̱ŋ East Kano Hausa well . . .

ga̱ma̱ ḵa̱sūwā Vd. rūwā B.9.

*ga̱mani̱ŋ because (= ga̱mā 2a).

ga̱ma̱ŋ Ḵa̱tar m. good luck (Vd. ga̱mō).

ga̱ma̱to̱rō m. (sg., pl.) large, dark caterpillar, with rows of whitish spikes (often found on kurna̱ tree).

ga̱ma̱ tsa̱kāni̱ m. mischief making x ~ ga̱rēshi̱ he's a mischief maker (cf. tsa̱kāni̱ 4).

ga̱ma̱ tsa̱yi̱ m. failure of corn to produce a head.

ga̱mayya̱ Kt. f. = gamaɗē 2.

gamba A. (gamba̱) f. (1) the grass Andropogon Guyanus (used for zānā-mats), cf. ḵyāra̱, a̱bu 10. (2) ~ girman darē ɗayā how quickly he has prospered ! (3) ḵarḵwanta̱ ~ Vd. a̱lgabba̱ 2.

B. (ga̱mbā) f. (1) belching or distension of the stomach from flatulence (= magwa̱s). (2) ci̱ da̱ yawa̱ shi̱ ya ka̱n sā ~ murder will out.

Gambaje̱ another form of the name Ga̱mbo.

gambara A. (gambara̱) f. (sg., pl.) type of cloth having alternate stripes of red and white or black and white.

B. (ga̱mbara̱) f. (sg., pl.) musical instrument like kōmō.

ga̱mba̱r haba̱ru̱ m. T. in a muddle.

ga̱mba̱ri̱ m. (pl. ga̱mba̱rai). (1) Zar. type of shirt. (2) ga̱mba̱rim Būzū Sk. type of long-legged ram, sheep, or goat (= ara̱-ara̱).

gam6asa A. (ga̱mɓasa̱) (1) Vb. 2 (p.o. ga̱mɓashē, n.o. ga̱mɓashi) broke off large chunk of T. (2) f. (a) flatulent distension (cf. ga̱mbā). (b) Sk. epigastric region.

B. (ga̱mɓa̱sā) Vb. 1C broke off large chunk of T. and gave P. x nā ~ masa̱ furā.

C. (ga̱mɓa̱sā) Vd. gamɓashī.

gamɓashī = gamɓashēshe̱ m. (f. gam-ɓashā = ga̱mɓa̱shā = ga̱mɓa̱sā) pl. gambas-ga̱mɓa̱s huge.

ga̱mɓata̱ f. = ga̱mɓasa̱ 2.

ga̱mɓi̱za̱ Vd. gami̱ 3c.

Ga̱mbo (1) name for child born after twins (= Lēko̱ = Gado). (2) Ga̱mbaŋ watanni (*said by women*) the month Rajab (*cf.* tagwai).

gambū *Sk. m.* door (= ƙyaurē).

gambūtu *m.*, *f.* (*sg.*, *pl.*) fool.

Gambya *f.* the Gambia.

gam da (1) *Vb.* 4A *x* yā ~ ni = yā gamshē ni it pleased me. (2) *Vd.* gam da *compounds.*
gam da hari = gan da hari.
gam da Katar *m.* good luck.
gamdaran = gamdiran.
gam da yāƙi *m.* (*sg.*, *pl.*) = gan da hari.
gamdiran = gamduran (1) *f.* fine quality bullam gown. (2) *adv.* fine and big *x* yārinya cē ~ she's a fine, strapping girl.

game A. (game) (1) *Vb.* 1A. (*a*) = gama 1*c* ; 1*d*.i, ii ; 1*m.* (*b*) sun ~ kai they indulged in sharp practice (*cf.* gama 1*k*). (2) *Vb.* 3A. (*a*) (i) became joined. (ii) kansu bai game ba they are not unanimous (= gamu 1*c*). (*b*) became stuck together.

B. (game) *m.* (1) *x* yā sā wandō gaman jā he put on the red-ended variety of the trousers called kāmun ƙafa (= daƙkē 2). (2) *Sk.*, *Kt.* (*a*) wearing two upper garments simultaneously (especially black and white ones) (= hadi 1). (*b*) *Kt.* joining two loads as one (*cf.* gwāmē).

C. (game) (1) *adv.* (*a*) together *x* muna ~ we're together. (*b*) joined together, stuck together *x* suna ~. (*c*) kansu bā game yakē ba they are not unanimous. (2) *prep.* with *x* yana ~ da su he's with them (= gami 2). (3) na ~ regarding *x* kōmē ya faru na ~ da ƙasar whatever occurs in regard to the country. māganī kō wani abu na ~ da cīwo medicine or other medical supplies.

ga'me-game" *m.* mischief-making (*cf.* gama 1*c*).

gamfa *m.*, *f.* (*sg.*, *pl.*) a " softy ".

gamfū *m.* (1) type of tree. (2) ~ ƙetara hūdā *epithet of* fine horse.

gam-gam A. (gam-gam) firmly *used in* yā kāma ~ it's firmly fixed. ƙōfa tā dannu ~ door frame is firmly embedded. yana tsaye ~ it stands firmly.

B. (gam-gam) (*with long interval*

between gam *and* gam) yanā tafiya ~ he's treading heavily.

gamhū = gamfū.

gami (1) *m.* (*a*) (*secondary v.n. of* gamā 1*c*) *x* tanā gaminsa = tanā gamā tasa she's abusing him. (*b*) joining *x* (i) inā gamina da shi what have I to do with him ? (ii) B yā yi wa A ~ da C the man B, who owed C money, arranged that his own debtor A should settle direct with C. yā yi mini ~ da banki I owed him, he owed bank, so I paid bank. (iii) gami daya, kō da kūrā ā yi there's no harm in trying everything once (gami = meeting, *cf.* gamu). (*c*) adulteration *x* an yi wa turārē ~ the scent's adulterated (= mārā 1*b*). bā shi da ~ it's unadulterated, undiluted. abin gamim māganī T. to mix with medicine. marag gami unequalled, peerless. (2) *prep.* with *x* yana ~ da sū he's with them (= game 2). (3) *compounds* : (*a*) gamim bāki (i) worn-out cloth repaired as in bī tsatsō *q.v.* (ii) *Vd.* gama 1*c*. (*b*) gamim bākin tsummā useless intrigue. (*c*) gamim bauta = gamin gambīza joining two incongruous things (*odd shoes, etc.*). (*d*) gamin sahū mischief-making.

gamji A. (gamji) *m.* (*pl.* gamuzza) gutta-percha tree (*Ficus platyphylla*) (*epithet is* ~ shā sārā).

B. (gamjī) *m.* (1) old cassava (= gantamau *q.v.*). (2) *Kt.* = gaujin.

gamjigo *m.* (*mining term*) Banka drill.

gamkā *Kt. f.* (1) one's equal. (2) one's contemporary.

Gamkai *epithet of* Sarkin dōgarai.

gamkō *m.* (1) meeting together of several persons. (2) one's equal or contemporary (= sa'a). (3) = gankō.

gamma *used in* (1) Alā gammana (*a*) *m.* wrinkles from old age. (*b*) au revoir ! (*c*) yā zamā Alā gammana he's a hard one to get a debt from. (2) Alā gammamu au revoir (*cf.* gama).

gammāyē *Vd.* gammō.

gammō = gammo *m.* (*pl.* gammāyē). (1) (*a*) (i) carrier's headpad (*cf.* ƙungurmī). (ii) yā yi gamman daukar hasāra he steeled himself to suffering casualties. (*b*) anything coiled (rope, snake, etc.). (2)

fee payable by jạkādạ for permission to collect tax. (*b*) yā kāwō ∽, zại d̃au bāshị (i) he's brought a present to smooth the way for asking for loan. (ii) he "threw a sprat to catch a whale". (*c*) an cịnyē masạ fạm 5, an yi masạ ∽ na fạm bīyū he lost £5 at gambling and then a further £2 which became debt, as he couldn't pay. (3) young gazelle (bạrēwā). (4) d̃aŋ gammọ *m.* the fish mạ̄rī. (5) ganịmạm fatạ̄kē type of pumpkin. (6) tā yi gurgụ̄ŋ gammō she had miscarriage (= zubar dạ 2).

gạmō *m.* (1) meeting *x* (*a*) (i) bạ̄ shi dạ dādịŋ ∽ he's a "ticklish customer". (ii) mūgụ̄ŋ ∽ *Vd.* kạciɓịs. (iii) yanạ̄ dạ lāyạr gạmō dạ mạnyā he has a charm to protect him on an encounter with the powerful. (*b*) gạman jinī tsạkāninsụ they like one another. (*c*) ∽ ya yi he encountered evil spirits. (*d*) gạman daŋga dạ gạrạ̄funī (= gạman rānā tsakạ) nē ya gamạ mu we're not related, but merely joined by some fortuitous fact (as being on same work, etc.). (2) gạmō = fariŋ gạmō (*a*) good luck *x* (i) ∽ yā fi lāyạ actual luck's better than religious charm for bringing luck ; a bird in the hand's worth two in the bush. (ii) gạmōna ạbụ kạzā my luck's dependent on such and such omen. (iii) ∽ dạ Sarkī yā fi ∽ dạ dạ̄munā gaining a Chief's favour carries one further than rains favourable to one's crops. (*b*) ∽ dạ   Kạtar = gạmaŋ Kạtar = fariŋ ∽ good luck (= sā'ạ 3 (= azzịkī 2*a*). (*c*) an yi gạman turmī, bạ ạ yi gạman taɓaryā ba they're unevenly matched, only one of the two being good (*x* husband and wife : Emir and Premier, etc.) (*cf.* turmī 7).

gạmrākạ *Sk. m.* (*f.* gạmrākịyā) *pl.* gạmrākī crested crane (*Balearica pavonina*), *Vd.* gạụrākạ.

gạmsai *m.* slime on water ; moss (= gạmsạkūkạ).

gạmsặkai *adv.* impolitely, disrespectfully (= sūmạ̄k̃ai).

gạmsạk̃ēk̃ẹ = gạmsạk̃ī *m.* (*f.* gạmsạk̃ēk̃ịyā = gạmsạk̃ā) *pl.* gạmsạk̃ai-gạmsạk̃ai tall and stout.

gạmsạkūkạ *f.* = gạnsạkūkạ.

gạmsamēmẹ = gamsamī *m.* = gạmsạk̃ēk̃ẹ.

gạmsạnsạŋ ; gạmsạrk̃ị ; gạmsarwạ *Vd.* gạnsạnsạŋ ; gạnsạrk̃ị ; gạnsarwạ.

gạmsạyī the fodder karmāmī 2 *q.v.*

gamshē pleased P. (*Vd.* gam dạ).

gạmshēk̃ā *f.* (*sg., pl.*). (1) black hooded cobra (= kwāk̃ị), *Vd.* makarī 1*c*, kụmurcī. (2) *Vd.* fasạ 1*p* ; turkụdī 3.

gamt- *Vd.* gant-.

gạmu *Vb.* 3B (1) (*a*) are (were) joined *x* suŋ ∽ bisạ gạ harshẹ they have the same language in common. suŋ ∽ bisạ gạ hālịn zamansụ har ạ̄ īyạ cẹ musụ irị d̃ayā nẹ̄ their standard of culture is so similar that they might be classed together. (*b*) ạ hadạ su, sụ ∽ ạ kā mix them in the right proportions ! (*c*) kạnsu yā gạmu they are unanimous (= gamẹ). an yi shāwarạ ạmmā k̃ại yā k̃i gạmūwā they deliberated but could reach no unanimity. kạm mutạ̄nạŋ yā k̃i gạmūwā they could come to no agreement together. (2) are (were) collected (= gamẹ 2*a*.ii). (3) met *x* (*a*) mụ ∽ ạ kā let's meet further along the road ! nā ∽ dạ shī I met him. (*b*) in sukạ kụskurạ, sukạ yi hakạ, zā sụ gạmu dạ shī if they are so rash as to do so, they will have to reckon with him. yā cẹ̄ duk wandạ ya yi ragwancị, sạ̄ gạmu he said he would punish anyone showing slackness. (*c*) A gạmu ạ Lāhirạ *Vd.* marịkịcī. (*d*) ạ̄ gạmu ạ kōmā *Vd:* arạ 2*b*.ii. (4) is (was) finished *x* shirịnsụ yā ∽ their preparations are complete.

gamuzzạ gutta-perchạ trees (*pl. of* gamjị).

gạmzāk̃ị *m.* the morning-star (*epithet is* ∽ mạrhạbar darē = ∽ ụban tạụrạ̄rī).

gạmzạrai (1) *m.* = gạmzạrō. (2) *Vd.* gamzạrī.

Gamzạrā *Vd.* ạlgazarụ.

gạmzạrī *m.* (*pl.* gạmzạrai) caterpillar damaging bulrush-millet (= minyạ 2 *q.v.* = wạiwạyī = *Kt.* yạ̄mau).

gạmzạrō *m.* detachment detailed to guard villages whose men have gone to war, from being looted.

gạmzō *m.* powerfully-built man.

gan A. (gan) *Vd.* ganī.

    B. (gaŋ) *m.* sound of drum.

gana A. (gānạ) *Vb.* 1A. (1) had a confidential chat with another *x* nā ∽ dạ Audụ. (*b*) bā ạ̄ gānạ̄wā dạ shī he's not one to listen to illicit proposals. (*c*) gānạ̄wā cẹ wụyā she's a nymphomaniac, ready for connection with any man she sees (= tạ̄barmā 4). (2) (*with dative*) caused to experience *x* yā ∽ matạ wụyā he ill-treated her. yā ∽ minị dādī he treated me well (*Vd.* jī 4C).

B. (ganạ) *Eng. m.* (*sg., pl.*) gunner.

ganad da A. (ganad dạ) *Vb.* 4A showed *x* nā ∽ shī takạrdā = nā ganasshē shị takạrdā I showed him the paper. yanạ̄ dạ wụyar ganạrwā its position si hard to distinguish.

B. (gānad dạ) *Vb.* 4A explained *x* yā ∽ mū (= yā gānasshē mụ) azancinsạ he explained its meaning to us. wụyar gānạrwā gạrēshị he's slow-witted.

gạ̄ nākạ *m.* (1) (*a*) poor hoeing. (*b*) poor manuring (each limited to base of crops (*both also called* gạ̄ nākị = gẹ̄wạyạ bạ̄kin rāmị ; *sense* (*b*) *also called* tạrfē), *cf.* dạurạ wạrkī 2. (2) axillary abscess (= jambadẹ *q.v.*). (3) *cf.* gạ̄ tạ̄wa ; gạ̄ nạ̄wa. (4) *Vd.* ạkạ̄wū 2. (5) gạ̄ nākị *Vd.* dọrinā 3.

ganam *x* kōwā, idạnsạ yạ ganam masạ everyone has been given eyes to see what is going on (*cf.* ganō).

gạnarkị *adv.* abundantly (*re* work, food, loads).

gạnasā *f.* yā ga ∽ he got a bargain ; got it for nothing.

dạŋ ganasō *m.* (1) (*in songs*) vagina. (2) type of cheap European cotton material.

ganasshe A. (ganasshē) *Vd.* ganad dạ.

B. (gānasshē) *Vd.* gānad dạ.

gạnau *m., f.* (*sg., pl.*) eye-witness.

gạ̄ nạ̄wa *m.* axillary abscess (= gạ̄ nākạ 2).

gancī *m.* smell or taste between astringent (barcī) and bitter (dācī).

ganda A. (gạndā) *f.* (1) feet and skin of head and mouth (dāɓụrī) of cattle sold for cooking. an shā ∽ food *as above* was eaten = *Kt.* lạŋgaɓū = kạ̄kụmā (*Vd.* ƙaurī 2). (2) poor meat sold in scraps (= dạfau 1 *q.v.*) (*epithet is*

Gạndā kim fi ƙurmusū). (3) (*said b woman to another woman*) kiŋ kām yị gạndā you seem to think yourself too fine to mix with people !

B. (gandạ) *f.* 1 (*a*) red earth used to adulterate snuff. (*b*) adulteration of dye (= daurī 3 *q.v.*). *2 yā yi ∽ he behaved obstructively.

gạndā *f.* (*sg., pl.*) the hard palate.

gạn'da-gạndē" *m.* combining things of different kinds (*cf.* gạŋgạndā).

gandạgaurạ *f.* (1) girl heavy in body or mind (*Vd.* gạndạƙai 1). (2) type of guinea-corn. (3) unexpected stiffness (*x* of leather which should be supple ; of girl not supple in bending backwards in dance, etc.).

gạn dạ harị *m.* (*sg., pl.*) (1) black stork (harbinger of war) *Ciconia nigra* (= jạ̄ yāƙị = gạm dạ yāƙị). (2) person bringing ill luck.

gan dạ idō *used in* dạ nī dạ shī sãi gan dạ idō it is no affair of mine.

gạndạƙai (1) *f.* girl not supple in bending back in dance (= gạndạgaurạ 1). (2) *adv.* (*a*) tā tsayạ ∽ she rudely stood, instead of curtseying when handing T. to man. (*b*) fāifãi yā yi ∽ pot-cover fits awkwardly.

gandạm *used in* gạ̄ rānā ∽ it's already round 7 a.m.

gandamẽmẹ = gandamẽmẹ = gandamī *m.* (*f.* gandamā = gandamẽmīyā, etc.) *pl.* gandaŋ-gandạŋ = gandaŋ-gandạŋ huge.

gandarā *f.* (1) yā saɓạ (= yā saɓō) ∽ he brought trouble on himself. (2) bandicoot's tail. (3) penis (*especially of animals*). (4) *Vd.* gandarērẹ ; gandarī.

gandạrạŋ *f.* fine bullạm gown, *etc.* (= gamdịrạŋ *q.v.*).

gandarērẹ = gandarī *m.* (*f.* gandarērīyā = gandarī) *pl.* gandar-gandạr huge.

gandarī (1) *Vd.* gandarērẹ. (2) unstrung bow. (3) gandarī = gạndarị (*a*) bandicoot's tail. (*b*) penis (*especially of animals*) (*Vd.* gandarā).

gan dạ yāƙị = gạn dạ harị.

gandạyau *Vd.* dilā.

gandạ̄yē *Vd.* gandū.

gạn'de-gạndē" = gạn'da-gạndē".

gạndī (1) *m.* variety of kola of the gōrạm

...type (*Vd.* **gōrọ** 1*c*). (2) *Kt. used in* ...uŋ **gandī** we're nonplussed.

...ạndīɗō *m.* silk-cotton (**rīmī**) seeds roasted (**sọ̄yayyē**) for eating.

gandịrạŋ *f.* fine **bullạm** gown, etc. (= **gamdịrạŋ** *q.v.*).

gạndōkī *m., f.* (*sg., pl.*). (1) over-excitable P. always " putting his foot in it " (= *Kt.* **uŋgōzọ̄mạ** 2). (2) *epithet of* 1 *is* " **Gạndōkī, mụ jē bịkī !** ", ta cē " zanẹna yā yi gạba kọ̄ ".

gandu A. (**gandū**) *m.* (*pl.* **gandāyē**). (1) (*a*) tax *x* an **sạ̄ musụ** ~ **sulẹ bịyar bịyar** they've been assessed at five shillings tax each (= **hạrājị**). (*b*) indemnity *x* an **sạ̄ musụ** ~ **bāyī** 300 the conqueror imposed an indemnity of 300 slaves on them. (2) (*a*) large farm. (*b*) **yā nōmẹ gandunsạ** he's dead. (*c*) **Gandun Sarkī, k̃ọsạ aikị** *epithet of* any drum. (*d*) (i) **bāwạ, gandụŋ aikị** what a hard worker ! (ii) *Vd.* **shạ̄** 1*b*. (*e*) **Na nāyẹ gandụŋ k̃ẹ̄tā** *epithet of* **Filạ̄nī**. (*f*) *Kt.* **Tūrạ hạwājọ, gandụŋ kudī** *epithet of* European, Arab, girl called **Bạtūrīyā**. (*g*) **gandụŋ gurjīyā dạ duhụ, ạmmā bābụ wurim ɓūyā, kō kạzā bā tạ̄ ɓūyā** *epithet of* wealthy miser (*Vd.* **fagẹ** 2*b*). (3) (*mining term*) daily task of casual labourers. (4) **tūwạŋ gandū** (*a*) staple, everyday **tūwō**. (*b*) **mạganạn nạŋ tūwạŋ** ~ **cẹ̄** this is an everyday expression (*b* = **tūwan sallạ**), *Vd.* **k̃ōfạ** 1*e*. (5) **ạ** ~ **yakẹ̄** his food is brought him ready-cooked by the P. whom he works for (*cf.* **gashị** 1*b*). (6) **gandụŋ k̃wạlamā** *Vd.* **jịrātạ**.

B. (**gandu**) slave in charge of his owner's **gandū-**farm.

gandụrạŋ = **gandịrạŋ**.

gane A. (**gānẹ**) *Vb.* 1A. (1) (*a*) understood T. (= **fạhimtạ**). (*b*) realized that *x* **k̃ạ̄k̃ạ kukạ** ~ 'yan Jạbū nẹ̄ how did you realize that they were counterfeit coins ? (2) noticed (visible T.). (3) appraised correctly *x* **nā** ~ **shi** = **nā** ~ **masạ** (i) I " saw through him ". (ii) I understood the object of it. **aŋ gānẹ dạbārạssụ har anạ̄ shan rịgạ kafị** they've been " rumbled " and precautions are being taken. **wannạŋ tạusạyī, bạ mụ** ~ **masạ ba** we do not see any reason for

this kindness. **bạŋ** ~ **zaman nạm ba** I see no point in remaining here. **sum fi** ~ **wạ tukwạnạŋ k̃arfẹ dạ irịn na dạ̄** they appreciate the superior value of metal pots over those of yore. (4) looked for and found (lost T. or T. previously unknown) *x* **sạ̄ yā ɓatạ, har yạnzu bạŋ** ~ **shi ba** I've not yet found the lost bull. **nā gānō makạ littāfịnkạ** I found your lost book for you. **suŋ** ~ **itātūwạ waɗandạ sukẹ̄ īyạ sāmụm mặĭ garēsụ** they discovered trees from which oil could be extracted. **yā** ~ **dạbārạr sāmụm mặĭ dagạ itātūwạ** he found a way of extracting oil from trees (*cf.* **ganī**). (5) **in nā yī, bạ nạ̄** ~ **ba** if I do it, I'll regret it. (6) *Vd.* **gānō**.

B. (**gānē**) *m.* testing bride's virginity = **būɗē** *q.v.*

C. (**Gạ̄nē**) *m.* (1) the month **Rạbī'ị lawwạl**. (2) name of P. born in that month. (3) **Sallạr** ~ = **Tākutạhā**.

D. (**gạnẹ**) *Vb.* 1A (*with dative*). (1) kept an eye on *x* **gạnẹ mini rịgā** keep an eye on my gown for me ! (2) (*only interrogatively or negatively,* in contemptuous sense) *x* **wạ̄ zại** ~ **miki** Woman, who'd spare you a glance ! **bạ wạndạ zại** ~ **mini** nobody would waste a glance on me (*cf.* **jīyẹ, sanẹ**).

E. (**gạnẹ, ganē**) *Vd.* **ganī** A.1. 7*b*, 7*f*.

gane-gane A. (**gạ̀'ne-gạ̀nē"**) *m.* repeatedly looking at.

B. (**gạ̄'ne-gạ̄nē"**) *m.* (1) repeated confidential chatting (*cf.* **gānạ**). (2) slanderous whisperings. (3) incoherent ramblings of delirious P.

ganga A. (**gạŋgā**) *f.* (*occasionally masc.*) *pl.* **gạngunạ** = *Sk.* **gạŋgummạ**. (1) (*a*) type of drum (= **kwaurẹ** 1*c*) (*cf.* **kifạ** 1*b*, **gandū** 2*c* ; **gạŋgamī** 2, 3 ; **gaŋ-gaŋ-gaŋ** ; **gạŋgummạ**). (*b*) ~ **nạ̄ tāshị** the drum is sounding. (*c*) **gạŋgar nōmā** = **kyạkkyarẹ**. (*d*) *Vd.* **marọ̄kī** 2. (*e*) **sum bugạ** (= **suŋ kaɗạ**) **gạŋgar yāk̃i sabọ dạ mū** they declared war on us. (*f*) *Vd.* **muryạ** 4. (2) (*a*) (i) barrel. (ii) anything barrel-shaped. (iii) **gạŋgar jịkī** trunk of the body. (iv) **kan zūcịyā tā yạrdā, gạŋgar jịkī bāwạ nẹ̄** where there's a will, there's a way. (*b*) **zanạntạ yā yi** ~ her bodycloth is broad enough, but too short. (c) yā ban nį ∼ bạ rufį he " sucked me dry ". (d) yanạ ganīna ∼ bạ rufį he thinks me a fool. (3) (a) halved bundle of guinea-corn (= gundūwā 2b), cf. gwammā. (b) bundle of bulrush-millet with stalks in centre and heads at each end (= gundūwā 2c), cf. gwammā. (4) Vd. gaŋgar mātā ; gaŋgar zōmō, gaŋgā-gaŋgā ; bạkiŋ ∼. (5) gaŋgar 'yaŋ wutā Vd. diluŋ 1a. (6) gaŋgar Auzunāwā Vd. gyārā 1f.

B. (gaŋga) (1) m. (sg., pl.) ganger on railway. (2) (a) Gaŋgạ ūwar tsį̄yā epithet of gambling (cācā). (b) yārǫ, bā kạ ∼ sại kā yi gaŋgạliɓi one learns from experience !

C. (gaŋgā) Sk. m. edge x (i) gaŋgaŋ hanyạ roadside. gaŋgaŋ kǫgī river-bank (= bạkī 3). (2) ạ kau dạ shī ∼ = ạ kau dạ shī ∼ dayā move it to one side (= wajē 1a). (3) gaŋgaŋ gidā environs of compound. (4) yanạ gaŋgaŋsạ he's near it.

ganga-ganga A. (gaŋgā-gaŋgā) adv. bale after bale (Vd. gaŋgā 2a.ii).

B. (gaŋ'ga-gaŋgā" used in aŋ hūrạ wutā ∼ = Kt. aŋ hūrạ wutā gaŋgā dạ kurkutu they've lit blazing fire.

gaŋgalabādī m. = gaŋgalabādīyā f. Kt. aimless roving (= gīlǫ).

gaŋgạliɓi Vd. gaŋgạ 2b.

gangama A. (gaŋgạmā) Vb. 1C int. from gamạ.

B. (gaŋgamạ) Vb. 2 int. from gạmā.

C. (gaŋgāmā) f. steep river-bank (= gāɓạ).

D. (gaŋgamā) Vd. gaŋgamēmẹ.

gaŋgạmạ sautu epithet of (1) the kite (shirwạ), (2) P. who upsets bargain of others (Vd. shūrẹ 1c).

gaŋgamau Kt. m. turmeric (= gaŋgamō).

gaŋgambū Sk. m. (1) broken-necked pot (= kururrumī q.v.). (2) collapsed well or hole.

gaŋgamē Vb. 1C int. from gamẹ.

gaŋgamēmẹ = gaŋgamī m. (f. gaŋgamēmįyā = gaŋgamā) pl. gaŋgaŋ-gaŋgaŋ huge.

gangami A. (gaŋgamī) (1) Vd. gaŋgamēmẹ. (2) m. (a) am bugạ ∼ drum's been sounded before proclamation. (b)

an yi masạ ∼ his secret's been re vealed. (c) tun dạ ka ji ∼, kạ tabbạt ạkwai maganạ ạ bāya no smoke without fire ! (d) Gaŋgamiŋ kudī dạŋ Asạntē epithet of kolanuts. (3) Sk. any drum (cf. gaŋgā 1a ; gaŋ-gaŋ-gaŋ).

B. (gaŋgāmī) m. steep riverbank (= gāɓạ)).

gaŋgamō m. turmeric.

gangan A. (gaŋ-gaŋ) (1) dạ ∼ adv. recklessly and indifferent to what may result, when acting provocatively, deceitfully, or carelessly x (a) yā kētạ dōkā dạ ∼ though knowing the law, he disobeyed it, careless of what might be done to him. yā ɓi ganī dạ ∼ he deliberately ignored it (= tākẹ 1c). (b) aikiŋ ∼ deliberately careless act. (c) wai dạ gaŋgaŋ, an cẹ dạ kạrē Mạhammạŋ what an impossible thing ! (2) dạ ∼ kakẹ you're doing it for a joke, you're not serious. (3) cf. tạkạnas ; nufị.

B. (gaŋ-gaŋ) (1) adv. yā kāmạ ∼ it's firmly fixed. sun tsarẹ wuriŋ gaŋ-gaŋ they guarded the place firmly (= gam-gam q.v.). (2) Vd. gaŋgamēmẹ.

C. (gaŋ-gan) kept on looking at (him, etc.) int. from ganī.

gaŋgancī m. act committed as in gaŋ-gaŋ.

gaŋgandā Vb. 1C (1) brought into play all one's various resources x sại dạ ya ∼, sạn naŋ ya ḳǫshi only after eating various foods did he become replete (= gararrạntā q.v.). (2) Vd. gaŋdạ-gạndē.

gaŋ-gaŋ-gaŋ m. sound of drum.

gangan-gaŋgaŋ Vd. gaŋgamēmẹ.

gaŋgānīmạ (1) f. spying. (2) ɗaŋ ∼ m. (pl. 'yaŋ ∼) spy.

gaŋgaŋkǫ m. meeting together of people in place.

gaŋgantā Vb. 1C acted as in gaŋ-gaŋ.

gaŋgạŋtsarạ f. showing-off, boastfulness x yanạ ∼ he's swanking.

gangara A. (gaŋgạrā) (1) Vb. 3A (person) descended ; (water) flowed down ; (thing) rolled down. (2) Vb. 1C x yā ∼ kwarī he descended into the valley. (3) cf. ạ gaŋgarō.

B. (gaŋgarạ) f. hawā dạ ∼ (1) (a) rising and falling ground. (b) act of

...nting and descending. (2) **yā sāmi** ∼ : got the upper hand. (3) *Vd.* **gangarę.**

C. (**gaŋgarā**) *f.* reducing sum payable to P. by sum. owed by him (= **zāmīyā** 2).

gaŋgarad dą (*Vb.* 4A caused to descend, flow down, roll down.

gaŋgarąfō *m.* burly man ; burly horse.

gaŋgarą-gaŋgar *m.* (1) thing's rolling about. (2) P. being forced to migrate from place to place. (3) *cf.* **ą gaŋgarō.**

gangaram A. (**gaŋgąram**) *m., f.* (*sg., pl.*) P. who has memorized all Koran perfectly and is teacher of those who write Koranic texts on slates (**ąllō**) : *cf.* **farī** 2*a*.iv.

B. (**gaŋgąram**) *m. and adv.* (1) forlornly *x* **yaną ząune** ∼ he's sitting forlornly (= **jųgum**). (2) **mąganą tā yi masą** ∼ = **yā ji mąganąr** ∼ he could not understand what was said. (3) *Vd.* **gaŋgarmēmę.**

gangare A. (**gaŋgąrē**) (1) *Vb.* 3A = **gaŋgąrā** 1. (2) *Vb.* 1C he sloped (a bank, *etc.*) = **zāmę.**

B. (**gaŋgarę**) *m.* (1) (*a*) falling ground. (*b*) **tudų dą** ∼ rising and falling ground (*Vd.* **gaŋgarą**). (*c*) **yā tąfi** ∼ he went downhill. (2) *Vd.* **tudų** 1*c, d.* (3) *Vd.* **samą** 1*g.*ii.

gaŋgārīyą *f. and adv.* (1) being undiluted, pure *x* **dāwą cē** ∼ **tatą** it's guinea-corn without admixture. **gąskīyā** ∼ absolute truth. **yā bā ni kudī** ∼ he paid me entirely in cash. **ƙaryā** ∼ a whopping lie (= **zallā** = **tantagaryā** 1*a*). **suląllā** ∼ just shillings. (2) fine, strapping girl.

gąŋgar mātā *f.* **Cinyą** ∼ *epithet of* thigh (because women laugh and slap their thighs).

gaŋgarmēmę = **gaŋgarmī** *m.* (*f.* **gaŋgarmēmīyā** = **gaŋgarmā**) *pl.* **gaŋgaraŋgaŋgaraŋ** = **garaŋ-gąraŋ** huge.

gaŋgarō *Vd.* **ą gaŋgarō, gaŋgara.**

gąŋgar zōmō *f.* (1) hard fungus at base of tree-trunks. (2) military felt hat.

gaŋgau *m.* (1) hole accidentally made in garment when beating it in lieu of ironing. (2) **gą̄ bābā, gą̄** ∼ he's good but is marred by some blemish.

gaŋgawārę (1) *m., f.* (*sg., pl.*). (*a*) strong P. (*b*) stubborn P. (2) *m.* thick end of grass used in aphrodisiacs (*cf.* **gagąi**).

gaŋgi *m.* (*pl.* **gaŋguną**). (1) type of **dumā-**calabash covered with membrane (**tantānī**) and used as drum for spurring on farm workers doing **gąyyā ;** it is beaten in company with the drums **kanzagī** and **kąŋkąrē.** (2) **aną̄** ∼ *the 3 drums mentioned* are being beaten.

Gaŋgū *used in* ∼ **yā kāmą ta** she's possessed by the **bǫrī** spirit *so called* (*supposed to cause leprosy*).

gaŋgummą (1) *m.* (*sg., pl.*) drummer. (2) *Vd.* **gąŋgā ; gaŋgi.**

gaŋguną (1) drums (*pl. of* **gąŋgā**). (2) *pl. of* **gaŋgi.**

gaŋhū = **gamfū.**

gani A.1 (**ganī**) *Vb.* (*Vd.* 7 *for conjugation. Vd.* A.2 *below for* **ganī** *used as v.n. and progressive*). (1) (*a*) saw *x* (i) **nā̄** ∼ I saw (him, it, etc.). (ii) **ką̄** ∼ (*etc., according to* **ka-***forms in* 7*e below*) well then, you'll be sorry ! (*cf.* 2*b*). (iii) **ąbin, sǎi wandą ya** ∼ it must be seen to be believed. (iv) **Māląm, mē ka ganị** Diviner, what did your divination (**dūbā**) reveal ? (v) **iŋ kaną̄ sǫ ką ga maƙīyiŋką** if you really want to know who is your enemy, then . . . (vi) **lā̄bāri bai zamā kąmaŋ ąbin dą ka** ∼ **dą idąŋką ba** ṣeeing is believing (= **ganī** A.2,2). (vii) **mų zubą, mų** ∼ we'll leave events to fate. (viii) **kų zō, kų** ∼ *Vd.* **zō** 3. (ix) **nā̄** ∼ **dą idǫna, nā rǎi tantamā** I know it is so, for I saw it myself. (x) **kōwā ya ga biri** *Vd.* **biri** 1*m.* (xi) **mų ganī a ƙas** *Vd.* **kąrē** 29. (xii) *Vd.* **ganō.** (xiii) **gą bāyan** *Vd.* **bāyā** 1*c, d.* (xiv) **ya ga dāmā** *Vd.* **dāmā** 1*b, c* ; 2. (xv) **dā ną̄ ganī** *Vd.* **tīląs** 1*e.* (xvi) **mų ganī ą ƙas** *Vd.* **tūwō** 21. (xvii) *Vd.* **tā ga rānā.** (xviii) **dą̄ kā ganī** *Vd.* **dą̄kārę.** (xix) **iŋ kā ga mųtųm** *Vd.* **mųtųm** 9*h.* (xx) **bąba baŋ gaŋ ką ba** *Vd.* **bą̄ba** 5. (xxi) **tā ga hannuntą** *Vd.* **hannū** 1*d.* (*b*) saw that *x* **aką ga dǎi lallē gą̄ hąlāmą bā ą̄ ciką gų̄rị** it looked as if their desire would not be realized. **muŋ ga wađansu sun cę̄** we saw that some people said that . . .

(2) looked at *x* (*a*) **yaną̄ ganina** he's

looking at me. (b) kā̰ ~ (= 7e below).
(i) look ! (ii) listen ! (cf. 1a.ii).

(3) (a) considered x a̱bi̱n da̱ na ~ my
opinion is that ... ganī yakḛ̄ ba̱n
sani̱ ba he thinks that I don't know.
i̱ŋ kuŋ ga kwā̰ īya̱ if you think yourselves capable of doing it. kada̱
ku̱ ga wanna̱ŋ ka̱mar wani a̱bi̱ŋ kirki̱
don't imagine this is something good !
ƙasā̰sha̱n da̱ aka̱ ga ka̱mar sū nḛ̄
Jāmu̱s zā su̱ fā̰ra̱ tā̰kala̱ the countries
which it seemed likely would be the
first to be provoked by the Germans.
ganiŋ ka̱nsa̱ yakḛ̄ dǎidǎi da̱ kōwā he
considers himself a match for everyone.
mū, bā ā̰ ganiŋ ka̱mar muna̱ rēna̱ shi
we are not regarded as people who
despise it. (b) took into consideration
x ta̱usa̱yinsu̱ da̱ aka̱ ji, sū bā sā̰ ganiŋ
haka̱ they took no account of the fact
that mercy had been shown them. ba̱ a̱
ga girmansa̱ ba no respect was shown
his rank. wa̱nda̱ ya ga Allā̰ he who
truly respects God.

(4) got x don ya̱ ga ƙwansa̱ that he
might get offspring.

(5) ŋ ga (lit. let me see !) m.,
f. (sg., pl.) person desirous of x ŋ ga ci̱ nē
he's a glutton. nī kaďǎi nḛ̄ ŋ ga sa̱ra̱uta̱?
am I the only seeker after office ?
Audu̱ ŋ ga kudī̱ nḛ̄ Audu is a money-
grubber.

(6) Vd. gā̰ ; gane̱ ; ganō ; ganam ;
gan da̱ ido̱ ; gāne̱ 4 ; ga̱nu.

(7) CONJUGATION : (a) past, progressive and v.n. without object ganī. (b)
past, with pronoun object gan = Sk. ganē
x nā gan shi̱ = Sk. nā ganē shi̱ = Kt.
nā gan sa̱ I saw him. (c) past with
noun object ga x nā ga Audu̱ I saw
Audu. (d) progressive or v.n., with
object ganin x yana̱ ganinsa̱ he's looking
at it. ganin dōki̱ da̱ wu̱yā it's hard to
see the horse. (e) imperative without
object ga̱nī = ka̱ ganī = kā̰ ga = ka̱ŋ
ga = kā̰ ganī = ka̱ŋ ganī = kā gā̰. (f)
imperative with pronoun object ga̱n shi =

gane̱ shi = ka̱ gan shi̱. (g) imperative
with noun object ga̱ dōki̱ (cf. gā̰) = ga̱nī
dōki̱ = ka̱ ga dōki̱ look at the horse !
(h) before dative, Vd. gane̱.

A.2 (ganī) m. (1) (progressive and v.n.
of ganī A.1 where Vd. 7a, d). (a) ganiŋ
haka̱, sǎi suka̱ gudu̱ when they saw
this, they fled. tō̰, ganim fa ya̱dda̱
gā̰ shi, bā yā̰ sa̱mmu̱, a̱mmā muka̱
ya̱rdā when we saw he did not like us,
we nevertheless agreed. (b) ana̱ ji̱,
ana̱ ~ har suka̱ gudu̱ they unexpectedly
fled. (c) mu̱tumi̱n na̱n da̱ kakḛ̄ ji̱
da̱ ~ the very person about whom we
are speaking. (d) ku̱nnē nā̰ ~, ƙa̱fō
yā yi tsīrā things develop imperceptibly
along their appointed lines. (e) ganin
Dā̰lā bā̰ shiga̱ birnī ba nḛ̄ don't count
your chickens before they're hatched !
(f) gurgu̱ yana̱ ~, a̱ sā̰ri sa̱ndā, a̱
yi masa̱ dūka̱ one must bow to circumstances. (g) dō̰miŋ ganiŋ hadiri̱,
bā nā̰ wa̱ŋkā da̱ kāshī = mā̰yē 2b.
(h) ha̱ŋka̱lī kḛ̄ ~, ido̱ gu̱lūlai nḛ̄
sometimes one's eye fails to see
through forgetfulness. (j) n nā̰ ganiŋ
kūrā da̱ rānā, ƙā̰ƙa̱ za̱n ya̱rdā ta̱ cǐjē
ni̱ nobody blunders into danger if he
can help it. (k) da̱ ganiŋ kūrā, an san
tā ci a̱kwīya̱ appearance is an index to
character. (l) ana̱ ganiŋ wuya̱m biri̱
Vd. biri̱ 1k. (m) kā ƙi ~ bīyū Vd.
bīyū 15. (n) bā̰ ganim mātā ba Vd.
fa̱tauci̱.

(2) act of seeing x (a) ~ yā fi ji̱ =
ganī yā kō̰ri ji̱ seeing is believing (=
1a.vi page 298). (b) (i) da̱ ji̱ da̱ ~ bā sā̰
ƙārḛ̄wā wonders never cease. (ii) Vd. ji̱
1c ; 1a.ii, iii. (c) ba̱cē mini da̱ ~ get out
of my sight ! (d) ganiŋ ido̱ bā yā̰ hana̱
ci̱ŋ ka̱ŋ friendship with a senior won't
save you if you're guilty. (e) (i) ya̱ba̱ŋ
ganiŋ ido̱ tsō̰rō nḛ̄ praising P. to his face
makes him distrustful. (ii) Vd. lāda̱ŋ
ganiŋ ido̱. (iii) ido̱ bābu̱ ~ Vd. banzā
1h. (iv) ganiŋ ido̱ Vd. ido̱ 1h. (f)
duk īyā̰kar ganīna as far as my eye
could reach. (g) kā̰fi̱ŋ ƙyiftā̰war ~ sǎi
suka̱ kāma̱ shi in the twinkling of an
eye they seized it.

(3) looking at x (a) ịnā rūwaŋ ~ dạ gạjīyạ (lit. mere looking should not tire one) merely look on, don't interfere ! (b) ~ bạ cị ba nẹ, dạ kạrē baị kwānā dạ yuŋwạ ba there's many a slip 'twixt cup and lip. (c) ~ gạ Wānẹ tā ịshi Wānẹ tsọraŋ Allạ example is taken from the misfortunes of others.

(4) faculty of sight x ganinsạ garma-garma nẹ his sight is weak.

(5) opinion x (a) ạ ganīna, yā fi kyau ạ barị in my opinion it would be better to give it up. gạ nāmụ ~ = mū ạ nāmụ ~ in our opinion (cf. gạ 2). (b) sū ganinsụ dăi, sụ hanạ mu they think their best course is to prevent us. (c) sunạ ganiŋ kạmar Audụ ạbōkinsụ nẹ they think Audu is their friend.

(6) Vd. ganō ; ganin compounds.

B. (Gạnī) m. = Gạnē.
C. (gānị) Zar. m. (1) having a con-fidential chat x munạ ~ = munạ gānạwa (Vd. gānạ). (2) gānịn zumạ collecting honey (= cī 13).
D. (gānī) (1) Kano Village Hausa = ganī. (2) m. (a) = ganī A.2,2 x jị dạ gānī hearing and seeing. (b) divination (= dūbā).
ganigịs = ginigịs.
ganīmạ Ar. f. (1) booty. (2) unexpected luck. (3) bargain.
ganim bạntaŋ Wạmbai m. an impossible thing.
ganim bīyū shạ bīyar m. contemptuous look.
ganin dafị Vd. zạkarạ 7.
ganin Dạlā Vd. ganī A.2,1e.
ganin dāmā Vd. dāmā 1b, c, 2.
gạnin dūkạ m. foresight.
ganiŋ gạrī m. (1) (lit. seeing the sky) (a) power of sight x mạkāfọ nẹ, bābụ ~ he's blind, without the power of sight. (b) Audụ, mạkāfọ bābụ ~ yakẹ yị Audu is a pushful P. (c) Vd. mạkāfọ 1c. (2) (lit. looking at the sky) (a) birị, kanạ ~, kạfịŋ kạ gan shị, yā rigạ yā gaŋ kạ never under-rate your opponent ! (b) ~ gạrēshị (i) he's very cute (= wạyō). (ii) he's indecisive. (3) Vd. bạfō 2g.

ganiŋ hadirị Vd. ganī A.2,1g.
ganiŋ hannū used in zạraŋ ~ = zạraŋ gāniŋ hannū m. cotton spun by bride for husband in early days of marriage.
ganiŋ idọ Vd. ganī A.2, 2d, 2e ; lādaŋ ganiŋ idọ.
ganiŋ kitsẹ Vd. kitsẹ 1b.
gāniŋ fudā m. x (1) munạ zamaŋ ~ dạ sū we're staring at them. (2) Vd. fudā 1e.
ganiŋ funtā = ganiŋ fwaf m. inquisi-tiveness.
ganiŋ kūrā Vd. ganī A.2,1j, k.
ganiŋ fwạnjī = ganiŋ fyạshī m. covetous-ness x yanạ ganiŋ fyạshiŋ ạbịn dạ Audụ ya bā nị he's jealous because Audu gave me it.
ganim mashẹfā ayā m. a contemptuous look.
ganim mātā Vd. fạtaụcī.
ganin rānā used in bā yạ ~ it finds a ready sale (= māsạ 2), cf. wutā 1f.iii.
ganiŋ wadạ yị m. imitating another (Vd. wadạ).
ganiŋ wataŋ kụrēgē m. person's trying to draw child's heel round its neck.
gāniŋyạ Ar. f. acme x yanạ kạŋ ~ tasạ it's at its acme (= gạufā 2 = gạbạ 2b = gāyạ 2a = hayyạcī), cf. kakị.
gạnjar (1) adv. (a) rānā ~ in the hottest part of day. (b) tā nifạ shi ~ she ground it coarsely (Vd. ganjạrā). (2) m. rānā tā yi ~ sun's blazing. (b) (sg., pl.) harnessed antelope (= mạzō) ; epithet is ~ mūgụn nāmạ. (3) m., f. (sg., pl.) cantankerous P.
ganjạrā Vb. 1C tā ganjạrạ nifạ she ground corn coarsely (= fantsạrā 1, 2 q.v.).
ganjare A. (ganjạrē) (1) Vb. 3A rānā tā ~ yau sun was scorching to-day (= fant-sạrē). (2) Vb. 1C kạrē yā ~ (= yā ganjarō) minị hakọrā the dog snarled at me (= fantsạrē).
B. (ganjạrē) m. coarsely ground flour (= fantsạrē).
gạnjạrtū m. type of fleeting rash (= gịr-gịrtū q.v.).
ganji A. (ganjị) m. (pl. gamuzzạ) gutta-percha tree (Ficus platyphylla) ; epithet is ~ shạ sārā.
B. (gạnjī) m. (1) old cassava (= gạn-tạmau q.v.). (2) Kt. = gạujiŋ.

gaṇjigāga *m.* (1) hannun rūwā kolas from Cameroons. (2) old cassava (= gaṇtamau *q.v.*). (3) poor tūwō. (4) sluggish horse.

gaṇkō *m.* (1) bā shi da abōkiṇ ～ he's unrivalled. (2) = gaṇgaṇko. (3) = gamkō.

gaṇnai *Sk. m. pl.* eyes (= ido).

gaṇnannē *m.* (*f.* gaṇnannīyā) *pl.* gaṇnannū esteemed (*Vd.* gaṇnu).

gaṇnī *m.* deep hollow between deep-set eyes.

gaṇnu *Vb.* 3B is (was) highly esteemed.

gano A. (ganō) (1) *Vb.* 1E (*d.f.* ganī) *x* (*a*) nā ～ shi daga nēsa (i) I saw him afar. (ii) I saw him coming from afar (1*a* = gānō 1), *cf.* tsiṇkāya. (*b*) mu ganō wa idammu let us see for ourselves! (*cf.* ganam). (2) *prep.* to *x* yā yi tafīye-tafīyē ～ ḳasāshē he made many journeys abroad.

B. (gānō) *Vb.* 1E. (1) nā ～ shi daga nēsa = ganō 1*a*. (2) foresaw T. happening to P. *x* nā ～ maka halaka (amfānī) I foresee death (some benefit) coming to you. (3) nā ～ maka azancinsa I thought out and explained the meaning to you. (4) *Vd.* gānę 4.

gā nōmā *Sk. used in* ɗaṇ ～ *m.* (*pl.* 'yaṇ ～) P. farming for wages (*cf.* ḳōdagō).

gansai *m.* = gansakūka.

gansaḳēḳe = gansaḳī *m.* (*f.* gansaḳēḳīyā = gansaḳā) *pl.* gansaḳai-gansaḳai huge.

gansakūka *f.* (1) green slime on water. (2) moss (1, 2 = lanyā 1*b* = fitsārī 8 = damsakūka).

gansamēmę = gansamī *m.* (*f.* gansamēmīyā = gansamā) *pl.* gansamai-gansamai huge.

gansaṇsaṇ *m.* hugeness *x* macę cē ～ = macę cē ～ da ita.

gansarḳi *m.* (*sg., pl.*) poor type of cloth like sāḳi but with woof of black thread instead of black and blue (= zābakō).

gansarwa *f.* (*sg., pl.*) circular stand for pot (*often consisting of neck broken off another pot* (katangga)).

ganshęḳā = gamshęḳā.

gantafalfalā (1) *f.* idle roving. (2) *m., f.* (*sg., pl.*) idle roamer.

gantakā *f.* good luck.

gantalī *m.* idle roving.

gantamā *Kt. f.* big axe used as weapon (especially to attack rival claimant in hunting dispute).

gantamau (1) *m.* tough cassava a year or more old (= ajiṇgirī = gaṇjigāga 2 = gaṇjī 1 = gaudę 2 = ḳārāza = akul 2*c*). (2) *m., f.* (*sg., pl.*) daft P.

gantarma *m.* (*sg., pl.*) big, oafish man.

gantasō (1) *m.* bargain. (2) what a bargain!

gantsara A. (gaṇtsara) (1) *Vb.* 2 is (was) bent in a curve (*x* bow; back of dancer), *cf.* magaṇtsarī. (2) *f.* curvature *x* ～ garēshi it forms a curve. (3) *Vb.* 2 ate much of T.

B. (gantsarā) (1) *Vb.* 1C. (*a*) (*with dative*) did excessively *x* yā ～ masa kāyā he overloaded it. yā ～ masa kibīya he seriously injured him with arrow. yā ～ masa sandā he gave him a severe beating with a stick. suṇ ～ masa ḳyūyā they refused his orders or proposal point-blank. yā ～ mini baḳar magana he roundly abused me. aṇ gantsara mutūwa a gidan naṇ there's been a death in this home. (*b*) tā gantsara tūwō she ground corn coarsely for tūwō (= fantsarā). (2) *Vb.* 3A yā ～ da gudu he fled.

gantsara gūtsū = gantsara giṇdī *m.* (1) badly-made tūwō. (2) tūwō made from coarse flour (*cf.* gantsarā 1*b*).

gantsarę (1) *Vb.* 1C. (*a*) yā ～ shi da kāyā (kibīya), *etc.* = gantsara 1*a*. (*b*) ate up all large amount of T. available. (*c*) tā gantsarę bāḳī she made sneering grimace (*only done by women*) = gātsinā. (2) *Vb.* 3A. (*a*) = gantsara 1. (*b*) fātar idansa tā gantsarō his eyelid's everted by illness (= burma 2*b*).

gantsarwā *f.* (1) curvature, convexity. (2) dōki nē mai ～ it's a horse with well-arched hindquarters (*cf.* bāyā 1*h*).

gantsaura *f.* a lead alloy.

gantsī *m.* disrespectful speech (= gautsī).

Gānū (place in Kano) yā jē ～ he understood (*with play on this place-name, and* gānu " is intelligible ", *cf.* gānę).

gānun dūka *m.* foresight.

gānuwā = gānwā *f.* (1) (*a*) rampart round town. (*b*) ḳaraṇ ～ *Vd.* ḳaren 4.

(2) mound round farm of corn, sugar-cane, or cassava, sometimes with **shiŋgē** on top, to keep off animals. (3) *Kt.* wall of town (= **gā̀rū**). (4) **yā dadę kạmar gānūwar Amīnạ** it's as old as the hills (*cf.* **mạndawạrī** 2). (5) **dan** ~ *m.* (*f.* **'yar** ~) *pl.* **'yaŋ** ~. (*a*) bastard (= **shēgę**1*a*). (*b*)*Kt.* seasonal immigrant (= **dāgirạ** *q.v.*). **gaŋwō** *Sk. m.* carrier's headpad, *etc.* (= **gammō** *q.v.*). **ganyau** A. (**gạnyau**) *m.*, *f.* (*sg.*, *pl.*) P. always grinning (*epithet is* **mun cạkarạ** ~). B. (ganyau-gạnyau) *x* **yanā̀ dạ ha-ɓ̣ōrā** ~ he has protruding teeth (= **gạyau**). **ganyē** *m.* (*pl.* **ganyā̀yē** = **ganyā̀yakī**). (1) (*a*) (i) leaf. (ii) foliage. (*b*) **yā kadạ masạ** ~ = **yā kadạ masạ kargō** it left him " all of a dither " ; he intimidated him (*Vd.* **kadạ** 1*m*). (*c*) **ịndạ akạ san darajạr gōṛọ, naŋ a kạn nēmam masạ ganyē** if T. is prized, it is looked after. (*d*) **kạ̀mạ ganyē** *Vd.* **shikạ rēshę.** (*e*) **rūwạ̀ ganyē** *Vd.* **samạ** 1*e*. (2) any shrub. (3) being well-dressed *x* **bạ̀ kyạu sukạ fī tạ ba,** ~ **sukạ fī tạ** it's not in *beauty* they excel her but in *dress.* **mụtụm nē kyạkkyāwā, sǎi dǎi bābụ** ~ he's handsome but ill-clad. (4) *Kt.* **sunā̀ d2anyaŋ** ~ they're close friends. (5) **ganyan cēdīyā** *m.* mediumly blue colour. (6) **ganyan tsāmīyā** type of **zạyyanạ.** **gạnzākị** *m.* morning-star (= **gạmzākị** *q.v.*). **gạnzạṛō** *m.* detachment left to guard villages (= **gạmzạṛō** *q.v.*). **gap** *x* **yanā̀** ~ **dạ kṑgī** it's near the river (*cf.* **gaf**). **gạptarạ** = **gạftarạ.** **gar** *Vd.* **garạ.** **gara** A. (**gārā**) *f.* (1) (*a*) wedding-presents given bride by her parents. (*b*) **gạbaŋ** ~ *m. x* **an sā̀ matạ rā̀gō ạ gạbaŋ** ~ a ram is at the head of her presents in the wedding-procession. (*c*) **raŋ** ~ *Vd.* **bịkī** 1*b*. (*d*) **bū dạ** ~ *Vd.* **bạbūdę.** (*e*) **dạgạ dạushe gārar kīshīyā** it's an ill wind which blows nobody any good. (2) extra-special food (particularly that

for guests) *x* **yā shā** ~ (*a*) he ate some very tasty food. (*b*) he received presents. (3) (*a*) **gārar bạ̀ɓī** food pre-pared for guests. (*b*) **yā kashę** ~ he ate (or gave guests) special food. (4) **yā maishē nị** ~ **dạ kā̀jī** = **yā yi jā̀kiŋ kai** ~ **dạ nī** he treated me as a fool (= **dā̀dị**). B. (**gāra** = **gā̀ra**). (1) it would be better to *x* ~ **kạ yi hakạ** you'd better do this (= **gwạmmạ** *q.v.*), (*cf.* **hāsạlī**). (2) ~ **kạ ci na ɓạzāmī** *Vd.* **bạ̀ɓī** 2*s.* (3) ~ **yā̀ɓē** *Vd.* **yā̀ɓē** 2*b.* (4) ~ **shimfịdạ fuskạ** *Vd.* **shimfịdā** 1*b.* (5) ~ **kạ jē dạ kaŋkạ** *Vd.* **tsịnī** 2. (6) ~ **baɓim bantē** *Vd.* **tsịrārạ** 1*b.* (7) ~ **ạ jā** *Vd.* **rịgā** 1*t.* C. (**garạ**) (1) *Vb.* 3A. (*a*) (scorpion, lizard, cycle) skimmed along *x* **kḕkē yanā̀ garā̀wā gar** the cycle is bowling along. (*b*) hastened to *x* **nā** ~ **kā̀sūwā** I hastened to market. (2) *Vb.* 1A. (*a*) rolled (circular T.) rapidly along. (*b*) rode (cycle), drove (motor) quickly. (3) (*a*) **Garạ** *m.*, *f.* (*sg.*, *pl.*) Igala. (*b*) **Attā** ~ Chief of the Igala (*Vd.* **kwā-kwạ̀** 4, **Attā**). D. (**gạrā**) *f.* (1) (*a*) (i) white ant. (ii) (*collective*) *x* **mạnyaŋ** ~ large termites. (*b*) **an yi gudụ̀ŋ** ~, **aŋ hayę zagō** out of the frying-pan into the fire ! (*c*) **watạ yā tsērę ɓaŋkancịŋ** ~ it's useless to slander P. of proved integrity. (*d*) **ūwar** ~ *f.* queen-termite. (2) **gidaŋ** ~ *m.* ant-hill (*cf.* **sūṛị, jiɓā**). (3) **cị̀ŋ** ~ *m.* being punctured in several places (*Vd.* **cị̀ŋ gạrā**). (4) *Vd.* **nāmạ** 5. (5) *Sk.* = **gạrē** (*cf.* **gạrai**). E. (**gạ̀rā**) *adv.* forlornly, dazedly *x* **yanā̀ tsạye** ~. **gārạcē** *Vb.* 1C *x* **nā** ~ **shi dạ wannạŋ** I prefer it to this. **gạrā̀funī** *m.* (1) the twining plant *Momor-dica balsamina* (*used for making* **fạtę̀-fatē** *and for cleaning metals*). (2) **gạman daŋgā dạ** ~ **ya gamạ mu** we're not related, but are fortuitously to-gether (*x* through common task, *etc.*), *Vd.* **gạmō** 1*d.* **gạrạ-gạrạ** *f. and adv.* **idạnsạ yā yi** ~ = ~ **yakę̀ ganī** he has weak sight. **gạrā̀hunī** *m.* = **gạrā̀funī.** **garai** A. (**garai**) *m. and adv.* clearness of sight, water, or mirror *x* **rūwā̀ yā** kwạntā ∽ water has settled and is now clear.

B. (gạrai) *Sk.* = gạrēshị *x* dạ kudī ∽ he has money (= dạ kudī gạrēshị), *Vd.* gạrā 5.

garai-garai *used in* ∽ mukạ bīyā we paid in full.

gạrājē *m.* (1) haste. (*a*) munạ aikị dạ ∽ we're hurrying on with our work. yanạ ∽ har yanạ gudụ he's in such a hurry that he's running. (*b*) ∽ bạ ƙarfī ba nẹ the more haste the less speed. (*c*) yārọ bạ gạrājē tsōfō nẹ a spineless boy is useless. (2) maị ∽ (*a*) *m., f.* P. acting quickly and carelessly (*epithet is* " Maị ∽, gạ damị ! ", sǎi ya cẹ " ạ zubạ mīyạ ! "). (*b*) *Vd.* gạjērē 2.

garaji A. (gārājī = *Kt.* gạ̄rājī) *Fil. m.* black sewing-thread.

B. (gārạjī) *m.* a fodder grass with edible grain.

garạ̄kā, garạ̄kē *Vd.* garkā ; garkẹ.

garạlī *m.* yā kashẹ garạlinsạ he achieved his aim (= garạrī).

garam *m.* (*sg., pl.*). (1) an sạ masạ ∽ prisoner has been secured to log (tūrụ 2) with staple (= gam 1*c*). (2) umbrella-stick. (3) *Vd.* gạŋgarmēmẹ. (4) *Kt.* (*a*) ɗaŋ ∽ *m.* (*f.* 'yar ∽) *pl.* 'yaŋ ∽ cadger. (*b*) yā zō minị garam he cadged from me.

gạrāmạ *f.* yā fasạ ∽ he got benefit, bargain, lucky find, *etc.*

gạrambūwā *f.* (*pl.* gạrambī) children's plaited grass-armlets, *etc.* (= dạrambūwā *q.v.*).

garam-garạm ∽ garaŋ-gạraŋ.

garancị *Vd.* 'yaŋ garancị.

garandạŋ (*or* gạrandạŋ) = garai ; garaigarai.

gạrandīyạ what long teeth ! (*cf.* gạraŋgị).

garaŋ-gạraŋ (1) *adv.* (*a*) forlornly ; dazedly *x* yanạ tsạye ∽ (= gạrạ). (*b*) yā būshẹ ∽ it's quite dried. (2) huge (*pl. of* gạŋgarmēmẹ) (2 = ragam-rạgam = rakam-rạkam).

gạraŋgarkị *m.* (1) big and strong man. (2) tall and strong man.

garaŋgātsạ (1) *f.* type of sugar-cane. (2) *m.* loud chatterer.

gạraŋgātsụmī = gạraŋhōtsạmī.

gạraŋgị what long, thick horns ! (*cf.* gạrandīyạ).

gạrangọ *used in* ɗaŋ ∽ *m. epithet of* indigo (shūnī).

gạraŋhōtsạmī *m.* (*f.* gạraŋhōtsạmā) *pl.* gạraŋhọ̄tsạmai. (1) pushful P. (*epithet is* ∽ mūgụm bạbba, anạ rạbō, yanạ cịŋ gāyā). (2) strong, unruly horse.

garara A. (gạrārạ) (1) (*rolled* -r-) *f.* hessian material (= ạlgarārạ). (2) *flapped* -r-). (*a*) *f.* yā yi ∽ he's blind though his eyes look normal. (*b*) *m., f.* (*sg., pl.*). (i) P. blind, *as in* 1*b*. (ii) maị idọ ɗayā yā fi mạkāfọ gōmạ duk dạ ụbansụ gạrārạ half a loaf is better than no bread. (iii) gạrārạ bā yā gōdẹ Allạ̄ sǎi yā ga mạkāfọ nobody appreciates his blessings till robbed of them.

B. (gạrarạ) *used in* yanạ yāwọ ∽ he's roving aimlessly.

gararambạ *f.* aimless wandering.

garari A. (gạrarī) *m.* (1) trouble *x* yā jāwō wạ kansạ ∽ he brought trouble on himself. (2) (*Ar.*) yā kashẹ gạrarinsạ he achieved his aim (= garạlī).

B. (gạrarī) *m.* aimless roving.

gararrạjē *Vb.* 3A *int. from* garjẹ.

gararrạntā (1) *Vb.* 1D brought into play all one's various resources *x* sǎi dạ ya ∽, sạn naŋ ya ƙōshi only after eating various foods did he become replete. yā gararrạntạ ạbiŋ hannunsạ, ya sạyi dōkị by realizing on all he could, he manạ̄ged to buy a horse (= gaŋgandā). (2) *Kt. Vb.* 3A hurried.

garas A. (gạrạs) *Sk.* = gạrai.

B. (gạrạs) (1) *x* fātạ tā būshẹ ∽ the skin has completely dried. (2) = gaŋgārīyạ.

gạrāsạ *Sk.* = gạrai.

gạrạs-gạrạs (1) *adv.* sunạ cịnsạ ∽ they're eating it (kolanut, cassava, *etc.*) crunchingly (*cf.* gạrzā). (2) *m., f.* (*sg., pl.*) witless P.

garau *m. and adv.* clearness of sight, water, or mirror (= garai *q.v.*).

gạrauniỵā *f.* aimless wandering about.

gạrawạ *f.* " throwing a sprat to catch a whale ".

gạrāyā *f.* (*pl.* gạrạ̄yū). (1) the musical instrument kōmō. (2) *Vd.* damō 3 ; gạ̄garạ 3*c* ; Gāgarẹ ; Ƙạtūrū.

Garāzạ *epithet of* P. holding office of Bardē 3.

garāzun-garāzụŋ *used in* maị cịŋ garāzuŋ-garāzụŋ receiver of stolen goods (= ɓạrāwạn zạune).

Garba A. (Garbạ) (1) name for any man called Ạbū bakạr. (2) *Vd.* yạyī 4. B. (garbạ) *f.* obsolete type of wedding-drumming.

garɓa A. (garɓạ) *Vb.* 1A tā ~ niƙạ she ground corn coarsely (= fantsạrā *q.v.*). B. (garɓā) *f.* coarsely-ground flour (= fantsạrē).

garbạlī *Kt. m.* fence of posts with bars across top.

garɓạlī *m.* a food of flour with boiling water and milk.

garɓẹ *Vb.* 1A ground ail (the flour) coarsely (*Vd.* garɓạ).

garɓị *m.* (1) (*secondary v.n. of* garɓạ) *x* tanạ̄ garɓịŋ gērō = tanạ̄ garɓạ gērō she's grinding the millet coarsely. (2) = gạrɓā.

garbịl *Zar. m.* = gạrbul.

gạrdā *f.* young pods of locust-bean tree (dǫrawạ).

gạrdagǫ = gạrdāgujī *m.* burly fellow.

gardamạ *f.* wrangle, dispute, *etc.* (= gaddamạ *q.v.*).

gardancị *m.* the profession of a gardị 1.

gardạndamī *Vd.* gaddamạ.

gạrdạntā *Vb.* 3A disputed, wrangled.

gạrdāwā *Vd.* gardị.

gạrdāyẹ (1) *m.* (*a*) obstinacy *x* yanạ̄ ~ he (P. ; horse) is obstinate or dogged. (*b*) *Kt. Acacia machrostachys.* (2) *epithet of a* Gạlādīmạ *q.v.*

gardị *m.* (*pl.* gạrdạ̄wā). (1) (*a*) (i) snake-charmer. (ii) Sarkịŋ ~ the head of the snake-charmers. (*b*) (i) hyena-tamer. (ii) shịgā rāmịŋ kūrā bạ̄ na ƙaramịŋ gardị ba nẹ̄ do not undertake T. that is beyond you ! (*c*) conjurer ; magician (*cf.* tirɗẹ). (2) pupil just beginning to memorize Koran (*cf.* kūrị). (3) obstinate or dogged P. or horse.

gardī *m.* (1) flavour of cassava, etc. (2) flavour of roasted ground-nuts *or of* roasted millet *or of* roasted beniseed. (3) *cf.* shạ̄ ~.

gạrdō = gar'do-gardō‖ = gạrdam bidạ *m.* (1) children's game of prodding heaps

of sand to find T. hidden there (*cf.* 'yā 5*b* ; bidạ 5) = dạgạbi-dạgạbī. (2) type of birdsnare.

gare A. (garē) *Vd.* gạ. B. (gārẹ) *f.* (*pl.* gārukạ). (1) gown without gusset (= wutsīyạr shirwạ). (2) gạ̄rạn 'yan Sarkī gown of hybrid type between gạ̄rẹ and gịrkē (= tạshi lāfīyạ). (3) *Vd.* falmạrạŋ. C. (garē) *m.* (1) any game of rolling discs along, *etc.* (*cf.* garạ). (2) gudụŋ ~ pattering run (as of guinea-fowl, lizard, *etc.* (*cf.* garạ).

gare-gare *used in* am bīyā shị ~ he was " paid on the nail " (liga-liga).

garẹ̄kanī cotton-plots, *etc.* (*pl. of* garkā).

garẹ̄manī hoes (*pl. of* gạrmā).

garēgạ *Vd.* lallẹ 2*a*.

garẹ̄rā *f.* (1) (*a*) *Kano* guinea-corn heads from which grain has been threshed. (*b*) *Kt.* bulrush-millet from which grain has been threshed. (*c*) *Kt.* guinea-corn heads stripped (tumẹ) for fodder (= *Kt.* sōshīyā 2). (2) *Kt.* fibrous vein in centre of frond of kabạ, giginyạ (= gạzarī), *cf.* karị.

garẹ̄rī *Sk. m.* = garẹ̄rā 2.

garẹ̄rīyā *f.* = garẹ̄rā 2.

garẹ̄wanī petrol-tins, *etc.* (*pl. of* garwā).

Garga A. (Gargạ) *epithet of man called* Ạlī *q.v.* B. (gargā) *Sk. Vd.* garkā.

gargada A. (gargadā) *f.* (1) bad wash-out on road. (2) mange of goats and sheep. B. (gạrgādạ) *Vb.* 2 *int. from* gādā.

gargadạ *Vb.* 2. (1) admonished *x* ạbịn dạ ya gạrgạdē kạ dạ nī the injunctions he gave you about me. (2) gạrgạdō well, if you insist on admonishing me, let's get it over !

gargadī *m.* admonition, warning *x* nā sạmi ~ I was warned. nạ̄ yi makạ ~ I'll give you some good advice. ~ nẹ̄ gạ wandạ ya jī shị " a nod is as good as a wink to a blind horse "

gargaji *int. from* gạji.

gạrgajīgạ (1) *f. x* yanạ̄ gạrgajīgạr aikị he is working steadily. (2) *m., f.* (*sg., pl.*) P. acting *as in* 1.

gargājīyā *f.* olden times *x* ạl'ādạn naŋ ta ~ cẹ̄ = ạl'ādạn naŋ tuŋ ~ cẹ̄ this is an ancient custom (*cf.* gạ̄dā).

Gạrgāmị *epithet of any man called* Ạlĩ *q.v.*
gar-gar *used in* (1) yanậ dậ ƙarfĩ ∼ it's
tough, strong (= gagar). (2) hatsĩ
yā kai ∼ corn's quite ripe.
gargara A. (gargarậ) *f.* yā kai ∼ (i)
P. or animal is in death-throes (= mậ-
gậgĩ 3 = kākārĩ 2 = muhutalậr = shậ-
rafậ), *Vd.* mutūwậ 1*a*.ii,iii. (ii) it
(garment) is worn-out (*Vd.* mutūwậ
1*a*.ii,iii ; mutụ 1*a*.i). (iii) cĩwọ yā kai ∼
crisis of the sickness is reached and
patient near death. yuŋwậ tā kai ∼
famine is at its worst point. (iv) hậƙurĩ
yā kai ∼ patience is exhausted (*Vd.*
kakị).
   B. (gạrgạrā) *f.* rashness.
gargarĩ *used in* jaŋ gargarĩ *m.* red clay
soil (= bậriŋgō).
gargasa A. (gạrgāsā) (1) *m., f.* hairy. (2)
m. a hairy bulrush-millet.
   B. (gargạsā) *Vb.* 1C *int. from* gasậ.
gargatsa A. (gạrgātsậ) *Vb.* 2 *int. from*
gậtsā.
   B. (gargậtsā) *Vb.* 1C. (1) *int. from*
gātsậ. (2) did T. incompletely.
gargaza A. (gargạzā) *Vb.* 3A *int. from* gazậ.
   B. (gạrgazā) *m.* the cichlid perch
(= karfasā).
gargẹ *Sk. m.* (*pl.* garuggậ) herd (= garkẹ
q.v.).
gari A. (gậrĩ) *m.* (1) (*a*) flour. (*b*) gậrin
niƙậ coarsely-ground millet flour for
mixing with water or milk. (*c*) ậ
ƙârậ wậ ∼ rūwậ ? debt on debt !
(*cf.* ậ 1*s*). (*d*) gậrim mậi rōwậ ậ farau-
farau ya kậŋ ƙârẹ miser always stints
himself. (*e*) yārọ dậ ∼ ậbōkin tậfĩyậr
mậnyā this is a lad equal in ability to an
adult. (*f*) talakậ ∼ nẹ̃ the poor are clay
in the hands of the rulers (*Vd.* talậkậ
2). (*g*) sun rabậ ∼ they've quarrelled
(= rabā-rậbậ). (*h*) gậrin sadakậ
Vd. sadakậ 1*b*. (*j*) *cf.* shậ gậrĩ. (*k*)
jikin dāwậ duk ∼ nẹ̃ an inferior
has no choice but to obey
orders. (*l*) ɓērā yā shanyẹ gậriŋ
kyaŋwā *Vd.* ɓērā 1*d*. (*m*) gậriŋ ậrauyẹ
Vd. ậrauyē. (*n*) gậriŋ gậyyā *Vd.* ribdị
1*b*. (*o*) gậriŋ wākē *Vd.* būtsậrĩ 3. (*p*)
ɓātậ ∼ *Vd.* wākē 9. (*q*) shanyậr ∼
Vd. yậmmā 2*c*. (*r*) ∼ ậbin dakậ *Vd.*
dakậ 2*g*. (*s*) dậ gậriŋkậ akẹ̃ tūwō *Vd.*

būƙẹ. (*t*) kậ bā dậ ∼ *Vd.* niƙậ 2*c*. (2)
powder *x* (*a*) gậrin tābậ powdered
tobacco, snuff. (*b*) tābậ tā bậmbantậ
dậ gậriŋ gērō *epithet of* any tobacco.
(*c*) = shāfị 3, 4. (3) gậrin yāƙị levy of
funds for war.
   B. (gậrĩ) *m.* (*pl.* garūrukậ = garū-
rūwậ = *Kt.* garurrậ = *Sk.* garurrukậ)
(1) (*a*) town (*cf.* birnĩ) *x* (i) gậrim
Makurdĩ the town of Makurdi. (ii)
yā shā ∼ he has lived long in the town
(*cf.* 3*c*.ii *below*). (iii) mậi ∼ = wậŋ ∼
Vd. Sarkĩ 2*b*. (iv) mậganiŋ ∼ mậi
nĩsā, tậfĩyậ effort brings success. (v)
ta sāfẽ ta yārọ, ậmmā in rānā tā yĩ,
sậi mutậnaŋ ∼ a new broom sweeps
clean. (vi) hājậr mậi ∼ *Vd.* dillancị.
(vii) ∼ bā yậ tậshị ? bậllē magậnậ ?
can any statement be regarded as
absolutely certain ? (viii) gậrin dādĩ
bậ kusa ba nẹ̃ one's ambitions are
always just beyond one's reach. (ix)
mutậnaŋ ∼ dậ wutsĩyậ *Vd.* wutsĩyậ 1*j*.
(x) ∼ dậ rīmĩ, jēmāgẹ bā yậ rasậ dākiŋ
kwānā go the right way to work !
(*b*) (note *pl. pronoun*). (i) zậŋ kōmậ
gậrimmụ I'll return to my home town
(*only chief of the town would say* zậŋ
kōmậ gậrīna). tā tậfi gậrinsụ she went
to her home town (*cf.* gidā 1*c*). (ii)
rận naŋ ya cẹ̃ " gậ gậriŋkụ naŋ " then
he died. (*c*) ɗaŋ ∼ (*f.* 'yar ∼) *pl.*
'yaŋ ∼ *x* (i) ɗaŋ ∼ nẹ̃, bậ bậƙō ba
nẹ̃ he's a local man, not a stranger, he's
expert not novice, he's no fool. (ii)
Vd. rābā 1*e*. (iii) *Vd.* 'yaŋ garancị.
(iv) 'yar gậrĩ *f.* type of cotton. (*d*)
azụmin dū ∼ *m.* the month Rậmalaŋ.
(*e*) ∼ nẹ̃ har dậ kậsūwā, sậi rashiŋ
ginị he's no ordinary P. (*cf.* ginị 4*b*).
(*f*) (i) yā ci ∼ he captured the town.
(ii) nā ci ∼ I've won (in game, bet,
etc.). (iii) nā ci gậrinsậ I've broken the
back of this task. (*g*) nā bā kậ ∼ I
gĩve up ! (when trying to guess the
answer to riddle, *etc.*). (*h*) (i) wannậŋ
lậbāri jiŋ ∼ nẹ̃ this news is mere
gossip. (ii) bậ ka dậ jiŋ ∼ = bā kậ
jiŋ ∼ you're disobedient. (iii) *Vd.*
3*c below*. (*j*) gamậ ∼ *m.* T. in common
use (*Vd.* gamậ gậrĩ). (*k*) gamậ ∼ *m.*
roving *x* gamậ ∼ gậrēshị he roves.

(*l*) bāyaŋ ∼ *Vd.* bāyā 2*c*. (*m*) ịnā
zamaŋ gạrī how's life with you ?
(*reply* Ạlhamdụ lịllāhị. *Women reply*
dạ gọ̄dīyā) = hạƙurī 1*b*. (*n*) iŋ
kā zō ∼ *Vd.* wutsīyạ 1*j*. (*o*) *Vd.*
sạnsạŋ ∼ ; zạuna gạriŋkạ. (2) (*a*)
na ∼, *etc.*, good (*Vd.* na gạrī). (*b*)
ạbiŋ ∼ shī akę̄ wạ gūɗạ one rejoices
at good things. (*c*) yārọ dạ ∼ nę̄
he's a sensible young fellow.
(3) (*no pl.*) (*a*) sky *x* (i) ∼ yā
wāyę day has dawned : troubles are
over. (ii) dọ̄mim munāfụkī ∼ bā
yā ƙịŋ wāyę̄wā intrigue comes to light
sooner or later. (iii) kō̄mē nīsan darē ∼
yā wāyę every cloud has a silver lining.
(iv) kō̄wā ya yi ƙaryar darē, ∼ yā
wāyę murder will out. (v) kulluŋ
gạriŋ Allā ya wāyę, mā ji aŋ gamạ
ƙīrạr wani jirgī every day we hear that
they've built another ship. (vi) *Vd.*
wāyę. (vii) ∼ yā gamạ girā = ∼ yā
rikịcē the sky is lowering (*cf.* 3*d below*).
(*b*) *Vd.* ganiŋ gạrī. (*c*) (i) yanā jịŋ ∼
he's feeling the pinch of poverty (*cf.*
1*h above*). (ii) yā shā ∼ he had a hard
time (*cf.* 1*a*.ii *above*). (*d*) ∼ yā yi ∼ =
gạrī yā rikịcē these are hard times !
(*cf. in this sense* bạrkạtai, cịkạ sạurā,
bazarā, ɗauriŋ kạlạŋgū, ɗauriŋ kanjau, ɗauriŋ kanzagī, ɗauriŋ kạtę̄-kạtę̄,
ɗauriŋ kuntukurū, ɗaurịn tākurī, ɗaurịn
rīdī, ˉdụgu-dụgu, gūgạ 3, kiki-kạkạ,
tsạye 4, tukkum, wāwại). (*e*) fādụ̄war ∼
Vd. fādụ̄wā 4. (4) sāmụŋ ∼ (= sāmụŋ wurī). kuturū gāɗā cikin ramạ
what a parvenu ! (4A) *Vd.* kạryạ ∼ (5)
Vd. gạrin. (6) type of fish.

*garībancị *Ar. m.* strangeness (*Vd.* gạrībị).

gạrībị *m.* (*f.* gạrībịyā) *pl.* gạrībai *Ar.* (1)
unusual. (2) stranger.

gạrīdō the word dọ̄garị transposed in
code-speech (zạurạncē).

*garīfị *m.* (*f.* gạrīfịyā) *pl.* gạrīfai handsome.

gari-gari A. (ga'ri-gạrī") *adv.* abundantly.
B. (gā'ri-gārī") *adj. m., f.* (*sg., pl.*)
powdery (*cf.* gā̄rī).

gārijī *m.* a fodder grass with edible grain.

gārịƙāƙi *m.* burly fellow.

gạrin (*derived from* gạrī). (1) *prep.* (*a*) (i)
in order to *x* sun zō ∼ ɗaukạŋ kāyā

they've come to take the loads (= dọ̄-
min). ∼ ƙāƙạ why ? (ii) because of *x*
gạriŋ hakạ because of this (= dọ̄min).
(*b*) while *x* ∼ hawan dōkị, rịgā tā
kēcę while mounting the horse, the
gown became torn. (2) *conj.* in order
that *x* sun zō ∼ sụ ɗauki kāyā they've
come to take the loads.

gārīyọ *m.* double-bladed Barebari
throwing-weapon.

gạrjāgumī *m.* grubby lout.

gạrjayyạ *f.* having great difficulty in
doing T.

garje A. (garję) *Vb.* 3A. (1) behaved obstinately. (2) kạrē yā ∼ (= yā garzō)
minị haƙọrā the dog snarled at me.
B. (garjē) *m.* (1) embroidery on gown
at right-angles to lịnzāmị. (2) *Sk.* the
type of eczema callẹd kircī 2.
C. (gạrjē) *Vd.* gạrzā.

garji A. (gạrjī) *m.* (1) gạrjin rānā
scorching heat of sun. (2) *Kt.* rubbing
indigo on body to give blue tinge to
gown (= shūnim battạ *q.v. under*
shūnī 3*a*, *b*).
B. (gạrjị) (1) what scorching sun !
(2) what perseverance at grinding, *etc.*
(*as in* gạrzā).
C. (gạrji) *Vd.* gạrzā.

garkā *f.* (*pl.* gạrāƙā = garēkanī). (1) fenced
plot of cotton, cassava, or tobacco
(*Vd.* fagē 2). (2) *Sk.* open space in front
of compound (= fage 1*b*). (3) ɗam bạŋ
∼ = *Sk.* ɗam bāyaŋ ∼ = *Sk.* ɗam
bāyaŋ gidā the son of a slave-girl, who
on death of her master, marries, she
previously having been freed on bearing
her master a child.

garƙa A. (garƙa) *Vb.* 1A did abundantly
x aŋ ∼ wutā (hayāƙī) they've made big
fire (smoke). aŋ ∼ dāwạ ạ gō̄nạr
there's big guinea-corn crop in that
farm. aŋ ∼ wạ dōkị lịnzāmị the bit's
too large for the horse.
B. (gạrƙā) *Vb.* 2. (1) ate much of.
(2) yā gạrƙi kāyā he took up a heavy
load.

garƙạmā *Vb.* 1C = garƙạ 2.

garkę *m.* (*pl.* gạrāƙā = garāƙē = *Sk.*
garukkạ). (1) (*a*) herd of cattle ;
flock of sheep or birds. (*b*) kạmar
garkyạm kīfī dạ garkyạn damō as

different " as chalk and cheese ". (2)
(a) cattle-pen. (b) yā yi ɗam bặ ƙặrạ,
gōdị̄yā dạ kwānaŋ ∼ he bitterly rued
his act when too late (= gọ̄be 3). (3)
dūbaŋ ∼ m. squint ; cast in eye (=
fạṛallī = dūbaŋ gọ̄rā 1). (4) garặkā,
'yā'yam Mūsā epithet of carriers
(lēburōrī). (5) hạṛāṛạ ∼ Kt. m. = 3.
(6) ūwar f. ∼ leader of herd or flock.
garƙẹ (1) Vb. 1A yā ∼ ƙôfạ he closed
door firmly (= dannẹ 1). (2) Vb. 3A
(crop) is dense.
garƙị (1) what a lot ! (as in garƙạ). (2)
how firmly door is closed ! (cf. garƙẹ).
gạrkī Vd. gạrkūwā.
garkọ m. used in (1) ạbiŋ yā yi ∼ = ạbiŋ
yā cệ ∼ it's a handsome thing. (2)
yā yi zūwạm fặrar Garkọ his coming was
a waste of time. (3) yā yi haƙan
rĩị̄yar Garkọ, yā wucẹ rūwạŋ he went
on " wild goose chase ". (4) Majị̄
garkọ epithet of any man named
Yūsufụ.
gạrkūwā f. (pl. gạrkī). (1) (a) any shield.
(b) sū nệ ∼ tasạ gạ ạzzạ̄lụmai they
protect him against tyrants. (c) suŋ
kārạ gạrkī they had altercation. (d)
type of insect with shield-like shell.
(2) film x (a) gạrkūwar kụnū film on
gruel (= kạdarkọ 2 = yānā 1 q.v.). (b)
gạrkūwar nōnọ (i) film on milk. (ii)
finger-ring with five-franc piece (shuŋkụ), etc., attached. (3) (a) ɗaŋ ∼ m.
(f. 'yar ∼) pl. 'yaŋ gạrkī young P.
full of good cheer and taking pleasure
in company of opposite sex. (b) 'yaŋ ∼
raiders (= 'yaŋ ƙwarbai). (c) Kt.
'yan ∼ professional beggars living by
threatening to do obscene acts unless
given alms (cf. mazậwọ̄yī). (d) 'yar ∼
f. prostitute (=kārụ̄wạ 2b).
gạrmā f. (pl. garẹ̄manī = garmunạ). (1)
(a) (i) large type of hoe (Vd. firị ;
maimai ; sassaryā ; baŋgajē ; ƙu-
hurtū ; gōjẹ). (ii) Gạrmā ƙặrẹ aikị
epithet of industrious P. (iii) bā ặ ƙwācẹ
wạ yārọ ∼ what a stupid and pointless
act ! (Vd. bịkī 1g). (b) x ∼ gōmạ suŋ
gudụ ten taxpayers have run away. (c)
∼ ūwar rufị, ɗam fannạ epithet of
secretive P. (d) ɗau gạlmā Vd. shā gặrī.
(e) Vd. dōƙị 3b. (f) tā tōnō gạrmā Vd.

ạllūrạ 4. (2) discrimination x (a) Allặ
bā yặ ∼ God's no respecter of persons.
an yi manạ ∼ we've been unfairly
treated. (b) inūwạr darē, bặ dạ ∼ epithet
of any Mụhammạŋ. (3) Vd. kạryạ ∼.
garma-garma = garmạ-garmạ superficial x ganinsạ ∼ nệ he has weak
sight. yanặ jị̂ ∼ he's hard of hearing.
haŋkạlinsạ ∼ nệ he's unintelligent.
mulkịnsạ ∼ nệ he has little authority.
kạrặtunsụ ∼ nệ their education's
superficial (= bisạ-bisạ).
gạrmahọ̄ m. (sg., pl.) gramophone.
garmājẹ m. (f. garmājị̄yā) pl. gạrmặzai
dull, loutish P.
gạrmākạ Sk. m. crown-bird (= gạurākạ
q.v.).
garmanī Sk. m. (1) garmanī = fariŋ ∼
the weed Sida cordifolia. (2) baƙiŋ ∼
the shrub kā fi ramạ.
gạrmạsil m. type of watered-silk.
gạrmặzai Vd. garmājẹ.
garmazō m. (poor) second tobacco-crop.
garmunạ Vd. gạrmā.
garnạƙā Vb. 1C used in aŋ garnạƙạ
hayặƙī there's dense cloud of smoke
(= tunnụƙā).
gạrnaƙaƙī (1) epithet of Chief. (2) what a
bad smell !
garnạƙē Vb. 3A dākị yā ∼ dạ hayặƙī =
hayặƙī yā ∼ ạ dākị house is full of
smoke (cf. garnạƙā).
gạrnannē m. esteemed (= gạnnannē q.v.).
gạrnu = gạnnu.
garnūwā Kt. f. head of hemp (= daŋgirā 1).
garsaƙēƙẹ = garsaƙī = gansaƙēƙẹ q.v.
garsamēmẹ = garsamī = gansamēmẹ q.v.
gạrshēƀā Kt. f. rich gravy ; rich soup
(= dạrmạsōsụ̄wā).
gartaƙēƙẹ = gartaƙī = gansaƙēƙẹ q.v.
gartsa A. (gartsạ = gạrtsā) m. the mud-
fish Polypterus senegalus.
B. (gartsạ) Vb. 1A yā ∼ minị haƙọ̄rā
he gave me a severe bite.
C. (gạrtsā) Vb. 2 Kt. yuŋwạ tanặ
gạrtsāta I'm famished.
gartsa-gartsa used in bākinsạ ∼ nệ its
mouth has serrated edge.
gartsẹ Vb. 1A. (1) yā ∼ ni dạ haƙọ̄rā
he bit me severely. (2) Vd. girtsẹ.
gặrū m. (pl. gāruƙạ). (1) wall round town

or compound (cf. bạŋgō ; gānūwā ; katạŋgā ; birnī 1, 5 ; daŋgā). (2) (a) gārụŋ ƙauyẹ corn four feet high or more. (b) gārụŋ ƙauyẹ yā sōmạ fādụ̄wā reaping has begun. (3) gārun d̃ā *epithet of* any father.

garugg**ạ** *Sk.* herds (*pl. of* gargẹ *q.v. under* garkẹ).

gārūjẹ *m.* (*f.* gārūjị̄yā). (1) fool. (2) glutton.

gārukạ (1) *pl. of* gạ̄rẹ-gown. (2) walls (*pl. of* gạ̄rū *q.v.*).

garukka A. (garukkạ) *Sk.* herds (*pl. of* garkẹ).
    B. (gārukkạ) *Sk.* walls (*pl. of* gạ̄rū *q.v.*).

gārụmā *f.* (1) the roof-support ḳiriny**ạ** 1. (2) the gown gạ̄rẹ.

garūrạ = gạ̄rūrạ *f.* (1) green or magenta dye-crystals. (2) tā yi ~ she rubbed tobacco-flowers on her teeth. (3) cap of imported cotton material with pattern bitten in by Hausas (= mạsạlạfō). (4) ɗaŋ ~ *m.* (*pl.* 'yaŋ ~) professional cadger carrying rattle, drum or gourd-bottle (būtạ) and slandering those not giving alms (cf. gụgụrūgụ).

garurrạ = garūrukạ = garūrūwạ towns (*pl. of* gạrī).

gạ̄ rūwā *used in* ɗaŋ gạ̄ rūwā seasonal immigrant (= dāgịrạ *q.v.*).

garwā *f.* (*pl.* garẹ̄wanī). (1) petrol tin ; kerosene tin (cf. galạŋ ; kwānọ). (2) tsōfaŋ ~ old cycle ; old motor car.

garwai (*sg., pl.*) *m.* (1) strong grinding-stone (cf. zụbau). (2) *Vd.* makōdā 2.

garwāshị = garwāshī *m.* (1) live embers (*also called* garwāshiŋ wutā) = gaushị. (2) yinạ̄ dạ idọ kạman jaŋ ~ he's a real *man.* (3) *Vd.* kạs ~.

garwạyā *Vb.* 1C *Sk.* = gaurạyā.

gạrzā *Vb.* 2. (1) ate much of (crunchy food), cf. gạras-gạras. (2) *used in* tā gạrji niƙạ she did much grinding. yā gạrji nōmā he did much hoeing (= ɓạrzā 2 *q.v.*).

garzạyā (1) *Vb.* 3A hastened. (2) *Vb.* 1C hastened to place x nā ~ kạsūwā.

garzō *Vd.* garjẹ.

gạs (1) *adv. emphasizes* excellence x wardị ~ fine rose-water. yārinyạ ~ fine girl. (2) *m.* type of imported scent.

gasa A. (gạsạ) (1) blast it ! (2) my word !
    B. (gạsā) *f.* (1) (a) rivalry, emulation x (i) yanạ̄ ~ dạ nī he's competing with me (= karabkīyā 1 = kạsayyạ = kīshị 2a = hạ̄mayyạ = tākarā). gạsar tāshị aviation contest. (ii) yā ga ạbịm bạ̄ gạsā ba it saw it was beyond him. (iii) gạsar nēmaŋ aurē *Vd.* nẹ̄mā 1a.ii. (b) yanạ̄ gạsar wāwā he's trying to compete with one far beyond him. (iii) *Vd.* awọ 3d. (c) *rich neighbours or rich co-wives* (kīshīyōyī) *with whom poor one foolishly competes, call to their slave-girl* Gạsar wāwā ! (*to which latter replies* rashịn sanịm mafị̄yī (*Vd.* mafị̄yī 2) *in the rival's hearing, to annoy*). (2) gạsar zūcī ambition.
    C. (gasạ) (1) *Vb.* 1A (*Vd.* gashị). (a) (i) grilled meat (for immediate eating by hanging it long over fire) (*Vd.* babbạkā). nāmạ yā fārạ gạsūwā meat's begun to grill. (ii) = ƙafẹ 2. (iii) wạ̄ zai gasạ wạ kạrē gadọ̄ who bothers about poverty-stricken P. ! (*Vd.* gadō 2b). (iv) ạbịn dạ akạ gasạ shi, yā ga wutā fīlị dạ fīlī = nāmạn dạ kẹ kusa dạ wutā, shī ya fi gạsūwā *Vd.* dafạ 1e. (v) *Vd.* gashị. (vi) ạbiŋ ~ gīwā *Vd.* rịnō 2. (b) (i) ~ dōyạ to bake yam in embers. (ii) to fry (wạinā, fụŋƙāsō, gụrāsạ) = dānạ 2a = tōyạ 1a. (c) ~ tukunyā to fire a pot (= tōyạ 2a). (d) ill-treated x yā ~ mạtā tasạ (= dafạ 3) (*Vd.* gyạ̃dā 4). (e) yā ~ masạ magana he spoke roughly to him. (f) yanạ̄ ~ akaifā he's eating tūwō *Vd.* gashẹ. (2) *Vb.* 3A yā ~ ạ gujẹ he fled.

gạsạƙē *m.* sitting silent and forlorn x yanạ̄ zạune ~ = yā yi ~ (= jụgum).

gāsāƙī *m.* (*f.* gāsāƙā). (1) burly P. (2) important P.

gasara A. (gāsạ̄rạ) = gạsạ.
    B. (gạsārā) *f.* flour, water, and tsāmīyā (tamarind) for making gruel (kụnū).

gāsasshẹnīyā *f.* = gạ̄sā 1a.

gāsạyā *f.* (1) the pot-herb *Gynandropsis pentaphylla* (= ụŋgūwā 4). (2) namijiŋ ~ the weeds *Amaranthus polygamus, Polanisia viscosa, Croton lobatus.* (3) gwạfar ~ *f.* useless P.

gashẹ *Vb*. 1A = gasạ 1 *x* ạ gashẹ, bạ mại ; ạ dafẹ, bạ rōmō neither fish, flesh, fowl, nor good red herring.

gashi A. (gāshi) *m*. (*pl*. gāsūsūwạ = gāsū = gāsūsukạ). (1) (*a*) (i) hair, hairs (*cf*. sụmā, gịzō). (ii) gāshin jīmạ goat's hair scraped off soaked skins by dyers. (iii) kō tụlū yā fī shị ∼ he's a useless P. (iv) fịkậfịkammụ sum fārạ ∼ we've begun to become strong. (*b*) gāshi = gāshin tsuntsū feather, feathers. (*c*) dūkịyā gāshịn hancị being deprived of one's goods is as painful as removal of hair from one's nostrils. (*d*) (i) gāshịm bậkī moustache. (ii) Gậshịm bậkī *epithet of* man with moustache. (iii) gāshịm bậkinsạ yā kwạntā he's got his way. (iv) *Vd*. diŋgạ 2*c*, (*e*) yā yi ∼ hair (feathers) have grown on it. (*f*) dam mại gāshịn hafōrī what a destitute person !, what a miser ! (*g*) (i) *Kt*. gāshịn tsịyā gạrēshị he has persistent ill-luck. (ii) *Vd*. tsịyā 1*b*, *c*. (*h*) dạŋ gāshịŋ ūwā bother you ! (*j*) yā karyạ ∼ = yā karyạ gāshịn tsūlịyā he borrowed (with or without leave) another's horse or donkey and went for a ride (*cf*. diŋgạ 2*c*). (*k*) yā karyạ gāshịn tsịyā he (poor P.) bought a horse. (*l*) zā tạ yi gāshịm bāyā she married too young and will soon wilt. (*m*) im bạ ki dạ gāshịŋ Wancẹ, kadạ kị yi kitsạŋ Wancẹ don't attempt the impossible ! (*n*) gịndiŋ ∼ place at back of head whence hair radiates. (*o*) yā tạfi, yā kōmō kạmar mại yā dạ ∼ he went and returned rapidly. (*p*) kō bại yi ∼ kōịnā ba *Vd*. buzurwā 4. (*q*) gāshịŋ kudī *Vd*. bịcịlmī. (*r*) gāshịn jịminā *Vd*. tsōfō 1*g*. (*s*) yaŋkaŋ ∼ *Vd*. yaŋkā 2*d*. (*t*) *Vd*. tūzad dạ gāshị, būzūzụ 3*b*, bạrạ gadō gāshị, būshẹ gāshị. (2) character *used in* (*a*) yanậ dạ mūguŋ ∼ he is cantankerous. (*b*) ịnā rūwaŋ azzịkī dạ mūguŋ ∼ nothing succeeds like success ! (3) hannuŋ ∼ *m*. = taurā.

B. (gāshī) *Kt*. *m*. the region round the sacrum bone.

C. (gashi) *m*. (1) (*a*) (*secondary v.n.* of gasạ) *x* (i) yanậ gashin nāmạ =

yanậ gasạ nāmạ he's roasting meat. (ii) wutar ∼ *Vd*. nāmạ 1*h*. (iii) duk rịgimạn naŋ, kō na ∼ bạ sụ dībạ ba in all this conflict they inflicted no casualties on us. (iv) kậmịŋ kạ sậmi na dạfūwā, nī mā nậ sậmu na ∼ I'll outdo you yet (*Vd*. gasạ 1*a*.iv). (v) bạ sụ rịnjậyē mụ ba sặi dạ mukạ dẹbi na ∼ dạ na dạfūwā dạ na sūyạ dagạ cikin sōjansụ they did not overcome us without our taking heavy toll of their troops. (vi) baraŋ ∼ *Vd*. tsịrē 2. (*b*) gashịŋ kạnsạ yakẹ yị he's his own master, independent (*cf*. gandū 5). (*c*) gashịŋ kaskō slightly roasting or frying meat (= birgimā 5). (*d*) gashịn tandạ grilling on grid a whole skinned ram (*cf*. tạnarī). (2) (*a*) anậ yi masạ ∼ hot sand is being poured over him (P. with smallpox). (*b*) gashịŋ kậcịyạ applying hot sand to heal wound of circumcision. (3) gashịŋ fumā playfully forcing P. down on to hot ground (= *Kt*. gishị 2). (4) gashịŋ kilịshī *Vd*. kilịshī.

gậshiŋgālā (1) *f*. (*a*) bargain *x* yā sậmi ∼ he got it easily or cheaply. (*b*) being simpleton. (2) *m*., *f*. (*sg*., *pl*.) simpleton.

gạskami *m*. (1) blocks of locust-bean pulp (*epithet is* ∼ kậsūwarkạ dayā for it soon goes bad). (2) *when exposed for sale* (tạllạ), *vendors' cry is* ∼ tūwō dạgạ rēshẹ !

gaskata A. (gaskạtā) *Vb*. 1C. (1) credited truth of T. (2) verified.

B. (gạskatạ) *Vb*. 3B. (1) (truth of T.) became substantiated. (2) P. became vindicated.

gaskatad dạ *Vb*. 4B = gaskạtā.

gạskẹ (1) (*a*) dạ ∼ extremely *x* munậ sō dạ ∼ we like it very much (= munậ sō fwarai dạ ∼). mūgụ nē fwarai dạ gạskyaŋ ∼ he's thoroughly evil. sặi yā yī dạ ∼ yakẹ īyạ kufucẹwā it is only with difficulty that he can escape. (*b*) dạ ∼ (*negatively*) not at all *x* bā mậ sō dạ ∼ we don't like it at all. (*c*) kạmar gaskẹ as if it were really being done. (2) (*as noun following genitive*) real *x* namijịŋ gạskẹ nẹ he's a real trier. yāfịŋ gạskẹ bitter war. (3) *Nor*. yes, indeed !

gaskīyā *f.* (1) (*a*) (i) truth. (ii) ~ tā fi jąkā = gaskīyā tā fi Tūrancī (*cf.* Bątūrę 3, 4) = gaskīyā tā fi lāyą truth is the best policy. (iii) ą mąganąr ~ as a matter of fact. (iv) ~ sūnantą ~ = ƙaryā tā shęƙarą ƙaryā ~ taną matsayintą truth always prevails. (v) ciƙį (= wuyą) dą ~, wuƙā bā tą yąnką shi the really honest P. is not in danger from slander. (vi) ~ ɗūwąiwai nę, dą kąntą yakę ząune truth needs no padding. (vii) ~ wųyar fądā gąrētą, in kā fadį, sąi ką hau ɗan dubū don't expect popularity if you tell people the truth ! (*b*) ąbin dą yakę yį, yaną dą ~ what he is doing is sensible. (*c*) (i) ~ nę = gaskīyā cę = gaskīyarką quite so ! (ii) ąl'amąrin ~ nę it is an actual fact. (*d*) baƙar ~ an unpalatable truth. (*e*) true state *x* rūbą tasą tā fi gaskīyarsą yawą his boasts are much above his capabilities. (2) (*a*) nā bā shį ~ (i) I believed in him. (ii) I devoted all my attention to it. (*b*) bạn gaskīyā *m.* (i) reliability of P. *x* Audų bạn ~ gąrēshį Audu's reliable P. bạn ~ hąkīkąr aikį dogged wins ! (ii) trusting in P. *x* nā yi masą bạn ~ I placed reliance in him. Audų bạn ~ gąrēshį Audu is a trustful P. (3) (*a*) yaną dą ~ (i) he's in the right. (ii) he's honest. (*b*) marąg ~ *adj. m., f. sg.* (*pl.* marąsā ~) dishonest ; untruthful. (*c*) rashin ~ *m.* dishonesty, untruthfulness. (*d*) yā sąmi ~ (i) he won his case. (ii) the truth of his statement is proved (= gira). (4) yā yi ~ he acted rightly. (5) na ~ *m.* (*f.* ta ~) *pl.* na ~ real *x* amincį na ~ real friendship. (6) ~ dą ~, māląm ya sai māląm both sides are telling the truth. (7) gidan ~ *m.* the next world (*cf.* ƙaryā 1*e*), = lāhirą. (8) shirū, kąmar mąganąr ~ sąi suką ɓullō then they suddenly appeared. (9) bạ̄ ki ~ *Vd.* alakwąyī. (10) aną karąn ~ dą gaskīyā a heroic struggle was in progress. (11) gaskīyar mąi shī *Vd.* tsāfį 3. (12) dą̄ dūnīyą dą ~ *Vd.* dūnīyą 2*h*. (13) *Vd.* ɗācī 4.

gasmā *Kt. f.* hoe (= gąrmā *q.v.*).

gasnannē = gannannē.

gasnu = gannu.

gąsō rōgo (1) *m., f.* (*sg., pl.*) fool. (2) ~ m bā ką ɓawō what a dolt !

gasu A. (gāsū) *Vd.* gāshį.
B. (gąsu) *Vd.* gasą.

gāsūsūwą *Vd.* gāshį.

gat *x* ~ dą near (= gaf *q.v.*).

gata A. (gātą) *adv.* three days hence.
B. (gātā) *m.* (1) support *x* yā yi minį ~ he was my support. · ųbā gātan ɗansą a father is the support of his son. Allą̄ gātam mąrāyą = Allą̄ gātam bāwą God is the refuge of the helpless. (*b*) hąną bįkī maraicį, są̄ bįkī ~ what a fussy busybody ! (*Vd.* hąną bįkī). (2) ɗan ~ *m.* (*f.* 'yar ~) *pl.* 'yan ~ child of rich parents. (3) *m.* keeping look-out for game or enemy *x* yā yi musų ~ he kept a look-out for them. (4) *m.* (*sg., pl.*) sentinel, look-out. (5) gātā = jąn gātā = gātam birį (*a*) large red monkey. (*b*) *Vd.* ɓąrnā 1*b*. (6) an yi masą ~ a use has been found for it. (7) Mąnyā, gātan wą̄sā hail, Owner of the thing which others lack ! (8) gātam bāyā *Vd.* wutsīyą 1*f*. (9) māganim mąi ~ *Vd.* shąrī'ą. (10) dindimįnką dą ~ *Vd.* dįndimī 3. (11) rąi bā ~ *Vd.* katąngalą.

gą̄ tanā (1) *f.* fable *x* zō, mų yi ~ let's go and tell each other fables ! (= tą̄tsūnīyā 1), *cf.* gą̄ 3*b*. (2) gą̄ tānạnkų, tā jē, tā kōmō = gą̄ tan, gą̄ tạnkų.

gātancį *m.* an yi masą ~ he has received favoured treatment.

gą̄ tan, gą̄ tạnkų = gą̄ tan, gą̄ tạnką = *Sk.* gą̄ tanarkų here begins the fable . . . (= gą̄ 3*b*), *cf.* gątanā.

gątarī *m.* (*pl.* gāturą = *Sk.* gāturrą). (1) (*a*) axe, hatchet (= masārī 2). (*b*) Allą̄ yą tsąri ~ dą nōmā what have we in common ! (*Vd.* tsąrā 2). (*c*) mūgun gątarinką yā fi " sąri ką bā nį ! " independence is best, no matter how modest (= mūgų 1*f* = guntū 3 = ƙą̄sarī 1 = sąre-sąrē = ąlhamdų 2 = ųngųlū 7). (*d*) im bą̄ ą ~ ba, ą ƙōtą one or other of the misfortunes is bound to happen ; the misfortune is bound to befall one of us. (*e*) im mųtųm yā cę ząi hąɗīyi ~ riƙē masą ƙōtą don't waste your breath on a person who thinks he

can do the impossible ! (*f*) ∼ mai
kwaɓīyā, wąhąl dą mai hawā bisą it's
a thorn in one's side. (*g*) *Vd.* nēmam
mai ∼. (*h*) bą̄kiŋ ∼ *Vd.* sārā 5. (*j*)
yā mąntā ∼ *Vd.* bāwą 1*h*. (*k*) bą̄ yā
dą ∼ *Vd.* ƙwąŋƙwąmbishī. (2) embroidery on left side of neck of gown
(= gāfīyā 1). (3) yā cī har ya yi ∼ =
yā cī har ya kai masaɓar ∼ he ate to
repletion. (4) gą̄tarinsą yā kwaɓę
he's sexually impotent (= gidā 1*d*.ii =
lą'īfī). (5) guntuŋ ∼ *m*. destitute P.
(6) Gą̄tarī *title of* two sąrautą at Katsina
(*hence, Kt. people claim that the word*
gāfīyā *is out of respect for the office*
Gą̄tarī, *used for* " axe " *in place of the
word* gą̄tarī). (7) gą̄tariŋ ąrādu stone
celt (= dūtsę 1*c*). (8) gą̄tariŋ Gwārī (*a*)
jack-of-all-trades. (*b*) Gūgą̄rą, gą̄tariŋ
Gwārī what a dauntless person ! (*c*) *Vd.*
dandōsą, dūsąrą. (9) gą̄tariŋ ƙurēgē *Sk.*
the lily baurērę. (10) gą̄tarin takǫbī the
unsharpened part of sword blade, near
the hilt. (11) gą̄tarin tūwō hand
(= hannū). (12) an yi masą jaŋ ∼ it
(tree) has been burned through, to fell
it (*epithet of this process is* jaŋ ∼ sāran
darē).

gą̄ tą̄wa *Kt.* (1) = rifą 1*c*. (2) *cf.* gą̄ ną̄wa.

gatǫ *m.* (1) vagina (= farjī). (2) *Sk.* base of
T. (= gindī). (3) ɗaŋ gatąŋ ūwā (*said to
male*) blast you ! 'yar gatąŋ ūwā
(*said to female*) blast you ! (= ūwā 1*c*.ii).

gatsa A. (gą̄tsā) *Vb.* 2 bit off.
B. (gą̄tsą) *Vb.* 1A bit at.

gątsą̄fū *Vd.* gaggāwā 2.

gątsąl-gątsąl *used in* (1) yaną̄ aikī ∼ he's
scamping the work. (2) suną̄ cī ∼
they're eating in an unmannerly way.

gatsaltsąlā *Vb.* 1E scamped (work), etc.,
as in gątsąl-gątsąl.

gątsē *m.* (1) sarcasm. (2) gątsaŋ kuŋkurū replying rudely and recklessly to
a superior (= tsūlīyā 3). (3) sąndaŋ ∼
Vd. sąndā 1*l*.

gą̄tsi bą̄ mą̄tāką *Vd.* baunī.

gą̄tsīką *f.* (1) *Kano Hausa* young baobob
or dwarf baobob. (2) *Sk.* young leaves
of baobob (kūką).

gą̄tsinā *Vb.* 1C tā gątsiną hancī she made a
sneering grimace (*only done by women*)
= gantsąrē 1*c* (*cf.* girɓunā, durɓunā).

gą̄tsinē *m.* woman's sneering grimace.
(*cf.* gą̄tsinā).

gą̄tsirā *Vb.* 1C tā ∼ masą bą̄kī she made
a derisive grimace at him (*only done
by women*) = gą̄tsinā.

gatsō-gątsō = gątsąl-gątsąl.

gą̄tsunā ; gą̄tsurā = gą̄tsinā ; gą̄tsirā.

gatu *Kt.* ɗaŋ gatuŋ ūwā = gatǫ 3.

gą̄turą axes (*pl. of* gą̄tarī *q.v.*).

gą̄tūtą *f.* children's game (= *Kt.* nārandę).

gą̄tūtu *Kt. m.* (*f.* gą̄tūtūwā) slow-witted P.

gau A. (gąu) *adv. emphasizes* deepness of
hue (= dąu *q.v.*).
B. (gau) *adv. emphasizes* sharp pain
x haƙōrīna yaną̄ cīwǫ ∼ I've a sharp
pain in my tooth. kunnēna yiną̄ cīwǫ
gau-gau I've ear-ache.
C. (gąu) *adv. emphasizes* hard blow
x yā mą̄rē ni ∼ (= fąu). (2) *Zar. m.*
type of fish.

gaucī *Kt. m.* brittleness (= gautsī *q.v.*).

gaudā *m.* = ɗaŋ ∼ *m.* type of food
made from beans.

gauɗa A. (gauɗą) *Vb.* 1A *x* yā ∼ masą
mārį he gave him a severe blow.
B. (gąuɗā) *Vb.* 2 *x* yā gąuɗē shi
dą mārį he gave him severe blow.

gauɗā-gauɗā *m.* = gauɗā.

gauɗę (1) (*a*) *m.* the shrub *Gardenia
erubescens* (*branches used for fences ;
wounds made by its thorns heal slowly, so
its epithet is* sāraŋ wāwā ; *one variety
has yellow fruit ; another makes cosmetic* kątąmbirį). (*b*) gauɗaŋ dūtsę
shrub *Gardenia Sokotensis.* (*c*) gauɗaŋ
kūrā shrub *Gardenia ternifolia* (*has
inedible fruit*). (*d*) cantankerous P.
(2) *adj. m.* (*f.* gauɗīyā) ripe but unexpectedly hard (*used only re* kaɗanyą ; dabīnǫ ; rōgǫ) *x* wannąŋ rōgǫ
gauɗę nē this cassava is old and tough
(= gąntąmau). dabīnaŋ naŋ gauɗę nē
these ripe dates are tough. kaɗanyąŋ
naŋ gauɗīyā cę these ripe shea-nuts
are tough.

gauɗi what a slap ! ; what a blow !

gauɗīyā *Vd.* gauɗę.

gaugai *Kt. m.* the weed ƙudujī *q.v.*

gau-gau = gau *q.v.*

gaugāwā *f.* hastening (= gaggāwā *q.v.*).

gauję *Vb.* 1A *x* yā ∼ ni dą sąndā he hit
me hard with stick (= gabję *q.v.*).

gaujī *m.* (1) fool. (2) Emir's jester (= **wā-wan Sarkī**).

gaujin *m.* a large-grained type of guinea-corn (= *Kt.* **gamjī 2**).

gaukā *f.* (1) eagerness to complete task. (2) apogee (= **gānīyą**) *x* **gaukar cīwo tā kārę** crisis of illness is past. **gaukar zamantą tā kārę** she's divorced.

gaulā *m.*, *f.* (*pl.* **gauląyē**) gaby.

gaurā = **gaudā**.

gaurai-gaurai *m.* heterogeneous crowd *x* ~ **nę** what a mixed lot! (*reply is* **hatsim barą** corn given as alms!).

gaurāką *m.* (*f.* **gaurākīyā**) *pl.* **gaurākī**. (1) crownbird (*Balearica pavonina*) = **kumąrē**. (2) **tsīgī yakę ɓarnā, aną fushī dą gaurāką** seniors have to bear the blame for their juniors' misdeeds (*Vd.* **ɓērü**). (3) **kā ajīyę tukkūwā kąman gaurāką?** you sport a tuft like a crownbird! (4) (*a*) *Vd.* **sąn** ~. (*b*) *Vd.* **kąntąkalai**.

gauraya A. (**gaurąyā**) *Vb.* 1C. (1) mixed. (2) stirred up (**mīyą, furā**, milk) to mix sediment with liquid before serving (= **kaurąyā** = **mōtsą**), *cf.* **dāmą**.
B. (**gauraya**) *Vb.* 3B is (was) mixed.

gaurąyē *Vb.* 1C. (1) = **gaurąyā**. (2) permeated *x* **har jąn yą gaurąyę fātą duką** till the red-dye fully permeates the leather.

gaurī *Kt.* *m.* (1) becoming firm (body of child or young animal). (2) fruit's becoming tough. (3) **bar yārinyąn nąn tą yi** ~ don't give this girl in marriage till she's more mature!

gausąsā *Vd.* **gaggausā**.

gaushi *m.* (1) live embers (= **garwāshi**). (2) *Vd.* **kąs** ~.

gautā *m.* (1) the bitter tomato *Solanum sp.* (*Kano and Zaria call it* **dātą** *also, but* **yālō** *is a different variety. Kt. uses* **yālō** *as alternative name for* **gautā**, *but* **dwātą** *is a different variety*). (2) (*a*) **wąsąn** ~ *m.* youths' and girls' games at the end of rainy-season. (*b*) the game **māgī**. (3) **gautąn kąjī** the weed *Solanum nodiflorum*. (4) **gautąn kūrā** the poisonous *Solanum incanum* (= **idon 16ɓ**). (5) **gautąn kwądō** the marsh-plant *Cardiospermum halicacabum*. (6) **hancin** ~ *m.* a mere nobody (*epithet*

is **in dą shī mīyą, im bābu shī mīyą**). (7) *Vd.* **musāyā 4**. (8) *Vd.* **ɓatąn** ~.

gautsą *Kt.* *m.* *used in* **tun yaną gautsąnshi** when he was young.

gaul̈sątsā *Vd.* **gaggautsā**.

gaul̈sī *m.* (1) brittleness. (2) **yā yi** ~ he died early as did his forbears (*cf.* **gaggautsā**). (3) **yaną dą gautsim bąkī** he speaks rashly or rudely.

gauzą *Vb.* 1A *x* **yā** ~ **ni dą sąndā** he hit me hard with a stick (= **gabzą** *q.v.*).

gāwā *f.* (*pl.* **gāwaiwai** = **gāwąwwakī**) (*Ar.* **jīfa**). (1) (*a*) (i) corpse of P., carcass of animal (*but not applied to carcass of animal slaughtered for food, this being called* **nāmą** (*cf.* **gudā 1c**) : *body of animal dying naturally or from disease is called* **gāwā** = **mūshę**). (ii) ~ **mai sūnan** ~, **ąbin yā fi gąban kabąrī** corpses lay about in large numbers. (iii) **ją, māgąnin gāwar dōkī** work conquers any task. (*b*) **Salląr** ~ *f.* funeral-service. (*c*) **kunnĕna rūwan** ~, **bąn ji ba, bąn ganī ba** (*said by women*) I know nothing about it and I don't want to! (2) *used in* **nā ga gāwarsą** I saw it was cheap. (3) ~ **dą makā** (*a*) bee, scorpion, snake, etc., pretending to be dead and then stinging. (*b*) deposed P. who plagues his successor (*cf.* **ąlkakai**). (4) **gāwar gāshi** becoming grey-haired early. (5) **gāwar zākī, gāwar gizākā** *Vd.* **gizākā**. (6) *Vd.* **tisą** ~, **bīyą** ~.

gawai *Sk.* *m.* = **gawąyī**.

gawainā = **gąyaunā**.

gāwaiwai *Vd.* **gāwā**.

gāwāro *m.* **yā yi** ~ it's become charred.

*gāwaryā *f.* red dot under letter in the Koran to show that vowel " a " is **imālą**, *i.e.* pronounced as " e "

gāwązą *Kt.* *m.* = **gāwurzą**.

gąwasą *f.* (*pl.* **gąwąsū**). (1) gingerbread-plum-tree (*Parinarium macrophyllum*). (2) **kamshin** ~ **yā fi shąntą dādī** T. or P. belying good appearance.

gawāshi *m.* live embers (= **garwāshi**).

gāwąwwakī *pl.* of **gāwā**.

gawąyī *m.* (1) charcoal (*cf.* **kiryą**). (2) *Vd.* **sēmā ; ąllī 2 ; kīrą 1j**.

gawo A. (**gąwō**) *m.* (1) *Acacia albida* ; *epithet is* **kā ki rūwan Allą** (*foliage is*

camel's food). (2) **halālīyar gundạ,
itạcaŋ ~** it's my *own*. (3) *Vd.*
hawainīyā.

B. (**gāwọ**) = **gāwu** *Sk. m.* lunged
mud-fish (= **gaiwā**).

gāwuji *m.* = **gauji**.

gāwurcē *Vb.* 3Ā = **gāwurtạ** *Vb.* 3B. (1)
(*a*) became large ; attained full
strength. (*b*) became abundant. (2)
(*a*) became important. (*b*) (affair)
became serious.

gāwurzạ *m.* silly lout (*epithet is* ~ **laifiŋkạ
ɓad dạ ạbiŋkạ**).

gāwustạ *Sk.* = **gāwurtạ**.

gāwuttạ = **gāwurtạ**.

gaya A. (**gayạ**) *Vb.* 3A. (1) (*a*) told *x*
nā ~ masạ I told him. **yā ~ mini
zại zō = yā ~ mini kạmar zại zō** he
told me he would come. (*b*) **ŋ ~ makạ**
as a matter of fact . . . (2) **wạ ya ~
makạ** how can you expect me to believe
such a thing? (3) **gayạ jinī " nā
wucẹ "** *epithet of* **bīsạlạmī**. (4) **yā ~
masạ ạbu** (*said by women*) he (teacher)
went over passage in book (especially
Koran) with him (= **bīyạ** 1*c*). (5)
gạyạ bạkō gidā, tạ kārẹ kạŋkạ (*lit.*
you who by crowing indicate house to
passer-by, so that you are killed to feed
him) *epithet of* cock (**zạkarạ**). (6) *Vd.*
mākwī. (7) **bā ạ ~ wạ kạrē gidam
bạkī** what a pointless act ! (8) **gạyạ
mại zucīyā bikī, bạ mại dūkīyā ba a**
good character is better than wealth.

B. (**gāyạ**) *m.* (*pl.* **gāyạyyakī**). (1) (*a*)
anything spherical *x* **watạ yā yi ~** the
moon is full (= **dawọ** 3), *cf.* **gụdā** 1*b*.
ii, iii. (*b*) **furan nạŋ tanạ dạ
~** undissolved lumps (*cf.* 1*d*, 2*d*)
have settled at bottom of this **furā**-
and-milk. (*c*) **gāyaŋ kōko** (*Vd.*
gụdā 1*a*.iii) the lumps made for eating
in gruel (*Vd.* **dạlạkī** 2). (*d*) **gāyam
furā** lumps of ̇**furā** specially left in
furā-and-milk = **kạdạɓulai** 2 (*cf.* 2*d
below*). (*e*) **~ dạ mại** cakes of roasted
beniseed (**nōmẹ**). (2) unaccompanied
x (*a*) **yā fīta gāyansạ** he (deposed chief,
etc.) left in a hurry quite unaccompanied. (*b*) (i) **gāyan tūwō = tūwō ~**
the food **tūwō** without any soup (=
kạmūrā 1 = *Sk.* **ɓagas** 2), *cf.* **kanzō** 2.

(ii) *Vd.* 2*f below* ; **ūwā** 1*j*. (*c*) **tūwaŋ
kwạdạyī yā fi dādī** ; **kō dạ ~, sǎi ạ ci** expectation exceeds realization. (*d*) **gāyam
furā** the food **furā** without any milk
(*cf.* 1*b*, 1*d above*) (= **dawọ** 1*a*), *cf.*
gāhūhu. (*e*) **gāyam farī** roll of **farī**-
cloth as it leaves the loom (= **zugū** 1).
(*f*) **wạndạ bā shi dạ ūwā ạ gidā, dōlẹ
wata rānā tūwansạ ~ zại** ci a man
without a patron is sure to come a
cropper. (*g*) **yanạ ciŋ gāyā** *Vd.* **gạraŋhōtsạmī**.

C. (**gāyạ**) *Ar.* (1) *f. or adv.* maximum,
very much *x* **yā yi kọkarī ~ = yā
yi kọkarī gāyạr kọkarī** he tried his
hardest. (2) *f.* (*a*) acme *x* **yanạ gāyạr
shakīyyancinsạ** he is at the apogee of
his wickedness (= **tsululū** 1 = **gā-
nīyạ** = **gaɓạ** 2*b* = **gāfī** 2). (*b*) **ạbiŋ
yā kai ~** the matter has become really
serious. (3) **~ wạ nihāyạ** yes, plenty
(*reply to e.g.* has he much money ?).

D. (**Gayā**) *Vd.* **dụdduru** 1.

*****gāyạdī** *Ar. f.* human excrement (*Vd.*
kāshī).

gaya-gaya A. (**gāya-gāya**) very much *x* **yā
yi kọkarī ~** he tried his hardest (=
gāyạ).

B. (**gāyạ-gāyạ**) *f.* = *Kt.* **gạigāyạ**.

gayāji *m.* type of guinea-corn.

gạyamnā *f.* = **gạyaunā**.

gạyaŋ-gayaŋ (1) *m.* the wild field-bean
Vigna membranacea. (2) *adv.* **yanạ
cị ~** he eats indiscriminately in public.

gayar dạ *Vb.* 4A = **gai dạ**.

gayau A. (**gạyau** = **gạyau** = **gayau-gạyau**)
m. and adv. **yanạ dạ hakọrā ~ = yanạ
~ dạ hakọrā** (i) he has protruding
teeth. (ii) he exposes his teeth.

B. (**gayau-gạyau**) *m.* (1) *used in a*)
wurī yā yi ~ the place is arid. (*b*)
dōki yā yi ~ horse's thin. (2) *Vd.* **gạyau**.

gạyaunā *f.* (*pl.* **gạyaunī** = **gạyaunū**). (1)
small farm owned by member of com-
pound privately and independently of
the householder *x* **Audu daŋ ~ nē** Audu
works for another, but has small farm
of his own. (2) **sun sōmạ ~** they
(boxers), etc., are having trial-round.

gāyạyyakī *Vd.* **gāyā**.

gayē *m.* (1) **an yi masạ ~** the folly of his
ways has been pointed out to him. (2)

yā saukę Alkur'an ammā da ∽ he's been right through Koran from text, not from writing-board (a̱llō) (= bi̱yē 2). (3) acting by head-boy of Koranic class as locum in absence of the teacher. *gāyi̱tsī Ar. m. human excrement (Vd. kā;hī).

gayya A. (ga̱yyā) f. (1) (a) (i) communal labour ; communal workers x yā tāra̱ ∽ he collected people for communal work (farming, etc.). (ii) he conscripted war-levies, etc., x ∽ tā tafō the conscripts arrived (cf. ji̱za̱ 2b ; ga̱yyata̱). (b) Vd. gayya̱ 4; sa6a̱ 5. (bb) sāran ∽ drumming-party given for workers in ga̱yyā (= kalankūwā 1a q.v.). (c) ga̱yyar ma̱kāfo̱, ma̱i nīshi̱ kā̱ shā gā̱rī he's succeeded by mere " bounce ". (d) Vd. Amsa̱ ga̱yyā. (e) gāri̱n gayyā Vd. ribdi̱ 1b. (f) ga̱ban ∽ (i) leader of gayyā-party. (ii) Vd. gōję 3. (g) balbēla̱ bā̱ ga̱yyā ba cę Vd. bi̱kī 1e. (h) fā;shi̱n ga̱yyā Vd. Dumau 2. (j) dayā ta ma̱i ga̱yyā mā̱ yi there's no harm in trying everything once. (k) fasa̱ ga̱yyā Vd. fasa̱ 3a. (l) ga̱yyar wō̱fī Vd. inna̱ri̱di̱di̱. (m) kā kadǎi ∽ Vd. gwa̱ntō. (2) an yi musu̱ ga̱yyar hakōrī busybodies interfered in their quarrel (= tā̱ran da̱ngi̱). (3) ga̱yyar bā̱kī (a) cadging from one's better-off relations. (b) = 2. (4) ga̱yyar wagairahum (a) performing ga̱yyā 1 for those themselves therein engaged. (b) being a busybody (epithet is da̱ngi̱n na uwāki̱) (wagairahum Ar. = " others ").

B. (gayya̱) f. (1) malicious conduct, dirty trick x yā yi mini̱ ∽ (= kari̱ 3d = har 1d.ii = hakunci̱ 3b = wa̱lā-wa̱lā = ta̱sha̱rē̱-tasharē = ra̱ba̱ ma̱kāfo̱ da̱ gōra̱ = bu̱ku̱lu̱). (2) kuturū ka̱n wa̱ ∽, bā̱ ma̱i yātsa̱ ba (said by women) that's no way to talk to me ! (3) (a) rā̱mūwar ∽ tā fi ∽ cīwo̱ malice will recoil on the doer ! (b) saurō ma̱i rā̱mar gayya̱ Vd. rā̱mā 2b. (c) Vd. fushī 1a.iv. (4) ga̱yyā ma̱i aiki̱n gayya̱, makyu̱ya̱cī kira̱m makē̱ta̱tā a slack boss must expect lazy and dishonest service. (5) Vd. tu̱ma̱ da̱ ∽.

ga̱yya̱cē Vd. ga̱yyata̱.

gayyara A. (ga̱yyara̱) Vb. 3B. (1) suffered trouble. *(2) Ar. became changed.

B. *(gayya̱rā) Vb. 1C Ar. changed T. ga̱yyata̱ Vb. 2 (p.o. ga̱yya̱cē, n.o. ga̱yya̱ci̱). (1) summoned P. to communal task x a̱n ga̱yya̱ci̱ ja̱ma'a̱ the people have been called upon to take part in joint farm-work, etc. (Vd. ga̱yyā). (2) invited P. to party x a̱n ga̱yya̱cē shi̱ sūnā (bi̱kī) (wā̱sā) he's been invited to naming-ceremony (feast) (games).

gaza A. (gaza̱) (1) Vb. 3A. (a) fell short ; failed (= kāsa̱ 1a). (b) sānīyā bā tā̱ gazā̱wā da̱ ka̱fanta̱ come what may, one must shoulder one's responsibilities. (c) sǎi kudi̱n yāro̱ su̱ gaza̱ Vd. saina̱. (d) īya̱ tā ∽ Vd. īya̱ 1d. (2) Vb. 1A. (a) fell short of x yā ∽ ni hakurī he has less patience than I have. (b) lacked x yā ∽ hakurī he has no patience.

B. (gāza̱) Kt. f. yelling while working with others.

gaza̱ ganī = gaja̱ ganī.

gā̱zā̱gūrū m., f. (sg., pl.) strong and indomitable.

ga̱zajjē m. (f. ga̱zajjīyā) pl. ga̱za̱zzū P. unequal to task (= gaji̱yayyē).

gā̱zal m. lamp-black, etc. (applied to eyes by women).

Gazama̱ epithet of any man called Bāwa̱.

gā̱zara̱ f. type of small-barbed arrow (it being the longest in the quiver).

gazar-gazar A. (gazar-ga̱za̱r) emphasizes bushiness x yana̱ da̱ gāshi̱ ∽ he has bushy hair.

B. (gaza̱r-gaza̱r) used in an dafa̱ rama̱ ∽ the hemp-leaves are not cooked enough.

gazari A. (ga̱zarī) m. (1) (a) fibrous vein in centre of frond of kaba̱ or gigi̱nya̱ (= Kt. garē̱ra̱ 2), cf. kari̱. (b) fruiting-head after dates stripped· off (used as broom). (c) Sk., Kt. shoot of deleb (gigi̱nya̱) = mu̱rūcī q.v. (2) kada̱ ka̱ yi mini̱ ∽ (a) don't double-cross me ! (b) don't cheek me ! (3) yana̱ wani ∽ he's agog with excitement.

B. (gāzārī) m. (1) abundance x yā yi ∽ a̱ kā̱sūwā it's to be had in abundance. aiki̱ yā yi mini̱ ∽ I've too much work. (2) type of hannun rūwā kolanut (cf. Gāzau 2).

Gāzau (1) ~ dabbar Allā epithet of hyena. (2) ~ dam babbaŋ itācē, bā sayaŋkạ akạ yi ba, săi kạ bā dạ kaŋwā, mại gidā yạ gamạ ka dạ yārọ dạ 'yar gōrạ, kạ karkaɗō (lit. it's not sold : all you need do is to give the owner some potash and he will lend you a lad and a stick for you to knock down the nuts) epithet of the kolanuts called gāzārī. (3) ~ mại ɗanyaŋ aikị̌ epithet of over-eager blunderer.

gazạ zamā m. fidgetiness.

gazgạyī Kt. m. bin of cornstalks and mats daubed with mud.

gạznannē esteemed (= gạnnannē q.v.).

gāzuŋ-gāzuŋ = gazar-gạzạr

gạznu = gạnnu.

gāzunzụmī Zar. m. (sg., pl.) bugs (= kudī 6a).

gēbẹ Sk. m. (pl. gyạbbā = gyạbbū = gẹbbā) stream, watercourse.

gēɓē m. doltish man.

gēcī Kt. = gētsī.

gēfẹ m. (pl. gēfunạ = gyạffā). (1) (a) edge (cf. fuskạ 1b.i). (b) kụ bi hanyạ ạ gēfẹ-gēfẹ keep to very edge of the road ! (cf. bākī 3). (2) first or last pages of book x gā fihịrisạ ạ ~ the index is at the beginning (or end). (3) (negatively) x ạ gayạ wạ kōwā bā ~ tell everybody without exception. bā shi dạ ~, yā kāmạ kōwạ it applies to all without exception. (4) Kt. hole where mats are woven (= kụrfī q.v.). (5) cf. gēfin.

gēfin (derived from gēfẹ) prep. and conj. on eve of x ~ zūwạŋ Audụ = ~ Audụ zại zō when Audu was on the point of arriving.

gēfunạ Vd. gēfẹ.

gega A. (gēgā) skirted x hanyạ tā gēgi gidansạ road skirts his compound. yākị yā gēgi Baucī the war came close enough to affect Bauchi. yā gēgē nị dạ maganạ he tried to " pump " me. B. (gēgạ) Vb. 1A. (1) yā ~ mini maganạ he tried to "pump" me. (2) Vb. 3A x suŋ ~ they've come to blows (= gōgạ q.v.).

gēgẹ Vb. 1A used in yā ~, yā cī he passed tip of little finger between ring and

cowrie in game dạrạmbūwā 3, showing interval was that required to win. wurī bạ zại gēgu ba interval (as above) is too small to allow of insertion of tip of little finger.

gēgu Vd. gēgẹ.

gēhẹ Kt. = gēfẹ.

gēlọ m. maŋ ~ m. the oil mạn funị q.v.

gēmai-gēmại used in ~ dạ kai, zā kạ yi hakạ ? is this the sort of conduct befitting a man of your years !

gēmụ = Sk. gēmẹ m. (pl. gyạmmā = gēmunạ = gēmummukạ). (1) (a) beard. (b) yā kafạ ~ he's growing a beard. (c) ~ bā yạ hanạ wạsā there is many a good tune played on an old fiddle. (d) iŋ kā ga gēmụn dạŋūwaŋkạ yā kāmạ wutā, shāfa wạ nākạ rūwā be warned by what has happened to others ! (e) gēmụm masạrā beard of maize-cob. (f) Vd. cạɓulạ ~, Mūsạ dạ ~. (2) (a) mại ~ m. adult male. (b) bā gemụn dạ zại yī no self-respecting grown male would act so. (c) ạbin dạ ya sạ na bar gidāna, kōwạnẹ ~ yā bar gidansạ I left my home for a reason that would cause any man of self-respect to do so. (d) ~ bā yạ bịŋ săi dạ ạmfānī nobody consorts with another except for some good reason. (e) inūwạr ~ Vd. mạkōgwạrō. (3) support of tauyị-beam. (4) ɗaŋ gēmụŋ ụbā (mild abuse among elders) bother you ! (cf. ụbākạ, ūwā 1c). (5) gēmụn cēdīyā red aerial roots of cēdīyā tree. (6) mọtsiŋ ~ m. groundnuts shelled, boiled, salted, then roasted (sōyạ) with inner skin left on (= mōtsạ 2c), cf. mọtsī 5. (7) gēmụŋ kụrkunū first part of guinea-worm to extrude. (8) gēmụŋ kwāɗī dirty marks on body from washing in muddy water. (9) gēmụŋ kwāɗō type of grass.

gēra-gēra f. (1) flowering spikes of the reed gyāranyạ. (2) bird-snare on corn-stalks. *(3) " laying trap " for P.

gēranyạ = gyāranyạ.

gērē Vd. dōdō 8.

gērō m. (1) bulrush-millet (Pennisetum typhoideum) = Kt. hatsī 2. (2) ɗaŋ ~ m. the food kā tụrārạ. (3) gēran tsuntsāyē (a) type of grass like kọmayyạ. (*b*) = gẹ̄rạ-gẹ̄rạ 1. (4) Gẹ̄rō, ạbōkin Sarkī *epithet of* any ạlkālī. (5) gāriŋ ∼ *Vd.* tābạ 1*a.* (6) *Vd.* cī dạ ∼, Cị ∼.

gĕshē *m.* (1) small, ornamented calabash scraped with fingers to produce musical sound. (2) vagina (= farjị). (3) *Yawuri Hausa* type of trickery.

gĕtsẹ (1) *Vb.* 1A. (*a*) snapped (string, etc.). (*b*) ∼ mạganạ to leave one's sentence unfinished. (2) *Vb.* 3A (string, etc.) snapped.

gĕtsī *m.* fistula on horse's withers.

gĕtsọ *m.* moist gravel showing proximity of water when digging a well.

gĕtsū *m.* = gĕtsī.

gẹ̄wai-gẹ̄wai = gẹ̄waiwaikọ *m.* = gẹ̄wai-wainīyā *f.* (1) repeatedly circling round place. (2) "beating about the bush".

gewaya A. (gẹ̄wạyā) *Vb.* 1C (kẹ̄wạyā *is alternative form*). (1) went round (place) *x* (*a*) yā gẹ̄wạyạ d̃ākị he made the circuit of his house (= zāgạ 1*a*). (*b*) yā ∼ mu he visited us in rotation. (*c*) yā kẹ̄wạyạ sōjạ he inspected the soldiers drawn up. (*d*) zaŋ gẹ̄wạyạ fuskạta I'll have a look at my face in the mirror (*Vd.* gẹ̄wạyạ 1*b*). (*e*) zaŋ gẹ̄wạyạ gōnāta I'll have a look round my farm (*Vd.* gẹ̄wạyạ 1*b*). (2) sur-rounded (= zōbẹ 1*b*). (3) went round to *x* yā gẹ̄wạyā bāyaŋ gidā he went round to the back of the house. yā gẹ̄wạyā bāyansụ he backed them up. tun dạ ta gẹ̄wạyā bāyaŋ ụbaŋkạ, yā kạmātạ kạ yi matạ sụturạ since she was your father's wife (or concubine), it is your duty to provide for her (= zāgạ 3). (4) went round place with *x* (*a*) aŋ gẹ̄wạyạ sạ ox for killing on morrow has been paraded round market (= *Kt.* nūnị 2). (*b*) aŋ gẹ̄wạyạ Ạlkụr'aŋ Koran has been taken round place of theft in belief this will lead to divine clues. (5) yā ∼ he has gone to latrine (= zāgạ 3) (*cf.* magẹ̄wayī). (6) dãākị yā ∼ dạ rạhōnīyā *said when* P. is helped or leniently treated by one owing to his connection with another whom one honours or likes. (*b*) aŋ ∼ masạ he's been leniently treated (= gẹ̄wạyẹ 1*c*).

(7) aŋ ∼ masạ tsiŋkē he's an utter boor. (8) *cf.* gẹ̄wayō.

B. (gẹ̄wạyạ) *f.* (1) making circuit *x* (*a*) zạ̄ ni ∼ I'll go and have a look round my farm. (*b*) fuskạ gōnā cẹ̄, sǎi dạ ∼ one's face requires attention just as does one's farm (*cf.* gẹ̄wạyā 1*d*). (2) an yi ∼ people have gone round *as in* gẹ̄wạyā 4. (3) yā yi ∼ pilgrim made circuit of Kạ'abạ. (4) tanā ∼ she has her monthly periods now (= hailạ). bạ tạ tabạ ∼ ba she's not reached age of menstruation. (5) yā yi ∼ = gẹ̄wạyạ bạ̄kin rāmị. (6) gẹ̄wayạr kạshī *Vd.* kạrē 36.

gẹ̄wạyạ bạ̄kin rāmị *m.* hoeing or manuring limited to base of crops (= gẹ̄wạyạ 5 = gạ̄ nākạ 1*a*, *b*).

gẹ̄wạyạ tsāmīyā *m.* the creeper d̃add̃ọrī *q.v.*

gewaye A. (gẹ̄wạyē) (1) *Vb.* 1C. (*a*) (i) = gẹ̄wạyā 1. (ii) dãākị yā ∼ dạ rạhōnīyā = gẹ̄wạyā 6. (*b*) yā gẹ̄wạyẹ hatsī he acted *as in* gẹ̄wạyạ bạ̄kin rāmị. (*c*) aŋ ∼ masạ he's been leniently treated (= gẹ̄wạyā 6*b*). (2) *Vb.* 3A. (*a*) took roundabout way. (*b*) behaved shiftily. (*c*) *Vd.* gẹ̄wayō.

B. (gẹ̄wạyē) *m.* (1) the circular embroidered-pattern mạnnē. (2) han-yan naŋ ∼ cẹ̄ this is a roundabout way = *Kt.* walaŋkēdũwā (*cf.* dọshē, tandarạ).

C. (gẹ̄wayẹ) *m.* (1) open-air corn-pile. (2) (*a*) circumference. (*b*) whole *x* gẹ̄wayaŋ garī in the whole town. (3) place screened off (= magẹ̄wayī).

gẹ̄wạyẹ bạ̄kin rāmị = gẹ̄wạyạ bạ̄kin rāmị.

gẹ̄wạye-gẹ̄wạyẹ *m.* = gẹ̄wai-gẹ̄wai.

gẹ̄wayō *Vb.* 3A (date, day, year, etc.) came round again (*cf.* gẹ̄wạyā ; gẹ̄wạyē).

geza A. (gẹ̄zā) *f.* (*pl.* gẹ̄zōjī = gẹ̄zạnnī). (1) mane. (2) any ornamental fringe (= *Sk.* rạbạjạ 1*c*). (3) fạriŋ gẹ̄zā *Vd.* sāri 2.

B. (gẹ̄zạ) *f.* (*pl.* gẹ̄zōjī). (1) (*a*) the shrub *Combretum sp.* (*b*) farar ∼ shrub *Combretum aculeatum.* (2) aŋ kullẹ musụ ∼ (i) heads of tall grass have been knotted together to impede cavalry. (ii) false charge has been made against them. (3) an yi masạ amaryar ∼ *Kt.* violent attack has been

made on him (P. ; malevolent horse)
by party of people (= **shāmakancī 1**).
(4) dībar ～ *Vd*. **dība** 2*e*. **(5) murūciŋ** ～
Vd. **sōlōbiyo**.

gēzannī *Vd*. **gēzā**.

gēzau *used in* **am bā shi tsōrō** ; **kō** ～ **bai yi
ba** all efforts to intimidate him proved
abortive. **kō gēzau kada ka yi** don't be
alarmed ! **tā yi gēzau** she was afraid.

gēzōjī *Vd*. **gēzā** ; **gēza**.

gēzūwā = gēzwā *f*. a small fish of the
catfish (**tarwadā**) family.

gibbā *Vd*. **gībi**.

gibcē (1) *m*. **nā yi masa** ～ I winked to
him to come. **(2)** *Vd*. **gibtā**.

gibī *Kt*. *m*. meddlesomeness.

gībi *m*. (*pl*. **gibbā = gīyābū = gībuna**).
(1) gap from loss of two or more teeth
(*cf*. **wushiryā**). (2) **an yi wa kudī** ～
there's some shortage in the money.

gibjēje *m*. huge ; plentiful (= **gabjēje** *q.v.*).

gibta A. (gibta) *Vb*. 1A crossed in front
of (= **gifta** *q.v.*).

    B. **(gibtā)** *Vb*. 2 *p.o*. **gibcē**, *n.o*. **gibci**) *x*
nā gibcē shi I winked to him to come.

gībuna *Vd*. **gībi**.

gibzai-gibzai *pl*. huge ; plentiful (*pl*. of
gabjēje *q.v.*).

gicci = gici *m*. crossing in front of P.
(= **gifci** *q.v.*).

giciya A. (gicīyā) *Vb*. 1C. **(1)** placed transversely *x* (*a*) **aŋ gicīya tābarmā** the
mat's been laid transversely (=
gindayā). (*b*) **aŋ** ～ **masa dōki** horse
has been led before him for inspection
or mounting (*cf*. **gitta**). (*c*) **kō karā ya**
～, **bā mai kētarēwā** he has despotic
power. **(2) yā gicīya maiwā** he sowed
maiwā transversely across furrows of
different seed (*Vd*. **gicīyē**). **(3) aŋ** ～
masa sandā he's been beaten. **(4) yā
gicīya karyā** he told a lie.

    B. **(gicīya)** *Vb*. 3B *x* **yā** ～ **hanya =
yā** ～ **kaŋ hanya** it lay across the road
(= **gindaya**).

gicīyad da *Vb*. 3B (butcher) laid out
(bound goats or sheep for slaughtering).

giciye A. (gicīyē) *Vb*. 1C. **(1) aŋ** ～ **shi da
sandā** he's been beaten. **(2) aŋ gicīye
maiwā** all the **maiwā** has been sown *as
in* **gicīyā 2**. **(3)** *Sk*. **yā gicīye hanya**
it (snake, root) lay across road.

    B. **(gicīyē)** *m*. *x* **sunā** ～ they're
sowing (beans ; **maiwā** ; millet) *as in*
gicīya 2 (= **dauranci**).

    C. **(gicīye)** *adv*. **(1) a** ～ crosswise (*cf*.
tsaye 6). **(2)** an **daure dabbōbī a** ～
the beasts are tethered head to tail
as in **harda 4**.

    D. **(gicīye)** *m*. **(1)** thing lying across
road (root, snake). **(2)** ～ **haunī** we
turn left here, Your Majesty !

gidā *m*. (*pl*. **gidājē = gidādūwa = *gidad-
dajī**). **(1)** (*a*) (i) compound. (ii) house
consisting of several rooms, whether
native-style or European (*cf*. **daki**).
(iii) **yā yi** ～ **a naŋ** he's set up house
here. (iv) **kaya tā yi** ～ *f*. corn on foot
ascribed to presence of unextracted
thorn. (iv.A) **an yi masa** ～ he has
married (*Vd*. 1*l*). (iv.B) **karfī yā yi** ～
bai shiga ba he has overgrown his
strength. (v) **kāmuŋ** ～ *m*. sending
ahead to arrange quarters for travelling
Chief. (vi) **yā kita** ～ he left home.
(vii) **gidam bīyū nē** there is this world
and the next (*cf*. 1*h*, *j below*). **gidan
tabbata** the next world (*Vd*. **tabbata**
2*a*.iii). (viii) **kō gidam mutum ka jē,
kā fī shi** *epithet of* **Sarkī**. (ix) **mutum
a gidansa Sarkī nē** everyone is master
at home. (x) **bā ā darē a** ～ if one has
means, other difficulties are trivial.
(xi) **in dā zā a bi shāwara tasa nē,
dā har** ～ **zā mu rika biŋ Jāmus** if we
listened to him, we should comply
with all the demands of the Germans.
(xii) **suŋ iske su har** ～ they (enemy)
pursued them right up to their homes.
(xiii) **hanya bā ta bariŋ** ～ what's
bred in the bone . . . (*Vd*. **turba 2**). (xiv)
lābāri yanā naŋ gidan jīya the news is
unchanged (*Vd*. **dafkā 2**). (xv) **a** ～
bā shi da na bīyū he has no equal so
long as nobody else competes with him.
(xvi) *Vd*. **giji**. (*b*) **gidam bikī** *Vd*. **tūwō
21**. (*c*) (*note plural pronoun*) **tanā gidansu**
she's at home. **yanā gidansu** he's at
home (*but* **yanā gidansa** he (house-
owner) is at home). **ki tafi gidaŋku** go
(*fem*.) home ! **ba zaŋ auri mace ban saŋ
gidansu ba** I won't marry a woman
whose people are unknown to me (*cf*. **garī**
1*b*). (*d*) **a** ～ at home *x* (i) **ba ta sāmē shi**

ạ ∼ ba she didn't find him at home.
yanạ̄ ∼ he is at home. (ii) bā yạ̄ ∼ he's
not at home, *or* he's sexually impotent
(*cf.* lạ'ĩfī). haŋkalinsạ bā yạ̄ ∼ he's " not
all there ". (*e*) kyaŋwā bā tạ̄ ∼ *Vd.*
ɓērā 1*c*. (*f*) tā shigō ∼ she's reached
puberty. (*g*) yau tā ci ∼ to-day he has
acted at home in the evil way he does
outside. (*h*) gidā bīyū lālạ̄tạ kạrē don't
have " too many irons in the fire "
(*cf.* 1*a*.vii, 1*j*). (*j*) ∼ bīyū māgạniŋ
gō̄barā " don't put all your eggs in
one basket " (*cf.* 1*a*.vii, 1*h*). (*k*)
ɗaŋ ∼ *m*. (i) freeborn member of
household (*f.* 'yar ∼, *pl.* 'yaŋ ∼), *cf.*
dākị 5. (ii) = dakō 1*b*. (iii) ɗaŋ gidaŋkạ
Vd. farkē. (*l*) maị ∼ *m*. (i) householder
(= magidạncī = musammạŋ 1*b* =
wạ̄ 3*b* = ụbaŋ gidā 1). (ii) maị ∼ nē̄
he's a married man (*Vd.* 1*a*.iv.*A*).
(iii) Maị ∼ (*term of respect*) my husband
x Maị ∼ bā yạ̄ naŋ my husband is not
at home. maị gidantạ her husband.
(iv) head of the house (*pl.* mạ̄sū gidā̤jē
househeads, householders, *but* mạ̄sū
gidā occupants of a compound under a
maị gidā). (v) Maị ∼ Sir ! *x* sạnnū
Maị ∼ good day, Sir ! Maị ∼ kadạ
kạ yī please don't do so, Sir ! (vi) maị
gidantạ *Vd.* ạlkāfụrā. (vii) maị ∼
ạ hakōrī *Vd.* dạddawā 1*b*. (viii) maị ∼
ɗayā wāwā *Vd.* Dōzạ. (ix) an yi wạ
maị ∼ kụnū *Vd.* sạ̄ B.4. (x) ạ bar wạ
ɗam maị ∼ kạrē *Vd.* tạ̄rā 2*b*. (xi)
sham maị ∼ *Vd.* budịrī. (xii) nāmạ nạ̄
maị ∼ *Vd.* tūwō 9. (xiii) săi na maị ∼
yā fārę *Vd.* ūdạ 1*b*. (xiv) gidaŋkạ ạ
rēshę *Vd.* kūlumī. (*m*) ụbaŋ ∼ master
of servant, etc. (*Vd.* ụbaŋ gidā, ụbaŋ
gijị). (*n*) (i) ūwar ∼ senior or only
wife. (ii) (*term of respect*) wife *x* ūwar ∼
tā cē̄ . . . (*x said by servant to his
master*) Madam said that . . . (= dākị
9*b*). (iii) sạnnū ūwar ∼ good day,
Madam ! (iv) *cf.* mạɗākị, ita 4, ūwar
gijịyā, kwārī. (v) tā dōki ūwar ∼ *Vd.*
būlālạ 3. (*o*) na ∼ (i) member of the
same household as oneself *x* baị san
na ∼ ba nē̄ he didn't recognize the
other as a member of the same household as himself. (ii) *Vd.* cịnnākạ 5.
(*p*) bāyaŋ ∼ *Vd.* bāyā 2*d*. (*q*) yạ yi

kūkaŋ gidansạ *Vd.* tsuntsū 6. (*r*) bā
ạ̄ darē ạ ∼ *Vd.* darē 2*m*. (*s*) Allạ̄ kaŋ
kāwō kị ∼ *Vd.* tạntabạrā. (*t*) bạ̄ ka
∼ *Vd.* arnę. (*u*) gạyạ bạ̄kō ∼ *Vd.*
gayạ 5. (*v*) gidantạ na tsāmīyā *Vd.*
ụŋgulū 6. (*w*) *Vd.* cikịŋ gidā, mijịŋ
gidā, kaŋ gidā. (*x*) tā tunạ kwānaŋ ∼
Vd. tsō̄fō 1*d*. (*y*) (i) ɗam bạbbaŋ ∼
the son of a rich family. (ii) *Vd.*
bạbbar ∼. (2) receptacle *x* (*a*) (i)
gidaŋ ạshānā matchbox (*Vd.* faŋkō 2).
(ii) gidan zumạ beehive (= amyạ).
(*b*) *cf.* ạkwạ̄tị. (3) portion *x* rạbā shi
gidā-gidā divide it into portions !
nāmạ ∼ bīyū two of the portions
(kashị) into which meat-on-sale (tạllạ)
is divided. (4) (*a*) gidaŋ kauyę *Vd.*
manōmī. (*b*) gidan tsīrā = lāhirạ.
(*c*) gidan jīyạ *Vd.* dạfkā 2. (*d*) gidam
bịkī *Vd.* tūwō 21. (*e*) *for other compounds
of* gidan, *Vd.* second word. (5) *for
compounds where* gidā *is second word*,
Vd. first word.

gidādancī *m.* the ways of a country
bumpkin, lack of *savoir faire*
(= kauyancī = kidāhumancị).
gidādạ̄wā *Vd.* bạgidā̤ję.
gidādūwạ *Vd.* gidā.
gidā̤jē *Vd.* gidā.
gidạncē *Vb.* 1C made receptacle for T. *x*
aŋ gidạncę takō̄bī they have made a
scabbard for the sword (*Vd.* gidā 2).
gidạ̄nīyā *f.* officiousness.
gidaunīyā *Sk. f.* (*pl.* gidaụnī) any calabash
(*Vd.* dumā).
giddigī *m.* (*f.* guddụgā) *pl.* guddụgai
cripple forced to move along on hands
and knees.
gidē *Hadejiya Hausa* fancy !
gididdiba A. (gididdịbā) *Vb.* 1D sliced up
(meat, fish, wood, etc.).
B. (gididdibạ) *Vb.* 2 yā gididdịbi
tūwō he ate much tūwō.
gīdīdī *adj.* *m.*, *f.* (*sg., pl.*) very narrow *x*
'yar tābarmā cē̄ ∼.
gidigat *x* nā fitō ∼, nā faɗạ masạ I told
him bluntly.
gidị-gidī (1) *m.*, *f.* (*sg., pl.*) busybody. (2)
m. (*a*) officiousness. (*b*) trembling from
age.
gidị-gidī *Kt.* *m.* paralysis of the head.
gidigir (1) sịllīyạ ∼ cē̄ it's thick silk-cord.

(2) *Kt.* yā ƙī ∼ he refused point-blank (= gidigat).

gidigit = gidigat.

gidigō *m.* (*sg.*, *pl.*). (1) large log-drum. (2) what thick cloth, paper !, *etc.* (3) ∼ ūwar faɗa *epithet of* any gun.

gidimi *m.* making preparations for T. (= ɗigimi *q.v.*).

gidiniyā *f.* = gidūniyā.

gidis *Kt.* = gīdīdī.

gidiwuri *Kt. m.* = gidū-gidū.

gidōga *Kt. f.* officiousness.

gidū-gidū *m.* paralysis of the head.

gidūniyā *f.* officiousness *x* yanā ∼ kaman wanda akē kaɗā da rūwaŋ hanji he's very officious (= giggīwa 3), *Vd.* rūwā B.8.

gifcē (1) *Vd.* gīftā. (2) *m.* nā yi masa ∼ I winked to him to come.

gifci A. (gifci) *m.* crossing in front of P. B. (gifci) *Vd.* giftā.

gifi *m.* meddlesomeness.

gifil *m.* smallness of garment (= figil *q.v.*).

gifta A. (gifta) *Vb.* 3A = gilma 1*a*, *b*. B. (giftā) *Vb.* 2 (*p.o.* gifcē, *n.o.* gifci) *x* yā gifcē ni he winked to me to come.

giga *f.* doubt *x* iŋ kanā ∼, zō mu jē mu gani if you doubt it, we'll go together so you can see for yourself. wannam, bā ∼ there's no possible doubt about it (= shakka).

gigala *f.* decrepit crone.

Gīgama (1) *epithet of* Emir. (2) *Vd.* gīgamī.

gīgamī *adj. m.* (*f.* gīgamā = gīgama) tall and broad (*re* P., animal, house, pot).

gīgar *m.* (1) shackles with bar, for fixing to ankles of slave or madman likely to run away (*epithet is* ∼ māganiŋ gudajjam bāwa) = *Sk.* malwa. (2) type of mnemonic.

gīgarā *Vb.* 1C = dādarā *x* yā ∼ masa wuƙā he ran blunt knife over it.

gige *m.* place (= guge *q.v.*).

giggīwa *f.* (1) wilfulness of child. (2) over-rating one's ability. (3) officiousness *x* yanā ∼ kaman wanda akē kaɗā da rūwaŋ hanji he's very officious (= gidūniyā).

gīgī *m.* (1) (*a*) meddlesomeness. (*b*) mai gīgī kā taɓa *Vd.* dāwa 5. (*c*)

Vd. cila. (2) (*a*) gīgim barcī heaviness on awakening from sleep (*cf.* girgijē 1*b*). (*b*) gīgin tsūfā (i) second childhood. (ii) gīgin tsūfā takē yi though old, she dresses like a girl (= bulāyī).

gīgīcē *Vb.* 3A became flustered, flabbergasted (*cf.* gāgā).

giginya *f.* (*pl.* giginyōyī = giginyū). (1) deleb-palm (*Borassus flabellifer*), *cf.* bambāmī ; kwangi ; azārā ; ƙwallō ; gazarī ; murūcī ; ƙōdago ; guntsū, gōdā. (2) inūwar ∼ na nēsa kā shā sanyī (*lit.* Shade of the deleb : the one afar is most likely to enjoy thy shade !) you neglect your family and favour strangers (= barēwā 1*b*), *cf.* indararō, hannū 1*m.* (3) an yi masa kundumiŋ ∼ he's been (*a*) robbed of his all. (*b*) irretrievably dismissed from his position. (4) *Kt.* one of the four slender, round columns occasionally made to support roof of Emir's council-chamber.

gigita A. (gigita) *Vb.* 3B became flustered, flabbergasted (*cf.* māmare 3*b*). B. (gīgīta) *Vb.* 1C. (1) flustered. (2) aŋ gīgīta aiki the back of the work's been broken.

gīgīta bāmī *m.* P. or T. which flusters people.

gīgītad da *Vb.* 4B flustered, flabbergasted.

gīgītau *m.* P. or T. which flusters people.

Gīgo (1) *epithet of* chief. (2) *epithet of* bridegroom (*said by girls*) = Kīgo.

gigyū *used in* yanā da tauri ∼ it's very tough.

gije *Sk. m.* nest (= shēƙā).

giji *m.* (1) = gidā 1 *x* (*a*) zā ni ∼ I'll be off home. (*b*) naŋ ∼ nē gārēka please make yourself at home ! (2) (*a*) 'yaŋ ∼ young people of the household. (*b*) sātar 'yaŋ ∼ *Vd.* sāta 2*d*. (3) mai ∼ nē he's a married man (= gidā 1*l.*ii). (4) *Vd.* ubaŋ giji. (5) (*a*) an yi masa shigar giji he (youth) was given virgin slave-concubine prior to marriage with 'yā (freeborn girl). (*b*) an yi masa shigar ∼ da bāyī bīyū the youth was married to two virgin slave-wives on same day. (6) waŋ ∼ *epithet of* cock. (7) *Vd.* a ∼ gīwā. (8) bōkaŋ ∼ bā yā cī nobody's a prophet at home ! (*Vd.* bōkā 1*c*).

(9) ~ tā zō he (she) is dead. **(10)** *Vd.* sǫ ~. **(11)** hannū yā san na ~ he's generous, but only to his family (*Vd.* giginyạ 2).

gijibgī **(1)** *m.* tā yi ~ nāmạn tsūfā she has the middle-aged spread. **(2)** abundantly *x* nāmạ yanạ̄ kạ̄sūwā ~.

giji-giji A. (gị̄'ji-gịjī^ıı) *m.* (*sg.*, *pl.*) woodborer insect attacking date-palm (*cf.* gundạ).
  B. (gịjị-gịji) *m.* *x* yā yi masạ ~ it put him in a panic.
  C. (gịjī-gijī = gịjī-gịjī) *m.* *x* yanạ̄ ~ he's having a hard time.

gijịrcē *Vb.* 3A lay on one's side (= kịshịngidạ).

gijirtạ *Vb.* 3B = gijịrcē.

gijiwārẹ *m.* **(1)** tough meat. **(2)** stiff task. **(3)** slow horse.

gijīyạ *f.* *used in* an yi masạ ~ he's been kindly treated.

*gīlạ *Ar.f.* *used in* kisạŋ ~ *m.* treacherous murder.

gilbōshị *Sk. m.* = gī6ị 1.

gilgijẹ *m.* rain-cloud (= girgijẹ *q.v.*).

gilgilwạ *Sk. f.* being shaky in its socket (= lage-lage).

gilgịzā *Vb.* 1C *Kt.* shook T. to and fro (= girgịzā *q.v.*).

gillạ *Vb.* 1A did excessively *used in* **(1)** yā ~ laumạ he broke off huge mouthful of tūwō. yā ~ ƙaryā he told "whopper". yā ~ kāshī he defæcated. rūwā yā ~ manạ kāshī we were drenched by the rain. aŋ ~ masạ kāshī (sandā) he's been thrashed.

gịllạ-gillạ *m.* small-girls' cloth (*from navel to knee*).

gịllau **(1)** *m.*, *f.* (*sg.*, *pl.*) liar. **(2)** what a "whopper" !

gillẹ *Vb.* 1A severed the head *x* **(1)** aŋ ~ masạ kǎi he was beheaded (sạ̄rā 1*b*.iii). **(2)** awākī suŋ ~ shūkạ goats ate heads off crops (*all* = ƙundụmē).

gillị *m.* **(1)** covert hatred. **(2)** what a "whopper" !

gilmạ **(1)** *Vb.* 3A. (*a*) *x* yā ~ gạbāna he crossed in front of me. (*b*) yā ~ kạŋ hanyạ it (snake, root, etc.) lay across road (= gịcīyạ), *cf.* giftạ. (*c*) passed by (= wucẹ). **(2)** *Vb.* 1A. (*a*) it (road, etc.) crosses over (place). (*b*) ~ takǫbī to

sling sword across body. (*c*) ~ tụrạ̄rē to pass perfume under one's nose.

gịlmayyạ *f.* constantly passing across.

gilme A. (gịlmē) *m.* method of plaiting sword-knot.
  B. (gilmẹ) *Vb.* 1A *Kt.* **(1)** yā ~ hanyạ = gilmạ 1*b*. **(2)** yā ~ itạ̄cē he cut down the tree. **(3)** yā ~ tūwō he " wolfed up " the tūwō.

gilmị *m.* **(1)** passing by, passing across (*as in* gilmạ). **(2)** ~ wạndạ bā yạ̄ karyạ Azụmī (*a*) passing snuff under nostrils in cursory way so as not to invalidate the Fast (*Vd.* karyạ 1*d*). (*b*) passing-by of woman during Fast, with only minimum of essential conversation and no levity.

gīlǫ **(1)** gīlǫ = yāwạŋ gīlǫ *m.* aimless roving (= sạ̄rā 1*m.* ii). **(2)** *m.*,*f.* (*sg.*, *pl.*) aimless rover.

Gimba *epithet of* any Cirǭmạ.

gimballạ = gimbillạ *Sk. f.* the sleeveless shirt bịŋgyal.

Gimbīyā **(1)** ~ 'yar zākị *epithet of* chief's daughter. **(2)** short, fat woman.

gimẹ *m.* religious exhortations by professional beggars (mạ̄sū gimẹ = hạdīsị 2) for payment.

gimgimta A. (gimgimtā) *Vb.* 1C *Kt.* *x* yā gimgimtạ mạganạr he " made a mountain out of a molehill ".
  B. (gịmgimtạ) *Vb.* 3B *Kt.* *x* mạganạr tā ~ matter's been given quite undue importance.

gimsā *Sk.*, *Kt.* = gịnsā.

gimshẹ *Vb.* 3A became mature.

gimshị *Kt.* abundant *x* yanā naŋ ~ there's plenty of it.

gimshịƙē *Vb.* 3A becàme mature.

gimshịƙēƙẹ = gamsaƙēƙẹ̄.

gimshịƙị = gịnshịƙị.

gimshimēmẹ = gimshimī tall (= ginshimēmẹ *q.v.*).

gimtsẹ *Vb.* 1A = gintsẹ.

gina A. (ginạ = *Sk.* gīnạ) *Vb.* 1A. **(1)** built with clay, brick, cement *x* yā ~ gạrī he built a town. rạ̄irayī bā yạ̄ ginūwā sand is not suitable for building purposes (*cf.* kafạ). **(2)** ~ tukwạ̄nē to make pots. **(3)** *Sk.*, *Kt.* (*a*) = gịnā 1. (*b*) *Vd.* rịjịyā 1*b*.
  B. (ginā) **(1)** *Vb.* 2 *Sk.*, *Kt.* dug

(hole) *x* (*a*) **yā gịni rāmị = haɓạ**.
(*b*) *Vd*. **rāmị** 1*d*, *e*, **rịjịyā** 1*b*. (2) *m*.
(*sg*., *pl*.). (*a*) large type of flying
termite (= **shịŋgē** = *Sk*. **suŋgẹ** 2).
(*b*) **gịnan shānū** small type of flying
termite (= **shịŋgē**). (*c*) *Vd*. **fịtar** ∼.
(3) *Sk. f*. act of digging (= **gịnị**).
C. (**gīnạ**) *Sk*. (1) = **ginạ** 1. (2) *f*. =
gịnā 3.
gincẹ *Kt*. = **gimtsẹ**.
gịncirạ (1) *Vb*. 3B *Sk*. (*a*) lay on one's
side (= **kịshịŋgidạ**). (*b*) died. (2)
bạ ∼, **makarịŋkị Allạ wadai** what a lie !
gincịrē *Vb*. 3A *Sk*. = **gịncirạ** 1.
gincirmī *Kt*. = **gintsilmī**.
gịndā *Kt. f*. (1) buttocks. (2) **yā yi kunyạ
har ya yi 'yar** ∼ he slunk off " with his
tail between his legs " (= **gịndī** 9).
gịndāgurī *m*. big, strong man.
gindǎi *Kt. m*. (*pl*. **gịndạ̄wā = 'yaŋ gindǎi**). (1) (*a*) cotton-seller. (*b*) salt-
seller. (2) **gịndạ̄wā** *pl*. salt-**kantụ** cut
up for sale to middlemen for resale in
villages.
Gịndau *used in* ∼ **ɓạtạ mọ̄rīyā** *epithet of*
(1) dog. (2) destitute P.
gịndạ̄wā *Vd*. **gindǎi**, **bạgindẹ**.
gindaya A. (**gịndayạ**) *Vb*. 3B **yā** ∼ **ạ
hanyạ** it (snake, root, etc.) lay across
the road (= **gilmạ** 1*b*).
B. (**gịndạyā**) *Vb*. 1C. (1) placed
transversely (= **gicīyā** 1). (2) arranged
in rows.
gịndạyē *Vd*. **gịndī**.
gindi A. (**gịndī**) *m*. (*pl*. **gịndinạ**). (1) (*a*)
base of T., bottom (= **gatọ = gūtsū**) *x*
(i) **gịndin tukunyā** base of pot. (ii)
gịndin turmī corn at base of mortar not
reached by pestle (*Vd*. **turmī** 9). (iii)
yā nẹ̄mi gịndin zamā he looked for a
good job. (iii.*A*) **yaŋkẹ** ∼ *Vd*. **yaŋkẹ**
1*c*.vii. (iv) **gịndiŋ gāshị** place at back of
head whence hair radiates. (v) **gịndin
rịgā** skirt of gown. (vi) **yā ɗaurẹ**
(= **yā ɗaurạ**) **minị** ∼ he helped me.
(vii) **gịndin ɗākị** house-floor. (viii)
hanyạ tā bi ta gịndin dūtsẹ the road
skirts the hill (*Vd*. 1*e*). (ix) **gịndiŋ itạcē**
Vd. **tūshẹ** 1. (x) *Vd*. **hawā** 1*a*.vii, **gịndī**
1*e*, 2. (xi) *Vd*. **kantụ**. (*b*) (i) buttocks
(*cf*. **kwạŋkwasọ**). (ii) **yā karyạ** ∼ he
shook his loins suggestively in dancing

(*Vd*. **gwātsọ**), he behaved shamelessly
x **yā karyạ** ∼ **yā cī** he (boy who jibbed
at going errand to bring his mother
ingredients for food) shamelessly ate
the food when ready, undeterred by
remorse. (iii) **tā ɗaurạ zanẹ ạ namijịŋ** ∼
her cloth was so short that it left her
buttocks exposed. (iv) **gịndiŋ kūrā
yā sābạ dạ rāɓā** he has had to learn in a
hard school and is not finicky. (v)
yā kāmạ musụ ∼ he helped them. (vi)
mum bī sụ ạ ∼ **ạ** ∼ we closely dogged
them. (vii) **maị būnū ạ** ∼ **bā yạ̄ zūwạ
gudụmmawar gọ̄barā** the pot should not
call the kettle black. (viii) **warkī**
dǎidǎi ∼ *Vd*. **warkī** 4. (ix) **gịndiŋ
kabạ** *Vd*. **tsịŋkẹ** 2*a*.iii. (x) **gịndiŋ
kargō** *Vd*. **damị** 6. (xi) **dạ** ∼ **kạn cī**
Vd. **cī** 11*p*. (xii) **gịndim bạkā** *Vd*.
bạkā 3. (xiii) **gịndiŋ gyạ̄rē** *Vd*. **gyạ̄rē**.
(xiv) **gịndin tāsạ** *Vd*. **tāsạ** 2*c*. (*c*) (i)
(*euphemism*) male or female genital
organs (*cf*. **ạzakạrī**, **farjị**). (ii) **haifụ̄wā
ɗayā fọ̄raŋ** ∼ **nẹ̄** one learns from experience (*Vd*. **haifụ̄wā** 3). (*d*) **yā
zaunạ dạ gịndinsạ** he's living happily
with assured status (*Vd*. 1*h*). (*e*)
gịndin *prep*. at the foot of *x* (i) **gịndin
dūtsẹ** at the foot of the hill. (ii) **gịndiŋ
itạcē** (*Vd*. 1*a*.ix) at the foot of the tree.
(iii) *Vd*. **gịndin**-compounds *alphabetically*. (*f*) **anạ̄ yi wạ ūwar gidā
dạnnar** ∼ senior wife is being diverted
by drumming from introduction of new
bride (*Vd*. **dạnnā** 4). (*g*) **yā ci gịndinsạ**
(i) he caught him by the waist. (ii) he
backbit him. (iii) **gịndin cịttā** *Vd*.
cịttā 5. (*h*) (i) **bạ shi dạ kǎi**, **bạ shi dạ** ∼
he's feckless ; it's illogical. (ii) **im bạ ạ
zaunạ dạ** ∼ **ba**, **bā ạ̄ zamā dạ kā** if
one cannot get on with relations, how
much less with strangers ! (*Vd*. 1*d*).
(iii) **yā ɓi kǎi**, **yā ɓi** ∼ *Vd*. **ɓi**. (2) root
of plants (*Vd*. 10*b below*, **tūshẹ** 1).
(3) counterfoil stump. (4) **gịndin
takạrdā** packet of two leaves of imported paper. (5) (*a*) **yā kafạ** ∼ he
sat down. (*b*) **yā kafạ gịndinsạ** (i)
he laid the foundations of it (house,
etc.). (ii) he started work on it. (6)
yā fī nị ∼ he's more influential than I
am. (7) **bāban nạm ·bạ shi dạ** ∼ this

indigo has not produced a good precipitate. (8) dākinsa yanā gindiŋ gidāna his house´ is inside my compound. (9) yā ji kunya har ya yi ɗaŋ ∼ he slunk off with "his tail between his legs" (= Kt. gindā 2). (10) (a) jaŋ gindiŋ gīwā māganiŋ hakin tsaye (lit. elephant dragging its bottom crushes grass) epithet of influential P. (b) jā ∼ m. sorting groundnuts left in the ground after pulling up of plants. (c) Vd. jā 1e.

   B. (gindī) m. (pl. gindāyē). (1) hobbling-rope. (2) yā tsiŋkę ∼ = yā tsiŋka ∼ = yā cira ∼ (a) it (horse) broke loose. (b) he ran away.

gindigiri = Kt. gindigīrī m. (1) useless thick end of rakē or takandā-sugar-cane (= ƙundugurū q.v.). (2) coccyx (cf. dandari).

gindīkwalọ m. pieces of yam or sweet-potato cooked in oil.

gindimēmę = gindimī m. (f. gindimēmīyā = gindimā) pl. gindiŋ-gindiŋ. (1) large and round. (2) long and fat.

gindin Vd. gindī 1e.

gindina Vd. gindī.

gindiŋ akwatō m. diamond-pattern in embroidery on tāgīya cap (cf. akwatō).

gindin baƙā used in an jūya masa gindim baƙā his friend has turned against him (= jūya 1d.iii).

gindin cittā m. cantankerous P. (= cittā 5 q.v.).

gindin daƙwalwā m. type of native cloth mainly grey and blue, with few white strips let in.

gindindiŋ m. hugeness x macijī nē ∼ da shī it's a huge snake (pl. macīzai nē gindiŋ-gindiŋ da sū).

gindiŋ guzumā used in ya yi mini gindiŋ guzumā = yā yi mini gindiŋ gyārē (1) he informed against me. (2) he left me in the lurch (= zagwaŋ ƙas).

gindiŋ kaba Vd. tsiŋkę 2a.iii.

gindiŋ kargō Vd. dami 6.

gindiŋ kūrā Vd. gindī 1b.iv.

gindiŋ ƙūru m. (1) = ƙundugurū.˅ (2) = ƙūrūwā. (3) Sk. maize-cob with few remaining grains given to child.

gindim murhu m. (1) fireplace for cooking (Vd. murfu). (2) mai ūwā a ∼ bā

yā cin tūwō gāyā = tūwō 13, (cf. ūwar tūwō).

gindin takardā Vd. gindī 4.

gindin tandū : gindin tāsa : gindin turmī : gindin zubọ Vd. respectively tandū : tāsa 2c : turmī 9 : zubọ.

ginę Vb. 1A finished building ; built completely (as in gina).

giŋgācē Vb. 3A. (1) became fully-grown. became an important P.

giŋgāta Vb. 3B = giŋgācē.

giŋgātau m., f. (sg., pl.). (1) fully-grown P. (2) important P.

giŋgiŋbōdi Kt. m., f. P. of drivelling talk (= kiŋkiŋbōdi q.v.).

giŋ-giŋ-giŋ m. x an ji ∼, anā kiɗa drumming was heard.

ginginta A. (giŋgintā) Vb. 1C Kt. yā ginginta maganar he made a "mountain out of a molehill".

   B. (giŋginta) Vb. 3B Kt. magana tā ∼ matter's been given undue importance.

giŋgirābai m. and adv. (1) left about carelessly ; thing left about carelessly. (2) kau da ∼ m. pilfering (= sānē).

giŋgiriŋ m. (1) x yā yi mini ∼ it was beyond me. (2) kansa yā yi ∼ his hair stood on end. (3) hugeness x kansa ∼ da shī he has a huge head (pl. kāwunansu giŋgiriŋ-giŋgiriŋ da sū).

gini m. (1) (secondary v.n. of gina) x yanā ginin dāki = yanā gina dāki he's building a house. (2) (a) being occupied in building x yanā ∼. (b) da sābaŋ ∼ gāra yābē (i) choose the lesser evil ! (ii) it's better to improve existent conditions than to make a clean sweep ! (3) sg., pl. any building or structure made of clay, cement, or brick (cf. kafa) x wannaŋ gini this edifice, building. (4) (a) rampart round town x "alkarya" garī nē bā ∼ the word alkarya means a town without rampart. (b) rashin gini Vd. garī 1e. (5) yā yi ∼ he remedied an omission ; added something lacking. (6) Sk., Kt. yanā ginin rāmi (rījiyā) he's digging hole (well) (cf. gina). (7) type of large fish. (8) ginim Buri m. top-heavy thing. (9) giniŋ gadō Vd. badō 2.

giniga *f. and vb.* 3B *x* aiki yā yi ~ = aiki yā ~ there's much work.

ginigis *m. and adv.* abundantly *x* mun yi aiki ~ we did much work. aiki yā yi mana ~ we've too much work to do.

ginis *Sk. m.* yā yi ~ da fuska he scowled. yā yi mini ~ he scowled at me.

ginki *m.* idol (= gunki *q.v.*).

ginsā *Vb.* 2 (*p.o.* ginshē, *n.o.* ginshi) *x* abincin nan yā ginshē ni = nā ginsu da abincin nan I'm surfeited with this food (= cinkishē). kā ginshi Audu Audu's has had as much as he can stand of you. zuma ~ garēshi honey soon cloys.

ginsāmī *Sk. m.* slaughtering and selling on credit (= watandā 1*a*).

Ginsau name for any man called Hārūna.

ginshe A. (ginshē) *Vd.* ginsā.
   B. (ginshe) *Vb.* 3A became mature.

ginshi A. (ginshi) *Vd.* ginsā.
   B. (ginshi) *Kt.* abundantly (= gimshi *q.v.*).

ginshikē *Vb.* 3A became mature.

ginshikēke *m.* tall and stout (= gamsakeke *q.v.*).

ginshiki *m.* (*pl.* ginshikai). (1) (*a*) pillar supporting roof (= al'amūdi). (*b*) basis *x* ginshikin aminci a dūnīya the principles underlying world security. (2) double thickness reinforcing gown (= sace). (*b*) reinforcement of loin-cloth. (3) strong P.

ginshimēme, *etc.* = ginshimī.

ginshimī *m.* (*f.* ginshimā) *pl.* ginshinginshin tall and stout.

ginsu *Vb.* 3B *Vd.* ginsā.

gintse *Vb.* 1A. (1) ~ rūwā to dam water for catching fish (= tare). (2) interrupt conversation, sleep, etc., of P. *x* yā ~ maganassu he interrupted their conversation. (3) yā ~ fuska he scowled.

gintsilmī = gintsirmī *m.* running short of supplies *x* zare yā yi mini ~ my thread came to an end. rūwā yā yi mana ~ the rains were not enough for our crops (= raba zanga 2 = *Kt.* tangaragātsā).

gir *abbreviation of* girme *x* nā gir masa I'm older than he is.

gira A. (girā) *f.* (*pl.* girare = girōrī). (1) (*a*) eyebrow. (*b*) yā daura ~ he frowned (= fuska 1*c*). (*bb*) daurin ~

m. (i) frowning. (ii) operation to cure blepharitis (*Vd.* daurin ~). (*c*) gama ~ *Vd.* gama 1*l.* (*d*) upward twist of eyelids (ectropion). (*d*) tā kada masa ~ she "gave him the glad eye" (= *Sk.* tā sāra masa ~), *Vd.* kada 1*k.* (2) (*a*) edge of top of building. (*b*) edge of gwandā-cloth. (*c*) edge of kantu of salt. (*d*) *Vd.* waddare 2. (3) white line below black storm-clouds. (4) marks left on bank by receding water. (5) sunā zaman ~ their work brings them (enemies) into forced contact. (6) (*a*) wākē yā jā ~ beans are nearly cooked. (*b*) tā saka katambiri, tā jā ~ she applied cosmetic to her eyebrows.
   B. (gira) *Vb.* 3B (*progressive* girā). (1) P. became vindicated ; turned out to have been speaking accurately, truly (= gaskīyā 3*d* = kunita = kwāce 1*b*.i). (2) kā ~ *m.* bribe given judge, etc.

girāgirī *Sk. m.* wild tigernut (= ayaaya).

girāgizai stormclouds (*pl. of* girgije).

girāre *Vd.* girā.

giraya A. (girāyā) *f.* (*pl.* girāyū) the musical instrument kōmō.
   B. (girāya) *Vb.* 2 preceded (= rigāya *q.v.*).

girba A. (girbā) *Vb.* 2 reaped *x* (1) an girbi hatsī the corn has been reaped (= sārā 1*g*). (2) bā sā yarda su tarbi fadan da ba zā su girbi rība ba they are not the people to engage in unprofitable strife. (3) shī zai girbā *Vd.* shūka 1*a*.ii.
   B. (girba) (1) *Vb.* 1A applied abundantly *x* yā ~ masa māri (wuka) he gave him severe slap (knife-thrust). yā ~ mini karya he told me a "whopper". (2) *Vb.* 3A yā ~ a guje he fled.

girbau *Vd.* shāgirī 3.

girbe (1) *Vb.* 1A. (*a*) reaped completely. (*b*) yā ~ shi da māri (wuka) (karya) = girba 1. (2) *Vb.* 3A yā ~ a guje he fled.

girbi *m.* (1) (*secondary v.n. of* girbā) *x* yana girbin dāwa = yana girbar dāwa he's reaping guinea-corn. (2) being occupied in reaping *x* (*a*) yana ~. (*b*) mūgun ~ *Vd.* falle 1*b.* (*c*) kidan ~ *Vd.* kida 1*c.*

girɓuna A. (girɓunā) *Vb.* 1C **yā girɓunạ fuskạ** he made a wry face (*cf.* **gātsịnā**).
B. (girɓunạ) *Vb.* 2. (1) **yā girɓuni fuskạ** = girɓunā. (2) **bạŋ ∼ ba** I don't care a jot !
girɗā *Vb.* 2 = **girɗẹ 1**.
girɗā-girɗạ̄ *Vd.* **girɗēɗẹ**.
girɗẹ (1) *Vb.* 1A. (*a*) (i) dislodged from socket. (ii) snapped off short. (*b*) sprained. (*c*) twisted out of shape (= **jirɗẹ** *q.v.*). (2) *Vb.* 3A. (*a*) became dislodged from socket. (*b*) became sprained. (*c*) became twisted out of shape.
girɗēɗẹ *m.* (*f.* **girɗēɗịyā**) *pl.* **girɗā-girɗạ̄** huge.
girɗigī *Vd.* **giḍḍigī**.
girēmạ *used in* ∼ **kạ̄kam marạsā** what a persistently unlucky person !
Girgạ *used in* ∼ **bạ̄ jạn sau, kōwā ya yī kạ, dạ̄munā tā shāshē shị** = . . . **dạ̄munā tā bāshē shị** *epithet of* guinea-worm (**kụrkunū**), *cf.* **shā dạ̄ 2***b*.
girgạ̄mō = **girgạ̄mau** = *Kt.* **girgạ̄mū** guinea-worm (= **kụrkunū**).
girgiɗā *Vb.* 1C = **girgiɗạ** *Vb.* 2. (1) shook T. to dislodge it from socket (*cf.* **girgiɗē**). (2) gave P. reason to fear dismissal.
girgiɗē *Vb.* 1C. (1) dislodged T. from socket. (2) dismissed P. suddenly (*cf.* **girgiɗā**).
gịrgije A. (girgịjē) *Vb.* 1C. (1) (*a*) shook off (dust, water, friends, *etc.*) *x* **yā ∼ ta** he shook it (gown) to get rid of dust. **kạrē yā girgịjẹ jịkinsạ** the dog shook itself. **yā girgịjẹ rūwā dạgạ jịkinsạ** it shook water off its body (= **zazzạgē 2**). (*b*) **yā girgịjẹ barcī dạgạ jịkinsạ** he shook off the heaviness of sleep (*cf.* **gīgī**). (2) **nā girgịjẹ mūdụ** I shook overfull measure to reduce contents level with rim (*cf.* **girgịjī, zazzạgā 3**). (3) *Vd.* **girgịzā**.
B. (girgije) *m.* (*pl.* **gịzạ̄gịzai** = **gịrạ̄gịzai**). (1) raincloud *x* ∼ **yā sạuka ạ arẹ̄wā** a raincloud has gathered in the north (= **san dōkị** = **zirnānịyā**), *cf.* **gạ̄jịmạ̄rē, jịidā**.
girgịjī *m.* *x* **yā bā nị mūdụ ukụ dạ̄ ∼** he gave me 3 piled-up measures

plus one level to the rim (*cf.* **kwạ̄ncīyā 6, tsōrō 2**).
girgịllā *Vb.* 1C *int. from* **gillạ**.
girgịr *used in* **wākyaŋ ∼ m.** type of bean.
gịrgịrtū *m.* fleeting but irritating guinea-worm rashı (= **gạnjạrtū**).
girgiza A. (girgịzā) *Vb.* 1C. (1) (*a*) shook to and fro (bottle, head, *etc.*) (*b*) **tā girgịzạ hannū** she made gesture of dissent. (*c*) **yā girgịzạ kạ̣i** he shook his head in assent or dissent. (2) shook off water, *etc.*, on to *x* **kạrē yā ∼ minị rūwā** = **kạrē yā girgịzạ rūwā ạ jịkīna** dog shook water off itself on to me (*cf.* **girgịjē**).
B. (girgiza) (1) *f.* (*a*) act of shaking itself by bird or animal *x* **rạ̄gō yanạ̄ ∼** ram's shaking itself. **kạ̄zā tanạ̄ ∼** chicken's shaking water (dust) off itself. (*b*) act of shaking tree to and fro *x* **kō dạ ∼ kurnạ tā fi magaryā** the one's far superior to the other. (2) *Vb.* 3B was shaken to and fro *x* (*a*) **zūcịyā tasạ bạ tạ ∼ ba** he did not blench. (*b*) **kasā tā girgịzạ** there was an earthquake.
giri *m.* deceit *x* **yā ɗaurạ minị ∼** = **yā yi minị ∼** he deceived me.
giribtū *Kt. m.* (1) (*a*) **tā yi ∼** she had an illegitimate child (*cf.* **shēgẹ**). (*b*) **ɗaŋ ∼ m.** (*f.* **'yar ∼**) yoù bastard ! (2) (*a*) look out for bad road in front, Chief ! (*b*) **'yaŋ ∼** those calling out as in 2*a* (= **kạramtū**).
girīdạ *f.* senselessness.
giri-giri *Sk. m.* wild tiger-nut (= **ạyạ-ạyạ**).
girịŋ *m.* (1) ∼ **dạ kạ̣i** = **girịŋ-girịŋ**. (2) ∼ **dạ rānī** type of hemp (**ramạ**) maturing in hot season (= **kōkạ rānī 2**).
girịŋgiɗịshī *m.* (1) " counting one's chickens before they're hatched " (= **daurī 1***b* = **warạbukkạ 1***b* = **murnạ 2***c* = **hadịrị 1***e*), *Vd.* **wạrkī 5 ; gaggāwā 1***c*. (2) **yanạ̄ girịŋgiɗịshinsạ** he's on tenterhooks about it.
girin-girin A. (girịŋ-girịŋ) *m.* (1) sound made by strings of **gạrāyā**. (2) **bạ̄ ∼ ba, maŋ** = **bạ̄ ∼ ba, ạ yi mạ̣i, kūrā tā ɗau gurmī** not words, deeds are required !
B. (girịŋ-girịŋ) *x* **yā zamā ∼** it's become a big matter.

C. (girịŋ-girịŋ) with the head shaking x yanǎ tafe dǎ kǎi ∼ he's shaking his head about as he walks. ∼ dǎ kā takę formula said when playing with baby (N.B.— f. agreeing with the synonymous rawar kǎi).

girịrị x anǎ jǎnsǎ ∼ ponderous T. is being hauled along.

girịrrịdǎ Vb. 2 int. from girdā.

girịrrịkā Vb. 1D int. from girkǎ.

girịrrịmā (1) Vd. girmā. (2) (Vb. preceded by pl. subject) suŋ ∼ they grew big.

girịs A. (girịs) adv. (1) x (a) yā nǔna ∼ it's quite ripe. (b) kǎttā ∼ lusty young fellows. (2) = girịs 1.

B. (girịs) (1) used in wutā tā hǎdu ∼ = garwāshị yanǎ naŋ ∼ fire is all glowing embers. (2) girịs-girịs crunchingly (= garǎs-garǎs q.v.).

girka A. (girkǎ) (1) Vb. 1A. (a) (i) tā ∼ tukunyā she put cooking-pot on fire (cf. saukę 1c ; saŋwǎ). (ii) = yā dǎ 3b, c. (b) yā ∼ rumbū he set bin on its platform. (c) ∼ ịgwā to lay piece of artillery. (d) ∼ dūtsǎn nikǎ to support grinding-stone on stones (cf. magirkī). (e) suŋ ∼ dāgā they're drawn up in line of battle. (f) ∼ ǎl'ādǎ to establish a custom. (g) schooled P. how to act (in evidence ; bǒrī, etc.) (cf. magantad dǎ 2). (h) Vd. dā'irǎ. (2) Vb. 3A. (a) yā ∼ ǎ gujẹ he fled. (b) Vd. girku.

B. (girkā) f. (1) an yi matǎ ∼ she's been initiated into bǒrī (cf. girkǎ 1g). (2) an yi masǎ ∼ he (adult) has been exorcized (cf. burgā).

girke A. (girkę) Vb. 1A. (1) put away (water ; furā ; tūwō ; etc.) in vessel for consuming later (Vd. ajịyē 5a.i). (2) upbraided. (3) yā ∼ manǎ dǎ kūkā he pestered us with his crying, complaints.

B. (girkē) m. (pl. girkunǎ). (1) type of gown (= shāyǎ 1b = sǎbadǎ 2), Vd. ǎlbadǎ, sǎŋgō 3. (2) Vd. dumaŋ girkē.

C. (girkē) m. x zō, mu yi ∼ (said by women) let's go and grind in line together ! (cf. girkǎ 1d).

girkị m. (1) act of putting cooking-pot on fire x (i) tanǎ ∼. (ii) anā ∼ dǎ kandīlō food can be cooked over fire of dried dung. (2) (secondary v.n. of girkǎ) x tanǎ girkịn tukunyā = tanǎ girkǎ tukunyā she's putting the cooking-pot on the fire. (3) dākịn ∼ kitchen (= dākịn dǎfūwā). (4) type of cloth of alternately coloured strips. (5) ∼ garēshị he (P., horse, etc.) is well formed.

girku Vb. 3B yā ∼ = girkị 5.

girkunǎ Vd. girkē.

girma A. (girmā) m. (1) (a) (i) bigness x dōkị yanǎ dǎ ∼ = dōkị yā yi ∼ the horse is (was) big. dōkị yā yi girịrrịmā = dawākī sun yi girịrrịmā = dōkị yā yi girmā = dawākī sun yi girmā the horses are (were) big. (ii) saŋ ∼ garēshị it (P., animal) has grown up quickly (abbreviation for sauriŋ ∼). (b) honoured position x (i) yā yi ∼ he became honoured, promoted. (ii) an yi masǎ ∼ he is honoured. (iii) kōyaushē akǎ yi masǎ wani dan kāyaŋ ∼ whenever one shows some favour to him. (iv) yanǎ dǎ girman dūnịyǎ he has an assured position. (v) bai saŋ girmaŋ kōwā ba sǎi kǎnsǎ he is arrogant. (vi) iŋ kā bā nị, wannaŋ girmaŋ kǎŋkǎ nē if you give it to me, it'll redound to your credit (cf. girmaŋ kǎi). (vii) girmansǎ yā fādị = girmansǎ yā kǎrai he's lost his good name. (viii) yā kā dǎ girmansu he caused them to lose prestige. (ix) nēmaŋ ∼ garēshị = haliŋ ∼ garēshị he's liberal. (x) Allǎ mǎi ∼ good heavens ! (xi) tā gamǎ masǎ kāyaŋ ∼ she provided him with the appurtenances of a P. of position. (xii) anǎ bā shị ∼ respect is paid him. (xiii) bǎ ǎ ga girmansǎ ba he was not looked up to. (xiv) yā yi minị baŋ ∼ he showed me respect. ban girman rūdị lip-service. (xv) kǎbakiŋ ∼ yā fi kǎbakiŋ kǎŋkanci a small gift willingly given is better than a large gift accompanied by humiliation. (xvi) dǎ hannū a kǎn saŋ ∼ ǎmmā bǎ fadǎ yị kǎrē ba character is shown by generosity, not by quarrelsomeness. (xvii) in dǎi rǎkumī dǎ ∼, kāyansǎ dǎ yawǎ the rich man has many calls on his purse. (xviii) sū girmaŋ kauyę nē

they are country bumpkins. (xix)
tūwaŋ ∼ mīyassa̧ nāma̧ power never
lacks zest. (xx) jiŋ ∼ m. being conceited. (xx.A) girman darē d̯ayā Vd.
gamba̧ 2. (xxi) girmam mahau̯ka̧cī Vd.
banzā 1a. (xxii) girman shūci̯ Vd.
banzā 1a. (xxiii) girmaŋ kūka̧ Vd.
rēna̧ 7. (xxiv) girman d̯inyā Vd.
yāro̧ 1b. (xxv) da̧ girmā, ba̧ dībā Vd.
fa̧ŋkō 4. (xxvi) yā da̧ girmā Vd. yā
da̧ 1h. (xxvii) girmanta̧ yā zubȩ Vd.
ma̧rakī 1b. (xxviii) Vd. sa̧ndaŋ girmā.
(c) good will, tractability x (i) bā sa̧
yī bisa̧ ka̧ŋ ∼ they don't do it with a
good grace. bā sa̧ yī bisa̧ ka̧ŋ ∼ sǎi
sun shā wu̧yā nȩ they only do it under
duresse. (ii) ba̧ ∼ aka̧ mai da̧ sū
zagaraftū they had perforce to slow
down. (iii) yā gudu̧ tun da̧ ∼ he fled
"while the going was good". (iv)
zā mu̧ rasa̧ ta, bābu̧ rǎi, bābu̧ ∼ we
shall lose her irretrievably. (v) girmā
da̧ azziķī Vd. azziķī 4b. (vi) Vd.
girma-girma. (d) Vd. girman-com-
pounds. (2) Vb. 3B. (a) grew up x
(i) har girmāna till I grow up. sa̧n da̧
yakȩ ∼ while he was growing up.
(ii) kā girmā da̧ gāga Vd. Turu̧ŋkū.
(iii) iŋ kā girmā Vd. sha̧ talē-talē.
(b) aŋ ∼ (i) he has been circumcized.
(ii) he has reached time for putting on
loincloth (ba̧ntē). (iii) he has married.
(c) increased x tāshi̧ŋ ha̧ŋka̧lī na̧ ta ∼
alarm is on the increase. (d) became
great x a̧ ∼, a̧ ci ka̧sa̧? should one who
has reached high estate beha̧ve like
one of low degree!
    B. (girmā) Vb. 2 x nā girmē shi̧ I'm
older than he is. nā girmē shi̧ da̧
shēkara̧ uku̧ I'm three years older than
he is (= girmȩ 1).
girma-girma x yā zō ∼ aka̧ bā shi̧ he
came and was given what he wanted,
but now ill-will has arisen (cf. girmā 1c).
girmama A. (girma̧mā) Vb. 1C. (1) (a)
showed honour to. (b) ba̧ shi da̧ gir-
ma̧māwā he is disrespectful. (2) promoted P.
    B. (girmama̧) Vb. 3B. (1) became
honoured. (2) became promoted.
    C. (girma̧mā) pl. persons of prestige.
girma̧me-girma̧mē m. dū yā tāra̧ ∼

honours have been showered on him.
girma̧nce used in a̧ ∼ in keeping with
one's self-respect.
girman damō used in yā shi̧ga ∼ he's in
prison (Vd. damō 10b).
girman darē d̯ayā Vd. gamba̧ 2.
girman d̯inyā Vd. yāro̧ 1b.
girmaŋ kǎi m. (1) conceit. (2) Vd. girmā
1b.vi. (3) ∼ rawa̧niŋ ki̧ya̧sūwā pride
comes before a fall.
girmaŋ ko̧rar rāmi̧ used in yā (tā) yi ∼ he
(she) did well till about seven years old
and then died in first illness.
girmaŋ kūka̧ Vd. rēna̧ 7.
girmaŋ kushēwā = girmaŋ ko̧rar rāmi̧.
girmam mahau̯ka̧cī Vd. banzā 1a.
girman ra̧i = girmaŋ kǎi 1.
girman shūci̯ Vd. banzā 1a.
girman 'yan d̯inyā used in yāro̧ da̧ fu̧lā,
ba̧bba da̧ fu̧lā ∼ said when disparate
persons imitate one another.
girmȩ Vb. 1A (with dative). (1) nā ∼
masa̧ = nā gir masa̧ I'm older than he
is (= girmā). (2) is (was) beyond one
x sā tāka̧lmī yā ∼ mini̧ I'm no longer
well enough to wear sandals. yā ∼
wa̧ aran ri̧gā he considers himself far
too fine to borrow a gown.
girōrī eyebrows (pl. of girā).
girsa̧ f. x ana̧ girsa̧r aiki̧ they're working
might and main.
girsā-girsa̧ pl. huge (re men, kolas, sticks,
etc.).
girshe Sk. unexpectedly x ∼ suka̧ zō they
came suddenly.
girsillē = girsillī (1) m. type of inferior dark
Bornu salt. (2) m., f. (sg., pl.) grubby P.
girtsa Vd. gartsa.
girtsȩ (1) Vb. 1A. (a) yā ∼ mini̧ hako̧rā
it gave me a severe bite. (b) yā ∼ musu
hanzarī he snubbed them. (2) Vb. 3A
he's desperate.
gi̧rtsī Sk. m. cartilage (= guru̧ŋguntsī).
gishā̧rē Vd. gishirī.
gishi̧ Kt. m. (1) = gashi̧. (2) ∼ kwa̧d̯d̯ī =
∼ kwa̧rdī playfully forcing P. down
on to hot ground (= gashi̧ŋ ku̧mā).
gishirī m. (pl. gishā̧rē). (1) (a) salt
(= a̧lkālī 4). (b) gishirim ba̧ŋgō
mildew used as ingredient for gunpowder (a̧lba̧ru̧s). (2) an zuba̧ masa̧ ∼
(a) he's been told flattering lies. (b)

he's heard T. which has alarmed him. (3) gishiriŋ giṇdī *epithet of* woman's girdle (jigidā). (4) mutụm dạ gishirinsạ, in yā sō, yạ dafạ ƙạfō one's property is one's own to do as one likes with. (5) kantụ bạ̄ ∼ ba nẹ̄ how can one pay without funds ? (*Vd.* kantụ 1*c*). (6) ƙanshiŋ ∼ yā fi ∼ zāƙī an underling often swanks more than a P. of real importance. (7) kōmē zā ạ yi, ạ sạ̄ ∼, an yi wạ maị gidā kuṇū whatever your hands find to do, do it with all your might ! (8) Allạ̄ shī kẹ̄ bạ̄ kūrā ∼, nāmạ kō ạ kạ̄sūwā tạ̄ sāmụ *epithet of* warrior, dogged worker. (9) hancị baị san dādiŋ ∼ ba what has it to do with you ? (10) kataŋgar ∼, kōwā ya daŋganạ, yā lạ̄sā what a liberal person ! (11) gishiriŋ gạba *Vd.* zạkaŋkaụ. (12) birị dạ ∼ *Vd.* birị 3. (13) gạbaŋ ∼ *Vd.* gạbā 5. (14) gishirin sautụ *Vd.* gūgạ 6.

gishū *m.* pleuropneumonia of sheep or goats.

*gisshị *m.* fraud (= ạlgụs).

git 1. *m.* yā yi ∼ he relapsed into silence. (2) *adv.* gạjērē ∼ very short. yā sạ̄ wạndō ∼ he put on very short trousers.

gitạbajẹ *Fil. m.* type of food.

gitātumī *m.* big, strong man (= kịtātumī *q.v.*).

gitērẹ *East Hausa m.* cullender-pot for steaming food (= madambacī).

gititiŋ *m.* (1) *x* kạ̄ina yā yi ∼ " my hair stood on end ". (2) yā yi minị ∼ it is (was) quite beyond me.

gitsāwạ *m., f.* (*sg., pl.*). (1) red-and-white goat (= kyallạ). (2) *Kt.* black-and-white goat.

gittạ (1) *f.* (*pl.* gittōcī). (*a*) battle-axe. (*b*) hunters' axe. (2) *Vb.* 3A *Kt.* = gilmạ. (3) *Vb.* 1A *Sk.* aŋ ∼ masạ dōkị horse has been led past him for inspection or mounting (= gicịyā).

gittērẹ *m.* very thick tūwō.

gittōcī *Vd.* gittạ.

giwa A. (gīwā) *f.* (*pl.* gīwạ̄yē). (1) (*a*) (i) elephant (*epithet is* Mạƙạsau = Mạrin dawạ (*Vd.* Wạmbai ; 1*v below*) = Rāƙạsạ̄ = Rākaụ). (ii) gīwan *m.* (gīwar *f.*) huge *x* gīwan jirgī huge boat (*pl.* gīwạ̄yan jirạ̄gē). gīwar mōtạ huge motor-

car (*pl.* gīwạ̄yam mōtōcī). (*b*) (i) ∼ tạ ci tsāmīyạ̄ ? haƙōrin zōmō yạ mutụ ? should one suffer for the crime of another ? (*cf.* haƙōrī 10*a*). (*c*) tọraŋ ∼ *m.* adult bull-elephant (*Vd.* 1*u*). (*d*) ạ ƙạ̄rạ wạ ∼ māsụ̄ ? debt on debt ! (*Vd.* ạ 1*s*). (*e*) ∼ tā haifụ (i) there's a sunlit shower. (ii) sun has a halo. (*f*) Gīwā ! *greeting used when addressing* Sarkī, Wạmbai, Ụban dawākī. (*g*) *Kt.* ∼ wuriŋ Audụ, kūsụ Audu is fearless. (*h*) in zā kạ yi tạfīyạ, kạ yi tạfīyar ∼, kadạ kạ yi tạfīyar kūrā don't beat about the bush ! (*j*) (i) bạ̄ kā dạ ∼ kẹ̄ dạ wụyā ba, kạ̄fiŋ ạ birkịcē ta, ạ fẹ̄dẹ ta (= . . . kạ̄fiŋ ạ birkịcē ta, ạ yaŋkạ ta) it's easy to begin anything, but hard to see it through to the end. (ii) *Vd.* karmāmī 3. (*k*) saŋ ∼ yā tākạ na rạ̄ƙumī important T. overshadows lesser T. (*l*) bāyaŋ ∼ săi barbajẹ săi cạrkī *epithet of certain great men.* (*m*) wurin dạ akẹ̄ bạbbakạr ∼ wạ̄ zaị kulạ dạ ƙaurim ƀērạ̄ who will heed a boy when elders are conversing ? (*n*) zōmō bạ̄ bāwạŋ ∼ ba nẹ̄, dājị ya tārạ su these persons are of different status (origin), but happen to be colleagues in the same work. (*o*) dạ ta tạrbacē ∼ ta fi kōwā girmā = jụ̄cē 2. (*p*) wurim ƀạrnar ∼ bā ạ̄ kulạ̄wā dạ ƀạrnar birị in face of serious misfortune, small woes pass unnoticed. (*q*) ∼ tā shā rūwā dạ yawạ, ballē tā yi azụmī he's cantankerous without provocation, so how much more if provoked ! (*r*) an ci ∼ mā tā ƙārẹ, ballē gạdā as he gave me no share in his great good luck, how much less have I any chance of a share in his smaller good luck ! (*s*) kō dājị yā ƀāci, ∼ tā fi gudụ nil desperandum ! (*t*) dạmunā tā yi shigar zōmō, tā yi fitar ∼ the wet weather set in scantily but later was abundant. (*u*) karọ ɗayā kō dạ tọraŋ ∼ ạ̄ bugạ try everything once ! (*Vd.* 1*c*). (v) Gīwā, mariŋkạ tūwō *Vd.* marin tūwō (*cf.* 1*a*). (*w*) ạbin gasạ ∼ *Vd.* riṇō 2. (*x*) jīzạr ∼ *Vd.* jīzạ 2*b*. (*y*) bạ̄baŋ ∼ *Vd.* bạ̄ba 3. (*z*) jaŋ gindiŋ ∼ *Vd.* gindī 10. (*z*) (i) gīwar Bạ̄sạ *Vd.* 9. (z) (ii) tausar ∼ *Vd.* tausā 2*b*. (z) (iii)

Gwauraŋ ∼ *Vd.* Galādīma. (z) (iv)
bargwaŋ ∼ *Vd.* bargō 2. (z) (v) nōnaŋ
∼ *Vd.* nōnọ 1*h*. (z) (vi) ƙashiŋ ∼ *Vd.*
guŋgumurƙi. (z) (vii) magājiŋ ∼ *Vd.*
Hasaŋ. (z) (viii) kulkim fōraŋ ∼ *Vd.*
gwantal. (z) (ix) *Vd.* makīyāyī 2,
kāshiŋ gīwā, tāfiŋ gīwā, baŋ gīwā,
takandar gīwā. (2) tūwan naŋ ∼
nẹ̄ this tūwō was made at about 3 p.m.
and so is neither really day-food or
night-food. (3) longest string of mōlō
(= amālẹ 1*c*), *cf.* magūdīyā 5. (4)
sun yi ∼ the picked storm-troops have
massed for the attack. (5) sun yi ∼
suŋ gudu beaten army with civilians is
fleeing *en masse*. (6) *x* Niŋgāwā sun
tūra wa Kanāwā ∼ the Ningi people
pushed hugh rock down on the Kano
soldiery. (7) two mats sewn together
for money or corn (*cf.* 14). (8) gīwar
alharīnị packet of the silky fabric
alharīnị (*cf.* war-war 2). (9) gīwar
Bāsa type of cloth with alternate strips
of farī and sāƙi. (10) gīwar fitọ raft of
tanned oxhide (ƙilābọ). (11) gīwar
garī notorious woman. (12) gīwar
kambā type of large, early guinea-
corn. (13) gīwar karā (*a*) large collection of corn-stalks (*cf.* 8). (*b*) *Kt.* pile
larger than ƙiriga. (14) gīwar kudī
load of cowries tied in untanned oxhide
(ƙilābọ), so dry that it can only be
opened with an axe (= ƙuŋƙūru 3,
Vd. 7 *above*). (15) gīwar rūwā Nile
perch (*Lates niloticus*). (16) hannuŋ ∼
(*a*) elephant's trunk. (*b*) *Sk.* while
holding load on one's head, helping up
another's load with one's free hand.
(17) kaŋ ∼ *Kt. m.* open space before
Chief's palace (= ƙōfar fāda). (18)
Vd. a giji gīwā.
   B. (Gīwa) *man's* name.
gīya *f.* (*Ar.* ji'a). (*a*) (i) native beer (*cf.*
bārāsā). (ii) *its epithet is* Gīya, madarar
arnā. (*b*) bā a ∼ sāi da dāwa " one cannot make bricks without straw ".
(*c*) *x* gīyar kudī the unbalancing effect
of wealth. (*d*) shaŋ ∼ na bāwaŋ
gōnā nẹ̄? = shaŋ ∼ bā na bāwaŋ
gandū ba nẹ̄ who are *you* to attempt
such a thing ! (*cf.* gandū 2*d*). (2) *Eng.*
gear *x* yā tāka ∼ he changed gear.

gīyābū *Vd.* gībị.
gīyayyā *f.* (1) the marsh-tree *Mitragyne
africana*. (2) *Kt.* chapping of the legs.
Gīyẹ (1) *epithet of* Chief. (2) Audu ∼
nē = Audu yā yi ∼ Audu is outstanding.
gizāgizai *Vd.* gizọ-gizọ, girgijẹ.
gizāgō *m.* (1) adze (= masassaƙī). (2) ∼
nẹ̄ = mai lāfīyar ∼ nẹ̄ he is a hypocrite
(*epithet is* ∼ kaifiŋka nā cikī). (3) ∼
da gēmu he is not my senior, so why
should he send for me his equal ?
(= Mūsa 2).
gizākā *f.* (1) (*a*) caterpillar whose hairs
come out on being touched and cause
irritation. (*b*) *Vd.* 2*b*. (2) gāwar ∼ =
mūshaŋ ∼ = gāwar zāƙi (*a*) (i) P.
once wealthy. (ii) big, dear gown now
ragged. (*b*) gāwar ∼ kim mutu, kinā
bā yārā tsōrō *epithet of* 1, 2*a*. (*c*) T.
illegally obtained. (*d*) Allā ya bā mu
mūshaŋ ∼ may we get plenty of
money !
Gizāmị *epithet of* gizọ 2.
*gizāzi *Ar. m.* a perfume-measure.
gizda A. (gizdạ) *Vb.* 1A. *Sk.* boiled T.
for long time.
   B. (gizdā) *Sk. f.* (*secondary v.n. of*
gizdạ) *x* tanā gizdarsa = tanā gizdạ
shi she is boiling it for long.
gizganyā *Vb.* 1C *Kt.* = gizgayā.
gizgāra (1) *m.*, *f.* strong, energetic P.
(2) Gizgāra, bāwan yāƙi *epithet for*
Emir's slave.
gizgayā (1) *Vb.* 1C turned T. diagonally,
placed T. diagonally (= bākatad dạ 1
q.v.). (2) *Vb.* 3A turned diagonally *x*
hadiri yā ∼ kudu the storm has veered
southwards. wata yā ∼ kudu new moon
now faces south. rānā tā ∼ sun has
passed meridian (= bākatar *q.v.*).
gizgiri *m.* (1) edible base of gōdā of dum
or deleb. (*b*) gizgiriŋ kaba thickened
root of young dum-palm. (2) head of
guinea-corn (dāwa) or millet (gērō)
before it opens out.
gizo A. (gizọ) (1) *m.*, *f.* (*sg.*, *pl.*) cute P.
(2) *m.* (*a*) (i) Spider, as personified in
fables as type of most cunning P.
(*epithet is* Gizāmị). (ii) *Vd.* gizọ-gizọ.
(iii) *Kt.* yā bāta ma ∼ yānā he took to
his heels (= gizọ-gizọ 1*d*). (iv) bā

naŋ gizọ kẹ̃ sāƙar ba this is not the real issue. bā̧ naŋ gizọ yakẹ̃ sāƙar ba, sāmu̧ŋ kuɗi̧ŋ it's easy to sell anything, but hard to get payment for it (cf. gizọ-gizọ 1c). (v) ba̧ a̧ kā da̧ ~ ba̧ ? a̧ cẹ̃ ƙōƙi̧ ta̧ tāsọ̄ ? don't begin a fresh task till the one in hand is completed ! (vi) Kt. spider (for Kt. does not use the word gizọ-gizọ for spider). (b) stratagem x yā ƙulla̧ ~ he hatched a plot. aŋ gānẹ giza̧nsu̧ they have been found out ; we know what they're up to. (c) ba̧kaŋ ~ m. (i) rainbow (= gā̧ji̧mā̧rē 1b = kya̧ŋkyẹ̃nau = sàgō 2 = mashā̧ 3b). ba̧kaŋ ~ shī bā̧ Allā̧ ba, ya ka̧ŋ hana̧ wa̧ Allā̧ rūwā a skinflint often prevents the liberal P. giving. (ii) ceiling-arch (cf. ɗauri̧ŋ gūgā). (iii) dog-in-the-manger ; acting as dog-in-the-manger. (iv) type of spirit living in wells. (v) Sk. = haƙōrim fā̧rā. (d) inspiring one with dread x kūrā tā yi (= tā zuba̧) masa̧ ~ seeing the hyena turned his blood cold (= arwā). (3) Vd. shibci̧ŋ gizọ, tēki̧ 5, āya̧ 4. (4) ūwar ~ Vd. ba'a̧. (5) hu̧dag ~ Vd. hu̧dā 2c. (6) ƙīra̧r ~ Vd. ƙīra̧ 1g.

B. (gizō) m. (1) man's long, dirty, matted hair, i.e. neglected su̧mā. *(2) gidaŋ ~ m. prison.

gizọ-gizọ m. (pl. gi̧zā̧gi̧zai). (1) (a) spider (= tau-tau̧). (b) cf. gizọ (especially 2a.vi). (c) sāƙar ~ f. spider's web (cf. gizọ 2a.iv). (d) yā ɗēbẹ yānar ~ he took to his heels (= gizọ 2a.iii). (2) Sk. gizọ-gizọ = Kt. gi̧zā̧gi̧zai used in yā ga̧mu da̧ ~ he has oriental sore-marks on his skin, ascribed to drinking water wherein spider had been (= tau-tau̧ 2a), cf. tau-tau̧ 2b.

gōba̧ Eng. f. (sg., pl.) guava.

gōbarā f. (1) (a) catching fire x (i) ga̧rī yā yi ~ the town was destroyed by fire. (ii) mā̧sū aiki̧ŋ kashẹ ~ members of the fire-brigade. (iii) gidā bīyū māga̧ni̧ŋ ~ don't put all your eggs in one basket ! (iv) ~ da̧ga̧ kōgī, māganī nāta̧ Allā̧ (said in song) only God can remedy a really serious calamity ! (v) dōmi̧ŋ ka̧rē, a̧ yi ~ the fullest investigation will be welcome to me, for

I'm not involved. (vi) Vd. būnū 3. (b) gōbarar ciki̧ diarrhœa ; scalding oneself with boiling drink. (vii) hana̧ gōbarā Vd. dā̧lī. (c) gōbarar ɗaka̧ loss of one's goods through slump or deterioration. (d) fi̧tila̧ tā yi ~ the oil and wick of the lamp are both consumed. (2) gōrọ yā yi ~ the kolas have deteriorated. (3) the gambling-game di̧kka̧ŋ 2. (4) gōbarar 6ērā Vd. kāma̧ hannū 2.

Gōbarcī m. (1) the Gobir dialect of Hausa. (2) Gobir face-markings (mouth to temple). (3) Vd. Gọ̄bir.

gọ̄be adv. and f. (1) to-morrow x (a) za̧i zō ~ he'll come to-morrow. (b) a̧ ragẹ (= a̧ cī, a̧ ragẹ) doŋ ~ put a bit away " for a rainy day ! " (Vd. ya̧u 1f). (c) ~ mā rānā cẹ̃ don't be too impatient ! (d) ~ ta Allā̧ cē nobody knows what the future holds. (e) da̧ ~ ka̧n ɗau bāshi̧ what temporization ! (f) rānar ~ f. Day of resurrection (= kīyāma̧ 1). (g) gidaŋ ~ m. the Next World. (h) gọ̄be-gọ̄be = Kt. gọ̄be gwaf to-morrow for certain. (j) (i) sunā̧ yī har ~ it's a common practice of theirs. (ii) har ~ da̧ sāfē, da̧ A da̧ B bā̧ shiri̧ akẹ̃ yī ba there is an irreconciliable breach between A and B. (k) a̧ yī ya̧u, a̧ yī ~, shī nẹ̃ aiki̧ perseverance conquers. (l) săi dăi Allā̧ yā kai ra̧i ~ unless God spares us. (m) ɗauka̧ (= fāɗa̧) kō ya̧u kō gọ̄be Vd. dami̧ 2. (n) gọ̄be dauɗa̧ Vd. farī 2g.iii. (o) Vd. Allā̧ kai mu̧ gọ̄be. (p) ma̧i sāmu̧ŋ gọ̄be Vd. mara̧shī 2. (q) tūwaŋ gọ̄be Vd. tūwo 11. (r) mawa̧dā̧ci̧ŋ gọ̄be Vd. matsi̧yā̧cī 4. (2) (a) wata̧ŋ ~ adv. and m. next month. (b) shēkara̧ŋ ~ the day after to-morrow (= jībi), Vd. shēkarẹ. (3) yā yi ɗam bā̧ gọ̄ban daɗa̧ he did an act which he had cause to repent (= gōɗīyā 3). (4) ya̧u da̧ ~ Vd. ya̧u 2. (5) tā yi masa̧ ~ da̧ kallō she stained his gown with indigo (shūnī) when sleeping with him (= shūnī 4). (6) yana̧ naŋ ~ ya̧ jīya̧ = yana̧ naŋ ~ ya̧ gurbi̧ he's a stick-in-the-mud. (7) ~ da̧ bi̧kī m. makeshift trousers formed by folding cloth, sewing, and slitting holes for feet, it being taken apart after the

festival and used again as bodycloth.
(8) Mālam, ∼ da̱ nīsā P. who kills
others by magic.

Gǫbir f. (1) Gobir Area. (2) Vd. Hausā,
Gōbarci̱.

Gōbirāwā Vd. Bagǫbirī.

Gōbircī = Gōbarci̱.

gǫce (1) Vb. 3A. (a) (i) swerved aside
(= baudę). (ii) rānā tā ∼ zūwa̱ arę̄wā
the sun turned north (= bākatar), cf.
gǭta̱. (b) (joint, limb) became displaced, dislocated (= gullę 2 =
gurdę). (c) tāga̱ tā ∼ = sa̱ndā yā
∼ a̱ tāga̱ the window-shutter closed
through removal of prop. (d) rūwā
yā ∼ rain fell in torrents. (e) su̱ŋ ∼
they've become out of alignment (cf.
gurdę). (f) in nā ∼ musu̱, n̄ jē i̱nā
if I separate from them, where am I
to go ? (2) Vb. 1A. (a) removed prop,
letting T. supported fall x (i) yā ∼
ru̱mbū he removed the prop of the bin-
cover. (ii) yā ∼ bindiga̱ he released
the trigger of the gun. (iii) su̱ŋ ∼
wutā they fired a fusillade. (iv) su̱ŋ ∼
ga̱ŋgu̱na̱ they broke into drumming.
(v) yā ∼ hīrā he chattered away. (vi)
hadiri̱ yā ∼ da̱ rūwā it poured in
torrents (cf. Mod. Gram. 177c). (b)
put things out of alignment (= gurdę
2b).

gǭ'ce-gǫce" m. (1) shifty excuses. (2)
shiftiness (1, 2 = zu̱ke-zu̱kē).

gǫcīyā f. (1) swerving x yana̱ ∼ = yana̱
gǫcę̄wā he's swerving (= baudīyā).
(2) ka̱u da̱ bā̱rā, a̱ gama̱ ta da̱ ∼ " trust
in God but keep your powder dry ! "

gǭdā f. (1) fruiting-head of dum (gǭruba̱),
deleb (giginya̱), date-palm (dabīnǫ) or
kaba̱, whence branches radiate (= Kt.
mu̱llī), Vd. gi̱zgiri̱. (2) ∼ ɗa̱ŋ kaba̱t
tsaka̱ epithet of rich boy. ∼ 'yar kaba̱t
tsaka̱ epithet of rich girl. (3) stem
(hanci̱) attaching fruit or leaves of
pumpkin (ka̱bę̄wa̱) to main-stem. (4)
Sk. (with pl. gǭda̱nnī) any bell.

gōdabę = gwadabę.

gǭda̱nnī Vd. gǭdā 4.

gōda̱yī = gwada̱yī.

gōdę Vb. 1A. (1) is (was) grateful x (a)
mu̱ŋ ∼ Allā̱ = mu̱ŋ ∼ wa̱ Allā̱ we
thank God. (b) nā ∼ a̱lhēri̱nsa̱ I'm

grateful for his kindness. (c) sānīyā
bā tā̱ ∼ jēji̱ he is so ungrateful for
benefits that he keeps on pestering his
benefactor. (d) kōmē ka sāmu̱, gǫdę
Allā̱ be grateful to God for whatever
you receive ! (e) ga̱rāra̱ bā yā̱ ∼ Allā̱
sǎi yā ga ma̱kā̱fǫ nobody appreciates
his blessings till bereft of them. (f)
bai̱ ∼ ba Vd. bā̱kī 1b.xvii. (g) Vd.
wa̱hala̱ 1e. (h) ɗan nā ∼ Vd. gurgurī.
(2) nā ∼ maka̱ (a) thank you ! (used by
superior thanking inferior for some
service or favour not part of his normal
and customary duties. But Chief
thanking inferior for a normal and
customary act (such as gift at time of
Festival) says mādallā (or sa̱lbarka̱),
the attendants adding kā ji mādallā, yā
gōdę), Vd. gǭdīyā 1c. (b) Chief says
nā ∼ wa̱ Jama'a̱ thank you my people !
(3) Vd. gǭdīyā.

Gǭdī Kt. epithet of penis (a̱zaka̱rī).

gǭdī Vd. gōdīyā.

gǭdīyā f. (pl. gǭdī = gwa̱ddī = gwa̱dɗai
= gōdīyōyī). (1) mare (epithet is Ta
Shēhu̱). (2) gǭdīyā = gōdīyar bǭrī (a)
woman possessed by bǭrī-spirit x
Fā̱tī gōdīyar Bagǫbirī cę Fati is possessed by the spirit Bagǫbirī q.v. (b)
halin̄ ∼, halim bǭrī there's not a pin
to choose between the two persons.
(3) yā yi ɗam ba̱ ka̱ra̱ ∼ da̱ kwāna̱ŋ
garkę he bitterly rued his act when too
late : he " locked the stable after the
horse was stolen " (= gǫbe 3 = dōki̱n
zūcīyā). (4) gōdīyar Jāka̱rā, cī bai̱ i̱shē
ki̱ ba, hawā yā i̱shē ki̱ epithet of
despised wife or servant. (5) bu̱durwar
∼ Vd. bu̱durwā 2. (6) haifu̱war ∼
f. hanging on branch and somersaulting. (7) ka̱da̱ŋ kā ga ∼ da̱ sirdi̱,
wani ta kāyar if you see an attractive
woman no longer married, you can be
sure there is some good reason : if
nobody wants a T. which looks good,
it is due to some hidden blemish. (8)
yārǫ yā sō aurē, gidansu̱ bābu̱ ∼ one
must exercise patience. (9) gōdīyar
Sarkim pāwa̱ Vd. wutā 1a. (10)
nōna̱ŋ ∼ Vd. nōnǫ 1j.

gǭdīyā f. (1) thanks, gratitude x (a)
munā̱ ∼ we're grateful. (b) mun yi ∼

bisą gą wannąŋ we're grateful for this.
(c) ∼ yakę yį he's expressing his
thanks, Chief ! (said by audience when
recipient of gift has thanked Chief), Vd.
gōdę 2. (d) bą shi dą ∼ he's ungrateful.
(e) ∼ kę są ƙārįŋ kyąutā showing
gratitude brings further gifts. (f)
Vd. dādī 1c.vii. (2) (reply to greeting),
Vd. gąrī 1m, dąwąinīyā, ƙąƙą 1c,
rānā 2c.

godo A. (gōdō) m. (1) yaną gōdansų he's
" having another shot " at getting their
consent. (2) gōdąŋkų (said by woman
without bucket at well to women with
buckets) I'll help you fill your pots
from your buckets if you in return fill
my pot !
B. (gōdǫ) m. (1) bowl of lōfę-
tobacco pipe. (2) small gǫrā-gourd
used as tobacco-jar. (3) Kt. seedpods
of tobacco (edible).

gǫdǫbō m. gonorrhœa (= cīwąn sanyī).

gōdǫgō m. (1) (a) faked gambling-cowrie
(= ągō q.v. = laffą 3), cf. tųlū 4, nįkē.
(b) kadą ką cī nį dą ∼ don't try to
intimidate me ! (= bųrgā). (2) huge
cock (epithet is ∼ ząkarąn tsāfį).

gǫdōsō = gųdōsō.

gǫfā = gwąfā.

Gǫfę jandārū name given any man called
Muhammadu.

gǫfī Vd. gwąfī.

gōfō = gōhō.

gǫfǫfǫ Vd. gǫhǫhǫ.

goga A. (gōgą) (1) Vb. 1C (with dative)
(a) rubbed T. on to x (i) nā ∼ masą mąi
I rubbed polish on to it = gōgę 1a.ii
(cf. gōgę 1c). (ii) nā ∼ ƙafątą jįkim
baŋgō I scraped my foot against the wall
(to rid it of mud, etc.). (iii) yā ∼ minį
kāshiŋ kązā = yā ∼ minį ląifī he foisted
false charge on me. (iv) yā ∼ minį
hąsārą he caused me to incur loss. (b) tā
∼ fųrē she rubbed tobacco-flowers on to
her teeth with sweeping movement (cf.
daddągā 2). (c) rubbed together (two
tųmfāfįyā-sticks to kindle fire). (2)
Vb. 3A suŋ ∼ = suŋ ∼ 'yar ƙąshī
they came to blows.
B. (gōgā) Vb. 2 (progressive uses
gūgą). (1) brushed against P. or T.
(2) (a) gąrī yā gǫgē shį he had a hard

time. (b) yāƙį yā gǫgi gąrimmų war
came on our town (1, 2 = zǫzā 1). (3)
yā gǫgi kąrątū he kept on repeating
text from Koran aloud to memorize it
(= gōgę 1f), he went over and over the
same part of the text.
C. (gōgā) m. (1) experienced donkey
(epithet is ∼ kā saŋ hanyą). (2) jaŋ ∼
" an old hand " (cf. gǫgu).
D. (gǫgā) m. building a bin, etc., with
clay not made into bricks (= daddǫrī
3 = mątsē = dǫrē 5 = Zar. jąnyē).

gǫgaggē m. (f. gǫgaggīyā) pl. gǫgąggū
skilled x gǫgaggyan sōją an experienced
soldier (Vd. gōgę 2b).

gōgai Sk. m. the weed ƙudųjī.

gǫgą māsū m. the weed Mitracarpum
scabrum used for itch (= hąrwatsī).

gǫgarmą m., f. (sg., pl.) dauntless person.

gǫgarmāyą f. (1) struggling with task or
P. (2) (in songs) wifeless man
(= gwaurō).

Gǫgau Vd. banzar birnī 2.

gǫgayyą f. (1) friction due to things
rubbing against one another. (2)
yaną shąŋ ∼ dą mutąnē he's involved
in quarrels.

goge A. (gōgę) (1) Vb. 1A. (a) rubbed T.
x (i) nā ∼ mōtą I rubbed the car to
clean it. (ii) nā ∼ shi dą mąi = gōgą 1a.i.
(progressive n ną gūgą tasą dą mąi).
(iii) nā ∼ haƙǫrā I cleaned my teeth.
(b) (i) scraped x sirdį yā ∼ dōkį the
saddle rubbed on the horse's back.
gōgę tąƙalmī dą wuƙā scrape (mud,
etc.) off the shoe with a knife ! (ii)
(sheep, etc.) damaged (fence) by rubbing
against it (= zōję 1) x suŋ ∼ dangā.
(iii) rubbed with indigo-leaves (the
bow tsirkįyā used in teasing cotton)
to prevent cotton sticking to it
(= Kt. zōję 2). (iv) nā ∼ shi dą
zartǫ I sawed or filed it (progressive n ną gūgą tasą dą zartǫ). (c)
(with dative) rubbed off x yaną ∼
masą ƙųrā he is rubbing dust off it
(cf. gōgą 1a). (d) aŋ ∼ masą farcę
" he has been taken down a peg ".
(e) Kązā, cī kį ∼ what an ingrate ! (cf.
bąkiŋ kązā). (f) ∼ kąrątū = kaftū =
gǫgā 3. (g) Vd. ą ∼. (2) Vb. 3A. (a) is
(was) quite ripe (re groundnuts, corn,

onions, dates, gujīyā), cf. bira. (b)
yā ~ a cikinsa he's " an old hand " at
it (= gōgu), cf. gōgā 2, kā kōmō 1,
gōgaggē.
   B. (gōgē) m. yā yi mata ~ he (old
man) slowly introduced his penis into
her (unmarried little girl).
   C. (gōgē) m. (1) large fiddle. (2) first
quality zugē-ink. (3) gōgyan damō
(a) the gum-tree Combretum sp. (b) Kt.
type of ear-ring.
goggo m. baboon, etc. (= gwaggo q.v.).
gōgin damō Sk. m. = gōgē 3.
gōgo = gwaggo.
*gōgōjirgo m. methylated spirit.
gōgu Vb. 3B yā ~ he's experienced
(= gōgę 2b), cf. gōgā 2.
gōgūwa f. = gūgūwa.
gōgwannī Vd. gwaggō.
gōgyan damō Vd. gōgē 3.
gōhō m. (1) grey donkey (cf. ęfau). (2)
large snail-shell used for ornament
(= gōrī 1). (3) sitting on heels and
bending forward, head on ground,
buttocks in air. (4) gōhan wuri
gambling cowrie. (5) gōham baka
Sk. excessive length of animal's lower
lip which prevents it cropping short
grass.
gōhōhō (1) babba ~ nē (a) he's a stupid
lout. (b) though entitled to seniority,
he's a mere puppet (epithet is Yāyā,
kāwō akushinka). (2) you fool ! x ~
kana barcī a hanya ? you fool, are you
actually sleeping on the road ? ʼ
gōję m. (1) central strip of the 3 metal
strips joining blade of hoe (garmā) to
handle (= dōki 3b). (2) bucket whose
large capacity enables ground-nut
buyers to defraud villagers who sell.
(3) (a) Gōję gaban gayyā epithet of
any Mādākī (Vd. gayyā 1f). (b) abin da
ya vi ~ ai shī yā yi Kaurā we'll sink
or swim together ! (4) any dog
(epithet ~ samārin tōkā).
gōjī Sk. m. pumpkin, marrow (= ka-
bēwa).
gōla-gōla Sk. m. trousers made from uncut
cloth.
Golkwas Gold Coast.
gōlō m. (pl. gōlāyē) testicle (= gwaiwā).
gōlōbō Kt. m. gonorrhœa (= cīwon 4).

gōma f. (1) (a) ten. (b) ~ shā daya
eleven. ~ shā bīyū twelve, etc. (2) (a) ~
ta marmarī first 10 days of Ramazan.
(b) ~ ta wuyā = ~ ta tīlas middle 10
days of Ramazan. (c) ~ ta dōkin
salla = ~ ta murnar salla final 10
days of Ramazan. (3) (a) yā yi mini ~
ta azzikī = yā yi mini ~ shā bīyū
ta azzikī he was generous to me. (b)
haka ya zō hannunsa ~ he came
empty-handed (= hannū 1q). (4)
gidan ~ shā bīyū an embroidery
pattern. (5) tsinkyan ~ mai karam
bīyar = ~ ta karam bīyar type of
arrow. (6) yā yi mini ~ da gōma both
events happened to me simultaneously.
(7) Vd. shanyē 2b, karē 24,
kwarmī 3. (8) karo da ~ Vd. kālācī.
(9) makāfo ~ Vd. garāra 2b.ii. (10)
mai mātā ~ Vd. dagara. (11) ʼyar
Sarkī ~ Vd. tūbę 1b. (12) karē ~ Vd.
mę 4. (13) bai cika ~ ba Vd. tara 3.
gōmīya Kt. f. (used in multiples of ten) x ~
tara ninety.
gōnā f. (pl. gōnakī = gōnakai = Sk.
gōnakkai). (1) (a) farm (cf. fagē 2a,
garkā, aljanna 2). (b) dībam gōnar rānī (i)
clearing large area in the dry-season
which proves beyond one's powers
during the rains. (ii) failure to keep
good resolutions. (iii) " biting off more
than one can chew ". (c) nā nōmę
gōnakinsu I followed their example.
(d) aikin ~ m. farm-work. kāyan
aikin gōnā farming implements. (e)
mai ~, bari tsōkī m. useless, stunted
corn. (f) gōnar bābā, da ita da biri,
sāi ganī don't try and get blood from a
stone ! (g) kisam mai ~ Vd. kisa 10.
(gg) shēgę kā jē ~ Vd. shēgę 5. (h)
gama ~ Vd. sankacę. (j) biri yā mutu
a ~ Vd. Allā 7m, addu'a 1c. (k) kai
tsōfō ~ Vd. bam magana. (l) Vd.
marin ~. (m) gōnar gwāzā Vd. biri 1h.
(n) dōdan ~ Vd. dōdō 6. (o) fuska ~
cę Vd. gēwaya 1b. (p) bāwan ~ Vd.
gīya 1d. (q) gōnar Barę Vd. barę 2c.
(r) mai nīsan ~ Vd. gaida, kādo. (2)
(a) " mine of " x gōnar karyā nē he's
a " mine of " lies. gōnar zancē nē he's
a chatterbox. yana da azancī gōnā-
gōnā he's a " mine of " intelligence. (b)

am bā shị ∼ yanā̰ jā̰ he has a large
crutch-piece (hantsạ) to his trousers. (c)
Kt. yanā̰ jạŋ ∼ he's wearing būjẹ-
trousers. (3) in sun yi ∼ ɗayā, bā̰ lāfīyạ
if they meet, there'll be strife.
gongolā *Vd.* gwaŋgwalā.
goŋ-goŋ *Vd.* gwaŋ-gwaŋ.
gora A. (gōrạ) (1) *f.* (*pl.* gōrōrī). (1) (a) (i)
bamboo.   (ii) ∼ maị kạŋ gwāzā big-
knobbed stick.   (b) yanā̰ jạŋ gōrạr sā̰
he is pulling on the rope attached to
led bull.   (c) yanā̰ jā masạ ∼ he is
leading him (blind man) = tạfi dạ 2b.
(d) *Vd.* jā̰ gōrạ.   (e) trunk of body or
tree. (f) gōrạr hancị bridge of the nose
(= karā 1g.i).   (g) dạ Kande dạ Zainabụ
sunā̰ ∼ Kande and Zainabu are friends
(= ƙawā).   (h) rubūtun nạŋ ∼ gạrẹshị
this is elongated writing.   (j) gōrạr
kitsọ top centre-line of dōkạ-coiffure.
(k) gōrạr ganyē vein of leaf (cf. ƙardẹ).
(l) *Vd.* gōrōrī.   (2) *Vb.* 1A mocked
(= gwạrtā *q.v.*).
   B. (gōrā) *m.* (*pl.* gōrunạ).   (1) (a)
large gourd used as float by persons
crossing river (= gurākạ) *x* yā hau ∼
(i) he supported himself on a gourd to
cross the river. (ii) he made a slip of the
tongue (= kwatā 2 = kōlī 2b).   (b) (i)
gourd-bottle   (= būtạ = jạllō = *Sk.*
gyạnɗamā).   (ii) soldier's waterbottle.
(iii) *Kt.* any small water-bottle, whether
of clay, gourd, or metal (*i.e. what is elsewhere called* būtạ, sạhānị, sintạlī, etc.).
(c) dā̰ dạ gōrāna *m.* the bird Black-
winged stilt (*Himanotopus*).   (d) (i)
yā shịga gōran dạ bā̰ fạ̄fạ̄ he can't
extricate himself from his fix (= *Sk.*
bạngō 4).   (ii) bā ā̰ fā̰fạ̄ ∼ *Vd.* fā̰fạ̄ 3.
(e) rūwaŋ ∼ *Vd.* rūwā B.6.   (f)
dauɗạr ∼ ạ cikī a kạn shā tạ " one
must take the rough with the smooth ".
(g) gōran rūwā (i) = 1b.ii,iii.   (ii)
aluminium (= sạmhōlọ). (h) nōnọ yā
zubẹ, ạmmā yā bar ∼ the child died,
but the mother lived.   (j) kōwā ya
kas kīfī, ạ gōransạ zaị sạkā he who
doesn't seek won't get.   (k) *cf.* tụmạ
dạ ∼. (l) gā̰ gōran zumạ, gā̰ na maɗācī
epithet of ạlkālī.   (m) *Vd.* dūbaŋ gōrā.
(2) woman's breast *used in* gāfiŋ ∼
gạrētạ she has rich milk in her breasts.

yārọ yanā̰ dạ ƙurjiŋ ∼ the baby lad
has pimples owing to poorness of his
mother's milk.   tanā̰ dạ mūgụŋ ∼
she has poor milk, thus causing pimples
in her suckling child.   (3) yārọ yanā̰
kạrāyạr ∼ *Vd.* kạrāyạ 2e.   (4) ƙurjī
yā yi ∼ a blister has formed.   (5) (a)
rānā tā yi ∼ the sun is just setting.
(b) rānā tā yiwō ∼ the sun has fully set
over the horizon (*cf.* fā̰dị 9a). (6) (a) jạŋ
∼ brown donkey (*cf.* ẹ̄faụ).   (b) maị jaŋ
∼ *Vd.* kōlị 1. (7) shēgyạŋ ∼ nẹ̄ he is no
· use to God or man. (8) dūbaŋ ∼ *m.* (a)(i)
squinting. (ii) cast in the eye (= dūbaŋ
garkẹ).   (b) closing one of the eyes
(= kạnnē).
gōrạ-gōrạ *f.* type of grass.
gōrạntā *Vb.* 1C mocked P. (= gwạrtā *q.v.*).
gōrạrrạkai *Vd.* gōrọ.
gori A. (gōrị) *m.*   (1) mocking *x* sun yi
masạ ∼ they mocked him. (2) hạnạ ∼
Vd. dūtsẹ 7a.ii.
   B. (gōrī) *m.* (1) = gōhō 2.   (2) type
of long arrow.
gōribạ = gōrubạ.
gōrīyạ *f.* (1) largest and best kolanuts
(= kạŋ wāgā).   (2) largest and best
guinea-corn grains.
gōrọ *m.* (*pl.* gwạrrā = gōrạrrạkai).   (1)
(a) kolanut (*epithet is* Gaŋgamiŋ kuɗī
ɗaŋ Asạntē), *Vd.* jā̰tau 2b, Ạjauru,
marsạ, gōrīyạ, dabgajā, sārā 4, Gwạnjā 3,
fạkānī, daushē.   (ii) (*collective*) *x* mạnyaŋ
gōrọ = mạnyaŋ gwạrrā big kolanuts.
(iii) wạndạ ya bā̰ kạ ɓārịŋ ∼, in yā saŋ
gụdā, yạ bā̰ kạ even a small gift shows
goodwill (saŋ = sā̰mi).   (iv) wạndạ
ya san darajạr ∼, shī ya kạm biɗam
masạ hūhụ = indạ akạ san darajạr ∼,
naŋ a kạn nēmam masạ ganyē if one
values a thing, one looks after it.   (v)
rạ̈i dạngịŋ ∼, hūtū yakẹ̄ sọ all work
and no play makes Jack a dull boy.
(b) gōrạn sā̰ rānā *Vd.* aurē 6d. (c) gōrạm
biri type of kolanut with several
sections (ƙwạr) and not staining mouth
like true kolas.   (d) namijịŋ ∼ false
kola (*used as medicine*).   (e) gōrạm
bikī small present of kolas announcing
forthcoming ceremony to guest. (f)
dakạ ∼ *Vd.* dakạ 1c. (2) (a) reward for
finding lost property. or in prospect of

receiving a favour x in nā nūnạ makạ indạ yakḕ, gōrạm mḕ zā kạ bā ṇị if I show you where your lost property is, what reward will you give me ? (b) (i) ạbin ciṇ ~ Vd. ạbụ 1aa.iii. (ii) Vd. cị gōrọ. (c) `yā bạ̄ Kanọ gōrạn yạŋkiṇ ḱasar Kạtsinạ he gave Kano a part of the Katsina territory as a sop. (d) Vd. ạlbishịr 2.

gōrōrī (1) Vd. gōrạ. (2) type of ɓarạ̄gē-cloth having alternate stripes of coloured silk and cotton.

gọ̄rubạ f. (pl. gọ̄rụbai = gōrubōbī). (1) (a) dum-palm (Hyphæne Thebaica), (cf. lallẹ 1j, gụntsū, cī 1c, marạbā 4, tantạliɓọ, ạ cī kạ ạ fḕre). (b) maị sạndā kạ̄ ci ~ name for horse. (c) ḱwācẹ ~ ạ hannuŋ kuturū bạ̄ shi dạ wụyā = ḱwācẹ ~ dạgạ hannuŋ kuturū bạ̄ aiḳị ba nḕ it's as easy as falling off a log. (d) Sk. ~ an zō so you, my husband, have come to the point of mocking me ! (2) ɗaŋ ~ obsolete sạrautạ at Kano. (3) Vd. gọ̄rụbai, bịrī.

gọ̄rụbai (1) Vd. gọ̄rubạ. (2) tassels sewn at corners of saddle-cloth (jạlālạ) = rīmī 6 = bị ni kạ lālạ̄cē. (3) tassels of sword-sling (hạmīlạ).

gōrunạ Vd. gọ̄rā.

gọ̄shī m. (1) (a) forehead, foreheads. (b) gọ̄shin on the eve of x gọ̄shin zūwạnsạ just before his arrival. gọ̄shiŋ kạ̄kā (sallạ) just prior to the harvest (Festival). (c) (:) askị yā zō gạbaŋ ~ it is within an ace of completion. (ii) ɗaŋ gạbaŋ ~ Vd. gạbā 9. (d) gọ̄shin yạ̄ḱi forefront of the battle. (e) gọ̄shin tudụ brow of hill. (f) gọ̄shin jirgī prow of boat. (2) ɗaŋ ~ m. leather ornament for horse's face. (3) gọ̄shim ɓaunā (a) sandals with ornamented strips. (b) = 5. (c) gọ̄shim ɓaunā gạ̄gạrạ shạ̄fā epithet of redoubtable P. (4) gọ̄shiŋ kūrẹ the coiffure hạnạ sallạ q.v. (5) gọ̄shin Sarḱī maị wụyar tạrā = gọ̄shin zāḱi it's best not to attempt it. (6) (a) (i) yanạ̄ dạ ~ he's auspicious. (ii) Audụ, ~ gạrēshị = Audụ yā yi ~ Audu is (was) lucky. (b) Gọ̄shī name given child whose birth is coincident with some luck.

gọ̄tạ Vb. 1A exceeded slightly x yā ~

su azzịkī he's slightly better-off than they are. rānā tā ~ sun's just passed the meridian (cf. gōcẹ).

gōtai m. rather brackish water.

gōtạ̄yē Vd. gōtō.

gōtō m. (pl. gōtạ̄yē). (1) ornamenting (bow, helmet, etc.) with ostrich plumes. (2) nā sakar masạ gōtansạ I didn't think he was up to it !

gọ̄tọ̄tọ used in yạ̄rọ ~ dạ shị ? fancy such a big boy still sleeping in his mother's room !, etc. ~ dạ shī fancy him having so little self-respect ! (= ḱọ̄tọ̄to q.v.).

goya A. (gọ̄yā) Vb. 2. (1) (a) carried (baby, P., load) on one's back (for progressive Vd. gōyō). (b) Bạrạ̄ḱumā, tā gọ̄yi mijị, tā gọ̄yi ɗā epithet of bạrạ̄ḱumā i.e. woman who has no periods while suckling child. (c) yā gọ̄yi bāyāna (i) he helped me (Vd. gọ̄yạ 2 ; bāyā 1f). (ii) he concurred with me. (2) ya gọ̄yē shị he treated him (a dependent) well. (3) yā gōyō tạụrārī he had stroke of luck. (4) kạ̄ gọ̄yi mạrāyạ type of children's game.

B. (gọ̄yạ) Vb. 1A. (1) = gọ̄yā 1a, 2. (2) yā ~ bāyāna he got me to use my influence on his behalf (Vd. gọ̄yā 1c). (3) bound T. on to T. to reinforce it x aŋ ~ wạ azạ̄rā watạ azạ̄rā the Ḃorassus (giginyạ) pole has been reinforced by another bound on to it.

gọ̄yạyyakī Vd. gōyō.

goye A. (gọ̄yẹ) Vb. 1A carried baby on back x tā ~ yạ̄rọ (for progressive Vd. gōyō).

B. (gọ̄ye) (1) yạ̄rọ yanạ̄ ~ the baby-boy is being carried on her back. (b) tanạ̄ ~ dạ yạ̄rọ she's carrying the baby-boy on her back.

gōyō (1) m. (pl. gōyạyyakī). (a) T. (especially baby) carried on the back x (i) gōyantạ yā mutụ her baby is dead. (ii) tanạ̄ dạ ~ she has a baby (= kwạrī 2 = ạ bạmbaŋ), cf. jinjịrī. (iii) bā ạ̄ rarrạbẹ fitsārim maị gōyō = jēgo 3. (b) (i) ɗaŋ ~ cloth for securing baby to woman's back (= matarī 1). (ii) ɗaŋ kụnāmạ nē, bạ̄ ɗaŋ ~ ba he's an " ugly customer ". Jāmụs bạ̄ 'yā'yaŋ ~ ba nḕ the Germans are " tough customers ". (c) gōyam masạrā

maize-cob (= **dāwą** 4*b*). (*d*) **ūwar** ～ *f*.
(i) maidservant whose work is to carry
child pick-a-back to relieve its mother
of this duty. (ii) **Allą yą bā shi ūwar
gōyō** may the dead child lack nothing
in the Next World ! (*formula of condolence to parents*). (2) *m*. (*a*) (*secondary
v.n. of* **gōyā** 1*a* *and* **gōyę**) *x* (i) **taną
gōyan yārǫ = taną gōyę yārǫ** she
(mother, etc.) is carrying child slung
on her back. (ii) **lādan** ～ *m*. sore on
woman's back from carrying baby
(= **tąyā ni** ～). (iii) **gōyansą yā ƙārę**
his days of babyhood are over. (*b*)
carrying T. on one's back or P. head
downwards. (*c*) **gōyaŋ ūwar wani**
woman's slinging child on her back with
cloth separating their flesh. (*d*) **tā
tąfi gōyan ciƙi** she (girl 7 months gone
in first pregnancy) went to her parents'
home to bear her child there (= **waŋkā**
5). (*e*) (i) **gōyō = gōyaŋ kūrā** lifting
one's wrestling-opponent right up and
then throwing him down. (ii) **gōyaŋ
kūrā** growing of one tooth over another.
(*f*) **bardaŋ gōyō** *Vd*. **bardē** 10.

gōzanci *m*. midwifery (*Vd*. **uŋgōzōmą**).

gōzō (1) what coarse spinning ! (2) *Vd*.
mītą.

gōzōmą *f*. midwife (= **uŋgōzōmą** *q.v.*).

gū *m*. (*pl*. **gurąrē**) place *x* **wani** ～ somewhere. **nā zō guŋką** I've come to speak
to you. **dą maciji ą guŋ** there's a
snake there (= **wuri** *q.v.*).

gubą *f*. (*pl*. **gubōbi**). (1) (*a*) any poison
(= **dafi**). (*b*) tainted or dirty food
(*Vd*. 3). (*c*) malevolence of the evil eye
x **sam masą ƙadaŋ, idǫ** ～ **nē** give him
(P. seeing another eating) a bit, lest
evil-eye fall on you ! **ką kiyąyi kąnką,
idǫ** ～ **nē** beware of stinginess, lest
evil-eye fall on you ! (2) love-philtre
x **tā shā dą shi** ～ she gave him love-
philtre to make him love her. (3)
kadą ki ci mu dą ～ (*a*) now, none of
your love-philtres ! (*b*) don't poison us
with your dud cooking ! (*c*) don't give
us food forbidden by religion ! (*cf*.
1*b*). (4) *Vd*. **dafi**.

guɓą *Vd*. **guɓąr**.

gubāji *m*. badly-woven **ƙari** *or* **sāƙi**-cloth.

gubālą *f*. lavish-living.

gubąncē *Vb*. 1C poisoned (*Vd*. **gubą**).

gubanta A. (**gubąntā**) *Vb*. 1C poisoned
(*Vd*. **gubą**).
    B. (**gubantą**) *Vb*. 3B **yā** ～ it (food)
is poisoned.

guɓąr ƙarē *f*. a disease of the gums (*cf*.
būɓu 2).

***gubba** A. (**gubbą**) *f*. (*pl*. **gubbōbi**) (*Ar*.
qubbā dome) mausoleum.
    B. (**gubbā**) (1) teeth (*pl*. *of* **gabǫ**).
(2) *Kt*. molars (*pl*. *of* **gubbi**).

gubbāri *m*. (*pl*. **gubbąrai**) wealthy man.

gubbi *Kt*. *m*. (*pl*. **gubbā**) molar tooth
(= **turmi** 4).

gubɗą *Vb*. 1A threw abundant condiments
on (= **gumbudā** *q.v.*).

gubdū *Kt*. *m*. leaves of custard-apple
(**gwandąr jēji**).

gubōbi *Vd*. **gubą**.

gubrą *Vb*. 1A. (1) = **gabzą** 2 ; **gwaɓą**.
(2) *cf*. **gubrę**.

gubrę (1) *Vb*. 1A hit hard *x* **yā** ～ **ni dą
sandä** he hit me hard with a stick
(= **gabję** 1). (2) *Vb*. 3A. (*a*) is (was)
impregnated with odour *x* **dāki yā** ～
dą hayāƙi the house is filled with smoke
(= **gūrę** 2*b*). (*b*) increased (= **gūrę** 2*c*).

gubri *Vd*. **gumri**.

guɓus *Kt*. *m*. colliding with (= **karǫ**).

guda A. (**gudā**) (1) *m*. (*pl*. **gudąji = gudad-
dąji**). (*a*) lump *x* (i) **tūwō yā yi** ～ the
tūwō is lumpy (= **gulūlu** 3), *cf*.
gwārāji. **kunū yā yi** ～ the gruel is
lumpy (= **rututu** 2), *cf*. **gwārāji**. (ii)
kaɗi yā yi ～ the spinning is lumpy.
(iii) **gudąjiŋ wannąŋ kōko gwārāji nę**
this gruel has specially-prepared lumps
in it (*Vd*. **gāyā** 1*c*, **ƙadąbulai, gwārāji**).
(iv) *Vd*. **mārą** 2*c*. (*b*) anything spherical
x (i) **gudaŋ ąlbasą** round onion (*contrasted with* leek). (ii) **gudan rānā** orb
of the sun (*cf*. **gāyā** 1, **kaskō** 5*b*). **idam bą
ką shā gudan dawǫ ba, kadą ką shā
gudan rānā** don't tempt the heat on
an empty stomach ! (iii) **gudaŋ watą**
moon's full orb. **watą yā cika gudansą**
the moon is full (= **gāyā** 1*a*). (iv) **ɗan
gudąn jini** *m*. (*f*. **'yar gudan** ～) *pl*. **'yaŋ
gudan** ～ small child. (*c*) anything intact
x **gudan rągō** the body of a slaughtered
ram not yet cut up (*cf*. **gāwā**). (*d*)
unit *x* **dōki** ～ = **dōki gudā ɗayą** one

horse. mụtụm ∼ gōmạ = mụtụm gōmạ
ten persons (*cf.* fallē). mụtụm ∼ wajaŋ
gōmạ = mụtụm wajaŋ gōmạ about 10
persons. ∼ nawạ how many ? ∼ gōmạ
ten of them. wannaŋ gụdaŋ *this* one.
bạ̃ kō rīgā gạ gụdansụ not one of them
had even a gown. (*e*) shī ∼ nẹ̃ ạ
cikinsạ *he* is the one who matters in
it (= rukụnī 2). (*f*) *x* iŋ kā yī,
sūnaŋkạ ∼ well then, do so and you'll
see what happens to you ! (*g*) Gụdāji
= Gụda *name for* any man called Taŋkọ.
(*h*) wurī ∼ *Vd.* tārạ 1a.i. (*j*) gụdaŋ wạinā
Vd. tạ̃rindọ. (2) *Vb.* 2 (*p.o.* gụjē, *n.o.*
gụji) prevented P. getting *x* yā gụjē nị
dạ al'amạrinsạ he would not take me
into his confidence.
  B. (Gụda) *Vd.* gụdā 1*g*.
  C. (gụdạ) (1) *Vb.* 3A. (*a*) it (spring-
water) welled up. yauna yā ∼, nā
ga nāmạ on seeing meat, my mouth
watered. (*b*) aikị yā ∼ work has
made good progress. (*c*) yanạ̃ gụdạ̃wā
he has diarrhœa (= zāwọ = zarmẹ 2),
Vd. gụdụn dawạ. (2) *Vb.* 1A hastened
to *x* gụda kạ̃sūwā hasten to the market !
gūdạ *m.* (*pl.* gū̃'dẹ-gụ̃dẹ̃''). (1) (*a*) joyful
shrilling by women. (*b*) sun yi masạ ∼
the people cheered him. (*c*) sạ̃i biri yā
zō hannum Mālạm ya kạn yi gūdạ.
in yā zō hannum Mạ̃guzāwā, sạ̃i yạ
yi kūkā when cat's away, mice play
(*because Maguzawa eat monkeys, but
Muslims not*). (*d*) *Vd.* gạɪ̃ 2*b*. (2)
Aŋgọ, bạ̃ ∼ *epithet of* bridegroom. (3)
cf. shạ̃ ∼.
gụdādạ *Vb.* 3B = gụdānạ 1.
gudad dạ *Vb.* 4B removed.
gụdaddạjī *Vd.* gụdā.
gụdaddē = gụjajjē.
gụdạ-gụdẹ *m.* the fodder-grass *Dacto-
loctenium ægyp.*
gūdạ̃i *Sk. m.* the tree iŋgidīdọ *q.v.*
gụdāji *Vd.* gụdā.
gụdālẹ *m.* (*f.* gụdālạ) short-legged, short-
horned ox.
gudana A. (gụdānạ) (1) *Vb.* 3B. (*a*) it
(spring-water) welled up. (*b*) flowed.
(*c*) (i) happened. (ii) yā tsai dạ gụdānạr
al'amạriŋ he blocked progress of the
matter. (2) *Vb.* 2. (*a*) avoided *x* yā
gụdạ̃nē shị he avoided it (him). gụdạ̃ni,

kadạ wani yạ jī take care nobody hears !
(*b*) *Sk.* hastened *x* yā tạfī ạ gụdạ̃ne he
hastened away (*Vd.* gụdạ̃nā).
  B. (gụdạ̃nā) *Vb.* 3A. (1) hastened *x*
gụdạ̃nā, kạ kōmō dạ saurī hasten back
quickly ! (*cf.* gụdānạ 2*b*, gudụ, gudānī 4).
(2) aikị yā ∼ work made good progress
(= gusạ 2).
gudānad dạ *Vb.* 4B. (1) caused to occur.
(2) caused to flow.
gudane A. (gụdạ̃nē) small pots (*pl. of*
gudunyā).
  B. (gụdạ̃ne) *Vd.* gụdānạ 2*b*.
  C. (gụdạ̃nē) *Vd.* gụdānạ.
gudānī *m.* (1) redyeing black material.
(2) confirming appointments made by
one's predecessor in office (*cf.* waŋkan
takọ̃bī). (3) yā yi wạ ransạ ∼ he ate
some tasty food. (4) *Kt.* hastening *x*
yanạ̃ ∼ yạ ƙārẹ he is speeding on with
his work (*cf.* gụdạ̃nā).
gudar dạ = gudad dạ.
guddạndanī small pots (*pl. of* gudunyā).
gụɗɗū *Sk. m.* field-rat (= bạrēwā 3).
guddụgī *Kt. m.* (*f.* guddụgā) *pl.* gụddụgai
cripple forced to move along on hands
and knees (= ụŋgurdụgī).
gudīdī smallness *x* ɗan yārọ nē ∼ dạ
shī he's a tiny lad (*pl.* 'yan yạ̃rā nẹ̃
gudi-gudi dạ sū).
gụɗiɗī *m.* anạ gụɗiɗinsạ there's an under-
current of rumour about it.
gudi-gudi A. (gudi-gudi) (1) *Vd.* gudīdī. (2)
cf. tụntsụrạ ∼.
  B. (gudī-gụdī) *adv.* *x* sạ̃i ∼ ta zo
naŋ she came here naked but for rag
round her loins.
gudil *m.* shortness *x* zanẹ nē ∼ dạ shī
it's a short cloth (*pl.* zannūwạ nē
gudil-gudil (*or* gudildil *or* gujiljil) dạ sū).
gụdiŋkā = gụdụŋkā.
gudinyā = gụdunyā.
Gụɗisā name for a short girl (= Kumbulā 2).
gudō *Vd.* gudụ 1*a* ; gudạ.
gụɗōsō *m.* (1) food made from ground-
nuts and yam, etc. (= *Kt.* sạkwạrā 2).
(2) obsolete type of girls' game.
gudụ (1) *Vb.* ran away. (*a*) yanạ̃ ∼ he's
running away (*cf.* 2*b*, 2*d.*ii). gụdu be
off ! gụdu ŋ wucẹ let me pass ! yā gudō
wurimmụ he fled to us (*cf.* gujẹ). (*b*) ƙasā

ta̱ gudu̱ ta̱ jē i̱nā̱ a P. and his nature are inseparable. (c) (before dative), Vd. guje̱. (2) noun m. running away x (a) (i) an yi wa̱ drōba̱ ∼ a prisoner has escaped from warder's custody. (ii) an̲ karya̱ musu̱ ƙa̱fa̱r ∼ they've been prevented from fleeing. (iii) ∼ da̱ ma̱rī bā ya̱ māga̱nim ba̱utā one must face realities. (iv) ri̱ga̱ ∼ Vd. Ba̱fīlāce̱. (v) zōmō yanā̱ ∼ Vd. aja̱lī 2e. (vi) bā̱ ∼ ba Vd. hanzarī 1d.ii. (vii) i̱n kā ganī wani nā̱ ∼ Vd. rēna̱ 9. (b) yi ∼ = 1 x dōki̱ yā yi ∼ the horse broke loose (= tsi̱nke̱ 2b.i). bāwa̱ yā yi ∼ the slave ran away (progressive bāwa̱ yanā̱ ∼), cf. 2d.ii. (c) yi gudu̱n forestalled, tried to avoid x (i) nā yi gudu̱n̲ kada̱ ya̱ fo̱rē ni̱ I tried to avoid doing what would cause him to upbraid me. (ii) don̲ gudu̱n zūci̱yar Audu̱, ba̱i amsa̱ ba he refrained from reply so as not to excite Audu's anger (Vd. gudu̱n zūci̱yā). (iii) yā yi gudu̱nsu̱ he fled from them. (iv) ga̱ya masa̱ gudu̱n she̱ƙara̱ da̱ she̱ƙa̱rū yā sa̱mē ni̱ tell him I am off and may never return ! (v) nā yi gudu̱n she̱ƙara̱ a̱mmā sǎi ya tarad da̱ nī I stood it as long as humanly possible. (vi) nā yi gudu̱n yayyafī, nā shi̱ga mā̱māko̱ out of the frying-pan into the fire ! (vii) gudu̱n lahīyā Vd. uku̱ 3b, kula̱ kā̱i. (viii) tsuntsū yanā̱ gudu̱n rūwa̱ Vd. tsuntsū 7. (ix) kā̱zā ke̱ gudu̱n shirwa̱ Vd. shirwa̱ 1d. (d) hastening x (i) yā ci̱ ∼ he had to run far (Vd. zōmō 4). (ii) yā yi ∼ he hastened. dōki̱ yā yi ∼ the horse galloped along (progressive dōki̱ yanā̱ gudu̱), cf. 1, 2b. yi ∼ ka̱ ta̱fi kā̱sūwā hasten to the market ! (iii) dūtsa̱n̲, bā̱ shi da̱ ∼ the grinding-stone is not adapted for speedy work. (iv) kōmē gudu̱m ba̱rēwā, tā bar dāji̱ = kōmē gudu̱m ba̱rēwā, a̱ hannum ma̱i dawa̱ zā ta̱ kwan̲ no subject can be fully mastered, there is no way of escaping fate. (v) bā ā̱ gama̱ ∼ da̱ sūsa̱r katarā = bā ā̱ gama̱ gudu̱ da̱ sūsa̱r ɗūwā̱wū don't fall between two stools !, oil and water won't mix. (vi) da̱ dāmā ne̱, ∼ da̱ awākī act in good time ! (vii) a̱ ko̱ri mutu̱m, a̱ ga iri̱n̲ gudu̱nsa̱ hardship shows the hidden reserves in a person. (viii) a̱ do̱kē

ka̱, a̱ hana̱ ka gu̱du̱ ? why should a double wrong be inflicted on a person ? (ix) maƙī̱ ∼ Vd. maƙī̱. (x) gīwā tā fi ∼ Vd. ɓāci̱ 2c. (xi) gaddama̱r ∼ Vd. gaddama̱ 4. (xii) kā ganī wani nā̱ ∼ Vd. rēna̱ 9. (xii) dōki̱ ɗayā ∼ ga̱rēshi̱ Vd. dōki̱ 1c. (xiii) kā fi ka̱rē ∼ Vd. a̱ bo̱ƙara̱. (xiv) i̱nda̱ ma̱i ∼ ya kai Vd. ha̱ƙura̱ 1d. (e) ∼ ci̱, tsaya̱ ci̱ one is between the devil and the deep sea. (f) da̱ ∼ quickly x yā fi̱ta da̱ ∼ he sped away. (g) Vd. Ta ∼. (h) Vd. gudu̱n-compounds. gu̱dūgu̱ Sk. m. yā karya̱ ∼ he secured his gown-sleeves behind his neck (= dā̱gu̱mī 4).

gudu̱m Vd. gudu̱n-compounds. gu̱duma̱ f. (pl. gu̱du̱mai = gudumōmī). (1) (a) hammer. (b) a̱ ƙāra̱ ∼ mā̱i ? = a̱ ƙāra̱ ∼ nawyī̱ ? debt on debt ! (Vd. a̱ 1s). (2) (a) hunters' hammer-shaped throwing-stick wrenched (ɓazge̱) off tree (cf. kērē). (b) i̱nda̱ aka̱ sa̱ri kērē, nan̲ aka̱ sa̱ri ∼ they're of the same status or relative family-importance, but differ greatly in means. (3) nice, plump woman. (4) ∼ ɗan Za̱mfara̱, ba̱ ta̱ bar kōwā ba epithet of fractious P. (5) the short stem (hanci̱) joining bean-blossoms, etc., to stalk. (6) yā yi ∼ he plunged the stirrer (muci̱yā) deep into the dye-pit.

gudu̱mmawā = gudu̱mmōwā = Sk. gu̱du̱mmūwā f. help x (i) yā yi mini̱ ∼ he helped me (epithet is Gudu̱mmawā kā̱ ko̱rar yāƙi̱). an yi musu̱ ∼ da̱ sōja̱ they were reinforced with troops. (2) Vd. zu̱rū 1d. (3) gudu̱mmōwar gōbarā Vd. būnū 3.

gudu̱n̲ an̲go̱ Kt. m. mock flight of bridegroom and his friends before wedding.

gudun ɓad da san doki (gudu̱m ɓad da̱ san dōki̱) m. playful flight of bride to parents' home after wedding.

gudun barewa (gudu̱m ba̱rēwā) Vd. ba̱rēwā 1c, d.

gudun biri (gudu̱m biri̱) m. (1) type of horse's gait (cf. tāki̱m biri̱). (2) = tiri̱ 2.

gudu̱n cētō Vd. cētō 1b.

gudu̱n dawa̱ m. diarrhœa (= zāwo̱ 1), Vd. guda̱ 1c.

guduŋ gaba *m.* (1) small, sleeveless shirt with charms sewn in and worn by infantryman in war. (2) ~, kwānā zaurẹ " first come are not always first served ". (3) kāyā yā yi ~ load on donkey has slipped forward.

guduŋ garā *m.* an yi ~, aŋ hayẹ zagō " out of the frying-pan into the fire ! "

guduŋ garē *m.* pattering-run (as of guinea-fowl or lizard).

guduŋ-gudụŋ huge = guruŋ-gụrụŋ *q.v.*

gụdụŋgumī *m.* (*pl.* gụdụŋgụmai). (1) broken shackle on one ankle of prisoner or slave. (2) stick tied to leg of ox to prevent escape (= tụŋgumạ 2). (3) gụdụŋgumin tsụmmā ragged garment.

gụdụŋgurḳi *m.* (*f.* gụdụŋgurḳīyā) burly P. or animal.

gudụŋ gyāran dagā = *Kt.* gudụŋ gyāran lāyū *used in* yā yi ~ he made strategic retreat.

gụdụŋkā *f.* doorstep (= dōkịŋ ḳōfạ).

gudụŋ ḳas *m.* kibīyạ tā yi ~ arrow ricocheted along the ground.

gudụŋ ḳōrē *Sk.* *m.* = gudụn ɓad dạ san dōkị.

gudụŋ ḳurnạ *m.* dumplings of wheat-flour, beanflour, or millet-bran.

gudụŋ ḳūrụ *Vd.* ḳūrụ.

gudụn rūwā *Vd.* ạgwāgwā.

gudụn san dōkị *m.* = gudụn ɓad dạ san dōkị.

gudụn tạ̄tsattsīyar ạkwīyạ *m.* running away when it is too late.

gudunyā = gudunyạ *f.* (*pl.* guddạndanī = gudạ̄nē = gudunyōyī). (1) small earthenware pot. (2) 'yar ~ maị saurin tạfasạ *epithet of* quick-tempered P. (3) *cf.* tụntsụrạ ~.

gudụn yạ̄yē *m.* wife's going to parents' home on weaning her first child.

gudụn zūcị̄yā *m.* ~ gạrēshị he's tactful (*Vd.* gudụ 2*c*.ii).

gudur-gụdụr coarse (= guzur-gụzụr *q.v.*).

gụdurmusụ *Sk. m., f.* (*sg., pl.*) poor P.

gufā *Vd.* gụhā.

gufạtạ *Zar. f.* large calabash for transporting loads (= agōfạtạ).

gufụrạmī *m.* = gūrạmī.

guga A. (gụ̄gā) *m.* (*pl.* gūgunạ). (1) (*a*) well-bucket of skin or gourd. (*b*) any small metal-bucket. (*c*) gụ̄gan yạ̄sā bạ

dạ shī a ḳạn shā rūwā ba when some people prosper, they shake off trusty old servitors. (*d*) rījị̄yā tā bā dạ rūwā, gụ̄gā yā hanạ the master was generous, but his servant intercepted the gift. (*e*) ~ tsai *Vd.* zạbạrī 2. (2) *Vd.* ɗaurịŋ ~. (3) hanyạ cē ~ it's a frequented road. (4) jạ̄ ~ *m.* new cassava.

B. (gụ̄gạ) *f.* (1) (*secondary v.n. of* gōgẹ 1*a*, gọ̄gā *q.v.*). (2) act of rubbing *x* sirdị yanạ̄ ~ saddle's rubbing on horse's back. tanạ̄ ~ she's rubbing tobacco-flowers on her teeth *as in* gōgạ 1*b*. (3) gạrī yanạ̄ ~ tasạ he's having a hard time. (4) kạ̄zā tanạ̄ gụ̄gạr ḳwǎi hen's turning her eggs over. (5) (*a*) nā kạrɓi kudīna, wurị nạ̄ gụ̄gạr wurị I was paid in full. (*b*) nā bīyā, wurị nạ̄ gụ̄gạr ɗạŋūwansạ I paid in full. (6) ~ māganịŋ gishirin sautụ what finely rubbed powder ! (7) na ~, marmarī dạgạ nēsạ marriage looks all right till you come to try it yourself ! (8) gụ̄gạr zānā *Sk.* foisting false charge on P. (9) yanạ̄ ~ he's acting *as in* gōgẹ 1*f*.

Gụ̄gạ̄rạ *used in* ~ gạ̄tarịŋ Gwārī *epithet of* dauntless P. (*Vd.* dandōsạ).

gugẹ *m.* place *x* gugyạŋkạ mukạ zō we've come to speak to you (= bụgē 3).

guggụɓā = guggụɓē *Vb.* 1C. (1) drank up sediment (tsạkī). (2) drank up remains of sloppy food.

gụggụɓī *m.* remnant or sediment (tsạkī) of food, riches, people, etc.

guggufīyā *f.* golloping up food.

gụggụrmāyạ *f.* (1) struggling with task or P. (2) (*used in songs*) wifeless man.

gugụ *m.* (1) first steps in doing T. *x* an sōmạ gugụŋ aikịŋ the work's been put in hand. (2) bạ̄ shi dạ ~ it's scanty.

gụ̄gụcē *Vb.* 1C. (1) = guggụɓē. (2) nā ~ masạ māganī I administered the medicine to it (horse) through the rectum.

gụ̄gụmaɗā *f.* empty display of wealth.

gụ̄gunạ buckets (*pl. of* gụ̄gā).

gụ̄gụrūgụ *m.* (*sg., pl.*) man living by slandering those who refuse to pay him to refrain (*cf.* mazạ̄wọ̄yī, gạrūrạ 4).

gụ̄gūtā *Vb.* 1C = gụ̄gụcē 2.

ʒūgūtū *m.* administering remedy to horse via rectum (*Vd.* jan sạiwā).

gūgūwạ *f.* (*pl.* gūgūwai = gūgūwe-gū-guwẹ). (1) whirlwind (*cf.* janzarị 2). (2) running away. (3) īyạ̄kaciŋ ~ tạ ɗau karmāmī, bạ zā tạ ɗau damịn dāwạ ba don't expect from P. more than he can do ! (4) *cf.* gyạttā.

gụhā *Vb.* 2 *Sk.* did the act gụhị with girl.

gụhī = gụhị *Sk. m.* mutual masturbation between boy and girl (= tsạ̄rạncē).

gụjajjē *x* gụjajjam bāwạ runaway-slave (*d.f. Vb.* gụdụ).

gụje A. (gụjẹ) *Vb.* 1A (*the form taken by* gụdụ *before dative*) ran away from *x* (i) bāwạ yā ~ minị slave ran away from me. yā ~ minị dạ kudīna he ran off with my money. gụje masạ avoid it ! (2) gụjẹ wạ dōkịŋ harị *Vd.* turkẹ 1*a*.ii.

B. (gụjẹ) *adv.* (1) speedily *x* yā zō ạ ~ he hastened here. yā fịta ạ ~ he sped out. (2) yā ịsa ạ ~ it's amply sufficient. (3) kāmụn na gụje *Vd.* sakị 2*f.* (4) rūwaŋ gụje *Vd.* bạ̄ƙō 2*b*.

C. (gụjē) *Vd.* gụdā 2.

gụji *Vd.* gụdā 2.

gujib *m.* shortness *x* dōkị nē ~ dạ shī it's a small horse (*pl.* dawākī nẹ gujibjib (= gujib-gujib) dạ sū).

Gujịbā name given short girl (= Ƙumbulā 2).

gujibjib *pl. of* gujib (*alternative with* gujib-gujib).

gujil = gujib.

gujiljil *Vd.* gudil.

gujīyā = gujjīyā *f.* (*pl.* guzạ̄yē). (1) (*a*) (i) Bambarra ground-nut(s) (*also called* duƙus = gujīyā duƙus = kwạ̄rūrū). (*b*) at *Kt.* it is called gujīyar ƙwarạs = ƙurigạ = gujīyā maị ƙọ̄ƙō *to distinguish from* 5. (ii) *Vd.* fạshē. (2) horny growths above ankles of ruminants (*eaten by boys*). (3) small enlarged neck-glands (*also called* gujī-yar wuyạ). (4) type of gambling. (5) *Kt.* ground-nuts (= gyạɗā), *cf.* 1*b above*. (6) the tree gurjīyā. (7) type of cloth with strips of various alternating colours. (8) gujīyar awākī = gujīyar dawākī = gyạɗā 6. (9) ɗaŋ ~ *m.* player of cācā (= cācā 3*a*).

gujub = gujib.

guƙƙụŋ *Sk.* (1) *m.* heavy bracelets. (2) kō anạ̄ yi makạ ~, anạ̄ yi makạ gạ̄ dạ̄misạ, bạ kạ̄ yi minị ạbin nạŋ ŋ ƙyālẹ ka ba no matter *how* great you may be, you do this to me at your peril ! (guƙƙụŋ = drumming for chief : gạ̄ dạ̄misạ = laudatory-rhythm for Chief's son in drumming).

guƙụŋ-guƙụŋ *adv.* in large numbers *x* sun tạ̄ru ~ they have gathered in large numbers.

gulạ *f.* (*pl.* gulōlī). (1) big-headed drumstick. anạ̄ mārịŋ kọ̄tsō dạ ~ the drum kọ̄tsō is being beaten with drumstick (*cf.* fụryā, makaɗī, kiɗạ). (2) hitting opponent in stomach with knee or elbow. (3) *Sk.* jaŋ ~ head drummer of jaujē, kạlạŋgū *or* kọ̄tsō drums. an yi maị jaŋ ~ he's been appointed head drummer *of such drum-type* (= kiɗạ 1*g*).

gulạ̄bē *Vd.* gulbī.

gulai *Vd.* kạryar gulai.

gulạnjē *m.* the food tūwō.

gulam A. (gulam) *used in* bạ̄kinsạ ~ he's toothless.

B. (gulam-gulam) *used in* taụnā tasạ ~ he's eating with toothless mouth (= mạ̄gul-mạ̄gul).

gụlāmạ-gụlāmạ *Kt. adv.* in large chunks (*re* meat).

gụlāmī *m.* toothless man.

gụlạndō *m.* any injury to toe or finger, especially one causing loss of nail.

gụlārạ *Nor. f.* type of bag (= gụrārạ *q.v.*).

gulƀẹ *Sk.* (1) *Vb.* 3A. (*a*) is (was) tired out. (*b*) yā ~ dạ zāwọ he has (had) diarrhœa. (2) *Vb.* 1A ạbincī yā ~ ni the food caused me diarrhœa.

gulbī *Sk.*, *Kt. m.* (*pl.* gulạ̄bē). (1) river. (2) pond. (3) water in borrowpit (kụduddufī). (4) wạ̄ zaị ga gulbī ; kō baị shā ba, yā yi waŋkā why waste chances ? (5) kadạ dăi gulbī baị cī nị ba, kụduddufī yạ cī nị as P. of position has not managed to do me harm, how can P. of no position do so ! (6) ịdaŋ gulbī yā hanạ ƙẹtarạ, bạ yā hanạ dāwọ̄wā ba if T. is beyond you, don't attempt it !

gulẹ *Vb.* 1A. (1) reached destination *x* jirgī yā ~ cikin tashạ train's reached station of its destination. **yā ~ cikiŋ Kanọ** he has entered Kano, his destination (= **ƙurẹ**). (2) **yā ~ cikin dākịnsạ** he withdrew into his house (= **kudẹ**). (3) **yā ~ jirgī** he moored up boat at its destination.

gulgulẹ *used in* **ɗaŋ ~ nē** it's scanty or tiny.

gulgulmadạ *f.* making mischief.

gulguzū *m.* red-sorrel seeds (= **gurguzū** *q.v.*).

gụllā *Vb.* 2 = **gullạ** *Vb.* 1A *Kt.* **yā gullạ tūwō** he golloped up the tūwō (= **wụllā** = **wullạ**).

gullẹ (1) *Vb.* 1A dislocated ; sprained. (2) *Vb.* 3A is (was) dislocated ; sprained (= **gōcẹ** 1*b*).

gụllī *m.* the small, striped gourd **gụrjī** *q.v.*

gulliyā *f.* dislocation, sprain.

gulma A. (**gulmā**) *f.* making mischief. B. (**gulmạ**) *Vb.* 1A. (1) **yā ~ ƙaryā** he told a " whopper ". (2) *Kt.* **yā ~ lōmạ** he put huge lump of tūwō into his mouth.

gulmẹ *Kt. m.* cudgel.

gulōlī *Vd.* **gulạ**.

gulụbā *f.* ripe-fruit of the fig-trees **cēdīyā** *or* **ƙạwarī**.

gulūlụ = *Kt.* **gūlūlụ** (*pl.* **gụlūlai** = *Kt.* **gūlūlai**). (1) (*a*) ball of earth at top of spinning-spindle (= **tụlū** 6). (*b*) *Vd.* **haŋkạlī** 2*l* ; **zūcịyā** 3. (2) cotton-boll. (3) **tūwō yā yi ~** the tūwō is lumpy (= **gụdā** 1*a*). *(4) Ar.* **cịŋ ~** embezzlement. (5) **gụlūlai** type of ornamentation of **jạlāla** (saddle-cover) = **jēmāgẹ˙**8.

gụlyā'ẹ̄ *Vd.* **waḍḍarẹ**.

gụm *adv. and m.* (1) **nā ji ƙanshī ~ I** smelt pungent odour. (2) **nā ji ~ I** felt wave of hot-air from fire.

guma A. (**gụma**) *Vb.* 3B (*progressive* **gụmā**) *x* **wurī yā ~ dạ ƙanshī** place became impregnated with pungent odour, smoke, etc. (= **ribɗẹ** 2*b*), *cf.* **musƙẹ**. B. (**gụmạ**) (1) *Vb.* 3A *x* **yā ci aiki har ya ~** he worked on till sick and tired of it. **kā cī, kā ~** you'll have your bellyfull of it (work, etc.) ! (= **rātạyā** 2*g*). (2) *Vb.* 1A. (*a*) *Kt.* **yā ~ shi ạ baƙạ** he threw it (flour, tobacco) into his

mouth (= **afạ**). (*b*) *Sk.* **tā ~ shịŋkāfā** she steamed rice prior to husking (= **zazzạɓā**), *cf.* **sulạ̄lā** 2. (*c*) *x* **ƙanshī yā ~ wuriŋ dū** the perfume pervaded the whole place. (*d*) **yā ~ wutā** it caused the fire to blaze up. (*e*) *Kt.* ill-treated (= **kumạ** 2 *q.v.*). C. (**gụmā**) (1) *Vb.* 2. (*a*) tired P. (*b*) disgusted P. (*c*) *Vd.* **gụmu**. (2) *Vd.* **gụma**.

gụmạ̄gụmai logs (*pl. of* **guŋgumẹ**).

gụmạ̄kā idols (*pl. of* **guŋkị**).

Gụmạl (1) Gumel District. (2) *Vd.* **banzā**, **Bạgumạlī**.

gumalẹ = *Sk.* **gumālẹ** *Fil. m.* hornless ox, ram, or goat (= **kụndumī** 3).

gụmāmạ *Vb.* 3B = **gumạ̄mē** *Vb.* 3A = **gụma** *q.v.*

gụmāri *m.* the incense **ạl'ụl**.

gụmātsọ *m.* fierce struggle.

gụmāzạ *f.* fierce struggle.

gụmbā *f.* (1) (*a*) pounded bulrush-millet (gērō) with water (= **bọlọ̄lō** 4 = **tsụ̄gē** 1). (*b*) in **nōnọ yanạ̄ dạ dādī ạ gụmbā, gụmbā mā tanạ̄ dạ dādī ạ nōnọ** benefit is mutual. (2) **yanạ̄ fāmā dạ ~** he has gonorrhœa (= **cīwọn** 4). (3) *Kt.* mixed clay, used for building before matured (= **tsụ̄gē** 2 *q.v.*). (4) (*a*) white bead (= **farar sa'ạ**). (*b*) saliva churned in mouth and then spat out by boys playing. (*c*) *Sk.* type of white mat.

gumɓā *f.* the stinking soup-base **lạ̄tụŋ**.

gumbẹ *m.* (1) short P. (2) short donkey.

gumbī *m.* name of several thorny plants, especially *Mimosa asperata*.

gụmbiri *m.* (1) **yā yi ~** he's in a temper. (2) (*also* **gụmbịrī**) *x* **yā yi masạ ~** he (spectator) urged him (boxer) on (*Vd.* **agạlandạ** 2).

gụmbụdā *Vb.* 1C. (1) threw much tobacco or flour into mouth (*cf.* **afạ**). (2) **yā ~ masạ shī** he scattered it (much oil, condiments, soil, etc.) on it.

gụmbụdē *Vb.* 1C threw all the large quantity available *as in* **gụmbụdā 1, 2**.

gụmburi *m.* = **gụmbiri**.

gụmdạ = **gụnɗạ**.

gụmdẹ *Vb.* 1A *Sk.* = **gụntsā** ; **guntsẹ**.

gumẹ *Vb.* 3A *x* **wurī yā ~ dạ ƙanshī** place is impregnated with perfume (= **gụma** = **ɗumẹ** 2*c*).

gumēdạ *f.* (1) mischief-making. (2) ụbaŋ ∼ one of the bọrī spirits living in wells (*epithet is* na rūwa rūwa) = rūwā A.23..(3) ụbaŋ ∼ *m.* (*f.* ūwar ∼) mischief-maker.

gumfạrē *Vb.* 3A. (1) became large. (2) became important (= ƙạsaitạ).

gumi A. (gumị) *m.* (1) (*a*) corn heaped ready beside grinding-stone. (*b*) ∼ shāshịn Sarkī *epithet of* any Mạ̄dākī. (*c*) bạbbaŋ ∼ bạ shī nẹ̄ niƙạ ba " it's not all gold that glitters ". (2) mortar full of furā.

B. (gụmī) *m.* (1) perspiration *x* (*a*) yā yi ∼ he's perspiring (= jịɓī = zuffạ). (*b*) yā yi ∼ kạshirɓạŋ = yā hadạ ∼ he's perspiring profusely (*we can for* kạshirɓạŋ *substitute* shịrkat = sharaf = shịrɓaŋ). (*c*) ƙurạrrajiŋ ∼ sum fēsō minị prickly-heat has broken out on me. (*d*) hadạ ∼ *Vd.* 1*b above ;* hadạ 1*f.* (2) (*a*) hot weather (= zuffạ 2). (*b*) *Vd.* surkạ 2. (3) *Sk., Kt.* heat *x* rūwan naŋ yanạ̄ dạ̄ sauraŋ ∼ this water is still hot (= zāfī).

C. (gụmi) *Vd.* gụmu.

gumị-gumị *adv.* in piles.

gụmīƙạ *f.* leather halter (ragạmā) ornamented with metal.

gumkạ *Vd.* gụŋkạ ; gumkị *Vd.* gụŋkị.

gummạ *Had. f.* a food of crushed bulrush-millet fried with butter and onions.

gumrẹ *Vb.* 3A. (1) *x* dākị yā ∼ dạ̄ hayāƙī house's filled with smoke (= gụma). (2) *Vd.* gubrẹ.

gumrī *m.* (1) being far-seeing. (2) Gubrī shạ̄ bạkọsanī *epithet of* any Gạlạ̄dīmạ.

gumsạ *Sk. f.* = tạntakwashī.

gụmtsā *Vd.* gụntsā.

gụmu *used in* ∼ tā ∼ kạ̈i it is of no use pretending to ability one does not possess.

gumụkkā idols (*pl. of* gụŋkị).

gumurzu A. (gumurzū) *m. used in* gumurzum fadạ fierce struggle.

B. (gụmurzū) *m.* chewing up corn by leper, etc., and then mixing with water or milk.

gụmụs *x* yanạ̄ dạ̄ dọ̄yī ∼ it has pungent stench (= bụs).

gumzạ *Kt.* (1) *f.* (*a*) roaring (of water,

bull, lion, ostrich). (*b*) loud crying. (*c*) angry recrimination. (2) *Vb.* = gunzạ.

gụmzayyạ *Kt. f.* fierce struggle.

gunạ *f.* (*pl.* gunōnī). (1) water-melon (*Citrullus vulgaris*). (2) gunạr shānū a *variety*, having green variegated stripes when unripe. (3) ạ cụ̄di ∼ dạ mạntạ giving P. a present from proceeds of transaction with him.

gunạ̄gunī *m.* (1) muttering in complaint (= tsị-tsị 2) *x* yā yi gunạ̄gunī gạ ạbin dạ akạ sạ̄ shi he grumbled against the task imposed on him (= ƙụŋƙụnī). (2) murmuring. (3) growling of dog.

gụnạ̄gụs evil-smelling *x* wardịn naŋ ∼ nẹ̄ this attar of roses smells bad.

gunce A. (guncẹ) *Vb.* 1A *Sk.* (1) broke piece off (= gutsụrē). (2) cut piece off *x* nā ∼ rawạnī I shortened turban by cutting piece off.

B. (guncē) *Vd.* gụntā.

gundạ *f.* (*pl.* gundōjī = gundạ̄rī). (1) (*a*) young fruit on marrow, pumpkin, cotton, locust-bean tree, etc. (*b*) mai ∼ shī kẹ̄ dạ kạbēwạ " many a mickle makes a muckle ". (*c*) *Vd.* dumaŋ kadạ. (2) Alexander's Lesser Honey-guide (*Indicator minor Alexanderi*). (3) *Kt.* type of small drum. (4) *Vd.* gundạ̄rī ; jạŋ gundạ.

gundạ *f.* (*sg., pl.*). (1) type of wood-boring insect(s) (= sạrī = *Sk.* sụ̄sūwạ 2), *cf.* kịcīcīyạ ; gịji-gịjī. (2) hạlā-līyạr ∼ itạ̄caŋ gạ̄wō it's *my own*.

gụndāgurī *m.* burly man.

gundạ̄rī (1) *Vd.* gundạ. (2) an dafạ wākē gundạ̄rinsạ they've cooked the beans unmixed with anything else (*Vd.* ƙūlū 1).

gundōjī *Vd.* gundạ.

gụndugụrū *m.* useless thick end of takạndạ̄ sugar-cane (= gịndigịrī *q.v.*).

gụndugwīlạ *f.* knuckle (of elbow, wrist, knee, etc.).

gundule A. (gundụlē) *Vb.* 1C broke piece off T. (= gutsụrē).

B. (gundụlẹ) *m.* fragment (= guntū).

gunduma A. (gụndumạ) (1) *f.* (*pl.* gundumōmī) one of the subdivisions, total of which compose area under a District head (hākịmī). (2) *Vb.* 2 broke off (territory ; much furā, etc.)

x aŋ gundumi ƙasar A, am bǎ B some of A's area has been transferred to B.

B. (gundumā) *Vb.* 1C. (1) broke off much of T. and handed to P. *x* nā ~ masạ furā I broke off much furā and handed it to him. aŋ ~ wạ B ƙasar A = gundumạ 2. (2) yā ~ mini ƙaryā he told me a " whopper ".

C. (gundumā) *Vd.* gundumēmẹ.

*gundumājē *Kt. m.* ɦyena.

gundumau (1) *m.* type of venereal disease. (2) what a lie !

gundumbulī *Sk. m.* (1) intact gourd. (2) intact fruit of baobob (kūkạ), *cf.* ƙundumāsạ 1.

gundumē *Vb.* 1C = gundumạ 2.

gundumēmẹ = gundumī *m.* (*f.* gundumēmīyā = gundumā) *pl.* gunduŋgunduŋ huge (*as in* gungumēmẹ).

gundunduŋ *m.* being huge (*as in* gungumēmẹ) *x* nā ga itạcē ~ da shī I saw a tall, stout tree.

gundun-gundun A. (gunduŋ-gundun) *Vd.* gundumēmẹ.

B. (gunduŋ-gundun) *adv.* (1) in large chunks. (2) zāgi yinạ fitā dagạ bāƙinsạ ~ filthy abuse is pouring from his mouth. (3) haƙạ hakaŋkạ ~ *formula said by boys curving hands at enemy as type of* ạmbōlạ.

gundura A. (gundurạ) (1) *Vb.* 2. (*a*) is (was) beyond one's capacity *x* aikiŋ yā gundurē ni the work's beyond my power. ạbincin naŋ yā gundurē ni I cannot eat this food (owing to amount ; distaste ; being tired of such food) = gāgarạ. (*b*) yā ~ he was *nulli secundus*. (2) ~ aikiŋ ayā *epithet of* cantankerous P.

B. (gundurā) *f.* = gundurū 1.

gundurad dạ *Vb.* 4B = gundurạ 2 *x* abūbūwạ māsū gundurad dạ mutạnē things which bore one.

gundurancī *Kt. m.* acting *as in* gundurū 3.

gundurū (1) *f.* (*pl.* gundurōrī). (*a*) stumpy, ugly woman (*epithet is* ~ ɗaukạr dufu). (*b*) *Zar.* slave-girl. (2) *m.* the tree *Pterocarpus esculentus* (*seeds are roasted and eaten*), *Vd.* ạ cī kạ ạ fẹrẹ. (3) *Kt.* ɗaŋ ~ *m.* P. habitually throwing gown-sleeve over shoulder, thus baring arm and side, considered

sign of dissolute P. (*derived from nam* Shēhu Ɗaŋ Gundurū), *cf.* gundurancī.

gunɗus *Sk. m.* fornication prior to dark ness.

gundūwā = gundwā *f.* (*pl.* gundūwōyī) (1) (*a*) slice (*of fish or meat*). (*b*) aɪ yi masạ ~ he's been cut in twain witɦ sword. (2) (*a*) type of drum, one end beaten with stick, the other with fingers. (*b*) halved bundle of guinea-corn (= gạŋgā 3*a*). (*c*) bundle of bulrush-millet with stalks in centre and heads at each end (= gạŋgā 3*b*). (3) gundūwa-gundūwa *adv.* in slices.

gungāmạ *m.* burly, fearless man.

gungu *m.* (1) (*a*) act of collecting *x* suŋ yi ~ they've gathered and form a crowd. (*b*) crowd ; group. (2) island (= tsibirī). (3) gungum mālạmī an unrivalled scholar.

gungucē *Kt.* = gungutsē *q.v. under* gungutsạ.

gunguma A. (gungumạ) *f.* (1) type of plant used for stupefying birds. (2) *Kt.* gungumạr bāƙī rinsing out the mouth.

B. (gungumā) *Vb.* 1C *Kt.* yā gungumạ bāƙī he rinsed his mouth (= kuskurē 1*c*).

gungumẹ *m.* (*pl.* gumāgumai). (1) (*a*) log. (*b*) yā wucẹ kạmaŋ gumāgumam bạra it's a thing of the past. (*e*) gungumaŋ ayạbạ tsōfwā nạ ganiŋkạ kẹ kwānā dạ ɗārī what a useless thing ! (*d*) Gumāgumai kạ kwānā dạ wutā ! ƙirārūwạ săi tōƙā only big people can handle big affairs. (*e*) arnā nẹ, gumāguman Jahannamạ they are scoundrels destined for hellfire. (*f*) *cf.* gungurai. (2) crocodile. (3) *m., f.* tall, ragged P. (4) gunguman dōƙi huge horse.

gungumēmẹ = gungumī *m.* (*f.* gungumēmīyā = gungumā) *pl.* gunguŋgungɪŋ (1) large and round. (2) long and stout (= gindimēmẹ).

gungumurƙi *m.* (*f.* gungumurƙīyā) burly man (*epithet is* ~ ƙashin gīwā nạ tsatso).

gungūnī *m.* (1) muttering ; murmuring (= gunāgunī = tukuburī). (2) growling of dog.

gungunturī *m.* = alagidigō.

gungurai x rūwā yā taflı da gumāgumai gungurai-gungurai the water rolled the logs along.

gungurci Kt. m. lameness (= gurguntā).

gungurkā f. ballast of well-bucket to sink it.

gungurtā Kt. f. lameness (= gurguntā).

gungurtsī m. cartilage.

gungurum m. (1) hugeness x kansa ∼ da shī he has huge head (pl. kāwunansu gungurum-gungurum da sū). (2) kansa yā yi ∼ his hair stood on end.

gungutsa Vb. 2 defamed (= fallasa).

gūnī m. (1) muttering. (2) murmuring. (3) growling of dog (all = gunāgunī).

gunji A. (gunji) m. roaring (= gumza 1 q.v.).

B. (gunjī) m. being of short length x wannan gāshin jiminā ∼ nē these are short ostrich plumes.

gunka Vb. 1A Sk. tā ∼ rūwā she inverted small k̦ōk̦ō-calabash on larger one full of water to prevent it spilling (= burma).

gunki (1) m. (pl. gumākā = gumākai = Kt. gumukkā = Kt. gumukkai). (a) (i) fetish (= tsāfi). (ii) idol. (b) an yi ∼ da shī (said by women) he's considered a perfect Nestor (Vd. kutī 3). (c) gunkim mālamī unrivalled scholar. (2) m. (a) reward for finding missing animal or slave. (b) Sk. tā yi gunkin rūwā she has inverted calabash as in gunka.

gunnusuru used in gunnusuru gunāsāsa what a stench !

gunōnī water-melons (pl. of guna q.v.).

gunsur m. abundance x kudī sun yi ∼ garēshi he has much money. al'amarinsa yā yi ∼ he's become important.

gunsurgumī m. burly man.

gunta Vb. 1A = guntā Vb. 2 (p.o. guncē : n.o. gunci) broke piece off T. (= gutsurē).

guntattakī, guntāyē fragments (Vd. guntū).

guntil m. shortness (= gudil q.v.).

guntsā Vb. 2 yā guntsi rūwā he filled mouth with water.

guntsārī m. sour-milk having lumpy curd.

guntse Vb. 1A yā ∼ bāk̦ī he willy-nilly closed his mouth (from anger, fullness, or when burning to blurt out something).

guntsī m. cartilage.

guntsū m. (1) seeds of baobob (= gwargwamī). (2) Sk. kernel of giginya or gōruba palms (butter is made from them) (2 = tantaliɓo = Sk. ɗan gurtsū).

guntū (1) adj. m. (f. guntūwā) pl. guntāyē = guntattakī short x guntum mutum short man. guntūwar macē short woman. guntūwar rīgā short gown. (2) noun m. fragment (of cloth or paper, etc.). (3) (a) guntun gātarī destitute P. (b) guntun gātarinka yā fı "sāri ka bā nı !" to use your own article, however inferior, saves the humiliation of borrowing (Vd. gātarī 1c). (c) guntun k̦īrı Vd. kūrā 28. (4) Vd. guntūwā.

guntulē Vb. 1C broke bit off T. (= gutsurē).

guntūwā f. (1) Vd. guntū. (2) fitinakerchief. (3) foot of kāmun k̦afa trousers.

gunya A. (gunyā) m. (1) (a) cream-dun horse. (b) bak̦in ∼ = ∼ kargō light bay horse. (2) rich broth (= darmasōsuwā). (3) yellow sandals. (4) Kt. saddle-cloth with yellow embroidery.

B. (gunya) f. (1) = bara gurbi 2. (2) (a) tsumman ∼ cloth on which infant lies. (b) tun yanā gunya from his childhood on.

gunza Vb. 1A (1) did loudly x yā ∼ kūkā he cried noisily. yā ∼ īhu he yelled. yā ∼ k̦arātū he read loudly. (2) filled mouth with crunchable food x yā ∼ gērō a baka. (3) Vd. gumza.

gunzayya Kt. f. fierce struggle.

gunzū m. (1) pig (cf. gadū). (2) P. who is a " whale for work ".

gūra (1) (flapped -r-) Vb. 1A. (a) ∼ wutā to cause fire to blaze up. (b) yā gūru he flew into a temper. (2) (rolled -r-) Sk. f. type of fish-trap.

gura'a = guri'a.

gurābū Vd. gurbi.

gurāgū lame persons (pl. of gurgu).

gura-gura f. (1) bad enunciation of " r " as " gh " (= kwatā = kōlī 2a). (2) yanā da ∼ = gurgu 1d.

gurāka f. large gourd used for crossing rivers (= gōrā 1a).

gūrạ kọ̄gō m. hawk (= **shāhọ**).
gūrạmī = Kt. **gūrạmī** m. (1) mat-wall or corn-stalk wall inside **tsạŋgayạ** to ensure privacy (= **bạbbākạ** q.v.). (2) earth-wall inside hut (**ƙagọ**) for privacy (= **gāgạrạ** 1c).
gụrārạ f. (pl. **gụrā̰rū** = **gụrā̰rī**). (1) (a) hide pannier for pack animal. (b) **yā bugạ ~ hẹ** made such pannier. (2) **tsạkāninsụ ɓāriŋ ~ nē** there's no difference between them.
gụrā̰rē Vd. **gṵ̄**.
gụrā̰rī Vd. **gụrārạ**.
gụrāsạ (Ar. **qurs**) f. (1) (a) type of wheaten-food. (b) Vd. **bugạ** 1d. (2) an embroidery pattern. (3) **yā sạ̄mi ạbinciŋ ~** he got quick profits.
gṵ̄rā̰yē belts (pl. of **gūrū** q.v.).
gurɓạ̄cē Vb. 3A x (1) **rūwā yā ~** sediment of water has become stirred up (= **tāshị** 1o). (2) **haŋkạlinsạ yā ~** his mind's in a whirl (= **rīƙịcē**). (3) **zāmạnī yā ~** the world is all at sixes and sevens.
gurɓata A. (**gụrɓātạ**) Vb. 3B = **gurɓạ̄cē**.
B. (**gurɓā̰tā**) Vb. 1C. (1) **yā gurɓā̰tạ rūwā** it stirred up sediment in the water. (2) **yā ~ minị haŋkạlī** it disturbed my mind.
gurbị m. (pl. **gụrā̰bū** = **gurābū** = **gurbunạ**). (1) (a) (i) any natural or artificial indentation of ground, floor, coin-edge, rock (x made by hen for eggs; old site (**kufai**); hole in draughts-board Vd. **darạ, kwaɗọ**). (ii) **tanā̰ jạŋ gurbị** it (pigeon) is making cries indicating it is about to lay eggs. (iii) **furạd dạ zā tạ zubẹ bā tạ̄ tạ̄rar gurbị** there's no fighting Fate. (iv) Vd. **bạrạ ~**. (v) **gọ̄be yạ ~** Vd. **gọ̄be** 6. (vi) **ạ nēmam mikị ~** Vd. **bạrgi-bạrgī**. (b) **yā ɓatar dạ kuɗinsạ bā ~** he spent his money to the last farthing. (c) **kadạ kạ bi gurbịnsạ** don't follow his bad example! (d) (i) **gurbịŋ idọ** eye-socket. (ii) **gurbịŋ idọ, idọ nḛ̄**? mere coincidence does not render the two identical (x one's namesake is not oneself). (2) place where P. or T. should normally be found.
gụrɓīyạ f. rich broth (= **dạrmạsōsṵ̄wā**).
gurbunạ Vd. **gurbị**.

gụrcē Vd. **gụrtā**.
gurɗẹ (1) Vb. 3A. (a) is sprained, dislocated (= **gọ̄cẹ**). (b) is twisted out of shape (cf. **gọ̄cẹ** 1e). (2) Vb. 1A. (a) sprained; dislocated. (b) twisted out of shape (= **gọ̄cẹ** 2b).
gurdụgī Kt. = **guddụgī**.
gurdumụ Kt. = **gurdumụs** Sk. m. fowllice (= **ƙuddumụs**).
gure A. (**gūrẹ**) (1) Vb. 1A. (a) hollowed out x **yā ~ rījịyā**. (2) Vb. 1A. (a) became hollowed out. (b) is (was) impregnated with odour x **ɗākị yā ~ dạ hayā̰ƙī** the house's filled with smoke (= **gubrẹ** 2a). (c) increased (= **gubrẹ** 2b).
B. (**gurẹ**) m. (pl. **gụrā̰rē**) (cerebral -r-, Mod. Gram. 5). (1) place x **wạnẹ ~** where? (2) (rolled -r-) Kt. m. migration of Filani herds in the hot season (= **tāshị** 2b).
gụrfā̰nạ Vb. 3B = **gurfā̰nā** Vb. 3A. (1) (camel) knelt. (2) (a) (woman at childbirth) lay with elbows and knees on the ground (= **gwīwạ** 1c). (b) **yā ~ he** sat with elbows on knees.
gurfā̰nad dạ Vb. 4B caused (camel) to kneel (Vd. **gụrfā̰nạ**).
gurgụ m. (f. **gurgṵ̄wā**) pl. **gụrā̰gū**. (1) (a) lame (permanently), limping (temporarily) x **~ nē** he's a lame man. **~ nē yạnzu** he (P. or horse, etc.) is lame at the moment. (b) **gurgṵ̄war dạbārạ** plan of doubtful value. (c) **~ yanā̰ ganī, ạ sā̰ri sạndā, ạ yi masạ dūkạ** one must bow to circumstances (Vd. **dọ̄kā** 2a.ii). (d) **yanā̰ dạ gụrā̰gū** his feet are swollen from travelling (= **gụrạ-gụrạ** 2). (e) **gurgṵ̄war tsanyạ dạ wurī ta kạn sōmạ tịlā** don't leave things till the last minute! (f) "**ạ zō gạrēnị**!", **ɗākị yā fā̰ɗạ wạ gurgṵ̄wā tạ̄re dạ ɗam mā̰sū gidā, tā cẹ̄ "im bạ kụ zō dọ̄mīna ba, kwā zō dọ̄min ɗaŋkụ**" (said by mai **tạllạ**) buy, buy! (g) **ạbin dạ kạmar wụyā, gurgṵ̄wā dạ auran nēsạ** what a difficult thing! (h) **mijiŋ gurgṵ̄wā** Vd. **maƙẹtạcī**. (2) **~ nạwā̰tạ mai ƙafạ** epithet of cantankerous P. or donkey which bites. (3) **tā yi gurgụŋ gammō** she had a miscarriage.

gurgudu ran time after time (*int. from* gudu).

gurguje A. (gurgujē) *Vb.* 1C kept on avoiding (*int. from* guje).

   B. (gurguje) *x* a gurguje rapidly.

gurguncē *Vb.* 3A. (1) is (was) lame. (2) limped (temporarily). (3) dabāra tā ∼ the plan proved useless.

gurgunci *m.* = gurguntā.

gurgunta A. (gurguntā) *f.* (permanent) lameness. (2) (temporarily) limping (1, 2 = dingishī).

   B. (gurguntā) *Vb.* 1C. (1) lamed. (2) caused to limp (temporarily).

   C. (gurgunta) *Vb.* 3B. (1) is (was) lame (permanently). (2) limped (temporarily).

gurguntaka *f.* = gurguntā.

gurgura A. (gurgura) *Vb.* 2 = gurgurā 1C. (1) gnawed at. (2) stripped (meat from bone with teeth, knife, or fingers). (3) *Vd.* gurguri gōruba.

   B. (gurgurā) *Vd.* gurgurī.

gurgure A. (gurgurē) (1) *Vb.* 1C gnawed off completely. (2) *Vb.* 3A gāshinta yā ∼ her hair's fallen out.

   B. (gurgure) *m.* strong, short man.

   C. (gurgurē) *Kt. m.* cutting short-grass (= kurkurē).

gurgurī *m.* (*f.* gurgurā) strong, short P. (*epithet is* ∼ dan nā gōde).

gurguri gōruba *m.* child's game of seizing hand of another and making him bite his own wrist.

gurgurkā *f.* = gungurkā.

gurgurūgu *m.* (*sg., pl.*) man living by slandering those who refuse to pay him to refrain.

gurgusā *Vb.* 3A kept on moving aside (*int. from* gusa).

gurguzū *m.* (1) seeds of red-sorrel (yākuwā) or hemp (rama), *cf.* lātun. (2) (*a*) crowd of persons of same type *x* (i) gurguzum mazā (mātā) group of males (females). gurguzum fatakē crowd of traders (= sū yē sū *q.v. under* yē). (*aa*) rundunā cē ta Lārabāwā gurguzunsu it is an army composed entirely of Arabs. 'yam bom nē gurguzunsu they are composed entirely of bombing-planes (= zallā). (*b*) *Sk., Kt.* plain boiled beans (= kulū).

guri A. (gūri) *m.* keen wish *x* (1) gūrinsa yā cika his desire's been fulfilled. (2) (*sometimes in plur. sense*) *x* yā cika manyan gūrinsa he has fulfilled his main desires. (3) gūrin nan dōgō nē this wish is far-fetched.

   B. (gurī)· *m.* (*pl.* gurārē) place (= wurī *q.v.*).

   C. (gurī) *m.* growling of dog.

guri'a *f.* (*Ar.* kur'a casting lots). (1) " pooling " one's resources to buy T., .etc. = gamadē *q.v.* (*cf.* kuri'a). (2) kōwā ya yi ∼ da shī, burmi zai dauka he's the prince of rogues.

guriduma *m., f.* (*sg., pl.*) short-headed P. (2) stumpy, short-horned goat.

gurigubjī = gurugubjī.

guringuntsī = guringutsī *m.* cartilage.

gurjāgi *m.* (1) unkempt man. (2) badly-done work.

gurjāgo *m.* (1) = gurjāgi. (2) difficult T. (3) (*a*) file, saw (= zarto). (*b*) blunt knife. (4) obsolete Maguzawa dance.

gurjagunda *Sk. f.* type of wild cat.

gurje A. (gurje) *Vb.* 1A. (1) yā ∼ auduga he ginned the cotton. (2) ∼ dōki to rein up galloping horse sharply (= zāme 1*a*). (3) (*a*) grazed (part of one's body). (*b*) scraped (hair from skins, etc.). (*c*) T. rubbed against (sore place). (4) *Vd.* gurzā.

   B. (gurje) *Vd.* gurzā.

gurji A. (gurjī) *m.* (1) the small, striped gourd *Cucumis melo* (*for soup*). (2) *Vd.* daddawā 1*c*.

   B. (gurji) *Vd.* gurzā.

gurjīyā *Sk., Kt.* (1) Red-flowered Silk Cotton Tree (*Bombax buonopezense*) = *Sk.* kuryā, *Vd.* rīmī. (2) = gujīyā.

gurlī *m.* = gurjī.

Gurma *Vd.* banzā.

gurmādē *m.* woman's washing body while keeping loins covered (= wankan Gwārī).

gurmāje *m.* (*f.* gurmājīyā) big dolt.

gurmāzau *m., f.* (*sg., pl.*) big dolt.

gurmī *m.* (1) small type of stringed instrument. (2) quarrelling. (3) pain *x* tā kwānā tana ∼ she spent the night in pain. (4) kūrā tā dau gurmī *Vd.* giringirin.

gurmu *Sk., Kt.* lame (= gurgu *q.v.*).

gurmudē (1) *Vb.* 1C sprained, dislocated, twisted out of shape. (2) *Vb.* 3A is sprained, dislocated, twisted out of shape (*Vd.* gurdę).

gurmujajjēnīya = gurmujējēnīyā *f.* struggling together.

gurmuje A. (gurmujē) *Vb.* 1C overcame P. B. (gurmujē) *Vd.* gurmuzą.

gurmuntā *Sk., Kt. f.* lameness, limping (= gurguntā).

gurmususu *m.* = gurmujajjēnīyā.

gurmuzą *Vb.* 2 (*p.o.* gurmujē, *n.o.* gurmuji) = gurmujē.

gurnąnī *m.* (1) purring. (2) growling.

gurnukā = garnakā.

*gurō *Sk. m.* = kuɓēwā.

gurōrī *Kt. Vd.* tsąkī 1a.

gursā-gursą *Vd.* gursumēmę.

gurshēkē *m. and adj.* used in gurshēkyan aiki a stiff task. gurshēkyam fadą severe quarrel. sun shā ⌢ they had a stiff task.

gursumēmę = gursumī *m.* (*f.* gursumēmīyā = gursumā) *pl.* gursun-gursun = gursā-gursą huge (*re* P., animal, round things).

gursungumī *m.* (1) strong man. (2) knuckle of elbow, knee, wrist, etc.

gursun-gursun *Vd.* gursumēmę.

gursunū *m.* (*pl.* gursunai) pig (*Vd.* gadū).

gurtā *Vb.* 2 (*p.o.* gurcē. *n.o.* gurci) is (was) eager to get T.

gurtsū *Sk.* used in dan gurtsū *m.* = guntsū 2.

guru A. (gūrū) *m.* (*pl.* gūrąyē). (1) (*a*) (i) tubular belt of leather or cloth (= *Kt.* kīrį 4 = *Sk.* kąrfū). (ii) *cf.* jirgī 2. (*b*) ornamental ridge on pottery. (*c*) yā yi kiɓa har ya yi gūrąyē he's got rolls of fat round his waist. (4) *Sk.* type of trap. (5) *Kt.* (*a*) = kulī-kulī cakes. (*b*) hide rope kīrį. (6) gūrun dākį = kangū 2. (7) lāfīyar ⌢ gąrēshį he's a hypocrite. (8) *Kt.* gūrąyan dąndī rolls of skin forming wrinkles on forehead from age or carrying loads. (9) dūką dę gūrū *Vd.* dūką 2*b*. (10) *Sk.* gūrun kązā cutting chicken crosswise.
B. (gūru) *Vd.* gūrą.

gūrūdau *m.* (1) bluster. (2) empty rumours.

gurugubjī *used in* sun yi gurugubjim fadą two strong men had a fierce tussle.

gurū-gurū large and round (= dakwā-dakwā *q.v.*).

gurumbąlī *m.* (*sg., pl.*) clove (= kąnum-fąrī).

gurumfa A. (gurumfā) *f.* straw-hat (= mąlafā).
B. (gurumfą) *used in* dan gurumfą (1) trader who travels rapidly, unencumbered by women or heavy baggage (= dam bōjūwā *q.v. under* bōjūwā). (2) (*said by women*) what a big head !

Gurungū *Kt. epithet of* hyena (kūrā).

gurungundumī *m.* (*f.* gurungundumā). (1) loutish. (2) important (*re* affair, news).

gurunguntsī = *Kt.* gurungurcī *m.* cartilage, gristle.

gurungurtsī *m.* cartilage, gristle.

gurun-gurun A. (gurun-gurun). (1) huge (*re* plural round-things). (2) yau garī ⌢ yakę sky's overcast to-day.
B. (gurun-gurun) *used in* idona ⌢ nakē jinsa I've got something in my eye.

guruntsį *Daura Hausa m.* type of dance.

gurunzumī *Sk. m.* refuse-pit.

gurus *m.* (*Egyptian Arabic* girsh) (1) Maria · Theresa dollar (= līyar). (2) type of thick red fez. (3) type of burnous (ąlkyabbą). (4) *Kt.* gurushin ąlkyabbą burnous-tassel.

Gurūzą *nickname for any man called* Āmadu.

guryā *f.* (1) a food made from cotton-seed. (2) *Kt.* cotton-seed (= angųryā).

gurzā *Vb.* 2 (*p.o.* gurjē, *n.o.* gurji) (1) = gurję. (2) garī yā gurjē shį he had a hard time.

gurzā-gurzą *pl. adj.* big *x* gurzā-gurzan sōją tall soldiers.

gurzau *m.* (*sg., pl.*). (1) strong man. (2) *Vd.* dāguri ⌢.

gurzayyą *Kt. f.* having great difficulty in doing T.

gusą *Vb.* 3A. (1) moved aside or away slightly. (2) *x* aiki bā yą gusąwā the work's not progressing (*cf.* gudąnā 2).

gusad dą *Vb.* 4B. (1) moved T. aside or away slightly. (2) removed *x* yā ⌢ dą ląrūrą he satisfied his necessity.

ɗaukaŋ kāyā mai nawyī yā ∼ budur-cintạ lifting the heavy load ruptured her maidenhead.

Gusau *f.* (1) place-name. (2) 'yar Gusau *f.* the dear prices of 1943.

gusɗẹ to sprain, etc. (= gurɗẹ *q.v.*).

gusgus *used in* yanā tạfīyạ gus-gus he (short, heavy man) is pounding along.

gushẹ *Vb.* 3A. (1) passed away *x* rūwā bā yā gushẹ̄wā the place's still water-logged. (2) *x* baŋ ∼ ba, kulluŋ n nā gayạ masạ I never cease impressing it on him. (3) haŋkạlinsạ yā ∼ his mind's in a whirl.

gushi *m.* (1) progressing *x* yanā gushiŋ gạba he's making progress. (2) tuntuɓẹ daɗiŋ gushiŋ gạba nẹ̄, im bạ kạ ji cīwọ ba what an unexpected bargain ! ; we got off lightly !

gusmā *Kt. f.* = guzumā.

gusụm *Kt.* south (= kudụ).

gutsāgutsai = gutsạ-gutsạ short (*re* plural *x* children, sticks, etc.).

gutsạttsarī *Vd.* gutsurẹ.

gutsi-gutsi = gutsāgutsai.

gūtsū = *Kt.* gūtsụ *m.* (1) bottom, base, foundation (= gindī). (2) ạ gūtsuŋ itạcē at foot of the tree. (3) (*a* privy parts. (*b*) haifūwā ɗayā gyāraŋ ∼ nẹ̄ one learns from experience. (4) yā yi mini gūtsuŋ guzumā he left me in the lurch.

gutsuŋ-gutsuŋ *adv.* in fragments *x* yanā aiki ∼ he's doing various, scattered, small jobs (= kutsuŋ-kutsuŋ).

gutsuntsunā *Vb.* 1D broke into fragments.

gutsụrā *Vb.* 1C = gutsurạ *Vb.* 2 = gutsụrē 1*a.*i, 1*b.*i, iii *q.v.*

gutsure A. (gutsụrē). (1) *Vb.* 1C. (*a*) (i) broke piece off T. (ii) dōki yā gutsurẹ gindī horse bit through the hobbling-rope. (*b*) (*with dative*) nā ∼ masạ tūwō (i) I broke a piece of tūwō off for him. (ii) I broke off and seized a bit of his tūwō. (iii) muŋ ∼ mukụ lạ̄bāri we have made a summary of the news for you. muŋ gutsụrā mukụ cẹ̄wā . . . we told you in brief that . . . (2) *Vb.* 3A yā ∼ it has a bit broken off it.

　　B. (gutsurẹ) *m.* (*pl.* gutsạttsarī) frag-ment ; piece broken off T.

gutsuriŋ gutsātsạ *m.* fragment of kolanut.

gutsụri tsọ̄ma *m.* harping on A.

gutsuttsụrā *Vb.* 1D. (1) *int. from* gutsụrā. (2) yanā ∼ magananạ he's harping on it.

guzā *f.* (1) water-monitor (= tsārī 3). (2) ∼ mai baŋ haushī *epithet of* can-tankerous P. (3) yā yi fitar bardaŋ ∼ he decamped (through fear, hunger, etc.). (4) baŋ ∼ *Vd.* ban 3*b*. (5) damō yanā zamā guzạ *Vd.* damō 5, 6.

guzāmē *Vd.* guzumā.

guzāmī *Kt. m.* eager haste.

guzāyē *Vd.* gujīyā.

guzgus *Zar. m.* cooked accạ.

guzu-guzu A. (guzū-guzụ̄) *x* zạrē ∼ coarse thread.

　　B. (guzu-guzu) *Kt. m.* type of tiger-nut (ayā).

guzumā *f.* (*pl.* guzāmē = guzạ̄mai = guzumōmī). (1) (*a*) old woman (= gyạ̄tumā). (*b*) old cow or female animal (*cf.* gwabtā). (2) kōwā ya kas guzumar wani, ạ bạ̄kin jūyạ tasạ if P. damages another's property, he must pay. (3) yā yi mini gūtsuŋ ∼ he left me in the lurch. (4) haifūwar ∼ *f.* making bad worse (*epithet is* haifūwar ∼, ɗā kwạnce, ūwā kwạnce). (5) am fakẹ dạ ∼, aŋ hạrbi kạrsanā reference was made to one P. by innuendo, using another as a mere blind.

guzurcē *Vd.* guzurtạ.

guzur-guzụr = guzū-guzụ̄.

guzurī *m.* (1) journey-provisions *x* yā yi ∼ he took provisions for his journey (= tạ̄kạlmi 3). (2) *Vd.* kūrā 40.

guzurta A. (guzurtạ) *Vb.* 2 (*p.o.* guzụrcē, *n.o.* guzụrci) *x* nā guzụrcē shi I took it as provisions for my journey.

　　B. (guzụrtā) *Vb.* 1C *x* nā ∼ masạ sulẹ gōmạ I gave him 10*s.* to provision himself for his journey.

gwab = gwaf.

gwaɓa A. (gwaɓạ) *Vb.* 1A. (1) hafted *x* nā ∼ gạ̄tarī ạ k̄otạ I hafted the axe (= kwaɓạ 1 = dōsạ). (2) *x* yā ∼ shi dạ Sarkī he involved him in trouble with the Chief. (3) *Sk.* yā ∼ matạ = gwaɓā.

　　B. (gwạɓā) *Vb.* 2 *Sk.* yā gwạɓē tạ he copulated with her (= cī 16*a* = gwaɓạ 3), *cf.* gwaɓi.

gwāɓāɓā *pl.* thick-set (*pl. of* gwąggwāɓā).

gwaɓalɓashē *Vb.* 1D *Sk.* thrashed soundly.

gwabcę = gabcę.

gwabdųwā *Sk. f.* white of egg (= gwaidųwā).

gwaɓę *m.* (1) gruel from wholemeal-flour and sour milk. (2) *Kt.* sedimentary liquid (*such as of* tsąkim furā *or* tsąkiŋ kųnū) = dągwadągō 1*a*, *cf.* dąląkī.

gwaɓi A. (gwāɓī) *m.* (1) solidity. (2) viscousness. (3) thick-setness.

    B. (gwaɓi) *Sk. m.* yā yi matą ~ he copulated with her (= gwąɓā).

gwabję *Vb.* 1A collided with and knocked over (= gabję *q.v.*).

gwaɓǫ *m.* " showing-off " *x* yaną̄ ~ dą kudī.

gwabra A. (gwabrą) *Vb.* 1A. (1) dōki yā ~ karǫ dą shī the horse collided with him (= gabzą 2 *q.v.*). (2) = gwaɓą 1, 2.

    B. (gwąbrā) *Vb.* 2 collided with (= gąbzā 1*a*, 2 *q.v.*).

gwąbrau *Sk.* native doctor (= gwąurau *q.v.*).

gwąbrayyą *f.* fierce struggle.

gwabrę *Vb.* 1A. (1) yā ~ shi dą sandā he beat him with stick (= gabję 1, 2 *q.v.*). (2) = gubrę.

gwabrō *m.* (*f.* gwabrūwā) *pl.* gwamąrē wifeless-man (= gwaurō *q.v.*).

gwabsa A. (gwabsą) *Vb.* 1A. (1) dōki yā ~ karǫ dą shī horse collided with it (= gwabzą 1, 2, 4 *q.v.*). (2) = gwaɓą 1; 2. (3) *f.* the tree *Cussonia nigerica.*

    B. (gwąbsā) *Vb.* 2 (*p.o.* gwąbshē, *n.o.* gwąbshi) *x* dōki yā gwąbshi gārū horse collided with wall (= gąbzā 1*a*).

gwabshe A. (gwąbshē) *Vd.* gwąbsā.

    B. (gwąbshę) *Vb.* 1A collide with and knock over (= gabję 1, 2 *q.v.*).

gwabsǫ *Kt. m.* (1) sun yi ~ they collided. (2) yā yi masą ~ he involved him in trouble with superior.

gwabta A. (gwabtą) *Vb.* 1A *x* nā ~ masą gātarī I wounded him deeply with axe, *etc.* (= gabtą *q.v.*).

    B. (gwąbtā) *Vb.* 2 *x* yā gwąbcē shi = gwabsǫ 2.

    C. (gwabtā) *m., f.* old horse, donkey, or P. (*cf.* guzumā).

gwabzą *Vb.* 1A yā ~ karǫ dą shī he collided with him (= gabzą *q.v.*).

gwabzǫ = gwabsǫ.

gwada A. (gwadą) *Vb.* 1A. (1) measured. (2) tested. (*a*) ąbiŋ gwadą̄wā. (i) T. for testing with or measuring with (*x* ruler, tape, etc.). (ii) T. to be measured, tested (*cf.* gwaji 2). (*b*) ką ~ ragąmar ą (= dą) kāwunąn dawākī try the halter on the heads of the horses till you find the right fit ! (*c*) kō bą ą gwadą ba, linzāmi yā fi bąkiŋ kązā it's obvious. (3) tried, attempted. (4) showed *x* (*a*) yā ~ mini shī he showed it to me (= nūną). (*b*) yā ~ zāruntą he exhibited bravery. (*c*) bā ą̄ gwadą masą kōmē he has not his equal. (5) inflicted *x* ya ~ matą wųyā he treated her cruelly. aŋ gwadą musų ązābą torture was inflicted on them (= nūną). (6) (*a*) yā ~ bindigą he aimed the gun (= auną 6). (*b*) adjusted *x* yā gwadą agōgō he set the watch. (7) (*negatively*) never has *x* bą tą ~ haifųwā ba she has never born a child (= taɓą 3).

    B. (gwądā) *Vb.* 2 (*p.o.* gwąjē, *n.o.* gwąji) = gwadą 1, 2.

    C. (gwądą) it would be better to *x* ~ ką yi haką you'd better do so (= gāra).

    D. (gwādā) = jaŋ ~ *m.* orange-headed male lizard (= gwąrgwādą = *Kt.* kutū = *Sk.* kiskī = *Kt.* jaŋ katakō).

gwadabę *m.* (1) highway. (2) ~ ąbim bīyā *Vd.* Wązīri.

gwaɗaɗa A. (gwāɗaɗā) *Vb.* 1C improved T.

    B. (gwāɗaɗą) *Vb.* 3B he, it, improved.

gwąɗaɗɗashī *m.* (*f.* gwąɗaɗɗąsā) *pl.* gwąɗaɗɗąsai handsome.

gwądaddē *m. adj.* measured, tested, etc. (= gwąjajjē).

gwadā-gwądā̄ huge (*re* plural round-things).

gwadai-gwadai (1) *used in* yārǫ gwadai-gwadai plump boy just beginning to walk (= dagwai-dagwai *q.v.*). (2) small (*pl.*), *Vd.* gwai-gwai.

gwądaŋgwarkę = gwąndagwarki.

gwadunnā = gwądannī *Vd.* gwądǫ.

gwādarą *f.* (1) type of bran-gruel. (2) youths' dance.

gwādarē *m.* (1) affectation. (2) ogling.

gwadạyī *m.* (1) the twiner *Hippocratea obtusifolia.* (2) ∼ bạ sāraŋkạ ba, jạŋ it's hard to get a stingy P. to fulfil promise.

gwaddạ *Sk. f.* pawpaw (= gwandạ *q.v.*).

gwạddī mares (*pl. of* gōdịyā).

gwaddunạ *Vd.* gwạdọ.

gwadẹ *Kt.* = gwajẹ.

gwadị *Kt.* = gwajị.

gwạdọ *m.* (*pl.* gwaddunạ = gwạdạnnī). (1) (*also called* fariŋ ∼) type of native-woven white cloth, often with blue stripes. (2) (*rustic*) the cloth bụnū.

Gwạdọ-gwadō *m., f.* (*sg., pl.*). (1) Bagirmi P. (*the word means* " gruel " *in Bagirmi*). (2) type of chicken.

gwaf *Kt. used in* gōbe gwaf to-morrow definitely.

gwạfā *f.* (*pl.* gwạfạnnī). (1) forked stick (= shisshikẹ = dirkạ 1 = *Sk.* 6ạrạntinnị) (*cf.* hamạtā 1*d*). (2) gwạfar gāsạyā useless P. *(3) = gwạfī 1.

gwāfẹ *Vb.* 3A sat down to eat while holding food-vessel.

gwạfī *m.* (1) nick at end of arrow. (2) yanạ bạkiŋ ∼ he's within ace of T. good or bad happening to him.

gwafsạ *Vb.* 1A collided with, etc. (= gwabzạ *q.v.*).

gwạfsayyạ *f.* fierce struggle.

gwafshẹ *Vb.* 1A collided with and knocked over (= gabjẹ 1, 2 *q.v.*).

gwāgẹ *Vb.* 3A yā ∼ cikịnsạ he's an " old-hand " at it (= gōgẹ).

gwaggọ (1) *m.* (*pl.* gwaggunạ). (*a*) white dog-headed baboon (= yimkị = bịkā). (*b*) a drink made from locust-bean (kūkạ) pods and tamarind (tsāmiyā) (= *Kt.* dāgalē = dạgwadạgō 2), *Vd.* bọlọlō 1. (2) gwaggọ = gwạggō *f.* (*pl.* gwạgwạnnī). (*a*) wife of father, except one's own mother. (*b*) father's sister. (*c*) mother's brother's wife. (*d*) (i) *Vd.* yạyā A.1, 2*h*. (ii) *Vd.* būsạ gwaggọ. (*e*) fadạŋ gwaggọ ạ Kọfā doing T. at unsuitable time. (Kọfā *is place-name*).

gwaggōfīyā *Sk. f.* (1) being uneven. (2) (vessel's cover) fitting badly.

gwaggunạ *Vd.* gwaggọ.

gwạggwā6ā *m., f.* (*pl.* gwā6ạ6ā). (1) solid. (2) viscous. (3) thick-set (*cf.* gwā6ī).

gwaggwạfē *Vb.* 3A monopolized conversation, work, etc. (= fiffịkē).

gwāgwā *Kt. f.* sieve (= marārakī).

gwāgwạdā *Vb.* 1C applied T. to eyes *x* (1) tā gwāgwạdạ kwạllī ạ idō she applied antimony to her eyes. (2) yā ∼ masạ bạrkọnō he treated him harshly (*cf.* gwāgwạgwā).

gwāgwạgwā *f.* having a hard time (*cf.* gwāgwạdā).

gwagwạmā *f.* = gwagwạmī *m. Kt.* quarter of corn bundle (dami), *cf.* gwammā.

gwạgwạnnī *Vd.* gwaggọ 2.

gwagwar *adv.* in sound condition (= gwargwar *q.v.*).

gwagwarcị *m.* being wifeless or husbandless (*cf.* gwaurō).

gwagwạrē (1) wifeless men ; husbandless women (*pl. of* gwaurō *q.v.*). (2) Gwagwạrē *Kt.* an inferior official appointment.

gwagwạrmāyạ *f.* (1) struggling with task or P. *x* an shā ∼ kạnsạ it (task) was troublesome. (2) (*used in songs*) wifeless man.

gwagwạrtakạ *f.* being wifeless or husbandless (*cf.* gwaurō).

gwāgwịyạ *Vb.* 2 = gwāgwịyē 1C gnawed at.

gwāgwịyi gọrubạ *m.* child's game of seizing hand of another and making him bite his own wrist.

gwạhī *Kt. m.* = gwạfī.

gwaidạ *Kt. f.* girl whose breasts are not formed (*younger than* bụdurwā) = bērạ (*epithet is* ∼ ta dạŋ alị mại dịmiŋ fụndū).

Gwạidam *m.* (*said by children*) Next World *x* yā tạfi ∼ he's dead.

gwaidụwā *f.* egg-yoke (= fwandụwā 2).

gwai-gwai A. (gwai-gwai) smallness *x* 'yar tukunyā cẹ ∼ dạ ita it is a small pot (*pl.* 'yan tukwạnē nẹ gwadai-gwadai dạ sū). B. (gwại-gwại) *m.* (*sg., pl.*) evil spirit.

gwainạ *used in* fwaŋ ∼ *m.* type of blue-green beads.

gwainō *m.* (1) yā yi ∼ ạ kạsūwā it's unsaleable (*cf.* māsạ 2). (2) Audụ ∼ garēshị Audu's a good-for-nothing.

gwaisạ *f.* type of draughts (darạ) played by women.

gwaiwā *f.* (1) (*a*) testicle(s) (= **tsūwę** = *Sk.* **gōlō** = **ƙwādạ 2** = **ƙwālā̧tai** = **maraịnā** = *Sk.* **tsigau** = **lunsayī**) (*this word is from same root as* **ƙwāi** ; *similarly in Arabic* **baiza** = egg, testicle). (*b*) (i) **yanā̧ dạ** ~ he has enlarged testicles (= **ƙābā**). (ii) **yanā̧ dạ 'yar** ~ he has scrotal hernia (= **ƙābā** = **mạjạƙwar**), *cf.* **būlụŋƙwīyạ** ; **zụlūlūwā** ; **dạbaibạyī 3** ; **rụkwākwạ** ; **ƙuŋƙū**. (*c*) **dạ mutūwạr gạbā, gāra** ~ better a slight misfortune than a big one. (*d*) **gwaiwar jā̧kī** (*said by boys*) shrub *Grewia sp.*, which has edible berries. (*e*) **gwaiwar mātā** prolapse (= **ƙwaịƙwāyạ**). (*f*) **ƙȩ̄tar gwaiwā** doing evil which recoils on oneself (*epithet is* **ƙȩ̄tar gwaiwā wạddạ ta kar ụbaŋgijịntạ**). (*g*) **gwaiwā dạ kudī cakī cȩ̄** people sin if it is advantageous to them. Even old man, if rich, can get young bride. (*h*) **kāyaŋ gwaiwā** *Vd.* **tīlạs 1***e*. (*j*) **gwaiwas sā̧** *Vd.* **canjạras**. (2) weight on irrigation-pole (**jīgọ**).

gwā̧jā = **gwā̧jābọ** *Kt. m.* (*sg., pl.*) ugly man.

gwajạ-gwajạ *f.* (1) barge. (2) sailing-boat.

gwajajjạ̄ƀā *Vb.* 1E **yā gwajajjạ̄ƀạ aiki** he botched the work.

gwạjajjē *adj. m* (*f.* **gwạjajjīyā**) *pl.* **gwạjạjjū** having been measured, tested (= **gwạdaddē**).

gwaje A. (**gwajȩ**) *Vb.* 1A completely measured or tested (*cf.* **gwadạ**).

    B. (**gwạjē**) *Vd.* **gwạdā**.

    C. (**gwājē**) *m.* surreptitious riding of donkeys by boys (*cf.* **karyạ 6**).

gwaji A. (**gwạji**) *Vd.* **gwạdā**.

    B. (**gwaji**) *m.* (1) (*secondary v.n. of* **gwadạ 1–3**) *x* **tanā̧ gwajịŋ hatsī** = **tanā̧ gwadạ hatsī** she's measuring corn. (2) **ạbiŋ** ~ T. for testing or measuring with (*x* ruler, tape ; *cf.* **gwadạ 2**). (3) **gwajịŋ tā̧kạlmī** sleeping with woman to see whether pleasurable to marry.

gwal A. (**gwạl**) *used in* **yanā̧ dạ idọ gwạl** he has protuberant eyes.

    B. (**gwạl**) *Eng. m.* (*mining term*) gold (= **zīnārīyā**).

gwalā *used in* **Gwalā mạntạ rīgā** thou blazing fire !

gwạlai (1) = **gwạl**. (2) *adv. and m.* in foul state *x* **tā sayō nāmạ** ~ she bought putrid meat.   **nāmạn naŋ** ~ **dạ shī** this meat's rotten.

gwalalō *m.* moat round town with raised margins (= **tạsạ mahạrā** = *Kt.* **tsanyạ 2** = **bādalā 1**).

gwạlam *adv. and m.* **yā yi** ~ **yanā̧ kallō** = **yanā̧ kallansạ** ~ his mouth " watered " when he saw him eating.   **yā yi** ~ **dạ idọ** he looked longingly at the food (= **ƙwạlam 1**).

gwạlamnīyā *f.* = **gwạlaŋ-gwalaŋ** *m.* = **gwạlaŋgwạlantū** *m.* speaking unintelligibly.

gwalaŋgwasō *m.* ogling ; affectation (*epithet is* ~ **gai dạ ūwar saurā̧yī ạ kā̧sūwā**).

gwạlannīyā *f.* = **gwạlantū** *m.* = **gwạlamnīyā** *q.v.*

gwale A. (**gwalȩ**) *Vb.* 1A. (*a*) ignored P. (*b*) snubbed P. (*cf.* **pf !**) = **kwạ̄ƀā**. (2) *m.* **tā cikạ yawạŋ** ~ she has dirty ways.

    B. (**gwālȩ**) *Vb.* 1A *x* **yā** ~ **idọ** he opened his eyes wide.

gwalȩ-gwalȩ *m.* speaking unintelligibly.

gwalgwạdā *Vb.* 1C *Kt.* kept on measuring, etc. (*int. from* **gwadạ**).

gwali *Sk. m.* leather-band worn round neck (= **ƙwā̧rō 5***b*).

gwālịtsā *Vb.* 1C. (1) squashed. (2) mixed together food with hand.

gwālịtsē (1) *Vb.* 1C = **gwālịtsā**. (2) *Vb.* 3A is (was) squashed.

gwaljȩ (1) *Vb.* 1A scraped (= **kūjȩ**). (2) *Vb.* 3A is (was) scraped (= **kūjȩ** *q.v.*).

Gwalkwạs *f.* Gold Coast (= **Gwạnjā**).

gwallī = *Kt.* **gwallē** *m.* affectation ; ogling (= **fēlēƙē**).

gwallọ *Sk., Kt. m.* = **gwammā**.

gwalmạ *f.* (1) cudgel (= **kulkī**). (2) throwing-stick.

gwalmạɗā *Vb.* 1C *Sk.* bent (a knife blade, hoe, etc.) = **kalmạɗā** *q.v.*

gwalmị *m.* cudgel (= **kulkī**).

gwālō *m.* grimace.

gwama A. (**gwamā**) *f.* (1) cudgel (= **kulkī**). (2) old hag (= **gyā̧tumā**).

    B. (**gwāmạ**) *Vb.* 1A (1) (*a*) put T. or P. on another of the *same* kind *x* (i) **yā** ~ **wani kāyā ạ kạnsạ** he put a second

load on the first load already on his head
= ɗōrą q.v. (but ɗōrą is not limited to
superimposing same kind). aŋ ∼ zaŋgǫ
kąn zaŋgǫ they travelled several stages.
yā ∼ mųtųm bīyū, yā kāyar he
(wrestler) downed two opponents simultaneously. aŋ ∼ littāfi kąn littāfi
one book was put on another. (ii)
yā ∼ dami bīyū he put sheaf on sheaf
and took them away (= riôanyā 1).
(b) put two or more things of the same
kind on another T. x yā ∼ yārǫ bīyū
ą kąn jąkī he mounted two boys on the
donkey, one behind the other (cf.
ɗōrą, ajīyē 4, azą, są). (2) yā ∼ lōmą
bīyū he ate two mouthfuls of food
together. (3) aŋ ∼ wutā big fire's
been made.

gwamąkkai Vd. gwaŋkī.

gwāmąncē Vb. 3A is (was) knock-kneed.

gwamārē Vd. gwaurō.

gwāmątsā = gwāmųtsā.

Gwambą Sk. used in Ta ∼ lāfīyąr cikį
epithet of (1) koko-yam (gwāzā). (2)
honest P.

gwambązā f. (sg., pl.) (1) Western waterbuck (Kobus defassa) (= yąkumbą =
Sk. ąmbęcī = daddōką). (2) Kt.
old P.

Gwąmbę = Kt. Gwąmbē. (1) Gombe.
(2) Vd. banzā.

gwąmē m. joining two bundles of corn
together (= dąfkē 1), cf. gwāmą,
gąmē 2b.

gwami A. (gwāmi) (1) m. (f. gwāmīyā)
knock-kneed. (2) Kt. m. (a) burning a
tree through. (b) aŋ yi ∼ = gwāmą 3.
B. (gwami) m. cudgel (= kulkī).

gwamkī Kt. m. (pl. gwąmąkkai) roan
antelope (= gwaŋkī q.v.).

gwamma A. (gwammā) f. (pl. gwammōmī
= gwammąmmakī). (1) portion of
large bundle of corn (= Sk. gwallǫ),
cf. gąŋgā 3 ; tąbashī ; gwagwąmā. (2)
(sarcastically) small bundle of corn.
B. (gwąmmą) (1) rather x ∼ jīyą
dą yąu we were better off previously
than now. ∼ mų yī we had better do
it (= gāra = gwąda). (2) ∼ dą wāwā dą
bābų wāwā, gāra dą wāwā " half loaf's
better than no bread. (3) gwąmmą
rānā dą kē Vd. bąkī 3o.

C. (Gwąmmā) name for girl born
after succession of only girls (cf.
Hakąmā).

gwammącē Vb. 1C preferred x (1) nā ∼
shi dą kanąnsą I prefer him to his
younger brother. (2) yā gwammącę
kidį dą kąrątū he threw away the
substance for the shadow. (3) kuŋ
gwammącę kǫshī Vd. bąrēwā 1b.

gwąmmą kāshī Kt. m. a tree (1) of the
kanyā type and (2) one of the kadanyą
type whose wood emits offensive smoke
if burned.

gwammąmmakī, gwammōmī Vd. gwammā.

Gwamną (pl. Gwamnōnī) Eng. m. (1)
Governor. (2) ɗaŋ ∼ mֶ. (f. 'yar ∼)
pl. 'yā'yaŋ ∼ Vd. 'yā'yā 2. (3) Vd.
kundī. (4) shānuŋ ∼ Vd. są A.2, 1g.

Gwamnati Eng. f. (1) (British) Government. (2) mąsū aikiŋ ∼ Government
officials (cf. Sarkī).

gwamrą Vb. 1A hit hard ; collided with
(= gabzą q.v.).

gwąmrau Kt. m. native doctor
(= gwaurau q.v.).

gwamrō Kt. m. (f. gwamrūwā) pl.
gwamārē wifeless man (= gwaurō q.v.).

gwāmųncē Vb. 3A is (was) knock-kneed.

gwamunta A. (gwāmųnta) Vb. 1C rendered
knock-kneed.
B. (gwāmųntā) f. being knock-kneed.

gwamutsa A. (gwāmųtsā) (1) Vb. 1C
mixed food together with hand. (2)
squashed.
B. (gwąmutsą) Vb. 2 (1) jostled P.
(2) Vb. 3B suŋ ∼ they form dense
crowd.

gwāmųtsē Vb. 1C jostled P.

gwąmząrō m. detachment detailed to
guard villages whose men have gone
to war, from being looted.

gwana A. (gwānā) Zar. f. farm (= gōnā
q.v.).
B. (gwąnā) (1) expert (f. of gwąnī q.v.).
(2) Vd. farar ∼.

gwanąncē Vb. 3A is (was) expert. suŋ ∼
gą yākį they're expert in war.

gwanāyē Vd. gwąnī.

gwanda A. (gwandą) f. (pl. gwandōjī) (1)
pawpaw (Vd. shā A.1e). (2) gwandąr
jēji wild custard-apple (Anona

senegalensis), *Vd.* gwaŋgwalē, gubdū. (3) shī bā abōkin shaŋ gwandata ba nē he's not an equal of mine (= tsādā 1*b*). (4) *Vd.* halak 2*c*.ii. B. (gwandā) *f.* (1) type of white-edged native cloth (*for epithet, Vd.* gwandā), *cf.* jākī 7. (2) *Kt.* name for child whose birth reconciled antipathetic husband and wife. C. (gwandā = gwanda) (1) rather *x* ~ ka tafi you had better go (= gāra). (2) ~ kē dā mūgun sākī *epithet of* gwandā-cloth. gwandacē *Vb.* 1C preferred (= gwammacē *q.v.*). gwandagwarkī *m.* (*f.* gwandagwarkīyā) burly P. or animal (*epithet is* ~ kashiŋ gīwā na tsatsō). gwandai *m.* (1) *Stylochiton Dalzielii* (a plant of arum lily family, whose leaves and root (kincīyā) are used for soup) (= kunnē 5), *cf.* kincīyā. (2) the cotton called bagwandarā. gwandarērē *m.* (*f.* gwandarērīyā) *pl.* gwandar-gwandar huge. Gwandāwā *Vd.* Bagwandē. gwandī *Kt. m.* the cotton called bagwandarā (= karfī 8). gwandō *Sk. m.* eel. gwandō *m.* eager anticipation. gwandōjī *Vd.* gwandā. Gwandū *f.* Gwandu. gwandūwā *Sk. f.* egg-yoke (= gwaidūwā). gwaŋga *Fil.* (1) yes, quite so ! (2) anā karaŋ ~ dā ~ a heroic struggle is going on. (3) *Vd.* bātal gwaŋga. gwaŋgiri *m.* rail(s) for railway (= kwaŋgiri). gwaŋgō *Kt. m.* (*pl.* gwaŋgunā) = gwaŋgwaŋ. gwaŋgwalā *f.* (1) midrib of raphia (tukurwā), used for roofing and canoe-poles (*cf.* mucīyā 3). (2) *Vd.* tukurwā. gwaŋgwalē *m.* flower(s) of gwandar jēji (custard apple). gwaŋgwama A. (gwaŋgwāmā) *f.* Canna plant (*seeds used for rosary*). B. (gwaŋgwāmā) *Vb.* 1C kept on superimposing (*int. from* gwāmā *q.v.*). gwaŋgwamarkī = gwandagwarkī. gwaŋgwamarsō *m.* huge T. ; huge affair ; huge lie, *etc.*

gwan-gwan A. (gwaŋ-gwaŋ) *m.* (*pl.* gwaŋgwāyē). (1) small tin (*x* as used for tinned-milk, cigarettes, tobacco, etc.). gwaŋgwanin sigārī tin of cigarettes ; cigarette-tin (= kwaŋkō = kwaŋ-kwaŋ = fam-fam). (2) *Zar.* = kwānō 1*b*. (3) tin for tinning food ; tin of food (= kwānō 3). gwangwani A. (gwaŋgwānī) *Sk. m.* meddlesomeness. B. (gwaŋgwani) *Vd.* gwaŋ-gwaŋ. gwaŋgwaraŋ = kwaŋkwaraŋ. gwaŋgwāyē *Vd.* gwaŋ-gwaŋ. gwanī *m.* (*f.* gwanā) *pl.* gwanāyē = *Sk.* gwannai. (1) (*a*) expert. (*b*) gwanin dōki, wandā ya hau = gwanin dōki, wandā kē kansā possession is nine points of the law. (*c*) Gwanī kā īyā, kā ki ka yī what a clever but contrary person ! (*d*) yau dā gōbe, jībi gwanin rawā yā fādi pride comes before a fall. (*e*) gwanin dā kē fagē *Vd.* fagē 1*d*.iii. (2) Gwanī *title of* P. having memorized the Koran and who is past-master in it (*Vd.* farī 2*a*.iv). (3) gwanin very *x* gwaniŋ kyau garēshi it is very good. gwanin dādī garētā she's very nice. gwanin yawa garēsu they are numerous. gwanim baŋ haushī garēsu they're vexatious persons. sū abiŋ gwanim ban tausayī nē they inspire great pity. (4) shuttlecock of chickens' feathers. (5) farar gwanā *f.* thrift, foresight (= tānadī). gwaninta *f.* (1) skill. (2) kā yi mini ~ your action suits me well. Gwanjā *f.* (1) the Gold Coast (= Gwalkwas). (2) *Vd* rākumī 1*f*, bagwanjā. (3) ~ kusa *f. generic name for* plants used as substitute for kolanuts (*x* alālē). gwanjance *x* a ~ yā yi pam bīyar it'll amount to at least £5. gwanjō *m.* (*sg., pl.*). (1) (*a*) sale for cash at knock-down price. (*b*) auction-sale *x* am bugā ~ auction, etc., has been held. (2) kadā ka buga mini ~ = kadā ka yi mini gwanjan tsīyā don't shame me ! nā buga gwanjansā " I gave him away " (*cf.* tsīyā 1*e*). (3) ~ yā yi pam bīyar = gwanjance. gwaŋkī *m.* (*pl.* gwaŋkāyē = *Sk.* gwamakkai). (1) Roan antelope (*epithet is* Shạ̃ bạ̃rā̃), *cf.* darị 3. (2) tsōfaŋ ~ nẹ̃ he's an "old hand" (hannū 2g). (3) *Vd.* wạ̃raŋ ~.

gwạnnai *Vd.* gwạnī.

gwănō = *Kt.* gwạnnō *m.* (*sg.*, *pl.*). (1) the stink-ant. (2) wāriŋ ~ = gyặtsā 4.

gwạnsō *m.* (*sg.*, *pl.*) type of guitarre.

gwantạl *used in* gwantạl, gwaɓạl, gwamạl, kulkim fọ̃raŋ gīwā ; iŋ akạ fọ̃rī saŋ gidā dạ shī, sǎi yaŋkā *laudatory epithet of* Emir *by* masạrtā (professional-beggars).

gwạntō *m.* (*pl.* gwantặyē). (1) *Nor.* village-head (= dagacị). (2) *Kt.* strong man (*epithet is* ~ kā kadǎi gạyyā).

gwanyọ *Kt. m.* = gwayyọ.

gwạnzạrō *m.* (*pl.* gwạnzạrai) = gwạmzạrō.

gwap *Kt.* *used in* gọ̄be ~ to-morrow definitely.

gwar = gwargwar.

gwarā = *Kt.* gwạrā. (1) *f.* (*sg.*, *pl.*) grey sparrow (= ɓantā). (2) = gwarē.

gwarāɓīyā *Kt. f.* rich soup (= dạrmạsō- sū̃wā).

Gwarabjāwā *used in* daŋ Gwarabjāwā *m.* cloth like bụnū.

gwārācī *Kt. m.* = gwārājī.

gwạraf *used in* yā fādị gwạraf he fell on his hands and knees.

gwārāgī = gwārājī.

gwarā-gwạrā̃ *pl.* large and round (= dafkwā-dạfkwā̃ *q.v.*).

gwarạ̃jē *Vd.* gwarzō.

gwaraji A. (gwārājī) *m.* extra-special lumps made for kōko (gruel) *x* gāyansạ ~ nẹ̃ the gruel contains *such lumps* (= kụbārācī = fkụlūlụ 2c), *cf.* gāyā 1c ; gụdā 1a.iii.
    B. (gwạrā̃jī) *Vd.* gwarzō.

Gwārạncē *Vb.* 3A acted *as in* Gwārancī 2 (= dabaibạyē 2c).

Gwārancī *m.* (1) Gwari language. (2) (*a*) Gwari ways. (*b*) ignorant, feckless behaviour.

gwạrạraŋ-gwạrạraŋ *m.* tinkling of large bell (*cf.* gyaraŋ).

gwararrạɓē *Vb.* 3A. (1) (overcooked meat) disintegrated. (2) became tired out (= rabkẹ).

Gwạ̃rā̃wā *Vd.* Bạgwārī.

gwạrạzzai *Vd.* gwarzō.

gwarē *m.* hitting one's head against another's.

gwargwada A. (gwạrgwādạ̃) *m.* male lizard (= gwādā).
    B. (gwargwạdā) *Vb.* 1C kept on measuring (*int. from* gwadạ̃).

gwạrgwadō *m.* (1) (*a*) what approximates to *x* yạ̃ yi gwạrgwadan dạrī there are roughly 100. (*b*) proportion, standard *x* kōwạcẹ sạna'ạ tā daŋgantạ dạ gwạrgwadaŋ hālịŋ fkasā every trade is dependent on the state of development of the country. kạrạ̃tunsạ yạ zō dǎidǎi dạ gwạrgwadaŋ wạ̃yansạ his studies should be adapted to his standard of intelligence. (2) gwạrgwadan *prep.* proportionate with *x* gwạrgwadaŋ ạbịn dạ ya īyạ̃ = gwạrgwadaŋ fkarfinsạ in keeping with his strength or abilities.

gwạrgwamī *m.* seeds of kū̃kạ (baobob) = gụntsū 1.

gwar-gwar *adv.* *x* yanạ̃ naŋ ~ he's fit and well. hatsī yanạ̃ naŋ ~ the corn's in sound state.

Gwārī (1) *m.*, *f.* (*sg.*, *pl.*). (*a*) (i) Gwari person *x* nā ga wata ~ tanạ̃ zạune I saw a Gwari woman seated (*for epithet Vd.* akurū). (ii) *cf.* jặkin 3. (*b*) *cf.* Bạgwārī. (*c*) ịnā rūwaŋ ~ dạ mijị ; bạ̃ba yā ịsa it's the stupid sort of thing one *would* expect from such a P. ! (2) *f.* (*a*) type of grass-hopper. (*b*) shunting-engine. (*c*) name for 'yar wābị (girl whose mother lost her previous infants). (3) an yi ta gwāri-gwāri it was stated bluntly. (4) gyạdar ~ *f.* = gyạdā 1b. (5) Birnịŋ ~ *Vd.* banzā. (6) (*a*) gặtariŋ ~ *m.* jack-of-all-trades. (*b*) Gūgạra gặtariŋ ~ *epithet of* dauntless P. (*Vd.* dūsạrạ̃ ; dandō̃sạ). (7) hājạr ~ woman's jịgịdā-girdle. (8) waŋkaŋ ~ *Vd.* gụrmặdē. (9) *Vd.* nāmạ 6. (10) kudịŋ ~ *m.* cowries (*cf.* farin bīyạ̃). (11) *Vd.* kundụmē 2a. (12) tukunyar Gwārī *Vd.* bạrgi-bạrgī. (13) cīwạŋ Gwārī *Vd.* dạŋgwạlōlọ.

gwạrjē *m.* (*sg.*, *pl.*). (1) (*a*) the type of bell suspended from neck of horse or donkey. (*b*) dūkạn rūwā bạ yạ̃ hanạ̃ gwạrjē amō ba envy cannot cause Fate to deviate. (2) cantankerous P. (*epithet is* ~ mại muryạ gōmạ ; kōwā ya taɓạ ka, yạ̃ ji amaŋkạ). (3) Gwạrjē *epithet of* any woman called Amịnạ̃ *q.v.*

gwarlōba̲ *Bauchi f.* yā yi ⁓ he tied his gown-sleeves behind his neck (= dā-gu̲mī 4).

gwarmai *m.* (1) yā d̶aura̲ mini̲ ⁓ = yā yi mini̲ d̶auri̲ŋ ⁓ he brought cleverly-concocted false charge against me. (2) d̶auri̲ŋ ⁓ *m.* tying twine, thread, etc., into puzzle difficult to undo.

gwarmī *Zar. m.* cudgel (= kulkī).

gwa̲rrā kola-nuts (*pl. of* gōro̲ *q.v.*).

gwa̲rtā *Vb* 1C (*with .dative*) *x* nā ⁓ masa̲ gidādancī I mocked him for his lack of *savoir-faire* (= za̲mbata̲ 1).

gwa̲rza̲ntaka̲ *f.* qualities possessed by a gwarzō.

gwarzō *m.* (*f.* gwarzūwā = gwarzwā) *pl.* gwa̲rājī = gwarzā̲yē = gwarā̲jē = *Sk.* gwa̲ra̲zzai = *Sk.* gwa̲ra̲jinni̲. (*a*) undaunted P. (*also called* jaŋ gwarzō). (*b*) don la̲ifī d̶ayā (= don la̲ifin rānā d̶ayā), bā a̲ k̶i̲ŋ ⁓ one fault shouldn't lead to dismissal. (*c*) *Vd.* d̶a̲ma̲l. (*d*) P. about 40 years old. (2) *m.* (*a*) first crop of indigo in plant's first or second season, *cf.* safe̲. (*b*) ku̲sūsu̲ŋ ⁓ *m.* second crop of indigo in plant's first season (*cf.* ku̲sūsu̲, safe̲). (3) ⁓ banzā making farm-ridges after rains, for spring-sowing (= fa̲ra̲-fara̲), *cf.* kunyā. (4) *Vd.* bī da̲ gwarzō. (5) gwarzūwā *f.* type of guinea-corn.

gwāsala̲ *Vb.* 2 = gwāsa̲lē *Vb.* 1C *Kt.* snubbed P. (= kwa̲ɓā).

gwaskā *f.* (1) sasswood (*pagans make bark into brew for ordeal by poison*). (2) ⁓ ha̲na̲ kyau *epithet of* cācā (gambling).

gwātī *m.*, *f.* (*sg.*, *pl.*) scatter-brained P.

gwatsaŋ-gwatsaŋ *adv.* in fragments.

gwātso̲ *m.* protruding one's bottom in dancing (= karya̲ gi̲ndī).

gwaura̲ *Vb.* 1A hit hard; collided with (= gabza̲ *q.v.*).

gwa̲ura̲ntaka̲ *f.* being wifeless, etc. (*cf.* gwaurō).

gwa̲urau *m.*, *f.* (*sg.*, *pl.*) (1) native doctor, witch-doctor (*Vd.* bōkā). (2) ⁓ ma̲i māga̲nī *epithet of* European doctor (likita̲) or native doctor. (3) ⁓ bōkan Tūrai *epithet of* European doctor (likita̲). (4) ⁓ ba̲ hā̲ (*a*) *m.* (*sg.*, *pl.*) European doctor. (*b*) yā ga̲mu da̲ ⁓ ba̲ hā̲ he

got syphilis (*epithet is* Gwa̲urau ba̲ hā̲, ki̲skō kā fi aiki̲m māla̲m), *cf.* māla̲mī 1*c*.iv, ha̲ 1*b*,*c*. (5) damaged kola-nuts.

gwaurā̲yē *Vd.* gwaurō.

gwa̲urīk̶i *name applied to* gwaurō (wifeless man) in songs.

gwaurō *m.* (*f.* gwaurūwā) *pl.* gwaurā̲yē = gwagwā̲rē. (*a*) (i) P. no longer married, *cf.* tu̲zūrū (*it is rude to apply this word to* P. *in his or her presence*). (ii) *epithet is* ha̲na̲ gārā ru̲ɓā. (iii) *Vd.* k̶udiga̲. (*b*) nik̶a̲, daka̲, mafarki̲ŋ ⁓ preparation of food is the bane of wifeless man. (*c*) fi̲d da̲ ⁓ tsa̲mmānī *epithet of* midnight crowing of cock (*i.e. as time too late to expect any mistress*). (*d*) fitsāri̲ŋ ⁓ *m.* boil on the knee (= k̶u̲runzūzūwa̲). (*e*) gwaura̲ŋ gidā detached compound. (*f*) Gwaura̲ŋ gīwā *epithet of any* Ga̲lādīma̲. (*g*) an yi masa̲ gwaura̲ŋ kira̲ he was loudly shouted to. (*h*) an yi masa̲ gwauram māri̲ he was slapped hard. (2) the isolated peg used by P. preparing thread for weaving (*Vd.* ma̲rī 3). (3) (*a*) largest of drums beaten simultaneously. (*b*) gwauran tuntū large tassel at top of burnous (a̲lkyabba̲). (4) gwauram mazā̲wari̲ duodenum. (5) *cf.* tāshi̲ŋ gwauran za̲ɓō; tsāmī 1*e*. (6) ⁓ da̲ yā̲yē *Vd.* shiga 1*g*.ii. (7) *Vd.* gwagwā̲rē.

gwausa̲ *Vb.* 1A hit hard; collided with (= gabza̲ *q.v.*).

gwauso̲ *m.* colliding with.

gwauta̲ *x* nā ⁓ masa̲ gā̲tarī I wounded him deeply with axe (= gabta̲ *q.v.*).

gwayyo̲ *Sk. m.* yā yi ⁓ = ⁓ nē P. or animal is full-grown.

gwaza A. (gwāzā) *f.* (*sg.*, *pl.*). (1) (*a*) (i) koko-yam (*epithet is* ta Gwamba̲ lāfīya̲r ciki̲ = ciki̲ lāfīya̲, baka̲ lāfīya̲). (ii) kō biri̲ yā saŋ gōnar gwāzā, sǎi ya̲ gēwa̲yē ta do not attack P. stronger than yourself! (iii) *Vd.* ri̲gā 1*m*. (*b*) ūwar ⁓, a̲ cī ka̲ da̲ lu̲rā *epithet of* Chief. (2) ulceration of scrotum (= a̲lbasa̲ 3 = *Sk.* zāgau). (3) *Sk.* bargain. (4) ba̲bbar ⁓ type of European cloth. (5) ba̲bbaŋ ⁓ *m.*, *f.* (*a*) prosperous but touchy P. (*b*) = 4. (6) gōra̲ ma̲i ka̲ŋ ⁓ big-knobbed stick.

B. (gwāzą) *Vb.* 1A *x* yā ⁓ masą
sạndā he thrashed him.

gwazai *used in* ɗaŋ gwazai (*f.* 'yar ⁓)
pl. 'yaŋ ⁓ officious P. (*epithet is* ɗaŋ
gwazai, lādaŋkạ wuri).

gwazạŋgwari *Sk. m.* over-eagerness.

gwāzarmạ *f.* (*pl.* gwāzạrmī = gwāzạrmü)
white grub of dung hills (= dōlẹ-
dōlẹ).

gwī *used in* tanā dạ ɗaŋ kại gwī (1) he
has a tiny head. (2) her hair's scanty
(*cf.* gwīyam).

gwī6ạ *f.* sediment, as of pot of water (*cf.*
dạlạkī 2 ; maŋ gyạɗā 3 ; dạgwadạgō).

gwī6ī *m.* (1) viscousness. (2) kōwā ya
dāmạ dạ gwī6ī, shī zại shā ạbinsạ as
you sow, so shall you reap.

Gwịde = Gwīdụ̄wā = Gwịdi = Gwịdo =
Gwīdụ *name for* short girl (= Kumbulā 2).

gwīdụ̄wā *Kt.* (1) = Gwịde. (2) *f.* big
laying-hen (= dakwalwā).

gwiggwī6ā *m., f.* viscous.

gwī-gwī = gwī.

gwịgwịyạ *Vb.* 2 ≐ gwīgwịyē *Vb.* 1C
gnawed.

gwịgwịyi gōrubạ *m.* child's game of
seizing hand of another and making
him bite his own wrist.

gwinji *m.* roaring (= gunji) *q.v.*

Gwīsạ name for short girl = Kumbulā 2
q.v.

gwīwạ *f.* (*pl.* gwīwōyī = gwīyāyū). (1)
(*a*) (i) knee. (ii) kōkwaŋ ⁓ knee-cap.
(iii) sanyiŋ ⁓ *Vd.* sanyī 4*c.* (iv)
gwīwạrsụ tā yi karfī they became
strong. (v) lạbāri mại kārạ karfiŋ
gwīwạ heartening news. (vi) kasā ạ
gwīwū *Vd.* kasā 1*j.* (*b*) yā yi sōsại
kafạ bā ⁓ it is perfectly straight. (*c*)
tanā kaŋ ⁓ she's in labour (*cf.* gụrfānạ
2). (2) (*a*) curve *x* gwīwạr hannū
elbow. yā yi ⁓ it has a bend in it. (*b*)
yā yō wạ zạncē ⁓ he introduced an
exception to what he'd said. gwīwạr
mạganạ matter introduced to form
exception to main statement. (*c*) sun
yi masạ baŋ ⁓ they threw him off the
scent (*literally or figuratively*) (= *Kt.*
walaŋkēdūwā 2). (3) dībaŋ ⁓ taking of
largest sweet-potatoes by broker as
her commission in kind. (4) gwīwạr

rạbō extra share taken by an appor-
tioner. (5) an yi wạ zānā ⁓ edging of
grass-mat is completed (*cf.* dājẹ).
(6) joining grass in lieu of string.
(7) type of darạ (draughts). (8) gwīwạr rānī (*said by women*) (*a*) fancy
you being so weak as to stumble
like this ! (*b*) thanks for your
joking obeisance ! (9) *x* rūwā yā
zō masạ iyā gwīwū the water reached
up to his knees. (10) hatsī yā kāmạ
gwīwạssạ he (P. or horse) became
strong again. (11) iyākacim mạcẹ
⁓ *Vd.* barkōnō 1*b.* (12) kạs ⁓ *Vd.*
daŋgwamī. (13) *Vd.* ạ tạgaji ⁓. (14)
ạ ⁓ yakẹ tạgumī *Vd.* tạgumī 2. (15)
karyạ ⁓ *Vd.* karyạ 8.

gwīyam smallness (= kwīyam *q.v.*).

gwīyāyū *Vd.* gwīwạ.

gyạbbā *Sk.* streams, watercourses (*pl. of*
gēbẹ).

gyạbjī *m.* the rodent gyạzbī.

gyạbtọ *Sk.* = gyautọ.

gyā6ucē *Vb.* 3A = (was) chipped.

gyā6urạ *Vb.* 3B = gyā6urē 3A is
chipped.

gyạc'ce-gyạccē" *m.* continual repairing.

gyaɗa A. (gyạɗā) *f.* (*sg., pl.*) (1) (*a*) (i)
ground-nut, monkey-nut. (ii) *for epithet*
Vd. Kwalci. (iii) *Vd.* alạndayạ ; gujīyā 5,
gēmụ 6. (*b*) gyạɗar Gwārī = gyạɗar
Tūrāwā the striped groundnut called
Bạgwārīyā (= bạbarbarẹ 3 = bạjạrī 2).
(*c*) *Vd.* maŋ ⁓. (*d*) mīyạr gyạɗā *Vd.*
sūkanā 1. (*e*) rākumiŋ gyạɗā *Vd.* rākumī
6. (*f*) *Vd.* ciŋ gạrā. (*g*) gyạɗar wuri
Vd. kạrā 2*b.*iv (2) harāwạr ⁓ haulm of
ground-nut plants. (3) type of red
bead. (4) *Kt.* anā gasạ matạ ⁓ ạ kā
she's being ill-treated (*Vd.* gasạ 1*d*).
(5) Allạ yā yi masạ gyạɗad dōgō he had
luck on luck. (6) gyạɗar awākī the
fodder weed *Crotolaria* of the various
species called *cylindrocarpa, atrorubens,
macrocalyx, maxillaris, etc.* (= gujīyā
8). (7) gyạɗar mīyạ fragrant kernels
for flavouring soup.

B. (gyaɗạ) *Vb.* 1A yā ⁓ kại he
(assenting P. or lizard) nodded.

gyādọ *m.* (*f.* gyādanyạ) *Sk.* wart-hog
(= gạdū).

gyạ'ɗu-gyạɗū" *m.* quivering.

gyafat *used in* 'yar rigā cê ~ da ita it's a tiny gown.

gyaffā margins (*pl. of* gêfê).

gyaggyaɓā *f.* = **gyaggyaɓī** *m.* trembling.

gyāgijê = **gyāzajê**.

gyal-gyal *m.* trembling.

gyambō *m.* (*pl.* gyambuna). (1) ulcer (= mīkī 1), *cf.* ribcê 2d. (2) tā zamā rǎi da rǎi, gyambam Mākurū she's inseparable from her husband. (3) fāmin ~ *Vd.* fāmi. (4) mai ~ yā ci karo *Vd.* ayyahaha. (5) ~ da lāya *Vd.* kwakwarē.

gyammā beards (*pl. of* gēmu *q.v.*).

gyamrō *Kt.* = gyaurō.

gyandai *m.* (*f.* gyandīyā) *pl.* gyandāyē *Kt.* (1) destitute P. (2) strong slave. (3) P. breaking fast instead of observing Ramadan (*cf.* karya 1d.i).

gyandamā *Sk. f.* (*pl.* gyandummā). (1) gourd water-bottle (= gōrā). (2) gyandamar yāji *Kt.* Melegueta pepper (= cittā). (3) *Vd.* fāfê 1b.

gyangyadā *Vb.* 3A nodded from drowsiness.

gyangyadī *m.* (1) nodding from drowsiness. (2) gyangyadin kunāma, kōwā ya taɓa, yā shā kāshī never be off your guard ! (3) yā ɓugê da ~ *Vd.* ɓugê 2.

gyan-gyan *Zar. m.* stroll.

gyangyarē *Vb.* 3A. (1) fell down in a faint. (2) fell dead.

gyara A. (gyārā) (1) *Vb.* 1A (*Vd.* gyārā) (*d.f. Ar.* khayyara). (*a*) repaired. (*b*) improved *x* an ~ al'amarin ƙasā tasu the administration of their country has been reformed. zā a ~ al'amuram māsu aikin Sarkī N.A. employees will now enjoy improved conditions of service. (*c*) yā ~ hancinsa he blew his nose (*cf.* gyārā 1l). (*d*) yā ~ murya he cleared his throat. (*e*) yā ~ bākinsa he spoke wheedlingly. (*f*) Allā dǎi yā ~ God preserved him from harm. (*g*) an ~ iskōkinsa he has been exorcized. (*h*) " gyarta kāyanka ! " yā zamā " sauke, mu raba ʔ" honest advice should not be resented (*Vd.* saukê 1a). (*j*) cut throat of animal in slaughtering (= yanka). (2) *m., f.* (*a*) tartar on teeth. (*b*) yā sāmi (= yā

san) haƙōrī, yā bar ~ he let it spoil. (3) *Vd.* gyārā.

B. (gyārā) *m.* (*sometimes f.*). (1) (*a*) (*secondary v.n.* of gyāra) *x* yanā gyāransa = yanā gyāra shi he's repairing it. (*b*) tsuntsū yanā gyārar fiffikê the bird is straightening its plumage. (*c*) gyāram fuska shaving the face (*cf.* aski). (*d*) gudun gyāran dagā = gudun gyāran kambū strategic retreat (*Vd.* dagā 4). (*e*) kada ka yi gyāran gidan Gahōta don't be penny-wise and pound-foolish ! (*f*) gyāran gangar Auzunāwā making matters worse. (*g*) ka yi gyāran zamā (i) sit in a more seemly way ! (ii) pull yourself together ! an yi masa gyāran zamā he's been given corrective punishment. (*h*) gyāran Samā'īlu *Sk.* ruining T. one is supposed to be repairing. (*j*) gyāram mālam crazy scholar. (*k*) gyāran lāya *Vd.* lāya 10. (*l*) gyāran hanci yā fi gyāran gōnā, kō mai gari kā kōrē ka a small loss is not so bad as a big one (*Vd.* gyāra 1c). (*m*) gyāram mīya *Vd.* wanê 2b. (*n*) gyāran gūtsū *Vd.* gūtsū 2b. (*o*) gyāram badi *Vd.* hūra 2a. (2) act of shaving or repairing *x* an yi masa ~ it's been repaired. wanzāmi yā yi mini ~ the barber shaved my face. (3) (*a*) an ga wani ~ a daftari an error has been detected in the court records. nā cī shi ~ I found him out in a mistake. (*b*) an sāmi ~ sign of punctuation (cītali) has been inserted in the writing. (4) (*a*) " makeweight " given by seller (= dadī 2), *cf.* jēfa 2b.ii, saki 2d, jēlā 2, yāfa 4, nashi 2. (*b*) gyāran ~ additional " makeweight " (4b = rakīya 2).

gyaran *m.* tinkling of small bell (*cf.* gwararan).

gyāranya *f.* the bulrush *Typha australis* (= kacala), *Vd.* bundu, gēra-gēra.

gyarcê *Vb.* 1A repaired all of, repaired completely.

gyare A. (gyārê) *Vb.* 1A = gyarcê.

B. (gyārē) *m.* (*sg., pl.*) (1) (*a*) large type of cricket (= tsanya). (*b*) yā yi mini gindin ~ (i) he informed against me. (ii) he left me in the lurch. (2) ban ~ *m.* (i) being cooked or ripe only on the outside. (ii) being only superficially healed. (iii) **mąganą tasą ɓaŋ** ~ his words are half true, half lies. (3) metal whistle. (4) pulling out 2 or 3 cassava-tubers and leaving remainder.

C. (**gyarę**) *Vb.* 3A *x* (1) **cinikī yā** ~ the transaction's repudiated. (2) *Vd.* **barąndą.**

gyąrgyąrtū *m.* = **bǫriŋ kurkunū.**

gyąrtā *Vb.* 1C. (1) = **gyārą.** (2) *Vd.* **gyąttā.**

gyartai *m.* (*sg., pl.*). (1) calabash-mender (*Vd.* **gyąttā**). (2) calabash-mending (*Vd.* **mędī**). (3) **karōfiŋ gyartai** *Vd.* **mufalląshī**).

gyāshī *Sk. m.* belching (= **gyątsā**).

gyat (1) *m.* **yā yi** ~ he relapsed into silence. (2) *adv.* **gąjērē** ~ very short. **yā są wąndō** ~ he put on very short trousers.

gyątsā *f.* (1) belching (*considered polite after guest has enjoyed your meal*). (2) **gyątsar kǫgī nę** it's been deposited on land by receded flood-tide. (3) **gyątsar ƙanshī** giving advice which cannot be followed (*x* telling penniless P. where goods are cheap). (4) **gyątsar macįji** unaccountable stench (= *Kt.* **wārī** 7).

gyātsę *Vb.* 1A. (1) cleansed dyed garment in ashes or potash. (2) (*also* **gyātsō** 1E) (*a*) belched. (*b*) vomited T. up (= **amāyad dą** 1). (*c*) recovered from a bad temper (= **gyāząjē** 3*a*).

gyąttā *Vb.* 1C. (1) = **gyārą** *q.v.* (2) **gyąttą ɓarī, magājiŋ gūgūwą** *epithet of* **gyartai** 1.

gyątumā = **gyātųm** *f.* (*pl.* **gyątųmai** = **gyątųmī**) crone (= **guzumā** 1 = **gwamā** 2 = **tasąkalą**).

gyaujī *m.* the rodent **gyązbī.**

gyąurō *m.* self-sown plants (= *Sk.* **yąbarī**), *cf.* **kųtūtų** 5*b*.

gyautǫ *m.* (1) **tā yi** ~ she wore her cloth round her armpits. (2) smooth plastering of exterior base of wall (= **wąndō** 2).

***gyąwaską** = **jąwaską.**

gyązā *Kt. f.* mane (= **gēzā** *q.v.*).

gyāząjē *Vb.* 3A. (1) recovered from illness and was as healthy as before (= **warkę** = **wartsąkē** = **murę** = **farfādō** = **mīƙę** 2*a* = **zāgę** 2*c* = **rēwąyē** 1*b*). (2)

became plumper. (3) (*a*) recovered from bad temper (= **gyātsę** 2*c*). (*b*) did not feel ashamed of a lapse any more (3 = **mārę**). (4) became " at home " in place or in topic previously strange to one.

gyązbī *m.* (*sg., pl.*) the rodent **kūsuŋ kyaurō.**

gyēgā = **gēgā.**

gyēgumą *Kt.* **ta** ~ = **gyātumā.**

H

ha A. (**hā**) (1) wait till ! (*derived from* **har**) *x* (*a*) ~ **ŋ gwadą** I'll try my luck (in gambling, etc.) ! = **tallątā** 3. (*b*) **hā ŋ ci ąbincī** wait till I've had my food ! **hā ŋ nūną mukų** let me show it you ! **hā kų cī** wait till you've eaten. (*c*) *Vd.* **har** 3*b*. (2) open your mouth wide, child !

B. (**hą**) (1) (*a*) what a fall ! (*b*) **ɓą** ~ *m.* (*sg., pl.*) expert boxer. (*c*) **gwąurau ɓą** ~ *m.* (*sg., pl.*) European doctor. (*d*) **yā gąmu dą gwąurau ɓą** ~ he got syphilis (*epithet is* **Gwąurau ɓą** ~, **ƙiskō kā fi aikįm māląm**), *cf.* **māląmī** 1*c*, **tųnjērē.** (2) *exclamation* by dice-thrower. (3) (*a*) *exclamation* by P. doing hard, manual work. (*b*) **kō dą** ~ **mazā**, ~ **mātā ną yī** however difficult, I'll manage it. (*c*) Oho ! (3) *f.* (*a*) *the letter* " h ". (*b*) ~ **ɓąbba** looped form of Arabic " h ".

haba A. (**habą**) (1) (*a*) come, come ! ; don't make such a fool of yourself ! (= **kai** 2*a* = **warą** 2), *Vd.* **nąi.** (*b*) **ąmmā habą wannąm bąi haną shi ba** nevertheless, this did not prevent him. (2) = **habā.**

B. (**habā**) (1) *now* I see what you mean ! ; *now* I see what's wrong ! ; good, all's O.K. now !

C. (**haba**) I'm sick and tired of it !

haɓą *f.* (*pl.* **haɓōɓī**). (1) chin. (2) *Vd.* compounds of **haɓar.** (3) **nā ƙētąrą** ~ I took small breakfast. (4) *Vd.* **tągumī** 2.

haɓaɓɓaka A. (**hąɓąɓɓaką**) *Vb.* 3B *int. from* **hąɓaką** *x* **wutad dą kę tsąkānimmų dą sū taną tsakīyąr hąɓąɓɓaką** bitter war is between us.

B. (hab̃ab̃b̃akā) *Vb.* 1D caused T. to keep on swelling *as in* hab̃akā.

haba-haba *f.* looking after *x* yanā̤ ~ dạ dōkị dạ kyaụ he's looking after the horse well (= d̃awainīyā 4).

hạbaịce *x* yā gayạ minị ạ ~ he told me by innuendo.

habaicī *m.* innuendo, hint (= shạ̄gub̃ē = jịrwāyē 4 = hạsạshē 1 = sāran shạnyē) *x* (1) yā yi musụ ~ wai sụ fitō ạ karạ he hinted they should come and fight. (2) yā shịga habaicī, ya cẹ̄ . . . he began to drop hints that . . . (3) maị ~ masọ fadạ nē : wandạ ya amsạ, yā fī shị maker of innuendo is bad enough, but P. replying to such a challenge is worse !

hab̃aka A. (hạb̃akạ) (rice, fire, river, etc.) expanded, swelled.

B. (hab̃ạkā) *Vb.* 1C caused to swell *as in* hab̃akạ.

hāb̃alancī *m.* the ways of autochtonous people (*Vd.* hāb̃ẹ).

hāb̃alōkī = hāb̃ẹ.

hāb̃ancī *m.* = hāb̃alancī.

hab̃ạr kadạ *f.* cap with points used to cover ears (= fạ̄tumạ).

hab̃ạr samạ *f.* (1) wealthy or influential P. (*epithet is* Hab̃ạr samạ, sǎi ạ kai mikị taụnā), *cf.* hạdīyạ 2. (2) ƙarfī gạreshị ƙamar ~ he is very strong.

hāb̃artā *Vb.* 1C = lāb̃artā.

Habashạ *f.* Abyssinia.

Habashāwā *Vd.* Bạhabashẹ.

habạ̄wā = habbạ = habạ *q.v.*

habdị *Sk. m.* ashes (= tōkā).

hāb̃ẹ *pl.* indigenous tribes (*pl. of* kādọ).

hab̃ị *m.* (1) swelling of domestic-animal's udder just prior to giving birth. (2) dạmunā tanạ̄ ~ wet season's near.

hab̃ọ *m.* (1) bleeding from the nose. (2) sāmụ ~ nẹ̄ wealth comes suddenly.

hạbrā *Vb.* 2 *Kt.* = hạrbā.

habshi *Sk.* = haushi.

Habu A. (Hạbū) *name for any man called* Ạbūbakar.

B. (hābụ) *Kabbi Hausa m.* kabạ-palm framework to keep off mosquitoes.

hāb̃ulōkī = hāb̃ẹ.

hacī *Kt. m.* corn (= hatsī *q.v.*).

had (*assimilated form of* har " till " *when followed by initial* " d " *of next word*).

had̃a A. (had̃ạ) *Vb.* 1A. (1) (*a*) joined *x* nā ~ su I joined them together. (*b*) suṇ ~ jịkī they've gathered in a party for some purpose. suṇ ~ kạ̈i they became amalgamated. ~ kạ̈i shī nẹ̄ ƙarfī unity is strength. suṇ had̃ạ ƙarfī dạ mū they joined forces with us. yā had̃ạ dạ sū he joined forces with them. suṇ ~ shāwarạ, sụ yī they've decided to do so. muṇ ~ tạfīyạ we travelled together. (*c*) kā ~ ƙwǎi dạ dūtsẹ you've yoked together the strong and the weak ! (*Vd.* dūtsẹ 1*j*). (*d*) Allạ̄ yạ ~ fuskōkimmụ may we meet soon ! (*Vd.* fuskạ 1*f*, *g*). (*e*) yā ~ wutā he piled wood on fire. (*f*) (i) yā ~ gụmī he had a hard time. (ii) *Vd.* gụmī 1*b*. (*g*) yā ~ A dạ B he brought A into touch with B (*friendly or hostile*). yā ~ mu fad̃ạ dạ sū he embroiled us with them. (*h*) yā ~ ƙib̃ạ he's grown stout. (*j*) aṇ ~ shi ạ lịkkafạnī he's been wound in shroud. (*k*) aṇ ~ ƙafạ *Vd.* bīkọ 5 ; hadị 4. (*l*) yā ~ kibīyạ (i) he mounted arrow on bow-string, to shoot (= d̃anạ = kutạ 2). (ii) he mounted arrow-head in shaft (kyaurō). (2) finished (= gamạ). (3) *Vd.* hạd̃u.

B. (hạd̃ā) *Vb.* 2 *Sk.* = hạdīyạ.

had̃ad dạ *Vb.* 4B *Kt.* = had̃ạ 1*a*. (2) *x* aṇ ~ shī cikin d̃ākị he's been taken into the house.

hạd̃add̃ē *m.* (*f.* hạd̃add̃īyā) *pl.* hạd̃add̃ū *x* bịkī ~ a thronged feast. yāƙị ~ a packed battle.

hạd̃a-had̃ā *f.* trade in ground-nuts or cotton *x* ~ tā tāshị ground-nut season has opened.

hạd̃ākā *f.* (1) T. shared in common *x* Kạ̄dūnā gạrī nẹ̄ na ~ Kaduna's a town of mixed tribes. gidā nẹ̄ na ~ several families inhabit the compound. (2) *Kt.* alien ; interloper (= shigēgẹ *q.v.*).

hạd̃alashi *Ar. m.* satin ; velvet (= mạlallạs).

hạd̃amạ *f.* greed (= zạ̄rī).

hạd̃amammē *m.* (*f.* hạd̃amammīyā) *pl.* hạd̃amammū greedy.

hạd̃amī *m.* overflowing of river *x* kōgī yā yi ~ (*cf.* cịkōwạ).

hạd̃aṇ *Zar.* if (= ịd̃aṇ *q.v.*).

hadạnī *Ar. m.* alertness.

hadaraŋ *adv.* without reason.
hadar da = hadad da.
hadarị = hadirị.
*hadạrī = hatsạrī.
*hadā'ụ = hatsā'ụ.
*hadāyā = hadayā *Ar. f.* gift.
hạdāyā *f.* satin ; velvet (= hạdalashī *q.v.*).
haddạ *f.* (1) incessant cooing. (2) memorization (*cf.* haddạcē).
hạddabạ *Vb.* 2 *Ar.* pestered ; perplexed.
hạddạbabbē *m.* (*f.* hạddạbabbīyā) *pl.* hạddạbạbbū pesterer.
haddạcē *Vb.* 1C. (1) memorized *x* (*a*) yā ∼ shi = yā ∼ shi ạ kā he memorized it. (*b*) yā haddạcẹ Ạlƙụr'ạ̣ŋ he memorized the Koran (= sạmā 1*e* = sịttīnīyạ 1*b*), *cf.* farī 2*a*.iv. (2) is (was) expert in *x* yā haddạcẹ ƙīrạ he's an expert smith (*cf.* shạitsạŋ 2).
hạddạjī *m.* T. (especially plaited wool-cord used for hạmīlạ) consisting of alternate coloured components (*cf.* kincē).
haddạsā *Vb.* 1C *x* yā haddạsạ bāsāsạ he started civil war.
haddị *Ar. m.* (1) limit *x* haddịŋ kudinsạ sulẹ gōmạ the limit of his money is ten shillings. (2) irreducible fixed sentence (as for murder) in Muslim Law. (3) yā ƙētạrẹ (= yā kētạ) ∼ he offended against law or etiquette. (4) *Vd.* bịlā.
haddị m. = dūbā 2.
hadẹ (1) *Vb.* 3A. (*a*) became angry. (*b*) became corpulent. (2) *Vb.* 1A. (*a*) = hạdīyạ. (*b*) Sarkī yā ∼ the Emir covered his face to show that the audience was at an end.
Hadẹjāwā *Vd.* Bạhadẹjẹ.
Hadẹjịyā *f.* Hadejiya.
hadị *m.* (1) wearing two gowns (especially black one and white) together (= *Sk.* gạmē 2). (2) adulteration *x* tụrạran nạŋ, an yi masạ ∼ this perfume is adulterated. (3) hadịm fadạ garēshi he's a mischief-maker. (4) the lintel-beam joining each half (ƙafạ 8*a*.ii *q.v.*) of arch (*Vd.* bīkọ 5).
hạdīdā *f.* idle gossip.
hạdīdīyạ *Vb.* 2 *int. from* hạdīyạ.
Hạdījạtụ = Hạdījạ *woman's name* (*Vd.* Dīzọ, Dịje, Bạŋgō 1, Gạdaŋgamā).

hadinī *Ar. m.* alertness.
hadirị *m.* (1) (*a*) storm (*epithet is* ∼ dāmạ kāsūwā = Dumāri, Tambạriŋ wạdā = Dụmau 2). an yi ∼ jīyạ there was a storm yesterday. (*b*) ∼ yā wātsẹ (= yā shārẹ = yā bajẹ) storm has blown away. (*c*) dọmiŋ ganiŋ ∼ bā nạ̣ yiŋ waŋkā dạ kāshī = mạyē 2*b*. (*d*) hadiriŋ ƙasā māgạnim mai kạbidọ the kirārị of Ạlīyụ, a deposed Sarkiŋ Kanọ who died at Lokoja. (*e*) ∼ bạ̣ rūwā ba nẹ̣, ạlāmạ nē counting one's chickens before they're hatched (= giriŋgidịshī). (2) (*a*) hadiriŋ kạkā dust-storm. (*b*) hōlōƙō, hadiriŋ kạkā *Vd.* hōlōƙō 2. (3) daurịŋ ∼ *m.* charm to stop rain which is hindering work. (4) yā yi minị dūbaŋ hadiriŋ kạjī he looked at me contemptuously (= dūbam mashẹ̣ƙā ayā). (5) yā yi minị ∼ he slapped my face.
hạdīsị = hạdīshị *m.* (*pl.* hạdīsai) *Ar.* (1) traditions about the Prophet Mohammed (*such as the book by* Al Bukhārī, etc.) = wạ̣ƙē. (2) mai ∼ *m.* (*pl.* mạsū ∼) beggar living by religious admonitions (*Vd.* fyādị 2, gimẹ). (3) ∼ ạ Kụlā exhortation meeting no response (Kụlā *is place-name*).
hạdīyạ (1) *Vb.* 2 (*a*) swallowed. (*b*) yā hạdīyi zāgị he " swallowed " the insult. (*c*) yā hạdīyē sụ they're no match for him. (*d*) (i) yā hạdīyi tabạryā he brought trouble on himself. (ii) kōwā ya hạdīyi tabạryā, yạ̣ kwānā tsạye evil recoils on the doer. (*e*) *Vd.* rifẹ 1*a*.iii. (2) *f.* (*a*) act of swallowing. (*b*) (i) suŋ sọ̣ ạ yi musụ taụnā, ạ yi musụ ∼ kumā they're " bone idle ". (ii) *Vd.* habạr samạ. (iii) macịjī yā yi ∼ bai hadīyē ba, am mātsẹ bạ̣kī, yā zubas (*Sk. song*) these Europeans came and put an end to oppression by the Filani rulers. (iv) hạdīyạr mạsū haŋkulạ *Vd.* tụbānī 3. (v) *Vd.* tạ̣kạ baŋgō. (3) wurị dạ ∼ *m.* (*a*) cowrie with hole into which smaller cowrie can enter. (*b*) female slave having infant when acquired. (4) bāwaŋ wurị dạ ∼ slave owning male or female slave.
hadīyē *Vb.* 1C = hạdīyạ.
Hạdīzạtụ = Hạdījạtụ.

hạɗu *Vb.* 3B (*a*) (i) is joined *x* **suŋ** ∼ they are joined together. **suŋ** ∼ **dạ shĩ** they are joined to it. (ii) **shāwarạrsụ tā hạɗu sọsǎi** they were unanimous. (*b*) **yā** ∼ he (it) is full-grown. (*c*) **yā** ∼ **cikim baƙin ciki** he's very distressed. (*d*) is connected with *x* **ạbịn dạ ya ạuku, yā hạɗu dạ fāɗụwar kạsūwā** what has happened is result of slump.

hafsạ *Eng. m.* (*pl.* **hafsōshĩ**). (1) Army officer. (2) **am bā shĩ hafsạ** he was promoted to an officer.

hafsancĩ *m.* cantering (= **rĩshĩ**).

hafshi = **haushi.**

hạgā *Vb.* 2 (1) *x* **suŋ hạgē shị wurintạ** they borrowed sum or got T. on credit from her without intention of paying (= **ƙōlị 4** = **kạurā 1***a*). (2) **A yā hạgi B** A borrowed sum or got T. on credit *as in* 1. (3) (*a*) **yā hạgi jạma'ạ** he tricked people into paying him respect due to another. (*b*) **Audụ yā hạgē nị** I mistook Audu for someone else.

hage A. (**hạgē**) *m.* acting *as in* **hạgā.**
     B. (**hage**) *Vb.* 1A = **hạgā 2.**

haggyạlạ I'll get even with you yet !

hagu *Kt.* = **hagun.**

hạgūgūwạ *f.* experiencing difficulties.

haguŋ (1) *f.* (*a*) **hannuŋ** ∼ (i) left-hand. (ii) left-hand side. (iii) **ạ haguŋ gạrēshị** on his left. (iv) **tụkar hagun** *Vd.* **tụkā 2***c*. (*b*) **hanyạr** ∼ = **hanyạ wajaŋ** ∼ the road to the left. (*c*) **ạbịn dạ dāma ta jūrẹ, hagum bạ tā jūrẹ ba** everyone's patience differs. (2) *prep.* on the left of *x* ∼ **dạ hanyạ** on the left of the road.

hạgunce *x* (1) **yā zō minị ạ** ∼ it was inconvenient to me, it was a proposal repugnant to me. (2) **sun ɗauki ạbịŋ ạ hạgunce** they misunderstood the matter.

hạguncĩ *m. x* **yā zaunạ a haguncĩna** he sat down on my left.

hạgunyạ *f.* (1) being left-handed. (2) concealing T. in left sleeve.

hạgurĩ *m.* type of epilepsy.

hai = **hai-hai** *m.* eagerness *x* **yanạ** ∼ **yạ zō** he's eager to come.

hā'ĩ *f. the letter* " h " (= **hạ 3** *q.v.*).

haibạ (*Ar.* **hāba** dreaded) *f.* being of respect-inspiring or redoubtable appearance (= **kwạrjinĩ** = **mụhibbạ 2**).

haifa A. (**haifā**) *Vb.* 2 (*progressive and v.n. use* **haifụwā**). (1) (*a*) (female) bore *x* **tā haifi Audu** she gave birth to Audu (*cf.* **haifụ 3**). **tā haifi 'yā'yā bịyar** she bore three children. **tanạ haifụwar 'yā'yā dạ yawạ** she's bearing many children. **wōkạciŋ haifụwā tasạ, Tụrāwā bạ sụ zō ba** at time of his birth the Europeans had not come (*Vd.* **haifụwā**). **tā haifi 'ya'yā dạ shĩ** she had children by him. **sạn dạ akạ haifē shị dạ watạ 5** . . . when he was 5 months old, then . . . (*b*) (*before dative*) **tā haifam masạ 'yā'yā bịyū** she bore him 2 children. **ạkwĩyạn naŋ tā haifam mini 'yā'yā bịyar** this nanny-goat has produced 5 kids for me. **yā haifā, akạ haifam masạ** he had children and the latter too bore children. (*c*) **bạ ạ haifi ūwar bạdūkụ ba** *Vd.* **bōrin tiŋkẹ.** (2) (male) procreated *x* **nā haifi 'yā'yā dạ ita** I have had children by her. (3) *cf.* **haifụ** ; **haifạ 1.**
     B. (**haifạ**) *Vb.* 1A. (1) *x* **tā** ∼ **masạ 'yā'yā bịyū** = **haifā 1***b*. (2) made pregnant *x* **nā** ∼ **ta** I had a child by her. **nā** ∼ **ta 'yā'yā bịyū** I had two children from her. (3) produced *x* **yā** ∼ **manạ sābaŋ aikị** he's given us extra work. **yā** ∼ **ƙaryā** he told lie. **gaddamạ tanā** ∼ **ƙĩyayyạ** wrangling causes bad feeling. (4) *cf.* **haifā** ; **haifụ.**

haifad dạ *Vb.* 3B = **haifa.**

haifaffē *m.* (*f.* **haifaffĩyā**) *pl.* **haifaffū.** (1) excellent (*cf.* **haifu 2**). (2) house-born (not stranger).

haife A. (**haifẹ**) *Vb.* 1A. (1) **tā** ∼ **cikintạ** she was delivered of her child. (2) produced completely (*cf.* **haifạ 3**) *x* **yā** ∼ **maganạssạ** he told the whole of his affair. (3) *Vd.* **cikị 3.**
     B. (**haifē**) *m.* (1) ∼ **gạrēshị** he's resourceful, inventive. (2) **am fitō da wani sābaŋ** ∼ a new idea or fashion's been introduced (= **salō 1**).

haifō *Vb.* 1E = **haifā.**

haifu A. (**haifụ**) *Vb.* (1) (*used without object*). (*a*) *x* **bạ tạ** ∼ **ba tụkụnā** = **bạ tạ tabạ haifụwā ba tụkụnā** she's had no children yet.   (*b*) **gīwā tā** ∼ (i) there's a sunny shower.   (ii) there's a halo round sun.   (*c*) **bāya tā** ∼ there have been later developments (*cf.* **gaba** 3*h*, 4).   (*d*) **zā ka** ∼ you'll procreate children (*cf.* **haifā** 2).   (*e*) *Vd.* **shaddā**. (2) **nā** ∼ **da** ita = **haifā** 2.   (3) **tā** ∼ **'yā'yā bīyar** she bore 5 children (= **haifā** but if *name* follows, we use **haifā** *q.v. 1st example*).

B. (**haifu**) *Vb.* 3B.   (1) **sun** ∼ they are abundant (= **bābut** *q.v.*).   **tunjērē yā** ∼ **a jikinsa** syphilis-pustules have appeared abundantly on him.   (2) **Audu yā** ∼ Audu is an excellent fellow (*cf.* **haifaffē**).

haifŭwā *f.* (1) (*a*) *Vd.* **haifā** ; **haifu**.   (*b*) **bā tā** ∼ **sai a shaddā** she's barren.   (2) (*a*) **am masa** ∼ = **an yi masa** ∼ birth's occurred in his family.   (*b*) **Allā bai bā shi** ∼ **ba** he was not lucky enough to have any children.   (3) ∼ **daya gyāran gŭtsū nē** = ∼ **daya foran gindī nē** one learns from experience.   (4) **haifŭwar gōdīyā** hanging on branch and somersaulting.   (5) **haifŭwar guzumā** making bad worse (*epithet is* **haifŭwar guzumā**, **dā kwance, ūwā kwance**).   (6) **haifŭwā māganim mutūwa** = **haifŭwā māganin takaici** the name of P. who has children lives on.   (7) **haifŭwar da da hakōrī** *Vd.* **dīyan** 2.   (8) **wābin haifŭwā** *Vd.* **wābi** 4.   (9) **bā yā haifŭwar da** *Vd.* **fushī** 1*a.*ii.   (10) **bā** ∼ **kē da wuyā ba** *Vd.* **kaurī** 2*c*.

hai-hai A. (**hai-hai**) *x* **yanā da bākī** ∼ he has huge mouth.   **kōfa tanā būde** ∼ door's wide open.

B. (**hai-hai**) = **hai** *q.v.*

haihāta = **haihāta-haihāta** *Ar.* never will it be *x* **da kai da shī** ∼ nevermore will you meet him again.

haihaya *Vb.* 1C kept on crossing over (*int. from* **haya** *q.v.*).

haika (1) *Vb.* 1A ascended incline (= **haya**).   (2) **haikāwā** Chief, be careful of the step or acclivity !

haika = **haikan** (1) exceedingly *x* **tanā sōna** ∼ she loves me very much.   (2) in large numbers.

*haikalī *Ar. m.* idolaters' temple.

haikē *Vb.* 1A (1) mounted (hill).   (2) (*with*

dative).   (*a*) **dōki yā** ∼ **wa gōdīyā** stallion " mounted " mare (*Vd.* **bāyē**).   (*b*) suddenly encountered *x* **nā** ∼ **wa macijī** I suddenly trod on or met a snake.   **jirgī yā** ∼ **wa dūtsē** boat struck reef (= **cim**).   (*c*) recoiled from *x* **nā** ∼ **wa kōgī, yā kāwō** I recoiled from the flooded river.   (*d*) **yā** ∼ **mini** he " went for " me.

haila *f.* **tanā** ∼ she's undergoing menstruation (= **wanki** 4), *cf.* **jinī** 2, **fādī** 8, **fāshi** 1*c*, **gēwaya** 4, **hūdā** 2*b*, **bī** 7*b*, **bata** 1*a*.iii, **al'āda** 2.

hā'inci *Ar. f.* (1) fraud.   (2) treachery (*cf.* **alhā'inī**).

hā'inta *Vb.* 2 *x* **yā hā'incē ni** he defrauded or was treacherous to me.

hā'intaccē *m.* (*f.* **hā'intacciyā**) *pl.* **hā'intattu.**   (1) dishonest P.   (2) treacherous P.

hairan (1) *used in* **abin da mutum ya shūka, shī zai girbā** : **in** ∼, ∼ ; in **sharran, sharran** " as you sow, so shall you reap ".   (2) *cf.* **walā hairu**.

hairāni (*Ar.* perplexed) *m.* (1) wrangling.   (2) **da wā kikē** ∼, **kika daura zarē a wuya** (*said by women*) oh, you (*one of our* " set ") have put on a necklace or forehead-band to-day !

hairu *Vd.* **walā** ∼ ; **hairan**.

haiwā *Nor. f.* the hoe **hauyā**.

hāja *f.* (*pl.* **hājōjī**) *Ar.* (1) (*a*) merchandise.   (*b*) (*often has pl. adjective*) *x* ∼ **lālātattū** damaged goods.   (2) **bakar** ∼ unsaleable goods.   (3) **hājar Gwārī** = **jigidā**.   (4) **hājar mai garī** *Vd.* **dillanci**.   (5) an **daure su da hājar Sarkim Makāfī** they're bound with ropes.

hajā-hajā abundantly *x* **abin dūnīya yā ishē shi** ∼ he's wealthy.   **sun cī** ∼ they're replete.   **sunā da kāyā** ∼ they've much property.

Hājara *Vd.* **bambarākwai**.

hajātū *m.* loud talking.

haji *Ar. m.* (1) pilgrimage to Mecca (*cf.* **alhaji, tadawwa'a**) = **salla** 2.   (2) **yā yi** ∼ (*a*) he made the pilgrimage.   (*b*) he had stroke of luck.   (3) **an yi masa** ∼ **da umrā** he's been doubly fortunate (*for details of pilgrimage and* **umrā**, *Vd.* Sale's *Koran* and Macdonald's *Muslim Theology*).

hajijīya *f.* (1) giddiness (= **jirī**).   (2) game

where children gyrate, saying ∼ ɗaᶙkạn
ni ! (= jᶙwā 2).

hajjạ *f.* = hājạ.

hajjalạ I'll get even with you yet !

hạjjạtū (*Ar.*) *m.* (= tattāshīyā) learning
to read in syllables (*i.e. the stage after*
farfarū *q.v., the latter following* babbaƙū
q.v., in baƙī B.2 3c).

hak *used in* yā yi kạmā dạ nī ∼ he's
exactly like me.

hakạ *Ar.* (1) (*a*) hakạ = ạ hakạ thus. (*b*)
gạriŋ ∼ = dǫmiŋ ∼ for this purpose,
because of this. (2) sǎi ∼ it occurred
for the following reason . . . (3) (*a*)
dạ ∼ sukạ rịnjāyē shị it was in this
way they overcame him. (*b*) *x* dạ ∼
sǎi sukạ gamạ = dạ hakạ hakạ sǎi
sukạ gamạ = dạ ∼, dạ ∼ har gā shi,
sukạ gamạ = anạ̄ nam fa ạ ∼ sǎi
sukạ gamạ = kạ̄miŋ ạ yi hakạ, sǎi
sukạ gamạ = dạ hakạ dǎi, har sukạ
gamạ then they gradually completed
it. (*c*) anạ̄ ∼ har yā ƙārẹ the upshot
was that it came to an end. (4) " dạ ∼
mukạ fārạ ", kuturū yā ga mại ƙyạsfī
learn from what has befallen *me* ! (5)
dud dạ ∼ nevertheless. (6) *Vd.* hakạ-
hakạ, hakạ naŋ.

haƙa A. (haƙạ) (1) *Vb.* 1A. (*a*) yā ∼
rāmị he dug a hole (*cf.* tōnẹ) = *Sk.*
ginā 1*a*. (*b*) (i) in zā kạ ∼ rāmiŋ
mᶙgᶙntā, hạƙā shi gạjērē, watakīlạ,
kai zā kạ fāɗạ take care you are not
hoist with your own petard ! (ii) *Vd.*
rāmị 1*d, e.* (*c*) yā ∼ daŋgā he dug holes
for fence-uprights. (*d*) (i) kanạ̄ haƙō
masạ gafīyạ, yanạ̄ haƙō makạ macịjī
he repays good with evil. (ii) dạgạ bạ̄
hạƙō ba *Vd.* tᶙnjērē 1*d.* (*e*) *Kt.* (i) yā ∼
bindigạ he cocked the trigger. (ii)
yā ∼ kibīyạ = yā ∼ bạkā he fixed
arrow to bow-string (= kutạ 2). kōwā,
bạkansạ ạ haƙe everyone is expecting
immediate outbreak of war. (iii) yā ∼
tarkō he set spring of trap. (iv) yā ∼
tsaikọ he erected roof-frame on to
house (= hau dạ 3*c*). (2) *m.* (*a*) (*secondary
v.n. of* haƙạ 1, hạƙā) *x* yanạ̄ haƙạn rāmị
= yanạ̄ haƙạ rāmị he's digging a hole.
yanạ̄ haƙạn daŋkalị = yanạ̄ hạƙar
daŋkalị he's digging up sweet potatoes.
(*b*) act of digging hole, digging up *x*

jīyạ an yi haƙạ. (*c*) yā yi haƙạn rījịyar
Garkọ, yā wucẹ rūwạŋ he " went on a
wild goose chase ". (*d*) ta kạm fārạ ∼
Vd. tsanyạ 1*c.* (*e*) wᶙyar ∼ *Vd.*
mᶙrūcī 2.

B. (hạƙā) *Vb.* 2 (1) dug up (sweet
potato, etc.). (2) yā haƙi ạbincī he
devoured the food.

haƙa-haƙạ (1) *x* nā gaŋ kạ ∼ I saw you
all of a dither (= dạmạ-dạmạ). (2)
Vd. hakạ 3*b*, jịkī 1*e*.

Hakạmā name for girl whose mother
bore only girls (*cf.* Gwạmmā).

hakạ naŋ thus (= hakạ).

hạƙannīyā = haƙannīyā *f. used in* tạ̄rī
yā tā dạ ∼ (*lit.* coughing aggravates
pleurisy) investigation of trivial crime
often shows it to be merely one facet of
larger crime.

hakanyạ *Sk. f.* = hakīyạ.

haƙạrƙarī *m.* (*pl.* haƙurƙurạ = hạƙạr-
ƙarai). (1) rib (= sarkī 4*a*). (2) cīwạŋ
∼ pneumonia. yā gạmu dạ haƙạrƙarī = yā gạmu dạ cīwạŋ haƙạrƙarī
he has pneumonia (= maɗaukī 2 =
Sarkī 4*b* = ƙwībạ-ƙwībā). (3) haƙạr-
ƙariŋ kīfī herring-bone pattern in
embroidery or tattooing.

hạƙarnīyā = hạƙannīyā.

haƙe A. (haƙẹ) (1) *Vb.* 1A. (*a*) dug up all.
(*b*) yā ∼ minị sạiwā he " has cut the
ground from under me ". (*c*) = haƙạ 1*e*.
(2) *Vb.* 3A is (was) perforated. (*b*) sat
disdainfully aloof. suŋ ∼, idạnsᶙ idạn
jam bạrōdō sǎi iccẹ they stood aloof,
glaring.

B. (hạƙē) *m.* roots of certain plants
sold as firewood.

C. (hạƙe) *x* munạ̄ kallansᶙ, munạ̄ ∼
dạ sū we're sitting disdainfully aloof
from them (*cf.* haƙẹ 2*b*), we are pretending to pay them no attention.

haki A. (hạkī) *m.* panting, gasping
(= shạsshẹ̄kā = *Kt.* hᶙkā 2).

B. (haki) *m.* (*pl.* hakūkūwạ). (1) (*a*)
(i) grass (= cịyāwạ). (ii) *Vd.* ɗanyē 2*b*.
(*b*) hakin dạ ka rēnạ, shī kạn tsōkạnē
(= tsōnẹ) makạ idọ " do not reckon
without your host ! " (= sạ̄barạ 2).
(2) (*a*) yā shā rūwā dạ ∼ (i) he was
detected in extortion. (ii) he's got
syphilis. (iii) " he bit off more than he

could chew ". (b) kōwā ya shā rūwā da ∼, im baɪ amai ba, yaɪ ƙaƙī refunding is the minimum penalty for defalcation. (c) Vd. yau 2c. (3) haƙiŋ wuya uvula (= bɛ̣̄lī). (4) (a) yā kashɛ ∼ he absconded. (b) kisaŋ ∼ m. leaving one's trail in the grass. (5) zūcīyāta tā yāyi ∼ I feel vexed. (6) māganiŋ ∼ Vd. gɪndī 10. (7) marau da ∼ Vd. marau. (8) = haƙīya. (9) wages (= hakki q.v.).

ḥaƙīƙa = ḥaƙīƙa Ar. (1) ∼ =̱ ∼ ƙam undoubtedly. (2) f. (a) true facts x (i) bisa ga ∼ adv. in actual fact, in truth. (ii) baŋ saŋ haƙīƙar magana ba I don't know the true facts of the case. bā mu da haƙīƙar lābāriŋ abiŋ da zā su yi we have no definite information as to what they will do (Vd. haƙīƙanī). (iii) haƙīƙar aiki Vd. baŋ gaskīyā. (b) (Ar. 'aqīqa) ram or goat killed at child's naming.

haƙīƙancē Vb. 1D = haƙīƙantā Vb. 1D. (1) is (was) positive about x nā ∼ zai zō I'm sure he'll come. (2) gave credence to x nā haƙīƙanta maganassa (i) I believe what he said. (ii) I have verified his words.

haƙīƙanī = haƙīƙanī (1) = haƙīƙa 2a q.v. x haƙīƙanin raŋ da zai zō, ba mu sani ba we do not know the exact date he'll come. (2) a ∼ in reality, in fact.

haƙīƙantad da Vb. 4B nā ∼ da maganassa = haƙīƙancē 2.

haƙīƙicē Vb. 3A (1) monopolized conversation. (2) determined to outdo all x yā ∼ cikin nōmā he's striving to "beat everyone hollow" at farming (1, 2 = tsagalgalē) (2 = fiffīƙē).

haƙīlō m. taking unnecessary trouble over T. : going on "wild goose chase".

hāƙimcē Vb. 3A (1) "gave oneself airs" (derived from hāƙimī) = sarauta 1h, cf. kākumē. (2) Vd. hāƙimta.

hāƙimci m. being a hāƙimī.

hāƙimī m. (pl. hāƙimai) (Ar. ruler). (1) District Head (Sk. uses ubaŋ ƙasā = ūwar ƙasā for District Head) = ƙasā 2e (cf. gundumą). (2) any of the officials Alkālī, Ma'aji, Wazīrɪ, Galādīma, Mādākī, etc. (they were originally in charge of town-wards, i.e. uŋgūwōyī). (3)

Sk. unsalaried head of town-ward (uŋgūwā). (4)ˈhāƙimā f. rich woman.

hakimta A. (hākimta) f. being a hāƙimī. B. (hākimtā) Vb. 1C appointed P. as hāƙimī. C. (hāƙimta) Vb. 3B. (1) = hāƙimcē. (2) was hāƙimī x yāyin da ya ∼ a naŋ during his tenure of office as District Head here.

haƙīya = Kt. hakinya f. leucoma, etc. (= karā 5 = cīyāwa 3).

haƙƙaƙē = hakīƙancē 1.

hakkaŋ = haƙƙaŋ = haƙƙuŋ = hakkuŋ Ar. undoubtedly.

hakki m. (pl. hakūkūwa). (1) (a) one's due x bā mai biŋ hakkim maganassa there's nobody to see he gets his due (money, etc.). abiŋ da kē cikiŋ hakkinsa what he's entitled to. mu bā shi hakkinsa we should pay him the respect due to him. (b) wages (= alhakī 4a). (c) fault x bā da hakkinsa ba through no fault of his. (2) yā dauki hakkiŋ īyāyansa he sinned against his parents (= alhakī q.v.). (3) In Muslim law, some offences (x accidental manslaughter) consist of (i) offence against Man, plus (ii) offence against God hakkiŋ Allā. If relatives pardon killer, there still remains hakkiŋ Allā.

haƙo A. (haƙo) m. (1) x suna haƙwansa they are waiting the chance to "trap" him. (ii) they are planning how to get possession of it. (2) Kt. (a) pit-trap. (b) roof-frame (= tsaiko). (3) Vd. dāwa 5. B. (haƙō) Vd. haƙa 1d.

haƙōrī m. (pl. haƙōrā). (1) (a) (i) tooth (= haurɛ 3b = gabo), cf. fīƙa, turmī 4, zaga 1. (ii) don su būda haƙōransu su dɪrƙaƙi Masar that they may assume a threatening attitude and attack Egypt in force. (iii) mai ∼ kɛ sha'awar furē, mai dāsōrī ya dūba da ido tastes differ. (iv) rubaɓɓuŋ haƙōrā sum fi bāƙī banzā half a loaf is better than no bread. (b) haƙōraŋ arō false teeth. (2) ivory (= 6a q.v.). (3) (a) an yi wa baŋgō ∼ earth was slapped on, to roughen surface of wall as base for plastering (= ƙarā-ƙarā 1). (b) ƙurjī yā yi ∼ the ulcer has begun to heal at the edge. (c) embroidered edging of garments. (4) haƙoriŋ Aręmî type of bead (cf. Aręmî). (5) haƙorim fârā (a) white turban with pink edge (= Sk. baƙā 8c). (b) herring-bone embroidery on trousers (= ƙwan fârā). (6) haƙoriŋ gîwā (a) ivory (= haurę). (b) faranti na haƙoriŋ gîwā m. European china-plate. (7) haƙoriŋ haŋƙąlî = haƙoriŋ girmā wisdom tooth (epithet is Maŋgadagullą, haƙoriŋ girmā). (8) haƙoriŋ kārūwą (a) staining only 2 upper or 2 lower incisors. (b) black grain among other light grains on maize-cob. (9) haƙorim macijî (a) type of bulrush-millet with spiked, tightly packed grains (= bąkim macijî). (b) the weed ƙaimiŋ ƙadaŋgarę. (10) (a) haƙorin zōmō m. P. of no account. (b) gîwā tą ci tsāmîyą? haƙorin zōmō yą mutu? should one suffer for the crime of another? (c) Vd. mutu 8. (11) (a) tsąkāniŋ harshę dą ~ a ƙąn sābą there's bound to be some friction between friends unless there is some " give and take ". (b) dą harshę dą ~ sunā sābąwā barē mutąnē to err is human, so one must pardon. (12) dą mun yardā, dą yąnzu inā muką ga haƙoran dąrîyą had we agreed, what a sorry position would be ours to-day! (13) sun sąmi haƙoran dąrîyā they became happy. (14) yā fitō bąƙî dą haƙōrā, ya cę ... then he said openly that ... (15) mai gidā ą ~ Vd. dąd-dawā 1b. (16) gąyyar ~ Vd. gąyyā 2. (17) Vd. gyārą 2b.

haku = hakuŋ.
hakūkūwą Vd. haki, hakki.
hakumtā Vd: hakuntā, hākimtā.
hakuŋ m. surprise x ąbiŋ ~ m. surprising T.

hakuncē Vd. hakuntą.
hakunci A. (hakunci) m. (1) authority, ruling. (2) (= mulki) sphere of authority x Baucî tanā cikiŋ hakun-cinsą Bauchi is a town under his authority. (3) (a) verdict (Vd. zartad dą, shąri'ą 4, yaŋkę). (b) yā yi miŋi ɗanyaŋ ~ he " played me a dirty trick " (= gąyyą). (c) yąu nā ga hakun-ciŋ Allą (i) fancy! (ii) bother! (4)

regulations x hakuncin ząkkā the rules governing payment of tithes. B. (hakunci) Vd. hakuntą.
hakunta A. (hakuntą) Vb. 2 (p.o. hakuncē, n.o. hakunci) = hakuntā 1. B. (hakuntā) Vb. 1C. (1) administered (place) as one's sphere of influence: possessed jurisdiction over. (2) gave verdict x (a) ąlkālî yā ~ shi the judge sentenced him. (b) aŋ ~ shi zā ą ɗaurę shi watą uku he's been sentenced to three months' imprisonment. (c) yā ~ su = yā ~ tsąkāninsu = yā ~ musu he adjudged between them (civil case). yā hakuntą mąganąr he gave judgment in that suit (cf. yaŋkę 1e.iii). (3) divided out x yā ~ maną ąlbāshî he divided out our pay amongst us.

haƙura A. (haƙurą) Vb. 3B. (1) (a) is (was) patient x haƙuri be patient! (b) (dative) haƙurar masą (i) be patient with him! (= jūrę 2). (ii) wait patiently for him! (c) zā su ~ dą zamā they will steel themselves to having to remain there (cf. 3). (d) indą mai gudu ya kai, iŋ aŋ ~, mai rarrąfē sǎi yą kai " slow but sure ". (e) iŋ aŋ haƙurą Vd. zāfî 1b.iv. (f) wandą bai haƙurą ba Vd. tągumî 3. (2) (followed by dą " with ") sǎi ką ~ dą shî be patient with him! (3) (followed by dą replacing dąga, Vd. dą 7) x nā ~ dą littāfiŋ I resigned myself to having to do without the book (cf. 1c, dąŋgana, numfāshî 2c). B. (haƙurā) Vb. 1A x haƙurā masą = haƙurą 1b.
haƙurad dą Vb. 4A enjoined patience on P. x nā haƙurshē shi.
haƙurarrē m. (f. haƙurarrîyā) pl. haƙu-rarrū patient P.; long-suffering P.; resigned P.
haƙurę = haƙurcē Vb. 3A = haƙurą 1a, b, q.v.
haƙurî m. (1) (a) patience, forbearance, resignation x ~ māganin dūnîyą patience is essential in life. (b) inā haƙurî how are you? (Vd. garî 1m). (2) ~ hatsin tukunyā nę = Kt. ~ tu-kunyar tsābą there's a limit to every-one's patience. (3) (a) Allą yą bā ką ~ God calm your anger! (b) " Allą

yą bā ką ∼ ! " bā tą cikạ jąkā fine words butter no parsnips. (c) nā bā shị ∼, ya ƙī I vainly tried to make him see reason. (4) Alą̄ bā dạ ∼ = Allą̄ yą bā ką ∼ = Alą̄ 4a sorry, I've nothing for you ! (said to beggar, i.e. ąlmājịrī). (5) ∼ shī nę niƙạ, wāƙạ tạŋkīyā cę patience conquers all (= wāƙạ 1a.ii). (6) wạndạ bại ci hạƙuriŋ wạhalạ ba, yaną̄ hạƙurin talauci̩ if a man does not work, neither shall he eat. (7) hạƙuriŋ kāyā sǎi jąkī what an energetic person ! (8) (a) damō Sarkiŋ ∼, kurụm tā gamshē kạ dạ kōwā, wạndạ ya cę kā cę̄, shī ya cę̄ what a patient person ! (b) Vd. damō 4. (9) mại ∼ shī kạn dafạ dūtsẹ har yạ shā rōmō patience wins. (10) cīwạŋ idọ sǎi ∼ Vd. cīwọ 2e. (11) mại ∼ kạ̄ shā shi̩ Vd. rūwā B.10.

hakurkura Vd. hakạrƙarī.

hakurkurad dạ int. from hakurad dạ.

hakurshē Vd. hakurad dạ.

hakụrtā Vb. 1A x nā ∼ masạ I was patient with him, I waited patiently for him. (Vd. hạƙurạ).

hal dialectal Hausa = har.

halą̄ = halāmạ 2.

halaccị m. behaving as honest P. should (Vd. halạk).

halạk (Ar. halāl) m. (1) (a) an act lawful by Muslim Code. (b) honest or respectable action. (2) ɗaŋ ∼ m. (f. 'yar ∼) pl. 'yaŋ ∼ (a) honest P., respectable P., reliable P. (b) legitimately born P. (c) (i) ɗaŋ ∼ kā ƙi ambatō ; dạ zārar aŋ ạmbạcē shi̩, sǎi ạ gan shi̩ (said by woman) talk of the devil . . . (ii) ɗaŋ ∼ iriŋ gwandạ, dạ zụŋgurạ sǎi ɗaukạ what an easy prey he is to cadgers ! (iii) ɗaŋ ∼ akę̄ zạrgī, bāwạ sǎi sandā a word to the worthy suffices, but beating must be used towards the worthless. (d) cf. hạrạm. (e) na ∼ m. (f. ta ∼) pl. na ∼ legitimate, lawful, respectable x an san sụ Sarākunạ na ∼ they are recognized as the rightful rulers.

halaka A. (halakạ) Vb. 3B Ar. perished, died.
    B. (halạkā) Vb. 1C killed, destroyed.

halakad dạ Vb. 4A x yā halakashē sụ he destroyed them (= halạkā).

halạk malạk = halạm malạk.

halạl Sk., Kt. = halạk.

halālīyạ f. = halāli̩ m. (1) T. to which one is entitled (especially religiously). (2) kōmē zā kạ nę̄mā ạ dūnīyạ, im bạ̄ halālị̆ŋkạ ba, banzā nę̄ if you seek T. to which you are not entitled, it will do you no good. (3) nī halālīyạr Audụ cę̄ I'm the lawful wife of Audu. (4) halālīyạr gundạ itạ̄caŋ gạ̄wō it's my very own. (5) cf. hạrāmīyạ.

halallī m. (1) = halālīyạ. (2) halạllĩŋ gundạ, itạ̄caŋ gạ̄wō = halālīyạ 4.

halạltā Vb. 1C = halạttā q.v.

halāmạ Ar. (1) f. (pl. halạ̄mai = halạ̄mū = halạ̄mī = halāmōmī) sign ; mark on T. ; indication x (a) an yi masạ ∼ mark's been made on it. (b) (i) dạ ∼ bā yạ̄ zūwạ it doesn't look as if he's coming. (ii) gạ̄ halāmạ bạ̄ ạbin dạ zại hanạ su it looks as if nothing can stop them. akạ ga dǎi lallē gạ̄ halāmạ bā ạ̄ cikạ gūri̩ it looked as if their desire would not be realized. gạ̄ ∼ bạ̄ ạbin dạ yakę̄ sọ sǎi yạ zō Kano it's clear that his only object is to come to Kano. gạ̄ ∼ dūnīyạ tā yi dāɗī it looks as if all is pleasant. (c) ạlāmạr ƙarfī nạ̄ gạ mại ƙībạ what a hard worker he is ! (d) jạwābị̩nsạ yā nūnạ halāmạ haƙạ his speech gives this impression. (e) ạlāmum bazarā ạ ƙōfạr ɗāki̩ akę̄ ganī coming events cast their shadows before them. (f) book-marker. (g) larger dividing-beads of rosary. (h) forehead-bumps from prayer-prostration. (2) adv. possibly.

halạm malạk = halālīyạ 1 x yā ci ạbincī ∼ he enjoyed his legitimate food. nāsạ nē̄ ∼ it's his very own.

halạmnīyā f. quick greedy eating by people.

halạmtā Vb. 1C x nā ∼ shi I marked it with a sign.

*halarā f. Friday afternoon prayers of Tijanis.

halạrtạ (Ar. hazara) (1) x yā halạrcē ni̩ he came to see me. (2) Vd. hallarạ.

halartad dạ Vb. 3A. (1) (judge, etc.) sent for P. (2) Vd. hallarā.

halạs = halạk.

halatta A. (halattạ) Vb. 3B (action) is

(was) in conformity with Muslim precept.

B. (**halattā**) *Vb.* 1C declared T. to be in conformity with Muslim precepts.

halattaccē *m.* (*f.* **halattaccīyā**) *pl.* **halattattū**. (1) T. which conforms to Muslim precept. (2) legitimately born P. (3) honest P.

halāwa *f.* type of sweet (= **alēwa** *q.v.*).

hālāyē *pl. of* **hāli** ; **halī**.

halbā *Vb.* 2 *Nor.* = **harbā**.

halbā-halbā *Kt. f.* *x* ~ **garēshi** he overcharges. **cinikin nan** ~ **nē** prices in this transaction are excessive.

halbi *Nor. m.* shooting, firing (= **harbi** *q.v.*).

hali A. (**hāli** = **hālī**) *Ar. m.* (*pl.* **hālāyē** = **hālullukā** = **hālullukai** = **hālūlūwā**). (1) state *x* **yanā nan a hālinsa yaddā na bar shi** it's in the same condition as I left it. (2) circumstances *x* (*a*) **cikin hālin haka** under these circumstances. (*b*) **săi abin da** ~ **ya yi** = **mu ga abin da** ~ **zai yi** we must await developments. (*c*) ~ **yā yi ku tafi gidā yanzu, ammā** ~ **yā yi ku zauna** you'd be justified in thinking that by past analogy it's time for you to go home now, but circumstances necessitate your staying here. (*d*) **hāli Sarkin kansa nē** circumstances alter cases. (*e*) **tambayar hāli** *Vd.* **asalā**. (*f*) *cf.* **alhāli**. (3) *Vd.* **hali**.

B. (**halī** = **hālī** = **hāli**) *Ar. m.* (*pl.* **hālāyē** = **hālullukā** = **hālullukai** = **hālūlūwā**). (1) character, temperament, disposition *x* (*a*) **kyan** ~ **garēshi** he has a good character. **yanā da mūgun** ~ he has bad character. (*b*) **halin girmā garēshi** he's liberal. (*c*) **bā shi da** ~ he has not a pleasant disposition. (*d*) **yā fāra dan hali** he's up to his tricks. (2) **da karfi nikē nēmā, kō da halin kaka** I'm seeking it with all my might. (3) ~ **wutsīyā nē** = ~ **bā kan sākē** = ~ **zānan dūtse, bā yā kankaruwā** character is inborn. (4) (*a*) **idan da** ~, **mūni kyau nē : idam bābu** ~, **kyau mūni nē** beauty is skin deep ; it's character that counts ! (*b*) **kyan hali** *Vd.* **mūni**. (5) **karfin** ~ = **jan** ~ *m.* (*a*) bracing up one's courage. (*b*)

courageousness. (6) **halin gōdīyā, halim bōrī** " there's not a pin to choose between the two persons ". (7) *Vd.* **hāli**. (8) **halin karē** *Vd.* **sani** 1*a*.viii. (9) **halin rūwā** *Vd.* **albasa** 2*a*. (10) **bā kau da halī** *Vd.* **yunwa** 1*a*. (11) *cf.* **shūka halī**.

halicce *Vd.* **halitta** 1, 2.

Hālidu *man's name.*

Halifa *Ar.* (1) *m.* (*pl.* **Halifai**) (*a*) Caliph. (*b*) successor *x* **Audu nē Sarkī zai nada halifansa** it is Audu that the Chief will designate as his successor. (2) *f.* succession. **Audu zai gāji halifa** Audu will succeed him as leader. **yā gāji halifar Alī** he succeeded Ali.

hālikī *Ar. used in* **dan** ~ *m.* (*f.* **halikā**) *pl.* **halikai** (*said by women*) person *x* **wannan dan** ~ **yanā da kyau** this is a good fellow.

Halīlu *man's name.*

halitta A. (**halitta**) *Ar.* (*derived from* **yalid** *pres. of* **walada**). (1) *Vb.* 2 created *x* (*a*) **Allā yā halicci dūnīya** God created the world. (*b*) **Sarkin da ya halicci Sarkim Musulmī shī ya halicci jābā** all God's creatures are subject to his will. (*c*) **abin da mutum zai sāmu, da wanda zai sāmē shi, tun ran halitta** Fate decrees luck both good and bad. (2) *m., f.* (*a*) P. or T. created by God *x* **dukan halittar Allā** all the creations of God. **kō karē halittar Allā nē** even a dog is one of God's creatures. **sū halicce-haliccan Allā nē** they're God's creatures. (*b*) form, shape *x* (i) **mai kyan** ~ well-formed (*Vd.* **halittu**). (ii) **babban** ~ **garēshi** = **babbar** ~ **garēshi** he has large penis.

B. (**halittā**) *Vb.* 1C = **halitta** 1.

halittu *used in* **yā** ~ he (P. or animal) is well-formed (*Vd.* **halitta** 2*b*).

hāliya *f.* = **halī**.

hallā-hallā *f.* (1) worshippers' incessant chorus of God's name in replying to " **Allā Allā** " said by prayer-leaders in Kadiriyya mosques on Thursday evening (*cf.* **wazifa** ; **bandiri** ; **māgīya**). (2) **masallācin** ~ (*said by women*) any Kadiriyya mosque. (3) *cf.* **allā-allā**.

hallaka = **halaka**.

hallakē *Vb.* 3A died.

hallara A. (hallarą) *Vb.* 3B (*Ar.* hazzara).
(1) (*a*) appeared (*x* when sent for by
judge, etc.). (*b*) maganiŋ ƙaryā ∼
presence of honest witness scotches
lies. (2) suŋ ∼ they have collected.
(3) *cf.* halartą.
   B. (hallarā) *Vb.* 1C. (1) (judge, etc.)
sent for P. (2) he collected (persons).
hālulluką *Vd.* hālī ; halī.
*halmų *Ar. m.* digestion.
halshę *Sk., Kt. m.* tongue (= harshę *q.v.*).
*halwą *Ar. f.* (1) being hermit. (2) illegal
cessation of cohabitation pending
divorce.
ham A. (hąm) *adv.* gapingly *x* yanā dą
bąkī ∼ he has huge mouth.   ƙōfą
tanā būɗe ∼ door is wide open.
   B. (hąm) *Eng. m.* motor horn.
hamą (1) *Eng. f.* hammer. (2) *Kt.*
yawning (= hammą *q.v.*).
Hamādą *Ar. f.* (1) Sahara Desert (*from
this word is derived Eng.* " harmattan "),
cf. huntūrų. . (2) gąriŋ naŋ ∼ nē that
is a huge town.
hamadą *f.* greed (= haɗamą).
hamago *m.* abundance ; hugeness.
hamąli *Ar. m.* load (= himilī *q.v.*).
hamąmą *adv.* abundantly *x* gōnā cę ∼ it's
a huge farm.
hamąmī *Ar. m.* pungent smell.
hamarjigo what a lot !
hamąs-hamąs = hamąs-hamąs *adv.* yanā
cī ∼ it (he) is wolfing up food.
hamątą *f.* (*pl.* hamątū = hamatōcī = *Kt.*
hamuttą = *Kt.* hamąttū = *Zar.*
hąmuttū) (*Ar.* ibtu). (1) (*a*) armpit. (*b*)
hamątar hannū inside bend of elbow.
(*c*) hamątar ƙafą inside bend of knee.
(*d*) hamątar sąndā fork in stick (*Vd.*
gwąfā). (2) (*a*) (i) n nā sō ką cirą (= ką
ɗagą) minį ∼ please give me loan ! (ii)
hamątāta bā ta dą kōmē sǎi wārī
sorry, I've no money to lend you !
(*b*) *Zar.* ką cirą minį ∼ kwānā bǐyu
please give me extension for paying
debt ! (*c*) *Kt.* kadą ku cirą hamątarku
" don't wash your dirty linen in
public ! "
Hamau *Vd.* fushī 4.
hamayyą *f.* (*Ar.* heat) rivalry. ∼ tā ąuku
tsąkāninsų rivalry broke out between
them (= gāsā = kąsayyą).

hambąląm *Nor.* hush-a-bye baby !
hambalātsųwā *f.* pointless talk (= sōki
burūtsū).
hambamā *f.* self-sown young corn plants.
hamɓarą *Vb.* 2. (1) kicked. (2) *Vd.*
hamɓarō ; harbā.
hamɓarad dą 4B (1) knocked over by
impact or by kick. (2) put out of
alignment *x* yā ∼ gāruŋ he built the
wall askew. (3) *x* nā ∼ Kano yąmmā
I left Kano on my left.
hamɓarā-hambarā *f.* = hambalātsųwā.
hamɓarē (1) *Vb.* 1A = hamɓarad dą 1.
(2) *Vb.* 3A is (was) out of alignment.
hamɓarō *Vb.* 1E (1) *x* yā ∼ minį pąm
bǐyar he found shortage of £5 in my
accounts. (2) *Vd.* hamɓarą.
hambątsai *adv.* in a muddle *x* dākiŋ ∼
yakē house's untidy (= bąrkątai).
hambulkį *Kt. m.* = hamburkį.
hamburiŋ hąyąm *m.* (1) useless abundance. (2) pointless talk.
hamburkį *m.* dry flour.
hamce A. (hamcę) (1) *Vb.* 3A. (*a*) ran
away. (*b*) zanąntą yā ∼ her cloth
gaped open. (2) *Vb.* 1A. (*a*) ate much
of. (*b*) yā ∼ bąkī he opened his mouth
wide. (*c*) iską yā ∼ zanąntą wind made
her cloth gape open.
   B. (hąmcē) *Vd.* hąmtā.
hamdalą *Ar. f.* (1) (*a*) saying Ąlhamdu
lįllāhį (Thank God !). (*b*) dą jiŋ wannąŋ,
muką yi ta hamdalą we rejoiced at
hearing this. (2) nā yi ∼ (*a*) I'm
replete. (*b*) I said " Thank God ".
hamfuɗą *Vb.* 2 (1) threw powdered T.
into mouth (= afą *q.v.*). (2) yā hamfuɗi
ƙasā (*a*) he bowed humbly in apology
(= hurwā). (*b*) he was knocked down, etc.
hamfuɗīɗį *m.* (1) baked millet (gērō)
flour. (2) flour of baked locust-beans
(dōrōwą) or of baked seeds of yākųwā
or ramą.
hami *adv.* (1) abundantly *x* yā kāwō
kāyā ∼ he brought huge load. (2)
what a lot !
hamila *f.* (*pl.* hamilū = hamilai = hami-
lōlī = *Sk.* hamillai). (1) sword-sling (*cf.*
gōrubai 3). (*b*) ∼ Bątambūtīyā fine
sword-sling of Timbuctoo pattern. (2)
leather-strap for carrying the prayer-
book Dąlā'ilu.

hąmīnyą *f.* = hąmayyą.

hąmirjigọ what a lot !

hąmīyyą *Ar. f.* rivalry.

hammą *f.* (1) act of yawning. (2) (*with pl.* hammōmī) gaping hole *x* dākịn nąŋ ~ gąrēshị this house is unroofed. hammąr tukunyan nąŋ tā fi ta waccąŋ this pot is broader-mouthed than that. (3) yaną hammąr bąkā he's in a tight corner.

hammadancī *m.* cantering.

hąmmāką *f.* = hąmmākị *m.* (1) large crowd. (2) abundance *x* hąmmākąr aikị large amount of work.

hammątā *Sk. f.* = hamątā.

hąmpērę *m.* fool.

hąmrā *Nor. Vb.* 2 = hąrbā.

hamsą *Ar. f.* (1) 5,000. (2) ~ wą mętaŋ 7,000 cowries, *i.e.* 2*s.* (*cf.* hąmsiŋ).

hamsakō = hansakō.

hąmsąminyą = hąmsąmīyą *Ar. f.* (1) 500. (2) 500 cowries, *i.e.* twopence and three-tenths of penny (*cf.* hąmsiŋ; hamsą).

hąmshāķị *m.* (*f.* hąmshāķịyā) huge.

hąmsiŋ *Ar. f.* (1) 50. (2) 50 cowries, *i.e.* two-tenths of penny plus 6 cowries (*cf.* hąmsąminyą ; hamsą). (3) ɗaŋ ~ *m.* (*pl.* 'yaŋ ~) man dressing like woman and speaking in falsetto voice (= ɗan tāɗą). (4) bąrkǫnaŋ hąmsiŋ *Vd.* dādī 5.

hąmtā *Vb.* 2 (*p.o.* hąmcē, *n.o.* hąmci) = hamcę 2.

hamtsą *Kt. f.* = hantsą.

hąmūķī *m.* (1) swagger. (2) vexation.

hąmus-hąmus *x* yaną cị ~ he (it) is wolfing up food.

hamutta A. (hamuttą) *Vd.* hamątā.
    B. (hamuttā) *Kt. f.* = hamątā.

hąmzā *Kt. f.* the tree ąnzā.

hamzarī *Sk., Kt. m.* excuse ; speed (= hanzarī *q.v.*).

han *Vd.* har 3*b.*

hana A. (hąną) *Vb.* 1A (*Ar.* mana'a). (1) prevented *x* yā ~ ni zūwą = yā ~ minị zūwą he prevented me coming. yā ~ ni sāmunsą he hindered me getting it. (2) forbid *x* aŋ ~ shąm bąrąsā drinking of spirits is forbidden. (3) regarded as illegal *x* shąrī'ą tā ~ iŋ aŋ gamą garkyąn dą dabbą ta gamę

the tithes law regards it as illegal if cattle of different owners are collected in the same pen. (4) refused *x* (*a*) yā ~ he refused.   yā ~ ni (= yā ~ minị) ąbincī he refused me food. nā ~ ka = nā ~ maką I refused it to you. (*b*) ~ wani, ~ kąi niggardliness recoils on the miser. (*c*) iŋ aŋ ~ mu *Vd.* bā B.1,4*b.* (5) *Vd.* hana-*compounds.* (6) muŋ ~ *Kt.* = ą bā mụ. (7) bā yą ~ ɓąrāwọ *Vd.* sakę 1*d.* (8) bā yą sąwā, bā yą hanąwā *Vd.* są F.3. (9) bā ą hana rānā *Vd.* shanyą 1*a.*ii. (10) ą ~ ka gụdụ ?   *Vd.* dǫkā 2*a.*iii. (11) sąnnū bā tą ~ zūwą slow but sure ! (12) bā yą ~ yaŋkaŋ kązā *Vd.* sąbō 3.
    B. (hąnā) *Vb.* 2 = hana 1, 2 *x* yā hąnē nị gą zūwą he prevented me coming.   aŋ hąni Mụsụlmī gą shąm bąrąsā Muslims are forbidden to drink spirits.

hąną aikị *Vd.* karan dą, mụsayyą, mąrkā.

hąną arō *epithet of* any needle (ąllūrą).

hąną barcī *Vd.* tụŋkwīyau 1*b,* ząķarnaķọ.

hąną bịkī (1) ~ maraicị = ~ sūlū *m., f.* (*sg., pl.*) uninvited guest at feast. (2) ~ maraicị, są bịkī gātā what a fussy busy-body !

hąną būrā *Vd.* tsātsą.

hąną cịn są *Vd.* gają ganī.

hąną dāfị *Vd.* dāfị 4.

hąną daką *m.* (*sg., pl.*) woman's large, metal finger-ring.

hąną gādā *used in* Aŋgọ ~ *epithet of* bridegroom (aŋgọ).

hąną gārā rụɓā *epithet of* wifeless man (gwaurō).

hąną gāyā rụɓā *m., f.* (*sg., pl.*) glutton.

hąną gōbarā *Kt. epithet of* the tree dąlī.

hąną gōrị cry (tąllą) of seller of grinding-stones (dūtsąn niķą).

hąną ķētarą *m.* type of arrow-poison.

hąną kīshīyā barcī *epithet of* any small bangle.

hąną kyau *Vd.* cācā.

hąną mąkarą *m.* (1) rattle on roof, to serve as "alarm-clock" when swayed by morning-breeze. (2) bird-scarer in date-tree.

hąną mātā *Vd.* cịnnāką 2, hąną mātā ząrē.

haŋa mātā zạrē *m.* (1) *epithet of* ɗinyā-fruit. (2) *cf.* **haŋa zạrē.**

haŋāna *Ar. f.* (1) compassion *x* **yā yi miŋi** ~ he had pity on me (= **tausạyī**). (2) *cf.* **haŋi** 2.

haŋạnī *Kt. m.* pungent smell (*Vd.* **wārī**).

haŋa nōmā *epithet of* any Muslim Chief.

haŋa rantsūwā *x* (1) **ạmmā** ~ but, to tell the truth . . . (2) ~ **sǎi jirgī gụdā kawại sukạ kai ƙasạ** the only exception to this statement is that they shot down one aeroplane.

haŋa rūwā gudụ *m. x* ~ **gạrēshị** he's a busybody.

haŋa sallạ (1) *m.* wisp of hair on forehead of Filani women (shaped like Egyptian uraeus) = **gọshī** 4. (2) *Vd.* **kwarạmī.**

haŋau *m., f. (sg., pl.)* (1) skinflint, dog-in-the-manger (= **ūwar** ~). (2) **dạ** ~ **gāra mạnnau** better a mean P. than a skinflint.

haŋa waŋkyaŋ gēfẹ *Vd.* **ƙardạjī.**

haŋa yārọ kwạrakā *m.* stormy, black night in the rains.

haŋa zạrē (1) *Sk. epithet of* **mụrɗakā.** (2) *cf.* **haŋa mātā zạrē.**

hanci A. (hancị) *m. (pl.* **hantunạ)** (*Ar.* **anfī).** (1) (*a*) nose (*cf.* **hancī, dakạn danshī**). (*b*) **yā kai hancinsạ har Kanọ** he got as far as Kano. (*bb*) **suŋ kāwō** ~ they arrived. (*c*) **ạbin dạ ya tafạ** ~ **idọ sǎi yạ yi rūwā** = **ạbin dạ ya tafạ** ~ **har idọ rūwā zại yi** what affects your family, affects yourself, the two react mutually. (*d*) ~ **bại san dāɗiŋ gishirī ba** what has it to do with you ! (*e*) **sạ** ~ *Vd.* **sạ** A.5. (*f*) **wandạ ya cịji hancịŋkạ, kai kạ cịji tsūlịyā tasạ, kadạ kạ ji ɗọyī** if anyone shows hostility to you, pay him back in his own coin ! (*g*) **sunạ cịŋ** ~ they are quarrelling, abusing one another. (*h*) **mại hancịm Bạtūrẹ** small two-holed cowrie. (*j*) **hancịŋ jirgī** prow. (*k*) ~ **bā kafā** *Vd.* **ạbụ 9.** (*l*) **yaŋạ hūrạ hancị** he is behaving conceitedly. (*m*) **ɗārī yā sakō hancị** the cold season arrived. (*n*) **tāshiŋ** ~ *m.* = **ạlfaharī.** (*o*) **yā sakō** ~ *Vd.* **sạkā** 2*a*.iii. (*p*) **gāshiŋ** ~ *Vd.* **dūkịyā.** (*q*) *Vd.* **shịgā** ~. (*r*) *Vd.* **bāƙī dạ** ~ ; **hancī 2.** (*s*) **kafar** ~ *f.* nostril. (*t*) **kyạŋ** ~ **kafā** don't

judge by appearances ! (*u*) *Vd.* **hancī.** (*v*) *Vd. compounds of* **hancịŋ** *in* **5-12** *below.* (2) (*a*) (i) loop slipped over knot of slip-knot *x* **hancịŋ tạrnaƙī** loop of hobbling-rope. (ii) **an yi wạ tụkā** ~ the matter's settled. (*b*) horse-hair loop of bird snare. (*c*) *Vd.* **mạƙōgwạrō 7.** (3) the part of sandal-strap fitting between toes. (4) short stem attaching some fruits or vegetables to main-stem (*Vd.* **kwantsạ** 2*c*). (5) **hancịŋ ạllūrạ** eye of needle (= **kafar ạllūra**). (6) **hancịŋ ɗanị** the vaulting called **ƙafạr kạzā** *q.v. under* **ƙafạ 8***b*. (7) **hancịŋ dāwạ** guinea-corn chaff (= **kōnọ**). (8) **hancịŋ gautā** a " nobody " (*epithet is* in **dạ shī mịyạ ; im bābụ shī, mịyạ**). (9) **hancịŋ kạbēwạ** *Kt.* type of incense. (10) **hancịŋ kaɗē** *Sk.* cloves (= **kạnumfạrī**). (11) **hancịŋ kạrē** perpetually moist soil (*Vd.* **malwạ**). (12) **hancịŋ wạndō** place where crutchpiece joins trouser-ankle.

   B. (**hancī**) (*the form of* **hancị** *optionally used after* **ạ**) *x* (1) **yā sọkē nị ạ hancī** = **yā sọkē nị ạ hancị** he pricked my nose. (2) **yaŋạ aiki bakạ dạ hancī** he's working might and main (*Vd.* **bāƙī dạ hancị**).

hancịŋ *Vd.* **hancị 5** *onwards.*

hancinī *m.* (1) any odour. (2) (*a*) squeamishness (= **ƙyạmā**). (*b*) restlessness. (*c*) " flogging a dead horse ".

handạƙa *Vb.* 2 = **handạƙē** *Vb.* 1C. over-ate T.

handarạ *Vb.* 2 *Zar.* = **handạƙa.**

handumạ *Vb.* 2 ate much of.

handụmau *m., f. (sg., pl.)* glutton.

handụmē *Vb.* 1C over-ate T.

handūwā *f.* (1) shoots at base of corn or pawpaw (*cf.* **'ya'yyạwā**). (2) sixth finger (= **shịdạnīyā**). (3) relations settled far off.

hanga A. (haŋgā) *Vb.* 2. (1) saw P. or T. afar off (= **tsiŋkāyạ** = *Kt.* **dạurārạ**). (2) **kadạ kōgī yạ haŋgi randā** *Vd.* **randā** 1*b*.

   B. (**haŋgạ**) *Vb.* 1A. (1) *used in* (*a*) **nā** ~ (= **nā** ~, **nā** ~), **baŋ gan shi ba** though I kept looking into the distance, I could not see him. (*b*) **mụ waiwạyā bāyạ, mụ** ~ **gạba** let us examine past and future ! (2) = **haŋgā.**

hangahǫ = haŋgahau = haŋgamō what a big opening ! ; what a huge mouth !

hạŋgarā *f.* (1) blister preceding issue of guineaworm (*cf.* kurman 2). (2) type of cantharides infesting beans and ramạ.

haŋgarmēmę = haŋgarmī *m.* (*f.* haŋgarmēmīyā = haŋgarmā) *pl.* haŋgarhạŋgạr = haŋgạrmai huge.

haŋgaurạ *Kt. m., f.* fool.

hạŋgē *m.* (1) (*secondary v.n. of* hạŋgā) *x* sunạ haŋgyansạ = sunạ haŋgassạ they're looking at him afar. (2) act of looking afar *x* (*a*) nā yi ∼ I looked into distance. (*b*) ∼ bā yạ kāwō na nēsạ kusa wishful thinking is useless. (*c*) hạŋgyan nēsạ *Vd.* burburwạ 2.

haŋgō *Vb.* 1E = hạŋgā.

haŋgū *m.* = hạŋguŋ.

haŋgūgu *m.* chips of adūwạ (desert date tree) used as soap (*Vd.* sạbulu).

hangula A. (hạŋgulạ) *Vb.* 3B blazed up *x* wutā tā ∼ fire blazed up. cīwǫ yā ∼ illness became worse. mạganạn naŋ tā ∼ this affair has assumed serious proportions (= buŋƙāsạ 1).
B. (haŋgulā) *Vb.* 1C haŋgulạ wutā to make fire blaze. haŋgulạ cīwǫ to aggravate an illness. haŋgulạ mạganạ to " make mountain out of molehill ". aŋ ∼ shi they've incited him.

hạŋguŋ *m.* mumps (*supposed cure is to shout down empty dyepit* " kē tukunyā, bi ki saŋ ∼ bạ ? kai Hạŋguŋ, bạ kạ san tukunyar bābā bạ ? ").

hạŋhai *adv.* gapingly *x* yanạ dạ bạ̄kī ∼ he has huge mouth.

hạŋhạmnīyā *f.* quick greedy eating by person.

hani *m.* prohibition (1) *x* an yi ∼ kadạ ạ yī = an yi ∼ gạ yịnsạ its doing has been forbidden. (2) haniŋ hạnānā acting " like a dog in the manger ".

hạnī'ạŋ *Ar. m.* contentment *x* Audu ∼ yakē Audu's contented.

hạnīnīyạ *f.* neighing.

hanjī *m.* (1) (*a*) (i) intestines. (ii) bāshị ∼ nē, yanạ cikiŋ kōwā debt is common to everyone. (iii) kadạ kạzā tạ yi murnạ dōmin tā ga anạ jạŋ hanjin 'yarūwā tatạ there but for the grace of God go I ! (iv) kauriŋ ∼ *Vd.* ạnnūrị 3*b*. (v) yā nadę ∼ he's miserly. (vi) sukạ jā

hanjinsạ they attacked him tooth and claw. (vii) rūwaŋ ∼ *Vd.* rūwā B8. (viii) *Vd.* ūwar ∼. (*b*) hanjiŋ agōgō works of watch. (*c*) inner tube for tyre. (2) hanjim fịtilạ lamp-wick (lạgwạnī). (3) hanjiŋ gōnā beans intersown with corn. (4) hanjiŋ hạmīlạ rags lining sword-sling. (5) hanjiŋ ƙōshīyạ bobbin-nipple. (6) hanjiŋ ƙudā (*a*) type of three-ply thread (= *Kt.* mạriŋ kūrā). (*b*) poor spinning by girl-novice. (7) hanjin rạ̄gō (*a*) type of white turban-cloth. (*b*) the twiner *Oxystelma bournouense.* (8) hanjin tạwadạ cow-tail-hairs put in ink-bottle to prevent contents spilling. (9) kālaŋ ∼ *m.* child born late in mother's life.

haŋkạɗā *Vb.* 1C. (1) lifted up edge of mat, cloth, etc. (= baŋkạɗā *q.v.*). (2) muŋ ∼ su bāya we repelled them.

haŋkạɗạbōɗō *m.* (1) being indecently dressed. (2) ∼ rufịŋ ƙōfạ dạ ɓạrāwǫ shutting door, not aware thief is indoors. (3) type of obscene dance by girls.

hạŋkākạ *m.* (*pl.* hạŋkākī). (1) (*a*) crow. (*b*) ∼ mại dạ ɗaŋ wani yạ zamā nākạ *epithet of* crow or liberal P. (*c*) kurmaŋ ∼ *Vd.* kurman 1. (*d*) ɓōyaŋ ∼ *Vd.* ɓōyō 4. (*e*) *Vd.* birgimā 4. (2) (*a*) gown with black upperpart and blue skirt. (*b*) type of cloth alternately black and white, with blue stripes. (*c*) type of black and white Nupe bead. (3) hạŋkākạ = hạŋkākạn takạ̄rạ fool. (4) hạŋkạ̄kī *pl.* alternate light and shade (*x* due to diffusion of sunlight through branches) *x* inūwạn naŋ tanạ dạ hạŋkạ̄kī (= *Kt.* tsạ̄kō 2*b*). (5) sạ̄ hạŋkạ̄kī dākǫ = hạŋkạ̄kī dākǫ the herb Polygala arenaria (*cure for syphilis, etc.*) = shạ ni kạ san nị. (6) takabar hạŋkạ̄kī *Vd.* takabạ 3.

haŋkạlā (*used in*) ạ ∼ carefully (= hạŋkạlī 3).

hạŋkạlcē *Vd.* hạŋkaltạ.

hạŋkạlgạnā *Kr. used in* yā maishē nị ∼ he took me for a fool.

hạŋkạlī *m.* (*pl.* hạŋkula = *Sk.* hạŋkullạ) (*d.f. Ar.* 'aqli). (1) intelligence *x* (*a*) bā shi dạ ∼ he has no sense. (*b*) yā yi rashịŋ ∼ he acted foolishly. (*c*) kạ yi

~ take care ! (d) haŋkąliŋką mę ya
bā ką what does your own sense incline
you to believe ? (e) haŋkąlīn darē Vd.
ßātą 1b. (2) x (a) suką kōmą cikiŋ
haŋkąlinsų so they came to their
senses. (b) haŋkąlinsą yā fịta he fainted.
(c) haŋkąlīna yā rąbu bīyū (i) I'm
distracted. (ii) my mind is on two
things at once. (d) haŋkąlinsą yā tāshị
he's worried. (e) haŋkąlinsą yā kwąntā
his mind's at rest. (f) mai dą ~ pay
attention ! (g) yā tā dą haŋkąlīna it
upset me. (h) yā ɗauki haŋkąlīna he
pestered me. (j) bą ni haŋkąliŋką pay
attention to what I say ! (k) haŋkąlinsą
dū wurim mātā yakę he thinks of
nothing but women. (l) ~ kę ganī, idọ
gųlūlai nę sometimes one's eye fails to
see through inattention. (m) hądīyąr
mąsū haŋkulą Vd. tųbānī 3. (3) ą ~ (a)
slowly, carefully. (b) gradually x
ƙarfimmų yanā daɗą rągūwā ą ~ ą ~
our strength is gradually decreasing.
(4) ~ kwąnce with an easy mind. (5)
mai ~ ɗayā m., f. one-eyed P.

haŋkaltą Vb. 2 (p.o. haŋkąlcē, n.o.
haŋkąlci) understood x nā haŋkąlci
mąganąssą = nā ~ dą mąganąssą I
understood what he said (= fąhimtą).

haŋƙarą Vb. 2 = haŋƙarē Vb. 1C
devoured greedily.

haŋƙarƙarī Kt. m. = haƙarƙarī.

haŋƙarnīyā = haƙannīyā.

haŋkątịlō Kr. m. (1) curved one-edged
sword (= bịsąlāmī q.v.). (2) one-eyed.

haŋkibịrī m. (f. haŋkibịrā) crack-brained
P. (= shāshąshā).

hankici Eng. m. handkerchief.

haŋkịɗā = haŋkąɗā.

haŋkọ Vd. kaŋkọ.

haŋƙōrō m. (1) showing fidgety impatience
x yanā ~ yą ci gąba he's eager to get on
at all costs. (2) struggling to break free.

haŋkufā f. the medicinal under-shrub
Waltheria americana.

haŋkulą pl. of haŋkąlī.

haŋƙurą Vb. 3B Sk., Kt. = haƙura.

hannanta A. (hannąntą) Vb. 1C handed x
yā ~ minị shī he handed it to me
(= tāfą 2a). yą hannantō mąką ką kāwō
let him hand it to you for me ! (cf.
daŋgwąrā 1).

B. (hąnnantą) Vb. 3B has been
handed over to.

hannāyē Vd. hannū.

hannū m. (pl. hannąyē = hannūwą) (1) (a)
(i) hand (Vd. gątarī 11). (ii) (for compounds where hannū is second word, Vd.
2: for compounds where hannun is first
word, Vd. the next entry, i.e. hannun).
(iii) Vd. 3 below for proverbs with
hannū. (iv) ąl'amąrinsų nā hannūna
I am in charge of their affairs. (v)
wadǫandą aką kāmą ą hannū ɗąrī nę
100 prisoners were taken (Vd. 1g). (vi)
bą shi dą hannū bisą kąmmų he has no
control over us. (vii) bą shi kō dą ~
cikinsą he has no share in it. bą ąbịn
dą bą su dą hannū ą cikī they have a
finger in every pie. (viii) bą mu dą
saurąŋ hannū mai ƙarfī we've no more
strength. (ix) yā shịga hannū it has
come into our possession. (x) kąfịn
dǟi ą cę maką sā'ą bīyū gąrī ya zamā
na hannū the town was captured in
less than two hours. (xi) kōmē ta daɗę,
ą hannū zā tą kwānā in the long run,
we'll be victorious. (xii) hannuŋką dą
na Audų be on your guard against
Audu ! (xiii) yā aiką da jąwābịnsą ta
hannuŋ Audų he sent his reply via
Audu. (xiv) suŋ waŋkę hannū sų yī
they're taking steps to do it (Vd.
waŋkịŋ hannū). (xv) nā bīyā ɗąrī ukų
ta 'yaŋ ~ Vd. wurị 1g, ɗąrī 3. (xvi)
hannun tękū a channel of the sea
(= wutsīyą 1g), cf. hanyą 1f.ii. (xvii)
sleeve, etc. Vd. hannun 7, 11.
(b) ~ gąrēshị (i) he's skilful. (ii)
he has many helpers, relatives.
(iii) he's liberal (cf. 4). (c) (i) yā shā
~ it's soiled ; it's passed through
many owners' hands. (ii) aŋ kashę ~
hand-marks made in building have
been obliterated. (d) tā ga hannuntą
girl began to menstruate for first time
(cf. 2b). (e) (i) hannunsą nē = hannum
bąkansą nē = kā ga iriŋ hannunsą that's
just in his line ! (Vd. hannun 1). (ii) ~
bąkā Vd. hannun 1. (f) sǟ ~ Vd.
sǟ B.1. (g) (i) yā kāmą hannuntą he
(bridegroom) consummated marriage
with virgin-wife. (ii) bą kāmą hannun
yārọ very much x anā rūwā b.k.h.y.

there's been much rain. suŋ gudu̱ b.k.h.y. everyone fled (= sun yi gǫbarar 6ērā). munā̱ aiki̱ b.k.h.y. we're working hard. (iii) suŋ kāma̱ hannun jūnā they helped each other. (iv) *Vd.* 1.*a*.v. (*j*) ri̱gā tanā̱ da̱ ∼ the gown's symmetrical. (*k*) yā shi̱ga a̱dā̱shē ∼ bīyū (uku̱) he took 2 (3) shares in the pool (*Vd.* a̱dā̱shē). (*l*) (i) ∼ da̱ ∼ *adv.* cash-down (= tsāba̱ 2*c*). (ii) ∼ da̱ ∼ ci̱nikim ma̱kāfo̱ cash is preferable to credit ; I'll not sell to you on credit ! (*cf.* hannun 5). (*m*) ∼ yā san na giji̱ he's generous but only to his family (*cf.* giginya̱ 2). (*n*) hannuŋka̱ mai̱ sandā̱ (i) blindman, go in the direction of the hand holding your staff ! suŋ gāne̱ wanna̱ŋ "hannuŋka̱ mai̱ sandā̱" da̱ ya yi musu̱ they understood what order he was giving them. (ii) be careful, here comes the very P. you are talking ill of ! (iii) yā kōma̱ hannunsa̱ mai̱ sandā̱ upstart's reverted to former status. (*o*) an yi mini̱ hannuŋka̱ mai̱ ka̱fada̱ they talked " at me ". (*p*) yā yi ∼ da̱ nī he shook hands with me. bā mā̱ yi̱ŋ ∼ da̱ shī he's too senior for us to shake hands with. (*q*) haka̱ ya zō hannunsa̱ gōma̱ (= hannunsa̱ rab-ba̱nā = hannunsa̱ wo̱fī) he came without bringing any gift (*Vd.* wo̱fī 2). (*r*) hannū duka̱ dāma *Vd.* duka̱ 7.

(2) *Compounds where* hannū *is second word.* (*a*) nā yi masa̱ ɗauri̱ŋ ∼ = nā ɗaure̱ masa̱ ∼ I applied charm to child to cure it of pilfering. (*b*) za̱raŋ ganiŋ ∼ = za̱raŋ gāniŋ ∼ *m.* cotton spun by bride for husband in early days of marriage (*cf.* 1*d*). (*c*) dabba̱r tā ka̱r6i hannunsa̱ animal thrived in his care. dabba̱r tā ƙi hannunsa̱ animal deteriorated in his care. (*d*) ka̱ŋwar ∼ ga̱rēshi̱ he's consistently lucky. (*e*) mai̱ ∼ da̱ shūnī prosperous P. (*f*) mai̱ tsawaŋ ∼ thief. (*g*) tsōfaŋ ∼ *m.*, *f.* (*pl.* tso̱fa̱ffiŋ ∼) " old hand at work " (= sa̱nē 2*b* = kā kōmō 1 = ƙūnā 2*b* = gōge̱ 2*b* = gwaŋkī 2), *cf.* dake̱ 2. (*h*) lāda̱ŋ ∼ trifle of meat given P. who holds it while being cut up for the pot. (*j*) *Vd.* ūwar hannū. (*k*) wuya̱ŋ hannun *m.* wrist. (*l*) baƙi̱ŋ hannū *Vd.* biri̱ 1*m*. (*m*) fari̱ŋ

hannū *Vd.* farī 2*d*. (*n*) kāma̱ ∼ *Vd.* 1*g above.* (*o*) mūgu̱ŋ hannū *Vd.* du̱ŋgū 1*b*. (*p*) *Vd.* waŋki̱ŋ hannū (*cf.* 1*a*.xiv *above*) ; baŋ ∼ ; tūwaŋ ∼. (*q*) gā hannūna *Vd.* mara̱bī 3. (*r*) sau da̱ hannū *Vd.* sau 1*a*.vi. (*s*) saki̱n na hannū *Vd.* saki̱ 2*f*. (*t*) shi̱ga ∼ *Vd.* 1*a*.ix. (*u*) 'yaŋ ∼ *Vd.* 1*a*.xv. (*v*) shā ∼ *Vd.* 1*c*.i. (*w*) kashe̱ ∼ *Vd.* 1*c*.ii. (*x*) sā̱ ∼ *Vd.* 1*f*.

(3) *Proverbs with* hannū. (*a*) hannū, banzā bā yā ɗauka̱ŋ wutā im bā̱ māga̱nī da̱ sha̱ri̱ftaka̱ nothing is done by a P. without reason. (*b*) hannuŋ wani bā ya̱ ɗēbar wa̱ ˙wani mīya̱ if you want a T. done, do it yourself ! (= hannun 9*b*). (*c*) hannū da̱ yawa̱ māga̱-niŋ ƙa̱za̱ntar mīya̱ many hands make light work. (*d*) hannuŋka̱ bā ya̱ ru6ēwā, ka̱ yaŋke̱, ka̱ yas one cannot but pardon the faults of one's dependents. (*e*) da̱ hannū a ka̱n saŋ girmā, a̱mmā bā̱ faɗa̱ yi̱ ka̱rē ba a good character is shown by generosity but not by quarrel-someness. (*f*) hannū bāwa̱m bā̱kī the hand carries food to the mouth. (*g*) hannū mai̱ kira̱ŋ na nēsa̱ yā fi ƙafa̱ ta̱fīya̱ fame for liberality spreads far, quickly. (*h*) iŋ hannuŋka̱ bai̱ i̱sa yā̱face̱ ba, yi kira̱ da̱ bā̱kiŋka̱ if you're not rich, practise economy ! (*j*) hannuŋka̱ shī kē jāwō maka̱ ƙa̱za̱mtā sometimes it is one of your nearest and dearest who betrays you. (*k*) hannū bā yā̱ kwancēwā *Vd.* bā̱kī 1*b*.xvi. (*l*) sa̱nda̱n da̱ kē hannuŋka̱ *Vd.* sa̱ndā 1*j*.

(4) length of a cloth *x* zana̱n na̱ŋ ∼ ga̱rēshi̱ this cloth is long. zana̱n na̱ŋ yā fi wanca̱ŋ ∼ this cloth's longer than that (*cf.* 1*b*). (5) the tree hanū. (6) the imported leaf yātsa̱ bīyar *q.v.* (7) *compounds of* hannun *Vd.* hannun *below.*

hannun (1) (*a*) hannum ba̱kansa̱ nē I'm not surprised at what you tell me of his evil ways (*cf.* hannū 1*e*). (*b*) hannum ba̱kā yā sa̱6ē shi̱ he thought himself cured, but illness has recurred to him. (*c*) *Vd.* hannū 1*e* ; ba̱kā 5. (*d*) hannū ba̱kā, hannū ƙwaryā *m.* (i) greedy eating. (ii) ceaselessly working. (2) hannum Bīnūwa̱i " posh " looking harlot (= ki̱lāki̱). (2A) hannun dāma *Vd.* dāmā 1*a*, *e*, *f*, *g*. (3) hannuŋ gāshį plaits above woman's temples (= taurā). (4) **hannuŋ gīwā** (*a*) elephant's trunk. (*b*) *Sk.* while holding load on one's own head, helping another's load up with one's free hand. (5) hannum mąkāfǫ *adv.* cash down (*cf.* hannū 1*l*). (6) **hannum marįnī** (*a*) type of bead. (*b*) type of bean. (7) **hannun rįgā** (*a*) gown-sleeve (*pl.* hannāyan rįgā). (*b*) **kąmar hannun rįgā sukę** they are exactly alike. (*c*) *Vd.* shirį 5. (*d*) *x* **dą A dą B, kąman hannun rįgā sukę** A and B are equidistant from here. (8) (*a*) hannun rūwā a pale type of kola-nut with 3–7 sections. (*b*) **yā dāmą** (= kwāβą) hannun rūwā he ate *this kind of kola* (*its epithet is* shą rąbō, na Ągwandō). (8A) hannun tękū *Vd.* hannū 1*a*.xvi. (9) hannuŋ wani (*a*) long stick with cross-bar to facilitate unrolling thatching-grass on to roof. (*b*) hannuŋ wani bā yā dēbą wą wani mīya " every one tub must stand on its own bottom " (= hannū 3*b*). (9A) mai hannun sąke *Vd.* dǫrawą 2. (10) hannun (= yātsun) 'yan Sarkī type of yākūwā (sorrel). (11) hannun zanę the end of woman's body-cloth.

hannūwą hands (*pl. of* hannū).

hanō *Sk. m.* = hanū.

hansą *f.* (*said by women*) 5,000 (= hamsą *q.v.*).

hansakō *m.* (1) yā dʼaukō ∼ he borrowed one bundle of corn in rains for two to be repaid at harvest (illegal by Muslim law) = markē 3 (*cf.* dʼaukē 2*b*, wāyę). (2) *Zar.* borrowing and repaying one bundle of corn.

hansąmīyą *f.* (*said by women*) 500 (= hąmsąmīyą *q.v.*).

hansari A. (hansąrī) *Sk. m.* immature beans or ground-nuts.
 B. (hansārī) *Sk. m.* snoring (= min-shārī).

hansiŋ *f.* (*said by women*) 50 (= hąmsiŋ *q.v.*).

hantą (1) *f.* (*pl.* hantuną). (*á*) (i) liver. (ii) wā zaį rabą ∼ dą jinį there's nothing to choose between them (*cf.* zāβē 3). (iii) **hantąr kūrā** *Vd.* malaką. (*b*) sun

jiką ∼ tasą (*Vd.* jiką 2) they treated him liberally. (*c*) one's most treasured possessions. (2) *f.* (*pl.* hantōcī). (*a*) = tąlhatąnā. (*b*) type of flint. (*c*) the antimony dąulā. (3) type of confectionery.

hantą-hantą *m.*, *f.* (*sg.*, *pl.*) P. talking through his nose.

hantą wuyą *f.* fried blood (= *Zar.* danjinī).

hantōcī *Vd.* hantą.

hantsą *f.* (1) (*a*) crutch-piece of trousers (*Vd.* gōnā 2*b*). (*b*) *Kt.* sagging of roof (= tēkį 2). (2) udder. (3) (*a*) tā yi ∼ she's full-breasted (*cf.* tāsą 2*c*). (*b*) dōkįnsą har ∼ yakę yį his horse is very podgy. (4) **hantsąr gądā** various Aroid plants. (5) **hantsąr gīwā** (*a*) the Sausage-tree (*Kigelia œlhiopica*) = rąhainā. (*b*) pineapple (= ąbąrbā). (*c*) the aloe kabąr gīwā.

hantsakī *m.* (*pl.* hantsuką). (1) pincers, tongs, forceps, tweezers, metal-snuffers (= mątsēfatą). (2) hantsakim biri device made of corn-stalk integument (tsirgāgįyā), for removing splinters (= mątsēfatąr biri). (3) hantsakiŋ karā unreliable P.

hantsę *Vb.* 3A naŋ ya kwānā har ya ∼ he slept late here (*Vd.* hantsī).

hantsī *m.* (1) (*a*) dą ∼ at the time between 8 a.m. and about 11 a.m. (*epithet is* ∼ kutųrim būshīyā), *Vd.* kutųrī 6. ∼ yā yį it's between 8 and 11 a.m. (*b*) dą kąramiŋ ∼ at between 7.30 and 8 a.m. (*c*) dą bąbbaŋ ∼ = dą ∼ ząwąl at between 10 and 11 a.m. (2) kibīyą tā yi ∼ the arrow transfixed him, it, etc. (= lękā 3). (3) Hąntsī kā lęką gidaŋ kōwā what a cadger ! (4) ∼ yā dūbi lūdąyī, bą kō fus P. is feeling mid-morning hunger. (5) *Vd.* rąbō 6*e*. (6) *Vd.* rawar gąbaŋ ∼, bą kūkaŋ hąntsī.

hantsuką pincers (*pl. of* hantsakī).

hantukųryą *f.* yā gąmu dą ∼ he has suppurating glands in the groin (*cf.* mąrūrų).

hantsųlā = wantsųlā.

hantuną *Vd.* hancį, hantą.

hanū *m.* (1) (*a*) the frankincense-trees, *Boswellia Dalzielii* and *B. odorata* (*used for compound fences, as lucky ; resin*

used medicinally and for fumigation) =
ararra6ī. (*b*) *Vd.* **tarmasīkạ.** (2) hand
(= **hannū** *q.v.*).

haŋwāwạ *Zar. f.* chameleon (= **hạwainlyā**
q.v.).

hanyạ *f.* (*pl.* **hanyōyī**) (1) (*a*) (i) road,
street, track, path (= **tafarkị** = **turbạ**).
(ii) **hanyạr lāfīyạ, bị ta dạ shękarạ** the
longest way round is the shortest way
home. (iii) **sạn dạ sukạ ga ~ tā tōshẹ,
sukạ nẹmi hanyạr lāfīyạ, kā sam bā
ta dạ nīsā** when they found the road
blocked, they took the longer, but
safer way. (iv) **mạganạr bā tạ̣ kạŋ ~**
the story is untrue. (v) **~ bā tạ̣ barịŋ
gidā** what's bred in the bone . . . (vi)
dūbạ ~ *Vd.* **dūbạ 5.** (vii) **ạlkālīŋ ~**
Vd. **ạlkālī 7.** (viii) **hanyạr ạbar bị**
Vd. **Wazīrị.** (*b*) **nā bā shị ~ I** made way
for him (*cf.* 2). **yā rōƙi azzịkī, yạ bā
shị ~ yạ wucẹ** he asked him as a
favour to allow him to pass through his
territory. (*c*) **Allạ̄ yā bā shị ~ it**
became possible to him. (*d*) **yā sạ̄
ni ạ ~** he saw me off. (*e*) **yā kāmạ ~**
he set out. **yā kāmạ hanyạr Kanọ** he
set out for Kano. **yā kāmạ hanyạr tsūfā**
he's getting old. (*f*) **hanyạr rūwā**
(i) watercourse. (ii) channel (*cf.* **hannū**
1*a.*xvi). (iii) canal. (*g*) **hanyạ = hanyạr
Makkạ** the milky way. (*h*) **~ tā dạukẹ nị**
I went astray (= **6atạ** 1*d*). (2) opportunity *x* (*a*) **yā sạ̄mi ~** he found a
means of getting his way (= **tafarkị**).
(*b*) **nā bā shị ~ I** sanctioned his doing
it ; I gave him chance to mention T.
or get profit, etc. **am bā sụ ~ sụ yi
ạbin dạ sukẹ sọ** they've been allowed to
do what they wish. **sầi mukạ ga ạbịn
bā ~** we saw it was out of the question.
nā bā shị ~ kwabọ bīyū I gave him the
chance of earning twopence. (3)
method *x* (*a*) **bā ~ ạ yī** there's no way
of doing it. **~ yạddạ zā mụ kọ̄yẹ shị**
the way in which we can learn it. (*b*)
ạkwai wata ~ har wạ yau there is also
another method. **ta wannạŋ ~** in this
way. **sun sā6ạ wạ hanyạrmụ** they have
different ways from us. **hanyạd dạ
zā sụ bi, sụ hanạ shi 6ạrnā** the way
they can prevent his depredations.
(*c*) **aŋ kashẹ wannạm mụmmūnar ~**

dạ akẹ saŋ kafạ̄wā an end has been
put to their evil policy. (*d*) **zā sụ
kōmạ kaŋ ~ gụdā dạ mū** they will be
of equal status with ourselves. (4)
tsāgẹwā ya yị ? is it (the wall) cracked ?
(*reply* n **nạ̄ tsạmmānị wurịŋ ~ nẹ** no,
I think it is an unrepairable crack due
to spirits). (5) sect (*Vd.* **Musulumcị**).
(6) beehive (= **amyạ**).

hạnzā *f.* the shrubs *Boscia angustifolia*
and *B. senegalensis* (*have edible berries ;
bark is mixed with cereals for food*).

*****hanzạizai** intestines (*pl. of* **hanjī**).

hanzarī *m.* (*Ar.* 'udhr). (1) (*a*) excuse
(= **uzụrī 1**). (*b*) **yā kāwō ~** he made
excuses. (*c*) **bā shi dạ ~** " he hasn't a
leg to stand on ". (*d*) (i) **gạjēraŋ ~ =
rạrraunaŋ ~** *q.v.* = **hanzariŋ ƙardā**
lame excuse (*epithet is* **Māyẹ, fạke dạ
agạ̄nā**). (ii) **dạ wani ~, bạ̣ gudụ ba**
naturally I don't refuse to obey, but
might I be allowed to say a word ?
(iii) **yā katsẹ minị ~ = yā yaŋkẹ
minị ~** he " snubbed me " (*Vd.* **katsẹ**).
(iv) **kạ̣ fi ganiŋ hanzarinsạ** *Vd.* **ạikā 1c.**
(2) speed *x* (*a*) **kạ kōmō dạ ~** come back
quickly ! (*b*) **hanzariŋ gidā, namijị dạ
sạyam bạrkọnam wurị** being flustered
over trifle ; useless haste. (3) health *x*
jikīna yā sạ̄mu ~ I feel better. **bạn
ji ~ ba** I feel ill !

hanzạrtā *Vb.* 3A (1) *x* **yā ~** he hastened.
(2) **yā hanzạrtạ aikị** he worked quickly.

hanzụgā *Vb.* 1C (1) incited P. (= **zugạ**).
(2) made (affair) worse.

har A. (**har**) (1) *prep.* (*a*) till *x* ~ **gọ̄be** till
to-morrow. **~ īyạ̄kar ganimmụ** as
our vision extended. (*b*) **~ yau ?** (i) that
into the bargain ! (ii) **har wạ yau kumā**
moreover. **har yau ƙumā, yā yịwu . . .**
moreover, it is possible that . . . (iii)
ạkwai wata hanyạ har wạ yau there is
also another method. (iv) *Vd.* **har ịlā
yau.** (*c*) up to *x* **dạgạ naŋ har Kanọ**
from here to Kano. **dạgạ manyā ~ yạ
zūwạ ƙanānạ** people both high and
low (*Vd.* **zūwạ**). **~ ịndạ zā ku** no
matter whither you may go. (*d*) (i)
(*with noun*) even *x* **nạ̄ bā kạ ~ wannạŋ**
I'll give you even this. **yā lạllạshẹ
tạ dạ mạganạ, har mā dạ kyạutā** he
coaxed her with words and even with

presents. (ii) **an yi masą ∼ ita** he has been played a dirty trick (= gayyą). (iii) **har dą** including x **Sarkiŋ Iŋgilą har dą Tụ̄rāwā** the King of England as well as the other Englishmen. **ganīmąr har dą jirāgē 100** the booty included 100 ships. **har dą su kōfụr, dą su samanją** both corporals and sergeant-majors. **har dą zumą** Vd. **anyą.** (e) even (with verb) x (i) **hat tā zō̧** ? what, she has come ! ∼ **yā kai gą cēwā** he went as far as to say that . . . **mun ji kụ̄wā har suŋ īyą** we've heard that they're actually able to . . . (Vd. 4). (ii) in . . . **har** x **yā ɗaukam mą kansą bąbbaŋ aikị, in dăi har yanā̧ sō̧ nē wai yą yi haką** he has taken on a big task if he aims at nothing less than doing this. **iŋ kụ̄wā mā har suŋ kai gidā** even if they reach home safely. (iii) **bąllē har** Vd. **bąllē** 1b. (f) during x ∼ **shēkarą bīyū** during two years. ∼ **kwānā ąrbạ'iŋ** for 40 days. **ąbin dą ya įsa kōyąrwā har shēkarą bīyū** what suffices for two years' teaching. (g) in spite of x ∼ **girmāna** in spite of my size. ∼ **tsūfan nąn nāką** in spite of your old age. (2) conj. (a) till (with past sense Mod. Gram. 147, a.i) x **suŋ ajịyē shi ∼ sum** (= **har suką) bukā̧cē shị** they put it away till they needed it. (b) so matters went on till . . . (147 a.i) x **har ya yi** (= **har yā yi) shēkarą bīyū yanā̧ sąrautą ; săi aką tū̧ȩ shi** things continued thus during his two years' rule, then he was deposed. **har gīwā ta zō = har gīwā tā zō** so matters remained till arrival of the elephant. (c) by the time that (past tense and sense Mod. Gram. 147 a.iii) ∼ **suŋ** (= ∼ **suką) įsa kā̧sūwā, bą sụ gam mụ ba** by the time they reached market, they'd not seen us : ∼ **hąntsī yā yī** (= ∼ **hąntsī ya yī) bąn jē ba** by about 9 a.m., I'd not arrived there. (3) conj. (a) till (subjunctive with future sense Mod. Gram. 147 a.i) x (i) **ajịyēshi ∼ ką bukā̧cēshị** put it away till you need it ! **ząn yi tą̧fīyą ∼ ŋ įsa kā̧sūwā** I'll go on till I reach the market = **kā̧min** 1c (cf.3c below). (ii) ∼ **ką kōmō =** ∼ **kā̧miŋ ką kōmō** till you return. (iii) **har ŋ kwąntā** Vd. **dāma** 1d.

(iv) **har yą mutụ** Vd. **mutụ** 1a.iv. (b) wait till x (i) ∼ **ŋ ci ąbincī = han ci ąbincī** let's wait till I've eaten my food ! ∼ **kụ cī = hā kụ cī** let's wait till you've eaten ! ∼ **ŋ nūną maką = han nūną maką** just wait till I've shown it to you ! (ii) Vd. **hā.** (c) will continue till x **im mun sakę ą nąŋ, ∼ Bątūrę yā̧ zō** (= **yą zō**) if we lounge about here, that will go on till the European comes (and then there'll be trouble). **ząn yi tą̧fīyą ∼ ŋ** (= ∼ **nā̧**) **įsa kā̧sūwā, san naŋ, ząŋ hūtą** I'll go on till I reach market, then I'll rest (cf. 3a). **ajịyē shi har kā̧** (= **har ką) bukā̧cē shị** put it away till you need it (and then you can take it out) ! (Vd. Mod. Gram. 147a.ii). (d) by the time that (future sense, Mod. Gram. 147a.iii) ∼ **kụ** (= **har kuką) įsa Kanǫ, kwā̧ sąmē shị** by the time you reach Kano you'll get it. (4) conj. (a) so much so that (past sense, Mod. Gram. 147b) x **yā girmąmā su ∼ sun** (= **har suką) ɗaukaką** he honoured them so much that they acquired high rank. ∼ **in dą darē nȩ** so that even at night they . . . **har mā sabo dą dąbārą tasą săi suką yąbē shị** so ingenious was he that they approved of him. (b) so much so that (future sense) x **bā̧ tąimakwąn dą ka yi maną ∼ dą zā mụ bā ką kyąutā** you have not helped us to such an extent that we should reward you. (c) so much so that (habitual sense, Mod. Gram. 147b N.B.) x **ya kąn sā mutụm fą̧rīyą har zại** (= **har yā̧ = har yą = har ya kąn = har yanā̧ = har yakē = yakȩ̄) rēną īyā̧yansą** it makes a person so haughty that he despises his parents. **azụrfā tanā̧ dą dāmā ∼ anā̧ likkāfą dą ita** silver is so abundant that even stirrups are made from it. **sunā̧ ta sai dą gō̧ŋąkinsụ har sunā̧ rasą wurin nōmā** they have sold their farms to such an extent that they now lack arable land. **yanā̧ dą ąmfānī har saurā kąɗaŋ yą shāfȩ wą̧halą tasą** it's so useful that its value renders negligible the trouble of acquiring it. **suŋ gąmu bisą gą hālin zamansụ ∼ ā̧ īyą cȩ musụ irị ɗayā nȩ** their standard of culture is so similar

that they might be classed together.
(d) so much so that (present sense) x
yā bā kạ mãmākį kakệ̣ (= kanậ = har
kakệ̣ = har kanậ) tâfạ hannū it surprised you into applauding. (5) conj.
even though x har yā tsūfā, ạmmā sãi
yạ fitō shạɲ iskạ even though old, he
goes (went) out walking. (6) Vd. 1e
above. (7) Vd. har ịlā yạu, yạnzu,
hā.
 B. (hạr) x sun tāshị ∼ they (crowd
or birds) got up simultaneously.
hạrā Vb. 2 (1) made for near place x
nā hạri gidạɲ Audụ I made for Audu's
compound. (2) tried to attain T. (3)
raided (Vd. harị).
hạrābạ f. (Ar. rạhaba). (1) enclosed space
round mosque. (2) site for house,
surrounded by wall. (3) gidan nạɲ
kạmaɲ ∼ nē this compound seems
ownerless.
harad dạ = haras dạ.
*harạfī m. (pl. harufạ = hạrạfai = hara-
fōfī) Ar. any letter of alphabet.
hạrāgạ f. thin, red-leather shoe-lining.
hạrāgāgạ Kt. f. uproar.
haraji A. (hạrạjị) Ar. m. (1) poll-tax
(= gandū = kasā 2d = Kt. tạusā). (2)
yanậ dạ ∼ he is rich. bậ shi dạ ∼ he
is poor.
 *B. (hārạjī) Ar. m. totting up number
of recurrences for theological statistics
x (1) Ạlkur'aɲ, an cirẹ masạ ∼ =
am fitam masạ dạ ∼ the number of
times important words recur in the
Koran has been totted up. (2) yā
saɲ ∼ he knows how many Fridays
there are since the Hijira.
hạram Ar. m. (1) (a) an act unlawful by
the Muslim Code ; disreputable or dishonest act (cf. hạlak). (b) (said in
reply) oh no !, no, not at all x shī
yanậ cẹwā " kē cẹ̄ ", ita tanậ cẹwā ∼
he was saying " it was you who did it ",
while she was replying " that is not
so ! " (= hạrāmīyạ 3a). (2) (a) yā ci ∼
he ate something religiously proscribed.
(b) (playfully said) bại sạmi ∼ ba he's
thin. (3) Vd. ịɲgarmạ. (4) gidan talakạ
hạrāmuɲ Vd. talạkạ 3. (5) cf. hạrāmīyạ.
haramạ f. (1) being on the eve of x yanậ
haramạr tạfīyạ he is preparing for a

journey. hadirị yañậ haramạr zūwạ
a storm is threatening. (2) Kt. (a) ∼
barậdệ̣ help, help, you peopłe ! (b)
∼ Manọmā attention, you farmers !
Harạmainị pl. m. Mecca and Medina.
harambē m. yā yi minị ∼ na sulẹ gụdā
he said one shilling was wrong in my
accounts (= bantẹ 2).
hạramcē Vd. hạramtạ.
haramci A. (haramcị) m. being unlawful
as in hạrạm.
 B. (hạrạmcị) Vd. hạramtạ.
*harạmī Ar. m. clothes put on by pilgrim
nearing Mecca.
hạrāmīyạ Ar. f. (1) x Kạnde ∼ tasạ cē
Kande is by consanguinity unlawful for
him as wife. (2) kai dạɲ ∼ blast you !
(= shēgẹ̣ 3a). (3) (a) hạrāmīyạta =
hạrạm definitely not ! (replying to
" did you do so ? ") (= hạrạm 1b).
(b) hạrāmīyạrkạ I refuse to give it you !
(3) cf. hạlālīyạ, hạrạm.
haramta A. (hạramtạ) Vb. 2, 3B is (was)
unlawful by Muslim Code x tā ∼
gạrēnị = tā hạramcē nị it's unlawful
for me to marry her.
 B. (harạmtā) Vb. 1C. (1) (a)
declared T. unlawful by Muslim Code.
(b) dīyaucị yā harạmtā, mụ yī shị
self-respect forbids us to do it. (2)
yā ∼ minị shī he refused it me ; didn't
give me T. to which I was by etiquette,
etc., entitled.
hạrāmuɲ Ar. m. = hạrạm.
harar▸A. (harậrā) Vb. 3A reflected about
T.
 B. (hạrārā) Vb. 2 (1) yā hạrārē nị
he glared at me (= kyậlā = zārẹ̣ 3).
(2) Vd. hạrāri. (3) hạrārạ bậ dūkạ
ba cẹ̄ = hạrārạ bậ mārị ba cẹ̄ hard
words break no bones. (4) f. (a) (i) =
hạrārā 1. (ii) = hạrārā 2 x yā wurgạ
musụ hạrārạ he glared at them.
(iii) hạrārạ garkẹ̄ Kt. m. cast in eye (=
fạrạllī). *(b) (Ar. heat) sanyinsạ ∼ nē he
likes cold weather, not hot (cf. bụrūdạ).
 C. (hạrārā) f. (1) (secondary v.n. of
hạrārạ) x yanậ ∼ tasạ = yanậ hạrārạ
tasạ he's glaring at him. (2) act of
looking angrily at x sun dakạ masạ ∼
they looked angrily at him.
harar dạ = haras dạ.

harari bungā *Kt. m.* type of facial tattooing.

harari kīshīyā *m.* dark type of imported cotton material.

hararrami *m.* uproar.

harāsā tongues (*pl. of* harshe).

haras da *Vb.* 4B vomited T. out (*Vd.* amai).

harāwa *f.* (1) fodder of stalks and leaves of beans, ground-nuts, or sweet-potato plants (*all these are saleable, but cf.* karmāmī). (2) bana nā yi harāwa *Vd.* bāra 1*d.* (3) *Vd.* damō 13. (4) *Vd.* jaŋ ∼.

harba A. (harbā) *Vb.* 2 (*Vd.* harbi). (1) (*a*) shot P. or animal. (*b*) sanyī yā harbē shi he caught a chill (*cf.* harbe 2). (*c*) infected *x* tā harbē shi da tunjērē she gave him syphilis. (*d*) aŋ harbi karē a wutsī, sǎi gidā let's be off, as our errand's done ! (*e*) yā harbi maganata he " queered my pitch " (= tsakūwa 4). (*f*) yā harbi kankī (i) he disparaged P., unaware latter was within earshot (*Vd.* kankī 2*b*). (ii) he " hustled " simpleton into buying. (*g*) yā harbē ni he embroiled me with my senior (= sārā 1*e*). (*h*) marakā tā harbē shi he has a new-born child (= rāgō 2). (2) (animal) kicked backwards (*cf.* shūrā, maŋgara). (3) (scorpion) stung (*cf.* sārā 1*c*, cīzā).

B. (harba) (1) *Vb.* 1A. (*a*) fired *x* yā ∼ bindiga he fired the gun. nā ∼ masa kibīya I fired arrow at him. yā ∼ harsāshi he fired a cartridge. (*b*) kǎina yanā harbāwā my head's throbbing. (*c*) yā ∼ mini shī he overcharged me for it. (*d*) *x* n na sō m bā shi ; gā shi yā ∼ I was about to give him it, but he spoiled his chances. (*e*) kyaŋ ganī garēta, ammā tā ∼ she's goodlooking, but is spoiled by lack of hair, defect of character, etc. yanā da kyau ammā yā ∼ he's good in the main, but is spoiled by a blemish (= harbar da 4). (2) *Vb.* 3A. (*a*) gwanda tā sōma harbāwā paw-paws have begun to ripen now (= bira *q.v.*). (*b*) hatsī yā sōma harbāwā corn's begun to ripen (= haska). (*c*) jikinta yā ∼ she's leprous.

harbar da *Vd.* 4B (1) kicked off *x* (*a*) sā yā ∼ igīya bull kicked off tie-rope. (*b*)

yā ∼ maganata after agreeing, he then rejected my proposal. (2) tā ∼ kibanta she's old. (3) turned diagonally *x* garin naŋ yā harbar yammā that town is further west than the other. wata yā harbar kudu horns of crescent moon point south (= bākatar). (4) kyaŋ ganī garēta, ammā tā harbar = harba 1*e*.

harbatsā *f.* (1) being crack-brained *x* Audu ∼ garēshi. (2) T. fecklessly done *x* zancan naŋ ∼ nē this talk makes no sense. aikinsa ∼ nē his work's done " all anyhow ".

harbatsai *adv.* fecklessly *x* zancan naŋ ∼ yakē = harbatsā.

harbau *m.* blackquarter (cattle-disease) = dāji 3.

harbe *Vb.* 1A (1) shot over *x* yā ∼ Audu he shot Audu down ; shot him dead. (2) sanyī yā ∼ shi he's got serious chill which has laid him low (*cf.* harbā 1*b*). (3) yā ∼ maganata = harbā 1*e*. (4) infected (= harbā 1*c*). (5) (animal) kicked him (it) over (*cf.* harbā 2).

harbi *m.* (1) (*secondary v.n. of* harbā) *x* yanā harbiŋ barēwā = yanā harbar barēwā he's shooting the gazelle. (2) (*a*) act of shooting or kicking *x* yā yi masa ∼ mai zāfī it gave him a severe kick. kunāma, zāfiŋ ∼ garēta a scorpion has a painful sting. (*b*) ∼ a wutsī yā fi kuskure " half a loaf's better than no bread ". (*c*) harbi ga dan jākī gādo nē what's bred in bone . . . (*d*) sǎi an shā harbi *Vd.* zuma 1*c.i.*

harbiŋ allūra *m.* magically shooting invisible enemy by means of needle in horn.

harbiŋ dāji = harbiŋ dawa.

harbiŋ dawa *m.* (1) disease of unknown origin attributed to the spirit Gajērē mai bakā (*cf.* dawa 5). (2) *Vd.* dāji 3.

harbiŋ iska *used in* dōki yanā harbiŋ iska horse is in fine fettle.

harbiŋ kankī *Vd.* harbā 1*f.*

harbiŋ kaskō *m.* magically shooting soul of enemy in pot of water.

harda = hadda 2.

harda *Vb.* 1A (1) interlocked *x* yā ∼ dawākiŋ jiŋkā he interlocked main roof-rafters (*Vd.* dawākī 2*a*). (2) crossed T. over *x* yā ∼ hamīla he crossed sword-sling over each shoulder. **yā ~ ƙafą** he sat cross-legged. (3) (*a*) **yā ~ mąganą** he complicated the matter. (*b*) **suŋ ~ masą mąganą = aŋ hardō shį** they intrigued against him, they threw suspicion on him (**= ząrgā** 2). (4) **aŋ ~ dabbą** the animals have been tethered head to tail (**= gįcįye** 2).

hardącē *Vb.* 1C memorized, *etc.* (**= haddącē** *q.v.*).

hardąjī = haddąjī.

harɗe A. (**harɗę** (1) *Vb.* 1A is (was) tangled, entangled. (2) *Vb.* 1A. (*a*) **yā ~ = yā ~ ƙafą** he sat cross-legged. (*b*) **yā ~ ƙōfą** he barred the door.
B. (**harɗē**) *m.* (1) type of **hąmīlą** (sword-sling). (2) over-crossing method of tying turban. (3) **an yi wą dabbą ~** the animals are tethered head to tail (**= gįcįyē** 2). (4) **yaną ~ = yaną zamaŋ harɗē** he's sitting cross-legged (**= zamam fāɗī = zaman 'yan Sarkī = zamaŋ kuntukurū**). (5) *Kt.* goat-house of interlaced sticks.

harɗį *m.* **an yi masą ~** he's been embroiled with his seniors.

harĕ *m. x* **yā yi minį ~ na sulę gųdā** he said 1*s.* was wrong in my accounts.

hąrgā *Vb.* 2 devoured much of T.

hąrgągī *m.* uproar; angry speech (**= kwąŋkwąmī = tarwātū = Kt. kūwą** 1*d*).

hargę *Vb.* 1A devoured all the large amount available.

hargį *m.* (*pl.* **haruggą**). (1) the fastening securing sword in sheath. (2) small harpoon.

hargitsa A. (**hąrgitsą**) *Vb.* 3B is (was) in muddle.
B. (**hargitsā**) (1) *Vb.* 1C muddled up. (2) *Vb.* 3A **suŋ ~** they've quarrelled.

hargitsai *adv. x* **tąkąrdū suną ~** papers are in muddle (**= bąrkątai**).

hargitsē *Vb.* 3A is (was) in muddle.

hargitsi A. (**hąrgitsī**) *m.* dissension.
B. (**hargitsi**) what confusion!

hąrgōtai *Sk. m.* uproar; angry speech.

hąrgōwą *f.* (1) uproar; angry speech. (2) *cf.* **Shā̧ ~** .

har-hąr *x* **nā gaŋ ką ~** I saw you all of a dither.

hari *m.* (*Ar.* **ghāra**). (1) raiding *x* (*a*) **sun tąfi ~** they've gone raiding. (*b*) **aŋ kai musų ~** they've been raided. **ą ƙauyuką yakę kāwō ~** it's the *villages* he is raiding. (*c*) **sun zubą wą Kanǫ ~** they raided Kano (*cf.* **sąmąmē**). (2) **dōkiŋ ~, ą gujē shį tun dągą shąmakį = dōkiŋ hari tun yaną turkę a ƙaŋ guję masą** don't leave things too late! (3) **sun yi īhu** (**= sun yi kūwą**) **bāyaŋ hari** " they locked the stable after the horse had gone." (4) **ɗaŋ hari** *m.* (*pl.* **'yaŋ ~**) raider. (5) (*secondary v.n. of* **hąrā**) *x* **suŋ yi hariŋ Kanǫ = suŋ hari Kanǫ** they raided Kano.

hąrigidǫ (1) *m.* (*a*) uproar; angry speech. (*b*) being feckless. (2) *m., f.* (*sg., pl.*) feckless P.

****hārijā** *f.* (*Ar.* goer-out) nymphomaniac (*cf.* **dāhįlā** ; **kakērę**).

har įlā yąu (*Ar.* up till today; *cf.* **har yąnzu** *under* **yąnzu**) in addition **~ dą wani ąbu** there's still something else (*Vd.* **har**).

****harīrī** *Ar. m.* " sly customer " (*derived from* **Al Harīrī** author of adventures of **Abū Zaidi** in his **Mąqāmāt**).

harką *f.* (*pl.* **harkōkī**) (1) *Ar.* (*a*) movement *x* **bā yą̧ ~ dą hannunsą** he has lost power of movement in hand. (*b*) affair *x* (i) **n nā̧ dą wata ~ cikiŋ gidā** I've a job to do at home. (ii) **yā kāmą ~ tasą** he is busy on his affairs. (iii) **sǎi harkąr gąbansų sukę yī** they are going about their affairs. **sų yi ta harkąr gąbansų** let them proceed as before! (*c*) business *x* **Baucī bābu ~ cikintą** there's no business going on in Bauchi. (*d*) **yaną̧ dą ~** he is rich. (2) (*a*) interior-ridge of cowrie. (*b*) tiny amount *x* **kō ~ bą̧ ni dą shī** I've none at all (2 = **ƙarfamfąnā**).

harƙīyā *f.* the fodder-grass *Digitaria debilis.*

harƙumā *Vb.* 3A **suŋ ~** they (wrestlers) clinched. **dūnīyą̧ tā ~ dą yāƙi** the world is enveloped in war.

harƙumē *Vb.* 1C **= harƙumā.**

harƙyallą *f.* slight extra adornment of the person.

har lau = har įlā yąu.

harmạ *Zar.* *f.* being on eve of, *etc.* (= **haramạ** *q.v.*).

harmē *m.* = **harē**.

harmutsa = **hargitsa**.

harmutsī *m.* dense crowd ; being flummoxed (= **firmitsī** *q.v.*).

harmụtsē = **hargịtsē**.

harsa A. (**harsạ**) *f.* white muslin fabric used for turbaning.
    B. (**harsā**) *Sk.* *f.* = **harzā 1**.

harsāshi = *Kt.* **harsāshẹ** *m.* (*sg.*, *pl.*) (*Ar.* **ar rasāsu** " lead "). (1) (*a*) bullet. (*b*) cartridge (*epithet is* ~ **māgạnim mai kwantō**). (*c*) shell (for gun). (2) (*a*) foundations of a building (= **ussị**). (*b*) **am fid dạ harsāshịnsạ** its foundations have been laid.

harshẹ *m.* (*pl.* **harsunạ** = **harạsā**) (*Ar.* **al lisāni** *from which also comes the word* **Hausā**). (1) (*a*) the tongue. (*b*) (i) **tsạkāniŋ** ~ **dạ haɓōrī a kạn sāɓạ** there's bound to be friction among friends, but there must be " give and take ". (ii) **dạ harshẹ dạ haɓōrī sunạ sāɓạwā, bạrē mutạnē** to err is human so one must pardon. (*c*) **harshẹ zāki nē ạ ɗaure** check your tongue ! (*d*) **kaifiŋ** ~ **gạrēshi** he's fluent, voluble, glib, pronounces clearly. (*e*) **harshạŋ wutā** flame. (*f*) (i) **harshạm būlālạ** tip of whip. (ii) **harshạn takōbī** sword-tip. (iii) **harshạŋ wuɓā** knife-tip. (iv) **harshạm bạntē** tip of loincloth. (2) (*a*) language. (*b*) pronunciation *x* **harshạnsạ bā yạ fịtā sōsǎi** he doesn't enunciate clearly. (*c*) **yā ɗaukạ** ~ he spoke loudly. (*d*) **dạ** ~ **yakẹ** he's verbose. (*e*) **baɓiŋ** ~ **gạrēshi** he casts the evil-eye = **yanạ dạ baɓiŋ** ~ **kạmar na tuŋkịyā**. (3) (*a*) **dạmunā tā yi** ~ wet-season's protracted. (*b*) **gāshịntạ yanạ dạ** ~ she has long hair. (4) **harshạn damō gạrēshi** (*a*) it's forked (whip ; double-headed bulrushmillet, etc.). (*b*) he's two-faced. (**5**) **harshạn tuŋkịyā** the twiner *Oxystelma bornouense*.

harsunạ tongues (*pl. of* **harshẹ**).

hartạtandẹ *Kt.* *m.* stomatitis of tongue (= ***ạbạtā**).

***harufạ** letters of the alphabet (*pl. of* **harạfī**).

haruggạ harpoons, etc. (*pl. of* **hargi** *q.v.*).

Hārūnạ man's name (*epithet is* **Gịnsau**).

harwatsa = **hargitsa**.

harwạtsại *adv.* in a muddle (= **hargịtsại** *q.v.*).

harwatsī the weed **gōgạ māsū**.

haryā *f.* type of small fish.

har yau = **har ịlā yau**.

harzā *f.* (1) pulp of **kạbēwạ** (= **tōtụwā 1***a*), *cf.* **tsōkạ**. (2) **harzar kīfī** gills.

harzuɓạ (1) *Vb.* 3B flew into a rage. (2) *f.* ~ **gạrēshi** he is hot-tempered.

has = **has-has** (1) move on, donkey ! (2) go and start up the prey, dog ! (*cf.* **as**, **hasạ 4**).

hasạ *Vb.* 1A (1) **yā** ~ **wutā** he lit a fire. (2) incited P. (= **zugạ**). (3) **aŋ** ~ **fadạ** a quarrel has been fomented. (4) **yā** ~ **kạrē** he urged dog to start up game in the bush (*cf.* **has**).

hasadạ *Ar.* *f.* (1) envy, jealousy. (2) ~ **gạ mại rạbō tāki** envy does not prevent you getting the lot God has assigned to you. (3) ~ **bā tạ hanạ bāwạ rạbō** envy cannot stop the good man succeeding. (4) **dạ azzịkī dạ** ~ **tạre sukẹ kwānā** (*said by* **marōɓā**) prosperity is often accompanied by niggardliness. (5) *cf.* **hassadạ**.

hasafạ *Nor.* = **hasaftạ**.

hasạfcē = **hasaftạ**.

hasạfī *m.* (1) small present (= **mụdārātị**) *x* **Audụ** ~ **gạrēshi** Audu gives small presents. (2) **lōmạr** ~ **tā fi kạɓakiŋ ɓaŋɓanci** a small gift willingly given is better than a big gift plus humiliation.

hasaftạ *Vb.* 2 (*p.o.* **hasạfcē**, *n.o.* **hasạfci**) (1) gave small present *x* **yā hasạfcē nị dạ gōrọ** he gave me a few kola-nuts. (2) *x* **yā hasạfcē nị** he notified me of birth, death, wedding, etc.; he invited me to *such* ceremony. (3) **aŋ hasạfci Audụ dạ shāwarạ** Audu has been consulted.

hasala A. (**hasalạ**) (1) *Vb.* 3B is (was) angry. (2) *f.* (*a*) anger. (*b*) *x* **Audụ** ~ **gạrēshi** Audu is bad-tempered.
    B. (**hasalā**) *Vb.* 1C = **hassạlā**.

hāsạlī *Ar.* (1) it would be better to *x* ~ **mā sule ukụ dạ sīsi** why not accept my offer of three and sixpence? ~ **mā, ŋgō** I won't pay the price you demand, you'd better take your goods away ! ~ **kạ kai masạ yạ ganī** why not take

Hasąŋ

380

hạsūm

it to him to see ? (*cf.* gāra). (2) luckily
x ⁓ mā yąnā cikim masǫyammų
luckily he's a friend of ours.
Hasąŋ (1) *man's name (epithet is* Magājiŋ
gīwā). (2) *twin-boys are named* ⁓ *and*
Husaini.
Hasanā (1) *woman's name.* (2) *twin-girls
are named* ⁓ *and* Husainą.
hạsārą *Ar. f.* (1) (*a*) loss due to some
unlucky incident (*cf.* tsaųtsąyī) *x* nā yi
(= nā shā = nā dauki) ⁓ I suffered a
loss, I had a stroke of bad luck (*epithet
is* dąfkąki mai ąkwai). (*b*) jirāgyąn dą
muką yi ⁓ the ships which we lost as
casualties. (*c*) ⁓ ta kąm bi tūwō ciki
to suffer a loss is most unwelcome.
(*d*) (*sometimes treated as pl.*) *x* mun yi ⁓
mąnyā we've had serious losses. (*e*) mun
yi ⁓ tasą he has become lost to us.
(2) hạsārąr haifūwā = 3. (3) hạsārą =
dąŋ hạsārą *m.* (*f.* 'yar ⁓) *pl.* 'yąŋ ⁓
feckless P. (= wābi 4). (4) hạsārąd
dōki săi Sarkī to the rich a serious loss
is a mere trifle. (5) idąŋ ⁓ *Vd.* tsōnę 3.
(6) masōmiŋ ⁓ *Vd.* tąfī 1*f.*i.
hạsārarrē *m.* (*f.* hạsārarrīyā) *pl.* hạsārąrrū
= hạsārą 3.
hạsāshē *m.* (1) making insinuations,
innuendoes (= habaicī). (2) acting on
analogy of something else (= kintącē 2).
hasạssakī *Vd.* haskē.
has-has = has.
*hāshīyą *Ar. f.* (1) marginal-commentary
(*cf.* sharhą). (2) edge of cloth, etc.
(3) outskirts of town.
hāsilā *Sk.* = hassạlą.
haską (1) *Vb.* 1A (*a*) ⁓ wutā to light
fire ; poke up dying fire. ⁓ tōcilaŋ to
shine electric-torch about. ⁓ fitilą to
light lamp (*all* = ƙyallą 1*a*). (*b*) fitilą
tā ⁓ wuriŋ the lamp illuminated the
place (*for* sun, moon, *cf.* haskąkā).
(2) *Vb.* 3A (*a*) rānā tā haskō sun shone
out from clouds (= ƙyallą 2*c*). (*b*) hatsī
yā haską corn's begun ripening (=
harbą 2*b*). (*c*) tā yi dąrīshi har ta ⁓
she was dressed in her " Sunday best "
(= ƙyallą 2*d*).
haskaikai *pl. of* haskē.
haskaka A. (haskąkā) *Vb.* 1C fitilą tā
haskąką wuriŋ the lamp illuminated
the place. rānā tā (watą yā) haskąką

wuriŋ the sun (the moon) illuminate
the place (*cf.* haską 1*b*).
B. (hąskaką) *Vb.* 3B (1) is (was
illuminated. (2) shone. (3) = haską 2*c*
haske A. (haskę) (1) *Vb.* 1A = haskąkā
(2) *Vb.* 3A = hąskaką.
B. (haskē) *m.* (*pl.* haskōkī=haskaiką
= hasąssakī) (1) (*a*) (i) light. (ii) yi ⁓
shone *x* fitilą tā yi ⁓ ƙąl lamp shon
brightly. fitilą tanā ⁓ lamp's shining
yā ga sąrautąr Sarkin nōmā ąkwai ⁓
he saw that to become Sarkin nōmą
would make him illustrious. (*b*) yą
dauki ⁓ it shone, glittered. (*c*) wat:
sābaŋ ⁓ nę the moon's newish (*x* 7 days
etc.) = watą 1*e*. ii. (*d*) zūcīyassą tanā d:
⁓ he's happy. (*e*) (i) yā yi ⁓ there's im
provement in it. (ii) tąurārąnsą yanā ⁓
he's being lucky.(2)*x*yanā dą⁓he's alert
C. (hąskē) *m.* (1) shaking torch (i.e
of stick or grass), to give a glimmer
(2) (*a*) yanā dą lāyąz zānā, bā yą ciŋ ⁓
as he possesses the charm lāyąz zānā
he's careful to avoid spoiling its potency
by looking into cooking-pot by arti
ficial light (*Vd.* lāyą 7, 8). (*b*) an yi w:
ąbincī hąskē food in pot was looked a
as in (*a*).
haskōkī *Vd.* haskē.
haso *m. used in* (1) nā zō ŋ dēbę maką ⁓
I've come to relieve your solitud
(= kēwā). (2) *Kt.* type of perfume.
hassą *f.* white muslin for turbans (=
harsą).
hassada A. (hassadą) *Vd.* hasadą.
*B. (hạssadą) *Vb.* 2 envied.
hạssafą *Nor.* = hạsaftą.
hassala A. (hạssalą) *Vb.* 3B is accom
plished *x* bą ąbin dą ya ⁓ nothing'
been clinched yet.
*B. (hạssalā) *Vb.* 1C accomplished :
bąŋ hạssalą kōmē ba I've accomplishe
nothing.
hassilā *Vb.* 1C *Sk.* = hassạlā.
hạsū *m.* (1) type of cloth-destroying moth
(2) *m., f.* (*sg., pl.*) wastrel (*epithet is* ⁓
ßątą kudī) *x* kai kąmaŋ ⁓ nę you wast
everything.
*hạsūfį = hųsūfį.
hạsūmą *Ar. f.* enmity.
hạsūmīyą *f.* (1) minaret. (2) tower.
hạsūmī *Damagaram Hausa m.* = hạsūmą

hatalashĭ = **adalashĭ**.

hatara = **hattara**.

hātimĭ *m.* (*pl.* **hātuma**) (1) seal *x* am **bugă masa** ∼ seal's been affixed or stamped on it (= **tambarĭ 3**). (2) **yă bugă** ∼ = **yă karyă** ∼ he made pattern (*x* chessboard-squares, Shield of David, etc.) for drawing augury (*such practitioner is called* **mālămĭ maį bugun** ∼), *cf.* **aufāku**. (3) birthmark supposed to prove P. so marked is true **Shărĭfį**. (4) *Vd.* **rĭjįyā 4**.

hatsabĭbancį *Ar. m.* sorcery, divination (*cf.* **hatsabĭbį**).

hatsabĭbį *m.* (*f.* **hatsabĭbĭyā**) *pl.* **hatsabĭbai** (*Ar.* attabĭbu " doctor "). (1) sorcerer ; diviner. (2) cantankerous P.

hatsa-hatsa *f.* mild quarrel.

hatsaįtsai *Vd.* **hatsĭ**.

hatsalashĭ = **adalashĭ**.

hatsānĭyā *f.* (*pl.* hatsānĭyōyĭ) wrangling.

hatsarĭ *m.* (*Ar.* khatari) (1) danger *x* **nā gamu da** ∼ I was in peril. **barkă da fįtar** ∼ congratulations on your escape from danger ! **shānū sună cikin hatsarin nāmun dāji** the cows are exposed to danger of wild beasts. (2) serious calamity *x* ∼ **yă sămē shį** serious calamity befell him. (3) hostility *x* **da wani** ∼ **tsakānimmu da Jāmus** there's a dispute between us and the Germans (*Vd.* danja). **sună tā da** ∼ they're having a row or dispute. **yă tayar minį da** ∼ he started altercation with me.

hatsa'u *Ar. m.* accident, sudden misfortune.

hatsāyā *f.* = **adalashĭ**.

hatsĭ *m.* (*pl.* hatsaįtsai) (*Ar.* hinta) (1) corn (*i.e.* guinea-corn (**dāwa**) or bulrushmillet (**gērō**), etc.). (2) *Kt.* = **gērō**. (3) (*a*) **hakurĭ hatsin tukunyă nĕ** there's a limit to everyone's patience (*Vd.* tukunyā). (*b*) *Vd.* **yau 2d**. (4) hatsim **bara** *Vd.* **gaurai-gaurai**. (5) ∼ **yă kāma dōkį** the corn upset horse's digestion. (6) ∼ **yă kāma gwĭwassa** he (P. or horse) became strong again. (7) **ba a yi cikį dōmin** ∼ **ba, săi dom ɓōyam magana** what a blabber ! (8) **tāshim marăh** ∼ **bă shi da wuyā** migration is no hardship if you have no property. (9) **kōwā ya ci hatsin rancē, nāsa ya**

ci borrowing is only putting off the evil day. (10) **hatsin tsărĭ** (*a*) bulrushmillet which after removal of bran is fermented and dried. (*b*) mixed crowd. (11) **yă dĭba da karfin** ∼ he took it by force (*Vd.* **karfĭ 1c**). (12) **inā wani hatsin** *Vd.* **daurō 2**. (13) **cikį bă** ∼ **ba** *Vd.* **cikį 7**. (14) **maį hatsin gōnā** *Vd.* **awo 3d**.

hatsi-hatsi *used in* **rĭgā tā yi** ∼ the gown has just a nice tinge of indigo-dye.

hattā *Ar.* even *x* an **săce masa kāyā**, ∼ **tăkalmĭ ba a bar masa ba** his property was stolen, even his sandals.

hattara (1) *f.* alertness. (2) (*said by followers to mounted Chief*) ride carefully !

hātuma *Vd.* **hātimĭ**.

hau A. (hau) (*progressive* yană hawā, *v.n.* hawā). (1) (*a*) (i) mounted *x* **yă** ∼ **dōkį** he mounted the horse (*cf.* **haura 1d**). **yā hawō** he mounted and came. **nā gan su, sună hawan dawākinsu** I saw them mounted (*or* mounting) their horses (Mod. Gram. 123*e*.ii). **yană hawan ităce** he's climbing a tree. (ii) **ta inda aka** ∼, **ta nan a kan sauka** stick to the man whom you serve ! (iii) *Vd.* **dă 1b**.ii. (iv) ∼ **dōkin zūcįyā** *Vd.* **zūcįyā 5**. (*b*) **yā** ∼ **gadō** (i) he got into bed. (ii) he succeeded to the rulership. (*c*) (i) **yă hau shį** = **yā** ∼ **masa** he " went for " him (= **fāda 2c**). **yā** ∼ **masa da bugu** he thrashed him. **yā** ∼ **masa da zāgį** he abused him. (ii) **sun** ∼ **musu** they attacked them (enemy, places). **yā** ∼ **musu da cį** he attacked them. **yā** ∼ **musu hannū baka, hannū kwaryā** he attacked them rapidly. **sun** ∼ **musu da bugu tįtim tįtim** they attacked them fiercely. (1A) (i) **yā** ∼ **dōran aɓōkan găbā** he attacked the enemy. (ii) *Vd.* **dōrō 4**. (1B) (i) **mun** ∼ **bisa kansu** we defeated them utterly. (ii) ∼ **dan dubū** *Vd.* **dubū 6**. (iii) **yā** ∼ **rĭmĭ** *Vd.* **rĭmĭ 1e**. (iv) ∼ **gōrā** *Vd.* **gōrā 1a**. (v) *Vd.* **bardē 7, 9**. (vi) *Vd.* **tăka, ka hau ; zăɓi ka hau ; dambū**. (vii) **ta inda aka hau** *Vd.* **inda 1a**.iii. (2) began *x* **yă** ∼ **kan aikį** he began work. (3) is (was) in excess *x* **sule bĭyū sun** ∼ there are two shillings too many. (4) **zō mu** ∼ let's be off ! (5) swelled *x* (*a*) **hannunsa yā** ∼ his hand is swollen. (*b*) **darajạrsụ tā** ∼ they have been promoted. (*c*) **kạnsạ yā** ∼ he's arrogant. (6) **kōgī yā** ∼ the river's in flood (= **kāwō**). (7) **rode** *x* **yā** ∼ **dạgạ Kanọ zūwạ tạran yāƙị** he rode from Kano to the battlefield. (8) *Vd.* **hawā, haurạ, haurẹ, hayạ, hayẹ**. B. (**hau**) (1) **jā** ∼ *adj.* scarlet. (2) **gạrī yā kāmạ wutā** ∼ the town is ablaze. C. (**hau**) *used in* **yā gạmu dạ** ∼ prediction of his misfortune has led to it occurring (= **bạkin dūnīyạ** *q.v.*).

hau dạ *Vb.* 4A (1) mounted P. on *x* **nā** ∼ **shī dōkị** = **nā haushē shi dōkị** I mounted him on a horse. (2) **Kạnde tā** ∼ **Zạinabụ** Kande began Zainabu's grinding for her. (3) (*a*) **nā** ∼ **rịgā** I've completed sewing of the gown (= **tā dạ** 2). (*b*) **nā** ∼ **hannun rịgā** I've joined sleeves to gown. (*c*) **an** ∼ **d̃āƙị** roof has been mounted on to house (= **hayị** 1*a* = **tā dạ** 1*e* = *Kt.* **haƙạ** 1*e*.iv). (*d*) **aŋ** ∼ **kibīyạ** arrowhead has been mounted on its shaft. (*e*) **aŋ** ∼ **tạkạlmī** uppers of shoes have been sewn on to soles. (*f*) **aŋ** ∼ **jạlālạ** the various parts of the saddle-cover have been assembled (*cf.* **hayạ**). (4) steamed (flour or rice) *x* **tā** ∼ **shiŋkāfā** (= **sulạlā** 2). (5) **yā dadạ** ∼ **shī** he improved it. (6) ∼ **Hawạ gadō gạrēshi** (*a*) he flatters. (*b*) he makes mischief. (7) **suŋ** ∼ **shī** they egged him on to do T. beyond his powers.

*haudạjī *Ar.* *m.* camel-howdah (=**dạr-būkạ**).

hau-hau *m.*, *f.* (*sg.*, *pl.*) a " softy ".

hauhawạ *used in* (1) **kōgī yanạ** ∼ river is in flood (= **cikōwạ**). (2) *Kt.* **yārọ yanạ** ∼ the boy is growing up quickly.

hauƙā *m.* (1) (*a*) (i) madness. (ii) ∼ **nạ ƙārẹwā, anạ̃ sāran tūrụ** " sheep behaving as lamb ". (iii) ∼ **daŋgi-daŋgi nē, kōwā dạ irin nāsạ** everyone has his own particular failing. (iv) **kạraŋ** ∼ *Vd.* **zạrā** 2*b*.iii. (v) **ạbin na kādọ hauƙā nẹ** ? is he mad that he acts so ? (*b*) folly *x* **yā yi** ∼ he behaved with folly (*epithet is* ∼ **jā, zūwạ ƙạsūwā, bạ hājạ, bạ hujjā** = ∼ **jā, hụlā dạrā, bạ wạndō, bạ rịgā**). (2) (*a*) ∼ **gạrēshi** he's " swollen-headed ". (*b*) **tukunyā tanạ** ∼ the pot is boiling over (= **ɓātạ** 6*a*).

(*c*) **tẹƙū bā tạ̃ rạbō dạ** ∼ the sea is always rough. (3) ferocity *x* **yā zō dạ haukạn nan nāsạ, yanạ̃ ta bugụmmụ** he attacked us with his usual ferocity. (4) (*a*) **hauƙạ̃** *cry made by* **kadạfkarạ**. (*b*) *x* *A says* " *let us swim the river !* ", *to which* B *replies* **hauƙạ̃** not likely, I can't swim ! *A rejoins an* **cẹ̃ dạ kadạfkarạ yạ shiga akurƙī bạ** ? if you can't, then you can't, but *I* will (*cf.* **bạ** ? 3). (5) *Vd.* **yā'ẹ**. (6) **dạ** ∼ **ƙạn nadẹ̃ ta** *Vd.* **tạbarmā** 3. (7) **bạllē kūrā tạ yi** ∼ *Vd.* **dạ̃** 1*c*.

haukạcē *Vb.* 3A (1) is (was) mad. (2) is (was) foolish. (3) is " swollen-headed ".

hau'ka-hauka" *m.* becoming " all of a dither ".

haukata A. (**haukatạ**) *Vb.* 3B (1) became abundant *x* **hatsī yā** ∼ **ạ ƙạsūwā** there's glut of corn. **cīwọ yā** ∼ the illness has become aggravated. (2) became " swollen-headed ". (3) **haukatạr bịkī, gayạ mijịm bāya, tārẹ̃wā** stupidly doing pointless act. (4) *cf.* **haukạcē**. B. (**haukạtā**) *Vb.* 1C (1) rendered mad. (2) flabbergasted. (3) rendered " swollen headed ". (4) **wannạŋ yā haukạtạ ƙạsūwar gyạdā** this livened up the trade in ground-nuts (*cf.* **hauƙā**). (5) **haukạtạ yārọ** *epithet of* **ƙōshī** ; **bạmmī** ; **zaƙạmī**.

haula A. (**haulā**) *f.* (1) branches of trees, of corn, or of horns. (2) progeny. B. (**haulạ**) (*Ar.* there is no power but with God) *x* **ạl'amạriŋ yā kai lā haulạ** the matter became serious.

haumā-haumā (1) *f.* (*a*) pointless talk. (*b*) senseless actions. (2) *m.*, *f.* (*sg.*, *pl.*) scatterbrained P.

hauni *m.* (1) (*a*) left-hand. (*b*) left-hand side. (*c*) *Vd.* **bịlāƙạ**. (2) executioner.

haura A. (**haurạ**) (1) *Vb.* 1A (*a*) climbed over. (*b*) (i) exceeded *x* **yā yi shẹƙarạ ạrbạ'iŋ har ya** ∼ he's 40 years old or more. (ii) remained over *x* **bạ̃ wạndạ ya** ∼ nobody survived (= **saurā**). (*c*) **yā** ∼ **sāƙạ** he (busybody) continued the weaving begun by another. (*d*) (i) **yā** ∼ **dōkị** he leapt on to the horse. (*e*) *cf.* **haurā;** **hau, haurẹ, hayạ, hayẹ**. (ii) **suŋ haurạ gạriŋ** they climbed into the town. (2) *Vb.* 3A (*a*) **kudinsạ suŋ** ∼ its price is

higher than before. (b) x hatsī yā ∼ corn's become very dear. gōrọ yā ∼ kolas are very dear now.
B. (haurā) Vb. 2 Sk. (1) (a) = harbā x yā hauri jąkī, ya wuce he gave the donkey a kick and passed on (cf. haurạ). (b) an haurē sụ, sụ dạuki bindigạ they have been forced to take up arms. (c) jąkī yā haurē shị donkey kicked him. (d) yā hauri tąkạlmī he kicked his shoes on to his feet. (2) yā hauri arẹ̄wā he died.

haurad dạ Sk. = harbad dạ.

haurāgīyā f. senseless speech.

haure A. (haurẹ) (1) Vb. 1A = haurạ 1a. (2) Vb. 3A (a) = haurạ 2. (b) yā ∼ he ran away. hanyạ tā ∼ road goes off at tangent. (c) rānā tā ∼ sun's blazing. (d) ƙasā tā ∼ soil's cracking. (e) Kt. dabbạ tā ∼ domestic animal died naturally (therefore religiously inedible), cf. mūshẹ. (f) Kt. tā ∼ she is dry-breasted. (3) m. (a) (i) (= haurạŋ gīwā) tusk of elephant. (ii) (= haurạŋ dọrinā) hippo ivory. (b) tooth (= haƙōrī). cīwạŋ ∼ tooth-ache. (c) Kt. mad dog.
B. (haure) x gạ̄ su cạŋ haure they are over there on one side.
C. (haurē) m. (1) dilapidated part of town wall where people climb over. (2) continuing weaving begun by another (done by busybody). (3) doing T. at most unsuitable moment x yā yi minị ∼ (x mentioning marriage-offer in the street).

hauri Sk. m. shooting, kicking, etc. (= harbi q.v.).

haurigīyā Nor. f. (= haurāgīyā).

Hausā (1) f. (a) Hausa Language x yạnā jiŋ ∼ he understands Hausa. (b) (i) Hausa-people x ạ ∼ in Hausa-country. ƙasar ∼ Hausaland : sạrautạr ∼ ruler-ship of the Hausas. (ii) Sokoto x mạganạn naŋ, caŋ ∼ akẹ̄ fạdā tasạ this word is used in Sokoto. yā tạfi ∼ he went into Sokoto Province. (c) ∼ bakwại the Seven Hausa States. In Kano, these are Kanọ ; Kạtsinạ ; Daurā ; Zạmfạrā ; Zazzạu ; Gọbir ; Ranō. In Katsina, these are Sakkwatō ; Arguŋgụ ; Zazzạu ; Zạmfạrar Hāɓẹ̄ ;

Kanọ ; Baucī ; Auyọ in Hadẹjīyā. In Sokoto, these are Sakkwatō, Kwạnnī in Adạr ; Arguŋgụ ; Gọbir ; Zạmfạrar Hāɓẹ̄ ; Kạcinạ ; Asbịn. (d) cf. banzā 3. (e) Jạllā bạbbar Hausā epithet of Kano. (2) hausā f. (pl. hausōshī = hausạssakī) (Ar. allisāna ; from same root is derived harshẹ). (a) any language x bā nạ̄ jiŋ hausā tasạ I don't understand his speech. (b) meaning x nā gānẹ hausarkạ I understand your meaning. hausarkạ, nī nā yi sātạ you're hinting I'm a thief. (c) rōwā gạrēshị har bạ tạ saŋ ∼ ba he is a miser. (d) in don sụ bā mụ tsọ̄rō sukạ fạdi hakạ, tọ̄ hausạr bạ tạ fịta ba if they said this to frighten us, then their plan failed.

hausạgī Zar. m. = ausạgī.

Hausạnce adv. kạ fạdạ minị mạganạ ạ ∼ (1) tell me it in Hausa ! (2) speak out frankly !

hausạssakī Vd. hausā 2.

Hausạ̄wā Vd. Bạhaushẹ.

haushē Vd. hau dạ.

haushi A. (haushī) m. (1) vexation x yạnā haushiŋ hanạ shi sạyē he's angry at being forbidden to buy. (2) (a) yā hūcẹ haushinsạ (i) he got his way despite opposition. (ii) he got his revenge. (b) suŋ hūcẹ ∼ bisạ kạmmụ they revenged themselves on us (Vd. hūcẹ 2). (3) (a) ạbiŋ ∼ m. vexatious T. (b) ạbiŋ ∼ mūshẹ jaŋ kạrē what an annoying person ! (4) haushin ragō, cīzạm bāƙī what a lazy person ! (5) haushin rashi, an cẹ̄ dạ mạkāfọ " gạ̄ idọ ! " ya cẹ̄ " mẹ̄ zạn yi dạ shī ạbu mại wārī " it is sour grapes ! (6) haushiŋ kīfī Vd. kīfī 8. (7) tūrạ ∼ Vd. tūrạ 5. (8) Vd. baŋ ∼.
B. (haushị) Ar. m. (1) barking of dog (= hafshị = waŋ-waŋ). (2) nā dạuki kạrē doŋ ∼ yā kōmō yanạ̄ tuŋkwuyī it was unsuitable for the purpose to which it was applied. (3) bā ka dạ rānā sǎi ta ∼ Vd. rānā 4d. (4) cīzọ bạ̄ ∼ Vd. mūminị 1b.

hausōshī Vd. hausā 2.

hautsuna A. (hautsunā) (1) Vb. 1C (a) mixed together (solids, powder, or grains) x tā hautsunạ nāmạ dạ gishirī she mixed salt with the meat (cf. dāmạ).

(b) muddled up x suŋ hautsụnạ kāyạ they've muddled up the loads. (2) Vb. 3A suŋ ~ they've quarrelled.
B. (hautsụnạ) Vb. 3B (1) are mixed (as in hautsụnā). (2) is in a muddle. (3) = hautsụnā 2.
hautsụnē (1) Vb. 1C = hautsụnā 1. (2) Vb. 3A = hautsụnā 2.
hautsuni A. (hautsụni) what a muddle! B. (hạutsunī) m. squabbling.
hauya A. (hauyā = hạuyā) f. (pl. hauyōyī = Sk. hạuyai) (i) type of small hoe (= fartanyạ). (2) Vd. hạuyā.
B. (hạuyā) f. (1) (a) score (re cowries) x kudī ~ 20 cowries. (b) (before multiplier, hạuyā becomes hauyā) x kudī hauyā ukụ 60 cowries. (c) N.B. with the advent of coinage, hạuyā is but little used. (d) Vd. sịttiŋ 2. (2) hạuyar Lārạbā the 20 cowries (nowadays a halfpenny) given by pupil to Koranic teacher on Wednesdays. (3) 'yar ~ small present of money. (4) hạuyar sadakạ contribution of about 1s. given mourner towards his expenses in giving usual alms. (5) (a) ṇ yi mạgạnạ P̣, ạ cẹ̄ " gạ̄ hạuyar zubịn lạllẹ P̣ " why should I make matters worse by making a fuss? (b) bạn cẹ̄ kōmē ba, bạllē ạ cẹ̄ " gạ̄ hạuyar zubịn lallẹ " I said nothing, so what penalty could I incur!
C. (hauyạ) Vb. 1A Kt. mixed together (= gaurạyā).
hawa A. (hawā) m. (1) (v.n. and progressive of hau q.v.) mounting on, riding on x (a) (i) yanạ̄ ~ dōkị = yanạ̄ hawan dōkị he's riding (or mounting) a horse (cf. Mod. Gram. 103d, 123e.ii). (ii) mạgạnin nạŋ yanạ̄ ~ kā this drug has strong fumes. (iii) kāyaŋ ~ m. vehicle. (iv) bạ̄ ~ bạ̄ sạukā, sǎi sukạ cẹ̄ they said straightway that . . . bạ sụ saŋ ~ ba, bạ sụ san sạukā ba, sǎi kawai sukạ gan sụ then unexpectedly they saw them. (v) zō, mụ yi hawan yạ̄kị let's go on a cavalry foray! bại tafạ hawan yạ̄kị ba he'd never been out on a cavalry foray. (vi) bā ạ̄ ~ samạ sǎi dạ tsānị to get on you require a powerful backer (cf. 1b). (vii) bā ạ̄ ~ itạ̄cē ta gịndī, ạ sạuka ta rēshẹ stick to the man

whom you serve! (viii) hawaŋ kūrā Vd. kūrā 35. (ix) mại sauriŋ ~ Vd. dambū. (x) yā rigā kị ~ Vd. wutā 1a.i. (b) bạ̄ ~ samạ epithet of bushcow (ɓaunā). (c) hawam bishīyạd dạɛwạ̄lẹ (i) climbing tree but being unable to descend. (ii) " biting off more than one can chew ". (d) hawam ɓọrī being devil-ridden (Vd. ɓọrī). (e) hawam mạkạ̄fin dawākī Kt. quarrelling. (f) for hawan preceding the following words, Vd. dạrē, daushē, dōkịn macịjī, dōkịn zūcịyā, gọrā 1a, ɛạhō, ɛāwạrā, tsịmā, tsịmē, tsōkạ, wāgā 4. (2) mounting or riding done by P. (Mod. Gram. 90a) x (a) hawaŋ aŋgwạ̄yē parading of bridegroom and his friends after wedding (= Kt. tạ̄ka aŋgọ). (b) hawam bardē riding without saddle (cf. wāgā 4). (3) dōkịn naŋ ~ gạrēshị this horse's broken in.
B. (Hawạ) f. (1) Eve (name for girl born on Friday) = Hạwwā (cf. Ādạmū) ; her epithet is ~ mại sūnan Jumma'ạ (she is often called Kulụmā). (2) hau dạ ~ gadō gạrēshị (a) he flatters. (b) he makes mischief.
C. (hạwā) f. (Ar. " air ") (1) kā bị hạwarkạ = kā bi hạwar rạŋkạ you acted merely to suit yourself. *(2) (a) sky. (b) yanạ̄ ~ it's high up in the sky.
hawai Vd. hạwāyạ.
*hạwā'ī m., f. (sg., pl.) irresponsible P.
hạwainịyā f. (1) chameleon (= Zar. hạŋwāwạ) (epithet is ~ hawạlaini). (2) hạwainịyarkạ tạ kịyạ̄yi ramạta = hạwainịyarkạ tạ kịyạ̄yi gạ̄wōna none of your tricks or you'll rue it! (Vd. hạwāyạ). (3) Vd. wutsīyạr ~.
hạwājọ Vd. gandū 1f.
hawạlaini Vd. hạwainịyā.
hawar dạ = hau dạ.
hawasshē Sk. = haushē q.v. under hau dạ.
hạwātsīmạ f. desertion by one's staff (= ạwātsīmạ q.v.).
hạwāyạ Vb. 2 (mainly used in imperative) kạ hạwạ̄yē shi = hawai shi be on your guard against him! gạya wạ Audụ " kīyē nị, hawai nị ! " tell Audu to mind how he behaves to me! hawai nị = hạwạ̄yẹ ni beware of me! nạ̄ hạwạ̄yē shi = hạwāyạ tasạ na yi I was

on my guard against him (*Vd.*
hawainīyā 2).
hawāyē *m.* (1) tear(s) *x* tā yi ∼ = tā
zubar dā ∼ she cried. nā kāwō kūkā
wuriŋkā, doŋ kā shārę minī ∼ I'm in
trouble and have come to you for help.
(2) hawāyam fannā type of Barebari
face-marking (3 lines on each side of
nose). (3) hawāyan zākī (*a*) marking
(*similar to* 2) done in Kano Province.
(*b*) natural lines on certain kinds of
būtā (bottle-gourd). (*c*) the tree
Anaphrenium abyssinicum.
hawēnīyā = hawainīyā.
*Hāwīyā *Ar. f.* the lowest of the 7
Hells of Islam.
hawō *Vd.* hau.
Hawwā = Hawā.
hayā (1) *Vb.* 1A (*a*) crossed over *x* yā ∼
kōgī he crossed the river. yā ∼ tarkō
he passed safely over the trap. (*b*)
exceeded (= haurā 1*b q.v.*). (*c*) = hau
dā 3. (*d*) spliced *x* igīyan naŋ tūkā
bīyu-bīyu nē, ā ∼, tā zamā ukų ukų
make this 2-ply string into 3-ply !
(= kutā = mayā 1). (*e*) kų ∼ samā =
ɗōrā 4. (*f*) nā ∼ Zazzau I crossed the
boundary (of Kano, etc.) and entered
Zaria Province (*cf.* hayę 1*d*). (*g*) hayā
manyā *Vd.* cąrkī 4. (*h*) *Eng.* rented ;
hired. (2) *f.* (*a*) (i) *Eng.* rent, hire.
(ii) yanā ∼ he rents the house. (iii) anā
hayarsā kamar lēburā people hire him
as a porter. (*b*) gidam bā ∼ *m.* public
latrine. (*c*) ɗaŋ ∼ *m. pl.* 'yaŋ ∼ hirer
out of cycles.
hayāgāgā *f.* uproar ; angry speech.
hayā-hayā = hayā-hayā-hayā *f.* =
hayānīyā.
hayākā *Vb.* 3B (1) became large. (2)
became important (= gāwurtā). (3)
dūnīyā tā ∼ the world is at strife.
hayākī *m.* (1) (*a*) smoke. (*b*) *Vd.* bākiŋ
wutā. (*c*) idan dā ya ga ∼, shī ya kąn
ɗēbō wutā everybody is best suited to
look after his own affairs. (*d*) *Vd.*
tābā 1*e*, murtukē. (*e*) mātarkā ∼
Vd. farkē. (2) ∼ fīd dā na kōgō
what a determined person ! what a
quarrelsome person ! (3) hayākī-hayākī
adj. brownish.
hāyam empty (= wāyam *q.v.*).

hayam-hayam *used in* yanā cī ∼ he's
eating quickly.
hayānīyā *f.* (1) hubbub *x* jama'ā fa akā
ɗauki ∼ the public raised an uproar.
(2) garrulity.
hayātū *Kt. m.* (1) = hayānīyā. (2) harping
on T.
hayayyafā (1) *Vb.* 2 *int. from* haifā.
(2) *Vb.* 3B (*int. from* haifu) *x* kurarrajī
suŋ ∼ ā jikinsā pustules are very
numerous on his body.
hayayyē *m.* (*f.* hayayyīyā) *pl.* hayayyū
well broken-in (*re* horse), *cf.* hawā 3.
haye A. (hayę) (1) *Vb.* 1A (*a*) = hayā 1*a-e.*
(*b*) mounted *x* (i) yā ∼ dōkī he mounted
a horse (= hau). (ii) yā ∼ gadō =
hau 1*b*. (iii) wani yā ∼ tudų, yā bar
na gaŋgarę dā lękē some outstrip others.
(iv) *Vd.* tāka, haye. (v) ∼ manyā *Vd.*
cąrkī 4. (*c*) yā ∼ masā " he went for
him", he attacked him in war (= hau 1*c*).
(*d*) nā ∼ Kano I crossed the boundary
of Kano Province (*cf.* hayā 1*f*). suŋ ∼ dā
mū kasar Masar they caused us to cross
the Egyptian frontier. (2) *Vb.* 3A
(*a*) cikinsā yā ∼ tim his stomach is
inflated. (*b*) bā zā sų ∼ ba they
(positions being attacked) will not be
able to hold out.
B. (hayę) *used in* ∼ nē bā gādo ba
his status is acquired, not hereditary.
hayēwā *f.* further side of depression or
streambed.
hayi *m.* (1) acting as in hayā 1*c, d.* (*a*) an yi
wā dākī ∼ (i) roof has been mounted on
to house (= hau dā 3*c* = tā dā 1*e*). (ii)
house has been thatched = jiŋkā 1 (*cf.*
kąi 2*b*, rufi 2*b*). (*b*) yanā hayin rīgā
he is assembling the gown. (2) state
resulting from 1 *x* rīgā tanā dā kyaŋ ∼
the gown is well assembled. (3) dākiŋ ∼
nē it is a round, thatched house (=
kago). (4) sōrō nē hayin tsaiko it is a
mud-topped building with vaulting
(ɗauriŋ gūgā). (5) side of river, gorge,
etc. *x* gā mu ā hayimmų, gā su kumā
ā nāsų we were on our side of the river,
they on theirs. yanā hayin kōgī it is
across the river. ā wannaŋ ∼ yakē it
is on this bank. ā ∼ yakē it is across
the border (*Vd.* kētarę). (6) (*a*) offal.
(*b*) *Sk., Kt.* liver, etc., put at top of

tsỊrē (spitted-meat), cf. hūlā 8. (7) hayịn tsaurē seam where cloth is several-fold.

hāyincị Ar. m. (1) fraud. (= hā'incį), cf. ạlhā'inĪ. (2) treachery.

hayyạ (1) hi ! (2) ~ alạs salā Come to prayer ! (the prayer-call from the minaret), cf. ạssạlā. (3) dạ ~ alạs salā sukạ zō they came only with difficulty.

hayyaci A. (hạyyạci) Vd. hạyyatạ. B. (hayyạcï) m. apogee x yanā cikiɳ hayyạcinsạ it's at its acme. kō cikiɳ hayyạcinsạ baị fĪ sulẹ ukụ ba at its dearest it never fetched above 3s. (= gānỊyā).

hayyạ-hayyạ = hayyạ 1.

hayyạlạ I'll get even with you yet ! (= haggyạlạ).

hayyạɳ (Ar. alive) used in yanā naɳ hayyạɳ he's in best of health.

hayyā̆sā̆ Zar. hi !

hạyyatạ Vb. 2 (p.o. hạyyạcē, n.o. hạyyạci) pestered.

hạyyạtaccē m. (f. hạyyạtaccīyā) pl. hạyyạtattū pesterer.

hāzā (1) Zar. f. jumping into water sitting (= dĪyạm). (2) Ar. ~ wasạlạm = ~ wasạlạmụ I remain your obedient servant . . . (Vd. wasạlam).

hạzāƙạ Ar. f. quick intelligence.

hazbĪyā f. (pl. hazbĪyōyĪ) (1) the Speckled pigeon (Columba guinea). (b) idạɳ ~ (i) type of embroidery on anklebands of trousers. (ii) coloured-rings painted round women's eyes. (iii) type of ornamentation of bracelets and leather goods. (2) stye (= Sk. bụnūnụ̄wā). (3) rỊgā tanā dạ ciɳ ~ a hole's been burnt in the gown.

hāziƙancị Ar. m. quick intelligence.

hāziƙĪ m. (f. hāziƙā) pl. hāziƙai Ar. of quick intelligence.

hazō m. (1) mist, haze. (2) hazan tụtū hot-season haze when locust-bean tree (dọ̄rōwạ) is in bloom.

hẹ̄ (1) you there ! (2) just mind how you behave !

hēdkwātạ Eng. m. headquarters.

hēlumạ = hēlumạɳ = hēlimạɳ Eng. "headman" (1) m. headman of male gang (Vd. agā 2). (2) f. woman in charge of female gang.

hērẹ to pare (= fērẹ q.v.).

he- if not found here, Vd. fe-.

hĪ Vb. 5 Sk. exceeded (= fĪ q.v.).

hiɗa (hịɗā) Vb. 2 Kt. said (= fạɗā q.v.). B. (hĪɗạ) Vb. 1A Kt. flayed (= fĪɗạ q.v.).

hi- if not found here, Vd. fĪ-.

hidimā Ar. f. serving a P.

Hijirā Ar. f. (1) year of the Prophet's flight from Mecca, whence Muslim calendar begins (A.D. 622) = ƙaurā 2a.ii. ~ tanā dạ shēkarạ 1278, akạ yĪ it was done in A.H. 1278. (2) 'yaɳ ~ those who followed the call of Shēhụ Daɳ Hōdīyọ in his jịhādị, and their descendants. (3) bạri mụ tā dạ ~ (a) let us start on this long journey of ours ! (b) let us be off to the war !

hĪkạ f. minute quantity x yā bā nị tụrā̆rē hĪkạn naɳ he gave me this little amount of perfume.

*hịkāyạ Ar. f. (pl. hịkāyū) (1) narrative. (2) maị dạ hịkāyạrkạ let's now hear your version ! (= dạ'ạwā).

hĪkị m. = hĪkạ.

*hịƙidụ Ar. m. envy.

*hikimạ Ar. f. wisdom.

hikkạ f. acme x cĪwo yā kai ~ illness is at apogee (= kakị q.v.).

hĪkụ m. = hĪkạ.

hĪlạ Ar. f. guile.

hịlạci Vd. hịlatạ.

*hịlāfạ Ar. f. (1) discrepancy. (2) bā̆ ~ undoubtedly. (3) sun yi ~ they quarrelled.

hi- if not found here, Vd. fĪ-.

hịlatạ Vb. 2 (p.o. hịlạcē, n.o. hịlạci) tricked P.

himị adv. (derived from himịlĪ) (1) abundantly x yā kāwō kāyā ~ he brought huge load. (2) what a lot !

himịlĪ Ar. (1) m. (a) pack-animal's load. (b) heavy load x yā ɗaukō himịliɳ kāyā = yā ɗaukō kāyā himịlĪ he brought a big load. (2) adv. in great quantity (all = shimịlĪ), cf. himị.

himmạ Ar. f. (pl. himmōmĪ) (1) energy, perseverance (epithet is ~ bā̆ ta gạ ragō). yā tā dạ ~ he strove hard. (2) sā̆ ~ Vd. sā̆ A1, B3. (3) maị dạ ~ pay attention !

hịmmantạ Vb. 3B x yā ~ kạɳ aikiɳ he

" put his back into the work. **yā ~ gạ taimakwansụ** he strove to help them. ɲimmantad **dạ** *Vb.* 4A caused P. to strive hard.

ɲimmạntu *Vb.* 3B = **hịmmantạ.**

ɲiŋ *Kt.* (1) here, this is a present (payment) for you ! (= **ŋgō**). (2) (*a*) look ! (*b*) listen !

ɟindancị *m.* Hinduism.

*hịndī *Ar. m.* (" Indian ") curved one-edged sword (= **bịsạlạ̄mī**).

ɟindụ *x* (1) **ƙasar ~** *f.* India. (2) **Bahạriŋ Hindụ** *m.* = **Tẹ̄kuŋ Hindụ** *f.* the Indian Ocean.

ɲiŋgō *Kt.* = **hịŋ 1.**

ɲinjirạ *Vb.* 3B *Sk.* became out of control (= **bịjirạ** *q.v.*).

'hinsarī = **hinsarū** *Ar. m.* little finger.

ɲinzīrị (1) = **ạlhạnzịr.** (2) *Vd.* **lālạ̄cē 3.**

ɲir stop it !

ɲi- *if not found here, Vd.* **ɟi-.**

ɲira A. (**hīrā**) *f.* (1) chatting (= **yạucī 2**). (2) **~ tā ci fụrē** = **~ tā ci shūnī** the chat became animated. (3) **yā tạfi ~ dạ ita** (*euphemism for*) man has gone to sleep with concubine (*Vd.* **kwānā A.2 7**). (4) **hīrar darē** night-work (= **kurgā**). **in nā yi ~, nạ̄ gamạ kạ̄miŋ gạrī yạ wāyẹ** (*said by tailor or scribe*) if I work through the night, I'll get the work done.

B. *Vd.* **fīrạ** canine-tooth, etc.

C. *Vd.* **fịra** *Sk.* bird whirred up into air.

ɲirdẹ *Vb.* 1A slit up completely, etc. (= **fardẹ** *q.v.*).

hirfạ *Ar. f.* (*pl.* **hirfōfī**) any skilled trade (= **sạna'ạ**).

hịrī *m.* = **hīrā.**

hirtī *m.* = **hīrā.**

ɟisābị *Ar. m.* (1) (*a*) working out spells mathematically. (*b*) **mālạmiŋ hịsābị** *m.* astrologer, soothsayer (*Vd.* **dūbā**). *(2) reckoning up good and bad deeds of P. on Judgment Day. *(3) science of mathematics. (4) **Allạ̄ yạ yi minị ~ dạ shī** may God judge between us !

ɟi- *if not found here, Vd.* **ɟi-.**

ɟīyānạ *Ar. f.* (1) deceit. (2) dishonesty.

ɟizīfī *m.* (*pl.* **hịzịfai** = *Kt.* **hizuffạ**) one of the 60 portions into which Koran is divided (*Vd.* **izịfī**).

---

hǭ *Sk., Kt.* (1) (*a*) greeting ! (*reply is* **hǭ kạdǎi** ! = *Sk.* **iŋgwại**). (*b*) **~ dạ aikị** greeting on your work ! (= **sạnnū 1b**). (2) **~ shēgẹ** = **~ arnẹ** what a rogue he is ! (3) *Vd.* **~ dạ yinị**.

hōƀẹ̄sạ̄ = *Kt.* **hoƀƀạ̄sạ̄** = *Kt.* **hoƀƀạ̄sạ̄rạ̄** (1) (*a*) up with the load ! (*said by carrier*) = **abbạ̄sạ̄** = **wacạbẹ.** (*b*) **yā yi ạbiŋ hōƀẹ̄sạ** he did an energetic act. (2) **hoƀẹ̄sạ̄ nē** he's related to meat-selling (**fāwạ**) families (*uncomplimentary expression*).

ho- *if not found here, Vd.* **fo-.**

hōƀịjạm fancy !

hōcẹ *m.* (*pl.* **hwạttā**) (1) small circular Asbin-salt cake (= **tạ̄fin rạ̄ƙumī** = **kātā 3**), *cf.* **zạwārạ.** (2) circular cake of **tūwō** (*cf.* **cūrị 2**). (3) *Sk.* small cake like **wạinā.**

hōɗạ *Vb.* 1A *used in* **yā ~ tābạ** he inhaled tobacco-smoke (*cf.* **zụ̄ƙā**).

hōdạ = **fōdạ.**

hǭ dạ yinị = **hǭ dạ inị** type of woman's greeting (= **hǭdēnị**).

hōɗẹ *Vb.* 1A = **hōɗạ.**

hǭdēnị type of woman's greeting (= **hǭ dạ yinị**).

hōdịjạm fancy !

Hōdīyọ, *i.e.* **Shēhụ Daŋ Hōdīyọ** name of leader of Filani conquest.

hǭgā *f.* type of salt from Hoga in Kabi.

hōgẹ *m.* (*pl.* **hwạggā**) (1) (*a*) clod, sod (= **sagị**). (*b*) **na dạkamạ, mạnzaŋkạ hōgẹ, bā kạ̄ jiŋ kirạ sǎi jīfạ** Deaf man, strong measures are needed with you ! (*epithet of* **kurmā**). (2) **dāwạ tā ɗaukō ~** guinea-corn germinated and pushed up soil. (3) *Sk., Kt.* head of guinea-corn *cf.* **zaŋgannīyā.** (4) *x* **hōgyạŋ Kanọ** all Kano Emirate.

ho- *if not found here, Vd.* **fo-.**

hǭgō *m.* cancelling project (= **hụ̄gū** *q.v.*).

hoho A. (**hōhọ**) (1) (*a*) **~ sạnnū** (i) condolences on the death in your family ! (*reply is* **hǭhǭ jūnā** = **hōhọ kạdǎi**). (ii) what bad luck for you ! (*b*) **wạndạ bại ji " bạri ! " ba, yạ̄ ji " hōhọ "** once bitten, twice shy ! (*c*) *Vd.* **hǭhǭ.** (2) *m.* (*a*) shells of beans, groundnuts, etc. (*b*) **hōhạŋ kīfī** fish-scales.

B. (**hǭhō**) *Kt.* the woman's greeting **afūwō** *q.v.*

C. (hōhō) (1) *used in* ∼ jūnā *q.v. in*
hōho 1. (2) *P. at work says to another
at work* bark̯a d̯a aik̯i ! (*reply is* hōhō
jūnā).
hōk̯ar̯a *Vb.* 3B *used in* yan̄ā ∼ he's
putting on airs.
hōk̯e = hōk̯i (1) *m.* work not profiting
the doer. (2) *m., f. (sg., pl.)* doer of
work profiting the doer in no way.
hōl̯a *Eng. f.* cigarette-holder (= kwal̯a 4
= k̯af̯ō 5 = mashāyī 2).
hōlamī *m. (f.* hōlamā) pure white sheep.
hōl̯e (1) *Vb.* 3A (*a*) (cyclist, motor-driver)
turned in small space, turned corner
(*cf.* kwan̯a). (*b*) went for jaunt (on
cycle or in motor). (2) *Vb.* 1A *x* yā
s̯ami K̯ande, yā ∼ ta he got Kande to
agree to sleep with him.
ho- *if not found .here, Vd.* fo-.
hōl̯ī *Eng. m.* (1) ku yi ∼ fall in ! yā yi musu
∼ he made them (soldiers, carriers)
fall in line. (2) *x* yan̄ā ∼ a k̯asūwā
y̯anzu this commodity is abundant just
now.
hōl̯o *m.* merry, noisy conversation of
several persons.
hōlōk̯ō *m.* (1) pseudo-storm of harvest-
season with overcast sky, but no rain
(= *Kt.* daranyā 2). (2) ∼ hadirin̄ k̯āk̯ā,
duhuns̯a b̯ā na rūwā n̯ē ba what a
broken reed he is ! (= kink̯imbōd̯i 3
= tsūlīyā 4), *cf.* wālā 2. (3) (*a*) kernel-
less groundnuts. (*b*) grainless corn-ears.
homa A. (hōmā) *f.* (1) boastfulness.
(2) ostentatious behaviour.
B. (hōmā) *Sk. f.* small fishing-net.
hōrā *Vb.* 2 (*Vd.* hōrō) (1) disciplined. (2)
trained *x* (*a*) yā hōri dōk̯i he broke in the
horse. dabb̯ad d̯a ak̯a ∼ d̯ōmin̄ aikin̄
gōnā cattle trained for ploughing. yā hōri
sōj̯a he trained soldiers. (*b*) t̯akark̯arī
kan̄ ∼, j̯akī yā sāb̯a d̯a kāyā what's
bred in the bone. . . . (3) punished.
(4) *x* nā hōrē shi d̯a zūw̯a I impressed
on him the importance of his coming.
(5) *cf.* hōr̯e.
hōramī *m.* twisted, iron bracelet, usually
with charms attached.
hōr̯e (1) *Vb.* 1A (*a*) disciplined (*as in* hōrā)
thoroughly *x* (i) s̯ābō yā ∼ mini k̯ōgī
experience has accustomed me to
crossing rivers. (ii) All̯ā shī ya ∼ w̯a

r̯ak̯umī k̯ay̯a it (difficult T.) has become
second nature to him. (*b*) yā ∼ k̯waryā
he cleaned out pulp from gourd by
shaking stones and water inside it.
(2) *Fil. used in* k̯ai ∼ k̯āwō bābā (*said
jokingly*) Come here, Bighead !
hōri *Vb.* (*only used in this form*) *Fil.*
(1) yā ∼ it (meat, etc.) went bad.
(2) *Kt.* yā ∼ it (cassava, sweet-potato,
dambū) resisted all efforts at cooking
it (= tsumburumburum), *cf.* k̯irīr̯ic̯ē 3.
(3) *Kt.* tukunyā tā ∼ pot refused to boil.
hōri ɓaid̯u *m.* type of large, leather bag
(= b̯ar ni d̯a ɓaid̯u).
hōrīy̯o *Fil m.* yā yi ∼ it resisted cooking
as in hōri 2, 3.
horo A. (hōrō) *m.* (1) (*secondary v.n. of*
hōrā) *x* an̄ā hōrōna = an̄ā hōrāta I'm
being disciplined. (2) act of training *x*
an yi mas̯a ∼ he's been trained. (3)
haif̯ūwā d̯ayā hōran̄ gindī n̯ē one learns
by experience (*Vd.* haif̯ūwā 3). (4) f̯ōran̄
All̯ā *Vd.* r̯āk̯umī 1*d.* (5) f̯ōran̄ gīwā
Vd. gwant̯al.
B. (hōr̯ō) *adv.* gapingly *x* k̯ōf̯a ∼
doorless doorway (*pl.* k̯ōf̯ōf̯ī horō-hōr̯ō).
nā ga rām̯i ∼ I saw a yawning hole.
hanc̯i horō-hōr̯ō wide nostrils.
ho- *if not found here, Vd.* fo-.
hōrōc̯e *Kt. m.* N.A. policeman.
hōtakā *f.* " popcorn ".
hōtō *m.* (1) d̯an̄ ∼ *m.* (*pl.* 'yan̄ ∼)
member of group of dancers attending
weddings and going from farm to farm
where they work and do sleight of hand
(*x* stabbing themselves with knives,
shivering knifeblade by breathing on it)
(*cf.* b̯uzūzu 6). (2) aikin̄ ∼ useless
work. (3) *Eng.* photo (*pl.* hōtun̄a) *x*
(*a*) an d̯auki ∼ a photo was taken.
(*b*) an d̯aukē shi a ∼ (i) his photo's
been taken. (ii) he's been " seen
through ".
hu *Vd.* huu.
hubbār̯e *Ar.-Fil.* (*Ar.* qubba dome) grave
of Shēhu D̯an̄ Hōdīy̯o.
*hubusī *m.* (*Ar.* imprisonment) property
held inalienably in mortmain (= wak̯af̯ī
5).
huce A. (hūc̯e) (1) *Vb.* 3A (*a*) T. cooled *x*
g̯arī yā ∼ weather's cooler. (*b*) temper
cooled *x* săi kā ∼ tukun̄ā let's leave the

matter till you're calmer in mind !
(= laf̣ = karyakō). (c) hadiri̦ yā ∼
storm abated. (d) rậina yā ∼ my mind
calmed down. (e) (i) hūcẹ̄wā dǎi ạbōkị̄
calm yourself ! (ii) hūcẹ̄wā dǎi, Shūgạbạ
please calm down ! (f) "ạ bari̦ yạ
hūcẹ !" shī ya kāwō rạbaŋ wani if you
let your chance slip another will take it.
(2) Vb. 1A (a) yā ∼ haushinsạ he got
his way despite opposition ; he got his
revenge. yā ∼ mini̦ haushīna he caused
me to get my way. suŋ hūcẹ haushī
bisạ kạmmu̦ they revenged themselves
on us. (b) bā yạ̄ hūcẹ zūcīyā Vd.
sạ̄k̃ō 1c.
B. (hūce) (1) derived from hūtạ) x yā
yī shi̦ ạ ∼ he did it at his leisure. yā
sạ̄mē shi̦ ạ ∼ he got it easily. (2)
(derived from hūcẹ) x yā sạ̄mē shi̦ ạ ∼
he found it had cooled down. (3) Vd.
hū̦tā.
C. (hucẹ) passed by (= wucẹ q.v.).
hu- if not found here, Vd. fu-.
huci A. (hū̦cī) m. (1) stertorous breathing.
(2) hū̦cin rānā wave of hot air. (3) yā
sạ̄ri ∼ he (galloping-horse, hurrying P.)
fell over.
B. (hū̦ci) Vd. hū̦tā.
huda A. (hū̦da) Vb. 3B (Vd. hū̦dā)
(1) budded ; blossomed (re locustbean
(ɗọ̄rawạ), date-palm (dabīnọ) (the verb
fạsu also being used ; but for other trees
and plants, Vd. hū̦dā 2). (2) wuri̦ŋ
yā ∼ place oozes moisture. (3) gōdīyan
nạŋ tā ∼ this mare's on heat (= fi̦ta 7
= lāmī 1d = Sk. kẹ̄lu). (4) bābā yā ∼
indigo-dye is nearly ready for use.
(5) lallẹ yā ∼ henna is well applied.✓
(6) yā ∼ he took to his heels. (7) hūdō
Vb. 3A appeared æ (a) yā hūdō mini̦
ta wajaŋ gabạs he appeared to me from
the east. surạyyā tā hūdō gabạs Sirius
rose in east. (b) nā rasạ ta indạ zaŋ
hūdō masạ I don't know how to
"tackle him". (c) im baŋ hūdō masạ
ta bāyaŋ gidā ba, bạ zā mu̦ shiryạ ba
unless I assert myself, we shan't get
on together.
B. (hū̦dā) f. (1) (v.n. and progressive
of hū̦da) x yanạ̄ ∼ it's budding,
blossoming (as in hū̦da 1). (2) (a) wākē
yā yi ∼ beans blossomed (yi hū̦dā

applies to any tree or plant except
date-palm, locust-bean, tobacco ;
Vd. hū̦da 1; fu̦rē). (b) tā yi ∼
she menstruated. tanạ̄ ∼ she's
menstruating (= hailạ). (c) Kt. hū̦dag
gizọ shallow water-holes in bank of
large stream (k̃ọ̄ramạ), etc. (= k̃uru̦r-
ru̦bai). (d) Vd. dumaŋ kadạ.
C. (hūdạ) (1) Vb. 1A (a) bored,
pierced. (b) aŋ ∼ masạ hanci̦ (i) its
(ox) nose has been pierced for rope.
(ii) he's been initiated. (c) x hū̦da mini̦
kạdaŋ give me an advance ! nā ∼ sulẹ
gu̦dā cikiŋ kudīna I took an advance
of 1s. (d) yā ∼, yā ga jinī he's back
"on his old stunt". (e) Sarkī yā ∼
gidansu̦ bana the chief has this year
forced them to conform to orders.
(f) cleared x yā ∼ dawaŋ naŋ he cleared
this bush. (g) suŋ hūdō Kanọ they
(enemy) burst into Kano. (h) bā ạ̄ hūdạ
ciki̦, ạ yi kirāri̦ don't cut off your nose
to spite your face ! (2) f. (pl. hūdōjī)
hole bored or pierced (= hūji̦) x
hanci̦ntạ yanạ̄ dạ hūdạ her nose is
pierced for fitting ornament.
huɗa A. (hūɗạ) Vb. 1A (1) ∼ dāwạ to bank
up grown guineacorn after completion
of firi̦ and maimai ; such hū̦ɗā replaces
sassaryā (Vd. hū̦ɗā; k̃wạ̄māzạ; nōmā).
(2) ∼ gwāzā (dạŋkali̦) to make ridges
for kokoyams (sweet potatoes).
B. (hū̦ɗā) f. (1) secondary v.n. of
hū̦ɗạ) x yanạ̄ hū̦ɗar gwāzā = yanạ̄ hū̦ɗạ
gwāzā he's making ridges for kokoyams.
(2) (a) acting as in hū̦ɗạ 1 x jīyạ sukạ
yi ∼ they banked up their grown corn
yesterday (Vd. nōmā). (b) yā fasạ ∼
he turned over the ground some 3
weeks after sowing by baŋgajē
(Vd. k̃u̦furtū ; hūɗạ). (c) Vd. k̃ūru̦ 1b.iii.
hū̦daddē = hū̦dajjē.
hudạ-hudạ Ar. f. Senegal hoopoe (=
ạlhudạhudạ).
hū̦dajjē m. (f. hū̦dajjīyā) pl. hū̦dạddū
pierced.
*Hudạmā Ar. f. the third of 7 Hells
of Islam.
hūdạs = hūdashẹ m. an illness blackening
and thickening the skin.
hūɗẹ Vb. 1A banked up, etc. (as in hūɗạ)
completely.

hŭdŏ *Vd.* hŭda 7.
hu- *if not found here, Vd.* fu-.
hŭdŏjĭ *Vd.* hŭdạ 2.
hudŭ *f.* (1) four *x* ∼ tā fi ukų 4 is greater than 3. (2) (*a*) na ∼ *m.* (*f.* ta ∼) *pl.* na ∼ the fourth *x* dŏkịŋ hudŭ the 4th horse. (*b*) hudun four times as many as (*cf.* bĭyū 3*b*). (3) ∼ dạ ∼ *f.* type of cācā (gambling). (4) hudu-hudu *adv.* four by four. (5) ∼ bĭyar *f.* tribal-marks consisting of 5 cuts on right cheek and 4 on left. (6) nā ƙārạ idọ ∼ dạ mutānē I came face to face with the people. (7) mai ƙafạ ∼ ya kạm fādị, bạllē mai bĭyū to err is human.
huduba *f.* sermon (= hutsubạ *q.v.*).
hųdum-hųdum *used in* yanā tạfĭyạ ∼ (1) he's travelling silently in the dark. (2) he (blind man) is feeling his way along.
huffị *m.* the slipper(s) called wuffị.
hūgŭ *m.* cancelling project *x* mun yi ∼ we've given up the idea. tạfĭyạ tā yi ∼ journey's cancelled. hadirị yā yi ∼ threatened storm failed to materialize.
huhhūdā *Vb.* 1C kept on piercing (*int. from* hŭda).
huhhūjē = fuffūjē.
hu- *if not found here, Vd.* fu-.
huhu A. hūhū (1) lung(s) (= *Sk.* sufệ). (2) sānĭyan nạŋ, ∼ takệ yĭ this cow has pleuro-pneumonia. (3) yā yi ∼ = yā kumbųrạ hūhunsạ he became angry. (4) bā shi dạ zūcĭyā ; kŏ ∼ bā shi dạ shĭ he's spiritless. (5) a food from cassava. (6) padding on upper side of saddle (= mạdạburọ), *cf.* zubkạ.
B. (hūhu) *m.* (1) (*a*) wrapping for kolanuts. (*b*) wạndạ ya san darajạr gŏrọ shĭ ya kạm bidam masạ hūhu one looks after a T. one values. (2) (*a*) package of kolas. (*b*) kā yi hūhum bakạ = bākịŋkạ hūhun yārọ your mouth's full of kola (*lit.* if boy got packet of kolas, he'd squander it). (3) hūhum mā'ạhū (*a*) empty kola-wrappings. (*b*) P. falling short of the expectations formed about him (= faŋkạm fayạu).
huhus *x* gyạdā tā yi ∼ ground-nut pods are kernel-less (*cf.* fụs).
hūjajjē = hūdajjē.

huje A. (hūjệ) *Vb.* 3A is (was) pierce (*cf.* hŭdạ).
B. (hūjē) *m.* hole pierced in upper c lower lip of pagans for inserting orna ment (*cf.* hūjị).
hūjị *m.* (1) (*a*) hole pierced in nose or ea for inserting ornament (*cf.* hūjē) *x* tan dạ hūjiŋ hancị = hancịntạ yanā dạ ∼ her nose is pierced for insertion « ornament. (*b*) hūjiŋ ƙōtạ hole pierce for hafting. (2) (*a*) an yi matạ ∼ sh (cow) has been inoculated. (*b*) an yi w Audụ ∼ Audu's cattle have been ir oculated (*cf.* lambạ 1*b*). (3) advance c pay (*cf.* hŭdạ 1*c*). yā yi ∼ cikĭ kudinsạ he took an advance of pay an yi masạ ∼ he was given an advanc of pay. (4) *Kt.* yā yi hūjịn dawạ h cleared the bush (*cf.* hŭdạ 1*f*).
hujjạ *Ar. f.* (*pl.* hujjŏjĭ) (1) reason (*a*) ịnā hujjạr wannạŋ what is the reaso of it ? (= dạlĭlị 1). (*b*) bā watạ ∼, b kūwā wani dạlĭlị without rhyme c reason (= gairạ 2*c*). (*c*) hujjạr mē, an c dạ kạrē yạ dạuki damị why attempt any thing unsuited to you ? (2) excuse *x* (bā shi dạ ∼ = hujjạ tasạ tā yaŋkệ " h hasn't a leg to stand on ". (3) mai ∼ m *f.* (*pl.* māsū ∼) rich P. (4) *x* mun yi ∼ dạ shĭ we imposed conditions on hir (*cf.* sharạdĭ 3).
hujjatạ *Vb.* 2 (*p.o.* hujjạcē, *n.o.* hujjạc imposed conditions on P.
hujjatayyạ *f.* laying down mutual cor ditions.
hukā *f.* (1) bronchitis, asthma,etc. (2) *Kt.* panting, gasping (= hạkĭ).
hukācē *Vb.* 3A (1) has (had) bronchiti asthma, etc. (2) (*a*) is (was) emaciate or weak (= karācē). (*b*) (land) is (wa exhausted by farming. (*c*) (cor« vegetables) are dried up and light i weight.
hukū-hukū *m.* puffiness *x* (1) fųŋkās yā yi ∼ the wheaten-cakes have rise well. (2) kumạtunsạ sun yi ∼ his cheek are puffed out with anger.
hųkųkų *used in* yanā tạfe ∼ he's walkin along, his body puffed up with rag tsuntsū yanā tạfe ∼ the bird is walkin along with feathers ruffled from col illness, etc.

hu- *if not found here, Vd.* fu-.
hukumci = hakunci.
hukuntā *Vb.* 1C = hukuntā *Vb.* 2 (*p.o.*
hukuncē, *n.o.* hukunci) = hakuntā *q.v.*
hul A. (hul) = fil.
    B. (hul) = fil.
hūlā *f.* (*pl.* hūlunā) (1) (*a*) cap (= tāgiyā).
(*b*) yā sā ~ he put on a cap. (*c*) (i) yā
cirę ~ = yā tūbę ~ = yā daukę ~ he
took off his cap. (ii) yā cirę musu ~
he saluted them, he congratulated them.
(iii) mun cirę musu ~ we say to them
bravo ! (*d*) dōmin kāi akę ~, har ƙyēyā
tā sāmu your dependents share in your
good fortune. (*e*) " ban sā ā kā ba "
n ji ɓarāwam ~ that is beyond my
capabilities. (*f*) sāmun kāi yā fi sāmun
~ health is better than wealth. (2)
buhun nan yā cika har an yi masā ~
this sack of groundnuts, etc., is so full
that, it being impossible to sew up the
top (*cf.* kunnē), a piece of Hessian has
to be sewn on. (3) farar ~ *Vd.* farī *2h.*
(4) yārō dā ~, babba dā ~, girman 'yan
dinyā why do these persons so different
in type imitate one another ? (5) hūlar
gōrọ the smaller of the two halves of
a kola-nut (*cf.* burmi) if it is very tiny.
(6) (*a*) hūlad dạrā fez. (*b*) haukā jā,
hūlad dạrā, bābu wandō what madness
to act so ! (*Vd.* haukā). (7) hūlar jiɓā
cap-like top of mushroom-shaped ant-
hill. (8) hūlar tsīrē tiny bit of fat on
end of stick of tsīrē (*cf.* hayi *6b*).
(9) hūlar sarautā crown.
hultsā transactions.
hūlū *Kt. m., f.* (*sg., pl.*) (1) fool. (2) yārọ
bābu tambaya, ~ (= jāki) nę a youth
relying on his own strength without
charms, is a nitwit.
hulū-hulū *m.* swelling of pimples, of
eyelids, of moist seeds, *etc.*
hu- *if not found here, Vd.* fu-.
hululu A. (hulūlu) *m.* silly gossip.
    B. (hulūlū) abundantly *x* sunā nan ~
they're abundant.
hūlulūwā *Kt. f.* (1) barren land or farm
(= shāɓuwā). (2) T. of poor quality.
hūlunā *Vd.* hūlā.
*hulūri *Ar. m.* religious ecstasy.
humhun *m.* lampblack, *etc.* (= fumfun
q.v.).

*humushī *Ar. m.* the fifth of the booty
allotted to leader of raid.
*humusī = humushī.
hunhun = humhun.
hunhungālā (1) *m., f.* (*sg., pl.*) (*a*) fat,
weak P. (*b*) P. falling short of one's
expectations of him (= fankam fayau).
(2) *m.* type of big hawk.
hungō here, this is a present (payment)
for you ! (= ngō).
hunƙumēmę = hunƙumī *m.* (*f.* hunƙumē-
mīyā = hunƙumā) *pl.* hunƙum-
hunƙum huge (*re* articles).
hunƙurmī *etc.* = hunƙumī.
hunsā mishkil (*Ar.* female-like) *m.* herma-
phrodite.
huntanci *m.* nakedness (= tsiraici).
huntāyē *Vd.* huntū.
huntū *m.* (*f.* huntūwā) *pl.* huntāyē
(1) naked (= tsirārā = uryan), *cf.* tik.
(2) kōinā huntū zā shi, da sanim mai rigā
he who pays the piper, calls the tune.
(3) *Vd.* rufa *2.* (4) ram biki akę ƙin
huntū, ran kwāɓar ƙasā ā nēmō shi
everything has its time and place.
(5) ~ yā bā gaskiyā gā itācē *Vd.* ạbu *2j.*
(6) *Vd.* dāriyā *3.*
huntukē *Vb.* 1C *Kt.* stripped P. naked.
hu- *if not found here, Vd.* fu-.
huntunci *m.* nakedness (= tsiraici).
hunturu *m.* harmattan (N.B. *the word*
" harmattan " *is derived from* Hamāda
" Sahara "), *cf.* dārī *3* ; muku muku :
būdā ; dungun *2.*
huntūwā *f.* (1) *Vd.* huntū. (2) stripping
off outer clothes for work.
huppi *m.* the slipper(s) called wuffi.
hura A. (hūrā) (1) *Vb.* 1A (*a*) blew on *x*
(i) yā ~ wutā he lit fire (*lit.* he blew
on fire) = rūrā *1a, cf.* zugā (i*A*) yā ~
wutā he drove car very fast. (ii) yā ~
mini wutā he made a fire for me ; he
pestered, upbraided me. (iii) yā ~
wutar kansā he's begun business for
himself. (iv) itācan hūrāwā *m.* firewood. (v) *Vd.* hūru. (vi) sukā ~ wutā,
sukā rāshę they took life easy. (vi) yanā
~ hanci he's behaving conceitedly.
(vii) gadū yanā ~ ƙasā the pig is
smelling over the ground. (*b*) (i) inflated
(bladder). (ii) yā ~ ākwiyā = salkā *1c.*
(iii) salkā a kan ~. kōwā ya ~ rāriyā,

bąkinsą yą yi cīwo don't waste your time on futilities ! (c) suŋ ∼ shi = suŋ ∼ masą kunnē they incited him (= zugą). (d) fomented (an affair). (e) tūsą bā tą hūrą wutā Vd. tūsą 4. (2) f. (a) an yi ∼ farm has for one season been planted with leguminous crop (x beans, cotton, or sweet potatoes) for fertilization (epithet is gyāram bądi). (b) after rains, making ridges for spring-sowing (= farą-farą). B. (hūrā) f. (1) head of ƙansūwā-grass. (2) Kt. ƙansūwā-grass. C. (hurā) f. the food furā q.v.

hūrą kǒgǒ m. hawk, etc. (= shāho).

hurąncē Vb. 1C did first-weeding (firį) of farm (= hurę).

hūrau m. larvae of digger-wasp (= būsau q.v.).

hu- if not found here, Vd. fu-.

hurdē used in dōkį ∼ dappled grey horse (= kįlį 2).

hurdį (1) black-faced piebald ox. (2) epithet of chief, lion, energetic P.

hure A. (hūrę) (1) Vb. 1A (a) ∼ ƙwaryā to scrape calabash to remove pulp (tǒtūwā). (b) hollowed out (a tree-trunk or wooden vessel). (c) burned up completely x aŋ ∼ itącē duką. (d) ąbincin nąŋ, ∼ cikį gąrēshį this food soon leaves one as hungry as if not eaten at all. (e) blew out x nā ∼ fitilą I extinguished the lamp (= būshę 2a). hūre minį cīyāwą ą ido blow the grass out of my eye ! (= būshę 2b). (2) Vb. 3A (a) cikįna yā ∼ I've a sinking feeling of hunger. (b) rījįyā tā ∼ well-mouth's crumbled.
B. (hurę) (1) Vb. 1A did first weeding (firį) of farm. (2) m., f. (sg., pl.) type of white cow.
C. (hųrē) pl. hųrąnnī flower (= furē q.v.).

hurhūdā Vb. 1C to keep on piercing (int. from hūdą).

hurhudū (1) four by four. (2) f. type of darą (draughts), Vd. ƙwado.

hurhūtā (1) Vb. 1C tā hurhūtą ąbincī she fanned food to cool it (= fīfītā 2). (2) Vb. 3A kept on resting (int. from hūtą).

huri Vd. firi ; furi.

hūrō Vd. hūru.

hu- if not found here, Vd. fu-.

hurtsą f. transactions.

hurtutū used in yā yi ∼ dą ƙasā his body is covered in dust, etc.

huru A. (hūrū) m. skin of ground-nuts.
B. (hųru) Vb. 3B (1) wutā tā ∼ the fire blazed up, took well (Vd. hūrą). (2) kǒ kā ∼ į wutā, bą zam bā ką ba urge as you may, I won't give it to you. (3) hūrō Vb. 3A x wutā tā hūrō the fire caught up and swept towards us.
C. (fųru) used (by women) in mē ya fųru what's happened ? (= fāru).

huruci Kt. m. speaking x yā yi ∼ he spoke = firįcī (cf. furtą).

*hūrųl'ainį Ar. pl. houris.

hurumī m. (pl. hurųmai) land outside town, reserved for communal purposes such as grazing, cemetery, forest-reserve, etc.

hu- if not found here, Vd. fu-.

hurunhurmī m. concealed hole.

hururu A. (Hūrūrų) used in shąn tābą gąrēshį ƙamar ∼ = kō ∼ bai fī shį shąn tābą ba he " smokes like a locomotive ".
B. (hųrųrų) boundlessly (= farąrą q.v.).

hųrwā f. (1) throwing earth over one's shoulder or putting it on one's head in repentance or obeisance (= cī 8 = hąmfudą 2a). (2) putting hot earth on smallpox patient.

Hųsaina (1) name for woman. (2) twin girls are named ∼ and Hasaną.

Hųsaini (1) name for man. (2) twin boys are named ∼ and Hasąŋ.

*hųsūfį Ar. m. eclipse of sun or moon (= kųsūfį q.v. = zązząɓī 2).

hųsūmą Ar. f. (1) quarrel. (2) enmity.

hųsūmīyą f. (1) minaret. (2) tower.

hut used in bą shi dą kō ∼ he has no means, no strength (= fus).

huta A. (hūtą) Vb. 3A (1) (a) rested. (b) in zā ką ∼, hūta ą bąbbar inūwą whatever you do, do it with all your might ! (c) Vd. gąji 1e. (d) iŋ aŋ gąji, kō ą rānā sǎi ą ∼ beggars cannot be choosers. (e) Vd. ∼ rōro. (f) ą bā kį, ą ∼ Vd. yuŋwą 1h. (g) yā ∼ dą rānā Vd. sąmmakō 1d. (h) nā ∼ dą ƙudā Vd. ƙashī 1d, rǎi 5a. (2) mų ∼ let's

postpone further work for the moment !
(= ajīyē 10). (3) yā ∼ dạ dūnīyạ
(a) he's dead. (b) he's retired from
work. (4) (a) sǎi sụ yī tạ, kōwā yạ ∼ let
them make an end of the job once and
for all ! aŋ ∼ we can now relax, as
there is nothing further to fear, nothing
further to do. (b) suŋ ∼ aikạ̄wā (= suŋ
∼ dạ aikạ̄wā) jirạ̄gyan yā̱ḳi they are
freed from the necessity of sending
warships. aŋ ∼ dạ hạsārạr Jạbū one is
freed from the anxiety of losses from
counterfeit coin. (5) hūtạ dạ (with dative)
relieved P. of pain, etc. x kạ ∼ minị dạ
wạhalạ give me alleviation of my
trouble ! dạ shạm māgạnin nạŋ sǎi ya ∼
wạ rạnsạ dạ cīwọ by drinking this
medicine he gave himself relief from
pain (cf. hūtad dạ).
B. (hụ̄tā) Vb. 2 (p.o. hụ̄cē, n.o. hụ̄ci)
x Allạ̄ yạ hụ̄ci zūcīyarkạ God allay your
anger ! Allạ̄ yạ hụ̄ci Sarkī, sǎi kạ hūcẹ
Chief, God allay your displeasure !
hūtaccē m. (f. hụ̄taccīyā) pl. hụ̄tạttū
(1) mild-tempered P. (2) well-off P.
hūtad dạ Vb. 4A gave rest to x yā ∼ nī =
yā hūtasshē nị he left me in peace ; it
rested me (cf. hūtạ 5).
hūtạlī m. = hūtạlā f. (1) leather-fringe for
horse's face. (2) kunyạr idọ hūtạlin
tsīyā " one must make the best of a
bad job ".
hūtạ rōrọ m. getting relief from one's
troubles.
hūtasshē Vd. hūtad dạ.
hūtsạncē Vb. 3A is (was) cantankerous.
hūtsancị m. cantankerousness.
hūtsantạ = hūtsạntakạ f. cantankerousness.
hūtsū m. (f. hūtsūwā = hūtswā) pl.
hūtsạ̄yē (1) cantankerous. (2) Hūtsạ̄yē
Kt. = Sarkin sạmạ̄rị q.v. under saurạyī
2.
hutsubạ Ar. f. (pl. hutsubōbī) (1) Friday
sermon in mosque. (2) whispering into
4-day old child's ear the name to be
given on 8th day. (3) hutsubạr
Shạitsạŋ senseless, boastful talk.
hūtsū Bạzazzạgī Zar. m. the dove kurcīyā
q.v.
hūtsūwā Vd. hūtsū.
hū- if not found here, Vd. fu-.

hutturụ Sk.-Fil. m. time between sunset
and lịshā (= magạribạ).
hūtū m. (1) (a) resting x (i) yanạ̄ ∼ he's
resting. yā yi ∼ he rested. (ii) yanạ̄
hūtuŋ gạjīyạ he's resting from fatigue.
(iii) am bạ̄ 'yam makarantā ∼ = holi-
days have been given to pupils of Govt.
or N.A. School (cf. ɓạ̄rī, tạshē). (b) hūtun
jạ̄kī dạ kāyā ạ kā (a) resting in the
blazing sun. (b) resting preparatory to
completing irksome task. (c) hūtum
bịkī, 'yar matsīyạ̄cī tā mutụ raŋ gārā
getting relief from one's troubles. (d)
hūtū yakẹ̄ sọ Vd. rạ̌i 1a.xi. (2) passing
wind (= tūsạ).
huturọ = hutturụ Sk., Kt., Zar. = hutturụ
q.v.
hututū used in yā yi ∼ dạ ɓasā his body's
covered with dust, etc.
huu x yā būsạ huu he blew loudly on
(motor-horn, etc.).
hūwạ̄cē Vb. 1C (1) Allạ̄ yā ∼ rạ̄ɓumī ɓayạ
he makes light of his heavy toil, his
troubles, etc. (= rạ̄ɓumī 1l). (2) Kt.
Allạ̄ yạ ∼ manị God preserve me from
it ! (= Allạ̄ yạ kīyāshē mụ).
*huzunụ Ar. m. (1) sadness. (2) dis-
pleasure.
hw commonly replaces f in Katsina, x
hwarī for farī ; hwādị for fādị ;
hwạrautạ for fạrautạ.
hwạggā clods (pl. of hōgẹ).
hwạlgabā rustic Hausa f. terror (=
fạrgạbā).
hwạttā round salt-cakes (pl. of hōcẹ).
hwī-hwī-hwī x kāyā ∼ light load looking
bulky.
hyạ̄dē Sk. m. type of girls' game.
hyạdɗạ Sk. f. screen for bride's bed
(= fyadɗạ).

I

i (ī) (1) Vb. (followed by dative) overcame
x dạ kyar mukạ ī masạ only with
difficulty did we persuade him over
(Vd. im). dạ kyar na ī wạ (= ī mạ)
dōkịna I had great difficulty in forcing
my horse to obey me. yā ī mạ (= ī wạ)
hannunsạ he's expert (= īyạ 2f.ii).

(2) (a) (i) yes ! (= na'ạm). (ii) bạ̈ shi dạ̈ Ikọ yạ̈ cẹ̈ " I " kō "ā'ạ̈" he is powerless. (iii) (negative-interrogatives which in English require reply "no", have reply "yes" in Hausa) x bạ̈ sụ tạfi bạ̈ ? have they not gone ? (reply, I " they've not gone ! " ; lit. " yes, you're right in thinking they've not gone "). (b) ~ ayyạ̈ = Il well, yes ! (reply assenting with reservation). (3) = yī did q.v. (cf. I dạ̈).

i (I) Kano Village Hausa (1) yes ! (replying when called) (= I 2a'.i). (2) Vd. ạfūwō 1.

i (I) well x dam mẹ̈ ka yī shi hakạ̈ why did you do it thus ? (reply, I, kạ̈kạ̈ zan yI " well, how should I have done it ? ").

i (i) (abbreviation of yạ) x (1) inạ̈ zūwạ̈ = yinạ̈ zūwạ̈ he's coming (cf. n). (2) (progressive in relative sense) x ạbin dạ̈ ikẹ̈ yI = ạbin dạ̈ yikẹ̈ yI what he's doing. (3) (past in relative sense) ạbin dạ̈ i yi = ạbin dạ̈ ya yi what he did.

i (i) like x (1) saurā kạdạn yạ̈ yI i gīwā girmā it's nearly as big as elephant (lit. little remains that it do like an elephant as to size). bạ̈ ni dạ̈ kafā kō i ta ạllūrạ̈ I've not a moment to spare (lit. I've not a hole even like the eye of needle). (2) Vd. yI.

Ibạ̈ abbreviated dialectal form of dlbạ̈ drew water q.v.

ibādạ̈ Ar. f. (1) (a) serving God by prayer and good life. (b) gidạn ~ m. place of worship. (2) ạl'ādạn nạn tā zamā ~ gạrēshi this habit has become second nature to him (= tābạ̈ 4).

*ibhāmi Ar. m. thumb.

ibi A. (ibi) (1) (Yor. obi) (1) type of kola-nut known to Hausa kola-dealers in Yorubaland. (2) Ibi f. place near Wukari so called.
   B. (Ibi) dialectal form = dẹ̈bi q.v. under dlbạ̈.

ibiliccị = ibilicị = ibiliscị m. perverseness, wickedness (Vd. Iblis).

ibinụ Ar. son of x Umarụ ~ Shēhụ Omar the son of Shehu.

Ibirāhīmụ = Ibirāhim Abraham (Vd. Dabọ 2, Ibiro).

Ibirīlụ m. April.

ibiro A. (ibirọ) = iburọ.

B. (Ibiro) name for any man called Ibirāhīmụ.

Iblis (Arabic-Latin diabolus) pl. Iblisai (1) (a) Satan (cf. Lis). (b) murtukū fadạn iblisai, yārọ bại ganī ba, bạllē yạ̈ rabạ̈ what Armageddon ! (2) iblīshim mụtụm (a) evil P. (b) unusually skilled P. (cf. shạitsạn, mạsīfạ̈ 3, māyẹ̈ 2, fitinạ̈ 2d). (3) anạ̈ kụrūrūwạr ~ it's a lying rumour. (4) cf. tunnukū 1b.

ibnụ = ibinụ.

ibo A. (Ibọ) m., f. (sg., pl.) an Ibo.
   B. (Ibō) abbreviated dialectal form of dẹ̈bō drew water q.v.

iburọ m. cereal like accạ̈.

icẹ̈ = Sk. iccẹ̈ m. wood, tree (= itạ̈cē). icạn wutā = icạn hūrạ̈wā firewood.

i da A. (I dạ̈) accomplished (= Iyar dạ̈ q.v.) x kạ̈ bā dạ̈ gōrọ, mụ I makạ̈ dạ̈ ạlbishirin give us some kolanut and we'll tell you the glad tidings !
   B. (Idạ̈) Vb. 1A = Iyar dạ̈.

idabạr = idabạrI (1) m. crosspiece of swordhilt. (2) idabạrI m. (f. idabạrā) white-mouthed grey donkey (cf. ẹ̈fau).

idạn (1) = in ; kạdạn. (2) idan dại Vd. dại 2. (3) idạn Vd. idọn.

idandẹ̈ = idandi Zar. = ạdandẹ̈ q.v.

idandunạ̈ eyes (pl. of idọ).

idānīyā f. (pl. as for idọ q.v.) eye.

idạ̈nü Vd. idọ.

idar dạ̈ = id dạ̈ Vb. 4B accomplished (= iyar dạ̈ q.v.).

idda A. (iddạ̈) Ar. f. (1) period during which woman is ceremonially unclean and may not remarry (this is 3 menstruations (hailạ̈) for free-woman ('yā) but 2 for slave-girl (bạ̈iwā)), cf. jinī 2. (2) iddạr takabạ̈ = iddạr wạfāti similar period before widow may remarry (this is 4 months and 10 days for 'yā, but 2 months and 5 days for bạ̈iwā).
   B. (Iddā) f. Idah.

idi A. (Idi) Ar. m. any religious festival. sun tạfi ~ they've gone to celebrate festival. yā hau idinsạ̈ he celebrated his festival. sun kōmō dạga ~ they've returned from observing the festival. sun saukō dạga ~ festival's over (Vd. sallạ̈).
   B. (Idi) m. (1) type of water-melon. (2) Vd. idī.

C. (īdī = ịdī) (1) *abbreviation of* Idịrīsụ *q.v.* (2) *Vd.* ịdī.

Idịrīsụ Enoch (*Vd.* īdī).

idọ *m.* (*pl.* idậnū, *Vd.* 1*a*.ii) = idandunậ = idậndanī = idānūwậ) (1) (*a*) (i) eye (= *Sk.* ijīyậ). (ii) (*the pl.* idậnū *is sometimes used in sing. sense*) *x* idậnunsậ yậ jicẹ his eye is bunged up. idậnunsậ yậ būdẹ he is no novice. (iii) (*after the pre-position a, the form* idō *is optionally used*) *x* hakị yậ fādậ minị ậ idō (= ậ idọ) a wisp of grass fell in my eye (Mod. Gram. 24). (iv) *Vd.* 2 *below for* proverbs *with* idọ.

(*b*) (i) nā zubậ masậ ∼ I looked out for him ; I looked intently at him ; I watched him closely. (ii) munậ zubậ idậmmụ gậ zūwậnsậ we are eagerly awaiting his arrival. (iii) (*regarding action of superior towards inferior*) *x* Audụ, Kậnde ya zubậ wậ ∼ Kande is the woman on whom Audu centres his affection, reliance, *but* Kậnde, Audụ yậ zubậ matậ ∼ Audu is utterly indifferent to Kande (*cf.* iv *following*). (iv) (*regarding action of inferior towards superior*) *x* Audụ, maị gidā ya zubậ wậ ∼ = maị gidā, Audụ yậ zubậ masậ ∼ Audu relies on his compound-head for all. (v) in dārī yậ saụka, dōlẹ sǎi ∼ if the cold season arrives, he'll have to take precautions (*this is abbreviation for* dōlẹ sǎi yậ zubậ idọ). (vi) kậ zubậ ∼ ậ ƙasậ keep your gaze riveted on the ground ! (*cf.* 1*p.*v below). (vii) zụba minị ∼ (*said to seller*) give me (buyer of butter) the present of sour milk customarily given ! = wutsīyậ 3.

(*bb*) mụ ganō wậ idậmmụ let us see for ourselves ! (*bb*1) sunậ yị, ∼ nậ ganiŋ ∼ they do it openly. (*bb*2) ∼ rūwā zaị yi *Vd.* hancị 1*c*. (*bb*3) mū yậnzu, idậmmụ idậnsụ, sǎi harbị now as soon as we espy them, we shoot at them. (*bb*4) kashẹ ∼ *Vd.* kashẹ 10. (*bb*5) tā kadậ masậ ∼ " she gave him the glad eye " (*Vd.* kadậ 1*k*). (*bb*6) idọ hudū *Vd.* hudū 6. (*bb*7) sụ wanƙẹ ∼, sụ ganī let them watch carefully ! (*Vd.* 1*s* below). (*bb*8) yậ kafậ ∼ gậrēsụ he watched them carefully.

(*c*) (i) mun sậ ∼ nē, mụ ga ậbịn dậ zaị yi we're waiting to see what he'll do. mụ sậ ∼ let us remain alert ! let us have a look ! nā sậ masậ ∼ I watched him closely. (ii) sun sậ wậ ậl'amậriŋ ∼ they waited events. mahaụkậcī duk dậ sukậ sậ wậ ∼ har yậ kuɓụcē, lallē sậ kūkā dậ kậnsụ if they stand by idly and let any crazy fellow escape, they'll rue it.

(*d*) ậ idậm mutậnē = ậ idận jậma'ậ publicly. ậ kậŋ idậmmụ sukậ yī they did it in our presence.

(*e*) ∼ yậ yī bậƙō the eye has got some dirt, etc., in it (*hence epithet of* eye Idọ ! bā kậ sam bậƙō = Idọ ! kā ƙi jinim bậƙō Eye, how you hate a guest ! ; *these epithets are also applied to* inhospitable P.).

(*f*) (i) ∼ yậ rēnậ fātậ he's landed himself in trouble. (ii) Idọ, wậ ka rēnậ *Vd.* rēnậ 4.

(*g*) ∼ bậ mūdụ ba, yậ saŋ kīmậ though the eye is not a vessel of measure, it can make a close estimate ; one can draw one's own deductions from the facts.

(*h*) (i) bậ ganiŋ ∼ ba, bậndậ kai bậ wandậ zaị īyậ hậƙurī dậ shī I don't say it to curry favour with you, but you're the only P. who could put up with him. (ii) *Vd.* 1*r below* ; ganī A.2 2*e, f.*

(*j*) (i) yậ būdẹ ∼ dậ ƙīrậ he learnt smithing as a small child. (ii) kudī, har būdẹ masậ ∼ sukẹ yị sabọ dậ yawậ wealth has unbalanced him. (iii) sum fārậ būdẹ ∼ gậ ậmfậninsậ they've begun to realize its value. (iv) yậ būdẹ musụ idọ he brought them to their senses.

(*k*) fịtilận naŋ, ɗaukar ∼ gậrēshị this lamp dazzles. tanậ ɗaukaŋ idọna it's dazzling me.

(*l*) gurbịŋ ∼ (i) eye-socket. (ii) gurbịŋ ∼, idọ nẹ̄ ? mere coincidence does not render the two identical (*x* one's namesake is not oneself).

(*m*) (i) yanā̀ nēmansà ∼ à rụfe he's seeking it eagerly. (ii) sum bī shì ∼ rụfe they obeyed him implicitly. (iii) sun rufę̀ ∼ sun rūgō gàba they (soldiers) charged fearlessly. (iv) àkwai abūbūwà wadàndà dōlę̀ mụ rufę̀ ∼ dàgà gàrēsụ there are matters to which we must turn a blind eye. (v) *Vd.* rụfà idō.

(*n*) sam masà kàɗaɲ, ∼ gubà nē give him (P. seeing you eating) a bit, lest the evil eye fall on you ! kà kịyā̀yi kà ɲkà, ∼ gubà nē beware of stinginess lest the evil eye fall on you !

(*o*) (i) gā̀ ịdọ ? gā̀ rā̀i ? doing brazenly or openly T. which should be done secretly. (ii) *Vd.* cę̀ 1*b*.

(*p*) (i) yā̀ yi ∼ cikiɲ kàrā̀tū he can now write the letters of the alphabet. (ii) yanā̀ idọ = aikinsà ∼ yakę̀ yị̀ = idọ gàrēshị = idā̀nū gàrēshị he's slacking. (iii) yanā̀ ∼ he is one who counts his pence before spending. (iv) yā̀ yị minị̀ ∼ he took the " lion's share " and only gave me a trifle, he imposed unfair share of work on me. (v) gērō yā̀ (dāwà tà) yi idọ = zubà idọ grains have formed in head of bulrush-millet (guinea-corn) = ƙwàntsī (*cf.* 1*b above*).

(*q*) rūwaɲ ∼ gàrēshị he can't make up his mind.

(*r*) (i) *x* idọna mài ganī kę̀ naɲ it is " just in my line ". idànsà kę̀ naɲ mài ganī that's " just in his line " (*cf.* shā̀ dà 2*b*). (ii) *Vd.* 1*h above*.

(*s*) (i) waɲkiɲ ∼ *m.* charm conferring on owner the power to see the invisible ; power to see the invisible. (ii) nā waɲkę̀ (= nā waɲkō) masà ∼ I slapped his face. (iii) baɲ waɲki ∼ ba tụkụnā I've not washed my face yet. (iv) *Vd.* 1*bb*7 *above*.

(*t*) suɲ wārę̀ ∼ they turned aside. (*u*) gamà ∼ *Vd.* gamà 1*h*. (*v*) tsauriɲ ∼ *m.* insolence, shamelessness. (*w*) bā̀ shi dà ta idō he has no sense of propriety.

(*x*) *Vd.* idō-ịdō.

(*y*) *Vd.* idọn-*compounds*.

(*z*) (i) idàntà bā̀ rāɓā *Vd.* rāɓā 1*b*. (*z*) (ii) tsōkànē idọ *Vd.* tsōkànē 1*b*, 2. (*z*) (iii) darē à ∼ *Vd.* darē 7. (*z*) (iv) idànsà bīyū *Vd.* bīyū 4. (*z*) (v) rashiɲ ∼ *Vd.* wadai 2. (*z*) (vi) cikà ∼ *Vd.* cikà 1*h*. (*z*) (vii) fariɲ ∼ *Vd.* banzā 1*h*. (*z*) (viii) cịyā̀wàr ∼ = hakīyà. (*z*) (ix) *Vd.* wutsīyàr idọ.

(2) *proverbs.* (*a*) (i) àbiɲ yā̀ zō dăidăi, mài ∼ ɗayā yā̀ lēƙà būtà what unexpected luck ! (ii) *cf.* 2*d*. (*b*) sài bā̀kī yā̀ cī, ∼ kę̀ kunyà P. who has accepted bribe reveals this by the shifts he adopts. (*c*) " Idọ, wā̀ ka rēnà " (*reply,* " wàndà nikę̀ ganī yau dà gọ̄be ") familiarity breeds contempt (*cf.* 1*f above*). (*d*) mài ∼ ɗayā yā̀ fi màkāfọ gōmà duk dà ụbansụ gàrārà half a loaf is better than no bread (*cf.* 2*a*). (*e*) iɲ ∼ zài ɓatà, yà ɓatà à tsakàr kā if you *must* squander your money, do so yourself rather than give it to some rogue to do so ! (*f*) (i) cīwaɲ ∼ sài haƙurī what cannot be cured must be endured. (ii) mài cīwaɲ ∼ *Vd.* tàmfā. (*g*) idàn dà ya ga Sarkī dọ̄miɲ Gàlā̀dīmà ɗàzu nē from pathos to bathos ! ; from the sublime to the ridiculous. (*h*) ∼ bā̀ yā̀ mutūwà, tōzàlī yà tā̀shē shì T. once spoiled never regains its pristine value. (*j*) idàn dà ya ga hayā̀ƙī, shī ya kàn ɗēbō wutā̀ everyone is best suited to look after his own affairs. (*k*) ganiɲ ∼ bā̀ yā̀ hanà ciɲ kā̀i friendship does not necessarily mean that one sacrifices one's own interests (*Vd.* 1*h above*). (1) bā̀ƙō nā̀ dà ∼ bā̀ na ganiɲ gàrī ba the novice differs greatly from the expert. (*m*) bā̀ƙō màkāfọ nē, kō yanā̀ dà ∼ a talented novice is still a novice. (*n*) haushin rashi, an cę̀ dà màkāfọ

" gǎ idǫ ! ", ya cę̌ " mę̌ ząn yi dą shī ąbu mąi wārį " it's sour grapes. (o) mąi zurfįŋ ∼ dą wurī yakę̌ sōmą kūkā a stitch in time saves nine. (p) kunyąr idǫ Vd. hūtąlī. (q) ∼ sǎi yą yi rūwā Vd. tańą 1b. (r) bā ą̌ wą ∼ Vd. shą̌-makį 3b.

idō-įdǫ x mun yi ∼ dą shī he and I saw one another.

idǫn-compounds (1) idąn dājį guide not needing to rely on roads or tracks. (2) idąn dōkį " chestnut " on horse's leg. (3) (re articles) x mąi kyąu nē na idąn dūnīyą it is excellent. fįtilą cē ta idąn dūnīyą it is a fine lamp. (4) idąŋ hannū distal end of the ulna. (4A) idąŋ hąsārą Vd. tsōnę 3. (5) idąŋ hazbīyā Vd. hazbīyā. (6) idąŋ itącē knot in wood. (7) idąn jawąrā = idąn zawąrā (a) type of black-and-blue native cloth (= ka-tąngā 3). (b) = 9A below. (c) one of the types of ząyyaną. (8) idąŋ ƙafą = idąn sau ankle. (9) idąŋ kwą̌dī very watery farau-farau. (9A) idąŋ kwar-tūwā lines of embroidered dots in kāmuŋ ƙafą trousers (= 7b above = ɗis-ɗis = ɗigē-ɗigē). (10) idąm mą̌gē = idąm mussą type of green bead. (11) idąm mōtą silver coins on woman's temples. (12) kudī sun yi ∼ muzūrū in gambling (cācā), all four cowries fell face-up. (13) ∼ rūwā (a) spring of water (= Sk. marmarō). (b) yā tsōnę idąn rūwā = yā tsōkąnę idąn rūwā he selected the " pick of the bunch " (= wāgā 3b). (c) Vd. tsōnę 2b. (14) ∼ safąrą cuteness of itinerant trader. (15) x (a) kwānā bīyū bąŋ ga ∼ sanį ba I've not seen any of my acquain-tances lately. Allą yą fid dą ∼ sanį may it not befall any acquaintance of mine ! (b) yā yi minį ∼ sanį he favoured me because of previous acquaintance with me. (16) ∼ sānįyā (a) type of glass marble with coloured heart. (b) the plant gautaŋ kūrā. (17) ∼ sau Vd. 8. (18) yā yi musu ∼ yāƙį he (P. familiar with the terrain) surprised his companions by preceding them at the destination, they thinking him far behind. (19) ∼ ząkarą the twiner tā ga rā̄nā or its seeds. (20) ∼ zawąrā

Vd. 7. (21) idąn zāki one of the types of ząyyaną.

ifē m. woven tukurwā-leaves for covering woman's load.

į'fe-įfē" m. loud clamour (Vd. īhu).

ifu = īhu.

īgbįrą f. Igbirra.

Igę Sk. name for any woman named Ƙande.

įgidī Sk. m. = kwarąmī.

igīyą f. (pl. igīyōyī = Kt. įgwai). (1) (a) rope. (b) kōwā ya bą̄ ∼, ∼ tą̌ bā shį if you deposit T. with an honest P., you will get it back safely. (c) Vd. azzįkī 1h, ciką 1c, tsīrā 1b.iii. (d) ɗaurą dą ∼ Vd. dąbārą 3. (e) yā zargą ƙaransą ∼ he has gone away. (f) igīyąr bąutā Vd. yąŋkę 1c.iii. (2) chevron of N.C.O. x yā ci ∼ gudą he's been promoted to lance-corporal (cf. cī 4a). (3) (a) yā warwąrę igīyąr ąlkāwąrī he broke his promise. (b) an rātąyā masą igīyąr laifī he has been falsely blamed. (4) ∼ taną wuyąŋką you cannot evade this duty. (5) tąfāshīyą-bark for medicine. (6) four lengths (ząr hudū) of thread for weaving. (7) igīyąr aurē = sądāki, i.e. money-present by bridegroom to bride (minimum is sixpence, but previously was 1,300 cowries) (igīyąr aurē is also called rubu dīną d.f. Ar. rub'u dīnārin), Vd. aurē 6c. (8) igīyąr dabīnǫ string of 100 or 200 dates. (8A) (i) row of beads in necklace x dūwą̌tsū ∼ gōmą ten rows of beads (= kurfō 4). (ii) Vd. kįlįshī 2. (9) igīyąr jinī vein, artery. (10) (a) igīyąr ƙasą any snake. (b) Vd. tańą 1f. (11) igīyąr rūwā current of the water. (12 igīyąr sāƙą = 6.

igōgī Vd. įgwā.

Igudą = Tąŋkǫ.

igwā m. (sg., pl.) pl. igōgī artillery-gun. mąnya-mąnyaŋ igwā guns of large calibre.

įgwai Vd. igīyą.

*įhįsānį Ar. m. kindness.

įhō = ę̌fau.

īhu m. (1) (a) shouting to call attention x yā bugą musu ∼ he shouted to them (= kūwą = kurūrūwą), cf. sōwą. (b) kadą ku yi ∼ haƙą don't kick up such a row ! (c) sun yi īhu bāyaŋ harį " they locked the stable after the horse had gone." (2) **ihụŋkạ banzā** dense bush (= **kūwạ le** = **ƙwaŋƙōlī 2**).

i'i A. (**ī'ị**) no !
    B. (**īī**) *Vd.* **ī 2b**.

ı'ici *m.* (1) affectation. (2) being busybody.

i"ijē *Vb.* 1C kept on pushing (*int. from* **ijẹ**).

ı'ınā *f.* stuttering.

ı'irıcī *Kt. m.* affectation.

i"izā *Vb.* 1C kept on pushing T. on to (*int. from* **izạ**).

ijābạ *Vd.* **sadakạ**.

ijārạ *Ar. f.* (1) (*a*) wages (= **lādā 1**). (*b*) **sun yi** ~ they've agreed on rate of wages to be paid. (*c*) commission (= **lạ'adạ**). (*d*) fee for sending court-messenger for witness.

ije A. (**ijẹ**) *Vb.* 1A. (1) pushed aside. (2) **aŋ** ~ **itạcē, yā ƙārẹ** all the firewood has been used up in the fire.
    B. (**ijē**) *m.* **yā yi makạ** ~ he hinted to stranger to look for quarters in your house (= **dōdạnā 5**).

iji *m.* (1) (*secondary v.n. of* **izạ**) *x* **yanạ ijiŋ wutā** = **yanạ izạ wutā**. (2) acting as in **izạ** *x* **yanạ** ~ he's pushing outer unburnt ends of firewood into centre of fire.

ijiyạ *Sk. f.* (1) eye (= **idọ** *q.v.*). (2) cowrie (= **wurı**). (3) **ijīyạr** *Vd.* **idọn**.

ijıyē *Vb.* 1C = **ijẹ**.

ijtihādi *m.* = **ittihādi**.

ıkacī *Kt. m.* (1) affectation. (2) contrariety. (3) meddlesomeness (= **fi'ilī**).

ikāyạ *f.* (1) appointment to meet P. (2) interval for paying debt (= **ajạlī**).

*****ikirārı** *Ar. m.* confession.

Ikkō *f.* Ikoyi, *i.e.* Lagos (*epithet in songs is* **Tābạ maị shigā zūcī**).

*****iklīmi** (*Ar.* " continent ") *m.* (1) independent area. (2) paramount Chief.

Ikọ *m.* (1) (*a*) power, control *x* (i) **yanạ cikiŋ ıkwaŋ Sarkiŋ Kanọ** he is under the authority of the Emir of Kano. (ii) **bạ shi dạ** ~ **yạ cẹ "ı" kō " ạ'ạ "** he is powerless. (iii) **maị** ~ *m.*, *f.* (*pl.* **mạsū** ~) leader, commander. (iv) **maị ıkwạn jirgī** ship's captain. (*b*) (i) **dạ** (= **bisạ gạ**) **ıkwaŋ Allạ** God willing . . . (ii) **ıkwaŋ Allạ** fancy !, how wonderful ! (iii) **kạmin sāmuŋ**

hạdā-hadā tạ yi kạmar dạ, sǎi wani ıkwạŋ Allạ it is only by some factor out of the ordinary that the ground-nut trade will reach its old high level. (2) (*a*) **yā nūnạ mini** ~ he behaved arrogantly to me. (*b*) **kạ kāwō mini ıkọ** ? what ! do you treat me with such arrogance ?

ikyakkyạrī *Kt. m.* the drum **kyakkyarē**.

ila A. (**ılā**) *Ar. f. Kt.* sudden misfortune.
    B. (**ılạ**) *name for any man called* **Sạmā'ılụ**.

Ilāhi *x* **yā Ilāhil arshi** God on high !

ılāhirı (*Ar.* **ılā ākhiri**) *m.* whole *x* **duk ılāhirinsạ** all of it.

ılai = **ılại kụwā** suddenly *x* **anạ zạncansạ sǎi** ~ **gạ shi** = **anạ zạncansạ sǎi ılai min lẹmō kụwā gạ shi** we were talking of him when hey presto, there he was !

ılājẹ = *Kt.* **ılājı** *m.* type of coloured silk.

ilallạ *used in* **tụtur ilallạ** for ever and ever, always (*Vd.* **tụtur**).

ılaulạyī *Kt. m.* = **laulạyī**.

*****ilgāzı** *Ar. m.* (1) allegory. (2) softening import of harsh message.

*****ilhāmı** *Kt. m.* = **ılhāmạ** *Kt. f.* instinct.

ilību = **ilībọ** (*Ar.* **lif**) *m.* type of rope.

*****ilimī** *Ar. m.* (1) knowledge (especially of Muslim Theology). **sunạ dạ** ~ **iriŋ nāsụ** they have their own sort of knowledge. (2) **makarantar** ~ *f.* school for higher Muslim studies after' leaving Koranic school (*cf.* **Alƙur'aŋ 3**).

illa A. (**illạ**) *Ar. f.* (*pl.* **illōlī**). (1) blemish. (2) crime, fault.
    B. (**ıllā**) *Ar.* except *x* **bạ ạbin dạ yakẹ sọ** ~ **wannạŋ** there is nothing he wants except this.
    C. (**illā īyạkā**) *Vd.* **īyạkā 5**.

illı *Sk. m.* = **irlı**.

ilmı = **ilimī**.

Ilọrī *f.* Ilorin.

ilụ *abbreviation of* **Ismạ'īlụ**.

im *Vb.* (*d.f.* **ı** *q.v.* *plus doubling of* '**m** ' *of following* **mạ**, *this process shortening the vowel of* **ı** *since now standing in close syllable*) overcame *x* **dạ kyar mukạ im masạ** we only overcame him with difficulty. **dạ kyar na im mạ dōkinạ** it was with difficulty that I controlled my horse (= **ı** *q.v.*, *but* **im** *cannot be followed by* **wạ**).

*ịmālạ *f.* the sound " ē " (*as in* ɓērā) written in the normal way, i.e., with dot below the letter and ạlịf jā above (*Vd.* gāwaryā).

*ịmāmị *Ar. m.* Imam (= lịmạŋ).

īmānị = *Sk.* ịmancị *Ar. m.* (1) having faith in Islam. Allạ̄ yạ bā mụ cikạ̄wā dạ ∼ God cause us to die in Islam ! (2) ạbịn dạ mukạ yi ∼ ạ kạnsạ what we trusted in, put our faith in.

ịmbẹcī *m.* waterbuck (= gwambạzā *q.v.*).

ịmmā *Ar.* one must either . . . or *x* ∼ kạ bīyā, ∼ kạ tāshị you mụst either pay or move off elsewhere !

in A. (in) if. (1) (*a*) in sun zō (= in dạ sun zō = in sukạ zō = in zā sụ zō = in dạ zā sụ zō) sǎi ṇ tạfī kạ̄sūwā (= ṇ tạfī kạ̄sūwā = zạn tạfī kạ̄sūwā = nạ̄ tạfī kạ̄sūwā) if they come, I'll go to the market (*Vd.* 2 *below*, dạ 14*b*, Mod. Gram. 186). (*b*) *Vd.* ịdaŋ, kạdaŋ. (*c*) (i) in dǎi *Vd.* 5 *below.* (ii) in dạ̄ *Vd.* 9 *below.* (*d*) *Vd.* iŋ kā girmā. (*e*) iŋ kụ̄wā even if *x* iŋ kụ̄wā mā har suŋ kai gidā even if they reach home safely (= kō 7*b*). (*f*) in . . . sạn naŋ if . . . then in that case *x* in ya sam mahạụkạcī nẹ̄, sạn naŋ yạ̄ sạ̄ shi wạzīrị ? if he knows him to be mad, would he appoint him prime-minister ? (*g*) tạrzọ̄mạr, im mā har tā ịsa ạ kirā tạ tạrzọ̄mā the dispute, *if* dispute it can be called. (*h*) if . . . must (Mod. Gram. 106A) *x* in yā zō, sǎi kạ tạmbayạ if he comes, you must ask (*cf.* 1*a above*). sạn dạ na zō, sǎi yạ tạfī kạ̄sūwā when I come, he must go to market. (*j*) sạn dạ ya zō sǎi nā tạmbayạ when comes, I'll certainly ask (Mod. Gram. 186*b*). sạn dạ na zō, sǎi yā tạfī kạ̄sūwā there's no question that he'll insist on going to market once I come. (*k*) im bā *Vd.* bā A.1*e.* (*l*) im bạ̄ . . . ba *Vd.* ba C.1 (*i.e* bạ̄ . . . ba), 2, 3, 4. (*m*) (*sometimes we find* nē *or progressive in one of the clauses*) *x* iŋ kā bā nị, n nạ̄ sọ̄ if you give me it, I'll be pleased. iŋ kā yi jạ̄yayyạ dạ shī, kai nẹ̄ ạ k̆asạ if you quarrel with him, *you* will get the worst of it. in yanạ̄ sọ̄ yạ yī if he wants to do it. iŋ anạ̄ ganin sōjạ, ạ ragẹ fịtinạ if they see soldiers appear, the clamour will die down. (*n*) (*sometimes act of 2nd clause is looked on as certain and put in past tense*) *x* iŋ kā fạɗā, kā fịta if you confess, then the matter is closed. (*o*) (*sometimes* in *is omitted*) *x* (i) kā ajịyē gạ̄lạ̄lạ̄, maị sọ̄ yạ̄ ɗaukạ if you leave it about carelessly, some passer-by may pick it up. (ii) (*sometimes omitted before emphatic word at head of sentence*) Bạhaushẹ mukạ ga dạ yanạ̄ kạrạ̄tunsạ if it is a *Hausa* whom we see reading it.

(*p*) proverbs (*alphabetically*). (i) iŋ A fịta *Vd.* ạ 1*c.* (ii) iŋ akạ sạ̄mi lāmụnī *Vd.* dọ̄dō 10. (iii) iŋ Allạ̄ yā k̆i ạddu'ạ *Vd.* ạddu'ạ 1*c.* (iv) iŋ aŋ gạji *Vd.* rānā 2*l.* (v) iŋ aŋ k̆i *Vd.* mạrāyạ 4. (vi) iŋ aŋ k̆i daụrō *Vd.* daụrō 2. (vii) iŋ A zaunạ tā cẹ̄ *Vd.* zaunạ. (viii) im bạ ạ gạmu ba *Vd.* arạ 2*b.*ii. (ix) im bạ̄ ạ gātarī ba *Vd.* gātarī 1*d.* (*x*) im bạ ạ ji cīwọ ba *Vd.* tuntuɓẹ 2. (xi) im bạ ạ rạgi darē ba *Vd.* rạgā 2. (xii) im bạ ạ zaunạ dạ gịndī ba *Vd.* zaunạ 1*d.* (xiii) ịdam bạ kạ shā dawọ ba *Vd.* shā A.1*d.* (xiv) kạdam tẹ̀ kạ tārạ cin tūwō bạ, *Vd.* shā 1*g.*iii. (xv) im bā kạ̄ yị̄ *Vd.* wurī 1*c.*v, gạba 3*a.*iii. (xvi) im bak̆ī zā kạ yi *Vd.* fafat 2. (xvii*A*) im bạ̄ kwạɗayī *Vd.* kwạɗayī. (xviii) im bạ̄ yāk̆i *Vd.* yāk̆i 1*k.* (xix) in dạ ạbịnk̆ạ *Vd.* ạbụ 2*h.* (xix*A*) in darē *Vd.* nāmạ 1*m*. (xx) in dǎi ɓērā dạ sātạ *Vd.* ɓērā 1*g.* (xxi) in ɗaŋūwaŋkạ yanạ̄ tụnjērē *Vd.* rigạ kafị 1*b.* (xxii) in doŋ ạ cī *Vd.* sayar dạ 4. (xxiii) iŋ hannuŋkạ baị ịsa ba *Vd.* yạ̄f̆ạcē. (xxiv) iŋ idọ zaị ɓatạ *Vd.* ɓatạ 1*d.* (xxv) in jạ̄kī yā ga tọ̄kā *Vd.* birgimā 2. (xxvi) in jīf̆ạ yā wucẹ *Vd.* wucẹ 2*a.*ii. (xxvii) iŋ kā ga aŋ kāmạ zōmō *Vd.* ajạlī 2*e.* (xxviii) iŋ kā ga bạbbar sānīyā *Vd.* mạrak̆ī 1*b.* (xxix) iŋ kā ga ɓarāwọ *Vd.* taskirā 1*b.* (xxx) iŋ kā ga ɓērā 1*c*, sak̆ị 2*b.*ii. (xxxi) iŋ kā ga farī *Vd.* birgimā 4. (xxxii) iŋ kā ga gēmụn *Vd.* gēmụ 1*d.* (xxiii) iŋ kā ga gōdīyā *Vd.* gōdīyā 7. (xxxiv) iŋ kā ga mak̆īyịŋkạ nạ̄ rānā *Vd.* rānā 2*f.*ĩv. (xxxv) iŋ kā ga mụtụm *Vd.* mụtụm 9*h.* (xxxvi) iŋ kā ga mụtụ̆m yanạ̄ rawā *Vd.*

rawā 1g. (xxxvii) iŋ kā ga rāƙumī Vd.
rāƙumī 1h. (xxxviii) iŋ kā ga wani nā
inūwą Vd. inūwą 1a.ii. (xxxix) iŋ kā
girmā Vd. shą talē-talē. (xl) iŋ kā
haƙą rāmį Vd. muguntā 3. (xli) iŋ
ƙąi dą tsōƙą Vd. tsōƙą 2b. (xliA)iŋ kā
ji " ą sansąnā " Vd. ƙanshī. (xlii) iŋ kā
ji mąkāƙo Vd. buge-bugē. (xliii) iŋ
kā ji mąrāyą Vd. mąrāyą 2. (xliiiA)
iŋ kā ƙi mąrāyą Vd. ƙī 2d. (xliv) iŋ
kanā cim ɓaurē Vd. ɓaurē 4. (xlv) iŋ
kanā dą kyau Vd. waŋkā 3. (xlvA) iŋ
kanā dą rąi Vd. rąi 1l. (xlvi) iŋ kanā
tsąye Vd. tsąye 5. (xlvii) iŋ kanā wą
Allā Vd. Allā 4a. (xlviii) iŋ kā rąbu dą
mutum Vd. rąbu 2g. (xlix) iŋ kā zō
garī Vd. wutsīyą 1j. (l) iŋ kunnē yā
ji mugunyąr mąganą Vd. tsērę 2c.
(li) im macįjī yā sąrē ką Vd. tsummā 3.
(liA) im mągē bā tą naŋ Vd. mągē 1b.
(lii) im mawądącī yanā dįŋgishī Vd.
dįŋgishī. (liii) im mūgųn tayį Vd.
ąlbarką 2b. (liv) im mūgūwar kązā
Vd. akurkī 3. (lv) im mutum yā cę
" ịnā zaŋ kwānā " Vd. mutum 9m.
(lvi) im mutum yā cę ząi bā ką rįgā Vd.
rįgā 1o. (lvii) im mutum yā cę ząi hądįyi
gątarī Vd. rikę 1a.iii. (lviii) in nā rēną
kązā Vd. rēną 10. (lix) in nā yi maką rānā
Vd. rānā 4l. (lx) in nōno yanā dą dādī
Vd. nōno 1c. (lxA) in rāƙumī yā ɓatą
Vd. kurątandū. (lxi) in rānā tā fitō
Vd. rānā 1d. (lxii) in rūwaŋką bąi
ịsa ąlwąlā ba Vd. rūwā C.8. (lxiii) in
rūwā yā ci mutum Vd. rūwā C.3.
(lxiv) in tā tāshį lālącęwā Vd. tururuwā.
(lxv) in tā yi rūwā Vd. rījịyā 1h. (lxvi)
iŋ ųŋgųlū tā bīyā Vd. ųŋgųlū 7. (lxviA)
in zā ką dąurę ąkwīyą Vd. magaryā.
(lxvii) in zā ką haƙą Vd. haƙą 1b.
(lxviii) in zā ką hūtą Vd. hūtą 1b.
(lxix) in ƶā ką yi līlo Vd. tsāmīyā 1d.
(lxx) in zā ką yi tąfīyą Vd. tąfīyą 2d.
(lxxi) in zāƙį yā san ząi sąmi nāmą
Vd. sarƙaƙƙīyā 2. (lxxii) in ząmānį
yā dįŋką rįgā Vd. rįgā 1j.

(2) when (same constructions as 1a
above) iŋ kā gamą aikį, ką zō come
when you finish your work ! in suŋ
kōmō, ząi bā sų he'll give them it
when they return (Vd. dą 14b).

(3) whether (i) (after certain verbs) x
ŋ ganī in nā īyą let me see whether I
can ! (= kō 3a.i). (ii) im bisą, iŋ ƙasą
whether on horseback or on foot
(= kō 3b.iv).

(4) in shā Ạllāhụ = Ạllāhụ in shā'ą
God willing . . . (cf. mā shā Ạllāhụ ;
mā shā'ą).

(5) (a) in dăi provided that x ịdaŋ
dăi bukātąssą tā bīyā provided his
wish is fulfilled. in dăi fįtiną tanā
ąukūwā if dissension must break out. in
dăi yanā dą rąi so long as he is at least
alive . . . (b) in dăi doŋ ą dąukę dāna,
săi ŋ ƙī if it's a question of taking away
my son permanently, then I utterly
refuse (Vd. don 3, 4). (c) im bā don
Vd. don 6.

(6) im bā haką ba = im bā hakąnam
ba . . . otherwise . . . sunā kōyō ta
wuriŋ ąbin dą sukę ganī ; im bā haką
ba, kōyad dą sū banzā nę they learn by
ocular proof, otherwise to teach them
would be useless.

(7) (negatively) = dā 4 q.v. x im bā
doŋ haką ba, dā nā yąrdā but for this,
I'd have agreed. duk dąyā nę, im bā
dăi don rashiŋ haŋkąlī ba it was the
same thing if they'd only had the sense
to realize it (cf. ba C1.3a).

(8) (negatively) = dā 1a.iv x im bąn
yi ba, nā tafō dą saurī haką ? had
I not done it, is it likely I'd have come
so soon ?

(9) in dā = dā 1a.iii x in dā 'yaŋ gādį
nē na sōsăi, dā suŋ kāmą ɓarāyįn naŋ
had they been real police, they'd have
caught those thieves.

(10) = dā 2 x in dā ząn sāmu, săi
m bīyā were I to get it, I'd pay.

B. (iŋ) Kt. (1) x gā shi ~ (a) look,
it's here ! (= naŋ). (b) look, it's over
there ! (= caŋ). (2) ~ dą ~ at once
(= naŋ dą naŋ).

C. *Vd.* ṇ that I may, *etc.*

ina A. (inā̱) (*progressive 3rd sg.*) *x* ~
zūwa̱ = yina̱ zūwa̱ he's coming (*N.B.*—
n na̱ zūwa̱ I'm coming).
B. *(ina̱) *f.* stuttering (= i̱'i̱nā).
C. (i̱nā) (1) (*a*) (i) where ? *x* ~ yakē =
yana̱ i̱na̱ where is it ? (*Vd.* kō 2*d*). (ii)
(at head of sentence i̱nā = a̱ i̱nā) *x*
a̱ i̱nā yakē = i̱nā yakē where is it ?
i̱nā (= a̱ i̱nā) ka ji wanna̱ṇ where did
you hear this ? (iii) i̱nā a̱bi̱n da̱ ya
gama̱ ka da̱ ni̱ what have I to do with
your affairs ? ~ a̱bi̱n da̱ ya sa̱ suka̱
yi̱ why did they do so ? (iv) yā cē
" i̱nā sū " he said " a fig for them ! "
(*cf.* don 2). (v) i̱nā wani wa̱nda̱ māla̱-
minsa̱ ya rūɗō shi̱ you're no match for
me ! (vi) sū " i̱nā Sarkī ya kwānā "
nē they're slackers. i̱nā za̱ṇ kwānā *Vd.*
mu̱tu̱m 9*m.* (vii) i̱nā yakē da̱ ka̱sūwa̱
where is it relatively to the market ?
(viii) i̱nā wani ya̱ bā ni̱ who would give
me it ? (ix) ~ da̱ mana̱ni̱ *Vd.* nāne̱.
(x) ~ ni̱, i̱nā hana̱ ka̱ who am *I* to
forbid you ! (xi) ~ akē ɗimi̱ *Vd.*
tsararrīyā. (xii) i̱nā da̱līli̱ *Vd.* da̱līli̱.
(xiii) i̱nā wani hatsi̱ṇ *Vd.* da̱urō 2.
(xiv) i̱nā tukunyar damō *Vd.* damō 6.
(xv) i̱nā a̱kwīya̱ za̱ ta *Vd.* tāki̱ 2*a.*ii.
(xvi) i̱nā a̱mfāni̱ṇ ƙiba̱ *Vd.* ta̱lōlō.
(xvii) i̱nā ƙābaṇka̱ *Vd.* ƙābā 2*h.*

(2) (Mod. Gram. 160*a*, 178*b*). (*a*)
whence ? *x* yā fitō i̱nā = i̱nā ya fitō
where has he come from ? (*b*) whither ?
x yā jē i̱nā = i̱nā ya jē where did he go ?
i̱nā zūwa̱ where are you off to ?

(3) how *x* (*a*) ~ za̱i jā su̱ fada̱ how
could he possibly provoke them ? ~ ga̱
kā ƙāra̱ bā su dāmā, su̱ṇ ƙāra̱ ƙarfi̱ (if
that is what has happened) whatever
would happen in the case where you gave
them more scope and they became more
powerful ! (*Vd.* ga̱ 10). (*b*) i̱nā sūna̱ṇka̱
what is your name ? (= wa̱nē 1). (*c*)
i̱nā lābāri̱ what's the news ? (*reply*
sǎi a̱lhēri̱ " fine ! "). (*d*) (i) i̱nā
(= kō i̱nā) da̱bāra̱ what's to be done ? (ii)
cf. kōi̱nā. (*e*) i̱nā gajīya̱ I hope you're
feeling rested ? (*reply* bā ga̱jīya̱ = sǎi ta

ya̱u = A̱lhamdu̱ = A̱lhamdu̱ li̱llāhi̱).
(*f*) (i) i̱nā ji̱n sanyi̱ how are you enjoying
the cold weather? (*reply* A̱lhamdu̱ li̱llāhi̱).
(ii) *Vd.* ƙāƙa̱ 1*c.* (iii) *Vd.* wa̱hala̱ 1*e.*
(*g*) ~ nakē i̱ya̱ zamā i̱nda̱ bābu̱ rūwa̱
how can I live where there is no water ?
~ ya̱dda̱ za̱n yi̱ what am I to do ?
i̱nā kuka̱ ga am mutu̱, a̱ṇ kōmō̱ how
could you possibly believe that the
dead return ? ~ ya̱dda̱ aka̱ yi̱ = i̱nā
ya̱dda̱ aka̱ yi wanna̱ṇ haka̱ how did
this happen ? yā yi ~ fasa̱li̱ haka̱
how was he able to organize it like
this ? (*h*) i̱nā rūwāna̱, *etc.*, *Vd.* rūwā G,
D4.

(4) (*a*) ~ aka̱ saka̱ = *Nor.* i̱nā i̱ṇka̱
aza̱ = *Nor.* ~ nika̱ saka̱ (*a*) type of
game. (*b*) *Vd.* ka̱ 2*b.*i. (*b*) yana̱ ~ aka̱
saka̱ da̱ ganinsa̱ he's in a flutter of
joyful excitement at unexpectedly
seeing him (Mod. Gram. 140*c*) =
ta̱raira̱ya̱ 1. (*c*) sun ɗa̱uki bāƙi̱ṇ ~
nika̱ saka̱, ~ nika̱ saka̱ they welcomed
the guests with open arms. (*d*) an yi
masa̱ ~ ka saka̱ = ɗauka̱n 'yam makarantā 1.

(5) ana̱ na̱ṇ, ra̱n na̱ṇ, ~ ya̱ Alla̱,
bābu̱ ya̱ Alla̱, sǎi ya sa̱mi da̱bāra̱
then one day, he suddenly bethought
himself of a plan (*cf.* yā 2).

(6) i̱nā (*a*) how can that be ! how on
earth can I ! where on earth could I get
it ! (*b*) a̱mmā i̱nā but to what avail ? (*c*)
kā ta̱fi fatauci̱ nē ? (*reply*, fatauci̱ fa i̱nā)
have you been away peddling ? (*reply*,
how *can* I have been !). (*d*) bā mu da̱
shī (*reply*, bā ku da̱ shī i̱nā) we have
none ! (*reply*, but you *must* have some !).
(7) i̱nā *Nor.* yes ! (*replying to P.
calling one*) = na̱'am.
*i̱na̱bī *Ar. m.* (*sg.*, *pl.*). (1) grape. (2)
vine. (3) rūwa̱ṇ ~ *m.* wine.
inci *Eng. m.* inch.
i̱nda̱ = i̱nda̱ (1) (*a*) where *x* (i) ba̱n sa̱ṇ
~ yakē ba I don't know where it is.
(ii) ~ ka sa̱ ga̱ba, nan nē hanya̱ if
you really want a thing, you can get
it by trying hard. (iii) ta ~ aka̱ hau,
ta na̱ṇ a ka̱n sa̱uka stick to the man

whom you serve ! (iv) ∽ akạ kạrɓi
dãrĩyar mạkãfọ, naŋ ya kạm fasạ
ƙwaryã if you like a person, he can do
no wrong in your eyes. (v) ∽ wutã
ta kãmạ, naŋ a kạm bĩ tạ, ạ ji dịmintạ
go where fortune awaits you ! (vi)
Vd. shã dạ 2b. (vii) ∽ wani ya ƙĩ Vd.
yinị 1a.iv. (viii) ∽ akạ san darajạr
gõrõ Vd. ganyē 1c. (ix) ∽ mại gudụ
ya kai Vd. hạƙurạ 1d. (x) ∽ akạ sạri
kērē Vd. kērē. (xi) ∽ ya tsịnci wurị
Vd. tsịntã 2b. (xii) ∽ fãtạ ta yi tabshĩ
Vd. jĩmạ 4. (b) (ịndạ can be used as a
noun) x bạ sụ sạmi ∽ yakē ba they did
not find the place where he was. (c)
(with dative-preposition) wannạm bugụ,
bạ wạndạ ya saŋ ∽ zã sụ kai wạ
nobody knows whither they will carry
this attack. (2) (a) whereby x sụ sạmi
aɓõkan cịnikĩ ∽ zã sụ riƙạ sãi dạ
kãyansụ let them seek business
associates whereby to market their
goods ! (cf. dạ 12a). (b) way whereby x
bạ ∽ zã kụ ƙãrạ tabbạtãwã sãi kuŋ
waiwạyã there's no better way of convincing yourself than by examining
into the question. (3) duk ∽ mukạ
nēmã, bạ mụ sạmē shị ba wherever we
looked we failed to find it. ∽ sukạ jē
dukạ, sãi suŋ gan shị wherever they
went, they saw him. ∽ duk ka lēƙạ,
sãi kạ ga . . . wherever one's eye falls,
one sees that . . . (Mod. Gram. 185).
(4) Sk. = wurin x nã zõ ∽ Sarkĩ I've
come to see the Chief. (4) Nor. indạ
where ? (= ịnã).

Indãɓọ f. (1) name of town in Kano
Province. (2) yã tạfi ∽ he's very angry.

indạhū Vd. darạs.

indạllãhị Vd. darạs.

indã-indã = ịndã-ịndã f. giving indecisive
replies.

ịndararõ m. (pl. ịndạrạrai). (1) roof-drain
of flat-topped houses (= mazurãrĩ 1a).
(2) shĩ ∽ nē, yanã bạ jējị rūwã he
neglects his family and favours
strangers (cf. giginyạ 2).

*ịndịkyã f. farming, wood-cutting, dyeing,
weaving, sewing, etc., for payment
(= yĩmạ).

Indõ Vd. yãyĩ 5.

ịndororõ m. = ịndararõ.

---

iŋ ga Vd. ganĩ A.1 5.

ịŋgãjirã f. large pot for storing corn, etc.
(= gãjirmĩ).

iŋgạlãlạ f. (1) cotton-fluff. (2) nap of
material.

iŋganci m. durability x sãƙạ mại ∽ well
woven material. yã fi wancạŋ ∽ this
one's the more durable. yanã dạ ∽
he's burly.

iŋganta A. (iŋgạntã) Vb. 1C strengthened,
reinforced.
    B. (ịŋgantạ) Vb. 3B. (1) is (was)
strong and durable. (2) lãɓãrịn naŋ
yã ∽ that report has become verified.

iŋgạntaccē = iŋgãtaccē.

iŋgaramci Kt. m. = iŋgarmanci.

iŋgạrfai Sk. m. clogs (= dạŋgạrạfai q.v.).

iŋgarmạ m. (f. iŋgarmĩyã = Nor. iŋ-
garamnĩyã) pl. iŋgạrmū = iŋgạrmai =
iŋgarmõmĩ. (1) large stallion. (2)
burly P. (3) ∽ gadõ = 1. (4) iŋgarmạ
gidan talạkạ hạrãmuŋ it's impossible. (5) kadạ dãi iŋgarmạ yạ rēnạ
gudụŋ ƙūrụ never despise a weak P.,
you may need him some day. (6)
Vd. sayar dạ 2.

iŋgarmanci m. being big and strong.

iŋgãtaccē m. (f. iŋgãtaccĩyã) pl. iŋgãtạttū
(1) durably made. (2) (re P.) (a)
healthy. (b) burly.

iŋgatūtạ (used in songs by young people)
penis.

iŋgidĩdọ m. tree Cratœva Adansonii (has
edible leaf) (= Sk. gūdãi).

iŋgijē Vb. 1C Kt. pushed over (= aŋ-
gajē q.v.).

Iŋgịlạ Eng. f. England.

Iŋgịlịs = Iŋgịlĩshị (1) m., f. (sg., pl.)
English P. (2) m. safety-matches
which are reliable as not being suddenly
inflammable.

iŋgiricĩ m. (1) hay (= Sk. tạttakã 3 =
Sk. barọ 3). (2) yanã dạ ∽ he has a
bit put by for a " rainy day ". (3) ∽
yã ci dõkị : karmãmĩ yã ci sãnĩyã
said when P. who'd normally expect
gift from another, has to provide gift
for the latter.

iŋgirĩkọ Kaffi Hausa m., f. bastard
(= shēgẹ).

iŋgirmạ Nor. = iŋgarmạ.

iŋgiza = aŋgaza.

iŋgō here is a present or what's owing to you ! (= uŋgō).

iŋgōzọ̄mạ = uŋgōzọ̄mạ.

iŋguddugī = guddugī.

iŋgụrnū m. type of potash.

*iŋgūwā f. (pl. iŋgūwōyī = iŋgwạnnī = Kt. iŋgunnị) town-ward (= uŋgūwā q.v.).

iŋgwại Sk. (1) Vd. hō, sabbinanị. (2) fine !

iŋgwallọ m. (1) hip-joint (head of femur-bone) = kụtōlọ = kwạtạŋgwalọ = agụdī. (2) socket in pelvis for femur-head.

iŋgwạyyā Sk. (1) fine ! (2) Vd. sabbinanị ; hō.

iŋ'ịnā f. stuttering.

injahạu = injihạu.

injarī m. stream.

injị Eng. m. (1) (a) engine. (b) yā tā dạ ⁓ he started up the motor. (c) suŋ hau injin tākalmạ they went at a fast pace. (d) sun sạki injị, bạ darē, bạ rānā they sped along incessantly. (2) spring of watch x (a) am bā shị ⁓ it (clock) has been wound up (= wānị 1 = rūwā A.21). (b) ⁓ yā yi sanyī spring's run down.

injihạu m. the cobra tsādạrākị (epithet is mại sārā ɗayā) = bạ kūkaŋ hạntsī.

Injīlụ m. (Ar.-Gk. euangelion) Gospels ; New Testament (= Lịnjīnā).

injiŋ m. = injị.

injīnīyạ Eng. m. (sg., pl.) engineer.

iŋ kā girmā, kạ rāmạ Sk. the game shạ talē-talē.

iŋkallạ Abbạ hallo, how are you ? I hear you're now a regular Crœsus ! (reply, Allā hạnī).

iŋkārị Ar. (1) x yā yi minị ⁓ he was dubious about the truth of what I said. (2) concluding x ⁓ mukạ yi zại zō yạu we came to conclusion he'd come to-day. *(3) denial.

iŋkẹ = iŋkị used in bạ ⁓ ba nẹ̄, bạ wai ba nẹ̄ = bạ wai ba, bạ ⁓ ba there's no possible doubt about it.

iŋkịs m. (Ar. anqasa) x yā sạ minị ⁓ he found objections to, found flaws in my argument (= Kt. sūkạn lạmīrī).

inna A. (innạ = ịnnā) f. (1) (a) mother ; maternal aunt, etc. (epithet is ⁓,

ūwā bạ̄ dạ mạ̄mā) = ūwā q.v. (b) Vd. yạ̄yā A.1, 2h ; īyạ. (2) Mother ! (3) (a) Innạ = Dōgwā name of a bọrī-spirit, mother of Bāwạ mạ̄kau, hence (b). (b) Innạ tā shạnyē masạ ƙafạ his leg's become paralysed (= dawạ 5a q.v.), cf. son 2, 7 ; zanzanā 3 ; bạfilātạnā 3. (c) anạ̄ tsọ̄raŋ Innạ, ṇ ji 'yā'yam mạyyā = anạ̄ tsọ̄ran nī dạ īyạ, ṇ ji 'yā'yam mạyyā (cf. nī dạ ūwā) " needs must when the devil drives ". (d) kalwā tā saŋ ⁓ ; ⁓ tā saŋ kalwā " watch your step how you act to me ! " (4) Zar. innạ here x gạ̄ shi ⁓ look, it's here !

B. (ịnnā) f. (1) testing probity or knowledge of P. (2) Vd. innạ.

innạcē Vd. innatạ.

innạhū x innạhū ạlā kulli shai'iŋ ƙạdīrụŋ God is omnipowerful !

innạ̄-ịnnạ̄ Kt. f. dilatoriness.

innānạhā = innānịhā = Kt. innānạhāyạ (Ar. annihāya) extreme x gwạnī nẹ̄ na ⁓ he's very skilled.

innạrididị used in tạ̄raŋ ⁓ gạyyar wọ̄fī crowd of useless parasites.

innatạ Vb. 2 (p.o. innạcē, n.o. innạci) tested probity or knowledge of P.

innīyā Nor. here x gạ̄ shi ⁓ look, here it is ! in shā Ạllāhụ Vd. in 4.

intạhā f. (Ar. end). (1) ạbin yā kai ⁓ matters have become serious. (2) yā kai nị ⁓ I cannot stand it any longer.

intāwō Vd. ṇtāwō.

intāyạ Zar. f. the cereal accạ.

inūwạ f. (pl. inūwōyī). (1) (a) (i) shade. (ii) iŋ kā ga wani nẹ̄ ⁓, wani yanạ̄ rānā = wandạ yakẹ̄ ⁓ bại saŋ wani yanạ̄ rānā ba one half of the world doesn't know how the other half lives. (iii) inūwạr gạbạ̄rūwā, gạ̄ sanyī, gạ̄ ƙayạ what a capricious person ! (iv) kōwā ya yi kāshī ạ ⁓ yạ̄ bar tạ if you spoil your chances, it is yourself you have to blame. (v) baƙar ⁓ gwạmmạ rānā dạ kẹ̄ better an honest stranger than a false friend. (vi) in zā kạ hūtạ, hụ̄ta ạ bạbbar ⁓ whatever your hand finds to do, do it with all your might ! (vii) kōmē ka shūkạ, kạ shā ⁓ tasạ bạndạ mụtụm only man is vile. (viii) inūwạr gēmụ Vd. mạƙōgwạrō 6.

(b) shadow x tĕkū tā kŏmą cikįŋ ∼ tasy their shadow fell over the sea. (c) reflection. (d) title for any man named Muhammadu. (2) inūwąr giginyą, na nēsą ką shā sanyī neglecting one's family and favouring strangers (Vd. Mod. Gram. 140b) = barēwā 1b. (3) nā yi masą ∼, yā yi minį rānā he repaid my good with evil (= rānā 4l). (4) (a) dą nī, dą shī săi inūwąd darē ta gamą mu he and I are deadly enemies. (b) Vd. garmā 2b. (5) Vd. shirįm, ząuna inūwą. (6) yaŋą babbar ∼ he has a powerful protector. (7) yā shā inūwąr māsū he is a great warrior. (8) yā nūną minį ∼ he told me a lie. zancan nąŋ ∼ nē this is a lie. (9) (a) yā shā ∼ = yā ji sanyįŋ ∼ he's skilled at his craft. (b) sanyįŋ ∼ yā dĕbē shį (i) he fell asleep. (ii) it was mere tittle-tattle on his part. (10) yā shā ∼ he told a lie. (11) gajērē nę kąmar inūwąr allī he is very short. (12) yā sąyi ∼ (i) he bought T. without having seen it. (ii) he " bought a pig in a poke ". (13) suŋ kāsąyę inūwąrsy they spoiled their chances.

inūwancē Vb. 1D = inūwantą Vb. 2 (p.o. inūwancē, n.o. inūwanci) shaded, gave shade to.

inūwantad dą Vb. 4B = inūwąncē.

inyāwarā f. West African genet (= rabbī 2 = alwąrā = murdīyā 2 = cimōlą = tąmaŋgulā).

*inzālį Ar. m. orgasm.

in zaram maku Vd. ŋ.

inzu Nor. = yąnzu.

irāmį Zar. = irāmę Kt. m. (lit. holemaker) the wasp zanzarō.

i're-irē" Vd. iri 10.

iri (1) m. (a) seed(s) (pl. also irūrūwą). (b) ą kai iri gidā Vd. māząyā. (c) nikę iri Vd. dąmunā 3. (d) bą iri ba cę Vd. mōdā 2. (2) offspring. (3) stock x Hausāwā duk ∼ gudā nę the Hausas are all of the same stock. kai wąnę ∼ nę of what tribe are you ? irinsy nē su kąŋ yi irįŋ ąl'ądun nąŋ it's the tribes related to them who observe these kind of customs.

(4) the kind (followed by pl. or sg.

noun) x sabo dą irįŋ kaşarsy because of the kind of country they live in. irįŋ abūbūwąŋ dą mukę sō the kind of things we like. wannąm bą irįŋ ąbincinsą kę nam ba this is not the sort of food to suit him. irįn dādįn dą nakę jį such delight as I'm experiencing.

(5) kind. (a) (" every ", " a certain ", " which ? ", " whatever ", (and, when they precede iri, " these " or " those "), correspond in gender and number NOT with irįn but with the noun following irįn) x wąnę irįm mutum what kind of person ? wącę irįm mącē what sort of woman ? wata irįn dabbą a certain kind of animal. wadansu irįm mutąnē certain kinds of people. wadąnnąŋ irįn sūnąyē these kind of names. yā yāfę minį dukąŋ irįn daŋgįn ąbįn dą na yi masą he pardoned me every kind of thing I'd done to him. duk irįŋ wa'ązįn dą kę bākiŋką whatever exhortations you're giving. kō-wącę irįŋ kūrā ta zō whatever kind of hyena comes. wannąŋ rīgā wącę iri cę what kind of gown is this ? wannąŋ ajīyą bą irįŋ wąddą dą kā sō shan dąbgē, săi ką dībą this is not the sort of deposit you can cash in order to " go on the spree ". (b) (i) (usually, contrary to the English order of the sentence, " this ," " that," " these," " those," and adjectives follow irįn, cf. 5a, 6b) x irįŋ wannąm matsayī this kind of status. irįŋ wadąnnąŋ these kind of things. irįŋ wannąŋ wąhalą that kind of trouble. irįm mąganąŋ nąŋ this kind of talk. kadą ką yi irįŋ wannąŋ do not do this sort of thing ! irįm mąnyam mąkąrantun naŋ kąmar su A the big type of schools like A, etc. irįn tsōfaffim ɓarāyįn naŋ the old-fashioned kind of thieves. irįn nāsą māi = irįm mąnsą his kind of oil. ą irįŋ halinsy in view of the nature of their character. zā sy riką kōyą mąną irįŋ kąrątunsy they will institute for us their type of education. fātū irįm māsū gajēraŋ gāshį the short-haired type of (goat) skins. irįŋ kōmįn naŋ

wadanda akē daukōwā cikim manyan jirāgē those kind of small boats which are carried on steamers (*note pl. relative*). (ii) (*but* duk *precedes* irin) *x* cikin duk irin wāsannī in all types of games.

(6) kinds (*if adjective precedes, it is* plural) *x* wadansu iri other kinds. wadansu irin jirāgē bīyū two kinds of boats. kōwadannē irim ma'aikatā all kinds of workmen. sauran irin wadannan others of the same kind. manyan irin abincinsu their principal types of food. da sauran irinsu da yawa there are many other kinds of them. irin abincin da mukē ci the various kinds of food which we eat. irinsu da yawa there are many kinds of them.

(7) *noun m.,f.* (*sg.,pl.*) one(s) like, that which is like, etc., *x* irin tāka one like yours. yanā da wani māganī, bābu irinsa he owns a drug which has no equal. ka kāwō irin wadannan bring some like these! irin kāyan zubin azurfā the kind of thing used for casting silver. irin halin nan nāku na cutar jama'a people of your type who trick the public. irinku people like you. irin zamansu the way they live.

(8) *adj., m., f.* (*sg., pl.*) who is like *x* Batūre irin Tūrāwan gabas a European like the Eastern Europeans. zānā kō irinta a woven grass-mat, etc.

(9) irin *prep.* like (i) wandō irin na dā trousers like the previous ones. rīgā irin ta yau a gown like to-day's. sānīyā irin tāka a cow like yours. bā wanda ya yanka mutānē irin Sīdi there's never been such a butcher of people as Sidi. fātū (= fātun) irim buzurwan nan skins like that of this long-haired goat. (ii) bā aikin da sukē, irin yi musu hari they devote all their efforts to raiding them.

(10) i're-irē" *x* kāwō ire-iransu = kāwō irinsu bring some like them.

(11) iri-iri of various sorts *x* littattāfai iri-iri = littattāfai iri-iri dabandaban various kinds of books.

(12) irim bā kwīyābā *m.* corn cadged ostensibly for sowing, but actually for eating.

īrīrī *Sk. m.* anā ~ da shī he's being disparaged, etc. (= dīdīdī *q.v.*).

irli *m.* (*Ar.* honour) *used in* an ci irlinsa = an kētā irlinsa he's been put to shame.

irurūwa *Vd.* iri 1.

is (1) kneel, camel! (2) get up, camel! (3) = kisha.

isa A. (isa) *Vb.* (1) (*no progressive*). (*a*) (i) yā ~ it is (was) sufficient. (ii) Allā yā ~ God will provide! (iii) " Allā yā isa " bā tā fādūwā kasa banzā he who trusts in God will not be disappointed. (iv) mun yi Allā ishē mu *Vd.* 2*b below*. (*b*) is worthy that, is (was) of the kind to *x* laifinsa yā ~ a tūbē shi his crime is serious enough for him to be deposed. bā wanda ya ~ ya yi haka nobody can (may) do so. shī bai ~ ka jē gidansa ba he's not the sort of man you need (ought to) visit. tarzōmar, im mā har tā ~ a kirā ta tarzōmā the dispute, if dispute it can be called (*cf.* 3*b below*).

(2) (*p.o.* ishē, *n.o.* ishi) (*no progressive*) sufficed for *x* (*a*) yā ishē mu = yā isam mana it is (was) enough for us. yā isa Audu = yā ishi Audu = yā isar wa Audu it suffices Audu. (*b*) mun yi Allā ishē mu we tasted the new season's crop (*cf.* 1*a above*). (*c*) Allā yā isam mana tsakānimmu da sū God can judge where the truth lies between them and us. (*d*) nā isar wa Audu I am Audu's representative. (*e*) tā ishi wānē *Vd.* ganī A.2, 3*c.* (*f*) yā ishī tāyi *Vd.* yankā 1*c.*

(3) *Vb.* 1A. (*a*) (i) reached *x* mun ~ gareshi we reached it. don su kai isā Masar that they may get as far as Egypt (*Vd.* isā). yā ~ can he arrived there. yā isō nan he reached here. barka da isōwā welcome! sunā isō Ingila yanzu = sunā isōwā Ingila yanzu

they're now reaching England (Mod.
Gram. 178a¹). (ii) **yā** (**tā**) ~ **mutum**
he (she) became adult (= **muddi** 2).
(iii) **nā** ~ **barka** my wish has been
fulfilled. (b) (no progressive) is (was)
equal to, fit for, worthy of x (i) **ba**
ka ~ **wannaŋ** **lādā** **ba** you're not
worth such high wages. **rāƙumī yā** ~
ɗaukar kāyammu duka the camel is
up to carrying all our luggage. **yā** ~
kōwane aiki he's up to every task.
dōki yā ~ **hawā** the horse is old enough
to ride. **ba ta** ~ **aurē ba tukunā** she's
not yet of marriageable age (cf. **auru**).
suŋ ~ **zakkā** they reach a taxable
amount. (ii) **lallē, wannaŋ yā** ~ **ba-**
ƙauye that is what one would expect of
a bumpkin ! **yā** ~ **mamāki** it is enough
to surprise anybody ! **yā** ~ **abim**
misāli kōwā ya īya ganī it is sufficient
example for anyone ! **yā** ~ **maguji** he's
a real sprinter. **yā** ~ **babbam maƙar-**
yacī he's nothing but a liar (cf. 1b
above). **tā isa mātar** " **kāwō rūwā** ! "
she is very pretty. (c) **isa da** x **ya isa da**
Audu = **yā isa kaŋ Audu** he has jurisdiction over Audu. **tanā isā gum**
mijinta she " bosses " her husband.

B. (**isā**) f. (1) (progressive of **isa** 3a,
3c) x **yanā isā tasha, jirgī nā tāshi** he
arrived at station just as train was
starting. (2) (a) arrogance x ~
garēshi = **nūna** ~ **garēshi** he's arrogant. (b) worth, high rank x (i) **mai** ~
P. of position. (ii) **wata** ~ **kaŋ wata** ~
gajiyāwā cē too many cooks spoil the
broth ! (3) **isar baka** = **isar banzā** =
isar ƙādāgī = **isar zūcī** making unauthorized statements ; baseless claim
to authority.

C. (**īsā** = **īsa**) (1) Jesus. (2) **īsā**
Almasīhu Jesus Christ. (3) Vd.
Dūgaji.

iṣad da Vb. 4A delivered x **yā** ~ **kuɗiŋ**
wurinsu he delivered the money to
them. **yā isō mini da lābārin naŋ** he
conveyed that news to me. **har maganar**
tā ~ **mū haka** ? = **har maganar tā**
isshē mu haka ? have matters come to
such a pitch between us ? **har cīwo yā**

~ **shī** (= **yā isshē shi**) **haka** ? is he
as ill as all that ?
Is'afrika f. East Africa.
isai used in 'yar ~ f. gown or cap (**tāgīya**)
of **sāƙi** cloth made in Yoruba country.
īsalī Kt. cause, x **inā īsalinsa** what's
the cause (use) of it ? (= **asalī**).
isam Vd. **isa** 2a.
isānī m. **bā shi da** ~ it's unlimited
(= **asānī** q.v.).
isar baka = **isar banzā** = **isar ƙādāgī** =
isar zūcī Vd. **isā** 3.
isasshē m. (f. **isasshīyā**) pl. **isassū** (1) (re P.).
(a) burly. (b) influential. (2) (re T.).
(a) solidly-made. (b) sufficient x
isasshaŋ abincī ample food.
ish (1) kneel, camel ! (2) get up, camel !
(3) = **ƙisha**.
isha A. (**isha**) f. kolanuts damaged by
heat, maggots, etc.
    B. (**isha**) = **ƙisha**.
*ishā'i** Ar. m. period between darkness
and midnight (= **lishā**).
*ishāra** Ar. f. indication, sign.
ishasshē = **isasshē**.
ishe A. (**ishe**) Vb. 1A. (1) (a) overtook x
nā ~ **shi a hanya** I overtook him on the
road. (b) x **nā** ~ **shi a Kano** I found
him at Kano (1a, b = **tarad da** =
iske = **sāmā** 1b) (1b = **riskā**). (2)
found that x **nā** ~ **bā yā gidā** I found
he wasn't at home (= **iske**). **mijinta**
yā ~ **ta budurwā** her husband found
she was a virgin (= **iske**). (3) **suŋ** ~
shi har gidā they (the enemy) pursued
him up to his home. (4) **tsaya, a** ~
ka Vd. **tsittsige**.
    B. (**ishē**) Vd. **isa** 2.
ishi A. (**ishi**) Vd. **isa** 2.
    B. (**īshi**) Katagum m. envy (= **ƙīshi**
q.v.).
ishirin Ar. f. 20.
ishirīnīya f. name of a book of Muslim
devotional songs.
*ishirwā** f. thirst (= **ƙishirwā**).
ishisshire Vb. 3A (1) sat sprawled out at
ease. (2) is (was) in undisputed control.
(3) lived a care-free life (cf. **mōre** 1, **būsā**
3a, **bējē** 2).
iska f. in Kano (masc. elsewhere) (1) (a)
(i) wind. (ii) **kō dā mā,** ~ **cē ta iske**
kaba nā rawa don't only blame the

one, for they are both equally involved ! (iii) **iskạr dūnīyạ tā kumbụrā shi** he's puffed up with pride. (iv) **an sakam masạ ~ lạmbạ wạŋ** chloroform was administered to him. (v) *Vd.* **būsā** 3. (*b*) **yā shā ~** (i) he went for a stroll, went to the country for a change of air. (ii) it (hot food) cooled a bit. (iii) it (wet, washed garment) dried a bit. (iv) he (P. or horse) feels in good form after a pleasantly long rest. **sun zō yāwạn shạŋ ~** they have come for a holiday. **yā tạfi dībạr ~** he's gone for a stroll. (*c*) (i) **~ tā fi zūwạ dạgạ yammā** the prevailing winds are westerly. (ii) **~ tā bugạ** wind blew. **~ tā bugō manạ dạgạ kudụ** the wind blew on us from the south. (*d*) **wayạr ~** *f.* wireless-telegraphy, radio. **yā yi musụ mạganạ cikiŋ wayạr ~** he addressed them on the radio. (2) **~ tā kai musụ** collective punishment was inflicted on them. (3) (*a*) **an sạmi baŋ ~** there's now a short, dry spell in the rains (= **būshị = bā dạ** 8), *cf.* **farị**. (*b*) **am bạ dōkị ~ kwānā bịyū** the horse has been given a few days' rest. (*c*) **yā bā mu ~** he's ceased visiting us lately, thank goodness ! (4) **an yi wạ rịgā ~** gown being dyed was taken out of dye after each dipping. (5) (*with pl.* **iskōkī**) spirits (especially those causing hysteria) *x* (*a*) **iskōkinsạ ɗanyū nẹ** the spirits have only just begun to take possession of him. (*b*) **aŋ gyārạ iskōkinsạ** he has been exorcized. (*c*) **iskōkī suŋ kaɗạ** (= **tabạ**) **shi** he has gone mad. (6) **dōkị yanạ harbiŋ ~** the horse is in fine fettle. (7) **turạran naŋ ~ ɗayā nẹ** this perfume is evanescent (*cf.* **shạshịmī, rạkạ ni uŋgūwā**.

iskākā *Sk. m. x* **yā zaunạ iskākāna** he sat down to windward of me.

skakkē *m.* (*f.* **iskakkịyā**) *pl.* **iskạkkū**. (1) pre-existent. (2) inherited, not acquired.

skandạrịyyạ *f.* Alexandria.

skarō *m., f.* (*sg., pl.*) idiot.

skẹ = **ishẹ**.

smạ'īlụ *Vd.* **Sạmā'īlụ**.

so A. (**isō**) *Vd.* **ịsa** 3, **isad dạ**.

  B. (**isọ**) *m. x* **ạ yi minị ~ wurinsạ** please announce my arrival to him !

isshē *Vd.* **isad dạ**.

istidrājị *Ar. m.* **an yi masạ ~** he, evil as he is, seems immune from divine punishment in this world.

istịhādị *Ar. m. Kt.* striving hard (= **ijtịhādị**).

istịhārạ *Ar. f.* asking divine counsel.

istiŋgifārị *Ar. m.* **yā kāmạ ~** he called on God's protection.

Isufụ (1) = **Yūsufụ**. (2) **Isufāwā** *Vd.* **fịtar ~**.

ita (*independent pronoun*) she *x* (1) **dạ shị dạ ~** he and she. (2) (*used after causal verb*) *x* **yā hau dạ ~ dōkị** he mounted her on a horse. **yā cīyad dạ ~** he fed her. (3) (*used as second of two objects*) **yā daŋkạrā minị ~** he compressed it (tobacco) for me. (4) (*in* " avoidance ", Mod. Gram., Appendix III, Section D) *x* **ita** *is used by man if referring to* chief wife (**gidā** 1*n*) *or* eldest daughter ('**yar fārị**). (5) **har ~** *Vd.* **har** 1*d*.ii.

itạcē *m.* '(*pl.* **itātūwạ**) (1) (*a*) tree. (*aa*) **abūbūwan naŋ sū nẹ itātūwạn shiŋgē na zạmānị** these things are the features of modern life. (*b*) **itạcan dạ a kạn yi cōkạlī dạ shī kamar cinyạ yakẹ, dạ sạssakạ yạ kạrẹ** slow but sure ! (*c*) **bā ạ hawā ~ ta gindī, ạ sạuka ta rēshẹ** stick to the man whom you serve ! (*d*) **~ ɗayā bā yạ kurmị** one swallow doesn't make summer. (*e*) **kōwā ya yi minị kaŋ karā, sǎi ŋ yi masạ na ~ yạ shẹkarạ yanạ kōŋạwā** I shall do as I am done by and even more. (*f*) **itạcaŋ kạdaŋgarẹ** *Vd.* **tạfīyạ** 4. (*g*) **bā yạ kā dạ ~** *Vd.* **sārā** 2*b*.ii. (*h*) **bā yạ kisạŋ ~** *Vd.* **sāram bisạ**. (2) (*a*) wood. (*b*) **itạcaŋ wutā** = **itạcaŋ hūrạwā** firewood. (*bb*) *Vd.* **ạbụ** 2*j*. (*c*) **yā shā** = he was beaten with a stick. (3) **itātūwạ** *pl.* sticks, twigs, pieces of wood, timbers.

itācịyā *f.* tree (= **itạce** 1).

ịtālịyā *f.* (1) Italy. (2) **mụtumiŋ ~ an** Italian man. (3) **ịtālịyāwā** the Italians.

itātūwạ *Vd.* **itạcē**.

itẹ *m.* thin cane strip to prevent broad piece of material becoming narrower in course of weaving.

ittịfākạŋ (*Ar.* by chance) *adv.* for sure.

ittịhādị (*Ar.* ijtihādi) *m.* striving hard.

iwa A. (īwa) *Sk. f.* the grass *Rhytachne congoensis* (*for screens*).
B. (iwā) (1) like *x* ~ nī like me. *(2) the " Dog " constellation.
*iwalī *m.* (*Ar.* 'iwazi) substitute *x* Allā ya mai da iwalinsa may God give you another child in place of that dead one !
iya A. (īya) (1) *f.* (*a*) (i) mother, maternal aunt, etc. (ii)*Vd.*yāyāA.1,2*h*,inna,ūwā, īyāye. (*b*) Mother ! (*c*) Mistress ! (*said by pagan slave-girl, but she says yāyā if, on her arrival, she finds the latter method of address in vogue*). (*d*) ~ tā gaza, bāba yā takarkarē yā yī making shift with what's available. (*e*) anā tsōran nī da ~ n ji 'yā'yam mayyā needs must when the devil drives (*cf.* Inna 3). (*f*) *Vd.* da ~. (2) *Vb.* (*followed by noun, v.n. or subjunctive*). (*a*) can, was able to *x* mun ~ = munā īyāwā we are able to do it. abin da mukē īyāwā = abin da muka īya what we can do. yā ~ aikin nan he can (was able to) do this work = yā ~ ya yi aikin nan. yā ~ tafīya (i) he has learned to walk. (ii) there is no obstacle such as slipperiness, etc., preventing him walking. (*b*) (*sense* (ii) *of last example, if negatived, requires progressive*) bā yā ~ tafīya he cannot walk (because tired, ground slippery, etc.) *but* bai ~ tafīya ba (child) cannot yet walk. bā yā ~ sū he cannot fish (*because river too deep, etc.*) *but* bai ~ sū ba he has not learned to fish (= rasa 2*b*.ii). (*c*) (" cannot " *with future sense requires future tense*) *x* ba zan ~ tafīya gōbe ba I cannot leave to-morrow. (*d*) Gwanī, kā ~, kā ki ka yī what a clever but contrary person ! (*e*) *x* yā ~ da mutānē he knows how to deal with people. (*f*) (i) iya bākinka guard your tongue ! (ii) yā ~ hannunsa he is expert (= i 1 *last example*). (*g*) ba ka ~ nōmā ba = mīya 10. (3) *Vd.* iye, īyāwā, īya rūwā, īya wurī.
B. (īya) (1) *m.* a sarauta at *Kt.* and *Zar.* (*this being called* dan ~ at Kano). (2) *East Hausa* = yanā *x* iya nan = yanā nan he is here.
C. (īyā) (*abbreviation of* īyākā). (1) (*a*) *prep.* up to *x* (*a*) rūwā yā kāwō

masa ~ gwīwū the water came up to his knees. (*b*) (*so for all parts of the body*) *x* rūwā yā kāwō masa ~ wuya (ciki) (gindī) the water came up to his neck (stomach) (waist), *but* rūwā yā shā kansa the water came over his head (= rūwā īyā dū), *cf.* kundumī 2, īyākā 2*a*.ii, kāi 1A *b*.iv. (*c*) rūwā īyā wuya māganim makī wankā needs must when the devil drives. (2) yā kāwō ~ wuya " he is fed up " (=īyākā 2*a*.i).
iyad da = īyar da.
iyākā *f.* (*pl.* īyākōkī). (1) (*a*) (i) īyākā *f.* = kan īyākā *m.* frontier, boundary. (ii) abin kan ~ *Vd.* abu 10. (*b*) sun yi ~ da Kano they live on the Kano border, they have a common frontier with Kano. (*c*) yā ci mini ~ (i) he encroached on my farm, compound. (ii) he seduced my wife. (2) (*a*) limit *x* (i) yā kai ~ he is " fed up " (*cf.* īyā 2). (ii) rūwā yā kōmō ~ gindī = rūwā yā kōmō īyākar gindī the water came up to his waist (*cf.* īyā 1*b*). (iii) īyākar bukātarsu, su gan ni nē all they want is to see me. (iv) yā nūna īyākar halinsa na jāruntaka he showed what he was capable of in the way of courage. (v) har īyākar rāina as long as I live. har īyākar ganimmu as far as our sight reaches. duk īyākar ganīna as far as my eye could see. īyākar sanimmu as far as we know. (vi) alhakī da rōmō, a shiga īyākar wuya people sin if it helps them. (vii) īyākā = ~ dāi in short, in fact *x* īyākā, sū dāi, sun yi nīyya all they purposed was to . . . (*b*) bā ~ abundantly *x* hatsī yanā nan bā ~ there's abundance of corn. (*c*) abim bā ~ *x* Allā yā nufē shi da kiba har abim bā ~ God made him immeasurably stout. (3) total *x* īyākar mutānan da aka yākā the total of the prisoners of war. (4) (*a*) maximum *x* yā san shi īyākar sani he knows all there is to know about it. yā bā shi īyākar amāna he trusted him implicitly. abin yā rūdē īyākar rūdēwā the matter became most involved. (ii) īyākar abin yabō, sun . . . their most meritorious act was that they . . . (iii) īyākar īyāwassu *adv.* to the limit

of their ability. mų yi ta yī̃, īyąkar zarąfī let us strain every nerve ! nā yi ƙǫƙarī īyąkar īyąwāta I put forth every effort. yā kąmātą sų yī̃, īyąkar yąddą yakę̃ yiwūwā they must do it with all their might. (iv) munā̃ yįŋ īyąkar zarąfī gą tąimakwansų we are doing our best to help them. yā bā dą īyąkar ƙǫƙarinsą yą gamą he did his best to finish it. sun yi īyąkar ƙǫƙarinsų they did their level best. mun yi īyąkar yįmmų we did our best. munā̃ īyąkar nāmų mų gamą we're striving our hardest to finish it. (b) adv. (at end of sentence) to the utmost x yā tąimąkē nį̃ ⌒ he did his utmost to help me. yā yi musų tsą̃yayyą̃ ⌒ he resisted them all he could. yanā̃ ta ƙǫƙarī nę̃ ⌒ he's striving his utmost. (5) illā ⌒ that's all I wanted, you may go ! (= shī kę̃ naŋ). (6) Vd. īyā̃kacī.

īyākącē Vb. 1D restricted x nā ⌒ masą bąkįŋ ąbįn dą ząi yi i̠ndicated to him the limits of his sphere of action. bąŋ ⌒ maką kōmē ba I imposed no restrictions on you.

īyākacī = īyākacī m. (1) = īyąkā but only usable in genitive form īyąkacin = īyąkacin x (a) īyąkacįŋ ąbįn dą na sanị kę̃ naŋ that's all I know about it. īyąkacįŋ ƙasąd dą suką ci every country which they conquered (cf. īyąkā 3). (b) īyąkacin rąi dą ająlī for ever and ever. (2) īyąkacin tiką tiką tik = īyąkacįŋ wąje ƙōfą well, that's the end of that ! (said after doing some decisive act to " kill or cure "). (3) īyąkacim mącē gwīwą Vd. bąrkǫnō 1b. (4) īyąkacįŋ gūgūwą Vd. gūgūwą.

īyākancē = īyākącē.

īyākątaccē m. (f. īyąkątaccīyā) pl. īyą̃-kątąttū restricted, limited.

īyākōkī Vd. īyąkā.

īyāli̠ (Ar. ahālī) (1) (f. sg. ; m. pl.) man's wife or wives and children ; those dependent on man for food, i.e. one's household x īyāli̠na bā tą̃ gidā my wife is not at home. bą̃ shi dą ⌒ he has no wife. īyāli̠na sunā̃ naŋ my wife and children are present. ⌒ sun yi minị yawą I have too many mouths to feed. ƙąƙą ka barō īyāli̠nką how are your

family ? (2) Kt. īyālịn tīląs Vd. Dǫrōgō. (3) tūwō na īyāli̠, nāmą na mąi gidā said by 'yam fǫtō in gaŋgị rhythm.

īyāli̠yā f. an only wife x zą̃ ni wurịŋ īyāli̠yāta I'm going to see my wife.

īya mąlēlēkųwā Vd. mąlēlēkųwā.

īyar dą Vb. 4B (1) accomplished x kā ⌒ sąƙōną ? did you deliver my message ?, ī nā īyar yes, I did (Vd. ī dą). (2) kadą ką fīgę kązā sąi tā ⌒ mutūwą await the psychological moment !

īyą rūwā m. (1) ability to swim (cf. īyọ). (2) ⌒, fid dą kại I have done my duty, what others do is their affair ; I have paid my share, I'm not concerned with others ; knowledge never comes amiss. (3) Vd. sąkainā 2.

īyau Daura Hausa that's O.K. !

īyą̃wā (1) (progressive and v.n. of īyą) x yanā̃ dą wųyar ⌒ it's a hard thing to master. (2) (a) ability x yā fī nị ⌒ he's more capable at it than I am. nā yi mąmākįŋ ⌒ tasą I'm amazed at his skill. yā kōyą minị īyą̃war yāƙị he taught me military skill. (b) nā yi ƙǫƙarī īyąkar īyąwāta I put forth every effort. īyąkar īyą̃wassų to the limit of their ability. (3) saŋ ⌒ gąrēshị he's meddlesome ; he " shows off ". (4) sāmų yā fi īyą̃wā Vd. sāmų 3a.

īyą wurī̃ m. ⌒ gąrēshị he has a glib tongue.

īyāyē pl. (1) (a) parents (Vd. īyą). (b) fadą dą ⌒ Vd. mąrāyą 3. (2) large, sweet potatoes. (3) large blebs of smallpox. (4) īyą̃yaŋ giji Vd. ųbaŋ gijị. (5) cf. ųbā 1c.

iye A. (īyē) Kano village Hausa yes ! (reply to P. calling one) = ną'am.

B. (īyę) (derived from īyą ; only used with dative) x bą zaŋ ⌒ masą ba I shan't be able to put up with him. bą̃ mąi ⌒ masą nobody can put up with his ways.

īyọ m. (1) swimming (= nịŋƙāyā). (2) īyąn tsąye swimming erect. (3) Vd. yaŋkę 1f, īyą rūwā.

izą Vb. 1A (1) (a) pushed (= tūrą 1a). (b) suŋ izą ƙyēyąrmų dą ƙarfī they forced us to do it. (c) Vd. izą wāwā. (2) incited, persuaded (= tūrą 1b). (3) yā̃ ⌒ wutā he pushed outer, unburnt ends of firewood into centre of fire (= tūrą 1a.ii).

iẓaŋ *if* (= **in** *q.v.*).

izā̱rā *f.* section of split tree (= **azā̱rā** *q.v.*).

iẓạ wāwā ri̱mā *m.* leaving P. " in the lurch ".

iẓazzạrī *Asb. m.* neck-ornament of horses, made of leather or string.

izgā *f.* (1) tail used as fly-switch. (2) yā yā dạ ⁓ = yā bugar dạ ⁓ (*a*) he's dead. (*b*) (*said jokingly*) he's asleep. (3) bow for playing mōlō *x* yā ji ⁓ tanạ̄ tāshi̱ he heard sounds of a gọ̄gē-fiddle (*Vd.* tambạrā ; tsagīyā).

izgi̱lī *m.* presumptuousness (= wạ̄sạnī 1 = *Sk.* ad̲d̲e).

izi̱fī *m.* (*pl.* i̱zụfai = *Kt.* izuffạ). (1) one of the 60 portions into which Ḳoran is divided. (2) the circle marking beginning of each *such portion*.

izi̱nī *Ar. m.* (1) permission. (2) izi̱nim biki̱ *Vd.* aurē 6. (3) takạrdar ⁓ *f.* warrant appointing Chief, ạlkālī, hā-ki̱mī, *etc.*

izọ *m.* (1) = iji̱. (2) *Vd.* bạ ⁓.

izụ (1) *m.* = izi̱fī. (2) izụ-izụ *m.* 60 successful throws of spinning-top (= sụ̄rū-sụ̄rū).

izụfai *Vd.* izi̱fī.

*izzạ *Ar. f.* haughtiness.

J

ja A.1 (jā) (1) *Vb.* 5. (*a*) (i) pulled, dragged along (*cf.* jạnyē). (ii) mạganạn nạŋ, k̲ạk̲ạ zā ạ jāwō tạ cikin zạncē give me an example of how this word is used ! (iii) yanạ̄ nēmā yạ jāwō Masạr wajansạ he's trying to win the support of Egypt. (iv) mun jāwō jirā̱gyan samạ dạgạ wancạm fagyan yāk̲i we have transferred aeroplanes from that theatre of war. (v) yā jāwō tsananiŋ ạbincī it has caused famine. (vi) yā jāwō mini rībạ it was profitable to me. (vii) yā jā bạkā he distended his bow. (viii) sukạ jā hanjinsạ then they attacked him tooth and claw. (ix) bạ su jā li̱nzāmi̱ ba they did not halt. (x) yā jā sūrạ he painted a picture. (*xi*) yanạ̄ jansạ jikạ-jikạ he is intimate with him. (xii) Allạ̄ yạ jā zạmāni̱ŋkạ long life to you !

(*b*) (i) tā jā rūwā she drew water (from well, etc.) = dībạ 1*a*.iv. (ii) k̲ụrjī yā jā rūwā the pustule is full of pus. (iii) *Vd.* tsuntsū 5.

(*c*) (i) yā jā ji̱ki̱, yā shi̱ga gidā he made his way painfully home. (ii) *cf.* jạnyē. (iii) *Kt.* yanạ̄ jạn ji̱kī he's slacking.

(*d*) yā jā aiki̱ sạnnu-sạnnu he worked at a snail's pace.

(*e*) (i) yā jā gi̱ndī he dragged himself along the ground. (ii) sãi dạ sukạ jā gi̱ndī wurin Sarkī, sạn naŋ sukạ sāmụ it was only by humbly entreating the chief that they got it. (iii) *Vd.* gi̱ndī 10.

(*f*) (i) yanạ̄ jạm fad̲ạ = yanạ̄ jạm bạ̄kī he's picking a quarrel. (ii) jā bạ̄kī shut up !

(*g*) (i) yā jā bak̲ī he read out passage from text for another to interpret or comment on. (ii) yā jā Fātihạ he read the first verse of the Koran.

(*h*) (i) maci̱jī yā jā ciki̱ the snake crawled along. (ii) *Vd.* jạn ciki̱.

(*j*) (i) ạbin naŋ dukạ, nī na jā = ạbin naŋ dukạ, nī na jāwō wạ kạ̄ina = ạbin naŋ dukạ, nī na jā wạ kạ̄ina, bạ̄kī = ạbin naŋ dukạ, nī na jā wạ kạ̄ina, mạgana I brought this trouble on myself. (ii) yā jāwō manạ wạhalạ he brought trouble on us. (iii) kwạ-d̲ayiŋkạ nē ya jāwō makạ you've brought ruin on yourself.

(*k*) (i) kōwā ya jā dạ nī, yā fād̲i̱ anyone who tries conclusions with me will get the worst of it. bạ zā sụ īyạ jā dạ mū ba they will be no match for us. yạ jā dạ kōwā ạ dūnīyạ he can hold his own with anyone. (ii) sun jā fagyē they fought a battle. (iii) sunạ̄ jạn yāk̲i they are waging war. (iv) yā jāwō gạbaŋ wannaŋ yāk̲i he is in command of this war. (v) yā jā sōjạmmụ he led our troops : he was the commander. (vi) *Vd.* dāgā.

(*l*) **yanā jāna dạ kākācị = yanā jāna dạ wạsā** he is quizzing me.

(*m*) (i) **tā sakạ kạtạmbirị, tā jā girā** she applied cosmetic to her eyebrows. (ii) **wākē yā jā girā** the beans are nearly cooked.

(*n*) **duk mạganạ tā jā kasā** it's all moonshine.

(*o*) (i) **yā jā masạ gōrạ** he led him (blind man) ; he took a pull on the rope attached to hind leg of ox. (ii) *Vd.* **jā̰ gōrạ**.

(*p*) (i) **hatsī yā jā karā** the corn is about 3 ft. high, *i.e.* it has begun to develop a stalk. (ii) **yanā jạn karan rụbūtū** he writes a bold, clear script.

(*q*) **yā jā minị zūcīyā** after raising my hopes, he left me in suspense.

(*r*) *Vd.* **jā̰ ; compounds of jā̰, jạn**.

(*s*) *Vd.* **cạzbị ; dạmarạ** 1*e*.iii ; **darē** 6 ; **dawạ** 3 ; **gōnā** 2*b* ; **gurbị** 1*a*.ii ; **kayạ ; kīrị**. (*t*) **jā dạ wạsā** *Vd.* **wạsā** 1*f*. (*u*) **jāwō dạgạ duhụ** *Vd.* **dạgạ** 1*a*.ii. (*v*) **jā zạmānị** *Vd.* **Allā̰** 3*g*. (*w*) **jā̰ dōkị** *Vd.* **ambụlī**. (*x*) **jā zūwạ kạsūwa ; jā hụlā dạrā** *Vd.* **hạukā**. (*y*) **jā wạ dangị cụtā** *Vd.* **tụŋkū** 1*b*. (*z*) **ạ jā shị ạ sạnnū** *Vd.* **sạnnū** 2*b*.ii.

(2) (*intransitive ; progressive* **yanā jā̰**) *Vd.* **bāya** 1*a, b, c*.

A.2 (**jā**) *adj., m., f.* (*pl.* **jājạyē = Kt. jajjạyē**). (*a*) (i) red *x* **jan zanẹ** red cloth. **jar rīgā** red gown. (ii) **jạŋ wau** *Vd.* **wau**. (iii) brown *x* **jan sukạr** brown sugar. (*b*) **jạŋ kudī** gold coins. (*c*) **jạŋ kidạ** *Nupe Hausa =* **gulạ** 3. (*d*) **itạcē maị jar wutā** blazing firewood. (*e*) **yanā dạ idọ kạman jạŋ garwāshī** he's a real *man*. (*f*) (i) **jā wur = jā̰ jir = jā̰ zir = jā̰ zur** scarlet. (ii) (**jā̰** *may remain unchanged in plural here, cf.* **fat**) *x* **yā yī sụ jā̰ wur** he made

them red-hot. (iii) **sǎi yākị akē yị jā̰ wur** but bitter war is in progress. (*g*) (i) **jā maị farin rūwā** pink. (ii) **jā maị bakin rūwā** dark red. (*h*) (i) **jāja** (*pl.* **jāja-jāja**) reddish. (ii) *Vd.* **jā̰jạ amā̰rē**. (*j*) **karfẹ yā yi jā̰ ạ wuta har ya yi farī** the iron became white-hot. (*k*) **fātạ tā yi jā har tanā̰ bakī** the skin is very dark red. (*l*) **hạukā ~, fụlā dạrā, bā̰ wạndō** what unseemly behaviour ! (*Vd.* **hạukā** 1*b*). (*m*) severe *x* (i) **jaŋ aikị** hard work. (ii) **jar wạhalạ** severe trouble. (iii) **jad dā̰rīyā** laughter covering mortification or anger. (*n*) **jaŋ halī** *m.* (i) **== jar zūcīyā** *f.* bravery. (ii) bracing up one's courage. (*o*) **tun dạ jājạyan sauna** from my birth onwards. (*p*) *Vd. compounds of* **jan, jar.** *Vd.* **jā na kūkạ, karāgọ, rịnō, sā̰** A.2, 1*h*. (*q*) **ạlịf ~** *Vd.* **alịf** 2.

A.3 (*a*) redness *x* **haɽ jạŋ yạ gaurạyẹ fātạ kōịnā** till the red dye permeates the skin everywhere. (*b*) (with *pl.* **jājạyē**) a European (*these being considered red, not white, but a light-skinned African is considered white* **farī**) *x* **lēburạ sun zō, har dạ jā ạ cikinsụ** some carriers have arrived with a European (*cf.* **jātau, bạtūrẹ**). (*d*) **bā̰ jā ba nẹ, Tūrancī. kōwā ya yi kudī, shī nẹ Abbạ** don't be misled by appearances ! (*e*) *Vd.* **mạn jā**.

B. (**jā**) (1) (*progressive and v.n. of* **jā**) (*a*) **yanā̰ jā̰** he is pulling (it). **yanā̰ jạn cạzbị** he's telling his beads. **yanā̰ jạnsạ** he's pulling it. (*b*) **jā̰, māgạniŋ gāwar dōkị** work conquers any task. (*c*) **kanā̰ jā̰, yanā̰ jạnkạ,** *Vd.* **azzịkī** 1*e*. (*d*) **kịn jā̰** *Vd.* **tsịŋkạ** 1*e*. (2) *Vd. compounds of* **jạn**. (3) *Vd.* **jā̰ gōrạ ; jā̰ gindī.**

jaɓa A. (**jāɓā**) *f.* (1) (*a*) shrew-mouse (*Myosorex sp.*). (*b*) **Allā̰ nā̰ mutā̰nē, jāɓā tā ga bạkim mijịntạ** (*said by women*) it's a case of the pot calling the kettle black. (*c*) **jāɓā bā tā̰ jịŋ wārin jịkintạ** those who live in glass houses shouldn't throw stones. (*d*) *Vd.* **Sarkī** 1*d* ; **rōmō** 3. (2) over-bearing P. (3) **bā̰kin ~ gạrēshi** he's uncircumcized. (4) **jāɓar rā̰fī** *epithet of* onion.

B. (jāɓa) *f.* monkey or other animal coloured like **jāɓā**.

C. (jaɓa) *Vb.* 1A. (1) put heavy articles on each other (*as two sacks of corn, two heaps of meat, etc.*) *x* **an ~ buhū kam buhū.** (2) (*with dative*) (*a*) put very heavy load on *x* **an ~ wa jāki kāyā.** (*b*) **an ~ masa shī** wet article was put on it.

D. (jaɓā) *Vb.* 2 affected P. other than the doer *x* **laifin A yā jaɓi B** the crime of A had repercussions on B (= **shāfā 2**).

jaɓai (1) *m.* (*sg., pl.*). (*a*) lout. (*b*) P. piling debt on debt. (2) (*a*) what a large heap of wet things ! (*b*) **wannan zane ~** what heavy cloth ! (*c*) **wannan aiki ~** what botched work !

jaɓā-jaɓā = jaɓē-jaɓē.

jaɓakan *m.* (1) lout. (2) sluggish P. (3) load of heavy or damp articles.

jaɓal *adv.* messily *x* **tā zub da shī ~** she threw it away in a wet, messy way.

jabar *m.* type of **dara** (draughts) with 30 holes, each player having 12 pieces.

jabarē = kisan ~ *m.* second weeding (**maimai**) of ground-nuts.

jā bāya = jā nā bāya 2.

jabba *f.* (*pl.* jabbōbī) *Ar.* kind of sleeveless gown.

Jaɓɓa = Jaɓɓo *man's name.*

*jaɓɓāma *Fil.* welcome ! (= **maraɓā**).

jabdari *m.* yellow Mexican poppy (= **kwarko**).

jaɓe *Vb.* 1A. (1) put very heavy load on *x* **an ~ jāki da kāyā = jaɓa 2a.** (2) (*a*) put aside (work, tools, articles for sale, etc.) from sloth or lack of present utility (= **jibze**). (*b*) **an ~ shi** he's been suspended from his duties ; he's been detained ; he's been ignored.

jaɓē-jaɓē *adv.* abundantly (*re* wet or heavy things) *x* **yā kōmō da nāma ~** he brought back quite a pile of meat.

jaɓētati (1) *m., f.* (*a*) lout. (*b*) sluggish P. (*c*) child slow in learning to walk. (2) *m.* **aiki yā yi ~** work's only progressing slowly.

jabgarē *Vb.* 1C = jaɓe 2a.

jabgaro *m.* (1) court-messenger (*epithet is ~ babbam bāko*). (2) dilatory P.

jāɓu *Vb.* 3B *x* **nā ~ da shī** I'm related to him.

Jabū (1) *m.* = 'yan ~ *m. pl.* counterfeit coin or coins (= fanko 3). (2) *cf.* jēbū.

jācē *m.* partially-worn garment = jātau.

jādarbī = jādarbū (1) **wani mai ~ nē** he's a fellow covered in those wretched face-markings that people have ! (2) lines of water on body of P. from water trickling from pot on head.

jā darē *m.* (1) name of a certain star. (2) reading aloud from writing-board (allō) by firelight.

jaddadā (*Ar.* renew) *Vb.* 1C *x* **zai jaddada wannan hanyar banzā** he will reform this bad system.

jad dāriyā *f.* laughter covering mortification or anger.

jafā'i *Ar. m.* (1) abusive or disrespectful language. (2) slander. (3) refusal to accept judgment of the court. (4) *cf.* albadā.

jāfi *m.* (1) shaking raised spear or hand when saluting superior (= jinjina). (2) *Vd.* riɓa 1c.

jaga *f.* **yā yi ~** he lasted out two bouts of game langa.

jagab *adv.* wetly *x* **yā jiɓa ~** it's very damp.

jā gaba *m., f.* (*sg., pl.*). (1) (*a*) guide. (*b*) leader *x* (i) **sū nē jā gaba ga wannan samāmē** *they* are the leaders in this raid. (ii) **yā yi jāgaba** he took the lead. (iii) *Vd.* shūgaba ; gaba 3*b, c.* (2) intermediary *x* **jā gaban aurē** marriage-intermediary (1, 2 = shūgaba), *cf.* jā gōra, aurē 6*b.*

jagade *Vd.* jan jagade.

jagai *used in* dan jagai *m.* type of native-woven cloth.

jagainiyā *f.* going hither and thither.

jagal = jagalgal.

jagalam *m., f.* (*sg., pl.*) destitute P. (*epithet is* kārūwa ba kudin kōko).

jagalē *m.* (1) itinerant trading in a little corn or other foodstuffs within small radius by dealer (called dan ~), carrying his own load. (2) 'yar ~ woman *thus* selling okro, pepper, eggs, etc., *x of* 1, 2 tana jagalam barkōnō. yanā jagalan hatsī (*Vd.* kwarami, kirī, kōli).

jagalgal *adv. and m.* in slushy state *x*

nā ga kāsūwā ～ = nā ga kāsūwā tā yi ～.

jagamī *m.* carrying small load on larger one.

jagap = jagab.

jagari *Kt. m.* buck duiker.

jagē-jagē abundantly (*re* articles exposed for sale).

jā gindī *m.* (1) gleaning ground-nuts left in ground after pulling up plants (*cf.* kwarcē ; rōrọ). (2) *Vd.* jā 1*e.* (3) jaŋ gindiŋ gīwā māganiŋ hakin tsaye (*lit.* elephant dragging its bottom crushes grass) *epithet of* influential P.

jagō-jagō *used in* sun yi ～ = sun tsaya ～ they (two opponents) are hesitating about their next move.

jā gōra *m., f.* (*sg., pl.*) (1) (*a*) (i) blind person's guide *x* Audu jā gōransa nē = Audu jā gōra tasa nē Audu is that blind person's guide (*Vd.* Mod. Gram. 8*e.*ii). (ii) ～ dau anīya, ka 6ad da makāfo what a misleading guide ! (iii) any guide *x* zan yi muku jā gōra zūwa Kanọ I will be your guide to Kano. (*b*) leader. (*c*) *cf.* jāgaba. (*d*) *Kt.* intermediary. (*e*) *Vd.* raba makāfo da ～. (2) *Vd.* jā 1*o.*

jā gūgā *m.* new cassava.

jāgula *Vb.* 1C spoiled (= dāgula *q.v.*).

jagwabe *m.* (1) meat from old cow. (2) unsound meat.

jagwaggwa6ā *Vb.* 1D. (1) gave P. severe jolting. (2) yā jagwaggwa6a aiki he botched the work.

jagwā-jagwā (1) *adv.* " in a sorry condition ". (2) kada ka yi mini ～ " don't try to come it over me ! "

jagwalam *Kt.* = jagalam.

jagwalgwalā *Vb.* 1D (1) soiled T. by handling (= lāguda). (2) yā jagwalgwala aiki he botched the work.

jagwar (1) yanā da dācī ～ it's very bitter. (2) yanā da tsāmī ～ it's very acid-tasting.

jāgwardọ (*Fil.* hardọ) *m.* (1) professional fomenter of litigation. (2) (*a*) Filani headman. (*b*) man in charge of migrating Filani. cattle. (3) jāgwardaŋ aurē marriage-intermediary (= shūgaba 2).

jāha (*Ar.* jiha). (1) *f.* direction *x* a wace ～ yake in what direction is it ? da

kōwace ～ everywhere ; on all sides. yanā jāhar yammā it is westwards. yanā jāhar Sarkī he's under the Emir's jurisdiction. (2) jāha-jāha area by area.

jahādi *Ar. m.* (1) war to propagate Islam *x* yā kāwō ～ he led out a jihad. (2) mun shā ～ da shī we had hard tussle with him (it).

Jahannama *Ar. f.* (*from Hebrew* gēy Hinnōm " Valley of Hinnom ") first of the seven hells of Islam, but loosely used for Hell (*cf.* lazzā, jahīmu, hudama, hāwīyā).

jahilci A. (jāhilci) *Ar. m.* ignorance. B. (jāhilci) *Vd.* jāhilta.

jāhilī *Ar. m.* (*f.* jāhilā) *pl.* jāhilai = *Sk.* jāhillai ignorant.

*Jāhilīyya *Ar. f.* time prior to institution of Islam.

*jāhilta *Vb.* 2 (*p.o.* jāhilcē, *n.o.* jāhilci) is (was) ignorant of.

Jahīmu *m.* = Jahīmi *m.* = Jahīma *f.* (1) *Ar.* sixth of seven - hells of Islam (*cf.* Jahannama). (2) kullūtan ～ *m.* tertiary syphilis (= kabbā).

*jā'iba *Ar. f.* misfortune *x* yā jāwō wa kansa ～ he brought misfortune on himself.

jaijaitọ *m.* = jējētọ.

*jā'irci *Ar. m.* shamelessness ; disrespectfulness.

jā'irī *m.* (*f.* jā'irā) *pl.* jā'irai *Ar.* (1) shameless. (2) disrespectful.

jā-ja (1) reddish (*Vd.* jā A.2*h*). (2) jā-ja amare *m.* (*a*) redness of setting sun. (*b*) slight staining of hands or teeth.

jājātā *Vb.* 1C. (1) reddened. (2) dyed red.

jājāyē *Vd.* jā A.2 ; jā A.3.

jaje A. (jājē) *m.* (1) *x* nā yi masa ～ I expressed my sympathy to him (*re* any misfortune except death ; *cf.* ta'azīyya) = *Sk.* tanzaŋkō. (2) making inquiries about T. lost *x* yanā jājan jākinsa he's seeking news of his lost donkey (1, 2 = jējētọ). B. (jājē) *m.* *x* an yi masa ～ it's been dyed red.

jāji *m.* (1) caravan-leader (= mādugū). (2) *Vd.* fargar ～.

jājiba (1) *Vb.* 2 led P. into some dangerous course with bad result *x* tā jājibē shi, tā sā masa tunjērē she led him into sleeping with her so that she gave him syphilis. (2) **jājibō** *Vb.* 1E (*with dative*) brought **P.** something involving trouble *x* **yā jājibō matā tsummā** he brought her a rag which later involved her in trouble. **kā jājibō manā sārautā** by accepting office, you've brought trouble on us. (3) **jājibe-jājibē** *m.* repeated acts *as in* **jājibō** *or* **jājibā** *x* **yā cikā jājibe-jājibē har wata rānā zāi jāwō ɓarāwō** he's always bringing home undesirable companions, so one day he's bound to bring a thief.

jājibērē = jājibir = jājibēraŋ gaskē = *Kt.* **jājibiriŋ garī duka** *m.* (1) day before either of the two main Muslim festivals. (2) **jājibēraŋ tsāmī =** *Kt.* **jājibirin surukkai** 2nd day before either of the two festivals. (3) **jājibēram ɓarāyī =** *Kt.* **jājibiriŋ aggulai** 3rd day before the two festivals.

jājibō *Vd.* **jājibā** 2.

jājircē *Vb.* 3A. (1) behaved obstinately. (2) persevered *x* **yā ∼ kaŋ aikinsa** he persevered at his work.

jājirmā *m., f.* undaunted or persevering **P.** (= **muzakkarī**).

jājirtā *Vb.* 3B = **jājircē**.

jajjā *Vb.* kept on pulling (*int. from* **jā**).

jajjāyē *Vd.* **jā** A.2.

jajjōgā *f.* cantering (= **kwakkwafā = kakkaftū**).

jaka A. (**jakā**) *f.* (*pl.* **jakuŋkunā**) (*Ar.* **ziqāqa**). (1) (*a*) bag (*cf.* **gafakā, zabīrā**). (*b*) **nāmansa nā ∼ Vd.** **rawā** 1*e.* (*c*) **babbar ∼ Vd.** **būrumā** 2. (*d*) **tā fi ∼** *Vd.* **gaskīyā.** (2) (*often equivalent to* **pam darī**) *x* **∼ ukū £300.** (3) **mācē dā ∼ abar tsōrō cē** woman with cyst in armpits brings her husband bad luck. (4) **babba dā ∼ m.** Saddlebill, *i.e.* African Jabiry (*Ephippiorhynchus Senegalensis*). (5) **yā kwancē bākin ∼** he's chattering away (*Vd.* **burgāmī** 2). (6) **jakar ƙwālātai** scrotum. (7) **jakar mālamī** first stomach of ruminant. (8) **jakar mātam fādā** woman's cloth made into corn-bag by rolling up and tying the ends (= *Kt.* **mātam fādā**). (9) *Vd.* **warwar**. (10) **kadā ka daurā mini jakar tsābā, 'yan tsākī su bī ni** don't cause me any unpleasantness ! (11)

(*labourers' talk*) **an rātayā masā ∼** he has had his food.
B. (**jākā**) *f.* (*pl. as for* **jākī**). (1) she-ass. (2) **kē ∼ you** silly woman ! C. (**jākā**) *Sk. f.* (1) = **jākā.** (2) tripping opponent in wrestling (= **tādīyā**).

jakādā *m.* (*pl.* **jakādū**). (1) tax-collector in pre-Administration times (*his epithet is* **Sādā garī**) = **jē ka fādā.** (2) *Vd.* **jakādīyā**.

jakadanci *m.* duties of a **jakādā**.

jakādīyā *f.* (*pl.* **jakādū**) female attendant at palace (*Vd.* **jakādā**).

jākai *Vd.* **jākī**.

jakancē *Vb.* 1C made T. into bag.

Jākarā *f.* (1) *name of a* stream rising in Kano City (*Vd.* **Jawal**). (2) **gōdīyar ∼, cī bai ishē ki ba, hawā yā ishē ki** *epithet of* wife or maidservant " getting more kicks than halfpence ". (3) **nī rūwan ∼ nē, kam ba a shā ni a Birnī ba, ā shā ni a ƙauyē** you may despise my help now, but one day you'll be glad of it ! (4) *Vd.* **bā ∼**.

jākī *m.* (*f.* **jākā** = *Sk.* **jākā**) *pl.* **jākunā = jākai.** (1) (*a*) donkey. (*b*) (*like* **dōki**, *it can in enumerations, be used in plural sense*) *x* **jākī yā yi 300** there are 300 donkeys. (*c*) **yāwaŋ jākai** meandering about the town. (*d*) **∼ bā yā wucē tōkā = in ∼ yā ga tōkā, sǎi birgimā** how apposite !, just in your (his, etc.) line ! (*cf.* **shā dā** 2*b*). (*e*) **harbi ga dan ∼ gādō nē** what's bred in the bone . . . (*f*) **mā wanyē hakā dan Sarkī a kaŋ ∼** one must take the second-best if the best is not available ! (*g*) **Jākī, bāwaŋ kāyā = haƙuriŋ kāyā sǎi ∼** what an energetic person ! (*h*) **am bar ∼ anā dūkaŋ tēki = dārārī** 2. (*j*) (i) **yanā ƙōƙarī ya fid dā ∼ dagā dumā** he's striving to clear himself of the charge. (ii) **a yi maza dǎi, a fitad dā ∼ dagā dumā** finish off that hard job and be clear of it once and for all ! (*k*) **yārō bābu tambaya ∼ nē** *Vd.* **hūlū.** (*l*) **dōki dā jākī ba su mutu ba** *Vd.* **mīki** 2*c.* (*m*) **kāyā bā yā rāɓar ∼ Vd.** **būtsarī** 2. (*n*) **∼ yā sābā dā kāyā** *Vd.* **takarkarī** 1*b.* (*o*) **mai ∼ yā fi mai tākalmī** *Vd.* **tākalmī** 1*e.* (*p*) **jākiŋ kai**

gārā *Vd.* gārā **4.** *(q)* lạifin ∼ *Vd.* diƙiŋ-diƙiŋ. *(r)* bǫrin ∼ *Vd.* bǫrī **10.** *(s)* tụmbin ∼ *Vd.* tụmbī **3.** *(t)* dāwạr jǎkai *Vd.* bụkū. *(u)* kụnnan ∼ *Vd.* kụnnē **5.** (v) *Vd.* tūsạr jǎkī, tāshịn jǎkin 'yan Rūmā, tsūwẹ. (2) first portion of hair secured when making woman's coiffure (= shịmfịɗạ). (3) kē jǎkā you silly woman ! (4) the cornstalk on which rests penis of circumcized boy (ɗan shǎyī), to save him from knocks (*there are in all, three sticks forming triangle,* jǎkī *being the one described*). (5) thieves' assistant (*cf.* jǎkin **5**). (6) carrier fitted to back of cycle. (7) bǎkin ∼ *m.* (*a*) white border of gwandācloth. (*b*) = alạwusại. (8) ∼ bisạ tudụ = ∼ dạ makǫrī type of coiffure (= kwạncīyā **4**). (9) *Vd.* jǎkincompounds.

jǎkin (1) ∼ maginīyā headstrong P. (*epithet is* ∼ maginīyā sǎi kā sō, a kạn ci kạsūwā), *Vd.* maginī. (2) ∼ bēnē lower storey of flat-topped house (*Vd.* sōrō 1*b*). (3) ∼ birnī bạ wutsīyạ look at that wretched Gwari woman carrying load on shoulder as they all do ! (4) ∼ dịllālị broker's assistant (*cf.* jǎkī **5**, samạ dōgō **2**). (5) jǎkin dōkị (*a*) mule = ạlfadarī. (*b*) half-caste (= barbaran yạnyāwạ). *(5*A*) ∼ fatahạ the letter aleph following "a" (fatahạ), and so used to lengthen it to "ā", *as in* mā. (6) jǎkiŋ gadō each of the beams (mashimfịdī) of bed. (7) jǎkiŋ gyạdā single-kernelled ground-nut. (8) yā saŋ Hausā kạmar jǎkiŋ Kanọ he's learnt Hausa thoroughly. (9) jǎkiŋ kutụr man carrying woman's load for her. (10) jǎkin tagwạyē boy born next after twins. (11) jǎkin tụrurūwā the spider mạkạrā. (12) ∼ kai gārā *Vd.* gārā **4.** (13) ∼ 'yan Rūmā *Vd.* tāshịn ∼.

akitị *Eng. m.* (*pl.* jakitōcī) any waistcoat-like garment.

ạkkā *f.* (1) *Kt.* (*from m.* jạkkī) *pl.* jạkkai donkey. (2) *Sk.* = jākā 2.

ạkumī *Kt. m.* small bag like sanhọ.

akunạ *Vd.* jǎkī.

akuŋkunạ *Vd.* jạkā.

ạ kutụr = jạ kutụrī 1 *m.* donkey crupper

(*made of kapok, but previously of rope*) = tundufụrī = ạddibịrī = jạ nạ bāyā 2*a.* (2) *Kt.* = janjạmī.

jạkwạtạŋ *m.* slackness *x* yanạ zạune ∼ dạ shī he's sitting idly.

*jalạbī *Ar. m.* (1) prayer for fulfilment of wish. (2) T. done with motive of advantage.

jạlạinīyā *f.* (*Ar.* jāla) going hither and thither.

jạlājạlai *Vd.* janjalō.

jạlālạ *Ar. f.* (*pl.* jạlālū) embroidered saddle-cover (= *Kt.* yifị 3).

*Jạlālainị *m.* book of Koranic commentaries by Jalālud dīn and Jalālus Suyūtī.

jalandị *Fil. m.* trouble ; anxiety.

*jalạutā *Vb.* 3A *Ar.* wandered about (*cf.* jạlạinīyā).

jalɓi *Fil. m.* threadworm *x* yā gạmu dạ ∼ he has threadworm (= ayạmbā).

jạlēnīyā *f.* (*Ar.* jāla) going hither and thither.

jālị *Sk. m.* trading-capital (= jạllī *q.v.*).

*jālisạm bil ạmānạ *Ar.* (1) yā zạunạ jālisạm bil ạmānạ he (horseman, etc.) sits firmly (= daɓạs 2). (2) dạ mā, bạ yāƙị akē yị ba, anạ zạune nẹ ∼ previously there was peace, not war.

jalkadạrī *Kt. m.* going hither and thither.

jalla A. (jallạ) *used in* (1) ∼ jurundụm (*said by women*) bad luck ! (2) Jallạ Sarkī mai īyạwā glory to God the All-powerful !

B. (Jạllā) *used in* ∼ bạbbar Hausā *epithet of* Kano.

jạllạ ku jạllē type of girls' game.

jallara A. (jạllarạ) *f.* trouble ; anxiety.

B. (jallạrā) *Vb.* 1C *x* yā ∼ minị tsiŋkē ạ idō = yā jallạrạ tsiŋkē ạ idọna he poked a bit of grass in my eye.

jallạrē *Vb.* 1C *x* yā ∼ minị idọ he poked me in the eye.

jạllī (*Ar.* jārī) *m.* (1) = jārị 1. (2) yā karyạ minị ∼ he kept me waiting long for payment of goods. (3) har tā kai mụ jallim fadạ haƙạ ? to think she'd involve us in such quarrel !

jạllō (*Fil.* jolloru) *m.* (1) gourd water-bottle (= gōrā). (2) yanạ nēmansạ, rūwā ạ ∼ he's seeking it might and main. (3) **ɗan** ∼ *m. contemptuous term for* Sokoto man. (4) *Vd.* **dịbgibarạ.**

jạlwāmī *Kt. m.* type of cloth worn mainly by **Bugạjē** women.

jam *Vd.* **tsallị.**

jạma'ạ *Ar. f. (pl.* **jạmạ'ū = jama'ō'ī**). (1) the public *x* **ạ idạn** ∼ in public. (2) crowd. (3) (*a*) community *x* **jạma'ạrmụ** our community; our "set". (*b*) inhabitants *x* **sauran jạma'ạr Tūrai** the other inhabitants of Europe. (4) = **jam'ị** 2, 3. (5) *Vd.* **yā** 2*c.*

Jama'ārẹ *f. Vd.* **banzā.**

jạ̄ mạkạ̄fī *m.* big cattle-track (**lāwạlī**).

jạmạkụtur *Daura Hausa m.* = **jạ̄ kutụr.**

*jạmālạ *Ar. f.* beauty.

*jam'ạntā *Ar. Vb.* 1C put (word) into the plural.

jama'ō'ī *Vd.* **jạma'ạ.**

*jama'u A. (jama'ụ) *Ar. m.* (1) **kạ̄ yi manạ jamạ'ụ**? will you punish us collectively for the fault of one of us? (2) **bạ̄** ∼ **ba, ạmmā** . . . I don't wish to make any odious comparisons, but . . . B. (jạmạ'ū) *Vd.* **jạma'ạ.**

jambaɗẹ *m.* abscess under armpit (= **gạ̄ nākạ** 2 = **gạ̄ nạ̄wa**), *cf.* **mạrūrụ.**

jam bạ̄ɓō *Vd.* **jan bạ̄ɓō.**

jạm bạ̄kī *Vd.* **jạn bạ̄kī.**

jam ɓạlī *Vd.* **jan ɓạlī.**

jạmɓạr = jạmɓạrɓạr.

jamɓạrā *Vb.* 1C daubed on much of (= **damɓạrā**).

jạmɓạrɓạr *adv. emphasizing* weight *x* **yā yi nawyī** ∼ it's very heavy.

jamɓare A. (jamɓạrē) *Vb.* 3A is (was) dilatory. B. (jạmɓạrē) (1) *m., f.* lout. (2) *m.* clumsily done T. *x* **aikịnsạ** ∼ **nẹ̄.**

jam baujē *Vd.* **jan baujē.**

jamfạ *Eng. f. (pl.* **jamfōfī**) jumper (garment).

jamhūrụ *Ar. m. x* **an yi minị** ∼ they intrigued against me.

*jam'ị *Ar. m.* (1) doing two devotions together. (2) gathering of persons for joint devotions. *(3) plural of words (*cf.* **mufurạdī**).

jāmị'ī *Ar. m.* (1) congregational mosque for Friday service. (2) director, manager (= **shụ̄gạba**).

*jạmīlị *m.* (*f.* **jạmīlịyā**) *pl.* **jạmịlai** *Ar.* handsome.

jam'īyyạ *Ar. f.* political party, club, society.

Jāmunancī *m.* (1) German language. (2) *Vd.* **Jāmụs.**

Jāmụs (1) a German (= **Bạjāmushẹ**). (2) Germans (= **Jāmusāwā**). (3) *f.* Germany. (4) *cf.* **Jāmunancī.**

jạnabạ *Ar. f.* (1) ceremonial impurity in Muslim law. (2) *Vd.* **waŋkan** ∼.

jạ̄ nạ̄ bāyā *m.* (1) baby acquired at same time as its slave-mother. (2) (*a*) = **jạ̄ kutụr.** (*b*) cord from woman's temples to back of head to fasten plaits.

jạ̄ nạ̄ ɓūtī = jạ̄ nạ̄ ɓūtū *m.* donkey-crupper (= **jạ̄ kutụr** *q.v.*).

Jạnairụ *m.* January.

jạnā'izạ *Ar. f.* funeral. **kāyan** ∼ *m* funeral appurtenances.

jā na kūkạ *m.* the insect **gạmạdīdī** *q.v.*

Janạr *Eng. m.* (*sg., pl.*) General (military)

jan baki A. (jam bạ̄kī) *m.* (1) Cardinal-bird (= **mulụfī**). (2) ∼ **bạ̄ mạitā** there's too little of it to be of any use. B. (yanạ̄ jạm bạ̄kī) he's picking a quarrel (*Vd.* **bạ̄kī** 2*w*, 2*x*).

jan bạɓō (jam bạ̄ɓō) *Sk. m.* = **jan baujē.**

jan ɓali (jam ɓạlī) *Kt. m.* = **jaŋ gargarī**

jan barodo (jam bạrōdō) *m.* (1) any cheap red clothing. (2) fair, penniless P. (3) = **bạrōdō** 1

jan bauje (jam baujē) = **baujē** *m.* the thatching grasses *Andropogon apricu* and *Andropogon exilis* (*they turn red when mature; Vd.* **jan raunō**).

jạn cikị (1) *x* **kō dạ** ∼ **mạ̄ ƙ̃etạrē** by hook or by crook we'll get across the river (2) *Vd.* **jā** 1*h*; **rạ̈i** 5*c.*

jạndal *x* **yā cịka** ∼ it's quite full.

jạndalạ *Vb.* 3B is (was) replete.

jan dọ̄rīnī *Vd.* **bạsarākẹ.**

jaŋ gạcī *m.* copper (= **tagụllā**).

jaŋgai *m.* adulteration of food *x* **an yi wạ ạbincin naŋ** ∼.

jaŋgạlā *Vb.* 1C = **jallạrā.**

jaŋgạlī *m.* cattle-tax. ∼ **yā tāshị** collection of cattle-tax has begun.

jaŋgalwā *f.* = **jagwaɓẹ.**

jaŋgarai *m.* place where **bọ̄rī** rites are done

jan gargarī *Vd.* **gargarī.**

jaŋ gātā *Vd.* **gātā** 5.

jan gạtarī *Vd.* **gạtarī** 12.

jaŋ garwāshī *Vd.* garwāshī.

jaŋ gindiŋ gīwā *Vd.* gindī 10.

jaŋ gōgā *Vd.* gōgā 2.

jaŋ gōrā *m.* (1) brown donkey. (2) maį jaŋ gōrā *Vd.* kōlį 1. (3) *cf.* ḕfau.

jaŋ gulạ *Vd.* gulạ.

jaŋ gundạ = dạ īyạ.

jaŋ gurbį *m.* tanā ⁓ pigeon is making cries indicating it is about to lay eggs.

jạngururu *used in* jạŋgururuŋ aikį heavy toil.

jaŋ gwādā *m.* orange-headed male lizard (= gwạrgwādạ = *Kt.* kutū = *Kt.* jaŋ katakō = *Sk.* kiskī).

jaŋgwạlā *Vb.* 1C = jallạrā.

jạŋgwam (1) (= jụgum) listlessly, flaccidly, despondently *x* yā zaunạ ⁓ he sat listlessly. sānįya tanā tsạye ⁓ cow is sitting flaccidly (*pl.* sunā tsạye jaŋgwam-jạŋgwạm). (2) *m.* misfortune *x* yā jāwō wạ kansạ ⁓ he brought misfortune on himself.

jaŋ gwarzō *m.* brave warrior (*Vd.* gwarzō).

jan hali *Vd.* jā A.2*n.*

jaŋ hạrāwạ *m.* type of horse's gait = *Zar.*

jįjįjigạ 2 (*cf.* sạnsạrạm, zụndụm-zụndụm).

Jạŋ hwạl *m.* (*Eng.* John Holts) trading in such trinkets, curios, etc., as Europeans will buy. ḍaŋ ⁓ *such* trader.

jā n̥ jā *m.* = jāyayyạ.

janjạ6ā *Vb.* 1C kept on overloading (*int. from* ja6ạ *q.v.*).

jaŋ jagadẹ *m.* anything troublesome. yā jāwō minį ⁓ he brought trouble on me.

janjalō *m.* (*pl.* jạlājạlai) pebble for breaking antimony (kwạllī).

janjạmī *m.* (*pl.* jạnjạmai). (1) horse-crupper made of farī *or* sāḱį cloth (*cf.* jā kutụr). (2) sergeant's sash.

janjancį *m.* (1) destructiveness of a child. (2) great skill in crafts (*cf.* ạljaŋ).

janjani A. (janjạnī) *m.* (*f.* janjạnā). (1) refractory P. (2) P. greatly skilled in a craft.
    B. (jạnjạnī) *m.* eking out one's supplies.

janjạnyē *Vb.* 1C kept dragging away (*int. from* jạnyē).

janjārẹ *m.* a red type of guinea-corn.

janjē (1) kept on going (*int. from* jē). (2) na ⁓ nī gidaŋ gwaurō type of children's game.

jaŋ kaŋkį *m.* setting fire to bush.

jaŋ ḱạrāgọ *Vd.* ḱạrāgọ.

jaŋ kạrē *Vd.* haushī 3*b.*

jaŋ ḱarfẹ *m.* copper (= tagụllā = gạcī).

jaŋ ḱạshī *m.* *x* ⁓ gạrēshį he has great endurance.

jaŋ katakō = jaŋ katakwāḍọ *Kt. m.* orange-headed male lizard (= jaŋ gwādā).

jaŋ ḱirạraŋ gyạtumā *Kt. m.* urging horse forward slightly, then reining it in sharply.

jaŋ ḱirạram makaunįyā *m.* reining in galloping horse so suddenly that it slithers (= *Kt.* kwāsaŋkarā).

jaŋ kudī *m.* gold coins.

jaŋ kwatakį = jaŋ kwatakwārẹ *Kt. m.* = jaŋ katakō.

jạnnā *Vd.* jēnẹ.

jannaį *m.* windpipe (= mạḱōgwạrō).

jan rāgō *m.* snoring (= minshārī).

jan raunō = jan ramnō = jan rannō = jan ranō *m.* the fodder grass *Andropogon exilis* (*Vd.* jan baujē) (*it reddens in autumn ; it is used for thatch and when chopped, is mixed with building clay*).

jan rįnō *Vd.* rįnō.

jan sā dạ abạwā *Vd.* abạwā 2.

jan sạiwā = *Sk.* jan sāyẹ *m.* the tree *Trichilia emetica* (*used for administering remedy to horse via rectum, i.e.* gūgūtū).

jan sau *Vd.* Girgạ.

jantādį *m.* a steel for sharpening knives.

jan takọbī *Vd.* takọbī 2.

jan taŋkō = *Kt.* jan taŋkā = *Sk.* jan twaŋkā *m.* (1) plain, cheap red cloth. (2) Cardinal bird (= mulụfī).

jantẹ *m.* feverish cold. ⁓ yā bụgē nį I have a feverish cold (= zạzzạ6ī 1*b*).

jaŋ waḍḍarẹ *Vd.* waḍḍarẹ.

jan wau *Vd.* wau.

jan yārọ *m.* (1) windpipe (= mạḱōgwạrō). (2) the Euphorbia tree *Hymenocardia acida.*

jạnyayyē *used in* jạnyayyaŋ aikį, an sā kuturū kụntar ạkwīyạ *epithet of* almost insuperable task.

janye A. (jạnyē) (1) *Vb.* 1C. (*a*) dragged away (*cf.* jā). (*b*) yanā jạnye dạ dōkį he's dragging the horse away (Mod. Gram. 80*d*.ii). (*c*) yā jạnyẹ jiki he withdrew from participation (*Vd.* jā 1*c*). (*d*) mun janye ƙafa daga garesu we cut ourselves off from them. (*e*) yā ∼ wando he hitched up his trousers for working. (2) *Vb.* 3A *x* (*a*) rūwā yā ∼ flood-water has subsided. wutā tā ∼ fire died down in centre. (*c*) sun ∼ da bāya they retreated (= jā 2).

B. (janye) *Zar. m.* building (bin, etc.) with clay not made into bricks (= gōgā).

janzari *m.* (1) one of the spirits taking possession of bōrī devotees. (2) lofty whirlwind (*cf.* gūgūwa).

jan zūcīyā *used in* jan zūcīyā gareshi he has a difficult disposition (*cf.* zūcīyā 11).

jar *adv. used in* yanā da ɗācī ∼ it's very bitter.

jaraba *Ar.* (1) *Vb.* 3B is (was) fascinated by *x* yā ∼ da ita he is very fond of her. (2) *Vb.* 2 caused P. to hanker after *x* Allā yā jarabē shi da san sarauta God inspired him with desire to become Chief. (3) *f.* (*pl.* jarabōbī = jarabū). (*a*) overmastering desire (*epithet is* ∼ mai kai mutum gadō tsirāra). tāba tā zamā ∼ gareshi he " is crazy " over smoking. yā gamu da ∼ by giving way to his desires, he has landed in trouble (*cf.* jarrababbē). an kōre musu ∼ temptation has been put out of their way. gā ∼ tanā shirin aukō mana our overweening ambition has marked us down. (*b*) calamity *x* Allā yā kaɗe mana jarabun nan God has warded these calamities off us. (4) *Vd.* jarrabā.

jarabcē *Vd.* jarabta.

jarabōbī *Vd.* jaraba 3.

jarabta A. (jarabta) (1) *Vb.* 3B = jaraba 1. (2) *Vb.* 2 (*p.o.* jarabcē, *n.o.* jarabci) = jaraba 2.

B. (jarabtā) *Vb.* 1C tested (= jarrabā *q.v.*).

jarabtu *Vb.* 3B = jaraba 1.

jarabū *Vd.* jaraba 3.

jarau *m.* archery-contest.

Jārāwā *Vd.* Bajārī.

jar dārīyā *Vd.* dārīyā 1*e*.

jarfā *f.* (1) tattoo-marks (*done at will, for ornament, not hereditary as is* askā).

(2) wanzāmi bā yā san ∼ nobody likes to be " hoist with his own petard ". (3) 'yar ∼ *f.* (*pl.* 'yan ∼) = bēra 2.

jar fīƙa *Vd.* fīƙa 1*b*.

jargō-jargō = jagō-jagō.

jari A. (jāri) *Ar. m.* (1) capital (whether in money, skill, or beauty, etc.) = dōki 2 = dūkīyā 3 = digi 2 = kudī 5*a*. (2) babbar dafūwā mai ƙare jārin yāro what a luscious looking woman ! (3) *Vd.* jallī.

B. (jari) *Had. m.* type of fish.

jarīda *f.* (*Ar.* palm-leaf) *pl.* jarīdū newspaper.

jarīri *m.* (*f.* jārīrīyā) *pl.* jārīrai infant (= jinjiri).

Jarma *East Hausa* an official position (sarauta).

jarmai *m.* (1) brave man (= jārumī). (2) *Vd.* ɗan kāma *under* kāma 9.

jarōgama = jarōgwamā *f.* going hither and thither.

jarraba A. (jarraba) = jaraba.

B. (jarrabā) *Vb.* 1C tested, examined P. or T. (*Vd.* jarrabāwā).

jarrababbē *m.* (*f.* jarrababbīyā) *pl.* jarrababbū P. fallen into trouble through surrendering to his desires (*cf.* jaraba 3).

jarrabāwā (*v.n. of* jarrabā) *f.* (1) testing, examining P. or T. (2) school examination *x* (*a*) da aka yi jarrabāwan nan, bai ci kōmē ba he got no marks at that exam. (*b*) an yi wa 'yam makarantā ∼ pupils have been set exam. (*c*) ya ci jarrabāwā he passed the examination. (*d*) yā shiga jarrabāwā he entered for the examination.

jar sānīyā *Sk.* blast you ! (*Vd.* ūwā).

jar sārā = jas sārā.

jārum *m.* (1) (police or military) guardroom. (2) (*a*) Government prison (*cf.* kurkuku). (*b*) ɗan ∼ *m.* (*f.* 'yar∼) *pl.* 'yan ∼ Government prisoner (*cf.* jēla, sarƙa 3*c*, ƙāmammē, bursuna, kurkuku).

jārumī *m.* (*f.* jāruma) *pl.* jārumai = jārumāwā brave man (*epithet is* Jārumī, ƙūsar yāƙi).

jārumta = jārunta = jārumtaka = jāruntaka *f.* bravery.

jar zūcīyā *f.* endurance, bravery.

jas sārā *f.* tool for sharpening saltseller's saw.

jāsūrẹ *m. Ar. m.* piles (hæmorrhoids) = bāsụr.

jāsūsụ = jāsūsị *Ar. m.* (*f.* jāsūsụ̄wā) *pl.* jāsūsai. (1) P. with biting tongue. (2) spy.

jā ta, kạ ffẹ́dẹ (1) *m.* food-animal useless because died of disease or naturally (= mūshẹ). (2) *f.* harlot.

jātan landẹ *Vd.* jātau 1*f.*

jātau *m.* (1) (*a*) (i) fair African. (ii) light brown dog. (*b*) gā ～ yā zō = gā ～ bagarẹ = gā bagarẹ mại jaŋ kāyā (*said in top-playing when as a forfeit, a player has his hand hit and blood drawn* (*cf.* dāwạ 3) ; *also said when blood is drawn in scuffle, wrestling, boxing), cf.* sāraŋ kọ̄fatọ 3. (*c*) type of arrow-poison. (*d*) Allā yā kāwō ～ (*said by potter*) the pottery has turned out the desired red colour. (*e*) *Sk.* type of rice. (*f*) jātan landẹ (i) red and white imported type of cloth. (ii) prawn. (2) (*a*) name of mythical tree, sight of which is said to portend wealth. (*b*) *epithet of* kolas, indigo, cassava as being means to wealth. (3) partially worn clothing *x* jātan rīgā. (4) forte *x* dịŋkị jātansạ nē tailoring's his strong point (= shā dạ 2*b*). (5) Jātau man's name.

jātumā *f.* crone (= gyātumā *q.v.*).

jā'u *Vb.* 3B *x* mun ～ dạ shī we're intimate with him.

jaụdā *Kabi Hausa.* (1) *m.* any monkey. (2) *disrespectful epithet by Kabi people for* Filani (*Vd.* Bạfilācẹ).

jaudạrī *m.* yellow Mexican poppy (= kwạrkọ).

jaụdī *Vd.* bardē 12.

jauhạ *Ar. f.* (1) close-fitting, thick gown, with wide tinsel-adorned sleeves. *(2) name of a star portending rain.

*jauhạrī *Ar. m.* (1) any jewel. (2) qualities innate in P. or T.

jau-jau A. (jau-jau) *Nor. m.* (*pl.* jaujāyē) = jaujē.
  B. (jaụ-jaụ) *m.* any imported, figured, cotton material dyed with indigo (= jọ̄jọ̄).

jaujāyē *Vd.* jau-jau.

jaujē *m.* (*pl.* jạwājạwai). (1) hourglass-drum, beaten at only one end (*it is beaten together with the smaller*

kōlō), *cf.* kạlạŋgū. (2) Sarkin ～ *Vd.* marọ̄ƙī.

jaulā *Nor. f.* = jaurā.

jaụnī *Vd.* kaŋkọ.

jaura A. (jaurā) *Ar. f.* (1) peddling. (2) dan ～ *m.* (*pl.* 'yan ～) peddler.
  B. (jaurạ) *f.* frigid part of harmattan (*epithet is* Jaurạ ūwar dārī, Jaurạ kạs itātūwạ).

jạwābị = jạwāƙị *Ar. m.* (*pl.* jạwābai). (1) (*a*) message. (*b*) an yi musụ ～ a message was sent to them. (*c*) an yi ～ message was sent. (2) reply *x* (*a*) yā mai dạ ～ he replied (= amsạ). (*b*) bindigōginsụ sunā mai dạ ～ their guns are firing back. (3) affair *x* jạwābịm bāshịn dạ nikẹ́ bịnsạ the matter of the money he owes me. (4) speaking, a speech *x* (*a*) yā yi ～ yā cẹ̀ he made a speech saying that . . . (= mạganạ 2*b*.ii). (*b*) yā yi ～ gạrēsụ he delivered a speech to them. (*c*) yā yi ～ ạ kạm mạganạn naŋ he touched on that point. (5) yā bar wạ 'yā'yansạ ạbin ～ he left a bad reputation behind him.

jạwājạwai *Vd.* jaujē.

jawạl *used in* dan ～ *m.* the sạrautạ at Kano whose holder is occupied with keeping the River Jāƙarā clean.

jawạlānị *Ar. m.* going hither and thither.

jāwandụ *m.* buying up scrap metal (*done by* dan ～).

jawạrā *f.* (*pl.* jawarōrī = jawarāwā = jạwạrū) woman no longer married (= zawạrā *q.v.*).

jawarcị being a jạwạrā.

jạwạrū *Vd.* jawạrā.

jạwaskạ *f.* essential flying-feathers of bird's wing (= wutā 4).

jāwō *Vd.* jā.

jāwụl *m.* gum-resin of *Balsamodendron myrrha*.

jāyạ *Vb.* 1A *Sk.* prolonged *x* (1) an ～ ajạlim bīyạm bāshị the time for paying debt has been enlarged. (2) an ～ aurē wedding's been postponed. (3) ～ mạganạ gạrēshị he makes everything into a long job. (4) Allā yạ ～ makạ kwānukạ God give you long life ! (*cf.* jāyāwā). (5) jāya manạ, mụ gānạ leave us to consult !

jāyāwā *f.* long way *x* **Kano tanā da** ~
Kano is far off (*cf.* **jāyā**).

jāyayya *f.* (1) controversy, dispute (*d.f.*
jā), *cf.* jīyayya. (2) *Vd.* ālēwa 1.

jāyayyē *m.* (*f.* jāyayyīya) *pl.* jāyayyū *x*
aiki ~ troublesome work (= janyayyē
q.v.).

jāye *Vb.* 3A = janyē 2.

jā'ye-jāyē" *m.* = jājiba 3.

*jazā'i *Ar. m.* retribution (*Vd.* ālhakī 1).

*jazam *m.* (*Ar.* lopping) mutilating and
nodular leprosy.

jazzā *Vd.* jēji.

jē (*Vb. without progressive, Vd.* 3 *for
imperative*). (1) (*a*) (i) went to *x* **gōbe
zan** ~ **Kano** to-morrow I'll go to Kano.
(ii) **gāra ka** ~ **da kanka** *Vd.* tsīnī 2.
(iii) **shēge kā** ~ **gōnā** *Vd.* shēge 5.
(*b*) (*before any noun but place-name, we
insert* **ga**) *x* **nā** ~ **ga Audu** I went to
Audu. (2) set out *x* (*a*) **ka** ~ **ka zāga
garī** go round the town ! (*b*) (i) **zō
mu jē** = **mu jē mū** let's be off ! (ii)
mu jē zūwa *Vd.* mahaukacī 1*a*.ii. (iii)
ammā mu jē zūwa dǎi let us cut the
cackle and get to the horses ! (*c*) " **Zā
ni** " **cē ta tad da** " **Mu jē mū** " do not
blame only the one, for both are equally
involved ! (*d*) *Vd.* tāshi, **mu jē mū**.
(*e*) (i) **majē gaba yā jē, na bāya sǎi
lābāri** east is east and west is west.
(ii) *Vd.* safe. (3) (*a*) *m.* **jē ka** (*f.* **jē
ki**) *pl.* **jē ku** (i) clear out ! (= *Sk.* **zō
ka**). (ii) **jē ka gidā abinka** be off ! (*b*)
(*imperative of* **jē**). (i) *m.* **ka jē kāsūwā** =
jē ka kāsūwā go to the market ! (ii)
f. **ki jē kāsūwā** = **jē ki kāsūwā** go
(*fem.*) to the market ! (iii) *pl.* **ku jē
kāsūwā** = **jē ku kāsūwā** go (*pl.*) to the
market ! (*c*) irin " **jē ka ka dāwō** "
nē it's an unreliably manufactured
thing needing continual spares. (4)
arrived at *x* **san da muka jē Kano** when
we arrived at Kano (*cf.* Mod. Gram.
180). **suna bī, suna bī, har suka** ~
ga dūtsan they kept on and on till
they reached the rock (*for* **ga**, *Vd.* 1*b
above*). **har hantsī ya yī, ba su jē ba**
by noonish they'd not arrived there.
(5) '**yam mu jē da nī** *m.* parasites
accompanying guest to some gathering.
(6) *cf.* **majē**. (7) *N.B.*—*the* -ō *form of*

jē *is* zō (*cf.* Mod. Gram. 70). (8) *Vd.* zō
2*b*, *compounds of* jē ka.

jēbū (1) *Sk. m.* worn-out hide bag (= *Kt.*
dību). (2) *Vd.* Jabū.

jēdā *f.* going hither and thither.

jefa A. (jēfa) *Vb.* 1A. (1) threw *x* (*a*)
yā ~ **māshi** he threw spear. (*b*) **tā** ~
gūgā a rijīyā she let down her bucket
into the well (= **sā** A.1*c* ; **saka**). (*c*)
jēfa āllūra rijīyā *Vd.* āllūra 9. (*d*) an
jēfa shi a tandum mǎi *Vd.* matsīyācī 2.
(*e*) sun ~ **kafa cikin Kano** they set foot
in Kano. (2) (*with dative*). (*a*) threw T.
at (= **jēfā**) *x* **yā** ~ **masa māshi** he
threw spear at him. (*b*) threw T. to,
for *x* (i) **yā** ~ **masa nāma** he threw meat
to it (dog). (ii) **tā** ~ **mini daya** she
(seller of butter, shea-oil, **wainā**-cakes)
gave me one extra as " make-weight "
(*cf.* gyārā 4*a* ; saki 2*d*). (3) *Sk.* **kāzā
tā jēfa kwǎi** hen laid eggs (*Vd.* kwǎi 1*c*).
(4) *Vd.* jēfu.

B. (jēfā) *Vb.* 2 (*progressive and v.n.
use* jīfa). (1) threw T. at *x* (*a*) **yā
jēfē ni da māshi** he threw spear at me.
nā jēfē shi da dūtse I threw a stone at
him ! (= **jēfa** 2*a* = *Sk.* **kādā**). (*b*) **yā jēfē
ni da sammu** he put spell on me (*Vd.*
jēfaffē). (*c*) **jēfi gafīya** *Vd.* gafīya 4.
(2) accused *x* **yā jēfē ni da sāta** he
accused me of theft. (3) *Vd.* jēfu.

jēfad da *Vb.* 4B. (1) threw away one T.
(2) threw things away one by one (*cf.*
zubar da). (3) *Vd.* **A** jēfas.

jēfaffē *m.* (*f.* jēfaffīyā) *pl.* jēfaffū P.
failing to prosper because cursed (*Vd.*
tsīne 2*a*) by his father, etc., or because
victim of spell (sammu).

jēfar da = jēfad da.

jēfas *Vd.* jēfar, **A** jēfas.

jefe A. (jēfe) *Vb.* 1C *x* **yā** ~ **shi da māshi**
he threw spear at him and so knocked
him over.

B. (jēfē) *m.* (1) small amount of
fresh butter added to soup (**mīya**),
because too little of the butter left for
any other purpose. (2) over-hand
swimming (= *Sk.* tsārī 1*c*). (3) **bā
nā cin** ~ I (P. seated) think it would
be more polite for you (P. passing) to
halt when you greet me ! (4) *Sk.*
portion of raw cotton *as in* saki 2*e*.

jêfi-jêfi often.

jêfu *Vb*. 3B (*d.f.* jêfā) *x* bā tā jêfūwā (1) it cannot be put up with. (2) it cannot be considered suitable.

jêgo *m*. (1) suckling of infant. (2) mai ∼ = amaryar ∼ *f*. nursing mother (*Vd*. amaryā 7). (3) bā sājē, fitsārim mai ∼ = bā ā rarrabē fitsārim mai gōyō slyly benefiting by coincidence (*Vd*. bā sājē).

jējē *m*. = jējētọ.

jējētọ *m*. (1) *x* nā yi masā ∼ I expressed my sympathy to him (*re* any misfortune except death ; *cf*. tạ'azīyya ; murnā 1*e* ; d'ēbē 4 ; gaisūwā 5 ; jājē). (2) making inquiries about T. lost *x* yanā jējētạn jākinsā he's seeking news of his lost donkey (1, 2 = jājē).

jēji *m*. (*pl*. jazzā). (1) (*a*) "the bush". (*b*) *Vd*. dāji ; dawā. (*c*) jēji bai kārē cin wutā ba *Vd*. barkā 8. (*d*) bā tā gōdē jēji *Vd*. sā A.2, 1*l*. (2) an yi masā d'aurin ∼ = an d'aurē masā ∼ he was given charm enabling him to pass safely through dangerous " bush". (3) *Vd*. būd'ad dawā. (4) yā ci ∼ (i) he travelled via the " bush". (ii) he ran away. (5) ciki ∼ nē ; bā abin dā bā yā haifūwā " all kind of fruit may grow on same tree ".

jējēgadi *m*. going hither and thither.

je ka A. (jē ka) *Vd*. jē 3 ; *Vd*. compounds *of* jē ka.

B. (jēkā) *Sk. f*. = jakādīyā.

jē ka dā kwạrinkā *used in* auran ∼ *m*. marriage where husband lives sometimes in wife's home, sometimes returning to own home for farming, etc. (= dauki sandankā).

jē ka fādā *m*. (*sg., pl*.) = jakādā.

jē ka fādīyā *Sk*. = jē ka fādūwā *Nor*. (*pl*. jē ka fādū) = jakādīyā.

jē ka hūdā *m*. wound ; bruise.

jēkalā *f*. going hither and thither.

jēkarēkarē *used in* an shā jēkarēkarē dā shī he gave much trouble.

jela A. (jēlā) (*word used mainly by women for* wutsīyā) *f*. (1) (*a*) tail of animal or bird. (*b*) tail of a cloth (*cf*. tsārā 1*c*) = *Sk*. mad'ēbī 2. (2) zuba mini ∼ give me (purchaser) the " dash " of sour milk, which is the perquisite of buyer of

butter ! (*Vd*. jēfā 2*b*.i). (3) *Kt*. going hither and thither.

B. (jēlā) *Eng. m*. (1) head-warder of Government prison. (2) gidan ∼ *m*. Government prison (*cf*. jarum).

jēlē *m*. (1) going hither and thither. (2) abin dā ya kai tsōfwā rawar kūkūmā, tā rē jēlanta (*lit*. the crone went to dance to the kūkūmā-drum in order to make her triceps dance) nobody acts without a motive (*as* " triceps ", jēlē *is only used in this proverb*).

jema A. (jēmā) (1) *Vb*. 1A (*progressive usually employs* jīmā) tanned. (2) *f*. (*a*) the scented grass *Vetiveria zizanioides* used for making darambūwā-armlets. (*b*) scented roots for perfuming soap, etc.

B. (jēmā) *Vb*. 2 tanned partly ; tanned some of the skins to be tanned.

jēmāgē *m*. pl. (jēmāgū) (1) (*a*) fruitbat. (*b*) dōmin jēmāgē, ā nad'ē kasā the fullest investigation will be welcome to me, for I'm not involved (= dōmin 2*f*). (*c*) bābu irin daran dā jēmāgē bai ganī ba fortune's wheel revolves. (*d*) ku bar kisạn jēmāgē, māganim macē madi the charm for a woman is money ; deeds, not words, are wanted (*N.B.*— bats are used for love-philtres). (*e*) gari dā rīmī, jēmāgē bā yā rasā d'ākin kwānā go the right way to work and your desires will be realized ! (2) " addenda " slip. (3) that part of gown where cūnā is made. (4) simultaneous falling of two mounted opponents while attacking each other (*cf*. zubar gadō). (5) part of back of slaughtered animal given barber removing uvula of seven-day-old infant (*cf*. wanzāmi). (6) bride's tray and cover made of two fāifāi. (7) peddling of haberdashery, cloths, etc., by d'an ∼ (= kirī *q.v.*). (8) type of adornment of jalālā (= gulūlu 5). (9) sore place on horse's ribs. (10) (*a*) riding on cycle as passenger. (*b*) riding on mudguard or running-board of car. (10) jēmāgē = ∼ mai kurungē type of children's game. (11) azumin jēmāgē *Vd*. azumī 3.

jēmau (1) *m*. the girl's game ā rausā. (2) (*a*) what sudden destitution has befallen him ! (*b*) fancy him (her) having thus lost eyelashes !

jẽmẹ (1) *Vb.* 1A tanned (= jẽmạ). (2) *Vb.* 3A. (*a*) became destitute after prosperity. (*b*) (hair or eyelashes) have fallen out from illness.

jẹ̃mõ *m.* (*sg., pl.*) elliptical calabash with natural spout (= zọ̃mọ̃dõ).

jẽnẹ (1) *Kt. m.* (*pl.* jạnnā) *f.* (*a*) row of reaped corn laid down on farm before heads cut off (= sạŋkacẹ). (*b*) *Vd.* ruɓa jạnnā. (2) *Sk. adv.* *x* ku tạfl ∼ walk in file !

jẽrạ *Vb.* 1A arranged in a row (= tsārạ 1).

jẽraŋgĩyā *f.* prolixity.

jere A. (jẽrẹ) *Vb.* 1A arranged all of them in a row (*cf.* jẽrạ).

B. (jẽre) *x* darē uku ạ jẽre three nights in succession. sunā jẽre dạ mū they're parallel, in the same line with us.

jẽrị *m.* (*sg., pl.*). (1) row *x* sun yi ∼ they've formed up in line. (2) jẽrị-jẽrị *adv.* in rows.

jẽrĩyā = jẽryā *f.* = jẽrị 1.

jẽsạ *f.* (1) (*a*) type of master-stroke in darạ (draughts). (*b*) an ɗaurạ masạ ∼ they've conspired against him. (2) Jẽsạ *epithet of* aŋgọ (bridegroom).

jẽtạraŋgū *m.* (1) trouble. (2) going hither and thither (= kạiwā dạ kāwọ̃wā).

jẽwā (1) going to and fro between two places. (2) hovering (*by bird of prey or by thief looking for chance*).

jẽwạyạ *Vb.* 1C made circuit of place, etc. (= gẽwạyā *q.v.*).

ji A. (jĩ) *Vb.* 5 (1) heard *x* (*a*) (i) bạ ni lạ̃bārị ṇ ji tell me the news that I may hear it (Mod. Gram. 84*). (ii) mụtumịn naŋ dạ kakẹ̃ jị dạ ganĩ the very P. about whom we are speaking (*cf.* iii *and* 1*c below*). (iii) anā jị, anā ganĩ har sukạ gudụ they suddenly fled (*cf.* ii *above*, 1*c below*). (iv) sū nẹ̃ kẹ̃ ɗadị ạ jĩ they are the ones in authority. ạ tẹ̃kū kụwā, mukẹ̃ ɗadị ạ jĩ it is on the *sea* that we're undisputed masters. (v) tọ̃, dạ wạnnē zãi jị by what considerations will he be swayed ? (vi) bạ̃ mại jị na wani nobody could hear anyone else speak

through the noise. (vii) kā ji, kā jĩ ạbịn dạ ya ạuku this and this befell. (viii) kụnnē yā jĩ ạmmā zūcĩyā bạ tạ kạrɓā ba it was heard but not believed. (ix) mun jĩ, muŋ kạrɓā (*said to superior*) we'll carry out your behests ! (*adaptation of* Arabic sam'an watā'atan). (x) nā ji (= nā jĩyõ) dạgạ bạ̃kim Mālạm A I studied under Malam A. (xi) *Vd.* jị ta, jị ta. (xii) kā ji mạnyan jārumāwā these I have mentioned are great heroes. kā ji mālạmĩ he's a scholar if ever there was one ! kā ji tạmbayạr banzā what a stupid question ! (xiii) bạ̃ba bạn ji ba *Vd.* bạ̃ba 6. (xiv) bā kạ̃ jịŋ kirạ *Vd.* dạkamạ. (*b*) heard that *x* (i) nā ji an sõ ạ kashẹ ka I hear that there is a plot to kill you. an ji yā cẹ̃ he was heard to say that . . . dạ jịntạ yanā zūwạ, sãi ta gudụ as soon as she heard that he was coming, she ran away. (ii) nā ji kạmar zại zõ I've heard that he's coming. (*c*) (i) yanā aikị bạ̃ jị, bạ̃ ganĩ he's working might and main (*cf.* 1*a*.ii, iii *above*). yā dọ̃kẹ̃ nị bạ̃ jị, bạ̃ ganĩ he beat me unmercifully. sunā kọ̃kārĩ bạ̃ jị, bạ̃ ganĩ they're trying their level best. (ii) jị dạ ganĩ *Vd.* ganĩ A.2, 2*a*, *b*. (*d*) (*preceded by subjunctive pronoun* ṇ) *x* ṇ jĩ shị he said that . . . (*lit.* let me hear him that . . .). ṇ ji bạtūrẹ the European said that . . . ṇ jĩ nị it is *I* who say that . . . ṇ ji wạ̃ who said so ? ṇ jĩ kạ ba says *you* ! kūrā ta cẹ̃ wạ kạrē yạ jẽ, yạ zãgẹ̃ sụ, yạ cẹ̃ "ṇ jĩ tạ" the hyena then said to the dog to go and abuse them and say " that's the hyena's message to you ! '". cẹ̃ musụ " ūwākạ dukạ ! " ṇ jĩ nị tell them I say to them " you bloody fools ! ". (*e*) ṇ jị dãi (*introduces question*) *x* ṇ jĩ dãi kā gạmu dạ shị ? did you meet him ? ṇ jị dãi bạ sụ gaŋ kạ ba ? did they not see you ? (*f*) kā jĩ = kạ̃ jĩ (i) look here ! (ii) listen ! (iii) Husband ! (iv) nĩ nẹ̃ Ụmarụ, kā jĩ, kā jĩ I'm Umaru and so forth and so forth. (*g*) wannạŋ dạbārạ tạ jĩwu (tạ̃ jĩyu) this plan is feasible. ạkwai magana mại jĩwūwā = ạkwai magạnạ mại jĩyūwā there is a tale worth hearing.

(2) understood x (a) nā ji ạbịn dạ ya cẹ I understood what he said (= fạhimtạ). (b) yā ji Hausā he understands Hausa. (c) yanā̰ jịn Hausā (i) = 2b above. (ii) he's getting to know Hausa (Mod. Gram. 180).

(3) listened (Mod. Gram. 180) x săi kạ jī dạ kyạu listen carefully ! (= kasạ kụnnē). yi minị wāƙạ ṇ ji sing me a song for me to hear ! (Mod. Gram. 84*).

(4) felt x (a) (i) nā ji zāfī I felt the heat. (ii) yā ji zāfī he was offended. (iii) yā ji cīwọ Vd. cīwọ 2, 3 ; kulẹ. (iv) nā ji tsọrō I was afraid. ji tsọraṇ Allā̰, kạ girmạmạ mahạifạnkạ fear God and respect your parents ! (Vd. tsọrō 1). (v) Vd. jịye-jịyē. (vi) ji wụuyā ; ji dādī Vd. wụuyā, dādī respectively. (vii) yā ji gạrī he suffered poverty (Vd. gạrī 1h, 3c ; jịṇ gạrī). (viii) ji jịkī Vd. jịkī 1e. (ix) tā ji kibīyạ ạ jịkintạ she felt the pain of an arrow having pierced her. (b) (i) ạ rặina n nā̰ jị̄ kạmar ṇ tākạ gidaṇ kōwā I feel as if I'd like to visit every home. (ii) sun ji kạmar zā ạ sā̰ su ạljannạ they felt delirious with joy. (iii) yā ji kạmar aṇ kāwō masạ wani sāban rặi he felt as if he had got new life. (c) n nā̰ jịn nā taɓạ ganinsạ I have an idea I have seen him (= sō 4). (d) (i) yā ji wutā he warmed himself by the fire. (ii) yā ji wutar makarantā he benefited by his schooling. (iii) yanā̰ jịṇ wutā it is unsaleable (cf. māsạ 2, ganin rānā). (e) yanā̰ jị̄ (i) he's conscious. (ii) he's perceiving what is occurring. yanā̰ jịnsu he's conscious of what they're up to. ƙāƙạ zā su jī in . . . how will they feel if . . . ? yā ji bạ saurā he realized that nothing was left. kō yā dadẹ, bại sāmi wani ạbincī săi madarā ba, bạ zại ji kōmē ba even if he has to go for long with nothing but milk, he'll feel no discomfort. bại ji zāƙī ba he did not notice it had a sweet smell (cf. 4A below). yi minị gidaṇ tụkụṇ ṇ ji

make the house for me first and then I'll see how I like it ! (f) yanā̰ jịṇ aikị he's working might and main. (g) bā sā̰ jịṇ ƙārẹwā they are innumerable. (h) ƙāƙạ ka ƙārạ jḭ̄ do you feel better ? (j) yā ji ị jḭ̄ (i) he's replete. (ii) he's famished. (iii) he's having much trouble. (iv) he is weary. (v) he has been abused. (vi) he has been beaten. baṇ kāmạ shi ba, ạmmā yā ji yạ jḭ̄ I didn't manage to seize him, but I got in a stinging blow. (k) ji rānā Vd. yārọ 1o. (l) ji mặi Vd. yāmụtsā. (m) ji dāmā Vd. dāmā 1b.i, 3, 6. (n) ji sanyī Vd. sanyī. (o) ji ɗārī Vd. ɗārī 1a.ii. (p) ji ɗācī Vd. ɗācī 2, 3.

(4A) tasted x nā ji zāƙinsạ I tasted its pleasant flavour. (4B) smelt x nā ji wārinsạ I smelt its stench, i.e. its smell obtruded itself on my notice (cf. shẹ̄ƙā 1a).

(4C) caused to feel x yā ji minị cīwọ (i) he offended me (cf. cụ̄tā 1b). (ii) it (thorn, etc.) gave me sudden pain (cf. jḭ̄ dạ 2 ; gānạ). yā ji masạ tạkạicī it made him indignant. Jāmụs sun ji wạ mụtụm hạmsiṇ the Germans inflicted 50 casualties.

(5) obeyed x (a) yā ji mạganạtạ he obeyed me. (b) yanā̰ jịn lịnzāmị he (person, horse) is tractable. (c) yanā̰ jịn lịnzāminsu he obeys them. yanā̰ jịn lịnzāmịntạ " he is hen-pecked ". (d) yārạn naṇ bā yā̰ jḭ̄ this lad's disobedient.

(6) (a) was concerned about x Audụ nikẹ̄ jḭ̄ it is Audu for whom I am concerned. n nā̰ jịn tạfīyạn naṇ I'm concerned about this journey. kanā̰ jịn zūwạ ? ka bari wōƙacī yạ wụcẹ ? you wanted to come, didn't you ? —then why did you let the time go by ? (Mod. Gram. 164b). iṇ kunā̰ jịn cī if you really want to eat it, then . . .

(b) (i) **yā ji ƙaina** he had mercy on me, felt sympathy for me. (ii) **Allā majī ƙam bāwą** Merciful God ! (iii) **Allā yą ji ƙansą = Allā yą ji ƙan rąnsą = Allā yą yi masą jin ƙai** God have mercy on his soul ! (iii) **Allā cikin jin ƙansą yā sā mun kuɓucē** God in his mercy has kept us safe. (c) **bā yā jin ƙan ųbansą** he's not a dutiful son to his father. **kōmē rashin jin ƙansą, mē ząi sā m̥ bųgē shi** however undutiful he be, why should I beat him ?

(7) (a) **sunā jin ƙansu** they're really fine. **rīguną bīyū māsū jin ƙansu** two gowns each better than the other. (b) **kārūwōyī māsū jin ƙansu** harlots who are full of confidence through prosperity. (c) **mųtum mai jin ƙansą** prosperous and self-confident man (= **tąbbątaccē** 2a). (d) Vd. **jin ƙäi**.

(8) Vd. **jin**-compounds ; **jīyō** ; **jīyar** ; **jī dą, jīyę**.

(9) Vb. intransitive condiments are of just the right amount x **gishirī yā ji ą ąbincin** there is just the right amount of salt in the food.

B. (**jī**) m. (1) (progressive and v.n. of **jī**) Vd. **jī**. (2) Vd. compounds of **jin**. (3) (a) power of hearing or of understanding x **jinsą ƙąɗan nę** (i) he is hard of hearing. (ii) he has but little sense. (b) act of hearing x (i) **ganī yā fi jī** = **ganī yā kōri jī** seeing is believing. (ii) **dą jī, dą ganī bā sā ƙārēwā** wonders never cease. (iii) Vd. **ƙī**. (4) **ąbin ~** things to be listened to.

jiɓa A. (**jiɓā**) Vb. 2. (1) x **mun jiɓē shi** = **mun jiɓu dą shī** we're related to him, etc. (= **jiɓintą** q.v.). (2) affected P. other than the doer x **ląifin A yā jiɓi B** the crime of A had repercussions on B. (= **shāfā** 2).
B. (**jiɓā**) f. (1) (a) small anthill made by **zagō** (cf. **sūri** ; **gąrā** 2). (b) **biri yā**

san jiɓad dą yakē wą kāshī everybody knows his own limitations. (2) **hųlar ~** caplike top of mushroom-shaped anthills. (3) **lądānin ~ m.** puffball-fungus.

jiɓādau m. epithet of big, heavy gown or big-made, middle-aged woman.

jiɓājē rubbish-heaps (pl. of **jūjī**).

jiɓbą Ar. f. (pl. **jiɓbōbī**) type of sleeveless gown.

jiɓcē Kt. m. "making a whip round" (= **jūcē** q.v.).

jibdą Sk. f. musk (= **jūdą**).

jibdą Kt. Vb. 1A **tā ~** she struck pestle on corn to pound it (= **jindą**).

jibdę Kt. Vb. 1A **tā ~** she pounded all the corn (= **jindę**).

jibdi Kt. pounding of corn (= **jindi**).

jiɓę Vd. **jaɓę**.

jibga A. (**jibgą**) Vb. 1A. (1) piled up loads on one another x **sun ~ kāyā**. (2) (with dative) x **an ~ masą kāyā** (a) it (animal) has been overloaded (= **nannągā** 2). (b) he's been given gift after gift.
B. (**jibgā**) (1) m., f. (sg., pl.) fat P. (2) **~ rąban duhų** what a large quantity ! (3) f. type of head-dress worn by certain followers of Emir.
C. (**jibgā**) Vb. 2 (1) beat P. (2) **yā shā ~** he was beaten.

jibgaro Sk., Kt. court-messenger (= **jąbgaro** q.v.).

jibgayyą f. struggling of two or more persons.

jibgę Vb. 1A (1) = **jibgą**. (2) put aside from sloth or lack of present utility (work, tools, articles for sale, etc.) = **jaɓę** 2a.

jibgi (1) what a pile ! (2) adv. **yanā nan ~** what masses of it there are !

jibi A. (**jībi**) (1) m. and adv. (a) day after to-morrow (= **wąn shēkarę** 1). (b) **yau dą gōbe, jībi gwąnin rawā yā fądi** pride comes before a fall. (2) **watąn ~ m.** month after next. (3) Zar. **shēkarąn ~** 3rd day hence (= **gātą**).
B. (**jībi**) m. any meal.

jiɓi A. (**jiɓī**) m. (1) perspiration (= **gumī**). (2) **marąg gąskīyā kō cikin rūwa yā yi ~** murder will out. (3) cf. **shā ~**. (4) **dą jiɓin gōshī suką kuɓucē** they escaped by the skin of their teeth.

B. (jiɓi̧) (1) abundantly. (2) relationship *x* i̧nā jiɓi̧ŋka̧ da̧ Wa̧zīri̧ what's your relationship to the Waziri ? (*reply*, da̧ nī da̧ ūwā tasa̧ a̧ɓo̧kaŋ wa̧sā his mother and I were playmates), *Vd.* jiɓinta̧.

jiɓinta A. (ji̧ɓinta̧) *Vb.* 2 (*p.o.* ji̧ɓi̧ncē, *n.o.* ji̧ɓi̧nci). (1) is (was) related to *x* nā ji̧ɓi̧ncē shi̧ wajaŋ ūwā I'm related to him on my mother's side. (2) is (was) connected with *x* yā ji̧ɓi̧nci aiki̧ŋ hukumci̧ he's connected with judicial work.
B. (ji̧ɓi̧ntā) *Vb.* 1C (1) considered as being related *x* yā ∼ ni da̧ Sarkī = yā ∼ mini̧ Sarkī he considered me related to the Chief. (2) *x* an ∼ masa̧ aiki̧ŋ hukumci̧ he's been put on to judicial, etc., work.

Jibir = Ji̧bi̧ri̧ŋ.

Ji̧bi̧ri̧ŋ Gabriel (*Vd.* Ma̧nzo ; Jibo̧ ; Ji̧bi̧r).

jibjī *Sk.*, *Kt.* *m.* dungheap (= jūjī).

jibjibta̧ *Sk.* *f.* vulture (= u̧ŋgu̧lū).

Jibo̧ *name for any man called* Ji̧bi̧ri̧ŋ (*any man so named is often called* Ma̧nzo).

jice A. (jicȩ) (1) *Vb.* 1A. (*a*) overwhelmed *x* (i) hadiri̧ yā ∼ rānā storm's blotted out sun. (ii) dāki̧ yā ∼ shi house fell on him. (iii) an ∼ shi da̧ ita̧cē he was thrashed with a stick. (iv) yā ∼ dōki̧ he's too broad for the horse. (v) an ∼ shi da̧ kāyā his load's beyond him. (vi) hāki̧mī yā ∼ talakāwā the district-head treated his subjects harshly. (*b*) yā ∼ gishirī he baked salt into cakes (kantu̧) (*cf.* jici̧). (2) *Vb.* 3A. (*a*) ga̧rī yā ∼ sky's angry looking. (*b*) ida̧nunsa̧ yā ∼ his eye's "bunged up".
B. (ji̧ce) yā fādi̧ a̧ ∼ he fell on his face (*cf.* ru̧b da̧ ciki̧).

jici̧ *m.* (1) baking European salt (kaka̧nda̧) into cakes (kantu̧), these often being adulterated with beans or farfarā. (2) *cf.* rufi̧ 4.

jī da̧ *Vb.* 3A (1) caused T. to be heard by *x* yā ∼ sū shȩla̧ he read out proclamation to them. (2) caused T. to be experienced by P. over long period (*cf.* jī 4C) *x* kada̧ Allā ya̧ jīshē mu̧ wanna̧ŋ may God not cause this to be endured by us ! yā ∼ nī dādī he was

constant source of pleasure to me. yā jīshē ni̧ wu̧yā he was constant source of worry to me. Allā̧ jīshē mu̧ a̧lhēri̧ God give us lasting happiness !

ji̧dā (1) *Vb.* 2 removed several persons or things to another place *x* sun ji̧di kāyā. (2) *f.* quickly-moving clouds (= *Kt.* farkē 2), *cf.* girgijȩ. (3) dam ba̧ ∼ *Daura Hausa* chief of hunters' guild, this being official post. (4) *Vd.* no̧mi-ji̧di.

ji̧da *Vb.* 3B (*progressive* ji̧dā) *Sk.* dismounted ; lodged (= sa̧uka = *Sk.* shi̧da). (2) mu̧sība tana̧ ji̧dā bisa̧ ga̧rēsu̧ misfortune's afflicting them. (3) (water, anger) subsided (= kwa̧ntā).

ji̧dad da̧ *Vb.* 4A *Sk.* = saukad da̧ *x* yā ∼ kāyā he put the load down off his head. yā ∼ nī = yā jisshē ni̧ he lodged me.

ji̧dadu̧ŋ *adv.* for ever.

ji̧dāla̧ *Ar.* *f.* (1) struggle, combat *x* ∼ ga̧rēshi̧ he's contentious. (2) muna̧ shan ∼ we're having trouble with it.

ji̧dāli̧ *Sk.* *m.* = ji̧dāla̧.

jid da̧ (*derived by assimilation from* jid da̧) *Vb.* 3A *Sk.* = jīdad da̧.

ji̧ddi̧ŋ always *x* fi̧ddi̧ŋ ∼ halinsa̧ kȩ̄ naŋ this is the sort of thing he always does ! fi̧ddi̧ŋ ∼ tu̧tur ilalla̧ absolutely *always* (*cf.* ilalla̧).

ji̧dȩ *Vb.* 1A removed (*as in* ji̧dā) all the persons, etc.

jī̧dȩ *Vb.* 1A *Sk.* = saukȩ *x* yā ∼ kāyā he put down the load off his head.

ji̧do̧ *m.* removing *as in* ji̧dā.

jī̧fa̧ *m.* (*less usually f.*). (1) (*the secondary v.n. generally used to form progressive and v.n. of* jȩfā) *x* suna̧ jīfa̧nsa̧ da̧ māshi they're throwing a spear at him. (2) (*a*) throwing shuttle in weaving. (*b*) dan ∼ *m.* weaver's bobbin (= kwark-warō 2 = dan tārīyā). (3) act of throwing *x* (*a*) suŋ kai masa̧ ∼ they threw (spear, etc.) at him. (*b*) daŋ kūka̧ shī kaŋ jā wa̧ ūwā tasa̧ ∼ the faults of the children recoil on the parents. (*c*) kōmē tsananin ∼ (= kōmē nīsan ∼) ka̧sa̧ yakȩ̄ fādu̧wā no smoke without fire, patience wins. (*d*) in ∼ tā wucȩ (= in ∼ tā kȩ̄ta̧rȩ) ka̧ŋka̧, kō kaŋ wa̧ ya̧ fāda̧ every tub must stand on its own bottom. (e) jīfan kūrā Vd. sandā 1f. (f) bi tsuntsū da ∼ Vd. masō 1. (g) kanā jin ∼ Vd. dakama. (h) abin jīfan yuŋwa Vd. wākē 5b. (4) jumping from height by bōrī devotee without injury. (5) ∼ gabas, ɗauka yammā I saw you over there, fancy you turning up here ! (6) jīfan duhu m. = jīfar duhu f. generous present to woman no longer married (bazawarā) by her suitor.

jiffo Sk. f. vulture (= uŋgulū = jigal).

jifirma f. Martial Eagle (Polemœtus bellicosus).

jigā f. (sg., pl.) jigger insect (= kwark--wata 2).

jigājigai pl. of jijjige.

jigal f. (sg., pl.) vulture (= uŋgulū).

jigānīyā Sk.,* f. anā shan ∼ da shī it's giving much trouble.

jigāta Vb. 3B Sk. suffered trouble (cf. jigānīyā).

jigāwa f. (pl. jigāyī = jigāwū). (1) sandy soil. (2) ∼ tārin Allā mai wuyar jiŋkēwā " Man proposes and God disposes ".

jigāwalā f. vulture (= uŋgulū).

jigib = jigibgib adv. emphasizing heaviness or dampness.

jigidā f. (pl. jigidū). (1) woman's hip-girdle (epithet is ∼ gishirin gindī), Vd. Gwārī 7, bōko 1c. (2) necklace made from shell of palm-kernel or coco-nut (1 being also made therefrom). (3) yā zame mini ∼ it (T. I wish to sell) is a " drug in the market ". (4) anā ∼ da shī he's being " dragged off his feet ".

jigina m. (1) elder brother or father of chief. (2) yā yi ∼ he (elder brother of or father of the Chief) is mere figure-head (as he should normally have been Chief).

jigindi m. large amount.

jigiriftū Vd. zagaraftū.

jīgo m. (pl. jīguna). (1) (a) pole of apparatus for irrigating lambū-farm (= Sk. kutāra), Vd. gwaiwā 2. (b) pole for hanging articles on. (c) (mining) underground pillars supporting roof. (d) tethering-post (= turke). (2) (a) leader. (b) ∼ ubam marātayā epithet of energetic P. (c) wannan taimakō yā

kāra babban jīgo ga nasara this help was a great contribution to victory.

jīgōjī veins (pl. of jījīyā q.v.).

jīguna Vd. jīgo.

jiha Ar. f. direction (= jāha q.v.).

jihādi Ar. m. war to propagate Islam (= jahādi q.v.).

jihirma Sk. f. = jifirma.

jije A. (jīje) Vb. 1A x yā ∼ tabō daga (= jikin) kafassa he scraped his foot clean of mud by drawing foot along ground, etc. (cf. jīza).
    B. (jijē) Vd. jīzā.

ji-ji A. (jī-jī) m. conceit x ∼ da kāi garēshi he's conceited (cf. jin kāi).
    B. (jī-jī) x munā ganinsa ∼ he seems to us conceited.

jiji A. (jījī) Vd. jīzā.
    B. (jīji) the sedge kājīji q.v.

jijigadi m. going hither and thither (= jējēgadi).

jījīyā f. (pl. jījīyōyī = jīgōjī = jīyōjī). (1) (a) (i) vein. (ii) artery. (b) muscle x an ɗaura wa sā kulkī don a kashe masa ∼ beam's been fixed to ox's neck to neutralize strength of its muscles. (c) Masar jījījā cē mai karfī Egypt is a vital position. Kano tanā wurī nē magamar ∼ Kano is a focal point. (2) nā ɗaure shi da jījīyar jikinsa I " blarneyed " him. (3) Audu ∼ bā nāma ba I'm surprised that the small, wiry Audu has proved so strong (= saurō 2).

jijjifī = jijjif m. (1) da ∼ at the pro-tracted period of brighter light preceding sunrise (Vd. Mod. Gram. 111d). (2) nā yi ∼ I set out at early dawn (= sammakō).

jijjiga A. (jijjigā) Vb. 1C. (1) shook T. to and fro. (2) tā jijjiga ɗanta she dandled her baby lad to hush him.
    B. (jijjiga) (1) Vb. 3B. (a) is (was) shaken to and fro. (b) (child) is (was) dandled x yā ki ∼ all dandling failed to hush the baby. (2) Zar. f. the horse's gait jan harāwa.

jijjige A. (jijjige) m. (pl. jigājigai). (1) (a) forked, upright beam(s) (wācila) supporting weak roof. (b) beam for wedging door (= gāgara 10d). (c) influential P. (d) = shisshikę 2. (2) the horse's gait bąsąngalā.

B. (jįjįįgē) m. dandling a child.
jik clear out, Vulture ! (= Kt. jit).
jika A. (jįkā) Kt. f. bag (= jąkā q.v.).

B. (jīką) m., f. (f. also jīkanyą) pl. jīkōkī = jīyōkī = jīkąnnī = jīkąnū. (1) grandchild (epithet is ~ mąyātą kąkā). (2) dan ~ = tąbą kunnē. (3) dafą wą jīkōkįnkį Vd. dadį 5.

C. (jiką) Vd. jįkī 2.

D. (jįką) used in ~ dą regarding x jįką dą sąrautą in reference to rulership.

jiƙa A. (jiƙą) Vb. 1A. (1) moistened. (2) sun ~ hantąssą they treated him liberally. ~ hantą f. generosity (cf. laimątā 1b).

B. (jįƙa) Vb. 3B (progressive jįƙā). (1) (a) became moist. (b) yā ~ it (cooked food) became flabby. (c) yā ~ (i) horse or P. has fattened out. (ii) horse is unsatisfied through shortness of gallop. (iii) yā sōmą jįƙūwā P. or horse has begun to fill out. (d) kąnwā bā tą jįƙā ą bąkinsą he's a windbag. (2) mąganąr Kano jiƙar kąnwā true I've had to wait long to find the apt retort, but now I've found it !

jiką dą jiką adv. very close together.
jika-jika A. (jįkā-jikā) m., f. (pl. jįkā-jįkai) fat x mųtųm ~ fat P. mātā jįkājįkai fat women.

B. (jiką-jiką) Vd. jįkī 2c.
jįƙā-jįƙā f. slapdash work.
jikąncē Vb. 1C Kt. made T. into bag.
jįkąnū ; jįkąnnī Vd. jīką.
jįkanyą Vd. jīką.
jiƙę (1) Vb. 3A. (a) = jįƙa 1a, b. (2) farar rīgā tā ~ white gown became indigo-tinged from dyed gown worn over it (Vd. ban shūnī). (2) Vb. 1A. (a) soaked thoroughly ; soaked all of. (b) suką jiƙę shi kaf they attacked him tooth and claw.

jįkī m. (pl. jikuną = jikuŋkuną = jikū-kūwą). (1) (a) body. (b) (i) yā jā ~ yā shįga gidā he made his way painfully home. (ii) yā jąnyę ~ he withdrew from participation. (iii) Kt. yąnā jąn ~ he's slacking. (c) tufą tā shā ~ the clothing

is worn out. (d) yā yi ~ he's become fat. (e) (i) n nā jįn ~ I feel very ill. (ii) n nā jįn ~ haką-haką (= . . . dąmą-dąmą = mąshąr-mąshąr) I feel out of sorts. (iii) mun ji ~ it was a serious misfortune to us. (f) wannąŋ yā zamā ~ gąrēshį this has become a habit with him. (g) ~ magąyī the strain will tell on you in the end ; don't fly in the face of providence ! (h) kibīyą ą jįkiŋ wani, kwąrī one P. does not really care what befalls another. (j) jįkim mųtųm type of okra, light-coloured and with smooth exterior. (k) mų kai ~ let's go close up ! (l) (i) suŋ hadą ~ they've collected in a group. (ii) aŋ gamą ~ they've come to blows (Vd. gamą 1g). (m) ƙin ~ m. energy. (n) yā mai dą ~ he's regained his former health. (o) jįkin taląką duk kudī nē = jįkin dāwą duk gąrī nē an inferior has no choice but to obey orders (Vd. taląką 2). (p) (i) ~ yā fi kunnē jį if P. won't listen to advice, he must learn in the hard school of experience. (ii) dą kunnē yā jī, dą ~ yā tsīrā forewarned is forearmed. (q) bā ąbin da zai dauką ą jikinsą he will get no profit. (r) jįkī yā yi sanyī Vd. sanyī 4. (s) yąnkę jikī Vd. yąnkę 1g. (t) ya sąki jikī Vd. sąkā 2d. (u) tārą jikī Vd. tārą 1b. (v) sąn jikī Vd. son 4. (w) jįkī dū dādī Vd. bųdurų. (x) bą ką ci jikī ba Vd. dųnjī. (2) (after prep. ą, the form jiką may be used) x (a) yā hąrbē shį ą jiką = yā hąrbē shį ą jįkī he shot him in the body. (b) (i) aŋ haląkā su dą jininsų ą jiką they were killed young. (ii) jinin jįkī Vd. jinī 7. (c) yanā jąnsą jiką-jiką he is intimate with him (cf. jįkā-jikā). (d) shēkarą bā tą fādūwā sāi ą jiką time leaves its mark on a P. (3) Vd. jikin.

jikkā Kt. f. bag (= jąkā q.v.).
jikkata A. (jikkątą) Vb. 3B is (was) reduced to straits.

B. (jikkątā) Vb. 1C reduced P. to straits.

jįkin prep. embedded in ; against the side of (derived from jįkī q.v.) x gwaŋ-gwaŋ yanā dą marįkī ą jikinsą the tin has a handle fixed to it. ƙūsą tanā ~

itącē the nail's sticking in the wood.
haƙōrī yanâ ∼ dāsąshī the tooth's in
the gums. fartanyą tanâ ∼ (= cikiɲ)
ƙōtą the hoe's fixed in its haft.   yā
dāfą tsāni ∼ baŋgō he leaned the ladder
against the wall.   nā gōgą mąi ą
jikinsą I rubbed polish on it.   yā
shāfą farar ƙasā ∼ baŋgō he whitewashed the wall.   anâ dībąm mąi
ą ∼ gyądā (= ą cikiɲ gyądā) oil's
extracted from ground-nuts.   gidāna
yanâ ∼ gidansą my compound adjoins
his. yā są kibīyą ∼ bąkā he put arrow
in bow.
jiƙọ m. (1) (a) marinī yā yi ∼ dyer made
indigo-infusion.   (b) tonic made from
infusion of herbs.   (2) sąi wani ∼
not now, another time ! (3) (a) kąrē yā
zubar dą tsāmīyar kūrā, ya cę " sąi
wani jiƙwąɲ ! " that won't be for many
a long day.   (b) sąi dąi wani jiƙọ,
kąrē yā zubad dą tsāmīyar kūrā that's
the end of the matter for the present.
jikuną Vd. jiƙī ; jiƙā.
jim Vd. jimą 1c.
jima A. (jīmą) f. (1) (secondary v.n. of
jēmą) x yanâ jīmąr fātą = yanâ jēmą
fātą he's tanning the skin.   (2) act of
tanning x yanâ ∼ he is a tanner.   (3)
kōrā jīmąr Allâ ringworm is the tanning
done by God.   (4) Sk. indą fātą ta hi
tabshī, naɲ akę mai dą ∼ one takes
line of least resistance (Vd. taushī).
(5) gāshiɲ ∼ goats' hair scraped off
soaked skins by dyers.
    B. (jimą) Vb. 3A (1) spent quite a
time at, on x (a) yā ∼ yanâ aiki he's
been working for some time.   (b) n
nâ zūwą iɲ aɲ ∼ I'm coming shortly.
(c) (i) jim kądaɲ (= dą aką jimą) sąi
ya kōmō after a while he returned. (ii)
bą ą ∼ ba, suką gudu soon they fled.
(iii) bāyan jimąwā kądaɲ suką yąrdā
it was not long before they agreed.
(iv) kąmiɲ jimąwā kądaɲ kumā suką
isō they arrived shortly afterwards.
(2) sąi an ∼ = sąi an jimąɲku au
revoir ! (3) ąbin naɲ jimąwā gąrēshi
this thing has durability. (4) tun dą
jimąwā (= tun dą jimąwā kę naɲ),
Jāmus ɲâ naɲ, suɲ wulākąntā (= sunâ
ta wulākąntā) su the Germans have

long been tormenting them. tun dą
jimąwā sukę zūwą they have been
coming since some time. (5) jimą dą
x (a) an ∼ dą fārą shi it was begun
long ago. (b) Sk. Allâ yą ∼ dą raŋką
long life to you ! (= dadę 2). (6) kō
bą dadę, kō bą jimą, zā ą yī it is bound
to be done sooner or later (= kul 2b).
    C. (jimą) f. mere rumour.
jimada A. (jīmādā) f. type of black and
white striped native cloth.
    B. (Jīmādą) Vd. tagwai.
*jimā'i Ar. m. (polite term, replacing the
vulgar cī 16a) = duhūli sexual intercourse (Vd. tārą 2, tąkā 1d).
jim bąkī Vd. jin bąkī.
jimɓirērę m. (f. jimɓirērīyā) pl. jimɓir-
jimɓir heavy.
jimɓirī (1) m. (f. jimɓirā) pl. jimɓir-
jimɓir heavy. (2) m. (a) moist beans,
ground-nuts, or Bambarra ground-nuts
(gujīyā). (b) unripe tamarind-pods
(tsāmīyā).
jimɓurɓur m. heaviness x ąbu nē ∼ dą
shī it's a heavy thing.
jimdą Daura = jindą.
jimfī m. (1) load of grass for horse. (2)
inā kakę ka kai jimfiɲką have you no
home so that you come and eat here ?
jimillą Ar. f. (pl. jimillū). (1) (a) total.
(b) an tārą ∼ tasu they've been added
up. (c) Vd. jimlą. (2) jimilląr hākimī
area or subjects of a District Head
(= kampąnī 2).
jimiltā Vb. 1C totalled up (Vd. lāsąftā).
jiminā f. (pl. jiminū = jiminai = jimi-
nōnī). (1) (a) (i) ostrich (epithet is
Tōri). (ii) cf. bąrōdō ; bīcilmī. (b)
dan tsąkwan jiminā, gągarą shāfą
dauką it's beyond one. (c) sū mąsū
saɲ kudī nę kąmar jiminā they are
terribly eager for money (N.B.—
ostrich likes crunching up cowries). (d)
gāshiɲ jiminā Vd. tsōfō 1g. (2) Kt. ∼
tā hąrbē shi he has a new-born child
(= rągō 2 q.v.).
jimirī m. (1) endurance, patience x yanâ
dą ∼ he's persevering.   itātūwąnsu
sunâ dą jimirin rąyūwā their trees are
hardy. (2) Vd. jiŋgā 1d. (3) mai
jimiriɲ as Vd. as. (4) jimirin shąwāgi
Vd. tsąrakā.

jimƙạ *Vb.* 1A gave P. handful of T., *etc.*
(= daŋƙạ *q.v.*).

jimlạ *f.* (1) = jimillạ. (2) (*a*) jimlạ-
jimlạ *adv.* portion by portion. (*b*)
kadạ kạ yanyạŋkạ ƙanānạ, yạŋkā
shi ～ cut it into big chunks !

jimlạtā *Vb.* 1C = jimịltā.

Jimmạ = Jimmai = *Kt.* Jimo name for
girl born on Friday (*Vd.* Jumma'ạ).

jịmōlạ *f.* (1) type of owl. (2) West
African genet (= inyāwarā).

jịmrau (1) *Kt. m., f.* (*sg., pl.*) patient P.
(= jụ̄rai *q.v.*). (2) *Sk.* type of reddish
rice.

jimrẹ *Sk., Kt.* is (was) long-suffering
(= jūrẹ *q.v.*).

jịnai (*Eng.-Ar.* guinea) *used for* pound
sterling *in Egypt*.

jina-jina A. (jịnạ-jịnạ) *f.* the weed majinācịyā *q.v.*
B. (jinā-jịnạ̄) (1) *adv. x* muŋ gan
sụ ～ we saw them (combatants) in
gory state. (2) *f.* severe struggle.

jịnạr *m.* = jịnai.

*jịnāyạ *Ar. f.* wounding.

jin baki (jịm bậ̄ƙī) *m.* quarrelsomeness *x* ～
gạrēshị he's quarrelsome. (2) yạnậ̄ ～
he's picking a quarrel (*Vd.* bậƙī 2*x*).

jinɗa A. (jinɗạ) *Vb.* 1A tā ～ she struck
pestle on corn in pounding.
B. (jịnɗā) *Vb.* 2 (1) tā jịnɗi hatsī
she pounded corn. (2) an jịnɗē shi
he's been thrashed.

jinɗẹ *Vb.* 1A pounded all the corn.

jinɗị *m.* (1) (*secondary v.n. of* jịnɗā) *x*
tanậ̄ jinɗịŋ hatsī = tanậ̄ jịnɗar hatsī
she's pounding the corn. (2) act of
pounding corn *x* tanậ̄ jinɗị.

jinga A. (jịŋgā) *f.* (1) (*a*) wages. (*b*) an yi ～
rate of wages has been agreed on (=
tsậ̄dā 3). (*c*) ɗan ～ *m.* (*pl.* 'yan ～)
daily labourer. (*d*) *Sk.* ～ jịmirī *epithet
of* P. learning barbering (*lit.* his wages
are the long-sufferings of his
customers). (2) earth embankment to
prevent water flooding farm or for
damming-in fish.
B. (jịŋgạ) *Vb.* 1A (*with dative*)
pierced *x* yā ～ masạ māshi he pierced
him with spear.   yā ～ masạ kibīyạ
he punctured him with red-hot arrow
to let out pus (*cf.* saƙīyạ).

jiŋgacē *Vd.* jịŋgatạ.

jiŋ garī *m.* (1) yịnậ̄ ～ he's feeling pinch
of poverty. (2) rumour *x* kō jiŋ garī
nẹ̄ mukạ jị ? was it mere rumour we
heard ? (Mod. Gram. 164*c* ; 165*b*). (2)
(*negatively*) bā yậ̄ ～ = bậ̄ shi dạ ～
he's disobedient.

jịŋgatạ *Vb.* 2 (*p.o.* jịŋgacē, *n.o.* jịŋgaci)
hired P. by the day.

jiŋgẹ *Vb.* 1A *x* yā jiŋgẹ shi dạ māshị =
jịŋgạ.

jiŋgịdạ *f.* leather bangle ornamented with
beads (= deŋgịdạ).

jingim A. (jịŋgim) (1) abundantly (*but
not re* liquids) *x* nā ga mutận̄ẹ ～ I saw
many people.   dāwạ tanậ̄ naŋ ～ there's
much money available. (2) *Vd.*
jịŋgiŋ.
B. (Jịŋgim) *epithet of* ajịŋgī *q.v.*

jịŋgimgim *x* yanậ̄ da nawyī ～ it's very
heavy.

jiŋgim-jịŋgim *m.* altercation (= dabar-
dạbar 1*a, b, q.v.*).

jịŋgiŋ (1) *Kt. x.* yanậ̄ jịŋgin dạ gidāna
it's near my home. (2) *Vd.* jịŋgim.

jingina A. (jịŋginā) (1) *Vb.* 1C. (*a*)
propped T. against *x* yā ～ shi dạ
baŋgō he propped it against the wall
(= daŋgạnā 1*b* = rāɓạ 3*a*). wạsīyyạ
ạbar jịŋgināwā gạ mạrậyū the will
referring to the orphans. (*b*) pawned *x*
nā ～ shi wurinsạ, nā kạrɓi 10*s.* I
pawned it with him for 10*s.* (= daŋgạnā 1*a*). (2) *Vb.* 3A leaned against
x nā ～ dạ baŋgō I leaned against wall.
B. (jịŋginạ) (1) *Vb.* 3B *x* nā ～ dạ
baŋgō I leaned against wall. (2) *f.*
pledge. (*a*) nā bā dạ shī ～ I gave it as
a pledge, pawned it (= daŋgạnạ 2*b*.i).
(*b*) yā kaɗạ ～ tasạ (i) he squandered
his substance. (ii) he spoiled his chances
(= daŋgạnạ 2*b*.ii, iii). (*c*) jịŋginạr
Kirụ (i) inability to redeem pawned
T. (ii) pawning T. useless to pawn-
broker. (iii) inability to fulfil promise.

jịŋginad dạ *Vb.* 4B pawned.

jịŋgine A. (jịŋginẹ̄) *Vb.* 1C ignored P.
B. (jịŋginẹ̄) *m.* (1) sitting horse
badly and so damaging it with spurs.
(2) adding room to main building and
utilizing existing wall.

jiŋgiŋgiŋ = jịŋgimgim.

jiŋgir *m.* (1) pounded gērō flour given mourners at funeral (= *Kt.* bīyạ gāwā). (2) *Daura Hausa* food given as alms 3 days after funeral.

jiŋ girmā *m.* being conceited.

jinī *m.* (1) (*a*) blood. (*b*) igīyạr ∼ *f.* vein ; artery. (*c*) (i) an yi masạ ∼ blood was drawn by the blow. yā tārạ masạ ∼ it bruised him. (*d*) nā būdẹ masạ ∼ I bled it (horse, donkey). (*e*) ∼ bā yạ̄ māganiŋ ƙishirwā = ∼ bā yạ̄ māganin yuŋwạ. finally, oppression brings one to grief. (*f*) rashin ∼, rashin tsāgạ̄wā getting T. without trouble (= tsiŋkạ 1*e* = kāmạ 1*a*.vi = ƙi 1*b*). (*g*) jinī bā yạ̄ wucẹ wuyạ everything has its own purpose. (*h*) dạ jinī ạ bakạ a kạn zubad dạ farin yau men being what they are, one must learn to pardon. (2) menstruation *x* taŋạ̄ ∼ she has her periods. bặiwā, jinintạ bīyū ; ạmmā 'yā, jinintạ ukụ nē slave-girl is free to marry after menstruating twice, but free-women cannot re-marry till after third menstruation (*cf.* iddạ). (3) murder *x* kadạ kạ bar ƙasā tạ shā jininsạ don't slay him ! nā bi jiniŋ Audụ I sought compensation for Audu, my murdered kinsman (*Vd.* bị jinī). (4) (*a*) yanạ̄ dạ farin ∼ = yanạ̄ dạ jinim mutạ̄nē he is popular (*Vd.* farin jinī). mutụm mại jinim mutạ̄nē popular or pleasant P. (*c*) bạ̄ shi dạ jinī = yanạ̄ dạ baƙin ∼ he's unpopular (= yagwan jinī = tazgarō). (*d*) yā ƙi jinīna he dislikes me. (*e*) *Vd.* bạ̄ƙō 1*c*. (*f*) baƙin jinim mụzūrū, mại kạ̄zā zāgị, marạk kạ̄zā zāgị give a dog a bad name and hang him ! (*cf.* farin jinī). (*g*) jinimmụ bại hạdu ba we don't get on together. (5) *Vd.* jinị-jinị. (6) jininsạ yā kōmạ ạ kụmbā he was terrified. (7) (*a*) yā shā jinin jiki he was on his guard (= *Kt.* tsạ̄rakạ). (*b*) sun shā jinin jikinsụ they became afraid. (*c*) aŋ halặkā su dạ jininsụ ạ jikạ they were killed while young. (*d*) *cf.* shạ̄ jinī. (8) sun yi kạrē ∼ biri ∼ they oppose each other fiercely. (9) kisạŋkị bā ∼ *Vd.* yuŋwạ 1*a*. (10) gạman ∼ *Vd.* gạmō 1*b*. (11) nēman ∼ *Vd.* bābẹ 2.

(12) rabạ hantạ dạ ∼ *Vd.* hantạ 1*a*.ii. (13) gạyạ ∼ *Vd.* bịsạlạ̄mī. (14) bugạ ∼ *Vd.* bugạ 1*h*. (15) gụdan ∼ *Vd.* gụdā 1*b*.iv. (16) sārạ ∼ *Vd.* sārạ 1*d*. (17) jiniŋ kāfụrī type of red bead for necklaces. (18) jiniŋ kạrē *Kt.* a dark maize. (19) jinin sạrautạ lineal descendant of Chief.

jinị-jinị *formula introducing children's game* wạ̄san jinī (*reply* jinī *is made when T. containing blood is mentioned*).

jịninị *Sk. m.* harping on past wrongs.

jiniya A. (jīnịyā) *f.* (*pl.* jīnīyōyī). (1) grass-roll on wall-top as cushion (purlin) for roof to rest on (= kalaŋkūwā 3). (2) grass-torch *x* yā daukō ∼, zạ̄ su cin zumạ he took and lit a grass-torch to smoke out the bees (= yūlā = *Kt.* mūshē = *Zar.* tụkwīmạ = bạ̄kiŋ wutā *q.v.*). (3) jīnịyā, dạu dākị = jīnịyā dạu daŋgi what a liberal P.!

B.. (jīnịya) *Eng. m.* (1) engineer (= injịnīyạ). (2) steam-syren. (3) cotton-ginning establishment. (4) wool tied round girl's neck as adornment.

jinjimī *m.* Sacred (white) Ibis (*Threskiornis œthiop.*) = tuntumī 1*a* = dịddifạ.

jinjina A. (jinjịnā) *Vb.* 1C. (1) tested. (2) pondered on.

B. (jinjinạ) *f.* (1) (*a*) shaking raised spear or hand in saluting superior (= jāfị). (*b*) *Vd.* riƙạ 1*c*. (2) preliminary drumming on beginning again after period of silence.

jinjinnịyā *Vd.* jinjịrī.

jinjirī *m.* (*f.* jinjinnịyā = jinjirnịyā = *Sk.* jirjirnịyā) *pl.* jirạ̄jịrai = fililiļkī = jạ̄rīrị) baby (*as opposed to bigger P.* ; but taŋạ̄ dạ gōyō she has a baby). (2) Jinjịrī, bạ kạ sam " bābu " ba *epithet of* persistent P.

jinƙā *m.*, *f.* (1) act of thatching *x* an yi wạ dākị ∼ (= hayị 1*a*.ii. = *Kt.* bặibayē). (2) the thatch *x* bā shi dạ ∼ it's not thatched (*cf.* rufạ 1*c*.ii ; rufị).

jiŋ kại *m.* (1) arrogance. (2) *Vd.* jī 7.

jiŋ ƙai *Vd.* jī 6*b, c*.

jiŋkakkē *m.* (*f.* jiŋkakkīyā) *pl.* jiŋkakkū (1) having been thatched. (2) weal'hy.

jiŋkẹ *Vb.* 1A. (1) yā ∼ dākị he thatched the house (= *Kt.* bặibayē 1), *cf.* rufạ

1c.ii, rufi, jita 3. (2) yā ∼ ni he gave me present. (3) mai wuyar jiŋƙēwā Vd. tāri 1b.

jiŋƙim = jiŋƙim = jiŋƙimƙim = jiŋƙiŋƙiŋ x yanā da nawyī ∼ it's very heavy.

jiŋkirī m. (1) tardiness x (a) yā yi ∼ da yawa he was very slow about it. (b) yā sā mana jiŋkirī wajan shiga yāƙi it caused us to delay in entering the war. (2) Allā ya bā mu ∼ God give us long life !

jinkirta A. (jiŋkirta) Vb. 3B is (was) tardy.

B. (jiŋkirtā) Vb. 1C. (1) postponed x mu ∼, kō sā isō let's postpone it in the hope they'll come ! (2) (with dative) nā ∼ masa (a) I waited for him. (b) I extended his time for paying debt.

jiŋkirtad da Vb. 4B caused to be delayed.

jiŋ kunnē m. rumour.

jiŋ rāi m. conceit.

*jinsi Ar. m. (1) kind. (2) grammatical gender. (3) sex of P. or animal.

jiŋ wutā m. used in ∼ akē yī da shī it's unsaleable (cf. wutā 1f).

jinya Sk. = jīyya.

jinyata Sk. jiyyata.

jippo Sk. f vulture (= uŋgulū).

jir used in jā jir scarlet (= wur).

jira A. (jirā) (1) Vb. (progressive and v.n. jira). (a) waited for x nā ∼ shi I waited for him (= dāƙatā = tsumāya). (b) (i) yā yi jiran ya ji lābāri he waited for news. (ii) mai jiran gadō heirapparent, second in command. (iii) wanda kē jiran kabaki dungum, ba yā kula da lōma ba important desires blot out trifling wishes. (iv) Vd. lōkacī 2. (v) jiran akwiya Vd. kūrā 36. (vi) yanā jiran gāwan shānū he's been kept waiting indefinitely (i.e. like cows waiting for gāwō fruit to fall). (c) (with dative) kept watch over x jira mini shī guard it for me ! yanā jiran gida he's guarding the compound. (d) rūwan jira mai haƙurī kā shā shi (said by woman) epithet of her younger ƙawā. (2) Vb. intransitive waited.

B. (jira) Vd. jirā.

C. (jirā) f. (sg., pl.) Weaver-bird (Ploceus luteolus ; Plesiosittagra cuc-

culatus ; Ptelia melba citerior) = Sk. būwa = gādō = Kt. mārai.

jirācē Vd. jirāta.

jirāgē Vd. jirgī.

jirāi Sk. m. gum (= ƙārō q.v.).

jirājirai Vd. jinjirī.

jirāta Vb. 2 (p.o. jirācē, n.o. jirāci). (1) waited for. (2) yā zamā jirāta saŋwa, gandun ƙwalamā = yā zamā jirāta saŋwa, kantar ƙwalamā he's one who hangs about near meal-time, hoping he will be invited to stay. (3) jirāci bābu Vd. batar da 5.

jirāya Vb. 2 waited for.

Jirāyē Kt. = Taƙāta.

jirbācē m. acting or speaking senselessly.

jirbayya f. hitting one another.

jirbō = jirƙō.

jirdā-jirdā Vd. jirdēdе.

jirdе (1) Vb. 1A. (a) dislocated, sprained (= girdе q.v.). (b) uprooted (tree, post). (c) mutūwa tā ∼ shi sudden death befell him. (2) Vb. 3A. (a) is (was) dislocated, sprained. (b) is (was) uprooted.

jirdēdе m. (f. jirdēdīyā) pl. jirdā-jirdā huge.

jirdi how heavy !

jirga (1) Vb. 1A. (a) slewed T. round (= jūya). (b) tilted (wide-mouthed vessel in which liquid has run low) x tā ∼ tukunyā, tā dēbе hatsī (= jirkicē 1a). (c) yā ∼ alkalamī he cut pen on the slant. (2) Vb. 3A. (a) slewed round x hadiri yā ∼ wajan kudu the storm's veered southwards. (b) moved aside a little. (3) cf. jirgе.

jirgad da = jirga 1c.

jirgai-jirgai used in yanā tafīya ∼ he (P. whose legs are of different length) is hobbling along.

jirganya Zar. f. boat, canoe (jirgī).

jirge A. (jirgе) (1) Vb. 1A. (a) tā ∼ turmī, tā yi zanе she (Asbin, Barebari, or Bararo woman) folded " piece " of akōkō or bāsuma cloth in half and sewed it to make a body-cloth. (b) tā ∼ rīgā, tā yi zanе she (as in 1) made kōrе-cloth into body-cloth. (c) x yā ∼ sulе bīyar a cikī he (debtor) deducted from it (debt) the five shillings owed him by creditor and paid him the balance (= zargę 1*f*). (*d*) = jirgą 1*c*. (*e*) tā ∼ gōyō = tā jirgō gōyō she hitched forward the baby on her back (= jirkįcē 1*b*). yā ∼ rįgā he (sitter) slipped off his gown by passing armhole over his head. (2) *Vb.* 3A. (*a*) bąkī yā ∼ mouth became contorted by illness. (*b*) kāyā (sirdį) yā ∼ the load on animal (saddle) slipped out of place (= jirkįcē 2*a*). (3) *cf.* jirgą. B. (jįrgē) *m.* (1) hitching baby round *as in* jirgę 1*c*. (2) pen cut on the slant (= dąwąyē), *cf.* kąfē.

jirgī *m.* (*pl.* jirągē) (1) (*a*) (i) jirgī = jirgin rūwā boat, canoe, steamer (*epithet of* steamer *is* Shątīmą, bąƙwan Tūrai). (ii) ∼ yā dąuki rūwā the boat is leaking, water has swirled into the boat. (iii) jirginsą yā dąuki rūwā he has been found out. (*b*) (i) jirgī = jirgių ƙasā railway-train. (ii) *epithets of train are* Mahąuƙącī dągą Tūrai = Sąkāką mąnzan Tūrai = Samamī yąnkę dawą = tąkarkąrī 1*c* = dōgō 1*a*.iii = shą'awą 2*b* = Shątīmą bąƙwan Tūrai = fasą 1*k*.iii. (iii) jirgin dąddawā slow (not express) train. (iv) mātansų sųŋ įsa mātan shįgā ∼ their women are very pretty. (v) *Vd.* kūkan jirgī. (*c*) yąnā bąkin ∼ he's at the railway station. (*d*) (i) hanyąr ∼ *f.* railway line, permanent way. (ii) hanyōyin jirągyaŋ ƙasąn naŋ the railway system of that country. (*e*) jirgin samą aeroplane. jirągyan samą 'yam fashį raiding aeroplanes. jirgin samą ɗam faɗą fighter plane. jirgin samą ɗam bọm bombing plane. jirągyan samąnsų their air-fleet. jirgin samą na rūwā seaplane. (2) (*a*) cattle-trough (= kōmī 1*b*). (*b*) metalworkers' mould. (*c*) (*mining*) sluice-box. (3) (*a*) line indented along swordblade. (*b*) jirgin dallą line down forehead, nose, or both, made by child as adornment by rubbing with cloth (= kantā 2). (4) the cloth wāwā. (5) pen cut on the slant (= jįrgē 2). (6) (*a*) Jirgių askā, wą zai tąri gōshinsą *epithet of* Mādākī. (*b*) *Vd.* askā 9. (7) jirgin danƙarō (*a*) motor road-roller (ūwar dąɓē). (*b*) dilatory P.

jirgīyā *f.* (1) deducting *as in* jirgę 1*c* (= zāmīyā). (2) *Kt.* seven gūrū belts joined for adornment, not as charm.

jirgō *Vd.* jirgę 1*c*.

jįrī *m.* (1)(*a*) neuralgia *x* ∼ yā tąskā masą he has neuralgia. (*b*) kąina yaną̄ ∼ I feel dizzy (= jų̄wā 1 = hąjįjīyą 1). (2) the tree sansamī.

jirif *x* ųngųlū tā sąuka ∼ vulture settled plonk !

jįrin dą rānī *Bauchi Hausa* type of hemp maturing in hot season (= girin dą rānī).

jirjirnīyā *Vd.* jinjįrī.

jirkįcē (1) *Vb.* 1A. (*a*) (i) tilted. (ii) tilted vessel in which corn run low *x* tā jirkįcę hatsī dągą tukunyā she tilted pot and let the corn run out (= jirgą 1*b* = *Kt.* margąyā 1). (*b*) tā jirkįcę gōyō = tā jirkitō gōyō she hitched forward the baby on her back (= jirgę 1*e*). (2) *Vb.* 3A (*a*) kāyā (sirdį) yā ∼ load on animal (saddle) slipped out of place (= jirgę 2*b*). (*b*) ƙwaryā (tukunyā) tā ∼ calabash or pot (*i.e.* wide-mouthed vessel) fell over, upsetting contents. tābą tā ∼ tin of tobacco fell over, upsetting contents. (*c*) changed in appearance *x* kąmā tatą tā ∼ her appearance is changed (*because of pregnanƈy, etc*). (3) *cf.* jirkįtā.

jirkįcin tumɓwīką *Kt.* = jūyį gātam farā.

jirkita A. (jirkitą) *Vb.* 3B = jirkįcē 2*c*. B. (jirkįtā) (1) *Vb.* 3A turned round (in changing one's direction). (2) *Vb.* 1C = jirkįcē 1.

jirkitad dą *Vb.* 4B threw away (liquid or grain) = zubar dą.

jirkitō *Vd.* jirkįcē.

jirƙō (1) *m.* (*sg., pl.*). (*a*) work requiring long time to do (*epithet is* ∼ aikįn sųrųkai). (*b*) slow worker. (2) (*a*) what a lengthy job ! (*b*) what a slow worker !

jirnąkō *Zar.* the hornet zįrnąkō *q.v.*

jirọ *Kt. m.* wall of round-house (kagọ) built of clay not made into bricks (*Vd.* gōgą).

jįrwāyē *m.* (1) trickling of water on to P. carrying leaking vessel. (2) leak in roof letting water trickle down (= bį baŋgō). (3) boiling over of water. (4) ∼ dạ kạmar waŋkā innuendo (= habaicī).

jĭshē Vd. jĭ dạ.

jisshē Sk. Vd. jĭdad dạ.

jit Kt. clear out, Vulture ! (= jĭk).

jitạ Vb. 1A. (1) put on much clothing x yā ∼ rĭgā he put on huge gown. (2) yā ∼ ạlkyabbạ he put on burnous (= yāfạ). (3) yā ∼ cĭyāwạ kạn tsaikọ he thatched the roof-frame (cf. jiŋkẹ). (4) yā ∼ gishirī he baked salt into cakes (kantụ) = jicẹ 1b (cf. jicị). (5) (with dative) yā ∼ minị rĭgā he gave me huge gown.

jĭ ta, jĭ ta (1) m. (a) mere rumour. (b) an zubạ musụ ∼ rumours have been spread amongst them. (2) adv. x an dadẹ anạ jĭm mạganạn nạŋ ∼ rumours about this have long been current.

jĭtāmạ (1) what a huge gown ! what numerous garments he's wearing ! (2) how the sun's clouded over ! (3) mutūwạ bạ ∼ sudden death (= mu-tūwạ 1f).

Jĭtau epithet of Paramount Chief.

jĭtō used in bā sạ ∼ they don't get on together. suŋ ƙi ∼ they won't come to terms " at any price " (cf. jĭtu).

jĭtu Vb. 3B is (was) on good terms x mun ∼ we're on friendly terms (cf. jĭtō).

jĭwārā m.,f. (sg., pl.) gullible P.

jĭwu Vd. jĭ 1g.

jĭwuyạ Vb. 3B turned back.

jĭyạ (1) f. and adv. (a) (i) yesterday. (ii) ∼ kā rabạ, yạu kạrɓā akẹ yĭ you must be content with the lot God has assigned to you. (iii) ∼ bạ yạu ba, tsōfwā tā tunạ kwānaŋ gidā oh, for the days of yore ! (iv) ciki bai saŋ kyạutar ∼ ba ingratitude is common to man. (v) gọbe yạ ∼ Vd. gọbe 6. (vi) gạ na ∼ Vd. bĭyạn dạddawā. (b) shēkarạn ∼ adv. and m. the day before yesterday. (c) watạn ∼ m. last month. (d) (i) munạ naŋ gidan ∼ we've made no progress. (ii) lạbārị yanạ naŋ gidan ∼ the news is unchanged. (iii) Vd. dạfkā. (e) mụtumịn ∼ a P. who is a " back number ". (f) dakạn ∼ kā ƙi tsāmī = Kt. dawạn ∼ kā ƙi tsāmī

epithet of thin, weak P. always looking the same age. (g) jĭyạ-jĭyạ quite recently. (2) Vb. 1A Sk. heard (= jĭ).

jĭyad dạ Vb. 3A = jĭ dạ q.v.

jĭyar x kụnnansạ yạ ∼ masạ let him listen with his full attention !

jĭyayyạ f. (1) x munạ ∼ we're on good terms (d.f. jĭ, cf. jạyayyạ). (2) dạ sū mukẹ ∼ it is with them that we are allied. (3) nā nẹmē shị ạ fuskạr ∼ I tried to settle my dispute with him in a friendly way (Vd. fuskạ 8).

jĭyẹ Vb. 1A wạ zại ∼ makạ who'd listen to you ! bạ wandạ zại ∼ makạ nobody would trouble to listen to you !

jĭ'ye-jĭyē" m. sensations x jĭye-jĭyan dādī sensations of pleasure (cf. jĭ 4).

jĭyō Vb. 1E (1) heard and came x jẹ ka, kạ ∼ manạ go and hear and then tell us ! (2) yā ∼ sụ he heard them from afar.

jĭyōjĭ Vd. jĭjĭyā.

jĭyōkĭ Vd. jĭkạ.

jĭyu Vd. jĭ 1g.

jĭyyạ f. (1) tending sick P. x tā yi masạ ∼ she nursed the patient. (2) dōkị bā yạ hạwūwā sǎi an yi ∼ tasạ the horse (not ridden for some time) will need attention before he is rideable. (3) yā tāshị dạgạ ∼ he got up from a sick-bed. (4) yā kwạntā ∼ he lay sick. (5) lādan ∼ m. few large marks on P. nursing a smallpox case. (6) mại ∼ m., f. (pl. mạsū ∼). (a) sick-nurse. (b) hospital patient (6a, b = majĭyyạcī). (7) mutūwạ bạ ∼ Vd. mutūwạ 1f.

jiyyata A. (jĭyyatạ (1) Vb. 2 (p.o. jĭyyạcẹ, n.o. jĭyyạci) tended sick P. (2) Vb. 3B lay sick.

B. (jĭyyạtā) Vb. 1C rendered ill.

jĭyyạtaccē m. (f. jĭyyạtaccĭyā) pl. jĭy-yạtạttū ill.

jĭzạ (1) Vb. 1A. (a) scraped T. off one T. on to another x yā zō nạŋ dạ tạɓō ạ ƙafạ, ya ∼ jikim baŋgō he came here with muddy feet and scraped the mud off on to the wall. (b) yā ∼ masạ kāshiŋ kạzā he brought false charges against him. (2) f. (a) buzz, hum of voices, any prolonged, indistinct sound (= ƙū-gi = sạmatạ 1 = dirī). (b) jĭzạr gĭwā collective-labour (gạyyā) done for owner of small farm by those doing **gayyā** on adjacent large farm.

jizi'ạ = jizīyạ *Ar. f.* poll-tax on conquered non-Muslims.

jōgōgūwā *f.* (1) unsaleable T. (2) baseless statement.

jōgurō (1) *f.* crone (= gyạ̄tumā). (2) *m.* old hack.

jọ̄jē *m.* earth used by Filani for whitening outside of calabashes for adornment.

jōji *m.* (*Eng.* judge) *pl.* jōji-jōji. (1) administrative officer. (2) judge (*cf.* cifjōji). (3) magistrate.

jọ̄jọ̄ *m.* any imported material then dyed blue (= jau-jau).

jọ̄lōlọ *m.* (*f.* jọ̄lōlụ̄wā) lanky, ugly P., animal, tree, *etc.* (= tsọ̄lōlọ).

ju6ā *f.* anthill (= ji6ā *q.v.*).

jubbạ *Ar. f.* (*pl.* jubbōbī) kind of sleeveless gown.

jụ̄cē *m.* (1) " whip-round " (*also* jụ̄cē-jụ̄cē) *x* ạ yi masạ ~ let everyone contribute a little for him ! (= tạrbạcē = kạ̄rō = kudī 4 = *Kt.* cạncạmnō). (2) dạ ~, dạ ~ (= dạ ta tạrbạcē) gīwā ta fi kōwā kibạ P. for whom " whip-round " has been made is afterwards often better off than those who contributed.

jūdạ *f.* (1) (*a*) musk from civet cat. (*b*) *Vd.* mụzūrū 1*d.* (2) jūdạr kas the twiner *Cissampelos Pareira* (*bitter root used for drug*).

jugudum = jugum.

jugum *adv. and m.* *x* yanạ̄ tsạye ~ = yā yi ~ he (P. or animal) is standing despondently or flaccidly (*pl.* sunạ̄ tsạye jungun-jungun *or* jugun-jugun = sun yi jungun-jungun *or* jugun-jugun) = jạngwam *q.v.* = gạngạrạm = kạsạkē.

juhụrmạ (*pl.* juhurmōmī) *f.* Martial eagle (*Polemœtus bellicosus*).

jūjī *m.* (*pl.* jūjāye = jibājē). (1) (*a*) rubbish-heap ; dung-heap. (*b*) bạbba jūjī nẹ̄, kōwā ya zō dạ shạ̄rā, yạ zubạ the noble person must be long-suffering (*Vd.* bạbba jūjī). (*c*) fụran jūjī *Vd.* fụrē 4. (*d*) *Vd.* ạ jūjī. (*e*) *Vd.* tsụmmā 2. (*f*) yabanyạr ~ *Vd.* wadai. (2) *Sk.* girl unpopular with men.

jūjū *m.* (1) (*a*) fetich. (*b*) spirit. (2) Audụ, ~ gạrēshi Audu's a P. of moods.

jūjūwā *f.* clump of date-palms growing from same base.

Jukunāwā Jukons (*pl. of* Bạjukụnī).

jūlā-jūlā *f.* any inferior garment.

Jumma'ạ *f.* (1) (*a*) Friday. (*b*) bạ̄ kullun rānā kẹ̄ ~ ba, you can't expect unbroken spell of luck (*Vd.* Aljumma'ạ 2). (*c*) kōwạcẹ Jumma'ạ ta farin ciki dạ ạl'amạrintạ coming events cast their shadows before them. (*d*) *Vd.* Jimmạ, Aljumma'ạ ; Hawạ ; Ādạmū. (*e*) bịkin ~ *Vd.* Alhạmis 3. (2) Masallācin ~ Friday congregational mosque.

jūnā *m.* (1) each other *x* sun ga ~ = sun ga jūnansụ they saw one another. sun zamā ạbọkan ~ they're friends. (2) tanạ̄ dạ ~ bīyū she's pregnant (*Vd.* kadai 3).

jungun-jungun *Vd.* jugum.

jūnī *only used in following type of expression* in jūninkạ sạn kīfī nẹ̄, kạ̄ ci, kạ̄ bari well, if it's *fish* you like, you'll have more than enough ! in jūninkạ fadạ, kạ̄ yi, kạ̄ gumạ if you're spoiling for a fight, you've come to the right place !

jūrạ *Vb.* 1A tā ~ hatsī she dried moist, new corn over fire before grinding it (*cf.* jūrē).

jūrai = jūrau *m.* (1) energetic, tireless P. or animal. (2) durable T.

jure A. (jūrẹ) *Vb.* 3A. (1) (*a*) showed fortitude. (= daure). (*b*) ạbin dạ dāma ta jūrẹ *Vd.* dāma 1*g.* (2) (*with dative*) nā ~ masạ (*a*) I bore with him. (*b*) I endured it (illness, trouble) with fortitude (= hạkurạ).

B. (jūrē) *m.* (1) drying *as in* jūrạ *x* tā yi ~ har ta taras she dried moist, new corn over the fire and ultimately got threshed corn (tsābạ). (2) (*secondary v.n. of* jūrạ) *x* tanạ̄ jūraŋ hatsī = tanạ̄ jūrạ hatsī. (3) working with unsuitable material (*x* building with clay not yet " set "). (4) jūran tukunyā pot-making in wet season, etc., when clay will not dry.

jūrụ *m.* strawberry-roan horse.

jurum *adv. and m.* yanạ̄ tsạye ~ = yā yi ~ = yā yi jurumī = jugum *q.v.*

jūshi *m.* the acacia dinshẹ 1.

jūwā *f.* (1) giddiness *x* kạ̄ina yanạ̄ ~ I

feel giddy (= jịrī 1*b*). (2) the game hạjījīyạ 2 *q.v.*

jūwīyạ *Vb.* 3B = jūyạ 2*a*.

juya A. (jūyạ) (1) *Vb.* 1A: (*a*) (i) turned T. round on its base (= jirgạ = markạɗā), *cf.* murɗạ. (ii) yā ⁓ hạŋkạlinsụ gạ kạrạtū he interested them in reading (*cf.* jūyẹ 1*b*). (*b*) (i) revolved, rotated T. (ii) turned T. over *x* an ⁓ shāfị the page has been turned. jūyạ shāfị P.T.O. (iii) kō an cūɗạ, an ⁓, mā ci nasarạ whatever vicissitudes we suffer, yet we'll be victorious. (iv) *Vd.* dambū. (*c*) " turned over " money *x* nā bar makạ kuɗịŋ, kạ ⁓ I leave the money in your hands as trading-capital (= sauyạ 1*e*). (*d*) yā ⁓ musụ bāyā (i) he turned his back on them. (ii) he ceased to back them up. (iii) he gave them the cold shoulder. yāfị yā ⁓ manạ bāyā the war went ill with us. (*dd*) ⁓ gịndim bạkā *Vd.* bạkā 3. (*e*) lent *x* yā ⁓ minị sulẹ bīyar he lent me five shillings (= rạntā = sauyạ 1*f*). (*f*) transformed into *x* tā ⁓ shi kạrē she (witch) changed him into a dog. zạn ⁓ shi dạ Lārabcī I'll translate it into Arabic. (2) *Vb.* 3A. (*a*) yā ⁓ he turned (away from the speaker). yā jūyō he turned (towards the speaker). yā jūyō kạnsụ he turned his attention to them. yā jūyō gidā he returned home. kibīyạ tasụ tā jūyō kạnsụ their arrow recoiled on themselves. (*b*) revolved, rotated. (*c*) yā ⁓ dạ bāya he withdrew, retreated (= bāya 1*a*.i *q.v.*). (*d*) became turned over *x* shāfị yā ⁓ the page was turned. (*e*) became transformed *x* kiɗạ ya ⁓ then matters took a different turn. (3) *f.* (*pl.* jūyōyī). (*a*) barren woman, cow, sheep, or goat (bạkạrārā). (*b*) ạ bạkin ⁓ tasạ *Vd.* guzumā 2. (4) jūyạ bạ̈i *m.* the feast so-called on 10th Muharram when each member of household eats a fowl (or in poor house, a goat's head) (*the feast is also called* sallạr cịŋ wutsīyạ *for ram's tail is kept from* layyā (10th Zụlhajjị) *till 9th Muharram, when it is cooked in soup* (mīyạ) *and a piece given to everyone in the house for them to do* jalạbī). (5) *cf.* jūyẹ.

B. (jūyā) *Vb.* 2 *x* nā jūyi takạrdā I copied the paper.

jūyad dạ *Vb.* 4A = jūyạ 1*a*.i, 1*e*.

jūyạta *Vd.* sạɓạta.

jūyạyī *m.* anxiety about *x* yanạ jūyạyīna he's anxious about me, sympathetic to me, *cf.* tạusạyī. n nạ jūyạyiŋ ganinsạ I feel trepidation about my coming interview with him.

jūyayyā *f.* transverse-furrow (*Vd.* kạdādā ; kạ̈i 7*e*).

jūyayyē *m.* (*f.* jūyayyīyā) *pl.* jūyạyyū. (1) mại jūyayyaŋ kạ̈i *m.* (*pl.* mạsū jūyayyaŋ kạ̈i) P. of sudden moods. (2) jūyayyīyā = jūyayyā.

juye A. (jūyẹ) (1) *Vb.* 1A. (*a*) turned T. inside out. (*b*) turned away *x* kạ ⁓ zūoịyassạ dạgạ gạrētạ divert his thoughts from her ! (*cf.* jūyạ 1*a*.ii). (*c*) (i) poured from one vessel into another *x* tā ⁓ rūwā cikin tukunyā she poured the water into the pot (= zubạ). kạ ⁓ minị mại ạ mōtạ pour the petrol into the car ! (= sauyẹ). (ii) ŋgō, jūyẹ, ban jạkạr you (a harlot) empty out the money and return the bag to me ! (said by unsophisticated man with plenty of money). (*d*) *x* yanạ sọ yạ ⁓ makạ kạ̈i he's trying to persuade you into a course harmful to you. sun nẹmi jūyẹ kạm mutạ̄nē they tried to seduce the people. (2) *Vb.* 3A. (*a*) became turned inside out. (*b*) became inverted *x* Garbạ yā kā dạ Audu, Audụ ya ⁓ Garba downed Audu (his wrestling-opponent), but Audu then twisted round and got on top. (*c*) (i) became changed *x* ạl'amạriŋ duk ya ⁓ then matters became entirely different. (ii) became changed into *x* bakī ya ⁓ farī = bakī ya ⁓ dạ farī black became changed into white. (iii) tsāmīyā tā ⁓ dạ mūjīyā " hoist with one's own petard ". (*d*) tā ⁓ she (woman, cow, sheep, goat) became barren (*cf.* jūyạ 3). (3) *cf.* jūyạ.

B. (jūyē) *m.* type of woman's bushy coiffure.

jū'ye-jūyē" *m.* (1) vicissitudes. (2) alternations.

jūyị *m.* (1) change of state or position *x* (*a*) an yi ⁓ " the tables were turned " ;

the situation became reversed. **mum mai dạ jūyị, muŋ kǫrē sụ** " we turned the tables on them " and routed them. (*b*) **sabǫ dạ jūyị** for the sake of variety. (*c*) **mun sākẹ jūyị** our affairs have changed. (*d*) **bā ạ yịn rawā bạ** ～ (*lit.* you can't dance without change of position) " one cannot make bricks without straw ". (*e*) **dūnīyạ jūyị-jūyị, kwạdō yā fādạ ạ rūwan dịmī** what an unlucky period ! (2) alternation *x* (*a*) **jūyịn rānī dạ dạmunā** alternation of hot and wet seasons. (*b*) **wannaŋ jūyị yāƙị yā ƙārẹ** war is over for the moment. (3) ～ **gātam farā** fancy a P. having money enough to acquire a good T. contenting himself with an inferior one ! (as P. able to buy horse, buying donkey ; P. able to live in a good house, living in a shack) (～ **'Yar Mạsau** *has same meaning* : when large number of guests suddenly arrived, householder, instead of entertaining them as guests, converted them into customers by saying **jūyị !** to his wife **'Yar Mạsau ;** she, falling in with his wishes, then began **tạllạ** to sell the guests food, saying **tūwō dạ mīyạ !**). (4) **jūyịm māsạ = jūyịŋ wạinā** (*a*) somersaulting into water (*cf.* **dīyạm**). (*b*) **dūnīyạ tā yi jūyịm māsạ** events took unfavourable turn.

jūyō *Vd.* **jūyạ.**

jūyōyī *Vd.* **jūyạ** 3.

jwai used in **zāƙī** ～ very sweet.

K

ƙ (*in Katagum,* **ƙ** *is dropped*) *x* **ōfạ** door (= **ƙōfạ**). **bạ̄ō** guest = **bạ̄ƙō**).

ka A. (**kā**) (1) (*masculine pronoun, past sense* " you " *singular*) *x* (*a*) **kā tạfi** you went. (*b*) (*sometimes* " you " *is respectfully put in 3rd singular*) *x* **in yā sō mā, kadạ kạ sạyā** if such is Your Honour's wish, then do not buy ! (*c*) **kā ci damị** *Vd.* **damị** 5, **tsīrukụ.** (*d*) **kā fī kạrē gudụ** *Vd.* **ạ bōƙarạ.** (*e*) **kā fī kūkā cīwǫ** *Vd.* **yạ̄ƙē.** (*e.*i) **kā kai kūkā** *Vd.* **kūkā** 1*a.*iv. (*f*) **kā fī sautụ** *Vd.* **gạidā** 3. (*g*) **kā kaďăi gạyyā**

Vd. **gwạntō.** (*h*) **kā kai cakī** *Vd.* **cakī** 3. (*j*) **kā ƙi cịn damō** *Vd.* **damō** 2. (*k*) **kā ƙi fādūwā** *Vd.* **cịwō.** (*l*) **kā ƙi rūwaŋ Allā** *Vd.* **gạ̄wō, kwạrkǫ.** (*m*) **kā yi dạ kunyạ** *Vd.* **fạrkā** 2*b.* (*n*) **kā yi rībạr ƙafạ, kūrā tā tākạ kwạdō** you've had unexpected luck. (*o*) *Vd.* **kā cī, kā rātạyā.** (*p*) **kā fī aikịm mālạm** *Vd.* **mālạmī** 1*c.*ivA, *Vd.* **kā fī mālạm.** (*r*) **kā cịkạ ?** *Vd.* **kwạndo.** (*s*) *Vd.* **kā fī amaryā, kā fī bōkā, kā fī ďā wụyā, kā fī ƙaryā, kā fī ramạ, kā fī 'yaŋ gyạdā, kā fī yārǫ, kā gịra, kā ƙi Bīmạ, kā ƙi rūwaŋ Allā, kā ƙi zūwạ, kā kōmō, kā lēƙạ, kā rātsạ, kā tụrārạ, kā tsirō.** (2) (*locative form of* **kại**) *x* (*a*) (i) **tā zubạ masạ ạ kā** she poured it over his head. **yanā dạ kāyā ạ kā** he has a load on his head (Mod. Gram. 24*a*). (ii) **in shēgạntakạ nā kā, săi sụ cẹ** if wickedness is uppermost in their minds, they say that . . . (iii) **săi sụ ci makạ tūwō ạ kā** *Vd.* **sakẹ** 2*b.* (iv) **bạn sạ̄ ạ kā ba** *Vd.* **tạ̄gīyạ** 3. (*b*) (*used as in* Mod. Gram. 24*d*). (i) **yā fādị dạ kā** he fell headlong. (ii) **yā ci dạ kā** he fell, hitting his head on the ground. (iii) **yā shiga ạl'amạrin naŋ dạ kā** he entered rashly on this affair, not realizing its implications. (iv) **bạ dạ kā sukạ tōnō fadạ ba** they started a quarrel without any preliminaries. (*c*) **kā bā yạ wucẹ wuyạ** everything has its own purpose. (*d*) **bạrā dạ kā** *Vd.* **bạrā** 3. (*e*) (i) **ạ kā** *Vd.* **gạmu** 3*a.* (ii) *Vd.* **haddạcē.** (iii) **ạ kā, ạ kā** continuously. (*f*) **ɓatạ a tsakạr kā** *Vd.* **ɓatạ** 1*d.* (*g*) **bā ạ zamā dạ kā** *Vd.* **gịndī** 1*h.*ii, **zaunạ** 1*d.* (*h*) **hawā kā** *Vd.* **hawā** 1*a.*ii. (*j*) **anā kāyaŋ kā** *Vd.* **rạtạyạ** 2*b.*

B. (**ka**) (*employed grammatically for* " you " (*masculine, singular*) *in the cases illustrated in the following examples*) (1) **zā ka Kanǫ** you'll go to Kano (Gram. 17). (2) **kanā zūwạ** you are (were) coming (Gram. 16). (3) **ka kạn zō** you are (were) in habit of coming (Gram. 15). (4) **bā ka zūwạ** you are (were) not coming (= **kā** 1) (*Vd.* Mod. Gram. 19*b*). (5) **bā ka dạ kudī** you have (had) no money (Gram. 22). (6) **ạbịn dạ ka ganī** (*relative usage*) what you saw (*Sk. may double following vowel x* ab̦in dạ kag ganī). lōkacin dạ ka zō when you came (Gram. 133*a**). yaushẹ ka zọ̄ when did you come? (160*b*). (7) nā kāmạ ka I seized you (Mod. Gram. 49*a*¹). (8) ka cẹ̄ *Vd.* cẹ̄ 9.

C. (kạ) (*employed grammatically for* "you" (*masculine singular*) *in the cases illustrated in the following examples*). (1) kạ zō come! yā kạmātạ kạ zō you ought to come (Gram. 13*a*). (2) kadạ kạ zō do not come! (13*a*). (3) zā kạ zō you will come (14). (4) bạ kạ zō ba you didn't come (20*a*). (5) (*relative past*) *used in* kikạ; mukạ; kukạ; sukạ; akạ *x* sạn dạ mukạ zō when we came (Gram. 133*a**). yaushẹ kikạ zọ̄ when did you (*f.*) come? (160*b*). (6) nā bā kạ I gave you (*Vd.* ka 7). (7) (*a*) nākạ *q.v.;* tākạ *q.v.* yours (48). (*b*) *Vd.* tākạ 1*b*. (8) makạ to you (50). (9) gạrēkạ in your possession, *etc.* (55*a*). (10) = kai̦. (11) ~ cici *Vd.* cici.

D. (kạ̄) (1) (*used to negative* "you" *masculine singular in progressive*) *x* bā kạ̄ zūwạ you're not coming; you were not coming. (2) (*a*) (i) (*future relative; Vd.* Mod. Gram. 140*b*) is the one who will *x* nī kạ̄ fạdā I'm the one who could tell a tale of woe! Inūwạr giginyạ, na nēsạ kạ̄ shā sanyī (*lit.* Shade of the deleb-palm, the one afar is he who will enjoy thy shade!) you neglect your family and favour strangers. (ii) (*future perfect relative*) *x* shī yakạ̄ cẹ̄ dạ sū, sụ fitō it must have been *he* who told them to go forth. (*b*) (*future relative used in rhetorical questions and negative sentences; Vd.* Mod. Gram. 140*c*). (i) wạ̄ yạ̄ īyạ = wạ̄ yakạ̄ īyạ who could possibly do it! wạ̄ kạ̄ ganẹ makạ who in the world would spare *you* a glance! inā nakạ̄ sakạ where on earth could I put it! (*Vd.* inā 4). inā takạ̄ sāmụ where on earth could she get it! (ii) *Vd.* kū kạ̄. (3) *Sk.* (*used for* kẹ̄ (Gram. 133*a**) *of relative present*) *x* rashin sani̦ kạ̄ sā mạkāfọ tākạ shimfid̦ạr it is lack of *knowledge* that makes a blind man tread on one's mat.

E. (kạ̄) (*used in indefinite future for* "you" *m. sg.*) *x* ~ zō nạ̦ gọ̄be you'll very likely come here to-morrow. (2) ~ fad̦ō kud̦i̦ hājạrkạ you'll have to sell off cheap! (3) ~ kạ̄ri nikạ *Vd.* nikạ 2*c*. (4) *Vd.* mạkwī. (5) ~ kạ̄ri kūkā *Vd.* kūkā 1*a*.v.

kạ̄ (1) how *x* ~ akạ yi̦ how was it done? (= kạ̄kạ *q.v.*). (2) kanạ̄ ai̦ki̦? are you working? (*reply,* im bā nạ̄ yi̦ ~ well, what does it *look* as if I'm doing!).

Kạ'abạ *Ar. f.* the holy, black stone at Mecca (= d̦āki̦ 3).

kaba A. (kabạ) *f.* (*pl.* kabōbī). (1) (*a*) young dum-palm or its fronds (used for mats, string, basket (lẹ̄fē), hats, etc.), *cf.* kari̦, gạzarī, kạibābạ, gọ̄dā. (*b*) kabạr gīwā the aloe called *Aloe barteri* (= hantsạ 5*c* = mōdạ). (*c*) gērō yā yi ~ the bulrush-millet is about a foot high. (*d*) har yạ mutụ bā yạ̄ kullạ ~ he's spineless (*Vd.* mutụ 1*a*.iv). (*e*) dami̦ yā tsi̦nkẹ ạ gindi̦ ~ = dạcē. (*f*) ~ nạ̄ rawā *Vd.* iskạ 1*a*.ii. (*g*) dạ̦ gạrī ~ nē *Vd.* rābā 1*e*. (*h*) kāyạ̦ ~ *Vd.* būtsātsạ. (*j*) kuduri̦ ~ *Vd.* tạsūbạlā 2. (2) *Eng.* taking cover *x* sun yi ~ dạ dūwạtsū they (soldiers) took cover behind the rocks.

B. *Vd.* Kạ'abạ.

kaba A. (kābā) (1) *Vb.* (*a*) is (was) angry. (*b*) is (was) conceited. (2) *m.* (*a*) (*progressive of* 1) *x* yanạ̄ ~ dạ kudī he's "swanking" because of his money. kudī sunạ̄ ~ ạ wurinsạ his wealth's steadily on the increase. (*b*) ~ yā saukō (= saukar) masạ he has enlarged testicles or scrotal hernia (= gwaiwā 1 *b*.i,ii. = d̦ad̦ali̦). (*c*) kābạn ci̦ki̦ dyspepsia. (*d*) kābạ̦ kạshī rheumatism. (*e*) kābam mārạ = kābam mātā various gynæcological affections. (*f*) ~ mai̦ kụmburī rheumatism accompanied by swelling. (*g*) kābạn yạnyạ̄yī perineal abscess in men. (*h*) inā kābạ̦kạ ya yi rūwạ̄; ạ sakạ makạ what business is it of *yours*! (3) *cf.* kạbbā.

B. (kābạ) *Vd.* kạ̄bạrạ 2.

ka6a A. (kạ6ā) *Vb.* 2. (1) collided with. (2) shook (*garment*) to rid it of dust (= ka6ẹ).

B. (kaɓą) *Vb.* 1A. (1) = **kaɓąncē** 1*a*.
(2) *x* yā ~ ƙwaryā ą bąkī he put his lips
to the calabash to drink (= **dōɓą** 1 *q.v.*).
ƙabąbą = ƙąbąbą = ƙąbąbąbą *f.* (1) yā yi
minī ~ it (stiff garment, burr, etc.)
chafed my skin. (2) ya tāsō **ƙąbąbąbą**
he set out at once. ya tāsō **ƙąbąbąbą,**
ya nufō su ~ then he plunged into the
attack against them.
kaɓad dą *Vb.* 4B = **kaɓąncē** 1*b*.
kaɓąkā *Vb.* 1C *x* tā **kaɓąką** ƙwaryā
kąŋ wata ƙwaryā she inverted the
calabash on another to prevent the
latter spilling.
kaɓā-kąɓą *adv.* in big pieces *x* nāmąŋ
yąŋkā nę ~ the meat's cut in large
lumps.
kąɓakī *m.* (*pl.* **kaɓuką** = *Kt.* **kaɓukką** =
kąɓąkai).   (1) (*a*) 5–10 mądurgujī of
tūwō brought in calabash called **masakī,**
then emptied on to a mat, cut up, bit
of raw meat (**kusuŋkusumī**) put on
each portion and shares given neighbours and relations on occasion of
naming or wedding.   (*b*) (Filani
practice) many **mądurgujī** of **tūwō**
brought in **akushī** *or* ƙwaryā, soup
(**mīyą**), milk and meat added and then
shared out *as in* 1*a*. (*c*) **kąɓakiŋ girmā**
yā fi **kąɓakiŋ ƙaŋƙancī** a small gift
willingly given is better than a big
gift accompanied by humiliation. (*d*)
wandą kē jiraŋ ~ ɗuŋgum, bą yā
kulą dą lōmą ba important desires blot
out trifling wishes. (*e*) **gāfarą ~** *Vd.*
gāfarą 1*c*. (*f*) mabī ~ *Vd.* **laƙai-**
laƙai. (2) **dōkī yā yi** ~ the horse now
has its upper and lower age-teeth.
kąbamā *Sk. f.* old mare (= **kąmbamā**).
kaɓąncē (1) *Vb.* 1C. (*a*) = **kaɓąkā.** (*b*)
dropped or knocked over wide-mouthed
vessel (*x* calabash) so that it falls,
spilling contents. (*c*) scooped up with
edge of calabash, etc., some spilled
grain or liquid in a single sweep (*if in*
several sweeps, we say **dīɓą** 1*c*.i). (*d*) =
kaɓę 1. (2) *Vb.* 3A became overturned,
capsized.
kaɓąntā *Vb.* 1C = **kaɓąkā.**
kaɓąntad dą = **kaɓąncē** 1*b*, *c*.
kaɓąnyą *Vd.* **kaɓǫ.**
kabara A. (**kabąrā**) = **kabbąrā.**

B. (**kabarą**) *Ar. f.* (1) yā tā dą ~ he
said **Ąllāhu ąkbar !,** thus beginning his
prayers (*cf.* kabbąrā). (2) *x* am **fādą**
masą dą ~ = an yi masą ~ he's suddenly been attacked.   (3) **māmantą**
yā tā dą ~ ząi fādī her breasts are about
to droop (*cf.* ƙirgą 2*b*, buŋƙusą).
kąɓarą *m.* (*pl.* **kąɓąrū**) tactless lout.
ƙąbąrą (1) blast you ! (*said by B to A,*
with whom he is angry, the moment A
addresses him) = **ƙąƙą** 2 = *Kt.* **shīɓōlī.**
(2) *the P. to whom* **ƙąbąrą = ƙąƙą =**
ƙāsararką = ƙąƙąrą = ƙąbą *is said,*
may retaliate by saying **ƙārō = ƙārō**
nę = mēlē nę = tsūlīyarką *to which B*
replies ą bąkiŋką yą daŋƙarē. *But, if A*
wishes to be conciliatory, he replies to the
original **ƙąbąrą** *by saying* Allą yą bā ką
hąƙurī = mę ya yi zāfī (*cf.* ƙāraŋ ƙąbą).
kābarai = **kābarē** *m.* (*pl.* **kąbąrai**).   (1)
Senegal   spotted-backed   weaver-bird
(*Plesiosittagra c. cucculatus*). (2) **kābaraŋ**
kabą Little Black-throated Weaver
(*Ploceus luteolus*).   (3) **gąbaŋ** ~ *Vd.*
gąban 10*a*.
kabari A. (**kabąrī**) *Ar. m.* (*pl.* **kaburburą**).
(1) (*a*) grave, tomb. (*b*) ~ yā rufą dą
sū the grave closed on them, *i.e.* they
died. (*c*) duhuŋ ~ *Vd.* duhu 1*b*. (2)
mątar mutum kabąrinsą nē fate decrees
inexorably the wife for you.
     B. (**kābarī**) = **kābarai.**
kaɓau A. (**kąɓau**) *m.* (*sg., pl.*) tactless lout.
     B. (**kaɓau**) *Vd.* karaŋ kaɓau, bąkiŋ
kaɓau.
Kabāwā *Vd.* **Bąkabę.**
ƙabbā *J.* (1) (*a*) tertiary syphilis (*cf.*
tunjērē, ƙābā) = **ƙullūtu** 2 *q.v.*   (*b*)
Vd. fashę 1*a*. (2) yā yi masą kāmuŋ
ƙabbą he got a stranglehold on him.
(*note tone!*) (3) **ƙabbar ƙazwā** type of
scabies. (4) **ƙabbar kurkunū** swelling
where guinea-worm extrudes.   (5)
ƙabbar ƙyąmbī a horse-disease.
kabbara A. (**kabbąrā**) *Vb.* 1C said **Ąllāhu**
ąkbar ! (*cf.* kabarą). yā kabbąrą sallą
he has begun his prayers.
     B. (**kabbarą**) = **kabarą.**
kabbąrtā = **kabbąrā.**
kabcę = **kafcę.**
ƙabdarō *epithet of* stingy P.
ƙabdōdǫ *m.* (1) the thorny shrub *Capparis*

tomentosa. (2) Preuss's Cliff Swallow (*Lecythoplastes preussi*) = **ƙarƙāɗǫ**. (3) *epithet of* stingy P. (4) small child dogging its mother.

kaɓę *Vb.* 1A. (1) (*a*) *x* **nā ~ rĩgā** I shook the gown to rid it of dust. (*b*) **nā ~ ƙūrā dąga jikin rĩgā** I shook dust off the gown (*Vd.* **kaɗę, karkąɗē**). (2) = **kaɓąncē** 1*b*. (3) (*plus dative*) *x* (*a*) **yā ~ minį shĩ** he knocked it out of my hand (= **kaɗę**). (*b*) **yā ~ minį cinikī** he " spoiled my market " (= **shūrę** 1*c*). (*c*) **yā kaɓę mana jąrąbū** he protected us from temptations (*cf.* **kakkąɓē**). (4) **kā ~ dąngana** " you've given yourself away ".

kąbēwą *f.* (*pl.* **kąbēyī**). (1) (*a*) marrow ; pumpkin (= *Sk.* **gǫjī**), *Vd.* **hąrzā, gǫdā 3**. (*b*) *Vd.* **shąn ~**. (2) **maį gundą shĩ kę dą ~** " many a mickle makes a muckle ". (3) *Kt.* **hancįn ~** *m.* type of incense.

Kabi-*Vd.* **banzā**.

kąbidǫ *m.* (*pl.* **kąbidai**). (1) double-matting worn over head as mackintosh. (2) **hadarįn ƙasā māgánim maį kąbidǫ** the **ƙirārį** of **Ąlīyų**, a deposed S. Kano who died at Lokoja.

kąbīlą *Ar. f.* (*pl.* **kąbīlū** = **kąbīlai** = **kabīlōlī**). (1) tribe. (2) one's relatives, dependents, followers.

ƙąbirī (1) *m.* (*a*) swelling. (*b*) increase (*cf.* **ƙābā**). (2) *adv.* abundantly.

kablę *Kt.* = **kaurę**.

kąblīyyą = **ƙąblīyyą** *f.* *(1) an addition to devotions, to make up for some involuntary addition (*cf.* **bą'ądiyyą**). (2) **yā sąn ~ dą bą'ądīyyą** he knows the world inside out. (3) **nā kāwō matą ~ dą bą'ądiyyą, ta ƙī** I tried hard to persuade her, but uselessly.

kabo A. (**kābǫ**) *Yor.* (*traders'* Hausa) **sulę ~** one and sixpence.
   B. (**kabǫ**) *Rustic Hausa* penny (= **kwabǫ** *q.v.*).

kaɓǫ (1) *m.* tactless lout. *(2) *m.* (*f.* **kaɓanyą**) young gazelle (**bąrēwā**).

kabōbī *Vd.* **kabą**.

kaɓō-kąɓǫ = **kaɓā-kąɓą**.

kabra *Sk., Kt.* = **kaura**.

ƙabrį *Zar. m.* = **kabąrī**.

kabsą *Sk., Kt.* = **kausą**.

kąbsayyą *f.* struggling.

kabtu *m.* = **kaftu**.

kąbudǫ = **kąbidǫ**.

Ƙābugą *used in* **ɗan ~** *m.* lime-fruit (*as there are many lime trees at the* **Ƙābugą** *Gate in Kano*).

ƙābugā *f.* cloth with hole in it, for passing over head to use it as gown.

kaɓuką *Vd.* **kąɓakī**.

kaburburą *Vd.* **kabąrī**.

***kąburū** *m.* large Gwari stringed-instrument.

kąbus = **kąbūshį** *m.* (1) variety of big, white marrow (= **rųgudū** = **rūgūgūwā 2**). (2) *used in* **ɗan wākē yā yi ~** bean-dumpling is uncooked in centre.

ƙābūwā *f.* = **ƙabbā**.

kącā *Nupe Hausa, used in* **~ mūgųn jībį** epithet of gruel (**kōkǫ**).

kącābą = **kącāɓą** (1) *f.* constantly changing one's clothes. (2) *m., f.* P. acting *as in* **1**. (3) what changing of clothes !

kacaca A. (**kącācą**) (1) *f.* cheap type of beer (**gīyą**). (2) how dirty !
   B. (**kącącą**) *m., f.* (*pl.* **kacā-kacā** = **kacā-kącą**) dirty.

kacaccąlā *Vb.* 1D attacked.

kącącē (1) *Vb.* 3A is (was) destitute. (2) *Vb.* 1C impoverished.

kaca-kaca A. (**kacā-kacā** = **kacā-kącą**). (1) *Vd.* **kącācą**. (2) *adv. and m.* (*a*) *x* **ɗakį yā yi ~** house's muddled and dirty. **yā yi tsųmmā ~** he was in filthy rags. **kąjī sun tantǫną wurī ~** fowls have scrabbled over the whole place. **jikinsa ~ dą jinī yakę** he's all gory. (*b*) **an yi masą ~** (i) he's been abused. (ii) his goods have been scattered or left in mutilated condition.
   B. (**kacā-kacā**) *adv. and f.* *x* **sun gudų ~** they fled helter-skelter. **mun yi musų ~** we routed them.
   C. (**kącą-kacā**) *adv. and f.* *x* **sunā magana ~** = **sunā nąn sunā ~** they are making a hubbub.

kącąkāmā *Nor. m.* (*pl.* **kącąkāmai**) favourite servant-lad.

kacakamcį *Nor. m.* being a **kącąkāmā**.

kącąkaurą (1) *epithet of* P. with large teeth. (2) type of rattle used in games (=**lālājǫ**).

kącąkurį *m.* tactless lout.

kacal *adv.* *emphasizing* contempt at trifling value *x* **don tarō ∼ zā kạ yi minị mạganạ** ? what a fuss over threepence ! (*Vd.* **don** 2 ; **kaɗāi** 4*a*.

kạcala *f.* (1) the bulrush *Typha australis* (= **gyāranyạ**). (2) *Kt.* **na ∼** *m.* the food **ɗaŋ wākē** exposed for sale.

Kạcallạ *Kr. m.* (1) head of **'yam bindigạ** (band of gunmen). (2) *title of* several slave-positions in former days *x* *title of* **Makạman ɗan rīmī** (*cf.* **Dākọ** 4), **Mạdākin ɗan rīmī, Cirọmạn Shạmakị,** *etc.*

kacancạnạ *Vb.* 1D divided into pieces or districts.

kacancạnē *Vb.* 3A (1) disintegrated. (2) became spoilt.

kacau-kacau *m.* (1) rattle (instrument). (2) rattling.

kạcaurạ *f.* protuberant teeth (= **cạkaurạ** *q.v.*).

kacawaiwại *m.* *used in* **yā yi minị ∼** it struck me " all of a heap "

kacē-kạcē = **kacā-kạcā**.

kạciɓis = **kạciɓus** *adv.* *and m.* (1) *x* **nā yi ∼ dạ shī** = **∼ na gạmu dạ shī** I met him all of a sudden (= **arbạ** 3 = **duŋguŋ** 2*b*). (2) **∼ mūguŋ gạmō** the less I see of him the better !

kạ cịci *Vd.* **cịci**.

kạcīcīyạ *f.* woodboring-insect, *etc.* (= **kịcīcīyạ** *q.v.*).

ka ci ka rataya A. (**kā cī, kā rātạyā**) *m.* band of plaited leather (= **ƙwạrō**).
B. (**kạ cī, kạ rātạyā**) *x* **aikịn naŋ, ∼** = **aikịn naŋ, kạ cī, kạ gumạ** you'll find this work too much for you.

kācịkāri *m.* lout.

Kạcinạ *Kt. f.* Katsina (*Vd.* **banzā**).

Kacinancī *Kt. m.* Katsina Hausa.

kạcirọ = **kịcirọ**.

kaciwaiwại = **kacawaiwại**.

kạcīyạ *f.* (1) (*a*) circumcision (= **kụgunū** = *Sk.* **kwīdọ**). (*b*) **an yi wạ yārọ ∼** the boy's been circumcised (= **sallātad dạ** = *Kt.* **tānā** 3*b*). (*c*) *cf.* **shā** D, **jāɓā** 3. (2) **gashịŋ ∼** applying hot sand to heal wound from circumcision. (3) **kaŋ ∼** *m.* glans penis. (4) *Kt.* **ɗan ∼** newly circumcised boy (= **ɗan shạyī**). (5) cutting groove round tree to kill it (= **mạgēdūwā** 3).

kạcōkaŋ *adv.* completely removed *x* **an ɗaukē su ∼** they have been removed *in toto.* **sun tāshị** they went away lock, stock, and barrel.

kada A. (**kadạ**) (1) *m.* crocodile = **kadọ** *q.v.* (2) **kadạ** = **doŋ kadạ** (*with subjunctive*) (*a*) do not ! *x* (i) **∼ kạ zō** do not come ! (ii) **∼ ạ ɗaurạ minị jạkar tsābạ, kạjī sụ riƙạ bī nị** don't falsely accuse me ! (iii) **∼ kạ zamẹ minị ạutam fikạfikī lạlātạ ạbōkin tāshị** don't play the dog in the manger ! (iv) **∼ kōwā yạ kūkā dạ wani ; yạ kūkā dạ kạnsạ** those who live in glass houses . . . (v) **∼ kạ yi tsạmmānịŋ ạlhēri ịndạ bạ kạ ga fuskạ ba** don't expect goodness from a hangdog-looking person ! (vi) **ɗaŋ ∼ kạ ƙārạ** *m.* (*f.* **'yar ∼ kạ ƙārạ**) *pl.* **'yaŋ ∼ kạ ƙārạ** spoiled child. (vii) **∼ kạ ạri bạƙīna, kạ ci minị ạlbasạ** — **wạrkī** 7. (viii) *Vd.* **kadạ kạ tākạ, kadạ tạ kwānā.** (viii*A*) **∼ kạzā tạ yi murnạ** *Vd.* **kạzā** 1*a*.viii. (ix) **∼ kạ fīgẹ kạzā** *Vd.* **fīgẹ** 1*b*. (x) **∼ kạ yi azụmī** *Vd.* **azụmī** 2. (xi) **∼ ịŋgarmạ** *Vd.* **ƙūrụ**. (xii) **∼ rạncē** *Vd.* **bāshị** 3. (xiii) **∼ dǎi kōgī** *Vd.* **rạndā** 1*b*. (xiv) **∼ kụ sakẹ** *Vd.* **sakẹ** 2*d*. (xv) **∼ Allạ yạ kāwō rānar yạbō** *Vd.* **yạbō** 5. (xvi) **∼ dǎi gulbī** *Vd.* **kụduddufī** 3. (xvii) **∼ kạ labtạ** *Vd.* **labtạ** 7. (*b*) *x* in **nā sō, ∼ ŋ īyạ** it's no concern of yours whether I can or not (*reply to* you cannot do it !). **∼ yạ yi kyạu mạŋ** it may be no good as you say, but what do *I* care about it ! (*reply to* it's no good !). (*c*) there is a risk that by so doing *x* **sunạ sạn nāmạ, ∼ sụ ɗaukạ, sụ kā dạ girmansụ** they want the meat, but there is cause to fear that if they take it, they may be disgraced. **∼ ạ zō, ạ yi manạ farmakị** there is a risk that they may attack us. (*d*) (*with subjunctive*) that not *x* **yā fi kyạu ∼ ạ yī** it is better that it be not done. **bạ sụ kulạ dạ kō sụ cī, kō ∼ sụ cī ba** they do not care whether they win or not. (*e*) **kadạ dǎi** *Vd.* **dǎi** 3.
B. (**kādạ**) *Vb.* 1A. *Sk.* = **kā dạ**.

kā dạ *Vb.* 4A. (1) (*a*) (i) felled (tree). (ii)

felled (opponent) = tand**ạ**rā = taushẹ
5. (b) (i) (animal) threw (rider) =
taushẹ 5. (ii) iɲ kā ga gōdị̄yā dạ
sirdị, tanā gudụ, wani ta kāyar if
nobody wants T. or P. apparently
good, then it must have a hidden
blemish. (iii) bā ~ gīwā kḕ dạ wụyā ba,
kāfiɲ ạ birkịcē ta, ạ yaŋkạ ta it's easy
to begin anything, but hard to see it
through to the end (Vd. karmāmī).
(iv) ~ gizọ Vd. gizọ 2a.v. (v)
tsūtsạ tā ~ kudī Vd. tsūtsạ 6. (vi)
Kā dạ baŋgō Vd. rịmā 2. (vii) bā
yā ~ itācē Vd. sārā 2b.ii. (c) shạrī'ạ
tā ~ shī he lost his case. aɲ ~ shī
he was worsted in argument. cīwọ
yā ~ nī illness laid me low. dāmunā
tā kāshē mụ the wet season was bad
for our crops. (2) collided with and
knocked over (cf. būsad dạ). (3) yā ~
girmansụ = yā kāyar musụ dạ girmā it
lowered their prestige.

kaɗa A. (kaɗạ) (1) Vb. 1A (a) yā ~
gạŋgā (i) he beat the drum (cf. kiɗạ).
(b) suɲ ~ gạŋgar yāƙị sabọ dạ mū
they declared war on us (= bugạ
1c.iii). (b) tā ~ nōnọ she churned
milk. ~ ƙwăi to whisk an egg. (c)
(i) stirred T. of thin consistency x
soup (mīyạ), cf. tūƙạ. (ii) tā ~ kūkạ ạ
kạn rōmō she added kūkạ (Vd. rōmō)
to rōmō thus converting it into mīyạ.
(a) ~ rịgā to shake garment on one's
body lightly to and fro from one's
chest, to create current of cool air
(cf. kaɗẹ). (e) ~ audụgā to spin
cotton. (f) yā ~ wutsīyạ it wagged
its tail (= rau dạ). (g) brandished.
(h) iskạ tā ~ itācē wind swayed the tree.
(j) yā ~ kăi (i) he nodded in assent.
(ii) he shook his head in dissent. (k) tā
~ masạ idọ = tā ~ masạ girā she gave
him the " glad eye " (= fạrī = Sk. sārạ
1k). (l) yā ~ dạŋganạ tasạ = yā ~
jịŋginạ tasạ (i) he squandered his
substance. (ii) he spoiled his chances.
(m) yā ~ su, suɲ kạɗu = yā ~ musụ
cikị = yā ~ musụ ganyē it left them
" all of a dither " (Vd. (o) below ;
rūwā B.8). yā kaɗạ masạ ganyē
= yā ~ masạ kargō he intimidated
him. (n) (i) nā ~ shi, nā rayạ shi,

ya ƙī I tried my hardest to persuade
him, but he was obdurate. (ii) zạtan
naɲ, ạ kaɗạ, ạ rayạ one must ponder
this idea carefully. (o) iskōkī suɲ
~ shi he's gone mad = taɓạ (Vd. (m)
above, rūwā B.8). (p) kāzā tā ~
ƙwan naɲ the chicken has sat too long
on these eggs and they are inedible.
(q) Vd. cakī ; kạŋgạrē ; kililī ; kōyạ ;
bạgullịyā. (r) kaɗạ ƙwạrkwatạ Vd.
mụtụm 9f. (s) Nor. yā ~ masạ
bējē he overthrew him in wrestling.
(2) Vb. 3A (a) x iskạ tā ~ yạmmā
wind has veered westwards. (b)
idạnsạ yā ~ his eyes are inflamed.
(3) cf. kaɗẹ ; kạɗạ ƙwaryā.

B. (kạɗā) Vb. 2 (1) x nā kaɗō
sulẹ ukụ I was given 3s. as drumming-
fee. (2) collided with and knocked
over. (3) knocked down a little fruit
from tree. (4) ~ dạ rūwaɲ hanjī Vd.
rūwā B.8. (5) ƙadar rāɓā begging for
bundles of millet (gērō) in villages
by scholars after garnering their own
millet (= ƙakkaɓạ 3).

C. (kāɗạ) Vb. 1A = ƙāɗā 1a.

D. (kāɗā) Sk. f. throwing T. at
x yā yi minị ~ dạ dūtsẹ he threw
stone at me.

E. (kạɗā) (1) Vb. 2 (1) (a) teased
(cotton). (b) Sk. threw T. at x yā
kạɗē shi dạ dūtsẹ he threw stone at
him (= jēfā). (2) f. (a) raw cotton
(= dunĝujī), Vd. sakạ 1f; tādạlī.
(b) furā tanā ~ the furā has become
mildewed (= fīyāyạ).

ƙadạbạrbạr = ƙadạbạr m. (1) stiffness of
leather or of cotton-fabric with much
" dressing ". (2) = katạbạrbạr.

ƙadạbarbạrī m. (f. ƙadạbarbạrā) stiff as in
ƙadạbạr.

ƙadạbạrī m. stiff leather, etc. as in
ƙadạbạr.

ƙadạbdạb = ƙadạddạb.

ƙadạbērẹ m. (f. ƙadạbērịyā) = ƙadabạrī.

kadạbkarạ Kt. f. = kadạfkarạ.

ƙadaɓọ how thick !

ƙadāɓụlai Sk. m. (1) lumps specially made
for gruel (kōko), Vd. gwārājī. (2)
furā-lumps specially left in mixture
of furā and milk (= gāyā 1d). (3)
gạri yanā dạ ~ sky's overcast.

kǎdādā *f.* (*pl.* **kǎdādū**) (1) (*a*) transverse ridge across furrows (**kunyā**) = *Kt.* **kīrā**, *cf.* **jūyayyā, dǎtsā 2**. (*b*) area between one transverse-ridge and the next *x* **yā yi** ~ **dayā, kunyā 20** he completed one such area containing 20 furrows (*Vd.* diagram *to* **kǎi** *7e*). (2) (negatively) **bǎ shi dǎ** ~ there's no limit to it, i.e. it's abundant. (3) **kǎdādar ƙaryā** *Vd.* **wai** *2b*.

kadad dǎ *Vb.* 4B = **kadę** *1a, d, e*.

kǎdaddǎb *m.* thickness *x* **ƙwaryan naŋ** ~ **dǎ ita** this calabash is thick.

kǎdaddǎɓī *m.* (*f.* **kǎdaddǎɓā**) *pl.* **kǎdaddǎɓai** (1) thick. (2) thick-set.

kadaddarē = **kacal**.

kadādunǎ crocodiles (*pl. of* **kadǫ**).

ƙadaf *Vd.* **dǎfūwā 3**.

kadǎfkarǎ *f.* (*pl.* **kǎdǎfkǎrū**) (1) Knorhaan Lesser Bustard (*Eupodotis senegalensis*). (2) *epithet of* stingy P. (3) **Kadǎfkarǎ, tǎfi dǎ ƙwaŋki** *epithet of* acutely distrustful P. (4) *Vd.* **haukā 4**.

ƙādāgā *Vd.* **ƙādāgī**.

ƙadagal *adv.* in full *x* **yā bīyā sulę ukų** ~ he paid the three shillings in full.

ƙadagar = **ƙadagargar** = **ƙadabarbar** *q.v.*

ƙādāgī *m.* (*f.* **ƙādāgā**) *pl.* **ƙǎdǎgai** (1) huge. (2) **isar** ~ *f.* making baseless claim to authority, making unauthorized statements.

ƙadāgirī *m.* (*f.* **ƙadāgirā**) *pl.* **ƙadāgirai** destitute P.

ƙadāgwī *m.* useless P. (*epithet is* ~ **kaŋwar ƙashī**).

kǎdǎi *used in reply to greeting x* **sǎnnū** greeting ! (*reply is* **sǎnnū** ~ greeting to you also !). **barkǎ dǎ ǎsųbǎ** greeting on the morning ! (*reply is* **barkǎ** ~).

kadǎi *adv.* (1) only *x* (*a*) **shī** ~ he alone. **sulę gudā** ~ only one shilling (= **kawǎi** *1e*). (*b*) **ǎf, doŋ wannaŋ** ~ **mē zǎi sǎ** well, what does *that* matter ! (*Vd.* **don 2**). (2) alone *x* **zamāna nī** ~ my remaining alone. **nā gan shi shī** ~ I saw he was alone. (3) **nā ga ǎlāmǎ bǎ ita** ~ **ba cę** she seems to be pregnant (*Vd.* **jūnā 2**). (3*A*) **kā** ~ **gayyā** *Vd.* **gwǎntō**. (4) (*a*) = **kacal**. (*b*) nonsense ! (5) = **kadanyǎ**.

kadǎicē (1) *Vb.* 3A sat, etc., apart. (2) *Vb.* 1C called P. aside.

kadǎici *m.* being lonely, solitary.

kadǎikǎ *f.* being an only child.

kadǎita A. (**kǎdǎitǎ**) *Vb.* 3B sat, etc., apart.

B. (**kadǎitā**) *Vb.* 1C (1) **yā kadǎitǎ Allǎ** he believed in, acknowledged, stated the unity of God. (2) set P. or T. apart by himself, itself.

kǎ'da-kǎdā" *f.* **furā tanǎ** ~ = **kǎdā** *2b*. **kadǎ kǎ tākǎ** *m.* **tūwō** made in early morning (*cf. next*).

kǎdǎ ƙwaryā *m., f.* quickly made, poor **tūwō** (*cf. previous entry*).

kadaŋ if (= **in** = **idaŋ** *q.v.*).

kǎdaŋ (1) (*a*) *adj.* a few *x* **bǎ mai sǎnsǎ sǎi mutǎnē** ~ only a few persons like him. (*b*) *m.* few *x* (i) **kǎdan nę dǎgǎ cikimmų wadǎndǎ bā sǎ īyǎ tǎimakō dǎ kōmē** there are but few of us who can help with nothing. **sauraŋ,** ~ **nę ya ragę** but *few* of them remain. (ii) **'yaŋ** ~ *pl.* very few indeed. (2) (*a*) slightly *x* (i) **yā īyǎ** ~ he can do it slightly. (ii) ~ **sukǎ dara ǎ cę musų hǎkimai** they are but little superior in status to District-heads. (*b*) **kǎdaŋ-kǎdaŋ** very slightly. (3) *m.* a little *x* (*a*) **yā yi** ~ it is too small ; there is not enough of it. (*b*) **yā yi mini** ~ I have not enough of it. (*c*) **marēnǎ** ~ **ɓarǎyī nę** ungrateful persons are like thieves. (4) *adj.* trifling *x* (*a*) (i) **ǎbų** ~ a trivial matter. **lǎifī** ~ a slight crime. (ii) **rānā** ~ in the early morning. (*c*) **ǎlhēri bǎ shi** ~ don't look a gift horse in the mouth ! (5) ~ **dǎ aikinsǎ** that is in keeping with his character ! (good or bad).

kadanā *used in* **daŋ** ~ *m.* = **tūgandē 1**.

kadǎndanī *Vd.* **kadǎnyǎ**.

kadǎndanī *Vd.* **kadǫ**.

ƙadandōnīyā *f.* (*sg., pl.*) reticulated millipede (= *Sk.* **daidayā 1**).

kadandunǎ *Vd.* **kadǫ**.

kadǎnē *Vd.* **kadǎnyǎ**.

ƙadaŋgarę *m.* (*f.* **ƙadaŋgarūwā**) *pl.* **ƙadaŋgarū** (1) (*a*) lizard (*cf.* **jaŋ gwādā**). (*b*) **tǎfīyar itǎcaŋ ƙadaŋgarę** what procrastination ! (*c*) **sǎi katangā tā tsāgę ƙadaŋgarę kǎn sam mashigā** when friends quarrel, this gives others matter for gossip. (*d*) *Vd.* **ǎlbarkǎcī** *3c*. (2) ~

shiga rūwa, ka zamā kadọ he has prospered beyond his former equals, stranger has become more at home than the townsmen. (3) kadangaram bākin tūlū, a kas ka, a kas tūlū, a bar ka, kā ɓāta rūwā = kadangaram bākin randā ; a kashẹ ka, a kas randā being between the devil and the deep sea. (4) kadangaran rūwā crocodile (= kadọ). (5) kadangarūwar jējị type of lizard (*from superstition, children seeing it say bā nī na gan kị ba !*). (6) *Vd.* māshị 6. (7) *Vd.* cịn ∼, cī kadangarū.

kadangatsẹ *m.* (1) corn to which thorough surfē has not been done and which was not properly wetted and left to dry slowly, object being to obtain food hastily. (2) abịn nan yā yi minị ∼ it came on me as sudden calamity. (3) yā yi minị ∼ it (commodity) suddenly gave out "on me". (4) mutūwar ∼ untimely death (*Vd.* mutūwa 1*f*).

kadanī *m.* rags used as woman's sanitary-towel (= kasankī 2).

kadankadafī *m.* crab-louse, etc. (= dankadafī *q.v.*).

kadannū crocodiles (*pl. of* kadọ).

kadanya *f.* (*pl.* kadānē = kadanɗanī = kadanyōyī = kadanyū) (1) a shea-tree or its fruit (*Vd.* kwāra ; tāɓọ). (*b*) *for cry of* talla-*girls, Vd.* cū. (*c*) *Vd.* ɗum bēla ; fyāɗị 4*c*. (*d*) kadanyam mēlẹ *Vd.* buruntunkusa. (*e*) cịn kadanyar Fulānī *Vd.* dimbala. (*f*) *Vd.* man ∼ ; kaɗē. (2) kadanyar rāfī = kadanyar rūwā the tree *Adina micro-cephala* (*but in Benue, it is a tree provid-ing rafters*). (3) namijịn ∼ = kujēmē. (4) leonine leprosy (*Vd.* kuturta).

kadara *Ar. f.* property ; goods.

kadaran kadahan (1) yā yi kadaran kadahan it's average in price, amount, temperature, etc. shī kadaran kadahan nē he's phlegmatic. (2) *adv.* at an average price, etc.

kadar da = kadad da.

kadarī *Ar. m.* value ; price.

kadarkọ *m.* (*pl.* kadarkī = kadarkuna = kadarkai = kadarkōkī) (*Ar.* qantara). (1) bridge (*cf.* gada). (2) film on gruel, etc. (= garkūwā 2).

kadar rāɓā *Vd.* kadā 5.

kadarta = kaddara.

kada ta kwānā *f.* (1) hastily made gown of European material, for selling. (2) urgent, through-mail (= mugunyar takarda).

kadaurā *f.* (*sg., pl.*) W. African copaiba-balsam tree (*Pardaniellia oliveri*) = mājẹ.

kadda do not ! (= kada *q.v.*).

kaɗɗā *pl. of* kādọ *q.v.*

kad da bis (*derived from* kasa) *adv.* (1) below and above. (2) nā nēmē shị ∼ I sought it everywhere.

kad dafị (*derived from* kas 3) *epithet of* shrub kirnī *q.v.*

kaddai *Vd.* kadọ.

kaddajī *m.* the thorny *Mimosa asperata* (*epithet is* ∼ hana wankyan gēfẹ) = *Kt.* kwīya 2.

kad dangị = kar dangị.

kaddara = kadara.

kaddara A. (kaddarā) *Vb.* 1C. (1) pre-destined *x* Allā yā ∼ masa wannan God ordained this should happen to him. (2) estimated *x* nā kaddara kudinsa sulẹ gōma I estimated its price at 10*s.* mu ∼ tafīyan nan tā yi kwānā 20 let's reckon this journey will take 20 days. (3) assumed *x* yā ∼ zā (= yā ∼ kamar zā) a ɓā shị he assumed he'd be given it. mu ∼ masa azancī kazā let's assume for sake of argument, it's meaning is such and such . . . !

B. (kaddara) *Ar. f.* (1) (*a*) fate. (*b*) abịn ∼, sāi al'amarịn duk ya jūyẹ fate changed the circumstances. (2) ∼ tā rigā fātā man proposes and God disposes (= Allā 1k.i. = munā 2).

kad dātsī *Vd.* kas 3*b*.

kad digādigī *m.* type of sandals (= faɗẹ).

kaɗɗū *Kt.* never, etc. (= daɗāi).

kadduna crocodiles (*pl. of* kadọ).

kaɗe A. (kaɗē) *m.* (1) (*a*) shea-tree (= kadanya). (*b*) man kaɗē bai sāɓa da tandū ba prosperity is alien to the poor (*Vd.* man kadanya). (2) *Sk.* hancịn ∼ clove(s) (= kanumfarī). (3) *Sk.* namijịn ∼ = kadanya 3.

B. (kadē) *m.* short grass cut for

fodder in first fortnight of wet-season (*cf.* yaŋke ; cire).

C. (kaɗe) (**1**) *Vb.* 1A (*a*) shook dust from garment *x* yā ~ ƙūrā dagà rīgā (*Vd.* kaɓe). (*b*) (i) itàcē yā ~ ganye tree's shed all its leaves. (ii) yā ~ har ganyansà he's squandered his substance ; he has spoiled his chances. (*c*) yā ~ daŋganà tasà = kaɗà 1*l*. (*d*) *x* nā dōkē shì dà sandā, săi ya ~ I aimed blow at him, but he parried the stick. (*e*) yā ~ dūkīyā tasà he squandered all his means. (*f*) yā ~ shi he collided with him and knocked him over. (*g*) tā ~ audugā she spun all the cotton. (*h*) *x* Allà yà ~ manà tsàutsayī (jarabà) may God fend off accident (calamity) from us. (**2**) *Vb.* 3A (*a*) became thin. (*b*) yā ~ it (indigo ; kōre-gown ; lēmà-gown) lost its gloss. (*c*) *Vd.* kaɗu ; kaɗà ; karkaɗē.

kādī *m.* *x* am bi kādim màganà it's been investigated.

kaɗi A. (kaɗì) *m.* spinning.

B. (kāɗì) *Sk. m.* throwing T. at *x* an yi kāɗinsà dà dūtsè stone was thrown at him.

kadīdi (*Ar.* qadīdi) *m.* spitted-meat (= tsìrē 1).

kādīfīrī *m.* (**1**) affection. (**2**) ogling (*both* = fēlēƙē).

kāɗirā *Vd.* kàdurū.

kàɗirai *Vd.* kàdurū.

Kādirancī *m.* (**1**) the tenets of the Kàɗirīyyà Sect. (**2**) *Vd.* Bàkādirè.

Kādirāwā *Vd.* Bàkādirè.

kadọ *m.* (*pl.* kaddunà = kadōdī = kàdannī = kàdannū = kadāduṇà = kadāduwà = kadanduṇà = kàdandanī = *Kt.* kàddai = *Kt.* kàdunnī) (**1**) crocodile (= kadà = *Sk.* cāwàrākì = ƙadaŋgaràn rūwā). (**2**) (*a*) an jēfà mini kāyā à bàkin kadọ = an jēfà mini kāyā à bàkin kadà kaɓau my property's been commandeered for a chief. (*b*) bàkin kadà *m.* type of long guinea-corn. (**3**) ƙaryar ~ ta rūwā cē, in yā fitō tudu, yā zamā nāmà the absence of one essential component renders the whole useless (= ƙaryā 1*h* q.v.). (**4**) *Vd.* à kōri kadà. (**5**) yā bayyànā wà

jamà'à gàskīyā, yā cē rūwaŋ dà ~ he told the public the truth and warned them to be on their guard. (**6**) *if flirtation* (tayì) *is going on between Audu and Kande, she coming from well with water on her head, may jokingly say* kōgī ! *If he replies* kadọ !, *she empties the water over him* (*or he may reply* ìnā kadọ, *in which case, she says* gà shi *and empties water over him*). *But if he does not want his clothes wetted or does not care for the girl, he does not reply to* kōgī ! *in which case, she says to him* kā kàrai = kā yi kàdaŋ (*N.B.—the sexes may be reversed, Kande being the one over whom the water is emptied*). (**7**) kà zamā ~ *Vd.* ƙadaŋgarè 2.

kādọ *m.* (*f.* kādūwā) *pl.* kàddā = hāɓe = hāɓulōkī = hāɓalōkī (**1**) original inhabitant of a country, as Hausas from the point of view of the Filani (*epithet is* ~ mai nīsaŋ gōnā = ~ kā dafè dà Filànī). (**2**) (*a*) stupid, backward P. (*b*) àbin na ~ haukà nè is he mad that he acts thus ? (*c*) kas ~ *Vd.* kaskamī. (**3**) ~ wāwā poor furā with mere film of milk (= *Sk.* samà dōgō 1).

kadōdī *Vd.* kadọ.

kaɗu A. (kaɗu) *Vb.* 3B yā ~ he's " in a fix " (*Vd.* kaɗà, kaɗe).

B. (kaɗū) *Kt.* never, etc. (= dàdăi).

kādū = kādī.

kàdunnī *Vd.* kadọ.

kàdurū *m.* (*f.* kāɗirā) *pl.* kàɗirai simpleton.

kādūwā *Vd.* kādọ.

kaf A. (kaf) *adv.* (**1**) completely *x* yā ƙārè ~ it is quite finished. sun yi mukù zōɓe ~ they completely surrounded you. sukà jiƙe shi ~ then they attacked him tooth and claw. yā shāfe su ~ he annihilated them. yā cinye ~ he ate it all up. sun tàru ~ the members of the meeting are all present. (**2**) yā kāmà shi ~ he held it tightly (*cf.* sàkwàf). (**3**) ~ dayà ya sàrē shi he felled him with one cut of the sword. (**4**) an ɗaure shi ~ it is tightly tied.

B. (kaf) *m.* nā ji ~ I heard the

sound of wood being chopped or felled.

ƙaf (1) *Vd.* **ƙafẹ** 1*a*. (2) **nāmạn nạŋ**, an yi masạ dạfūwar ∼ this meat was cooked for so long that all the gravy became richly soaked into it (*Vd.* dạfūwā 3).

kafa A. (**kafā**) *f.* (*pl.* **kafạ̃fẽ = kafõfĩ = kafạifai**) (1) (*a*) small hole *x* (i) **kafar ạllūrạ** eye of a needle (= **hanci** 5). (ii) **bạ̃ ni dạ ∼ kõ i ta ạllūrạ** I've not a moment to spare. (iii) **kafar hanci** nostril. (iv) **hanci bạ̃ ∼** *Vd.* **ạ̃ƀụ** 9. (*b*) *cf.* **ƙõfạ**. (2) chance *x* **bạn sạ̃mi kafar zūwạ ba I** didn't get a chance to come (= **zarạ̃fĩ**). (3) cheapness *x* **rĩgan nạŋ tanạ̃ dạ ∼** this gown is cheap (= **arạ̃hā**). (4) blemish *x* **nā ga ∼ tasạ** (*a*) I saw it had a blemish, defect. (*b*) I despise him. (5) lack *x* **zā sụ cikạ kafar dạ sukạ barị** they will make up for the lack they caused.

B. (**kafạ**) *Vb.* 1A (1) (*a*) built, erected (*apart from building with* mud, brick, *or* cement, *for which Vd.* **ginạ**) *x* **yā ∼ laimạ** he put up a tent. **yā tāsam mạ kafạ zaŋgo** he set about making an encampment. **suŋ ∼ ịgwā** they set up the artillery-guns. (*b*) founded *x* ∼ **kạ̃sūwā** *Vd.* **kạ̃sūwā** 1*b*. **yā ∼ gịndim makarantā** he founded a school (= **shimfị̃dã** 2). (2) fixed *x* (*a*) (i) **kạ ∼ shi ạ baŋgõ** nail it on to the wall ! (ii) *Vd.* **fẽgị**. (*b*) **yā ∼ gẽmụ** he has started growing a beard. (*c*) (i) **yā ∼ gịndinsạ** he set to work on it with a will. (ii) *Vd.* **gịndĩ** 5. (*d*) **yā kafạ yātsū ạ garịŋ** it (army) stood firm in the town. (*e*) **yā ∼ gõshĩ** he put his forehead to the ground in prayer. (*f*) **yā ∼ kạ̃i** = *c*.i *above*. (*g*) **yā ∼ kạ̃i ạ būtạ** he put his mouth to the edge of the gourd-bottle to drink (*cf.* **dõƀạ**). (*h*) **yā ∼ masạ idọ** he fixed his gaze on it ; he stared at him. **yā kafạ idọ garẽsụ** he watched them closely. (*j*) **yā ∼ õdạ = yā ∼ dõkā** he issued an order. (*k*) **yā ∼ aminci ạ dūnīyạ** he maintained security in the world. (*l*) **suŋ ƙārạ ∼ shaidạrsụ dạ wạsĩƙạ** they strengthened their testimony with a letter. (*m*) **zā mụ**

fārạ kafạ̃wā mụ shịga aikị, săi mukạ jĩ am fãsạ we were arranging to begin work when we heard it was cancelled. (*n*) **suŋ ∼ māsunsụ ạ Kanọ** they made war on Kano. (*p*) **bạri ŋ ∼ makạ, kạ cirẹ** *formula used in* **ạlkāfụrā** (somersaulting). (*q*) (i) **yā ∼ ƙạfansạ** he embedded in the ground the left horn of the animal to be slaughtered. (ii) *Vd.* **ƙạfõ** 10. (*r*) **yā ∼ būzū** he pegged out the skin to dry (= *Kt.* **kẽrẹ** 2). (*s*) **yā ∼ mạtassạ** he used a charm on his wife to prevent her abandoning him. (*t*) **yā ∼ gidansạ** he put a protective charm on his home. (*u*) **yā ∼ gāwā** he washed the corpse and placed it on its right side eastwards for final prayers (= **kaifạfã** 1*b*). (*v*) **nā ∼ masạ mārị** I gave him a slap. (*w*) **yā kakkạfā minị cụ̃tā** he did me an injury. (*x*) **aŋ ∼ tamạninsạ** its price has been fixed. **tamạnĩ kạfaffẽ** a fixed price. (*y*) **tā ∼ dõkạ** *Vd.* **dõkạ.** (*z*) *Vd.* **tsirrạ.**

C. (**kāfạ**) *f.* blancmange wrapped in leaves.

ƙafạ *f.* (*pl.* **ƙafạ̃fū = ƙafāfūwạ = ƙafõfĩ**) (1) (*a*) (i) foot, leg (*cf.* **sau**). (ii) **yā tạfi dạ ∼ = yā tạfi ạ ∼** he went on foot (= **ạ ƙasạ**). (iii) **zā mụ mĩƙẹ bisạ ƙafāfūwạmmụ** we shall regain our strength. (iv) **suŋ kāmạ ƙafạrmụ dạ kõkawạ** they attacked us (*Vd.* 5). (v) **Kanọ tanạ̃ ƙarkashiŋ ƙafāfūwạnsụ** Kano is in their power. (vi) **mun tạfi ƙafạta, ƙafạrkạ** you and I went together. **ƙafạrkụ, ƙafạrmụ** your interests and ours are identical. **gạ̃ ƙafạrsụ, gạ̃ tāmụ cikiŋ wannạm fagyam fāmā** they and we are sharing this campaign. (vii) **aŋ karyạ musụ ƙafar gudu** they have been prevented from fleeing. (viii) **sunạ̃ jin dādim mĩƙẹ ƙafạrsụ** they are having a good time. (ix) **mukạ cirạ ∼** then we got the upper hand (*Vd.* **cirạ** 1*e*). (x) **bạ shi dạ ∼** he's lame, he's a cripple. (xi) **ƙafạssạ tā būɗẹ** his foot turns outwards from disease. (xii) **mum bi ƙasạ̃shansụ, mun rirrịƙẽ musụ ƙafāfūwạ** we went to their countries and seized the bases there. (xiii) **shịgā sukẹ kạ̃i dạ ∼** they are penetrating everywhere without let or hindrance. (xiv) yā bautā masa ƙăi da ~ he obeyed him implicitly. (xv) yā ɗauki ƙansa da ƙafāfūwansa, yā cẹ̆ bai saŋ kōwā ba săi Sarkiŋ Kano he stated categorically that he follows no overlord but the Emir of Kano. (xvi) wani ƙafa-ƙafa a tripod. (xvii) ƙafar wandō ankle-band of trousers. (b) bā̆kī yā īya ɗaurẹ ~ ya yaŋka wuya guard your tongue, it can lay you low! (c) kōwā ya yi ~ yā răi jan cikĭ if you have a dog, you don't bark yourself. (d) kā yi rībar ~ kūrā tā tāka kwāɗō you've had an unexpected piece of luck. (e) farar ~ garēshĭ (i) his feet have very white soles (considered unlucky). (ii) he's very unlucky. (f) ūwā tā sā yāranta a ~ the mother put the baby-lad across her feet to urinate or defecate (= tsugunad da). (g) (i) ~ ita ƙaŋ kāwō ƙasā a tābarmā someone must have done it, for things don't do themselves. (ii) ƙafa tā jā ƙasā Vd. matsīyācī 2. (h) ƙafar uŋgulū mai ɓāta mīya what a horrible person! (j) ~ bā ta zamā inda bābu ƙasā nobody can realize his desires till the chance offers. (k) ƙafar wani mai wuyar arō, im ba ta yi tsawō ba, tā yi gajērē it's hard to wear borrowed plumes. (l) sā ~ Vd. sā B.11. (2) yā yi ~ he's found a helper. (3) yā yi masa ~ (i) he kicked him. (ii) he helped him. (iii) he gave him a chance to state his case. (iv) he gave him trading-capital. (4) yā īya ~ (i) he's an expert foot-fighter. (ii) he's expert at making kāmuŋ ƙafa embroidery. (5) (a) nā kāma ~ tasa (i) I supplicated his help. (ii) I asked him for pardon. (b) kō kāma ~ tasa ba ka yi ba you're far inferior to him. mū, kō kusa, ba mu kāma ƙafarsu ba wurin shaŋ kōfĭ they drink far more coffee than we do. Vd. 1a.iv; kāma 11. (6) Vd. bā̆ ni ~. (7) (a) yā ɗauki ~ tasa Vd. ɗauka 1a.x, xi. (b) ~ tā ɗaukē = sau yā ɗaukē it is dead of night. (c) yā ɗaukẹ ~ it (animal)

is lame. (d) ya ɗaukẹ ~ daga garēshĭ he has ceased doing it. (e) yā ɗaukē masa ~ (i) he cheated him. (ii) he brought false charge against him. (f) yā ɗauka ~ he " put his best foot foremost ". (8) (a) (i) each stick of ɗauriŋ gūgā 1 (such stick is also called ƙafar gūgā). (ii) each half of arch in bakaŋ gizo or ɗauriŋ gūgā 2 (the latter may have 4–36 such ƙafa) x sōrō nẹ̆ ɗauriŋ gūgā ~ gōma shā bīyū it is a mud-topped house with vaulting consisting of 12 half-arches (Vd. rījīya 2, kafĭ 3, hadĭ 4). (b) ƙafar kāzā vaulting consisting of two joined half-arches with another half-arch added at right angles, to their centre (= tāƙalmī 7a = ɗanĭ 4). (c) Vd. ƙafar kāzā. (9) time x ƙafata uku gidaŋka I've been 3 times to your home (= sau 1b). (10) ~ da lallẹ obtaining goods on false pretences by some speciously attractive offer. (11) ƙafar kẹke (i) wheel of cycle. (ii) tyre of cycle. ƙafar mōta motor-wheel, motor-tyre. (12) ƙafa bā gwīwa Vd. gwīwa 1b. (13) ƙafa huɗū Vd. huɗū 7. (14) săi ya hūcẹ ƙafa Vd. sāƙō 1c. (15) ba ka ci ƙafa ba Vd. cūrĭ 4. (16) (a) yanā rawā da ƙafar wani Vd. rawā 1f. (b) Vd. rawar ƙafa. (17) Vd. bā̆kī ƙanaŋ ƙafa; fĭtar ƙafa; barci. (18) Vd. ƙafar-compounds.

ƙāfaɗa f. (pl. ƙāfaɗū) (1) (a) shoulder. (b) tā yi ~ da nī (i) she stood beside me. (ii) she helped me. (c) suna yiŋ ~ da mū they are on our side, they support us (= wajan). (d) sun yi ~ da ~ da aɓōkansu they fought side by side with their allies. (2) rāgō yā yi ~ the ram has a sore shoulder and cannot walk (cf. karfata). (3) an yi mini " hannuŋka mai ~ " " they talked at me ". (4) Vd. allō 3. (5) ƙas ~ Vd. dunjī. (6) Vd. ƙarya ƙāfaɗa.

ƙāfāfa f. putting on airs.

kafāfĭ Vd. kafā.

kafaffagī = ƙafaffagē m. (f. ƙafaffagā) wide-mouthed (re vessel) x masakī ~.

ƙafaffagō (1) m. (f. ƙafaffagā) = ƙafaffagī. (2) the fig-like tree Uapaca guineensis (fruit used for poison).

ƙafāfū feet (*pl. of* ƙafa *q.v.*).

kafaifai *Vd.* kafā.

ƙafan *Vd.* ƙafō.

kafara A. (ƙafārą) *Ar. f.* (1) (*a*) (i) atonement-penalty for breach of Muslim precepts *x* yā yi azumiŋ ~ kwānā ukụ he fasted for 3 days as atonement for breach of Muslim Law. (ii) *cf.* shā E. 2*a*; mūdanabị. (*b*) yā fïd dą ~ = *Sk.* yā ɗēbę ~ (*cf.* kōnō 2) he's fulfilled *such penalty.* (2) yā yi (= yā shā) rantsūwar ~ he perjured himself (= rantsūwā 3).

B. (kafarą) *f.* earthenware basin (= kwątarnịyā).

ƙafar birnī *Vd.* ąrąhā 4.

ƙafar fąkarā *f.* the grass *Chloris breviseta* which has edible seeds (= ƙafar gaurāką = saŋ gaurāką).

ƙafar gaurāką *f.* (1) *Vd.* kąntāƙalai. (2) = ƙafar fąkarā.

ƙafar gūgā *f.* (1) each stick in ɗauriŋ gūgā 1 (= ƙafa 8*a*.i *q.v.*). (2) = ƙafa 8*a*.ii.

ƙafar Kanọ *f.* flat-footedness (= madaɓi 1*b*).

ƙafar kązā *f.* (1) tattooing where there are three marks at each corner of mouth. (2) *Vd.* ƙafa 8*b*. (3) ciŋ ~ cramp *x* ciŋ ~ nę ya sā hannūna ya ƙagę cramp made my arm stiff (= maƙyūyącī 2).

ƙafar shąmūwā *f.* type of red sugar-cane (tąkandā).

ƙafar tsuntsū = san tsuntsū.

ƙafar uŋgulū *f.* *Vd.* ƙafa 1*h*.

ƙafar wālā *Vd.* wālā 2.

ƙafar yāƙi *x* nā kāmą ~ I got part of the required sum.

kāfataŋ *Ar.* (1) *adv.* entirely *x* ~ gąrni naŋ duką in the whole of this town. (2) kāfatąnī *m.* entirety *x* kāfatąniŋ gąrin naŋ.

ƙafau *Vd.* ƙafō.

kafce A. (kafcę) *Vb.* 1A (1) hoed up deeply the whole farm. (2) yā ~ ƙafa dą fartanyą he accidentally hacked his foot with hoe, whilst hoeing. (3) = kaftā 1.

B. (ƙafcē) *Vd.* ƙąftā.

kaf dą kaf exactly *x* ƙyaurē yā rụfu ~ door fits exactly. yā yi minị

~ it (commodity) lasted as I'd reckoned.

ƙafe A. (ƙafę) (1) *Vb.* 3A (*a*) yā ~ it (pond, well, river) dried up. yā ~ ƙaf it (pond, etc.) is quite dried up. (*b*) nāmą yā ~ meat is roasted *as in* 2. (2) *Vb.* 1A roasted (meat) thoroughly on skewer (tsiŋkē) by fire till cooked ready to eat (= *Kt.* kawącē = *Sk.* kērę 4), *cf.* ƙafē, ƙyāfę, gasą, tsịrē.

B. (ƙafē) *m.* (1) chicken or large piece of meat skewered and left long by the fire (*Vd.* ƙafę 2). (2) maƙąŋwącī bā yā ~ (*lit.* the ravenous P. will not delay to roast meat by the fire for the long time necessary) it is a case where speed counts more than carefulness.

kafe A. (kafę) (1) *Vb.* 3A (*a*) became embedded in mud, etc. (*b*) behaved resolutely *x* yā ~ kaŋ aikị he stuck to his work. (*c*) behaved obstinately *x* yā ~ kaŋ wannąŋ he has persisted in his attitude. (2) *Vb.* 1A (*a*) erected (*as in* kafa) all of. (*b*) yā ~ laimą he set up a tent (= kafą 1*a*). (*c*) = kafą 2*c*.i, 2*f*, *q*, *r*, *s*, *t*, *u*. (*d*) nā ~ shi dą mārị I slapped him.

B. (kafē) *m.* (1) verandah (shirāyī) fixed to house wall. (2) pen with point cut at right angles (*cf.* jịrgē, kafiŋ ąlkaląmī).

C. (kafē) *used in* 'yar ~ (*pl.* 'yaŋ ~) decoy-bird.

kaffą-kaffą *f.* = kaf-kaf.

kąffārą = kąfārą.

kafi *m.* (1) hut of cornstalks (= tsąŋgayą). (2) (*a*) kafị = kafiŋ gąrī stockade. (*b*) town surrounded by stockade-fence. (*c*) *Vd.* 4. (3) kafiŋ ƙafą (*a*) securing the beams with which ƙafą 8*a*.ii is made (= sūką 2*b*, *q.v.*). (*b*) each of the shorter beams placed alternately with kafi 3*a*, to reinforce. (4) kafiŋ gąrī (*a*) buried charm for prosperity of town. (*b*) *Vd.* 2. (5) anā kafịm būzū the skin has been pegged out to dry. (6) nā sau ~ I've been proved wrong, so give way. (7) *Vd.* kafiŋ ąlkaląmī.

kā fi amaryā *m.* the fragrant herb ɗaɗɗōyą.

kā fi bōkā _m._ the convolvulus Ipomaea argentaurata.

kā fi dā wuyā _m._ type of coloured bead.

kā fi ƙaryā _m._ hair left growing below lower lip (= tsai da magana).

ƙāfillō _m._ (1) affectation. (2) ogling (_both_ = fēlēƙē).

kā fi mālam _m._ the herb _Evolvulus alsinoides (used for charms or drugs),_ _Vd._ mālami 1_c._iv.

kāfin = ƙāfin _conj._ (1) before (= kamin _q.v._). (2) tun ~ _Vd._ tun 1_cc._

kafin alkalamī _m._ first instalment paid for charm, rest being payable when charm " works " (_cf._ kafē 2).

kāfirai _Vd._ kāfirī.

kā fi rama _m._ the undershrub _Urena lobata (bark gives fibre)_ = ramānīyā = garmanī 2.

kāfircē _Vb._ 3A (1) became kāfirī. (2) horse became vicious.

kāfirci _m._ (1) being neither Muslim nor one of the " People of the Book " (Kitābi _such as_ Christian, Jew, etc.). (2) deliberately acting or speaking with intent to annoy. (3) yāƙi irin wanda ka sani na kāfirci bitter war (_cf._ kāfirī 2). (4) kāfircim māgē, alwalā bā salla _epithet of_ T. which P. undertaking has no intention of doing.

kāfirdō _used in_ yā īya ~, namijin kāfirī he's a regular rogue.   kada ka yi mini ~ now, none of your knavery ! kāfirī _m._ (_f._ kāfirā) _pl._ kāfirai = kāfirāwā (1) (_a_) non-Muslim _such as described in_ kāfirci. (_b_) annabi da kāfirī _Vd._ annabi 3.   (2) _emphasizes quality_ x kāfirim bābā excellent indigo. kāfirin dōki (i) speedy horse.   (ii) vicious horse. kāfirar tābā strong tobacco. harbin kunāma, da kāfirin zāfi yakē sting of scorpion's very painful.   (3) Audu kāfirī kashe mai salla that accursed Audu !

kāfirta _Vb._ 3B = kāfircē.

kafīyā _f._ behaving resolutely or obstinately.

kā fi 'yan gyadā _m._ type of cloth.

kā fi yāro _m._ forehead-ornament of woman with dōka coiffure.

kaf-kaf A. (kaf-kaf) _m._ yanā ~ da shi he's looking carefully after it.

B. (kaf-kaf) yanā kwakkwafā ~ he's cantering tap ! tap !

ƙafō _m._ (_pl._ ƙahōnī = ƙahunhuna = ƙahwanni). (1) (_a_) horn (_b_) horn for blowing (_cf._ marōƙi). (_c_) nī kē rike ~ wani yanā tātsā I'm merely his catspaw. (_d_) munā sā ido, ran da muka ga ~ mā gaya muku we're on the watch and when we see a sign, we'll tell you.   (_e_) yā dafa ~ _Vd._ gishirī 4.   (_f_) sānīyā bā tā gazāwā da ƙafanta _Vd._ sā A.2 1_k._ (_g_) ~ yā yi tsīrā _Vd._ tsīrā 1_b._iv.   (_h_) ƙafan taurī _Vd._ taurī 2_c._   (_j_) _Vd._ zīnārīyā da ~.   (_k_) hawan ~ wrestling of man with bull.   (2) an yi masa ~ (_a_) he's been cupped.   (_b_) the ƙahō-tattooing has been done on him. (3) (_a_) ƙafam fārā antennæ of grasshopper or locust.   (_b_) dōhilō, ƙafam fārā da tsīnī, bā sūka what a fool !   (4) (_a_) destitute P. (_b_) miser (_epithet is_ ~ sāi būsa = ~ bā ka mīya). (5) ƙafan sigāri cigarette-holder (= hōla).   (6) ƙafam barēwā (_a_) type of large kuɓēwā (okro).   (_b_) type of large trousers. (7) ƙafan Dandi warming one's back before fire after rubbing it with oil.   (8) ƙafan karo (_a_) reinforcement of upper part of gown both in front and behind (_cf._ addā 3). (_b_) type of flat building (sōrō).   (9) ƙafan zūcī = ƙafan zūcīyā place behind breastbone where heartbeats are visible (= murfī 1_b_).   (10) (_a_) yā kafa mini ƙafan zūkā he pestered me.   (_b_) _Vd._ kafa 2_q._ (11) _Vd._ rīgar ƙafō.

ƙafō _m._ (1) deep mud. (2) yā fāda ~ = yā shiga ~ he's " in a fix ".

kafōfī _Vd._ kafā.

ƙafōfī _Vd._ ƙafa.

kafta A. (kafta) _Vb._ 1A. (1) dug ground deeply for planting cassava, tobacco, sugar-cane (rakē), hemp (rama), sorrel (yākūwā), etc. (_cf._ farce 3_a_). (2) yā ~ magana he spoke in an unseemly way. (3) nā ~ masa shī I swung it (sword, axe, hoe, etc.) at him.   nā ~ garmā a ƙafassa I hacked his foot with the hoe. (4) (_a_) nā ~ masa shī I gave him large share of it. (_b_) Sarkī yā ~ masa ƙasā the Chief put him in charge of large area.

B. (kaftā) _Vb._ 2 (_p.o._ kafcē, _n.o._

ḳaɓci). (1) = kaftạ 1. (2) took large share of.

ḳaftaŋ m. (1) = ḳaftānị. (2) Nor. (French capitaine) French military officer administering station in military occupation.

ḳaftānị Ar. m. caftan, i.e. long type of tagūwā.

kaftu A. (ḳaftū) m. (secondary v.n. of kaftạ) x yanạ̄ ḳaftuŋ ɓasā = yanạ̄ kaftạ ɓasā.

B. (kaftū) m. repeating the Koran aloud to memorize it (= gōgẹ 1f = ḳiskādị).

kāfū = kāhū.

ɓạfullō = ɓạfillō.

kāfur = kāfurī Ar. m. camphor.

kāfurcē = kāfircē.

ɓaga A. (ɓāgạ) (1) f. " the pick of the bunch ". (2) Vb. 1A. (a) (i) invented x aŋ ∼ irịn sāban jirgī a new kind of ship has been invented. (ii) yā ∼ ɓaryā = yā ∼ mạganạ he told a lie. (b) yā ∼ minị ɓaryā he told a lie to me, against me. yā ∼ minị mạganạ he brought a false charge against me. (c) yā ∼ littāfị he composed a book.

B. (ɓāgā) Vb. 2 = ɓāgạ 2.

C. (ɓagā) used in aŋ kāmō shị dạ ∼ (lit. when seized as a slave, he was a pagan wearing a leather apron) how he has made his way in the world !

ɓagal adv. and m. rising suddenly x yā tāshị ∼ = yā yi ∼ yā tāshị he suddenly stood up, departed.

kagarā f. (1) x yā ga ∼ he got a bargain. yā sāmē shị ạ ∼ he got it cheap. (2) f. zareeba.

ɓagarạ Vb. 3B = ɓagautạ.

ɓagau m. (1) bucket jammed in well (= sạgau 2). (2) the charm sạgau q.v.

ɓagautạ Vb. 3B is (was) eager to x yā ∼ ạ bā shị hanyạ he is eager to receive leave to depart.

ɓage A. (ɓagẹ) (1) Vb. 3A. (a) yā ∼ it (arm, leg) became temporarily stiff or permanently paralysed (cf. ɓamẹ 2, dagẹ 2a, daŋgalē 2). (b) (i) T. became caught in branches, etc. (= sarɓafē). (ii) kudīna suŋ ∼ ạ wurinsạ I cannot get him to pay me what he owes. (iii) gūgā yā ∼ bucket became jammed in

well (1a, b = sagẹ = maɓalē). (c) P. sent on errand delayed inordinately (= maɓalē). (2) Vb. 1A. (a) dārī yā ∼ ni cold weather's made me stiff. (b) nā ∼ shi I prevented his (its) departure (of P. ; of horse by securing reins ; of bucket left hanging in well ; of cloth left hanging in dye-pit, etc.). (c) yā ∼ minị kudīna = 1b.ii above.

B. (ɓāgē) m. (1) yā yi minị ∼ he lied to me, against me (= ɓāgạ 2b = yaŋkē 2 = sartsẹ 3a). (2) Audụ, ∼ gạrēshị Audu's a liar.

C. (ɓāgē) inventing x shī nẹ̄ ya yi ɓāgyansạ it was he who invented it (cf. ɓāgạ 2).

kaggā round-houses (pl. of kagọ).

kagguna Vd. kagọ.

kā gira m. bribe to judge, etc.

kago A. (kagọ) m. (pl. kaggā = kagguna). (1) round, thatched house = hayị 3 (cf. dākị). (2) (a) man of perseverance (epithet is ∼ nē ; anạ̄ rūwa, kanạ̄ tsạye). (b) an dadẹ anạ̄ rūwa, kagọ yanạ̄ tsạye it's useless to slander P. of proved integrity (cf. dadẹ 1c).

B. (kāgọ) Eng. m. cargo-steamer.

ɓāgwā = ɓāgūwā f. (pl. ɓāgwōyī = ɓāgū-wōyī). (1) crab. (2) blacksmith's pincers. (3) tạfīyạr ∼ f. boys' walking on hands, feet in air.

Ḳạhartụm f. Khartoum.

kaharụ = ɓaharụ Ar. m. yā yi minị ∼ he falsely accused me.

ɓahō = ɓafō.

ɓahō m. = ɓafō.

kahu (kāhū) m. (1) numnah of padded, embroidered cloth garnished with pieces of coloured leather. (2) " lame excuse " (= rạrraunaŋ hanzarī).

ɓahuŋhunạ Vd. ɓafō.

ɓāhurgumī m. (f. ɓāhurgumā) big and fat.

ɓahwạnnī Vd. ɓahō.

kai A. (kai) (1) (a) (said to male) you there ! (but kai mai tạfīyạ hi, you passer-by !). (b) ∼ kā saŋ indạ darē ya yi makạ don't be nosey ! (2) (more emphatically said than 1 and tone falling much lower) (said to both sexes) (a) come, come !, now behave yourself ! (= habạ). (b) fancy ! (c) oh dear ! (d) well ! x tā cẹ̄ mạsụ " kai, mẹ̄ zại

sǎ kụ bĭ nị " she said to them " well,
why are you willing to go with me ? ".
(3) ∼ barị, hakǎ sukǎ yi in short, this
is how they acted. (4) ∼ nǎ ƙĭ, bạ ạ
taɓạ jịn irịn wannạm ba the like of this
has never been heard. (5) (a) = kǎ
yi you will do it. (b) Vd. Mǎlikị.

B. (kǎi) m. (genitive kạn) pl.
kāwunạ = kāyūwạ = kānū = kāyukạ.
(1) (a) (i) head. (ii) kạn kẹƙyan dịnƙị
actuating-wheel of sewing machine.
(iii) ƙọƙwaŋ ∼ m. skull, cranium. (iv)
cikạ ∼ rūwā Vd. rūwā A.17c. (v) ∼
dạ ∼ Vd. 7d. (vi) ạ kǎi, ạ kǎi Vd. 7c.
(vii) ci ∼ ; shā ∼ Vd. 1A below. (viii)
for proverbs with kǎi, Vd. 1B below. (ix)
kạnsụ yā fārạ wāyẹ̌wā they've begun to
gain experience. (x) yā kai kạnsạ
caŋ he went there. suŋ kāwō ∼ they've
turned up. dặmunā tā kāwō ∼ the
rains have come (Vd. kāwō 2g,' 4).
(xi) yā ɗauki kạnsạ dạ ƙafāƙūwạnsạ, yā
cẹ bai saŋ kōwā ba sǎi Sarkịn Kano he
stated categorically that he follows no
overlord but the Emir of Kano. ɗaukẹ
kǎi Vd. ɗaukē 1e. (xii) kạnsụ yā gạmu
they are unanimous. dạ mū, dạ sū
duk, ∼ yā zō ɗayā they and we are
unanimous. kạnsụ ɗayā nẹ gạ yinsạ
they are unanimous that it should be
done (cf. 1m below). kạnsụ bǎ gạme
yakẹ ba = kạnsụ yā ƙi gạmūwā =
kạnsụ bai gamẹ ba they could come to no
unanimity. gamạ kǎi Vd. gamạ 1k.
(xiii) aɓōkaŋ gǎɓā sum bǎ dạ ∼ the
enemy surrendered (cf. bǎ ni ∼).
(xiv) yā bautā masạ ∼ dạ ƙafạ he
obeyed him implicitly. shịgā sukẹ ∼
dạ ƙafạ they are entering everywhere
without let or hindrance. (xv) Vd.
kạn-compounds. (xvi) suŋ ƙi ∼ Vd.
ƙĭ 1c.iv. (xvii) Vd. nēmaŋ kǎi. (b) (i)
magạnạŋ naŋ, bǎ ∼, bǎ gịndī this talk
is all at sixes and sevens. (ii) bǎ shi
dạ ∼, bǎ shi dạ gịndī he's senseless (cf.
1f.iii. (iii) mun rasạ kạnsụ, mun rasạ
gịndinsụ we're at a loss how to deal
with them. (c) kạnsạ yā hau he's
arrogant. (d) Vd. fāɗịŋ ∼. (e) tāshịn ∼
= jịŋ ∼ m. arrogance (Vd. 5j). (f)

(i) mại farịŋ ∼ m., f. (pl. mǎsū farịŋ ∼)
educated P. (ii) mại baƙịŋ ∼ m., f.
(pl. mǎsū baƙịŋ ∼) ignorant P. (iii)
keen intelligence x yanǎ dạ ∼ he's
" sharp ". bǎ shi dạ ∼ he's " dull ",
senseless (cf. 1b.ii). (g) kạn rǎƙĭ m.
source of stream. (h) ∼ bĭyū yā
fi ∼ ɗayā kō na zīnārịyā two heads
are better than one ! (j) yā tsayạ
∼ dạ fātạ bai yi ba he firmly maintained that he did not do it. (k)
bai kōmạ ta kạnsụ ba (i) he troubled
no further about them. (ii) he was not
anxious about them. (iii) he didn't go
to see them. (iv) Vd. kạn 5b. (l) (i)
yanǎ cirạ ∼ he's arrogant (= ɗagạ 1d).
(ii) bǎ wandạ ya isa cirạ ∼ gạrẹshị
he's too powerful to resist. (m) kạnsụ
ɗayā nẹ they are of the same age (cf.
1a.xii above). (n) yā bar kạnsạ (i)
he is unmanageable. (ii) the thing is
useless. (o) Allǎ yạ barạ kạnsạ ạ
sāmụ (said by women visitors to woman
after her confinement) long life to your
baby son ! (p) sun yi kạnsạ they
crowded round him. (q) (i) kạn Sarkĭ
head on coin. (ii) mẹ ka bị, dạmarạ ?
kō kạn Sarkĭ heads or tails ? (r) kǎi
tsạye adv. at once. (s) fitar dạ ∼ Vd.
fitar dạ 2. (t) (i) jẹ ka, yạ kāmạ makạ
kạnkạ go to him that he may charm
away your headache ! (ii) kǎmạ kǎi
m., f. (sg., pl.) assistant. kǎmạ kạnsạ
his assistant. (u) (i) yā karyạ kǎi, yā
yi tạƙīyạ tasạ he refused and went on
his way. (ii) cīwọ yā karyạ ∼ the illness has passed its crisis. (v) kạnsạ
yanǎ cīwọ Vd. cīwọ 4c. (w) aɓịŋ ∼
zō kammụ now we're in for it ! (x)
tạɓạ kǎina Vd. taɓạ 1c. (y) kạnkạ ạ
dǎme Vd. akurū. (z) dǎidǎi dạ kạŋ
kōwā Vd. daŋkwarā. (z) (i) zūwạŋ ∼
Vd. zūwạ 5. (z) (ii) ƙwarịŋ ∼ Vd.
ạdụrūkụ. (x) (iii) duhụŋ ∼ Vd. duhụ
5. (z) (iv) dāɗịŋ ∼ Vd. dāɗī 6. (z) (v)
ɓōyaŋ ∼ Vd. ɓōyō 5a. (z) (vi) Vd.
mūgụŋ kǎi, bụɗar kǎi. (z) (vii) kạn dạ
bǎ idǎnū Vd. kụrtū. (z) (viii) kyaŋ ∼
Vd. kyau 2. (z) (ix) Vd. kau dạ 5.

1A. (a) yā shā ƙǎi he got ahead of the
others. (b) yā shā (= yā ci) kạnsụ =

yā shā musu kǎi (i) he managed to get ahead of them (= gạba 3*l*). (ii) he headed them off, he outflanked them (= gạba 3*l* = fanyā 2*b*). (iii) *Kt.* it overtopped them. (iv) it (river) was over their heads, they were out of their depth (*Vd.* īyā 1*b*). (v) it was too much for them. (vi) he outwitted them. (vii) he pared their edges (calabashes). (viii) it (liquor, tobacco, etc.) stupefied them. (*c*) mun shā (= mun shāwō) kansạ we persuaded him over. (*d*) kāyan yạrdā (= kāyan rā'ị) bā yạ̌ cin kǎi what one does voluntarily does not irk. (*e*) yā ci kansạ he hemmed it (= kalmạsā), *Vd.* cī 23*b*, *bb.* (*f*) yanạ̌ shāwō kǎi he's bubbling over with excited talk. (*g*) mẹ̌ ya shā makạ kại what has come over you ? (*h*) sunạ̌ cin kansụ they are squabbling. (*j*) kāyā yạ ci minị kǎi the load I carried made my head sore. kāyan nạn, cin kǎi gạrēshị carrying this load makes one's head sore. (*k*) lạ̄bārin nạn yā shā musụ kǎi this news disturbed them.

1B. *proverbs with* kǎi :—(*a*) (i) sāmụn ∼ yā fi sāmụn hūlā = sāmụn ∼ yā fi sāmụn askị health is better than wealth. (ii) dọ̄min kǎi akẹ̌ hūlā *Vd.* dọ̄min 2*e.* (*b*) in ∼ dạ tsōkạ, kōwā yạ tabạ nāsạ yạ ji if a P. says generosity is an easy quality to display, let us see what he himself gives ! (*c*) kīwạn ∼ yā fi kīwạn dabbạ one must learn self-control before one can control others. (*d*) (i) sạ̌ ∼ ạ ukụ *Vd.* ukụ. (ii) *Vd.* sạ̌ B.5*b.* (*e*) ∼ bạ̌ ma'aji ba nẹ̌, bā yạ̌ ajịyẹ kōmē săi mājinā one is likely to forget unless one jots a thing down. (*f*) dạ ∼ dạ kāyā mạllakạr wuyạ nē what one's dependents own is the same as what one owns oneself. (*g*) kạnkụ akẹ̌ jī, mahạukạcī yā fādạ rījịyā what have I to do with what you are saying ? (*h*) săi an dāfạ kansạ *Vd.* dāfạ 1*a.*ii. (*j*) kǎi bā yạ̌ fashẹwā ạ banzā *Vd.* rōtsị 2.

(2) top (*a*) kan takạrdā the top of the paper. kan dūtsẹ summit of rock. kan littāfị beginning of a book. kan izụfī top of a paragraph. (*b*) kan ɗākị

roof of kagọ (round house). kan sōrō roof of flat-topped building (*cf.* hayị 1*a.*ii ; rufị 2*b*). (*c*) yā mai dạ kansạ ƙasạ he turned it upside down.

(3) tip (*a*) kan ạllūrạ point of needle. kam būlālạ whip-tip (*Vd.* nōnọ 2*b*). (*b*) penetrating voice *x* lạ̄dānin nan, ∼ gạrēshị that muezzin's got a penetrating voice. n nạ̌ jin kansạ dạgạ nan his voice carries right over here.

(4) (*a*) chief *x* shī nẹ̌ kammụ he's our Chief, our leader, our senior. (*b*) *Vd.* kānū.

(5) self. (*a*) nī dạ kǎina I myself. sụ tạfi dạ kansụ let them go themselves ! (*b*) (i) yi ta kạnkạ be on your guard ! (ii) ta kǎina nakẹ̌ yị I'm relying on myself alone. (iii) ta ∼ nikẹ̌ I've all I can do to look after *myself*, so how can I help *you* ! (*reply to* " please help me ! "). (iv) anạ̌ ta ∼ *Vd* 5*h*, ta 1*d.* (v) kụ yi ta kạnkụ mind your own business. (*c*) yā kạmātạ kụ nẹ̌mi ạbin kạnkụ you should earn your own living. (*d*) don kạnkạ ka fitạ ạikị ? was it of your *own* accord you gave up work ? (*e*) gạban ∼ becoming independent *x* yā yi gạban kansạ he followed his own counsel. yā sạ̄mi gạban kansạ he's started his own household. tā sạ̄mi gạban kantạ (i) she's now married. (ii) she is living on her own. (*f*) sạ̄mi kansạ (kantạ) *Vd.* sạ̄mā 1*g.* (*g*) maganạ tā yi kantạ it's turned out satisfactorily. (*h*) yā yi ta kansạ he took to his heels. mụ yi ta kammụ let's clear out ! (*Vd.* ta 1*d*). (*j*) sunạ̌ jin kansụ they're really fine. rīgunạ bīyū mạ̄sū jin kansụ two gowns, one even better than the other. kāruwōyī mạ̄sū jin kansụ harlots full of confidence through prosperity (*cf.* 1*e*). (*j*) don sạn ∼ from selfish motives (*Vd.* sọ̄ 2*c*). (*k*) *cf.* rǎi 4. (*l*) sạ̌ kǎi ukụ *Vd.* ukụ 3. (*m*) gāra kạ jē dạ kạnkạ *Vd.* tsịnī 2. (*n*) don kạnkị *Vd.* nōmā 1*b.*ii.

(6) particulars *x* bạn ji kam mạganạn nam ba I don't follow the drift of that ; I do not see " what's at the bottom of

it ". (*b*) yau, baŋ ga ƙanta (= ƙansa) ba I don't see where my next penny's to come from. (*c*) babbaŋ abin da ba mu saŋ ƙansa ba an important affair which we can't solve. (*d*) yā nẹmi kam magana he tried to get at the root of the matter.

(7) unit *x* (*a*) (i) kaŋ itącē a load of wood (*Vd.* karā 1*e*). rūwā ~ ukụ 3 head-loads of water. itącē yanā naŋ kăi-kăi wood is there in bundles. (ii) *Vd.* ƙundụmāsa. (iii) kaŋ karā bundle of corn-stalks (*Vd.* karā 1*e*). (iv) im mụtụm yā yi minị kaŋ karā, n̥ yi masa kaŋ itącē, ya shẹkara, yanā ƙōnāwā whatever a P. does to you, good or bad, outdo him in return ! (v) 'yaŋ ~ and a bit *x* ukụ da 'yaŋ ~ three and a bit. bāyan shẹkara gōma da 'yaŋ ~ after 10 years and a bit (= abụ 4). (*b*) yā yi barcī ~ gụdā he had a snatch of sleep. (*c*) anā zūwa a kăi a kăi they are coming in steady succession, continually (= agufi-agufi). (*d*) (i) abiŋ yā zō ~ da ~ shūkạr matsụkī it happened appositely. (ii) sun yi ~ da ~ they are evenly matched. (*e*) unit of

hoeing *as shown on diagram at foot of page.*

(8) *Vd.* (*a*) kạn. (*b*) kạn-*compounds.*

C.1 (kai) *Vb.* 1B. (1) reached *x* (*a*) (i) yā ~ Kanọ = yā ~ ga Kanọ he reached Kano. doŋ sụ ~ ga isā Masạr that they may get as far as Egypt. yā ~ gạrinsụ he reached his native town. sunā ~ kāsūwā = sunā kaiwā kāsūwā they're reaching the market (*Vd.* Mod. Gram. 178*a*). yā ~ kunyā he reached the end of the furrow which he was hoeing. (ii) rūwā yā ~ the wet season is protracted (*Vd.* dāmunā). (iii) ba ta ~ ba = ba ta ~ bantē ba she was not virgin at marriage (*said because previously, village-girls kept on* bantē *till marriage and then changed it for a* mụkurū) = budurcị 3. (iv) yā ~ Kuncī = yā tafi Kuncī (*cf.* ƙuncī 3) he became angry. (v) tā ~ dăi fagyạm bā yā jiŋ ƙaŋ ubansa things went so far that he forgot his filial duty. anā naŋ dăi har ya ~ ga fagyạŋ yanā cị, hannū yanā rawā matters reached such a pitch

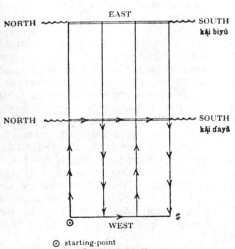

NORTH ~~~   EAST   ~~~ SOUTH
     kăi biyū

NORTH ~~~   ~~~ SOUTH
     kăi dayā

     WEST

⊙ starting-point
— kunyā (west to east)
= kadādā (north to south)
⚡ finish of one kăi
→ direction of work

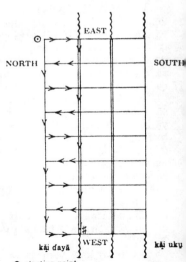

   EAST

NORTH   SOUTH

kăi dayā   WEST   kăi ukụ

⊙ starting-point
— kunyā jụyayyịyā (north to south)
= kadādā (east to west)
⚡ finish of one kăi
→ direction of work

that he couldn't take food without his hand trembling (*Vd. 2c*). (vi) **karansạ yā kai = karansạ yā kai tsaikọ** he realized his ambition (*Vd.* **tsaikọ** 1*c*). (vii) **yā ~ ƙarfinsạ = shẹ̄ƙạrunsạ suŋ ~** he's in his prime (20–30 years of age). (viii) **iŋ aŋ ga ƙọ̄ƙarim mụtụm yā ~ ƙwarai** if a man shows exceptional energy. (ix) **ạl'amạriŋ wannạŋ yāƙi yā ~ ịndạ ya ~ = bạ̄ ịndạ bai ~ ba** this war is a matter of widespread anxiety. (*x*) **dōki bạ zại ~ wannạm fagē ba** the horse will not last out this lap. (xi) **kụ tarẹ, kadạ yạ ~** cut him off so that he does not escape! (xii) **yā kai tạfī** *Vd. 3j below*. (xiii) **yā kai yā dōkẹ** *Vd.* **dōkẹ** 3. (xiv) **tụ̄rā tā kai baŋgō** *Vd.* **tụ̄rā** 2*b*. (xv) **ịndạ mại gudụ ya kai** *Vd.* **hạƙurạ** 1*d*. (xvi) **birnī yā ~ ƙasạ** the town fell (in war).

(*b*) sufficed *x* (i) **bạ zại ~ ba** it will not suffice. (ii) **tsawō yā ~** the wall of house (**dāki** *or* **sōrō**) is finished and only awaits roof (= **kashẹ** 4*a last example*). (iii) **hatsī yā ~ gar-gar** the corn is quite ripe. (*c*) went so far as *x* (i) **ạbịŋ zại ~ gạ ɓạrnā** it will lead to trouble. (ii) **ạl'amạriŋ yā ~ gạ yāƙi** the affair led to, ended in war. (iii) **ạbịŋ yā ~ gạ dōlẹ ạ daurẹ** su it became indispensable to imprison them. (iv) **har yā ~ gạ cẹwā** he went as far as to say that ... (v) **yā wucẹ ạbụ̄tā, yā ~ ạ cẹ̄ masạ zụmụntā** this surpasses friendship and enters the realms of relationship-affection. (vi) **yā ~ gạ zuŋgụrimmụ** he has begun even to provoke us. (vii) **har ạbụ yā ~ sukạ zạ̄ɓē shi yạ zamā shụ̄gạbansụ** matters finally reached the point where they elected him as their ruler. (viii) **akạ ~ har gạ yịŋ ƙullī dạ ƙullī** matters came to hand to hand fighting. (*d*) amounted to *x* (i) **mutạ̄nē suŋ ~ 400** the people amounted to 400. (*e*) equalled *x* **bạ̄ wạndạ ya ~ shi** girmā it has not its equal in size, he has not his equal in power. **bai ~ Kanọ azziƙī ba wajaŋ gyạɗā** it is no match for Kano in groundnuts.

(2) caused to reach *x* (*a*) **yā ~ bạ̄ƙī, zại dība** he put his mouth to the vessel to drink. **ạbịn dạ ya ~ ni watạ gụdā** what is (was) enough to last me a month. (*b*) **Alạ̄ ~ mụ = Alạ̄ ~ mụ gọ̄be** may God cause us to see to-morrow! (*c*) **har yạnzu yā ~ ni fagyạŋ** I own it up to the present (*cf.* 1*a*.v). (*d*) **ạ kai dambē** *Vd.* **dambē** 6. (*e*) **kai dā nēsạ** *Vd.* **dumā** 3. (*f*) **kai yạ̄rā makasā** *Vd.* **tụŋkū** 1*e*. (*g*) **bạ̄ yạ̄ kai tsōfō** *Vd.* **bam mạganạ** 2, 3.

(3) took, took to *x* (*a*) (i) **yā ~ tạ Kanọ** he took her to Kano. (ii) **mẹ̄ ya ~ kạ yāwọ dạ fitilạ** what has led you to wander about with a lamp? (iii) **kadạ dại mụ ~ kạ dạ nīsā** let us not exaggerate! (iv) **muŋ ~ sụ ƙasạ** we felled them. **muŋ ~ jirạ̄gyansụ ƙasạ** we have sunk their ships. (v) **yā ~ kansạ caŋ** he went there. (vi) *cf.* **ạ ~ cikī**. (vii) **aŋ ~ shi** he (corpse) has been buried (= **binnẹ**). (viii) **yā ~ musụ yāƙi** he made war on them. (ix) **yā ~ kansạ ịndạ Allạ̄ bai ~ shi ba** he " put on side ". (*b*) (i) **yā ~ ƙārā** he cried out, wept. (ii) **yā ~ ƙārā wurinsạ** he took his complaint to him (*Vd.* **ƙārā** 2). **nā ~ kūkāna wurinsạ** I took my trouble to him. (*c*) **yā ~ aikinsạ dạ bakạ** he exaggerated. **kadạ kạ ~ ni dạ bakạ** don't exaggerate about me! (*d*) **yā ~ ayā matsukā** he " put his head in the lion's mouth ". (*e*) **yā ~ takạrdā** he died (= **tikiti** 2). (*f*) **ạ ~ kāshin dōki birnī ? = ạ ~ dambē Kạtsịnạ ?** taking coals to Newcastle. (*g*) **yā ~ kallō** he attracted attention. (*h*) **yā ~ raunī** he bent back, touching the ground with his hands. (*j*) **yā ~ tạ̄fī = yā ~ tạ̄fī baŋgō** he " came out into the open " (*d.f. testing fairness of gambling-cowries*). (*k*) (i) **suŋ ~ rūwā rānā** they're engaged in a bitter quarrel. (ii) **kạ̄miŋ ạ yī, ạ ~ rūwā rānā** much water will flow under the bridges before that is done (*Vd.* **rūwā** A.18). (*l*) **bạri mụ ~ jịkī** let's go close up! (*m*) **yā ~ karā maƙauracī** he's dead (*Vd.* **karā** 7). (*n*)

kai kūkā *Vd.* mutūwạ le. (*o*) ạ kai
irị gidā *Vd.* māzạyā. (*p*) kai shị d̶akạ
Vd. d̶akạ ld. (*g*) kạ kai cakī *Vd.* cakī 3.
(*r*) kạɳ kai kạsūwā *Vd.* sọ̄ lc.

(4) kai dạ kāwō. (*a*) yā kai, yā kāwō =
yā kai, yā dōkẹ he's big-made. (*b*)
kọ̄gī yā kai, yā kāwō the river is in
flood. (*c*) yā cikạ kạiwā dạ kāwọ̄wā he's
a mischief maker. (*d*) sāi dạ akạ kai,
akạ kāwō, akạ yī it was only accomplished after much trouble. (*e*) kạiwā
dạ kāwọ̄wā *f.* going hither and thither,
going to and fro *x* suɳ hanạ manạ
kạiwā dạ kāwọ̄wā ạ hanyạr = suɳ
hanạ manạ kai dạ kāwō ạ hanyạr they
hindered us passing along that road
(= rạ̄gayạ 2 = rētọ 2*a* = Sạfā 2 =
wad̶arī lc = wạcạ̄-wạcạ̄ 1 = jẹ̄tạrạɳgū
= d̶ạbdalạ 3 = zụrubtū = tsụgụni, tạshi
2 = zịrgạ̄-zirgā). (*f*) (i) kā san yạddạ
yakẹ kai, yanạ̄ kāwọ̄wā you know his way
of going to and fro. yā hanạ su kai dạ
kōmọ̄wạn naɳ he prevented them from
their journeys to and fro. jirạ̄gyammụ
sunạ̄ ta kạiwā, sunạ̄ kāwọ̄wā ạbinsụlāfīyạ
= sunạ̄ ta kai, sunạ̄ ta kōmọ̄wā, *etc.*, our
ships go about their business safely.
(ii) iɳ kā ga 6ērā, yanạ̄ kạiwā, yanạ̄
kāwọ̄wā, kyạɳwā bā tạ̄ gidā when the
cat's away, the mice play. (*g*) kai kāwō
m. sentry-go. mại kai kāwō *m.* (*pl.*
mạsū kai kāwō) sentry. (*h*) *Vd.* tā
kai tā kāwō. (*j*) tā kai, tā kōmō *f.* = *Kt.*
tā kai, tā kāwō *f.* = fạtalạ *q.v.*

C.2 (kai) (*independent pronoun, masc.*
sing., Mod. Gram. 46). (1) (*a*) (i) ~
nẹ̄ it is you. (ii) dạ nī, dạ ~ both you
and I. (iii) dạ nī, dạ kai *Vd.* shēgẹ 4.
(*b*) yā nēmar minị ~ he sought you for
me (Mod. Gram. 76*a*.ii). (*c*) yā gajīyad
dạ ~ it tired you (Mod. Gram. 167).
(2) ~ nẹ̄ d̶āi that's just the sort of bad
behaviour one would expect of you !
(3) *Vd.* kại la ; kai kạ̄ cikạ ; kai ka
sō ; kai ka zō. (4) ~ nại *Vd.* nại. (5)
fād̶ạ nạ̄ caɳ, kai wạ̄, kai wạ̄ the palace
was involved in bickerings. (6) kō
kai na Allạ̄ *Vd.* Allạ̄ 1*h.*

D. (kại) (1) (*contradictory particle*)
x kā d̶ēbō kạd̶aɳ ~ no, you didn't,
you only drew a little water ! (*reply to*
" I drew a lot of water from the well ").
kā zō dạ rānā kạ = kā zō dạ rānā
kại no you didn't, you came late in the
day ! (*reply to* " I came early ").
(2) *Sk.* = kẹ̄ yị *x* mẹ̄ ka kại = mẹ̄ kakẹ̄
yị what are you doing ?

kai *Vd.* jī 6*b*, 6*c* ; k̶an dạ.
k̶aibābạ *f.* (1) thorny leaf-stem of kabạ.
(2) yā d̶aukō ~ = yā d̶ēbō ~ he
brought trouble on himself.
kaicō = kaitō.
k̶ā'idạ = kā'idạ *Ar. f.* (*pl.* k̶ā'idōdī =
k̶ā'idōjī). (1) law *x* an yạɳkẹ ~ watạ
bīyū ạ gamạ hạrājị order's been given
to complete tax-collection in two
months. (2) method *x* yanạ̄ aikị, bạ̄ ~
he's working unmethodically. ~ tasạ
its guiding principle. (3) limit *x* (*a*)
yā wucẹ k̶ā'idạd dạ akạ yi masạ he
exceeded the scope given him.
(*b*) suɳ wucẹ ~ they're innumerable.
(4) etiquette *x* yā saɳ ~ he observes
etiquette. (5) bạ tạ saɳ k̶ā'idạ ba *Vd.*
tīlạs 2*d.*
k̶aidajī *m.* the mimosa k̶addạjī *q.v.*
kaidị *Ar. used in* ạl'amạrī nẹ̄, sạk̶e bạ̄ ~
it's left to one's discretion ; it is
unrestricted, unlimited (*Vd. next*).
kā'ịdī *m.* (*negatively*) bạ̄ shi dạ ~ it's
unrestricted, unlimited, left to one's
discretion (*Vd.* kaidị).
k̶ā'idōdī *Vd.* k̶ā'idạ.
kaifafa A. (kaifạfā) (1) *Vb.* 1C. (*a*)
sharpened. (*b*) yā kaifạfạ gāwā he
washed corpse and placed it on right
side eastwards for final prayers (= kafạ
1*u*). (*c*) turned T. askew for it to pass
through narrow entrance. (2) *Vb.* 3A
turned oneself sideways *as in* 1*c*. (*Cf.*
kaikạitā, kạikạice).
B. (kaifạ̄fā) *pl.* sharp (*pl. of*
kạkkaifā).
kaifī *m.* (1) (*a*) sharpness *x* (i) yanạ̄ dạ ~
it's sharp. (ii) kaifīm bīyayyạrkụ
gạrēnị your zealous obedience to me.
(iii) rānā tanạ̄ dạ ~ sun's blazing.
(iv) kaifīm bạ̄kī (= kaifịɳ harshẹ)

gạrēshị he is voluble, glib. (b) Vd. 3 below). (c) cutting-edge x (i) kaifin takọ̄bī edge of sword (Vd. rūwā C.3). (ii) maị ~ ɗayā one-edged. (iii) ɗaŋ ~ bīyū m. (f. 'yar ~ bīyū) pl. 'yaŋ ~ bīyū P. born from parents both of same kind (x both malams, Filani, slaves, etc.)(cf. yẹ̄). (iv) dōlẹ mụ zā̀ɓi ɗayā, kaifī kō tsīnī we are forced to adopt one of the two alternatives. (v) kaifiŋkạ nā̀ cikī Vd. gịzā̀gō 2. (vi) Vd. kạs ~. (2) alertness x yārọ yā fi sauransụ ~ the boy's "sharper" than the rest. dōkịna yinā̀ dạ ~ my horse quickly answers the rein. (3) dearness x (a) yā shā ~ (i) he has had to pay high price, been overcharged. (ii) he has had a bad time. (iii) he has been slashed (cf. 1 above). (b) munā̀ shạŋ kaifinsụ we're suffering at their hands. (4) type of tool for cutting leather.

kaifīyaŋ Ar. m. (1) certain cure (= sạdīdạŋ 1a). (2) adv. unquestionably. (3) adj. x ~ nē kạman yaŋkaŋ wuƙā it's absolutely certain.

Kaigamạ Kr. epithet of any Mā̀dākī.

kaikạ (1) fancy! (2) bother! (3) how tired I am!

kai kạ cikạ m. (Mod. Gram. 140) part of stolen goods, finding of which renders P. at whose house found, liable for total of goods stolen.

ƙaiƙai Sk., Kt. m. = ƙaiƙayī.

kaikạice sideways x yā tạmbạyē nị ạ ~ he asked me in a roundabout way. yā dụ̄bē nị ạ ~ he looked at me askance (cf. kaikạitā).

ƙaiƙaikūwā f. prickly type of self-sown yāƙụ̄wā (sorrel).

kaikainịyā Sk., Kt. f. (pl. kạikạinū = kāyẹ̄kāyī) plaits at side of woman's temples (= taurā).

kaikaita A. (kaikạitā) = kaifạfā 1b, c; 2. B. (kạikaitạ) Vb. 2 (p.o. kạikaicē, n.o. kạikaici) x tā kạikaici idạnsạ she caught him off his guard (= fạkā).

kai ka sō m. used in tūwō yā yi ~ the tūwō is too hot to eat.

ƙaiƙayī m. (1) (a) chaff. (b) dust rising when winnowing. (2) (a) (i) itching (= yanyārẹ̄). (ii) Vd. sūsạ 2c. (b) (i) ƙaiƙayin zūcịyā vexation. (ii) munā̀

jiŋ ƙaiƙayim mạganạssạ we feel "hurt" by what he said. (3) (a) the fruit-tree Parinarium polyandrum. (b) (i) ~ kọ̄mạ kạm mashēƙịyā the hairy weed Indigofera astragalina, brew of which is said to cause harmful spell (sammụ) to recoil on P. who set it in action. (ii) yā yi minị ~ kọ̄mạ kạm mashēƙịyā his hostile act to me recoiled on his own head. ~ kọ̄mạ kạm mashēƙịyā hoist with one's own petard! (4) ƙaiƙayim bā̀kī blurting T. out. (5) macịjiŋ ~ sāri kạ nōƙẹ what a treacherous person!

kai ka zō m. peg against which treadle of loom rests, so liable to trip P. (= Alā̀ 10a).

ƙaimī Ar. m. (pl. ƙayā̀mē) (1) (a) spur of cock. (b) spur for urging on horse. (c) yā sạ̀ masạ ~ (i) he spurred it (horse) on. (ii) it spurred him on, excited him to action. (2) yā cikạ minị ~ = yā cikạ minị dạ ~ he pestered me. (3) sallamạr ~ f. cursory leave-taking. (4) ƙaimiŋ ƙạdaŋgarẹ the spiky-flowered weed Achryanthes aspera (= haƙōrī 9b = Kt. māsuŋ ƙạdaŋgạrū).

*ƙā'ịmī Ar. m. (f. ƙā'ịmā) pl. ƙā̀'ịmai householder.

kainaị = kainanaị (1) stop it! (2) shut up! (cf. kẹ̄ naị).

kai na wārī used in bạ zā ạ ƙārạ jiŋ ~ ba nothing more will ever be heard of the matter.

kā'ịn dạ nā'ịŋ = kā'ịn nā'ịŋ.

kā'ịn nā'ịŋ adv. and m. (1) completely full x kọ̄gī yā cịkạ ~ river's in flood. hadirị yā ɗaurō ~ sky's black all over with impending storm. wā̀sā yā cịkạ ~ the game, theatre, spectacle is (was) packed. (2) ạbụ yā yi ~ the matter's become serious.

kainūwā f. the floating plant Pistia stratiotes (salt is obtained from its ash), cf. zạkaŋkau.

kaitạrạŋ m. leather strip securing girthstrap to saddle (= Kt. asasā̀shī).

kaitō = kạitō (1) (a) (said sympathetically to P.) bad luck! (b) bā̀ ka dạ ~ you've only yourself to blame! kōmē ya sạ̄mē sụ, bā̀ su dạ ~ whatever befalls them is their own fault. kōmē ya sạ̄mē shị, bā̀ ~ whatever happens to him will

serve him right ! (2) damn you ! (3)
Vd. aras 3.
kǎi tsąye *Vd.* kǎi 1*r.*
kaiwa A. (kaiwā) *f.* present for which
return-present is expected (mainly
applies to present of food taken by
woman to her woman-friend (ƙawā)
or her bązawąrī).   (2) *Sk.* fruit of
kanyą-tree.
     B. (kąiwā) *Vd.* kai C.1 4*e.*
kaiwą-kaiwą *f.* vituperative quarrelling.
ƙąjęnīyā *f.* (1) trouble.   (2) going hither
and thither.
ƙaji (1) kō kā yi furfurā i̧ ta ƙaji̧, sǎi kā
bīyā you *shall* pay come what may !
*(2) arnā sum tam mą ⁓, sǎi mīyau
(*lit.* pagans attacked the reed-buck,
but all they got was spittle) in spite of
their machinations I ousted them all.
kąjī *Vd.* kązā.
kąjiji̧ *m.* the sedge *Cyperus articulatus*
(*fragrant root used for incense*).
kajinjirī *m.* (*pl.* kąji̧nji̧rai) the palm
kijinjirī *q.v.*
kąjiiƙī ƙaƙƙarfī *adv.* with might and main
(*d.f.* kąs jiƙī, kąs ƙarfī).
kaka A. (kąkā) (1) *f.* (*a*) harvest. ⁓ tā
yī it's harvest-time.   wōƙąci̧ŋ ⁓ *m.*
harvest-time.   Baucī tā fi Kąno ⁓
Bauchi has cheaper, more abundant
crops than Kano.   (*b*) d̄ari̧ŋ wākē *is
first part of cold season and is followed by
d̄ari̧ŋ kąkā, then by harmattan* (hun-
tūru̧).   (*c*) Hōlōƙō hadiri̧ŋ ⁓, duhu̧nsą
bą na rūwā nę ba what a broken reed he
is !   (= tsūlīyā 4).   (*d*) kąkar ąlbasą
onion-harvest.   kąkag gērō bulrush-
millet harvest.   (*e*) kąkam mǎi *Vd.*
ąyū.   (*f*) bābaŋ ⁓ *Vd.* cābǫ.   (1A) yā
yi kąkam Fąrū dą dūkīyā tasą he made
" ducks and drakes " of his money.
(2) *m.* (*pl.* kąkąnī).   (*a*) grandfather.
(*b*) kąkąni̧ŋ kąkąnimmu̧ our ancestors.
(*c*) (i) ku̧nnē kąkan dūnīyą one accepts
tradition though not present oneself.
(ii) *Vd.* dūnīyą 1*b.*ii.   (*d*) kąkam marō-
wątā *Vd.* zumbu̧lī.   (*e*) Mąyątą ⁓ *Vd.*
mayątā 2.   (*f*) kąkam marąsā *Vd.*
girēmą.   (*g*) kąkan tsāfi̧ *Vd.* bągirō,
bi̧jirō.   (*h*) bi bāshi̧ŋ ⁓ *Vd.* kąrąmbąnī
(3) *f.* (*pl.* kąkąnī) grandmother.
     B. (Kąka) (1) *name for* girl (less

commonly, for boy) born at harvest-
time (= ƙǫsau).   (2) d̄aŋ ⁓ *name for*
boy born at harvest-time. (3) *cf.* Kąkalę,
Kąkandi.
     C. (kąką) *Vd.* ƙąƙą 1*d.*
     D. (kaką) *Sk.* = ka (*relative past
for* " you " *masc. singular*) *x* yąushę
kaką zǭ = yąushę ka zǭ when did you
come ?
ƙaƙa A. (ƙąƙą) (1) (*a*) (i) how ? *x* ⁓ suką
sani̧ how do (did) they know ? (= yąyą
q.v.).   (ii) ⁓ har yakę dą bąkim musu̧
dą su̧ how can he possibly stand out
against them ?   (iii) ⁓ bąn shā nōnąŋ
ūwāta *Vd.* dība 1*j.* (iv) ąbi̧ŋ yā zamam
mini̧ " ƙąƙą niką̄ yi̧ " the matter was
beyond me. (v) sun zamę mini̧ " ƙąƙą
naką̄ yi̧ " they are a thorn in the flesh to
me.   (*b*) (*in the following* = *English*
what ?)   *x* ⁓ sūnaŋką what is your
name ? ⁓ ząn yi dą shi̧ what am I to
do with him ?   what am I to do about
it ? ⁓ kę̄ nąŋ what's to be done ? (*c*)
(*used in greetings*) (i) ⁓ ci̧nikī ya yī
yąu how was business to-day ?   (ii) ⁓
mukę how are you ? (*reply,* lāfīyą lau).
(iii) ⁓ gidą̄ = ⁓ ka barō i̧yāli̧ŋką = ⁓
ahali̧ how are your folk at home ?
(*reply,* lāfīyą lau).   (iv) ⁓ wąhalą I
hope you're not too troubled ? (*reply,*
dą gōdīyā = dą saukī), *Vd.* wąhalą 1*e.*
(v) ⁓ ka ji yąu I hope you feel better to-
day? (*reply,* dą saukī).   (vi) ⁓ ka ƙārą ji̧
do you feel any better ? (*cf.* i̧nā 3*e, f*).
(vii) ⁓ aką ji dą dādi̧ŋ Allą̄ *Vd.* dādī
1*c.*vii.   (viii) ⁓ ka ji dą ƙafą is your
foot better ? (*reply,* dą saukī).   (ix) ⁓
rūwā = i̧nā rūwą̄ how does the rain
suit your crops ? (a greeting in the
rainy season : *reply is* dą saukī =
rūwā yā yi gyārā = kwānąkinsą nē =
rūwā dą gōdīyā), *Vd.* sanyī 1*a.*ii,
ąlhīmī, rānā 2*c.* (x) *at Zar.* ƙąƙą *is
regarded as impolite in such greetings
as quoted above, and* yąyą *is substituted
x* yąyą mukę *replaces* ƙąƙą mukę.
(*d*) kąƙą gidā *m.* (i) children born to
Hausas who have migrated away from
Hausaland (*these people mispronouncing*
ƙąƙą gidą̄ *as* kąƙą gidā).   (ii) slaves
set free by order of Europeans and
placed in a settlement or in the charge

of a responsible P. (*e*) **kana̱ a̱iki̱** ? are you working ? (*reply* **im bā na̱ yĭ** ~ well, what does it *look* as if I'm doing ?). (*f*) ~ **tsārā = ƙa̱ƙa̱ tsārā** ~ *measure played on drums or wind-instruments and signifying* we're ready to join battle, join **ga̱yyā**, etc., so are you our rivals, competitors ready too? (*reply is* **sǎi lāfīya̱, ma̱i ga̱ngā**). (*g*) *Vd.* **kō ƙa̱ƙa̱**. (2) (*a*) **= ƙa̱ba̱ra̱**. (*b*) **yā yi ka̱mar yā ce̱ " ƙa̱ƙa̱ ! "** **sabo̱ da̱ murna̱** he was overjoyed.

kaka̱ *Vd.* **kaka̱-kaka̱**.

ƙaƙaba A. (**ƙa̱ƙaba̱**) *Vb.* 2 pestered.
B. (**ƙāƙabā**) *Vb.* 1C (*with dative*) infected *x* **tā** ~ **masa̱ cīwo̱** she infected him with disease. **a̱ŋ** ~ **masa̱ la̱ifī** he has been falsely accused.

kăkābi̱ *m.* surprise *x* **a̱bin** ~ wonderful T. **nā yi ka̱kābi̱nsa̱** I wondered at it.

kākāce̱ *Vb.* 3A reached harvest-time *x* **in a̱ŋ** ~, **na̱ bīyā** I'll pay after harvest.

kākāci̱ *m.* (1) joke. (2) joking. (3) **a̱na̱ ja̱nsa̱ da̱** ~ he's being quizzed ; they're " pulling his leg ".

kākad da̱ *Vb.* 4A **yā** ~ **ma̱jinā** he spat out phlegm from throat.

kakaf = ƙaƙaf completely finished (= **kaf** *q.v.*).

kaka gida A. (**ƙa̱ƙa̱ gida̱**) *Vd.* **ƙa̱ƙa̱ 1***c.*iii.
B. (**ƙa̱ka̱ gidā**) *Vd.* **ƙa̱ƙa̱ 1***d.*

kaka̱ kaka̱ *x* **a̱na̱ ta̱ yī kaka̱-kaka̱-kaka̱-kaka̱** they're doing it might and main.

ka̱ka̱kī *m.* (*sg.*, *pl.*) (1) (*a*) long metal horn blown for chiefs (*cf.* **famfamī**). (*b*) funnel for pouring liquids (= **mazurarī**). (*c*) T. funnel-shaped. (*d*) **fu̱re̱ yā yi** ~ tobacco-flowers have opened. (2) **yā kafa̱ kǎi a̱ būta̱, yana̱** ~ he's drinking in gulps from the gourd-bottle. (3) **ka̱kākin Sarkim Faga̱ŋ** useless P. or T.

ƙāƙalabā the Great Famine of 1913–1914 (= **sude̱** 1*c*).

kakale A. (**kăkale̱**) *m.* make-believe claims about T. *x* (1) (*a*) **kākalan da̱ngi ga̱rēshi̱** he's always claiming fictitious relationship with the influential (= **nēman da̱ngi**). (*b*) **yana̱ kākala̱ŋ aiki̱** he's pretending that his job can only be done by a quick worker like himself. (*c*) **yana̱ kākalan cīwo̱** he's malingering (*all* = **kālā**), *cf.* **da̱'a̱wā 2** ; **ƙāƙaro̱ 3**.

(2) (*a*) " making up " to people *x* **yana̱** ~ **gu̱ŋ Wa̱zīri̱** he's " sucking up " to the Waziri. (ii) **tā cika̱ kākalam maza̱** she gives men "the glad eye" (= **fa̱rī**). (*b*) **kākalam fada̱ ga̱rēshi̱** he picks quarrels (= **kālā**). (*c*) **kākalam ma̱gana̱ ga̱rēshi̱** (i) he is querulous (= **kālā**). (ii) he picks quarrels (= **kālā**).
B. **Ka̱kale̱** (1) *name for* girl called after her grandfather. (2) *name for* girl born at harvest-time (= **Ka̱ka**).

kakanda̱ *m.* (1) European salt (*Vd.* **kantu̱** ; **ya̱ŋke̱** 1*c.*ii)). (2) **sha̱ŋ** ~ **shī ya sa̱ wu̱yar nāku̱da̱** eating European salt has caused her difficulty in bearing the child (*N.B.—so Hausas believe, but real cause is* **zi̱rzir** *q.v.*).

Ka̱kandi *name given* girl born at harvest-time (= **Ka̱ka**).

ka̱kan Fa̱rū *Vd.* **ka̱kā 1A**.

ka̱ka̱nī grandparents (*pl. of* **ka̱kā 2, 3**).

ka̱ka̱nnīyā = ka̱ka̱rnīyā.

kakara A. (**kāka̱rā**) *Vb.* 1C (*with dative*) *used in* (1) **yā** ~ **masa̱ wuƙā** he cut it with knife. (2) **yā** ~ **masa̱ ƙaimī** he spurred it (horse).
B. (**ka̱kara̱**) *Vb.* 2 **= kāka̱rā** *x* **yā ka̱ka̱rē shi̱ da̱ wuƙā**.
C. (**kakarā**) *f.* small ivory tusk.

ƙaƙara A. (**ƙāƙa̱rā**) *Vb.* 1C (1) **yā ƙāƙaro̱ ma̱jinā** he cleared his throat of phlegm. (2) **yā ƙāƙa̱ra̱ haƙo̱rā** he picked his teeth (= **sa̱kata̱·3**). (3) (*with dative*) (*a*) **= kāka̱rā 2**. (*b*) **a̱ŋ** ~ **masa̱ la̱ifī** he's been falsely accused of crime. (3) *Vd.* **ƙāƙaro̱**.
B. (**ƙa̱ƙara̱**) *Vb.* 2 **= ƙāƙa̱rā 1, 2**.
C. (**ƙāƙara̱**) *Vd.* **ƙa̱ba̱ra̱**.

ƙa̱ƙārāko̱ = ƙa̱ƙārāto̱ *m.* cackling of frightened cock.

kākāre̱ *Vb.* 3A became jammed *x* **ƙa̱shī yā** ~ **masa̱ a̱ ma̱ƙōgwa̱rō** a bone stuck in his throat.

ƙa̱ƙa̱re̱ *m.* the side-plaits below **taurā**-plaits.

kākārī *m.* (1) snoring (= **minshārī**). **yā jā wani** ~ **ma̱i ƙarfī** he gave a loud snore. (2) death-rattle in throat of dying, slaughtered animal or of P. (= **gargara̱**).

ka̱ka̱rnīyā struggling with difficulties (= **fāmā**).

ḳ̄āḳarō *Vb.* 1E (1) *Vd.* ḳ̄āḳạrā. (2) yā ~
mạganạn nạŋ dukạ he invented the
whole thing, " it's mere moonshine " of
his (= kālā). (3) pretended about *x*
yanā̧ ~ tạ̄rī he's pretending to have
a cough (= kālā), *cf.* kākalē.

kakas *m.* sound of rustling of cornstalks
in contact.

kakat A. (kạkat) *used in* sun zamā ~
kụnnan dōkị they're as like " as two
peas ".
    B. (kakat) thoroughly *x* yā wạŋku ~
it's washed specklessly.   yā shārẹ
wurịŋ ~ he swept the place thoroughly.
yā zạzzā̧gē shị ~ he abused him
roundly.

ḳ̄āḳā̧tā *Vb.* 1C *used in* yā ḳ̄āḳā̧tạ dā̧rīyā
he roared with laughter (= fashẹ 1*b*).

kākātū *m.* (1) loud laughter.   (2) uproar
of talk or of quarrel.

kakau *adv.* *used in* (1) yā tsērẹ ~ he
" got clear away ".   (2) ḳasan nạŋ
taurī gạrētạ ~ this ground's as " hard
as iron ".

kạkautū *m.* trouble *x* yanā̧ ~ he's having
trouble.

ḳ̄āḳā̧yā *Kt.* *f.* the shrub Grewia (=
shīḃōlị).

kake A. (kāḳẹ) *Vb.* 1A yā ~ mā̧jinā he
spat out phlegm from his throat.
    B. (kakẹ̄) (*used for* " you ", *masc.*
sg. *in present relative sentence with*
positive sense) lōkạcịn dạ ~ zūwạ when
you're coming.   yạushẹ ~ yị when do
you do it ? (*cf.* ḳȩ̄ 1 ; Mod. Gram.
133*).

kakērẹ *m.* excessive development (hyper-
trophy) of clitoris = dạŋgwạrạ
dạḃē (*this is said to cause nymphomania ;*
cf. hārịjā).

kaki A. (kā̧kī) *m.* (1) kā̧kī = kā̧kim
mā̧jinā throat-phlegm.   (*b*) kōwā ya
shā rūwā dạ hakị, im bạị amai ba,
yạị ~ refunding is *minimum* penalty
of defalcation.   (*c*) kạmarsạ ḍayā
dạ ta ụbansạ yak kạmar ~ he's the
" dead spit " of his father. (2) (*Persian-*
Urdu-Eng. " clay-coloured "). (1) khaki-
cloth.   (2) military uniform.
    B. (kākị = kākịn zumạ) *m.* (1)
empty honeycomb (= totụ̄wā 1*b*.ii),
cf. zumạ. (2) wax.

C. (kakị) *m.* apogee of seriousness *x*
(1) cīwǫ yā kai ~ the illness has
reached its most serious stage (=
gargạıạ). tsā̧dā tasạ tā kai ~ it's " fire-
dear ".   mạganạ tā kai ~ affair's
become unmanageable. (2) yā kai nị ~
he exasperated me (= ḳwadǫ 2*b* =
hikkạ), *cf.* gānīyā, munzị̄lī.

kā̧kibẹ *m.* = kā̧kidẹ.

kā ḳi Bị̄mạ = kā ḳi zūwạ Bị̄mạ *m.* saddle-
cover (jạlālạ) highly ornamented with
silver-wire round border (= fạntamạ).

kā̧kidẹ *m.* beef or mutton dripping.

ḳ̄āḳil *adv.* (1) in full condition *x* yā
cịka ~. (2) abundantly *x* gā̧ mutā̧nē ~
ạ kā̧sūwā market's thronged.

kạkiŋ *used in* yā yi ~ he pricked up his
ears.

kā ḳi rūwaŋ Allā̧ *epithet of* kwạrkǫ-
poppy *and* gā̧wō-tree.

kā ḳi zūwạ Hausā (= kạlạŋgạ) *m.*
large soft mat made by Yorubas from
banana or palm leaves.

kạkkaḃạ *Vb.* 2 (1) drank much of.   (2)
shook garment to rid it of dust *x*
yā kạkkạḃi rị̄gā (*cf.* kaḃẹ).   (3) kạk-
kaḃạr rāḃā begging for bundles of
millet (= kạdā 5 *q.v.*).

kakkạḃē *Vb.* 1C (1) = kạkkaḃạ 2.   (2)
x (*a*) yā kakkạḃẹ ḳụ̄rā dạgạ jịkin
rị̄gā he shook dust off the gown.
(*b*) suŋ kakkạḃẹ hannunsạ they re-
strained him.   (*c*) har yạnzu bạ ạ
kạkkạḃẹ hannunsụ dạgạ Kanǫ ba it
has not yet been possible to shake
them off from Kano (*cf.* kaḃẹ). (*d*) aŋ
kạkkạḃē musụ yuŋwạ they are freed
from want.

kạkkabrā *Sk.*, *Kt.* thick (= kạkkaurā
q.v.).

ḳ̄āḳḳạbtā̧wā *Kt.* = ḳaḳḳạutā̧wā.

kakkabtu A. (kakkabtū) *m.* cantering
(= ḳwạkkwạfā).
    B. (kạkkabtū) *m.* trouble *x* yanā̧ ~.

kakkafa A. (kạkkạfā) *f.* cantering (=
kwạkkwạfā).
    B. (kakkạfā) *Vb.* 1*c intens.* of kafạ *q.v.*

kakkafī *m.* (1) insistence.   (2) persistence
(*cf.* kafẹ 1*b*).

kakkafīyā *f.* deep mud (*cf.* kafẹ 1*a*).

kakkaftū *m.* cantering (= kwạkkwạfā).

kakkālụmē = kā̧lumạ.

ḳaḳḳamsā *m. f.*, (*pl.* ḳamsāsā) fragrant (*cf.* ḳamshī).

ḳaḳḳarai (1) *m.* whitlow. (2) *adv.* without reason *x* ~ (= ą ~) yā mąrē nị he hit me without provocation. yā ɓatar dą kuɗinsą ~ he squandered his money uselessly. (3) (*a*) ɗaŋ ~ = mụtumịŋ ~ *m.* (*f.* 'yar ~) *pl.* 'yaŋ ~ = mutānaŋ ~ worthless P. (*b*) ɗaŋ ~ you useless fellow! (*c*) ąbịŋ ~ valueless T.

ḳaḳḳarfā *m., f.* (*pl.* ḳarfāfā) strong (*cf.* ḳarfī).

kakkārụmē = ḳālumą.

kakkaryā *f.* small guinea-corn stalks or bean plants which are poor and so cut near harvest-time for fodder (= 'ya'y-yąwā).

ḳaḳḳaurā *m., f.* (*pl.* kaurārā) thick (*cf.* kaurī).

ḳaḳḳausā *m., f.* (*pl.* kausāsā) rough to the touch (*cf.* kaushī).

ḳaḳḳautāwā (*only negatively*) incessantly *x* sunā wuçēwā bą ~ they're passing incessantly.

kakkawa A. (ḳaḳḳāwā) *f.* selling meat on credit (= wątandā).

    B. (ḳaḳḳāwą) *f.* loud laughter of men (= kāwą).

kakkụ *m.* squabble.

ḳāḳọ *m.* insect-pest of potatoes (= sąŋḳąrā 3) *x* dąŋkalị yā yi ~.

kā kōmō *m.* (1) "old hand" (= hannū 2*g*). (2) returning caravan *x* munā tārū, sū sunā ~ we were the outward caravan, they the incoming one.

ḳāḳụmā *f.* the poor meat called gąndā 1 *q.v.*

kākụmē *Vb.* 3A sat haughtily or sulkily among others or apart (*cf.* ḳaurąçē ; ḳauyąçē ; hāḳịmce ; tsibịrcē).

ḳāḳụmē *Vb.* 1C gripped (garment of P.) with both hands *x* nā ḳāḳụmę rịgā tasą (= ribçę 1*a*), *cf.* dądumą.

kaḳuŋ-kaḳuŋ *adv.* batch by batch.

ḳāḳụrundū *m.* type of guinea-corn.

ḳāḳūzą *m.* plucky, persevering P., horse, etc. (= ḳwāmāzą 3).

ḳāḳyau (1) *adv.* (*a*) well. (*b*) *Vd.* dāma 3*a*. (2) ~ zāḳị *said by retainers of chief if he changes posture.*

kal *adv.* (*pl.* kal-kal) whitely *x* yanā dą farī ~ it's snow-white. yā wąŋku

~ it's specklessly washed. watą yā fitō ~ moon's brilliant. yā gōgę haḳọrā kal-kal he cleaned his teeth spotlessly. an shārę gidā ~ compound's well swept : rūwā yā kwąntā ~ sediment settled, leaving clear water.

ḳal A. (ḳạl) *x* fịtilą tanā haskē ~ lamp's bright.

    B. (ḳal = ḳạl) *Vd.* karyę.

kala A. (kālā) *m.* (1) gleaning (= *Kt.* rọ̄rō). (2) kālam mąganą = kālan taŋkīyā = kālam bąkī = kālam fadą quarrelsomeness. (3) = kākalē 1, 2*b*, 2*c*. (4) yā yi kālam mąganąŋ naŋ duką he invented the whole thing, it's "all moonshine". yanā kālan tąrī he's pretending to have a cough (4 = ḳāḳarō). (5) kālaŋ hanjī child born late in mother's life. (6) yanā kālan cīyāwą he's cutting very short grass at harvest-time (= ḳwalanjē 4) (7) fụraŋ kālā *Vd.* tsīgī 2, māḳilā 2*b*. (8) *Sk.* fishing-float (= kąŋgwalī).

    B. (kalą) *used in* ą = = ą ~, mụ ga tsawam bāyā = ą ~, ą bā mụ wurī be off and leave us in peace ! ḳālą *used in* bą sụ ịyą çę masą ḳālą ba they dared not oppose him.

kalace A. (kālącē) *Vb.* 1C (1) (*a*) gleaned whole (of crop). (*b*) gleaned all (of farm). (*c*) took whole of *x* yā kālącę ąbincī dū he "scoffed up" all the food.

    B. (ḳālącē) *Vd.* ḳālatą.

kalaci A. (kālącī) *m.* (1) (*a*) any meal. (*b*) yā yi ~ he took food. (*c*) karịŋ ~ *m.* breakfast (= karịŋ kụmallō), *cf.* 2. (2) *Kt.* breakfast (*cf.* 1*c*). (3) *Kt.* kwānąkịŋ ~ time of food-scarcity. (4) Karọ dą gōmą ḳālącin sāfē what a mighty warrior !

    B. (ḳālącī) *Vd.* ḳālatą.

*kal ądam (*Ar.* as if non-existent) *x* yā shịga ūwā dūnịyą ~ he vanished completely.

kalaf *used in* cikị yā yi kalaf stomach's sunk in from hunger.

kalahaddī *m.* big bull.

ḳalai = kal.

ḳalailaiçē *Vb.* 1D (1) examined minutely. (2) put finishing touches to *x* yā ḳalailaiçę aikịŋ. (3) yā ~ dą ąbin naŋ he's expert ịn this.

ƙalā-ƙalā *m.* (1) clear water.   (2) *Vd.* mashā 1.

ƙalalau = ƙalau.

kalallamē *Vb.* 1D flattered ; coaxed (*derived from* kǫlāmị).

ƙalālūwaị-kǫlālūwaị *x* yanā aikị ~ he's slacking at his work.   yanā tǫrīyǫ ~ he's walking slowly, as does P. who is ill or tired.

kalǫmadị *m.*, *f.* (*sg.*, *pl.*) chatterbox.

kǫlamfǫrī *Nor. m.* clove(s) (= kǫnumfǫrī).

kalamfatē = kalamfatai *m.*, *f.* (*sg.*, *pl.*) of thin texture (= fale-fale).

kǫlāmị *Ar. m.* (1) (*a*) word ; words ; speech *x* kǫlāminsǫ kē nan those were his words (= mǫganǫ), *Vd.* kalmǫ. (*b*) mūgun ~ (i) unseemly speech.   (ii) expressing wish that ill befall P.   *x* yā yi minị mūgun ~.   (2) *x* Audu, ~ gǫrēshị = Audu dādịn ~ gǫrēshị Audu's all things to all men.

kalǫngǫ *f.* the mat kā ƙi zūwǫ Hausā.

kalǫngū *m.* (*pl.* kalǫngai = kalangunǫ = *Sk.* kǫlǫnginnị = *Sk.* kǫlǫngunnị) (1) (*a*) hourglass-drum (*cf.* jaujē) used largely by meat-sellers and beaten in company with kuntukurū and dundufǫ drums (*Vd.* kuryā, tillǫ).   (*b*) Sarkịn ~ *Vd.* marǫƙī.   (2) yā yi ~ he (traveller) rolled up trousers and suspended them from neck by string (= zāgē 1*d.*ii).   (3) an yi masǫ (matǫ) ~ tattooing has been done near his (her) cheekbones (*this is sometimes tribal-mark* (askā), *sometimes mere tattooing* (jǫrīā) *for adornment*).   (4) yārinyǫ cē maị ɗaurịn ~ = yārinyǫ cē maị ƙirǫr ~ she's slender girl with good hips (*Vd.* ƙirǫ 1*e*).   (5) garī yā yi masǫ ɗaurịn ~ he's having a hard time.

kalankūwā *f.* (1) (*a*) an yi manǫ ~ jīyǫ last night drumming party was held for us who start gǫyyā (collective-work) to-day (drums used are kanzagī, gǫngị, and gǫngǫrē) = sāran gǫyyā.   (*b*) 'yam mātǫ sunā yi manǫ ~ girls are singing to us at gǫyyā, to lighten our toil (*Vd.* saurǫyī 3).   (2) horizontal cornstalks (karā) reinforcing perpendicular ones in fence.   (3) roof-cushion (purlin) = jīnịyā.   (4) the adornment of women called yartǫnī.   (5) an yi wǫ

sōrō ~ roof of mud-topped house has been enclosed by extending edges slightly upwards (= rawǫni 3*b*).   ,(*b*) sun yi musu ~ they surrounded them.   (*c*) (i) levelling the edges of wǫrkī-loincloth.   (ii) reinforced edge of wǫrkī (= dājịyā 2*b*).   (*d*) evasive talk.   (*e*) hanyǫ tā yi ~ road twists.

kalap = kalaf.

kǫlatǫ *Vb.* 2 (*p.o.* kǫlǫcē, *n.o.* kǫlǫci) gleaned (*cf.* kālǫcē).

ƙalau (1) *m.* or *adv.* (1) (*a*) spotlessly = kal *q.v.*   (*b*) *x* (i) rūwan nan yā yi sanyī ~ this water's ice-cold.   (ii) *Vd.* sanyī 1*b*.v.   (*c*) ~ yakē = lāfīyǫ ~ yakē = ~ dǫ shī = ƙalau-ƙalau dǫ shī he's in fine form ; it's in good order.

ƙalāwǫ *f.* greed.

kǫlāwǫrī *Fil. m.* a Filani milk-measure.

kalcī = ƙalcī *Sk. m.* astringent taste (as of green dates, kolas, potash, etc.) = daurī 2.

Kālę *used in* ɗan ~ *m.* black and blue striped cloth (*made at* Kālę *in Kano• Province*).

ƙale A. (ƙalę) (1) *Vb.* 3A became jammed in *x* gūgā yā ~ ǫ rịjịyā bucket stuck in the well (= maƙalē).   (2) *Vb.* 1A *x* nā ~ shi dǫ sǫndā I hit him down with stick.

   B. (ƙalē) an ɗaurǫ ~ they're playing *the following game: boy seeing another eating T., playfully crosses little finger over 4th finger and says x* Audu, nā ƙalę ; *in reply, Audu crosses little finger over 4th, saying kā ƙali ƙalallę ? But if Audu replies before crossing finger, he must, as forfeit, give what's left of the food* (*game is also called* rǫbǫ dāidǫi).

kalēfatē = kalamfatē.

kā lēƙǫ *epithet of* P. deposed after short tenure *x* Ǫlkālī ~ that judge of short tenure !

kale-kale *adv.* stretched out *x* yanā kwǫnce ~ he's lying sprawled out.   rūwā yā kwǫntā ~ water lay everywhere (*both* = kyalē-kyǫlę).

kalfu = kalhu.

kalgō *Sk.*, *Kt.* (1) the tree *Bauhinia reticulata* (= kargō *q.v.*).   (2) *Vd.* sāri kalgō.

kalhū m. yā zubą masą ~ he " led him on " with wild talk.

kalīhu = kalīfu Ar. m. (1) P., animal, etc. entrusted to one's care x Audu kalīhunā nē (= tallafī 3). (2) x munā ~ garēką, ą sabō lāfīyą best wishes for a safe journey !

kalīlan m., f. (sg., pl.) Ar. small x (1) an daurę shi don abu ~ he was imprisoned for merest trifle (Vd. don 2). (2) an sayar dą shī kudī ~ it was sold at " knockdown price ".

kālīyārę Kt. used in na ~ spongers, parasites.

kalkada Sk., Kt. = karkada.

kalkafī Sk. m. kalkafin zanę small piece of cloth.

kalkala A. (kalkalą = kalkalą) x (1) ~ tā yi sūrūtu my word, how she talks ! (2) yā īyą aski ~ what a close shaver that barber is! (cf. kalkalu).
B. (kalkalā) Vb. 3A yā ~ dą gudu he took to his heels.

kalkalē = kalkalę Vb. 1C (1) shaved P. close. (2) swept (place) clean.

kalkalī = kalkalī m. (1) act of shaving P. close. (2) sweeping (place) clean.

kalkalu Vb. 3B (1) is shaved close. (2) is swept clean.

kalkashī Sk., Kt. below (= karkas, karkashī q.v.).

kalkashī Sk., Kt., m. the plant karkashī.

kallą (1) ą ~ Ar. at least (= ąkallą q.v.). (2) Vb. 1A x yā ~ kūkā he burst out crying (= kwallą q.v.).

kallabī m. (pl. kallubą) (1) woman's kerchief (= ąlhūtą). (2) dōki mai ~ white-faced horse. są mai ~ white-faced bull. (3) Vd. abu 2b. (4) kallabī tsąkānin rawuną she's a woman who is as capable as a man (= mącę 8).

kallace A. (kallącē) Vb. 1C looked at.
B. (kallącē) Vd. kallatą.

kallafā Vb. 1C Ar. (1) enjoined, imposed x an ~ musu aikin nan that work's been imposed on them (= lāząmtā). (2) Vd. kallafō.

kallafa A. (kallafā) Vb. 1C (1) an ~ masą laifī he's been falsely accused. (2) yā kallafą ransą ą kan (= yā k. ransą wajan) sāmunsą he's eager to

get it. tā dauki rantą, tā ~ kan Audu she's very " keen on " Audu.
B. (kallafą) Vb. 3B x rantą yā ~ kan Audu she is very " keen on " Audu.

kallafō Vb. 1E. (1) headed off (flock, herd). (2) turned (horse) = tarę 2. (3) persuaded P. over. (4) Vd. kallafā.

*kallamī Kr. m. tūwō put aside as alms.

kallatą Vb. 2 (p.o. kallącē, n.o. kalląci) looked at.

kallę Vb. 1A (1) shaved P. close. (2) washed T. cleanly.

kallę Vb. 3A snapped (= karyę q.v.).

kallēmū m. (1) hindlegs of grasshopper. (2) tangs on arrow. (3) thorny stick.

kalli (1) m. fishing-float (= kangwalī = Sk. kālā 8). (2) yā wanku ~ it is specklessly washed.

kallō m. (1) looking at x (a) munā kallansą we're looking at it. (b) zā ką ji barāyī sum bullą tsakīyar gidanką kai dan ~ then you hear that thieves have broken into your home but you're powerless to do anything about it. (c) yawan ~ ya kan jāwō rēni = dāmisą 2. (d) sunā ta ~ sąke dą bąkī they stared doltishly (Mod. Gram. 80d.ii). (2) abin ~ m. (a) T. worth looking at, sights of the town, etc. (b) illustrated journal. (c) theatre, public games, etc. (d) makantąrką abin ~ Vd. dindimī 3. (3) kōfą mai kallan kudu the door which faces south. (4) yā kai ~ = yā kāwō ~ he attracted attention. (5) yā yi mini kallan hadirin kājī he looked at me contemptuously (= dūbam mashękā ayā). (6) tā yi masą gōbe dą ~ she stained his gown with indigo (shūnī) when sleeping with him (= shūnī 4). (7) bar ta kallan kai apart from you x bar ta kallan kai, kō wandą ya fī ką bą zai yi mini haką ŋ kyālę ba I would not suffer such treatment from your superior, far less from you.

kallubą Vd. kallabī.

kalmą Ar. f. (pl. kalmōmī). (1) word, words, speech (= mąganą), Vd. kalāmi. (2) kalmą = kalmar shahādą title of creed-formula whereby P. acknowledges that he is Muslim (this formula in Arabic is called kalimatush-shahādati *and begins* aṣhhadu an lā ilāhạ ill'Ạllā-hu). yā bugạ ~ he recited *this creed* (= sạlātị = zikịrī), *cf.* ạṣalātụ, ạssạlā, sallạ.

kalmaɗa A. (kalmạdā) *Vb.* 1C bent over (tip of knife, hoe-blade) (= malƙwạsā), *cf.* kalmạsā, kalmạshē.

B. (kạlmaɗạ) *Vb.* 3B. (1) it (hoe-blade, knife-tip) is bent over (= naɗẹ 2d = malƙwạsạ), *cf.* kạlmasạ, kalmạshē. (2) wuƙan naŋ tanạ dạ ~ tip of this knife is bent over.

kalmaɗai-kalmaɗai *x* yanạ tạfīyạ ~ he's walking with legs aquiver.

kalmạɗē *Vb.* 3A = kạlmaɗạ 1.

kalmạ'iŋ that ends the matter in dispute ! ; there's nothing more to be said ! (= shī kẹ naŋ = dīyaŋ 3).

kalmạjaraŋ (1) *m.* quite definite *x* wannaŋ ~ nē that proves it without doubt. (2) = kalmạ'iŋ.

kạlmạndōsō *Sk., Kt. m.* wastrel (= kạrmạndōsō).

*kalmantakō = kalmuntakō.

kalmasa A. (kalmạsā) *Vb.* 1C. (1) (a) turned down edge of T. (*cf.* kalmạdā). (b) hemmed (= taushẹ 4 = kại 1A.*e*). (2) yā kalmạsạ harshẹ he spoke tactfully or persuasively. (3) yā kalmạsạ zūcịyā he contained himself. (4) tā kalmạsạ gāshị she did her hair preparatory to kitsọ (coiffure).

B. (kạlmasạ) (1) *Vb.* 2 (*p.o.* kạlmạshē, *n.o.* kạlmạshi) = kalmạsā 1. (2) *f.* hem (*cf.* kạrbū ; lāfị).

kalmashe A. (kalmạshē) *Vb.* 1C. (1) = kalmạsā 1 (*cf.* kalmạdā). (2) devoured.

B. (kạlmạshē) *Vd.* kạlmasạ.

kalmashi A. (kạlmashī) *m.* (1) = kạlmasạ 2. (2) acting *as in* kalmạsā 4.

B. (kạlmạshi) *Vd.* kạlmasạ.

kạlmāzūrū *m.* reins (= kạ̄māzūrū).

kalmẹ *Sk., Kt. m.* type of small hoe.

kalmōmī *Vd.* kalmạ.

kalmuntā *f.* bush resembling tā ga rānā, but former grows in compounds, not wild.

*kalmuntakō *m.* sulphur (= farar wutā).

kalo A. (kạlō) *m.* (1) (a) Red-headed Love-bird (*Agapornis pullaria*) = tsiryā 2. (b) Scarlet-bellied Senegal Parrot (*Poicephalus senegalus versteri*). (c)

Orange-bellied Senegal Parrot (*Poicephalus senegalus mesotypus*). (2) dud dạ ~ ạ cin daŋƙọ ? you busybody !

B. (kạ̄lō = kạ̄lō) (*Eng.* coal-tar) *m.* (1) tar. (2) black paint. (3) tarred hessian.

*kaltịbētạ *Eng. f.* plough.

*kālū *Kr. m.* soup (= mīyạ).

kạ̄lūlūwạ *f.* swollen glands, especially in armpit or groin.

kaluma A. (kạ̄lumạ) *Vb.* 2. (1) *x* yā kālumō ganyē dạ harshạnsạ it (grazing ruminant) lapped its tongue round grass. (2) devoured quickly. (3) *x* gạ abịn dạ ta kālumō here are the various things she's trapesed round and got.

B. (kālụmā) *Vb.* 1C. (1) *x* yanạ kālụmạ ganyē dạ harshạnsạ it (grazing ruminant) is lapping tongue round grass. (2) yanạ kālụmạ ạbincī he (toothless man) is eating. (3) nā kālụmạ harshẹ I passed my tongue round my mouth to clear away food adhering (= lālamō 2).

kālụmē (1) *Vb.* 1C = kālụmạ. (2) kālumō *Vd.* kālụmạ ; kālụmā.

kālụme-kālụmē *m.* yā cikạ ~ he's always collecting odds and ends ; always bringing home guests.

kalwā *f.* (1) (a) (i) seeds of locust-bean tree (dọ̄rawạ). (ii) *Vd.* manukī. (b) ~ kin sābạ dạ wutā *epithet of* persevering P. (2) ƙūnā yā yi ~ burn healed quickly without forming blister (bạrōrọ). (3) raunim farcẹna yā yi ~ the injury to my nail caused suffusion of blood under nail and then healed. (4) bāyan dōkị yā yi ~ horse's back began to ulcerate from galling of saddle (if then saddled, ulcer becomes ƙaŋƙū). (5) ~ tā saŋ Innạ, Innạ tā saŋ ~ " watch your step how you act to me ! " (6) tsạriŋ kalwā *Vd.* tsạrī 1*b*.

kạlyẹ *m.* proclamation (= shẹlạ).

ƙam *x* yā ƙamẹ ~ it (leather) dried rigidly.

kam A. (kam) (1) if *x* ~ yā zō if he comes (= kan ; in *q.v.*). (2) nā gan shị, yā fi sau ~ = nā gan shị ~ dạ yawạ I've often seen him. (3) securely *x* aŋ kullẹ ƙōfạ ~ door's securely locked.

B. (kạm) x nā mạ̄rē shị ~ I slapped him hard.

C. (kạm) indeed x nī ~ bạn san shị ba as for me, I don't know him (= kụ̄wa).

kama A.1 (kāmạ) Vb. 1A. (1) (a) (i) seized hold of x kạ̄ma minị dōkị hold the horse for me, catch the horse for me ! (ii) captured x wad̯andạ akạ ~ ạ hannū, d̯arī nẹ̄ 100 prisoners were captured. yā ~ su bursụnạ he took them prisoner. (iii) = kāmẹ 1c.i. (iv) ạbịn dăi, bạ wajạŋ kāmạ̄wā the matter is incomprehensible. yā rasạ wạddạ zại kāmạ he is at a loss how to act. sun tạmbayi dạlīlị, bạ sụ sạ̄mi mại ƙwārī na kāmạ̄wā ba they asked the reason, but received no definite reply. (v) Vd. ƙīfī ; kạ̄mu. (vi) ƙịŋ kạ̄mūwā, ƙịn jạ̄wūwā = jinī 1f. (b) kadạ kạ ~ mạganạssạ don't believe a word he says ! (c) (i) zō, kạ ~ minị come and help me ! (Vd. kāmạ hannū). (ii) yā ~ musụ gịndī he helped them. (iii) suŋ ~ hannun jūnā they helped each other. (d) arrested. (e) shạrī'ạ zā tạ ~ shi he'll be prosecuted. (f) kạ̄mạ ganyē Vd. shikạ rēshẹ. (g) kạ̄mạ tōzō Vd. sạkị zārī. (h) aŋ kāmạ zōmō Vd. ajạlī 2e. (j) kā kāmạ kaŋ gabạ you've done just the right thing. (k) d̯ārī yā kāmạ ni Vd. d̯ārī 1a.ii. (l) kāmạ ạ cūnạ Vd. cūnạ 2c. (m) Vd. gạjī. (n) ~ cikịn yārọ Vd. kạ̄mụ. (2) yā ~ hannun dansạ har wajạŋ kạ̄kansạ he took his son to his grandfather. (3) (a) included x bạ̄ shi dạ gēfẹ, yā ~ kōwā it includes all without exception. dōkan naŋ tā ~ kōwā this law is binding on everyone. (b) religious duty is incumbent on x Aljumma'ạ bạ tạ ~ shi ba he's not bound to attend Friday mosque-service (as he is stranger on his way through, etc.). azụmī yā ~ ni I must fast in Ramadan, as nothing (such as old age, youth, etc.) exempts me. (4) (plus noun) began (= fārạ) x (a) suŋ ~ aikị (i) they've begun work., (ii) they've begun quarrelling. yā ~ shirin yāƙị he prepared for war. (b) suŋ ~ ƙad̯ạ

quarrel has broken out between them. muŋ ~ ƙad̯ạ dạ sū we began hostilities with them. (c) yā ~ mulkị he began to reign. suŋ ~ hawansạ they began to climb it. suŋ ~ shẹ̄lạ gạ jạma'ạ they began a proclamation to the public. suŋ ~ kōkawạ they began a struggle. (d) iŋ kā ~ dạgạ Sarākunạ har zūwạ talakāwā, bạ mại ƙị̄ whether high or low, nobody would refuse. (e) aŋ kāmō dạgạ "Sabbih", akạ kāwō "Nāsi" reading of the Koran was begun at the word "Sabbih" and continued to the word "Nāsi" (Vd. kạ̄mē 3). (5) (a) yā ~ bạ̄kī he kept silence. (b) Vd. bạ̄kī 2b. (c) Vd. bạ̄kin dūnīyạ. (6) aŋ ~ aŋgọ (amaryā) the bridegroom (bride) has been hennaed (Vd. lallẹ 1d). (7) kạ̄ma naŋ ! Kano form of riƙạ 1c. (8) (a) kōwā yā ~ gạbansạ each went his own way. (b) sukạ ~ gạbaŋ kansụ so they went their respective ways. (c) Vd. gạba 3a. (9) d̯aŋ ~ m. (pl. 'yaŋ ~) minstrel who catches in his mouth the largesse thrown from afar (epithet is Jạrmai). (10) (a) yā ~ hanyạ he set out. yā ~ hanyạr Kanọ he set out for Kano (= daukạ 1a.xv). yā ~ hanyạr tsūfā he's getting old. (b) extends, extended x ƙasarsạ tā ~ (= tā kāmō) dạgạ arẹ̄waciŋ Asbịŋ, ta yiwō kudụ his land extends from the north of Asbin to the areas southwards. ạbin dạ ya ~ dạgạ naŋ har kạ̄sūwā the area extending from here to the market (= daukạ 1p). (11) (a) nā ~ ƙafassạ I supplicated his help, asked him for pardon. (b) kō ~ ƙafạ tasạ bạ kạ yi ba you're far inferior to him. yawạmmụ bại ~ ƙafạr yawạnsụ ba they far outnumbered us (Vd. ƙafạ 5b). (c) yā ~ ƙafạ he refused to come when sent for. (d) suŋ ~ ƙafạrmụ dạ kōkawạ they attacked us. (e) cf. kāmụŋ ƙafạ (separate entry) and 14 below. (12) (a) (i) jẹ̄ ka, yạ ~ makạ kaŋkạ go to him that he may charm away your headache ! (ii) Vd. kǎi 1t ; ~ kǎi ; kāmụŋ kǎi. (b) yā īyạ kāmụŋ kụnāmạ he can charm away scorpion stings. (13) (a) hatsī yā ~ dōkị the corn upset the horse's digestion. (b) hatsī ỵā ~ gwīwạssạ he

(P. or horse) became strong again. (14) yā ∼ ƙafar wālā he trusted to a " broken reed " (cf. 11 above, wālā). (15) yā ∼ rūwā he washed his genitals after urination or defecation (= taɓa 2b). (16) kāma kunyā Vd. kunyā. (17) yā ∼ gōnā Kt. he cut down trees on edge of new farm to mark boundaries. (18) (a) yā ∼ da nī he attacked me. (b) bā wanda zai ∼ da shī no one would try conclusions with him. (19) wutā tā ∼ gidā = gidā yā ∼ wutā the house caught fire. (20) Vd. kāma kāi ; kāma karya ; kāma kunnē.

A.2 (kāma) Vb. 3A. (1) lallę (bābā) yā ∼ the henna (indigo) has " taken " well on the place where applied. dashē yā ∼ the transplanted seedling is thriving. (2) (a) wutā tā ∼ the fire has caught up well. (b) Vd. wutā 1m. (3) (a) wata yā ∼ = tsaya 1f. (b) watan Agusta yā ∼ the month of August has begun. (4) gōdīyā tā ∼ the mare is pregnant. (5) sun ∼ = kāma A.1.4b.

B. (kāmā) f. (1) an yi masa ∼ they (beans, ground-nuts, or sweet potatoes) have been roasted in trench (= da-fūwā 4). (2) an yi masa ∼ his foot has been buried in a trench heated and then filled with leaves, to reinduce circulation of blood stopped by severe fall from tree, etc. (if pain not so severe, lalas is done) (cf. acūraƙī). (3) sabo da ∼ a ƙan ci ƙasā one puts up with annoyance for another's sake.

C. (kama) (Ar. ka mā according as) f., m. (pl. kamannī). (1) similarity x (a) sun yi ∼ they're similar. (b) wannan yā yi ∼ da wancan this one is like that. (c) kamarsa dayā da ta ubansa he's just like his father. (d) ∼ da Wānę, bā Wānę ba nę the similarity of two objects, etc., is far from saying they're both the same (cf. 5). (e) mai ∼ da nī one resembling me. da nī, da kai

kamammu dayā you and I closely resemble one another (= shiga 1c.iii). (2) (a) a thing like, the like of, the equivalent x kō nawa mutānē suka ajīyē, Gwamnati zā ta ƙāra musu kamarsa the Government will double whatever deposits people make. (b) a person such as x kamarsa one like him. kaman nī ba zai yi haka ba = kaman nī ba zan yi haka ba one like myself would not behave so. kamar kū (= kamarku) ba zā ku yi haka ba one like you would not behave so (Vd. tankā, kaman). (3) appearance x (a) yā sākę ∼ he looks different, he has changed his clothes (= shiga 1c.ii = sūra). (b) mai farar ∼ one dressed in white. (c) yā fita daga ∼ tasa = Kt. yā fita ∼ tai he looks poverty-stricken these days. (d) abin da kamar wuyā, gurgūwā da auran nēsa what a difficult thing ! (e) rēna ∼ Vd. rēna 2. (4) Sk. kada mu kuskura mu yi abin da ba shi yi ∼ ba let us not behave unfittingly ! (5) (a) kamā da prep. like x rūri ∼ da na dāmisa a roar like that of a leopard. (b) Vd. kaman, kamā 1d.

kamaca = kamacca Zar. f. mother (= ūwā).

kamācē, kamāci Vd. kamāta.

kāmadānī m. (1) wooden bin-support. (2) P. on whom one relies.

kamādisinō m. (1) food consisting of mixture of cassava and ground-nuts (word is used jokingly by labourers) = kwado 2. (2) Vd. ƙarā-ƙarā.

kāma hannū (1) yā kāma hannunta he consummated marriage with a virgin. (2) bā kāma hannun yāro very much x sun gudu, bā kāma hannun yāro they fled full pelt (= sun yi gōbarar ɓērā). anā rūwa b.k.h.y. it's raining " cats and dogs ". munā aiki b.k.h.y. we're working might and main. (3) Vd. kāma 1c, 2, hannū 1a.v, 1g.iii.

ƙamailā f. (1) quid of powdered tobacco (gārin tāba) for sucking (Vd. kōmē 3, daka 1a.ii, būzūzu 8). (2) (a) expression of surprise about food not provided with enough soup (mīya) or fat (mǎi) x

tūwan naŋ ∼ how short of oil this
tūwō is ! (b) what a stingy person ! (c)
what small breasts she has ! (d) tuŋkịyan
naŋ ∼ what a skinny sheep !

ƙāmājī m. (f. ƙāmājịyā) huge x ƙāmājin
ɗākị huge house.

kặma kặi m., f. (sg., pl.). (1) assistant x
kặma kansạ nē he is his assistant.
(2) Vd. kāmạ 12a, kāmuŋ kặi.

kặṁā-kặmā x (1) ∼ sǎi ya fitō he suddenly
* came out. (2) ∼ sukạ tsērẹ they fled
full pelt.

kặ'ma-kặmē" m. making random guesses,
talking at random.

kặma, kạrya x yanặ ∼ he's selling off at
knockdown price, to get ready cash.

kặmạ kunnē type of game.

kamalta = kammala.

ƙặmặmạ used in yā ciwō ∼ (1) he ate T.
which upset his digestion. (2) he did
T. which brought trouble on him.

kặmammē m. (f. kặmammīyā) pl.
kặmạmmū. (1) (a) prisoner of war
(= rịbạtaccē = bursunạ 2). (b) Government or N.A. prisoner (cf. sarƙạ,
kụrkukụ, jặrum, bursunạ). (2) P. of
dignity.

kạman = kạmar (1) prep. (d.f. kạmā)
like x (a) (i) bābụ 'yā mai kyạu kạmantạ
= bābụ 'yā mai kyạu kạmā tatạ there
is no other girl as good (pretty) as she
is. munặ dạ dūkịyā kạman shī = munặ
dạ dūkịyā kạmansạ we're just as rich
as he is (Vd. kạmā 2). ạbịn dạ zại sǎ
kạ tabạ ạjīyạn naŋ, sǎi fa ∼ dom
bīyạŋ kāyan jạnā'izạ you can only
cash this deposit as, for example, where
it is needed to defray funeral-expenses.
(ii) anặ hayạrsạ ∼ lēbụrạ people hire
him as a porter. (iii) ∼ gạskē as if it
were really being done. (iv) sunặ kīwạn
tumākinsụ kusaŋ ∼ Filặnī they tend
their herds much like the Filani do.
(v) kạmar mịsālịn dǎi yạddạ mukẹ̀,
hakạ sū mā they are just like ourselves.
(vi) mun ɗạukị mịsālị, Ạlī shī nẹ̀ ∼
mụtumịŋ Kano for the sake of example,
let us take Ali as a typical Kano man.
(vii) Vd. shigē 2, su 5. (b) mai kạmaz
zūwạ kạŋ ạikā what a hard worker he
is ! (c) bặ kạman . . . ba Vd. bặ C.1. 8.
(d) " kạman dạ ƙasā " ŋ ji mai cīwạŋ

idọ why, of course ! (e) ạbịŋ dạ kạmar
wuyā Vd. kạmā 3d. (g) dạ kạmar waŋkā
Vd. jịrwặyē 4. (f) kạman dadị Vd.
dadị 6. (h) kạmar garkyạŋ kīfī Vd.
garkẹ 1b. (j) Vd. kumbọ. (2) prep.
about x ạshē, bāyaŋ ∼ watạ ukụ
after about three months (= mịsālịn =
wajan). (3) it is (was) as if x (a) ∼
nā fitō dạgạ wutā it seemed as if I'd
come out of the fire. yā mōtsạ musụ
haŋkạlī ∼ zā sụ gwabzạ this so disturbed them that it seemed likely that
they would come to blows. ∼ bāshi
nē akạ bā kạ it is as if it is a loan which
they have granted you. (b) kạmar
mụtụm yạ tịŋkặri kōgī Vd. tịŋkārạ. (c)
kạmaŋ ƙayạ bạ tạ sōkạ ba Vd. ƙayạ 1g.
(d) ∼ karā akạ tsāgạ they're as like as
two peas. (4) conj. as if x (a) yā yi
kwạncē ∼ yā mutụ he lay as if he were
dead. sukạ kōmạ magạnạ ∼ sunặ
gidặjansụ then they resumed their
normal way of speech as if they were
at home. (b) yanặ dạ kyạu ∼ ạ ƙwācẹ
it's excellent. (c) nā ji haushī ∼ m
mutụ I felt mortally offended (lit.
as if it is necessary that I die, cf. 8).
(d) yā yi kạmar yā yi shirū he pretended
to be silent. (5) conj. that (after certain
verbs, cf. cẹ̀wā 3, wai), x (a) suŋ gayạ
musụ ∼ zại zō they told them that he
would come. (b) sun yi kịrạ ∼ " tạfō ! "
they called out " come ! ". (c) yā ji
lặbārị ∼ tā mutụ he heard that she
was dead. (d) yā yi zạtō (= yā zạci)
∼ in yā zō, mặ̀gan shị he thought that
if he came, we should see him. (e) nā
ji ∼ yāƙị yā tāshi I heard that war
had broken out. (f) kuŋ ga ∼ ạl'amạrī
yā yi dādī you see that the matter
turned out well. yā ga ∼ sunặ naŋ he
thought that they were available. (g)
sun cẹ̀ ∼ " kadạ kạ zō ! " they said
" do not come ! ". (h) Allặ yā
ƙaddạrā ∼ zại zamā bāwạ God had
ordained that he should be a slave.
(j) Vd. bayyạnā. (k) wai kạmar Vd.
wai 3h. (l) kạmar wai Vd. nūnạ. (6)
∼ yạddạ according as x yanặ naŋ ∼
yạddạ mukạ bar shị it is in the same
state as we left it. ∼ yạddạ sukạ fạɗā
in accordance with what they said.

(7) yanā dạ kyau ∼ mē = yanā dạ
kyau kạmak kạmam mē it is excellent.
(8) in such a way that x zā ạ ɓatar dạ
kudᶖn naŋ ∼ sụ kyautạtạ cᶖnikimmụ
that money will be spent in such a way
that it may benefit our trade (cf. use of
subjunctive in 4b, c above).
kamạndishᶖnō = kamādisᶖnō.
kạmạnnī Vd. kạmā.
kamạntā Vb. 1C (1) described, illustrated
x yā ∼ minᶖ yạddạ yakē he described to
me what it's like. (2) imitated x kā
ɕī shᶖ sanᶖ you know more than he does
(modest reply, munā kamạntāwā dặi
I'm trying to copy his example).
kạmar Vd. kạman.
kāmārī = ɕāmārī m. (1) abundance x
yanā dạ kāmārin dūkīyā he is wealthy.
(2) mạganạ tā yi ∼ matter became
serious.
Kạmạrụ Cameroons.
kamas Vd. kạmạs-kạmạs.
ɕamas x yā tāshᶖ ∼ he got up suddenly
(= ɕazam q.v.).
ɕamạsagᶖ m. (1) T. which revolts one
(= ɕāmụsāyī q.v.). (2) dā yā zō naŋ,
dạgạ shī sặi ɕamạsagiŋ wạrkinsạ from
being penniless, how he's got on !
kamasho A. (kạmashọ) Eng. m. commission on sales (= lạ'adạ).
    B. (kamashō) (1) m., f. (no pl.) weak.
(2) m. shrivelled ground-nuts (= mōtsī 3).
kạmạs-kạmạs = kamạs-kamạs x yanā
cᶖ ∼ he's wolfing up food.
ɕamạs-ɕamạs = ɕāmāmạ.
kạmātạ (1) Vb 3B is (was) seemly x (a)
yā ∼ kạ yī shᶖ you ought to do it.
yā ∼ gạ Sarkī yạ kai wạ kāɕirai yāɕi
it behoves a Muslim ruler to war against
infidels. (b) yā ɕi kạmātạ yạ zō dạ
kạnsạ it is more suitable that he should
come in person. (c) kạmāci kạmātạ,
kwādō yā yi dụrɕusō kạman na niɕạ
do everything at the right time and
place ! (2) Vb. 2 (p.o. kạmāċē, n.o.
kạmāci) befitted x ɓai kạmāċē kạ, kạ
yi ba it does not befit you to do it.
kā matsō m. T. one has no option but to
buy dear.
ɕāmayamạyạ = ɕāmāmạ.
kāmāzūrū m. reins.

kạmɓai m. coil of dried hemp (ramạ) or
kargō.
kambakarē m. odds and ends (= karẹ).
ɕambāɕī m. lack of appetite after childbirth.
kambalē m. paralysis.
kambama A. (kạmbamā) f. old mare.
    B. (kạmbamạ) f. boastfulness ; os-
tentatious behaviour.
    C. (kambạmā) Vb. 1C showed honour
to P. (= girmạmā).
kạm ɓạrāwọ Vd. kạn ɓạrāwọ.
kambarī m. type of Argungu spear.
kạm bāyī Vd. shāmakᶖ 2a.
*kambī m. (1) (used only in translations
from Ar.) kambin sạrautạ appurtenances of royalty (such as turban,
ạlkyabbạ and where applicable, crown
such as that of King of Egypt, England,
etc.). (2) kambim bakạ = kambū.
kạm birᶖ Vd. kạn birᶖ.
*ɕambōrī m. (pl. ɕambōrai). (1) claw ;
talon. (2) pincer of earwig, etc.
kamɓōrī m. (1) shell of x (a) kamɓōriŋ
gyạdā shell of ground-nuts. (b) kamɓōriŋ ɕwặi egg-shell (1 = ɓamɓarōkᶖ).
(2) kamɓōriŋ kīfī fish-scales. (3)
kamɓōrin raụnī scab. kamɓōrim bāɕī
scales on mouth due to cold drying up
one's skin (all = ɓāwō).
kạmbōsamā f. big, unkempt woman.
kambu A. (kạmbū) m. (pl. kambunạ). (1)
bangle-charm worn on forearm (= dagā q.v.), cf. mundūwā. (2) hoop-shaped
ɕulī-ɕulī cakes (= Kt. gūrū).
    B. (kambū) used in yā yi minᶖ
kambum bakạ he cast evil eye on me
(Vd. ɕishạ 2).
kamce A. (kamċē) m. = kamcī.
    B. (kạmċē) Vd. kạmtā.
kamci A. (kamcī) m. cornering market
as in sārā 2a.i q.v.
    B. (kạmci) Vd. kạmtā.
kamdạrē Vd. kandạrē.
kame A. (kāmẹ) (1) Vb. 1A. (a) (i) =
kāmạ 1a.ii. (ii) ∼ bāɕī = kāmạ A.5a.
(iii) ∼ ɕafạ = kāmạ A.11d. (iv) yā ∼
ɗansạ (dōkᶖnsạ) he took back forcibly
his son (horse) entrusted to another.
(b) sewed up rent x yā ∼ wurin naŋ
he sewed up this place where garment
was torn. (c) (i) yā ∼ kạnsạ = yā

~ yi gą̃ndā (*cf. 2c*) he showed self-restraint. (ii) yā wąjabą ƙą tsarę jikiᶇką cikin daurêwā dą kāmêwā you should keep yourself chaste. (*d*) tā ~ ƙąntą dągą yāwǫ she refrained from roving. (*e*) yā ~ gaɓuɓɓąnsą he has no vices. (2) *Vb.* 3A. (*a*) stuck together *x* tąkąrdū suᶇ ~ papers stuck together. (*b*) ƙurjī yā ~ sore place is nearly healed. (*c*) (i) withdrew and sat aloof superciliously. (ii) (*said by woman to another woman*) kiᶇ kāmę yi gą̃ndā you seem to think yourself too fine to mix with people ! (*cf. 1c.*i).

B. (ƙą̃mē) *m.* (1) *x* 'yaᶇ gādi sunā ~ N.A. police are going on rounds at night to arrest suspicious characters. (2) (*a*) impressing forced labour for carriers, etc. (*b*) (*of olden days*) Chiefs' sending out to seize women for forced fornication. (3) reading last section of Koran, then reading each previous section till beginning reached *x* aᶇ kāmō dągą " Sabbih ", aką kāwō " Nāsi ", kumā dągą " 'Amma " zūwą " Sabbih " reading of Koran was begun at the word " Sabbih " and continued to the word " Nāsi ", then from word " 'Amma " to " Sabbih " (*Vd.* kāmą 4*e*).

C. (ƙą̃me) *x* yanā ~ dą hannuntą he's holding her hand.

ƙamę *Vb.* 3A (1) yā ~ (*a*) it (fruit, leather) dried and became stiff (*cf. ƙam*). (*b*) matter from sore place dried and hardened, indicating healing and end of pus. (2) yātsątą tā ~ my finger became stiff from cold (*cf. ƙagę*). (3) (*a*) yā ~ he (soldier, etc.) stood rigidly " at attention " (= būshę). (*b*) tsǫ̃rō yā kāmą shi har ya ~ he was petrified with fear.

ƙą̃ˡme-ƙą̃mēˡˡ *m.* making random guesses.

ƙąmƙā *adv.* thereupon . . .

ƙamƙā *f.* (1) (*a*) iri (dąshē) yā yi ~ seed (transplanted seedling) failed to grow (= kōrā 4). (*b*) gōnā tā yi ~ farm's failed in places. (*c*) zā mǫ kashę ~ we'll re-sow where seed's failed (= ƙwāƙī). (*d*) haifǫ̃wā tā yi matą ~ she's ceased to bear children. (2) any lack *x* hatsī yā yi ~ there's shortage of corn.

kamface A. (kamƙącē) *Vb.* 1C *x* yā ~ mini hatsī he took out a lot of my grain. B. (ƙąmƙącē) *Vd.* ƙamƙatą.

ƙąmƙallī *Sk. m.* shoulder-blade (= ąllō 3).

kamƙąnī = kampąnī.

kamƙāsi = kampāsi.

kamfata A. (ƙąmƙatą) *Vb.* 2 (*p.o.* ƙąmƙącē, *n.o.* ƙąmƙąci) took out much (water or grain). B. (kamƙątā) *Vb.* 1C. (1) *Kt.* poured too much fluid into *x* tā kamƙatą rūwā ą tukunyā she poured too much water into the pot (= kandą̃mā 3). (2) (*with dative*) took out much (water or grain) and gave P. *x* yā ~ mini hatsī he took out and gave me much corn. yā ~ mini gōnā he gave me a large slice of his farm. aᶇ ~ musǫ aiki much work has been given them. (3) yā ~ masą fartanyą he gave him a blow with the hoe.

kamƙē *m.* short trousers as short as a bąntē.

kamƙuną *Vd.* kampąnī.

kāmilaᶇ *Ar. adv.* completely.

kāmilī *Ar. m.* (*f.* kāmilā) *pl.* ƙąmilai perfect.

ƙą̃miᶇ = ƙą̃min (1) *conj.* (*with subjunctive*) before (*a*) (*past sense*) *x* ~ ᶇ zō, suką (= suᶇ) gąma they had finished before I came. ~ mǫ jē Kanǫ, sąi aką shiga ɗaką before we reached Kano the people had retired to rest. kāfin sǫ isō, dą̃ mā aᶇ aikō dą mąnzaᶇ the messenger had already been dispatched before they even arrived. (*b*) (*future sense*) *x* (i) mǫ tāshi ~ watą yą fitō let us start before the moon rises ! (ii) kāfiᶇ ą cê suᶇ gamą shiri, ɗārī yā shigō winter will come before they've finished their preparations. kāfin dăi ą cê maką sā'ą bīyū, gąrī ya zamā na hannū the town was captured in less than two hours. (*c*) *conj.* until (*future sense*) *x* dą̃kątą ~ (= dą̃kątą har) ᶇ gamą wait till I have finished ! (2) *prep.* before *x* (*a*) (i) ~ jimąwā kądaᶇ kumā, suką isō they arrived before long. ~ ƙyiftą̃war idǫ, suką kāwō masą sǫ̃rā in a twinkling they swooped on it. (ii) tuᶇ kāfiᶇ yāƙiᶇ before the war. (*b*) ką gamą ~ ƙarfę bīyar finish it by five o'clock !

(3) *conj.* *(with subjunctive)* by the time that *x* ∽ sụ gamạ kạnsụ, ạ sakam musụ mulkịŋ ạbinsụ by the time they have settled their differences, they should be given their independence ! (4) *Vd.* kạn tạ fargā.

kamịslikạ *x* Kanọ, ita cḙ ∽ alfụŋ. Yārọ ! kō dạ mḙ ka zō, am fī kạ Kano is peerless.

kam-kam securely (= **kam** 3).

kammạ *Vb.* 1A *Nor.* seized (= kāmạ *q.v.*).

kạm māgē = kạŋ kyạŋwā.

kạm maƙḙrā *Vd.* kạn maƙḙrā.

kammala A. (kammạlā) *Vb.* 1C *Ar.* (1) finished *x* aŋ kammạlạ aikị the work's finished (= gamạ). (2) completed up to the desired total *x* bạ nạ̄ kạrɓi kudịŋ sǎi kā ∽ ba I won't accept payment till you make it up to the required total. ạ kammạlạ mutạ̄nē, ạ kāwō sụ collect the total men required and bring them ! B. (kammạlạ) *Vb.* 3B. (1) is finished. (2) is complete (*as in* kammạlā 2).

kạm mazarī *Vd.* kạn mazarī.

ƙamnā *Sk. f.* love (= ƙaụnā *q.v.*).

kạmnḙkū *Zar. m.* flour of cassava or yams.

kampạnī *Eng. m.* (*pl.* kampunạ = kạmfạnai). (1) company of soldiers or police *or* their living-quarters. (2) *Kt.* kampạniŋ hākịmī area or subjects of a District Head (= jịmillạ).

kampāsị *Eng. m.* canvas honeycomb netting for uppers of slippers after insertion of wool.

kạmpāwụl (*Eng.* compound) the compound at Kano, near Nasarawa Gate, where school-boarders live. ɗaŋ ∽ *m.* (*pl.* 'yā'yaŋ ∽) *such* boarder.

kamrạrā *Sk., Kt.* = kaurạrā

ƙamsạ̄sā *pl.* fragrant (*pl. of* ƙạƙƙamsā).

ƙamshī *m.* sweet smell (= ƙanshī *q.v.*).

kạmsịr = kạmsīrị = kạmsịl cartridge case (*cf.* kạrtūshị).

ƙamsūwā *f.* the grass *Pennisetum pedicellatum.*

kạmtā *Vb.* 2 (*p.o.* kạmcē, *n.o.* kạmci) bought up *as in* kamcī.

kamtsạ *Vb.* 1A blurted out (= kwantsạmā *q.v.*).

kamu A. (kạ̄mu) *Vb.* 3B. (1) watạ yā ∽

moon's in eclipse (*Vd.* kụsūfị). (2) *Vd.* kāmạ 1*a*.vi.

B. (kạ̄mụ) *m.* the food of guineacorn or millet (gḙrō) flour, which, mixed with water, makes gruel (kōko) ; *epithet is* ∽ mại kāmạ cikịn yārọ.

C. (kāmụ) *m.* (1) (*secondary v.n.* of kāmạ, kāmḙ 1*c*) *x* anạ̄ kāmụnsạ he's being seized. (2) act of seizing *x* (*a*) tarkwạŋ yā yi ∽ the net has made a haul. (*b*) wannạŋ lallḙ ∽ gạ̄rēshị this henna " takes " well. (3) favourite T. *x* ạbincin naŋ kāmụnā nḙ this is my favourite food (= mōwạ 3 = kyarmā). (4) kāmụna kḙ naŋ yạnzu it is my turn now (= shịgā 1*d*). (5) (*a*) measure of 18 inches (*Vd.* cikị 11, dụŋgū 3, dara'ạ 2, saɓị 1, saɓạ 4*a*). (*b*) yā yi minị kāmụŋ kạ̄sūwā he gave me short measure. (6) wạndō mại ∽ trousers embroidered with kāmụŋ ƙafạ. (7) *Vd.* kāmụn-*compounds.*

kāmụn dạcē *Vd.* dạcē.

kāmụŋ gafịyạ *Vd.* bịyụ byụ̄.

kāmụŋ gidā *m.* sending ahead to arrange for quarters for travelling Chief.

kāmụŋ gōnā *Kt. Vd.* kāmạ 17.

kāmụŋ ƙabbạ *m.* yā yi masạ ∽ he got a stranglehold on him.

kāmụŋ ƙafạ *m.* (1) (*a*) embroidered ankle-band of trousers (*cf.* mạhallitsạ). (*b*) wạndō mại ∽ trousers with embroidered ankle-band (= kāmụ 6 = Dōmạ 2). (2) *Vd.* kāmạ 11.

kāmụŋ kại (1) *Vd.* kāmạ 12*a*, kāmạ kại. (2) *m.* self-restraint (*cf.* kāmḙ 1*c*).

kāmụŋ kaŋkị *m.* talking disparagingly of P. when unaware he is within earshot (= harbịŋ kaŋkị).

kāmụŋ ƙwaryā *Vd.* ƙwaryā 1*d*.

kāmụn lūdayī *m.* *x* mụ ga kāmụn lūdayinsạ = mụ ga irịŋ kāmụn lūdayinsạ let us see what he is like !

kāmụn na gạba *Vd.* sakị 2*f*.

kāmụn na gụje *Vd.* sakị 2*f*.

kāmụn 'yan tsạ̄kī *m.* novice's overturning top with thumb and first finger of both hands.

ƙamūrā *f.* (1) tūwō, etc., without any soup with it (= gāyā 2*b*.i). (2) (*a*) thin P. (*b*) destitute P. (*c*) miser (*epithet is* ƙanƙamịŋ ƙamūrā).

ămṵsḁyī *m.* (1) food, etc., which one finds nauseating. (2) filthy place *x* yārọ yā tḁfi cikiṇ ~, ya zaunḁ.

ămūwā *f.* seizing property in lieu of debt (*cf.* zāmīyā).

tḁ̄ mwīyā-mwīyḁ̄ = ḵ ̣ḁmḁ̄mḁ.

tḁm wuyḁ *Vd.* kḁṇ wuyḁ.

tamzō *Vd.* ḵ ̣anzō.

tan A. (kḁn) (1) (*particle indicating habitual action* ; *Vd.* Gram. 15) *x* (*a*) na ~ zō I come ; I used to come. bḁ na ~ zō ba I don't come ; I used not to come. (*b*) *Vd.* diṇgḁ ; yḁn. (2) (*a*) before (= kḁ̄mịn *q.v.*). (*b*) *Zar.* kḁn dḁ before *x* kḁn dḁ yḁ zō before he comes (= kḁ̄mịn). (*c*) *Vd.* ~ tḁ fargā.

B. (kan) (1) (*a*) if (= in *q.v.*). (*b*) (*negatively*) provided not *x* kḁ gayḁ minị kam bḁ̄ ḵ ̣aryā ba tell me it provided it's not a lie ! (2) (*a*) yā kan nị he killed me (*assimilation of* yā kas nị). (*b*) *Vd.* kḁn ni ; kash ; kas. (3) (*abbreviation of* kāyan) *Vd.* kan sallḁ.

C. (kḁn) (*derived from* kḁ̄i). (1) *prep.* (*a*) on *x* (i) ḁjịyē shi ~ ḁkwḁ̄tị put it on the box ! ḁ ~ īyḁ̄kā on the frontier (*Vd.* ḁbṵ 10). (ii) tanḁ̄ ~ gwīwḁ she is in labour (*cf.* gṵrfānḁ 2). (iii) ḁbịn dḁ mukḁ yi ịmānị ḁ kansḁ what we trusted in, put our faith in. (iv) mḁganḁr bā tḁ kḁṇ hanyḁ the story is untrue. (*b*) dḁgḁ ~ from on *x* yā fādị dḁgḁ ~ dōkị he fell off the horse. (*c*) sukḁ zaunḁ ~ hakḁ so they remained on those terms. (*d*) *x* ḁbịn nḁṇ yanḁ̄ kḁmmṵ this is incumbent on us. (*e*) ḁ ~ idḁmmṵ sukḁ yī they did it in our presence. (2) *prep.* regarding *x* bḁ̄ wḁddḁ akḁ̄ sọ̄ sǎi ita ḁ ~ kirkị she has no equal in goodness. wannḁṇ, sǎi an dḁṇkwḁfē nị ḁ kḁn ? sḁ do you think I need *telling* not to do it ! yā yi shā- warḁ dḁ sū ḁ ~ zaman 'yaṇūwansṵ he consulted with them about the living conditions of their kinsmen. dḁ̄ munḁ̄ cḁ̄wā sū arnā nḁ̄, ḁshē sū Mṵsṵlmī nḁ̄ ḁ kḁn Jāmṵs previously we thought them scoundrels, but we find they are paragons compared with the Germans. (3) *prep.* (*a*) because of *x* bḁ̄ ḁ kḁn sḁnsḁ takḁ̄ zūwḁ ba it is not by *his* wish that she is coming. an shā fāmā

ḁ kansḁ trouble was caused on its account. (*b*) ḁ kḁm mḁ̄ ya zḁ̄gē kḁ why did he abuse you ? (4) *conj.* (*a*) because *x* (i) sun shịga gidan Sarkī ḁ kḁn suṇ ga yanḁ̄ kḁrɓaṇ kudịṇ hḁrājị they entered the Chief's compound, because they saw him collecting tax. (ii) ḁbịn nḁṇ na kḁm (= mḁganḁn nḁṇ ta kḁm) bḁị sanị ba this occurred because he didn't know. ḁbịn dḁ nakḁ̄ fḁḍā na kḁm bḁ mu dḁ shirị I say so, since we are unprepared. (*b*) in regard to the fact that *x* munḁ̄ bāyansḁ ḁ kḁn ḁ yī we share his opinion that it should be done. yā shḁ̄warcē sṵ ḁ kḁn yā kḁmātḁ sṵ yī he consulted them on the expediency of doing it. (*c*) to the effect that *x* suṇ ḵ ̣ullḁ sharḁdī ḁ kḁn zā ḁ bā sṵ they have contracted to give them it. suṇ aikō manḁ dḁ tḁkḁrdū ḁ kḁn zā sṵ tḁịmḁkē mṵ they've written to the effect .that they will help us. (*d*) (*with subjunctive*) in order that *x* yā yī ḁ kḁṇ amincịmmu yḁ ḵ ̣arfafḁ he did so in order that our friendship might become ratified. (5) ta kḁn *x* (*a*) bḁị kōmḁ ta kḁnsṵ ba *Vd.* kḁ̄i 1*k.* (*b*) zā mṵ fārḁ ta kḁm farin lḁ̄bārị we'll begin with the good news. (6) *Vd.* kḁn-*compounds.*

ḵ ̣an *Vd.* jī 6*b,* ḵ ̣an dḁ.

kana A. (kanḁ̄) *x* kanḁ̄ zūwḁ you're coming (Mod. Gram. 15).

B. (kānḁ) then (1) *x* cī tṵkuṇ, ~ kḁ tḁfi have your food and then go ! (2) (*follows* " it is only after " *with future sense* ; Mod. Gram. 107*c*) *x* sǎi an shā fāmā dḁ shī tṵkunā, ~ yḁ fịta it cannot be got outside without great effort. sǎi kā zō, ~ mṵ tḁfi only after you come will we go. (3) (follows " it was only after ", Mod. Gram. 181*d*) *x* sǎi dḁ akḁ yi tḁfīyḁ tṵkuṇ, ~ mukḁ isa kḁ̄sūwā it was only after travelling some way that we reached the market. (4) in addition *x* ~, gḁ̄ ḵ ̣arfịṇ halī gḁrēshị in addition, he is resolute. (5) *Zar.* thus *x* ~ nḁ̄ it's thus (= hakḁ nḁ̄).

kḁṇ ḁddā *Vd.* ḁddā 3.

kanagōgọ *m.* (1) *x* shī ~ nḁ̄ he's become a fixture. (2) yā yi minị ~ = yā yi minį ~ kadamɓarɓar he kept the thing I had lent him, indefinitely.

kaŋ ̦akwīyą m. roots of sąbarā, kargō used as firewood in times of stress (= kwantai 1).

kąnamfąrī m. clove(s) (= kąnumfąrī).

ƙanāną pl. small (pl. of ƙaŋƙanę, ƙąramī).

Ƙąnąnce used in ą Ƙąnąnce adv. in Kano Hausa.

Kanancī m. Kano Hausa.

kaŋ ̦aŋgayā Vd. ̦aŋgayā.

kanannaƙa A. (kąnąnnaƙą) Vb. 3B. (1) curled oneself up (sleeper, snake). (2) zanę yā ~ cloth is crumpled.

B. (kanannąƙā) Vb. 1D rolled T. up ; coiled T. up.

kanannąƙē Vb. 3A = kąnąnnaƙą.

kąnannaƙọ m. type of bean with curly pod.

ƙanantą f. yā ciką ~ he's a mean-minded or undignified person (cf. ƙaŋkanci ; kąramī 2).

kąnąnzir = kąnąnzīrį Eng. m. kerosene.

Kanąr Eng. m. Colonel.

kąnąrī Eng. m. (pl. kąnąrai) (1) canary. (2) (playfully) ita ~ bą kējį cē she's a whore.

Kanāwā Kano-people (pl. of Bąkanọ).

kąm ɓąrāwọ m. the herb Leonotis pallida.

kąm bāyī Vd. shąmakį 2a.

kąm birį m. small bundle of seed-millet (gērō).

kąncąr = kancąrcąr x tā niƙą ~ she ground coarsely (= fąntsąrtsąr).

kancī = kamcī.

kąncikulkųl m. the trailer-plant Cucumis prophetarum with prickly gooseberry-like fruit.

kancilkō m. (1) huckster's odds and ends carried in pack for sale. (2) woman's toilet oddments.

kąn ̦dą Zar. before Vd. kąn 2b.

ƙan ̦dą = ƙąn ̦dą = ƙąn ̦dą (1) how x bąn saŋ ~ ząŋ ̃īyą yį ba I do not know how I shall manage to do it. Allą mąi ƙąn ̦dą ya sō God is all-powerful. (2) Vd. jį 6b.

kandąbārā how thick ! how fat P. is ! how thick-lipped !

kąn dabbōbī Vd. afąlalų.

kąn daɗį ; kąŋ ūwar daɗį Vd. rufį 7.

kąndągąrkī m. (1) protection x nā yi

masą ~ I protected it (him). (2) protector x Sarkī kąndągąrkimmų ne

Kandalā name for any woman called Kąnde (epithet is Kandalą mąƙąsau because she has elder brothers to protec her).

kąndam = ƙąndam abundantly (re liquids).

kandama A. (kąndamą) Vb. 2 (1) = kąmfatą. (2) yā kąndąmi hayį = kandąmā 2.

B. (kandąmā) Vb. 1C (1) = kamfątā 1, 2. (2) yā kandąmą hayį he tied thatch to roof-frame (tsaikọ) = sūką 2a, ii. (3) tā kandąmą rūwā ą tukunyā she poured much water into the pot.

kąndąmę m. (1) oval, arched-window or doorway. (2) type of large wąrkī. (3) yā yi ~ he tucked end of wąrkī intc front of waistband = sąnƙē (cf. ƙunzugū).

kandamēmę m. (f. kandamēmįyā) pl. kandam-kąndąm abundant (re fluids).

kandami A. (kandąmī) m. large pond (epithet is bąbbaŋ ~ shą wąnkā).

B. (kandamī) m. used in aŋ kafą kandaminsą (1) they scolded him. (2) they backbit him.

kandam-kąndąm Vd. kandamēmę.

ƙandarą Vb. 3B = ƙandąrē.

kandarę m. (f. kandarįyā) contrary P. (epithet is ~ sǎi kā sō).

ƙandąrē Vb. 3A (1) yą ~ he (P., animal) became thin. (2) fātą tā ~ skin became rigid.

ƙandas m. and adv. being devoid of required moisture x wannąŋ tūwō ~ what oil-less tūwō ! rījįyan nąŋ ~ dą ita this well's waterless. yā zamā ~ kaŋwar ƙąshī he (it) "isn't up to much ".

kąndāshirī m. (f. kąndāshirā) dirty, un-kempt P.

kandąyē Vd. kandū.

Kąnde name for girl borŋ after two or more boys (cf. Kandalā ; Bąrauką 2 ; Igę ; dēlą ; Dūdų).

kandi A. (kandį) m. the milk daƙąshį q.v.

B. (Kandi) (1) name for any woman called Sąlāmatų (cf. sallą 1j). (2) Vd. saŋhọ 4.

kandīdạ *f.* (1) kernel of **kurnạ**-fruit. (2) (*a*) P. with penetrating voice. (*b*) what penetrating voice ! (*c*) what chatter !

kandīlō *m.* dried dung of cattle or donkey used for cooking food. **sun tạfi** ~ they've gone out collecting *such dung.*

kạndīri *m.* (*pl.* **kạndīrai**) staff of malam or chief, etc.

kạndirmō *m.* the milk **kịndirmō** *q.v.*

kandū *m.* (*pl.* **kandạyē** (1) a white stone used in necklaces. (2) **yā rāmẹ har ya yi** ~ he's so thin that his collarbone protrudes. (3) *Kt.* **kandum bakạ** = **kambum bakạ.**

kạn dūkīyā *m.* trading-capital (= **jārị**).

kanẹ *m.* (*f.* **kạnwạ**) *pl.* **kạnnē** = **kannūwạ** = *Sk., Kt.* **kạnnai** (1) (*a*) younger brother, etc. (*b*) (i) Būzū **kạnạn kạrē, ạn kọrē kạ, kanạ kūwwạ, barē in kai nẹ ka yi kọrā** *epithet of Būzū.* (ii) *Vd.* **farkē.** (*c*) **ɓērā yā ɓātạ kạnwạ tasạ, yā cẹ har jịkīna yā yi sanyī** getting small gift instead of the large gift expected. (2) **kanạn rānā** boyfriend of young man, former among other things, helping at feast (**bịkī**) at latter's wedding (*cf.* **rānā** 3). (3) **kạnwạr rānā** young bridesmaid (= *Sk.* **yạrō**). (4) **kanạn kanạn Audu nē** he's very much younger than Audu (= **baicī** 4*b*). (5) (*a*) **kōwā mā yanạ dạ** ~ everybody has some dependent. (*b*) **kōwā yanạ dạ** ~, **ạbọ̄kạrạ kanạn jirgī** (*phrase in girls' song*) everyone has someone dependent on him : why, the train has the pumptrolley ! (6) *Vd.* **yạyyē.** (7) **bạbbạn** ~ **mahūtar haushī** = *Kt.* **bạbbạn** ~ **madēbar haushī** what a grand helper ! (8) **kanạm ɓạrāwọ** *Vd.* **tugu** 2. (9) **nẹmạ kạnkạ kanẹ** *Vd.* **būbụ** 3. (10) **mụtụm dạ kanạnsạ** (*in zạurạncē*) one and sixpence. (11) *Vd.* **bạ̄kī kanạn kafạ ; bạ̄i kanạnkạ.**

kanē-kạnē *m.* "taking too much for granted" (*x* lolling about to discomfort of another ; monopolizing conversation ; making free with another's property).

kạnẹnẹ contemptuously *x* **yā dụbē nị** ~ he looked at me contemptuously (*cf.* **kāniyā**).

kanga A. (**kạngạ**) *Zar. f.* type of knife made by pagans.

   B. (**kạngạ**) *Vb.* 1A (1) (*a*) screened off *x* **ạn** ~ **magēwayī dạ zānā** latrine's been screened with grass-mat. **ạn** ~ **zānā** grass-mat's been put up as screen. (*b*) *x* **yā** ~ **rịgā, yā kạrɓi** 10*s.* he produced another's gown " as a blind ", so managing to borrow 10*s.* (2) (*with dative*) screened with *x* **ạn** ~ **masạ lạifī** his crime's been hushed up. **ạn** ~ **wạ Sarkī rịgā** chief was screened from view by raised gown-sleeve of another. (3) *cf.* **kạngā ; kạngẹ.**

   C. (**kạngā**) *Vb.* 2 *x* **ạn kạngi shānū** the cattle have been partially gathered in one place, to prevent dispersal (*cf.* **kạngẹ**).

kạn gadō *m.* (1) good sense *x* **yanạ dạ** ~ he's sensible. **bạ shi dạ** ~ he's a feckless P. **yā ki** ~ he refused to listen to reason. (2) aim, object *x* **bạn gānẹ kạn gadam mạgạnạr ba** I don't grasp what underlies the matter. **nā rasạ kạn gadansạ** I can't make " head or tail " of it, of his actions.

kạngalē *used in* **dạn** ~ *m.* (*f.* **'yar** ~) *pl.* **'yạn** ~ fomenter of strife.

kạngamas *adv.* (1) brusquely and shamelessly *x* ~ **sãi ya fādạ masạ dạ fadạ** he attacked him without a moment's warning. (2) shamefacedly *x* **yā tāshị** ~ he stood up with a hangdog look (= **kyamas** 2 = **muzū-mụzū** 1).

kạngamēmẹ = **kạngamī** *m.* (*f.* **kạngamēmịyā** = **kạngamā**) *pl.* **kạngamkạngam** broad (*re* house or receptacle).

kạngạngạn unexpected meeting, etc. (= **kạnkạnkạn** *q.v.*).

kạngar *m.* (1) fermented infusion of roots with dash of cattle-urine, this being used to give " tang " to milk. (2) (*a*) the forfeit whereby one hits (**an sạ masạ** ~) fellow player with a top (**kạtantạnwạ**) on side of finger or wrist (instead of on hand-back) if his top falls on its side (*cf.* **dāwạ** 3). (*b*) **kạtantạnwạ tā yi** ~ top fell *as in* 2*a* (*cf.* **sụrū**).

kangara A. (**kạngarạ**) *Vb.* 3A. rebelled.

B. (kaŋgarā) Vb. 1C caused to rebel.
kaŋgarad ɗa Vb. 4B = kaŋgarā.
kaŋgarai = kaŋgarē.
ƙaŋgaraŋ = ƙaraŋgaŋ.
kaŋgararrē m. (f. kaŋgararrīyā) pl.
kaŋgararrū (1) rebel. (2) P. or horse,
etc., refusing obedience; insubordinate.
ƙaŋgarau = ƙaŋgararau x yā būshe ~
it's now quite dry. an sōya (tōya) shi ~
it's well fried.
kangare A. (kaŋgarē) (1) Vb. 3A (a)
rebelled, became insubordinate, became
out of hand (= tandarē = gāgara). (b)
jikinsa yā ~ his body became rigid
from cold (1a, b = sandarē). (2)
Vb. 1C (with dative) suŋ ~ masa
they rebelled against him, behaved
insubordinately to him.
    B. (kaŋgarē) m. (1) aŋ kaɗa masa
~ he was submitted to the torture of
sandwiching his ears between bow
and bowstring and then twanging (=
Kt. ɗamriŋ kirū). (2) aŋ kaɗa masa ~
admonition had effect of goading him
on to T. which he was enjoined to
refrain from.
kaŋgarī m. = kaŋgar.
kaŋgarwā f. and adv. T. lacking its normal
concomitants x yā hau ~ he rode
saddle without trappings. allūra ~
suka kāwō they brought unthreaded
needle. yā kāwō takōbī ~ tasa he
brought sword lacking scabbard. kaŋ-
garwar mace (i) husbandless woman.
(ii) bride without gārā (trousseau).
~ ya zō he came alone (cf. ƙaryā 1h).
ƙaŋgayau (1) yā būshe ~ it's now quite
dry. (2) yā rāme ~ he's become
very thin.
kaŋgāyē Vd. kaŋgō.
kange A. (kaŋge) Vb. 1A (1) (a) segregated. (b) aŋ ~ shānū cows have
been herded together to prevent them
dispersing. (c) made exception of T.
or P. (= tōge 2). (d) screened place
with T. x aŋ ~ magēwayī the latrine's
been screened off. (2) acted as in
kaŋge.
    B. (kaŋgē) m. tacking material pre-
paratory to sewing or dyeing (cf.
lallaƙcē).
kaŋgī m. = kaŋgē.

ƙaŋgi m. leather thong made of ƙiri, to
secure travelling slaves by the neck.
kaŋ gidā m. used in kaŋ gidansu nē it's
their totem-animal; it's an animal
taboo to them.
kaŋ gīwā Kt. m. open space before Emir's
palace (= ƙōfar fāda).
kaŋgō m. (pl. kaŋgwāyē = kaŋgāyē) (1)
adj. empty x kaŋgwaŋ akwāti empty
box. kaŋgwaŋ gidā deserted compound;
tumbledown compound. (2) m. un-
inhabited place x kaŋgwaŋ Allā mai
wuyar jiŋkewā = kaŋgwaŋ Allā bā
yā jiŋkewā what a feckless P. ! (3)
kaŋgwan sirdi saddle-frame without
coverings (cf. ƙuŋgurmī 1b) = ƙashin
sirdi.
    B. (kaŋgo) m. type of infusion (cf.
gabārūwā), to cure sores or syphilis (=
maɗi 3).
ƙaŋgū m. (1) band round drum to keep
skin taut (= dauri). (2) core of wood
or grass at apex (wuyan ɗāki) of round
house (kago) around which rope is
coiled and which is then joined to
vertical ropes to keep thatch firm
(= bārōgī = gūrū 6).
kaŋ gwādā m. type of embroidery on
tāgīya.
kaŋgwalī = Sk.   kālā   8   (= kalli =
kwaŋgalī).
kaŋgwāyē Vd. kaŋgō.
kaŋ gwāza Vd. gōra 1a, ii.
kāni then = kāna q.v.
ƙani Zar. younger brother (= ƙane).
ƙā nikā yi m. = ƙaƙa nikā yi.
ƙanir used in nā ƙōshi ƙanir I'm quite
replete.
kānīyā (a low expression) you blasted
swine !
ƙanjamē Vb. 3A became thin.
kanjau m. (1) (a) long, narrow Barebari
drum held between legs and beaten
standing. (b) type of Filani drum. (2)
yāro, gindī kamam makaɗiŋ ~ a
small-buttocked boy. (3) garī yā
yi masa ɗauriŋ ~ he's having a hard
time.
ƙanjau-ƙanjau x yana tafīya ~ he (thin
P. or animal) is walking along.
ƙanjiƙī m. unhealthy state of blood delaying healing of even minor sore.

kanjīlō *m.* = kandīlō.

kanjū *m.* a little sour milk in gourd to hasten fresh milk turning sour when poured in.

ƙanƙa *f.* (1) P. "sticking to one like leech" (= alƙaƙai = ƙaŋƙamō 3). (2) bā ni da ∼, bā ni da ƙaŋƙazōbę I've no physical defect.

kaŋ kācīya *m.* glans penis.

kaŋ ƙadaŋgarę *m.* = kaŋ gwādā.

kaŋkajērē *m.* (1) trouble. (2) kaŋkambą ∼ *f.* going hither and thither.

kankama A. (kaŋkāmā) (1) kept on catching (*int. from* kāmą). (2) suŋ ∼ they are busily at work. (3) yāƙi yā ∼ war is going on in real earnest. amincį yā ∼ goodwill became firmly established.

B. (kaŋkāmą) suŋ ∼ = kaŋkāmā 2.

kankambą *Vd.* kaŋkajērē.

ƙaŋƙamē *Vb.* 3A yā ∼ minį he stuck to me "like a leech".

kaŋkamę *Sk.*, *Kt.* *m.* frond of gōribą (dum) or giginyą (deleb) = karį 1.

ƙaŋƙamī *m.* (1) = ƙaŋƙamō. (2) ƙaŋƙamiŋ ƙamūrā *epithet of* stingy P.

ƙaŋƙamō = kaŋkamō *m.* (1) (*a*) useless guinea-corn. (*b*) desiccated fruit on tamarind, date-tree, dum-palm (gōribą) or kanyą (ƙaŋƙamō = ƙarmō 1). (2) ƙaŋƙamaŋ ƙammūrā *epithet of* stingy P. (3) yā zamę minį ∼ he stuck to me "like a leech" (= alƙaƙai).

kan-kan A. (kaŋ-kaŋ) (1) tightly *x* yā rifę shi ∼ he held it tightly. (2) yā tsayą ∼ bai yąrdā ba he refused point-blank. (3) *Vd.* shūnī 6.

B. (kaŋ-kaŋ) = kaŋ kaŋ kaŋ.

kaŋkanā *f.* (1) type of red-pulped watermelon. (2) 'yā'yaŋ ∼ *pl.* *m.* type of small red beads resembling tąlhātąnā.

ƙankana A. (ƙaŋkaną) *Vd.* ƙaŋkanę.

B. (ƙaŋƙānā) *Vb.* 2 reviled P. by saying ƙānīyā.

ƙaŋƙanāną *Vd.* ƙaŋkanę, ƙaramī.

ƙankance A. (ƙaŋƙancē) *Vb.* 3A became small.

B. ƙaŋƙancē) *Vd.* ƙaŋƙantą 2.

ƙankanci A. (ƙaŋƙancį) *m.* (1) humiliating a P. *x* an yi masą ∼ he's been humiliated. yā shā ∼ he was humiliated. (2) suną ∼ they are insulting

each other. (3) ɓarāyī sun yi masą ∼ thieves made serious inroads on his property. (4) ƙaŋƙancįŋ gąrā *Vd.* tsērę 2*b*. (5) *cf.* ƙanantą, ƙarantą, ƙarancī.

B. (ƙaŋƙanci) *Vd.* ƙaŋƙantą.

ƙaŋƙaŋ da kąi *m.* humility.

kaŋƙānē = kyaŋkyēnē.

ƙankane A. (ƙaŋƙanę) (1) *adj.* *m.* (*f.* ƙaŋƙanūwā) *pl.* ƙanāną = ƙaŋƙanāną = ƙaŋƙanāną = ƙaŋƙaną small *x* yārǫ ƙaŋƙanę = ƙaŋƙanaŋ yārǫ little boy. (2) *m.* a little *x* yā bā nį ∼ he gave me a little. (3) sum fārą 'yaŋ ƙanānąm mągaŋgąnū they entered on despicable talk. (4) *adv.* slightly *x* bā ni dą shī kō ∼ I haven't any at all (= bā ni dą shī kō kądaŋ). yā gutsurį tūwō ∼ he broke off a little tūwō.

B. (ƙaŋƙānē) *Vb.* 1C = ƙaŋƙāną.

ƙaŋƙani *Zar.* = ƙaŋƙanę.

kaŋ-kaŋ-kaŋ *m.* (1) mun yi ∼ dą shī we met him unexpectedly (= kącibīs). (2) sun yi ∼ (*a*) they're evenly matched. (*b*) they're quits. (3) *cf.* kaŋ-kaŋ.

ƙaŋƙannā *Kt.* *f.* (*pl.* ƙannąnā) nursing-mother (= ƙannī 2).

ƙankanta A. (ƙaŋƙantą) *f.* (1) smallness (*cf.* ƙaŋƙancį, ƙanantą, ƙarantą). (2) kų bar ganiŋ ∼, allūrą ƙarfę cē "good things are wrapped up in small parcels"; "don't look a gift-horse in the mouth!"

B. (ƙaŋƙantā) *Vb.* 1C = ƙaŋƙantą 2.

C. (ƙaŋƙantą) (1) (*a*) became humiliated. (*b*) lost importance. (*c*) became smaller. (2) *Vb.* 2 (*p.o.* ƙaŋƙancē, *n.o.* ƙaŋƙanci) (*a*) humiliated. (*b*) reduced size of. (*c*) mai hągē yā ƙaŋƙancē nį my fraudulent debtor ran away without paying me.

ƙaŋƙantad dą *Vb.* 4B humiliated, humbled.

kankara A. (kaŋkąrā) *Vb.* 1C = kaŋkąrē 1, 2.

B. (kaŋkąrą) *Vb.* 2 = kaŋkąrē 1, 2.

ƙankara A. (ƙaŋƙąrā) *Vb.* 1C made well *x* yā ƙaŋƙąrą rīgā he made the gown well.

B. (ƙaŋƙąrą) *f.* (1) (*a*) flint *x* aną sāmuŋ wutā jikiŋ ∼ fire is struck by flint and steel (*cf.* masaɓī). (*b*) flint of flintlock-gun. (c) ～ bā ki malāsā what a stingy person ! (2) (a) (i) hail. (ii) snow, ice. (b) ƙaŋƙarar maitā glass beads produced from mouth by conjurer and thought to be solidified saliva. (c) ŋgō, mai da ƙaŋƙararka here, take a taste of this ! (3) (a) cadger. (b) yā zuba minī ～ he cadged from me. (4) brownish fowl. (5) prominent Adam's apple.

C. (ƙaŋƙara) = kaŋƙarē.

kaŋ karā Vd. karā 1e.

kaŋkaraŋ-kaŋkaraŋ Vd. kaŋkarmēmę.

ƙaŋƙararrē adj. m. (f. ƙaŋƙararrīyā) pl. ƙaŋƙararrū x ƙaŋƙararran jā'irī an utter rogue (= ƙwaŋgwararrē).

kankare A. (kaŋkarē) Vb. 1C (1) hoed hard ground lightly (= farcę 3a), cf. kafta. (2) (a) scraped T. to remove dirt, weeds, bark, writing, fish-scales, etc. (= farcę 3b), cf. kātsę, maƙaŋwacī. (b) a wurinsa, zancaŋ Audu bā yā kaŋkarūwā he takes everything Audu says as Gospel-truth. (3) mahaifīyarka, kō kuturwā cę, bā tā kaŋkarūwā your mother is your mother whatever she does. (4) cf. ƙaŋƙarē.

B. (kaŋkarē) m. (1) nōmaŋ ～ m. during a dry spell in rains (a) hoeing hard farmland, (b) scraping round base of corn (= karcē). (2) type of drum made from dumā (Vd. gaŋgi).

C. (kaŋkarę) m. (pl. karākarai) (1) scrapings of loose tūwō from cooking-pot (cf. ƙanzō). (2) portion of tūwō which is perquisite of cook who made tūwō for large gathering.

kaŋ karē m. ～ bā ka da masāyar tāgīya epithet of contentious P.

ƙaŋƙarē Vb. 1C (1) = kaŋkarē 2a. (2) yā ƙaŋƙarę kōrę he opened out the kōrę-gown which had been treated with indigo and gum, rolled it up and left it to dry. (3) (a) ba mu ƙaŋƙarę maganarmu ba tukunā we've not settled point at issue between us yet. (b) tā yi " kōma, mu～ ! " she's re-married her husband, but it won't last long.

kaŋ kari adv. just appositely ; at the psychological moment (Vd. kari).

kaŋkarmēmę = kaŋkarmī m. (f. kaŋ-

karmēmiyā = kaŋkarmā) pl. kaŋkaraŋ-kaŋkaraŋ broad (re house, horse, etc.).

kaŋ karōfī Vd. karōfī.

kaŋki m. (1) West African hartebeeste. (2) (a) kaŋki ! look out, here comes the very P. we're talking about ! (b) yā harbi ～ (i) he disparaged P. unaware latter was within earshot (= makwarwā 3 = badō 3 = sārā 3 = kāmuŋ kaŋki = ƙunshi a baraka), cf. dūba 5b.ii. (ii) he " hustled " simpleton into buying. (3) jaŋ ～ setting fire to bush. (4) simpleton ; unsophisticated P. ; village bumpkin (= bagidāję).

kaŋkọ used in wā nē kaŋkọ (= wā nē haŋkọ), ballē jaunī how could you possibly have imagined you could do it !

ƙaŋƙū Vd. kalwā 4.

kaŋ ƙudā m. (1) daddawā in course of preparation. (2) the tiny metal-bosses on harness (= ƙwārō 7). (3) minute amount. (4) negro woolly hair (= karaŋgīyā) x sūmā tasa ～ cę he has negro-hair (cf. layā-layā).

kaŋ kyaŋwā m. (1) small piece of tūwō. (2) an sayi auduga kamaŋ ～ a little cotton was bought.

kam maƙērā m. anvil (Vd. maƙērā 2).

kam masābā m. type of guinea-corn.

kam mazarī m. thread on spindle (= bāƙī 6a q.v.).

kanna Vb. 1A overcharged for x yā ～ minī rīga he overcharged me for the gown (= līƙa 2).

kannacē Vb. 1C = karnacē.

ƙannai Kt. younger brothers (pl. of ƙanę q.v.).

kannakancī m. = karnakancī.

ƙannānā Vd. ƙaŋkannā.

kanne A. (kannę) Vb. 3A (1) closed one eye to look at T. or from illness (= kashę 10a). (2) steeled oneself.

B. (kannē) m. acting as in kannę 1 (= dūbaŋ gōrā 2).

ƙannē (1) younger brothers (pl. of ƙanę q.v.). (2) Vd. yayyē.

kannī m. = karnī.

ƙannī m. (1) smell of blood, fish, bad meat, dirty nursing-mother, etc. (cf.

ḳārī, wārī, ḳaurī). (2) (*a*) amaryar ∼
f. nursing-mother (*Vd.* amaryā 7). (*b*)
aŋgwaŋ ∼ *m.* man whose wife is
nursing-mother. (3) kudī nā wurinsa,
har sun yi ∼ he's wealthy.

ḳan ni ḳa ga Sarkī = ḳashē ni ḳa ga
Sarkī *m.* (*sg., pl.*) importunate P.
bringing trouble on those not avoiding
him (*Vd.* kashe 1*b*).

kannikancī *Vd.* karnakancī.

ḳan ni ḳa tūɓe *f.* (1) poor type of ḳuŋ-
ḳumā-gown. (2) woman with milkless
breasts.

ḳan nōno *m.* nipple.

kannuḳa *Vd.* ḳarē.

kannukancī *m.* = karnakancī.

ḳannūwa *Vd.* ḳane.

Kano *f.* (1) Kano. (2) ḳaḳar ∼ *f.* flat-
footedness (= madaɓī 1*b*). (3) Jallā,
ɓabbar Hausā *epithet of* Kano. (4)
Vd. Allā 7*g.* (5) Kano, ita cē kamislika
alfuŋ. Yāro ! kō da mē ka zō, am fī
ḳa Kano is peerless. (6) kā jī, ɗaŋ
Kano da ɗaŋ Ḳatsina Greek met
Greek. (7) *Vd.* yāḳi 1*k* ; jāḳin 8 ;
jiḳa 2 ; lābāri 3.

Kanōmā (*name of village*) used in ɗaŋ
∼ *m.* (1) cerebro-spinal meningitis (=
Saŋḳarau). (2) relapsing fever.

ḳan rumbū *used in* ɗaŋ ∼ *m.* grass roof
of corn-bin (= bākīre *q.v.*).

ḳansaisai *Vd.* ḳanshī.

ḳansakalī *m.* (*pl.* kansakula = Kt.
kansakulla) (1) any sword (= takōbī).
(2) *Vd.* waŋkaŋ ∼.

kan sallā *m.* (*abbreviation of* kāyan sallā)
presents given on the two Festivals
by parents to married daughters.

ḳan Sarkī *m.* (1) postage-stamp. (2)
head (*on coins*) *x* mē ka bī : damara ?
kō ḳan Sarkī heads or tails ?

ḳansasa A. (ḳansasā) *Vb.* 1C rendered
fragrant.
    B. (ḳansāsā) *pl.* fragrant (*pl. of*
ḳaḳḳansā).
    C. (ḳansasa) *Vb.* 3B became fragrant.

ḳanshī *m.* (*pl.* ḳansaisai) (1) (*a*) fragrant
smell (*cf.* wārī). (*b*) iŋ kā ji "a
sansanā !", bā ḳanshī empty vessels
make the most noise. (*c*) ḳanshiŋ arziḳī
yā fi ḳanshiŋ wainā to sniff round
a lucky P. is more profitable than

sniffing at cakes. (2) gyātsar ∼
f. giving advice which cannot be
followed (*x* telling penniless P. where
goods are cheap). (3) kō ḳanshin
lābārinsa ban ji ba I've not any news
of him. (4) yā shā ḳanshim biḳī he heard
news feast was being held and came to
cadge. (5) 'yaŋ ∼ roasted kernels of
bagārūwā. (6) ḳamshin zōmō *Vd.*
ɓabbaka 2. (7) ḳanshiŋ gishirī *Vd.*
gishirī 6. (8) *Vd.* gawasa.

ḳansūwā *f.* the coarse grass *Pennisetum
pedicellatum* (= ḳyāsūwā *q.v.*).

kantā *f.* (1) callus (*x* on hand from
pulling rope ; on knee from constant
prayer-kneeling). (2) kantar salla line
down forehead or nose or both, made
by child as adornment by rubbing
with cloth (= jirgī 3*b*). (3) becoming
ingrained *x* tsīyā tā yi masa ∼ he
is inured to poverty. yanā alfarmā
har ta yi ∼ arrogance is second nature
to him.

ḳan ta fargā *f.* bead of red sealing-
wax in imitation of red coral (murjāni) ;
epithet is ∼ bā rōba ba cē.

ḳan tāfī *m.* (1) carrying T. on upturned
palm of hand (*epithet is* ∼ masōmiŋ
hasāra). (2) bar ∼ da ranka don't
rush into needless danger !

ḳan tafīya *m.* advance-party.

kantāḳalai *used in* kantāḳalai ḳaḳar
gaurāka what stingy P. ! (*cf.* saŋ
gaurāka).

kantaḳarā *f.* the gum-tree taraunīyā.

kantakarmēme = kantakarmī *m.* (*f.*
kantakarmēmīyā = kantakarmā) *pl.*
kantaḳarmai huge.

ḳan takōbī *m.* (1) knob of sword-hilt.
(2) wuḳan naŋ, ∼ cē this knife's made
from sword-point.

kantamēme = kantamī *m.* (*f.* kanta-
mēmīyā = kantamā) *pl.* kantaŋ-
kantaŋ broad.

kantara A. (kantara) *Vb.* 3B *Ar.* (1)
is (was) crooked. (2) hanya tā ∼ road
winds.
    B. (kantarā) (1) *Vb.* 1C (*a*) made
crooked. (*b*) yā ∼ mini ḳaryā he told
me brazen lie. yā ∼ musu ḳyūyā he
brazenly refused to comply with them.
(2) *Vb.* 3A diverged towards *x* hanya

tā ∼ arēwā = hanya tā ∼, tā yi arēwā road swung off northwards.

kantarē *Vb.* 3A = **kantara.**

kantauza *m., f.* (1) lout. (2) rough-skinned P.

kantē *m.* type of coloured cloth (*also called* ɗaŋ ∼).

kantī *Eng. m.* (*pl.* **kantuna**). (1) European-shop. (2) groundnut-buying by firms *x* an sōma ∼ groundnut-buying season has opened.

kantōma = **kantōmati** *m.* (*Eng.* cantonment). (1) Local Authority. (2) **karyar** ∼ *f.* harlot.

kan tsaka *m.* = **kaŋ gwādā.**

kantsama *Vb.* 1C yā ∼ cikim mutānē he went about blurting out secrets (= **kwantsama**).

kantsarā = **kwantsama** 2.

kantu *m.* (*pl.* **kantuna**). (1) (*a*) block of Asbin-salt (**maŋgul**), block of sugar or sesame (**rīdī**) (*it consists of base* (**gindī**) *and tapering top* (**wutsīya**) ; *it is first cut into two longitudinal sections* (**tsāgi**), *these being then divided into semicircular sections* (**zawāra**)), *cf.* **yaŋkę** 1*c*.ii, **fasa** 1*g*, **turūzu**, **gaba** 5*a*, **diri, dire.** (*b*) cake of European salt (**kakanda**) made by **jici** *q.v.*, then cut into **zawāra** (*cf.* **yaŋkę** 1*c*.ii, **kaskō** 5). (*c*) **kantu ba gishirī ba nę** how can one pay without funds ? (*Vd.* 3). (2) a food made of beniseed (**rīdī**). (3) **yā cinyę bāshi, yā yi** ∼ he brazenly refused to pay debt (*epithet is* ∼ **ba gishirī ba, kana ɗaka, a kan shā lāmī**), *Vd.* 1*c above.*

kantuna *Vd.* **kantī ; kantu.**

kantūshi (*French* " cartouche ") *m.* cartridge case (= **kamsir**).

kānū *pl. of* **kāi** " head "). (1) heads of the community. (2) the best kolas (= **kaŋ wāgā** *q.v.*).

kanumfarī *Ar. m.* (*sg., pl.*). (1) clove (= **gurumbalī** = *Sk.* **kaɗē** 2). (2) *Vd.* **zaiti** 2.

kaŋ ūwar daɗi *Vd.* **rufi** 7.

kaŋwā *f.* (1) (*a*) (i) potash (**farar** ∼ for food, animals, soap-making ; **jar** ∼ for medicine). (ii) **da suka ji wannan kaŋwar tā fayę yāji, sǎi suka bari** when they found this too tough a job, they gave it up. (iii) **Masar ba kaŋwar**

lāsā ba cę Egypt is no easy prey. (*b*) **ɗauki kaŋwar baki, ba awākim baki** paying debt by borrowing from another ; being generous at another's expense. (*c*) **zamā da maɗaukā** ∼ **shī ya sa fariŋ kāi** becoming like P. through long association. (*d*) ∼ **tā kas tsāmī, kwarnafī yā fāda** the matter's settled, there's nothing more to be said ! (*e*) **yā zamā kandas, kaŋwar kashī** he (it) isn't up to much (*cf.* **kadāgwī**). (*f*) (i) ∼ **ba tā jika a bākinsa** he cannot keep a secret. (ii) *Vd.* **jika** 2. (*g*) ∼ **mai kyēya** = ∼ **mai gāshi** (*formerly*) slave for sale. (2) *Kt.* meal of goat-meat and ground-nuts, etc., given mother on day before naming-ceremony of child (= **kaurī** 2*a*) or given lad (**ɗan shāyī**) after circumcision. (3) **kaŋwar hannū garēshi** he's a lucky P. (4) *Kt.* **kaŋwā ! kaŋwā !** *said by* Sarkin **samārī** to call people to gathering where girl will choose **tsārancē**-partner, or where harlot will choose lover by selecting the article belonging to the man she prefers from things heaped together on mat and belonging to the various aspirants (*Vd.* **kāsūwā** 2). (5) *Vd.* **takanda.**

kanwa A. (**kaŋwa**) *f.* younger sister (*Vd.* **kane**).

B. (**kaŋwā**) *f.* (1) great eagerness to eat meat. (2) keen desire for (= **gūri**).

kaŋwacē *Vd.* **kaŋwata.**

kaŋ wāgā *m.* (1) best kolas (= **kānū** 2 = **gōrīya**). (2) " pick of the bunch " (= **idon** 13*b*).

kaŋwā kaŋwā *Vd.* **kaŋwā** 4.

kaŋwāta *Vb.* 2 is (was) eager for *x* **yā** ∼ **da sarauta** = **yā kaŋwāci sarauta** he was eager to obtain rule.

kaŋ wurī *Sk. m.* = **kaŋ gīwā.**

kaŋ wuya *m.* type of bead-necklace.

kanya *f.* (*pl.* **kanyōyī**). (1) African ebony tree (*Diospyros mespiliformis*) noted for brittleness of its wood (*Vd.* **kaiwā** 2). (2) **kanya**-fruit (*Vd.* **baro**). (3) **wāyan a cī, aŋ kōri karē daga gindiŋ** ∼ succeeding by guile (*Vd.* **wāyō** 1*b*). (4) **sandaŋ** ∼ *Vd.* **bāmī.** (5) **kilī** ∼ dark-grey horse. (6) (*said by woman and lads*) **ɗaŋ** ∼ = **ɗaŋ kanyo** clitoris.

kanyọ *Vd.* kanyạ 6.

kanzagī *m.* (*pl.* kạnzạgai). (1) small drum, closed at one end only, and beaten with sticks in company with drum gaŋgi *q.v.* (2) gạrī yā yi masạ ɗauriŋ ∼ he's having a hard time. (3) *Vd.* kazagī.

kạn zagō *m.* variety of large-grained guinea-corn.

kanzạm unexpectedly *x* ∼ sǎi mukạ gan shi we suddenly caught sight of him.

kạnzịl *used in* bạn cẹ̈ dạ shī ∼ ba I did not address a word to him (= uffạŋ).

kanzō *m.* (1) (*a*) rice, tūwō, etc., burned on to cooking-pot (*cf.* kaŋkarẹ). (*b*) mucus dried on eyelids. (*c*) *Vd.* kụnnē 1*d.* (2) cake such as gụrāsạ eaten with nothing to accompany it (*cf.* gāyā 2*b*).

kap = kaf.

kar A. (kạr) (1) do not ! *x* ∼ kạ yī don't do so ! (= kadạ *q.v.*). (2) yā bụgē shi ∼ ạ kā he hit him hard on head.

B. (kar) (1) *used in* ∼ tā saŋ ∼ = ∼ nạ̈ ganiŋ ∼ they're evenly matched. (2) (*abbreviation of* kashẹ " killed " = kas) *Vd.* example in gwaiwā 1*f*.

ƙar *rustic Hausa* = ƙas *x* yanạ̈ naŋ ạ ∼ there it is on the ground !

kara A. (kạrā) *f.* (1) being screened off *x* wuriŋ yā yi ∼ the place is screened off. (2) (*a*) *x* an yi masạ ∼ (i) he's been leniently dealt with (= ragạ 2*b*). (ii) his feelings have been respected. (iii) ạlkunyạ has been used instead of his real name. (*b*) mutual respect *x* (i) dạ ∼ tsạkānimmụ we show one another mutual respect. (ii) kạrarsụ bạ tạ būɗẹ ba they're still on good terms. (iii) yā būɗẹ minị ∼ he shamed me. (iv) Kạtsina dākiŋ ∼ : ạ ci gyạɗar wuri, ạ waŋkẹ hannū Katsina is place of genteel poverty. (3) " eyewash " *x* kibīyạn nạm, bā ta dạ ạmfānī ; sǎi ∼ nikẹ̈ dạ ita this arrow is not intended for shooting, I merely carry it as " eyewash " (*i.e. to frighten robbers*). (4) " making compliments " (= fīlākọ). (5) 'yaŋ ∼ devotees of bọrī. (6) *Vd.* ɓōyō 5*b*.

B. (kārạ) *Vb.* 1A. (1) *x* aŋ ∼ wuriŋ dạ zānā = aŋ ∼ zānā ạ wuriŋ the place has been screened with a grass-

mat (= sāyạ). (2) (*a*) aŋ ∼ masạ = kạ̈rā 2*a*. (*b*) aŋ ∼ masạ lạifinsạ his crime has been leniently dealt with (= sākạyā 2 = sāyạ). (3) suŋ ∼ gạrkī they have had an altercation. (4) ạ ∼ rūwā ạ murfụ put the water by the fire to get warm ! (5) Allạ̈ yạ ∼ God protect us from it !

C. (kārā) *m.* (*pl.* karạ̈rē = *Kt.* karā-rūwạ). (1) (*a*) stalk (especially corn-stalk) *x* (i) karan dāwạ guinea-corn stalk. karaŋ ạlbasạ onion stalk. karaŋ hūrạ wutā corn-stalks used by the poor as substitute for firewood (itạ̈caŋ hūrạ̈wā). (ii) suŋ karyạ ∼ they've quarrelled. (iii) kạmar ∼ akạ tsāgạ they are identical. (iv) *Vd.* bạ̈ zāƙẹ. (v) aŋ ƙētạrẹ karaŋ dạ ya gittạ they dis-obeyed his orders. (vi) kō dạ ∼ ạ̈ dōgạrā *Vd.* sạndā 1*e*. (vii) kō ∼ ya gicīyā *Vd.* gicīyā 1*c*. (viii) hạntsakiŋ ∼ *Vd.* hạntsakī 3. (ix) *Vd.* dōkịŋ karā, cī dạ karā. (*x*) shā ∼ *Vd.* shā A.1*l*. (x) kau dạ ∼ *Vd.* kau dạ 10. (*b*) gīwar ∼ *Vd.* gīwā 13. (*c*) karan sịgārị cigarette. sịgārị ∼ hạmsiŋ fifty cigarettes. (*d*) dōkịŋ ∼ child's hobby-horse. (*e*) (i) wạndạ ya yi makạ kạŋ ∼ kạ yi masạ kạŋ itạ̈cē yạ shẹkạrạ yanạ̈ ƙōnạ̈wā take two eyes for an eye and two teeth for a tooth !, recompense generosity with even greater generosity ! kōwā ya yi minị kạŋ ∼ sǎi ṇ yi masạ na itạ̈cē yạ shẹkạrạ yanạ̈ ƙōnạ̈wā I'll do as I'm done by and even more ! (ii) kạŋ ∼ *Vd.* kạ̈i 7*a.*iii. (*f*) (i) hatsī yā jā ∼ the corn is about 3 ft. high, *i.e.* has begun to develop stalk. (ii) yanạ̈ jạŋ karaŋ rụbūtū he's writing a bold, clear script. (*g*) karaŋ hancị bridge of the nose (= gōrạ 1*f*). (ii) hancịnsạ yanạ̈ dạ ∼ he has a shapely nose. (iii) yanạ̈ dạ karan jịkī he has a shapely body. (*h*) karam mạcārā = *Kt.* karam bụshārā child's rattle made from reed. (*j*) karaŋ wutsīyạ penis (= ạzakạrī). (*k*) ∼ zụbe (i) leaderless people. (ii) type of poor embroidery. (2) (*a*) jīyạ an yi sātạ, har an yi ∼ lots were drawn to see who committed yesterday's theft. ∼ yā nūnạ ɓạrāwọ the lots drawn indicated the thief. (*b*) zō, kạ yi manạ ∼ come and fix the ownership for us ! (*i.e.* as we could not determine the relative sizes of the heaps into which the commodity to be shared among us had been divided, we called a passer-by : he asked each of us for something belonging to us and put one on each heap, this determining ownership of such heap). (3) one of the draughtsmen which one **darą** (*q.v.*) player uses, his opponent having **dũtsę**-pieces. *(4) am fid dą ∼ sign of omission has been inserted in writing (= **cītąlī** = **tātąlī**). (5) **idąnsą yā yi** ∼ he shows signs of leucoma (**hakīyą**). (6) (*a*) **yā yi** ∼ he had luck. (*b*) **karansą yā kai** = **karansą yā kai tsaikǫ** he realized his wish. (*c*) *Vd.* **tsaikǫ** 1*c*. (7) (*a*) **yā kai** ∼ **maƙauracī** he's dead. (*b*) **ą kai** ∼ **maƙauracī tuŋ gąbaŋ ƙaurā bą tą zō ba** (*said by beggars* **marǫƙā**) give me alms and so lay up treasure in the next world ! (8) **na 'yaŋ** ∼ inferior quality *x* **tābąn naŋ ta 'yaŋ** ∼ **cę** this is inferior tobacco. (9) (*a*) **karam mąmā** = **karan nōnǫ** large, pendulous breasts. (*b*) **karam mąmā yā gudą** milk's gathered in her breasts. (10) *Vd. compounds of* **karan.** (11) ∼ **hąną aikį** *Vd.* **karan dą.**

D. (**karą**) (1) *Vb.* 3A collided *x* (*a*) **muŋ** ∼ we collided. (*b*) **muŋ** ∼ **dą sū** (i) we collided with them. (ii) we quarrelled with them. (iii) we warred with them (*cf.* **karǫ**). (2) *Ilorin Hausa f.* place screened off as latrine, etc. (= **magēwayī**).

ƙara A. (**ƙārā**) (1) *Vb.* (*uses* (2) *for v.n. and progressive*). (*a*) cried out. (*b*) **an tsąttsǫ̧kąnē shi, ya** ∼ after constantly being irritated, he could contain himself no longer (= **ɓamā** 2). (2) *f.* (*a*) (i) crying out *x* **yā kai** ∼ he cried out ; he wept. (ii) noise. (iii) sound *x* **ƙārar bindigą** report of a gun. (*b*) complaining of P. to one in authority such as **ąlkālī**, European or N.A. officer *x* **yā yi ƙarar Audu** he made a complaint against Audu. **yā kai** ∼ **wurin Sarkī** he took his grievance to the Chief. **aŋ kai Audu** ∼ **gąbaŋ ąlkālī** a charge against Audu was laid before the native judge.

B. (**ƙārā**) (1) *Vb.* 2. (*a*) finished *x* **bąŋ ƙari zarąfī** (= **bąŋ ƙāri bukātą**) **dą shī ba tukunā** I'm not done with it yet (*as in reply to* please lend me this book !). (*b*) **ku ƙārē mu, mu ƙārē ku** let us help one another ! (*c*) (i) **ką ƙāri kūkaŋką, ką dēną** (*said by mother*) you fretful child, devil take you ! (ii) **ką ƙāri niƙą, ką bā dą gąrī** rant on to your heart's content, what do I care ! (*d*) **ąbin dą zaŋ ƙārē ką dą shī, ką zō dą saurī** what I would impress on you is that you must come quickly. (*e*) **zaŋ yi haką har Allą yą ƙāri kwānāna** I'll do so till God brings my life to an end. (*f*) *Vd.* **ƙāri wąllāhį.** (2) *f.* end *x* (*a*) **gǫbe ząi kai ƙārar littāfį** to-morrow he'll reach the end of the book. (*b*) **yā kai** ∼ " he's done for ". (*c*) **ƙārar kwānā tā zō** = **ƙārar kwānā tā sąmē shį** he died.

C. (**ƙārą**) *Vb.* 1A (1) increased *x* (*a*) (*with noun following*). (i) **suŋ** ∼ **minį aikį** they gave me more work (= **dadą** 1*a q.v.*). **zaŋ** ∼ **ƙōƙarī** I'll try harder, redouble my efforts. **yā** ∼ **mąi** he (driver) increased the speed of the car, he (walker, worker) speeded up his pace. **suną ƙārō rąncąŋ** they are contributing further loans. (ii) **ą** ∼ **sadaką** *Vd.* **sadaką.** (iii) **lą̄bārį mąi** ∼ **ƙarfiŋ gwīwą** heartening news. (iv) **ką** ∼ **dą waŋkā** *Vd.* **waŋkā** 3. (v) **ą** ∼ **dąmisą kāyą** ? *Vd.* **dąmisą** 4. (vi) **ą** ∼ **gudumą** *Vd.* **gudumą** 1*b*. (vii) **ą** ∼ **dawākį** ? *Vd.* **Bąrnō.** (viii) **ą** ∼ **wą gārī** *Vd.* **gārī** 1*c*. (ix) **ką** ∼ **masą wutā** *Vd.* **rānā** 2*f*.iv. (x) **yą** ∼ **wą kǫgī rūwā** *Vd.* **Allą** 7*l*. (*b*) (*with v.n. following*) *x* **tā** ∼ **tąfīyą** she went on further. **ƙāƙą ka** ∼ **jį** do you feel any better ? (*c*) (*with adjective following*) *x* **ąl'amąrī yā** ∼ **baƙī** matters became worse. (*d*) (*with noun understood*) *x* **aką ƙārą, suką zamā sįttiŋ** then they were increased to sixty. (*e*) (*followed by v.n., etc., from intransitive verb* = English comparative) *x* **suŋ** ∼ **ƙarfafą** they became stronger. **yāƙį yā** ∼ **tsananī** the war became fiercer. **muną** ∼ **ƙiba** we're becoming fatter. **ku** ∼ **gąba** go forward ! **nā** ∼ **mąmākinsą** I wondered

more and more at it.   yā ∽ fusātą
he became angrier still.   in sun ∽
girmā, ą yi bįkī when they are older
let a marriage-banquet be made for
them ! su ∽ nīsā gāreshį let them keep
as aloof as possible from him ! bā
įndą zā ku ∽ tabbatąwā sǎi kun wai-
wąyā you have no better way of
convincing yourselves than by investigating it.   (f) added to x sun ∽
bisą gą ąbįn dą suką zō dą shī they
added to the amount they had brought.
bąi ga ąbįn dą wannąn amincį ya ∽
masą ba he did not see how this friendship benefited him.   mun kāmą
mąkąmai, mun ∽ cikin nāmu we captured munitions and added them to our
own.   (2) (a) repeated x bąn ∽ ganinsą
ba I have not seen him again.   bąn ∽
ganintą ba sǎi dą aką shēkarą uku I
did not see her again for three years.
yā ∽ cēwā he repeatedly said that . . .
(= dadą 1b).   (b) bą nā ∽ ba I promise
not to do it again !   (c) yā yi ɗam bā ∽
gōdįyā dą kwānan garkę he rued his
act when too late (= gōbe 3).   (d)
kadą ką ∽ Vd. kadą 2a.vi.

karaɓą (d.f. karɓā) Vb. 3B became universal x ginį ya kąn ∽ wōkącim bazarā
building is universal just before the
rains.   lābārįn nan yā ∽ ą gąrī that
news is (was) common knowledge.

karaɓaɓā f. self-sown yākuwā.

karābāję m. (f. karābājįyā) huge.

karaɓąs m. collision (= karǫ).

kārabką Sk. f. high road (= kārauką q.v.).

kārąbkī m. (1) slender posts for fence
(= tsąrnū).   (2) Sk. big crocodile. (3)
pl. of kārabką.

karabkīyā f. (1) competing x sunā ∽ ą
kąntą they're competing for her favour
(= hāmayyą).   (2) (a) noise of clashing
of weapons together or of clashing of
buckets, etc.   (b) bandicoot-trap of
pieces of calabash (sąkainā), or pieces of
pot (tsįngārǫ) and noose (ząrgē) which
rattle if bandicoot touches them
(= māshākǫ).

karabsū Kr. m. calyx of red-sorrel
(= sōɓarōdǫ).

karącē Vb. 3A is (was) emaciated, weak
(= hukącē 2).

karącē Vd. karātą.

kārad dą Vb. 4B x Allą yą kārad dą
mąsīfąn nan may God ward off that
calamity ! (cf. kąrā).

kārad dą Vb. 4B.   (1) bą nā kārar ba I
feel far from sure about it.   (2) an ∽
lābārį news has been disseminated
(both = dōrar).

Karądūwą Kt. used in na ∽ m. epithet of
murūcī (= Kt. marąshī).

karaf suddenly x ∽ sǎi muką gan shį we
suddenly saw him.

karąfā metals (pl. of karfę q.v.).

karāfīyą = karāhīyą.

karafkīyā = karabkīyā.

karaftū m. constant lauding of Emir by
retainers, in his presence.

karagą f. (pl. karągū = karągai = karagōgī) couch of corn-stalks, sticks, etc.

karagągą (1) f. roving about.   (2) adv.
rovingly x tanā yāwǫ ∽ she roves
about. (3) m., f. (sg., pl.) roving P.

karągē pl. (1) profligates (pl. of kargį).
(2) Vd. tree kargō.

karągǫ = jan karāgǫ m. (1) (a) kulī-kulī
cakes.   (b) cakes made from gujīyā.
(2) new season's kolas.

karagōgī Vd. karagą.

karā hąną aiki Vd. karan dą 3.

karāhīyą (Ar. thing loathed) f.   (1) ∽,
cįnkį banzā, barįnkį banzā epithet of
bandicoot (gafīyą).   *(2) (Muslim law)
T. not actually forbidden, but dis-
recommended.

karai A. (kąrai) Vb. (only used in past)
(d.f. karāyą).   (1) (a) lost heart (= sārę
2c).   (b) nā ∽ dą shī (i) I felt uncertain
of my power to get the better of him.
(ii) I'm doubtful of his chances of
recovery.   (c) Vd. kadǫ 6.   (2) snapped
x (a) hannunsą yā ∽ = yā ∽ ą hannū
his arm is broken (= karyę).   (b)
azzįkinsą yā ∽ his luck is over.   (c)
kuɗinsą sun ∽ his money is all spent,
his fortune no longer exists.   (d) girmansą yā ∽ " he lost face ".   (e) cf.
karai dą.   (f) Vd. ąlwąllā, lallę 1g.
(3) hannunsą yā ∽ dą shī he's expert
in it.   (4) harshąnsą yā ∽ he is in the
delirium which precedes death.   (5)
hakǫransą sun ∽ his milk-teeth have
fallen out (cf. karāyą 2g).

B. (ƙārai̱) *Nor.* *m.* crocodile
(= kado̱).

ƙarai *x* sanyī ~ ga̱rēshi̱ it (water, etc.) is
ice-cold.

karai da̱ *used in* (1) yā ~ kǎi̱, yā yi
ta̱fīya̱ssa̱ he refused and went on his
way. (2) cīwo̱ yā ~ kǎi the illness has
passed its crisis (= karya̱ 11).

ƙarai̱rai *Vd.* ƙaryā.

karairaya A. (ka̱rai̱raya̱) *Vb.* 3B gave oneself airs, strutted about.

     B. (karairayā) *Vb.* 1D *int. from*
karya̱.

ka̱rai̱ra̱yau *m.* the grass *Andropogon
arthrolepsis.*

karaira̱yē *Vb.* 3A su̱ŋ ~ they snapped in
succession (*int. from* karye̱).

ƙarai̱rayī *Vd.* ƙaryā.

ƙārājī *m.* (1) loud talking. (2) crying out
in pain.

kara̱kǎi *m.* (1) showing fidgety impatience.
(2) struggling to get free (1, 2 = ha̱ŋ-
ƙōrō).

kara̱kainā *f.* (1) abundance *x* yā yi ~
it is abundant. (2) = karabkīyā 1.

kara-kara Λ. (karā-karā)*f.* any uncovered,
rickety motor-lorry.

     B. (ka̱ra̱-karā) *f.* inhabited-area near
city (= ka̱rkarā *q.v.*).

     C. (ka̱rā-ka̱rā) A sends B to bring
ingredients for kamādisi̱nō (= kwaɗa̱m
baka̱), giving him merely a halfpenny :
B says banteringly, Ba̱tūre̱ yā sō ~
what prodigality !

ƙa̱rā-ƙa̱rā *f.* (1) an yi wa̱ ba̱ŋgō ~ earth
was slapped on to roughened surface of
wall as base for plastering (= haƙōrī
3a). (2) (a) eating snack of cassava
plus ground-nuts (*Vd.* kamādisi̱nō) at
time of la̱'asa̱r or ha̱ntsī. (b) yana̱
nēma̱ŋ ~ he's " out for pickings of
food ". (3) the corn-stalks (karā)
fitted between the main beams (dawākī) of tsaiko̱ (= zu̱zzu̱bā).

ka̱rāka̱rai scrapings of pot (*Vd.* ka̱ŋ-
kare̱).

ka̱'ra-ka̱rē'' *m.* scolding (*derived from*
snapping of " dog ", *i.e.* ka̱rē).

kǎra̱kkī *Sk.* = kǎra̱bkī 2.

kara̱m = kwara̱m.

ka̱rāma̱ *Ar. f.* (1) bountifulness ; cheerful
disposition *x* yā nūna̱ musu̱ ~ he

behaved kindly to them (*cf.* 2). mu̱tu̱m
mai̱ ~ generous man. (b) ~ bāyan
zilla̱ relenting towards P. whom one has
treated harshly. (2) nūna̱ ~ ga̱rēshi̱
he (saint, *i.e.* wa̱lī) has magic-powers
(*Vd.* mu̱'u̱jiza̱), *cf.* 1 *above.*

ƙarama̱ *f.* small (*Vd.* ƙaramī).

ka̱ramba̱ *f.* rosary (ca̱zbī) of black wooden
beads.

karambāna̱ *m., f.* (*sg., pl.*). (1) busybody.
(2) *Vd.* ka̱ramba̱nī.

ka̱ramba̱nī *m.* (1) meddlesomeness (*epithet*
is ~ ƙauya̱ŋ hanya̱). (2) mai̱ ~ shī ya
ka̱m bīyā bāshi̱ŋ ka̱kansa̱ a̱ lāhira̱
epithet of busybody. (3) ka̱ramba̱ni̱ŋ
ka̱zā, auram mu̱zūrū don't be officious !
(4) ka̱ramba̱ni̱ŋ a̱kwīya̱, gai da̱ kūrā
it's attempting the impossible. (5)
ka̱ramba̱nim ba̱ƙō ya̱ cu̱di ma̱tai̱
ma̱sū gidā what impertinence !

ƙaramba̱ŋ-ƙa̱ramba̱ŋ *m.* yā yi ~ it's too
large to enter doorway, etc. (= bara̱ŋ-
ƙam-ba̱ra̱ŋƙa̱m *q.v.*).

karamba̱ta̱ *f.* (1) Black-crested Hawk-
Eagle (*Lophœtus occipitalis*). (2)
African Mountain-Kestrel (*Falco tin-
nunculus*).

kara̱m batta̱r ƙarfe̱ *Vd.* karo̱.

ka̱ram ɓikī *Vd.* karen 1.

ka̱rambūsa̱ *f.* (1) inferior T. (2) ugly
dirty woman.

karamci̱ *m.* generosity.

ka̱ra̱mē *Vd.* karmā.

ƙaramī *m.* (*f.* ƙarama̱) *pl.* ƙanāna̱, etc
(*as for* ƙaŋƙane̱). (1) (*a*) (i) small
(ii) ƙaramar salla̱ *Vd.* salla̱ 1*d*. (iii)
ƙaramar shūka̱ *Vd.* shūka̱ 2c.iii. (iv)
ƙarami̱ŋ a̱lhakī *Vd.* a̱lhakī 3. (v)
ƙaramim mai̱ lāfīya̱ *Vd.* banzā 1*a*
(vi) ƙaramas sa̱ŋwa̱ *Vd.* sa̱ŋwa̱ 4
(vii) ƙaramin sani *Vd.* ƙuƙumī. (*b*)
ƙaraminsu̱ the smallest of them. (*c*)
younger, youngest *x* ƙaramin ɗansa̱
his younger, youngest son. (*d*) junio
ƙaramarsu̱ the junior wife, the younges
sister among them. (2) ƙaramim mu̱tu̱m
mean-minded P. ; undignified P. (*cf*
ƙanana̱). (3) ƙaramar tsanya̱, da̱ wur
ta ka̱m fāra̱ haƙa̱ a stitch in time saves
nine.

karammata̱ = karamba̱ta̱.

ka̱rammuskị *m.* (1) the scarlet, velvety

spider seen in rainy season (= dą̊-munā 9 = bōkā 4). (2) velvet (the word comes from Persian ḳirmizī, which gives us French " cramoisi " and English " crimson ").

ḳaramnīyā f. (pl. ḳarạmnū) white mat made from young dum-palm (kabạ) leaves (= kēsọ 2).

ḳarạmnīyā = ḳarạunīyā.

ḳaramtạ = ḳarantạ.

ḳaramtū used in ḳaramtū ~ Chief, be careful of the road ! (this is said by 'yaŋ ḳaramtū), cf. maŋkō, gịribtū.

ḳarą̊mūzạ f. inferior P. or T.

karan A. (karan) (genitive of karā) Vd. karan compounds alphabetically.

B. (ḳaran) (genitive of ḳạrē) Vd. karen compounds alphabetically.

karan bara (karam bą̊rā) m. (1) target x an są̊ ~ target (this usually being a stick) has been set up. (2) an są̊ shi ~ he's ruler elect. (3) karam bą̊ram mutūwạ an elder (= dattījọ).

karạn battạr ḳarfę Vd. karọ.

karan bazarā (ḳaram bazarā) Vd. karen 2.

karan бiki (ḳaram бikī) m. (1) jackal. (2) Vd. ạlbasạ 7.

karan bushara (karam bụshārā) Kt. m. type of rattle made from a reed (= mạcārā).

karance A. (karạncē) Vb. 1C read, studied all of.

B. (ḳarạncē) Vd. ḳarantạ.

ḳarancī m. (1) smallness. (2) (a) small amount (cf. ḳaŋḳancị). (b) x tụrą̊rē yā yi ~ there is shortage of scent.

karan dạ (1) = karantad dạ. (2) ḳarạn dạ masạnā epithet of learned man. (3) karaŋ hạnạ aikị = karā hạnạ aikị Study, thou hinderer of work ! (epithet of ḳạrą̊tū).

karan dafị m. red leaf-sheaths of a guinea-corn (used for dyeing red, leather and dum-palm (kabạ) products).

karan d'orị Vd. d'orị 2.

ḳaraŋgạ f. (1) P. or T. one cannot get rid of x yā zamę minị ~ (= ạlḳaḳai). (2) German 3-mark piece.

ḳarạŋgaŋ m. (1) yā zamę minị ḳarạŋgaŋ (= ḳaŋgaraŋ) = ḳaraŋgạ 1q.v.). (2) ḳyaurē yā yi ~ it's impossible to shut the door.

ḳaraŋ gānūwā Vd. karen 4.

karaŋ gạrkūwā m. handle of shield.

ḳarạŋgīyā f. (1) prickly burrs from the grass Cenchrus catharticus. (2) gāsh-jnsạ ~ nę̊ he has the negro woolly hair (= kaŋ ḳudā (cf. layā-lạyạ)). (3) ḳarạŋgīyar Asbịŋ a prickly grass.

karaŋ hạnạ aikị Vd. karan dạ 3.

karan hancị Vd. karā 1g.

karan jịkī Vd. karā 1g.

ḳāraŋ ḳą̊bạ = ḳāraŋ ḳą̊bą̊rạ (said by women) blast you ! (Vd. ḳą̊bạrạ, ḳārō).

karaŋ kaбau m. the grass Andropogon sp. nov.

karaŋ kad'ạ mīyạ m. nonentity.

karaŋkarmạ = ḳarạŋkarmạ m. collar-bone or neck-hollow above it (= ḳạshim bạri wallē).

karaŋḳạtsā Vb. 1D used in yā karaŋ-ḳạtsạ 'yā'yā he, it (animal, tree) was very prolific.

karan mạcārā = karā 1h.

karan maroḳa (ḳạram marọḳā) Vd. karen 5.

karan masallaci (karam masallācī) m. (1) the leafless plant Caralluma Dalzielii (is transplanted into malallautā). (2) quadrangular bead.

karan mota (ḳạram mōtạ) Vd. karen 6.

ḳạran rārīyā Vd. karen 8.

karan rụbūtū Vd. karā 1f.

karan Sarkī m. sugar-cane (= rạḳē).

karanta A. (karạntā) Vb. 1C. (1) read (cf. dūbạ 6). (2) studied.

B. (ḳarantạ) (1) Vb. 2 (p.o. ḳarạncē, n.o. ḳarạnci). (a) read. (b) studied. (2) Vb. 3B yā ~ he's well-read (= ḳạrạntu).

C. (kārạntā) Vb. 1C aŋ ~ masạ = ḳạrā 2a.

ḳaranta A. (ḳarantạ = ḳạrạntā) f. (1) yā cikạ ~ he's mean-minded ; he is an undignified P. (2) insufficiency x ạbincī yā yi masạ ~ (cf. ḳaŋḳancị).

B. (ḳarạntā) Vb. 1C. (1) diminished. (2) used insufficient of T.

C. (ḳarantạ) Vb. 3B. (1) became diminished. (2) is (was) insufficient.

karantad dạ Vb. 4A yā ~ nī = yā karan-tasshē nị he educated me, taught me to read.

ḳạrantṣayī = ḳạrantṣạyē m. (1) (a) yanḳ̣

da ⏜ it has a rent in it. kaya tā yi mini
⏜ a jikin rīgā thorn tore my gown. (b)
da ɓatan rīgā, gāra karantsayī better
slight loss than big. (2) Audu yā yi ⏜ =
an yi wa Audu ⏜ Audu's been dismissed.
karantu Vb. 3B x sun karantu cikin
ilimī they are versed in knowledge
(= karanta 2). yā karantu he is well-
trained in knowledge.
karan wutsīya Vd. karā 1j.
karap = karaf.
karaptū = karaftū.
karara f. the climber Mucuna pruriensis
(pods are covered with hairs, causing
irritation to body of P. touching it).
karara A. (karara) f. and adv. rustling of
clothing as P. moves.
    B. (karara) used in (1) rūwā yana
da sanyī ⏜ water's ice-cold. (2) rūwā
nē ⏜ it's clear water.
    C. (kārara) pl. stinking (Vd. kar-
karā).
kararau used in yā būshe ⏜ it's now quite
dry. an sōya (tōya) shi ⏜ it's well
fried.
kārar da = kārad da.
karāre stalks (pl. of karā, q.v.).
karāre glass-bangles, etc. (pl. of karau
q.v.).
kararī m. (1) clear water x a kōre rūwā, a
shā da ⏜ push aside water-weeds and
drink underlying clear water ! (b)
" a kōre, a shā da ⏜ " yake yī he's
bringing feeble excuses (= kusassarī).
(2) slight remaining utility x zanan nan
yana da ⏜ there's still a little wear left
in this cloth.
kararrawa f. P. or T. whose quality is
inferior to its appearance x mē zā a yi
da wannan ⏜ of what use is this article
which merely looks good ? (cf. fankam
fayau)
kararrawā f. (1) bell. (2) bell-like appen-
dage of porcupine (begwā) sounded
when angry. (3) Tunkū da ⏜, mai jā
wa dangi cūtā epithet of P. who is
nuisance to his family.
kararre m. (f. kararrīyā) pl. kararrū adj.
(1) (a) finished. (b) kararre fararre no
sooner said than done ! (2) worn-out
(cf. kāre 1b.ii).

karārūwa Vd. karā.
kārasā Vb. 1C. (1)(a)(i) finished T. (= kāre
2). (ii) maganan nam ba ta kārasa fita
daga bākinsu ba săi aka ji hardly had
they uttered these words when we heard
that . . . (b) yunwa tā ⏜ shi hunger
finished him off. (2) x bā kā bari har n
kārasa ? can't you even wait till I'm
dead !
kāras da Vd. kārad da.
karashe A. (kārashē) Vb. 1C = kārasā 1.
    B. (kārashe) m. x nā gama, saurā ⏜
I've completed it except for just the
finishing touches.
karas-karas m. the sound heard when P.
eats raw kola, raw dankali or raw
groundnuts, etc., x nā ji ⏜.
karasū Kr. m. calyx of red sorrel (= sōɓarōdo).
karatā Vb. 1C read, studied (= karantā
q.v.).
karata A. (karata) (1) Vb. 3B approached.
(2) Vb. 2 (p.o. karacē, n.o. karāci)
approached (P., place, etc.) x yā
karāci Kano.
    B. (karata) x yā ⏜ kusa da shi
he approached him.
    C. (karata) used in kā ⏜ rant on to
your heart's content, what do I care !
(= kārā 1c.ii).
kā rātsa f. oversewing along length of
cloth to create appearance of tuck.
karātū m. (Ar. qirā'atun) (1) (secondary
v.n. of karantā) x yana karatunsa =
yana karantā shi he's reading it ;
studying it. (2) education x (a) bā
shi da ⏜ he's illiterate. (b) nā bā shi ⏜
I educated him. yana bā da ⏜ he's
teaching ; he's a teacher. (c) yā
dauki karātū wurin Audu he studied
under Audu. (d) ā kōyi ⏜ ran tukuri !
don't leave things till last minute !
(e) karātū, farkwanka madācī, kar-
shanka zuma there is no royal road to
knowledge (= Tōri, mōriyarka da nīsā).
(f) Vd. karan da. (g) Vd. babbāwa 3.
(h) kidi da karātū Vd. gwammace.
karau (1) (with cerebral " r " ; Vd. Mod.
Gram. 5). (a) m. (i) glass bangle (cf.
mundūwā ; sā da kūkā). (ii) any small
bottle x karan turāre scent-bottle
(= wakīyya). karan tadawa small

bottle of ink. (iii) an ɗaurą masą ∼ ta ƙafą he " has his cross to bear " (x false charge, bad wife, etc.). (b) rūwaŋ ƙarau Vd. rūwā B.11. (c) = ƙalau. (2) (with rolled " r " ; Vd. Mod. Gram. 5) yā būshę ∼ it's now quite dry. yā sǫyu ∼ it's thoroughly fried (2 = raƙau).

kārauką f. (pl. ƙąrąukū = kāraukōkī = ƙąrąukī) high road (= tumfushī).

ƙarau-ƙarau = ƙarau 2.

ƙąrąukī (1) pl. of kārauką. (2) m. slender posts for fence (= tsąrnū). (3) Sk. large crocodile.

kąrauniyā f. (pl. kąrąunū) white mat made from young dum-palm (kabą) leaves (= Kt. kēsǫ 2).

ƙąrauniyā f. (1) rattling x nā ji ƙąrauniyar ąshānā ą ąljīfunsą, ąmmā bai bā ni ba I heard rattling of matches in his pocket, but he said he had none. (2) muną ∼ dą shī go where we may, there's no means of shaking him (it) off.

ƙarauzayą f. = ƙarauzayi m. (1) lumpiness (such as T. badly pounded ; gravelly place ; stalks of grass left by horse after eating soft parts ; poorly woven mat, etc.) x dōki yā cinyę mai laushī, ya bar ∼. (2) how lumpy !

kąrāwąlī Fil. m. a Filani milk-measure (= ƙąlāwąrī).

kąrāyą Vb. 3B (1) = kąrai (but kąrāyą has progressive and v.n. while kąrai has not). (2) f. (a) (i) yā yi ∼ he lost heart (= 1 above), Vd. rauni. (ii) ∼ gąrēshi he's spineless, he's a whiner. (b) kąrāyąr zūcīyā hąsārąr namiji " faint heart never won fair lady ". (c) kąrāyą gąrēshi when guests come, he doesn't offer food (= sārę 2d). (d) wąsaŋ ∼ Vd. làdǫ. (e) yārǫ yaną kąrāyąr gǫrā = kąrāyąr mąmā = kąrāyąr nōnǫ baby lad has diarrhœa. (f) aną kūkan targaɗę, gą ∼ tā zō " out of frying-pan into fire ! ". (g) haƙǫransą suną ∼ lad's shedding milk-teeth (= fąmfarą 1 = Sk. fīrą 3), cf. kąrai 5, karyą 9.

ƙąrāyā f. (1) type of spiky-finned fish. (2) T. or P. " thorn in one's flesh " x yārąn naŋ yā zamę mini ∼ try as I

may, I cannot shake off this boy (= ąlƙaƙai).

Kārąyē (1) name of town in Kano Province. (2) bą cǖǘ, bą bōkǫ, bą guduŋ wutā, ɗaŋ ∼ here is the best Karaye shea-oil for lamps, buy, buy ! (said by girls exhibiting it, i.e. tąllą, hence ɗaŋ ∼ m. the best shea-oil). (3) gąludayą, tąlląm mutąnaŋ ∼ epithet of aimless wandering.

ƙąrāzą f. old cassava (= gąntąmau).

kąrāzanā f. assiduity.

karā zubę Vd. karā 1k.

karɓa A. (kąrɓā) (1) Vb. 2 (but progressive and v.n. uses 2). (a) received (= riƙą 1d). (b) baŋ kąrɓi mąganąrką ba I don't believe you. (c) mun jī, muŋ ∼ (said to superior) we'll carry out your behests ! (adaptation of Arabic sam'an watā'atan). (d) ransomed a slave (= fąnsā) x tā kąrɓi kąntą she (slave) ransomed herself (= sąmā 1g). (e) took over duty from another, i.e. relieved (= mąyā 1). (f) suited x rīgąr tā kąrɓē ką the gown suits you. dabbąn naŋ tā kąrɓi hannunsą this domestic animal is thriving with him (= sō 2d), cf. hannū 2c. (g) yā kąrɓi gąba he got the lead. (h) indą aką kąrɓi dąrīyā Vd. dąrīyā 2. (j) yā kąrɓi takąrdā Vd. tikiti 2. (k) Vd. kąrɓi ą jiką. (2) f., m. (v.n. of 1). (a) (i) yaną kąrɓansą = yaną kąrɓassą he's receiving it. (ii) fātansą bai sąmi kąrɓā ba his wish was not realized. (iii) bā yą kąrɓar saurī sài lūrā it requires careful consideration, not hasty action. (iv) sun tąfi kąrɓaŋ aiki they've gone to relieve those on duty. (b) sun jē kąrɓar sūnā they've got to infant's naming-ceremony (Vd. sūnā). (c) ąbiŋ ∼ acceptable T. (d) mągąniŋ ∼ charm or drug to enable beggar or cadger to get alms, gifts, or loans. (e) yā fi sauransų ∼ he gets more favours than the others. (f) kudī nikę sǫ, bą ∼ ba I want cash, not payment in kind (cf. farin bīyą ; fariŋ kudī ; tsābą). (g) wani dą kąrɓar rīgā Vd. tūsą 3.

B. (karɓą) Vb. 1A Sk., Kt. (1) replied to call or greeting x (a) ya karɓą musu, ya cę . . . then he replied

to their greeting, saying that . . . (b)
n nā karɓāwā greeting to you also !
(*reply to greeting*). (2) (a) aŋ ∼ masa he
received favourable reply. (b) suŋ karɓa
yāƙi they accepted the challenge to war.
C. (karɓā) *Sk.* = karɓā 2f.

karɓaɓɓenīyā f. alternation by relieving
each other of load, duty, etc. turn and
turn about, *cf.* mayayya.

karɓā-karɓā f. (1) = karɓaɓɓenīyā. (2)
māgani ∼ nē circumstances alter cases.

karɓayya f. = karɓaɓɓenīyā.

karɓe *Vb.* 1A. (1) received all of. (2)
rūwā yā ∼ wuriŋ water's enveloped the
place. (3) deprived *x* yā ∼ masa shī
he took it away from him.

karɓeɓenīyā f. = karɓaɓɓenīyā.

karbī *rustic Hausa* m. leather-bucket
(= wasaƙī).

karɓi a jika m. (1) burying pauper shroud-
less and/or without the pots or logs for
keeping earth off corpse (= Kt. diɓgē).
(2) unexpected happening " flummoxing " P. (= firmitsī).

karɓū m. (1) selvedge, *i.e.* made by
hemming rough-edge of weaving (*cf.*
kalmasa). (2) seam consisting of
junction of two selvedges. (3) upper
and lower margins of eyelids (*i.e.*
place where they meet when eye
closed and where galena (tōzalī) is
applied). (4) yā ɗau ∼ he pulled up
chin-piece of turban over mouth and
nose (*Vd.* amāwalī).

karce A. (karcę) (1) *Vb.* 1A. (a) = kaŋkarē 1, 2. (b) abraded, causing slit in
material or skin of P. = kūję 1 =
farce 3c (*cf.* zāgę). (2) *Vb.* 3A yā ∼ a
guje he took to his heels.
    B. (karce) (1) m. = kaŋkarē 1. (2)
Vd. karta.
    C. (karcē) *adv.* diligently *x* nā nēmē
shi ∼ I sought it keenly. yanā aiki ∼
he's working hard.

karci *Vd.* karta.

ƙardā f. (1) Ƙardā bāƙwan tīlas, am ram
maka, ka kōmō *epithet of* unwelcome
visitor. (2) hanzariŋ ∼ lame excuse
(*Vd.* hanzarī 1d).

kardāda *Vb.* 2. (1) went direct to. (2)
estimated (both = kintāta).

kardādā *Vb.* 3A squeezed one's way

through crowd, small opening, etc., *x*
yā ∼, ya wucę he squeezed his way
through (= firmitsā).

kardādę m. narrow corridor between
places.

kardādō m. acting *as in* kardāda.

ƙardajī m. the thorny *Mimosa asperata*
(*epithet is* ∼ hana waŋkyaŋ gēfę).

ƙar daŋgi m. (1) type of arrow-poison. (2)
Chestnut-capped Weaverbird (*Ploceus
vitellinus*. (3) *Vd.* zabgai.

ƙardę *Fil.* m. (1) veins of leaf of dum-
palm (kaba) *or* locust-bean (dōrawa)
(*both also called* mēdī). (2) veins of
leaf of corn-plant or of feather. *N.B.—
leaf-vein in general is called* gōrar
ganyē.

ƙardi = ƙardę.

ƙardūwā f. undersized woman or goat.

kare A. (karē) (*Ar.* kalb) m. (f. karyā)
pl. karnuka = kannuka = karnai =
karnau = karnāwū (1) (a) (i) dog
(*epithet is* Nasadaru, baƙiŋ kīwo, bā
ka da dāki, kanā faɗaŋ gidā =
Gindau), *cf.* tarę 1c.ii, tōkā 7, shā rānī
2, ƙaurā 3, gōję 4, durwā. (ii) *Vd.* karyā.
(b) karam mōta chauffeur's assistant
(*cf.* mōtar karē *under* mota 2). (c) (i)
kai ɗaŋ ∼ you worthless fellow ! (ii)
ɗaŋ karan *x* ɗaŋ karaŋ kyau garēshi
he's very good.   ɗaŋ karan tsōrō
garēshi he's very timid (*Vd.* nēmā 7c).
(d) Karē, bā ka da rānā, sāi ta haushi
what a useless person ! (*Vd.* rāna
4d). (e) yā sāmē ni da zāgi, abiŋ kō
karē ba yā ci ba he attacked me with
insufferable abuse.   (f) yā cika ci
kaman na ∼ he is a greedy oppressor.
(2) a ɗauki ∼ ram farauta ? don't leave
things till the last moment ! (3) (a)
Jāmus sunā shaŋ kōrar ∼ the Germans
are being routed. an yi musu kōrar ∼
they've been driven away (*Vd.* fata-fata ;
47 *below*. (4) karan rārīyā nē he's a
tramp, casual worker (*Vd.* karen 8). (5)
mun yi musu na bāya ∼ kē cīzo we reduced them to helter-skelter panic. (6)
yā ranta a na ∼ = Kt. yā dība cikin na
∼ he took to his heels (*Vd.* barę 2c).
(7) kā shāfi baƙiŋ ∼ a rigarka you've
soiled your gown on the cooking-
pot. (8) ∼ da zōmō da maharbī

Orion. (9) kōwā yai dārīyar ∽ ā̀ bar shi show firmness and people won't molest you ! (10) da̧ kūrā da̧ ∽ bā sā̧ gama̧ mazaunī oil and water won't mix. (11) a̧ ta̧ru, a̧ kas mahau̧ka̧ciŋ ∽ he cadges from the generous without making any return. (12) aŋ ha̧rbi ∽ a̧ wutsī, sǎi gidā the job is done, so let's be off ! (13) (a) da̧ wani ∽ bā̧ Barȩ ba̧ ? it's six of one and half a dozen of the other. (b) Kt. yā ci nōmaŋ ∽ = barȩ 2c. (14) (a) hanci̧ŋ ka̧rē m. perpetually moist soil. (b) nōna̧ŋ ∽ Vd. nōno̧ 1k. (15) ka̧raŋ hau̧kā Vd. za̧rā 2b.ìii. (16) a̧biŋ haushī, mūshȩ, ja̧ŋ ∽ what an annoying person ! (17) ri̧k̃e ka̧raŋka̧ doŋ ka̧raŋ gida̧ŋ wani meet a P. with his own weapons ! (18) rāgō da̧ wutsīya̧r ∽ Vd. rāgō 6. (19) dōmi̧ŋ ∽ a̧ yi gōbarā the fullest investigation will be welcome to me for it will prove me innocent. (20) a̧ aiki ∽, ya̧ aiki wutsīya̧ ? what right have you to depute another to do your task ? (21) sabo̧ da̧ ka̧raŋ gida̧ŋka̧ ka ka̧ŋ ga ka̧raŋ gida̧ŋ wani like attracts like. (22) kōwā ya ga da̧misa̧, yā sam bā̧ ∽ ba nȩ it is obvious. (23) aŋ saŋ haliŋ ∽, ka̧n d'aukō shi one must take the good with the bad. (24) mȩ̄ ∽ gōma̧ yakā̧ yi̧ da̧ kūrā̧ what have they in common ? (25) ba̧ri murna̧ doŋ ka̧raŋka̧ yā kāma̧ zāki̧ don't count your chickens before they're hatched ! (26) sun yi ∽ jinī, biri̧ jinī they opposed each other fiercely. (27) bā ā̧ gaya̧ wa̧ ∽ gidam bā̧k̃ī what a pointless act ! (28) yā cȩ̄ za̧i yi musu̧ kwā̧sar ka̧ram mahauka̧ci̧yā he was sure it would fall an easy prey to him. (29) an cȩ̄ da̧ ka̧rē " tūwō yā yi yawa̧ a̧ gidam bi̧kī ", yā cȩ̄ " mu̧ ganī a̧ k̃as ! " seeing is believing. (30) aŋ k̃i ci̧ŋ ∽ aŋ kōmō an ci kwi̧kwīyo̧ straining at a gnat and catching a camel. (31) nā d'au̧ki ∽ doŋ haushi̧, yā kōmō, yanā̧ tu̧ŋkwu̧yī it was unsuitable for its purpose ; things turned out the reverse of what was expected. (32) hujja̧r mȩ̄, an cȩ̄ da̧ ∽ ya̧ d'au̧ki dami̧ why attempt the impossible ? (33) da̧ hannū a ka̧n saŋ girmā, a̧mmā bā̧ fad'a̧ yi̧ ∽ ba character

is shown by generosity, not by quarrelsomeness. (34) wai da̧ ga̧ŋgaŋ. an cȩ̄ da̧ ∽ Ma̧hammaŋ what an impossibility ! (35) ∽ yā zubar da̧ tsāmīyar kūrā, ya cȩ̄ " sǎi wani ji̧k̃wa̧ŋ " that won't be for many a long day ! (36) ∽ nā̧ naŋ, nā̧ kȩ̄wāya̧r k̃ashī state of indecision prevails. (37) kāshin turmī bā̧ na wa̧daŋ ∽ ba nȩ don't attempt what's beyond you ! (38) in da̧ a̧biŋka̧ anā̧ k̃au̧narka̧, in bābu̧ a̧biŋka̧ ∽ yā fī ka̧ only the rich are courted. (39) kula̧ kǎ̧i ∽ da̧ gudu̧n lahīyā he's too big for his boots (Vd. uku̧ 3b). (40) kōmē tsananin tā̧rā, ā̧ bar wa̧ d'am ma̧i gidā ∽ no smoke without fire ! (41) tūwaŋ k̃as na ∽ nȩ̄ = 40 (cf. tūwaŋ k̃asā). (42) bā ā̧ sani̧m murna̧r ka̧ran da̧ bā̧ shi da̧ wutsīya̧ destitute P. cannot realize his desires. (43) bā̧ kisa̧ŋ ∽ ba, ja̧ŋ to begin is one thing, to persevere, another. (44) an sa̧yi ∽ Vd. tsu̧gu̧nō. (45) a̧turȩ bā yā̧ raba̧ ∽ da̧ kūrā desperate affairs need desperate remedies. (46) k̃anaŋ ∽ Vd. būzū, farkē. (47) aŋ kōri ∽ Vd. wa̧yō 1b (cf. 3 above). (48) ∽ yā shā tāba̧ Vd. tāba̧ 2. (49) wā̧ za̧i gasa̧ wa̧ ∽ Vd. gadō 2b. (50) yā zarga̧ ka̧ransa̧ igīya̧ he's gone away. (51) ∽ ba̧i kwānā da̧ yu̧ŋwa̧ ba Vd. ganī A 2, 3b. (52) ajīyȩ ka̧raŋka̧ Vd. ajīyȩ 7b.ii. (53) kā fi ∽ gudu̧ Vd. a̧ bō̧k̃ara̧. (54) ∽ ba̧ ya̧ ci ∽ ba Vd. mara̧bī 2. (55) aŋ k̃i ci̧ŋ ∽ = damō 2. (56) ka̧ram Māguzāwā Vd. biri̧ 1b.ii. (57) ja̧ŋ ∽ Vd. haushī 3b. (58) ka̧ryar ka̧ntōma̧ Vd. ka̧ntōma̧, ka̧ryā. (59) ka̧ryar daŋgi Vd. a̧jūzā, ka̧ryā. (60) lā̧lā̧ta̧ ∽ Vd. bīyū 11. (61) ∽ ya̧ sā̧mu̧ ? Vd. kūrā 21. (62) tā̧ yi gu̧zurī da̧ ∽ Vd. kūrā 40. (63) bā ā̧ bā̧ ∽ dillanci̧ Vd. kūrā 53. (64) ∽ sǎi lȩ̄k̃ē Vd. kūrā 55. (65) a̧ljanna̧r ∽ Vd. tsa̧ka-tsaka̧. (66) āya̧r ∽ Vd. āya̧ 4. (67) Ba̧dau̧ri̧ŋ ∽ Vd. Ba̧dau̧rī. (68) dārīyar ∽ Vd. dārīyā 4. (69) malaka̧r ∽ Vd. malaka̧. (70) mōta̧r ∽ Vd. mōta̧ 2. (71) nōna̧ŋ ∽ Vd. nōno̧ 1k. (72) Vd. ka̧n ka̧rē, mūmi̧niŋ ka̧rē, Barka̧.

B. (karȩ) (1) Sk., Kt. (cerebral " r ", Vd. M.G. 5) (a) stalk (= karā q.v.). (b)

Vb. 3A (i) lost heart (= kạrai *q.v.*). (ii) snapped (= karyẹ *q.v.*). (2) (*rolled* " *r* ", *Vd.* M.G. 5) odds and ends (= liƙe-liƙē = tạrkạcē).

C. (kārẹ) *Vb.* 1A (1) guarded *x* kạrē ya kạŋ ~ gidā a dog protects a compound. (2) screened off *x* (*a*) zānā tā ~ magēwayī grass-mat screens off the latrine. aŋ ~ wuriŋ the place has been screened off. (*b*) yā kārẹ su gạ Kano it shut them off from Kano. (3) aŋ ~ shi he's been treated leniently (= kạrā 2*a*). (4) aŋ ~ dūtsạn niƙạ dạ mạgirkai the grinding-stone has been supported underneath with small stones. aŋ ~ ƙwaryā dạ ɗan dūtsẹ small stone's been put under calabash to steady it. (5) yā ~ ƙōfạ he put the door " to ".

D. (kārē) *m.* any gambling (= cācā).

ƙare A. (ƙārẹ) (1) *Vb.* 3A (*a*) is complete, is ready *x* aikị yā ~ the work is (was) complete. ạbincī yā ~ the food is cooked ready to eat (*cf.* 1*b*). (*b*) (i) has (had) come to an end *x* ạbincī yā ~ there's no more food (*cf.* 1*a*) = sārẹ 2*b*. (ii) yā ~ fat it is completely finished. (iii) is (was) worn out *x* wuƙā tā ~ the knife is worn out. (iv) Audu dū yā ~ Audu is as thin as a skeleton. (v) tā fạru, tā ~ *Vd.* damị 7. (vi) bā sạ jiŋ ƙārẹwā they are innumerable. (vii) ƙārẹwā mā dǎi finally. (viii) ƙārẹwā tạ yi ƙasạ *Vd.* bisạ 1*a*.iii. (ix) *Vd.* ƙārẹwā da ƙārō. (x) sǎi na mai gidā yā ƙārẹ *Vd.* ūdạ 1*b*. (xi) ƙạre dạ " wạllāhi " *Vd.* fạdā 1*g*. (2) *Vb.* 1A (*a*) finished *x* aŋ ~ aikị they've completed the work (= ƙārạsā 1*a*.i). (*b*) yā ~ su he killed them off. (*c*) yā ~ minị kallō he stared at me. (3) *Vd.* ƙạrẹ-compounds. (4) mai ~ ƙarfī *Vd.* zāwọ 3. (5) ƙạrẹ aikị *Vd.* gạrmā 1*a*.ii. (6) ƙārẹ jārin yārọ *Vd.* dạfūwā 1*d*. (7) tạ ~ kạŋkạ *Vd.* gayạ 5.

B. (ƙārē) *Vd.* ƙārā.

ƙārẹ aikị *used in* gạrmā ~ *epithet of* industrious P.

ƙārẹ daŋgi *m.* = ƙar daŋgi.

karēfatū shoulders of meat (*pl. of* karfạtā).

ƙārẹ kāmụ *m.* end, completion.

kạ're-kạrē‖ *m.* scolding (*derived from snapping of* " dog " kạrē), *cf.* karnak-ancī.

karēmanī profligates (*pl. of* karmā).

karen (kạran) (*genitive of* kạrē) (1) ~ ɓikī (*a*) jackal. (*b*) *Vd.* ạlbasạ 7. (2) ~ bazarā shuttle-cock (*made of pith of corn-stalk* (tōtụ̄wā) *and feathers*). (3) ~ fạrautạ hunting-dog. (4) ~ gānūwā = 8. (5) ~ marōƙā beggar's tout. (6) (*a*) ~ mōtạ driver's apprentice. (*b*) mōtạr kạrē *Vd.* mōtạ 2. (7) ~ ramạ (*a*) type of children's toy. (*b*) useless P. (8) ~ rārīyā (*a*) " pi-dog ". (*b*) *Vd.* rārīyā 2*b*. (9) ~ rūwā West African otter (*Aonyx pœnsis*).

ƙarērā *f.* part of stomach of ruminants.

ƙarērē lies (*pl. of* ƙaryā).

kạ̄rēre *m.* (1) acting *as in* kārạ 4. (2) aŋ ƙārạ masạ ~ he's been allotted small extra task. (3) an yi minị ~ I've been entrusted with commission to carry out on my way. nā yi makạ (= nā bā kạ) ~ zūwạ gạ Audu as you were going that way, I gave you errand to see to for me at Audu's (= sautụ).

ƙārẹwā dạ ƙārō *Kt.* = ƙāriwạllai 2.

karfạ *f.* (1) an yi masạ karfạr baƙạ a false charge has been brought against him. (2) charm to bring P. into disfavour *x* an yi matạ ~ charm has been set in motion to make her husband hate her.

ƙarfafa A. (ƙarfạfā) *Vb.* 1C (1) strengthened. (2) encouraged P. (3) urged *x* nā ~ masạ yạ yī I urged on him the necessity of doing it, I emphasized the importance of his doing it (= urincē 2). (4) emphasized *x* aŋ ƙarfạfạ lābāriŋ Kano the history of Kano was stressed, emphasized.

B. (ƙarfafā) *Vb.* 3B (*a*) became strong *x* zūcīyātā tā ~ I felt encouraged. (*b*) lābārị yā ~ the news proved true. (2) *Vb.* 2 forced *x* nā ƙarfạfē shi yạ yī I forced him to do it.

C. (ƙarfạfā) *Vd.* ƙaƙƙarfā.

ƙarfamfạnā *f.* = harkạ 2*a*, *b*.

karfasā *f.* (1) Cichlid perch (*Tilapia nilotica*) = gạrgazā. (2) *Nupe* ~ būƙū big type of perch.

karfashe *m.* = karfasā.

karfạtā *f.* (*pl.* kạrfatōcī = kạrfạtai = karēfatū = *Sk.* kạrfạttai) shoulder of meat (*cf.* kạ̄fadạ 2).

ƙarfę *m. (pl.* ƙarāfā = ƙarfuną = *Kt.* ƙaruffą)* (1) *(a)* (i) metal. (ii) ƙarāfū nę kawąi, bą ą gamą su ba tukunā they are mere pieces of metal not yet joined together. (b) dōkįŋ ∼ *m.* bicycle (= bāsukur). *(c)* baƙįŋ ∼ (i) iron. (ii) ą wurin Jāmus, sū duką baƙįŋ ∼ nē in the view of the Germans they are of inferior quality. (d) farįŋ ∼ zinc, tin, brass, etc. (e) jaŋ ∼ copper (= tagullā = gącī). (f) ƙarfąŋ hannū bangle, bracelet, armlet. (g) ƙarfąŋ ƙafą anklet (cf. 6 below). (h) ∼, lakā, itącē, gārī *epithet of* ɗan taurī (who breaks knives against his stomach). (j) ∼ ɗayā bā yą amō it takes two to make a quarrel ; remove the mote from your own eye ! (2) *(a)* (i) money. (ii) x ∼ uku three shillings. (b) (cry of beggars, i.e. marōƙā) mai ƙarfī, mai ∼, mai ƙarfįŋ halim bāyąrwā ! (3) o'clock (from beating iron-rods to indicate the time) x ∼ uku at three o'clock. ∼ uku dą rabį at 3.30. ∼ uku na ąsubą = ∼ uku na darē at 3 a.m. (4) wannąm magana ∼ cē this is perfectly true. (5) strong T. or P. x (a) Audu ∼ nē (i) Audu is a vigorous worker. (ii) Audu is stingy (epithet is ∼ mai ƙįn jiƙā = bidą ƙī tąŋƙwasą). (b) tsōfwā dą yārinyą, wātō ƙarfąŋ dą ta kātākwąŋ a crone and a girl, i.e. one fresh and one worn out. (6) ƙurjī yā yi masą ƙarfąŋ ƙafą he has ulcers round both ankles (cf. 1g above). (7) Vd. ƙarfę dą ∼. (8) ąllūrą ∼ cē Vd. ąllūrą 5. (9) mahūrįŋ ∼ Vd. yuŋwą 1a. (10) ƙarfąŋ askā Vd. tsaurī 1. (11) tsābar ∼ Vd. tsābą 2b.

ƙarfę dą ƙarfę x (1) hadirį yā kāmą ∼ the sky is black with thunder-clouds. (2) kōgī yā kāwō ∼ river's level with the banks. (3) fādą yā cika ∼ Chief's audience-chamber is packed.

ƙarfī *m.* (1) *(a)* strength x (i) yanā dą ∼ = yā yi ∼ he is strong. (ii) yā fārą ∼ = yā fārą yįŋ ƙarfī he's begun to become strong. (iii) mai ∼ *m., f. (pl.* māsū ∼) strong. (iv) bā mu dą sauraŋ hannū mai ∼ we have no more strength. (v) yā fi ƙarfinsą it's beyond him. (vi) bą su ji ƙarfin yinsą ba they did not feel

up to doing it. (vii) bą mu bā dą ∼ gą sāmunsą ba we did not exert ourselves to get it. (viii) săi ƙarfī ƙarfī sukę yį they are waxing stronger and stronger. (ix) anā ta yį ∼ dą ∼ they're doing it might and main (cf. ą rausą). (x) yā tārą ƙarfinsą wurī gudā he concentrated his troops in one place. suŋ hadą ∼ dą mū they joined forces with us. (b) (i) yā kāwō ∼ he's in his prime (20-30 years of age). (ii) yā kāwō ∼ he became strong. (c) (i) dą ∼ by force. (ii) yā ƙwąci kansą dą ∼ he behaved insubordinately. (iii) yā dībą dą ƙarfin hatsī = yā dībą dą ƙarfin tūwō he took it by force (Vd. tūrą 1a.ix. (d) dą ƙarfin yājį with all one's might. (e) fįŋ ∼ aką yi masą Vd. fįŋ ƙarfī. (2) reason x rashįŋ kudī, shī nę ƙarfin zūwąmmų shortage of money is our motive for coming. (3) maganar tanā dą ∼ this is important or serious. (4) (a) ąl'ādąn nąŋ tā yi ∼ yąnzu this custom is in vogue. (b) hatsī yā yi ∼ ą kąsūwā corn is scarce. (5) ƙaramįŋ ∼ gąrēshi he's not well off, he holds only a small position. (6) ƙarfįŋ halī = ƙarfin rąi = ƙarfin zūcīyā (a) (i) courage. (ii) bracing up one's courage. (b) yā tsayą dą ƙarfįŋ halī he resisted strongly. (7) (a) rashįŋ lāfīyą yā cī ƙarfinsą ill-health weakened him. (b) mun ci ƙarfįŋ aiki we've " broken the back of the work ". (c) yā yi aikį cįŋ ƙarfinsą he worked might and main. (d) an ci ƙarfinsą he's been held in an iron grip. (8) 'yar ∼ f. the cotton gwąndī. (9) sābaŋ ∼ Vd. badarę. (10) ∼ yā yi gidā Vd. gidā 1a.iv. (11) ƙarfįŋ gąbā Vd. bābę 3. (12) Vd. ƙarfę 2b. (13) Sarkiŋ ∼ Vd. yawą 4. (14) ąlāmąr ∼ Vd. hąlāmą 1c. (15) kim fi ƙarfin yārọ Vd. gabārą.

ƙarfīyaŋ = ƙaifīyaŋ.

ƙąrfū *Sk. m. (pl.* karfuną) tubular belt of leather or cloth (= gūrū).

ƙarfunā Vd. ƙarfę.

karfunā Vd. ƙąrfū.

ƙargagę *m.* (1) contrary P. (2) " bilker ".

ƙargąmē *Vb.* 3A stuck to, stuck in x ƙąshī yā ∼ minį ą wuyą the (fish)

bone stuck in my throat. **ƙaya̱ tā** ~ **mini̱ a̱ ri̱gā** the thorn stuck in my gown.
kargō (1) *m.* (*pl.* **karā̱gē**) (*a*) (i) tree *Bauhinia reticulata* (*bark used for rope : root for reddening women's lips: previously used as substitute for kola when dear : leaves used for wrapping foods* **gaudā** *and at Katsina* **kulē̱lę̄**). (ii) **dami̱ yā tsi̱ŋkę̱ a̱ gi̱ndi̱ŋ kargō** = **dā̱cē**. (*b*) slow-moving little boy is asked **kanā̱ sō̱ ka̱ hau dōki̱ŋ kargō̱?** and if he agrees, he is playfully flicked along with twig (= *Kt.* **dōki̱ŋ wuya̱**). (*c*) **aŋ kada̱ masa̱** ~ he's been frightened, intimidated (*Vd.* **kada̱** 1*m*). (2) **kargō** *m.* (*f.* **kargūwā** = **kargwā**) *pl.* **karā̱gē** brown (*re* donkey, pigeon, sheep) *x* **jā̱ki̱ŋ na̱ŋ** ~ **nē̱** this donkey's brown. **tuŋki̱yan na̱ŋ kargūwā cē̱** this sheep's brown. (*b*) **gunyā** ~ *m.* light bay horse.
ƙarhȩ *Kt. m.* metal = **ƙarfȩ** *q.v.*
ka̱rhū *Sk., Kt.* = **ka̱rfū**.
kari̱ *m.* (*derived from* **karya̱**; **karyȩ**) (1) frond of dum (**gō̱riba̱**) or deleb (**giginya̱**), *cf.* **kaba̱**; **kaŋkamȩ**; **ga̱zarī**. (2) (*a*) crease (*unintentionally made or from being ironed into crease x trousers*) (= **makarī** 2*a*). (*b*)*four* ~ (*i.e. folds of cloth*) *make up one* **ƙwaryā** *of the cloth* **sāƙi̱**, *thus* **nā sa̱yi sāƙi̱ ƙwaryā da̱yā da̱** ~ **bi̱yu** I bought 6 folds of **sāƙi̱**. (*c*) **yā kwa̱ntā** ~ **uku** he lay with his knees gripped up against his chest, to keep out the cold. (3) (*a*) profit *x* (i) **nā ci kari̱nsa̱** I benefited or made gain of money by it. (ii) **kā yā da̱** ~ you missed your chance. (*b*) **a̱ ka̱ŋ** ~ **ya zō** he came appositely, at the psychological moment (= **makarī** 2*b*). (*c*) **a̱ kari̱m banzā** inapposi̱tely, at the wrong moment. (*d*) **kari̱ŋ ka̱rē** (i) dirty trick (= **gayya̱**). (ii) belated arrival of P. one wished to help. (4) usage of word *x* (*a*) **kari̱nsa̱ yā zamā ka̱zā da̱ ka̱zā** it (word) is applied thus and thus (*speaker replacing* **ka̱zā** *and* **ka̱zā** *by actual examples*) (= **makarī** 2*c*). (*b*) **kari̱** = **kari̱m maganā̱** (i) idiom. (ii) proverb. (*c*) **kari̱ŋ wāƙa̱** text and rhythm of song. (5) the **tūwō** called **duŋgurȩ**. (6) (*a*)

yā yi mata̱ ~ he gave present to girl-dancer and she passed it on to the drummer. (*b*) **sun yi masa̱** ~ they (guests at wedding-feast, i.e. **bi̱ƙī**) gave him (bridegroom or eulogizing-beggar, i.e. **marō̱ƙī**) a present. (*c*) *Kt.* presents by bridegroom to bride on day of **bū̱da̱r ka̱i** (*they dancing together to drumming at* **la̱'asa̱r** *time*). (7) *after doing the ablutions-preceding-prayers* (**a̱lwa̱lā**), *if P. urinates, breaks wind, or defecates, this is* **ƙarami̱ŋ** ~ *and necessitates repetition of* **a̱lwa̱lā**, *as does involuntary ejaculation whether* **ma̱zīyyi̱** *or* **wa̱dīyyi̱**; *if, however, ejaculation is intentional* (**don ji̱n dādī**), *then this is* **ba̱bbaŋ** ~ *and complete bath* (**waŋkā**) *must be done before proceeding to pray* (*Vd.* **karya̱** 1*d*). (8) **kari̱ŋ ka̱lā̱cī** = **kari̱ŋ ku̱mallō** breakfast.
ƙari A. (**ƙārī**) *m.* odour of sour-flour, urine, or dirty P. (= **zārī** = **zarnī**), *cf.* **ƙannī**.
B. (**ƙa̱rī**) *m.* (1) increase, addition *x* (*a*) **an yi masa̱** ~ addition has been made to it. (*b*) **bugu̱ da̱ ƙāri̱ bā yā̱ bari̱ŋ ƙāto̱ tsa̱ye** persistence wins. (2) *Vd.* **kō̱gī** 1*e*.
C. (**ƙa̱ri**) *Vd.* **ƙa̱rā**.
D. (**ƙari̱**) *m.* (1) (*a*) sting possessed by bee, wasp, or scorpion. (*b*) **zāgi̱ bā yā̱ ƙari̱** abuse does not kill. (2) (*a*) ganglion. (*b*) **iŋ kā yi haka̱, sa̱i cībi̱ ya̱ zamā** ~ if you do so, there's no end to the hullabaloo that'll be raised. **ņ yi ma̱gana̱, cībi̱ ya̱ zamā ƙari̱?** why should I make matters worse by making a fuss?
ka̱rikiki̱ = **ka̱riƙiƙi̱** *adv.* *emphasizing weight x* **yanā̱ da̱ kāyā** ~ (1) he has heavy load. (2) he has swollen testicles (= **gwaiwā**).
kā̱riki̱tai *m.* odds and ends (= **karȩ** 2).
ka̱ri̱mbau *m.* eruption like 'yar rānī.
karimci̱ *m.* = **karamci̱**.
karimi A. (**ka̱rīmi̱**) *m.* (*f.* **ka̱rīmi̱yā**) *pl.* **ka̱rīmai** *Ar.* generous P.
B. (**kārimī**) *used in* **an ci kārimi̱nsa̱** he was held in iron grip.
kari̱ŋ *compounds Vd.* **kari̱**.
ƙāri̱ wa̱llāhi̱ = **ƙāri̱ wa̱lla̱i** (1) = **kalma̱'i̱ŋ**. (2) type of oath (*Vd.* **ƙārȩ̄wā**).

kariya A. (kārīyạ) *f.* screening off = ƙ̧ạrā 1, 2*a q.v.*

     B. (ƙ̧ārīyạ) (*Eng.* carrier) (1) **Ƙārīyạ shānuɳ gwamnạ** *epithet of* porter (*Vd.* (lēbụrạ). (2) **Ƙ̧ārīyạ** epithet of **Shạ̄makį.**

karkābụ *Kt. m.* falsely accusing P.

karkạce *Vb.* 3A (1) is (was) crooked. (2) swerved *x* **hanyạ tā** ∼ road deviates, is full of curves. **hanyạ tā** ∼, **tā yi kudụ** road bends off south. **Audụ yā** ∼ Audu is lax in religion. (3) made incorrect statement. (4) **hanyạn naɳ tā karkạcē wạ iriɳ halimmụ** this way of acting is contrary to our ways.

karkacįkkē *Vb.* 1D *Nor.* = **karkạcē.**

karkạdā *int. from* **kaɗạ.**

karkạdē *Vb.* 1C (1) shook off dust *x* **yā karkạɗẹ ƙụ̄rā dạgạ ṝgā** he shook dust off the gown (*Vd.* **kaɗẹ ; kakkạɓe**). (2) **yā** ∼ **kunnūwạnsạ** he pricked up his ears.

ƙ̧ạrƙādọ *m.* Preuss's cliff-swallow (= **ƙabdōdọ** 2 *q.v.*).

ƙ̧ạrƙaf *x* **yā kārẹ** ∼ it's completely finished.

*****karkạndạ** = **karkạndạm** *f.* (*Ar.* **karkaddan**) rhinoceros.

ƙar-ƙar *Kt.* = **ƙwar-ƙwar.**

kar-kar *Vd.* **kar-kar-kar.**

karkara A. (kạrkarā) *f.* (1) inhabited area near city. (2) **yā yi wạ kạnsạ** ∼ he made a reputation for himself. (3) **dawạɳ wani, kạrkarar wani** people differ in ability or knowledge (*cf.* **dōkạ** 1*e*).

     B. (karkạrā) *Vb.* 1C *Kt.* = **kaɳkạrē** 1, 2.

ƙ̧ạrƙara A. (ƙ̧ạrƙārạ) (ƙ̧ạrƙārạ) *f.* (1) the very thorny *Acacia campylacantha* (*yields gum*) = **ƙụmbā** 4. (2) *Vd.* **kạrkī.**

     B. (ƙ̧ạrƙārā) *m., f.* (*pl.* **ƙ̧ārg̣rā**) stinking (*Vd.* **ƙ̧ārį**).

karkare A. (karkạrē) *Kt.* = **kaɳkạrē.**

     B. (kạrkạrē) *Kt.* = **kaɳkạrē.**

     C. (karkarẹ) *Kt.* (1) = **kaɳkarẹ.** (2) **kā ci gụdā dạ** ∼ = **ƙạrugāgī.**

ƙ̧ạrƙarfā = **ƙạ̧ƙƙarfā.**

ƙ̧ạrƙarī *m.* (1) eagerness. (2) trying to get T.

kar-kar-kar *x* **jikinsạ yā ɗạụki** ∼ he began to tremble violently.

karkarwạ *f.* trembling.

ƙ̧ạrƙas A. (ƙạrƙas) *adv.* underneath.

     B. (ƙạrƙas) *adv.* a little lower *x* **sạ̄ shi** ∼ put it a little lower down !

karkạshē *Vb.* 1C *int. from* **kashẹ.**

ƙ̧ạrƙashī (1) *m.* (*a*) under-side. (*b*) **iɳ kā tōnạ ƙ̧ạrƙashinsạ** if you investigate it. (*c*) **ƙ̧ạrƙashin zūcīyarsạ yanạ̄ sọ̄** he wishes from the bottom of his heart to. . . . (2) *adv.* underneath. (3) **ƙ̧ạrƙashin** *prep.* (*a*) under. (*b*) **Kano tanạ̄ ƙ̧ạrƙashiɳ ƙafāfūwạnsụ** Kano is trampled underfoot by them. **munạ̄ ƙ̧ạrƙashin tạ̄kạlminsụ** we're in their power.

karkashī *m.* (1) the herb Ceratotheca sesamoides whose leaves are used for soup (= **yauɗō**), *Vd.* **nōmẹ** 3, **rīdī.** (2) *Vd.* **tạwadạ** 3.

karkata A. (karkạtā) (1) *Vb.* 3A = **karkạcē** 1, 2. (2) *Vb.* 1C (*a*) (i) twisted T. out of shape. (ii) caused to swerve *x* **suɳ karkatō kunnūwạnsụ gạ saụrāraɳ kūkammụ** they've turned their attention to our complaints. (*b*) swerved towards, veered towards *x* (i) **hanyạ tā** ∼ **kudụ** the road bends off south. (ii) **mụ karkatō Masạr** let us turn our attention to Egypt !

     B. (kạrkatạ) *Vb.* 3B (1) = **karkạcē** 1, 2. (2) **yā** ∼ **kạmar zại dōƙē nị** he stood with body flexed to strike me. (3) swerved *x* (*a*) **hanyạ tā** ∼ **zūwạ kudụ** the road veers south. (*b*) **zūcīyassạ tā** ∼ **kan saɳ kudī** he's eager for money. (*c*) **sunạ̄ kallō, su ga ịndạ ƙ̧ại-ƙ̧ại zại** ∼ they're " waiting to see which way the cat jumps " (*Vd.* **ƙ̧ại-ƙ̧ại**).

karkatad dạ *Vb.* 4B caused to deviate, caused to swerve.

kạrkāzạ *m.* industrious P.

ƙ̧ạrƙē *Vb.* 1C *Nor.* finished (= **ƙ̧ārẹ**).

kạrkī *Kt. m.* = **ƙ̧ạrƙārạ** (*epithet is* ∼ **bạ̄ hawā dạ kilābụ**).

kạrkīyā *f.* (1) forked stick in which is fixed (*a*) neck of led dog, (*b*) horse's neck to prevent it biting galled back, (*c*) neck of prisoners or travelling slaves (*epithet of* 1*a is* ∼ **lạ̄lātạ kạrē,** *cf.* **lālātā** 1*c*). (2) forked stick put lengthwise between knees of newly circumcised boy *x* **an yi masạ̄** ∼ .

ƙ̧arƙō *m.* (1) durability *x* **yā yi** ∼ it gives long service. **bạ̄ yạ̄** ∼ it is not a durable article. (2) munạ saņ ƙarƙwan dabīnọ, bạ ƙarƙwaŋ gạbạrūwā ba all's well that ends well (*for dates are first bitter, then on ripening, become sweet, while gạbạrūwā follows the opposite process*). (3) mụmmūnaŋ ~ ạ yi ƙarƙwaŋ kīfī, dạgạ rūwā sǎi wutā all's bad that ends badly. (4) Allạ yạ fisshē kạ tsakạ mại wụyā, bạ ƙarƙō ba, ƙarƙō may you always remain virtuous ! (5) ƙarƙwan rūwā, kwarị the evil come to a bad end. (6) ƙarƙwantạ gambạ *Vd.* ạlgabbạ 2.

karmā (1) *m.* (*pl.* karẹ̄manī = karạ̄mē) (*a*) infantryman in pre-Administration days (= dạ̄kārẹ 1). (*b*) **Sarkin ~** = sātī 1. (2) *m.*, *f.* (*pl. as in* 1) profligate P. (3) *m.* profligacy *x* **yanạ** ~ he's profligate. (4) ɗaŋ ~ *m.* professional wrestler.

karmạɗā *Vb.* 1C bent over (tip of knife, etc.) = kalmạɗā *q.v.*

***Ƙạrmāmạ** *used in* zāmạniŋ ~ in the time of the great famine Karmama (*N.B.— This expression is only vaguely understood*).

karmāmī *m.* (1) leaves of dāwạ *or* gērō, these not being saleable, as is hạrāwạ (**karmāmin dāwạ** *is eaten by cows and donkeys*; **karmāmiŋ gērō** *is made into ash for* cụ̄sā *of horse*). (2) stunted corn-plants (= 'ya'y'yạ̄wā) useful only for horse or donkey fodder (= gạmsạyī). (3) **Karmāmī, kā dạ gīwā** = ~ kā dạ gīwa thou David who hast overcome a Goliath !

karmancị (1) *m.* profligacy. (2) 'yaŋ **karmancị** *m.* being a professional wrestler (*Vd.* karmā 4).

kạrmạndōsō *m.* wastrel.

ƙarmanjē *m.* trouble.

***karmantakō** *m.* sulphur (= kalmuntakō *q.v.*).

ƙarmạshē *Vb.* 3A became emaciated.

karmatsa A. (**karmạtsā**) *Vb.* 1C (1) yā karmạtsạ aikị he did work hastily and badly. (2) yā karmạtsạ rụbụ̄tū he wrote badly cramped hand-writing (*cf.* cụ̄shē).

B. (**kạrmatsạ**) *Vb.* 2 unexpected event " flummoxed " P. *x* zūwạm bạ̄ƙī yā kạrmạtsē nị unexpected arrival of guests " flummoxed " me (= fịrmitsạ).

kạrmạtsē *m.* (1) hurried, careless work.

(2) badly cramped writing (*cf.* cụ̄shē, matsạ 1*b*).

ƙarmō (1) desiccated fruit on tamarind (tsāmīyā) or kanyạ tree (= ƙaŋƙamō). (2) **Ƙarmō ɗan tsāmīyā, kā nụ̄na, kā ƙi fāɗụ̄wā** *epithet of* miser.

karmụntā = kalmụntā.

karnạ *f.* (1) cord used by Arabs for tying up loads. (2) *such* cord covered with leather for stirrup-leathers.

kạrnai *Vd.* kạrē.

karnakancī = karnikancī = karnukancī (1) quarrelsomeness. (2) profligacy (*the word is d.f.* karnukạ " dogs "), *cf.* kạre-kạrē.

karnēnē *m.* yā yi minị ~ he kept T. I had lent him.

karnī *m.* (1) inside white-layer of hide or skin (*cf.* fuskā). (2) **an ci karninsạ** meat has been scraped off dressed hide.

karnikancī *Vd.* karnakancī.

karnukạ *Vd.* kạrē.

karnukancī *Vd.* karnakancī.

karo A. (**karọ**) *m.* (1) (*a*) (i) collision *x* **yā ci ~ dạ sū** he collided with them, met them unexpectedly, came to blows with them (= rạbsagọ). **yā ci ~ dạ sā'ạ** he was lucky. (ii) attack, onslaught, charge, battle, campaign. (iii) ~ **ɗayā kō dạ tọraŋ gīwā ạ bugạ** there's no harm in trying everything once. (iv) *Vd.* tạ̄rō 3. (v) **anạ karaŋ gạskīyā dạ gạskīyā** = anạ karaŋ gaggā dạ ƙaggā = anạ karạm mazā dạ mazạ̄jē a mighty struggle is in progress. (*b*) ~ **dạ gōmạ, kạ̄lạcin sāfē** what a mighty warrior ! (2) **karaŋ dūtsẹ sǎi dạwayạ** = karaŋ dūtsẹ bạ dạwayạ discretion is the better part of valour. (3) **karạm battạr ƙarfẹ** struggling together of two strong men. (4) ~ **sǎi rạ̄gō dạ rạ̄gō, ɗaŋ ạkwīyạ bạ zại īyạ ba** don't fight against impossible odds ! *(5) male-camel (*only used in translating Arabic* fahl). (6) **Karọ** name for any man called Bạ̄ƙo (*Vd.* Dārārī). (7) **ƙạfaŋ karọ** *Vd.* ƙạfō 8. (8) **mại wụyar karọ** *Vd.* bana 1*c.* (9) **yā ci karọ dạ turmī** *Vd.* ayyạhạhạ.

B. (**kāro**) *m.* (1) = ƙạrērẹ 2, 3. (2) parents' entrusting bringing up of child to another (*cf.* tallạfī). (3) owner's entrusting animal to be reared in another's care.

C. (ƙạ̄rō) *m.* (1) " whip-round "
(= jūcē *q.v.*). (2) da ∽ gı̄wā tā fi
kōwā ƙibạ *Vd.* jūcē 2. (3) *Nor.* an
sạ̈ musụ ∽ tax has been imposed on
them (= harājị̣).

ƙārō *m.* (1) (*a*) gum (= *Sk.* jı̣̄rǎi). (*b*)
sun tạfi cị̣ṇ ∽ they've gone out collecting gum. (2) *angry retort to* ƙạ̈bạrạ
q.v. (3) *cf.* ƙārę̈wā dạ ∽; ƙāraṇ ƙạ̈bạ.

karōfı̄ *m.* (*pl.* kạrǫ̈fai). (1) dye-pit (*cf.*
rạndā 4). (2) daṇ kạṇ ∽ cover for dye-
pit (= *Kt.* majicı̄ = *Sk.* daṇ kụtuƀı̣̣).
(3) *cf.* tsāmı̄yā 4. (4) karōfị̣ṇ gyartai
Vd. mụfallashı̄.

ƙạ̄rō-ƙạ̄rō = ƙạ̄rō.

karǫn battạr ƙarfę̈ *Vd.* karǫ 3.

ƙarǫ̈rā *f.* mere stalks of beans after all
leaves gone.

kạrsanā *f.* (*pl.* kạrsạnū = karsanōnı̄). (1)
heifer (*i.e.* virgin cow). (2) am fakę̈
dạ guzumā, aṇ hạrbi ∽ reference was
made to P. by innuendo, using another
P. as mere blind.

Kạrsanı̄ *used in songs, as laudatory
epithet of* Chief.

kạrsạshı̄ *m.* (1) rejoicing. (2) handsome
appearance.

ƙạrshē *m.* (1) end *x* ƙạrshaṇ (= ạ̈ ƙạrshaṇ)
watạ at end of the month. (2) on last
occasion of *x* ƙạrshan zūwạnsạ the
last time he came here. (3) *x* ƙạrshaṇ
ạbị̣ṇ, yạ tsayạ tı̄lạs finally he's forced
to halt. (4) na ∽ *m.* (*f.* ta ∽) *pl.*
na ∽ final *x* mạganạd dạ ya yi ta
ƙạrshē his last speech. (5) tip *x* ƙạrshaṇ
Ạfirkạ the tip of Africa.

karta A. (kartạ) (1) *Vb.* 1A scraped *as in*
karcę̈ *q.v.* (2) *Vb.* 3A. (*a*) cikị̣na yanạ̄
kartạ̈wā I have gripes (*cf.* ƙullę̈ 2).
(*b*) yā ∽ dạ gudụ he fled. (3) *Eng. f.*
(*a*) playing-cards. (*b*) card-playing.

B. (ƙạrtā) (1) *Vb.* 2 (*p.o.* kạrcē,
n.o. kạrci) scraped *as in* karcę̈. (2)
f. (*a*) cikị̣na yanạ̄ ∽ I have gripes.
māgạnin nạṇ ∽ gạ̈rēshị̣ this medicine
gives one the gripes (*cf.* ƙullę̈ 2). (*b*)
kạrtaƙ ƙasā (i) excited pawing or
scraping up of ground by angry animal.
(ii) impatient eagerness (hạṇƙōrō).
(*c*) type of implement for teasing
raw cotton (shiƀạ̈). (*d*) competition,
rivalry (= gạ̄sā).

C. (kartā) *f.* = kạrtā 2*a.*

ƙạrtā *Vd.* ƙạ̄tǫ̈.

ƙạrtaf yā ƙạ̄rę̈ ∽ it's completely finished.

kartājı̣̄yā *f.* integument of corn-stalk
(= tsirgạ̄gı̣̄yā).

kartakạrā *f.* the gum tree tạraunı̄yā.

kartakēkę̈ = kartakı̄ *m.* (*f.* kartakē-
kı̣̄yā) *pl.* kartakai-kạrtạ̈kạị̈ huge.

kạrtaƙ ƙasā *Vd.* kạrtā 2*b.*

ƙạrtap = ƙạrtaf.

Kạrtau *epithet of* dauntless farmer.

kạrtūshị̣ *m.* (*sg., pl.*) cartridge (*cf.* kạ̈msị̣r).

ƙạ̄ru *Vb.* 3B (1) increased *x* mutạ̄nē suṇ ∽
people have become more numerous.
aikị̣ yā ∽ amount of work has increased.
sǎi ƙarı̄ kę̈ ƙạ̄rūwā gạrēmụ wajan sōjạ
our strength in soldiers goes on growing
(*cf.* ƙạ̄rạ). (2) made progress *x* (*a*)
nā ∽ I've benefited (by tuition, in-
formative talk, etc.). (*b*) muṇ ∽ dạ
lạ̈bāri we've received some news. (*c*)
yā ∽ dạ sha'anōnị̣ṇ ƙasammụ he became conversant with, familiar with the
affairs of our country. (*d*) sun yi ƙạ̄rūwā
they have made progress. (*e*) wannạṇ
duk ƙạ̄rūwā nę̈ all this is progress. (*f*)
yā ∽ dạ kudı̄ he became richer.

ƙaruffạ̈ metals (*pl. of* ƙarfę̈ *q.v.*).

kạ̈rugạ̄gı̣̄ *epithet of* glutton.

kạrumƀạ̈ *f.* struggle, collision.

kạ̄rụmē *Vb.* 1C = ƙạ̄lumạ.

kạ̄rụme-kạ̄rụmē = ƙạ̄lụme-ƙạ̄lụmē.

Kārūnạ *Ar.* (1) man known for generosity
(*such as was the Arab of that name in
Arabic literature*). *(2) daṇ ∽ *m.* type
of okro.

kạ̄rūrūmạ̈ *f.* (1) mere rumour. (2) (*a*)
kạ̄rūrūmạr mutạ̄nē mixed crowd, crowd
of idlers. (*b*) kạ̄rūrūmạr mātā crowd of
harlots.

kārūwạ (1) *m.* thief (*also* baƙị̣ṇ ∽). (2)
m., f. (*pl.* kạ̄rūwai). (*a*) profligate man.
(*b*) harlot (*epithet is* tsụmmā, maƙunsar
cụ̈tā) = gạrkūwā 3*d.* (*c*) kārūwạ ƀạ̄
kudị̣ṇ kōko *Vd.* jạgạlam. (3) haƙōrị̣ṇ ∽
m. (*a*) staining two upper or two lower
incisors. (*b*) black grain among other
light grains on maize-cob. (4) what a
self-controlled man of the world !

ƙạ̄rūwā *Vd.* ƙạ̄ru.

kạ̄rūwai *Vd.* kārūwạ.

kārūwancı̣ *m.* (1) profligacy, harlotry.

(2) Audu ~ gareshi Audu is self-controlled.
karwā *Vd.* minya 2.
karwayā *Vb.* 1C = kaurayā.
karya A. (ƙaryā) (1) *f.* (*a*) bitch (*cf.* ƙarē). (*b*) *Vd.* karyar-*compounds.* (*c*) harlot. (*d*) termagant. (*e*) fracture of limb *x* ~ tasa bā ta ɗōri ba cē his fracture is not settable (*cf.* 2). (2) *Vb.* 2 (*a*) snapped T. off *x* yā karyi gōro he broke off a piece of kola. (*b*) sun karyar masa arahā they sold it to him cheaply (= karya 17 = karyad da). B. (karya) *Vb.* 1A. (1) (*a*) (i) snapped T. across (*cf.* fasa). (ii) an ~ musu ƙafar gudu they are prevented from fleeing. (iii) kalmōmī irim māsū ~ wuya expressions which demolish a person's case, which confound him. (iv) lābārin nan yā ~ shi this news discouraged him. (v) sun yi su ~ mu they did their best to smash us. (vi) ba su ~ ƙarfimmu ba they could not make us give ground. (vii) karyayyar ƙōta deposed P. giving trouble to his successor. (*b*) sun ~ linzāmi they took to their heels. (*c*) yā ~ alkāwarī he broke his promise (*Vd.* alkāwarī 1g). (*d*) (i) yā ~ azumī he violated the Fast of Ramadan and must expiate this by ƙafāra if done deliberately (*cf.* shā E.2*a*; gyandai; gilmi 2). (ii) yā ~ addīni he offended against religion. (iii) yā ~ lāya he did an act which invalidated his magic charm (*cf.* ritsē, kari 7). (*e*) kā ~ shi (i) you sold it at a knock-down price when hard pressed for ready cash (= tanƙwarā 2), *cf.* 17 *below*; karyad da; arahā 1*c.* (ii) you squandered his substance. (*f*) folded *x* kā ~ takardā look, you've bent over the edge of the paper. yā ~ zane uku he folded the cloth into three. (2) yā ~ baƙi he made a mistake in speech or writing. (3) bāwa yā ~ fansā *Vd.* fansā 1*b.* (4) tā ~ fatala she did karyē. (5) sun ~ gari they took the town by storm. (6) yā ~ gāshi = yā ~ gāshin tsūlīyā (*a*) he borrowed (with or without leave) another's horse or donkey and went for a ride (*cf.* gwājē). (*b*) *Vd.* tsīyā 1*b, c.* (7)

yā ~ gindī (*a*) he shook his loins suggestively in dancing (= gwātso). (*b*) he acted shamelessly *x* yā ~ gindī yā cī he (boy who jibbed at going errand to bring his mother ingredients for food) was so shameless that when invited to eat, he did so unashamed. (8) (*a*) yāro yā ~ gwīwa the baby lad is trying to crawl. (*b*) yā ~ gwīwa he reduced the price. (*c*) *Vd.* karya gwīwa. (9) yā ~ haƙōrā he has shed his milk-teeth (= famfara). (10) *Vd.* hātimī 2. (11) (*a*) yā ~ kai yā yi tafīya tasa he refused and went on his way. (*b*) cīwo yā ~ kai the illness has passed its crisis (11 = karai da kai). (12) sun ~ karā they've quarrelled. (12*a*) yā ~ kumallō he breakfasted. (13) yā ~ kusurwā he turned the corner (= kwana). (14) *Kt.* yā ~ kwībi, yā bugan he flexed his body to strike me. (15) (*a*) kada ka ~ māganī sai gōbe do not, by taking food, spoil the effects of the medicine, till to-morrow! (*b*) yā ~ dafi it was an antidote to the poison (*cf.* makarī). (16) (*a*) sun ~ tsinkē *Vd.* tsinkē 1*b, c.* (*b*) yā karyō tumu he got syphilis. (17) yā ~ masa wuri he sold it at a knock-down price (= karyad da), *cf.* 1*e above.* (18) yā ~ 'yanci he behaved scandalously. (19) veered off *x* yā ~ yā yi kudu he turned off south (= ƙarkata). (20) alkarya sai an ~ *Vd.* alkarya 2. (21) ~ dāgumī *Vd.* dāgumī 4. (22) ~ gadō *Vd.* bōsarā. (23) yā ~ hannunsa *Vd.* raƙwas 24. (24) *Vd.* jallī 2. (25) *Vd. compounds of* karya. (26) *cf.* kari.
ƙaryā *f.* (*pl.* ƙarērē = ƙarairai = *Kt.* ƙarairayī = ƙaryacē-ƙaryacē). (1) (*a*) (i) lie (= yanƙē 1). (ii) *epithet is* zūƙi tā mallaƙi. (iii) jawābin ~ ba? naturally, it's a lie isn't it? (iv) yana shāra musu ƙarairai he's feeding them with lies. (v) ~ ta shēkara ~, gaskiyā tana matsayinta truth prevails finally. (*b*) yā yi (= yā shā = yā yanƙa) ~ he told a lie. yā yi (= yā yanƙa) mini ~ (i) he told me a lie. (ii) he lied against me. (*c*) na ~ *adj. m.* (*f.* ta ~) *pl.* na ~ false, imitation. (*d*) (i) ƙaryarka tā shā (= tā yi) ƙaryā =

ƙaryarḳ tā shā kāshī be sure your crime (lie) will recoil on you ! (ii) kōwā ya yi ƙaryar darē, g̣arī ỵā wāỵe murder will out. (e) gidaŋ ∽ m. this world (cf. g̣askīyā 7). (f) kōwā ya yi ∽, na gidā ỵā zō = rāmịŋ ∽ ƙurarrē n̤e a lie is soon detected. (g) ji ƙaryar banzā what a lie ! (h) ƙaryar ƙīrị ta ṃại cē = (said by women) ƙaryar r̤ạƙumī ta zūẉa Asbịn cē, ̣ammā ḅa zại jē Gẉanjā ba = ƙaryar kaḍa ta rūwā c̤ē, in yā fitō tuḍu, yā zamā nāṃa the absence of one essential factor renders the whole thing useless (cf. kaŋgarwā). (j) kōwā ya ṃantā ụbaŋgijịŋ ∽, shī ya yī ṭa if anyone tells you he forgets who told him some lie, be sure he invented it himself. (k) ∽ akē̤ yị, tūṣa bā t̤ā hūṛa wutā don't lean on a broken reed! (l) ƙaryar azzịkī shịgar rụmbuŋ ayā ḍa igīỵa it's beyond him, but he doesn't realize it. (m) Vd. kā fi ƙaryā. (n) ḳadādar ƙaryā Vd. wai 2b. (o) kōwā yan̤ā ḍa ∽ Vd. ḅabba 2d. (p) rānā bā t̤ā ƙaryā Vd. rānā 4c.ii. (q) māg̣anịŋ ∽ Vd. ḥallaṛa 1b. (2) ∽ g̣arēshị (a) he makes himself out to be richer than he is (by aping superiors, giving lavish presents, etc.) (b) he's a liar. (c) the statement is false. (3) (a) the pink-flowered shrub Adenium Honghel (called " lie " because useless). (b) its epithet is ∽ fụrē takē̤ yị, bā ṭa 'yā'yā.

karyad ḍa Vb. 4B (1) yā ∽ shī he sold it at a knock-down price (= karỵa 17, 1e.i, ḳaryā 2b). (2) ∽ k̤ại = karỵa 11.

ḳarỵa g̣arī epithet of brave warrior.

ḳarỵa g̣armā epithet of any hard-rooted plant.

ḳarỵa gwīẉa epithet of any calf = ṃaraƙī (Vd. karỵa 8).

ḳarỵa k̤ạfaḍa used in tā yi ∽ she hung the silken cord sịllīỵa round her neck.

ḳarỵa ƙashī epithet of horseman's servant.

karyakō used in fushinṣa yā ∽ his anger's cooled (= hūc̤e).

karyar ḍa = karyad ḍa.

Ḳarỵa rānā epithet of muezzin (l̤āḍaŋ).

ḳaryar daŋgi Vd. ̣ajūzā.

ḳaryar daẉa f. hyena (= kūrā).

ḳaryar gulai (1) mischief-making woman. (2) shameless female-slave (kụyaŋg̣a).

ḳaryar ḳantōṃa f. harlot.

ƙaryata A. (ƙarỵatā) Vb. 1C. (1) disbelieved. (2) (a) contradicted. (b) yā zamā ƙ̣arỵaṭa bōkā he is one who falsifies predictions. B. (ƙarỵaṭa) Vb. 3B x l̤ābārị yā ∽ the news proved false.

ḳarỵa ṭambaỵa m. (1) counter-charm (cf. ṭambaỵa 2 ; māg̣anī 2 ; lāỵa ; sammụ). (2) = sḥā ḍādaḷa.

ḳaryayyē m. (f. ḳaryayyīyā) pl. ḳarỵayyū adj. (1) snapped off. (2) ḳaryayyīyar ƙōṭa deposed P. thorn in side of his successor.

karye A. (kary̤e) Vb. 3A. (1) yā ∽ it (limb, stick) snapped (for thread, rope Vd. tsiŋk̤e), cf. cir̤e 2a, fash̤e. yā ∽ ƙal (= ƙ̣al) it snapped snap ! (2) = ḳarai except ƙ̣arai 3 x zūcīyasṣa tā ∽ he lost heart. (3) kudịnṣa suŋ ∽ his wealth's vanished. (4) baƙī yā ∽ mistake in writing or speaking has been made. (5) lāỵa zā ṭa ∽ amulet will become invalid. ̣alẉalā tā ∽ ceremonial ablutions became void (as e.g., by karị 7). (6) Vd. karyō. B. (ḳary̤e) m. woman's tying round her head a kerchief (f̤ataḷa) made into narrow band.

karyō used in (1) Kt. jịɓī yā ∽ perspiration broke out on P. (2) Vd. tuṃu 3.

kas (1) bother ! (= kash). (2) adv. ỵā yi farī ∽ it's snow-white. yā ẉanƙu ∽ it's specklessly washed. (3) (abbreviation of kash̤e) x (a) ḳashē shi tum bại kas ḳa ba kill it before it kills you ! (b) yā kad ḍatsī he took to his heels. (c) (i) nā ∽ ɓāƙī I've completed my work. (ii) kuɓē̤wā tā ∽ ɓāƙī the okro ceased fruiting. (iii) ṃagaṇa tā ∽ ɓāƙī the matter is settled. (iv) Vd. kash̤e 5. (d) yā ∽ (= yā kats) tsakā he got a bargain, he was lucky (= g̣amō). (e) aŋ ∽ rūwa, laŋg̣a tā mutụ Vd. rūwā K. (f) banzā tā ∽ ẉo̤ĩ, ɗaŋ kōlị yā kash̤e ḍillāli Greek met Greek. (g) Vd. kash̤e. (h) ḳas k̤ạfaḍa Vd. dụnji. (j) kas tsāmī Vd. kaŋwā 1d. (k) ḳat tākalṃa Vd. Ḅaṛarō, kata, fata-fata 2. (l) kas kād̤o Vd. kaskamī. (m) kōwā ya ∽ kīfī Vd.

gōrā 1*j*.　(*n*) ƙas madafīyā *Vd.* ƙulū.
(*o*) *Vd.* kan, kar, kash, ƙad digãdigī, ƙad
dafi, ƙas kaifī, ƙajjiƙī, ƙan ni ƙa ga
Sarkī, ƙan ni ƙa tūɓe, ƙas gwīwa, ƙas
gaushi, ƙas garwāshī, ƙas-ƙas.
ƙas A. (ƙas) *abbreviation of* ƙasa) *x* (1)
nã gan shi a ～ I saw it on the ground.
(2) aƙwīya kudiŋ ～ cē a goat com-
mands a ready sale.　(3) mu ganī a ～
Vd. tūwō 21.　(4) *Vd.* ƙad da bis.
(5) mai kāshī a ～ *Vd.* maurǫ.　(6)
tūwaŋ ƙas *Vd.* tūwō 15, tūwaŋ ƙasā.
(7) *Vd.* ƙasā, ƙas-ƙas.
　　B. (ƙas) yā karye ～ it snapped snap !
kasa A. (kasa) (1) *Vb.* 1A.　(*a*) (i) arranged
in small heaps (kashi).　(ii) yā ～ su
kashi-kashi he arranged them (ground-
nuts, etc.) in small piles for sale.　(iii)
sunã naŋ, ba a ～ da sū ba it is none of
their business.　(iv) haŋkalinsa yā
ƙasu he's bewildered.　(*b*) yā ～ ya
tsare (i) he (ɗaŋ kōli) is exposing his
wares and awaiting customers to come
and ask the price (*cf.* talla).　(ii) he's
waiting his chance.　(*c*) nã ～ wa mai
rīgā sule gōma I held out ten shillings
to seller of gown to take or leave without bargaining.　aŋ ～ mini awalaja cash
was proffered me (seller), to take or
leave.　(*d*) = kashe 2.　(*e*) (i) yā ～ kunnē
he pricked up his ears (= jī 3).　(ii) ƙasa
idǫ take a sharp look at it !　(2) *Vb.* 3A.
(*a*) rānã tā ～ sun is low on the horizon.
(*b*) dara tā ～ the game of draughts is
won and over.　(*c*) yā ～ yā yi yammā
he turned off westwards.　(*d*) yā ～ a
guje he took to his heels.
　　B. (kāsa) (1) *Vb.* 3A.　(*a*) fell short
(in amount, capability, ability to finish
task or journey, etc.) = sāre 2*a* =
rafƙe 1*b* = gaza = rasa 1.　(*b*) (garment)
wore out. (2) *Vb.* 1A is (was) unable to do
x (*a*) yā ～ numfāshī he was unable to
breathe (*Vd.* kāsa ganī).　(*b*) kā kāsa
ɗaukar ƙwãyā *Vd.* dami 5 ; tsīruƙu.
(*c*) yā kāsa ƙunda *Vd.* tsInī 1*b*.　(3)
m., *f.* (*without pl.*).　(*a*) one's inferior in
ability, etc.　(*b*) one's junior *x* nī
kāsansa nē I am junior to him in rank
(= kāshi 1).
　　C. (kāsa) *f.* (1)　puff-adder.　(2)
falkãwar ～ *f.* being wise after the

event.　(3) kūkaŋ ～ *m.* sound made
when clearing throat of bit of kola-nut.
　　D. (kāsā) *f.* (*sg.*, *pl.*) rough, woollen
Timbuctoo blanket (= saƙalā).
ƙasa A. (ƙasā) *f.* (1) (*a*) earth, soil (*cf.*
ƙasa).　(*b*) yā ci ～ he did humble
obeisance (= hurwā).　(*c*) ～ kē kirãna
I'm doomed. (*d*) (i) farar ～ whitewash.
(ii) yā shāfa farar ～ jikim baŋgō he
whitewashed the wall. (*e*) duk magana tā
jā ～ " it's all moonshine ".　(*f*) ～
cē ta kai (= ta kāwō) shi he died abroad
(*Vd.* ajalī 2*c*).　(*g*) (i) sun tãru ƙamar ～
they've gathered in crowds.　(ii) yā
yiwu ?　ī, tamfad da ～ can it be done ?
(*reply*, yes, as easy as winking).　(iii)
" ƙaman da ～ " n ji mai cīwaŋ idǫ
why, of course !　(*h*) (i) an tãra masa ～
Vd. tãra 1*a*.iii.　(ii) *Vd.* tãra ～.　(*j*)
ban yi ～ a gwīwū ba " I didn't let the
grass grow under my feet ".　(*k*) kūrā
tā wuce, ～ aka zãgā back-biting a
person.　(*l*) ～ ta gudu, ta jē inã P.
and his nature are inseparable.　(*m*)
ƙafa ita ƙan kāwō ～ a tãbarmā someone must have done it, for things don't
do themselves !　(*n*) bā ā tsayãwā sãi
da ～ = ƙafa bā tã zamā inda bābu ～
nobody can realize his desires till the
chance offers.　(*o*) wanda duk kē bisa
～ everyone in the world.　(*p*) an tila
masa ～ a idō he has received a curt
refusal, been humiliated.　(*q*) Jāmus
sun dēbi ƙasā, sun rike a hannū, sunã
cēwā " duk dūnīyan naŋ, ban zāɓe ba "
the Germans have challenged the whole
world to fight (*person takes handful of
earth plus some of his spittle, turns and,
with his hand behind his back, says*
taŋkwaɓe !　*If the other knocks it out
of his hand, he says* ƙãƙa ban shā
nōnaŋ ūwāta, nā ƙōshi ba ?　zā ƙa
zubar mini ?　*The other replies insultingly*
da kai da ūwar tāka, kazaŋ ūwāƙu).
(*r*) ～ dōkiŋ kōwā *Vd.* kōwā 1*b*.　(2)
(*pl.* ƙasãshē = ƙasaisai = ƙassai) (*a*)
(i) country, district.　(ii) (*sometimes
used as pl.*) *x* manyaŋ ƙasā na cikim
mulkimmu the big countries under our
rule (*note the masc. na*).　(*b*) an yi masa
ɗauriŋ ～ = an ɗaure masa ～ he's
been given a charm which has the effect

of seven-league boots. (c) yā bi ∼ he went by land. (d) kuɗiŋ ∼ pl. tax (= haraji). (e) mai ∼ man in charge of district (= hakimi). (ƒ) Audu ∼ nē, dōkiŋ kōwā Audu is long-suffering. (g) Audu ∼ mai girmaŋ ƙai nē Audu is conceited. (3) yā yi mini ∼ he did sand-divining for me (= dūbā), Vd. bugā 4. (4) ∼ tā taɓa ni a snake bit me (Vd. ƙasa 1g, taɓa 1ƒ). (5) ɗaŋ ∼ m. (ƒ. 'yar ∼) pl. 'yaŋ ∼ (a) native of the country (cf. ƙasa 12). (b) = muturū. (6) itinerant traders (ƙataƙē) seeing the ants kwarkwāsā on P., say " ƙasā " ; those hearing this, reply " rawā ƙasa " and stamp to shake off (kaɗe) the ants from their bodies. (7) Vd. saŋ ∼ ; tūwaŋ ƙasā ; dōkiŋ kōwā. (7) māganiŋ ƙasā mai taurī Vd. dāgi. (8) dōraŋ ƙasā Vd. dōrō 4. (9) kō ƙasā tanā saŋka Vd. shūnī 1b. (10) cf. ƙasa ; ƙasa-ƙasa.

B. (ƙasa) adv. (1) (a) on the ground, down below x (i) yanā ∼ it is on the ground ! it is down below. ajiyē shi a ∼ put it on the ground ! yā zuba shi ∼ he poured it on to the ground. (ii) yā fāɗi a ∼ = yā fāɗi ∼ he fell over. (iii) yā mai da kansa ∼ he turned it upside down. (iv) maganā tasa bā tā fāɗūwā ∼ banzā his words have weight. (v) ka zuba ido a ∼ keep your eyes fixed on the ground ! (vi) sǎi gā Jāmus nē ∼ the Germans lost the battle, war. (b) (i) halin yāƙi nē, a yi ∼, a yi sama war has its ups and downs. (ii) jirgī yā yi ƙasa the ship sunk. (iii) an yi ∼ da gindim māto the tail-boards of the lorry have been lowered. (c) (i) muŋ kai su ∼ we felled them. (ii) muŋ kai jirāgyansu ∼ we sunk their ships. suŋ kai jirgin sama ∼ they shot down the aeroplane. (iii) birnī yā kai ∼ the town fell (in war). (d) (i) ∼ da bis above and below. (ii) nā nēmē shi ∼ da bis = nā nēmē shi sama da ∼ = nā nēmē shi ƙad da bis I sought it high and low. (e) aɓin da babba ya ganī yanā ∼, yāro kō yā hau rīmī, ba zai gan shi ba a young P. has not the judgment of an older P. (ƒ) kōmē tsananin jīfa, ∼

yakē fāɗūwā no smoke without fire. (g) igīyar ∼ ƒ. = aɓiŋ ∼ m. snake (cf. ƙasā 4). (h) yā kōma ∼ he was demoted, degraded. (j) kōmē ta bisa ƙārēwā tā yi ƙasa no smoke without fire. (k) sama bā tā kōmō ƙasa har aɓadā, tudu bā yā kōmō gangare east is east and west is west. (l) tāshi ∼, kōma daɓē the two are identical. (2) (a) ƙasa-ƙasa slightly downwards x jirgin samaŋ yā yi ƙasa-ƙasa the aeroplane began to descend. muŋ gan su ƙasa-ƙasa we saw them quite low down. ƙasa-ƙasa kaɗaŋ a little lower down. (b) Vd. ƙasa-ƙasa (separate entry). (3) (a) yā zō a ∼ he came on foot (= ƙafa 1a.ii). (b) tafīya a ∼ journeying on foot (cf. sama 2c, bisa 2c). (4) na ∼ (ƒ. ta ∼) pl. na ∼ adj. the lower. (5) batūre yā tafi ∼ the white man has returned to Europe (cf. tudu). (6) cīwo yā kai shi ∼ illness has laid him low. (7) wanda yakē ∼ da shī (a) he who is junior to him (cf. sama 4). (b) that which is lower than it. (8) (a) daga ƙasansa (i) below it. (ii) in its lower part. (b) a ƙasan shāfi na bīyū at the foot of page 2 (note masc. -n of ƙasan). (9) iŋ kā yi jāyayya da shī, kai nē a ƙasa if you have a tussle with him, you will get the worst of it. (10) sarautar garin naŋ tanā ∼ har yanzu the post of Chief of this town is still vacant. (11) tanā ∼, tanā dabo it still " hangs in the balance ". (12) (a) ɗaŋ ∼ m. man on foot accompanying horseman. (b) ɗaŋ ∼ = ɗākāre 1a, b. (c) (in bōri parlance) 'yaŋ ∼ = aljaŋ. (d) cf. ƙasā 5. (13) cf. ƙasā ; ƙas. (14) rawā ∼ Vd. ƙasā 6.

C. (ƙāsā) (1) bother ! (2) fancy ! kāsa aiki Vd. shā gārī.

kasabi x yanā kasabinsa he is engaged in earning his living (cf. kasaƙī) = tsuwurwurī.

kasabtā = kasaƙtā.

kasada (1) ƒ. (a) pluck, " grit " (= kasai). (b) bargain-lot of remnants sold off at shop or by European going home. (2) Vb. 3B was plucky.

kasaƙi = kasaƙtā.

kasaƙī m. (1) being occupied in x yanā

kasafiŋ gabansa he's occupied in his affairs. **tana kasafin nōno** she's occupied in milk-selling (= **sha'anī**). (2) *cf.* **kasabī**.

kasaftā *Vb.* 1C shared T. out among people *x* **yā ∼ mana gōro** he divided out the kolas amongst us.

kāsa ganī *m.* inquisitiveness, meddlesomeness (= **gaja ganī**).

kasai *used in* **yā yi ∼ da ransa** he pluckily risked his life (= **kasada** *q.v.*).

kasaisai *Vd.* **kasā** 2.

kāsaita *Vb.* 3B. (1) became fully-grown. (2) became important. (3) assumed serious proportions *x* **kāsaitaccīyar kōkawa** bitter struggle.

kasa-kasa A. (**kasa-kasa**). (1) *f.* corn-sweepings *x ∼* **bā cīmad dawākī ba cē** corn-sweepings are not fit food for horses. (2) *adv.* **suna cācā ∼** they're gambling surreptitiously without mat (= *Kt.* **kwarya-kwarya**).
B. (**kasa-kasa**) *adv.* lower down *x* **a yi ∼ da shī** put it lower down ! **ku yi ∼ da muryarku** talk a bit more quietly ! **suna magana ∼** they're talking in an undertone. **gindin kūrā tā yi ∼** hindquarters of a hyena droop. (2) **∼ tā fi kas** (= **kasa-kasa yā fi kasa**) ; **mai jākī yā fi mai tākalmī** better small loss than big. (3) *Vd.* **kasa** 2.
C. (**kasa-kasa**) (1) *adj.* earth-coloured, khaki. (2) **an yi ∼ da shī** he's been man-handled. (3) **yana yāwo ∼** he's travelling far and wide.

kasakē *pl. of* **kaskō**.

kasakē *adv. and m. x* **yana tsaye ∼ = yā yi ∼** he (P. or animal) is standing despondently, flaccidly (= **jugum**).

kasāla *Ar. f.* languidness, apathy (= **la'asar** 4).

kasambarā = *Kt.* **kasambarā** *f.* a Filani dish of steamed guinea-corn flour (or rice-flour) with milk and butter or gravy (= **sambarā**).

kasam-kasam = **kasam-kasam** *m.* sound of movement in grass.

ka san *Vd.* **ka saŋ, ka saŋ**.

kasancē *Vb.* 3A (= **zamā**). (1) is, was *x* **nā ∼ da shī** I have it. **kasancēwā tasa bā shi da kyau** the fact that it is no

good . . . (2) became *x* **dōmiŋ ka ∼ da shina yana zūwa** that you may know he is coming. **al'amarin naŋ yā ∼ this** occurred. (3) proved true *x* **lābārin naŋ yā ∼ this** news has proved true (*Vd.* **kashe** A.2).

kasangalī *m.* (*pl.* **kasangalai**). (1) shin. (2) calf (*both* = **shā rābā** *q.v.*).

kasaŋkama (1) what a forward woman ! (2) what a wandering animal ! (3) (*beggar's cry*) what an important woman you are !

ka saŋ, ka saŋ = ka saŋ, ka sanĭ guess what I have in my hand ! (= **cĭci** *q.v.*).

kasaŋkĭ *m.* (*pl.* **kasaŋkai**). (1) rags for wrapping feet or hands in henna or for wrapping up cotton goods (= **mulumbucī**). (2) **kasaŋkiŋ al'āda** sanitary-towel (= **kadanī**).

kāsarā *used in* **kāsararka** blast you ! (= **kābara** *q.v.*).

kasarbo = kasharbo.

kāsare contemptuously *x* **yā dūbē nĭ ∼** he looked at me contemptuously.

kāsarī *m.* (1) dom furar wani mai nōno, sā **kāsariŋka gōrā** independence is best on no matter how small a scale (= **gātarī** 1c). (2) *Kt.* (*a*) **furā** with water instead of with milk (*cf.* **gāhūhu**). (*b*) water in which pounded grain has been washed (= **tsārī** 1).

kasāshē countries (*pl. of* **kasā** 2 *q.v.*).

kāsashī *m.* wet autumn-mist (= **kāsunsumī**).

kasassabā *f.* ill-effects of wrongful act or senseless act *x ∼* **tā sāmē shi** retribution befell him. **kudinsa sun yi ∼** he's on road to bankruptcy through his senselessness.

kasassawā *f.* type of long spear.

kāsasshē *m.* (*f.* **kāsasshīyā**) *pl.* **kāsassū**. (1) P. overthrown (*derived from* **kā da**) = **kāyayyē**. (2) P. who has fallen short (*derived from* **kāsa**).

kasau *Vd.* **sululū ∼**.

kasausawā = kasassawā.

kāsayad da *Vb.* 4B voided T. in excrement (= **zāwayad da**).

kāsaye *Vb.* 1C. (1) defiled with excrement (*d.f.* **kāshī**) = **zāwaye**. (2) **suŋ kāsaye inūwarsu** they spoiled their chances.

kạsayyạ *f.* competition, rivalry (= hạ̃mayyạ).

kạs dafị (*d.f.* kas 3) *epithet of* poison-antidote kirnī *q.v.*

kạs digạ̃digī *m.* type of sandals (= fadẹ).

kasfīyā *f.* the tree *Crossopteryx Kotschyana* (= kāshiŋ awākī 2).

kạs gaushị = kạs garwāshī *m.* fat meat ; fat chicken.

kạs gwīwạ *Vd.* daŋgwamī.

kash (1) bother ! (= a'ạhā). (2) (*the form of* kas, *itself abbreviation of* kashẹ " killed ", *used before* sh- ; *cf.* kan) *x* Wānẹ, cẹ̃ dạ mụtụm " Bạ̄ba ! " kạ kash shị *epithet of* polite hypocrite.

kasha-kasha *adv.* (1) yā yi aikị ⁓ his work is poorly done. (2) yā sạ̃mē shị dạ ạrạhā ⁓ he got it " dirt-cheap ".

kashamō (1) *m.*, *f.* (*no pl.*) weak. (2) *m.* shrivelled ground-nuts (= mọtsī 3).

kashaŋgarē = kashaŋgarai *used in* yanạ̃ kwạnce ⁓ he's lying sprawling with his back against wall.

kạsharɓọ *m.* (1) gravy (mīyạ) or tūwō even more flavourless than if called lāmī. (2) tactless blurter (= cạ̃ɓālọ).

kasharkamạ *Kt. f.* Emerald Cuckoo, *i.e. Chrysococcyx cupreus* (*according to Wellman*) but Eritrean Shikra (*Accipiter badius*) *according to Bannerman.*

kạshayyạ *f.* competition, rivalry.

kashe A.1 (kashẹ) *Vb.* 1A. (1) (*a*) (i) killed. (ii) *Vd.* kas, kash, kan. (iii) ạbiŋ kashẹ̃wā = ạbiŋ kisạ weapon whereby one kills ; P. or T. to be killed (Mod. Gram. 90*c*). (iv) ⁓ rūwā *Vd.* kas 3*e*, langạ. (v) kō aŋ kashẹ birị, yā rigā yā yi ɓarnā shutting the stable-door after the horse is stolen. (vi) haunī yā ⁓ shi the executioner beheaded him (*Vd.* sạ̣̄rā 1*b*.iii). (vi.*A*) Sarkī yā ⁓ shi the Chief ordered his execution (= yaŋkạ). (vii) yā rantsẹ dạ ạbin dạ zai ⁓ shi he swore a mortal oath that . . . (viii) suŋ kasō jirạ̣̃gyan samạ they shot down aeroplanes. (ix) sunạ̃ ⁓ na kashẹ̃wā, sunạ̃ kāmạ na kāmạ̃wā they killed some and captured others. (x) sun cẹ̃ " ạ kashẹ ! " they said " go to the devil ! " (= sun cẹ̃ " ạ dafạ ! " = sun cẹ̃ " ạ cī ! " = sun cẹ̃ " ạ yaŋkạ ! "). (xi) yā ⁓ dịllālị *Vd.* wọ̃fī 2*d.* (xii) aŋ ⁓ bạ ạ sārẹ kạm ba *Vd.* banzā 1*g.* (xiii) ⁓ cịnnākạ *Vd.* cịnnākạ 4. (*b*) kạshē ni, kạ ga Sarkī = kạshē ni gạ Sarkī = kạn ni kạ ga Sarkī *m.*, *f.* (*sg.*, *pl.*) P. bringing trouble on those having anything to do with him. (*c*) yā ⁓ shi dạ mārị he gave him a hard slap.

(2) worsted *x* (*a*) anạ̃ darạ dọ̃miŋ ạ kasạ nē people act so as to gain advantage. (*b*) yā ⁓ ạbōkinsạ he beat his opponent (at darạ, dambē, langạ, courting (tashị), seeking-office, etc.). yā ⁓ mazā he's ousted his rival (*cf.* kasō).

(3) cancelled, withdrew T. from use *x* (*a*) (i) aŋ ⁓ bạutā slavery has been abolished. (ii) aŋ ⁓ rạndar daka, ta wạje bạ tạ shigō ba don't throw away dirty water till you've got clean water ! (*for one pot is kept inside house and another outside*). (*b*) aŋ ⁓ aurē divorce has been pronounced. (*c*) yā ⁓ fịtilạ he extinguished the lamp. (*d*) muŋ ⁓ tạfīyạ dạ yawạ we have travelled far. (*e*) yā ⁓ gidā he let his home fall into disrepair. (*f*) aŋ ⁓ hanyạ (i) road is disused, road is temporarily closed. (ii) a stick has been put at cross-roads at mouth of road which those coming behind are not to follow. (*g*) (i) yā ⁓ kạ̣sūwā he spoiled his chances. suŋ ⁓ masạ kạ̣sūwā they spoiled his chances. (ii) yā ⁓ kạsūwar gọbe he spoiled his chances for the future. (iii) *Vd.* burā-burā. (*h*) (i) yā ⁓ kudī he spent money (= ɓatar dạ). (ii) ⁓ kudī, fasạ fushī *epithet of* train. (*hh*) furā tā ⁓ masạ jịkī the furā he ate made him feel languid. (*j*) yā ⁓ tufạ he wore out his clothes. (*k*) (i) yā ⁓ wutā he extinguished the fire. (ii) kạshe wutā tun tanạ̃ ɓaramā " nip things in the bud ! " (iii) yā ⁓ ɓaryạn naŋ he scotched that lying rumour. (iv) auraŋ kisạŋ wutā *m. used in* sải tā yi auraŋ kisạŋ wutā kānạ tạ kōmạ gidam mijịntạ now that her husband has given her a triple divorce (sakịm battạ) she cannot resume the

marriage till she has in between, married another. (*l*) **yā ∼ zarāfī** he wasted his time, he lost his chances. **yā ∼ mini zarāfī** he wasted my time uselessly. (*m*) **yā ∼ muryą tasą** he disguised his voice. (*n*) **kashę ƙishi** *Vd.* zartsī.

(4) finished off (work), put a stop to *x* (*a*) **aŋ ∼ hayi** the thatching is finished. **aŋ ∼ baŋgō, saurā hayi** the wall is ready for thatch. **aŋ ∼ sōrō, saurā aząrā** the walls of the mud-topped building are ready for roofing with rafters (= **tsawō** 2*a*). (*b*) **aŋ ∼ mąganą** the matter is settled. (*c*) **an ɗaurą wą są kulkī, doŋ ą ∼ masą jījīyā** beam has been fixed to bull's neck to neutralize power of its muscles. (*d*) **tābą (gīyą) (ɗọrōwą) tā ∼ shi** = **tā ∼ jikinsą** excessive use of tobacco (beer) (locust-bean flour, *i.e.* **gąrin ɗọrōwą**) has made him feel dizzy.

(5) (*a*) **suŋ ∼ bąkinsą** they bribed him to keep him quiet. (*b*) **yā ∼ bąkin tąbarmā** he made a selvedge round the mat (*also applied to* **gwąɗọ, zānā, shirąyī** *as is* **kitsę** 2*b q.v.*). (*c*) **kā ∼ maną bąkinsą** thank goodness, you've reduced him to silence ! (*d*) **kubęwā tā kas bąkī** the okra has ceased fruiting. (*e*) **nā kas bąkī** I've finished off my work. (*f*) **mąganą tā kas bąkī** the matter is settled.

(6) **yā ∼ gārā** he ate extra-special food ; he gave guests extra-special food. (7) **yā ∼ gararinsą** he achieved his aim. (8) (*a*) **yā ∼ haki** he absconded. (*b*) *Vd.* **kisąŋ haki**. (9) **aŋ ∼ hannū** hand-marks made in building have been obliterated. (10) (*a*) **yā ∼ idọ** he screwed up his eye (= **kannę**). (ii) **tā ∼ idọ** " she gave the glad eye " (= **ƙarī**). (iii) **haskę yā ∼ mini idọ** the light dazzled me. (11) **yā ∼ kunnē** it (animal) put back its ears prior to biting or kicking.

A.2 (**kashę**) *Vb.* 3A = **kasąncē** *q.v. x* (1) **tun dą ya ∼ mūgu nē** in view of the fact that he is evil. **yā ∼ nāmu**

nē it is ours. (2) **kashęwā ą zūcīyar marąbī** (= **kashęwā ą zūcīyar mąi rąbō**) **tā fi " Wānę, gą hannūna !** " it is better to be remembered than to have to ask for a share.

B. (**kashē**) *m.* warning (= **kashēdi**).

C. (**kashē**) *m.* each competitor in **dīdībākọ** taking her share of cotton prior to starting work.

kashēdi *m.* warning *x* **an yi masą ∼ kadą yą yī** he's been warned not to do it (= *Kt.* **kwandọ**).

kashęgąrī (1) *adv.* on the following day. (2) day after event (= **wąn shēkarę** 2).

kashēji *m.* = **kashēdi**.

kashēkā *f.* (1) **Kąshēkā** an office among Emir's slaves. (2) *Kt.* means of getting *x* **yā yi mini ∼ ŋ sāmu** he provided me with the means of getting it (= **dąlīli** 3).

kashēkarā *f.* tendon at back of the neck.

kashē ni gą Sarkī = **kashę** 1*b*.

ƙashēshę *Kt. m.* (1) peeled stems of hemp (**ramą**). (2) the tree *Heeria insignis* (*both* = **ƙēƙashēshę**).

kashi A. (**kāshī**) *m.* (1) (*a*) (i) excrement (*Vd.* **nąjasą**). (ii) **kōwā ya yi ∼ ą inūwą, yą bar tą** if you spoil your chances, it's your own fault. (iii) **kāshin turmī bą na wądaŋ ƙarē ba nę** don't attempt what is beyond you ! (iv) **kōmē lālącęwar māsą, tā fi kāshin shānū** half a loaf is better than no bread. (v) **bariŋ ∼ ą ciki bā yą māgąnin yuŋwą** speak out when the time comes ! (vi) **dọmin ganiŋ hadari bā nā yin waŋkā dą ∼** = **mąyē** 2*b*. (vii) **māgąnim maƙī gudu, baŋ ∼** some persons need to be goaded on. (viii) **biri yā san jiɓad dą yakę wą ∼** = **tuŋkū yā san sūriŋ dą yakę ∼** everyone knows his own limitations. (ix) **tuntuɓąŋ ∼ yā ɓātą uku. yā ɓātą raŋ, yā ɓātą ƙafą, yā ɓātą hannū** what an intractable person ! (x) **bą kōmē ą tsūlīyar mąi dōki săi ∼** what a broken reed he is ! (= **hōlōƙō** 2). (*b*) **ą kai kāshin dōki birnī** ? taking coals to Newcastle (*Vd.* **kai** 3*f*). (*c*) **kāshiŋką yā bushę** you've given yourself away, you've let the cat out of the bag. (*d*) **yą kwāshę kāshinsą ą hannū** he'll curse the day he was born. (*e*) **lallę**

yā ɕi ∼ the henna failed to "fix".
(ii) ɕiŋ ∼ gąrēshi he has foolish ways.
(f) bą nagąrĭ ą ∼ ƙō na tūwan shiŋ-
ƙāfā don't look for good where no good
can be ! (2) (a) rūwā yā bā ni ∼ rain
soaked me. (b) am bā shi ∼ = an
daƙą masą ∼ = an niƙą masą ∼ he
was given a bad time, he was beaten.
(c) yā shā ∼ he was drenched by rain,
beaten, given a bad time, had trading-
loss, etc. (d) Vd. ƙaryā 1d. (e) an yi bą
ta ∼ an affray occurred. (f) bą
ɗansą ∼ Vd. mōtsą 1a.ii. (g) Vd.
bō'ę. (3) ŋgō kudĭna, ką yi mini ∼
take this money and gamble with it for
me ! (4) ūwar ∼ epithet of the bovine
stomach tubųrā. (5) kuną jiŋ ∼ Vd.
tsūlĭyā 7. (6) wųyar baŋ ∼ Vd. tirɗę.
(7) ɗaŋ ∼ Vd. rąƙumĭ 1e. (8) zūwąŋ
ƙąi dą ∼ Vd. dĭyaŋ. (9) bē'ę bą ∼
Vd. dēwą yā'ę. (10) mai ∼ ą ƙas Vd.
maurọ. (11) Vd. kāshin-compounds,
dumaŋ kāshĭ.
　B. (kāshi) m. (d.f. kāsą) (1) junior of
P., inferior to x Audụ kāshinā nę Audu is
my junior (= kāsą). (2) kāshiŋ
girmā smallmindedness. (3) kāshiŋ
hąƙurĭ impatience (cf. gajaŋ hąƙurĭ).
　C. (kashi) m. (1) (a) heap x ą kasą
su kashi-kashi divide them into heaps !
(Vd. kasą). ą yi ∼ bĭyar make five
heaps ! (b) (i) section, fraction x iŋ
kā kasą ƙasąshan Lārabāwā ∼ tą-
lātiŋ, Birniŋ ƙudụs yą yi ∼ gųdā
ɗayā kaɗāi if you divide the Arab
countries into 30 parts, Jerusalem
will form only one-thirtieth. (ii) cikiŋ ∼
huɗū, sū sun yi ∼ they form a fourth
part of it. (2) Sk. aną kashinsą he's
being killed (= kisą q.v.).
ƙashĭ m. (pl. ƙasūsūwą = ƙasussą =
ƙassā = ƙassai = ƙassą). (1) (a) bone.
(b) ƙashiŋ kĭfĭ large fishbone with four
corners (used for ornament in boy's belt),
Vd. ƙayą 2. (c) kąrē ną naŋ, ną kęwa-
yąr ∼ a state of indecision prevails. (d)
yā yas dą ∼ yā hūtą dą ƙudā I've paid
and am clear of the matter. (Vd. rąi
5a). (e) ƙashiŋ ąbiŋ dą ya fąɗā the
outline, summary of what he said.
(f) naŋ ∼ Vd. ciląkōwą. (g) gōgą ∼
Vd. gōgą 2. (h) kaŋwar ∼ Vd. ƙadāgwĭ,

ƙandas. 　(j) ƙashiŋ gĭwā Vd. gųŋ-
gụmurƙi. 　(k) gąjēraŋ ∼ Vd. gąjērē 4.
(l) dōgwaŋ ∼ Vd. dōgō 1a.ii. 　(m) Vd.
agānar ∼, ƙąryą ∼. (2) yaną dą ∼ =
ƙashĭ gąrēshi he's a lucky P. ƙashinƙą
nē that's the thing in which you're
always lucky. ƙashiŋ gafĭyą gąrēshi =
bą shi dą ∼ = bą shi dą ƙashiŋ azziƙĭ
he's persistently unlucky (= ƙashim
mĭnąwa). 　(3) ƙashinsụ yā hąɗu they
(servant and master, husband and
wife, etc.) are now sharing in each
other's good luck after previous
penury. 　(4) mąnyaŋ ∼ gąrēshi he is
big-boned. 　yā fĭ sụ mąnyaŋ ∼ he's
bigger-boned than they are (cf. kāwō
1d.i ; ɓarągē 2). 　(5) jaŋ ∼ gąrēshi he
has great endurance. 　(6) māyę yā saką
masą ∼ cikiŋ ƙurjĭ evil spirits have
put bone into ulcer to prevent him
getting better (= ajĭyą 6). 　(7) Vd.
ƙashin-compounds. 　(8) ∼ dą ∼ m. type
of native-woven cloth. 　(9) 'yar ∼ f.
shin-bone of animal or ostrich used
(a) as tethering-post, (b) as a child's
toy (= tsanā 2), (c) secured to well-
rope near the calabash for drawing
water, in order to tilt the latter and so
dip up water. 　(10) suŋ gwadą 'yar ∼
they've had a fight. 　(11) cf. yārọ 3.
ƙashiŋ ąŋkyarō Vd. ąŋkyarō.
kāshiŋ awākĭ m. (1) first blossom on
locust-bean tree (cf. kāshin rāƙumą)
(2) the tree kasfĭyā. (3) Vd. ƙwadọ 1,
samną.
ƙashiŋ bąkin tukunyā " between the devil
and the deep sea ".
ƙashim bąri wallē = ƙashim bąri wargĭ m.
collarbone (= karąŋkarmą).
kāshim ɓaunā m. corn not fully ripe.
ƙashim bāyā m. (1) spine. 　(2) an yi wą
Jāmus ɓarnā wąddą ta karyą musụ ∼
a crippling blow was inflicted on the
Germans.
kāshim ɓērā m. grass from which is made
dąrąmbūwā.
ƙashiŋ gafĭyą Vd. ƙashĭ 2.
ƙashiŋ gaiwā m. persistent ill-luck.
ƙashiŋ gąrĭ m. (1) type of native-woven
cloth. (2) Vd. Gąlādĭmą.
ƙashiŋ gaskĭyā m. the unvarnished truth
(= zallā 1b).

kąshiŋgiɗą *Vb.* 3B reclined on one's side.

kāshin girmā *Vd.* kāshi 2.

kāshiŋ kąjī *Vd.* kāshiŋ kązā.

kāshiŋ gīwā *m.* heaps (bụŋgā) for sowing corn.

kāshiŋ hąƙurī *Vd.* kāshi 3.

kashiŋ ƙamfā re-sowing places where seed not germinated (= ƙwāfi).

kāshiŋ kązā *used in* yā gōgą masą ~ = yā jīzą masą ~ = yā zōzą masą ~ = yā shāfą masą kāshiŋ kąjī he accused him falsely (= ząmbō 3).

ƙąshiŋ ƙurus *m.* persistent ill-luck.

kāshim maƙērā *m.* slag from smithy (= ƙwą).

ƙąshim mīnọ = ƙąshim mīnąwā *m.* persistent ill-luck.

ƙąshim mundirīƙi *m.* persistent ill-luck (= mīnąwā).

kāshin rāƙumą *m.* blossom on locust-bean tree (ɗọrawą) before appearance of bobble (tuntū) *x* ɗọrōwą tā yi ~ (*cf.* kāshiŋ awākī).

ƙąshin sirdi *m.* saddle-frame without coverings (= kaŋgō 3).

kāshin tamā *m.* slag from smithy.

kāshin tānā *m.* worm-casts.

ƙąshin tsīyā *m.* persistent ill-luck.

kāshin tūjẹ *m.* (1) kind of white potash (kaŋwā). (2) yā yi ~ he joined the small piles of ground-nuts (*cf.* tsąkō 2*d*) into large heaps on the farm for seven days (*cf.* kịrigą).

ƙąshiŋ ụmbụsū *m.* persistent ill-luck (= *Sk.* ụmbụsū).

kāshiŋ watą *Kt. m.* hard fungus at base of certain trees or ant-hills (sūri).

kāshin yąwō *m.* type of thorny grass.

kąshirɓaŋ *adv.* copiously (*re* perspiring or weeping) *x* yā yi gụmī ~ he perspired profusely.

ƙashīyą *f.* (1) lower part *x* ƙashīyąr dūtsẹ foot of hill. ƙashīyąr ɗākị mud-wall of house. ƙashīyąr hannun rịgā lower end of gown-sleeve. (2) inferior part *x* ƙashīyąr gōrọ the smaller kolas. (3) origin *x* ƙashīyąr mąganą the origin of the matter.

*ƙąsīɗą *f.* (*Ar.* collection of poems) pamphlet ; booklet.

Kāsiŋ *used in* ɗaŋ ~ *m.* type of imported perfume.

kąsindilā *f.* cotton-spinning as livelihood (= sịndịlē).

kąsirit *m.* (1) mun ji ~ (*a*) we noticed that the noise had relapsed into silence. (*b*) we found way out of difficulty. (2) har mun ji ~, an cirẹ wą shēgyąn ɗā kụnnē (*said by woman*) that fretful baby's now silent !

kaską *f.* (1) (*a*) tick. (*b*) kaską tā mutụ dą haushiŋ kīfī rejoicing at another's misfortune. (*c*) kaską bā tą kōmē dą bịjimī, sāi tą shā jinī tą tāshi what a parasite ! (2) kaskąg gīwā tick found on cow, horse or donkey. (3) ~ maɗamfarịyā *epithet of* tick or cadger. (4) P. sticking to one " like a limpet " (= ąlƙaƙai).

kas kāɗọ *Vd.* kaskamī.

kąs kąfaɗą *Vd.* dụnjī.

kąs kaifī *m.* the plant *Uraria picta*, brew of which is for rendering skin temporarily impervious against cutting-weapons (*used by 'yan taurī who thus become shą dąɗalą*) (= shāfi 4 = gārī 2*c*), *cf.* kicịŋ, taurī 2.

Kaskamī ~ kas kāɗọ *epithet of* fearless man.

ƙas-ƙas = ƙarƙas.

kąs-kąs *adv.* yaną sāraŋ itącē ~ he's chopping much wood (*cf.* ƙwas-ƙwas).

ƙasƙascị = ƙasƙancị *m.* reducing status *x* ~ yā cim masą his status has been lowered.

ƙasƙas dą kąi *m.* humility.

ƙasƙasta A. (ƙasƙąstā) *Vb.* 1C. (1) lowered. (2) reduced status of P. (3) yā ƙasƙąstą kansą he behaved modestly. (4) humiliated.
   B. (ƙąsƙastą) *Vb.* 3B. (1) became lowered in status or humiliated. (2) *Vd.* ƙasƙastō.

ƙasƙastaccē *m.* (*f.* ƙasƙastaccīyā) *pl.* ƙasƙastąttū nincompoop ; unpopular P.

ƙasƙastad dą *Vb.* 4B = ƙasƙąstā.

ƙasƙastō *Vb.* 3A (1) (P., T., or time) approached. (2) *Vd.* ƙasƙasta.

kąskawąmẹ *m.* (1) shrub *Psorospermum senegalense* (*used as remedy for* ƙazwā). (2) kąskawąmąn ƙātọ burly man. (3) how huge ! (4) how rough the skin on soles of your (his, etc.) feet is !

kaskō *m.* (*pl.* kasąkē) (1) (*a*) (i) small, earthenware, bowl-shaped vessel. (ii) ɗanyaŋ kaskō bā yą kai rūwā ban ɗāḳị *epithet of* one of the Sarkim Mụsụlmī. (iii) kụnāmą tā hạrbi kaskō, tā cę 'yam bakạ what a chattering girl ! - (iv) rūwaŋ ∼ *Vd.* ạlbarkạcī 3*c.* (*b*) gashịŋ ∼ *m.* slightly roasting or frying meat (= birgimā 5). (*c*) harbịŋ ∼ *m.* magically shooting soul of enemy in pot of water. (*d*) potsherd of large size (*i.e. either* kaskwan tụlū *or* kaskwan tukunyā) used for bringing fire or for covering cooking-pot (*N.B.*—kaskō *is larger than* tsịŋgārọ *which is too small to use for any purpose*). (*e*) ką nẹmi ∼ wurịn dą ka fĭ tụlū, sǎi ą fasą tụlụŋ, ą bā ką kaskwąŋ (*lit.* if you seek a big shard from P. too liberal to you to trouble about loss of ewer, etc.) if you ask him for a trifle he gives you a large gift. (2) brave man. (3) mạrūrụ yā yi ∼ boil has come to a head (= tukunyā 2*a*). (4) bą zạm bīyā ba sǎi ḳasā tā yi ∼ I'll not pay till rains are over. (5) (*a*) kaskwam mạŋgụl small round cake of mạŋgụl-salt (*cf.* kantụ). (*b*) kaskwan rānā sun's orb just above horizon at rising or setting (*cf.* gụdan rānā). (6) *Vd.* mutūwą 1*gg.* (7) tumụŋ ∼ *Vd.* tumụ 4.

ḳas madaɗīyā *Vd.* ḳūlū.

ḳasnī *Sk., Kt. m.* smell of blood, etc. (= ḳannī *q.v.*).

kaso A. (kasō) *Vb.* 1E (1) yā ∼ nị he defrauded or robbed me. (2) ą ∼ dą mặi may your hunt be good ! (3) yā ∼ nị it pleased me (*Vd.* kashẹ 2, 1*a.*viii). B. (kasọ) *Nor. m.* (*French* incarcerer) prison.

ḳassā bones (*pl. of* ḳashī *q.v.*).

ḳassai A. (ḳassai) *Vd.* ḳasā 2. B. (ḳạssai) *Vd.* ḳashī.

kạssūwā *Nor. f.* market (= ḳāsūwā *q.v.*).

kastā *f.* competition, rivalry (= hạmayyą).

ḳas tākalmą *Vd.* kas 3*k.*

kas tsāmī *Vd.* kaŋwā 1*d.*

ḳạsu *Vd.* kasą 1*a.*iv.

kạsundulā *f.* cotton-spinning as livelihood (= sụndụlē).

kạsunni *Vd.* ḳāsūwā.

ḳạsunsụmī *m.* wet autumn-mist (= ḳāsạshī).

ḳāsurgumī *m.* (*f.* ḳāsurgumā) huge (P. or animal).

ḳasussą ; ḳasūsūwą bones (*pl. of* ḳạshī).

kāsūwā *f.* (*pl.* kāsūwōyī = *Sk.* ḳāsunnị = *Sk.* ḳāsụ̄wai). (1) (*a*) (i) market (*for epithet, Vd.* Lūmọ). (ii) sǎi suką cę " ą kai ḳāsūwa !" they said " it is not in our line ". (iii) kāyaŋ ḳāsūwā market commodities. (*b*) (i) aŋ ḳāsūwā market's been established. (ii) aŋ kafą ∼ tasą = aną cịŋ ∼ tasą he's being maligned. (iii) ḳāsūwar wani mại dāɗin cị it's pleasant to backbite people. (*c*) (i) yā tąfi cịŋ ∼ he's gone marketing. (ii) yā ci ∼ he bought goods at market ; he sold goods at good profit. (iii) ∼ taną cị market's going on. gọ̄be zā ą ci ∼ market will be held to-morrow. (iv) suną cịŋ ∼ there's a hubbub. kụ dēną cịŋ ∼ stop that noise ! (*d*) trade *x* (i) rashịŋ ∼ *m.* lack of trade. (ii) Alą yą bā dą ∼ *Vd.* Alą 7*b.* (iii) yā yi ∼ = yā sąmu ∼ he's found a sale for his goods, sold at a satisfactory price. (iv) ḳāsūwā tā fāɗị there's a slump. ḳāsūwar gyạɗā tā fāɗị ground-nuts are not in demand. (*e*) *x* gā rīgā, mụ yi ∼ look, there's a gown, let's go and bargain for it ! (*f*) ∼ tā hau shị he's a trader whose goods are in great demand. (*g*) fāɗą ḳāsūwą cę ? *Vd.* fāɗą 5. (*h*) kashẹ ∼ *Vd.* kashẹ 3*g.* (*j*) kai zōmō ∼ *Vd.* banzā 1*f.* (*k*) dāmą ∼ *Vd.* hadirị. (*l*) ḳāsūwarką ɗayā *Vd.* gạskamī. (*m*) kąŋ kai ∼ *Vd.* sọ 1*c.* (*n*) yaną rawā ą ∼ *Vd.* rawā 1*g.* (*o*) gạmą ∼ *Vd.* rūwā B.9. (*p*) gạrī dą ∼ *Vd.* gạrī 1*e.* (*q*) tụŋkuŋ ∼ *Vd.* tụŋkū 2. (2) *Kt.* an yi ∼ tā ɗạuki Audụ she chose Audu as her lover by method of kaŋwā 4. (3) *if A is buying e.g., kolas from B and the kola-nut falls, then A says* ɗaŋ kōlị yā fāɗō dạgą kąŋ gadō, sǎi ya cę ∼ may this bad luck be balanced by great good luck ! (4) (*a*) ɗaŋ ∼ *m.* (*f.* 'yar ∼) *pl.* 'yaŋ ∼ = 'yaŋ kāsūwōyī market-trader. (*b*) 'yar ∼ *f.* small market (*pl.* 'yaŋ kāsūwōyī). (*c*) yā kāwō 'yaŋ ∼ he brought back foodstuffs from market for household use. (*d*) 'yaŋ kāsūwancị *m.* market-trading.

(5) ~ dạ gadō (a) taking a "month of Sundays" to do T. (b) tardy P. (6) (a) dạ ~ dạ Sarkī dạ gulbi, bā ạ̄ bāyar dạ lạ̄bārịnsụ it is unwise to jump to conclusions, for often circumstances change overnight. (b) Vd. kọ̄gī 1b, c.

kāsūwancį m. market-trading.

kat (1) yā wạŋku ~ it's washed speck-lessly (= ƙal q.v.). (2) yā tsiŋkẹ ~ it snapped snap !

ƙat completely x (1) yā ƙārẹ ~ it is quite finished. nā ƙọshi ~ I'm quite replete. (2) bạndạ kai, bạ̄ wạndạ zại fitō ~ yạ gayạ masạ you're the only one who would speak out to him so bluntly. (3) nạ̄wa nẹ̄ ~ (a) it's my very own. (b) he's a pal of mine.

kata A. (kạtạ̄) used in dạ rānā ~ in broad daylight.
   B. (kata) used in 'yar ~ f. girl employee, in milk-trade (tākudẹ) ; mocking epithet is kata-kata kạs tākalmạ (cf. kātā).
   C. (kātā) m., f. (1) small, shallow calabash used by sellers of milk or honey (cf. kata) = Sk. cendị. (2) kạmar Kumbọ, kạmar kātantạ how in keeping the two are ! (Vd. kumbọ 1b.ii). (3) the circular salt-cake hōcẹ. (4) Kt. broad, thin section of kola-nut.

kạtā'ạrē m. meddlesomeness.

kataɓalɓạl m. "being neither fish, flesh, fowl, nor good red herring ".

kạtaɓạrɓạr adv. and m. thickly (re liquid or clothes) x (1) tufạn nạm mại kaurī cẹ̄ ~ these clothes are thick. (2) an dāmạ furan nạŋ ~ = furā cẹ̄ ~ dạ ita it's thick furā. (3) ƙwaryan nạŋ ~ dạ ita this is a solid calabash.

kataɓērē m. trouble.

katabsạ Kt. f. rope-ladder, etc. (= katausạ q.v.).

kạtabtạb = kạtaɓạrɓạr.

katāɓur (1) = katāɓus. (2) x tā shigẹ katāɓur-kạtạ̄ɓur big-bottomed woman passed by.

kạtaɓurnā (1) what big-bottomed P. ! (2) m., f. big-bottomed P.

katāɓus = kạtāɓus energetic behaviour (only used negatively) x (1) bạ̄ shi dạ ~ "he's spineless ". ạbọ̄kạŋ gạ̄bā bạ sụ yi wani ~ bā sọ̄săi no real resistance

was offered by the enemy. (2) im bạn cị ba, bạ̄ ni ~ ; in nā cī, bạ̄ ni tāɓusạ kōmē (said by woman) what a feckless fool !

katad dạ = katar dạ.

kạtāfārẹ m. (f. kạtāfārịyā) huge.

kạtafī-katafī (1) m. frequent change of residence. (2) m., f. (sg., pl.) P. frequently changing residence.

kạtaftạf = kạtaɓạrɓạr.

kạtagạŋganā Vd. ɓatạn.

Kạ̄tāgum Vd. banzā.

Kātāgumāwā Vd. Bạkạ̄tāgụmī.

kạtāhū used in dạŋ ~ m. type of hannun rūwā kola-nut.

Kā tākalō Kt. name for boy born after successive girls (= Taŋkọ).

katakaŋkaŋ x yā riƙẹ shi ~ he held it tightly.

katakas (1) = katāɓus. (2) nā yi ~, ūwar 'yā tā sạyi tsintsịyā (said play-fully by woman) yes, I fear I've been very slack in doing it !

kata-kata A. (kạtā-kạtā) f. first efforts of child at walking.
   B. (kata-kata) Vd. kata.
   C. (kạtạ-kạtạ) with difficulty.

katakau used in yā tserẹ ~ (1) he managed to escape. (2) he won easily (1, 2 = fau).

kạtakī m. (f. kạtakā). (1) burly. (2) much x kạtakiŋ aiki much work.

katakiŋ walakiŋ m. and adv. once and for all x an yi ~ dạ sū a clean sweep's been made of them. zā mụ yi ~ dạ shī we're going to "pay off old scores against him ". sun rạbu ~ they've parted once and for all.

katakis = katāɓus, katakas.

katakkā Kt. f. fierce struggle.

katako A. (kātākō) Yor. m. (pl. kạ̄tạ̄kai). (1) plank. (2) Vd. ƙarfẹ 5b. (3) kātāk-wan jirgịn naŋ the remains of that ship.
   B. (katakō) Kt. used in jaŋ ~ orange-headed male lizard (= jaŋ gwādā).

kạtạ̄ƙō Vd. ƙịƙō.

katakōrẹ m. (f. katakōrịyā) burly P.

kạ̄tạ̄kōrō m. huge P. or animal.

kạtạkū m. sack or bag for kolas (= bustạ 2).

katakwādọ Kt. m. jaŋ ~ = katakō.

katala A. (katalā) *f.* type of antidote (makarī) for arrow-poison (= takalā). B. (kạtala) *m.*, *f.* spendthrift (*epithet is ɓạd dạ nākạ, ɓạd dạ na wanī = ɓạ̄tạ nākạ, ɓạ̄tạ na dangį*).

kạtạllū = kạtạllī *m.* adornment. daŋ ~ *m.* (*f.* 'yar ~) *pl.* 'yaŋ ~ well-dressed P.

kạtạmbirį *m.* (1) tree *Gardenia ternifolia*. (2) face-cosmetic from fruit of 1 or other tree (*epithet is* ~ kā fi zanạŋ arō), *Vd.* gaudẹ. (3) tā sakạ ~, tā jā girā she applied cosmetic to her eyebrows.

kạtạnas *Kt.* expressly *x* ya tạfi ~ he went expressly for that purpose (= tạkạnas *q.v.*).

*kātancį *m.* hugeness.

katanga A. (kạtangạ) *f.* (*pl.* kạtạngū = kạtạngī). (1) complete neck (wuyạ) broken off ewer (tūlū), *cf.* kụrurrumī. (2) potsherd (= tsịngārọ). (3) Kạtangạ bā ki tsạutsạyī *epithet of* reckless P. who is " like cat with nine lives ". (4) fạsūwar kạtangạ *Vd.* fạsu 2.

B. (katangā) *f.* (*pl.* kạtạngū = kạtạngī). (1) (*a*) (i) house-wall. (ii) wall round compound (*both* = bangō), *cf.* gā̱rū. (*b*) sǎi katangā tā tsāgẹ fạdạngarẹ kạn sam mashigā when friends quarrel, this gives others matter for gossip. (*c*) katangar gishirī, kōwā ya dạnganạ, yā lạ̄sā what a liberal P ! (2) daŋ ~ *m.* type of cloth (= idọn 7*a q.v.*).

katangalạ *f.* (1) *m.*, *f.* P. without visible means of subsistence or relatives (*epithet is* ~ rạ̈i bā gātā). (2) (*a*) being P. as in 1. (*b*) am bar shį ~ it's been left about as if unwanted (= gā̱lạ̄lạ).

kạtạngī *Vd.* kạtangạ ; katangā.

kạtānīyā *f.* struggling with task (= dạwạinīyā *q.v.*).

kạtạŋkatạnā *f.* *x* yā yi minį ~ it's put me in a dilemma.

katantạŋwạ *f.* (*pl.* kạtạntạŋwū = kạtạntạnyī). (1) snail in shell = *Sk.* alkwatō (*cf.* dọ̄dō 12). (2) (*a*) snail shell (these are used as spinning-top = kōdį), *cf.* dāwạ 3 ; cībīyā 6*e.* (*b*) yanā̱ ~ (i) he's playing top (= *Kt.* raŋwā). (ii) it's gyrating. (*c*) *Kt.* spinning-top made from gourd-stem (bạ̈kim būtạ). (3)

anything spiral (*x* whirlpool, spiral-staircase, etc.). (4) kạtantạŋwạr kūrā large snail-shell used as charm.

kạtạŋwạ *used in* daŋ ~ (*f.* 'yar ~) *pl.* 'yaŋ ~ contentious P.

kạtạptạŋ = kạtạɓarɓạr.

Kạtar *used in* yā gạmu da ~ = yā yi gạmō dạ ~ = yā yi gạmaŋ ~ he had luck.

katarạ *f.* (*pl.* kạtạttarī = katarōrī). (1) (*a*) outside of thigh. (*b*) ạbiŋ arō bā yā̱ rufẹ katarạ *Vd.* ạbụ 2*n.* (*c*) *Vd.* buzurwā. (2) gā̱ shi ạ katarạrkạ look, it's near you ! (3) an illness of woman nearing confinement. (4) gyạdfā tā yi ~ groundnuts are beginning to scorch.

katar dạ *Vb.* 4A Allā̱ yā ~ shī = Allā̱ yā katarshē shi he had good luck.

katari A. (kạtarī) *m.* (1) (rolled " r ") = kạtar. (2) (cerebral " r ", Mod. Gram. 5) bent, unserviceable distaff (mazarī) still useful as spindle to hold much thread (*smaller than* tạŋgōrī). B. (katarī) *Kt.* *m.* = katarạ.

katarōrī *Vd.* katarạ.

katarshē *Vd.* katar dạ.

*kạtartạ *Vb.* 3B P. was lucky (*cf.* kạtar).

kataryạ *f.* (1) throwing opponent by knee-lock in wrestling. (2) *Kt.* winning one's lawsuit by trick.

katạttarī *Vd.* katarạ.

kạtātumī *m.* (*f.* kạtātumā) *pl.* kạtạ̄tụmai burly P.

katauję *m.* trouble, difficulty.

katausạ *f.* (1) rope-ladder. (2) Filani woman's forehead or neck-ornament of rows of grass or beads.

kạtāwạ *f.* snare for rats (*made of* bạkan shiɓạ).

kạtayạrī *m.* meddlesomeness.

katē *Kt.* *m.* (1) = tākudẹ 1 (*cf.* kata). (2) gambling by P. who has already lost all his money.

kate-kate *m.* (1) an daurạ gūgā ~ ropes have been passed in umbrella-shape round gourd-bucket. (2) gourd-bucket with its ropes as in 1 (*Vd.* daurịŋ gūgā 1). (3) *Vd.* daurịŋ ~.

kātị *m.* (1) playing cards. (2) card playing.

kātịbī *m.* (1) *Nor.* five-franc piece = shuŋkụ. *(2) *Ar.* scribe.

kătiɓĭrĭ *m.* struggling with task.

katiɓtịb *m.*, *f.* (*sg.*, *pl.*) simpleton.

kạtĭfạ *f.* (*pl.* kạtĭfŭ = kạtĭfai = katĭfŏfĭ) mattress.

kạtĭnĭ *used in* 'yar∼*f.* type of guinea-corn.

kătintĭnā *f.* = kătuntunā.

kā tịrārạ = kā tụrārạ.

ƙătǫ *m.* (*f.* ƙătūwā) *pl.* ƙattā = ƙartā = ƙattai = ƙattĭ *noun or adj.* (1) huge (*epithet of* huge T. or P. *is* sặ mārar kāyā). (2) *Vd.* gặ ƙătǫ. (3) bā yặ barịn ∼ *Vd.* bugu 1*c*.

kạtŏɓarā *f.* ill-judged talk.

ƙạtŏ-ƙạtŏ *used in* yā zaunạ ƙạtŏ-ƙạtŏ he waited interminably.

kats (1) *used in* yā tsiŋkẹ kats it snapped snap ! (2) *Vd.* kas 2*d*.

katsa A. (kātsạ) *Vb.* 1A = kặtsā *Vb.* 2 = kātsẹ *q.v.*

B. (kātsā) *f.* cikịna yanặ ∼ I have gripes (= kartạ 2*a*).

C. (katsạ) *Vb.* 1A (1) (*a*) snapped T. (thread, rope) (= tsiŋkạ). (*b*) plucked (fruit, etc.). (2) yā ∼ adŏ he " togged himself up ". (3) aŋ ∼ masạ mārị he received a good slap. (4) caused sediment to settle *x* tsāmĭyā, ∼ kụnū gạrĕtạ tamarind causes gruel to settle, so becoming watery and poor. (5) yā ∼ rụbūtū he wrote well (*all* = tsiŋkạ 1*a*).

katsa'ạŋ suddenly *x* ∼ săi ya zặgĕ nị he began to abuse me without warning.

*kạtsạlandạŋ = kạtsạrandạŋ.

katsam A. (kạtsạm) abundantly (= kwạtsạm *q.v.*).

B. (katsạm) = katsa'ạŋ.

kā tsāmẹ *m.* a soup-stuff made from seeds of baobob (kūkạ), *cf.* dạddawā 1*d*.

katsam-katsam *adv.* yanặ aikị ∼ he's working hurriedly and slapdash.

kạtsạm-katsạmĭ *m.* (*f.* kạtsạm-katsạmā) worker *as in* katsam-katsam.

kạtsạrandạŋ = kạtsạrantạŋ *m.* meddle-someness.

kạtsarĭ *m.* the acacia *Albizzia Chevalieri*.

katse A. (kātsẹ) *Vb.* 1A (1) scraped (food, etc.) off pot, etc., by running finger along it = shāfẹ 1*a*.ii (*cf.* kaŋkạrĕ). (2) yā ∼ itặcĕ he planed wood. (3) yā ∼ ƙwaryā he scraped interior of new calabash with mahūrĭ to smoothen it.

B. (katsẹ) (1) *Vb.* 1A (*a*) interrupted *x* (i) yā ∼ minị zạncĕ he broke into what I was saying. (ii) an ∼ masạ hanzarĭ he was " left without a leg to stand on " ; he was prevented finishing what he was doing or saying. (iii) mutūwạ tā ∼ masạ hanzarĭ death put an end to his schemes. (*b*) aŋ ∼ shi dạ mārị = katsạ 3. (2) *Vb.* 3A. (*a*) yā ∼ it (material) ran short before work was finished (= sārẹ 2*b*). (*b*) igĭyạ tā ∼ rope snapped (= tsiŋkẹ 2). (*c*) (i) hanyạ tā ∼ the road is empty of people. (ii) kŏgĭ yā ∼ the river has become shallow. (iii) hatsĭ yā ∼ ạ kặsūwā corn has become scarce (= tsiŋkẹ 2*e*). (*d*) kụnū yā ∼ gruel is thin (*as in* katsạ 4) = tsiŋkẹ 2*e*. (*e*) *Sk.* ripened *as in* bịra. (*f*) *Vd.* tsiŋkẹ.

kātsị *m.* dried sediment of dye-pit (karŏfĭ) made into lāsǫ-cement (= *Kt.* zạrtā 2).

Kạtsinạ *f.* (1) Katsina. (2) *Vd.* kặrā 2*b*.iv, Kanǫ 6, burburwạ 2*b*, dambĕ 6.

Katsinancĭ *m.* Katsina Hausa.

Katsināwā *Vd.* Bạkatsinẹ.

kā tsirŏ *m.* making innovations in religion, etc. (*Vd.* tsịrā).

kạtsū (*Ar.* qattu) *x* (1) ∼ hakạ halinsạ yakẹ̆ thus he always behaves. (2) ∼ bạn saŋ wannạm ba I never got to know this (= daɗǎi *q.v.*).

kạttā *f.* competition, rivalry (= hạmayyạ).

ƙạttā *Vd.* ƙătǫ.

kattājĭyā *f.* integument of corn-stalk (= tsirgāgĭyā).

kạt tākalmạ *Vd.* kas 3*k*.

kattakạrā *f.* the gum-tree tạraunĭyā.

ƙattĭ *Vd.* ƙătǫ.

kātukạ *Kt.* (1) *adv. and f.* south *x* yanặ ∼ dạ shĭ it's south of it (= kudụ). (2) *f.* Kātukạ an obsolete sạrautạ.

kạtukụ *m.* cock-pigeon (*cf.* tạntabạrā).

Kạtūmā *used in* Kạtūmā wạrkiŋ aikị, *epithet of* any Mặdākĭ.

kạtuntunā *f.* an amber-coloured necklace-stone (= tặtātunā 1).

kā tụrārạ *m.* kind of dumpling of millet (gĕrŏ) made in times of scarcity (= gĕrŏ 2).

Kạtūrū name for any man called Garbạ.

ƙătūwā *Vd.* ƙătǫ.

kau A. (**kau**) (1) *Vb.* (*no progressive*) *x* (*a*) suŋ ~ ɗagạ naŋ they've migrated from here. (*b*) ~ ɗagạ naŋ clear out ! (2) *adv.* nā ji zāfī ~ I felt sharp pain. .rānā tā yi zāfī ~ sun's blazing. ƙasā tā yi taurī ~ ground's very hard. sābō ~ brand-new. yā tsērẹ ~ he got " clean away ". B. (**kau**) (1) yā yi haskē ~ it shone brightly. (2) *Sk.*, *Kt.* indeed (= kụ̄wā *q.v.*). C. (**kau**) yā mạ̄rē nị ~ he gave me a hard slap. **ƙau** (1) rūwā yā yi sanyī ~ water's ice-cold. (2) rānā tā yi zāfī ~ sun's blazing. (3) sābō ~ brand-new. (4) ƙarƒẹ ~ cash down.

kaucẹ (1) *Vb.* 3A. (*a*) (i) dodged aside (= **baudẹ**). (ii) nā ~ masạ I dodged it. (iii) kōwā, kạnsạ kaucẹ yakẹ̄ yị everyone is avoiding it. (*b*) changed one's version of events. (2) *Vb.* 1A hoed up deeply the whole (farm) = **kafcẹ** *q.v.*

kaucị *m.* (1) the tree-parasite *Loranthus pentagona* and other species of *Loranthus*. (2) bāshị yā yi masạ ~ he's weighed down with debt. (3) (*a*) kaucịŋ kabạ shạ̄ nēmā *epithet of* popular P. or T. (*b*) nemaŋ kaucịŋ kabạ seeking the unobtainable.

ƙaucī *m.* eagerness *x* yanạ̄ ƙaucin yạ sāmụ he's keen to get it.

kaucīyā *f.* dodging aside (= **baudīyā**).

kaudạ (1) *f.* desiccated T. (*x* fruit, marrow, kolas, meat). (2) *Vb.* 1A nā ~ masạ mārị I gave him a hard slap.

kauda A. (**kauda**) *Sk.*, *Kt.*, *Vb.* 1A = **kau dạ**. B. (**kau dạ**) *Vb.* 4A (1) altered position of T. (2) (*a*) removed to another place. (*b*) muŋ kawad dạ shī ɗagạ ạbin dạ yakẹ̄ sọ̄ we have diverted him from his aim. (*c*) zạncaŋ Kanāwā bạ̄ shi ạ littāfị, ạmmā littāfị bā yạ̄ ~ shī the Kano wit is racy colloquial and though unwritten, equal in quality to any book. (*d*) rūwā dạ iskạ bạ̄ maị kaushē sụ water and wind are irresistible. yanạ̄ cikiŋ irim mutạ̄nē, waɗ̀andạ rūwā dạ iskạ bā sạ̄ kaushē sụ he is one of those men undeterred by anything. (3)

yā ~ ganī = yā ~ idọ (*a*) he turned his eyes away. (*b*) made mistake in copying. (4) yā ~ idạm mutạ̄nē he withdrew from sight. (4A) yā ~ jị he did not hear clearly. yā ~ ganī he did not see clearly. (5) (*a*) yā ~ kạ̄i (i) he turned his head aside. (ii) he ignored P. (iii) he used euphemism. (*b*) ạ kau dạ kạ̄i, ạ sārẹ tōƙā forcing one-self to do shameful T. publicly. (6) yā ~ ạbincī maị yawạ he " wolfed up " much food. (7) yā ~ mayaŋkā he changed his previous statement to avert trouble. (8) kau dạ bạ̄rā *m.* charm against being wounded (*epithet is* ~ ạ gamạ ta dạ gōcīyā " trust in God, but keep your powder dry ! "). (9) kau dạ giŋgirạ̄ɓai *m.* pilfering (= **sạ̄nē**). (10) kau dạ karā bạ̄ aikị ba nẹ̄ it's " mere child's play ". (11) bạ̄ kau dạ halī *Vd.* yuŋwạ 1*a*.

ƙaudē *Kt.* *m.* changing place of enclosure for herd or flock.

kaudī A. (**kaudī**) *m.* verbosity. B. (**kaudị**) (1) how hot ! (2) what a sharp pain ! (3) what verbosity !

ƙaudōdọ *m.* = **ƙabdōdọ**.

kau-kau *Sk.* *m.* Grey Plantain-eater (*Crinifer piscator*).

***ƙaukạ̄wā** *f.* selling meat on credit (= **ƙạkkạ̄wā** *q.v.*).

***kaulā** = **kalwā**.

kạulē *m.* type of stone used for necklaces.

***kaulị** *Ar.* *m.* yā īyạ kaulịm mạganạ he's good at repartee.

ƙaunā *f.* (1) (*a*) love, liking *x* (i) yanạ̄ ~ tatạ he loves her. (ii) bābụ ~ tsạkāninsụ there's no affection between them. (*b*) nā ɗēbẹ (= nā yaŋkẹ) ~ ɗagạ garēshị = nā yaŋkẹ masạ ~ I no longer hanker after it, I've abandoned hope of getting it, I no longer love him, I feel no further interest in it. bā ạ ɗēbẹ ~ gạ rahamạr Allạ̄ one need never despair of God's mercy. nā ɗēbẹ (= nā yaŋkẹ) ~ dạ zūwạ gidansạ I'm determined not to visit him again. (*c*) mum fid dạ ƙaunar zā sụ sākẹ wani ạbiŋ kirkị we've ceased to expect any good behaviour from them. sum fid dạ ~ ɗagạ zūwạ they have given up all idea of coming (*Vd.* zūcịyā 1*c*.ii). (*d*) yā yi mini yaŋkaŋ ~ he refused me my desire. (e) in dạ ạbiŋkạ, anạ ƙaunarkạ, im bābụ ạbiŋkạ, kạrē yā fī kạ only the rich are sought after. (2) nā yi ƙaunar Muntasạr ạ Dạwạnau my hopes were vain. (3) kō ƙasā tanạ ƙaunarkạ Vd. shūnī 1b.

ƙaunacē Vd. ƙaunatạ.

ƙaunatạ (1) Vb. 2 (p.o. ƙaunạcē, n.o. ƙaunạci). (a) loved, liked. (b) ƙaunatō Vb. 1E nā ƙaunatō kạ I'm depending on you, I've come to ask you a favour.

kaura A. (kaurạ) (1) Vb. 1A. (a) (i) nā ~ masạ mārị I gave him a hard slap. (ii) nā ~ karọ dạ shī I collided hard with it. (iii) nā ~ tuntuɓẹ I stumbled hard against it. (b) cf. kạurā, kaurẹ. (2) Vb. 3A. (a) suŋ ~ they collided hard. (b) raŋ kaurạwā f. day of battle. (3) Rustic Kano Hausa f. potsherd used as missile to knock down fruit or bird.

B. (kạurā) (1) Vb. 2. (a) suŋ kạurē shi wurinsạ they borrowed sum, got T. on credit from him without intention of paying. (b) A yā kạuri B A borrowed sum or got T. on credit from B as in (a) (both = hạgā). (2) f. (a) acting as in 1 (epithet is ~ bạ jin cīwọ). (3) ụbaŋ ~ = ūwar ~ head of the local bọrī who is usually followed by many women and a pimp (= ūwar kusfā = ajiŋgi q.v.).

ƙaura A. (ƙaurā) (1) Vb. 3B. (a) migrated. (b) died. (2) m., f. (a) (i) (v.n. and progressive of 1) x yanạ ~ he is migrating. (ii) ƙauraŋ Ạnnabị = hijirā 1. (b) yā yi ~ = 1a, b. (c) Audụ, ƙaurar zūcī gạrēshị Audu's mind is elsewhere. (d) ạ kai karā maƙauracī tuŋ gạbaŋ ~ bạ tạ zō ba (said by marọƙā) give me alms and so lay up treasure in the next world! (3) m. (a) any dog. (b) Kt. nā gạmu dạ ~ = ƙaurā yā zạgē nị = nā zạgi ~ I got syphilis (= tụnjērē). (c) (i) Ƙaurā epithet of any Mādākī. (ii) nā nẹmē shi Ƙaurā Wạmbai = nā nẹmē shi Ƙaurā gạ waitakạ, ban sāmụ ba I looked for it high and low, but in vain. (iii) yā ɓatạ Ƙaurā gạ waitakạ it is completely lost. (iv) Vd. gōjẹ 3. (v) Ƙauran zugū an evil spirit in bọrī (Vd. kiŋkimbōdị).

B. (ƙaurạ) f. (1) type of red guinea-corn. (2) best native writing paper. (3) returning to one's original position in game raunin dịrē after having bent back till hands touch ground. (4) swelling on back of hand (= dāwạ 3).

ƙaurạcē (1) Vb. 3A x yā ~ manạ (a) he's left our district, (b) ceased visiting us, (c) died. (2) (a) sat haughtily or sulkily among others or apart (= kā-kụmē). (b) refrained from mixing with others through feeling of inferiority.

kaurara A. (kaurạrā) Vb. 1C thickened. B. (kạurarạ) Vb. 3B. (1) became thick. (2) mutạnē suŋ ~ ạ naŋ people have increased here. C. (kaurạrā) pl. thick (pl. of kạkkaurā).

ƙaurạrā Vb. 1C fried (meat) cursorily (= tānạnā 1), cf. babbạkā.

ƙaurare A. (ƙaurạrē) Vb. 1C = ƙaurạrā B. (ƙaurạrē) m. ground-nuts fried (sōyạ) in their shells (cf. tạnạnē).

kaurạyā Vb. 1C (1) stirred up (x mīyạ, milk, furā) so as to mix sediment with liquid before serving (= gaurạyā = mōtsạ), cf. dāmạ. (2) searched through-out x nā kaurạyạ dākịŋ, ban sāmụ ba though I searched throughout the house, I couldn't find it. (3) yā kaurạyạ wurịŋ dukạ he wandered over the whole place.

kaurạyē Vb. 1C (1) = kaurạyā 1. (2) spread over x cīwọ yā kaurạyẹ ƙasar naŋ the sickness spread over all this area.

kaurẹ (1) Vb. 1A. (a) A yā ~ B = kạurā 1b. (b) nā ~ shi dạ mārị I gave him a hard slap. (2) Vb. 3A increased in volume x rūwā yā ~ ạ kọgī water increased in river. fadạ yā ~ quarrel became serious. gidā yā ~ dạ fadạ compound was filled with squabbling. kidạ yā ~ drumming became deafening. kạsūwā tā ~ market's packed. gōrọ yā ~ dạ tsạdā kolas became expensive. hīrā tā ~ the conversation became ani-mated.

kauri A. (kaurī) m. (1) (a) thickness. (b ạnnūrim fuskạ, kaurịŋ hanjī a shining face is due to a full belly. (c) kauri ɗákĭ *Vd.* dạɓē 4. (2) *x* naŋ sukạ fi ∽ *that's* where they excel.

B. (kauri̧) (1) what a slap ! (2) what loud thunderclap !

ƙaurĭ *m.* (1) (*a*) smell of burnt hair, rags, flesh, etc. (*cf.* wārĭ). (*b*) *Vd.* ƙūnā 1*b.* (*c*) ƙaurim ɓērā *Vd.* bạbbakạ 3. (2) (*a*) an yi wạ mai jēgọ ∽ cattle-feet and dāɓurĭ, etc., have been stewed for the nursing-mother (= gạndā = *Kt.* kaŋwā 2) *x* mai jēgọ tā shā ƙaurĭ. (*b*) *Rustic Kano Hausa* stewed fowl or goat's head for nursing-mother or newly-circumcised boy (ɗan shāyĭ). (*c*) bạ haifũwā cẹ dạ wụyā ba, kạji̧ŋ ƙauri̧ŋ it's easily got, but hard to use. (3) *Kt.* zạrē yā yi ∽ thread's too tightly spun (= tsaurĭ 5*a*).

kausạ *Vb.* 1A set about *x* suŋ ∽ faɗạ they fell to fighting. gạ ri̧gā ta sayạrwā, zō mụ ∽ let's set about bargaining for that gown that's on sale !

kạusạ-kạusạ *f.* small plant (*leaves used for cleaning writing-slate, i.e.* ạllō).

Kạusarā Ar. f. one of the rivers of Muslim paradise.

kausasa A. (kausạsā) *Vb.* 1C (1) roughened. (2) yā ∽ mini̧ mạganạ he spoke harshly to me.

B. (kạusasạ) *Vb.* 3B became rough. C. (kausạsā) *pl.* rough (*pl. of* kạk-kausā).

kaushē *Vd.* kau dạ.

kaushĭ *m.* roughness.

kạusūwā *Sk. f.* market (= kạsūwā *q.v.*).

kauta = kafta.

ƙauyạcē *Vb.* 3A sat apart *as in* ƙaurạcē 2*a, b.*

ƙauyancĭ *m.* ways of country bumpkins (= gidādancĭ).

ƙạuyạwā *Vd.* bạƙauyẹ.

ƙauye A. (ƙauyẹ) *m.* (*pl.* ƙauyukạ). (1) (*a*) village. (*b*) country (*as opposed to* birnĭ town) *x* (i) tā fi̧ta zạ ta ∽ she went out of the town, intending to go into the country. yanạ ∽ he lives in the country. bạ mai zūwạ birnĭ dạgạ ∽ nobody comes into town from the country. (ii) girmaŋ ∽ ya yi he is a mere country bumpkin. sū girmaŋ ∽ nē they're rustics. (iii) bạ ka gidā săi ∽ *Vd.* arnẹ. (iv) *Vd.* tāshi̧ŋ ∽. (*c*)

birni̧ŋ (= gāruŋ) ∽ yā sōmạ fāɗụwā reaping has begun. (*d*) yanạ yāwạŋ ∽ (i) he is talking at random, he is making random guesses. (ii) he's licking his lips after toothsome morsel (= ki̧lĭsạ 3). (*e*) ƙawar ∽ *Vd.* ƙawā 1*d.* (*f*) gidaŋ ∽ *Vd.* manōmĭ. (*g*) *Vd.* tāshi̧n dagaci̧ŋ ∽, tāshi̧m Magạji̧ŋ ∽. (*h*) *Vd.* Sạrạkaŋ ƙauyẹ *under* Sarkĭ 4. (2) *adv.* on the edge *x* yanạ zạune caŋ ∽ he's sitting over there at the edge. (3) *Kt. m.* (*pl.* ƙawạyyā) edge *x* (*a*) ƙauyạŋ kạsūwā the edge of the market. (*b*) ƙauyạŋ hanyạ *Vd.* kạrạmbānĭ. (*c*) yanạ shaŋ ƙauyạm fạtẹ-fatē = *Kt.* yanạ shaŋ kunuŋ ƙawạyyā " he is beating about the bush ".

B. (ƙauyē) *Kt.* ɗaŋ ∽ *m.* little finger (= ƙurĭ 2*a*).

kạwa A. (kạwa) (1) *Vb.* 3B. (*a*) moved away (= zākụɗā). (*b*) *Kt.* died. (2) *Kt. adv.* indeed (= kụwā *q.v.*).

B. (kawạ) *Kt. f.* roasting (meat) before fire (= ƙafẹ), *cf.* kawạtā.

C. (kāwạ) *f.* loud laughter of *men* (*cf.* shēwạ).

ƙawa A. (ƙawā) *f.* (*pl.* ƙawạyē). (1) (*a*) girl's or woman's female pal (= gōrạ 1*g* = ạmakạlĭ = rūwā A.24, B.10), *Vd.* sọ 3. (*b*) ƙawar kunyạ *such pal* with whom she remains from morning till night so absorbed in conversation that they are not distracted by hunger or calls of nature (*cf.* ƙwārĭ 6). (*c*) *Vd.* yạyyē. (*d*) (i) tā tsayạ sạrọrọ yạ ƙawar ƙauyẹ she stood agape like a gaby. (ii) *Vd.* ƙyẹrẹrẹ. (*e*) ƙawar ƙawā *Vd.* ɗọri i̧hirĭ. (*f*) ∽ dạ mazạ *Vd.* kidinā. (2) yā yi ∽ it (he) is handsome.

B. (ƙāwạ) *f.* great eagerness *x* yanạ ji̧ŋ ƙāwạr nāmạ he feels overmastering desire for meat (*cf.* ƙawạ zūcĭ).

kawạcē *Vb.* 1C *Kt.* roasted (meat) before fire (= ƙafẹ).

kawad dạ = kau dạ.

kawai (1) (= hakạ ∽) *adv.* without reason *x* kā zāgē ni̧ ∽ you abused me without provocation. nā ga ∽ mun zubẹ I saw we were routed for no explainable reason. sunạ dạ Sarkĭ nẹ kawai they have a Chief who is such in name only.

(b) merely x hōlōk̄ō isk̄ cē ∼ the storm
hōlōk̄ō is wind and nothing else. ̣
bar m̦agan̦ar ∼ leave the matter as
it is ! (c) without warning x sǎi ∼ suk̄
ji mury̦asș they suddenly heard his
voice. (d) silently x sǎi ∼ suk̄ jī
they listened in silence. (e) (i) only (=
kad̄ǎi 1a). (ii) (followed by relative construction) is the only one who isxmū nạ̄ŋ
k̄asar kawa̦i k̄ē za̦une lāfīy̦ we in this
country are the only people at peace.
Aud̦u nē kawa̦i b̄ sōj̦ ba Audu is the
only one not a soldier (cf. kur̦um 2a). (2)
m. yā yi∼he kept silence, became silent.
yi ∼ be quiet ! (= shirū = kur̦um).
kawaici m. (1) keeping silence. (2)
reticence, reserve.
k̄waita̦ Vb. 3B (1) became silent. (2)
remained silent.
kawaitad d̦ Vb. 4B reduced to silence.
kawalci̦ Ar. m. acting as k̄wāli̦.
k̄wāli̦ Ar. m. (f. k̄wālīyā) pl. k̄wā̄lai
P. who arranges assignations between
man and woman for copulation (cf.
magājīyā).
k̄walwalnīyā = k̄walwalnīyā f. visible
evaporation from hot soil ; mirage
(= 'yā'yā 5).
k̄awany̦ f. (pl. k̄awa̦ŋwanī = k̄awā̄nē =
k̄awanyōyī). (1) any small metal ring.
(2) circular spread of hair at back of
head of some persons (= cībīyā 5).
(3) k̄awany̦ar kunnē = k̄awany̦ar kunnē
ear-ring. (4) sun yi ∼ they're in a
circle. (5) an yi maș ∼ (a) they
surrounded it. (b) made circuit of it.
(6) z̦arē yā yi ∼ thread's twisted owing
to over-tightness of ply (tsaurī).
k̄awarā f. temporary fence made at
harvest-time (k̄āk̄ā) for storing crops
till bin (r̦umbū) is made in hot-season
(rānī) ; in Kt., it is made of stakes, but
in Kano, of cornstalks (karā).
k̄āwārā f. (1) the fish Characin (Alestes
Nurse). (2) an ci ∼, yin̄ G̦adas when
what he wanted was available, he
wasn't there to enjoy it (G̦adas is town
in Zaria). (3) yā yi mini hawaŋ ∼ he
unexpectedly " went for me ".
kawar d̦ Vb. 4A = kau d̦.
k̄awarī used in k̄warī, ma̦i g̦abā tsạye
epithet of reckless P.

k̄awarī m. the large type of fig-tree Ficus
kawuri (Vd. gul̦ubā).
kawata A. (kawā̄tā) Vb. 1C Kt. = kawā̄cē.
B. (K̄wātā̦) epithet of any Ma'aji.
k̄awata A. (k̄wātā̦) Vb. 3B is (was)
beautiful.
B. (k̄awā̄tā) Vb. 1C beautified.
k̄awā̄yā used in ya̦u, k̄ fad̦̄ (= ya̦u, k̄
gay̦) k̄awā̄yaŋk̄ to-day's likely to be
a trying day for you ; to-day you'll be
sorry you were ever born ! = m̄akwī).
k̄awā̄yē Vd. k̄awā.
k̄awa̦yyā Vd. k̄auy̦ 3c.
k̄̄w̄ zūcī m. (1) greed. (2) undue persistence (cf. k̄āw̦).
kāwō (1) Vb. 3 (a) arrived. (b) k̄ōgī yā ∼
the river is in flood (= shāf̦ 1b.v = hau
6 = cik̄ōw̦). (c) yā∼he had ejaculation
of semen (Vd. zūwā 5). (d) (i) yā kai,
yā ∼ he's big-made (cf. k̄ashī 4). (ii)
k̄ōgī yā kai, yā ∼ the river's in flood.
(iii) sǎi d̦ ak̄ kai, ak̄ ∼, ak̄ yī it was
only accomplished after much trouble.
(iv) yā cik̄ kạiwā d̦ kāwōwā he's a
mischief-maker. (v) kạiwā d̦ kāwōwā
f. going hither and thither (Vd. kai
4e, f). (vi) kai k̄āwō m. sentry-duty.
ma̦i kai k̄āwō m. (pl. m̄asū kai k̄āwō)
sentry. (vii) Vd. tā kai tā kāwō ; kai
4j. (2) Vb. 1D. (a) brought x (i) yā ∼
mini shī he brought it to me. (ii) m̄
ya ∼ k̄ naŋ how do you happen to be
here ? (iii) ab̄in d̦ ya ∼ ni wuriŋk̄,
nā ∼ k̄ārar hāk̄imī k̄ naŋ I've come to
you because I wish to complain against
the District Head. (iv) y̦anzu z̦amāni
yā ∼ m̦u we must move with the times.
(v) tā isa m̄atar " k̄āwō rūwā ! " she is
very pretty. (vi) yā ∼ he reined (in)
his horse sharply (= zām̦ 1a.i). (vii)
k̄āwō akushiŋk̄ Vd. gōh̄ōh̄ō. (b)
k̄āwō kudī very well, I'll sell at the
figure you name, so where is your
money ? (c) kōwā yā ∼ tāș everyone
stated his opinion. (d) k̄āk̄ zā ̣ ∼
shi cikin z̦ancē give me an example of
how the word is used ! (e) k̄ōgī yā ∼
rūwā = 1b. (f) yā ∼ k̄ǎi he turned up.
(g) sall̦ tā ∼ k̄ǎi = sall̦ tā ∼ jik̄ī
the festival is at hand. d̦āmunā tā ∼
k̄ǎi the rainy season has come (Vd.
4 below). (h) arrived at x yā ∼ Kano =

yā ∼ gạ **Kanọ** he arrived at Kano (*cf.*
Mod. Gram. 130). (*j*) yā ∼ īyā wuyạ
he's " fed up to the teeth ". (*k*) kạ̄wō
bābā *Vd.* hōrẹ 2. (*l*) dūkạn kạ̄wō wuƙā
Vd. wuƙā 1*e*. (3) *m.* (*a*) the mahogany
Afzelia africana. (*b*) kai mại ∼ ho,
you drummer there ! (4) (*a*) kạ̄wō kại
m. lopping standing corn (= fạllē *q.v.*).
(*b*) *Vd.* 2*f*, *g above.* (5) kạ̄wō ƙwaryā
m. exchange of food by women (= *Sk.*
dẹ̄gīyā 1).
kāwụ = kạ̄wū *Fil. m.* (*pl.* kạ̄wụnai). (1)
maternal uncle (= rāfạ̄nī). (2) *cf.*
kujẹ̄rā 5.
kāwunạ heads (*Vd.* kại).
kạ̄wụnai *Vd.* kāwụ.
kawwạ *Kr. f.* (1) laterite (= marmarā). (2)
Chief, be careful of that stone on the road!
ƙawwạmā *Vb.* 1C *Kt.* divided out *x* yā ∼
manạ gōrọ he divided out the kola-
nuts amongst us (*cf.* ạ ƙawwạmā).
kawwạmē (1) *Vb.* 3B = ƙaurạcē. (2)
Vb. 1C set apart.
kaya A. (kāyā) *m.* (*pl.* kāyạyyakī). (1) (*a*)
(i) load. (ii) dạ kại dạ ∼ mạllakạr wuyạ
nē what one's dependents own is the
same as what one owns oneself. (iii)
wani ∼ sǎi amālẹ abilities differ. (iv)
rānar ∼ ạkwīyạ bạ bisā ba cẹ don't
attempt the impossible ! (v) in dǎi
rạ̄ƙumī dạ girmā, kāyansạ dạ yawạ a
rich P. has many calls on his purse.
(vi) kāyan sạmmakō, dạ wurī a kạn
daurẹ shi forewarned is forearmed.
(vii) Jạ̄kī, bāwạn ∼ = hạƙurin ∼ sǎi
jạ̄kī what an energetic person ! (viii)
wani ∼ sǎi Bạnufē, wạccẹ Ạyāgī mại
dan dōrọ (*said by woman*) who am *I*
to be able to do it ! (ix) ạ sǎi dạ ƙūrụ, ạ
yi wạ ịngarmạ ∼ one P. has been
deprived of his share to give it to a
favourite. (x) tạkarkạrī kạm fọ̄rā,
jạ̄kī yā sābạ dạ ∼ what's bred in the
bone . . . (xi) tsīrā dạ ∼ *Vd.*
2*b.*viii; tsīrạ. (xii) anạ̄ kāyạn kā *Vd.*
rạ̄tayạ 2*b.* (xiii) kāyan yārọ *Vd.* yārọ 1*e.*
(xiv) mārar ∼ *Vd.* mārā 3. (xv) kāyạn
kabạ *Vd.* būtsātsạ. (xvi) kā ci kāyạn
kōwā *Vd.* dawạ 7. (xvii) sāmụn ∼ *Vd.*
sāmụ 2*c.* (xviii) sạnnū dạ ∼ *Vd.* sạnnū 4.
(xix) rạ̄ƙumī bā yạ̄ kūkā don ∼ mại
yawạ *Vd.* mạruhū. (xx) ạ ƙārạ dạmisạ

∼ *Vd.* dạ̄misạ 4. (xxi) ∼ bā yạ̄ rạ̄6ar
jạ̄kī *Vd.* būtsạrī 2. (*b*) (*often treated as if
plural*) *x* nauyạ̄yan kāyā = nauyạ̄yan
kāyạyyakī heavy loads. wadansu ∼
some loads. kāyan jīmạ, sū nẹ̄ gạbạ̄-
rūwā dạ bābā dye-stuffs are Egyptian
mimosa and indigo. kāyan nạn,
ạjīyē su dǎi-dǎi put down these loads
one by one ! (Mod. Gram. 9*d N.B.* ;
176*d*). (2) property *x* (*a*) yā shā ∼ he
received many gifts (*cf.* 3*d*, 5*a below*).
(*b*) wadansu ∼ dạ yawạ many
belongings. wadạnnạn ∼ = wannạn
∼ these goods. (*c*) 'yan kāyansụ their
small property. (3) outfit. (*a*) yā yi
farạ̄ran ∼ he put on white clothes. (*b*)
dan sạndā yā sạ̄ farin ∼ the policeman dressed in mufti (as disguise).
(*c*) tā gamạ masạ kāyan girmā she
gave him an outfit in keeping with his
rank. (*d*) dōki yā shā ∼ the horse is
gaily caparisoned (*cf.* 2*a above*, 5*a
below*). (*e*) kāyan yāƙi field-service
uniform, battle-dress. (*f*) yā shiga
kāyan sōjạ he put on uniform. (*g*)
kāyan dāki furniture. (*h*) kāyạn
kạsūwā market commodities. (*j*)
kāyam fadạ arms, accoutrements. (*k*)
kāyan ciki *Vd.* ciki 1*c.* (*m*) *Vd.* kāyan.
(4) (*a*) yanạ̄ dạ ∼ = yanạ̄ dạ kāyam
mazā he has enormously enlarged
scrotum (= *Kt.* ạjīyạ 8*b*). (*b*) kāyạn
gwaiwā *Vd.* tīlạs 2*e.* (*c*) bā yạ̄ rạbūwā
dạ kāyam mazā he's energetic. (5) ∼
gạrēshi (*a*) he has a heavy load (= shā
B.11*a*), *cf.* 2*a*, 3*d above.* (*b*) he can carry
heavy loads. (6) kāyan yạrdā (= kāyan
rā'ị) bā yạ̄ cin kại what one does
voluntarily does not irk one. (7) ∼
dạ yāni bad P. seeming good. (8) ∼
rūwa *m.* short pack-donkey (*cf.* kāyan
5). (9) *Vd.* kan sallạ, kāyan-*compounds.*
(10) anạ̄ ta kại, wạ̄ yakẹ̄ ta kāyā *Vd.*
ta B.1,1*d.*
B. (kāyạ) *used in* kōkawạ tā ∼
(1) as one of the opponents is thrown,
the wrestling bout is over. (2) the
matter's settled.
C. (kayạ = kayạ-kayạ) *f.* sound of
movements in grass.
ƙayạ *f.* (*pl.* ƙayōyī = *Kt.* ƙayāyūwạ). (1)
(*a*) (i) thorn. (ii) yā zamam mini ∼ he

is a nuisance to me. (iii) tạfị-tafị tā fị zamā kō ∾ ka tākạ *Vd*. tạfịfịyạ. (iv) iŋ kā ga rạƙumī yanạ̄ cịŋ ∾, bạ̄ dǫmin dādī yakē cị ba acting under compulsion. (v) kōwā ya jā ∾, ƙayạ tạ̄ jā shị if you plot, your plot will recoil on you. (vi) arzịkī rịgar ∾, kanạ̄ jạ̄, yanạ̄ jạŋkạ prosperity brings many onerous duties. (vii) yā hōrę wạ rạ̄ƙumī ∾ *Vd*. rạ̄ƙumī 1*l*. (viii) kā fị ∾ tsịnī *Vd*. fịƙē 2*b*. (ix) *Vd*. hūwạ̄cē. (x) bạ̄ ki ƙayạ *Vd*. cēdīyā. (xi) cịre minị ∾ ṃ fị kạ gudụ it's a case of the pupil excelling the master ! (*Vd*. cịre minị ƙayạ). (*b*) (*sometimes treated as plural*) *Vd*. 1*d*. (*c*) farar ∾ the gum-yielding *Acacia sieberiana*. (*d*) rụɓaɓɓịyar ∾ deposed P. who is thorn in the side of his successor (= tsụmmā 2). rụɓạɓɓuŋ ƙayạ disaffected persons. (*e*) Kayạ, bị kị san na gijị ba *epithet of* evil P. (*f*) (i) (*said to P. of limited means*) ạ rabạ dạ ∾ may you live long to wear this new garment ! (*cf*. tsōị̄ę). (ii) (*if said to P. of position, he may reply* nī matsịyạ̄cị nẹ̄ ? why say " may it last long ? " am I a pauper that I should wear the same garment for ever !). (*g*) kạman ∾ bạ tạ sōkạ ba *Kt*. suffering a reverse, then getting compensatory benefit. (*h*) ∾ tā yi gidā corn on foot supposedly due to unextracted thorn. (2) ƙayạr kịfị small, sharp fish-bone (*large one is* ƙashī 1*b q.v.*). (*b*) (i) ƙayạr būshīyā hedgehog quill. ƙayạr bēgwā porcupine-quill. (ii) bēgwā (būshīyā) tā tā dạ ƙayạ porcupine (hedgehog) erected its quills. (iii) yā tāyar minị dạ ƙayạr bāyā he showed enmity towards me. (3) *Vd. compounds of* ƙayạr.

kaya-kaya A. (kayạ-kayạ) *Vd*. kayạ.
    B. (kāyā-kāyā) *adv*. load by load.
kạ'ya-kạyē‖ *m*. carrying food-utensils indoors, as storm impending or dogs about.
Kayạmạ *f*. Kayama.
ƙayạ̄mē spurs (*pl. of* ƙaimī).
kāyan (*genitive of* kāyā). (1) ∾ adō articles for adorning the body. (2) ∾ aikị tool(s). (3) ∾ cikị entrails. (4) ∾ dōkị saddlery, bridle, saddle-cover,

etc. (5) kāyan rūwā yakē yị his sight's bad (*cf*. kāyā 8). (6) *Vd*. kāyā 3.
ƙayanta A. (ƙạ̄yantạ) *Vb*. 3B is (was) beautiful.
    B. (ƙạ̄yạntā) *Vb*. 1C beautified.
ƙạ̄yantad dạ *Vb*. 4A (1) beautified *x* dạ ƙạ̄yantạrwā yakē it's beautiful. wannạŋ yā fị ƙạ̄yantạrwā this is the most beautiful. (2) is (was) pleasing to P.
ƙayạr Allạ̄ *f*. corn on the foot (= ƙọ̄ƙīyā).
kạyararā *used in* yanạ̄ kwạnce kạyararā he's confined to his bed (= shịrkat).
ƙayạr ɓērā *f*. = ƙayạr ƙạdaŋgarę.
kāyar dạ *Vb*. 4A = kā dạ.
ƙayạr gīwā *f*. the plant zāzar gīwā.
ƙayạr Gōbirāwā *f*. the weeds *Trianthema monogyna* and *Trianthema pentandra*.
ƙayạr ƙạdaŋgarę *f*. the plant *Asparagus Pauli-Guilelmi*.
ƙayạr kūsụ *f*. the twiner kwạraŋgā.
kāyā rūwa *Vd*. kāyā 8 ; kāyan 5.
ƙayạr tụnjērē *f*. yaws-sores on hands or feet.
ƙāyata = ƙāyanta.
ƙāyatad dạ *Vb*. 4A = ƙāyantad dạ.
ƙayau (1) yā būshę ∾ it's now quite dry. (2) yā sọ̄yu (tọ̄yu) ∾ it's well fried.
ƙayau-ƙayau (1) = ƙayau. (2) *m*. (*a*) ạbin nạŋ ∾ nẹ̄ this is well fried. (*b*) crumbs of the cakes wạinā *or* ƙōsǎi.
ƙayāyūwạ *Vd*. ƙayạ.
kāyạyyaki loads (*pl. of* kāyā).
kạ̄yayyē *m*. (*f*. kạ̄yayyīyā) *pl*. kạ̄yạyyū. (1) having been taken (*d.f*. kai). (2) having been brought (*d.f*. kāwō) *x* kạ̄yayyan tūwō yā rịƙi mụtụm ? can a man live for ever on free food brought him through his poverty, from other houses ? (3) having been overthrown (*d.f*. kā dạ) = kạ̄sasshē.
kaye A. (kāyẹ) *m*. (1) yā yi ∾ he got the better of me (in wrestling, lawsuit, etc.). (2) jạ̄kī yā yi ∾ donkey threw off its load. jạ̄kī yā yi minị ∾ my donkey threw off its load. (3) kụrkunū yā yi ∾ guinea-worm has laid P. low. (4) mun yi fạrautạ, mun yi ∾ we went hunting and got prey. (5) kō yā yi ∾ *Vd*. bạ̄rē 2.
    B. (kayẹ) *Vb*. 3A suŋ ∾ they (crowd, market, etc.) have dispersed.

ƙāyẹ *m.* (1) arrogance (= ạlfarmā) *x*
yā cikạ ~ he is arrogant. (2) yā yi ~
it is beautiful.,
kạ'ye-kạyē" = kạ'ya-kạyē".
kāyẹkāyī *Sk. m.* woman's plaits (*pl. of*
kaikainịyā).
kāyị *East Hausa m.* (1) head (= kặi *q.v.*).
(2) changing place of enclosure for
flock or herd.
kạyō *used in* ɗaŋ ~ Bạmāgujẹ *name of*
a bọrī-spirit.
ƙayōyī *Vd.* ƙayạ.
kāyūwạ *Vd.* kặi.
kạyyā = kayyā = kayyạ (1) (*a*) bother !
(*b*) alas ! (2) come, come !, behave
yourself ! (= habạ). (3) now, buck up !
(4) ho, you there ! (5) bad luck ! (6)
I doubt it ! (*as in reply to* do you think
it likely ?).
ƙayyạdē *Vb.* 1C *Ar.* (*cf.* ƙā'idạ). (1)
passed order or law that *x* aŋ ~ kwānā
ukụ zại bīyā an order has been passed
that he must pay in three days. (2)
passed order about *x* aŋ ƙayyạdẹ aikị
rules have been drawn up as to how the
work is to be done. Gwamnạtị yā
ƙayyạdẹ kuɗiŋ gishirī gạ masạyā
buhunạ Government has fixed sale-
price to buyers per sack of salt.
kaza A. (kặzā) *f.* (*pl.* kặjī). (1) (*a*) (i) hen.
(ii) sābō dạ ~ bại hanạ yaŋkantạ ba
familiarity with a judge doesn't mean
you can count on his favouritism. (iii)
kōmē yakẹ cikin ɗaŋ ~ shāfọ yā daɗẹ
dạ saninsạ teaching one's grandmother
to suck eggs. (iv) yārọ maŋ ~, in yā
ji rānā, săi yạ narkẹ the young have no
staying power. (v) ~ mại 'yā'yā ita
kẹ gudụn shirwạ the P. of property is
the one who hates risks (*cf.* 2*a*). (vi)
im mūgūwar ~ tā shịga akurkī, kō-
wạccē ta zō, săi tạ sārē tạ no fellow-
wife (kīshīyā) is welcomed by the
others. (vii) ~ tarạ tā ịsa lahīyā săi
kō im fātạ akẹ sọ if the best is not
available, take what offers ! (viii)
kadạ ~ tạ yi murnạ dọmin tā ga anạ̄
jạŋ hanjin 'yarūwā tatạ there but for
the grace of God go I. (ix) in nā rēnạ ~
Vd. rēnạ 10. (x) ~ mại jimiriŋ as
what a headstrong person ! (xi) ~ jạŋ
ƙunduŋ ạbūyạ what a slanderer !

(xii) ạlbarkạciŋ ~ *Vd.* ạlbarkạcī 3*c.*
(xiii) farar ~ *Vd.* bịkī 1*e.* (xiv) dạgạ ~
ya fārạ *Vd.* bạrāwọ 1*b.* (xv) kặjī sụ
rifạ bī nị *Vd.* ɗaurạ 1*a.*iv. (xvi) kặjiŋ
haifūwā *Vd.* ƙaurī 2*c.* (xvii) kō ~ bā
tạ̄ būyā *Vd.* gandū 2*g.* (xviii) kặzar
tsāfị *Vd.* fiŋgi. (xix) fīgẹ ~ *Vd.* īyar
dạ 2. (xx) mại ~ zāgị *Vd.* mụzūrū 1*f.*
(xxi) kặjim birnī *Vd.* awāyẹ. (xxii) ~
tā̄ fi dōkị *Vd.* sayar dạ 4. (xxiii)
kạrạmbạniŋ ~ *Vd.* mụzūrū 1*e.* (xxiv)
~ kạnkị *Vd.* ạlmụtsụtsai. (xxv) yā
fi ~ ạ sạke *Vd.* tallē 1*b.* (xxvi) an
yabạ wạ ~ mịƙā *Vd.* mịƙā 2*b.* (xxvii)
Vd. tūsạr kặjī, dūbaŋ hadiriŋ kặjī.
(*b*) săi ạ bar ~ cikiŋ gāshịntạ let
sleeping dogs lie ! (*c*) Kặzā, gạmạ
kạnkị dạ dūtsẹ how he overrates his
ability ! (*d*) (i) Kặzā, cī kị gōgẹ what
an ungrateful person ! (ii) bặkiŋ ~ nẹ̄
he's an ingrate, he's unreliable (*for
fowl eats, rubs mouth, and forgets*). (iii)
bặkiŋ ~ gạrēshị he's a breaker of
promises. (iv) lịnzāmị yā fi bặkiŋ ~
Vd. lịnzāmị 1*a.*ii. (*e*) yā gōgạ minị
kāshiŋ kặjī he slandered me (*Vd.*
kāshiŋ kặzā). (*f*) wạndạ ya ci ~
shī kẹ̄ dạ ita possession is nine points of
the law. (*g*) (i) wặcẹ̄ kặzā, tạ amsạ
kūkam burtụ̄ how can the weak vie
with the strong ? (ii) wạcẹ nị̄, ~ ạbiŋ
gyāram mīyạ (*said by wife when
husband buys cloth for new wife*) it's
more than I can bear ! (*h*) Kặzā,
ƀātạ wuriŋ kwānaŋkị how he spoils his
chances ! (*j*) (i) mum fịta tuŋ kặjī
dukū-dukū̄ we started at earliest dawn.
(ii) sunā yiŋ kặjī dukū-dukū̄ villagers
are eating dawn-meal of Ramadan
(*Vd.* sạhụr). (*k*) Uŋgulū, bạ̄ kặzar
kōwā ba *Vd.* uŋgulū. (*l*) Kặzā, kạnkị
dạ mọtsī what nonsensical talk ! (2)
(*a*) ~ dạ 'yā'yā pleiades (= tạrsōwạ =
surạyyā). (*b*) *cf.* 1*a.*v. (3) kặzar gēzạ
Allen's Reed-hen (*Porphyrula alleni*),
black crake. (4) kặzar dūtsẹ Stone
Partridge (*Ptilopachus petrosus*). (5)
kặzar rūwā African Little Grebe (*Polio-
cephalus ruficollis capensis*), Cape Red-
necked Grebe (*Podiceps ruficollis capensis*), Lesser Moorhen (*Gallinula angulata*). (6) kặzar Yarạbā duck

(= ạgwạ̃gwā). (7) saŋ ~ m. = washẹ̃-
washī. (8) ḳafạr ~ = tạ̃kạlmiŋ ~
Vd. ḳafạ 8b, c, tạ̃kạlmī 7a, b. (9) cf.
nāmạŋ ~.
B. (kạzā) Ar. (1) adj. such and such
x mụtụm ~ So-and-so. ạbụ ~ such-
and-such a thing. sạu ~ so and so
many times. ~ dạ ~ so and so forth.
(2) bạ̃ wani ~ dạ ~ it's no use your
making excuses. (3) (a) ɗaŋ kạzaŋ
ūwā = ɗaŋ kạzar ūwā damn your
eyes ! (but it is not such coarse abuse
as ūwākạ which it replaces). (b) yā
yi minị ɗaŋ kạzaŋ ūwan dūkạ he
abused me coarsely (Vd. ūwā 1c, dībạ 1j).
kazạb = kazạf = ḳazạf Ar. m. yā yi
minị ~ he accused me falsely.
kazagam m. sudden attack.
kazagī m. (1) the drum kanzagī. (2)
an yi musụ kazagim bakạ they have
been flattered.
ḳazạ-ḳazạ m., f. Kt. energetic P.
kazạllahạ f. meddlesomeness.
ḳazam m. and adv. hastily rising or setting
out x yā yi ~ = ~ sǎi ya tāshị.
ḳazāmī (1) (a) adj. m. (f. ḳazāmā) pl.
ḳazạ̃mai = ḳazạ̃mū dirty. (b) "ḳazā-
mị̃, mẹ̃ ka ci gidaŋkụ", ya cẹ̃ "ḳụ
dūbi bạkīna !" everything is known
by its characteristics. (c) gāra kạ ci na
ḳazāmī Vd. cī 26l. (d) shạ̃rạ ḳazāmā
ɗāki Vd. būjẹ. (2) m. abundance x
yanạ̃ dạ ḳazāmiŋ kyau it's very good.
yanạ̃ dạ ḳazāmiŋ kudī he's rich. yanạ̃
dạ ḳazāmin tsạ̃dā it's dear. sun tạ̃ru
mạsū ḳazāmin yawạ they've collected
in large numbers (= ḳazạntā 2).
ḳazạmtā ~ ḳazạntā.
kạzaŋ if (= in q.v.).
ḳazanta A. (ḳazạntā) f. (1) (a) dirtiness.
(b) hannū dạ yawạ, māganiŋ ḳazạntar
mīyạ many hands make light work.
(c) mẹ̃ ya kai furā zanẹ why did you
act so ? (reply, ḳazạntar dāmụ from
lack of ability). (d) hannuŋkạ (or
wạrkiŋkạ) shī kẹ̃ jāwō makạ ḳazạmtā
sometimes it is one of your nearest and
dearest who betrays you. (2) abundance x yā yi yawạ, har ya yi ~ it's
very abundant (= ḳazāmī 2).
B. (ḳazạntạ) Vb. 3B (1) is (was)
dirty. (2) is (was) abundant.

ḳazantad dạ Vb. 4A dirtied.
kazạrkayạ f. restlessness.
ḳazat = ḳazam.
Kāzaurāwā Vd. Bạkāzaurẹ.
Kạ̃zaurē Vd. banzā.
ḳạ̃zāzạ f. (1) lumbar spinal deformity
(= ḳụsumbī). (2) Vd. bisọ 4.
ḳazazzam = ḳazazzat = ḳazam q.v.
kazganyạ f. virgin-sheep.
kazgị East Hausa m. illiterate P.
kạ̃zịbai (Ar.) liars.
ḳạzḳaznā Kt. f. (pl. ḳaznạ̃nā) nursing-
mother (= ḳannī 2).
ḳaznī m. = ḳannī.
kạ̃zunzụmī m. (sg., pl.) bug.
ḳazwā f. (1) scabies, crawcraw (= Kt.
sọsōnị = bạ̃ sūsạ 1). (2) wākē yā sōmạ
~ beans are in blossom. (3) ḳazwar
lallẹ skin-eruption due to application
of henna. (4) ḳazwar birnī syphilis
(= tụnjērē).
ke A. (kē) (independent pronoun, feminine
singular). (1) kē cẹ̃ it's you (Mod.
Gram. 46). dạ kē dạ nī both you and I.
yā nēmar minị ~ he sought you for me
(76a.ii). yā gajīyad dạ ~ it tired you
(167). (2) ~ cẹ̃ ɗǎi that's the sort of
bad conduct I'd expect of a woman
like you ! (3) kē nai Vd. nai.
B. (kẹ̃) (1) (a) (used to indicate
relative sentence with present positive
sense, Mod. Gram. 133*) x ạbin dạ
nikẹ̃ bā sụ what I am giving them.
mutạ̃nan dạ sukẹ̃ (= mutạ̃nan dạ kẹ̃)
zūwạ the people who are coming
(Vd. nikẹ̃, nakẹ̃, kakẹ̃, kikẹ̃, yakẹ̃
yikẹ̃, ikẹ̃, shikẹ̃, takẹ̃, mukẹ̃, kukẹ̃
sukẹ̃, akẹ̃). (b) (past sense) x har yạnzu
ɗǎi kanạ̃ naŋ ịndạ kakẹ̃ you've made no
progress (lit. you are where you were).

(2) (emphasizing word placed at head of
sentence, Mod. Gram. 137a) x wạ̃si
sukẹ̃ yị̃ it's play they're engaged in
wani ạbụ Audụ kẹ̃ sọ nẹ̃ ? is there anything else Audu wants ?

(3) (kẹ̃ naŋ emphasizes whole preceding
sentence) x (a) ạbin dạ nikẹ̃ gayạ makạ kẹ̃
naŋ that is what I keep on telling you
nā gayạ makạ kẹ̃ naŋ well, I've warned
you. yā sạ̃mi kudī kẹ̃ naŋ he's really

wealthy. bā iriŋ abincinsa ba kē naŋ it is not the food for *him.* abin da aka yi kē naŋ cikin zāmaninsa *these* are the events of his time. (*b*) wani mutum kē naŋ, yanā zaune a Kano there was once a man living at Kano. (*c*) (i) ago *x* aŋ kafa gariŋ yau shēkara gōma kē naŋ the town was founded 10 years ago. shēkara gudā kē naŋ akē jiŋ tausayinsa a year ago one felt sorry for him (*Vd.* shēkara). (ii) since *x* shēkara hamsiŋ kē naŋ sunā buga jarīda they have been printing the newspaper for 50 years. yau shēkara bīyū kē naŋ sunā ta yāƙiŋ jūnā war has now been going on between them for two years. (*d*) *Vd.* 6 *below.*

(4) shī kē naŋ *x* (*a*) shī kē naŋ thanks, that's all I wanted you for ; that's O.K. = wasalam (Mod. Gram. 137*a*). shī kē naŋ ? was this what you wanted me for ? ; are matters all right thus ? (*reply,* ī, shī kē naŋ yes, I need nothing more). anā tsammāni tun da aka bā shi, shī kē naŋ it was thought that as he had been given it, the matter was at an end. shī kē naŋ, sǎi mu rinjāyē su we shall overcome them if this occurs. kō mun rinjāyē su, bā shī kē naŋ ba yāƙi yā ƙāre even if we overcome them, it doesn't mean that the war is over. shī kē naŋ, sǎi suka kāma faɗa so they began to quarrel. shī kē naŋ, sǎi su zamā bā su aiki ? does that mean to say they (coins) are out of circulation ? (*b*) = shirū 2.

(5) (*used in interrogative sentence introduced by inherently interrogative word*) *x* mē sukē yi what are they doing ? inā kakē tafīya where are you going ? yaushe yakē aiki when does he work ?

(6) (*followed by* sǎi *with relative past, or relative past without* sǎi) when . . . then *x* (*a*) yā fāra hawā kē naŋ, sǎi gā ƙanansa yanā saukōwā when he began to mount the stairs his younger brother was descending. suŋ kāwō bāƙiŋ kōgī kē naŋ sǎi muka gan su we saw them when they reached the river bank.

yā zō kē naŋ, ya kwānā bīyū cikiŋ Kano when he had come he spent two days at Kano. (*b*) shiga tasu kē da wuyā sǎi suka gam mu as soon as they entered, they saw us. (*c*) *Vd.* 3 *above.*

keɓa A. (kēɓā) *Vb.* 2 = kēɓe.
    B. (kēɓa) *Vb.* 1C *x* yā ~ musu wurī he marked off a place for them.
kēɓance = kēɓantā *Vbs.* 1C = kēɓe.
kēɓanci *m.* = kēɓi.
kēɓe *Vb.* 1A (1) (*a*) set aside for some purpose *x* yā ~ wajansa he screened off his quarters. yā ~ shi daban he set it aside. (*b*) aŋ kēɓe shi he has been treated with great distinction. (*c*) suŋ kеɓe runduná they cut off the army from escape. (*d*) Allā ya kēɓe mana masīfa may God fend misfortune off us ! (2) excepted *x* baŋ ~ kōwā ba I've not excepted, exempted anybody. (3) put (writing) in brackets.
kēɓi *m.* (1) section of area *x* yanā kēɓiŋ yammā it's in the western part of the place. a shūka shi a kēɓiŋ caŋ it must be planted in that part over there. (2) T. or P. excepted *x* Audu kēɓiŋ Allā nē Audu is one exempted by God from some calamity, etc.
kē bi (*derived from* letters K.B. *abbreviation of* kamam Baitulmal that which has accrued to Native Treasury as no heirs to property). yā sāmu na ~ he got bargain.
kece A. (kēcē) *Vd.* kētā.
    B. (kēce) (1) *Vb.* 3A. (*a*) is split, torn (= tsāge 2*a*). (*b*) yā ~ da dārīyā he burst out laughing = yā ~ da shēwa (= fashe 1*b*). (2) *Vb.* 1A. (*a*) (i) tore T. (= tāɓe 1*a* = yāge). (ii) gāra a jā, ta ~ *Vd.* ƙwāce 1*a*.vi. (*b*) yā ~ rēni he had a " jolly good time " (= ishisshirē). (3) *Vd.* kētō.
kēci *Vd.* kētā.
keftiŋ *Eng. m.* (*pl.* keftōcī) Captain.
kēgā *f.* (1) old woman. (2) old animal.
kēgē *m.* (1) wuƙā tā yi ~ knife-edge's worn away. (2) *Kt.* (*a*) rough edge of cakes or chameleon's head. (*b*) ƙēgyan zakara comb of cock (= zaŋkō).
kēji *Eng. m.* (*pl.* kējōjī) bird-cage.
ƙeƙasa A. (ƙēƙasa) (1) *Vb.* 3B yā ~ it

(soil, clothes) dried. (2) *f.* yā fi wancan ~ it's become drier than that one.
B. (ƙeƙasā) *Vb.* 1C dried (washed clothes). (2) cured (meat or fish). (3) yā ƙeƙasa ƙasā, yā ƙi he refused point-blank.

*ƙeƙasa ƙuru *m.* halo round sun or moon = sansanī.

ƙeƙasa kwaɓa *used in* maginī yā yi mini ~ builder inconvenienced me by not coming at time arranged.

ƙeƙasasshe *Vd.* wutā 1*o*.

ƙeƙashe (1) *Vb.* 3A = ƙeƙasa 1. (2) *Vd.* wutā 1*o*.

ƙeƙasheshe *m.* (1) peeled stems of hemp (rama) = sīyāye. (2) name of various weeds. (3) *Kt.* the tree *Heeria insignis*.

ƙeƙe *m.* (*pl.* keƙuna) (1) (*a*) bicycle. (*b*) ƙeƙyan shānu ox-cart. (*c*) ƙeƙyan diŋki sewing-machine. (*d*) ƙeƙyan rubutū typewriter. (*e*) ƙeƙyam fitila wheel actuating wick of hurricane-lamp, etc. (*f*) ƙeƙyan lema umbrella-spring. (2) (*a*) *the following are* mayāfi *of joined cloths of two kinds.* (i) ƙeƙyaŋ gwandā 20 pieces of baƙī joined to 20 of gwandā. (ii) ƙeƙyan sāƙi 20 baƙī joined to 20 sāƙi (= *Sk.* zambāgī). (iii) ƙeƙyaŋ kudī 20 baƙī joined to 20 kudī. (iv) ƙeƙyan dan katangā 20 baƙī joined to 20 dan katangā. (*b*) tana ƙeƙe she gives birth alternately to boys and girls.

ƙeƙe *used in* ƙeƙe da ƙeƙe sun gamu "Greek met Greek".

ƙeƙedarī *m.* (*f.* ƙeƙedarā) skinny goat or P.

ƙeƙemuƙe *m.* (1) stinginess. (2) half-hearted refusal.

keƙuna *Vd.* ƙeƙe.

ƙeƙuwā *f.* (1) (*a*) barren spot (= faƙo). (*b*) fitsāriŋ ƙeƙuwā *Vd.* fitsārī 6. (*c*) ƙeƙuwā sāi zōmō *Vd.* rūwā C.17. (2) (*a*) poor man. (*b*) stingy man.

keli *m.* (1) spring-balance (= sikeli). (2) 'yaŋ ~ skin-buyers.

ƙeli *Kt. m.* (1) affectation. (2) coquetry; ogling; simpering (= feleƙe).

kelu *Sk.* used in gōdiyā tā ~ mare's on heat (= huda 3).

kema *Vb.* 3A went in search of profit or advantage *x* yā ~ cikiŋ garī.

ƙemadagas = ƙemagadas = ƙememe *q.v.*

kemanta *Vb.* 3A = kema.

ƙememe (1) *adv.* yā ƙi ~ he refused point-blank. (2) *m.* yā yi ~ he is stingy. yā yi mini ~ he was niggardly to me (2 = mursīsī).

kemō *m.* (1) farī-cloth dishonestly woven very narrow. (2) slightly-built P.

ke nai (*said by woman to another*). (1) shut up ! (2) stop it ! (*cf.* kai nai).

ƙenau-ƙenau = ƙenau-ƙenau *used in* yana tafiya ~ (1) he's slinking along. (2) he (skinny P.) is walking past.

ke naŋ *Vd.* ke.

*kera (*used in translating from Arabic*) kūkaŋ kera professional wailing after a death.

ƙera *Vb.* 1A (*Vd.* ƙira). (1) (*a*) forged, smithed (metal). (*b*) manufactured *x* (i) aŋ ƙera jiragyan rūwā ships were built. (ii) bā ma saŋ a ƙerō wani sāban tāshiŋ haŋkalī we do not wish a fresh disturbance to be created. (2) yā ~ ƙaryā he forged a lie. (3) yā ~ gidā he built fine home. tā ~ 'yā tata she "togged up" her daughter. (4) yanzu na ~ ka if you don't look out, I'll give you a thrashing ! ƙerarre *m.* (*f.* ƙerarrīyā) *pl.* ƙerarrū well-built horse or P.

ƙerau-ƙerau *m.* wrangling.

kere A. (kere) *Vb.* 1A. (1) overtopped. (2) *Kt.* yā ~ būzū he pegged out the skin to dry (= kafa 2*r*). (3) *Kontagora Hausa* lashed P. to post with arms outstretched. (4) *Sk.* dried meat by the fire (= ƙafe).

B. (kere) *m.* (1) (*a*) hunters' throwing-stick, shaped like figure 7 and slashed (sarā) off a tree (*cf.* guduma). (*b*) *its epithet is* Kere mūguŋ sandā, kaŋ wuya, kaŋ hannū. (*c*) inda aka sari guduma, naŋ aka sari ~ they are of the same status or relative family-importance, but differ greatly in means. (2) (*a*) yā yi mini ~ he boggled with me. (*b*) yana ~ (i) loser in gambling (cācā) is refusing to pay. (ii) he's refusing from shyness (= filāko).

ƙere *Vb.* 1A forged all of the things, forged completely.

ƙe're-ƙeꞁreꞁꞁ *m.* (1) various acts of smithing, manufacturing. (2) wuriŋ *m.* factory.

ƙẹ̀rẹ̀rẹ̀ *used in* yā tsaya ∼ he stood disrespectfully (= zẹ̀ƙẹ̀ƙẹ̀ 2b).

kẹ̀ri *m.* exaggerating amount really bid for one's article.

kẹsạ *Vb.* 1A (1) (a) went direct through (place, crowd, etc.) x yā ∼ tạrō he forced his way through the crowd. yā ∼ daŋgā, yā wucẹ he passed through hole in fence (= rātsạ). (b) yā ∼ yā yi kudụ he turned off south (= bākatar). (2) yā ∼ gidāna he entered my compound without a by-your-leave. (2A) *cf.* kẹ̀tạ. (3) Bardē, bạ̄ kẹsạ̄wā *epithet of* any Bardē.

Kẹ̀sau = kẹsạ 3.

ƙẹshạm *Kt. m.* rumours (= ƙishiŋƙishiŋ).

kẹsọ *m.* (*pl.* kẹsunạ = kyạssā). (1) (a) (i) old grass-mat. (ii) *Vd.* kwānaŋ ∼. (iii) kōwā ka ganī dạ ɗaŋ kẹsạnsạ, wurin shimfiɗāwā yakẹ̄ nẹ̄mā do not mistake a malefactor for a P. in want ! (b) kẹsạŋ kuɗī load of 20,000 cowries. (c) *Vd.* zūcị̄yā 13c. (2) *Kt.* = kạram-nị̄yā mat. (3) kyạssā *pl.* worn-out footwear.

keta A. (kẹ̀tạ) *Vb.* 1A. (1) (a) split, tore (= tsāgạ 1a). (b) tore off. (c) yā ∼ hanyạ (i) he cut a road through the place (= tsāgạ 1b). (ii) he forced his way through. bạ sụ yạrdā aŋ ∼ su ba they did not let the enemy break through them. jirạ̄gē suŋ ∼ tẹ̄kū tạạ the ships clove their way through the sea. (d) *Vd.* irlị. (2) = kẹsạ 1, 2. (3) infringed x (a) yā ∼ haddị = yā ∼ shạrī'ạ he infringed the order, he offended against etiquette. (b) yā ∼ ịyạ̄kar Allạ̄ he offended against religion. (4) ∼ kōmā *Vd.* bargị 2.

B. (kẹ̀tā) *Vb.* 2 (*p.o.* kẹ̀cē, *n.o.* kẹ̀ci) = kẹ̀tạ.

ƙẹ̀tā *f.* (1) malicious injury. (2) wickedness. (3) dạ̄rīyar ∼ malicious laughter, schadenfreude. (4) ƙẹ̀tar gwaiwā doing evil which recoils on oneself (*epithet is* ƙẹ̀tar gwaiwā waɗɗạ ta kar ụbaŋgijintạ). (5) *Vd.* gandū 2e. (6) lūdạyiŋ ƙẹ̀tā *Vd.* gāgọ 4b. (7) cịŋ ƙẹ̀tā *Vd.* rụ̄zū 1a.

ƙetara A. (ƙẹ̀tạrā) *Vb.* 1C. (1) stepped over T. (2) crossed border and reached x yā ƙẹ̀tạrạ Dạurā he crossed over the

border into Daura territory. (3) yā ƙẹ̀tạrạ habạ he ate a small breakfast. (4) bẹ̄rā yā ∼ ni I went to bed supperless (*Vd.* dẹ̄tạrā 2). (4) *Vd.* ƙẹ̀tạrē, ƙẹ̀tạrạ shiŋgē.

B. (ƙẹ̀tara) *f.* (1) (a) act of crossing (*Vd.* ƙẹ̀tạrē, ƙẹ̀tạrā). (b) *Vd.* gulbī. (2) omission in reading or writing (*cf.* tsallē 2). (3) skin-disease said to be due to passing over place where charm (ajịyạ 6b) is buried to cause death of another.

ƙẹ̀tarad dạ *Vb.* 4A (1) (a) ferried across (= fitar dạ 6). (b) caused to pass a frontier. (2) x hatsī yā ∼ nī the corn tided me over.

ƙẹ̀tạrạ shiŋgē *m., f.* (*sg., pl.*) slave who has escaped soon after being bought (= shạ̄fạ gadaŋkạ).

ƙetare A. (ƙẹ̀tạrē) *Vb.* 1C. (1) (a) crossed (road, river, border). (b) *Vd.* ƙūrụ 1b.iii. (c) in jịfạ tā ƙẹ̀tạrẹ kaŋkạ, kō kaŋ wạ̄ yạ fāɗạ every tub must stand on its own bottom. (d) bạ̄ mai ƙẹ̀tạrẹ̄wā *Vd.* gicị̄yā 1c. (e) ƙẹ̀tạrẹ karā *Vd.* karā 1a.v. (2) omitted T. in reading or writing. (3) yā ƙẹ̀tạrẹ haddị = kẹ̀tạ 3. (4) ∼ dạ = ƙẹ̀tarad dạ x aŋ ∼ dạ shī ịyạ̄kā he has been taken across the border.

B. (ƙẹ̀tare) *m.* (1) ƙẹ̀tạraŋ kọ̄gī river-bank. (2) yanạ̄ wannaŋ ∼ he's on this bank. (3) yanạ̄ ∼ = yanạ̄ wancạŋ ∼ he is on the further bank (= hayị 5).

Kẹ̀tau epithet of any barber (wạnzāmị).

kẹ̀tō *Vb.* 3A tun dạ ạlfijir ya ∼ from earliest dawn. . . . kẹ̀tọ̄war rānā sunrise (*Vd.* kēcẹ).

kẹ̀tū *m.* quarrelling ; struggling

kẹ̀turmus (1) *adv.* yā ƙī ∼ he refused point-blank. (2) *m.* (a) speaking out bluntly. (b) yā yi ∼ he brazenly did shameful act. an yi masạ ∼ he's been humiliated ; he's been dismissed from his post.

kẹ̀wā *f.* yā ɗẹ̄bẹ minị ∼ he came to relieve my solitude or grief (= hasọ), *Vd.* ɗẹ̄bẹ 4.

kẹ̀wai-kẹ̀wai *m.* = kẹ̀waiwainị̄yā *f.* (1) constant circling round place (= gẹ̄waigẹ̄wai). (2) " beating about the bush "

kewaya A. (kēwạyā) *Vb.* (1) (*a*) went round place (= gēwạyā *q.v.*). (2) *Vd.* kēwayō.
B. (kệwaya) *f.* (1) making circuit (= gệwayạ *except* 5). (2) ƙệwāyạr ƙashī *Vd.* kạrē 36.
kệwạyạ bạ̀kin rāmị = kệwạyệ bạ̀kin rāmị.
kệwạyạ tsāmīyā *m.* the creeper ɗaɗɗọ̄rī.
kewaye A. (kēwạyệ) went roundabout way, *etc.* (= gēwạyē *except* 1*b*).
B. (kệwạyē) *m.* embroidered circle on gown (= gệwạyē *q.v.*).
C. (kēwayệ) *m.* circumference, *etc.* (= gēwayệ).
kệwạyệ bạ̀kin rāmị *m.* hoeing or manuring limited to base of crops (= gạ̄ nākạ).
kệwạye-kệwạyē *m.* = kệwai-kēwai.
kēwayō *Vb.* 3A (day, night, year, etc.) came round again (= gēwayō).
ƙi A. (ƙị) (1) *m.* (*sg., pl.*) *Eng.* key fitted to fishplate on railway-metals. (2) *Kt.* *x* ∼ zō you'll probably come (= kyā).
B. (ƙi) (ƙị) you *fem. sing.* (*employed grammatically, as illustrated by substituting* ki *for* ka, *and* ƙị *for* kạ *in entry* ka 1-7, *and* kạ 1-8).
C. (ƙị) *m. and adv.* (1) nā ji ∼ I heard the sound of a T. being dragged along. (2) an jā shị ∼ it was drawn along with a swishing sound.
ƙi A. (ƙī) *Vb.* 5. (1) (*a*) (i) refused (*i.e.* said "no ! "). (ii) ạbụ yā ∼ nothing came of the matter, it was impossible of execution. (*b*) refused to accept *x* (i) Allạ̄ yā ƙi ạddu'ạrsạ God failed to grant his prayer. (ii) kōwā ya ƙi yawạ, Allạ̄ yā ƙī shị God helps him who helps himself. (iii) ƙi huntū *Vd.* bịkī 1*k.* (iv) an ƙi dụngū *Vd.* dụngū 1*b.* (v) ƙi dạngi *Vd.* dạngi 1*b.* (vi) an ƙi dạurō *Vd.* dạurō 2. (vii) bā yạ̄ ƙin sanhọ *Vd.* tụmbī 1*b.* (viii) kā ƙi rūwan Allạ̄ *Vd.* gạwō, kwạrkọ. (ix) bā ạ̄ ƙin dādī *Vd.* wụyā 1*g.* (x) bā yạ̄ ƙim mại *Vd.* dādī 1*b.* (*c*) refused to do *x* (i) sun jạnyē, sun ƙi taịmakwammụ they stood aside and refused to help us. (ii) ạbịn yā ƙi rība the matter turned out badly. (iii) shiri yā ƙi dādī tsạkāninsụ they did not get on well with one another. (iv) sun ƙi gạba, sun ƙi

bāya, sun ƙi kạ̀i, sun ƙi gịndī they behaved mulishly. (v) mun ƙi yạrdā true as it is, it seems incredible. (vi) kại, nā ƙī, bạ ạ tabạ jịn irịn wannạm ba the like of this has never been heard. (vii) an ƙi cịn kạrē *Vd.* kạrē 30. (viii) ạkwai rānar ƙin dillancị, ran dạ hājạr mại gạrī ta ɓatạ the day of reckoning finally comes. (ix) kōwā ya ƙi jị, yạ̄ ganī he who won't take advice, will live to rue it. (x) kā ƙi cịn damō *Vd.* damō 2. (xi) kā ƙi fāɗụ̄wā *Vd.* cịwō. (xii) yā ƙi ambatō *Vd.* hạlạk. (xiii) tā ƙi cịn tūwō *Vd.* dadị 5. (xiv) kā ƙi tsāmī *Vd.* dakạn jīyạ. (xv) yā ƙi nōmā *Vd.* warạbukkạ. (xvi) indạ wani ya ƙī *Vd.* yinị 1*a.*iv.
(2) disliked *x* (*a*) (i) yā ∼ shị = yā ƙi jininsạ he hated him. (ii) *Vd.* bạ̀ƙō 1*c*, jinī 4*d.* (*b*) kạmar yạddạ yakệ ƙim mutūwạ tasạ, hakạ yakệ ƙinsụ he hates them like poison. (*c*) bạ ạbin dạ ya kwānā ƙī irịn wannạn there is nothing he hates so much as this. (*d*) in kā ƙi mạrāyạ dạ rīgar būzū, wata rānā ạ̄ gan shị dạ ta ƙarfệ poor to-day, rich to-morrow. (*e*) tạ̄shi sad dạ ka ƙī, kạ isa sad dạ kakệ sọ̄ work hard at the outset and you'll be able to rest later !
(3) yā ƙi hannūna it (domestic animal) did not thrive in my care. (4) *Vd.* ƙị bugụ ; kun ƙi cị ; ƙị ; mun ƙī.
(5) ƙī sạ̄bō = kā ƙi gani bīyū *Vd.* dạ̄misạ 2.
B. (ƙị̄) (1) (*a*) (*progressive and v.n. of* ƙī). (*b*) ƙin kạmūwā, ƙin jạwūwā = ƙin jā, ƙin tsiŋkạ̄wā = jinī 1*f q.v.* (*c*) ƙin dillancị *Vd.* ƙī 1*c.*viii. (2) (*a*) ƙin jị garēshi he's disobedient. (*b*) ƙin jịkī energy. (3) ∼ dạ sọ̄ = ∼ dạ ƙị̄ willy-nilly. (4) ƙin ƙi *Vd.* kuturū 2. (5) *Vd.* ƙin-*compounds.*
C. (ƙị̄) abundantly *x* sun tafō ∼ they came in large numbers.
ƙibạ *f.* (1) fatness *x* (*a*) yā yi ∼ he is (was) fat. yanạ̄ ∼ = yanạ̄ dạ ∼ he is fat. (*b*) munạ̄ ƙārạ ∼ we're becoming fatter. (2) ạ sararī, ƙibạr dōkị that is obvious ! (3) sun jē nēman ∼ sukạ sāmō rạ̄mā it's a case of the biter bit. (4) hạlāmạr ƙarfī nạ̄ gạ mại ∼ what a hard worker he is ! (5) ịnā ạmfạ̄nin ƙibạ *Vd.*

tạlōlō. (6) gīwā ta fi kōwā ƙibạ Vd. jūcē.

kibai Vd. kibīyạ.

ƙibạ-ƙibā m., f. (pl. ƙibạ̃ƙibai) fat P.

kibau Vd. kibīyạ.

kibbụ = Kt. kibbụŋ adv. and m. x mạganạn naŋ ~ cē there's no doubt about it. yā yị̃? did he do it? (reply, kibbụ yes, for sure!).

ƙibcē m. (1) blinking. (2) yā yi minị ~ he winked at me. (3) Vd. ƙibtā.

kibɗayyạ f. struggling together.

*kibịrītị Ar. m. sulphur (= wutā 1b.v).

kibīyạ f. (pl. kibīyōyī = kibau = Kt. kibai). (1) (a) arrow (epithet is Kyallạ, bạ̃ rụfan cikị). (b) date-stone used in game (Vd. ɓallē). (c) tā harbar dạ kibantạ she's old. (d) ~ ạ jịkiŋ wani, kwạrī nobody cares what happens to another. (2) (a) kibīyạr bạdūkụ leather-worker's awl. (b) kibīyạr kitsọ instrument used for woman's coiffure. (c) kibīyạr sakīyạ instrument for puncturing abscess (= Sk. cịŋkẹ 2). (3) cịcị kibau Vd. cịcị.

kibrītị = kibịrītị.

ƙibta A. (ƙibtạ) (1) yā ~ he blinked. (2) yā ~ minị idọ he winked at me. (3) kạmar ƙibtạwā dạ bịsmillạ̃ sǎi sukạ yī they did it in twinkling of an eye.
B. (ƙibtā) Vb. 2 x yā ƙibcē nị he winked at me.

ƙị bugụ Sk., Kt. m. the charm sạgau.

kicẹ Kt. m. fat (= kitsẹ q.v.).

kịcīcīyạ f. auger-beetle (cf. gunɗạ).

kicịfī Kt. m. = kitịfī.

kicik Kt. = kicin.

kicī-kịcī = kicị-kici = kịcị-kicī m. struggling to do long journey, hard task, support family, etc. (= ɗawạinīyā). (2) adv. x yanạ̃ aikị ~ he is struggling with lengthy task.

kịcīmạ Vb. 3B Sk., Kt. assumed serious proportions x faɗạ yā ~ quarrel grew serious. ạl'amạrī yā ~ matter grew grave.

kiciŋ m. charm to render P. permanently invulnerable (cf. shạ̃ dạdalạ; kạs kaifī).

kicincine A. (kịcincinē) x yā yi minị ~ it (work, etc.) is beyond me.

B. (kicincịnē) Vb. 1D yā ~ minị it (work, etc.) is beyond me.

kicịnīyā f. = kịcī-kịcī 1.

kiciŋ-kiciŋ m. ạnd adv. being deeply involved in x yā ɗaurẹ fuskạ, yā yi ~ he scowled. yā shiga mạganạ ~ he interfered deeply in it. yā yi tsụmmā, yā yi ~ he's in tatters. zaman dūnīyạ yā yi masạ ~ he's destitute. yā ci (= yā shiga) ɗạmạrū ~ he's armed to the teeth.

kịcirọ m. (1) carelessly-built hut for trivial guests (= kụsugụ 1). (2) any low wall. (3) thick-set P. or horse, etc. (4) (a) what a stubborn P. or horse! (b) how hard and uncookable this food is!

kiɗạ m. (1) (a) (i) drumming with drumstick (gulạ), cf. mārị, kọ̃tsō. (ii) injịn na mōtạ yanạ̃ kiɗị dṇ dṇ dṇ the engine of the car is vibrating. (iii) kiɗạ yạ jūyạ matters took a different turn. (iv) Sarkiŋ ~ Vd. marọ̃ƙī. (b) ạbiŋ ~ generic name for drum (epithet is Gandun Sarkī, ƙọsạ aikị), cf. gạŋgā. (c) bā ạ̃ nēmar wạ kiɗạŋ girbị dādī don't come "butting in" like this! wạnẹ kiɗạŋ girbị sukẹ nẹ̃ what the devil are they interfering for! (d) kiɗạŋkạ na jiyō epithet of busy-body. (e) kạ̃ gwammạcẹ ~ dạ kạrạtū you'll be throwing away the substance for the shadow. (f) (i) yā yi kiɗạnsạ, yā yi rawassạ shī kaɗǎi he did alone what really requires essential collaboration of another. (ii) Jāmụs sun yi mukụ kiɗạ, kunạ̃ rawā ạ gabạs the Germans incited you to attack the east. (g) jaŋ ~ Nupe Hausa the drummer gulạ 3 q.v. (h) sarkiŋ ~ Vd. marọ̃ƙī. (j) cf. shạ̃ kiɗị. (k) kiɗạm fạrautạ Vd. zōmō 2b. (l) kuɗiŋ ~ Vd. dạbaŋ 1b. (m) sạmmakwaŋ ~ Vd. sallạ 1m. (2) whisking, churning x kiɗạn nōnọ churning milk (= tugū̃wā), cf. tụntsụrē.

kidạ̃ɓạ how thick!

kidāhumancị m. ways of bumpkin (= gidādancī).

kịdāhụmī m. (f. kịdāhụmā) pl. kịdāhụmai bumpkin.

ƙidaya A. (ƙidạ̃yā = Kt. ƙidạnyā) Vb. 1C counted up x yawạnsụ yā fi gạbaŋ

a ƙidayā they were countless (= ƙirga, ƙididdiga 2), cf. lāsafta.
B. (ƙidaya) f. (secondary v.n. of ƙidayā) x munā ~ tasu = munā ƙidayā su we're counting them.
C. (ƙidaya) (1) Vb. 2 counted some out x yā ƙidayi 10 daga cikinsu he counted out ten from them. (2) f. x an yi mini ~ da gidansa I've been given a rough indication of the position of his home. (3) an cika ~ da sū they're included in the total. (4) Vd. tanƙā 1b. (5) dan ~ Vd. ƙunƙuru.
ƙidayɛ̃ Vb. 1C counted all of.
kidi Sk., Kt. m. = kida.
ƙididdiga A. (ƙididdigā) (1) Vb. 3A x nā ~ a rāina I reflected, pondered. (2) Vb. 1D counted up (= ƙidayā).
B. (ƙididdiga) f. (1) yanā ~ he's reflecting, pondering. (2) (secondary v.n. of ƙididdigā) x anā ~ tasu = anā ƙididdigā su they're being counted.
ƙididdigɛ̃ Vb. 1D (1) counted all of (= ƙidayɛ̃). (2) investigated fully. (3) x kā ~ da shi ? are you fully au fait with it ?
ƙidīdi Kt. adv. abundantly ; in large numbers.
ƙidigāle m. (f. ƙidigālīyā) destitute.
ƙidima A. (ƙidimā) Vb. 1C flustered.
B. (ƙidima) Vb. 3B is (was) flustered.
kidimī m. noise and bustle of festive occasion, etc. (= digimī q.v.).
kidinā f. deceitfulness (epithet is ~ ƙawā da mazā).
kidin girbi Vd. kida 1c.
kifa Vb. 1A. (1) (a) inverted T. on another x tā ~ ƙwaryā kan wata she inverted one calabash on another. (b) tana ~ kantu = tana kifin kantu she's marking beniseed cakes, turning them out and slapping them down on mat, in inverted position. (c) (i) yā ~ ciki he lay on his stomach. (ii) yā ~ ciki kan abim mutānɛ̃, yā cɛ̃ nāsa nɛ̃ he made false claim to article (cf. kifɛ ciki). (2) yā ~ ni he (trader) tricked me. (3) yā ~ da baka he fell forwards on to the ground (= cī 20). (4) Vd. kifa ƙwandō.
kifad da Vb. 4B (1) threw away liquid or grain (= zubar da). (2) yā ~ azzikinsa he squandered his means. (3) dropped

T., spilling its contents. (4) mōta tā ~ nī motor jolted me out of it.
kifa ƙwandō m. (1) defrauding P. (2) Zar. pagan Chief's seizing P. and family and selling as slaves (cf. tūwā).
kifar da = kifad da.
*kifāya Vd. farlu.
kīfāyɛ̃ Vd. kīfī.
kifɛ (1) Vb. 1A. (a) inverted. (b) mōta tā ~ da mū motor overturned, pinning us underneath. (c) (i) yā ~ kāi yanā shirū he bowed his head in shame. (ii) yā ~ kāi he covered his head with kabido or skirt of gown (to keep off rain or sun). (d) Kt. yā ~ ciki (i) he concealed the true facts. (ii) he wriggled out of his previous statement (= sauya 1h), cf. kifa 1c. (iii) yā ~ mana ciki he hid the truth from us. (2) Vb. 3A became inverted.
kiffɛ m. extreme round-shoulderedness with feet turning inwards (meeting such P. is considered unlucky, i.e. shu'umī).
kīfī m. (pl. kīfāyɛ̃) (1) (a) any fish. (b) irin zaman kīfāyɛ̃ sukɛ yi they behave like cannibals. (c) jirgin nan, kīfāyɛ̃ sun sōma ƙwāi kansa that ship has sunk. (2) kīfin rījīyā untravelled P. (= maƙāfo 1d). (3) an tāra ~ da ƙwādō "not separating the grain from the chaff". (4) (a) bā ā nēman ~ a faƙo he's a skinflint. (b) a rūwa a kan nēmi ~, a ƙēƙūwā sāi zōmō go the right way to work ! (5) garkyan ~ Vd. garkɛ 1b. (6) masōyin ~ bā na ƙwādō ba nɛ̃ tastes differ. (7) kōwā ya kāma ~ (= kōwā ya kas ~), a gōransa zai saka he who does not seek, will not get. (8) kaska tā mutu da haushin ~ rejoicing at another's misfortune. (9) ƙarƙwan ~ Vd. ƙarƙō. (10) yā san kīfinsa Vd. tāri 1d.ii. (11) Vd. lausa, Musulmī.
kiffīya f. turtle.
ƙifl m. love-philtre smeared on the eyes.
ƙifl-ƙifl used in yanā ~ da ido he (child on verge of tears, sleepy P., P. thought asleep but really eavesdropping) is blinking.
kifin kantu Vd. kifa 2.
ƙifta = ƙibta.

kifugu *m.* deceitfulness.

ƙigaga *f.* load tied on to bull when cattle migrate.

kigē *m.* the instrument **kuge** *q.v.*

Kịgo = **Kịgo** (1) *epithet of* Chief *or* bridegroom. (2) *Vd.* **dǫgarị.**

ƙihịhịyạ *Kt. f.* turtle.

kijẹ *Vb.* 3A sat disdainfully aloof, *etc.* (= **kākụmē** *q.v.*).

kijinjirī = **kijijjirī** *m.* (*pl.* **kijịnjịrai**) the palm *Phœnix reclinata* (*fronds are used for mats* (*Vd.* **tạbarmā** 1*b*) *and hats* ; *women stain teeth with its fruit*).

kikạ *Vd.* **kạ** 5.

ƙīƙạ *Vd.* **tạrī** 2.

ƙịƙạm *used in* **yā tsayạ ƙịƙạm** (1) he stood boorishly silent. (2) he stood listlessly from long wait. (3) hungry horse stood despondently = **ƙyǧrǧrǧ** (*cf.* **kikyū-kịkyụ**).

ƙịƙatạ *used in* **ƙịƙatạ,** **auran sǫ, bạ hatsin cị** working for another who then fails to pay one.

kikẹ A. (**kikẹ**) *Vb.* 1A finished, completed.
B. (**kikẹ**) (*used for* you (*fem. sg.*) *in present relative sentence with positive sense*) *x* **lōkạcịn dạ** ~ **zūwạ** when you (*fem.*) come. **yạushẹ** ~ **zūwạ** when do you (*fem.*) come ?

kiki-kạkạ = **ƙiƙi-ƙạƙạ** *f.* (1) **yā yi minị** ~ it nonplussed me. (2) **gạrī yā yi** ~ these are hard times.

kikī-kịkị *m.* (1) brazenness (= **ƙirī-ƙịrị**). (2) **am matsạ shi sǎi ya yi** ~ he was " left without a leg to stand on ".

ƙīƙịƙī *m.* (1) type of cloth. (2) miser. (3) creaking of loose chair or of bare saddle (**kạŋgwan sirdị**).

kikịrī *m.* (1) flesh (**tōtụwā**) of gourd become dry and hard. (2) **kikịrin dumā mại taurī** *epithet of* miser or of unconquerable P.

kịkirịkij = **ƙịƙirịƙ** *m.* (1) sound of crowing of cock. (2) **ya zamẹ musu ƙịƙirịƙ mūgụn zạkarạ** he was a thorn in their sides.

ƙịƙō destitute P. (*epithet is* **kạtạƙō** ~).

ƙiƙyu *used in* **yaŋ dạ taurī** ~ it (food) is hard and uncookable.

kikyū-kịkyụ *m.* **yā yi** ~ he stood alert (from danger or to listen), *cf.* **ƙịƙạm.**

kịkyụnīyā *f.* = **ƙirịnīyā.**

ƙil (1) *m.* tininess *x* **wạndō nǧ** ~ **dạ shī** they're tiny trousers. (2) *adv.* *x* (*a*) **bīyū ƙil** only two. (*b*) **ƙasassu caŋ takẹ gēfẹ gụdā ƙil** theirs is a small, isolated land.

kila A. (**kịlā**) *Vb.* 2 to thrash.
B. (**kīlạ**) (*Ar.* " was said "). (1) perhaps. (2) **sunạ cikin kīlạ wạ kālạ** they are in a state of doubt (*Vd.* **wạtạkīlạ**).

kịlābọ *m.* (*pl.* **kịlạ̄bai**) tanned ox-hide (*cf.* **ƙirgị**).

kilābụ *Vd.* **kạrkī.**

kịlāgạ *f.* one of the stomachs of ruminants (= **tubụrā**).

kịlāgọ *Sk., Kt. m.* (*pl.* **kịlạ̄gai** = **kịlạggai**) = **kịlābọ.**

kịlākị (*Eng.* clerk) *m., f.* (*pl.* **kilākāwā**) (1) well-dressed harlot (= **hannun** 2). (2) overdressed lad. (3) **gyạdā tā yi** ~ the ground-nuts have white skins, but no kernels (= **bụgau** 3).

ƙịlạ̄ƙilai *m.* (1) Long-tailed Glossy Starling (*Lamprotornis caudatus*) = **ƙyạ̄rī-ƙyạ̄rī.** (2) the bird kakelaar (*Phœniculus erythrorhynchus guineensis*).

kịlạ̄sạmadụ *m.* the bit-strap **marāyā** 1 *q.v.*

ƙịlạ̄wại contemptuously *x* **yā dụbē nị** ~ he looked at me contemptuously (= **shẹ̄ƙẹ̄ƙẹ**).

ƙilga *Sk., Kt.* = **ƙirga.**

kịlị *m.* (*f.* **kịlịyā**) *pl.* **kịlịyai.** (1) light-grey horse. (2) ~ **kanyạ** dark-grey horse (= **hụrdē**). (3) ~ **ƙwǎi** = ~ **magō** = ~ **bạmasạrī** cream-coloured horse. (4) *Vd.* **dụŋgụn dạ mại kịlị.**

ƙịlī *used in* **ƙilim bạlagạ** precocious flirting.

ƙịlīlī *m.* (*pl.* **ƙili-ƙili**) any tiny object.

kịlilī *m.* pollen of male date-palm.

kịlịs *Sk. m.* = **kịlịshī.**

kịlīsạ *f.* (1) **yā hau** ~ he went for a ride on horse, donkey, or in car. (2) **dōkịnsạ,** ~ **gạrēshị** his horse is trotting regularly. (3) **harshạnsạ yaŋạ** ~ = **yanạ̄ kịlīsạr bạ̄kī** he's licking his lips after pleasant food (= **ƙauyẹ** 1*d.*ii).

kilishi A. (**kịlịshī**) *m.* (1) thin strips of meat dried in sun, sprinkled with pounded ground-nuts (**tsōmịn gyạdā** *q.v.*) or pounded tigernuts (**tsōmịn ayā**), redried in sun, dipped in ground-nut decoction (**tsōmịn gyạdā**), then re-dried in sun and finally re-dried (gashi) before fire (= *Sk*. yąwarā). (2) ∼ igīyą bīyū two strips of dried meat *as in* (1).

    B. (kilīshī) type of wool-rug.

    C. (Kilīshi) the official charged with spreading Emir's rug.

ɓillą *Vb*. 1A yā ∼ ɓaryā he told a lie.

killącē *Vb*. 1C screened off (= kārę 2).

ɓillāgǫ *Kt. m.* destitute P.

ɓillę *Vb*. 1A severed *x* aŋ ∼ masą hannū his hand's been cut off. aŋ ∼ masą kǎi he's been beheaded (= ɓallę 2*b q.v.*).

ɓillī how small !

ɓilū *m.* (1) smallness *x* ɗaŋ wąndō ∼ small trousers (= ɓil). (2) ∼ tā jāwō bąu " it's the thin edge of the wedge ".

kiluhū *m.* (1) young child, animal, or plant. (2) finely-ground flour.

kilmisō *Kt. m.* bow-leggedness of horse.

kim huge *x* jirgin rūwā ∼ a huge ship.

kima A. (kīmą) (1) *adv.* slightly *x* (*a*) ɗębō minį rūwā ∼ draw me a little water ! (*b*) gā zāfin rānā fīye dą ∼ the sun was unusually hot. sunā san su yi haką fīye dą ∼ they're very keen to do so. (*c*) gąba dą ∼ *Vd.* gąba 2*b*. (2) *f.* (*a*) any medium-sized T. *x* wannąŋ ∼ nē, bā ɓātǫ ba this is medium-sized, not big. (*b*) (*Ar.* qīma price) (i) estimating value or amount (*cf.* kintātą 2). (ii) suŋ wucę ∼ they're innumerable. (iii) *Ar.* judicial appraisal of value *x* ą yi masą ∼ let its price be judicially assessed ! (iv) mąi ∼ *m.* official appraiser. (v) ąbiŋ ∼ *m.* T. to be judicially appraised. (vi) idǫ yā saŋ ∼ *Vd.* mūdu 1*c.* (*c*) etiquette *x* yā saŋ ∼ he knows etiquette (= dā'ą). (3) *pl. sense.* (*a*) *noun* a few *x* ∼ dągą cikinsu a few of them. anā ɗębō ∼ dągą cikinsu a few of them are being transferred, drawn upon. sun sā 'yaŋ ∼ ą kaŋ lyākā they stationed a few men on the frontier. yawąnsu bąi wucę ∼ ba they only reach a modest total. (*b*) *adj.* a few *x* mutąnē ∼ a few persons.

    B. (kimą) *Vb*. 1A yā ∼ rawanī he put on a huge turban. tā ∼ fątalą she put on a huge headkerchief.

    C. (kima) *Vb*. 1B (*progressive* kimā). (1) yā ∼ it (food, kolas) went bad. (2) yā ∼ he trembled with rage. (3)

cikina yā ∼ my stomach gurgled. (4) ɓurjī yā ∼ ulcer seemingly healing has eaten in further.

kīmą *f.* = kīmą 2*b, c*.

Kimallē *Sk. used in* ɗaŋ ∼ an .obsolete sąrautą among slaves.

kīmanin = kīmmānin.

kīmąntā = ɓīmąntā *Vb*. 1C. (1) estimated, appraised *as in* kīmą 2*b*. (2) took moderate amount of (condiments to add to food, etc.).

kimbā *f.* (1) (*a*) the pepper *Xylopia æthiopica* (*used for condiments and purgative*) = ą gōgę. (*b*) kimbar maharbā the under-shrub *Lantana salvifolia*. (2) dūnīyą tā shā ∼ these are hard times. (3) the black and blue cloth ą gōgę. (4) quick-tempered P. (*epithet is* Kimbā, ą gōgę : shā yąnzu, māganī yąnzu). (5) (*said by women*) ɗaŋ ∼ *m.* baby's penis.

kimę *Vb*. 3A (1) = kima 1, 2. (2) sat aloof or silent in company through disdain or vexation (= kākumē).

ɓīmī *used in* ɓīmin dōki huge horse.

kimmānin *prep.* about *x* ∼ bīyar about five (*cf.* kīmą).

kimsa A. (kimsą) *Vb*. 1A. (1) tidied one's things *x* yā ∼ kāyā he prepared his loads for journey. bą zan tāshi ba sǎi nā ∼ I shan't set out till I've set my affairs in order (*x* packed, had a meal, garnered crops, etc.) = kintsą. (2) (*a*) sat in Hausa way with feet drawn in (= kintsą). (*b*) *Vd.* kintsą 2. (3) stuffed T. into (*as* cotton into bag ; food into mouth, etc.) *x* (*a*) yā ∼ zaŋgarnīyā he stuffed corn-heads into bin (= cūsą 1). (*b*) yā ∼ kǎi dawą he fled to the " bush ". (*c*) yā ∼ cikin dūnīyą he vanished. (*d*) yā ∼ kǎi ɗāki he entered without a " by-your-leave " (= cūsą 2). (4) yā ∼ ɓaryā he told lie. (5) (*a*) yā ∼ masą wuɓā he stabbed him with knife. (*b*) yā ∼ masą naushi he punched him. (*c*) tā ∼ masą tunjērē she gave him syphilis.

    B. (kimsā) (1) *Vb*. 2 (*p.o.* kimshē, *n.o.* kimshi) *x* yā kimshē shi dą naushi he gave him punch, *etc.* (= kimsą 5). (2) *f.* yā shā ∼ he was punched, stabbed, etc., *as in* kimsą 5.

kimshe A. (kimshẹ) *Vb.* 1A tidied completely ; stuffed in all, etc. (*cf.* **kimsạ** 1, 3).

B. (kịmshē) (1) *Vd.* **kịmsā. (2)** stuffing corn-heads into bin *as in* **kimsạ** 3 (*epithet is* ∼ **mai hanạ saurin sātạ**).

kimshi A. (kimshị) what fine packing ! (*as in* **kịmshē** 2).

B. (kịmshi) *Vd.* **kịmsā.**

kimtsạ *Vb.* 1A = **kimsạ** 1, 2.

ƙịn *Vd.* **ƙị.**

kin A. (kin) (*fem. pronoun past tense*) *x* **(1) kin zō** you (*fem.*) came. **(2) kim fi dākị** *Vd.* **rugā** 1*a.*

B. (kịŋ) *Rustic Kano Hausa x* **shī** ∼ yes, *he* is the one I mean (= **ɗŋ-ŋ**).

kinạ̄ (1) *x* **kinạ̄ zūwạ** you (*fem.*) are coming (Mod. Gram. 16). **(2)** *f.* imitation musk (*epithet is* **kinạ̄ nạm, bạ mạ̄ yi kunyạ ba**).

kịnạ̄mī *m.* leather cords attached to stirrups.

kịnarā *Kt.* the cactus *Euphorbia kamerŭnica* (= **kyạranā** *q.v.*).

kịnāyạ *f.* **(1)** trickery. **(2)** *Ar.* (*a*) = **ạlkunyạ.** (*b*) metaphor.

Kịncākirī *Kt. epithet of* any *ɗan taurī.*

kince A. (kincẹ) *Kt. m.* destitute man.

B. (kincē) *m.* **(1)** cord of **ạlhạrīnị** made by stretching on one's foot and plaiting ; it is either (*a*) red *or* (*b*) multi-coloured (*b* = **hạddạjī**). It is used for the cap **habạr kadạ** *or* for neckadornment of women (*cf.* **ƙuŋgu, sịllīyạ**). **(2)** *Vd.* **kuncē.**

kincīyā *f.* root of plant **gwandai** used in dearth.

kịndạ̈i type of **lẹ̄fẹ̄**-basket (= **zubā**).

ƙịn dangị *Vd.* **darạŋgamị** 2.

ƙịndịgīrị *m.* (*pl.* **ƙịndịgīrai**) destitute.

ƙịn dillancị *Vd.* **ƙī** 1*c.*viii.

ƙịndim = **ƙindim (1)** abundantly (*re* liquids) = **ƙạndam. (2)** (*a*) **kindima** = **kandama.** (*b*) **kindimẹ̄mẹ** = **kandamẹ̄mẹ.**

ƙịndirmō *m.* sour milk with its full curd and cream (= **fadandẹ**).

kịndōjị *m.* early Victorian shilling.

ƙịndū-ƙịndū *adv.* in rags.

ƙịn fāsạ̄wā *Vd.* **fāsạ** 1*e.*

kịŋgī *Sk., Kt. m.* remainder (= **saurā**).

kinī *m.* one like ; those like *x* **bābụ kininsạ** he has no equal. **kinịn dạ**

bạ̄ nāsạ ba those not of the same type as himself.

kịnịbabbē *m.* (*f.* **kịnịbabbīyā**) *pl.* **kịnịbạbbū** deceitful P. ; mischief-maker.

kinibībị *m.* deceitfulness ; mischiefmaking (= **shịgi dạ fịci** 2).

kinīnịyē *Vb.* 1D **(1)** importuned. **(2)** impeded P.

ƙịn jạ̄ *Vd.* **tsịŋkạ** 1*e.*

ƙịn jī ; **ƙịn jịkī** *Vd.* **ƙī.**

kiŋkạ *Sk.* = **kikạ.**

ƙịŋ ƙị *Vd.* **kuturū** 2.

ƙịŋƙịhū *m.* **(1)** stingy P. **(2)** crop too hard to cook.

kinkima A. (kịŋkimạ) *Vb.* 2. **(1)** carried heavy T. short distance with the hands. **(2) yā kịŋkịmi dōkị** he made horse prance and rear. **(3) yā kiŋkimō bāshị** he incurred big debt. **(4) yā kịŋkimō ạbin dạ ya fi ƙarfinsạ** he's undertaken T. beyond him.

***B. (kịŋkịmā)** *f.* **(1)** bragging. **(2)** attempting T. beyond one.

kịŋkịmbōɗị (1) *m.* P. of drivelling talk. **(2)** ∼ **nānạ̄nā, Kauran zugū** (*words of song*) oh, those **bọ̄rī** people ! (*Vd.* **ƙaurā** 3*c.*v). **(3) kịŋkịmbōɗị bọ̄kọ̄ƙọ̄ bạbbaŋ hadarị bạ̄ rūwā sǎi iskạ** = **hōlōƙō hadariŋ kạ̄kā.**

kiŋkimẹ̄mẹ = **kiŋkimī** *m.* (*f.* **kiŋkimẹ̄mịyā** = **kiŋkimā**) *pl.* **kiŋkiŋkiŋkiŋ** huge.

kinkimo *Vd.* **kiŋkimạ.**

ƙịnnī used in **bāwạ** ∼ (*f.* **bǎiwā** ∼) P. born in slavery of slave-parents (= **bạcūcanẹ** *q.v.*).

kinnī *m.* the shrub **kirnī** *q.v.*

kinsạ = **kimsạ.**

kịntācē (1) *Vd.* **kịntātạ. (2)** *m.* **nā yi** ∼ I did so acting on analogy of similar act (= **hạsạ̄shē** 2).

kintata A. (kịntātạ) *Vb.* 2 (*d.f.* **kīmạ** 2*b*) **(1)** went direct to (= **dọ̄sā**). **(2)** reckoned out *x* **nā kịntạ̄ci zūwạ̄nsạ yau** I reckoned he'd come to-day. **na kạŋ kịntạ̄ci ƙarfẹ bīyar** I estimate roughly when it is 5 o'clock. **nā kịntạ̄ci ạbin dạ zai kai nị watạ gụdā** I estimated what I would need for a month's supply. **(3)** reckoned that, conjectured that *x* **nā** ∼, **nạ̄ ga zūwạ̄nsạ yau** I reckon he'll come to-day.

B. (kintạ̄tā) *Vb.* 1C = **kịntātạ.**

C. (kįntātā) *f.* *x* bā̧ shi da̧ ∽ he's muddle-headed.

kintįkě *Vd.* kuntųkě.

(kintin fakirin) *used in* kintįm fākirįm, makądin zįgįdir (= k.f. makądin zįndir) *epithet of* destitute P.

kįntįŋkau *Kt.* yā tsērę ∽ he got " clean away ".

kįntįŋkirī *m.* (1) tā daura̧ ∽ she put on neck-ornament of knotted cotton or abā̧wā. *(2) thread fastening edge of length of imported cloth.

kintsa̧ (1) *Vb.* 1A = kimsa̧ 1, 2. (2) sāi ka̧ kįntsu pull yourself together ! (*Vd.* kimsa̧ 2, kįntsattsē).

kįntsattsē *m.* (*f.* kįntsattsīyā) *pl.* kįnt-sa̧ttsū methodical P.

kintsį *m.* orderliness (of mind or place).

kįntsu *Vd.* kintsa̧ 2.

fįnzįgě *Vd.* fįunzųgě.

kippę *m.* round-shoulderedness (= kiffę *q.v.*).

fįir *used in* n nā̧ ganī ∽ I'm seeing clearly. idā̧nunsa̧ ∽ he is wide-awake.

kira A. (kirā) *Vb.* (*Vd.* kira̧). (1) called to P. (2) (*a*) summoned. (*b*) Allā̧ yā ∽ shį = fįasā tā ∽ shį he died. (3) invited *x* yā ∽ nį dīna̧ he invited me to dinner.

B. (kira̧) *m.* (1) (*progressive and v.n. of* kirā) *x* (*a*) anā̧ kira̧ŋka̧ you're being called. an yi masa̧ ∽ ka̧man " ta̧fō ! " he was called to come. (*b*) hannū mai kira̧n na nēsa̧ *Vd.* nēsa̧ 4. (*c*) bā yā̧ jįŋ ∽ *Vd.* nīsā 1*h*. (*d*) bā ka̧ jįŋ ∽ *Vd.* da̧kama̧. (*e*) gwaura̧ŋ ∽ *Vd.* gwaurō 1*g.* (*f*) tsōra̧ŋ ∽ *Vd.* barį 4*e.* (*g*) yi ∽ da̧ bā̧kiŋka̧ *Vd.* yā̧fa̧cě. (*h*) yā yi kira̧ŋkį sa̧u dayā *Vd.* ta alakō. (2) fįasā kȩ̌ kira̧na my days are num-bered. (3) wani ∽ yā fi " gā̧ ni na̧ŋ " death is no respecter of persons. (4) kira̧ŋ kā̧sūwā seller's announcing bargain-prices to get quick turnover. (5) kira̧ŋ kurtū getting P. to return to place by magic (*cf.* kira̧nyē).

C. (kįrā) *Kt.* *f.* transverse-ridge (= ka̧dādā *q.v.*).

fįira A. (fįira̧) *f.* (1) (*a*) (*progressive and v.n. of* fįera̧) *x* yana̧ fįira̧r fartanya̧ = yana̧ fįera̧ fartanya̧ he is forging a hoe. (*b*) fįīra̧r bā̧kī ga̧rēshį he is a profes-

sional panegyrist (*i.e.* makȩ̌rim bā̧kī = da̧ŋ fįīra̧ = baka̧ 6*b*.i ; *such P. does not blow horn* (būsa̧) *or do drumming* (kida̧) *such as is done by* marō̧fįā), *Vd.* marō̧fįī, ma̧'abba̧, ma̧gana̧ 2*d.* (*bb*) sa̧ŋ fįīra̧ (i) chief of professional panegyrist-beggars. (ii) head of smiths. (*c*) da̧ kya̧ŋ ∽ ga̧rēshį he is well-built. (*d*) fįīra̧r fįaryā ga̧rēshį he's an inveterate liar. (*e*) yārinya̧ cě mai fįīra̧r ka̧la̧ŋgū she's a slender girl with good hips (= maya̧ŋkā 2 = ka̧la̧ŋgū 4 = zųm-bū́tu̧ 2 = *Kt.* za̧nzarō 2). (*f*) fįīra̧r darě broad, hinged, white metal brace-let (fįawanya̧). (*g*) fįīra̧r gizo̧, kada̧ ka̧ tsīna̧nā, kada̧ ka̧ dumba̧bā = fįīra̧r gizo̧, kada̧ ka̧ tsīna̧nā, kada̧ ka̧ dausa̧sā what a cantankerous person ! (*h*) *Kt.* yārinya̧ cě mai fįīra̧r za̧nzarō = 1*e.* (*j*) im bā̧ ∽, mȩ̄ ya ci gawa̧yī if the transaction is not likely to materialize, let's call it off at once ! (*k*) fįīra̧r sanyī *Vd.* ba̧rhō. (2) metal bangles or anklets. (3) correcting error in writing by scratching out and writing over it. (4) fįwaryar ∽ *f.* cosmopolitan town.

B. (fįira̧) (1) *Vb.* 1A. (*a*) yā ∽ fįaryā he told a lie. (*b*) *East Hausa* severed. (2) *East Hausa m.* *x* anā̧ fįira̧ŋka̧ you're being called (= kira̧).

kirā̧fě *Vd.* kurfō.

fįirā̧gā *Vd.* fįirgį.

fįirāję *m.* type of fish.

kira̧-kira̧ *f.* type of starling.

kira̧nyē *m.* (1) an yi masa̧ ∽ = shī ∽ nę̧ he's been caused to return to place by charms (*cf.* kira̧ 5). (2) challenge by boxer in the ring via words of marō̧fįā-beggars.

fįirare A. (fįirā̧rē) *m.* (1) (*a*) twigs for fire-wood (= būbu̧). (*b*) *Vd.* fįirārūwa̧. (2) ja̧ŋ fįirā̧ra̧ŋ gyā̧tumā *Kt.* *m.* urging horse forward slightly, then reining it in sharply. (3) ja̧ŋ fįirā̧ram makaunīyā reining in galloping horse so suddenly that it slithers.

B. (fįirā̧rē) *Vd.* fįirį.

kįrāre-kįrā̧rē *m.* numerous acts *as in* kirāri.

kirāri *m.* (1) *descriptive epithet x* bā̧ gūda̧ *used in* A̧ŋgo̧, bā̧ gūda̧ Bridegroom, causer of joyful shrilling ! (*cf.* lafįabī,

ƙiꞬāre-ƙiꞬārē). (2) (a) boasting x
sunā ~ sun rinjāyē mu they're boasting
that they have overcome us. kō dā
jirgī dayā tak sukā harbe, yā isa Jāmus
~ even if they have shot down only
one aeroplane, it is a cause of boasting
for the Germans. (b) reputation x
yā tunā dā tsōfan kirārin nāsā he
remembered what vogue he used to
enjoy. (c) kirārin tallā Vd. tallā 1b.
(3) jubilation x (a) a nan nē sukē ta ~
they are jubilant about that. abin
~ na gaskīyā real cause for rejoicing.
(b) bā ā hūdā cikī a yi ~ don't cut off
your nose to spite your face !
ƙirārūwa f. (1) twigs for firewood (= ƙi-
Ɡārē). (2) Gumāgumai, ka kwānā dā
wutā ! ~ sǎi tōkā only big persons can
handle big affairs.
kirāwō Vb. 1D = ƙiꞬāya Vb. 2 called
(= kira 1 q.v.).
ƙiꞬāzā Vd. ƙiꞬjī.
kirɓa A. (kirɓā) Vb. 1A. (1) pounded
moist substance in mortar x (a) nā ~
bābā I pounded indigo. tā ~ furā she
pounded grain for furā (= nausā 1b).
(b) kō an ~ a turmī, mai yawan rǎi
sǎi ya fita if you're gifted with nine
lives, nothing can harm you. (2) yā ~
masā wuƙā he stabbed him.
    B. (kiꞬɓā (1) Vb. 2 beat P. (2) f.
yā shā ~ he's been beaten.
kiꞬɓaɓɓēnīyā = kiꞬɓayya f. hitting one
another.
kirɓe A. (kirɓe) Vb. 1A. (1) pounded (as
in kirɓā) all of. (2) yā ~ shi dā wuƙā
he stabbed him with a knife.
    B. (kiꞬɓē) m. soup of new baobob-
leaves (= laffo).
kiꞬɓēɓēnīyā = kiꞬɓaɓɓēnīyā.
kirɓi (1) m. (secondary v.n. of kirɓā)
x (1) (a) munā kirɓim bābā we're
pounding indigo. (b) munā kirɓim
furā = naushi 3. (2) what a stab !
kirbullē certain (= kibbu q.v.).
kirɓunā Vb. 1C Kt. yā kirɓunā fuskā
he frowned (= girɓunā q.v.).
kircī m. (1) eczema on cow, etc. (= kur-
kūzau 1). (2) eczema on human buttocks (2 = tā zāgā = Sk. garjē 2).
kiꞬdādā Vb. 2 Kt. (1) estimated. (2)
went direct to (1, 2 = kintātā).

ƙire A. (ƙire) (1) Vb. 1A Sk., Kt. severed.
(2) Vb. 3A East Hausa yā ~ it (rope)
snapped.
    B. (ƙirē) m. slandering P. = ƙiryē.
kirfā (1) (Ar. qirfa) f. cinnamon. (2) Vb.
1A. (a) folded x nā ~ shi ukụ I folded it
in three (= ninkā 1). (b) yā ~ ƙaryā
he told lie. (3) yā ~ masā mārị he
slapped him.
kirfị m. type of tree.
kirfō m. (pl. kiꞬāfē) whip (= kurfō q.v.).
ƙirga A. (ƙirgā) Vb. 1A counted up
(= ƙidāyā), cf. lāsāftā.
    B. (ƙirgā) (1) Vb. 2 counted out
some of x yā ƙirgi bīyū dagā cikinsụ
he counted out 2 from them. (2)
f. (a) an yi minị ~ dā gidansā I've been
given rough indication of position of
his home. (b) tā sōmā ƙirgad dangi
her breasts have begun to develop
(= ƙusāshī), cf. kabarā 3. (c) yanā
ƙirgar (= yanā ƙidāyar) tanƙā he's
unable to sleep (through hunger, etc.).
ƙirge A. (ƙirge) Vb. 1A counted all (Vd.
ƙirgā).
    B. (ƙirgē) m. (1) bā tā ~ it's not
permissible to count them ! (in games
darar shānū and 'yā), cf. nūnē, sākē.
(2) cf. tantalaminya.
    C. (ƙirgē) m. act of counting.
ƙirgi m. (pl. ƙirāgā). (1) (a) untanned ox-
hide (cf. kilābo). (b) dā sannū sannū
a kan ci ƙirgim bijimī slow but sure !
(c) Vd. shimfidā 4. (2) yā cikā ~ he's
become fat or important. (3) sun gama
~ they've formed a party for some
purpose. (4) Vd. kōrā 1e.
kiri A. (kīrī) m. (1) sun shūki ~ they've
sown their crops immediately after
first rains (cf. tātūwā ; kīrīyā). (2)
stunted P.
    B. (kirī) m. peddling haberdashery,
cloths, etc., by dan kirī (kirī = jēmāge
7), cf. jagalē, kwaramī, kōlị, bōjwā).
ƙiri A. (ƙīrị) m. (pl. ƙiꞬārē = ƙirrā). (1)
(a) hide rope (= Kt. gūrū 5b). (b)
kūrā tā zō dā guntun ~ " falling into
trap dug for another ". (2) abin dā
bai isa a jā dā abāwā ba, ā jā dā ƙiri ?
" making mountain out of molehill ".
(3) ƙaryar ~ ta mǎi cē the absence of
one essential factor renders the whole

thing useless (= ķaryā 1*h*). (4) *Kt.*
tubular belt of leather (= gūrū 1*a*).
B. (ķiṛī) *m. and adv.* (1) (*a*) yā yi ~
dą idǫ = yā kwānā ~ he couldn't sleep
(through hunger, etc.). (*b*) yaṇā barcī,
ąmmā idąnsą yaṇā ~ he's sleeping
"with one eye open" (= zōmō 3). (2)
idąnsą ~, kō kunyą bā yą jị he's
brazen. (3) idąnsą yā yi ~ he has protuberant eyes ; his eyes were "bulging
out of his head". (4) yaṇā tsąmmānị
yā ɓuyā, ąmmā gą shi ~ "like the
ostrich, he thought himself hidden".
(5) (*a*) yā ķī ~ dą mųzū he refused
point-blank. (*b*) ya fītō ~ dą mųzū,
ya gayą masą he spoke out bluntly to
him. (*c*) ~ dą mųzū suką cịnyē, suką
haną ni they ate it up shamelessly
without offering me any. Jāmųs
suṇ ķwācę ķasąr ~ dą mųzū the
Germans "'swallowed up" the country
in a trice. (6) *Vd.* ķirī-ķiṛī.
ķiribzą *f.* old P., old T.
kirif *adv. and m. x* (1) mīyą tā yi ~ =
mīyą tā yi kitib the soup is thick. (2)
ķyaurē yā rųfu ~ the door is firmly shut.
ķirigą *f.* (1) stack of firewood. (2) (*a*)
(i) pile of ground-nuts (October) or rice
(September) made on farm *x* yaṇā dą
shịṇkāfā ~ ukų he has three piles of
rice (= bāgą = dabą). (ii) *in the case of
ground-nuts, the piles called* kāshin tūję
are left for 7 *days, then amalgamated
to make* ķirigą. (*b*) pile of millet (gērō)
on farm in late August (= bāgą =
dabą), *Vd.* zōgarī, būshīyā 4*b.* (*c*) pile
of guinea-corn on farm (= bāgą =
dabą), *Vd.* būshīyā 4*c.* (*d*) *Vd.* gīwā 13*b.*
ķirigigi *m.* type of large owl.
ķiriķinjū *m.* the wild hunting-dog
kyarķęcī.
ķiri-ķiri A. (ķirī-ķiṛī) (1) *m. and adv.* = ķiṛī.
(2) *adv.* (*a*) n nā ganiṇką ~ I can see
"what you're up to". (*b*) dą rānā ~ in
broad daylight. (3) *Vd.* kiki-kikị.
B. (ķiṛī-ķiṛī) *m.* (1) wilfulness of
child. (2) over-rating one's ability
(*both* = giggīwą).
C. (ķiˈri-ķiṛīⁱⁱ) *m.* Dub-grass (*Cyno-
don dactylon*) = tsirkīyā 3.
ķiṛi ķǫrē *Kt.* ~ ɓēran taṇkā *epithet of*
shameless boy.

ķirin (1) (*a*) (i) baķī ~ jet-black (= sidiķ
= sil = sit = tilik = tilim), *cf.* subul.
(ii) (*adj. referring to plural or fem.
noun may stand in masc. before* ķirin)
x Hąmādą baķī ķirin the deadly Sahara.
lāɓarai sunā naṇ baķī ķiriṇ (= baķąķē
ķiriṇ) there is very bad news (*cf.* ƒat).
(iii) iṇ an cę musų "baķī", sǎi sų
cę "ķirin" they are yes-men. (*b*)
yā yi duhų ~ it's pitch dark. (2) duk
ąlhērịn dą Allą ya yi masą, yā yi masą
baķī ~ all the good fortune God had
lavished on him, seemed to him in-
significant.
ķiriṇgimą *Kt.* meddlesomeness.
ķiṛinīyā *f.* (1) officiousness ; meddlesomeness (= fēlēķē). (2) affectation ;
coquetry ; simpering (= fēlēķē). (3)
Kt. (*a*) disobedience by child. (*b*) idling
by child who should be at work. (4)
Vd. sąrā 1*m.*
ķirinjịjīyą = *Kt.* ķirinjịjīyą *f.* Whistling-
teal (*Dendrocygna viduata*).
ķiriṇkī *m.* meddlesomeness.
ķirinyą = kirinyą *f.* (1) the circular
reinforcement inside apex of conical
thatch-roof (= gārųmā 1). (2) ring on
tethering-post, attached to rope, to let
goat move or sleep without rope
coiling round post (*cf.* tālālā). (3)
reinforced edge of lęfę-basket.
kirip = kirif.
ķiṛīrị *m.* (1) coccyx (= dąndarị). (2)
ą ~ ta ɗaurą zanąntą she's wearing
cloth too short to cover her buttocks
(*cf.* sāɓulancī). (3) nā ķī I refuse !
(*reply,* kā yi ~ ; mątarką tą ķī ką
bother you ! *this reply being playful
abuse to male by woman or boy*).
ķiṛīrịcę *Vb.* 3A (1) yā ~ he's brazen (*cf.*
ķiṛī). (2) idǫna yā ~ I cannot sleep
(through hunger, etc.) ; *cf.* ķiṛī. (3)
wāķē yā ~ beans are too hard to cook
(*cf.* hǫri).
ķiris *m. and adv.* (1) bą ni dą shī kō ~ I've
none of it at all. (2) yā bā nị ~ he
gave me a tiny amount of it.
Kiṛistą *m., f., sg., pl.* a Christian (= Bąna-
sārę).
kīrīya *used in* sun shūką kīrīyar gyąɗā
ground-nuts have been intersown with
millet (gērō) about 15 days after kīrī.

kiriya kōrē ɓeran taŋkā *epithet of* shameless boy.

kirjī *m.* (*pl.* kiɽāzā) (1) (*a*) chest. (*b*) tā daurę ～ = tā yi dauriŋ ～ she for the first time secured cloth above her breasts (*done by Filani at age of seven, but others give feast 3 months after marriage, when bride first secures cloth above breasts*). (2) square of thread-adornment between each tsadarī 2. (3) bugi kirjī *Vd.* bugā 2.

kirkā *f.* (1) Vervet-monkey (*Cercopithecus pygerythus*). (2) Patas-monkey (*Cercopithecus patasi*).

kirki *m.* (1) excellence *x* (*a*) abiŋ ～ good T. yā bā ni abiŋ ～ he gave me something good. an shiga shāwara kamar abiŋ kirki deliberations began as if all were well. (*b*) yā yi mini abiŋ ～ he treated me well. (*c*) kā yi ～ you behaved well. (*d*) muna ～ (= munā abiŋ ～) da shī he and I get on well. (2) abiŋ ～ *m.* satisfactory amount *x* bai shā abiŋ ～ ba he didn't drink much. (3) abar kirki *Vd.* gabāruwā 1*c*.

kirkintā *Vb.* 1C looked carefully after (= ādanā).

kirkira A. (kirkirā) *Vb.* 1C. (1) invented (*cf.* kēra). (2) yā ～ masa laifī he falsely accused him.

　　B. (kirkira) *Vb.* 2 = kirkirā 1.

kirkitsa *int. from* kitsa.

kirma A. (kirma) *Vb.* 1A. (1) overfilled with fluid *x* tā ～ rūwā a tukunyā she over-filled cooking-pot with water. (2) (*a*) yā ～ kāi dawa he fled to " bush ". (*b*) yā ～ kāi cikiŋ gidā he entered without a " by your leave " (= rāka 1*a*). (3) yā ～ shi da kasā he threw him down. (4) yā ～ masa wukā he stabbed him. yā ～ masa naushi he punched him.

　　B. (kirmā) *Vb.* 2 (1) drank much of *x* yā kirmi rūwā. (2) yā kirmē shi da wukā (naushi) = kirma 4.

kirmę *Vb.* 1A yā ～ shi da wukā (naushi) = kirma 4.

kirmijī *m.* huge P. or T.

kirmis completely *x* yā kōnę ～ it's completely burnt. yā cinyę ～ he ate it all up. yā kī ～ he refused point-blank.

kirmitsā *Vb.* 1C did hastily and badly (= karmatsā).

kirmuŋ *m.* sleeping-sickness (= cīwam barcī).

kirnī *m.* the shrub *Briedelia ferruginea* and brew from it which is said to ward off arrow-poisons and syphilis = riga kafi 1 (*epithet is kad dafi*).

kirrā hide-ropes (*pl. of* kiri).

kirsa *Vb.* 1A = kirshę 1.

kirshę *Vb.* 1A (1) tā ～ zananta she tucked up her cloth round her waist to do work. yā ～ warkinsa he tucked up his leather loin-cloth round his waist, so as to leave his body free for work. (2) yā ～ he's sticking at his work.

Kirsimati = Kirsimēti *Eng. m.* (1) Christmas. (2) sāi jira mukē mutum ya daga kafa, mu sā a yi Kirsimēti bā da shī ba if we see anyone move, we'll " bump him off ".

kirtānį *m.* string ; twine.

kirtif (1) *x* mīya tā yi ～ the soup's thick. (2) garī yā yi ～ the sky's overcast, black with storm-clouds.

kirtikēkę *Vd.* kurtukēkę.

kiru A. (kirū) dōki yā yi ～ horse put its ears back in fright (= riŋkyū-riŋkyū).

　　B. (Kiru) jinginar ～ inability to redeem pawned T., *etc.* (*Vd.* jingina 3*c*).

　　C. (kirū) *Kt.* damriŋ ～ the torture kangarē 1.

kirū-kirū *m.* = kirū.

kirwadī *used in* daŋ kirwadī *m.* (*f.* 'yar ～) *pl.* 'yaŋ ～ young (*re* child, animal, beans, ground-nuts, etc.) = tirwadī.

kirya *f.* (1) the tree *Prosopis oblonga* (*used for charcoal, i.e.* gawayī *or* stockade, *i.e.* kafiŋ garī). (2) namijiŋ ～ *m.* the tree *Amblygonocarpus Schweinfurthii.* (3) the eulogistic drumming, *etc.*, called tākē.

kiryē *m.* slandering P.

kis = kiris.

kisa *m.* (1) (*a*) (*secondary v.n. of* kashę *q.v.*) *x* kisaŋ aurē divorce (*Vd.* kashę 3*b*). kisaŋ gararī achieving one's aim (*Vd.* kashę 7). kisaŋ kāi murder. tāba tanā kisa = tāba tanā kisaŋ jikī tobacco taken in excess makes one dizzy (*Vd.* kashę 4*d*). (*b*) ～ yakē cikiŋ cinikī he is a dishonest trader, he overcharges. (*c*) *x* Audu kisaŋ gōrǫ nē Audu is addicted to kola-nuts. (2) bā kisaŋ karē ba, jaŋ to start is easy, but it is hard to persevere. (3) zamaŋ kisaŋ dąɓē *m.* overstaying one's welcome (= zauną gąriŋką 2 = daŋgwamī 2). *(4) kisaŋ gīlą *Vd.* gīlą. (5) kisaŋ haki *Vd.* haki 4*b.* (6) kisąm mųmmųkē *Vd.* mųmmųkē. (6*A*) kisąn rāɓā stunted sheep or goat. (7) kisaŋ wutā *Vd.* kashę 3*k.*iv. (8) kisąn damō haŋkąlī nę, īyąwā nę act cautiously ! (9) kų bar kisaŋ jēmāgę, māgąnim mącę madi the charm for women is money (*for bats are used for love-philtres*), deeds are required not words. (10) dōkį yā fi kisąm mąi gōnā *epithet of* shą dądalą. (11) kisąŋkį bą jinī sąi yaushī *epithet of* yuŋwą. (12) kisąm macįjim mātā *Vd.* banzā 1*g.* (13) bā yą kisaŋ itącē *Vd.* sāram bisą.

kisāgārę *m.* (*f.* kisāgārįyā) burly.

*kisāsį *Ar. m.* lex talionis.

*kisfę *Vb.* 3A *Ar.* sun (moon) was eclipsed (*Vd.* husūfį).

kishą (1) I've found it ! (*said in game* 'yā *where aim is to find in which heap T. is hidden*) = ish 3. (2) kishą = ∼ tųbarkallą no, don't praise my child, horse, etc., like this ! (for, if you do, evil eye, *i.e.* kambum baką, may fall on him) = sitilaŋ.

kishi A. (kīshį) *m.* (1) (*a*) (i) jealousy. (ii) ∼ ya kąŋ kai mųtųm makasā jealousy may cause one's destruction. (iii) kuŋgurmin dājį māgąnim mąi kīshi don't be jealous where there's no cause for jealousy ! (*b*) bakiŋ ∼ bitter jealousy. (*c*) kīshįm birnī concealing by co-wives (kīshįyā) of mutual jealousy. (2) (*a*) emulation, rivalry (= gąsā). (*b*) kīshįn zūcī ambition. (*c*) suną kīshįn sąurī = *Kt.* suną kīshin sąmrī wives of two brothers are vying together.

    B. (kishį) *Sk., Kt. m.* (1) thrashing *x* yā shā ∼ he was thrashed. (2) (*with pl.* kishi-kishį) section, portion (= kashį).

kishi A. (kīshį) *m.* (1) thirst (= kīshirwā). (2) *Vd.* zartsī 2*b.*

    B. (kīshī) *m.* excellence *x* mųtumįŋ ∼ good P. (= kirkį).

kishimį sąi bągō epithet of decrepit old male gazelle or old man.

kishiŋ = kishiŋ-kishiŋ.

kishiŋgidą *Vb.* 3B reclined on the elbow = gijįrcē = kwąncīyā 8 = shągidą = *Sk.* gįncirą).

kishiŋgįdē *Vb.* 3A = kishiŋgidą.

kishiŋ-kishiŋ *m.* (1) rumours *x* mun ji ∼ wai yaną shirįn yāki we've heard that he's planning war. (2) rumours about *x* nā ji ∼ mąganąn naŋ I heard rumours about this.

kishin rūwā = kishiŋ ruwā *Sk.* m. thirst (= kishi).

kishirwā *f.* (1) (*a*) thirst. (*b*) watąŋ ∼ *m.* Ramadan (the month of fasting, *i.e.* azumī). yaną ∼ he's fasting. (*c*) ∼ tā sąmi rūwan shą person's wish was fulfilled. (*d*) *Vd.* zartsī. (*e*) jinī bā yą māgąnįŋ kishirwā in the end, tyranny brings one to grief. (*f*) *Vd.* tandą 2. (2) shortage *x* kishirwar gōrǫ scarcity of kolas. bą ząi kashę musų ∼ ba it will not make up to them for the deficiency. (3) *x* muną kishirwar ganin-tą we're longing to see her.

kīshįyā *f.* (*pl.* kīshīyōyī). (1) (*a*) co-wife (*epithet is* ∼ bą haushī ; aną ganįŋkį, kąn zągi mijį), *cf.* baranyą. (*b*) Azagandį, mugunyąr ∼ *epithet of* bad co-wife. (*c*) bā tą sǫ ą yi (= ą kai) matą ∼ she does not want her husband to bring another wife home. (*d*) dą zamąm banzā gwąmmą aikiŋ ∼ (*lit.* it's better to work for one's co-wife than to do none) any work's better than idleness. (*e*) hąrąri ∼ *m.* dark type of imported cotton. (*f*) an sawō matą ∼ poor man with one wife, bought horse (*i.e.* as not able to pay for both 2nd wife *and* horse). (*g*) kīshįyar mąi dōrō *Vd.* bųkū-bųkū 3. (*h*) gārar kīshįyā *Vd.* dąushe 2*b.* (*j*) bāwąŋ kīshįyā *Vd.* fąrkā 2*b.* (*k*) kīshįyar kǫnannīyā *Vd.* saurā 1*f.* (*l*) ūwar ∼ tā mutų *Vd.* kūkā 1*b.*iv. (2) rival *x* an yi wą Audų ∼ part of Audu's duties have been delegated to another. kąsūwarmų tā zamā kīshįyar tākų our market's the rival of yours. (3) opposite of *x* (*a*) baki kīshįyar fąrī nę black is the opposite of white. (*b*) tsaiwā kīshįyar tąfīyą resting retards a journey. (5) yā yi wą dōkįnsą cikiŋ ∼ he hobbled his horse near-hindleg to off-foreleg, *etc.* (*Vd.* ycikįŋ kīshįā).

*kisima A. (kisi̱mā = ƙisi̱mā) *Vb.* 1C *Ar.* divided into portions.
    B. *(kisima̱ = ƙisima̱) *Ar.f.* portion, part.
*kisira̱ *Ar. f.* Arabic vowel sign for " i " (*Vd.* fādu̱wā 8).
ki̱sīsina̱ *f.* underhand ways.
ki̱skādi̱ *Kr. m.* repeating Koran aloud to memorize (= kaftū = gōgę 1*f*).
kiskī *Sk., Kt. m.* (1) (*a*) Orange-headed male lizard (= jaŋ gwādā). (*b*) kā ci kiskī *Vd.* damō 2. (2) destitute P.
kiski̱rī *m.* first stages in the making of a mat.
ki̱skō *used in* Gwau̱rau ba̱ hā̱, ki̱skō yā fi aiki̱m māla̱mī epithet of syphilis (tu̱njērē).
kisnī *Kt. m.* the shrub kirnī *q.v.*
*kisra̱ *f.* = kisira̱.
kissa̱ *f.* (1) tact *x* yā īya̱ ∼ he's tactful. (2) (*with pl.* kissōshī) intrigue.
ƙissa̱ *Ar. f. x* kada̱ ka̱ amsa̱ ja̱wābi̱ sāi kā saŋ ∼ tata̱ do not reply to a matter till you know what it's really about !
*kiswa̱ *Ar. f.* the holy carpet for the Ka̱'aba̱ sent annually by Egypt.
kita A. (ki̱ta̱) *x* yā fādi̱ ∼ he fell flat. yana̱ kwa̱nce ∼ he's lying flat.
    B. (kīta̱) *Sk., Kt. f.* (1) a tear, rip (*cf.* kēta̱). (2) sum ba̱nkę wanna̱m ba̱bbar kītar ƙi̱yayya̱ wa̱dda̱ kę̄ tsa̱kāninsu̱ they've patched up the bitter hostility between them.
ƙī tāɓȩ̄wā *m.* small grass tubers whose smoke is said to prevent poverty.
kitābi̱ *Vd.* kāfi̱rci̱.
ki̱ta̱-ki̱ta̱ *f.* staggering.
ƙītā-ƙītā̱ *pl.* huge *x* dammuna̱ ∼ huge corn bundles (= tīƙā-tīƙā̱).
ki̱tāla̱ *Ar.f.* struggle *x* sāi an shā ∼ da̱ shī tu̱ku̱nā ya̱ bīya̱ he'll only pay after one's had endless trouble with him.
ki̱ta̱mau *Kt. m.* meddlesomeness ; senseless behaviour.
ƙī ta̱nƙwasa̱ *Vd.* bida̱ 3.
ki̱ti'a̱ *Ar. f.* fragment.
kitib = kirif.
ki̱ti̱btib thick (= ka̱ta̱ɓarɓar *q.v.*).
kitifī *m.* conspiring.
ki̱tījǫ *Fil. m.* Bararo Filani who pronounces the incantations called su̱rkullē.

kitikā-ki̱ti̱ƙā̱ *pl.* huge.
kitikō *m̩.* (1) mischief-making. (2) ūwar ∼ *f.* mischief-making, scandalmongering woman. (3) u̱baŋ ∼ *m.* scandalmongering, mischief-making man.
kitikwa̱ *Zar. f.* bundle of millet (gērō) with stalks plaited together.
ki̱ti̱mbō *Vd.* shā̱ ∼.
ki̱ti̱ŋkā *f.* mischief-making (= kinibi̱bi̱).
kitsa̱ *Vb.* 1A (1) = kitsę 2*a*. (2) aŋ ∼ ma̱gana̱ lying story's been fabricated.
kitsanya̱ *f.* a boil.
kitsę (1) *m.* (*a*) suet. (*b*) gani̱ŋ ∼ akȩ̄ wa̱ rōgǫ it belies its good appearance. (*c*) kitsę mūgu̱n nāma̱ ba̱ ka̱ nu̱na ba, kā kashȩ wutā *playful epithet of* Filani. (*d*) har ya̱ mutu̱ bā yā̱ fid da̱ kitsę a̱ wuta what a spineless person ! (*e*) kalla̱bi̱ŋ ∼ *Vd.* a̱bu̱ 2*b*. (*f*) *Vd.* bu̱rgumā.
    (2) *Vb.* 1A (*a*) tā ∼ mata̱ ka̱nta̱ she did coiffure for her. (*b*) aŋ ∼ ka̱n zānā edge of grass-mat has been finished off. aŋ ∼ ka̱ŋ gwa̱dǫ edge of gwa̱dǫcloth has been finished off. aŋ ∼ ka̱n shi̱rāyī top of covered-corridor has been finished off. aŋ ∼ ka̱n ta̱barmā edge of mat's been finished off (= dājȩ = kashȩ 5*b*).
kitsǫ *m.* (1) (*a*) woman's coiffure. (*b*) im bā̱ ki da̱ gāshi̱ŋ Wancę, kada̱ ki̱ yi kitsa̱ŋ Wancę don't attempt the impossible ! (*c*) i̱nā rūwaŋ u̱ŋgulū da̱ ∼ what do I care ! (*d*) kada̱ a̱ yi kitsǫ da̱ kwa̱rkwata̱ act honestly in all you do ! (*e*) lā̱bāri̱ŋ ∼ *Vd.* kundumī. (2) finishing off *as in* kitsę. (3) kitsa̱ŋ rama̱ plaiting scanty hair of woman, with hemp.
ki̱ttāni̱ = ki̱rtāni̱.
ƙiwā *f.* = ƙyu̱yā.
kiwata A. (kīwa̱ta̱) *Vb.* 1C (1) tended P. or animal *as in* kīwǫ. (2) grazed, fed (animal).
    B. (kīwata̱) *Vb.* 2 (*p.o.* kī̱wa̱cē, *n.o.* kī̱wa̱ci) = kīwa̱tā.
kīwǫ *m.* (1) (*a*) tending P. or animal *x* anā̱ kīwa̱ŋ Ka̱nde Kande is being provided for, supported, subsisted, looked after. yana̱ kīwa̱n ta̱lo-ta̱lō he keeps turkeys (*Vd.* ajīyȩ̄ 7*b*). yā̱ yi kīwa̱n dōki̱nsa̱ da̱ kya̱u̱ he looked

well after his horse. (b) lādaŋ ∼ m. one of the young goats given P. tending another's goat, etc. (c) kōwā dạ kīwạn dạ ya kạrɓē shị, maƙwạbcin ạkwīyạ yā sạyi kūrā everyone for himself. (2) (a) feeding by animals x dōki (sā) yanā ∼ the horse (bull) is grazing. (b) pecking up food by birds (= ƙọtō) x kạjī sunā ∼ the poultry are feeding. (3) being on one's guard against x (a) n nā kīwạnsạ I'm on my guard against him. (b) mālạmī ạbin ∼ in yā kịyạyī kạnsạ a scholar, as one knowing spells, is to be feared provided he behaves as he should. (c) zạn yi kīwạn zūwạŋkạ I'll be on the look out for your arrival (cf. kịyāyạ). (d) mutạ̄nē akē ∼, bạ dabbạ ba always be on your guard against people, but an animal can be safely left to graze alone. (e) kīwạŋ kại yā fi kīwạn dabbạ one must learn to control oneself before one can control others. (4) kīwạn lāfīyạ hygiene. (5) (a) yā yi masạ kīwạn tsawō he underfed it (child, animal). (b) nīsaŋ ∼ Vd. nīsā 1d. (6) rabạ dạ kīwạŋ awākī Vd. ạkwīyạ 1s. (7) kīwạn tsabtạ; kīwạn yạrdā Vd. bardō, tạntabạrā. (8) (a) kīwạm ɓatạ Vd. tạntabạrā. (b) Vd. kyallạ 2. (9) ạbōkin ∼ Vd. burtū 5. (10) ɓạtạ ∼ Vd. ɓātạ 9. (11) Vd. wāwaŋ kīwọ.

ƙīyạ Vb. 1A Sk. refused (= ƙī).

kīyā dạ Vb. 4A protected x nā ∼ kạrēna kadạ kūrā tạ kāmạ I protected my dog against the hyena. Allạ̄ yạ ∼ mū = Allạ̄ yạ kīyāshē mụ God forbid ! (= kịyāyạ 1b = Kt. hụ̄wạ̄cē 2).

kīyad dạ = kīyā dạ.

kīyai Vd. kīyē.

kīyā-kịyạ x yā yi adō ∼ he togged himself up.

kịyāmạ Ar.f. (1) raŋ ∼f. Day of resurrection (= narkō = gọ̄be 1f). (2) yā tạfi ∼ he is dead.

kīyārạ Kt. m. black horse (= akawạlī).

kīyar dạ = kīyā dạ.

*kīyāri m. type of guinea-fowl.

kịyạsai Vd. kịyāshī.

kīyāshē Vd. kīyā dạ.

kīyāshī m. (sg., pl.) (pl. kịyạsai = kịyạsū) (1) type of small ant (cf. ƙyạshī). (2) pale, undyed flecks on cotton. (3)

spots on embroidery where lower material shows through. (4) mại ∼ m. European velveteen.

*kịyāsi Ar. m. analogy x ạ kạŋ ∼ by analogy.

kịyạstā Vb. 1C Ar. assumed that (Vd. kịyāsi).

kịyạsū Vd. kīyāshī.

kiyaya A. (kịyāyā) Vb. 1C = kīwạtā.
   B. (kịyāyạ) (1) Vb. 2 (a) = kīwạtā. (b) protected x Allạ̄ yạ kịyāyē mụ God forbid ! (= kīyā dạ). kạ kịyāyi kạŋkạ be on your guard ! (Vd. idọ 1n). (c) was on guard against x kạ kịyāyē nị dạ wạ̄sạnnī none of your tricks ! kạ kịyāyē shị be on your guard against him ! (d) paid attention to x kạ kịyāyi mạganạtạ attend to my words ! (2) Vb. 3B yā ∼ animal or P. is well fed. (3) cf. kịyāyē, hạwainīyā 2.

kịyāyayyē Vd. kịyāyē 1b.

kịyāyē (1) Vb. 1C (a) = kịyāyạ 1b-d. (b) x shānū suŋ kịyāyẹ gōnā the cattle have denuded the farm. kịyāyayyīyar gōnā farm denuded by cattle. (c) memorized. (d) nā kịyāyō shị wurin Audụ I heard this from Audu. (e) ∼ dạ knew accurately x suŋ ∼ dạ kuɗin dạ zā sụ sāmụ they know the exact sum they are to receive. (2) Vb. 3A garkar audụgā tā ∼ the cotton-plot has ceased bearing. (3) cf. kịyāyạ.

kịyayyạ f. (1) mutual hatred. (2) Vd. rạbu 2k.

kīyē used in ∼ nị, hawai nị = kīyai nị, hawai nị mind how you behave towards me ! (Vd. hạwāyạ).

kīyẹ Vb. 1A (the form of ƙī used before dative) x rụbụ̄tū yā ∼ mini kyạu I'm out of form with my writing. kạ̄sụ̄wā tā ∼ musụ their business is not a success. jikī yā ∼ mini dāɗin azancī I feel ill at intervals.

kīyī m. (1) hubbub (= jīzạ). (2) ∼ yā dạukē shị he meddled.

kīyọ Sk. m. = kīwọ.

ƙīyọ Kt. m. used in yārinyạn naŋ ∼ takẹ this girl dislikes the husband chosen for her.

ko A. (kō) (1) (a) or x baƙī ∼ farī black or white. wạndạ ya cẹ " ī " kō kọ ya cẹ̄ " ā'ā̀ ", bābu kōmē gạrēshi he who says " yes " or he who says " no ", is guilty of no offence. (b) either . . . or x kāwō ~ tūlū kō tukunyā bring either a ewer or a cooking-pot ! (Vd. 3b).

(2) (a) (introduces question, Mod. Gram. 165b) x (i) kō zā kạ zọ̄ ? = kō zā kạ zọ̄ will you come ? kō yā kāwọ̄ shị ? = kō yā kāwō shị did he bring it ? kō Audu nẹ̄ ? = kō Audu nẹ̄ I wonder if it is Audu I see ? nā ji mọ̄tsī, kō bạtūrẹ nẹ̄ ? = nā ji mọ̄tsī, kō bạtūrẹ nẹ̄ I hear a noise, I wonder if it is the European ? (cf. kọ̄). (ii) nā tạmbạyē shị kō sum bīyā̀ ? = nā tạmbạyē shị kō sum bīyā̀ I asked him whether they had paid ? (Mod. Gram. 166b, 166c). dạ garī ya wāyẹ, yanā̀ cẹ̄wā kō yā kusa dạ Kạnọ ? = kō yā kusa dạ Kano when day dawned, he wondered whether he were near Kano ? kā sạnị ? kō sun zọ̄ ? = kā sạnị ? kō sun zọ̄ do you know whether they have come ?

(b) (introduces alternative question, Mod. Gram. 165a, 165b) x (i) kā nẹ̄mē shị ? kō bạ kạ nẹ̄mē shị bạ did you look for it or not ! zā kạ zọ̄ ? kō bạ zā kạ zō bạ will you come or not ? (ii) (sarcastically) zā kạ zō (= zā kạ zọ̄ ?), kō bạ zā kạ zō bạ well, make up your mind whether you'll come or not ! (iii) zā kạ zọ̄ ? kō kụ̄wā = zā kạ zọ̄ ? kō kọ̄ will you come or not ? (cf. kọ̄). (iv) kō kụ̄wā Vd. kụ̄wā 2. (c) (i) bā ā̀ sam magana dạ " kō " nobody likes uncertainty. (ii) Vd. kō tā kwānā̀ ? (d) (kō is sometimes used optionally before inherently interrogative words, Gram. 160) x inā dạbāra = kō inā dạbāra what is to be done ? bạ ạ san jirgī gudā nawạ gạrēsu ba = bạ ạ san jirgī gudā nawạ gạrēsu ba it is not known how many ships they have. yanā̀ ta tụnānī mẹnēnẹ̄ (= kō mẹnēnẹ̄) nufinsạ he was reflecting as to what was its meaning. (e) Vd. 10 below, mẹ̄.

(3) (a) whether x (i) bạn san kō zại zō ba I don't know whether he'll come

(cf. in 3). (ii) Vd. 2a.ii. (iii) x n cẹ̄ kō dǎi (= na cẹ̄ kọ̄ ?) sun saŋ kại nẹ̄ ? I wonder if they knew it was you ? (Vd. cẹ̄ 10). (b) kō . . . kō whether . . . or x (i) kō yā zō, kō bại zō ba, ọ̄hō I don't care whether he comes or not. (ii) x bạ su kula dạ kō su cī, kō kadạ su ci ba they did not care whether they won or not. (iii) kō bạ dadẹ, kō bạ jima, zā ạ yī it is bound to be done sooner or later (= kul 2b). (iv) kō bisạ, kō k̃asạ whether on horseback or on foot (= in 3). (v) Vd. 1b above.

(4) (a) perhaps x kō Allā̀ yā̀ yāfẹ muku who knows, maybe God will pardon you. iŋ kō n nā̀ tạfīyạ if I happen to be travelling. (5) (with future or subjunctive) in the hope that mu jiŋkịrtā kō sā isō let's postpone it in the hope that they may come ! sun sạki bọm kō su kashẹ Sarkī they dropped bombs hoping to kill the King. yā harạrē su kō sū mā wai zā su yi caffạ he behaved menacingly to them with intent that they might give in to him. n nā̀ zubạ idọ kō wạtạkīlạ zaŋ ga nāmạ ŋ harbā I'm keeping a look out in the hope of finding game to shoot. (6) (with past or future according to sense) (a) to see whether x ku dụ̄bi hanyạr " Gạskīyā " kō kīlạ muŋ k̃ạru dạ lābāri look out in future issues of the newspaper " Gaskiya " to see whether we have had any further news. kạ lụ̄rā dạ tufāfīna kō wạtạkīlạ ạnīnī yā cirẹ attend to my clothes to see whether a button has come off ! (b) in case x don su tạimạki Masạr kō watạ ḟiṭina tā tāsam musu that they may help Egypt in case of further dissension. yā yi tānạdī kō dạ zại yi 6atạŋ k̃ại he took steps in case he should lose his way.

(7) (a) kō = kō dā̀ even x (i) kō nī bạn san shi ba even I don't know it. yā̀ dẹ̄bi kō karkashī let him take even a trifle like beniseedleaves ! kō sū (= kō dā̀ sū) suŋ kạrai even they have lost heart. dạ aŋ ga

mutum kō dā dā takardā ā hannū if they
see anyone with even a newspaper in
his hand. (ii) kō kūrā tā san turmī ā
wāje yakē kwānā have more sense
than to press a destitute P. to repay
a debt ! (ii*A*) kō ā Kwārā *Vd*. tsibirī 1*b*.
(ii*B*) kō kai na Allā *Vd*. Allā 1*h*. (ii*C*)
kō biri yā saŋ gōnar gwāzā *Vd*. biri 1*h*.
(ii*D*) kō ƙasā tanā saŋkā *Vd*. shūnī 1*b*.
(ii*E*) kō yanzu rūwā *Vd*. rūwā C. 21.
(iii) (*negatively*) not even *x* bā sā kō
sō ā san sūnansu they do not even
want their names known. bā zai bā
su kō dā kwabo ba he won't give them
even a penny. hā shi dā sauran sāmuŋ
kō dā wuƙā he can no longer obtain
even a knife. kō dā dā yādi gudā bā
su ci gāba ba they did not advance
even so much as one yard. bā kō dā
yāƙi ba even without war. tā yi hakā
bā dā kō tā tabā jinsā ba she did this
without even having heard of it (*cf*.
bā C.14). (iv) kō gēzau kadā kā yi don't
be alarmed ! (*b*) *conj*. even if (such-and-
such occurs) *x* (i) kō nā sāmu, bā zam
bā kā ba even if I get it, I shall not give
you any (= in 1*e*). (ii) kō ā rūwa ka
tākā, sǎi ā cē kā tā dā ƙūrā they blame
you whatever you do. (iii) kō dāji
yā ɓāci, gīwā tā fi gudu nil desperandum ! (iv) kō an ci birniŋ kūrā, bā
ā bā kārē dillanci whatever happens,
there are always seniors and juniors.
(v) kō aŋ kōri kūrā, tā yi guzurī dā
kārē = iii *above*. (vi) kō ƙaya ka tākā
Vd. tafifīya. (vii) kō aŋ kirɓā ā turmī
Vd. rǎi 1*q*. (viii) kō aŋ kashē biri *Vd*.
biri 1*c*. (ix) kō biri yā karyē *Vd*.
ruŋhū 2. (x) kō an ci birnī *Vd*. cī 11*e*.
(xi) *cf*. 8. (*c*) there is not even *x* ammā
har yau kō lābāri there is no news of it
even yet.

(8) (*a*) kō dā = kō 7*b*.i (*with
past or present sense*) even if, though *x*
kō dā jirgī ɗayā tak sukā harbe, dā
isa Jāmus kirāri even if they have shot
down only one aeroplane, it is a cause
of boasting for the Germans. kō dā
mukā jē, bā mu gan shi ba = kō mun
jē, *etc*., though we went, we didn't
see him. kō dā yakē yanā naŋ, bā mu

gan shi ba though he's here, we did
not see him. kō dā sukē naŋ even
though they are here . . . bā yā jin
tsōraŋ kōwā, kō dā Sarkī nē he fears
nobody, not even the Emir. (*b*) *cf*.
7*b above*. (*c*) even if it had been so
x kō dā mukā sani kanā naŋ, bā mā jē
ba even had we known you were there,
we should not have gone (*cf*. dā 1 *a*.i).

(9) kō dā (*a*) when *x* kō dā
sukā zō, sǎi mukā gan su we saw
them when they came (= lōkacin dā).
(*b*) *for* kō dā *Vd*. 8.

(10) (*a*) *prefix conveying sense*
" every ", *used in* kōwā, kōmē
(*cf*. kōmē), kōmēnēnē, kōyaushē,
kōnawā, kōƙāƙā = kōyāya, kōinā,
kōwanē, kōwānēnē, kōwannē *q.v.*
x kōwā yā san shi everybody
knows him. (*b*) *prefix giving indefinite
sense* " ever " *in the case of the words
quoted in* (a) *above, q.v. alphabetically x* (i)
kōinā mukā jē, sǎi muŋ gan shi where-
ever we went, we saw him. (ii) (*preposition may be interposed between* kō
and mē, *etc*., *in sense* (b) *x* kō dā mē,
kō dom mē, zā mu ci nasarā come what
may, we shall be victorious ! kō ta
ƙāƙā, bā zā su bar mu ba in any event,
they'll not leave us in peace. *Vd*.
kōwā 2, kō ƙāƙā 5. zā su yī, kō dā wanē
hāli they'll do it at any cost (*cf*. 2*d above*).
(11) wai doŋ kō = kō wai *Vd*. wai 3*d*.

B. (kō) (1) isn't that so ? ; don't
you agree with me ? (2) (*placed at
end of sentence, forms question*) *x* zā
kā zō, kō will you come ? yā kāwō
shi, kō did he bring it ? = kūwā 1 (*cf*.
kō 2 : kō P).

C. (kō ?) (*expresses surprise at speed
of occurrence*) zā kā tafi, kō P do you
mean to say you're off *already* ? kā zō,
kō P what, you're here *already* ! har kā
ji, kō P fancy you hearing the news so
soon ! (M.G. 165*c*) = kūwā 2. (2) *Vd*. kō
3*a*.iii ; kō.

D. (kō) (1) = kūwā 1 *x* zā kā zō P

kō will you come or not ? yā kāwǭ
shi̧ ? kō kǭ did he bring it or not ?
(M.G. 165b). (2) Sk., Kt. indeed x
nī kǭ as for me . . . wanda̧ ya cę̄ " ī "
kō kǭ ya cę̄ " ā'ā̧ ", bābu kōmē ga̧rēshi̧
he who says " yes " or he who says
" no " is guilty of no offence (= ƙųwā).
kō a̧ i̧nā = kōi̧nā.
ƙǭbara̧ Vb. 3B = ƙōba̧rē Vb. 3A is (was)
bowed down by age or load.
kōba̧yaushē Vd. ba̧yaushē.
kǭbira̧ f. small horn blown by carriers
(may also be made of wood or neck of
būta̧-bottle) = bindī 1.
kǭbiro̧ m. = kǭbira̧.
ƙōbōbō m. (1) yā yi ∼ (a) he is round-
shouldered and bent. (b) he is bowed
down by age or load. (c) he's crouching
with head close to knees. (2) m., f.
person as in 1.
kǭbura̧ ; kǭburo̧ = kǭbira̧ ; kǭbiro̧.
koda A. (kōda̧) f. (1) women's work for
payment (x grinding, pounding, etc.),
cf. ƙōdagō. (2) mai ∼ bā tā̧ sa̧m mai ∼
nobody likes a rival.
  B. (kō da̧) Vd. kō 7.
koda A. (kōda̧) Vb. 1A (Vd. kūda̧) (1) (a)
sharpened (edge of knife, axe, fartanya̧,
lauję) by beating with grinding-stone
(dūtsa̧n niƙa̧) = wāsa̧ 1a = ɗāda̧ (cf.
akara̧s). (b) roughened a grinding-
stone (dūtsa̧n niƙa̧) by beating (=
wāsa̧ 3). (2) " puffed " one's wares or
P. one wants to succeed (cf. akara̧s) x
yā ∼ ka̧nsa̧ " he blew his own trumpet." (= wāsa̧ 3). (3) yā ∼ ƙaryā he lied.
(4) (a) yā ∼ sukūwā he galloped hard.
(b) ana̧ ∼ rānā sun's blazing. (5) (a)
yā ∼ shi da̧ ƙasā he flung him down.
(b) yā ∼ masa̧ māri̧ he slapped him.
(c) yā ∼ masa̧ askā he cut him in
shaving him.
  B. (kōdā) Vb. 2 (1) muŋ kōɗi
rānā = rānā tā kōɗē mu we've had
blazing sun. (2) yā kōɗi rūwā he drank
up much water. (3) yā kōɗi ta̧fīya̧ he
travelled far.
ƙōda̧ f. (pl. ƙōdōjī) (1) kidney (Vd. ƙwāda̧).
(2) kūkan ∼ rumbling noise some
horses make when in motion.
ƙodago A. (ƙōdagō) m. (1) farming for
wages = Kt. fāɗim bāyā (cf. kōda̧ ;

aika̧tau). (2) ɗaŋ ∼ (pl. 'yaŋ ∼) P.
farming for wages (= ɗaŋ gā̧ nōmā).
  B. ƙōdago m. (pl. ƙōda̧gai) (1) stone
of deleb (giginya̧) or dum-palm (gǭruba̧)
= ƙwallō. (2) (a) fine and big (P.
or horse) x ƙōdagwa̧n dōki̧ fine, big
horse. (b) big and round. (3) ci̧rar ∼
(a) Kt. attaining higher status. (b)
Sk. seizing foot of wrestling opponent,
throwing him up, then dashing him
down (= ci̧rar ƙwallō).
ƙōdai Kt. m. plant similar to rūjīya̧.
kō da̧ yaushē = kōya̧ushē.
kǭɗayya̧ f. struggling together.
kōɗę (1) Vb. 3A (a) (colour) faded (=
kūję = ƙwāƙę). (b) (shoe) wore through.
(c) tsa̧kāninsu̧ yā ∼ they've " fallen
out ". (d) kāsūwassa̧ tā ∼ it's no longer
in demand. (e) dūnīya̧ tā ∼ times have
changed for the worse. (f) a̧l'ama̧rī yā
∼ matter's become manifest. (g)
hadiri̧ yā ∼ rain is about to fall, as
wind-clouds have passed, revealing
the rain-clouds (= kōrę 2a.ii). (2)
Vb. 1A (a) = kōɗa̧ 1. (b) yā yi ku̧ŋkurū,
bai ∼ ba he made cryptic remark
(Vd. ku̧ŋkurū 4).
kōɗi (1) ∼ nā shā rānā phew, I felt the
heat ! (2) m. zō, mu̧ yi ∼ let's go and
play top ! (ka̧tantaŋwa̧).
ƙōdōjī kidneys (pl. of ƙōda̧).
ƙōfa̧ f. (pl. ƙōfōfī) (1) (a) (i) doorway (cf.
ƙyaurē). (ii) wa̧je ƙōfa̧ Vd. īyākacī 2.
(iii) tsa̧raŋ ƙōfa̧ Vd. tsa̧rō 2. (iv)
rūwa̧ŋ ƙōfa̧ Vd. rūwā B.12. (b) ƙōfa̧r
fāda̧ open space before Emir's palace
(= Sk. ka̧ŋ wurī = Kt. ka̧ŋ gīwā). (c) yā
yi ∼ he made for the door. (d) yanā̧
bā̧ki̧ŋ ∼ it's by the door. (e) a̧ ƙōfa̧r ɗāki̧
yakę it's an everyday occurrence ; it's a
word in common use ; it's a T. easily
obtainable (Vd. gandū 4). (f) dōki̧ŋ ∼
doorstep (= dandama̧lī). (g) ƙōfa̧r fi̧tā (i)
exit. (ii) way out of trouble or dilemma.
(h) ∼ ka̧ sam fi̧tassa̧ he's vanished.
(j) an ɗaura̧ ∼ = an ɗaurę ∼ lintel's
been fitted to doorway. (2) (a) breach
(x in fence). (b) (i) hole bored in bead
(cf. kōgō). (ii) hole in roof (cf. rāmi̧ ;
kafā). (c) yā sa̧mi ∼ he " sees his way
clear ". (d) yanā̧ ganiŋ ƙōfa̧ta he has
the cheek to compare himself with me.

(3) intermediary between P. and one more influential, patron (= **tsān̲i** 2 = **tafarki̲** 2a = **ragạmā** 2). (4) **kǫ̃fạr** ragō, **kǫ̃fạr** ragō head the animal off ! (5) **yan̲ą kǫ̃fōfī** he's making lame excuses (= **kusạssarī**).

Kǫ̃fǎ used in **faɗạŋ gwaggǫ ạ** ∼ doing T. at unsuitable time (**Kǫ̃fǎ** is placename).

kǫ̃fatǫ m. (pl. **kǫ̃fạtai**) (1) (a) hoof (= **tạ̄kō** 4a). (b) an **sạri** ∼ hoof has been pared (Vd. **sạrā**). (c) **kǫ̃fatạŋ** kudī Vd. **alkālāwā**. (2) head of cattle x **yanā dạ** ∼ **gōmạ** he has ten head of cattle. (3) (boys' slang) **kǫ̃fatạŋ gạdā** vagina (= **farji̲**), cf. **tạ̄kō**.

kǫ̃fę̃ Kt. m. bark of any dried tree.

kǫ̃fī Eng. m. (1) coffee. (2) Vd. **ạkạrạ̄** 3

ƙofi A. (**ƙōfī**) m. (1) inspiring feeling of helpless fear x **kūrā tā yi** (= **tā zubạ**) **min̲i** ∼ seeing the hyena petrified me with fear (= **arwā**). (2) **yā yi min̲i** ∼ he cast spell on me by incantation (= **arwā**), cf. **sammu̲**, **lāyạ**.
  B. (**ƙofi̲**) m. = **ƙwāfi̲**.

kǫ̃fǫ = **kōhǫ**.

ƙōfōfī Vd. **ƙofą̃**.

kǫ̃fu̲r Eng. m. Corporal.

ƙōgạlē Vb. 3A became emaciated.

kōgamā f. old woman, old cow, old mare, etc. (= **kwazgamā**).

kōgạwą f. rope for securing prisoners of war (= **tāmāgę**).

kǫ̃gī m. (pl. **kōgun̲ą**) (1) (a) (i) river (cf. **rạ̄fī**, **ƙǫramạ**). (ii) **kōgin tụn̲ạ̄nī** a welter of reflections. (iii) Vd. **wutsīyạr kǫ̃gī**. (b) **kạsūwā** ∼ **cę** a market like a river is sometimes full, sometimes empty. (c) (i) **dạ** ∼ **dạ Sarkī dạ kạsūwā, bā ạ̄ bā dạ lạ̄bārin̲su** a river, a Chief and a market are too capricious to make definite prognostications about. (ii) **dạ dōki̲, dạ** ∼ Vd. **ạmān̲ą** 8c. (d) (i) **Audu̲** ∼ **nę̃** Audu is a mine of knowledge. (ii) **Kǫ̃gī matuƙar tayi̲** Vd. **tayi̲** 4. (e) ∼ **bā yạ̃ ƙin̲ ƙari̲** = **kadạ dǎi** ∼ **yạ hạngi rạndā** one can never have too much of a good thing. (f) **gōbarā dạgạ** ∼ Vd. **gōbarā** 1a.iv. (g) **kōgin Sarkī** Vd. **wutā** 1v. (h) ∼ **kạn cika** Vd. **yayyafī** 2. (j) **yạ tiŋƙạri** ∼ Vd. **tiŋkārạ**. (k) **yạ ƙārạ wạ** ∼ **rūwā** Vd.

Allą̃ 7l. (l) Vd. **mạ̄tar** ∼. (2) (a) **yan̲ą̃ bạ̄kiŋ** ∼ it's on the riverbank (= **gacī** 1). (b) 'yar **bạ̄kiŋ** ∼ = 'yar **bạ̄kin rạ̄fī** f. onion (= **ạlbasạ**). (c) Vd. **cilạndō**.
(3) for game **kǫ̃gī**, Vd. **kadǫ** 6.

kǫ̃gō m. (1) cavity x **kǫ̃gwaŋ itạ̄cē** hollow in tree, hollow tree. **kǫ̃gwan dūtsę** hollow rock, hollow in rock. **kǫ̃gwaŋ haƙōrī** hollow in tooth, hollow tooth (cf. **ƙōfạ** 2). (2) dishonest P. (3) **kǫ̃gwaŋ kạ̃i gạrēshi̲** he is loud-voiced (= **kūwạ** 1f). (4) **kǫ̃gwaŋ gaƙi̲** Vd. **gaƙi̲**. (5) **kǫ̃gwam madạ̄cī** Vd. **madạ̄cī** 2. (6) **fid dạ** ∼ Vd. **hayāƙī**.

kōgun̲ą Vd. **kǫ̃gī**.

kǫ̃gwaɗō m. (1) hollow in stream-bank (suitable lair for crocodiles). (2) **kǫ̃gwaɗaŋ idǫ gạrēshi̲** he has deep-set eyes.

kōhę̃ Kt. m. bark of any dried tree.

kōhǫ m. husk of beans or ground-nuts (= **ɓāwō**).

ƙōhwą f. (pl. **ƙōhōhī**) = **ƙōfạ**.

kōin̲ā (1) **kōin̲ā** = **kō ạ in̲ā** = **ạ kōin̲ā** = **kōin̲ā dạ in̲ā** everywhere x **an̲ạ̃ ganinsạ** ∼ it is to be seen everywhere. (2) (negatively) nowhere x **bā ạ̄ ganinsạ kōin̲ā** it is nowhere visible. (3) wherever x (a) **kōin̲ā mukạ jē**, **sǎi muŋ gan shi̲** wherever we went (go), we saw (see) him (M.G. 185) = **dukạ** 3. (b) **kōin̲ā huntū** (= **kōin̲ā mai̲ arō) zạ̃ shi̲, dạ sanim̲ mai̲ rīgā** he who pays the piper, calls the tune. (c) cf. **in̲ā** 3d.

koje A. (**kōjē**) m. (1) Niger Common Bulbul (Pycnonotus barbatus). (2) bead coloured like 1.
  B. (**kōję**) Vb. 3A faded as in **kōdę̃** q.v.

koka A. (**kōkạ**) (1) Vb. 1A x **yǎ** ∼ **bāyaŋ Audu̲** he assisted the family of his dead friend Audu. (2) Vb. 3A (a) **yan̲ą̃ kōkạ̄wā** he's longing for the good old times (= **nīsạ** 1b). (b) **rạbansạ yā** ∼ he's benefited by somebody's death. (3) Vd. **kōkạ rānī**.
  B. (**kōkā**) Vb. 2 x **nā kōki arzikiŋkạ kạ tạimạkē n̲i** I beg you to help me.

ƙōƙā prep. like x ∼ **kai** like you. ∼ **shī** like him (= **kaman**).

ƙōƙafē Vb. 3A behaved resolutely x **yā** ∼ **kaŋ aiki̲** he persevered in the work (= **kafę̃** 1b).

kō̰kai = dą kō̰kai (1) there is, there are, there was, there were *x* ~ kudī there is (was) some money (= ąkwai). (2) 6ąd dą kō̰kaī, jirąci bābu what a wastrel ! kō ƙą̰ƙą (1) in every possible way *x* aną̰ sāmųŋ kudī ~ men earn their living in every possible way. (2) (*negatively*) in no way *x* bą zā ką īyą yįnsą ~ ba you won't be able to do it in any way at all. (3) no matter how *x* (*a*) ~ ka bā nį, yą̰ įshē nį whatever you give me, much or little, will suffice me. ką bā nį ƙądaŋ ~ give me as little as you like ! ~ ya sāmų, sǎi yą hąƙurą no matter how rarely (how unsatisfactorily) he gets it, he must think himself lucky to get it at all. ą yī shį ~ I don't care *how* it's done as long as it *is* done. (*b*) ~ rūwan zartsī ząi kashę ƙishį, bą̰ kąman na dādī ba a substitute is never like the real thing. (4) however *x* ~ suką yī, sǎi sun yi dą kyaụ (Mod. Gram. 185) however they used to do it, it was well done. (5) (*in senses* 3 *and* 4, *preposition may be interposed between* kō *and* ƙą̰ƙą) *x* (*a*) kō dą ƙą̰ƙą, ą tafō dą shī it must be brought by hook or by crook. kō ta ƙą̰ƙą bą zā sụ bar mụ ba come what may, they'll not leave us in peace. tun dą na sąmi dōkį, in nā sō, ŋ hau shį kō ta ƙą̰ƙą as I have a horse. I can ride it at my pleasure. (*b*) dą ƙarfī nikę̰ nēmā kō dą haliŋ ƙą̰ƙą I'm looking for it might and main (*cf.* kō 10*b*.ii).

kō̰kantō *m.* = kō̰kwantō.

kō̰karā *f.* the tough tree Dalbergia used for cudgels.

kō̰ką rānī *m.* (1) (*a*) chameleon (hąwēnįyā) which has exceptionally outlived the hot season. (2) the hemp (ramą) called girin dą rānī.

ƙō̰ƙarī *m.* (1) effort *x* (*a*) yaną̰ ~ yą gamą he's striving to finish it. (*b*) ~ yakę̰ yī wai yą sāmu he's trying to get it. (*c*) n nā̰ ƙō̰ƙarīna I'm doing my best. (*d*) ząŋ ƙārą ~ I'll try harder. (*e*) sǎi ką yi ~ ką bīyā shi ąlbāshinsą yaụ please oblige me by paying him his salary to-day. (2) (*a*) suną̰ ~ bā jį, bą̰ gani they're trying might and

main. (*b*) yaną̰ ~ duk yąddą ząi īyą yą yī he's trying his utmost to do it. (*c*) yā bā dą īyą̰kar ƙō̰ƙarinsą yą gamą he did his best to finish it (*Vd.* bā dą 6). (*d*) sun yi īyą̰kar ƙō̰ƙarinsụ they did their level best. (*e*) yaną̰ ta ~ nę̰ īyą̰kā he's striving his utmost. (3) ąllūrą bā tą̰ ~ *Vd.* ąllūrą 6.

ƙō̰ƙartā *Vb.* 3A exerted oneself (*as in* ƙō̰ƙarī) = turzą̰.

kō̰kawą *f.* (1) (*a*) wrestling. (*b*) ɗaŋ ~ *m.* (*pl.* 'yaŋ ~) wrestler (= makō̰kō̰wī = makųncī = ɗaŋ kuncē). (*c*) wąndą ya yi ~ ą bą̰rē, kō yā yi kāyę̰, ą̰ jūyę̰ shi it's hard to be popular abroad. (*d*) yā sa6ą ~ he (wrestler) lifted opponent prior to throwing ·hiṃ down. (*e*) suŋ kāmą ~ they have begun a struggle together, they are at war with one another. (*f*) ~ dą dą6ē *Vd.* tirįjī. (2) striving *x* yaną̰ ~ dą aikį he's struggling with the work. yaną̰ ~ yą gamą he is trying hard to finish it. (3) kō̰kąwe-kō̰kąwē constant struggling.

kō̰kē *m.* (1) plaint *x* yā kāwō kō̰kyansą wurīna he brought me the matter troubling him, for me to help him. (2) kō̰'ke-kō̰kē ‖ *Vd.* kūkā.

ƙō̰ƙę *Vb.* 3A *Kt.* faded (= ƙwāƙę).

ƙō̰ƙi (1) (*a*) wife of mythical spider Gizọ. (*b*) bą ą kā dą gizọ bą ? ą̰ cę̰ ~ tą tāsō̰ ? don't start on a new task till the first is completed ! (*c*) *Vd.* bųllųŋ ~. (*d*) *cf.* dāƙirin. (2) ƙō̰ƙi-ƙō̰ƙi type of mantis (*Vd.* masą̰rī-masą̰rī, dōkįŋ Allą̰).

kō̰kiną *Kt. f.* begging for food at midday by young scholars.

ƙō̰kīyā *f.* (1) the trees *Strychnos spinosa, Strychnos alnifolia, Strychnos triclisioides* (*acid-pulp is edible and shell* (ƙō̰ƙwaŋ ƙō̰ƙīyā) *is used for storing women's knick-knacks for titivation*). (2) corn on the foot (= ƙayą̰r Allą̰). (3) rą̰kumī yā fid dą ~ the male camel protruded red-gland when on heat (= wutā 6 = kurcīyā 4).

koko A. (kō̰kō) *Eng. m.* cocoa.

B. (kōko) *m.* (1) gruel (= kųnū 1*a q.v.*) (*epithet is* Kącā, mūgųŋ jībį). (2) *Vd.* Bąnufē, gāyā 1*c*, tantį 3, ąyagį. (3) lūdąyiŋ ~ *Vd.* fąŋkō 4. (4) kudiŋ ~ *Vd.* jągąlam. (5) *Vd.* ą shā lāfīyą 2.

ƙǫ̆ƙō *m.* (*pl.* ƙǫ̆ƙunʠ) (1) (*a*) small calabash. (*b*) an yi mini̧ ɗaŋ ~ I (buyer of
kola-nuts) have been swindled. (2)
ƙǫ̆ƙwam barʠ (*a*) type of white shell
used as baby's neck-ornament. (*b*)
horse given by Chief and then paraded
by recipient in villages, etc., to get
further gifts. (3) ƙǫ̆ƙwaŋ gwīwʠ
kneecap. (4) ƙǫ̆ƙwaŋ kǎi̧ cranium
(= ƙwaryā 6). (5) gujīyā ma̧i̧ ~ *Kt. f.*
Bambarra ground-nut (= *Kt.* ta ƙuriga̧).
(6) bʠ ~ *Vd.* galʠmaɗi̧. (7) *Vd.*
dōki̧ŋ ~, tābaŗ ~.
ƙǫ̆ƙǫbirǫ = ƙǫ̆ƙǫburǫ (1) *m.* type of
woodpecker. (2) what a thin person !
kōkōci̧kō *m.* the rattle cikōkō.
kǫ̆kōwʠ = kǫ̆kawʠ.
ƙǫ̆ƙunʠ *Vd.* ƙǫ̆ƙō.
ƙoƙwa A. (ƙō̆ƙwā = ƙō̆ƙūwā) *f.* (1) (*a*)
ƙō̆ƙwar ɗāki̧ apex of round thatched-
roof (= wuyʠn ɗāki̧). (*b*) ƙō̆ƙwar
tʠgīyʠ top-part of cap tʠgīyʠ. (*c*)
ƙō̆ƙwam ma̧lʠfā top-section of straw-
hat. (*d*) ƙō̆ƙwar ʠlkyabbʠ top-section
of burnous (*cf.* ƙōli̧). (*d*) yā shi̧ga
ƙō̆ƙwā Chief put burnous (ʠlkyabbʠ)
over head instead of draping over
shoulders (yāfʠ). (2) maximum *x*
ƙō̆ƙwar kuɗinsʠ sulʠ ɗarī limit of his
cash is £5. ƙō̆ƙwar tsawansʠ gʠbā 3
its highest point is 3 gʠbā.
    B. (ƙō̆ƙwā = ƙō̆ƙūwā) *Kt. f.* (*pl.*
ƙō̆ƙunʠ) = ƙō̆ƙō 1.
kǫ̆kwai = kǫ̆kai.
ƙǫ̆ƙwan *Vd.* ƙǫ̆ƙō.
kǫ̆kwa̧ntā *Vb.* 3A felt doubtful.
kǫ̆kwantō *m.* doubt *x* n nʠ̆ kǫ̆kwantan
zūwʠnsʠ I'm doubtful whether he'll
come (= shakkʠ).
ƙōlʠ *Vb.* 1A = ƙwālʠ.
ƙōlamī *Sk., Kt.* stingy (= ƙūlumī *q.v.*).
kōlāyē *Vd.* kōlō.
kōlej *Eng. m.* college.
koli A. (kōli̧) *m.* (1) (*a*) peddling small
wares by ɗaŋ ~ (= *Kt.* mashi̧mfi̧ɗī),
Vd. kirī, kwara̧mī. (*b*) *his epithet is*
ɗaŋ ~ ma̧i jaŋ gō̆rā. (*c*) ɗaŋ kōli̧ yā
kashʠ ɗi̧llāli̧ *Vd.* wǫ̆fī 2*d.* (*d*) *Vd.*
mʠtar ɗaŋ kōli̧. (2) *if A. is buying,*
e.g., kolas from B. and the kola falls.
A. says ɗaŋ ~ yā fādō dagʠ kaŋ
gadō, sǎi ya cʄ̆ " ƙʠ̆sūwā " may this

bad luck be balanced· by great gooɗ
luck !
    B. (kōli̧) *m.* (1) an yi ~ dʠ̆ shī he'.
been flung down or discarded. (2) (*a*
harshʠnsʠ yanʠ̆ ~ he lisps (= gurʠ-
gurʠ *q.v.*). (*b*) yā yi ~ = harshʠnsʂ
yā yi ~ he made slip of the tongu·
(= gō̆rā 1*a.*ii).
ƙoli A. (ƙōli̧) *m.* (1) top *x* yā hau ~ h·
climbed to top (of hill, ladder, tree
etc.), *cf.* ƙō̆ƙwā. (2) hatsī yā (= kuɗi·
hatsī sun) tʠfi ~ corn is " fire-dear ".
    B. (ƙōli̧) *Kt. m.* (1) = ƙōlī. (2
yā harbʠ kibīyʠ ~ he shot the arrov
into the sky. (3) sun yi ~ they stooɗ
up and raised their voices in alterca
tion. (4) sun yi mini̧ ~ they borrowe·
sum or got T. on credit from m·
without intention of paying (= hʠgʠ 1)
kōlō *m.* (*pl.* kōlāyē) (1) type of smal·
drum (*Vd.* jaujē). (2) any dog. (3
Sk. vulture (= u̧ŋgu̧lū).
ƙōlōlwā = ƙōlōlūwā *f.* (1) top (= ƙōlī)
(2) yā tʠfi ƙōlōlūwar dūnīyʠ he's gon·
to a far place.
koma A. (kōmʠ) (1) *Vb.* 3A (*a*) returne·
(in that direction). kōmō returne·
(in this direction), *Vd.* kōmō. (*b*) yā ·
bāya = yā ~ dʠ bāya (i) he went back
wards, retreated. (ii) (speed, progress
illness) has lessened (*Vd.* bāya 1*a*). (iii
~ bāyansʠ *Vd.* bāyā 1*f.* (*c*) yā ~ ·
(child few days old) died. (*d*) kōmʠ ~
kōmō became *x* (i) yā kōmō tik he'·
become penniless. zʠi ~ mijintʠ he'·
become ber husband. yā ~ uku i·
has become three (= tāshi̧ 1*g*). ma·
kīfī dʠ maŋ gyʠɗā su kaŋ ~ sǎi k·
cʄ̆ iri̧ ɗayā nʄ̆ fish-oil and ground-nu·
oil become indistinguishable from on·
another. yā ~ dʠ arʠhā it has becom·
cheap. (ii) alallʠmī dʠ kʠmar lall·
bʠ zā kʠ ~ lallʄ ba *epithet of* an·
pretence or makeshift. (*e*) becam·
again *x* nā ~ mu̧tu̧m I've becom·
a human being again after meta
morphosis. (2) *Vb.* 1A (*a*) returned ·
(in that direction). kōmō returned t·
(*in this direction*) *x* (i) yā ~ Kʠtsin·
he went back to Katsina. san d·
na ga̧mu dʠ shī, yakʄ̆ ~ Kʠtsinʠ ·
san dʠ na ga̧mu dʠ shī, yakʄ̆ kōmʠ̆w·

Ҟatsinạ he was returning to Katsina when I met him (M.G. 178*b*²). **sǎi sukạ ~ magana sǫsǎi** then they again spoke normally. **yā tāshị kōmạwā gidā** he set out for home. **yā ~ wạ aikịnsạ** = **yā ~ aikịnsạ** he returned to his work. (ii) *Vd.* **Ҟaŋҟarē** 3*b*. (iii) **kǫma daɓē** *Vd.* **tāshị** 1*a*.vii. (*b*) went off to *x* (i) **ya ~ Kano** from there he went to Kano (where he had not necessarily ever been before) (= **zāgạ** 4). **sukạ ~ arēwā** then they went northwards. **dạ jirgī zại nutsẹ, sukạ ~ gạ 'yaŋ ҟanānạn jirāgē** when the ship was about to sink, they had recourse to the lifeboats. (ii) **murnạ tā ~ cikī** happiness came to an end. (iii) **yā ~ bāyāna** he helped me. (iv) **fushinsạ yā ~ kaŋ ҟanạnsạ** his anger became directed towards his younger brother. (v) **dạlīlịn dạ ya sạ mutānē sukạ ~ wạ dalmạ, ta fi saukịŋ kudī ainụ** people have turned to tin-trading because it's an easy way of making money. (vi) **yā ~ zagaraftū** he changed his pace to a canter. (vii) **an yi manạ kyautar "kǫma ban daki, kạ yi kūkā!"** they gave us a thing they required themselves. (*c*) *Sk., Kt.* repeated *x* **baŋ ~ ganinsạ ba** I've not seen him again. **bạ ni ~ kwānā dạ mạtāta** I'll never again sleep with my wife (2*c* = **kumạ**).

B. (**kōmā**) *f.* (*pl.* **kōmāyē**) (1) small fishing-net. (2) **an yi masạ ~ it** (prey, prisoner, etc.) has been headed off. (3) **kētạ kōmā** *Vd.* **bargị** 2. (4) **ā gạmu ạ kōmā** *Vd.* **arạ** 2*b*.ii.

komaɗa A. (**kǫmaɗạ**) (1) *Vb.* 3B became buckled up *x* ҟwaryā tā ~ calabash from which pulp (**tōtūwā**) had been cleaned out (**hūrẹ**), buckled becoming elliptic (*it is called* ҟwaryā mại san dōkị ; *cf.* **kōmō 2**) = **mōdẹ** 2*b*. (2) **mụ tā dạ ~** let's appease our hunger !

B. (**kōmạɗā**) buckled T. (*Vd.* **kǫmaɗạ**).

kōmad dạ *Vb.* 4A (1) restored *x* **nā ~ shī garēshị** I returned it to him. (2) replaced *x* **an ~ dạ shī wurinsạ** it's been put back in its place.

kōmạɗē *Vb.* 3A = **kǫmaɗạ** 1.

kōmai = **kōmē**.

komar dạ = **kōmad dạ**.

kǫmạtsǎi collection of odds and ends.

kōmāyē *Vd.* **kōmā** ; **kōmī**.

kǫmayyạ *f.* (1) the fodder-grass *Eragrostis tremula* (= **burburwạ**). (2) *x* **kō ҟwāyar ~ bại bā nị ba** he gave me absolutely nothing.

kome A. (**kōmẹ**) *Vb.* 1A (*with dative*) resumed act previously given up *x* **cīwọ yā ~ masạ** illness thought cured has returned to him. **aŋ ~ masạ** matter thought closed has been reverted to. **tā ~ masạ** wife who had left him remarried him.

B. (**kōmē**) (1) (*in interrogative sentence*) *x* **~ ya ɓatạ?** is anything (something) lost ? (*cf.* **kōmē** 1*a*). **kā ga ~ ạ hanyạ? = ~ ka ganī ạ hanyạ?** did you see anything (something) on the road ? (M.G. 174 ; *cf.* **kōmē, wani** 5*a*, 1*a*). (2) **kō . . . mẹ** *Vd.* **mẹ, kōmē** 6.

C. (**kōmē**) (1) (*a*) **kōmē** = **kōmē dạ kōmē** *m.* (*but cf.* 1*d*, *e*, 4*b*, 5*b*, *c*, *d*) everything *x* **Allạ yā saŋ ~** God knows everything. **kā sạyi kōmē?** have you bought everything ? **~ yā ɓatạ?** is everything lost ? (*cf.* **kōmē** 1). (*b*) **dabbōbī bạ sụ ishē mụ ~ dạ ~ na bukātạrmụ ba** the cattle do not satisfy our total requirements (*Vd.* 3*b below*). (*c*) **in dạ raŋkạ, ~ kạ ganī** marvels never cease. (*d*) **nạ jē, nạ bugạ, ~ tạ tạfasạ, tạ ҟōnẹ** death or victory ! (*e*) **~ ta bisạ ҟārēwā tā yi ҟasạ** no smoke without fire ! (2) *Vd.* **kōmē**. (3) (*negatively*) nothing *x* (*a*) (i) **bā ~ wandạ na sāmụ** there is nothing which I got (*Vd.* **wani** 5*a*). **ban sāmi ~ ba** I got nothing. **wạ zại bā nị kōmē** who would give me anything ! (i.e. nobody), *cf.* **wani** 5*a*. **bā shi dạ ~** he has nothing. (ii) **wandạ ya yi hakạ, bā ~ garēshị** he who acts so, is guilty of no offence. (iii) **sun yi bạ doŋ ~ ba nē sǎi sụ yaudạrē mụ** they did so with the express purpose of deceiving us (*Vd.* **dōmin** 2*b*). (iv) **kō sun yī, kō bạ sụ yi ba, wannạm bại sạ ~ ba** whether they do it or not does not matter. (v) **bạ ạ yi ~ ba, an ɗannẹ kạm boɗarī, am bar shākịrā** the mischief is scotched, not killed. (b) dabbōbī bạ sụ ishē mụ ~ na bụkātạrmụ ba (= bạ sụ ishē mụ ~ bụkātạrmụ ba) the cattle do not at all meet our requirements (lit. not as to anything), cf. 1b above, Mod. Gram. 175. bạ ~ jịkinsạ (= bạ ~ na jịkinsạ) ịllā ḳashī there is nothing of his body but mere bone. (c) not at all x bạ sụ tsayạ ~ ba they halted nowhere. (4) whatever x (a) ~ sukạ fạďā, ḳaryā nẹ̄ whatever they say (said), is (was) a lie (= dukạ 3). ~ ya yī, kyạu whatever happens, it's all right (Mod. Gram. 185). ~ ya fạ̄ru na gạme dạ ḳasạr whatever happens in regard to the country. ~ zại yi, yanạ̄ tunạ̄wā yā kạmātạ whatever he does, he recalls that one must. . . . (b) ~ ta yī whatever happens. (c) yanạ̄ sọ̄ ạ yī, kōmē akẹ̄, ạ yī he wants it done at all costs. in yā sō, kōmē akẹ̄ yị̄, ạ̄ yi let him do his worst! (d) proverbs (alphabetically) (i) ~ ďācī, ~ baurī, bā mạ̄ dạŋganạ sǎi muŋ ga ḳwaďọ we shall persevere till the bitter end. (ii) ~ dāďin tālālā Vd. tālālā 2b. (iii) ~ dāďin tūwō Vd. dāďī 1b. (iv) ~ ďākị ya sāmụ Vd. ạlbarḳạcī 3b. (v) ~ gudụm bạrēwā Vd. bạrēwā 1c. (vi) ~ kạ̄ ganī Vd. 1c above. (vii) ~ ka shūkạ Vd. shūkạ 1a.iii. (viii) ~ kẹ̄ cikin ďan tsạ̄kō Vd. tsạ̄kō 1d. (ix) ~ lālạ̄cẹ̄war māsạ Vd. lālạ̄cē 2. (ixA) ~ nīsan darē, gạrī zại wāyẹ every cloud has a silver lining. (x) ~ nīsan jīfạ, ḳasạ zại fāďị patience wins. (xi) ~ ta bisạ Vd. 1e above. (xii) ~ tạ tạfasạ Vd. 1d above. (xiii) ~ tsananin darē Vd. tsananī 1d. (xiv) ~ tsananin tạ̄rā Vd. tạ̄rā 2b. (xv) ~ tsananin jīfạ (tạ̄rā) Vd. tsananī 1b. (xvi) ~ tsūfan dōkị Vd. tạ̄kạlmī 1d. (xvii) ~ wạ̄yaŋ amaryā Vd. wạ̄yō 1d. (xviii) ~ yakẹ̄ cikin ďan tsạ̄kō Vd. shāhọ 1c. (xix) ~ yakẹ̄ cikiŋ kạ̄zā Vd. kạ̄zā 1a.iii. (xx) ~ zā ạ yi Vd. gishirī 7. (xxi) ~ zurfin rūwā Vd. yạ̄shī 1b. (5) no matter how much, however much x (a) ~ wụyā tasạ, sǎi nā yi oh no, no matter how hard it is (was), yet I can (could) do it (reply to " it is beyond you ", Mod. Gram. 184). kōmẹ̄nēnẹ̄ bạ mại

yị̄, sǎi nā yī no matter what is beyond others, yet I shall manage to do it! (b) ~ ta daďẹ, ạ hannū zā tạ kwānā in the long run, we'll be victorious. (c) ~ ta daďẹ, Jāmụs kẹ̄ bisạ for the time being, the Germans have the upper hand. (d) ~ ta daďẹ, hakạ zā ạ yi this will be done in the end. (6) (in senses 4, 5, preposition may be interposed between kō and mẹ̄) x kō kạm mẹ̄ wutā ta fāďạ, bạ sụ shā rūwaŋ kụlā ba they didn't care a straw what places were bombarded. kō dạ mẹ̄, kō dom mẹ̄, zā mụ ci nasarạ come what may, we shall be victorious (Vd. kō 10b.ii).

C. (kọ̄mē) m. (1) resuming act previously given up (Vd. kōmẹ) x tā yi ~ = sun yi ~ they've remarried. cīwọ yā yi masạ ~ sickness thought cured has recurred to him. (2) redyeing. (3) quid of tobacco (ḳamailā) re-chewed, as one has got no new tobacco (= Kt. shạn shā). (4) detritus from wall heaped up at its base by rain. kōmẹ̄nēnẹ̄ (1) = kōmē. (2) kō mẹ̄nēnẹ̄ Vd. mẹ̄nēnẹ̄.

komi A. kōmī (1) m. (pl. kōmạ̄yē) (a) (i) any native boat. (ii) (also collective) x ḳanānaŋ ~ = ḳanānaŋ kōmạ̄yē small boats. (b) boat-shaped trough for cattle (= jirgī 2). (c) kōmin darạ draughtboard. (d) bed for crops in irrigated farm (lạmbū) = faŋgalī 3. (e) mould for casting metal (= zubị 2c). (2) Sk., Kt. = kōmē. B. (kōmī) Sk., Kt. = kōmē. kōmĩnēnẹ Sk., Kt., = kōmẹ̄nēnẹ.

kōmŏ (1) (a) Vd. kōmạ, dāwō. (b) Allạ̄ yạ ~ dạ kai lāfīyạ may you return here safely! (c) ạbin dạ ya ci, yā ~ dạ shī he vomited up what he had eaten (= amāyad dạ). (d) Vd. tā kai tā kōmŏ. (e) kā ~ m. (i) " old hand ". (ii) returning caravan x mū, muŋ tārū : sū, sunạ̄ kā ~ we were outward-caravan, they inward one. (2) m. (a) calabash which has buckled elliptically after removal of pulp (Vd. kọ̄maďạ). (2) ellipse = mōlō 3a. (3) an elliptical musical instrument (= gạrāyā). (4) yanạ̄ dạ kōmaŋ kạ̄i he has a long head. (5) fariŋ ~ m. weak P.

kōṇạ (1) Kt. f. = kōnọ. (2) Kōnāwā (from sing. Bạkōnẹ) aborigines of Zaria, the Kōfạr Kōṇạ and Līmạŋ Kōṇạ being named after them.
ƙōṇạ Vb. 1A = ƙọnā Vb. 2 (1) = ƙōnẹ 1. ʹ(2) yaṇạ̄ ƙōṇạ farcẹ he's eating tūwō (= tūwō 1b). (3) yā ~ mini māi he delayed or pettifogged me (cf. ƙōnẹ 1c).
ƙọnannē x (1) ƙọnannaŋ wạ̄yō excessive cuteness. (2) kīshīyar ƙọnannīyā Vd. saurā 1f.
Konawa A. (Kōnāwā) Vd. kōṇạ 2.
  B. (kōnawạ) Vd. nawạ 2, 3.
ƙōnẹ (1) Vb. 1A (a) burned (= tōyạ 2b). (b) yaṇạ̄ ~ mini māi ạ banzā = ƙōṇạ 3. (c) yā ~ māi he used up petrol. (d) jaurạ tā ~ ganyē the cold part of the harmattan nipped the foliage. (e) kōwā ya ~ rụmbunsạ, yā saŋ indạ tọ̄kā takẹ kudī nobody acts without a motive. (2) Vb. 3A (a) (i) became burned. (ii) fêtụr yā ~ the petrol became used up. (iii) nāmạ yā ~, yā bar rōmō what a hypocrite! (b) kọ̄gī yā ~ the river has dried up. rījīyā tā ~ the well is dried up. nōnạntạ yā ~ her breasts have shrivelled. (c) idạnsạ yā ~ he's brazen. (d) rūwā yā ~ ạ tukunyā water in the pot has boiled away. (e) (i) yā ~ tum bại tạfas ba he (boy) is too precocious. (ii) Vd. tạfasạ 1c.
kōni Sk. come, come! now, behave yourself! (= habạ).
kōni-kōni m. (1) being half-hearted. (2) being indecisive.
kono A. (kōnọ) m. (1) chaff of guineacorn (= ƙaiƙayī = hanci 7). (2) Kt. = kōnō 1. *(3) bowl (= kwānọ q.v.).
  B. (kōnō) m. (1) Sk. yā kāwō zạkkar ~ = yā kāwō fid dạ kāi. (2) Sk. yā kāwō ~ mūdụ kạzā he's given in charity so-and-so many measures of corn as expiation (= yā fid dạ kạfārạ q.v. under kạfārạ). (3) kadạ kạ yi dāmạ ~ take care you don't let your clothing become burnt by tobacco or match falling on it!
kora A. (kọrā) (1) Vb. 2 (a) (i) drove away (cf. kōrạ). (ii) yā kọri fagē he drove back the spectators crowding into the

place where contest was being held. (iii) kō aŋ kọri kūrā, tạ yi gụzurī dạ kạrē nil desperandum! (iv) ganī yā kọri jī seeing is believing. (v) ạ kọri mụtụm, ạ ga iriŋ gudụnsạ hardship shows the mettle of a person. (vi) ạbin dạ ya kōrō ɓērā har yā sạ̄ yā fādạ wuta, tọ̄, yā kụ̄wā fi wutạr zāfī desperate causes need desperate remedies. (b) = sạllamạ 2. (c) ạ kọri kadạ m. children's water-game. (d) ƙaƙạ zā ạ kōrō mạganạn naŋ cikin zạncẹ how is this word applied in conversation? (e) Alạ̄ kōrō Vd. Alạ̄ 7. (2) f. (a) (progressive and v.n. of 1) x yaṇạ̄ kọrā tasụ he's driving them away. (b) yā yi ~ he has diarrhœa (= zāwọ). (c) act of driving away x (i) ~ dạ halī tā fi ~ dạ karā black looks are worse than blows. (ii) ~ tā mīƙẹ har Kano the pursuit was carried on right up to Kano. (iii) Jāmụs suṇạ̄ shaŋ kọrar kạrē the Germans are being routed (Vd. fata-fata; 2c.xi below). (iv) yā (tā) yi girmaŋ kọrar rāmi he (she) flourished till seven years old and then died in his (her) first illness. (v) kōwā ya kwānā wurim fadạ, shī ya yi ~ effort prevails. (vi) yā sạ̄mi ~ he got the upper hand (= taushi 3). (vii) yā rabạ ~ he sent his goods to several markets, he sent to several places for what he required. (viii) aŋ kọ̄rē kạ kanạ̄ kūwwạ Vd. būzū 2. (ix) banzā tā kọri wọ̄fī Vd. banzā 1e. (x) aŋ tausạ kọrā Vd. tausạ 1c. (xi) aŋ kọri kạrē Vd. wạ̄yō 1b (cf. 2c.iii above). (xii) Mạtsạ kọrā Vd. matsạ 1g. (xiii) kọrar yāƙi Vd. gudụmmawā. (xiv) ci kōrō Vd. ạllaŋ ~. (xv) Vd. ạ kọri kadạ.
  B. (kōrạ) (1) Vb. 1A (a) drove animal in front of one x yaṇạ̄ ~ tumākī (= tạfi dạ 3a), cf. kọrā. (b) nā ~ masạ zōmō I finished my share of work before he'd finished his (= zōmō 6). (c) yā ~ rūwā (i) he drank water on the sly during the Fast (azụmī). (ii) he drank alcohol. (iii) he kept drinking water to clear mouth of fat sticking to it. (d) yā ~ tābạ he smoked tobacco; he took pinch of snuff. (e) dạ kōrạ̄wā,

ɗaŋ ƙirgi yā ci āfu a fine profit, I *don't*
think ! (2) *Vb.* 3A aiki yā ∼ the
work has progressed.

C. (kōrā) *f.* (1) (*a*) ringworm (*epithet
is* ∼ jīmạr Allā). (*b*) askā tā ɓacę
mại korā *Vd.* birinciŋ kulạ. (2)
zāɓūwā tā fasạ ∼ guinea-fowl's begun
to get big (*marked by horny excrescences
on head*). yā fasạ ∼ he's getting on in
the world. *(3) space between columns
of verse. (4) iri yā yi ∼ seeds have not
germinated (= ƙamfā 1).

ƙŏrạĩ *m.* (1) querulousness ; fussing
at slightest pain or inconvenience. (2)
ubaŋ ∼ *m.* (*f.* ūwar ∼) querulous P.

ƙọrai calabashes (*pl. of* ƙwaryā *q.v.*).

kọrakā *f.* cadging meal by ɗaŋ ∼ i.e.
P. always hanging about when meals
of others are being served.

ƙọramạ *f.* (*pl.* ƙọrạmū = ƙọrạmai) (1) (*a*)
large stream (bigger than rāĩ, but
smaller than kōgī). (*b*) shiŋkāfā cę
ɓabbar ƙọramạr ƙāsan naŋ ta azziki
rice forms the main source of wealth
of this country. (2) head of the women-
traders in cereals and foodstuffs sold
by measure (mūdụ) = *Sk.* sạrāki 3.

*kọramī *Kt. m.* pen-case.

kọrarrē *m.* (*f.* kọrarrīyā) *pl.* kọrạrrū
fugitive.

Ḳọrau (1) (= Būwāyī) *epithet of* any
Shāmaki. (2) *Kt. epithet of* any Chief
(Sarkī).

kōrāwā *Vd.* kōrạ 1*e*.

kore A. (kōrę) (1) (*rolled* " r ", Mod.
Gram. 5) (*a*) *adj. m.* (*f.* kōrīyā) *pl.*
kwạrrā (i) grass-green, emerald-green
(= algashī), *cf.* baƙī. (ii) ∼ shar bright
green. (*b*) *noun m.* greenness *as in* 1*a*.i
x (i) ciyāwạ tā yi ∼ the grass is green.
(ii) nāmạ yā yi ∼ the meat has begun
to stink (= gaisūwā 7). (iii) (*with pl.*
kwạrrā) type of glossy, very dark
indigo-dyed gown (*cf.* lēlā 4, dōmōsō 4).
(2) (*cerebral* " r ", Mod. Gram. 5) (*a*)
Vb. 3A hadiri yā ∼ (i) storm has
passed. (ii) rain is near, as dark wind-
clouds have passed and lighter rain-
clouds are visible (*both* = wāshę 2*g*),
cf. kōɗę 1*g*. (*b*) rāina bại ∼ ba my
mind's not at rest about it. (*c*) *Vb.*
1A (i) drove away (= kọrā). (ii)

ạ ∼ rūwā, ạ shā dạ ƙararī push aside
the waterweeds and drink the underlying clear water. " ạ ∼, ạ shā dạ
ƙararī " yakę yī he's adducing feeble
excuses (= kusạssarī). (iii) aŋ ∼ musụ
jạrabạ temptation has been put out
of their way.

B. (kōrē) *m.* (1) beating up birds or
animals for marksman. (2) touting
for mālạmī who does spells, magic, etc.
(tsubbụ). (3) cock-pigeon's (ƙatukụ)
chasing hen-pigeon (tạttabạrā).

C. (kọrē) *m.* long-distance trading
in cattle, sheep, or goats.

ƙọrē calabashes (*pl. of* ƙwaryā).

kōrinō *m.* (1) Cambridge blue dye. (2)
such colour. (3) leather so dyed. (4)
dụsar ∼ *Vd.* dụsā 3.

kōrīyā *Vd.* kōrę 1*a*.

kọrīyọ *m.* bottle (būtạ) made of plaited
frṏnds of young dum-palm (kabạ) or
of fibre (yāwā), used by Barebari
travellers for dry flour (gārī) or flour
mixed with water (= mạruhū 2).

kōrō *Vd.* kọrā 1*a*.vi, 1*d*, 1*e*.

ƙọrọsō = kọrọsō *m.* jingling anklet(s)
of dancers (= cạccạkai = akayau), *cf.*
barambajau, cạkansamī, cịkạ sạurā 2.

ƙọrukạ, ƙọrunạ calabashes (*pl. of*
ƙwaryā).

kōsạ *m.* (1) kōsạ = na ∼ type of chalk
got by burning clay (*cf.* ạllī). (2)
Kōsạ *epithet of* any Sarkin dawākī.

ƙosa A. (ƙōsā) *Vb.* 2 (*only* negatively,
but cf. ƙōshi, ƙōshī) *x* haŋkạlī bại
ƙōshē shi ba he has no sense. lāfiyạ
bạ tạ ƙōshi Audụ ba Audu does not
enjoy good health.

B. (ƙōsạ) (1) *Vb.* 1A (*a*) satisfied
appetite *x* ạbincin naŋ yā ∼ ni this
food satisfied my appetite. (*b*) wạhalạ
tā ∼ ni I've a peck of trouble. aiki
yā ∼ ni I'm sick and tired of work.
(*c*) enriched. (2) *Vb.* 3A (*a*) yā ∼ he
became exasperated. ƙōsạ̄wā gạrēshi
he's bad-tempered. bā yạ̄ ƙōsạ̄wā dạ
mutā̄nē he's not easily " put out ".
(*b*) Gandun Sarkī, ƙōsạ aiki *epithet of*
any drum. (*c*) became ripe (*re* round
things growing in the ground *x* gourd,
onion, cassava, sugarcane), *cf.* nụ̄na,
bịra. (*d*) became adult, full-grown.

(e) looked well-fed. (f) is (was) well-off.

ƙọsạ aiki̱ Vd. gandū 2c.

ƙōsad dạ Vb. 4B = ƙōsạ 1.

ƙōsǎi m. (sg., pl.) (1) (a) cake made from bean-flour (= sọ̄tō = arai). (b) sāri̱ŋ ∼ bạ shi dạ rība love's labour lost. (2) nāmạ yā sọyu, yā yi bāyaŋ ∼ the meat is just nicely fried.

ƙōsar dạ = ƙōsad dạ.

ƙọsau (1) epithet of Sarkin nōmā. (2) name for child born at harvest-time (= Ƙạka).

ƙoshi A. (ƙọshi) Vb. (progressive and v.n. are ƙọshī q.v.) (1) (a) became replete. (b) kōwā ya ∼, yạ ragẹ put a bit away for a rainy day! (c) " Bạ dādī " tanạ̄ gidaŋ " Nā ƙọshi " it is the rich man who grumbles at loss, not the poor man. (d) mai̱ tạunā ya ka̱ŋ ∼ Vd. tạunā. (e) Vd. gāgọ 4b. (2) yā ∼ hạŋkạlī = yā ∼ dạ hạŋkạlī he's sensible. bại ∼ lāfīyạ ba he does not enjoy good health (cf. ƙōsā). (3) did constantly x nā ∼ faɗạ masạ I'm always telling him so. nā ∼ yi̱ I'm always doing it (= di̱ŋgạ).

B. (ƙọshi) m. (1) (progressive and v.n. of ƙọshi). (2) ample sufficiency (epithet is ∼ hạuƙạtạ yārọ). (a) bana, dạ ∼ there is ample food this year. (b) shaidạr ∼ saurā only the rich have a surplus. (c) yanạ̄ dạ ƙọshin sāmu̱ he's well-off. yanạ̄ dạ ƙọshi̱ŋ hạŋkạlī he's sensible. bạ shi dạ ∼ he's witless (cf. ƙọsā). (d) tanạ̄ dạ ƙọshin ɗāki̱ she is liberally treated by her husband. (3) ku̱ŋ gwammạcẹ ∼ Vd. bạrēwā 1b. (4) ƙọshin nāmạ Vd. bari̱ 7b.iii. (5) ƙọshi̱ŋ wạhalạ Vd. masọ̄ 2. (6) ∼ yā mai dạ tsōfō yārọ Vd. yārọ 1h.

ƙọshīyạ = kọshīyạ f. (pl. ƙọshīyōyī) (1) wooden ladle (= tạmōlạkā). (2) shuttle. hanji̱ŋ ∼ bobbin-nipple. (3) scalpel for removal of uvula (bẹ̄lī). (4) ∼ tasạ tanạ̄ kạn dawọ he's popular with his superior; he's wealthy and liberal. (5) gạmshẹ̄ƙā tā yi ∼ cobra raised its hood (= fasạ 1p). (6) yanạ̄ ∼ he's taking a lot of soup (mīyạ).

ƙọsọ̄sọ (1) ∼ dạ kai, ạ gọ̄yẹ̄ kạ ? fancy

a big child like you expecting still to be carried on your mother's back! (2) ∼ kā shi̱ga mini̱ ɗāki̱ ? fancy you bursting in, in this loutish way! (3) foolhardiness x ∼ gạrēshi̱ he's foolhardy (= ku̱ndu̱mbālā q.v.). Vd. ƙọ̄tọ̄tọ.

ƙọtạ f. (pl. ƙōtōcī) (1) (a) haft (= Sk. ɓōtạ 2a), Vd. kwaɓạ; kwaɓẹ. (b) cf. rūwā J. (2) im bạ̄ ạ gạ̄tarī ba, ạ ∼ one or the other of the two misfortunes is bound to befall; the misfortune's bound to befall one of us. (3) im mu̱tu̱m yā cẹ̄ zai hạɗīyi gạ̄tarī, ri̱ƙe masạ ∼ don't waste your breath on P. who thinks he can do the impossible! (4) kạryayyīyar ∼ = fạsasshīyar ∼ deposed P. thorn in flesh of his successor.

ƙōtai m. the plant ƙwātai.

kō tā kwānạ̄ ? I challenge you to race, competition of liberality (cf. ạljạmā) or quarrel! (reply accepting is har ta yi tsāmī).

ƙọtō m. (1) pecking up food by birds x kạjī sunạ̄ ∼ poultry are pecking up food (= kīwọ 2b). (2) bā dạ ∼ gạrēshi̱ he provides amply for his family or guests. (3) ƙọtaŋ kạzā = ƙọtaŋ kurcīyā (i) twice rapidly placing forehead on ground in prayer, instead of doing so in the quiet dignified way enjoined with raka'ạ between each. (ii) type of children's game.

ƙōtōcī hafts (pl. of ƙọtạ).

ƙọtọ̄kō Kt. m. (1) large cock. (2) Ƙọtọ̄kō, zạkarạm mạsū gạrī epithet of strong wrestler or boxer.

ƙọ̄tọ̄tọ used in yārọ, ∼ dạ shi̱ ? fancy such a big boy still sleeping in his mother's room, etc.! ∼ dạ shi̱ fancy him having so little self-respect! (= gọ̄tọ̄tọ = ƙọsọ̄sọ q.v. for further examples).

ƙọ̄tsạ Vb. 1A (1) did abundantly (= kwantsạmā q.v.). (2) yā ∼ yau he (toothless P.) weakly ejected saliva.

ƙọtsạnnī Vd. ƙọtsō.

ƙọtsẹ Vb. 1A x nā ∼ shi dạ sạndā I hit him with stick.

ƙọtsō m. (pl. kōtsunạ = ƙọtsạnnī). (1) (a) type of drum beaten with the fingers x anạ̄ māri̱ŋ ∼ the drum ƙọtsō is

being beaten (cf. kiɗa). (b) Sarkin ~
Vd. marōkī. (2) Kōtsō mai muryā
gōma epithet of P. whose voice changes
rapidly from base to falsetto (= macē
6).
kōtu Eng. m. Local Authority's court.
yā taɓi ~ = yā hau ~ he went to
court.
kowa A. (kōwā) (1) (a) everyone x (i) kōwā
yā sani = duk kōwā yā sani everyone
knows it. (ii) yā san ~ dā ~ he knows
everyone. (iii) bā ~ nē ya zō ba not
everyone came. bā ~ yakē zūwā ba not
everyone's coming (cf. 3). (b) (i) dōkin
~ zan hau I'll go on Shank's pony. (ii)
ƙasā, dōkin ~ epithet of helpful P.
(c) kōwā dā rānā tasā everyone has his
speciality. (d) kōwā dā kīwan Vd.
akwīyā 1t. (e) kōwā yā san indā
ɗāki Vd. yayyō. (f) kōwā yanā sō
yā gāji ubansā Vd. matsīyācī 3. (g)
kōwā yā taɓā nāsā Vd. tsōkā 2b. (2)
Vd. kōwā. (3) (negatively) nobody x
bā ~ wandā ya zō nobody has
come. (cf. 1a.iii). ban ga ~ ba
I saw nobody. kadā kā bā ~ sǎi shī
don't give it to anyone but him!
kadā ~ cikinsu yā yi jāyayyā none of
them must offer opposition! inā
zan sāmi kōwā where shall I find anyone (i.e. nowhere) (Vd. wani 5a),
cf. kōwā. (4) whoever x (a) ~ ya bā mu
(= duk ~ ya bā mu), sǎi mun yi
murnā whoever gave (gives) us, we
were (are) pleased (Mod. Gram. 185).
~ kē sō, ā bā shi whoever wants it will
be given it (= dukā 3). (b) Vd. kōwā 2.
(5) proverbs (alphabetically). (a) ~ bai sā
rīgā ba Vd. dōmin-dōmin. (b) ~ ka ganī
dā kēso Vd. shimfiɗā 1c. (c) ~ ya ajīyē
Vd. ajīyē 5a.ii. (d) ~ ya bā igīyā Vd.
igīyā 1b. (e) ~ ya bā kā fāwā (fiɗā)
Vd. fincē 2. (f) ~ ya cē "ā yi duffā!"
Vd. duffā. (g) ~ ya cē dūnīyā Vd.
dūnīyā 1h. (h) ~ ya ci albasā Vd.
albasā 1b. (hh) ~ ya ci amānā Vd.
amānā 4. (j) ~ ya ci dā mǎi Vd. ā
cī dā mǎi. (k) ~ ya ci hatsin rancē
Vd. rancē 2b. (l) ~ ya cikā bikī Vd.
Alhamis 3. (ll) ~ ya ci lādan kuturū
Vd. kuturū. (m) ~ ya cikā ci Vd. amai
1b. (n) ~ ya cikā kǎi rūwā Vd. rūwā

A.17c, cikā 1j. (o) ~ ya ci kāzā Vd.
kāzā 1f. (p) ~ ya ci shinkāfā Vd.
shinkāfā 1b. (q) ~ ya ci tūwō dā shī
Vd. shā 1g.iv. (r) ~ ya ci zōmō Vd.
zōmō 4. (s) ~ ya daɗe Vd. daɗǎi. (t) ~
ya dakā Vd. dakā 1b. (u) ~ ya dāmā
Vd. dāmā 1c. (v) ~ ya ɗauki bāshim
barcī Vd. bāshi 5. (w) ~ ya ɗaurē
kūrā Vd. ɗaurē 1a.v. (x) ~ ya ɗēbō
Vd. zāfī 1d. (y) ~ ya fāsā Vd. shēgē 4.
(z) ~ ya ga biri Vd. baƙī B.1.1e. (z)
(i) ~ ya ga dāmisā Vd. dāmisā 8.
(z) (ii) ~ ya ginā rījīyā Vd. rījīyā 1b.
(z) (iii) ~ ya hau gaggāwā Vd. gaggāwā 1d. (z) (iiiA) ~ ya ga shāmūwā
Vd. shāmūwā 3. (z) (iv) ~ ya hūrā
rārīyā Vd. rārīyā 3c. (z) (v) ~ ya jā
ƙayā Vd. ƙayā 1a.v. (z) (vA) ~ ya
ji zāfin wuƙā Vd. ƙudūrū. (z) (vi) ~
ya kāmā kīfī Vd. sakā 4. (z) (vii) ~
ya kas Vd. guzumā 2. (z) (viii) ~ ya
kas kīfī Vd. gōrā 1j. (z) (ix) ~ ya ƙi
jī Vd. ƙī 1b.ix. (z) (x) ~ ya ƙi yawā
Vd. ƙī 1b.ii. (z) (xi) ~ ya ƙōnē rumbū
Vd. tōkā 2. (z) (xii) ~ ya ƙōshi Vd.
ƙōshi 1b. (z) (xiii) ~ ya kwānā wurim
faɗā Vd. kōrā 2c.v. (z) (xiv) ~ ya
mantā Vd. ƙaryā 1j. (z) (xv) ~ ya
rēnā gajērē Vd. tākā 2aa.v. (z) (xvi)
~ ya rēnā mai lābāri Vd. rēnā 9. (z)
(xvii) ~ ya rēnā mōtsinkā Vd. rēnā
11. (z) (xviii) ~ ya rēnā watā Vd.
rēnā 8. (z) (xix) ~ ya rigā ki hawā Vd.
wutā 1a.i. (z) (xx) ~ ya sāmu Vd.
sāmā 1a.vii. (z) (xxi) ~ ya sāmu Vd.
barā A.2.1d. (z) (xxii) ~ ya sāmi rānā
Vd. shanyā. (z) (xxiii) ~ ya sau kā
Vd. afalalu. (z) (xxiv) ~ ya shā ɗayā
Vd. gāgo 4b. (z) (xxv) ~ ya shā rūwā
Vd. haki 2. (z) (xxvi) ~ ya taɓā
nāsā Vd. tsōkā 2b. (z) (xxvii) ~ ya
tunā bāra Vd. tunā 1a.ii. (z) (xxviii) ~
ya yi aɓutā dā biri Vd. sandā 1h. (z)
(xxviiiA) ~ ya shā inūwā Vd. maƙōg-
warō. (z) (xxix) ~ ya yi cīzo Vd.
cīzo 2b. (z) (xxx) ~ ya yi darē Vd.
Burungū. (z) (xxxi) ~ yai dārīyar
ƙarē Vd. dārīyā 4. (z) (xxxii) ~ ya yi
guri'ā Vd. burmi 3. (z) (xxxiii) ~
ya yi ƙafā Vd. rǎi 5c. (z) (xxxiv) ~
ya yi kan karā Vd. itācē 1e. (z) (xxxv)
~ ya yi ƙaryā Vd. ƙaryā 1f. (z) (xxxvi)

~ ya yi ƙaryar darē *Vd.* darē 4*q.*ii. (*z*) (xxxvii) ~ ya yi kāshī *Vd.* inūwą 1*a.*iv. (*z*) (xxxviii) ~ ya yi kirąŋki sąu dayā *Vd.* ta alakō. (*z*) (xxxix) ~ ya yi sąmmakō *Vd.* sąmmakō 1*d.* (*z*) (xl) ~ ya yi wāwan zamā *Vd.* wāwan zamā. (*z*) (xli) ~ ya zubar mini *Vd.* tsāmīyā 1*f.*

B. (kōwą̄) (*in interrogative sentences*). (1) anyone, someone *x* ~ ya zō̜ ? has anyone (someone) come ! kā ga ~ ą hąnyą ? = kōwą̄ ka ganī ą hąnyą ? did you see anyone (someone) on the road ? (*cf.* kōwā 3, wani 1*a,* 5*a*). (2) (*a*) kō kąŋ wą̄, etc. *Vd.* kō 10*b.*ii. (*b*) kō kąŋ wą̄ yą fādą *Vd.* wucę 2*a.*ii.

C. (kōwą̄) *f.* bean-pods.

kōwąnę = kōwąną *m.* (*f.* kōwącę = kōwącą) *pl.* kōwądąnnę = kōwądąnną. (1) (*a*) every *x* (i) kōwąnę mutum everybody. kōwącę rīgā every gown. kōwąnę dayammu every one of us men. kōwącę dayarmu every one of us women. kōwądąnnę ƙasąshē all countries. (ii) kōwącę Jumma'ą̄ ta farin ciki dą ą̄l'amąrintą coming events cast their shadows before them. (iii) kōwąnę tsuntsū yą̄ yi kūkąŋ gidansą let the cobbler stick to his last ! (iv) kōwącę ƙwaryā *Vd.* murfī 1*a.*ii. (v) kōwąnę bąkiŋ wutā *Vd.* bąkiŋ wutā. (vi) kōwąnę allązī *Vd.* āmą̄nū. (*b*) both of *x* kōwąnę hannunsą both his hands. (*c*) any *x* yā̄ wucę indą kōwąnę mutum ya tafą̄ zūwą he has gone beyond where anyone has ever gone before. bā ą̄ yą̄rdā kōwąnę yārǫ yą rąbu dą gidā sǎi yā sąmi yąrdāta no servant may be absent from the house without my leave. bą̄ mā kwądayim mulki, kō dūkīyā, kō kōwąnę ą̄bu dąbaŋ they have no desire for rule nor wealth nor anything else (*cf.* kōwąnnē 3). (2) whatever *x* (*a*) kōwącę hanyą muką̄ bi, sǎi muŋ gąji whatever road we follow (followed), we tire (tired) (Mod. Gram. 185). kōwącę iriŋ kūrā ta zō whatever kind of hyena came (Mod. Gram. 64*b.*ii. *Vd.* iri 5*a*). (*b*) (*in this sense, prep. can be interposed between* kō *and* wąnę) *x* zā su yī, kō dą wąnę hāli they'll do it, cost what it may (*Vd.*

kō 10*b.*ii). (3) no matter which *x* kōwącę 'yar ƙīrą suką ganī, sǎi sun yi no matter what trifle of smithing is required, *they* are up to it.

kōwą̄nēnę̄ *m.* (*f.* kōwą̄cēcę̄). (1) everyone = kōwā *q.v.* (2) no matter *who* it is *x* iŋ am bą̄ wani sąrautą, ~ ku kashę shi if anyone is appointed ruler, kill him, no matter *who* he is !

kōwąnnē *m.* (*f.* kōwąccē) *pl.* kōwądąnnē (1) everyone *x* (*a*) kōwąccē ta kąn yi hailą every woman has menstruations. kōwądąnnē su yi haką let all do this ! kōwądąnnansu each of them. (2) whoever, whichever *x* kōwąnnē ya bā mu, sǎi mun yi murną whichever one he gave (gives) us, we were (are) pleased (Mod. Gram. 185). (3) anyone of them at all *x* bąri zą̄ɓē, ką daukō kōwąnnē take *any* of them it may be without picking and choosing ! (4) *Vd.* kōwā.

kōwąsshē = kōyąushē.

koya A. (kōyą) (1) *Vb.* 1A taught *x* yā ~ mini kąrą̄tū he taught me to read ; educated me. (2) *f.* (*pl.* kōyōyī). (*a*) red-earth and the red ink made from it. (*b*) yā kadą ~ it began ripening (= bira *q.v.*).

B. (kōyā) *Vb.* 2 (*Vd.* kōyō) learned *x* nā kōyē shi I learned it.

ƙōyā *Sk. f.* a grain of T. (= ƙwą̄yā *q.v.*).

kōyąushē (1) always *x* (*a*) aną̄ sāmun dāwą ~ guinea-corn is always obtainable. (*b*) fīyē dą kōyąushe more than ever. (2) (*negatively in progressive with habitual sense*) never *x* bą̄ shi dą ąmfānī kōyąushē it is never advantageous. bā ną̄ ganinsą ~ I never see him. (3) whenever *x* ~ na zō, sǎi nā gan shi whenever I came (come), I saw (see) him (= duką 3). ~ na zō, bā ną̄ ganinsą whenever I came (come), I didn't (don't) see him (Mod. Gram. 185). (4) no matter when *x* ~ muką ga dāmā, sǎi mun yī no matter *when* we want to (wanted to), we'll manage it (we managed it) (Mod. Gram. 184). (5) *cf.* yąushę, bayąushē.

kōyāyą *Vd.* yą̄yą 2.

kōyi *m.* imitating *x* (1) yaną̄ ~ dą Audu he's imitating Audu. (2) ąbiŋ ~ *m.* example (*cf.* kwąikwayą).

kọyō *m.* (*secondary v.n. of* kọyā) *x* yanā̀ kọyaŋ kàrā̀tū = yanā̀ kọyar kàrā̀tū he's learning to read.

kōyōyī *Vd.* kōyā̀ 2.

ƙōzō *m.* (1) type of frog (*epithet is* ~ mūgụŋ kwā̀ɗō : kōmē zurfin rūwā, idaŋkà yanā̀ wàje). (2) (*a*) the spinal deformity ƙụsumbī. (*b*) *epithet of* P. afflicted with 2*a*.

ƙụ *Vd.* ƙụụ.

ku A. (kū) (*independent pronoun, plural,* Mod. Gram. 46). (1) ~ nḕ it is you (*pl.*). dā̀ ~ dā̀ mū both you and we. yā nēmar minị ~ he sought you for me (Mod. Gram. 76.*a*.ii). yā gajīyad dā̀ ~ it tired you (Mod. Gram. 167). (2) kū nḕ dǎi that's the sort of conduct one would expect of you. (3) *Vd.* kū kā̀. (4) kū yḕ kū *Vd.* yḕ.
B. (ku) (kụ) (1) (*employed gram-matically for* " you " (*plural*) *as illus-trated by substituting* ku *for* ka, *and* kụ *for* kā̀ *in* ka 1-7 *and* kā̀ 1-8). (2) *Vd.* kụ aunā̀ ; Kụ yī ; sụ 4 ; kụ tarę ; kụ cī, kụ bā nị. (3) bā̀ ā̀ yi wani yāƙị ba na " kụ zō, kụ ganī ! " no important war has occurred.
C. (kū) (1) come, come ! ; behave yourself ! (= habā̀). (2) *Kt.* = kwā̀ *x* kụ zō gọ̀be you'll probably come to-morrow.

kụ aunā̀ *x* nā yi ~ dā̀ shī I met him suddenly (= aunē).

kụb *m.* type of rosary (cā̀zbī). ~ ɗinsā̀ his rosary.

kūbā̀ *f.* (*pl.* kūbōbī). (1) iron door-lock for outside (*cf.* sā̀katā̀). (2) lock inside door of European house. (both = makullī 2).

kụbạnnī *Vd.* kụbē.

kụbārācī *m.* extra-special lumps made for kōko (gruel). gáyansā̀ ~ nḕ the gruel contains *such* lumps (= gwārājī).

*kubbā̀ *f.* (*Ar.* dome) *pl.* kubbōbī mauso-leum.

kubcę *Vb.* 3A = kuɓụcē.

kubcikkē *Vb.* 3A *Sk.* =ƙuɓụcē.

kụbē *m.* (*pl.* kụbạnnī). (1) sheath (for knife or razor). (2) bā̀kinsā̀ yā shiga ~

he was reduced to silence. (3) kyaŋwā̀ tā mai dā̀ farā̀utā ~ the cat drew in its claws. (4) dāwā̀ tā yi kụbaŋ askā̀ guinea-corn failed.

kuɓę̀ *Kt. m.* = ku'ę̀.

Kūɓe *used in* Kūɓę, kā yi bạbba dā̀ kạŋkā̀ " he's too big for his boots ".

kuɓę̀wā *f.* (*pl.* kụɓę̀yī). (1) okro. (2) ạrādụ tā̀ yi minị yaŋkaŋ ~ I swear I didn't do it ! ; I swear I won't do it ! (= ā̀bassamā̀ 2).

kūɓōbī *Vd.* kūbā̀.

kụɓōrọ *m.* ferrule of spear or digging-stick (dāgị).

kụɓūbūwā̀ *f.* (1) any viper (= gā̀jērē 3). (2) mụtụm ~ *m.* quick-tempered P.

kuɓụcē (1) *Vb.* 3A escaped (*also* kuɓutō), *cf.* kụɓutā̀. (2) *Vb.* 1C (*with dative*) *x* (*a*) nā ~ masā̀ I escaped from it, him. (*b*) yā kuɓụcē masā̀ (i) it became lost to him. (ii) it slipped out of his hand.

kuɓul = kuɓulɓul.

ƙubul *m.* small and round *x* ạlbasā̀ cē ~ dā̀ ita it's a small onion (*pl.* albasōshī nḕ ƙubul-ƙubul dā̀ sū).

kuɓulɓul = kuɓul *m.* squatness *x* gā̀jērē nḕ ~ dā̀ shī he's podgy (*pl.* 'yaŋ gā̀jērū nḕ kuɓul-ƙuɓul dā̀ sū).

ƙubulbul = ƙubul.

ƙubul-ƙubul *Vd.* ƙubul.

kuɓur-kuɓur = kuɓul-kuɓul *q.v. under* kuɓulɓul.

kụɓurọ *m.* one-stringed instrument, made of oval gourd covered with skin and played with fingers (is considered blind man's instrument).

kụɓutā̀ *Vb.* 3B. (1) = kuɓụcē 1. (2 slipped from one's grasp *x* madūbī yā̀ ~ dā̀gā hannūna.

kuɓutad dā̀ *Vb.* 4A. (1) enabled P. to escape. (2) shạrī'ā̀ tā ~ dā̀ shī he wa̱ acquitted.

kụɓutai = *Kt.* kụɓuttai *m.* the slipper kụfụtai *q.v.*

kuca *Nor.* yā fāɗị ~ he suddenly fe̱ down.

kucā̀-kucā̀ = kucā̀kucī = kucīcī *q.v.*

kuccę *Vb.* 3A = kuɓụcē.

kuccīyā *f.* the dove kurciyā *q.v.*

ƙụcē (1) *m.* making click of annoyanc (= ƙwā̀fā). (2) *Vd.* ƙụtā.

kuci *m.* (1) (*secondary v.n. of* kụtā̀

x anā kuciŋ hancin tarnaƙi = anā kuta hancin tarnaƙi loop of hobbling-rope is being spliced (= haya). (2) place in rope, daram-būwā-armlet, etc., where they are spliced. (3) an yi wa maƙā ~ archer's thumb-ring has been padded with leather-strips to fit him (= kuta 4). (4) yā īya kucim magana he's too glib.

ƙu ci *Vd.* ƙu-cī-ƙu-bā-ni.

ƙuci *Vb.* ƙutā.

kucici A. (kucīcī) *m.* (1) stuntedness *x* ɗan yāro nē ~ da shī he's a stunted boy (*pl.* 'yan yārā nē kuci-kuci da sū = kuca-kuca da sū = kucaƙucī da sū). (2) *pl.* kuci-kuci odds and ends.
B. (ƙucīcī) (1) *used in* ~ mūguŋ tarkō *epithet of* P. " with finger in every pie ". (2) *Vd.* fitar ƙucīcī.

ƙu cika *Kt. f.* back-door (= madudduƙā).

ƙu-cī-ƙu-bā-ni *used in* 'yaŋ ƙu-cī-ƙu-bā-ni rag, tag, and bobtail.

kuci-kuci A. (kuci-kuci) *Vd.* kucīcī.
B. (ƙucī-ƙucī, *etc.*) = ƙicī-ƙicī.

kucincinā *Vb.* 1E broke pieces off tūwō, etc. (= gutsurā).

ƙucīnīyā *f.* = ƙicī-ƙicī.

kuciŋ-kuciŋ *m.* (1) small bits pinched off tūwō, etc. (2) = kuci-kuci.

ƙudā *m.* (*pl.* ƙudājē). (1) (*a*) fly ; flies. (*b*) hanjiŋ ~ (i) type of 3-ply thread (= *Kt.* mariŋ kūrā). (ii) poor spinning by girl novice. (*c*) fitsāriŋ ~ *m.* (i) fly-marks. (ii) honey (= zuma). (*d*) *Vd.* kaŋ ƙudā. (*e*) (i) yārā suŋā dūbaŋ ~ = yārā suŋā gāniŋ ~ boys are playing game of staring each other out. (ii) munā zamaŋ gāniŋ ƙudā da sū we're staring at them. (*f*) har nā ci ~ bai zō ba I got tired of waiting for him and went away. (*g*) ƙudan zuma bee (*Vd.* zuma 2). (*h*) *Vd.* rīgar ƙudā. (*j*) yā hūta da ~ *Vd.* ƙashī 1*d*. (*k*) mutum ƙudā nē *Vd.* sēmā 2. (*l*) dārīyar ƙudā *Vd.* dārīyā 5. (2) foresight of rifle.

kūda (1) *f.* (*a*) an yi wa dūtsan niƙa ~ grinding-stone has been roughened (= kōda 1*b q.v.*). (*b*) an yi masa ~ it's been sharpened *as in* kōda 1*a q.v.* (*c*) yā yi masa ~ he " puffed " them (his wares) or P. he wants to get on (*cf.* akaras) = kōda 2. (*d*) (*secondary*

v.n. of kōda) *x* anā kūdar wuƙā = anā kōda wuƙā knife's being sharpened *as in* kōda 1*a*. (*e*) kunnansa (haƙōrinsa) yanā ~ he has ear-ache (tooth-ache). (*f*) yā ɗanɗana kūdarsa he "had a bad time ". (*g*) *Vd.* bīsalāmī. (2) (*a*) how hot ! (*b*) how painful !

ƙudābu *m.* (1) wannaŋ rātsē ~ nē this ford has certain known spots where water is over one's head. (2) yā jāwō mini ~ he brought trouble on me by my acting on information which he had distorted.

kudaɗɗakī *Kt.* = kudī 1*a*.

ƙudaddarī knots (*pl. of* ƙudurī).

kudaɗē *Vd.* kudī 1*j*.

ƙudāgirī = ƙudāgī *m.* (*f.* ƙudāgirā) *pl.* ƙudāgirai destitute person.

kudaiɗai *Vd.* kudī 1*j*.

ƙudājē *Vd.* ƙudā.

kūdaku *Sk. m.* sweet-potato (= daŋkali).

kudancī *m.* (1) area lying to south of *x* kudanciŋ Kano (*Vd.* kudu 3). (2) ways or speech of southern districts.

kudandamī *m.* (*pl.* kudandamai). (1) the rufēwā type of bin, but always built *outside* house. (2) *Sk., Kt.* round house built in same way as rufēwā-bin. (3) *cf.* kudandaŋ.

kudandaŋ *m.* (*pl.* kudandanī (*cf.* 1*b*)). (1) (*a*) round house with clay walls and flat clay roof. (*b*) kudandanīna my *ditto* (*cf. plural above*). (*c*) ~ ɗauriŋ gūgā *ditto* (1*a*) with vaulted roof. (2) *cf.* kudandamī ; sōrō.

kudandandarīya sound of opening rhythm of drumming done at farming-levy (gayyā).

kudandani *Vd.* kudandaŋ.

ƙudandōnīyā *Kt. f.* (*sg., pl.*) reticulated millipede (= ƙadandōnīyā *q.v.*).

kudāsa untrustworthy P. (*epithet is* ~ ci na marac cī).

kuɗau *m.* (*sg., pl.*) type of small water-beetle.

kuɗɗī *Kt. pl. m.* bugs (= kudī).

ƙuddumus *m.* (1) (*a*) fowl-lice (= ƙumā 2 = *Kt.* gurdumu). (*b*) ~ yā kāma kāji the deadly disease *so called*, due to fowl-lice, has attacked the poultry. (2) an yi masa ~ he's been cheated out of his all.

kudᶑę (1) *Vb.* 3A. (*a*) macıjı̣̄ yā ⁓ cikin rāmı̣ snake drew back into its hole. ɓērā yā ⁓ rāmı̣ rat withdrew into its hole. kaŋ kuŋkurū yā ⁓ tortoise has gone back into its shell. yā ⁓ cikiŋ ᶑākı̣ he withdrew into his house (*all* = nōᶄę) (*cf.* gulę 2). (*b*) wuyạnsạ yā ⁓ his neck has sunk into his chest through fat (= nōᶄę). (*c*) Sarkı̄ yā ⁓ Emir pulled head of burnous over his head (= sụŋᶄum 3). (*d*) tsạ̄rı̄ (kạran rūwā) yā ⁓ monitor (otter) dived into the water (kudᶑę *also applies to* crocodile or hippopotamus). (2) *Vb.* 1A *x* kuŋkurū yā ⁓ kạnsạ tortoise drew its head back into its shell.

kudı̄ *m.* a black-bordered, red cotton material (= bạkunāshę), *Vd.* agēdu̳ ; tayạ ragō.

kudı̄ (*pl. of* wurı̣ *q.v.*). (1) (*a*) (i) money *x* ⁓ sum ɓacę minı̣ I lost my money. (ii) *Vd.* ᶑạrı̄ 3. (iii) rūwaŋ ⁓ *Vd.* rūwā B.13. (iv) ci ⁓ *Vd.* cı̄ 5. (v) sạ̄ ⁓ *Vd.* sạ̄ B.13. (vi) kashę ⁓ *Vd.* kashę 3*h*. (*b*) fariŋ kudı̄ = tsābạr kudı̄ payment in cash (not in kind), *Vd.* fariŋ kudı̄. (*c*) jaŋ ⁓ gold coins.   (*d*) gidaŋ ⁓. (i) bank.   (ii) Government Treasury (*cf.* bạitu̳lmạl). (*e*) zạncansạ wani ⁓, wani bāshi̳ his statement is half-true, half-false. (*f*) kudiŋ aurē *Vd.* aurē 6*a*. (*g*) kudiŋ tunı̣ *Vd.* aurē 6*b*. (*h*) kudiŋ 'yam mātā *Vd.* aurē 6*d*. (*j*) kudạᶑē = *Sk.* kudᶑaiᶑai sums of money.   (*k*) kudim fitọ (i) ferry-fee. (ii) levy on caravans (now obsolete). (*l*) (i) kudiŋ ᶄasā tax (= hạrājı̣ *but mainly used at Kt.* in this sense). (ii) *Vd.* ᶄas. (*m*) kudim masạr type of small cowries. (*n*) kudiŋ zaurę (i) fee paid village-head after arranging marriage or settling quarrel. (ii) fee paid mālạmı̄ who officiates at a marriage (*Vd.* aurē 6*c*). (iii) fee paid village-head to cover up a delinquency. (*o*) (i) an tsarę amaryā sabọ dạ kudim mararrabā friends of bridegroom, by convention, stopped the bride on the road and wouldn't let her pass till she had given them the customary present. (ii) *Vd.* mararrabā 2*a*. (*p*) kudiŋ Gwārı̄ cowries (*cf.* farin bı̄yạ). (*q*) Mại ⁓ *name for* boy born on a

Tuesday and so considered lucky (*cf.* Bạtūrı̣yā, Tạlātạ).   (*r*) kudim mại cūtā na mại māgạnı̄ nę P. wanting T. will go to any lengths. (*s*) kudiŋ kidạ *Vd.* dạbaŋ 1*b*. (*t*) kudin sāᶄı̣ *Vd.* sāᶄı̣ 1*b*. (*u*) sǎi kudin yārọ sụ gazạ *Vd.* sainạ.   (*v*) mại ⁓ shı̄ kȩ dạ mạganạ he who pays the piper calls the tune. (*w*) kōwā ya yi ⁓ shı̄ nȩ Abbạ *Vd.* Tūrancı̄ 1*c*. (*x*) kudiŋkạ ạ mārạ *Vd.* yạ̄fȩ 2. (*y*) māgạniŋ kudin zạmānı̣ *Vd.* ạlgazarụ. (*z*) wani ⁓ wani bāshı̣ *Vd.* bāshı̣ 7. (*z*) (i) im bạ mại ⁓ *Vd.* Sarkı̄ 1*e*. (*z*) (ii) kōwā ya cı̄ dạ mǎi, kudinsạ *Vd.* ạ cı̄ dạ mǎi.   (*z*) (iii) tsōfō mại ⁓ *Vd.* tsōfō 1*h*.   (*z*) (iv) duk ⁓ nȩ *Vd.* talạkạ 2. (*z*) (v) bạkiŋkạ dạ ⁓ *Vd.* ạlkalạmı̄ 1*a*. (*z*) (vi) kōfatạŋ ⁓ *Vd.* alkālāwā.   (*z*) (vii) gāshiŋ ⁓ *Vd.* bıcılmı̄.   (*z*) (viii) ⁓ farat dᶑayạ *Vd.* farat 2.   (*z*) (ix) ganduŋ ⁓ *Vd.* gandū 1*f*. (*z*) (x) gwaiwā dạ ⁓ *Vd.* cakı̄.   (*z*) (xi) kudin tukı̣ *Vd.* tukı̣ 2. (*z*) (xii) kudiŋ kōko *Vd.* jạgạlam. (2) price *x* kudinsạ nawạ how much is it ? (3) yā yi ⁓ it is expensive.   gyạdᶑạ yā yi ⁓ ground-nuts fetch a good price. (4) mụ yi kudi-kudi, mụ sạyā let's club together (= jūcē) and buy it ! (5) ūwar ⁓ *f.* (*a*) capital (= digi̳ 2), *cf.* ūwā 2, arụgumạ. (*b*) large shell on end of strop, held between toes of barber when stropping (wāshę) razor. (*c*) *Vd.* dalạ 5. (6) (*a*) kudı̄ = kudin cīzọ bug, bugs (= gāzunzụmı̄). (*b*) *Vd.* fādı̄ 1*c*.

ᶄudigạ *used in* na ⁓ tụ̄lū mại santsim bāyā *opprobrious epithet of* wifeless man (gwaurō).

ᶄudijı̄ = ᶄuduju̳ı̄.

kudindirā = kudundurā.

kudᶑin *Vd.* kudı̄.

kudu̳ (1) *adv.* southwards *x* yā tạfı̣ (= yā yi) ⁓ he went south. ⁓ sak due south (= *Kt.* gusụm = *Kt.* kātukạ). yanạ̄ ⁓ masọ gabạs gạrēmụ it is south-east of us. ⁓ tasọ yạmmạ south-west. (2) *prep. x* yanạ̄ ⁓ dạ Kanọ = yanạ̄ dạgạ ⁓ Kanọ = yanạ̄ ⁓ gạ Kanọ it is south of Kano. (3) *f.* regions south of *x* yā tạfı̣ kudụŋ Kanọ = yā tạfı̣ kudanciŋ Kanọ he went south of Kano. ᶄasạ̄shansụ na ⁓ gạ Cādı̣ their territories south of Chạ̌d ƙūdū *m.* a foot-disease of horses and donkeys (periostitis).

ƙūdubē *Vb.* 1C cut or snapped corn or tree, etc., off at vital point.

kududdufī *m.* (*pl.* kududdufai). (1) borrow-pit. (2) kududdufim barƙōnō iyāƙacim macē gwīwa women are very cautious. (3) kada dāi gulbī bai cī ni ba, ~ ya cī ni as P. of position has not done me harm, how can a person of no position do so! (4) *Vd.* Allā 7*l.*

kududdurā *Kt. f.* = kudundurā.

ƙududdurā *Vb.* 1D *int. from* ƙudurā.

kududdurī *Kt. m.* = kudundurā.

kududdusā *m., f.* short in stature (*re* woman) *x* kududdusar yārinya short girl.

ƙudugāle *m.* (*f.* ƙudugālīyā) destitute.

ƙudugu *Kt. m.* fowl with permanently ruffled feathers (= fingi).

ƙudugum *m.* (1) stripping P. of his possessions *x* an yi masa ~, an yi wa mai dame dayā sāta he's been robbed of all his possessions. (2) deposing P. (3) *Vd.* magēdūwā 2*b.*

ƙuduji *m.* (1) the red weed *Striga senegalensis,* considered destructive to guinea-corn (*Kt.* marin gōnā = wutāwuta = gaugai = dōdō 7), *cf.* yaryādī 2. (2) *epithet is* ƙudujī, ɓata ragō gōnā. (3) *Vd.* alkataf.

*kudukūki = kudukuki = kūdukuki = kundukuki *q.v.*

kudumī *m.* = tafki 1.

kudumnīyā *Kt. f.* looking hither and thither (= fāfutukā *q.v.*).

kudundun *m.* = kudandan.

kudunduna A. (ƙudunduna) *Vb.* 3B = ƙudundunē 1.
   B. (ƙudundunā) *Vb.* 1E = ƙudundunē 2.

kudundune A. (ƙudundunē) (1) *Vb.* 3A. (*a*) lay curled up. (*b*) zane yā ~ the cloth is crumpled. (*c*) gāshinsa yā ~ he has the negro woolly hair (*cf.* yālōlo). (2) *Vb.* 1E. (*a*) tā ~ shi, tā sā cikin lēfanta she screwed it (her cloth) into a ball and put it in her basket. (*b*) yā ƙudundune magana (i) he dissembled. (ii) he made a précis of the matter.
   B. (ƙudundune) (1) (*noun of state from* ƙudundunē) *x* yanā ~ it is

crumpled, etc. (2) yā cī shi a ~ he tricked him.
   C. (ƙudundunē) *m.* (1) lying curled up *x* yā yi ~ he's lying curled up. (2) *cf.* shigā hanci da ~.

kudundurā *f.* (1) knife for women to cut meat, okro, etc. (*it has no protective metal-band* (gaban wuƙā) *round handle, nor any sheath* (kubē)) = *Kt.* māshinjirī (*cf.* tsūrā). (2) any worn-out tool. (3) short, ugly woman.

kudundurī *m.* (1) = kudundurā 1. (2) kudundurin īya (*a*) type of tall grass with sharp leaf-edges, growing among rice (= *Kt.* alwanzan). (*b*) evil spirit living in rivers and coming out at night to beg alms (bara).

ƙudungurum = kudungurum (1) *m.* = ƙudugum. (2) *adv.* completely removed *x* an dauke ~ it's been completely removed.

ƙudun ƙurna *Kt. f.* dumplings (= gudun ƙurna *q.v.*).

ƙudura A. (ƙudura = kudura) *Ar.* my word! ; fancy!
   B. (ƙudurā) *Vb.* 1C. (1) (*a*) knotted (= ƙulla 1*a*). (*b*) nā ƙudura alkāwari da shī I made him a promise. (*c*) yā ƙudura annīya he tried his hardest. (*d*) yā ƙudura jāri he sold up his effects to get capital. (2) decided to *x* an ƙudura maganar tafīyarmu our journey's been arranged, decided on. nā ~ sāi nā yī = nā ~ n yī = nā ~ a zūcī zan yī I've decided to do it. abin da ya ~ what he decided on.

ƙudurē *Vb.* 3A became knotted (= ƙulle).

ƙuduri *m.* (*pl.* ƙudaddarī) (1) (*a*) knot (= ƙulli). (*b*) fillet of thick thread (abāwā) or bark of kaba *or* kargō, with spittle (tōfī) inside, as remedy for toothache, headache, or eye-affection. Audu, ~ garēshi Audu is expert in teaching use of *this charm.* (*c*) charm to cause return of runaway slave or lost animal, property (*it is buried at* turke, *etc., of lost animal*). (*d*) Audu mūgun ~ garēshi Audu's malevolent. (2) *x* nā yi ~ a zūcī n yī I decided to do it. (3) ƙudurin kaba *Vd.* tasūbala. (4) *Vd.* ƙulli.

ƙudurtā = ƙudurā.

ƙụdūrū *m.* (1) *Abuja Hausa* cutting off both hands of P. as previously done by Abuja chiefs *(local custom, not connected with Koranic law of amputation for theft).* (2) kōwā ya ji zāfiŋ wuƙā, bạ̄ yą̣ ~ ba making fuss about nothing (yą̣ " like ") = ƙ̣ōrą̣fī.

ƙudus A. (ƙudus) *used in* yā shịga rāmị ~ it (rodent) popped like lightning into its burrow *(cf.* kuḍ̣ẹ).
   B. (Ƙudụs) *x* Birniŋ Ƙudụs Jerusalem. ƙasar B.Ƙ. Palestine.

ku'ẹ *m.* kernel of fruit of danyā-tree.

kụf *m.* type of rosary (cą̣zbī). ~ dinsą̣ his rosary.

kụfaḍ̣ą̣ *f.* valley (= kwarị).

kufai *m.* (1) (*a*) abandoned site. (*b*) *Vd.* dą̣ɓaŋ kufai (2) scar. (3) kufam mą̣i yā fì kufan rūwā breeding tells, even though one is poor. (4) bụtụlū kufaŋ wutā expect nothing from P. of low breeding !

ƙụfēgērẹ *m.* (*f.* ƙụfēgērịyā). (1) ragged, destitute P. (2) Ƙụfēgērẹ, yaŋkā *epithet of* ḍan taurī in drum-rhythm (kiḍ̣ą̣).

ƙụfērē *m.* (*f.* ƙụfērịyā) = ƙụfēgērẹ 1.

kufì A. (kufì) *m.* black dye for leather (= kwalōḳọ).
   B. (kufị) (1) *m.* food vessel left unwashed overnight. (2) *adv.* sun zō ą̣ ~, ą̣ ~ they came in quick succession (= ą̣ ƙą̣i, ą̣ ƙą̣i).

ƙụfī *m. and adv.* yā yi ~ dą̣ idọ he couldn't sleep through hunger, etc. = ƙịrī 1*a, b. q.v.*

kuftą̣ *f.* coat-sleeved, short, embroidered gown.

kụftirī *m.* poor quality millet-heads (= bụturī).

kụ̄fū *m.* = kụ̄hū.

kụfulą̣ (1) *Vb.* 3B. (*a*) became enraged. (*b*) is (was) quick-tempered. (2) *f.* yā ciką̣ ~ he's touchy.

kụfulụ *m.* type of black burnous (ą̣lkyabbą̣).

kụfuŋgū *m.* destitute P.

ƙụfurtū *m.* (1) = bą̣ŋgą̣jē *but* with use of fartanyą̣-hoẹ (*so too* am fasą̣ ~ = am fasą̣ bą̣ŋgą̣jē), *Vd.* bą̣rjē 2*b.* (2) preparing ground with fartanyą̣-hoe in hot-season for sowing in first rains.

kụfụtai *m.* backless native slippers, usually yellow, but sometimes red = wuffị.

ƙūgą̣ *Vb.* 1A (1) (*a*) aŋ ~ wutā big fire's been made. (*b*) aŋ ƙūgą̣ shi cikim mulkị he obtained wide dominion. (*c*) aŋ ƙūgą̣ shi kụrkukụ he was " jammed into prison ". (2) (*with dative*). (*a*) aŋ ~ masą̣ wutā fire's been set to it (house, bush). (*b*) aŋ ~ masą̣ sātą̣ he's been seriously robbed. (*c*) nā ~ masą̣ kirą̣ I called him loudly.

kụgē *m.* " V "-shaped metal instrument, used like gong.

ƙūgẹ *Vb.* 1A aŋ ~ itą̣cē ą̣ wuta all large amount of wood available has been piled on, to make big fire (*cf.* ƙūgą̣).

ƙūgị *m.* (1) roaring of ostrich ; bellowing of bull. (2) (*a*) (i) buzzing of bees. (ii) ịdaŋ kā ji zumą̣ yaną̣ ƙūgị, yā yi rūwā nẹ if you hear a friend has made some profit, visit him ! (*b*) hum of voices. (*c*) any prolonged indistinct sound (= jīzą̣).

ƙūgịyā *f.* (*pl.* ƙūgīyōyī). (1) any hook. (2) hooked spring-balance.

ƙūgụ *Sk., Kt. m.* rear lumbar region (= kwą̣ŋkwasọ), *cf.* gịndī.

ƙugum *m.* (1) aną̣ ~ pounding or drumming is going on. (2) sound of pounding or drumming *x* nā ji ~.

kụgunū *m.* (1) circumcision (= ƙą̣cīyą̣). (2) *Kt.* ḍaŋ ~ circumcized boy (= ḍan shą̣yī).

ƙụhī = ƙụfī.

kụ̄hū *m.* lung ; lungs (= hụ̄hū *q.v.*).

kụhulą̣ = kụfulą̣. kụhulụ = kụfulụ. kụhungū = kụfuŋgū. ƙụhurtū = ƙụfurtū. kụhụtai = kụfụtai.

kūjẹ (1) *Vb.* 1A. (*a*) frayed, abraded, causing slit in material or skin of P. (= karcẹ 1*b* = zāgẹ 1*c*). (*b*) dōkị yā ~ ni jịkim baŋgō horse scraped me against the wall (= kurzą̣). (2) *Vb.* 3A. (*a*) (i) is (was) abraded (*as in* 1). (ii) yā fìtō kō kūjẹ̄wā he got away " without a scratch ". (*b*) it (colour, cloth) faded (= kōḍ̣ẹ). (*c*) became destitute.

ƙujẹ *Sk. m.* fly (= ƙudā *q.v.*).

kūje-kūjē *Vd.* kūrā 25*a.*

kụjēmē *m.* Meni oil tree (*Lophira alata*) (= kaḍ̣anyą̣ 3).

kujẹ̄rā = kujērạ *f.* (*pl.* kujẹ̄rū = ku-
jẹ̄rī = kujērōrī = *Sk.* kujẹ̄rinnị) (*Ar.*
kursiyya). (1) chair. (2) preventing P.
in court, etc. wandering from the
point in giving evidence or information.
(3) ɗaŋ ~ *m.* (*pl.* 'yaŋ ~) P. employed
by owner of dye-pit as his deputy. (4)
kujẹ̄rar kurciyā type of guinea-corn
(= shẹ̄ƙā 6). (5) kujẹ̄rar mạtar kạwū
woman's red kerchief (now obsolete).
ƙujịjī *m.* the weed ƙudụjī *q.v.*
kuka A. (kūkā) (1) *m.* (*pl.* kọ'ke-kọ̄kē")
(*a*) (i) weeping, crying. (i*A*) crying out,
lamenting.   (ii) mai kwạrmiŋ idọ
(= mai zurfiŋ idọ) dạ wurī yakẹ̄ sōmạ ~
a stitch in time saves nine. (iii) kōwā
ya rēnạ mọ̄tsiŋkạ, yạ yi ~ never under-
rate a person's potentialities !   (iv)
kā kai ~ gidam mutūwạ it's a case of the
blind leading the blind.   (v) kạ ƙạ̄ri
kūkaŋkạ, kạ dēnạ (*said by mother*) devil
take you, you snivelling little brat !
(*b*) complaint, complaining *x* (i) nā
kai kūkāna wurinsạ I put before him
the matter which was troubling me.
(ii) sunạ kūkaŋ (= sunạ ~ dạ) wulākancị they are complaining of being
oppressed. (iii) kūkan ɗārī *Vd.* ạbụ 2*j.*
(iv) bạ kūkāna ba, ūwar kīshīyā tā
mutụ (*said by woman*) what do *I*
care !   (v) anạ kūkan targaɗẹ, gạ̄
kạrāyạ tā zō out of the frying-pan into
the fire !   (vi) kā fi kūkā cīwọ *Vd.*
yạ̄ƙẹ̄.   (vii) rāƙumī bā yạ kūkā *Vd.*
mạruhū.   (viii) yạ sōmạ kūkā *Vd.*
dūnīyạ 1*h.*   (ix) birị ya kạn yi kūkā
Vd. birị 1*b.*   (x) ạkwīyạ tā yi kūkā
Vd. ạkwīyạ 1*c.*   (xi) *Vd.* bạ kūkaŋ
hantsī. (xii) *cf.* sā dạ kūkā. (xiii) bạ
kūkā *Vd.* bōkōnị.   (*c*) cry of animal
(= rūrị 1) *x* (i) yā yi kūkaŋ kūrā he
behaved menacingly.   (ii) dạ kūkaŋ
kūrā, dạ ɓacẹ̄war ạkwīyạ dukạ ɗayā
nẹ̄ these two things are cause and
effect. (*d*) cry of bird (= rūrị 1) *x* (i)
kōwạnẹ tsuntsū yạ yi kūkaŋ gidansạ
let the cobbler stick to his last ! (ii)
tsạ̄da bā tạ kukam burtū abilities differ.
(*d*) rumbling of stomach.   (*e*) *Vd.*
kūkan-*compounds.* (2) *Vb.* used in (*a*)
kōwā ya yi hakạ, yạ ~ dạ kạnsạ
anyone acting thus has only himself to

blame.   (*b*) kadạ kōwā yạ ~ dạ wani,
yạ ~ dạ kạnsạ those who live in glass-
houses should not throw stones !
   B. (kūkạ) *f.* (*pl.* kūkōkī). (1) baobob-
tree, pods or leaves (*Adansonia digi-
tata*) (*leaves* (mīyạ 2) *are used for making
flour for soup* (gạ̄riŋ kūkạ = dụŋkū 2)
and for cụ̄sā. *The bark is made into*
gindī-*rope and strings* (tsirkīyā) *of
musical instruments. The acid pulp
is eaten fresh*), *Vd.* Lely, Plate 9 and
frontispiece.   *Vd.* kumbạlī, gụntsū,
gwaggọ 1*b*, gạ̄tsīkạ, ƙwamẹ, ɓakkọ. (2)
~ ạ gicịye mai dāɗiŋ hawā what an
easy-going person !   (3) jā na ~ the
insect gạmạɗīdī *q.v.* (4) ciŋ kūkạr rēmā
m. fortitude during distressing times.
(5) yā yi minị dakạŋ ~ *Vd.* dakạŋ kūkạ.
(6) ɗaŋ ~ shī kạn jā wạ ūwā tasạ jīfạ̄
the faults of the children recoil on the
parents.   (7) rẹ̄nạ girmaŋ ~ gạbạ̄rūwā
tā fī tạ don't place good on a level with
evil ! (8) ukụ ~ *Vd.* ukụ 7*b.*   (9)
mīyạr ~ bạ̄ wạdā ba nẹ̄ *Vd.* mīyạ 9*b.*
(10) yā zamẹ manạ kūkạr " saụke mụ
rabạ ! " it is a bone of contention
between them and us (*Vd.* saukẹ 1*a*).
(11) bọ̄riŋ kūkạ *Vd.* bọ̄rī 9.
   C. (kukạ) *Vd.* kạ 5.
   D. (kūkạ̄) (*future relative*, Mod. Gram.
140*c*) *x* ịnā ~ sạ̄mi gidā kụ fakẹ *where,*
I ask you, could you find a compound to
shelter in !
   E. (kū kạ̄) (*Vd.* Mod. Gram. 140*a*).
(1) kū kạ̄ cī shị *m.* the food tūwō
with yesterday's remains mixed into it.
(2) kū kạ̄ shā tạ, furar Naitọ the food
furā with stale-furā (*i.e.* kwantai)
mixed into it.
kūkan-*compounds* (1) ~ amaryā (*a*) formal
wailing of bride and her friends when
she is about to go to her husband's house
(tārẹ). (*b*) rūwā yā sōmạ kūkaŋ amaryā
water on the boil has begun to " sing ".
(2) (*a*) kūkam burtū *Vd.* burtū 4.
(*b*) kūkam mūjīyā = 2*a.*   (3) kūkan
jirgī (*a*) whistling of railway-engine.
(*b*) sixpence (= sīsị) (*because* 3*a* sounds
to Hausas like sī . . . sī). (4) kūkaŋ
kạ̄ị lamenting another's death and
knowing one's own death is near.
(5) kūkaŋ kāsā sound made when

clearing the throat of a bit of kola-nut. (5A) kūkam mūjīyā Vd. 2b above. (6) kūkan tsirkīyā (a) whining to escape punishment. (b) aggressor's pretending to be the injured party. (7) kūkan zūcī whining, cringing (= kạrāyạ 2a.ii). (8) Vd. ƙōdạ 2. (9) kūkan dārī Vd. rufa 2. (10) Vd. also kūkā.

kū kä̀ shā tạ Vd. kū kä̀.

kuke A. (kukẹ) Vb. 1A finished, completed (= ƙurẹ).

　B. (kukẹ̄) (used for you (pl.) in present relative sentence with positive sense) x lōkạcin dạ ∼ zūwạ when you (pl.) are coming. yạushẹ ∼ yị̄ when do you do it ? (cf. ƙẹ̄ 1).

ƙuke A. (ƙukẹ) Vb. 1A yā ∼ minị (1) it nonplussed me. (2) gạrī yā ∼ masạ he's " in low water ".

　B. (ƙūkẹ) Vb. 3A persevered (= nācẹ).

ƙuƙī m. and adv. yā yi ∼ dạ idọ he couldn't sleep through hunger, etc. (= ƙirī, 1a, b q.v.). (2) cf. ƙuƙī-ƙuƙī.

ƙuƙī-ƙuƙī (1) idạnsạ yā yi ∼ (a) he has protruberant eyes. (b) his eyes were bulging out of his head. (2) idạnsạ ∼, kō kunyạ bā yạ̄ jī he's brazen (= ƙirī 2, 3). (2) cf. ƙuƙī.

kukkub̃ā f. (1) cracked cooking-pot. (2) Vd. kukkub̃ī.

kukkub̃ē Vb. 1C drank up sediment (tsạkī) of ; drank up (remains of sloppy food) (= gugguḅē).

kukkub̃ēb̃ẹ = kukkub̃ī m. (f. kukkub̃ēb̃īyā = kukkub̃ā) fat (re P., child, or animal).

kukkūkị m. the gum-tree Sterculia tomentosa.

ƙuƙƙurnā m., f. sg. short and thick-set (re P. or horse).

ƙuƙƙūsā m., f. (pl. ƙūsạ̄sā) short and thick-set (P. or horse).

kukkūtsạ Vb. 2 upbraided (= kurkūtsạ q.v.).

kūkōkī Vd. kūkạ.

kūku Eng. m. (pl. kūku-kūku) European's cook.

ƙū-ƙū m. (1) (a) sound made by intestines of P. with scrotal hernia (mạjạƙwar). (b) rumbling of stomach of some horses in motion. (2) the fish (a) ƙurungu, (b) ramfai.

ƙuƙū-ƙuƙū = ƙuƙī-ƙuƙī.

ƙuƙum x yā zaunạ ∼ he sat in sulky silence.

kūkūmạ f. (1) small type of gōgē-fiddle. (2) ạbin dạ ya kai tsōfwā rawar ∼, tạ rẹ̄ jēlantạ nobody acts without a motive.

ƙuƙumcē = ƙuƙuncē.

ƙuƙumī m. (1) an yi masạ ∼ he (prisoner) has one hand tied round his neck (= mạriŋ wuyạ). (2) ƙạramin sanị ∼ nẹ̄ a little learning is a dangerous thing. (3) Vd. tạ̄gumī 3. (4) b̃ērā dạ ∼ Vd. dūnīyạ 1l.

ƙuƙuncē Vb. 1C (1) tied prisoner (as in ƙuƙumī). (2) yā ƙuƙuncẹ kạnsạ he was the very one who brought trouble on himself.

kukụru kukụ m. (1) cockadoodledoo ! (2) bā saurạŋ kukụru kukụ ; arnẹ yā kāmạ kurcīyā that's the end of the matter.

ƙuƙurūtụ m. boastfulness.

ƙuƙụs (genitive ƙuƙushin) (1) (a) grass growing among and resembling rice (its grains become mixed with the rice-grains, are uncookable and injure the teeth). (b) wạ̄ kä̀ rabạ shịnkāfā dạ ∼ " they're as alike as two peas ". (2) Kt. hard, uncookable beans or kalwā (= tsarar-rīyā 2 q.v.).

ƙuƙut (1) adv. Audụ ạbōkinsạ nē ∼ Audu's a close friend of his. d̃ạŋūwānā nẹ̄ ∼ he's a close relation of mine. (2) m. smallness x d̃an d̃ākị nē ∼ dạ shī it's a tiny house (pl. 'yan d̃ākunạ nē ƙuƙut-ƙuƙut dạ sū).

ƙūƙūtạ Vb. 3A (1) yā ∼ he strove his hardest. (2) yā ∼ cikin tạ̄rō he forced his way through the crowd (= firmịtsā 2a).

kūkūtū m. loud clamour.

kul (1) = ạkul. (2) (a) ∼ kwānan dūnīyạ always (= kulluŋ). (b) kul bạ jimạ, kul bạ d̃ad̃ẹ, zā ạ yī it'll be done sooner or later (= jimạ 6).

ƙul (1) m. sound of light blows of pestle against small mortar in pounding (cf. ƙulƙulā ; tuŋgwal). (2) mại d̃aŋ kä̀ị ∼ P. with tiny head.

kula A. (kulạ) (1) *Vb.* 3A (*a*) paid attention *x* baŋ ∼ ba I took no notice ; I don't care. (*b*) mutạnansạ, baị kulạ dạ kō nawạ sukạ mutụ ba he did not care however many of his people met their death. baị kulạ ba kōmē ya aụku he didn't care what happened. (*c*) (*negatively, followed by subjunctive*) does (did) not care whether *x* bạ sụ ∼ dạ kō sụ cĭ, kō kadạ sụ ci ba they don't care whether they win or not. (*d*) *Vd.* kulạ kại ; ḳwālạ 3 ; bịrinciŋ kulạ, shākulātị̣. (*e*) bịkiŋ kulạ *Vd.* bịkī 4. (2) *Vb.* 1A *x* nā ∼ shi = nā ∼ dạ shī I paid attention to it ; I looked well after it (him). bā yạ̄ ∼ dạ aikịnsạ = bā yạ̄ kulạ̄wā gạ aikịnsạ he pays no attention to his work. (3) *f.* the water-container kwalạ *q.v.*

B. (kụlā) *Vb.* 2 (1) = kulạ 2 *x* nā ∼ dạ shī. bā yạ̄ ∼ dạ aikịnsạ. (2) (*a*) kō kạm mę̄ wutā ta fāḍạ, bạ sụ shā rūwaŋ kụlā ba they didn't care what places were bombarded (*Vd.* shākulātị̣). (*b*) ịnā kụlātạ what do I care ? what business is it of mine ? (= rūwā G.1).

C. (Kụlā) *x* hạdīsị ạ Kụlā unheeded exhortation (Kụlā *is place-name*).

ḳụlāfạcī *m.* eager desire.

kulạ kại *used in* ∼ ḳụrguŋgụmā dạ gudụ̣ŋ shāfọ = ∼ ḳạrē dạ gudụ̣ŋ lahīyā " he's too big for his boots " (*Vd.* ukụ 3*b*).

kulạ̄kē *Vd.* kulkī.

ḳụlạ̄ḳụlai *Vd.* ḳụlūlụ.

ḳūlamī *Sk.* = ḳūlumī.

ḳūlạ̄yē *Vd.* ḳūlū.

kulɓạ *f.* (*pl.* kulɓōɓī) skink-lizard (= lindō).

kule A. (kulẹ) (1) *f.* cat (= kyạŋwā). (2) kulẹ = kulạŋkạ Playmate, may I throw it at you ? (*reply* cạs " yes " *or* jịn cīwọ rāmūwā " no ").

B. (kūlẹ) = kullẹ.

ḳulẹ (1) *Vb.* 3A (*a*) = kuɗẹ 1. (*b*) flew into a rage. (2) *Vb.* 1A = kuɗẹ 2.

kulẹlẹ *m.* steamed cakes of bean-paste.

kụlēlẹ̄nē *m.* (1) boggling. (2) half-hearted refusal.

kụlērē *m.* wooden-headed arrow.

ḳulī-ḳulī *m.* (1) (*a*) small fried cakes made from residue (tụḳā) after expressing oil from ground-nuts to make 1*b* (= mạrgīshị 1 = aụtā 2 = cạzbī 2 = *Kt.*

gūrū 5*a* = ḳạrāgọ 1), *Vd.* burụjī 4, markạdā 2, barbaɗēɗẹ. (*b*) maŋ ∼ ground-nut oil (*Vd.* maŋ gyạɗā). (2) cakes of pounded, unprepared indigo-leaves.

ḳụlīyạ = kụlīyạ *used in* ∼ mạntạ sạ̄bō *epithet of* ạlkālī.

kulkī *m.* (*pl.* kulạ̄kē) (1) (*a*) (i) cudgel (= wạ̄ ya zạ̄gi bạ̄bạ = gwamā = *Kt.* gulmẹ = *Zar.* gwarmī). (ii) yā ḍạuki kulkim bugụnsụ he opposed them. (iii) kulạ̄kē sun sāmụ weapons are available. (iv) kulkim fọraŋ gīwā *Vd.* gwantạl. (v) *Vd.* bạ̄ ta kulkī. (*b*) block of wood on neck of vicious bull to prevent use of its neck-muscles when being moved from place to place (= bugụ 8*b*). (2) destitute P. (3) kulạ̄kē *pl.* parts of the giraffe-trap tubau.

ḳulḳụlā *Vb.* 1C pounded *as in* ḳul *q.v.*

ḳụlḳụlē *m.* pounding *as in* ḳul *q.v.*

ḳul-ḳụl-ḳul (*used only in songs*) venereal disease.

ḳụlḳụllā *Vd.* tạmalmạlā.

kulkushẹ *Kt. m.* an irritating disease of the feet in the wet season (= ḳushạ̄-ḳushī).

kullā *f.* the parasite *Thonningia sanguinea* (*root used as spice*).

ḳulla A. (ḳullạ) *Vb.* 1A (1) (*a*) (i) knotted (= ḳudụrā) *x* yā ∼ zạrgē he made a slip-knot. (ii) dạ kyar yakẹ̄ ∼ rịgā he has the greatest difficulty in providing himself with a gown. dạ kyar ta ∼ zanẹ she had much difficulty in finding money to buy a cloth. ūwā tatạ bạ tạ ∼ matạ kōmē ba her mother had not the wherewithal to buy her (her daughter) any clothing. (iii) har yạ mutụ, bā yạ̄ ∼ kabạ he's spineless. (iv) sū kaɗ̆ai sukạ ∼, sukạ kwancẹ they are autocrats. yā bā sụ mạgaŋạ don sụ ∼ sụ warwạrē tạ̄rẹ he advised them to act in concert. (v) aŋ ∼ musụ dạbārạ they've been plotted against. (vi) dạbārạ tā ḳi ḳullūwā no plan of action could be decided on. (vii) yā ∼ mini rịkicī he intrigued against me. (viii) yā ∼ mini sharrị he did me evil. (ix) suŋ ḳullạ amincị dạ mū they have made friends of us. (x) suŋ ḳullạ ạbụ̄tā they became friends. (xi)

aŋ ƙullạ aminci security has been established. (xii) hadari yā ƙullu a storm is impending (*Vd.* ƙullẹ 2). (xiii) ƙullạ ạsīrī *Vd.* ạsīrī 1*e*. (2) made (pact) *x* suŋ ∼ sharạdī ạ kạn zā sụ yi hakạ they've concluded a pact to do so. yā ∼ ạmānạ dạ sū he made an alliance with them. (3) aŋ ∼ musụ gẹ̄zā (*a*) heads of tall grass have been knotted together to impede cavalry. (*b*) false charge has been made against them. (4) planned, decided *x* anạ̄ ƙullạ̄wā zā ạ cụ̄cẹ̄ shị they're conspiring to deceive him. sharuɗaŋ kạmar yā ∼ nē the stipulations are those he decided on. (5) organized *x* yā ∼ rụndunar sōjạ he organized an army. (6) *Vd.* ƙullẹ.
     B. (ƙullā) *Vb.* 2 = ƙullatạ.
ƙullące *Vd.* ƙullatạ.
ƙullallēnịyā *f.* (1) setting out darạ-pieces so that opponent cannot put down his last piece (= *Sk.* bạtsātsạ). (2) playing the " confidence trick " on a person.
ƙullallīyā *f.* plot, intrigue.
ƙullatạ *Vb.* 2 (*p.o.* ƙullạcē, *n.o.* ƙullạci) *x* yā ƙullạcē nị he feels malevolent to me.
kullạ yaumịŋ *Ar. adv.* day in and day out.
kulle A. (kullẹ) (1) *Vb.* 1A locked *x* yā ∼ ƙōfạ, he locked the door. (*b*) locked P. in *x* aŋ ∼ shi cikin ɗākị he's been locked in the house. (*c*) (i) yā ∼ bāịwā he took slave-girl (sạ̄ɗakạ) as concubine (ƙwarƙwarạ). (ii) yā ∼ ta he kept free-born woman ('yā) in purdah (tsarẹ) as his wife (*but note that the word* makullīyā *q.v. refers only to* concubine). (2) = kulẹ 2.
     B. (kụlle) *noun of state from* kullẹ *x* ƙōfạ tanạ̄ kụlle the door is locked. tanạ̄ kụlle she is in purdah *as in* kullẹ 1*c*.
     C. (kụllē) *m.* (1) keeping woman in purdah *as in* kullẹ 1*c x* Kanāwā sunạ̄ ∼ Kano men keep women in purdah. (2) gidaŋ ∼ *m.* storehouse.
     D. (kullē) *Vd.* bịris ∼.
kullẹ (1) *Vb.* 1A (*a*) = ƙullạ. (*b*) yā ∼ hannū he clenched his fist (= duŋƙulē). (*c*) = kullẹ 1. (*d*) rūwā yā ∼ shi = zụ̄rā.

(2) *Vb.* 3A became knotted (*cf.* ƙullạ 1*a* xii) *x* (*a*) gaddamạ tā ∼ tsạkāninsụ strife broke out between them. (*b*) cikịnsạ yā ∼ he has a cutting pain in his stomach and is constipated (*cf.* kartạ 2, kạrtā 2).
ƙullēlēnịyā *f.* = ƙullallēnịyā.
kullẹ̄rū *used in* kullẹ̄ruŋkạ = kulẹ 2.
ƙulli A. (ƙullī) *m.* (1) punching with the fist *x* yā tīƙạ masạ ∼ he punched him. (2) = ƙullū.
     B. (ƙullị) *m.* (1) = ƙudurị 1, 2. (2) enough powdered tobacco to make a quid (ƙamailā). (3) single-nutted ground-nut (= ƙumbulā). (4) ƙullịn dạbaibạyī slight umbilical hernia (*cf.* mạjaƙwar).
*ƙullīyạ *f.* entirety *x* ∼ tasụ all of them.
kullu A. (kullū) *Kt. m.* būtạ-bottle for ceremonial ablutions (ạlwạlā).
     B. (kụllū) *used in* daŋ ∼ *m.* (*pl.* 'yaŋ ∼) mendicant scholar.
ƙullu A. (ƙụllū) *m.* (1) ingredients for wainā-cake *x* tā kwāḅạ (= dāmạ) ∼ she mixed flour and water to make wainā. (2) mixture of flour and water added to partly-prepared gruel (kōko).
     B. (ƙullu) *Vd.* ƙullạ.
kullumẹ *m.* catfish (= tarwaɗā).
kulluŋ (1) (*a*) always. (*b*) bạ̄ ∼ akẹ kwānā ạ gadō ba, wata rānā kō ạ ƙasạ sāi ạ kwạntā = 2*b*. (2) (*followed by noun denoting* time) every *x* (*a*) ∼ sāfīyā sāi ƙarfī kẹ̄ ƙạrūwā gạrēmụ wajan sōjạ all the time we are become stronger in soldiers. ∼ shẹ̄karạ every year. (*b*) bạ̄ ∼ sāfīyā takẹ̄ Aljumma'ạ ba not every day brings luck. (3) whenever *x* ∼ sukạ tāshị, sāi sụ nụfi itạ̄caŋ whenever they flew up, they sought that tree. ∼ mukạ yi kirạŋkụ, bā kwạ̄ amsạ manạ sāi dạ " nạ'am " whenever we called you, you responded willingly. ∼ gạriŋ Allạ̄ ya wāyẹ, mạ̄ ji aŋ gamạ ƙīrạr wani jirgī every day we hear that they have built another ship.
ƙullūtụ *m.* (*pl.* ƙullụ̄tai). (1) swelling, cyst. (2) ƙullụ̄tan Jạhīmụ tertiary syphilis (= ƙabbā = matārin lāyū = ƙwạ̄lạ̄tai 2), *Vd.* ƙūlū 2.

kulōdǫ = kulūdụ.
kulōkǫ *m.* the dye kwǎlōkǫ *q.v.*
ƙūlū *m.* (1) (*a*) beans cooked alone (= gundǎrī = *Sk.* gurguzū 2*b* = gǎkaiwǎ = mǎrǎ bǎkiŋkǎ = ƙwāmā). (*b*) *epithet is* ∼ ƙǎs madafīyā. (2) ƙūlū, Sarkin sharrị *epithet of* ƙụllūtụ 2. (3) malicious P.
kulụɓūtụ *m.* (*pl.* kulụɓūtai) the long type of dumā called zụŋgụrū.
kulūdụ *m.* (1) tricking unsophisticated people in trading or in a type of gambling done with a piece of dry grass (tsiŋkē) and noose (zǎrgē) = ǎlhōwǎ 2. (2) *Vd.* sūkǎŋ ∼.
ƙulụfītǎ *children's name for vegetable* gautā *in riddle.*
ƙulū-ƙụlū *pl.* (1) large and round (*re* eyes, onions, or fruit. (2) idǎnunsǎ sum fitō ∼ his eyes are starting out of his head.
ƙụlūlụ *m:* (1) = ƙụllūtụ. (2) ƙụlǎƙụlai *pl.* (*a*) " bobbles " of locust-bean tree (= tuntū 1). (*b*) loops (mǎɗaụkai) on portable ink-pot. (*c*) lumps made for kōko (gruel) = gwārājī. (*d*) pom-poms (tukkū) on sword-sling (hǎmīlǎ) or saddle-cloth (jǎlālǎ).
Kulụmǎ (1) name for any woman called Hǎwwā. (2) *Vd.* dirịndāsǫ.
kulụmbūwǎ *f.* large hide shield.
ƙūlumī *m.* (*f.* ƙūlumā) *pl.* ƙūlụmai. (1) stingy P. (*epithet is* ∼ gidaŋkǎ ǎ rēshę). (2) ƙūlumin jējị large area of bush.
kulunduŋ abundantly (*re* fluids) *x* kōgī yā cịka ∼ river is in flood.
ƙulụŋƙulụfītǎ = ƙulụfītǎ.
kulụntuɓị fat P., etc. (= lukụntuɓị).
kum A. (kum) = ƙul 1.
  B. (kụm) *adv.* resoundingly.
ƙum *Vd.* ƙumǎ.
kuma A. (kumā) (1) (*a*) also *x* nī ∼ I also. (*b*) (*often inserted without affecting existing construction of sentence*) *x* gamę ∼ dǎ yǎrdar rai voluntarily too (*cf.* mā ; kụwā). (2) ∼ dǎi that's *just* the sort of bad conduct I'd expect of you ! (3) kumǎ ? that into the bargain !
  B. (kụmǎ) *Vb.* 1A. (1) repeated *x* yā ∼ yị he did it again (= kōmǎ 2*c q.v.*). (2) aŋ ∼ masǎ baƙin cikị P.

helpless to retaliate or reply has been harshly treated (= *Kt.* gumǎ 2*e*). (3) aŋ ∼ masǎ jinī (i) he has bruise from being thrashed (*cf.* ƙurmā ; tārǎ 1*a.*iv). (ii) = 2 *above.* (4) aŋ ∼ masǎ sātǎ he's been seriously robbed.
ƙuma A. (ƙumā) *f.* (*sg.*, *pl.*). (1) white flea (= tụŋkwīyau 1). (2) = ƙuddumụs. (3) gashịŋ ∼ *m.* playfully forcing P. down on hot soil (= *Kt.* gishị 2).
  B. (ƙumǎ) *Vb.* 1A hit hard *x* aŋ ∼ kǎnsǎ ƙum his head's been hit hard. aŋ ∼ masǎ kǎi gǎ ƙasā his head's been hit hard on the ground.
ƙūmājī *Kt. m.* struggling.
kumǎkumī *m.* (*pl.* kụmǎkụmai) corslet worn by 'yan lifidǎ of Chief.
kụmallō *m.* (1) nausea ; biliousness ; faintness from hunger (especially in early morning). (2) yā karyǎ ∼ he breakfasted. (3) fariŋ ∼ biliousness due to food disagreeing with P. (4) baƙiŋ ∼ vomiting from illness (*cf.* amai). (5) kụmallō-kụmallō *adj.* bright greenish (= tsaŋwa-tsaŋwa).
kụmāmǎ *m.*, *f.* (*pl.* kụmǎmī = kụmǎmū) feeble P.
kumāmancị *m.* = kumāmǎntǎ *f.* feebleness.
kumǎmmatū cheeks (*pl. of* kuncị).
kumǎncē *Vb.* 3A became feeble.
kụmannīyā *f.* = kụmunnīyā.
kumanta A. (kụmǎntǎ) *f.* feebleness.
  B. (kumǎntā) *Vb.* 1C enfeebled.
  C. (kụmantǎ) *Vb.* 3B became feeble.
kumantaka A. (kụmǎntakǎ) *f.* feebleness.
  B. (kụmantakā) *f.* (1) belt (= ɗamarǎ). (2) leather arm-shield worn in shancī (*cf.* baurǎ).
kụmǎrē = *Kt.* kụmǎrai *m.* crownbird (= gǎurākǎ).
kụmǎrī *m.* plumpness *x* yā yi ∼ he's plump.
kumǎrmatū cheeks (*pl. of* kuncị).
ƙụmǎrǫ *m.* (1) destitute P. (2) the purse alabę *q.v.* (3) grass bag slung over shoulder by herdsmen to hold kabǎ for making fǎiƙǎi-mats while watching herds.
kumǎsǎ *used in Sk.* ɗaŋ ∼ *m.* = durụmī.

kumątū (1) cheeks (*pl. of* **kuncį**). (2) **mąi** ~ *f.* type of rice.

ƙumbā = **ƙumbā** (*pl.* **ƙumbuną**). (1) mussel-shell (*used for storing musk*) = **mąkaŋkarī**. (2) talon of wild-animal or bird of prey. (3) *Kt.* (*a*) fingernail (= **farcę**). (*b*) **jininsą yā kōmą ą ƙumbā** he was terror-stricken. (4) **ƙumbar shāfǫ** the acacia **ƙąrƙārą** *q.v.*

kumbąlī *m.* flower-buds or flowers of baobob (**kūką**).

kumbąli-kumbąli *m.* mendicancy (**barą**), especially that done by scholars.

ƙumbīyą̄-ƙumbīyā *f.* " beating about the bush " = **gēwąi-gēwai**.

kumbǫ *m.* (*pl.* **kumbuną**). (1) (*a*) calabash-basin made by cutting (**fāfę**) the round type of **dumā** called **ƙwaryā** *across* (**ą gįcīye**). (*b*) (i) **kąmar Kumbǫ, kąmar kātantą** how in keeping the two are ! (ii) **bą̄ shąnyē mąn kumbǫ akę̄ jį ba, mai dą kātąn akę̄ jį** its pleasant to receive gifts but not quite so pleasant to have to make return-gifts. (2) **sārąn** ~ (i) cutting gourd across, to obtain 1. (ii) **an yi masą sārąn** ~ he was cut in two at waist.

kumbųcē *m.* woman's hasty, make-shift coiffure (*cf.* **lallą̄ɓā** 3*b*).

kumbudŭwā *used in* **sārąn kumbudŭwā na yi** I've cracks under my toes.

ƙumbulā (1) *f.* single-kernelled groundnut = **ƙullį** 3 = **ƙwąllī** 1 = **ƙwąndī**. (2) **Ƙumbulā** *name given any* short girl (= **Gudīsā** = **Gujįbā** = **Gwįde** *q.v.* = **Gwīsą** = **Kundųrkū**).

ƙumbųlą̄cī *m.* = **ƙumbulā** 1.

kumbuną *Vd.* **kumbǫ**.

ƙumbuną *Vd.* **ƙumbā**.

kumbura A. (**kumbųrā**) *Vb.* 1C. (1) (*a*) caused to swell. (*b*) **iskąr dūnīyą tā** ~ **shi** he's puffed up with pride. (*c*) *Vd.* **hų̄hū** 3 ; **kumburō**.

B. (**kumburą**) *Vb.* 3B. (1) swelled. (2) *Vd.* **kumburō**.

kumburą fagē *m.* the herb *Vernonia Kotschyana* (*medicine for fattening horses is made from it*).

kumbųrē *Vb.* 3A swelled (= **kumburą**).

kumburī *m.* (1) (*a*) swelling. (*b*) ~ **ą mōwą, sakīyą ą bōrą** = *Kt.* ~ **gą dōkį, sąkīyą gą jąkī** " kissing goes by favour ".

(*c*) **kųmburiŋ kūką** swelling of lim**ɓ** affected by guinea-worm before suffere is wholly incapacitated. (*d*) **kųmburiŋ kīshīyā** type of cloth (*now obsolete*) (*e*) **yą̄ yi kųmburī** *Vd.* **amai** 1*b*. (*f* **fasą kųmburī** *Vd.* **fasą** 1*k*.i, v. (2 vexation *x* **kųmburim mę̄ kakę̄ y** what's " put you out " ? **yaną̄ cįcciką yaną̄** ~ he's vexed.

kumburō (1) *Vb.* 1E **yā** ~ **ƙasā** it (ger minating seed) pushed up ground. (2 *Vb.* 3A. (*a*) food swelled in pot. (*b* germinating seed swelled. (3) *Vd* **kumbura**.

kumbusū *m.* type of okro (**kuɓę̄wā**) with red capsules.

kumcį *Sk. m.* (*pl.* **kumųttā**) cheek (= **kun-cį** *q.v.*).

kume A. (**kumę**) *Vb.* 3A. (1) **rąunī yā** ~ wound closed up. (2) **cikįnsą yā** ~ his (adult's) stomach became distended and constipated (*cf.* **kųmē**).

B. (**kųmē**) *m.* **yārąn nąn yaną̄ kųmąŋ girmā** this baby lad has the constipation common to growing children (*cf.* **kumę**).

ƙumę *Vb.* 1A (1) hit hard *x* **aŋ** ~ **kąnsą ƙum** his head's been hit hard (= **ƙumą**). (2) despoiled P. by trickery or force.

kumfa A. (**kumfā**) *m.* (*pl.* **kumfąįfai** = **kumfąffakī**). (1) froth ; scum ; foam. (2) *Vd.* compounds *of* **kumfā**.

B. (**kųmfą**) then . . .

kųmfalalō *m.* used in **gyądā tā yi kųm-falalō** the ground-nuts have no kernels (= **fųs**).

kumfan-compounds (1) ~ **mąi** butter which has not been fried (**tōyą**). (2) ~ **mālīyą** cuttle-fish (= **gājįmą̄rē** 3). (3) ~ **rūwā** (*a*) = **kumfā**. (*b*) a small, marked pebble for adornment. (4) ~ **wākē** " cutting off one's nose to spite one's face " (= **fushī** 4). (5) ~ **zīnā-rįyā** gold tinsel (= **dųsā** 1*b*).

ƙumi A. (**ƙūmī**) *m.* conceit.

B. (**ƙumį**) what a hard blow ! (*Vd.* **ƙumę**).

ƙųmīnīyā *f.* (1) dilly-dallying. (2) shilly-shallying in replying (= **mųƙwīnīyā**).

kųmircī *m.* = **kųmurcī**.

kumma-kumma *Kt. adv.* in batches ; in piles.

*kumsạ *f.* (*Ar.* khumsā) sign marking end of every 5th (*i.e. 5th, 15th, 25th, 35th, etc.*) verse (āyạ) of Koran (*cf.* kurī).

ƙumsa = ƙunsa.

ƙumụ *Zar. m.* waiting for.

ƙụ̄mūmụ̄wā *Kt. f.* struggling together.

kụmunnīyā *f.* hole in ground for burying garbage.

kụmurcī *m.* black-hooded cobra (= gạmshẹ̄ƙā).

kumuryā *f.* over-filling mouth with kola or roasted millet (= zugạ̄zugī 2 = tēkị 4), *cf.* tụmuƙụ 2.

kumụttā *Vd.* kumcị.

ƙụmwịnīyā *Kt. f.* = ƙụmịnīyā.

kumyạ *Sk. f.* = kunyạ.

kun A. (kun) (1) (*plural pronoun for* "you" *past tense*) *x* kun tạfi you went (Mod. Gram. 12*a*). (2) *Vd.* dārạ, kuŋ ƙi cị, kun tạru. (3) kuŋ gwammạcẹ ƙọshī *Vd.* bạrēwā 1*b*.
B. (kụn) *Kt.* = kwạ̄ *x* kụn zō gọ̄be you'll probably come to-morrow.

kunạ̄ *x* (1) ~ zūwạ you (*pl.*) are coming (Mod. Gram. 15). (2) ~ barịn damō *Vd.* damō 5. (3) ~ baƙạ *Vd.* baƙạ 1*f.* (4) ~ dafạ wākē *Vd.* barẹkatạ.

ƙuna A. (ƙūnạ) *f.* (1) great heat *x* rānā tanạ̄ ~ = rānā tanạ̄ dạ ~ the sun is blazing. (2) yā yi minị ~ it vexed me.
B. (ƙūnā) (1) *Vb.* (*progressive and v.n. uses* 2). (*a*) became burnt. (*b*) (i) yā ~, bạ shi shạ̄yịŋ ƙaurī = yā ~, bạ shi shạllịŋ ƙaurī = yā ~, bạ shi tạ̄rar ƙaurī = yā ~, bạ shi tsọraŋ ƙaurī he's an "old hand" (= hannū 2*g*). (ii) *Vd.* shạllī. (2) *m.* (*a*) (*progressive and v.n. of* 1). (*b*) ƙūnā = ƙūnan rūwā = ƙunārī *q.v.* (*c*) ƙūnam baƙiŋ wākē = ƙūnan dāgā reckless courage (= kạsadạ).
C. (ƙụnā) *f.* used in ƙụnar halī inquisitiveness.
D. (ƙūnā) used in ƙunā rūwā = ƙunārū.

kụnāmạ *f.* (*pl.* kụnạ̄mī = kụnạ̄mū = kunāmōmī). (1) (*a*) scorpion (*cf.* mạiramụ). (*b*) ~ tā hạrbi kaskō, tā cẹ 'yam baƙạ what a chattering girl! (*c*) gyạŋgyạdịŋ ~, kōwā ya tabạ, yạ̄ shā kāshī never be off your guard! (*d*) baị tākạ ~ ba *Vd.* gạjērē

1*b.*ii. (*e*) kụnāmạr ƙạdaŋgarẹ *Vd.* cịŋ kụnāmạr ƙạdaŋgarẹ. (2) (*a*) ɗaŋ ~ "dangerous customer". (*b*) ɗaŋ ~ nē bạ̄ ɗaŋ gōyō ba "he's an ugly customer". (3) yā īyạ kāmạ ~ he can charm away scorpion-stings. (4) namijịŋ ~ *m.* large, quick spider with hairy legs. (5) kụnāmạr rūwā type of water-beetle.

ƙūnan *Vd.* ƙūnā.

ƙụnantạ = ƙụnā.

ƙụnar halī *Vd.* ƙụnā.

ƙunārī = ƙunārū *m.* plain water without addition of flour = ƙūnā 2*b* (*cf.* faraufarau).

ƙụnātạ *f.* = ƙụnā.

ƙunātō *m.* perseverance, persistence (= nācị).

ƙunau *m.* = ƙunārī.

kunce A. (kuncẹ) = kwancẹ.
B. (kuncē) *Daura Hausa m.* (1) wrestling (= kọ̄kawạ). (2) ɗaŋ ~ *m.* (*pl.* 'yaŋ ~) wrestler (= ɗaŋ kọ̄kawạ). (3) yā gạmu dạ 'yaŋ ~ he is treading on slippery soil (= santsī). (4) *Vd.* kincē ; cācā 4.
C. (kụncē) *Vd.* kwạncē.

kunci A. (kuncị) *m.* (*pl.* kumạ̄tū = kumạrmatū = kumạmmatū = kumạrmacị). (1) cheek ; side of face. (2) *Vd.* cācā 4.
B. (kụnci) *Vd.* kwạnci.

Kuncī A. (Kuncī) place-name used in yā kai ~ = yā tạfi ~ he became angry (*cf.* ƙuncī 3).
B. (ƙuncī) *m.* (1) constrictedness (*a*) *x* yā yi ~ its area's constricted. (*b*) wurịŋ yā yi musụ ~ "the place is too hot to hold them". (2) slight dearth (= matsị). (3) bad temper *x* yā fāyẹ ~ he's bad-tempered. mại ƙuncin zūcịyā bad tempered (*cf.* Kuncī). (4) *Kt.* = duhūwạ.

kuncịŋ ạkwīyạ *m.* type of okro (kuƙẹ̄wā) with short, thick capsules (= kuruskuƙạ).

ƙundạ *f.* (*pl.* ƙundōjī). (1) blunt arrow made from tamarind (tsāmīyā) and fruit of desert-date (adūwạ) and used by boys for throwing at birds (= adụllū). (2) gạrin nēman tsịnī, yā kāsạ "throwing away the substance for the shadow".

kundāyē *Vd.* kundī.

kundi A. (kundī) *m.* (*pl.* kundāyē). (1) wad of small sheets of paper with notes on them. (2) Kundī, ạbin cikiŋ ạljīfū *epithet of* confidential servitor. (3) dạ kundī dạ tạdawạ bā sạ tā dạ Gwamnạ, sǎi Mạdī yā zō one must bow to circumstances.

    B. (kụndī) *Vd.* daudụŋ ∾.

kundī = kundīlā = kumbulā 1 *q.v.*

kundọ *Kt. m.* section of sugar-cane or bamboo lying between two joints (gaɓạ).

kundōjī *Vd.* kundạ.

kundu A. (kụndū) *m.* (*pl.* kundunạ). (1) (*a*) (i) gizzard of chicken or ostrich (= bạrōrọ 1). (ii) kạzā jạŋ kundụŋ ạbūyạ what a slanderer. (*b*) (i) tā yi ∾ she's pregnant. (ii) tā fasạ kunduntạ she's been delivered of a child. (*c*) *Vd.* gwaidạ. (*d*) (i) yā cikạ kundunsạ he's had good meal. (ii) *cf.* tạttạrạ kundunạ. (*e*) kundụŋ kạzaŋ ūwarkạ blast you ! (*said by* Māguzāwā), *cf.* kạzā. (2) (*a*) kundụŋ gidā the part of compound where bulk of residents live (= cikiŋ gidā), *cf.* tụrākā. (*b*) kụndụŋ gạrī "heart of the town". (3) kụndụŋ kạzā dish of corn and beans cooked together. (4) ∾ wạje shallow compound or hut.

    B. (kundū) *m.* nā ci kundunsạ I just missed it or him (*re* shooting, opportunity, T. desired, P. sought) = turạ 2.

kunduɓā *f.* = kumbulā 1.

kụndugurū *m.* useless thick end of rạkē or tạkạndā-sugar-cane (= gịndigịrī = gịndiŋ kūrụ = *Kt.* kụtūtụ 5*a* = wạlạ-bābạ).

kụndukukị = kụndukūkị *m.* (*pl.* kụndụkūkai) *only used in translations from Arabic* cheek-bone.

kundū-kundū = cī dạ gērō 2.

kụndum (1) abundantly (*re* liquids). (2) *Vd.* shā ∾.

kunduma A. (kundumạ) = kundumī.

    B. (kundụmā) *Vb.* 1C poured out much fluid.

kunduma A. (kụndumạ) *Vb.* 2 (animal) ate off heads of standing corn.

    B. (kundụmā) *Vb.* 1C yā ∾ minị zāgị he insulted me.

kụndụmāsạ *f.* (1) whole gourd (gụdan dumā) whose pulp (tōtụ̄wā) has not been removed (hūrẹ) = *Sk.* gụndumbulī 1 = bụmbū. (2) large bundle (damị) of dry grass (shūcị) cut in handfuls (dạŋkị-dạŋkị) from time of guinea-corn harvest up to February with scythe (lạujē) : when yantā is done, one kụndụmāsạ forms four kại, these being evened up (dirẹ) and sold for thatching (hayị) ; *cf.* kurshẹ ; damị 1*b*.

kụndumbạ *f.* the move in darạ (draughts) called bạtsātsạ.

kụndụmbālā *f.* (1) foolhardiness (*epithet is* ∾ shịgar mạkāfọ kōgī). (2) foolishly giving away all one owns. (3) diving full-tilt into river to find T. fallen in, etc.

kundume A. (kundụmē = kundụmē) *Vb.* 1C. (1) cut off branches of tree, pollarded. (2) (*a*) aŋ kundụmẹ kạntạ girl's hair has been cut off because of kazwā, her parents then playfully calling her Gwārī. (*b*) aŋ kundụmẹ kạntạ weaned girl's head has been shaved (= dauriŋ gụ̄gā 3 *q.v.*), *cf.* askị. (3) aŋ ∾ shi he's been stripped of his all.

    B. (kundụmē) *Vb.* 1C. (1) = kụndumạ. (2) aŋ ∾ masạ kại he's been beheaded (= gillẹ). (3) *Vd.* kundụmē.

kundumēmẹ *m.* (*f.* kundumēmīyā) *pl.* kundum-kụndụm abundant (*re* fluids).

kundumēmẹ *m.* (*f.* kundumēmīyā) *pl.* kundum-kụndụm. (1) large and round. (2) long and fat (= gundumēmẹ).

kụndumī = kundumī *m.* (1) (*a*) acting as in kundụmē 1, 2*a*, *b* ; *hence* :—(*b*) ạ tạmbayi maị ∾ lạ̄bāriŋ kịtsọ ? don't waste time seeking information from the ignorant ! (*c*) aŋ yi masạ kụndumiŋ gigiinyạ he's been robbed of his all ; he's been irretrievably dismissed from his position. (*d*) *Kt.* bịkiŋ wani kundumī, bịkiŋ wani dōkạ, bịkiŋ wani kwạmbē "tastes differ". (2) *Kt.* rūwā yā yi minị kundumī water was so deep it was over my head (*cf.* īyā 1*b*). (3) *m., f.* (*sg., pl.*) hornless ox, goat, ram (= gumalẹ).

kụndunạ *Vd.* kụndū.

Kundụrkū name for short girl (= Kumbulā).

ƙụnduttū *m.* = ƙụndụmbālā.

kun fạ yạkūnụ *Ar.* God said " let it be ! " and so it was.

kungạ *used in* nā kuŋgạ, nā kuŋgạ, bạn sāmụ ba I searched and searched, but couldn't find it (= kuŋkụŋgā).

kụŋ'ge-kụŋgē" *m.* looking hither and thither for T or P.

ƙuŋgīyā *f.* = ƙunjīyā.

ƙuŋgu *m.* (1) forked stick (gwạ̄fā) on which sịllīyạ-cord is knitted by men (*cf.* tsiŋkē 5). (2) brick (= tūbạlī). *(3) = ƙaŋgū 2.

ƙụŋgurgụmā *f.* the beetle ƙụrguŋgụmā *q.v.*

ƙuŋgurmī *m.* (1) (*a*) yā ɗạụki kāyā ạ ⁓ he carried load without headpad (gammō). (*b*) ƙuŋgurmiŋ gadō bed without mat on it (*cf.* kaŋgō 3). (2) (*a*) burly lout. (*b*) (*with f.* ƙuŋgurmā) notorious *x* (i) ƙuŋgurmim bạrāwọ notorious thief. ƙuŋgurmin jējị large area of bush with unsavoury reputation. ƙuŋgurmim matsīyạ̄ci utterly destitute P. (ii) ƙuŋgurmin dājị māgạnim maị kīshị don't be jealous where there's no cause for jealousy (*cf.* ƙuŋƙuzū ; kuntukurmī).

ƙụŋgūrụ *m.* the rear lumbar region (= kwạŋkwasọ).

ƙuŋgurus *Sk., Kt.* = ƙụrụŋƙus.

ƙụŋgwītū (1) *adv.* tanạ̄ dạ kạ̈i ⁓ she has skimpy hair. (2) *f.* woman with skimpy hair.

kuni *Eng. m.* quinine.

kunīkạ *f.* = kwanīkạ.

ƙụnī-ƙunī *m.* = ƙụmīnīyā.

ƙụnīnīyā *f.* = ƙụmīnīyā.

kụnitạ (1) (*derived from* kwancẹ) *Vb.* 3B became vindicated, shown to be in the right ; became exonerated (= gịra). (2) *f.* yā sạ̄mi ⁓ = 1.

ƙụnjī *Sk., Kt. m.* (1) gizzard (= ƙụndū). (2) ƙụnjim bụrgū type of kụnun dọ̄rawạ. (3) *cf.* tạttạrạ ⁓ ; ƙwạnjī.

ƙunjīyā *f.* (1) collection, crowd of T. or P. (2) sun yi ⁓ they travelled together.

ƙuŋkạ out and out *x* mālạmi nē ⁓ he's a thorough scholar. namijị nē ⁓ he's a " he-man ". kārụ̄wạ cē ⁓ she's an out-and-out whore.

kuŋkạ *Sk.* = kukạ.

kụŋkēlị a small, round shield (gạrkūwā).

kuŋ ƙi cị *m.* (*sg., pl.*) weevil (*found in sacks of corn*).

ƙuŋkū *m.* (1) slight scrotal hernia (*cf.* mạjạƙwar). (2) *Sk.* brick (= tūbạlī). (3) *Kt.* debris of ant-hill (sūrị).

kuŋkụmā *Vb.* 1C *int. from* kumạ.

ƙuŋƙuma A. (ƙuŋƙumā) *f.* (1) skimpy, embroidered, sleeveless gown. (2) small-breasted grown-up girl or woman (*cf.* lūbīyā 2). (3) date-palm with skimpy clusters of fruit.

B. (ƙuŋƙumā) *Vb.* 1C. (1) pounded a little *x* tā ƙuŋƙumạ ɗaŋ hatsī she pounded a little corn. (2) yā ƙuŋ- ƙumạ rīgā he lightly beat (*a*) washed gown (= sansạ̄mā = lallạsā), (*b*) kōrẹ- gown to freshen it up. (3) aŋ ⁓ shi he's been given slight thrashing (= lal- lạsā).

kunkumbura A. (kuŋkumbụrā) *int. from* kumbụrā.

B. (ƙụŋƙụmburạ) *int. from* kụmburạ.

ƙụŋƙụmē *m.* (1) slight beating (*cf.* ƙụŋƙụmā; lạllạshē). (2) (*a*) a little pounded tobacco or pounded mixed condiments (*x* for journey). (3) (*a*) petty thefts. (*b*) small raids. (*c*) secret gambling. (4) lạ̄bārịn naŋ ⁓ nẹ̄ this is a piece of news, not public but shared only with a friend.

kuŋkumēmẹ = kuŋkumī *m.* (*f.* kuŋ- kumēmīyā = kuŋkumā) *pl.* kuŋkụŋ- kụŋkụŋ (1) huge. (2) notorious (= ƙụŋgurmī 2 *q.v.*).

kuŋkumī (1) *Vd.* kuŋkumēmẹ. (2) *Kt. m.* (= *Sk.* tūrū 2) type of drum (*for adult, it is made of skin-covered gourd* (dumā), *but for child, of top* (bạ̄kī) *of waterpot, i.e.* jẹmō *covered with skin*).

kinkimo *Vd.* kuŋkumạ.

ƙụŋƙūnē *m.* = ƙụŋƙūnī.

kuŋkụŋgā *used in* nā ⁓, nā ⁓, bạn sāmụ ba I searched and searched, but couldn't find it (= kuŋgạ).

ƙụŋƙūnī *m.* (1) muttering in complaint. (2) murmuring. (3) growling of dog (*all* = gunạ̄gunī).

kuŋkụŋ-kụŋkụŋ *Vd.* kuŋkumēmẹ.

kụŋkunnīyā *f.* soot inside top of house (*Vd.* fụmfuŋ).

ƙụŋƙuntā *m., f.* (*pl.* ƙuntạ̄tā) limited *x*

(1) ƙuŋƙuntaŋ gidā compound with restricted space. (2) ƙuŋƙuntar yārinya short-tempered girl (derived from ƙuncī).

kuŋkurū m. (pl. kuŋkura = kuŋkurai). (1) (a) (i) tortoise. (ii) rabaŋ ∼ bā ya hawā sama = shāfo bā ya ciŋ rabaŋ ∼ everyone has his separate destiny. (iii) ragō bai san ragō ne shī ba sǎi yā ƙōri ∼ yā tsēre the sluggard only learns from lethargy greater than his own. (iv) ∼ yana san dambē, damtsansa yā gaza don't attempt the impossible ! (v) " ∼ ta inā akē ciŋka ", ya cē "ta tsūlīyā " = 1b. (vi) Vd. gādā 1e. (b) gatsaŋ ∼ replying rudely and recklessly to a superior (= 1a.v). (c) Vd. baŋ ∼. (d) ∼ shī ya sam makāmar mātā tasa let him gang his own gley ! (e) kuŋkuruŋ kudu (i) P. from Southern Nigeria (= Cāƙiri). (ii) steam-shovel. (2) structure on which weaver's cotton thread rests. (3) round cushion. (4) (a) dyed garment or cloth not yet beaten in lieu of ironing. (b) yā yi mini ∼ = yā bar ta ∼ yā wuce = yā yi ∼ bai kōɗe ba he made a cryptic remark to me.

ƙuŋƙurū m. (1) putting aside one out of every 100 cowries counted, as token (such token being called ɗaŋ ƙidāya). (2) mu sā ∼ let us (gamblers) balance up winnings and losses ! (3) ƙuŋƙūruŋ kudī load of cowries tied up in a hide (= gīwā 14).

ƙuŋƙurus = ƙuruŋƙus.

ƙuŋƙuzū (1) = kuŋkumēme (but only used with masculine noun, cf. ƙuŋgurmī) x ƙuŋƙuzuŋ ƙāto huge, fearless man. ƙuŋƙuzum ɓarāwo notorious thief. (2) nothing but x yā kāwō fam ɗarī, kwabo kwabo ƙuŋƙuzunsa he brought £100 all in coppers (= zallā).

kuŋkyāra Sk. = kwākyāra.

kunna A. (kunna) Vb. 1A. (1) (a) yā ∼ fitila he lit the lamp, he switched on the light. (b) yā ∼ masa wutā ɦe set it on fire. aŋ ∼ wa rījīyōyinsu wutar bōm their wells have been bombed. (c) yā ∼ masīfa a ƙasarsu he brought calamity on their land. (2) yā ∼ ƙǎi

ɗaka he entered without a by-your-leave. inda ya kunnō hanci where he poked his nose in, meddled. (3) yā ∼ musu bāƙō (ɓarāwo) he gave quiet hint to stranger (thief) of their premises as being a place likely to suit him as lodging (house to rob) = dōdana 5. B. (kunnā) used in nā kunni wutā a wurinsa I got fire from him.

ƙunnai Kt. m. = ƙuŋƙūnī.

kunne A. (kunnē) m. (pl. kunnūwa = kunnāyē). (1) (a) (i) ear (after prep. a, we have e.g. a kunnē = a kunnē in the ear). (ii) yā rūɗa kunnūwansu he misled them. (iii) ∼ nā ganī, ƙaƙō yā yi tsīrā imperceptibly things develop along their appointed lines. (iv) dā ∼ yā jī, dā jiki yā tsīrā = iŋ ∼ yā ji mugunyar magana, wuya yā tsēre yaŋkā forewarned is forearmed. (v) jiki yā fi ∼ jī if P. won't listen to advice, he must learn in the hard school of experience. (vi) ∼ ƙāƙan dūnīya one accepts tradition though not present oneself. (b) (i) yā kasa ∼ he listened carefully, pricked up his ears. (ii) kunnansu yana wajan lābārin yāƙi they are listening tensely for war-news. (iii) kōwā, kunnansa nā kan abin da zā mu faɗā all are keyed up to hear our words. (iv) muka sā ∼, yau mā ji lābāri, gōbe mā ji, shirū we felt sure we should hear news any day now, but there was none. (v) muna kunnē Vd. baka 1f. (c) bā mai jiŋ ∼ nobody could hear himself speak owing to the noise. (d) yana da ∼ kamar baraukiŋ ƙanzō he has huge ears. (e) ɗaŋ kunnaŋ ūwā bother you ! (Vd. ūwā 1c). (f) jiŋ ∼ m. mere rumour. (g) kunnēna rūwaŋ gāwā, ban ji ba, baŋ ganī ba (said by woman) I'm not concerned in the matter ! (h) A, having heard rumour, asks B if he too has heard it, by saying kunnaŋka nawa to which B replies kunnēna bīyū, A then saying ƙāra na uku, ka shā lābāri and tells him the rumour. (j) Vd. hūra 1c. (k) kunnan dōki Vd. ƙakat. (l) cf. taɓa kunnē ; būɗar ∼. (m) kashe ∼ Vd. kashe 11. (n) dōdaŋ ∼ Vd. dōdō 11. (2) (a) (i) each of the prongs of forked stick

(gwaҭā). (ii) barb of an arrow (Vd. 6).
(b) Sarkī yā yi naɗi ɗa kunnūwa Chief
put on turban arranged in two " horns "
(Vd. filāfili). (c) first leaf of plant to
sprout. (d) an yi masa ⁓ it (very full
sack) has had its top-ends sewn up so
as to enable it to be lifted. (3) ƙunnam
ɓērā (a) narrow cake (cūri) of ɗaddawā. (b) poor selvedge (ƙarbū) in
novice's weaving (sāƙar bāmī). (4)
ƙunnam būlāla thong of whip (= kurfō).
(5) ƙunnan jāƙī the plant gwandai.
(6) ƙunnaŋ kibīya barb of arrow. (7)
ƙunnan Shaitsan (a) auricular appendices of the heart. (b) nā jī ka ɗa
ƙunnan Shaitsan what low talk you
employ ! (8) ƙunnam samfo handle of
bag samfo. (9) ƙunnan shēge =
ƙunnaŋ ūwar shēge pretending not to
hear what was said. mun yi wa lābārai
ƙunnaŋ uwar shēge we turned a deaf ear
to the news (i.e. as mother of bastard knows
all are discussing her shame, she pretends
not to hear). (10) Kt. dōƙi mai ƙunnan
tarauniyā lop-eared horse. (11) ƙunnan zōmō the ginger-like herb Cadalvena
Dalzielii. (12) ƙunnan tandū handle of
tandū-vessel.

B. (kunne) Vb. 1A aŋ ⁓ mai duka
whole of oil in lamp has been consumed.

ƙunnīyā f. crowd, etc. (= ƙunjīyā q.v.).
ƙunnū m. the insect-pest ƙurnū q.v.
kunnūwa Vd. ƙunnē.
ƙunsa A. (ƙunsa) Vb. 1A. (1) (a) yā ⁓
shi a hannun rīgā he wrapped sleeve of
his gown round it, to carry it (cf.
maƙe 2b). (b) tā ⁓ shi a zananta she
wrapped her body-cloth round it, to
carry it on her shoulder. (c) (i) made T.
into parcel. (ii) abin ɗa na ƙunsa
cikin jawābina, n nā muku gōdīyā
my thanks to you form the subject of
my speech. (2) tā ⁓ lalle she encased
her hands or feet in henna (cf. ƙunshi ;
lalle). (3) yā ⁓ gārin tāba he took a
pinch of powdered tobacco wrapped in
paper, to use as snuff or suck as quid
(ƙamailā). (4) yā ⁓ ƙai ɗaka he
entered without a " by-your-leave ".
(5) yā ⁓ dōƙi he galloped into the
crowd. (6) (with dative) (a) nā ⁓

masa naushi I punched him. (b) yā ⁓
mata cūtā (i) he infected her with
venereal disease (= sunna 1b). (ii)
he robbed her. (c) aŋ ⁓ wa mārūru
māganī the boil on buttocks was
syringed out. (7) yā ⁓ a guje he fled.
(8) Vd. ƙunsu.

B. (ƙunsā) Vb. 2 (p.o. ƙunshē,
n.o. ƙunshi). (1) = ƙunsa 1. (2) yā
ƙunshi rūwā a baka he filled his mouth
with water. (3) yā ƙunshi maganan
naŋ he stored this in his mind to bring
shame on P. by bandying it about
later.

ƙunshe A. (ƙunshe) Vb. 1A = ƙunsa 1,
ƙunsā 3. (2) tā ƙunshe lalle she used
up all the henna (acting as in ƙunsa 2).

B. (ƙunshē) Vd.) ƙunsā.

C. (ƙunshe) x (1) yanā ⁓ ɗa kuɗī
he's holding the money wrapped as in
ƙunsa 1. (2) Vd. sai mā ⁓.

ƙunshi A. (ƙunshi) Vd. ƙunsā.

B. ƙunshi m. (1) (secondary v.n. of
ƙunsa 1) x yanā ƙunshinsa = yanā
ƙunsa shi. (2) (a) an yi mata ⁓ bride's
been hennaed (Vd. lalle) ; cf. labū,
duŋgū 2. (b) tā yi ⁓ she encased herself in henna (for feast, etc.). (c) (i)
kōwā ya ga shāmūwā, ɗa ƙunshinta
ya gan ta everybody is as God made
him. (ii) ya yi wa shāmūwa ⁓ Vd.
lalle 1h. (3) bundle ; parcel. (4) zā
mu ⁓ we're going to wedding-festival.
(5) dāwa tā yi ⁓ guinea-corn's about to
produce ears (= ɗaure 1d.ii), cf. māƙara 2b. (6) nā yi ⁓ a ɓaraka I spoke
against him unaware he was within
hearing or unaware P. to whom I
spoke was his friend (= ɓallīyā 3 =
kaŋki 2b.i).

ƙunsu Vb. 3B aŋ ⁓ cikin ɗāƙi house's
thronged. yā ⁓ a ɗaka he delayed
long in the house (cf. ƙunsa ; ƙunsā).

kunta A. (kunta) Vb. 1A untied (= kwance
q.v.).

B. (kuntā) Vb. 2 (p.o. kuncē, n.o.
kunci) = kwanta.

C. (kuntā) f. (1) dōƙinsa yā cika ⁓
his horse bites through tethering-rope
(gindī). (2) an yi masa ⁓ the horse,
etc., lent him has been taken back by
the owner. (3) ɗaŋ ⁓ nē he's a Don

Juan on the sly, roving at night. (4) gāgara ƙuntā Vd. gāgara 9.

ƙuntā used in ganiŋ ƙuntā garēshi he's inquisitive.

ƙuntace A. (ƙuntacē) Vb. 3A is (was) restricted in area (cf. ƙuntata).
B. (ƙuntacē) Vd. ƙuntata 2.

ƙuntar = ƙuntāri m. (1) shī ~ nē (i) he's a burly lout. (ii) he's a feckless wastrel. (iii) he's skilful at his trade. (2) (with fem. ƙuntārīyā) x ƙuntārim ɓarāwo notorious thief (= ƙuŋƙuzū). ƙuntārīyar kārūwa thorough whore. *(3) Ar. (a) weight of 1 cwt. (b) big tusk of ivory (2a, b only used in trading with Arabs).

kun tāru used in wurin naŋ yanā da ~ this place is notorious (as haunted, full of disease, etc.).

ƙuntata A. (ƙuntata) (1) Vb. 3B. (a) is (was) restricted in area (= ƙuntacē). (b) is (was) poor. (2) Vb. 2 (p.o. ƙuntacē, n.o. ƙuntaci) (a) pestered P. (b) " cramped his style " x aŋ ƙuntacē shi.
B. (ƙuntatā) Vb. 1C. (1) restricted (area of place). (2) aŋ ~ masa = ƙuntata 2.
C. (ƙuntātā) constricted (pl. of ƙuŋƙuntā).

ƙuntataccē m. (f. ƙuntataccīyā) pl. ƙuntatattū restricted in area, circumscribed.

ƙuntigi m. type of small, one-stringed musical instrument (mōlō).

ƙuntū m. (pl. kuntuna) brown blanket (as issued to soldiers, prisoners), cf. bargō.

kuntu bıllāhi Ar. ~ ban yi ba I swear I didn't do it. ya tsaya ~ bai yi ba he firmly denied doing it.

ƙuntugi = ƙuntugu m. = ƙuntigi q.v.

ƙuntuƙā Vb. 1C did abundantly x yā ƙuntuƙa ƙaryā he told a " whopper ". aŋ ~ masa sāta he was seriously robbed. aŋ ƙuntuƙa fada there was serious altercation. aŋ ƙuntuƙa hayāƙī a dāki = kuntuƙē last example.

kuntuƙē Vb. 3A x fada yā ~ there was serious altercation. kāsūwā tā ~ market's thronged. dāki yā ~ da hayāƙī = hayāƙī yā ~ a dāki room's full of smoke.

kuntukū = kuntukurū.

kuntukurmī m. (f. kuntukurmā) pl. ƙuntuƙurmai. (1) notorious x kuntukurmim ɓarāwo notorious thief. kuntukurmin jēji large area of bush with unsavoury reputation (= zunzurūtu = rantsattsē 2 = ƙuŋgurmī 2 q.v.). (2) kuntukurmim matsīyāci = ƙuntuƙūru.

kuntukuru A. (kuntukurū) m. (1) small, round drum made of wood hollowed out, and covered with skin (is beaten in company with kalaŋgū and tūdarā drums) = kurkutū. (2) cake (cūri) of prepared indigo. (3) zamaŋ ~ m. = hardē 4. (4) Vd. daurin ~.
B. (ƙuntuƙūru) used in ƙuntuƙūrum matsīyāci P. in direst poverty.

kuntumēme = kuntumī m. (f. kuntumēmīyā = kuntumā) pl. kuntuŋkuntuŋ huge.

kuntuna Vd. ƙuntū.

kunū m. (1) (a) (i) gruel (= kōko). (ii) epithet is Kunū, mai ɓāta uku Gruel, waster of flour, water, and wood ! = Kunū na ciki, ku kwānā da yuŋwa. (iii) N.B.—gruel is made preferably with guinea-corn flour, but if none available, then with maiwā, and failing that, with gēro. It is flavoured with tamarind-juice (tsāmīyā) and honey or sugar. As seen from its epithets above, kunū is disliked and is substitute for tūwō or furā for the sake of speed. (b) kōmē zā a yi, a sā gishirī, an yi wa mai gidā ~ whatever your hand finds to do, do it with all your might ! (c) dōmiŋ auki akē yiŋ ~, ya kōmō ya rasa auki the expectation was not realized. (d) ~ kō yā kwānā Vd. tsīnanā 1b.ii. (e) Vd. rāgaya 1e. (f) arahar ~ Vd. arahā 5. (g) dāwar ~ Vd. dāwa 6. (h) kunuŋ ƙawayyā Vd. ƙauye 3c. (2) kunuŋ kaŋwā gruel flavoured with potash (for nursing-mother (i.e. mai jēgo) or circumcized-lad (i.e. dan shāyī)). (3) kunun dōrawa gruel made from locust-bean pods. (4) kunun zāƙī gruel with sweet-potato, wheat, etc., added and used as a drink. (5) kunuŋ arauyē Vd. arauyē.

kunuŋgurū m. the fodder-weed spiderwort (Commelyna nudiflora) = balasanā 2.

kunya A. (kunyạ) *f.* (1) modesty *x* (*a*) ~
tā hanạ ni fạdā modesty forbids me to
say it. (*b*) bạ̄ shi dạ ~ he has no sense of
propriety. (*c*) bạ̄ ka dạ kụnya ? you
shameless person ! (*d*) rashịŋ ~ *m.*
impudence, shamelessness. (2) feeling
ashamed *x* (*a*) (i) nā ji (= nā ci) ~
I feel (felt) ashamed, I was put to
shame. (ii) bā kạ̄ jịŋ kụnya ? aren't
you ashamed to act thus ? (*rude reply
is* ~ nạ̄ gōnā mind your own business !),
cf. iii *below.* (iii) tsọrō nạ̄ dāji, ~ nạ̄
gidā the jungle is the place for fear, but
the dwellings of man, for civility. (iv)
bā yạ̄ kunyạr kōwā ạ fagyam fadạ
he is intrepid in battle. (v) sunạ̄
aikạtāwā, bạ̄ ~, bạ̄ tsọrō they are
acting contrary to the dictates of
humanity. (vi) sǎi bạ̄kī yā cī, idọ kẹ̄ ~
P. who has accepted a bribe reveals the
fact by the shifts he is driven to adopt.
(vii) kā yī dạ ~ *Vd.* fạrkā 2*b.* (viii)
ịnā rūwam mạkāfọ dạ ~ *Vd.* rūwā
G.4. (ix) tạ̄barmar ~ *Vd.* tạ̄barmā 3.
(x) kunyạr idọ *Vd.* hūtạlī. (*b*) yā yi ~
(i) he did a shameful T. (ii) expert
fell short of his best. (*c*) yā bā nị ~
(i) he humiliated me (= tānạdī 4). (ii)
he shocked me. (iii) baŋ ~ kạman
tūsạ ạ jạma'ạ being humiliated makes
one feel as if " one would like to sink
through the floor ". (*d*) yā yi yawạ,
har kunyạr gọ̄dīyā nikẹ̄ yị̄ you've done
so much that my mere thanks are inadequate. (*e*) kadạ kạ sạ̄ wạ kạŋkạ
wani jịŋ ~ cikī don't " make compliments ! " (= fīlākọ). (*f*) sun tāshi
dạ ~ they left " with their tails between
their legs ". (3) fawar ~ girl's or
woman's female pal with whom she
remains from morning to night so
absorbed in conversation that they
are not distracted by hunger or calls
of nature. (*cf.* fwārī 6). *(4) tail of
Arabic final " n " written backwards,
to show that the case-ending " n "
(tanwīn) is assimilated in sound to
following " b " or " f " and so pronounced " m " (= ạlkunyạ 2).
    B. (kunyā) *f.* (*pl.* kunyōyī = kun-
yạyyakī). (1) (*a*) ridge on which to plant
crops in farm = *Sk.* kwīyyạ (*Vd.*

kạdādā ; kwarị ; kạ̄i 7*e* ; gwarzō 3 ;
jụyayyā). (*b*) kạ kāmạ kunyạn naŋ, kạ
kōmạ (= kōmō) dạ ita hoe along that
ridge, then hoe back in this direction !
(2) kunyar gizọ *Kt. m.* ridges left on
ground by receding water.

kụnyạce *used in* ạ ~ *adv.* feeling
thoroughly ashamed.

kụnyạ̄-kunyā *Kt.* (1) nā ạmsā ~ I
accepted it, but felt I had not been
fairly remunerated. (2) yā zō ~ he
came thoroughly abashed (= kụnyạce).

kunyata A. (kunyạtā) *Vb.* 1C shamed P.
    B. (kụnyatạ) *Vb.* 3B is (was)
ashamed.

kunyatad dạ *Vb.* 4B shamed.

kunyạyyakī *Vd.* kunyā.

kunyōyī *Vd.* kunyā.

funzụgē (1) *Vb.* 1C yā funzụgẹ bạntē
he tucked end of loin-cloth into his
waist-band (= saŋfẹ). (2) *Vb.* 3A
persevered.

funzugū *m.* (1) tucking in *as in* funzụgē
1 (= saŋfẹ = kạndạmē). (2) = sọ̄kē 1.

kunzụmā *Vb.* 1C poured out too much
fluid, *etc.* (= kandạmā *q.v.*).

kup *m.* type of rosary (cạzbī) : ~ dinsạ
his rosary.

kụptirī = fuftirī.

kur (1) come here, donkey ! (2) sound of
frogs' croaking at dusk. (3) kụrwā
tasạ kur he is alive and kicking.

fur *Vd.* fur dạ fūnạ.

kura A. (kūrā) *f.* (*pl.* kūrạ̄yē). (1) (*a*) male
or female hyena = kạryar dawạ (*cf.*
kūrẹ) (*epithets are* Amīnạ̄ 3 = Dạ̄gwị̄-
yau = Būrụ, ạljanad darē = Burụŋgū
ạljanad darē ; kōwā ya yi darē, baraŋ
ụbaŋkị nē = Gạzau = Shạ̄ hạrgōwạ =
Fauru, dạ̄gwị̄yau, dabbạr Allạ̄ = *Kt.*
Gurụŋgū). (*b*) yā yi kūkaŋ ~ he
behaved threateningly. (*c*) ladạbịŋ ~
Vd. ladạb 1*d.* (*d*) yā sạ̄ kūrar zạncē
while chatting, he suddenly asked for
a loan. (*e*) sunạ̄ yịŋ " ~ yākị ~ ! " =
sunạ̄ wạsaŋ ~ they (young actors or
actresses) are imitating a hyena at
tạ̄shē games (= bạ̄bạ̄kērē 3). (*f*)
sạrautạr ~ *f.* mere self-seeking rule.
(*g*) *Vd.* rakīyạr kūrā. (*h*) tạfīyạr kūrā
Vd. tạfīyạ 6. (*j*) kwạllịŋ kūrā = tōzạlịŋ
kūrā *Vd.* kwạllī 4. (*k*) *for* kūrā *idioms,*

Vd. 18–62 *below.* (2) (*a*) kūrab bāya, māganiŋ gudummōwạ warriors left behind to fight rearguard action. (3) (*a*) many-pronged hook for retrieving bucket from well (*cf.* zạbạrī). (*b*) tool for opening battens on bales. (4) luggage-trolley. (5) (*a*) yā cī nị kūrar sulẹ gōmạ he (broker) cheated me (owner of goods) out of ten shillings. (*b*) kā ci ∼ dạ fadạ you (broker) are talking incessantly to owner of goods to divert attention from your defalcations. (6) yā ci kūrar kạnsạ he " made compliments " (= filākọ). (7) *Kt.* figar ∼ tearing skin of chicken when skinning it (= tạyā 2). (8) rawạnī daŋ ∼ type of turban. (9) kūrar shānū (*a*) ox with drooping horns (= bijāyẹ). (*b*) dwarf-cow (= muturū). (10) kūrar ƙudā type of large fly. (11) kūrar yārā child's toy, like bull-roarer (*made of corn-stalk or* tsiŋgārọ). (12) Sallạr kūrā *Vd.* bạrgi-bạrgī. (13) gōyaŋ kūrā *Vd.* gōyō 2*e.* (14) *Vd.* cībīyar kūrā. (15) *Vd.* tōzạliŋ kūrā. (16) mai kashẹ kūrā *Vd.* sĩyākī. (17) Kūrā *name of any woman named* Amīnạ (*Vd.* Amīnạ 3).

(18) *idioms and proverbs with* kūrā. (*a*) yā fitō dạgạ dākiŋ ∼ he has passed out of danger. (*b*) dākiŋ kūrā sải 'yā'yantạ it is a dangerous place best avoided. (19) dạ mā yạyạ lāfīyạr kūrā, ballē tạ yi haukā things were bad enough before, so what will they be like now! (20) kā yi rībạr ƙafạ, kūrā tā tākạ kwạdō you've had an unexpected piece of luck. (21) ∼ tanạ sọ, kạrē yạ sạmu? hands off! (22) ạturẹ bā yạ rabạ kạrē da ∼ desperate affairs need desperate remedies. (23) sải dāi wani jiƙọ, kạrē yā zubad dạ tsāmīyar ∼ that's the end of the matter for the present. (24) dạ ∼ dạ kạrē bā sạ gamạ mazaunī oil and water won't mix. (25) (*a*) bạ shigar rāmiŋ ∼ kẹ dạ wuyā ba, fitọwạr dōmiŋ kụwā sải dạ kūje-kūjẹ = gaddamạ 4. (*b*) shigạ rāmiŋ ∼ bạ na ƙaramiŋ gardi ba nẹ don't attempt what is beyond you! (26) ∼ tā cinyẹ ɓạrāwọ the biter bit!

(= burum 3). (27) an yi manạ " tạya Kūrā, mụ ci ạkwīyạ ! " an attempt wa made to trick us. (28) ∼ tā zō dạ guntuŋ ƙīrị oneself falling into th trap one dug for another. (29) mạ wạsā dạ ∼ wata rānā rạgwantạ n shī don't play with fire! (30) an yạbaŋ ∼, tā ɓarkẹ dạ zāwọ praising P who then acts in way showing th praise was undeserved. (31) ∼ tan māganin zạwọ? tạ yi wạ kạntạ mạn Physician, heal thyself! (32) rāmiŋ ∼ mai wuyar lēƙạwā what a sly customer (33) mẹ kạrē gōmạ yakā yị dạ kūr what have they in common! (34) sur zamā gạbạ ∼, bāya dạmisạ they'r between the devil and the deep sea (35) dạbārạ nạ gạ mai hawaŋ ∼ it' for *him* to extricate himself from th mess he's got himself into. (36) b ạ bạ ∼ jirạŋ ạkwīyạ = bā ạ bạ ∼ ạjīyạr nāmạ one does not set a wolf t guard a lamb. (37) mai ạkwīyạ bi darē, ballē mai kūrạ if the rich ma feels apprehension, how much more th poor man! (38) dōkiŋ ∼ im bại sạwư ba, tạ ci ạbintạ unsold food is no loss as vendor will eat it himself. (39) d kūkaŋ ∼ dạ ɓacēwar ạkwīyạ duk dayā nẹ they are cause and effect. (40 kō aŋ kọri ∼, tạ yi guzurī dạ·kạrē n desperandum. (41) gindiŋ ∼ yā sāb dạ rāɓā he has had to learn in a har school and is not finicky. (42) n n ganiŋ ∼ dạ rānā, ƙaƙạ zạn yạrd tạ cịjē nị nobody blunders into dange with his eyes open. (43) ∼ tā fi dāgum sải sarƙạ he's brazen. (44) ∼ tā wucẹ ƙasā akạ zāgạ backbiting a person. (45 sạndan jīfạŋ ∼ sải dạ sāfē a kạ daukō shi do things at the right time (46) gami dayā kō dạ ∼ ạ yi there's n harm in trying everything once. (47 aŋgwaŋ ∼ kanā dakạ a kạn daur aurē, iŋ kā fitō wạje, aurē yạ mut when the cat is away the mice play (48) kō ∼ tā san turmī ạ wạje yak kwānā have more sense than to press destitute P. to pay a debt! (49) kōw ya daurẹ ∼ yạ san yạddạ zại yi y kwancẹ ta look before you leap! (50) ∼ tā ga sānịyā tanạ lāshẹ dīyā tatạ, *et*

Vd. ạbụ *2b.* (51) in zā kạ yi tạfīyạ, kạ yi tạfīyạr gīwā, kadạ kạ yi tạfīyạr ⁓ don't beat about the bush ! (52) lạifī duk na ⁓ nẹ ạmmā bạndạ sātạr wadạrī give a dog a bad name and hang him. (53) kō an ci birniŋ ⁓ bā ạ̄ bạ̄ kạrē dillanci whatever happens, there are always the rulers and the ruled. (54) dạ ganiŋ ⁓ an san tā ci ạkwīyạ appearance is an index to character. (55) kūrā nạ̄ shạn rūwā, kạre sǎi lẹ̄ƙē don't compete with superiors ! (56) Allạ̄ shī kẹ̄ bạ̄ ⁓ gishirī, nāmạ kō ạ kạsūwā tạ̄ sāmụ *epithet of* warrior or dogged worker. (57) kōwā dạ kīwạn dạ ya kạrɓē shị, maƙwạbciŋ ạkwīyạ yā sạyi ⁓ everyone for himself ! (58) kạrạmbānịŋ ạkwīyạ, gai dạ ⁓ it's impossible. (59) ⁓ dạ kallạbiŋ kitsẹ *Vd.* ạbụ *2b.* (60) kūrā tā ɗau gụrmī *Vd.* giriŋ-giriŋ. (61) yā hau ⁓ *Vd.* mahạụkạcī 1*a*.ii. (62) ⁓ tā mutụ, aŋ hūtạ our troubles are over.
B. (kurạ) *Vd.* ạbbānī.
ƙura A. (ƙụrā) *f.* (1) (*a*) dust. (*b*) sunạ̄ yāƙị, bā ạ̄ kō ganiŋ ⁓ tasụ they are at war afar. (*c*) (i) an tā dạ ⁓ a noisy quarrel is afoot. (ii) bā nạ̄ bị sǎi an tā dạ ⁓ I won't give in without a struggle. (iii) dūnīyạ duk tā ga an tā dạ ⁓ everyone saw they had offered resistance. (iv) kō ạ rūwa ka tākạ, sǎi ạ cẹ̄ kā tā dạ ⁓ they blame you for whatever you do. (*d*) kanạ̄ gạ ƙūrā *Vd.* yāƙị 1*l*. (2) mụ yi shirū har ⁓ tā kwạntā let's keep silence till the hue and cry has died down ! (3) dạ ⁓ ạ bāya there's more than meets the eye. (4) *Vd.* tilạ 2. (5) bindigạr ⁓ *f.* flit-gun.
B. (ƙurạ) *Vb.* 1A *x* yā ⁓ idạnsạ ƙurr (= rwai) ạ kạnsụ (i) he stared at them. (ii) he devoted all his attention to them. bạ̄ ịndạ sukạ fi ⁓ wạ idọ kạmar Masạr they were preoccupied with Egypt.
ƙura'ạ *f.* = ƙuri'ạ.
ƙurạcē = ƙurạshē.
kurạdā *f.* (*sg., pl.*) (1) small hatchet for chopping fodder (= masārī 3), *cf.* ƙurshẹ 2. (2) one of the patterns of zạyyanạ.
kurạfē *Vd.* kurfō.

kurạfū *Vd.* kụrfī.
ƙurạjē *Vd.* ƙurjī.
kūra-kūra *f.* yanạ̄ ⁓ he's timid.
ƙura-ƙura *x* ganinsạ yā yi ⁓ he has dim sight.
kụrākụrai *Vd.* kurẹ.
kurạmā *Vd.* kurmị.
kūrạm Bạ̄dau *Vd.* kūrẹ.
kurạmē *Vd.* kurmā ; kurmị.
kụrangạ *f.* (*pl.* kụrạngū = kụrạngī). (1) rope-ladder. (2) *Kt.* wooden ladder (= tsānị). (3) the twiner *Smilax Kraussiana.*
kụrạngẹ̄dū *m.* boggling ; lame excuses.
kūrar bāya *Vd.* kūrā 2.
kụrạrī *m.* intimidation (= bụrgā).
ƙurạrrajī pimples, etc. (*pl. of* ƙurjī *q.v.*).
ƙurasa A. (ƙụrāsạ) *Vb.* 2 (*p.o.* ƙụrāshē, *n.o.* ƙụrāshi) dipped out dregs of water from well or water-pot (= ƙwạrfatạ).
B. (ƙụrāsā) *Vd.* ƙurshẹ.
ƙurashe A. (ƙụrāshē) (1) *Vb.* 1C. (*a*) = ƙụrāsạ. (*b*) yā ⁓ shi he over-worked it (horse). (2) *Vd.* ƙurshẹ.
B. (ƙụrāshē) *Vd.* ƙụrāsạ.
kurạsū *Vd.* kurshẹ.
kurạtā *Vd.* kurtụ.
kurạtandū *m.* small hide container for antimony (tōzạlī) = tandū 5. (2) in rạ̄kuminkạ yā ɓatạ, nẹ̄mạ shi har cikiŋ ⁓ if you lose T. seek it high and low !
kurawa A. (kūrạ̄wā) *Vd.* kūrị.
B. (Kurāwạ) *epithet of* any Sarkin yāƙị.
kūrạ̄yē *Vd.* kūrā.
kụrɓā (1) *Vb.* 2 sipped *x* yā kụrɓē shị he sipped it. bạri dǎi ŋ ⁓, lūdạyī ukụ let me sip three ladlefuls. (2) *f.* a sip.
ƙurbạ̄bẹ *m.* (*f.* ƙurbābịyā). (1) small P. (2) *adj.* of small area.
kurcīcī (1) yanạ̄ dạ cikị ⁓ he's pot-bellied (= tirtsītsī). (2) dāƙị ⁓ very small round hut (kagọ).
kurcīyā *f.* (*pl.* kurcīyōyī = kurtạttakī). (1) (*a*) Senegal Blue-winged Dove (*Stigmatopelia senegalensis*). (*b*) Vinaceous Turtle-dove (*Streptopelia semitorquata*) (*b* = wālā 1*b*). (*c*) (i) an yi masạ ⁓ charm (lāyạ) has been tied to dove's leg, with aim that one's enemy may be caused to follow it and go away.

(ii) yā yi kạmar wạndạ akạ yi wạ ~ he has vanished. (d) yā nūnạ ~ bạkā he gave P. hint of the inner state of affairs. (e) dạ ~ dạ ạbūyạ, t̄āre su kạn jē k̄ōtō they are friends, like David and Jonathan. (f) ~ mai ɖạmarạ Shelley's Mourning-dove (Streptopelia decipiens shelleyi). (g) kurcīyar jēj̣i Rose-grey Turtle-dove (Streptopelia roseogrisea). (h) kurcīyar dụddurụ (i) Black-billed Wood-dove (Turtur abyssinica delicatula). (ii) when alluding to P. who is a hypocrite, A says kurcīyar dụddurụ cē to which B concurring, replies mụnạ̄fuffuk. (j) barịŋ kurcīyar gij̣i k̄ōshin nāmạ if P. lets a chance slip, he has " better fish to fry ". (k) bạ̄ saurạŋ kụkụru kukụ, arnẹ yā kāmạ ~ that's the end of the matter. (l) kurt̄att̄akī fạɖạn dụddugā Kt. epithet of rivalry. (m) nōnạŋ ~ Vd. nōnọ 1l. (n) Vd. bambamī 2. (2) large spool of cotton-thread, but smaller than matārī. (3) pommel, etc., of saddle (= kwaccīyā q.v.). (4) rạ̄k̄umī yā fid dạ ~ the male camel on heat protruded red gland from mouth (= wutā 6).

kurɖ̣a Vb. 3A (1) made a detour. (2) (a) yā ~ he sought his aim in a roundabout way, by devious means. (b) he made devious excuses. (3) yā ~ ta k̄ōfạ, ya fịta he squeezed his way out through the door (cf. kụrɖ̄ē).

k̄ur dạ k̄ūnạ adv. and m. yā yi ~ yā fạɖạ masạ = ~ ya fạɖạ masạ he spoke out bluntly to him.

kụrdānị m. large kerchief used for carrying food in.

kụrɖ̄ē m. (1) by-way (= kusfā 1). (2) making a detour. (3) seeking one's aim deviously x yā jē Sarkī ta ~. (4) yā fịta ta ~ he went out by the back door (= k̄ōfạr bạ̄i q.v. under bạ̄i 2a.ii). (5) making devious excuses. (6) squeezing through narrow place (cf. kurɖ̣a, kurɖ̣ị).

kurɖi A. (kurɖ̣ị) m. (1) = kụrɖ̄ē 1. (2) screened off portion of compound (= magēwayī). B. (kurɖī) = kudī.

kurɖị-kurɖ̣ị = kusfā 4.

k̄urdumụs = Kt. k̄urdumụ m. (1) (a) fowl-lice. (b) ~ yā kāmạ k̄āj̣ī the deadly disease so called, due to fowl-lice, has attacked the poultry. (2) an yi masạ ~ he's been cheated of his all.

kure A. (kūrẹ) m. (1) (a) male hyena (Vd. kūrā, ambụlī). (b) Kūrẹ = Kūrạm Bạ̄dau = Kūrạn shānū epithet of any Ṣarkim pāwạ. (2) farịŋ ~ mai rērọ type of children's game. (3) gọ̄shiŋ ~ type of coiffure. (4) darạŋ ~ Vd. darē 10. (5) gạ̄garạ ~ Vd. gạ̄garạ 10. B. (kurẹ) m. (pl. kụrạ̄kụrai) mistake (= kuskurẹ).

k̄urẹ (1) Vb. 3A. (a) is (was) constricted x (i) lōkạcī yā ~ there is little time left. wurī yā ~ the place is constricted. (ii) sunạ̄ sọ sụ yī, wurī yā ~ they wanted to do it, but it was too hard for them. (iii) ɖ̄ārī yā ~ masạ the cold is too much for him. (iv) wurī yā ~ mini I'm at my wits' ends, I've found no way out of doing T. which I don't want to do. (b) rāmịŋ k̄aryā k̄urarrē nẹ̄ a lie is soon detected. (c) arrived at limit or at destination x jirgī yā ~ the train has reached its destination (= gulẹ 1). (d) Vd. magaryā 2. (2) Vb. 1A. (a) cornered P. x aŋ ~ masạ he is cornered, " floored." (b) yā ~ aikịnsạ he completed his work. (c) reached limit of x (i) yā ~ mālamịnsạ he has learned all his master has to teach him. (ii) rāmịŋ k̄aryā bạ̄ shi dạ wụyar k̄urē̄wā = 1b above. (iii) yā ~ rēshẹ, wạ̄ zai bā shị tsānị he's got into a fix by his own fault, let him find a way out! (iv) Vd. mụtụm 9g. (3) Vd. k̄urē̄wā.

kụrē̄cī m. ringworm (= mạkērọ), cf. kyạsfī, mawaŋkī 2.

kụrēgē m. (pl. kụrē̄gū). (1) groundsquirrel (= bụzại 1), Vd. Dōzạ. (2) ganịŋ watạŋ ~ person's trying to draw child's heel round its neck. (3) cīzạŋ ~ Vd. cīzọ 3. (4) ạnnạshụ̄war ~ f. false air of benevolence in miser.

kụrēgēgẹ Kt. m. lame excuses (= kusạssarī).

k̄urē̄wā (v.n. of k̄urẹ) f. extremity x yanạ̄ caŋ k̄urē̄war gạrī it's at the extremity of the town.

kurfai m. (1) wādaŋ ∾ = kurfaŋ wādā knee-boots for riding. (2) kurfai = 1 with leather extension up to waist, for riding (cf. sufādu, sāfā). (3) kurfaŋ wādā nĕ it's too big for lad and too small for man (= wādā 2).

kurfa-kurfa = kusfā 4.

kurfi A. (kurfī = Kt. kurfi) m. (pl. kurāfū). (1) (a) lair of wild animal. (b) (said playfully) zaŋ kōma kurfīna I'll be off home ! (= shĕkā 3b). (2) (not Kt. ; Vd. B) hole in ground where mat-makers work (cf. tĕri).
    B. (kurfī) Kt. m. hole in ground where mat-makers work (= Kt. gēfĕ 4), cf. kurfī 2.
    C. (kurfī) m. (1) type of small chisel. (2) Kurfī dātsau epithet of evil P.

kurfi-kurfi = kurfi-kurfi = kusfā 4 q.v.

kurfō m. (pl. kurāfē). (1) any whip, including būlālą or kwaraŋgwamā. (2) būlālą mai ∾ bīyū whip with two thongs (kunnē). (3) whipping x an yi masą ∾ he's been whipped. an yi masą ∾ gōmą he's been given 10 strokes. (4) row of beads in necklace x dūwatsū ∾ gōmą 10 rows (igīyą 8A.i) of beads.

kurgā f. infantile diarrhœa (= bayammā 3). (2) working by night (= hīrā 4).

kurguŋgumā f. (1) type of beetle feigning death when touched (= Kt. mącĕ 27). (2) Vd. kulą kăi.

kurhō = kurfō.

kuri A. (kūri) m. (pl. kūrāwā). (1) man in training to become mālamī (so P. addressed as Mālam ! often modestly replies kūri) ; cf. gardi. (2) Vd. tōzō 1b.
    B. (kūrī) m. bluster (= burgā).
    C. (kurī) m. (1) circle used to mark every tenth verse (āyą) of Koran, i.e. 10th, 20th, 30th, etc. = ashar 1 (cf. kumsą). (2) multicoloured cap or turban worn by P. who has done pilgrimage (haji) = makāwuyą.

kuri A. (kurī) (1) Vd. kuryą. (2) ɗaŋ ∾ m. (a) little finger (= autā 3). (b) 'yar ∾ Kt. = kwantą kurī. (3) 'yaŋ ∾ pl. two superimposed rings worn on the little finger.
    B. (kuri) adv. idąnsą ∾, kō kunyą bā

yā ji he's brazen, etc. (= kirī 2. 3, 4 q.v.).

kuri'ą Ar. f. (1) divination. *(2) casting lots in lottery (cf. guri'ą).

kurigą = 'yar kurigą f. small Gwari hoe made by Kuriga people.

kurigą or ta ∾ Kt. f. Bambarra groundnut = gujīyā q.v. (Vd. kōkō).

kuri-kuri A. (ku'ri-kurī[n]) Kt. m. small beetle attacking calabashes.
    B. (kuri-kuri) (1) m. shortness x yārinyą ∾ dą ita = 'yar ∾ short girl. 'yan yārä- ∾ dą sü = 'yaŋ ∾ short children. (2) adv. yanā tąfīyą ∾ he (short P.) is moving along briskly.

kuri-kuri A. (kurī-kurī). (1) x idąnsą ∾, kō kunyą bā yā ji he's brazen = kirī q.v. (2) = kurū-kurū 3.
    B. (kurī-kurī) Kt. m. Cassia absus = fidilī (but Dalziel gives this as Bauhinia Thonningii, both being Cæsalpinaceæ) = kurū-kurū.

kurillą f. (1) stinginess. (2) inquisitiveness.

kurimī used in shā kurimiŋką shut up !

kuriŋgą Sk., Kt. ladder (= kuraŋgą q.v.).

kuriŋgĕdū Kt. m. lame excuses (= kuraŋgĕdū).

kurīridą f. lame excuses ; boggling (= kusąssarī).

kurirribī = kururrubī.

kurirrīcī m. striving hard.

kuritau m. shamelessness.

kurjī m. (pl. kurąrrajī = kurājē). (1) (a) pimple, pustule, boil, abscess (cf. mārūru). (b) gā kurjī yā fitō ą bākim mawākīyā he's at a loss what to say. (2) kurąrrajiŋ gumī sum fēsō mini I've prickly-heat. (3) dăidăi rūwā, dăidăi ∾ everyone acts according to his ability = dăidăi ∾, dăidăi rūwansą. (4) kurjim birnī syphilis (= tunjērē).

kurkīyā Sk. f. unmarried girl of marriageable age (= budurwā).

kurkudu m. sandhopper (= rākumī 8).

kurkuku = kurkuku m. (1) (a) Native Administration prison. yā yi kurkuku watą shidą he was imprisoned for 6 months. (b) ɗaŋ ∾ m. (f. 'yar ∾) pl. 'yaŋ ∾ N.A. prisoner (cf. jārum). (2) cf. tsūtsą 3.

kurkullā Vd. tąmalmąlā.

kurkunū m. (1) guinea-worm (epithet is Girgą, bą jaŋ sau). (2) gēmuŋ ∾ m.

first part of guinea-worm to extrude.
(3) *Vd.* **kurman 2** ; **mạriŋ** ∼ ; **gịr-**
gǎmō. (4) **bǒriŋ kµrkunū** *Vd.* **bǒrī 8.**

kur-kur *Vd.* **kµrwā 3***a, b* ; **kur kµrwātạ.**

ƙur-ƙur *m.* shortness *x* **ɗaŋ gạjērē nē** ∼ **dạ**
shī he's short (*pl.* **'yaŋ gạjērū nē ƙur-**
ƙur ƙur-ƙur dạ sū).

kurkµrā *Vb.* 1C. (1) (*a*) **yā kurkµrạ bậkī**
he rinsed out his mouth. **yā kurkµrạ**
māgạnī ạ̣ bakạ he rinsed his mouth out
with medicine. (*b*) *Vd.* **azµmī 2.** (2) =
kuskµrā.

ƙurƙurā *f.* the type of guinea-corn called
lạ̌tị̄yā.

kurkure A. (**kurkµrē**) *Vb.* 1C = **kurkµrā 1.**
    B. (**kurkurẹ**) = **kuskurẹ.**

ƙµrƙµrē *m.* (1) cutting short grass. (2) (*a*)
pilfering. (*b*) **ɗaŋ** ∼ *m.* pilferer.

kur kµrwātạ (1) *used in* **kur kµrwātạ,**
nāmạna dạ dācī *said by boys to ward*
off dung-beetle (**būzūzµ**). (2) *Vd.*
kµrwā 3.

kurkusa (1) *prep.* **yanậ** ∼ **dạ Kanọ** it's
near Kano. (2) *m.* **yā yi** ∼ it's very
near (*cf.* **kusa**).

kurkushē *m.* irritating disease of feet or
hands in wet-season (= **ƙushậƙushī**).

kurkutsa A. (**kµrkūtsạ**) *Vb.* 2. (1) **yā**
kµrkµtsē nị dạ zāgị he abused me. (2)
yā kµrkµtsi dōkịnsạ he spurred on his
horse (*cf.* **kǔtsā**).
    B. (**kurkūtsā**) *Vb.* 1C (*with dative*)
yā ∼ **minị zāgị** = **kµrkūtsạ 1.**

kurkutu A. (**kµrkutµ**) *Kt.* = **kµrkudµ.**
    B. (**kurkutū**). (1) *m.* the drum **kun-**
tukurū. (2) **ɗaŋ** ∼ small *x* **ɗaŋ kur-**
kutun dākị tiny house. **ɗaŋ kurkutuŋ**
gidā tiny compound. **ɗaŋ kurkutun**
rāmị small hole in ground. (3) *Vd.*
ɗauriŋ ∼.

kµrkµzau *m.* (1) eczema on cow (= **kircī**
1). (2) mange on dog or donkey.

kurma A. (**ƙurmā**) *m., f.* (*pl.* **kurậmē** =
kurmāyē). (1) deaf (*Vd.* **dạkamạ**). (2)
P. with no tribal marks (**askā**) on face.
(3) *Vd.* **kurman** *compounds.*
    B. (**kurmạ**) *Vb.* 1A did abundantly
(= **kwarmạ** *q.v.*).

ƙurma A. (**ƙurmā**) *f.* (1) thicket (= **sar-**
ƙaƙƙīyā). (2) **an dǒkē shị har jinī ya yi**
masạ ∼ he was beaten so hard that
bump was raised.

    B. (**ƙµrmā**) (1) *Vb.* 2 bit (= **cị̄zā**). (2)
f. a bite.

kurmājẹ *Kt. m.* two small tribal-lines cut
on temples of **Rūmāwā, Yaruβāwā** and
Alibāwā Filani clans of *Kt.* and *Sk.*

kurmạncē *Vb.* 3A became deaf.

kurman (*genitive of* **kurmā**). (1) ∼ **hạŋ-**
kākạ P. who talks so much himself
that he never listens to objections of
others (*epithet is* **anậ tsāwā, yanậ saµkā**)
(2) ∼ **kµrkunū** guineaworm-swelling
without blister preceding extrusion of
worm (**hạŋgarā**). (3) *Vd.* **kyaŋkyandī ;**
lāyạ 1*c* ; **rµmbū 1***e.* (4) ∼ **rūwā**
Vd. **rūwā** A.16. (5) (*a*) ∼ **wurị** unbored cowrie. (*b*) ∼ **zōbẹ** ring with no
join (**magamī**) in it.

Kµrmānµ *m.* (*sg., pl.*) Kroo-boy.

kµrmậwā servants of **Saŋ kurmị** (*pl. of*
bạkurmẹ).

kurmậyē *Vd.* **kurmā.**

kurmē *m.* (1) (*a*) **yậrā sun tạfī** ∼ children
are playing in water. (*b*) **ɗan** ∼ *m.*
boy playing in water. (2) **rūwạn dạ**
ya isa kurmē, dạ fādậwā cikinsạ an
sanị one learns by experience.

ƙurmẹ *Vb.* 1A lopped *x* **aŋ** ∼ **kạn dāwạ** =
gillẹ.

kurmị *m.* (*pl.* **kurậmē** = **kurậmū** =
kurậmā). (1) (*a*) thickly-wooded gully.
(*b*) thickly-wooded country (*cf.*
duhūwạ). (*c*) **itậcē dayā bā yā** ∼ *Vd.*
itậcē 1*d.* (*d*) *Vd.* **wāwaŋ kurmị.** (2)
yā tạfī ∼ he's gone to Southern Provinces to bring back things (*x* kolas)
to sell (*cf.* **Dạndī**). (3) **Kurmị** (*a*) =
Saŋ kurmị *q.v. under* **san 2***b.* (*b*) Native
Administration warder in charge of
District prison. (*c*) *Kt.* Market-head
(= **Sarkin kạsūwā**).

ƙurmus (1) **yā ƙōnẹ** ∼ it's completely
burnt up (= **mµrƙus**). (2) **dạ shī, dạ**
dōkịnsạ sum fādị ∼ (= **sun yi** ∼) he
and his horse fell headlong.

ƙurmµsā *Vb.* 1C. (1) **yā** ∼ **su cikinsạ**
he stuffed them into it (= **murƙµsā**).
(2) **aŋ** ∼ **ta** immature girl has been
married off.

ƙurmµshē = **murƙµshē** *Vb.* 1C. (1) (*a*)
threw P. down (= **kā dạ**). (*b*) weighed
down *x* **kạbēwạ tā ƙurmµshẹ dāki**
heavy pumpkin caused roof to sink in

(2) x ịndạ ya ∽ where he forced his way in (Vd. ụŋgūwā 3).

ırmusū m. (1) niggardliness. (2) yā yi minị ạdạ'ar ∽ he behaved ungratefully to me. (3) Vd. gạndā.

ụrmutsạ Vb. 2 = ƙurmụshē 1b.

ırmụ̄wā f. (1) yanạ̄ ∽ dạ kantụ ạ kā he's presumptuous (= izgilī). (2) Kt. = kurmē.

ırnạ f. (1) (a) the thorny tree Zizyphus Spina-Christi (Vd. kandīɗạ). (b) kurnạn Nạsārā = kurnạm Masạr tree Melia Azedarach. (c) kō dạ girgizạ, ∽ tā fi magaryā the one's far superior to the other. (d) gudụ̣n ∽ dumplings of wheat-flour, of bean-flour, or of millet-bran. (2) ∽ maị zụbā garrulous P. (3) yā ci ∽ he was put to shame (said by women or children).

ırnū m. (1) insect-pest of gourds. (2) stunted P. (3) hard lump of fūrā.

ırr Vd. ƙurạ.

ụrrā Vd. ƙūrụ.

ırsạ f. the paper called ɗạba'ạ.

ırsā-ƙụrsạ̄ Vd. ƙursumēmẹ.

ırshẹ = Kt. kurshẹ m. (pl. ƙurạ̄sā = Kt. kurạ̄sū). (1) ƙurshạŋ igīyạ hank of thatching-rope made of kabạ. (2) ƙurshạn cịyāwạ̄ small bundle of grass cut in wet-season for chopping with kurạ̄dā-hatchet and making into dạ̄tsē-fodder for horse or cattle (cf. ƙụndụ-mācạ). (3) Kt. kurshạm masạrā small bundle of maize-cobs. (4) kurshạŋ harāwạ bundle of bean-leaves made like a mat (anạ̄ nadẹ harāwạr wākē) after gathering in the crop (rōrọ) ; the stems are taken 5 by 5. (5) ƙurshạŋ gyạdā bundle of ground-nut leaves (after the leaves (harāwạr gyạdā) are plucked off (tsịŋkā), they are evened up and tied together).

ırsumēmẹ = ƙursumī m. (f. ƙur-sumēmīyā = ƙursumā) pl. ƙursā-ƙụrsạ̄ huge.

ụrsụnsụ̣n used in (1) ƙụrsụnsụ̣n dạ kai, ạ gọ̄yẹ kạ ? fancy a big child like you expecting still to be carried on your mother's back ! (2) ∽ kā shịga minị dạ̣kị ? fancy you bursting in on me thus ! (= ƙọ̄sọ̄sọ).

:urtạ Vb. 1A marked out ground with

---

magirbī-tool for building tsạŋgayạ-hut, after making circle on ground (Vd. shātạ).

kurtạttakī doves (pl. of kurcīyā).

kurtsītsī smallness (= kurcīcī q.v.).

kurtu A. (kụrtū) m. (pl. kurtunạ). (1) (a) round gourd as receptacle for milk, seed, shūnī-indigo, honey, etc. (b) kụrtun tạwadạ gourd used for ink-pot (cf. tukunyā 1h). (c) (i) ∽ bīyū gạrēshị : gạ̄ na zumạ, gạ̄ na madạ̄cī = kụrtun zumạ gamị dạ madạ̄cī what a capricious P. ! (ii) Vd. zumạ 1b. (2) kirạŋ ∽ m. getting P. to return to place by magic (cf. kirạnyē). (3) kạn dạ bạ̄ idạ̄nū, ∽ nẹ̄ of what use is a blind man like you ! (4) kụrtun cikị gạrēshị he's pot-bellied. (5) ạbin nạŋ shī kaɗ̃ai nẹ̄ ạ wurīna, rạ̃ina ∽ I can't part with this, as it's the only one I've got (Vd. rạ̃i 1o).

B. (kurtụ) Eng. m. (pl. kurạ̄tā) recruit to army, etc.

kụrtuf x mīyạ tā yi ∽ the soup's thick (= kịrtif q.v.).

kurtuka A. (kurtụkā) Vb. 1C = kuntụkā.

B. (kurtukā) Vd. kurtukēkẹ.

kurtukēkẹ = kurtukī m. (f. kurtukēkīyā = kurtukā) pl. kurtukai-kụrtụkai stout (re stick, etc.).

kurtunạ Vd. kụrtū.

kụrtup = kụrtuf.

kuru A. (kūrụ) m. (pl. kūwạ̄rū) narrow Maguzawa drum tapped with fingers.

B. *(kụru) used in kā ∽ you had a narrow escape !

C. (kurụ) Vd. tạbạ̄ ∽.

D. (kụrū) Vd. sạkatạ 2c.

ƙuru A. (ƙūrụ) m. (f. ƙūrụ̄wā) pl. ƙūrunạ = ƙụrrā = ƙūwạ̄rū. (1) (a) (i) pony. (ii) ạ sai dạ ƙūrụ ạ yi wạ iŋgarmạ kāyā one P. has been deprived of his share to give it to a favourite. (b) (i) tāshịŋ ∽ = gudụ̣n ∽ making good start, then tailing off (= būbūƙụ̄wā 2). (ii) kadạ dạ̃i iŋgarmạ yạ rēnạ gudụ̣n ƙūrụ never despise a weak P., you may need him some day ! (iii) banzạ̄ gudụ̣n ƙūrụ, bạ zaị ƙētạrẹ hụ̄ɗā ba he thinks himself cleverer than he is. (2) ƙūrụ = gindịŋ ƙūrụ (a) useless, thick end of rạkē or tạkạndā-sugar-cane (= ƙụndu-gụrū q.v.). (b) gindịŋ ƙūrụ = ƙūrụ̄wā.

(c) *Sk.* gịndiŋ ƙūrụ maize-cob with few remaining grains given to child. (3) ƙūrụm bāƙī being afraid to make known one's real wishes from fear or foolishness (= ƙwaurọ 2). (4) ∼ dạ lifịdī much soup (mīyạ) with but little tūwō in time of dearth (= lifịdī 2c). (5) *Vd.* mutūwạ 1h.
B. (ƙụrū) *m.* (1) reckless courage (= kạsadạ). (2) *Vd.* ƙurū-ƙụrụ̄ 1. (3) dạ ƙụrū gạdā tā yi sūnā fancy his being able to do that !

ƙụrụ̄cīyā = *Kt.* ƙụrụccīyā *f.* (1) youthfulness (*epithet is* ƙụrụ̄cī (= ƙurūcẹ) daŋgịŋ haụkā). (2) mutūwạr ∼ *f.* dying young. (3) ƙụrụ̄cīyar ɓērā pilfering (= sạ̄nē). (4) ƙụrụ̄cīyar ụŋgụlū slap-dashness of youth.

ƙụrụffai *Kt.* = ƙụrfai.

kurū-ƙụrụ̄ *m.* tying sack (bụhū) or hide bag (taiƙị) on to mule, donkey, or pack-ox (tạkarkạrī) after disposing of contents.

ƙuru-ƙuru A. (ƙụrū-ƙụrū) *m.* the *Cassia* ƙụrī-ƙụrī *q.v.*
B. (ƙurū-ƙụrụ̄) (1) dạ ƙụrū a kạn ci ∼ persistence pays. (2) = ƙurī-ƙụrị. (3) clearly *x* anā ganinsạ ∼ : yā zō, yā ɗaukạ he took it openly. yā fạdi gạskīyā ∼ he told the whole truth.

ƙụrullạ *f.* (1) stinginess. (2) inquisitiveness.

kurum A. (kurụm) (1) *f.* (a) silence (= shirū = kawaị 2). (b) yi ∼ = *Kt.* shā kurụmiŋkạ shut up ! (c) ∼ mā mạganạ cē silence gives consent. (d) ∼ tā gamshē kạ = ∼ tā rabạ ka dạ kōwā *Vd.* dattịjọ 1a. (e) kurụm tā gamshē kạ dạ kōwā *Vd.* damō 4b. (2) (a) (*following the word to be emphasized*) only *x* (i) ukụ ∼ three only. dōkị mẹtaŋ ∼ sukạ rasạ they lost only 200 horsemen in the battle (*cf.* 2c *below*) = kaɗăi. (ii) barịm bāƙī ∼ shī ya kāwō jịn yuŋwạ cause and effect ! (b) (*following verb to be emphasized merely x* yā tạmbạyē nị ∼ he merely asked me. (c) (*following the word to be emphasized*) merely in regard to, apart from other things *x* dōkị ∼ sun rasạ mẹtaŋ they lost 200 in the battle, in cavalry alone (*cf.* 2a). (3) suddenly

x ∼ sǎi mukạ gan sụ we suddenl caught sight of them. (4) motionlessl *x* tsạya ∼ stand still ! (5) silently *x* (∼ mun zaunạ ∼ we remained silent. (∼ mụtụm ∼ mūgụ nē a silent P. is ofte meditating deceit.
B. (kurum) (1) very *x* ƙạŋƙanẹ nē ∼ it's very small. (2) (*negatively*) not a all *x* bạn ji ba ∼ I don't unde̱ stand at all. ∼ kurum bābụ there' none at all.

ƙụrumbạsallīyā = ƙụrumbạshallīyā reckless courage (= kạsadạ).

kụrumbọ *m.* (1) gourd-vessel deeper tha̱ kumbọ *q.v.* (*used as corn-measure, etc.* (2) solid clog, *i.e.* with no side-holes suc as ɗạŋgạrfai has. (3) cycle gear-cas̱ǫ

kurụmcē = kurụncē.

kurụmī *used in Kt.* shā kurụmiŋkạ shu up ! (= kurụm 1b).

kụrụm-kurum *Vd.* kụrụŋ-kuruŋ.

kụrumtạ = kụruntạ.

kurun *Vd.* kurum.

ƙūrunạ *Vd.* ƙūrụ.

ƙūrụn bāƙī *Vd.* ƙūrụ 3.

kurụncē *Vb.* 3A (1) became deaf. (2 turned deaf ear to entreaty, etc. (3 yā ∼ he (expert, horse), etc., has los skill (= taurī 1e.ii).

kurunci *m.* deafness.

ƙụrụngē *Vd.* jēmāgẹ 10.

ƙụrụŋgụ *m.* (1) spotted synodont catfis̱ (*Synodontis batensoda*). (2) Ƙụrụŋgụ dạmạ dạddawā dạ kā what a big-heade̱ǫ fool !

ƙụrụŋgus = ƙụrụŋƙus.

kụrụŋ-kuruŋ *m.* meddlesomeness.

ƙụrụŋƙus (1) ∼ kạn ɗam ɓērā = ∼ kạ̱ kūsụ here ends the fable ! (*so, abbreviate̱ǫ into* ƙụrụŋƙus " that's the end of tẖ matter ! " ; *Vd.* kyaŋ-kyạ̄ŋ-kyaŋ). (2 completely *x* yā ƙārẹ ∼ it's quiṯ finished.

ƙụrụŋƙusai *m.* natural lumps of dry cla̱y lying in place.

ƙụrụŋƙushēwā *f.* the shrub *Gymnospori̱ senegalensis.*

ƙụrụŋƙushīyā *Kt. f.* = ƙụrụŋƙushēwā.

kurunta A. (kụruntạ) *Vb.* 3B = kurụncē
B. (kuruntạ) *f.* deafness.

ƙụrunzūzūwạ *f.* boil on the knee (= fit sārī 10).

kururrubạ *Vb.* 1D kept on sipping (*int. from* kurɓā).

ɓ̣ururrubai *m.* shallow water-holes in banks of large-stream (ɓ̣ōramạ), *etc.* =kwīyạkā = *Kt.* hụdag gizọ.

ḳururrubī *used in* kō kā shā kururrubī dạ ɓ̣ūnạ ? kạ̄ yi hạ̄ḳạ ? you'd never manage it " in a month of Sundays ".

ɓ̣urrurrụ̄cī *m.* striving hard.

kururrumī *m.* (*f.* kurrurrumā) *pl.* kururrụmai. (1) (*a*) broken-necked *x* kururrumin tụ̄lū broken-necked ewer. kururrumar tukunyā broken-necked pot =*Sk.* gaŋgambū (*cf.* kạtaŋgạ). (*b*) kururrumin rāmị deep hole in ground (= fạ̄fuŋgạ *q.v.*). (*c*) kururrumim bạ̄kī toothless mouth. (2) ～ bā yạ̄ rasạ kaskwan rufị ugly or deformed P. will even so get wife or husband.

kururu A. (kụrūrụ) *m.* (1) crop of bird, etc. (= bạrōrọ *q.v.*). (2) longitudinal (ạ tsạye) lining of sạ̄cē-gown (*cf.* ạlgabbạ).
B. (kụrurụ) abundantly *x* (1) yanạ̄ mạganạ ～ he's chattering. (2) yanạ̄ cịnikī ～ buyer pretended to be eager to buy, but in reality only wasted the seller's time.

ɓ̣ururū *m.* (1) Scops Owl (*Otus senegalensis*). (2) Abyssinian Spotted Eagle-owl (*Bubo africanus cinerascens*).

ɓ̣ụrūrụ̄cī *m.* striving hard.

kụrūrụ̄rụ̄ (1) come and look ! (2) hear ! (3) help !

kurūrụ̄tā *Vb.* 1D exaggerated (= zagaigạitā).

kụrūrūwạ *f.* (1) shouting to call attention *x* yā bugạ musụ ～ he shouted to them (= īhụ 1*a*), *cf.* sōwạ. (2) anạ̄ kụrūrūwạr Iblịs it's a lying rumour.

kurus *used in* ～ sǎi ya shịga he (it) suddenly entered.

ɓ̣urus *m.* (1) sound of crunching. (2) ɓ̣ashiŋ ～ gạrēshị he is persistently unlucky (= ɓ̣ashim mundịrīɓ̣i).

kuruskubạ *f.* the okro called kuncịŋ ạkwīyạ *q.v.*

ɓ̣urus-ɓ̣urus = ɓ̣urus.

ɓ̣uruwa A. (ɓ̣ūrūwā) *used in* hụ̄lā tā yi ～ the two edges of the cap are uneven and need trimming (= ɓ̣ūrụ 2*b*).
B. (ɓ̣ūrụ̄wā) *Vd.* ɓ̣ūrụ.

kụrwā *f.* (1) (*a*) (i) soul. (ii) kụrwā tasạ kur he is alive and kicking. (*b*) ghost *x* yā ji ～ he heard ghost (*N.B.*— *ghosts are not considered visible*). (2) bạ̄ shi dạ ～ he's out of sorts, worried. (*b*) gōnassạ bạ̄ ta dạ ～ banạ his youngcorn (yabanyạ) isn't thriving this year. (3) (*a*) kur-kur, kụrwātạ, kadạ kị ci ạbịn dạ bạn ci ba (i) what a fine smell, I'm only sorry I can't have any ! (ii) I certainly thought I noticed that sweet odour, but I must have been wrong ! (*b*) kur-kur kụrwātạ, nāmạna dạ ɗācī, bạ̄ ạ̄ cī nị ba = ɓ̣ishạ 2. (*c*) *Vd.* kur kụrwātạ. (3) type of small bat.

ɓ̣uryạ *f.* (1) (*a*) wall of house opposite door (= sāɓ̣ọ 2) *x* yā shigō ～ bạ̄ izịnī he penetrated into the house without a " by your leave ". (*b*) back of bed, *i.e.* near wall. ạ ～ = ạ ɓ̣urī at the wall-end of the bed (*cf.* bạ̄kiŋ gadō). (2) yā tsarẹ ～, yā tsarẹ bạ̄kiŋ gadō his knowledge is encyclopædic.

kuryā *f.* (1) (*a*) type of drum, beaten with kạlaŋgū, as war-challenge. (*b*) ～ nẹ̄, " kạɗa ạ mutụ ! " *epithet of* mischief-maker. (2) tukunyā tasạ tā yi rawar ～ (*a*) much meat has been cooked for him making rich gravy. (*b*) he's spent all his money on rich food or gambling. (3) *Sk., Kt.* the tree gurjīyā *q.v.*

kurzạ *Vb.* 1A dōkị yā ～ ni jịkim baŋgō horse scraped me against the wall (= kūjẹ 1*b*).

ɓ̣urzunā *f.* leprosy with small nodules (= bạkaɗānīyā 2), *Vd.* kuturtạ.

ɓ̣urzunū *m.* type of warty gourd.

ɓ̣us *m.* yā yi ～ he was silent from shame or fear (= mwī-mwī).

kusa A. (kusa) (1) *m.* (*a*) nearness *x* (i) yā yi ～ it's near. (ii) yanạ̄ ～ dạ Kanọ = yanạ̄ ～ gạ Kanọ it is near Kano. munạ̄ kusa dạ gạrī we're near the town now (= 2*a below*). (iii) yanạ̄ kusa-kusa dạ sū it is very near them. (iv) ɓ̣auyukạŋ ～ dạ gạrī the villages near the town. (v) waɗansu mutạ̄nē̄ ～ dạ gidansạ sukạ cẹ̄ then some persons who lived near his home, said . . . (vi) wani ɗaŋūwaŋkạ na ～ a close relative of yours. (vii) yā rasạ ạbịŋ kusa *Vd.* shịmfiɗạ 1*d*. (*b*) yā yi kusaŋ ƙārẹ̄wā it is nearly finished (*cf.* 1*d*). (*c*) kō kusa (*with negative*) not in the least *x* kō ∽, bạ̄ mū mukạ bā sụ ba *we* are far from having given them it. baị kai ba, kō ∽ (i) he's not nearly arrived there. (ii) it's far inferior to the other. (iii) he's far from being up to it. (*d*) kusan *adv.* almost *x* kusan rabịṇ ạbịn dạ yakẹ̄ sāmụ, akẹ̄ karƃẹ̄wā it is almost *half* his earnings that are taken in tax. kusaṇ kōwạnẹ darē nearly every night. kusam bạ̄ hanyạ there is hardly any road. kusam bạ̄ sauraṇ wani jirgī nạ̄ fatauci ạ bahạr hardly any ships trade at sea now. kusan sū kaɗǎi sukạ yī they were almost the only ones to do so. (*e*) *conj.* (*with subjunctive*) it is almost the case that *x* kusam mụ cẹ̄ one can almost say that . . . kusan tạ dạṇganci ƙasammụ wajan yanạyī it nearly corresponds with our country in climate. (2) *Vb.* approached *x* (*a*) muṇ ∽ dạ gạrī we are near the town (= 1*a*.ii *second example above*). (*b*) sallạ tā ∽ the Festival is near. (*c*) (*followed by v.n.*) almost *x* yā ∽ ƙārẹ̄wā it is nearly finished. aṇ ∽ kai shị caṇ it has almost been delivered there.

B. (kụ̄sā) *Vb.* 2 (*p.o.* kụ̄shẹ, *n.o.* kụ̄shi) *x* yā kụ̄shē nị he found fault with me (= kūshẹ).

C. (kūsā) *Vd.* kūsụ.

ƙūsạ *f.* (*pl.* ƙūsōshī). (1) (*a*) nail. (*b*) ∽ maị barīmạ screw. (2) ∽ māgạnim ɫamfarīyā = Jārụmī, ƙūsạr yāƙi what a brave man! (3) *x* (*a*) ƙūsōshiṇ gạrī chief persons of a town. (*b*) garịn naṇ, shī nẹ̄ bạbbar ƙūsạrmụ ạ gabạs that town is our pivotal position in the east.

kusaci A. (kụsạ̄ci) *Vd.* kụsātạ.

B. (kusācị) *m.* (1) nearness. (2) close relationship.

kụsailamā = kụsailamạ (*word used by women*) *f.* deceitfulness; mischief-making (*cf.* musạilamạ).

kusan *Vd.* kusa.

kusanta = kusata.

kūsanyạ *Vd.* kūsụ.

ƙūsạ̄sā short and thick-set (*pl. of* ƙụƙƙūsā).

ƙụsạ̄shī *m.* tā yi ∽ her breasts have begun to develop (= ƙịrgā 2*b q.v.*).

kusạssarī lame excuses (*pl. of* kusụrwā corner *q.v.*) = ƙōɗạ 5.

kusata A. (kụsātạ) *Vb.* 2 approached *x* yā kụsạ̄cē mụ = yā kusātō mụ he approached us. suṇ kụsạ̄ci gidā they've nearly reached home. nā kụsạ̄ci gamạ aikị I've nearly finished the work. sallạ tā kusātō the Festival's almost due.

B. (kụsātạ̄) *Vb.* 1C brought near *x* (*a*) ạ̄ddịnị ya kạṇ kusạntạ mụtụm gạ Ubạṇgijị religion brings a man near his God. (*b*) suṇ ∽ manạ gạrī dạ bakạ they pretended to us that the town was near.

kūsạ̄yē *Vd.* kūsụ.

kusfā *f.* = kusfī *m.* (1) (*a*) by-way (= kurdị). (*b*) wạcẹ kusfā ya yị where on earth's he gone? (2) gap made in fence for passage of persons. (3) yā yi ∽ " he made compliments ". yā cikạ ∽ " he makes compliments " (= fïlākọ). (4) yā saṇ gạrin naṇ kusfa-kusfa he knows all the ins and outs of this town. (5) ūwar ∽ = ụbaṇ kạurā *q.v. under* kạurā 3.

ƙushạ̄ƙushī = kushạ̄kushī Kt. *m.* an irritating disease of feet or hands in wet season (= kurkushē).

kushe A. (kūshẹ) *Vb.* 1A found fault with *x* yā ∽ minị he found fault with me. nā kai masạ, ya ∽ I took it to him but he found fault with it. wannạṇ rạkē, aṇ ∽ masạ zāƙinsạ they find fault with the lack of sweetness in this sugar-cane. yā ∽ ni wuriṇ Audụ he reported me to Audu.

B. (kụ̄shē) (1) *m.* fault-finding *x* an yi masạ ∽ they " picked holes in it " (= makalạ̄mā). (2) *Vd.* kụ̄sā; shạ̄ ∽; makūsā.

kụshēkarā Kt. *f.* tendon at back of the neck (= kạshēkarā).

kụshēwā *f.* (*pl.* kụshẹ̄yī). (1) grave. (2) gạ̄ kụshēwar Barkạ, gạ̄ ta kạransạ the two are inseparable like David and Jonathan. (3) an yi ∽, bạ̄ mụtụm *said when* P. makes ridiculous statement or acts ridiculously. (4) kụshēwar bạdi, săi bạɗi though some seem like cats with seven lives, it's because their time hasn't come. (5) *cf.* tạ̄kạ kụshẹ̄yī; girmaṇ kụshēwā.

kụshēyā = kụshēwā.

kụshi *Vd.* kụsā.

kushinā how ugly !

ƙụshịnīyā *f.* = ƙus-ƙus.

ƙushiŋ-ƙushiŋ *m.* rumours (= ƙishiŋ-ƙishiŋ *q.v.*).

kush-kụsh *Ar. m.* the food kus-kụs 2.

kụskụndā *f.* lame excuses (= kusạssarī).

kuskura A. (kụskurạ) (1) *Vb.* 2 missed P. or T. when shooting (*cf.* kuskụrē). (2) *Vb.* 3B. (*a*) escaped from danger or punishment (*also* kuskurō). (*b*) acted rashly *x* kadạ kạ ∼ kạ yi hakạ don't be so unwise as to act thus ! wạnda ya ∼ ya yi hakạ, ā yi masạ hukumci anyone foolish enough to act thus, will be charged before the court.

    B. (kuskụrā) *Vb.* 1C yā kuskụrạ bāƙī = kuskụrē 1*c*.

kuskure A. (kuskụrē) (1) *Vb.* 1C. (*a*) (i) nā ∼ shi I missed him (P. whom I wanted to find, etc.). (ii) made a mistake about *x* yā kuskụrę abin dạ kę gạ zukātammụ he mistook our intentions. (*b*) = kụskurạ 1. (*c*) yā kuskụrę bāƙī he rinsed out his mouth (= *Kt.* guŋgụmā). (2) *Vb.* 3A made a mistake.

    B. (kuskurę) *m.* (1) a miss in shooting. (2) mistake *x* (*a*) yā yi ∼ he made a mistake. (*b*) iŋ kā yi kuskurạŋ abụ kạɗaŋ if you make the smallest error. (*c*) yā fi kuskurę *Vd.* harbi 2*b*.

kus-kụs *m.* (1) white-patterned turban. (2) *Ar.* a wheaten food.

ƙus-ƙus *adv. and m.* talking in a sibilant whisper *x* nā jī sụ, sunā ∼ I heard them talking *thus*. sunā zạncē ∼ they're talking *thus*.

kụsōgōgọ *m.* yā yi minị ∼ he talked scandal about me.

ƙūsōshī nails (*pl. of* ƙūsạ *q.v.*).

kūsụ *Sk. m.* = kūsā. (*f.* kūsanyạ) *pl.* kūsāyē (1) (*a*) rat, mouse (= ɓērā). (*b*) ƙurụŋkus kaŋ ∼ *Vd.* ƙurụŋkus. (2) penis (*vulgar term*). (3) kūsụm bisạ squirrel (= ɓēram bisa). (4) kūsụŋ kyaurō *Sk.* type of rodent = gyazbī (*cf.* mafịcī). (6) *cf.* ūwar kūsā ; mạriŋ kūsụ ; gīwā 1*g* ; tsụgunniŋ kūsụ. (7) bạrēwar kūsā *Vd.* bạrēwā 3.

*kụsūfị *Ar. m.* eclipse of sun or moon (= darē 5 = ɓūyā 2*b* = zạzzạɓī 2 =

hụsūfị), *Vd.* mạshasshara 3, kậmu, kisfę.

kụsugụ *m.* (1) carelessly built hut for trivial guests (= kịcirọ). (2) burly P. (3) ugly T. or P.

kụsum *adv. and m.* (1) all, entirely *x* yā ɗạuki ∼ he took it all. yā ɗạukē sụ ∼ he took them all. (2) ∼ dạ gụdā akạ ajịyē masạ his (absent person's) share was put aside for him.

kụsumạ *Kt. f.* conceit.

ƙụsumbī *m.* lumbar spinal deformity (= ƙāzāzạ = ƙōzō 2*a*).

kụsụmbōɗị *m.* (1) game of jumping high and dropping down flat on one's buttocks. *(2) *epithet of* dolt.

kusumɓụdē *Vb.* 3A *Kt.* yā ∼ P., crops, etc., deteriorated.

kụsumburwạ *f.* (1) (*a*) self-sown guinea-corn (= magargạrā). (*b*) guinea-corn spoilt before maturity. (*c*) the corn-stalk flute sịrīƙi. (2) *epithet of* unmarried girl, no longer virgin (*cf.* bụdurwā 2).

kụsuŋkụsumī *m.* intact (gụdantạ) body of goat or sheep, skinned and head cut off and entrails ('yan cikị) removed (*cf.* gāwā ; kạɓakī).

kụsunnīyā *f.* fidgetiness, restlessness (= mụtsụnīyā).

kusurī *Sk. m.* dark corner, hidden place (= luŋgụ).

kusurū *Kt. adv.* yā sậmē shị ∼ he got it easily.

kụsụrwā *f.* (*pl.* kusurwōyī = kusạssarī). (1) (*a*) (i) corner. (ii) yā karyạ ∼ he turned the corner (= yi kwanạ). (*b*) angle. (*c*) kusụrwar arēwā dạ gabạs = kusụrwar arēwā masọ gabạs = kusụrwar arēwā tasọ gabạs the north-east. (*d*) (i) ∼ huɗū the four points of the compass. (ii) mun nēmē shị ∼ huɗū, bạ mụ sậmē shị ba we looked for him high and low, but vainly. (*e*) kusụrwar daŋgā (= *Kt.* kusụrwar dạrnī) mai ƙamar mụtum P. seeming honourable, but not so. (*f*) kusụrwar hannū elbow. (2) (*a*) yā cikạ ∼ he's deceitful. (*b*) kadạ kạ yi minị ∼ don't deceive me ! (*c*) kusạssarī lame excuses (= ƙōfạ 5 = rạrraunā 2*b*).

kụsussurī *Kt. m.* = kusụrwā 2*c*.

kụsūsụ (1) *m.* (*a*) second crop of indigo,

okro, henna, or pepper got by reaping
crop and leaving stump to re-sprout *x*
ƙusūsuŋ saƒẹ 2nd crop of indigo
(*Vd.* saƒẹ ; ƙutūtu 5*b*). (*b*) ƙusūsuŋ
gwarzō second crop of indigo in plant's
first season (*cf.* gwarzō). (2) ƙusūsu
m. (*f.* ƙusūsūwā) hypocrite.
ƙut *x* Audu ạbōkinsạ nē ~ Audu's his
close friend (= ƙuƙut *q.v.*).
kutạ *Vb.* 1A (1) (*a*) yā ~ igīyạ he spliced
a rope (= hayạ 1*d*). (*b*) yā ~ dạrạmbūwā he spliced grass to make the
armlet dạrạmbūwā. (*c*) yā ~ hancịn
tạrnaƙī he spliced the hobbling rope,
making loop at each end (*v.n. of*
1 *is* kucị). (2) *Kt.* yā ~ kibīyạ he
fitted arrow to bow-string, to shoot
(= ɗanạ = haɗạ 1*l* = haƙạ). (3) yā ~
izgā (ūlu) he spliced giraffe-hair (wool)
to make woman's neck-ornament (tạl-
hātạnā-stone *sometimes being added*).
(4) aŋ ~ mạƙā strip of leather's been
added inside of archer's thumb-ring
to make it fit finger (= kucị 3). (5)
suŋ ~ gạ̄bā tsạkāninsu they've begun
quarrelling. (6) (*a*) yā ~ ƙaryā he
concocted a lie. (= sāƙạ 1*b*.ii). (*b*)
yā ~ kinibībị he has caused dissension.
(*c*) yā ~ mutạ̄nē su yi bọrē he incited
the people to rebellion. (7) aŋ ~ masạ
mạganạ he's been prompted to tell
lying story (*cf.* magantad dạ). (8)
aŋ ~ masạ ƙaryā he's been maligned.
ƙuta A. (ƙutā) *Vb.* 2 (*p.o.* ƙucē, *n.o.*
ƙucị) *Sk.* broke off bit of *x* yā ƙucị
furā he broke off a bit of furā (=
gutsurạ).
    B. (ƙutạ) *Vb.* 3A made click indi-
cating annoyance (= ƙwạƒā).
kutạ̄kē *Vd.* kutukī.
ƙūtạmā *f.* an yi masạ ~ loss has been
inflicted on him (by theft, dismissal,
or dirty trick).
ƙutaŋ *adv.* (1) = ƙut. (2) plainly *x*
gạ̄ shi ạ sararī ~ there it is plainly
visible. ya fitō sararī ~, ya faɗạ
masạ then he told him it bluntly.
kutārạ *f. Sk.* pole of irrigation-plant
(= jīgọ).
kutare A. (kutạ̄rē) lepers (*pl. of* kuturū).
    B. (ku tarẹ) *m.* (*sg., pl.*). (1) (*a*)
thief *x* tsōƒaŋ ~ an old hand at theft.

(*b*) ku tarẹ, ku tarẹ stop thief ! (2)
any dog.
ƙutārọ *m.* (1) poor man. (2) wifeless
man.
kutī *m.* (1) (*a*) dog (*only in the following*)
im bạ̄ haƙạ ba, ṇ zamā ~ if I'm lying,
devil take me ! (*b*) *cf.* kuti-kuti. (2)
(*a*) gidaŋ ~ juju-house of Gwari (= gidan tsāƒị). (*b*) arnẹ yā shā ~ the pagan-
Gwari swore by his juju (tsāƒị). (3)
an yi ~ dạ shī he's considered a perfect Nestor (*Vd.* guŋkị 1*b*).
kuti-kuti come here, dog ! (*cf.* kutī 1).
kutịŋkā *f.* mischief-making.
kutōlọ *Kt. m.* hip-joint (= agụdī).
kutsa A. (kūtsạ) (1) *Vb.* 3A. (*a*) " barged
in " *x* mại kūtsạ̄wā nē = ~ kại gạrēshị
he's a busy-body, know-all. (*b*)
rushed into *x* yā ~ ɗākị he rushed into
the house (= burmạ 1*f*). (*c*) muŋ
kūtsạ musu bạ̄ salamạ dạ rundunarsu
we attacked their army fiercely. (*d*)
yā ~ cikiŋ ạl'amạrī = yā ~ kại cikiŋ
ạl'amạrī (i) he interfered in conversation or project unasked. (ii) he
entered on " wild-cat scheme ". (*e*)
(*transitive*) *x* suŋ ~ rūwaŋ dạ jirạ̄gyan
yāƙị they launched ships into the sea,
etc. (2) yā ~ ạ gụje he fled. (3) *cf.*
kūtsē.
    B. (kūtsā) *Vb.* 2 yā kūtsē nị = yā
kūtsē nị dạ zāgị he reviled me.
    C. (kutsạ̄) *Kt.* yā fāɗị ~ he fell
sprawling.
kūtsạ̄nīyā *f.* meddlesomeness.
kūtsayyạ *Kt. f.* meddlesomeness.
kutse A. (kūtsē) *m.* (1) acting *as in* kūtsạ
x yā yi minị ~ he burst in on me uninvited. (2) tạƒīyạn naŋ tā yi minị ~
sudden necessity for this journey
flustered me (= titsē = firmitsī 2),
cf. tōtsạ 1*c*.
    B. (kụtsē) *m.* seed-vessel of plant *x*
kubẹ̄wā (kạbēwạ) tā yi ~ the okro
(pumpkin) developed ovaries. (3)
wata tanạ̄ ~, wata tanạ̄ 'yā'yā things
keep popping up one after the other
(= ƒụrē 3).
kutsu *Vd.* ƒitar kutsu.
ku tsumạ̄yē nị *m.* stunted goat (= tsu-
mạ̄yaŋ = *Kt.* mẹtsō).
kutsuŋ-kutsuŋ *adv.* in fragments *x* yanạ̄

aiki ∼ he's doing various scattered small jobs = gutsuŋ-gutsuŋ.
kutta Vb. 1A = kutt‍ukā.
kuttō Vb. 3A escaped (= ku6utō q.v. under ku6ucē).
kuttu A. (kuttu) m. used in yanā shaŋ ∼ he's sad.
B. (kuttū) m. = kurtū.
kuttukā Vb. 1C yā ∼ mata bakin ciki he treated her harshly.
kuttukē x fada yā ∼ there was serious altercation, etc. (=kuntukē q.v.).
kuttukū m. the drum kuntukurū q.v.
kutū Kt. m. Orange-headed male lizard (= jaŋ gwādā).
kutu6i Sk. used in daŋ ∼ m. (1) cover of dye-pit (= karō6i 2). (2) roof of corn-bin (2 = bākīre q.v.).
kutu6ū Kt. used in daŋ ∼ = daŋ kutu6i.
kutu6ur6uri m. (f. kutu6ur6urā) pl. kutu6ur-kutu6ur thick-set P.
kutubyalbyal Kt. m. turning somersaults (= alkāfurā).
kutuf (1) tsō6ō ∼ tottery old man (= tukuf = cukup). (2) Kt. (a) bagidāje ∼ m. ignorant rustic (= futuk). (b) the gecko sāri kutuf.
kutufānī m. large, round shield of tanned hide.
kutu6ī m. (1) band of plaited leather worn over shoulder and breast of horseman, with whip attached. (2) type of bead necklace.
kutukullē Vd. biris.
kutukuŋ-kutukuŋ pl. huge (re round things, persons, horses, boxes, etc.).
kutu-kutu m. conspiring.
kutumā blast you !
kutumba thick-set P. or animal.
kutumbutsu Kt. m. dilapidated grasshut, roof, etc. (cf. kwābatsē).
kutuŋgu6us Kt. nā yi ∼ da shī I met him unexpectedly (= kaci6is).
kutuŋgwīla f. mischief-making (= kinibībi).
kutuŋkā f. mischief-making (= kinibībi).
kutuŋkū (1) kutuŋkum 6aunā big bullbuffalo (= tōrō 2). (2) kutuŋkum 6arāwo notorious thief (= kuntukurmī). (3) Kutuŋkū, dan tsīyā na fāri epithet of debt (bāshi).
kutuŋkushāri m. dirty lout.

kutup = kutuf.
kutur = kuturī m. (1) (a) hindquarters of horse or donkey. (b) tā fi Kande ∼ she has finer buttocks than Kande. (c) Vd. ja ∼. (2) yā sā ni a ∼ he mounted me (tired P.) behind him on horse. (3) (a) yā kōma ∼ (i) he rode on hindquarters of horse with another P. in front. (ii) he has become subordinate to P. previously junior to him in same work (especially master and servant). (iii) he's gone down in the world. (b) yā maishē ni a ∼ it was a set-back for me. (4) seed-vessel of tobacco-flower (furē). (5) jākiŋ ∼ m. man carrying woman's load for her. (6) yā zō naŋ hantsī yā yi kuturim būshīyā he came here between 7 and 8 a.m.
kuturcē Vb. 3A to become a leper.
kuturī Vd. kutur.
kuturta A. (kuturtā) Vb. 1C. (1) rendered P. a leper. (2) yā ∼ ni he (son, agent, P. to whom T. entrusted) impoverished me.
B. (kuturta) Vb. 3B became a leper.
C. (kuturta) f. (1) (a) leprosy (= albaras = zāfī 1c.iii), cf. kadanya 4, kuturū, jazam, kurzunā, dāfi. (b) Vd. gāgara 11. (2) a blight on gērō-millet.
kuturtad da Vb. 4A = kuturtā.
kuturū m. (f. kuturwā) pl. kutārē. (1) (a) leper (Vd. dāgāra, kuturta). (b) kōwā ya ci lādaŋ ∼ yā yi masa aski if you undertake a task, you must see it through. (c) ∼ bā bākwam mīki ba nē don't teach your grandmother to suck eggs ! (d) ∼ yā ga mai kyasfī, ya cē " da haka muka sōmu " be guided by what has befallen me ! (e) kwācē gōruba daga hannuŋ ∼ bā aiki ba nē it is an easy thing to do. (f) Vd. raŋgyana. (g) ∼ mā yanā yī Vd. tūwō 19. (h) an sā ∼ kuntā Vd. janyayyē. (j) ∼ kaŋ wa gayya Vd. gayya 2. (k) ∼ dāra makāfo Vd. dārīyā. (l) ∼ gādā Vd. gādā 4. (2) kin kī, ∼ guje māye destitute woman foolishly running away from husband eager to get rid of her. (3) kuturuŋ yā yi maka (a) he's suddenly gone up in the world. (b) he has suddenly become expert. (4) kōwā yanā sō ya gāji ubansa banda

ɗaŋ ∼ one wants to go up in the world, not down (= matsīyācī 3). (5) Ąkū ∼ *epithet of* parrot. (6) kuturun daŋgi poor relation. (7) kuturuŋ gērō blighted millet. (8) kuturuŋ kinibībi blatant deceit. (9) kuturwā type of grasshopper. (10) kuturwar ūwā, ą zaunạ dạ kē dōlę it's a poor article, but there's no choice! (11) *Vd.* tāfiŋ ∼.

kututturę *m.* (*pl.* kututtụrai). (1) tree-stump. (2) thick-set person.

kututturọ *Kt. m.* = kututturę.

kutūtụ *m.* (1) pulp of gourd (= tōtụ̄wā). (2) core of boil *x* kutūtụm mạrūrụ core of boil on buttocks, etc. (3) kutūtụm masạrā cob after removal of maize-grains (= tōtụ̄war masạrā). (4) tsịyā tā yi masạ ∼ he's very poor. bāshi yā yi masạ ∼ he's heavily in debt (= tạtạtūrū). (5) *Kt.* (*a*) kutūtụn rạkē useless, thick end of rạkē. kutūtụn tạkạndā useless, thick end of tạkạndā (5a = gindigịrī). (*b*) short stems of dāwa, gyạdā *or* gērō left in ground after crop reaped, to sprout and form second crop (= gyạurō), *cf.* kụsūsụ.

ƙụụ *x* yā jā burkị ∼ he came to a dead stop.

kuwa A.1 (kụ̄wā). (1) (*a*)(*i*) indeed, as for *x* shī ∼ bai yạrdā ba as for him, he did not agree. ɗan Sarkī nē shī kụ̄wā but he was a prince. kuŋ ∼ sanị well, you know that . . . (*ii*) fạɗi dạ ∼, ƙạre dạ " Wạllāhi !" speak clearly and swear to the truth of what you say! (*b*) (kụ̄wā *often leaves the same construction as if it were not present, cf.* dǎi, mā, kumā) lōkạciŋ ∼ dạ sukạ zō at the time they came indeed . . . (2) kō ∼ well, why not . . . *x* kō ∼ kụ tạfi tạre well, why not go together ? (3) *Vd. next entry.* (4) gūrịnsụ sụ zō, sǎi dạ kụ̄wā sukạ zō they were determined to come, cost what it might. (5) iŋ ∼ *Vd.* in 1*e*.

A.2 (kụ̄wạ) *interrogative form of* kụ̄wā *above*). (1) (*used in second part of alternative interrogative question*) zā kạ zō ? kō ∼ will you come or not ? yā kāwọ shi ? kō ∼ did he bring it or not ? (Mod. Gram. 165*b*) = kọ̄ 2. (2) kụ̄wạ ? (*expressing surprise at speed of*

occurrence) har zā kạ tạfi ∼ what yo are starting out *already* ? kā zō ∼ what, you're here so soon ? har k jī ∼ fancy your hearing the news s soon ! yā tạfi ∼ has he gone after all (= kọ̄ ?).

B. (kūwạ) *f.* (1) (*a*) shouting to ca attention *x* (i) yā bugạ musụ ∼ h shouted to them (= īhụ 1*a*), *cf.* sōwạ (ii) sun yi ∼ gidā, akạ ƙārō musụ gud ụmmawā they sent for and got reinforce ments. (*b*) yā yi ∼ bāyaŋ hari h " locked the stable after the horse ha gone ". (*c*) aŋ kọ̄rē kạ, kanạ̄ ∼ *Vd* Būzū 2*a*. (*d*) *Kt.* kụ̄wạtai *pl. m.* uproar angry speech (= hạrgāgī). (*e*) kūwạrkạ banzā dense bush (= īhụ 2). (*f*) ma kạŋ ∼ loud-voiced (= kọ̄gō 3). (2)(*Ar* quwwa) strength or power enough to ạ bạ shi dạ kūwạr ɗaukạnsạ = bạ shi dạ ∼ yạ ɗaukạ he's not strong enough t lift it. bạ shi dạ kūwạr zūwạ he ha no authority to come.

kụ̄wạce-kụ̄wạcē *m.* repeated shouting (*cf* kūwạ).

Kuwạ̄rạ *Kt. f.* River Niger (= Kwạ̄rạ).

kūwạrū *Vd.* kūrụ.

ƙūwạrū *Vd.* ƙūrụ.

kụ̄wạtai *Vd.* kūwạ 1*d*.

kūwwạ *Vd.* kūwạ.

kụyā̀fạ *Sk. f.* any spoon (= cōkạlī).

kuyạ-kuyạ *m.*, *f.* (*sg.*, *pl.*) small P.

Kụyambanā *Vd.* banzā.

kuyạŋgạ *f.* (*pl.* kụyạŋgī). (1) (*a*) female slave (= bạ̄iwā = ạgidi = tamaŋ-kwarō), *cf.* magụdạncī, kạryar gulai. (*b*) yanạ̄ sātạr ∼ he is using slave-girl as concubine but without kụllē. (2) yautạ kuyạŋgī = rụ̄dạ kụyạŋgī redness of sun just before setting.

kuyạŋgancị *m.* serving a superior *x* yanạ̄ ∼ ạ wurīna he's in my service (*Vd.* kụyạŋgạ).

kuyarī *m.* (*f.* kụyarā). (1) slender P. (2) kụyarī harmattan-wind (= sạ-rārạ 2).

kū yẹ̄ kū *Vd.* yẹ̄.

Kụ yī *name for* any dog.

kụyī-kụyī *m.* type of spear.

kuza A. (kụzạ) *f.* tin (as mined), *cf.* darmạ.

B. (kūzạ) *Vb.* 1A poured much fluid

into or on to *x* aŋ ~ rūwā ạ tukunyā much water's been poured into the pot.

kūzad dạ *Vb.* 4A threw much fluid away (*cf.* **zubar dạ**).

kụzārī *m.* being energetic *x* **yā cikạ** ~ he's energetic. **bā shi dạ** ~ he's "spineless". **kụ zō, kụ ganī** *Vd.* **kụ 3.**

kūzū *m.* swanking *x* **yanā** ~ **dạ kudī** he's swanking about his wealth.

kụzunzumī *used in* **kụzunzumin rāmī** big hole in ground (= **fāfuŋgạ**).

kwā (1) (*used in indefinite future for* "you" *plural*) *x* (*a*) ~ **tạfi gōbe** you'll probably go to-morrow. *Vd.* **kwā shā.** (2) **nā ji** ~ I heard sound of water being poured out.

kwā *f.* (1) slag (= **ƙwan maƙērā** = **kāshin tamā** = **kāshim maƙērā**). (2) plucky, persevering P. or horse. (3) (*in children's game*) A says **sam minī kạɗaŋ** "give me a little!" B says **cẹ̄ne** ~ "take it by force!" A then says ~, to which B replies **ƙwāce minī** "take it from me!" (*cf.* **turmī 8, sā A.2 2** *page* 573).

kwaɓa A. (**kwāɓā**) **(1)** *Vb.* 1A (*a*) mixed T. into paste *x* **yā** ~ **ƙasā** he mixed clay for building. **tā** ~ **ƙullū** she mixed flour and water to make **wạinā**-cake (**kwāɓā** = **dāmạ** *except that only* **dāmạ** *is used in case of* **furā, kụnū, sạlạlạ**; *cf. b below*). (*b*) **tā** ~ **tūwō** she made bad **tūwō** (= **dāmạ**; *cf.* **tā tūƙạ tūwō** she made **tūwō** well). (*c*) muddled up an affair, puzzled P. (= **dāmạ**). (*d*) **yā** ~ **hannun rūwā** he ate the kola-nut called **hannun rūwā** (= **dāmạ 4**). (2) **yanā kwāɓạ̄wā** he is prosperous (= **dāmạ 3**).

B. (**kwāɓā**) *f.* (1) (*secondary v.n. of* **kwāɓạ**) *x* (*a*) **yanā kwāɓar ƙasā** = **yanā kwāɓạ ƙasā** he's mixing clay for building. (*b*) *Vd.* **bịkī 1***k***, turmī 6.** (2) act of mixing clay for building *x* **yā yi** ~ **turmī ukụ** he mixed clay or cement enough for three spells of work.

C. (**kwāɓạ**) *Vb.* 1A. (1) hafted *x* **yā** ~ **gātarī ạ ƙotạ** he hafted the axe (= **gwaɓạ 1**), *cf.* **kwaɓẹ.** (2) **yā** ~ **ni da Sarkī** he embroiled me with the Chief. (3) **mạganạ kạɗaŋ, sǎi yạ** ~ **ta ạ ƙōtạ** "he makes mountains out of

molehills". (4) **aŋ** ~ **masạ mārī** he has been shackled.

D. (**kwạɓā**) (1) *Vb.* 2. (*a*) knocked T. out of person's hand *x* **yā kwạɓi gōrọ ạ hannūna** he knocked the kola-nut out of my hand. (*b*) **aŋ kwạɓē shi** he has been snubbed, prevented finishing what he was saying, prevented doing what he wished to do, interfered with (= **siŋƙāƙē 1***c* = *Kt.* **gwāsalạ** = **gwalẹ 1***b*). (2) *f.* rebuke *x* **anā masạ** ~ he's being rebuked. **bā shi dạ** ~ he is undisciplined (*Vd.* **kwạɓō**).

kwababbā *Vd.* **kwabọ.**

kwạɓạl *adv.* in big splodge (*re* saliva, mucus, excrement).

kwaɓalɓalē *Vb.* 3A **gyambō yā** ~ ulcer grew bigger, more purulent (= **kwạk-kwabtạ** = **caɓalɓalē**).

kwạbạrō *Nor.* ten-centime piece.

kwābạtsē *Vb.* 3A *Kt.* **yā** ~ it (grass-hut, roof) became dilapidated (*cf.* **kụtumbutsụ**).

kwabbunạ, kwạbbai *Vd.* **kwabọ.**

kwaɓe A. (**kwāɓẹ**) (1) *Vb.* 1A mixed all (*Vd.* **kwāɓā 1***a*). (2) *Vb.* 3A (*a*) became muddled *x* **ạl'amạrī yā** ~ the affair is at sixes and sevens (= **dāmẹ**). **ạl'amạrī ya tạru, ya** ~ **minī** I felt completely nonplussed. (*b*) (i) **idọ yā** ~ the eye has become purulent. (ii) **hanyạ tā** ~ road became slushy. **jikinsạ yā** ~ **dạ tạɓō** his body is muddy. (iii) **gyạmbō yā** ~ the ulcer has become purulent. (iv) **rụbūtū yā** ~ the writing has become smudgy (2*b* = **cāɓẹ 1** = **dāmẹ**).

B. (**kwạ̄ɓẹ̄**) *m.* (1) the way **rụ̄dē** is prepared (= **dạ̄mē**). (2) mixture of bran and water given to animals (= **dạ̄mē**).

C. (**kwaɓẹ**) (1) *Vb.* 1A. (*a*) unhafted *x* **yā** ~ **gātarī ạ ƙotạ** he unhafted the axe (= **famfạrē 2***a*), *cf.* **kwaɓạ, dōsạ.** (*b*) (i) deposed. (ii) dismissed. (iii) pushed (animal) away. (*c*) = **tūɓẹ 2.** (*d*) drew out one from bundle (*x* mat) = **zāmẹ 1***c*. (*e*) prevented *x* **zā mụ** ~ **su dạga ƙētạrẹ̄wā** we shall prevent them crossing. (*f*) (*with dative*) protected P. from *x* **Allạ yạ** ~ **manạ wannạm mạsīfạ** God ward this misfortune off us! (2) *Vb.* 3A (*a*) became unhafted

(= *Kt.* famfarē 1*c*). (*b*) (nut, bolt) became loose (2*a.b* = kwalę = salę). (*c*) gātarinsạ yā ⌣ he's sexually impotent (= gidā 1*d*.ii = lạ'ịfị). (*d*) kọ̄fatọ yā ⌣ hoof fell away through disease (3) *m.* mụ ɗaurạ ⌣ let us play the game kwaɓę !

kwăɓị *m.* (*secondary v.n. of* kwăɓạ 1*a, b*) *x* yanạ̄ kwăɓịŋ ƙasā = yanạ̄ ƙwăɓạ ƙasā he's mixing clay for building.

kwạ̄birạ *f.* small horn blown by carriers (*may also be made of wood or neck of* būtạ-*bottle*).

kwaɓīyā *f.* (1) *x* gātarin nạŋ ⌣ gạrēshị this axe is liable to frequent unhafting. (2) Gātarī mại kwaɓīyā, wạhạl dạ mại hawā bisạ it's a " thorn in one's side ".

ƙwabkạ̄ina = ƙwafkạ̄ina.

kwabo A. (kwabọ) *m.* (*pl.* kwabbunạ = kwạbbai = kwabumbunạ = *Sk.* kwabạbbā (*Eng.* copper). (1) (*a*) penny (= dalạ 6 = wạ̄wạ̄gī). (*b*) sīsịŋ ⌣ *m.* half penny. (2) Kwabọ mại girman banzā what a useless person ! (3) (*a*) unmarried girl no longer virgin (= bụdurwā 2). (*b*) mȩ̄ akạ sāmụ what sex was the child she bore (*reply*, kwabọ " a boy ") (*this is said by women, cf.* dalạ 6).

B. (kwăbọ) *m., f.* (*sg., pl.*) P. talking drivel (= cạ̄ɓālọ 1).

kwạɓō *used in* mại rạban dūkạ bā yạ̄ jiŋ ⌣ the P. charged with administering corporal punishment is not hindered by rebukes. Alạ̄ bā dạ hạƙurī, bā yạ̄ kwạɓaŋ kōwā permit me to say with all due respect that he rebukes nobody (*Vd.* kwạɓā 2).

ƙwạbrī *Kt.* = ƙwaụrī.

kwabsa A. (kwabsạ) *f.* large, stringed instrument.

B. (kwạbsā) = kwạfsā.

kwabumbunạ *Vd.* kwabọ.

kwạ̄burạ = kwạ̄birạ.

kwacciyā *f.* (*pl.* kwaccāyē) *Sk.* (1) type of small calabash. (2) shell of tortoise. (3) kwacciyar gạba pommel of saddle (= kurcīyā 3). (4) *Kt.* kwacciyar bāya cantle of saddle.

ƙwace A. (ƙwăcȩ) (1) *Vb.* 1A. (*a*) took by force *x* (i) yā ⌣ kudīna = yā ⌣ minị kudī = yā ⌣ kudī dạgạ hannūna he took away my money. (ii) suŋ ƙwātō

ạbinsụ they managed to wrest their property from those who had seized it (iii) duhụ yā ⌣ = duhụ yā ⌣ ganī = darē yā ⌣ it's too dark to see. (iv) wạlƙīyā mại ⌣ ganī dazzling lightning (v) bā ạ̄ ⌣ wạ yārọ gạrmā. *Vd.* gạrmā 1*a*.iii. (vi) dạ ạ ⌣ yārọ rīgā, gāra ạ jā tạ kȩ̄cȩ it's better for a T. to become spoiled than for it to be taken from you and given to another. (vii) ⌣ gọ̄rubạ ạ hannuŋ kuturū bạ̄ shi dạ wụyā = ⌣ gọ̄rubạ dạgạ hannuŋ kuturū bạ̄ aikị ba nȩ̄ it's as easy as falling off a log. (viii *cf.* ƙwạ̄ 3, turmī 8, sạ̄ A.2.2 (*page* 753) (*b*) yā ⌣ kạnsạ (i) he managed successfully to defend himself (= gịra) (ii) he turned his head away. (iii) he behaved rebelliously, provocatively (*al-* 1*b* = fịzgā 1*c*). (*c*) yā ⌣ shi he (commander, etc.) relieved him of his post Sarkī yā ⌣ rawạninsụ the Chief dismissed them from office. (*d*) *Vd.* ƙwạ̄tā. (*e*) kạ ⌣ *Vd.* turmī 8. (*f* yā ⌣ kạn dōkịnsạ he led his horse apart. (2) *Vb.* 3A exceeded *x* nawyinsạ yā ⌣ it is the heaviest. (*b*) (i) took the lead. (ii) *Vd.* gạba 3*k*. (*c*) escaped *x* yā ⌣ ạ hannunsụ he escaped from them (3) ƙwạ̄cȩ ragō gōnā *epithet of* yaryạ̄dī

B. (ƙwạ̄cē) *m.* (1) (*a*) plundering property *x* an yi minị ⌣ = fịzgē. (*b Vd.* taubāshī. (2) *Kt.* thinning out guinea-corn and replanting (*cf.* cịrā 1*b*, 2*b*). (3) *Vd.* ƙwạ̄tā.

ƙwạ̄ci *Vd.* ƙwạ̄tā.

kwaɗa A. (kwāɗạ) (1) *Vb.* 1A did abundantly *x* yā ⌣ masạ māri he slapped him hard. yā ⌣ ƙaryā he told a " whopper ". yā ⌣ adō he togged himself up. ⌣ kại gạrēshi he's a braggart. aŋ ⌣ rānā yạu it's been blazing hot to-day. aŋ ⌣ rūwā it rained heavily. muŋ ⌣ tạfīyạ we travelled far. (2) *Vb.* 3A yā ⌣ ạ gụjȩ he took to his heels.

B. (kwạ̄ɗā) *Vb.* 2 = kwāɗạ *x* yā kwạ̄ɗē shi dạ māri he slapped him hard

ƙwada A. (ƙwạda) it would be better to *x* ⌣ mụ tạfi we had better go ! (= gāra)

B. (ƙwāɗạ = ƙwādā) *f.* (*pl.* ƙwādōjī Kt.* (1) kidney (= ƙōdạ *q.v.*). (2 testicle (= gwaiwā *q.v.* = *Sk.* ƙwāɗō) ƙwādagō *Kt. m.* farming for wages (*cf.* ƙōdạ, ạiƙạtau).

kwaɗagwam *adv. and vn.* (1) yā rāmẹ ∼ = cikịnsạ yā yi ∼ he's become emaciated. (2) rūwā yā fāɗạ ∼ water-level in river is now low. rījịyā tā yi ∼ water-level of well's low. rūwā yā yi ∼ ạ tukunyā little- water remains in the pot. (3) idạnsạ yā fāɗạ ∼ his eyes have sunk into their sockets from illness. (4) yā kwānā ∼ = ƙwạɗagwam.

ƙwạɗagwam (1) yā kwānā ∼ he went to bed supperless. (2) yā bar mātā tasạ ∼ he left his wife unprovided for.

kwạɗai *Sk. m.* = kwạɗayī.

kwaɗaita A. (kwạɗaitạ) (1) *Vb.* 2 desired eagerly *x* nā kwạɗạicē shị = nā ∼ dạ shī I eagerly desire (desired) it. (2) nā kwaɗaitō ganinsạ I eagerly desire (desired) to see him.
B. (kwaɗaịtā) *Vb.* 1C rendered eager *x* shī nẹ ya ∼ minị zūwạ it was *that* which made me so eager to come.

kwạɗaịtụ *Vb.* 3B *x* nā ∼ dạ shī = kwạɗaitạ 1.

ƙwādā-ƙwạɗā *pl.* large and round *x* gwạrrā ∼ large kolas. rūwā yā sakō ∼ the rain (*e.g.* harvest-rain) fell in large drops (= daƙwā-dạƙwā).

kwạɗāƙwạɗai *Vd.* kwarkwaɗā.

ƙwādalēlẹ = ƙwādalī *m.* (*f.* ƙwādalēlịyā = ƙwādalā) *pl.* ƙwādal-ƙwạɗạl large and round (= daŋƙwalēlẹ).

kwaɗam *adv. and m.* = kwaɗagwam.

kwaɗan *Vd.* kwaɗọ.

ƙwạɗaŋgwạɱiyọ (1) *adv.* yā kwānā ∼ = ƙwạɗagwam. (2) *epithet of* miser.

ƙwạɗaŋgwam = ƙwạɗagwam.

kwaɗantā *Vb.* 1C. (1) tā kwaɗạntạ nāmạ she made kwaɗọ for meat. (2) yā kwaɗạntạ magạnạ he talked irrelevantly (*cf.* kwaɗọ 3) = sọ̄ki burụ̄tsū.

kwạɗayī *m.* (1) keen desire (= ƙwạlamā) *x* (*a*) yanā̄ kwạɗayintạ he's eager to get her. (*b*) kwạɗayinsụ nē ya jā sụ it was their greed which ruined them. (*c*) kwạɗayiŋkạ ya jāwō makạ you've brought ruin on yourself. (2) im bā ∼, bā wulākancị envy leads to abuses. (3) tūwaŋ ∼ yā fi dādī ; kō dạ gāyā, săi ạ ci expectation exceeds realization.

(4) răị dạ ∼ zại mutụ so long as one is alive one feels desires.

ƙwad dạ *Vb.* 4B *Sk.* satisfied (one's appetite) = ƙōsad dạ *q.v.*

kwạɗɗō *Kt. m.* frog (= kwạ̄ɗō *q.v.*).

kwāɗẹ *Vb.* 3A = kwāɗạ.

kwāɗī *Vd.* kwạ̄ɗō.

kwạɗọ̄ *m.* fuel-bricks made from refuse (dạlạkī) of ƙwaŋƙōnī (*Vd.* maŋ gyạɗā 3).

kwaɗo A. (kwạ̄ɗō) *m.* (*pl.* kwạ̄ɗī = kwāɗunạ = *Kt.* kwạɗɗī). (1) (*a*) (i) frog. (ii) kạmạci kạmātạ, ∼ yā yi durƙusō kạman na niƙạ everything has its time and place. (iii) bā ạ sakẹ̄wā dạ ∼ ạ warkī even the smallest anxiety torments one. (iv) rạbaŋ ∼ bā yā̄ hawā samạ everyone has his own limited destiny. (v) dūnịyạ jūyị-jūyị, ∼ yā fāɗạ ạ rūwan ɗịmī what an unlucky period ! (vi) masọ̄yiŋ kīfī bā̄ na ∼ ba nẹ̄ tastes differ. (vii) rībạr ƙafạ, kūrā tā tākạ ∼ even the most trifling advantage is useful. (viii) Kwạ̄ɗō bā kạ cīzaŋ ɗaŋ kōwā what a mild person ! (*b*) *cf.* tālibambam. (*c*) idạŋ kwạ̄ɗī *Vd.* idọn 9. (*d*) kwạ̄ɗan sēsē = dạ̄tạnnīyā 4. (*e*) *Vd.* makạɗim kwạ̄ɗō. (2) padlock. (3) frog-shaped embroidery on back of gown-neck. (4) part of flintlock-gun. (5) woman's silver neck-pendant. (6) crown-badge of sergeant-major. (7) zanạntạ yā yi matạ ∼ her cloth flapped open (= ɓantạrē 2). (8) fitsāriŋ ∼ *Kt. m.* slimy red growth on water-surface (= lanyā 1*b*). *(9) kwạ̄ɗaŋ harshẹ (*only used in translating from Arabic*) root of tongue.
B. (kwaɗọ) *m.* (1) dạddawā or ground-nuts pounded, mixed with water and condiments, and poured cold over meat (= *Sk.* ɗatọ), *Vd.* maŋ gyạɗā 1. (2) (*a*) kwaɗam bakạ food consisting of mixture of cassava and ground-nuts (= kamādịsinō = mandaƙō = guɗōsō = *Kt.* sạkwạrā 2 = sạ mai gidā tsallē), *Vd.* kạrākạrā. (*b*) *epithet is* Kwaɗam bakạ, māgạnim mai ƙwạlamā). (3) kwaɗam magạnạ irrelevant talk (= sọ̄ki burụ̄tsū). (4) yā fi ∼ *Vd.* gạbā 5*b*.

ƙwado A. (ƙwadọ) (1) (*a*) ∼ gidaŋ wani shạ type of draughts (darạ) played on board (kōmī) with 12 holes (gurbị),

the pieces ('yā'yā) being 4 kāshiŋ awākĭ in each hole (*one part of this game is called darạr shānū, another part is darạr kūrā*). (*b*) *the game is also called* hurhuɗú = darạr kāshiŋ awākĭ. (2) .*m.* (*a*) am mọ̈rē shị har ƙwadạnsạ the last ounce of use has been got out of it (him). (*b*) yā kai nị ~ he tried my patience (= kakị). (*c*) *Vd.* barcĭ 4*b*.
B. (ƙwādō) *Sk. m.* (*pl.* ƙwādōjĭ) testicle (= gwaiwā = *Kt.* ƙwādā).

ƙwādōjĭ testicles (*pl. of* ƙwādạ ; ƙwādō).

kwaɗon *Vd.* kwaɗọ ; kwạ̈ɗō.

ƙwadọ shạ = ƙwadọ 1*a*.

kwāɗunạ *Vd.* kwạ̈ɗō.

kwaf A. (kwaf) *used in* ganiŋ kwaf *m.* inquisitiveness.
B. (kwạf) *Eng. m.* cup *x* Kanọ tā ci ~ Kanọ won the cup (for football, etc.).

kwafạ *Vb.* 1A (1) = kwakkwạfā 1*a* ; kwakkwạfē. (2) hafted (= kwabạ *q.v.*).

ƙwafa A. (ƙwāfạ) *Vb.* 1A. (1) yā ~ hatsĭ ạ gōnā tasạ = ƙwāfị. (2) yā ~ tsạ̈kāninsụ he forced his way among persons already crowded together. (3) aŋ ~ ɗākị tsạkānin ɗākunạ house was squeezed into already overbuilt area. (4) aŋ ~ kabạ ạ tạ̈barmā fronds of young dum-palm were inserted to increase breadth of mat (*Vd.* ƙwāfị).
B. (ƙwạ̈fā) *f.* (1) muŋ kafạ ~ săi mun sāmụ we've set our heart on getting it. (2) sum mai dạ ~ tasụ gạ Kanọ they have turned (transferred) their attention to capturing, etc., Kano.
C. (ƙwạfā) 1 *f.* *x* yā yi ƙwạfā he made a clicking sound expressive of anger (= ƙụcē). (2) *Vb.* 3B made click indicative of anger (= ƙutạ). (3) *Vb.* 2 *x* yā ƙwạfē shị he made click of anger and so sent him away.

kwạfạrō *Nor. m.* ten-centime piece.

ƙwāfạtā *Kt.* yā ɗaŋ ~ he did slight work (= ƙwāƙwạtā).

ƙwāfẹ (1) *Vb.* 1A yā ~ hatsĭ ạ gōnā tasạ he completely re-sowed *as in* ƙwāfị. (2) ƙwāfẹ = kwāfẹ *Vb.* 3A sat apart alone (= kākụmē).

kwafe A. (kwafẹ) *Vb.* 1A = kwakkwạfē.
B. (kwāfẹ) *Vd.* ƙwāfẹ 2.

ƙwaffĭ *Kt. m.* putting spell on P. (= ƙōfĭ *q.v.*).

ƙwafi A. (ƙwafĭ) *Kt. m.* = ƙwaffĭ.
B. (ƙwāfị) *m.* (1) (*secondary v.n. of* ƙwāfạ) *x* yanạ̈ ƙwāfịŋ gōnā = yanạ̈ ƙwāfạ gōnā he's re-sowing places where seed not germinated (= kashịŋ ƙamfā = ƙamfā 1*c*). (2) increasing length of rope by adding kabạ.

kwāfinĭ *Kontagora Hausa m.* second crop of okro (= kụsūsụ).

ƙwaf kạ̈ina *x* ạbincin naŋ ~ nẹ̈ this food is enough for one P. only. azzịkinsạ ~ nẹ̈ he shares his money with nobody.

kwafsa A. (kwafsạ) *f.* a large, stringed instrument.
B. (kwạfsā) = kwạsfā.

kwạfsō *m.* = kwạsfā.

kwaftara A. (kwaftạrā) *Vb.* 1C yā ~ masạ sạndā he thrashed him with a stick.
B. (kwạftarạ) *Vb.* 2 yā kwạftạrē shị dạ sạndā = kwaftạrā.

kwāgirĭ (1) cane, switch (= tsumāgĭyā). (2) imported walking stick.

kwagwam *m.* sound of stroke on drum.

ƙwăi *m.* (*pl.* ƙwāyạ̈yē = ƙwăi). (1) (*a*) egg. (*b*) kạ̈zā tā ɗau ~ = *Kt.* tā ajĭyẹ ~ the hen is about to lay eggs. (*c*) (i) kạ̈zā tā sakạ ~ = tā jēfạ ~ = tā yi ~ the hen laid an egg, eggs (= *Kt.* tā nasạ ~), *cf.* zazzạgē 4. (ii) kạ̈zā tā zubạ ~ the hen has laid many eggs. (*d*) ~ ạ bakạ yā fi kạ̈zā ạ akurkĭ = ~ gụdā ɗăi tallē, yā fi kạ̈zā ạ sạke a bird in the hand is worth two in the bush. (*e*) kịlị ~ *m.* cream-coloured horse (*Vd.* kịlị 3). (*f*) (i) bạtūrẹ yā tafi shaŋ ~ (*labourers' slang*) the European has gone on tour (*but* nā ci ~ I ate an egg, eggs). (ii) sōjạmmụ sun shā ƙwăi our soldiers got booty. (*g*) yā yi shạ̈mọmọ kạmaŋ ~ yā fashẹ wạ kạ̈zā ạ cikị he has a dejected look. (*h*) sum fasạ manạ ~ ạ kā they foiled us. (*j*) jirgịn naŋ, kĭfạ̈yē sun sōmạ ~ kạnsạ that ship has sunk. (*k*) gạ̈ ~ *Vd.* alaŋƙōsạ̈. (*l*) nĭ bā nạ̈ ~ săi dạ zạkarạ it is not mere gossip, for I can produce a reliable informant. (*m*) (i) ~ tsạkānin dūtsẹ = ~ tsạkānim makōdĭ P. interfering between disputants who

then band against him. (ii) ~ dạ
dūtsẹ bā sạ hạɗūwā wurī ɗayā oil and
water won't mix. (iii) kā haɗạ ~ dạ
dūtsẹ you have yoked the strong with
the weak. (n) ~ mā yā yi wạyō, bạllē
ɗan tsạ̄ƙọ̄? you think yourself very
smart, but you're not the only pebble
on the beach ! (nn) ~ tarạ Vd. tsīnạ̄nā.
(o) cf. Sarkiŋ ~. (p) ạ barạ darị
ƙwansa Vd. darị 2. (q) ƙwam mạkaunīyā
Vd. ciŋ ~. (r) Vd. ƙwam maƙērā. (s)
ƙwam mulụfī Vd. dạ̄lō 4b. (t) ƙwan
dạ̄lō Vd. dạ̄lō 4b. (2) (a) globe of hurri-
cane lamp. (b) bulb of electric light.
(3) Vd. ƙwan-compounds.

kwaifạ 1 f. rich soup or gravy (= dạr-
mạsōsụ̄wā). (2) (a) what rich soup !
(b) how clearly the child speaks !

kwai-kwai m. being prone to illness
(= laulạyī).

ƙwăi-ƙwăi = ƙwăi-ƙwăi-ƙwăi.
ƙwăi-ƙwăi-ƙwăi used in yārọ nē ~ dạ shī
he's a sensible lad. yārinyạ cē ~ dạ
ita she's a sensible lass.

kwạikwayạ Vb. 2 imitated (cf. kōyị).

***ƙwạiƙwāyạ** f. prolapse (= gwaiwar
mātā).

kwạikwayē m. kernel(s) of fruit of desert-
date (adūwạ).

kwạikwayō m. (secondary v.n. of kwạikwayạ) x yanạ̄ kwaikwayansụ = yanạ̄
kwạikwayạ tasụ he's imitating them.

kwailọ m. (1) affectation. (2) ogling ;
coquetry ; simpering (= fēlēƙē).

ƙwaiŋ used in zāƙī ~ very sweet. yanạ̄
sạntạ ~ he loves her very much. rānā
tā būɗẹ ~ sun's blazing.

ƙwạinānụ̄wā f. alert, young girl.

ƙwājājā (1) m., f. thin P. with pot-belly.
(2) adv. yanạ̄ dạ kạ̈i ~ he has huge
head on small neck.

ƙwājiɓō what ugly P. or T. !

ƙwājirạ Vb. 2 scratched (= yạ̈kusạ =
ƙwạrzanạ).

ƙwāƙẹ Vb. 3A (colour, cloth) faded
(= kōɗẹ).

ƙwaki A. (kwākī) m. cassava-flour.

B. **(kwāƙị)** m. black-hooded cobra
(= gạmshēƙā).

C. **(kwakī)** Kt. m. well-informed old
man.

:wāƙị m. faded indigo-dyed cloth.

kwākịyā Kt. f. = kwāƙị.

ƙwāƙịyā f. = ƙwāƙị.

kwakko Kt. m. = kōko.

kwakkọ̄mā Vb. 3A int. from kōmạ.

ƙwaƙƙọ̄nā Vb. 3A intensive from ƙōnạ.

kwakkwạbcē Vb. 3A = kwạkkwabtạ.

kwakkwabta A. (kwạkkwabtạ) Vb. 3B
gyạmbō yā ~ ulcer increased, grew
purulent (= kwaɓalɓạlē = caɓal-
ɓạlē).

B. **(kwakkwạbtā)** Vb. 1C yā kwak-
kwạbtạ gyạmbō it (scratching, etc.)
caused ulcer to spread, grow purulent.

kwakkwaɗī m. = kwailọ.

kwakkwafa A. (kwạkkwạfā) f. cantering
(= jạjjọ̄gā = kakkabtū).

B. **(kwakkwạfā)** Vb. 1C. (1) (a)
yā kwakkwạfạ fēgị he drove a peg into
ground. (b) yā kwakkwạfạ itātūwạ
cikin damịŋ icẹ he knocked peg into
bundle of wood to prevent bundle
falling apart. (2) ạ ~, ạ hanạ rụ̄ɗẹ
kadạ yạ zubẹ dip up ladlefuls of rụ̄ɗẹ
and pour them back, to prevent overflowing ! (3) (with dative) impressed on
P. urgency x nā ~ masạ ạbin nạŋ
I impressed on him the urgency of this
(= nānạtā 2 = kwarkwạrtā 2). (4)
yā kwakkwạfạ sāƙạ he banged down
weaving-comb to make woof-threads
lie close together.

C. **(kwạkkwafạ)** Vb. 2. (1) impressed
on P. that x nā kwạkkwạfē shị don yạ
lụ̄rā dạ shī I urged him to pay attention
to it (cf. kwakkwạfā 3). (2) trained up
child the way it should go (= họ̄rā).

kwakkwạfē Vb. 1D tapped, hit (bundle,
etc.) on ground to even up the ends
(= dirạ).

ƙwaƙƙwafī m. yā bi ƙwaƙƙwafim mạganạ
he investigated the matter.

kwakkwal = kwakwal.

ƙwạƙƙwārā = ƙwạrƙwārā.

B. ***(ƙwaƙƙwārā)** f. (only used in
translating from Arabic) doing P. a
kindness, but then repeatedly reminding
him of it.

ƙwaƙuce A. (ƙwạ̄ƙucē) Vb. 1C = ƙwạ̄ƙulạ.

B. **(ƙwạ̄ƙucē)** Vd. ƙwạ̄ƙutạ.

ƙwaƙula A. (ƙwạ̄ƙulạ) Vb. 2. (1) yā
ƙwạ̄ƙuli kunnē he scraped wax out of
his ear with his finger. (2) yạrā sunạ̄

ƙwạƙulạr rōgọ (gyạɗā) boys are stealing cassava (ground-nuts) by scrabbling in ground-nut ridge (kunyā). (3) yā ƙwạ̄ƙụli jūdạ he scraped musk from pot with little stick (tsiŋkē), cf. lạ̄katạ, sạ̄katạ. (4) cf. ƙwāƙụlē.

B. (ƙwāƙụlā) Vb. 1C. (1) inserted T. to scrape out x yā ƙwāƙulạ tsiŋkē ạ jūdạ = ƙwạ̄ƙulạ 3. (2) tsōfō yā ƙwāƙulạ yārinyạ = gōgē.

ƙwaƙule A. (ƙwāƙụlē) Vb. 1C. (1) = ƙwạ̄ƙulạ. (2) kūrā tā ƙwāƙụlẹ gāwā hyena disinterred corpse. (3) yā ∼ shi he investigated it. (4) cf. ƙwalƙwạlē.

B. (ƙwāƙulē) m. (secondary v.n. of ƙwạ̄ƙulạ ; ƙwāƙụlē) x yanạ̄ ƙwāƙulan jūdạ = yanạ̄ ƙwạ̄ƙulạr jūdạ he's scraping musk from pot.

ƙwāƙụmē Vb. 1C gripped garment of P. with both hands x nā ƙwāƙụmẹ rị̄gā tasạ (= ƙāƙụmē q.v.).

ƙwạƙurạ Vb. 2 yā ƙwạƙuri dōkịnsạ he galloped his horse (= sụkwānạ).

kwākutā = kwākwatā.

ƙwaƙuta A. (ƙwāƙutạ) Vb. 2 (p.o. ƙwāƙụcē, n.o. ƙwāƙụci) = ƙwạ̄ƙulạ.

B. (ƙwāƙụtā) Vb. 1C = ƙwāƙụlā.

kwa-kwa A. (kwā-kwạ) f. (1) oil-palm (epithet is Kwā-kwạ, bā ạ̄ sạ̄ mikị lōkọ). (2) for oils, Vd. alayyạɗī ; mạn jā. (3) yā ci ∼ he had a bad time. (4) kwākwạr ạttā garạ (a) coco-nut palm or fruit. (b) type of woman's girdle (jịgidā), cf. Garạ. (5) Vd. ∼ lāgị.

B. (kwạ̄-kwạ̄) used in anạ̄ rūwa ∼ it's raining heavily.

ƙwạ̄-ƙwā f. inquisitiveness x yā cikạ ∼ he's " nosey ".

ƙwāƙwạcē = ƙwāƙụlē.

kwạkwai there is (= ạkwai).

kwakwal = ƙwaƙwal x yā wạŋku ∼ it's washed specklessly (= kal q.v.).

ƙwaƙwala A. (ƙwạ̄ƙwala) = ƙwạ̄ƙulạ.

B. (ƙwāƙwạlā) = ƙwāƙụlā.

kwā-kwạ lāgị m. fuel-logs for railway-engine or steamer (derived from kwā-kwạ and English " log " ?).

ƙwaƙwạlē = ƙwāƙụlē.

ƙwaƙwalwā f. the brain (= kwanyā = Sk. ɓōɓwā).

*kwakwanā Zar. used in ɗaŋ ∼ m. (pl.

'yaŋ ∼) upper stone for grinding ground-nuts.

*kwākwanyạ f. = kwantsạ.

kwakwar Kt. adv. in sound condition (= gwagwar).

kwā-kwạ rāgị = kwā-kwạ rākị m. = kwā-kwạ lāgị q.v.

kwā-kwạr ạttā garạ Vd. kwā-kwạ 4.

kwakwarē used in ạbiŋ kwakwarē, gyạmbō dạ lāyạ what unusual excellence ! kwạkwạrō Nor. m. durability (= ƙarƙō).

kwākwashā f. bargain x nā sạ̄mi ∼ I got it cheap.

kwākwatā f. (pl. kwākwatōcī) Zar. ; Nu. gown with neck-opening like tagūwā, lined sleeves and wide skirt.

ƙwāƙwạtā Vb. 3A yā ɗaŋ ∼ he did a little manual work (x farming, building, etc.).

kwạ̄kwāzọ m. exaggerated fuss (= kwạrmatọ 2).

kwạ̄kyārạ used in ɓạriŋ kwạ̄kyārạ m. (1) blurting out what one ought not to have said. (2) extravagance.

kwal A. (kwal) (1) adv. (a) yā wạŋku ∼ it's specklessly washed (= kal q.v.). (b) Vd. kwallẹ "abused". (2) (contraction of kwānā " passed the night ") x (a) ∼ lāfiyạ I hope you slept well ? (reply, ∼ lāfiyạ = n nạ̄ lāfiyạ = munạ̄ lāfiyạ to which 1st speaker says lāfiyạ several times). (b) mụ ∼ lāfiyạ good night ! (reply, Allạ̄ yạ sạ̄ = mụ kwạncē = ạsụbạ̄ ta garī = ạsụbạ̄ ạlhẹr). (c) Vd. kwānad dạ. (d) kōwā ya yi hakạ, bạ yā ∼ lāfiyạ ba anyone who does so will not sleep with an easy conscience. (3) ∼ lāfiyạ Mụsụlmī type of plover.

B. (kwạl) Eng. m. coal.

ƙwal A. (ƙwal) adv. (1) = kwal 1a. (2) alone x nā iskẹ shi ∼ I found him alone. (3) ɗaŋ ạbụ ∼ dạ shī tiny thing. (4) (a) yā askẹ minị kạ̄i ∼ he completely shaved my head. (b) kạntạ ∼ yakẹ (i) she has skimpy hair. (ii) her head's been shaved (due to illness, etc.).

B. (ƙwạl) yā fāɗō ∼ sound of its falling was audible.

kwalạ (Eng. cooler) f. (1) double-spouted ewer. (2) soldier's (a) water-bottle. (b) bandolier. (3) collar. (4) cigarette-holder (= hōlạ).

kwala A. (ƙwãlậ) *Vb.* 1A. (1) yã ~ shi dậ ƙasã he threw him to the ground (= kã dậ). (2) (*a*) yã ~ kũkã he cried out. (*b*) aŋ ~ rãnã yậṵ it was blazing-hot to-day. (*c*) yã ~ wãƙậ he burst into song. (3) yanậ ~ kậi he's arrogant (*cf.* ƙwãlậ kậi). (4) kậ ~ blast you! (= lậyã). (5) yã ~ minị sậndã he thrashed me with stick.

B. (ƙwậlã) (1) child says ŋgõ "here's something for you!" and when the other child is about to take it, says kậ ƙwậlã " well, I'm not giving it to you " (*cf.* ƙwậlẽlẽ ; dõdọ 3) = kwậyã 2 = *Kt.* kwậrã 3. (2) *f.* seeds of water-lily (badọ) = dãwậ 2 (*cf.* mậiwã 1*d*).

kwalabã (1) *f.* (*pl.* kwalậbẽ = kwala-bõbĩ) (*a*) glass-bottle (= tũlũ 1*b*). (*b*) *Eng.* crowbar. (2) *m.* ~ dậ nõnọ child's drink made from milk and baobob-pulp (= *Kt.* zullụ).

kwalaf = kwalap *adv. and m.* cikịnsậ yã yi ~ = cikịnsậ yã fãɗậ ~ his stomach is shrunken (from hunger or illness).

kwalailậicẽ *Kt.* examined minutely, *etc.* (= ƙalailậicẽ *q.v.*).

wãlậ kậi (1) ~ ƙurguŋgụmã dậ gudụn shãfọ = ~ kậrẽ dậ gudụn lahĩyã *epithet of* P. " too big for his boots ". (2) *Vd.* ƙwãlậ 3 ; ukụ 3*b*.

walã-ƙwậlậ large and round (= daƙwã-dậƙwậ *q.v.*).

wậlậkwậlai *Vd.* kwalkwalĩ.

walậlã = ƙwalậlã *Vb.* 1C poured out abundantly (= kwarậrã 1*a*).

walam A. (ƙwalam) (1) yã cịnyẽ ~ he ate it up greedily. (2) *m.* yã ci ~ dậ kuɗinsậ = yã ci ~ dậ mãƙụlậshẽ he spent his money on luxurious, but unsatisfying food (*x* fried cakes of English flour *i.e.* fậŋkẽ, or cakes *i.e.* kyật).

B. (ƙwậlam) (1) *adv. and m.* yã yi ~, yanậ kallõ = yanậ kallansậ ~ his mouth watered when he saw him eating. yã yi ~ dậ idọ he looked longingly at the food (= gwậlam = ƙwậl-ƙwậl). (2) yanậ zậune ~ he's sitting penniless and solitary. (3) *Vd.* ƙwậl-ƙwậl.

wậlamã *f.* (1) keen desire for (= kwậ-ɗậyĩ). (2) ƙunshị yã yi ~ henna has only "taken" patchily. (3) idậnsậ ~ gậrẽshị his eyes become affected merely

by seeing other affected eyes. (4) *Vd.* kwaɗọ 2*b*. (5) gandụŋ ƙwậlamã *Vd.* jịrãtậ.

kwalaŋgwasõ *Kt. m.* ogling ; affectation (= gwalaŋgwasõ).

ƙwalanjẽ *m.* (1) yanậ fãmaŋ ~ he's having to go short of T. (2) meanly stinting oneself. (3) hankering after (= kwậɗậyĩ). (4) cutting very short grass at harvest-time (= kãlã 6).

kwậlậŋkwalmậ (1) *m.* (*pl.* kwậlậŋkwậlmai) part of loom for weaving narrow width. (2) *m.*, *f.* (*a*) obscene dancer (*i.e.* mậi karyậ gịndĩ). (*b*) rogue. (*c*) *Kt.* tall P.

kwalaŋkwancị *m.* shameless conduct.

ƙwậlậŋƙwasọ *Kt.* kõ ~ bậi bã nị ba he didn't give me even a scrap.

kwalap = kwalaf.

kwalậrĩ = *Kt.* kwalậrẽ *m.* affectation ; ogling ; coquetry (= fẽlẽƙẽ).

ƙwậlậtai *m.* (1) (*a*) testicles (= gwaiwã *q.v.*). (*b*) jậkar ~ scrotum. (2) ƙwậlậ-tan jậhĩmị = ƙụllũtụ 2.

kwậlãwậrĩ *Fil. m.* a Filani milk-measure.

kwalbã bottle *Vd.* kwalabã.

kwalbậ A. (kwalбậ) *Vb* 1A = kwamбậlã.

B. (kwậlбã) *Vb.* 2 *Kt.* = kwalбẹ.

kwalбad dậ *Vb.* 4A = kwamбậlã.

ƙwalbata A. (ƙwalbậtã) *Vb.* 3A *Kt.* yã ɗaŋ ~ he did a little manual work (*x* farming, building, etc.) = ƙwãƙwậtã.

B. (ƙwậlbatậ) *Kt. f.* yanậ ~ he's doing a little work *as in* ƙwalbậtã.

kwalbatị *Eng. m.* (1) culvert (= *Kt.* sagị 3*b*). (2) crowbar (= kwalabã).

kwalбẹ *Vb.* 1A *Kt.* aggravated sore place by scratching it.

Kwalcị *used in* Kwalcị, birĩjị, gandun dãdĩ : bậ doŋ kin yi yawậ ba, sãi 'yan Sarkĩ *epithet of* ground-nuts.

*kwalcọ *Sk. used in* ɗaŋ ~ jackal (= dilã).

kwale A. (kwalẹ) (1) *Vb.* 1A. (*a*) yã ~ ta he had sexual connection with her (= cĩ 16*a* *q.v.*) (*b*) *Kt.* ignored P. ; snubbed P. (= gwalẹ). (2) (*a*) became unhafted. (*b*) (nut, bolt) became loose (2*a*, *b* = kwaбẹ 2).

B. (kwậlẽ) *m.* tã yi ~. (1) she put on her cloth in Yoruba fashion. (2) she has below each eye one tribal-mark (askậ) *or one such mark* made with the cosmetic kậtậmbirị.

ƙwālẹ *Vb.* 1A yā ∼ ni dạ sandā he beat me with stick (= ƙwālạ 5).

kwale-kwale A. (kwạlẹ-kwạlẹ) *m.* small, round-bottomed Kakạndạ-canoe.

B. (kwạ'le-kwạlẹ") *x* sun yi kwạle-kwạlẹ dạ shī they ignored it.

kwalẹkwalī *Vd.* kwalkwalī.

ƙwạlẹlē (1) ƙwạlēlaŋkạ (*a*) I refuse to give you what you're asking for ! (*b*) you can't have it ! (*said after proffering T. and then withdrawing hand ;* cf. dōdọ ; ƙwạlā ; dạŋgōlī), *Vd.* lallẹ 2c. (2) ạbin naŋ ƙwạlēlansạ dạ shī this is his, but he won't get it back !

kwạlfā (1) *Vb.* 2 = ƙwạrfatạ. (2) *Kt. f.* = kwạsfā.

kwālī *m.* (1) (*Eng.* card) cardboard. (2) tie-on luggage-label. (3) ɗaŋ ∼ *m.* type of velvet cloth.

ƙwālị *used in* ɗaŋ ∼ *m.* (*pl.* 'yaŋ ∼) bobbin placed in shuttle by weaver.

ƙwālịsạ *f.* (1) affectation. (2) ogling, coquetry (*both* = fēlēƙē).

kwālīyā *f.* dishonestly " loading " hides and skins with earth and blood, to increase weight.

ƙwalƙōlūwā *f.* summit (= ƙōlōlūwā *q.v.*).

kwạlkotạ *Kt. f.* louse (= kwạrkwatạ *q.v.*).

kwalkwaɗā *Sk. f.* = kwarkwaɗā.

kwal-kwal = kwal 1.

ƙwạl-ƙwạl (1) *adv. and m.* yā yi ∼ dạ idọ = idạnsạ yā yi ∼ = ƙwạlam. (2) yārọ yā yi ∼ the lad looked as if about to cry.

ƙwalƙwala A. (ƙwạlƙwalạ) *Vb.* 2. (1) yā kwạlƙwali rūwā he dipped out small remainder of water from pot, well, etc. (2) yā ƙwạlƙwali tsōkạ he stripped remnants of meat from bone. (3) *Kt.* = ƙwạ̄kulạ.

B. (ƙwalƙwạlā) *Vb.* 1C *Kt.* = ƙwā̄ƙulā.

ƙwalƙwale A. (ƙwalƙwạlē) *Vb.* 1C. (1) yā ∼ shi he investigated it (= ƙwā̄ƙulē 3). (2) = ƙwạlƙwala 1, 2. (3) rūwā yā kwalƙwạlẹ gạ̄rū water undermined wall (= zāgẹ). (4) *cf.* ƙwā̄ƙulạ ; ƙwāƙulē.

B. (ƙwạlƙwạlē) *m.* = ƙwalanjē 1, 2.

kwalkwalī *m.* (*pl.* kwalẹkwalī = kwạlā̄kwạlai = kwalkwalōlī) type of cap (tạ̄gīyạ) made of rags covered with

multicoloured cloth and with ostrich-feather stuck in (*it is worn by* 'yaŋ lifidạ *who are therefore called* 'yaŋ kwalkwalī).

ƙwalƙwā̄sā *Kt. f.* driver-ant (= ƙwarƙwā̄sā *q.v.*).

kwalkwashē *Vb.* 3A *Kt.* yārọ yā ∼ chil child deteriorated.

kwạlkwatạ *Kt. f.* louse (= kwạrkwatạ).

kwạllā (1) *Vb.* 2 = kwallẹ. (2) *f.* yā shā ∼ (*a*) he was abused. (*b*) it (garment) w‍: well washed.

ƙwalla A. (ƙwalla) *Vb.* 1A = ƙwālạ 2.

B. (ƙwạllā) yā yi dạrīyā har yā yi ∼ he laughed till he cried. yā shā furā har yā yi ∼ he took furā till he could eat no more.

ƙwạllạfā *Vb.* 1C = ƙwạllafạ *Vb.* 3B longed for (= ƙallafa).

ƙwạllam abundantly (*re* fluids).

ƙwạllā̄tai *Kt.* = ƙwā̄lā̄tai.

ƙwạllạtu *Vb.* 3B is (was) replete (= ƙōshi).

ƙwạllā̄yē *Vd.* ƙwallō.

kwallẹ *Vb.* 1A. (1) yā ∼ ni kwal he abused me. (2) (*a*) shaved well. (*b*) swept well. (*c*) washed well.

kwalli A. (kwạllī) *m.* (1) galena (*i.e.* silver-lead = tōzạlī) (*is applied to eyelids and eyebrows ;* cf. kurạtandụ, daulā mishī ; *is used as blood-tonic, i.e.* mā̄gạnin jinī ; *is mixed with indig‍ and beaten into* sā̄ƙị *to freshen up*). (2 nā yi ∼ dạ shī I perceived him (= tōzạlī). (3) tunkīyan naŋ, ∼ gạrēt‍ this sheep has black-ringed eye‍ (= tōzạlī). (4) kwạlliŋ kūrā blacl deposit left by flood.

B. (kwallị) how well washed ! (*cf* kwallẹ) = kwalliŋ kwatanā.

ƙwalli A. (ƙwallị) (1) how hot ! (2) how bright ! (3) how white !

B. (ƙwạllī) *m.* (1) ƙwạlliŋ gyaɗ‍ single-nutted ground-nut (= ƙumbulā) (2) cotton-boll. (3) bā ni dạ shī kō ∼ I've none at all.

kwalliŋ kwatana = kwallị.

kwallīyā *f.* bathing and sprucing onese‍ up.

ƙwallo A. (ƙwallō = ƙwallọ) *m.* (*p‍ ƙwallā̄yē*). (1) (*a*) stone of any fruit ƙwallaŋ giginyạ ; ƙwallaŋ gọrubạ ƙwallam maŋgwạrọ (*cf.* ɗā 6a, b ɓallē ; tsōkạ ; ƙọ̄dagọ). (b) giginyạ mại ∼ bīyū = ƙwạr 3. (2) any ball. (3) ƙwallō = ƙwallan dōƙị (q.v. under ƙwallō B.). (4) yā ci ∼ (a) he won the horse race. (b) he was lucky. (5) bạ̄ ni dạ shī kō ∼ I've none at all. (6) cịrar ∼ f. (a) seizing foot of wrestling opponent, throwing him up, then dashing him down. (b) suddenly dismissing P. and reducing to destitution. B. (ƙwallō) m. (f. ƙwallūwā) pl. ƙwallạ̄yē. (1) handsome x ƙwallan dōƙị handsome horse. ƙwallūwar yārinyạ pretty girl. (2) ƙwallan shēgẹ thorough rogue. (3) ƙwallaŋ ƙātọ burly lout.

ƙwallūwā (1) Vd. ƙwallō B. (2) f. ƙwallūwar kại cranium.

kwalmạɗā bent over (tip of knife, etc.) = kalmạɗā q.v.

ƙwạlōkọ m. black dye for leather (= kufī).

kwalo-kwalo A. (kwạlō-kwalō) m. (1) breaking one's word. (2) after making offer (tayị) and its acceptance (an sallạmā), then offering less (epithet is ∼ cịnikin Yarabāwā) (1, 2 ⇐ sụkū-sukū 1). B. (kwạlō-kwạlō) = kwạlē-kwạlē.

ƙwalwā Kt. f. the brain (= ƙwaƙwalwā).

kwam A. (kwạm) (1) adv. and m. yanạ̄ dạ dọ̄yī ∼ it stinks. nā ji ∼ I smelt a stench. (2) = kwạraŋ 2. B. (kwam) m. (1) nā ji ∼ I heard axe-blows. (2) jẹ̄ ka har ∼ you can go to the devil !

ƙwāmā f. beans cooked alone (= ƙūlū).

ƙwạ̄mạ̄cālī Kt. m. odds and ends (= karẹ).

ƙwamama A. (ƙwāmạmā) Vb. 1C = ƙwạ̄mamạ Vb. 2 importuned x yā ƙwāmạmā ni sǎi m̀ bā shị = yā ƙwạ̄mạmē nị sǎi m̀ bā shị he importuned me to give him it. B. (ƙwạ̄mạ̄mạ) used in yā ciwō ∼ (1) he ate T. which upset his digestion. (2) he did T. which brought trouble on him.

ƙwạmandạ Eng. m. Commander.

ƙwạmashọ Eng. m. commission on sales (= lạ'adạ).

ƙwamāyē Vd. kwamī.

ƙwạ̄māzạ f. (1) slacker's banking up corn with gạrmā-hoe without weeding (cf. hụ̄ɗā). (2) (a) stiff leather. (b) food

without oil or butter x tūwaŋ ∼. (c) = ƙwāmā. (3) strong, energetic P. or horse, etc. (= ƙạ̄ƙūzạ).

ƙwạmazgị m. big lout.

kwạmbalạ f. unsavoury-looking soup (cf. kwamɓạlā).

kwamɓala A. (kwamɓạlā) Vb. 1C. (1) spattered place with x yā kwamɓạlạ mạjinā (yau) (tābạ) ạ naŋ he spattered this place with phlegm (saliva) (tobacco-juice). (2) tā kwamɓạlạ mīyạ ạ tūwō she poured unsavoury-looking gravy over the tūwō (cf. kwạmbalạ). B. (kwạmɓalạ) what unsavoury-looking gravy !

kwambalē = kwạmbạlē m. blot in writing (= dạŋgwạlē).

kwạmɓar = kwamɓar Kt. am bar shị ∼ he's been left penniless.

ƙwambara A. (ƙwạmbarạ) Vb. 3B is (was) bent with load, age, etc. (2) = ƙwambạrē. B. (ƙwambạrā) Vb. 1C bent (back of P. or animal) as in ƙwạmbarạ 1. ƙwambạrē Vb. 3A. (1) = ƙwạmbarạ. (2) is buckled (re leather T. having become wet).

kwạmbē m. (1) shaving hair above temples and forehead of labourers, thus making circle from ear to ear. (2) bịkiŋ wani sārīyā, bịkiŋ wani ∼ tastes differ.

kwambịlō m. (1) type of game. (2) Vd. kwaŋ kwambịlō.

ƙwambọ m. (1) (a) ostentatiousness, boastfulness (= ạlfahạrī). (b) yā tākạ ƙwambọ he behaved conceitedly. (2) (labourers' slang) female pudenda (= farjị).

kwamcẹ Vb. 1A Kt. yā ∼ ni dạ mārị he slapped me.

*ƙwamẹ m. ƙwamaŋ kūkạ fruit of baobob.

kwạmfạ thereupon (= kụmfạ).

kwạmfalalō Sk., Kt. gyạɗā tā yi ∼ the groundnuts have no kernels (= kụmfalalō).

kwamī Kt. m. (pl. kwamāyē) any native boat (= kōmī).

ƙwamī m. (f. ƙwamā) x dōƙị ∼ burly horse. yārinyạ ƙwamā burly girl.

kwammā f. (1) old guinea-fowl. (2) Kt. portion of large bundle of corn (= gwammā q.v.).

fwammạ *Vb.* 1A aŋ ~ masạ mārị he's been slapped.

fwammạtā *Vb.* 3A had to content oneself with inferior T.

fwạmrī *Sk., Kt.* = fwạurī.

kwạmsō *Sk., Kt. m.* sheath (= kwạnsō *q.v.*).

kwan A. (kwan) *abbreviation of* kwānā *q.v.* (*cf.* kwal, kwạn 3, 4).
  B. (kwạn) (1) = kwạm. (2) ~ dạ kạmar wannạŋ yakẹ̃ yị he's copying that out. (3) ~ gạba, ~ bāya gạrẹshị he's inconsistent. aikịn nạŋ, ~ gạba, ~ bāya this work's not progressing. (4) Cụ̃tā, makwạn dạ yārọ tsōfō = Cụ̃tā makwạn dạ tsōfō rāmị hunger thou devastator ! (*cf.* kwan).

kwana A.1 (kwānā) *Vb.* (*for progressive, Vd.* A.2. 3 *below*). (1) spent the night *x* (*a*) (i) ịnā zā kạ ~ yạu where will you pass the night, where will you sleep to-night ? ạ zaurẹ yakẹ̃ ~ he passes the night in the entrance-porch. jīyạ nā ~ ạ Kanọ yesterday I slept at Kano (*cf.* barcī, kwạntā, kwānā A.2. 3*a*). jīyạ nā ~ n nạ̃ aikị I worked all last night. nā ~ bạn yi barcī ba I couldn't sleep at night. (ii) nā ~ dạ yuŋwạ I went to bed supperless (*Vd.* tūwō 16). (*b*) kā ~ lāfīyạ ? did you have a good night ? (*reply* lāfīyạ lau). (*c*) kạ kwānā lāfīyạ sleep well ! (*d*) aŋ ~ lāfīyạ ? = kwạncē 2. (*e*) kōwā ya yi hakạ, bạ yā ~ (= bạ yā kwan) lāfīyạ ba nobody so acting will sleep with an easy conscience (= kwal 2*d*). (*f*) ~ lāfīyạ dūkīyā it is a great asset to pass a peaceful night. (*ff*) sai rugā ta kwānā lāfīyạ *Vd.* rugā 1*b*. (*g*) fịtilạ tā ~ tanạ̃ cị̃ the lamp burned all night. (*h*) rạn naŋ, kō aŋ ~, kō bạ ạ ~ ba, sǎi ya yi musụ jạwābị he addressed them on that day or the next. (*j*) ạ hannū zā tạ ~ *Vd.* hannū 1*a*.xi. (*k*) kwānā gidā *Vd.* ạlbasạ 6. kwānā birgāmị *Vd.* ạlbasạ 6. (*l*) kwānā tsạye *Vd.* tabaryā 1*b*. (*m*) kwānā wạje *Vd.* kūrā 49. (*n*) bạ kulluŋ akẹ̃ ~ ạ gadō ba, wata rānā kō ạ kasạ sǎi ạ kwạntā the world is full of vicissitudes. (*o*) im mụtụm yā cẹ̃ " ịnā zạŋ kwānā ", ạ yi darē wait and see

instead of asking unnecessary questions ! (*p*) ~ bukkạ yā fi ~ sōrạn dạ bạ kudī better a modest competence than making a big show when one has not the funds. (*q*) ịnā Sarkī ya kwānạ̃ *Vd.* Sarkī 1*r*. (*r*) yā kwānā wurim fadạ *Vd.* fadạ 1*f*.iv. (2) (*a*) remained, spent time (*cf.* kwānā A.2.5) *x* (i) kun ji ịndạ lạ̃bārịŋ ya ~ you've heard how the matter stands. (ii) bạ ạbin dạ ya ~ ƙị irịŋ wannạŋ there is nothing he hates so much as this. bạ wạndạ ya ~ dạ ƙị ạ zūcịyassạ kạmar Audụ Audu is his *bête noire.* (iii) sạndāna yạ kwam bisạ *Vd.* sạndā 1*g*. (*b*) food was left standing for a day or two and became stale *x* (i) furā tā ~ the furā went stale from standing. (ii) gōrọ bại ~ ba the kolanuts found a ready sale. (iii) kụnū yā ~ *Vd.* tsīnạnā 1*b*.ii. (2) since *x* nā ~ bīyar, bạŋ gan shị ba = ~ bīyar kẹ̃ naŋ, bạŋ gan shị ba it's five days since I saw him. nā ~ bīyar, n nạ̃ ganinsạ kōwạcẹ rānā I've seen him each day for the last five days. (3) yā ~ dạ ita he had connection with her (*by day or night ; cf.* A.2. 3) (= cī 16*a q.v.*). (4) *on reaching* darạs-*sign in Koran, the reader postpones going on and says* iŋ an zō darạs, ạ kwānā. (5) yā ~ bīyū ạ naŋ he's been here some time. dạ akạ kwam bīyū after a while. nā kwam bīyū " I wasn't born yesterday ! " sǎi aŋ ~ bīyū au revoir. (6) rushed into *x* yā ~ ạ rūwa he jumped into the water. yā ~ ạ wutā he leapt into the fire. sǎi ya ~ cikịŋ ạbōkaŋ gạbā he rushed against the enemy. (7) jīyạ nā ~ ạ turkẹ I got some food or money last night bại ~ ạ turkẹ ba he spent the night out with a woman. (8) kwạ̃nā, tạshi = ạ kwānā, ạ tāshị (= kwānā A.2. 4 gradually *x* ạ ~, ạ tāshị, dārī yạ tsạnantạ gradually, the cold became intense (= kwạnci 1), *cf.* yạu dạ gōbe (9) *Vd.* kō tā kwānā ; kadạ tạ ~.

A.2 (kwānā) *m.* (*pl.* kwạ̃nạkī = kwānạkī = kwānukạ = *Kt.* kwānukkạ). (1

night-time (*Vd.* A.1. 1 *above*) *x* wunina
bĭyū, kwānāna ɗayā ą Kano I spent a
day and a night at Kano and left
late on the following day. (2) (*in
merely speaking of* " so and so many
days " *without emphasis on distinction
of day or night, we can use either*
kwānā, yini, *or* wuni *at will*) *x* (*a*) ～ukụ
baŋ gan shi ba I've not seen him for
three days. kwānammụ (= wunimmụ)
huɗū muną aikinsą we've been working
on this for four days. yau ～ kąman
nawą mukę sąurąre we've been waiting
a long time for news. yau kwānāna
gōmą rąbōna dą gąrimmụ I have been
away from my home-town for ten days.
(*b*) shękarą ～ cę in dą rąi gąba delay
doesn't matter provided success
follows. (*c*) yā yi kwąnąkĭ caŋ he spent
some days there. yā yi 'yaŋ kwąnąkĭ
ą gidāna he spent a few days at my
home (*Vd.* kwąnąkĭ 3). (*d*) ～ dą
kwąnąkĭ for a long time *x* nā yi ～
dą kwąnąkĭ, n ną nēmansụ I looked for
them for long (*Vd.* kwąnąkĭ 2). (3)
(*progressive and v.n. of* A.1) *x* (*a*) yaną
～ = yaną barcĭ he is asleep (whether
by day or night, *cf.* kwānā A.1. 1).
(*b*) ang kwānan zaune *Vd.* zaune 3.
(*c*) ɗākiŋ ～ *m.* bedroom. (*d*) taną
kwānaŋ hanyą ą wuriŋ ądąshē she's
late in paying her contribution to the
communal " pool " (*Vd.* ądąshē). (*e*)
gą indą nakę ～ = kā ga wuriŋ kwānāna you despised me. (*f*) nā tąmbąyi
kwānansą I asked after his health. (*g*)
dą kwānāna gąba na mĭkę after a few
days I recovered. (*h*) ～ ą dāji *Vd.*
bāwą 8*b*. (*j*) naŋ yakę sō dą ～ *Vd.*
wani 4*e*. (*k*) wani yakę sō dą ～ *Vd.*
yini 1*a*.iv. (*l*) ～ bukką *Vd.* bukką.
(*m*) ～ dą yuŋwą *Vd.* tūwō 16. (*n*) ～
nēsą *Vd.* sąnnū 2*a*.ii. (*o*) wuriŋ kwānaŋki *Vd.* bātą 1*c*. (*p*) (i) tā tuną
kwānaŋ gidā *Vd.* tsōfō 1*d*. (ii) *Vd.*
kwānaŋ gidā. (*q*)kwānaŋ garkę *Vd.*garkę
2*b*. (*r*) *Vd.* baŋ kwānā. (4) ～ dą tāshi =
～ tāshi = kwānā A.1. 8 *q.v.* (5) period
(*cf.* kwānā A.1. 2) *x* (*a*) kwānan naŋ
at present. kwānan naŋ at that time.
(*b*) kwānan nąm fa, bą mā kwānan
nąm ba, raŋ ukụ gą watą just recently,

no I'll be more precise, actually on the
3rd of the month. (*c*) kwānā-kwānan
naŋ (i) at this present time. (ii) quite
recently. (*d*) kwānā-kwānan naŋ
during all that long period. (*e*)
kwānam bāya *Vd.* kwąnąkĭ 1. (*f*) *Vd.*
kwąnąkĭ 3. (6) ～ wąje (i) (*said by
town gate-keeper*) I'm about to close
the town gate ! (ii) Hi ! gate-keeper,
don't close up ! (iii) Hi ! ferryman,
there are still passengers waiting before
you go for the night ! (7) (*a*) ƙwąrą-
ƙwąrai bā ą bā sụ ～ concubines are
not entitled to the fixed rotation of
nights for cohabitation as is the case for
real wives (mātaŋ aurē) by Muslim
law, *so it is said* bą ta dą ～ she (concubine) only has the right of her man
staying a short time at night with her
(*cf.* hĭrā 3) before sleeping with the real
wife whose turn it is for conjugal rights
(kąmin yą tąfi ɗākin dą ząi kwānā).
(*b*) yau kwānaŋ Kande nę to-night is
Kande's turn to sleep with her husband.
(*c*) wājibĭ nę miji yą rabą (= yą
dāidāitą) kwānā it is enjoined on a
husband to devote an equal number of
nights to every wife. (8) nā yi baŋ ～
dą shĭ I took leave of him. (9) *Vd.*
kwąnąkĭ, kwānąkĭ, kwąnąkĭ ; *compounds of* kwānan.

B. (kwaną) *Eng. f.* (1) yā yi ～ he
turned round the corner (= karyą
13 = mālĭyō 2), *cf.* hōlę 1*a*. (2) hanyą
tā yi ～ road bends sharply. (3) yā
yi ～ cikin ząncansą he went off at a
tangent in his conversation.

kwānad dą *used in* Allą yą kwanshē
ką lāfĭyą good night ! (*said to superior*)
(*reply is* ąmiŋ, mụ kwal lāfĭyą), *Vd.*
kwal 2.

kwanaki A. (kwąnąkĭ) (*pl. of* kwānā A.2).
(1) kwąnąkĭ = ą kwąnąkĭ = kwānam
bāya = kwąnąkim bāya = tuŋ kwąnąkĭ *adv.* a few days ago *x* kwąnąkĭ
muką gąmu dą shĭ we met him recently.
(2) kwānā dą kwąnąkĭ it's long since *x*
kwānā dą kwąnąkĭ baŋ gan shi ba I've
not seen him for a long time. muną
nēmansą kwānā dą kwąnąkĭ we have

long been looking for it (*Vd.* **kwānā**
A.2. 2*d*). (3) period *x* **kwāṇakin d̄arī
suŋ kusa ƙārẹ̄wā** the cold period is
nearly over. **kwāṇakin dā̧** of old *Vd.*
kwānā A.2. 2*c* ; **kwānaķī** 3 ; **ƙā̧ƙa̧**
1*c*.ix.

  B. (**kwānaķī**) *m.* (1) = **kwā̧naķī** 1,
3 *x* **a̧ kwānaḳim bāya** : **kwānaḳin
d̄arī** : **kwānaḳin dā̧**. (2) **wani ~** . . .
wani ~ sometimes . . . sometimes. (3)
ina̧ rūwā̧ what news of the rains?
(*reply*, **ruwā kwānaḳinsa̧ nē** " as one
would expect, for this is the rainy
season "), *Vd.* **ƙā̧ƙa̧** 1*c*, **kwā̧naķī**
3.

  C. (**kwā̧naki**) *m.* = **kwānaḳī** 1, 2.

kwānaŋ aurē *x* **tā jē ~** according to a
custom considered shameless, woman
on marrying again (**ba̧zawa̧rā**) spent one
night (in villages, 7 nights) with
husband and then returned home till
time fixed for her officially to join
husband (**tārẹ**).

kwānaŋ azancī *m.* great cuteness.

kwānan gidā (1) *used in* **tā yi kwānaŋ
gidā** she slept at her paramour's house.
(2) *Vd.* **kwānā** A.2. 3*p*.

kwānaŋ kēso̧ *x* **yā (tā) yi ~** he (she) was
not buried till next day.

kwa̧nanta̧ *Vb.* 3B **hanya̧ tā kwa̧nanta̧**
the road bends (*cf.* **kwana̧**).

kwānaŋ wa̧sā *used in* **nā saŋ kwānaŋ
wa̧sā** I know what you refer to.

kwānan za̧une *m.* the jollifications at
bridegroom's house, night before bride
is taken there (**tārẹ**), *Vd.* **za̧une** 3.

kwānā rawā *m.* (1) tinkling ear-pendant.
(2) *Kt.* = **ba̧ra̧mba̧jau**.

kwana̧rī *Kt.* *m.* = **kwala̧rī**.

ƙwānarya̧ *f.* (1) tree whose seeds are used
for making rosary (**ca̧zbī**). (2) **yā yi ~**
horse (donkey) has abscesses on back
(= **cu̧l**).

kwance A. (**kwancẹ**) (1) *Vb.* 1A. (*a*) (i)
untied (= *Sk.* **sancẹ**). (ii) **hannū
bā yā̧ kwancȩ̄wā** *Vd.* **bā̧ķī** 1*b*.xvi. (iii)
ya̧dda̧ za̧i yi ya̧ ~ kūrā *Vd.* **kūrā** 49A.
(*b*) **yā ~ bā̧kim burgāmi̧** = **yā ~ bā̧kin
ja̧kā** he's chattering away. (*c*) **yā ~
mini̧ ciki̧m ma̧gana̧** he explained the
matter to me. (*d*) **nā ~ la̧rūra̧** (i) I
satisfied my need for connection with

a woman. (ii) I relieved myself by paying a call of nature. (iii) I explained my
needs to P. (*e*) **yā ~ a̧lkāwa̧rī** he broke
his promise. (2) *Vb.* 3A. (*a*) became
untied. (*b*) **dōķi̧ yā ~** horse broke loose
(= **tsiŋkẹ** 2*b*). (*c*) **yā ~ mini̧** (i)
he's gone down in my estimation. (ii)
it has slipped my memory. (*d*) **da̧bāra̧
tā ~ mini̧** I'm at my wits' end.

  B. (**kwa̧nce**) *m.* (1) (*d.f.* **kwancẹ**) (*a*) (i)
discarded garment. (ii) **yā zuba̧ masa̧
kwa̧ncaŋ girmā** he gave him some fine,
slightly-worn clothes. (*b*) a discarded P.
x **Ka̧nde kwa̧ncaŋ Audu̧ cē** Kande is
Audu's discarded wife or mistress.
tā zamā kwa̧ncan Tu̧rā̧wā she's a
European's cast-off mistress. **kwa̧ncan
Sarkī (mālami̧) (a̧ttāji̧rī)** divorced wife
of Chief (scholar) (rich man) (*these are
not popular among those seeking wives*).
(*c*) **Audu̧ kwa̧ncaŋ hau̧kā nȩ̄** Audu is a
cured lunatic. (2) lying position (*d.f.*
kwa̧ntā) *x* (*a*) **yā yi ~** he lay down. (*b*)
yanā̧ da̧ga̧ ~ he's lying down. (*c*)
yā tāshi̧ da̧ga̧ ~ he rose from lying
position. (*d*) **fitsāriŋ ~ yakȩ̄ yi̧** he's
a bed-wetter (= **ama̧lāla̧**). (*e*) **yanā̧ ~**
he's lying down. (*f*) **yanā̧ ~ d̄ai-
d̄ai** he's lying sprawled out. (*g*) *Vd.*
kwa̧ncīyā. (*h*) **d̄ā kwa̧nce** *Vd.* **guzumā**
4. (3) (*a*) **yanā̧ ~** it's untied (*d.f.*
kwancẹ). (*b*) **ha̧ŋka̧lī kwa̧nce** with an
easy mind (*cf.* **kwa̧ncīyā** 1A).

  C. (**kwa̧ncē**) *Vd.* **kwa̧ntā**.

  D. (**kwa̧ncē**) (1) *Vd.* **kwal** 2*b*. (2)
aŋ ~ lāfi̧ya̧ ? good morning ! (*said by
village women*) = **kwānā** A.1. 1*d*.

ƙwa̧ncē *Sk.* *m.* ginning cotton without
first teasing it (= **tĩtsē**).

kwa̧n'ce-kwa̧ncē" *m.* making ready to *x*
yā yi ~, **ya d̄irƙa mini̧ sa̧ndā** then he
took up an attitude and " laid into me
with stick ". **yā kwa̧ntā ~**, **ya shȩ̄ƙa̧
musu̧ ƙaryā** he told them a carefully
prepared lie. **an yi ~**, **aƙa̧ shȩ̄ƙa̧
rūwā** it rained heavily.

kwanci A. (**kwa̧nci**) (1) **~**, **tā̧shi** gradually
= **kwānā** A.1.8 *x* **~**, **tā̧shi, sǎi suka̧
yi girmā** they gradually grew up. (2)
~, **tā̧shi, bābu̧ wu̧yā** how the time has
sped ! (3) *Vd.* **kwa̧ntā**.

  B. (**kwanci̧**) *Sk.* *m.* = **kwa̧ncīyā**.

C. (kwancī) *m.* (1) kāzā tanā ~ hen's sitting on eggs. (2) an yi wa̱ karōfī ~ dye-pit's been filled with water prior to inserting the indigo. **kwançiyā** *f.* (1) lying position *x* yanā̱ ~ he's lying down (= kwa̱nce 2*e*). yā yi ~ tasa̱ he lay down (= kwa̱nce 2*a*). yanā̱ ~ da̱ ita he sleeps with her (= kwa̱nce 2). (1*A*) ha̱nka̱linsa̱ bā yā̱ ~ sai yā gan ta̱ his mind was not at rest till he saw her (*cf.* kwa̱nce 3*b* ; kwa̱ntā 4*a*). (2) yi mini̱ zānā ~ bi̱yū make me a mat double the length of recumbent P. with arms stretched beyond head ! (3) gya̱ra masa̱ wuri̱n ~ get his bed ready ! (4) ~ da̱ masō̱yī (*a*) type of woman's coiffure (= ja̱kī 8). (*b*) type of tattooing. (5) yā sa̱mi kwançiyar ha̱nka̱lī (*a*) he's in easy circumstances. (*b*) his mind's calmed down. (*c*) kwançiyar ra̱mmu̱ our peace of mind. (6) kwançiyar kado̱ vessel slightly less full than gi̱rgi̱jī. (7) kwançiyar kwi̱yā̱kwi̱yai persons lying curled against each other for warmth. (8) yā yi kwançiyar migirbī he reclined on elbow (= ki̱shi̱ngida̱). (9) kwançiyar rā̱i *Vd.* 5.

kwanda A. (kwa̱ndā = ƙwa̱ndā) *f.* (1) (*a*) Maguzawa fetish consisting of bivalve-shell (*placed on farm, is considered to paralyse fingers of thief*). (*b*) ~ tā sa̱mi ɓa̱rāwo̱ such fetish paralysed fingers of thief. (*c*) **Kwa̱ndā ka̱s na gi̱ji̱** *epithet of* (i) such charm, (ii) evil man. (2) *Kt.* *f.* (*a*) biceps (= ƙwandu̱wā). (*b*) ƙwa̱ndātā cē it's my very own.

B. (ƙwanda = ƙwa̱nda) it would be better to . . . (= gāra).

kwanda̱ *Vb.* 1A *x* yā ~ mini̱ māri̱ he slapped me. a̱n ~ rānā ya̱u sun was blazing to-day.

ƙwanda̱fā *Vb.* 1C = ƙwa̱nda̱fa̱ *Vb.* 2 *Kt.* dipped out small remainder of water (= ƙwa̱lƙwala̱ 1).

ƙwa̱nda̱fē *Kt.* *m.* (*secondary v.n. of* ƙwa̱nda̱fa̱) *x* tanā̱ ƙwa̱nda̱fan rūwā = tanā̱ ƙwa̱nda̱fa̱r rūwā = tanā̱ ƙwa̱nda̱fa̱ rūwā.

ƙwandage̱ *m.* large, thick rings usually of silver or white metal (fari̱n ƙarfe̱),

on finger or slung by cord round neck.

ƙwan dāle̱ *Kt.* *m.* = ƙwan mulu̱fī 2.

ƙwandalēle̱ = ƙwandalī *m.* (*f.* ƙwandalēli̱yā = ƙwandalā) *pl.* ƙwandal-ƙwa̱nda̱l large and round (= da̱n-ƙwalēle̱).

ƙwa̱ndam *adv.* abundantly (*re* fluid).

ƙwanda̱rē *Vb.* 3A = ƙwamba̱rē.

ƙwanda̱rōso̱ *m.* (1) type of bent, dried, smoked fish. (2) yā yi ~ he acted deceitfully.

ƙwa̱ndasa̱ *Vb.* 2 (*p.o.* ƙwa̱nda̱shē, *n.o.* ƙwa̱nda̱shi) = ƙwa̱nda̱fa̱.

ƙwa̱nda̱shē *m.* = ƙwa̱nda̱fē.

kwande̱ *Vb.* 1A. (1) scraped out *x* a̱n ~ aku̱shī (*a*) food-bowl's been scraped out (= sude̱). (*b*) food-bowl's been licked clean (= *Kt.* tande̱). (2) a̱n ~ shi da̱ māri̱ he's been slappe̱d.

kwandi̱ (1) (*a*) what hot sun ! (*b*) what fine soup ! (*c*) how sweet ! (2) water game, where potsherd (tsi̱ngāro̱) is sent skimming along water. (3) tum ba̱ a̱ yi ɗarē (= ɗaras) ba, aka̱ yi ~ you're " trying to teach your grand-mother to suck eggs ".

ƙwa̱ndī = ƙwandī *m.* single-nutted ground-nut (= ƙumbulā 1).

kwandīɗa̱ *f.* (1) kernel of kurna̱-fruit. (2) (*a*) P. with penetrating voice. (*b*) what penetrating voice ! (*c*) what chatter !

kwando A. (kwa̱ndō) *m.* (*pl.* kwandu̱na̱). (1) basket. kwa̱ndan shā̱rā wastepaper-basket. (2) (*military*) good conduct stripes. (3) *Sk.*, *Kt.* = kwa̱ndo. (4) ornamented inside-apex of kago̱ (made from wood of gēza̱) (= *Kt.* taskirā 2). (5) tsāra̱n kwa̱ndō *Vd.* tsārā.

B. (kwa̱ndo) *used in* ɗa̱n ~ type of eulogist (maro̱ƙī *q.v.*) wearing many turbans (*people say playfully to him* kā ci̱ka̱ *to which he replies* n na̱ nēma̱n ƙāri̱).

C. (kwando̱) *Kt.* *m.* yā yi mini̱ ~ he warned me (= ka̱shēdi̱).

kwandu̱na̱ *Vd.* kwa̱ndō.

ƙwandu̱wā *f.* (1) biceps. (2) yolk of egg (= gwaidu̱wā).

ƙwan fara (ƙwam fa̱rā) *m.* herring-bone embroidery on trousers (= haƙōrim fa̱rā).

kwạngạlï *m.* fishing-float (= **kạngwạlï** *Sk.* **kālā** 8), *cf.* **kwạŋgwạlï**.

ƙwaŋgē = *Kt.* **ƙwaŋgē** = *m.* (occasional) pilfering (*cf.* **dạuke-dạukē**).

kwaŋgērẹ *used in* **tsōfaŋ kwaŋgērẹ** *m.* very old man.

kwaŋgi *m.* (1) = **kwaŋgērẹ**. (2) wood from lower, hard part of **giginyạ** palm (*i.e. part below* **bambạmï**). (3) *Kt.* hollowed-out (**hụrarrē**) trunk of **giginyạ** used for beehive (**amyạ**).

kwaŋgilā *f.* (1) contract for construction-work (*x* building, stone-cutting, etc.) *cf.* **kwantạrāgi**. (2) **maï** ～ contractor *as in* **1.** (3) **daŋ** ～ *m.* (*pl.* **'yaŋ** ～) contractor's labourer.

kwaŋgiri *m.* rail(s) for railway (= **gwạŋgiri**).

ƙwaŋ gwainạ *m.* type of blue-green stone used for adornment.

kwaŋgwalā *f.* midrib of raffia (**tukurwā**) used for roofing or canoe-poles (= **gwạŋgwalā**).

kwaŋgwalam *m.* emptiness *x* **wannạŋ ạkwạti** ～ **dạ shï** this box is empty (*pl.* **wadạnnạŋ akwātunạ kwaŋgwalam-kwạŋgwạlam dạ sū**).

kwạŋgwạlï *used in* **kwạŋgwạlï dạ rặi, māyẹ yā ci tsōfwā** boasting or fussing about mere trifle (*cf.* **kwạŋgạlï**).

ƙwangwara A. (**ƙwạŋgwạrạ**) *f.* type of oblong, white shield. B. (**ƙwạŋgwạrạ**) *Vb.* 2. (1) woman rapped (child on head) with knuckles *x* **tā ƙwạŋgạri dạntạ**. (= **dạŋƙwasạ**). (2) P. rapped (his head) to relieve itching from lice, etc. *x* **yā ƙwạŋgwạɹi kạnsạ**. (= **dạŋgwarạ** 1*b*).

ƙwạŋgwạrarrē *m.* (*f.* **ƙwạŋgwạrarrïyā**) *pl.* **ƙwạŋgwạrạrrū**. (1) notorious. (2) cute.

kwaŋgwarẹ *used in* **tsōfaŋ** ～ very old man.

ƙwạŋgwạrẹ *m.* (1) small amount of work. (2) = **ƙwaŋgē**.

kwanïkạ *f.* (1) conceiving before previous child weaned *x* **Kạnde, kwanïkạ takẹ yï** Kande often conceives while still a nursing-mother (= *Sk.* **rurrutsā**). (2) *Vd.* **cạncạŋ** ～. (3) **daŋ** ～ *m.* (*f.* **'yar** ～) child conceived before mother has weaned previous one (*so considered puny*). (4) *cf.* **kwanïkāwā ; kwanïkanci**.

kwanïkancị *m.* unseemly behaviour (*cf.* **kwanïkāwā**).

kwanïkāwā *pl.* (1) jokers. (2) untrustworthy persons (*pl. of* **bạkwanïkẹ**). (3) *cf.* **kwanïkạ ; kwanïkancị**.

ƙwạnjï (1) **ganiŋ** ～ covetousness. (2) *Sk. m.* crop of bird (= **bạrōrọ**). (3) *Vd.* **tattạrā** 1*d*, **ƙundū, ƙunjï**.

ƙwaŋ kadọ *m.* long cake (**cūrị**) of **tūwō** (= **malmalā**).

kwạŋkē *Vb.* 3A *Sk.* returned *x* **cïwọ yā** ～ **masạ** illness returned to him.

ƙwaŋƙi *m.* = **ƙwandagẹ**.

ƙwaŋƙirō *Kt. epithet of* stingy P.

kwaŋkọ *m.* (*pl.* **kwaŋkunạ**) = **gwaŋgwaŋ**.

ƙwaŋƙōlï *m.* (1) summit. (2) **ƙwaŋƙōlin dājị** dense bush (= **dōkā** 1*d* = **kūwạ** 1*e* = **ïhụ** 2).

ƙwaŋ ƙọmas-ƙọmas *used in* **yā yi ƙwaŋ ƙọmas- ƙọmas** he brought trouble on himself.

ƙwaŋƙọnā *Vb.* 1C kept on burning (*int. from* **ƙōnạ**).

ƙwaŋƙōnï *m.* dark oil got from residue of **maŋ rūrūwạ** (*Vd.* **maŋ gyạdā**).

ƙwaŋƙōshai = **gujïyā** 2.

kwaŋkunạ *Vd.* **kwaŋkọ ; kwaŋ-kwaŋ**.

kwạŋkwadạ *Vb.* 2. (1) quickly drank much of. (2) **yā kwạŋkwạdi tạfïyạ** he travelled far. (3) **kwạŋkwạdi gïwā, kwạŋkwạdi zākị, yạu mā, gạ ƙwaryā wọfï** now my child, drink up your food !

kwạŋkwạdē *Vb.* 1C (1) drank greedily all of. (2) = **kwandẹ** 2.

kwạŋkwadō *m.* (1) defaced coin (*cf.* **similikạ**). (2) 4 in. U-shaped pin used by woman for scratching head (**masōshï**). (3) **'yaŋ** ～ Maguzawa minstrels drumming on fragment of gourd (**sạkainā**) ; *epithet is* **Kwạŋkwadō na magạjï**.

kwạŋkwamā *Kt. f.* cave.

ƙwạŋƙwạmai *pl.* evil spirits causing madness (= **iskōƙï**).

kwạŋkwambịlō (1) **yā tạfi** ～ he's disappeared. (2) **sūnansạ yā tạfi har** ～ he's famous everywhere.

ƙwạŋƙwạmbishï *m.* type of small, black biting-ant (*epithet is* **Kwạŋƙwạmbishï, bạ yā dạ gạtarï**).

kwaŋkwąmĭ *m.* (1) (*a*) yā yi ～ he raised voice in anger (= hąrgāgĭ). (*b*) yā cikạ ～ he's a raucous P. (*c*) mụtụm mại ～ loud voiced P. ƙūrụ mại ～ pony with loud neigh. (2) kwaŋkwąmiŋ kāshĭ, dĕbĕwā = kwaŋkwąmiŋ kāshĭ, kwāshĕwā if T. *must* be done, better get it over and done with ! (3) exaggerated fuss (= kwąrmatọ).

kwan-kwan A. (kwaŋ-kwąŋ) *m.* (*genitive* kwaŋkwąnin) *pl.* kwaŋkunạ = gwaŋgwaŋ. B. (kwąŋ-kwąŋ) (1) *adv.* with excessive fuss. (2) ～ dạ dūbā look carefully for it !

kwankwani A. (kwąŋkwanĭ = kwąŋkwąnĭ) *m. Strophanthus hispidus ; S. sarmentosus* (*seeds used for arrowpoison*). B. (kwaŋkwąnĭ) *Vd.* kwaŋ-kwąŋ.

ƙwąŋƙwantō *m.* investigation.

kwaŋkwaramēmẹ = kwaŋkwaramĭ *m.* (*f.* kwaŋkwaramēmĭyā = kwaŋkwaramā) *pl.* kwaŋkwaraŋ-kwąŋkwąrąŋ huge (*re* P., horse, house).

kwaŋkwąrąŋ (1) *m.* yā yi ～ it's huge (= kwaŋkwaramēmẹ). (2) *adv.* yanġ tsạye ～ he's standing lankily. nā ga gidā ～ I saw a desolate, large compound (= gwąŋgwąrąŋ).

ƙwąŋƙwąrarrē = ƙwąŋgwąrarrē.

kwaŋkwarmēmẹ = kwaŋkwaramēmẹ.

ƙwanƙwasa A. (ƙwaŋƙwąsā) *Vb:* 1C. (1) (*a*) yā ƙwaŋƙwąsạ ƙōfạ he knocked at door (= dakạ 1*d.*v). (*b*) yā ƙwaŋƙwąsạ tukunyā he tapped pot to test it. (*c*) tested knowledge of P. B. (ƙwąŋƙwasa) *Vb.* 2 (*p.o.* ƙwąŋƙwąshē, *n.o.* ƙwaŋƙwąshi) = ƙwąŋƙwąsā.

kwaŋkwasọ *m.* rear lumbar region (= tsatsọ = ƙuŋgūrụ = *Sk.* ƙūgụ = *Sk.* tamrō), *cf.* gịndī.

kwaŋkwątsā *Vb.* 1C (1) shattered (= fasạ). (2) perforated (garment) = fasạ.

kwaŋkwątsē (1) *Vb.* 1C = kwaŋkwątsā. (2) *Vb.* 3A (garment) is perforated.

kwaŋkwatsĭ *used in* ạrādụ tạ yi minĭ ～. (1) I swear I did not do it ! (2) I swear I won't do it ! (= ạbassamạ 2).

ƙwaŋƙwōnĭ = ƙwaŋƙōnĭ.

ƙwam maƙērā *m.* slag (= ƙwạ 1).

ƙwam mulụfĭ *m.* (1) small, bluish bead. (2) type of blue burnous (ạlkyabbạ).

ƙwąnnąfĭ *m.* (1) flatulence (= sūyạ 3). (2) *Vd.* kaŋwā.

Kwạnni *Vd.* Hausā.

kwānọ *Yor. m.* (*pl.* kwānōnĭ = kwānunnukạ). (1) (*a*) any metal bowl or basin. (*b*) small tin basin used as cornmeasure (= gwaŋ-gwaŋ 2). (2) headpan. (3) tin of tinned food *x* kwānạŋ kīfĭ a tin of fish. kĭfiŋ ～ tinned fish (= gwaŋ-gwaŋ 3). (4) tinplate. (5) corrugated iron. (6) fariŋ ～ dạ kāshĭ ạ ryfe "whited sepulchre". (7) mụtụm mại ～ P. of wealth. (8) *cf.* gwaŋ-gwaŋ ; kwaŋ-kwąŋ ; kwaŋkọ ; fam-fạm ; garwā ; galạŋ. (9) sạmạriŋ kwānọ *Vd.* bōjwā.

kwanshē *Vd.* kwānad dạ.

ƙwạnsō = kwạnsō *m.* integument (*x* nut, shell, pod, cartridge-case, cotton-boll), *Vd.* kwạsfā.

kwanta A. (kwạntā) *Vb.* 3A. (1) (*a*) lay down (for sleep or otherwise), *cf.* barcĭ, kwānā A.1, kwānā A.2. 3*a*. (*b*) yā ～ cĭwọ he lay sick. (*c*) har ŋ ～ dāma *Vd.* dāma 1*d.* (*d*) iŋ kanạ zạune, kạ ～ *Vd.* tsạye 5. (2) yā ～ kwạn'cekwạncē", ya shēƙạ musụ ƙaryā he told them carefully prepared lie. (3) kạdarkọ yā ～ bridge has fallen in. (4) (*a*) (i) haŋkạlīna yā ～ my mind is now at rest (= lafạ). (ii) haŋkạlīna bại ～ dạ shĭ ba I don't trust him. (*b*) cikịntạ yā ～ she mistakenly thought herself pregnant (= tsirgạ 3 *q.v.*). (*c*) gāshịm bạkinsạ yā ～ he's got his way. (5) (affair, dispute, fire, wind, pain, etc.) subsided (= wāshẹ 2*h.*ii) *x* iskạ tā ～ the wind has abated (= rimạ 1 = lafạ). mạganạ tā ～ (*a*) the matter's settled (= lafạ = tsirgạ 2). (*b*) the matter is in abeyance. (6) (*a*) rūwā yā ～ sediment of water has fallen to the bottom. an yi rūwạ ? has there been rain ? (*reply,* ĭ, har yā ～ yes, and it has left puddles). (*b*) = wāshẹ 2*h.*i. (7) azzịkinsạ yā ～ his luck is out. (8) yā ～ minị it has slipped my memory. B. (kwantā) *f.* (1) (*a*) dōkịnsạ yā cikạ ～ his horse bites through the tethering-rope (gịndī). (*b*) gạgạrạ ～

Vd. gągąrą 9. (2) an yi masą ∼ the horse, etc., lent him has been taken back by the owner. (3) ɗaŋ ∼ nē he's a Don Juan, roving at night. (4) *Kt.* undoing woman's coiffure (= tsĪfą). C. (kwantą) *Vb.* 1A untied (= kwancę *q.v.*). D. (kwąntā) *Vb.* 2 (*p.o.* kwąncē, *n.o.* kwąnci). (1) untied (= kwancę *q.v.*). (2) an sā kuturū kuntā *Vd.* jąnyayyē.

kwąntaccē (1) *m.* tanā dą ∼ she has abdominal affection, attributed to fœtus failing to develop (*cf.* kwąntā 4, Shā tąmbayą, Shā rubūtū, Shēkąra, Shēkąrau). (2) kwąntaccē *m.* (*f.* kwąntaccīyā) *pl.* kwąntąttū lying, stagnant *x* rūwā ∼ stagnant water.

kwantad dą = kwantar dą.

Kwąntągōrā *f.* (1) Kontagora. (2) Sarkiŋ ∼ Emir of Kontagora (= Sarkin Sūdaŋ).

Kwantagōrāwā *Vd.* Bąkwąntągōrę.

kwąntą gwĪwū *Kt.* *f.* = kwąntą ƙurī.

kwantai *m.* (1) roots of sābarā *or* kalgō used as substitute for firewood (= kaŋ ąkwĪyą). (2) (*a*) (i) perishable food left unsold at end of day. (ii) nā yi ∼ I returned home with some perishable food unsold (= *Kt.* tsāwā 3). (*b*) kwantam furā stale furā. (3) dįllālį yā yi ∼ broker had some of the garments specially made for Festival, left unsold. yā yi kwantaŋ hāją gōmą he had ten *such garments* left unsold (= bą izǫ).

kwąntą kądā *m.* wastrel (= ragō).

kwąntąkī *m.* high road (= kārauką).

kwąntą ƙurī = 'yar kwąntą ƙurī *f.* small girl chaperoning girl going to tsārąncē (= ƙurī 2*b*).

ƙwantąlā *Vb.* 1C *Kt.* (1) yā ƙwantąlą masąrā he picked open a maize-cob to see if ripe. (2) dōkį yā ƙwantąlą ƙasā horse kicked up earth while in motion. (3) yā ∼ ą gujē he fled.

ƙwąntallę *Sk.*, *Kt.* *m.* contents of one cotton-boll.

kwantąrā *Vb.* 1C (1) yā ∼ ni dą ƙasā he threw me down. (2) did abundantly (= kwantsąmā 3).

kwantar dą *Vb.* 4A *x* yā kwantasshē shį he laid it down.

kwąntą rāfī *m. sg.*, *pl.* reedbuck.

kwantąrāgį *Eng. m.* contract for future supply of nuts, hides, skins, etc., at price stipulated in contract (*cf.* kwaŋgilā).

kwantarērę = kwantarī *m.* (*f.* kwantarērīyā = kwantarā) *pl.* kwantarkwąntąr huge.

kwantasshē *Vd.* kwantar dą.

kwantō *m.* (1) eavesdropping. (2) (*a*) ambushing (= *Kt.* fąkō). (*b*) ɗaŋ kwantō *m.* (*pl.* 'yaŋ ∼) sniper, ambusher. (*c*) māgąnim mąi ∼ *Vd.* hąrsāshį. (3) stealthy movements. (4) bending down to avoid missile.

kwantsą (1) *Vb.* 1A = kwantsąmā 3. (2) *f.* (*a*) idǫ yā yi ∼ eye had mucous discharge (= tsēfą). (*b*) har idǫna yā yi ∼ I had a bad time. (*c*) kwantsąr ƙąrē germinating part of ground-nut (= hancį 4).

kwantsąmā *Vb.* 1C (1) yā kwantsąmą mąganą he blurted out information, spoke tactlessly. (2) tā kwantsąmą ɓąrī she let her load fall, muddling up contents. (3) did abundantly *x* yā kwantsąmą 'yā'yā it (tree) fruited abundantly ; he had many children. yā ∼ masą mārį (sąndā) (gātarī) he dealt him blow with hand (stick) (axe). yā ∼ masą zāgī he abused him. yā ∼ masą jĪfą he threw missile at him.

kwantsąmē (1) *Vb.* 1C yā ∼ shi dą mārį = kwantsąmā 3. (2) *Vb.* 3A became emaciated.

kwantsąmi what abundant fruit on tree, *etc* !

kwantsąrā *Vb.* 1C = kwantsąmā.

kwantsąrē *Vb.* 1C = kwantsąmē 1.

kwantsąri = kwantsąmi.

kwantsę *Vb.* 3A = kwantsąmē 2.

ƙwąntsī *m.* hatsī yā yi ∼ corn has young ears (= idǫ 1 *p.v.* = tąutsī 1).

kwānuką days (*pl. of* kwānā A.2).

kwānunnuką *pl. of* kwānǫ.

kwanyā *f.* (1) occiput (= ƙyēyą). (2) the brain (= ƙwaƙwalwā). (3) flesh on occiput (especially of ram).

ƙwąnyar *used in* rānā tā būdę ƙwąnyar the hot-season (bazarā) sun is blazing.

ƙwanyạrē *Vb.* 3A rānā tā ∼ = ƙwạnyar.

kwạnzạgọ *m.* (1) plaited-grass bag used by wives of itinerant traders (fatāƙē) for carrying goods (*resembles* samfọ). (2) load *so packed.*

ƙwap kậina *x* ạbincin nạŋ ∼ nē this food is enough for one P. only. azzịkinsạ ∼ nē he shares his money with none.

ƙwar A. (ƙwar) *adv.* n nā ganī ∼ I can see perfectly. dumā yā ƙōsạ ∼ gourd's quite ripe. wāyō gạrēshị ∼ he's very cute. wannạŋ gōrẹ yanā dạ ƙwārī ∼ this kola's sound and hard.

B. (ƙwạr) *m.* (1) segment of kola-nut having more than two segments *x* gōrọ mại ∼ uƙụ kola with 3 segments (*cf.* azārā ; tagwāyē 3, ƙwārạ 1c). (2) ∼ uƙụ nē he's a Syrian, *i.e.* Kwạrạ (*referring to their cuteness*), *Vd.* ƙwaras-ƙwaras. (3) *Kt.* giginyạ ∼ bīyū deleb-palm whose stone consists of 2 segments (*the usual form being* 2-3) = ƙwallō 1b. (4) ∼ wạje slave-girl with whom owner sleeps, though not regular concubine.

kwara A. (kwārạ) (1) *Vb.* 1A did abundantly *x* aŋ ∼ rūwā much water's been poured on it ; it's rained heavily. aŋ ∼ masạ kudī it's expensive. aŋ ∼ masạ mārị he's been slapped. (2) Kwārạ = Kwārạ.

B. (kwārā) *Vb.* 2 (1) (*referring to obsolete practice now replaced by* canjạ) *x* nā kwārị sulẹ bīyū da kudīna 5,200 I received coined money for my 5,200 cowries. (2) *Kt.* stripped off (bark, etc.) = tāyā. (3) *Kt. child says* ŋgō (here is something for you !) *and when the other child is about to take it, says* kā kwārā well, I'm not giving it to you ! (*cf.* dōdọ 3, ƙwālēlē) = ƙwạlā 1. (4) *Vd.* kwārẹ.

C. (Kwārạ) *f.* (1) River Niger. (2) kō ạ ∼ dạ tsịbirī there's nowhere without somebody of importance. (3) *Vd.* mōdā 3.

D. (Kwạrạ) = ƙwạrạ.

ƙwara A. (ƙwārạ) (1) *f.* (*pl.* ƙwārōrī). (*a*) shea-nuts (*Vd.* kaɗanyạ). (*b*) bīkilī ∼ *m.* bay horse. (*c*) *Kt.* grain of (= ƙwāyā), *cf.* ƙwạr. (2) *f.* (*no pl.*) large size *x* gōrạn naŋ yanā dạ ∼ these are large kola-nuts. zạrē mại ∼ coarse thread.

rụbūtū mại ∼ thick writing. (*b*) strand *x* zạrē mại ∼ bīyū two-ply thread (*cf.* murjị, tūkā 2b, sịlī). (*c*) *name for* one of twins (*Vd.* tagwāyē).

B. (ƙwārā) (1) *Vb.* 2. (*a*) overloaded. (*b*) overcharged. (*c*) overcame *x* rūwā yā ƙwārē nị water made me choke. aŋ ƙwārị Jamụs the Germans have been overcome. (*d*) underpaid P. (2) *f.* iŋ kā ganī dạ ∼ kạ barị if you think it is beyond you, give it up !

C. (Kwạrạ) *m.*, *f.* (*sg.*, *pl.*) Christian Syrian (*Vd.* ƙwạr 2).

ƙwarai (1) *adv.* very much *x* yanā dạ girmā ∼ it's very big. iŋ aŋ ga ƙōƙa-rim mụtụm yā kai ƙwarai if a man shows exceptional energy. yanā dạ kyạu ∼ dạ gạskē = yanā dạ kyạu ∼ dạ ạnīyạ = yanā dạ kyạu ƙwarai-ƙwarai = yanā dạ kyạu ƙwarai dạ gạskyạŋ gạskē it's extremely good. (2) *m.* excellence *x* aikị na ∼ good work. mụtumịŋ ∼ good P.

kwạrakā *Sk.*, *Kt.* *f.* cadging a meal (= kōrakā *q.v.*).

kwara-kwara A. (kwarā-kwạrā) *f.* (*sg.*, *pl.*) mat made from thin strips of stem of raffia (tukurwā).

B. (kwạrā-kwạrā) *f.* stilts *x* sunā hawaŋ ∼ they're on stilts (= tāk-warākwạrā = *Sk.* ɗaŋkwarō).

kwạrākwạrai spindles (*pl. of* kwarkwarō *q.v.*).

ƙwạrāƙwạrai concubines (*pl. of* ƙwạr-ƙwạrạ).

kwaram A. (kwarạm) (1) suddenly *x* (*a*) sāi gā kyaŋwā ∼ a cat suddenly appeared. (*b*) gạrī yanā wāyẹwā sāi akạ ga ∼ sun isō they unexpectedly came at dawn. (*c*) kwarạm mụ wāyi gạrī, sāi mukạ ji . . . then on waking up one day we suddenly heard that . . . (2) sound of calabashes knocked together. (3) *Vd.* kwarạmī.

B. (kwạram) = kwạraŋ.

kwarami A. (kwarạmī) *m.* buying corn in villages and selling in towns (*epithet is* Kwarạm, hanạ sallạ), *cf.* sārā 2a.i ; jagalē ; kirī ; bōjūwā ; jēmāgẹ 7 ; taŋkū ; ạgịdi 2b.

B. *(kwạramī) East Hausa m.* pen-case (= *Kt.* kōramī).

kwaramnīyā *f.* = **kwaraŋ**.

Kwaran A. (Kwaraŋ = Kwaraŋ) *used in* ~ haną sallą *Vd.* kwaramī.

B. (kwaraŋ) (1) *adv.* ang ząncansą ~ cikiŋ garī his name's being bandied about. (2) watąn ~ ɗayā yakę, na bīyū săi zągąrī people discuss one another for a while, then forget. (3) *Vd.* bąkin turmī.

ƙwarąncē *Vb.* 3A has improved (*cf.* ƙwarai) = ƙwarę.

kwarąngā *f.* (1) the twiner *Smilax Kraussiana* (= ƙayąr kūsų). (2) ladder (= kųrąngā *q.v.*).

kwarąngwādī *Kt. m.* meddlesomeness (= kąrąmbąnī).

ƙwarąngwam *adv.* yā rāmę ~ he's emaciated.   są yang tsąye ~ ox is standing fląccidly (= jųgum).

ƙwarąngwamā *f.* (1) whip of ox-hide or hippo-hide (= būlālą = kurfō). (2) old woman, cow, or mare.

kwarąngwatsǫ = **kwarąngwatsąi** *m.* (1) blurting out T. best kept secret. (2) odds and ends (= karę).

kwarąnkwacį *m.* odds and ends (= karę).

kwaraŋ-kwaraŋ *m.* noisy packing up of belongings by senseless P. in a hurry.

kwarąnkwatsąŋ *x* tā zubar dą kāyā ~ she let fall her load containing tins or other sounding articles.

kwarąnkwatsī *used in* ąrādų tą yi minį ~ (1) I swear I didn't do it ! (2) I swear I won't do it ! (= ąbassamą).

kwarąnnīyā *f.* = **kwarąŋ**.

kwaranya A. (kwarąnyā) *Vb.* 1C threw away (liquid, grain) = zubar dą.

B. (kwarąnyą) *Vb.* 3B flowed.

kwarąnyē (1) *Vb.* 1C eroded (= zāgę). (2) *Vb.* 3A (*a*) rūwā yā ~ river receded. (*b*) *x* rūwā yā ~ ą ƙas dągą tukunyā water leaked out of pot ; pot overflowed or boiled over (= tsīyągē = sąrārą). (*c*) rūwā yā kwaranyō cikin ɗākį (i) water leaked into house (= fęshī, yǫyō). (ii) water flowed through house.

kwarara A. (kwarągrā) (1) *Vb.* 1C. (*a*) poured out much fluid (= ƙwaląlā). (*b*) did abundantly *x* yā kwarągrą tąfīyą he travelled far.   yā kwarągrą dōkį he galloped horse hard (*cf.* kwarągrą 1*b*). aŋ kwarągrą rūwā it rained hard.   yā

kwarągrą īhų he shouted to another. aŋ kwarągrā masą mārį (būlālą) he's been slapped (whipped). (2) *Vb.* 3A. (*a*) rūwā yā kwarārō cikin ɗākį = kwarąnyē 2*c*. (*b*) yā ~ ą gųje he fled.

B. (kwarągrą) (1) *Vb.* 2. (*a*) brought task near to completion *x* yā kwarągri aikį he's nearly finished the work.   yā kwarągri gąrī he has nearly reached the town. (*b*) yā kwarągri dōkį he overrode the horse (*cf.* kwarągrā 1*b*). (*c*) suŋ kwarągrē shį they cadged from him. (2) *Vb.* 3B. (*a*) flowed (= kwarąnyē). (*b*) yā ~ a gųje he fled.

ƙwārągrā *pl.* strong (*pl. of* ƙwąƙƙwārā).

kwarārad dą *Vb.* 4A threw away (liquid, grain) = zubar dą.

kwarąrai *Vd.* kwararǫ.

kwarare A. (kwarągrē) *Vb.* 3A = kwarąnyē 2*a–c*.

B. (kwarągrē) *m.* (1) long journey. (2) *Kt.* = kwącī 2.

kwararo A. (kwararō) *m.* (1) alley. (2) *Kt.* yā yi minį ~ it (ring, bracelet) is too big for me.

B. (kwararǫ) *m.* (*pl.* kwarągrai) = kwarōrǫ.

kwararrąƃē = **kyararrąƃē**.

kwarąrrąƃī *Kt. m.* type of snake.

kwarągrrąƃi how old it is !

kwararrąƃǫ *m.* old P. or T.

ƙwararrafcī *m.* beating kōrę-gown to make it shiny.

kwararrąsā *Vb.* 3A cracked the finger-joints.

ƙwarąrrē *m.* (*f.* ƙwąrarrīyā) *pl.* ƙwarąrrū. (1) expert. (2) sly.

kwaras *x* gidansą ą cikim birnī ~ yakę his home is right inside the city.

ƙwarąs *used in* gųjīyar ƙwarąs *Kt. f.* Bambarra ground-nuts (*Vd.* gujīyā).

kwarashē *Eng. m.* crochet-needle.

ƙwaras-ƙwaras (1) Christian Syrian (*allusively used*), *Vd.* ƙwąr 2. (2) farar kaŋwā cę ~ it's very white potash.

kwarątē profligates (*pl. of* kwartō).

kwarāwąlī *m.* type of Filani milk-measure.

kwarāyą *Kt. f.* (1) the contest shancī. (2) *Vd.* dambē.

kwarbā *f.* threadworms (= ayąmbā).

ƙwarbai *m.* (1) ang shąŋ ~ dą shī he'

giving much trouble. (2) ɗaŋ ∼ m.
(pl. 'yaŋ ∼). (a) warrior, raider (=
garkūwā 3b). (b) shameless P. (=
dākārę).
warcē m. bewitching P. by T. rubbed on
him or buried (= sammu).
warce A. (ƙwarcē) m. second gleaning of
ground-nuts done by poor P. in farm
of owner (is subsequent to jā gindī).
B. (ƙwarcę) Vb. 3A acted as in
ƙwarcē.
kwarɗo Fil. m. (1) bark. (2) integument
of corn.
wārę (1) Vb. 1A. (a) (i) stripped off x
iskạ tā ∼ jiŋkā wind stripped off
thatch (= yāyę). iskạ tā ∼ masạ
rīgā wind lifted up his gown. yā ∼ rīgā
he lifted his gown (to urinate, etc.). (ii)
yā ∼ mini yānā he slapped me over the
eyes. (b) yā ∼ jikinsạ he bared his
body (x by pulling up sleeve to cool arm).
(c) aŋ ∼ halinsạ he's been " exposed ".
(d) (i) aŋ ∼ magana matter's been
cleared up. (ii) yā kwārę wannaŋ
kwạsfā he removed that obstacle. (e)
aŋ ∼ masạ bāyā (gindī) he's been left
in the lurch. (ƒ) = kwārā 1. (g) Kt.
stripped off (bark) = kwārạ. (h) Kt.
aŋ ∼ shi dạ zāgi he's been abused. (2)
Vb. 3A. (a) ƙwaryā tā tuntsurē, rūwā
ya ∼ calabash overturned and water
was spilled (= kyālạyē). (b) garī
yā ∼ sky has cleared. (c) jiŋkā tā ∼
thatch has been stripped off by wind.
ware A. (ƙwārę) (1) Vb. 3A yā ∼ dạ
rūwā he " choked " when drinking
water. yā ∼ dạ gōrọ kola-nut· " went
down wrong way " and made him
splutter (= sarƙę 1e). (2) Vb. 1A
rūwā (gōrọ) yā ∼ ni water (kola-nut)
made me " choke " (= sarƙę 2b).
B. (ƙwarę) Vb. 3A has improved (cf.
ƙwarai).
warfa Vb. 2 = ƙwarfatạ.
warface A. (ƙwarfacē) Vb. 1C dipped
out all the small remainder of liquid.
B. (ƙwarfacē) Vd. ƙwarfatạ.
warfatạ Vb. 2 (p.o. ƙwarfacē, n.o.
ƙwarfaci). (1) dipped out small remainder of liquid (= ƙwalƙwalạ =
ƙurāsạ). (2) bailed out (boat) =
kwāsạ 2.

ƙwargwam = ƙwargwam adv. and m. yā
rāmę ∼ = yā yi ∼ he's emaciated.
kwari A. (kwari) m. (pl. kwarūrūwạ).
(1) (a) valley (= kufadạ) ; depression
in ground. (b) ƙarƙwan rūwā, kwari
the evil come to a bad end. (2) furrow
(cf. kunyā).
B. (kwạrī) m. (pl. kwarūrūwạ =
kwarūrukạ). (1) (a) quiver for arrows.
(b) kibīyạ ạ jikiŋ wani ∼ nobody cares
what happens to another. (2) tanā
dạ ∼ she has a baby (= gōyō). (3)
ɗam bāwạ mai kwarin tābarmā, wạndan
tarō, mazāgim fạtakạ epithet of labourer.
(4) kwạrim miji Vd. sani 1a.iii. (5)
sāi kwạrī yā cikạ Vd. zāgīyā 1b.
C. (kwārī) kwāriŋ gidā ƒ. senior wife
(= gidā 1n).
ƙwari A. (ƙwārī) m. (1) (a) strength. (b) (i)
gōnā mai ∼ a fertile farm. (ii) sun
tạmbayi dạlīli, bạ su sāmi mai ƙwārī
na kāmāwā ba they asked the reason,
but received no definite reply. (c)
ƙwāriŋ ạbōkaŋ gābā sun tāsam musu
the bulk of the enemy have attacked
them. (2) soundness (literally or
metaphorically) x maganan naŋ tanā
dạ ∼ it's a sound statement. (3) (a)
ƙwāriŋ kại garēshi he's stubborn
(= tauriŋ kại). (b) ƙwāriŋ kại Vd.
ạdụrūkụ. (4) sunā zamaŋ ƙwārī (a)
they're behaving bravely. (b) they're
on bad terms. (5) (a) = arwā q.v. (b)
yā zubạ masạ ∼ he put a spell on him.
(6) sunā zạune, sunā dībaŋ (= sunā.
zubạ) ∼ they're sitting absorbed in
chatting for long time, without eating
or being distracted by call of nature
(cf. kunyạ 3).
B. (ƙwārī) (1) insects (pl. of ƙwārō).
(2) gā ∼ kam bābā there is froth on the
indigo in the vat.
kwarjallē m. (1) cloth tied round corpse
or round loins of man (especially at
pilgrimage-rites). (2) wrapping trousers
round loins as cloth.
kwarjinī m. (1) being of respect-inspiring
or redoubtable mien (= haibạ =
marawwạ 2). (2) being of good
appearance. (3) kwạrjinin dawạ hakị
a big entourage ensures respect.
kwạrkọ m. yellow Mexican poppy (Ar-

gemone mexicana) : *used for staining teeth* (*epithet is* Kwạrkọ, kā ƙi rūwaŋ Allạ̄) = jabdạrī.

kwarkŏḍumō *m.* scalp-eczema of girls, causing hair to fall out.

kwarkwaḍā *f.* (*pl.* kwạḍạ̄kwạḍai). (1) top of horse's head between ears. (2) gāshiŋ ∼ the hair on 1 which hangs down face. (3) *Kt.* top of human occiput.

ƙwar-ƙwar *adv.* (1) very well *x* yanạ̄ dạ kyau ∼ it's very good. yanạ̄ ganī ∼ he has good sight (= ƙwarai). (2) exactly *x* gōmạ ∼ exactly ten.

ƙwarƙwara A. (ƙwạrƙwārā) *m.*, *f.* (*pl.* ƙwārạ̄rā). (1) strong. (2) in sound condition (*d.f.* ƙwārī).

B. *(ƙwarƙwārā) *f.* = *ƙwaƙƙwārā.

C. (ƙwạrƙwarạ) *Vb.* 2 dipped out small remainder of liquid (= ƙwạl-ƙwalạ).

D. (ƙwạrƙwarạ) *f.* (*pl.* ƙwạrạ̄ƙwạrai) concubine-slavegirl (bạ̄iwā) = sạ̄ḍakạ = makullīyā (*Vd.* sōrō 3, maçẹ̄ 4).

kwarkwarce A. (kwarkwạrcē) *Vb.* 1C wound all the thread on to kwarkwarō (*cf.* kwarkwạrtā).

B. (kwạrkwạrcē) *Vd.* kwạrkwartạ.

ƙwạrƙwạrē *m.* dipping out small remaining liquid.

kwarkwarō *m.* (*pl.* kwạrạ̄kwạrai). (1) (*a*) spindle (mazarī) with much coarse thread (abạ̄wā) wound on it. (*b*) act of winding on abạ̄wā *as in* 1a (= tārīyā). (2) weaver's bobbin (= tārīyā 2 = jīfạ 2b). (3) kai " yạŋke sāƙạ ! " nē, bạ̄ " kạ̄wō kwarkwarō ! " ba *you* are the one in charge. kai kwarkwarō nẹ̄, bạ̄ "yạŋke sāƙạ ! " ba *you* are empowered to act on your own responsibility. (4) kwar-kwaran lạbarbạr chamber of revolver. (5) gold or silver ornament suspended from neck (especially of rider) or secured to turban. (6) double iron device on bit, to prevent horse seizing reins in mouth (cījẹ). (7) kwarkwaram bạrgā hole to drain off horse's urine from tethering-place.

kwarkwarta A. (kwarkwạrtā) *Vb.* 1C. (1) wound abạ̄wā on *as in* kwarkwarō 1a, b. (2) (*with dative*) impressed on *x* nā ∼ masạ kadạ yạ mạntā I urged on

him not to forget it (= nānạtā 2 = kwakkwạfā 3).

B. (kwạrkwartạ) *Vb.* 2 *x* nā kwạr-kwạrcē shị kadạ yạ mạntā I impressed on him not to forget it (*Vd.* kwar-kwạrtā 2).

kwarkwasa A. (kwạrkwasạ) *f.* (1) affectation. (2) ogling ; coquetry ; simpering (*all* = fēlēƙē).

B. (kwarkwạ̄sā = kwạrkwāsạ) *f.* (1) (*a*) driver-ant, · driver-ants (*epithet is* Kwarkwạ̄sā, fịd dạ mai gijị). (*b*) *Vd.* ƙasā 6. (2) yā zamẹ minị " Kwarkwạ̄sā, fịd dạ mai gijị " guest made my life a misery, so I left my house to him.

kwạrkwashī *m.* (1) dandruff (= amōsạniŋ kā). (2) kwạrkwạshiŋ ƙazwā flakes of skin peeled off through scabies. kwạr-kwạshin tụnjērē *ditto* through syphilis (*both* = bạrbạshī 2).

kwạrkwatạ = ƙwạrkwatạ *f.* (1) louse ; lice (= *Sk.* ƙyāyạ). (2) kwạrkwatạr ɓutẹ (*a*) jigger-insect (= jigā). (*b*) kwạrkwatạr ɓutẹ = kwạrkwatạr mātā crab-louse (= ḍạŋkạḍafī 1). (3) bạri mụ jē, mụ fịd dạ kwạrkwatạr idọ let's go to the public spectacle ! ḍēbẹ kwạrkwatạr idọ mukẹ̄ we're enjoying the public entertainment. (4) kadạ ạ yi kitsọ dạ kwạrkwatạ act honestly in all you do ! (5) mụtụm bai fī ka tsụmmā ba, bạ zai kaḍạ makạ kwạr-kwatạ ba junior should not lord it over senior.

kwạrkwạtsaŋ *adv. and m.* in muddle *x* am bar kāyā ∼ = kāyā yā yi ∼ the things are in a muddle.

kwarma A. (kwarmạ) (1) *Vb.* 1A. (*a*) yā ∼ īhụ he shouted out to another. yā ∼ ƙaryā he told " whopper ". tā ∼ rūwā she poured too much water into pot. yā ∼ ƙại cikiŋ ḍākị he entered " without a by-your-leave ". (2) *Vb.* 3A yā ∼ ạ gụjẹ he fled.

B. (kwạrmā) *f.* (1) gauge of ring, bracelet, etc. (2) fitting loosely (circular T.) *x* ạ yi wạ dōkị gindī mai ∼ fit the hobbling rope slackly to the horse's leg !

kwarmạḍā *Vb.* 1C bent over (knife-tip) = kalmạḍā *q.v.*

ƙwarmạsā *Vb.* 1C (1) crumpled up (piece

of paper, etc.). (2) yā ƙwarmạsạ aikị he did the work hastily and carelessly.

ƙwarmạshē *Vb.* 3A is (was) crumpled.

kwarmạtā *Vb.* 1C *x* yā ∼ minị he " blabbed " it to me (*cf.* kwạrmatọ).

kwạrmatọ *m.* (1) " blabbing ". (2) fussing (= kwặkwāzọ = kwạrōkwạrō = zuŋgumī) ; *epithet is* ∼ dạ ƙạshī, māyẹ yā ci tsồfwā. (3) cackling of alarmed poultry (= cẹ̄tō = kwạrōkwạrō).

kwạrmī *used in* (1) mại kwạrmiŋ idọ *m.*, *f.* P. with deep-set eyes. (2) mại kwạrmiŋ idọ dạ wurī yakẹ̄ sōmạ kūkā stitch in time saves nine ; don't leave things till the last minute ! (3) mại kwạrmiŋ idọ bạ yặ ga watạ ba sǎi yā kwānā gōmạ shặ bīyar (*song*) poor man who has nothing to give should keep away from feasts.

ƙwạrnạfī *m.* (1) flatulence. (2) *Vd.* kaŋwā 1*d.*

kwarnō the dye kōrinō *q.v.*

ƙwaro A. (ƙwặrō = *Sk.* ƙwārọ) *m.* (*pl.* ƙwặrī) (1) (*a*) insect. (*b*) ƙwặrạn dạ ya jạrabạ dạ wākẹ̄, dạ shī a kạn dafạ su no amount of warning will divert P. prey to overmastering desire ; if two plot together, the fate of one will be the fate of the other. (2) thief. (3) wizard (= māyẹ). (4) hyena, hippo, crocodile *x* rūwan nạŋ yanặ dạ ∼ this water has hippo or crocodiles in it. jējịn nạŋ, dạ ∼ there are hyenas in this bush. (5) *Kt.* (*a*) wick. (*b*) lanyard (= lạgwạnī = kā cī kā rātạyā). (6) large-headed pin-ornament in woman's ṭaurā. (7) ƙwặrī *pl.* metal bosses ornamenting harness, bridle, or saddle (= kạŋ ƙudā). (8) yā ɓallẹ ƙwặran lifịdī he unhooked metal fastening of armour. yā ɓallạ ƙwặrạn lifịdī he hooked up metal fastening of armour. (9) *Vd.* ƙwặrī. (10) ƙwặrō mại kặi *Vd.* ạlmụkwīdạ.

B. (ƙwārō) *Kt.* *m.* gum (= ƙārō *q.v.*).

kwạrō-kwạrō *m.* = kwạrmatọ 2, 3.

kwạrọ̄rai *Vd.* kwạrọ̄rọ.

ƙwārōrī shea-nuts (*pl. of* ƙwārạ).

kwạrọ̄rọ *m.* (*pl.* kwạrọ̄rai). (1) bag woven

from kabạ-leaves or grass. (2) penis-sheath as worn by Plateau pagans. (3) *cf.* kwararō.

kwạrrā *pl.* (1) green. (2) kōrẹ-gowns (*pl. of* kōrẹ *q.v.*).

kwartakēkẹ = kwartakī *m.* (*f.* kwartakēkịyā = kwartakā) *pl.* kwartakaikwạrtạkại hefty.

ƙwạrtanạ *Vb.* 2 dipped out small remaining liquid (= ƙwạlƙwalạ).

kwartancị *m.* fornication ; adultery (= zịnā).

ƙwartane A. (ƙwạrtạnē) *Vb.* 1C dipped out all small remainder of liquid.

B. (ƙwạrtạnē) *m.* dipping out small remainder of liquid.

kwartō *m.* (*f.* kwartūwā) *pl.* kwartặyē = kwarặtē). (1) *x* kwartantạ nē he's her paramour. kwartūwā tasạ cē she's his paramour. (2) *Vd.* kwartūwā.

ƙwạrtō *Kt.* *m.* gleaning *as in* ƙwarcē *q.v.*

kwạrtōwạ *f.* pulp (tōtụwā) of bitter type of gourd. wannạŋ yanặ dạ dācī kạmar ∼ this is " as bitter as gall ".

kwartūwā *f.* (1) *Vd.* kwartō. (2) blunt-pointed tool for patterning metal. (3) idạŋ ∼ type of embroidery-pattern (= idạn zawạrā).

kwặru *m.* (*obsolete*) changing cowries into money (*Vd.* kwặrā).

ƙwặru *Vb.* 3B (1) = ƙwārẹ 1. (2) became replete.

kwặrūrū *m.* Bambarra ground-nut (= gujīyā *q.v.*).

kwarūrukạ, kwarūrūwạ valleys (*pl. of* kwarị). (2) quivers (*pl. of* kwạrī).

kwarwạ *f.* (1) sun ɗaurạ ∼ they (touts) " puffed " their master's goods. (2) *Sk.*, *Kt.* female knob-billed goose (*Sarkidiornis melanotus*), *cf.* ɗanị.

ƙwạr wạje *Vd.* ƙwạr 4.

ƙwaryā *f.* (*pl.* ƙọ̄rē = ƙōrukạ = ƙōrunạ = ƙọ̄rai = *Kt.* ƙōrukkạ). (1) (*a*) (i) any circular gourd (dumā), *cf.* gịdaunịyā, kumbọ, dặshīyạ. (ii) ạl'amạrin nạŋ ∼ rụfe kẹ̄ nạŋ this matter is a mystery. (iii) hannū ∼ *Vd.* bakạ 2*a*.ii. (iv) shī mā zại bī mụ, cikiŋ ∼ ɗayā zā mụ ci ạbincī he will be our close ally. (*b*) rūwā akẹ̄ kạmar dạ bặkiŋ∼it's "pouring cats and dogs ". anặ rūwa, kạmar dạ ∼ akạ yī shị there were torrents of rain.

(c) kŏwạcẹ ~ tanạ̈ dạ murfinsạ everyone has the chance to decide what suits him and what does not. (d) maị kāmụṇ ~ f. woman bǫrī-devotee on whom another woman relies (= dạ̈fe 2), cf. 10 below. (e) dūkạṇ ~ akẹ̈ yi matạ one wife is denying rival wife or latter's child, proper share of food (= daŋgwạrī 2 = 9a below). (f) ḳwaryä = n nạ̈ ~ I'm having my food (said to P. calling one). (g) munạ̈ ~ (said to P. arriving while one is eating) come and join me! (reply is ạlhamdụ lịllāhị " thanks " or ạ ɗau ạnīyạ " no thanks, I've already eaten "). (h) yä fī nị ~ he gets more to eat than I do. (j) gạ̈ yārọ (dōkị) (rạ̈gō) bạ̈ ~ what a tiny boy (horse) (ram)! (also gạ̈ yārọ, har yārọ bạ̈ ~). (k) baị mai dạ ~ bịkī ba he did not reciprocate the kindness. (l) ~ tagạrī tanạ̈ rạ̈gayạ (i) there's more than meets the eye. (ii) respectable women don't rove about. (m) ~ tạ bi ~, in tä bi akụshī, sãi tạ fashẹ don't tackle what is beyond you! (n) yä fallạ ~ he told a whopping lie. (o) (i) fasạ ~ Vd. dạ̈rīyä 2. (ii) bä ạ̈ fasạ ~ Vd. mạ̈yē 2b. (iii) fạsūwar ~ Vd. fạsu 3. (p) ḳwaryar fādạ Vd. sintạlī. (q) masụdiṇ ~ Vd. masụdī 2. (r) Vd. bạ̈ ni ~. (s) kạ̈wō ~ Vd. kāwō 5. (t) bīkwạṇ ~ Vd. bīkọ 7. (u) zumạr ~ Vd. zumạ 2f. (v) dǭdaṇ ~ Vd. dǭdō 9. (w) ḳwaryar rōrọ Vd. gạba-gạba. (x) Vd. zụbe baṇ ḳwaryāta. (2) (a) sixteen cubits (kāmụ) of farī-cloth. (b) eight kāmụ of sāḳi (Vd. turkụdī, karị 2b, rūwä B.4b). (3) (a) breadth of cloth x zannūwạ mạ̈sū fādiṇ ~ cloths of great breadth (cf. ạlbadạ, cf. 9b below). (b) measurement across diameter of round-house x ḳwaryar wannaṇ ɗāḳị (= ḳwaryar wannaṇ kagọ) tāḳị ạshịriṇ this roundhut is 20 paces across (= shạ̈ 4). (4) ḳwaryar kụṇkurū shell of tortoise. (5) (a) ḳwaryar ạllūrạ 100 needles. (b) ḳwaryar cịttä 100 pods of Melegueta pepper. (c) ḳwaryar fātạ ten sheepskins or goat-skins. (d) ḳwaryar gōrọ 100 kola-nuts. (e) ḳwaryar shūnī 100 cakes of prepared indigo. (f) ḳwaryar tạfannūwä 100 bulbs of garlic. (g)

ḳwaryar Yarạbä 200 kola-nuts. (6) ḳwaryar kại cranium (= ḳǭḳō 4). (7) ḳwaryar ḳīrạ cosmopolitan town. (8) ḳwaryar kǭgī bed of river. (9) 'yar ~ f. (a) = 1e above. (b) narrowness of cloth (cf. 3a above). (10) 'yar riḳwạŋ ~ woman who is bǫrī-novice (cf. 1d).

ḳwạryạ-ḳwaryạ Kt. sunạ̈ cācā ~ they're gambling surreptitiously without a mat (= ḳasạ-ḳasạ).

ḳwạrzabạ Vb. 2 Kt. (1) pestered. (2) treated harshly.

ḳwarzana A. (ḳwạrzanạ) (1) Vb. 2. (a) made scratch on surface of T. (= ḳwạ̈jirạ = yạ̈kusạ). (b) yä ḳwạrzạnẹ̈ nị = yä ḳwạrzạni rạ̈ina it annoyed me. (c) P. rubbed sore place (= sūsạ). (d) yä ḳwạrzạnẹ̈ nị m bī shị he tapped me lightly on arm, as sign for me to follow him. (2) f. scratch x ḳayạ tä yi minị ~. B. (ḳwarzạnä) Vb. 1C = ḳwạrzanạ 1.

ḳwarzạnẹ̈ Vb. 1C = ḳwạrzanạ 1.

kwarzạntä Vb. 3A (1) tried one's hardest. (2) spruced oneself up.

kwasa A. (kwāsạ) Vb. 1A (1) dipped out some of x tä ~ bīyū she dipped 2 calabash-dipperfuls (mārä) of tūwō from pot (tukunyä) into food-bowl (akụshī). tä ~ masạ tūwō she dipped him out some tūwō. yä ~ masạ gōrọ he took out some kolas and gave them to him. (2) yä ~ rūwä dạgạ jirgī he baled out the boat (= ḳwạrfatạ 2).

B. (kwạ̈sä) (1) Vb. 2 (p.o. kwạ̈shē, n.o. kwạ̈shi). (a) = kwāsạ. (b) collected and removed (= kwāshẹ 1b) x jirạ̈gē suṇ kwāsō kāyä the ships brought goods. (c) yä kwạ̈shi gudụ = yä kwạ̈shi jịkī he ran away. (d) kwạ̈shi, ṇ yi makạ gyārä m. anything cheap. (e) yä kwạ̈shē nị (i) he joked with me. (ii) I mistook him for someone else. (f) jirgī yä kwạ̈shi rūwä water poured into the boat. (g) yä kwạ̈shi ạrạhä he availed himself of cheap prices. (h) yä kwạ̈shi rawä buḳwī-buḳwī he began to jump for joy like a hunchback. (j) yä cẹ̈ zaị yi musụ kwạ̈sar kạram mahaukacīyä he was sure they would fall an easy prey to him. (2) f. (a) tanạ̈ ~ she's dipping out tūwō from pot (**tukunyā**) into food-bowl (**akụshī**). (*b*) **yā maishē nị dặdịŋ** ~ he took me for a fool.

C. (**kwāsā**) *Sk.*, *Kt. f.* = **kwặsā** 2*a*.

D. (**kwasā**) *f.* type of loosely-woven material.

kwạsabrọ *Kt.* = **kwạsaurọ.**

ƙwasai-ƙwasai *x* **yā yi** ~ he looks clean and tidy.

kwạsā-kwạsā *f.* pink-backed pelican‑(*epi-thet is* ~ **dāmạ rūwā**) = *Sk.* **būbū-ƙūwā** 3.

kwạsamrọ = **kwạsaurọ.**

kwāsaŋkarā *Kt. f.* reining in galloping horse so suddenly that it slithers (= **jạŋ ƙirặram makaunịyā**).

ƙwasara A. (**ƙwặsarạ**) *Vb.* 2 = **ƙwạrzanạ.**

B. (**ƙwāsặrā**) *Vb.* 1C (1) = **ƙwạrzanạ.** (2) teased (**kặdā**) cotton carelessly.

ƙwặsạrē *m.* (*secondary v.n. of* **ƙwāsặrā** 2) *x* **yanặ ƙwặsạraŋ audụgā** = **yanặ ƙwā-sạrạ audụgā** he's teasing cotton carelessly.

kwạsaurọ (1) what a pot-belly ! (2) *Kt. m.* basket made of **kabạ.**

kwạsfā *f.* (1) outer covering (*x* nut-shell, cartridge-case, setting for jewel ; *Kt.* egg-shell) = **ɓāwō** (*Vd.* **kwạnsō, kamɓōrī**). (2) (*a*) **yā kwārẹ wannaŋ kwạsfā** he removed this obstacle. (*b*) **mum ɓārẹ kạmmụ dạgạ cikiŋ wannạŋ kwạsfā ta "wai munặ zamaŋ ặmānặ"** we swept from our minds the false assumption of being at peace.

kwặ shā *x* **zạn jūyạ gạrēsụ, ŋ sặmē sụ, kwặ shā, kwặ shā, kwặ shā** I'll turn my attention to them and capture them and what bombardment I'll subject them to ! (*Vd.* **kwặ**).

kwasha-kwasha *adv.* (1) poorly-done (work). (2) **yā sặmē shị dạ ạrạhā** ~ he got it " dirt-cheap "

ƙwashal *Kt.* **yā wạŋku** ~ it's specklessly washed.

kwashe A. (**kwāshẹ**) (1) *Vb.* 1A. (*a*) dipped out (**tūwō**, etc. ; *cf.* **kwāsạ**). (*b*) collected and removed (= **kwặsā** 1*b*). (*c*) **yā** ~ **rūwā dạgạ jirgī** he baled out the boat (= **kwāsạ** 2). (*cc*) **yā** ~ **dōkị** he abruptly reined in his horse (= **zāmẹ**). (*d*) **yặ** ~ **kāshinsạ ạ hannū** he'll rue the day he was born ! (*e*)

dukꞋ yā ~, **yā fạɗā** he told the whole affair. (*f*) **yā** ~ **mutặnē** he took prisoners of war. (*g*) **barcī yā** ~ **shi** he fell asleep (= **daukạ**). (*h*) **santsī yā** ~ **shi** he slipped (= **daukạ**). (2) *Vb.* 3A. (*a*) **yā** ~ **ạ gụje** he fled. (*b*) **wadạnnaŋ dặi, tāsụ tā kwāshẹ** these people are done for.

B. (**kwặshē**) (1) *Vd.* **kwặsā.** (2) *m.* (*a*) type of button-hole stitch in embroidery. (3) *Kt.* the reaping-instrument **magirbī.** (4) drawing bow with all the fingers stretching bow-string, for greater force. (5) offal, etc., for making soup (**mīyạ**).

kwặꞋshe-kwặshē꞊ *m.* (1) buying odds and ends. (2) = **kwặshē** 4.

kwặshi *Vd.* **kwặsā.**

kwashiɓō how ugly !

kwāshịkkē *Vb.* 1C *Sk.* = **kwāshẹ.**

kwặshi kwạrạf *m.* (1) ~ **kwặshē** 4. (2) old or useless P. or T.

kwạskwạrīmạ (1) *f.* **kōrạn naŋ** ~ **nē** this **kōrẹ**-gown has been furbished up. (2) how he has scratched his scabby skin !

ƙwas-ƙwas (1) = **ƙwasai-ƙwasai.** (2) **yanặ sāraŋ itặcē ƙwas-ƙwas-ƙwas** he's chopping a little wood.

kwāsō *Vd.* **kwặsā.**

kwat A. (**kwạt**) *m.* court of Local Authority.

B. (**kwat**) *adv.* **yā wạŋku** ~ it's washed specklessly (= **kwal** 1*a*).

kwata A. (**kwatā**) *f.* (1) bad enunciation of " r " as " gh " (= **gurạ-gurạ**). (2) slip of the tongue (= **gọ̄rā** 1*a*.ii). (3) edge-trimmings left over after cutting out cloth or leather, or after preparing **kilịshī.**

B. (**kwatạ**) *Eng.* (1) *f.* (*a*) quarter of a yard of European patterned-cloth (**sạndā**). (*b*) third of a yard of plain white European cloth (*x* **alawayyọ**) = *Sk.* **dara'ạ** 3. (*c*) town (*as opposed to village*) *x* **mụ jē** ~ let's go into " town " ! (= **birnī** 2*b*). (2) *Vb.* 3A played double or quits (*x winner says* " you owe me twopence : shall we play so that we're quits or you owe me fourpence ? " (**ŋ kwatạ bīyū dạ biyū ?**) : if opponent agrees, he says **I, kwata !**). (3) *Vd.* **ạ** ~.

C. (kwậtā) *f.* (1) quay ; mooring-place for boats. (2) *Lokoja Hausa, etc.*, place in River Niger, etc., near big town, where washing is done or water drawn. (3) (*a*) place near railway-station (*x* shēdị), quay, etc., where donkeys are loaded or unloaded by 'yaŋ kwậtā. (*b*) transporting loads by donkey or porter to or from vicinity of railway station (*x* shēdị) or quay for fee.

ƙwata A. (ƙwậtā) *Vb.* 2 (*p.o.* ƙwậcē, *n.o.* ƙwậci). (1) took by force (= ƙwācẹ *q.v.*). (2) yanậ ƙọƙarī yậ ƙwậci girmā he's seeking fame. yā ƙwậci gậbaŋ kansậ he got the leadership (*cf.* ƙwācẹ 1*c*). (3) yā ƙwậci kansậ dậ ƙarfī he behaved insubordinately.

B. (ƙwatā) *f.* type of children's game played in sand.

kwatagādi *Eng. m.* quarter-guard.

kwậtagwaŋgwậmā *f.* false accusation.

Kwậtậhū *used in* ɗaŋ ∼ = Kậtậhū *q.v.*

kwatai *adv.* yā wậŋku ∼ it's specklessly washed (= kwal).

ƙwātai *m.* a plant mixed with henna and applied to hand as charm (māgậnī) to get gifts.

kwātakēkẹ = kwātakī (*f.* kwātakēkịyā) *pl.* kwātakai-kwậtậkai huge.

kwataki A. (kwatakị) *Kt.* jaŋ ∼ = kwatakwārẹ.

     B. (kwātakī) *Vd.* kwātakēkẹ.

kwatakwārẹ *m.* jaŋ ∼ Orange-headed male lizard (= jaŋ gwāɗậ).

kwatakyas (1) bậ shi dậ ∼ " he's spineless " or penniless. (2) *Kt.* yā yi ∼ " he hasn't a leg to stand on ". (3) yā gậji ∼ he's fatigued.

kwatal *adv.* yā wậŋku ∼ it's specklessly washed (= kwal).

kwậtamāsậ *Eng. m.* (1) marine quarter-master. (2) rudder.

kwậtamī *m.* (1) sink. (2) sump.

kwatanā *Sk. f.* beads, etc., round woman's hips (*now replaced by* jịgịdā) = ala-gidigō.

kwậtancē *m.* yā yi minị ∼ he gave me a rough description of it.

kwatanci *m. pl.* (kwậtậnce-kwậtậncē). (1) comparison. (2) = kwậtậncē. (3) yā yi minị ∼ he gave me an example,

illustration. (4) bậ shi dậ ∼ it's unrivalled.

kwatancịn *prep.* resembling ; about *x* mụtụm ∼ gōmậ about 10 persons.

kwậtaŋgwalọ *m.* hip-joint (= ịŋgwallọ).

kwậtaŋkwậcī *m.* (1) comparison *x* bậ shi dậ ∼ it's unrivalled (= kwatancị). (2) kwậtaŋkwậcin = kwatancịn.

Kwậtaŋkwarō *Vd.* banzā 3.

kwậtannịyā *f.* = kwậtarnịyā.

kwatậntā *Vb.* 1C (1) compared *x* yā kwatậntậ wannaŋ dậ wancaŋ he compared this one with that. ậmfậninsậ bā yậ kwậtậntūwā dậ kōmē its advantages are immeasurable. (2) gave a rough idea *x* kậ ∼ minị shī give me a rough idea of it. yā kwatậntậ ukụ dậ hannunsậ he made a sign with his hand, indicating that " three " were meant. (3) endeavoured to emulate *x* nā kwatậntậ aikịŋ ụbāna. (*b*) anậ sậrautậ yậnzu (= yậnzụ ?), kō anậ kwậtậntāwậ is there any such thing as rule at the moment or is one merely playing at it ? (Mod. Gram. 165*a*).

kwậtarnịyā *f.* (*pl.* kwậtậrnī) earthenware basin (= kậfarậ).

kwatashi A. (kwậtashī) *Sk. m.* (*pl.* kwậtậsai) small lidded basket of woven grass (= tậkwashī = kwīkwītậ).

     B. (kwậtashị) *m.* upper storey of European house *x* an ginậ ∼ (= samậ 1*g*.iii) upper storey's been built. yā hau ∼ he went upstairs (*cf.* bēnē, sōrō 1*c*).

kwậ'ti-kwậtī" *m.* white-breasted, little hornbill.

kwậtịrậ *Kt. f.* importunity.

ƙwātō *Vd.* ƙwācẹ.

kwatsa· A. (kwātsậ = kwatsậ) *Vb.* 1A did abundantly (= kwantsậmā 3 *q.v.*).

     B. (kwậtsā) *Vb.* 2 *Kt.* snubbed, rebuked (= kwậ6ā 1*b*).

kwatsa-kwatsa = dātsa-dātsa.

kwatsam A. (kwatsậm) *m.* noise of falling odds and ends.

     B. (kwậtsam) *adv.* (1) abundantly. (2) anậ yị dậ shī ∼ cikịŋ gậrī his name's being bandied about.

kwậtsâtsậ *f. used in* kwậtsâtsậ gậrēshị he's a tactless blurter.

kwatsi̱ what a muddle the dropped things are in !

kwaura A. (kwaur**ạ**) *Vb.* 1A. (1) knocked T. against. yā ∼ k**ạ**ns**ạ** he banged his head. yā ∼ ƙaf**ạ** ji̱kin dūts**ẹ** he hit his foot against a stone.   yā ∼ tuntuɓ**ẹ** he stubbed his foot.   (2) a**ŋ** ∼ mas**ạ** māri̱ he's been slapped.   B. (kwa**ụ**rā) *Vb.* 2 collided with *x* yā kwa**ụ**ri gā̱rū he collided with the wall (= g**ạ**bzā).

kwaur**ẹ** (1) *m.* (*pl.* kwauruk**ạ** = kwaurun**ạ**). (*a*) dead tree (*especially if still standing*). (*b*) destitute P. (*c*) the drum g**ạ**ŋgā. (2) *Vb.* 1A collided with and knocked over (= gabj**ẹ**).

ƙwa**ụ**rī *m.* (*pl.* ƙwauruk**ạ**). (1) calf. (2) shin (*both* = sh**ạ̱** rāɓā).

ƙwaur**ọ** *m.* (1) niggardliness. (2) ƙwaur**ạ**m bā̱kī hesitating to express one's real wishes, from fear or foolishness *x* bā s**ạ̱** ∼ they're not afraid to speak out (= ƙūr**ụ** 3).

kwauruk**ạ** *Vd.* kwaur**ẹ**.

ƙwauruk**ạ** *Vd.* ƙwa**ụ**rī.

kwaurun**ạ** *Vd.* kwaur**ẹ**.

kwāw**ạ** *f.* bean-pods (= kōw**ạ**).

kwā̱yā *Vb.* 2 (1) stripped off (bark), *etc.* (= tā̱yā *q.v.*). (2) child says ŋgō " here's something for you ! " and when the other is about to take it, says k**ạ̱**˙∼ " well, I'm not giving it to you ! " = ƙw**ạ**lā 1 (*cf.* ƙw**ạ**lēlē ; dōd**ọ** 3).

ƙwā̱yā *f.* (*pl.* ƙwāyuk**ạ** = ƙwāyuyuk**ạ** = ƙwāyōyī). (1) (*a*) (i) grain (of corn, rice, etc.) (= *Kt.* ƙwār**ạ**). (ii) b**ạ** m**ụ** ji ƙwā̱yar d**ạ**līli̱n wann**ạ**ŋ **ạ**l'am**ạ**rī ba we have ˙not heard the slightest reason for this. (iii) kā ci dami̱, kā kās**ạ** ɗaukar ƙwā̱yā what an idle lout !   (iv) ƙwā̱yar zarr**ạ** *Vd.* zarr**ạ**. (v) All**ạ**ŋ ƙwā̱yā *Vd.* tsīruk**ụ**. (vi) ya bā d**ạ** ƙwā̱yā *Vd.* z**ạ**kar**ạ** 2. (*b*) single tuber *x* ƙwā̱yar d**ạ**ŋkali̱ sweet-potato tuber. rōg**ọ** yā yi ∼ cassava has formed tubers (= s**ạ̱**iwā 1*b*). (2) part of embroidery of cap or gown *x* t**ụ**mbin jā̱kī m**ạ**i ∼. (3) *in top-playing* (k**ạ**tantaŋw**ạ**), *it is said* an yi mas**ạ** ∼ " his hand's been struck as forfeit ", *to which reply is made* w**ạ**c**ẹ** iri̱ c**ẹ̱** : dā̱w**ạ** ? kō gēr**ọ** is

it a large swelling ? (*Vd.* dā̱w**ạ** 3). (4) fine P. or T. (5) ƙwā̱yar g**ạ**skīyā absolute truth (= zallā 1*b*). (6) ƙwā̱yar id**ọ** ball of eye ; pupil of eye. (7) *Kt.* ƙwā̱yar mā̱rūr**ụ** core of boil on buttocks or thigh. ƙwā̱yar b**ạ**n ni d**ạ** mūg**ụ** core of acne in pubert boys.

Kwāyamāwā *pl.* members of the small-statured Katagum Barebari Clan so named (*pl. of* B**ạ**kwāy**ạ**mī).

ƙwāyā̱y**ẹ̱** eggs (*pl. of* ƙwǎi *q.v.*).

kwā̱y**ẹ** *Vb.* 3A became stripped (= tāy**ẹ** *q.v.*).

ƙwāyōyī *Vd.* ƙwā̱yā.

ƙwāyuk**ạ** *Vd.* ƙwā̱yā.

kwaz**ạ** *Vb.* 3A took to one's heels.

ƙw**ạ**zab**ạ** *Vb.* 2 *Kt.* (1) pestered. (2) treated harshly.

ƙwāz**ạ**ntā *Vb.* 3A tried one's hardest (= kwarz**ạ**ntā).

ƙwā̱z**ạ**ntak**ạ** *f.* striving hard.

kwāzārī *m.* (1) first rains (= *Kt.* mashā̱-ri̱yā). (2) ∼ yā kāwō first water has appeared in river after dry-season (= mashāri̱yā = mā̱gūw**ạ**). (3) ∼ yā ɓāt**ạ** rīji̱yā water's flowed down into well and made it turbid. (4) yā zub**ạ** mak**ạ** ∼ he " led you (seller) on " by overbidding for it (= rūwā A.13*a*).

kw**ạ**zazzab**ọ** *m.* (*pl.* kw**ạ**z**ạ**zz**ạ**bai). (1) gorge. (2) deep channel cut by water (*epithet is* ∼ g**ạ**ba yak**ẹ̱** ci̱).

kwazgi̱ *Kt. m.* old man.

kwazgwamā = kwazgamā *f.* old woman, cow, mare, etc.

ƙwā̱zō *m.* diligence ; pluck.

ƙw**ạ**zzab**ạ** *Kt.* = ƙw**ạ**zab**ạ**.

kwi̱ (1) come, come ! ; behave yourself ! (= hab**ạ**). (2) *Vd.* c**ạ̱**.

ƙwĭ *m.* sound of breaking wind (*Vd.* tūs**ạ**).

ƙwĭɓ**ạ**-ƙwĭɓ**ạ** *f.* pneumonia (= haƙar-ƙarī 2).

kwiɓi̱ *m.* (*pl.* kwiy**ạ**ɓā = kwiyāɓū = kwi̱-ɓun**ạ** = kwiɓōɓī). (1) (*a*) side of the body between thorax and hips. (*b*) *Vd.* kary**ạ** 14. (2) kwiɓi̱ŋ kurēg**ẹ** (*a*) bean with white stripe. (*b*) type of cloth with white stripe.

kwĭd**ọ** *Sk. m.* circumcision (= kā̱cīy**ạ**).

ƙwĭ-ƙwĭ *x* tan**ạ̱** d**ạ** ciki̱ ∼ she (old woman) has abdominal swelling.

kwïkwïtạ f. the basket kwạtashï.
kwïkwïyọ m. (pl. kwịyạ̈kwịyai). (1) (a)
puppy ; lion-cub ; hyena-cub. (b)
kwịyạ̈kwịyai pl. small children. (c)
kwạncïyar kwịyạ̈kwịyai persons lying
curled up against one another for
warmth. (d) ạlhakï ~ nẹ̈ : ụbạŋgi-
jịnsạ yikẹ̈ bị a crime recoils on its
doer. (e) mại ~ shï nẹ̈ dạ kạrē children
one day grow up and then help their
parents. (f) aŋ ƙi cịŋ kạrē, aŋ kōmō
an ci kwïkwïyọ straining at a gnat and
swallowing a camel.
ƙwïtā f. passing wind (= tũsạ 1).
*kwïwā f. Adenodolichos sp. (stalks used
for purlins ; medicine for scorpion bite
is got from this shrub).
ƙwïyạ (1) ạ ~ in the open, exposed. (2)
Kt. the mimosa ƙaddạjï q.v. (3) cf.
kwïyyạ.
kwïyạ̈bā Vd. kwïbị.
kwịyạ̈fạ Sk., Kt. spoon (= cōkạlï).
ƙwïyạkā f. (pl. ƙwïyakōkï) shallow water-
hole in banks of large stream (ƙọramạ),
etc. (= ƙụrụrrụbai).
kwïyạ-kwïyạ m., f. (sg., pl.) small P.
kwịyạ̈kwịyai Vd. kwïkwïyọ.
kwïyam (1) m. smallness x ƙạŋƙanẹ nē ~
dạ shï he's small (pl. ƙanāņạ nē
kwïyam-kwïyam dạ sū). (2) adv. x
yanạ̈ zạụne ~ small P. is sitting
huddled up pensively. 'yar fuskạ ~
tiny features.
kwïyas-kwïyas used in yanạ̈ tạfïyạ ~
slight P. is bustling along.
kwïyat = kwïyam.
kwïyātọ m., f. small P.
kwïyātū m. (1) hubbub. (2) garrulity.
kwïyï-kwïyï m. type of multi-barbed
spear.
kwïyyạ Sk., Kt. f. (pl. kwïyyōyï =
kwïyyai = kwïyyạyyakï). (1) farm-
ridge (= kunyā). (2) cf. ƙwïyạ.
kwọbsā f. sheath (= kwạsfā q.v.).
kwọrōrọ Zar. m. penis-sheath, etc. (= kwạ-
rōrọ q.v.).
kyạ̈ (used in indefinite future for " you "
feminine) x kyạ̈ zō gọ̈be you (fem.)
will probably come to-morrow.
ƙyạ̈ adv. and f. yā fịta ~ = yā yi ~ he's
" togged up ". nā ga zanạn nạŋ ~
this seems to me a fine cloth.

ƙyafa A. (ƙyāfạ) f. toasting (grilling)
meat or fish on skewer (tsiŋkē) near
fire or in pot (to keep it from going bad :
this process lasts longer than babbạkā :
when meat, etc., is done on one side,
skewer is turned round) ; cf. ƙafẹ ;
gadẹ.
B. (ƙyạfā) f. (1) type of small bird.
(2) aŋ kāmạ ~ ạ tarkō " he has met his
match ".
ƙyạ̈fạcē (1) Vd. ƙyạ̈fatạ. (2) yā yi minị
~ = yā ƙyạ̈fạcē nị (Vd. ƙyạ̈fatạ).
ƙyafal used in kō ~ (negatively) not in the
least x kō ~ bạn yi barcï ba I didn't
sleep at all.
ƙyạ̈fatạ Vb. 2 (p.o. ƙyạ̈fạcē, n.o. ƙyạ̈fạci)
called person's attention by stealthy
touch or sign x yā ƙyạ̈fạcē nị. (= yạ̈-
fatạ).
ƙyafe A. (ƙyāfẹ) (1) Vb. 1A toasted as in
ƙyāfạ. (2) Vb. 3A. (a) dried oneself at
fire. (b) (meat) became toasted as in
ƙyāfạ. (c) (clothing) became dried by
fire. (d) P. cooled down after work, etc.
(= hūcẹ).
kyāfị Eng. m. (1) (a) (military) Captain.
(b) " captain " of mining-camp. (2)
leader. (3) manager. (4) handsome P.
ƙyạ̈firfịtā f. (sg., pl.) sandfly (= ƙyạshï 2).
ƙyāƙẹ Vb. 3A Kt. (1) kọ̈gï yā ~ river
became in spate. (2) P. is replete. (3)
is (was) beside oneself with rage. (4)
sobbed loudly.
ƙyāƙïlā Vd. ƙyāƙyịlā.
kyakkẹ̈cē Vb. 1C kept on tearing (int.
from ƙẹcẹ).
ƙyạ̈ƙƙẹgạ Vd. ƙyạƙƙyẹgạ.
kyakkyaƙï m. trembling ; shivering.
kyạkkyarẹ Kt. m. small, flattish drum
always accompanied by dumā (= gạŋgā
1c = Kt. dịkyakkyarị).
ƙyạƙƙyạstū m. tribal-marks tattooed on
face (cf. shạsshāwạ).
kyakkyạụtā Vb. 1C kept on doing T.
well (int. of kyạutā).
kyạkkyāwā m., f. (pl. kyāwạ̈wā). (1)
good. (2) handsome. (3) Vd. ƙarƙō ;
mũnị.
ƙyạƙƙyẹgạ Kt. f. lame excuses ; boggling
(= kurïridạ).
kyạkkyĕwạ Kt. f. loud laughter of men
(= kāwạ = ƙạkkāwạ).

ƙyāƙyācē *Vb.* 3A = ƙyalƙyālẹ.

ƙyaƙyạlā *used in* mại idạŋ ƙyaƙyạlā nẹ " he's got sight like a hawk " kyākyārī = kākārī.

ƙyāƙyạtā *Vb.* 3A = ƙyalƙyạlā.

ƙyaƙyila A. (ƙyāƙyịlā) *Vb.* 1C did slightly *x* tā ƙyāƙyịlạ adō she put on slight adornment. yā ƙyāƙyịlạ gōrọ he took a trifle of kola-nut.

B. (ƙyāƙyilā) *f.* slight amount *x* tā yi ~ she put on slight adornment.

ƙyal A. (ƙyạl) = ƙyạl-ƙyạl.

B. (ƙyal) (1) *adv.* (*a*) yā bā nị sulẹ ~ he gave me 1*s.* exactly. (*b*) kā ƙyālẹ ni ~, kai mā ~ you ignored me, so I ignore you. (2) *m.* (*a*) shī bạ̈ ~ ba nẹ don't under-rate him for *he* is one to be reckoned with (= dādī 6*b*). (*b*) sound of falling of ·small metal article.

ƙyala A. (ƙyạlā) *Vb.* 2. (1) glared at P. in reproval = harārạ (*cf.* kyạrā). (2) *Vd.* lallẹ 2*b*.

B. (ƙyalạ) *Vb.* 1A yā ~ wutā he struck fire from steel and flint (= ƙyallạ 1*b*).

ƙyālạcē *Vd.* ƙyạlatạ.

kyalala A. (kyalạlā) *Vb.* 1C poured out much fluid *x* (1) tā kyalạlạ mại cikin tūwō she poured much butter on the tūwō. (2) jīyạ aŋ kyalạlạ rūwā it rained heavily yesterday.

B. (kyalālā) *x* rūwā yā yi fẹshī ~ much rain blew through the doorway.

kyalạ̄lẹ *Vb.* 3A flowed out abundantly *x* rūwā yā ~ dagạ cikiŋ gōrā water poured out of the gourd.

ƙyạlatạ *Vb.* 2 (*p.o.* ƙyạlạcē, *n.o.* ƙyạlạci) = ƙyạlā.

kyālạyē (1) *Vb.* 1C *x* rūwā yā kyālạyẹ wuriŋ water spread all over the place (= malạ̄lẹ). (2) *Vb.* 3A *x* ƙwaryā tā tuntsụrē, rūwā ya ~ calabash overturned and water was spilled (= kwārẹ 2*a*).

kyālẹ = kyālạyē.

ƙyale A. (ƙyālẹ) *Vb.* 1A. (1) *x* kạ ~ shi (*a*) don't bother about it ! (*b*) take no notice of him ! (2) nā ~ ka I won't be cross with you this time. săi kạ ~ shi don't be cross with him ! (3) ba

zā ạ ~ ba it won't be passed over in silence. (4) *Vd.* ƙyạle mōɗā.

B. (ƙyalẹ) *Vb.* 1A. (1) hit with missile and knocked over. (2) severed (= gillẹ).

kyalē-kyạlẹ *x* yanạ̈ kwạnce ~ he's lying sprawled out. rūwā yā kwạntā ~ water lay everywhere (*both* = kalekale).

ƙyạlē-ƙyalē *m.* yanạ̈ ~ " he's hard up ".

ƙyạle mōɗā (*lit.* " don't bother about the water-dipper ! "). (1) furā or flour mixed only with sour milk (*i.e. undiluted with water, so only possible to the prosperous*). (2) dāmụŋ ~ the mixing of 1.

ƙyạlī *m.* (1) plaits behind ears of women (*cf.* taurā). (2) *x* tā yi ~ dạ sīsi she attached a sixpence to 1.

kyaliya A. (ƙyālīyā) *f.* *x* ~ garēshị he never bothers (*cf.* ƙyālẹ).

B. (ƙyalīyā) *f.* dōkịnsạ yanạ̈ dạ ~ his horse kicks its foreleg with its hindleg (= ƙyạstū).

kyalkẹcī *Kt. m.* the animal kyarkẹcī.

ƙyalƙyạcē *Vb.* 3A = ƙyalƙyālẹ.

ƙyal-ƙyal A. (ƙyal-ƙyal) exactly *x* yā bīyā nị kudīna ~ he paid me my money exactly.

B. (ƙyạl-ƙyạl) (1) *x* yanạ̈ wạlƙīyā ~ it's glittering brightly. (2) *Vd.* ƙyạl-ƙyạl banzā.

ƙyalƙyạlā *Vb.* 3A yā ~ dạ dạrīyā he laughed loudly.

ƙyạl-ƙyạl banzā *m.* (1) showy but useless T. or P. (2) type of bead.

ƙyalƙyạlē *Vb.* 3A yā ~ dạ dạrīyā he laughed loudly.

ƙyạlƙyạlī *m.* (1) twinkling. (2) (*a*) glittering. (*b*) ƙyạllin sulạllā kẹ rūɗạ su they are being deceived by appearances. (3) = ƙyạl-ƙyạl banzā 2.

ƙyalƙyạtā *Vb.* 3A yā ~ dạ dạrīyā he laughed loudly.

kyallạ *f.* (1) (*a*) red and white goat (= gịtsāwạ). (*b*) anạ̈ rabạ ka dạ kīwạŋ awākī, kanạ̈ ɓaɗị kyallạ tā haifụ don't keep on talking about a P. whom nobody wants to hear about ! (2) Kyallạ, kīwạm ɓatạ *epithet of* pigeons (tạttabạrā). (3) Kyallạ, bạ̈ rụfan cikị *epithet of* arrow.

ƙyallạ (1) *Vb.* 1A. (*a*) yā ∼ wutā (i) he lit fire. (ii) he poked up dying fire. (iii) = ƙyanƙyasā 3. yā ∼ tōcilan he shone electric torch about. yā ∼ fitilạ he lit lamp (*all* = haskạ 1*a*). (*b*) yā ∼ wutā he struck fire from flint (ƙanƙarā) with steel (masaɓī) = ƙyastạ. (*c*) yā ∼ idọ he screwed up his eye to look at T. or P. (2) *Vb.* 3A. (*a*) wutā tā ∼ nearly dead fire burned up. (*b*) idansạ yā ∼ sleeper's eyes opened. (*c*) rānā tā ƙyallō sun shone out from behind clouds (= haskạ). (*d*) yā ∼ he " togged himself up " (= haskạ).

ƙyallạrā *Vb.* 1C = ƙyallạ 1.

ƙyallē *m.* (1) small piece of cloth (= guntū = ɓarkị 2). (2) = ƙyalīyā. (3) = ƙyal 2*a*.

ƙyallạ *Vb.* 1A yā ∼ idọ = ƙyallạ 1*c*.

ƙyallī *m.* = ƙyalƙyalī 1, 2.

ƙyạl'li-ƙyạllī^{ll} *m.* (1) = ƙyạlƙyạlī 1, 2. (2) ƙyạlli-ƙyạllin tsādạ, kyan gidā dạgạ baicī he seems well-off, but his family go short.

ƙyallō *Vd.* ƙyallạ.

ƙyạllū *m.* firefly (= mạƙēsūwā).

kyam *x* yā mīƙẹ ∼ it's quite straight. yā kai kāyā ∼ he took the load straight there.

ƙyāmā *f.* (1) feeling of aversion *x* Iŋgịlīshi sunạ ƙyāmar zālunci the English feel aversion from tyranny (= tsantsanī 1*b* = yancanī = tsāgināginī). (2) fastidiousness *x* yanạ jin ∼ he's fastidious (2 = tsāgināginī = tsantsanī 1 = *Sk.* tsandạ).

ƙyamama *Kt.* an zubạ masạ kudī ∼ = yā yi kudī ∼ heavy price has·been fixed for it (= tsababa = *Kt.* ƙyatata).

kyamārē arrow-shafts (*pl. of* kyaurō).

ƙyamārē doors (*Vd.* ƙyaurē).

ƙyamas (1) *m.* rustling sound *x* nā ji ∼ cikin ganyan nan I heard a rustling in that undergrowth. (2) *adv. and m.* yā tāshi ∼ he stood up shamefacedly. ∼ sukạ zō they came brazenly (= ƙangamas).

kyạmbā *used in* 'yan kyạmbā the plant *Curcuma sp.* which gives yellow dye (= rāwayạ 1*a*).

ƙyạmbā *f.* = ƙyạmbī *m.* horse-yaws.

ƙyamị = *Kt.* ƙyamẹ *m.* (1) section of

split giginyạ used for roofing (*cf.* azạ̄rā). (2) stingy P. (3) the bat with intermittent tinkling note, commonly heard at night on trees.

ƙyāmirī *m.* = ƙyāmurī.

ƙyāmọ *m., f.* P. with small buttocks (= tāmīlō).

ƙyamrē *Sk., Kt. m.* door (= ƙyaurē *q.v.*).

ƙyāmurī *m.* (1) one-centime piece. (2) short, slight P.

ƙyāmushē *Vb.* 3A became emaciated or stunted.

ƙyāmụs-ƙyāmụs *adv.* yanạ tạfīyạ ∼ thin P. is walking along.

kyan A. (kyaŋ) *m.* ringing-sound of metal. B. (kyan) *Vd.* kyaụ.

kyānạ *f.* (1) inferior T. (2) fraud.

kyạnarā *Kt. f.* = kyạranā.

ƙyandā = *Kt.* ƙyandạ *f.* (1) measles (= *Kt.* gạidā 2). (2) chicken-pox (1, 2 = tumfụs).

ƙyandal *adv.* abundantly (*re* fluid).

ƙyandạlā *Vb.* 1C poured out much fluid.

ƙyạndam = ƙyạndal.

kyandir *Eng. m.* (*sg., pl.*) European candle (= ạbēlạ).

ƙyangamas = ƙyamas 2.

kyangạrē *Vb.* 3A (1) died. (2) remained long motionless as if dead (from hunger, etc.).

kyạnƙẹnau *Vd.* kyạnkyẹnau.

ƙyạnƙyamạ *Vb.* 2 drank much of.

ƙyạnƙyạmbishī *m.* medium-sized, red kola-nut.

kyan-kyan exactly *x* gōmạ ∼ ten exactly.

kyankyandī *m.* (*pl.* kyạnkyạndai) bag made from gwạdọ-cloth for use as kit-bag. kurman ∼ kit-bag filled with kit.

kyan-kyạn-kyan *m.* (1) clanking of hoes against each other. (2) ƙurụnƙus kạn kūsụ, bābụ sauran ∼, dịllālịm farētani yā mutụ the matter is settled !

kyạnkyạntā *f.* (1) whining. (2) wheedling. (3) taking advantage of person's kindness. (4) spoiled child's fractious ways (1–4 = shikạm bạkī = shạgwaɓạ), *cf.* kyankyẹnē. (5) ɗan ∼ *m.* (*f.* 'yar ∼) *pl.* 'yan ∼ wheedler, whiner.

ƙyanƙyasa A. (ƙyạnƙyasạ *Vb.* 2 (*p.o.* ƙyạnƙyashē, *n.o.* ƙyạnƙyashi). (1) hatched (eggs). (2) yārạn nan ∼ yaƙẹ this week-old lad has a small sore.

B. (ƙyaŋƙyạsā) *Vb.* 1C. (1) (*a*) tapped (egg to test hardness before the game fashē *q.v.*). (*b*) (i) ya ƙyaŋƙyạsạ ƙōfạ he knocked on the door. (ii) bạ zạtō, bạ tsạmmāni, bạ sallamạ, bạ ƙyaŋƙyạsạ ƙōfạ săi mukạ gan sụ we caught sight of them quite unexpectedly. (2) yā ∼ mini lạbārin naŋ he told me this "on the q.t." (= ƙyasạ 2). (3) hit torch (bạkiŋ wutā) to knock off burnt end and make it glow (= ƙyallạ).

kyaŋkyạsai *Vd.* kyạŋkyasọ.

ƙyanƙyashe A. (ƙyạŋƙyạshē) *Vd.* ƙyạŋ- ƙyasạ.

B. (ƙyaŋƙyạshē) (1) *Vb.* 1C. (*a*) hatched all (the eggs). (*b*)=ƙyaŋƙyạsā 3. (*c*) mụ ƙyaŋƙyạshẹ mạganạr cịnikin naŋ let us make this into a " firm " transaction. (2) *Vb.* 3A (*a*) yā yi wạyō har yā ∼ he's very cute. (*b*) ƙurạrrajī suŋ ∼ pimples have burst (= ɓārẹ 2).

C. (ƙyaŋƙyashẹ) *m.* (1) red embers falling from torch *as in* ƙyaŋƙyạsā 3. (2) small amount *x* nā ji ƙyaŋƙyashạm mạganạ I heard some rumours (= kishiŋ-kishiŋ). dạ sauraŋ ƙyaŋ- ƙyashạm mạganạn naŋ a small part of this affair remains still to settle. (3) tiny hole (ƙōfạ) in indigo-dyed garment.

kyạŋkyasọ *m.* (*pl.* kyạŋkyạsai) cockroach.

kyạŋkyẹnau *m.* (1) rainbow (= gizọ 2*c*). (2) officious P.

kyaŋkyẹnē *Vb.* 3A (1) is (was) officious. (2) monopolized conversation or work (= fiffịƙē), *cf.* kyạŋkyạntā.

kyạŋwā *f.* (*pl.* kyaŋwōyī). (1) (*a*) cat (= mạgē *q.v.* = kulẹ 1 = mussạ = dạ̄- dīyạ = ụllē). (*b*) *male is* mụzūrū. (*c*) *epithet is* Fạtu (= Fạtu kulẹ) wutsīyạ dạzạzạ = Adamạ). (2) (*a*) leopard (= dạmisạ). (*b*) dạmisạ wuriŋ Audụ ∼ Audu's fearless. (3) Kyạŋwā, kạshẹ rạ̄ƙumī, kị ci kụnnē benefiting another unselfishly, without profit to oneself. (4) kaŋ ∼ (*a*) small piece of tūwō. (*b*) an sạyi audụgā kạmaŋ kaŋ ∼ a little cotton was bought. (5) kyạŋwar tantạl civet cat = mụzūrun jūdạ. (6) *cf.* sạsariŋ ∼. (7) kyạŋwā bā tạ̄ gidā *Vd.* ɓērā 1*c*. (8) gạriŋ kyạŋwā *Vd.* wạndạ 2*b*.

kyar A. (kyar = ƙyar) (1) dạ ∼ with difficulty *x* dạ ∼ mukạ sāmụ we only just managed to get it (= shạjarạ mạjarạ 2). (2) *x* bạ̄ wani " dạ ∼ "; zai ịsa sọsăi there's not the slightest doubt that it's ample.

B. (kyạr) *x* zanẹ yā kēcẹ ∼ cloth ripped zip !

kyara A. (kyārạ) (1) *Vb.* 1A poured out much fluid. (2) *East Hausa f.* black horse (= akawạlī).

B. (kyạ̄rā) *Vb.* 2 (1) glared at P. in reproval (= ƙyạlā). (2) rebuked P.

ƙyara A. (ƙyạ̄rā) *Vb.* 2 took aim at (= ạunā).

B. (ƙyạ̄rạ)*f.* (1) the grass *Cymbopogon Ruprechtii* (*it is first grass to ripen in harvest-season, followed by* gambạ : *used for making* zānā *and* tufānịyā. (2) yā kas ∼ he fled. (3) *Kt.* duhụŋ ∼ " broken reed " (*Vd.* duhụ 6).

kyārad dạ *Vb.* 4B threw away (liquid, grain) = zubar dạ.

ƙyaraŋ = *Kt.* ƙyaramā *f.* type of bearded, pendulous guinea-corn (= yalaŋ).

kyạranā *f.* the cactus *Euphorbia Barteri etc.* (*for fences*), *Vd.* kịnarā.

ƙyarạŋƙyashi *used in* daŋ ∼ *m.* (*f.* 'yar ∼) *pl.* 'yaŋ ∼ slightly-built P.

kyārar dạ = kyārad dạ.

kyararrạɓē *Vb.* 3A (1) P. became decrepit. (2) P. became dilapidated (*both* = ragwargwạjē).

kyararraɓọ *m.* (1) decrepit P. (2) dilapidated T.

ƙyạ̄ratạ = ƙyạ̄rā.

kyārẹ *Vb.* 3A T. became upset *x* rūwā yā ∼ (= tuntsụrē).

ƙyạ̄rī-ƙyạ̄rī (1) *m.* (*a*) the bird ƙịlạ̄ƙilai 1. (*b*) putting on bright clothes, bright beads or ornaments. (*c*) glitter. (2) *m.*, *f.* (*sg.*, *pl.*) P. dressing *as in* 1*b*.

kyarkẹcī *m.* (*pl.* kyạrkẹtai) a wild hunting dog (= ƙirịƙinjū).

kyarkū = kyarkō (1) daŋ ∼ *m.* (*pl.* 'yaŋ ∼) brass-rods (*used still for payment of dowry in such areas as Idoma, etc.*). (2) yārọ daŋ ∼ cute lad. yārinyạ 'yar ∼ cute girl.

kyarkyarā *f.* (1) kạ̄zā tā sōmạ ∼ hen cackled before laying eggs. (2) tanạ̄ ∼ dạ mazā she ogles men (= fạrī).

kyar-kyar-kyar *m.* cackling.

ꝁyąrꝁyąrtŭ *m.* = ꝁyąsꝁyąstŭ.

kyarmā *f.* (1) one's favourite T. *x* ąbincin nąŋ kyarmātā nę̃ this is my favourite food (= kāmu 3). (2) shivering, trembling.

kyarmŏ *Kt. m.* arrow-shaft (= kyaurŏ *q.v.*).

ꝁyas (1) (*negatively*) nothing at all *x* kŏ ~, bą̃ mu dą lą̃bārị we have no news whatsoever. bai bā nị kŏ ~ ba he gave me absolutely nothing (= ꝁiris). (2) on the quiet *x* mun ji ~ sun ɗaurą ąnĩyąr su yĩ we've heard rumour they intend doing it.

ꝁyasą = ꝁyāsą *Vb.* 1A. (1) = ꝁyastą. (2) yā ~ minị lą̃bārịn nąŋ he told me this on the " q.t." (= ꝁyaŋꝁyąsā 2).

kyąsfĩ = kyąsbĩ *m.* (1) (*a*) disease like ringworm on face, chest, and neck (*cf.* kurę̃cĩ). (*b*) kuturŭ yā ga mąi kyąsfĩ, yā cę̃ "dą haką muką sõmu" be guided by *my* fate ! (2) (*a*) shameless P. speaking to annoy (*cf.* cą̃ɓālǫ). (*b*) *epithet is* Kyąsfĩ, cị fuską.

ꝁyą̃shĩ *m.* (1) ꝁyą̃shĩ = ganịŋ ꝁyą̃shĩ *m.* (*a*) jealousy *x* yaną̃ ꝁyą̃shịŋ (= yaną̃ ganịŋ ꝁyąshịŋ) ąbịn dą Audu ya bā nị he's jealous because Audu gave me it. (*b*) ꝁyą̃shin tŭbąlĩ *Vd.* dą̃lā 2*b*. (2) sandfly ; sandflies = ꝁyą̃fịrfịtā (*cf.* kĩyāshĩ).

kyas-kyas = ꝁyas-ꝁyas quickly (*re* gait or movements).

ꝁyąsꝁyąstŭ *m.* tribal marks tattooed on face (*cf.* shąsshāwą).

kyąssā old grass mats (*pl. of* kẽsǫ *q.v.*).

ꝁyastą *Vb.* 1A yā ~ wutā (1) he lit a match. (2) he struck fire from flint (ꝁąŋꝁarā) and steel (ꝁyąstŭ) = ꝁyallą 1*b*.

ꝁyąstŭ *m.* (1) the steel used *as in* ꝁyastą *x* nā bugą ~ I struck fire from steel (= masaɓĩ). (2) dõkị yaną̃ dą ~ the horse kicks its foreleg with its hindleg (= ꝁyalĩyā).

ꝁyą̃sŭwā *f.* (1) the coarse grass *Pennisetum pedicellatum* (= ꝁąnsŭwā). (2) girmaŋ kăi rawąnịŋ ~ pride comes before a fall.

kyat A. (kyat) = kyar.

B. (kyąt) *Eng. m.* (*sg., pl.*) English cake.

ꝁyatą *Vb.* 3A = ꝁyątā *Vb.* 3B *Sk.* made click indicative of anger (= ꝁwąfā).

ꝁyatata *Kt.* = ꝁyamama.

ꝁyattą = ꝁyastą.

ꝁyąttŭ = ꝁyąstŭ.

kyau (*genitive* kyąn) (1) (*a*) (i) goodness, beauty *x* yaną̃ dą ~ = mai ~ nẽ he is good, he is handsome (*Vd.* dūnĩyą̃ 1*o*). (ii) ꝁasąd dą ta yi ~ dą ginị earth which is good for building purposes. (*b*) mąi ~ Sarkĩ im bą̃ mąi kudĩ kusa in the country of the blind, the one-eyed is king. (*c*) iŋ kaną̃ dą ~ ką ꝁārą dą waŋkā ability or prosperity without good character is insufficient. (*d*) mūnị dą kyaŋ halĩ yā fị kyąkkyāwā handsome is as handsome does. (*e*) kyąn ɗā *Vd.* ɗā 1*b*. (*f*) taną̃ dą kyąn ganĩ = mąi kyąn ganĩ cę̃ she is pretty. (2) (*a*) kyąŋ kăi gąrẽshị he's intelligent or amenable. (*b*) yaną̃ dą kyąŋ kăi he brings luck (= alfālu). (3) yaną̃ dą kyąn dirị = yaną̃ dą kyąŋ ꝁĩrą he's well-built. (4) kyąn zŭcĩyā being phlegmatic, tolerant. (5) dą ~ very well !, O.K. ! (6) kyąm banzā *Vd.* banzā 1*a*.i. (7) kyąn rawā *Vd.* rawā 1*d*. (8) kyąm mazā *Vd.* dąɗą kyau. (9) hąną ~ *Vd.* cācā. (10) kyąŋ ąlwāshĩ = kyąŋ ąlkāwąrĩ *Vd.* ąlwāshĩ 4.

ꝁyaurę m. (*pl.* ꝁyamą̃rę = ꝁyawą̃rę) door (*made of* ꝁyamị, tukurwā, karā, wood, planks, iron, etc.) = *Sk.* gąmbŭ (*cf.* ꝁõfą). (2) ꝁyauraŋ gabąs type of white alloy (= cịŋkąl).

ꝁyaurĩ *m.* (1) type of thin grasshopper. (2) ~ nę̃ mūgum bābę this boy or girl is undergrown.

kyaurŏ *m.* (*pl.* kyamą̃rę). (1) the grass *Saccharum spontaneum* (*used for arrow-shafts*). (2) arrow-shaft. (3) *Vd.* shā B3, shẽmę 2. (4) ɓeraŋ ~ *Vd.* ɓerā 6.

kyauta A. (kyąutā) *f.* (1) liberality *x* yā bā nị ~ he gave me a present (*cf.* rĩbą 1). (2) kyąutar ubā *Vd.* aurę 6*c*. (3) gŏdĩyā kę̃ sā ꝁārịŋ ~ showing gratitude brings further gifts. (4) cikị bai saŋ kyąutar jĩyą̃ ba ingratitude is common to Man. (5) an yi mąną kyąutar "kõma ban ɗākị, ką yi kūkā ! "

they gave us a T. they required them-selves. **(6)** biḳī bạ̄ ∼ ba nẹ̄ *Vd.* biḳī 1*j*.
(7) kyạutar "dẹ̄bi ! " *Vd.* dībạ 1*a*.vi.
(8) yabạ ∼ *Vd.* tukwīcị.

B. (**Ƙyạuta**) **(1)** *name for any* ɗaŋ wābị male or female (= Ạ jẹ̄fas *q.v.*).
(2) *name for* 1st child born to oldish woman (= **Daran tūwō** *q.v. under* darẹ̄ 1*k*).

C. (**kyạutā**) *Vb.* 1C **(1)** (*with dative*) was kind to *x* yạ̄ ∼ minị (*a*) he did me a kindness. (*b*) he reduced price to me. (*c*) he gave me more for my money. **(2)** (*a*) Allạ̄ yạ ∼ manạ God favour us ! (*b*) Allạ̄ yạ̄ ∼, bạ̄ ạbịn dạ ya sạ̄mē sụ thank God, no harm befell them. (*c*) Allạ̄ yạ kyạutạ yịŋ *Vd.* mālạmī 1*c*.ix. **(3)** did well *x* aŋ ∼ shi (*a*) it has been well done. (*b*) it has been given a good appearance. Allạ̄ yạ kyạutạ ƙạrshansạ God bless him ! tun dạ kukạ yi hakạ, kuŋ ∼ since you acted thus, you did well. **(4)** *Vd.* kyạutu.
ƙyautạ = ƙyiftạ.
kyautata A. (kyautạtā) *Vb.* 1C = kyạutā 3.
B. (**kyạutatạ**) *Vb.* 3B became improved.
kyạutu *Vb.* 3B is (was) suitable *x* iŋ kā yi hakạ, bạ zaị ∼ ba if you do so, it will not be a good act (*cf.* kyạutā 3). mạganạŋ nạm bạ tạ ∼ ba this is impolite ; this is not correctly ex-pressed. wannạŋ dạbārạ bạ tạ̄ ∼ ba this plan is useless.
ƙyawạ̄rẹ̄ *Vd.* ƙyaurẹ̄.
kyāwạ̄wā *Vd.* kyạkkyāwā.
kyāwụ *Sk. m.* goodness (= kyau *q.v.*).
ƙyāyạ *Sk. f.* louse, lice (= kwạrkwatạ).
ƙyạzganạ *Vb.* 2 made scratch on surface of (= ƙwạrzanạ *q.v.*).
ƙyēmēmē niggardliness, *etc.* (= ƙēmēmē *q.v.*).
ƙyẹ̄rẹ̄rẹ *x* yạ̄ tsayạ ∼ he stood boorishly silent = ƙiƙạm *q.v.* (*epithet is* rẹ̄rẹ ƙawar ƙauyẹ).
ƙyẹ̄yạ *f.* **(1)** (*a*) occiput (= kwanyā). (*b*) yạ̄ ga ∼ tasụ the enemy fled from him. sun tasō (sun tūrạ = sun taŋkạdạ) ƙyẹ̄yạr rụndunā tasạ they routed his army. (*c*) suŋ izạ ƙyẹ̄yạrmụ dạ ƙarfī they forced us to do it. (*d*) yạ̄ dāfẹ ∼ he fled. (*e*) *Vd.* hụ̄lā 1*d*. **(2)** bā ạ̄

aikạtạ ∼ sǎi gọshī it is done not sin-cerely, but merely for effect. **(3)** " dạ̄ nā shinạ " ∼ cē, ạ bāya takẹ̄ it's no good crying over spilt milk (= dạ̄ 1*b*). **(4)** kaŋwā maị ∼ (*formerly*) female slave for sale. **(5)** ∼ tạ sāmụ *Vd.* dọmin 1*e*. **(6)** fuskạ tā fı̣ ∼ *Vd.* sạ̄re-sạ̄rẹ̄. **(7)** nāmạŋ ∼ *Vd.* alạgwaidạ.
ƙyẹ̄yī *used in* ɗaŋ ∼ (*pl.* 'yaŋ ∼) woman's tress large enough to hang down her back.
ƙyibta = ƙyiftạ.
ƙyifce A. (ƙyifcẹ) *Vb.* 1A. **(1)** yạ̄ ∼ idọ he blinked. **(2)** yạ̄ ∼ minị idọ he winked at me.
B. (**ƙyịfcē**) *m.* **(1)** blinking. **(2)** winking *x* yạ̄ yi minị ∼ he winked at me (= ƙyifcẹ 2).
ƙyifta A. (ƙyịftạ) *Vb.* 1A. **(1)** yạ̄ ∼ idọ he blinked. **(2)** yạ̄ ∼ minị idọ he winked at me. **(3)** *x* kạ̄mịŋ ƙyiftạ̄war idọ sǎi ya kōmō = kạmaŋ ƙyiftạ̄wā dạ bịsmillạ̄ sǎi ya kōmō he returned " like lightning ".
B. (**ƙyịftā**) *Vb.* 2 yạ̄ ƙyịfcē nị he winked at me.
kyǔū *m.* sun yi ∼ they waited in silent anxiety (= tsūū).
ƙyụ̄yā (*derived from* ƙi wụyā) *f.* (*pl.* ƙyụ̄yạce-ƙyụ̄yạcē) indolence, laziness *x* **(1)** yanạ̄ jịŋ ∼ he feels slack. **(2)** yạ̄ kantạrā musụ ∼ he brazenly refused to comply with their orders. **(2)** *cf.* yārọ 4 ; bạlagạ 2.

L

lā (*Ar.* " no ") **(1)** *x* ∼ bạn ji ba I really did not hear it (= lā lā *q.v.*). **(2)** *cf.* lā ịlāhạ. **(3)** *cf.* haulạ.
lạ'adạ *Ar. f.* (*derived from* ạl'ādạ " cus-tom " ; *cf.* Urdu dastūr " custom ", dastūri " commission "). **(1)** com-mission on sales (= kạmashọ = ịjārạ 1*c*). **(2)** lạ'adạ wạje *Vd.* wạje 1*b*.
lạ'akạrī *m.* carefulness *x* bạ̄ shi dạ ∼ he's careless.
*lạ'allạ *Ar.* perhaps.
lạ'anạ *Ar.* **(1)** *f.* (*a*) crime, fault. (*b*) *Vd.* sạmmakō 1*c*. **(2)** *Vb.* 2 *used in* Allạ̄ yạ

la'anē shi God render him accursed !
(thief, etc.) = la'anta.

la'annē m. (f. la'anniyā) pl.
la'annū used in la'annan Allā
scoundrel.

la'anta A. (la'anta) (1) Vb. 2 (p.o.
la'ancē, n.o. la'anci) = la'ana 2. (2)
Vb. 3B is accursed.

    B. (la'antā) Ar. (derived from lahanī)
Vb. 1C. (1) " picked holes in P.". (2)
shamed P.

la'antaccē m. (f. la'antacciyā) pl.
la'antattū = la'annē.

la'ārī = la'ārī Ar. m. feeling of panic.

la'arkance used in yanā la'arkance da
shī, he's keeping an eye on it.

la'asar = la'asariya Ar. f. (1) da la'asar
between 4 p.m. and sunset (Vd.
dada kyau 2). (2) da la'asarim fāri
soon after 4 p.m. (3) Vd. lis ; līshā.
(4) jikina yā yi ~ I felt languid,
apathetic (= kasāla). (5) yā yi la'asariya tasa he spruced himself up and
went out in evening. nā kāwō maka
la'asariya I've come this evening to
spend a while with you.

laɓa Vb. 3A = laɓāɓā.

laɓaɓa A. (laɓāɓā) Vb. 3A walked stealthily
(= sadada = sandā).

    B. (laɓāɓa) adv. yanā taɓe ~ he's
walking stealthily.

    C. (laɓāɓa) Vb. 2 pursued stealthily
(= sandā).

laɓādīya f. (1) yanā shiɓkal ~ he's
wandering aimlessly. (2) Kt. yanā ~
he's wandering aimlessly.

laɓai f. (1) type of soft cotton (= taushī
3a). (2) sūtul ~ m. useless P.

Laɓaran Ar. m. (1) the month of Ramalan.
(2) man's name.

lāɓāri m. (Ar. alkhabari) pl. lāɓārū =
lābārūruka = lābarruka = lāɓārai. (1)
(a) (i) news, information. (ii) (in the
following, lāɓārai can be treated as sing.)
lāɓārai mai yawa = laɓārai māsū yawa
much news. (iii) nā ji ~ = nā shā ~
I heard some news. (iv) nā sāmi ~
cēwā I heard that . . . (v) yā bā ni
lāɓārinsa he informed of it. yā bā
da ~ wai an yī = yā bā da ~ an yī
he brought news that it had been done.
(vi) kun ji inda ~ ya kwānā you've

heard how matters stand. (vii) kō
dayā bai kai ~ ba they perished to the
last man. (viii) lāɓārin zūciya a
tambayi fuska one's face shows what
is in one's heart. (ix) ~ bai zamā
kaman abin da ka ganī da idanka ba
seeing is believing. lāɓārin kitso ,Vd.
kundumī. (b) inā ~ how are you ?
(reply, lāfīya = sāi alhēri " very
well, thanks ! "). (2) (a) bā ~ (i)
there's no news. (ii) that's bad news !
(= mayana = sha'anī 2). (b) bā ~
sāi muka gan su then we suddenly saw
them. (c) bā adō, bā lāɓāri Vd. adō 1d.
(3) ~ nē = lāɓārin Kano, nāma yā
ƙōne, yā bar rōmō tell that to the horse
marines ! (4) (a) kōwā ya rēna mai
lāɓāri Vd. rēna 9. (b) mai ~ Vd.
sūdā 1b. (5) Vd. shāfa lāɓāri shūnī.
(6) lāɓārin wutā Vd. sōya 2.

labarbar Eng. m. (sg., pl.) revolver.

lābartā Vb. 1C nā ~ masa shī I informed
him of it.

lābartad da Vb. 4B nā lābartam masa
da shī = lābartā.

laɓɓā lips (pl. of lēɓe).

labbāti = labbāni = Kt. labbāshi m. imported Tripoli numnah, placed on
horse's mashimfidī.

labbātīyo m. local imitation of labbāti.

labce A. (labce) Vb. 1A took much x
yā ~ nāma da yawa.

    B. (labcē) Vd. labtā.

labda Vb. 1A = labdancē Vb. 1C did
well ; arranged (articles) well.

labdantā Vb. 1C = labda.

labdi m. methodicality, orderliness,
symmetry (= fasalī).

laɓe A. (laɓe) (1) Vb. 1A. (a) x yā ~ da
bangō he crouched behind wall (for
eavesdropping, etc.) = rāɓa 1a. (b)
yā ~ da cīwo he malingered (= faka
2c). (2) Vb. 3A sheltered ; concealed
oneself (= faka 1).

    B. (laɓe) x (1) yanā ~ he's sheltering,
concealed. (2) a ~ secretly.

    C. (lāɓe) Vb. 3A it (meat, potato,
fruit, etc.) became squashy from over-
ripeness or over-cooking (= lāguɓe).

laɓe-laɓe A. (laɓē-laɓe) soggy.

    B. (la'ɓe-laɓē") (1) m. slinking along.
(2) cf. lafe-lafe.

lābị *m.* = lāwụlī.

lā biddị = lā buddạ.

labkī *Kt. m.* softness (= laushī *q.v.*).

lạblạbtū *m.* act of tacking cloth (= lạl-lautū).

laɓo-laɓo *adv.* (1) loosely (tied or socketed). (2) auransụ ∼ nẹ their marriage won't last. (3) = lạɓẹ-laɓẹ.

lạbsụr *m.* Cress (*Lepidium sativum*), *Vd.* algarịf.

labta A. (labtạ) *Vb.* 1A loaded up P., animal, or lorry *x* an ∼ kāyā ạ jạkī donkey's been loaded. yā ∼ kāyā ạ lōrị he loaded the lorry. (2) an ∼ masạ baƙar maganạ (zāgị) he's been spoken to angrily (abused). (3) an ∼ masạ būlālạ (tsumaŋgīyā) he's been whipped (caned). (4) yā ∼ minị kudī he overcharged me. (5) tā ∼ tụrạ̄rē ạ jikạ she "smothered" herself in scent. (6) an ∼ rūwā it rained heavily. (7) kadạ kạ ∼ *m.* racketeering by village-ħead, who refuses to let goods be loaded up till given " rake-off ".

  B. (lạbtā) *Vb.* 2 (*p.o.* lạbcē, *n.o.* lạbci) took much of.

lạbtū *m.* (1) swaying. (2) (*a*) (*secondary v.n. of* labtạ) *x* anạ lạbtun rāƙumạ = anạ labtạ wạ rāƙumạ kāyā the camels are being loaded. (*b*) pack-animal's load.

la bu A. (lā bụ) *Kt.* = lā buddạ.

  B. (labū) *m.* native twine (red and blue or red and white) for tying woman's limbs in henna (ƙunshị).

lạɓūɓụ *m.* (*f.* lạɓūɓụ̄wā). (1) new-born. (2) tūwan naŋ ∼ nē this tūwō is flabby. furan naŋ lạɓūɓụ̄wā cẹ this furā is soggy.

lạɓụcē *Vd.* lạɓụtạ.

lā buddạ *Ar.* for sure ; definitely.

lābūjẹ *m.* type of superior kola-nuts (*from Nupe*).

laɓu-laɓu A. (laɓu-laɓu) = laɓo-laɓo.

  B. (lạ'ɓu-lạɓū") *m.* type of game played by children on river-bank, using formula ∼ kạ̄mạ jijjigẹ, kakkafīyā rịƙyạŋ ƙafạ.

lābulẹ *m.* (1) curtain. (2) yā shiga ∼ he's busy fornicating at the moment.

laɓuna A. (lāɓụnā) *Vb.* 1C. (1) did insecurely (*re* tying, embedding, joining two things) *x* nā lāɓụnạ igīyạ I tied string loosely. (2) placed lightly in soil (*x* cassava, sweet potato). (3) sun lāɓụnạ aurē their marriage won't last long (= laŋgạrā). (4) (*with dative*). (*a*) nā ∼ masạ igīyạ I tied string loosely round it. (*b*) smeared on *x* an ∼ wạ kibīyạ dafị poison's been smeared on arrow. yā lāɓunō minị laifī he falsely accused me.

  B. (lạ̄ɓunạ) *Vb.* 2 poked out (ointment, musk, etc.) from pot with finger or small stick (tsiŋkē) = lākatạ (*cf.* ƙwạ̄ƙulạ).

lạ̄ɓunē *m.* acting *as in* lāɓụnā 2.

lạ̄ɓutạ *Vb.* 2 (*p.o.* lạ̄ɓụcē, *n.o.* lạ̄ɓụci) = lạ̄ɓunạ.

lacam *Kt. used in* yā jiƙa lacam it's sodden.

lācẹ *Kt.* = lātsẹ.

lādā *m.* (*Kt. fem.*). (1) lādā = lādaŋ aikị wages (*cf.* ạlbāshī ; sātī 2*a*) = gaɓạ 3 = ịjārạ 1*a*. (2) reward *x* (*a*) ạbin sāmun ∼ any pious act (*antithesis of* ạlhakī). (*b*) Allā yạ bā dạ ∼ God reward you ! (*Vd.* gaisūwā 5). (*c*) Allā bā yā aikị doŋ ƙaunar ∼ God dispenses justice to rich and poor alike. (*d*) kōwā ya ci lādaŋ kuturū, yā yi masạ askị if you undertake to do T., you must see it through. (3) *Vd. compounds of* lādan. (4) lādaŋkạ wurị *Vd.* gwazai. (5) zōɓẹ lādā *Vd.* zōɓẹ 2*b*.

ladab = ladạbī.

ladạbāwā *Sk. f.* = ladạbī 2*a–c*.

ladạbī *m.* (1) the humble posture assumed before a superior. (2) (*a*) politeness *x* yā yi minị ladạbī he was courteous to me. (*b*) good manners. (*c*) etiquette (= dā'ạ). (*d*) yā yi minị ladạbiŋ kūrā he paid me mere lip-service. ladạbinsạ ladạbiŋ kūrā nẹ he merely pretends politeness. (*e*) yā yi rashin ∼ he behaved impolitely (= ta'ạddā 1). (3) slight punishment as a warning not to repeat (*x* slapping P. ; knocking off (tūrẹ) his turban ; a day or two's imprisonment.

ladạbtā *Vb.* 1C yā ∼ ni = ladạbī 2*a*.

ladạfī = ladạbī.

lạdāmạ = nạdāmạ.

lādaŋ = lādāni *m.* (*pl.* lạ̄dāṇai). (1) muezzin = wazanạ 2 (*epithet is* Kạryạ

rānā = Dǫdaŋ ạsụbạ̄). (2) cock.
(3) long cylindrical bead at head of
rosary (cạzbị). (4) (a) first pock-mark
on forehead or nose in smallpox or
syphilis. (b) swelling on forehead due to
excessive prayer-prostration. (5) Vd.
compounds of lạ̄dānịn.

lādaŋ askā x nā ci (= nā sha) lādaŋ askar
Audụ I playfully slapped Audu on his
head, recently shaved.

lādancị work of lạ̄dạŋ.

lādaŋ ganiŋ idǫ m. small portion of T. one
is eating, given to onlooker (= mai
dạ 2j).

lādaŋ gōyō m. sore on woman's back from
carrying baby (gōyō) = tạyā ni gōyō.

lādaŋ hannū m. trifle of meat given P.
who holds it while it is being cut up for
the pot.

lạ̄dānị Vd. lạ̄dạŋ.

lạ̄dānịn jiɓā m. puffball-fungus.

lādan jīyyạ m. few big marks on P.
nursing small-pox case.

lādaŋ kīwǫ m. one of the young given P.
tending another's goat, etc.

laddạ Kt. f. = ladạbī 2a–c.

Lādị = Lạ̄dị f. (1) Sunday (= Lahạdị).
(2) Lādị = Lạ̄dị = Lạ̄dī = Lạ̄dịŋgō =
Sk. Lạ̄dindimā name for girl born on a
Sunday (cf. Landō). (3) ɗan Lādị =
ɗan Lạ̄dị name for boy born on Sunday
(cf. Landō).

Lạ̄dīdī = Lạ̄dị 2.

lādiŋ kǭgī m. Egyptian plover (Pluvianus
ægyptius) = mạtar kǭgī.

Lado A. (Lạ̄dō) = Lạ̄dī 2.
B. (lādǫ) m. a children's game
(epithet is Lādǫ, wạ̄san darē = Lādǫ,
wạ̄saŋ kạrāyạ ; kōwā ya ɓatạ, yạ
shā dūkạ).

lafa A. (lafạ) Vb. 3A (1) died down (wind,
fire, dispute, illness) (= kwạntā). (2)
Audụ yā ∼ Audu's temper has cooled
down (= hūcẹ).
B. (lāfạ) Vb. 1A (1) an ∼ masạ
lạifī he's been falsely accused. (2) an ∼
azancịn naŋ kạŋ wannạm mạganạ
that sense has been applied to this
word.

lafafa A. (lāfạ̄fā) Vd. lāfīyạ 1f.
B. *(lạfạ̄fạ) Ar. f. shroud (= lịkkafạnī).

Lạfại f. Lapai.

lafā-lạfạ̄ pl. broad and thin (= falā-
falā).

*lafạzī m. speech ; pronunciation x
lafạziŋ Kanǫ = Kanancī.

lafcạkā Vb. 1C yā ∼ minị mạganạ he
addressed me in vulgar slang.

lāfẹ (1) Vb. 1A. (a) x yā ∼ hannun rịgā he
turned down the edge of the gown-
sleeve and sewed another piece of
material (often red) over it to make
hem (cf. kạlmasạ ; kạrbū). (b) dōkị
yā ∼ kunnūwạnsạ horse laid ears back
in temper. yā ∼ kunnūwạnsạ, ya fādạ musụ dạ fadạ he " went for " them.
(2) Vb. 3A. (a) = laɓạ̄ɓā. (b) = laɓẹ 2.

lafe-lafe A. (lafē-lạfẹ̄) = lafā-lạfạ̄.
B. (lafe-lafe) adj. m., f. (sg., pl.) thin
and flimsy.

lạfẹ̄rū m. the large pad placed over
akumạ̄rī on donkey or mule (sometimes
used as cushion in house), cf. manadạrī.

laffạ f. (1) ornamentation cut from thin
tin and applied to door (ƙyaurē) or bed.
(2) the thin sheet of tin hermetically
sealing inside of top of tin of cigarettes
or tobacco. (3) the faked gambling
cowrie gǭdǫgǭ.

laffǫ m. (1) = lamfǫ. (2) mīyạr ∼ f.
soup of new baobob-leaves (= kịrɓē).

lafi A. (lāfị) m. hem as in lāfẹ 1a.
B. (lạfī) vol-planing of bird (= lạyī).

lāfintạ = lāfindạ Eng. f. lavender-water.

lafiya A. (lāfīyạ) (Ar. al'āfiya). (1) f.
(a) (i) health x munạ̄ ∼ we're well.
(ii) dạ̄ mā yạ̄yạ lāfīyạr kūrạ̄, bạllē
tạ yi hạukạ̄ things were bad enough
before, so what will they be like now ?
(b) (i) inā ∼ how are you ? (reply,
sǎi ạlhērị). (ii) Vd. lau ; lāmī. (c)
gạrī yā yi ∼ = gạrī yanạ̄ ∼ all's well
with the town. (d) Allạ̄ yạ bā mụ ∼
well, we'll wait and see what happens !
(e) Vd. kwal 2. (f) Allạ̄ yạ bā mụ
kwānā lāfạ̄fā God give us prosperity !
(g) mụtụm mại ∼ nē = yanạ̄ dạ ∼
kạmar bạntē he is easy-going (= sāliŋ
āliŋ 1a). (h) zạ̄ ni n dūbạ ∼ tasạ I'll
go and see how he is. (j) safety x (i)
hanyạr ∼ bị ta dạ shẹ̄karạ the longest
way round is the shortest way home. (ii)
san dạ sukạ ga hanyạ tā tōshẹ,

sukạ nẹmi hanyạr ∼, kā sam bạ ta
dạ nīsā when they found the road
blocked, they took the longer but
safer way.   (k) ƙaramim maị ∼ Vd.
banzā 1a.   (l) ∼ dạ sạnnū takẹ shịgā
Vd. sạnnū 2b.iv.   (m) bạ ∼ Vd. tābạ 2.
(n) kwānā ∼ Vd. dūkịya 1c.   (o) yā
sāmạ matạ ∼ Vd. sāmạ 1c.   (p) ạ
zaunạ ∼ Vd. zaunạ 1e. (q) Vd. gịzạ̄gō 2.
(r) lāfīyạr gūrū Vd. gūrū 7.   (s) lāfīyạr
ūwar tsandō Vd. tsandō 2.   (2) adv.
safely x (a) kā zō lāfīyạ ? have you
arrived safely ? ∼ kakẹ tạfīyạ yạnzụ ?
is there anything the matter that I
see you about here now ?   (b) cikị ∼,
bakạ ∼ epithet of koko-yam (gwāzā),
mild P., T. not dangerous.   (c) cf. ạ
shā ∼, tạshi ∼.   (d) ∼ kukạ aikạtạ
ạbịŋ hakạ ? did you do well to act
thus ?
     B. (lāfīyā) f. type of late-sown
guinea-corn (= ƙurƙurā).
lạ̄fīyayyē m. (f. lạ̄fīyayyīyā) pl. lạ̄fīyạyyū.
(1) healthy P.   (2) sound T.   (3) mild
P.
lafƙạcē Vb. 3A is (was) soggy.   (2) has
(had) no reserve of health.
lafkī Kt. m. softness (= laushī q.v.).
lạflạftū m. act of tacking cloth (= lạl-
lạutū).
lạfsụr m. Cress (Lepidium sativum), cf.
ạlgạrif.
laftạ Vb. 1A loaded (= labtạ q.v.).
lagạ Vb. 1A yā (tā) ∼zanẹ he (she) threw
cloth round body, covering one
shoulder.
lagab = lagabụ used in farī ∼ narrow,
loosely-woven farī material, undyed or
dyed with indigo.
lạgạdam adv. and m. (1) yanạ̄ tsạye ∼ he
(P. or animal) is standing despondently,
flaccidly (pl. sunạ̄ tsạye lagadam-
lạgạdạm).   (2) wilting of corn through
lack of rain.
lagaf adv. (1) yā jiƙa ∼ it's sodden. (2)
jiƙīna yā yi ∼ I'm feeling out of
sorts.   (3) yārọ (tsōfō) yā yi ∼ child
(old man) is emaciated.
lagai used in farin lagai m. type of mạŋgụl
salt.
lạgē m. draping cloth as in lagạ.
lage-lage m., f. (sg., pl.).   (1) loose in

socket x yanạ̄ ∼ it is loose in its socket
(= Sk. gilgilwạ).   (2) unsteady on its
base (x pot on fire, stool on floor,
marriage) = laŋge-laŋge (cf. daƀas).
laggyạlbālị Fil. m. type of medicine.
lagọ m. (1) holding right-foot with left-
hand or vice-versa in game laŋgạ.
(2) nā ci lagwạnsạ I (his opponent in
laŋgạ) seized the hand with which he
was holding his foot. (3) an ci lagwạnsạ
they got the better of him.   (4) nā
san lagwạnsạ I know something which
gives me a hold over him.
lāgụƀē Vb. 3A it (meat, potato, fruit, etc.)
became squashy from over-ripeness or
over-cooking (= lāƀẹ).
lāgụdā Vb. 1C (1) soiled by handling
(= jagwalgwạlā).   (2) kneaded T. to
soften it (= lailạyā).
lagwadā f. (1) pleasant-looking P. or T.
(2) yanạ̄ shạn ∼ he is partaking of T.
with pleasant flavour.
lạgwai-lạgwai m., f. (sg., pl.) flabby.
lạgwạnī m. lamp-wick (= hanjī 2 = Kt.
ƙwạ̄rō 5).
laha Kt. = lafa.
Lahạdị (1) Ar. f. Sunday. (*2) m. = lahạdụ.
*lahạdụ Ar. m. niche in grave, pointing to
Mecca.
lahại-lahại = lạhai-lạhai adv. yanạ̄ yāwọ
∼ tun dạ sāfē he's been wandering
since early morning without food.
lạhainīyā f. wandering as in lạhai-lạhai
(epithet is Lạhainīyā, cikị bạ kōmē).
lahạŋ Sk., Kt. m. = lahạnī.
lahạnī Ar. m. (1) flaw, blemish. ƙarạiran
nạŋ sunạ̄ dạ ∼ ga bụkātarmụ these
lies adversely affect the fulfilment of
our wishes.   fạdịnsạ yā yi bạbban ∼
what he said did much harm.   (2) distressing occurrence.
lahanta A. (lahạntā) (1) Vb. 1C spoiled.
(2) cf. la'ạntā.
     B. (lạhantạ) Vb. 3B is (was) spoiled.
lā haulạ Vd. haulạ.
lāhẹ Kt. = lāfẹ.
lạhẹrū = lạfẹrū.
lāhịr Vd. tagwai.
Lāhira (Ar. alākhira) (1) the Next World
(= maƙauracī 2 = makōmā 2 = gạskīyā
7 = tsāmīyā 5 = tsīrā 2b.ii) (antithesis is
dūnīyạ).   (2) ran ∼ dạ mạganạ the

mills of God grind slow but exceeding sure. **(3) ạ gạmu ạ ~ tā fi dubū** *epithet of* **mariƙicī. (4) bi bāshị ạ ~** *Vd.* **kạrạmbạ̄nī. (5)** *Vd.* **bạlạ̄hịrā. (6) mabị kạɓakī ~** *Vd.* **laƙại-laƙại.**
lahiya A. (lāhīyạ) *Kt.* = **lāfīyạ.**
   B. (Lahīyā) = **Layyā.**
lạhū bother it all (= **ạp).**
*la'ịfcē *Vb.* 3A became sexually impotent (*Vd.* **lạ' īfị).**
*la'ifcị = **la'ibcị** *m.* man's being sexually impotent (*Vd.* **lạ'īfị).**
lạifī *m.* (*pl.* **laifōfī** = **laifufukạ** = *Kt.* **laifuffukạ). (1)** (*a*) crime, fault *x* **yā yi ~** he did wrong. **bạ̄ shi dạ ~** he's not to blame. (*b*) **an yi masạ ~** (i) a wrong has been done him. (ii) baby has been weaned (= **yāyẹ).** (*c*) **an sạ̄ masạ ~** he's been unjustly accused. (*d*) **don ~ ɗayā** (= **don lạifin rānā ɗayā) bạ̄ ạ̄ ƙịn gwarzō** one fault shouldn't lead to dismissal. (*e*) **~ tudụ, kā tākạ nākạ, kā ganō na wani** everyone is blind to his own shortcomings. (*f*) **~ bạ̄ shi dạ ụbandākị** a criminal always says another is guilty. (*g*) **~ duk na kūrā nẹ, ạmmā bandạ sātạr wadạrī** give a dog a bad name and hang him! (*h*) **rịgar ~ dạ̄ mā bạ̄ ɗịnkạ takẹ̄ dạ wụyā ba, sạ̄wā** nobody admits to a crime (*Vd.* **rịgar lạifī).** (*j*) **tsọrạŋ lạifiŋkạ** *Vd.* **tsọrō** 3. (*k*) **lạifiŋkạ ɓad dạ ạbiŋkạ** *Vd.* **gāwụrzạ.** (*l*) **lạifin jạ̄kī** *Vd.* **diƙiŋ-diƙiŋ. (2)** blemish *x* (*a*) **lạifin rịgan nạŋ gajartạ** the defect of this gown is its shortness. (*b*) **ịnā lạifị** it's not too bad. (*c*) **ạl'amạrimmụ bạ̄ ~** our affairs are prospering. **(3) kadạ kạ zaunạ ạ fariŋ watạ, kanạ̄ dạ ~** do not sit in the moonlight, seeing you've previously had syphilis, lest it recur (*i.e.* **kadạ ƙabbā tạ tāshị)!**
lạ'īfị *Ar. m.* (*pl.* **lạ'ịfai)** sexually impotent man (= **ɗakạ** 2 = **gạ̄tarī** 4 = **bạ̄bā** 2 = **sanyī** 8 = **gidā** 1*d*.ii).
*lạ'iftạ *Vb.* 3B = ***la'ịfcē.**
laifufukạ *Vd.* **lạifī.**
lạ'īhị *Kt.* = **lạ'īfị.**
lailā *f.* = **lelā.**
lā ịlāhụ illạllāhụ (*Ar.*) there is no God but Allah! (*cf.* **tạụhīdị, wạzīfạ, lā).**
*lailạŋ wa nạhārạŋ *Ar. adv.* continually.

lailaya A. (lailạyā) *Vb.* 1C. **(1)** kneaded into balls. **(2)** kneaded T. to soften (= **lāgụdā). (3)** shook together slabs (**cūrị**) of **tụ̄wō** to make them coalesce. **(4)** shook churned milk, for butter to collect in one place on surface. **(5)** rubbed child's bump or bruise "to make it well".
   B. (lạilayạ) *Vb.* 2 = **lailạyā.**
lailaye A. (lailạyẹ̄) *Vb.* 1C completely smoothed over (fresh cement or freshly-beaten mud-floor (**dạɓē)).**
   B. (lailayẹ) *m.* ball of **furā** (= **cūrị).**
laimạ *f.* **(1)** dampness of ground or house (= **danshī** = **rịmā** = **nạ̄sō** = *Kt.* **dambạdā** 1). **(2)** flattery with a view to swindling P. **(3) nā ji bạ̄kiŋkạ yanạ̄ laimạ-laimạ** I hear you munching in the dark. **(4)** (*a*) (i) **an yi wạ rịgā bugụn ~** the particular type of beating gowns called **bugụn ~** has been done to this gown. (ii) *Vd.* **bugụ** 9. (*b*) **laimạ ɗanyā** *Vd.* **ɗanyē** 7. **(5)** (*Ar.* **al khaima**) *pl.* **laimōmī** a tent (= **tantị).** (*b*) umbrella (= **bazarā** 3). (*c*) sunshade (= **shạmsīyyạ).** (*d*) parachute.
laimạcē (1) *Vb.* 3A (house, soil) became damp. **(2)** *Vb.* 1C **yā ~ masạ** = **lai-mạtā** 1*b*.
laimạtā *Vb.* 1C **(1)** (*a*) wetted. (*b*) (plus dat.) *x* **yā ~ minị** he gave me small presents (*cf.* **jiƙạ** 2). **(2)** received small presents *x* **yanạ̄ laimạtāwā gụnsụ** " he's receiving small presents from them ".
laje-laje = **lage-lage.**
lak = **tak.**
laka A. (lākā) *f.* **(1)** (*a*) spinal cord. (*b*) **bạ̄ shi dạ ~** he's apathetic = **shī kạmaŋ an zārẹ masạ ~ nẹ̄** he became terrified. (*c*) **an sạ̄mi ~ tasạ** he was attacked when defenceless. (*d*) **ƙarfẹ, lakā, itạ̄cē, gạ̄rī** *epithet of* **ɗan taurī** who breaks knives on his stomach. **(2)** three longitudinal straps joining front and rear of saddle.
   B. (lākā) *f.* **(1)** (*a*) mud (= **tạɓō).** (*b*) **kadạ kạ sạ̄ ƙafạ ạ ~** = **kadạ kạ shiga ~** keep out of trouble! **(2) ɗan ~** *Kt. m.* = **ɗan rinị** *q.v. under* **dạ̄** 4. **(3)** *Vd.* **banzā** 3.
   C. (lạkā) *used in* **ɗan ~** type of hannun rūwā kola-nut (*its epithet is*

ɗan ~ shā rabō, na Agwandō) (Agwandō *is town-name*).

lakabī *m.* nickname *x* Mai Kano (*cf.* kirārī).

lakace A. (lākace) *Vb.* 1C (1) scraped out all (*as in* lākata). (2) (*plus dative*) = lākata 2.

B. (lakace) *m.* (1) staring like a gaby. (2) kai ~ what a gaby you are ! (*said by* abōkin wāsā).

lakaɗā *Vb.* 1C did abundantly *x* nā ~ masa kāshī I drubbed him. an lakaɗa rūwā da yawa it rained heavily. rūwā yā ~ mu rain drenched us.

lakaɗakawas *used in* ~ da aikim mālan God forbid !

lakadan *adv.* (1) (*Ar.* nakdan) cash down (*cf.* ajalī 3). (2) undoubtedly (= hakīka).

lakaf = lakap.

lakafanī *m.* = likkāfanī.

lakai (1) *adv.* *x* gārī yā yi laushī lakai the flour is finely ground. (2) *m.* *x* gārī yā niku, yā yi lakai the flour is finely ground.

lakaikai = lakai.

lakaikai-lakaikai = lakai-lakai.

lakai-lakai A. (lakai-lakai) = lakai.

B. (lakai-lakai) languidly, apathetically.

C. (lakai-lakai) parasitic glutton (*his epithet is* ~ mabī kaɓakī lāhira).

lakaka loosely *x* yā saki linzāmi ~ he held the reins slackly.

lakakī *m.* indolence.

lakamī *m.* (*pl.* lakamai) (1) wooden bit for horse or donkey, to guard growing crops from being eaten. (2) halter tied round horse's lower jaw.

lakan always.

lakan *m.* lucky charm (lāya) for bridal couple.

lakap *used in* cikinsa yā ɗākalē, yā yi ~ i na Badaurin karē he's become as thin as a rake.

lakata A. (lākata) *Vb.* 2 (1) scraped out (sticky T. *x* butter, man kaɗanya, etc.) from pot *x* yā lākaci jūda he scraped out musk from the pot (= kwākula 3 = lāɓuna), *cf.* sākata. (2) yā lākaci (= lākatō) hancina (i) he pressed me back by putting a finger against my

nose (to provoke me). (ii) he provoked me.

B. (lākatā) *Vb.* 1C (*plus dat.*). (1) smeared T. on to *x* yā ~ masa māi he smeared butter on it. (2) *x* an ~ masa laifī he has been falsely accused (1, 2 = lātunā = shāɓunā). (3) yā ~ mini kaɗan he gave me a trifle.

lakatar *x* yā saki bākī lakatar (= lakataf) he stared like a gaby.

lakayī = lakamī.

lake A. (lake) *Vb.* 1A (1) rapidly ate up small, tasty amount of. (2) (*a*) rapidly overcame. (*b*) knocked down.

B. (lakē) (1) *m. and adv.* yā yi ~ = yā zauna ~ (*a*) he remained lost in meditation. (*b*) he was terror-stricken. (3) *Vd.* sadaki ~.

lakē-lakē *m.* despondency.

lakī *m.* overlapping (= rakī *q.v.*).

lākin (*Ar.* but) for *x* ~ nī bā bāwanka ba nē for I am not your slave.

lakīyā *f.* not sharing with anyone outside one's household the meat of the ram killed for the festival layyā.

lakkā *Kt.* *f.* spinal cord (= lakā *q.v.*).

lakkanā = lakkanā *Vb.* 1C prompted *x* nā ~ masa abin da zai faɗā I prompted him (= magantad da).

lakkata = lākatā *q.v.*

lakkin (1) = lak. (2) not even *x* kō ~ bābu not even a particle is left.

lakō = lakē.

*lakōkō *used in* ɗan ~ *m.* (*pl.* 'yan ~) the fish mārī.

lako-lako A. (lako-lako) loose in socket, etc. (= lage-lage *q.v.*).

B. (lakō-lakō) apathetically (= lakai-lakai).

lakō-lakō *m.* despondency (= lakē-lakē).

lākucē = lākacē.

laku-laku A. (lāku-lāku) (1) loose in socket (= lage-lage *q.v.*). (2) *m.* carelessness.

B. (laku-laku) loose in socket (= lage-lage *q.v.*).

lākuma lākuma lēlē *m.* type of children's game.

lākumē = lankwamē.

lākuta = lākata.

Lakwaja *f.* Lokoja.

lałwā-lałwā *pl. adj.* large and round (*x* eyes, fruit, etc.).

lałwas *m.* (1) despondency, exhaustion, flabbiness. (2) **an tạmbạyē shị sǎi ya yi ∽** he was asked, but failed to reply.

lala A. (lạ̄lā) *f.* (*a*) indolence. (*b*) **tsịyā tā yi aurē dạ ∽, sū sukạ haifi hạgē dū dạ bāshị** destitution and idleness can only engender misery.

B. (lālạ) *used in* **mẹ̄ ya yi minị na ∽** how does it concern me ?

C. (lạ̄lā) *Kt. f.* boys' whooping-cough (= **tạ̄rī 2**).

D. (lā lā) *x* ∽ **bạn yi ba** I swear I didn't do it. ∽ **bạ zạŋ yi ba** I'll never, never do it (= **alạlā** = **lā lạ̄ lā** = **lā**).

lālaba = lāluba.

lālạ̄cē *Vb.* 3A (1) (*a*) T. or P. deteriorated ; T. became spoiled (*cf.* **lạ̄lātạ**). (*b*) **duk ạl'amạrī yā lālạ̄cē** everything has gone wrong. (2) **kōmē lālạ̄cẹ̄war māsạ, tā fi kāshin shānū** half a loaf is better than no bread. (3) **kō zākị yā lālạ̄cē, yā yi łarfịŋ hịnzīrị** a P. with hereditary dignity, no matter what happens to him, will not sink to the bottom (= **birị 1g**). (4) **in tụrurrūwā tā tāshị lālạ̄cẹ̄wā, sǎi tạ yi fikạ̄fikī** if a wife begins to show temper, it means she wishes to leave you.

lālācị *m.* laziness (*cf.* **lālạ̄cē**, **lạ̄lātạ**).

lalai (1) *m. and adv.* effortlessly *x* (*a*) **yā sạ̄mē shị ∽** (= **ạ ∽**) he got it without trouble. (*b*) -**kanạ̄ shạn ∽** you get all your desires fulfilled (*Vd.* **mashạ̄ 2**). (2) *adv.* = **lalas**. (3) submissive P. (*his epithet is* ∽, **nāmạŋ kạ̄zā**).

lālājọ = lālājẹ̄ = lālājị rattle used in Filani games (= **cạkaurạ 1b** = *Kt.* **takkyatẹ**).

lā lạ̄ lā = lā lā.

lalama A. (lālamạ) *f.* (1) flattery (= **lal-lamī** *q.v.*). (2) goodwill *x* **zā mụ shiryạ dạ ∽, bạ dạ tāshịŋ haŋkạlī ba** we'll settle our quarrel peaceably (= **lịmānạ**).

B. (lạ̄lamạ) flattered (= **lạllaɓạ**).

lạ̄lạmẽ *m.* kind of gruel (= **lạ̄mạmẽ**).

lālamō *Vb.* 1E (1) found with difficulty T. vanished into large area (as vanished into pocket, fallen in pond, etc.). (2) **yā ∽ bạ̄kinsạ** he swept his tongue round

his mouth to clear it of food-particles (= **kālụmā 3**).

lā larrạ wạlā lịrārā (*Ar.* there's no evil) there is no deception about it !

lalas A. (lalạs) *m.* (1) cauterizing sore with red-hot knife. **lalạshịn dạ akạ yi masạ yā yi ạmfạ̄nī** the cauterization done to him was beneficial (*cf.* **kạ̄mā 2 ; acū-rạkī**). (2) applying warmth of heated pit to sick P. on whom oil has been rubbed and who lies in the pit covered with cloths (= *Sk.* **zōbā**).

B. (lalas) (1) finely ground *x* **yā nịłu ∽.** (2) **yā dọku ∽ a** he's been been drubbed.

lalạshī *Vd.* lalạs.

lalata A. (lạ̄lātạ) *f.* (1) bad conduct. (2) badly done work. (3) immorality, fornication, adultery (= **zịnā**), *cf.* **lālācị, lạ̄lātaccē.**

B. (lālạ̄tā) (*a*) spoiled a T. (*b*) brought shame on, disgraced *x* **mun lālạ̄tā shi dạ tạrkạcansạ na Jāmụs** we have brought him low, together with his German crew of cut-throats (= **mu-gụntā**). (*c*) (i) **gidā bīyū lạ̄lātạ kạrē** don't have too many irons in the fire ! (ii) *Vd.* **kạrkīyā.**

lạ̄lātaccē *m.* (*f.* **lạ̄lātaccīyā**) *pl.* **lạ̄lātạttū** (*a*) a spoiled T. (*b*) wastrel. (*c*) **lạ̄lātaccạŋ kāyā, darē ạ bī dạ shī** dishonourable acts can only be done on the sly.

lālātad dạ *Vb.* 4B spoiled a T. (= **lālạ̄tā 1a**).

lale A. (lạ̄lẹ̄) (1) **lạ̄lẹ̄** = **lạ̄lẹ̄ turụm** welcome, Visitor ! (2) a cry by boys jumping into water (= **bạ̄hẹ̄**).

B. (lālẹ̄) *Vb.* 1A (1) **yā ∽ shi** he (child) playfully hit him (friend). (2) shuffled (cards).

C. (lālē) *Zar.* for sure (= **lallē** *q.v.*).

lạ̄lẹ̄gọ *m.* Filani children's dancing-game.

lạ̄lẹ̄manā *f.* type of female dance.

lālẹ̄mọ *Sk. m.* type of thatching-grass.

lāliba = lāluba.

lạ̄līṭạ *f.* (*pl.* **lạ̄līṭai**) long, narrow, cotton money-bag (= **rạ̄rīṭạ**).

lallaɓa A. (lallạɓā) *Vb.* 1C. (1) (*a*) smarmed, flattered. (*b*) soothed (angry P.). (*c*) encouraged (tired traveller). (2) drank much of. (3) (*a*) repaired temporarily. (*b*) **tā lallạ̄ɓạ gāshịntạ**

(woman) made makeshift coiffure (ḳumbu̱cē) = taushe̱ 4A. (c) tied slackly as temporary measure. (4) smeared on x tā lalla̱6a̱ lalle̱ a̱ ƙafa̱ she smeared henna on her foot. (5) Vd. lalla6ō.
B. (la̱lla6a̱) Vb. 2 = lalla̱6ā 1.
lallabce = lallafce.
lalla6e A. (la̱lla̱6ē) m. woman's makeshift coiffure (= ḳumbu̱cē).
B. (lalla̱6ē) intensive of la6e̱.
la̱llab̲ƙā Kt. finely-ground (= la̱llausā q.v.).
la̱lla̱6ō x la̱lla̱6ō dǎi (1) pull yourself together ! (2) come along carefully !
lallabta = lallafta.
lallafce A. (lalla̱fcē) Vb. 1C tacked material (cf. ka̱ŋgē, lalla̱ftā).
B. (la̱lla̱fcē) Vd. la̱llafta̱.
la̱llafsā Kt. m., f. (pl. lafsa̱sā) = la̱llausā.
lallafta A. (lalla̱ftā) Vb. 1C tacked T. on to material x yā lalla̱fta̱ a̱ljīfū = yā ∽ wa̱ zana̱ŋ a̱ljīfū he tacked the pocket on to the cloth (cf. lalla̱fcē).
B. (la̱llafta̱) Vb. 2 = la̱llafcē.
la̱llaftū m. (1) act of tacking (Vd. lalla̱fcē). (2) part where cloth is tacked.
la̱llaga Vb. 2 lapped up.
la̱lla̱ga kunnē m. ear-ring ; ornament for ear-lobe (= cililligā 2).
lallagē = lallagī m. (1) act of lapping (Vd. la̱llaga̱). (2) leaf budlets and branch-tips.
lalla̱gōwa̱ f. = lallakī.
lallai Skt., Kts. = lallē.
lallakī m. sprouting of leaves.
la̱llama̱ Vb. 2 flattered (= lalla̱6ā).
lalla̱mē Vb. 1C flattered (= lalla̱6ā).
lallamī m. (1) flattery (= malmal). (2) da̱ ∽ ka̱n d̃au bāshi̱, rānar bīya̱ a̱ shā dambē loans are got by flattery, but on payment day there are blows.
lalla̱n Vd. lalle̱.
lalla̱ntā Vb. 1C rendered incumbent x an ∽ musu̱ shī it has been rendered compulsory to them (Vd. lallē).
la̱llaptū = la̱llautū.
lalla̱s Kt. m. = lala̱s.
lallasa A. (lalia̱sā) Vb. 1C beat slightly (= ƙuŋƙumā 2a, 3 q.v.).
B. (la̱llāsa̱) Vb. 2 (1) (a) appeased, fondled (= ra̱rrāsa̱). (b) persuaded x yā la̱llāshē su̱ bisa̱ su̱ had̃a̱ kǎi he

persuaded them to come to terms. (2) kept on licking (intens. from lǎsa̱).
lallashe A. (lalla̱shē) Vb. 1C = la̱llāsa̱.
B. (la̱lla̱shē) Vd. la̱llāsa̱.
C. (la̱lla̱shē) m. act of lightly beating clothing (= ƙuŋƙu̱mē q.v.).
lallashi A. (lallāshī) m. (1) act of coaxing (= ta̱rairaya̱ 2 = rarrāshī) (Vd. la̱llāsa̱). (2) rarrāshī bā ya̱ yi musu̱ sǎi sa̱ndā coaxing is useless—force must be used against them.
B. (la̱lla̱shi) Vd. la̱llāsa̱.
C. (lalla̱shi) Kt. = lala̱shī.
la̱llausā m., f. (pl. lausa̱sā). (a) finely-ground. (b) pliable, supple.
la̱llautū m. act of tacking material (cf. lalla̱fcē)'
lalle A. (lallē) (1) adv. for sure x ∽ za̱i zō he's sure to come. (2) (with subjunctive) it is essential that x ∽ ka̱ bā ni̱ you must give me without fail. suka̱ ga ∽ su̱ sākē̱ wurī they considered it essential to migrate. yā san lallē ya̱ cī mu̱ kō ya̱ lāla̱cē he knows he must either defeat us or " go to the wall ". (3) a̱bin lallē Vd. fa̱rkā 2b.
B. (lalle̱) m. (1) (a) (i) henna, Egyptian privet (used for staining women's hands and feet ; root serves for aperient and abortion). (ii) its epithet is Mara̱ndā, kā fi bābā kāmu̱. (iii) Vd. alalla̱mī ; mara̱ndā. (b) (i) hannū yā ci ∽ the henna-stain on the hands has become well fixed. (ii) ƙafa̱ tā ci ∽ the henna-stain on the feet has become well fixed. (iii) ƙafa̱ da̱ lalle̱ Vd. ƙafa̱ 10. (c) tā ƙunsa̱ ∽ she encased her hands or feet in henna (cf. ƙunshi̱). (d) an sā ta (shi) a̱ ∽ she (bride) (he, bridegroom) is undergoing the 5 days (for bridegroom 1–2 days) application of henna just prior to the bi̱ki̱ŋ aurē (Vd. aurē 6d, bu̱d̃ar kǎi, kāma̱ 6). (e) ga̱mā lalle̱ henna, buy, buy ! (f) gōro̱ yā yi ∽ the kola-nut has become discoloured. (g) lalla̱nsa̱ yā ka̱rai (i) his prosperity has declined. (ii) the crisis of his illness is over (= a̱lwa̱llā 2). (h) (i) ka̱ bar ni̱ don Sarki̱n da̱ ya ya yi wa̱ shāmūwā ƙunshi̱, ba̱ da̱ lalla̱nta̱ ba for goodness' sake, leave me in peace ! (ii) kōwā ya ga

shǎmuwā, dạ lallạntạ ya gan tạ everybody is as God made him. (iii) *Vd.*
4 *below.* (*j*) gǒrubạ tā sōmạ ∼ the dum fruit has begun ripening (*cf.* nǔna).
(*k*) zubịn ∼ *Vd.* hạ̣uyā 5. (2) (*a*) lallạŋ garēgạ nē it's in demand but unobtainable. (*b*) naŋ ganī, naŋ ƙyǎlā, lallạŋ garēgạ best give it up as a bad job ! (*c*) lallạŋ garēgạ = ƙwạlēlē 1. (3) lallạn jiɓā = lallạn sūrị the shrub *Feretia canthioides.* (4) lallạn shǎmūwā the red-rooted weed *Gisekia pharnaceoides* (*Vd.* 1*h above*). (5) *Vd.* saŋhọ 5.

lalleƙū *m.* (1) summit, apex (= lēƙū). (2) *Kt. used in* yā yi minị ∼ dạ shī he proffered it to me, but then withdrew it (= daŋgōlī *q.v.*).

*lallọ *m.* ceremonial ablutions (= ạlwạlā).

lallōkī *m.* (*pt.* lạllọ̄kai). (*a*) inner room. (*b*) women's quarters (*cf.* tụrākā). (*c*) cul-de-sac. (*d*) *pl. of* lōkọ 2.

lālọ *m.* (1) jute (*Corchorus tridens* ; *Corchorus trilocularis*) used as potherbs (= tụrgunnǔwā). (2) type of bird.

laluba A. (lālụbā) *Vb.* 1C *x* yā ∼ ạ dākị he groped about the house (= fāfạkā).
B. (lạlubạ) *Vb.* 2 groped for T. (= fạ̄fạkạ).

lālụɓā = lallạɓā 3*c.*

lalube A. (lālụbē) groped over the whole of (place).
B. (lạ̄lụbē) *m.* act of groping (*Vd.* lāluba).
C. (lālubē) *m.* boys' catching fish with the hands after fishermen have fished already there (= taɓē 2 = *Kt.* dạ̄fē 2).

lạluma A. (lạlumạ) *Vb.* 2. (1) = kạlumạ. (2) = lāluba.
B. (lālụmā) = kālụmā.

lạlūrạ *f.* = lạrūrạ.

lạlūrī *m.* = lạrūrī.

lāluwai *x* yanạ̄ aikị ∼ he's slacking at his work (= kạlālūwai-kạlālūwai *q.v.*).

lam *used in* bā ∼, bā tsam = sīdīdī.

lamai = lamai-lamai *used in* wannạŋ tūwō yā yi laushī ∼ this tūwō is finely-ground and buttery.

lạmā-lạmā = lạmē-lạmē.

lamama A. (lamama = lạmạmạ) *adv.* (1) abundantly (*re* water in pool or on ground) *x* rūwā yā kwạntā ∼ the water lay in great amount, in pools, etc. (= malala = lamē-lạmē = malēmạlẹ̄). (2) yā kwạntā ∼ he lay exhausted and sprawled out. (3) *Vd.* lạmạmạ.
B. (lạmạmạ) (1) = sạmạmạ. (2) *Vd.* lamama.
C. (lạmāmạ) (1) = lamama 1. (2) what a lot of water ! (*used in same sense as* lamama, *i.e.* on ground or in pool).

lạmạmē *Kt. m.* kind of gruel (= lạ̄lạmē).

Lạmạrūdụ *Ar.* the giant Nimrod.

lạ̄mạ̄sūrū *m., f.* a good-for-nothing.

lamba *f.* (*pl.* lambōbī) (English number). (1) (*a*) (i) token (*i.e.* beacon, signpost, crest, medal, badge, etc.). lambạr jārụntakạ medal for valour. (ii) trade-mark (= wutā 5). (iii) flag (= tūtạ) *x* lambạr asịbitị Red Cross sign, Red Cross flag. (iv) sum mai dạ shī lạmbạ kāshī they have rendered it valueless. (*b*) an tsāgạ masạ ∼ he's been vaccinated (*cf.* hūjị 2). mālạmin ∼ vaccinator (*cf.* dasạ 2). (2) *Vd.* lạmbạ tụ ; lạmbạ wạŋ ; matsạ 1*c.*i.

lamɓai *Kt.* = lạmɓau.

lạmba kāshī *Vd.* lambạ 1*a.*iv.

lamɓạnā (*plus dative*) *x* an ∼ masạ mạganạ he has been falsely accused.

lamɓạnē (1) P. has become slacker. (2) P. has become weak.

lạmbạ tụ (*Eng.* number two, *cf.* lamba) *m.* (1) gutter, drain. (2) horse coming in 2nd in race. (3) second-grade (*re* cotton, hides, skins, etc.). (4) *cf.* lạmbạ wạŋ.

lamɓau *m. and adv.* (*a*) lying comfortably (baby, cat, dog) *x* yārọ yạ̄ yi ∼ = yārọ yā kwạntā ∼ the little boy lay tranquilly. (*b*) rūwā yā kwạntā ∼ the water settled on the ground. (*c*) gāshịnta yā kwạntā ∼ = gāshịntạ yā yi ∼ her hair lay smoothly. (*d*) furā tā yi ∼ = furā tā dạmu ∼ the furā is smoothly mixed.

lạmbạ wạŋ *m.* (*Eng.* number one). (1) horse coming in first in race. (2) firstgrade (*re* cotton, hides, skins, etc.). (3)

cf. **lambạ** ; **lạmbạ tụ̄.** (4) (*a*) **yā yi** ~ he's skilled at it. (*b*) **wajan niŋƙāyạ, yanā̆ cikin** ~ he's an expert swimmer. **yanā̆ cikim masọ̄yammụ** ~ he's one of our best friends. **suŋ kōmạ ạmīnammụ lạmbạwạŋ** they have become our best friends. **wajaŋ gudụ yā yi** ~ he's a sprinter. (5) **an sakam masạ iskạ lạmbạwạŋ** chloroform was administered to him.

lạmbē *Sk. m.* children's water-game (= **'yā 5***a*).

Lạmbēsā a *Kt.* **sạrautạ.**

lambō *m.* (*a*) querulousness, fussing at slightest pain or inconvenience (= **ƙōrạfī**). (*b*) **sōrō, yawạn** ~ **gạrēshị** a flat, mud-roofed house needs constant repair.

lambo-lambo *Sk. m.* = **lạmbē.**

lạmbū *m.* (*pl.* **lambunạ**) irrigated farm (= **rạfī 2**).

lamcẹ *Vb.* 3A *Kt.* was slushy, purulent, *etc.* (= **cāɓẹ** *q.v.*).

lạmē-lạmē = **lamē-lạmē** = **lamama** *q.v.*

lamfọ *m.* (1) new foliage on lopped trees. (2) re-sprouting of trees pruned during **sạssạɓē**, etc. (= **tattọ̄fī**). (3) *cf.* **lạmpọ.**

lami A. (**lāmī**) *m.* (1) (*a*) (i) insipidity of food (= **salab** = *Kt.* **sallaɓī**), *cf.* **sāliŋ āliŋ.** (ii) *Vd.* **kantụ 3.** (*b*) being second-rate *x* **bịkin nạŋ** ~ **nẹ̄** this feast is boresome. (*c*) **dōkịŋ yā yi** ~ (i) the horse needs potash. (ii) the horse is ill-trained. (*d*) **gōdịyar tā yi** ~ the mare is on heat (= **hūda 3**). (2) ~ **lāfīyạ** = **lāfīyạ lau** *q.v. under* lau.

B. (**Lạ̄mī**) (1) *name given* girl born on a Thursday (**ạlhạmis**). (2) **dan** ~ *name given* boy born on a Thursday.

lạmīrị *m.* (*Ar.* **zamīr** thought, idea). (1) intention *x* **lạmīrịŋ zūcịyāta** my intentions, inclinations. **yanā̆ dạ kyạkkyāwan** (**mụmmūnan**) ~ he has good (bad) character. **yanā̆ dạ lạmīrịŋ sạrautạ** he has kingly ways. **bā̆ lạmīrịŋ tạfīyạ** there seems no prospect starting out. (2) good prognostication *x* (*a*) **zạncansạ bā̆ shi dạ** ~ he harps on calamities past and future. (*b*) *Vd.* **fātā 2, sūkạn lạmīrị.** **(3)* personal pronoun.

lam-lam *m.* **yā yi minị** ~ **dạ bā̆kī** he flattered me (= **mal-mal** *q.v.*).

lampo A. (**lạmpọ̄**) *m.* (*French* l'impôt) *Nor.* tax (= **gandū**).

B. (**lampọ**) = **lamfọ.**

lamsạ *f.* (*sg., pl.*) type of fish.

lamshī *Kt.* = **laushī.**

lamunce A. (**lāmụncē**) *Vb.* 1C (*with dative*). (1) *x* **nā** ~ **masạ** I accredited him as my representative (= **wakịltā 1**). (2) gave permission *x* **nā** ~ **masạ yạ shigō** I gave him leave to enter. (3) *cf.* **lāmụnī.**

B. (**lā̆mụncē**) *Vd.* **lā̆muntạ.**

lāmụnī *m.* (*pl.* **lā̆mụnai**) (*Ar.* **al amīni** the trusted one). (1) surety, bail, standing guarantee for *x* (*a*) **mai** ~ **shī kẹ̄ dạ bīyạ** the guarantor is the one responsible for payment. (*b*) **hājạn nạŋ,** ~ **nẹ̄ mukạ ɗaukạ** it was on credit that we took these goods (= **ajạlī 3**), *cf.* **lakadạŋ.** (2) **iŋ kā sạmi** ~ **gạ dọdō, sãi kạ shiga rūwa lāfīyạ** = **gạmō 2***a.i.*

lamunta A. (**lā̆muntạ**) *Vb.* 2 (*p.o.* **lā̆mụncē,** *n.o.* **lā̆mụncī**). (1) went bail for P. (*as in* **lāmụnī**) *x* **nā lā̆mụncē shị** I went bail for him. (2) **nā lā̆mụncē shị sulẹ gōmạ** I sold him ten shillings' worth of goods on credit (*cf.* **lāmụnī 1***b*). (3) **nā** ~ well, I agree (= **yạrdā**).

B. (**lāmụntā**) *Vd.* 1C **nā** ~ **masạ sulẹ gōmạ** = **lā̆muntạ 2.**

lāmushē *Vb.* 1C (1) devoured. (2) folded (garment). (3) (woman) tidied (hair preparatory to **kitsọ**).

lāmushī *m.* hair-tidying *as in* **lāmushē 3.**

lamyā *Kt.* = **lanyā.**

lando A. (**landō**) *m.* **kulɓạ**-lizard.

B. (**Landō**) *name for* boy or girl born on a Sunday (*cf.* **Lādị**).

langa A. (**lạŋgạ**) = **lạŋgā̆** *f.* (1) a children's game where player holds one foot with opposite hand (**lagọ**), *Vd.* **ɗanạ 5, jạgạ, cōgē.** (2) **aŋ kashẹ rūwa** (= **aŋ kas rūwa**) *Vd.* **rūwā K.**

B. (**laŋgạ**) *used in* na ~ **mại mucịyar karā, mại gidā bā yā̆ cẹ̄wā ạ yī** *epithet of* **fạtẹ̄-fatē 1***a.*

laŋgạɓē *Vb.* 3A (1) (meat, potato, fruit, etc.) became mushy from over-ripeness or over-cooking (= **lāgụɓē**). (2) drooped, was (is) flaccid.

langaɓũ *Kt. m.* the meat gaṇdā 1 *q.v.*

langa-langa *m.* (1) batten on bales. (2) long, slender P. or T.

langarā *Vb.* 1C (1) suṇ laṇgarạ aurē = sun lāɓuṇạ aurē. (2) yā ~ miṇi kyaụtā he gave me a small gift.

langarẹ *m.* small amount *x* yā bā ṇi ɗan laṇgaraṇ ạbincī he gave me a trifle of food (*cf.* langē, laṇgyanē).

langē *m.* (1) small portions of meat distributed at festival or naming ceremony *x* am bā ṇi ɗan ~ (*cf.* langarẹ, laṇgyanē). (2) small native-made salt-bag.

lange-lange (1) *adj.* loose in its socket (= lage-lage *q.v.*). (2) cock's comb (= zaṇkō 2).

langwai *m.* (1) sexually impotent man (= lạ'ĩfị). (2) (*a*) querulousness (= ƙõrạfĩ). (*b*) ụban ~ querulous man. (*c*) ũwar ~ querulous woman.

laṇgwạmĩ *m.* = langwai 2.

laṇgyanē *adj.* small *x* ɗan laṇgyanaṇ ƙurjī small pimple (*cf.* langē).

lanhọ = lamfọ.

lanƙafa A. (laṇƙạfā) = laṇƙạyā.

B. (laṇƙạfạ) *Vb.* 3B yā ~ dạ nĩ = laṇƙạfē.

laṇƙạfē *Vb.* 3A *x* yā ~ miṇi he stuck to me like a limpet (= ɗafẹ).

laṇƙai-laṇƙai *adv.* languidly (= lạƙailạƙai).

lankandī *m.* good-for-nothing P. *x* Kạnde ~ cẹ Kande is a useless woman.

laṇkạyā = laṇƙạyā *Vb.* 1C tā laṇkạyạ furā (tũwō) she made good furā (tũwō).

laṇƙạyā *Vb.* 1C (1) an ~ masạ mạganạ he's been falsely accused (= ɗāfạ). (2) = laṇkạyā.

laṇƙạyē = laṇƙạfē.

laṇƙẹ *used in* bā ni dạ shī kō ~ I've none at all.

lanƙi = laṇƙẹ.

lanƙo A. (laṇƙọ) = laṇƙẹ.

B. (laṇƙõ) *Kt. used in* kā ci ~ you've taken the lion's share (*cf.* ƙawwạmā).

laṇkwạmē (1) *Vb.* 1C ate greedily, gulped down. (2) *Vb.* 3A became diminished in bulk (cooked food, deflated tyre, etc.).

lanƙwasa A. (laṇƙwạsā) *Vb.* 1C bent (flexible T.) = taṇƙwạsā.

B. (laṇƙwasạ) *Vb.* 3B (flexible T.) became bent (= taṇƙwasạ).

laṇƙwạshē (1) *Vb.* 3A = laṇƙwasạ. (2) *Vb.* 1C = laṇƙwạsā.

Laṇƙwayạ *Vd.* wutā 1*v.*

lantamĩ *m.* tongue of a shoe.

lantana A. (lạntanạ) *f.* brown stone used as jewellery.

B. (Lantạnā) *girl's name* (derived from portion of Koran so called).

lạntirki *m.* = lạntịrĩkị *Eng. m.* electric light.

lạntõ *x* zanạn naṇ ~ nẹ this cloth is a dụngũ to which a piece one yard long has been joined, making it thus three yards long (*N.B.*—a normal body-cloth (zanẹ) is 4 yards long).

lanyā *f.* (1) (*a*) spawn of frogs (lanyar kwạdĩ) or fish (lanyar kĩfĩ). (*b*) the slime gansạkũkạ *q.v.* (*c*) skin forming on curdled (barcī) milk and used for making butter. (*d*) film on eyes of P. going blind. (*e*) *cf.* yānā. (2) (*a*) tying rope round and round T. (*b*) an yi wạ ɗākị ~ rope has been tied down over the roof made of thatch (*cf.* lanyạcē).

lanyạcē *Vb.* 1C (1) tied string round and round T. (2) yā lanyạcẹ ɗākị he tied rope down over the thatch-roof. (3) made thread into skein (sũlũ), *cf.* warwạsā.

lapƙī = laushī.

lappạ = laffạ.

lapsụr = lausụr.

lapta = labta.

Lạrạbā *f.* (*Ar.* fourth) (1) Wednesday (*Vd.* bāwạ 8*a*.i). (2) *name for* girl born on a Wednesday (*cf.* Bạlā, Bạlārabẹ).

Lārabāwā Arabs (*pl. of* Bạlārabẹ).

Lạrạbce *x* ạ ~ in Arabic.

Lạrạbganā *f.* the last Wednesday of a lunar month (*it is considered unlucky, especially that at the end of month* Safạr ; *on* lạrạbganā, *no travelling, bathing, or shaving is done*).

laraḅī *m.* (*Ar.* a'raba explained). (1) exegesis *x* an zubạ masạ ~ it (Muslim religious text) has been explained. (2) soothsaying *x* nā bụgi ~ I cast a horoscope in sand (= bụgā 4*b*).

larǧdē *Vd.* lardi̦.

Lārai (1) = Bǧlā. (2) = Lǧrǧbā 2.

lardi̦ *m.* (*pl.* larǧdē) (*Ar.* al arz) district, locality.

larę (*word used by children*) *x* yā ∼ dǧ shī he realized it (= lu̦rā).

lǧrūrǧ *Ar. f.* (*pl.* larūrōrī = lǧrūre-lǧru̦rē). (1) (*a*) necessity. (*b*) ∼ kō cikiŋ ido̦ sǟi tǧ kwānā necessity knows no law. (*c*) nā kwancę ∼ I satisfied my need for going to the lavatory, sexual intercourse, etc. (*d*) nā kwancę masǧ lǧrūrǧta I explained my requirements to him. (2) living-expenses *x* yanǧ dǧ ∼ dǧ yawǧ he has heavy expenses. (3) affair, business *x* n nǧ dǧ wata ∼ cikin dāki̦ I've something to attend to in the house. yā tsarę lǧrūrǧr (= yā dau̦ki lǧrūrǧr) mai gidansǧ he looked after his master's affairs.

lǧrūrī *m.* (*Ar.* al 'urud hour of the night) the period between lǧ'asǧr lis and actual sunset (mǧgǧribǧ).

lǧru̦wai *m.* (1) string or strings held in the hand to balance load on one's head. (2) loops on pannier (wāgā) for pack-animal, to facilitate securing it on to animal's back.

larwai *Eng. m.* railway (= jirgiŋ ƙasā).

lasa A. (lǧsā) *Vb.* 2 (*p.o.* lǧshē, *n.o.* lǧshi). (1) (*a*) licked up (liquid). (*b*) (i) defeated utterly (= lāshę). (ii) Masǧr bǧ kaŋwar ∼ ba cę Egypt is no easy prey. (*c*) *Vd.* katangā. (2) licked (receptacle) *x* yā lǧshi lūdǧyī he licked the ladle (1, 2 = *Kt.* tǧndā). (3) (*a*) yā lǧshi bǧki̦ he licked his lips. (*b*) yanǧ lǧsar bǧki̦ he's lost in eager anticipation. (*c*) bǧ lǧsar bǧkī *Vd.* cǧrkwai 4. (4) (*a*) yā lǧshi tōkā gǧbansǧ he swore fealty to him. (*b*) sun lǧshi banati̦ they swore fealty (*Vd.* lāsǧ). (5) yā lǧshi 'yar rībǧ he's got a small profit (*cf.* lāshi̦). (6) bābu̦ "tǧndi!" bǧrē "lǧshi!" there is no advantage whatever. (7) wǧndō mai lǧsā the trousers malǧshī.

B. (lāsǧ) *Vb.* 1A = lǧsā 1–4 *x* sun ∼ takō̦bin Sarkī ǧ kǧn zā su̦ yī they swore to the Chief to do it (*Vd.* lǧsa 4).

C. (lāsā) *f.* potash for cows to lick.

lāsǧƙcē = lāsǧftā.

lāsǧ̄ī = li̦ssāƙi̦.

lāsǧftā *Vb.* 1C = lǧsaftǧ *Vb.* 2 (*p.o.* lǧsǧƙcē, *n.o.* lǧsǧƙci) reckoned up (figures, totals), counted up (= tārǧ 1*a*.v), *cf.* zānǧ 4, jimi̦ltā, ƙidǧyā, ƙirgǧ.

lāsaŋ *x* nā sǧmē shi̦ ǧ ∼ I got it cheaply, easily.

lǧsau *m. x* ƙafǧta tā yi ∼ my foot is chafed by my sandal (*cf.* dādę).

lāsau̦tā = lāsǧftā.

lashe A. (lǧshē) *Vd.* lǧsā.

B. (lāshę) (1) *Vb.* 1A (*a*) completely licked (*Vd.* lǧsā) *x* bai ∼ su tāshi̦ dayā ba he didn't mop them (enemy) up at the first attempt (= lǧsā 1*b*.i). (*b*) tanǧ lāshę dīyā *Vd.* ǧbu̦ 2*b*. (2) *Vb.* 3A wuƙā tā ∼ the knife-blade is worn down.

lǧ'she-lǧshē" *m.* (1) continual licking. (2) ∼ dǧ tǧrō shī nę bi̦kī plenty to eat and good company is as good as a banquet.

lashi A. (lǧshi) *Vd.* lǧsā.

B. (lāshi̦) *m.* (1) act of licking. (2) small profit *x* yā sǧmi dan ∼ he got a small profit (= lǧsā 5). dǧ lǧshi̦ ? is there any profit ?

lasiŋ *Eng. m.* licence *x* yā karɓǧ wǧ bindigǧ tasǧ ∼ he took out a licence for his gun.

laso A. (lāso̦) *m.* cement for sealing roofs and dye-pits (*Vd.* kātsi̦, dāfārā).

B. (laso̦) *m.* twenty.

lasso̦ *Sk.* = laso̦.

lā tǧ'addu̦ = lā tu̦'addu̦.

lātsǧ *Vb.* 1A (1) *x* yā ∼ kadanyǧ (maŋ-gwǧro̦) he squeezed the shea-nut (mango) to test its ripeness. yā ∼ dǧŋkali̦ (rōgo̦, *etc.*) he squeezed the sweet-potato (cassava, *etc.*) to see whether fully cooked (*cf.* mātsǧ). (2) tā ∼ furā she (seller) marked the furā with finger-impress to indicate it was already sold. (3) squashed T. (4) *x* yā ∼ bai sāmu̦ ba he sought in vain.

lātsę (1) *Vb.* 1A. (*a*) = lātsǧ. (*b*) tā ∼ yāro̦ she overlaid her baby-boy. (2) *Vb.* 3A became squashed.

lǧ'tse-lǧtsē" *m.* (1) looking hither and thither (*Vd.* lātsǧ 4). (2) dǧ ∼ jēmāgę ya kǧn saŋ ǧbincī he who seeks finds. (*N.B.*—sam = sǧmi.)

lātsū *m.* any thin material.

lātsụnā *Vb.* 1C = lātsunạ *Vb.* 2 = lātsạ *q.v.*
lātsụnē = lātsẹ 1, 2.
lattị *m.* (*Eng.* late) lateness *x* kadạ kạ yi ∼ don't come late (= mạkarạ).
agōgō yā yi lattịm mantị gōmạ the clock is ten minutes slow.
lattọ *Nor. m.* time (= lōtọ *q.v.*).
lā tụ'addụ (*Ar.* it is not counted). (1) abundantly *x* mutạ̄nē sunạ̄ naŋ ∼ there are crowds of people. (2) frequently *x* zūwạ sukẹ̄ yị̄ ∼ they often come.
lạ̄tụŋ *m.* = dạddawar lạ̄tụŋ *f.* type of dạddawā made from putrid meat, bones, etc., and gurguzū (= gumbā).
latuna A. (lạ̄tunạ) *Vb.* 2 scraped out (*as in* lạ̄katạ *q.v.*).
   B. (lātụnā) *Vb.* 1C (*with dative*) smeared T. -on ; falsely accused (*as in* lākạtā 1, 2 *q.v.*).
lau A. (lau) (1) *used in x* yanạ̄ naŋ lāfīyạ ∼ = lau yakẹ̄ he is in the best of health. (2) what ! (= ạp). (3) har ∼ up to now.
   B. (lau) (1) *used in* rạssā sunạ̄ rạusayạ ∼ the branches are swaying in the breeze. barcī yā dạukē shị ∼ he (drowsy P.) is swaying with sleep. (2) yā yi ∼ yā kai raunī he bent over backwards touching the ground.
lā ụbālī = lā ụbādī (*Ar.* I care not) *x* nā yi ∼ dạ shī I treated it as of no account.
lạujē *m.* (*pl.* laujunạ) small, curved sickle.
laukī = laushī.
laulạ *f.* type of girls' game.
laulāwạ *Sk. f.* bicycle (= bāsụkụr).
lạulaya A. (lạulayā) *Kt. f.* well-mixed furā and milk.
   B. (laulạyā) = lailạyā.
laulạyī *m.* (*Ar.* al a'lāli) *x* Audụ yawạn ∼ gạrēshị Audu is prone to every illness (= kwai-kwai).
laumạ *f.* (*pl.* laumōmī) (1) mouthful of tūwō *x* yā fayẹ ∼ he takes large mouthfuls of tūwō. (2) laumạr hasạfī tā fi kạbakiŋ kaŋkancị a small gift willingly given is better than a big gift accompanied by humiliation.
laumạcē *Vb.* 1C ate in a single mouthful (the entire remaining trifling amount of tūwō).

lau'ne-laụnē'' = launị-launị.
launị *m.* (*pl.* launōnī) (*Ar.* colour). (1) (*a*) colour. (*b*) dye *x* an yi masạ launịm bakī it has been dyed black. (2) style *x* (*a*) yā fitar dạ wani launịn diŋkị he introduced a new fashion in sewing (= salō 1 = ficē). (*b*) bạn san launịm mạganạr ba I do not follow the meaning. (3) launịŋ wākạ tune, rhythm.
launị-launị *adv.* (1) variegatedly. (2) multifariously *x* sunạ̄ naŋ ∼ they're of various kinds (= salō 4 = wafilạŋ).
lausạ *f.* type of fish (*epithet is* ∼ Mụsụlmiŋ kīfī).
lausạ̄sā *Vd.* lạllausā.
lạusayạ = rạusayạ.
laushī *m.* (*Ar.* lauth flabby). (1) (*a*) softness. (*b*) tenderness of meat (1 = taushī). (2) flexibility. (3) amenableness *x* mụtụm mai laushiŋ halī tractable P. (4) fineness (of powder). (5) kạrạ̄tunsạ yanạ̄ dạ ∼ he can read his lesson but has not memorized it. (6) wākạ tā yi ∼ the singing is excellent. (7) *Vd.* tantị 3.
lạusur = lạusurụ *m.* Garden Cress (*Lepidium sativum*), *cf.* ạlgạrịp.
lạutū (1) swaying by camel or drowsy P. (2) person's swinging on branch.
lauyạ (1) *Vb.* 1A. (*a*) bent (pliable T.) into an arc. (*b*) (*plus dative*) yā ∼ minị he accused me falsely (= dāfạ 1*c*). (*c*) (i) yā ∼ he turned back and went there (= kōmạ). (ii) yā lauyō he turned back and came here (= kōmō). (2) *m.* (*pl.* lauyōyī) *Eng. x* yā hayạ ∼ he engaged a lawyer. (3) *f.* false charge *x* sun yi minị ∼ they brought a false charge against me (= dāfạ 1*c*).
lauyẹ *m.* pliable T. bent in an arc.
lauyō *Vd.* lauyạ 1*c.*ii.
lāwạlī *m.* (*pl.* lạ̄wạlai) *Fil.* cattle-path fenced in with trees (= burtạlī = jạ̄ mạkạfī).
lạ̄wānị *m.* (*pl.* lạ̄wạ̄nai) *Nor.* village-head (= dagacị).
lawạshī *m.* onion-tops (*when pounded* (kirbạ), *they are called* gabū *in Sk.*).
lāwạ̄yē *Vd.* lāyạ.
lạ̄wụ̄ = lau 2.
lāwur *m.* (1) sweet-potato (= dạŋkalị).

(2) short type of early-ripening bulrush-millet. (3) the trousers **wandō mai kāmuŋ ƙafa**.

lāwurjĕ *m.* trouser-string (= **mazāgī**), *cf.* **kubāka**.

Lawwal (1) *man's name.* (2) *Vd.* **tagwai**.

laya A. (**lāya**) *f.* (*pl.* **lāyū** = **lāyōyī** = **lāwāyĕ**). (1) (*a*) (i) written charm (*it contains the words* **Bismillāhi-rrahmāni-rrahim** ; *cf.* **sammu, ƙōfī**. *It is of the class* **māgani 2**, *but* **sammu** *being evil charm, is not.* **lāya** *is antidote* (**makarī**) *to* **sammu** *and is also for driving away fever, evil spirits, and thieves, cf.* **kurcīyā** 1*c*). (ii) **yanā da lāyar gamō da manyā** he has a charm to protect him on an encounter with the powerful. (iii) **gaskīyā tā fi** ∼ truth is more powerful than any charm. (iv) **babbal** ∼ *Vd.* **bagajigī**. (v) **dūka da** ∼ *Vd.* **dūka** 2*b*. (*b*) **lāyar dantsĕ nē** he is a nincompoop (= **lāyun dantsĕ**). (*c*) **kurman** ∼ charm sewn in leather but without suspender (**hanci**). (*d*) ∼ **tā yi kyan rufi** all is in fine order. (*e*) **gyambō da lāya** *Vd.* **kwakwarĕ**. (2) the Koran *x* (*a*) **aŋ gĕwaya** ∼ = **gĕwayā** 4*b*. (*b*) (i) **yā ci** ∼ = **yā saɓa** ∼ he swore on the Koran. (ii) *Vd.* **saɓa** 1*b*, *c*. (*c*) **yā bugi** ∼ *Vd.* **bugā** 2. (3) an **yi masa lāyū** (*a*) the ornamentation called **lāya** has been made to the rooms or calabashes. (*b*) the gown is ornamented *as in* **askā** 3*b*. (4) **tā ďaura 'yan lāyū** she has adorned each of her temples with two small white-metal (*or* **kōrinō** 3) ornaments. (5) **matārin lāyū** syphilitic gummata (= **ƙullūtu** 2). (6) (*a*) **yā yi** ∼ he became invisible. (*b*) **yā yi musu** ∼ he gave them the slip. (7) **lāyar zānā** = **lāyaz zānā** (*a*) charm which, when bitten or squeezed, makes one invisible. (*b*) **yā yi lāyaz zānā** = 6*a above* (*possessor of* **lāyaz zānā** *says* **bā nā ciŋ amshē** *if, whilst eating with others, one of them is called and replies, for if possessor were to go on eating, the charm would lose its efficacy*) (*Vd.* **haskĕ** 2*a*). (8) **lāyaz zānar ƙarĕ** hiding like an ostrich (= **āya** 4). (9) (*rustic*) any folded letter. (10) (*a*) **gyāran** ∼ *m.* making one's preparations. (*b*)

Vd. **guduŋ gyāran dagā**. (11) *Vd.* **lāyun**-*compounds*.

B. (**lāyā**) *used in* **kā** ∼ blast you ! (= **ƙwāla** 4 = **ūwā** 1*c*.ii).

lāyacē *Vb.* 3A *Kt.* = **lāya** 6.

layā-laya *x* **gāshi gareshi** ∼ his hair has been left to grow long (*i.e.* the straight hair of Arabs, **Barĕbarī**, Tuareg Amenokal), *cf.* **kaŋ ƙudā** 4.

layi A. (**lāyi**) *m.* (*pl.* **lāyi** = **lāyūyuka** = **lāyi-lāyi**) *Eng.* (1) (*a*) line, row. (*b*) rank *x* **ba su ɓāta** ∼ **ba** (i) they (soldiers) did not break ranks. (ii) they stood firm. (2) Native Court. (3) market consisting of cement or clay stalls.

B. (**layī**) *m.* (1) reeling of drunken P. (**taŋgadī**). (2) planing of bird or aircraft (= **lafī**). (3) **yā saki** ∼ he behaved unconstrainedly.

lāyō = **yālō**.

lāyuŋ āmata *Vd.* **āmata**.

lāyuŋ awākī *m. pl.* the two wattles hanging from goat's lower jaw (*cf.* **rĕrō, lāyun tumākī, lĕ6ĕ** 4).

lāyun dantsĕ *m. pl. x* **yanā ganina kaman** ∼ he holds me of no account (= **lāya** 1*b*).

lāyun tumākī *m. pl.* the two wattles of a sheep (*cf.* **lāyuŋ awākī**).

lāyūyuka *Vd.* **lāyi**.

layyā *f.* (*Ar.* al azhā) (1) **layyā** = **sallar layyā** *f.* the Festival so called on the 10th **zulhaji** (= **lahīyā** = **salla** 1*c*). (2) **Watan** ∼ the month of **zulhaji**. (3) *Vd.* **kula kāi** ; **kāzā** 1*a*.vii. (4) **anā** ∼ **da dōki nĕ ?** it is impossible. (5) **gudun lahīyā** *Vd.* **uku** 3*b*.

layya'a *Vb.* 1C treated P. or T. cruelly, carelessly, or disrespectfully (= **wulā-kanta**).

layyace A. (**layyacē**) = **lanyacē**.

B. (**layyacē**) *Vd.* **layyata**.

layyata *Vb.* 2 (*p.o.* **layyacē**, *n.o.* **layyaci**) *Vd.* **lanyacē**.

lazamta A. (**lāzamta**) (1) *Vb.* 2 (*p.o.* **lāzamcē**, *n.o.* **lāzamci**) (1) (*a*) frequented *x* **yā lāzamci fāda** he constantly went to the palace. **nā san shi sabo da yawan** ∼ **tasa** I know him from his frequent visits. (*b*) ∼ **cē ta sā suka fahimta** familiarity enabled them to understand. (*c*) is characterized by *x* **yā lāzamci hali**

kazā he has such-and-such a character (= **fayę**). (2) is (was) incumbent *x* **cī dą įyāli yā ~ kam mąi gidā** support of the household is incumbent on the householder.

B. (**lāząmtā**) *Vb.* 1C rendered incumbent *x* **yā ~ mini shī** he rendered it obligatory to me (= **kallafā**).

lāzįmī = **lāzụmī**.

lāzimta = **lāzamta**.

lāzụ = **lāzụŋ** *m. x* **wannąm mąganą ~ cē** this is an actual fact.

lāzụmī *Ar.* (1) *m.* T. incumbent on P. *x* **ąbin nąŋ lāzụmīnā nę** this is obligatory on me. (2) *m.* (*with f.* **lāzụmā**) *pl.* **lązụmai** constant companion.

Lązzā *Ar. f.* one of the seven Muslim Hells (*cf.* **Jąhannamą**).

lē (*meaningless suffix used by women and children*) *x* **mąi sūnaŋ ụbālē** (= **mąi sūnaŋ ụbālę**) **yā zō** someone of the same name as my father has come (*Vd.* Mod. Gram.,-D. of Appendix 3). **mąi sūnaŋ ūwąlē tā zō** somebody of the same name as my mother has come (*cf.* **ąlkunyą**).

lēɓāɓę *m.* (1) protrusion of contents of load, rick, etc., such contents threatening to fall. (2) overflowing the proper margin (as riders overflowing on to verge of road).

lēɓąn *Vd.* **lēɓę**.

lēbąrą = **lēbụrą**.

lęɓątū *Vd.* **lēɓę**.

lēɓę *m.* (*pl.* **lēɓụną** = **lạɓɓā** = **lēɓōɓī** = **lęɓątū**). (1) lip. (2) **shī lēɓąn rąƙumī nę, yaną dą kamar fādụwā** he's pleasant-spoken, but stingy (= **bąkin rąƙumī 3**). (3) **tā yi lēɓąŋ ūwar miji** she crossed her cloth over her breast and let it hang down so that it made flapping noise (**tambarin shaitsąŋ**) as she walks. (4) **lęɓątū** *pl.* (*a*) wattles of cock or turkey (*cf.* **lāyuŋ awākī**). (*b*) dewlap of cow (= **bakwąlī**). (*c*) lobe of the ear (= **cililligā**). (*d*) the part of a mat projecting beyond bed-end or beyond another mat. (*e*) **tā yi lęɓątū** = 3 *above.*

lēbụr *Eng. m.* levelness *x* **hanyą tā yi ~** the road has been levelled (*cf.* **sādą 4**).

lēbụrą = **lēbąrą** *m.* (*pl.* **lēbụrōrī**) *Eng.* (1) labourer, porter (= **są̄ A.2 1g** *page* 753) ;

Vd. **garkę 4, kąrīyą.** (2) **yā yi mini ~** he worked for me as a porter.

lēburancī *m.* labourers' slang.

leccą *f.* (*Eng.* lecture) *x* **sun yi masą ~** they (police) cross-questioned him (prisoner) = **zōlayą.**

lēcę *m.* bed of **tukurwā** plus **asabąrī.**

lęcęcę *x* **yaną dą bą̄kī ~** he is pendulous-lipped.

lęfē *m.* (*pl.* **lēfuną**) (1) basket made of **kabą** or **kijinjirī** (= **fąlfąlā**). (2) **aŋ kāwō lęfantą** the cloths customarily given a bride have been given her (bride).

lef-rę *Eng. x* **an yi mācịnsą lef-rę, lef-rę** they were marched along in step.

lęhē = **lęfē.**

leƙa A. (**lęƙā**) *Vb.* 2 (1) (*a*) peeped at. (*b*) *Vd.* **lēƙą.** (2) **lēƙō** *Vb.* 1E peeped at in this direction. (3) **aŋ hąrbē shį dą kibīyą har tā lēƙō** he has been transfixed with an arrow (= **hąntsī 2**).

B. (**lēƙą**) (1) *Vb.* 1A (*a*) = **lęƙā 1a**. (*b*) **idǫ dayā yā ~ būtą** *Vd.* **ąbụ 5g**. (*c*) **ą̄ lēƙą** *Vd.* **wāwan zamā.** (*d*) *Vd.* **hąntsī 3.** (2) *Vb.* 3A peeped about. (3) *Vd.* **kā lēƙą.**

lęƙą tukunyā *m.* woman's or boy's plait hanging over forehead.

lęƙē *m.* (1) act of peeping. (2) **yā bar shị dą ~** *Vd.* **tudụ 1c.** (3) **kūrā ną̄ shan rūwā, kąrē sāi ~** don't compete with those superior to yourself !

Lēkǫ *name given* child born after twins (= **Gąmbo**).

lēƙū *m.* (1) summit. (2) **yā yi mini ~** he proffered it to me, but then withdrew it (= **dąŋgōlī** *q.v.* = **lạllęƙū 2**).

lēƙūwā *f.* = **lēƙū 1.**

lēlā *f.* (1) base of cone of **mąŋgụl** salt (*used for* **mīyą**). (2) type of night-drumming at house of rich man. (3) *Kt.* **kidƒąn lēlā** type of day or night dance with drumming in which women participate (= **gādā 3**). (4) **yā sąmi kōrę, yaną ~ ą cikī** he's wearing a black gown for it to colour his body with indigo (*cf.* **ban shūnī**).

lele A. (**lęlē**) *m.* (1) **aną lęlansą** he (child) is being coddled. (2) **dan ~** *m.* (*f.* **'yar ~**) *pl.* **'yan ~** a favourite (= **gąbā**

9 *q.v.*). (*b*) a spoiled child. (*c*) cloth of mixed **gwandā** and **sāƙị**.

B. (**lēlē**) *m.* (1) unpatterned, white, European material (especially a type of calico) = **alawayyọ** = **zạwwātị**. (2) **na ∼, na ạtị̱jō** anything of prime quality.

lẹ̀lẹ̀gajị̱ *m.* (1) dithering about. (2) bedvalance (= **barankaɓa**). (3) **yanā** lẹ̀lẹ̀gajị̱n cĩwọ he's constantly fingering his sore. (4) *Kt.* a suggestive dance by girls accompanied by drumming.

lēmạ = **laimạ**.

lẹ̱mō = lẹ̱mū *m.* (1) (*a*) lime tree. (*b*) lime fruit (*Vd.* **shā** A.1*e* ; **Ƙạ̱bugạ**). (2) ∼ **mai zāƙĩ** orange. (3) **lẹ̱mam Masạr** citron. (4) **Kutumbāwā** tribalmarks (2 horizontal marks, plus 2–4 vertical). (5) the fits and starts of a horse suddenly reined in (**zāmẹ**). (6) (*a*) **wạsā dạ lẹ̱mū** man's toying with woman's breasts. (*b*) **wạsā dạ ∼ yā fi shạnsạ dādĩ** anticipation is better than realization.

Lẹ̱rē = Lẹ̱rĩ *f.* (town in Bauchi Province) *used in* ɗan ∼ *m.* (*pl.* 'yan∼) (1) type of mat. (2) type of horse girthstrap (**majāyĩ**).

*li̱'abbị *m.* (*f.* li̱'abbĩyā) *pl.* li̱'ạbbai *Ar.* brother by different mother (= ɗạ̱nạ̱bā), *cf.* li̱'ummị, shạƙĩƙị, ɗạnūwā, tụrākạ 2.

libbạn = lụbbạn.

li̱ɓōsō *m.* = lūbĩyā.

libtū = liftū.

lĩcĩ *Kt. m.* looking carefully after T. (= **tattalĩ**).

lif A. (**lif**) *m. and adv.* (1) *x* **yā kwạntā ∼** he lay quietly. (2) **dōkị yā yi ∼** the horse is docile (*cf.* **luf-luf**). (3) ∼ **Zāƙị** bend down, Chief ! (to avoid branch, top of doorway, etc.), *Vd.* **faram**.

B. (**li̱f**) = lĩfị *Eng. m.* **yā dạ̱uki ∼** he went on leave. **bā sạ̱ zūwạ Tūrai ∼** they do not go to Europe on leave.

li̱fāfạ *f.* = li̱kkafạnĩ.

lĩfị = lif.

lifị̱dĩ *m.* (*pl.* lifidạ = *Kt.* lifiddạ) (*Ar.* libd felt-material) (1) protective quilting for cavalry and cavalry-horses. (2) ɗan ∼ (*pl.* 'yan ∼). (*a*) cavalryman dressed in 1 (*Vd.* kumạ̱kumĩ, kwalkwalĩ). (*b*) ɗan ∼ small bits of intestines

---

spitted on stick and enveloped in ƙulĩƙulĩ to conceal bad quality (= butārĩ 1), *cf.* ṭsị̱rē. (*c*) = ƙūrụ 4. (3) rị̱gar ∼ *f.* = sạ̱fā 2. (4) yā shị̱ga ∼ he's sulking. (5) (*a*) yanā̱ ∼ he has refused to acknowledge losing at **cācā** till two throws of the dice made. (*b*) kạ̱zā tā shị̱ga ∼ the sick chicken is drooping. (6) *Kt.* thimble (= sāfĩ). (7) ạbị̱n yā ci mātan lifidạ it is very difficult. (8) *Vd.* ạlbarkạ 2, sukụ̄wā 2. (9) bạntan ∼ *Vd.* bạntē 13.

liftu A. (**liftū**) *m.* exercising horse by long ride.

B. (**li̱ftu**) *Vb.* 3B dōkị yā ∼ horse has been exercised by long ride.

liga-liga (1) yanā̱ kwạnce ∼ he's lying sprawled out (= mina-mina 2). (2) completely *x* yā kạrɓi kuɗinsạ ∼ he was paid in full. sōjạmmụ sụn kōmạ gidā ∼ all our soldiers have returned home.

ligis = laƙwas.

lihị̱dĩ *Kt.* = lifị̱dĩ.

li̱'imạ *f.* prosperity (= nị'imạ *q.v.*).

*li̱'irabị *m.* = larạbĩ 1.

lĩƙạ *Vb.* 1A (1) (*a*) caused to adhere *x* an ∼ takạrdā jị̱kim bangō the notice has been pasted to the wall. nā ∼ shi gạ ɗạnūwansạ I stuck them together (= mannạ 1). (*b*) yā ∼ minị laifĩ he falsely accused me (= mannạ = ɗạ̱fạ 1*c*). (2) sun ∼ masạ dōkị dạ tsạ̱dā he has sold the horse at an extortionate price (= mannạ 2 = kannạ). (3) yā ∼ minị ƙạnƙanẹ he gave me a trifle. (4) an ∼ shi dạ ƙasā he's been felled to the ground.

li̱kārĩ *m.* (*pl.* li̱ƙạrai) *Vd.* farĩ 2*a*.iv.

lĩƙẹ (1) *Vb.* 1A. (*a*) stopped up (orifice) = tōshẹ. (*b*) sun ∼ hanyạ they (enemy) have blocked the road (= tōshẹ). (2) *Vb.* 3A sun ∼ they (papers, etc.) became stuck together. (*b*) yā ∼ masạ it stuck to it. (*c*) (orifice) became stopped up (2*c* = tōshẹ 2).

li̱'ƙe-lĩƙē" *m.* (1) constantly sticking to. (2) personal odds and ends (= karẹ 2) *x* ∼ tōshin 'yan kōlị pedlars give small trinkets to their girl-friends.

lĩƙi *m.* (1) action of stopping up orifice. (2) stopped-up orifice *x* tụlun nạ̱n yanā̱ dạ ∼ the hole in this pitcher has been mended by stopping it up. (3) how small ! (4) how dear !

līkimō *m.* (1) keeping oneself out of the way. (2) *Kt.* an yi masą ~ he's been thrashed.

lißis = lakwas.

likitą = l̹ikitą *m.* (*pl.* likitōcī = likitōtī) *Eng.* doctor (*cf.* gwaurau).

l̹ikkāfą *f.* (*pl.* l̹ikkąfū) *Ar.* (1) stirrup. (2) sauna ą ~ I'm just about to start out. (3) ~ tasą tā yi gąba he's got on in the world. l̹ikkāfąr kāfircị tā yi gąba heathenism is on the increase. (4) sun yi ~ ɗayā they rode abreast. (5) farar ~ descendant of Filani Chief or ruler.

l̹ikkafąnī *m.* (*pl.* l̹ikkąfąnai) *Ar.* shroud *x* aŋ hadą shi ą ~ he has been wound in his shroud (= lạfāfą).

lißyas = lakwas.

l̹il̹ī *used in* ɗan ~ *m.* lad's penis.

lilis *m. and adv.* (1) (*a*) yā dąku ~ = yā dąku, yā yi ~ (i) it (flour) is well pounded. (ii) he's been thrashed. (*b*) yā nißu ~ it (flour) is finely ground (= tilis = tuɗas = ɗaɗas = ruɓus 1), *cf.* ɓarzą, fantsąrā. (2) nā gąji ~ = jikīna yā yi ~ I'm tired out (= tilis).

lillaŋ ąlaihịŋ *Kt.* undoubtedly (= nāną ąlaihịŋ).

lilliɓī = lulluɓī.

līlọ *m.* (1) (*a*) dangling, swinging *x* yā yi ~ he (child) went and had a swing (= rētọ = rąɓęnīyā). (*b*) in zā ką yi ~, ką yi ą tsāmīyā ; iŋ kā kāmą tąwatsā, tā karyę don't lean on a broken reed ! (*cf.* wālā 2). (2) wandering about (= gīlọ). (3) type of small plant with edible berries.

lịmąm = lịmāmī = lịmaŋ *m.* (*pl.* lịmąmai) *Ar.* (1) officiating Muslim priest. (2) ɗan ~ *Vd.* bąmmī.

lịmāną *f.* (*Ar.* al amāna confidence). (1) goodwill, friendship. (2) ɗaukąr bāshi dą ~, bīyą dą hąyāgągą there is goodwill when money is borrowed, but repayment leads to recrimination.

līmancị *m.* office and work of a lịmąm.

lịmānị = lịmąm.

limę = lumę.

limmąkaifą = lummąkaifą.

limshī = lumshī.

lindō *m.* the lizard kulɓą *q.v.*

liŋgąɓū *Kt. m.* new leaf-buds (= lallagē 2 *q.v.*).

Lịnjīnā *f.* = Ịnjīlụ.

linka = ninka.

lịnzāmị *m.* (*pl.* lịnząmai) (*Ar.* lijāmi). (1) (*a*) (i) bridle, bit. (ii) kō bą ą gwadą ba, ~ yā fi bąkiŋ kązā it is obvious. (iii) sūnā ~ nē hearing one's name spoken arrests one's attention. (iv) yaną tąunar ~ ząi yī he's bragging that he'll do it. (*b*) zubę ~ *Vd.* zubę 1c. (*c*) aną jin lịnzāmịŋ Audụ they obey Audu (*Vd.* jī 5). (*d*) bą sụ jā ~ ba they did not halt. (*e*) suŋ karyą ~ they took to their heels. (*f*) (i) dōkị yaną cịn ~ the horse is biting its reins. (ii) yārọ yaną cịn ~ the suckling lad is moving his mouth as if still sucking the breast. (2) brake of cycle or motor-car *x* yā są ~ he put on the brake. yā kwancę ~ he released the brake (= burkị). (3) yaną dą ~ ɗąrī he has 100 horses. (4) embroidery on right of gown's neckopening.

liptū = liftū.

lis A. (lis) (1) dą lą'asąr ~ just before sunset (= sąkālịyā = sanyī 1*b*.ii). (2) *Kt.* jikīna yā yi minị ~ (*a*) I felt languid (= lą'asąr 4). (*b*) I felt tired.

B. (Lịs) *used in* (1) ɗan ~ the devil (= iɓlịs). (2) ɗan ~ (*with f.* 'yar ~, *pl.* 'yan ~) devilish P.

lịsąfī = lịsāfị = lịssāfị *q.v.*

lịshā *Ar. f.* period from darkness till towards midnight (*cf.* mągaribą, lą'asąr).

Lịslāmą *Ar. f.* Islam, Mahommedanism (= Mụhąmmądīyyą).

lissąfcē = lāsąfcē.

lịssāfị = lịssąfī *m.* (*Ar.* al hisābi). (1) act of reckoning up. (2) (*a*) yā yi ~ he counted them up. (*b*) sum fi ~ they're innumerable. (3) arithmetic, mathematics *x* yā īyą ~ he knows mathematics. (4) bill, account, list, inventory. (5) (*a*) bą shi dą ~ (i) he is senseless. (ii) he has no sense of propriety. (*b*) dą kā yi ~, dą bą ką yi hakạ ba had you considered, you'd not have done so.

līta *Kt. f.* = lītārę.

lītārẹ *Fil. m.* small calabash drilled for its carrying-string.

Lịtịnịŋ = Lịttịnịŋ.

littāfị *m. (pl.* lịttạttāfai == lịttāfai == littạttafī) (*Ar.* al kitābi). (1) book. (2) Littāfịŋ Allā the Koran (= Ạlkur'ạŋ). (3) būɗe ∼ *Vd.* mālạmī 2.

littāfịyā *f.* = littāfị.

Lịttịnịŋ *f.* (*Ar.* yaumul ithnaini) Monday. Lịttịninịn naŋ on that Monday (Mod. Gram. 10*d*).

*lị'ummị *m.* (*f.* lị'ummịyā) *pl.* lị'ummai brother by different father (*cf.* lị'abbị).

lịwasạ *Sk. f.* = ạlwasạ.

lịyāfạ *f.* (*Ar.* diyāfa) hospitality.

lịyā-lịyā = layā-lạyā.

lịyạr = lịyārị *m.* (*pl.* lịyārai) (*Italian* lira). (1) Maria Theresa dollar (= dalạ 3 = mụtạr = gurụs 1). (2) *Vd.* sūrạ 1*c.*

lịzāmị = lịnzāmị.

lizimta = lazamta.

lịzzāmị *Kt.* = lịnzāmị.

lō (1) yā yi ∼ it is handsome. (2) *adv.* expertly *x* yanā hawā ∼ he's a fine horseman. yā īyạ Hausā ∼ he's expert at Hausa.

loɓa A. (lōɓā) *f.* foreskin (= *Sk.* sịllī = *Kt.* tānā 3*a*).
  B. (lōɓạ) (1) *Vb.* 1A. (*a*) dented. (*b*) gave bad advice to. (*c*) tricked P. (2) *Vb.* 3A became dented.

lōɓạnā = lāɓụnā.

lōɓē *m.* (1) bad advice. (2) trickery.

lọdā *m.* (1) the plant *Rogeria adenophylla* (*used for same purpose as* dāfārā). (2) the plants dāfārā, bāba rọdō (*q.v. under* bāba 8), shẹkarạ tsạye. (3) the tree danyā (*cf.* luddẹ).

lōdị *Eng. m.* (1) load (for lorry, etc.). (2) anā yi wạ lōrị ∼ the lorry is being loaded.

lōfẹ *m.* clay smoking-pipe (tukunyā), *cf.* gōdọ.

lōgạ *f.* root of the matter *x* kạ shāwō minị lōgạr zạncạŋ explain the root of the matter to me ! yā bi lōgạr mạganạr he investigated the matter.

lō̃kạ (*vulgar*) *Vb.* 1A *Kt.* had connection with (woman) = cī 16.

lōkạcī *m.* (*pl.* lọkạtai) (*Ar.* al waqti). (1) (*a*) time, period (= yạ̄yī). (*b*) lōkạcinsạ yā yī it's now the time for it. har lōkạcin tạfīyạ yā yī, bại isō ba by the time it was

necessary to set out, he had not appeared. ∼ yā yī dạ ya kạmātạ ạ yī the time has come to do it. (*c*) sun sācī ∼ sụ fạdi gạskīyā they secretly told the truth. (2) jirạn ∼ yakē he's at the point of death. (3) lōkạcī ∼ sometimes. (4) ∼ bịyar *Vd.* bịyar 2. (5) (*a*) lōkạcin dạ when (= sā'ạ 5 *q.v.*). (*b*) *Vd.* dukạ 3. (6) *Vd.* lōtọ.

lōkọ *m.* (1) (*a*) place where porters halt for a rest *x* sun yi ∼ = suŋ kai ∼ they (carriers) have halted for a rest. (*b*) mụ yi ∼ let us (persons at any work) rest a bit ! (2) (*a*) yā sā ∼ he (carrier) has put his load up in a tree resting on a pole. (*b*) *Vd.* kwā-kwā. (3) *Vd.* yā dạ 3*e.* (4) iroko tree (*Chlorophora excelsa*). (5) (*with pl.* lallōkī) dark recess, cubby-hole (= luŋgụ).

lōmạ = laumạ.

lōrẹ = lōrị *m.* (*pl.* lōrōrī) *Eng.* lorry.

loto A. (lōtọ) *m.* (1) time (= lōkạcī *q.v.*). (2) lōtọ-lōtọ from time to time. (3) dạrīyā bā ∼ *Vd.* dạrīyā 8.
  B. (lọ̄tō) *m.* (1) (*mining term*) overburden. (2) (*with fem.* lọ̄tōtụ̄wā) fool.

lototo A. (lọ̄tọtọ) *m.* (*f.* lọ̄tọ̄tụ̄wā) fool.
  B. (lọ̄tọ̄tọ̄) *m. and adv. x* yā yi ∼ dạ bākī = yā zaunạ ∼ dạ bākī he stared like a gaby.

lōtsạ (1) *Vb.* 3A became concave under weight or stress *x* ɗākị yā ∼ the thatch-roof caved in. bāyan jākī yā ∼ the donkey's back sank down under the weight of the load. (2) *Vb.* 1A caused to sink down *as in* 1.

lōtsẹ = lōtsạ.

lōtsō *m.* (1) becoming concave *as in* lōtsạ. (2) yā yi ∼ he gave up (struggle, journey, etc.) = kạrai.

lub = luf.

lụbarbạr *Eng. m.* revolver.

lụbayyạ *Kr. f.* business (= cịnikī).

lụbbạŋ = lụbbānị *m.* (*Ar.* lubnā storax). (1) a gum used for incense. (2) rosary made from 1.

lubcẹ *Kt.* = lumshẹ.

lūbẹ *Kt. m.* = lūbịyā 3.

Lụ̄beyyạ *f. the place* Al 'Ubaid.

lūbịyā *f.* (1) soft, ripe fruit (*x* date, mango, ɗinyā, kaɗanyạ, etc.) = lugụbā == liɓōsō. (2) ∼ bin dạ zugụ what a

massive, bosomy, ugly woman ! (*cf.*
ƙuŋƙumā 2). (3) type of tree.
lub-lub A. (lub-lub) (1) *adv.* itācĩyan naŋ
tā yi ganyē ∽ this tree is very leafy.
(2) *m.* (*a*) ga̱rī yana̱ ∽ the sky is overcast (= lumshe̱). (*b*) yā tāka̱ sōrō, yā
ji ∽ the flat roof yielded to his tread.
(*c*) ƙurjī yā yi ∽ the swelling contains
pus. (*d*) gāshi̱nta̱ yā yi ∽ she has
thick hair (= tōfu).
B. (lub-lub) *m. and adv.* tā yi ∽ da̱
zane̱ = tā yi lullu6ī ∽ she enveloped
herself completely in her body-cloth
(*Vd.* lullu̱6ā).
lubtū = liftū.
lu6u-lu6u A. (lu6u-lu6u) *m.* (1) (*a*) *x*
'yā'yan naŋ sun yi ∽ these fruits are
soft and ripe (*cf.* lūbi̱yā 1). (*b*) *Vd.*
lu6us. (2) = lu̱6u-lu̱bū.
B. (lu̱'6u-lu̱6ū") *m.* sogginess *x* wurin
naŋ yā yi ∽ this place is soggy.
C. (lu6ū-lu̱6u̱) *m.* = lu6u-lu6u 1.
lu6us *m.* (1) = lu6u-lu6u 1*a*. (2) sū
ta̱6ā ni ∽ nē̱ they're lazy.
lu̱dārī *m.* fool (= sōko̱).
lūda̱yī *m.* (*pl.* lūwa̱dū = lūdaya̱). (1) (*a*) a
type of dumā and i̱ts fruit. (2) (*a*)
ladle made from split fruit of 1. (*b*) ∽
ga̱dā, i̱ŋ kā kāma̱, ka̱ ba̱ da̱ŋūwaŋka̱,
ya̱ kāma̱ take heart for luck comes to all
in turn ! (*c*) lūda̱yiŋ kōko *Vd.* fa̱ŋkō 4.
(*d*) lūda̱yiŋ ƙe̱tā *Vd.* gāgo̱ 4*b.* (*e*) *Vd.*
wutsīya̱r ∽. (*f*) *Vd.* kāmu̱n ∽. (*g*)
Vd. ha̱ntsī 4.
lu̱ddai *Sk. m.* (*pl.* ludduna̱) = lūda̱yī.
ludda̱yī = lūda̱yī.
ludde̱ *m.* fruit of danyā (*cf.* lo̱dā 3).
luf *Vd.* lif, luf-luf.
lu̱fāfa̱ *f.* = li̱kkafa̱nī.
lu̱fāfi̱ *Kt. m.* = li̱kkafa̱nī.
luf-luf *x* ƙa̱ŋƙarā tā rufe̱ ƙasā ∽ snow
(hail) blotted out the face of the
ground (*cf.* lif).
luftū = liftū.
luga̱ = lugga̱.
lugga̱ *f.* (*Ar.* lugha word) deep, elevated
speech.
lūgu̱ *Kt. m.* = luŋgu̱.
lugub-lugub = lugub *x* nāma̱ yā da̱fu ∽
the meat is tenderly cooked. maŋgwa̱ro̱
yā nu̱na ∽ the mango is squashy.
lugu̱bā = lūbi̱yā 1.

lu̱gu̱bai *m.* blandishment.
lu̱gu̱dē *m.* (1) (*a*) pounding in rotation by
women at same mortar. (*b*) ita gwa̱nar
∽ cē̱ har tā īya̱ salō she is expert at
pounding in rotation and can dance
away from the mortar, strike her
pestle on the ground and return in
time to get in her stroke rhythmically
at the mortar. (2) hitting of same iron
by smiths in rotation (1, 2 = sa̱ma̱m-
ma̱ncē). (3) suŋ hau masa̱ da̱ ∽ they
hit him in turn, one after the other.
lu̱gudi̱ = lu̱kudi̱.
luguf = lugub.
lugwīgwi̱tā *Vb.* 1D (1) kneaded T. to
soften it (= laila̱yā). (2) rubbed
(pounded contents of mortar with
pestle to soften) = *Kt.* nanna̱gā. (3)
yā lugwīgwi̱ta̱ ma̱gana̱ tasa̱ he repeated
what he had said, to avoid misunder-
standing.
luhū-lu̱hu̱ *m.* being large and round *x*
ida̱nsa̱ yā yi ∽ his eyes are swollen.
'yā'yaŋ itāca̱ŋ naŋ ∽ sukē̱ this tree
has big fruit. ƙura̱jē sun yi ∽ the
pimples are large and round (= luƙū-
lu̱ƙū).
lu̱jē = la̱ujē.
lu̱jīya̱ = ru̱jīya̱.
lūƙa̱ *Vb.* 1A *Kt.* (1) yā ∽ masa̱ wuƙā he
stabbed him. (2) = luŋƙumā.
lu̱ƙa̱-lūƙā (1) *m.* feckless P. (2) *f.* fecklessness.
lu̱kudi̱ *m.* potion to become rich quickly
(*said to have evil results whether
efficacious or not*).
lu̱ku̱ku̱ *m. and adv. x* yā yi ∽ = yā yi
jiki̱ ∽ he is a lumping P. yana̱ ta̱fe ∽
he's walking heavily.
luƙū-lu̱ƙū = luhū-lu̱hū.
lukuntu6ī (1) ∽ ka̱ran rārīyā what a fat
person ! (*cf.* lu̱ku̱tuttu̱6ī). (2) gruel
made by bride's girl-friends.
lu̱ku̱tuttu̱6ī *m.* (*f.* lu̱ku̱tuttu̱6ā) fat P. (*cf.*
lukuntu6i̱).
lu̱ƙwāso̱ *used in* da̱ lu̱ƙwāmī, da̱ ∽ it's a
case of P. needing help seeking it from
P. as little able to help as he himself
(= sa̱hōramī da̱ sa̱hōrō = ruŋgu̱me ni
mu̱ fādi̱).
lukwī = luƙwī (1) *m.* Bambarra ground-
nuts (gujīyā) shelled and cooked. (2)

adv. (*a*) (i) yā nị̄ƙu ⁓ it (flour) is finely ground. yā daku ⁓ it is finely pounded (= lilis). (*b*) yā bugu ⁓ he's been thrashed. (*c*) = lukwi-lukwi. (*d*) aŋ gyārạ ⁓ it has been well repaired.

luƙwĭƙwị̄yā *Vb.* 1D ground or pounded finely.

lukwi-lukwi *x* yā yi ƙibạ ⁓ he is very fat.

luƙwi-luƙwi = lukwi 2*a, b.*

lūlạ *Vb.* 3A. (1) (*a*) fled. (*b*) (missile) went far. (*c*) P. went on long journey. (2) *Vb.* 1A shot (missile) far *x* yā ⁓ kibĭyạ he shot the arrow far. (3) *Eng. f.* (*a*) ruler (for ruling lines). (*b*) roller for road (= rūlạ).

lulai *x* yā tạfi, yā yi zamansạ ⁓ he remained away a long time.

lụ̄lạ̄yē *m.* a food made of crushed, boiled beans.

lullu6a A. (lullụ6ā) *Vb.* 1C *x* tā lullụ6ạ zanẹ she completely covered herself with a mayāfĭ cloth.

B. (lụllu6ạ) *Vb.* 3B *x* tā ⁓ dạ zanẹ she is completely covered with a mayāfĭ cloth.

lullụ6ē *Vb.* 1C = lullụ6ā.

lullu6ĭ *m.* covering oneself *as in* lullụ6ā.

lụllụmĭ *m.* garĭ yā yi ⁓ the sky is overcast (= lumshẹ).

lụ̄lū = lụ̄lū *m.* (*sg., pl.*) small glass bottle for ink or scent (= wạkĭyyạ).

lūlụ̄cē *Vb.* 3A = lālạ̄cē.

lūlụ̄lū *m.* = lụ̄kạ̄-lūkā.

lum *x* yā lumẹ cikin rūwa ⁓ it vanished in the water. yā tạfi ⁓ he went very far.

lụmānạ = lịmānạ.

lum6ụ *f.* (1) plump young woman, plump chicken, plump horse, etc. (*epithet is* ⁓ kashẹ wutā). (2) any big, round fruit (*cf.* luntsumā).

lụm'bu-lụmbū" *m.* (1) = lụ̄kạ̄-lūkā. (2) deceitfulness.

lụm6wĭ = lạm6au *d.*

lumẹ *Vb.* 3A vanished into (water, dense bush, etc.), *cf.* lum.

lụ'me-lụmē" *m.* the embroidery-pattern dạshi-dạshĭ 2.

lumfạrfashĭ = numfạrfashĭ.

lumfạsā = numfạsā.

lumfāshĭ = numfāshĭ.

lummạkaifạ (1) bai cẹ ⁓ ba he uttered no word at all (= uffạŋ). (2) yā cẹ " ⁓ bạn sanị ba " he said " I am ignorant of the matter " (= alạmusurụ).

Lūmọ *x* ⁓ gạyyar Allạ̄ *epithet of any* market.

lumsạ̄shē *Kt.* = lumshẹ 1.

lumshẹ (1) *Vb.* 3A. (*a*) garĭ yā ⁓ the sky is overcast (= rụmfā 5). (*b*) idạnsạ yā ⁓ his eyes are heavy with sleep. (2) yā ⁓ idạnunsạ he closed his eyes in drowsiness.

lumshĭ *m.* garĭ yā yi ⁓ = lumshẹ 1*a.*

lụmtā = lụntā.

lụmụmụ *m. and adv.* rūwā yā shigō dā̆kị ⁓ water swirled into the house. sạn dạ na tā̆kạ, sǎi na ji ⁓ as I trod, I felt the place was soggy.

lumus *x* yā yi laushĭ ⁓ it is very soft.

lụncē *Vd.* lụntā.

lụngạ = luggạ.

lụŋ'ge-lụŋgē" *x* ƙasā tā yi ⁓ the country is angular in shape (*cf.* lungu).

lụŋgu *m.* (*pl.* lụnguna = luŋgōgĭ = lụŋ'ge-lụŋgē"). (1) dark or out-of-the-way recess, cubbyhole or district = *Sk.* kusụrĭ (*cf.* sāƙọ). (2) kudĭ sun durƙusā ạ wani ⁓ the funds have been misappropriated. (3) sharp bend in river, land, or farm *x* ƙasạ̄shạn dạ ƙẹ lụŋgụŋ gabạs the countries in the eastern bulge. (4) *Vd. previous entry.*

lụŋgụ6ūtụ (1) what squashy fruit ! (2) what tenderly cooked meat ! (*cf.* lugub).

lụŋkạ = nịŋkạ.

lụŋƙumạ *Vb.* 1C put large, soft T. into the mouth *x* yā luŋƙumạ nāmạ ạ bặkinsạ he p t a large lump of meat into his mouth.

lụŋƙumē *Vb.* 3A *x* idạnsạ yā ⁓ his eyelids are swollen from a sting.

lụŋkwĭ = lụŋƙwĭ = lạm6au *q.v.*

lunsạyĭ *m.* (*pl.* lụnsạyai) (*Ar.* al unthayaini) testicle (= gwaiwā).

lụntā *Vb.* 2 (*p.o.* lụncē, *n.o.* lụnci) exercised (horse by riding it far).

luntsuma A. (luntsumā) *f.* = lum6ụ' (*cf.* luntsumēmẹ).

B. (luntsụmā) = luŋƙumā.

luntsumēmẹ *m.* (*f.* luntsumēmĭyā) plump *as in* lum6ụ.

luntū = liftū.

luntumē *Vb.* 3A **(1)** was tired. **(2)** was famished.

lūrā **(1)** *Vb.* 3B. (*a*) (i) paid attention *x* **yā riƙa yī, yanā** ⁓ he acted cautiously. (ii) **săi ka** ⁓ **da shī** attend to it carefully ! **săi ka** ⁓ **da abiŋka** you must look after your own affairs ! **ka** ⁓ **da tufāfina, kō watakīla anīnī yā cirę** attend to my clothing to see whether a button has come off ! (*b*) realized that *x* **yā** ⁓ **ba'a akę yi masa** he realized he was being derided. (*c*) took charge of *x* **am bā shi** ⁓ **da mayaƙā** he was given charge of the soldiers. **(2)** *f.* carefulness *x* (*a*) **bā shi da** ⁓ he is inattentive, careless, regardless of the consequences. (*b*) **sun jē da** ⁓ they proceeded carefully. (*c*) **babbaŋ abin** ⁓ **ga jawābinsa** the point to observe about his speech is that . . . (*d*) **a cī ka da** ⁓ *Vd.* **tubānī** 3.

lūrad da *Vb.* 4B = **lūrā** 1*a*.ii.

lūrę *x* **nā** ⁓ now I understand !

lurra *Zar. f.* = **larūra.**

lūrū *m.* (*pl.* **lūrāyē**) type of black and white striped native cloth.

lūsarī *m.* (*f.* **lūsarā**) *pl.* **lūsarai** feckless P. (= **sōƙo**).

lutsa A. (**lūtsa**) *Vb.* 1A. **(1) yā** ⁓ **masa haƙōrā** he dug his teeth into it. **(2) yā** ⁓ **masa wuƙā** he dug a knife into it. B. (**lūtsā**) *Sk.* **'yan na** ⁓ *pl.* young pigeons (= **'yan shila**).

lūtsu *m.* (*Ar. word for the Biblical man* Lot) sodomy.

lututu = **lututu** *x* **yanā da yauƙī** ⁓ it is very slimy.

*lu'u-lu'u *m.* (*pl.* **lu'ulu'ai**) *Ar.* pearl.

lūwādū *Vd.* **lūdayī.**

luwaidi *m.* native macaroni (= **tālīya** 1), *cf.* **tsūtsa** 1*c.*

lūwai-lūwai *x* **yanā da jiƙī** ⁓ he's very smooth-skinned.

lwas = **laƙwas.**

lwī-lwī **(1)** = **luƙwī** 2*a*, *b.* **(2)** *Nor.* **ɗan** ⁓ *m.* = **lūlū** 2.

lwīlwīyā = **lailaya.**

M

m **(1)** (*a*) yes ! (*b*) **yā zauna bā̧ m, bā̧ m m̧** he remained mum (= **uffaŋ**), *cf.* **m m̧.**

(2) well ! *x* **m, kada ka tsai da nī** well, don't delay me !

ma A. (**mā**) **(1)** in fact, indeed *x* **nī** ⁓ **nā jī** I in fact heard it. **kō da** ⁓ **nā faɗa maka** as a matter of fact, I told you about it long ago. **yanzu** ⁓ at the present time indeed . . . **n nā̧ māmākin da ba ta tafi ba** (*reply,* **mū** ⁓ **haka**) I'm surprised she did not go (*reply,* so are we as a matter of fact). **(2)** (**mā** *stands after the word it emphasizes, but does not affect the construction which remains as if* **mā** *were not present*) *x* **lōkacim mā da suka shigō** when indeed they entered . . . **garin naŋ shī nę ya hau mā wa** it is *this* very town which he attacked. **ban tafa jim mā** (= **ban tafa jī mā**) **am faɗā ba** I've never even heard it said that . . . **bā mā su zāki kō dāmisa kaɗăi ba har kyaŋwā zā mu kashę** it is not only animals such as lions and leopards that we shall kill, but also those such as cats (*for other words thus inserted without affecting construction cf.* **dăi, kw̧ā, kumā**). **(3)** *Vd.* **da** 5, **da** 1*b*, 1*c*, 2.

B. (**ma**) **(1)** to (Mod. Gram. 50) *x* **maka** to you. **mini** to me. **(2) ma** = **mā** (*contraction of* **maka** *in* 1 *above*) *x* **nā gaya ma** I told you. **(3)** (*prefix, accompanied by suffix* -**ī**, *denoting agent,* Mod. Gram. 103) *x* **maƙērī** smith. **mahaifīyā** mother. **(4)** (*prefix, accompanied by suffix* -**ī**, *denoting tool,* Mod. Gram. 104) *x* **mabūdī** key. **(5)** (*prefix, accompanied by suffix* -**ā** *or* -**ī**, *denoting* place, Mod. Gram. 104) *x* **mahautā** abattoir. **madafi** kitchen.

C. (**ma**) *Sk.* to (= **wa** *q.v.*) *x* **ita cę maganad da suka tāsam ma** = **ita cę maganad da suka tāsar wa**. it is this on which their attention is concentrated. **mutānan da suka fāɗa ma** = **mutānan da suka fāɗa wa** the persons on whom they made an onslaught. **(2)** *Kt.* (*both* **ma** *and* **wa** *inserted*) *x* **wā zan kai ma wa** who shall I take it to ? (*Vd.* **wā** 3, **wa** 2*d.*i *last example*).

D. (**mā**) **(1)** *Vd.* **ma** 2. **(2)** we shall probably (Mod. Gram. 118) *x* (*a*) **mā zō** we shall most likely come. (*b*) *Vd.* **wanyē** 3. (*c*) **mā ga dabo** *Vd.* **dabo** 5.

(d) mā ga tsīram būshīyā *Vd.* tsīrā 1*b*.
vii.

mą'abbą = ɗam mą'abbą *m.* (*pl.* 'yam
mą'abbą) beggar who recites panegyrics
(ƙīrąr bąkī) but has no drum (*Vd.*
ƙīrą 1*b*, marōƙī).

*mą'ądūdį *m.* (*f.* mą'ądūdīyā) *pl.*
mą'ądūdai (*Ar.* mahdūd) limited *x*
kwānaŋką dūnīyą ⁓ nē (*words of a
song*) Man's life is but a fleeing moment
of time.

ma'aibąncī *m.* (*f.* ma'aibancīyā) *pl.*
ma'ąibąntā disgraceful.

ma'aikaci A. (ma'aikacī) *m.* (*pl.*
mą'ąikątai) any tool.
    B. (ma'ąikącī) *m.* (*f.* ma'aikacīyā)
pl. ma'ąikątā worker.

ma'aikata A. (ma'aikatā) *f.* (*pl.* mą'ąikątai) work-place.
    B. (ma'ąikątā) *Vd.* ma'ąikącī.

ma'ąikī *m.* (*pl.* ma'ąikā). (1) messenger
(= māsįnją = mąnzō). (2) Ma'ąikiŋ Allą
the Prophet Mahommed (*Vd.* ąnnabį).

ma'aji A. (ma'ajī) *m.* (*pl.* mą'ąjīyai). (1)
store. (2) *cf.* mazubā.
    B. (ma'aji) *m.* (1) Native Adminis-
tration treasurer = ąjīyą 4 (*epithet is
Kąwātą*). (2) gidam ⁓ *m.* N.A. treasury
(= bąitųlmąl). (3) kąi bą ⁓ ba nę,
bā yą ajīyę kōmē sǎi mąjīnā one is likely
to forget unless oné writes a thing down.

ma'ajīyā *f.* = ma'ajī.

ma'ajīyi = ma'aji.

mą'ąlūfį *m.* (*pl.* mą'ąlūfai) needle-case.

mą'āmalą *Ar.* *f.* (1) transactions, business *x*
muną ⁓ dą sū we do business with
them, we have transactions with them
(= mųbāsharą 1 = mųwālātį = sabgą).
(2) bā ną ⁓ dą shī I have nothing to do
with him.

mą'āmilą = mą'āmillą = mą'āmalą *q.v.*

ma'amrā *Kt.* = ma'aurā.

mą'ąnā *f.* (*pl.* ma'anōnī) *Ar.* (1) meaning
x įnā ⁓ tasą what does it mean ? (2) (*a*)
sense *x* mąganąn nąm bą tą yi ⁓ ba
this word makes no sense, it is wrongly
used. (*b*) symmetry *x* shirįn nąm bąi
yi ⁓ ba this arrangement is useless
(= fasąlī 1). (3) pleasantness *x* ąbincin
nąŋ yā yi ⁓ this food is nice. *(4) įnā
azancinsą wajam mą'ąnā what is its
metaphorical sense ? (*cf.* zāhįrī 3*b*).

ma'ąnītā *Vd.* namijį 1*c*.

ma'arā *f.* (*pl.* mą'ąrai) place where T. is
borrowable.

*ma'arafancī *m.* (*Ar.* ma'rūf known) *x*
wannąm mąganą tanā dą ⁓ this word
enjoys great currency.

ma'ąrī *m.* (*f.* ma'arīyā) *pl.* ma'ąrā (1)
borrower, *cf.* ąrā. (2) kōįnā ⁓ zą
shi, dą shinąm mąi rįgā no subordinate
is a free agent.

ma'ąrzųcī *m.* (*f.* ma'arzucīyā) *pl.* ma'ąr-
zųtā rich. (2) Ma'ąrzųcim bāyī God,
Man's Refuge (*cf.* arzųtā).

mą'āsī *m.* (*Ar.* mu'āsāt rebellion) adultery
(= zįnā).

ma'ąskī *m.* (*pl.* ma'ąskā). (1) barber. (2)
ma'ąskin darē spirit to whom bald
patch on one's head is attributed
(= wąnzāmį 4).

ma'auna A. (ma'ąunā) *Vd.* ma'ąunī.
    B. (ma'aunā) *f.* (*pl.* mą'ąunai) place
where corn is sold by measure (awǫ).

ma'auni A. (ma'aunī) *m.* (*pl.* mą'ąunai)
(1) any measure. (2) scales, balance
(= wayą 2*b*). (3) weighing-machine
(= sįkēlį). (4) ma'aunin sakūwą *Vd.*
dąsharē.
    B. (ma'ąunī) *m.* (*f.* ma'aunīyā) *pl.*
ma'ąunā P. selling corn by measure
(*cf.* awǫ).

ma'aurā *f.* *x* tā tąfi ⁓ she (bride)
has moved to her husband's home
(= tārę 2).

ma'ąurī *m.* (*pl.* ma'aurā). (1) man looking
well after his household (*cf.* ąurarrē,
ma'aurīyā). (2) *Vd.* radą 2*c*.

ma'aurīyā *f.* good wife (*cf.* ma'ąurī).

mabā *m.*, *f.* (*sg.*, *pl.*) (*this word must be
followed by a noun, cf.* mafį). (1) giver.
(2) ⁓ dą ƙalai native oculist (*cf.* ƙalau).

mabą'ąncī *m.* ˙ (*f.* maba'ancīyā) *pl.*
mabą'ąntā mocker.

mabagā *f.* (*pl.* mąbągai) place of ambush.

mabākacī *m.* (*pl.* mąbąkątai) *Sk.* =
matąŋkadī.

mabāƙųncī *m.* (*f.* mabāƙuncīyā) *pl.*
mabąƙųntā strange *x* ląntįrīkį ⁓ nē
electricity is a wonderful thing.

mabaƙunta A. (mabąƙųntā) *Vd.* mabą-
ƙųncī.
    B. (mabāƙųntā) *f.* (*pl.* mąbąƙųntai)
lodging-place for guests.

mā̆bā̆lē *Kt. m.* large, leather apron for Rahazāwā.

mā̆ɓallī *m.* (*pl.* mā̆ɓā̆llai). (1) fastener (*x* loop, button, etc.). (2) heelstrap of sandal.

mā̆ɓamɓara *f.* bā̆ ka dā̆ ∼ you have no means of escape.

mā̆ɓannā̆cī *m.* (*f.* mā̆ɓannacīyā) *pl.* mā̆ɓannā̆tā. (1) spendthrift. (2) damager.

mā̆ɓārā *f.* (*pl.* mā̆ɓā̆rai) place on kola-nut where it is splittable.

mabā̆rā̆cī *m.* (*f.* mabaracīyā) *pl.* mabā̆rā̆tā beggar (*Vd.* barā̆).

mā̆barā̆s = mā̆barā̆shī = mū̆barrā̆shī *q.v.*

mabā̆rā̆yī *m.* (*f.* mabārayīyā) *pl.* mabā̆rā̆yā P. taking part in Māguzāwā funeral-games (bārayā̆).

mabā̆rcī *m.* (*f.* mabarcīyā) *pl.* mabā̆rtā. (1) creditor. (2) debtor.

mā̆ɓarnā̆cī = mā̆ɓannā̆cī.

mā̆barrā̆s = mā̆barrā̆shī = mū̆barrā̆shī.

mabarta A. (mabā̆rtā) *Vd.* mabā̆rcī.
    B. (mabartā) *f.* (*pl.* mā̆bā̆rtai) sleeping-place.

mabatā *f.* (*pl.* mā̆bā̆tai) *Sk.* chatting-place (*d.f.* batā̆).

mā̆bāyi'ā̆ *Ar. f.* swearing fealty (= caffā̆ *q.v.*).

mabī̆ *m., f.* (*sg., pl.*) (*this word must be followed by a noun, cf.* mabī̆yī). (1) P. who follows. (2) ∼ jī̆kī *m.* (*a*) type of crawcraw. (*b*) rheumatic pains. (*c*) *Kt.* serious chill. (3) ∼ jinī *m.* paraplegia. (4) ∼ kā̆ɓakī *Vd.* lā̆kā̆i-lā̆kā̆i.

mabirkī = maburgī.

mabī̆yī *m.* (*f.* mabī̆yīyā) *pl.* mabī̆yā (*this word may stand alone or be followed by a noun, or stand in the genitive, cf.* mabī̆). (1) younger brother. (2) (*a*) loyal, obedient. (*b*) servant. (*c*) retainer, follower. (3) mabī̆yīyā *f.* afterbirth (= mahaifā 2 = ūwā 9). (4) mabī̆yā *pl.* the spirits supposed to cause hysteria (= ā̆bū 11 = mā̆kā̆rai).

mā̆ɓōyā *f.* = mā̆ɓōyī *m.* (1) hiding-place. (2) tsārī̆yā bā̆ ∼ cē̆ ba there is no way of evading justice.

mā̆ɓuɓɓ̆ugā *f.* (*pl.* mā̆ɓuɓɓ̆ugai) spring of water.

mabū̆dī *m.* (*pl.* mā̆bū̆dai). (1) key (= mā̆ɓullī). (2) type of obsolete Kano

sā̆rautā̆. (3) the beam matōkarī 3 *q.v.*
    (4) mabū̆dīn kwānō tin-opener.

mabuga A. (mabū̆gā) *Vd.* mabū̆gī.
    B. (mabū̆gā) *f.* (*pl.* mā̆bū̆gai). (1) (*a*) log on which washed clothing is beaten. (*b*) place where beating *as in* 1*a* is done. (*c*) place where corn is threshed. (2) rolling from side to side on ground by donkey, horse, or boy pretending sickness (= birgimā). (3) takō̆bī yā̆ yi ∼ the sword is bent. (4) ∼ hū̆tā *Kt. f.* type of black and blue European cloth.

mabū̆gī *m.* (*f.* mabugī̆yā) *pl.* mabū̆gā. (1) P. who beats (*especially as in* mabugā 1*a*). (2) P. threshing corn.

mabū̆kā̆cī *m.* (*f.* mabukācī̆yā) *pl.* mabū̆kā̆tā. (1) P. requiring T. (2) extravagant P.

mabū̆nkū̆sā kasā *m. pl.* any root-crop (*x* onion, cassava, etc.).

maburgī *m.* (*pl.* mā̆bū̆rgai) swizzle-stick.

maburkākī *m.* (*pl.* mā̆bū̆rkā̆kai) *Sk.* (1) = maburgī. (2) the inflorescence burū̆dē̆.

maburkī = maburgī.

maburmī *m.* (*pl.* mā̆bū̆rmai). (1) = makamfacī. (2) the inverted calabash dam burmī̆ *q.v. under* burmī̆.

mabusa A. (mabū̆sā) *Vd.* mabū̆shī.
    B. (mabū̆sā) *f.* (*pl.* mā̆bū̆sai). (1) = sī̆rī̆kī̆. (2) = sā̆rē̆wā̆.

mabū̆shī *m.* (*pl.* mabū̆sā) trumpeter, horn-blower.

mā̆ɓuyā = mā̆ɓōyā.

mā̆caccakū *Sk. f.* = mā̆tsattsā̆kū.

mā̆caccē̆ *m.* (*f.* mā̆caccīyā) *pl.* mā̆tattū dead (= mā̆taccē̆ *q.v.*).

macakī *m.* (*pl.* mā̆cā̆kai) (1) tool for piercing. (2) long digging-rod (dāgī̆) for making holes for cotton-seed, etc. (3) piece of stick for poking into cake (*x* dā̆n wākē̆) to pick it up without touching it (= macōkī).

mā̆cakō̆ *f.* type of red guinea-corn.

mā̆cā̆kwar *Kt. f.* scrotal hernia (= mā̆jā̆kwar *q.v.*).

mācanjā̆ *Nor.* = māsinjā̆.

mā̆cārā *f.* (1) hollow reed for mouthpiece of ā̆lgaitā̆. (2) *Vd.* karā 1*h*.

mā̆ccē̆ *Sk.* = mā̆cē̆.

mace A. (mā̆cē̆) *f.* (*pl.* mātā = mātā̆yē̆ = mātattakī = mā̆tā̆ikū = mā̆tē̆kū). (1)

(a) (i) woman. (ii) wife (both = mātā).
(iii) mātar Garbā = macan Garbā
Garba's wife. mātā tasā = macansā
his wife (in genitive, the form mātar is
commoner than macan). mātan Garbā
the wives of Garba. (b) (i) mātar
mutum marufar asīrinsā Vd. marufā 3.
(ii) mātar mutum kabarinsā nē Vd.
kabari. (iii) mātar mutānē cē she is
another's wife, not yours. (c) tāram
mātā bābu karo, banzā what an idle
crowd has gathered ! (d) babban abu
shī nē, ~ tā rigā mijintā bawalī (said
by labourers) what a serious affair ! (e)
mun yi sāfiyar mātā we got up safely
in the morning (cf. sāfiyā 1f). (f) (i)
mātansu sun isa mātan shigā jirgī
their women are very pretty. (ii) tā
isa mātar "kāwō rūwā ! " she is very
pretty. (2) female of animal x macan
akū = tamatar akū female parrot (Vd.
tamatā). (3) (a) bim mātā Vd. bī 3b.
(b) nēmam mātā Vd. nēmā. (4) mātan
aurē the four legally allowed contemporary wives (cf. kwarkwarā). (5) (a)
'yā macē Vd. 'yā 1a.i. (b) 'yam mātā
Vd. yārinyā. (6) mai muryar mātā =
kōtsō 2. (7) dākī yā zaunā a mātā the
house is well proportioned. tukunyā
(kwaryā) a mātā a symmetrical pot
(calabash), cf. namiji 3. (8) macē dā
kamar mazā, kwarī nē bābu Woman,
you are almost as brave or skilful as a
man ! (= namiji 1c = rawanī 1d). (9)
macijim mātā Vd. maciji 2. (10) Na
mātā (a) = Tanko. (b) na mātā = na
mātā, na mātā, madaukā mātā lēfē
man over-frequenting society of women.
(11) dā kōgī, dā macē Vd. amānā 8c.
(12) bā ganim mātā ba Vd. fataucī.
(13) mātarkā hayākī Vd. farkē. (14) Vd.
hanā mātā zarē. (15) mai mātā gōmā
Vd. dagarā. (16) bā mātākā Vd. baunī.
(17) īyākacim macē gwīwā Vd. barkōnō
1b. (18) mazarim mātā Vd. mazarī 5.
(19) kyam mātā Vd. dadā kyau. (20) Vd.
ūwar mātā. (21) macē a tsugune (a)
type of potash. (b) cone-shaped cake of
daddawā. (c) Kt. type of gujīyā. (22)
macē dā cikī epithet of P. or T. whose
value is still unknown. (23) macē
dā gōyō type of coiffure. (24) gangar

mātā Vd. cinyā. (25) macē dukus
type of guinea-corn. (26) macē kadan
name for girl born tiny (= Afīrē). (27)
mātā mīyāgū Kt. m. the beetle kurgun-
gumā. (28) macē tsundumī pied Kingfisher (Ceryle rudis). (29) mātā kurāsā
Woman, thou temptress ! (30) māganim ~ Vd. jēmāgē 1d. (31) Vd.
mātan-compounds, Vd. mātar-com-
pounds.

B. (macē) (1) Vb. 3A died (= mutu)
x rīgāta tā ~ my gown is worn out.
(2) (the form of mutu used before dative) x
kāzan nan, kwăi yā macē matā a
cikī this hen is suffering from having a
broken egg in her. bākin wutā yā
macē masā a hannū he has fallen below
the rank of his ancestors. (3) Vd.
mace ; mace-macē.

C. (mace) x kō a raye, kō a mace
alive or dead (cf. macē).

D. (macē) Kt. m. the stirrups makē.

E. (mācē) Kt. m. cooked sorrel-
leaves (= mātsē q.v.).

maceci A. (macēcī) m. (pl. macētai) place
of refuge.

B. (macēcī) m. (f. macēcīyā) pl.
macētā rescuer.

ma'ce-macē" m. x anā ~ many deaths
are occurring.

maceta A. (macētā) f. = macēcī.

B. (macētā) Vd. macēcī.

maci A. (macī) m., f. (sg., pl.) eater (this
word must be followed by a noun, cf.
macīyī). (2) ~ amānā yanā tāre dā
kunyā defalcation is shameful. (3) ~ na
wuyā the kingfisher cī na wuyā.

B. (mācī) Eng. m. (1) act of marching.
(2) marching people along x (a) an yi
mācinsu lef-rē, lef-rē they were marched
along in step. (b) an yi mācinsu zūwā
kurkuku they were marched off to
prison. (3) anā mācin gidammu our
compound is being searched for thieves.

maciga Kt. f. rendezvous of idlers
(= makwallā).

maciji m. (f. macijīyā) pl. macīzai. (1) (a)
(i) any snake = sagō. (N.B.—though
the word derives from cīzā "bit",
yet " snake bit " is sārā.) (ii) tsākāninsu
bā kō "gā maciji ! " they hate each
other (= shēgē 4). (iii) epithet of

snake is Sukuku m̧aķaķą = Ş̣ululu na
būnū. (b) ∼ yā yi hạdīyą bại hadīyē
ba, am mātsę bą̄kī yā zubas (Sk. song)
the European came and put an end to
the oppressions of Filani rulers. (c)
im ∼ yā sąrē ķą, iŋ kā ga baķin
tsųmmā, săi ķą gudụ once bitten,
twice shy. (2) (a) macijim mātā =
 farim macījī Vd. dakō 2. (b) banzā
kişąm macījim mātā, aŋ kashę, bạ ą
sārę ķam ba half measures are no good.
(3) (a) macījī = macījiŋ ķą̄iķąyī deceitful P. (b) macījiŋ ķą̄iķąyī, şąri
ķą nōķę what a treacherous person !
(4) bą̄kim ∼ = haķōrī 9. (5) ky̧am ∼
Vd. banzā 1a. (6) mūgųm ∼ Vd.
wųji-wųjī. (7) wuy̧am ∼ Vd. wuy̧ą 5.
(8) gą̄ ∼ kwąnce Vd. dą̄rą̄rī 2. (9)
gy̧ātsar ∼ f. unaccountable stench. (10)
w̧arkim ∼ Vd. w̧arkī 8. (11) Vd.
dōķim macījī. (12) macījim baķą
accidentally spurting out saliva while
speaking or reading aloud (= tsartūwā 2b). (13) macījin ciķi intestinal
round worms (= dauḑąr ciķi), cf.
ay̧ambā.
Mācikā f. one of the Katsina şąrautą.
mącīlilī dą maŋ kaḑany̧ą m. riding a cock-
horse (= tą̄cūcū 2), cf. dōķiŋ karā.
maciya A. (macīyā) f. (pl. mącīyai). (1)
wayside little market. (2) edible part
of T. x ķashin nąm bą̄ shi dą ∼ there
is nothing edible on this bone. (3) (a)
advantage. (b) cī kaķę ganī ą wurinsą,
ąlhālī bā ∼ he's too smart for you.
(c) profit x gōrąn nąm bą̄ shi dą ∼
there's no profit on these kola-
nuts.
B. (macīyā) Vd. macīyī.
maciyi A. (macīyī) m. (f. macīyįyā) pl.
macīyā. (1) eater (this word may stand
alone or in the genitive, Vd. macī) x
tūwan nąm bą̄ shi dą ∼ there is nobody
to eat this tūwō. (2) a glutton. (b)
rȩną aiķim ∼, kō yā yī, zại ciny̧ē nȩ
he eats up more than the value of his
work. (3) (a) dependent x macīy̧ansą
gōmą nē he has ten mouths to feed.
(b) macīyiŋķą bā y̧ą̄ ganin rąmakķą
P. to whom you habitually give gifts
cannot realize you can ever be short of
money yourself.

B. (macīyī) m. (pl. mącīyai) Kt.
the tool mishī.
mącīzai Vd. macījī.
macōkī = macakī.
macų̄cī m. (f. macūcįyā) pl. macų̄tā.
(1) rogue, deceiver. (2) any biting or
stinging insect.
Mą̄dā (1) name for slave-girl. (2) ģąrī
yā yi ḑaurịn rīdim ∼ these are hard
times.
madabā f. (pl. mądąbai) hunters' campingplace (Vd. dabą).
maḑāba'ā f. (pl. maḑāba'ō'ī) Ar. printing-
press.
*mądabbąr = mudabbąr.
mada6ī A. (madą̄6ī) m. (f. mada6īy̧ā) pl.
madą̄6ā P. who beats mud-floor (dą6ē).
B. (madą6ī) m. (pl. mądą6ai = ma-
du6ą = Kt. madu6ba = Kt. mądų66ai).
(1) (a) implement for beating mud-
floor (dą6ē). (b) yaną̄ dą ķafą ķąmam
∼ = ķafąr Kanọ. (2) shoulder or
foreleg of butcher's meat.
mądąburọ m. padding on upper side of
saddle (= hūhū 6), cf. zubķą.
madą̄cī m. (f. madācįyā) pl. madą̄tā
child of 8–10 years old.
maḑācī m. (pl. mądą̄tai). (1) African
mahogany tree. (2) Allą̄ y̧ą 6ōy̧ę shi ą
kȯgwam ∼ = . . . ą kȯgwan ḑācī (said
by women to mother of new-born baby)
long life to your baby lad ! (3) ∼ yaną̄
raḑąn dumā = dumā yaną̄ raḑąm ∼
the pot is calling the kettle black. (4)
ķąrą̄tū, farkwaŋķą ∼, ķąrshaŋķą zumą
there is no royal road to knowledge.
(5) (a) gą̄ gōran zumą, gą̄ na ∼ epithet
of ąlkālī. (b) Vd. ķurtū 1c.
maḑācįyā f. gall-bladder (= mątsar-
mamā).
madądī m. (Ar. help) P. who is one's
representative, relief, or locum tenens
(= wąkīlị = muķaddąshī).
maḑāḑīyā Kt. f. bird-scaring whip.
madafa A. (madąfā) f. (pl. mądąfai). (1)
place for cooking, kitchen. (2) place
for brewing. (3) place for smelting
(1–3 = madąfī).
B. (mądāfą) f. (pl. mądąfai) (Ar.
madāfī' guns, artillery) muzzle-loading
cannon.
C. (madāfā) f. (pl. mądąfai). (1)

place to lean on. (2) yā rasa ∼ he has no one to help him.

madafi A. (madafī) m. (pl. madafai) = madafā 1–3.
B. (madafī) m. (f. madafīyā) pl.
madafā. (1) cook. (2) kas madafīyā Vd. kūlū.
C. (madāfī) Vd. dōkin dam ∼.

madāgā f. (pl. madāgā = madāgai) x madāgā māsū aminci strong battle-positions.

madāgulā = majāgulā.

madaha m. (Ar. madh praise) scholar earning his living by reciting books like Ishirīnīya which eulogize Mahommed.

madahanci m. earning one's living as in madaha.

madahu m. = madahanci.

madāidāicī m. (f. madāidāicīyā) pl. madāidāitā. (1) of medium size. (2) correct. (3) exact. (4) corresponding with x kāwō wani ∼ da wannan bring one resembling this one!

madāidāicī m. (f. madāidāicīyā) pl. madāidāitā widespread x lābārin nam ∼ nē this news is widespread.

madakā (1) bā ku tārar ∼ Vd. dōgari. (2) Kt. na ∼ you blasted fellow! ta ∼ blast you, Woman!

Mādākancī m. office and work of a Mādākī.

Mādākantaka f. = Mādākancī.

madākatā f. (pl. madākatai) = mabagā.

Mādākī m. (1) an important title and sarauta (cf. Kaurā 3c, Gōje 3a, Gumi 1b, Jirgī 6, Kacalla, Kaigama, Gāgū, Katūmā) = Sk. Uban dawākī. (2) equivalent x (a) sūmā mādākim mutūwa fainting is the twin-brother of death. tsārancē mādākin zinā the tsārancē custom is virtually fornication. (b) mādākin tilas Vd. sulhu 2b.

madāki f. (d.f. mai dāki) madākina my senior wife (= ūwar gidā).

madakūki m. (f. madakūkīyā) pl. madakūkai. (1) = mudukūki. (2) Kt. miser.

mādākullē m. short-necked P. (= dāmākullē).

mādallā (Ar. thanks be to God!). (1) splendid! (2) (a) thank you! (b) Vd. gōde 2. (3) yā yi ∼ tir he behaved ungratefully.

madambaci A. (madambacī) m. (pl. madambatai). (1) pot with big hole (kōfa) in the bottom over which kēso is put, for use as a steamer (= rigāna = Kt. masulālī), cf. madigī. (2) Kt. madambacin Tūrai m. penny (because pierced).
B. (madambacī) m. (pl. madambatā). (1) boxer. (2) mūgum ∼ nē he's a tough customer.

madamfarī m. (f. madamfarīyā) pl. madamfarā. (1) child inseparable from its mother (= makēke 2). (2) madamfarīyā f. tick (= kaska 3 q.v.).

madāmī m. (pl. madāmai). (1) large calabash (but not so big as masakī). (2) the ladle makamfacī q.v.

madamrī Kt. = madaurī.

madangale m. (pl. madangalai) Kt. shin or calf of leg (= shā rāɓā).

madangarci Kt. m. delight (= badangarci).

madangare Kt. = madangale.

madangarī Nor. m. = magirbī.

madānīyā Kt. f. (1) struggling. (2) difficulty. (3) wrangling.

madankwalī Had. m. bird-snare.

madannī m. (pl. madannai) = jijjige 1b.

madarā f. (Ar. tamaddara milk co-agulated). (1) (a) fresh milk (cf. nōno 1a, m). (b) tsōma bākī a ∼ Vd. tsōma. (2) loose European salt (i.e. not made into cūri which is adulterated with bean-flour). (3) (a) pure musk. (b) pure silver. (5) Vd. gīya 1.

madārāti = mudārāti.

madārī m. kum maishē ni ∼ you've made me a laughing-stock (= dādin kwāsā).

madas = madashī m. any deadly poison administered by the mouth (cf. dafi).

madatsa A. (madātsā) f. (pl. madātsai) rendezvous of idlers.
B. (madatsā) f. (pl. madatsai) place for making a dam.

madau adv. sufficiently applied x yā ji gishirī ∼ it (food) is sufficiently salted. an sā kwallī ∼ the right amount of galena has been applied to the eyes.

madauci A. (Madaucī) a Zaria sarauta.
B. (madaucī) Nor. m. = madāwacī.

madauka A. (madaukā) Vd. madaukī.
B. (madaukā) f. (pl. madaukai). (1)

place where T. is lifted (*Vd.* maɗaukī).
(2) maɗaukar zāfī *Vd.* gaban 6.
maɗaukai *Vd.* maɗaukā, maɗaukī.
madaukakī *m.* (*f.* madaukakīyā) *pl.*
madaukakā P. sticking to one like a
limpet (= malizimcī).
maɗaukakī *m.* (*f.* maɗaukakīyā) *pl.*
maɗaukakā. (1) (*a*) highest. (*b*) best.
(*c*) most important. (2) Allā maɗaukakin Sarkī God Almighty. (3) intense *x*
maɗaukakīyar himma intense efforts.
yanā da murya maɗaukakīyā he has a
loud voice.
maɗauki A. (maɗaukī) *m.* (*pl.* maɗaukai).
(1) (*a*) handle. (*b*) loop for lifting portable ink-pot (kurtun tawada) = ƙulūlu
2*b.* (*c*) *Vd.* cī ∼ ; maɗaukā. (2)
maɗaukai *pl. x* yā gamu da maɗaukai he
has pneumonia (= haƙarkarī 2).
B. (maɗaukī) *m.* (*f.* maɗaukīyā) *pl.*
maɗaukā. (1) taker, lifter. (2) maɗaukim magana mischief-maker (= algungumī). (3) *Vd.* kaŋwā 1*c.*
maɗauri A. (maɗaurī) *m.* (*f.* maɗaurīyā)
pl. maɗaurā P. who ties.
B. (maɗaurī) *m.* (*pl.* maɗaurai) T.
used for tying.
madāwacī *m.* (*pl.* madāwatai) farm
reserved for guinea-corn (dāwa).
Mādawākī *Kt.* = Mādākī 1.
madawwamī *m.* (*f.* madawwamīyā) *pl.*
madawwamā *Ar.* (1) permanent. (2)
Allā ∼ God Eternal.
madawwarī *m.* (*f.* madawwarā) *pl.* madawwarai *Ar.* (1) round. (2) *m.* circle.
madda *Ar. f.* (1) line over letter alif to
lengthen this vowel. (2) dilatoriness.
maɗe A. (mādē) *m.* affectation (= fēlēƙē).
B. (maɗe) *Vb.* 3A (1) is (was) extinguished. (2) died.
maɗebi A. (maɗēbī) *m.* (*pl.* maɗēbai). (1)
vessel for dipping out (*x* ladle, shovel,
etc.). (2) *Sk.* tail of a cloth (= jēlā 1*b*).
B. (maɗēbī) *m.* (*f.* maɗēbīyā) *pl.*
maɗēbā P. who draws water, dips out
liquid, etc.
madēgu *used in* 'yar ∼ *f.* hunger (= yunwa).
madeideicī *Vd.* madāidāicī.
madi A. (madi) *Vd.* furā 6, tsāmīyā 5.
B. (Mādī) (1) = Mahadī. (2) *Vd.*
tawada 1*b.*

maɗi *m.* (1) (*a*) a sweet drink made from
juice of sugar-cane (takanɗā) and
various trees (*x* dinyā, kanya, ɗōrawa).
(*b*) *Vd.* jēmāgę 1*d.* (*c*) sautum ∼ *Vd*
galamaɗi. (2) the blight darɓā *q.v.* (3)
the infusion kaŋgo *q.v.* (4) *cf.* maɗimaɗi.
madībī *Sk.* = madūbī 1.
mādīdī *m.* type of blancmange made from
rice-flour and sold wrapped in leaves
(*cf.* agidi 2).
maɗiga *f.* (*pl.* maɗigai) fontanelle.
mādiga *Vd.* mādugū.
maɗigī *m.* (*pl.* maɗigai). (1) pot (tukunyā)
or calabash (ƙwaryā) pierced with small
holes (ƙōfa) for percolating ash-water
(= matarārī), *cf.* madambacī. (2)
type of lēfē basket for percolating
(diga) fruit-juice (maɗi).
mādigō = mādigō *m.* sapphism with
artificial penis (talōlō 4), *Vd.* dāɓa.
maɗigyallē *Kt. used in* ɗam ∼ *m.* type of
dance.
mādillā = mādallā.
maɗi-maɗi *m.* (1) idansa yanā ∼ his eyes
are winking with sleep. (2) fitila tanā ∼
the lamp is flickering preparatory to
going out.
mādindimī = mādindimī *m.* (1) blindman's buff (= *Kt.* māmuŋga 2), *cf.*
burum-burum. (2) small duck-like
bird. (3) ignorant P.
maɗiŋkī *m.* (*f.* maɗiŋkīyā) *pl.* maɗiŋkā.
(1) tailor. (2) maɗiŋkīyā *f.* needle
(= allūra).
madō *m.* (1) an yi mata ∼ she (virgin)
has been violated. (2) Madō *abbreviation
of name* amadu.
madōbīyā *f.* (*pl.* madōbai). (1) African
Rosewood tree (*Pterocarpus erinaceus*).
(2) the tree *Andira inermis*. (3) madō-bīyar rāfī (*a*) the tree *Albizzia Brownei*.
(*b*) the tree *Albizzia zygia*.
madōdōwa *Kt. f.* (1) writhing, reeling. (2)
struggling (1, 2 = magōwa).
madōgarā *f.* (*pl.* madōgarai). (1) prop.
(2) one's means of support, one's means
of livelihood *x* Allā madōgarar bāwa
God brings a means of livelihood to Man.
madōgarī *m.* (*pl.* madōgarai) = madōgarā.
madoki A. (madōkī) *m.* (*pl.* madōkai).
cudgel (= kulkī).

B. (madǫ̆kī) *m.* (*f.* madōkīyā) *pl.* madǫ̆kā. (1) P. who hits. (2) abiŋ yā zamā ∼ kusa, macę̆cī nēsạ one must remain friends with one's immediate senior in rank.

madǫ̆rī *m.* (*pl.* madǫ̆rā) bone-setter.

madōshī *m.* (*pl.* madǫ̆sai). (1) punch (tool). (2) (*a*) branding-iron (= acūraḳī). (*b*) tool for burning holes in wood.

madu6ạ *Vd.* mada6ī.

madubi A. (madūbī) *m.* (*pl.* madūbai). (1) glass (material). (2) mirror (2 = matsōkacī). (3) madūbī = madūbiŋ idǫ spectacles, eyeglass (= munzạrī = magānī 3 = tabā̯rau). (4) ∼ mai kāwō nēsạ kusa telescope, binoculars.

B. (madūbi̯) *m.* (*pl.* madūbā) soothsayer, fortune-teller (*cf.* dūbā).

maduddukā = maduddukῙyā *f.* (*pl.* madụddụḳai) back door (= bặi 2*a*.ii = *Kt.* kụ cikạ).

madūdụ (1) *m.* large amount. (2) *adv.* abundantly.

māduganci *m.* work of a mạdugū.

mạdugū *m.* (*f.* mạdugā = mạdigā) *pl.* mạdugai. (1) headman of caravan (= ụban tạfīyạ = jāji). (2) jirā̯gē sun yi iriŋ tạfīyạn nan na ∼ the ships travelled in convoy.

mādugwai = mādigō.

mạdụnd'umī = mādindimī.

mad'ụ̆ŋkī = madiŋkī.

mạdurgujī *m.* (*pl.* mạdụrgụzai) *Kt.* large tūwō-cake (*cf.* kạ6akī).

madurkusa *f.* (*pl.* mạdụrkụsai). (1) camelstation. (2) protector.

madwạccī *Sk. m.* = madʹ̆cī.

mafạ *Vb.* 1A *x* yā ∼ tsummā ạ jikin rīgā tasạ he added a patch over the worn part of the garment (*Vd.* mahǫ).

mạfādạ *m.* (*pl.* fād'ā̯wā) = bạfādạ.

mafadʹa A. (mafad'ā) *Vd.* mafadʹī.

B. (mafādʹā) *f.* (*pl.* mạfād'ai) place of falling *x* (1) bạn sam mafādʹar magan̯ạ ba I don't know how the affair will end (= makwantā). (2) mafād'ar rānā sunset.

mafạdʹ̆cī *m.* (*f.* mafadʹācīyā) *pl.* mafạd'ātā quarrelsome, vicious.

mafad'ī *m.* (*f.* mafadʹīyā) *pl.* mafạdʹā. (1) (*a*) speaker. (*b*) im mafạd'im magan̯ạ wāwā nę̆, mai jī yan̯ā dạ haŋkạlī don't believe all you hear ! (*c*) bạ ạ

rasạ ∼ ba, săi majῙyī akạ rasạ he was told but wouldn't heed. (3) yāran̯ nạm bạ shi dạ ∼ this lad has no mentor.

mafakā = mafakaitā *f.* (*pl.* mạfạkai = mạfạkạitai) place of shelter.

mafalkī = mafarkī.

mafallā = makwallā.

mạfallạs = mạfallashī = mafallạshī *m.* (*f.* mạfallạs = mạfallashīyā = mafallashīyā) *pl.* mafạllạsā = mạfallạsā (1) (*d.f.* fạllasạ) blabber. (2) (*d.f.* fallạsā) spendthrift.

mafạraucī *m.* (*pl.* mafạrautā) hunter.

mafarauta A. (mafạrautā) *Vd.* mafạraucī.

B. (mafarautā) *f.* (*pl.* mạfạrautai) hunting-ground.

mafārī *m.* (1) beginning, origin. (2) reason *x* mafāriŋ dạ Kanǫ ta fi kōin̯ā bābā mai kyaụ kę̆ naŋ this is why Kano has better indigo than anywhere else.

mafạrkạcī *m.* (*f.* mafarkacīyā) *pl.* mafạrkạtā immoral P.

mạfạrkạnce *x* ạ mạfạrkạnce during the course of a dream.

mafarkī *m.* (*pl.* mạfarkai = mafạrkemafạrkē). (1) (*a*) (i) dream (*cf.* falkạ). (ii) mafarkin dʹārī *Vd.* sūtai. (iii) mafarkiŋ gwaurō *Vd.* gwaurō. (*b*) ambition *x* mę̆ sukę̆ īyā̯wā ; dạgạ mafarkin Sarkinsụ what can *they* do ? it is nothing but an idle dream on the part of their king. kuŋ gạ cikim mafarkinsạ this is his real ambition. sunặ mafarkiŋ wai zā sụ ci dūnīyạ they dream of conquering the world. (2) yārǫ tum bại yi ∼ ba before a lad reaches puberty (*cf.* balagạ).

mafashī *m.* (*pl.* mafạsā) highwayman.

mafạtạrcī *m.* (*f.* mafatarcīyā) *pl.* mafạtạrtā. (1) miser. (2) impoverished P.

mafạucī = mahaucī.

mafe A. (māfę̆) *Sk.* = makạrē.

B. (mafę̆) *Vb.* 1A (1) yā ∼ rīgā dạ tsummā he added a patch over the worn part of the gown (*Vd.* mahǫ). (2) Sarkī yā ∼ garī dạ dawākī the Chief filled the town with cavalry.

mafi A. (mafῙ) *m.*, *f.* (*sg.*, *pl.*) in excess of, superior to (*this word must be followed by a noun, cf.* mafīyī) *x* wannạm ∼ tsawō nę̆ this one is longer ; this one is the longest. dōkī ∼ tsā̯dā dạ nặwa a horse dearer than mine. **abūbūwạ** ~ **wannaŋ tsạnạnī** things more unpleasant than this.

B. (**mafị**) *m.* (1) adding patch over worn part of garment (*cf.* **mafẹ**, **mahọ**). (2) stopping up orifice in beehive with perforated **sạkainā**. (3) stopping up mouth of **burdụmī** bag with **kabạ**. (4) the articles employed for **2, 3** *above*.

mafici A. (**maficī**) *m.* (*pl.* **mafịtai**): (1) ford (*cf.* **fitọ**) = **mashigī** = *Sk.* **matuzgī**. (2) **shinạm maficim bạra** being out of date in one's information.

B. (**maficī**) *Sk.* = **mahūcī**.

C. (**maficī**) *m.* (*f.* **maficīyā**) *pl.* **mafịtā**. (1) temporary, transitory. (2) "**wụyā maficịyā** " **ṇ** ji kūsụŋ kyaurō trouble does not last for ever.

mafifici A. (**mafīfīcī**) *m.* (*f.* **mafīfīcīyā**) *pl.* **mafīfītā** superior.

B. (**mafīfīcī**) *m.* (*pl.* **mafịfịfịtai**) fan (= **mahūcī**).

mafilficē *Kt.* = **mafīfīcī**.

mafita A. (**mafịtā**) *Vd.* **maficī**.

B. (**mafitā**) *f.* (*pl.* **mafịtai**). (1) means or place of exit or escape. (2) **Wānẹ, dam** ~ **nẹ** = **Wānẹ yanạ̄ dạ bạbbar** ~ (*said by rich* **kīshīyā** *to poor one*) of what account are you !

mafịtai *Vd.* **maficī**, **mafịtā**.

mafitịnī *m.* (*f.* **mafitinīyā**) *pl.* **mafịtịnā** trouble-maker.

mafitsārā *f.* (*pl.* **mafịtsạrai**) bladder (*cf.* **fitsārī**).

mafịyī *m.* (*f.* **mafīyịyā**) *pl.* **mafịyā** (*this word can stand alone or be followed by a noun or stand in the genitive, cf.* **mafị**) in excess of, superior to *x* (1) **abūbūwạ mafịyā wannaŋ, tsạnạnī** things more unpleasant than this. (2) **rashịn sanịm** ~ failing to acknowledge P. as one's superior (*Vd.* **gạsā 1c**).

mafọ = **mahọ**.

mafyādī *m.* (*pl.* **mafyạ̄dai**). (1) piece of wood supported in two forked sticks for making **rụmfā**, **rụmbū**, or to serve as lavatory seat. (2) any stick used for threshing.

magạ̄ *m., f.* (*sg., pl.*) (*this word must be accompanied by noun, cf.* **mafị**) *used in* (1) ~ **ịsā** P. authorized for any purpose.

(2) ~ **takạrdā** *sg., pl.* (*pl. also* ~ **tạkạrdai**) N.A. scribe (= **mālạmī 1e**). (3) ~ **watạ** *name for* P. born at new moon. (4) ~ **yākị** *Kt.* one of the **sạrautạ**. (5) ~ **rawar wani, gạ̄ tākạ** don't gloat, it'll be your turn next ! (6) **Magạ̄** *name for* slave.

magạbạcī *m.* (*f.* **magabācīyā**) *pl.* **magạbạ̄tā** (1) one's official superior. (2) **bạ̄ hawam magạbạ̄tā** *Vd.* **bakarị**.

magạbcī *m.* (*f.* **magabcīyā**) *pl.* **magạbtā** (*d.f.* **gạ̄bā**) enemy.

magạ̄dā *Vd.* **magạ̄jī** ; **magạ̄jīyā**.

mạ̄gāgạ *Kt. f.* (1) **giginyạ** having only one **ƙwallō**, there normally being two or three (*cf.* **ƙwạr**). (2) **an yi masạ cịm** ~ (*a*) he's been humiliated. (*b*) it (work) has been polished off.

magạ̄gạcī *m.* (*f.* **magạ̄gācīyā**) *pl.* **magạ̄gạ̄tā** foolhardy.

magāgarī *m.* (*pl.* **magạ̄gạrai**). (1) file (= **zartọ 1b**). (2) *Vd.* **zartọ 2**.

magạggaucī *m.* (*f.* **magaggaucīyā**) *pl.* **magạggạutā** impetuous.

mạ̄gāgị *m.* (1) dazedness. (2) **mạ̄gāgim barcī** (*a*) dazedness on awaking. (*b*) sleep-walking by child. (3) **mạ̄gāgim mutūwạ** death-throes (= **gargarạ**). (4) *Vd.* **asharā**.

magaji A. (**magạ̄jī**) *m.* (*f.* **magājīyā**) *pl.* **magạ̄dā**. (1) (*a*) heir. (*b*) *Vd.* **bạrạ magạ̄dā**. (*c*) **bịkim** ~ *Vd.* **bịkī 6b**. (2) ~ **magạjīyī nẹ** one's successor is often inferior to oneself. (3) **Magạ̄jin Rụmfā** *epithet of* any Emir of Kano (*as* **Rụmfā** *was one of the Emirs who built Kano*). (4) *Kts.* elder brother *x* **magạ̄jintạ yā zō** her elder brother has come (= **wạ̄**), *cf.* **magạ̄jīyā 2**. (5) *Kt.* **magạ̄jin B** the village-head (**dagacị**) of the hamlet B (*cf.* **Magạ̄ji 3**). (6) *Vd.* **magạ̄jīyā**. (7) *cf.* **tāshịm magạ̄jiŋ ƙauyẹ**. (8) **magạ̄jiŋ gūgūwạ** *Vd.* **gyạttā**.

B. (**Magạ̄ji**) *m.* (*pl.* **Mạgạ̄dai** = *Kt.* **Mạgạ̄ddai**) an official position and its title (*epithet is* **Gādọ**). (2) **Magạ̄ji** = **Magạ̄jiŋ Gīwā** *epithet of any man named* **Hasạn**. (3) **Magạ̄jiŋ gạrī** (*a*) **sạrautạ** at Kano and Katsina (*cf.* **magạ̄jī 5**). (*b*) **mai Magạ̄jiŋ gạrī** type of cloth.

magājīyā *f.* (*pl.* **magạ̄dā**). (1) woman inheriting, heiress (*Vd.* **magạ̄jī**). (2)

elder sister (cf. magājī 4). (3) Magājịyā (a) *title for* Chief's mother or his elder sister or his father's younger sister. (b) *title for* senior procuress, cf. kạwālịyā, ̣Ạlgājē. (4) Zar. princess.
magajịyị m. (f. magajịyịyā) pl. magạjịyā. (1) P. falling short of a task, P. giving up effort. (2) Vd. magājī 2.
magamā f. (pl. magamai) = magamī.
magạ̄-magạ̄ x yanạ̄ tạfịyạ ~ he's reeling along (= tagạ̄-tagạ̄).
magamāmī m. (pl. magamạ̄mai) appointment to meet P. x mun yi ~ ạ kạsūwā we arranged to meet each other at the market.
magamī m. (pl. magamai). (1) place where people assemble. (2) place fixed for rendezvous. (3) (a) junction, confluence. (b) Kanọ tanạ̄ wurī nẹ̄ magamar jịjịyā Kano is a focal point.
magana A. (maganạ) f. (pl. magạŋganū = mʌganōnī). (1) (a) word. (b) ~ bīyū gạrēshị he's two faced. (c) zạn yi makạ ~ bīyū ? shall I give you a word of advice ? (2) (a) speech. (b) (i) thing said x ~ tasạ what he said. (= fạdā 2). (ii) act of speaking x yā yi ~ he spoke (= jạwābị 4 = Sk. bạtū 1). yā yi mạganạr kudī he spoke of money. (c) mại kudī shī kẹ̄ dạ ~ he who pays the piper calls the tune. (d) dam ~ m. (pl. 'yam ~) panegyrist beggar talking rapidly (cf. kịrạ 1b, marọkị). (e) shī mukẹ̄ yi wạ ~ he is the one to whom we refer. (f) (in negative sentences with sense it's better not talked about !) x gạrin nạŋ dạ dārī yakẹ̄ how cold this town is ! (reply, dārī, bā ạ̄ ~ yes, it is terribly cold !). jịyạ an shā rūwā mạnạ what rain we had yesterday ! (reply, rūwạm, bā ạ̄ ~ yes, what rain !). zākịm, bạ̄ ~ akẹ̄ yị ba it is indescribably sweet. (g) mụtụm shidạ sụŋ halakạ, bā ạ̄ mạganạr wadạndạ sukạ yi raunī seven persons died apart from the wounded. (h) sum fārạ 'yaŋ kanānạm mạgaŋganū they entered on despicable talk. (j) gạrī bā yạ̄ tạshị ? bạllē mạ-ganạ ? can any statement be inflexible ? (k) bạ̄ ki ~ Vd. alakwạyī. (l) Vd. bam mạganạ. (m) Vd. tāshịm mạganạ. (3) (a) affair (= Sk. bạtū 2). (b) ~ mại nauyī an

important affair. (c) n nạ̄ dạ ~ I've something to tell, ask you. (d) ịnā mạganạr tāshị setting out is out of the question. (e) daurạ ~ Vd. daurạ 1a.ii, d, f. (4) Vb. (not used in progressive) x in yā gạji, yạ̄ ~ when he comes to the end of his endurance he'll speak out (= magạntu 3). B. (magānā) f. (pl. magạ̄nai). (1) place in public view x yanạ̄ dạ gidā ạ ~ his compound is very exposed. (2) kyạn rawā, ạ kai tạ ~ there's a time and place for everything.
magạ̄nai Vd. magānā.
magancayyạ = magantayyạ.
magance A. (magancē) Vb. 1C = magantad dạ 2.
B. (māgancē) Vb. 1C x tā ~,shi she put a spell (sammụ) on him, to act as love-philtre (= dabạrcē = tsub-bạcē = nēmẹ), cf. lāyạ, makạrī.
C. (māgancē) Vd. māgantạ.
magan dạ = magantad dạ.
mạ̄gane-māgạnē m. constantly giving drugs (Vd. māganị).
magaŋgamā f. (pl. magaŋgamai) = magamī.
magaŋganū Vd. magana.
magaŋgarā f. = magaŋgarī m. (1) place of descent. (2) (a) path over decayed town wall (= mahaurā). (b) path downhill. (3) declivity. (4) watercourse flowing over hillside.
magani A. (māganị) m. (pl. māgụŋgunạ = Kt. māgụŋgunnạ). (1) (a) (i) medicine. (ii) anạ̄ yi masạ ~ he (sick P.) is being treated. (iii) Vd. kạrɓā-kạrɓā. (b) ~ in yā kị shạwūwā, bạ yạ̄ kị zubạrwā ba if T. is beyond you, don't attempt it ! (c) Vd. karyạ 15. (d) mại ~ m. (pl. māsū ~) doctor, soothsayer (cf. 2). (e) kudịm mại cụ̄tā na mại ~ nẹ̄ P. really desiring T. will go to any lengths. (f) wụyar ~ Vd. shịkịŋkịmī. (g) cf. ūwar māgụŋgunạ. (h) Vd. 4 below. (2) (a) charm, amulet x yā sạ̄ ~ he put on an amulet (cf. lāyạ). (b) tā yi masạ ~ = māgancē. (c) Vd. kạrɓā 2d ; tạmbayạ 2 ; sammụ. (3) means against, means of avoiding x (a) rịgar rūwā māganịn rūwā cẹ̄ a mackintosh is a protection against rain. (b) māganịŋ aikị, yị the only way to dispose of work is to do it.

(c) māganin̲ ḁllōbā Vd. rạ̈i 1q. (d) māganim biri̲ Vd. biri̲ 1b.ii. (e) māganin d̲ārī Vd. rānā 2j.iv. (f) māganin daud̲ạ Vd. rūwa C.21. (g) māgạnim famfaryā Vd. famfarīyā. (h) māgạnin̲ gạrī mai̲ nīsā Vd. tạfīyạ 1g. (j) māgạnin̲ gōbarā Vd. bīyū 10. (k) māgạnin̲ iskạ prophylactic against hysteria. (l) māgạnin̲ ƙarƒẹ charm guarding one against harm from weapons (cf. 4). (m) māgạnin̲ ƙasā mai̲ taurī Vd. dāgi̲. (n) māgạnin̲ ƙi̲yayyạ Vd. rạbu 2k. (o) māgạnin̲ kud̲in zạmāni̲ Vd. ḁlgazaru̲. (p) māgạnim mai̲ dangi̲ Vd. cācā 1b. (q) māgạnim mai̲ gātā Vd. shạrī'ạ. (r) māgạnim mai̲ ƙwārin̲ kạ̈i Vd. ḁdu̲rūku̲. (s) māgạnim makalạ̄mā Vd. dāma 1e. (t) māgạnim maƙī̲ waŋkā Vd. rūwā C.11. (u) māgạnim mugunyạr dạƒūwā Vd. yun̲wạ 1c. (v) māgạnin̲ wata rānā Vd. ḁjīyạ 2f. (w) (i) māgạnin yun̲wạ Vd. yun̲wạ 1g ; 3z.i below. (ii) māgạnin̲ gāwā Vd. gāwā 1a.iii. (iii) māgạnin̲ haki̲ Vd. gi̲ndī 10. (iv) māgạnim mai̲ kwantō Vd. hạrsāshi̲. (v) māgạnim macẹ Vd. jēmāgẹ 1d. (vi) māgạnim mai̲ ƙwạlamā Vd. kwad̲ọ 2b. (vii) māgạnin̲ ƙaryā Vd. hạllarạ 1b. (y) (i) māgạnin zāwọ remedy against diarrhœa (cf. 4c). (ii) kūrā tanạ̄ māgạnin zạ̈wọ ? tạ yi wạ kạntạ manạ physician, heal thyself ! (z) Allạ̄ yā yi matạ ∼, Sarkin̲ Kanọ dạ ganim ƙạ̄rā (said by women) only God can lighten our troubles. (z) (i) bari̲n̲ kāshī̲ ạ ciki̲ bā yạ̄ māgạnin yun̲wạ speak out when the time comes ! (cf. 3w above). (z) (ii) māgạnim maƙī̲ gudu̲ ban̲ kāshī̲ some persons need to be goaded on. (4) method of obtaining x (a) nā yi māgạnin̲ ḁbīna I knew how to look after my affairs. (b) māgạnin̲ ƙarƒī (i) means of obtaining strength. (ii) aphrodisiac. (c) māgạnin zāwọ purgative (= shạ̄rā 2d), cf. 3y above. (5) bạ̄ ni dạ shī kō na ∼ I've absolutely none of it.
  B. (magānī) m. (pl. mạgānai). (1) mirror. (2) eye. (3) spectacles (= madū-bī 3).

maganōnī Vd. mạganạ.

maganta A. (magạntā) Vb. 1C spoke x
  (1) nā ∼ masạ ạbi̲n dạ zā mu̲ yi I

told him what we should do. in̲ kā ∼ sạ̈i ạ yī if you state your wishes they' be executed. (2) Vd. mạgạntu.
  B. (māgạntā) Vb. 1C (with dative) bai ∼ mini̲ kōmē ba it (medicine) di me no good (cf. cī 19).
  C. (mạgantạ) Vb. 2 (p.o. mạgạncē n.o. mạgạnci) x likitạ yā mạgạncē sh the doctor treated him.

magantad dạ Vb. 4B (1) governed administered, had authority over Audu̲ kẹ mai̲ magantạrwā Audu is th one in authority. ∼ jạma'ạn na wu̲yā gạrētạ that community is hard t rule. (2) prompted x yā ∼ sū ạbi̲ dạ zā su̲ ƒạdā he prompted them what t say (cf. kutạ 7, girkạ 1g, mạgạntu) = zancẹ = lakkạnā = tạ̈ƙamā 1b.ii.

mạgạntayyạ f. x mun yi ∼ dạ sū we con versed with them.

magạntsạrī (1) ectropion of the eyelic (2) (with pl. magạntsạrā) (a) type o professional dancers who dance t piping of 'yam bāƒọ (cf. gạntsarạ). (b upper grinding-stone with conve working surface (cf. d̲ā 5a). (c) bạkā ∼ bow shaped like the letter " B ".

mạgạntu Vb. 3B (1) x yā yi ƒushī, bā yạ mạgạntūwā he's angry and will no listen to reason (d.f. magạntā). (2 bā yạ̄ mạgạntūwā he's not one who ca be prompted (d.f. magantad dạ 2) = zancẹ 1b. (3) in yā gạji yạ̄ ∼ = mạganạ 4.

mạgạnu = mạgạntu 3.

māgaraṃ = māgē 1.

magạ̄rē Vd. magaryā.

magargạrā f. self-sown guinea-corn (= ku̲-sumburwạ 1a).

mạgạriba = mạgạrubạ Ar. f. time betweer sunset and li̲shā q.v. (= Sk. hutturu̲).

magaryā f. (pl. magạ̄rē) (1) (a) (i) Jujub tree (Zizyphus jujuba). (ii) in zā kạ d̲aurẹ ḁkwīyạrkạ, kạ d̲aurẹ ta magaryā when you speak, speak th truth ! (iii) magaryab bisạ Vd. bugu̲ 7 (b) magaryar kūrā Buffalo-horn shru (Zizyphus mucronata). (c) Vd. gi̲rgizạ 1b ; sạ̈shē. (2) maganạ tā kai magaryạ tiƙẹ̄wā the matter has reached its utmost extension (x lawsuit referre to highest court of appeal) = ƙurẹ 1c.

magaucī = magabcī.

magaugaucī *Kt.* = magaggaucī.

mạgauji *m.* the hoe bạgǭdā *q.v.*

magayī *Vd.* jịkī 1*g.*

mạ̈gē *f.* (1) (*a*) cat (= kyạŋwā *q.v.*). (*b*) im ∼ bā tạ̄ naŋ, ɓērā sǎi yạ sakę when the cat is away, the mice play. (*c*) *Vd.* bazarā 5 ; kāfircị 4. (*d*) ạlēwạr ∼ *Vd.* cịŋ ạlēwạr ∼. (*e*) dōram ∼ *Vd.* dōrō 5. (2) ∼ dạ wurị a simply-dressed and apparently respectable wife who commits adultery on the sly. (3) idạm ∼ *Vd.* idǫn 10.

mạgēdūwā *f.* (1) large, striped beetle with long antennæ. (2) (*a*) the disease ainhum. (*b*) ƙudugum, ∼ dạgạ kā taking away all a person's property is like beheading him, *cf.* ƙudugum. (3) cutting groove round tree to kill it (= kạ̄cīyạ 5).

magewayi A. (magēwạyī) *m.* (*f.* magē-wayịyā) *pl.* magē̱wạyā military spy, reconnoitrer (*cf.* rạhōtǫ 2*b*).

B. (magēwayī) *m.* = magēwayā *f.* (*pl.* mạgē̱wạyai). (1) place screened off for latrine, bathroom, etc. (= makēwayī = kurdị 2). (2) *Vd.* makē-wayī.

mạ̈gī *used in* yāwạm ∼ *m.* jollifying from village to village (yāwǫ) by young people dressed in adults' clothing (gautā 2*b*).

magịdancī *m.* (*pl.* magịdạntā) house-holder (= gidā 1*l*).

*magịftai *m. pl.* eyes (*cf.* ƙyiftạ).

mạgimfā *f.* the shrub *Tephrosia Vogelii* (*used for drugging fish*).

magini A. (maginị) *m.* (*f.* maginịyā) *pl.* maginā. (1) builder. (2) (*a*) potter. (*b*) jạkim ∼ sǎi kā sō, kạn ci kạ̄sūwā what a stubborn person ! (*as unwilling donkey may break pots on way to market*).

B. (maginī) *m.* (*pl.* mạ̄ginai) = dāgị 1.

magirbi A. (magịrbī) *m.* (*f.* magirbịyā) *pl.* magịrbā reaper.

B. (magirbī) *m.* (*pl.* mạgịrbai). (1) type of harvesting tool shaped like ƒartanyạ (= mạsassabī = *Kt.* kwạ̄shē 3). (2) *Vd.* kurtạ. (3) kwạncīyar ∼ *Vd.* kwạncīyā 8.

magirkī *m.* (*pl.* mạgịrkai) = sạ̄ƙō 4 (*cf.* girkạ 1*d*).

magịrmī *m.* (*f.* magirmịyā) quickly-grow-ing lad or girl (= mashạ̄ 3*a*).

magirō = bạgirō.

māgīyạ *f.* *x* ạlmạ̄jịrai mạ̄sū rǭƙō sun cịkạ ∼ mendicants reiterated mention of God's name (*cf.* hạllạ̄-hallā).

magō *m.* (*sg., pl.*) cream-coloured horse (= kịlị 3).

magōgī *m.* (*pl.* mạgōgai) 1 grater for kola-nuts for use by toothless persons. (2) brush (especially for horse). (3) eraser for writing in pen or pencil. (4) stone used by Nupes in polishing tsạ̄kīyạ-stones, etc., for necklaces, etc.

magǭrī *m.* (*pl.* magǭrā) (1) peddling herbalist (mainly selling love-philtres, i.e. sammụ). (2) *Vd.* būrūƙụ.

mạgōwạ *f.* (1) reeling. (2) writhing in pain. (3) *cf.* mạ̄gūwạ.

maguda A. (magudā) *f.* (*pl.* mạgụdai) place of refuge.

B. (magụdā) *Vd.* magụjī.

māgụdā *Vb.* 1C (toothless P.) chewed.

mạgụdai *Vd.* magujī.

magudādā = magudānā.

magudānā *f.* (*pl.* mạgụdạ̄nai) (1) = magu-dā. (2) watercourse.

magụdancī *m.* (*pl.* magụdạntā) slave-lad (= majị 2), *cf.* kụyaŋgạ.

mạgudī *m.* (1) dishonestly adulterating food, etc. (2) scamping work. (3) what toothless chewing ! (*cf.* mạ̄gụdā).

magūdīyā *f.* (*pl.* magụ̄dā) (1) woman who makes the shrilling-noise gūdạ at ceremonies. (2) = mukurūrūcịyā. (3) shortest string (tsirkīyā) of the three strings in a mōlō (*cf.* tambạrī 5, amālę 1*c*, shạ̄ kidị).

maguji A. (magujī) *m.* (*pl.* mạgụdai) = magudānā 2.

B. (magụjī) *m.* (*f.* magujịyā) *pl.* magụdā (1) fugitive. (2) runaway slave. (3) fast horse.

māgụlā = māgụdā.

mạgul-mạgul *x* taụnā tasạ ∼ he chews with a toothless mouth (= gụlam-gụlam), *cf.* mạ̄gụdā.

māgumę *m.* (1) stocky P. (2) horse of medium height and age (= faf dạ jiɓā).

māguŋguŋạ *Vd.* māgạnī.

magurjī = mugurjī.

m̧ạgūwạ *f.* (1) = m̧ạgōwạ. (2) ~ tā zō the first flood-water has arrived (= mashārịyā = kwāzārī).

Māguzancị *m.* rites practised by the Māguzāwā (*Vd.* Bạmāgujẹ).

Māguzāwā *Vd.* Bạmāgujẹ.

magwaji A. (magwạjī) *m.* (*f.* magwajịyā) *pl.* magwạdā P. who measures.
   B. (magwajī) *m.* (*pl.* mạgwạdai) (1) measuring-rod. (2) magwajin tākạlmī boot-last (= gālịbī).

magwạs *m.* yā yi ~ he (flatulent P.) belched (= gạmbā).

māgyārē *f.* type of meaningless singing (*epithet is* ~ wạddạ bā ta dạ āyạ).

m̧ạgyāzọ *m.* (*f.* m̧ạgyāzụwā) (1) stunted P. or animal (= tsụmbụrarrē). (2) ɗam ~ *m.* (*f.* 'yar m̧ạgyāzụwā) (*a*) stunted P. or T. (*b*) small billy-goat.

mahạbā *rustic* = marhạbā.

mahaɗā *f.* (*pl.* mạhạɗai) = magamī.

mahạɗạncī *m.* (*f.* mahaɗancịyā) *pl.* mahạɗạntā glutton (*d.f.* haɗịyē).

mahạddạcī *m.* (*f.* mahaddacịyā) *pl.* mahạddạtā (1) P. having memorized the Koran (= marụbụcī 2 = makạrạncī 1), *cf.* farī 2*a*.iv. (2) pigeon cooing incessantly (= zạķāķụrī). (3) *Vd.* ạlhudạhudạ.

Mạhạdī *Ar. m.* (1) The Mahdi. (2) *Vd.* tạwadạ 1*b*.

mahadī *m.* = mahaɗā.

Mạhạdīyyạ *Vd.* Ạlīyyạ.

mahaifa A. (mahạifā) *Vd.* mahạifī.
   B. (mahaifā) *f.* (*pl.* mạhạifai) (1) womb. (2) afterbirth (= mabịyī 3). (3) (*a*) birthplace. (*b*) sạm ~ *m.* patriotism (*d.f.* sọ̄).

mahạifī *m.* (*f.* mahaifīyā) *pl.* mahạifā (1) parent. (2) bịm mahạifā *m.* filial conduct. (3) *Vd.* kạŋkạrē 3.

mahạihạyī *m.* (*f.* mahaihayịyā) *pl.* mahạihạyā (1) lofty *x* mahạihạyim bịgirẹ a lofty place. (2) superimposed on *x* dūwạtsū mahạihạyan jūnā stones superimposed on each other (*x* ɗagwarwā).

mahạķī *m.* (*pl.* mạhạķai) digging-stick (= dāgị).

mahạķụncī = mahụķụncī.

mahạķụrcī = mahụķụrcī.

mạhạl *Ar. m.* (1) a lie. (2) craftiness, dishonesty.

mahạlbī *Kt.* = mahạrbī.

Mahạlịccī *m.* The Creator (*d.f.* hạlittạ).

mạhālịyạ *f.* = mạhạl.

mạhạllị *Ar. m.* (*pl.* mạhạllai) (1) place *x* ạ wạnẹ ~ yakẹ̄ in what place is it ? (2) place of residence. (3) an yī matạ ~ jīyạ she was married yesterday. (4) context *x* ịnā mạhạllịŋ wannạm m̧agạnạ in what usage is this word employed ? ạ nạm, bā shi dạ ~ it (expression) is not applicable here.

mạhạllidạ = mạhạllitsạ.

mạhạllitsạ *f.* (*Ar.* makhlūta " mixed ") (1) assortment of variegated articles (including variegated threads for making trouser ankle-bands (kāmụŋ ķafạ)). (2) indiscriminate dealings.

Mạhạmūdụ *m.* (1) *man's name.* (2) *Vd.* Mallē, Mạ̄mūdụ, Mụhammadụ.

mahaŋgā *f.* (*pl.* mạhạŋgai) *x* gạrin nạ̄ŋ yanạ̄ dạ ~ (1) this town is visible from afar. (2) from this town one can see far. 3 *cf.* mahaŋgī.

mạhạŋgai *Vd.* mahaŋgā, mahaŋgī.

mahangi A. (mahaŋgī) *m.* (*f.* mahaŋgịyā) *pl.* mahạŋgā (1) P. who looks into the distance. (2) P. of forethought.
   B. (mahaŋgī) *m.* (*pl.* mạhạŋgai) (1) = madūbī. (2) *cf.* mahaŋgā.

mahani A. (mahạnī) *m.* (*f.* mahanịyā) *pl.* mahạnā hinderer, forbidder.
   B. (mahanī) *m.* (*pl.* mạhạnai) (1) obstacle. (2) veto.

mahaŋkạlcī *m.* (*f.* mahaŋkalcịyā) *pl.* mahạŋkạltā sensible P.

mahạrbī *m.* (*f.* maharbịyā) *pl.* mahạrbā (1) P. who shoots. (2) kạrē dạ zōmō dạ ~ Orion. (3) mahạrbī (= mahạrbin darē) yā hạrbē shị (*a*) he has disease of unknown origin (= gạjērē 2 *q.v.*). (*b*) = dājị 3. (4) mahạrbiŋkạ yanạ̄ samạ (*a*) what a well-developed woman ! (*b*) *Vd.* ɓaunā 1.

mahạrdạcī = mahạddạcī.

mahạrẹ *x* idạŋ Kạnde ~ nē̄ Kande's eyes lack pigment.

mahạrī *m.* (*pl.* mahạrā) (1) raider. (2) *cf.* tạsạ mahạrā.

mạharramạ (*Ar.* muhammara " reddened ") *f.* any thin, patterned, cotton material, reddish with white stripes (*sometimes used in barter*, cẹfạnē 2, etc.) = masarcī 2.

mahạssạdī *m.* (*f.* mahassadīyā) *pl.* mahạssạdā *Ar.* (1) jealous. (2) mahạssạdā sunạ zạtam farị, Allạ yā sakō rūwā he has prospered to the discomfiture of his enemies. (3) (*a*) mahạssạdā kụ jē kụ mutụ you are thoroughly disgraced, so much for you ! (*b*) mahạssạdā sụ jē sụ mutụ may our ill-wishers " come to a sticky end " !

mahạucī *m.* (*pl.* mahạutā) (1) butcher i.e. meat-seller (= mạsau 1 = bạrinjẹ 2 = baŋgārọ), *cf.* mahautā ; fāwạ ; mālạmī 1*h.* (2) kụrkununsạ ∼ nẹ he has guinea-worm with bleeding. (3) syphilis with bleeding. (4) mahaucīyā *f.* wife or daughter of 1.

*mahạlūkị *m.* (*pl.* mahạlụkai) *Ar. m.* any of God's creatures.

mahauhạwī = mahaihạyī.

mahaukạcī *m.* (*f.* mahaukacīyā) *pl.* mahaukạtā (1) (*a*) (i) mad P. (*Vd.* wạlī 4*b*). P. acting senselessly. (ii) mụ jē zūwạ, ∼ yā hau kūrā " you're all at sea ". (iii) " nī nā sanị " sautụm mahaukacīyā what an unintelligible way to deliver a message ! (iv) shịkiŋkịmī yā fi ∼ wụyar māgạnī what a loony ! (v) ∼ bā yạ warkẹwā sǎi raŋgwamẹ character does not change. (vi) kạŋkụ akẹ jị, ∼ yā fādạ rịjịyā what have I to do with what you're saying ? (vii) kạram mahaukacīyā *Vd.* kạrē 28. (viii) ạ rinạ, an sạci zanạm mahaukacīyā stolen goods must finally be disgorged. (ix) banzā girmam ∼, ƙaramī mai wạyō yā fi shị better a sensible boy than a foolish adult. (x) tsọram ∼ *Vd.* fāsạ 1*e*. (*b*) Jirgiŋ ƙasā ∼ dạgạ Tūrai *epithet of* train (*Vd.* jirgī). (2) *x* ạbincī mai mahaukạcin dādī most delicious food. yanạ dạ mahaukạciŋ gudụ he (P., horse, etc.) runs like the wind.

mahaurā *f.* (*pl.* mahạurai) place where one climbs over (*cf.* magaŋgarā 2*a*).

mahauta A. (mahautā) *Vd.* mahạucī.
    B. (mahautā) *f.* (*pl.* mạhautai) (1) abattoir. (2) place in market where meat is sold (*cf.* mahạucī).

mahawā *f.* (*pl.* mạhạwai) incline, place where one climbs up.

mạhāwarạ *Ar. f.* disputation.

mahawāyī *m.* (*pl.* mạhạwạyai) place or P. inspiring fear and caution.

mahaya A. (mahayā) *Vd.* mahạyī.
    B. (mahayā) *f.* = mahayī.

mahayi A. (mahạyī) *m.* (*pl.* mahạyā) (1) good rider. (2) mahạyin dōkị = mahạyī dōkị P. mounted on horse. (3) dōkị yā sam mahạyinsạ everyone knows his own business best.
    B. (mahayī) *m.* (*pl.* mạhạyai) (1) ford (= mashigī). (2) = mahaurā.

mahẹ = mafẹ.

mạhibbạ = mụhibbạ.

mahịhịcī *Kt.* = mafịfịcī.

mahịmmạncī *m.* (*f.* mahimmancīyā) *pl.* mahịmmạntā energetic.

mahọ *m.* (1) an yi masạ ∼ it (worn part of clothing) has had a patch superimposed (= baŋkị = dafkị), *cf.* fitọ 2*b*, tirị 2. (2) an yi wạ daŋgā ∼ fence has been reinforced (*as in* bumạ 2*b*).

mahōmạcī *m.* (*f.* mahōmacīyā) *pl.* mahọmạtā boastful, swanker.

mahọrī *m.* (*f.* mahōrīyā) *pl.* mahọrā educator, trainer.

mahūcī *m.* (*pl.* mạhụtai) fan (*d.f.* fītạ) = mafīfīcī, *Vd.* marạu.

mahūjī *m.* (*pl.* mạhụdai) gimlet, awl, etc.

mahụkụncī *m.* (*f.* mahukuncīyā) *pl.* mahụkụntā administrator.

mahukuntā *f.* (*pl.* mạhụkụntai) (1) law-court. (2) magạnạn nạm bā ta dạ ∼ no legal question is involved in this matter.

mahụƙurcī *m.* (*f.* mahuƙurcīyā) *pl.* mahụƙurtā (1) patient, longsuffering P. (2) ∼ mawạdạcī patience is a virtue.

mahūrī *m.* (*pl.* mạhụrai) (1) sharp, curved, two-handled tool for cleaning out pulp (tōtụwā) from gourds. (2) mai mahūriŋ ƙarẹ *epithet of* hunger (yuŋwạ).

mạhụtai *Vd.* mahūcī.

mai A. (maị) (1) he, she who owns (Gram. 51) *pl.* mạsū *x* (*a*) ∼ dōkị (i) groom. (ii) owner of horse. (iii) *Vd.* dōkị 1*a*.iii. (*b*) ∼ gạrī Chief of town. (*c*) ∼ tạfīyạ traveller. (2) (*forms adjective when prefixed to noun*)

x (*a*) ∼ kyąu good. ∼ girmā big.
∼ hankąlī sensible. (*b*) nāma ∼ mǎi
rich meat (= maiƙọ 2 = māyā =
rǎi 3*b*), *Vd.* mǎi 1*a*.iii. (3) ∼ gidā *Vd.*
gidā 1*l*. (4) *Vd. other compounds of*
mąi *under second word.*
　　B. (mai) *Kt.* to him (= masą *q.v.*).
　　C. (mǎi) (1) (*a*) (i) oil, fat, grease.
(ii) nāmą mąi ∼ rich meat (= maiƙọ 2
= māyā = rǎi 3*b*). (iii) rība mąi ∼
rich profit (*cf.* maiƙọ). (*b*) nā tōyą ∼
nā mąncē dą ąlbasą the details were
attended to but the important part
neglected.　　(*c*) yā shāfą masą ∼ ą
baką (= ą bąkī) he flattered him. (*d*)
tūwō bā yą ƙim ∼ *Vd.* dādī 1*b*. (*e*) (i)
shą ∼ *Vd.* dąngī. (ii) ą shā mąntą
Vd. wąyō 1*d*. (*f*) bąllē yą sąmi ∼ *Vd.*
tūyą 2.　(*g*) ji ∼ *Vd.* yāmųtsā.　(*h*)
kąkam ∼ *Vd.* ayū.　(*j*) tandum ∼
Vd. matsīyącī 2.　　(*k*) auram ∼ dą
wutā *Vd.* ąlƙaƙai. (*l*) rūwam ∼ *Vd.*
rūwā B. 14. (*m*) mąn wuri *Vd.* ɓakyąlcē.
(*n*) *Vd.* girin-girin.　　(2) ∼ baƙī =
baƙim mǎi *q.v.* (3) (*a*) kōwā ya cī dą ∼
kuɗinsą (i) P. can do as he likes with
own property. (ii) how deservedly his
efforts have been rewarded.　(*b*) *Vd.*
ą cī dą ∼. (4) bąkīna yā yi ∼ my mouth
watered. (5) (*a*) petrol. (*b*) yā ƙārą ∼
(i) he (driver) increased speed of car.
(ii) he (pedestrian, train, ship) speeded
up its pace. (*c*) yā ƙōnę mini ∼ he
delayed me, cf. ƙōnę 1*c*. kā ƙōnę
mini ∼ ą banzā you’ve wasted my
time (= zarąfī 1*b*). (6) (*a*) butter *x*
mīyą dą ∼ dą nāmą broth, butter and
meat.　(*b*) mąn shānū butter.　(7)
pliability of leather (*Vd.* ƙaryā 1*h*,
fātą 1*a*.ii). (8) *Vd.* mąn-*compounds.*
(9) *Vd.* ∼ birim. (10) bą ∼ *Vd.* rōmō 1*c*.
mai’ą *f.* the spice stacte.
mǎi birim *m.* type of coloured bead (=
masąrā 3 = wayą 3).
mai da A. (mai dą) *Vb.* 4A (*p.o. also*
maishē) (1) (*a*) put T. back in its place
(*cf.* mayą, mąyā). (*b*) bą sų ∼ mū ba
they were unable to repulse us.　(2)
(*a*) restored T. to P. *x* (i) yā mayar
mini dą shī he gave it back to me. (ii)
yā ∼ amsą he replied.　(iii) yā ∼
mąganą tasą he set out his side of the

case (*Vd.* dą’ąwā).　(iv) bindigōginsų
suną ∼ jąwābi their guns are firing
back.　(v) bā yą mąyūwā it is not
restorable.　(*b*) ∼ kātąn *Vd.* shąnyē
1*b*.　(*c*) *Vd.* ąmfąnannē.　(*d*) ∼ rūwā
rījīyā bą ɓąnnā ba nę there’s no harm
in handing unsold goods back to the
supplier. (*e*) yā ∼ bidą he repaid the
loan.　(*f*) yā ∼ jikī he’s regained his
former health.　　(*g*) ∼ māshi ran
gąbā tsǭrō nę don’t be in too much of a
hurry to retaliate, your time will come !
(*h*) *Kt.* yā ∼ arō he (relation) has
brought back to her father the bride
whom the former took to his house for
two days, for application of henna.
(*j*) mąi dą yanką = *Kt.* mąi dą mīyanką
here, looker-on, take a morsel of this
tasty thing I’m eating (= lādąn ganin
idọ), *cf.* yau. (*k*) ∼ ƙwaryā bikī *Vd.*
ƙwaryā 1*k*. (3) (*a*) changed into, converted into *x* (i) am ∼ ąkwąti ąbin
zamā the box has been made to serve as
a seat. (ii) mąi dą ąbōkī barą *Vd.* barą
A.2 1*e*. (iii) mąi dą ąbin wani nāką *Vd.*
wąjiri. (iv) ∼ ągąnā cīwọ *Vd.* ągąnā 2. (*b*)
converted P. *x* sum ∼ arnā gą Lislāmą
they converted the pagans to Islam.
(4) applied *x* ką ∼ himmą do your
best !　yā ∼ hankąlī (= yā ∼ kąnsą)
gą ƙarątū he applied himself seriously
to study.　yā ∼ wąiwąyē he referred
again to the matter. (5) transferred
x (*a*) ịnā zā ką ∼ sirdịnką where are
you going to transfer your saddle ?
ząi ∼ sōjąn Afirką sų kōmą gidā he’ll
transfer the soldiers serving in Africa,
to the home-establishment.　suną
sọ̄ sų ∼ dūnīyą tą kōmą cikim baƙin
duhų they want to put the world back
into the dark ages.　am maishē shi
Kanọ he has been transferred to Kano.
(*b*) yā ∕ kąnsą ƙasą he turned it upside
down.　　(*c*) mum ∼ jūyi, mųn kǭrē
sų we turned the tables on them by
routing them.　(*d*) am mayar dą shī
fādą he’s been made a member of the
cabinet.　(*e*) zā ą sąmi wadąndą zā
ą mayar mąimakwansų we shall find
others to replace them.　(*f*) bą wąndą
ya kąmātą ą mayar ą matsayinsą sǎi
Audų nobody but Audu is worthy to

take his place. (6) put x inā akạ ∼ shī where has it been put ? (= ajīyē 1a) (for conjunction of senses 1 and 6 in same verb, Vd. kōmạ). (7) considered as being x nā maishē shị wāwā I considered him a fool. yā maishē nị kạmar ụbansạ he treated me as his father. (8) vomited out x yā ∼ ạbincinsạ he vomited up his food (= maishē = maisō = amai).
  B. (maidạ) Sk. Vb. 1A = mai dạ.
  C. (Maidạ) = Maidā name for posthumous child (= ạbăicī 2).

maidō Vb. 1E Sk. (d.f. maidạ) transferred hither x sum ∼ jirāgyansụ nạŋ they have transferred their ships here.

Maidụgurī f. the town of Maiduguri.

maikad dạ Vb. 4 Nor. = mai dạ.

maikị m. (f. maikīyā) pl. maikōkī = maikīyōyī. (1) = mīkị. (2) Kt. bặkim ∼ type of broad arrow. (3) Kt. maikīyā kạ kitsạ tuft left on centre of head.

maikọ m. (1) (a) greasiness, oiliness x rīgan nạŋ tanặ dạ ∼ this gown has an oily stain (= masĸī). (2) richness of meat, etc., x (a) nāmạ maị ∼ rich meat (= mặi 1a.ii). (b) aikị maị ∼ "a fat job" (cf. bụsasshē). (c) Vd. shặ ∼ ; sāri 2. (d) sặ bặkī ∼ Vd. farī 2d. (e) ūwar ∼ Vd. zịnā 2. (3) maiĸwạn jịkī sweatiness of face, neck, etc. (= ạnnākīyā q.v.). (4) Kt. = ᵇīkọ 7.

mạil = mịl.

maimā f. x gōrọ yā yi ∼ the kola-nuts have internal blemish.

mai-mai m. (d.f. maimạitā). (1) (a) second weeding of farm. (2) second hoeing (with fartanyạ), Vd. nōmā, firị, bạŋgạjē. (b) Vd. firị 2, 3. (3) inadvertently making same entry twice in the register.

maimạitā Vb. 1C (1) repeated (doing, saying, etc.) = sākẹ 1h = Kt. mayạ 1b, cf. maimạicē. (2) Vd. Alặ 6.

maimạkī = maimako.

maimakō m. (1) (a) substitute x yā bā nị maimakwạŋ wannạŋ he gave me a substitute for this. (b) representative, locum tenens x wặ kẹ̆ maimakwạŋ Audụ who is Audu's deputy ? kadạ kạ sặ wani maimakwạŋkạ cikiŋ wannạŋ aikị do not delegate this work to anyone else ! zā ạ sặmi wad̃andạ zā ạ mayar

maimakwansụ we shall find others to replace them (1 = madạdī = mamạyī = matsayī 1a.ii = wạkīlị = mụkaddạshī = mụsāyā 3c = canjị), cf. mạyā, bạgayẹ. (2) maimakwan prep. (a) instead of. (b) in exchange for x muŋ ĸullạ sharạdī dạ sū ạ kạn zā mụ bā sụ matsayin jirặgē, maimakwansạ kumā sụ bā mụ jirặgyan yāĸi we have made a treaty with them to cede them a harbour in exchange for warships which they will give us. (3) maimakwan conj. (followed by subjunctive) instead of the fact that x maimakwan sụ rạgu, ĸārūwā sukạ yi instead of decreasing they increased. maimakwaŋ kụ aikạ dạ hatsī kwặ yạrdā kụ sayạr ? will you agree to sell corn instead of sending it ?

maimakwan sụ bā shị hanyạ, sukạ (= săi sukạ) tirjẹ far from acceding to his request, they resisted doggedly. (4) Maimakō name for posthumous child (= Ạbăicī).

Maimūnạ f. woman's name.

mạ'iŋ = kạlmạ'iŋ.

Mainạ = Mạinạ East Hausa. (1) name for son of Chief. (2) cf. mặtar ∼, Mairạŋ.

mạinadạrī m. type of pad for pack-animal.

mạiramụ m. (1) (a) young scorpion. (b) small scorpion. (2) Mạiramụ (Ar. Maryamu) Mary, Miriam (by a play on senses 1 and 2, any woman called Mạiramụ, Mạryamụ, or Mạirō has title 'yar kụnāmạ).

Mairạŋ East Hausa (1) name for daughter of Chief (cf. Mainạ). (2) Vd. shūnī 5.

mạirō = mạiramụ.

maisad dạ Vb. 4 Nor. = mai dạ.

maishē Vd. mai dạ.

mạishē m. vomiting (= amai).

maisō m. vomiting (= mạishē).

mạitā f. (1) witchcraft. (2) jam bặkī bā ∼ there's too little of it to be of any use.

maiwā = mạiwā (1) f. (a) the millet Pennisetum spicatum (= daụrō). (b) the colour of such millet. (c) a good type of sword. (d) the best type of the seeds ĸwạlā 2. (e) damịm ∼ Vd. zōᵇīyā 2. (2) m. used in maiwan tsōfō old man behaving childishly.

majặ m., f. (sg., pl.) (this word must be followed by another noun, cf. majặyī) puller, *used in* (1) ∼ cikį any snake (macįjī). (2) ∼ hanyạ guide.

mājāgulā = *Kt.* mạjāgulạ *f.* making a muddle of a T.

*mạjạhūlịlhālį *Ar. m.* cantankerous P.

majai = majāyī.

mạjajjawā *f.* (1) sling for throwing missile. (2) anạ̄ ∼ dạ shī it gives much trouble.

mạjạƙwar *f.* scrotal hernia (= gwaiwā 1*b*.ii *q.v.*), *cf.* ƙullį 4.

mạjạlisạ *f.* (*pl.* mạjạlịsai). (1) law court. (2) council. (3) council-hall. (4) dattījạm ∼ the president of the council. (5) Sarākunạnsạ na ∼ his cabinet-ministers.

mạjạmfạrī *m.* = rại dɔ̣rē.

mạjāmi'ạ *f.* = masallacī 1*b*.

*mạjạnūnį *m.* (*f.* mạjạnūnįyā) *pl.* mạjạ-nụ̄nai mad.

mạjau *m.* type of eczema attacking fore-arm and lower leg.

mạjaujawā = mạjajjawā.

majayi A. (majāyī) *m.* (*pl.* mạjạ̄yai). (1) girth-strap. (2) extra cloth securing gōyō-child on back of woman carrying it.
    B. (majāyī) *m.* (*f.* majāyįyā) *pl.* mạjạ̄yā puller (*this word is employed either alone or before a noun, or stands in genitive, cf.* majạ̄).

mạjāzạ = mụjāzạ.

maje A. (mājẹ) *m.* (1) (*a*) Copaiba balsam tree (*Pardaniellia Oliveri*) = kadaurā. (*b*) ƙāram ∼ *m.* type of West African copal (ƙārō) used as medicine and scent (*cf.* gạlhaŋgạ). (2) Mājẹ, rįƙẹ ganyaŋkạ *epithet of any miser* (*as this tree does not shed its leaves*).
    B. (majẹ̄) *m., f.* (*sg., pl.*) (*this word must be followed by a noun, cf.* mafį). (1) the P. who went (jē) to *x* (*a*) (*i*) ∼ gạba yā jē, na bāya sǎi lạ̄bārį east is east and west is west. (ii) majẹ̄ gạba *Vd.* safẹ 1. (*b*) ∼ Sakkwatō yā kāsạ ạ Wạtạrī he was put to shame. (2) (Mod. Gram. 103*e*) *x* ∼ hajį the P. who died on the pilgrimage to Mecca. ∼ Baucī the P. who died on the way to Bauchi.

majẹ̄fī *m.* (*f.* majẹ̄fįyā) *pl.* majẹ̄fā. (1) thrower. (2) ∼ bɔ̣m *m.* (*pl.* majẹ̄fā bɔ̣m) bomber-aeroplane.

majema A. (majẹmā) *Vd.* majẹmī.
    B. (majẹmā) *f.* (*pl.* mạjẹmai) tannery.

majemi A. (majẹmī) *m.* (*f.* majẹmįyā pl.* majẹmā. (1) tanner. (2) in d gạbạ̄rūwā ạbar kirkį cē, bạ ạ̄ bạ̄ ma jẹmā ita bạ there's more than meet the eye. (3) *Vd.* gạbạ̄rūwā 1*e*.
    B. (majẹmī) *m.* (*pl.* mạjẹmai scraping-tool used by tanners.

maji A. (mạ̄jī) *Sk. m.* = mạ̄zō.
    B. (majį) *m., f.* (*sg., pl.*) (*this wor must be followed by noun, cf.* majįyī hearer, feeler, *used in* (1) ∼ ƙari strong P. or animal. (2) *Sk.* ∼ kir slave-lad (= magụdạncī *q.v.*). (3 Allạ̄ ∼ ƙam bāwạ Merciful God ! (*Va* jī 6*b*, *c*). (4) (*a*) ∼ dādī = gạbā 9*a*. (*b Sk.* one of the sạrautạ. (5) *Vd.* garkɔ̣ 4

Mạ̄jiɓārį *used in* fushim ∼ *m.* cutting o one's nose to spite one's face (*Va* fushī 4).

majiɓincī *m.* (*f.* majiɓincįyā) *pl.* majį ɓintā. (1) related to. (2) connecte with *x* majiɓinciŋ aikiŋ hukumcį on engaged in administrative or legal work (3) *cf.* makụsạcī.

majicī *m.* (*pl.* mạjįtai) *Kt.* conical thatch top for dye-pit (= karōfī 2 = bākīrẹ).

majīdī *m.* (*pl.* mạjị̄ɗai) *Sk.* lodgin (= masaukī).

majigi A. (mạ̄jigī) *m.* camwood (produce red dye).
    B. (mājịgį) (*Eng.* magic) *m.* (1) cinem (*cf.* Sụlaimnụ). (2) ∼ lantị magic lanter

mạ̄jinā *f.* (1) (*a*) phlegm. (*b*) nose-mucu (*cf.* tạsōnō). (2) yā fācẹ ∼ he blew hi nose. (3) *Vd.* ma'aji 3.

majinācīyā *f.* (*pl.* mạjinạ̄tai). (1) (*a vein. (*b*) artery. (2) type of red juiced weed (= jinạ-jinạ).

majiŋginī *m.* (*pl.* mạjiŋgị̣nai) pillo (= matāshiŋ kạ̄i).

majinyạcī = majįyyạcī.

mạ̄jira *Vd.* ạlmājirī 1.

majirạ̄cī *m.* (*f.* majirācįyā) *pl.* majirạ̄tā (1) watchman. (2) bird-scarer.

majiya A. (majįyā) *Vd.* majįyī.
    B. (majįyā) *f.* (1) yā jī shi ạ ∼ h heard it from a reliable source. (2 an dɔ̣kē shį har yā jī ạ ∼ he wa severely thrashed.

majįyī *m.* (*f.* majįyįyā) *pl.* majįyā. (1 hearer, feeler (*this word may be use either alone or followed by a noun or in genitive, cf.* majī). (2) saurąyī majīyī ƙarfī = saurąyī majīyiŋ ƙarfī an able-bodied young fellow.

majīyyącī *m.* (*f.* majīyyacīyā) *pl.* majīyyątā. (1) sick-nurse. (2) hospital-patient.

majiyyata A. (majīyyątā) *Vd.* majīyyącī. B. (majīyyatā) *f.* (*pl.* majīyyątai) hospital.

maka A. (maką) (1) to you (Gram. 50). (2) maką Māląm *Vd.* māląmī 1*c*.viii. (2) Maką = Makką.
B. (mąkā) *Vb.* 2 *Kt.* (1) beat (= dǫkā) *x* yā mąkē ni dą sąndā he beat me with a stick. (2) hit down (fruit or leaves from tree).
C. (māką) *Vb.* 1A *Kt.* (1) yā ∼ minī sąndā he beat me with a stick (= mąkā). (2) added much liquid *x* (*a*) tā ∼ rūwā cikin nōnǫ she added much water to the milk. (*b*) jīyą am ∼ rūwā it rained heavily yesterday.
D. (mākā) *Sk. f.* bean-leaves (*these form remedy for headache*).

maƙa A. (maƙą) *Vb.* 1A. (1) (*a*) fixed T. into *x* yā ∼ madūbī ą idąnsą he put on spectacles, he fixed monocle in his eye. yā ∼ ąlkaląmī ą ƙunnansą he stuck the pen behind his ear. (*b*) yā ∼ mąƙā he (archer) put on protective-ring. (*c*) nā ∼ masą dūbā = nā ∼ masą idǫ I stared at him. (2) = maƙąlā. (3) (*plus dative*) put T. under another's arm or chin *x* nā ∼ masą sąndā I put a stick under his arm.
B. (mąƙā) *f.* (1) thumb-ring worn by archers. (2) kuturuŋ yā yi ∼ (*a*) he has got on in the world. (*b*) he has suddenly become expert. (3) *cf.* gāwā 3.

makąbcē *Sk.* = makąncē.
makąbcī *m.* (*pl.* mąkąbtai) = magirbī.
mąkąbtą *Sk.* = mąkantą.
mąkąbūli *m.* (*Ar.* thing received) *x* (1) yanā dą ∼ he has a P. who looks after him (= wąƙīli 2). (2) an yi matą ∼ she has been found a husband. (3) an yi masą ∼ a good place has been found for it.
makądǟicī *m.* (*f.* makadǟiciyā) *pl.* makądǟitā peerless *x* makądǟicin ząmāninsą

the outstanding man of his day. **Allą** makądǟicin Sarkī the One God.

mąkaddąs = mąƙaddąs = muƙaddąs *q.v.*

makadi A. (makądī) *m.* (*pl.* makądǟ). (1) (*a*) drummer. (*b*) Sarkim makądǟ *Vd.* marǫƙī. (*c*) ∼ kąm bi *Vd.* fagē 1*d*.iii. (*d*) makądiŋ kwądǫ *Vd.* tąlibambam. (*e*) shigę ∼ dą rawā *Vd.* shigę 2*b*.ii. (2) *Vd.* kanjau 2, gąl-gal.
B. (makadī) *m.* (*pl.* mąkądai). (1) drum-stick (*cf.* gulą, furyā). (2) yā kąmātą kōwā yą sabę makadinsą nobody should molest his fellow-man. (3) makadin tambąrī stump of būlālą-whip.
C. (mākādī) = mąkādī (1) *m. and adv.* abundantly. (2) *adj.* large. (3) (*a*) how large ! (*b*) what abundance !

*mąkądīru *Ar. m.* Fate *x* mąkądīruŋ Allą, bą shi dą māgąnī it is no good carping at Fate.

mąƙąfąrī *Sk. m.* (1) = mahǫ. (2) mending a calabash (= gyartai 2).

makafcī *Sk.* = makabcī.

mąkāfǫ *m.* (*f.* makaunīyā = *Kt.* makamnīyā) *pl.* mąkąfī (*Ar.* makfūf). (1) (*a*) blind. (*b*) ịndą aką ƙąrɓi dąrīyar ∼ naŋ ka kąm (*or* naŋ ya kam) fasą ƙwaryā a favourite can do no wrong. (*c*) ∼ bābu ganiŋ gąrī (i) seeking T. where it cannot possibly be. (ii) type of children's game. (iii) *Vd.* ganiŋ gąrī. (*d*) na ząune ∼ an untravelled P. is ignorant of the world (*cf.* kīfī 2). (*e*) ąn cę dą ∼ "gą idǫ !", ya cę "dą dǫyī " it's sour grapes ! (*Vd.* rashị 1*l*). (*f*) bąƙō ∼ nē, kō yanā dą idǫ even a talented novice is still a novice. (*g*) ∼ bai saŋ anā ganinsą ba sǎi an dāfą kansą it's no good playing the ostrich. (*h*) mǫtsa, mu jī ką, ∼ yā sō bą ɗansą kāshī let's hear what *you* have got to say about it ! (*j*) an ɗaurę su dą hājąr Sarkim mąkāfī they're bound with ropes. (*k*) iŋ kā ji ∼ yā cę ą yi wąsam bu'ge-bugē", yā kāmą sąndā nę there's more than meets the eye ! (= duffą 2). (*l*) dūba minī hanyą, ∼ yā sō tsēgumī take care you don't speak evil of a P. when he can hear you ! (*cf.* kaŋkị 2*b*). (*m*) fushī yanā haifūwar ∼ *Vd.* fushī

1a.ii. (n) kuturū dārą ∼ Vd. dārīyā 3. (o) ɗinyar ∼ Vd. ɗinyā 4. (p) rąbą ∼ dą gōrą Vd. rąbą mąkāfǫ. (q) ∼ dą wąiwayą Vd. aikį 1a.iii. (r) ban tą̄fim ∼ Vd. tą̄fī 1e.ii. (s) cācar ∼ Vd. cabkącaɓę. (t) cįnikim ∼ ; hannum ∼ Vd. hannun 5 ; hannū 1l.ii. (u) ịnā rūwam ∼ dą kunyą what the eye does not see, the heart does not grieve for. (v) ∼ gōmą Vd. gąrārą 2b.ii. (w) săi yā ga ∼ Vd. gąrārą 2b.iii. (x) gąyyar ∼ Vd. gąyyā 1c. (2) (a) (i) makauniyā blind woman. (ii) ignorant woman (= bągidājịyā). (iii) ƙwam makauniyā Vd. cịɳ ƙwam makauniyā. (b) dąsham makauniyā Vd. dąshē 6. (c) ɗūrar ɗam makauniyā Vd. ɗūrā 2c. (d) makauniyar hāją buying T. of unknown value (forbidden by Muslim law). (3) Vd. bąrim makauniyā. (4) mąkāfąɳ ƙudā type of biting fly. (5) ɗam mąkāfąm birnī m. blind beggar singing slanderous songs and accompanied by his refrain-assistant (mąi amshị) who sings the words Allą̄ nārị gōdę. (6) hawam mąkāfin dawākī Kt. m. quarrelling. (7) Vd. ją̄ ∼. (8) shịgar ∼ kō̜gī Vd. ƙundųmbālā.

mąkaftą Sk. = mąkantą.

mąkagaucīyā Sk. f. cramp (= ƙafąr kązā 3).

mąkāhǫ = mąkāfǫ.

mąƙai m. yā gąmu dą ∼ = mąƙai yakę yị he has severe constipation necessitating removal of impacted fæces with matsēfatā.

mąƙaifų m. the disease būsau q.v.

makaka A. (makaka) noun and adj. big and broad x tą̄barmā cę̄ ∼ = tą̄barmā cę̄ ∼ dą ita it is big, broad mat. zanę ∼ = zanę ∼ dą shī a big, broad cloth.
   B. (mąkąką) = sąmąmą.
   C. (maką̄kā) Vb. 1C. (1) yā maką̄ką kăi cikin ɗākị he entered the house unceremoniously. (2) = māką 2. (3) yā ∼musų he entered their house unceremoniously. (4) rūwā yā makākō cikin ɗākịmmų much water penetrated into our house.

mąƙąƙī m. (1) astringent feeling in throat after swallowing astringent T. (2) feeling offended x n ną̄ jịm mąƙąƙiɳ

ąbịn dą ta yi minị I'm offended at what she did to me. (3) Vd. cąrī.

mąƙąlā Vb. 1C (1) caused to become lodged in tree, etc., x yā ∼minị sąndāna he caused my stick to become lodged in the tree. (2) yā mąƙąlą ƙafą̄fū ą jąkī he (rider) hooked his feet together under the donkey. (3) foisted T. on P. x tā ∼ minị ɗantą she foisted her child on me. (4) = mąƙą 1a. (5) mąƙalō = mąƙatō.

makalą̄mā (Ar. mukālama conversation). (1) x an yi masą ∼ fault has been found with him (= kūshē). (2) Vd. dāma 1e.

mąƙąlē (1) Vb. 3A. (a) became lodged in (x stick in tree, bucket in well, boat in rushes, etc.). (ii) Vd. sąndā 1h. (b) yā ∼ he (P. sent on errand) dallied. (c) yā ∼ wurinsą it (debt owing) is long outstanding. (d) it (arm, leg) became (i) temporarily stiff. (ii) permanently paralysed (all 1 = ƙagę). (e) (with dative) clung to x ɗantą yā ∼ matą her baby-boy clung to her. (f) Vd. mąƙę. (2) Vb. 1C. (a) = mąƙąlā 1, 2, 3. (b) yā ∼ jąkī dą ƙafą = mąƙąlā 2.

mąƙalƙąlā Vb. 1D intens. from mąƙąlā (= mammąƙąlā).

makąlkąlī m. (pl. mąkąlkąlā) (1) (a) barber. (b) mąkąlkąlim makąlkąlā what a fine barber ! (2) lad who scrapes out cooking-pots.

makallacīyā f. the corn-stalk spindle consisting of sillē q.v.

mąkąlūtą f. = mąkąlūtų m. = mąƙatą 1 q.v.

makama A. (Maką̄mā) m. (1) one of the sąrautą (epithet is Tōgai, rųmfar Sarkī = Gābị). (2) Vd. maką̄mī ; Kącallą 2.
   B. (makāmā) f. (pl. mąkąmai). (1) place where one catches hold .of T. (x handle). (2) ząncan nąm bą̄ shi dą ∼ this affair is nebulous. (3) Rūwā, bą̄ ká ∼ what fecklessness ! (4) (a) an sąmi ∼ tasą his weak point has been discovered. (b) kųɳkurū shī ya sam makāmar mą̄tā tasą let him gang his own gley ! (5) ʰą ni dą ∼ I've no distrainable property.

makąmąncī m. (f. makamancīyā) pl. makąmąntā similar x sū makąmąntā dą jūnā nē they are similar to one another. (2) *m.* replica *x* makamancinsa a replica of it.

makāmashī *m.* twigs, grass, etc., for starting a fire.

makamfacī *m.* (*pl.* makamfatai). (1) big ladle or calabash (maburmī) used as dipper (= madāmī 2). (2) *for epithet, Vd.* fankō 4*b*.

makami A. (makāmī) *m.* (*f.* makāmīyā) *pl.* makāmā P. who seizes.
B. (makāmī) *m.* (*pl.* makāmai). (1) (*a*) any weapon (= makashī). (*b*) sum fārā wāsā makāmai a kan Jāmus they (the army) have begun making their preparations to attack the Germans. (2) yā yi minī ∼ he wounded me with a weapon. (3) makāmin karē *Vd.* mazāgī 2.

makāmī *m.* (1) *x* (*a*) rīgā mai ∼ finely-made gown. (*b*) yanā da ∼ (i) he is well-dressed. (ii) he is influential. (2) yā shigē makāminsa he exceeded his authority.

makamnīyā *Vd.* makāfo.

makancē *Vb.* 3A became blind.

Makanci *m.* (1) office and duties of a Makāmā. (2) the town-ward where a Makāmā lives.

makangarī *m.* (*f.* makangarīyā) *pl.* makangarā. (1) (*a*) rebel. (*b*) perverse. (2) Makangarā the tribe *so called* in Niger Province.

makani *m.* (1) raised, roofed-platform (*used as store, and as sleeping-place when mosquitoes are numerous*) = rūdu = *Kt.* tantāmī. (2) *Vd.* dākī 6*a*.

makānīkī *m.* (*pl.* makānīkai) *Eng.* mechanic.

makankancī *m.* (*f.* makankancīyā) *pl.* makankantā. (1) P. given to humiliating others. (2) quarrelsome P.

makankara A. (makankarā) *Vd.* makankarī.
B. (makankarā) *f.* (*pl.* makankarai). (1) place where scraping is done. (2) maganam nam bā shi da ∼ this affair is immutable.

makankari A. (makankarī) *m.* (*f.* makankarīyā) *pl.* makankarā P. who scrapes.
B. (makankarī) *m.* (*pl.* makankarai) mussel-shell used for storing

musk or scraping out food-vessels (= kumbā), *cf.* mawankī 3.
C. (makankarī) *m.* (*pl.* makankarai) tool for scraping or erasing.

makanta A. (makantā) *f.* (1) blindness. (2) makantarka abin kallō *Vd.* dindimī 3.
B. (makantā) *Vb.* 3B became blind.

makanwacī *m.* (*pl.* makanwatai) place where potash exists in the soil *x* anā kankarar kanwā a ∼ potash is being scraped out of the potash-deposit.

makanwacī *m.* (*f.* makanwacīyā) *pl.* makanwatā. (1) greedy P. (2) ∼ bā yā kafē *Vd.* kafē 2.

makara A. (makara) (1) *Vb.* 3B (*a*) delayed, dallied. (*b*) was late. (2) *f. x* yā yi ∼ (*a*) he delayed. (*b*) he came late (= latti).
B. (makarā) *f.* (1) (*a*) bier (= anna'ashī). (*b*) Makarā dau duka *epithet of* (i) bier. (ii) liberal P. (2) type of acakwa tray made of gwangwalā, kwāgirī-cane, and rope, for carrying kolas. (3) type of spider preying on tururrūwā ants and carrying them on its back (= rākumī 10 = jākin 11 = dōkin tururrūwā = tāgūwa 2).

makara A. (mākarā) *Vb.* 1C. (1) = mākara 1*a.i.* (2) filled brimful *x* dawākī sun mākara garī (*a*) horsemen have overcrowded the town. (*b*) cavalry have invaded or garrisoned the town in vast numbers. (3) kā mākara wurin you've monopolized all the space. (4) tā mākara dūtse a wuyanta she tied her necklace firmly round her neck (*cf.* mākarē).
B. (mākara). (1) *Vb.* 2. (*a*) (i) strangled (= mākura = shākē). (ii) rūwā nē ya sā shi ∼ *water* made him choke. (iii) *Vd.* mākarē. (*b*) bijimī yā fi ∼ sǎi yankā do not oppose your superiors !, don't fly in the face of Fate ! (2) (*a*) was brimful *x* garī yā ∼ da mutānē the town is (was) packed with people. yā ∼ da fushi he ·is (was) choking with rage. tukunyā tā ∼ the cooking-pot is brimful. (*b*) dāwā tā ∼ the guinea-corn is within a week of producing ears (*cf.* kunshi 5) (2 = shākē 2).

C. (makārā) f. (1) = makārī. (2) Vd. tantalaminya.

makarācī m. (pl. makarātā) = makaranci. makarai pl. the spirits mabiyā q.v. under mabiyī 4.

makarai Vd. makarū.

makarana = makarina.

makaranci m. (f. makaranciyā) pl. makarantā. (1) = mahaddacī. (2) well-read P.

makaranta A. (makarantā) Vd. makaranci.

B. (makarantā) f. (pl. makarantai = makarantū = makarantōcī = Sk. makarantinni). (1) (a) (i) school. (ii) its epithet is Makarantā gidan tsoran Allā. (b) yā yi ~ a Kano he attended school at Kano. a Kano sukē ~ they're at school at Kano. (c) makarantarsu daya da ta Jāmus their methods are the same as those of the Germans. (d) takardar ~ f. school-certificate. (2) Vd. Alkur'an 3. (3) (a) dam ~ m. (f. 'yar ~) pl. 'yam ~ school-pupil. (b) dam ~ m. (pl. 'yam ~) (i) writing-slate (= allō). (ii) the bird alhudahuda. (c) an yi masa daukan 'yam ~ (i) he (pupil) has been lifted up to receive a caning. (ii) two to four persons lifted it up, each holding one side of it (ii = rūwā A. 7b = Kt. cālī-cālī).

makararai-makararai adv. very slowly (re gait of hungry P. or idler).

makarau m., f. (sg., pl.) dilatory P.

makarau m. (1) quinsy, diphtheria, etc. (2) hæmorrhagic septicæmia. (3) (a) anthrax. (b) blackquarter disease (affecting neck of cattle).

makārayī m. (f. makārayiyā) pl. makāraya complainant at law, plaintiff.

makarbiyā f. (pl. makarbā). (1) midwife (= ungōzōma). (2) Vd. ūwā 1h.

makardādā f. (pl. makardādai). (1) place of refuge. (2) narrow corridor between places (= kardādē). (3) means of escape from dilemma.

makarē Vb. 3A = makara 1.

makare A. (mākarē) (1) Vb. 1C. (a) = mākarā 2, 3. (b) oppressed. (2) Vb. 3A was choked, strangled.

B. (makarē) m. (1) necklace sitting

firmly round the throat (cf. mākarā 4, sakē 2b).

makarfafā f. (pl. makarfafai) vital spot in the body x yā kāma shi a ~ he caught hold of him in a vital spot (= makasā).

makarfo m. (1) (a) the hard-wooded tree Afrormosia laxiflora. (b) bakim ~ the hard-wooded tree Burkea africana. (2) miser (= marōwacī). (3) the disease fūrau.

makari A. (makarī) m. (1) (a) (i) antidote x yā shā ~ he took an antidote (cf. katalā). (ii) Vd. karya 15b ; gincira. (b) epithet of warrior or Chief. (c) Bakī, bā sham ~ epithet of the cobra gamshēkā. (d) means of escape x makarinka gudu your only way of avoiding it is to run away. (2) (a) crease (= kari 2a q.v.). (b) a kam ~ ya zō it happened appositely ; he came at the psychological moment (= kari 3b). (c) usage of word x makarinta yā zamā kaza da kaza it (word) is applied thus and thus (= kari 4a q.v.).

B. (makarī) m. love-philtre x an yi masa ~ he has been bewitched (= sammu = māgancē).

C. (makārī) m. (pl. makārai) = sākō 4.

makari A. (makārī) m. (1) (d.f. kārē) boundary, limit, end. (b) Vd. bakwai 5. tantalaminya. (2) (d.f. kāra) increase x gidan nam bā shi da ~ this compound cannot be enlarged as no space is available.

B. (mākarī) act of strangling (Vd. mākara).

makārina = makārina f. (Ar. muqārana accompanying) meeting x mun yi ~ a kasūwā we met (by appointment or by chance) in the market.

makarkarī Kt. = makankarī.

makarkashiyā f. (1) = bandar kasa 1 (2) yā yi mini ~ he secretly gave me a hint of T. likely to affect me adversely, so as to give me a chance to make my plans.

makarrabai (Ar. favoured P.) (1 m. trusty counsellor. (2) pl. (a members of one's household (= iyāli) (b) Chief's retinue.

makaru A. (makaru) *m.* = **makạ̄rī.**
B. (mākāru) *Kt. m.* **furā** mixed with water instead of with milk (*Vd.* **gāhūhu**).
mak̟ạ̄rū *m.* (*pl.* **mak̟ạ̄rai**). (1) point of the jaws. (2) inside-top of cooking-pot.
mak̟aryạcī *m.* (*f.* **mak̟aryacīyā**) *pl.* **mak̟aryạtā** liar.
mak̟as *x* **yā cika** ⌣ it is brimful.
makạs *m., f.* (*pl.* **makạsā**) (*this word must be followed by a noun, cf.* **makạshī**). (1) P. who kills. (2) ⌣ **bīyū** (*a*) thick (**mai gwībī**) **farau-farau** (*as it appeases* (**kashẹ**) *both hunger and thirst*). (*b*) " killing two birds with one stone ". (3) *Vd.* **agazạrī.** (4) **makạs ạbōkin kīwo** *Vd.* **burtū 5.**
makasa A. (makạsā) *Vd.* **makạshī.**
B. (makasā) *f.* (*pl.* **makạsai**). (1) (*d.f.* **kashẹ**). (*a*) vital spot in the body (= **mak̟arfafā** *q.v.* = **marāyā 3c**). (*b*) place where P. perishes *x* **kīshị ya kạn kai mutụm** ⌣ jealousy brings a P. to where he perishes. (*c*) *Vd.* **tụnkū 1e**. (2) (*d.f.* **kasạ**) place where articles (*x* ground-nuts, pepper, etc.) are displayed in small heaps for sale.
makạsai *Vd.* **makashī ; makasā.**
Mak̟ạ̄sau *epithet of* (1) elephant, (2) burly P., (3) influential man. (4) *Vd.* **Kandalā.**
makashi A. (makashī) *m.* (*pl.* **mak̟ạsai**). (1) any weapon (= **makāmī**). (2) *Vd.* **gafīyạ 3.**
B. (makashī) *m.* (*f.* **makashīyā**) *pl.* **makạsā** (*this word may stand alone, or be followed by a noun, or stand in the genitive, cf.* **makạs**). (1) killer. (2) **zōmō bā yạ̄ fushī dạ makạshiņsạ sǎi dạ marātạyinsạ** being beaten or arrested is not so bad as being mocked. (3) **makạshim mazā, mazā kạ̄ kash shị** he who lives by the sword shall die by the sword. (4) *Vd.* **makạs, dọ̄rawạ.**
makassạrī *m.* (*f.* **makạssạrā**) *pl.* **makạssạrai** (*Ar.* **maksūr**) cripple (= **gurgụ**).
makạsūdị *m.* (*pl.* **makạsūdai**) *Ar.* (1) one's aim, T. desired (= **murādị**). (2) meaning (= **mạ'ạnā**).
makatạ = **mak̟atạ** *f.* (1) hooked stick (= **makạlūtạ**), *cf.* **mazuņgurī.** (2)

hannunsạ kạmam ⌣ **nē** he has a permanently bent arm.
makatau = **makɛatau** *m. and adv.* *x* **nā ạikē shị, ya yi** ⌣ = **nā ạikē shị, har yạnzu makatau-makatau bại zō ba** I sent him on an errand but he has dallied there.
makɛatō *Vb.* 1E pulled down (branch) with hooked stick (**makɛatạ**) = **makɛalā 5.**
***makạtūbị** *Ar. m.* anything committed to writing.
makạtūlụ *Kt. m., f.* = **agọ̄lạ̄.**
mākau *Vd.* **bāwạ.**
makạau *m.* (1) **gūgā yā yi** ⌣ the bucket has become jammed in the well (= **sạgau 2**). (2) **audụgā tā yi** ⌣ cotton-crop has been damaged by boll-worms.
makauniyā *Vd.* **mak̟āfọ 2.**
makɛauraci A. (makɛaurạcī) *f.* **makɛauracīyā** (*pl.* **makɛaurạtā**) migrant.
B. (makɛauracī) *m.* (*pl.* **mak̟aurạtai**). (1) **yā sākẹ** ⌣ he's moved his quarters. (2) (*a*) The Next World (= **lāhirạ**). (*b*) **ạ kai karā** ⌣ **tuņ gạbaņ kaurā bạ tạ zō ba** lay up a store of good deeds here as an earnest for the Next World ! (*said by* **marọ̄kā**). (*c*) **yā kai karā** ⌣ he is dead.
makawā *f.* (*d.f.* **kau dạ**) *used in* **bạ̄** ⌣ *x* **bạ̄** ⌣ **sǎi an yī** there's no way of avoiding doing it. **hakuncịn nạm bạ̄ shi dạ** ⌣ there's no way of evading this judgment. **ạzal bạ̄ ta dạ** ⌣ one cannot fight Fate. **bạ̄** ⌣ **mun yi gaddammạssạ** we denied it categorically.
makɛāwạcī *Sk.* = **makɛạņwạcī.**
makɛāwạlī *m.* (*f.* **mak̟āwalīyā**) *pl.* **makɛ̟ạ̄walai** stingy (= **marọ̄wạcī**).
mak̟āwuyạ = **mak̟āwīyạ** (1) multi-coloured cap or turban worn by wealthy man. (2) the cap **kurī 2** *q.v.*
makɛ̟āyạncī *m.* (*f.* **makɛ̟āyancīyā**) *pl.* **makɛ̟āyạntā.** (1) handsome. (2) haughty P.
Mākayẹ kā fi dākọ *epithet of any* Chief.
makɛazạncī *m.* (*f.* **makɛazancīyā**) *pl.* **makɛazạntā** dirty.
makɛe A. (makɛẹ) (1) *Vb.* 3A. (*a*) = **makɛalē 1.** (*b*) **bā yạ̄ makɛẹwā ạ bisạ** *Vd.* **ạbụtā 2.** (*c*) hid oneself (= **labẹ 1**). (*d*) **nōnạntạ yā** ⌣ her milk-flow ceased. (2) *Vb.* 1A (*a*) = **makɛalē 2b.** (*b*) tucked T. under

one's arm (= sāyẹ), *cf.* ꞗunsạ. (*c*) hid
T. (*d*) looked after T. carefully.
  B. (mạꞗe) (1) *x* yanā ∼ it (stick)
is stuck in the tree, etc. (*Vd.* maꞗạlē).
(2) ∼ nạṇ, rāꞗe cạṇ har sukạ zō they
came up stealthily.
  C. (mạꞗē) *m.* (*sg., pl.*) type of Asbin
stirrup.
mākẹ *Vb.* 1A *Kt.* thrashed.
maꞗēꞗashīyā = farā maꞗēꞗashīyā *f.*
pernicious anæmia (= bạyạmmā 1).
mākēkẹ *m.* (*f.* mākēkīyā) long and broad.
maꞗēꞗẹ (1) stingy. (2) child inseparable
from its mother (= madạmfạrī).
mạꞗē-maꞗē = dạmē-damē.
maꞗera A. (maꞗērā) *Vd.* maꞗērī.
  B. (maꞗērā) *f.* (*pl.* mạꞗērai =
mạꞗērū = maꞗērōrī). (1) smithy. (2)
maꞗērā *f.* = kạm maꞗērā *m.* = ūwar ∼
f. anvil. (3) kāzan nạṇ ∼ cē this hen is
dark grey. (4) bạ zại bīyā ba săi ạ ∼
he won't pay unless forced.
maꞗērī *m.* (*pl.* maꞗērā) (1) (*a*) smith. (*b*)
maꞗērim babbaꞗū iron-smith. maꞗērim
farfarū smith of white metals. (2)
clicking beetle. (3) Vieillot's West
African Barbet (*Lybius Vieilloti
rufescens*). (4) Guinea Little Woodpecker (*Dendropicos lafresnayi*). (5)
type of bat. (6) maꞗērim bākī professional beggar (*Vd.* ꞗīrạ 1*b* ; marōꞗī).
(7) maꞗērim budurcị yā hau tạ =
maꞗērim budurcị yā zō wurintạ her
(young girl's) unattractive appearance
has improved (= masạssạꞗī 2).
maꞗērīyā *f.* flat-headed tool of smiths.
mạꞗērọ = mạꞗērọ *m.* ringworm (= kụ-
rēcī *q.v.*).
mạꞗēsū *m.* = mạꞗēsūwā *f.* firefly
(= ꞗyạllū = wutar 'Yōlạ = wutar
baṇgō = wutar fạdamạ).
maꞗētạcī *m.* (*f.* maꞗētacīyā) *pl.* maꞗē-
tạtā (1) malicious (*epithet is* ∼ mijịṇ
gurgūwā, anā gudụ, kanā sai dạ jākā
you are so malicious that you sell the
she-ass on which your lame wife
rides).
maꞗetara A. (maꞗētạrā) *Vd.* maꞗētạrī.
  B. (maꞗētarā) *f.* = maꞗētarī *m.* (1)
(*a*) crossing-place. (*b*) fording-place *x*
maꞗētarinsụ the place where they cross
(road, river, etc.). (2) forked stick

(gwạfā) at entrance to cattle-garkẹ, to
restrict passage of animals.
maꞗetari A. (maꞗētarī) *m.* = maꞗētarā.
  B. (maꞗētạrī) *m.* (*f.* maꞗētarīyā) *pl.*
maꞗētạrā P. who crosses (road, river,
etc.).
makewayi A. (makēwayī) *m.* = makē-
wayā *f.* (*pl.* mạꞗēwạyai). (1) roundabout way (= gēwạyē). (2) place
fenced off as bathroom, lavatory, etc.
(= magēwayī = kurdị 2).
  B. *Vd.* magēwạyī.
maki A. (mākị) *Eng. m.* (1) direction-
mark on bales of goods (*cf.* kwālī). (2)
the fraud kụlūdụ *q.v.*
  B. (makị) *Vd.* mikị.
maꞗī *m., f.* (*sg., pl.*) (*this word must be
followed by a noun, cf.* maꞗīyī). (1) P.
who refuses, hates. (2) māgạnim ∼
waṇkā *Vd.* rūwā C.11. (3) (*a*) ∼ ganī,
yā kau dạ idānū in view of his present
strong position, what does he care for
his enemies ! (*b*) Maꞗī ganī *name for*
male slave. (4) ∼ sạkē persevering P.
(5) māgạnim ∼ gudụ, baṇ kāshī some
persons need to be goaded on. (6)
Vd. nasarạ.
makicīyā *Kt.* = makitsīyā.
mạkīdạ *f.* (*pl.* makīdōdī) *Ar. f.* (1) wiliness.
(2) *Kt.* indolence.
mạkīdị *m.* (*f.* mạkīdīyā) *pl.* mạkīdai
Ar. crafty (= mākirī).
māꞗil *adv.* abundantly *x* kōgī yā kāwō ∼
the river is in flood. mutānē ∼ many
people.
māꞗilā (1) *Vb.* 1C *x* yā ∼ masạ kạdaṇ he
gave him a trifle. (2) *f.* (*a*) stunted girl
(= māꞗilātūwā), *cf.* māꞗilātọ. (*b*) yā
bā shị ∼ fụraṇ kālā = 1 (*Vd.* fụrē 1*a.*ii,
kālā 7).
māꞗilātọ *m.* stunted boy (*cf.* māꞗilā 2*a*).
māꞗilātūwā = māꞗilā 2*a*.
māꞗilō *m.* = māꞗilātọ.
mākirci *m.* wiliness (*cf.* mākirī).
mākirī *m.* (*f.* mākirā) *pl.* mākirai *Ar.*
crafty.
māꞗis *Kt.* = māꞗil.
maꞗishirwạncī *m.* (*f.* maꞗishirwancīyā)
pl. maꞗishirwạntā thirsty.
makitsīyā *f.* (*pl.* makitsā). (1) coiffeuse
(*cf.* kitsọ). (2) 'yar ∼ *f.* work carefully
done. (3) *Vd.* ạsīrī 3.

maƙịwạcị = maƙyụ̄yạcị.

makịyāyā ƒ. (pl. mạkịyạ̄yai). (1) pasturage. (2) the large intestine = ūwar hanjị (cf. tubụrā).

makịyạyị m. (ƒ. makịyāyịyā) pl. makịyạ̄yā. (1) herdsman. (2) makịyạ̄yị̃ɳ gịwā a " yes-man " (= sassạlƙịyādị).

maƙịyị m. (ƒ. maƙịyịyā) pl. maƙịyā. (1) enemy (this word can be used alone or followed by a noun or stand in genitive, cf. maƙị). (2) iɳ kā ga maƙịyiɳkạ nặ rānā, kạ ƙārạ masạ wutā kick your enemy when he is down ! (3) maƙịyiɳkạ bā yặ yạbaɳkạ kō kā kāmạ dặmisạ kā bā shị a bitter enemy remains implacable. (4) shirị dạ ~ Vd. shirị 2b.

Makkạ ƒ. (1) Mecca (= Makạ). (2) hanyạr ~ ƒ. the Milky Way. (3) tặkạlmim ~ m. prickly-pear.

mạkkanạ Vb. 3B (1) (Ar. makịn) is (was) definite, certain. (2) (Ar. mumkin) is (was) possible.

mākǫ m. week x mākwạn nan na farkwan Dịsambạ the first week of December. mākwạn naɳ ukụ dạ sukạ wucẹ in the past three weeks.

maƙǫ m. (1) stinginess. (2) stingy. (3) what stinginess ! (4) = maƙēƙẹ 2.

makoɗa A. (makǫ̆ɗā) Vd. makǫ̆ɗị.
   B. (makǫ̆ɗā) ƒ. (1) Kt. rocky place from which stones for roughening grinding-stones (dūtsạn niƙạ) are hewn (cf. makǫ̆dị). (2) ɗam Makǫ̆ɗā m. (pl. 'yam ~) (a) best nether grinding-stone (from Makǫ̆ɗā in Kano Province). (b) its tạllạ is Garwai, dūtsạn niƙạ.

makoɗi A. (makǫ̆dị) m. (pl. mạkǫ̆ɗai). (1) stone for roughening surface of grinding-stone (dūtsạn niƙạ). (2) ɗam ~ m. (pl. 'yam ~) = 1. (3) shirwạ bā tặ bạrar ~ sǎi dạ tsōkạr nāmạ ạ jịkinsạ nobody acts without reason.
   B. (makǫ̆dị) m. (pl. makǫ̆ɗā). (1) man who hews out (haƙạ) stones for roughening grinding-stones (cf. makodị, makǫ̆ɗā). (2) makǫ̆dịyā ƒ. (pl. makǫ̆ɗā) woman who roughens grinding-stones.

mạƙōgwạrō = Kt. mạƙōgạrō m. (1) windpipe (= jan yārǫ = jannại). (2) throat. (3) neck of jar (= wuyạ 1d). (4) (a) waterpipe (= mēsạ). (b) mạƙōgwạraɳ ịndạrạrō the place where the rain-spout (ịndạrạrō) springs from the roof. (5) mạƙōgwạran dāwạ yā bụ̆dẹ the guinea-corn has grown sturdily. (6) kōwā ya shā inūwạr gēmụ, bặ kạmam ~ ba nobody is ever such a favourite as P. in close touch with one (x one's wife, son, etc.). (7) an dasạ (= haɗạ) mạƙōgwạraɳ (= hancịɳ) wạndō tailor has inserted triangle of cloth where hantsạ joins lower trouser-leg.

makoki A. (makōkī) m. (1) (a) yanặ zamam ~ he is passing the three-day period after a death and receiving callers as in 1b. (b) daɳgi sun shārẹ ~ relations called to offer condolences (gaisūwā 5) as in 1a (Vd. sadakạ 1b). (2) an yi ~ ạ gidansạ he's recently bereaved. (3) aɳ kāwō ~ dagạ Kano news of a bereavement at Kano has arrived.
   B. (makǫ̆kī) m. (ƒ. makōkīyā) pl. makǫ̆kā. (1) mourner x (a) ~ nẹ̆ he is in mourning (Vd. makōkī). (b) makǫ̆kim mutūwạr ụbansạ nē he is in mourning for his father as in makōkī. (2) (a) one who is crying. (b) fretsome, querulous, whiner. (3) small orphan importuning callers during makōkī (= tặkạ makǫ̆kā). (4) makǫ̆kāna (said by old parent) these youngsters of mine who will soon be orphans.

mặƙōƙǫ m. (1) (a) goitre. (b) wen on throat. (c) double chin (1 = mạlōlǫ). (2) (a) fatness on throat of young animals denoting good health x yā ƙōshi har yanặ ~ it (young ram or sheep, etc.) is chubby and full-throated. (b) sǎi ūwā tā ƙōshi, ɗantạ kẹ̆ ~ (i) it is obvious he (or she) belongs to rich parents. (ii) one cannot indulge oneself unless one has the means to do so. (3) ~ dạ rōwạ yakẹ̆ what a miser he is !

makǫ̆kǫ̆wị m. (pl. makǫ̆kǫ̆wā) wrestler (= ƙōkawạ 1b).

makōmā ƒ. (1) relatives, supporters, helpers. (2) The Next World (= Lāhirạ).

mặƙǫ̆-maƙǫ̆ m. (1) niggardly P. (2) (a) niggardliness x yanặ ~ dạ ạbinsạ he is stingy with what he has (= mạƙǫ̆nịyā = mạtsǫ̆-matsǫ̆). (b) reticence. (c) being self-reserved.

makǫmĭ *Vd.* ąnĭyą 4.

makoniya A. (makōnĭyā) *f. used in* ịdaŋ am bi ta halinsą, kō wutā ∼ bą ą bā shị ba if his true character were known, he'd be shunned. B. (makǫnĭyā) *f.* = makǫ-makō 2*a*.

makori A. (makǫrĭ) *m.* (*f.* makōrĭyā) *pl.* makǫrā. (1) driver of donkey, cattle, etc. (*Vd.* kōrą). (2) bą ka ∼ sǎi makashĭ thou warrior who wouldst die rather than retreat ! (= mālĭyō 3). (3) *Vd.* burgą 5. B. (makōrĭ) *m.* (*pl.* makǫrai) T. for driving away flies, birds, etc. (*x* stick, fly-swatter, etc.).

makǫsanĭ *Kt.* = bakǫsanĭ.

makōshĭ *Sk. m.* (*pl.* makǫsai) throat (= makōgwąrō).

makǫyĭ *m.* (*f.* makōyĭyā) *pl.* makǫyā learner, beginner, novice.

makụ *Vd.* mukụ.

makuba *f.* (1) (*a*) empty pods of locust-bean tree (ɓāwan 'yā'yan dǫrōwą) pounded to make plaster for walls or beaten-floor (dąɓē). (*b*) dąɓē yā ji ∼ deserving P. was successful as his merits deserved. (2) *epithet of* makubą is Makubą ɓātą farĭ. (3) *cf.* cąfē.

makublĭ *Sk.* = makullĭ.

makublĭyā *Sk.* = makullĭyā.

makudunū *m.* ugly P.

makụląshē *m.* luxurious food.

makulĭ (*rustic*) = makullĭ.

makullā *Vd.* makullĭyā.

makullĭ = makullĭ *m.* (*pl.* makụllai = makụllai). (1) key (= mabūdĭ). (2) lock (= kūbą) (1, 2 = daŋ makullĭ).

makullĭyā *f.* (*pl.* makụllā) concubine-slavegirl (*Vd.* kullę 1*c*, kwąrkwarą).

makul-makul = gụlam-gụlam.

makụ-makū = makǫ-makō.

makụmbē lumpy, ugly boy or girl.

makụncĭ *m.* (*pl.* makụntā) wrestler (= daŋ kuncē = makǫkǫwĭ).

makụnĭyā *f.* niggardliness (= makǫ-makō).

makunsā *f.* (*pl.* makụnsai). (1) bit of cloth wherein or place in garment wherein T. can be tied up = makunshĭ *q.v.* (2) *Vd.* kārūwą 2*b*.

makunshĭ *m.* (*pl.* makụnsai) = makunsā 1

x makunshiŋ gishirĭ, kā fi gishirĭ zākĭ he trades on his master's position.

makụntā (1) *Vd.* makụncĭ. (2) *f.* slipperiness (= santsĭ).

makụnyącĭ *m.* (*f.* makunyacĭyā) *pl.* makụnyątā self-respecting P.

makurą *Vb.* 2 = makụrā *Vb.* 1C = makarą *q.v.*

makụrarrē *m.* (*f.* makụrarrĭyā) *pl.* makụrarrū stumpy P.

makurdā *f.* = makurdĭ *m.* (*pl.* makụrdai). (1) (*a*) pass through hills or mountains. (*b*) narrows of river, (*hence*, sense 2). (2) Makurdĭ the town *so called.* (3) place only large enough for one to squeeze oneself into (= matsāfā 2).

makụrē *Vb.* 3A sat huddled up.

makụrē (1) *Vb.* 1C. (*a*) strangled (= makarą). (*b*) filled *as in* makarā 2. (2) *Vb.* 3A. (*a*) P. became choked. (*b*) P. was strangled.

makuri A. (makụrĭ) *m.* (1) act of strangling P. (2) experiencing choking sensation. B. (makurĭ) *m.* end, limit (= makārĭ).

makurū (1) what a short-necked person ! (2) *Vd.* gyąmbō 2.

makụrundū *m.* = makụmbē.

makurūrūcĭyā = mukurūrūcĭyā.

makūsā *f.* (*pl.* makụsai) blemish = aibụ (*cf.* kụshē).

makụsącĭ = makusąncĭ *m.* (*f.* makusacĭyā, etc.) *pl.* makụsątā, etc. (1) near *x* wani kauyę ∼ dą Kanọ a village near Kano. (2) relative *x* Audụ makụsącīnā nę Audu is a relative of mine. (4) similar *x* abūbūwą makụsąntā dą jūnā things resembling each other. (5) *cf.* majiɓịncĭ.

makusanta A. (makūsantā) = makūsā. B. (makụsąntā) *Vd.* makụsąncĭ.

makūwā *f.* (1) forgetfulness (= maŋkō). (2) going astray.

makwąbcē *Vd.* makwabtą.

makwabci A. (makwąbcĭ) *m.* (*f.* makwabcĭyā) *pl.* makwąbtā. (1) (*a*) neighbour. (*b*) wata mĭyą, sǎi ą makwąbtā (i) if T. is beyond you, seek help ! (ii) *f.* type of cloth. (2) makwąbciŋ ąkwĭyą *Vd.* kĭwọ 1*c*. B. (makwąbci) *Vd.* makwabtą.

makwabta A. (makwabtā) *Vd.* makwabcī.
B. (makwabtā) *Vb.* 2 (*n.o.* makwabci, *p.o.* makwabcē) bordered on, is
(was) neighbour of (= makwabtata).
makwabtaka *f.* (1) being adjacent *x*
sunā makwabtaka da Kano they live
near Kano. (2) being a neighbour of.
makwabtata *Vb.* 2 (*n.o.* makwabtaci, *p.o.*
makwabtacē) = makwabta.
makwadāici *m.* (*f.* makwadāiciyā) *pl.*
makwadāitā greedy P., one eagerly
desirous, cadger.
makwafī *m.* (*pl.* makwafai). (1) proper
place for T. or P. (= matsayī). (2)
makwafin instead of *x* an sā shi a
makwafīna he has been appointed in
my stead. an aikō ni makwafinsa I've
been sent instead of him.
makwaiwa *f.* variety of the ant
kwarkwāsā.
makwakkafī = makwakkafō *m.* (*sg., pl.*).
(1) Fine-spotted Woodpecker (*Cam-
pethera punctuligera*). (2) Yellow-
breasted Barbet (*Trachyphonus mar-
garitatus*). (3) hawk (= būra kōgō).
makwakwancī *m.* (*f.* makwakwanciyā) *pl.*
makwakwantā P. looking on but doing
no work ; P. whose work is a sinecure
(= zurū 1*b*.i).
makwallā *Kt. f.* resort frequented by
idlers.
makwan *Vd.* kwan.
makwancī *m.* = makwantā *f.* (*pl.* makwantai). (1) (*quizzically*) sleeping-place.
(2) (*a*) lair. (*b*) mūgu yā sam makwan-
cim mūgu (i) Greek met Greek. (ii)
evil consorts with evil. (3) (*a*) grave
(= kabarī). (*b*) makwantai *pl.* cemetery.
(4) = mafādā 1.
makwarārā *f.* = makwarārī *m.* (*pl.* mak-
warārai) water-course (= magudāna =
mazurārī).
makwarē *Vd.* makwarwā.
makwarkwadā *Kt. f.* = kwarkwadā.
makwarmaci *m.* (*f.* makwarmaciyā) *pl.*
makwarmatā. (1) mischief-maker,
blabber. (2) fusser. (3) makwarmaciyā *Kt. f.* = matsēgunci 2.
makwarwā *f.* (*pl.* makwarē = makwark-
warī = makwarwai = makwarwōyī).
(1) bush-fowl ((*a*) Double-spurred
Francolin, *i.e. Francolinus bicalcaratus.*

(*b*) Clapperton's Francolin, *i.e.*
Francolinus clappertonis) = fakarā. (2)
epithet of 1 *is* Mīya bīyū = Fayau. (3) an
yi shūka a idam ∼ he spoke against a
P. not realizing that the latter could
hear or see him (= kanki 2*b*.i).
makwarwā *f.* one gulp *x* nā shā rūwā ∼
uku I took three gulps of water.
makwasa *Sk. f.* favourite wife
(= mōwa 1).
makwauci = makwabcī.
makwayo *Kt. m.* village-head (= dagaci).
mākwi *used in* yau, kā fada ∼ = yau
kā gaya ∼ you'll have a bad time to-
day ! (= kawāyā).
makyali = makyallī *Nor. m.* = masabī *q.v.*
*makyangyamā *f.* shin (= kwaurī *q.v.*).
mākyararē *used in* dam ∼ *m.* (*f.* 'yar ∼)
pl. 'yam ∼ (1) stunted P. or animal.
(2) spy.
makyarkyatā = makyarkyata *f.* act of
trembling.
makyūyaci *m.* (*f.* makyūyaciyā) *pl.*
makyūyatā. (1) slacker, indolent. (2)
makyūyaciyā *f.* cramp (= kafar
kāzā 3).
mala A. (malā) = mulā.
B. (mālā) *Zar. f.* (1) type of satchel
(= gafaka). (2) nā sā shi a ∼ (*said by
propounder of riddle when his friend
after saying* n ga " let me think a bit ! "
gives it up) well, I'll tell you the
answer ! (3) nā batar da kudīna a ∼
I've wasted my money.
malabā *f.* (*pl.* malabai) place of refuge.
malafā *f.* (*pl.* malafū = malafōfī = malfōfī = maléfanī = malfuna = *Sk.*
maluffa) (*Ar.* malfūfa " plaited "). (1)
(*a*) straw-hat (= gurumfā). (*b*) yā
sā ∼ he put on a straw-hat. (*c*) yā
cirē ∼ = yā tūbe ∼ = yā kwabe ∼ he
took off a straw-hat. (2) helmet. (3)
large oval mat made from kaba and
kijinjirī (= tāfin gīwā = wundī). (4)
malafar sambo obsolete type of woman's
kerchief.
malaha *f.* (*pl.* malahōhī) sandal-sole consisting of one thickness of hide.
malā'ika *m.* (*pl.* malā'ikū) *Ar.* (1) angel.
(2) dam malā'ikan Allā new-born child.
(3) malā'ikan 'yan Adan bloodthirsty P.
malaidūwā = malēdūwā.

malakạ *used in* malakạr kạrē dạ hantạr kūrā = malakạrkạ you'll get it when the moon turns into green cheese !

malala A. (mạlālạ) flowed into, on to, over, pervaded *x* rūwā yā ∼ cikin dākịnsụ the water flowed into their house. yā malālō cikin d̃ākịmmụ it flowed into our house. B. (malālā) (1) *Vb.* 3B = mạlālạ. (2) *Vb.* 1C poured T. into, on to, over *x* am malālạ mặi kạŋ ạbincī oil has been poured over the food. yā malālạ rūwā ạ wurin nạŋ he has poured, spilled much water here (*cf.* malālē).

C. (malala = mạlālạ) abundantly *in sense of* malālā *x* rūwā yā kwạntā ∼ pools of water lay everywhere (= lamama).

malālācī *m.* (*f.* malālācīyā) *pl.* malālātā idler, lounger (*Vd.* lālācị). (2) malālācīyā *f.* pernicious anæmia (= bạyammā 1 *q.v.*).

malale A. (malālē) (1) *Vb.* 3A flowed out, leaked out (*cf.* mạlālạ, malālā). (2) flowed into, on to, over, pervaded entirely *x* rūwā yā malālẹ wurịŋ water covered the whole place. sọ̃jī sum malālẹ k̃asā dukạ soldiers have overrun the whole land. B. (mạlālē) *m.* place for water to flow off mud-roof without necessity of fitting ịndạrạrō.

Mạ̃lālī *m.* the famine of 1913–14 (= sụd̃e mụ gaisạ *q.v. under* sụd̃ẹ 1c).

malallabtā *Kt.* = malallautā.

malallafī = mạlallạfī *m.* martingale.

mạlallạs *m.* satin (= ạd̃alashī).

malallautā = malallōtā *f.* (*pl.* mạlạllạutai, etc.). (1) place for religious ablutions (ạlwạlā). (2) upper limit of ceremonial ablution of feet *x* nā shịga rūwa īyạ ∼ I entered the water ankle-deep.

Mālạm *Vd.* mālạmī.

mālạmā *Vd.* mālạmī.

malā-mạlā = malala.

mạlāmạlai *Vd.* malmalā.

mālamancī *m.* using abstruse language (*cf.* mālantạ).

mālạmī *m.* (*f.* mālạmā) *pl.* mạlạmai = *Sk.* mālumạ = *Kt.* mālummạ (*Ar.* mu'-allim " teacher "). (1) (*a*) (i) literate P. (ii) teacher (*Vd.* sō sō banzā, kūrị, gardị, rạuhānī). (*b*) ịnā wani wạndạ mālạminsạ ya rụ̃d̃e shị you're no match for me. (*c*) (mālạmī *as vocative* " Teacher ! '", *or as in* iv, vi, viii, x, xi, xii " You, O Teacher ", *or as title, becomes* Mālạm) *x* (i) Mālạŋ (= Mālạm) kadạ kạ yi fushī dạ nī please don't be cross with me, Teacher ! (ii) Mālạm Mạmūdụ (= Mālạŋ Mạmūdụ) yā zō Mamudu the Teacher, Clerk, etc., has come. (iii) *Vd.* wạdā 1*a.* (iv) sanịnsạ yā gạgạri Mālạm, yā gạgạri bōkā it is unknown to all (*lit.* it is beyond you, O Teacher !) (iv*A*) kā fi aikịm Mālạm *Vd.* Gạikau, Gwạurau. (iv*B*) bụ̃wạ̃yạ mạlạmai *Vd.* ạlkālī. (iv*C*) *Vd.* kā fi mālạm. (v) Mālạm, nā zō tạmbayạrkạ nē Scholar, I've a *query* which I'd be obliged if you'd elucidate ! (*reply is* Allạ̃ yạ sanasshē mụ !), *Vd.* tạmbayạ 1*b.*ii. (vi) sặi ạ k̃ārạ wạ Mālạm sadakạ, ạddu'ạ tạ gamu dạ ịjābạ trust God, but keep your powder dry ! (vii) Mālạm, kā ji aikịn 'yā'yā what an achievement ! (viii) makạ Mālạm (= Mālạm makạ) sukạ gīgītạ well then, they became all of a dither. wạsa-wạsā makạ Mālạm sặi akạ gan sụ then they suddenly turned up. (ix) bạ kạ saŋ ạbim mạ̃mākị ba, Allạ̃ yạ kyautạ yịŋ, Mālạm, ạshē . . . well the strangest thing of all is that . . . (x) Allạ̃ yạ gāfạttạ Mālạm *Vd.* gāfạrtā, nạ'am. (xi) būzum birị nēsạ gạ Mālạm how am I concerned with such a thing ! (xi*A*) birị yā zō hannum Mālạm *Vd.* birị 1*b.* (xii) (*sometimes politely used for* " you ") *x* lallē Mālạm bại mạntā ba . . . of course you have not forgotten that . . . (xiii) rāgō dạ wutsīyạr kạrē, d̃am Mālạm what a protligate scholar ! (xiv) Mālạŋ yā k̃i nōmā *Vd.* warạbukkạ. (xv) Mālạm, gọ̃be dạ nīsā *Vd.* gọ̃be 8. (*d*) Mālạmī bạfādạŋ Allạ̃ ! *address to scholars by* marọ̃k̃ā. (*e*) scribe (of court, tax-registers, etc) (= mag̣ạ 2). (*f*) (i) mụtụm duk mālạmiŋ kạnsạ nē everyone is the best judge of his own affairs (= yạyyō 2). (ii) ∼ dạ kudịŋ kid̃ạ *Vd.* dạbaŋ 1*b.* (*g*) mālạmiŋ ạlkūkị student taking notes which he never consults. (*h*) the official Muslim slaughterer (= mayạŋkī), *cf.* mahạucī. (*j*) the dignitary before whom marriage-ceremony is performed

(*Vd.* aurē 6*c*). (2) Mālạm Bēbị = Mālạm, būɗe littāfị *m.* (*sg., pl.*) butterfly. (3) mālạmin dawạ *Vd.* dilā. (4) jạkar ∼ *f.* first stomach of ruminant. (5) *Vd.* tạfī dạ mālạminkạ. (6) Mūgụm ∼ *Vd.* dạḍumạ.

mālancị *m.* = mālantạ.

mālaŋkōcī *m.* = zāƙī banzā *q.v.* under zāƙī 8.

malanta A. (mālantạ) *f.* (1) scholarship *x* yanạ̄ dạ ∼ he is learned. (2) work of a mālạmī. (3) *cf.* mālamancī.
   B. (mạ̄lantạ) *Vb.* 3B is literate, is learned.

malāsā *f.* (1) utility *x* ạbin nạŋ ∼ gạrēshị this thing is useful. (2) ƙạŋ ƙarā bạ̄ ki ∼ what a stingy person!

malāshī *m.* wạndō ∼ trousers with crutchpiece (hantsạ) reaching to the ground (= lạ̄sā 7).

malāshīyā *Kt. f.* expertness in embroidery, building, hairdressing, etc.

malau-malau *adv.* zigzag *x* macịjī yanạ̄ tạfīyạ ∼ the snake is following a zigzag course.

malē (*formerly used in women's songs at Kt.*) na ∼ *m.* vagina (= *Sk.* māmạrūsụ).

mạlēɗūwā *Kt. f.* the vine dāfārā *q.v.*

malēfanī *Vd.* mạlạfā.

malēƙū *m.* summit (= lēƙū).

mạlēlēƙūwā *f.* (1) *x* hatsī yanạ̄ ∼ the corn is waving in the breeze. (2) hanyạn nạm ∼ cē̳ this is a roundabout way. (3) īyạ ∼ type of children's game.

malē-mạlē = malala.

malēmalī *Vd.* malmalā.

mạlfā *Kt.* = mạlạfā.

malfōfī *Vd.* mạlạfā.

mạlgā *Kt.* = mạrgā.

mạlīhūlīyā = mạlūhūlīyā.

Mālikāwā *Vd.* Bạmālikī, Mālikīyyị.

Maliki A. (Mālikị) (1) the angel in charge of hell-fire. (2) kō kai ∼ nē̳, kai (*insult to a* Sharīfị, *such being considered immune from hell-fire*) Sharifi or not, you'll have to do it ! (kai = kā̳ yī).
   B. (Mālikị) *name of the* founder of the Mālikīyyạ School of Muslim Law.

Mālikīyyạ the Malikiyya School of Muslim Law *x* yanạ̄ ƙạm ∼ he is a follower of the Malikiyya School (*the other orthodox ones being the* Hanafi, Hanbali, Shafi'i *apart from the unorthodox* Shi'i), *cf.* Mālikī, Bạmālikī.

Mālikīyyị *m.* (*f.* Mālikīyyīyā) *pl.* Mālikāwā = Bạmālikī.

malīlā *f.* niggardliness.

Mālīyạ *f.* (*Ar.* māliha "salty") (1) Bạhạr ∼ = Bạhạrụl ∼ *m.* (*a*) Red Sea. (*b*) Mediterranean Sea. (2) kumfam ∼ *Vd.* kumfan 2.

mālīyō *m.* (*Ar.* māla) (1) wheeling one's horse. (2) yā yi ∼ he turned the corner (kwanạ 1). (3) bạ ạ tabạ ganim mālīyansạ ba he is a warrior who never retreats (= makọ̄rī 2).

malizimcī *m.* (*f.* malizimcīyā) *pl.* malizimtā P. or T. sticking to one like a limpet.

malkā *Kt.* = mạrkā.

malkạɗā *Kt.* = markạɗā.

malkē *m.* = hạnsakō.

malƙwasa A. (malƙwạsā) *Vb.* 1C bent over tip of knife or hoe-blade (= kalmạɗā).
   B. (mạlƙwasạ) = kạlmaɗạ.

malƙwashē = kalmạshē, kạlmaɗạ.

mạllakạ (1) *Vb.* 2 (*a*) possessed. (*b*) got possession of. (*c*) ruled over. (*d*) *x* yā mạllạkē mụ ạ kạnsụ (ạ kạŋ ƙasarsụ) he gave us dominion over them (over their country). (2) *f.* (*a*) what is within one's jurisdiction *x* dạ kạ̄i dạ kāyā dū mạllakạr wuyạ nē̳ (i) a P. is responsible for his household as well as for himself. (ii) everyone can deal with his possessions as he thinks fit. (*b*) isā dạ ∼ yakē̳ yị he's abusing his authority. (*c*) type of small plant.

mallạƙā *Kt.* = maƙạlā.

mallạƙē *Kt.* (1) = maƙạlē 1. (2) tucked T. under one's arm (= sāyē̳).

mallạƙē *Vb* 1C (1) = mạllakạ 1*a–c*. (2) yā ∼ shi he stuck to it (T. lent him).

mallạƙī *m.* property *x* mallạƙīna nē̳ it belongs to me.

mallạmī *Sk.* = mālạmī.

Mallē *name given any man called* Mạhamūdụ.

Mallērị *used in* dājịm ∼ the traditional Sokoto place of execution (*cf.* Durūmạ).

malmal *used in* ∼ dạ bakạ *m.* flattery.

(= lam-lam = sạlē6ạ 3 = balmạ 2 = lallamĭ = rōmō 4).

malmalā f. (pl. malēmalĭ = mạlāmạlai = Sk. mạlmạlinnị) long cake of tūwō (= ƙwaŋ kadọ).

malmō m. (1) the tree Eugenia owariensis. (2) profligate man (epithet is Malmō, gịndiŋkạ yanạ rūwa).

mạlōlọ m. (1) = mạƙōƙọ 1. (2) bird's crop.

maltị m. grey baft (= ạkōkō q.v.).

mạlūfị = mạ'ạlūfị.

mạlūhūlịyā f. (Ar. malankhūliyā from Greek) (1) vicious behaviour or talk. (2) false statement x yā gạmu dạ ∼ he is the victim of slander.

mālumạ Vd. mālạmī.

malumbucī = mulumbucī.

mạlụm-mālum f. gown having 'yaŋ asạkē embroidery (Vd. askā 3b).

malwạ f. (1) Sk. the shackles gĭgar q.v. (2) Kt. ∼ cē, hancịŋ kạrē it's a never-drying spring of water.

mạmā (1) m. (a) breast (= nōnọ 2b). (b) yārọ yā kāmạ mạmansạ the baby-lad has begun suckling (mạmansạ = " the breast provided for him by God "). (c) mạmantạ yā tā dạ kabarạ, zại fādị her (maiden's) breasts are about to droop (cf. ƙịrgā 2b). (d) rūwam mạmā Vd. rūwā B.15. (e) mūgụm mạmā Vd. dākālẹ 3. (2) Vb. 2 Kt. = mạmayạ.

mamạcī m. (f. mamacịyā) pl. mamạtā (1) the deceased x ịnā dam mamạcịŋ where is the son of the deceased? (2) Vd. sadakạ 1d.

mamạdī (rustic) = madạdī.

mạmākị m. (pl. mạmạ̄kai) (1) (a) being surprised x yā bā nị ∼ he surprised me. (b) yā yi ∼ he was surprised. yā yi mạmākịnsạ he was surprised at it. (2) (a) ạbim ∼ m. wonder, marvel. (b) ạbim ∼ bā yạ ƙārēwā ạ dūnịyạ wonders never cease. (c) sun nūnạ ạbim ∼ they did splendidly. (d) bạ kạ saŋ ạbim ∼ ba, Allạ yạ kyautạ yiŋ, Mālạm, ạshē ... well, the strangest thing of all is that. . . . (3) bạ ∼ Vd. ạsīrī 5.

mạmākọ (1) adv. abundantly x an yi rūwā ∼ it rained heavily. tạfīyạ cē ∼ the travellers were many. bịkĭ

nē ∼ it's a crowded banquet. gōnā cē ∼ it's a huge farm. (2) adj. m. (f. mạmākụwā) x (a) mạmākụwar tạfīyạ cē = 2nd example in 1. mạmākụwar īskạ a mighty wind. (b) nā yi gudụn ciccifī, nā shịga ∼ I fell out of the frying-pan into the fire! (3) epithet of any Emir.

mạmạrē m. (1) groping (= fạfạkē). (2) endeavouring x yanạ ∼ yạ shiryạ su he's trying to reconcile them. yanạ mạmạram fadạ he is trying to cause a quarrel. (3) mạmạre-mạmạrē (a) constant groping, etc., as in 1, 2. (b) being flustered, flabbergasted (cf. gĭgītạ).

māmạrūsụ (used in women's songs) Sk. na ∼ m. vagina (= Kt. malē).

mamạtā Vd. mamạcī.

mamaya A. (mạmaya) Vb. 2 (1) attacked P. unawares. (2) flummoxed (= fịrmitsạ).

B. (mamạyā) Vd. mamạyī.

mamạyācī m. (f. mamayācịyā) pl. mamạyātā destitute.

mamạyī m. (f. mamayịyā) pl. mamạyā substitute, representative, deputy, etc. x aŋ kāwō mamạyinsạ his locum tenens has been brought (= mạimakō = madạdī).

mạmē Kt. m. (1) (sec. v.n. of mạmayạ) x anạ mạmansạ = anạ mạmayạssạ he is being suddenly attacked. (2) sudden attack.

mam funị Vd. man funị.

mạmĭ f. (Eng. " mammy ") (1) woman. (2) European woman. (3) native mistress of European. (4) sulẹ mại ∼ Victorian shilling. (5) mạmĭ = rĭgar ∼ f. woman's short jumper with pleated top.

mạmmā Sk. = mạmā.

mammaƙalā = maƙalƙalā.

mạmmaskā m., f. (pl. masƙạ̄ƙā) (1) rich (of meat). (2) greasy (re clothing), cf. mại 1a, maiƙọ.

mammōrā f. (1) (a) liberality. (b) marạm ∼ m., f. (pl. marạsā ∼) stingy. (2) Kt. rōman rōgọ bạ ka ∼ how useless! (cf. tsạrī 1b).

mamu A. *(māmū) (d.f. Ar. imām, Hausa lịmạm) P. imitating postures of a prayer-leader (līmạm) = mamūmị.

B. mamụ *Sk.* to us = manạ *q.v.*

Māmūdụ (*Ar.* Mahmūdụ "Praised") *man's name* (= Mūdī 2), *Vd.* Mahamūdụ, Mụhammadụ.

māmụlā *Vb.* 1C (toothless P.) chewed T.

mạmul-mạmul = gụlam-gụlam.

māmulkō = mạmulkọ *m., f.* (*sg., pl.*) (1) toothless P. (2) *m.* toothless mouth.

*māmūmạ *f.* (*Ar.* " having been wounded in the brain ") deep wound inflicted on the head (*cf.* mūlihạ).

*māmūmị = *māmū.

mạmunga *f.* (1) = mạmạrē. (2) *Kt.* = mādịndịimī.

mạmurạ *f.* = mạmạrē.

man A. (mạn) (1) *Vd.* mặi. (2) *Vd.* mṇ.

B. (mạn) = manạ.

mana A. (manạ) to us.

B. (manạ = mạn) well, indeed *x* tạfi ∼ = jē ∼ now be off ! zō ∼ now come along ! bạ ni ∼ come now, give me it ! sam mṇ ∼ come now, give me a bit ! zā ạ yị ? will it be done ? (*reply* sǎi ạ yī ∼ of course it will !). hakạ nē ∼ yes, that *is* how the matter stands ! in nā sō, kadạ ṇ īyạ ∼ it's no concern of yours whether I can or not ! (*reply to* you cannot do it !).

manadạrī *m.* type of pad for pack-horse or pack-donkey (*the* lạfẹrū *is put over it*), *cf.* akumạrī.

manadi A. (manadī) *m.* (*pl.* mạnạdai) (1) cloth-strip wound round T., bandage, etc. (2) manadịn kafạ puttee.

B. (manạdī) *m.* (*f.* manadīyā) *pl.* manạdā (1) P. who winds T. round T. *as in* nadẹ. (2) *Vd.* ạ shā dạ ∼.

managarcī *m.* (*f.* managarcīyā) *pl.* managạrtā reliable.

mạn alayyạdī *m.* oil from palm-kernels (*cf.* mạn jā).

manạnị *Vd.* nānẹ 1*d.*

*mạnārạ *f.* (*Ar.* " minaret ") steps up to place whence prayer-calls are made (*cf.* mumbạrī).

mạnạwai *m.* (*sg., pl.*) (*Eng.* " man-of-war ") warship.

*mạnāzarạ *Ar. f.* reading to oneself (*cf.* dūbạ 6).

mạncē *Vb.* 1C forgot *x* (i) nā ∼ shi =

nā ∼ dạ shī I forgot it (= mạntā). (2) nā ∼ dạ albasạ *Vd.* tōyạ 1*c.* (3) ∼ gātarī *Vd.* bāwạ 1*h.*

mancịkkē *Nor. Vb.* 1C = mạntā.

mandā *f.* (1) a dark Bornu salt used medicinally. (2) dạddawa gayạ ∼ bafī it's a case of the pot calling the kettle black. (3) *cf.* yārọ 6.

mandafō = kwadọ 2*a.*

mạndawạrī *m.* (1) type of braiding on gown-neck (= sharabạ). (2) (*a*) *name of an* old market in Kano City. (*b*) fankanẹ dạ shī, ạmmā shẹkarạ kạman gānūwar Mạndawạrī it looks small but is very ancient (*cf.* Amīnạ 2).

mạndẹwā = mạndīwā *f.* the tree *Maerua angolensis* (= *Kt.* cịcịwā).

mandō *m.* (*sg., pl.*) the aphis causing the blight darβā.

manẹmī *m.* (*f.* manēmịyā) *pl.* manẹmā seeker.

man funi (mạm funị) *m.* (1) a stinking oil made from ground-nuts, cotton-seed (anguryā), physic-nuts (bị ni dạ zugū), red sorrel (sōβạrōdọ), bulrush-millet (gērō) or castor-oil plant (zụrmạn) (*it is used for rubbing on camels for mange, for driving off the* tụrurrūwā *ants and sometimes drunk by P. as eczema cure*) = mạn gēlọ. (2) *Kt.* = fumfuṇ.

manga A. (mạngā) *Sk. f.* (*pl.* mạngạ̄yē) the plaits taurā *q.v.*

B. (Mạngạ) (1) ∼ ūwar shānū *epithet of* βaunā. (2) Mụhammạm ∼ title (lạfabī) for any man named Mụhammadụ *q.v.*

C. (mạngā) *Vd.* sọ ∼.

Mạngạdagullạ *used in* ∼ hafōriṇ girmā *epithet of* wisdom-tooth.

mạngaje = bạngaje.

mạngalạ *f.* (*pl.* mạngalōlī) bag made of plaited dum-palm (gōribạ) leaves (*for pack-animals to take manure to farm or bring maize, okro, etc., from farms into the town*).

mangara A. (mạngarạ) *Vb.* 2 (1) P. gave sideways kick at (*cf.* harbā, shụrā). (2) animal kicked at *as in* harbā, shụrā. (3) hit P. with fist of outflung arm.

B. (mạngarā) *Vb.* 1C (*with dative*) *x* yā ∼ masạ fafạ he (person) kicked him sideways (*cf.* mạngarạ).

maŋgarē m. (1) (a) acting as in maŋgarạ. (b) (Sec. v.n. of maŋgarạ) x yanạ maŋgaransụ = yanạ maŋgarạssụ he's kicking them sideways. (2) ε sideways kicking game (Vd. tsạgyan tsạyī, wartsahū) = Sk. dōrọ.

maŋgarī m. (= maŋgarē 1) x yanạ maŋgarinsụ = yanạ maŋgarạssụ he's kicking them sideways.

maŋgaribạ = magaribạ.

maŋgartū = maŋgartū m. x sunạ maŋgartunsạ they are longing for him (absent P.) = bẹgē.

maŋgasạ Vb. 2 (p.o. maŋgashē, n.o. maŋgạshi) Kt. = maŋgarạ.

Maŋgāwä Vd. Bạmaŋgẹ.

maŋgạyē Vd. maŋgā.

maŋgaza = baŋgaza.

maŋ gēlọ = man funị.

maŋgōsọ m. sore place (mīkị) on hindquarters (kutụrī) of pack-animal due to rubbing of akumạrī.

maŋgụl m. type of Bornu salt (cf. kaskō 5 ; lēlā, kantụ).

maŋgwarọ Eng. m. (sg., pl.) mango fruit or tree (Vd. cī 1c ; shā A.1e).

maŋ gyạɗā m. ground-nut oil of the following kinds :—(1) maŋ fulī-fulī (obtained by slightly roasting (sōyạ) ground-nuts, the residue (tịfā = tụŋkūzạ) being made sometimes into the fulī-fulī cakes and sometimes into kwaɗọ (Vd. markạɗā 2) : it is a pale oil used for pouring on or for frying (tūyạ) food). (2) (a) man rụrūwạ (= bafim mặi q.v.) (this oil is dark, bitter, and cheap ; it is obtained by roasting (sōyạ) the nuts till black and is used for frying (tōyạ) and lamp-oil ; in Katsina, man rụrūwạ is not this oil (bafim mặi), but is maŋ fulī-fulī, i.e. 1 above). (b) Vd. barcī 3c. (3) by further roasting of residue (gwībạ) of man rụrūwạ (2a above), we get fwaŋfōnī, a dark oil ; the dạlạkī = tịfā = dạgwadạgō = tụŋkūzạ (residue) of fwaŋfōnī is mixed with shells of groundnuts and made into kwạɗọ-fuel.

mani A. (manị) Sk. to me = minị q.v.

  B. *(manị) = manīyyị.

mānị'Ī m. (Ar. " preventing ") obstacle x wani ~ yā hanạ ni zūwạ a hindrance

prevented me from coming. wannaⁿ bạ ~ ba nẹ that is no good reason.

mani'imcī m. (f. mani'imcīyā) pl. manị'. imtā fertile (land).

manīsancī m. (f. manīsancīyā) pl. manị santā distant.

manịtsī m. = munụtsī.

manīyyị Ar. m. semen (= zūwạ 5b), cᵢ mazīyyị.

man jā m. (1) palm-oil obtained from tʰ cortex (cf. maŋ alayyạdī). (2) Vᵢ bạmmī. (3) dāɗin dōyạ dạ ~ whᵉ superficial friendship !

manjạ = manjọ Eng. m. (1) Major (Arm rank). (2) anything handsome.

manjạgarạ f. (sg., pl.) rake. (2) sā ᵣ kạ yạyā you seem to think mone grows on the tops of trees !

maŋ kaɗăi = maŋ kaɗē = maŋ kaɗany m. (1) shea-butter. (2) maŋ kad bai sābạ dạ tandū ba prosperity unknown to the poor. (3) Vd. fạtị fatē 2.

maŋkanī West Hausa m. type of kokᶜ yam (gwāzā).

maŋkạrā = mạkạrā.

maŋkas (1) used in yā tạfi, yā yi zamans ~ he dallied a long time when senⁱ (2) = maŋfas.

maŋfas used in yā cịka ~ it is chock full (= fal).

maŋ kạzā Vd. narfẹ.

maŋkishị Ashanti Hausa m. matches (= ạshānā).

maŋkō m. (1) used in bạ ~, bạ sakẹwᵉ dạ linzāmị (said by attendant whᵒ precedes a horseman, i.e. ɗaŋ kạramtū) don't relax your bridle ! (2) forgetfulness x nā yi ~ I forgot (= makūwā).

maŋ fulī-fulī Vd. maŋ gyạɗā 1.

mannạ Vb. 1A (plus dative) (1) (a) gummed T. on to x am ~ takạrdā jikim baŋgō a notice has been affixed to the wall (= lifạ 1a). (b) yā ~ minị laifī he falsely accused me (= lifạ 1b). (2) x yā ~ minị dōki he overcharged me for the horse (= lifạ 2), cf. mīfẹ 1e. (3) gave a trifle x yā ~ minị 'yar kyautā he gave me a small present. yā ~ manạ he gave us a trifle. yā ~ minị tarō he gave me threepence.

mannau *used in* dạ hạnau, gāra mạnnau better half a loaf than no bread.

manne A. (mannẹ) (1) *Vb.* 3A stuck to *x* yā ⁓ gạrēshị = yā ⁓ ạ jịkinsạ it stuck to it. (2) *Vb.* 1A stopped up *x* rịgā tā tsāgẹ, akạ ⁓ the gown became torn and was sewn up.
 B. (mạnnē) *m.* round, embroidered pattern on gown (= gḕwạyḕ 1 = tambạrī 2), *cf.* dạmɓạrē.

manomi A. (manọmī) *m.* (*f.* manōmịyā) *pl.* manọmā farmer (*Vd.* nōmā).
 B. (manōmī) *m.* (*pl.* mạnọmrai) farm-settlement (gidạŋ ƙauyẹ), some distance from one's home in a town.

mạn rụrūwạ *Vd.* mạŋ gyạdā 2 ; barcī 3c.

mạn shānū *m.* butter (= mại 6).

mạntā *Vb.* 1C forgot *x* (1) nā ⁓ shi = nā ⁓ dạ shī I forgot it (= mạncē). (2) *Vd.* Ạ mạntā ; ḳulịyạ.

Mantai *name given to female* 'yar wābị (= Ạ mạntā), *cf.* Ạ jēfas, Mạntau.

mạntạnfas *f.* (*sg.*, *pl.*) muzzle-loading cannon.

mạntạsạlā *f.* (1) being forgetful (= mantūwā). (2) dilly-dallying (= sakacẹ).

Mạntau *name given to male* ɗaŋ wābị (*cf.* Mantai).

mạntạ ūwā *m.* (1) *Crotolaria arenaria* (plant). (2) *Ansellia congoensis* (*both plants are medicines for weaned children*).

manti *m.* (*pl.* mantōcī) *Eng.* (1) minute of time. (2) kō dākạtāwar ⁓ ɗayā bạ zā mụ yi ba we won't delay a moment.

mantūwā *f.* forgetfulness (= mạntạsạlā).

manukī = manukiŋ kalwā *m.* calabash-sieve used for fermenting dạddawā (*Vd.* nuḳạ).

mạŋ wurị *m. Vd.* ɓakyạlcē.

mạnyā *Vd.* bạbba.

mạnyantạ *Vb.* 3B (1) P. has become important. (2) P. has attained the age of 50–60 (*d.f.* mạnyā).

mạn zạitụŋ *m.* olive-oil (*Ar.* zaitūn " olive ").

mạnzạnni *Vd.* mạnzō.

manzạrī *Ar. m.* (*pl.* mạnzạrai) (1) pair of spectacles, eyeglasses. (2) monocle (1, 2 = tạbārau, madūbiŋ idọ).

mạnzil *m.* type of incense.

manzo A. (mạnzō) *m.* (*pl.* mạnzạnnī)

(1) (*a*) messenger (*cf.* ma'aikī, mātinjạ). (*b*) mạnzan Tūrai *Vd.* sạkākạ. (*c*) mạnzạŋkạ hōgẹ *Vd.* dạkamạ. (2) *Vd.* Ajạlạ.
 B. (Mạnzo) *name for any man called* ādạmū *q.v. or* Jịbịrịŋ.

map *Eng. m.* (*sg.*, *pl.*) map (*cf.* matạƙaicī).

mar A. (mạr) (*rolled* " r ", Mod. Gram. 5) to him = masạ *q.v.*
 B. (mar) (*cerebral* " r ", Mod. Gram. 5) *Kt. x* (1) bạ ạ ⁓ masạ ba it has not been used (= mọrā). (2) yā ⁓ minị he deceived me.

mara A. (mārạ) (1) *Vb.* 1A *used in* am ⁓ masạ bāyā (*a*) he has progressed through influence. (*b*) he has received help from powerful friends (*Vd.* bāyā 1*f*). (*c*) *Vd.* tạka m mārạ. (2) *f.* (*a*) lower part of the stomach. (*b*) rịgā māganin ciki dạ ⁓ (i) fine feathers make fine birds. (ii) fair without and foul within. (*c*) tūwantạ (kaɗintạ) gụdā dạ ⁓ her tūwō (spinning) is uneven, *cf.* gụdā 1*a*. (*d*) kuɗiŋkạ ạ mārạ *Vd.* yạ̄fē 2. (*e*) namijị dạ ⁓ *Vd.* ɗạkwạrī.
 B. (mārā) (1) *Vb.* 2 (*Vd.* mārị *for progressive*) (*a*) (i) slapped. (ii) am mạri tsōfam banzā *Vd.* zaunạ 1*e.* (*b*) yā mạri tụrạrē he adulterated the scent (*cf.* gamị 1*c*). (2) *Vd.* mạri ki tāshị, mārạ bāḳiŋkạ, mārō. (3) *f.* odd number *x* ukụ ⁓ cẹ three is an odd number (*cf.* cịkā 2*e*). kuɗin nạŋ sunạ dạ ⁓ this sum of money is not complete.
 C. (mārā) *f.* (*pl.* mārōrī = mārạrrakī = mạrāḳū) (1) (*a*) fragment of cala-bash for dipping out (dība) tūwō from cooking-pot (*Vd.* shạrif 2, ạlkālī 5). (*b*) (i) mại wụyar kwāshḕwā dạ ⁓ *Vd.* tūwō 7. (ii) *cf.* sạkainā. (2) cake of tūwō (*cf.* cūrị 2). (3) sạ̄ mārar kāyā *epithet of* pack-ox (tạkarkạrī) or burly P. (ƙātọ).

maraba A. (marạbā) (*Ar.* marhaban) (1) (*a*) marạbā = marạbā turụm welcome ! (= jaɓɓāmạ). (*b*) *Vd.* mạrhạbā. (2) *m., f.* welcoming *x* (*a*) marạbaŋkạ = marạbā dạ kai welcome ! (= 1 *above*). (*b*) yā yi minị ⁓ = yā yi ⁓ dạ nī he welcomed me. (*c*) *Vd.* bạ̄ƙō 2*d.* (3) dagạ marạbar Sarkim pạ̄wạ ? kumfạ zāƙim mịyạ ? taking advantage of a chance full-pelt ; how can you expect such quick results ! (4) ∼ dạ rānā *Kt. f.* old dum-palm (gọrubạ) leaves useless for string-making. (5) ∼ dạ wutā *f.* small twigs for firewood (= būbụ). (6) marạbā (*cerebral* " r ", Mod. Gram. 5) *Vd.* marạbī.

B. (marabā) *f.* (*pl.* mạrạbai) (1) (*a*) place where travellers' ways diverge. (*b*) cross-roads (= mararrabā). (*c*) munɡ̣ nēmam ∼ we're seeking a way of parting from one another. (*d*) suɲ gạmu, bạ̄ ∼ they're indissolubly joined. (2) halfway-point *x* yā yi marabar littāɦɲ he's read half the book. (3) difference *x* ịnā marabar ạlịf dạ alịf what is the difference between the word ạlịf and the word alịf ?. dạ bạbbar ∼ tsạkāninsụ there's a great difference between them. ịndạ sukẹ̄ dạ ∼ kẹ̄ naɲ *that* is where they differ.

marāɓā *f.* (*pl.* mạrạɓai) place of refuge.

mạ̄rạ bākiɲkạ *m.* beans cooked alone (= ɓulū).

marabi A. (marabī) *m.* = marabā.

B. (marạbī) *m.* (*f.* marabīyā) *pl.* marạbā (1) distributor. (2) kạrē bạ yạ̄ ci kạrē ba sǎi dạ mūgụm ∼ he would not dare to act thus unless sure of strong backing. (3) kashẹ̄wā ạ zūcịyar ∼ tā fi " Wānẹ gạ̄ hannūna ! " it's better to be remembered than to have oneself to ask for a share.

marāɓīyā *f.* the spleen (= saifạ).

marạbkạnī *m.* (*f.* marabkanīyā) *pl.* marạbkạnā forgetful, liable to make mistakes.

mạrābụs = mụrābụs.

Marādāwā *Vd.* Bạmarādẹ.

maradi A. (marạdī) *m.* (*f.* maradīyā) *pl.* marạdā (1) slanderer. (2) (*said by women*) bạ̄kim ∼ ạ wuta what a slanderer !

B. (Marādī = Maryādī) *f.* the town of Maradi.

marạfīyạ *f.* cap of European material with bitten-in pattern.

marạfkạnī = marạbkạnī.

marāgadī *m.* (*pl.* mạrạ̄gạdai) (1) long stick for probing hole for depth or testing whether rat, etc., inside. (2) ramrod (= marwāshī). (3) stalk for

hollowing out cornstalk-flute kụsumburwạ 1*c* (1–3 = marāraki). (4) *Vd.* marāgadīyā.

marāgadīyā *f.* (1) = marāgadī. (2) hunger.

mạ̄rai *Kt. m.* = the bird gạ̄dō *q.v.*

maraice A. (mạrạicē) *m.* late evening. dạ ∼ in the late evening.

B. (marạicē) *Vb.* 3A became orphaned (= mạraitạ 1), *cf.* mạrāyạ.

maraici *m.* orphanhood.

maraina A. (marạinā) *f.* (1) testicles (= ɓwạ̄lạtai). (2) *Vd.* marẹ̄nī.

B. (marainā) = marēnā.

marạinī = marẹ̄nī.

marainiya A. (mạrainīyā) *Vd.* mạrāyạ.

B. (marainīyā) *Vd.* marẹ̄nī.

marairaịcē *Vb.* 1D coaxed, wheedled.

mạrạiraitạ *f.* act of coaxing, wheedling.

maraita A. (mạraitạ) *Vb.* 3A (1) = marạicē. (2) started out in the late evening (*Vd.* mạrạicē). (3) died (*only re* person).

B. (marạitā) *Vb.* 1C orphaned a P.

mạrạɓā *Vd.* mạrạɓī.

maraki A. (marạkī) *m.* (*f.* marakīyā) *pl.* marạkā (1) P. escorting one. (*b*) ∼ bạ̄ ạbōkin tạfīyạ ba nẹ̄ P. escorting one a short way is not the same as being one's fellow-traveller. (2) *Kt.* pall (= bạrmūshị).

B. (marākī) *Kt.* = marārakī.

mạrạɓī *m.* (*f.* mạrạɓā) *pl.* maruɓạ (1) (*a*) calf (= kạryạ gwīwạ). (*b*) iɲ kā ga bạbbar sānīyā tsạkānim maruɓạ, girmantạ yā zubẹ anyone who associates with inferiors, lowers his dignity. (*c*) ɗam ∼ *m.* (*f.* 'yar mạrạɓā) *pl.* 'yam maruɓạ = 1*a*. (2) mạrạɓā tā hạrbẹ̄ shị, he has a new-born child (= rạ̄gō 2). (3) an yi manạ ɗauriɲ 'yam maruɓạ we've been given something to divide with another P. (= *Kt.* daɲgwạlī 2).

mạ̄rạɓū *Vd.* mārā.

marā-mạrạ̄ *pl.* beautiful (*re* eyes, writing) = gadā-gạdạ̄.

mạ̄rạ̄marai *Vd.* marmarā.

maramfakā *f.* (*pl.* mạrạmfạkai) place of refuge.

marạndā (1) *f.* small leaves of Egyptian privet (lallẹ) such as are gathered in the dry-season. (2) *Vd.* lallẹ 1*a.*iii, ii.

marantsā *f.* (*pl.* **mạrạntsai**) breast of camel (= **masaɓā** *q.v.*).

marạr = **marạs**.

mararaki A. (**mārārakī**) *m.* (*pl.* **mạrārạkai**) (1) native sieve = **rārīyā** 3*a* = *Kt.* **gwāgwā** (*cf.* **marēgī, matạŋkadī** 2, **minikī**). (2) = **marāgadī** 1–3.

B. (**marārạkī**) *m.* (*f.* **marārakīyā**) **mạrārạkā** (1) cadger (= **zāwọ** 3). (2) *cf.* **hạntsī** 3.

mạrārạŋ = **mụrārạŋ**.

mạrạrē = **mạrạrī** *m.* enjoyment *x* **tanā mạrạriŋ ganimmụ** she's overjoyed to see us.

mararraba A. (**mararrabā**) *f.* (*pl.* **mạrạrrạbai**) (1) cross-roads (= **marabā** 1*b*). (2) *Kt.* kuɗim ∼ money thrown down at cross-roads, so that an enemy may pick it up and, through magic, fall ill (*Vd.* **cịrak ƙayạ**). (3) an **tsarẹ amaryā sabọ dạ** kuɗim ∼ *Vd.* kuɗī 1*o.i*.

B. (**mạrạrrạbā**) *pl.* opposites (*x* black and white).

mararrabī *m.* = **mararrabā**.

mararrafī = **malallafī**.

mārạrrakī *Vd.* **mārā**.

maras A. (**marạs** = **marạr**) *m., f., sg.* (*pl.* **marạsā** = *Kt.* **marạssā**) (*this word must be followed by a noun, cf.* **marạshī**). (1) lacking in. (2) (-r, -s *usually become assimilated to the following consonant*) *x* **marạk kunyạ** = **marạs kunyạ** *m., f., sg.* shameless. **marạh haŋkạlī** = **marạr haŋkạlī** *m., f., sg.* senseless. **marạ' 'ạmfạnī** = **marạs ạmfạnī** *m., f., sg.* useless (*in the last example, we see that where the following word begins with a vowel, the glottal stop is inserted, then doubled*). (3) *Vd.* **marạshī**. (4) **rịgā marạr wuyạ** *Vd.* **rịgā** 1*n*. (5) ∼ **ạbụ** *Vd.* **ạbụ** 2*b*.

B. (**maras**) (1) **yā būshẹ** ∼ it's become as dry as a bone. (2) **yā gạsu** ∼ it is well roasted.

marạsā *Vd.* **marạs, marạshī**.

marashi A. (**marạshī**) *m.* (*f.* **marashīyā**) *pl.* **marạsā** (*this word can stand alone or in genitive, cf.* **marạs**) lacking in *x* (1) (*a*) **marạshiŋ haŋkạlī** *m., sg.* senseless. (*b*) **marashīyar haŋkạlī** *f., sg.* senseless. (*c*) **marạsā haŋkạlī** *pl.* senseless (1*a*, 1*b* = **marạh haŋkạlī**).

(2) **marạshin yau shī nẹ mại sāmụŋ gọ̄be** life has its ups and downs. (3) **kạ̄kam marạsā** *Vd.* **gịrēmạ**.

B. (**marāshī**) *Kt.* na ∼ *epithet of* **mụrūcī** (= **Karạ̄ɗūwạ**).

maratayi A. (**marạ̄tạyī**) *m.* (*f.* **marātayịyā**) *pl.* **marạ̄tạyā**. (1) one who ties up. (2) *Vd.* **makạshī, jịgọ** 2*b*. (3) unmounted traveller (= **dạ̄kārẹ** 1*b*).

B. (**marātayī**) *m.* (*pl.* **mạrạ̄tạyai**). (1) T. on which another T. is to be hung (*x* strap, peg). (2) hanging-place (*x* shoulder in reference to sword). (3) *Sk.* receptacle hanging from rafters (**rạ̄gayạ**).

marau = **maras**.

marạu dạ hakị *m.* (*sg., pl.*) (**bọ̄rī**-*language*) fan (= **mahūcī**).

marạunạcī *m.* (*f.* **maraunacīyā**) *pl.* **marạunạtā** wounded person.

maraurayī *m.* (*pl.* **mạrạurạyai**) *Kt.* = **marārakī**.

mạrawwạ *f.* (*Ar.* **murū'at**). (1) (*a*) respectfulness (= **mutuncị** 1*a*). (*b*) **bạ̄ shi dạ** ∼ he lacks respect for the feelings of others (= **mutuncị** 3*b*). (2) being of redoubtable or respect-inspiring mien (= **kwạrjinī**).

maraya A. (**mạrāyạ**) *m.* (*f.* **mạrainịyā**) *pl.* **mạrāyū**. (1) orphan. (2) **iŋ kā ji** ∼, **ragọ** " scratch an orphan and you will find a wastrel ". (3) **mạrāyạn zākị, faɗạ dạ mā̄sū īyạ̄yē** what an energetic orphan ! (4) **iŋ aŋ ƙi** ∼ **dạ rịgar būzū, wata rānā sǎi ạ gan shi dạ ta ƙarfẹ** don't despise a poor man for one day he may be richer than you ! (5) *Vd.* **marāyā** 3*b*, **zūcịyar** ∼, **aŋgarā**.

B. (**marāyā**) *f.* (*pl.* **mạrạyai**). (1) strap along jaw securing a horse's bit (= **kịlạsamadụ**). (2) any unwalled town (= **ạlkaryạ**). (3) (*a*) place of safety or well-being *x* **yā sạ̄mi** ∼ he has found a place of safety (*d.f.* **rạ̈i**). (*b*) ∼ **nẹ, bạ̄ mạrāyạ ba** he supports others, he is not one who needs *their* support. (*c*) any vital spot *x* **tā kāmạ shi ạ** ∼ she caught hold of him by the genitals (3*c* = **makasā**).

C. (**mārạyā**) *f.* (*pl.* **mārayŏyī**). (1) Western cob (*Adenota cob*). (2) *Zar.* **bāyam** ∼ type of thatching grass.

marāyancī *m.* the cocksureness of townspeople (*Vd.* marāyā 2) = birnancī, *cf.* zāmanancī.

mārayōyī *Vd.* mārayā.

marāyū *Vd.* marāya.

mārę (1) *Vb.* 1A slapped P. so hard that he fell over (*Vd.* mārā). (2) *Vb.* 3A recovered (from illness, disgrace, fright, indigence, etc.) = mārō = gyāzajē 3 = farfādō. (3) *cf.* mārō.

marēcē = maraicē.

marēdī *m.* (*pl.* marędai = *Sk.* marędinni). (1) lower grinding-stone (= dūtsan nika). (2) dam ⁓ *m.* (*pl.* 'yam ⁓) upper grinding-stone (= dā 5a).

maredi A. (marēdī) *m.* (*pl.* marędai) tool for trimming leather, etc. (*Vd.* rędā).
     B. (marędī) *m.* (*f.* marēdīyā) *pl.* marędā P. who trims leather.

marēgā *f.* (*pl.* marēgai) sifting-place (*Vd.* rēga). (2) *Kt.* (*a*) spy-hole. (*b*) any aperture through which one can see.

marēgī *m.* (*pl.* marēgai) sieve (*cf.* marārakī).

marēmarī *Vd.* marmarā.

marena A. (marēnā) = marainā.
     B. (marēnā) *f.* T. inspiring scorn *x* bā shi da ⁓ he has no vices.

marēnī *m.* (*f.* marēnīyā) *pl.* marēnā. (1) (*a*) despiser, scoffer. (*b*) marēnā kadam, barāwo nē ungrateful persons are like thieves (*d.f.* rēna). (2) P. looking after child on behalf of its mother (*Vd.* rēnō).

marēta = maraita.

marfa *used in* an yi masa ⁓ a trap has been laid for him.

marfī *Kt.* = murfī.

marfīya = marafīya.

margā *f.* the tree gama fada *q.v.*

margal *x* yā yi ⁓ it is excellent.

margayā *Vb.* 1C *Kt.* (1) tilted *as in* jirkicē 1a. (2) rolled T. along (= mirginā 1a).

margayē *Kt.* = mirginē.

margīshi *m.* (1) the cake kulī-kulī. (2) *Kt.* (*used abusively, or by women and children allusively* (alkunya)) vagina (= farjī).

margōwa *f.* small herb used by Filani for flavouring milk.

marhabā (1) = marabā. (2) ⁓ bika ashar

welcome. to you ! (3) marhabar darē *Vd.* gamzāki.

*marhabin = marhabun = marhabā *q.v.*

mari A. (mārī) (1) (*a*) (*used to form progressive of* mārā *in replacement of regular form*) *x* yana mārinsu he is slapping them. (*b*) *Vd.* gula. (2) (*a*) a slap *x* yā yi mini ⁓ he slapped me (*Vd.* gwaurō 1*h*). (*b*) harāra bā ⁓ ba cē hard words break no bones. (3) ki shā mārī *Vd.* tsārā 1*c*. (4) *Vd.* mārin *compounds.*
     B. (marī) *m.* (*pl.* marūrūwa). (1) (*a*) fetter, shackle. (*b*) gudu da ⁓ bā yā māganim bautā one must face realities. (2) (*a*) yana cikim ⁓ he has no clothing but a ragged gown and so is ashamed to appear in public (*Vd.* cūri 4). (*b*) marin tsummā = 2*a*. (*c*) *Vd.* marin tākamā, marin tūwō. (3) (*a*) ⁓ da gwaurō the single peg (gwaurō 2) and the farther pair of pegs used in wadarī. (*b*) yā kai ⁓ yā kai gwaurō he's been scurrying about. (4) *Vd.* daukar marī. (5) *Vd.* marin *compounds.*
     C. (mārī) *m.* (*sg., pl.*) type of fish (= dan lakōkō = gammo 4 = rambōshī).

mari bākinka *Kt.* = māra bākinka.

mari ka tāshi = māri ki tāshi *m.* (1) cadging food from village to village. (2) quick act of fornication without the usual appurtenances (*x* without mat, in the open, etc.).

mariki A. (marikī) *m.* (*f.* marikīyā) *pl.* marikā one who holds, supports P., etc. (*Vd.* rike).
     B. (marikī) *m.* (*pl.* marikai) handle.

marikicī *m.* (*f.* marikicīyā) *pl.* marikitā. (1) (*a*) intriguer. (*b*) *his epithet is* A gamu a Lāhira tā fi dubū. (2) peevish (*re* child).

marīli *m.* (*f.* marīlīyā) *pl.* marīlai (*Ar.* marīz) ill.

marī-marī *Sk.* = mirī-mirī.

marina A. (marinā) *f.* (*pl.* marinai) (1) dyeing-place. (2) *cf.* tsāmīyā 4.
     B. (marinā) *Vd.* marinī.

marin baka (marim baka) *m.* empty promises.

marin dawa *used in* Gīwā ⁓ *epithet of* (1) elephant, (2) any Wambai.

marin fizgau (marim fizgau) *m.* twisting the sense of a person's words.

mariŋ gōnā *Kt. m.* the weed ƙudujī *q.v.*

marinī *m.* (*f.* mariniyā) *pl.* marinā. (1) dyer. (2) hannum ∼ *Vd.* hannun 6.

mariŋ kūrā *Kt. m.* the three-ply thread called hanjiŋ ƙudā.

mariŋ kurkunū *m.* guinea-worm in both legs.

mariŋ kūsu *Kt. m.* = mariŋ kūrā.

marin tāƙamā *m.* an ɗaura masa ∼ = an ɗaura masa marī it (horse) has been taught the gait tāƙamā of the type where horse is continually reined in and then let out.

marin tsummā *Vd.* marī 2*b.*

marin tūwō *m.* (1) small slave-child. (2) idle P. always greedy for the food of others (*epithet is* Gīwā, mariŋka tūwō).

mariŋ wuya *m.* the type of imprisonment called ƙuƙumī *q.v.*

mārīri *m.* (*pl.* mārīrai) White Oryx (= warwājī).

Māris *m.* month of March.

Mārīsūwā *f.* (1) the epidemic dundū 4. (2) obsolete type of girls' song. (3) type of obsolete native cloth.

mārīyā *f.* horse's throwing back head and hitting rider.

marjawo *Kt. m.* the eczema majau *q.v.*

marka A. (markā) (1) (*cerebral* " r ", Mod. Gram. 5) a sarauta at Daura. (2) (*rolled* " r ", Mod. Gram. 5). (*a*) (i) period from middle to end of wet season (dāmunā). (ii) *its epithet is* Markā, hana aiki. (*b*) wet day *x* yau an yi ∼ it's been wet to-day. (*c*) abundance *x* yanā markar sāmu he's making a fine income. bāƙī sunā markar zūwa gidansa he receives many visitors.

B. (Marka) *name for* girl born during markā 2*a.*

marƙabū *m.* intrigue.

markaɗā *Vb.* 1C. (1) twisted T. round on its base (= jūya). (2) ground the cereal dāwa slowly with water to get fine flour (*this process is common west of Kano, to make* furā *from* dāwa *when no* gērō *is available; the method of making* ƙulīƙulī *is similar*). (3) = markaɗē 2.

markaɗe A. (markaɗē) *Vb.* 1C. (1) ground completely *on method of* markaɗā 2.

(2) shānū suŋ markaɗe wuriŋ cows have dropped manure and enriched the soil of that place.

B. (markaɗē) *used in* furar ∼ *f.* furā made *as in* markaɗā 2.

marƙayā = maƙalā.

marƙayē = maƙe.

markē *m.* (1) Chew-stick tree (*Anogneissus leiocarpus*). (2) (*a*) wiry P. or horse. (*b*) *Vd.* maza-maza 2. (3) yā ɗaukō ∼ he borrowed *as in* hansakō *q.v.*

markū = markuf *used in* wuffi ∼ *m.* slippers (*cf.* wuffi).

marmace *Vb.* 3B *intensive of* mutu died (= murmutu).

marmaɗā = barbaɗā.

marmadī = marmadī *m.* " giving the glad eye " (= farī).

mar-mar = mar-mar *x* yanā ∼ da ido he's blinking, winking (*also applied to* fluttering of heart, lips, etc., palpitation, throbbing).

marmarā *f.* (*pl.* marāmarai = *Kt.* marēmarī). (1) laterite (= kawwa 1). (2) *Vd.* wākē 5*b.*

marmarcē *Vd.* marmarta.

marmarī *m.* (1) desire *x* yanā marmarin sarauta he's eager to obtain an official position. (2) abim ∼ any luxury, delicacy. (3) gōma ta ∼ the first 10 days of the month Ramalan (*Vd.* gōma 2). (4) ∼ daga nēsa *Vd.* gūga 7.

marmarō *Sk. m.* spring gushing out of rock (= idan rūwā).

marmartō *Vb.* 1E = marmarta 2 (*n.o.* marmarci, *p.o.* marmarcē) longed to get.

marmartū *m.* act of trembling.

marmarwā *f.* act of trembling.

marmasā *Vb.* 1C = marmasa *Vb.* 2 (*n.o.* marmashi, *p.o.* marmashē) = murtsuka 1*a.*

marmashe A. (marmashē) *Vd.* marmasa.

B. (marmashē) *Vb.* 1C = murtsuƙā.

marmashī *m.* = ɓarɓashi.

marmasō *used in* ta ∼ *f.* roasted groundnuts.

marmātà *f.* (*d.f.* mazā mātā) supposedly sexually-impotent man with falsetto voice and lack of beard (= mātā mazā).

marmatsiŋ kimbā *m.* pinching playfellow's wrist.

marmazā (*d.f.* maza-maza) very quickly (= maza-maza).

mārō *Vb.* 3A (1) recalled forgotten detail.
(2) = mārę 2.

mạrŏ́dŏ́dọ *m.* (1) (*a*) eagerness *x* yanā̀ ~
tạ zō he's eager for her to arrive. (*b*)
Na ~ sarkin dōki what an over-eager
person ! (2) nā shā ~ I felt a sharp
pain (*cf.* mạrŏ́gadị̀).

mạrŏ́gadị̀ (1) *m.* = mạrŏ́dŏ́dọ. (2) (*a*)
what a sharp pain ! (*b*) what tasty
meat, tasty gravy !

marŏ̄k̠̄ī *m.* (*f.* marŏ̄k̠̄īyā) *pl.* marŏ̄k̠̄ā. (1)
requester, pleader. (2) (= masạrcī *q.v.*)
i.e. professional beggar *of the type
described eight lines below* (*the* Bamba-
d̠āwā *do not blow* (būsạ) *horns nor drum*
(kid̠ạ), *but they eulogize in Filani, while
the* mak̠ḕram bā̀kī = *Kt.* bakạ 6*b.*i (*Vd.*
k̠īrạ 1*b*) *do so in Hausa. These are both
official positions* (sạrautạ). *The* 'yan
durbai *are mostly Filani ex-slaves and
neither blow horns nor drum. The*
marŏ̄k̠ā, *on the other hand, blow and
drum and are headed by the* sạrautạ-
holder *the blower* Sarkim būsạ *with the*
sạrautạ-*holder* Gạlā̀dīmạm būsạ *under
him, these being drummed to by* (*a*)
Sarkiɲ kid̠ạ = Sarkim makạd̠ā (*who is
in charge of* gạŋgā *and* k̠ạhō *and whose
work is called* sā̀rā). (*b*) Sarkiɲ kạlaŋgū.
(*c*) Sarkin jaujē. (*d*) Sarkiɲ kŏ̄tsō (*a–d
being* sạrautạ). *When any of the above*
sạrautạ-*holders go out eulogizing persons,
this is called* rā̀rakạ). *Vd.* kwạndo,
mạ'abbạ, mạganạ 2*d*, mālạmī 1*d*,
agạlandạ, ạlmājirī 2, mawā̀k̠ī, gulạ 3.
(3) marŏ̄kin rūwā Malochile Kingfisher
(*Corythornis cristata*).   (4) kạram
marŏ̄k̠ā *Vd.* karen 5.

mārōrī *Vd.* mārā.

marŏ̄wạcī *m.* (*f.* marŏ̄wạcīyā) *pl.* marŏ̄-
wạtā. (1) miser, stingy P. (*for epithet
Vd.* fạŋkō 4*a*). (2) *epithet is* (*a*) k̠wạ-
dạŋgwafīyọ = māję 2. (*b*) *Vd.* gandū
2*g.* (3) kạ̄kam marŏ̄wạtā *Vd.* zumbụli.

*marrạrā *Vb.* 1C *Ar.* did repeatedly.

marsạ *m.* (1) the largest kolas (*cf.* mịnū,
marsŏshī). (2) hefty youths.

marshę *Vb.* 3A *Kt.* loiterčd.

Mạrsīlīya *f.* Marseilles.

ma·sŏshī *pl.* = marsạ 1.

martabạ *Ar. f.* (*pl.* martabŏbī) high rank.

martạnī *used in* yā̀ mai masạ dạ ~ on

being successful, he taunted them with
having prophesied failure for him.

māru *Vb.* 3B = mārō 1.

marūbạcī *m.* (*f.* marūbacīyā) *pl.* marūbạtā
boaster, overweening P. (*Vd.* rūbạ).

marụbūcī *m.* (*f.* marubūcīyā) *pl.* marụ-
būtā. (1) good writer. (2) = mahaddạcī
1. (3) *East Hausa* scribe (= mālạmī).

marūdī *m.* (*f.* marūdīyā) *pl.* marū̠dā
deceiver, trickster.

marufā *f.* (*pl.* mạrụfai). (1) place of concealment.   (2) Darē marufar ạsīrī
Night, concealer of secrets ! (*Vd.*
darē 1*a.*ii). (3) mạtar mụtụm marufar
ạsīrinsạ a man's wife is the repository
of his secrets.

marufī = murfī.

mạ̄ruhū *m.* (1) corn-stalk peg for securing
threads while weaving. (2) the bottle
kŏ̄rīyọ *q.v.* (3) (*a*) short stick inserted to
tighten camel's load. (*b*) rā̀kumī bā
yā̀ kūkā doɲ kāyā mại yawạ, s̀ài dom ~
it's the last straw that breaks the
camel's back.

maruk̠ạ *Vd.* mạrak̠ī.

mạ̄rūrụ *m.* boil on buttocks or thigh (*cf.*
jambad̠ę, hạntukụryạ, k̠urjī).

marūrūwạ *Vd.* mạrī.

Marūsa *Kt. f.* a Katsina sạrautạ.

marwa A. (mạrwā) *f.* (1) tangling of
several well-ropes let down simultaneously by different persons into
deep well (tinyạ). (2) bickering.
     B. (Marwạ) *f. Vd.* Sạfā.

mạrwāshị *m.* (*pl.* mạrwāsai) ramrod
(= marāgadī 2).

Maryādī = Marādī.

Maryamạ = Maryamụ = Mạryamụ
(*Hebrew-Ar.*). (1) Mary, Miriam (= Mạiramụ).   (2) azzịkim ~ prosperity
accompanied by niggardliness.

marzạyē *Vb.* 1C = mārę 1.

mas A. (mas) on, horse ! on, donkey !
(= has).
     B. (mạs) to him = masạ *q.v.*

masa A. (masạ) to him.
     B. (māsạ) *f.* (*pl.* māsŏshī). (1) (*a*)
the cake wạinā̀ *q.v.* (= mạshē). (*b*)
Vd. jūyị 4 ; lālạ̄cē 2. (2) yanā̀ kạmam
~ it finds a ready sale (= ganin rānā),
cf. jī 4*d.*iii, dạddawā 4, d̠ịmī 5, gwainŏ̄.
(3) ā̀ ci ~ dạgạ tsạkạ ? putting the cart

before the horse. (4) ～ **wąje** *f.* type of short-sleeved gown.

masaba A. (**masą̄bā**) *f.* (*pl.* **mąsąbai**) (*Ar.* mirzabba) blacksmith's hammer (*cf.* maskō).

B. (**masābā**) *f.* (*pl.* **mąsą̄bai**) place to which one is accustomed.

masaɓā *f.* (1) masaɓā = masaɓar **lāyą** (*d.f.* saɓą 1*b*.ii) camel's breast (*because if on rising, it hits its chest with its knee, this is a sign that the load is not too heavy*) = marantsā. (2) yā cī har yā kai masaɓar **gą̄tarī** he ate to repletion (= gą̄tarī 3).

masąbaucī *m.* (*f.* masabaucīyā) *pl.* **masąbąutā** quarrelsome.

masąbbącī *Kt.* = masąbąucī.

masaɓī *m.* (1) steel for flint and tinder (= ƙyąstū), (*cf.* ƙąŋƙarą 1*a*). (2) *Kt.* the spinning-bow **bąkā 10** *q.v.*

masabkī = masaukī.

mąsāfahą = mąsāfihą *Ar.* *f.* shaking hands with P.

masąfąrcī *m.* (*f.* masafarcīyā) *pl.* **masą̨fą̄rtā** (*Ar.* safar "journey") itinerant trader (= farkē).

masafartā *f.* (*pl.* **mąsąfą̄rtai**) trading-area of a **masąfą̄rcī**.

mąsągā *f.* Bida glass-bangles and beads.

masai *m.* (*sg., pl.*). (1) cesspit (*d.f.* **sāyę**) = sargā. (2) *Vd.* **rījįyā** 1*h*.

masakā *f.* (*pl.* **mąsąkai**). (1) place for putting T. (*d.f.* saką). (2) *Kt.* grazing-place (*d.f.* **sąkā**).

masāƙā *f.* (*pl.* **mąsą̄ƙai**) weaving-place.

masąkē *Vd.* maskō.

masakī *m.* (*pl.* masuką = mąsąkai = *Sk.* masukką) (*Ar.* masƙāt). (1) very large calabash (*cf.* madāmī). (2) wārįm ～ bą̄ ka dą ąbōkim burmį Thou peerless one ! (3) ta ～*f.* (*a*) doing dyeing at home in calabashes (*b*) swimming by resting oneself on a calabash. (4) *Vd.* cįką ～ ; nitsǫ 3.

masą̄ƙī *m.* (*f.* masā̄ƙīyā) *pl.* **mąsą̄ƙā** weaver.

mąs'alą = mątsalą.

mąsąląfō *m.* (1) a type of cheap, white, patterned European cotton fabric. (2) the cap gąrūrą *q.v.*

mąsalahą = mąsąlahą *Ar.* *f.* (1) reconciliation *x* **sun yi** ～ they have become

reconciled. (2) yā yi **minį** ～ he gave me good advice.

mąsąląhō = mąsąląfō.

masaląŋ *Ar.* (1) for example. (2) (*introducing change of mind*) *x* ～ **ną̄** yī dą kąina no, on second thoughts, I'll do it myself. yāką ～ ję̄ ka, ną̄ tąfi dą kąina *you* come ! no, I will go *myself*. bą̄ ni sulę gōmą ～ gōmą shą̄ bīyar give me ten shillings, or rather fifteen ! (3) *cf.* mįsālį, mįsālįŋ.

mąsąlce-mąsąlcē *Vd.* mįsālį.

masallaci A. (**masallācī**) *m.* (*pl.* **mąsąllątai**) (*d.f. Ar.* salāt " prayer ", *Hausa* sallą). (1) (*a*) mosque. (*b*) masallācin Jumma'ą̄ Friday congregational mosque (= mąjāmi'ą̄). (2) sun saukō dągą ～ the Friday-service at the mosque is over. (3) *cf.* masąllą̄cī. (4) ɓēram ～ *Vd.* ɓērā 2.

B. (**masąllą̄cī**) *m.* (*f.* masallācīyā) *pl.* masąllą̄tā P. who prays (*cf.* masallācī).

masallātā *f.* = masallācī.

mas'alōlī *Vd.* mątsalą.

masąltā = misįltā.

mąsammąŋ = mųsammąŋ.

masąnī *m.* (*f.* masanīyā) *pl.* masąnā. (1) P. who knows. (2) knowledgeable P. (3) learned P. (4) expert P.

masaŋkī *East Hausa* = masaukī.

Masąr *f.* (*Hebrew* Mitsrāyim " The Two Egypts ", *Ar.* masr " province "). (1) Egypt. (2) Cairo (*Ar.* Masru'l qāhira). (3) kudīm ～ *m.* small cowries. (4) ɓēram ～ *Vd.* ɓērā 5.

masąrā *f.* (*d.f.* Masąr). (1) (*a*) masąrā = dāwąr ～ maize. (*b*) *Vd.* gēmų 1*e*, burūdę, gōyō 1*c*, kųtūtų 3. (3) the bead mąi birįm.

masąraucī *m.* (*pl.* masąrąutā). (1) P. occupying official position (sąrautą) = bąsarākę *q.v.* (2) masąraucīyā = bąsarākę 3.

masarautā *f.* (*pl.* mąsąrąutai) place of government, area of jurisdiction.

Masarāwā *Vd.* Bąmasąrī.

masarci A. (**masąrcī**) *m.* (*f.* masarcīyā) *pl.* **masą̄rtā** professional beggar, whether marǭƙī or dąŋ ƙirą (*Vd.* marǭƙī).

B. (**masarcī**) *m.* (*pl.* mąsąrtai). (1) comb (*Vd.* sarcę) = mashācī. (2) the material mąharramą.

---

masārī *m.* (*pl.* maṣārai). (1) pick-axe (*Vd.* sārā) = digā. (2) axe (= gātarī). (3) the small hatchet kurādā *q.v.*

masārī-maṣārī (*only used in boys' songs*) the mantis ḳōḳi-ḳōḳi.

maṣarūfi (*Ar.* " expended ") *used in* ạbim ∼ ingredients for soup (*cf.* cē-fạnē).

maṣassabī *m.* (*pl.* maṣassạbai) the harvesting tool magirbī.

masassaḳa A. (masassaḳā) *f.* (*pl.* maṣạssạḳai). (1) carpenters' shop. (2) chippable place in timber.

B. (masassaḳā) *Vd.* masassaḳī.

masassaḳī A. (masassaḳī) *m.* (*pl.* masassaḳā). (1) carpenter. (2) masassaḳim budurci yā hau tạ her (girl's) unattractive appearance has improved (= maḳērī 7).

B. (masassaḳī) *m.* (*pl.* maṣassaḳai) adze (= gizāgō).

maṣassarā *Sk.* = maṣhasshará.

masạssaucī *m.* (*f.* masassauciyā) *pl.* masạssautā wastrel, slacker, feckless P.

masau A. (māsau) *m.* (*sg.*, *pl.*). (1) = mahaucī. (2) *Vd.* jūyi 3.

B. (maṣau) = faufau.

masaukī *m.* (*pl.* maṣaukai) lodging-place.

masạusaucī *Kt.* = masạssaucī.

masaya A. (masayā) *f.* (*pl.* maṣayai) buying-place (*d.f.* sayā).

B. (masāyā) *f.* (*pl.* maṣāyai). (1) place for putting T. (*d.f.* sā). (2) kaŋ kạrē bā̱ ka dạ masāyar tāgīyạ what a contentious person.

C. (masayā) *Vd.* masayī.

masayi A. (masayi) *m.* (*f.* masayiyā) *pl.* masayā buyer (*d.f.* sayā).

B. (masayī) *Zar.* = masai.

masgayā = mazgayā.

maṣhā̱ *m.*, *f.*, *sg.*, *pl.* (*must be followed by noun*, *cf.* maṣhāyī) drinker of, *used in* (1) ∼ ḳalā-ḳalā P. in easy circumstances, because he has a patron (*cf.* ḳalā-ḳalā). (2) ∼ lalai = 1 (*cf.* lalai 1*b*). (3) ∼ rūwā (*a*) *m.*, *f.*, *sg.*, *pl.* quickly growing lad (= magịrmī), *cf.* rūwā A.2. (*b*) *m.* rainbow (= baḳā 8*a*). (*c*) *Vd.* dilā, cịlē. (4) ∼ mīyạ *Kt.* beggar (*Vd.* shā 1*g*).

mā shā'ạ *x* bā sā̱ yịŋ kōmē sǎi mā shā'ạ

---

they spend their time in pleasures (*cf.* mā̱ shā Ạllāhu ; Ạllāhu 2).

mā̱ shā Ạllāhu *Ar.* bravo ! (= yạwwā), *cf.* mā sha'ā̱.

mashācī *m.* (*pl.* maṣhātai) *Kt.* comb (*d.f.* shātā) = matsēfī = masarcī.

mashāfī *m.* (*pl.* maṣhāfai). (1) duster (*d.f.* shāfę). (2) handkerchief (= ạdīko 1).

maṣhagūli *m.* (*f.* maṣhagūliyā) *pl.* maṣhagūlai (*Ar.* " distracted from doing T."). (1) forgetful (= shạgalallē). (2) absent-minded.

mashahūranci *m.* being well-known, famous.

maṣhahūri *m.* (*f.* maṣhahūrīyā) *pl.* maṣhahūrai *Ar.* well-known, famous. ∼ nē gạ īyạ yịnsạ he is well-known as being able to do it.

mashaidī *m.* (*f.* mashaidīyā) *pl.* mashaidā witness (= shaidạ).

mashaijī = mashaidī.

mā̱shāḳo *m.* (1) bronchitis (*d.f.* shāḳę). (2) the trap karabkīyā 2*b* *q.v.*

mā̱shallērā *East Hausa* *f.* the bird tsạttsēwạ.

mashancīyā *Vd.* dilā.

mashanyā *f.* (*pl.* maṣhanyai) rock (pā) whereon are dried clothing, okro, corn, pepper, etc. (*d.f.* shạnyē).

mā̱sharā̱rē *m.* = mā̱sharērā *f.* the bird tsạttsēwạ *q.v.*

mashārī *m.* (*pl.* maṣhārai) (1) rake. (2) type of wooden farm-broom (= mayā-yī). (3) mashārin rūwā windscreen-wiper.

mashārīyā *f.* *x* ∼ tā zō the first flood water has arrived (= mā̱gūwạ = kwāzārī 1).

maṣhar-maṣhar *x* jịkīna ∼ yakē̱ I feel out of sorts (= dạmạ-dạmạ).

maṣhā̱ rūwā *Vd.* maṣhā̱ 3.

mā̱shāshā (1) *adv.* *x* gōnā cē̱ ∼ it is a huge farm. (2) *adj.* big, thronged *x* mā̱shāshaŋ garī a large town. mā̱shāshan yāḳi a mighty war. mā̱shāshar gōnā a huge farm. (3) *epithet of any* great chief.

maṣhā̱shā̱cī *m.* (*f.* maṣhāshācīyā) *pl.* maṣhā̱shā̱tā huge.

maṣhasshará *f.* (*pl.* maṣhassharū). (1) (*a*) feverishness (= zạzzạḃī). (*b*) mạs-

hassharā = ∼ mai fitā = ∼ mai rūwā
smallpox (= yāyī 3 = agānā = rānī
5). (c) Vd. rūwā A.10b. (d) ūwar ∼ f.
large smallpox-pustules. (2) farar ∼
anæmia (= farā). (3) watā yā yi ∼
the moon is in eclipse (cf. zazzafī 2) =
kusūfi q.v.

mashātai Vd. mashācī.

mashau-mashau Kt. = mashar-mashar.

mashāwarcī m. (f. mashāwarcīyā) pl.
mashāwartā adviser, consultant,
counsellor.

mashawarta A. (mashāwartā) Vd. mashāwarcī.

B. (mashāwartā) f. (pl. mashā-
wartai). (1) council-chamber. (2)
conference.

mashaya A. (mashāyā) f. (pl. mashāyai).
(1) drinking-place. (2) watering-place
for animals. (3) watering-trough. (4)
place of resort x mashāyarsu dayā
they both frequent the same school,
workplace, woman, etc.

B. (mashāyā) Vd. mashāyī.

mashāyai Vd. mashāyā, mashāyī.

mashayi A. (mashāyī) m. (f. mashāyīyā)
pl. mashāyā (can stand alone or be
followed by noun or stand in genitive,
cf. mashā). (1) drinker x mashāyin
tāba a smoker of tobacco. (2) drinker
of alcohol (contrary to Muslim precept).
(3) habitual drunkard.

B. (mashāyī) m. (pl. mashāyai). (1)
the hollow-branched shrub Cleroden-
dron capitatum (branches used for making
pipe-stems). (2) cigarette-holder
(= hōlā).

māshē = māsa 1a.

masheka A. (mashēkā) f. (pl. mashēkai)
winnowing-floor.

B. (mashēkā) Vd. mashēkī.

mashēkarī m. (pl. mashēkarai) wet-
season pasturage (= tāshi 2b = galbi),
cf. cin rānī.

mashēkī m. (f. mashēkīyā) pl. mashēka.
(1) winnower. (2) Vd. dūbam mashēkā,
kaikayī 3b.

mashēru Vd. dungū 8.

mashi A. (māshi) m. (pl. māsū = māsū-
suka). (1) (a) (i) spear. (ii) yā yā da ∼
Vd. yā da 3d. (iii) sun kafa māsunsu a
Kano they made war on Kano (b)

yā shā inūwar māsū he's a great
warrior. (c) mai da ∼ ran gābā, tsōrō
nē don't be in too much of a hurry to
retaliate, your time will come ! (d)
tsinim ∼ Vd. tsinī 2. (e) sūkam ∼
Vd. daurarrīyar magana. (f) Vd. bā
ni māsū. (2) mai ∼ yā harbi shānummu
our cattle have been attacked by blackquarter disease (harbin dawa =
maharbī) attributed to the spirit
Gajērē mai baka. (3) māsun zagāgē a
sarauta the holder of which is responsible for the two spears which, wrapped
in red and green material, form part of
the insignia of the Emir of Kano. (4)
shooting-star. (5) yā yi ∼ he stood
upright on his hands. (6) māsun
kadangarū the shrub kaimin kadangarē. (7) bīkwam māshi Vd. bīko 8.

B. (mashi) Sk. to him (= masa).

C. (mashī) = mishī.

mashīdī m. (pl. mashīdai) Sk. = masaukī.

mashigī m. (pl. mashigai). (1) ford
(= mahayī = maficī = Sk. matuzgī).
(2) kada a rigā mu ∼ let us not be
forestalled !

mashimfidi A. (mashimfidī) m. (pl.
mashimfidai) (1) numnah (Vd. sūka 7).
(2) Vd. jākin 6.

B. (mashimfidī) m. (pl. mashimfidā)
pedlar (= dan kōli), Vd. shimfida 2.

māshin m. (sg., pl.) Eng. machine.

māshingau m. type of children's game.

māshinjirī Kt. m. the knife kudundurā q.v.

māshirārē Zar. the bird tsattsēwa.

mashirīrīcī m. (f. mashirīrīcīyā) pl.
mashirīrītā P. who makes empty
promises.

mashīyyī = mishī.

*māsī m. (1) vowel-points in Arabic
script (= wasalī). (2) Vd. tafī da ∼.

masība = masīfa.

masīdi Nor. m. (pl. masīdai) (Ar. masjidi)
mosque (= masallācī).

masīfa f. (Ar. musība) (1) misfortune. (2)
troublesomeness x yāran nan da ∼
yakē this little lad is fretful. Audu ∼
garēshi Audu is quarrelsome. hatsī
yanā da ∼ corn is expensive, scarce.
(3) x tanā da masīfar kyau she's extra-
ordinarily handsome (cf. shaitsan 1b,
iblis 2b.

masihircī *m.* (*f.* masihircīyā) *pl.* masihirtā (*Ar.* sāhir) sorcerer, magician, sooth-sayer.

masillā = basillā.

māsinja = mātinja.

*maskana *f.* (*Ar.* " poverty ") a minute gift.

maskī *m.* greasiness = maiko *q.v.*

maskin A. (maskiŋ) why, that's just what I wanted !

B. (maskiŋ) = maskīni.

maskīni *m.* (*f.* maskīnīyā) *pl.* maskīnai *Ar.* destitute.

maskō *m.* (*pl.* masākē) large, blacksmith's hammer (= *Kt.* sallēta) *cf.* masābā.

masō *m.*, *f.*, *sg.*, *pl.* (*d.f.* sō) (*must be followed by another word, cf.* masōyī) one who likes, loves, *used in* (1) ~ dan tsuntsū shī ya kam bī shi da jīfa no effort is too much for the really eager P. (2) sam ~ wani kōshiŋ wahala affection is wasted on P. who doesn't like you. (2A) ~ fada *Vd.* habaicī. (3) ~ bīyū, daya nē nāsa don't put all your eggs into one basket ! (4) (*used to denote the intermediate points of the compass*) *x* arēwā ~ gabas north-east. kudu ~ yammā south-west (= tasō).

masōkī *m.* (*f.* masōkīyā) *pl.* masōkā. (1) one who stabs, pricks. (2) masōkīyā *f.* spasm in kwībā.

masomī A. (masōmī) *m.* (*pl.* masōmai). (1) (*a*) beginning. (*b*) masōmiŋ hasāra *Vd.* tāfī 1*f.*i. (*c*) masōmim fada *Vd.* dakūwa 2. (2) place of origin.

B. (masōmī) *m.* (*f.* masōmīyā) *pl.* masōmā. (1) one who begins. (2) novice.

māsōrī *m.* snoring (= minshārī).

masōrō *m.* black pepper (*for food and cough-cure*).

masoshi A. (māsōshī) *Vd.* māsa.

B. (masōshī) *m.* (*pl.* masōsai) big pin with which women scratch their heads (= tsiŋkē 2 = *Kt.* ciŋkē 3).

masōyī *m.* (*f.* masōyīyā) *pl.* masōyā = masōwā (*stands alone or is followed by a noun or stands in genitive, cf.* masō). (1) one who likes or loves *x* masōyin dāwa one who likes dāwa. masōyiŋ Kande one in love with Kande. (2) masōyiŋ kīfī bā na kwādō ba nē =

masōyin dam fāri bā na auta ba nē tastes differ. (3) masōyiŋka bā yā ganiŋ aibuŋka everyone is perfect in the eyes of one who loves him. (4) masōyiŋ wani *Vd.* sō 1*d.*

mastūrī *m.* (*f.* mastūrīyā) *pl.* mastūrai *Ar.* well-dressed.

masu A. (masu) *Sk.* to them = musu *q.v.*

B. (māsū) *Vd.* māshi.

C. (māsū) *Vd.* mai.

masudī *m.* (*f.* masudīyā) *pl.* masudā. (1) P. who scrapes out a pot to eat the scrapings. (2) masudiŋ kwaryā bai ki ta dāme ba P. wanting a T. has no scruples.

masufurcī *m.* (*f.* masufurcīyā) *pl.* masufurtā (*d.f.* suhurī). (1) hirer, tenant. (2) hirer-out.

masuka *Vd.* masakī.

masukwani A. (masukwānī) *m.* = masukwānā *f.* (*pl.* masukwānai) galloping-place, hippodrome, race-course.

B. (masukwānī) *m.* (*f.* masukwānīyā) *pl.* masukwānā. (1) swift horse. (2) P. travelling fast, speedy P.

masulālī *Kt.* *m.* the pot madambacī *q.v.*

masūnā *Zar.* *f.* gonorrhoea (= sanyī 12*b* = sūnā 9 = sai A.1. 1*b*).

masuncī *m.* (*pl.* masuntā). (1) fisherman (*d.f.* sū). (2) bāwam ~ *Vd.* fatsā 1*b.*

masunta A. (masuntā) *Vd.* masuncī.

B. (masuntā) *f.* (*pl.* masuntai) fishing-ground (*d.f.* sū).

masussukā *f.* (*pl.* masussukai). (1) threshing-floor. (2) barar ~ cadger's finding before him the very T. he intended cadging (*Vd.* bara A.1).

masussuki A. (masussukī) *m.* = masus-sukā.

B. (masussukī) *m.* (*f.* masussukīyā) *pl.* masussukā thresher.

māsusuka *Vd.* māshi.

mata A. (mātā) (mātā) *Vd.* mace.

B. (mata) (1) to her. (2) *Vb.* 1A (*re weaving, sewing, etc.*) *x* sai ki rika ~ hannū cikiŋ kadiŋki = ki rika matāwā do your spinning, etc., skilfully ! (3) *Vb.* 3A *used in* bari rānā ta ~ kadaŋ wait till the sun's a bit cooler !

matabbaci A. (matabbacī) *m.* (*f.* matab-bacīyā) *pl.* matabbatā. (1) permanent. (2) reliable (*re news, etc.*).

B. (matabbacī) *m*. *x* dūnīyạ bạ ∼ ba nẹ this world is not one's permanent place of abode.

matabbata A. (matạbbạtā) *Vd*. matạbbạcī.

B. (matabbatā) *f*. = matabbacī.

mataɓī *m*. chalk got from lime or burned bone (= ạllī), *cf*. kōsạ.

mạ̄tạ̄būbū *m*. great trouble *x* yanạ̄ ∼ dạ cīwạn cikị he's suffering from severe stomach-ache. anạ̄ ta ∼ dạ shī he's giving a lot of trouble.

mạtaccē *m*. (*f*. mạtaccīyā) *pl*. mạtạttū (*d.f*. mutụ). (1) dead. (2) *Vd*. askā 8.

matạfī *m*. (*f*. matafīyā) *pl*. matạfā *Kt*. ⇌ matạfīyī.

matạfīyī *m*. (*f*. matafīyịyā) *pl*. matạfīyā traveller, walker.

matạhī *Kt*. = matạfī.

mạtā'ī *Ar*. *used in* ∼ mạ'ī my property is in my possession.

mạ̄taikū *Vd*. mạcẹ̄.

mataimaka A. (matạimạkā) *Vd*. matạimạkī.

B. (mataimakā) *f*. (*pl*. mạtạimạkai). (1) means of helping. (2) place of helping.

matạimạkī *m*. (*f*. mataimakīyā) *pl*. matạimạkā. (1) helper. (2) matạimạkīna gạ kashẹ su my helper in killing them.

matạ̄kạ *m*., *f*. (*sg*., *pl*.) (1) P. who treads on. (2) ∼ yārọ rụmā *Vd*. bạsarākẹ.

matạƙaicī *m*. (*f*. matạƙaicīyā) *pl*. matạƙaitā. (1) restricted *x* wurī nẹ̄ ∼ the place is of limited area. lōkạcī ∼ short space of time. wōkạcimmụ ∼ nẹ̄ our time is limited. (2) reduced in scale (map, photo, etc.) *x* ƙasar Kanọ matạƙaicịyā a map of Kano (= mạp).

matākalā = matākarā *f*. (*pl*. mạtạ̄kạlai, etc.) flight of steps, stairs (= matākī = safạragō).

mạtạ̄kashī = bạtạ̄kashī.

matākī *m*. (*pl*. mạtạ̄kai). (1) (*a*) = matākalā. (*b*) matākim bēnē stairs leading to upper storey. (*c*) dūnīyạ matākim bēnē there's always someone below and someone above you. (2) (*a*) sole of foot. (*b*) *Sk*. ox-feet on sale. (3) leather mat on which a woman spinning, revolves the spindle (mazarī) inside the taskirā *q.v*.

matạlaucī *m*. (*f*. matalaucịyā) *pl*. matạlautā poor.

matamācī *m*. (*pl*. mạtạmạ̄tai) iron-stratum (*d.f*. tamā).

mạ̄tạ̄ mazā = mạrmātạ.

matambaya A. (matạmbạyā) *Vd*. matạmbạyī.

B. (matambayā) *f*. (*pl*. mạtạmbạyai) *x* yā yi ∼ he asked a question.

matạmbạyī *m*. (*f*. matambayịyā) *pl*. matạmbạyā. (1) inquirer, asker, questioner. (2) ∼ bā yạ̄ ɓatạ it is better to ask for elucidation than to make a mistake.

matạmkạcī *m*. (*f*. matamkacịyā) *pl*. matạmkạtā. (1) P. of keen desires. (2) *Kt*. miserly P.

matamnī *Kt*. = mataunī.

matan fada (mātam fādạ) *Kt*. *pl*. (1) woman's cloth made into corn-bag by rolling up and tying the ends (= jạkā 8). (2) *Vd*. mạ̄tar fādạ.

*matanī *Ar*. *m*. text.

mạtaŋkadī = mataŋkadī *m*. (*pl*. mạtạŋkạɗai). (1) large, round tray of kabạ for separating coarse-flour (tsạkī) from fine flour. (2) European sieve (*cf*. marārakī).

mātan lifidạ *used in* ạbin nạŋ yā ci ∼ this has become a serious matter (= bụŋƙāsạ).

matara A. (matārā) *f*. (*pl*. mạtạ̄rai). (1) collecting-place. (2) rendezvous. (3) emporium, entrepot. (4) *Vd*. Tụrạ̄kī.

B. (matarā) *Vd*. matạrī.

matarārī = mạdigī.

mạ̄tar ɗaŋ kōlị *f*. gourd-bottle (= būtạ *q.v*.).

mạ̄tar fādạ *f*. (1) middle-aged concubine of deceased Emir to whom she bore a child. (2) *Vd*. mātam fādạ.

matari A. (matārī) *m*. (*pl*. mạtạ̄rai). (1) (*a*) large spindle for thread. (*b*) large spool of thread (*cf*. kurcīyā 2). (2) = matārā. (3) matārin lāyū = ƙullūtụ 2.

B. (matarī) *m*. (*pl*. mạtạrai). (1) the cloth gōyō 1*b* (*d.f*. tarẹ). (2) matarin lāyạ = ƙullūtụ 2.

C. (matạrī) *m*. (*f*. matarīyā) *pl*. matạrā. (1) opponent (*d.f*. tarẹ). (2) bạ̄ shi dạ ∼ he's unequalled.

D. (mạtạrī) *m*. extreme eagerness (= dōƙī).

mātar kāwū Vd. kujērā 5.

mātar kōgī f. the bird lādiŋ kōgī q.v.

mātar Maiṇạ f. (1) type of sugar-cane, very juicy but not sweet. (2) thread like shūṇayyạ. (3) type of bead. (4) obsolete type of festival-singing by female voices.

mātar makī gudụ Vd. nasarạ.

mātar mazā f. (1) woman no longer married (= bạzawạrā). (2) cadger (= marārạkī). (3) Vd. nasarạ.

mạtarnīyā f. = mạtạrī.

mātar watạ f. planet Venus (= zāharatụ).

matashi A. (matāshī) m. (pl. mạtậsai). (1) matāshī = matāshiŋ kậi cushion, pillow. (2) in the case of opposite Arabic pages, writing the first word of the second page in small script at the foot of the first page (cf. matậshī 3).

B. (matậshī) m. (f. matāshīyā) pl. matậsā. (1) riser. (2) yārọ nē ∼ he's a growing lad. (3) x nā yi masạ matāshīyā I gave him a reminder (cf. matāshī 2).

mātattakī Vd. mạcē.

matattarā f. (pl. mạtạttạrai) = matārā.

mạtattū Vd. mạtaccē.

mataunī m. (pl. mạtaụnai) molar tooth (= turmī 4).

mātāyē Vd. mạcē.

matayī m. (f. matayīyā) pl. matạyā. (1) P. making price-offer for goods (d.f. tayị). (2) bậ ta dạ ∼ " she is a wallflower ", " is on the shelf."

mātēkū Vd. mạcē.

Mậtī name for boy born after girls (= Taŋkọ q.v.).

mātinjạ m. (pl. mātinjōjī) Eng. Messenger officially employed in Government and some N.A. offices (cf. mạnzō).

matizgī Sk. m. steep place.

mato A. (matō) Vb. 3A had feeling of longing for T. or P.

B. (mātọ) m. (pl. mātōcī). (1) Eng. motor-car (= mōtạ). (2) Mātọ = Mậtī.

matōkarī m. (pl. mạtōkạrai). (1) prop. (2) forked-prop (gwạfā) of corn-bin, used to open it in order to take out corn. (3) the beam gāgạrạ kūrẹ q.v. under gāgạrạ 10d.

matōnī m. (pl. mạtōṇai) the metal-shod digging-stick dāgị.

matōshī m. (pl. mạtōṣai). (1) cork, stopper, bung. (2) matōshim bậkī bribe (= rashawạ).

matoya A. (matōyā) Vd. matōyī.

B. (matōyā) f. (pl. mạtōyai) fryingplace.

matōyī m. (f. matōyịyā) pl. matōyā P. who fries.

matsa A. (mātsạ) Vb. 1A. (1) squeezed out x (a) (i) nā ∼ lēmū = nā ∼ rūwā dạgạ lēmū = nā ∼ rūwan lēmū I squeezed out juice from the lime-fruit (= digạ 2), cf. lātsạ. (ii) nā ∼ maŋ gyạɗā I extracted oil from the groundnuts (1a.ii = nạnnagạ). (iii) tā ∼ zanẹ she wrung out the cloth (= murdạ 1b). (b) pressed together (x pile of papers to reduce their bulk). (c) bạ ạ fịta rūwa ba, bā ậ ∼ wạrkī don't be in too much of a hurry!; don't count your chickens before they're hatched! (2) massaged (1, 2 = mātsẹ 1. 2 = tausạ 1e). (3) yā ∼ ạbincinsạ he eked out his food. (4) yā ∼ dōkịnsạ he made his horse prance by reining it in sharply (= taf̣ạ 1l). (5) = matsạ 1d. (6) cf. matsạ 1e.

B. (mātsā) Vb. 2 = mātsạ 1a, 4.

C. (matsạ) (1) Vb. 1A. (a) pinched together, squeezed together x (i) yā ∼ bậkin zōbẹ he squeezed together the two ends of the metal ring to make them join (cf. tāfẹ 1a.ii). (ii) hạntsakī yā ∼ miṇị hannū the pincers nipped my hand. (iii) yā ∼ shi dạ baŋgō he pressed him against the wall. (iv) sum ∼ ƙyaurē they put the door " to ". (v) nā ∼ fịŋ ạ jịkin takạrdā I stuck the pin into the paper. (vi) yā ∼ rūbūtū he cramped his writing (cf. matsị 2). (b) yā ∼ hannū, yā yi cūshē through shortage of paper, he wrote tiny, fine characters (cf. kạrmạtsē). (c) hemmed in, pestered, worried x (i) yā ∼ ni = yā ∼ miṇị = yā ∼ miṇị lambạ he badgered me (= tākụrā 3c) (cf. matsị 1b). (ii) ạbịn dạ ya ∼ manạ kạnsạ what he pressed us to do. (iii) garī yā ∼ masạ he's poor, in trouble. (iv) Vd. mạtsu. (v) dōgạrai sum ∼ ɓạrāwọ the N.A. police hemmed in the thief (= dāfạ 1b). (vi) yuŋwạ tā ∼ ni hunger rendered me desperate (cf. matsi 1a). (vii) kāshī yā ~ ni I urgently required to defecate. (viii) fitsārī yā ~ ni I urgently required to urinate. (d) nā ~ dami I pulled the rope tight when binding the sheaf (= mātsa 5). (e) cf. mātsa, matsā, mātse, matse, kā matsō. (f) sum ~ shi = 2a below. (g) Matsa kŏrā epithet of any brave P. (h) matsa runguma m. (sg., pl.) button (= anīnī 2). (j) matsa sarākī = muntsuna sarākī. (2) Vb. 3A. (a) sum ~ (= sum matsō) kusa da shī = sum ~ wajansa they approached him (= 1f above = matsā). ku matsō kusa-kusa, ku jī come close and listen! (b) da matsawā it's only a short distance from here (= tafāwā). (c) moved away x Tūrāwā sum ~ daga gōnāta the Europeans have moved their quarters away from the vicinity of my farm. D. (matsā) Vb. 2 x sum matsē shi they approached him (= matsa 2a).

matsabtacī m. (f. matsabtacīyā) pl. matsabtatā. (1) clean, clean P. (2) economical P.

matsafa A. (matsāfā) Vd. matsāfī. B. (matsāfā) f. (pl. matsāfai). (1) fetish-place (Vd. tsāfi). (2) place only large enough for one to squeeze oneself into (= makurdī 3). (3) one's usual sitting-place. (4) Vd. Tōya ~.

matsāfī m. (f. matsāfīyā) pl. matsāfā fetish-worshipper (Vd. tsāfi).

matsafīyo m. short, slim male (cf. matsarī).

matsaftacī = matsabtacī.

matsagī = matsattsagī.

matsakaicī m. (f. matsakaicīyā) pl. matsakaitā adj. of moderate size, of moderate wealth (= tsaka-tsaka 2).

matsakancī = matsakaicī.

matsala = matsala f. (pl. matsalōlī) (Ar. maslaha) affair.

matsalu m. miser.

matsanancī m. (f. matsananciyā) pl. matsanantā severe (re calamity, trouble, etc.). yanā da wuyā matsananciyā it is of extreme difficulty.

matsara A. (matsarā) Vd. matsarī. B. (matsarā) f. (pl. matsarai) place

occupied by outposts, those on guard, etc.

matsari A. (matsarī) m. (f. matsarīyā) pl. matsarā watchman, watcher, lookout, picquet, outpost. B. (matsarī) f. (1) short, slim female (cf. matsafīyo, matsaro). (2) Matsarī name given to 1.

matsarkakī m. (f. matsarkakīyā) pl. matsarkakā clean, pure.

matsarmamā f. (1) gall-bladder (= madāciyā = dātannīyā 3). (2) the medicinal weeds Physalis angulata and Physalis minima.

matsaro m. (1) = matsafīyo. (2) Matsaro name given to matsafīyo.

mātsatsa Vb. 3B was crowded x hanya tā ~ the road is (was) crowded (= matse 2).

matsatsī = matsi 2.

matsattsagi A. (matsattsāgī) = tsattsāgī. B. (matsattsagī) m. (pl. matsattsagai) stick for ramming earth.

matsattsakū f. (sg., pl.) leech (= Zar. cakwā).

matsattsē m. (f. matsattsīyā) pl. matsattsū x matsattsan wurī a restricted place.

matsautacī = matsabtacī.

matsawā f. used in (1) inā matsawātā what am I to do? (2) ban sam matsawad da nikē cikī ba I don't know how to solve my difficulty (= matsirgā 2).

matsayī m. (pl. matsayai). (1) (a) (i) place where T. or P. remains, stands, etc. (= makwafī). (ii) a sā (= a mai da) Audu a matsayin Garba put Audu in place of Garba! (= maimakō). ka zauna a matsayīna take my place! (iii) bā wanda ya kamātā a mayar a matsayinsa săi Audu nobody but Audu is worthy to take his place. (iv) gaskīyā tanā matsayintā Vd. karyā 1a.v. (v) matsayin jirgin rūwā harbour. (vi) matsayin jirgin sama aerodrome. (b) site. (c) geographical position. (d) an daure shi matsayin ransa he's been imprisoned for life. (2) (a) rank, status. (b) yā ga matsayinsa it's more than he can stand. (3) (a) an kai shi mūgum ~ he's been arrested. (b) yā kai su mūgum ~ it caused litigation between them.

matse A. (mātsę) *Vb.* 1A = mātsạ 1,
2. (2) yā ⌣ rawạnī he firmly wound on
his turban. (3) (*a*) yanạ̄ mātsẹ̄wā he's
enjoying life. (*b*) bạri ŋ kwạntā, m̩ ⌣
kạɗaŋ I think I'll have a snooze.
B. (matsę) *Vb.* 3A. (1) = matsạ 2*a*
x sum ⌣ shi they approached him. (2)
is (was) crowded *x* hanyạ tā ⌣ the
road is crowded (= mātsatsạ). (3)
mạtsu *Vb.* 3B (*a*) wurī yā mạtsu the
place is congested. (*b*) (i) nā mạtsu I'm
harassed, I'm in difficulties. (ii)
mạtsūwā tā zō difficulties have arisen.
(iii) bạbbar mạtsūwā crisis. (iv) *Vd.*
ta alakō. (*c*) *cf.* matsạ 1*c*.
C. (mãtsē) *m.* = gọ̄gạ̄.
mạtsēfatạ *f.* (*pl.* mạtsẹ̄fạtai). (1) pair of
tweezers (= hạntsakī). (2) mạtsēfatạr
birị an instrument made of tsirgāgịyā
for extracting splinters (= hạntsakī 2).
matsēfī *m.* (*pl.* mạtsẹ̄fai). (1) comb (= *Kt.*
mashācī). (2) part of a loom.
matsẹ̄guncī *m.* (*f.* matsẹ̄guncịyā) *pl.*
matsẹ̄guntā. (1) scandalmonger (*Vd.*
tsẹ̄gumī). (2) matsẹ̄guncịyā *f.* raised
ground just inside house-door near
dandamạlī (= *Kt.* makwạrmạcī 3).
matsegunta A. (matsẹ̄guntā) *Vd.* mat-
sẹ̄guncī.
B. (matsēguntā) *f.* (*pl.* mạtsẹ̄guntai).
(1) resort of scandal-mongers. (2) =
matsẹ̄guṅcī 2.
mạ'tse-mạtsē'' *m.* *x* yanạ̄ ⌣ dạ ạbinsạ
he's taking great care of his property.
matsị *m.* (1) (*a*) food shortage = ƙuncī 2
(*cf.* matsạ 1*c*.vi). (*b*) yā yi musu ⌣ =
yā yi ⌣ gạrēsu he pestered them, he
treated them with harshness (*cf.* matsạ
1*c*.i). (2) being crowded *x* rụbūtun
naŋ ⌣ gạrēshị this writing is crowded
together (*cf.* matsạ 1*a*.vi). (3) the
suppository ɗaukē 2 *q.v.* (4) *Kt.* =
gạbaŋ wuƙā *q.v.* *under* gạban 13.
matsirā *f.* (*pl.* mạtsịrai) sprouting-place.
matsirgā *f.* (*pl.* mạtsịrgai). (1) place where
water falls on a rock. (2) *x* bạn sam
matsirgam mạganạn nạm ba I don't
know how to solve my difficulties
(= matsawā).
mãtsirgạ̄gī = ɗam ⌣ *m.* (*f.* 'yar ⌣)
pl. 'yam ⌣ slightly-built P. or animal.
matsirgī *m.* = matsirgā.

matsirī *m.* = matsirā.
matsīwạcī *m.* (*f.* matsīwacịyā) *pl.* matsī-
wạtā. (1) insolent. (2) brave *x* shī irịm
matsīwạtan sōjạn nan nẹ dạ he is one oí
those intrepid soldiers who . . .
matsīyạ̄cī *m.* (*f.* matsīyācịyā) *pl.* matsī-
yạ̄tā. (1) poor (*for epithet Vd.* Gịndau).
(2) ⌣ kō kā hau dạ shī kạn rạ̄ƙumī,
ƙafạ tasạ tā jā ƙasā = ⌣ dǎi, kō an
jēfạ shi ạ tandum mặi, sǎi yạ fitō dạ
firī put a beggar on horseback and he'll
ride to the devil! (3) kōwā yanạ̄ sǫ
yạ gạ̄ji ụbansạ bạndạ ɗam ⌣ everyone wants to go up in the world, not
down (= kuturū 4). (4) (*a*) matsī-
yạ̄cin yau shī nẹ mawạdạ̄ciŋ gọ̄be poor
to-day, rich to-morrow! (*b*) ⌣ ya
karyạ mawạdạ̄cī *Vd.* dịŋgishī. (5)
'yar ⌣ tā mutu *Vd.* bịkī 1*b*. (6) zại
mutu ⌣ *Vd.* dọ̄min-dọ̄min.
matsō *used in* kā ⌣ *m.* T. which one has
no option but to buy dear.
matsōkacī *m.* (*pl.* mạtsọ̄kạtai) mirror (=
madūbī 2).
mạtsō-matsō *m.* (1) = mạƙō-maƙō 2*a*.
(2) yā shịga ⌣ (i) he entered a big
crowd. (ii) he mixed himself in a
serious quarrel. (3) gidansạ yanạ̄ ⌣
his home is in an isolated spot.
matsọ̄rạcī *m.* (*f.* matsōracịyā) *pl.* matsọ̄-
rạtā one who fears, frightened P.,
coward.
matsorata A. (matsọ̄rạtā) *Vd.* matsọ̄rạcī.
B. (matsōratā) *f.* (*pl.* mạtsọ̄rạtai)
place inspiring fear.
mạtsu *Vd.* matsẹ 3.
matsubbạcī *m.* (*f.* matsubbacịyā) *pl*
matsubbạtā magician.
matsubbata A. (matsubbạtā) *Vd.* matsubbạcī.
B. (matsubbatā) *f.* (*pl.* mạtsubbạtai)
place of magic rites.
matsuka A. (matsukā) *f.* (*lit.* crunching-
place) *used in* yā kai ayā ⌣ " he pul
his head in the lion's mouth ".
B. (matsukā) *Vd.* matsụkī.
matsụkī *m.* (*f.* matsukịyā) *pl.* matsụkā.
(1) cruncher. (2) ạbịŋ yā zō kặi dạ
kặi, shūkạr ⌣ it happened appositely.
mãtsurutai *pl.* entrails of ram killed on
naming day (ran sūnā) and given to
midwife (ŋgōzọ̄mạ) and neighbours.

mātūci *m.* (1) (*a*) female pudenda (= farji). (*b*) pistil of flowers. (2) fact of being a woman. (3) the character inherent in women (*cf.* mazakūta). (4) Allā wadam ∼ (*a*) I wish I were not a woman ! (*b*) bother women ! matufkī *m.* (*f.* matufkīyā) *pl.* matufkā rope-maker (= matūkī).

matūkā *Vd.* matūkī.

matuka A. (matukā) (1) *f.* (*a*) end, limit, boundary. (*b*) matukar tayi *Vd.* tayi 4. (*c*) matukar wuyā *Vd.* bī tsatsō. (*d*) matukar yāwam bākō *Vd.* darē 1*a.* (2) *adv.* entirely *x* yā gaji ∼ = yā gaji matukar gajīya he is (was) tired out. harshansa yā fitō ∼ he speaks clearly. hankalinsa yā tāshi ∼ he's in a state of great perturbation. yā wahala ∼ he suffered extreme trouble.

B. (matūkā) *Vd.* matūkī.

matūkī *m.* (*f.* matūkīyā) *pl.* matūkā rope-maker (= matufkī).

matuki A. (matūkī) *m.* (*f.* matūkīyā) *pl.* matūkā (1) (*a*) poler or paddler of canoe. (*b*) matūkā *pl.* ships-crew. (2) driver of car.

B. (matūkī) *m.* (*pl.* matūkai) (1) paddle or pole for canoe (= filāfilai). (2) driving-wheel of motor. (3) lever for rotating coil of woven material on loom. (4) stirring-rod for ink.

matūkkī *Kt.* = matūkī.

mātumburī *m.* (*f.* mātumburā) (1) stunted P. or animal. (2) ɗam ∼ *m.* = 1.

mātunci *Kt.* = mātūci.

mātunta = mātūta.

maturārī *m.* (*pl.* maturārai) = madambacī.

maturzai *Sk. pl.* calf of leg (= dambūbu 1).

matusgī = matuzgī.

mātūta *Vb.* 3B became apprehensive (*d.j.* mātā).

mātūwā *Sk. f.* (1) she-ass. (2) (*said playfully*) woman.

matuzgī *Sk. m.* (*pl.* matuzgai) ford (= mashigī).

mau = tamau.

maucī *m.* being favourite *as in* mōwa *x* maucin Kande the fact of Kande being his favourite wife.

mauɗa *Vb.* 1A *x* yā ∼ masa sandā he beat him with a stick (= dōka).

mauɗe *Vb.* 1A = dōke.

mauje = mauɗe.

mauro *m.* (1) poor man, " the man in the street " (= talaka). (2) *his epithet is* Mauro, mai kāshī a kas.

mautara A. (mautara) *Vb.* 2 *x* yā mautarē shi da sandā he hit him hard with a stick (= dōkā).

B. (mautarā) *Vb.* 1C (*with dative*) *x* yā ∼ masa sandā he hit him hard with a stick (= mautara = dōka).

mautarē *Vb.* 1C = dōke.

mauyā = mauyā *f.* = maiwā.

mawā *f.* = munzili 2 *x* tsakānimmu da shī har tā kai mawar zāgi things went as far as the exchange of filthy abuse between us.

mawadācī *m.* (*f.* mawadācīyā) *pl.* mawa-dātā (1) wealthy (= attājirī). (2) *Vd.* mahukurcī, matsīyācī 4.

mawāfaka = muwāfaka.

mawākī *m.* (*f.* mawākīyā) *pl.* mawākā (1) = marōkī. (2) gā kurjī yā fitō a bākim mawākīyā he's at a loss what to say.

mawankā *f.* part of house-floor raised solidly for use as bed.

mawanki A. (mawankī) *m.* (1) one who washes T. (2) corpse-washer. (3) washer of bride or bridegroom before first marriage.

B. (mawankī) *m.* (*pl.* mawankai) (1) washing-place for pots. (2) a skin-disease like ringworm (kurēcī) but appearing anywhere on the body. (3) *Kt.* (*a*) stripped millet heads (sōshīyā), stripped guinea-corn heads. (*b*) the shell called makankarī, used for scraping out food-vessels.

mawarganci *m.* (*f.* mawargancīyā) *pl.* mawargantā = mawāsancī.

mawāsancī *m.* (*f.* mawāsancīyā) *pl.* mawā-santā playful, joker.

mawōfinci *m.* (*f.* mawōfincīyā) *pl.* mawō-fintā (1) fool. (2) (*a*) empty *x* wurin nam ∼ nē this place is empty. ∼ daga mātā nē it is devoid of women. (*b*) an sācē kāyāna, am bar ni ∼ thieves stripped me to the bone.

mawuyācī *m.* (*f.* mawuyācīyā) *pl.* mawu-yātā difficult, troublesome.

maya A. (maya) (1) *Vb.* 1A (*a*) spliced *x*
igīyan naŋ, tŭkā bīyu-bīyu nȩ, a ∼ ta,
ta zamā ukṵ-ukṵ make this 2-ply
string into 3-ply ! (= haya 1*d*). (*b*)
Kt. repeated doing T. (= maimaitā).
(2) *Kt.* (*a*) maya returned there, went
there (= kōma). (*b*) mayō returned
here, came here (= kōmō). (3) *cf.*
mayā, mai da.
　　B. (mayā) *Vb.* 2 (1) *x* yā mayi
Audu = yā mayi wuriŋ Audṵ he took
the place of Audu, relieved Audu,
was locum tenens, deputy of Audu
(= karɓā 1*e*), *cf.* maimakō. (2) dis-
possessed a P. (3) succeeded P. in office.
　　C. (māyā) *f.* richness of meat *x*
nāma mai ∼ rich meat (= mǎi 1*a*.ii).
mayācē *Vb.* 3A became poor.
mayad da = mai da.
mayādī *m.* (*pl.* mayāɗai) skimmer.
mayāfī *m.* (*pl.* mayāfai) (1) large cloth
covering woman's head or man's
shoulders (*Vd.* kȩkē 2). *(2) an yi
masa ∼ = bargō 3.
mayāɓī *m.* (*f.* mayāɓīyā) *pl.* mayāɓā 1
warrior, soldier. (2) *Vd.* bǎi ∼.
mayalwacī *m.* (*f.* mayalwacīyā) *pl.* mayal-
wata (1) abundant. (2) extensive.
mayā-mayā *f. and adv. x* yā yi ∼ da
tufāfi = yā yi tufāfi ∼ he put on many
clothes.
mayamfaɗī *m.* (*pl.* mayamfaɗai) type
of mat serving as door-covering.
mayana *used in* bā ∼ that's bad news !
(= lābāri 2*a*.ii).
mayānī *m.* (*pl.* mayānai) (1) handkerchief (= adīkọ). (2) *Kt.* = alhūtsa.
mayanka A. (mayaŋkā) *Vd.* mayaŋkī.
　　B. (mayaŋkā) *f.* (*pl.* mayaŋkai) (1)
(*a*) abattoir. (*b*) yā kau da ∼ he
changed his previous statement, to
steer clear of trouble. (2) yārinya cē
mai ∼ she's a slender girl with good
hips (= kīra 1*e*).
mayaŋkī *m.* (*pl.* mayaŋkā) (1) the official
Muslim slaughterer (= mālamī 1*h*),
cf. mahaucī. (2) mayaŋkiŋ gishirī cutter-
up of jici or kantṵ of salt (*Vd.* yaŋkȩ).
mayaŋkwanīyā *f.* (1) pernicious anæmia
(= bayammā *q.v.*). (2) a type of
rectal complaint.
ᵐayar da = mai da.

mayata A. (mayāta) (1) *Vb.* 3B became
poor (= mayācē). (2) *f.* poverty.
　　B. (mayātā) *Vb.* 1C (1) impoverished
a P. (2) Mayāta kākā *epithet of* any
grandson (jīka).
Mayau = Abǎicī 2 (*cf.* mai da).
mayaudarī *m.* (*f.* mayaudarīyā) *pl.* mayau-
darā trickster.
mayautā *f.* (*pl.* mayautai) place for strolling
or change of air (*cf.* yāwọ).
mayawa A. (mayāwā) *f.* (*pl.* mayāwai) =
mayautā.
　　B. (mayāwā) *Vd.* mayāwī.
mayawaci A. (mayāwacī) *m.* (*f.* mayā-
wacīyā) *pl.* mayāwatā stroller (=
mayāwī).
　　B. (mayāwacī) *m.* (*pl.* mayāwatai) =
mayautā.
mayawata A. (mayāwatā) *Vd.* mayāwacī.
　　B. (mayāwatā) *f.* (*pl.* mayāwatai) =
mayautā.
mayāwatai *Vd.* mayāwācī, mayāwatā.
mayāwī *m.* (*f.* mayāwīyā) *pl.* mayāwā
stroller (= mayāwacī).
mayāyī *m.* (*pl.* mayāyai) the broom
mashārī 2 *q.v.* (*d.f.* yāyȩ 1*b*).
mayayya *f.* (1) alternation. (2) = karɓaɓɓenīyā.
maye A. (māyȩ) *m.* (*f.* mayyā) *pl.* māyū
(1) (*a*) sorcerer (= kwārō 3). (*b*) ana
tsōraŋ Inna, n ji 'yā'yam mayyā =
anā tsōran nī da īya, n ji 'yā'yam
mayyā needs must when the devil
drives (*cf.* nī da ūwā). (*c*) ∼ yā cī
shi he died in delirium. (*d*) ∼ yā ci
tsōfwā *Vd.* kwaŋgwalī. (2) extra-
ordinarily skilful P. (= iblis 2 *q.v.*).
(3) *Vd.* hanzarī 1*d*.
　　B. (māyē) (1) (*a*) intoxication (*cf.*
bugu 1). (*b*) bā ∼ *Vd.* dagara. (2)
swanking about T. *x* (*a*) yanā māyaŋ
kudī he's swanking with his money
(= tākamā 2). (*b*) dom māyan diŋki
(= don tākamar diŋki) bā ā fasa kwaryā
(*lit.* one doesn't shatter a calabash
merely to show how well one has repaired it (gyartai)) don't cut off
your nose to spite your face ! (= ganī
A.2 1*g*). (3) n nā māyansa I'm relying on
him, etc. (*x* on father, mother, etc.) =
tākamā 4. (4) gērō yā yi ∼ the bulrush
millet is backward due to over-manur-

ing, but will later produce heavy crop.
(5) dāwą tā yi ∼ the guinea-corn has
been spoiled by banking-up (hūdā
q.v.) or by lack of manure.
  C. (mayę) (1) Vb. 3A returned (=
mayą). (2) Vb. 1A relieved P. (=
mąyā).
mą́'ye-mąyēǁ Sk. m. the food fątē̩-fatē.
mayi̩ m. acting as in mayą 1a.
Māyibi̩ m. month of May (= Māyu̩).
mayō Vd. mayą.
mayu A. (Māyu̩) m. = Māyibi̩.
  B. (māyū) Vd. māyę.
  C. (mąyu) Vd. mai dą 2a.v.
mayu̩ŋwącī m. (f. mayu̩ŋwacīyā) pl.
mayu̩ŋwątā hungry.
mąyyā Vd. māyę, bąbba.
maza A. (mazā) (1) males (Vd. namiji̩).
(2) husbands (Vd. miji̩). (3) Vd.
mazan compounds.
  B. (maza) (1) (a) quickly. (b) (i)
maza-maza very quickly. (ii) yi
maza-maza go quickly ! hasten ! act
quickly ! (c) yā yi ∼ he acted quickly,
hastened. yā yi ∼, yā gamą he finished
it quickly. (d) ą yi ∼ dǎi, ą fitad dą
jąkī dągą dumā let's finish off that
hard job and be clear of it ! (Vd.
jąkī 1j.) (2) ∼ daya instantly x ∼
daya sǎi ya amsą he replied without a
moment's hesitation (= farat 1).
mazāḃa f. (pl. mązāḃai) good quality x
bą shi dą ∼ he has no good qualities.
mązāburą = mązāfarą = mązāfirą =
mązāfurą = Kt. mązāhirą energy x
bą shi dą ∼ he is not energetic, he's
spineless (= himmą).
mazaga A. (mazągā) Vd. mazągī.
  B. (mazągā) f. (pl. mązągai) (1)
(d.f. zągą) detour. (2) (d.f. zągā) that
which causes one to be abused x bą
su dą ∼ no blame attaches to them.
mazagi A. (mazągī) m. (f. mazāgīyā) pl.
mazągā abuser.
  B. (mazāgī) m. (pl. mązągai) (1)
trouser-string (= lāwu̩rjē = mazargī =
zārīyā), cf. zāgę 1d, kubāką. (2)
mazāgiŋ kąrē dog-leash used by pagans
(= makāmiŋ kąrē). (3) horse's leading-
rope (= asalwąyī).
mązągwądī m. extreme eagerness (=
dōkī).

mązāhirą Vd. mązāburą.
mazaiki̩ m. (f. mazaikīyā) pl. mazaikā (1)
comer. (2) guest. (3) mazaikin darē =
mijin darē. (4) Cf. mazō̩, maząyī.
mazaizai Vd. miji̩, namiji̩.
maząjē Vd. miji̩, namiji̩.
mązakkąrī = mu̩zakkąrī.
*mązākuci̩ m. = mązākutą.
mazākudā f. (pl. mązākudai) place whereto migration is made.
mązākutą = mązākūtą = mązākuntą f.
(1) penis. (2) manliness. (3) character
inherent in males (cf. mātūci̩).
mązallakọ Vd. ząllim ∼.
maza-maza A. (maza-maza) Vd. maza.
  B. (mązą-mązą) m., f., sg., pl. (1)
tirelessly energetic, dauntless (= mu̩za-
kkąrī). (2) mązą-mąząm markē epithet
of 1.
maząmbącī m. (f. mazambacīyā) pl.
maząmbątą rogue.
mazamnī Sk. = mazaunī.
mazanci̩ used in 'yam ∼ m. fearlessness,
perseverance (d.f. namiji̩).
mazan du̩ŋku̩lą pl. (1) dung-beetle (=
būzūzu̩). (2) cooked beans kneaded
into ball.
mazani A. (maząnī) m. (f. mazānīyā) pl.
maząnā P. who adorns.
  B. (mazānī) m. (pl. mązānai) patterning tool.
mazantā f. (pl. mąząntai) chatting-
place (Vd. ząncē).
mazanya A. (mazanyā) f. the stingless
bee gallā.
  B. (māzanyą) Vd. mązō.
maząrē (1) Vd. mazarī. (2) Vd. namiji̩
1b.ii. (3) maząrē ! the street-cry of
hawkers of spitted-meat (tsi̩rē).
mazargī = mazāgī.
mazarī m. (pl. mazą̄rē) (1) (a) (i) spindle
(cf. taskirā, matākī 3). (ii) ∼ bą ą
san gąbąŋką ba how mysterious !
shī ∼ bą ą san gąbąŋką ba " he's a
closed book ". (iii) cf. arnā 2b. (b)
kąm ∼ m. = bąkī 6a. (c) Vd. dūnīyą
2h. (2) Vd. namiji̩ 1b. (3) trembling,
shivering. (4) dragon-fly. (5) mazarim
mātā the skink shą̄rindọ. (6) Vd.
mazą̄rē.
mąząrḱwailą f. brown sugar.
mąząrō m. eagerness (= dōkī).

mazaudā *f.* (*pl.* mḁzaṵɗai) = mazākuɗā.

mazauni A. (mazaṵnī) *m.* (*f.* mazauni̱yā) *pl.* mazaṵnā (1) sitter. (2) dweller.
B. (mazaunī) *m.* (*pl.* mḁzaṵnai) (1) (*a*) seat. (*b*) (i) dwelling-place. (ii) dḁ kūrā dḁ ḵḁrē bā sḁ gamḁ ∼ oil and water won't mix. (*c*) deep part of river bed. (2) involuntary seminal discharge (mḁzīyyi̱) of woman who has dḁŋgwarḁ dḁɓē 2 or who has long been without coitus with a male *x* dḁ ∼ ji̱kin zanḁntḁ *such* seminal discharge has stained her bodycloth.

mazāwari̱ *m.* (1) descending colon and rectum. (2) gwauram ∼ duodenum.

mazāwọ̆yiŋ ḵāsūwā *m.* (*pl.* mazāwọ̆yaŋ ḵāsūwā) man threatening to defecate in market unless his blackmail succeeds and he is paid not to do so (= *Kt.* būdi̱ 8), *cf.* gḁrkūwā 3*c*, gūgu̱ ūgu̱.

mazaya A. (mazayā) *f.* (mḁzḁyai) (*d.f.* zō) place of resort (*cf.* mazḁyī).
B. (mazḁyā) *Vd.* mazḁyī.
C. (māzḁyā) *Vb.* 3A (1) went off at a tangent (= bākatar). (2) (*a*) ḁ ∼ ḁ kai iri̱ gidā (*originally said by* Sarkiŋ Gọbir) let's give up the battle ! (*b*) sun yi ḁ ∼ ḁ kai iri̱ gidā they retreated.

mazḁyī *m.* (*f.* mazayi̱yā) *pl.* mazḁyā = mazai̱kī.

mazgḁ *Vb.* 1A *x* nā ∼ masḁ sḁndā I beat him with a stick (= dōkḁ).

mazgḁyā = māzḁyā.

mazgḛ *Vb.* 1A beat and knocked over (= dōkḛ).

mazinācī *m.* (*f.* mazinācī̱yā) *pl.* mazi̱nḁtā adulterer, fornicator (*cf.* zi̱nā).

mḁzīyyi̱ *Ar. m.* seminal discharge due to experiencing a shock (*cf.* mazaunī 2, wḁdīyyi̱, mḁnīyyi̱).

mazo A. (mḁzō) *m.* (*f.* māzanyḁ) harnessed antelope (*Tragelophus scriptus*) = gḁnjar 2*b q.v.*
B. (mazọ) *m.*, *f.* (*pl.* mḁzọ̄wā) P. in hereditary succession *x* (1) ∼ nē gḁ sḁrautḁ he belongs to the ruling classes. sḁrautḁ bḁ tḁ ḵamācē shi̱ ba, sabọ dḁ bḁ ∼ ita ba nḛ he is not fitted for an official position as he was not born to it. (2) sū mḁzọ̄wā fatauci̱ nē they're hereditary traders. (3) mḁzọ̄wā gḁri̱ the inhabitants of a town. (4) *Cf.* mazai̱kī.

mazubā *f.* (*pl.* mḁzu̱bai) place where several things are put (*cf.* zubḁ) *x* mazubar tākalmḁnsu̱ the place where they throw off their shoes (*cf.* ma'ajī).

mazubī *m.* (*pl.* mḁzu̱bai) (1) matrix for casting. (2) = mazubā.

mazuŋgurī *m.* (*pl.* mḁzu̱ŋgu̱rai) (1) stick for removing from tree such fruits as dọ̄rōwḁ, gwandḁ, etc. (*cf.* mḁḵatḁ). (2) *Kt.* pointed stick for digging holes or forcing rat out of hole.

mazuŋkuɗīyā *f.* maggot (tsūtsḁ) ravaging ripe bulrush-millet (= tu̱ŋku̱ɗau = zu̱ŋku̱ɗau), *cf.* minyḁ 2.

mḁzūrai = mu̱zūrai.

mazurārī *m.* (*pl.* mḁzu̱rārai) (1) (*a*) = i̱ndararō. (*b*) watercourse (= makwarārā). (*c*) place where water flows over rock. (*d*) children's slide over rock. (2) gourd-funnel for pouring out liquid (= bōtọ). (3) = būtūtū 2 = ḵāḵāḵī 1*b*.

mḁzūru̱ *Nor.* = mu̱zūru̱.

mazza = maza.

mbōlḁ *f.* = ḁmbōlḁ.

mḛ *m.* what ? (= *Sk.* mi̱) *x* (1) (*a*) ∼ kaḵḛ sọ = kanḁ sḁm mḛ what do you want ? (*b*) *x* tọ, ∼ nē na ri̱njāyḁrmu̱ what is this talk of conquering us ? (*c*) (kō *may optionally precede*) *x* bḁ mu̱ saŋ kō kam mḛ zā mu̱ fāɗḁ we don't know upon what we may fall (*cf.* kō 2*d*). (*cc*) ∼ ya rabḁ *Vd.* dambē 5. (*d*) ∼ ka shūkḁ *Vd.* gajaŋ hḁḵurī (*e*) ∼ ya kai furā *Vd.* ḵazḁntā 1*c.* (2) *x* ∼ aḵḁ yi̱, aḵḁ yi̱ karnukḁ what are mere dogs ! (3) kō na ∼ not in the slightest *x* bḁ shi dḁ kyau̱ kō na ∼ it is not the slightest good. (4) ∼ ḵḁrē gōmḁ yakḁ yī dḁ kūrḁ what have they in common ? (5) yanḁ dḁ kyau̱ ḵamar ḵamar ∼ it is extremely good (6) *x* ∼ ya yi masḁ zai̱ bā mu̱ why should he give us it ? (7) *Vd.* mḛnēnḛ mḛ ya fi rāi̱na. (8) *cf.* kōmē, kōmḛ.

mḛcēcḛ *Vd.* mḛnēnḛ.

mḛdī *m.* (1) fibre from root of dum (kabḁ and locust-bean (dọ̄rōwḁ) used fo mending broken calabashes (gyartai and for making the fish-net calle ashu̱tā. (2) *Vd.* ḵardḛ.

mēkị = mīkị 2.

mẹl = mēlẹ.

mele A. (mēlē) (1) (a) botheration ! (b) Vd. ƙābạrạ. (2) m. depigmentation (= wuyạ 5). B. (mēlẹ) Eng. m. (1) mail (letters). (2) mail-steamer. (3) kaɗanyạm ∼ Vd. bụrụntụŋkusạ.

mẹli Vd. mẹlu.

mẹlu Vb. 3b = Kt. mẹli x in nā ∼ nạ̄ yī if I feel inclined, I'll do it.

mēmā f. = maimā.

mẹnẹ̄ = mẹnēnẹ̄.

mẹnēnẹ̄ m. (f. mẹcēcẹ̄) (1) = mẹ̄. (2) what is it ? x (a) yanạ̄ dạ maganạ he has something to tell you (reply mẹcēcẹ̄ " well, what is it ? "). (b) ∼ shī dạ zại yi minị hakạ who does he think he is to treat me so ! mẹcēcẹ̄ ita dạ zā tạ ƙī who is she to refuse ! (c) (kō is sometimes used before inherently interrogative words) x yanạ̄ ta tụnạ̄nī kō mẹnēnẹ̄ nufịnsạ he was reflecting as to what was its meaning (Vd. kō 2d). (3) ∼ hakạ why did you do so ?

nẹnu = mịnu.

nẹrẹ x ạ ∼ uselessly (= ạ banzā).

nēsạ f. (pl. mēsạ̄yē = mēsōshī) (1) python. (2) hose (= maƙōgwạrō 4).

nẹshe Kt. = maishē.

nẹtaŋ f. = Kt. mẹtiŋ (Ar. mi'ataini) 200.

nẹtsō Kt. m. stuṅted goat, etc. (= kụ tsụmạ̄yē nị).

nẹ̄ ya fi rạ̄inạ since I want to buy this luxury, why not, one only lives once.

nẹ̄yẹ̄ what is ? x ∼ maganạrkụ what do you wish to say ? (= mẹnēnẹ̄).

ṇhm (1) well ! (2) (in reply to P. greeting one) greeting to you too ! (Vd. sạnnū, sabbinanị).

ṇị Sk., Kt. (1) (a) = mẹ̄. (b) Vd. mig. (2) Vd. mị nạ̄ Wānẹ ; mị ƙạ̄ cī nị ; mị ya hi rạ̄inạ.

nicīyā = macīyā.

nidiɗɗiƙē Kt. = maɗaɗɗạƙē.

nidil Eng. f. Middle-school.

nidir Kt. firm (not soft) = ninnir.

nig (in Sk., mị ya may become mị and double following consonant) x mịg gamạ ku dạ sụ̄ = mị ya gamạ ku dạ sụ̄ what

have you in common with them ? (cf. na 8b.ii, ni 4).

miji A. (mijị) m. (pl. mazā = mazạ̄jē = mazạizai these also serving as plurals of namijị q.v.) (1) (a) husband. (b) bạbbaŋ ạbụ shī nẹ̄, mạcẹ̄ tā rigā mijịntạ bawạlī (said by labourers) what a serious affair ! (c) Vd. namijị. (2) the small amount of dạddawar batsọ which one mixes (gaurạyē) into the making of ordinary dạddawā. (4) kwạrim mijị Vd. sanị 1a.iii. (5) bạ̄kim mijịntạ Vd. Allạ̄ 7f. (6) mijịm bāya Vd. bịkī 1g. (7) ūwar ∼ Vd. dadị 5. (8) ịnā rūwaŋ Gwārī dạ mijị Vd. Gwārī 1c. (9) mijịŋ gurgụ̄wā Vd. maƙẹ̄tạcī. (10) Vd. mijịn-compounds. B. (mijị) = majị.

mijicī = majicī.

mijinācịyā = majinācịyā.

mijịn darē used in tā ga ∼ she had an erotic dream (x where she seems to commit incest with her father-in-law ; this is supposed to result in miscarriage and future sterility).

mijịŋ gidā m. entrance-hut (= zaurẹ q.v.).

mijịŋ kaɗanyạ m. the tree kụjēmē.

mijịm mazā m. (1) strong man. (2) brave man.

mika A. (mīkạ) (1) Vb. 1A (a) stretched out x masạ̄ƙī yā ∼ zạrē the weaver stretched out the thread in the loom for weaving (Vd. mīƙị). (b) yā ∼ sāƙạ he paid no attention to what was being said. (c) yā ∼ ƙafạ (i) he stretched out his leg. (ii) he went for a stroll. (iii) Vd. mīƙẹ 1b. (d) yā ∼ sau " he put his best foot forward " (= ɗagạ 1e). (e) mai mīƙạwā m., f. (pl. mạsū mīƙạwā) generous P. (f) am ∼ hanyạ the road has been straightened. (g) (plus dative) handed x yā ∼ musụ shī he handed, offered it to them. (h) yā ∼ sauransụ he outdistanced the other travellers. (j) Vd. mīƙẹ 1. (2) Vb. 3A (a) extended x (i) hanyạ tā ∼ the road goes on endlessly. kōgịŋ yā ∼ har tẹkū this river empties into the sea. ƙasarsụ tā ∼ cikim bahạr kamar ƙafạ their country forms a promontory. (Vd. mīƙẹ 2d). (ii) shūkạ tā ∼ the crops grew high

(= ɗagà 2a q.v. := mīƙè 2d q.v.).
(b) lằbārịŋ yā ∼ the news spread. (c)
continued on one's way x bạri mụ ∼
let's go on our way ! sum ∼ har suƙạ
ịsa Kanọ they went on their way till
they reached Kano. (d) set out x bạri
mụ ∼ let us set out ! (e) became
expensive x gōrọ yā ∼ kola-nuts have
become dear (= ɗagà 2a) (Vd. mį̀ƙā
1).
B. (mį̀ƙa) Vb. 3B (Vd. mį̀ƙā 1)
ạbịŋ yā ∼ the affair has become
protracted.
C. (mį̀ƙā) f. (1) (progressive and v.n.
of mį̀ƙa) x ạbịŋ yanā ∼ the affair is
becoming protracted. (2) stretching
oneself (as done by animal or P. after
sleep, etc.) x (a) yā yi ∼ he stretched
himself (= mimmī̀ƙē 1). (b) an yabạ
wạ kạzā ∼ sǎi ta cē "gā cinyạ !"
person's being so overjoyed that he is
ready to do anything for you. (3)
one pace (= tāƙị 2b). (4) ornament for
baby's loins.
mį̀ ƙā cī nị Kt. used in yā shịga rĭgar ∼ =
dạfā ni 2.
mīkạntā Vb. 1C x yā yi masạ rạunī
har ya ∼ shi he wounded him in a
way that caused the wound to form an
ulcer.
mīƙe A. (mīƙè) (1) Vb. 1A (a) = mīƙạ
1a. (b) yā ∼ ƙafạ (i) = mīƙạ 1c. (ii)
he's independent and can give such
orders as he wishes (= mimmī̀ƙē 2).
(iii) sunā jịn dāɗim ∼ ƙafạịsụ they're
having a good time. (iv) yā ∼ ƙafạ,
ya zamā shụgạba he was promoted to
leader. (c) (i) sun sā mụ ∼ wuyạ they
gave us courage. (ii) yanā ∼ wuyạ,
yanā sọ yạ ci dūnịyā he's ambitious
to conquer the whole world. (iii)
ạbōkaŋ gạbā sum mīƙō wuyạ the
enemy surrendered. (d) unrolled (mat,
rope-coil, etc.). (e) overcharged x
yā ∼ ni he overcharged me (cf. mannạ
2). (2) Vb. 3A (a) recovered from illness (= gyāzạjē q.v.). (b) became
stretched out x ƙafạ tasạ tā ∼ his foot
became stretched out. tābarmā tā ∼
the mat is unrolled, stretched out. (c)
(i) yā mīƙè = yā ∼ tsạye = yā ∼
tsawō = yā ∼ tsawansạ he stood up ;

he stood up to his full height ; he
exerted all his strength. (ii) ạ nạ
ka tākụrạ ? kā ∼ if you think you'l
get some advantage here, you're makin
a great mistake ! (iii) dā̀, yā ∼ tsạye
cikim mụgụntā, yạnzu yā suŋkwịyĭ
he has repented of his former bad
ways. (d) = mīƙạ 2a.i x hanyạ tā ∼
the road goes on endlessly. zạị ∼ tu
dagạ Masạr har yạ gamạ dạ Tūnạs i
will extend from Egypt to Tunis
kṑrā tā ∼ har Kanọ the pursuit wa
carried on as far as Kano. zā mụ ∼
bisạ ƙafafūwạmmụ we shall regai
our strength. yā ∼ it (plant x beans
spread (= yạ̀ɗō = mīƙạ 2a.ii q.v.)
(e) anā sọ sụ ∼ sụ yĭ we want them t
exert themselves and do it. (f) =
mīƙa. (g) = mīƙạ 2e. (h) Vd. mim
mīƙē.
B. (mīƙē) m. (1) anything handed
over fence or through doorway o
window (considered an unlucky ac
as it will karyạ lāyạ). (2) bā nā̀ cịm ∼
(a) no thanks, I don't want foo
handed me through the door, etc.
(b) don't greet me from so far away
(said to P. who greets one withou
troubling to come up to polite speaking
distance).
miki A. (mīkị) (1) m. (pl. mīyākū) (a) (i
ulcer (= gyạmbō). (ii) kuturū b
bā̀kwam ∼ ba nḕ don't teach you
grandmother tó suck eggs ! (b) mīkị
cikị (i) pancreas. (ii) T. grieving o
annoying one x yā yi minị mīkịn cikị i
annoyed, grieved me. (2) m. (f. mīkĭyạ
pl. mīkōkī = mīkĭyōyī (a) Ruppell'
griffon (Gyps ruppellii). (b) Mīkĭyā
bā̀ ki sạukā sǎi dạ dạlīlị nobody ac
without cause. (c) zāmạnịn dạ dṑ
dạ jākī bạ sụ mutụ ba, mḕ mīkĭyā
ci, ta yi rằi (said by woman) you Fellov
wife, you were a poverty-stricke
creature before you came here !
B. (mikị) to you (fem.), cf. makạ.
mĭkị m. weaver's stretching thread in loo
for weaving.
mīkịntā = mīkạntā.
mikitsị̄yā = makitsị̄yā.
mīkĭyā Vd. mīkị 2.
mīƙọ Kt. = mīƙị.

mīkōkī *Vd.* mīkį 2.

mil A. (mįl) *m.* (*sg., pl.*) *Eng.* mile (= maịl).

B. (mil) *used in* yā ɓatạ ~ = yā tạfi ~ he has vanished from sight.

mịlyạŋ *m.* (*sg., pl.*) *Eng.* million.

mīlā *Kt.* = mạlā 2.

mįlī *m.* being in a daze (= sāɓạ 2*f*).

mīlīlī (1) *adj. m.* (*f.* mīlīlịyā) *pl.* milī-mili small and round (*re* fruit) *x* 'yar ạlbasạ mīlīlịyā a small round onion. (2) *noun* 'yar ạlbasạ mīlīlī dạ ita it's a tiny onion.

milkẹ *Kt.* = buɗuɗɗukē 2.

millạ (1) *Vb.* 3A travelled far. (2) *Vb.* 1A (*a*) projected (missile) far. yā ~ ɓaryā he told a whopping lie. (*c*) tā ~ tūwō she made fine tūwō (= sillạ). (*d*) *Kt.* tā ~ zanẹ she fastened her cloth well round her body.

millẹ *Kt.* (1) *Vb.* 1A = millạ 2*d*. (2) *Vb.* 3A *x* yā ~ dạ gardamạ he became involved in a heated quarrel.

mįlmītạ *f.* (*pl.* milmītōcī) millimetre-gun.

mįlu = mēlu.

mimmįɓē = mįɓā 2*a*, mīɓẹ 1*b*.ii.

mįŋ *Vd.* mŋ.

mina A. (mįnā) *Sk.* what is it ? (*masc.*) = mẹnēnẹ.

B. (Mįnạ) *f.* the town Minna.

mina-mina *adv.* (1) (*a*) ~ mukạ bīyā we paid in full (= garai-garai). (*b*) Audụ kudī nẹ ~ Audu pays up in full. (2) yanā kwạnce ~ he's lying sprawled-òut (= liga-liga).

mīnạnā *Sk.* what is it ? (*masc.*) = mẹnēnẹ.

mīnạwā *used in* ɓashim ~ persistent ill-luck (= ɓashim ʌnundịrīɓi).

mị nā Wānẹ *Kt. used in* yā yi minị ~ he treated me with contempt.

mincịnā *Kt.* = muntsụnā.

mincịrīcị = mincịrītị *Kt. used in* ɓashim ~ = mīnạwā. b

mindạ *f.* (*pl.* mindōjī) *Eng.* medal (= dalạ 4).

mịndawạrī = mạndawạrī.

mịndịɓis = mịndịŋɓis *x* yā ɓi ~ he refused point-blank. yā cịnyē shi ~ he devoured it all. yā yi zamansạ ~ he stayed very long, he took his time.

ɱindōjī *Vd.* mindạ.

mịnẹ̄ = mịnēnẹ̄ *Sk.* what is it ? (*masc.*) = mẹnēnẹ̄.

mịnēcẹ̄ *Sk.* what is it ? (*fem.*) = mẹcēcẹ̄ *q.v. under* mẹnēnẹ̄.

miŋgịrē = mirgịnē.

mịŋgyau = askā 5.

minị to me.

minikī *m.* (*pl.* mịnịkai) sieve for dạddawā (*cf.* marāraki).

mini-mini = mitsi-mitsi.

mīnīnī = mīlīlī. •

mịnịtsī *m.* = munụtsī.

mịnjau = mịŋgyau.

minjiryā *f.* (*sg., pl.*) (1) electric catfish (*Malapterus sp.*). (2) limb's going to sleep. (3) coral tree (*Erythrina seneg.*).

mīnọ = mīnạwā.

minshārī *m.* snoring (= masōrī = jạn rạgō = kākārī 1).

mintị *Eng. m.* (1) mint (= fẹlụ̄). (2) minute of time.

minu A. (mịnū) *m.* (1) tiny kolas, dates, cịttā-peppers (*cf.* marsạ). (2) mịnuŋ Asbịŋ wiry Asben horse.

B. (minu) *x* ɓạŋɓanẹ nē ɗam ~ dạ shī it is tiny.

minukī = minikī.

minyạ *f.* (*Ar.* mi'a) (1) *used in the compounds* ạrɓạmīyạ = ạrɓạminyạ 400. hạmsạminyạ 500. alịf wạ minyạ = alụ wạ minyạ 1100. alịf (= alụ) wạ ạrɓạminyạ 1400. alịf (= alụ) wạ hạmsạminyạ 1500. ạlfyaŋ gairạ minyạ 1900. (2) ~ wạ karwā = minyạ wạ karwai the caterpillar gamzạrī *q.v.* (*cf.* mazuŋkudīyā).

minzạrī = munzạrī.

mịrārạŋ = mụrārạŋ.

mirɗạ = murɗạ.

mirgina A. (mirgịnā) (1) *Vb.* 1C (*a*) rolled T. along (= *Sk.* ɓiŋgịrā 2 = *Kt.* margạyā 2). (*b*) yā mirgịnạ lūlạ he drove the steam-roller along. (2) mirginō *Vb.* 3A (farmer) turned on reaching end of furrow. (3) *Vd.* tā ~.

B. (mịrginạ) *Vb.* 2 = mirgịnā 1.

mirgine A. (mirgịnē) (1) *Vb.* 3A (*a*) T. rolled over, rolled away (= tuntsụrē 2*a*). (*b*) toppled over (= tuntsụrē 2*b*). (2) *Vb.* 1C rolled T. aside (= tuntsụrē 1).

B. (mịrginē) *m.* (1) hoeing (nōmā) farm in sections (*x first the north, then the south).* **(2)** villager's removing to near-by compound (*N.B. townspeople do not often move their abode*). **(3)** travelling by District Head, etc., only short daily distance when on tour.

C. (**mirginē**) *m.* rolling one's self along to reach place to commit theft.

mirginī what a huge sheaf! (**damị**).

mirgiŋ-mirgiŋ *adv.* rollingly *x* **yanạ̄ tạfīyạ** ~ he (stout man) is lurching along.

mirginō *Vd.* **mirginā 2.**

miri-miri A. (**miri-miri**) = **mitsi-mitsi.** B. (**mịrī-mịrī**) *m.* **(1)** (*a*) line of fish-hooks. (*b*) floating mines. **(2)** maggot ravaging baobob (**kūkạ**) leaves.

miriri = **mitsitsi.**

mirirrịdā *Kt.* kept on twisting (*intens. of* **murdạ**).

mirmijē = **murmụjē.**

mịrshē = **mụrshē.**

mirsīsī = **mursīsī.**

mịsālị *m.* (*pl.* **mịsālai** = **mịsạlce-mịsạlcē** = **misịlce-misịlcē** = **mạsạlce-mạsạlcē**) *Ar.* **(1)** copy of T. **(2)** replica. **(3)** one like *x* **kạ̄wō minị mịsālịnsạ** bring me one like it! **ịnā mịsālịnsạ** 'what is it like? of what kind is it? **(4)** (*a*) parable, pattern, example, illustration *x* (i) **zạn yi makạ** ~ I'll quote you an example. (ii) **nā bi mịsālịnsạ** I followed his example. (iii) **mun dạuki mịsālị Ạlī shī nē̦ kạmar mụtumịŋ Kano** for the sake of example, let us take Ali as a typical Kano man! (iv) **ƙasar Habashạ ita cē̦ bạbbar** (= **bạbbaŋ**) **ạbim mịsālị** Abyssinia is a case in point. (*b*) **yawạnsụ yā wucẹ** ~ their number is indescribable. **dōkạrtạ tā wucẹ** ~ her coiffure (**dōkạ**) was something extraordinary. (*c*) **gạ̄gạrạ mịsālị** *Vd.* **būwạ̄yī 2.** **(5)** **yanạ̄ dạ kyau na** ~ it is extremely good. **(6)** *adv.* for example *x* ~ **kadạ kạ yi hakạ** for example, do not do that! ~ **kadạ ạ yī** . . . e.g. one must not do. . . . **(7)** *Vd.* **mịsālin, masalạŋ, mụsịlī.**

mịsālin **(1)** about *x* ~ **ạshịriŋ** about 20. ~ **ƙarfẹ ukụ** at about 3 o'clock (= **wajan** = **kạman**). **kwānā** ~ **bịyar** about 5 days. **(2)** like *x* (*a*) **kạ̄wō**

minị dōkị mịsālịnsạ bring me a horse like it! (*b*) **kạmar** ~ **dǎi yạddạ mukē̦, hakạ sū mā** they are just like ourselves (**1, 2** = **mụsịliŋ**). (**3**) *cf.* **mịsālị, masalạŋ.**

misạltā = **misịltā.**

Mịsau = *Kt.* **Misạu** *Vd.* **banzā 3.**

mishi A. (**mishị**) *Sk.* to him (= **masạ**). B. (**mishī**) *m.* bone antimony-pencil.

*mịshirịkī = **mụshirịkī.**

mishīyī = **mishī.**

misịlce-misịlcē *Vd.* **mịsālị.**

misịltā *Vb.* 1C compared *x* **dạ mē̦ zā ạ misịltạ girmaŋ gīwā̦** with what can the size of an elephant be compared? **bā yā̦ misịltūwā** no comparison can be drawn with it, it's incomparable.

misissikā = **masussukā.**

mịskālị = **mịsƙālị** *m.* (*Ar.* **mithƙāl** weight) **(1)** unit for measuring perfume. **(2)** **kō mịskālịn zạrratịŋ bābụ** there is absolutely none of it (*cf.* **zạrrạ**).

miskị *Ar. m.* musk.

mịskilạ *Vb.* 2 pestered (*cf.* **miskịlī**).

miskilancị *m.* contrariness in P. (*cf.* **miskịlī**).

miskịlī *m.* (*f.* **miskịlā**) *pl.* **mịskịlai** (*Ar.* mushkil difficult) **(1)** puzzling. **(2)** difficult P., contrary P.

mịskiŋ *Ar.* = **mịskīnị.**

mịskīnị *m.* (*f.* **mịskīnīyā**) *pl.* **mịskīnai** destitute P.

mịslī = **mịsālị 3.**

mịsliŋ = **mịsālịŋ.**

mita A. (**mịtạ**) *f.* **(1)** grousing, grumbling (= **sallạllamī** = **tạsạlīmạ** = **zūgūgụ**). **(2)** *epithet* (*in songs*) *is* **Na Gō̦zō**, sarkim **mītạ.** B. (**mītạ̄**) = **mītạ̄tạ̄** *Sk.* what is it? (*fem.*) = **mē̦cē̦cē̦** *q.v. under* **mē̦nē̦nē̦.**

mitsilī *m.* (*f.* mitsilā) *pl.* mitsil-mitsil *x* **yạrọ nē̦ dam mitsilī** he's a small lad. **yạrinyạ cē̦ 'yar mitsilā** she's a tiny little girl. **yạ̄rā nē̦ mitsil-mitsil** they're tiny tots.

mītsītsī = mitsītsī *m.* (*f.* **mītsītsịyā**) *pl.* mitsī-mitsī = mitsilī.

mīyạ *f.* **(1)** (*a*) soup or gravy made from meat and leaves of **kuɓēwā**, **karkashī**, etc. (*cf.* **rōmō̦**). (*b*) '**yam** ~ *m.* certain seeds imported from the Southern Provinces for making **1a.** **(2)** leaves of baobob (kūkạ). (3) ạ ɓātạ zūcīyas sâ etc., *Vd.* ɓātạ 8. (4) in dạ shī, ∼ *Vd.* hancị 8. (5) (*a*) kạdam bạ kạ tārạ cịn tūwō dạ mụtụm ba, bạ kạ san shạm ∼ tasạ ba you cannot know a P. till you have lived with him = bạ ạ sam macị tūwō ba sǎi ∼ tā ƙārę (*Vd.* tūwō 14). (*b*) *Vd.* 11 below, shā A.1*g*, shậ mīyạ 2. (*c*) kōwā ya ci tūwō dạ shī, ∼ ya shā he's a tough customer. (*d*) bậ ni, ṇ shā ∼ lend me it, them! (clothes, adornment, horse, etc.). (*e*) yā shā ∼ he (rich P.) is ageing. (6) kậzā ạbiṇ gyāram ∼ *Vd.* wạnę 2*b*. (7) mīyạr gyạɗā *Vd.* sụkanā 1. (8) wata ∼ sǎi ạ maƙwạbtā (i) if T. is beyond you, seek help! (ii) *f.* type of cloth. (9) (*a*) mīyạr gạɗạukūkạ *Vd.* baurērę. (*b*) tūwan dāwạ, mīyạr kūkạ bậ wạdā ba nę. kuturū mā yanậ yị (*said by husband in reply to taunts of wife*) you accuse me of ingratitude, but what price yourself! (*c*) hannuṇ wani bā yạ ɗebar wạ wani ∼ if you want a thing done, do it yourself! (*cc*) ƙạzạntar mīyạ *Vd.* hannū 3*c*. (*d*) "Mại gạrậjē, gậ damị," sǎi ya cę ạ zubạ ∼ running before one can walk. (*e*) dạgạ "Mạrhạbā Sarkim Pậwa?" sǎi zāƙim mịyạ? how can such a course of action produce the desired result! (*f*) tūwaṇ girmā, mīyạ-ssạ nāmạ power never lacks zest. (*g*) ƙafạr ụngụlū mại ɓātạ ∼ what an undesirable person! (*h*) bậ ka ∼ *Vd.* ƙạfō 4*a*. (9*A*) ạlkālim ∼ *Vd.* ạlkālī 4. (10) kā tākạ ∼ sorry, but you're too late to share our meal! (= nōmā 1*f*). (11) (*a*) shā ∼ servant *x* shậ mīyạnā nę he is my servant. shậ mīyạtā cę she is my servant (*Vd.* 5 *above*, shā A.1*g*, shậ mīyạ 2). (*b*) mīyạ ya shā *Vd.* shā 1*g*.iv. (*c*) *Kt.* mashậ ∼ *m.*, *f.* (*sg.*, *pl.*) beggar. (12) tanậ tūwō dạ ∼ she's making tūwō for sale (*cf.* tậkạ bangō, sâfalā). (13) ∼ ɓīyū epithet of the bushfowl (makwarwā) = Fayau. (14) mīyạr rūwā watersnake. (15) *Vd.* minyạ.

mīyạ̄gū (1) *Vd.* mūgụ. (2) mīyậgum bậƙī *Vd.* barękatạ.

mị ya hi rậinạ *Kt.* = mę ya fi rậinạ.

mīyākū *Vd.* mīkị 1.

mīyau *m.* (1) *Sk.* saliva = yau *q.v.* (2) *Vd.* mai dạ 2*j*, arnę 3.

mịyū *Kt.* = mịnū.

mīyu-mīyu = mitsi-mitsi *q.v. under* mītsītsī.

*mīzānī *m.* (*pl.* mịzānai) *Ar.* weighing-scales.

mṃ (1) no! (= ā 'ậ). (2) yā zaunạ bậ m, bậ ∼ he remained mum. (3) *cf.* m.

mmạ (*two syllables, high followed by low*) = ṃmā (*low then high syllable*) = ummạ = mmạmạ (*high, low, low*) *Ar.* *f.* (1) mother *x* mmạtạ my mother. (2) cikịm mmạtā nę he's my full-brother (= ɗạṇūwā). (3) mmạ-mmạ bīyū tā fi mmạ-mmạ ɗayā two heads are better than one. (4) dakạ na ummạ *Vd.* Dakạrkarī.

mṇ to me (= minị).

mōdạ *f.* the aloe Aloe Barteri (= kabạr gīwā).

modạ A. (mōɗā) *f.* (*pl.* mōɗậyē) (1) gourd for dipping water out of pot. (2) ∼ bậ irị ba cę there is no harm in appointing a P. to an official position even though not hereditary to him. (3) Mōɗā, kō ạ Kwậrạ sǎi an dannạ what a stubborn person! (4) azụmim ∼ merely pretending to fast (*Vd.* azụmī).

B. (mọɗā) *Vb.* 2 gulped down.

mōdę (1) (*a*) gulped down all of liquid. (*b*) yā ∼ bậkī he sucked in his lips. (2) *Vb.* 3A (*a*) (cheeks) sank in. (*b*) = kōmaɗạ 1.

mōdị *m.* gambling (= cācā).

mōkạɗā = kōmạɗā.

mōkaɗạ = kōmaɗạ.

mōkạɗē = kōmạɗē.

mōlạƙē = kōmạɗē.

*mọlạnce *x* ạ ∼ yakę it is ellipse-shaped (*Vd.* mōlō 3).

mōlậyē *Vd.* mōlō.

mọlī = mọlī-mọlī *Kt. f.* the bird tsậda.

mōlō *m.* (*pl.* mōlậyē) (1) three-stringed guitarre (= tafậshē 2*a*), *Vd.* izgā 3, magūɗīyā. (2) protracted howling of dog especially at night. (3) (*a*) ellipse (= kōmō 2). (*b*) mōlaṇ kậi gạrēshị he is dolichocephalic.

mora A. (mǫrā) *Vb.* 2 (*Vd.* mǫrō) made use of P. or T. (*cf.* mar). B. (mǫrā) *Vd.* mōri. mōre (1) *Vb.* 3A felt enjoyment *x* ṇ saki jiki, m ∼ let me relax and enjoy life ! (*cf.* ishisshịrē 3). (2) *Vb.* 1A (*with dative*) *x* mum ∼ wa idammụ kallam mājịgi we feasted our eyes on the cinema. (*b*) *Kt.* (i) yā ∼ mini he deceived me (= mar 2). (ii) sum ∼ mukụ they got the upper hand of you.

mori A. (mǫrī) *m.* type of white, hard-grained guinea-corn (= mǫri mātarka). B. (mōri) *m.* (*pl.* mǫrā) (1) stable (= bargā 1). (2) dam ∼ *m.* (*pl.* 'yam ∼) (*a*) a favourite (= mōwa 2 *but there is no form* 'yar ∼ *with sense of* mōwa 1), *cf.* gabā 9. (*b*) boy who is favourite of rich man or Chief and acts as mounted messenger.

mǫrīyā *f.* (1) usefulness, value *x* (*a*) bā shi da ∼ it is of no use. (*b*) nā sāmi ∼ a wurinsa = nā ci ∼ tasa I found it useful. sun ci mǫrīyar nasarammụ they benefited by our victory. (*c*) *cf.* karātū 2*e.* (2) maram ∼ *m.*, *f.* (*pl.* marasā ∼) (*a*) useless. (*b*) slacker. (*c*) miserly. (3) *cf.* yārǫ 7, Zangi, Gindau.

mǫrō *m.* (1) (*Sec. v.n. of* mǫrā) *x* yanā mǫransa = yanā mǫrā tasa he is using it. (2) a ci ∼ (*said by children playing*) let's knock down (baje) his sand-castle !

mōta *f.* (*pl.* mōtōcī) *Eng.* (1) (*a*) motor-car (= mutuka). (*b*) *Vd.* bāwa 8*b.* (2) (*a*) yā zō a mōtar karē he came on foot. (*b*) yā hau mōtar karē he ran away. (*c*) karam ∼ *Vd.* karen 6. (3) idam ∼ *Vd.* idǫn 11.

mōtǫ *m.* = mōta.

mōtsa (1) *Vb.* 3A (*a*) moved *x* (i) kada ka ∼ don't move ! yā ∼ gaba he moved forward. (ii) mǫtsa, mụ jī ka, makāfǫ yā sō bā dansa kāshī let's hear what you've got to say about it ! (*b*) set out on journey. (*c*) was in ferment *x* (i) garī yā ∼ = garī yā mǫtsu the town was excited. fada yā mǫtsu tsakāninsụ quarrel arose between them. (ii) kāsūwā tā ∼ business is brisk. (iii) yāƙin da ya tāshị mōtsāwā the war which has broken

out fiercely. (iv) haŋkalinsa yā ∼ his mind is disturbed ; he is angry ; he is mad. (v) azakarinsa yā ∼ his penis is in erection. (vi) gindinsa yā ∼ he (small boy) wants to pass water. (*d*) cīwansa yā ∼ his pain has re-appeared. (*e*) jikinsa yā ∼ = jikinsa yā mǫtsu he is not feeling well. (*f*) bangō yā ∼ = bangō yā mǫtsu the wall is beginning to crack, beginning to subside. (*g*) (i) tsiminsa yā mōtsa the tonic has invigorated him. (ii) *Vd.* saiwā 4. (*h*) *Vd.* mǫtsu. (2) *Vb.* 1A (*a*) moved T. (*b*) affected *x* kamar bā abin da ya ∼ su as if nothing has affected them. ba sụ ∼ wani abu a tsārin zamansụ ba no change was made in their organization. (*c*) a mōtsa *m.* = mǫtsiŋ gēmụ. (*d*) (*plus dative*) *x* yā ∼ masa haŋkalī = yā ∼ masa rāi it disturbed his mind, it angered him. (*e*) (*plus dative*) nā ∼ masa maganar I reminded him of the matter. (*f*) (i) stirred up (soup, etc., *as in* kauraya *q.v.*). (ii) yā ∼ rigima he stirred up dissension.

mǫtsattsē *m.* (*f.* mǫtsattsīyā) *pl.* mǫtsattsū mad.

mǫtsī *m.* (1) (*a*) movement, motion. (*b*) cikina yanā ∼ my stomach feels queasy. (*c*) inda yāƙi ya fi ∼ where the war is most active. (*d*) mai rāi bā yā rasa ∼ while there's life there's hope. (*e*) *Vd.* rēna 11. (2) akwai wani ∼ tsakānimmụ da shī there is a dispute between us and him. (3) shrivelled ground-nuts (= kamashō 2 = kashamō 2). (4) cī da mǫtsiŋ wani *Vd.* balbēla. (5) mǫtsiŋ gēme *Kt.* ground-nuts shelled, roasted (sōya), skinned, salted and peppered, and then again roasted. (5) mǫtsiŋ gēmụ ground-nuts shelled, boiled, salted, then roasted (sōya) with inner skin left on (= mōtsa 2*c*).

mōtsǫ *m.* = mǫtsī 3.

mǫtsu *Vb.* 3B (1) *Vd.* mōtsa 1. (2) im mutụm yā ∼ săi a kashe shi if anyone shows opposition, he is killed.

mōwa (1) (*a*) *f.* favourite wife (= *Sk.* makwasa), *cf.* bōra. (*b*) kumburī a ∼, sakīya a bōra kissing goes by favour. (*c*) bā a ∼ săi da bōra there must be more than one before one can make comparisons. (d) tūlum $\sim$ Vd. tūlū 6. (2) m., f. (a) who or what one prefers x tūwō mōwₐnsₐ nē what he prefers is tūwō. furā mōwₐssₐ cē his favourite dish is furā (= kāmu 3). (b) a favourite (= mōrį 2), cf. gₐbā 9.

mȯyį = mōwₐ.

mu A. (mū) (1) (independent pronoun, Mod. Gram. 46) we x (a) mū nȩ it is we. mū nȩ mukₐ zō it is we who came. (b) (used as direct object when dative precedes, Mod. Gram. 76a.ii³) x yā nēmar musu mū he sought us for them. (2) mū yȩ̄ mū Vd. yȩ̄. (3) (dialectal) x mū zō = mun zō or mukₐ zō. (4) Vd. mū dukₐ, zā 5.

B. (mu) (1) (objective pronoun after low tone in previous verb, Mod. Gram. 49a¹) us x yā kāmₐ mu he seized us (cf. mu). (2) Vd. mukȩ̄, mukₐ, munā. (3) (first pl. pronoun used after zā Mod. Gram. 17 and bā Mod. Gram. 19b) x zā mu kₐsūwā we're off to market. bā mu zūwₐ we're not coming.

C. (mu) (1) (objective pronoun after high tone in previous verb, Mod. Gram. 49a¹) us x suŋ gam mu they saw us (cf. mu 1). (2) (subjunctive pronoun, first pl., Mod. Gram. 13a) x (a) mu tₐfĭ let us go ! yanā sō mu zō he wants us to come. munā sō mu tₐfĭ we want to go. (b) mu ganĭ ₐ ƙas Vd. kₐrē 29. (c) mu ga ta fādĭ Vd. tsūtsₐ 6. (d) mu jē mū Vd. zā 5. (e) mu jē zūwₐ Vd. mahₐukₐcĭ 1a.ii. (3) our x (a) dōkįmmu our horse (Mod. Gram. 47b). (b) (after v.n. of changing verbs and after sec. v.n.). (i) ₐikarmu = aikįmmu the sending us (Mod. Gram. 47c). nēmammu the looking for us. tₐmbayₐ mu the asking us. sunā nēmammu they're seeking us. kunā tₐmbayₐrmu you are asking us. (ii) (gives continuous sense in cases like the following) mun yi zamammu cikin dākin naŋ well, we went on living in that house. munā tₐfĭyₐrmu sài . . . while we were on our way, then . . . munā yāwₐmmu sài . . . while wandering about, we . . . (4) zaŋ kōmₐ garimmu I'll return to my town (only Chief of town would say

zaŋ kōmₐ garĭna), Vd. Mod. Gram. 47e. (5) Vd. nāmu. (6) (following zā) we shall (Mod. Gram. 14) x zā mu zō we shall come. bₐ zā mu zō ba we shall not come (Mod. Gram. 20a). (7) we (in negative past, Mod. Gram. 20a) x bₐ mu zō ba we did (have) not come.

D. (mū) Kt. = mā x mū zō we shall probably come.

mu'ālātu = muwālātu.

mu'āmalₐ = mu'āmilₐ = mu'āmillₐ = mₐ'āmalₐ q.v.

*mu'annₐsā Ar. f. feminine in gender (Vd. muzakkₐrĭ).

Mu'āzu man's name.

mubarrₐs = mubarrₐshĭ m. (pʹ. mubₐrrₐsai) thin, white turban-fabric.

*mubāsharₐ Ar. f. being in relations with x munā $\sim$ dₐ sū (1) we have dealings with them (= mₐ'āmalₐ). (2 we embrace them (= ruŋgumₐ).

mubāya'ₐ = mubāyi'ₐ = mₐbāyi'ₐ q.v.

mubazzarancį m. being spend-thrift (Vd. mubazzₐrĭ).

mubazzₐrĭ m. (f. mubazzₐrā) pl. mubₐzzₐrai Ar. spend-thrift, prodigal.

mubįyĭ = mabįyĭ.

mubugĭ = mabugĭ.

muburmĭ = maburmĭ.

muci-muci x idₐnunsₐ $\sim$ sukȩ̄ he's nearly blind (= dushi-dushi).

mucĭyā = mūcĭyā f. (pl. mucĭyōyĭ = mūcĭyōyĭ). (1) (a) stick for stirring tūwō. (b) zō, kₐ ci $\sim$ come here, Child, and I'll give you the tūwō-scrapings (cf. kātsȩ) from the mārā ! (2) pole for stirring dye in dye-pit (karōfĭ). (3) canoe-pole (= gwaŋgwalā). (4) stick for stirring sweets when being boiled. (5) mūcĭyar karā Vd. langₐ.

mudₐ Vb. 1A Kt. used in (1) bₐi $\sim$ bₐ̄kĭ ba he uttered no reply. (2) bā shi dₐ ta mudₐ̄wā he's stumped for a reply.

*mudabbar Ar. m. contract by owner that slave becomes manumitted on the former's death (Vd. *mudabbₐrĭ).

*mudabbₐrĭ m. (f. mudabbₐrā) pl. mudₐbbₐrai slave granted contract as in mudabbₐr.

mudafā = madafā.

mūdₐnabį = Kt. mūdunnabį m. (d.f. mūduŋ ₐnnabį, cf. mūdu 1b) a measure

containing four handfuls (tāfī) of corn
(*four such measures, i.e. one* sā'ī *q.v. are
due to every* P. *as alms at end of* Azųmī),
Vd. fįd dą kąi, kąfārą, mūdų 1b,
cakwalǫ, dăi dą zakką.

*mųdārātį Ar. m. small present (=
hasąfī).

mųdawwąrī = mądawwąrī.

mūdąyē Vd. mūdų.

muddą Ar. (1) f. (a) period x muddąr
zamāna ą Kanǫ during the period of my
stay at Kano. (b) Vd. muddį. (2)
muddąr conj. (a) when (*with past
sense*) muddąr muką zō, muką gan shį
when we came, we saw him (= sā'ą
5a q.v.). (b) if (i) (*with progressive tense*)
x yąyą zā mų mąntą dą shī muddąr
muną tunąwā dą rąn dą ya yi fāmā
dą Jāmųs how can we ever forget him if
we recall the day when he stood out
against the Germans? kadą ku
yąrdā muddąr kuną dą sauran numfāshī never agree as long as you live!
(ii) (*followed by past tense or subjunctive*)
x muddąr kā nadą ni Sarkī, ną bī ką if
you appoint me Chief, I shall acknowledge your sway. muddąr dăi yą sąmi
girmā provided only that he becomes
powerful.

muddį (1) = muddą 1a. (2) yā kai
muddįm mutąnē he became adult
(= įsa 3a.ii).

mūdī m. (1) type of harmless snake
(= gidā 1k.ii). (2) Mūdī *another form
of the name* Mąmūdų q.v.

mūdų m. (pl. mūdąyē) (Ar. mudd). (1) (a)
vessel of standard capacity for
measuring out corn (cf. fąfąkī). (b)
yā fįd dą ~ he gave a mūdąnabį of
corn Vd. fįd dą kąi, kąfārą. (c) idǫ
bą ~ ba, yā sąŋ kīmą though the eye is
not a vessel of measure, it can make a
close estimate; one can make one's
own deductions from the facts. (d)
fasą ~ Vd. fasą 1l. (2) dam ~ m. (a)
(pl. 'yam ~) small type of 1a. (b)
(no plural) (i) an yi dam ~ there was
a slight famine. (ii) dam ~ gąrēshį
he's niggardly. (3) dāwą dą ~ maize-
cobs (= gōyō 1c).

mududdukįyā f. back-door (= maduddukā).

mū duką f. metal bracelet or anklet
(*epithet is* Mū duką 'yan Sarkī).

mūdukārę Kt. m. Rahazāwā type of
cloth (white with black stripe).

mųdųkūkį m. (f. mųdųkūkīyā) pl. mų-
dųkūkai. (1) sullen P. (2) cloddish P.
(3) dirty, slovenly P. (= dųnsurmą).

mūdųnnabį Kt. = mūdąnabį.

mudus-mudus x fįtilą taną cį ~ the lamp
is dim.

mųfalląs = mųfalląshī.

mųfalląshī m. (f. mųfallashīyā) pl. mų-
fąlląsai. (1) spend-thrift (d.f. falląsā).
(2) (a) mischief-maker (d.f. fąllasą).
(b) epithet is Mųfalląs, karōfįŋ gyartai.

*mufurądī Ar. m. being of the singular
number (cf. jam'į), the singular number
x namijį ~ nę the word " namijį " is in
the singular.

mufųtī m. (pl. mųfųtai = Sk. mųfųttai).
Ar. (1) judicial assessor (*two such sit
with* ąlkālī), Vd. fątąwā. (2) scribe
attached to a hākįmī.

mųgāmą f. (Ar. maqāmą) staying at a
place during a journey.

mų ganī ą kas Vd. kąrē 29.

mųgaribą = mągaribą.

mūgų m. (f. mugunyą = mūgūwā) pl.
mīyągū = mūgąyē. (1) (a) bad, evil (=
mųmmūnā). (b) ~ shī ya sam makwantar
~ Greek met Greek. (c) mūgųn yārǫ
kā yi barcį? are you going to cease
your evil ways? (*he is supposed to
reply, threatening to denounce the speaker,
in the words* n ną jį, kā zągi Sarkī). (d)
bā ą mūgųn Sarkī, săi mūgųm bąfādę
the Emir is not evil but he has evil
counsellors. (e) im mūgūwar kązā
tā shįga akurkī, kōwąccē ta zō, săi tą
sąrē tą no kīshīyā is welcomed by the
others. (f) mūgųn nāką yā fi bąrē
na wani better my own than a borrowed
thing! (= mūgųn gątarī = gątarī 1c
q.v.). (g) Dųngū mūgųn hannū, iŋ
aŋ kī ką, bą wani make the best of a
bad bargain! (h) rįgar mūgų Vd.
darē 1a.ii. (j) Vd. bąn ni dą ~. (k)
mīyągum bąkī Vd. barękatą. (2) Vd.
compounds of mūgųn, mugunyąr. Vd.
mųmmūnā. (3) mugunyą f. pus
(= dīwą 1 = sųrkāmī = Kt. bardį).

mugųdįancī = magųdįancī.

mụgụḍụ̃wã *f.* short woman, short fowl (*cf.* ḍụ̃ngu-ḍụ̃ngū).

mūgụ̃n babba *Vd.* garạ̃nhõtsạmī.

mūgụ̃n bābẹ *Vd.* bābẹ 5.

mūgụ̃n bạ̃kī *Vd.* bạ̃kī 2*p.*

mūgụ̃n bạ̃k̃õ *Vd.* barẹkatạ.

mụgụ̃nce-mụgụ̃ncē *Vd.* mụgụ̃ntā.

mūgụ̃n ḍã *m.* thief, wastrel, debauchee (*cf.* mūgụ̃n 'yancị).

mūgụ̃n dawạ *m.* wart-hog (= ạlhạnzịr).

mūgụ̃ŋ gạmõ *Vd.* kạciɓis.

mūgụ̃ŋ gāshị *m.* (1) cantankerousness. (2) *Vd.* azzịkī 8.

mūgụ̃ŋ gãtarī *used in* mūgụ̃ŋ gãtarịŋkạ yā fi " sạ̃ri kạ bā nị ! " independence is best on no matter how modest a scale (= mūgụ̃ 1*f*).

mūgụ̃ŋ girbị *Vd.* fạllē 1*b.*

mūgụ̃ŋ gõrọ *Vd.* dabgajã.

mūgụ̃ŋ hannū *Vd.* dụ̃ngū 1*b.*

mūgụ̃ŋ kại *m.* perversity.

mūgụ̃ŋ macịjī *Vd.* wụ̃ji-wụ̃jī.

mūgụ̃n mālạmī *Vd.* dạ̃dumạ.

mūgụ̃n mạ̃mā *Vd.* ḍãkālẹ 3.

mūgụ̃n matsayī *Vd.* matsayī 3.

mūgụ̃n nāmạ *Vd.* kitsẹ 1*c* ; gạnjar 2*b.*

mūgụ̃n rūwā *m.* *x* tanạ̃ ∼ she's in mourning for her husband (= takabạ *q.v.*).

mūgụ̃n sạndā *Vd.* kẽrẽ 1*b.*

mūgụ̃n Sarkī *Vd.* Sarkī 1*q.*

mūgụ̃n sirdị *Vd.* bukurū.

mugunta A. (mụgụ̃ntā) *f.* (1) badness, wickedness. (2) (*a*) evil act (*pl.* mụgụ̃nce-mụgụ̃ncē). (*b*) *epithet of* 2*a is* Mụgụ̃ntā, fitsārim fạ̃k̃ọ (*cf.* fitsārī 6). (3) iŋ zā kạ hạk̃ạ rāmịŋ ∼, hạk̃ā shi gạjẽrẽ ; watakīlạ, kai zā kạ fāḍạ = rāmịŋ ∼ ạ ginạ shi gạjẽrẽ take care you are not hoist with your own petard ! (4) suŋ ginạ rāmịŋ ∼ they did evil.

B. (mụgụ̃ntạ) *Vb.* 3B became bad, evil (= mụ̃nanạ).

C. (muguntā) *Vb.* 1C. (1) slandered (= mụ̃nanā 1). (2) disgraced (= lā-lạ̃tā 1*b*).

mūgụ̃n tarkõ *Vd.* kụcīcī.

mūgụ̃n tayị *Vd.* ạlbarkạ 2*b.*

mūgụ̃n tūwõ *m.* type of guinea-corn making dark tūwõ.

mugunyạ *Vd.* mūgụ.

mūgụ̃n 'yancị *m.* theft, immorality, etc. (*cf.* mūgụ̃n ḍã, 'yancị).

mugunyạr dạfūwā *Vd.* yuŋwạ 1*c.*

mugunyạr rawā *Vd.* rawā 1*b.*

mugunyạr takạrdā *f.* overland mail (= kadạ tạ kwānā).

mugunyạr yuŋwạ *Vd.* sạndi.

mūgụ̃n zạkarạ *Vd.* k̃ĩk̃irịk̃ij.

mugurjī *m.* (*pl.* mụgụrzai). (1) stone whereon cotton is hand-ginned (*Vd.* gurjẹ). (2) ḍam ∼ (*pl.* 'yam ∼) = bidạ 2*a, b.*

mụgwāmạ *Kt.* = mụgāmạ.

mụhālīyạ *f.* (*Ar.* muhāl " impossible "). (1) superstition. (2) deceit *x* an yi masạ ∼ he has been wronged, deceived.

mụhallị = mạhallị.

mụhalliḍạ = mạhallitsạ.

Mụhammạdīyyạ *f.* (1) (*a*) (i) the Muslim religion (= Lịslāmạ = Musuluncị). (ii) *Vd.* Musuluncị 2. (*b*) yāk̃iŋ yā wucẹ na ∼ it was a terrible battle. (*c*) ạbịŋ yā wucẹ na ∼ it was too much to bear. (*d*) jạ̃ dạ bāya irịn ta ∼ = dagā 4. (2) Muhammadan affairs (*x* law, history, traditions, etc.). (3) makarantar ∼ *f.* Koranic school.

Muhammadụ (1) Mohammed (*Vd.* ạnnabị 2*b*, shụ̃gạba 3). (2) Amīnạ 1*b* = Inūwạ 1*d* = Taɓaryad dạshī = Tārī = Tụrạ̃re = Sayyạdī = Gõfe jandārū *is name for any man called* Mụhammadụ. (3) *Vd.* Mạhạmūdụ, Mạ̃mūdụ, Muham-mạ̃ŋ, Maŋgạ, gạŋgaŋ 1*c*, ạnnabị, ma'ạik̃ī.

Mụhammạ̃ŋ (1) = Mụhammadụ. (2) *Vd.* garmā 2*b*, gạŋgaŋ, Maŋgạ.

mụhammarạ = mụharramạ.

Mụharrạm *m.* 1st Muslim month (*Vd.* wọwwõ, wutsīyạ 1*d*, cịkạ cikị).

mụharramạ *f.* (*Ar.* hammara " dyed red ") any thin, patterned, reddish cotton fabric.

mụharrạmī *m.* (*f.* mụharramā) *pl.* mụ-harrạmai (*Ar.* muharram " ritually forbidden ") P. forbidden to one in marriage through closeness of blood-ties.

mụhāwarạ = mụhawwarạ *Ar. f.* disputation, discussion.

mụhibbạ *f.* (1) (*Ar.* mạhabbat) love *x* dạ ∼ yak̃ẹ he is popular (= farin jinī).

(2) (*Ar.* hāba) being of respect-inspiring or redoubtable mien (= haibạ).

muhimmį *m.* (*f.* muhimmįyā) *pl.* muhįm-mai *Ar.* important (*re* affair) = mu-sammạŋ 1*c.* ∼nē gạrēsụ it is important to them.

muhūci = mahūcī.

muhūjī = mahūjī.

muhukuncī = mahukuncī.

muhūrī = mahūrī.

muhutai *Vd.* mufutī.

*muhutalạr *m.* (*Ar.* muhtazar) *x* yā kai ∼ he's in the death-throes (= gargarạ).

mui let us do ! (= mụ yī).

mujaddạdī *m.* (*pl.* mujạddạdai) (*Ar.* " renewer ") religious reformer (*x* the Mạhạdī ; Shēhụ Ụsụmānụ ɗaŋ Hōdīyọ, etc.).

mujāzạ *f.* (*Ar.* ajāza "he allowed ") means whereby *x* Audụ nē mujāzạr auran naŋ it was through Audu that the marriage was arranged. nā yi masạ mujāzạr wannạŋ aikį I was the means of his getting this job.

mūjīyā *f.* (*pl.* mūjīyōyī). (1) owl. (2) yā yi minį kūkam ∼ he gave me a present (= kūkan 2). (3) tsāmīyā tā jūyẹ dạ ∼ *Vd.* tsāmīyā 1*b*.

mūjizạ = mu'ujizạ.

mukạ we (*past relative verbal prefixed pronoun*) *x* sạn dạ mukạ zō when we came (Mod. Gram. 133, 181, 182).

mukạ A. (mụ̄kā) *Vb.* 2 hit *x* nā mụ̄kē shi dạ sạndā I hit him with a stick (= ɗōkā).
　　B. (mūkạ) *Vb.* 1A (*with dative*) *x* nā ∼masạ sạndā I hit him with a stick (= ɗōkạ, mụ̄kā).

*mukābalạ = mukābilạ *Ar. f.* collating of manuscripts.

mukaddạm = mukaddạs.

mukaddạs = mukaddạs = mukaddạshī = mukaddạshī *m.* (*pl.* mukạddạsai, etc.). (1) deputy, relief, representative (= ma-dạdī = maimakō). (2) Deputy Chief *x* Mụkaddạshin ɗōgạrai the Deputy Chief N.A. police-head. (3) Baitįl ∼ *m.* Jerusalem (*Ar.* Baitu'l Maqdis).

mukaddasancī = mukadassancī *m.* office and duties of mụkaddạs.

mukaddasantad dạ = mukaddasantad dạ *Vb.* 4 appointed P. as mụkaddạs.

mūkā-mūkā *Vd.* mūkēkẹ.

mukạmukī *m.* (1) lower jaw (= mum-mukẹ). (2) mukạ̄mukai *pl.* the upper and lower jaws.

mūkẹ *Vb.* 1A *x* nā ∼ shi dạ sạndā I hit him with a stick (= mụ̄kā).

mūkēkẹ *m.* (*f.* mūkēkīyā) *pl.* mūkā-mụ̄kā long and thick.

mūkį what a hard blow ! (*cf.* mūkẹ).

mukụ to you (*pl.*).

mukụddū *m.* (*f.* mukuddụwā) bull-necked P. or jug.

mukullī = makullī.

mụkū-mụkū (1) *m.* mụkū-mụkun ɗārī the part of the cold-season when the harmattan (hụntūrụ *q.v.*) is thick. (2) *adv.* *x* Allạ yā saukad dạ sanyī ∼ the cold season came with thick harmattan.

mụ'ku-mụkū" = mụkū-mukū *m.* (1) being reserved, reticence (= zurfī 2). (2) sunạ ta ∼ tukuŋ they're lying low at present. (3) sun yi ta mụku-mụkuŋ ạbiŋ they spread news about it surreptitiously.

mụkūnīyā = mụkwīnīyā.

mukụrdū = mukuddū.

mụkurū *m.* (*pl.* mukurạ) woman's loin-cloth (= fạ̄tạ̄rī *q.v.*).

mukurūrūcīyā *f.* cereal's head being about to appear (= magūɗīyā).

mukus *m.* *x* yā yi ∼ he was silent through fear, shame, etc.

mukūsā = makūsā.

mukut-mụkụt *m. and adv.* (1) *x* nā ji ∼ I heard a gulping-noise. (2) yā haɗīyē shi ∼ he swallowed it gulpingly.

mụkwīnīyā *f.* (1) dilly-dallying. (2) shilly-shallying in replying (= kumį-nīyā).

mul *m. and adv.* (1) yā ɓatạ ∼ he has completely vanished. (2) (*a*) zanẹ yā yi ∼ dạ shūnī his cloth is well-stained with indigo. (*b*) an yi tūwō ∼ dạ shī some excellent tūwō has been made.

mụlā *Vb.* 3B (1) vanished. (2) was in-toxicated (= bụgu).

*mụliddį *m.* (*f.* muliddīyā) *pl.* mụliddai (*Ar.* muzidd " adversary ") cantan-kerous P.

mūlihạ *f.* (1) yā kai ∼ the affair has become serious (= bụŋkāsạ). *(2) severe head-wound (*cf.* māmūmạ).

mụlī = mụlī-mụlī = mōlī *q.v.*

mulka A. (mulkā) f. (1) rubbing indigo (shūnī) on one's body. (2) Had. rubbing shūnī on edges of shoe-soles. (3) Kt. yā shā ~ he was beaten.
  B. (mulkā) (1) = mallakạ. (2) Nor. = mū̃kā.
  C. (mulkạ) Nor. = mū̃kạ.
mulkẹ Nor. = mū̃kẹ.
mulkị Ar. m. (1) (a) ruling, governing, government. (b) sunā̃ ~ dạ ƙasạn naŋ = sunā̃ mulkịŋ ƙasạn naŋ they rule that country. (c) Gabasāwā tanā̃ cikim mulkịnsạ G. District is under his authority, jurisdiction (= hakuncị). ƙasā̃sham mulkịn Sarkī countries ruled by the King. (d) Afirkạ ta kudụ tā sā̃mi mulkịŋ kạntạ = tā sā̃mi mulkịŋ ạbintạ South Africa has acquired independence (Vd. mụsammạŋ 1a). (2) option x yanā̃ cikim mulkịnsạ it's within his option to do it or not. (3) (a) yanā̃ zubạ ~ he's making a show of authority. (b) ~ gạrēshị he is arrogant (= ạlfarmā).
mullạ = millạ.
mụllī Kt. m. fruiting-head (= gō̃dā q.v.).
mulmula A. (mulmụlā) Vb. 1C kneaded T. between the fingers.
  B. (mụlmulạ) Vb. 2 = mulmụlā.
mulmule A. (mulmụlē) Vb. 1C = mulmụlā.
  B. (mulmulẹ) m. kneaded-ball x mulmulạm furā ball of furā (= cūrị 2).
mulụfī m. (1) Scarlet Bishop Bird (Pyromelana flammiceps) = dā̃lā = jan bā̃kī 1 = jan taŋkō. (2) (a) red flannel or serge, etc. (= jan taŋkō). (b) farim ~ white flannel, serge, etc. (so for other colours, the name of the colour being prefixed) (2a, b = ạl'akạrī). (c) Vd. dā̃lō 4b.
muluk = mul.
mulumbucī m. the rags kasaŋkī q.v.
mụmbarạs = mụbarrạs.
mumbạrī m. (pl. mụmbạrai) (Ar. minbar). (1) type of embroidery on gown. (2) pulpit of Friday Congregational Mosque (masallācin Jumma'ạ), cf. mạnārạ.
mūminī = mumminī m. (f. mumminā, etc.) pl. mụmmịnai, etc., Ar. (1) (a) true believer, i.e. Muslim. (b) mūminịŋ kạrē underhanded P. (epithet is Mūmi-

niŋ kạrē, cīzọ bā̃ haushị). (2) (Ar. amīn) trustworthy P. (3) Vd. rịgar mū̃mịnai.
mummuƙe A. (mummuƙẹ) m. = muƙā̃muƙī.
  B. (mụmmuƙē) m. (1) kisạm ~ ill-treating P. whom one pretends to like. (2) an yi musụ cịm ~ = an yi musụ kisạm ~ they have been oppressed (all = tumụ 4).
mụmmūnā m., f. (pl. mūnā̃nā). (1) (a) bad, evil (= mūgụ q.v.). (b) mụmmūnaŋ ƙarƙō ạ yi ƙarƙwaŋ kīfī, dạgạ rūwā sǎi wutā all's bạd that ends badly. (2) ugly. (3) Vd. mūgụ.
mummụnī = mummịnī.
mumur used in tūwō yā yi ~ = tūwō ~ dạ shī nẹ̃ it is good tūwō.
mun A. (mun) we (verb-prefix of past tense, Mod. Gram. 16) x (1) mun zō we came, we have come. (2) Vd. mun dạɗu, muŋ hanạ, muŋ ƙī. (3) ~ cạkarạ Vd. gạnyau.
  B. (mụn) Sk. = mā̃ (Mod. Gram. 118) x mụn zō we'll probably come.
muna A. (munā̃) we are (verb-prefix of progressive, Mod. Gram. 16) x (1) munā̃ zūwạ we are coming. (2) munā̃ tāmụ, Allā nā̃ tāsạ = ƙạddarạ 2. (3) munā̃ kunnē Vd. bakạ 1f. (4) ~ ƙwaryā Vd. ƙwaryā 1g.
  B. (munạ) Sk. to us = manạ q.v.
munāfincị = munāfuccị.
munāfuƙī m. (f. munāfuƙā) pl. mụnā̃fụkai = Kt. mụnā̃fụkkai Ar. (1) (a) hypocrite (= tā̃wịlallē). (ii) cf. mụnā̃fuffuk. (b) traitor. (c) dō̃mim ~ gạrī bā yā̃ ƙịŋ wāyẹ̃wā intrigue comes to light sooner or later. (d) Vd. rịgar mū̃mịnai. (2) mat like asabạrī.
munāfuccị = munāfuncị m. (1) hypocrisy (= rịyā). (2) (a) treachery. (b) ~ dō̃dō, ụbaŋgijịnsạ ya ƙạn ci evil recoils on the doer. (3) intrigue.
mụnā̃fuffuk m., f., sg., pl. (1) hypocrite (= munāfụkī 1a). (2) epithet is Mụnā̃fuffuk, kurcīyar dụddurụ (cf. kurcīyā 1h).
mụnā̃funtạ Vb. 2 (n.o. mụnā̃fụncị, p.o. mụnā̃fụncē) x sum mụnā̃fụncē mụ they played the hypocrite to us.
munana A. (mūnā̃nā) Vd. mụmmūnā.
  B. (mūnā̃nā) Vb. 1C. (1) x am ~

masạ he has been slandered (= mu-
gụntā). (2) made ugly, spoiled *x*
am ∼ masạ it has been spoiled.
C. (mụnanạ) *Vb.* 3B. (1) became bad,
spoiled *x* halinsạ yā ∼ his character
has deteriorated (= mụgụntạ). (2)
became ugly.
mụnãrạ = mạnãrạ.
*mụnãzarạ *Ar. f.* referring to a book of
reference.
mụnbarạs = mụbarrạs.
mun dạďu *m., f.* (*sg., pl.*) bastard.
mundāyē *Vd.* mundūwā, mundū.
mundirĩkị *Vd.* ƙashim mundirĩkị.
mundū *m.* (*pl.* mundāyē). (1) hammer
resembling masạbā. (2) large mundūwā.
mundūwā -ƒ. (*pl.* mundāyē). (1) torque
bangle (*Vd.* hanạ kĩshĩyā), *cf.* ƙạmbū,
ƙarau, dạrạmbūwā. (2) mundūwā =
mundūwar ƙafạ torque anklet (=
mụrďē).
mụngạribạ = mạgạribạ.
mụngulā *Kt. f.* (*sg., pl.*) type of bush-cat.
mụngulēlẹ = mụngulĩ *m.* (*f.* mụngulē-
lĩyā = mụngulā) *pl.* mụngul-mụngụl
big and round.
muŋ hanạ *Kt. m.* = ạ bā mụ.
mũnị *m.* (1) ugliness (*cf.* mụmmūnā). (2)
(*a*) vice, evil, wickedness *x* bạ ∼ gạ
mụtụm dạ ya fi yạ ƙi bịm mạganạr
ĩyạ̃yansạ there is no greater wickedness
than unfilial conduct. indạ ạbịŋ ya
fi ∼ the place where the situation is
at its worst. (*b*) ∼ dạ kyạŋ halĩ yā
fi kyạkkyāwā handsome is as handsome
does. (*c*) *cf.* tạyā ni ∼. (*d*) ∼ tudụ nē,
sãi kā tãkạ nãkạ kạ ganō na wanĩ
those who live in glass houses should not
throw stones !
munịtsĩ = munụtsĩ.
muŋkạ *Sk.* = mukạ.
Muŋkar *Vd.* Walạkĩrị.
muŋ ƙĩ *used in* yā yi masạ "muŋ ƙĩ"
he turned his back on him ; he refused
to accept it.
munsạ'alạ = mạs'alạ.
muntạ *Sk. f.* anus (= dubụrā).
muntạlagạ = muntạragạ *f.* small hammer.
Muntasạr *used in* nā yi ƙaunar ∼ ạ
Dạwạnau my hopes were vain.
muntsinā = muntsụnā.
muntsuna A. (mụntsunạ). (1) *Vb.* 2 (*a*)

pinched. (*b*) pinched off a bit of T.
(= *Kt.* tsụngulạ). (2) *f.* pinching.
B. (muntsụnā) *Vb.* 1C (*with dative*)
x yā ∼ minị ƙạďaŋ he pinched off a
bit and gave it to me.
mụntsụnạ sạrạkĩ *m.* (*sg., pl.*) type of small
biting insect.
muntsunẹ *m.* bit pinched off *x* tā bā nị
furā ∼ gụdā she gave me a bit of furā
(= *Kt.* tsụngulĩ).
munukĩ = minikĩ.
munụtsĩ *m.* small worn-out loincloth
(bạntē) = tsạlãlạ 2 = zĩrĩ 1*a*.
munzạrĩ *Ar. m.* (*pl.* mụnzạrai) pair of
spectacles (= madūbĩ = tạbạrau).
munzịlĩ *Ar. m.* (1) time for *x* yā ịsa
munzịliŋ kōmọ̃wā he is now due to
return. (2) limit of abuse or illness *x*
tsạkānimmụ dạ shĩ har tā kai munzịlin
zãgị we're on such bad terms that we
descend to mutual abuse. tā kai
munzịlim bā sạ gaisạ̃wā they dislike
each other so much that they don't
even greet one another on meeting.
cĩwạnsạ yā kai munzịlim bā yạ̃ cịŋ
ạbincĩ he's too ill to eat (= mawā), *cf.*
kakị.
mụr *m.* (*Ar. from Greek muron*) myrrh.
mụrạ *f.* cold in the head, catarrh, bronchial
cold.
*mụrabbạ'ĩ *m.* (*f.* mụrabbạ'ā) *pl.* mụ-
rạbbạ'ai *Ar.* (1) *adj.* square. (2) *m.*
(*a*) a square, rectangle. (*b*) ∼ mại dãrị
an oblong.
mụrābụs *m.* (*Ar.* irtabathū "they
separated "?) *x* yā yi ∼ dạ sạrautạ he
resigned, abdicated from his official
position.
mụrãdị *Ar. m.* (1) a desire *x* mụrãdịna yā
bĩyā my wish has been fulfilled (*Vd.*
bĩyā 2). (2) a necessity, requirement *x*
n nạ̃ dạ ∼ ạ gidā I've something to
attend to at home.
*mụrãfịkĩ *m.* (*f.* mụrãfịƙā) *pl.* mụrãfịƙai
(*Ar.* rāhaqa) P. about twelve years of
age.
mụrãfū *Vd.* murfụ.
mura-mura = muri-muri.
mụrãrạŋ *adv.* (1) (*Ar.* mar'ā ainin "seeing") *x* (*a*) nā gan shị ∼ I saw it with my
own eyes. (*b*) bạ̃ wạndạ zại fitō mụrãrạm-
mụrãrạŋ yạ fạďạ masạ nobody would

have the courage to tell him outright.
*(2) (*Ar.* mirār "several times")
frequently.

murɗa A. (murɗ̧a) *Vb.* 1A. (1) (*a*) (i)
twisted (*cf.* jūy̧a). (ii) yā ∽ faŋķa
he set the electrical fan revolving. (*b*)
wrung out (= mātsa̧ 1*a*.iii). (*c*) twisted
out of shape *x* cīwo̧ yā ∽ bāķinsa̧ =
cīwo̧ yā ∽ masa̧ bāķī disease distorted
his mouth. (*d*) sprained a limb (*Vd.*
murɗȩ 2*c*, targaɗȩ). (2) am ∽ gaddama̧
a hot dispute arose. (3) *Vd.* dagā
3.
   B. (mu̧rɗā) *Vb.* 2. (1) twisted T.
away from, out of *x* yā mu̧rɗi zūcīyar
kaba̧ he twisted the heart out of the
young dum-palm. (2) zūcīyā tā mu̧rɗē
shi̧ in a rage he committed a wrongful
act.

murɗaɗɗakī *Vd.* mu̧rɗē.

mu̧rɗaɗɗāwa̧ = mu̧rɗaɗɗēnīyā *f.* (1)
surging to and fro (stragglers). (2)
writhing backwards and forwards (*x*
dying snake).

mu̧rɗakā *f.* binding used on inner apex of
beehive-shaped roof of hut (*this consists
of a coil of the grass* dīwa̧, *tied with*
rama̧ *and darkened with mud* (ta̧ɓō) :
its epithet in Sokoto is Ha̧na̧ za̧rē) =
Kt. dārumā.

murɗā-mu̧rɗ̧ā *Vd.* murɗēɗȩ.

murɗe A. (murɗȩ) (1) *Vb.* 1A. (*a*) =
murɗa̧ 1, mu̧rɗā 2. (*b*) deposed (= tūɓȩ
1*a*). (*c*) am ∽ aurē the proposed
marriage has been cancelled. (*d*) cīwa̧n
ciķi yā ∽ shi he had gripes. (2) (*a*) (i)
became twisted *x* igīya̧r dōķi̧ tā ∽ the
horse's tethering-rope has become
twisted. (ii) yāķi̧ yā murɗō wajan
dāɗi̧n the war turned in our favour.
(*b*) dōķi̧ yā ∽ = 2*a*.i *above*. (*c*) (limb)
became sprained (*cf.* murɗa̧ 1*d*).
   B. (mu̧rɗē) *m.* (*pl.* murɗuna̧ = mur-
da̧ɗɗakī) = mundūwā 2.

murɗēɗȩ *m.* (*f.* murɗēɗīyā) *pl.* murɗā-
mu̧rɗ̧ā = murɗum-mu̧rɗu̧ŋ burly,
massive.

mu̧rɗēɗēnīyā = mu̧rɗaɗɗēnīyā.

mu̧rɗēɗēwa̧ = mu̧rɗaɗɗēnīyā.

murɗi̧ *m.* argumentativeness (= gad-
dama̧).

murɗīyā *f.* (1) part of embroidery of
saddle-cover (ja̧lāla̧). (2) genet (= inyāwarā).

murɗō *Vd.* murɗȩ 2*a*.ii.

mu̧rɗōɗōnīyā *Kt.* = mu̧rɗaɗɗēnīyā.

mu̧rɗōɗōwa̧ = mu̧rɗaɗɗēnīyā.

murɗukēķȩ *m.* (*f.* murɗukēkīyā) *pl.*
murɗuk-mu̧rɗu̧k burly, massive
(= murɗēɗȩ).

murɗum-mu̧rɗu̧ŋ *Vd.* murɗēɗȩ.

murɗuna̧ *Vd.* mu̧rɗē.

murȩ *Vb.* 3A recovered from illness,
poverty, etc., *x* tum ba̧ su̧ ∽ wanca̧m
bugu̧ ba before they recover from the
effects of that blow (= gyāza̧jē *q.v.*).

murfī *m.* (*pl.* mu̧rfai). (1) (*a*) (i) cover, lid,
stopper (*d.f.* rufȩ) = marufī. (ii)
kōwa̧cȩ ƙwaryā tana̧ da̧ murfinsa̧
everyone has the chance to choose what
suits him and to leave what does not
suit him. (*b*) = ƙafō 9. (2) walls of
abdomen of cow, etc. (*these are given as
wages to* P. *skinning the animal*), *cf.*
tantānī.

murfu̧ *m.* (*pl.* mu̧rāfū = murāfū = mur-
funa̧). (1) (*a*) (i) the three stones which
form native cooking-place. (ii) ma̧i
ūwā a̧ ∽ bā ya̧ ci̧n tūwō gāyā one
"needs a friend at court" (*Vd.*
tūwō 13). (*b*) iron-tripod replacing 1*a*.i.
(*c*) *Vd.* gi̧ndim murfu̧ ; fādūwar ∽. (2)
combination of three persons or things
x (*a*) yā yi ∽ a̧ gidan Yāri̧ he went to
prison three times. (*b*) aŋ ƙulla̧ ∽ a
tripartite pact has been made. (*c*)
ita cē cikwa̧m murfu̧n Jāmu̧s that
country is the third of the German
axis-partners. (*d*) yā yi ∽ he has three
wives. (*e*) (i) tā yi ∽ she is shu'uma̧,
so thrice widowed. (ii) tā yi ∽, sa̧i
tukunyā takē nēma̧, ta̧ ɗōra̧ she's now
seeking a fourth husband. *(3) murfu̧
uku̧ 3,000 cowries.

murginā = mirginā.

murgu̧ *m.* payment made by slave to his
owner in lieu of working personally
(= galla̧ 1).

murguɗā *Vb.* 1C (1) = murɗa̧ 1. (2) bar
mu̧ ∽ ɗan tūwō let's make some tūwō !

murguɗe (1) *Vb.* 1C = murɗa̧ 1. (2)
Vb. 3A = murɗȩ 2.

murgwī *m.* type of horse-ailment.

murhu = murfu̧.

mūrị = mōrị 1.

muri-muri A. (muri-muri) *used in* 'yan yārā ∼ small children.

  B. (mụrī-mụrī) = mịrī-mịrī.

mūrịyā *f.* anus (= dubụrā).

mụrjajjē = mụrzajjē.

mụrjānị *m.* (*Ar.* marjān). (1) red coral. (2) mụrjānịm fụr fine red coral.

murje A. (murjẹ) (1) *Vb.* 1A. (*a*) = murzạ 2, 3. (*b*) dịd completely act denoted by murzạ 1. (2) *Vb.* 3A = murẹ.

  B. (mụrjē) (1) *m.* (*a*) flour mixed with milk, honey, and butter for journey-provisions. (*b*) twisted-thread (*as for necklace, etc.*) = dạrjē, *cf.* murzạ. (*c*) rubbing one's eyes on rising in lieu of ritual-washing (ạlwạlā) = mụrtsụkē. (*d*) *cf.* murjị. (2) *Vd.* mụrzā.

murji A. (murjị) *m.* (1) rolling together two strands of cotton between the hands, to make thread (*cf.* tụ̄kā). (2) two-ply thread (*thus one* murjị = *one* sịlī *and consists of two* kwārạ, *cf.* tụ̄kā).

  B. (mụrji) *Vd.* mụrzā.

Mụrkā *f.* a Daura sạrautạ.

mụrkus (1) *adv. used in* yā kōnẹ ∼ it was completely burned up (= kurmus). (2) *m. used in* dạ shī, dạ dōkị sun yi ∼ he and his horse fell in a heap.

murkụsā *Vb.* 1C stuffed T. into (= kur-mụsā *q.v.*).

murkụshẹ *Vb.* 1C (1) = kurmụshē. (2) horse at turkẹ bit P.

murkụshēshẹ *m.* (*f.* murkushēshịyā) *pl.* murkus-murkus huge.

mụrkụshēshēnịyā *f.* struggling of two wrestlers on the ground.

mụrkụsusū *m.* = mụrdạddēnịyā.

mụrlī *Kt.* = mụllī.

murmụjē *Vb.* 3A = murẹ.

mur-mur *m.* (1) = mumur. (2) kāshī yā yi ∼ the fæces are impacted.

murmura A. (mụrmurạ). (1) *f.* a soft, sweet type of guinea-corn, eaten before it ripens (= tsẹ̄fē). (2) *Vb.* 2 yā mụrmuri dāwạ he rubbed parched (gasạ) guinea-corn between his hands (*cf.* tumạ, zạgā).

  B. (murmụrā) *Vb.* 1C = mụrmurạ 2.

murmure A. (mụrmụrē) *m.* (1) act of

rubbing *as in* mụrmurạ 2. (2) *Kt.* = mụrmurạ 1.

  B. (murmụrē) *Vb.* 3A = murẹ.

mụrmushī *m.* smiling, a smile *x* yā yi ∼ he smiled. yanạ ∼ he's smiling.

murmutụ *Vb.* died one after another (*d.f.* mutụ) = marmạcē.

murnạ *f.* (*pl.* mụrnạce-mụrnạcē). (1) (*a*) (i) gladness. (ii) nā yi ∼ dạ sukạ zō I'm delighted they have come. (*b*) ạbim ∼ *m.* cause for rejoicing. (*c*) yā ɗauki ∼ = yā yi murnạ he is (was) happy. yanạ ∼ he is happy. (*d*) ∼ ta kōmạ cikī joy turned into sadness. (*e*) nā yi masạ ∼ I congratulated him (*cf.* jẹ̄jētọ). (2) (*a*) murnạr kạrē = murnạr kạran Yarạbā showing pleasure at seeing P. but giving him nothing. (*b*) bā ạ̄ sanịm murnạr kạran dạ bā shi dạ wutsịyạ a destitute P. cannot realize his desires. (*c*) bạri ∼ dọŋ kạraŋkạ yā kāmạ zākị don't count your chickens before they're hatched ! (= girịŋgịdịshī). (*d*) murnạr sallạ *Vd.* gōmạ 2. (*e*) kạzā tạ yi ∼ *Vd.* kạzā 1*a*.viii.

murrụ = mụr.

mụrsạ *Vb.* 2 (*p.o.* mụrshē, *n.o.* mụrshi) ate (much corn or nuts) with crunching sound.

murshe A. (mụrshē) (1) *Vd.* mụrsā. (2) *m.* a drink made from pulp (gạrī) from inside of pods of locust bean (dọ̄rōwạ), plus millet-flour, condiments, and juice of tamarind (tsāmịyā).

  B. (murshẹ) (1) *Vb.* 1A. (*a*) did completely the act denoted by mụrsā. (*b*) *x* tā ∼ zanẹ she wore out her cloth, caused her cloth to fade. (2) *Vb.* 3A zanẹ yā ∼ the cloth is worn out, faded.

mursīsī *m.* niggardliness = kēmēmē 2 *q.v.*

murtsuka A. (mụrtsukạ) *Vb.* 2. (1) yā mụrtsụki hannū he rubbed his palms together (after eating, etc.). (*b*) yā mụrtsụki idọ he rubbed his eyes hard. (2) felt enjoyment from *x* yā mụrtsụki dōkịnsạ he enjoyed riding his horse. yanạ mụrtsukạr dūnịyạ he is enjoying life (= mụrzā).

  B. (murtsụkā) *Vb.* 1C. (1) (*a*) crumbled up brittle T. with the fingers (x salt, chalk (ạllī), tsạkin tābạ, dạddawā for kwaḍọ, etc.) (= murzạ = marmạsā). (b) screwed up (paper to throw it away). (2) tā murtsᶷkạ furā she mixed furā with her hands.

murtsuke A. (murtsᶷkē) (1) Vb. 1C. (a) = murtsᶷkā 1, 2. (b) yā murtsᶷkẹ maḳīyinsạ he crushed his enemy. (c) = mᶷrtsukạ 1. (d) trampled on (= tākạ). (2) Vb. 3A (a) became crumpled. (b) became crushed.

B. (mᶷrtsᶷkē) m. = mᶷrjē 1c.

murtsukū Kt. m. blepharitis (= amōḍạrī).

mᶷrtuk used in (1) rūwā yā yi ⌒ the water is turbid. (2) ḳūrā tā yi ⌒ dust rose. hayāḳī yā yi ⌒ smoke-cloud arose. (3) fuskạssạ tā yi ⌒ he frowned (= ḍaurẹ 2b). (3) faḍạ yā yi ⌒ the quarrel became fierce. (4) cf. murtᶷkē, murtᶷkā.

murtᶷkā Vb. 1C stirred up dust, etc., as in mᶷrtuk x am murtᶷkạ hayāḳī dust has been raised (= musḳạ = dinnᶖkā). anạ murtᶷkạ yāḳᶖ fierce fighting is going on (cf. murtukū). yā murtᶷkạ fuskạ he frowned.

murtᶷkē (1) Vb. 1C = murtᶷkā. (2) Vb. 3A (dust, etc.) was stirred up as in mᶷrtuk x ḳūrā tā ⌒ dust-cloud arose. hayāḳī yā ⌒ (a) smoke cloud arose (= dinnᶖkē = musḳẹ). (b) fierce fighting is in progress. hayāḳī yā ⌒ har bā ạ̄ īyạ ganiᶇ iriᶇ kᶷnᶷn dạ akẹ dāmạ̄wā such fierce fighting is in progress that the result cannot yet be seen.

murtukū (1) m. serious quarrel, mighty combat (epithet is Murtukū, faḍạᶇ iblīsai Vd. 2c below), cf. mᶷrtuk, murtᶷkā, murtᶷkē. (2) (a) what clouds of smoke ! (b) what a quarrel ! (c) Murtukū (= tunnuḳū) faḍạᶇ iblīsai, yārọ bại ganī ba, bạllē yạ rabạ what Armageddon ! (Vd. 1 above).

murᶷbạcī = marᶷbạcī.
murᶷbᶷcī = marᶷbᶷcī.
mᶷrūcī = Kt. mᶷruccī. (1) shoot of the deleb (giginyạ) nut = Sk. gạzarī 1c (Vd. Karạ̄dūwạ, marạshī). (2) birᶖ bại ḳi ⌒ ba, sȧi dȧi wᶷyar hakạ all seek success, but it is hard to attain. (3) Vd. sọlọ̄bīyọ.
murᶷdī = marᶷdī.

murufā = marufā.
murufī = murfī.
muru-muru = muri-muri.
murus = mᶷrkus.
mᶷrūwwạ = mạrawwạ.
muryạ f. (pl. muryōyī). (1) (a) voice. (b) sunạ̄ sạurārạm ⌒ gᶷdā they all obey one master. (c) sun sākẹ muryạr wākạ (i) singers changed their melody, rhythm. (ii) people changed their tone. (d) bạ̄ yạddạ zại sạ̄mi tāsạ ⌒ ta kạnsạ he has no means of getting his opinions heard. (e) yā gyārạ ⌒ he cleared his throat. (f) musical tone (pitch) in speech. (2) yanạ̄ dạ ⌒ he has a nice voice. (3) mại muryạr mātā Vd. kọtsō 2. (4) (in riddle, the following is asked) dạgạ nēsạ nā ji muryạr kawāta from afar I (girl) heard my girl-friend's voice, what do I mean by these words ? (reply, gạᶇgā " you mean a drum "). (5) throat extracted from chicken.

murza A. (murzạ) Vb. 1A. (1) rolled some thread as in murjᶖ 1 (= Kt. burᶷntā). (2) (a) rubbed T. between one's palms (= murjẹ). (b) yā ⌒ dūnᶖyạ he made wide conquests. (3) (wife) massaged (husband's) limbs to remove tiredness as in tạusā 2 (= murjẹ).

B. (mᶷrzā) (1) Vb. 2 (p.o. mᶷrjē, n.o. mᶷrji) = mᶷrtsukạ 2. (2) f. (a) (secondary v.n. of murzạ 3) x tanạ̄ mᶷrzar ḳafạssạ = tanạ̄ murzạ ḳafạssạ she's massaging his leg. (b) massaging as in 2a above (= tạusā 2).

mᶷrzajjē m. (f. mᶷrzajjīyā) pl. mᶷrzạzzū well-fed, sleek.

mus (1) = mᶷrkus. (2) bạn cẹ dạ shī ⌒ ba I did not address a word to him (= uffạᶇ).

Musa A. (Mūsā) Ar. m. (1) Moses. (2) Garạkā 'yā'yam ⌒ epithet of porters (lēbᶷrạ).

B. (musạ) Vb. 1A contradicted x wā zại ⌒ wannạᶇ who will contradict this ? (cf. musᶷ).

C. (Mūsạ) used in (1) ⌒ gēran tākᶖ epithet of any ạlkālī. (2) ⌒ dạ gēmᶷ = gizạ̄gō 3. (3) Vd. Dạᶇkō.

mᶷsāfahạ = mᶷsāfihạ Ar. f. yā yi ⌒ dạ nī he shook hands with me (= baᶇ hannū = sunnạtā).

musai dạ = musāyad dạ.

Musạilamạ (*famous heretic of the early days of Islam*) *Ar. m.* hypocrite (= Usạilamạ), *cf.* kụsailamā.

mụsammạŋ (1) *adj.* (*a*) independent *x* (i) Sarkī nẹ̄ ∼ he's a paramount chief (= Sarkin yạŋkā 1), *Vd.* mulkị 1*d.* (ii) ƙasā cẹ̄ ∼ it is a sovereign state (*Vd.* mulkị 1*d*). (*b*) Audụ mụtụn nẹ̄ ∼ Audu has a house of his own (= gidā 1*l*). (*c*) ạbin nạm ∼ nẹ̄ this is very important (= mụhimmị). (2) *adv.* (*a*) expressly *x* ∼ ya zō don yạ sạyē shị he came on purpose to buy it (= tạkạnas). (*b*) *Kt.* mụsammạm-mụsammạŋ only occasionally.

mụsāmụsai *pl. m.* (1) long temple-locks of Afzin men and Jārumāwā slaves. (2) *Kt.* long, curled moustaches of Barẹ̄barī and slaves of the Emir of Katsina.

mụsanyā = mụsāyā.

musaya A. (mụsāyā) *f.* (1) exchanging one T. for another *x* yanạ̄ nēmam ∼ he's desirous of exchanging it for something else. yā yi mụsāyar dōkị dạ jạ̄kī he exchanged a horse for a donkey. (2) barter. (3) (*a*) change for money (= canjị). (*b*) transferring P. *x* an yi masạ ∼ he's been transferred elsewhere (= canjị). (*c*) relief, deputy *x* ∼ tasạ tā zō his relief has come (= canjị = mạimakō 1*b*). (4) mụsāyar gautā exchanging T. for T. of equal value. (5) mụsāyar kạsūwā selling T. and buying another of the same kind, whether cheaper or dearer (*x selling one horse and buying another, selling guinea-corn and buying millet, etc.*).

B. (mụsāyạ) *Vb.* 2 exchanged *x* yā mụsāyi dōkị dạ jạ̄kī he exchanged a horse for a donkey.

C. (mụsāyā) *Vb.* 1C. (1) = mụsāyạ *x* yā mụsāyạ dōkị dạ jạ̄kī. (2) yā mụsāyạ tufāfịnsạ he changed his clothes.

mụsāyad dạ *Vb.* 4 = mụsāyạ.

mụsāyē *Vb.* 1C exchanged completely, exchanged all the articles (*Vd.* mụsāyạ).

mụsayyạ *f.* (*d.f.* musụ) mutual disputations (*epithet is* Mụsayyạ, hạnạ aikị).

mushe A. (mūshẹ) *m.* (*d.f.* mutụ). (1) (*a*) (i) carrion (= ụŋgụlū 10), *cf.* yạŋkā

2*c* ; buŋgā 3*a* ; jạ̄ ta, haurẹ 2*e*. (ii) *x* mūshạm mạrakī body of calf found dead, body of calf died of disease. (*b*) *Vd.* gāwā 1*a.* (2) (*a*) mūshạŋ gizākā *Vd.* gizākā. (*b*) mūshạŋ gizākā, kim mutụ, kinạ̄ bạ yạ̄rā tsọ̄rō *epithet of* gizākā. (3) ∼ jạŋ kạrē *Vd.* haushī 3*b*.

B. (mūshē) *Kt. m.* torch (= yūlā = bạ̄kiŋ wutā *q.v.* = jīnịyā 2).

mụshirikī = mụshurụkī = mụshurịkī *m.* (*f.* mụshirịkā, etc.) *pl.* mụshirịkai, etc., *Ar.* polytheist, fetish-worshipper.

mushīyī *m.* bone antimony-pencil (= mishī).

mụsībạ = mạsīfạ.

mụsilī (1) *m.* (*Ar.* mithli). (*a*) a replica, counterpart. (*b*) one's equal (*cf.* mịsālị, masalạŋ). (2) mụsịliŋ *prep.* like = mịsālịŋ *q.v.*

musƙa A. (musƙạ)· *Vb.* 1A *x* am ∼ hayāƙī much smoke has been raised (= dinnịƙā = murtụkā).

B. (mụsƙā) *Kt. f.* yā yi ∼ he put so much food into his mouth that it puffed out his cheeks.

musƙạ̄ƙā *Vb.* 1C = musƙạ.

musƙẹ *Vb.* 3A *x* dạ̄kị yā ∼ dạ hayāƙī the room became filled with smoke (= murtụkē = dinnịƙē), *cf.* gụma.

musƙẹdē *Vb.* 1C *Kt.* yā ∼ shị dạ sạndā he hit him with a stick (= dōƙẹ).

musƙī (1) what clouds of smoke ! (2) *Kt.* what eating ! (*as in* musƙā).

musƙụdā *Vb.* 3A (1) fidgeted about. (2) (seated P.) changed position of his body, moved aside to make room, edged away (= shāgịdā 2*b*). (3) migrated short distance (= *Sk.* tizgạ) (2, 3 = zākụdā 2*a*). (4) waddled, owing to stoutness.

musƙụrumị = *Kt.* musƙụmurị owl (= mūjịyā).

musƙụtā = musƙụdā.

mus-mus *m.* ɓērā tanạ̄ ∼ dạ bạ̄kī the rat's mouth is twitching (= mwīmwī 2).

mussạ *f.* (1) domestic or wild cat = kyạŋwā *q.v.* (2) *Vd.* amam mussạ. (3) idạm ∼ *Vd.* idọn 10.

mussai *Kt.* = mūshẹ.

musshẹ *Sk.* = mussạ.

musụ (1) to them. (2) *m.* (*a*) contradicting P., disputing, denying the facts to be as stated by another. (b) in kanā ∽ sǎi ka tambayi wani if you don't believe me, then ask someone else ! (c) ƙāƙa har yakē da bākim ∽ how can he possibly resist them ? (d) bākī da tsawō na mai ∽ nē rather than reply angrily and bring trouble on yourself, keep silent ! (3) musun gafiya pointless contradiction.

musukwānā = masukwānā.

musulce-musulcē Vd. misāli.

musulimta = musulumta.

Musulmī m. (f. Musulmā) pl. Musulmī = Musulmai (Ar. Muslim, cf. Urdu Musulmān). (1) (a) a Moslem. (b) ∽ duk na dūnīya mai-mai da gabā gabas sun yardā all the Moslems of the world (i.e. who turn towards the qibla in prayer) agreed. (c) ƙasar ∽ f. Mohammedan countries. (d) ∽ māsū zūwa haji Moslems who go on the pilgrimage to Mecca and Medina. (e) dā munā cēwā sū arnā nē, ashē sū ∽ nē a kan Jāmus previously we thought them scoundrels, but now we find they are paragons compared with the Germans. (2) Kīfī, Musulmin nāma (a) Fish, thou ceremonially pure thing ! (b) what an equable person ! (3) Vd. Sarkim Musulmī, lausa.

Musulumce = Musulunce x kōmē nāsa dǎi a ∽ all his behaviour is dignified.

Musulunci = Musulunci m. (1) = Muhammadiyya. (2) al'amarim ∽ ta hanyar Wahhābāwā the Wahhabi Sect of the Mahommedans.

Musulumta = Musulunta Vb. 3B became a Mahommedan.

musur-musur = busur-busur.

musuru f. = muzūrū.

mutakabbarci Ar. m. conceit.

mūtalar = muhutalar.

mutānē Vd. mutum.

mutar m. (d.f. Ar. bitair " with the image of a bird on it ") Maria Theresa dollar (= līyar), Vd. sūra 1c.

Mutawallī m. a sarauta at Katsina, Daura, Hadejiya, etc.

mutsi-mutsi = mitsi-mitsi.

mūtsu Sk. used in dam ∽ m. (pl. 'yam ∽) type of fish.

mutsulī = mitsilī.

mutsū-mutsū m. = mutsūnīyā f. (1) (a) restlessness, fidgetiness (= kusunnīyā = sukurnīyā = gaja zamā = tsumwīnīyā). (b) mun shiga ∽ we're in a state of disorganization. (2) imbroglio.

muttsuka = murtsuka.

mutu Vb. (for progressive, Vd. mutūwa 3a, 1a.ii, iii) (Ar. yamūtu " he will die "). (1) (a) (i) he died, it (animal) died (Vd. rasu), cf. mutūwa. wandō ya ∽ the trousers are worn out (= gargara ii). rīgā tā ∽ the gown is worn out. itācē yā mutu the tree is withered (Vd. mutūwa). (ii) watan Agusta yā ∽ August is over. (iii) wata yā ∽ the moon has reached the last day of the month. (iv) har ya ∽ bā yā fid da kitse a wuta = har ya ∽ bā yā ƙulla kaba he's a spineless P. (v) zāmanin da dōki da jākī ba su ∽ ba, mē mīkīyā ta ci, ta yi rǎi (said by woman) Fellow-wife (kīshīyā), you were a poverty-stricken creature before you came here ! (vi) mai dōki ya cē ya ∽ bare dan ciyāwa ? if you refuse good advice, don't afterwards blame your adviser ! (vii) akwiya tā ∽, tā bara fāta wuyā he has been left in the lurch. (viii) mahassadā su jē, su mutu may our ill-wishers " come to a sticky end " ! (ix) mahassadā, ku jē, ku mutu you are thoroughly disgraced, so much for you ! (x) ∽ a gōnar arne Vd. addu'a 1c. (xi) 'yar matsīyācī tā mutu Vd. bikī 1b. (xii) zai ∽ matsīyācī Vd. dōmin-dōmin. (b) Vd. shā rānī. (2) rānā tā ∽ the sun has set. (3) wutā tā ∽ the fire has gone out. fitila tā ∽ the lamp has gone out. (4) (a) hanya tā ∽ the road's fallen into disrepair, disuse. (b) (i) aurē yā ∽ their marriage is dissolved. (ii) Vd. ango 6. (5) jikinsa yā ∽ he has become indolent. (6) bākinsa yā ∽ he is (was) stumped for a reply. yanzu bākī yā ∽ words fail. (7) magana tā ∽ the matter is now shelved, unworthy of attention. (8) (a) haƙōrinsa yā ∽ (i) his tooth is jarred, chilled, on edge. (ii) his tooth is decayed (ii = zuma 1d.iii). (b) Vd. haƙōrī 10b. (9)

Vd. mutūwạ, mạtaccē, marmạcē, murmutụ, macẹ.

mutukạ *f.* (*Eng.* motor-car) *pl.* mutukōkī. (1) motor-car (= mātọ = mōtạ). (2) steam-roller (= ūwar dạ6ē).

mụtụm = mụtụŋ *m.* (*genitive* mụtumịn) *pl.* mutặnē. (1) (*a*) man, male (= namijị *whose fem. is* mạcẹ). (*b*) bạbbam ~ adult man. bạbbar mạcẹ adult woman. (2) person, human being *x* (*a*) ~ nē yạ kōwā he's a human being like everyone else. ~ cē yạ kōwā she's human like everyone else. (*b*) mụtụm dạ yawạ = mutặnē dạ yawạ many people. (*c*) yā (tǎ) ịsa ~ he (she) has become adult (= muddị 2). (*d*) mụtụm maị sūnā mụtụm wạndạ ya kashẹ the true number of persons whom he murdered. (*e*) mụtumịn naŋ dạ kakẹ jị dạ ganī the very P. we're talking about. (*f*) *Vd.* yā 2*c.* (*g*) ~ bīyū *Vd.* bīyū 13. (3) *for proverbs with* mụtụm *Vd.* 9 *below.* (4) (*in genitive, with fem.* mụtūnīyar). (*a*) inhabitant of *x* mụtumịn Kanọ *m.* (*f.* mụtūnīyar Kanọ) *pl.* mutặnaŋ Kanọ an inhabitant of Kano (= Bạkanọ). (*b*) pal *x* Audụ mụtumīnā nẹ Audu is my pal (*cf.* 5 *below*). ita mụtūnīyātā cẹ (i) she's my paramour, mistress. (ii) she's a crone with whom I trade. (*c*) mụtumịn kirkị good fellow. mụtūnīyar kirkị decent sort of woman or girl. mụtumịm banzā good-for-nothing fellow. mụtūnīyar banzā useless girl or woman. (5) yā yi ~ dạ nī he treated me like a friend (*cf.* 4*b above*, mutuncị 4). (6) (*used in* zạurạncē) shilling *x* (*a*) yā bā nị ~ bīyū he gave me two shillings. (*b*) ~ dạ ƙanạnsạ one shilling and sixpence (*cf.* 1ụmfā 3). (7) (*a*) dạ A dạ B ~ yạ ~ A and B are equals. (*b*) Audụ dạ Ạlī ~ yạ ~ Audu followed the example of Ali (*Vd.* yị 1*h*). (8) *Vd.* mụtumī, bạkim mụtụm, ụbam mutặnē. (9) *proverbs with* mụtụm :—(*a*) ~ duk mālạmiŋ kạnsạ nē everyone is the best judge of his own affairs. (*b*) ~ ạ gidansạ Sarkī nẹ everyone is master at home. (*c*) ~ dạ gishirinsạ, in yā sō, yạ dafạ ƙạfō everyone can do what he likes with his own property. (*d*) ạbim ~, ạbiŋ

wạsansạ training makes perfect. (*e*) ~ ɗayā bā yạ ɗaukạr ɗākị many hands make light work. (*f*) ~ baị fī ƙạ tsụmmā ba, bạ zaị kaɗạ makạ kwạrkwatạ ba a junior must not lord it over a senior. (*g*) mutặnan dūnīyạ in sun sạmi dōkị dạ sukụ̄wā, sǎi sụ ƙurẹ shi don't overwork the willing horse! (*h*) iŋ kā ga ~ bạr shi ịndạ ka gan shị if you don't know a person's object, don't interfere! (*j*) im ~ yā cẹ zaị bā ƙạ rịgā, dụ̄bạ ta wuyạnsạ if a P. makes you a promise watch how he treats others! (*k*) ~ bā yạ tū6ẹ minị rịgā ạ kạ̄sụ̄wā, san naŋ yạ kōmō gidā, yạ cẹ zaị sạ minị (*said by woman*) I won't stand *that* from my husband! (*l*) mutặnē su kạm mai dạ ɗinɗimī cīwọ some people fuss over a trifle. (*m*) im ~ yā cẹ "ịnā zạŋ kwānạ̄", ạ yi darẹ dǎi wait and see instead of asking foolish questions! (*n*) mutặnan dūnīyạ iŋ kā sakẹ, sǎi sụ ci makạ tūwō ạ kā give him an inch and he'll take an ell. (*o*) mụtụm ƙudā nẹ *Vd.* sēmā 2. (*p*) mụtụm tarạ yakẹ *Vd.* tarạ 3. (*q*) bạndạ mụtụm *Vd.* shūkạ 1*a*. (*r*) ịndạ ya shā mutặnē *Vd.* shā dạ 2*b*.ii. (*s*) mụtụm ạ gwīwạ tasạ *Vd.* tạ̄gumī 2. (*t*) mutặnē bā sạ san yiŋ ạbụ *Vd.* ạbụ 5*d*. (*u*) Allạ̄ nạ̄ mutặnē *Vd.* Allạ̄ 7*f.* (*v*) mutặnē akẹ kīwọ *Vd.* dabbạ 3. (*w*) ạ kọ̄ri ~ *Vd.* gudụ 2*d*.vii. (*x*) ạ sam ~ *Vd.* c̣nikī 4.

mutụ mātā *Kt. m.* uxorious husband.

mutumcị = mutuncị.

mutumī *used in* ɗam ~ *m.* = mụtummụtumī.

mụtum-mụtumī *m.* effigy of person, horse, etc. (*x* as scarecrow, doll, idol, etc.).

mutụ-mutụ *adv.* vastly *x* yanạ̄ kūkā ~ he's crying bitterly. kāyā nẹ ~ it is a heavy load. yā ci ạbincī ~ he golloped up much food. yanạ̄ nēmansụ ~ he's seeking them hither and thither.

mụtụŋ = mụtụm.

mutuncị *m.* (1) treating others with due respect (= mạrawwạ 1*a*). (2) yā yi minị ~ he treated me with due respect. (3) (*a*) yā ci mutuncịnsụ he treated them disrespectfully. (*b*) yanạ̄ cịm mutuncịm mutặnē he treats everyone like dirt (= marawwa 1b). (4) mung ~ da shi he and I are close friends, cf. mutum 5). (5) bā ki ~ Vd. alakwayī. (6) tsīrā da mutunci Vd. tsīrā 2b.viii. (7) cf. mutuntaka.

mutūnīyā Vd. mutum 4.

mutuntaka f. (1) human nature with all its frailties x tŏ ~ cē well, it's only to be expected ! (soothing P. complaining of ingratitude). (2) kada ka yi mini ~ don't treat me boorishly, unkindly ! (3) cf. mutunci.

muturū m. (pl. muturai) the small, humpless cattle of the Benue and the Southern Provinces (= kūrā 9b = kasā 5b).

mutūwa f. (1) (a) (i) death x mutūwar Audu the death of Audu (cf. rasūwā). (ii) yang nēmam ~ he is dying, it is dying (re persons, animals, trees, garments-wearing-out, cf. 3a, 3b below ; gargara). (iii) yā daukō ~ it is dying = 3a below q.v. (iv) ram ~ bā bākī death puts an end to all. (v) kamar yadda yakē kim ~ tasa, haka yakē kin Jāmus he hates the Germans like poison. (b) anā ~ many deaths are occurring. (c) mutūwar kurūcīyā dying young. (d) Mutūwa, yanke būri Death, severer of cravings ! (e) kā kai kūkā gidam ~ it's a case of the blind leading the blind. (f) ~ bā jīyya = mutūwar fuja'a = ~ bā jitāma sudden death. (g) mutūwar kadangatse untimely death. (gg) mutūwar kaskō (i) simultaneous death of two persons. (ii) stalemate (cf. zubar gadō). (h) mutūwar kūwārū = 1gg above. (j) mutūwar tsaye (i) becoming blind. (ii) gradual emaciation. (iii) gradual loss of wealth. (iv) being dazed by a blow. (k) mutūwar tsōfwā (i) infantile convulsions (= ta-fīya 7). (ii) type of children's game. (l) mutūwar gabā Vd. gabā 2b. (2) becoming worn out x mutūwar rīgā the becoming worn out of the gown. (3) (progressive of mutu used as follows): (a) yang ~ it is dying (re animals, trees, and plants only, not re persons) = 1a.iii above, cf. 1a.ii. (b) wandō yang ~ the trousers are worn-out (= 1a.ii

above). (c) ido bā yā ~ tōzali ya tāshē shi T. once spoilt never regains its pristine value. (4) feeling eagerness for x yang mutūwar dōkin he's keen to get that horse. (5) turākar ~ Vd. zanzanā 3. (6) idar da ~ Vd. idar da.

mu'ujiza f. (pl. mu'ujizai = mu'ujizōjī) miracle done by a Prophet (cf. karāma).

muwa A. (mūwā) Sk., Kt. we = mū q.v. B. (mūwa) Zar. we shall = mā q.v.

muwāfaka Ar. f. (1) (a) good luck (= sā'a 3). (b) lucky guess. (2) x A yā yi ~ da B A corresponds with B.

muwālāti Ar. m. (1) transactions, dealings (= ma'āmala). (2) abōkim muwālātinā nē he is my companion, my partner.

muwālātu m. = muwālāti.

muwambal m. type of coloured silk fabric.

mū yē mū Vd. yē.

muzābura = muzāfura = mazābura q.v.

muzakkaranci = muzakkarci m. (1) tireless energy. (2) dauntlessness.

muzakkarī m. (f. muzakkarā) pl. muzak-karai Ar. (1) very energetic P. (2) dauntless P.

mūzancē Vb. 3A behaved like a simpleton.

mūzanci = mūzancī m. behaving like a simpleton.

mūzanta Vb. 3B = mūzancē.

muzanyā Kt. f. the stingless bee gallā.

muzgudā = muskudā.

mūzī m. (1) simpleton (= bagidāje). (2) (Ar. mu'thi) evildoer.

muzū Vd. kirī 5c.

muzū-muzū (1) m. looking sheepish (= kangamas 2). (2) adv. yā yi gāshi ~ he's very hairy (= buzū-buzū).

muzunkudīyā = mazunkudīyā.

muzūrai Vd. muzūrū.

muzurarī = mazurarī.

muzūrū m. (pl. muzūrai) (1) (a) male cat, domestic or wild (fem. is kyanwā). (b) Vd. Fātu 2 ; dakū. (c) azzikim ~ m. prosperity accompanied by niggardliness (= azzikī 7). (d) muzūrun jūda civet cat (= kyanwā 5). (e) karambānin kāzā, auram ~ don't interfere in what doesn't concern you ! (f) bakin jinim ~, mai kāzā zāgi,

marẹk kẹzā zāgị give a dog a bad name and hang him ! (g) anẹ ~ Vd. zẹkarẹ 1e. (h) idẹm ~ Vd. idọn 12. (2) (a) sunẹ mụzụrai they're staring about (cf. zụrū). (b) sunẹ mụzụran jūnā they're gazing silently at each other in anger or embarassment. (3) Mụzūrū epithet of any talẹkẹ. (4) cf. tukkum ~.
mwẹ we shall = mẹ q.v.
mwī-mwī m. (1) being silent from shame or fear. (2) ɓērā tanẹ ~ dẹ ɓẹkī the rat's mouth is twitching (= mus- mus).

N

n (1) (genitive suffix) Vd. na. (2) (a) (Gram. 16a*) x (i) n nẹ zūwẹ I am coming (cf. i 1). (ii) n nẹ ganịn kūrā dẹ rānā, ƙẹƙẹ zạn yẹrdā tẹ cịjē nị nobody blunders into danger if he can help it. (b) n cẹ Vd. cẹ 10, kō 3a.iii.
ṇ (subjunctive verbal-prefix for 1st singular, Gram. 13a*) x (1) ṇ zō let me come ! bẹri ṇ tẹfi gẹrī let me go to town ! (2) ṇ jī kẹ ba says you ! (3) Vd. ṇ compounds.
ŋ (M.G. 127c) the one in question (masc. nouns, and fem. nouns not in -a suffix -ŋ, while fem. noun in -a suffixes -r which Kt. may replace with -ai) x (1) yā bā nị dōkịŋ he gave me the horse in question. bakịŋ the black one. bẹ mụ ga gōdīyẹr (= Kt. gōdīyẹi = Kt. gōdīyẹl) ba we did not see the mare. yārinyẹr (= Kt. yārinyẹi = Kt. yārinyẹl) the girl in question. Audụŋ yes, the Audu whom we know (reply to which Audu ?). Kẹndaŋ yes, the Kande (woman's name) whom we know (Vd. naŋ 1b, d). (2) (-ŋ can be suffixed to noun accompanied by demonstrative) x ẹ wannaŋ wōkẹcịŋ at this time. (3) (-ŋ can be suffixed to noun accompanied by " some ", " other ") x iŋ kā ƙi dāwẹ, ịnā wani hatsịŋ if you refuse guinea- corn, where is any other corn to be found ? wadạnsu Jāmusāwaŋ the other Germans. wadạnsu mutẹnaŋ some people. wani ẹl'amẹrịŋ . . . wani

kūwā one affair . . . another, cf. wani 3a.ii. (4) (-ŋ can be suffixed to noun accompanied by possessive pronoun) x irịn nāsụ halịŋ a character like theirs, Vd. M.G. 127e, nāmụ 2, tāsẹ 1a.i. (5) (-ŋ can be suffixed to noun in genitive) x fāman na kāmẹ Masẹr the struggle to take Egypt. zamạn na kōwạcẹ ƙasā hakẹ yakẹ this is the condition of every country. wancạŋ tẹrạn na Kanāwā that crowd of Kano people. kạntịn na dẹ the previously-existing shop (in the last four examples -ŋ has become -n by assimilation to the initial n- of the following na). (6) (-ŋ can be suffixed to whole sentence) x wadạndẹ sukẹ ji rạunịŋ those who were wounded. wadạndẹ akẹ zẹɓan naŋ (from wadạndẹ akẹ zẹɓā) those who were chosen. mẹsū kāmẹ shịŋ Vd. naŋ 1d. (7) (-ŋ can be suffixed to adverb) wadạndẹ sukẹ jā dẹ bāyaŋ those who retreated. (8) all the above = naŋ 1d q.v.
na A. (na) of (1) (a) (-n which is con- traction of na, is suffixed to masc. noun to give sense of genitive " of ") x dōkịn Daudẹ = dōkị na Daudẹ David's horse. (b) (-au, -ai become -an) x kẹi head, kẹn Daudẹ David's head. littẹttẹfai books. littẹttẹfansẹ his books. sau footprint, san Daudẹ David's footprint. (c) (in Kano -on, -en become -an) nōnọ breast, nōnẹn Sāratụ Sarah's breast. fụrē tobacco, fụran tābẹ tobacco-flower. (d) (-ken, -gen become -kyan, -gyan) fagē open-space, fagyaŋ wẹsā playground. (e) (-ko, -go become -kwan, -gwan) x kōko gruel, kōkwan dāwẹ guinea-corn gruel. kạngō derelict, kạngwan ɗākị derelict house. (f) (nouns ending in con- sonant, suffix -in) x kạnạnzịr kerosene, kạnạnzīrịnsẹ his kerosene. Ạlhẹmis Thursday, Ạlhẹmīshịn naŋ on that Thursday. (2) (-r which is contraction of ta, is suffixed to fem. nouns ending in -a : those not ending in -a, suffix -n like masc. nouns of 1 above) Vd. ta B.2 3a.iii. (3) (the -n of 1 above and the -r of 2 above, can for emphasis be replaced by the full forms na and ta respectively, but must be so replaced

when the two nouns standing in genitival relationship are separated *from one another*) x (a) (i) bābu wani abu na muguntā = bābu wani abim muguntā there is no evil in it. al'amuran dūnīya da na mutānē the affairs of the world and those of men. wasīyyar nan ta Daudā this last will of David's. abu yā zamā na Audu Audu became top dog. anā ta magangganū iri-iri na abin da zai fāru various opinions are being expressed about what will happen. kāwō alkalamī kō nākā kō na wani bring a pen, either your own or another's. (ii) *Vd.* nāsā 3. (b) (na, *etc.,* may precede adverb) x kōmē ya fāru na gáme dā kasar everything which occurs regarding the country. (c) (na *etc.,* in sense in order to *may precede* verb) x bā tarkwan dā ba a kafa masā ba na a kāma shi no pitfall to catch him was neglected. maimakwan ya ragu, kārūwā ya yi instead of its lessening, it increased. sun yi shāwarar su yi sātā they decided to commit theft. (d) (na, *etc., may precede conjunction introducing verb*) x sunā jin tsōran kadā a tōna laifinsu they're afraid their secrets may be revealed. nā yi gudun kadā ka fōrē ni I was careful not to act so that you would reprove me. alkāwarimmu na in Jāmus sum fādā mukū, mū zā mu aukam musu our pact that if the Germans attack you, *we* shall attack them. kōwanē tānadī zā a yi na wannan yāki, a yi na kamar zā a shēkara uku anā yāki whatever preparations are made for this war should be made on the assumption that it will last three years. (e) (*the following type of construction may be used for all verbs*) x sum bar na bari they spared some. sunā cin na cī they're eating some of it. (4) (a) (*genitive may refer to action done by the subject*) x gudun kūru running done by a pony (*i.e.* making a good start and then tailing off). (b) (*genitive may refer to action done to the object*) x nā yi gudun garā I ran away from the white ants. (c) (*sometimes two nouns follow the genitive, the first referring to action done to the object, the second*

to action done by the subject) x banzā kisam macijim mātā the way women kill a snake is useless. tafīyar itācan kadangarē the way a lizard climbs a tree. (d) (*genitive may mean both* in order to get *and* in order to avoid) x māganin karfī means of securing strength. māganin rūwā protection against rain (*as* raincoat, etc.). (5) *Vd.* n 5, nā 2. (6) (a) (*genitive is used before suffixed personal pronouns, and in case of 1st singular, no pronoun-suffix at all is used*) x dōkina my horse. rīgāta my gown. dōkinsa his horse. dōkimmu our horse. (b) (-na, -ta " my " *become* nā, tā *respectively before* nē, cē) x dōkinā nē it is my horse. rīgātā cē it is my gown. (c) *Vd.* nā 2. (6A) (*genitive is used before* " this ", " that ", Gram. 125–7) x dōkin nan this horse. māsū kāma shin nan those who captured him (*cf.* nan 1b). (7) (*genitive is used before relative* dā, M.G. 133) x abin da ya ganī what he saw. gōdīyar dā ta cijē ni the mare who bit me. mātar dā takē (= mātar dā kē) zūwā the woman who is coming. (8) (a) *Vd.* nakē. (b) (*1st sing. relative past*, M.G. 133*) x (i) abin da na ganī what I saw. (ii) (*Sk. may double initial consonant of verb*) x abin da yag ganī = abin da ya ganī what he saw. abin da tag ganī = abin da ta ganī what she saw. abin da nag ganī = abin da na ganī what I saw (*Vd.* ni 4). abin da mug ganī = abin da muka ganī what we saw. abin da ag gani = abin da aka ganī what people saw (*cf.* mig). (9) *Vd.* na cē.

B. (nā) (1) (*1st sing. past tense*) x (a) nā tafi I went, have gone. (b) nā dauki karē don haushi, yā kōmō yanā tunkwuyī it was unsuitable for the purpose to which it was applied ; things turned out the reverse of what was expected. (c) nā yi gudun tsattsafī *Vd.* tsattsafī 1b. (d) Nā kōshi *Vd.* dādī 1d. (e) nā tōya mai *Vd.* mai 1b. (2) (*except for 1st sing., for which vide* nā 1, *the word* nā *is used to form independent personal pronominal adjectives referring to masc. noun*, tā *being*

used when fem. noun is referred to,
Gram. 48) *x* (*a*) jąkin nąn nāką nē
this donkey is yours. ƙwaryan nąŋ
tāsų cē this calabash is theirs. (*b*)
Vd. nāmų 2, nāsą 3. (3) *Vd.* na 6*b*.
    C. (nā̧) (1) (*used in 1st sing. of
independent personal pronominal adjectives referring to masc. noun, tā̧ being
used when fem. noun is referred to,*
Gram. 48) *x* jąkin nąn nā̧wa nę̄ this
donkey is mine. rįgan nąŋ tā̧wa cę̄
this gown is mine (*Vd.* nā̧ 2). (2) *x*
bā ~ sǫ I do not wish (Gram. 19).
(3) (*a*) (*suffix of the continuous*, Gram.
16) *x* n nā̧ zūwą I am coming. kanā̧
zūwą you are coming. (*b*) (*after sing.
or pl.* noun, *we can use* nā̧ *instead of the
full forms*, Gram. 16*b*) *x* Mūsā nā̧
zūwą = Mūsā yanā̧ zūwą Moses is
coming. (4) *Sk.* is (*after masc. noun*) =
nē *x* gą̄rī nā̧ it is a town (*N.B.—tone
varies as for* nē), *cf.* tā̧.
    D. (ną̄) *East Hausa* = ŋ (1) *x* bą̄ri ną
tąfi let me go !
    E. (nā̧) (Gram. 118–121) *x* nā̧ zō
I shall probably come.
na afutū *Vd.* **afutū.**
Na akurū *Vd.* **akurū.**
Na ąlōlō *Vd.* **Bąnufē.**
na'am A. (na'ąm) yes ! (*affirmative reply*)
= ī.
    B. (ną'am) yes ! (*reply when called,
but reply to senior calling one is* rąŋkai
dadę, *and to* māląmī *is* Allā̧ yą gāfąttą
Māląm). (2) (*a*) (i) yā yi ~ dą jąwābi
he assented to the proposal.   (ii)
kullum muką yi kirąŋkų, bą kų amsą
sāi dą " ną'am " ba whenever we called
you, you responded willingly. (*b*) yā yi
~ dą shī he took a liking to him. (*c*)
dūnīyą tā yi ~ dą shī he has made his
way in the world. (3) = **na'ąm.**
ną'ą-na'ą = ną'ą-na'ų *m., f.* = rūhųn
ną'ą-na'ą *m.* mint (= fę̄lų).
na bāgarā *Vd.* **bāgarā 2.**
nąbba'ą *Vb.* 3B *Ar.* (1) became replete
(= ƙōshi). (2) *x* ką jirā sāi nā ~ wait
till I have more leisure, feel more easy
in mind !
na bįlbis *Kt. Vd.* **gąl-gal 2.**
nąbīsǫ used in kiɗąn ~ *m.* type of Zaria
drumming.

na bōbą *Vd.* **būbų 3.**
na būnū *Vd.* **būnū 5, 6.**
nā̧ɓųwā *f.* = dāɓųrī 3.
nācę̧ *Vb.* 3A (1) persevered, persisted. (2)
    yā ~ minį he kept on at me.
na cę̄ *Vd.* **ƙō 3***a*.iii, **cę̄ 10.**
nācị *m.* perseveringness, persistence (=
    zų̄gā 2*a*).
nācīyā *f.* = nācị.
Nā cōcę̧ *m. name of* goblin believed to
live in locust-bean trees.
naɗa A. (naɗą) *Vb.* 1A (1) (*a*) yā ~
    rawąnī he wound on (put on) a turban
    (= niŋką). (*b*) yā ~ kā̧i dą rąggā (i)
    he put forth every effort (= niŋką).
    (ii) he bought T. far beyond his means.
    (*c*) an ~ masą būlālą he was severely
    whipped.   (*d*) an ~ wą jąkī kāyā the
    donkey was heavily laden. (2) officially
    appointed P. *x* (*a*) Sarkī yā ~ shi the
    Emir has given him office. (*b*) an ~
    masą sąrautą = an ~ shi Sarkī he
    has been appointed Chief.   zā ą ~
    shi Sarkịn Kano he will be appointed
    Emir of Kano. Wązīrịn Sakkwatō yā ~
    Sarkin Zazząu the Sokoto Wązīrī
    installed the Emir of Zaria. aką naɗą
    Sarkim Baucī Ųmarų then Umaru
    was installed as Emir of Bauchi. (*c*)
    an ~ masą sąrautą he has been given
    office (= rātąyā 2*e*). an ~ masą
    Gąlādīmą he has been appointed Gąlā-
    dīmą. (3) Audų yā ~ shi Audu gave
    him clothing.
    B. (nąɗā) *Vb.* 2 (1) = naɗę 1*a*.
    (2) (*a*) yā nąɗi ąbincī he ate much
    food.   yā nąɗi rūwā he drank much
    water (*cf.* naɗę 1*e*). (*b*) yā nąɗi kāyā
    (*a*) he carried a heavy load.   (*b*) he
    (marǭƙī) managed to cadge many gifts,
    clothes, etc.
na dāgā̧rą *Vd.* **dāgā̧rą.**
na dā̧ƙilą *Vd.* **dā̧ƙilą.**
nądāmą (*Ar.*) *f.* (1) regret, remorse.   (2)
    being worried *x* n nā̧ nądāmąr wurịn
    kwānā I'm worried as to where to pass
    the night. yanā̧ nądāmąr mā̧tassą he's
    worried about his wife.
nādąrī = **nādịrī.**
na Dāyē *Vd.* **Dāyē.**
naɗę (1) *Vb.* 1A (1) (*a*) (i) rolled up (mat,
    turban, etc., to put away) = niŋką 1*d*

= **nạɗā** 1. (ii) **dạ haụkā kạn** ～ **ta**
Vd. **tạ̄barmā** 3. (iii) **an** ～ **shi** = **an** ～
masạ kāyā he has been robbed of his
all. (*b*) (i) folded up (letter, etc.) =
niṇkạ. (ii) **yā** ～ **hannū** he (boxer)
is milling wth his fists preparatory to
engaging. (*c*) (i) wrapped up *x* **yā** ～
shi cikin takạrdā he wrapped it up
in paper. (ii) **yā** ～ **lāyạ** he wrapped the
charm round in thread. (iii) **yā** ～
kại dạ būzū *Vd.* **būzū** 1*b*. (iv) **yā** ～
hanjinsạ he's miserly. (*c*) (i) tied up
(prisoner). (ii) **cīwọ yā** ～ **shi, shẹkarạ
bīyū bā yạ̄ tāshi** illness has immobilized
him for two years (*cf.* **2***a*). (*d*) **yā** ～
rawạnin nạŋ dukạ he enturbaned himself in the whole of the cloth. (*e*) **yā** ～
rūwā dukạ he drank up all the large
amount of water available (*cf.* **nạɗā 2***a*).
yā nadẹ ạbincī dukạ he ate up all the
abundant available food. (*f*) **dọ̄min
jẹmāgẹ ạ** ～ **ƙasā** the fullest investigation will be welcome to me for I'm
not involved. (*g*) **yā** ～ **shi dạ ƙafạ**
he kicked him. **yā** ～ **shi dạ sạndā** he
knocked him down with a stick. (*h*)
yā ～ **ƙafạ** he has joined the army. (*j*)
an ～ **jạ̄kī dạ kāyā** = **naɗạ 1***d*. (2)
Vb. 3A (*a*) **yā** ～, **yā ƙi tāshi** he would
not rise from his bed through exaggerating to himself the importance of his
slight indisposition (*cf.* **1***c*.ii). (*b*) **yā** ～
ạ ɗakạ he remained indoors. (*c*) **yā** ～
mini he (cadger, etc.) clung to me.
(*d*) = **kạlmadạ 1**. (3) **nạɗe dạ mạ̄i**
used in ～ **mukạ ci** we went to bed
supperless.

naɗi *m.* (1) (*a*) act of winding on *as in*
naɗạ 1*a* ; rolling up, folding, etc., *as in*
naɗẹ. (*b*) **tūrẹ Būzū naɗi** *Vd.* **būzū 2***c*.
(2) *Vd.* **ạtụmurmụr 2**. (3) *Vd.* **Sō sō
banzā**.

nādịrī *Ar.* (1) *m.* (*f.* **nādịrā**) *pl.* **nạ̄dịrai**
rare. (2) *m.* (*pl.* **nạ̄dịrai**) a rarety. (3)
rarely *x* **bā ạ̄ sāmụnsạ sǎi** ～ it is only
rarely to be found.

na Dọ ọ̣̄ō *Vd.* **Dọ ọ̣̄ō**.

nāfila *Ar. f.* (*pl.* **nāfilōlī** = **nāfịlfịlī**)
supererogatory prayers (*cf.* **fạrillạ**).

ua gạl-gal *Vd.* **gạl-gal 2**.

nagạrī (*d.f.* **gạrī**) (1) *m.* (*f.* **tagạrī**) *pl.*
nagạrgạrū (*a*) good. (*b*) *Vd.* **gạrī 2** ;

sạye 3 ; **zạ̄ɓē 5**. (2) *m.* (*a*) goodness *x*
yanạ̄ dạ ～ it is good (= **nạgạrtā**).
(*b*) **bạ̄** ～ **ạ kāshī kō na tūwan shịŋkāfā**
don't look for good where no good canbe !

nạgạrtā *f.* (1) goodness (= **kyaụ** = **nagạrī**
2*a*). (2) **yā ƙi** ～ it (horse) is not so
speedy, untiring, etc., as before.

naggẹ *Sk. f.* (*pl.* **'yan** ～) cow (= **sānịyā**
Vd. **sạ̄ A**.2 *page* 753.

na Gọ̄zọ̄ *Vd.* **mītạ**.

nahawụ *Ar. m.* (1) (*a*) **yā sōkạ** (= **sạ̄**)
mini ～ he contradicted me. (*b*) **kadạ
kạ sạ̄** ～ **cikin zạncạŋ** don't bring this
affair into dispute ! *(2) grammar.

nạhīsā *Ar.* (1) *f.* (*a*) ill-omen, inauspicious-
ness (*cf.* **alfālụ**). (*b*) **yā gạmu dạ** (=
yā tākạ = **yā tạ̄ki**) ～ he met with misfortune. **sum fitō cikin sā'ạr nạhīsā**
they were unsuccessful. (2) *adv.* *x*
yā fịta ～ going at an inauspicious
time, he met with ill-luck.

nahīsanci *Kt. m.* quarrelsomeness (=
nashittạ).

nạhīshi *Kt. m.* (*f.* **nạhīshịyā**) quarrelsome
P. (= **nạshīshi**).

nāhīyạ *Ar. f.* (*pl.* **nāhīyōyī**) region,
district.

nai A. (**nại**) *used in* **kai** ～ (*said by woman
to man*), **kē** ～ (*said by woman to
woman*) come, come ! now then ! (=
habạ).

B. (**nai**) (1) (*Eng.*) *m.* ninepence. (2)
Sk. his (*after masc. noun*) *x* **dōki** ～
his horse (= **dōkịnsạ**). (3) *Sk.* = (*a*)
nā yī I did. (*b*) **na yi** *x* **dạ nai hakạ**
when I did so.

nā'ibanci *m.* duties or office of a **nā'ịbī**.

nā'ịbī *Ar. m.* (*pl.* **nạ̄'ịbai**) (1) deputy
lịmaŋ. (2) *Vd.* **bạmmī**.

Nạijērīyạ *f.* Nigeria.

nā'ịŋ *Vd.* **kā'ịŋ nā'ịŋ**.

Nainō *man's name.*

Naitọ *Vd.* **kū kạ**.

na janjē *Vd.* **janjē**.

najadụ *Vd.* **tsōfō 1***n*.

nạjasạ *Ar. f.* (1) human excrement (= **tūtụ**
1 = **rātsị 1***a* = **bāyā 2***d*.ii), *cf.* **kāshī,
tạrōsō, gāyạdī, artai**. (2) anything
rendering one ceremonially unclean in
Islam.

nāka (*independent possessive pronoun,*
Gram. **48**) yours (*referring to singular*

masc. possessor of masc. thing possessed) x **(1)** (*a*) **dōkin nạn** ∼ **nē** this horse is yours. (*b*) **gā** ∼ *Vd.* **ạkạwū 2.** (*c*) **ci** ∼ *Vd.* **rōwạ 1***b*. (*d*) *Vd.* **mūgụ 1***f*. **(2) nākị** yours (*referring to singular female owner of masc. thing possessed*) x **zanạn nạn nākị nē** this bodycloth is yours. **(3)** *cf.* **tākạ, tākị. (4)** *Vd.* **nāmụ 2, nāsạ 3.**

na kạcalạ *Vd.* **kạcalạ 2.**

naƙace A. (naƙācē) *Vb.* 1C **(1)** (load) weighed P. down. **(2)** *Vd.* **awọ 2.**
    B. **(naƙācē)** *Vd.* **nạƙātạ.**

Nạkādạ *m.* type of **bọrī**-spirit x ∼ **yā hau kạntạ** = **tanā dạ** ∼ she is possessed by this spirit.

nạƙạlcē *Vd.* **nạƙaltạ.**

naƙạlī *Ar. m.* instructions x **yā yi minị naƙạlim māganịŋ** he gave me instructions how to use the charm.

na kạlīyạrē *Vd.* **kạlīyạrē.**

nạƙalta A. (naƙạltā) *Ar. Vb.* 1C explained (= **bayyạnā**).
    B. **(nạƙaltạ)** *Vb.* 2 (*p.o.* **nạƙạlcē,** *n.o.* **nạƙạlci**) x **nā nạƙạlcē shị wuriŋ Audụ** I learned of it from Audu.

na· Karạɗūwạ *Vd.* **Karạɗūwạ.**

naƙasa A. (naƙạsā = **nakạsā)** *Vb.* 1C *Ar.* rendered of less account.
    B. **(nạƙasạ** = **nạkasạ)** *Vb.* 3B became of less account.

nạƙasụ *Ar. m.* blemish, defect (= **aibị**).

naƙata A. (naƙạtā) = **niƙạtā.**
    B. **(nạƙatạ)** *Vb.* 2 (*p.o.* **nạƙạcē,** *n.o.* **nạƙạci**) **(1)** = **niƙạtạ. (2)** (*a*) harassed. (*b*) *Vd.* **awọ 2.**

Nạƙạtau *epithet of* Emirs.

nakē = **nikē.**

naki A. (nākị) *Vd.* **nākạ.**
    B. **(nạkī)** *m.* slackness, dilatoriness.

*Nạkīrī = ***Walạkịrị.**

nạkīyạ *f.* **(1)** a confection made from flour (of rice, guinea-corn or millet) and honey and peppers (= **dạndakwạryạ** = **dawọ 4). (2)** gelignite.

naƙƙạlā = **naƙạltā.**

nakkạsā = **nakạsā.**

na kōsạ *Vd.* **kōsạ.**

Nā ƙōshi *Vd.* **dādī 1***d.*

nākụ (1) (*independent possessive pronoun,* Gram. 48) yours (*referring to plural possessors of masc. thing possessed*) x

(*a*) **dōkin nạn** ∼ **nē** this horse is yours. (*b*) **kun yi nākụ, kun yi na ragō** you did more than your share. (*c*) **tākụ** yours (*referring to plural possessors of fem. thing possessed*) x **rīgan nạŋ tākụ cē** this gown is yours. **(2)** *Vd.* **nāmụ 2, nāsụ 3.**

nāƙudạ *f.* **(1) tanā** ∼ she (pregnant woman) is in labour. **(2)** slackness, slowness in work **yā cikạ** ∼ he is dilatory (= **nạwā).**

na ƙudigạ *Vd.* **ƙudigạ.**

na langạ *Vd.* **langạ.**

nalhụ *m.* (*Ar.* nazaha) **(1)** sprinkling water on T. **(2) ɗan** ∼ *m.* small present.

na lūtsā *Vd.* **lūtsā.**

nam *Vd.* **naŋ 3.**

nāmạ *m.* (*pl.* **nāmū** = **nāmōmī) (1)** (*a*) (i) meat, *Vd.* **gāwā 1***a*, **tsōkạ 1***d*, **1***b*.i (*epithet is* **Nāmạ** (= **Dāgū) cịmar zākị). (ii) ạbin cịn** ∼ *Vd.* **ạbụ 1***aa*.iii. (iii) **nāmạnsạ nā jạkā** *Vd.* **rawā 1***e*. (*b*) **cịn nāmạm mutạ̄nē gạrēshị** he defames people. (*c*) **yā zamā** ∼ he was easily beaten (in draughts, '**yā, langạ,** etc.). (*d*) **gyạmbō yā yi** ∼ = an **sā wạ gyạmbō** ∼ = **ạjīyạ 6.** (*e*) (i) **sanyin** ∼ **gạrēshị** he is lethargic (= **sanyī 4***e*). (ii) **zāfin nāmạ gạrēshị** he is quick in his movements. (*f*) (i) **kitsẹ mūgụn** ∼, **bạ kạ nụna ba, kā kashẹ wutā** *playful epithet of* Filani. (ii) **mūgụn** ∼ *Vd.* **gạnjar 2***b*. (*g*) **nāmạn dạ kẹ̄ kusa dạ wutā shī ya fi gạsũwā** *Vd.* **gasạ 1***a*.iv. (*h*) **wani yā sạ̄mi** ∼ **yā rasạ wutar gashị, wani · yā sạ̄mi wutạr, bai sạ̄mi nāmạn gasạ̄wā ba** one lacks ability while another has it without opportunity to use it. (*j*) **nāmạ yā ƙōnẹ, yā bar rōmō** (i) what a hypocrite ! (ii) tell that to the horse marines ! (*k*) **tūwạŋ girmā mīyạssạ** ∼ power never lacks zest. (*l*) **in zākị yā san zại sạ̄mi** ∼ **yanā cikin sarƙaƙƙīyā, bā yạ̄ ƙītā wạje** nobody undertakes trouble uselessly. (*m*) **in darē yā yi darē, būzūzu** ∼ **nē** at night all cats are grey. (*n*) **Allā shī kẹ̄ bạ kūrā gishirī,** ∼ **kō ạ kāsũwā tạ̄ sāmụ** *epithet of* warrior, dogged worker. (*o*) **bā ā bạ kūrā ạjīyạr** ∼ don't set a thief to catch a thief ! (p) **tsūtsąn** ~ **ita mā** ~ **cē** the two are identical. (q) **mąi wųyar ban** ~ Vd. **agǫlą̄.** (r) ~ **ną̄ mąi gidā** Vd. **tūwǒ** 9. (s) **bą̄** ~ **ba nę̄** Vd. **amǒ.** (t) **nāmąŋ wāką** Vd. **ąyū.** (u) **ƙǫshin** ~ Vd. **barį** 7b.iii. (v) **nāmąn dǒkį** Vd. **cī** 11p. (w) **nāmąŋ ƙązā** type of mushroom. (2) (a) flesh. (b) **yā yi** ~ he has become fat. (c) **zanąn nąŋ** ~ **gąrēshį** this cloth is of stout material. **rįgan nąŋ** ~ **gąrētą** this is a solidly-made gown (Vd. **ąrąfīyą** 4). (d) Vd. **tsōką** 1d, 1b.i. (e) **nāmąŋ ƙyēyą** Vd. **alągwaidą.** (3) animal x **nāmąn dājį** wild animal. **nāmun dājį** wild animals. **nāmąŋ gidā** an edible domestic animal. **namąn rūwā** any fish. (4) ~ **bą̄ ƙąshī** Kt. Vd. **tūwǒ** 1a. (5) **nāmąŋ gąrā** (a) = 6 below. (b) human corpse. (6) **nāmąŋ Gwārī** generic name of several fungi. (7) **nāmąŋ uŋgųlū** carrion (= **mūshę**). (8) cf. **nāmū**

na madakā Vd. **madakā.**

namądǒtąl zagin zagą̄gē m. nincompoop.

na malē Vd. **malē.**

na **māmąrūsų** Vd. **māmąrūsų.**

na **marąshī** Vd. **marąshī.**

na **mąrǒdǒdǫ** Vd. **mąrǒdǒdǫ.**

na mātā Vd. **mącē** 10.

namijį m. (pl. **mazā** = **mazą̄jē**) (1) (a) (i) male = **mųtųm** 1a q.v. (Vd. **tamątā**). (ii) **kyąm mazā** Vd. **dądą kyąų.** (b) brave man x (i) **yāƙį shī nę̄ ąbincin** ~ war is pleasant to the brave man (Vd. **yāƙį** 1a.ii). (ii) **mazā nę̄ bą̄ mazą̄rē ba** they are real men. (iii) **makąshim mazā, mazā ką̄ kash shį** he who lives by the sword shall die by the sword. (iv) **mazą̄jan jirą̄gyan yāƙimmų** our brave warships. (v) **mazā bisą kąŋkų** look out, the enemy are attacking ! (vi) **mun yi sāfīyar mazā** we went to war (cf. **sāfīyar mātā**). (vii) **karǫ nē na mazā dą mazą̄jē** it is a heroic struggle. (viii) Vd. **mijįm mazā.** (ix) **mazan dawą** Vd. **Aibǒ.** (x) **mazā bą̄ tsǒrǒ** Vd. **Tūlą.** (xi) **tā dą mazā tsąye** Vd. **bazarā** 2. (c) **mazą̄jam fāmā** = **mazā ma'ąnītā** = **mącē** 8 q.v. (d) **tā daurą zanę ą namijįŋ gįndī** her cloth

was so short that it left her buttocks exposed. (e) Vd. **tirdę.** (2) **mazam bāya** (a) people of old. (b) **sąŋ ą shiną yį na gayą mazam bāya tārę̄wā** m. meddlesomeness (= **ƙąrąmbąnī**), Vd. **sanį** 1a.iii. (3) **dāƙį yā yi ą mazā** the house is high compared with its area (Vd. **mącę̄** 7). (4) **bįm mazā** Vd. **bī** 3b. (5) **Mazā mąsū jirąn tsąmmānį** epithet of **uŋgųlū.** (6) **yā shā mazā ciƙį** (= **ą ciƙį**) he's a redoubtable P. (cf. **cī** 17a). (7) 'yam **mazā damįn gujīyā nę̄, sǎi am fasą,** a **kąn sam bįdī** (a) all is not gold that glitters. (b) it takes time to know a P. (8) (a) **namijį bąrkǫnǒ nę̄, sǎi an tauną zā ą san yą̄jįnsa** = 7b above. (b) ~ **dą bąrkǫnąŋ wurį** Vd. **hanzarī** 2b. (9) **sąbam mazā fadą** dissension among real men is a necessary preliminary to friendship ; disputes lead to the appreciation of the good in people. (9A) **įnā rūwam mazā** Vd. **bīƙį** 2. (10) **namijįŋ kųnāmą** Vd. **kųnāmą** 4. (11) **namijįn daką** = **dąŋkarǒ** 1. (12) **namijįŋ kadanyą** Vd. **kadanyą** 3. (13) **namijįŋ kadē** Sk. = 12 above. (14) **namijįn tsādą** Vd. **tsādą** 3. (15) **namijįŋ gōrǫ** Vd. **gōrǫ** 1d. (16) cf. **mazan**-compounds. (17) Vd. **mątar mazā ; bąmbąrākwąi.** (18) ~ **dą mārą** Vd. **dąkwarī.** (19) **namijįŋ gįndī** Vd. **gįndī** 1b.iii.

nāmōmī vd. **nāmą.**

namu A. (**nāmū**) (1) Vd. **nāmą.** (2) m. small cyst on horse's face.

B. (**nāmų**) (1) (independent possessive pronoun, Gram. 48) ours (referring to masc. thing possessed) x (a) **dǒkįn nąn** ~ **nę̄** this horse is ours. (b) **tāmų** ours (referring to fem. thing posssesed) x **rįgan nąŋ tāmų cē** this gown is ours. (2) (preceding noun, it can replace suffixed possessive pronoun) x (a) **ƙāƙą zā mų yi dą nāmų tsǒfąffiŋ kudį** what shall we do with our old money ? (= **tsǒfąffiŋ kudimmų**), Vd. M.G. 127e, ŋ 4. (b) (noun is sometimes omitted) (i) **ą lōkąciŋ ąmāną mukē** ~ it is in time of peace that we carry on our work. (ii) **muną̄ īyą̄kar nāmų mų gamą** we're doing our best to finish it. (3) Vd. **nāsą** 3.

Nąmūzų *Vd.* **ąkōkō.**

nan A. (nąŋ) *adj.* (1) this, these (near at hand) *(used when tone of preceding noun is high,* M.G. 125a) *x (a)* **gąrin nąŋ** this town. **gōdīyan nąŋ** this mare. **kāyan nąŋ** this load. **dawākin nąŋ** these horses. *(b) Vd.* **nąŋ, wannąŋ.** *(c) (sometimes added to vocative) x* **kai kŭwā ɗan tsuntsun nąŋ** you little bird ! *(2)* = **nąŋ** 3*a.*

B. **(nąŋ)** (1) *adj. (a)* (i) this, these (near at hand) *(used when tone of preceding noun is low,* M.G. 125b) *x* **dōkįn nąŋ** this horse. **jākunąn nąŋ** these donkeys. (ii) *(sometimes replaces possessive pronoun) x* **dōgō ŋ̄, gāshįn nąŋ bakī** he is tall and his hair is black. *(b) Vd.* **nąŋ, wannąŋ.** *(c) Vd.* **nąŋ** 1*c.* (2) *(a)* here *x* **yanā̀ nąŋ** it is here. **zō nąŋ** come here ! **yā bīyō ta nąŋ** he passed through here. **gā̀ ni nąŋ** here I am ! *(to P. calling one, cf.* **nąŋ** 2b.i). *(b)* **kāyan nąŋ** the load here. *(c)* **yanā̀ dąga nąŋ** he is here. **kā̀wō shi nąŋ** = **kā̀wō shi dąga nąŋ** bring it here ! *(d)* **bā nąŋ, bā cąŋ** neither fish, flesh, fowl, nor good red herring. *(e)* **nā yi nąŋ, nā yi nąŋ** I looked hither and thither.

C. **(naŋ)** (1) *adj. (a)* that, those (in near or far distance, but visible). *(b)* the one in question, those referred to *(in both* 1*a* and 1*b, if preceding noun ends in high syllable, this becomes falling tone) x* **dōkin naŋ** that horse over there *(=* **cąŋ**). **gąrin naŋ** that town over there *(=* **cąŋ**). **dōkin naŋ** the horse in question *(=* **cąŋ**). **ą cikin shĕkarąn naŋ** in that year *(=* **cąŋ**). **Ạlhạmīshįn naŋ** on that Thursday in question *(=* **cąŋ**). **gąrin naŋ** that town referred to *(as speaker at Kano referring to* Bauchi). **mąsū kāmą shįn naŋ** those who captured him *(Vd.* 1*d below,* **na** 6). *(c) Vd.* **wąnnaŋ, wąncaŋ.** *(d) (often* **naŋ** *is omitted,* Mod. Gram. 127c) *x* **yā bā nį dōkįŋ** he gave me the horse in question. **bakįŋ** the black one *(Vd.* Mod. Gram. 127c, d, e). **mąsū kāmą shįŋ** those who captured him *(all the examples meaning* " in question " = **ŋ** *q.v).* (2) *(a)* (i) there (visible = **cąŋ**). (ii) there (distant and

not visible = **cąŋ**). (iii) available (Mod. Gram. 128) *x* **yā bi ta naŋ** he passed through there *(=* **cąŋ**). **nā gan shį naŋ** I saw him there *(as Kano speaker referring to Kaduna =* **cąŋ**). **kāyan naŋ** the load there. **kudī sunā̀ naŋ** money is to be had, is available. *(b)* (i) **gā̀ ni naŋ** *(to P. calling one)* I'm busy on this for the moment *(cf.* **nąŋ** 2a). (ii) **wani kirą yā fi gąbaŋ** " **gā̀ ni naŋ !** " death is no respecter of persons. (iii) **naŋ ganī** *Vd.* **lallę** 2b. *(c)* **haŋkąliŋką bā yā̀ naŋ** it was because your thoughts were elsewhere. *(d)* (i) **naŋ gąba** in the future. (ii) **gąba ŋ̄ naŋ** to-morrow is another day. *(e)* **kanā̀ naŋ įndą kakę** you've made no progress. *(f)* (i) then *x* **naŋ aką ji ąbim mā̀mākį** then a wonderful thing was heard of *(=* **cąŋ**). (ii) **dąga naŋ sǎi aką ji ąbim mā̀mākį** = 2f.i *above.* (iii) **anā̀ naŋ, anā̀ naŋ sǎi aką ji ąbim mā̀mākį** = 2f.i *above.* (iv) **anā̀ naŋ, rąn naŋ sǎi aką ji ąbim mā̀mākį** = 2f.i *above.* (v) **naŋ kŭwā, aką ji ąbim mā̀mākį** = 2f.i. *(g)* **kę̄ naŋ** *Vd.* **kę̄** 3–6. *(h)* **naŋ dą naŋ** at once *x* **naŋ dą naŋ sǎi suką gudų** at once they fled. *(j)* **nam fa ɗayā** *Vd.* **ɗayā** 7. (3) *(abbreviation for imperative of* **nē̆mā** *before dative) x (a)* **naŋ (nam) minį rūwā** seek some water for me ! *(=* **nąŋ** 2). **naŋ wą Audų rūwā** seek some water for Audu ! *(ly dropping of* -a, **nē̆ma** *becomes* nem, *this by* Mod. Gram. 10a.iii *becoming* nam, **naŋ** *cf.* **Māląm Mā̀mūdų** = **Māląŋ Mā̀mūdų**). *(b) Vd.* **būbų** 3.

nana A. (nana) = **nąŋ.**

B. **(Nāna)** (1) = **Nānā** 1. (2) 'yar ~ type of bọ̄rī-spirit.

C. **(nānạ)** (1) **Nānạ** name *(as ạlkunyą)* given to daughter named after her mother. (2) *Vb.* 1A caused to stick to *x (a)* **yā** ~ **shi dą kasā** he felled him *(=* **kā dą**). *(b) (plus dative).* (i) **yā** ~ **masą tąɓō jikin rīgā tasą** it caused mud to stick to his gown. (ii) **yā** ~ **min̦ lạifī** he falsely accused me. (iii) **yā** ~ **masą tsā̄dā** he overcharged him. (iv) **tā** ~ **masą cīwọ** she infected him with venereal disease. (v) **yā nānạ wą jāk**

wutā he branded the donkey, he cauterized the donkey to cure sickness. (3) *Vb.* 3A **yā ~ ạ gụje** he took to his heels (= **shēkạ**).

nănạ alaihịɳ nā tabbạtā . . . I feel quite sure that . . .

nạnạɳgā *Sk.* = **naɳ**.

nānạtā *Vb.* 1C (1) did repeatedly. (2) **nā ~ masạ ạbin naɳ** I impressed on him the urgency of this (= **kwakkwạfā** 3).

nānẫyē *expression used in children's songs* (*Vd.* **ạrauyē**).

na nāyẹ *Vd.* **gandü** 2e.

naɳ dạ naɳ *Vd.* **naɳ** 2h.

nānẹ (1) *Vb.* 1A (a) sealed up (broken place, jar, etc.). (b) stopped up (hole). (c) corked *x* **an ~ bạkinsạ** it (bottle) has been corked up. (d) (boy prior to noisily smashing **bindigạr ƙasā** says **ịnā dạ manạnị**) reply is **gạ wani yā nānẹ** (if gun makes no report, they say **wōhọ yā ci tsōfwā**). (2) *Vb.* 3A (a) stuck to *x* **tạkạrdū sun ~ dạ jūnā** the papers stuck together. **yā ~ gạ Audụ** he stuck to Audu like a leech. **yā ~ masạ** he stuck to him like a leech (= **ɗafẹ** 1a). (b) **yā mayar, yā ~** his prosperity has returned. (c) (nose, eye) became stopped up.

nānị *m.* (1) = **nānīyā**. (2) broken place (in waterpot, etc.) which has been stopped up.

nānịƙē *Vb.* 3A (1) = **nānẹ** 2a. (2) **hancịnsạ yā ~** his nose has no bridge.

nānīyā *f.* stopping up *as in* **nānẹ** 1a–c (= **nānị**).

naɳkarwā *f.* (1) = **fạsō** 1. (2) wrinkles on stomach and breasts of woman who has borne children, due to breasts returning to normal size after cessation of lactation.

nạnnafā *Sk. f.* = **nạnnahō**.

nannaga A. (**nannạgā**) *Vb.* 1C. (1) massaged (stomach of corpse to prevent swelling). (2) **yā ~ masạ kāyā** he overloaded it (animal) = **jibgạ**. *(3) strained (beer being prepared). (4) *Kt.* = **lugwīgwītā** 2.

B. (**nạnnaga**) *Vb.* 2 expressed (oil from seeds) = **mātsạ** 1a.ii.

nạnnạgē *m.* acting *as in* **nạnnagạ, nannạgā** 1, 3, 4.

nạnnahō *m.* the weed *Celosia trigyna* (remedy for tapeworm) = **bōkā** 5.

nạnnauyā *m., f.* (pl. **nauyẫyā**). (1) heavy. (2) important.

nannīyā *Sk.* = **naɳ** 2.

nānum used in **bạn ci ~ ba, ~ bạ tā cī nị ba** even if I get no advantage, I shall not be the loser.

Nạrạbā *Sk.* = **Lạrạbā**.

Nārai *Sk.* name for girl born on a Wednesday (= **Bạlārabạ**).

nārandẹ *Kt. m.* = **gạtūtạ**.

na rārạ *Vd.* **bōdạrī**.

nardẹ = **nardị** *Fil.* **sạ ~** *m.* black-and-white ox. **sānīyā ~** black-and-white cow.

narẹ *Vb.* 3A (**zạurạncē** expression) **yā ~** he is fully alive to what is going on. **yā ~ dạ sū** he knows what they're up to.

Na rēgạ *Vd.* **Dōzạ** 2.

Nārikāwā = **Bārikāwā**.

narkạ *Vb.* 1A to melt T. (*Vd.* **narkẹ** 2).

narkad dạ *Vb.* 4 = **narkạ**.

narkẹ (1) *Vb.* 3A. (a) became melted. (b) **yārọ maɳ kạzā, in yā ji rānā, sǎi yạ ~** the young have no staying-power. (c) **kalmōmin naɳ sun narkẹ, suɳ kōmạ Hausā sọsǎi** these words have become acclimatized in Hausa. (2) *Vb.* 1A = **narkạ** *x* **mun narkẹ kalmōmịn naɳ, mum mai dạ sū Hausā** we've adapted those words into Hausa form.

narkị used in **~ mun shā rānā** how hot it has been !

narkō used in **rānar ~** *f.* the Judgment Day (= **kịyāmạ** 1).

narkōkọ *m.* = **shạrạndaƀọ** 1a,b,c.

nasa A. (**nāsạ**) (1) (independent possessive pronoun, Mod. Gram. 48) his (referring to masc. thing possessed) *x* (a) **dōkịn naɳ ~ nē** this horse is his. (b) **tāsạ** his (referring to fem. thing possessed) *Vd.* **tāsạ**. (2) *Vd.* **nāmụ** 2. (3) (this form is used when suffixed pronoun is separated from its noun) *x* **irịn tsọran dạ akẹ jī nāsạ** the fear felt of him (= **tsọransạ**).

B. (**nasạ**) *Vb.* 1C (1) **tā ~ furā** she put balls of **furā** in the cooking-pot. (2) **dumā yā ~ ɗā** the gourd is getting young fruit. (3) **tā ~ minị dayā** she

(seller of food) gave me one free as "make-weight" (= gyārā 4), *Vd.* nashi 2. (4) an ∼ masa mashi a spear was thrown at him. (5) *Kt.* kāzā tā ∼ ƙwăi the hen laid an egg (= saka = sā).
    C. (nasā) *Vb.* 2 (*p.o.* nashē, *n.o.* nashi) *x* rānā tana nasar gōran nan the heat is spoiling these kola-nuts. rānā tā nashē shi the heat of the sun overcame him.

nasaba *Ar. f.* (1) relations by blood or marriage. (2) fellow-countrymen.

Nasadaru *Vd.* kare 1*a.i.*

nasara A. (nasara) *f.* (*pl.* nasarōrī) *Ar.* (1) victory, success (*epithet is* Nasara, mātar maƙi gudu = Nasara, mātar mazā). (2) (*a*) yā ci ∼ he was victorious, successful. (*b*) sun ci nasarar wannan yāƙi they won this war. (*c*) mun sāmi nasara a kansu we were victorious over them. (3) Allā ya bā ka ∼ *Vd.* tara 2*c.*
    B. (Nasārā) (1) *pl. Vd.* Banasāre.
(2) *m., f.* (*pl.* nasārū) = Banasāre.

Nasārancī *m.* (1) Christianity. (2) language or customs of Europeans.

Nasāranta *Vb.* 3A (1) became converted to Christianity. (2) aped the ways of Europeans.

Nasarawa A. (Nasārāwā) *Vd.* Banasāre.
    B. (Nasārāwā) *f. place-name* (*x* European quarter at Kano).
    C. (Nasārāwa) *f. place-name* (*x* Emirate of that name in Jama'a).

nāsārī *Kt. m.* snoring (= minshārī).

Na shāci *Vd.* dilā.

nasba *Sk. f.* = nasaba.

nashāda = nashātsa *f.* = nishātsi *q.v.*

nashādi = nashātsi *m.* = nishātsi *q.v.*

nashe A. (nāshē) (1) *Vb.* 3A. (*a*) (i) (clothing) became greasy with perspiration, etc. (ii) mǎi yā ∼ oil spread (on clothing) (1*a.*ii = nīsō 2). (*b*) ɗāƙi yā ∼ = ɗāƙi yā nāsō the house is very damp. (2) *Vb.* 1A *x* (*a*) rimā tā ∼ ɗāƙi = rimā tā nāsō ɗāƙi = tā nasu a ɗāƙi damp permeates the house. mǎi yā ∼ rigan nan oil has spread over this gown. (*b*) magana tā ∼ har ya jē ga Audu the matter spread till it reached the ears of Audu. (*c*) *Vd.* nasu.

    B. (nashē) *Vb.* 3A an ∼ shi da mashi = nasa 4.
    C. (nashē) (1) *m.* (*a*) good fura for personal use, not for sale (= saƙē 2*c*), *cf.* buntsura 4. (*b*) fraud taking the form that *x* if five pounds is brought, the receiver counts out twenty-one shillings into each of four piles and asks for the four shillings short in the fifth pile, to be made up (= zirē = zurārē 2). (2) *Vd.* nasā.

nashi A. (nāshi) (1) *m.* type of imported, indigo-dyed material. (2) *Sk.* his (= nāsa).
    B. (nashi) *m.* (1) acting *as in* nasa 1. (2) "make-weight" given *as in* nasa 3 (= gyārā). (3) da ∼, da kāmun gōra conceiving very soon after marriage.
    C. (nashi) *Vd.* nasā.

nashīshi *m.* (*f.* nashīshīyā) cantankerous P. (= *Kt.* nahīshi).

nashitta *f.* cantankerousness (= *Kt.* nahīsanci).

nasīha = nasīyya *Ar. f.* advice.

nas-nas *m.* greasiness of mouth after eating oily food.

naso A. (nāsō) *Vd.* nāshe.
    B. (nasō) *m.* (1) (*a*) = rimā. (*b*) nasō ba a san shigarka ba = rimā 2, sandī. (*c*) *Vd.* bi ∼. (2) rigā tā yi ∼ the gown is stained with perspiration.

nassi *Ar. m.* (1) text of Koran, etc. (2) yā karantad da mū babban nassi he taught us a valuable lesson.

nasu A. (nāsu) (1) (*independent possessive pronoun*, Mod. Gram. 48) theirs (*referring to masc. thing possessed*) *x* (*a*) dōkin nan ∼ nē this horse is theirs. (*b*) tāsu theirs (*referring to fem. thing possessed*) *x* rigan nan tāsu cē this gown is theirs. (2) *Vd.* nāmu 2, nāsa 3.
    B. (nasu) *Vb.* 3B (1) *Vd.* nāshe. (2) addininsu yā nasu har Masar their religion spread as far as Egypt.

nāsūrū = nāsūre = nāsūri *m.* = bāsur *q.v.*

nata (1) (*a*) (*independent possessive pronoun*, Mod. Gram. 48) hers (*referring to masc. thing possessed*) *x* zanan nan ∼ nē this cloth is hers. (*b*) tāta hers (*referring to fem. thing possessed*) ƙwaryan nan tāta cē this calabash is hers.

(c) Vd. nāmu 2, nāsạ 3. (2) f. early
crop of kola-nuts (epithet is Nātạ, mại
nątaccaŋ kudī).
nātī m. type of blue-dyed cloth.
natsạ = nitsạ.
na tsīruku Vd. tsīruku.
na Turuŋkū Vd. Turuŋkū.
nau Sk. mine x ạbin naŋ ~ nā this is
mine (= nāwa).
naunaya = nauyaya.
nā'ūrạ Ar. f. (1) machine. (2) typewriter. (3) diŋkin ~ garment made by
sewing machine. (4) bugun ~ printed
matter.
nausa A. (nausạ) (1) Vb. 1A (a) yā ~
masạ ƙullī ạ idō he punched him in the
eye. (b) tā ~ furā = kirɓạ 1. (2)
Vb. 3A x yā ~ dạ gudu he fled. yā ~,
yā yi arẹwā he went northwards. yā ~
kạnsạ jēji he fled to the bush.
    B. (nausā) Vb. 2 (Vd. naushi) (p.o.
naushē, n.o. naushi) punched (cf. dundū 2).
naushe A. (naushẹ) Vb. 1A punched P.
so hard that he fell over.
    B. (naushē) Vd. nausā.
naushi A. (naushi) Vd. nausā.
    B. (naushi) m. (1) punch x yā yi
masạ ~ he punched him. (2) (secondary
v.n. from nausā) x yanā naushinsạ =
yanā nausassạ he is punching him.
(3) acting as in kirɓạ 1a (= kirɓi 1b).
nausi vulgar pronunciation of naushi.
nauyaya A. (nauyayā) Vb. 1C.   (1)
rendered heavy. (2) rendered burdensome x yā ~ mini aiki (a) he made my
work burdensome. (b) he gave me an
unwelcome task (= naunayā).
    B. (nauyaya) Vb. 2 x wannaŋ aiki yā
nauyayē ni this work is burdensome to
me (= naunaya).
    C. (nauyāyā) Vd. nannauyā.
nauyī m. (1) (a) heaviness. (b) yanā dạ ~
dạ gaskē (i) it is very heavy. (ii) he
has a large family to support. (c)
yā zubạ masạ ~ he put him to a lot
of trouble. (d) ~, bāƙwam mại dōki
shī yạ cī, dōkinsạ yạ cī it is beyond one.
(e) nauyin jikī gạrēshi = jikinsạ yā
yi ~ (i) he's a sluggish P. (ii) he
feels slack. jikinsu nā yi musu ɗan
nauyī they're feeling uneasy.   (f)

nauyim bākī gạrēshi (i) he's unready
of speech.   (ii) he has a clumsy pronunciation.   (g) nauyiŋ harshẹ = f
above. (h) nauyiŋ hannū gạrēshi he's a
slow worker. (2) mạganạ mại ~
important affair. (3) n nā jin nauyinsạ
I feel shy of him.
nawa A. (nāwa) (1) (independent possessive
pronoun, Mod. Gram. 48) mine (referring to masc. thing possessed) x (a)
dōkin nan ~ nẹ this horse is mine.
(b) tāwa mine (referring to fem. thing
possessed) x rīgan naŋ tāwa cẹ this
gown is mine. (2) Vd. nāmu 2, nāsạ 3.
(3) n ci nāwa Vd. rōwạ 1b.
    B. (nāwā) f: slackness, slowness in
work (= nāƙudạ 2). nạwar mācinsu
the slowness of their march.
    C. (nawạ) (1) (a) (preceded by sin-
gular noun).   (i) how much x gārī ~
how much flour ?   (ii) how many ?
x mutum ~ how many persons ?
mutum ~ sukạ zọ how many persons
came ? (Mod. Gram. 160b).   kā sạyi
gōrọ ~ how many kola-nuts did you
buy ?   sau ~ how many times ?   sum
fī mu yawạ sau wajan nawạ they outnumber us greatly.   (b) gudā ~ how
many ?   (c) kudī ~ how much money ?
kudī ~ sukạ sạyā at what price did
they buy ?   (d) kā sạyi gōrọ na nawạ
how much did you spend on kolas ?
(e) nawạ ka sạyā Vd. bāwạ 12.   (2)
(kō may optionally precede nawạ) x
mutānansạ, bại kulạ dạ kō nawạ
sukạ mutu ba he did not care however
many of his people met their death.
bạ ạ saŋ kō jirgī gudā nawạ gạrēsu
ba it is not known how many ships they
have (Vd. kō 2d). (3) kō ~ (a) however many x kō ~ sukạ bā ni, yā yi
kyau however many they give me will
do. (b) no matter how many x kō ~
sukạ cẹ m bā kạ, săi m bā kạ no matter
how many they tell me to give you, I
will give you them. zā su īyạ tsarẹ
ƙasarsu dạgạ sōjạ kō nawạ waɗandạ
mukạ īyạ kāwọwā they will be able to
protect their country from however
many soldiers we bring. (c) no matter
at what price x kadạ kạ sayas, kō ~
sukạ sạyā do not sell no matter what

price they offer you ! (d) no matter how much x kō nawạ sukạ bīyā = duk kō nawạ sukạ bīyā whatever sum they paid.

nạwằcĕ Vd. nạwātạ.

nạwātạ Vb. 2 (p.o. nạwằcĕ, n.o. nạwằci). (1) importuned. (2) Vd. gurgu 2.

nawaya = nauyaya.

nạwu Sk. = nằwa.

nawyī = nauyī.

nāyẹ Vd. gandū 2e.

nazạrī Ar. m. (1) (a) looking at. (b) seeing x nā dadẹ bạn yi nazạrinsạ ba it is long since I saw him. (2) reading silently to oneself (cf. dūbạ 6).

n cẹ̆ Vd. kō 3a.iii, cẹ̆ 10.

*ṇdikyā = *iṇdikyā.

ne (nĕ is used after previous low tone, but nẹ̆ after previous high tone of masc. noun : similarly, we use cĕ or cẹ̆ in the corresponding cases of fem. nouns). (1) is, are, was were x shī nẹ̆ it is he. dōkị nĕ it is a horse. ita cẹ̆ it is she. mạcẹ cĕ = mạcạ cĕ it is a woman. dạ Ạnnabi Daudạ dạ Ạnnabi Sulạimānu Yahūdāwā nẹ̆ the Prophets David and Solomon were Jews. (2) (optionally used in relative construction of emphasis, Mod. Gram. 137) wạ̄sā nẹ̆ sukẹ̆ yị = wạ̄sā sukẹ̆ yị they're playing. Audu nĕ yakẹ̆ zūwạ = Audu yakẹ̆ zūwạ Audu is the one who is coming. Audu nĕ ya zō = Audu ya zō it is Audu who came. ita cẹ̆ fa mukẹ̆ kirạ ƙasar Masạr that is the land which we call Egypt. (3) (a) (nẹ̆ ? can be suffixed to sentence to render it interrogative, Mod. Gram. 163b.ii) x nā sanị nẹ̆ ? do I know anything about it ? kanạ̄ sọ kạ kashẹ tạ nẹ̆ ? do you want to kill her ? (b) (nẹ̆ can be otiosely suffixed to sentence containing interrogative word) x mẹ̆ ya dạ̄mē shị nẹ̆ = mẹ̆ ya dạ̄mē shị what troubled him ? (4) (for emphasis) x mū nẹ̆ bạ mu lụ̄rā ba we don't know the reason why. kō yā yi tạfīyạr kwānā gōmạ nĕ even if he travels for ten days. mū nẹ̆, bạ mu sanị ba we do not know. zạn zō nẹ̆ ṇ shiryạ ku I'll come with the special purpose of reconciling you people. mum fitō nẹ̆ dạgạ birnī we've come from the town. yā sạyē shị nĕ

tum bạ ạ yi yāƙị ba he bought it before the war. (5) it is because x nā sanị nĕ it is because I know. kanạ̄ sọ kạ kashẹ tạ nẹ̆ you act thus, because you want to kill her. haṇkạlī nẹ̆ bā yạ naŋ it is because he is not in his right mind that he acted thus. ạbin dạ ya sạ̄ ta kirā kị, n nạ̄ sạŋ kị nē dạ aurē the reason why she called you is because I wish to marry you. ạbin dạ ya sạ̄ mukạ yi kirạŋkị, mukạ ji lạ̄bārịŋkị nĕ it's because we'd heard all about you that we sent for you.

nema A. (nẹ̆mā) (1) Vb. 2 (but Vd. nēmā for progressive) (cf. naŋ 3). (a) (i) looked for (= bịdā). (ii) yā nẹ̆mē tạ dạ aurē he sought her in marriage (Vd. aurē 6c). nēmaŋ aurē m. courting. gạ̄sar nēmaŋ aurē f. rivalry in courting girl. (iii) yā nẹ̆mē tạ dạ zịnā he wanted to commit adultery, fornication with her. (iv) ya kạn nẹ̆mi mātā he fornicates, commits adultery (cf. bī 3). (v) sun nēmō dạlīlai, sum bā mu they adduced reasons to justify themselves to us. (vi) Vd. zumuncị 5. (b) yā nẹ̆mi yaddạ zại yi he sought a way to do it. (bb) (i) a kạn nẹ̆mi kīfī Vd. rūwā C.17. (ii) yā nēmō kạ Vd. afạlalu (iii) nẹ̆mạ kạŋkạ ƙanẹ Vd. būbụ 3 (c) requested x zạn nẹ̆mi ragi gạ mạsụ jirgī I'll ask the boatmen for a rebate yaddạ sukạ nẹ̆mā in accordance with their request. (d) wanted to, tried tọ x yā nẹ̆mi shiryạ su he tried to makẹ peace between them. (e) tā nẹ̆mē sḅ wurim mālạmī she got a love-philtrẹ from the soothsayer to make him lov⟨ her (Vd. sạ̄mā 1a.iii, nēmẹ). (2) f adultery x yā yi ~ dạ ita he committe⟨ adultery with her (= Sk. nēmā 6).

B. (nēmā) m. (1) (used to forṃ progressive of nẹ̆mā) x (a) (i) aṇ nēmansạ he is seeking it. (ii) V⟨ nēmaŋ aurē. (b) yanạ̄ nēmansạ rūw⟨ ạ jạllō he's seeking it might and mair (c) yanā ~ yạ jāwō sụ cikin yāƙ he's trying to involve them in war (c nẹ̆mā 1d). (d) nụ̄nạ mai nēmaŋkị V Yaŋgạ. (e) nēmam faɗạ Vd. faɗạ 1 (f) nēmaŋ kīfī Vd. rūwā C.17. (ẹ yanạ̄ nēmam mutūwạ he (person) dying, it (animal, tree) is dying, (garment) is worn-out (Mod. Gram. 113*b*), *Vd.* mutūwặ, *cf.* dauko̯. (3) tsananin ~ bā yặ kāwō sāmụ effort does not always end in success. (4) maị sāmụ yā rigā maị ~ one P. is rich and another seeks to emulate him. (4*A*) ạgwặgwā cikin rūwa takę̆ nēmā *Vd.* ạgwặgwā 2. (5) maị ~ yanặ tặre dặ sāmụ he who seeks, finds. (6) *Sk.* = nę̆mā 2. (7) dan ~ *m.* (*a*) *Sk.* bother you ! (*b*) (*with fem.* 'yar ~) bastard (= shēgę̆). (*c*) dan nēmaŋ kyau (tsǫ̆rō) gặrēshị he is very good (afraid), *cf.* kặrē 1*c*.ii. (8) *Vd.* nēman-*compounds*.

C. (nēmặ) *Vb.* 1A. (*a*) (*the form of* nę̆mā *used before dative*) *x* nā ~ (= nē-mar) masặ shī I sought it for him. (*b*) nā ~ nā ~, bạn sāmụ ba I looked carefully but could not find it (= *Kt.* tādặ). (2) *Kt.* yā ~ he took to his heels. nēmaŋ aurē *Vd.* nę̆mā 1*a*.ii. nēmaŋ azziķī *m.* *Vd.* ạzzimmặ 2, aurē 6*c*. nēmam bặķī *Vd.* bặķī 2*x*. nēman daŋgị = kākalē 1*a*. nēmam fadặ *Vd.* fadặ 1*c*. nēmaŋ girmā *Vd.* girmā 1*a*.ix. nēman jinī *Vd.* bābę̆ 2. nēmaŋ kặi *m.* ~ yakę̆ yī dặ shī he'll sell it " for a song ". nēmaŋ kaucị *Vd.* kaucị 3. nēmaŋ ƙibặ *Vd.* ƙibặ 3. nēmaŋ ƙīfī *Vd.* rūwā C.17. nēmam maị gặtarī *m.* not being able to see the nose on one's face (*x* seeking spectacles and not realizing one is wearing them) = tặfī 1*e*.ii. nēman tsịnī *Vd.* tsịnī 1*b*. nēmę̆ *Vb.* 1A tā ~ shi she won his love by a philtre (= dabặrcē), *cf.* nę̆mā 1*e*, sặmā 1*a*.iii. nēmō *Vd.* nę̆mā. nēsặ (1) *adv.* far away *x* (*a*) yanặ ~ it is far off (= nīsā 2). (*b*) tun dagặ nēsặ = dagặ nēsặ (i) from afar. (ii) *Vd.* muryặ 4. (*c*) (i) to afar. (ii) kai dā ~ *Vd.* dumā 3. (2) ~ dặ = ~ gặ *prep.* far from *x* (*a*) yanặ ~ dặ Kano it is far from Kano (= nīsā 3). (*b*) būzum biri ~ gặ Mālặm how is one concerned with such a thing ! (3) (*a*) san rặƙumin

yặrā dagặ ~, in yā zō kusa, sǎi gudụ liking T., but fearing to accept it when the chance offers. (*b*) kwānā ~ *Vd.* sạnnū 2*a*.ii. (4) that which is afar *x* (*a*) madūbī maị kāwō nēsặ kusa tele-scope, binoculars. (*b*) (i) na ~ *m.* (*f.* ta ~) *pl.* na ~ *adj.* far *x* gạrī na nēsặ distant town. (ii) ạbin ~ *Vd.* shịm-fīdặ 1*d.* (*c*) bābụ ~ gặ Allặ to God all is possible. (*cc*) hannū maị kirạn na ~ yā ƙafặ tạfīyặ fame for liberality spread far and fast. (*d*) ạbịŋ dặ kạmar wụyā, gurgūwā dặ auran ~ what a difficult thing !

ŋ ga *Vd.* ganī A.1 5. ŋgantā *Vd.* iŋgantā. ŋgas the Angass people (*epithet is* askā dayā, mạganặ dayā). ŋgiricī *Vd.* iŋgiricī. ŋgo (1) here's a present for you ! (*epithet is* ~ ita cę̆ ta būdę̆ ƙōfạr ạljannặ) (= *Kt.* hiŋ). (2) (*a*) catch hold !, hold this for me !, keep this for me ! (*b*) " ~ riƙe minị ita ! " tā zamā bāshị give him an inch and he'll take an ell. (3) *Vd.* dǫ̆rinā 3 ; ƙạŋƙarặ 2*c*. ŋgōzǫ̆mặ *Vd.* ụŋgōzǫ̆mặ. ŋguddụgī = guddụgī. ŋgụdūdụ *Kt.* = iŋgidīdọ. ŋgụlū = ụŋgụlū. ŋgurdụgī = guddụgī. ŋgụrnū = ụŋgụrnū. ŋgūwā = ụŋgūwā. ŋgwaị = iŋgwaị. ŋgwallọ = iŋgwallọ. ŋgwayyā = iŋgwayyā. ŋhwānặ *Kt.* = ạmfānặ. ŋhwạnī *Kt.* = ạmfạnī. ni A. (nī) (1) (*independent pronoun*, Mod. Gram. 46). (1) *x* ~ nę̆ it is I. ~ nę̆ na zō it is *I* who have come. bặ ~ ba not I. (2) (*used as direct object when dative precedes*, Mod. Gram. 76*a*.ii) *x* yā nūnặ musụ ~ he showed me to them. (3) *Vd.* nī dặ ūwā ; shēgę̆ 4. (4) nī kę̆ riƙę̆ ƙạfō *Vd.* riƙę̆ 1*a*.ii. (5) nī nā sanị *Vd.* sanị 1*a*.vi.

B. (ni) (1) (*objective pronoun after low tone in previous verb*, Mod. Gram. 49*a*) me *x* yā kāmặ ~ he caught hold of me (*cf.* nị). (2) *Vd.* nikặ, nikę̆. (3) (*1st sg. pronoun used after zặ* Mod.

Gram. 17, *and* bạ̄ Mod. Gram. 19*b*) *x*
zạ̄ ～ gidā I'll be off home, bạ̄ ～ zūwạ
I am not coming. (4) *Sk.* = na 8*b*
q.v. (*it doubles following consonant*) *x*
ạbin dạ nig ganī what I saw.   ạbin
dạ nif fadi what I said.   ạbin dạ nib
bā shị what I gave him (*cf.* mịg).

C. (nị) (1) (*objective pronoun after
high tone in previous verb*, Mod. Gram.
49*a*[1]) me *x* yā gan nị he saw me (*cf.*
ni 1). (2) *Vd.* minị.

D. (nị) *Sk.* = nạ̄ *x* nị bā kạ I'll probably give you it.

nī dạ ūwā *m.* (1) big dạddawā-lumps. (2)
cf. innạ 3*c*.

nīgā (*d.f. metathesis of* gānẹ *in* zạurạncē) =
gānẹ understood.

nīgạncē *Vb.* 1C = nīgā.

nīgẹ *Vb.* 1A = nīgā.

nigirạ *Vb.* 3B *Nor.* = lụ̄rā.

nigircē = nigirtạ *Nor.* = lūrẹ.

nigirtad dạ *Nor.* = lūrad dạ.

nịhāyạ *Vd.* gāyạ 3.

ni'imạ *f.* (*pl.* ni'imōmī = nị'imū) *Ar.* (1)
(*a*) prosperity. (*b*) fertility. (*c*) wurī
maị ～ (i) fertile place. (ii) cool,
shady place. (2) (*a*) ～ tā saukō the
rainy season has begun. (*b*) gōrạn
nạŋ bā shi dạ ～ these kolas have no
dampness in their wrappings.

nị'imcē *Vd.* nị'imtạ.

ni'imta A. (nị'imtạ).   (1) *Vb.* 2 (*p.o.*
nị'imcē, *n.o.* nị'imci) rendered prosperous *x* Allạ̄ yā nị'imcē shị God has
showered blessings on him.   jirgiŋ
ƙasā yā nị'imci gạrimmụ the railway
has been a great boon to our town. (2)
Vb. 3B became prosperous, fertile.

    B. (ni'imtā) *Vb.* 1C = nị'imtạ 1.

nikạ = nukạ.

niƙa A. (niƙạ) (1) *Vb.* 1A. (*a*) ground up
(*cf.* fasạ 1*a*.i).   (*b*) an ～ masạ kāshī
he has been thrashed.   (2) *m.* (*a*)
(*secondary v.n. from* niƙạ 1) *x* tanạ̄ niƙạ
gạ̄rī = tanạ̄ niƙạŋ gạ̄rī she is grinding
flour. (*b*) being occupied in grinding *x*
tanạ̄ ～ she is grinding.   (*c*) kạ̄ ƙạ̄ri ～,
kạ̄ bā dạ gạ̄rī rant on to your heart's
content, what do I care ? (*d*) wụyar ～
fashi, iŋ am fasa, yā ƙārẹ the first step
is the hardest.   (*e*) dūtsạn ～ (i) *Vd.*
dūtsẹ 7.   (ii) dūtsạn ～ kā fi gạbaŋ

ạljīfū what an important person !
(*f*) wāƙạ ɗayā bā tạ̄ ƙārẹ ～ patience
conquers all. (*g*) *Vd.* gumị 1*c* ; gwaurō
1*b* ; haƙurī 5.

    B. (niƙā) *Vb.* 2 vexed, annoyed.

niƙace A. (niƙạcē) *Vd.* niƙātạ.

    B. (niƙạcē) *Vb.* 1C *Sk.* = niƙātạ.

niƙāka *Vd.* nuƙākạ.

niƙata A. (niƙātạ) *Vb.* 2 (*p.o.* niƙạcē,
n.o. niƙạci).   (1) approached *x* yā
niƙạci gạrī he (usually P. of importance)
approached the town.   (2) yā niƙạci aiki he has nearly finished the work.
(3) *Vd.* nạƙātạ.

    B. (niƙātā) *Vb.* 3A. (1) (usually P.
of importance) went in certain direction *x* (*a*) gīwā tā ～, tā yi kudụ the
elephant turned south.   (*b*) ɗārī
(hadari) yā niƙātō the cold weather
(storm) is approaching.   Sarkī yā
niƙātō the chief is approaching (*cf.*
nīsō 1).   (2) in aŋ ～ zại fi wancạŋ if
progress is made he will surpass that P.

Niƙātau *epithet of* Emir.

niƙau *m.* grinding done for payment
(*cf.* aikạtau).

nike A. (nikẹ̄) (*used for* " I " *in present
relative sentence with positive sense,*
Mod. Gram. 133) *x* lōƙạcin dạ nikẹ̄
zūwạ when I come.   yạushẹ ～ yị
when do I do it ? (*cf.* kẹ̄).

    B. (nikẹ̄) *m.* (1) gambling-cowrie
deceitfully loaded with lead (*cf.* agō).
(2) wax used for sticking down skin of
kōtsō.

    C. (nikẹ) *Vd.* nukẹ.

niƙẹ *Vb.* 1A (1) (*a*) ground all of. (*b*) ～
iri *Vd.* dạmunā 3.   (2) overloaded *x*
an ～ jāƙī dạ kāyā the donkey is overloaded.

niƙi what a heavy load !

niƙiƙī-niƙiƙī = niƙi-niƙi = niƙī-niƙī *used
in* yā ɗauki kāyā ～ he carried a heavy
load.

nikọ = nukọ.

nina *Kt.* = nūna.

Niŋgāwā *Vd.* Baniŋgẹ.

Niŋgī *f.* Ningi in Gombe.

niŋkạ *Vb.* 1A (1) (*a*) folded *x* yā ～ shi
ukụ he folded it in three (= rifịyā =
kirfạ 2*a*). (*b*) yā ～ rawạnī = naɗạ 1*a*.
(*c*) yā ～ kại dạ raggā = naɗạ 1*b*.i.

(d) = naɗę 1a.i, 1b.i. (2) sąu uƙu suką ∽ hanyąn naŋ they passed three times to and fro over that road. (3) exceeded by so and so many times x sōjąnsu sun ∽ nāmu shidą = sun ∽ nāmu sąu shidą they have six times as many soldiers as we have. yā ∽ na dą̄ sąu shidą ƙę̧ naŋ it is six times as much as before (= riɓą 3 q.v.). (4) = riɓą 2.

niŋƙāyā f. swimming (= īyǫ).

niŋkę Vb. 1A = niŋką 1.

niŋki m. = riɓi 1.

niŋkim bą niŋkin used in yā yi masą ∽ he gave him present after present.

niŋƙir m. used in kāyan naŋ ∽ yakę̧ = kāyan naŋ yā ciƙa ∽ this load is heavy.

niŋƙira A. (niŋƙirā) Vb. 1C an ∽ masą kāyā he is heavily laden (= niƙę).

B. (niŋƙirą) Vb. 2 yā niŋƙiri kāyā he took heavy load.

niŋƙirērę m. (f. niŋƙirērīyā) pl. niŋƙir-niŋƙir very heavy.

ninnir = nirnir m. (1) hardness of a swelling. (2) tūwō yā yi ∽ the tūwō is nice and firm.

nisa A. (nīsą) (1) Vb. 3A. (a) groaned. (b) yaną̄ nīsą̄wā = kōką 2a. (c) hadiri yā ∽ storm is rumbling afar (Vd. nīsō). (d) (wall) cracked and threatened to fall. (2) Vb. 1A kept on thinking regretfully of dead or absent P., etc., x yaną̄ ∽ tąfīyąn naŋ he keeps regretfully thinking of that pleasant journey now in the realms of the past.

B. (nīsā) (1) m. (a) (i) distance x nīsammu dą fagyam fāmā our great distance from the theatre of hostilities. (iii) Vd. wāwan ∽. (b) yā yi ∽ it is far away. yā yi mini ∽ it became far from me ; it's too far for me. dą ∽ tsąkāninsu they are far from each other. (c) yā yi ∽ cikin kąrą̄tū (hąƙurī) he is very learned (long-suffering). (d) yā yi nīsaŋ kīwǫ he (messenger) has been long away. (e) dą nīsaŋ haŋkąlī yakę̧ he is far-seeing (= tsiŋkāyā 2). (f) kōmē nīsan darē, garī yā̧ wāyę̧ every cloud has a silver lining. (g) Allą̄ yą̧ bā mu nīsaŋ kwānā God give us a long life ! (h) wąndą ya yi ∽ bā yā̧ jiŋ kirą P. firmly given over to a

habit cannot break away from it. (j) kōmē nīsan jīfą, ƙasą zą̄ shi = . . . ƙasą ząi fāɗi every cloud has a silver lining. (k) mąi nīsaŋ gōnā Vd. gąidā ; kāɗǫ. (2) dą ∽ adv. afar x (a) yaną̄ dą ∽ it is far off (= nēsą 1). (b) kadą dāi mu kai ką dą nīsā let us not exaggerate ! (3) dą ∽ dą prep. far from x iŋ kā tąfi dą ∽ dą Kanǫ if you go far from Kano (= nēsą 2). (4) mąi ∽ m., f. (pl. mą̄sū ∽) (a) distant. (b) māganiŋ garī mąi nīsā, tąfīyą effort completes work.

nīsāce = nīsancē.

nisance A. (nisąncē) Vd. nisantą.

B. (nīsancē) Vb. 1C x nā ∽ masą I avoided him (= nisantą).

nisanta A. (nīsantą) Vb. 3 (p.o. nisąncē, n.o. nisąnci) avoided x nā nisąncē shi = nisąncē.

B. (nīsantā) Vb. 1C separated x an ∽ shi dą ita he has been kept away from her.

nīsantad dą Vb. 4 = nīsąntā.

nīsāta = nīsanta.

nishāɗą = nishātsą f. = nishātsi q.v.

nishāɗi = nishātsi m. feeling happy about something (= ąnnąshūwā), cf. fąra'ą̧.

nishi m. (1) groaning, grunting. (2) mąi ∽ ką̄ shā gārī Vd. gąyyā 1c.

niskę (1) Vb. 3A deteriorated x kyąnsą yā ∽ its quality has deteriorated. (2) Vb. 1A surpassed.

nīsō Vb. 3A (1) approached x yā ∽ he (usually important person) is approaching (cf. nīsą 1c, niƙą̄tā 1b). (2) = nāshę̧ 1a.ii. (3) rījīyā taną̄ nīsǭwā = rūwā yaną̄ nīsǭwā ą̧ rījiyā water is flowing into the well. (4) (grease-spot on washed garment) reappeared.

nitsą Vb. 3A (1) (a) (wind, trouble) abated. (b) wurī yā nitsą things settled down. (2) penetrated x yā ∽ ą̧ rūwa he jumped into the water (= fāɗą 2). yā ∽ cikin ƙasā he penetrated far into the country. (3) vanished x (a) yā ∽ ą̧ rūwa he vanished under the water. (b) iŋ kā ∽ ką̧ tāsą you always turn up like a bad penny. (c) tąlōlō yą̧ nitsę̧ Vd. tąlōlō.

nitsattsē m. (f. nitsattsīyā) pl. nitsattsū P. of reflection (cf. nitsę̧ 2).

nitse A. (nitsę̧) Vb. 3A = nitsą 3a.

B. (niṭse) *x* ạ yĭ shị ạ ~ reflect before doing it ! (*cf.* niṭsattsē).

nitso A. (nitsọ) *m*. (1) vanishing below the water. (2) swimming under water. (3) yaṇ̃ ~ ạ masakī he thinks his faults hidden. (4) (*a*) yaṇ̃ ~ ạ tsandaurī = 3 *above.* (*b*) bā ạ̄ yịn ~ ạ tsandaurī don't knock your head against a stone ! B. (niṭsō) *m*. = niṭsūwā.

niṭsu *Vb*. 3B yā ~ (1) he has come to his senses. (2) he is in good spirits.

niṭsūwā *f*. being P. of foresight, being P. of reflection (= tsịṇ̃kāyā).

nīyā *Sk*. (*independent personal pronoun*) I (= nĭ).

nīyyạ (*Ar. f.*) = ạnīyạ.

ṇjarī = ịnjarī.

njị = injị.

n ṇ̃ (*progressive,* Mod. Gram. 16) I am *x* ~ zūwạ I am coming.

nōcẹ *Sk*. = nitsẹ.

nōk̃ẹ *Vb*. 3A (1) withdrew. (2) (*a*) (snake, tortoise) drew in head (= kudẹ 1*a*). (*b*) *Vd*. ṩạri kạ nōk̃ẹ. (*c*) *Vd*. k̃aik̃ạyī 5. (*d*) = kudẹ 1*b*. (3) backed out of statement.

noma A. (nōmā) *m*. (1) (*a*) (i) farming (*this consists of* nōmam firị (*Vd*. firị), *then* mai-mai *or for* dāwạ *and* beans sassaryā *replacing* mai-mai): (*if soil lacks manure, Vd*. baṇ̃gajē). (ii) *for epithet Vd*. dǔk̃e 2. (*b*) (i) Sarkin ~ head-farmer (*epithet is* k̃ọsau). (ii) 'yā tā k̃i auran Sarkin ~ (*reply,* don cikiṇ̃kị = doṇ kaṇ̃kị) acting contrary to one's own interests. (*c*) *cf*. firị, mịrginē, gạ̄ nōmā, yāk̃ị 1*a*.ii. (*d*) yā k̃i ~ *Vd*. warạbukkạ. (*e*) Allạ̄ yạ tsạri gạ̄tarī dạ nōmā *Vd*. tsạrā 2. (*f*) bạ kạ ĩyạ ~ ba = mĭyạ 10. (2) (*secondary v.n. from* nōmạ 1*a, c*) *x* yaṇ̃ nōmaṇ gōnā = yaṇ̃ nōmạ gōnā (*a*) he is tilling his farm. (*b*) he is weeding his farm. (3) *Vd*. nōmā-*compounds.*

    B. (nọ̃mā) *Vb*. 2 = nōmạ 1.
    C. (nōmạ) (1) *Vb*. 1A (*Vd*. nōmā 2). (1) (*a*) tilled, worked (farm). (*b*) yā ~ gōnar Audụ he imitated Audu. (*c*) weeded (farm, road). (*d*) *Vd*. barẹ 2*c*. (2) *Vb*. 3A yā ~ ạ gụje he took to his heels.

nōmam Barẹ *Vd*. barẹ 2*c*.
nōmaṇ Barkạ *Vd*. Barkạ 2.
nōman cịrā = cịrā 2*b*.

nōman dụrwā *Vd*. dụrwā 3.

nōmam firị *m*. *Vd*. firị.

nōmaṇ kaṇ̃kạrē *Vd*. kaṇ̃kạrē.

nōmaṇ kạrē *Vd*. kạrē 13*b*.

nōmẹ (1) *Vb*. 1A (*a*) tilled all of, weeded all of (*cf*. nōmạ). (*b*) yā ~ gandunsạ he's dead. (*c*) nā nōmẹ gọ̄nạ̃kinsụ I followed their example (= nōmạ 1*b*). (2) *Vb*. 3A yā ~ ạ gụje he took to his heels (= nōmạ 2). (3) *m*. the beniseed *Sesamum indicum,* which has red flowers and darker seed than rīdĩ *q.v., but the two names are often interchanged* (*cf*. karkashī, gāyā 1*e*).

nōmị *Kt. m.* = nōmẹ 3.

nọ̄mi-jịde = nọ̄mi-jịdi *Kt. m.* living in ạ tax-area different from where one farms.

nōnạn-*compounds Vd*. nōnọ 1*h–l*.

noṇnā *Vd*. nōnọ.

nōnọ *m*. (*pl.* nōnạ̃yē = noṇnā). (1) (*a* sour milk (*cf*. madarā, fadandẹ). (*b* nōnạn wurị kō na kudī gōmạ, farins̃ dayā cut your coat according to you cloth ! (*cf*. 1*e*). (*c*) in ~ yaṇ̃ dạ dād ạ gụmbā, gụmbā mā taṇ̃ dạ dādī ạ ~ the benefit is mutual. (*d*) cịnik̃i dūnīyạ dībạn ~ nē as you act t others, so they will act to you. (*e* ạmfạ̃nin ~ farī it is utility one require not mere beauty (*cf*. 1*b*). (*f*) ~ y zubẹ ạmmā yā bar gọ̄rā the child die but its mother is alive. (*g*) kōwā y zubar mini dạ tsāmīyāta, sǎi ṇ zub masạ dạ nōnạnsạ I'll not be outdo in repaying good for good and evil f evil. (*h*) nōnạn gīwā *Kt*. fruit ṛahainā. (*j*) nōnạn gōdīyā fou pointed spur for horses. (*k*) nōṇ kạrē gạrētạ she has pointed breas (*l*) nōnạn kurcīyā the weed *Euphorb hirta.* (*m*) (i) milk (in breast or udde (ii) *Vd*. ꞗatạn ~. (2) (*a*) (i) breast. (ii nōnạn ūwāta *Vd*. dībạ 1*j*. (iii) V ạlbarkạ 3*b*. (*b*) kạn ~ nipple (= mạ̃m (*bb*) *Vd*. mạ̃mā 1*c*. (*c*) (i) rūwan nō *Vd*. rūwā B.15. (ii) *Vd*. shạ̃ nō (*d*) udder. (3) cluster (of dates, dọ̃rōw pods, etc.). (*b*) fins below head of f

nọs-nọs = nạs-nạs.

nōwạ *f*. ulcerative gingivitis (*cf*. ꞗubụ

ṇtāwō *m*. red variety of kola-nut from Gold Coast.

nūcę *Kt.* = nitsą.

nųfā *Vb.* 2 (1) intended *x* ąbin dą suką ~ their intentions. bąn sąŋ ąbin dą ya ~ ba I don't know what he intended to do. yā nųfē shi dą mūgųŋ ąbu he intended evil to him. (2) went to destination *x* yā nųfi gidā he set out for home. yā nufō wajammu he came in our direction. mun nųfē su taimakō we set out with help for them. (3) destined *x* suŋ isa indą muką nųfē su dą zūwą they have reached the destination which we fixed for them. Allą yā nųfā sunā dą shūgąba God ordained that they should have a leader. nā gōdę wą Allą dą ya nųfā suką zō I thank God for destining them to come (*cf.* są *construction* Mod. Gram. 159*a*). iŋ Allą yā ~ if God so wills. Allą yā nųfē shi dą zūwą nąŋ God destined him to come here.

nųfātą *Vb.* 2 (*p.o.* nufācē, *n.o.* nųfąci) = nųfā.

Nufāwā *Vd.* Bąnufē.

Nufē *f.* (1) Nupe-land. (2) *Vd.* banzā.

nufi *m.* (1) intention *x* dą nufinsą, bą ząi tsayą kōinā ba his former intention was to halt nowhere. ąbin dą sukę ~ their intentions (*cf.* nųfā). (2) dą ~ purposely (= tąkąnas), *cf.* gąŋgaŋ.

Nūhu Noah.

nuka A. (nuką) *Vb.* 1A. (1) ripened (fruit by storing), *Vd.* nūna. (2) *x* tā ~ dąddawā she fermented the locust-bean seeds (*Vd.* kalwā, nuka 3). (3) rānā tā ~ shi the sun made him perspire freely. B. (nuka) *Vb.* 3B (*progressive* nukā). (1) (fruit) ripened by being stored. (2) yā nuku (*a*) fruit (stored to ripen) is now fully ripe. (*b*) he is perspiring freely from the heat of the sun. (3) (indigo, shea-nuts, dąddawā) became fermented (= nukāką).

nukāką *Vb.* 3B (1) P. perspired freely. (2) T. became mildewed from overheating (= nuka 3).

nukākē *Vb.* 3A = nukāką.

nukę *Vb.* 3A = nuka 2*b*.

nuko *m.* = rifi 2.

nuku *Vb.* 3B *Vd.* nuka.

nukūli *Ar. m.* hesitation.

nukū-nukū *m.* dilly-dallying.

nukurą *Ar. f.* hostility *x* yanā ~ dą ni he is hostile to me.

nukurkusa A. (nukurkusā) *Vb.* 1D yā ~ ni he kept putting off paying me. B. (nukurkusą) *Vb.* 2 (*p.o.* nukurkushē, *n.o.* nukurkushi) *x* ząncan nąŋ yanā ~ tasą he wants to speak of the matter troubling him but he does not dare to reveal it.

nukurkushe A. (nukurkushē) *Vb.* 1D = nukurkusā. B. (nukurkushē) (1) *Vd.* nukurkusą. (2) *m.* anā nukurkushansą it is being spoken of on the quiet.

nukurkushi *Vd.* nukurkusą.

nukus *m.* dampness *x* yā yi ~ it (garment, house, etc.) is damp.

nukusaŋ = nukusāni = nūsaŋ *q.v.*

nukushē *Vb.* 3A (gown, house, etc.) became damp.

numfąrfashī *Vd.* numfāshī.

numfāsā *Vb.* 3A (1) breathed. (2) rested a while.

numfāshī *m.* (*pl.* numfąrfashī). (1) (*a*) breathing (= shędā). (*b*) (i) breath. (ii) kadą ku yąrdā muddąr kunā dą sauran numfāshī never agree as long as you live! (2) (*a*) numfāshinsą yā dąukē he (trumpeter, P. crying, etc.) emitted long-drawn sound (= shīdę 2). (*b*) yā dąukę ~ he held his breath. (*c*) yā dąukę numfāshinsą dąga sāmųnsą he gave up hope of getting it. (*d*) yanā dąukąn ~ (boxer, charging bull, etc.) is waiting his chance. (*e*) nā fąki numfāshinsą, nā bā shi magąną I waited for the right moment and then proffered my request to him. (3) *Vd.* tąrā 2. (4) numfąrfashī *pl.* panting.

nuna A. (nūną) *Vb.* 1A (1) (*a*) (i) showed *x* yā ~ mini shī he showed it to me (= gwadą). yā nūną wą dūnīyą bā yą jin tsǫrō he showed the world that he is not afraid. (ii) sun nūną mąną yawą they outnumbered us. (iii) exhibited quality *x* yā nūną dattākǫ he behaved with dignity. sun nūną ąbim mąmāki they did marvellously. yā nūną īyąkar halinsą na jąruntaką he showed what he was capable of in the way of courage. sun nūną tąusąyī they showed mercy. (iv) sunā nūną cęwā they maintain that ... (v) yịŋ hakạ yā nūnạ cẹ̄wā the fact of this having been done proved that ... (b) farkwam fadạ, ~ hannū coming events cast their shadows before them. (bb) (i) nūnạ shi akẹ̄ Vd. sạndā 1m.ii. (ii) nūnạ maị nēmaŋkị Vd. Yaŋgạ. (c) ~ ịsā gạrēshị he's arrogant. (d) yā ~ kạnsạ he has shown himself in his true colours (good or bad). (e) yā ~ kạrfī he behaved threateningly. (f) (i) yā ~ kạmar wai bā yā̰ sọ̄ he pretended not to want it. (ii) yā nūnạ wai yā yi fushī he pretended to be angry. (iii) sunā̰ nūnạ (= sunā̰ nūnā̰wā) sū nẹ̄ zā sụ ci nasarạ they are pretending they will be victorious. (iv) yā nūnạ manạ bạndạ dǎi yạ yi bāya he pretended to us that he was not going to retreat. (g) yā ~ kurcīyā bạkā he gave P. a hint of the inner state of affairs. (h) yā ~ minị inūwạ he told me a lie. (2) pointed T. at x yā ~ masạ bindigạ he pointed the gun at him (= nūnā 1).

B. (nūnạ) Vb. 3B (progressive nūnā). (1) became ripe (cf. bịra ; kōsạ 2c ; rịka 3; lallẹ 1j, nukạ). (2) became fully cooked. (3) kōmē yā ~ all is arranged. (4) Vd. cịwō ; dinyā 4. (5) Vd. nūnā 2.

C. (nūnā) (1) Vb. 2 pointed T. at x yā nūnē shị dạ bindigạ (= nūnạ 2). (2) f. (v.n. of nūna) x yanā̰ ~ it's becoming ripe. (b) nūnar rānā (i) false appearance of being ripe in case of withered fruit of gwandạ, kanyạ, kadanyạ, etc. (ii) jịkintạ nūnar rānā nẹ̄ her body shows first signs of leprosy.

nune A. (nūnẹ) Vb. 3A = nūna.

B. (nūnē) m. used in bā tā̰ ~ it must not be shown (used in game darạ, etc., cf. sākē, kịrgē).

nunguri = nungurō m. (1) feeling slack. (2) feeling dejected.

nūnị m. (1) an yi wạ gōdīyā ~ the mare has been covered by a stallion (cf. bā̰yē). (2) Kt. an yi nūnịn sā̰ = gēwạyā 4a. (3) Kt. = nūnīyā.

nūnīyā Kt. exhibiting woman's wedding-outfit.

nuŋkạ = niŋkạ.

nuŋkufurcị m. pent-up rancour.

nūrā Sk. = lūrā.

nūsad dạ Vb. 4 showed x yā ~ shī (= yā nūshē shi) hanyạ he pointed out the road to him. yā nūshē shị kạrạtū he tutored him.

nūsaŋ (Ar. nuqsān " decrease ") m. (1) watạ yā yi ~ it is a 29-day month (cf. farillạ 2b). (2) yā yi ~ he has vanished.

nūshē Vd. nūsad dạ.

nūshị Sk. = naushị.

nụssaŋ Kt. nūsaŋ.

*nusụfī (Ar.) m. half (= rabị).

*nụsuhạ f. (pl. nusuhōhī) Ar. writing an alternative reading of an Arabic text in the margin.

nūtā Sk. = nitsạ.

nutsạ, etc., Vd. nitsạ.

nutsọ = nitsọ.

Nuwambạr = **Nuwambạ** (Eng.) m. November.

nụwātạ = nạwātạ.

nwardẹ = nardị.

nwạs-nwạs = nạs-nạs.

nyạm-nyam m., f. (sg., pl.) cannibal.

nyạr Vd. tsīkạ 2.

nyawarā = īnyawarā.

ṇ zaram makụ Kt. f. woman who uses up her husband's resources in helping her children from previous marriage.

O

o (1) (indicates motion towards speaker) x yā tạfi he went, yā tafō he came. yā jē he went, yā zō he came (Mod. Gram. 129–132). (2) (abbreviation of -ūwā, Mod. Gram. 113a²) x bā yā̰ yịwō = bā yā̰ yịwūwā it is impossible. (3) (indicating anger) x bā̰ ni rīgan naŋ give me this gown ! (reply) rīgō = rīgō matạ I'm bothered if I do ! mẹ̄ kakẹ̄ yị̄ ạ naŋ what are you doing here ? (reply) jirạ nakẹ̄ yị̄ I'm waiting, (reply) jirō = jirō matạ why the devil are you waiting ! (3) Sk. quite so ! (= āwō).

ōbạ̄sạ = ōbā̰sạrạ = ōbẹ̄sạ = abạ̄sạ q.v.

ōdạ f. (pl. ōdōjī = Kt. ōdōdī) (Eng. order). (1) order, command x yā kafạ ~ he issued an order. yā kị bịŋ ~ he disobeyed the order. yā

yi ōdạr kāyā he ordered some goods.
(2) **wuriŋ** ∼ nē access to the place is
forbidden. **wurī mai** ∼ forbidden place.
yā shiga ∼ he entered a forbidden place.
(3) set time for paying debt (= **ajạlī**) x
yā yi ∼ **kwānā gōmạ m̩ bīyā** he gave
me ten days to pay. (4) term of
imprisonment x **yā cikạ** ∼ he has
completed his sentence. **an yi masạ** ∼
kwānā gōmạ he was sentenced to
ten days' imprisonment. (5) dilatoriness. (6) **yā yi** ∼ (a) he (bugler)
blew a call. (b) he (cyclist) sounded his
bell. (c) he (motorist) blew his horn.
(7) East Hausa = **ƙōdạ**.
ōdạlẹ = **ōdilẹ** m. (pl. **ōdalōlī**) Eng. (1)
orderly (military). (2) **ōdilaŋ Gwamnạ**
Private Secretary to Chief Commissioner, etc.
ōdōdī, ōdōjī Vd. **ōdạ**.
ōfạ East Hausa = **ƙōfạ**.
ōfiis = **ōfishī** m. (pl. **ōfisōshī**) Eng. (1)
Provincial Office, Divisional Office,
Resident's Office, etc. (2) business-office.
ọhō (1) (a) what do I care ! (b) **kō yā zō, kō
bai zō ba** ∼ I don't care a straw whether
he comes or not. (c) Vd. **ọhō'ō'ō**. (3) **daŋ-
giŋ** ∼ m. useless relatives (= **daŋgi** 5).
ọhō'ō'ō (1) = **ọhō** (1) x **yạnzu kō yāyạ,
ọhō'ō'ō** what is to be done at this
juncture I neither know nor care. (2)
ọhō'ō'ō, karim bē'ē'ē (said by women)
what is it to do with me ?
ọkēlē f. Okene.
Oktōbạ Eng. October.
ōlō m. (1) grunting of camels being
loaded. (2) angry shouting.
ōlōlō = **ōlō**.
ōnẹ East Hausa = **ƙōnẹ**.
o'ọ (said by women) So-and-so x **kadạ su** ∼
su jī take care that So-and-so and So-
and-so do not hear ! (cf. **Wānẹ**).
ọshi (East Hausa) = **ƙōshi**.

P

p Vd. **f**.
pf (said by placing upper incisors well
behind lower lip and expelling air
sharply) your opinion is worth nothing,
so keep your mouth shut ! (Vd. **gwalẹ**).

R

-r Vd. **ta**.
rā f. Arabic letter " r ".
rā'asu Ar. m. leader (= **shūgạba**).
ra'ạyī Ar. m. (1) opinion x **nā bi ra'ạyinsạ**
I followed his opinion. (2) **yā yi
mini** ∼ he treated me with the respect
due to me. (3) cf. **rā'i**.
rab (1) = **rab-rab**. (2) Kt. (abbreviation of
rạbu) x **yā rab dạ ita** he's divorced
her.
raba A. (**rabạ**) Vb. 1A (1) (a) divided,
separated. (b) **bạ su** ∼ **ƙwaryā dạ
ubansu ba** they had never before
eaten apart from their father. (c) **doŋ
Allā, rạbā mu dạ wannạm mạganạ**
don't bother me about this ! (d) **ạlkālī
yā** ∼ **su** = **ạlkālī yā** ∼ **auransu** the
judge has pronounced them divorced.
(e) **ạ** ∼ **dạ ƙayạ** Vd. **ƙayạ** 1f. (f)
anạ ∼ **ka dạ kīwaŋ awākī, kanạ
fadi kyallạ tā haifu** don't keep on
speaking of a T. which nobody wants
to hear about. (g) **ạ** ∼ **dạ dubū** Vd.
dubū 5. (h) **ạ gidansạ mukạ** ∼ **darē**
we spent the whole evening at his
house. (j) **an** ∼ **ciki** they've shared
the loss. (k) **yā** ∼ **kōrā** he sent his goods
to several markets, he sent to several
places for what he required. (l) **yā** ∼
dayā bīyū he unfairly treated one of
his relations. (m) **wannạŋ yā rabạ
musu haŋkạlī bīyū** this made them
hesitate. (n) ∼ **hantạ dạ jinī** Vd. **hantạ**.
(o) Vd. **ram** 2a. (2) divided out x (a)
an ∼ **musu gōrọ** the kolas have been
divided out amongst them. **nā** ∼ **shi
tsạkāninsu** I divided it out among
them (= **rabad dạ** 1 = **rarrạbā**). (b)
(i) **yā zamẹ manạ kūkạr " saukẹ mu
rabạ ! "** it is a bone of contention
between them and us. (ii) **dūtsạn**
(**kwariŋ**) **" saukẹ mu rabạ ! "** a lonely
hill (valley) exposed to danger from
bandits. (iii) Vd. **saukẹ** 1a.iii. (c)
an ∼ **harājī** tax has been announced,
assessed. **an** ∼ **musu harājī** they have
been assessed for tax, each has been
informed of how much tax he must pay.
(d) **jīyạ kā** ∼ **yạu kạrɓā akẹ yī** Fortune's
wheel turns. (e) **sun** ∼ **gạrī** they have

quarrelled (= rabā-rᶐbā̤). (f) fᶐrā kᶐ̤ ~ Vd. fᶐrā 2d. (2A) (a) distinguished x mᶒ̣ ya ~ sụ what differentiates them ? (b) mᶒ̣ ya ~ dambē Vd. dambē 5. (c) wᶐ̤ zᶐi rabᶐ̤ Vd. wᶐ̤ 1e.vii, viii. (3) settled x (a) yā ~ faḍᶐ̤ he settled the quarrel. yā ~ gaddamᶐrsụ he settled their dispute. (b) Vd. sᶐndā 1b ; rᶐbō 2b. (c) murtukū (= tunnuɓū) faḍᶐŋ iblīsai, yārọ bᶐi ganība, bᶐlle yᶐ rabᶐ̤ what Armageddon ! (4) sun ~ ᶐbim fᶐḍā they're no longer on speaking terms. (5) Vd. rᶐbᶐ̤-compounds. (6) darē yā ~ it is midnight.

B. (rᶐba) used in ~ dᶐ̤ since x nā daḍᶒ̤ ~ dᶐ̤ ganinsᶐ̤ I have not seen him for a long time (= rᶐbe 1 = rᶐbō 4b).

raɓa A. (rᶐ̤ɓā) Vb. 2 (1) went close along x yā rᶐ̤ɓi bᶐkiŋ kọ̄gī he followed the riverbank (= zāgᶐ̤ 2 = rāɓᶐ̤ 1b = rᶐ̤ɓu = rātsᶒ̣ 3). (2) was close to (a) gidansᶐ̤ yā rᶐ̤ɓi kọ̄gi his compound is near the river (= rāɓᶐ̤ 1c). (b) kāyā bā yᶐ̤ rᶐ̤ɓar jᶐkī Vd. būtsᶐrī 2. (3) (a) yā rᶐ̤ɓi Audụ he (cadger) stuck to Audu like a leech (= rāɓᶐ̤ 1d). (b) rᶐ̤ɓi, kị kashᶒ̣ Vd. shirinyᶐ̤. (4) (a) approached x mun rᶐ̤ɓē shị we approached it (= rāɓᶐ̤ 3). (b) bᶐ̤ mᶐi ~ tasᶐ̤ nobody will have anything to do with him.

B. (rāɓᶐ̤) (1) Vb. 3A (a) concealed oneself behind x yā ~ jịkin daŋgā he hid behind the fence (= rāɓᶒ̣ 1, rāɓᶐkā 1 = laɓᶒ̣ 1a). (b) yā ~ dᶐ̤ kọ̄gī = rᶐ̤ɓā 1. (c) gidansᶐ̤ yā ~ dᶐ̤ kọ̄gī = rᶐ̤ɓā 2. (d) yā ~ dᶐ̤ Audụ = rᶐ̤ɓā 3. (2) approached x (a) yā ~ wajansᶐ̤ = yā rāɓᶐ̤ gᶐrēshị he approached him (= rᶐ̤ɓā 4a). (b) kadᶐ̤ mụ rāɓᶐ̤ wani ᶐbụ wᶐndᶐ̤ zᶐi taɓᶐ̤ mulkịŋkụ let us not take any action likely to encroach on your prerogative of rule. (3) Vb. 1A (a) leaned T. against x yā ~ shi dᶐ̤ baŋgō he propped it against the wall (= jịŋginā 1a). (b) tā ~ hannū ᶐ kᶐfadᶐ̤ tasᶐ̤ she put her hand on his shoulder. (c) rịgan naŋ, an ~ ta ᶐ jikᶐ̤ this gown has been worn a few times. (4) Vd. rāɓa-compounds.

C. (rāɓā) f. (1) (a) dew. (b) idᶐntᶐ̤

bᶐ̤ ~ she has bold eyes (cf. rāɓā-rāɓā). (bb) Vd. bᶐ̤ ~. (c) kisᶐn ~ m. stunted sheep or goat. (d) gịndiŋ kūrā yā sāɓᶐ̤ dᶐ̤ ~ he has had to learn in a hard school and is not finicky. (e) bᶐ̤ɓō ~ nᶒ̤, ḍaŋ gᶐrī kabᶐ̤ a stranger is a mere bird of passage (cf. rūwā B.7b). (f) cf. shᶐ̤ rāɓā. (2) disease of sheep and goats where sacs of fluid like dewdrops form in the stomach. (3) rāɓar gwāzᶐ small, plain glass bead (= rᶐ̤irᶐyī 3). (4) kᶐḍar ~ Vd. kᶐḍā 5.

raɓaɓa used in sun zuɓō ᶐ ɓas ~ it (fruit) has fallen abundantly off the tree.

raɓaɓɓaka A. (raɓaɓɓᶐ̤kā) Vb. 1D = zaɓaɓɓᶐ̤kā 2. B. (rᶐ̤ɓaɓɓakᶐ̤) Vb. 3B = zᶐ̤ɓᶐ̤ɓɓakᶐ̤ 2.

raɓaɓɓᶐ̤kē (1) Vb. 1D = zaɓaɓɓᶐ̤kā 2. (2) Vb. 3A = zᶐ̤ɓᶐ̤ɓɓakᶐ̤ 2.

rᶐ̤bᶐ̤ dᶐidᶐi m. (1) yā yi minị ~ he (broker) overcharged me by a half. (2) = ɓalē.

rᶐ̤ɓᶐ̤ dᶐrnī m., f. (sg., pl.) boy or girl who keeps aloof from games.

rabad dᶐ̤ Vb. 4 (1) divided out x nā ~ gōrọ I divided out the kola-nuts. nā rabam musụ dᶐ̤ gōrọ I divided the kolas amongst them (= rabᶐ̤ 2). (2) Sk. left P. x (a) mun ~ shī ᶐ kᶐ̤sūwā we separated from him in the market. (b) mun rabar we've got a divorce. (c) yā rabshē tᶐ̤ he divorced her (2 = rᶐbu), cf. rabᶒ̣ 5.

rāɓad dᶐ̤ Vb. 4 (1) concealed. (2) sold (defective T.) on the quiet.

rᶐ̤ɓagwᶐnō m. (1) soup where meat is boiled to shreds. (2) decrepit P.

rᶐ̤bajᶐ̤ (1) f. (a) spreading far x gᶒ̤zā tā yi ~ the mane spreads out. (b) = yᶐ̤ḍō. (c) Sk. plaited-fringe (gᶒ̤zā 2). (2) adv. yā yi rᶐssā ~ it has spreading branches (cf. rabajē-rᶐbajē̤).

rabajā-rᶐbajᶐ̤ = rabajē-rᶐbajᶒ̣ adv. spreadingly (re plural) x yā yi rᶐssā ~ it has spreading branches (cf. rᶐbᶐjᶐ̤ 2).

raɓaka A. (rāɓᶐkā) Vb. 3A (1) concealed himself behind x yā ~ jịkin daŋgā he hid behind the fence (= rāɓᶐ̤ 1a). (2) = faka 1. B. (raɓᶐkā) Vb. 1C Sk. = raɓaɓɓᶐ̤kā.

C. (rạɓakạ) *Vb.* 3B *Sk.* = rạɓạɓɓakạ.
raɓake A. (rāɓạkē) *Vb.* 3A = rāɓạkā.
   B. (raɓạkē) *Sk. m.* = taushē 1.
rabam *Vd.* rabad dạ.
rạbạ mạkāfọ dạ gōrạ *m.* (*used negatively*)
   kadạ kạ yi minị ~ do not play me a
   dirty trick ! (= rạsạsā-rasasā), *cf.*
   gayyạ.
rạbantạ = rạbbantạ.
raba-raba A. (rabā-rạbā) sun yi ~ they
   have quarrelled (= rabạ 2e).
   B. (rạbā-rabā) (1) *f.* forking of
   roads. (2) *adv.* = rạbạ tsakạ.
raɓa-raɓa A. (raɓā-rạɓā) = raɓē-rạɓē.
   B. (rāɓā-rāɓā) *f.* shyness, diffidence
   (*cf.* rāɓā 1b).
rạɓạrɓasạ *Vb.* 2 (*p.o.* rạɓạrɓashē, *n.o.*
   rạɓạrɓashi) = rạgạrgazạ 1a.
rabar dạ = rabad dạ.
rāɓar gwāzā *Vd.* rāɓā 3.
rạbạ tsakạ *adv.* halfway *x* yā zō ~ sāi
   ya gam mụ he saw us when he had come
   half-way (= rạbā-rabā 2).
rạbạzai = rạbạjā.
rạbạ zạngā *m.* (1) = rạbạ mạkāfọ dạ
   gōrạ. (2) = gintsilmī.
rạbbai *Vd.* rạbō.
rabbana A. (Rabbạnā) *Ar.* Lord God !
   (= Rabbị).
   B. hakạ kā zō minị hannuŋkạ
   rabbạnā ? have you no shame in
   coming to me thus empty-handed ?
   (= wọ̄fī 2b).
rạbbantạ *Vb.* 3B nā ~ I've had luck
   (*Vd.* rạbō).
rabbi A. (rạbbī) *m.* (1) the hunting
   leopard (*Acinonyx jabatus*) = *Sk.*
   ạrginị. (2) 'yar ~ = inyāwarā.
   B. (Rabbị) (*Ar.*) = yā Rabbị =
   Rabbạnā A. *q.v.*
rạb'bi-rạbbī" *adj.* spotted.
rabe A. (rạbẹ) *Vb.* 1A. (1) distinguished *x*
   kā ~ tsạkānịnsụ ? did you distinguish
   one from the other ? (= rarrạbē 1).
   (2) bạn ~ dạ shī ba I did not recognize
   him (= fitar dạ 3). (3) yā ~ dạ
   ạl'amạrịŋ he is familiar with the
   matter. (4) *Vd.* rarrạbē 2. (5) *Kt.*
   mun ~ dạ shī we've separated from
   him (= rạbu = rabad dạ 2). (6) *Vd.*
   bā ~.
   B. (rạbe) (1) *adv.* *x* (a) nā dadẹ ~

dạ ganinsạ = rạba. (b) dạ nī, dạ shī,
   mun dadẹ ~ I have not seen him for a
   long time. (2) (*noun of state from* rabạ)
   x sunā ~ they're separate.
raɓe A. (rāɓẹ) *Vb.* 3A. (1) hid behind *x*
   yā ~ jịkin dạngā = rāɓạ 1a. (2) ~
   dạ = rāɓạ 1b, c, d. (3) = fakạ 1.
   B. (rạ̄ɓe) (*noun of state*) *x* (1) yanā ~
   he is hidden (*cf.* rāɓạ 1a). (2) yanā ~
   dạ Audụ he sticks to Audu like a
   leech (*cf.* rạ̄ɓā 3). (3) sạndā yanā ~ dạ
   baŋgō the stick is leaning against the
   wall (*cf.* rāɓạ 3a). (4) (a) mạƙe nạŋ,
   rạ̄ɓe cạŋ har sukạ zō they came up
   stealthily. (5) ƙasạshē cạŋ rạ̄ɓe ạ
   wata kwanạr dūnīyạ distant, isolated
   countries (*cf.* rāɓạ 1a).
rạɓẹnīyā *f.* being dangling (*cf.* raɓe-
   raɓe) = līlọ.
raɓe-raɓe A. (rạ̄'ɓe-rạ̄ɓē"). (1) going
   along nervously, furtively. (2)
   chicanery.
   B. (raɓẹ-raɓẹ) *adv.* in a dangling
   position.
   C. (raɓē-rạɓē) *adv.* *x* tanā dạ nōnọ ~
   she has pendulous breasts.
rabga *Kt.* = rafkạ.
rạbgayyạ *Kt. f.* mutual hitting (= bụ-
   gayyạ).
rabgẹ *Kt.* = rafkẹ.
rabị (1) *m.* (a) half. (b) wajan rabịŋ
   watạn nạŋ half-way through this
   month. (c) mun yi rabịn zạŋgo =
   mun yi rabịŋ hanyạ we're half-way.
   (d) yā bar shi dạ gūrị rabị dạ rabị it
   left him with his designs only half
   fulfilled. (b) portion (= shāshị). (2)
   rabịn between *x* munā rabịm Mīnạ
   dạ Kanọ we live between Minna and
   Kano.
raɓi A. (rāɓị) (1) *m.* ɗan ~ *m.* small
   piece. (2) rāɓịn *prep.* near *x* gōnassạ
   tanā nạŋ rāɓịmmụ his farm is near us.
   B. (rạɓī) *Kt. m.* = bạrạŋgwajē.
Rạbī'ị *m.* (1) ~ lawwạl the 3rd Muslim
   month (= Gạ̄nē). (2) ~ lāhịr the
   4th Muslim month. (3) *Vd.* tagwai.
rabịn *Vd.* rabị 2.
rāɓịn *Vd.* rāɓị 2.
rabīyạ *f.* (1) yā jē ~ he has gone to settle
   their dispute or fight. (2) (a) nā yi
   musụ rabīyạr zannūwạ I gave them

(women of my household) presents of cloths at the Festival. (b) **Sarkī yā yi wą matsįyąta** ~ the Chief gave largesse to the poor. **rabką** (1) = **rafką**. (2) Sk. = **dōrą** 1a. **rąbkaną** = **rąfkaną**. **rąbkayyą** = **rąbgayyą**. **rabkę** = **rafkę**. **rąbō** m. (1) sharing out x **yąną rąban dūnīyą gą masǫyansą** he is dividing up the world among his cronies. (b) **kashęwā ą zūcįyar maį** ~ **tā fi " Wānę gą hannūna ! "** it is better to be given than to have to ask. (c) **rąbaŋ gādǫ** (i) dividing out deceased's estate. (ii) spurting out of boiling contents of pot. (d) **wannąŋ rąban duhu nę** this is an unfair dividing-out (Vd. **jibgā** 2). (e) **aną** ~ Vd. **gąrąŋhōtsąmī**. (f) **gwīwąr** ~ Vd. **gwīwą** 4. (2) (a) settling a dispute x **yąną rąbam fadąnsu** he's settling their dispute. (b) **maį rąbam fadą yā dauki sandą ?** he does the very thing which he tells others not to do (Vd. **sąndā** 1b, **rabą** 3). (3) **shą** ~ Vd. **hannun** 8b. (4) separation x (a) **rąbōna dą Kano shękarą uku** I left Kano three years ago. **yau kwānāna gōmą rąbōna dą gąrimmu** I have been away from my home-town for ten days (cf. **rąbu** 2c). (b) **nā dadę rąbōna dą ganinsą** = **rabą**. (c) **kārą nīsā kę nan rąbammu dą gidā** this but increases our line of communications. (5) **yā īyą** ~ he knows how to do division-sums (cf. **sau** 1b.ii). (6) (a) luck. (b) (i) **yā ci rąbansą** his luck was short-lived. (ii) Vd. **cin rąbō**. (c) **Allą yā nufi bą rąbansą yą sāmu** he was not destined to be lucky. (d) **bą** ~ **ba, daŋ wābi yā fadą rijįyā** what bad luck ! (e) **darē gą maį** ~ **hantsī nę** all that some people touch turns to gold. (f) **rąbansą yā rantsę** he has been lucky. (g) Vd. **kōką** 2b, **tākį** 2a.iii, **tātī**. (7) (a) share. (b) **rąbaŋ wani bą nāką ba** don't steal what is not yours ! (c) (i) " **ą bari, ą hūcę ! "** shī ya kāwō **rąbaŋ wani** procrastination gives your adversary his chance. (ii) **rąbaŋ kuŋkuru** Vd. **shāhǫ** 1b. (iii) **haną bāwą** ~ Vd. **bāwą** 1j. (d) **rąbansą yā kārę** (i) he has

died. (ii) he has lost prestige. (e) **rąbaŋ kwądō (rąbaŋ kuŋkuru) bā yą hawā samą** everyone has a different fate. **rąbo** A. (rābǫ) m. (1) (cerebral " r ") soft excrement. (2) (rolled " r ") Kt. type of infantile disease.
B. (rabǫ) m. adolescent of 15–16 years old, not yet reached full development.
rab-rab used in **jikīna yąną** ~ I'm trembling (from fever, etc.). **rąbsagǫ** m. collision (= **karǫ**). **rabshe** A. (rabshē) Vd. **rabad dą**.
B. (rabshę) = **raushę**. **rabshi** Kt. = **raushi**. *****rabtō** = **lą'ifi**. **rąbu** Vb. 3B parted from x (1) (a) **mun** ~ we are divorced. (b) **haŋkąlinsą yā** ~ **bīyū** he is distrait, his thoughts are elsewhere (cf. **bīyū** 1a.ii). (2) (a) **nā** ~ **dą shī** I'm keeping aloof from him. (b) **haŋkąlinsą yā** ~ **dą shī** he's mad. (c) **nā** ~ **dą Kano tuŋ kwānā uku** I left Kano three days ago (cf. **rąbō** 4a). (d) **nā** ~ **dą ganinsą** I've not seen him for a long time. (e) **mun** ~ **dą Kano sai muką gan shi** hardly had we left Kano when we saw him. (f) **bā ką rąbūwā dą wąsā** you're full of fun. (g) **iŋ kā** ~ **dą mutum, kadą ką tąmbąyi halinsą, tąmbąyi ąbin dą ya sāmu** circumstances may change, characters never. (h) **rąbu dą shī** (i) let's change the subject ! (ii) give him up as a bad job ! (j) **rąbu dą wannąm mąganą** don't bother me with this affair ! (k) **māgąniŋ kiyayyą rąbūwā** if you can't get on with a P., it is best to part. (l) cf. **rabad dą**. **rąbu** Vb. 3B x **yā** ~ **dą kǫgī** = **rąbā** 1. **rāci** Kt. = **rātsi**. **rąciŋ gigamą** Kt. m. (1) extortion of supplies without payment, by member of Chief's retinue (cf. **gąbazgą**). (2) abusing one's position to obtain from P. property of one of one's relatives. **rada** A. (rādą) Vb. 1A **yā** ~ **masą sandā** he beat him with a stick.
B. (rądā) Vb. 2 **yā rądē shi dą sandā** = **rādą**.
C. (radą) (1) Vb. 1A (a) **yā** ~ **masą** he whispered to him. **suną radąwā**

they're whispering together. (b) an raɗa masa sūnā name has been whispered into child's ear on naming-day. an ∼ masa sūnā Mūsā the child has been named Moses (cf. zāna 5). (c) rānar ∼ sūnā child's naming-day (= sūnā 5a). (2) m., f. (a) whispering x sunā ∼ they're whispering. (b) (secondary v.n. from raɗā) x sunā raɗarsa = sunā raɗarsa = sunā masa raɗa they're slandering him. (c) raɗar ma'aurā a " frame-up " to cheat a victim. (d) Vd. dumā 1d.

D. (raɗā) Vb. 2 (Vd. raɗa 2b) slandered P.

raɗaɗa f. and adv. (1) nā ji ∼ = nā ji tōyī ∼ I heard the crackling of a bush-fire. (2) nā ji ∼ = nā ji cīwo ∼ I felt slight stinging pain, slight irritation. (3) nā ji ∼ I smelt roasting meat.

raɗaɗī m. (1) smarting-feeling. (2) agony, torture.

raɗam Kt. = raɗau.

raɗau = rau.

raɗdawā (rustic) gā raɗdē, gā ∼ term used in talla for daddawā.

rāɗe Vb. 1A yā ∼ shi da sandā = rāɗa.

raɗēraɗī Kt. m. (1) whispering by several persons. (2) anā raɗēraɗinsa rumours are current about it.

rāɗi = rā'i.

rāɗo Kt. m. = lāɗo.

raf A. (raf) m. and adv. yā yi ∼, yā kāma shi = yā kāma shi ∼ he snatched it up.

B. Vd. raf-raf.

rafa A. (rāfa) = rāfanī.

B. (Rafa) Kt. an obsolete sarauta.

*raf'a = *rafa'a (Ar.) f. = *fataha.

rafaifai-rafaifai used in yanā tafīya ∼ he (sick, tired P.) is walking with difficulty.

rafaffakā Vb. 3A walked as in rafaifai-rafaifai.

rāfānī m. (pl. rāfānai) (1) maternal-uncle (= kāwu). (2) lobe of ear (= cililligā).

rāfasa (1) plant used as remedy for tapeworm. (2) kada kunya ta hana sayan ∼ a birnī don't make compliments ! (cf. filāko).

rafi A. (rāfī) m. (pl. rāfuka = rāfuffuka = rāfuna = Kt. rāfukka). (1) stream, brook (cf. kōgī, korama). (2) =

lambū. (3) 'yar bākin ∼ Vd. kōgī 2b.

B. (rāfī) m. planing of bird (= layī = lafī).

rafka A. (rafka) (1) (with dative) hit with implement x yā ∼ masa sandā he hit him with a stick. (2) (a) yā ∼ adō he togged himself up. (b) yā ∼ īhu he yelled. (c) tā ∼ shēwa she laughed loudly. (d) yā ∼ karyā he told a whopping lie. (3) cf. rabka.

B. (rafkā) x yā rafkē shi da sandā = rafka 1.

rafkana (1) Vb. 3B made a mistake. (2) f. (a) mistake. (b) (Eng.) ready-reckoner.

rafkananē m. (f. rafkananīyā) pl. rafkanannū careless P.

rafkanūwā = Kt. rafkannūwā f. (1) = rafkana 2a. (2) yā yi mini ∼ one expense after another has come on me thereby.

rafke (1) Vb. 3A. (a) became old, thin, withered. (b) became tired out (= kāsa = sike 1b = tabke). (c) deteriorated. (d) (meat in soup) disintegrated. (2) Vb. 1A yā ∼ shi da sandā = rafka 1.

rafki yā rafku (1) how thin !, how tired out ! (as in rafke). (2) what a beating ! (as in rafka 1).

rafōgō = rufēwā.

rafōnīyā = rahōnīyā.

rafōto = rahōto.

raf-raf x sun ɗauki tafī raf-raf-raf they applauded unanimously.

rafshi = raushi.

raftā (1) f. worn-out T. (2) m. (a) famine-refugees from French territory. (b) Nor. an obsolete sarauta. *(c) = la'īfī.

*raftō = la'īfī.

rāfuka Vd. rāfī.

rāfuna Vd. rāfī.

rafusa Kt. = ruhusa.

raga A. (ragā) (1) reduced (= rage). (2) im ba a ragi darē ba, ā ragi rānā nobody knows the hour of his death.

B. (raga) Vb. 1A (1) reduced speed of x yā ∼ mōta he slowed down the motor-car. yā ∼ linzāmi he slowed down his horse. (2) (with dative) x nā ∼ maka sule uku I will reduce the price for you by three shillings (= rage). (b) an ∼ masa he's been leniently dealt with (= kārā 2a.i).

C. (rāgā) *f.* (*pl.* rāgōgī). (1) net securing contents of woman's load. (2) fishing-net. (3) large snare for guinea-fowl, etc. (3) hammock. (4) liana-bridge. (5) *Vd.* ɓarāwọ 3.

ragab = ragam.

ragaɗa A. (rāgaɗā) *Vb.* 1C = zuŋgụrā. B. (rāgaɗa) *Vb.* 2 = zuŋgụra.

ragadāda *f.* = ɗafau 1.

rāgaɗē *Vb.* 1C = zuŋgụrē.

ragadī *m.* pleasantness *x* yā yi ∼ it is pleasant.

ragagā *used in* yanā tafīya ∼ he (tall, thin P.) is walking flaccidly.

ragai A. (ragai) *m.* = ragē 2. B. (rāgai) *adv.* (1) yanā tafīya ∼ he's wandering about aimlessly. (2) *Kt.* yā dụbē ta ∼ he looked at her contemptuously (= shẹ̄ḳẹ̄ḳẹ̄).

rāgaita *f.* = yāwan ∼ *m.* (1) aimless roving. (2) *Vd.* zụrū 3.

ragam = ramau 1, rau 3, 4.

ragamā *f.* (*pl.* ragamōmī). (1) halter (= zaŋgọ 5). (2) ragamar mutānē tanā hannunsa he is an intermediary *as in* ḳōfa 3. (3) (*a*) an sakam musụ ragamar mulki they've been given home rule. (*b*) kun sā ragamar shūgabanci a hannūna you have entrusted me with rule.

ragam-ragam = garaŋ-garaŋ 2.

raga-raga *x* sun yi wa kadarkọ raga-raga they demolished the bridge.

ragargaje A. (ragargajē) *Vb.* 3A (1) became shattered. (2) (meat) disintegrated from over-cooking (2 = zaɓaɓɓakē). (3) (garment) became dilapidated. (4) *cf.* ragargaza. B. (ragargajē) *Vd.* ragargaza.

ragargaza A. (ragargazā) *Vb.* 1D. (1) (*a*) shattered T. (*b*) spoiled (gown being beaten to impart gloss). (2) (*a*) nā ∼ masa sandā I gave him a good thrashing. (*b*) nā ∼ masa zāgi I abused him. (3) *cf.* ragargajē. B. (ragargaza) *Vb.* 2 (*p.o.* ragargajē, *n.o.* ragargaji). (1) (*a*) yā ragargaji itācē he broke up much firewood (= raɓarɓasa). (*b*) ate much of *x* yā ragargaji nāma he ate much meat. (2) nā ragargajē shi da sandā (zāgi) = ragargazā 2. (3) *cf.* ragargajē.

ragargazau (1) how dilapidated ! (2) how shattered it is !

ragas (1) = ramau. (2) wutā tā yi garwāshī ragas the fire is all embers.

rāgaya *f.* (*pl.* rāgayū = rāgayōyī) (1) (*a*) receptacle for calabashes (*made from* kaba-*string and suspended from roof :* *it is considered article of adornment and there may be many* rāgaya *hanging inside house, cf.* sagā). (*b*) *epithet is* Rāgaya, māganiŋ gāgararrun yārā. (*c*) ɗāki yā tāshi ?, ∼ tā zauna ? does a servant remain after the departure of his master ? (*d*) ɓwaryā tagarī tanā ∼ (i) there's more than meets the eye. (ii) respectable women don't wander about. (*e*) yā tūrō kụnū a ∼ his intrigues brought trouble on him. (2) going hither and thither (= kaiwā da kāwọwā). (3) rāgayar dūtsẹ unscrupulous P. (*epithet is* Rāgayar dūtsẹ, ajalim mai ɗāki).

ragayya *f.* *x* tsakānimmụ da shī da ∼ I owe him much respect (= ragōwa 2).

ragaza *f.* rope preventing pack-animal's load slipping backwards (*cf.* cindufụrī).

rage A. (ragẹ) (1) *Vb.* 1A. (*a*) (i) reduced, shortened, lessened (= taḳaicē) *x* yāḳin naŋ bai ∼ mutum ɗayā a cikinsụ ba that war did not reduce them by even one person (*cf.* (*d*) *below*, rasa 2*d*). (ii) kụ ∼ magana don't talk so loudly ! (iii) yā ∼ tsawō (= fasa 3*b*) he sold an article, bought a cheaper kind, and had balance over (= *Kt.* sabka 2). (iv) yanzu suŋ hūta da ragẹ murya they've now given up blandishment. (*b*) (*with dative*) *x* (i) yā ∼ mini kuɗīna he reduced my pay. (ii) nā ∼ maka sulẹ ukụ I'll make you a reduction of three shillings (i, ii = raga) (ii = sauḳaḳā 1). (*c*) fell short of by *x* sun ∼ Kanọ mil 40 = sun ∼ Kanọ da mil 40 they got within 40 miles of Kano. ḳarfẹ bīyar yā ∼ manti 3 it is 3 minutes to 5 o'clock. (*d*) left over *x* (i) yā ∼ mini ukụ he left three for me. yāḳin naŋ bai ∼ mutum ɗayā a cikinsụ ba the war did not spare one person among them (*cf.* 1*a*.i *above*). (ii) ba ka ∼ mini kōmē ba you grudged me nothing. (iii) bai ∼ mini kōmē ba he told me every detail.

(iv) ạ ~ dǫmiŋ gǭbe *Vd.* cī 26*e.* (*e*) left behind *x* sun ragę sōjạ ạ gidā they have left behind some soldiers in reserve. (2) *Vb.* 3A. (*a*) remained over *x* mę̄ ya ~ cikiŋ ajạlịŋ how much of the appointed period still remains ? (= rạgu 1 = wạnzu). (*b*) fell short *x* mę̄ ya ~ ạ lịssāfịŋkạ by how much is your reckoning short ? watạ yā ~ dạ kwānā ukụ, mukạ fịta we set out when three days of the month were left. mantị ukụ sun ~ ạ ƙarfę̄ bịyar it is three minutes to 5 o'clock (= 1*c* above). (*c*) *Vd.* rạgu.

B. (rạgē) *m.* (1) young ramạ-plants thinned out from farm and offered for sale. (2) type of gruel made from water off tūwō (= ragai).

C. (rāgę) = rāję.

rạggạ *f.* (*pl.* raggōgī = *Sk.* raggaɗūɗạ) rags (= tsụmmā).

raggō *Sk. m.* (*f.* raggūwā) *pl.* raggā̰gē = raggā̰yē = raggwā̰yē = ragō *q.v.*

ragi A. (ragị) *m.* (1) reduction. (2) yā nę̄mi ~ he wished to give up the fight, he asked for quarter.

B. (rạgī) *m.* (1) *x* ukụ dạ ~ three and a bit (= rārā 1*b*, ạbụ 4), *cf.* zaŋkō 4, 'yā'yā 1*f*, fā̰fạkī. (2) *Kt.* = rạgē 2.

rāgīyā = rājīyā.

rago A. (rā̰gō) *m.* (*f.* tuŋkīyā) *pl.* rāgunạ. (1) ram. (2) ~ yā tụŋkwịyē shị he has a new-born child (= jịminā 2 = mạraƙī 2). (3) hanjin ~ *Vd.* hanjī 7. (4) jạn ~ snoring (= minshārī). (5) (*a*) jạ̄ dạ bāya gạ ~ bạ̄ gudụ ba nę̄ reculer pour mieux sauter (*Vd.* dagā̰ 4). (*b*) karǫ sǎi ~ *Vd.* karǫ 4. (6) Rā̰gō dạ wutsīyạr kạrē, ɗam Mālạm what a profligate scholar ! (7) rā̰gwan rūwā type of fish. (8) wata rānā rā̰gwantạ nē shī *Vd.* kūrā 29. (9) rā̰gwaŋ arnā *Vd.* Ajạlā̰. (10) rā̰gwan sūnā *Vd.* yaŋkạ 1*a.v.*

B. (ragō) *m.* (*f.* ragūwā) *pl.* rag-wā̰yē. (1) (*a*) slacker (*epithet is* Ạbin shā̰ rānī). (*b*) (i) haushin ~, cīzạm bā̰kī what a lazy person ! (ii) *Vd.* dārạ 2*b.* (*c*) ~ bai san ~ nę̄ shī ba sǎi yā kǫri kuŋkurū yā tsę̄rę̄ a sluggard only learns from sluggardliness greater than his own. (*d*) kun yi nāku, kun

yi na ragō you did more than your share. (*e*) iŋ kā ji mạrāyạ, ragō *Vd.* mạrāyạ 2. (*f*) bạ̄ ta gạ ~ *Vd.* himmạ. (*g*) bā̰tạ ~ gōnā *Vd.* ƙudujī. (2) *Vd.* tayạ ragō. (3) ragwaŋ azancī lack of judgment. (4) ragwam mazā Senegal Coucal (*Centropus senegalensis*) = *Kt.* ɗan ragūwā. (5) ragwan jinī = yagwan jinī.

rāgōgī *Vd.* rāgā.

rạgōwạ *f.* (1) (*a*) remainder (= saurā). (*b*) rạgōwạr kōmiŋ nāsụ gụdā bīyū their remaining two canoes. (2) tsạ̄-kānimmụ dạ shī dạ ~ = rạgayyạ. (3) rạgōwạr cikị one's existent property realizable in case of need, for selling for food. (4) yanā̰ ƙaryā kạman rạgōwạr yā̰ƙị he lies like a trooper.

rạgu *Vb.* 3B (1) = ragę 2*a.* (2) decreased *x* ạbin dạ ya dạɗu dạ ạbin dạ ya ~ the increase and decrease.

rāgunạ *Vd.* rā̰gō.

ragūwā *Vd.* ragō 4.

ragwaɗā *used in* yanā̰ shạn ~ (1) he's enjoying himself. (2) he's eating rich food.

ragwaggwaɓa A. (ragwaggwạɓā) = zaɓaɓ-ɓạkā 2.

B. (rạgwạggwạɓạ) = zạɓạɓɓạkạ.

ragwaggwạ̄ɓē *Vb.* 3A (1) = zaɓaɓɓạkē 2. (2) P. became decrepit.

ragwan *Vd.* ragō.

ragwạncē *Vb.* 3A became a slacker, deteriorated.

ragwancị *m.* = rạgwạntakạ *f.* being a slacker, laziness.

ragwanta A. (ragwạntā) *Vb.* 1C caused to become a slacker.

B. (rạgwantạ) *Vb.* 3B = ragwạncē.

ragwargwạjē = ragargạjē.

ragwā̰yē *Vd.* ragō.

rạgwazǫ *m.* = ragō.

rahạ *Ar. f.* (1) pleasant chatting. (2) rukǫ ~ type of gambling stakes.

rạhainā *f.* (*sg., pl.*) (1) the Sausage-tree (*Kigelia œthiopica*) (= hantsạ 5*a*). (2) *Vd.* nōnǫ 1*h.*

rahamạ *Ar. f.* (1) mercy. (2) nā sạyē shị dạ ~ I bought it cheaply.

rahamad dạ *Vb.* 4 *used in* Allā̰ yạ rahamshē shị God have mercy on his soul !

Rahāzāwā *Vd.* Bạrahāję.

rạhōgō *m.* = rụfēwā.

rąhōnįyā *f.* (*pl.* rą̈hǫnī). (1) small clay corn-bin in house for storage of tsābą (*such bins are hardly ever seen now except in villages*), *cf.* rųfēwā, rųmbū. (2) *Vd.* dākį 4.

rąhōtǫ *m.* (*Eng.* report) (1) school-report *x* māląmī yā yi rąhōtąŋ Audu the teacher sent a report on Audu. (2) (*a*) report rendered by spy, informer. (*b*) dan ~ *m.* (*pl.* 'yan ~) spy, informer (*cf.* magēwąyī).

rąhūmą *Kt.* *f.* (1) odds and ęnds. (2) odds and sods.

rąhusą *Kt.* = rųhusą.

rą̈i *m.* (*pl.* rāyuką = rāwuką = *Kt.* rāyukką). (1) (*a*) (i) life. (ii) yā ji kąmar aŋ kāwō masą wani sāban rą̈i he felt as if he had got new life. (iii) Allą̈ yā dąuki rąnsų they died. (iv) sǎi dǎi Allą̈ yā kai rą̈i gǫbe unless God spares us. (v) īyą̈kacin rą̈i dą ająlī for ever. (vi) iŋ am bar sų dą dan rą̈i-rą̈i if they are allowed to retain any strength. (vii) ya kōmą rą̈i gą Allą̈ he became helpless. (viii) yaną̈ naŋ dą rąnsą na Allą̈ he is safe and sound. (ix) fādą ą Masąr sai dą rą̈i nē ą filī Egypt can only be attacked at great risk to life (*cf.* sąyar dą). (x) muŋ gayą mukų irin rāyukąn dą kē fādūwā we have told you of the great number of casualties. (xi) ~ dąŋgin gōrǫ, hūtū yakē sǫ all work and no play makes Jack a dull boy. (xii) bą̈ ~ *Vd.* bądi 1*c*. (xiii) mąi rąm banzā *Vd.* dą̈kārę. (xiv) ~ bą̈ gātā *Vd.* katąŋgalą. (*b*) mąi ~ *m.*, *f.* (*pl.* mą̈sū ~) (i) living, alive. (ii) *Vd.* sįlikį 2. (*c*) mąi ~ bā yą̈ rasą kǫ̈karī = mąi ~ bā yą̈ rasą mǫtsī while there's life there's hope. (*cc*) ~ dą kwądąyī *Vd.* kwądąyī. (*d*) ~ yā fi dūkįyā life is more valuable than wealth. (*e*) ką yi minį ~ (i) spare my life ! (ii) help me ! (*f*) jįn ~ *m.* conceit. (*g*) fādin rą̈i = girman rą̈i = 1*f above*. (*h*) (i) kąrą̈tū yā ci rąnsą he devoted all his attention to study. (ii) *Vd.* cįn rą̈i. (*j*) (i) dauri ~ dą ~ life-sentence. (ii) zā ą yi maką dauri muddįn rą̈ina dą nāką (*said by Emir*) I sentence you to imprisonment for as long as I live ! (iii) *Vd.* gyąmbō 2. (*k*) (i) ząm babbąkā shi dą ~ I'll roast him

alive. (ii) am binnę tsōfwā dą ~ *Vd.* binnę 2. (*l*) in dą rąŋką, kōmē ką̈ ganī = iŋ kaną̈ dą ~, bą̈ ąbin dą bą ką̈ ganī ba truth is stranger than fiction. (*m*) rąŋkai dadę *Vd.* dadę 2. (*n*) rąnsą ą farcę yakę (i) he is quick-tempered. (ii) he's at the point of death. (*o*) *x* bą̈ shi dą kōmē sǎi ąkwīyą gudā, rą̈ina kųttū he has only one goat and *that* is his darling, *that* is his sole treasure (*Vd.* kųrtū). (*p*) shę̈kąrą kwānā cę in dą ~ gąba delay doesn't matter, provided success follows. (*q*) (i) kō aŋ kirbą ą turmī, mąi yawąn ~ sǎi yą̈ fįta if you are gifted with nine lives, nothing can harm you = yawąn ~ mągąniŋ ąllǫbā. (ii) *Vd.* dą̈shī 2. (*r*) ~ kąŋ ga ~, Bąnufē yā ga kōko that's just in his line (= shā dą 2*b*). (*s*) bą̈ rą̈i, bą̈ girmā *Vd.* girma 1*c*.iv. (2) mind *x* (*a*) mun sā ~ kąn sāmųnsą we've set our minds on getting it (*cf.* są̈ B.10). (*b*) ąbin dą na ganī ą rą̈ina my opinion is that. . . . mun dauką ą rāyukąmmų ą kąn zā ą shę̈kąrą bįyar we assume that five years will be required for its completion. (*c*) rąnsą yaną̈ sąnsą he wants it. (*d*) kų yī shi dą ~ do it energetically ! (*e*) yā kąrfąfą rąnsų it strengthened their resolve. (*f*) (i) rą̈ina yā tǫfu = rą̈ina yā yi farī I feel happy. (ii) *Vd.* dādī 2. (*g*) zāfįn ~ *Vd.* zāfī 3*c*. (*h*) dācin ~ unpleasant disposition. (*j*) bakin ~ *Kt.* evil character. (*k*) *Vd.* mę̈ ya fi rą̈ina. (*l*) *Vd.* yallą. (*l*) *Vd.* bątą 5 ; bącį. (3) richness *x* (*a*) gąrin nąŋ yā yi ~ this town is flourishing. (*b*) nāmą mąi ~ rich meat (= rąirāyā 1 = mąi 1*a*.ii). (*c*) gōrǫ mąi ~ kolas in good condition (= rąirāyā 1). (4) = zallą *x* yā fądi gąskīyā rąntą he told only the truth. nōnąŋ, rūwā nę̈ rąnsą the milk is practically all water (*cf.* kąi 5). (5) *Vb.* used in (*a*) nā yā dą kąshī, nā ~ kudā I've got rid of that bane (= yā dą 1*j*) (*Vd.* kąshī 1*d*). (*b*) nā ganī dą idǫna, nā ~ tantamā as I have seen it, I'm in no doubt about it. (*c*) kōwā ya yi kąfą, yā ~ jąn cikį if you have a dog, you don't bark yourself.

rā'ị *Ar. m.* willingness *x* (1) iŋ kā yi ∼ kạ zō, im bạ kạ yi ∼ ba, kadạ kạ zō come if you so wish, but do not come if you don't wish ! rā'iŋ zūcịyāta (= rā'iŋ kạina) the fact of my being willing. (2) kāyan ∼ bā yạ ciŋ kặi what one does willingly does not irk. (3) *cf.* ra'ạyī.

rặi dǭre *m. Cassia occidentalis (cure for fever)* = mạjạmfạrī = rặi-rặi = tạfạsā 3 = *Sk.* saŋgā-saŋgạ), *cf.* dǭrẹ.

rạigargạdī *m.* going by roundabout route (*cf.* gẹ̄wạyē).

raina = rena.

rainị = rēnị.

rạinō *m.* (1) caring for (child, animal) = *Kt.* tāwai. (2) *cf.* tạyā ni ∼.

rainūwā = rēnūwā.

rairạ = rērạ.

rai-rai A. (rặi-rặi) *Sk. m.* = rặirạyī.
    B. (rặi-rặi) *m.* = rặi dǭre.

rạiraŋ = rẹ̄raŋ.

rairaya A. (rạirayạ) *Vb.* 2 sifted.
    B. (rạirāyā) *m., f. (no pl.).* (1) sound *x* nāmạ ∼ rich meat.   gōrọ ∼ kolas in good condition (= rặi 3). (2) inūwạ ∼ cool shade.

rairaye A. (rạirạyē) *Vb.* 1C = rạirayạ.
    B. (rạirayẹ) *m.* siftings of corn.

rặirạyī *m.* (1) fine sand (*cf.* tụrɓā, yạshī). (2) rặirạyin cikị gạrētạ she has handsome children. (3) rặirạyiŋ Ạljannạ = rāɓā 3. (4) birnin ∼ *Vd.* birnī 7.

rạirō = rẹ̄rō.

***rạ'īyyạ** *Ar. f.* (1) subjects of Emir. (2) one's dependants or relatives.

rạjā *Vb.* (*only used in this form*) *x* yā ∼ kan sāmụnsạ he's eager to get it. nā ∼ kạnsạ I like it very much.

Rajạb *m.* the 7th Muslim month (*Vd.* azụmī 5 ; gạmbo 2).

***rạjamụ** *Ar. m.* stoning P. for adultery by Muslim law.

rājẹ (1) *Vb.* 1A. (*a*) eroded (= zāgẹ 1*b*). (*b*) yā ∼ masạ kặi dạ sạndā he wounded him in the head with a stick. (*c*) tied (package) with rope passing round it in different directions. (2) *Vb.* 3A (*a*) (wall, etc.) became eroded (= zāgẹ 2*a*.i). (*b*) (wall, etc.) collapsed.

rājī *m.* (1) delightfulness *x* zūwạnsạ yā yi minị ∼ his arrival delighted me. wạ̄san naŋ, bạ ∼ ạ cikinsạ this game

is not interesting. (2) eagerness *x* sunạ̄ ∼ yạ zō they're eager for his arrival.

rạjị'ī *Vd.* shikạ ∼.

rajịmantị *Eng. m.* regiment.

rājīyā *f.* (1) type of tiny, red-tailed fish. (2) tying *as in* rājẹ 1*c*. (3) brittleness.

rak (1) exactly *x* ukụ ∼ exactly three. (2) yanạ̄ dạ d̶ācī ∼ it is very bitter.

raka A. (rakạ) (1) *Vb.* 1A. (*a*) escorted P. on journey (= tākạ 2*g*). (*b*) *Vd.* watạ 1*e*.vii. (*c*) rạkạ yārọ indạ yakẹ sǭ = rạkạ bāwạ gạriŋ dạ yakẹ sǭ one must often be insincere to preserve friendly relations. (*d*) *Vd.* ram 2*b*. (2) *Vb.* 3A. (1) lasted *x* rịgan naŋ tạ̄ ∼ watạ gụdā this gown should last another month. (2) mụ ∼ kạdaŋ, mụ ganī (*a*) let us go on a bit and wait for him ! (*b*) though things have not yet turned out as expected, let's wait a bit longer ! (3) *Vd.* rạkạ-*compounds*.
    B. (rākạ) (1) *Vb.* 1A (*a*) yā ∼ kặi cikiŋ gidā he entered the compound without a " by your leave " (= kirmạ 2*b*). (*b*) yā ∼ masạ sạndā he beat him with a stick (= dōkạ). (*c*) *Kt.* yā ∼ ayā he sifted ayā to remove earth. (2) *Vb.* 3A *Kt.* took to his heels (= shēƙạ).

raka'ạ *Ar. f.* (*pl.* rạkạ'ū) bending down during prayers (*x at ạzahạr prayers, 4* raka'ạ *are compulsory during devotions and 2 are optional at beginning and 2 at end. At* lạ'asạr *prayers, 4* raka'ạ *are compulsory at end of devotions and 2 are optional at beginning*).

rākạɓā = rāɓạkā.

rākạɓē = rāɓẹ 1.

rạkạcạm *adv. and m.* untidiness, untidily *x* lāyū sun yi ∼ ạ wuyạnsạ = lāyū sunạ̄ wuyạnsạ ∼ he has a profusion of charms round his neck. d̶āƙị yā yi ∼ = d̶āƙị yanạ̄ ∼ the house is littered up.

rākādī *m.* (1) loud-voicedness. (2) loudly raising one's voice.

rạkaf *adv.* completely collected *x* kāyā yā hạdu ∼ the articles are gathered complete.   yanạ̄ zạune cikin daŋginsạ ∼ he is living among a crowd of relations.

rạkạ mại gijị *m.* part of fence at entrance, screening from view the interior of

compound (= tsai dǝ bǎ̱kō), *cf.* babbākǝ,
sābi̱, gūrǝmī.

rǝkǝ matǝfīyā *m.* two projecting sidewalls
outside town gate to prevent animals
falling into gwalalō.

rǝ̱kambǝ *adv. and f.* profusion of small
articles *x* (1) yā yi ⁓ dǝ kāyā he is
loaded with small articles = yā dǎukō
kāyā ⁓. (2) yā wō ⁓ dǝ bāshi̱ he is
overburdened with debts.

rakam-rǝkǝm = garaṇ-gǝrǝṇ.

rǝkǝncǝmai *x* dǎki̱ yanǎ̱ dǝ ⁓ = rǝkǝcǝm.

rǝkǝ ni u̱ṇgūwā *m.* type of scent with
evanescent perfume (*cf.* iskǝ 7).

rǝkap = rǝkaf.

rāƙǎsǎ̱ (1) what a strong person ! (2)
what a tall person ! (3) *Vd.* Shǎmaki̱
2*a*, gīwā.

rākātū = rākādī.

Rǎkau *Vd.* gīwā.

raƙau = ƙarau 2.

rakǝ wāwā *Vd.* watǝ 1*e.*vii.

rake A. (rākę̱) *Vb.* 1A (1) yā ⁓ shi dǝ
sǝndā = rākǝ 1*b.* (2) *Kt.* = rākǝ 1*c.*
　　B. (rǝkē) *m.* sugar-cane = karan
Sarkī (*cf.* tǝkǝndā, bǝ̱ zāƙę̱).

raƙē-raƙē = rēƙē-rēƙē..

raki A. (rāki̱) *m.* (1) cowardice. (2)
querulousness (= ƙōrǝfī).
　　B. (rākī) *Sk. m.* (1) rags (= tsu̱mmā).
(2) rākin ri̱gā ragged gown.
　　C. (rǝkī) *m.* yā yi ⁓. (1) it overlaps.
(2) it sags (2 = *Kt.* sǝkī).

rakiya A. (rakīyǝ) *f.* (1) (*a*) escorting P. on
journey *x* yā yi musu̱ ⁓ he escorted
them on their way. (*b*) dǝn ⁓ tasǝ
the P. escorting him. (2) = gyārā 4*b.*
(3) rakīyǝr bǝzawǝrā type of gait taught
to horse. (4) rakīyǝr kūrā traveller
escorting back P. who has escorted
himself.
　　B. (Rakīyā) *f. woman's name* (*Ar.*
Raqiyyatu).

rakki̱ṇ = rak.

rakō *m.* (1) = rakīyǝ 1*a.* (2) *Vd.* dadi̱ 8 ;
dakǝn ⁓.

rāku̱ɓē = rāɓǝkē.

rǝ̱ƙumī (*d.f. Ar.* rakūba) *m.* (*f.* rǝ̱ƙumā) *pl.*
rāƙumǝ. (1) (*a*) (i) camel (*cf.* amālę̱,
tǎgūwǝ). (ii) *for epithet, Vd.* sǝnnū 2*a.*ii.
(*b*) wutsīyǝr ⁓ tā yi nēsǝ dǝ ƙasā fancy
his thinking he is up to doing it ! (*Vd.*

wutsīyǝr ⁓). (*c*) in ⁓ yā ɓatǝ *Vd.*
kurǝtandū. (*d*)Rǎ̱ƙumī fǫraṇ Allǎ̱ Camel
made by God tractable ! (*e*) Rǎ̱ƙumī mai̱
dǝṇ kāshī what trashy gifts this rich man
gives ! (*f*) ƙaryar ⁓ ta zūwǝ Asbi̱n cē,
ǝmmā bǝ zai̱ jē Gwǝnjā ba (*said by
women*) = ƙi̱ri̱ 3. (*g*) in dǎi ⁓ dǝ girmā,
kāyansǝ dǝ yawǝ the rich man has
many calls on his purse. (*h*) i̱ṇ kā
ga ⁓ yanǎ̱ ci̱ṇ ƙayǝ, bǝ̱ dǫmin dādī
yakę̱ ci̱ ba acting under compulsion.
(*j*) san rǝ̱ƙumin yǝ̱rā dǝgǝ nēsǝ, in
yā zō kusa, sǎi gudu̱ liking thing, but
fearing to accept it when the chance
offers. (*k*) saṇ gīwā yā tāka na ⁓ an
important T. overshadows a lesser T. (*cf.*
sau). (*l*) Allǎ̱ shī ya hōrę̱ wǝ̱ ⁓ ƙayǝ (=
hūwǎ̱cē 1) it (difficult T.) has become
second nature to him. (*m*) rǝ̱ƙumī bā
yǎ̱ kūkā *Vd.* mǝruhū. (*n*) kō kā hau dǝ
shī kǝn ⁓ *Vd.* matsi̱yǎ̱cī 2. (2) *Vd.*
lēɓę̱ 2, Tǝṇgǝ, shǝn rūwan rāƙumǝ,
kāshin rāƙumǝ, zaman rāƙumǝ, wutar
⁓, bǝkin ⁓. (3) tǎfin ⁓ = hōcę̱.
(4) rǝ̱ƙumin dǝṇgi̱ P. always financing
his relatives. (5) rǝ̱ƙumin dawǝ
giraffe (*cf.* du̱ṇgī). (6) rǝ̱ƙumi̱ṇ gyǝdǝ̱
ground-nut with three kernels. (7)
rǝ̱ƙumi̱ṇ karā type of toy. (8) rǝ̱ƙumi̱ṇ
ƙasā = kurkudu̱. (9) rǝ̱ƙumi̱n rūwā =
tǎgūwǝ 1*b.* (10) rǝ̱ƙumin turwā =
mǝkǝrā 3.

rǝ'ku-rǝkū" *Kt.* weak *x* rǝ'ku-rǝkun"
ri̱gā flimsy gown. mai̱ rǝ'ku-rǝkuṇ"
ƙarǝtū an indifferent scholar.

rakūwā *f.* (1) type of small, stingless bee
(= gallā). (2) *cf.* tukunyā 7.

rakwǝcǝm = rǝkǝcǝm.

rakwakkaɓa = ragwaggwaɓa.

rǝkwǝncǝmai *x* dǎki̱ yanǎ̱ dǝ ⁓ = rǝkǝcǝm.

rǝ̱kwǝs *m. and adv.* (1) hannunsǝ̱ yā yi
⁓ = yā karyǝ hannunsǝ̱ ⁓ he made
cracking sound with his finger-joints
(= raṇƙwǝsā 2). (2) sound of squashing
lice, etc.

rakwas *Sk. m.* mat consisting of interlaced strips.

rakwǝtō *m.* = rākādī 1.

ram (1) (*with rolled* " r " Mod. Gram. 5).
(*a*) = rau 3 *x* shiri̱ sukę̱ yi̱ ram they
are on the best of terms. kalmōmi̱n

naŋ sun zaunạ ram dạ gịndinsụ those words have come to stay, are firmly established. ạbụ̄tā ram (= ạbụ̄tā ramau) tsạkāninsụ kạmar sā rabạ fạ̄rā there is the closest friendship between them. (b) = ramau 1. (2) (with cerebral " r ") (Vb. plus dative and only in this form) (a) x kwabǫ ɗayā yạ̄ ∼ makạ dạ yụŋwạ ? will one penny remove you from hunger ! (d.f. rabạ 1a). (b) escorted x nā ∼ masạ I escorted him on his journey (= rakạ 1a).

rama A. (rạ̄mā) (1) Vb. 3B = rāmẹ 1. (2) Vb. 2. (a) repaid action of P. (with good for good or evil for evil), took revenge for T. x yā rạ̄mi gayyạ he paid back in the same coin the dirty trick played on him (= rāmạ 2a). (aa) Vd. rāmạ 1, 2. (b) saurō mại rạ̄mar gayyạ = jījịyā 3. (3) f. (a) emaciation. (b) macịyiŋkạ bā yạ̄ ganin rạ̄makkạ a P. whom you habitually treat liberally cannot realize that you can ever be in difficulties yourself.

B. (rāmạ) (1) Vb. 3A (a) retaliated, made requital (good for good or evil for evil. (b) Vd. bīyū 13. (2) Vb. 1A (a) (i) repaid action of P. (with good for good or evil for evil) x yā ∼ gayyạ he paid back in the same coin the dirty trick played on him (= rạ̄mā 2a). yā rāmạ bugụ he met force with force. (ii) mại fushī bā yạ̄ ∼ gayyạ revenge is attained by quiet pondering, not by rage. (iii) made up for (fast broken through illness, etc., as in shā E.2a). (b) (with dative). (i) retaliated on P., requited P. (with good for good or evil for evil) x nā ∼ masạ ạbin dạ ya yi minị I retaliated on him for his evil action to me. nā ∼ masạ aikịn dạ ya yi I rewarded him for the work he did for me (2b.i = sākạ q.v.). (ii) compensated x nā ∼ masạ jạkinsạ I compensated him for the harm I had done his donkey.

C. (rāmạ) f. (1) (a) Indian hemp (Hibiscus cannabinus) (cf. rạgẹ ; dịrin ; sīyāyẹ ; daŋgịrā ; gurguzū). (b) dạgạ fakẹ rūwā, kụmfạ shūkạ rāmạ ? why make matters worse ?, give him an inch

and he'll take an ell. (c) tsạ̄gar ∼ f. hewing P. in two with sword in war. (2) Vd. waŋkan ramạ. (3) ramạr kitsǫ dyed hemp-fibre used for making tresses of false hair. (4) Vd. rạmạ-ramạ ; Cị̄ ∼ ; kā fi ∼. (5) gāɗā ạ ∼ Vd. gāɗā 4. (6) Vd. hạwainịyā.

Rạmạdaŋ = Rạmạlaŋ = Rạmạlaŋ Ar. m. (1) Muslim fast-month of Ramadan (Vd. azụmī 6). (2) man's name.

ramai = ramau.

Rạmạlaŋ Vd. Rạmạdaŋ.

rạmānīyā f. = kā fi ramạ.

rạmạ-ramạ f. = kā fi ramạ.

ramas = ramau.

Rạ̄matụ f. woman's name (= Rạ̄mū).

ramau adv. (1) yā būshẹ ∼ it (leaf, wood, clothing, etc.) has become very dry (= ram 1b = ragam). (2) yā gạsu ∼ it (meat) is well roasted. (3) cf. ragas.

rambạɗā Vb. 1C (1) raised voice x tā rambạɗạ gūɗạ she uttered a shrill cry. (2) (with dative). (a) kụnāmạ tā ∼ masạ harbị the scorpion stung him. yā ∼ minị sạndā he beat me with a stick. (b) added right amount of, added too much (of condiments, antimony, etc.) x tā rambạɗạ gishirī ạ mīyạ (rambạɗā 2 = ranɗạ).

rạmbạɗē Kt. m. making implement from pieces of old metal (cf. rạ̄wạyē).

rambạɗi (1) how salty ! (2) how sweet !

ramɓasa A. (rạmɓasạ) Vb. 2 (p.o. rạmɓashē, n.o. rạmɓashi). (1) snapped x yā rạmɓashi karā he snapped the cornstalk across. (2) yā rạmɓashē nị dạ sạndā he thrashed me. (3) yā rạmɓashē nị he collided with me.

B. (ramɓasā) Vb. 1C x sun ramɓasạ karǫ they collided.

ramɓashe A. (rạmɓashē) Vd. rạmɓasa.

B. (ramɓashē) Vb. 3A (cornstalk, etc.) snapped.

ramɓashēshẹ m. (f. ramɓashēshịyā) pl. ramɓas-rạmɓạs huge in body.

ramɓas-rạmɓạs Vd. ramɓashēshẹ.

rạmɓashi Vd. rạmɓasa.

rạmɓatsai = rạmɓatsau adv. and m. = rạkạcam.

ramɓo m. (1) = akạrɗạ̄. (2) yā shā ∼ he jumped into shallow water thinking it deep, and so hurt himself.

rạmbōshī *m.* = mạ̄rī.

rạmcē *Kt.* = rạncē.

ramdạ *f.* brown ostrich or its feather(s).

rame A. (rāmẹ) (1) *Vb.* 3A (*a*) became thin, emaciated (= rạ̄mā 1), *Vd.* wutsīyạ 1*e.* (*b*) wukā tā ∼ the knife-blade is worn down. (2) *Nor. m.* = rāmị.
  B. (ramẹ) *m.* fewness *x* hatsī yā yi ∼ there is little corn.

ramẹ-ramẹ *Kt. m.* = ramẹ.

ramfai (1) *m.* type of fish. (2) (*a*) how hot ! (*b*) what a severe sting !

ramfạkē = rāẞạkā 1.

ramfạyā = rambạdā 2*b.*

ramgạdā = rạngạdā.

rāmị *m.* = *Kt.* rạ̄mī (*pl.* rāmunạ = rāmū = rāmummukạ). (1) (*a*) hole in the ground, wall, or earth-floor (*cf.* ḳōfạ, kafā, kurfī 2, tērị). (*b*) *Vd.* hakạ 1*a, b.* (*c*) rāmịŋ karyā kurarrē nẹ̄ a lie is soon detected. (*d*) suŋ ginạ rāmịm mugguntā they did evil. (*e*) rāmịm mugguntā, ạ ginạ shi gạjērē take care you don't fall into the trap you lay for another ! (*f*) ẞērā nạ̄ ganin rāmịnsạ, bā yạ̄ yạrdā wutā tạ cī shi everyone looks after number one. (*g*) rāmịŋ kūrā *Vd.* kūrā 32. (*h*) arnạn ∼ *Vd.* gafīyạ. (*j*) *Vd.* girmaŋ ḳọrar ∼. (2) (*rustic*) town *x* yanạ̄ cikin rāmịnsạ he's at his town. (3) aŋ kai shị ∼ he's in prison. (4) rāmịŋ ūwar wani hole playfully dug by lads at ford for passers to fall in.

ramkạ *Sk.* = rāmạ.

ramnana *Kt.* = raunana.

ramni *Sk.* = rauni.

ramnō *Sk.* = jan raunō.

ram-ram *Kt.* = rumu-rumu.

ramta *Kt.* = ranta.

ramu A. (Rạ̄mū) = Rạ̄matụ.
  B. (rāmū) *Vd.* rāmị.

rāmummukạ = rāmunạ *Vd.* rāmị.

rāmūwā *f.* (1) (*a*) retaliation, rewarding (*as in* rāmạ). (*b*) rāmūwar gayyạ *Vd.* gayyạ 3. (2) *Vd.* kulẹ. (3) yā bīyā wadansu rāmūwā wạddạ Kạnde ta ci he paid for the gifts received by her from her first suitor and now to be returned to the latter.

ran A. (rạn) (1) *Vd.* rặi. (2) *Vd.* rānā 6*c.*

B. (ran) (1) day of (*genitive*), *Vd.* rānā 6. (2) wata ∼ = wata rānā some day, another day.

rānā *f.* (1) (*a*) sun. (*b*) fitọwar ∼ *f.* sunrise. (*c*) fādụwar ∼ *f.* sunset. (*d*) in ∼ tā fitō, tạ̄fiŋ hannū bā yạ̄ rufẹ ta a thing once public cannot be concealed. (*e*) gụdan ∼ (i) the orb of the sun. (ii) *Vd.* shā A.1*d.* (*f*) watạ yā bi ∼ there's no moon to-day. (*g*) bā yạ̄ ganin ∼ it finds a ready sale (= māsạ 2), *cf.* wutā 1*f.*iii.
  (2) heat of the sun *x* (*a*) yạu anạ̄ ∼ the sun is very hot to-day. (*b*) (i) ∼ tā yī the sun is well up. (ii) ta sāfē ta yārọ, ạmmā in ∼ tā yī, sǎi mutạ̄naŋ gạrī a new broom sweeps clean. (iii) in ∼ tā yī, sǎi fạ̄rā sụ tāshị *Vd.* sāfē 1*b.* (*c*) kạ̄kạ akạ ji dạ rānạ̄ how is the hot season treating you ? (*reply*, dạ gōdīyā = kwānạkintạ nē well, thank you !), *cf.* kạ̄kạ 1*c.* (*d*) yā hūtạ dạ ∼ *Vd.* sạmmakō 1*d.* (*e*) in yā ji ∼ *Vd.* yārọ 1*o.* (*f*) (i) iŋ kā ga wani nạ̄ inūwạ, wani yanạ̄ ∼ *Vd.* inūwạ 1*a.*ii, v. (ii) gwamma ∼ dạ kē *Vd.* bakī 3*o.* (iii) bại saŋ anạ̄ ∼ ba *Vd.* dūtsẹ 1*l.* (iv) iŋ kā ga makīyiŋkạ nạ̄ ∼ kạ kạ̄rạ masạ wutā kick your enemy when he is down ! (*g*) kōwā ya sạ̄mi ∼ sǎi yạ yi shanyạ make hay while the sun shines ! (*Vd.* shanyạ 1*a.*ii). (*h*) kai rūwā ∼ *Vd.* kai 3*k*, rūwā A.18. (*j*) (i) yanạ̄ wạje ạ tsakạr rānā (= yanạ̄ wạje ạ tsakar rānā Mod. Gram. Appendix 1, 24) he is outside in the heat of the sun. (ii) yā zō ạ tsakạr (= ạ tsakar) rānā he came when already advanced in life. (iii) *Vd.* gạmō 1*d.* (iv) ∼ tsakạ māgạnin dạ̄rī a friend in need is a friend indeed. (*k*) yā shā ∼ (i) he travelled through the heat of the day = yā dạuki ∼ (*cf.* 4*n*). (ii) it (garment) was aired, dried in the sun. (*l*) iŋ aŋ gạji, kō ạ ∼ sǎi ạ hūtạ beggars cannot be choosers.
  (3) (*a*) dan ∼ = dāki 5. (*b*) 'yar ∼ = dīyā 4. (*c*) *Vd.* ūwar ∼. (*d*) 'yā'yan ∼ = kạwalwalnīyā. (*e*) *Vd.* wan ∼; kạnẹ 2, 3.
  (4) (*pl.* rạnēkū = rạnaikū = rạnạkū). (*a*) (i) day. (ii) *for* days of week, clock-time, sun-time, *Vd.* Mod. Gram. Appendix 1. (*b*) sạ̄ ∼ *Vd.* sạ̄ B.3, F.

(c) (i) **dᶐ rānartᶐ ᶐ kā** her marriage-
date is fixed. (ii) **~ bā tᶐ ƙaryā, sǎi
ūwar 'yā** occasions arrive, but people
are dilatory. *(d)* **bᶐ shi dᶐ ~** he is a
useless P. *(epithet is* **Ƙᶐrē bᶐ ka dᶐ ~
sǎi ta haushị).** *(e) Vd.* **tā ga ~.** *(f)*
**bᶐ hanyᶐr gudụ bᶐllē sụ tunᶐ dᶐ
rānarsụ** there is nowhere to flee, so
of what use to remember their custom
of running away ! *(g)* **sun sᶐki injị,
bᶐ darē bᶐ ~** they sped along
incessantly. **haƙᶐ dǎi bᶐ darē, bᶐ ~
har sukᶐ gamᶐ kᶐi** this (discussion)
went on uninterruptedly till they
reached agreement. *(h)* **ᶐ rᶐgi ~** *Vd.*
rᶐgā 2. *(j)* **yā gᶐmu dᶐ ~ =** **rānā tā
taɓᶐ shi** it (baby) has illness which is
accompanied by diarrhœa, piles, etc. **=
bᶐyᶐmmā 2** *(cf.* **bāsụr).** *(k)* (i) **sǎi wata
~** adieu ! (ii) **māgᶐniɳ wata ~** *Vd.* **ᶐjīyᶐ
2f.** *(l)* **in nā yi makᶐ ~ kadᶐ kᶐ yi minị
darē** do not repay my kindness to you
with evil ! *(Vd.* **inūwᶐ 3).** *(m)* **~ yị ta
yᶐu** *Vd.* **yị 1f.** *(n)* **yā dᶐuki ~** he fixed
a date for doing T. *(cf. 2ƙ.i).* **(5)** lucky
day *x* *(a)* **kōwā dᶐ ~ tasᶐ** everyone
has his own speciality. *(b)* **rānarkᶐ kē
naɳ** this is your chance ! *(c)* **yᶐnzu
zᶐi yi rānassᶐ** this is his chance to use
his abilities ! *(d)* **yā sᶐmi ~** he secured
an auspicious time (= **sā'ᶐ 4e),** he had
a lucky day. *(e)* **~ tā ɓacᶐ masᶐ** he
has had bad luck. *(f)* **ɓācịn ~** *Vd.*
ɓācị A2.3. **(5A)** *Vd.* **ƙaryᶐ ~.**

(6) ran = rānar *(genitive)* day of *x*
(a) **bᶐn san rᶐn (= rānᶐd) dᶐ zā sụ
zō ba** I don't know what day they will
come. **sum fid dᶐ rᶐn dᶐ zā sụ ci
nasarᶐ** they have fixed the day when
they will be victorious. *(b) Vd.* **ran.**
(c) (i) **rᶐn naɳ** on that day. (ii) *x*
anᶐ naɳ, ran naɳ sǎi ya sᶐmi dᶐbārᶐ
then one day he thought of a plan.
(d) **duk rānar Allᶐ** every day. *(e)*
ran (= rānar) Jumma'ᶐ Friday, on
Friday. **ran Lārᶐbar 3.5.1941,** on
Wednesday 3.5.1941. *(f)* **ran sāfiyar
wannᶐɳ ciɳ ᶐmānᶐ** on the morning
on which he committed this depredation. *(g)* **ran cikwᶐn rānā ta ukụ** on
the third day. *(h)* **ran sūnā** *Vd.* **sūnā 5.**

(7) *proverbs with* **ran, rānar :—**(a)

**dᶐ rānar ƙịn dillancị rᶐd dᶐ hājᶐr
mᶐsū gᶐrī ta ɓatᶐ** the pitcher goes to
the well once too often. *(b)* **ram bịƙī
akᶐ ƙịm huntū, raɳ kwᶐɓar ƙasā
ᶐ nēmō shị** everything has its own
time and place. *(c)* **rānar kāyā ᶐkwīyᶐ
bᶐ bisā ba cᶐ** don't attempt the impossible ! *(d)* **rānar yᶐbō** *Vd.* **yᶐbō 5,
bā 4.** *(e)* **raɳ gōbe** *Vd.* **gōbe 1f.** *(f)*
rānar sallᶐ *Vd.* **sallᶐ 1m.** *(g)* **rānar
sāmụ** *Vd.* **bāwᶐ 8a.** *(h)* **rānarkᶐ ɗayā**
Vd. **sụɳgumī.** *(j)* **ram mutūwᶐ** *Vd.*
mutūwᶐ 1a.iv. *(k) Vd.* **yᶐmmā 2c.**
(l) **raɳ aurē** *Vd.* **budịrī.** *(m)* **rānar
waɳkā** *Vd.* **cībịyā 2.** *(n)* **rānar tᶐfīyᶐ**
Vd. **fāfᶐ 3.** *(o)* **ran lāhirᶐ** *Vd.* **lāhirᶐ 2.**

(8) dᶐ rānā *(a)* (i) during daylight.
(ii) openly. *(b) cf.* **zᶐ 6.** *(c)* **wᶐndᶐ
bᶐi ɓatᶐ dᶐ darē ba, bᶐ yā ɓatᶐ dᶐ
rānā ba** if one is able to cope with
something difficult, how much more
so with an easy thing ! *(d)* **su kᶐn
cī dᶐ rānā** *Vd.* **ᶐbụ 2b.** *(e)* **dᶐ rānā
kō dᶐ karā ᶐ dōgᶐrā** *Vd.* **sᶐndā 1e.** *(f)*
dᶐ rānā akᶐ awo, dᶐ darē sǎi ᶐ ci tūwō
(labourers' slang) don't buy a pig in
a poke !

(9) *Vd.* **rana-rana.**

rᶐnᶐiƙū, rᶐnᶐkū *Vd.* **rānā 4.**

rana-rana A. (rᶐnᶐ-rānᶐ) (1) *adv. x* **dᶐ
~ muƙᶐ zō** we came rather late in the
morning. **(2)** *f. (a)* **wannᶐɳ aiƙị ~
nē, muɳ mᶐkarᶐ** as we started it late in
the morning. *(b) Vd.* **sallᶐ 1m.**

B. (rāna-rānᶐ) occasionally (= **sā'ᶐ
1b).**

rᶐncaccē *past participle from* **(1) ranta,
rancᶐ. (2)** *Kt.* **rantsᶐ.**

rance A. (rancᶐ) *Vb.* 1A **(1)** borrowed all
of *(cf.* **rᶐntā). (2)** *Kt.* = **rantsᶐ.**

B. (rᶐncē) (1) *Vd.* **rᶐntā. (2)** *m. (a)*
borrowing for a short time money or
T. not *itself* to be returned *(cf.* **arō,
bāshị)** *x* (i) **nā yi rᶐncan sulᶐ ᶐ wurinsᶐ**
I borrowed a shilling from him (=
rᶐntā). (ii) **nā bā shị rᶐncan sulᶐ** I lent
him a shilling (= **rᶐntā).** *(b)* **kōwā ya
ci hatsin ~, nāsᶐ ya ci** borrowing is
only putting off the evil day *(Vd.*
shiɳkāfā 1b). *(c)* **kadᶐ ~ yᶐ zamā
bāshị** *Vd.* **bāshị 3.**

rąnci *Vd.* rąntā.

rąndā *f.* (*pl.* randunạ) (1) (*a*) large water-pot. (*b*) kadạ dăi kǫgi yạ hạŋgi ~ one can never have too much of a good thing. (*c*) aŋ kashẹ rạndar ɗakạ, ta wạje bạ tạ shigō ba don't throw away dirty water before you've got clean ! (*d*) ~ tanā ɗakạ *Vd.* tūlū 1*b*. (*e*) tsụmmā ạ rạndā *Vd.* sạkatạ 1*b*. (2) cistern, tank. (3) money-safe. (4) large karōfī. (5) large drum shaped like tandū. (6) hadarị yā kāmạ ~ = hadarị yā zaunạ ạ ~ a storm has gathered in the north-east or south-east.

randạ *Vb.* 1A = rambạɗā 2.

rạn dạ kwaŋ = ciɓụs 2.

rạndam *x* gā su ạ jẹre ~ they are in a line.

randạmā = rambạɗā.

randẹ *Fil. m.* any tethering-rope for oxen (*cf.* tạŋgē).

randị (1) how hot the sun is ! (2) what a severe sting !

randunạ *Vd.* rạndā.

rạnẹkū *Vd.* rānā 4.

ranfạkē = rāɓạkā 1.

rangạɗā (1) *Vb.* 3A = raŋkạyā. (2) *Vb.* 1C = rambạɗā.

rangādị (*Eng.* round-guard) *m.* (1) bush-touring *x* jōjị yā tạfi ~ the Administrative Officer has gone out on tour. (2) policeman's beat.

rangajī *m.* = rạŋgwaɗạ.

raŋgalēlẹ *x* yanā dạ kăi ~ he has a huge head.

rạŋgạlgạl *x* yanā dạ kăi ~ he has a huge head.

rạŋgamā *f.* paying for T. in kind instead of in cash (*cf.* fụrfụrē).

raŋgamad dạ *Vb.* 4 sold T. and was paid in kind, not cash (*cf.* fụrfụrạ, raŋgamō).

raŋgamō *Vb.* 1E got goods by false pretences (*cf.* raŋgamad dạ).

rạŋgạ-raŋgạ *adv.* dangling flaccidly (*x* limbs of unconscious or sick P. being carried).

rạŋgazạ *f.* contagious bovine pleuro-pneumonia (= bạlāgirō 2).

rạŋgwaɗạ *f.* (1) swaying (of branch, camel, etc.). (2) swaggering (1, 2 = rạụsayạ). (3) *Vd.* rigā 3.

raŋgwamẹ *m.* (1) (*a*) reduction in price (= sịyāsạ 2). (*b*) cheapness. (2) (*a*) clemency. (*b*) yā yi minị ~ he did me a favour (2*a*, *b* = sịyāsạ). (*c*) ạ yi minị ~ (*said by woman-petitioner to judge or her husband*) please grant me.divorce ! (*d*) mitigation of sentence or of madness, illness, etc. *x* ạmmā dạ raŋgwamạŋ ạlkālī but the judge has the option of reducing the maximum sentence laid down. bābụ ~ gạ irịŋ wannạŋ lạifī but in the case of a crime of this nature (*x* kisạŋ gīlạ) the Muslim Code gives the judge no power of reducing the sentence enjoined. (*e*) ɗagạ hannū raŋgwamạŋ dūkạ nē (i) what an unexpected bargain ! (ii) we've got off lightly ! (*f*) mahạụkạcī bā yā warkẹwā săi ~ character does not change.

rangwangwan A. (raŋgwaŋgwạŋ) *m.* (1) weak but quarrelsome P. (2) magic medicament making it fatal for one's opponent to touch one's head in fray.
 B. (rạŋgwạŋgwạŋ) *m.* yā rāmẹ yá yi ~ he (fat man) has now become thin.

raŋgwanta A. (raŋgwạntā) *Vb.* 1C reduced (price).
 B. (rạŋgwantạ) *Vb.* 3B (price) has been reduced.

rạŋgwazạ *Kt.* = rạŋgazạ.

rạŋgyanạ *f.* (1) querulousness. (2) querulous P. (*epithet is* Rangyanạ, kutạran Tākai, bā ā cẹ musụ " jẹ ku gạba ! ").

rānī *m.* (1) (*a*) the hot-season (*epithet is* ~ bā yā hanạ rīmī tǫhō). (*b*) sạba dạ mại fitọ tun ~ *Vd.* sābạ 3. (*c*) *Vd.* wạhalạ 1*e*.iv. (*d*) mạkārar ~ *Vd.* watạ 2*o*. (2) yā sā masạ ~ he shared a friend's food which was only enough for one in reality. (3) (*a*) cịn ~ taking cattle to where pasturage is good during hot season = cị rānī (*cf.* tāshị 2*b*, mashēkarī, ɓạrtī). (*b*) yā tạfi cịn ~ in order to eke his corn out, he has gone to spend the hot season elsewhere in exercise ọf his trade. (4) *Vd.* gōnā 1*b*. (5) 'yan ~ *pl.* smallpox (= agānā 1). (6) 'yar ~ *f.* (*a*) type of late sugar-cane. (*b*) = 5 *above*. (7) *Vd.* shā rānī, gwīwạ 8, kǫkạ rānī.

rankai A. (raṇkai) in a straight line *x* sun jĕru ~ they're in a line.

B. (raṇkai) *Vd.* alĕnīyạ.

raŋƙāsō = riŋƙāsō.

ᴊaŋƙạtā *Vb.* 1C (1) aŋ ~ shi dạ ƙasā he has been felled. (2) aŋ ~ masạ sạndā he was thrashed with a stick.

raŋkạtsā = raŋkwạtsā.

raŋkạyā *Vb.* 3A departed unceremoniously.

raŋƙạyā *Vb.* 1C = ƙāgạ 2*b*.

raŋki (*Eng.* rank) *m.*, *sg.*, *pl.* porter(s), carrier(s).

raŋkō *m.* = rāmūwā 1*a*.

raŋƙwalĕlẹ = riŋgimēmẹ.

rạŋƙwạlƙwạl = riŋgiŋgiŋ.

raŋƙwasa A. (raŋƙwasạ) *Vb.* 2 (*p.o.* rạŋƙwạshē, *n.o.* rạŋƙwạshi) = daŋƙwasạ.

B. (raŋƙwạsā) *Vb.* 1C (1) = daŋƙwasā. (2) yā raŋƙwạsạ yātsū = rạƙwạs 1. (3) *Kt.* yā raŋƙwạsạ tạbarmā he broke rolled-up or folded mat by stepping on it.

raŋƙwashe A. (raŋƙwạshē) *Vb.* 1C = daŋƙwasạ.

B. (raŋƙwạshē) *Vd.* raŋƙwasạ.

ranƙwashi A. (raŋƙwạshi) *Vd.* raŋƙwasạ.

B. (raŋƙwạshī) *m.* = daŋƙwạshī.

raŋkwạtsā *Vb.* 1C yā raŋkwạtsạ 'yā'yā he has many children.

Ranō *Vd.* hausā, jan raunō.

ranta A. (rạntā) (1) *Vb.* 2 (*p.o.* rạncē, *n.o.* rạnci) (*a*) borrowed *as in* rạncē 2*a x* nā rạnci sulẹ ạ wurinsạ I borrowed a shilling from him (= rạncē 2*a*.i). (*b*) yā rạnci darē jīyạ he went to bed late last night. (*c*) yā rạnci hanyạ he did a " moonlight flit ". (2) *Vb.* 3B yā ~ = Barẹ 2*c*, 2*d*.

B. (rạntā) *Vb.* 1C lent *as in* rạncē 2*a x* nā ~ masạ sulẹ I lent him a shilling (= rạncē 2*a*.ii = jūyạ 1*e*).

rantạɓā *Vb.* 1C (1) yā ~ mini lạɓārị he told me an improbable story (= zubạ 9). (2) yā ~ ni dạ ƙasā he felled me.

rantaɓēɓẹ *m.* (*f.* rantaɓēɓịyā) tall and big.

rạntạltạl = raŋgạlgạl.

rantsad dạ *Vb.* 4 put P. on oath.

rạntsattsē *m.* (*f.* rạntsattsīyā) *pl.* rạntsattsū (1) of good quality *x* bindigạ rạntsattsīyā a reliable gun. yanạ dạ ɗā ~ he has a fine son. (2) shạkīyyị ~ a thorough rogue. maƙaryạcī ~ thoroughpaced liar (2 = kuntukurmī).

rạntsattsēnīyā *f.* mutual swearing (*x* by plaintiff and defendant).

rantsẹ *Vb.* 1A (1) (*a*) took an oath (= *Sk.* wallạcē), *cf.* saɓạ, bạkantạ. (*b*) (i) yā ~ dạ Allạ he swore by God (= wallạcē). (ii) yā ~ dạ tsāfị he (pagan) swore by his fetish. (iii) yā rantsẹ dạ ạbịn dạ zại kashẹ shi he swore a mortal oath that . . . (iv) nā rantsẹ dạ girman dạttịjạntakạta (*said by labourers*) I swear it is true. (2) assumed great proportions *x* kạsūwā tā ~ the market became (*a*) filled, (*b*) large. (3) rạbansạ yā ~ he has been lucky. (4) rūwā yā ~ it is raining heavily.

rantsụ̄wā *f.* (1) taking an oath (*Vd.* rantsẹ, bạkạncē). (2) yā yi ~ = yā shā ~ = yā ɗauki ~ he took an oath. sun yi rantsụ̄wā kaŋ hakạ they swore to this. (3) yā yi rantsụ̄war ƙaryā he committed perjury (*cf.* zur ; kạfārạ 2). (4) ạmmā, hanạ rantsụ̄wā but, to tell the truth. . . . hanạ rantsụ̄wā, sại jirgī gụdā kawại sukạ kai ƙasạ the only exception to this statement is that they shot down one aeroplane.

raŋwā *Kt. f. x* zō, mụ yi ~ let's have a game with a spinning-top ! (= kạtantaŋwạ 2*b*.i).

ranyạ *Vb.* 3A yā ~ dạ gudụ = ranyẹ.

ranyẹ *Vb.* 3A took to one's heels.

raptā = raftā.

rara A. (rạrā) *f.* acting *as in* rārẹ 1*a*, *b*.

B. (rārā) *f.* (1) (*a*) surplus *x* nā yi ~ I have a surplus. rashịŋ haŋkạlī gạrēshị har yā yi ~ he's abysmally stupid. (*b*) = rạgī 1. (2) *Kt.* = rạ̄rā.

C. (rạ̄-rạ̄) *f.* (*sg.*, *pl.*) (1) Glossy Ibis (*Theristicus hagedesh*). (2) Greater Hammerkop (*Scopus umbretta bannermanni*) (2 = shaidạ 4*c*).

D. (rārạ) (1) *Vb.* 1A (*a*) = rārẹ. (*b*) *Kt.* = rērạ. (2) Na ~ *Vd.* bōdạrī.

rarai *Kt.* yā kārẹ ~ it is completely finished.

rạ̄rạikū *Vd.* rārīyā.

raraka A. (rạ̄rakạ) (1) *Vb.* 2 (*a*) drove

away *x* an rārąki ąbǫkaŋ gąbā the enemy have been routed. kąrē yā rārąki ąlmājįrī the dog drove away the beggar (= rārę 1*d*). (*b*) prodded (rat, etc.) out of hole *x* yā rārakō ɓērā = zuŋgųrā 2*a*. (*c*) stripped (leaves from cornstalks prior to storing). (*d*) hollowed out (*x* pith from cornstalk). (*e*) cadged *x* yā rārąki sįgārį ą wurīna he cadged a cigarette from me. (*f*) yā rārąki dōkįnsą he galloped his horse (= sukwąnā). (2) *f.* cadging (*Vd.* marǭkī).
    B. (rārąkā) *Vb.* 1C (1) = zuŋgųrā 1*a*, *b.* (2) = rāraką 1*f.*
    C. (rārakā) (*rustic*) *f.* potash as used at accouchement.
rārąkē (1) *Vb.* 1C (*a*) completely stripped (leaves from cornstalks prior to storing), *cf.* rāraką 1*c*. (*b*) completely hollowed out (*x* pith from cornstalk), *cf.* rāraką 1*d*. (2) *Vb.* 3A (*a*) cikįna yā ~ my stomach is empty (from hunger, etc.). (*b*) mīkį yā ~ the ulcer has become deeper (*opposite of* cikō 3 *q.v.*).
rārakō *Vd.* rāraką 1*b*.
rārātū *m.* loud raising of the voice in anger.
rārauką *f.* diffidence.
rārę (1) *Vb.* 1A yā ~ rįgā he (*a*) unwrapped new black gown or turban from its paper and unfolded it ready to wear, (*b*) put on new black gown or turban, *(c)* put on any new garment *x* yā ~ sāban tufą. (*d*) = rāraką 1*a*. (*e*) = fąllasą. (*f*) = zuŋgurą 2. (2) *Vb.* 3A (*a*) took to his heels (= shēɓą). (*b*) lost shyness (= yā dą 1*b*).
rārīną *f.* loquacity.
rārītą = lālītą.
rārīyā *f.* (*pl.* rārīyōyī = rāraikū) (1) (*a*) drainage-hole in wall (= *Kt.* sagį 3*a*). (*b*) rārīyar ɓasą underground drain. (2) (*a*) any street in a town. (*b*) kąran rārīyā nę̄ (i) he's a tramp, casual worker. (ii) *Vd.* kąren 8. (3) (*a*) sieve (*Vd.* marā-rakī). (*b*) sąlkā a kąŋ hūrą, kōwā ya hūrą ~, bąkinsą yą̄ yi cīwǫ don't waste your time on a futile person ! (*c*) kōwā ya sai ~ yā san tą̄ zubad dą rūwā what's bred in the bone comes out in the flesh (*Vd.* sai 2). (4) bleeding a *person*

from calf of the leg (*cf.* sārą 1*d*). (5) rārīyar hannū gąrēshį (*a*) he's unlucky with his money (= zųbau 2). (*b*) he never has anything to show for his money.
rarraba A. (rarrąbā) *Vb.* 1C (1) shared out *x* yā rarrąbā shi gąrēsų he divided it among them. an ~ musų gōrǫ the kola-nuts have been divided out among them (= rabą 2*a*). (2) kadą kų rarrąbą ąbįn dą muką shar'ąntā mukų do not abrogate what we have enjoined on you by Muslim Law ! (*Vd.* rabą 1).
    B. (rąrrąbā) *Kt. f.* = wątandā 1.
rarrąbcē *Kt. Vb.* 1C = rabę 1–3.
rarrąbē *Vb.* 1C (1) = rabę 1–3. (2) bā ą̄ rarrąbę̄ fitsārim maį gōyō = jēgǫ 3.
rarrąfā *Vb.* 3A (1) (lizard, snake, baby) crawled. (2) yā gąji, yaną̄ rarrąfāwā he is tired and proceeding very slowly.
rąrrąfē *m.* (1) (*a*) crawling *as in* rarrąfā 1, 2. (*b*) *Vd.* hąkurą 1*d.* (*c*) bąrēwā tą̄ yi gųdų P ɗantą yą̄ yi rąrrafę̄ P "like breeds like". (*d*) dą ~ yārǫ ya kąn tāshį from little acorns mighty oak-trees grow. (*e*) sum mai dą ɓasąn naŋ gą rąrrąfē they (enemy) have brought that country to her knees. (2) mąsū ~ *pl.* those who crawl (*x* babies, reptiles, etc.).
rąrramnā *Kt.* = rąrraunā.
rąrrāsą = ląllāsą.
rarrāshī = lallāshī.
rarrątsā *Kt.* = famfątsā.
rąrraunā *m., f.* (*pl.* raunąnā) (1) wounded. (2) (*a*) weak. (*b*) rąrraunaŋ hanzarī weak excuse. (2*b* = sukųrkurī = taŋgardą 2 = tāwīlį = hanzarī 1*d* = ɓararī 1*b* = kusųrwā 2*b*).
rąruką *Sk.* = rāraką.
rąrumą *Vb.* 2 grabbed.
rārųmē *Vb.* 1C = rārumą.
ras A. (ras) *adv. and m.* (1) (*a*) yā karyę ~ it snapped with a crashing sound. (*b*) nā̄ ji ~ I heard a rending sound. (2) itącē yā būshę ~ the tree is dried up.
    B. (rąs) *m.* (1) gąbāna yā yi ~ my heart turned to water. (2) = ras 1*b*.
rasa A. (rasą) (1) *Vb.* 3A yā ~ he found himself unable to cope with the situation (= kāsą 1). (2) *Vb.* 1A (*a*) (i) lacked, was short of. (ii) săi wani yā ~, wani

kạn sāmu one man's gain is another's loss. (iii) Bạhaushẹ yạ̄ ∼ Hausạ̄? is it possible for a Hausa not to understand Hausa? (iv) yā rasạ ạbiŋ kusa *Vd.* shimfiɗạ 1*d.* (v) bā yạ̄ ∼ mọtsī *Vd.* rạ̈i 1*c.* (vi) bạ tā̀ rasạ wurim barcī ba *Vd.* tīlạs 2*c.* (vii) bạ yạ̄ ∼ sallamạr gidā ba = bạ yạ̄ ∼ tạmbayạr hālị ba *Vd.* asạlā. (b) is unable to, was unable to *x* (i) nā̀ ∼ ạbin dạ zạn yi I do (did) not know how to act. mun rasạ kạnsu, mun rasạ gindinsu we're at a loss how to deal with them. yā rasạ wạddạ zại kāmạ he is at a loss how to act. (ii) nā̀ ∼ ganinsạ I cannot see it. yā ∼ yạddạ zại rịnjāyē su he saw no way of overcoming them. (*Vd.* īyạ 2*b.*) (*c*) (*negatively*) for sure *x* bā ạ̄ ∼ jirạ̄gyan samạmmu sunạ̄ biŋ ƙasạn naŋ our aeroplanes are certainly attending to that country. dạ dōyạ ạ Kạnọ? are there any yams at Kano? (*reply* bạ ạ̄ ∼ ba of course there are !). bạ zại rasạ kūkā ba he's sure to cry out. (*d*) ceased to possess *x* sun ∼ dōki dạrī they lost a hundred cavalry in the battle (*cf.* ragẹ 1*a.*i). zā mụ rasạ ta bābụ rạ̈i, bābụ girmā we shall lose her irretrievably. (*e*) felt the loss of *x* bā sạ̄ harbẹ manạ jirạ̄gyan samạ sắi ɗải-ɗải, ạbin dạ bā ạ̄ rasạ̄wā they are not shooting down many of our aeroplanes —no very severe loss. (3) *Vd.* rạsu.   B. (rạsā) *Vb.* 2, *Vd.* rạshi.

rạsạsạ̄-rasasā *f.* = rạbạ mạkāfọ dạ gōrạ.

rasga = razga.

Rashạ *f.* Russia.

rashā-rashā = rashashā *adv.* (1) yā zaunạ ∼ he sat sprawled out. (2) yā fāɗị ∼ he fell headlong.

rashawạ *Ar. f.* bribe *x* yā ci ∼ he accepted a bribe (= tōshị 3).

rashẹ A. (rāshẹ) *Vb.* 3A (1) loitered, lingered, was dilatory. (2) sukạ hūrạ wutā, suka rāshẹ so they took life easy.   B. (rạshē) *Vb.* rạsā.

rashi A. (rạshi) = rasạ 2*b.*ii *x* nā̀ ∼ ganinsạ I cannot see it.   B. (rashị) *m.* (1) (*a*) lack *x* (i) anạ̄ rashịŋ hatsī there is a shortage of corn (= talauci 4). (b) bạbban rashịn dāɗiŋ ạbiŋ kumā but the worst of the matter is that . . . (*c*) rashịn jinī, rashịn tsāgạ̄wā getting T. without trouble. (*d*) ∼ bạ̄ yị dạ kạɗaŋ however small a loss is, it is still a loss. (*e*) rashịŋ ạlbarkạ = rashịn kunyạ shamelessness, impudence (= tsīwạ). (*f*) rashịn azzịkī (i) = 1*e above.* (ii) ill-luck. (*g*) rashịm fariŋ watạ, taụrārọ kẹ̄ haskē any port in a storm. (*h*) rashịn ƙarfī weakness. (*j*) rashịŋ kunyạ *Vd.* 1*e above.* (*k*) rashịn lāfīyạ illness. (*l*) rashịn rashị, an cẹ̄ dạ mạkāfọ "gạ̄ idọ", ya cẹ̄ "mẹ̄ zạn yī dạ shī ạbụ mại wārị" it's sour grapes (*Vd.* mạkāfọ 1*e*). (*m*) *Kt.* rashịn ta mại barạ = 1*e above.* (*n*) rashịn tūwō ạ ci wākē ạ kwānā make the best of a bad job! (*o*) mại rashịn yaụ shī nẹ̄ mại sāmụŋ gọ̄be life has its ups and downs. (*p*) kadạ kạ yi wannạŋ rashịŋ hạŋkạlī don't be so stupid as to act like this! (*q*) rashịn sanị yā fi darē duhụ nothing is worse than ignorance. (*r*) rashịŋ ạbiŋ wutā *Vd.* shịŋkāfā 1*c.* (*s*) rashịn tayị *Vd.* tayị. (*t*) rashịn ūwā *Vd.* ūwar rānā 2. (*u*) rashịŋ idọ *Vd.* wadai 2. (*v*) rashịŋ gini *Vd.* gạrī 1*e.* (2) yā yi ∼ he has suffered a loss. (3) bereavement *x* (*a*) an yi ∼ a death has occurred. (*b*) an yi rashịŋ Audụ Audu died. (*c*) *Vd.* gaisūwā 5.

rashwạ = rashawạ.

rạsịt = rạsītsị *Eng. m.* receipt for money paid.

raskwamā *f.* the feeble (*x* women and children).

rạssā = rạssū *Vd.* rēshẹ.

rạsu *Vb.* 3B (1) is in short supply. (2) (*person*) died (*cf.* mutụ). (3) *cf.* rasạ.

Rạsūlụ *Ar. m.* envoy, *used in* Muhammadụ Rạsūlụllāhị Mohammad The Apostle of God.

rạsūwā death of person *x* (1) an yi ∼ = rashị 3. (2) ∼ ya yi = Allạ̄ yā yi masạ ∼ he has died (*cf.* mutūwạ).

rātā *f.* (1) = tazarā. (2) tạfi gạba, nā bā kạ ∼ (*a*) you'd better leave before I do, so as to give yourself a start. (*b*) I'll give you a start in the race as handicap to myself.

ratąl *Ar. m.* measure of weight (15¾ ounces in Egypt, but 5 lb. in Syria).

ratata A. (ratata) *x* 'yā'yaŋ itącē sun zubŏ ∼ much fruit has fallen off the tree. mutąnē suŋ wątsu ∼ the people have scattered.

B. (rątątą) *adv. and f.* (1) 'yā'yaŋ itącē sun zubŏ ∼ = sun yi ∼ = ratata *q.v.* (2) rūwā yā zubō ∼ = rūwā yā yi ∼ water dripped off the leaves drop by drop. (3) suną ząncē ∼ they're chattering.

ratattaka A. (ratattąkā) *Vb.* 1D = ragargązā 1*a*.

B. (rątattąką) *Vb.* 3B = ratattąkē.

ratattąkē *Vb.* 3A = ragargąjē 1.

rataya A. (rātąyā) *Vb.* 1C (1) hung up (*x* picture). (2) (*a*) hung T. from shoulder *x* (i) yā rātąyą wąndansą he (traveller) slung his trousers from his shoulder. (ii) yā rātąyą gafakąrsą, yā gudu he's taken to his heels. (*b*) (i) yā ∼ he is ready to set out (2*a*, *b* = rątayą). (ii) yā fi ą rātąyā *Vd.* są A4. (*c*) (*labourers'* *talk*) an ∼ masą jąkā he has had his food (*cf.* rątayą 2*c*). (*d*) an ∼ masą ląifī = an rātąyā masą igīyąr ląifī he has been falsely accused (= ƙāgą). (*e*) an ∼ masą sąrautą = nadą 2*c*. (*f*) yā ci dūką har yā ∼ he was well thrashed. (*g*) (i) kā cī, kā ∼ you'll have your bellyful of it (work, etc.) ! = gumą 1. (ii) *Vd.* kā cī kā ∼.

B. (rątayą) (1) *Vb.* 2 = rātąyā 2*a*, *b*. (2) *f.* (*a*) (i) hanging a T. *as in* rātąyā 2*a*. (ii) T. hung *as in* rātąyā 2*a*. (*b*) aną kāyaŋ kā, a kąn yi ∼ the busy P. always has time for more ; P. with many calls on his purse can still find something for charity. (*c*) dōkin naŋ bąi sąmi ∼ ba this horse has not yet been fed (*cf.* rātąyā 2*c*). (*d*) bą ą san rątayąd dą Allą ya yi masą ba nobody knows what destiny God has in store for him (mad, destitute, etc., P.). (3) *Vb.* 3B (*a*) hung down from one's neck *x* bą zaŋ kashę ka, ką ∼ ą wuyąna ba I won't kill you and so have your death on my conscience. (*b*) refers to *x* takąrdarku wąddą ta ∼ dą sha'ąnim mąi mutūwą your letter in reference to the deceased. (*c*) is, was dependent

on *x* įyālįm mųtųm sun ∼ dą shī = sun ∼ gąrēshį = sun ∼ gųnsą a mai is responsible for the support of hi● dependents.

rataye A. (rātąyē) *Vb.* 1C (1) = rātąyā 1 2*f.* (2) hung (a criminal).

B. (rątąyē) *m.* charms, beads, etc. hung from the neck (*but falling lowe●* *than* sąkē 2*b*).

C. (rątąye) (*noun of state from* rātąyī 2*a*) (1) yaną ∼ dą takǫbī he is wearing a sword (M.G. 80*d*.ii). (2) ząkarą ą ∼ bā yą cārā the underdog has to ea● humble pie.

rātsą *Vb.* 1A (1) (*a*) passed through ą (i) nā ∼ gąrī I passed through the town (= fētsą 1*a* = kēsą). (ii) nā ∼ kǫgī I forded the river (ii = fįta 11) (*b*) dǫmiŋ kā ∼ rūwā, im bąi ∼ k● ba, banzā nę half-measures are use less. (2) yā ∼ ni he abused me (= zągā), *cf.* rątsattsīyā. (3) (*a*) nā ∼ Kanǫ I turned aside towards Kan● (*cf.* rātsę). (*b*) in tsąutsąyī yā rātsą i an accident occurs. (4) *Vd.* nā ∼.

rątsattsīyā *f.* unseemly speech or conduc (= tądadðīyā).

ratse A. (rātsę) *Vb.* 3A (1) (*a*) yā ∼ dąg● hanyą = yā ∼ hanyą (i) he swerve● off, strayed from the road (= fandąrē : = *Sk.* tādę 2). (ii) he committed breac● of religion (= rątsē 2). (*b*) = fandąrē 2 (2) = tsugunā 1*b* (*cf.* rātsį). (3) (*wit● dative*) followed edge of *x* yā ∼ w● gidaŋ Audu he passed along the edg● of Audu's compound (= rąβā 1).

B. (rątsē) *m.* (1) kǫgī yā zamā ∼ the river is now fordable (*cf.* rātsą 1*a*.ii) (2) swerving from path *x* Allą yą fissh● mų rątsē God keep us from backsliding (*cf.* rātsę 1*a*,*b*).

rātsę gidā *m.* type of mąngųl-salt causin● diarrhœa.

rātsį *m.* (1) (*a*) = nąjasą 1 (*cf.* rātsę 2). (*b* yā jē ∼ = tsugųnā 1*b*. (2) stripe ● farī nę dą rātsįn jā it is white with ● red stripe.

rattąbā *Vb.* 1C *Ar.* (1) arranged symmetri cally. (2) yā ∼ minį mąganąr he relate● the matter to me in its proper sequence

rattąfā *Kt.* = rattąbā.

rau A. (rau) *adv.* (1) well *x* yā įyą mągan●

~ = bāḳinsạ ~ yaḳḕ he speaks well,
clearly. zg̣nan nạŋ yā ḟịta ~ this
pattern is well done. tukunyan nạŋ ~
taḳḕ this pot is sound. (2) yan̄ạ
mạg̣anạ ~ he is speaking out without
reserve or fear. (3) mīyạ tā ji gishirī ~
the soup is nicely salted. gishirī
yā ji ~ the salt in the food is just
right (= ragam = ram 1a q.v.). tōzạlī
yā kāmạ ~ ạ idāṇunsạ = idạnsạ yā
ji tōzạlī ~ his eyes are nicely smeared
with galena. (4) sun̄ạ zạụne ~ they're
on good terms (4 = ragam). (5) nā
ji zāḟī ~ I felt a sharp sting. (6) yā
būshḕ ~ it is quite dry.

B. (rạụ) adv. and m. (1) yā yi ~
it is handsome. (2) = rau 1 x zg̣nan
nạŋ yā ḟịta ~ this pattern is well
done.

C. (rạụ) (1) m. sun̄ạ ~ they're
exactly similar to each other. (2)
adv. yā ḳwālạ minị sạndā ~ he gave
me resounding blow with a stick.

rau dạ Vb. 4 shook x (1) iskạ tā ~ dạ
shī = iskạ tā raushē shị the wind swayed
it. (2) yā ~ ḍansạ he dandled his
baby-son. (3) yā ~ wutsīyạ it (dog,
etc.) wagged its tail (= kaḍạ 1f). (4)
marạu dạ haḳị Vd. marạu.

rạuhānī (Ar. rūh soul) m. (pl. rạuhg̣nai) (1)
mại ~ m. = mālạmī. (2) yā nḕmi
rạuhg̣nai he invoked night-spirits to
carry out his wishes (if mistakes made,
it is considered there is risk of madness
or even death).

rauka Kt. = rafka.

rạukanạ Kt. = rạfkanạ.

rạụmạ fādạ = rụmạ fādạ.

raunạna A. (raunāṇā) Vd. rg̣rraunā.

B. (rạunanạ) Vb. 3B (1) became
weak. (2) kạsūwạ tā ~ the market has
fallen off. (3) hujjạrkạ tā ~ your
excuse is weak.

C. (raunạnā) Vb. 1C weakened.

rauni A. (rạụnī) m. (pl. raunukạ) (1) (a)
wound. (b) yā yi ~ = yā shā ~ he is
wounded. jirgī yā shā rạụnī the ship
suffered damage. (c) yā yi masạ ~ ạ
kā it wounded him in the head. (d)
jirgin ḍaukg̣m māsū ~ hospital ship,
hospital train. (2) Rạụnī jḕ ka dawạ
m. skinflint.

B. (raunị) m. losing heart (= kạrāyạ
2a.i).

C. (raunī) m. (1) suppleness (of
body, twig, etc.). (2) (a) yā kai ~
he bent backwards touching the ground
with his hands. (b) yā kai raunin
dịrē he turned his body to form a
bow, resting on hands and feet (cf.
dịrē). (3) (a) weakness. (b) lg̣bārịn
nạŋ ~ gạrēshị this is a doubtful report.
(4) cīwọ yan̄ạ raunịŋ watạ the disease
thought cured recurs monthly. (5)
raunịŋ karā type of children's game.

raunō = jan raunō.

raunukạ Vd. rạụnī.

rau-rau A. (rau-rau) = rau.

B. (rạu-rạu) used in idạnsạ yā yi ~
(1) his eyes filled with tears. (2) his
eyes were starting out of his head with
eagerness.

raurawa A. (rạụrawạ) Vb. 3B (1) quivered
x rēshḕ yan̄ạ ~ the branch is swaying.
(2) (a) zūcịyassạ tan̄ạ ~ he's terrified.
(b) gg̣rī yā ~ the town was panic-
stricken. (3) (a) became emaciated.
(b) (money) became reduced. (c)
(intelligence) became blunted.

B. (raurạwā) Vb. 1C caused to
quiver x yā raurạwạ rạŋ kōwā he
terrified everyone.

raurawad dạ Vb. 4 caused to quiver, etc.,
as in rạụrawạ.

rạụrayạ Kt. = rạirayạ.

rausa A. (rausạ) Vb. 1A did abundantly
x (1) yā ~ itg̣cē ạ wuta he piled wood
on the fire. (2) sun ~ murnạ they were
overjoyed. (3) sun ~ karọ they collided.
yā ~ kg̣i dạ baŋgō he banged his head
against the wall. yā ~ kūkā he cried
out. (4) Vd. ạ rausạ.

B. (rausā) Sk. yā ~ tạ he divorced
her (= Sk. rabad dạ).

rausạsā = tausạsā.

rạusayạ f. (1) swaying (of body, branches,
etc.). (2) swaggering (1, 2 = rạŋwadạ).

raushe A. (rạushē) m. = ạ rausạ.

B. (raushḕ) (1) Vb. 1A yā ~ kg̣i
he banged his head (cf. rausạ 3). (2)
Vb. 3A yā ~ dạ kūkā he cried out
(= rausạ 3).

C. (raushē) Vd. rau dạ.

raushi A. (raushị) m. (1) two persons

mutually hitting palms of right hands together in enjoyment of remark, joke. (2) mutual enjoyment of conversation, friendship (2 = anọ 1).
  B. (rạushī) *m.* hot, fine ash (= ribidī).
  C. (raushī) *m.* = laushī.
rautā *Kt.* = raftā.
rawā *m.*, *f.* (*pl.* rạ'ye-rạyē") (1) (*a*) (i) dancing, a dance. (ii) Jāmụs sun yi mukụ kiɗạ, kunā̀ rawā ạ gabạs the Germans incited you to attack the east. (iii) sun sauyạ rawā they've changed their policy. (iv) yạu dạ gọbe, jībi gwạnin rawā yā̀ fādị pride comes before a fall. (v) sunā̀ ta ∼ they are dancing, jubilating. (*b*) dạ mugunyạr ∼ gāra ƙin tāshị it's best to leave well alone. (*c*) yā kwā̀shi ∼ he danced for joy (*Vd.* kwā̀sā 1*h*). (*d*) kyạn ∼ ạ kai tạ magānā don't hide your light under a bushel ! (*e*) yanā̀ ∼, nāmansạ nā̀ jạkā he has nothing to worry about. (*f*) (i) yanā̀ ∼ dạ ƙafạr wani he lives on reflected glory. (ii) *Vd.* bạzā 2. (*g*) iŋ kā ga mụtụm yanā̀ ∼ ạ kā̀sūwā, bā̀ ran naŋ ya fāra ba habit is second nature. (*h*) magā̀ rawar wani, gā̀ tākạ those who live in glass houses should not throw stones. (*j*) bā ā̀ yịn ∼ bā̀ jūyị you can't make bricks without straw. (*k*) *Vd.* jēlē, shigẹ 2*b*.ii. (*l*) ∼ ƙasạ *Vd.* ƙasā 6. (2) (*a*) drilling. (*b*) rawar dājị manœuvres. (3) trembling *x* (*a*) (i) rawar ɗārī trembling with cold. (ii) jịkinsạ yā ɗạuki ∼ he's trembling (= rawar jịkī). (*b*) haƙōrīna yanā̀ ∼ my tooth is loose. (*c*) azzịkinsạ yanā̀ ∼ his luck is on the wane. (4) *Vd.* rawar-compounds.
rawad dạ *Vb.* 4 = rau dạ.
rawad dūnīyạ = rawar dūnīyạ.
rawạncē *Vb.* 1C finished off (top of mudwall or sōrō *as in* rawạnī 3*a*, *b*).
rawạnci *Vd.* rạwantạ.
rawạnī *m.* (*pl.* rawunā̀ = *Kt.* rawunnā̀) (1) (*a*) (i) turban. (ii) yā ajịyẹ rawạnī he has resigned office. (iii) yā ajịyẹ wạ Sarkī rawạnī he sent in his resignation to the chief. (iv) yā warwạrẹ rawunạnsụ he dismissed them from

office. (v) sun tū6ẹ rawạniŋ wazircị dạgạ kạnsạ they deposed him from being prime minister. (vi) Sarkī yā ƙwācẹ rawạninsụ the chief dismissed them from office. (*b*) yā cirẹ ∼ = yā tū6ẹ ∼ he took off his turban. (*c*) girmaŋ kā̀i, rawạniŋ ƙyā̀sūwā pride comes before a fall. (*d*) kallạbī tsạkānin rawunā̀ she's a woman who is as skilful as many a man (= mạcẹ̄ 8). (2) any official appointed by an Emir (= bạsarākẹ). (3) (*a*) top of compound-wall. (*b*) an jā wạ sōrō ∼ = kalaŋkūwā 5*a*.
rạwantạ *Vb.* 2 (*p.o.* rạwạncē, *n.o.* rạwạnci) = rawạncē.
rawar dạ *Vb.* 4 = rau dạ.
rawar dūnīyạ *f.* earthquake.
rawar gạbaŋ hạntsī = rawar hạntsī *f.* used in yā kaŋ hanạ minị ∼ he gives me no peace.
rawar idọ *f.* quivering of one's eyelid (*considered to be sign of arrival of stranger; women wet blade of grass and place it on the eyelid to prevent it quivering*).
rawar jịkī *f.* trembling *x* yā shịga ∼ = yanā̀ ∼ he's trembling (= rawā 3*a*.ii).
rawar ƙafạ *f.* used in bā nā̀ ∼ dạ ạbīna I'll find a purchaser all right.
rawar kā̀i *f.* (1) quivering with eagerness. (2) (*a*) shaking one's head when speaking. (*b*) Paralysis agitans. (3) going elsewhere than the place whither one was sent.
rawar kuryā *Vd.* kuryā 2.
rawar zūcị̄yā *f.* palpitation of the heart.
rā̀wayạ (1) *f.* (*a*) the shrub *Cochlospermum tinctorium* whose yellow root yields dye (= zạbībị = kyạmbā). (*b*) yellow dye from 1*a* (= zạbībị). (*c*) yellow-colour. (2) *m.*, *f.* (*pl.* rā̀wayōyī = rā̀wạyū) *adj.* yellow *x* (*a*) rā̀wayạn rawạnī yellow turban. rā̀wayạr rīgā̀ yellow gown (2 = 'yarạnī). (*b*) yā halịccē sụ rā̀wayạ = yā halịccē sụ rā̀wạyū God created them yellow.
rā̀wạyē *m.* (1) repairing old hoe-blade with fresh metal (*cf.* rạmbạɗē, rēwạyē 2). (2) hoe repaired *as in* 1.
rāwukạ *Vd.* rā̀i.
rawunạ *Vd.* rawạnī.

raya A. (rāyą) gave life to x (1) **Allā yą** ~ **shi** (*a*) may God give him long life ! (*b*) may God cause him (child) to grow up ! (*c*) may God resurrect him ! (*d*) may God restore him to health ! (2) (*a*) (rain) revived (drooping plant). (*b*) **kąsūwā tā** ~ **gąrin nąŋ** the market has restored the languishing trade of this town. (3) re-erected (collapsed building). (4) *Vd.* **rāyu**.

     B. (rayą) *used in the following* (1) **dągą bana bą kyā** ~ **ba** (*in song addressed to girl soon to be married*) your dancing-days are over ! (2) *Vd.* **kądą** 1*n*, **jēlē**.

rāyąt (*Eng.* right) *m.* **an sā** ~ it has been ticked as correct (*cf.* **ēkįs**).

rayau x **yā būshę** ~ it has become quite dry.

rąye x **kō ą rąye, kō ą mące** *adv.* alive or dead.

rąye-rąyē *Vd.* **rawā**.

rāyį = **rāi**.

rāyu *Vb.* 3B prospered x **ąlbasą bą zā tą** ~ **ba sãi ą ląmbū** onions do not prosper except in irrigated plots (*Vd.* **rāyą**). **sun rāyu cikin shēkąrųn nąŋ** they lived safely through those years.

rāyuką *Vd.* **rāi**.

razana A. (rāząnā) *Vb.* 1C terrified.

     B. (rāzaną) (1) *Vb.* 3B became terrified. (2) *f.* terror.

rāzanad dą *Vb.* 4 = **rāząnā**.

rāząnī *m.* terror.

rāząnzaną *Vb.* 3B kept on becoming terrified.

Rāzdąŋ *Eng. m.* Resident of a Province.

razga A. (rązgā) *Vb.* 2 snapped off much (x sugar-cane, cassava, branches, crunchable food, etc.).

     B. (razgą) *Vb.* 1A **yā** ~ **itącē ą wutą** he put much wood on the fire (= **gabzą** 3).

razgę *Vb.* 1A (1) snapped off all the large amount available (*Vd.* **rązgā**). (2) burned up all the large amount of wood available (*cf.* **razgą**).

rę *Vd.* **jēlē**.

rēbū *Sk. m.* meat from side of cow, sheep, goat, etc.

rędā *Vb.* 2 (1) = **rįdā**. (2) *Sk.* ground (= **niką**).

reda A. (rēdą) (1) (*with rolled* " r ", M.G. 5) *Vb.* 3A went away. (2) (*with cerebral* " r ") *Vb.* 1A = **rędā** 2.

     B. (rędā) *Vb.* 2 (*Vd.* **rīdą**) (1) pared x **an rędi bąkiŋ kwaryā** shavings have been pared from the calabash. (2) (*a*) **an rędi nāmą jįkim fātą** (**kąshī**) meat has been scraped from the hide (bone). (*b*) **an rędi nāmą** meat has been cut off in thin, broad strips to make **kiļįshī** (= **yanyąnā** 3).

rēdę *Vb.* 1A *Sk.* ground all of (*cf.* **rędā**).

rēdę *Vb.* 1A (1) = **rędā**. (2) cut all (the meat) into strips (*cf.* **rędā** 2*b*).

rędūwā *f.* part of branch which is too weak to bear weight of P. (= **bį ni ką lālącē** 1).

refata A. (rēfątā) *Vb.* 1C (1) dipped out small amount of (corn, water, etc.). (2) **yanā rēfątāwā** he's eking out his supplies (= **cancąnā**).

     B. (rēfątą) *Vb.* 2 (*p.o.* **rēfącē**, *n.o.* **rēfąci**) = **rēfątā** 1.

rega A. (rēgą) (1) *Vb.* 1A (*Vd.* **rīgą**) (1) (*a*) shook (corn, rice, etc.) with water to rid it of sand, etc. (*b*) *Sk.* peeped into (= **lēką**). (2) **Na rēgą** *Vd.* **Dōzą, cīzǫ** 3.

     B. (rēgā) *Vb.* 2 shook part of (*cf.* **rēgą** 1*a*).

rēgądā *Vb.* 3A went away.

rēgargądī *m.* going by roundabout way (*cf.* **gēwąyē**).

rēgę *Vb.* 1A shook all of (*cf.* **rēgą** 1*a*).

rēkē-rēkē (*Ar.* raqīqi) slender x **tanā dą wuyą** ~ she has a slender neck.

rēmā *m.* (*pl.* **rēmąyē**) (1) coney, hyrax (= **agwadā**). (2) **bunsurun** ~ *m.* male hyrax. (2) *Vd.* **cįŋ kūkąr** ~.

rena A. (rēną) *Vb.* 1A (1) (*a*) despised x **yā** ~ **ni** = **yā** ~ **minį** he despised me. (*b*) **idǫ yā** ~ **fātą** he's landed himself in trouble. (2) **ąbin nąŋ rēną kąmā nę** this is better than it looked. (3) **kōwā ya rēną gąjērē bąi tāką kunāmą ba nę** one learns from experience. (4) " **Idǫ, wā ka rēną** ". " **wandą nikē ganī yąu dą gǫbe** " familiarity breeds contempt. (5) **rēną aikįm macįyī ; kō yā yī, ząi cįnyē nę** he eats up more than the value of his work. (6) **mąi rēną kądaŋ, ɓąrāwǫ nē** ungrateful P. is like thief. (7) rę̄ną girmaɲ kūką ; gaɓarūwā tā fī tą don't place good on a level with evil ! (8) kōwā ya rę̄ną tsayą̄war watą, yą hau yą gyārą shi don't criticize if you cannot remedy ! (9) kōwā ya rę̄ną maį lą̄bārį, iɲ kā ga wani nǎ gudụ, shī nę̄ he who spurns advice will be the first to suffer. (10) in nā rę̄ną ką̄zā, kō rōmantą bā nǎ sǫ *(said by woman)* what a horrible kīshįyā I have to put up with ! (11) kōwā ya rę̄ną mǫtsiɲką, yą̄ yi kūkā never underrate a person's potentialities ! (12) *Vd.* ƙūrụ. (13) hakįn dą ka ~ *Vd.* tsōkąnē 1*b.*

B. (rę̄nā) *Vb.* 2 looked after (child, animal, etc.), *Vd.* rąinō.

rēnį *m.* (1) (*a*) contempt. (*b*) yā ciką ~ he's arrogant (= shąƙawą). (*c*) *Vd.* dūban ~. (*d*) (i) są̄baɲ idǫ shī kę̄ sǎ ~ familiarity breeds contempt (*Vd.* kallō 1*c*). (ii) *Vd.* wą̄sā 1*p.* (2) yā kēcę ~ he had a jolly good time. (3) sąukā ~ *Vd.* tsīgī 3*a.*

rę̄nō = rąinō.

rēnūwā *f.* (1) being discontented with smallness of a gift. (2) = rūwā B9.

rērą *Vb.* 1A (1) sun ~ wāƙą they raised a song. (2) *Vd.* shą̄fa mụ ~.

rę̄rai *Kt.* = rą̄irąyī.

rę̄raɲ = rę̄ras *adv.* taking up much space *x* gidąjē, gǎ su caɲ ~ there are the compounds spread about over there ! yā fādį ~ he fell sprawling. sunǎ kwąnce ~ they're lying sprawled out.

rere A. (rērę) (1) *m.* (*a*) friendly chat. (*b*) *Vd.* tąfī dą rērę. (2) what a lie ! B. (rę̄rę) *Vd.* ƙyę̄rę̄rę.

*rę̄rētō *m.* = lallāshī.

rę̄rēyą = rą̄irayą.

rę̄rō *m.* (1) long hair hanging from ram's chin (*cf.* lāyuɲ awākī). (2) maį ~ *m.* game like Fox-and-geese.

rēshę *m.* (*pl.* rąssā = rēshiną = *Kt.* rąssū) (1) branch. (2) yā ƙurę ~, wǎ ząi bā shi tsānį he's got into a fix of his own accord and must get himself out as best he can. (3) yā yaɲkō minį ~ he got me into trouble (= ɓazgā 2), *Vd.* yąɲkā 1*a.*ii. (4) *Vd.* shiką rēshę. (5) sąuka ta ~ *Vd.* hawā 1*a.*vii. (6) gidaɲką ą ~ *Vd.* ƙūlumī.

rę̄tau *adv. and m.* yanǎ ~ = yanǎ yāwǫ ~ he's wandering aimlessly.

rētǫ *m.* (1) (*a*) dangling, swinging (= līlǫ = shillǫ). (*b*) yā ga ~ kusa da ƙasǎ he mistakenly thought T. cheap. (2) (*a*) going hither and thither (= ką̄iwā dą kāwǫwā). (*b*) yā shā ~ he was sent hither and thither.

rę̄wai = rę̄tau.

rewaye A. (rēwąyē) (1) *Vb.* 3B (*a*) put up with *x* mą̄ ~ haką we'll put up with it thus. (*b*) = gyāząjē 1. (2) *Vb.* 1C (*a*) repaired (old hoe-blade with fresh metal), *cf.* rą̄wąyē. (*b*) *Kt.* = yanyąnā 1–3.

B. (rę̄wąyē) = rą̄wąyē.

rị *x* sun tāshį ~ they left in a body.

riba A. (rībą) *f.* (*pl.* rībącē-rībącē) (*Ar.* ribh) (1) (*a*) (i) money-profit (*this is legal by Muslim law, whereas rįbā 1 is illegal ; to cloak illegality, it is often called* kyąutā). (ii) yā jāwō minį ~ it was profitable to me. (iii) ~ maį mǎį rich profit. (iv) ąbįɲ yā ƙi rībą the matter turned out badly. (v) rībą tasą tā kōmą fādụwā his profit became loss. (vi) Allǎ yą kōrō ~ *Vd.* Allǎ 7. (vii) *Vd.* sārį 2. (viii) rībą kim fi ūwǎ *Vd.* arugumą. (*b*) advantage. (*c*) yā ci ~ he got (i) profit, (ii) advantage. (*d*) cin ~ *Vd.* rigē 2. (2) rībar ƙafą. kūrā tā tāką kwą̄dō even the smallest advantage is useful. kā yi rībar ƙafą. kūrā tā tāką kwą̄dō you've had an unexpected piece of luck. (3) bīyąm bukātą yā fi cin ~ fulfilment of wishes is better than profit.

B. (rįbā) (*Ar.* ribh) *f. x* yā ci ~ (1) he charged interest on the money = rōmō 3 (*Vd.* rībą 1*a*). (2) he dishonestly sold T. not yet paid for.

riɓa A. (riɓą) *Vb.* 1A (1) = ruɓą. (2) (*d.f.* riɓį) multiplied T. *x* ką ~ ukụ gōmą multiply 3 by 10 ! ząi ~ miɲ shī he will double it for me (= niɲką 4) (3) exceeded by so-and-so many times ; sōjansụ sun ~ nāmụ shidą = niɲkạ 3 *q.v.* sun riɓą mu yawą they outnumbered us. sun riɓą nāmụ sąu dạ yawą they far outnumber us. yawansụ yā riɓą yawąmmụ they exceed us in numbers. (4) *cf.* riɓąnyā.

B. (rįɓa) = rųɓa.

riɓaɓɓąnyā *Vb.* 1D *intensive from* riɓąnyā.

rįɓā̧bē *m.* (1) superficially-healed sore.
(2) yā yi minį ∼ he defrauded me. (3)
Sk. nearly-ripe fruit.

ribace A. (rīɓącē) *Vb.* 1C = rįɓatą.
B. (rįɓącē) *Vd.* rįbatą.

rįɓące-rįɓącē *Vd.* rīɓą.

rįɓąci *Vd.* rįbatą.

*ribādī *Kt.* = *ribātsī.

rįɓāgo (1) *m.* anything stinking. (2)
what a stink !

rībąncē = rībącē.

rįbantą = rįbatą.

riɓąnyā *Vb.* 1C (*d.f.* riɓį) (1) = gwāmą 1*a.*
(2) repeated *x* yā bā nį kyąutā, yā
kumą riɓąnyāwā he gave me a present,
then another. (3) folded (= riɓįyā).
(4) = riɓą 2, 3.

riɓąnyē *Vb.* 1C = riɓąnyā.

rįbatą *Vb.* 2 (*p.o.* rįɓącē, *n.o.* rįɓąci) got
the better of P.

rįɓataccē *m.* (*f.* rįɓątaccīyā) *pl.* rįɓątąttū
(1) prisoner of war (= ką̄mammē 1*a*).
(2) evil P.

*ribātsī *Ar.* *m.* awaiting attack on the
alert, being on outpost duty.

ribcę (1) *Vb.* 1A (*a*) = k̄āk̨umē. (*b*)
= cafę 2. (2) *Vb.* 3A became deeply
involved *x* (*a*) sun ∼ dą kōkawą they
(wrestlers) are in a clinch. (*b*)
sun ∼ dą fadą they're involved in
a serious quarrel. (*c*) idąnsą yā
∼ dą kūkā tears are pouring from
his eyes. idąnsą yā ∼ dą hayāk̄ī his
eyes are watering from the smoke.
(*d*) k̄afąssą tā ribcę his foot is badly
ulcerated (*cf.* gyąmbō). (*e*) (i) gąrī
yā ∼ the town is poverty stricken. (ii)
gąrī yā ∼ = gąrī yā ∼ dą rūwā storm
is following on storm. (*f*) yā ∼ dą
kūkā he burst out crying, burst into a
shout (*Vd.* fashę 1*b*).

ribɗa A. (rībɗą) (1) *Vb.* 1A (*a*) did much
of *x* yā ∼ gidā he built a large compound. yā ∼ bindigą he fired the gun
loudly. (*b*) = rįbɗā 1*d.* (*c*) (*with
dative*) applied much of *x* an ∼ masą
wuk̄ā· he has been deeply stabbed.
an ∼ masą sąndā he's been severely
thrashed with a stick. an ∼ masą
sātą he's been victim of serious robbery.

an ∼ masą zāgį he's been much abused.
(2) *Vb.* 3A (*a*) took to one's heels
(= shēk̄ą). (*b*) = rūshę 2*a.*
B. (rįbɗā) (1) *Vb.* 2 (*a*) demolished,
caused to collapse (= rūshę 1). (*b*)
yā rįbɗē nį dą k̄afą he kicked me
severely. yā rįbɗē nį dą sąndā he
beat me severely. (*c*) ate much of. (*d*)
an rįbɗi hatsī much corn has been
pounded (for furā). (2) *f.* yā shā ∼
he has been severely beaten.

ribdā-rįbɗą̄ *Vd.* ribɗēdę.

rįbɗayyą *f.* severely striking each other.

ribɗę (1) *Vb.* 1A. (*a*) = ribɗą 1*c x* an ∼
shi dą wuk̄ā. (*b*) = rįbɗā 1*a.* (2) *Vb.*
3A. (*a*) = rūshę 2*a.* (*b*) wurī yā ∼
dą k̄anshī = gųma.

ribɗēdę *m.* (*f.* ribɗēdįyā) *pl.* ribɗā-
rįbɗą̄ tall and broad, long and broad.

ribɗį (1) *m.* (*a*) first pounding of corn
(*Vd.* daką). (*b*) *epithet is* Gą̄rin gąyyā.
(2) (*a*) what a large amount ! (*b*) what
a severe thrashing ! (etc., *as in* ribɗą).

riɓe *Vd.* ruɓe.

ribga A. (rįbgā) *Vb.* 2 *Kt.* = dōk̄ā 2*a.*i.
B. (ribgą) *Vb.* 1A *Kt.* = dōk̄ą 2.

ribgēgę = dibgēgę.

riɓį *m.* (1) (*a*) thickness of cloth when
more than one thickness is present *x* ∼
uk̨u threefold (= ninkį), *cf.* falan. (*b*)
fold *x* kōmē ya yi minį, sāi n̄ yi masą
riɓinsą whatever he does to me (good
or bad), I'll outdo him in return (*cf.*
riɓą). (*c*) ∼ dą ∼ = *Kt.* ∼ dą bank̨į =
ninkįm bą ninkįn̄ *q.v.* (2) fermenting
(of indigo, shea-nuts, dąddawā, etc.)
(= nuko), *Vd.* ruɓą 1.

rįbibī *m.* (1) (*a*) clamouring for *x* ang̈
rįbįbin hatsī people are clamouring
round the corn to buy it. sung̈ ta
rįbibin sāmō shi they're clamouring to
get it. (*b*) k̄asarsų tā fādą rįbįbī their
country became involved in insurrec-
tion. (2) crowd *x* yā shiga ∼ he
entered the crowd.

ribidī *m.* (1) = rąushī. (2) pounded flour.

rįɓinjī *m.* (1) glut *x* hatsī yā yi ∼ there
is a glut of corn. (2) wastrel (= ragō).
(3) ragged garment.

riɓis = ruɓus.

riɓįyā *Vb.* 1C folded (= ninką 1*a*), *cf.*
riɓą, riɓąnyā 3.

ribiyĕ = niŋkę.

ribje A. (ribję) (1) Vb. 1A. (a) pushed forcibly. (b) hit x yā ∼ shi dą sąndā. (c) abused. (d) collided with. (2) Vb. 3A = rūshę 2a.
B. (ribjē) Vd. ribzā.

ribkā (1) Vb. 2 = cafę 2. (2) f. yā kai masą ∼ he clutched it (moving object, animal, etc.).

ribkę Vb. 1A = cafę 2.

ribshī m. = raushī.

ribtą Vb. 1A = ribcę 2a x sun ∼ kŏkawą.

ribza A. (ribzā) Vb. 2 (p.o. ribjē, n.o. ribji) = ribję 1.
B. (ribzą) (1) Vb. 3A = rūshę 2a. (2) Vb. 1C x yā ∼ karo dą shī he collided with him (= ribję 1d). yā ∼ masą sąndā = ribję 1b.

*ricā = kwatsąm.

ricīcī Kt. = rītsītsī.

ridą A. (rīdā) Vb. 2 grabbed at x yā rīdi kāzā he clutched at the hen (= wą̄warą).
B. (rīdą) f. (1) clutching at x yā kai wą kązā ∼ = rīdā. (2) loitering about (to seize an opportunity, to steal, etc.).
C. *(ridą) f. = kąragą.

rīdą (1) (with cerebral " r ", Mod. Gram. 5) f. (secondary v.n. from rĕdā) x yaną rīdąr fātą = yaną rĕdar fātą he is paring the leather. (2) (with rolled " r ") yā ∼ ni dą ƙasā he felled me (= kā dą).

rīdad dą Vb. 4 = rīdą 2.

riddā Ar. (1) f. apostasy x yā yi ∼ (a) he apostasized. (b) he became perverted. (2) Vb. (used only in this form). (a) apostasized. (b) became converted to some new custom x 'yam mātā sun ∼ gą shąn sigārį girls have taken to smoking.

riddad dą Vb. 4 (1) caused to become an apostate. (2) perverted.

ridaddē = ridajjē m. (f. ridaddīyā = ridajjīyā) pl. ridąddū apostate.

rīdī m. (1) (a) the white-flowered beniseed Sesamum indicum (Vd. nōmę 3, kantų). (b) rīdim bąrēwā the wild Sesamum alatum. (c) Vd. dąskin dą ∼ ; ɗaurin ∼. (2) (a) type of native-made cloth. (b) rīdiŋ kado = rīdiŋ kadą another type.

rididdigā Vb. 1D seriously tore (garment), Vd. rididdigĕ.

rididdigĕ Vb. 3A (1) (garment) became seriously torn, ragged. (2) became shattered. (3) (fruit) rotted: (4) (meat) became over-cooked.

ridįdī x suną gudų ∼ they're running away in a body.

ridī-didī = ridįdī.

rididī-didįdī x sun dikąkē shi rididīdidįdī they attacked him en masse.

ridī-rįdī adj. pl. huge x awākī ∼ huge goats.

rif adv. (1) yā rufę ∼ it is fully shut. (2) as many as x dųbi ƙwaŋ kązāta har ukų ∼ look, my hen has laid as many as three eggs ! tarą ris a full nine. (3) Vd. dąki ∼.

rifa = rufa .

rifcę = ribcę.

rifka = ribka.

rifshī = ribidī.

riftą = ribtą.

riga A. (rīgā) f. (pl. rīguną = rīgunōnī). (1) (a) (i) man's gown (cf. tagūwā 1). (ii) rīgar rūwā mackintosh. (b) (i) woman's garment as in tagūwā 2. (ii) tā sąmi — Vd. sōrō 3. (c) (i) yā są ∼ = yā są ∼ ą wuyą he put on a gown. (ii) yā cirę ∼ = yā kwaɓę ∼ = yā tūɓę ∼ he took off his gown. (d) ūwar ∼ f. body of gown. (e) fuskąr ∼ f. embroidery on front of gown. (f) ∼ taną dą hannū the gown is symmetrical. (g) kąmar hannun rīgā sukę they are exactly alike (Vd. hannun 7). (gg) shiriŋ hannun ∼ Vd. shiri 5. (h) Mai ∼ name for child born with a caul (Vd. rīgar haifųwā). (j) in ząmānį yā diŋką ∼, yā kąmātą ą saką one must bow to fate. (k) (i) rīgar Sarkī Government uniform (x of police, soldiers), cf. fariŋ kāyā. (ii) Sarkī yā shiga rīgā tasą the Chief is riding mounted among his horsed bodyguard. (iii) rīgar Sarkī, dōkį an Emir is surrounded by horsemen. (l) darē rīgar mūgų Vd. darē. (m) Gwāzā, rīgarkī ɗayā you, though welloff, never wear two gowns at once as others do ! (n) ∼ cę marąr wuyą, iŋ kā ga tā yi maką dăidăi, săi ką są ą wuyą " if the cap fits, wear it ! "

(*said when in reply to* habaicĩ, *person* asks " are you referring to *me* ? "). (*o*) im mutum yã cę zai bã ka ⁓, dūbą ta wuyąnsą if a P. makes you a promise, watch how he treats others ! (*p*) wani dą tūsą, wani dą karɓar ⁓ *Vd.* tūsą 3. (*q*) azzikĩ bã ⁓ ba, ballē 'yaŋūwã su tūɓę prosperity entails responsibilities = azzikĩ rĩgar kayą (*Vd.* azzikĩ 1*e*). (*r*) ⁓ farã bã tą bã 'yarūwã tatą shūnĩ don't lord it over your equals ! (*s*) kõinã mai huntū (= mai arõ) zã shi, dą sanim mai ⁓ he who pays the piper calls the tune. (*t*) (i) dą ą kwãcę yãrǫ ⁓, gãra ą jã, tą kēcę it's better for a thing to become spoiled than for it to be taken from you and given to another. (ii) dą ɓatan rĩgã *Vd.* ɓatą 2*b*. (*u*) rĩgã mãganin ciki dą mãrą *Vd.* mãrą 2*b*. (v) iŋ aŋ ki mąrãyą dą rĩgar būzū, wata rãnã sãi ą gan shi dą ta karfę don't despise poor P., for one day he may be richer than you ! (*w*) (i) *Vd.* daɓǫ 2. (ii) rĩgar daɓansą tã kēcę he has been "rumbled" (*cf.* daɓǫ). (*x*) rĩgar laifĩ, dą mã bã diŋką takę dą wuyã ba, sãwã nobody admits to a crime. (*y*) bã yã tūɓę mini ⁓ *Vd.* mutum 9*k*. (*z*) *Vd.* shamągē. (*z*) (i) fuską mai sai dą ⁓ *Vd.* fuską 5. (*z*) (ii) *Vd.* rĩgar-compounds. (*z*) (iii) *Vd.* ąɓąkwą 2. (2) skin of edible bird (*x* chicken, ostrich ; *for animal* fãtą *is used*).

B. (rĩgą) *f.* (*secondary v.n. from* rēgą) *x* yaną rĩgar hatsĩ = yaną rēgą hatsĩ he's shaking corn *as in* rēgą *q.v.*

C. (rĩgã) *Vb.* (*used only in this form*). (1) *transitive* (*a*) preceded *x* (i) yã ⁓ mu zūwą he came before we did. (ii) yã ⁓ nūnã it was the first to ripen. (iii) tã ⁓ mijintą *Vd.* ąɓu 5*f.* (iv) kõwã ya ⁓ ki hawã *Vd.* wutã 1*a*. (*b*) arrived at before P. *x* (i) yã ⁓ tą gõnã he arrived at the farm before her. (ii) kadą ą rĩgã mu mashigi lest we be forestalled. (2) (*intransitive*) already *x* (*a*) yã ⁓ yã tąfi he has (had) already gone. an ⁓ am fãrą = an ⁓ fãrąwã they have (had) already begun. bą ą ⁓ am fãrą ba = bą a ⁓, bą ą fãrą ba they have (had) not yet begun. (*aa*) *cf.*

yaŋką 1*e*, yãdą 2. (*b*) duk kasąd dą suką rigã, suką kuɓutar every country which they had previously liberated (*cf.* są *construction*, Mod. Gram. 159). (3) rĩgą ta rąŋgwadą *m.* forestalling P. (*x* by asking loan from P. about to ask one for loan). (4) *Vd.* rĩgą kafi ; rĩgą gudu.

D. (rĩgã) (1) *Vb.* (used only in this form) = rigã 2 *x* yã ⁓ yã tąfi he has already gone. (2) = rigã 1*a*.i *x* yã rigē mu zūwą he came before we did. rĩgãgę *m.* forestalling P. (= rigē *q.v.*). rĩgą gudu *Vd.* Bąfilãcę. rigai *Kts.* (1) = rigã. (2) = rigē. rĩgą kafi *m.* (1) (*a*) = kirnĩ. (*b*) in dąŋūwaŋką yaną tunjērē, kai kǫ ką shã ⁓ when trouble befalls your neighbour, look out for yourself ! (2) prevention *x* (*a*) aŋ gãnę dąbãrąssu har aną shan rĩgą kafi they've been " rumbled " and precautions are being taken. (*b*) rĩgą kafim muguntã, rashin yĩ wą wani the best way of preventing evil being done you is not to do it to another. rĩgãną *f.* = madambacĩ. rĩgar " dąfã ni " *Vd.* dąfã ni. rĩgar dõmin-dõmin *Vd.* dõmin-dõmin. rĩgar haifūwã *f.* caul (*Vd.* rĩgã 1*h*). rĩgar kafõ *f.* (1) imaginary gown delicate enough to fit into horn. (2) kǫ yã są ⁓ bą zã tą sõ shi ba no matter what he does, she will never love him. rĩgar kudã *f.* the film between layers of an onion. rĩgar laifĩ *f. used in* ⁓ mai wuyar sãwã nobody will admit himself in the wrong (*Vd.* laifĩ 1*h*). rĩgar mūgu *Vd.* darē. rĩgar mūminai *f.* yã są ⁓ he's a hypocrite. munãfukĩ, ⁓ yakę arõ the hypocrite pretends to be an honest man. rĩgar rūwã *Vd.* rĩgã 1*a*.ii. rĩgar Sarkĩ *Vd.* rĩgã 1*k*. rĩgar uɓã *Kt. f.* a shilling given by bridegroom to guardian (walĩ) of his bride (= rĩgar walĩ). rĩgar walĩ = rĩgar uɓã. rĩgą ta rąŋgwadą *Vd.* rigã 3. rĩgãwã *Zar. f.* = tūrē 5.

rigāyǝ (1) *Vb.* 3B = rigā 2. (2) *Vb.* 2 = rigā 1 *x* yā rigāyē mụ zūwǝ he came before we did.

rigē *m.* forestalling *x* (1) munā ~, mụ kai Kanǫ we're racing along in competition as to which of us will reach Kano first. mụ yi ~ let us try and outrace one another ! (= rigyaŋgyātǫ). yākin rigyan tārǝ mǝkǝ̃mai a war consisting of who is first to amass munitions. (2) rigyaŋ kǝ̃sūwā bǝ̃ shĩ nē̃ cin rĩbǝ ba if T. is fated for you to get, you are bound to get it, not otherwise.

rigēgǝ = rugēgǝ.

rigēgēnĩyā *Sk.* *f.* = rigyaŋgyātǫ.

rigif *adv.* (1) yā dǝfu ~ it is fully cooked. (2) yā tsūfā ~ he is very old.

rigigĩ *used in* kāyā ~ (1) a heavy or bulky load. (2) many loads. (3) *Vd.* rigĩ-rigĩ.

rigijā (1) *f.* (*a*) itǝ̃cē yā yi ~ the tree gives broad, leafy shade. (*b*) yā yi ~ he is wearing many clothes. (2) *adv.* yā fādị̃ ~ he fell with a crash.

rigijim = rigijā.

rigijinjim = rigijā.

rigimǝ *f.* (*pl.* rigimōmĩ = rigimai). (1) uproar, tumult. (2) (*a*) being occupied in noisy task (*x* preparations for feast). (*b*) one's mind being in a whirl (through taking on too many tasks, living beyond one's means, being busy body, etc.).

rigimĩ *m.* = digimĩ.

rigimō *Vb.* 1E bought T. without being able to pay for it.

rigiŋgincē 1) *Vb.* 1D misrepresented what P. said *x* yā ~ ni. (2) *Vb.* 3A (*a*) lay on one's back. (*b*) mǝganǝ tā ~ the matter thought settled has failed to materialize.

rigiŋgine (*noun of state from non-existent* rigiŋginē). (1) (*a*) yanā ~ = ǝ ~ yakē he's lying on his back. (*b*) ǝ ~ yakē kwānā he's a miser. (2) yā gayǝ mini wannǝŋ ǝ ~ he told me this confusedly. (3) *Vd.* bǝbba ~.

rigiŋgintā *Vb.* 1D = rigiŋgintad dǝ.

rigiŋgintad dǝ *Vb.* 4. (1) laid P., etc., on his back. (2) = rigiŋgincē 1.

rigip = rigif.

rigĩ-rigĩ = rigigĩ *x* kadǝ kǝ dauki yākin naŋ ~, kǝ yi tsǝmmāni wani

dibgēgyaŋ karǫ nē̃ akē̃ yĩ do not take this war too seriously and think it is a big campaign !

rigis = rigis *used in* wutā cē̃ ~ it's a blazing fire.

rigizǝ (1) *f.* big sack for corn or groundnuts. (2) *Vd.* ayā.

rĩgōjĩ *Vd.* rĩjĩyā.

rĩgunǝ *Vd.* rĩgā.

rigyā = rigā.

rigyaŋgyātǫ = rigyaŋgyantǫ *m.* = rigē 1 *q.v.*

rigyaŋgyēnĩyā *f.* = rigē 1.

rigyāwā = rigāwā.

rigyāyǝ = rigāyǝ.

rihēwā *Sk.* *f.* = rufēwā.

rija A. (rijā) *Kt.* = rǝjā.

B. (rijā) *x* rijā sǝi gā̃ su sukǝ zō = sǝi rijā sukǝ zō they suddenly came.

rijā-rijā *adv.* danglingly *x* an daukē shi rijā-rijā he was carried along with his body drooping down.

rijau *Eng.* *m.* reserves (military).

rijib = rijif = rijip *adv. and m.* sun rufǝ shi ~ = sun yi masǝ ~ they crowded around him.

rĩjĩyā *f.* (*pl.* rĩjĩyōyĩ = rĩgōjĩ = rĩgōzai = rugōjĩ = *Kt.* rĩyōjĩ). (1) (*a*) well (*cf.* tinyǝ 2). (*b*) (i) figurative trap to catch P. (ii) kōwā ya ginǝ ~ don daŋũ̃wansǝ yǝ fādǝ, shĩ kē̃ fādǝ̃wā cikĩ if you lay a trap for another, you may fall into it yourself (*cf.* 1*e* ; 1*j*). (*c*) yā zurǝ ƙafǝ ǝ ~ he became involved in intrigue (= zubǝ 5). (*d*) (i) ~ tā bā dǝ rūwā, gũgā yā hanǝ the master was generous but his servant intercepted the gift. (ii) rĩjĩyad dǝ bǝ̃ rūwā miser (= marǫ̃wǝcĩ). (iii) mai dǝ rūwā ~ *Vd.* mai dǝ 1*d.* (*e*) bǝ̃ rǝbō ba, ɗaŋ wābị yā fādǝ ~ what bad luck ! (*cf.* 1*b* ; 1*f* ; 1*j*). (*f*) kaŋkụ akē̃ jị, mahaụkǝcĩ yā fādǝ ~ what have *I* to do with what you are saying ! (*cf* 1*e*). (*g*) dǝ rūwan cikĩ a kǝn jā na ~ nothing succeeds like success. (*h*) in tā yi rūwā ~, im bǝ tǝ yi ba, masǝi some use at least will be found for it if unsuited to its present purpose. (*j*) 'yar sadakǝ tā fādǝ ǝ ~ *Vd.* sǝdarrǝdai (*cf.* 1*e above*). (*k*) *Vd.* ǝllūrǝ 9. (*l*) an zarcǝ ~ *Vd.* dabĩnǫ 3. (*m*) haƙan rijiyar Garko *Vd.* garko 3. (2) circular or square " navel " from which radiate each of ƙafa 8*a*.ii. (3) ɗaurin ~ = (*rustic*) gadan ~ ledge formed by lessening width of well. (4) rijiyar hatimi blank space on charm for inserting the wish one wants realized. (5) string-puzzle like cat's cradle.

riƙa A. (riƙa) (1) *Vb.* 1A. (*a*) (i) (*followed by v.n.*) kept on doing (= dinga 1*a*) *x* sǎi ka ~ zūwa keep on coming ! (ii) (*followed by noun*) *x* sun riƙa baƙin ciki they were sad. yā ~ kūkā he kept crying out. (iii) (*followed by noun used as if it were verbal noun*) *x* yā riƙa ɓarnar ƙasā he kept on devastating the land. (iv) Alla ya taimake shi riƙawā God enable him to execute his duties faithfully ! (*b*) held (= riƙe). (*c*) *Kt.* riƙa man nan (*said playfully with raised arm in imitation of jinjina*) greeting, Chief's Son ! (*reply is* yawwā) = *Kt.* tāwa 4 = kāma 7. (*d*) received *x* yā riƙa kwabo he received a penny (= ƙarɓā). (2) *Vb.* 1A tā ~ it (cow, mare, donkey) became pregnant.

B. (riƙa) *Vb.* 3B (*progressive* riƙā). (1) (P. or animal) became full-grown. (2) became prosperous, powerful. (3) (kuɓewā, dumā) became ripe (*cf.* nuna 1).

C. (riƙa) (1) *Vd.* riƙa. (2) *Vb.* 2 (*Vd.* riƙo 1). (*a*) looked after well *x* ya riƙi gidansa he looked well after the inmates of his compound. yā riƙi aikinsa da kyau he paid proper attention to his work (*cf.* riƙo 1). (*b*) supported, nourished (*cf.* riƙo 1). (*c*) (i) was mindful of (advice). (ii) bore in mind (= riƙe 1*c*). (iii) memorized. (*d*) Audu yā riƙe ta wurin ubanta Audu bespoke her (young girl) from her father as his wife for when she would be marriageable (*cf.* rufi 6). nā riƙar wa Audu ita I got her bespoken for Audu as his wife when she should reach marriageable age. (*e*) staked (so-and-so much in gambling), *cf.* riƙo 2.

riƙe A. (riƙe) (1) *Vb.* 1A (*Vd.* riƙo 1) (*a*) (i) held. (ii) nǐ kē ~ ƙafō, wani yanā tātsā I'm merely his catspaw. (iii) im mutum yā cē zai haɗiyi gātari, riƙe masa ƙota if P. makes a ridiculous claim, don't contradict him ! (iv) riƙe karanka don karan gidan wani *Vd.* karē 17. (v) yā riƙe ɓaki he showed surprise. (*aa*) clung to (belief, opinion, etc.) *x* sun riƙe addininsu da gaskiyā they followed their religion perfectly. (*b*) = riƙā 2*b*. (*c*) = riƙā 2*c*, ii. (2) *Vb.* 3A. (*a*) = riƙa. (*b*) *Kt.* became over-ripe.

B. (riƙe) (*noun of state from* riƙe 1*a*, riƙā 2*b, c*) *x* yanā ~ da takōbi he's holding a sword (Mod. Gram. 80*d*.ii). yanā ~ da ubansa he supports his (indigent) father. yanā ~ da gargaɗin ubansa he observes the admonitions of his father.

riƙi (1) *m.* (*a*) beam across corner of room as saddle-support. (*b*) *Zar.* = ruƙunsumai 1. (2) *adv.* yā ɗaukō kāyā ~ what a heavy load he has brought !

rikica *Vd.* cirin.

rikicē *Vb.* 3A (1) (thread, etc.) became tangled (*cf.* zarge 2). (2) (*a*) (P., affair) became confused *x* hankalinsa yā ~ = gurɓacē 2. (*b*) (*followed by dative*) dūnīya tā rikicē mana our affairs are all awry (= rikitō 1*b*). (3) gari yā ~ (*a*) the sky is overcast. (*b*) these are hard times. (4) *cf.* rikitō.

rikici *m.* (1) being tangled *x* igiya tā yi ~ the rope is tangled. (2) intrigue, deceitfulness. (3) *Vd.* mariƙici.

rikiɗa A. (rikiɗā) *Vb.* metamorphosed *x* yā ~ ni kūrā he changed me into a hyena.

B. (rikiɗa) *Vb.* 3B. (1) became metamorphosed into *x* yā ~ kūrā he changed into a hyena. (2) ba ~ kē da wuyā ba, a yi wutsīya it's not hard to begin, but it's hard to finish.

rikiɗad da *Vb.* 4 = rikiɗā.

rikiɗē *Vb.* 3A = rikiɗa.

rikijā = rigijā.

rikijin = rikijā.

rǐkiki *m.* type of small, reddish beads.

rikiki = rigigi.

rikimba = raƙamba.

rikī-rikī = rigigi.

rikirkicē *Vb.* 3A *intensive from* rikicē.

rikirkiɗa *Vb.* 3B *intensive from* rikiɗa.

rikirkita A. (rikirkitā) *Vb.* 1D *intensive from* rikitā.

B. (rįkįrkitą) *Vb.* 3B *intensive from* rįkitą.

rikita A. (rikįtā) *Vb.* 1C. (1) tangled (thread, rope, etc.). (2) muddled up (affair). (3) (*a*) yā rikįtą maganą he introduced deceit into the matter. (*b*) yā ∽ yā sąmi dōkį he got a horse by fraud. (4) *Vd.* rikitō.
B. (rįkitą) *Vb.* 3B. (1) = rikįcē. (2) maganą tā rikitar the matter is puzzling.
rikitad dą *Vb.* 4 = rikįtā.
rikitar *Vd.* rįkitą.
rikitībą *used in* wannąŋ rōmō ∽ what rich gravy ! (= ritībą).
rikitō (1) *Vb.* 3A (*a*) fell down from height. yākį yā rikitō dą sū the war went ill with them (= rikįcē 2*b*). (2) *Vb.* 1E = rigimō. (3) *cf.* rikįcē, rikįtā.
rikizā *Kt. f.* any large, thick, ragged gown.
rikǫ *m.* (1) (*secondary v.n. of* rikę, rįkā) *x* yaną rikwąnsą = yaną rikę shi he's holding it. yaną rikwąŋ (= rįkar) aikįnsą dą kyau he's paying proper attention to his work. yaną rikwąn sha'ąnim mulkįnsų he's in charge of governing them (*Vd.* rįkā 2*a*). dą ganimmų sǎi suką cę '' muną rikǫ '' on seeing us they said '' we're close behind you to support you '' (*cf.* rįkā 2*c*). (2) gambling-stake *x* rikwąnsą kwabǫ ukų he has staked threepence (*cf.* rįkā 2*e*). (3) yā sąmi ∽ he has obtained an official position (= sąrautą 1*b*). (4) yaną rikǫna he bears me malice. (5) (*a*) tūwan ∽ *m.* paste used by leatherworkers. (*b*) daŋkwąn ∽ *Vd.* daŋkǫ 7.
rim A. (rįm) *adv. and m.* (1) suną zaune ∽ they're sitting silent and despondent. gidansą yā yi ∽ his household is enveloped in silence and gloom through illness or grief there. (2) yā fādį ∽ it (house, horse, etc.) fell with a crash.
B. (rįm) (1) *adv.* = rįm 2. (2) *m.* (*a*) nā ji ∽ I heard a crash (caused by a fall, explosion, etc.). (*b*) gidansą yā yi ∽ his compound is crowded with buildings.
rima A. (rįmā) *f.* (1) = laimą 1. (2) Rįmā ką dą baŋgō what a deceitful person ! (nąsō 1*b*), *Vd.* sąndī. (3) matąką yārǫ ∽ *Vd.* bąsarākę.

B. (rimą) *Vb.* 3A (1) (wind, temper, crying, etc.) subsided (= kwąntā). (2) had a nap.
rįmą fādą = rųmą fādą.
rįmānā = rųmānā.
rīmąyē *Vd.* rīmī.
rimcī *Kt.* = runtsī.
rįmfā = rųmfā.
rīmī *m.* (*pl.* rīmąyē) (1) (*a*) (i) White Silk Cotton Tree (*Eriodendron orientale*) from which kapok is obtained (*cf.* gurjīyā). (ii) bā yą hang ∽ tǫhō *Vd.* rānī 1. (*b*) (i) audųgar ∽ *f.* kapok. (ii) Audųgar ∽ fąsu, kōwā yą sāmų what a liberal person ! (iii) *Vd.* gąndįdō. (*c*) gąrī dą ∽, jēmągę bā yą rasą dākįŋ kwānā go the right way to work and you'll realize your desires ! (*d*) Allą yā gyārą ∽, cēdīyā tą bar fushī one must take things as one finds them. (*e*) ąbįn dą bąbba ya ganī yaną kasą, yārǫ kō yā hau ∽, bą ząi gan shį ba young P. has not the judgment of an older P. (2) sun yi ∽ they struggled together. (3) yā yi ∽ (*a*) he rose to his feet in anger or excitement. (*b*) he stood on his hands. (*c*) it (horse) reared up (*c* = tąbaryā 2). (4) type of pattern bitten into cap (*cf.* cīzǫ 2). (5) type of children's game. (6) rīmąyē *pl.* = gǫrubai 2. (6*a*) rīmįŋ gafīyą = 2 *above.* (7) rīmim Masąr thornless type of 1*a above.* (8) rīmin saųrī = rīmin sąmąrī = 5 *above.* (9) *Vd.* Kącallą 2.
rimis *used in* sum būshę ∽ they (leaves, strips of kilishī) are now quite dry.
rįmis-rįmis (1) *m.* noise of food being crunched. (2) *adv.* crunchingly.
rimtsą (1) (*with cerebral* '' r '') = rintsą. (2) (*with rolled* '' r '') *Kt.* = rūtsą.
rina A. (riną) *Vb.* 1A (1) (*a*) dyed with indigo (*cf.* tiri). (*b*) dyed (beard with henna). (2) slandered. (3) (*a*) yą ∽ he's the sort of P. who might have done it (*as in reply to* '' did *Audu* do it ? ''). (*b*) ą riną, an sąci zanąm mahaukacįyā stolen property must ultimately be disgorged.
B. (rinā) *f.* (*sg., pl.*) (1) (*a*) type of hornet. (*b*) gidan ∽ *m.* (i) hornet's-nest. (ii) type of embroidery. (2) dą sauran ∽ ą

kabạ the matter is not yet ended. (3) yā yiwō minị ∼ he " went for me " rinau m. dyeing for wages.

rincā6ē Vb. 3A (1) assumed serious proportions x fadạ yā ∼ the fight became serious (= gāwurtạ). (2) became abundant x 'yā'yā sun ∼ masạ he has many children.

rincā6i how huge !

rindāwā Vd. barinjẹ.

rindị m. (1) = ribdị 1. (2) = kāraukạ.

rindimēmẹ = rindimēmẹ m. (f. rindimēmịyā, etc.) pl. rindiŋ-rindịŋ huge and round.

rindimī = rindimī m. (f. rindimā, etc.) pl. rindiŋ-rindịŋ huge and round.

rindindịŋ = rindindịŋ huge roundness x yanā dạ cikị ∼ he has a huge paunch.

rindiŋ-rindịŋ Vd. rindimēmẹ.

rindumēmẹ = rindimēmẹ.

rindumī = rindimī.

rindundụŋ = rindindịŋ.

inẹ (1) Vb. 1A. (a) dyed all of (cf. rinạ). (b) = rinạ 1b. (2) Vb. 3A (a) idansạ yā ∼ his eyes are inflamed. (b) gabạs tā ∼ the eastern sky is full of storm-clouds.

iŋgāsā f. nā sạmi ∼ I got a bargain, I got it cheap.

iŋgēshē m. (1) = rạŋgwadạ 2. (2) Damagaram Hausa reclining on the elbow (cf. kishiŋgịdē).

iŋgī m. a remainder, surplus (= saurā).

iŋgidī m. (1) = rạŋgwadạ 2. (2) feeling pleasure x anā riŋgidin zūwạnsạ people are pleased that he will come.

iŋgimbạ Kt. f. = rạkambạ.

iŋgimēmẹ = riŋgimī m. (f. riŋgimēmịyā = riŋgimā) pl. riŋgin-riŋgịŋ used in yanā dạ kại ∼ he has a huge head.

ŋgiŋgiŋ used in yanā dạ kại ∼ he has a huge head.

ŋgu = ruŋgu.

ni A. (rinị) m. (1) (a) dyeing with indigo (cf. tirị). (b) rinịn tạ6ō dyeing cotton-yarn with black-earth infusion. (2) Vd. dā 4.
B. (rīnī) Sk. m. = rīmī.

njāyạ (Ar. rajaha) (1) Vb. 3B (a) preponderates, preponderated x na dāma yā ∼ the right-hand pan of the

scale descended. cinikiŋ gyạdā yā ∼ ạ Kanọ Kano specializes in the groundnut trade. wạnẹ cinikī ya fi ∼ ạ Kanọ what's the main trade at Kano ? (b) zūcịyāta tā ∼ kaŋ Kạnde I prefer Kande. (2) Vb. 2 (a) overpowered (= bụwāyạ 2b). (b) persuaded over.

rinjāyayyē m. (f. rinjāyayyīyā) pl. rinjāyạyyū preponderant.

rinjāyẹ m. preponderance x bạ halāmạr ∼ gạ kōwā there was no sign of one side being more powerful than the other.

rinjāyō Vb. 1E = rinjāyạ 2.

rinjẹ = rinzạ.

rinjị (1) m. temporary coiffure as in rinzạ. (2) Vd. barinjẹ, rugā 1b.

riŋkāsō Vb. 3A approached (= gabātō).

riŋkị m. (1) collection (of persons, trees, animals). (2) = ụŋgūwā.

riŋkisō = riŋkāsō.

riŋkyū m. disease of horses and donkeys causing paralysis of ears (= ciŋkau-ciŋkau).

riŋkyū-riŋkyū m. dōkị yā yi ∼ dạ kụnnē the horse put back its ears (through anger, fright, etc.) = kịrū.

rinō m. (1) skewer or two- or three-pronged fork for toasting meat. (2) Jan ∼, ạbiŋ gasạ gīwā epithet of Emir of Kano.

rintọ m. cheating, dishonesty.

rintsạ Vb. 3A x yanā rintsạwā he's sleeping. bari ŋ ∼ I'll go and have a sleep. jīyạ nā kwānā, baŋ ∼ ba I couldn't get to sleep last night. yā sạmi rintsạwā he (sick P., sleepless P.) has managed to get a bit of sleep.

rintsẹ = runtsẹ.

rintsī = runtsī.

rintuma = runtuma.

rinzạ Vb. 1A tā ∼ gāshiŋ (= kaŋ) Kạnde she coiffured Kande's hair temporarily.

rirịcī used in rirịciŋ gūdạ yā fi na kūkā it's better to be happy than sad.

rirịrī Vd. fatattạkā 5.

rirịs adv. yā fādạ aikị ∼ he fell to work with a will. yanā ta kūkā ∼ he's screaming lustily.

rirịtā Vb. 1C eked out.

rirītī m. eagerness (= dōkī).

rirrịkē intensive from rikẹ.

rirriskạ = rụrrufkạ.

ris (1) = rẹ̃raŋ. (2) = rif 2.

Risãlạ f. (1) the standard text-book of Maliki law. (2) Vd. gãfarạ 1c.

ris6ạ = riz6ạ.

rishĩ m. type of canter (= hafsancĩ = zagaraĩtũ q.v.).

rishwạ = rashawạ.

riskã (1) Vb. 2. (a) = ishẹ 1b x nã riskẽ shị ạ Kanọ I found him at Kano. (b) clutched hold of x yã riski kạ̃zã he clutched the hen. (c) was present during x nã riski (= nã riskõ) sạn dạ yakẹ̃ Kanọ I was present at Kano at the same time as he was there. (2) f. yã kai wạ kạ̃zã ⌢ = 1b above.

riskẹ Vb. 1A = riskã 1.

rịs'ke-riskẽ" m. steadily endeavouring to do T. = rụfke-rụfkẽ (cf. rịrriskạ).

rĩtĩ m. = rĩrĩtĩ.

rĩtĩ6ạ f. (1) rich gravy. (2) wannạŋ rõmõ ⌢ what rich gravy!

rits Vd. ritsạ.

ritsạ Vb. 1A hemmed in x (1) an ⌢ shi = an ⌢ dạ shĩ he is hemmed in. an ⌢ su rits they're completely hemmed in. (2) kãmụ yã ritsạ dạ shĩ arrest " cramped his style ".

ritse A. (ritsẹ) Vb. 1A = ritsạ.

B. (rịtsẽ) bã nạ̃ shạn ⌢ (said by warrior) I must not drink at the well from this pot which is not yet full for it will nullify my magic charms (karyạ lãyạ) and expose me to harm from the weapons of my enemies (Vd. karyạ 1d).

ritsĩ-ritsĩ m. odds and ends.

rĩtsĩtsĩ = rindindiŋ.

riya A. (rĩyã) Ar. f. deception, hypocrisy (= munãfucci).

B. (rĩyạ) (Ar. ra'y opinion). (1) came to conclusion that x nã ⌢ dạgạ Kanọ sukạ zõ I concluded that they'd come from Kano. (2) decided x nã ⌢ ŋ yĩ = nã ⌢ zạn yĩ I intend, have decided to do it. (3) falsely claimed that x yã ⌢ yanạ̃ bịna bãshị he falsely asserted that I owe him money (= dạ'ạwã 2).

rĩyạl = rĩyãlị = lịyãrị q.v.

rĩyạ-rĩyạ adv. sun tãshị ⌢ they've gone on a " wild-goose chase ". suŋ kõmõ ⌢ they've returned from a " wild-goose chase ".

rĩyõjĩ Vd. rĩjịyã.

riz6ạ Vb. 3A = rũshẹ 2a.

riz6ẹ Vb. 3A = rũshẹ 2a.

rizgã f. the small edible tuber Plectranthus sp.

rizmạ = Kt. rizimạ Ar. f. (pl. rizmõmĩ) packet of 500 sheets of writing-paper (cf. daŋkạ).

roba A. (rọ̃bã) f. type of tall marsh-grass. B. (rõbạ) (Eng. rubber) f. (1) (a) rubber. (b) india-rubber. (c) tyre. (2) (a) sealing-wax, vulcanite, bakelite, etc. (b) beads or bangles made from 2a. (3) Vd. kạn tạ fargã.

rõcẹ Kt. = rõtsị.

rõdị-rõdị x zanẹ nẽ ⌢ dạ shĩ = zanẹ nẽ mại ⌢ it is a cloth with dense speckled pattern (cf. dabbarẹ-dabbarẹ).

rọ̃ĩõgõ = rạhõgõ.

rõgạjẽ (1) Vb. 3A. (a) melted. (b) (meat, wall, etc.) disintegrated. (2) Vb. 3A caused to melt, disintegrate.

rõgọ m. (1) (a) cassava (= dõyạ 1a.ii), cf. bana 2d; tạibạ; gạntạmau, gũgã 4. (b) for epithet, Vd. jạtau 2b. (2) Kt. rõman ⌢ bạ̃ ka mammõrã what a useless person! (3) rõgwạn dãjị = rõgwạn dawạ = rõgwạn jẽjị (a) type of thick-rooted vine. (b) the wild yam Dioscorea sp. (4) duhụn ⌢ Vd. duhụ 6 (5) Vd. gạsõ rõgọ. (6) ganiŋ kitsẹ akị wạ ⌢ it belies its good appearance.

rõhọ m. (1) yã yi ⌢ (a) it is handsome (b) it tastes good. (2) = nịshãtsị.

rọ̃hõgõ = rạhõgõ.

rọ̃kã Zar. f. (1) conversation. (2) n nạ̃ ⌢ dạ kai I want a word with you.

rokạ A. (rọ̃kã) Vb. 2 (Vd. rõkọ). (1 beseeched, requested x nã rõkẽ shị yạ yĩ I requested him to do it. (2) askeẹ P. for x gạ̃ ạbịn dạ ya rõkã garẽnị thi is what he begged of me. nã rõkẹ shị gõrọ = nã rõkị gõrọ garẽshị asked him for some kola-nut (= rõkạ 1) (3) Vd. marõkĩ.

B. (rõkạ) Vb. 1A (with dative). (1 asked P. for x nã ⌢ masạ gõrọ = rọ̃kã 2. (2) nã ⌢ masạ I prayed for hir (3) asked for T. for P. x nã rõkạ masạ gõrọ I asked for some kola for hir

rọ̃kõ m. (1) (secondary v.n. usuall replacing rọ̃kã for progressive and v.n.

x (a) **yanā rōkōna** he's beseeching me.
(b) **rōƙwaŋ ǔbā wurį** Vd. **zạllim**. (2) (a)
begging x **yā yi minį** ∼ he (beggar =
marǫƙī q.v.) begged off me. (b) **rōƙō bā
yā sā kyautā, sǎi don sǫyayyạ** gifts go to
those you like, not to those who ask.
(c) Vd. **rārakạ 2, ạlmājįrī 2**. (3) re-
questing, beseeching x **Allā shī nē
ạbin rōƙō** God is the one to invoke.
munā rōƙō, Allā yạ tạimạkē shį we
pray that God will help him.

rōkō-rōkō = **rōdį-rōdį**.

Rōmạ f. Rome (= **Rum** 2a.i).

rōmō m. (1) (a) broth (provided not
thickened with **karkashī, kuɓēwā,** etc.
If so thickened (**kadạ**), it is called
mīyạ). (b) **rōman rōgǫ** Vd. **rōgǫ** 2. (bb)
nāmạ yā ƙōnę, yā bar ∼ (i) tell that
to the horse marines! (ii) what a
hypocrite! (c) **ạ gashę bā mǎi, ạ dafę
bā** ∼ neither fish, flesh, fowl, nor good
red herring. (d) **in nā rēnạ ƙāzā, kō
rōmantạ bā nā sǫ** what a horrible
kīshīyā I have to put up with! (e)
kō rōmantạ bā nā sǫ Vd. **rēnạ** 10.
(2) advantage x (a) **ạlhaƙī dạ** ∼ **ạ
shįga īyākar wuyạ** people sin if it
is advantageous to them. (b) Vd.
zụnubį. (3) **rōman jāɓā** (a) = **rįbā**.
(b) ill-gotten gains. (4) **rōmaŋ kunnē
sukạ yi minį** what they told me was
mere "eyewash" (= **mal-mal**).

rōmūwā Sk. f. = **rōmō**.

rǫrā Vb. 2 (1) harvested (beans, etc.,
as in **rōrō**) x **nā rǫri wākē** = **nā rǫri
fagyaŋ wākē**. (2) collected (debt,
tax).

rōrę Vb. 1A (1) harvested all (beans, etc.,
cf. **rǫrā**) = **tsīnę** 1c. (2) collected all
(debts, tax), cf. **rǫrā** 2. (3) **tā** ∼ **kantạ**
she tidied her hair (cf. **rōrīyā**). (4)
mahạrā sun ∼ **ƙasạr** the raiders
stripped the land bare.

rōrīyā f. (1) woman's tidying her hair
= **fīshī** 1 (cf. **rōrę** 3). (2) sewing
kāmụŋ ƙafạ to finish it off with
cįŋ kǎi, i.e. **dājīyā** 2b. (3) **bāyaŋ kyautā
akạ yi minį** ∼ after receiving a
present, I was also given a smaller
one.

rōrǫ m. (1) harvesting beans, ground-nuts,
or **gujīyā** (cf. **jā gįndī**). (2) Vd. **gạba-**

gạba ; hūtạ ∼. (3) **yā yi rōrạŋ wākē**
he stumbled and almost fell.
B. (**rǫrō**) Kt. m. = **kālā**.

rōsạ Kt. = **rūsạ**.

rōshę Kt. = **rūshę**.

rōtsạ Vb. 1A (1) broke (brittle T. x egg,
gourd). (2) injured P. in the head.

rōtsį m. (1) injury to the head x **an yi
masạ** ∼ he has received an injury
to his head. (2) **kǎi bā yā fashēwā ạ
banzā, im bā ƙabbā ba, sǎi an yi** ∼
nobody acts without an object.

rōwạ f. (1) (a) miserliness (= **talaucį** 3).
(b) "ci nākạ n ci nāwa!" bā ∼ **ba
nē, mūgụn zamā nē** let each of us go
our own way! (c) **gārim mai** ∼ **ạ
farau-farau ya kạŋ ƙārę** the miser
always stints himself. (2) **ạkwai** ∼
ạ jikinsạ it (new-born infant) has patch
of deep pigment (supposedly due to the
mother when pregnant not having been
offered some of the food being eaten by P.
in her presence).

rōzạyē = **rāję** 1a, 2.

rōzō = **rōzōzō** = **rōzo-rōzo** = **rōzōzōnī**
m. (sg., pl.) type of large, swift spider.

rūbạ Ar. f. (1) boasting. (2) bluster,
arrogance, intimidation (= **bụrgā** 2a).

ruɓa A. (**ruɓạ**) Vb. 1A (1) (a) fermented T.
as in **riɓį** 2. (b) fermented (building-
clay by wetting it, adding horse-dung
and grass, mixing (**kwāɓạ**), leaving three
days, then again mixing, then leaving
two days and then again mixing).
(c) fermented (tobacco-leaves), cf. **sạŋkā**
1. (2) = **riɓạ** 2, 3. (3) folded (**niŋkę**),
cf. **riɓīyā, riɓạnyā**.
B. (**rụɓa**) Vb. 3B (progressive **rụɓā**)
(1) putrefied. (2) became fermented
as in **ruɓạ** 1. (3) cf. **ruɓę**.

rụɓaɓɓē (past participle from **rụɓa**) m.
(f. **rụɓaɓɓīyā**) pl. **rụɓạɓɓū** (1) (a)
putrid, fermented. (b) decayed (tooth).
(c) x **rụɓạɓɓum bāyinsạ** his wretched
slaves. (2) **rụɓạɓɓīyar ƙayạ** = **tsụmmā**
2. (3) **rụɓạɓɓuŋ haƙǫrā sum fi bāƙi
banzā** half a loaf is better than no
bread.

rụɓāɓē = **rįɓāɓē**.

rụɓāɓī Kt. m. = **rįɓāɓē** 3.

rubace A. (**rūɓạcē**) Vb. 1C intimidated
P. by bluster, etc., as in **rūɓạ**.

B. (rūḅ̣acē) *Vd.* rūbatạ.

ru6a jạnnā = ruḅạ jạnnā *Sk. m.* = ru6a saŋkacẹ.

ru6ạnyā = ri6ạnyā.

ru6a saŋkacẹ *m.* = rūwā B 16.

rūbatạ *Vb.* 2 (*p.o.* rūḅ̣acē, *n.o.* rūḅạci) = rūḅ̣acē.

ruḅau *m.* = bạrạ gurbị 2.

rubcẹ = ribcẹ.

rubḍạ = ribḍạ.

ruḅ dạ cikị (1) *m.* yā yi ~ he lay face downwards. (2) *adv.* yā fāḍị ~ he fell face-down (*cf.* jịce, rufạ 1*a*.ii).

rubḍị = ribḍị.

ru6e A. (ru6ẹ) *Vb.* 3A (1) (*a*) = ruḅa. (*b*) hannuŋkạ bā yạ̄ ru6ẹ̄wā, kạ yaŋkẹ, kạ yas one must overlook faults of one's dependents. (2) bạ̄kinsạ yā ~ his mouth is in purulent condition. (3) *Kt.* = nuka 1.

    B. (ru6ē) *m. x* wannạŋ tạntabạrā ~ yakẹ yị this cock-pigeon causes eggs to become addled.

ru6ị = ri6ị.

ru6ịyā = ri6ịyā.

rubjẹ = ribjẹ.

rubkā = riskā.

ruḅu *Vd.* igīyạ 7.

rububbūtā *Vb.* 1D *intensive from* ruḅūtā.

ruḅubī = riḅibī.

rubuce A. (ruḅūcē) *Vb.* 1C wrote completely (*cf.* ruḅūtā).

    B. (ruḅūcē) *Vd.* ruḅūtạ.

rubudī = ribidī.

ruḅu dīnạ *Vd.* igīyạ 7.

*ruḅu'ī *Ar. m.* (1) quarter of. (2) *Vd.* igīyạ 7, sạdākị.

ru6us A. (ruḅus) *adv. and m.* nā ji ~ I heard sound of P. walking on sand, etc.

    B. (ru6us) *adv.* (1) yā nịku ~ = lilis 1*b*. (2) Auḍu kuḍī nẹ̄ ~ Audu is a prompt payer.

    C. (ru6us) *Vd.* ci6us.

ru6ushi A. (ruḅushī) *m.* = ribidī.

    B. (ruḅūshị) *m.* (1) type of wheat-food. (2) type of pastry.

rubuta A. (ruḅūtā) *Vb.* 1C (*Vd.* ruḅūtū) (1) wrote. (2) sun ruḅūtā wai ... they wrote to say that ... (3) ruḅūtā dạ nī cikim masọyaŋkạ include me also among your well-wishers !

    B. (ruḅūtạ) *Vb.* 2 (*p.o.* ruḅūcē, *n.o.* ruḅūci) wrote part of.

ruḅūtū *m.* (1) (*sec. v.n. of* ruḅūtā) *x* yanạ̄ ruḅūtunsạ = yanạ̄ ruḅūtā shi he is writing it. (2) act of writing. (3) written matter *x* wannạŋ Ạlḳur'ạŋ ruḅūtuŋ hannū nẹ̄ this Koran is hand-written (*cf.* bugu 2*a*). (4) *Vd.* Shạ̄ ruḅūtū.

rubza = ribza.

ruḍa A. (rūḍạ) (1) *Vb.* 1A (*a*) bewildered, perplexed *x* yā ~ minị tụnānī he bewildered me (= dāmạ 2*a*). (*b*) muddled T. up *x* (i) ạ̣bịn dạ ya ḳārạ rūḍạ ạ̣bịŋ what further complicates the matter. (ii) yā rūḍạ kunnūwạnsụ he misled them. (*c*) tā ~ tsạkī she put the first flour into hot water in the pot when making tūwō (= talgạ), *cf.* afạ 2. (2) *Vb.* 3A *Kt.* yā ~ cikịŋ gạrī he went wandering in the town.

    B. (rūḍā) *Vb.* 2 (*Vd.* rūḍị) (1) deceived. (2) mālạminsạ ya rūḍō shi *Vd.* mālạmī 1*b*.

rūḍaḍḍē *m.* (*f.* rūḍaḍḍīyā) *pl.* rūḍaḍḍū (1) (*past participle from* rūḍā). (2) slow-witted, addle-pated (*Vd.* rūḍẹ 1).

rūḍạ kuyaŋgī *m.* = yautạ kuyaŋgī.

rūḍāmạ *f.* = ruḍāmī *m.* (1) loquacity. (2) conflict, welter, confusion.

ruḍḍā *Vd.* rūḍu.

ruḍe A. (rūḍẹ) (1) *Vb.* 3A (*a*) P. became bewildered, puzzled. (*b*) T. became in a muddle *x* (i) ạ̣bịŋ yā ~ īyạ̄kar rūḍẹ̄wā the matter became very involved. lạ̄bārị sại ḳārạ rūḍẹ̄wā yakẹ yị the news becomes more and more involved. ạl'amạrin tsạkāninsụ yā ḳārạ rūḍẹ̄wā relations became worse between them. gidansạ yā ~ his compound is involved in quarrelling. (ii) cikịnsạ yā ~ his inside is upset. (iii) (*with dative*) ạl'amạrī yā ~ masạ the matter is beyond his comprehension, beyond his power to deal with. maganạ tā rūḍẹ masạ he has been unsuccessful. (2) *Vb.* 1A = rūḍạ 1*a, b*.

    B. (rūḍē) *m.* (1) acting *as in* rūḍạ 1*c*. (2) mixture resulting from action *as in* rūḍạ 1*c* (= talgē), *Vd.* dạ̄mē 1.

rūḍị *m.* (1) (*sec. v.n. of* rūḍā) *x* sunạ̄

rūdinsa = sunā rūdā tasa they're
deceiving him. (2) deception, trickery.
rūdu *m.* (*pl.* ruddā = rūduna) *Sk.* =
makani.
*ruɗūba *Ar. f.* soft fæces.
rududdugē = rididdigē.
rūduna *Vd.* rūdu.
rudū-rudū *m.* jikinsa yā yi ~ his body
is swollen from weals, insect-bites,
etc. (*Vd.* birdidi).
rūdwā = rūdūwā *f.* (*pl.* rūdūwōyī) (1)
woman's load of utensils packed ready
for transporting (= angayā 1 = faggo 1).
(2) bride's load of calabashes, bowls,
etc. (3) *Vd.* dūban ~.
ruf *Vd.* rufe 2c.
rufa A. (rufa) (1) *Vb.* 1A (*a*) (i) covered
x yā ~ ƙwaryā da fǎifǎi = rufe 1a.i.
zā a rufa ta, a kai ta gidam mijinta
cover her head and take her to her
husband's home ! (ii) yā ~ cikinsa he
lay on his stomach (*cf.* rub da ciki).
(*b*) = rufā 1a. (*c*) (i) (*with dative*)
covered x yā ~ masa zane he covered
it with a cloth. yā ~ fǎifǎi a ƙwaryā he
covered the calabash with a mat-cover.
(ii) roofed (except with thatch) x
yā ~ sōrō he roofed the house with a
mud-top (*cf.* jiŋkā, jiŋke). an ~ ɗāki
da kwāno pan-roof has been put on
the building. an ~ mōta da fāta the
car has a leather hood. an ~ rumfar
mōta da zāŋā the garage has grass-
mat roof. (*d*) concealed x (i) Allā
ya ~ mana asīrī may God not allow
us to be put to shame ! (*cf.* Alā 8). (ii)
kōwā ya ~ asīriŋ wani, Allā yā ~
nāsa he who does not shame another
will not himself be put to shame. (iii)
Vd. būde 1k. (*e*) (i) bari n ~ ido, n
tafi I'll try and go (= runtse 1b.ii). (ii)
rufa ido, ka bā ni do your best to give
it to me ! (iii) *Vd.* rufa ido. (iv)
Vd. rufe 1b.iii. (2) *Vb.* 3A (*a*) became
round-shouldered (2a = rufu). (*b*)
kabarī yā rufa da sū the grave closed
on them, i.e. they died.
B. (rufā) (1) *Vb.* 2 (*a*) deceived x
yā rufē ta he deceived her (into thinking
he would marry, buy from her, etc.) =
rufa 1b (*cf.* rufā-rufā). (*b*) (i) covered
(= rufe 1a). (ii) Allā ya rufi asīrimmu

= rufa 1d.i. (*c*) concealed T. from x
yā rufē ni, bai gaya mini zai zō ba
he hid from me the fact that he would
come. (*d*) garin naŋ, sun rufam masa
they (soldiers) have invested the town
(= rufe 1e). (2) *Vd.* rufa.
C. (rufa) *Vb.* 3B (*progressive* rufā) is
wrapped in x (1) yā ~ da alkyabba
he is wearing a burnous. wannam
bargō bā shi da dāɗin rufā it is not
pleasant to wrap oneself in this blanket.
(2) mai abin rufā shī kē kūkan dārī,
huntū yā bā gaskīyā ga itace often rich
P. fusses over trifling expense.
rufa idō *m.* (1) (*a*) charm (lāya) or
potion rendering one invisible. (*b*)
power of rendering oneself invisible x ~
garēshi. (*c*) using 1b above x 6arāwo ~
ya yi mana the thief by charm, etc.,
robbed us without our being able to
see what was going on. (2) *Vd.* rufa 1e.
rufā-rufā = rufa-rufā *f.* deceiving P.
x kada ka yi mini ~ don't try to
deceive me ! (*cf.* rufā 1a).
rufam *Vd.* rufā 1d.
rufce = ribce.
ruf da ciki = rub da ciki.
rufe A. (rufe) (1) *Vb.* 1A (*a*) (i) covered x
yā ~ ƙwaryā da fǎifǎi he covered the
calabash with a mat-cover (= rufa 1a.i,
rufā 1b.i). (ii) sun ~ kǎi da būzū,
sǎi suka . . . they screwed up their
courage and . . . (iii) yā ~ katarā
Vd. abu 2n. (iv) bi ki ~ cībīyā ba
Vd. falmaraŋ. (*b*) concealed x (i) bā
mā rufe muku kōmē we are not hiding
anything from you. duhun da ya ~
mu yā wāshe the darkness which
enveloped us has dispersed. (ii) = rufa
1d. (iia) rufe ido, ka bā ni = rufa 1e.ii.
(iii) yā ~ ido he closed his eye(s).
akwai abūbūwa waɗanda dōle mu
rufe ido daga garēsu there are matters to
which we must close our eyes. sun
rufe ido, sun rūgō gaba they (soldiers)
charged fearlessly (*cf.* rufe 1, 2). (iv) tarō
sun ~ mu the people crowded round
us (*cf.* rufu). (*c*) sun ~ shi he has been
put in the lock-up pending trial. (*d*)
an ~ shi he has been buried. (*e*)
sun ~ gariŋ they (soldiers) have
invested the town (= rufā 1d). (*f*)

gishirin Tūrāwā yā rufẹ nāmụ European salt has displaced, rendered ours obsolete. (g) (i) sun ~ masạ bāyā they protected, helped him. (ii) sun rufẹ bāyansạ they followed him as escort. (2) Vb. 3A became covered, concealed x (a) rānā tā ~ the sun is enveloped in clouds. (b) idạnsạ yā ~ (i) his eyes are closed. (ii) his attention is wholly absorbed. (c) yā ~ ruf it is completely concealed. (d) (i) ƙōfạ tā ~ doorway has been covered by door. (ii) wannạn ƙōfạ tā rufẹ musụ that avenue is closed to them.

B. (rufe) (noun of state from rufẹ) x (1) yanạ̃ nēmansạ idọ ạ ~ he's seeking it eagerly. (2) sum bī shi idọ rufẹ they obeyed him implicitly (cf. rufẹ 1b.iii). (3) ạl'amạrin nạn, ƙwaryā rụfe kẹ̃ nạn this matter is a mystery.

rufẹnĩ Vd. rufēwā.

rufēwā f. (pl. rufẹ̃yī = Sk. rụfẹnĩ, rụfẹnũ) (1) large outdoor clay corn-bin used for storing zaŋgannĩyā or tsābạ, though sacks are now generally used for tsābạ (it has no hayị, but the clay is continued upwards in funnel shape, capped with dan bōtọ) = rạhōgō = rụmbū 1c (cf. rạhōnĩyā ; rụmbū ; kụdandạmī). (2) its epithet is Rụfēwā maị baŋ haushī (because not portable like the zānā-type of rụmbū).

rufị m. (1) (sec. v.n. of rufẹ, rufạ) x yanạ̃ rufịn sōrō = yanạ̃ rufạ sōrō he is roofing the mud-topped building (cf.rufạ 1c. ii). rufịŋ ạsīrī sài Allạ̃ only God can save one from discomfiture in this world (cf. rufạ 1d). (2) (a) lid. (b) roof as in rufạ 1c.ii x an yi wạ sōrō ~ roof has been made for the mud-topped building (cf. hayị 1a.ii). mōtạ bā ta dạ ~ the car has no hood. (c) sheath, casing. (d) bā ~ Vd. gaŋgā 2c. (3) Audụ ~ gạreshị Audu is (a) secretive, (b) treacherous. (4) double inverted jicị of indigo or salt. (5) completing ridges in corn-farm after fẹ̃dẹ̃ 1. (6) dạ Audụ dạ Kạnde an yi musụ ~ = an yi musụ auran ~ Audu and Kande were by Barạrō custom betrothed as children (cf. rịƙā 2d). (7) rufịŋ kạn dadị = rufịŋ kạŋ ūwar dadị becoming so

involved in details as to forget the main point. (8) sun yi wạ ƙasạr rufịŋ tandũ they crushed the country entirely. (9) bā kyā̀ ~ Vd. ạkũ. (10) ūwar ~ Vd. gạrmā 1c.

rufkā Vb. 2 clutched (= rịskā 1b).

rufkẹ Vb. 1A = rụfkā.

ruf'ke-rufkē" m. steadily endeavouring to do T. (= rịske-rịskē), cf. rụrrufkạ.

rufōgō Kt. (1) rạhōgō. (2) = asūsụ 1.

rufōtọ = rạhōtọ.

rufu Vb. 3B (1) = rufạ 2. (2) sun rụfu gạ ƙasạn naŋ they massed against that country (cf. rufẹ 1b.iv).

*rufu'ạ Ar. f. (1) Arabic symbol for vowel " u ". (2) Vd. fādũwā 8.

ruga A. (rūgạ) (1) Vb. 3A rushed x (a) sài ya ~ yāƙị then he rushed into the battle. (b) yā ~ he fled ; he rushed off. ya rūgō then he raced up. sun rufẹ idọ, sun rūgō gạba they (soldiers) charged fearlessly. (2) Vb. 1A (a) yā ~ kầi dawạ he took to his heels (b) yā rūgō kầi d̓ākị he entered unceremoniously (cf. rụgu). (c) yā ~ shi ạ bakạ he popped all of it into his mouth.

B. (rūgā) Vb. 2 (1) drove away (= kōrā). (2) drove (animal) along (= kōrạ).

C. (ruga) f. (pl. rugāgē) (1) (a) Filani cattle-encampment (epithet is Rugā kim fi d̓ākị). (b) sài ~ tā kwānā lāfịyạ, rinjị kẹ̃ kwānā lāfịyạ one's master's misfortune is one's own. (c sai dạ bābā ạ ~ taking coals to Newcastle. (2) maị yā tạfi ~ the milk has reached boiling-point.

rugage A. (rugāgẹ) m. forestalling P. (= rigẹ q.v.).

B. (rugāgē) Vd. rugā.

rugānạ f. = madambacī.

rugẹ m. half-witted P.

rugēgẹ m. (f. rugēgĩyā) huge x rugēgyạ̀ karọ a huge struggle.

ruggā Nor. m. = rugā 1.

rūgō Vd. rūgā.

rugōjī Vd. rījĩyā.

rūgu Vb. 3B several persons unceremoniously pushed their way in (cf rūgā 2b).

rugụbnĩyā = rugụmnĩyā.

rugụdū m. = kạbụs 1.

rugudūmạ f. (1) rich meat-gravy. (2) = dạfau 1. (3) = ruguntsumī 2.

rugugī m. rumblings (x of stomach, thunder, engine, etc.).

rugugū m. = rugugī.

rugugun = rugugī.

rūgūgūwā f. (1) rushing about x yanā̃ ∼ yạ ƙārẹ aikinsạ he's in a ferment to finish the work. sunā̃ rūgūgūwar fītā they are rushing out. (2) = kạbus 1.

rugujē Vb. 3A = ragargạjē.

rugum = rugum adv. and m. nā ji ∼ I heard boom (of gun, collapsing building, etc.). yā fādi ∼ it (wall, meteorite, etc.) fell with a thud. an yi ∼ house has collapsed, etc.

rugumnīyā f. (1) = rugugī. (2) confused babel intermingled with sound of drumming and horns (cf. ruguntsumī 2).

rugundumī Kt. = ruguntsumī.

rugunguntā Vb. 3A = ruguntsumā 1 x sun ∼ sun kāmạ shi they made a rush and seized him.

rugunnīyā = rugumnīyā.

ruguntsumā Vb. 3A (1) they rushed in a body. (2) sun ∼ fadạ they became engaged in a noisy quarrel.

ruguntsumē Vb. 3A (1) wurī yā ∼ the place was a seething mass of people. (2) = bunƙāsạ. (3) sun ∼ dạ fadạ = ruguntsumā 2.

ruguntsumī m. (1) big melée. (2) indiscriminate drumming (= rugudūmạ 3), cf. rugumnīyā 2.

rugurgujē = ragargạjē.

rugurguza = ragargaza.

rugu-rugu A. (rugū-rugū) (1) pl., adj. huge and round x dạnkali ∼ huge sweet-potatoes.

B. (rugu-rugu) (1) yā kakkạryē ∼ it was completely shattered. (2) m. an yi musu rugu-rugu they have been destroyed.

rugus = rugus adv. yanā̃ nan ∼ it is broken in small pieces.

ruguzum adv. (1) yanā̃ dạ ciki ∼ he is pot-bellied. (2) yā fādi ∼ he fell headlong.

ruguzunzumī m. (f. ruguzunzumā) pl. ruguzun-ruguzun burly.

ruhōgō Kt. m. (1) = rạhōgō. (2) = asūsu 1.

ruhōnīyā = rạhōnīyā.

rūhun na'ạ-na'ạ = nạ'ạ-na'ạ.

ruhusạ Ar. f. cheapness.

ruī = rwī.

rūjīyạ f. a herb of the Asclepiadeae family.

rujuf = rijif.

ruƙāƙē Vd. ruƙuƙī.

ruko Vd. rahạ 2.

rukuɓu Sk. m. (1) = zāƙī 8. (2) child which has overgrown its strength.

*rukuɓūjẹ = rukuɓūji = bạrạngwạjē q.v.

rukucạ-rukucạ used in gōrọ ∼ kola-nuts of inferior size.

rukuki m. (1) type of tree. (2) walking-stick made from 1.

ruƙuƙī m. (pl. ruƙāƙē) (1) = sarƙaƙƙīyā 1. (2) yā shiga ∼ (a) he's lying in ambush. (b) he's involved in intrigue and cannot extricate himself.

ruƙumạ (1) Vb. 2 came to grips with (in fight, lawsuit) x sun ruƙumē shi they've come to grips with him. (2) Vb. 3B sun ∼ they came to grips.

ruƙumē Vb. 1C = ruƙumạ 1.

rukunī Ar. m. (pl. rukunai) (1) (a) group, section, party. (b) share x am bā shi rukuninsạ he has been given his share. (2) shī ∼ gudā nẹ ạ cikinsạ he is the P. who matters in it (= gudā 1e).

ruƙunsumai pl. (1) bundle of charms hung round neck or at entrance to compound or tomb (= Zar. riƙi 1b). (2) pocket full of odds and ends.

rukunzumī m. (f. rukunzumā) big and useless.

ruƙū-ruƙū = rugu-rugū.

*ruƙū'u Ar. m. = raka'ạ.

rukwādọ Kt. m. wastrel.

rukwākwạ f. orchitis (cf. gwaiwā 1b).

rūlạ = lūlạ 3.

rum A. (rum) = rim.

B. (rum) (1) = rim. (2) (a) Rum f. (i) Rome (= Rōmạ). (ii) Byzantium. (b) Bahạr ∼ m. the Mediterranean.

ruma A. (ruma) = rima.

B. (rūmā) Vd. tāshin jạ̄kin 'yan rūmā ; Bạrūmạyī.

rūmạ̄cē m. (1) = akạrdā. (2) rūmạ̄can zạncē senseless drivel. (3) Vd. shạn rūmạ̄cē.

rumądā *Vd.* barinję.

rumą fādą *f.* Sweet broom weed.

rumąmā *Vb.* 3A = rimą 1.

rumānā *f. generic name for various edible-bulbed* gladioli.

Rūmāwā *Vd.* Barūmąyĭ.

rumbącē *Vb.* 1C grabbed.

rumbū *m.* (*pl.* rumbuną) (1) (*a*) outdoor corn-bin of clay or corn-stalks. (*b*) rumbun zānā outdoor corn-bin made of grass-mats (*used only for storing* zaŋ-ganniyā). (*c*) rumbuŋ ƙasā = rufēwā. (*d*) *cf.* rąhōniyā. (*e*) kurman ∼ full corn-bin. (*f*) ɗaŋ kąn ∼ = bāƙĭrę. (2) kōwā ya ƙōnę rumbunsą, yā saŋ indą tōkā takę kudĭ nę don't cut off your nose to spite your face! (3) ƙaryar azzikĭ shigar rumbuŋ ayā dą igĭyą it's beyond him but he does not realize so. (4) rumbun tsąmmāni, dą baƙin ciki akę ciką shi don't build castle in the air! (5) dąrĭyā ą ∼ *Vd.* bam mąganą. (6) *cf.* būɗą ∼. (7) bąkin ∼ *Vd.* dami 2. (8) fāɗūwar mąi ∼ *Vd.* fāɗūwā 6.

rumbujē = ruŋgujē.

rumbumą *Vb.* 2 = rumbuzą.

rumbuzą *Vb.* 2 (*p.o.* rumbujē, *n.o.* rumbuji) clutched.

rumcę *Kt.* = runtsę.

rumfā *f.* (*pl.* rumfuną = rumfōfī) (1) grass-shed (= dabi 1). (2) *Vd.* magąjĭ 3, Makąmā. (3) (*in* ząurąncē) ɗāki dą ∼ 1500 cowries (*cf.* mutum 6). (4) rumfar mōtą (*a*) garage. (*b*) hood of motor. (5) rumfar wākē sky being overcast (= lumshĭ). (6) Rumfā shą shirgi what a willing person! (7) rumfar ganyē *Vd.* bąkō-bakō.

rumfū = ruŋhū.

rumhwā *Kt. f.* = rumfā.

rūmi *m.* collection of silk thread of various colours.

rummaŋ = rummāni *Ar. m., sg. and pl.* pomegranate.

rum-rum = rumu-rumu.

rumtsą *Kt.* = rintsą.

rumurmusą *Vb.* 2 (*p.o.* rumurmushē, *n.o.* rumurmushi) crunched (food).

rumurmushe A. (rumurmushē) *Vb.* 1D crunched all of (*cf.* rumurmusą).

B. (rumurmushē) *Vd.* rumurmusą.

rumu-rumu *m.* suną ∼ dą jūnā they're intimate friends (= *Kt.* ram-ram).

rumus *adv.* (1) yā būshę ∼ it (meat, leaves, etc.) is completely dried up. (2) *Kt.* kō ∼ ban yi barcī ba I didn't sleep a wink.

rumus-rumus *adv. and m.* nā ji ∼ I heard a crunching sound. yaną cĭ ∼ he's eating with a crunching sound.

rumwi-rumwi = rumu-rumu.

rundąwā *Vd.* barinję.

rundi *m.* (1) = ribɗi 1. (2) = ƙārauką.

runɗumēmę = rinɗimēmę.

rundunā *f.* (*pl.* rundunōni) (1) (*a*) army, multitude. (*b*) rundunar rahamą tą saukam maną may God be merciful to us! (2) gą mutānē rundunā-rundunā there are crowds of people.

runɗunɗuŋ = rinɗinɗiŋ.

runfū = ruŋhū.

ruŋgu *Vb.* (*used only in this form*) remained over (= rągu).

ruŋgudē *Kt.* = rikicē.

runguje A. (ruŋgujē) *Vb.* 1C forcibly pushed over (*Vd.* ruŋguzā).

B. (ruŋgujē) *Vd.* ruŋguzą.

runguji A. (ruŋguji) *m.* habitual butting.

B. (ruŋguji) *Vd.* ruŋguzą.

runguma A. (ruŋgumą) *Vb.* 2 (1) embraced. (2) carried T. by clasping it. (3) x yā ruŋgumi ƙasąshąŋ dą mākirci he got possession of those countries by trickery. (4) mątsą ruŋgumą *Vd.* matsą 1*h*.

B. (ruŋgumā) (1) *Vb.* 1C put all of T. into one's mouth. (2) *Vb.* 3A x sun ∼ sun tąfi wurinsą they went in a body to him.

ruŋgumammēniyā *f.* mutual embracing.

ruŋgumą ni, mu fāɗi = ruŋgumąn ni, mu fāɗi = ruŋgumę ni, mu fāɗi *m.* "what a broken reed!" (*cf.* wālā 2, luƙwąsǫ).

rungume A. (ruŋgumē) *Vb.* 1C = ruŋgumą.

B. (ruŋgumę) (*noun of state from* ruŋgumą) x yaną ∼ dą hāją he is clasping the goods (M.G. 80*d*.ii).

C. (ruŋgumę) *m.* bundle (of corn-heads, wood, stalks, etc.).

ruŋgumi *Kt. m.* = ruŋgumę.

ruŋgun dāji *m.* tireless farmer.

ruŋgunɗumĭ *Kt. m.* = ruguntsumĭ.

ruŋgutsā *Vb.* 3A = **ruŋgumā** 2.

ruŋgutsē = **rūdę** 1.

ruŋgutsumą *Nor. f.* = **ruguntsumī**.

runguza A. (**ruŋguzā**) *Vb.* 1C (1) ˥pushed into, on to *x* **yā ∼ ni cikin rāmi** he pushed me into a hole. (2) **yā ∼ musu ąrąhā** he sold to them cheaply.

B. (**ruŋguzą**) *Vb.* 2 (*p.o.* **ruŋgujē**, *n.o.* **ruŋguji**) butted, collided with.

ruŋhū *m.* (1) the tree *Cassia goratensis*. (2) **kō biri yā karyę, yą hau ∼** = **zāki** 1*f*.

runję *Vb.* 1A = **rinzą**.

runji *Vd.* **Bąrinję**.

runƙaƙa A. (**ruŋƙāƙą**) *Vb.* 2 (1) drove away (= **ƙōrā**). (2) drove (animal) along (= **kōrą**).

B. (**ruŋƙāƙā**) *Vb.* 3A went away, vanished.

ruŋki = **riŋki**.

ruŋƙumą *Kt.* = **ruƙumą**.

ruŋkwī (1) *m.* children's game of embracing each other. (2) *adv.* (*a*) **taną dą ciki ∼** she (woman about to bear) has huge stomach. (*b*) **yaną dą kāyā ∼** (i) he has heavy load. (ii) he has big testicles. (*c*) **taną dą gōyō ∼** she is carrying heavy child on her back (*cf.* **ruŋkwī-ruŋkwī**).

ruŋkwīkwī = **ruŋkwī**.

ruŋkwī-ruŋkwī *adv.* (1) **yaną tąfīyą dą kāyā ∼** (i) he's staggering along with heavy load. (ii) he's walking awkwardly through large testicles. (2) **taną tąfīyą ∼** she's staggering along with a heavy child on her back (*cf.* **ruŋkwī**).

runsynā *Kt.* = **rusynā**.

runto = **rinto**.

runtsą = **rintsą**.

runtsę (1) *Vb.* 1A (*a*) **yā ∼ shi ą hannū** he gripped it tightly. (*b*) (i) **yā ∼ ido** he screwed up his eyes. (ii) **bąri ņ ∼ ido, ņ tąfi** = **rufą** 1*e*.i. (2) *Vb.* 3A **kąsūwā tā ∼** the market is crowded.

runtsī *m.* (1) **kąsūwā tā yi ∼** = **runtsę** 2. (2) **rubūtun naŋ yaną dą ∼** this writing is crowded together.

runtuma A. (**runtumā**) (1) *Vb.* 1C (*a*) **an ∼ masą sandā** he was thrashed with a stick. (*b*) **an ∼ shi dą ƙasā** they felled him. (*c*) **sun runtumą fadą** they engaged in a struggle. (2) *Vb.* 3A

(*a*) **sun ∼, sun tąfi** they went off in a body. (*b*) **sun ∼ dą gudu** they fled en masse.

B. (**runtumą**) *Vb.* 2 drove away (= **ƙōrā**).

runtumē (1) *Vb.* 1C **an ∼ shi dą sandā** = **runtumā** 1*a*. (2) *Vb.* 3A **sun ∼ dą fadą** they attacked each other.

runtumēmę *m.* (*f.* **runtumēmīyā**) *pl.* **runtuŋ-runtuŋ** huge.

runtumī (1) *m.* (*f.* **runtumā**) *pl.* **runtuŋ-runtuŋ** = **runtumēmę**. (2) *m.* irascibility, wrangling.

runtuntuŋ *m.* hugeness *x* **yaną dą kąi ∼** he is huge-headed.

runzą = **rinzą**.

rūrą (1) *Vb.* 1A (*a*) **yā ∼ wutā** he blew up the fire (= **hūrą** 1*a*.i), *cf.* **zugą**. **wutā tā rūru** the fire has been made to burn up. (*b*) incited (= **zugą**). (*c*) (i) wailed. (ii) (P. or animal) uttered a cry (*Vd.* **rūri**). (iii) he (lądaŋ) uttered Muslim call to prayer. (iv) **yā ∼ īhu** he shouted. (2) *f.* (*a*) the small tree *Parinarium curatellaefolium*. (*b*) *Sk.* angrily reprimanding an inferior.

rūrau *m.* (1) rotten place on pumpkin. (2) = **bųsau** 1.

rūrę (1) *Vb.* 3A (*a*) became hollowed out. (*b*) **ƙafąssą tā ∼ ulcer** (**gyąmbō**) has burrowed into his foot (= **zaɓaɓɓąkē** 1), *cf.* **rūrau** 2. (2) *Vb.* 1A hollowed T. out.

rūri *m.* (1) cry (of lion, ox, camel, ostrich, etc.) = **kūkā** 1*c, d*. (2) roaring of fire. (3) wailing. (4) shouting. (5) *Sk.* angrily reprimanding an inferior.

rurrūbącē *intensive from* **rūbącē**.

rurrubką = **rurrufką**.

rurrubūtā *intensive from* **rubūtā**.

rurrufką (1) *Vb.* 2 *intensive from* **rufkā**. (2) *Vb.* 3B put forth sustained effort (= **ririską**), *cf.* **riske-riskē**.

rurrutsā *Sk. f.* = **kwanīką** 1.

ruruma A. (**rūrųmā**) *f.* (1) (*a*) clamour. (*b*) clamouring crowd *x* **yā shiga rūrųmar kąsūwa** he entered the noisy market-crowd. (2) **yā mutu ą ∼** he died at a time of heavy mortality.

B. (**rurumā**) *Vb.* 3A took a sleep *as in* **rurumī**.

rurumī *m.* short sleep before dawn by P. who has travelled all night.

rụ̄rūtạ *Vb.* 3B *x* ƙurjī yā ∽ the abscess has become deep-set.

rụ̄rūwạ *used in* mạn ∽ *q.v. under* mạŋ gyạdā 2 ; barcī 3*c*.

rus *x* itạ̄cē yā būshẹ ∽ the tree became dried up.

rusa A. (rūsạ) (1) *Vb.* 1A (*a*) = rūshẹ 1. (*b*) nā ∽ masạ sạndā I thrashed him with a stick. (2) *Vb.* 3A = rūshẹ 2. B. (rụ̄sā) (*p.o.* rụ̄shē, *n.o.* rụ̄shi) *Vb.* 2 (1) *x* yā rụ̄shi gōrọ he crunched up much kola-nut. (2) yā rụ̄shi kūkā he cried bitterly.

rūsā-rụ̄sạ̄ *Vd.* rūshēshẹ.

rusɓạ *Vb.* 3A = rūshẹ 2.∽

rūshe A. (rūshẹ) (1) *Vb.* 1A demolished, caused to collapse (house, wall, etc.) = rịbɗā. (2) *Vb.* 3A (*a*) collapsed (= rịbɗạ 2*b*). (*b*) yā ∽ dạ nī it collapsed under my weight. B. (rụ̄shē) *Vd.* rụ̄sā.

rūshēshẹ *m.* (*f.* rūshēshịyā) *pl.* rūsā-rụ̄sạ̄ huge.

rushi A. (rūshị) (1) how huge ! (*cf.* rūshēshẹ). (2) what a lot of crunch-able food has been eaten ! (*cf.* rụ̄sā). B. (rụ̄shi) *Vd.* rụ̄sā. C. (rụ̄shī) *m.* = rạushī.

rushu'ạ = rashawạ.

rụskā = rịskā.

rụskụ (1) what a huge paunch ! (2) Rusku *name for* slave.

rụskwī = rụŋkwī.

rụskwīkwī = rụŋkwīkwī.

rusụnā *Vb.* 3A (1) bent forward in greeting or obeisance. (2) knelt before one's superior.

rutsa A. (rūtsạ) (1) *Vb.* 1A yā ∽ matạ wuƙā he stabbed her with a knife. (2) *Vb.* 3A yā ∽ ạ gụje he took to his heels. B. (rutsạ) = ritsạ.

rutsẹ = ritsạ.

rutsō *Vb.* 3A = riskō *q.v. under* rịskā.

rutsụkkē *Vb.* 1C *Sk.* = ritsạ.

rututu A. (rututu) abundantly (*re* per-sons, fruit, insects, pimples, crops, etc.) *x* itạ̄cạn yā yi 'yā'yā ∽ the tree has much fruit. mutạ̄nē sum fitō ∽ many persons have come out. B. (rụtụtụ) *m.* (1) jịkinsạ yā yi ∽ he has a form of dermatitis. (2) kụnū yā yi ∽ the gruel is lumpy (= gụdā 1*a*.i).

rūtụ̄tūwạ *f.* crowd *x* rūtụ̄tūwạr jirāgē a mass of ships.

rụ'ụyā *f.* (*Ar.* vision) dream (= mafarkī).

rūwā *m.* (*pl.* rūwạ̄yē = rūwạiwai, *cf.* D 5*b below*). Paragraph A *gives general and idiomatic usages of* rūwā *in the* sense water. Paragraph B *gives* rūwan-compounds. Paragraph C *gives* pro-verbs. Paragraph D *gives sense* rain. Paragraph E *gives sense* juice. Para-graph F *gives sense* colour. Paragraph G ịnā rūwan . . . Paragraph H *gives sense* interest on money. Paragraph J *gives sense* blade. Paragraph A.1*b* and Paragraph K rūwa (*with short final vowel*). Paragraph L rūwa-rūwa, rụ̄wạ-rūwạ.

A. water *x* (1) (*a*) ∽ Sarkī nẹ, bā yā zamā sǎi dạ shịmfidạ *epithet of* water. (*b*) (*final vowel is shortened so that* rūwā *becomes* rūwa, *when we have preposition* ạ *stated or understood before it*) *x* (i) yā fāɗạ ạ rūwa he fell into, dived into the water. yā shịga rūwa he entered the water. yā fịta rūwa he came out of the water. (ii) *Vd.* Paragraph K *below*. (iii) *Vd.* 2*d*, 23, 25, C 17, D3 *below*. (2) (*a*) yā shā ∽ (i) he drank water. (ii) (*euphemism*) he drank beer. (iii) jīyạ an shā ∽ it rained heavily yesterday (*cf.* shā B 9*a*). (*b*) yā shā ∽ dạ hakị *Vd.* hakị 2. (*c*) a tạfīyạ tā shā ∽ the journey has been abandoned (= fāsạ 2 = sha 1*l*) (*d*) kạmaŋ ạ rūwa sukạ shā (i) what rapid progress they have made ! (ii) how thin and hungry they remain no matter what they eat ! (*e*) sunạ̄ dạ sauran shạn ∽ they have got a respite (*f*) mā zubạ ∽ ạ ƙas, mụ shā dom murnạ we shall rejoice. (*g*) kō kạn mē wutā ta fāɗạ, bạ sụ shā rūwaŋ kụlā ba they didn't care what places were bombarded. (*h*) *cf. below* B 10, B 24 C 9*b*, C 9*d–l*, C 23, K 2*b*. *Vd.* shạ rūwā mashạ̄ 3. (3) (*a*) tā dẹ̄bi ∽ = tā jā ∽ she drew water from well, stream, etc (*b*) ƙurjī yā jā ∽ = ƙurjī yā yi ∽ the abscess is full of pus. (*c*) *Vd.* tsuntsū 5 (4) zạn taɓạ ∽ (*euphemism*) I'll go and pass water (= 12*b*). (5) yanạ nēmansạ ∼ ạ jạllō he's seeking it might and main. **(6) yā bi** ∼ it is lost, vanished ; it has all come to nothing. **(7)** (a) **ɗaukạr** ∼ f. = **tạr̃īyạ 7.** (b) **an yi masạ ɗaukạn** ∼ two to four persons lifted it, each holding one side of it (= **makarantā** 3c.ii). (c) **jirgī yā ɗạuki** ∼ the boat is leaking, water has swirled into the boat. (d) **jirginsạ yā ɗạuki** ∼ he's been found out. **(8) igīyạr** ∼ f. current of a stream or river. **(9)** (a) **jirgin nạŋ, cikin rūwam Masạr yakẹ** this ship is in Egyptian waters. (b) **hanyạr** ∼ f. channel, canal. **(10)** (a) **mại** ∼ = **bindigạ mại** ∼ f. machine-gun. (b) **yā gạmu dạ** ∼ = **yā gạmu dạ mại** ∼ (i) he got smallpox (= **mạshasshārā** q.v.). (ii) it (ox, etc.) got febrile cattle-disease rendering carcass watery. **(11) ɗaurịn** ∼ m. (a) charm used by 'yam **f̣ōtō** or pagans to cause storm to pass. (b) charm to bring luck in fishing. **(12)** (a) **yā kāmạ** ∼ he washed his genitals after urination or defecation. (b) (euphemism) **zạŋ kāmạ** ∼ (= 4 above). (c) ∼ **yā kāmạ dōki** the water upset the horse's digestion. (d) **Rūwā bạ ka makāmā** what fecklessness ! **(13)** (a) **yā bā kạ** ∼ he "led you (seller) on " by overbidding for it (= **kwāzārī 4**). (b) **nā bā shi** ∼ (i) I (boxer) dodged to avoid his blow. (ii) I (darạ-player) made a move which gave me the advantage. (iii) I ducked him. (c) Vd. **ban rūwā.** (d) **shūci yā bā dạ** ∼ the grass that was being used, slipped out of place during thatching (= **zūk̃ẹ** 2d). (e) Vd. A 20, 21, C 42, C 18 below. **(14) ɗaŋ gā** ∼ m. (pl. **'yaŋ gā** ∼) = **dāgirạ. (15) bak̃in** ∼ (a) clear water, drinking water. (b) **madūbī mại bak̃in** ∼ a clear mirror. (c) Vd. F 2 below. **(16) kurman** ∼ (a) dangerous bog (= **ɗạmbā**). (b) calm-looking water with dangerous undertow. (c) treacherous P. or T. (epithet of 16 is **Shịgar mại gāgā**). **(17)** (a) **yā cikạ** ∼ too much water has been added to it. (b) **K̃ande tā cikạ** ∼ K̃ande's thread came to an end before she had completed doing her **waɗạrī,**

cf. B 4b below. (c) **cikạ** ∼ **gạrēshị** (= **cikạ kậi** ∼ **gạrēshị**) he brags, he over-rates his powers (epithet is **kowā ya cikạ kậi** ∼, **yā ragẹ**). **(18)** (a) **sǎi aŋ kai** ∼ **rānā dạ shī, kānạ yạ bīyā** he only pays debts when hounded down. (b) **suŋ kai** ∼ **rānā** they're engaged in a bitter quarrel (Vd. **kai** 3k). **(19)** (a) **yā wātsạ** ∼ he used foul language. (b) **dōki yā wātsạ** ∼ the horse kicked, bucked, waved its tail, etc. (c) **jậkī yā wātsạ** ∼ the donkey bucked. **(20) bạ bạrẹyī** ∼ **gạrēshị** he's a great liar. **(21) am bạ agōgō** ∼ (Vd. **injị** 2) the watch has been wound up (Vd. A 13 above). **(22) yanạ̄ dạ ɗan rūwā** he is a small, wiry P. (= **tsābạ** 5b = Kt. **tsagē** 2). **(23) ɗan rūwa** one of the **bọrī**-spirits living in wells (= **gumēdạ** 2 q.v.), Vd. 25 below. **(24) 'yar rūwan sanyī** f. (a) woman's female pal (k̃awā) or the latter's daughter, Vd. B 10, C 10 below ; **dịyā 5.** (b) type of food. **(25) 'yan rūwa** pl. (a) pl. of 23. (b) mosquito, etc., larvae and pupae (as they breed in stagnant water). **(26) shī** ∼ **nẹ mại aikịn sạnnū** Vd. **sạnnū** 3a.ii. **(27)** Vd. **sāran** ∼ ; hannun ∼. **(28) rījịyạd dạ bạ** ∼ miser (= **marọwạcị**). **(29)** (a) **yā shāfạ wạ kạnsạ rūwā, yā yi shirū** he thought discretion the best part of valour and so kept silent. (b) Vd. **wutā** 1r. **(30)** (a) **rūwā dạ iskạ bạ mại kaushē sụ** water and wind are irresistible. (b) **yanạ̄ cikiŋ irịm mutạ̄nē, waɗạndạ rūwā dạ iskạ bạ sạ̄ kaushē sụ** he is one of those men undeterred by anything. **(31) yā bayyạnā wạ jạma'ạ gạsk̃īyā, yā cẹ rūwaŋ dạ kadạ** he told the public the truth and warned them to be on their guard. **(32) tā isa mạ̄tar "k̃ạwō rūwā ! "** she is very pretty. **(33)** Vd. **mūgụn** ∼.

B. rūwan-compounds (alphabetically). **(1) rūwaŋ Allạ** Vd. **gạwō. (1A) rūwaŋ ạwazạ** thin layer of meat on breast of animal. **(1B) rūwam bazarā** Vd. **bazarā 2. (2)** (a) **rūwan cikị** centre of abdomen x **yā dọkē nị ạ rūwan cikị** he hit me in the centre of the stomach. (b) tum bạ ạ yi rūwan cikiŋkạ ba na saŋ wannaŋ I knew this long before you were even born. (c) dạ rūwan ciki kạn jā na rijịyā nothing succeeds like success (cf. C 7)' (3) rūwan dādī (a) water pleasant to the taste. (b) an opaque, white stone used in women's ornaments. (3A) (a) rūwan darē mại gamạ gạrī epithet of wanderer (mại yāwọ). (b) Vd. darē 4p. (3AA) rūwan dịmī Vd. dịmī 2. (4) rūwam fagē (a) remainder consisting of crumbs, wisps, grains (= dịddigā). (b) fagyantạ (= rūwam fagyantạ) ƙwaryā shidạ nē she has six ƙwaryā of thread to do in wadạrī (Vd. ƙwaryā 2), cf. A 17b above. (5) rūwaŋ gāwā (a) hard bean which fails to become cooked (= tsararrīyā 2). (b) kụnnēna rūwaŋ gāwā, bạn ji ba, bạŋ ganī ba (said by women) I know nothing of the matter, and I don't want to! (6) rūwaŋ gọrā daily subsistence-money given to dependents by traders (fatạƙē). (7) rūwaŋ gụje (a) transitory T. (b) temporary guest x bạ̄ƙō rūwaŋ gụje nē a stranger soon passes on (cf. rā6ā 1e). (8) kanạ ƙamar wạndạ akẹ ƙạdā dạ rūwaŋ hanjị ? (a) you're a bit dotty ! (b) Vd. gịdūnīyā. (9) rūwaŋ idọ gạrēshi he's one who can never make up his mind (epithet of such P. is Mại rūwaŋ idọ, gạmạ ƙạsūwā dạ yāwọ)= rēnūwā 2. (10) rūwan jirạ, mại hạƙurī ƙạ shā shị (said by woman) epithet of her younger female pal (ƙawā), cf. A 24 ; A 2 above. (10A) Vd. Jạ̄karā. (11) rūwaŋ ƙạrau cataract of the eyes. (11A) rūwaŋ kaskō Vd. ạlbarƙạcī 3c. (12) rūwaŋ ƙōfạ (a) house-doorway. (b) gateway of a town. (13) rūwaŋ kudī (a) = rūwā H below. (b) cash x in yā ga rūwaŋ kudī, sāi yạ sallạmā if he is offered cash, he will sell. (14) rūwam mại (a) butter which has melted through heat of sun, etc. (cf. E below). (b) gyạɗan naŋ tanạ dạ rūwam mại these ground-nuts are rich in oil. (15) gạrētạ rūwam māmā = gạrētạ rūwan nōnọ she (nursing mother) has rich milk in

her breasts (= gāfī 1a). (16) rūwan ruɓas saŋkacẹ heavy rain after cutting of bulrush-millet (= ruɓa saŋkacẹ = Sk. ruɓa jạnnā). (17) (a) rūwan rūwā ŋ ji birị why, the raindrops are falling on us off the trees ! (b) Vd. C 1 below. (18) rūwan shạ drinkẽng-water. (19) rūwan shiɓạ teased cotton. (19A) rūwan tsạrī Sk. = jẹfē 2. (20) rūwan tsīrā abundant rain at end of wet-season, favourable to crops (cf. 21). (21) n nạ̄ mạganạ, n nạ̄ mạganạ, bại saŋ Allạ̄ yā yi rūwan tsịrāta ba I spoke to him again and again but he ignored me (cf. 20). (21A) rūwan zāfī (a) hot water. (b) = dāfị 1. (c) Vd. C 10 below, A 2 above. (22) rūwan zartsī Vd. zartsī 2. (23) rūwan zumạ honey (Vd. E below). (24) Vd. shạn rūwan rāƙumạ (Vd. A 2).

C. Proverbs using rūwā.

(1) (a) rūwan rūwā wạndạ birị bā yạ̄ sọ humiliation can be borne from superiors, but not from their servitors. (b) Vd. B.17.a above. (2) kōmē zurfin rūwā, dạ yạ̄shī ạ cikī there's an end to all things. (3) in ~ yā ci mụtụm, kō am bā shị bịsalạ̄mī (or kō am bā shị kaifin takọ̄bī) sāi yạ kāmạ a drowning man clutches at a straw ; any port in a storm. (4) rūwạn dạ ya ịsa kurmē, dạ fādạ̄wā cikinsạ an sanị one learns by experience. (5) ~ bạ̄ · tsārạŋ kwạndō ba nẹ̄ oil and water won't mix. (6) Vd. ịyạ rūwā. (7) (a) in tā yi ~, rījịyā im bạ tạ yi ba, masai if unsuited to its destined purpose, be sure it will be put to some other use (cf. B.2c above). (b) rījịyā tā bā dạ ~, gūgā yā hanạ Vd. rījịyā 1d. (c) mai dạ ~ rījịyā Vd. mai dạ 1d. (8) in rūwaŋkạ bại ịsa ạlwạlā ba, sāi ƙạ yi tạịmamạ ƙạ tāshị if you're not rich, you must practise economy. (9) (a) dăidăi ~, dăidăi ƙurjī = dăidăi ƙurjī, dăidăi rūwansạ everyone acts according to his ability. (b) yārọ shā ~ dăidăi dạ cikiŋkạ don't try what is beyond you ! (cf. A.2). (c) rūwaŋ kaskō Vd. ạlbarƙạcī 3c. (d) kūrā nạ̄ shạn ~ Vd. kūrā 55. (e) an shā ~, yạnzu yā

kąmātą ą kōmą wąsā they have had a
breathing-space and must now return to
the task. (f) gīwā tā shā ~ dą yawą,
bąllē tā yi azųmī he's cantankerous in
any case, how much more so if provoked ! (g) bā ą cę yą shā ~ Vd.
wākē 4. (h) Vd. yąsā. (j) yā shā, tā
fi cikįnsą Vd. ciki 1h. (k) Vd. 23 below.
(l) shā ~ dą haki Vd. kąkī. (10) ąbin
dą rūwan zāfī ya dafą, iŋ aŋ hąkurą,
sǎi rūwan sanyī yą dafą time remedies
all (cf. B.21a, A.24). (11) ~ īyā
wuyą māgąnim makī waŋkā needs must
when the devil drives (cf. wuyą 1g).
(12) rūwan ciki Vd. B.2c above. (13)
bą ą fįta rūwa ba, bā ą mātsą wąrkī
don't count your chickens before they're
hatched ! (14) ~ bā yą tsāmī banzā
nobody acts without some good reason.
(15) rūwan darē, gamą gąrī what a
wanderer ! (Vd. darē 4p). (16) rūwam
bazarā Vd. bazarā. (17) (a) ą rūwa a
kąn nęmi kīfī, kękūwā sǎi zōmō go the
right way to work ! (b) nēmaŋ kīfī ą
fako Vd. fako 5. (18) sǎi ~ yā yi
saurā, a kąm bā dōki the poor get
nothing till the rich have a surplus. (19)
rūwąn dą ya dąkē ką shī nę ~ con-
centrate all your efforts on your bene-
factors ! (20) hadari bą ~ ba nę =
13 above. (21) kō yąnzu ~ ną māgąnin
daudą essentials do not change. (22) (a)
dūtsę bā yą zamā ~ you cannot make a
silk purse out of a sow's ear. (b)
dūtsąn dą kę cikin rūwa Vd. dūtsę 1l.
(23) shan ~ yā fi barįnsą half a loaf
is better than no bread ; hungry dogs
eat dirty pudding (cf. A.2). (24) (a)
an dadę ąnā rūwa, kago yąnā tsąye it's
useless to slander a P. of proved
integrity (Vd. D3). (b) Vd. kago 2 ; dadę
1c. (25) ągwągwā cikin rūwa takę nēmā
Vd. ągwągwā 2. (26) dūkąn ~ Vd. dūką
1b, c. (27) shāfa wą gēmųŋką ~ Vd.
gēmų 1d. (28) har ido ~ ząi yi ~ Vd.
hanci 1c. (29) (a) bā ą tāką ~ Vd. tāką
2aa.ii. (b) kō ą rūwa ka tāką, sǎi ą
cę kā tā dą kūrā you are blamed whatever you do. (30) ą dųbi ~ ą dųbi
tsąkī Vd. tsąkī 1b. (31) tsuntsun dą
ya jā ~ Vd. tsuntsū 5 (cf. A.3 above).
(32) kai ~ rānā Vd. rānā 2h. (33)

halin ~ Vd. ąlbasą 2a. (34) bą tā
sąbu ba, bindigą ą rūwa, Vd. sąbą 3b.
(35) yākin ~ Vd. sąkainā 1b. (36)
sakīyąd dą bā rūwā Vd. sakīyą. (37)
dągą ~ sǎi wutā Vd. karkō. (38) rąndā
tā sąmi ~ Vd. tųlū 1c. (39) tūwan
dan daŋgi bā yą ~ Vd. tūwō 18. (40) yą
kārą wą kōgī ~ Vd. Allą 7l. (40A) ą kārą
wą gąrī rūwą ? Vd. gąrī 1c. (41) tūyą
wąinā dą ~ Vd. tūyą 2. (42) Allą yā
bā ki ~ Vd. alkamą (cf. A.13 above).
(43) mai dāki yā saŋ įndą ~ yakę
zum masą Vd. dāki 9.

D. rūwā = rūwan samą rain x (1)
rūwā yā dąukē (a) the rain has stopped
(Vd. samą 1e). (b) the rainy season is
over. (c) ya kąŋ haną wą Allą ~
Vd. bąkā 8d.ii. (2) rīgar ~ f. raincoat.
(3) (a) an yi ~ rain has fallen. (b)
ąnā rūwa it is raining (Vd. C.24, 26).
(c) ąnā rūwa, kąmar dą kwaryā aką
yī shį there are (were) torrents of rain.
(d) Vd. tsūlīyā 7. (4) kāką rūwą =
įnā rūwą how does the rain suit your
crops ? (a greeting in the rainy season),
reply is dą saukī = rūwā yā yi gyārā =
kwānąkinsą nē = rūwā dą gōdīyā.
(5) (a) shower. (b) (sg. can in collective
sense be preceded by pl. adjective) x
mąnyan rūwā = mąnyan rūwāyē big
showers. (c) Vd. rūwāyē, tsīrā 2b.vi.

E. juice x (1) wannąŋ lęmū bą shi
dą rūwā this lime-fruit has no juice.
(2) Vd. B.14, 15. (3) rūwan zumą
honey.

F. colour x (1) yā fi wancąŋ kyaŋ
rūwā it is of a better colour than that
one. rūwansą irįn na wannąn nē it
has a colour like this one. mai jan ~
nę it is of a red colour. (2) (a) yā fi
wancąŋ bakin ~ it is darker in colour
than that one (cf. A.15). (b) Vd.
azųmī 2. (3) wannąŋ ąlkaląmī jā nę
mai bakin ~ this pen is dark red,
dark brown. (4) jā nę mai farin ~
it is pink. algąshī mai farin ~ light
green.

G. (1) (a) inā rūwāna what do I care ? what business is it of mine ? (== shākulāti == shigaďda 2 == shū da == kulā 2b). inā rūwansa what business is it of his ?, etc. (b) Vd. azziki 8 ; biki 2 ; Gwāri 1c. (2) (a) bā rūwāna it is no business of mine. (b) bā rūwāna, bā rūwan dangina what is it to do with me ? (c) Vd. bā rūwāna. (d) bā rū-wanki Vd. biki 1h. (e) bā rūwansa cikin wannan this is no concern of his. (3) (a) inā rūwanka why do you interfere ? (reply, da rūwāna, har da tsakina it is my affair). (b) Vd. tsaki 1b.i. (c) yā yi rūwā, yā yi tsaki he acted the busybody. (4) inā rūwam makāfo da kunya what the eye does not see, the heart does not grieve for. (5) Vd. ungulū 4 ; ganī A.2 3a.

H. (1) interest on money. (2) Vd. B.13.

J. Any handleless (marak kwōta) blade x rūwan takōbī sword-blade (apart from hilt). rūwan wukā blade of knife (apart from handle). rūwam fartanya blade of hoe (apart from haft).

K. (rūwa (short final vowel) (1) Vd. A.1b above. (2) f. one of the players in langa-game x (a) an kas (or an kashe) rūwa, langa tā mutu (i) the child playing the part of rūwa· has been caught, so the game is over. (ii) one's troubles are at an end. (b) rūwa tā shā the rūwa has reached the goal (cf. A.2 above).

L. (1) rūwa-rūwa adv. (a) in rather watery state x an dāma furan nan ~ this fura is rather waterily mixed (== tsararō 3). (b) almost within one's grasp x gā kudī rūwa-rūwa zā a bā ni, kumā bā su tabbata ba the money seemed almost within my grasp, but the matter fell through. (c) Vd. gumēda 2. (2) rūwa-rūwa m. immature P. or T. (x lad, crops).

rūwaitā Vb. 1C (1) x yā rūwaita lābāri he spread, related news.   yā ~ mini lābāri he related the news to me (cf. rūwāya). (2) nā ~ a rāina zan yī shi I decided to do it.

rūwaiwai Vd. rūwā.

rūwan-compounds Vd. rūwā B.

rūwa-rūwa Vd. rūwā L.1.

rūwa-rūwa Vd. rūwā L.2.

rūwāya f. (pl. rūwāyū) (1) (rolled " r ", Mod. Gram. 5) Ar. news, story. (2) (cerebral " r ") dispute, disagreement.

rūwāyē (1) Vd. rūwā D.5b. (2) the equine disease quittor.

rūzū m. (pl. rūzuna) (1) (a) small, but capacious knitted bag (epithet is Rūzū, mai cin kētā). (b) cī garēshi kaman ~ he has insatiable appetite. (2) type of darning.

ruzuma f. = rizma.

rwī x (1) yā kasa kunnē ~ he listened attentively. (2) yā zuba ido ~ he stared.

S

sa A.1 (sā) Vb. 1A put. (Para. A. below deals with " put in ". Para. B., " applied T. to." Para. C., " put on." Para. D., " put." Para. E., " put down." Para. F., " appointed, fixed." Para. G., " caused." Para. H., " supposed."). Vd. page 753, foot of Column 1, for sā A.2 onwards.

A. put T. or things in x (1) (a) yā ~ shi cikin akwāti he put it in the box (= ajiyē 7a), cf. zuba 2, zurma. tā ~ tūwō a akushī she put food into the wooden food-bowl. (b) yā ~ takardā a bosta he dropped the letter into the letter-box, he posted the letter. (c) tā ~ gūgā a rījiyā she let her bucket down into the well (= jēfa). (d) yā ~ fatsā a rūwa he let down his fishing-line into the water (a–d = saka). (e) yā ~ ďansa makarantā he put his son to school. (f) Vd. saka. (2) an sā a lallē Vd. lallē 1d. (3) an ~ ta a ďaka Vd. ďaka 1c. (4) (a) ~ a baka yā fi a rātaya a bird in the hand is

worth two in the bush. (*b*) *Vd.* **a̦bu̦**
1*aa*.iv. (*c*) *Vd.* **baka̦'**1*b, c*. (5) **yā sa̦mi**
wurin̄ ∼ han̄ci̦ he's found a chance of
advantage. (6) **ba̦ mu̦ sā da̦ sū cikin**
li̦ssāfi̦ ba we've not included them in
the total. (7) **ta̦ ∼ ka dawa̦** *Vd.* **son 7.**

B. (*with dative or similar prep.*)
applied T. to *x* (1) (*a*) **yā ∼ masa̦**
han̄nū (i) he took part in it. (ii) he
interfered in it (*cf.* 7, 11*a below*).
kada̦ ka̦ ∼ han̄nū ciki̦n̄ a̦l'ama̦rinsa̦
don't interfere in his affairs ! **yā ∼**
han̄nū cikim ma̦gana̦n na̦n̄ he took a
part in this affair. **tun da̦ wani ya ∼**
han̄nū, nī ba̦ za̦n yi ba since someone
else has had a finger in it, I'll have
nothing to do with it. (iii) took a
hand in *x* **sun sā han̄nū ga̦ riī̦wa̦n̄**
iī̦asa̦r they've begun to administer the
country. **mun sā han̄nū ga̦ ta̦imakwansu̦**
we've set about helping them. (*b*) **yā ∼**
mini̦ han̄nū what happened to me was
due to him (good or bad). (*c*) **yā ∼**
han̄nū a̦ bābā he's begun using new dye-
pit. (ii) **bābā yā nū̦na, gōbe zā a̦ ∼**
han̄nū dye is sufficiently infused to
start work to-morrow. (*d*) **Sarkī yā**
∼ masa̦ han̄nū the Emir has turned his
attention to him (favourably or unfavourably). (*e*) **zō ka̦ ∼ mana̦ han̄nū**
come and help us ! **yā sā mini̦ han̄nū**
he helped me. (*f*) (i) **yā ∼ han̄nū a̦**
taka̦rdā he signed the letter, document.
(ii) **yā ∼ masa̦ han̄nū** he signed it. (iii)
yā sā han̄nū cikim bāca̦ he signed the
voucher. (iv) **sun ∼ han̄nū a̦ ka̦n sun**
yi a̦lkāwa̦rī ba̦ zā su̦ sāke̦ yi̦n yāiī̦i ba
they have signed an undertaking to the
effect that they will never again make
war. (*g*) **zā mu̦ sā han̄nū a̦ fāta̦** we'll
begin work . . . (*h*) **ma̦i wu̦yar ∼**
han̄nū *Vd.* **a̦ljīfū 2.**

(2) **∼ sūnā** *Vd.* **sūnā 3, 4.**

(3) (*a*) **yā ∼ masa̦ himma̦** he devoted
his attention to it. (*b*) **∼ himma̦ yā**
fi ∼ rānā starting work is better than
fixing a day to start (*cf.* F. *below*). (*c*)
cf. 5*b*, 10 *below*.

(4) **kōmē zā a̦ yi, a̦ ∼ gishirī, an**
yi wa̦ ma̦i gidā ku̦nū whatever your
hands find to do, do it with all your
might !

(5) (*a*) **∼ ka̦i uku̦** *Vd.* **uku̦.** (*b*) (i)
yā ∼ masa̦ ka̦i = 3*a above*. (ii) took
part in *x* **bā sā sō su̦ ∼ ka̦nsu̦ ga̦**
rigima̦ they don't wish to participate
in the tumult.

(6) **∼ ido̦** *Vd.* **ido̦** 1*c*.

(7) **∼ bāiī̦ī** *Vd.* **bāiī̦ī** 2*t and cf.* B.1
above.

(8) (*a*) **an sā musu̦ gandū bāyī**
d̦arī uku̦ indemnity of 300 slaves was
imposed on them. (*b*) *Vd.* **gandū** 1*a*.
(*c*) **an ∼ ha̦rāji̦** tax has been imposed :
tax-collection has been ordered (8 =
saka̦).

(9) **yā ∼ musu̦ aminci̦** he pacified
them.

(10) *x* (*a*) **mun ∼ rāi ka̦n sāmu̦nsa̦**
we have set our hopes on getting it (*cf.*
3, 5*b above*, 12 *below*). (*b*) **mu̦ sā rāi**
ga̦ nasara̦ we must count on victory.
(*c*) **sā rāi ga̦ ci̦, shī ke̦ kāwō ji̦n yu̦n̄wa̦**
thinking of food makes one hungry
(= 12*b below*).

(11) (*a*) **yā ∼ iī̦afa̦ ciki̦n̄sa̦** = B.1*a*
above, 1*st example*. **yā sā iī̦afa̦**
a̦ iī̦asarsu̦ he set foot in their
country. (*b*) **kada̦ ka̦ ∼ iī̦afa̦ a̦ lākā**
don't involve yourself in trouble !

(12) (*a*) **mun ∼ zūcīyā ga̦ sāmu̦nsa̦** =
10 *above*. (*b*) **∼ zūcīyā a̦ ci̦, shī ya**
kāwō ji̦n yu̦n̄wa̦ thinking of eating
makes one hungry (= 10*c above*).
(*c*) *cf.* **ajīyē** 13 (*for, here* **sā,** **ajīyē**
differ in sense, cf. C. *below*). (*d*) **sun**
sā zukāta̦n̄ amin̄cēwā ga̦rēshi̦ they
trusted him implicitly.

(13) (*a*) *x* **wanna̦n̄ rīgā, an ∼ mata̦**
kudī the price of this gown has been
fixed (= **ya̦n̄ka̦** 1*d*,i. *q.v.*). (*b*) **mu̦ ∼**

kudī ạ kạnsạ let us bet on it ! (c) an ∼
kudī ạ kạntạ her bride-price has been
fixed (Vd. sạdākị 2).

(14) ∼ wutā Vd. wutā 1e.

(15) sā gạba Vd. gạba 3g.

(16) sā fuskạ Vd. fuskạ 1a.

(17) sā kụnnē Vd. kụnnē 1b.

(18) sā kặi ukụ Vd. ukụ 3.

C. (1) put on (clothing) (= sakạ =
shịga 1a.ii) x (a) (i) yā ∼ rịgā (wạndō,
hụlā, mạlạfā) he put on a gown
(trousers; fez, straw hat), cf. cirẹ. (ii)
∼ rịgar dọmin-dọmin Vd. dọmin-
dọmin. (b) bạn ∼ ạ kā ba, ṇ ji ɓạrāwạn
hụlā (= . . . ṇ ji ɓạrāwạn tạgīyạ) I
have no prospect of getting it. (2)
put T. or P. on (cf. ajịyē 4, azạ, ɗōrạ,
gwāmạ) x yā ∼ shi bisạ ạkwạtị he
put it on the box (= ajịyē 4 q.v.).

D. put x (1) sā shi ạ nạṇ put it here !
(= ajịyē 1). (2) an ∼ shi dạ mutānē
men were sent out with him (x to
help in a search, investigation, etc.).
(3) yā ∼ takọbī, yā sārẹ shi he put out
his sword and beheaded him. (4)
Vd. sā manjạgarạ. (5) kō sun yī, kō
bạ sụ yi ba, wannạm baị sā kōmē ba
whether they do it or not doesn't
matter.

E. put down x (1) yā ∼ kāyā he
(carrier) put down his load (= ajịyē 2).
(2) Vd. sakạ.

F. appointed, fixed x (1) (a) yā
sā rānā he has fixed a day, the day (cf.
B.3b above). an sā musụ rānā gạ zūwạ
a date has been fixed for their coming.
(b) Vd. aurē 6d. (2) sun sā shi Sarkī
they made him their Chief. kadạ kạ
sā wani maịmakwạṇkạ cikiṇ wannạṇ
aikị do not delegate this work to any-

one else ! an ∼ Audụ shī nẹ bạbbaṇkụ
they have appointed Audu your leader.
wā ya ∼ kạ. nī, nā ∼ kặina who set
you to do it ? (reply), I did it of my own
accord. (3) bā yā sāwā, bā yā hanāwā
he is quite uninfluential, of no account.

G. caused (1) (followed by noun or by
pers. pronoun in accusative or dative) x
yuṇwạ tā ∼ ka fushī hunger has put
you in a bad temper. yuṇwạ tā
∼ Audụ fushī hunger irritated Audu.
mē ya ∼ shi ạrạhā what has made
it so cheap ? rashịṇ waṇkā ya sā
minị ƙyāyạ it is being dirty that has
made me louse-ridden. mē ya sā shi
wannạṇ aikị what caused him to take
this step ? mē ya sā su yāƙị what caused
them to go to war ? yā sā ni cīwạn
cikị it gave me stomach-ache. yā yi
gunāgunī gạ ạbịn dạ akạ sā shi he
grumbled against the task imposed
on him. (2) (sā followed by verb which if
it has future sense, requires latter to
be in subjunctive) Allā yạ ∼ may God
bring it about ! Allā yạ ∼ kạ dāwō
lāfiyạ may God cause you to return
safely ! yā tāshị sāwā ạ yi yāƙị he set
about causing war. (3) (when sense of
second verb is progressive, then we
can use progressive (cf. 4b below)
or subjunctive) x yā sā sunā
yiṇ gōnạkī = yā sā sụ yi gōnạkī he
caused them to make farms. yanā
sāwā anā yi (or ạ yi) masạ furā he is
causing people to make furā for him.
(4) (a) (with past sense, sā in the past
tense requires the following verb to be
in the past tense also. But if sā is in a
relative tense (Mod. Gram. 133*),
so is verb following sā) x (i) Sarkī yā
sā aṇ kashẹ su the Emir caused them to
be executed. Sarkī nẹ ya sā akạ
kashẹ su it was the Emir who caused
them to be executed. sū nẹ sukạ sā
akạ yi hakạ it was they who caused this
to be done. mē ya sā sukạ zọ what led
to their coming ? sǎi akạ sā mạnzō ya
kirā shị then a messenger was sent to
summon him. ạbịn dạ ya sā sukạ yī
their reason for doing so. (ii) (a further

explanatory clause may follow, preceded by conjunction or conjunction understood). ḁbiṇ dḁ ya sḁ sukḁ īyḁ, don suṇ isō dḁ wuṛī what made them able to do it was because they arrived early. ḁbiṇ dḁ ya sḁ na kirā kḁ, dọ̄miṇ kḁ taimḁkē ni what led me to sending for you was the wish that you might help me. ḁbiṇ dḁ ya sḁ mukḁ kirā kḁ, n nḁ̄ sọ̄ ṇ yi mḁganḁ dḁ kai what caused us to call you was because I wanted to speak to you. *(b)* (i) *(when* sḁ *is in* relative past, *and* following verb has progressive *sense, following alternatives are possible)* *x* sai ya sḁ sunḁ̄ yiṇ gọ̄nḁkī = sḁi ya sḁ su yi gọ̄nḁkī = sḁi ya sḁ sukḁ̄ yiṇ gọ̄nḁkī then he caused them to make farms. shī ya sḁ akḁ̄ sọ̄, etc., *this* is why one wants to. (ii) *(progressive in both clauses) x* dḁ wani bḁbban dḁlīlị wandḁ kḁ̄ sḁ sukḁ̄ yị (= sunḁ̄ yị = sḁ yī) there is a good reason for their doing so. (5) sḁi ya sḁ tswḁffī sukḁ tḁfi wurinsḁ then he caused the old men to go to him *(here* tswḁffī *is noun and object of* sḁ, *while* sukḁ *is subject-pronoun of verb* tḁfi. *If, however, as in* mḁ̄ ya sḁ sukḁ zọ̄ *in* 4 *above, the subject-pronoun of the second verb contains the object of* sḁ *understood, this* pronoun-object *may alternatively be expressed as follows) x* mḁ̄ ya sḁ su sukḁ zọ̄ what led to their coming ? mḁ̄ ya sḁ ki kikḁ zọ̄ what led to your coming, woman ? nā sḁ su sun tḁfi I caused them to go. ḁbiṇ dḁ ya sḁ (= sḁ ni) na zō, n nḁ̄ cḁ̄wā why I came was because it seemed to me that . . .

H. supposed *x* bḁn sḁ zai yi minị hakḁ ba I never supposed, expected he would act so to me. ḁ sḁ mu tḁfi Kano let us assume we are going to Kano !

J. *Vd.* sḁ bḁbba sātḁ, sḁdakḁ, sā dḁ kūkā, sḁ fḁ̄rū jikkā, sḁ hḁnkḁ̄kī dākọ, sḁ mai gidā tsallē, sā ṇ sḁ, sḁ dōrō, sḁ bḁ̄kī maiƙọ.

sa A.2 (sḁ̄) (1) *m.* (*f.* sāṇīyā = sānūwā) *pl.* shānū = shḁ̄nḁkai = shānḁnnakī =

Sk. 'yan naggḁ̄) (*a*) ox, bull (*epithet is* Tūnārḁ̄ = Zīnārīyā dḁ ƙḁfō). (*b*) yā yi fuskḁr shānū he scowled, frowned (*Vd.* fuskḁ 1*c*). (*c*) ḁ ɓātḁ zūcīyas ∼, sḁn naṇ mīyḁ tḁ yi dādī = sḁi zūcīyas ∼ tā ɓācị, mīyḁ kḁn yi zāƙī everyone acts on the principle "devil take the hindmost ! ", desperate causes need desperate remedies. (*d*) ∼ mārar kāyā *Vd.* mārā 3. (*e*) ta ∼ dḁbaṇ, ta sāṇīyā dḁbaṇ = ta ∼ kūwā bḁ̄ kḁmar ta sāṇīyā ba natures differ. (*f*) (i) yā bi shānun Sarkī = yā shigḁ shānun Sarkī it has become lost or untraceable (= tḁ̄kū 2). (ii) saniṇ shānū *Vd.* sanị 2*b*.v. (*g*) shānuṇ Gwamnḁ labourers, carriers (= lēburḁ), *Vd.* kḁ̄rīyḁ. (*h*) *Sk.* sāṇīyā = jar sāṇīyā blast you ! (*j*) iṇ kā ga bḁbbar sāṇīyā tsḁkānim maruƙḁ, girmantḁ yā zubḁ̄ he who associates with inferiors lowers himself. (*k*) sāṇīyā bā tḁ̄ gazḁ̄wā dḁ ƙḁfantḁ come what may, one must shoulder one's responsibilities. (*l*) sāṇīyā bā tḁ̄ gōdḁ̄ jējị he is so ungrateful for benefits that he keeps on pestering his benefactor. (*m*) saṇīyar dawḁ = sāṇīyar sḁkē buffalo (= ɓaunā). (*n*) sāṇīyar tḁ̄tsā (i) milch-cow. (ii) profitable T. (*o*) turbḁr shānū ɓad dḁ bḁ̄ƙō, yārọ yā bi, bai sanị ba he has brought a hornet's nest about his ears. (*p*) bḁ̄ shānū *Vd.* shigḁ sharọ. (*q*) jan ∼ dḁ abḁ̄wā *Vd.* abḁ̄wā. (*r*) sāṇīyā tanḁ̄ lāshḁ̄ *Vd.* ḁbu 2*b*. (*s*) bịkin sḁ̄ *Vd.* bịkī 1*j*. (*t*) cin sḁ̄ *Vd.* gajḁ ganī. (*u*) idḁn sāṇīyā *Vd.* idọn 16. (2) *(in children's game)* (*a*) A. says sam minị kḁdaṇ give me a little ! B. says cḁ̄ne ∼ take it by force ! A. then says ∼, to which B. replies sḁ̄cē minị take it from me by theft ! (*cf.* ƙwḁ̄ 3, turmī 8). (*b*) sāṇīyā ! *Vd.* dḁkū.

sa A.3 (sḁ̄) (Mod. Gram. 118) *x* (*a*) sḁ̄ zō they'll probably come (= *Sk.* swḁ̄). (*b*) *Vd.* ḁikā 2. (*c*) *cf.* sā'ḁ.

B. (sḁ) (1) his. (*a*) dōkịnsḁ his horse (Mod. Gram. 47*b*). rịgarsḁ = rịgassḁ =

rĩgã tasạ his gown (Mod. Gram. 47*b*) =
shị 3. (*b*) (*after v.n. of changing verbs
and after secondary v.n.*). (i) ạikarsạ =
aikịnsạ the sending him (Mod. Gram.
47*c*). nĕmansạ the looking for him.
tạmbayạrsạ = tạmbayạssạ = tạmbayạ
tasạ the asking him (Mod. Gram. 47*c*).
munạ̃ nĕmansạ we are looking for him.
munạ̃ tạmbayạssạ we are asking him.
(ii) (*gives continuous sense in cases like
the following*) yā yi zamansạ cikin
d̃ākịn naŋ well, he went on living in
that house.   yanạ̃ tạ̃fīyạ tasạ sǎi . . .
while he was on his way, then . . .
yanạ̃ yāwạnsạ sǎi . . . while wandering
about, he . . .   (*c*) *Vd.* sụ 4.   (*d*) *Vd.*
tāsạ 1*a*.ii.   (*e*) nãsạ his (*after masc.
noun*) *x* jạ̃kin naŋ nāsạ nĕ this donkey
is his.   tāsạ his (*after fem.*) *x* rĩgan naŋ
tāsạ cĕ this gown is his.   (2) *Vd.* masạ.
(3) *Sk.* him (*object of changing verb*,
Mod. Gram. 49*a*¹) *x* sun nĕmāsạ they
looked for him = sun nĕmĕ shị (*Vd.*
sa).

C. (sa) *Sk.* him (*objective pronoun
after low tone in previous verb*, Mod.
Gram. 49*a*¹) *x* suŋ ginạ sa they built
it (*cf.* sạ 3).

sa'a A. (sā'ạ) *f.* (*pl.* sā'ō'ī) (*Ar.*) (1) (*a*)
(i) hour, time *x* ạ wạcẹ ∼ sukạ zọ̃
at what time did they come ? = ạ
wạnẹ sā'ị sukạ zọ̃.   (ii) sun yi sā'ạ
ạrbạ'iŋ caŋ they spent 40 hours
there.   (iii) wannạŋ ita cẹ̃ sā'ạ ta
sọ̃sǎi this was the appointed hour of
death.   (*b*) sā'ạ-sā'ạ *adv.* occasionally,
from time to time (= rāna-rāna).
(2) clock, watch.   (3) (*a*) good luck
(= gạmō 2 = mụwāfakạ) *x* kā yi ∼
you were lucky.   yā tạ̃ki ∼ he was
lucky.   (*b*) Allạ̃ yạ̃ bā dạ̃ ∼ good luck !
(*c*) mugunyạr ∼ bad luck.   (*d*) sā'ạrsụ
tā 6ācị their luck was out.   (4) propitious time for setting out, doing T.,
etc. (*a*) yā d̃aụki ∼ he ascertained what
was a propitious day.   (*b*) *Vd.* fitar dạ̃
4*b*.   (*c*) yā nẹ̃mi ∼ he sought a propitious day (*cf.* burụjī).   (*d*) yā bā nị ∼

he (diviner) told me of propitious day
to set out, etc.   yā īyạ̃ bā dạ̃ ∼ he can
cast horoscopes to find out propitious
times.   (*e*) yā sạ̃mi ∼ he hit on a propitious time (= rānā 5*d*).   (5) saŋ
dạ̃ = sad dạ̃ = sā'ạn dạ̃ = sā'ạd dạ̃
when *x* (*a*) (i) saŋ dạ̃ mukạ jẽ Kano,
(sǎi) mukạ gan shị = saŋ dạ̃ mukạ
jẽ Kano, muŋ gan shị when we went to
Kano we saw him (*Vd.* Mod. Gram.
181*a*.i).   (iA) *Vd.* dukạ̃ 3.   (ii) (*with progressive sense*) *x* saŋ dạ̃ suŋ̃ yārā = saŋ
dạ̃ sukẹ̃ yạ̃rā during their boyhood.   (*b*)
saŋ dạ̃ na yi magana dạ̃ Audụ, Daudạ̃ yā
fịta = sad dạ̃ na yi magana dạ̃ Audụ,
Daudạ̃ yā rigā yā fịta at the time I was
addressing Audu, David had already
gone out (Mod. Gram. 181*c*).   (*c*) saŋ dạ̃
mukạ zō, yanạ̃ kạrạ̃tū (*less commonly*
yakẹ̃ kạrạ̃tū) he was reading when we
came (Mod. Gram. 181*c*).   (*d*) tạ̃shi
sad dạ̃ bā kạ̃ sọ̃, kạ̃ ịsa sad dạ̃ kakẹ̃
sọ̃ work hard at the outset and rest
later !   (*e*) (*future sense*) saŋ dạ̃ sukạ
zō, zaŋ tạfi kạ̃sūwā = . . . sǎi ṇ tạfi
kạ̃sūwā, etc., when they come, I shall
go to market (Mod. Gram. 186).
(6) saŋ naŋ = sā'ạn naŋ (*a*) then
x (i) bạ tạ̃ kai marī ba, saŋ naŋ
zạrạŋ ya k̃arẹ she'd not yet reached the
spacing-peg when the thread gave out
(Mod. Gram. 182*a*).   yā yi zụ̃k̃ā ukụ,
saŋ naŋ tāba ta k̃arẹ he took three
whiffs, then the tobacco came to an
end.   (ii) dạgạ raŋ dạ̃ akạ yi wannạŋ
dōkā, saŋ naŋ tạ̃ kāma kōwā dạ̃ kōwā
this law will apply to everyone from the
day it is promulgated.   (iii) saŋ naŋ
zāmanin Tụ̃rāwā ya fạ̃ru it was *then*
that the European occupation of the
country began.   (iv) sǎi dạ̃ ya shā
tukụnā, saŋ naŋ akạ bạ̃ k̃anānā it was
not till he *himself* had drunk that the
little ones were served.   (*b*) in that case
x im muŋ ga sulẹ̃ bạ̃ kan Sarkịŋ Iŋgilạ̃,
saŋ naŋ bā mạ̃ kạr6ā if we see a shilling
which does not bear the effigy of the
head of the King of England, in that
case we do not accept it.   ạ sā'ạn naŋ,
sǎi yạ̃ bā mụ in that case he must give
us it.   in sum fādạ̃ manạ, ạ saŋ nam
bạ̃ sauran zamā if they attack us, we

shall take immediate action. **in yā sam mahaukạcī nē, sạn naŋ yā̀ sā shi wạzịrì** ? if he knows him to be mad, would he appoint him prime minister ? (c) so *x* **shī kạnsạ ạzābạ nē, sạn naŋ in** it is a torture in itself, so if into the bargain . . . (d) in addition *x* **gā̀ haliŋ kirkị, sạn naŋ gā̀ wạyō** he has a good character and cuteness in addition. (7) the measure **sā'ị** *q.v.*
B. (**sa'ạ̀**) *m., f.* (*pl.* **sa'ō'ī**) *Ar.* (1) P. of about one's own age (= *Sk.* **wā̀rī = zumụ 1 = dīyyạ**). (2) *cf.* **farar sa'ạ̀**.

saba A. (**sābạ**) *Vb.* 3A became accustomed *x* (1) (a) **nā ~ dạ wannạŋ** I'm accustomed to this. (b) **bisạ gạ yạddạ sukạ sābạ** according to their habit. (c) **gịndiŋ kūrā yā ~ dạ rāɓā** *Vd.* **kūrā 41.** (d) **jā̀kī yā ~ dạ kāyā** *Vd.* **tạkarkạrī 1b.** (e) **yā ~ ɓacēwā** *Vd.* **ạ̀bụ 2k.** (2) **sā̀ba dạ wụyā, d'am balbēlạ** you must reconcile yourself to the fact that you'll have a stiff time ! (3) **sā̀ba dạ mai fitọ tun rānī** don't leave things till the last minute !, forewarned is forearmed.
B. (**sabạ**) *Vd.* **sabạ dạ.**

saɓa A. (**sāɓạ**) *Vb.* 3A. (1) *x* **mun ~** we missed one another by following different routes. (2) **dayansụ yā ~** one of them projects beyond the others. (3) quarrelled *x* (a) **mun ~.** (b) (i) **tsạkāniŋ harshẹ dạ haƙōrī a kạn ~** there's bound to be friction between friends, but there must be some give and take. (ii) **dạ harshẹ dạ haƙōrī sunā̀ sāɓạ̀wā, barē mutā̀nē** to err is human so one must pardon. (4) (a) varied *x* **sum bā nị lā̀bārịn naŋ, bạ sụ ~ ba** they informed me of this, their versions not varying. **mạganạd dạ ka yi minị tā ~** what you told me is not in accordance with the circumstances. **hāliŋkạ yā ~** your behaviour is not the same as before. (b) **kā ~ = kā sāɓạ ạlkāwạrī** you have broken your promise. **Audụ yā ~** Audu has not kept his word. (5) (a) **yā sāɓạ musụ** he disobeyed them (= **sā̀ɓā 2**), *cf.* **sāɓị, sāɓō.** (b) **bạ mụ sāɓạ musụ bisạ gạ wani ạbin dạ sukē sọ̀ ba** we did not oppose them in any of their wishes. (c) **sun sāɓạ wạ**

hanyạrmụ they have different ways from us.
B. (**sā̀ɓā**) (1) *f.* (a) sloughed-off skin of snake or lizard. (b) **yanā̀ ~** (i) it (snake, etc.) is sloughing its skin. (ii) his (feverish P.) skin is peeling off (*all* = **zā̀nā**). (2) *Vb.* 2 disobeyed *x* **yā sā̀ɓē sụ** he disobeyed them (= **sāɓạ 5** *q.v.*).
C. (**saɓā**) *Vb.* 1A (1) (a) **yā ~ Alƙur'aŋ** he swore on the Koran (**rantsūwā** *q.v.* is any type of oath). (b) **yā ~ lāyạ** (i) = **1a.** (ii) camel hit its chest with its knee (considered sign it will deliver load at destination safely) (*cf.* **masaɓā**). (c) **furā (wạinā) tā ~ lāyạ** the furā (wạinā-cakes) are unsold at this late hour, so chance is slight of disposing of them to-day. (2) slung T. over the shoulder *x* (a) **yā ~ bindigạ** he shouldered his rifle : **yā ~ hannun rịgā** he flung the sleeve of his gown on to his shoulder. (b) *Vd.* **makadī 2.** (3) (a) **yā ~ bindigạ** he fired the rifle. (b) **bạ tā̀ saɓu ba, bindigạ ạ̀ rūwa** it's impossible. (4) (a) measured T. out in cubits (*Vd.* **kāmụ 5a**). (b) **yā ~ gōnā** he measured the farm by pacing (*Vd.* **tākị 2b, saɓị 1**) or 6 ft. staff. (5) **an ~ gạyyā** people have been summoned to collective labour. (6) **yā ~** (= **yā saɓō**) **gandarā** he brought trouble on himself. (7) *Vd.* **kōkawạ 1d.** (8) **an ~ masạ sā̀bulụ** soap has been rubbed on it (clothing, body, etc.) (= **saɓẹ 1c**). (9) **tā ~ shiɓạ** she flicked cotton with bow-string. (10) (a) **yā ~ mịsālị** he gave an example. (b) **yā ~ mịsālị dạ shī** he used it as an illustration. (11) **yā ~ cācā** he threw gambling-dice (*cf.* **saɓẹ 1d, saɓad dạ**). (12) **yā ~** he (darạ-player) got three of his pieces in a row, thus huffing his opponent. (13) **yā ~ wutā** he made fire with flint, steel, and tinder. (14) **sun ~ wạsōsụ** *Vd.* **wạsōsọ.** (15) *Vd.* **saɓō.**
D. (**saɓā**) *Vb.* 2 (1) (heat, air, liquor, etc.) had overpowering effect on P. *x* (a) **rānā tā saɓē shị** the sun overpowered him. **hūcịn dōkị yā saɓē nị** I fell over through the air-disturbance caused by the passing horse. (b) *Vd.*

hannun 1b. (2) sạɓi, zạrce m. telescoping together x (a) doing two days' journey in one, doing without food till evening when not compelled to by azụmī, etc. (b) Jāmụs sunā nufịn yi wạ Masạr sạɓi zạrce the Germans intended to pass through Egypt at whirlwind speed. (c) bilking trader by giving him the slip and leaving by back door.

saba'ạ f. 7,000.

sabạb (Ar.) used in bā gairạ, bā ~ without rhyme or reason (Vd. sabạbī).

sạbābạ (1) f. forefinger (= alị). (2) Sạbābạ name for any man named Sambọ q.v.

sā bạbba sātạ m. (sg., pl.) type of large bean (= sakạ bạbba sātạ = yārọ 6).

sābạbbī Vd. sābō.

sabạbī Ar. m. (1) (a) reason, cause (cf. sabạb). (b) Vd. gairạ 2c. (2) wrangling. (3) kadạ kạ jā minị ~ don't bring trouble on me ! (4) sabạbin prep. on account of, because of.

sạbạbīyyạ f. = sabạbī 1.

sabạd (1) = sabạb. (2) Sk., Kt. sabạd dạ because of (= sabọ dạ).

sạbadạ f. (1) immature ɗọrōwạ-pods. (2) girkē-gown.

sabạ dạ Sk. because of (= sabọ dạ).

sabạd dạ Vd. sabạd.

saɓad dạ Vb. 4 yā ~ kuɗinsạ he gambled away his money (cf. saɓạ 11).

sạbạ'iŋ f. 70.

sabạk = sabạb.

sā bākī maikọ Vd. farī 2d.

sạbạlikịtā m., f. good-for-nothing P.

sāɓānī m. (1) mun yi ~ dạ shī we missed each other through following different routes (= sāɓạ 1). (2) disagreement x mun yi ~ we've fallen out (= sāɓạ 3a). (3) varying from x wannạŋ sāɓānim mạganạrkạ ta jīyạ cē this is different from your statement of yesterday (= sāɓạ 4). (4) a thief's charm to avoid harm (= sạmātsī 1). (5) the plant Tephrosia elongata (= sạmātsī 3).

sabạr = sabạb.

sạbarạ f. (pl. sạbạrū). (1) (a) the plant Guiera senegalensis (pounded, dried leaves used for piles (bāsụr) ; its wood-smoke keeps flies off cattle, Vd. duɗɗạlī 3 ; from roots (bạrbartā) comes

decoction for nursing-mother and infants). (2) wani zōmō ạ ~ kạm bar shi " don't reckon without your host ! " (= hakị 1b). (3) Sạbarạ tā taɓạ shi he has disease of unknown origin supposed due to spirit Gạjērē (for Sạbarạ is wife of Gạjērē 2 q.v.).

sabarbaɗẹ m. (pl. sạbạrbạɗai). (1) = tsạrnū. (2) (with f. sabarbaɗīyā) tall, strong youth, horse, etc.

saɓar dạ = saɓad dạ.

sāɓar tākạlmī Kt. f. (1) treading on heels of P. (= dundūnịyā 2). (2) junior's insubordinately preventing carrying out of work ordered by his superior.

saɓā-sạɓā x tanā da yātsū ~ she has tapering fingers (applied also to girls, leeks, etc.).

saɓas dạ = saɓad dạ.

sạɓatạ jūyạta f. trading in odds and ends.

sabbananị = sabbinanị.

sạbbātụ Kt. = sạmbātụ.

sạbbī Vd. sābō.

sabbinanị = Alā sabbinanị Long life to you ! (a greeting to superiors), reply is iŋgwai = iŋgwayyā = mādạllā = āmiŋ = mhm = yạwwā).

sabbunanị = sabbinanị.

sabce (1) = safce. (2) Vd. bị sạbcē.

sạbci fạɗi Kt. m. pointless talk (= sọki bụrūtsū).

saɓe A. (sāɓẹ) (1) Vb. 1A (a) abraded x yā fāɗị, yā ~ kafạ he fell and abraded his foot. (b) pounded (wood first heated in fire (babbạkā 4), to remove bark). (2) Vb. 3A (a) became abraded. (b) yā kāmạ ɓērā ạ wutsīyạ, wutsīyạ tā ~ having caught the rat by the tail, the rat escaped leaving the tail in his hand.

B. (saɓẹ) (1) Vb. 1A. (a) (i) = saɓạ 2. (ii) Vd. makaɗī 2. (b) made saɓīyā. (c) rubbed soap on to clothing, body, etc., x yā ~ fuskạ tasạ dạ sạbulụ he rubbed soap on to his face (= saɓạ 8). (d) (i) yā ~ he (gambler) lost all his stakes. (ii) yā ~ kuɗiŋ Audụ he (gambler) won Audu's stakes (cf. saɓạ 11). (e) measured whole of (as in saɓạ 4). (f) flicked all the cotton (as in saɓạ 9). (2) Vb. 3A (a) became emaciated. (b) = sacẹ.

C. (saɓe) *x* sunā saɓe da bindiga they've sloped arms.

sabga *f.* (*pl.* sabgōgī). (1) affairs, business (= mu'āmala) *x* munā ∼ da shī we're doing business with him. (2) aɓōkin ∼ confrere, business-associate, close friend.

sāɓī *Vd.* sābō.

saɓi A. (sāɓị) *m.* (1) *x* sāɓịm mutānē garēshị he does wickedness to people (= saɓō, *cf.* saɓā 2). (2) two zānāmats, or mats of stalk (karā) which overlap to provide entry ¯or exit (= baɓɓa ka raka mai gijị), *cf.* raka mai gijị.

B. (saɓị) (1) cubit (= kāmu 5*a*). (2) (*a*) (*secondary v.n. of* saɓā 4) *x* yanā saɓịŋ gōnā = yanā saɓa gōnā. (*b*) act of measuring (*as in* saɓa 4) *x* jīya an yi wa gōnā saɓị. (3) act of soaping (*as in* saɓa 8) *x* rịgan naŋ, ∼ bīyū aka yi mata da saɓulu this gown has been twice soaped. (4) act of throwing dice (*as in* saɓa 11) *x* Audu bai īya ∼ ba Audu does not know how to throw dice. (5) move in dara (*Vd.* saɓa 12). (6) *Sk., Kt.* = shiɓa.

saɓīlị (*Ar.* " road ") *used in* (1) saɓīlịn *prep.* on account of *x* saɓīlịm mē on account of what, why ? (2) saɓīlị da (*a*) = sabo da. (*b*) *conj.* on account of the fact that.

saɓīya *f.* second row of stitching when making seam (= taushị 5).

saɓi zarce *Vd.* saɓā 2.

sabka *Kt.* (1) = sauka. (2) saɓkar sirdị = rage 1*a*.iii.

sabke A. (sabkę) *Kt.* = sauke.

B. (saɓkē) *Kt. m.* (1) hunting guineafowl in early morning. (2) boy's setting out in early morning for work on gayaunā (= *Kt.* taɓē 3). (3) saɓke huce = sauke huce.

sabkō (1) = sammakō. (2) = saukō *q.v. under* sauka.

sabo A. (sābō) (1) *m.* (*f.* sābūwā = sābwā) *pl.* sāɓaɓɓī = saɓɓī = sāɓī new. (*a*) yāro nē sābwar haifụwā he's a newborn lad. (*b*) sāban zūwa nē he's a newcomer. ita sābwar zūwa cē she's a new-comer. sū sāɓaɓɓin (= sāban) shigā nę they're new to the service (police, soldiers, etc.), *cf.* Mod. Gram.

89*c*[1]. (*c*) ∼ pul brand new (= saŋkā 3). (*d*) ƙwăi bā sābō ba nę the egg is not fresh. (*e*) sāban tākalmī *Vd.* tākalmī 1*d*. (*f*) da sābaŋ ginị *Vd.* yāɓē 2*b*. (*g*) *Vd.* alkāwarī 2. (*h*) sābaŋ ƙarfī *Vd.* badarę. (*j*) sābaŋ ganī *Vd.* aŋgọ. (*k*) *Vd.* sābwā. (2) *m.* new ground-nuts.

B. (saɓō) familiarity with *x* (1) (*a*) saɓō yā hōrę minị kōgī experience has accustomed me to crossing rivers. (*b*) ∼ turkyaŋ wāwā don't be a stick-in-the-mud ! (2) sābam mazā fada disputes lead to appreciation of the good in people : dissension among *real* men is a necessary preliminary to friendship. (3) (*a*) ∼ da kāzā bā yā hana yaŋkanta friendship with a senior won't help you if you do wrong. (*b*) manta ∼ *Vd.* alkālī. (*c*) ƙị ∼ *Vd.* dāmisa 2. (4) bā sābam ba he's not really to blame as he's still unaccustomed to it. (5) sābaŋ idọ shī kę sa rēnị familiarity breeds contempt. (6) cịn dādī ∼ *Vd.* dādī 5.

C. sabo da (1) (*a*) on account of *x* ∼ haka muka zō it was because of *this* that we came. (*b*) (*we can also use* don ∼) *x* bā don sabo da haka muka zō ba it was not owing to *this* that we came. tun da yakę suŋ hakīkance da wannaŋ, sabo da haka suka zō they came in view of the fact that they are sure of this. (*c*) ∼ karaŋ gidaŋka ka kaŋ ga karaŋ wani like attracts like. (2) *conj.* because of the fact that *x* ∼ nā san shị because of my knowing him.

saɓo A. (sāɓō) *m.* (1) sinning (*cf.* sāɓị, sāɓā 2). (2) *Sk.* a quarrel.

B. (saɓō) *used in* (1) saɓō lāfīya a ∼ lāfīya may you return safely ! (2) kā ∼ lāfīya ? have you returned O.K. ? (= barka da zūwa). (3) *Vd.* saɓa 6.

sabo da *Vd.* sabo.

sabrō *Kt.* = saurō.

saɓu *Vd.* saɓa.

sāɓu *Vb.* 3B (1) = sāɓa. (2) = shāƙu.

saɓuhānallāhị (*vulgar pronunciation*) = subhānallāhị.

sāɓula *Vb.* 2 (1) = tūɓe 2. (2) (*a*) stripped skin from beans, rizga, etc.; stripped off corn-sheath (tsirgāgīyā) = sulluɓe 1*b* = tūɓe 3. (*b*) nā saɓulị tsịrē

I stripped meat off skewer on which spitted. (3) *Vd.* sāɓulē.

sāɓulancī *m.* wearing trousers in a way exposing much of the buttocks (*cf.* ƙirīrị 2).

sāɓulē *Vb.* 1C (1) = sạɓulạ. (2) yā sāɓulẹ tākalmạ he kicked off his shoes.

sạbulu *m.* (*Ar. from Italian* sapone). (1) (*a*) soap (*Vd.* hạŋgūgu). (*b*) sạbulun salō type of Nupe soap. (2) yā shā ~ he was abused. (3) sạbulun kuyạŋgī = sạbulun 'yam mātā the herb *Zornia diphylla.*

sabunta A. (sābuntā) *Vb.* 1C renewed.

B. (sạbuntạ) *Vb.* 3C became renewed.

C. (sạbuntā) *f.* newness.

sạbuntakạ *f.* = sạbuntā.

sābwā (1) *Vd.* sābō. (2) wata ~ (*a*) *f.* type of gambling. (*b*) sằi gạ wata sābwā then a fresh event occurred.

sạcaccē *adj.* stolen = sạtaccē.

sace A. (sācẹ) *Vb.* 1A. (1) stole. (2) yā ~ jịkī he slunk away. (3) *Vd.* sạ̄ A.2 2 (*page* 753).

B. (sạ̄cē) (1) *Vd.* sạ̄tā. (2) *m.* (*pl.* sātunạ = sātuttukạ) double thickness of material let into back and front of gown (= ginshiƙị 2 = ballō), *cf.* ƙurūru 2.

C. (sạ̄ce) *x* ạ sạ̄ce on the quiet.

D. (sacẹ) *Vb.* 3A (1) subsided *x* hannunsạ yā ~ swelling in his hand has subsided. ƙumburī yā ~ the swelling's gone down. rōbạ tā ~ tyre is deflated. iskạ tā ~ the wind subsided (*all* = saɓẹ 2*b*). (2) *Kt.* became emaciated.

sạci *Vd.* sạ̄tā.

sācīyāf. passing intestinal wind (= tūsạ 1).

sad *Vd.* sā'ạ 5.

sādạ *Vb.* 1A (1) caused to meet *x* (*a*) Allạ̄ yạ ~ mu dạ ạlhērị (i) may we meet again safely ! (ii) God prosper us ! (*b*) Allạ̄ yạ ~ ka dạ gidā lāfīyạ may you reach home safely ! (2) delivered *x* nā ~ takạrdā dạ hannunsạ I delivered the letter to him. (2A) *Vd.* sādad dạ. (3) yā ~ ta he ruptured her perineum (= sājẹ 2). (4) *x* ạ ~ wurịŋ yạ dạ̄idā itạ let the place be filled in till it is level ! (= sājẹ 2), *cf.* lēbur. (5) Sādạ garī *Vd.* jạkādạ.

sādạ *Vd.* sīdīdī.

sadạb *Ar. m.* mother-of-pearl.

sadad = sadar.

sad̳adạ A. (sādādā) *Vd.* sīdīdī.

B. (sad̳ādā) *Vb.* 3A went stealthily, crept along (= laɓạ̄ɓā).

C. (sạdādạ) *Vb.* 2. (1) stalked. (2) tried to get P. off his guard (to cheat him, etc.), *cf.* sad̳ādā.

D. (sad̳adā) (1) *f.* yā yi ~ he acted stealthily. (2) stealthily *x* tanạ̄ tạfīyạ ~ she's walking stealthily.

sad̳adaf = sad̳adā 2.

sadad da A. (sādad dạ) *Vb.* 4 = sādạ 1, 2 *x* kạ ~ dạ magạnạn nạŋ garēshị deliver this message to him ! zā ạ ~ hanyạr dạ Kanọ this road will be linked up with Kano.

B. (sadad dạ) *Vd.* sadar dạ.

sad̳af-sad̳af = sad̳adā 2.

Sādạ garī *Vd.* sādạ 5.

sadag dạ = sadar dạ.

sạdajjē *adj. of state, from* sājẹ.

sadak dạ = sadar dạ.

sadaka A. (sadakạ) *Ar. f.* (*pl.* sadakōkī = sạdake-sạdakē). (1) (*a*) (i) charity, alms (= zạkā 2 = *Kt.* takkūwā). (ii) sằi ạ ƙārạ wạ Mālạm sadakạ ạddu'ạ tạ gạmu dạ ịjābạ trust God but keep your powder dry ! (*b*) gạrin ~ the gumbā-flour divided out at death-feast. (*c*) kāyansạ duk, yā rabạ ~ he gave away all his wealth in charity. (*d*) sadakạr mamạcī alms given on 3rd, 7th, and 40th day after death of one's father, etc. (*e*) 'yar ~ (i) = baịwā 3*c*. (ii) *Vd.* sạdarrạdak. (2) yā yi ~ dạ rạnsạ he risked his life, he sold his life dearly.

B. (sạdạkā) *Damagaram* = zakkạ 1.

sạdạkạ *f.* (*pl.* sạdạkū = sādakōkī) concubine slave-girl (= ƙwạrƙwarạ *q.v.*), *Vd.* dạkạ 1*c*.

sạdạkī = sạdạkī *m.* (1) money given by bridegroom to wạlị of his bride to buy her goat, sheep, cow, necklace, etc. (the minimum used to be 1,300 cowries, *i.e.* rubu'in dīnārị, but is now sixpence or much more, *Vd.* aurē 6*c*) = igīyạ 7. (2) an yaŋkẹ (= an sạ̄) minị ~ sulẹ shidạ the sum (*as in* 1) I have to pay is six shillings.

sạdạki lạƙē *m.* giving to one's household food originally intended for sadakạ 1*a.*i.

sạ̄dạku *Vd.* sạ̄dakạ.

sā dạ kūkā *m.* tight ƙarau bracelet put on wrist by means of lubrication with soap.

sạdarạ *f.* (*pl.* sạdạrū) *Ar.* line of writing, line of print (*cf.* zạ̄nē).

sadar da A. (sādar dạ) = sādad dạ.

    B. (sadad dạ) *Kt.* *x* nā ∼ Allạ̄ I put my trust in God (dạŋganạ).

sạdarrạdak (1) mun rạbu ∼ (*a*) we separated, neither of us owing the other anything. (*b*) I came away from him empty-handed. (2) ∼ 'yar sadakạ tā fādạ ạ rījīyā how disappointing to receive no gift !

sadas dạ = sadar dạ.

sadā-sạdạ̄ = saɓā-sạɓạ̄.

Sạ̄dau name for boy or girl born after divorced mother has returned to husband because found to be pregnant.

sadạukā gave as charity *x* (1) nā sadạukạ kudī I gave money in alms. (2) nā ∼ makạ shī I give it you as charity, *cf.* sadakạ. (3) = sadaukad dạ.

sadaukad dạ *Vb.* 4 = sadạukā 1. (2) (*a*) mutạ̄nạn dạ ya sadaukar ạ fagyam fāmā the lives he squandered in war. (*b*) yā sadaukam musu dạ ransu he spared their lives.

sạdạukạntakạ *f.* bravery (*cf.* sadaukī).

sadaukī *m.* (*f. only used by* ạlmājịrai, *is* sadaukā) *pl.* sạdạukai. (1) brave warrior. (2) Sadaukī name for any Ạbū Bakạr.

sad da A. (sad dạ) *Vb.* 4 = suŋkwīyad dạ.

sādẹ *Kt.* = sājẹ.

sadī *m.* (1) stick passed through loops of loads to hang them on a pack-animal. (2) stick put into woman's rāgā to hold it firm.

sạdīdạn (1) *m.* (*a*) sure remedy (= kạifī-yạn 1). (*b*) reliable statement. (*c*) unalloyed T. (*x* metal). (2) *adv.* in unalloyed state, etc., *x* yā bā nị māgạnī ∼ he gave me a sure cure.

sạ̄ dōrō *Vd.* bugu 1*b*.

sạ̄du *Vb.* 3B (1) met *x* mun ∼ ạ Kano. (2) suited *x* haŋkạlīna dạ nāsạ bạ su ∼ ba our temperaments are opposed. (2) reached *x* yā ∼ dạ Kano he reached Kano. takạrdā tā ∼ dạ hannūna the letter reached me.

sạdūdạ *Vb.* 3B *x* yā ∼ he has become calm in mind.

safa A. (sāfā) *f.* (1) (*a*) leek(s). (*b*) spring-onion(s) (= ạlbasạ 8). (2) nincompoop.

    B. (sạ̄fā) *f.* (*pl.* sāfạmfamī). (1) soft-soled riding-boots reaching to knee = sụfādu (*cf.* kụrfai). (2) quilted garment worn by warriors and serving as armour (*cf.* lifịdī, sụlkē). (3) (*a*) sock(s). (*b*) stocking(s). (*c*) glove(s).

    C. (safạ) *Vb.* 1A. (1) (*a*) increased slightly (length, price, etc.), *cf.* sạfē. (*b*) Allạ̄ yạ ∼ azzịkī may God prosper us ! (2) exceeded T. slightly (= ɗarạ). (3) *Kt.* began T.

    D. (Sạfā) *f.* (1) during Pilgrimage at Mecca, worshippers proceed from Mt. ∼ to Mt. Marwạ. (2) yanạ̄ ∼ dạ Marwạ he wanders to and fro (= kạiwā dạ kāwọ̄wā).

sāfạcē *Sk.*, *Kt.* *Vb.* 3A dodged away, slipped away (= baudẹ).

sạfai (*only negatively*) *x* bạ̄ ∼ ya kạn zō ba he does not come often.

sāfalā *f.* tūwō made for sale (*Vd.* mīyạ 12).

sāfạmfamī *Vd.* sạ̄fā.

Safar *Vd.* lạ̄rạbgạnā.

safarạ *Ar. f.* (1) = fataucị. (2) *Vd.* idọn 14. (3) *cf.* Sạhārạ. (4) ūwar ∼ *Vd.* dụmbā.

safạragō *m.* = matākī.

sạ̄ fạrū jịkkā = sạ̄ fạrū jịkā *Kt. m.* fool.

safce A. (safcẹ) yā ∼ gōnā he completed first light hoeing to produce straight furrow, prior to deeper digging, *cf.* sạftā.

    B. (safcē) (1) *Vd.* sạftā. (2) *m.* acting as in sạftā.

safe A. (sāfē) (*Ar.* subh). (1) *adv.* (*a*) dạ ∼ in the morning (*cf.* sassāfē). (*b*) dạ sāfē a kạn kāmạ fạrā, in rānā tā yī, sǎi su tāshị the early bird catches the worm. (*c*) ta sāfē ta yārọ, ạmmā in rānā tā yī, sǎi mutạ̄nạn gạrī a new broom sweeps clean. (*d*) sǎi dạ ∼ a kạn ɗaukō *Vd.* sandā 1*f.* (*e*) tūwan ∼ *Vd.* sụkūnị 2*b.* (*f*) sǎi dạ ∼ adieu till to-morrow ! (*reply*, Allạ̄ yạ kai mụ !, *to which is replied* ạ̄miṇ). (2) *m.* = sāfīyā.

    B. (safẹ) (1) *m.* (*f.* safịyā) colt about three years old (*epithet is* Safẹ majẹ gạba). (2) *m.* (*a*) first indigo-crop in its first season (*Vd.* kụsūsụ, gwarzō 2).

(b) **safaŋ gēmụ** beginning of a beard. (c) *Vd.* **safīyā.**
C. (**sạfē**) *m.* (1) **yā yi minị** ～ he over-charged me. (2) leaving unshaven line on head of girl of 8–12 years old, to allow growth of hair previously shaven too far back (*cf.* **ɗaurịŋ gūgā 3**).

sāfī (1) *m.* (a) thimble (= *Kt.* **lifịdī 6**). (b) oxtail-hide covering of matchet-handle, etc. (2) *adj.* (*Ar.*) pure *x* **rūwā** ～ pure water. **azụrfā** ～ un-alloyed silver. **zạncē** ～ true account. **mụtụn nē** ～ he's honest.

sạfīfạ *Ar. f.* braid on **jabbạ, kạftānị,** etc., and on neck of **ạlkyabbạ** (= **ạmārạ**).

sāfịrcē *Vb.* 3A said **ạstạgfịrụllāhạ** (1) *q.v.* (*cf.* **sāfirullạ**).

sāfirullạ (*Ar.* astaghfiru'llāha) may God forgive me ! (for unintentional perjury, etc.), *cf.* **sāfịrcē, ạstạgfịrụllāhạ.**

safiya A. (**sāfīyā**) *f.* (1) (a) morning (*cf.* **sāfē**). (b) *Vd.* **sallạ 1e.** (c) ran **sāfīyar wannạŋ cịŋ ạmānạ** on the morning he committed this depredation. (d) **nasarạr sanyin sāfīyā** easy victory. (e) **mun yi sāfīyar mātā** we got up safely in the morning (*cf.* **sāfīyar mazā**). (f) **mun yi sāfīyar mazā** we went to war (*cf.* **sāfīyar mātā**). (2) *adv.* (a) **sāfīyar Allạ dukạ** = **kullụŋ sāfīyā** *adv.* daily. **kullụŋ sāfīyā sầi ƙarfī ƙē ƙạrụwā gạrēmụ wajan sōjạ** all the time we are becoming stronger in soldiers. (b) *Vd.* **Ạljumma'ạ.**
B. (**safīyā**) *f.* (1) *Vd.* **safẹ.** (2) beginning of swelling of scrotum.

sạfīyọ (*Eng.*) *m.* (1) surveying. (2) relaying of railway-line.

safka = **sauka.**

sạfōramī *Vd.* **sạhōramī.**

sạftā A. (**sạftā**) *Vb.* 2 (*p.o.* **sạfcē,** *n.o.* **sạfci**) **ya sạfci gōnā** he did first light hoeing in farm to get straight furrows prior to deeper digging (= **fēdạ 3** = **shērị** = **tsạgē 1**), *cf.* **rufị 5.**
B. (**sạftạ**) *Vb.* 1A = **sạftā.**

saftụ = **sautụ.**

safū = **sahū.**

saga A. (**sāgā**) *f.* adult woman.
B. (**sagā**) *f.* shelf suspended from rafters and mainly used by village crones (fire-wood, stalks, etc., are kept

in it and as it is made from old well-rope, etc., it is considered inferior in dignity to **rạgayạ**).

sagạdā-sagadā (1) *m., f.* wastrel (= **shā-shạshā**). (2) unreliable behaviour *x* **kadạ kạ yi minị** ～ don't behave to me with your usual fecklessness.

sạgạgī *m.* uncultivated land near village or town (= *Kt.* **sụŋƙūrụ**).

sagạlabị *Kt. m.* fool.

sạgarā *f.* pullet.

sagaraftū *m.* = **rīshī.**

sāgạrcē *Kt.* = **saŋgạrcē.**

sạgau *m.* (1) charm (**lāyạ**) in form of leather wrist-bangle, supposed to stiffen arm of opponent striking one (= **ƙagau** = **ƙī bugụ**). (2) **gūgā tā yi** ～ bucket has jammed in well (= **kạgau** 1), *cf.* **sagẹ.**

sagẹ (1) *Vb.* 3A = **ƙagẹ 1a, b.** (2) *Vb.* 1A stiffened, paralysed (= **ƙagẹ 2** *q.v.*).

sagi *m.* (1) clod, sod (= **hōgẹ**). (2) **tsạkānimmụ dạ ɗan** ～ there's a balance of debt outstanding between us. (3) *Kt.* (a) = **rārīyā 1.** (b) = **kwalbạtị.** (c) hunter's platform in tree (*cf.* **bạgō**).

sāgịdā *Kt.* = **shāgịdā.**

sagō *m.* (1) any snake (= **macịjī**). (2) rainbow (= **bạkā 8a**). (3) **sagwan cikị** = **tānā 1b.**

sagwabạ *Sk.* = **shạgwabạ.**

***Sạhābī** *m.* (*pl.* **Sạhạbai**) one of the Companions of the Prophet (*cf.* **sāhịbī**).

sạhānị *m.* (*pl.* **sạhạnai**) (*Ar.*) kettle.

sā hạnkạ̄kī dāko type of herb with drastic, purgative qualities.

Sạhārạ *f.* (1) the Sahara. (2) *cf.* **safarạ.**

***sahhạhā** *Vb.* 1C (*Ar.*). (1) did (work, etc.) well. (2) proved, confirmed.

sāhịbī *m.* (*f.* **sāhịbā**) *pl.* **sāhịbai.** (1) close friend (*cf.* **Sạhābī**). (2) **Sạhịbansạ dạ tābị'īnạ** His (Muhammad's) Companions and followers.

***sahīhancị** *m.* sincerity, truthfulness.

sạhīhị *m.* (*f.* **sạhīhịyā**) *pl.* **sạhīhai.** (1) sincere, honest, truthful. (2) healthy. (3) handsome.

sạhōramī *m.* (1) good-for-nothing P. (2) *Vd.* **lụƙwāsọ.**

sạhōrō *m.* (1) = **sạhōramī.** (2) *Vd.* **lụƙwāsọ.**

sahu A. (sahū) *m.* (*Ar.* saff). (1) row, line.
(2) sahū-sahū in rows, lines.
B. (sạhū) *Vd.* gamị 3*d.*
sg̣hūhụ *m.* (*f.* sg̣hūhụ̄wā) *pl.* sg̣hụ̄hwai
Kt. fool.
sạhụr *Ar. m.* pre-dawn meal during
azụmī (*Vd.* duƙū-duƙū 2).
sg̣hūrụ *Kt.* = sg̣hūhụ.
sai A.1 (sai) (1) *Sk. m.* (*a*) urine *x* yā
yi ∼ he urinated (= sanyī 12*a*). (*b*)
cīwạn ∼ = sanyī 12*b.* (2) (*a*) (i) yā ∼
shị he bought it (= yā sạyē shị). yā ∼
dōkị he bought a horse (= yā sạyi
dōkị). (ii) *Vd.* rārīyā 3*c.* (*b*) = sayạ.

A.2 (sǎi) A. *prep.* except (*after nega-*
tive) *x* (1) (*a*) bā mai yịnsạ ∼ kai there's
nobody to do it but you. wanīna bā
yg̣ yịnsạ ∼ nī nobody would do it except
myself. (*b*) (*quasi-verb following*
negatived verb in preceding clause) and
there is nothing except *x* im muŋ
ga bā kạn Sarkiŋ Iŋgịlạ, ∼ kạn Sarkin
Jạbū, bā mg̣ kạrɓa if we see it (a coin)
does not bear the effigy of the King of
England, but merely that of the King
of Ijebode, we will not accept it.
Kanāwā bā sg̣ ƙaryā ∼ daɗi the Kano
people do not lie, they merely
exaggerate. (2) (*if negative is under-*
stood, not stated (like it is in 1*a*), *then*
sǎi = there is nothing except, there is
nobody except) *x* (*a*) fansar bāwạ, ∼ dạ
kudī only with money can a slave be
redeemed. ∼ g̣bịn dạ ka cẹ it's for you
to give the order and for me to obey (*lit.*
there's nothing but what you say). ∼
haƙạ this is how it happened . . . kudī
nẹ̃ kạmar waɗannạŋ, sǎi dǎi ƙan sāban
Sarkī gạrēshị it is money just the same
as this, the only difference is that it
bears the head of the new King.
(*b*) dg̣gạ nī ∼ kai *Vd.* dg̣gạ 3*b.*i
(*c*) wani wạndạ im bā Audụ sǎi
shī a colleague of Audu's. (3)
except (*after positive*) *x* Tg̣rābụlụs duk
hg̣mādạ cē ∼ ta wajan tẹ̃kū Tripoli is
all desert except along the coast. (4)
Vd. G.2 *below.*

B. nothing is (was) done except
(*quasi-verb used when first clause is*

negative and sǎi *introduces second clause*
which contains a verb). (1) (sǎi *followed by*
subjunctive *indicating* habit) *x* bā
wạndạ ya īyạ jinyạr mg̣sū cīwọ, ∼ g̣
bar gidansụ bg̣rkạtai (= sǎi dǎi ang̣
barịŋ gidansụ bg̣rkạtai) nobody knew
how to care for the sick, so their
quarters were left higgledy-piggledy.
sg̣ƙō bā yg̣ hūcẹ zūcīyā, ∼ yạ hūcẹ
ƙafạ a message sent by a chance-
traveller does not comfort the mind, it
cools nothing but one's foot. (2) (*when*
second clause has past sense, *then* sǎi
introduces verb in past) *x* bā sụ sạki
bọm ba, ∼ sun sạki jạrīdạ they did
not drop bombs, but merely news-
papers. bā don sunā tsg̣mmānị zā
g̣ yi yāƙị ba, ∼ dǎi don suŋ ganī . . .
it is not because they thought there
would be war, but merely because they
saw . . . bā dom mā arzịkinsụ ba kaɗǎi,
sǎi dōmin sū . . . not only because· of
their wealth, but also because they . . .
bā wannạŋ ya bā mụ haushī ba, sǎi dǎi
dạ sukạ yi kuskurẹ it was not *this*
which annoyed us, but it was because
they made a mistake. (3) (*sometimes*
where sense verges on both habitual and
past, sǎi *may introduce either* subjunctive or past) *x* bā sụ tafạ cịn
nasarạ ba ∼ aŋ kǭrē sụ (= ∼ g̣ kǭrē
sụ) they have never been victorious,
but always been defeated.

C. then (1) (*stands before second*
clause with verb in relative form, *first*
clause meaning " when ") *x* (*a*) sạn dạ
mukạ jē Kanọ ∼ mukạ gan shị when
we went to Kano, we saw him (Mod.
Gram. 181*a*.i). dạ mukạ gabācē sụ, ∼
sukạ gudụ (= sǎi dạ sukạ gudụ) when
we approached them, they fled (Mod.
Gram. 181*a*.i), *cf.* H. *below.* (*b*) tun
dạ mukạ bạlagạ, ∼ mukạ sōmạ aikị
we began to work from the time we
reached puberty (Mod. Gram. 181*a*.i).
(*c*) tum bai zō ba, ∼ na gamạ aikị I'd
finished work before he came (181*a*.i).
kg̣mịm mụ jē Kanọ, ∼ akạ shigạ
ɗakạ before we reached Kano, the
people had retired to rest (191*a*.i), *Vd.*
E.3 *below.* (*d*) ịndạ mukạ jē ∼ mukạ gan

sụ we saw them at the place we went to (181*a*.ii). (*e*) bāyạn dạ sukạ gịrbi hatsī, ~ sukạ hūtạ after reaping the corn, they rested. (*f*) ạbịn dạ sukạ bā nị, ~ na ƙi I refused the one they offered me (181*a*.ii). (*ff*) bā zāgị yakẹ̄ mā ba, har kūkā sǎi dạ ya yi not content with abuse, he even proceeded to bawling out. (*g*) duk dạ wannạn, sǎi sukạ yi ta cẹ̄wā in spite of this, they said that . . . (*h*) yạddạ sukạ yi, sǎi sukạ gamạ dạ saurī their method was to finish quickly. (*j*) dạ jịnsạ ~ ya yi fushī as soon as he heard it, he became angry. (*k*) sun shịga kẹ̄ naŋ, ~ sukạ gam mụ as soon as they entered, they saw us (181*e*). (*l*) būdẹ̄ bākimmụ kẹ̄ dạ wụyā, ~ sukạ kwạɓē mụ hardly had we opened our mouths before they snubbed us (181*e*). (*m*) mazansụ sun sạkē sụ, dạgạ naŋ ~ sukạ yi ta yāwọ after their husbands had divorced them, they went wandering about (182). (*n*) yā yi zụ̄ƙā ukụ, ~ tābạ ta ƙārẹ he took three whiffs, then the tobacco came to an end (182). (*o*) naŋ dạ naŋ (= bā lāɓārị) ~ sukạ harbē nị dạ ƙafạ they kicked me unexpectedly. (*p*) (*progressive in first clause*) *x* yanā shịgā, sǎi ya gan tạ no sooner had he entered than he saw her. darē nā̀ yī, sǎi sukạ tāshị night was falling when they set out. (*q*) (*subjunctive in first clause*) *x* mụ wāyi garī, sǎi gā̀ ạbịn dạ ya bā mụ mā̀mākị we woke up one fine morning to encounter a surprising thing. (*r*) (sǎi *with verb understood*) yạmmar fārị sǎi gidaŋ ụbantạ in the early evening she went to her father's house. (2) *Vd*. Mod. Gram. 183 for " then ", after " while " in first clause. (3) sǎi *can be replaced by* sǎi dạ. (*a*) *Vd*. *second example in* C.1*a above*, C.1*ff*, G.2, H, J, L.2 *below*. (*b*) gūrịnsụ sụ zō, sǎi dạ kụ̄wā sukạ zō they were determined to come, cost what it might. (4) (" then " *is sometimes put in the form of a rhetorical question, though no interrogative sense is implied*) *x* rạn naŋ bā sǎi akạ ji bạ ? then on that day they heard it. sukạ bi maƙịyammụ, bā ~ sukạ yā̀ƙē mụ

bạ ? then they went over to our enemies and made war on us (*cf*. J.1 *below*).

D. nevertheless (1) (*after* " no matter how much " *etc*., *in first clause, we have* sǎi *with past tense in second clause*). (*a*) kōmē wụyā tasạ, ~ nā̀ yi oh no, no matter *how* difficult it is (was), yet I can (could) do it (*reply to* it's beyond you), *Vd*. Mod. Gram. 184. (*b*) (*first clause is often omitted*) ~ nā̀ dọ̄kē tạ yes, I *will* beat her (*reply to* whatever you do, don't beat her !), 184. (*c*) (*if second clause has* habitual sense, sǎi *is followed by* subjunctive) *x* kō ita tā yi fushī, ~ yạ dịŋgạ bā tạ magạnạ no matter how angry she gets, he always calms her (184). (2) (*after* whatever, whoever, wherever, *etc*.). (*a*) (*if sense is* past *or* present, sǎi *requires* verb *in* past tense *or* subjunctive, Mod. Gram. 185*a*) *x* kōịnā mukạ jē, ~ muŋ gan shị wherever we went (go), we saw (see) him (= ịndạ mukạ jē dukạ, ~ mụ gan shị). duk ịndạ na nẹ̄mā, ban sā̀mē shị ba wherever I sought, I didn't find him (*negative second clause cannot have* sǎi). (*b*) (*if sense is* future, sǎi *requires verb in* subjunctive) *x* kōyạushē mukạ tạfi (= kōyạushē zā mụ tạfi), ~ mụ gan shị we'll see him whenever we go (Mod. Gram. 185*b*). (3) sǎi dǎi *x* sǎi dǎi dạ wani ạbụ mại bā mụ mā̀mākị nevertheless, there is one thing which surprises us. sǎi dǎi bā yā̀ īyạ yị̄ however, he's not up to doing it.

E. in that case (*when* " if " *stands in first clause we have* sǎi *with* subjunctive, *etc*., *in second clause*, Mod. Gram. 186*a*) *x* (1) in sun zō, ~ ṇ tạfi kā̀sūwā if they come, I'll go to market. in yā zō, ~ kạ tạmbayạ if he comes, you must ask (*here*, sǎi *is that of* F. *below*). iŋ kā fạɗi wata magạnạ, garī nā̀ wāyẹ̄wā, ~ kạ ga 'yan sandā sun zō if you talk any more and the dawn comes, the police will arrive. (2) (*similar to* D.1 *above*) *x* in yā zō, ~ nā̀ tạmbayạ if he comes, I'll most certainly ask (Mod. Gram. 186*b*). (3) kā̀mịn yạ zō, ~ ṇ gamạ by the time that he

comes I shall have finished, *Vd.* 1*c*
in C. *above* (Mod. Gram. 186*e*).
(4) (*unfulfilled condition*) *x* dạ̈ an
ţambąyē nị, ~ ņ yạrdā had I been
asked, I'd have agreed (Mod. Gram.
187*a*). (5) (remote possibility) *x* dạ̈
ạ̈ ţambąyē nị, ~ ņ yạrdā if I were to be
asked, I'd agree (Mod. Gram. 187*b*).

F. must (*quasi-verb followed by* subjunctive) *x* (1) (*a*) ~ mụ yī dạ saurī
let us do it quickly ! ~ kạ ţạfī yạnzu
you must go now ! ~ kạ fadạ masạ
you'd better tell him ! (*b*) ~ kạ bar
wurī bạ̈ shạ̈rā you're just the kind that
would leave the place unswept ! (Mod.
Gram. 106A.*a*). (*c*) sǎi ạ ƙārạ wạ
Mālạm sadakạ *Vd.* mālạmī 1*c*.vi. (*d*) ~
ạ barạ darị ƙwansạ *Vd.* darị. (*e*) sǎi
ạ bar kạ̈zā *Vd.* kạ̈zā 1*b*. (*f*) *Vd.*
E.1 *above*, G.1*b below*. (2) (*this* sǎi
is often used with cẹ̈ " said ") *x* ƙarfī
gạrēshị ~ kạ cẹ̈ zākị he's as strong as
a lion (Mod. Gram. 106A.*b*), *Vd.* cẹ̈ 3.
(3) (*in subordinate clause*) *x* kō dạ ya
sạ̈mi wannạņ ụmụrnī ~ yạ zō when he
received this order to come.

G. (1) (*a*) than (*from* F. *above, is derived
sense* " than " *with* future *meaning*) *x*
bạ̈ ạbịn dạ ya fi ~ mụ kōmạ gạrimmụ
there's no better plan than for us to
return home. (*b*) (*exact construction
of* F.1 *above*) *x* ạbịn dạ ya fī, sǎi mụ
hūtạ we had better rest. dạbārạd dạ
tà fī, sǎi sụ ţạru the best thing would be
for them to gather. (2) (*from* A.
above, is derived sense " than " *with*
past *meaning*) *x* bạ̈ ạbịn dạ ya fi
fạrạntā manạ zūcīyā ~ dạ mukạ gan
sụ nothing pleased us better than seeing
them (*lit.* except that we saw them).

H. when (sǎi dạ) *x* sǎi dạ mukạ jē
Kanọ, sǎi mukạ gan sụ when we went
to Kano, we saw them. sǎi dạ darē
ya yī, akạ būsạ kạ̈kạ̈kī when night came,
the trumpet was blown (Mod. Gram.
181*d*³), *cf.* C.1*a above*.

J. only when (sǎi = sǎi dạ). (1)
(*negative usage*) not only after *x* kun

sam mạ'ạnar wannạņ, bạ̈ ~ mum fadạ
mukụ ba you know (knew) the meaning
of this without it being necessary for us
to tell you (*cf.* C.4 *above*). (2) (past
sense positive *uses* relative *construction
in both clauses, but if* sǎi (*not* sǎi dạ) *is
used, relative construction is not used
in first clause*) *x* sǎi dạ akạ kashẹ su
ţukụnā mukạ zō it was only after they'd
been killed that we came (Mod. Gram.
181*d*). ~ yā gā yā ci mịl tarạ,
sạn naņ ya jūyō gidā it was only after
he saw he'd covered nine miles that he
turned homewards. (3) (*a*) (*future
sense uses* subjunctive *in second clause*)
x sǎi an shā fāmā dạ shī ţukụnā yạ
fịta it cannot be got outside without
great effort. sǎi kā zō kānạ mụ ţạfi it
is only after you have come that we will
go (Mod. Gram. 107*c*). (*b*) (*construction
of* 3*a above sometimes* omits second
clause) *x* in zā sụ fịta, ~ sun ţambạyē
shị izịnī when going out, it is only after
asking permission (that they do so).
(*c*) (*for future sense, we can also use
various alternatives*) *x* kạ̈mịn yạ fịta, ~
an shā fāmā dạ shī = sǎi an shā fāmā
dạ shī, zại fịta = sǎi an shā fāmā dạ
shī, yakẹ̈ fịtā = 3*a above, first example*.
(*d*) sǎi bạ̈ki yā cī *Vd.* bạ̈kī 1*b*.xiii. (*e*)
sǎi aņ kai rūwā rānā *Vd.* rūwā A.18*a*.
(*f*) sǎi rūwā yā yi saurā *Vd.* rūwā C.18.
(*g*) sai rugā tā kwānā lāfīyạ *Vd.* rugā 1*b*.
(*h*) sai wani yā rasạ *Vd.* sạ̈mā 1*a*.vi.
(*j*) sǎi katạngā tā tsāgẹ̈ *Vd.* tsāgẹ̈ 2*b*.
(*k*) *Vd.* yāmụtsā 1*a*.ii. (*l*) sǎi kwạrī
yā cịka *Vd.* zāgīyā 1*b*. (*m*) sǎi dājị
yā yi yawạ *Vd.* zākị 1*d*. (*n*) sǎi am fasạ
Vd. bịdī 5. (*o*) sǎi birị yā zō hannum
Mālạm *Vd.* birị 1*b*. (*o*) sǎi kā sō *Vd.*
kandarẹ.

K. unless (*with future sense*) (sǎi
with subjunctive) *x* bạ̈ zā kạ ɗagạ
ɗagạ nạm ba ~ kạ bīyā you don't
leave here unless you pay (Mod. Gram.
106B), *cf.* L.1*a fifth example*.

L. till (*with past or future sense*) (sǎi
with past tense) *x* (1) (*a*) ~ kā zō
adieu ! (*lit.* till you come !). ~ mun

dāwō adieu ! (*lit.* till we return !). ajīyē shi ~ mum bukācē shi put it away till we need it ! yā ajīyē shi ~ mum bukācē shi he put it away till we needed it. ba zā ka ɗaga daga nam ba ~ kā bīyā you don't leave here till you pay (*cf.* K.), Mod. Gram. 107*a*. sannū sannū ~ kā gā bā sauran tsōfaffin kudī this will go on till gradually there is no more of the old money. (*b*) (săi in *sometimes is used for* " till ") *x* ba zā mu taimakē su ba săi in sum bar kashe jūnansu we shall not help them till they cease killing each other. (*c*) săi dăi wani jiƙo, karē yā zubad da tsāmīyar kūrā that's the end of the matter for the present. (2) (săi da *with relative form of verb can also be used*) *x* sun tsare garinsu săi da suka gā bā dāmā they defended their city till they saw there was no further chance. (3) (*verb already mentioned is often understood negatively before* " till ") ~ yā gama salla tukunā no, (do not call him) till he has finished praying ! (*reply to* shall I call him ?), Mod. Gram. 107*b*. săi dăi an kāwō tukun no, (we shan't eat) till it's brought (*reply to* are you going to eat now ?). audugarsu ~ sun gama ta da rama they (don't use) cotton till mixed with hemp. zā a bā ka ammā ~ an kai an kāwō they'll give it to you, (but not) until after much delay. (4) *Vd.* har.

M. only (*a*) (*usually emphasized word heads sentence preceded by* săi *and followed by* relative form of verb) săi ƙōƙarin yim maƙāmai sukē yī it is only *weapons* that they are striving to manufacture, Mod. Gram. 137. (*b*) abin da zai sā ka taɓa ajīyan nan, ~ fa ƙamar dom bīyan kāyan janā'iza the only thing permitting you to use this deposit is, for example, the provision of funeral appurtenances.

N. habitual sense (**1**) (*alternatively with* kan, *we can use* subjunctive *with or without* săi *when there are* two or more contrasted habitual clauses or clauses of sequence which balance one another)

x (*a*) shunku (săi) ya hau, (săi) ya sauka the 5-franc piece rises and falls in value (Mod. Gram. 106D). wani sā'i (săi) ya zō nan, wani sā'i (săi) mu jē gidansa sometimes he comes here, sometimes we go to him. in an kāwō abincī, a cī, san nan a shā when food is served, one eats and then drinks. binī-binī săi wani mutum ya tāshi, ya cē constantly men get up and say . . . (*b*) (*second of clauses may be replaced by* progressive) *x* mutānan Kano da Katsina, săi a kāma hannun jūnā, anā ɗaga ƙafa gaba ɗayā, anā tafīyar abūtā bisa tītī the people of Kano and Katsina shake hands together, keep pace together and walk in a friendly way in the streets. (2) (*provided* kullun, wani sā'i, binī-binī, *etc.*, *appear, we can use* săi *with either* past tense *or* subjunctive *in cases where* second *of the* contrasted clauses *is omitted, or where there is only* one habitual clause) *x* (*a*) shunku wani sā'i săi yā hau = shunku wani sā'i săi ya hau = shunku wan sā'i ya kan hau the 5-franc piece sometimes rises (Mod. Gram. 106D.*b*). kullun săi sun zō nan = kullun săi su zō nan = su kan zō nan kullun they always come here. nan dūnīya, kullun săi wani mutum ya tā da fitina, etc. there is always someone in the world who stirs up strife. (*b*) (săi *can be omitted, cf.* N.1 *above*) *x* kullun mu fita farauta nēman abincī we always used to go out hunting in search of food.

sa'i A. (sā'ī) *m.* (*Ar.* sā'). (**1**) the four mūdanabi given by every member of a household to beggar (almājirī), *cf.* sā'i 1. (2) (*a*) assessor of jangalī appointed by Muslim religious law (shar') to assess tithes (zakā). (*b*) Zar. one of the sarauta.

B. (sā'i) *m.* (**1**) (*Ar.* sā', *cf.* sā'ī) measure equivalent to 16 handfuls (= sā'a), *Vd.* zakka, sā'ī 1. (2) hour (= sā'a) *x* wani sā'i sometimes (*Vd.* 2 *in* săi N).

saiɓāɓā *Vd.* sassaiɓā.

saiɓī *m.* (**1**) ill-luck (including not finding P. to marry). (2) an wanke saiɓinta (saiɓinsạ) = an yi matạ (masạ) waŋ-kan ∽ ablutions have been done for her (him) who has at last managed to get married.

sai da A. (sai dạ) = sayar dạ.
    B. (saidạ) *Vb.* 1A. (1) *Sk.* = sayar dạ. (2) *Kt.* = shaidạ.

*sạ'īdạ *Ar. f.* good luck (= sā'ạ) *x* ạbiŋ yā zō manạ dạ sạ'īdạ we were successful in it.

sā'idī *used in* sā'idiŋ dạ when *x* sā'idiŋ dạ mukạ zō when we came (= sā'ạ 5).

saidụ *used in* ụban ∽ = ajiŋgi.

saifạ *f.* spleen *x* ∽ tasạ tā kụmburạ he has enlarged spleen (= marāɓịyā).

Sạifī *name of a* book of devotions.

sā'ilī *used in* sā'iliŋ dạ = sā'idiŋ dạ.

saima A. (saimā) = sēmā.
    B. (saimạ) = sainạ.

sai mā fụnshe *m.* (1) T. only apparently good. (2) P. only apparently good or merely appearing to be simpleton. (3) statement not really complete, but needing further elucidation.

saimō *m.* unfertile ground (= shạ̄ɓūwā), *cf.* fafọ.

sainạ *f.* (1) A. offered for sale. (2) ∽ bā tạ fārēwā sǎi kuɗin yārọ sụ gazạ it's purchase-money which is always lacking, not goods on which to spend it. (3) ɗan ∽ (*f.* 'yar ∽) *pl.* 'yan ∽ seller.

sainō = saisainō.

*Sạ'īrā *Ar. f.* one of the Muslim hells.

saisai *Vd.* sēsē.

saisainạ *Kt. f.* = sainạ.

saisainō *m.* tūwō made from flour of bulrush-millet (gērō) or wheat, less solid than but resembling bụrạbuskọ.

saisaitā (1) *Vb.* 3A took a rest. (2) *Vb.* 1C. (*a*) fanned (food) to cool it (= fīfītā 2). (*b*) yā saisaitạ muryạ he lowered his voice (= sassautā 2).

saisayạ *Vb.* 2 *x* an saisạyi gāshinsạ his (man's) hair has been cut, its (sheep's) coat has been sheared. an saisạyi gēzā tasạ (kụnnansạ) (gāshiŋ kọ̄fatạnsạ) they have sheared its mane (horse's ear-hair) (horse's hoof-hair).

saisayē *Vb.* 1C sheared all of (*as in* saisayạ).

saishē *Vb.* sayar dạ.

saisụ̄wā *Kt.* = sayạrwā.

sạiwā *f.* (*pl.* saiwōyī) (1) (*a*) root (*cf.* tūshẹ 1). (*b*) = fwạ̄yā 1*b*. (*c*) sū nẹ̄ saiwōyim fịtinạ *they* are the instigators of the rising. (2) yā yi ∽ ạ wuriŋ he has become permanently resident. (3) yā hafẹ mini̱ ∽ he "has cut the ground from under my feet". (4) ∽ tasạ tā mōtsạ he's quivering (i) from rage, (ii) from drinking tsimi to become invulnerable (*Vd.* mōtsạ 1*g*.i). (5) sạiwar sạlā (*x*) even-tempered. (*b*) not pungent (*x* onion). (6) *Vd.* jan ∽.

sājạ *m.* (*pl.* sājōjī) (*Eng.*) (1) sergeant. (2) sạ̄jạmanjạ *m.* sergeant-major (*cf.* manjạ).

sạjādạ = sụjādạ.

saje A. (sājẹ) (1) *Vb.* 3A (*a*) *x* wuriŋ yā ∽ the place has been filled in to level it. (*b*) kụduddufī yā ∽ dạ hanyạ the borrow-pit has been levelled up with the road. (*c*) yā ∽ cikin jạmạ'ạ he mixed with the crowd. (*d*) imitated *x* bạgidājẹ nē ạmmā yā ∽ dạ mutạ̄nam birnī he's a rustic but he imitates townsmen. (*e*) resembled *x* tā sā tufāfim mazā, tā ∽ dạ sū she put on male attire and so resembled men. (*f*) *cf.* bạ̄ ∽. (2) *Vb.* 1A = sādạ 3, 4. (3) = sājạ.
    B. (sạ̄jẹ) *m.* (1) side-whiskers (*cf.* wạhābā). (2) sạ̄jam bisạ *Kt.* shaving head except narrow line over top of head between temples.

sāji = sājạ.

sājōjī *Vd.* sājạ.

sak (1) *adv.* *x* (*a*) arẹ̄wā ∽ due north. gabạs ∽ due east. (*b*) yā mīfẹ ∽ he went in a bee-line. (2) *m.* yā yi ∽ he remained motionless.

saka A. (sākạ) *Vb.* 1A. (1) recompensed (good for good or evil for evil) *x* nā ∽ masạ ạlhēriṇ dạ (= nā ∽ masạ bisạ gạ ạlhēriṇ dạ) ya yi mini̱ I recompensed him for his goodness to me (= rāmạ 2*b*.i = waiwạyā 2*a*), *cf.* sạ̄kạmakō, fansā 2. Allạ̄ yạ ∽ dạ ạlhēri may God give a good reward! (2) nāmạn naṇ yanạ̱ sākạ̄wā this meat is beginning to stink.
    B.' (sakạ) *Vb.* 1A (1) = sạ̄ A.1*a*, *b*, *c*, *d*; B.8; C.1*a*.i; F. (2) (*a*) kạzā tā ∽ fwǎi the hen has laid an egg (= jēfạ = *Kt.* nasạ), *cf.* sạ̄ E., zazzạgē 4. (*b*)

kạbēwạ tā ⁓ ɗā the marrow put forth ɪruit. (c) hantsạ tā sakō the udder has increased in size. (d) Kt. ạkwīyạ tā fārạ sakạ̄wā goat's udder has begun to become big. (e) yā ⁓ bịdī his hair is greying (= bịdī 3). (f) tā ⁓ kạ̄dā she has put into the basket as much raw cotton as she can tease (cf. sakị 2e, sakẹ 1). (g) tā ⁓ minị ɗayā = jēfạ 2b.ii (cf. sakị 2d). (3) ịnā akạ ⁓ ; ịnā ka ⁓ Vd. ịnā 4. (4) yā ⁓ ạjīyạ he has leucoma. (5) wurin naŋ dạ rūwā, ạ ⁓ masạ there's pus here, so the place should be incised (Vd. sakīyạ). (6) Vd. sạkạ bạbba sātạ ; sạkạ 6urnā.

C. (sạkā) Vb. 2 (Vd. sakị, shikạ). (1) (a) released x an sạki bursụnạ the prisoner has been released. yā sakō musụ daŋginsụ he set their relatives free (cf. ạsakō). (b) divorced (a wife) x yā sạki mạ̄tạ tasạ he divorced his wife (Vd. shikạm battạ, ạsakō 3). (2) (a) (i) let go of x yā sạki bindigạ he fired the rifle. yā sạki ịgwā he fired the artillery-gun. yā sakam masạ kibīyạ he fired an arrow at him. yā sakam masạ bindigạ he fired a rifle at him. sun sakam musụ hạrsāshị shạạạ they fired volleys of cartridges at them. (ii) an sakar wạ injịŋ wutā they speeded up. sun sạki injịŋ they sped along. sun sạki injị bạ darē, bạ rānā they made forced marches, they went at full speed. ya sạki wutā he put on speed. (iii) ɗārī yā sakō hancị the cold season arrived. (iv) an sakam masạ iskạ lạmbạ wạŋ chloroform was administered to him. (v) Vd. gōtō. (b) sạki ɗanē, kạ kai tạ̄fī (in cācā) show me your dice ! ('yā'yan cacā) before you throw, because I suspect you of using doctored cowries ! (c) yā sakō minị 6aurē he threw down the fig to me from the tree. (d) (i) kadạ kạ sạki jịkī do not get slack !, do not sit in a slovenly way ! (ii) yā sạki jịkī he feels easy in mind, is in easy circumstances, is acting in natural unconstrained way, behaved indolently. kadạ kụ sạki jịkī dạ kāyaŋkụ don't be careless with your things ! kadạ kụ sạki jịkī kulluŋ zā kụ īyạ . . . don't run away with the

idea that you'll always be able to . . . sạki jịkiŋkạ make yourself at home !, do not feel nervous ! (iii) yā sạki jịkī dạ nī he behaved to me without formality (all 2d = sakẹ 2 q.v.). (e) yā sạki fuskạssạ he assumed a pleasant expression (Vd. shikạm fuskạ, sakịm fuskạ, sạke 2, ạlhērị 3c). (ee) 6ērā yā sakẹ Vd. 6ērā 1c. (f) dropped purposely x sun sạki bọm ạ Masạr they dropped bombs on Egypt. (3) renounced x (a) yā sạki gōnā tasạ he gave up farming. rịgạd dạ ka jiŋgịnā minị, kā sạkạ ? have you renounced claim to the gown which you pawned with me ? yā sạki auransạ he divorced his wife, annulled his marriage. an sakam musụ ragạmar mulkị they've been given home-rule. an tāsam mạ dăi sakam musụ ḵasarsụ the aim is to give them control of their own land. (b) yā sạki dọ̄kā he disobeyed the law. (4) kōwā ya kāmạ kīfī (= kōwā ya kas kīfī), ạ gōransạ zai ⁓ he who doesn't seek, won't get. (5) Vd. sạki lẹcẹcẹ, sạki nā dāfẹ, sạki zārī, sạko tumākī.

sāḵạ (1) Vb. 1A. (a) wove. (b) (i) pondered on, planned T. (= aunạ 6b, cf. 2f below). (ii) yā ⁓ mạganạ he concocted a lie (= kutạ 6a). (iii) yā tūḵạ, yā sāḵạ, ạbụ yā ḵi ḵullūwā he strained every nerve but couldn't accomplish it. (c) (i) put T. between two others x yā ⁓ shi tsạkāninsụ. (ii) yā ⁓ yā shịga cikin tạrō he forced his way into the crowd. (2) f. (a) any weaving. (b) (secondary v.n. of 1) x yanạ̄ sāḵạr tạbarmā = yānạ̄ sāḵạ tạbarmā he's weaving a mat. (c) (i) A. woven. (ii) Vd. mīḵạ 1b. (iii) yā ɗōrạ ⁓ he's started weaving a new cloth. (iv) yạŋke ⁓ Vd. kwarkwarō. (d) honeycomb (cf. zumạ 1a.iii). (e) (i) sāḵạr gizọgizọ spider's web (= yānā 3a). (ii) bạ naŋ gizọ kẹ sāḵạr ba this is not the real issue. bạ naŋ gizọ yakẹ sāḵạr ba, sāmuŋ kudịŋ it's easy to sell T., but hard to get paid. (f) sāḵạr zūcī pondering, planning, being disturbed in mind (cf. 1b.i above). (g) chafing of inside of thigh (of fat people, from walking).

sąkąb = sąkwąf.

sąką bąbba sātą *m.* = są bąbba sātą.

sakabu *used in* nā zō ∼ I've come (temporarily or permanently) to sleep at your house as there's no room in mine.

sąką 6urnā bą 6urnā *Kt. f.* big-buttocked woman.

sakace A. (sākącē) *Vb.* 1C = sākatą. B. (sākącē) (1) *Vd.* sākatą. (2) act of picking the teeth *x* yaną ∼ he's picking his teeth (*Vd.* sākatą 3). C. (sakacē) *m.* dilly-dallying (= mąntąsalā = sąkē).

sakaci A. (sākąci) *Vd.* sākatą. B. (sakacī) *Sk. m.* = sakacē.

sakad dą *Vb.* 4 *Sk.* = sąkā.

sąkainā *f.* (1) (*a*) fragment of calabash (*cf.* mārā). (*b*) yākin rūwā yā tad dą ∼ don't blame the one for they're both equally to blame. (2) cute rogue (*his epithet is* Sąkainā mąi īyą rūwā). (3) tąką ∼ *Kt. f.* quarrelling.

sakaka A. (sākāką). (1) abundantly *x* shānū ∼ many cows. (2) *adj.* big *x* gōnā cē ∼ it is a large farm. sākākąr gōnā big farm. sākākąn dōkī a big horse. dōkī nē ∼ it is a big horse. B. (Sąkāką) (1) *epithet of* Emir (*cf.* dįkāką). (2) ∼ mąnzan Tūrai *epithet of* train. C. (sąkąką) *x* an sąkē su ∼ they (cattle) have been left to roam about. yaną tąfīyą ∼ he's roaming idly about.

sąkąką *x* yā shigō ∼ he entered without a by-your-leave.

sakakī *Kt. m.* = sakacē.

sąkakkē *m.* (*f.* sąkakkīyā) *pl.* sąkąkkū (*past participle passive*) (1) *from* sąkā, sąką, (2) *from* sakę *x* (*a*) well developed in body. (*b*) ill-behaved.

sąkąlā *f.* (1) cotton blanket. (2) rough woollen Timbuctoo blanket (= kąsā).

sąkālį *m.* (*f.* sąkālįyā) *pl.* sąkąlai good-for-nothing P.

sąkālįyā (1) *Vd.* sąkālį. (2) da lą'asąr ∼ just before sunset (= lis).

sākąmakō *m.* requital, recompense (good for good and evil for evil), *cf.* sāką. Allą Sarkin sākayyą O God, the requiter !

sąkąmārį *m.* knuckle-duster used in boxing

(dambē) or wrestling (kōkawą) and consisting of ring with sharp points.

sąkandamī *m.* (1) (*a*) markings other than black ring, on dove's neck. (*b*) necklace of tāgōdę. *(2) metal-hafted axe. *(3) chart indicating destiny of P.

sakaŋkąncē *Vb.* 1D knew for certain *x* nā ∼ ząi zō I'm sure he'll come. bąn ∼ indą (= dą indą) ya tąfi ba I don't know for sure where he's gone (= tantąncē). nā ∼ dą shī I'm sure of it.

sakaŋkįlaŋ *Eng. m.* second-class (in train, etc.).

sākąr-*compounds, Vd.* sāką.

*Sakąrā *Ar. f.* one of the Muslim hells.

sakaraftū *m.* = rīshī.

sākarai *m., f.* (*pl.* sākąrkarī = sākarōrī) feckless P.

sākarcį *m.* fecklessness.

sakar dą *Vb.* 4 *Sk.* = sąkā.

sākarē = sākarai.

sākąrkarī *Vd.* sākarai.

sakata A. (sākątą) *Vb.* 2 (*p.o.* sākącē, *n.o.* sākąci). (1) poked, hunted (rat, P.) out of place, hole, etc., *x* yā sākatō 6ērā = zuŋgurā 2*a.* (2) dislodged T. firmly embedded in matrix (*x* stiff honey from hole in tree, kola-nuts from their hūhu-packing, etc.), *cf.* lākatą. (3) yā sākąci hakōri he picked his teeth (= kākąrā 2, *cf.* kwąkulą, tsattsągē 3). B. (sąkatą) (1) *Vb.* 3B. (*a*) = sąkā 2*d.* (*b*) (*said by woman to another woman*) ŋ kwąntā, ŋ ∼, ŋ yąryādą I'm going to relax and have a good rest (*reply,* ī, kąmar tsummā ą rąndā). (2) *f.* (*pl.* sąkątū = sakatōcī). (*a*) two or three superimposed beams across door for securing it (*cf.* gągarą 1, 10 ; kūbą). (*b*) = gągarą 10*c.* (*c*) yā shiga sąkatąr kurų = yā shiga sąkatąr ūwar kurų he's got into difficulties. C. (sąkątā) *f.* (*sg., pl.*) type of yam.

Sakatarę *Eng. m.* Secretary (of N.P., S.P., or Nigerian Secretariat).

Sąkątārīyą *Eng. f.* Secretariat.

sąkątū *Vd.* sąkatą 2.

sąkątubu *m.* (*Ar.* she will write) gown covered with charms.

sakaucī *m.* petty larceny from a house.

sākąyā *Vb.* 1C (1) = sāyą 1, 2. (2) an ∼ masą ląifinsą = kārą 2*b.*

sakayau (1) *adv.* *x* kāyā nē ∼ it is a light load. (2) *m.* nā ji ∼ I felt it was light.
sakaye A. (sākąyē) *Vb.* 1C = sāyą 1, 2.
  B. (sąkąyē) *m.* concealment *x* yā cę bą kō ∼ he said openly that . . .
sąkayyą *f.* = sąkąmakō.
sake A. (sākę) (1) *Vb.* 1A. (*a*) changed *x* yā ∼ kąmā his appearance is altered (= sauyą 1*j*). yā ∼ ąl'ādą he changed his ways (= sauyą). yā ∼ mąganą he contradicted himself (= sauyą 1*h*), *cf.* 1*g below.* mun sākę jūyį our affairs have changed. (*b*) yā ∼ shāwarą he changed his opinion (= sauyą 1*k*). (*c*) yā ∼ wurī (i) he migrated. (ii) he changed his quarters. (*d*) yā ∼ minį fuską he suddenly became angry with me. (*e*) changed clothes *x* yā ∼ rįgā he put on another gown (= sauyą 1*c*). (*f*) gave T. or P. in place of existing one *x* an ∼ mąną sāban Sarkī we have been given a new Chief (*cf.* sauyą 1*a*). sum fid dą kąunar zā mų ∼ wani ąbiŋ kirkį they've given up hope of our behaving better. (*g*) sąke mąganą ! rot ! (*cf.* 1*a above*). (*h*) repeated *x* yā ∼ tąfīyą he went again. yaną sǫ yą sākę irįn ta dą he wants to return to his old tricks (= maimąitā). (2) *Vb.* 3A became changed *x* kąmassą tā ∼ his expression changed (= sauyą 2).
  B. (sākē) *m.* *used in* bā tą̄ ∼ = bąndą ∼ you've had your throw (made your move) and that's the end of the matter ! (*said in dice-throwing* (cācā), darą, 'yā, kątantaŋwą 2), *cf.* nūnē, kirgē.
  C. (sakę) (1) *Vb.* 1A (*a*) tā ∼ she put out all the cotton to be teased (*cf.* saką 2*f*). (*b*) *Sk.* = sąkā *x* yā sakę kīfī he let go of the fish. (2) *Vb.* 3A = sąkā 2*d q.v.* *x* (*a*) yā sakę he feels easy in mind, is in easy circumstances, behaved indolently. (*b*) mutānan dūnīyą iŋ kā sakę, sǎi sų ci maką tūwō ą kā if you give him an inch he'll take an ell. (*c*) *Vd.* ɓērā 1*c*. (*d*) " kadą kų ∼ ! " bā tą̄ hang ɓarāwǫ yįn sātą " be careful of your goods ! " being said to you, isn't itself sufficient to prevent your being robbed. (*e*) bā ą̄ sakēwā *Vd.* wąrkī 3.

  D. (sąkē) (1) *Vd.* sąkā. (2) *m.* (*a*) (i) slackness (*cf.* sakę 2) = sakacē. (ii) *Vd.* tālālā 2. (*b*) necklace. falling as low as chest (*cf.* mą̄kąrē, rą̄tąyē). (*c*) the furā called nąshē. (*d*) *Vd.* kaidį, są A.2 1*m* (*page* 753).
  E. (sąke) (*adj. of state from* sąkā) *x* (1) (*a*) dąurarrē yaną ∼ the prisoner has been released. (*b*) *Vd.* dǫrawą 2. (2) fuskąssą ą ∼ takę he has a pleasant expression (*cf.* sąkā 2*e*), bąsąke cikį. (3) muną naŋ bą̄kī sąke we stood open-mouthed in wonder. suną ta kallō sąke dą bą̄kī they stared doltishly (Mod. Gram. 80*d*.ii). (4) yā fi kązā ą ∼ *Vd.* tallē 1*b*.
sake A. (sā̃kę) *Vb.* 1A wove all of (*cf.* sā̃ką).
  B. (sąkē) *m.* *x* yā yi ∼ he sat pensively (*cf.* tą̄gumī).
sake-sake A. (sąˈke-sąkēⁱⁱ) *m.* (1) repeated acts of weaving. (2) various bits of woven material.
  B. (sąkē-sąkę̄) *m.* ąbincin naŋ yā yi minį ∼ ą cikī this food is lying heavy on my stomach.
saki A. (sąki) *Vd.* sąkā ; sąki-*compounds*.
  B. (sąkī) *Kt. m.* = rąkī 2.
  C. (sakį) 1 (*a*) (this replaces sąkā 1, 2*a*, 3 *when latter has its object understood*) *x* yā sąkę̄ shį ? has he released him ? ī, yā sakį yes, he has let him go. yā sakį, ąrąhā he sold it cheaply. yā sakį he gave it up as a bad job. bą dāmā sų sakį they have no chance to give up (fighting, effort, etc.). duk dūnīyą, kōwā yā sakį, bą mai kudī kąmansą all are agreed that in the whole world, he has no equal for wealth. (*b*) is loose *x* (i) hakōrī yā sakį the tooth is loose. (ii) tūwō yā sakį the tūwō is sloppy. (iii) kujērā tā sakį the chair is rickety (sakį 1*a*, *b* = shiką). (2) *m.* (*a*) (i) divorce *x* saurin ∼ gąreshį he often divorces = shiką 2*c* (*cf.* sąkā 1*b*). (ii) yā yi matą ∼ ukų = shikąm battą. (*b*) (i) yā yi sakį = yā yi sakįn jikī he behaved indolently, led carefree life, etc. (*as in* sąkā 2*d*). (ii) iŋ kā gā ɓērā yaną sakį, kyaŋwā bā tą̄ gidā when the cat's away, the mice play. (iii) *Vd.* ąkwīyą

1*h.* (iv) Sakịm fuskạ *Vd.* ạlhērị 3*c*, sạke 2, sạkā 2*e*, shikạm fuskạ. (*c*) (*secondary v.n.* of sạkā) *x* sunạ sakịm bọ:n ạ Masạr they are dropping bombs on Egypt (= shikạ). sunạ sakịm mai rūwā shạạạ they're firing volleys from the machine-guns (*Vd.* sạkā 2*a*.i). (*d*) makeweight thrown in by seller (= gyārā 4, *cf.* jẹfạ 2*b*.ii ; sakạ 1*g*). (*e*) portion of raw cotton (*as in* sakạ 2*f*) = *Sk.* jẹfẹ 4. (*f*) sakịn na bāya, kāmụn na gạba = sakịn na hannū, kāmụn na gụje throwing away dirty water before one has got clean (= shịkạ rẹshẹ = sạki zārī). (*g*) *Vd.* bịdā 2, tālālā 2*b*.

D. (sākī) *m.* (1) *dialectal pronunciation of* Sarkī. (2) *Sk.* = sīyākī.

sāƙị *m.* (1) (*a*) cotton material of black and blue strands woven into tiny check pattern (= *Sk.* zạ̄bō 2*c*), *cf.* gansarƙī. (*b*) kudịn ~ bambaŋ dạ na farī they're as different as chalk and cheese. (2) wurin nạŋ dạ ~ look out what you say, there's an enemy here !

sạki lẹcẹcẹ *m.* = tālālā 2*a*.

sạki nā dāfẹ *m.* (1) exchanging T. (*x* work) for better one. (2) acting so as to leave surplus or savings.

sakiŋkịlạ = sakaŋkịlạŋ.

sakīyạ *f.* (1) puncturing abscess (with hot arrow-head, etc.) to let out pus (*cf.* sakạ 5 ; jiŋgạ). (2) *Vd.* kụmburī 1*b*. (3) an yi masạ sakīyạd dạ bā rūwā he's had an unpleasant experience.

sạki zārī, kạ̄mạ tōzō = saki 2*f*.

sakkarāwā *Vd.* bạsakkarẹ.

sạƙƙwatạ *Vb.* 2 (*p.o.* sạƙƙwạcẹ, *n.o.* sạƙƙwạci) *Sk.* pecked P., pecked at T.

Sakkwatancī *m.* the Sokoto dialect of Hausā.

Sakkwatāwā *Vd.* Bạsakkwacẹ.

Sakkwatõ *f.* (1) Sokoto. (2) *Vd.* hausā, majẹ 1*b*, Sạrkim Mụsụlmī, Shēhụ 3*c*, Bạsakkwacẹ.

sako A. (sākọ) *m.* (*f.* sākụ̄wā) one's next younger brother or sister by same mother. tsạkāninsụ ~ dạ ~ they are full brothers (or sisters) with no intervening child of their mother born between them.

B. (sạkō) dense undergrowth (= sarƙaƙƙīyā).

C. (sakō) *Vd.* sạkā 2*c*, 1.

saƙo A. (sāƙọ) (1) (*a*) (i) niche, nook, crevice, hiding-place (*cf.* luŋgụ). (ii) mun sạ su ạ sāƙọ we've got them " in a cleft stick ". (*b*) yā shịga ~ he has been ambushed. yā sạ mu sāƙọ he ambushed us. (2) = ƙuryạ 1*a*.

B. (sạ̄ƙō) *m.* (1) (*a*) message sent to P. *x* nā yi masạ ~ I sent him a message (*cf.* ạikẹ, sautụ, sạllahụ). (*b*) sạ̄ƙwan ~ passing on a message received. (*c*) ~ bā yạ̄ hùcẹ zūcịyā, sǎi yạ hùcẹ ƙafạ if you want a thing done well, do it yourself ! (2) T. handed P. to hand on to another. (3) asking P. to buy and bring back T. (4) sạ̄ƙō = dan sạ̄ƙō small stone placed on smaller of three cooking-stones used for oven, to raise height of former for pot to rest on (= makārī = magirkī = dạgạjinā), *cf.* girkạ 1*d*.

C. (sạƙō) *m.* = sạƙẹ.

sako-sako (1) *adv.* an daurẹ ~ it is loosely tied. (2) *m.* (*a*) ~ yakẹ̄ = daurịnsạ ~ nẹ̄ = 1. (*b*) yā yi ~ he's a slacker. (*c*) ~ nẹ̄ he's a slacker.

sạƙo tumākī *m.* good-for-nothing P.

sakurạ *Sk. Vd.* sạurā.

sạ̄kutạ = sạ̄katạ.

sākụ̄wā *Vd.* sākọ.

sākwạcē *Kt.* = sākạcē.

sạkwạf *m.* (1) (*a*) A. light in weight. (*b*) being light *x* yā yi ~ it is light. (2) becoming loose *x* yā yi ~ it (T. tied) has become loose (*cf.* kaf). (3) ~ nẹ̄ ạiki, dịndịn nạ̄ rawā *epithet of* Adamāwā Filani.

sạkwaf dạ lạkwaf = cibụs 2.

sakwalkwạcē *Kt.* = sakwarkwạcē.

sạkwạp = sạkwạf.

sạkwạrā *f.* (1) pounded yams. (2) *Kt.* pounded sweet-potato (dạŋkalị) or cassava (rōgọ) with ground-nuts (= kwadọ 2).

sakwarkwạcē *Vb.* 3A (1) (T. tied tightly) became slack. (2) P. became slack. (3) showed signs of age.

sạkwāti *m.* (*sg., pl.*) railway-sleeper.

sạkwạtọ = *Kt.* sạkwạtō *m.* (1) shorts worn by Filani herdsmen. (2) = tọ̄bī. (3) trousers without crutchpiece (hantsạ), but with roomy legs, worn by labourers.

sākyal *Kt.* = sākē.

sal *x* yā wạŋku ∼ it's been washed snow-white.   farī ∼ snow-white.   aŋ askẹ kạnsạ ∼ he's been shaved bald.

sala A. (sālạ) *f.* long, thin slice of raw meat (= saŋkẹdā 1).
    B. (sạlā) *Vd.* sạiwā 5.

salab *m.* insipidity *x* namạŋ ∼ yakẹ the meat is insipid (= lāmī).

salahạ = salhạ salak = salab.

sạlạlạ *f.* type of thin medicinal gruel (= *Kt.* shẹgē 2).

salam A. (salam) = salab.
    B. (sạlạm) (1) *m.* dōgō nẹ ∼ dạ shī he's tall and well-made. (2) *adv.* yanạ dạ wuyạ ∼ he (it) has a handsome neck (spout), *Vd.* santalēlẹ.

salama A. (sạlāmạ) *Ar. used in* ∼ ạlaikạ (1) greeting ! (2) may I come in ? (*reply*, ạlaikạ sạlāmụ) (*if more persons than one are greeted, we say* ∼ ạlaikụŋ *and reply to more than one is* ạlaikụŋ sạlāmụ). (2) *Vd.* sạlāmụŋ, salamạ, ạlēkạ, ạlēkụŋ, ạfūwō, asạlā.
    B. (salamạ) *f.* (1) *x* (*a*) munạ ∼ we are greeting you by saying sạlāmạ ạlēkạ at your door tọ ask your leave to enter (*Vd.* sạlāmạ). (*b*) sōjạmmụ sun yi shigan naŋ tāsụ bạ sallamạ our soldiers made a rapid entry. (*c*) muŋ kūtsạ musụ bạ salamạ dạ rụndunarsụ we attacked their army fiercely. (*d*) sại sukạ hau musụ bạ salamạ, bạ bịsmillạ then they attacked them forthwith. (2) *x* yā tạfi kō ∼ bại yi ba he went off without saying good-bye (= baŋ kwānā). (3) (*a*) mun yi salamạ dạ shī we took leave of him. (*b*) yā sạmi ∼ he's been given leave to depart (by Emir, etc.). (*c*) *Vd.* ḳaimī, sạllamạ. (*d*) *Vd.* wāwā 1*e*. (*e*) am bā shị ∼ tasạ he's received his parting-gift. (4) completion of prayers *x* (*a*) in yā yi ∼ kạ cẹ dạ shī yạ zō when he has finished his prayers tell him to come here ! (*b*) sōrō ∼ yakẹ yị this mud-ceiling is about to collapse. (*c*) d̃arī yā sōmạ ∼ the cold season is (i) approaching, (ii) about to finish. (5) a sạrautạ held by one of slaves of Emir of Kano (1–5 = sallamạ). (6) *cf.* sallạmā, sạllamạ, asạlā.

salạmainị *Kt.* = talạtainị.

Sạlāmatụ woman's name (*Vd.* Kandi, sallạ 1*j*).

sālạmīnạ ālạmīnạ = sāliŋ āliŋ.

sạlạm nagō *Kr. greeting by women when entering compound, cf.* ạfūwō.

sạlāmụ = sạlāmạ.

sạlāmụŋ (1) = sạlāmạ. (2) (*used as follows at beginning of letter, where* gaisūwā 3 *q.v. is unsuitable, as letter is not to a senior*) dạgạ Sarkiŋ Kanọ, Audụ d̃am Mụhammadụ, sạlāmụŋ zūwạ Hākịmiŋ Gēzāwā, Ạbū Bakạr. Bāyaŋ hakạ . . . (3) *x* zā mụ shiryạ mạganạ sạlāmụŋ sạlāmụŋ we'll arrange the matter peacefully.   anạ naŋ hakạ sạlāmụŋ-sạlāmụŋ they're on good terms.

sạlạŋgạdạmū *m.* type of child's game.

Sạlātị (*Ar.* salātu) *m.* (1) yā bugạ ∼ he recited the Muslim creed (= kalmạ *q.v.*). (2) invoking blessing on the Prophet as part of the regular prayers *x* yā yi ∼ bisạ Mụhammaŋ he said Ạllạhummạ ! sạlli 'ạlā Mụhammadịŋ wa 'ạlā ālịhi wa sạllim. (3) *cf.* tārukụ, ạsạlātụ, ạssạlạ̄, sallạ, ạddu'ạ.

Sạlātụ *Kt.* = Sạlāmatụ.

salbarkạ = mādạllā *q.v. under* gōdẹ 2.

sale A. (sālẹ) (1) *Vb.* 3A *x* hannū yā ∼ the hand peeled, became abraded (= sālụ6ẹ). (2) *Vb.* 1A abraded T. (3) Sālẹ = Sālihụ.
    B. (salẹ) *Vb.* 3A = kwa6ẹ 2*a, b.*

sạlē6ạ *f.* (1) yā yi ∼ he let kola-nut juice stain outside of his lips (= ālạ 2). (2) *Kt.* dribbling by sleeper (= yau 1*b* = barcī 1*d*). (3) sạlē6ạr zumạ empty words, flattery (= malmal dạ bakạ).

salẹkanī *Vd.* sạlkā.

salgā = sargā.

salhạ *f.* European cotton-goods.

Sālihụ *man's name.*

sālịhī *m.* (*f.* sālịhā) *pl.* sạlịhai *Ar.* honest.

sāliŋ āliŋ (1) *m.* (*a*) even-tempered (= lāfiyạ 1*g*). (*b*) insipid (food), *cf.* lāmī. (2) *adv. x* mun rạbu ∼ we parted on good terms (1, 2 = sālạmīnạ ālạmīnạ).

Sālịyō *f.* Sierra Leone.

sạlkā *f.* (*pl.* salẹkanī = salkunạ). (1) (*a*) water-bottle made of untanned (hairy)

skin, this being stripped off like sheath
from slaughtered goat after slitting the
neck (*cf.* **tandawara**, **sulluɓē 1***c*,
agadōdā). (*b*) ~ **a kaŋ hūra**. **kōwā
ya hūra rārīyā, bākinsa yā yi ciwọ** don't
waste your time on a futile person !
(*c*) *Kt.* **an yi wa akwīya** ~ they have
blown up entire dead goat prior to
pulling off its skin (**tūɓē 3***b*) to separate
latter from the meat (= **būsa 1***d*.ii =
hūra 1*b*.ii). (2) **yā yi** ~ his (smallpox patient's) skin entirely peeled off.
(3) *Kt.* ~ **da rūwā**=**ɗaukan 'yam makarantā**. (4) **salkar ciki** drinking a great
deal in anticipation, because one has
been given much food for one's journey,
but has no container for liquid.

*salƙa = **sarƙa**.

salkuna *Vd.* **salkā**.

salla *f.* (*Ar.* **salātu**). (1) (*a*) (i) each of the
five Muslim daily series of prayers. (ii)
Vd. **sallācē**, **tūwan** ~. (*b*) **yana** ~
(i) he's now praying. (ii) he's a Muslim.
(*bb*) **yau ana salla** it is the festival to-day.
(*c*) **babbar** ~ = **layyā 1**. (*d*) **ƙaramar** ~
festival on 1st of **Shawwal** following
fast-month of **Ramalan**. (*e*) **sāfīyar** ~
f. 1st of **Sha'aban**. (*f*) (i) **Na sallar
tsọfaffī** *m.* month of **Sha'aban**. (ii)
watan ~ the month of **Shawwal**. (*g*)
sallar ciŋ wutsīya = **jūya bai** *q.v.*
under **jūya 4**. (*h*) **Na** ~ name for boy
born during any festival (= **Sallau**).
(*j*) **Ta** ~ name for girl born during any
festival (= **Salāmatu** = **Ta salluwā**).
(*k*) *Vd.* **Cika ciki Gānē 3**, **Tākutahā**,
tashē 3, **gāwa 1***b*, **Wowwō**, **adaŋkīyā**.
(*l*) *Vd.* **kan** ~. (*m*) **rana-rānar** ~ **tā
fi sammakwaŋ kiɗa** better late praying
than early drumming. (*n*) **Audu kāfirī
kashe mai salla** that accursed Audu !
(*o*) **sallar kūrā** *Vd.* **bargi-bargī**. (*p*)
fāshin ~ *Vd.* **fāshi 1***c*. (*q*) **gōma ta** ~
Vd. **gōma 2**. (2) pilgrimage to Mecca
(= **hajj**) *x* **shēkara ɗaya muka yi** ~ **da
shī** it was in the same year that he and
I did the pilgrimage. **yā tafi Maka**,
ammā bai sāmi ~ **ba** he went to Mecca,
but did not perform the pilgrimage-
rites. (3) (*a*) **yā yi** ~ **da kā** he fell
headlong (= **cī 20***b*). (*b*) **suƙuwar** ~
attack on P. by number of persons.

(4) *cf.* **Salāti**, **asalātu**, **assalā**, **addu'a**,
sallāta, **salla-salla**, **sallātad da**, **īdi**.

sallaɓī *Kt. m.* = **lāmī**.

sallace A. (**sallācē**) *Vb.* 3A *x* **yā** ~ **a
ƙauye** = **yā yi salla a ƙauye** he spent
the festival (**salla 1***c*, *d*) in the country.
B. (**sallācē**) *Vd.* **sallāta**.
C. (**sallace**) *Vb.* 3A *Sk.*, *Kt.* = **sāne 1**.

sallāci *Vd.* **sallāta**.

sallahu *m. x* **nā bar** ~ **a gidansa** I left a
message for him at his house (*cf.* **sāƙō**,
sautu, **aikē**).

sallaƙe *m.* morsel *x* **bābu kō** ~ there's not
an atom of it.

sallallāhu *Vd.* **annabi**.

sallallamī *m.* fussing, grousing (= **mīta**).

sallama A. (**sallama**) = **salama**.
B. (**sallamā**) *Vb.* 1C. (1) agreed to
sell at price offered (**tayi**) *x* **yā** ~ **mini
rīgā** (*cf.* **sallamī**, **sallame**, **albarka**). (2)
surrendered T. *x* (*a*) **mun sallamā musu
garī** we surrendered the town to them.
(*b*) **munā gaddama**, **ammā nā** ~ we
were disputing, but I gave way. **a
kam maganar tājirci an** ~ **wa Alhasaŋ**
Alhasan is universally admitted as the
richest. (3) *cf.* **salama**, **sallama**.
C. (**sallama**) *Vb.* 2 (1) senior gave
inferior leave to depart *x* **Bature
(Sarki) yā sallame shi** (*Vd.* **salama 3***b*).
(2) (*euphemism for* **kōrā 1***b*) dismissed
P. from one's employ (*re* servant, clerk,
etc., *cf.* **tūɓe**).

sallame *m.* agreeing to accept price offered
(**tayi**) for T. *x* **yā yi mini** ~ (*cf.* **sallama**,
albarka, **sallamī**).

sallamī *m. x* **nā sāmi sallamin rīgan naŋ**
I (broker) have received permission
from my principal to sell this gown at
the price you offer (**tayi**) ; *cf.* **sallama**,
sallame, **albarka**.

salla-salla *f.* bedecking oneself, *cf.* **salla**.

sallāta *Vb.* 2 (*p.o.* **sallācē**, *n.o.* **sallāci**).
(1) performed one of the five Muslim
daily prayers (**salla 1***a*) *x* **yā sallāci
azahar** he performed the 2–3 p.m.
prayer. (2) **yā sallāci gāwā** he performed the funeral-service over the
corpse.

sallātad da *Vb.* 4 (1) circumcized (a boy) =
kāciya 1*b*. (2) *x* **liman yā** ~ **da jama'a**
the imam led the people in prayer.

sallątsā *Vb.* 1C (*Ar.* sallata). (1) caused to rule over *x* Allā yā sallątsą Filānī kąŋ Hąusāwā God set the Filani over the Hausas. (2) *x* an ∼ musu ąbin dą yā fi ƙarfinsu more was imposed on them than they could cope with. Sąllau = sallą 1*h*. sallētą *Kt. f.* = maskō. sąllīyą = sillīyą. sallōto *m.* good-for-nothing P. Sąllūwā *used in* in Ta ∼ = sallą 1*j*. salō *m.* (1) fashion *x* (*a*) sāban ∼ a new fashion, new pattern. (*b*) muŋ ga wani sāban ∼ yąu to-day we've seen something new to us (*a, b* = ficē = launi = sauyi = haifē 2).. (*c*) salaŋ kiɗą = sąŋgalī 2*a*. (*d*) salan rawā = sąŋgalī 2*b*. (2) (*a*) cleverness *x* Audu ∼ gąrēshi Audu is a smart fellow. (*b*) *Vd.* lugudē 1*b*. (3) sąbulun ∼ type of Nupe soap. (4) salō-salō *adv.* of different kinds (= launi-launi 2). salubbą *Sk. f.* = sąmbątsai. sālu6ē *Vb.* 3A (1) = sālę 1. (2) = sullu6ē 2. sāluŋ āluŋ = sāliŋ āliŋ. salwąncē *Vb.* 3A became lost (= 6atą). sąlwantą *Vb.* 3B = salwąncē. sam (1) = sāmi obtained *q.v. under* sāmā (*cf. examples under* lā'tse-lątsē", 6āri 1*b*, 6atąŋ gautā). (2) (*abbreviated imperative from* sāmą) *x* (*a*) sam mini kąɗaŋ give me a little ! (= *Sk.* ɗam). (*b*) *Vd.* sā A.2 2. (*page* 753). (*c*) *Vd.* tąntąląminyą. (3) *adv., used in* shēkarą ∼ for a complete year. sama A. (sāmą) *Vb.* 1A (1) (*with dative*) gave *x* (*a*) yā ∼ (= sāmō) mini kudī he gave me some money. (*b*) *Vd.* sam 2. (*c*) yā sāmą matą lāfīyą he divorced her. (2) = sansāmā.
B. (sąmā) *Vb.* 2 (*but when object is understood,* sāmu *replaces* sąmā *usually ; when noun-object follows, we use* sąmi = sāmu ; *progressive is formed with* sāmu 2*a q.v.*). (1) (*a*) (i) obtained *x* kā sąmē shi did you get it ? ī, nā sāmu = ī, nā sąmā yes, I did get it. (ii) *Vd. c.*iv *below*. (iii) tā nēmę shi tā sąmē shi she bewitched him into loving her (*Vd.* nēmā 1*e*, aikącē 3). (iv) yā sąmē su he managed to persuade

them. (v) kōwā ya sāmu, ą sāmu dą shī if you prosper, then your dependants also prosper. (vi) sǎi wani yā rasą, wani kąn sāmu one man's gain is another's loss. (vii) kōwā ya sāmu *Vd.* barą A.2 1*d*. (viii) wani yā sąmi nāmą yā rasą wutar gashi, wani yā sąmi wutąr, bąi sąmi nāmąŋ gasąwā ba one lacks ability and another lacks the chance to use it. (ix) yā sąmi dūnīyą *Vd.* dūnīyą 2. (*b*) chanced on *x* nā sąmē su sunā barcī I found them asleep (= tarad dą = ishę = iskę). (*c*) (i) befell *x* wani mūguŋ ąbu yā sąmi (= sāmu) Audu a misfortune has befallen Audu. (ii) mē ya sąmē ką what is the matter with you ? (iii) overtook *x* ci gąba, ną sąmē ką go on in front, I'll overtake you (= tarad dą). (iv) dą ąbin dą zā ką sāmu, dą ąbin dą ząi sąmē ką, tun rānar hąlittą yakē what you'll get (1*a above*) and what will befall you, is predestined. (*d*) hit (in aiming) *x* (i) nā jēfē shi, ąmmā ban sąmē shi ba I threw a stone at it, but did not manage to hit it. (ii) kirki gąrēshi, sǎi dǎi ą wurī ɗayā aką sąmē shi he has good character but one defect. (iii) yā sąmē ni dą zāgi, ąbin kō kąrē bą yā ci ba he attacked me with insufferable abuse. (iv) nā sąmē shi dą dūką I thrashed him. (*e*) yā sąmi Alƙur'aŋ = haddącē 1*b*. (*f*) *Vd.* saukī 2*c*, hanyą 2*a*, tafarki, gąskīyā 3*d*. (*g*) yā sąmi kąnsą (i) he has got clear of trouble (*x* clearing himself from charge). (ii) he ransomed himself (slave). tā sąmi kąntą (i) she is over her troubles (*x* having born child safely). (ii) she has ransomed herself from slavery (= kąr6ā 1*d*). (2) managed to *x* (*a*) ban sąmi ganinsą ba I didn't manage to see him. nā sąmi shigā I managed to obtain an entrance. sun sāmu su yī they managed to do it. in yā sąmi yą kashę shi if he manages to kill him. sun sąmi sai dą kāyansu they managed to sell their goods = sun sāmu sunā sai dą kāyansu. (*b*) *x* sǎi suką bi duhun darē, suką sāmu, suką kai then they managed to escape at night. (3) *Vd.* sāmu, sąmu, sam.

C. (sama) (1) *m., f.* (*pl.* sammai) *Ar.*
(*a*) sky, heavens (*cf.* samānīya). (*b*)
ta sama *Vd.* 1*h below.* (*c*) turbar ∿
săi tsuntsū skill is required for it.
(*d*) rūwan ∿ *m.* rain. (*e*) (i) bā dūkan
rūwan ∿ kē da cīwo ba, rūwan ganyē
it is the humiliation put on one by an
understrapper that irks, not that to be
borne from a superior. (ii) *Vd.* dūka 1*b*.
(*f*) *Vd.* kwādō 1*a*.iv. (*g*) top *x* (i)
samansa its top. (ii) ∿ bā tā kōmō ƙasa
har abadā, tudu bā yā kōmō gangare
east is east and west is west (*cf.* tudu
1*c*). (iii) gidan ∿ *m.* = kwatashi. (iv)
kamar daga ∿ săi aka ji yā cē he was
suddenly heard to say that . . . bā
săi aka ji kamar daga ∿ ba ? wai sum
fāɗa wa Masar ? then suddenly the news
came that they had attacked Egypt (*cf.*
săi C.4). (v) yā yi ∿ he went up-
stairs ; it (aeroplane) rose into the
air ; it (aeroplane) went up higher.
(vi) halin yāƙi kē nan, a yi ƙasa, a yi
sama war has its ups and downs. (vii)
sun yi ∿ they're wrangling. (*h*) ta ∿ =
bayammā 3. (*j*) *Vd.* tantabarā. (2)
adv. up above *x* (*a*) (i) yanā ∿ he's up
above, on top. (ii) sū nē a sama *they*
are the winners. (*b*) a ∿ yakē he's in a
rage (*cf.* 1*g*.vi *above*). (*c*) yā zō a ∿,
bā a ƙasa ba he came on horseback, not
on foot, *cf.* ƙasa 3, bisa 2*c*. (3) *adv.*
upwards *x* tun daga mai albāshim fam
uku har ∿ those receiving salary of
£3 upwards. (4) sama da *prep.* above
x yanā sama da shī (i) it is above it.
(ii) he is senior to him, *cf.* ƙasa 7. (5)
Vd. sama-sama, sama dōgō, sama
jannatū.
    D. (sama) *Vb.* 1A *Eng.* yā ∿ shi he
summoned him, *cf.* samāci.
samāci *Eng. m.* court-summons *x* yā yi
samācinsa he summoned him (= sami).
sama dōgō *m.* (1) *Sk.* = kāɗo wāwā (*Vd.*
kāɗo 3). (2) *Kt.* tā yi masa ∿ she stole
T. off head of his (broker's) servant
(jāƙin dillāli).
sāmāgī (1) *m.* powerful ruler. (2) *m.*
(*f.* sāmāgīyā) strong P., slave, horse,
etc. (3) *Kt.* Sāmāgī, babbar macē what
a burly woman !
sā mai gidā tsallē *m.* = kwaɗo 2.

Samā'īlu = Ismā'īlu (1) Ishmael. (2)
Vd. gyārā 1*h* ; ila ; īlu.
sama jannatū = sama jannati *f.* small
gown worn by some zealots (sleeves
supposed to act as wings to heaven).
sāmājīrī *Kt.* huge (*re* living T.).
samama A. (samama) (1) *adv. x* sunā
wucēwā ∿ they (crowd) can be heard
passing. (2) *f.* nā ji ∿ I heard the
noise of crowd passing or of snake in
undergrowth.
    B. (samama) abundantly *x* shānu
sunā nan ∿ there are many cattle.
samāmē *m.* (1) raiding (hari) done by
small bands. (2) ɗan ∿ = mai ∿
(*pl.* 'yan ∿ = māsū ∿) raider *as in* 1.
samamī (1) *Vd.* jirgī 1*b*.ii. (2) *Vd.* Dankō.
samammance *m.* (1) = lugudē. (2)
alternating various actions in dance (*cf.*
taƙai).
samammē *m.* (*f.* samammīyā) *pl.* samam-
mū (*past participle from* sāmu) available,
obtainable.
samance *Vb.* 1C summoned P. (*cf.* sama,
samāci).
samanī *Ar. m.* (1) = tamanī. *(2) =
sumunī.
samānīya *Ar. f.* = sama 1*a*, g.i.
sāmanja = sāja 2.
sā manjagara *Vd.* manjagara 2.
samantā *Vb.* 1C = samance.
samārama *m., pl.* vagabonds, wastrel lads.
samārī (1) *pl. of* saurayī. (2) samārī =
kai samārī now then, lad ! (*cf.* yārinya
2). (3) (*a*) short length of tsarnū. (*b*)
thin sticks of firewood. (4) samārin
tōkā any dog. (4) *Vd.* zōgalagandi. (5)
samārin aduwa ragged clothing. (6)
samārin kwāno *Vd.* bōjwā.
samartaka *f.* (1) youthful ways of lads.
(2) har yanzu bai askē ∿ ba he still
behaves as if he were a lad.
samaryā *Kt. f.* (1) = taɓaryā 2. (2) rising
up to engage in struggle.
sama-sama (*d.f.* sama 2). (1) (*a*) superficial *x* saninsa ∿ nē his knowledge is
superficial. (*b*) ∿ nē he's " dotty ".
(2) superficially *x* yanā numfāshī ∿
he's scarcely breathing.
samata *f.* (1) buzz, hum of voices, any
prolonged, indistinct sound (= jīza 2*a*).
(2) sound of any movement. (3) *x*

nā ji ∼ tasạ yanạ̄ Kanọ I've heard a rumour that he's at Kano.

sạmātsī *m.* (1) = sạ̄6ānī 4. (2) yā cikạ ∼ he's persistently unlucky = yā gạmu dạ ∼ (*cf.* shu'ụmī). (3) the plant *Tephrosia elongata* (= sạ̄6ānī 5).

sạmā'ụ *m.* = samạ 1*a*.

sạ̄mayyạ *f.* *x* yā sāmō ∼ he got a present (*d.f.* sạ̄mā).

sạ̄mazādawạ *m.* (1) type of sạndā 3 with linear pattern. (2) one of the patterns bitten into a cap (*cf.* cịzā 2).

sam6alēlẹ *m.* (*f.* sam6alēlīyā) *pl.* sam6al-sạm6ạl tall and well-formed.

sam6alī *m.* (*f.* sam6alā) *pl.* sam6al-sạnɪ6ạl = sam6alēlẹ.

sambanāwā *Vd.* bạsambānẹ.

sạmbạ̄nī *m.* metal clappers, two pairs being played together.

sam6arā *f.* (1) = kạsam6arā. (2) piece of corn-stalk (karā) rubbed between hands as accompaniment to fiddle (*hard exterior is split into strips and pith is removed*). (3) large slab of tūwō.

sạmbarkạ = sạlbarkạ.

sambātātạ *f.* (1) = tạ̄fī 1*e*.ii. (2) pointless talk *x* zạncạnkạ yā yi ∼ you're talking senselessly (= sọ̄ki bụrūtsū).

sạmbạ̄tsai *pl.* ornamented sandals with cross-bands of red leather (= *Sk.* salub6ạ).

sạmbạ̄tū *m.* pointless talk (= sọ̄ki bụrūt-sū).

sam 6ērā *m.* type of embroidery-pattern (*d.f.* sau na 6ērā).

sạmbẹ̄rū *m.* the poisonous herb *Lasiosyphon Kraussii* (= tụrurrụbī).

Sambọ (1) (*a*) *name for any man called* Mụhammadụ (= Sạbābạ). (*b*) *name given to* second son (= Tạbārị), *cf.* Dikkọ. (2) ∼ yā hau kạntạ the bọ̄ri-spirit Sambọ took possession of her.

samcī *Kt. m.* = santsī.

sạmfạlwā *f.* type of cylindrical, blue bead.

samfạrā *Nor. f.* apron (wạrkī) of undressed white leather.

samfẹ̄rā *f.* unpounded leaves (*x* tobacco, kūkạ, lallẹ, etc.), *Vd.* shanshẹ̄rā.

samfọ *Kt. m.* (*pl.* samfunạ) = sạnhọ.

sạmfōlạ *f.* = sạmfōlọ *m.* (1) anything light in weight. (2) aluminium (= gọ̄rā 1*g*.ii).

samfụr = sampụr.

samgēgẹ *m.* (*f.* samgēgīyā) huge (*re* living T.).

sạmhōlạ = sạmfōlạ.

samhwạn *Vd.* sạnhọ.

samị *m.* = samācị.

sạ̄mịyyạ *f.* (1) type of dermatitis. (2) = bọ̄rịn kụrkunū.

samjị *Kt. m.* (1) any long, large load for women. (2) ɗaurịn ∼ tying T. up to form load *as in* 1.

sam6e = sạn6e.

sammạcē *Vb.* 1C bewitched (*Vd.* sammụ).

sammācị = samācị.

sammāgī = samāgī.

sạmmai *Vd.* samạ 1.

sạmmakō *m.* (1) (*a*) yā bụgi (= yā yi) ∼ he made an early start with work or journey (= asubancī = jijjifī 2 = dubtū). (*b*) kāyan ∼, dạ wurī a kạn ɗaurẹ forewarned is forearmed. (*c*) yinị yā ịsa aikị, ∼ lạ'anạ nē an early start is a nuisance, for there are enough hours of daylight for work. (*d*) kōwā ya yi ∼ yā hūtạ dạ rānā a stitch in time saves nine. (2) azzịkī yā yi masạ ∼ he prospered early in life. (3) *Vd.* būbū6ụ̄wā 2, sallạ 1*m*.

sammarịn *Eng. m.* (*sg.*, *pl.*) submarine-boat.

sạmmātsī = sạmātsī.

sammorẹ *m.* trypanosomiasis in cạttle (*cf.* cīwọn 2).

sammụ (*Ar.* poison) *m.* *x* yā yi masạ ∼ he bewitched him (with buried charm (lāyạ) or drugs rubbed on body, etc.) = makạrī, (*cf.* jẹ̄fā 1*b*, jẹ̄faffē, arwā, 6ōfī, 6wārī 5, lāyạ, aikị 1*h*, māgạnī 2, tạmbayạ 2).

samnạ *Sk. m.*, *f.* (*pl.* samnōnī) feckless P. (*epithet is* Samnạ kāshịn awākī).

sampụr *m.* (*pl.* sampurōrī) *Eng.* (1) sample. (2) sun sākẹ ∼ they tried a new plan.

sạmrā *Sk.* = sạurā.

samrạyī *Sk. m.* (*pl.* sạmrī = sạmạrī) = saurạyī.

samri A. (samrī) *Sk.* = saurī.

  B. (sạmrī) *Vd.* samrạyī.

samrō *Sk.* = saurō.

samsạm *Sk.* = sansạn.

sạmsamtsā = sạnsantsā.

samshẹ̄rā = shanshẹ̄rā.

samtsĭ *Sk.* = santsĭ.

samu A. (sāmụ) (1) *Vd.* sąmā. (2) *m.* (*a*) (*v.n.* and progressive of sąmā) yaną sāmụnsạ he is getting it. yaną dạ wụyar sāmụ it is hard to get. (*b*) barkạmmụ dạ sāmụm bąkĭ *greeting used on morning after completion of azụmĭ.* (*c*) sāmụɳ kại yā fi sāmụɳ askị (= ... yā fi sāmụɳ hụ̄lā = ... yā fi sāmụɳ kāyā) health, freedom, etc., is better than wealth. (*d*) sāmụɳ dạlīlị *Vd.* dạlīlị 4*c*. (*e*) (i) sāmụɳ ạbincī earning one's living. (ii) sāmụɳ ạbincin ɗan tsạ̄kō, bą sāmụɳ kẹ̄ dạ wụyā ba, wurin cị it's easy to get but where can it be kept ? (*f*) mại sāmụɳ gōbe *Vd.* marạshī 2. (3) act of getting *x* (*a*) ∼ yā fi ĭyąwā, hawan dōkịm macịjī possession is nine points of the law. (*b*) mại nēmā yaną tạ̄re dạ ∼ he who seeks, finds. (*c*) mại ∼ yā rigā mại nēmā one P. is rich and the next seeks to emulate him. (*d*) tsananin nēmā bā yą̄ kāwō ∼ effort does not always succeed. (4) earnings, wealth *x* (*a*) yạnzu bābụ ∼ there is no money to be made now. yaną dạ ∼ he is wealthy (*Vd.* zarạfī 2). sāmụna bại ịsa ạ bā kạ lādā hakạ ba I can't afford to pay you those high wages. shẹ̄karạ ɗayā sāmụɳkạ mịsālịn nawạ nẹ̄ about how much do you earn in a year ? (*b*) *Vd.* habọ. (5) rānar sāmụ *Vd.* bāwạ 8*a*. (6) sāmụɳ gạrī, kuturū gāɗā, etc. = sāmụɳ wurī, kuturū gāɗā ạ tsĭdau = gāɗā 4 *q.v.*

B. (sạmu) (1) *Vd.* sąmā. (2) *Vb.* 3B. (*a*) is obtainable *x* hatsĭ yā ∼ corn has been got, is obtainable (= wạnzu 3). (*b*) occurred *x* faɗạ yā ∼ there is a fight in progress. ịɳ hakạ tā ∼ if this occurs, in this case (= wạnzu 2).

sāmụkẹ̄ *Vb.* 1C (1) = saɳkẹ̄. (2) devoured (food).

san A. (san) (1) (*a*) footstep of (*Vd.* sau). (*b*) *Vd.* san-*compounds*. (2) Chief of (*abbreviation of* Sarkin) *used in* (*a*) Saɳ Kaɳo the Emir of Kano. (*b*) Saɳ kurmị = Kurmị obsolete sạrautạ *i.e.* controllership of main Kano market (kạ̄sūwar kurmị) and prison (*Vd.* kurmị 3). (*c*) Saɳ ƙịrạ *Vd.* ƙịrạ 1*bb*. (*d*) *Vd.* Tụrāķĭ. (3) *Vd.* sanị, saɳ girmā. (4)

(*the form taken by* sam 1 *before* k-, g-) *cf.* ɓārị 1*b*.

B. (sạn) *Vd.* sọn-*compounds*, sọ̄, sā'ạ 5, 6.

sạnā *Vb.* 2 = sānẹ 2.

sạna'ạ *Ar. f.* (*pl.* sana'ō'ī). (1) (*a*) one's occupation, trade, profession. (*b*) ∼ tā fi dūkịyar gādọ having an occupation is better than to inherit wealth. (*c*) *Vd.* bạbba 2*d*. (2) lip-service.

sanabē *m.* (1) = ficē 1. (2) yā cikạ ∼ he treats people like dirt.

sanad dạ *Vb.* 4 (1) informed *x* yā sanad dạ mū, yā cẹ̄ ... he informed us that ... nā ∼ shī wannạɳ = nā sanasshē shị wannạɳ = nā sanshē shị wannạɳ I informed him of this. (2) *Vd.* tạmbayạ 1*b*.ii, mālạmī 1*c*.v.

sanạdī *Ar. m.* (1) (*a*) cause *x* Audụ nẹ̄ sanạdịn dạ na sāmụ Audu was the cause, means of my getting it (= dạlīlị 3 = silạ). (*b*) = dạlīlị 4*a*. (2) cause of misfortune *x* rạbu dạ shī, kadạ yạ yi makạ ∼ keep clear of him lest he bring trouble on you !

sạnạntạkayyạ *Sk. f.* = sạnayyạ.

sanar dạ = sanad da.

saɳ ạ shinạ *Vd.* namijị 2*b*, sanị 1*a*.iii.

sanasshē *Vd.* sanad dạ.

sạnayyạ *f.* *x* dạ ∼ tsạkāninsụ there is mutual acquaintance between them.

san ɓērā *Vd.* sam ɓērā.

sance A. (sancẹ) *Vb.* 1A *Sk.* untied (rope, etc.), released P. (= kwancẹ).

B. *(sancē) m.* = sincē.

sanda A. (sạndā) (*m. at Kano, f. at Kt.*) *pl.* sandunạ. (1) (*a*) stick. (*b*) force *x* (i) rarrāshī bā yą̄ yi musụ sǎi sạndā coaxing is useless—force must be used against them. bą wụyā munạ̄ ĭyạ sạ̄ sạndā it would be easy to use force. bą ạbin dạ kẹ̄ tsạkāninsụ sǎi sạndā they're deadly enemies. (ii) ɗan hạlas akẹ̄ zạrgī, bāwạ sǎi sạndā a word to the worthy suffices, but beating has to be used for the worthless. (iii) mại rabạ faɗạ yą̄ ɗau sạndā ? it is useless for a mediator to use force (*Vd.* rạbō 2*b*). (*c*) hannụɳkạ mại sạndā *Vd.* hannū 1*n*. (*d*) mại ∼ kạ̄ ci gọruba *name for* horse. (*e*) dọ̄min darē akẹ̄ ∼, dạ rānā ko dạ karạ ạ̄ dōgạrā desperate causes need desperate remedies (*Vd.* dōgąrā 2*a*). (*f*) sandan jīfąŋ kūrā săi dą sāfē a kąn daukō shi do things at a suitable time! (*g*) bā ną̄ ąbụ̄tā dą biri, sandāna yą kwam bisą it is no good being a favourite if one cannot get one's desires fulfilled. (*h*) kōwā ya yi ąbụ̄tā dą biri, sandansą bā yą̄ mak̄ẹ̄wā ą bisą if one is in the swim, one can get what one wants done. (*j*) sandan dą k̄ẹ̄ hannuŋką, dą shī ak̄ẹ̄ dūką (i) every pot must stand on its own bottom. (ii) one must cut one's coat according to one's cloth (=tągunī2). (*k*) sandaŋ gąbąrūwā black-and-brown goat. (*l*) sandaŋ gątsē reliable P., T., horse, etc. (*m*) sandaŋ girmā (i) staff of office. (ii) sandaŋ girmā nūną shi ak̄ẹ̄, bā ą̄ dōkąwā a nod's as good as a wink to a blind horse. (*n*) sandan 'yam bọrī the herb *Tacca pinnatifida*. (*o*) yā sąri ～ *Vd.* sąrā 1*m*. (*p*) *cf.* shą̄ ～. (*q*) sandaŋ kanyą *Vd.* bāmī. (*r*) yā kāmą ～ *Vd.* bụge-bụgē. (*s*) *Vd.* dąuki ～. (*t*) mūgụn ～ *Vd.* kērē 1*b*. (2) (*a*) dan ～ *m.* policeman (*pl.* 'yan ～) (= bụhū 3*b*). (*b*) shẹ̄-karąssą shidą ą dan ～ he has six years' service in the police. (*c*) dan sandan cikī member of the C.I.D. (3) any kind of European cotton-goods (*but in Kano means* patterned cotton goods, *i.e.* bāsumą), *cf.* alawayyọ. (4) (*a*) *unit of length* (*yard*) for measuring ląbbāṭi, mulụfī, etc., not in form of turmī (*the word* yādi *being used for the latter*). (*b*) tsąiwā ～ bīyū two plaited-string door-curtains. (5) (*a*) tēkị yā yi ～ the hide-bag is very full. (6) *Vd.* sandą-sandą.

    B. (Sandą = Sanda) *name for any man called* Ụmarụ *q.v.*

san dą *Vd.* sā'ą 5.

sanda A. (sandā) (1) going along stealthily *x* ɓąrāwọ (mụzūrū) yā tafō yaną̄ ～ the thief (cat) came up stealthily. (2) (*secondary v.n. of* sandā) *x* yaną̄ ～ tasą = yaną̄ sandā tasą he's stalking it.

    B. (sandā) *Vb.* 2. (1) (*a*) stalked (= ląɓāɓą). (*b*) tried to "trap" P. (2) farā taną̄ nēmā tą sandē shi he's showing signs of anæmia.

sandąl *Ar. m.* (1) sandalwood. (2) sandalwood-oil.

sandąlī = sandąlū *m.* large, pale kola-nut of hannun rūwā type.

sandarą *Vb.* 3B = sandąrē.

sandąrarrē *m.* (*f.* sandąrarrīyā) *pl.* sandąrąrrū. (1) *past participle from* sandąrē. (2) sandąrąrrū inanimate objects.

sandąrē *Vb.* 3A (1) = daskąrē. (2) = kaŋgąrē 1*a, b.*

sandą-sandą *m.* (1) cik̄ịnsą yā yi ～ he had cutting pain in stomach rendering bending down painful. (2) tēkị yā yi ～ = sandā 5.

sandī *m.* treacherous P. (*his epithet is* Sandī, mugunyąr yuŋwą, ną̄sō bą ą san shịgarką ba), *Vd.* rịmā 2.

sandō *Kt. m.* = sandā.

san dōkị *m.* (*d.f.* sau na dōkị). (1) = gizągizai *q.v. under* girgijẹ̄ 1. (2) (*a*) being oval *x* k̄waryā tā yi ～ the calabash is oval. (*b*) *Vd.* kọmadą.

sandōkọ *m.* (*f.* sandōkụ̄wā) (1) feckless P. (2) *Vd.* fitsārī 9.

sandūk̄ị *Ar. m.* (*pl.* sandụ̄k̄ai) box.

sanduną *Vd.* sandā.

sane A. (sānẹ̄) (1) *Vb.* 3A became used up through extraction of juice (*x* kola-nut, tsāmīya, farm-soil, etc.) = *Kt.* sulą̄lē 1*b* = *Sk.* sallącē (*cf.* fąŋkō). (2) *Vb.* 1A stole *as in* sąnē.

    B. (sąnē) *m.* (1) daylight pilfering from the person or goods of a P. = giŋgirą̄ɓai 2 (*cf.* dąuke-dąukē). (2) dan ～ *m.* (*f.* 'yar ～) *pl.* 'yan ～ pilferer *as in* 1.

    C. (sanẹ) *Vb.* 1A (*with dative*) (*d.f.* sanị) *x* wą̄ ząi ～ maką who will take any notice of you? nī nā ～ mąsą? am *I* in his counsels?

    D. (sąnē) *m.* (1) sagacity. (2) tsōfan dōkị mąi ～ (*a*) knowing horse. (*b*) old hand (= hannū 2*g*). (*c*) *Vd.* tsōfō 1*g* ; tsūfā 2.

    E. (sąne) *x* muną̄ ～ dą shī we're aware of it (*cf.* sanị 1*d.*ii).

saŋgā *x* yā sąmē shi ą ～ he got it easily, cheaply (= ą banzā).

saŋgalaɓi *Kt. m.* fool.

saŋgalī *m.* (*pl.* saŋgąlai). (1) calf, shin-bone (= shą̄ rāɓā *q.v.*). (2) (*a*) saŋgaliŋ ƙidạ any drum-rhythm accompanying 2b (= salō 1c). (b) saŋgaliŋ rawā any dance-rhythm performed to 2a (= salō 1d). (c) (i) yā ɗạuki ~ he (dancer) danced to the drum-rhythm. (ii) sun ɗạuki saŋgalinsạ they imitated his example, copied him.

saŋgamẽmẹ m. (f. saŋgamẽmịyā) pl. saŋgam-saŋgạm huge (re living T.).

saŋgamī m. (f. saŋgamā) pl. saŋgam-saŋgạm = saŋgamẽmẹ.

Saŋgamin tamā Vd. Ụsụmạŋ.

saŋgạrcē Vb. 3A = saŋgartạ.

saŋgarmẽmẹ m. (f. saŋgarmẽmịyā) tall and strong.

saŋgarmī m. (f. saŋgarmā) tall and strong.

saŋgartạ Vb. 3B (1) P. deteriorated. (2) (P., horse) strayed about.

saŋgartad dạ Vb. 4 demoralized.

saŋgā-saŋgā Sk. f. = rạ̃i ɗọrē.

saŋ gạurākạ f. (d.f. sau). (1) = ƙafạr fạkarā. (2) Vd. kạntạ̃ƙalai.

saŋgayā f. (1) one selvedge of material being longer than other. (2) acting or speaking diffidently, reluctantly.

saŋgẽgẹ = samgẽgẹ.

saŋ girmā m. (d.f. sauriŋ girmā) x ~ gạrēshị he (domestic animal, P.) has grown up quickly.

saŋ gīwā m. (d.f. sau) used in saŋ gīwā yā tākạ na rạ̃ƙumī important T. over-shadows lesser T.

saŋgō m. (1) elephant-harpoon (= Kt. bumạ 1d). (2) Mại ~ epithet of any man called Ạlī. (3) yā sạ̃ ~ (said mock-ingly) he has put on worn-out girkẽ-gown. (4) name of Yoruba idol.

saŋgwamī = suŋgumī.

saŋhọ m. (pl. saŋhuŋạ). (1) (a) two-handled bag of woven grass. (b) Vd. kụnnē 8. (2) tụmbī bā yạ̃ ƙin ~ they're identical. (3) yā ɗau ~ he became angry. (4) saŋhwạŋ kandi useless lout. (5) saŋhwạn lallẹ = 4.

saŋhōramī = sạhōramī.

saŋhuŋạ Vd. saŋhọ.

sani A. (sanị) (1) Vb. (when object follows, san replaces sanị. Vd. 2a below for progressive : cf. shinạ). (a) (i) knew x nā san shị I know him, knew him. (ii) Allā yạ sạ̃ yạ sam mụ, mụ san shị

may God cause this baby to grow up safely ! (iii) saŋ ạ sanị, yājị dạ kwạrim mijị (mockingly) he hates this wife so that if she hadn't taken his bow, he wouldn't even know she had gone out ! (= santarantaŋ 2) (N.B.—saŋ is d.f. sọ̃), cf. 1a.x. (iiiA) Vd. namijị 2b. (iv) an san shị dạ sātạ he is known as a thief. (v) dạ̃ nā sanị Vd. dạ̃ 1b. (vi) " nī nā sanị " sautụm mahaukacịyā what an unintelligible way to deliver a message ! (vii) dạ hannū a ƙạn saŋ girmā Vd. girmā 1b.xvi. (viii) an saŋ haliŋ ƙạrē, ƙạn ɗaukō shị if one needs a P., one must put up with his defects. (viiiA) ạ sam mụtụm Vd. cịnikī 4. (ix) ƙại, saŋ ịndạ darē ya yi makạ don't be nosey ! (x) kōwā yā san dạ sanị bā mạ̃ yạrdā everybody well knows that we shan't agree to it (cf. 1a. iii). (xi) bạ ạ saŋ gạbaŋkạ ba Vd. mazarī 1a.ii. (xii) bạ ạ san shịgarkạ bā Vd. sạndī. (xiii) bạ ạ san cikịŋkạ ba Vd. tādạlī 1, 2. (xiv) yā saŋ kīfinsạ Vd. tārị 1d. (xv) Vd. shāhọ 1c. (xvi) bạ ƙạ san na gidā ba Vd. cịnnākạ 5. (xvii) bại san " nā gạji " ba Vd. ɗaukạ wuyạ. (xviii) bại san zaman dạ rāŋā ba Vd. dūtsẹ 1l. (xix) yā san dubū Vd. dubū 4. (xx) dūnīyạ ta san shị Vd. dūnīyạ 1j. (xxi) bạ ƙạ san tarkō ba Vd. gạ̃dō. (xxii) Vd. ƙạ saŋ, ƙạ saŋ. (b) got to know x jīyạ mukạ san shị it was yesterday we got to know it (M.G. 180). (c) knew that x nā sanị yanạ̃ zūwạ I know (knew) that he is (was) coming. (d) knew of the existence of x (i) iŋ ƙā saŋ ƙayạ gạrēshị if you know that there are thorns in it. (ii) sun san dạ shī they are aware of it (cf. sạne). (e) recognized as x an san sụ sarākunạ na hạlas they are recognized as the rightful rulers. bạ sụ san dādī ba they don't know what's nice when they see it. (f) thought that x nā san zại yi hakạ I thought he would act so. (g) Vd. ta B.1 1f, zaman. (2) m. (a) (v.n. and progressive of 1) x yanạ̃ saninsạ he is getting to know it (cf. 1b above). (b) (i) knowledge (= shinạ 2). (ii) Vd. zāmạnī 3b. (iii) Vd. idọn 15. (iv) nā san shị farin sanị I know him well. (v) yā san shi saniṇ shānū he knows it superficially. (vi) ạmfąnin ∽ aikąwā knowledge is useless if not applied. (vii) rashiṇ sani̩ yā fi darē duhụ nothing is worse than ignorance. (viii) rāyukąd dạ sukạ hạlakạ, wannąŋ sǎi ạ bar wạ Allą̄ saṇi God alone knows how many perished! (ix) bā ą̄ saniṃ murnạr kạrē Vd. murnạ 2b. (x) k̩ạramin ∽ Vd. k̩uk̩ụmī.

B. (sāni̩) m. that (x lemon, potash, salt, madi̩, tsāmīyā, tea, etc.) which has lost its savour (as in sānẹ q.v.) x tsāmīyan nạ̩ŋ ∽ cē = Kt. tsāmīyan nạ̩ŋ tā yi ∽ this tamarind has lost its original goodness, through infusion (= Kt. sụlālẹ).

saŋ innạ Vd. son inna.

sānịyā f. cow (Vd. sạ̄ A.2 page 753).

sanji̩ (Eng.) m. small change, cf. sanzạ.

san ji̩kī Vd. son jiki.

sanka A. (saŋkā) (1) f. (pl. saŋkạ̄yẹ) (a) bunch of fermented (ruɓạ) tobaccoleaves. (b) Kt. fool. (2) Kt. (no pl.) boiled tạfạsā-leaves. (3) adv. sābō ∽ brand new (= pul).

B. (saŋka) Vb. 3B East Hausa = saukạ.

saŋkacẹ m. (pl. saŋkạtū = saŋkạtai) (1) row of cut corn on farm, laid down for cutting off heads (= Kt. jēnẹ) (epithet is Saŋkacẹ gamạ gōnā). (2) Vd. ruɓạ saŋkacẹ.

saŋkacēcẹ m. (f. saŋkacēcị̩yā) pl. saŋkamsạ̩ŋkạm huge (living T.).

saŋ kǎi Vd. son kai.

saŋkạlmạkal (1) adv. empty-handed. (2) m. (sg., pl.) (a) P. without adornment. (b) traveller without journey-equipment.

saŋk̩ạmē (1) Vb. 3A (a) sat bolt upright, held oneself erect. (b) cikiṇsạ yā ∽ he found it painful to bend through stomach-ache. (2) Vb. 1C x cīwọ yā saŋk̩ạmẹ wuyąntạ illness stiffened her neck.

saŋkam-sạ̩ŋkạm Vd. saŋkacēcẹ.

sankara A. (sạ̩ŋkạrā) f. (sg., pl.) (1) insect boring into kola-nuts (epithet is Saŋk̩ạrā, cị̩ gōrọ). (2) P. eating kola-nuts excessively (epithet as for 1). (3) = k̩āk̩ọ.

B. (Saŋkarạ) Vd. saŋkarancī.

saŋkarancī = sankarcī m. face-tattooing done by people of Saŋkarạ in Kano Province.

Saŋk̩ạrau used in ạllọ̄bar ∽ f. cerebrospinal meningitis (= Kanōmā 1).

saŋk̩ạrē = saŋk̩ạmē.

saŋ k̩asā m. late supper of tūwō, in azụmī (d.f. sau na k̩asā).

saŋkạtū Vd. saŋkacẹ.

saŋkạ̄yē Vd. saŋkā.

saŋ kạ̄zā m. (d.f. sau) tukunyā tā yi ∽ = washẹwashī.

sank̩e A. (saŋk̩ẹ) Vb. 1A (1) yā ∽ wạrkī (wạndō) he pulled end of leatherloincloth (trousers) through his legs and tucked it into his waistband (= durwạcē), cf. durwā, k̩unzugū, kạndạmē, sọ̄kē, tụ̄rē 3, sansạŋk̩ē. (2) yā ∽ wutsīyạ it (dog, horse) put its tail between its legs. (3) saŋk̩ẹ wạrkiŋkạ m. type of sensitive plant (= Kt. tạuyẹ wạlkiŋkạ).

B. (saŋk̩ẹ) m. tucking in as in saŋk̩ẹ.

saŋk̩ẹdā f. (1) = sālạ. (2) x kạbēwạ ∽ gụdā one slice of marrow (on sale). (3) single pod of locust-bean (dọ̄rōwạ) or tamarind (tsāmīyā). (4) single segment of orange, etc.

saŋ'k̩e-saŋk̩ē ‖ m. = dạmē-dạmē 1.

saŋk̩ẹ wạrkiŋkạ Vd. saŋk̩ẹ 3.

Saŋ k̩īrạ Vd. k̩īrạ 1bb, san.

saŋkị̩yā f. type of fish-trap.

saŋk̩ō m. (1) (a) baldness. (b) bald patch ((b) = Kt. sulại 3b). (2) shaving hair over eyes in V-shape.

saŋk̩ōlamī m. (f. saŋk̩ōlamā) good-fornothing P.

Saŋ kurmi̩ Vd. san 1b.

san naŋ Vd. sā'ạ 6.

sạnnū (1) (a) greeting! (reply is ∽ kạdǎi = mhṃ). (b) sạnnuŋkạ dạ aiki̩ = ∽ dạ aiki̩ greeting to you in your work! (reply as in 1a) = Sk. họ̄ 1b. (c) ∽ dạ gajīyạ I hope you'll soon feel rested! (reply as in 1a). (d) ∽ dạ hūtạ̄wā I'm glad to see you're resting! (reply as in 1a). (e) ∽, Allạ̄ yạ sauk̩ak̩ē allow me to condole with you on your trouble (or injury)! (reply as in 1a). (f) Mại zamā, ∽ I'm glad to see you are enjoying the shade!

(*said to unknown P.*) (*reply as in* 1*a*).
(*g*) " sạnnū ! " bā tā warkẹ cīwọ sǎi dǎi
kā ji dādī a zūci soft words butter no
parsnips (*said by P. whom one has
insulted or hit and then to calm him,
said* sạnnū *to him : before he says* (*g*),
he may say sạnnū mẹ what's the good
of your saying sạnnū to me ?). (*h*) *Vd*.
Bạtūrẹ 2. (*j*) ∼ dạ rashị *Vd*. gaisūwā 5.
(*k*) = 2 *below*. (2) sạnnū sạnnū (*a*) (i)
slowly *x* yanā tạfīyạ s.s. he's walking
slowly. (ii) tạfīyạ s.s. kwānā nēsạ Camel
thou slow goer but traveller far ! (iii)
yaushẹ zaị zọ when will he arrive ? (*reply*,
sǎi sạnnū not just yet). (iv) 'yan dūnīyạ
sǎi sạnnū alas, Man's ways never
improve ! (*b*) gradually *x* (i) sạnnū sạnnū,
sǎi gā shi bā sauran tsọfaffịn kudī then
little by little the old money went out
of circulation. sạnnū sạnnū Allā ya
taịmakē shị then as the days went by,
God mitigated his trouble. (ii) al'amạrin
dūnīyạ, a jā shị a sạnnū moderation in
all ! (iii) dạ sạnnū sạnnū a kạn ci
ḳirgịm bịjimī slow but sure ! (iv) lafīyạ
dạ sạnnū takē shịgā recovery of health
is a slow matter. (3) *f*. (*a*) slowness
(*cf*. 2*b*.ii–iv *above*) *x* (i) ∼ bā tā hanạ
zūwạ slow but sure ! (ii) shī rūwā nẹ
maị aikịn ∼ he is a deliberate P.
(*b*) carefulness *x* sǎi kạ yi ∼ dạ shī
be on your guard against him ! (*c*) *cf*. 1*g*
for further use of sạnnū *as fem. noun*.
(4) ∼ dạ kāyạ *m*. (*a*) A. out of fashion,
old-fashioned. (*b*) cheap imitations. *(5)
Sk. = Dārịgō.

san raḳumin yārā *Vd*. son raḳumin yara.

sā n sā *m*. mutually bandying words
(= fạdi m fạdā = *Kt*. shẹrayyạ).

sansama A. (sansāmā) *Vb*. 1C (1) =
ḳunḳumā 2*a*, 3. (2) threshed (corn).
    B. (sạnsāmạ) intensive from sāmā.

sansāmē *m*. acting *as in* sansāmā.

sansami A. (sạnsāmī) *m*. (1) *Kt*. leaves.
(2) sạnsāmin tābạ leaf-tobacco.
    B. (sansamī) *m*. the tree *Stereo-
spermum kunthianum* (= jịrī 2).

sansạn *m*. (1) = fịd dạ hakūkūwạ.
(2) *Vd*. sạnsạn garī.

sansana A. (sansạnā) *Vb*. 1C (1) smelt at.
(2) in kā ji " a sansạnā ! ", bā ḳanshī a
good wine needs no bush.

    B. (sạnsanạ) *Vb*. 2= sansạnā 1 *x* sukạ
fārạ sạnsanạr yā tạfi then they began
to suspect he had gone away.

sansạncē *Vb*. 3A = sakaŋḳạncē.

sạnsạn garī *m*. (1) being *au fait* with
town or subject. (2) ∼ yị bāwạn gādọ
what a know-all ! (*d.f*. sanị).

sansanī *m*. (1) (*a*) war-camp. (*b*) (*sometimes used as plural*) *x* wadạnsu sạnsanī
some camps. (2) (*a*) halo round moon
(*portends war*). (*b*) halo round sun
(*portends birth of elephant*).

sansaŋḳē *Vb*. 3A (1) on meeting a superior,
pulled one's gown close round one and
covered one's folded arms with it (*cf*.
tārạ 1*b*). (2) = saŋḳẹ 1, 2.

sansannạ *Kt*. *f*. *x* nā dau ∼ shī nẹ ya
yī I feel certain *he* is the one who did it
(= sakaŋḳạncē).

sansantsā *m.f*. (*pl*. santsātsā) (1) slippery
(*cf*. santsī). (2) sly. (3) worn-out (soil).

sansanyā *m*., *f*. (*pl*. sanyāyā (1) cold.
(2) halī ∼ patient disposition. (3)
sạnsanyar magạnạ pleasant speech.

sansạram-sạnsạram *m*. noise made in the
gait jạn harāwạ.

sanshē = sanasshē *q.v. under* sanad dạ.

sanshẹrā *Kt*. = shanshẹrā.

sansōmā *Vb*. 1C *intensive from* sōmạ.

sạnsōmī *m*. initial stages in deterioration
x sạnsōmin lālācẹwā yā sāmē shị it is
showing first traces of deterioration.
sạnsōmịn haukā zub dạ yau dribbling is
first stage in madness (= sarẹsarī 2).

sạntaccē *m*. (*f*. sạntaccīyā) *pl*. sạntạttū
past participle from sancẹ.

santalēlẹ *m*. (*f*. santalēlīyā) *pl*. santal-
sạntạl (1) handsome (*cf*. salạm). (2)
santalēlạn dōkị = sạntịlō.

santalī *m*. (1) *f*. (santalā) *pl*. santal-sạntạl
= santalēlẹ. (2) *m*. (*pl*. santulạ) =
sintalī.

sạntambul *f*. (1) Stamboul, Constantinople
(*Ar*. Islāmbul). (2) ḳasar ∼ *f*. Turkey.

santarantạn (1) empty-handed. (2) ∼ yājị
bā bikọ = sanị 1*a*.iii.

sạntī *Kt*. = fanyā 3.

sạntịlō *used in* ∼ dōkịn Asbịn this horse
is as fine as if it came from Asben
(= santalēlẹ 2).

sạntōlaɓī = sạntōlạmī *m*. (*f*. sạntōlạɓā)
good-for-nothing P.

santōlǫ = santōrǫ *m.* (*f.* santōlůwā = santōrůwā) = santōląɓī.
santsątsā *Vd.* sąnsantsā.
santsī *m.* (1) (*a*) slipperiness (= tąlālāɓīyā).
(*b*) ∼ yā ɗaukē shi = ∼ yā kwāshę shi he slipped, slipped over. (2) smoothness *x* takąrdā tanā dą ∼ the paper is glossy. (3) mąi santsim bāyā *Vd.* tůlū 3.
san tsuntsū *m.* type of grass with edible leaf (*d.f.* sau).
san turākī *Vd.* turākī.
sānůwā *Vd.* sā A2 (*page* 753).
sąŋ ūwar dawą *Vd.* son uwar dawą.
saŋwą *f.* (1) tā girką ∼ = tā yi ∼ = tā azą ∼ = tā sā ∼ she put water in cooking-pot on fire to boil (*cf.* giɪką). (2) an yi ∼ all preparations for task have been made. (3) tā ciką ∼ she buys in small quantities for cheapness. (4) ƙaramas ∼ gąrēshi he's tall and slender. (5) *Vd.* jirātą.
sanya A. (sanyā) = ūwar māgunguną.
　B. (sąnyā) *Vb.* 1C put, etc. = sā 1 *q.v.*
sanyaya A. (sanyąyā) *Vd.* sąnsanyā.
　B. (sanyąyā) (1) *Vb.* 1C (*a*) cooled T. (*b*) appeased, soothed (angry P.). (*c*) *x* yā ∼ mini zūcīyā = yā ∼ mini rąi he comforted me. (*d*) Allā yą ∼ maną = Allā yą sanyąyą zūcīyarmų may God give us His comfort ! (2) *Vb.* 3A (*a*) took a rest *x* yā tąfi ƙauyę don yą ∼ he's gone to the country for a rest. (*b*) yā sąmi wurin sanyąyąwā he's now having an easier time.
sanye A. (sąnye) (*d.f.* sąnyā) *x* sunā sąnye dą kāyan Sarkī they are dressed in uniform.
　B. (sąnyē) *Vb.* 1C (*with dative*) *x* nā ∼ masą I gave him permission.
sanyī *m.* (1) (*a*) (i) damp coldness (*cf.* ɗārī) *x* dākiņ naŋ da ∼ yakę this room is cold and damp (*cf.* *b*.iii below). (ii) ƙāƙa aką jī dą sanyī how does this damp cold weather suit you ? (*reply* dą saukī = Alhamdų lillāhi quite well, thanks !). *Vd.* ƙāƙa 1*c*. (iii) wurī yā fayę musų sanyī the place is too cold for them. (iv) sun riką sanyī they held aloof. (*b*) (i) chilly weather (= ɗārī *q.v.*). (ii) dą sanyin yąmmā = lis 1.

(iii) dākiŋ naŋ dą ∼ yakę this room is chilly (*cf.* 1*a above*). (iv) ∼ yā shigō cold weather has set in. (*v*) yā yi ∼ ƙalau the weather is bitterly cold (*Vd.* ƙalau 1*b*). (vi) yā sąmē shi cikin sanyī ƙalau he got it easily. (vii) nasarąr sanyin sāfīyā easy victory. (*c*) a chill *x* (i) ∼ yā kwantad dą nī the chill I caught has temporarily incapacitated me. (ii) ∼ yā kāmą ni = ∼ yā hąrbē ni I have caught a chill (*cf.* ɗārī 1*a*.ii). (2) ban ∼ *m.* cooling iron in sand. (3) hannunsą yā yi ∼ his arm is (*a*) cramped, (*b*) stiff with cold, (*c*) paralysed, withered. (4) slackness *x* (*a*) ∼ gąrēshi he is a slacker, sluggish P. yā yi sanyī gą shirin yāƙi he was slack in preparing for war. sum fārą sanyī cikiŋ ąl'amąriŋ they've begun to get slack in the matter. (*b*) bąi yi ∼ ba he didn't slacken his efforts. (*c*) kadą ką yi sanyiŋ gwīwą don't give up effort, hope ! (*d*) (i) jīkīna dū yā yi ∼ I lost heart. (ii) jikīnā yā yi ∼ *Vd.* ɓērā 1*h*. (*e*) sanyin jikī (i) indolence, lethargy = sanyin nāmą (*cf.* zāfin nāmą). (ii) *Vd.* ɓōrī 2*a*. (*f*) *x* yā yi ∼ ą harbi his shooting is no longer so good. (*g*) yā yi ∼ cikiŋ aikinsą he's sick of his work. (*h*) ƙūsą tā yi ∼ the rivet has become loose. (*j*) inji yā yi ∼ the clockwork has run down. (5) sanyī gąrēshi yau he's out of sorts to-day. (6) Audų ∼ gąrēshi Audu is an equable P. (7) (*a*) ∼ gąrēshi he does not feel well in cold weather. (*b*) *sanyinsą bųrūdą nē cold weather is bad for him. *sanyinsą hąrārą nē hot weather is bad for him. (8) yā yi ∼ he has become sexually impotent (= lą'īfi). (9) sanyiŋ halī forbearance, being long-suffering. (10) sanyim mąganą gąrēshi he (sick P.) is speaking in faint voice. (11) ji sanyiŋ inūwą *Vd.* inūwą 9. (12) (*a*) urine (= bawąlī). (*b*) cīwąn ∼ *m.* gonorrhœa (= sai A.1 1*b* = sūnā 9 = *Zar.* mąsūnā). (13) rūwan sanyī (*a*) cold water. (*b*) *Vd.* rūwā A.24, B.10, C.10 ; dīyā 5. (14) sun ji indą kę dą sanyi-sanyi they hit on a weak spot. (15) ƙīrąr ∼ *Vd.* bąrhō.
sanyō *Vb.* 1E *Sk.* put, etc. = sā 1.

sanzą *Vb.* 1A *Eng.* changed (money), *cf.*
sanji.
sanzad dą *Vb.* 4 = sanzą.
san zūcįyā *Vd.* son zuciya.
sā'ǫ (*rustic*) *x* muną ~ we wish (= sǫ).
sa'o'i A. (sā'ō'ī) *Vd.* sā'ą.
  B. (sa'ō'ī) *Vd.* sa'ą.
sąr *Vd.* sąr-sąr.
sara A. (sąrā) (1) *Vb.* 2. (*a*) yā sąri itącē
(i) he felled the tree. (ii) he chopped firewood (1*a* = sārę 1*a*). (*b*) (i) slashed,
hacked at. (ii) hacked off (= sārę 1*a*), *cf.*
sārą 1*b*, sārę 1*b*). (iii) haunī yā sārē shį
the executioner beheaded him (= kashę
1*a*.vi = *Sk.* dēbę 9 = bugę kąnsą
(*q.v. under* bugę 2) = fallę 2*b* = gillę
1), *cf.* yąŋką 1*a*.iv. (*c*) (i) macįjī
yā sārē ni the snake bit me (*cf.* cįzā,
hąrbā 3). (ii) *Vd.* tsųmmā 3. (*d*) kązā
tā sārē ni the hen pecked me. (*e*)
yā sārē ni he maliciously accused me to
embroil me with my superior = hąrbā
1*g* (*cf.* sārā 3). (*f*) an sąri kǫfatǫ the
hoof has been pared (*by placing edge
of knife on hoof and striking with wood*),
cf. yąŋkę 1*c*.vi, sāraŋ kǫfatǫ. (*g*) an
sąri gįndiŋ hatsī the corn has been
reaped (= gįrbā), *cf.* yąŋkę 1*b*. (*h*)
bought rural produce (corn, milk,
pepper, salt, dąddawā, etc.) as it
arrived in town from village, in order
to corner market and sell when
scarce and prices high = sārad dą
(*cf.* kwarąmī, sārā 2*a*). (*j*) yā sąri
gōnā he cleared " bush " to make new
farm = sassąbē (*Vd.* shēmā, sāraŋ
gōnā). yā sąri gąrī (masallācī) he
cleared site for town (mosque). (*k*)
yā sąri dundūnįyā tasų he trod on their
heels (= dundūnįyā 2). (*l*) dōkį yā
sąri hųcī he (galloping-horse, hurrying
P.) fell over. (*m*) *x* (i) yā sąri sandaŋ
kąrątū = yā sārar wą kąrątū sandā
he has become immersed in study.
Hądįją tā sārar wą kįrįnīyā sandā
Hadija does nothing but rove about
looking for men (= gīlǫ 1). cācā
(sātą) suką sārar wą, sandā they gave
over all their time to gambling (theft).
(ii) *Vd.* dǫkā 2*a*.ii. (*n*) sąri ką bā ni
Vd. gątarī 1*c*. (*o*) *Vd.* sāran-*compounds*,
sąri-*compounds*, sārą, sārā, sārę, sārē-

sārē. (2) *f.* (*a*) (*negatively*) *x* sǎi dą
na ga bą ~ ba, na barį I only gave up
when I saw there was no advantage to
be gained. (*b*) custom *x* (i) sārarką,
musų it is your way to contradict. (ii)
sū nę suką bā dą wannąŋ ~ it was
they who introduced this custom. (iii)
aką dąuki ~, kōwā ya ga ąbim mąmākį,
sǎi yą yi īhų then the custom was
adopted that anyone who saw anything strange, should shout out. (*c*)
suną ~ they (the marǫkā *q.v. under*
marǫkī 2*b*) are performing the
Thursday-evening drumming for the
Emir (= wāzą). (*d*) kāyā yā yi ~ the
load is ill-balanced on head of carrier.
  B. (sārą) (1) *Vb.* 1A. (*a*) = sārā
1*a*.i, ii, *b*.i *x* an sārą hanyąr rūwā a
canal was cut. (*b*) yā ~ kǫfą (tāgą) he
cut hole in wall for door (window), *cf.*
sārā 1*b*.i. (*c*) yā ~ kasā, yā kwābą
he cut out earth (with pick, etc.) and
mixed it into clay. (*d*) (i) an ~ wą
dōkį jinī vein has been opened in
horse's leg to let out old blood and gain
strength (*cf.* rārīyā 4). (ii) yā ~ masą
jinī he cadged something from him. (*e*)
divided into portions *x* an ~ rōgǫ
(nāmą) ukų the cassava (meat) has
been divided into three portions. (*f*)
an ~ masą kudī = yąŋką 1*d*.i (*cf.*
sārē 3). (*g*) yā ~ masą he (soldier, etc.)
saluted him. (*h*) yā ~ ąlēwą he broke
off piece of ąlēwą-sweets. (*j*) yā ~
mini bąkī (i) he made unauthorized
statement on my behalf (*cf.* yąŋką
1*d*.ii). (ii) he (friend) advised me how
much to offer for the article (*cf.*
sāram bąkī). (*k*) *Sk.* tā ~ masą girā
she gave him " the glad eye " (*Vd.*
kadą 1*k*). (*l*) *Vd.* sāran-*compounds*,
sąrā, sārā, sārę. (2) *Vb.* 3*A x* rįgā tā ~
the gown is showing signs of wear. (*b*)
kąina yā ~ my head is beginning to
ache. (*c*) yā ~ yā tąfi he set off.
  C. (sārā) *m.* (1) (*secondary v.n. for*
sąrā *and* sārą *provided these are not
used with dative as is, e.g.,* sārą 1*d*) *x*
yaną sāraŋ itącē = yaną sārar itącē
he's chopping firewood (= sąrā 1*a*).
macįjī yaną sārāna = yaną sąrāta the
snake is biting me (sąrā 1*c*.i); mąi~dayā

Vd. ịnjihaụ. yanậ sāraŋ gōnā = yanậ sậrar gōnā he's clearing " bush " to make new farm (sậrā 1*j*), etc. (2) (*a*) (i) acting *as in* sậrā 1*h* (= sōkē = dakẹnō = sōdọ̄rē = kamcī = cīdọ = sārị), *cf.* tākudẹ, taŋkū, cikọ 3, kwarạmī. (ii) dan ∼ (*f.* 'yar ∼) *pl.* 'yan ∼ P. acting as in 2*a.i.* (*b*) (i) acting *as in* sậrā 1*b.*i *x* aŋ kai (= kāwō) masạ sārā he was slashed. (ii) sārā dayā bā yậ kā dạ itậcē Rome wasn't built in day. (iii) *Vd.* sạssakạ 2*b.* (iv) bậ sāraŋkạ ba *Vd.* gwadạyī. (*c*) acting *as in* sậrā 1*j x* (i) an yi sāban sārā a new farm has been made. (*d*) *Vd.* sāran-*compounds.* (3) yậ yi ∼ dạ mutụm ạ bisạ = harbā 1*g* (*cf.* sậrā 1*e*). (4) gōran naŋ yanậ dạ ∼ these kola-nuts are big. wannaŋ gōrọ yậ fi ∼ this kola-nut is the biggest. (5) yanậ ∼, yanậ dūbam bậkiŋ gậtarī he's hesitating as to whether this is too difficult for him to do.

D. (sarạ = sạrạ) (1) = shẹ̄ḵẹ̄ḵẹ̄. (2) dāki ∼ yakẹ̄ this roof lets in the sun. (3) *Vd.* cậsau 2.

sarad da A. (sārad dạ) *Vb.* 4 = sậrā 1*h.*

B. (sarad dạ) *x* yā ∼ wuriŋ he is familiar with the place, frequents the place.

sạraf-sạraf = sararaf.

sậ rāgaitạ *Vd.* zụrū 3.

sarai A. (sarai) excellently *x* yanậ ganī ∼ he can see well. nā gānẹ ∼ I understand perfectly. yā īyạ ∼ he is well able.

B. *(sarai) *Vb.* (*not in progressive*) fell (= fādị, *but only used in translating from Arabic*).

C. (sạrai) = sạrạ.

sạrakạ *Kt. Vb.* 3B (1) = sarkẹ̄ 1*a.* (*b*) sun ∼ cikim fadạ = sarkạ 2*b.*

sạrậkai *Vd.* (1) Sarkī, Sạrậkī, bạsarākẹ̄. (2) *Vd.* Sarkī 4.

sạrậkī (1) *m.* = bạsarākẹ̄. (2) matsạ sạrậkī = muntsunạ sạrậkī. (3) *Sk. f.* = ḵōramạ 2.

sarakullē *Kt.* = sụrkullē 3.

sarākunạ *Vd.* sarkī, bạsarākẹ̄.

sạrakutạ = sarakutạ = sạrạkuntạ *f.* in-law relationship (*cf.* sụrukī, sạrạkūwā).

sạrạkūwā *f.* (*for pl. Vd.* sụrukī). (1) mother-in-law. (2) daughter-in-law. (3) younger brother's wife. (4) sạrạ-

kūwarkị ạ turmī (*said by woman to woman*) please come and give me a hand with my pounding ! (5) sạrạkūwar saurō = dạddōyạ.

sạrạm *x* nā ji dọ̄yī ∼ I smelt an awful stench.

sāram bậkī *m.* (1) marking out line to show where to begin farm-work (= *Kt.* sāraŋ gōnā). (2) acting as in sậrạ 1*j.*

sāram barhō *m.* (1) yanậ dạ ∼ it (kola-nut) has been damaged by knife used in removing outer pod. (2) kolas damaged *as in* 1.

sāram bisạ *m. used in* ∼ bā yậ kisạn itậcē a small loss is not ruin.

sāran b.... *Vd.* sāram.

sāran darē *m.* (1) stealing fencing at night for firewood. (2) *Vd.* gậtarī 12.

sāran daurī *m. used in* ∼ bậ dậ *Vd.* daurī 1*b.*

sāraŋ gạbā *m.* overcharging for T. sold.

sāraŋ gạyyā *m.* = kalaŋkūwā 1*a.*

sāraŋ gōnā (1) acting *as in* sậrā 1*j* (= sạssạbẹ̄). (2) *Kt. Vd.* sāram bậkī 1.

sāraŋ kọ̄fatọ *m.* (1) acting as in sậrā 1*f.* (2) staining merely edges of teeth (= bậkin cạrkī 2), *cf.* shịŋkāfā 2. (3) *Zar.* hitting player on finger-nail in katantaŋwạ 1*b.*i (*cf.* jậtau 1*b*, dāwạ 3).

sāraŋ kumbọ *Vd.* kumbọ 2.

sāraŋ kụmbudụ̄wā *Vd.* kụmbudụ̄wā.

sāran rūwā *used in* ạ shẹ̄karạ ∼ săi tạmfạtsē he's in too firm a position to be injured by slander.

sāran shạnyē *m.* = habaicī.

sāran shūkạ *m.* (1) making holes with suŋgumī for hoeing. (2) yanậ tạfīyạ, yanậ ∼ he has contracted Achilles tendon (= cōbẹ̄).

sāran sụ̄mā *Kt. m.* shaving baby's head on naming-day (ran sūnā).

sāran tūjī *m.* young men's voluntarily going round countryside when summoned by drumming, to weed roads in towns and villages (= tūjī 2).

sāran tūrụ *m.* (1) haụkā nậ ḵārẹ̄wā, anậ sāran tūrụ " sheep behaving as lamb ". (2) needle with small eye (*cf.* ạllūrạ, asirkā 2).

sāraŋ wāgā *m.* kola-nuts of assorted sizes.

sāraŋ wāwā *m.* (1) *Vd.* gaudẹ̄. (2) cutting green wood and leaving it to dry.

sarara A. (sarārā) *Vb.* 3A. (1) took short rest. (2) *x* yau anā sarārā ɗārī it is blowing very cold to-day.

  B. (sarārā) (1) *Vb.* 3B (*a*) = kwaranyē 2*b*. (*b*) hancinsa yanā ～ he has a heavy cold and his nose is dripping. (2) cold harmattan-wind (= kuyarī).

  C. (sarārā) *x* yanā yāwo ～ he's roving aimlessly.

sararaf A. (sararaf) *m.* acting like lightning *x* yā yi ～ yā sācę masa zanę he stole gown from him, whipping it away like lightning.

  B. (sarāraf) *m.* slip-slopping noise of sandals.

sararī *m.* (*pl.* sararai) (1) (*a*) open space, cleared space, open country (= fīlī). (*b*) (i) fītō mana a ～ speak out frankly ! (*Vd.* taŋkā 2). (ii) abu a ～ *Vd.* gabagabā. (*c*) (i) garī yā yi ～ storm has cleared away. (ii) *x* a barī sǎi garī yā yi ～ postpone it till after the wet season ! (*d*) ka yi rubūtū da ～ do not crowd your writing ! (= tsakānī-tsakānī). (*e*) (i) fuska tasa bā ta da ～ he looks worried. (ii) sararin rǎi garēshi he's a cheerful P. (iii) sararin zūcīyā a tambayi fuska one's face shows what is in one's heart. (iv) *Vd.* subhaŋ. (2) opportunity, leisure *x* (i) bā ni da ～ yau I've no time to spare to-day (= dāmā 1*a*.i). (ii) na waje shī kę ganin ～ *Vd.* dambē 2. (3) yā fi Audu ～ he's quicker in the uptake than Audu (*cf.* 4). (4) mai ～ nę he's well-off. yā fi Audu ～ he's better-off than Audu (*cf.* 3). (5) ɗan ～ nę he's profligate.

sararracę *intensive from* sarcę.

sararrakā *Vb.* 3B is interlinked, intertwined *x* sun ～ duka they are all interrelated. harshę yā karai, hakōri yā ～ he (dying man) cannot move his tongue or jaws (*cf.* sarkę, sarka).

sararrakē *Vb.* 3A = sararrakā.

sara-sara A. (sarā-sarā) *f.* (1) sāka tā yi ～ it is of open weave. jiŋkā yā yi ～ it is not densely thatched. (2) kāsuwā tā yi ～ the market is sparsely attended. (3) *cf.* sarau-sarau.

  B. (sarā-sarā) = zarā-zarā.

sarau A. (sarau) *Vb. invariable.* yā ～ (1) he has been appointed to official position (sarauta) = sarautu. (2) he lives " like a lord ".

  B. (sarau) = shękękę.

sarauce A. (saraucē) *Vb.* 1C = sarauta 2.

  B. (saraucē) *Vd.* sarauta 2.

Saraunīyā *Vd.* Sarkī.

sarau-sarau *m.* (1) = sarā-sarā. (2) kunū yā yi ～ the gruel is thin.

sarauta A. (sarauta) (1) *f.* (*pl.* sarautū) (*a*) being the ruler, having sovereignty (*cf.* Sarkī 1). (*b*) (i) official position to which P. is appointed (*x* Wazīrī, Galādīma, Mādākī, etc.) by the holder of 1*a* (*cf.* Sarkī 2) (= rikō 3). (ii) yā yi sarautū iri daban-daban he held many different offices. (iii) yā ajīyę sarauta he resigned office. (*c*) kāyan ～ *m.* emblems of chieftainship, royal insignia. (*d*) bikī dǎi bā ～ ba nę all is not gold that glitters. (*e*) (i) yanā ～ he's ruling. yanā sarautar Kano he's the Emir of Kano. (ii) sarautar kūrā mere self-seeking governing. (iii) Sarkin sarauta Almighty God ! (*f*) (i) yā ci ～ he succeeded to the rule. (ii) *Vd.* cī 10. (*g*) *Vd.* nada. (*h*) talakan naŋ da ～ yakę what airs this fellow gives himself ! (= hākimcē). (*j*) Sarkin naŋ jin ～ garēshi this ruler is arrogant (= jiŋ kǎi). (*k*) *Vd.* waŋkan～. (2) *Vb.* 2 ruled over *x* yā saraucē su he ruled them. yā sarauci Kano he ruled Kano.

  B. (sarauta) *Vb.* 1C (1) appointed P. as chief (*Vd.* sarauta 1*a*). (2) appointed P. to official position (*Vd.* sarauta 1*b*).

sarautu A. (sarautū) *Vd.* sarauta 1.

  B. (sarautu) *Vb.* 3B he has become chief, he has become office-holder (*Vd.* sarauta 1*a*, 1*b*).

*saraya *Vb.* 3B = *sarai.

sārayya *f.* behaving mutually *as in* sārā.

sarɓa *f.* unconsidered talk (= ɗanyē 4*a*).

sarɓaɗa *Vb.* 3A roved aimlessly.

sarɓaɗai = sarɓaɗę (1) yanā yāwo ～ he's roving aimlessly. (2) = shękękę.

sarɓai = sarɓandai.

sarɓaŋ = sarɓandai.

sarɓandai *x* yā mīkę ～ he stretched out his legs.

sarbu pardon me, inexpert as I am, doing this task in the presence of a specialist like you !

sarcẹ (1) *Vb.* 1A (*a*) combed (hair, beard, mane). (*b*) yā ~ kabạ he removed leaves from dum-palm, to make tạ̄barmā-mat. yā ~ ganyaŋ gambạ don yạ yi zānā he removed leaves from Andropogon grass to make zāna-mat (1*a* = shācẹ 1*b* = tsēfẹ 1) (1*b* = fẹ̄tsā 1*c*). (2) *Kt.* = sartsẹ.

*sạrcē-sạrcē = ƙarga-ƙarga.

Sardaunā *Sk.* one of the sạrautạ.

sardị *Nor.* = sirdị.

sạrdō *Kt. m.* = shāyạ 1*c*.

sare A. (sārẹ) (1) *Vb.* 1A. (*a*) = sạ̄rā 1*a*.i, ii, *b*.ii. (*b*) *x* yā ~ shi dạ taƙọbī he slashed him dead with a sword (*cf.* sạ̄rā 1*b*). (*c*) bought up all the available rural produce *to act as in* sạ̄rā 1*h*. (*d*) yā ~ wạ ƙạrạ̄tū sạndā = sạ̄rā 1*m*. (*e*) ạ ~ tōfā *Vd.* tōfā 2. (2) *Vb.* 3A (*a*) yā ~ he (traveller, horse, etc.) became tired out and unable to proceed without a rest (= kāsạ 1*a*). (*b*) (material) became used up *x* hatsī yā ~ ạ ƙạsūwā corn ceased to be on sale. fẹ̄tụr yā ~ masạ ạ hanyạ his petrol gave out before he had finished his journey (= ƙārẹ 1*b*.i = katsẹ 2*a*). (*c*) lost heart (= ƙạrai). (*d*) he failed to ask guest to take food (= ƙạrāyạ 2*c*).
  B. (sạ̄rē) *m.* (1) roughly-cut doorway. (2) = fadandẹ. (3) an yi masạ ~ = sārạ 1*f*. (4) *Kt.* half *x* sạ̄raŋ ƙwaryar gōrọ half a ƙwaryā (*Vd.* ƙwaryā 5*d*) of kolas.

sạrēfā *Kt.* = shạrēfā.

sarẹkanī = sạrƙā.

sarẹrā = shanshẹ̄rā.

sare-sare A. (sarē-sạrẹ̄) = zarā-zạrḡ̣.
  B. (sạ̄'re-sạ̄rē‖) *m.* ƙuskạ dạ ~ tā fī ƙyēyạ = gạ̄tarī 1*c*.

sarẹsarī *m.* (1) cause *x* kā yi masạ sarẹsarim ɓatạ you have done what may cause it to get lost. (2) = sạnsōmī.

sạrēwạ *f.* (1) type of flute made from cornstalk (karā) or bamboo (= mabūsā = shẹ̄shē). (2) unmarried girl no longer virgin (= bụdurwā 2).

sarfạ (1) *Ar. m.* generous P. (*cf.* tasarrụfī). *(2) *Ar. f.* a star in Leo.

sargā *f.* (*pl.* sargunạ) cesspit (= masai = shạddā = *Kt.* sihịrdā).

sargafa *Kt.* = sarƙafa.

sạrgantạ *Kt.* = sạlwantạ.

sargunạ *Vd.* sargā.

sari A. (sāri) *m.* (1) chestnut horse. (2) ~ fạriŋ gẹ̄zā = ~ kalgō = ~ maiƙọ fawn-coloured horse (= daƙūwạ 3 = shẹ̄jị 1). B. (sārị) *m.* (1) = sārā 2*a*.i. (2) sārịŋ ƙōsǎi bạ̄ shi dạ rībạ love's labour lost. (3) ɗan ~ = sārā 2*a*.ii. C. (sạrī) *m.* = gundạ.

sạ̄ri bạ̄ mạ̄tākạ *epithet of* baunī (= gạ̄tsi bạ̄ mạ̄tākạ).

sạ̄ri, dọ̄sa (1) makeshift hoe-haft consisting of tree-branch. (2) = shigēgẹ.

sạ̄ri kạ bā nị *Vd.* gạ̄tarī 1*c*.

sạ̄ri, kạ nōƙẹ = *Kt.* sạ̄ri, kạ dōnẹ *m.* (1) type of snake. (2) crafty P.

sạ̄ri kutuf *m.* type of gecko-lizard (tsakā) with adhesive discs on toes (*though harmless, is considered harmful*) = *Kt.* kutuf.

sārịŋ ƙōsǎi *Vd.* sārị 2.

sārīyā *f.* (1) shaving front of head from ear to ear. (2) = fạskạrē 2*a*. (3) wrestlers' shaving hair into three parts.

sarka A. (sạrkā) *f.* (*pl.* sarkunạ = sarẹkanī) = sạlkā.
  B. (sarkạ) *Kt. f.* = sarƙạ.

sarƙa A. (sarƙạ) (1) *Vb.* 1A. (*a*) interwove, interlaced *x* yā ~ itạ̄cē cikiŋ itạ̄cē he interlaced the sticks (= sarƙạfā *q.v.*). (*b*) yā ~ magana he told a contradictory story. (*c*) yā ~ magana cikin zạncēna he interposed in my conversation. (2) *Vb.* 3A *x* sun ~ (*a*) they are close friends (*cf.* sạrƙu). (*b*) they are bitter enemies. (3) *f.* (*pl.* sarkunạ = sarƙōƙī) (*a*) chain (= sạsarī 1). (*b*) = sạsariŋ kūrā. (*c*) ɗan ~ *m.* (*f.* 'yar ~) *pl.* 'yan ~ prisoner (for crime, whether Government or N.A.), *cf.* jạrum, ƙạmammē, bursunạ, ƙurkukụ. (*d*) kūrā tā fī dāgụmī sǎi ~ he's brazen.
  B. (sạrƙā) *Vb.* 2 frequented constantly P. or place.

sarƙafa A. (sarƙạfā) (*Kt.* sarkạfā) *Vb.* 1C (1) = sarƙạ 1*a q.v. x* an sarƙạfā igīyạ jịkiŋ kāyā string has been interlaced round the load. (2) hooked T. on to, round another T. *x* yā sarƙạfạ tạragụ jịkin dạŋūwansạ he coupled the railway-waggon on to another. (3) yā sarƙạfạ zūcīyā tasạ gạ sāmụnsạ he's eager to get it. (4) jạwō ƙōfạ, kạ ~ ta pull the

door to and chain it, fasten its hasp to its staple !
B. (sarƙafa) *Vb.* 2 = sarƙafā.
sarƙaƙē = *Kt.* sarƙafē (1) *Vb.* 1C = sarƙafā. (2) *Vb.* 3A (*a*) became tangled. (*b*) = ƙagę 1*b*.i. (*c*) became hooked on, caught on *x* rīgāta tā ⁓ ą ƙusą my gown caught on a nail.
sarƙaƙƙē *m.* (*f.* sąrƙaƙƙīyā) *pl.* sąrƙaƙƙū. (1) (*past participle from* sarƙę). (2) wayą sąrƙaƙƙīyā *f.* barbed wire.
sarƙaƙƙiya A. (sąrƙaƙƙīyā) *Vd.* sąrƙaƙƙē. B. (sarƙaƙƙīyā) *f.* (1) dense thicket (= ƙurmā = sąkō = ruƙuƙī = surƙuƙī), *cf.* duhūwą, sarƙę. (2) in zāki yā san ząi sąmi nāmą, yaną cikin ⁓, bā yą fitā wąje nobody undertakes trouble uselessly.
sąrkantaką *f.*, *used in* (1) (*a*) 'yan ⁓ the arrogant ways of princes. (*b*) yā yi halin 'yan ⁓ he behaved arrogantly. (2) yā yi halin 'yan ⁓ he behaved liberally (*cf.* ɗan sarkī).
Sarkāwā *Vd.* Bąsarkę.
sarkę (1) *m.* = bōtǫ 2*b*, *cf.* tsaikǫ. (2) *Kt.* = sarƙę.
sarƙę (1) *Vb.* 3A. (*a*) (country) is densely-wooded (*cf.* sarƙaƙƙīyā). (*b*) became interlaced, intertwined. (*c*) gōnā tā ⁓ dą hatsī farm is thick in corn. (*d*) (i) sun ⁓ dą faɗą = saɪƙą 2*b*. (ii) sun ⁓ dą kǫkawą they (wrestlers) have clinched. (*e*) = ƙwārę 1. (*f*) choked with rage. (*ff*) became incoherent through stuttering-fit. (*g*) haƙǫransą sun ⁓ he (dying man) cannot move his jaws. (2) *Vb.* 1A. (*a*) = sarƙafā. (*b*) = ƙwārę 2. (3) *m.* two intertwined kabą leaves.
Sarkī *m.* (*f.* Saraunīyā, *Vd.* 6 *below*) *pl.* Sarākuną = Sąrākai (*cf.* bąsarākę, Sąrākī). (1) (*a*) (i) Emir. (ii) *epithet is* Sukuku mąkąką = Dįrkąkau = Tōyą matsāfā = Wąndarą = tayi 4 = gwāzā 1*b* = gwantąl (*cf.* sąrautą 1*a*, ąlfandā). (iii) Audu bąi yi Sarkim Baucī ba Audu was not Emir of Bauchi. (iv) sun są shi Sarkī they made him their Chief. (v) Sarkinsu wannąm mąi cį the reigning Emir. (vi) yąnzu Audu ną Sarkī Audu is the present ruler. (vii) yā Sarākuną O Chiefs ! (viii) Sarkin Sąrautą = Allą Sarkī Almighty God ! (ix) Jallą Sarkī

mąi īyąwā glory to God the All-powerful ! (x) Allą shī nę ⁓ God's will be done ! (xi) *Vd.* wutā 1*v.* (*b*) idąn dą ya ga⁓, dǫmiŋ Galądīmą ɗązu nę from pathos to bathos. (*c*) dą dāmā, ⁓ ą kąn jąkī if the best is not available, one must take the second-best. (*d*) Sarkįn dą ya hąlicci Sarkim Mųsųlmī, shī ya hąlicci jāɓā all God's creatures are subject to his will, God is no respecter of persons . (*Vd.* Sarkim Mųsųlmī). (*e*) mąi kyąu ⁓ im bą mąi kudī kusa in the country of the blind, the one-eyed is king. (*f*) mųtųm ą gidansą⁓ nę a man is a lord in his own home. (*g*) hąsārąd dōki sǎi ⁓ big loss is trivial to the rich. (*h*) (i) 'yan ⁓ *Vd.* mū duką. (ii) zaman 'yan ⁓ = hardē 4. (iii) *Vd.* 7. (iv) 'yan ⁓ gōmą *Vd.* tūɓę 1*b.* (v) ɗan ⁓ ą kąn jąkī *Vd.* jąkī 1*f.* (*j*) *Vd.* kąn Sarkī. (*k*) gǫshin ⁓ *Vd.* gǫshī 5. (*l*) gandun ⁓ *Vd.* ƙōsą 2*b.* (*m*) mąsū aikįn ⁓ = en'ę. (*n*) yā sąuki ⁓ *Vd.* sąukā 1*b*.ii. (*o*) kā zągi ⁓ *Vd.* mūgų 1*c.* (*p*) hāli Sarkįn kąnsą nę circumstances alter cases. (*q*) bā ą mūgųn ⁓ sǎi mūgųm bąfādę the Chief is not evil but has evil counsellors. (*r*) sū " įnā ⁓ ya kwānā " nē they are slackers. (*s*) *Vd.* rūwā 1*a.* (*t*) dawākin ⁓ *Vd.* agaząrī. (*u*) nōman ⁓ *Vd.* yāƙi 1*a*.ii. (*v*) ąbōkin ⁓ *Vd.* ąlkālī. (2) (*a*) headman of town or village (*Vd.* dagaci), *cf.* sąrautą 1*b.* (*b*) *epithet is* wąŋ gąrī = wąn dawą. (*c*) head of guild. (3) *Vd.* San, *compounds of* Sarkin. (4) Sąrākaŋ ƙauyę *pl.* (*a*) ribs. (*b*) yā gąmu dą Sąrākaŋ ƙauyę he has pneumonia (4*a*, *b* = haƙarkarī 2). (5) ⁓ ukų the cloth mayāfī of the type consisting of 20 baƙī (*Vd.* baƙī B.6) plus 10 gwandā plus 10 sāki. (6) Saraunīyā *f.* (*a*) chieftainess. (*b*) head of female bǫrī-devotees. (*c*) evil spirit supposed to cause partial sexual impotence. (7) hannun (= yātsun) 'yan ⁓ *Vd.* hannun 10 (*cf.* 1*h above*). (8) kǫgin ⁓ *Vd.* wutā 1*v.*
Sarkim bąkā *m.* Head of the Hunters (*Vd.* baushę 4).
Sarkim bērą *Vd.* bērą.
Sarkin Būsą *Vd.* marǫƙī.

Sarkin darē = Sarkin sa̱urī.

Sarkin dawa̱ *Vd.* dawa̱ 11.

Sarkin dawākī *Vd.* Sarkin dōki̱.

Sarkin dōga̱rai *Vd.* Gamkai.

Sarkin dōki̱ *Vd.* dawākī 5, ma̱rōɗōɗo̱ 1*b*, ba̱rgā 3, Kōsa̱.

Sarkim fāda̱ *m.* (1) Emir's chief counsellor (*epithet is* Tu̱kura̱). (2) = fa̱ta̱rī.

Sarkim fāwa̱ *Vd.* fāwa̱ 1*c*.

Sarkiŋ gardi̱ *Vd.* gardi̱ 1*a*.ii.

Sarkiŋ ha̱ƙurī *Vd.* damō 4.

Sarkin jaujē *Vd.* marō̱ƙī.

Sarkiŋ ka̱la̱ŋgū *Vd.* marō̱ƙī.

Sarkiŋ Kano̱ *Vd.* Alla̱ 7*g*.

Sarkiŋ kā̱sūwā market-head (= *Kt.* kurmi̱ 3*c*).

Sarkiŋ kiɗa̱ *Vd.* marō̱ƙī.

Sarkiŋ kō̱tsō *Vd.* marō̱ƙī.

Sarkiŋ ƙwăi *m.* type of beetle with hard wing-case.

Sarkim maka̱dā *Vd.* marō̱ƙī.

Sarkim ma̱ka̱fī *Vd.* ma̱kāfo̱ 1*j*.

Sarkim mīta̱ *Vd.* mīta̱ 2.

Sarkim Mu̱su̱lmī *m.* (1) Head of the Nigerian Muslims, *i.e.* Emir of Sokoto. (2) *Vd.* Sarkī 1*d*.

Sarkin nōmā *Vd.* nōmā 1*b*.

Sarkim pāwa̱ *Vd.* fāwa̱ 1*c*.

Sarkin sa̱kayya̱ *Vd.* Alla̱ 2*b*.

Sarkin sa̱urī *Vd.* saura̱yī 2.

Sarkin sharri̱ *Vd.* ƙūlū 2.

Sarkin Sūda̱ŋ *m.* Emir of Kontagora (Kwa̱nta̱gō̱rā).

Sarkin turākū *Vd.* turākū.

Sarkiŋ wata̱ *Vd.* aŋgo̱.

Sarkiŋ wuƙā = Sarkin ya̱ŋkā 1.

Sarkin yāƙi̱ *m.* (*pl.* Sarākuna̱n yāƙi̱). (1) military General (= yāƙi̱ 1*f*). (2) *cf.* bardē 2, Kurāwa̱.

Sarkin 'yam mātā = Sarkin sa̱urī *q.v. under* saura̱yī 2.

Sarkin ya̱ŋkā *m.* (1) Emir with power of life and death (= wuƙā 2 = mu̱sam-ma̱ŋ 1*a*.i). (2) head executioner.

Sarkin Yāri̱ *Vd.* Yāri̱.

Sarkin yawa̱ *Vd.* yawa̱ 4.

sarƙō̱ƙī *Vd.* sarƙa̱ 3.

sa̱rƙu *Vb.* 3B *x* nā ∼ da̱ shī I'm intimate with him. mun dadɛ da̱ sa̱rƙūwā we have long been intimates (*cf.* sarƙa̱ 2*a*).

sa̱rkullē = su̱rkullē.

sarkuna̱ *Vd.* sa̱rkā.

sarƙuna̱ *Vd.* sarƙa̱ 3.

sarmada̱ŋ always, for ever.

sa̱rmāɗawa̱ *f.* (1) dice provided by head of gambling-party to prevent use of doctored cowries. (2) = gīlo̱ 1, 2.

sa̱rma̱nɗai *x* yā mīkɛ ∼ he stretched himself out at full length.

*sa̱rma̱ndaunā *f.* (1) slippery place. (2) (*a*) sinning. (*b*) apostasy.

sa̱rma̱ntaka̱ *Kt. f.* = sa̱ma̱rtaka̱.

sarma̱yī *Kt. m.* = saura̱yī.

saro A. (sa̱rō) *m.* (1) (*rolled* " r ", Mod. Gram. 5) (*a*) long, close-fitting, narrow-sleeved gown. (*b*) type of fa̱tala̱. (2) (*cerebral* " r ") some kinds of fish dried in sun, for use in soup.

B. (sa̱rō) *emphasizes* uncovered orifice *x* ƙōfa̱ ∼ cɛ (*pl.* ƙōfōfī sarō-sa̱rō̱ nē) it is a doorway without a door.

sa̱rō̱rō̱ *x* (1) muna̱ ganinsa̱ sa̱rō̱rō̱ we are biding our time to deal with it. (2) tā tsaya̱ sa̱rō̱rō̱ ya̱ ƙawar ƙauyɛ she stood agape like a gaby.

sarra̱fā *Ar. Vb.* 1C (1) ruled over. (2) li̱nzāmi̱ yana̱ sarra̱fa̱ dōki̱ the bit controls the horse well. (3) (*a*) yana̱ sarra̱fa̱ i̱yāli̱nsa̱ he rules his household firmly. (*b*) tana̱ sarra̱fa̱ miji̱nta̱ she henpecks her husband. (4) dōki̱ yana̱ sa̱rra̱fūwā the horse is tractable. (5) yā sarra̱fa̱ Hausā he has mastered Hausa. (6) yana̱ sarra̱fa̱ ku̱ɗinsa̱ he's turning over his money in trading.

sa̱r-sa̱r *x* (1) yana̱ hawa̱yē ∼ he's crying steadily. (2) jinī yana̱ ɓullō̱wā ∼ the blood is flowing steadily (= tsa̱r-tsa̱r). (3) idan rūwā yana̱ ɓullō̱wā ∼ the spring is steadily gushing forth (= tsa̱r-tsa̱r).

sartsɛ *m.* (*pl.* sarutsa̱) (1) (*a*) splinter. (*b*) *cf.* fi̱ da̱ ∼. (2) kada̱ a̱ yi mini̱ ∼ I hope no parasitic P. attaches himself to me ! (3) an yi masa̱ ∼ (*a*) = ƙāgē. (*b*) he has been somewhat cheated.

sa̱ru kutuf = sa̱ri kutuf.

sa̱rūru̱ *m.* (*f.* sa̱rūru̱wā) nincompoop.

sarutsa̱ *Vd.* sartsɛ.

sa̱sāgumī *m.* (*f.* sa̱sāgumā) huge (*re* living creatures).

sa̱sa̱ka̱i *adv. x* yā bar gidansa̱ (i̱yāli̱nsa̱) ∼ he left his home (family) uncared for (= wa̱wai).

sāsaṇtā *Vb.* 1C divided T. out in shares (*cf.* shāshị).

sāsarī *m.* (1) = sarḳạ 3*a*. (2) sāsariŋ kūrā type of creeping plant (= sarḳạ 3*b*). (3) sāsariŋ kyaŋwā rags (= tsummā).

sashe A. (sāshẹ) (1) *m.* (*pl.* sạssā). (*a*) = shāshị 1. (*b*) district *x* ạ sạssaŋ arệwā yakẹ it's in the northern part. (2) *Vb.* 1A = shāshẹ 1.

B. (sāshē) *Kt. m.* dried magaryā-leaves.

sāshị = shāshị.

sāsir = sāsum.

sạssā *Vd.* sāshẹ.

sạssạbānī *m.* = gạbạ̄rūwā 4.

sassạbcē = sassaụcē.

sassạbe A. (sassạbē) *Vb.* 1C cleared land for farming (= sạ̄rā 1*j*).

B. (sạssạbē) *m.* action *as in* sassạbē (= sāraŋ gōnā 1).

sassāfệ *used in* dạ ~ in the very early morning (*cf.* sāfệ).

sạssaiɓā *m., f.* (*pl.* saiɓạ̄ɓā). (1) unlucky (including not finding marriage-partner), *cf.* saiɓī. (2) slow worker or speaker.

*sạssạḳā *f.* jog-trot (of horse, P.).

sassaḳa A. (sassạḳā) *Vb.* 1C. (1) carpentered *x* (*a*) yā sassạḳạ kujệrā he (carpenter) made a chair, *cf.* masạssạḳī. (*b*) yā sassạḳạ turmī he hollowed out a mortar. (*c*) *Vd.* sạssạḳō. (2) *x* yā sassạḳạ itạcē he adzed bark off tree.

B. (sassạ̄ḳā) *Vb.* 1C (*intensive* of sāḳạ) *x* sun sassạ̄ḳā wạ jạma'ạ ḳaryā they lied to the public.

C. (sạssaḳa) *Vb.* 2 (1) (*a*) = sassạḳā. (*b*) dạ ~ yạ ḳārẹ *Vd.* cōḳalī 2. (2) (*a*) jeered at. (*b*) ~ tā fi sārā cīwọ carping at one is worse than being really punished.

sassaḳe A. (sassạḳē) *Vb.* 1C carpentered all (*cf.* sạssạḳā).

B. (sassaḳẹ) *m.* (*sg., pl.*) chip of wood.

sạssạḳō (*imperative*) (1) *Vd.* Gạikau. (2) sạssạḳō dẹbō = *Kt.* sạssạḳō ginō *m.* medicinal herbs, chips, etc.

*sassạlḳiyādī *m., f.* (*Ar.* salisu'l ḳiyādi) " yes "-man (= makịyạ̄yī 2).

sạssạrē *Vb.* 1C acted *as in* sassaryā.

sạssạrfā *f.* (1) making successive

stumbling-steps (P., horse, etc.), *cf.* tuntuɓẹ. (2) yā yi ~ he made a *faux pas.*

sassaryā *f.* the final weeding before harvesting, done with fartanyạ (*Vd.* nōmā, bạŋgạjē).

sạssātau *Vd.* ɓạrau.

sassaụcē *Vb.* 3A (1) it (T. tied) became loose. (2) P. became slack. (3) became emaciated. (4) became diminished. (5) became cheaper.

sassauci *m.* (1) slackness *as in* sassaụcē 1, 2. (2) cheapness.

sạssauḳā *m., f.* (*pl.* sauḳạ̄ḳā). (1) easy. (2) easygoing P. (3) cheap (*d.f.* sauḳī).

sassauta A. (sạssautạ) *Vb.* 3B = sassaụcē.

B. (sạssaụtā) *Vb.* 1C. (1) rendered (P., T. tied) slack. (2) diminished. (3) cheapened. (4) = saisạitā 2*b*.

sāsuḳạ *Vb.* 2 drove away (= ḳọrā).

sāsụḳē *Vb.* 1C = sāsuḳạ.

sāsum *x* yā cịka ~ it (bag) is chock-full. ḳafạ tasạ tā kụmburạ ~ his foot is very swollen.

sāsụmē *Vb.* 3A became swollen.

sāsur = sāsum.

sata A. (sạtā) *Vb.* 2 (*p.o.* sạcē, *n.o.* sạci). (1) stole (*cf.* sātạ). (2) sun sạci lōḳạcī sụ fạdi gạskịyā they secretly told the truth. (3) ạ rinạ, an sạci zanạm mahaukacịyā stolen property must ultimately be disgorged (*Vd.* rinạ).

B. (sātạ) *f.* (1) (*secondary v.n. to* sạtā) *x* yanạ sātạr kudī = yanạ sạtar kudī he is stealing money. (2) (*a*) theft. (*b*) sātạr fagē *Vd.* fagē 9. (*c*) *Vd.* kụyaŋgạ 1*b*. (*d*) sātạr 'yaŋ gijị (i) the bringing by women-guests of gọ̄rā of flour, etc., to bride, this then being shared out. (ii) bringing portion of farm-produce and sharing it out *as in* (i). (*e*) sātạr wađạrī *Vd.* kūrā 52. (*f*) bā yā hanạ sātạ *Vd.* sakẹ 1*d.* (*g*) an yi wạ mại damị ɗayā sātạ *Vd.* damị 7. (*h*) in dǎi ɓērā dạ ~ *Vd.* ɓērā 1*g*.

*sātạ'izạŋ (*d.f.* Ar. sā'ata *on model of* waqta'izin) at once.

satampạ *Eng. f.* distemper-paint.

sạtārạ = sạttārạ.

satā-sạtā = saɓā-sạɓā.

sātī *m.* (1) war-leader of infantry (dāḳạ̄rū *q.v.*). (2) (*Eng.* " Saturday ") (*a*)

weekly wages (*cf.* albashī, lādā). (*b*)
Saturday (*b* = Asabar = Subdu). (*c*)
(*with pl. sense, preceded by pl. adj.*) *x*
cikiŋ wadannaŋ sātī bīyū during these
two weeks. wadannaŋ sātī da suka
wuce these last few Saturdays.
satsara = sadara.
sattāra *f.* ornamented jalāla.
sattiŋ = sittiŋ.
sātū *Vd.* farī 2*a*.iv.
Satumba = Sitamba.
sātuna = sātuttuka *Vd.* sācē.
sau A. (sau) (1) *m.* (*genitive* san) (*pl.*
sāwāyē) (*a*) (i) foot, sole of foot, footprint (*cf.* kafa). (ii) ka bi sansa follow
him !, spoor it (animal) ! (*Vd.* wāwan
∼). (iii) *Vd.* bī bī san dōkī ; gudun
san dōkī. (iii*A*) *Vd.* batar da 3. (iv)
yā dauki sansa *Vd.* dauka 1*a*.x. (v)
sau yā daukē *Vd.* kafa 7*b*. (vi) sum
bī shi ∼ da hannū they obeyed him
implicitly. (vii) *Vd.* san-*compounds*,
farin sau (*q.v. under* farar kafa), zuba 5.
(viii) ciŋ sau *Vd.* alkāmura. (ix) bā
jan sau *Vd.* Girga. (*b*) (i) times *x*
sauna uku gidaŋka I've been to your
home three times (= kafa 9). (ii)
yā īya ∼ he can do multiplication (*cf.*
rabō 5). (iii) (*only used with ordinals*)
x ∼ na uku the third time, ∼ na
hudū the fourth time (*cf.* sau). (iv)
x uku da ∼ three times (= sau 1).
(*c*) a move in dara. *(d) Sk.* twenty-
cubit skein of thread or length of woven
fabric. (2) yā yi ∼ it got lost. (3)
verb invariable (*a*) = saka. (*b*) *Vd.* sau
ta ga wāwā ; kafī 6. (*c*) kōwā ya ∼
ka *Vd.* afalalu.
  B. (sau) times (*only used with car-
dinals, cf.* sau 1*b*) *x* (1) sau uku three
times (= sau 1*b*.iv. = *Sk.* ajī 4). (2) ∼
da yawa = ∼ tāre = sau da dāmā *adv.*
often. (3) sum fī mu yawa sau wajan
nawa they greatly outnumber us.
sum fī mu yawa ∼ shida they're six
times as many as we are. (4)
kōwā ya yi kiraŋkī ∼ dayā *Vd.* ta
alakō.
sauce = safce, sabce.
*saufa-saufa = *sōfa-sōfa.
sauga = sabga.
sauka A. (sauka) *Vb.* 3B (*Vd.* saukā 2*a*).

(1) (*a*) descended (from horse, tree,
train, etc.) *x* (i) yā ∼ a dōkī he got down
from the horse. yā ∼ daga itācē he
descended from tree. (ii) bā ki saukā
sāi da dalīlī *Vd.* mīkī 2*b*. (*b*) (i) arrived
x yā ∼ a Kano he arrived at Kano
(= shiga 1*j* = *Sk.* shīda). (ii) ka ∼
lāfīya may you arrive safely ! (*reply*,
Allā ya sā !). (iii) dārī yā sauka the
cold season has come. dāmunā tā ∼
the wet season has begun (= tāgūwa
3*b*). (iv) yaushe aka sauka how long
have you been waiting here ? (*c*)
rūwā yā ∼ = rūwā yā saukō rain fell.
(*d*) ta naŋ a kan ∼ *Vd.* inda 1*a*.iii.
(2) lodged *x* yā ∼ a gidāna he lodged
with me (*Sk.* shīda). (3) recovered
(from temper, hysteria, woman from
confinement, etc.). (4) diminished
x (*a*) (fever, pain of sting, etc.)
subsided (= fādī 5*c*). (*b*) (i) kāsūwā
tasa tā ∼ it is no longer in
demand. (ii) kāsūwā tā ∼ daga kansa
he is no longer lucky in trade. (*c*)
kudinsa sun ∼ it has gone down in
price. (5) (*a*) yā ∼ = saukā 1*d*.
(*b*) *Vd.* masallācī 2. (6) (*before dative*,
Gram. 114) yā saukam masa (*a*) he
arrived at it (*x* house, place) (*cf.* 1*b*.i
above). (*b*) he lodged with him (*cf.* 2
above). (*c*) he besieged it. (7) ∼ rēni
Vd. tsīgī 3*a*. (8) *Vd.* saukā, saukē,
saukad da.
  B. (saukā) (1) *Vb.* 2. (*a*) *x* nā saukē
shi I helped him (carrier) down with his
load (= saukę 1*b*), *cf.* saukad da 2. (*b*)
(i) nā saukē shi I lodged him (guest) =
saukad da 1 = *Sk.* shīdad da. (ii) yā
sauki sarkī he got syphilis. (*c*) brought
down (fruit, leaves) from tree *x* yā
sauki 'yā'yaŋ kūka (*cf.* saukę 5, saukar
dōrawa). (*d*) yā sauki Alkur'aŋ he has
completed reading of Koran (= sauka
5*a*, saukę 2). (2) *f., m.* (*a*) (*v.n. and progressive of* sauka) *x* yana saukā he is
descending. Sarākuna sun jē su ga
saukar Gwamna the chiefs went to
greet the Governor on his arrival (*Vd.*
sauka 1*b*). (*b*) act of descending *x* (i)
saukar yaushe = sauka 1*b*.iv. (ii)
bā hawā, bā saukā, sāi suka cę . . . then
they said straightway that . . . (iii)

bạ sụ saŋ hawā ba, bạ sụ san saụkā ba,
sǎi kawại sukạ gan sụ then unexpectedly
they saw them. (c) yā kāwō minị ~ he
(host) brought me (guest) customary
present of food on my arrival (=gaisūwā
6b). (d) act of completing reading of
Koran (1d above). (e) Vd. saụkar-
compounds, saụka, saukad dạ, saukẹ.
saukad dạ Vb. 4 (1) = saụkā 1b.i. (2) (a)
lifted T. down, brought T. down x
load from lorry, cf. saụkā 1a, shīɗad dạ.
(b) Allạ yạ saukō manạ dạ rụndunarsạ
ta rahamạ God send down on us his
mighty mercy ! (3) took (pupil) right
through Koran x ạ gūna ya yi kạrạtū
har nā saukasshē shị (= saukad dạ
shī) he studied with me right up to
completion of reading through the
whole Koran (cf. saụkā 1d). (4) Vd.
saụka, saụkā, saukẹ.
saukad ɗọrōwạ = saụkar ɗọrōwạ.
saukạkạ A. (saukạkā) Vb. 1C. (1) reduced
x (a) an saukạkạ kuɗinsạ its price has
been reduced. yā ~ musụ aikị he
reduced their work. (b) māganị yā ~
masạ cīwọ the medicine relieved his
pain (= ragẹ 1b). (2) an ~ masạ leniency
has been shown to him. (3) enabled to
do x duk ạbin dạ Allạ ya ~ manạ all the
success that God has endowed us with.
(4) Allạ yạ ~ (a) God forbid ! (b) God
lighten your trouble ! (Vd. sạnnū 1e).
 B. (saụkạkạ) Vb. 3B became
diminished.
saukạkẹ A. (saukạkē) Vb. 1C. (1) Allạ
yạ ~ = saukạkā 4. (2) reduced (as in
saukạkā 1–3) completely x yā ~
masạ kuɗiŋ he absolved him of
necessity of paying the money.
 B. (saụkạkẹ) x yanạ ɗaukan dūnīyạn
naŋ ạ saụkạkẹ he behaves simply and
unaffectedly.
saụkakkē m. (f. saụkakkīyā) pl. saụkakkū
(past participle from saụkā 1d) P. who
has read right through Koran.
saụkan Vd. saụkar.
saukar dạ = saukad dạ.
saụkar ɗọrawạ f. = saụkan ɗọrawạ m.
(1) gathering locust-bean pods (cf. saụkā
1c). (2) (a) talking wildly x kadạ kạ yi
minị ~ don't tell me a long, senseless
rigmarole ! (b) zạncan saụkaɗ ɗọrōwạ

= hutsubạ 3. (3) simultaneous chatter
of several people. (4) Kt. = saukẹ 3.
saukasshē Vd. saukad dạ.
saukẹ Vb. 1A (1) (a) (i) put down (one's
load). (ii) yā zamẹ manạ kūkạr " saụke
mụ rabạ ! " it is a bone of contention
between them and us. (iii) gyạrtạ
kāyaŋkạ, bạ yạ zamā " saụke mụ
rabạ " ba I've advised you for your
own good, so don't get cross ! (iv)
dūtsạn (kwariŋ) " saụke mụ rabạ ! "
a lonely hill (valley) exposed to danger
from bandits. (b) = saụkā 1a. (c)
took cooking-pot off the fire (cf.
girkạ) x saụke, mụ cī take the pot off
the fire and let us eat ! (2) = saụkā
1d. (3) yā saukẹ minị bāriki he (cadger)
is waiting inexorably at my house. (4)
x nā ~ = askẹ 2a. (5) x yā ~ kūkạ =
saụkā 1c. (6) saụke, hụce = saụke,
hụta m. (sg., pl.) thong securing stirrup-
strap to a ring on the saddle.
saukī m. (1) lightness. (2) (a) (i) easiness.
(ii) cikin saukī adv. easily. (b) dạ ~ (i)
easily. (ii) Vd. kạkạ 1c. (c) (i) yā sạmi ~
he has recovered. (ii) duk rigimạr sǎi ta
zō dạ saukī the commotion " ended in
smoke ". (d) yanạ dạ saukiŋ kại =
yanạ dạ saukin ɗabī'ạ he is tractable,
amenable. (3) cheapness x wannạŋ
yā fi saukiŋ kuɗī ainụŋ this one is far
the cheapest. (4) scarcity x kanạ dạ
kuɗị ? have you any money ? dạ ~
not much ! can mutạnē dạ ~ there
are not many people there. rūwā yā
yi ~ water is scarce. (5) nā yi makạ ~
I forgive you. (6) Kt. agility x dōkiŋ
naŋ yanạ dạ ~ this is an energetic horse
(= zāfin nāmạ).
saunạ Kt. = samnạ.
saurā A. (saurā) (1) m. (a) (i) remainder
(= rạgōwạ 1 = Sk. kiŋgī). (ii) waɗạn-
naŋ saurā these remaining persons.
(iii) mum mai dạ sū saurā kạmar
gōmạ we've reduced them to about
10. (iv) shaidạr kōshī ~ only the rich
can save. (b) sauran tūwō Vd. tūwō 4.
(c) sǎi rūwā yā yi ~ a kạm bạ dōki
the poor get nothing till the rich have a
surplus. (d) (in genitive) x (i) tun
sauran shẹkarạ ɗarī ạ haifi Ạnnabị,
Yahūdāwā kẹ dạ Birniŋ Kudụs the

Jews owned Jerusalem from 100 years before the birth of the Prophet (*Vd.* tun 3*a*.iv, v). (ii) bạ mu dạ sauraŋ kō dạ kōmī we have nothing at all left. bạ shi dạ sauran sāmuŋ kō dạ wuƙā he can no longer obtain even a knife (*Vd.* kō 5). (iii) cikin sauraŋ watạ shidạ during the remaining six months. (iv) 'yan sauram mutạnē the few remaining people. (v) bạ sauram mụtụm gụdā wạndạ zā ạ īyạ kāmạ̄wā nobody still remains to be caught. (vi) sunạ̄ dạ sauran shạn rūwā they have got a respite. (vii) Allạ̄ yā sạ̄ yanạ̄ dạ sauran cịm burōdị God spared his life. (viii) in sun yī, bạ̄ mu dạ sauran zamā if they do so, we cannot ignore it. (*dd*) (*genitive followed by subjunctive*) *x* bạ̄ sauraŋ ạ bar sụ dạ 'yancịnsụ there is no chance of their being left free men. bạ̄ sauram mụ dạ̄mu there is no longer any question of our losing our wits. Allạ̄ yā nụfē shị dạ sauran yạ yi yāƙị God has granted him a further span of life to wage war (*cf.* 2*b below*). (*e*) (*in genitive followed by singular noun with plural sense*) (i) other, the other *x* sauran jạma'ạr Tūrai (the) other races of Europe. sauraŋ al'ummạ the other nations. yā yi masạ sauraŋ hidimạ kumā he also performed other services for him. (ii) (*plural sense but noun used in singular*) some (= wadʼansu) *x* ạkwai sauran sōjạ ạ Masạr there are some soldiers in Egypt. (iii) (*negatively*) not any (*singular sense*) *x* bạ̄ sauraŋ wani mại shakkạ there are no longer any sceptics. bạ̄ sauraŋ wani lallāshī the time for appeasement has gone by. bạ̄ sauraŋ ịndạ yakē bụkātạ he has no further desire for territory. (*f*) bạ nạ̄ īyạ sauraŋ wutā ba, ṇ ji kīshīyar ƙọnannīyā (*said by one kīshīyā as habaicī to another*) *some* people are outsiders, you for instance ! (*g*) sauran rinā *Vd.* rinā 2. (2) *Vb.* 3B. (*a*) (i) (has) remained over. (ii) = haurạ 1*b*.ii. (*b*) (*followed by subjunctive*) *x* ~ ƙamar shēkarạ ạrbạ'iṇ kē naŋ yạ mutụ it happened about 40 years before his death (*cf. d below, 1dd above.* (*c*) *x* bạ ạ ragẹ darajạr tsọ̄fạffịŋ kudī ba, ~

yā ƙamātạ mạsū sū, sụ yi canjịnsụ the old coinage has not depreciated in value, but one simply exchanges it for the new. (*d*) saurā ƙaɗaŋ (*followed by subjunctive*) almost *x* saurā ƙaɗaŋ yạ yi ị gīwā girmā it is nearly as big as an elephant. saurā ƙaɗaŋ yạ zō he will soon come. saurā ƙaɗaŋ yạ mutụ he nearly died. (*e*) saurā, ạbịn dạ ya saurā musụ, shī nē sụ ci gạba all they now have to do is to advance.

B. (saụrā) *f.* (*pl.* saurukạ = *Sk.* sakurạ). (1) disused farm. (2) (*a*) tā yi ~ she cannot find a husband. (*b*) *Kt.* yā yi ~ he cannot find a wife. (3) *Vd.* cịkạ ~.

*saụrantạ *Vb.* 3B = saurā 2*a, b*.

saurara A. (saurạ̄rā) (1) listened attentively, waited quietly *x* kụ ~, kụ ji ạbịn dạ nakē fạdā listen till you have heard what I have to say ! (2) *x* sẵi mụ ~ ƙaɗaŋ let's rest a while ! (3) *x* sẵi kụ ~ masạ take no notice of him ! (*cf.* saụrārē 2*b*).

B. (saụrārạ) *Vb.* 2 listened attentively to, waited quietly for *x* bạ kạ saụrāri mạganạtạ ba you paid no attention to what I was saying (*cf.* saụrārē 2*b*). sunạ̄ saụrāram muryạ gụdā they all obey one master.

saụrārē = saụrārō = saurārō *m.* (1) (*secondary v.n. to* saụrārạ) *x* n nạ̄ saụrārran zūwạnsạ = n nạ̄ saụrārạr zūwạnsạ I'm waiting for him to come. (2) (*a*) act of listening attentively, etc., *x* n nạ̄ yịm mạganạ dạ shī, yanạ̄ ~ I was speaking to him and he was listening attentively (*cf.* saụrārā 2). (*b*) n nạ̄ mạganạ dạ shī ạmmā yanạ̄ ~ I was talking to him but his attention was devoted to listening to someone else (*cf.* saụrārā 3). (*c*) sunạ̄ saụrāram muryạ gụdā they all obey one master.

saụrayī *m.* (*pl.* sạmạ̄rī = saụrī). (1) (*a*) (i) young man (*f. is* bụdurwā). (ii) ūwar ~ *Vd.* gwalaŋgwasō. (*b*) Audụ saụrayintạ nē Audu is her masturbation partner in tsạ̄rạncē (*Vd.* bụdurwā 3 ; dạƙū ; gāgọ 2*b*). (*c*) *Vd.* sạmạ̄rī. (*d*) *Vd.* aŋgọ 1*b*. (2) Sarkin saụrī head of the young girls for arranging work, play, and assignations = Sarkin darē = Sarkin saurī = Kt. hūtsū 2 (cf. Takāta). (3) saurī wōho (said by girls during kalaŋkūwā 1b) on you lads with your gayyā !

sauri A. (saurī) Vd. saurayī.
   B. (saurī) m. (1) (a) quickness. (b) da ~ quickly. (c) aiki yārọ indạ ya sō, kā ga saurinsạ the willing horse is the best worker. (d) bā yā karɓar saurī sǎi lūrā it requires careful consideration, not hasty action. (e) saurim bākī sukạ yi they spoke prematurely. (f) mai sauriŋ hawā Vd. dambū. (2) (a) yā yi ~ (i) he hastened. (ii) he has come early. (b) im bạ kạ yi ~ ba if you don't look sharp, then . . . (c) kạ yi ~ hurry up ! (3) (followed by subjunctive) is in hurry to x yanā ~ yạ rigā sụ he's in a hurry to get ahead of them. sunā saurī sụ sullụɓē they're in a hurry to escape. (4) saŋ girmā garēshi it (animal, P.) has grown up quickly (san = saurin).

saurō m. (sg., pl.) (1) mosquito. (2) ~ mai rāmar gayyạ = jījīyā 3. (3) gidan ~ m. mosquito-net. (4) Vd. sạrakūwar saurō.

sauruka Vd. saurā.

sausaucē = sassaucē.

sau ta gạ wāwā f. girl whose first marriage came to speedy end.

sautarērẹ = sautaretarẹ m. asking P. to buy T. and promising to refund cost when he brings it (= sautụ 3), cf. sautụ 1.

*sauti Ar. m. (1) voice. (2) any sound.

sautụ m. (1) commissioning P. going somewhere, to buy one something, cost being prepaid to him x nā yi masạ ~ (= nā bā shi ~) yạ sayō mini tābạ I asked him to buy and bring me back tobacco when he returned from his journey. (2) Vd. sạllahụ, sāƙō, aikē, kārērẹ 3. (3) sautụm bakạ = sautarērẹ. (4) kā fi sautụ Vd. gaidā 3. (4) Vd. mahaukacīyā 1a.iii. (5) sautụm madị Vd. galamadị. (6) gishirin ~ Vd. gūgạ 6.

sauya A. (sauyā) Sk. = saiwā.
   B. (sauyạ) (1) Vb. 1A. (a) exchanged x nā ~ dōkị dạ dōkị I exchanged one

horse for another. nā ~ jākī, nā karɓi dōkị I gave a donkey and got a horse in exchange (cf. sākẹ 1f). (b) nā ~ su I changed the position of the things. (c) yā ~ rīgā he changed his gown, putting on another (= sākẹ 1e). (d) yā ~ al'ādạ he has changed his ways (= sākẹ 1a). (e) yā ~ kudī he turned over his money in trading (= jūyạ 1c). (f) x yā ~ mini sulẹ ukụ he lent me three shillings (= jūyạ 1e). (g) yā ~ bākī he changed over from one language to another. (h) yā ~ maganạ he contradicted himself (= Kt. kifẹ 1d = sākẹ 1a). (j) (i) yā ~ kamā his appearance is altered (= sākẹ 1a). (ii) duk wannaŋ gajīyạ, bạ sụ sauyạ fuskạ ba in spite of all their fatigue, they did not give up. (k) yā ~ shāwarạ he changed his opinion (= sākẹ 1b). (l) sun sauyạ rawā they've changed their policy. (m) yā sauyạ fǎifǎi he changed his tone. (n) akạ sauyạ wāƙar yāƙi they changed their song to a war-song. (o) Vd. sākẹ. (2) Vb. 3A became changed (= sākẹ 2).

sauyẹ Vb. 1A = jūyẹ 1c.i.

sauyi m. (1) changing x shēkarạ ta gōmạ dạ yiŋ wannaŋ sāban sauyi the 10th year since this change was made. (2) exchanging x yā yi sauyim mōtạ tasạ dạ wata he has exchanged his car for another. (3) an yi sāban ~ new system has come into vogue (= salō). *(4) homonym.

sạwābạ f. (1) (a) easiness. (b) cheapness (a, b = sauƙī). (2) (Ar. sāba hit the target). (a) yā yi ~ he said (did) the correct thing. (b) yā fadi maganạr ạ kan ~ he gave a true account of what happened. *(3) (Ar. thawāba) religious merit.

sạwai = shēkẹkẹ.

sawai-sawai x ƙwaryā cē ~ it is a fine, delicate calabash (also applied to bowls, pots, etc.).

*sawānā Ar. Vb. 1C = 'yantā.

sawarwarī m. (1) carelessness. (2) misfortune.

sāwāyē Vd. sau.

sawo A. (sāwō) Vb. 1E put and brought (from sā).

B. (sawō) *Vb.* 1E bought and brought = sayō *q.v. under* sąyā.

sawu A..(sąwu) *Vb.* 3B. (1) is saleable (*cf.* sąyā 1*c*). (2) *Vd.* kūrā 38.

B. (sāwu) = sau 1.

*sąwwā (*Ar.* equal) (1) *adv.* (a) x mun rąbu ∼ we parted neither owing the other anything. (b) yā zō ∼ he came at just the right moment. (2) *f.* equality x dą shī dą Audu ∼ sukę he and Audu are on a par.

sawwąkā = saukąkā.

saya A. (sąyā) *Vb.* 2 (*for progressive, Vd.* sąyē). (1) (a) (i) bought x yā sąyē shi he bought it (= sai). yā sąyi dōki he bought a horse (= sai). (ii) *cf.* fąnsā 3. (b) sayō = sawō bought and brought. (c) sąyu *Vb.* 3B is buyable (*cf.* sąwu). (d) nā ∼ sulę = nā ∼ ą sulę = nā ∼ ą kąn sulę I bought it for a shilling. (e) nā sąyā gąrēsu I bought it (i) from them, (ii) for them (*cf.* gą 6*b*). (f) nawą ka sąyā *Vd.* bāwą 12. (g) an sąyi kąrē *Vd.* tsugunō. (h) sąyi tsintsīyā *Vd.* katakas. (2) dam bą ką ∼ ba *Kt. m.* a fragrant gum obtained from dąshī. (3) yąddą aką sayō, haką aką sayar (a) stolen goods have now been stolen from me ! (b) tit for tat. (4) *Vd.* inūwą 12.

B. (saya) *Vb.* 1A (*with dative*) x yā ∼ mini shī he bought it for me (= sai).

C. (sāya) *Vb.* 1A. (1) yā ∼ ƙōfą he put the door ajar, shut it but did not lock it (= sāyę). (2) = sāyę 1*b, c, d.* (3) = kārą 1, 2.

sąyākī = siyākī.

sąyā ląyā *f.* = sąiwā 5.

sąyan *Vd.* sąyē.

sāyąncē *Vb.* 3A *Kt.* (limb) withered = sāyę 2, *cf.* sąyī.

sąyąntą *Vb.* 3B *Kt.* = sāyąncē.

sayar dą *Vb.* 4 (1) (a) sold x nā ∼ shī = nā saishē shi I sold it. yanā sayąrwā he is selling it. (b) sun ∼ gōnā gąrēshi = sun sayar masą dą gōnā they sold the farm to him (sun sayar masą dą gōnā *also means* they sold the farm for him). (c) yā ∼ rąnsą he showed great bravery. sai dą rąŋ yā yi yawą the risk to life is considerable. fādą ą Masąr sai dą

rąi nē ą fīlī Egypt can only be attacked at great risk to life. (d) an sayar yąddą aką sayō = sąyā 3. (2) ą sai dą ƙūru ą yi wą iŋgarmą kāyā one P. has been deprived of his share to give it to a favourite. (3) fuską mąi sai dą rįgā *Vd.* fuską 5*b.* (4) in don ą cī, bą ą sayar ba, kązā tā fi dōki value of T. depends on what it is to be used for. (5) sai dą bābā *Vd.* rugā 1*c.* (6) *Vd.* są̄i mā ƙunshē. (7) ∼ biri *Vd.* tsugunō 1*a.*ii.

sayarwā *f.* (1) *Vd.* sayar dą 1*a.* (2) sale x kąran nąŋ na ∼ nę this dog is for sale. ąkwīyąr bą̄ ta ∼ ba cę̄ the goat is not for sale.

sayas dą = sayar dą.

sayau *m.* (1) lightness x wannąŋ rįgā cę̄ ∼ dą ita this is a gown of light weight. (2) nā ji ∼ I " breathed more freely ".

sayau-sayau = sawai-sawai.

sayąyā *Vb.* 1C = sanyąyā.

sayāyę = sīyāyę.

sąyayyą *f.* x zą̄ ni kąsūwā ŋ yi ∼ I'm going to market to make some purchases.

sai dą = sayar dą.

saye A. (sąyē) *m.* (1) (*v.n. and progressive of* sąyā) x yanā sąyansą he is buying it. yanā sąyan dōki he is buying a horse. (2) *Vd.* bąkī 2*y*, furā 5. (3) sąyaŋ ąbu nagąrī mai dą kudī gidā nę̄ buying reliable T. is like bringing one's money home again.

B. (sayę) *Vb.* 1A bought all of.

C. (sāyę) (1) *Vb.* 1A. (a) = sāyą 1, 3, makę 2*b.* (b) yā ∼ kansą (i) he covered his head with his gown-sleeve. (ii) he hid himself (= sāyą). (c) ką ∼ fįtiląn nąŋ shade the light of this lamp ! (= sāyą). (d) fenced in (*cf.* masai) = sāyą. (2) *Vb.* 3A = sāyąncē. (3) *Sk. m.* (*pl.* sāyū = sąyyū) = sąiwā.

D. (sāye) (1) (*noun of state from* sāyę 1) x ąllansą yanā ∼ his slate is tucked under his arm (sāyę 1*a*). (2) (*noun of state from* są̄) x (a) rįgā tasą tanā ∼ his gown has been put on. (b) yanā ∼ dą rįgā he is wearing a gown (Mod. Gram. 80*d.*ii).

sayi A. (sāyi) *m.* (1) an yi wą wuriŋ ∼

the place has been fenced in. (2) fenced-in place. (3) (a) A. carried tucked under one's arm (cf. sāyę 1a). (b) A. carried on hand or head and covered with a cloth (b = yānį).
B. (sąyī) Kt. m. withering of a limb (cf. sāyąncē).
ąyintą Vb. 3B Kt. = sāyąncē.
ayo A. (sayō) Vd. sąyā 1b.
B. (sāyō) -ō form from sāyą, sāyę.
ayu A. (sāyū) Vd. sāyę 3.
B. (sąyu) Vd. sąyā 1c.
ʂayyądī Ar. m. (1) (f. Sayyądā) used by beggars in įnā wani Sayyądī kō wata Sayyądā where is any charitable Muslim? (in Ar., Sayyid = descendant of the Prophet). (2) name for any man called Mųhammadų. (3) My lord! (addressing superior). (4) (preceding man's name, is honorific) x ~ Ąbū Bakąr noble Mr. Abu Bakar! (5) cf. Sīdį, Sayyų, Shąrif.
ayyu A. (sąyyū) Vd. sāyę 3.
B. (Sayyų) honorific form of address to Shąrif (cf. Sayyądī, Shąrif).
ei Vd. sǎi.
ēmā f. (pl. sēmōmī). (1) receptacle made of laced corn-stalks (karā) and shaped like amyą, for transporting kūką-leaves, tobacco-leaves, tamarind-fruit (tsāmīyā), bean-pods, etc. (cf. ącąkwą). (2) mųtųm ƙudā nę, bā yą bin sēmar gawąyī nobody acts without a motive. (3) Vd. sainą.
ēsē used in kwądan ~ = dątąnnīyā 4.
ēmō Vd. saimō.
ēnį Vd. Alą 11.
ha I (shā) Vb. 5 (for progressive Vd. sha III).
A. drank (1) yā ~ rūwā he drank water. yā ~ tābą (a) he smoked. (b) he chewed powdered tobacco (gārin tābą), Vd. tābą 1–3. (c) yārọ, ~ rūwā dǎidǎi dą cikįnką don't attempt what is beyond you! (Vd. k below). (d) įdam bą ką ~ gudan dawọ ba, kadą ką ~ gudan rānā don't tempt the heat on an empty stomach! (e) (i) ate certain fruits x lęmū, gwandą (we can use either shā or cī 1c q.v. for dinyā, tābọ q.v., mangwąrọ, ayąbą). (ii) Vd. gwandą 3. (iii) shā zumą Vd.

cī 13b, zumą 1c, d. (iv) cf. furā 1b. (v) ~ ƙwǎi Vd. ƙwǎi 1f. (f) (i) nā tąfi shąŋ iską I went for a stroll. (ii) yā ~ iską he went for a stroll; he went to the country for a change of air; it (hot food) cooled a bit; it (wet, washed garment) dried a bit; he (P. or horse, etc.) feels in good form after a pleasantly long rest. (g) (i) yā ~ mīyą he (rich P.) is getting old. (ii) bą ni ŋ ~ mīyą lend me it, them! (clothes, horse, adornment, etc.). (iii) kądam bą ką tārą cin tūwō dą mųtum ba, bą ką san shąm mīyą tasą ba Vd. mīyą 5, 11 ; shā mīyą 2. (iv) kōwā ya ci tūwō dą shī, mīyą ya ~ he's a tough customer. (v) Vd. shā mīyą, (vi) ą ~ mąntą Vd. wąyō 1d. (h) Vd. mashā 4. (j) ~ wutar is accustomed to x yā ~ wutar fādą (makarantā) he has long been at court (school). (k) shā rūwā Vd. rūwā A.2. (l) tąfīyą tā shā karā the journey has been abandoned (= rūwā A.2c). (m) (i) shā ąrādų Vd. ąrādų 2, 5. (ii) ~ rantsūwā Vd. rant-sūwā. (n) yā ~ mazā cikį (= yā shā mazā ą cikį) he's a redoubtable P. (o) yā ~ lągbārį he has heard some news. mun ~ lągbārį mąi dādī we've heard good news (cf. shąnyē). (p) yā ~, tā fi cikįnsą " he bit off more than he could chew ". (q) (i) rūwā yā ~ kąnsą the water came over his head (Vd. īyā 1b). (ii) Vd. kǎi 1A. (r) takąrdan nąŋ laifintą shā this paper causes the ink to spread, lets the ink through, Vd. shā III 2c. (s) (i) kadą ką bar ƙasā tą ~ jininsą don't slay him! (ii) sun ~ jinin jikinsu they became afraid. (iii) Vd. jinī 7. (t) ƙąƙą bąn ~ nōnąŋ ūwāta Vd. dībą 1j. (u) cf. E.5 below; ą shā lāfīyą. (v) tā ~ cįttā Vd. cįttā 3. (x) Vd. dākālę 3. (y) dą nā ~ = dąrmąsōsūwā. (z) Vd. shā-compounds, shąn-compounds. (z) (i) kōwā ya ~ dayā Vd. gāgọ 4b.

B. underwent (often interchangeable with cī 15, cf. shąnyē 1c, d). (1) (a) yā ~ kaifī (i) he has had to pay a high price, been overcharged (= 3b *below*). (ii) he has had a bad time. (iii) he has been slashed. (*b*) **muṇ shaṇ kaifinsu** we're suffering at their hands. (2) (*a*) **yā ~ ḍạriyā** he split his sides with laughter (= **fashẹ** 1*b*. (*b*) **yā ~ ḍācī** he laughed jeeringly (*Vd*. **ḍācī** 2). (3) **yā ~ kyaurō** (*a*) he was wounded with an arrow. (*b*) he has been overcharged (= 1*a*.i *above*). (*c*) he has venereal disease. (4) (*a*) **yā ~ wạhalạ** he has suffered trouble. (*b*) **yā ~ wụyā** *Vd*. **wụyā** 2. (5) **yā ~ rānā** (*a*) he travelled through the heat of the day. (*b*) it (garment) was dried, aired in the sun. (6) **nā ~ zamā** I've waited a long time. (7) **yā ~ tạfiyạ** (= **yā ci tạfiyạ**) he has travelled far (*cf*. **cī** 15). (8) **yā ~ gạrī** (*a*) he has lived long in the town. (*b*) he has had a hard time. (9) (*a*) **yā ~ kāshī** (i) he was drenched by rain (*Vd*. **rūwā** A.2*a*.iii). (ii) he was beaten. (iii) he was given a bad time. (iv) he had a trading-loss. (*b*) *cf*. D.2*b*.ii *below*. (10) (*a*) **yā ~ itạcē** he was beaten with a stick. (*b*) **yā ~ jibgā** = **yā ~ dūkạ** he was beaten (= **cī** 15). (11) (*a*) **yā ~ kāyā** (i) he carried a heavy load. (ii) he received many gifts. (*b*) **dōki yā ~ kāyā** the horse is gaily caparisoned. (12) **yā ~ ḍaurị** he was imprisoned. (13) **tufạ tā ~ jikī** the clothing is worn out. (14) **~ inūwạ** *Vd*. **māshị** 1*b* ; **inūwạ** 9, 10. (15) **yā ~ dādī** = **yā ji dādī** he felt happy. (16) (*a*) **bạ irim faḍạn dạ bạ su ~ ba** there is no type of combat which they have not taken part in. (*b*) **yā ~ yāḳị** he waged war. (17) **yā ~ bambaṇ dạ shī** it differs from it. (18) **yā ~ ḍārī** *Vd*. **ḍārī** 1*a*.i, **ḍārī** 4. (19) **~ wạṇkị** *Vd*. **suluf**. (20) **zạn jūyạ gạrēsu ṇ sạmē su, kwạ ~, kwạ ~, kwạ ~** I'll turn my attention to them and capture them and what a bombardment I'll subject them to ! (21) **yā ~ dūnīyạ** *Vd*. **dūnīyạ** 1*j*. (22) **~ hannū** *Vd*. **hannū** 1*c*.

C. has often *x* **nā ~ jị** I have often heard. **yā ~ zūwạ** he has often come. **nasarạd dạ sukạ shā cị** the victory which

they had so often won. **mun shā gạ mukụ** we have often told you that .

D. (sense of cutting) (1) (*a*) circu: cised (*cf*. **shạsshāwạ, kạcīyạ,** III 3 *belou* (*b*) **an ~ mụ, muṇ warkẹ** we're fr from anxiety on that score. (*c*) **sha mại gidā** *Vd*. **budịrī**. (2) (*a*) (i) **shātạ** 1*a*. (ii) *Vd*. **shạ** 4. (*b*) (i) **yā ḳaryā** he told a lie (= **ḳaryā** **shātạ** 1*b*). (ii) **ḳaryarkạ tā ~ ḳaryā ḳaryarkạ tā ~ kāshi** be sure your crin (or lie) will recoil on you ! (*cf*. B *above*). (*c*) *Vd*. **dāgā**.

E. various (1) **nā ~ dạ nī akẹ** guessed it was *I* who was being referre to. (2) (*a*) **yā ~ azụmī** he was forc to break the Fast through illnes essential journey, etc. (it must be ma up for (**rāmạ** 2*a*.iii) later, but expiation (**kạfārạ**) is exacted), **karyạ** 1*d*. (*b*) **yā yi ạshịriṇ, yā ~ gōn** he fasted for twenty days, but was th compelled to abstain from the Fast the final ten days (*as in* 2*a*). (3) **~ gạbansu** *Vd*. **kạị** 1*A*. (4) *Kt*. **kurụmiṇkạ** shut up ! (5) **dam n suka hau masạ dạ bại ci musụ b bại shā musụ bạ** why did they atta him who had never harmed them (6) *cf*. **ạ ~ dạ manạnī**. (7) **~ bamba** *Vd*. **bambaṇ**. (7) **~ ḟanyā** *Vd*. **ḟanyā**

II. (**shā**) (*intransitive, only used this form*). (1) became dry *x* **bạ itạcan naṇ yạ ~** leave this wood dry ! (2) *Vd*. **rūwā** K.2*b*. (3) **ạ zāg farī, yạ ~** unroll the white wove strip and ease its tension !

III. (**shạ**) *m*. (1) (*v.n. and progressi: of* **shā** I) *x* (*a*) **yaṇạ ~** he is drinkin (it). **yaṇạ shạnsạ** he is drinking yaṇạ **shạn rūwā** he is drinking wate (*b*) **shạn gīyạ bạ na bāwạṇ gandū nẹ** its beyond his status (*cf*. **gand** 2*d*). (*c*) **shạn rūwā yā fi barịnsạ tsirit mā shạ nẹ** half a loaf is better tha no bread. (2) act of drinking *x* (*a*) **rūwā don sha̱n yan sarƙa̱** water for the prisoners to drink. (*b*) **gidan ~** *m.* European or African clubhouse. (*c*) **taka̱rdan na̱ŋ tanā̱ da̱ ~ = shā** A.1*r*. **tū̱lun na̱ŋ yanā̱ ~** water percolates through this new pot. (*d*) **yā yi ~** he's been boozing. (*e*) **a̱bin shā̱** *m.* beverage (*cf.* **a̱bincī**). (3) *Kt.* **an yi masa̱ ~** he has been circumcized (*cf.* D. *above*). (4) (*a*) *Vd.* **shā** D.2 *above*. (*b*) (i) **sha̱ŋ wanna̱ŋ ɗāki̱ tāki̱ a̱shiriŋ** this round hut is twenty paces across. (ii) **ma̱i ka̱man sha̱n ɗāki̱** *adj.* round. (iii) **ma̱i ka̱man sha̱n sōrō** *adj.* square, rectangular (*all* (*b*) = **shāci̱ 1***c*). (5) *Vd.* **shā-***compounds*, **sha̱n-***compounds*.

shā'a̱ *Vd.* **mā shā'a̱ ; A̱llāhu̱ 2.**

sha̱a̱a̱ *x* **sun sakam musu̱ ha̱rsāshi̱ sha̱a̱a̱** they fired volleys of cartridges at them. **sunā̱ saki̱m ma̱i rūwā sha̱a̱a̱** they're firing volleys from the machine-guns (= **shu̱u̱u̱**).

Sha̱'a̱ba̱ŋ *Ar. m.* (1) (*a*) name of one of the Muslim months. (*b*) *Vd.* **salla̱ 1***e*, *f.* (2) name for boy born during **1**.

sha̱'afa̱ *used in* **nā ~ da̱ shī** it has slipped my mind.

shā̱ a̱lwāshī *m., f.* (*sg., pl.*) braggart.

sha'a̱nī *m.* (*pl.* **sha'anōnī = sha'anunnūwa̱ = sha'anunnuka̱**). (1) affair (= **shaga̱lī**). (2) **bā̱ ~** (*a*) there's no news ! (*b*) that's bad news ! (= **lā̱bāri̱ 2***a*). (3) business *x* **sha'a̱niŋ aurē** wedding-festivities or preparations. **nā yi ~ da̱ sū** I had dealings with them. **sunā̱ ~ da̱ abūbūwa̱ ka̱mar su ci̱ttā** they deal in articles like pepper, etc. **bā mā̱ sha'a̱niŋ kōmē da̱ shī** we have no transactions with him (= **shaga̱lī**). (4) **n nā̱ da̱ ~ da̱ yawa̱ tu̱ku̱nā** I'm busy at present (= **shaga̱lī**). (5) **yanā̱ ~ ya̱u** he's giving lavish presents to-day (*cf.* **shaga̱lī 2**). (6) **am bar su̱, su̱ yi ta sha'a̱niŋ ga̱bansu̱** they've been left to manage their own affairs.

sha̱'awa̱ *f.* (*pl.* **sha̱'a̱wa̱ce-sha̱'a̱wa̱cē**). (1) acquisitiveness *x* **yā cika̱ ~ = kōmē ya ganī, yanā̱ ~ tasa̱** he covets everything he sees. (2) (*a*) **nā yi sha̱'awa̱r Audu̱ = n nā̱ sha̱'awa̱r Audu̱** I like Audu. (*b*) **bā kā̱ sha̱'awa̱r hanya̱r kōwā, kada̱ kōwā ya̱ yi sha̱'awa̱r tāki̱** *epithet of* train (**jirgī 1***b*.i *q.v.*). (*c*) **ma̱i haƙōrī kē̱ sha̱'awa̱r fu̱rē, ma̱i dāsōrī sāi ya̱ dūba̱ da̱ ido̱** tastes differ.

sha̱'ayyē *Kt. m.* = **shūnī.**

shāba̱ *f.* = **zurārē 1.**

shaɓa = shabta.

Shā̱ ba̱ƙō̱sanī *Vd.* **Ga̱lā̱dīma̱ 1.**

Sha̱ba̱ŋ = Sha̱'a̱ba̱ŋ.

Shā̱ bā̱rā *epithet* (1) *of* **gwaŋkī ; dari̱ 3,** (2) (*at Kt.*) of **ɓaunā.**

***shabba̱** (*Ar.* **sabiyya**) *f.* fine girl (*cf.* **shabba̱ŋ**).

sha̱bba̱l Ya̱ma̱ŋ *Ar. m.* sulphate of iron (*used as medicine for teeth and eyes*).

***shabba̱ŋ** (*Ar.* **sabiyy, sabiyya**) (1) **yāro̱ nē ~** he's a fine lad. **yārinya̱ cē ~** she's a fine girl (*cf.* **shabba̱**). (2) **~ wa ~** a fine couple (lad and girl spouses).

shabce A. (**shabce̱**) *Vb.* 1A. (1) **yā ~ shi da̱ wuƙā** he cut him with a knife (= **sha̱btā**). (2) cut off large portion of.

B. (**sha̱bcē**) *Vd.* **sha̱btā.**

shabcēce̱ *m.* (*f.* **shabcēci̱yā**) *pl.* **shabtā-shabtā̱** huge.

sha̱bci *Vd.* **sha̱btā.**

shāɓe̱ = shabce̱.

shāɓi̱ *m.* meat from shoulder of ox.

shā̱ biri̱ *m.* type of bird.

shabka̱ = shauka̱.

shabta A. (**shabta̱**) *Vb.* 1A. (1) **yā ~ masa̱ wuƙā = shabce̱ 1, sha̱btā.** (2) **yā ~ ɗanyā** he spoke, acted foolishly.

B. (**sha̱btā**) *Vb.* 2 (*p.o.* **sha̱bcē,** *n.o.* **sha̱bci**) **yā sha̱bcē shi̱ da̱ wuƙā = shabce̱ 1.**

shabta̱kūlū (1) *m.* feckless P. (2) how damp it is ! (wood, room, etc.). (3) what badly cooked **tūwō** !

shabtare = shaftare.

shabtā-shabtā̱ *Vd.* **shabcēce̱.**

shāɓunā *Vb.* 1C = **lāka̱tā 1, 2.**

shā̱ɓu̱nē *m.* (1) wiping nose on back of hand (= *Kt.* **dā̱ji̱nē**). (2) **tā yi ~ da̱ jūda̱** she smeared musk on her face from bottom of nose outwards (*in sweep like* **billē**).

shā̱ɓūwā *f.* (1) unfertile land, *cf.* **faƙo̱.**

(2) sandy soil useless for building or farm (= saimō = hūlulūwạ).

shace A. (shācẹ)(1) *Vb.* 1A. (*a*) marked out all, fully *as in* shātạ. (*b*) combed (hair) = sarcẹ. (2) *Vb.* 3A (wall, etc.) cracked. B. (shāce) *Vd.* shạ̄tā.

shaci A. (shāci) *Vd.* shạ̄tā. B. (shāci) *m.* (1) (*a*) marking out ground plan of building, playground (fagē), etc. (*cf.* shātạ). (*b*) a marked-out site for a building. (*c*) (i) shācịn wannạŋ dāki tāki ạshịriŋ = shā 4*b*.i. (ii) kạman shācịn dāki = shā 4*b*.ii *x* anạ̄ wạ̄sā kạman shācịn dāki they're playing in a circle. (iii) kạman shācịn sōrō = shā 4*b*.iii. (2) shācịŋ gidansạ the whole of his compound. (3) ~ gạndạyau *Vd.* dilā.

shạ̄ cūdā *Vd.* wạrkī.

shādạ *Vb.* 1A *Sk.* = shā dạ.

shā dạ *Vb.* 4 (1) (*a*) gave water to *x* (*a*) yā ~ dōkịnsạ he watered his horse. yā ~ shī = yā shāshē shị he watered it (horse). nā ~ lạmbū I let water into the irrigated-farm. rījịyan nạŋ ta kạn ~ gạrimmụ dukạ this well suffices for the water of our whole town. (*b*) mạcẹ̄ mại shāyạrwā nursing-mother. (2) did injury to, deceived *used in* (*a*) Girgạ *q.v.* (*b*) (i) jndạ ya ~ arnā (mutānē) kẹ̄ naŋ that is where he shines, that's just in his line (= tōkā 3 = rại 1*r* = hannū 1*e*.i. = idọ 1*r* = jątau 4 = shēmā 2). (ii) jndạ ya ~ arnā (= mutānē) bạ̄ shi dạ karyạ his strong point is that he does not lie (*cf.* jạkī 1*d*).

shādạ (1) *f.* = gīlọ. (2) *Vb.* 1A = shaudạ.

shạ̄ dạ̄dalạ P. invulnerable through potions (= kạryạ tạmbayạ 2 = taurī 2*c*), *Vd.* kạs kaifī.

shạdarạ = sạdarạ.

shạ̄ darē *m.* an insect damaging nearly-ripe bulrush-millet (*cf.* shạ̄ gardī) = bọ̄bō.

shạdarī = shẹdarī.

Shạ̄ dārī *name given* child born during cold season (*Vd.* dārī 1*a*.ii, 4).

shadda A. (shạddā) *f.* (*pl.* shaddōdī). (1) cesspit (= sargā). (2) bā tạ̄ haifūwā sǎi ạ ~ she is barren. B. (shaddạ) *f.* (1) type of European silk-fabric. *(2) (*Ar.*) doubling a consonant and the sign representing it.

shaddada A. (shaddạdā) *Vb.* 1C *Ar.* yā ~ minị he pestered me. B. (shạddadạ) *Vb.* 3B *Ar.* is seriou *x* yuŋwạ tā ~ yạnzu the famine ha now become serious.

shaddōdī *Vd.* shạddā.

shādị *m.* = sharọ.

shạ̄ dụndū *m.* (*sg., pl.*) the mutilla insects resembling tụrurrūwā (*the* travel in pairs and children hit them wit their fists (dụndū)) = bāwạ 6 = *Kt.* shạ tīkā.

shaf *x* (1) yā mạntā ~ he forgot entirely (2) an shāfẹ shi ~ it is completel wiped out.

shafa A. (shạ̄fā) *Vb.* 2. (1) (*a*) (i) wiped (ii) passed the hand over, strokei (= shāfạ). (*b*) coaxed, persuaded appeased. (2) affected P. other than th doer *x* lạifin A. yā shạ̄fi B. the crime o A. affected B. wannạm mạsīfạ tị shạ̄fi kōwā this misfortune affect everybody (= jạɓā). B. (shāfạ) *Vb.* 1A. (1) (*a*) wiped stroked *x* yā ~ bāyan dōki he wiped thi horse's back (= shạ̄fā 1*a*). (2) (*wit* dative stated or implied*) (*a*) (i) yā ~ tụrārē he smeared scent on his body. (ii yā ~ masạ farar kasā he plastered i (wall). (iii) an ~ masạ bakim fentị = shāfẹ 1*a*.iii. (iv) *Vd.* fātihạ 2. (*b* yā ~ masạ mại ạ bakạ (= ạ bạkī he flattered him. (*c*) yā ~ wạ haŋ kạlinsạ tōkā he flew into a temper (*d*) (i) yā shāfạ wạ kạnsạ rūwā, yi yi shirū he thought discretion the bette part of valour and so kept silent. (ii shạ̄fa wạ gēmụŋkạ rūwā *Vd.* wutā 1*r* (*e*) *Vd.* kāshiŋ kạjī, zạmbō. (3) *Vd* shāfa-*compounds*.

shafa'ạ *Kt.* = shạ'afạ.

shạ̄fạ gadaŋkạ *m.* (1) = kẹ̄tạrạ shiŋgē (2) prostitute taken as wife.

shafal *m.* lightness *x* kāyā nẹ̄ ~ dạ sb it's a light load. rīgā cẹ̄ ~ dạ itạ it's a light gown. rīgunạ nē shafal-shạfạ dạ sū they are gowns of light weight.

shafạlā = cafạlā.

shạ̄fạ lạ̄bārị shūnī *m., f.* (*sg., pl.* exaggerator (*cf.* shūnī 1*e*).

shạ̄fa mụ rērạ = shạ̄fi mụ rērạ *m.* typ of hypnotism enabling possessor ti touch others so that they follow him like the Pied Piper.

shā fannōnī *Vd.* fannī 1*c.*

hāfā tābarmā shūnī *f.* wife sterile through previous prostitution (*cf.* shūnī 1*e*).

hafe A. (shāfē) (1) *Vb.* 1A. (*a*) rubbed, wiped *x* (i) ka ~ kāyan dākị dust the furniture ! (ii) tā ~ hannunta bākin dumā she ran her hand to and fro across edge of the gourd, to scrape off food (= kātse). (iii) yā ~ jịkinsa da turārē = shāfa 2*a.* yā ~ bangō da farar k̲asā = shāfa 2*a*.ii). an shāfe shi da bak̲im fentị it is painted black (= shāfa 2*a*. iii). (*b*) wiped away, effaced (= shārę 1*b*) *x* (i) zā ta ~ hawāyanta she will wipe away her tears : her affairs will improve (*cf.* shārę 1*b*.ii). (ii) wutā tā ~ g̱arī fire destroyed the town. yā ~ su = yā shāfę su kaf he annihilated them. (iii) yanā da amfānī har saurā kadan ya ~ wahala tasa it's so useful that its value renders negligible the trouble of getting it. (iv) yā dūba k̲asā, ya ~ he made divination-lines on the sand, then drew his nail along to efface them. (v) rūwā yā ~ kōgī the river is in flood (= kāwō 1*b*). (vi) yā ~ kudī he spent the money (= 6atar da). (vii) yā ~ abincī he golloped up the food (= shārę 1*c*). (*c*) exceeded, excelled *x* (i) yā ~ su he surpassed them. bā wanda ya ~ shi a dūnīya there is not his equal anywhere. (ii) bā ā ~ masa zānē = *c*.i. (*d*) yā ~ mini bāshị he cancelled the debt I owed him. (*e*) shāfę bākinka (*euphemism*) adjust your dress, for you're exposing your person ! (2) *Vb.* 3A became effaced *x* alāma tasa tā ~ all trace of it has disappeared. g̱arī yā ~ da wutā = 1*b*.ii *above*. kōgī yā ~ da rūwā = 1*b*.v *above*.

B. (shāfē) *m.* (1) plastering *x* an yi wa bangō ~ the wall has been plastered. (2) smearing floor with cow-dung. (3) corn-stalk bed which lies flat on the ground (= shịmfịdē).

C. (shāfe) (*noun of state from* shāfa 2*a*) *x* bangō yanā ~ da farar k̲asā = farar k̲asā tanā ~ a bangō the wall is plastered.

shaffai *Vd.* shēhu.

shāfị *m.* (*sg., pl.*) (1) (*a*) lining of skirt of gown or sleeve of gown (*cf.* waddare, algabba, k̲urūru). (*b*) reinforcement of jalāla with paper, rag, etc., as temporary measure, to prevent it puckering while being sewn. (2) (*a*) one side of a slate. (*b*) (i) one page (*i.e.* half a leaf (warak̲a) of paper). (ii) alk̲āwaran nan, sāban shāfị nē aka būda na abūta tsakānimmu these promises form a new basis of friendship between us. (iii) an rage yawan ~ the total number of pages has been reduced. (3) slight dressing used for stiffening calico, etc. (= g̱ārī). (4) = kas kaifī. (5) food *x* yā sāmi ~ he had a meal. (6) feckless P.

shā fịrjī *m.* fringed halter.

shāfo = shāho.

shaftare A. (shaftarē) *m.* (1) green firewood, put to dry. (2) driveller (*epithet is* shaftaran ayyarā mai wuyar būshēwā). (3) shaftaram magana ill-considered talk (= danyar magana).

B. *(shaftarē)* *Vb.* 3A *x* rīgā tā ~ the gown has become drenched (with dew, rain, urine, etc.).

shagala *Vb.* 3B *Ar.* (1) became diverted from *x* don santa yā ~ da aik̲insa his love for her diverted him from his work (*cf.* dauka 1*c*.iii). (2) occupy oneself with *x* kōwā ya ~ da abiŋ kansa let everyone look after his own affairs !

shagalad da *Vb.* 4 *x* santa yā ~ nī daga aik̲ina = santa yā shagalshē nị daga aik̲ina my love for her has diverted me from my work.

shagalallē *m.* (*f.* shagalallīyā) *pl.* shaga-lallū = mashagūlị.

shagalcē *Vb.* 3A = shagala.

shagalce-shagalcē *Vd.* shagalī.

shagalī *m.* (*pl.* shagulgula = shagalce-shagalcē) *Ar.* (1) = sha'anī 1, 3, 4. *(2)* extravagance *x* yanā ~ balangē he's having a good time, spending plenty of money (*cf.* sha'anī 5).

shagalshē *Vd.* shagalad da.

shagaltad da = shagalad da.

shā gardī *m.* large, black insect which damages stored corn (= shanyau), *cf.* shā darē.

shā g̱ārī *m.* (1) wastrel (*epithet is*

Shā gārī, kāsa aiki). (2) mai nīshi kā shā gārī *Vd.* gayyā 1*c*. (3) shā gārī, ḍau galmā (*a*) what payment " on the nail " ! (*b*) what a favourable and quick verdict from this bribed judge ! (*c*) how quickly he has returned the service done him !

shaggā *Vd.* shēgę.

shagiḍa A. (shāgiḍā) (1) *Vb.* 1C (*a*) x yā shāgiḍa rawanī (hūlā) he put on the turban (cap) askew. (*b*) a yi maka magana sǎi ka ∼ mini bāki ? is it right for you to look sour when given an order ? (2) *Vb.* 3A (*a*) = shāgiḍē. (*b*) = muskuḍā 2, 3. B. (shāgiḍa) *Vb.* 3B = kishiŋgiḍa.

shāgiḍē *Vb.* 3A became askew x rawaninsa yā ∼ his turban is askew. bākinsa yā ∼ (*a*) his mouth is crooked. (*b*) he looks sour.

shāgirī *m.* (*pl.* shāgirai) (1) glabrous, beardless man. (2) shāgirā *f.* (*pl.* shāgirai) glabrous woman with hairless genitals. (3) shāgirī girbau *Kt.* feckless P.

shāgo *m.* (1) = fyādī. (2) = tēbur 1*b.*

shagū *Kt. m.* = shakka.

shāgubē *m.* = habaicī.

shā gūḍa *m*ι = magūḍīyā 3.

shagulgula *Vd.* shagalī.

shagwaba A. (shagwaba) *Vb.* 1C coddled, spoiled (child). B. (shagwaba) *f.* = kyaŋkyantā.

shahāda *Ar. f.* (1) death while warring for Islam or accidentally, etc. (2) *Vd.* kalma 2.

shahara *Vb.* 3B *Ar.* is well known.

shā hargōwa *epithet of* (1) hyena, (2) dishonest P.

shahhai *Vd.* shēhu.

shāhi = asshāhi.

shahidi *A.* (shahīdi) *m.* (*f.* shahīda) *pl.* shahīdai P. who met his death *as in* shahāda 1. *B.* (shāhidī) *m.* (*f.* shāhidā) *pl.* shāhidai = witness (= shaida).

shāho *m.* (*pl.* shāhuna) (1) (*a*) hawk, falcon, any of the Accipiter family. (= būra kōgō). (*b*) shāho bā yā cin raban kuŋkurū everybody has his allotted destiny (*Vd.* kuŋkurū 1*a.*ii). (*bb*) anā ∼ *Vd.* zakara 1*e.* (*c*) kōmē

yakē cikin ḍan tsākō, shāho yā daḍę da saninsa = kōmē yakē cikin ḍaŋ kāzā, shāho yā daḍę da saninsa teaching one's grandmother to suck eggs. (*d*) bā tsārakā ga shāho, kai dǎi a yι jimirin shāwāgi nothing is obtained without effort. (*e*) gāgara ∼ *Vd.* tsākō 1*c.* (2) farin ∼ (*a*) Chanting or Neumann's Goshawk (*Melierax metabetes neumanni*). (*b*) Little Goshawk (*Melierax gabar*). (3) shāhwam barēyī = gaggāfā 1.

shahūlā *adj.* very thin (*re* fabric).

shāhuna *Vd.* shāho.

shā'i *Ar. m.* tea.

shai'aŋ *Ar.* (1) *used in* ban cē da shī ∼ ba I did not address a word to him (= uffaŋ). (2) *Vb.* shai'iŋ.

shaida *A.* (shaidā) *Vb.* 1C (1) bore witness. (2) informed x (*a*) jē ka ka ∼ masa ni nā nēmansa go and tell him I am looking for him ! (*b*) (Gram. 18) a ∼ maka I am instructed to inform you that . . . (*formula used in official letters*). (3) recognized x nā haŋgē shi ammā ban ∼ shi ba I espied him far off, but didn't recognize him (= fitar da 3). (4) x dūkan da ya yi mini yā ∼ the beating he gave me left a mark behind. B. (shaida) *Ar. m., f.* (*pl.* shaidū) (1) (*a*) evidence, testimony x suŋ kāra kafa shaidarsu da wasīka they strengthened their testimony with a letter. (*b*) shaidar zur perjury. 2 (*a*) mark, sign by which T. may be recognized. (*b*) shaidar kōshī saurā only the rich can save. (3) shaida = mai shaida witness. (4) (*a*) Black-headed Weaver Bird. (*b*) Lesser Hammerkop (*Scopus umbretta*). (*c*) Greater Hammerkop (*Scopus umbretta bannermanni*) 4*c* = rārā 2.

Shaidaŋ = Shaitsaŋ.

shaidū *Vd.* shaida.

*shaidī = shaida 2*a.*

shaihu = shēhu.

shai'iŋ *Ar.* (1) *used in* bi gaira bi ∼ = gaira 2*c.* (2) *Vd.* shai'aŋ.

*sha'ir *Ar. m.* barley.

Shaitsaŋ = Shaitsānī *Ar. m.* (1) Satan. (2) (*with f.* shaitsānīyā) *pl.* shaitsānai = shaitsānū (*a*) cantankerous P. (*b*) very skilful P. (*cf.* ạljan, ịblịs 2, haddạcē 2 mạsīfạ 3, māyẹ 2, gāgarạ 3*b*, fịtinạ 2*d*). (3) (*a*) kụnnan ~ auricular appendices of the heart. (*b*) nā jī kạ dạ kụnnan ~ what low talk you employ! (4) tambạrin ~ *Vd.* tambạrī 10.

haitsanạ *f.* = shaitsancị *m.* (1) cantankerousness (*cf.* shạitsạŋ 2*a*). (2) great skill (*cf.* shạitsạŋ 2*b*).

haitsantạ *f.* = shaitsanạ.

hạjarạ mạjarạ *Ar.* (1) yanạ̄ aikị ~ he's working might and main (= gạdugạdu 2). (2) ~ sukạ isō it was only with the utmost difficulty they got here (= dạ kyar).

hạ̄ jạ̄yayyạ *Vd.* ạlēwạ 1.

hạ̄ jịɓī *m.* small garment worn next to the skin.

hạ̄ jinī *m.* (1) plant used as remedy for headache. (2) *Vd.* jinī 7.

hak̄a A. (shākạ) (1) throttled, choked (= mạ̄kurạ). (2) an ~ shi = an ~ wuyạnsạ he was seized by the throat. (3) *Sk.* = shēk̄ạ. (4) *Vd.* shạ̄ku.
  B. (shạ̄kā) *Vb.* 2 = shākạ 1, 2.

hakaf *m.* (1) (*a*) lightness in weight. (*b*) tūwō yā yi ~ the tūwō is sloppy. (2) *adv.* danyē ~ very moist.

hạ̄k̄āk̄ī *m.* long distance x tsạkāninsụ ~ nẹ̄ they're a long way apart. sāmụŋ warkē̆wā gạrēshị ~ it'll be long till he recovers.

hạ̄kālẹ *m.* = *Kt.* shākālạ (*f.* shạ̄kālị̄yā) *pl.* shạ̄kālai good for nothing P., rover (= gīlọ).

hakạlī *Ar. m.* vowel-sign.

haka-shaka = kwasha-kwasha.

hāk̄atā *Vb.* 3A (1) took short rest. (2) (*a*) kạ ~ mụ ganī let's wait and see! (*b*) hạr ạ īyạ yịŋ hakạ, ạ̄ shāk̄atā it'll take some time before this can be done. (3) *Kt.* dạ shāk̄atạ̄wā = taɓạ̄wā.

hā kạ tạfi *m., f.* (*sg., pl.*) roving man or woman, prostitute.

hakạwạ *f.* request x yanạ̄ shạkạwar rạncē he's seeking a loan (= fạtạwā 2).

hạk̄awạ *f.* arrogance (= rēnị 1*b*).

hāk̄ẹ (1) *Vb.* 1A (*a*) = shāk̄ạ 1, 2. (*b*) filled chock-full x yā ~ bāk̄insạ dạ gōrọ he filled his mouth with kola-nut. (2) *Vb.* 3A = mạ̄k̄arạ 2. (3) *Vd.* shạ̄k̄u.

shạ̄ kidị *m.* the medium-length string of mōlō (*cf.* magūdị̄yā 3).

*shak̄īk̄ancị *m.* being a shạk̄īk̄ị.

*shạk̄īk̄ị *m.* (*f.* shạk̄īk̄ịyā) *pl.* shạk̄īk̄ai *Ar.* full brother or sister (*cf.* danụɓā, danụ̄wā, lị'abbị, lị'ummị).

shākịrā *f.* (*pl.* shạ̄kịrai) (1) anus. (2) bā ạ̄ gamạ gudụ da sūsar ~ *Vd.* gudụ 2 *q.v.*

shạ̄kịrce = shạ̄kịre = shẹ̄k̄ẹ̄k̄ẹ̄ *q.v.*

shạ̄ kịtịmbō *m., f.* fool.

shakīyyancị *m.* being a shạkīyyị.

shạkīyyị = shạk̄īyyị *m.* (*f.* shạkīyyị̄yā, *etc.*) *pl.* shạkị̄yyai, *etc.* *Ar.* shameless rogue (*cf.* shēgẹ).

shakkạ *f.* (1) doubting x n nạ̄ ~ tasạ I'm in doubt about it. yā sạ̄ kōwā shakkạ wạtạkīlạ . . . it made everyone wonder whether . . . kōwā nạ̄ shakkạ lallē k̄aryā nẹ̄ everyone suspects that it is a lie. (= k̄ọ̄kwantō = tantamā = gīgạ = wahạmī = tāɓāɓạ). (2) fearing x mum fārạ shakkạ kadạ sụ rịnjāyē mụ we're nervous lest they may conquer us. an yi shakkạr kīlạ sū mā hakạ zā sụ yi it was feared that perhaps they might do so. yā fārạ shakkạr kīlạ zại fāɗị he has begun to feel nervous lest he be defeated. bā yạ̄ shakkạr kōwā he fears nobody. (3) bạri ~, ita shēgị̄yā cẹ̄ *m.* = shēgẹ 5.

shakkatạ *Vb.* 2 (*n.o.* shạkkạcē, *p.o.* shạkkạcị) doubted.

shakkū *m.* = shakkạ.

shạ̄k̄ō *m.* wannạŋ sịrīk̄ị bā yạ̄ ~ this flute makes no sound at intake of breath.

shạ̄ku *Vb.* 3B x mun ~ dạ shī we're intimate with him (*cf.* shāk̄ẹ).

shākulācị = shākulātị *used in* shākulātịna what has it to do with me? (= rūwā G.1). shākulātịŋkạ what has it to do with you? (*Vd.* kụlā 2).

shā kụndum (1) what a rich person! (2) what a fine town! (3) what a learned person!

shāk̄ụrā *Vb.* 1C *Sk.* = shāk̄ạ.

shạ̄ kụshē (1) *m.* P. belittled by those whom he benefits. (2) *Vd.* dạŋkali.

shākutū *m.* fool.

shak̄ụ̄wạ *f.* yā yi ~ he hiccoughed.

shal *Kt.* x mun rạbu ~ we separated, I having got nothing out of him.

shalallēkū *m.* = tsalallēkū.

shallā *Vb.* 3B *Kt.* yā ~ dạ gudu he took to his heels.

shallạkē *Vb.* 1C *x* yā ~ shi dạ ƙafạ tasạ he threw his leg over him in fun (*cf.* shạ talē-talē).

shallālancị *m.* being a shạllālị.

shạllālị *m.* (*f.* shạllālīyā) *pl.* shạllālai fool.

shạllē *Kt. m.* = shạllū.

shạl'le-shạllē" *m.* = shạllū.

shạllī *used in* kạdam mutum yā ƙūnā, bā yā shạlliŋ ƙaurī habit is second-nature (*Vd.* ƙūnā 1*b*).

shạllīyē-shạllīyē = shạllū.

shạllū = shạllū-shạllū *m.* the children's game like catch-as-catch can (= allam bā ku).

shalmạ *m., f.* sleek, well-dressed P.

sham A. (sham) *x* (1) yā mīƙẹ ~ he stretched himself out to his full length. (2) yā tạfi ~ he went off without a word to anyone.

B. (Shạm) *Ar. f.* (1) Syria. (2) Palestine.

shamagē bạbbar rīgā (*said by* marōƙī) largesse, noble one !

shạ mǎi *Vd.* dạŋgī.

shạ maiƙo *m.* big type of gaŋgī.

*shạ mạ jikạ = huƙā.

*shāmakạncē *Vb.* 1D partitioned off.

shamakanci A. (shāmakancị) *m.* (1) being shāmakị. (2) office (sạrautạ) of shạmakị.

B. (shāmakancī) *m.* (1) sun yi masạ ~ (*a*) they (number of people) fell upon him (P. or malevolent horse) with blows. (*b*) they (N.A. police) seized P. at order of Emir, to maltreat him. (2) taking two ladlefuls each (lūdạyī bīyu-bīyu) by persons who are sharing food.

shāmakị *m.* (*pl.* shạmạkai) (1) (*a*) stables, tethering-place in compound (= bạrgā = mōrị = bạrāyā 1), *cf.* turƙẹ. (*b*) dōkịŋ harị ạ yi gudụŋkạ tuŋ kanạ ~ forewarned is forearmed (*Vd.* harị 2). (2) (*a*) Stablemaster (*he was Head-slave with epithet* Kōrau kạm bāyī = Būwạyī = Cizgārī 7 = Kạrīyạ = Bạrgā 3 = Rāƙạsạ = Agudīmạ). (*b*) *Vd.* Kạcallạ. (*c*) shāmakịn dalạ penny. (3) (*a*) partition. (*b*) bā ạ̄ wạ idọ ~ a cat can look at a king. (*c*) protector.

shamɓara A. shamɓarā = shamɓarērīyā *f. pl.* shamɓar-shạmɓạr bosomy young woman.

B. (shamɓạrā) *Vb.* 1C (1) spread T on damp ground. (2) yā shamɓạrạ magana he spoke disrespectfully (*cf.* danyē 4*a*).

C. (shạmɓarạ) *Vb.* 2 sat on damp ground.

shạmɓạrɓạr *x* yārinyạ cē ~ dạ ita she's a bosomy girl.

shamɓar-shạmɓạr *Vd.* shamɓarā.

shamgēgẹ *m.* (*f.* shamgēgīyā) huge (*re* the living).

shāmigidī *m.* feckless P. ; gadabout (= gīlọ).

shạ mīyạ *m.* (1) *Vd.* mīyạ 11, shā A.1*g.* (2) material used for shāƙị.

shạmmạcē *Vd.* shạmmātạ.

shammāgīyā = shamɓarā.

shạmmātạ *Vb.* 2 (*p.o.* shạmmạcē, *n.o.* shạmmạci) deceived, tricked.

shāmọmọ *m.* (1) dejectedness. (2) *Vd.* ƙwǎi 1*g.*

*shạmsīyyạ *Ar. f.* (1) umbrella, sunshade (= laimạ). (2) solar year (*Ar. antithesis is* qamariyya). (3) Arabic letters with which previous " l " of al (*Arabic definite article*) assimilates.

shā mu dōrạ *m., f.* (*sg., pl.*) rover (= gīlọ).

shāmụƙē *Vb.* 3A procrastinated.

shāmụlallē = tāmụlallē.

shā mu shā *m., f.* (*sg., pl.*) rover (= gīlọ).

shāmūwā *f.* (1) Abdim's White-bellied Stork (*Sphenorhynchus abdimii*) which is harbinger of rainy season. (2) *Vd.* lallẹ 1*h.* (3) kōwā ya ga shạmūwā, dạ ƙunshịntạ ya gan tạ everybody is as God made him. (4) kōmē ya sāmi shāmūwā, watạm baƙwại nē ya jāwō matạ whatever has happened to him is through unfamiliar milieu (*Vd.* watạ 2*o*).

shan *Vd.* shā III.

shạ̄nạkai *Vd.* sạ̄ A.2 (*page* 753).

shanana = danana.

shānạnnakī *Vd.* sạ̄ A.2 (*page* 753).

shancī *m.* (1) the contest done by Māguzāwā with armlet baurạ (= *Kt.* kwạrāyạ), *cf.* kumantakā. (2) *Vd.* baurạ 2.

shan dạbgē *m.* luxurious living.

Shạndam *f.* Shendam.

Shangai furad dāwą what a daft person !
shąŋ gīyą *Vd.* gīyą 1*d.*
shąŋ gwandą *Vd.* gwandą 3.
shą̄ ni ką san ni *m.* = hąŋkāką 5.
shaŋką6ē *Vb.* 3A became soaked.
shąŋ kąbēwą *m.* (1) festival to celebrate ripening of pumpkins. (2) *Sk.* pagan custom four months after rains, to propitiate rain-gods.
shąŋ kauyę *Vd.* kauyę 2*c.*
shą̄ nōnǫ *m.* (1) (*a*) white type of guinea-corn. (2) = tandarą 1.
shan mąi gidā *Vd.* budiri.
shan rų̄mą̄cē *Kt. m.* = būdē 1.
shan rūwā (1) *Vd.* rūwā A.2. (2) shąn rūwan rākumą *used in* zūwąmmu ～ nē we only come now and then.
shan shā *Kt. m.* = kǭmē 3.
shąnshą̄nī *m.* (1) flat centipede with painful sting. (2) rover (= gīlǫ).
shāshancį *m.* acting witlessly (*cf.* shā-shą̄shā).
shanshērā *f.* (1) beans without pods removed. (2) unhusked ground-nuts, gujīyā, or rice. (2) unpounded, dried leaves of kūka, tobacco, etc. (*cf.* samfērā).
shan tā6ǫ *Vd.* tā6ǫ.
shantąkē *Vb.* 3A (1) procrastinated. (2) danshī yā ～ ą dākin nąŋ this house is always damp.
shantąlī = sintąlī.
shan tsādą = shąŋ gwandą *q.v. under* gwandą 3.
shąntū *m.* (*pl.* shantuną) long gourd-trumpet used by women and Filani.
shānū *Vd.* są̄ A.2 (*page* 753).
shąŋ watą *m.* = ząwārą 1.
shanya A. (shąnyā) *Vb.* 1C. (1) dried (*x* clothing in sun, *Vd.* shanyą). (2) yā ～ su he beat, killed them. (3) ką̄zā tā ～ 'yā'yantą ą sararī the hen left her chicks in the open exposed to hawks. (4) yā ～ bą̄kī, yaną̄ kallō he stared open-mouthed.
   B. (shanyą) *f.* (1) (*a*) (i) washed clothes put to dry. (ii) ąbin ～ bā ą̄ haną rānā take the chance when it offers ! (*b*) act of drying dąddawā (*cf.* fitǫ 3). (*c*) act of drying clothes *x* kōwā ya sąmi rānā, săi yą yi ～ make hay while the sun shines ! (3) (*secondary v.n.*

of shąnyā) *x* (*a*) taną̄ shanyąr tufāfį = taną̄ shąnyā tufāfį she's drying clothes.
   (*b*) shanyąr gą̄rī *Vd.* yąmmā 2*c.*
shąnyau *m.* = shą̄ gardī.
shanye A. shąnyē (1) *Vb.* 1C (*a*) yā ～ = yā ～ fat he drank up completely.
   (*b*) bą̄ shąnyę mąŋ Kumbǫ akē̦ jį ba, mai dą kātąŋ akē̦ jį it's pleasant to receive gifts but not quite so pleasant to have to make return-gifts. (*c*) sun shąnyę mąganą they ignored the matter. (*d*) mun shąnyę lą̄bārį we bore the news patiently (*cf.* shā A. 1*o*, B.). mun shąnyę dūką we bore our flogging bravely. (*e*) 6ērā yā shąnyę gą̄rī *Vd.* wandą 2*b.* (*f*) shąnyę hannū *Vd.* son 7. (*g*) shąnyę kafą *Vd.* inną 3*b.* (*h*) yā dāmę, yā ～ *Vd.* dāmę 1*c* (2) *Vb.* 3A (*a*) (i) (washed clothing, limb, etc.) shrunk. (ii) an dadę aną̄ rūwa, kasā taną̄ shąnyēwā let sleeping dogs lie ! (*b*) behaved with fortitude (*especially Filani during* sharǫ, *who, when challenged, says* săi gōmą give me ten more blows !).
   B. *Vd.* sāran shąnyē.
shan zumą *m.* (1) = tā6ǫ 2. (2) *Vd.* cī A.13*b.* (3) *Vd.* zumą 1*c, d.*
shar A. (shar) *Vd.* kōrę, tsaŋwā.
   B. (shąr) *x* 'yā'yaŋ itą̄cē sun zubō ～ the fruit fell off the tree with a rattling sound (*also applied to pouring out of small, hard objects like cowries, etc*).
shara A. (shārą) (1) *Vb.* 1A. (*a*) (i) swept T. on to *x* yā ～ musu kū̦rā ą kā it (galloping horse, etc.) covered them with dust. (ii) shą̄rą kązāmā *Vd.* būję. (*b*) did much of *x* yā ～ barcī he slept a lot. yā ～ karyā he told many lies (= shą̄rā). yaną̄ shārą musu karairai he is feeding them with lies. (2) *Vb.* 3A yā ～ = yā ～ dą gudu he took to his heels (1, 2 *have cerebral* -r-). (3) shą̄rą *f.* = kudin shą̄rą *m.* (*with rolled* -r-) money claimable from 10th Muḥarrąm onwards (*nine* ąnīnī *or a penny*) between ąbǭkaŋ wą̄sā (*this being* grand-child claiming from grand-parent ; one taubą̄shī *q.v.* from another ; hunter from mą̄ląmī ; barber from shąrīf or blacksmith ; native of Gobir from one of Kano,

Katsina, or Zaria ; Barebari from Filani, etc.), *cf.* tsintsīyā 1*e*.

B. (shārā) (1) *Vb.* 2. (*a*) swept (place) (= shārę). (*b*) cleared (a road), *cf.* shārā 2*f*, shārarrē. (*c*) *Vd.* 2*f below*. (*d*) = shārą 1*b* *x* yā shāri barcī. (2) *f.* (*a*) (i) act of sweeping *x* sun yi ∼ they've done the sweeping. (ii) tsintsīyā ɗayā bā tā ∼ unity is strength. (iii) tāran tsintsīyā bā ∼, banzā people are collected idly. (*b*) (i) sweepings (= shāre-shārē 2). (ii) kwandan ∼ *m.* wastepaper basket. (iii) babba jūjī nē, kōwā ya zō dą ∼, yą zubą the noble person must be long-suffering (*Vd.* babba jūjī). (*c*) watą yā yiwō ∼ the moon is about to rise. (*d*) māganin shārar cikī *m.* purgative (= māganī 4*c*). (*e*) shārar fagē = shārad dātsą clearing open space for drummers, to accompaniment of music and feasting. (*f*) shārar hanyą (i) clearing a road. (ii) making one's preparations (*cf.* shārę 1*a*.i).

C. (shārā) *Kt.* *m.* = shārā 2.

shara'ą *f.* = sharī'ą.

sharabą *f.* = mandawąrī.

shā rāɓā *f.* (1) (*a*) calf of leg (= *Sk.* maturzai). (*b*) shin (*both* = dambūbu = *Kt.* madangalę = sangalī = kwaurī = kąsangalī = tikātikī = *Sk.* dumtsī = *Kt.* futushī). (2) metal ornamental point to sheath of knife or sword.

shā rąbō *Vd.* hannun 8*b*.

sharąɗā *Vb.* 3A *Ar.* (1) *x* mun ∼ we have made conditions. kąmar sun ∼ in accordance with the conditions they imposed. (2) *x* mun ∼ dą shī zā mu gamu gōbe we've arranged to meet him to-morrow.

sharąɗī *m.* (*pl.* shąrąɗai = sharuɗą = sharaɗōdī) *Ar.* (1) agreement, arrangement *x* sun kullą ∼ ą kan zā ą bā su they have made a pact, treaty, contract to give it to them. (2) reason *x* im bai zō ba, dą ∼ if he has not come, then there is some good reason (= dalīlī). (3) (*a*) condition *x* ąmmā dą ∼ but it's dependent on a condition. (*b*) bisą ∼ *adv.* conditionally (*cf.* hujją 4). *(4) conditional mood. (5) bet.

sharaf A. (sharaf = sharaf-sharąf) *x* yā

yi gumī ∼ he's drenched in perspiration (*Vd.* gumī 1*b*). yā jikę ∼ it's sodden.

B. (shąraf) (1) *adv.* (*a*) yā fādī ∼ he (tall P. ; snake on tree) fell headlong. (*b*) yā zauną ∼ he sat down limply. (2) (*a*) nā ji ∼ I heard the juicy sound of sugar-cane being cut up or eaten. (*b*) yaną cin tūwō shąraf-shąraf he is eating tūwō slushy with mīyą. (*c*) yaną sham mīyą shąraf-shąraf he is noisily drinking soup (*cf.* shąrɓā). (*d*) ∼ dą mąi = ą cī dą mąi 1.

*shąrafą *Vb.* 3B *Ar.* yā ∼ = yaną ∼ he's at point of death (= gargarą 1).

shąrąfī *Ar.* *m.* (1) (*a*) enjoying a vogue, being in favour *x* tābą taną ∼ yanzu tobacco is in vogue now. yaną tsak ą dą sharąfinsą he's at the acme of his power. (*b*) *Vd.* furę 1*a*.ii). (2) lallę yā ɗaukō ∼ henna-stain is fading from body of P.

sharaf-sharaf *Vd.* sharaf, shąraf 2*b*, *c*.

shąrandaɓō (1) *m.* (*a*) sloppy tūwō. (*b*) tactless P. (*c*) unkempt, dirty P. (1*a*–*c* = narkōkǫ). (*d*) damp house. (2) what a lot of water has been added to this corn which is to be pounded !

shā rānī *m.* (1) (*a*) collective hunt during dry season. (*b*) yā mutu ą ∼ (i) he died from accident during collective hunt. (ii) he met his death through his own fault. (2) ąbin ∼ *m.* (*a*) black dog. (*b*) what a wastrel ! (*Vd.* ragō 1*a*).

sharap = sharaf.

shārarrē *m.* (*f.* shārarrīyā) *pl.* shārarrū (*past participle from* shārā, shārę). (1) swept. (2) shārarrīyā *f.* European-made road (*cf.* shārā 1*b*).

sharatsī = sharaɗī.

sharau = sharǫ.

sharbą = sharabą.

sharɓa A. (shąrɓā) *Vb.* 2. (1) *x* yā shąrɓi mīyą he noisily drank soup (*cf.* shąraf 2*c*). (2) cut (unripe corn, green wood, etc.).

B. (sharɓą) *Vb.* 1A. (1) an ∼ mutū-wą someone has died in his prime. (2) (*with dative*) (*a*) an ∼ masą takōɓi he has been slashed with sword. an ∼ masą būlālą he's been whipped. (*b*) an ∼ masą rikicī he's been tricked. (*c*) yā ∼ minî magana he spoke disrespectfully to me.

sharɓe A. (sharɓē) m. (1) weeping silently. (2) Kt. = shaftarē.

B. (sharɓẹ) Vb. 1A drank completely as in sharɓā.

sharɓilā what sloppy tūwō ! (also indicates surprise at any of the factors mentioned in sharandaɓọ).

sharcẹ = sarcẹ.

hare A. (shārẹ) (1) Vb. 1A. (a) swept x (i) ka ∼ daɓē sweep the floor ! (= shārā 1a). (ii) yā cẹ kada mu shārẹ wurī, mu zauna he told us not to relax our efforts. (iii) Vd. shārā 1e. (b) (i) wiped away, effaced (= shāfẹ 1b q.v.). (ii) nā kāwō kūkā wurinka doŋ ka ∼ minî hawāyē I'm in trouble and have come to you for help (cf. shāfẹ 1b.i). (iii) Vd. makōkī 1b. (c) = shāfẹ 1b.vii. (d) in yā yi haka, ba zai ∼ ba if he does this, he'll rue it. (e) Vd. fagē 1a.iii. (f) yā ∼ shi da mārî he slapped him. (2) Vb. 3A hadarî yā ∼ the storm has dispersed (= wātsẹ 1c). (3) Sk. m. portion (= shāshi).

B. (sharẹ) Vb. 3A. (1) evacuated one's bowels. (2) Kt. = ƙwarẹ.

harēfā f. lie x yā zuba minî ∼ he told me a lie.

hâ're-shārēˮ m. (1) sweeping continually. (b) = shārā 2b.i.

hargallē m. tactless P.

sharha f. (pl. sharhōhī) Ar. (1) written commentary x an yi masa ∼ an exegesis has been written on it (religious book), cf. hāshīya, tafsīri, tafī da mālaminka. (2) yā yi minî ∼ he amplified the details of his statement for me.

sharhancē Vb. 1A wrote commentary (sharha) on (religious book).

sharhi m. = sharha.

harhōla f. lie x yā zuba minî ∼ he told me a lie.

hārî (1) what a lot ! (2) what speed !

hari'a = sharī'a f. (pl. sharī'ō'ī) Ar. (1) Muslim law (epithet ∼ māganim mai gātā). (2) wurin ∼ m. Muslim law-court. (3) yā yi ∼ he administered justice. (4) yā yanƙẹ ∼ = yā zartad da ∼ he passed sentence, gave verdict (= yanƙẹ 1e.iii, zartad da, cf. hakunci,

hakuntā). (5) Vd. kētâ. (6) gāgara ∼ Vd. gāgara 15.

Sharif = Sharīfi m. (f. Sharīfīyā) pl. Sharīfai. (1) P. claiming descent from Alī, son-in-law of the Prophet (cf. Sayyu, Sayyadī, Sīdi, hātimī 3, Mālikî 2). (2) sharīfīyā (said playfully) = mārā 1a. (3) sharīfin cācā skilful gambler.

Sharifci m. = Sharifta = Shariftaka f. (1) being a Sharif. (2) the qualities of a Sharif. (3) Vd. hannū 3a.

shārindọ m. (1) = zaryā 1. (2) ∼ da gudaŋ wainā Kt. = cilandō. (3) Vd. wutsīyar ∼.

sharīri m. (f. sharīrīyā) pl. sharīrai Ar. evil, wicked.

sharkaf = sharkat. (1) = sharaf. (2) Kt. = shirkat.

*sharƙīyya Ar. f. (1) the cursive Arabic script as written in Arabia, Syria, Turkey, India, Persia, etc., in a flowing hand (contrasted with the slow, careful script of Nigeria), cf. tafīya 8b. (2) italic script.

sharkwata Vb. 1C (1) defeated in any unsuitable place. (2) yana sharkwata zāwo he has diarrhœa. (3) yā ∼ minî zāgi he covered me with abuse (cf. asharkwatōta). (4) yā ∼ minî tūwō he gave me much tūwo of sloppy quality.

sharọ m. (1) Filani youths' undergoing test of endurance consisting of flogging from which they must not flinch (= fyādi 3 = shādi = dudɗalī), cf. agalanda. (2) Vd. shiga ∼.

sharraŋ Vd. shūka 1a.ii.

sharri Ar. m. (1) wickedness. (2) Sarkin sharri Vd. ƙūlū 2.

Shāru name for boy or girl born in Ramalaŋ.

Shā rubūtū name for child considered to be kwantaccē and whose mother had hard confinement necessitating prayers for her safe delivery (= Shā tambaya = Tambai).

sharuda Vd. sharadī.

shā rūwā Kt. f. = tsātsa rūwā (cf. rūwā A.2).

shā sanda m. ridge of plaited hair on fore-head to neck of Filani youths.

shā sārā Vd. gamji.

shāshad dạ *Kt.* = shā dạ.
shāshāgọ *m.* (1) big receptacle for bạmmī. (2) saw used in calabash-making.
shāshakancị = shāshancị *m.* roaming about for gossip or fornication.
shāshạntā = shāshạtā.
shāshạshā *m., f. (pl.* shạshạshai) witless fool (= sūsụsū).
shashata A. (shāshạtā) *Vb.* 1C. (1) treated as a fool. (2) diverted P. from topic in hand.
B. (shạshātạ) *Vb.* 3B increased, became general.
shāshātad dạ *Vb.* 4 = shāshạtā 1.
shạshạtau *m.* (1) the weed *Jussiœa villosa,* supposed to ward off results of wrong-doing if put in mouth of criminal or water in which he bathes. (2) malefactor who jokes about his crimes. (3) small insect attacking leaves of corn, etc.
shashe A. (shāshē) *Vd.* shā dạ.
B. (shāshẹ) (1) *Vb.* 1A (*a*) effaced previous flavour in T. *x* nā ∼ bạkīna I washed out my mouth, etc., to rid it of certain flavour. nā ∼ turmī I pounded bran in mortar aftẹr pounding henna there, prior to pounding corn in it. nā ∼ ƙwaryā I removed previous flavour left in calabash. (*b*) yā ∼ askā he (newly circumcised lad) indulged in sexual intercourse as soon as healed, to efface remembrances of the pain. (2) *m.* = shāshị.
shāshị *m.* (1) portion *x* shāshịm mutạnē kawại suṇ kulạ dạ shī only a section of the people obeyed his orders (*cf.* Mod. Gram. 9*d*) (= sāshẹ = rabị). (2) *x* (*a*) sāshịnā nẹ he is my pal (*girl says* sāshịṇ boy-pal !). (*b*) *Vd.* gumị 1*b.*
shạshịmī *m.* (1) a cheap perfume with evanescent scent (*epithet is* Shạshịmī iskạ ɗayā), *cf.* iskạ 7. (2) witless P. (3) prostitute.
shạ shirgị *Vd.* rụmfā 6.
shạ shūnī *f.* white garment coloured by being worn in contact with another dyed with indigo (shūnī).
shasshā *Vb. intensive from* shā.
shasshạbtā *Vb.* 1C (1) = shasshạutā. (2) *intensive from* shabtạ.
shasshakā *f.* = ạ cī dạ mại 1.

shassharē (1) *Vb.* 1C clinched (affair) = yaŋkẹ 1*e.*i. (2) *Vb.* 3A sun ∼ they have reached agreement.
shasshạutā *Vb.* 1C (1) cut shạsshāwạ on P., scarified P. in cupping, made small cuts in. (2) lanced (swelling).
shạsshāwạ *f.* (1) hereditary tribal-marks cut or tattooed on face or body (= askā 4), *cf.* jạrfā, ƙyạsƙyạstū. (2) yạushẹ daraṇ ya yī har ∼ takẹ ɓatạ is it right that prosperity should make you despise your friends ? (shạsshāwạ *d.f.* shā I.D).
shasshē *Vd.* shā dạ.
shạsshẹkā *f.* panting, gasping (= hạkī).
shata A. (shạtā) (1) *Vb.* 2 (*p.o.* shạcē, *n.o.* shạci) combed (hair) = shācẹ 1*b.* (2) *f.* mạganạn naṇ ∼ cẹ this is mere surmise.
B. (shātạ) (1) *Vb.* 1A. (*a*) marked out outline of pattern, marked out ground-plan of house, playground etc. = fasạltā 1 (*in case of* kagọ *or* tsạŋgayạ, *this is done with a stick in centre with rope passed round it, to use like compasses: for* kagọ, *next operation is* fid dạ hạrsāshị, *but for* tsạŋgayạ, *is* kurtạ) = shā D.2*a, cf.* shā 4. (*b*) yā ∼ ƙaryā he told a lie = shā D.2*b.* (*c*) yā ∼ bạntē he cut out a loincloth (= yaŋkạ 1*c.*iii). (*d*) *Vd.* dāgā 1. (2) *Vb.* 3A (*a*) hadarị yā ∼ storm stretches across heavens. (*b*) *Kt.* = shācẹ 2.
C. (shātā) *f.* (1) open-work style of weaving. (2) cloth woven *as in* 1.
shataf = shatap (1) ɗanyē ∼ very moist (wood, etc.). (2) yā yi ɗanyar mạganạ ∼ he spoke in ill-considered way (*cf* ɗanyē 4).
shạ talē-talē *m.* (1) children's game, where one passes his leg over the head of another (*cf.* shallạkē) = *Sk.* iṇ kā girmā, kạ rāmạ. (2) (*a*) taking round-about route. (*b*) beating about the bush.
Shạ tạmbayạ = Shạ rụbūtū.
shạ tīƙā *Kt. m.* = shạ dụndū.
Shạtīmạ *m.* (1) a minor sạrautạ originally held by slave. (2) *Vd.* jirgī 1*b.*i.
Shatụ = Shạtu *abbreviation of name* ā'ịshatụ.

Shạtumbạr *m.* September.
shạtụnē *m.* = billē 1.
shaud’a A. (shaudạ) *Vb.* 1A an ⁓ masạ
būlālạ he has been whipped.
  B. (shạudā) *Vb.* 2 an shạudē shị dạ
būlālạ = shaudạ.
shaukạ *f.* type of gown with embroidered
back and front, mainly worn by Arabs.
*shaulạ *Ar. f.* stars in tail of Scorpio.
shaụnī *m.* procrastination (= sakacē).
shaurā = saurā.
*shạurantạ = *saụrantạ.
shauraŋ wutā *Vd.* saurā 1*f.*
shaurãrā = saurãrā.
*shạurī *Kt. m.* type of spindle (mazarī)
for cotton.
shau-shau A. (shau-shau) *used in* ạrādụ
⁓ = tarnatsā.
  B. (shạu-shạu) (1) *m., f.* = shā-
shãshā. (2) hawãyē sunã zụbā ⁓ the
tears are flowing profusely. jinī yanã
zụbā ⁓ the blood is flowing freely.
shaushạutā *Vb.* 1C *Sk.* = shasshạutā.
shaushāwạ = shasshāwạ.
shãwāgị *m.* (1) (*a*) hovering about (by P.
or bird of prey, etc.). (*b*) *Vd.* tsãrakā.
(2) anã shãwāginsạ " one has to handle
him with kid gloves ".
Shāwai (*name given child born in time of
trouble*) = Shã wụyā.
shã waŋkā *Vd.* kandạmī.
shāwarạ *Ar. f.* (*pl.* shāwạrwarī = shāwarōrī = shãwạrce-shãwạrcē). (1) (*a*)
advice. (*b*) yā bā nị ⁓ ŋ yī he advised
me to do it. (*c*) nā bi ⁓ tasạ I followed
his advice. (*d*) yā ƙi ⁓ he refused to
accept advice, insisted on following
his own course. (*e*) yā kāwō ⁓
tasạ he put forward his own view
for consideration. (*f*) ⁓ tasụ ạ kaŋ
wannaŋ their opinion on this matter.
(*g*) yā bā dạ ⁓ kaŋ wannaŋ abụ he gave
advice about this. (*h*) biŋ wannaŋ ⁓
dạ wụyā this course of action is hard.
(*j*) shāwarạ, d’aukạr d’ākị where there's
a will there's a way. (2) (*a*) deliberating,
reflection *x* kunã shāwarạr mẹnēnẹ what
are you pondering on ? (*b*) yā kāmạ
shāwạrwarin dạ ạbin dạ zai yi he
reflected on how to act. (*c*) ạbin dạ ⁓
ta bāyar the results of deliberating. (*d*)
yanã ⁓ zại yī he's thinking of doing so.

(*e*) zā ạ yi ⁓ ạ ƙārạ musụ kud’ī they will
consider the question of increasing their
salaries. (*f*) kạ yi shāwarạ kaŋ wannạŋ
reflect on this ! mun yi ⁓ ạ kaŋ
ạl'amạrinsụ we have given thought to
their affair. (*g*) bā nã cikin shāwarạ
tasạ I'm not in his confidence. (3)
decision *x* sun yi ⁓ yā kạmātạ sụ yī
they have decided that they ought to
do so. sukạ yi ⁓ bā ạ sākẹ yāƙị they
decided never again to go to war.
shāwarạrsụ tā had’u sōsăi they were
unanimous. suŋ gamạ shāwarạ ạ
kaŋ yaddạ zā sụ taimaki jūnā they came
to agreement together how best to help
one another. sun yi shāwarạ yā fi kyaụ
ạ kashẹ shi they decided to kill him.
wandạ ya yi wannaŋ shāwarạ, yā yī
tụnãnī this was a good idea. an yi ⁓ ạ
yī they've decided to do so. (4) consultation *x* nā yi matạ ⁓ I consulted
with her. (5) yā gạmu da ⁓ he was
affected (*a*) by the disease bạyạmmā
1, 2. (*b*) by discoloration of the con-
junctivæ from fever, etc. (*c*) *cf.*
danyā 3.
shāwạrākị *m.* (*pl.* shãwạrãkai) fool =
shāwạrākim Bạdau.
shãwạrcē *Vd.* shãwartạ.
shāwạrī *m.* = shāwarạ 1–4.
shāwarōrī *Vd.* shāwarạ.
shawarta A. (shãwartạ) *Vb.* 2 (*p.o.*
shãwạrcē, *n.o.* shãwạrci) *x* nā shãwạrcē
shị (1) I consulted him. (2) I advised
him (2 = shāwạrtā 2). yā shãwạrcē sụ
ạ kan yā kạmātạ sụ taimaki Iŋgilạ
(1) he consulted them on the expediency of helping England. (2) he
advised them to help England.
  B. (shāwạrtā) *Vb.* 1C (1) deliberated
on. (2) (*with dative*) advised *x* nā ⁓
masạ I advised him (= shãwạrtạ 2).
shāwạrwarī *Vd.* shāwarạ.
shāwō *Vd.* shā.
shāwụd’ā *Vb.* 1C hung T. across (shoulder,
etc.) = rātạyā.
shāwụrākị = shāwạrākị.
Shã wụyā (1) = Shāwai. (2) *Kt.* shã
wụyā = wācilạ 1.
Shạwwālụ = Shạwwạl *m.* (1) name of a
Muslim month. (2) *Vd.* sallạ 1*d, f.*
shāyạ (1) *f.* (*a*) = binjimā. (*b*) = gịrkē.

(c) children's game with water-lilies (= Kt. sạrdō). (d) Purple Glossy Starling (*Lamprocolius purpureus*). (2) Vb. 1A Kt. = shātạ 1.

shāyad dạ = shā dạ.

shạ̈'ye-shạ̈yē" m. (1) onions boiled whole, with rōmō made of ground-nuts. (2) repeated drinking x (a) shāye-shāyaŋ Kirsịmatị sun rūɗẹ shị the Christmas libations had " put him off his stroke ". (b) shạ̈'ye-shạ̈yan dạ akẹ wạ gallā, bā ạ̈ wạ zumạ don't reckon without your host ! (c) Vd. dạgarạ.

shayi A. (shạ̈yī) m. (1) (a) misgiving. (b) duk dūnīyạ, Ịblịs kawại sukẹ shạ̈yī ạ kạn rashịŋ īmānị in the whole universe they are second to none but Satan in evil. (c) Vd. ƙūnā 1b. (2) ɗan ∼ m. (pl. 'yan ∼) circumcised boy (cf. shāyị).
B. (shāyị) m. (1) (a) = shācị. (b) cf. shạ̈yī 2. (2) (Ar.) tea (= ạsshāhị = shāhị).

shạ̈ zumāmị m. (sg., pl.). (1) sugar-ant. (2) horse of flea-bitten grey colour.

*shazzị Ar. m. unreliable statement.

shēbur = shēburī m. (pl. shēburōrī) Eng. shovel (= tēbur).

shēɗā f. breathing (= numfāshī).

Shēɗaŋ = Shạitsaŋ.

shēɗarạ Kt. = sạɗarạ.

shēdarī m. mat of reeds, grass, or gigịnyạ (for curtain or sitting on).

shēɗẹ Vb. 3A. (1) was delayed immeasurably. (2) kākācị yā ∼ the joke went too far.

shedi A. (shēdī) m. (1) any pattern x zanẹ mại ∼ patterned cloth. *(2) = *shạidī.
B. (shēdị) Eng. m. railway goodsshed, where goods are received or dispatched.

shēfẹ m. being mainly husk with scanty grain (re rice, nōmẹ, ịburọ, etc., cf. ɓuntụ) x shịŋkāfan naŋ tā yi ∼ this rice is mainly husk.

Shēfụ = Shēhụ.

shẹ̈gā f. = shēgạntakạ.

shēgạntā Vb. 1C treated P. as a shēgẹ, called P. a shēgẹ.

shēgạntakạ f. (1) impudence, rascality. (2) ridicule x (a) yā shā ∼ he ridiculed

people. (b) yā shā ∼ = an yi masạ ∼ he was ridiculed.

shege A. (shēgẹ) m. (f. shēgīyā) pl. shēgū = *shēgunạ = Kt. shạggū = shạggā) (d.f. Ar. shaqiyy, cf. shạkīy-yị). (1) (a) bastard (= gānūwā 5 = daɗạ 1c.ii). (b) (i) tā yi cikịn ∼ she had an illegitimate child (cf. gịribtū). (ii) Vd. ɗaurayẹ 2. (c) ḳunnan ∼ = ḳunnaŋ ūwar ∼ pretending not to hear what was said x mun yi wạ lạ̈bạ̈rai ḳunnaŋ ūwar shēgẹ we turned a deaf ear to the news (i.e. as she knows all are discussing her shame, she pretends not to hear). (2) (a) impudent P., rascal. (b) shī shēgū nẹ he is a thorough rascal. (3) (a) Shēgẹ you bastard ! (an abusive term actionable in Muslim courts), Vd. gịribtū ; hạrāmīyạ 2, fạrkā 2c. (b) cf. shẹ̈gē 3. (4) ∼ kạ̈ fāsạ m. = dạ nī dạ kai, kōwā yạ fāsạ, shēgẹ nē (a) tsạkānịnsụ ∼ kạ̈ fāsạ there is bitter enmity between them (= macịjī 1a.ii). (b) = 5 below. (5) ∼ kạ̈ jẹ gōnā m. bands of beads worn just below the knee by loose women (= tạ̈ka kạ hau = shakkạ 3 = bạri tantamā = shēgẹ 4b above). (6) Vd. gọ̈rā 7.
B. (shẹ̈gē) m. (1) (a) water in which furā was cooked. (b) Vd. buntsụrā 4. (2) Kt. = salạlạ. (3) ∼ ragē = shēgẹ 3a, but veiled by zaụrạncē.

shēgi ŋ shēgā m. tricking P. who has already tricked oneself.

shēhụ m. (pl. shẹ̈hụnai = shēhunạ = shēhōhī = shẹ̈hannai = Kt. shạffai = Kt. shạhhai) Ar. (1) shēhụ = shēhuŋ mālạmī deep scholar. (2) Vd. dilā 1a (3) Shēhụ (a) the ruler of Bornu. (b name for any man called Ụsmạŋ. (c na ∼ mạ̈sū ạmsā the Sokoto people (4) Ta ∼ Vd. gōdịyā 1. (5) Vd. Hōdīyọ.

shējị m. (f. shējịyā) (1) = sāri 2. (2) ∼ mại tsạyayyạ obstinate P.

shēkā f. piece of waste land inside compound.

sheƙa A. (shēƙạ). (1) Vb. 1A. (a) winnowed. (b) poured T. into vessel (= zubạ), cf. shēƙẹ 1b. (c) did well x yā ∼ naɗị he put his turban on well tā ∼ adō she has adorned herself nicely. (d) did much of x (i) yā ∼ masạ kuɗī he charged a high price fo it. **bana an ~ rūwā** we had a protracted wet season this year. **yā ~ ḳaryā** he told a whopping lie. (ii) **yā ~ dạrīyā = būshẹ** 1*e*. (iii) **yā ~ kāwạ** he laughed loudly (*Vd.* **kāwạ**). (*e*) smelled at (= **shẹ̃ḳā** 1*a q.v.*). (*ee*) *Vd.* **tābạ** 1*d*. (*f*) (*with dative*). (i) **yā ~ masạ rūwā** he splashed, poured water on it. (ii) **yā ~ masạ mārị** he slapped him (= **shẹ̃ḳẹ** 1*c*). (2) *Vb.* 3A **yā ~ dạ gudu = yā ~ ạ gujẹ** he took to his heels. **sun shẹ̃ḳạ cikiŋ gạrī** they fled into the town. **yā shẹ̃ḳō ạ gujẹ** he rushed up hither.

B. (**shẹ̃ḳā**) (1) *Vb.* 2. (*a*) smelḷed at (= **shẹ̃ḳạ** 1*e*), *cf.* **jī** 4B. (*b*) **nā shẹ̃ḳi numfāshinsạ** I've become accustomed to him. (2) *f.* (*a*) act of inhaling *x* **yā yi ~ uku** he took three puffs (of tobacco). (3) *f.* (*pl.* **shẹ̃ḳunạ**) (*a*) nest (= *Sk.* **gijẹ**). (*b*) (*playfully*) **zạŋ kōmạ shẹ̃ḳāta** I'll be off home now! (= **ḳurfī** 1*b*). (4) **gōrọ yā yi ~** the kola-nut has a hole where the worm entered and went out, but is not damaged elsewhere. (5) **wutsīyạr dōkị tā yi ~** the horse's tail has a natural tangle (*considered lucky*). (6) *Vd.* **shẹ̃ḳar kurcīyā.**

shẹ̃ḳad dạ *Vb.* 4 (1) poured away. (2) threw away (several things) = **zubad dạ.**

shekara A. (**shẹ̃ḳarạ**) (1) *f.* (*pl.* **shẹ̃ḳạrū**) (*a*) year. (*b*) **Bạlārabīyar ~** year of 354 days (*cf.* **bạbbāwạ**). (*c*) (i) **shẹ̃ḳarạrḳạ nawạ = shẹ̃ḳaruŋḳạ nawạ** how old are you? (ii) **yanā dạ shẹ̃ḳarạ 14, ụbansạ ya mutu** when he was 14 years old, his father died. (iii) **yā bā nị shẹ̃ḳarạ uku** he is three years older than I am. (*d*) **shẹ̃ḳạrunsạ suŋ kai** he's in his prime (20–30 years old) (= **kai** 1*a*.vii). (*e*) **~ tasạ shidạ cikin sōjạ = ~ tasạ shidạ yanā sōja** he has been six years in the army. (*f*) (i) **shẹ̃ḳạrunsạ na haifụ̄wā** (= **shẹ̃ḳạrunsạ dạ haifụ̄wā**) **ạshirin nẹ** he's 20 years old. **yạu shẹ̃ḳạrum birnī 1,000 dạ kafạ̄wā** it is 1,000 years since the town was founded. (ii) **shẹ̃ḳạrunsạ ạshirin ạ sạrautạ** he's been ruling for 20 years. (*g*) years since, ago *x* **yạu ~ dạrī** (= **yạu ~ dạrī kẹ naŋ**) **sukẹ riḳe dạ ḳasạr** they have been in

possession of the country for 100 years. **yạu shẹ̃ḳarạ uku kẹ naŋ dạ ta zō** it is 3 years since she came. **ita cẹ̃ sukạ kāmạ ta, shẹ̃ḳarạ 3 kẹ̃ naŋ** she is the one whom they captured 3 years ago. **tun rạn dạ ya kāmạ ni, yạu shẹ̃ḳarạta uku kẹ̃ naŋ** it is 3 years since he captured me. **gạriŋ, yạu shẹ̃ḳarạrsạ 1,000 dạ ginạ̄wā** the town is 1,000 years old. **shẹ̃ḳarạ hạmsiŋ kẹ̃ naŋ sunā bugạ jạrīdạ** they have been printing the newspaper for 50 years. **ạbin dạ ka yi, shẹ̃ḳarạ shidạ dạ sukạ wucẹ** what you did six years ago. **tun shẹ̃ḳarạ ạlfyaŋ dạ sukạ wucẹ** since the last 2,000 years. **yạu shẹ̃ḳarạ gōmạ dạ akạ gan sụ, sại . . .** when they were seen 25 years ago, then . . . (*Vd.* **tun** 1*b*, **yạu** 1*c*, **wucẹ** 1*c*.ii). (*h*) *Vd.* **bana** 2*b*, **dāḳị** 8. (*j*) **~ kwānā cẹ̃** in dạ rạ̈i gạba delay doesn't matter provided success follows. (*k*) **~ bā tạ̃ fāḍụ̄wā sại ạ jiḳạ** time leaves its mark on one. (*l*) **hanyạr lāfịyạ, bị ta dạ ~** the longest way round is the shortest way home. (*m*) **~ dạ shẹ̃ḳạrū** during years and years. **tun ~ dạ shẹ̃ḳạrū** since a long time. (*n*) time of the year *x* **in ~ tā yi kusa ta fid dạ zạkā** if the season for paying tithes approaches. (*o*) **ɗan ~ tạḷātin nẹ̃** he's 30 years old (*f.* **'yar ~ 30 cẹ̃**) *pl.* **'yan ~ 30 nẹ̃.** (*p*) **shẹ̃ḳạrum bāya a** few years ago. (*q*) (i) **ạ cikin 'yan shẹ̃ḳạrun naŋ** in the last few years. (ii) **tun 'yan shẹ̃ḳạrun naŋ sukẹ̃ ta aiḳị** they've been working for the last few years. (*r*) (*in dates,* **shẹ̃ḳarạ** *can be omitted*) *x* **aŋ haịfē shị cikin 1880** he was born in the year 1880. (2) *Vb.* 3A. (*a*) (i) spent a year *x* **baŋ ḳārạ ganintạ ba sại dạ akạ shẹ̃ḳarạ uku** I did not see her again till after 3 years. (ii) **ạ ~ sāran rūwā, sại tạmfạtsē** he's in too firm a position to be harmed by slander. (*b*) = **shẹ̃ḳarē.**

B. (**Shẽkạra**) name given girl supposed to have been a year in the womb (*cf.* **kwạntaccē, Shẽkạrau**).

shẽkaraŋ cittạ *adv.* five days hence (*Vd.* **shẽkarẹ**).

shẽkaraŋ gōbe *Zar.* *adv.* day after tomorrow (= **jībi**), *Vd.* **shẽkarẹ.**

shēkaraŋ jīya *adv.* the day before yesterday (*Vd.* shēkarę).

shēkara tsaye *Kt. m.* = bāba rǫdō *q.v. under* bāba 8.

Shēkarau name given boy supposed to have been a year in the womb (*cf.* kwantaccē, Shēkara).

shēkar da = shēkad da.

shekare A. (shēkarē) *Vb.* 3A (nomad Filani) spent wet season (= shēkara 2*b*).

B. (shēkarę) *Vd.* waŋ ∼, shēkaraŋ.

shēkar kurcīyā *f.* = kujērā 4.

shēkę (1) *Vb.* 1A (*a*) winnowed completely (*cf.* shēka). (*b*) poured out money, kolas, etc., on to the ground (*cf.* shēka 1*b*). (*c*) yā ∼ shi da māri = shēka 1*f.*ii. (2) *Vb.* 3A (*a*) (boy) got out of hand. (*b*) became spilled, poured away.

shēkękē contemptuously *x* sunā dūbansa ∼ they're looking at him contemptuously.

shēkī *m.* glossiness (= walkīyā).

shēkuna *Vd.* shēka 3*a*.

shēla = shēlā *f.* (1) proclamation (= yēkūwā = kalyē = *Sk.* wākurwa). (2) an yi ∼ wai su yī = an yi shēla a kaŋ su yī proclamation was made that they do so.

shēlantā *Vb.* 1C made proclamation.

shēmā *f.* (1) an yi ∼ ground has been cleared for sowing (*Vd.* shēmę, sārā 1*j*). (2) ∼ tasa kę naŋ this is his forte (= shā da 2*b.*i).

shēmę (1) *Vb.* 1A (*a*) cleared (ground) for sowing (= sārā 1*j*, *Vd.* shēmā). (*b*) thrashed. (2) *m.* type of reed for making kyaurō.

shęmęmę *used in* yā kwantā ∼ he lay sprawled out.

shera A. (shēra) *Vb.* 1A yā ∼ karyā he told a lie.

B. (shērā) (1) *Vb.* 2 *x* tā shērē ni her appearance was attractive to me. (2) *f. x* yā yi ∼ yau he has dressed himself very attractively to-day.

shērārę *m.* (1) mistake. (2) fault of conduct, misdemeanour.

shęrayya *Kt. f.* = sā n sā.

shērę *Vd.* shērā.

shēri = fędē 1.

shęshē *m.* the flute sarēwa.

Shętsaŋ = Shaitsaŋ.

shętsara *Kt. f.* = sadara.

Shetu = Shatu.

shēwa *f.* (1) (*a*) loud laughter of women *x* tā rafka ∼ she laughed loudly (*cf.* kāwa). (*b*) tūsa tā kārę a bōdari sǎi ∼ evil P. is at end of his tether. (2) *Kt.* yanā ∼ he is whistling (= fītǫ). (3) shēwar dilā dispersing of several persons.

shę'we-shęwē" *m.* = shēwa.

shi A. (shī) (1) (*independent pronoun,* Mod. Gram. 46) he *x* (*a*) (i) wānēnę who is it ? (*reply*) shī nę it is he. ī, da shī yes, there is some. bābu shī no, there is none (*both in reply to* is there any water ?, *i.e. a masculine noun*), *cf.* ita. (ii) shī nę . . . *i.e.* (*b*) (*used as direct object when dative precedes,* Mod. Gram. 76*a.*ii[3]) *x* yā karantā mini shī he read it to me. (3) = shin. (4) *Sk.* (*a*) = ya yi *x* Alla (= Alā) shī maka albarka God bless you ! (*b*) *Vd.* albarka 1. (5) shī kę naŋ *Vd.* kę 3, 4, 6.

B. (shi) (1) (*objective pronoun after low tone in previous verb,* Mod. Gram. 49*a*[1]) him *x* nā kāma shi I seized him (*cf.* shi). (2) *Vd.* shikę. (3) (*3rd sg. masc. pronoun used after* za Mod. Gram. 17, *and* ba Mod. Gram. 19*b*) *x* za shi kāsūwā he's off to the market. ba shi zūwa he's not coming.

C. (shi) (1) (*objective pronoun after high tone in previous verb,* Mod. Gram. 49*a*[1]) him *x* nā gan shi I saw him (*cf.* shi). (2) *Sk.* = ya (Mod. Gram. 13) *x* sǎi shi zō let him come ! (3) = sa 1*a* (Mod. Gram. 47*b*) *x* dōkinshi = dōkinsa his horse. (4) *Sk.* ba shi *sometimes* = bai (Mod. Gram. 20*a*) *Vd. example in* kama 4.

D. (shi) *Sk.* = ya (Mod. Gram. 118) *x* shi zō he'll probably come.

shiɓa *m.* (1) teasing cotton with bakan shiɓa (*Vd.* baka 10). (2) cotton *so teased* (= rūwa B.19). (3) (*a*) bā a gama wutā da ∼ oil and water won't mix. (*b*) yā mai da sū kamar wutā da shiɓa he brought them to loggerheads with each other (= annabi 3). (4) tāka ∼ *Vd.* Agaddabū.

shibce A. (shibcę) *Vb.* 1A. (1) cut off
much *x* yā ∼ cīyāwą he cut much grass
(*cf.* shibtą). (2) *x* yā ∼ hannunsą dą
wuƙā he cut him severely in the hand
(= shibtą 1*b*).
B. (shibcē) *Vd.* shibtā.
shibcēcę = shabcēcę.
shibci A. (shibcį) *Kt. m.* (*pl.* shifąttā =
shifittai). (1) = shūcį. (2) what a
severe cut! (*cf.* shibcę 2). (3) shibcįŋ
gizǫ = shiftāmą.
B. (shibci) *Vd.* shibtā.
shibką *Sk.* = shūką.
shīɓōlį, *Kt.* (1) *m.* the shrub Grewia
(= ƙāƙąyā). (2) = ƙąbąrą.
shibrā *Sk.* = shūrā 2.
shibta A. (shibtą) (1) *Vb.* 1A (*a*) did much
of *x* yā ∼ mantūwā he is (was) very
forgetful. yā ∼ ƙaryā he told whopping
lie (*cf.* shibcę). (*b*) yā ∼ masą wuƙā ą
hannū = shibcę 2. (2) *Vb.* 3A yā ∼
yā tąfi he raced away. yā shibtō yā
tafō he came here at great speed. (3)
f. yā bā nį ∼ he dictated T. for me to
copy down.
B. (shibtā *Vb.* 2 (*p.o.* shibcē, *n.o.*
shibci). (1) = shibcę 1. (2) tā shibci
tūwō (*a*) she served up much tūwō.
(*b*) she ate much tūwō. tā shibtar maną
tūwō she served us with much tūwō
(*cf.* gutsųrā).
shibtą-shibtā *f.* = shiftāmą.
shidą = *Sk.* shiddą *f.* (1) six *x* mųtųm ∼
six persons. (2) na ∼ *m.* (*f.* ta ∼)
pl. na ∼ sixth.
shīda *Sk. Vb.* 3A dismounted, arrived at,
lodged at (= sąuka = *Sk.* jīɗa).
B. (shīdā) *f.* (1) wata ∼ tā ɗaukē nį
I felt trepidation. (2) *Sk.* (*a*) lack of
judgment. (*b*) (*v.n. and progressive of*
shīda) *x* yaną ∼ ą gidāna he's lodging
at my house.
shīdad dą *Vb.* 4 *Sk.* = sąuƙā 1*b*.i, saukad
dą 2.
shidānī *Kt. m.* = shidąnīyā.
shidąnīyā *f.* sixth finger or toe (= cindǫ
1 = ɗąŋgōlī = handūwā 2).
shiddą *Vd.* shidą.
shiddānī *Kt. m.* = shidąnīyā.
shīdę *Vb.* 3A (1) ceased *x* numfāshinsą
yā ∼ his breath ceased, *i.e.* he died.
(2) yā ∼ he (trumpeter, P. crying, etc.)

emitted long-drawn sound (= siƙę
1*c* = numfāshī 2*a*).
shifādų *m.* = sųfādų.
shifąttā *Vd.* shibci.
shifcę = shibcę.
shifci = shibci.
shifī-shifī = shifit-shifit *used in* yā tsirō
∼ it (young corn) sprouted abundantly.
shifittai *Vd.* shibci.
shifką *Kt.* = shūką.
shiftāmą (1) ill-considered speech (ɗanyar
mąganą) or act (= shibci 3). (2) *m., f.*
(*sg., pl.*) tactless P.
shiftā-shiftā *f.* = shiftāmą.
shiga A. (shiga) *Vb.* 3B (*but also has
transitive sense*) (*for progressive Vd.*
shigā). (1) (*a*) (i) entered. (ii) put on
(clothing) *x* yā ∼ yauƙī he dressed in
silk. yā shiga kāyan sōją he put on
uniform (= są C.1), *Vd.* burtū 2, shigā
1*c*, dąfā ni. (*b*) *x* (i) tā ∼ gōnā = tā ∼
cikiŋ gōnā she entered the farm. yā ∼
ɗāki = yā ∼ cikin ɗāki he entered
the house (= shigę 2*c*). (ii) yā ∼
birninsą = shigę 2*e*. (iii) yā shiga
tāwāyę he entered on revolt. (iv)
yā shiga gąbam mutānē he assumed the
leadership. (v) yā shiga jarrąbāwā
he entered for examination. (vi)
ą shiga īyąkar wuyą *Vd.* ąlhaƙī 1*f.*
(vii) zā mų są yą shiga sirdį we will
bring him to his senses. (viii) an yi
masą " shigō, shigō, bą zurfī ! " they
" led him on ". (ix) tā shigō gidā
she's reached puberty. (*x*) ∼ bąŋgō
Vd. bąŋgō 4. (xi) yā ∼ dūnīyą he
went abroad. (*c*) yā ∼ hannummų
it came into our possession. yā shiga
hannū it has come into our possession.
(*cc*) bazarā tā shigō the hot season came.
(*d*) ƙāƙą zai ∼ cikin ząncē how is it
(expression, word) used? (*e*) yā ∼
tsąkānī he took a hand in the affair,
he interposed. (*f*) yā ∼ cinikī he
began trading (*cf. k below*). (*g*) (i) yā ∼
uƙu he has got into difficulties, he is in
a dilemma (*cf.* shigā 2*a*). (ii) shigā
uƙu, kąman na gwaurō dą yąyē *is
epithet of* shigā uƙu. (iii) shigā uƙu
gąrēshi he's a busybody. (*h*) *Vd.*
duhūwą 2. (*j*) arrived *x* gōbe yaną
shigōwā he'll arrive to-morrow (=

iso̱ = sa̱uka 1b.i). (k) began to (cf. (f) above) x yā ∽ rawar ji̱ki̱ he began to tremble. yā shi̱ga habaici̱, ya cẹ̈ ... he began to drop hints that ... maḵẹ̄rā sun ∽ gyārạ maḵạ̄mai the smiths have begun to repair weapons. (1) Vd. shi̱ga-compounds, shi̱gar-compounds. (m) Vd. shi̱gā 2c. (n) (with dative (i) yā shigam musụ he entered them (a crowd). (ii) yā shigam musụ = yā shigam musụ dạ bugu he attacked them with blows. (iii) yā shigam mini̱ ḏāki̱ he entered my house (= shigẹ 2f). (2) nā ∽ da shī I agree to it. (3) shi̱ga tạffā Mālạm = shi̱ga atạfā Mālạm (said jokingly for gāfạrtā 2a). (4) ∽ zūcī Vd. I̱kkō.

B. (shi̱gā) (1) f. (a) (v.n. and progressive of shi̱ga) x (i) yanạ̈ shi̱gā he is entering. yanạ̈ shi̱gā ḏāki̱ = yanạ̈ shi̱gar ḏāki̱ = yanạ̈ shi̱gā cikin ḏāki̱ he's entering the house. (ii) ∽ rāmi̱n kūrā bạ na ḵaramin gardi̱ ba nẹ̈ don't attempt what is beyond you ! (iii) bạ shi̱gar rāmi̱n kūrā Vd. kūrā 25a. (b) act of entering x (i) ba̱n ga ∽ tasạ ba I did not see him enter. (ii) bạ a san shigarkạ ba Vd. sạndī. (iii) shirin shi̱gā ḏārī preparations for wintering. (iv) yā sạ̄mi ∽ he has got into favour : he has managed to get audience with judge or senior to present his petition or complaint. (v) cf. ta̱yā ni ∽. (c) appearance x (i) yā yi ∽ mai kya̱u he has dressed himself well (cf. shi̱ga 1a.ii). (ii) tā sākẹ ∽ her appearance has changed (= shigē = ka̱mā 3a). (iii) ∽ tasụ ḏayā they closely resemble one another (= ka̱mā 1e = shigē). (d) turn x shi̱gāta kẹ̈ nan it is my turn (= kāmụ 4). (e) Vd. shi̱gar-compounds. (2) Vb. 2 (a) yā shi̱gē sụ = shi̱ga 1g.i (sụ refers to ukụ). (b) has visited (place) x nā shi̱gi Kano sa̱u ḏayā I've been to Kano once. (c) has lived in x gidan na̱n, nā shi̱gē shi̱ (= nā shi̱ga gidan na̱n) tu̱n watạ ukụ I have been living in this house for three months. (d) Vd. sọ̄ki 2.

C. (shīgạ) = sīga.

shigad dạ Vb. 4 (1) caused to enter x

nā ∽ shī = nā shigasshē shi̱ I caused him to enter. yā ∽ shī cikin ạkwạ̄ti̱ he inserted it in the box. (2) mẹ̈ ya ∽ ni̱ = Sk. mi̱sh shigasshē ni̱ what business is it of mine ? (= rūwā G.1).

shi̱gā hanci̱ dạ ḵu̱du̱ndu̱nē m. annoying persistence x mun yi masạ shi̱gā hanci̱ dạ ḵu̱du̱ndu̱nē we attacked him like a whirlwind.

shigam Vd. shi̱ga 1n.

shigar dạ = shigad dạ.

shi̱gar gi̱ji̱ f. Vd. gi̱ji̱ 5.

shi̱gar mai gāgā Vd. rūwā A. 16c.

shi̱gar ma̱kāfo̱ ko̱gī Vd. ḵu̱ndu̱mbālā.

shi̱gā sharo̱ bạ shānū f. meddlesomeness (= ka̱ramba̱nī).

shi̱gar shirgi̱ f. (1) meddlesomeness (= ka̱ramba̱nī). (2) meddlesome P., busy-body.

shi̱gar 'yam mātạn amạ̄rē f. entering of a number of people into presence of superior in a crowd instead of in file.

shi̱gar zōmō Vd. zōmō 10.

shi̱'ga-shi̱gā'' f. meddlesomeness (= ka̱ramba̱nī).

shigasshē Vd. shigad dạ.

shi̱gau m. = shi̱gēgẹ.

shige A. (shigẹ) (1) Vb. 3A passed by x ya̱nzu nẹ̈ sukạ ∽ they passed by just now (= wucẹ). (2) Vb. 1A (a) passed beyond (place). (b) (i) exceeded. (ii) yā yi ∽ makạdī dạ rawā he exceeded his powers, arrogated to himself status of his superior. (c) entered x yā ∽ ḏāki̱ he entered the house (= shi̱ga 1b.i). (cc) passed through x (i) sun shigẹ shi̱ suluf they passed clean through it (town). (ii) mun shigẹ wạtạnnin nan we passed through those months. (d) went deeply into x kibīya̱ tā ∽ cikin ji̱kinsạ the arrow deeply pierced his body. (e) (i) yā ∽ birninsạ he's in congenial company (= shi̱ga 1b.ii). (ii) Vd. Dạ̄lā 2c ; birnī 4. (f) yā ∽ mini̱ ḏāki̱ he entered my house (= shi̱ga 1n.iii). (g) a̱bi̱n yā shigẹ manạ duhụ the affair mystifies us.

B. (shigē) m. (1) gusset(s) let into gown to make lower part wider than upper. (2) yā yi matạ ∽ he crept into her house to get her to lie with him (*cf.* fạdē).

C. shigē *m.* (1) appearance = shigā 1*c q.v.* (2) shigyan *prep.* like (= kạman).

shigēgę *m.* P. following non-hereditary trade ; intruder (= bạrē 1*b* = sạri dǫsa 2 = *Sk.* tsịrgē), *cf.* hạdākā 2.

shigen (shigyan) *Vd.* shigē 2.

shi'ge-shigē" *m.* = shiga-shigā.

shiggạba *Kt.* = shūgạba.

shiggai *Kt. m.* = shịgē 1.

shịgi dạ fịci *m.* (1) restlessness. (2) mischief-making (= kinibĪbị).

shịgifạ *f.* (*pl.* shịgifū = shigifōfĪ = shịgifai) (1) *Kt. Vd.* sōrō 2. (2) *Zar.* = shịrāyĪ.

shigō *Vd.* shịga.

shigyan *Vd.* shigē 2.

shikạ (1) *Vb.* 1A = sakị 1, sạkā. (2) *m.* (*a*) (*sec. v.n.* of sạkā) yanạ̃ shikạm bindigạ = yanạ̃ sạkar bindigạ he's firing the rifle (*Vd.* sạkā 2*a*) = sakị 2*c*. (*b*) becoming loose *x* tūwō yā yi ∼ = sakị 1*b*.ii. kujērā tā yi ∼ = sakị 1*b*.iii. (*c*) = sakị 2*a*. (3) *Vd.* shikạ-*compounds*, shik ạn-*compounds*.

shĪkạ (1) *f.* (*a*) wini)wing. (*aa*) shĪkạd dakạ *Vd.* dakạ 4. (*b*) bạkin ∼ *m.* poor grains, perquisite of the winnower (= gạban shĪkạ), *cf.* zubǫ 2, bạkiŋ wukā. (*c*) (i) roving (= gĪlǫ). (ii) shĪkạl lạbādĪyạ roving. (*d*) *Vd.* tạrĪ 2. (2) what fine quality !

shikạ battạ = *shikạ battị = shikạm battạ *q.v.*

shikạm bạkĪ *m.* fractious ways of spoiled child (= kyaŋkyạntā).

shikạm battạ *m.* (*Ar.* albattata entirely) divorcing wife by saying three times nā sạkē kị, it then being impossible by Muslim law to remarry her till she has married and been divorced by another (= sakị 2*a*.ii), *Vd.* aurē 3.

shikạm fuskạ *m.* having a jovial expression, behaving in unconstrained way (*Vd.* sạkā 2*e*).

*shikạ rạji'Ī *m.* divorce revoked before woman's second hailā, when it would come into force.

shịkạ rēshę, kạmạ ganyē *m.* = sakị 2*f*.

shịkāshịkai *Vd.* shisshikę.

shikē *Sk.* = yakē *x* ạbịn dạ ∼ yĪ what he is doing (Gram. 133*a**).

shĪ kę naŋ *Vd.* kę 3,4,6.

shịkĪkị = shạkĪkị.

shịkimị (*playfully said*) = kịshimị.

shịkiŋkịmĪ *m.* (*f.* shịkiŋkịmā) *pl.* shịkiŋkịmai loony, dolt (*epithet is* ∼ yā fi mahaụkạcĪ wụyar māgạnĪ).

shikkạ *Kt.* = shūkạ.

shilạ *f.* (*pl.* shilōlĪ) (1) young pigeon (*Vd.* lūtsā). (2) dan ∼ *m.* (*f.* 'yar ∼) *pl.* 'yan shilōlĪ = 1. (3) *Vd.* cilạ.

shillạ = cillạ.

shillǫ = *Kt.* shịllō *m.* swinging, dangling, hanging down (= lĪlǫ = rētǫ).

shimạggā *Vd.* shiŋgē.

shịmāgǫ *m.* (1) huge P. or T. (2) shịmāgwaŋ kāyā huge load (*x* of grass, etc.), *cf.* shịmị.

shimfidạ A. (shimfịdā) *Vb.* 1C (1) (*a*) spread (mat, etc.). (*b*) gāra shimfịdạ fuskạ dạ shimfịdạ tạbarmā it's better to be welcomed than received grudgingly. (*c*) kōwā ka ganĪ dạ daŋ kēsạnsạ, wurin shimfịdāwā yakē nēmā don't mistake a dangerous person for one in want ! (2) founded *x* yā shimfịdạ mulkị he established rule. yā shimfịdạ makarantā he founded a school (= kafạ). (3) did much of *x* yā shimfịdạ nōmā he did much farming. (4) *Kt.* an ∼ masạ danyaŋ kirgị he's been deceived and led into trouble.

B. (shịmfidạ) *f.* (*pl.* shịmfịdū = shimfidōdĪ = shịmfịde-shịmfịdē) (1) (*a*) (i) A. spread out (mat, mattress, etc.). (ii) kun ji shịmfịdạr ạl'amạrĪ you've heard the details of the affair. (*b*) bạ zaŋ shā ba sǎi nā yi ∼ I won't drink till I've had something to eat. (*c*) rūwā SarkĪ nę, bā yạ̃ zamā sǎi dạ ∼ *epithet of* water. (*d*) wạndạ ya wucę ∼ tasạ dạ tsayạ̃wā, yā rasạ ạbịn kusa bạllē na nēsạ be satisfied with what you've got ! (2) = jạkĪ 2. (3) 'yan ∼ (*only pl.*) peddlars (= 'yaŋ kōlị = mashịmfịdā).

shimfide A. (shịmfidē) *m.* = shạfē 3.

B. (shimfịdē) *Vb.* 1C = shimfịdā 1*a*, 2.

shimfidēdę *m.* (*f.* shimfidēdĪyạ) *pl.* shimfidā-shịmfịdạ̃ extensive.

shimge A. (shimgē) *Kt. m. (pl.* shim**ą̄**gā = shim**ąggā**) = shiŋgē.
 B. (shimgē) = shiŋgē.
shimi A. (shimi) = himi.
 B. (shimī) *Eng. f.* (1) chemise. (2) woman's short jumper with pleated top *(is of* tagūwā *type).*
shimįlī = himįlī.
shimiryā = shimuryā *f.* raft consisting of two gourds joined by plank.
shiŋ = shiŋ I wonder *x* ~ dą̄ rūwą̄ ? I wonder whether there's any water ? ~, Jāmus mę̄ sukę̄ cikī nę̄ I wonder what the Germans are up to ?
shina A. (shiną̄) = yaną̄ *x* shiną̄ zūwą he is coming (Gram. 16).
 B. (shiną) (1) *Vb. (only used in this form and no object must be expressed after it) x* ī, nā shiną yes, I know ! *(Vd.* sanį). (2) *m.* knowledge (= sanį 2*b*.i).
shinākā *Sk. f.* type of thatching-grass.
shinąn shānū = sanį 2*b*.v.
shiŋgālīyą *f.* roving (= gīlọ).
shinge A. (shiŋgē) *m. (pl.* shiŋgąigai = shiŋgą̄yē = shiŋgōgī = *Kt.* shimąggā = *Kt.* shimą̄gā) (1) fence round farm, etc. *(cf.* gānūwā 2). (2) *(a)* Audu shiŋgyammu nē Audu is our protector. *(b)* shiŋgyam Masąr yā bū̄wą̄yi Jāmus kētą̄wā the Germans were unable to break into Egypt. (3) abūbūwąn nąn sū nę̄ itātūwąŋ shiŋgē na ząmānį these things are the features of modern life.
 B. (shiŋgę) *Vb.* 1A fenced (farm, etc.).
 C. (shiŋgē) *Sk., Kt. m. (sg., pl.)* winged termite(s) = ginā 2*a,b.*
shiŋgī *m.* (1) remainder (= saurā). (2) *x* ~ kądaŋ yą mutu he nearly died (= saurā 2*d*).
shiŋgilwą *f.* elder sister under influence of younger one *(cf.* shiŋgilwancī).
shiŋgilwancī *m.* roaming about for gossip or fornication *(cf.* shiŋgilwą).
shinį *Nor.* = shiną.
shininnikī *m.* sloth, dilatoriness.
shį'ni-shįnī" *m. (used negatively) x* kō ~ bā ni dą shī I have none at all. kō shįnishįnin zūwą bąi yi ba there's no sign of him coming.

shiŋkāfā *f.* (1) *(a)* (i) rice. (ii) fądamą shiŋkāfā paddy-field. *(b)* kōwā yą ci shiŋkāfar rąncē, tāsą ya ci borrowing is only putting off the evil day *(Vd.* rąncē 2*b*). *(c)* bą̄ darē gą mąi ~, sąi dąi rashįŋ ąbiŋ wutā if one has means other difficulties are trivial. *(d* wą̄ ką̄ rabą ~ *Vd.* ƙuƙus. (2) woman's staining teeth and then removing stain with slithering movement (dirję̄) by sand so that only sides of teeth are left coloured *(cf.* sāraŋ kọ̄fatọ 2).
shiŋkau *(m. and adv.) x* (1) itą̄cē yā yi ~ = itą̄cē yā būshę̄ ~ the tree is almost dried up. (2) yā yi ~ he's about to faint, collapse.
shiŋƙim = jiŋƙim.
shiŋƙimēmę̄ *m. (f.* shiŋƙimēmīyā) *pl.* shiŋƙim-shiŋƙim very heavy.
shiŋkiŋƙiŋ *m.* heaviness *x* kāyan nąŋ ~ dą shī this load is very heavy.
shiŋkiŋkimī *m. (f.* shiŋkiŋkimā) weak-minded P.
shiŋkitą̄-shiŋkitā *f.* = shįftāmą.
shiŋkitįmbau *m.* = shįftāmą.
shiŋkitįhū *Kt. m.* = shįftāmą.
shiŋku = shuŋku.
shinshimēmę̄ *m. (f.* shinshimēmīyā) *pl.* shinshim-shįnshim huge.
shinshimī *m. (f.* shinshimā) *pl.* shinshim-shįnshįm huge.
shintąlī = sintąlī.
shipcę̄ = shibcę̄.
shipką = shūką.
shiptą = shibtą.
shirą *Kt. f.* guinea-corn heads poor in corn *(cf. Kt.* bū̄sau 2).
shirąyī *m.* (1) mud-walled, thatched rectangular house (= *Zar.* shigifą). (2) *Vd.* ką̄fē.
shirɓa = sharɓa.
shirɓą̄cē *m.* acting or speaking senselessly.
shirɓaŋ = sharaf.
shirbicī = shirbucī = shįftāmą *q.v.*
shirɓuŋ = sharaf.
shirɓunā *Vb.* 1C *(with dative) x* nā ~ masą mąi = nā shirɓuną mąi ą jikinsą I rubbed oil on his body.
shirɓunē *Vb.* 1C *x* nā ~ shi dą mąi = shirɓunā.
shirɓuni what a lot of oil has been rubbed in ! *(cf.* shirɓunā).

shirga A. (shirgạ) (1) Vb. 1A did much of x (a) an ∼ masạ kāyā he's been given (i) a huge load to carry. (ii) many presents. (b) an ∼ masạ kudī (i) he has been overcharged. (ii) big sum has been charged for it. (c) an ∼ masạ sạndā he has been thrashed. (2) Vb. 3A yā ∼ ạ gụje he took to his heels. B. (shịrgā) Vb. 2 did much of x (1) an shịrgē shị dạ sạndā = shirgạ 1c. (2) yā shịrgi kāyā he carried a huge load. yā shịrgi barcī he slept a lot.

hirgẹ Vb. 1A piled up.

hirgị (1) m. large amount, pile. (b) large collection x shirgịn lịttạttạfai bookshelf. (c) fool. (2) adv. abundantly x gạ̈ kāyā ∼ what a lot of stuff! (3) shirgị what a lot of stuff! (4) shịgar ∼ f. (a) meddlesomeness (= kạrạmbạnī). (b) busybody. (5) Vd. rụmfā 6.

hirgīyā f. (1) pile of the wood collected in clearing farm. (2) piles of stones for throwing down on enemy. (3) = tọtsīyā 3. *(4) in pause (wakạfī), inserting Arabic letter wāw in red ink, after previous short "u", the latter being indicated in red by two "u" signs over the consonant x in the sentence lahu mā fi'ssamāwāti, the wāw is written in red between lahu and mā and two red small wāw are written over -h of -hu.

hiri A. (shirị) m. (1) (a) preparing to x (i) yanạ̈ shirịn sallạ he's getting ready to pray. (ii) shirịn zạune yā fi na tsạye the prospect of rest is more alluring than the prospect of work. (iii) gāra mụ zaunạ dạ ∼ we'd better be prepared! sụ zaunạ dạ ∼ let them remain on the alert! (aa) aikịn shirịn sōjạ the work of training soldiers. (b) being about to x dạ̈ ạbin dạ nakẹ ∼ ŋ gayạ mukụ kẹ̈ naŋ it is just what I was about to say to you. yanạ̈ shirịŋ kūkā he's about to cry. sunạ̈ shirịn yị = sunạ̈ shiri zā sụ yī they're about to do so. (2) being on good terms with x (a) bạ̈ ∼ sōsǎi tsạkāninsụ there is no proper concord between them. sunạ̈ ∼ dạ Jāmụs they are on

good terms with the Germans. rashịn shirịnsụ dạ mū the lack of cordiality between them and ourselves. tsạkāninsụ, bạ̈ shirị kō na ạnīnī they hate the sight of one another. shirị yā ƙi dādī tsạkāninsụ they did not get on well with one another. shirị sukẹ̈ yị ram they are on the best of terms. (b) tīlạs ita kẹ̈ sạ̈ shirị dạ maƙịyī needs must when the devil drives (Vd. shịryạ 3). (3) settling x shirịŋ gaddamạ settling the dispute. (4) threading (beads). (5) shirịŋ hannun rịgā adult who behaves childishly. B. (shịrì) (only used in this form) went away.

shịrīƙị = sịrīƙị.

shịrịm used in (1) gạ inūwạ ∼ look, there's some good shade! (2) ∼ nẹ̈ bạ̈ inūwạ he's prosperous but niggardly. (3) an nūnạ musụ ạshē ∼ bạ̈ shī nẹ̈ inūwạ ba it was demonstrated to them that all is not gold that glitters, that the vaunted prowess, etc., is built on sand.

shirim-shirịm adv. abundantly.

shirịŋkitạ = shịftāmạ 1, 2.

shirịŋkịtịbō = shịrịŋkịtịhū = shịrịŋkịtịmbō = shịrịŋkịtịmbau = shịftāmạ 1, 2 q.v.

shịrinyạ f. type of fig-tree which twines round and kills another (epithet is Shịrinyạ, rạ̈6i kị kashẹ̈).

shirīrịcē Vb. 3A deteriorated (cf. sharrị) = lālạ̈cē.

shịrīrịtā f. (1) (a) chicanery, double-dealing (= tạshạrẹ̈-tasharẹ̈) (epithet is Shịrīrịtā yị ta zanẹ dạ ạljīfū). (b) kōwạcẹ shịrīrịtā cẹ̈ kumā ta sạ̈mẹ̈ sụ, sǎi sukạ sākẹ shāwarạ through whatever stratagem it may have been, they changed their plans. (2) tā yi wạ zanạntạ shịrīrịtar mutūwạ she has worn out her body cloth (cf. shirīrịcē).

shirīrịtad dạ Vb. 4 rendered useless, invalidated x yā ∼ zạncaŋ he invalidated the whole matter. yā ∼ nī, ban tạfi ba his actions led to cancellation of my projected journey.

shịrịyạ (1) Katagum went away (= shịri). (2) Sk. = shịrinyạ.

shirkạ Ar. f. partnership x mun yi ∼

dạ sū ạ kạnsạ we possess it in common with them.

shirkat A. (shirkat) *used in* yanā̧ kwạnce ~ he's lying down too ill to rise.

B. (shịrkat) = shịrkit = shạrkaf *q.v.*

*shirkụ *Ar. m.* idolatry, polytheism.

shirma A. (shịrmā) *Vb.* 2 = shịrgā̧.

B. (shirmạ) = shirgạ̧.

shịrmē *m.* = shịftāmạ̧ 1.

shirū (1) *m.* (*a*) silence (= kurụm 1*a* = kawại 2). (*b*) yā yi ~ he kept silence. (*c*) ạbụ yā yi ~ no news came (*cf.* shiru-shiru 2). (*d*) sunā̧ dạ ịgwā dạ su mại rūwā sǎi ạ yi ~ they have countless artillery and machine-guns. (*e*) mun ji shirū we've heard no news. (2) well, there is nothing to be done ! (*said when insuperable obstacle arises x* defendant dying before case comes on, materials giving out before work is completed, etc.) = shī kȩ̄ naṇ. (3) *Vd.* shiru-shiru.

shiru-shiru *m.* (1) taciturnity *x* Audụ ~ gạrēshi Audu is a man of few words. (2) ~ sǎi shȩ̄karạ̧ bīyū sukạ̧ wucẹ no news (of him, etc.) was heard for two years (*cf.* shirū 1*b*). tun dạ ya tạfi har yạnzu ~ nothing has been heard of him since he went.

shirwạ *f.* (*pl.* shirwōyī) (*epithet is* Gạ̧ŋ-gạmạ sautụ = sūrau). (1) (*a*) African black kite (*Milvus migrans parasiticus*). (*b*) Ricour's or swallow-tailed kite (*Chelictinea ricourii*). (*c*) ~ bā tā̧ bạrar makōdī sǎi dạ. tsōkạr nāmạ̧ ạ jịkinsạ̧ nobody acts without good reason. (*d*) kạ̧zā mại 'yā'yā ita kȩ̄ gudụn ~ the P. of property is the one who hates risks. (*e*) ɗan zạkarạ̧ wạndạ̧ zại yi cārā, ~ bā tā̧ ɗaukạ̧ let the cobbler stick to his last ! (*f*) *Vd.* dạ̧fū. (2) dark dun horse. (3) energetic, agile P. (3) dạngịn ~ *m.* tyrant. *(4) *Sk.* ɗam bā̧ ~ = mazā̧wō̧yiṇ kā̧sūwā. (5) *Vd.* wutsīyạr ~

shirya A. (shiryạ̧) *Vb.* 1A (1) (*a*) prepared T. (*b*) kụ ~ make your preparations ! (2) (*a*) arranged T. (*b*) arranged to *x* nā̧ shiryạ̧ dạ zạn tạfi I have arranged to go. (3) (*a*) settled quarrel or affair *x* yā shiryạ̧ = yā ~ tsạkāninsụ he recon-

ciled them. an ~ su dạ Lārabāwā good relations have been established between them and the Arabs. (*b*) bạ sụ ~ dạ mū ba they are not on good terms with us (*cf.* shirị 2).

B. (shịryā) *Vb.* 2 = shiryạ̧ 1*a*, 2*a*.

shịryayyē *m.* (*f.* shịryayyīyā) *pl.* shịryạyyū *adj.* arranged, in good order *x* kā ga ạbụ kạmar shịryayyē matters moved like greased lightning.

shīshị̣tā *Vb.* 1C *Kt.* = cūnạ̧ 1*b*.

shịsshiftạ̧ *f.* *x* ~ mukạ̧ yi it slipped our memory.

shisshiga A. (shịsshịga = shịsshigạ̧) *intensive from* shịga.

B. (shịsshigā) *Vd.* firfītā.

shisshigī *m.* (1) meddlesomeness (= kạrạmbā̧nī). (2) an yi bạbban shisshigī gạ̧ haddōdiṇ Ụbaṇgịjị the precepts of God were violated.

shisshikẹ *m.* (*pl.* shị̣kā̧shị̣kai) (1) = gwạfā 1. (2) T. essential to religion (= jịjjigẹ 1*d*).

shisshinị̣yā *Sk.*, *Kt.* (1) = gwạfā 1. (2) cịrar ~ (*a*) rearing-up of horse (= taɓaryā). (*b*) lifting P. high in the ai as warning.

shītạlī *Fil. m.* = cītạlī.

shịttā = shị̣btā.

shị̣wākā *f.* the shrub *Vernonia amygdalina* (*root is used as* ạsạwākị).

shīyā *Sk.*, *Kt.* he (= shī).

shị̣yā̧gạbạnnī *Vd.* shūgạba.

shị̣yākī *Zar. m.* = sīyākī.

shị̣yyạ̧ *f.* direction (= wajē).

shọ̄mọ̄mọ̄ = shā̧mọ̄mọ̄.

shu A. (shū) *m.* silence. (= shiru).

B. (shū̧) *m.* *Eng.* shoe(s).

C. *Vd.* shuụụ.

Shū'ạrā (*Ar.* poets) *f.* *(1) *title of a* Arabic book of poems by* Imru'l qais etc. (2) ~ tā kāmạ̧ ta she has a nic figure.

*shūcẹ *Vd.* shibcẹ.

shūcị *m.* (1) dry grass for thatching (= *Kt.* cifcị). (2) Shūcị, kā bạịbạyi kōw (*said by beggars*) largess, noble one (3) *Vd.* shibcị. (4) girman ~ *Vd* banzā 1*a*.

shū dạ *Vb.* 4 mȩ̄ ya ~ nị̣ = mȩ̄ ya shūsh nị̣ what business is it of mine ? (= rūwā G.1).

shūdạ *m.* weak-witted P.

shuɗa A. (shūɗạ) (1) *Vb.* 1A dyed blue.
(2) *Vb.* 3A passed by, on (= wucẹ).
B. (shū̃ɗā) *Vd.* shūɗī 2.

shuɗɗā *Vd.* shūɗị 2.

shūɗẹ *Vb.* 3A = shūɗạ 2.

shūɗị (1) *m.* act of dyeing blue. (2) *m.*
(*f.* shūɗīyā) *pl.* shuɗɗā = shū̃ɗā
blue. (3) shūɗị-shūɗị blueish.

shụfādụ = sụfādụ.

shū̃gạba *m.* (*pl.* shū̃gạbannī = shū̃wā̃gạ-
bannī = shị̄yā̃gạbạnnī) (1) leader =
jā̃gạba *q.v.* = wainị), *cf.* gạba 3*b*;
jā̃ gōrạ. (2) shū̃gạbạŋ aurē the man or
woman *described in* aurē 6*b* (= jā̃-
gạba 2 = jāgwarɗọ 3), *cf.* ạlwalị.
(3) Shū̃gạbạŋ Annabāwā the Prophet
Muhammad. (4) shū̃gạbam mạjalisạ
president of a council. (5) shū̃gạban
yā̃kị military General. (6) shū̃gạban
yā̃kịn tẹ̄kū admiral. (7) shū̃gạbạŋ
gāwā = wạlị 3.

shū̃gạbancị *m.* leadership *x* (1) Audụ yā
ɗaukị ~ = yā kāmạ ~ = yā kạrɓi ~
Audu took over the leadership (*Vd.*
shū̃gạba 1). (2) kun sā̃ ragạmar shūgạ-
bancị ạ hannūna you have entrusted
me with rule.

shū̃gạbantad dạ *Vb.* 4 appoint P. as
shū̃gạba.

shuggạba = shū̃gạba.

shūkạ (1) *Vb.* 1A (*a*) (i) sowed. (ii) ạbịn
dạ mụtụm ya ~ shī zai girbā : iŋ hairạŋ,
hairạŋ, in sharrạŋ, sharrạŋ = ạbịŋ dạ
ka shūkạ, shī zā kạ girbẹ as a man
sows, so he shall reap. (iii) kōmē ka ~
kạ shā inūwạ tasạ bandạ mụtụm
only man is vile. (iv) shūkạ ramạ *Vd.*
ramạ 1*b*. (*b*) yā ~ ɓarnā he did evil.
(*c*) buried (person) = binnẹ. (2) *f.*, *m.*
(*a*) (*sec. v.n. of* 1) *x* (i) yanā̃ shūkạr
wākē = yanā̃ shūkạ wākē he's sowing
beans. (ii) ạbịŋ yā zō kại dạ kại shūkạr
matsụkī it happened just appositely.
(*b*) act of sowing *x* (i) yā yi ~ he did
the sowing. (ii) an yi shūkạ ạ idạm
makwarkwā *Vd.* makwarwā 3. (iii)
shūkạn yārā *Vd.* dandạŋginā. (iv)
~ ạ fakọ *Vd.* fakọ 2. (v) mẹ̄ ka ~
Vd. gajaŋ hạkurī. (*c*) (i) crops *x*
shūkạnsụ yā yi kyaụ = shūkạssụ
tā yi kyaụ their crops did well. (ii)

Vd. sāran shūkạ. (iii) bạbbar ~ crops
which have ripened early in a district
(contrasted with kạramar shūkạ). (iv)
bā̃ dạshē ba nẹ̄, ~ nẹ̄ he's not a new-
comer but of local birth.

shū̃kạ halī = shū̃kạ haliŋkạ *m.* (i) =
zōgalagandị. (2) *Nor.* = gạbā̃rūwar
Masạr.

shūkạlīyạ *f.* idle roving (= gīlọ).

shukạr = shukạrī *Eng. m.* sugar (=
sukạr).

shūkẹ *Vb.* 1A sowed all of.

shukụr *Eng. m.* = sukạr.

shukurạ *Ar. f.* (1) giving thanks *x* mun
yi ~ gạ Allā̃ we thank God. (2)
gratitude *x* munā̃ ~ we are grateful.

shul *used in* ɗaŋ kại ~ a tiny head.

shū̃mā̃gạba *m.* (*pl.* shū̃mā̃gạbạnnī) =
shū̃gạba.

*shūnā̃ = cūnā̃.

shū̃nayyạ (1) *adj. m., f.* mediumly dark
blue. (2) *f.* mediumly dark blue
thread (= sūsīyạ 1).

shūnī *m.* (1) (*a*) indigo prepared from
plant bābā and sold in cones or lumps
(*it is beaten into dyed cloth to deepen
hue : is remedy for bite by bụsau :
is used by women in hairdressing and as
contraceptive and abortifacient : is given
horses and donkeys through nostril as
solution for stomach-troubles*) = *Sk.*
bū̃tū̃kū 2. (*b*) *its epithet is* ɗaŋ gạraŋgọ
= Shūnī, kō kasā tanā̃ sạŋkạ = *Kt.*
Shūnī, kō kasā tanā̃ kaunarkạ =
ɗan dattījọ. (*c*) (i) shā ~ *f.* white
garment coloured by being worn in
contact with another dyed with shūnī.
(ii) *Vd.* ban shūnī. (iii) *cf.* 3 *below*.
(*d*) ạljamā tā ci ~ (i) they are competing
in alms-giving, liberality. (ii) the
party is in full swing. hīrā tā ci ~ the
conversation is in full swing (*Vd.*
hīrā 2). wạsā yā ci ~ play is in full
swing. (*e*) (i) shūnịn dạ ya shāfạ
musụ, yā kāmạ his propaganda has
borne fruit. (ii) *Vd.* shāfạ tạbarmā
shūnī ; hannū 2*e* ; bạrạ gadō shūnī.
(iii) rīgā farā bā tạ̄ bā 'yarūwā tatạ
shūnī " don't lord it over your equals ! "
(iv) tākạ ~ *Vd.* ụŋgụlū 3*a*. (v) *Vd.*
shāfạ lạ̄bārị shūnī. (2) yā zubạ minị ~
he told me a lie. (3) shūnim battạ (*so*

called because the indigo is mixed
(kwāɓạ) _in a_ battạ) (_a_) rubbing indigo
and milk on one's body to impart
bluish tinge to gown (_cf._ 1c _above_) =
bashinō == garjī == _Kt._ tinigạ), _Vd._
bụrsụnē. (_b_) sprinkling mixture of
indigo and dusar gērō or sand on to
white garment to give impression
it has been worn next to indigo-dyed
one (= garjī == ban shūnī 2 == bụgē).
(4) shūnin dōkā == gōbe 5. (5) shūnim
mairạŋ cubes of English blue (=
bulụ == zạrgīnạ == 6 _below_). (6) shūniŋ
kaŋkaŋ _Kt._ = 5 _above_. (7) _Vd._ warɓā
2_b._ (8) yau ~ _Vd._ farī 2_g._iii.
shuŋkạ _Kt._ _used in_ yā yi ~ he kept
silence.
shuŋkọ == shuŋkụ _m._ (_pl._ shuŋkunạ)
five-franc piece (== dalạ 2 == cuŋkụ ==
Nor. kātibī).
shura A. (shūrā) (1) _Vb._ 2 (_a_) yā shụ̄rē
nị he (P. or animal _x_ camel) kicked me
with forward motion (_cf._ harbā, maŋgarạ). (_b_) yā shụ̄ri tākalmạnsạ he
kicked on his shoes. (2)_f._ first bulrush-
millet of season to ripen.
    B. (shūrạ) (1) _Vb._ 1A (_a_) yā ~
ƙafạ he kicked forward his foot (_Vd._
shūrā 1_a_). (_b_) yā harbē shi, kō shūrạ̄wā
bai yi ba he shot it and it never even
gave a kick. (2) _Vb._ 3A (_a_) went away.
(_b_) garin naŋ yā ~ yạmmā this town
is farther to the west than the other
(== bākatar).
shūrārạ _Nor._ == saurārạ.
shūrẹ (1) _Vb._ 1A (_a_) kicked P. or T. with
forward motion and knocked over
(_Vd._ shūrā). (_b_) == tūɓẹ 1 (_c_) Audụ
yā ~ magana Audu by his interference.
prevented the matter coming to successful conclusion (== kaɓẹ 3_b_ == sōkā 1_b._i),
_Vd._ Gaŋgamạ sautụ. (2) _Vb._ 3A yā ~
(_a_) it (domestic animal) died. (_b_) (_said
playfully_) person died.
shūri _m._ (1) (_sec. v.n. of_ shūrā) _x_ yanạ̄
shūrinsạ == yanạ̄ shụ̄rassạ he is kicking
him (_as in_ shụ̄rā _q.v._). (2) a kick, act
of kicking _x_ yā yi minị ~ he kicked
me. (3) _Nor._ == sūri.
*shurkụ == *shirkụ.
shurū == shiru.
shūshē _Vd._ shū dạ.

shū-shū-shụ̄ _x_ ~ baŋ gan shị ba I've
not seen him for a long time.
shu'umī _m._ (_f._ shu'ụmā) _pl._ shụ'ụmai _Ar._
P., T. or place of ill omen (_cf._ sạmātsī 2,
alfālụ).
shu'ụmtā _Vb._ 1C considered P., etc., to
be shu'ụmī.
shụụụ _x_ (1) harsāshị sunạ̄ wucẹ̄wā shụụụ
cartridges are being discharged in
quick succession (== shạạạ). (2) _cf._
shu.
shụ̄wạ̄gạbạnnī _Vd._ shụ̄gạba.
shụ̄wākā == shiwākā.
shūyị _m._ type of patterned cloth.
sị _x_ santsī yā ɗaụkē shị ~ he slithered
along the wet ground.
sībō _m._ theft (== sātạ).
siddabarụ _m._ conjuring (== dabọ 1).
siddīkụ (_Ar._ truthful) name for any man
called Ạbū Bakạr.
sidẹ == sudẹ.
Sīdi (_abbreviation of Ar._ Sayyidī) (1)
refers to Sīdi Ạbdụl Kādiri Jẹ̄lāni. (2)
man's name. (3) == Sayyụ. (4) God
ward it off ! (5) _cf._ Sayyạdī (_the word
from which_ Sīdi _is derived_).
sīdị == sīdīdī _used in_ bạ sīdīdī, bạ sādādā ==
bābụ sīdị barē sādạ uselessly
(== ɓalak == cas 2 == lam == tạndi ==
zarētā == tsalam 1).
sidiƙ _used in_ baƙī ~ == baƙī ƙirin _q.v._
under ƙirin.
*sifạ == *siffạ.
*siffạ _f._ (_pl._ siffōfī) _Ar._ (1) likeness
picture, photo (== kạmā). (2) description, details. (3) adjective.
*siffạtā == *siffạntā described (_Vd._ *siffạ)
sifilī _m._ (1) == sifirī 2. (2) an yi wạ wāgā ~
the pannier has been lined with leaves
before being filled with kola-nuts.
sifircē _Vd._ sifirtạ.
sifirī _m._ (1) (_a_) hiring (animal, etc.)
renting _x_ nā yi sifirinsạ (i) I hired it
(ii) I rented it (house). (_b_) hiring out
renting out _x_ nā bā dạ sifirinsạ (i) I
hired it out. (ii) I let it (house). (2)
_Ar._ *(_a_) zero, nought-figure. (_b_) yā
sạ̄mi ~ (_school-language_) he got no
marks, he got out for a duck in cricket
*(3) _Ar._ volume of book.
sifirtạ _Vb._ 2 (_p.o._ sifircē, _n.o._ sifirci)
hired rented _x_ nā sifirci jạ̄kī I hired a

donkey. nā sifircē shi ạ wurinsạ I rented it (house) from him.

*sīgạ *Ar. f.* (1) appearance. (2) case of noun. (3) tense of verb.

sịgārạ *f.* = sịgārị *m. Eng.* (a) cigarette (= karan ~). (b) ~ karā ukụ three cigarettes.

sịgārịyā (used by hawkers of cigarettes and in songs) = sịgārị.

*sihircē *Vb.* 1C *Ar.* bewitched (cf. *sihirī) = sammạcē.

sihịrdā *Kt. f.* = sargā.

*sihịrī *Ar. m.* (pl. sịhịrce-sịhịrcē) magic, sorcery.

sikạr = sikạrī = sukạr *q.v.*

sikẹ (1) *Vb.* 3A. (a) was speechless with rage. (b) became dead-tired (= rafkẹ 1b). (c) = shīdẹ 2. (d) wutā tā ~ fire went out. (2) *Vb.* 1A yā ~ ni he wore me out with his importunity.

sịkēlị *Eng. m.* weighing-machine, scales (= ma'aunī = kēlị *q.v.*).

sikịr = sikịrī = sukạr *q.v.*

sịkkī *m.* unfertilized dates become dried up on tree.

sil used in baƙī ~ jet-black (= ƙirin).

silạ *Ar. f.* = dạlīlị 3, 4 x yā yi minị ~ har nā sāmụ it was through his good offices that I got it.

silại = sulại.

silạ̄lā = sulạ̄lā.

silạ̄lē *Vb.* 1A = sulạ̄lē.

sịlālị = sịlīlị.

silāmụ = sạlāmụ.

sile A. (silẹ) = sulại.

B. (Silẹ) = Sulẹ.

sịlī *m.* (1) *Vd.* murjị. (2) mụ bi jạwābịnsạ sịlī-sịlī let us follow his speech detail by detail.

silīfạ *Eng. f.* slipper(s) not enclosing heel.

sịliki *m.* (pl. sịlịkai). (1) silk-thread, mercerized cotton. (2) ~ mai rặi silk-thread which will not take native dye. (3) ~ ạfạtạ̄tū cheap silk-thread (*Vd.* ạfạtạ̄tū).

sịlīlị *m.* (pl. sịlīlai) (1) = sịlī. (2) yā yi minị tọ̄nan ~ = banƙạdā 2. (3) nēman ~ gạrēshị he picks quarrels.

sịlī-sịlī *Vd.* sịlī 2.

sịlīyạ = sịllīyạ.

sịlkē = sụlkē.

silla A. (sillạ) *Vb.* 1A = millạ 2c.

B. (sịllā) (1) *Vb.* 2 x yā sịlli tūwō he ate much good tūwō (= sụmụlmulạ). (2) f. yā shā ~ he has been abused.

sịllāyē *Vd.* sillē.

sille A. (sillẹ) (1) *Vb.* 1A. (a) yā ~ jịkinsạ he washed himself well. (b) yā ~ shi dạ zāgị he roundly abused him. (c) = sạ̄ɓulạ 2a. (d) yā sillẹ tūwō dukạ he ate up all the large amount of good tūwō (= sumulmulē). (2) *Vd.* 3A = sullụɓē 2a–c.

B. (sịllē) *m.* wearing gown without trousers or loincloth.

C. (sillē) *m.* (pl. sịllāyē) top section of corn-stalk (used after removal of the corn, by woman as makallacịyā).

sịllī *Sk., Kt. m.* (1) foreskin (= lọ̄ɓā). (2) uncircumcised penis.

sịllīyạ *f.* (pl. sịllīyū). (1) (a) the red variety of kincē. (b) *Vd.* turkụdī 4 ; kạryạ kạ̄fadạ. (2) fair African woman (= farī 2b.ii).

sịmī *m.* being tongue-tied through nervousness.

simil *Vd.* sumul.

simịlikạ how worn this coin is ! (cf. kwạnkwadō 1, sumul 1).

simịlmilạ = sịllā 1.

similmịlē = sillẹ 1d.

simintị = sumuntị.

sịmī-sịmī x yanạ̄ tạfīyạ ~ he's slinking along.

sịnādạrī *m.* (1) (a) solder. (b) flux for solder. (2) an zubạ gishirī ~ = an zubạ gishirī don ~ a little salt has been added to it.

sịnāsịr = sịnāsạr = sịnāsụr *Kt. m.* small cake of guinea-corn, maize, bulrush-millet or rice-flour fried (tọ̄yạ) and eaten with mīyạ or honey.

Sīnāwā *Vd.* Bạsīnị.

since A. (sincẹ) = sancẹ.

B. *(sincē) *m.* wrestling (= kuncē *q.v.*).

sịndịlē *m.* = kạsindịlā.

sịngịlạ *f.* = sịngịlatị *Eng. m.* (1) singlet. (2) narrow-sleeved shirt of native make.

sinƙạ = sunƙạ.

sinƙaƙa A. (sịnƙạ̄ƙā) *Vb.* 3A yā ~ ạ gujẹ he took to his heels.

B. (sịnƙāƙạ) (1) *Vb.* 2 drove away

(= ƙọ̄rā). (2) *Vb.* 3B yā ∼ ạ guje = siŋƙā̧ƙā.

siŋƙaƙe A. (siŋƙā̧ƙē) (1) *Vb.* 1C. (*a*) covered *x* yā siŋƙā̧ƙę fuskạssạ he covered his face by drawing down his turban over his eyes and its end up over his nose. (*b*) included *x* littāfin naṇ yā siŋƙā̧ƙę wancaṇ this book contains all that the other does. fam shidạ zại siŋƙā̧ƙę al'amạrin naṇ dukạ six pounds will cover all those expenses. (*c*) = kwạɓā 1*b*. (*d*) cīwọ yā ∼ shi = tun-nuƙē 2*a*. (2) *Vb.* 3A = dinniƙē 1*a*.
B. (siŋƙā̧ƙę) *adj. m.* huge.

siṇ'ke-siŋkē" *m.* = ɗạmȩ̄-ɗamē 1.

siŋkọ = siŋku = shuŋku *q.v.*

sintali A. sintạlī *m.* (*pl.* sintulạ) metal water-jug.
B. (Sintạli) one of the sạrautạ (*epithet is* Dumau, ƙwaryar fādạ).

sintaliƙō *m.* type of climbing-plant (*root is said to give power of invisibility but not to be findable till tree climbed and oil poured over it*).

siṇtī *Sk. m.* = fanyā 3.

sintilī = sintạlī.

siṇtsir *x* buhū yā cikạ ∼ the sack is stuffed full. yā yi ƙibạ ∼ he's very stout.

sintulạ *Vd.* sintạlī.

*sippạ = siffạ.

sirā *used in* yā yi fitar ∼ = fitar fīgạ.

sirā̧dā *Vd.* sirdi.

sirādī = sirātsī *Ar. m.* the narrow bridge over hell from which sinners fall.

sīrancē *Vb.* 3A = sīrīrạncē.

sīrā̧rā *Vd.* sīrīrī.

sirā̧rē = surā̧rē.

sirdi *m.* (*pl.* sirā̧dā = surā̧dā = *Kt.* sirid-dā) (*Ar.* sarji). (1) (*a*) saddle. (*b*) iṇ kā ga gōdīyā dạ ∼ tanā̧ gudu, wani ta kāyar if nobody wants T. or P. apparently good, it is because of hidden blemish. (*c*) zā mu sā̧ yạ shiga sirdi we will bring him to his senses. (*d*) mūgun ∼ *Vd.* bukurū. (2) sidebone of bird. (3) kā̧zā (zạkarạ) mại ∼ white hen (cock) with brown feathers on the back.

sịrī = sịlī.

siriddā *Vd.* sirdi.

sirīdī *m.* meddlesomeness (= kạrạm-bā̧nī).

siriki = suruki.

sīrīƙi *m.* (*pl.* sīrīƙai) type of flute made of corn-stalk (= mabūsā = kusumburwạ 1*c*).

sīrīrai *Vd.* sīrīrī.

sīrīrạncē *Vb.* 3A (1) became° thin. (2) decreased.

sīrīrạntā *Vb.* 1D (1) caused to become thin. (2) reduced T.

sīrīrī = sịrīri *m.* (*f.* sīrīrīyā = sịrīrīyā) *pl.* sīrā̧rā = sịrīrai = sirī-sirī) slender, slim.

sirī-sirī *Vd.* sīrīrī.

*sirkāmi *m.* pus (= mugunyạ).

sirri = sirru *Ar. m.* = ạsīrī.

sīsi *m.* (1) *Eng.* (*a*) sixpence (= kū'ran 3). (*b*) sīsiṇ kwabọ halfpenny (= adajjō = bạɗarę). (2) (*a*) yā bi sīsim magana he investigated the matter.

sissika = sussuka.

sit *used in* baƙī ∼ jet-black (= ƙirin).

Sitambạ *f.* September.

sitārạ = sạttārạ.

sitāti *Eng. m.* (1) starch. (2) yā yi ∼ he washed and spruced himself up. yanā̧ sitāti he's all togged up (= sukōlạ). (3) ɗan ∼ *m.* (*f.* 'yar ∼) *pl.* 'yan ∼ spruce P.

sitilaŋ *used in* Allā̧ ∼ = ƙishạ 2 = kurwā 3*b*.

sitirạ *Ar. f.* (1) (*a*) clothing *x* yā yi sābwar ∼ he has put on new clothing (*cf.* (*b*) *below*). (*b*) (*sometimes preceded by pl. adj.*) *x* yā yi sā̧bạbbin ∼ = (*a*) *above*. (*c*) darē ∼ nē at night all cats are grey. (2) mutum mại ∼ man of correct behaviour. (3) (*a*) doṇ Allā̧ kạ yi mini ∼ don't put me to shame ! (*b*) *Vd.* dā'imī. (4) zā mu yi masạ ∼ we are off to bury him. (5) *Vd.* buƙū-buƙū 3.

*sitircē *Vb.* 1C clothed.

sitiri *Vd.* buƙū-buƙū 3.

sitọk (*Eng.*) *m.* store (= taskạ).

sitsirạ *f.* = sạdarạ.

sittạ *Ar. f.* (1) six thousand. (2) *Sk.* (*obsolete word*) one and sixpence.

sittārạ = sạttārạ.

sittiŋ *Ar. f.* (1) sixty. (2) ∼ dạ hauyā̧ uku = ciɓus 2. (3) (*a*) ∼ ta Alƙur'aṇ

the sixty chapters (izufi) of the Koran,
i.e. the whole Koran. (b) nā rantsę dą ~
I swear by the Koran ! (cf. sittīnīya).
sittīnīya f. (1) (a) = sittiŋ 3. (b) sittīnīyạr
Alkur'aŋ tanā kạnsạ he has memorized
the whole Koran (= haddạcē q.v.). (2)
Vd. ạlhamdu 2.
sịwākī = ạsuwākị.
sịyākī m. (pl. sịyạ̄kai). (1) striped hyena
(epithet is Sịyākī, mai kashę kūrā). (2)
gạba kūrā, bāya ~ it's a case of being
between the devil and the deep sea.
sịyāsạ (Ar.) f. (1) (a) clemency. (b) yā
yi minị ~ he did me a favour, he made
me a concession (= raŋgwamę). mutum
mai ~ a kind man. (2) reduction in
price (= raŋgwamę).
sịyāyę m. (1) peeled stalks of ramạ (cf.
dạ̄yā) = ƙeƙashēshę. (2) torch (Vd.
bạ̄kiŋ wutā) made of 1 (smeared with
maŋ kạɗanyạ and used by thieves).
so A. (sō) Vb. 5 (Vd. sǫ). (1) (a) wanted.
(b) ạbin dạ ransạ ya ~ what he desired.
(c) in yā sō, kōmē akę yị, ạ yi let him do
his worst ! (d) kō yanā sǫ, kō bā yā
sǫ willy-nilly he .... (e) im munā sō, bā
wata wuyā if we wish to do so, there is
no difficulty. (f) indạ ya ~ Vd.
aikā 1c. (g) ạbin dạ mai dōkị kę̄ sǫ
Vd. dōkị 1k. (2) (a) loved, liked. (b)
wạndạ ya ~ kạ dạ ạbinsạ, kai yakę̄
sǫ if P. gives you a thing, it is because
he likes you. (c) (i) kā kuskurạ, ạmmā
Allā yā ~ kạ you had lucky escape
from consequences of your rashness.
(ii) cf. son 7. (d) dabbạŋ naŋ tā ~
hannunsạ this domestic animal thrived
with him (= kạrɓā 1f). (2A) was willing
to x tā sō tạ zō she was willing to come.
(3) (a) (i) intended x tuŋ kwānam bāya
mukạ ~ mu gayạ makạ we intended to
tell you some time ago. (ii) aŋ kashę
musu mutạ̄nē dạ yawạ har sun ~ su
ƙārę so many of them were killed that
it looked as if they would be annihilated.
(b) are (were) about to x kalmōminsu
sun sō su ruɗē mụ their words were on
the point of convincing us. mutạ̄nē
sunā sǫ su yi masạ ƙarancī the forces
at his disposal are tending to decrease.
(4) nā ~ ŋ taɓạ ganinsạ I have an idea
I've seen him (= jī 4c). (5) Vd. kai

ka sō, sǫ gijị, masǫ, sǫ maŋgā, sō
sō banzā. (6) sǎi kā ~ Vd. kandarę.
B. (sǫ) m. (1) (v.n. and progressive of
sō) x (a) n nā saŋ kudī I want some
money. yanā santạ he loves her. saŋ
kudī garēshị he is eager for money.
ạbin dạ akę̄ ~ gạ Musulmī, zumuncị
the sine qua non among Muslims is
solidarity between relations. (b) bā
wạndạ akę̄ ~ sǎi ita ạ kaŋ kirkị she
has no equal in goodness. (c) anā ~
kaŋ kai kạsūwā it's a case of the
cobbler's wife going without. (d) sạm
masǫyiŋ wani ƙōshiŋ wạhalạ ·it's a
waste of time to love one who loves
another (= ạljamā 3). (e) (i) mai saŋ
ạbiŋkạ wandạ ya fī kạ dạbārạ epithet of
thief. (ii) sạd dạ bā kā̧ sǫ Vd. tāshị
1a.vi. (iii) kō ƙasā tanā sạŋkạ Vd.
shūnī 1b. (iv) bā sā̧ san yiŋ ạbu Vd.
ạbu 5d. (v) naŋ yakę̄ sǫ dạ kwānā
Vd. wani 4e. (f) (i) nā fī saŋ wannạŋ
I prefer this one (Vd. fī). (ii) gạskīyā
cę̄, bā̧ fin ~ ba it is the truth without
bias. (iii) bā̧ ạbin dạ sukę̄ ~ kạmar
su sāmu their greatest desire is to get
it. (iv) fātun jājạyaŋ awākī sum fī ~
wurin Tūrạ̄wā Europeans prefer the
skins of red goats. (2) (a) affection. (b)
yā sạ̄mi ~ = fādạ 2. (c) ~ dukạ ~
nē, ạmmā saŋ kạ̄i yā fī no matter how
much one loves anyone, one always
studies one's own interests first (Vd.
son 5). (d) ạbin ~ anything or anybody
liked, loved. (3) dạ Kạnde dạ Shatu
sunā ~ Kande and Shatu are pals (=
zamā 2a.viii) (Vd. ƙawā). (4) Vd. sǫn-
compounds, wā kạ sǫ.
C. (sǫ) = sau.
sōɓạrōdọ m. calyx of yākụ̄wā (= barę̄-
katạ = kạrasū = zōɓạrōdọ).
sōcị Eng. (1) sock(s), stocking(s). (2)
jersey, shirt.
sōdị = gīlọ 1, 2.
sōdō = sǫdǫrē = sārā 2a.i q.v.
sōfanę m. patch of colour different from
that of rest of animal's coat.
sōfạ-sōfạ (1) slowly and carefully. (2)
half-heartedly x kanā̧ wani ɗan sōfạ-
sōfạ you're acting half-heartedly.
sǭfōfụ̄wā f. (1) empty honeycomb. (2) A.
puffed out (x bladder).

sōgā *f.* type of gown of poor quality.

Sọ̄ giji *name for boy or girl born soon after the mother's return home after longish absence.*

sōjạ = **sōji** *Eng. m.* (*sg.*, *pl.*, *but pl. also* **sōjōji**). (1) soldier(s) *x* **sōjạmmụ** = **sōjōjimmụ** our soldiers (= **yāḳi** 1*e*). **yanḡ sōjạ** = **yanḡ sōjạnsạ** he is a soldier. (2) **ɗan** ∼ *m.* (*pl.* '**yan** ∼) = 1. (3) military employ *x* **shẹ̄karạssạ shidạ cikin** ∼ he has been six years in the army. **ya fāɗạ sōjạ** then he entered the army. (4) military training *x* **aŋ kōyạ masạ** ∼ he has been trained as a soldier.

soka A. (**sōkạ**) (*plus dative or equivalent prep.*) *x* **an** ∼ **masạ wuḳā** he has been stabbed with a knife (= **sọ̄kā**). **tā** ∼ **ạllūrạ ạ zanẹ** she stuck a needle into the cloth. **suŋ sōkạ ḳại cikim Masạr** they thrust their way into Egypt. **sun sōkō wạ Kanọ ta gabạs** they burst into Kano from the east.
　　B. (**sọ̄kā**) *Vb.* 2 (*but progressive is usually formed with* **sūkạ**). (1) (*a*) pierced, stabbed *x* **an sọ̄kē shi dạ wuḳā** he has been stabbed with a knife (= **sōkạ**), *cf.* **tsīrẹ** 1*a*, **6usạ**. (*b*) (i) **yā sọ̄ki cịnikī** by his interference he prevented the transaction coming to a successful conclusion (= **sōkẹ** 1*d*, **shūrẹ** 1*c*). (ii) **sun sọ̄ki shaidạ tasạ** = **sōkẹ** 1*e*. (2) *Vd.* **sōkō**.

*sōkabō *m.* weak-minded P.

sōḳai-sōḳai *x* **yanḡ tạfīyạ** ∼ he's slinking along (= **sōmại-sōmại**).

sōkanabọ *m.* = **sōkọ**.

soke A. (**sōkẹ**) (1) *Vb.* 1A. (*a*) pierced *x* **an** ∼ **shi dạ wuḳā** he has been stabbed with a knife (= **sọ̄kā** 1). (*b*) killed by transfixing. (*c*) **yā** ∼ **nāmạ ạ tsiŋkē** he skewered **tsīrē..** (*d*) = **sọ̄kā** 1*b*.i. (*e*) **sun** ∼ **shaidạ tasạ** they contradicted his evidence (= **sọ̄kā** 1*b*.ii). (*f*) cancelled *x* **yā** ∼ **shi cikin lissāfi** he deleted it from the list. **mun sōkẹ sūnansạ cikin Sarākunạ** we've deleted him from among the Chiefs (*cf.* **tumbuḳē**). (2) *Vb.* 3A *x* **magạnạ tā** ∼ the affair has not been brought to a successful conclusion.
　　B. (**sọ̄kē**) *m.* (1) securing cloth round body by twisting corners together and

tucking in (= **ḳunzugū** 2). (2) **yā ci sọ̄kyansạ** he (wrestler) seized him (opponent) round the waist. (3) **hanyạn naŋ** ∼ **cẹ̄** this is a direct road (= **dọ̄shē**), *cf.* **gẹ̄wạyē**. (4) = **sārā** 2*a*.i.

sọ̄ki *m.* (1) (*a*) ∼ **yā shịga gōnā** = **gōnā tā yi** ∼ blight, drought, insect pest has attacked the farm. (*b*) **dạmuna tā yi** ∼ the rains have spoiled the crops. (2) ∼ **yā shịgē shi** = **yā gạmu dạ** ∼ he has a wasting disease.

sọ̄ki bụrūtsū *m.* pointless chatter (*cf.* **bụrūtsū**).

soko A. (**sōkō**) *Vb.* 3A. (1) budded, sprouted, etc. (= **tsịra**). (2) *Vd.* **sōkạ**.
　　B. (**sōkọ**) *m.* (1) fool. (2) (*a*) type of **marọ̄ḳī**. (*b*) the **rọ̄ḳō** done by 2*a*. (3) sprouting, budding (*cf.* **sōkō**).

soḳoḳo A. (**sọ̄ḳōḳọ** *m.* (*f.* **sọ̄ḳōḳ̣ūwā**) fool.
　　B. (**sọ̄ḳọ̄ḳọ̄**) foolishly *x* **yanḡ tsạye** ∼ he's standing like a gaby.

sōlī *m.* adding many bricks to worn-out wall.

sọ̄lọ̄6ịyọ *m.* slacker (*epithet is* **Sọ̄lọ̄6ịyọ mụrūciŋ gēzạ**).

soma A. (**sōmạ**) (1) *Vb.* 1A. (*a*) began (= **fārạ** *q.v.*). (*b*) **ta kạn sōmạ tịlā** *Vd.* **tsanyạ** 1*d*. (2) *Vb.* 3A began (*intransitive*) (= **fạ̄ru**).
　　B. (**sọ̄mā**) *Vb.* 2 was the first to do = **fạ̄rā** 1 *q.v.*

sōmại-sōmại = **sōḳai-sōḳai**.

sọ̄ mạngā *m.* = **tạfā-tạfā**.

sōmẹ *Vb.* 3A *Kt.* = **sūmā** 1.

sōmị *m.* beginning (= **masōmī**).

son (*v.n. of* **sō**) *used in following compounds.*
(1) **saŋ ạ sani** ; **saŋ ạ shinạ** *Vd.* **sani** 1*a*.iii, **namiji** 2*b*. (2) **saŋ innạ** = 7 *below*. (3) **saŋ īyạ̄wā** showing-off. (4) (*a*) **san jịkī** slackness, inertia. (*b*) (i) **mại san jịkī** *m.*, *f.* slacker. (ii) *Vd.* **bọ̄rī** 2*a*. (5) **saŋ ḳại** (*a*) selfishness, egoism. (*b*) *Vd.* **sọ̄** 2*c*. (6) **san rạ̄ḳumin yārā** wanting T. only so long as unobtainable (*Vd.* **rạ̄ḳumī** 1*j*). (7) **saŋ ūwar dawạ** insincere friendship (= 2 *above*), *epithet is* **tạ sō kạ, tạ shạnyē makạ hannū** = **tạ sō kạ, tạ sā ka dawạ** (*Vd.* **ūwar dawạ**). (8) **yā bi san zūcịyā** (*a*) he gave way to his baser instincts. (*b*) he stole. (*c*) *Vd.* **aurē** 2*a*. (9) **san zumunci gạrēshi**

he's kind. (10) sąm masǫ wani *Vd*.
sǫ 1*d*. (11) mại sąŋ ąbiŋką *Vd*. ɓąrāwǫ
1*a*. (12) sąm fici *Vd*. fici.
sōrō *m*. (*pl*. sōrāyē) (1) (*Kano*). (*a*) rectangular flat-topped house (or round
house with cupola-top) where walls and
roof are made of mud. (*b*) lower storey
of such rectangular building (= jąkim
bēnē). (*c*) sōrō = sōram bēnē upper
storey *of such building* (*cf*. kwątashị,
samą 1*g*.iii). (*d*) gidansą ~ dą bēnē
nę his home contains an upper storey.
(*e*) gidansą sōrāyē dą bēnāyē nę his
home consists of several rooms on the
ground-floor with others on the first
floor. (*f*) = zaurę 1*b*. (*g*) *Vd*. ɗākị,
hayịn tsaikǫ, ɗaurịŋ gūgā 2, bąkā 8,
kudąndąŋ, tākąlmī 7, tōzō 2*c*. (2) *Kt*.
sōrō *has sense of* 1*c above*, and shịgifą
replaces *the word* sōrō *in the sense of* 1*a
above*. (3) 'yar sōrō (*pl*. 'yan sōrō) one
of the four or five slave-girls (ƙwąrā-
ƙwąrai) who were personal attendants
of an Emir and brought him water, etc.
(= tųrākā 3 = bąrāyā 4) : the head-
girl was called ūwar sōrō and each of
the girls had a sleeping-place allotted
in the palace, but if one of them became
pregnant by the Emir, it was said am
fíd dą ita dągą sōrō, tā sąmi ɗākị = am
fíd dą ita dągą sōrō, tā sąmi rịgā.
(4) an tārą shi har yā yi ~ it was piled
up. (5) sōrąn dą bą kudī *Vd*. bukką.
sǫrǫm *x* nā ji ɗǫyī ~ I smelt an awful
stench.
sōsą *Vb*. 1A (*but progressive is usually
formed with* sūsą) scratched (irritating
place, etc.) *x* ką ~ minị bāyāna scratch
my back for me !
sǫsăi (1) *adv*. (*a*) (i) well, correctly *x*
yā īyą ~ he can do it well. nā ji ~ I
understand (understood) perfectly well.
suŋ kōmą mąganą ~ they spoke in their
normal way again. (ii) sǫsăi dą sǫsăi
quite correctly. (iii) yā bayyąnā minị
shī sǫsăi dą sǫsăi he explained it to me
in detail. (*b*) in a straight line *x* hanyą
tā mīƙę ~ the road stretches in a
straight line. hanyą, sǫsăi takę zūwą
cikịŋ gąrī the road leads straight to the
town. (2) *m*. (*a*) straightness, correctness *x* wannąŋ itącē yā yi ~ this wood

is straight (= ɗąrkwai). (*b*) wannąŋ ita
cę sā'ą ta sǫsăi this was the appointed
hour of death.
sōshę (1) *Vb*. 3A (garment) is nearly worn-
out. (2) *Vb*. 1A thoroughly scratched
as in sōsą.
sōshịyā *f*. (1) (*a*) heads of guinea-corn or
bulrush-millet from which the grains
have been stripped (tumę) not threshed
(bugu), or have been eaten by birds or
shą darē (= *Kt*. zaŋgarę). (*b*) iŋ
kā zō gąrī kā iskę mutąnaŋ gąrī dą
wutsīyą, kai kǫ bą ka dą ita, nęmi
sōshịyar gērō ką kafą at Rome do as
Rome does. (2) *Kt*. = garērā 1*c*. (3)
ą bar sōshịyā *Vd*. ząɓē 5.
sǫsō *m*. (1) (*a*) the loofah-gourd (*Luffa
ægyptiaca*, the climber from which 2*a*
is obtained). (*b*) sǫsan yąmmā a
species (*Luffa acutangula*) which has
better fruit than 1*a*. (2) (*a*) loofah
(*obtained from* 1). (*b*) sponge. (3) a
white, English honeycomb-material
used by women as fątalą.
Sō sō banzā mại ɓabban nadị (*used at
Yąwuri*) *epithet of* māląmī.
sǫsōnị *Kt*. *m*. = ƙazwā 1.
sōsūwā *f*. = sōshịyā 1.
sǫtō *m*. = ƙōsăi.
sōwą *f*. sun yi ~ = sun ɗauki ~ they
shouted out (*only re several persons*), *cf*.
ihụ.
sōyą *Vb*. 1A (1) fried (meat ; ground-nuts,
etc. in the juice exuding from them, if
necessary, supplementing this with a
dash of oil) (*cf*. tōyą). (2) ąbin dą aką
dafą dą wandą aką sōyą, duk lābārịŋ
wutā suką ji ; ąbin dą aką gasą shi, yā
ga wutā fīlī dą fīlī what went before
was nothing, but now this is a titanic
battle (*for in* dafą *or* sōya, *the pot is
interposed between food and fire, whereas
in* gasą *the meat is in contact with the
fire*), *cf*. sūyą 5.
sōyayyą *f*. mutual affection.
soye A. (sōyē) *m*. (1) flour of roasted
guinea-corn, bulrush-millet, or maize
used as journey-provisions (guzurī) =
bąragadą 5. (2) pieces of fried meat (*cf*.
tsịrē).
   B. (sōyę) *Vb*. 1A = sōyą.
stok *Vd*. sitǫk.

su A. (sụ) (1) *m.* (*a*) fishing. (*b*) ~ bābụ
tsặrakā wạhalạ nē you cannot make
bricks without straw. (2) *Kt.* = sặ A.3
(*page* 753) *x* sụ̄ zō they'll probably come.
B. (sū) (1) (*independent pronoun*
Mod. Gram. 46) they *x* (*a*) ~ nē it is
they. ~ nē sukạ zō it is *they* who
came. bābụ ~ there are none of them
to be had. dạ ~ some are available. (*b*)
(*used as direct object when dative
precedes*, Mod. Gram. 76*a*.ii) *x* yā
karặntā minị ~ he read them to me.
(2) sū yē̦ sū *Vd.* yē̦. (3) (*dialectal*) *x*
sū zō = sun zō, sukạ zō.
C. (su) (1) *Vd.* su wặnē̦, su wặnēnē̦,
Wānē̦, su wạ. (2) (*objective pronoun
after low tone in previous verb*, Mod.
Gram. 49*a*[1]) them *x* nā kāmạ ~ I
seized them (*cf.* sụ). (3) *Vd.* sukē̦,
sukạ, sunặ. (4) (*third pl. pronoun used
after* zặ Mod. Gram. 17, *and* bặ Mod.
Gram. 19*b*) *x* zặ ~ kặsūwā they're off
to market. bặ ~ zūwạ they're not
coming. (5) (*a*) (*repeated before each
of series*) such as *x* ạkwai nāmōmin
jējị kạmar ~ zākị, su dặmisạ, su kūrā
there are wild animals, *e.g.* lions,
leopards, and hyenas. (kū suwặnēnē̦
kukạ zō̦ which of you came ?) *reply*,
mū su Audụ, su Mūsā, su Nūhụ our
number include Audu, Musa, Nuhu,
etc. su Wānē̦ dạ su Wānē̦ So-ånd-so
and So-and-so (Mod. Gram. 52A). (*b*)
(*used with only one noun, etc.*) *x* sharudạ
dặi kạmar su Sarkiṇ Ịṇgilạ sukạ ƙullạ
nē they are stipulations like those made
by the King of *England* and other such
authorities. su ịyālịna sun zō my wife
and those with her have come. ~ mū
naṇ zā mụ tạfi the various ones of us
who are here will go. maṇ su fētụr
petrol and similar oils.
D. (sụ) (1) (*objective pronoun after
high tone in previous verb*, Mod. Gram.
49*a*[1]) them *x* nā gan ~ I saw them (*cf.*
su 2). (2) (*subjunctive pronoun third
pl.*, Mod. Gram. 13*a*) *x* (*a*) ~ zō let
them come ! yanặ sō̦ ~ zō he wants
them to come. sunặ sō̦ su zō they want
to come. (*b*) (sụ *is sometimes replaced
by the word* ạ) *x* mutānam Masạr dạ
sū, săi ạ kāmạ hannun jūnā the Germans

and they are shaking hands together.
(3) their (*a*) (i) dōkịnsụ their horse
(Mod. Gram. 47*b*). (ii) jạkā tasụ =
jạkarsụ = jạkassụ their bag (Mod.
Gram. 47*b*[1]). (*b*) (*after v.n. of changing
verbs and after secondary v.n.*) (i)
ạikarsụ = aikịnsụ the sending them
(Mod. Gram. 47*c*). nēmansụ the looking
for them. tạmbayạrsụ = tạmbayạssụ =·
tạmbayạ tasụ the asking them (Mod.
Gram. 47*c*). munặ nēmansụ we are
looking for them. munặ tạmbayạssụ
we are asking them. (ii) (*gives continuous sense in cases like the following*)
sun yi zamansụ cikin d̦ākịn naṇ well,
they went on living inthat house. sunặ
tạfīyạ tasụ săi . . . while they were on
their way, then . . . sunặ yāwạnsụ
săi . . . while wandering about, they . . .
sunặ nōmansụ, sunặ d̦iṇkịnsụ, sunặ dăi
dukạn sha'ạninsụ they're farming,
tailoring, and carrying out all their
occupations without disturbance. (4)
yā tạfi gạrinsụ he went to his home-
town (yā tạfi gạrinsạ *would only be
said of* Chief of Town). tanặ gidansụ
she is at home (*cf.* yanặ gidansạ the
house-holder (mại gidā) is at home).
yanặ gidansụ he (*i.e.* man *not* house-
owner) is at home (Mod. Gram. 47*e*).
(5) *Vd.* nāsụ. (6) *Vd.* musụ. (7) they
will (Mod. Gram. 14) *x* zā ~ zō they
will come. bạ zā ~ zō ba they will not
come (Mod. Gram. 20*a*). (8) they
(*negative past*, Mod. Gram. 20*a*) *x*
bạ ~ zō ba they did (have) not come.
E. *Vd.* sụụ.
sụ̄bād̦ad̦ā *m.* bletherer.
sụ̄bādī *m.* blethering, empty chatter.
*sụbāhị *Ar. m.* = ạsụbặ.
sụ̄b̦alē (1) *Vb.* 1C = sullụb̦ē 2. (2)
Vb. 3A = sullụb̦ē 1.
subbạ *Sk. f.* wading through deep water.
subcẹ *Kt. Vb.* 3A = sub̦ucē.
Subdụ *Kr. f.* Saturday (= Ạsabạr =
Sātī).
sụbhạṇ = sụbhānạ (1) *used in* sararin ~
dạ yawạ, kặ zaunạ wurī d̦ayā kạ
ƙuntạtạ ? don't stick in one place when
the world is before you ! (2) *Vd. next
entry.*
sụbhānạllāhị (1) Good heavens ! (2) *f.*

saying " Good heavens ! " $x \sim$ tā ḳọri lāḍaŋ hearing someone say " Good heavens " made the muezzin run away. (3) *Vd.* ṣubhaŋ.

subtū *Kt.* = sūtū.

suɓucē *Vb.* 3A = sulluɓē 2.

***suɓu 'ī** *Ar. m.* one-seventh.

suɓul A. (suɓul) *adv.* (1) well-washed x jikinsạ yā fịta $\sim$ = yā yi waŋkā $\sim$ he bathed himself clean. (2) easily x yā fịta $\sim$ (*a*) it slipped easily out of its handle. (*b*) he has escaped safe and sound. (3) yā warḳẹ $\sim$ he has completely recovered (1–3 = sumul). (4) baḳī $\sim$ very black and glossy.

B. (ṣuɓul) *m.* (1) yā yi ṣuɓul dạ hạrsāshị he fired a shot. (2) yā yi $\sim$ dạ baḳạ (*a*) he made a slip of the tongue (*cf.* ṣuɓur). (*b*) he acted ill-advisedly.

ṣuɓurạ = ṣumɓurạ.

ṣuɓur dạ bāḳī *m.* angry child's pouting (*cf.* ṣuɓul 2).

suɓū-ṣuɓū *pl.* huge and round (*x* cheeks, fruits).

ṣuɓutạ *Vb.* 3B (1) = sulluɓē. (2) ṣuɓutạr bāḳī = ṣuɓul 2.

sūdā *f.* (1) (*a*) Senegal Bush Shrike (*Pomatorhyneus Senegalus*) = zụmụntā 2. (*b*) *epithet is* Sūdā maị lābārị, fạɗi bạ ạ tạmbạyē kị ba (*cf.* fạɗā 1*b*). (2) (*a*) chatter-box. (*b*) scandalmonger, gossip.

sụdā *Vb.* 2 wiped one's finger round vessel to gather remains of food sticking to it x yā sụdi ḳwaryā (*cf.* kwanɗẹ).

sudan A. (Sūdạŋ) (*Ar.* black ones) *f.* (1) the Sudan. (2) Sarkin $\sim$ the Emir of Kwạntạgōrā.

B. (sudạŋ = suddạŋ) *adv.* without cause (= ạ banzā).

suɗẹ *Vb.* 1A (1) (*a*) wiped up all *as in* sụdā (= kwanɗẹ). (*b*) (i) yā $\sim$ shi he has worn it (garment) out. (ii) yā rigā yā suɗẹ sōjạnsạ he has used up all his available troops. (*c*) Suɗe mụ gaisạ *m.* the famine of 1913–14 (= Mạlạlī = ḳāḳalabā). (2) *Vb.* 3A. (*a*) kạntạ yā $\sim$ much of her hair has fallen out. (*b*) ḳafạ tā $\sim$ his feet are skinned from travelling with rough sandals.

suɗị *m.* (1) remains of food left in vessel for dependants. (2) ita sụdịŋ Audụ cē she was once Audu's wife.

***sudụsī** *Ar. m.* one-sixth.

sụfādụ *m.* (1) = sạfā 1. (2) type of slippers.

sufạrī *Nor.* = sifịrī.

sufcẹ *Kt.* = suɓucē.

sufẹ *Sk. m.* (1) lungs (= hụhū). (2) good-for-nothing P. (= ragō).

***Sūfī** *Ar. m.* (*pl.* Sūfāyē) Sufi mystic.

sufụlī = sifịlī.

sufụrī = sifịrī.

sụfurtạ = sịfirtạ.

sugạ *Eng. f.* sugar (= sukạr).

sugulmudī *m.* (1) = alguŋgumancị. (2) = fēlēḳē.

sụhānị = sạhānị.

sụhụr = sạhụr.

suhụrī = sifịrī.

sui = sụ yi x sui nạdāmạ let them repine ! **sụjadạ** = *Sk.* sụjudạ *Ar. f.* religious prostrations.

suka A. (sukạ) they (*past relative verbal prefixed pronoun*) x (1) mutạ̄nạn dạ $\sim$ zō the people who came (Mod. Gram. 133, 181, 182). (2) $\sim$ cē *Vd.* cē 6.

B. (sūkạ) *m.* (1) (*secondary v.n. of* sōkā) x yanạ̄ sūkạnsạ = yanạ̄ sōkassạ he's piercing it. (2) (*a*) (i) act of sewing x Audụ dōgwan $\sim$ gạrēshị Audu has a long stitch. (ii) tying thatch to roof-frame (= kandạmā 2). (*b*) an yi $\sim$ bīyū, sǎi haḍị the beams have been overlapped and secured and it is now time to join the sides and form the building-arch (= kafị 3*a*). (3) (*a*) (i) act of piercing. (ii) kọ̄inā $\sim$ *Vd.* būtsātsạ. (iii) sūkạm māshị *Vd.* ɗạurarrīyar mạganạ. (iv) an yi masạ $\sim$ through malicious interference his transaction has fallen through (= sọ̄kā 1*b*.i). (*b*) stabbing pain. (4) (*secondary v.n. of* sōkẹ 1*e*) x anạ̄ sūkạnsạ cikin lịssāfị = anạ̄ sōkẹ shi cikin lịssāfị it is being deleted from the list, bill. (5) slaughtering a camel. (6) method of finishing kitsọ. (7) $\sim$ dubū *m.* type of numnah (mashimfidī). (8) *Vd.* sūkạn-*compounds*.

sukana A. (sukạnā) *Sk.* = sukwạ̄nā.

B. (sụ̄kanā) *m.* (1) fool (*epithet is* Sụ̄kanā mīyạr gyạɗā ran sallạ). (2) = sọ̄ki burūtsū. (3) = *Kt.* sūtai.

sūkaŋ kulūdu m. (1) a gambling game with leather. (2) Vd. kulūdu.

sūkan lamīri Kt. m. = iŋkis.

sukānyā Kt. = sukwānā.

sukar = sukari (Eng.) m. sugar.

sukē (present relative verbal prefixed pronoun) they x mutānan da sukē zūwa the people who are coming (133).

sukē = sikē.

sukōla (Eng. " scholar ") m. (1) schoolboy. (2) (a) yā (tā) yi ~ he (she) togged himself (herself) up (= sitāti 2). (b) kāyan ~ m. (i) articles of adornment. (ii) toilet preparations (x soap, powder, etc.).

sukuf A. (sukuf) (1) adv. gōnā tā yi hatsī ~ the farm is thick in corn. tanā da gāshī ~ she has abundant hair. (2) m. gōnā tā yi ~ da hatsī = 1.
B. (sukuf) = sukukuf-sukukuf.

sukuku x yanā zaune ~ = yā yi ~ he's sitting despondently.

sukūkūcē = sakwarkwācē.

sukukuf-sukukuf x gā shi sukukuf-sukukuf he is moping.

Sukuku makaka epithet of (1) snake, (2) Emir (2 = Dirkākau).

sukum Kt. = kusum.

sukum-sukum = sukuŋ-sukuŋ.

sukūni Ar. m. (1) leisure. (2) (a) having sufficient to live on. (b) ~ shī kē sā tūwan sāfē sufficiency of means leaves a calm mind.

sukunnīyā = sukurnīyā.

sukuŋ-sukuŋ = sukuŋ-sukuŋ m. and adv. (1) (a) nā ji ~ I heard a rustling-sound. (b) macījī yanā tafīya ~ the snake is rustling along. (c) yanā tafīya ~ he's travelling on silently, he's travelling on alone in the dark (cf. sumumu). (2) abin da ka ji yanā ~ cikin cīyāwa, iŋ kā zuba ido, zā ka ganī nē coming events cast their shadows before them.

sukup = sukuf.

sukūrīya f. (1) eagerly searching for T. (x rat fossicking for food in larder). (2) Eng. Government or N.A. School x (a) makarantar ~ f. Government or N.A. School. (b) dan ~ m. (f. 'yar ~) pl. 'yan ~ pupil of Government or N.A. School.

sukurkucē = sakwarkwācē.

sukurkurī m. lame excuse (= rarraunā 2b).

sukurnīyā f. fidgetiness (= mutsūnīyā).

sukūru = sukūrīya.

sukurwā = kusurwā.

suku-suku A. (sukū-sukū) m. (1) = kwalō-kwalō. (2) slackness of P. (3) = sukuŋ-sukuŋ.
B. (sukū-sukū) = sukuŋ-sukuŋ.
C. (sukū-sukū) m. = sukū-sukū 2.

sukutī Ar. (1) m. keeping silence. (2) adv. silently.

sukutum A. (sukutum) entirely.
B. (sukutum) m. and adv. (1) mutum ~ nē da shī he's a fat P. mace cē ~ da ita she'a a stout woman. dōki yanā tsaye ~ the horse as it stands there looks very fat. (2) gizō garēshi ~ he has a huge, unkempt poll.
B. sukutum sukutum dōki (said to children) clackety-clack go the hooves of my horse !

sukūwā f. (1) (a) galloping. (b) yā yi ~ he galloped. (c) bā ā yiŋ aikin naŋ da ~ this work cannot be done at lightning speed. (d) mutānan dūnīya in sun sāmi dōki da ~ sāi su kure don't overwork the willing horse ! (e) sun sāmi fīlin sukūwā they " got a clear field ". (2) yā yi mini ~ da lifidī he gave me more than I expected. (3) sukūwar salla number of persons attacking another P. (4) Vd. amaryā 9.

sukwana A. (sukwānā) Vb. 1C galloped (a horse) x yā sukwāna dōkinsa (= rāraka 1f = sukwāna 1a).
B. (sukwāna) (1) Vb. 2 (a) galloped (a horse) x yā sukwāni dōkinsa (= sukwānā = kwakura). (b) galloped over x dōki yā sukwāni fagyan naŋ the horse galloped over that course. (c) pillaged (in war). (2) Vb. 3B galloped away.

sukwānē Vb. 1C (1) pillaged completely (in war), cf. sukwāna 1c. (2) marōkā suŋ sukwānē garī the marōkā q.v. have cadged the town dry.

sukwāti = sakwāti.

sul used in bakī ~ jet black (= kirin).

sulai A. (sulai) m. used as follows dūtsē nē mai santsī ~ da shī it is a smooth rock. dūwātsū nē māsu santsī sulai-

sulai dą sū they are slippery stones
(= sumul 1).
  B. (sulai) *m.* (*pl.* sulūlūwą = *Sk.*
suląllā). (1) *Eng.* (*a*) shilling. (*b*)
dą A dą B, kąman ∼ dą ∼ A and B
are as like as two peas. (*c*) ∼ mąi
mąmį Victorian shilling. (*d*) (i) money
(in- general). (ii) ƙyąllin suląllā kę
rūdą su they are being deceived by
appearances. (iii) mąi ∼ nē he's
wealthy. (2) = Sulaimānu 1. (3) (*a*)
russet horse or ox with white patches.
(*b*) *Kt.* = saŋƙō 1*b*.
Sulaimānu (1) *Ar.* Solomon (= Sulai 2). (2)
(*Eng.* " cinema ") gidan ∼ cinema-
house (= mājigi).
sulala A. (sulālā) *Sk. Vb.* 1C. (1) warmed
up (tūwō) = zāfąfā 2, *cf.* suląlē. (2)
cooked (rice, nearly-cooked tūwō) by
steaming (2 = turārā 2), *cf.* zazząɓā,
hau dą 4.
  B. (sulālą) *Vb.* 3B *Sk.* (1) (tūwō)
was warmed up (*cf.* suląlā 1). (2)
(rice, nearly-cooked tūwō) was cooked
by steaming (*cf.* sulālā 2) = turārą 2.
(3) suną sulālą suu kąŋ kąŋkarā they
(skaters) are skimming over the ice.
sulale A. (sulālē) (1) *Vb.* 3A (*a*) (food)
cooled. (*b*) *Kt.* = sānę 1. (3) *Kt.* =
surārē. (2) *Sk.* = sulālā 2.
  B. (sulālę) *Kt. m.* = sānį.
suląllā *Vd.* sulai.
sulance A. (sūląncē) (1) *Vb.* 3A ąl'amąrī
yā ∼ the affair came to nothing.
(2) *Vb.* 1C = sūląntā.
  B. (sūląncē) (1) *m.* = sūlū 1. (2)
Vd. sūlantą.
sulanta A. (sūląntā) *Vb.* 1C. (1) made
(thread) into sūlū. (2) yā sūląntą
ąl'amąrī it caused the affair to end in
failure.
  B. (sūlantą) *Vb.* 3B = sūląncē 1.
sūlāyē *Vd.* sūlū, sullūwā.
sulɓā *Kt. f.* yā shā — he was abused.
sulɓę = sullųɓē.
sulɓī *m.* slipperiness.
Suldaŋ = Suldānį *m.* (*pl.* Suldąnai) Emir,
Sultan.
sule = sulai.
Sulęmānu = Sulaimānu.
sulhu *Ar. m.* (1) peace. (2) (*a*) reconciliation. (*b*) Sulhu mądākin tīląs Thou

arbitration hard to bear ! (*re litigants
being forced to submit to arbitration as court cannot decide where truth
lies*).
sulhuntā *Vb.* 1C. (1) made peace between
x an ∼ su. (2) forcibly arbitrated on
(litigants *as in* sulhu 2).
sulkē *m.* (*pl.* sulkuną) (1) chain-armour
(= bądaudī). (2) *cf.* sąfā 2.
sulkumī *m.* (*pl.* sulkumą) = asulkumī.
sulla = silla.
sullāyē *Vd.* sullūwā.
sulle = sille.
sullī = sillī.
sullųɓē (1) *Vb.* 1C *Kt.* (*a*) washed substance from exterior of T. (*b*) = sąɓulą.
(*c*) yā sullųɓę ąkwīyą he cut off the
goat's head, taking out the entrails
through that hole, and used the skin for
sąlkā. (*d*) abused. (2) *Vb.* 3A (*a*) it (T.
tied) became loose, slipped. (*b*) T.
slipped from one's hand *x* yā ∼ dągą
hannūna. (*c*) he (prisoner) slipped from
captor's custody (2*a–c* = sumɓulē =
sillę 2 = surārē 1). (*d*) it (skin injured
by a burn) peeled off (2 = sālųɓē).
sullūwā *f.* (*pl.* sullāyē = sūlāyē = sullū-
wōyī) type of bangle.
sulmīyą *Vb.* 3B (1) slipped off T., fell off
T. (2) slipped into, fell into (hole,
water, etc.).
sulmīyē *Vb.* 3A = sulmīyą.
sūlū *m.* (*pl.* sūlāyē) (1) in the process
wadąrī, skein of white thread of length
required for weaving narrow width
material or dyeing = wadąrī 2 (*cf.*
lanyącē 3). (2) (*a*) good-for-nothing P.
(= ragō). (*b*) ąl'amąrī yā yi ∼ the
affair came to nothing. (*c*) sūlum mazā
= 2*a above.*
suluf (1) *adv.* (*a*) yā wąŋku ∼ it's washed
snow-white. (*b*) an zāgē shi ∼ = yā
shā wąŋki ∼ = aŋ wąŋwąŋkē shi ∼
he's been roundly abused (*cf.*
wąŋkā). (2) *m.* an yi masą ∼ = 1*b
above.*
suluki = siliki.
sululū (1) *m.* = sukuŋ-sukuŋ 1*a.* (2)
Sululū na būnū *epithet of any* snake or
lizard. (3) *adv. x* yā shigō sululū he
entered noiselessly (= sulu-lululū).
sululū kąsau = faŋkąm fayąu 2.

sụlụ-lụlụlụ silently (= sụlụlụ 3).

sulūlūwạ *Vd.* sulại.

sulum *x* kadạ yā fādạ rūwa ∼ crocodile leaped into the water.

sụlụŋgụdum *adv.* (1) yā tạfi ∼ he went unarmed. (2) hakạ akẹ bịkī sụlụŋgụdum ? is it fitting to give a feast like this without drumming ?

sulup = suluf.

*sụlụsāni *Ar. pl. m.* two-thirds.

*sulụsī *Ar. m.* one-third.

sūlūwā = sullūwā.

sum A. (sụm) = sọrọm.

B. (sum) *adv.* (1) completely *x* shẹkarạ ∼ sukạ yī shị they did it for a whole year. yā dạukẹ kāyā ∼ he removed all the loads. (2) yā fịta ∼ he went away without taking leave.

suma A. (sūmā) (1) *Vb.* 3B (*a*) fainted. (*b*) became dazed (from shock, blow, etc.). (*c*) became speechless (from fear, etc.). (*d*) withered (*d* = yạŋkwanạ). (2) *m., f.* fainting-fit.

B. (sụmā) *f.* (1) hair of the head (*cf.* gāshị, gịzō). (2) *Kt.* sāran ∼ *m.* shaving baby's head on naming-day (ran sūnā).

sụmākại = gạmsạkại.

sūmạncē *Vb.* 3A = sūmā 1.

sumba A. (sumbạ) (1) what a paunch ! (2) what a stench ! (3) *Vd.* bardē 1.

B. *(sumbā) *f.* kiss.

*sumbạcē = sumbạncē *Vb.* 1C kissed.

*sụmbantạ *Vb.* 2 (*p.o.* sụmbạncē, *n.o.* sụmbạnci) kissed.

sụmbattā *f.* muzzle for animal (= tạkuŋkụmī 2).

sumbāyē *Vd.* sumbū.

sụmbitạ = sụmbwitạ.

sumbū *m.* (*f.* sumbūwā) *pl.* sumbāyē debilitated P.

sumbụdē *Vb.* 3A became weak.

sumbụlē = sullụbē 2*a–c*.

sụmbụr dạ bạkī = sụbụr.

sụmbụrạ *Vb.* 2 yā sụmbụri bạkī he (angry child) pouted (*Vd.* sụbụr).

sụmbụrē (1) *Vb.* 1C = sụmbụrạ. (2) *Vb.* 3A bạkinsạ yā ∼ he has swollen lips.

sụmbwitạ *f.* stoutness of middle-aged women *x* tā sōmạ ∼ she is getting the middle-aged spread.

sụmfuk = sụmfut = sụkụf *q.v.*

sụmī = sịmī.

summat (*Ar.*) *used in* wạllāhị, ∼ Ạllāhị I swear by God !

sumul (1) *m.* (*pl.* sumul-sumul) = sulai. (2) *adv.* (*a*) yā fịta ∼ = suɓul 1, 2. (*b*) yā warkẹ ∼ = suɓul 3.

sumụlikạ = simịlikạ.

sụmụlmulạ = sịllā 1.

sumulmụlē *Vb.* 1D = sillẹ 1*d*.

sumumu silently (= sụkụŋ-sụkụŋ 1*c*).

*sumụnī *Ar. m.* one-eighth.

sumuntị *Eng. m.* cement, concrete. dākịn ∼ house of permanent brick, etc., construction.

sụmwī = sụmī.

sun A. (sun) (1) they (*verb-prefix of past tense,* Mod. Gram. 12) *x* ∼ zō they came, have come. (2) *cf.* sụ 2*b*.

B. (sụn) *Sk.* = sạ (Mod. Gram. 118) *x* sụn zō they'll probably come.

suna A. (sunạ) they are (*verb-prefix of progressive,* Mod. Gram. 16) *x* ∼ zūwạ they are coming.

B. (sūnā) *m.* (*pl.* sūnạyē = *Kt.* sūnạnnakī). (1) (*a*) name. (*b*) *x* mụtụm mại sūnā mụtụm wạndạ ya kashẹ the true number of persons whom he murdered. jimlạr dạŋ Adạŋ mại sūnā dạŋ Adạŋ wadạndạ sukạ mutụ the real total of persons dead. (2) ịnā sūnạŋkạ = wạnē sūnạŋkạ what is your name ? (3) (*a*) an sạ (= yi) masạ ∼ he was named. (*b*) mẹ akạ sạ masạ sūnạ what name was he given ? sun sạ wạ birnịŋ sūnansạ they named the town after him. (*c*) an yi masạ ∼ Mūsā he was named Moses. (4) kạ sạ ∼ suggest a price for selling your article so that we can bargain ! (*cf.* tayạ). (5) (*a*) ran ∼ = rānar radạ ∼ *m.* naming-day of child (seventh day after birth). (*b*) sun jē kạrɓar ∼ they've gone to infant's naming-ceremony. (*c*) sunạ ∼ they're occupied in the naming-ceremony (*cf.* ụŋgōzọmạ, wạnzāmị, yinị 1*c.*ii, zānạ 5, būdar kụnnē, radạ, zụbe baŋ kwaryāta). (*d*) rạgwan ∼ *Vd.* yạŋkạ 1*a.*v. (*e*) sūnan yạŋkā *Vd.* yạŋkạ 1*b*, fitọ 6. (6) (*a*) (i) yā yi ∼ he became famous *x* yā yi ∼ cikin dịŋkị = yā yi sūnan dịŋkị he is a famous tailor. (ii) *Vd.* ɓātạ 1*b*. (*b*) dạ kụrū gạdā tā yi ∼ fancy his being

able to do that !   (c) kạrātū gạrēshi
he is learned (reply, kạrātū ? kō sūnā
learned or merely so called ?)   (7) ~
linzāmi nē hearing one's name spoken
arrests one's attention.   (8) sun tārạ ~
they're namesakes (Vd. tạkwạrā).   (9)
maị ~ Zar. m. gonorrhea (= mạsūnā).
C. (sūnā) f. any grain about a year or
more old.

sunāsạr = sunāsụr = sịnāsịr q.v.

sūnāyē Vd. sūnā.

sunce A. (suncẹ) = sancẹ.
B. (suncē) Vd. suntā.
C. *(suncē) = *sincē.

sunci Vd. suntā.

*sundĭyā Fil. f. instrument used in kitsọ.

sundūƙi Ar. m. (pl. sundūƙai) box.

sundulē m. = kạsundulā.

sundum = sundum = suŋƙum q.v.

sundụmē = suŋƙụmē.

sundumēmẹ m. (f. sundumēmĭyā) pl.
sunduŋ-sundụŋ big and swollen (re
round, hard T.).   (1) x kụmburĭ ~ a
hard swelling on the body. dạŋkalị ~
big potato.   (2) cf. sundụndụŋ.

sundumĭ m. (f. sundumā) pl. sunduŋ-
sundụŋ = sundumēmẹ.

sundundun A. (sundụndụŋ) (1) m. being
swollen (as in sundumēmẹ) x ƙafạ
tasạ ~ dạ ita his foot is very swollen.
(2) adv. ƙātọ nē ~ he's a huge lout.
ƙāfạ tasạ tā kụmburạ ~ his leg is
very swollen.   (3) Vd. sụŋkuf.
B. (sundundụŋ) used in dạɓē bạ̄
wāƙạ ~ (said by women) if we do
floor-beating without a song, it is
dull work.

sunduŋ-sundụŋ Vd. sundumēmẹ, sundumĭ.

sunfuk = sunfut = sụkụf q.v.

sunga A. (suŋgā) Vb. 2 Kt. x yā suŋgē
shị dạ māshị he threw a spear at him
(= jēfā).
B. (suŋgạ) Vb. 1A (with dative) Kt.
x yā ~ masạ māshi he threw a spear
at him (= suŋgā = jēfạ).

sungẹ (1) Vb. 1A Kt. x yā ~ shi dạ
māshị = suŋgā.   (2) Sk. m. = gịnā
2a.

suŋgumạ Vb. 2 (1) lifted (large or heavy
load).   (2) took without permission.

suŋgụmē Vb. 1C = suŋgumạ.

sungumēmẹ m. (f. suŋgumēmĭyā) pl.
suŋguŋ-suŋgụŋ = sundumēmẹ.

sungumi A. (suŋgumĭ) m. (f. suŋgumā) pl.
suŋguŋ-suŋgụŋ = sundumēmẹ.
B. (suŋgumĭ) Kt. m. (1) long-handled
wooden hoe to which blade (rūwā) is
joined and which is only used on the
day of sowing corn (epithet is Suŋgumĭ
rānarkạ dayā).   (2) Vd. yā dạ 3f.

suŋgụŋgụŋ = sundụndụŋ.

sungun-sungun A. (suŋguŋ-suŋgụŋ) Vd.
suŋgumēmẹ, suŋgumĭ.
B. (suŋguŋ-suŋguŋ) = zuŋgwĭ-
zuŋgwĭ.

sunkạ Sk. = sukạ.

sunƙạ Vb. 1A put too much (food) into
the mouth.

suŋƙāƙạ = sịŋƙāƙạ.

suŋƙạƙē = suŋkwĭyā.

suŋ'ƙe-suŋƙē" = dạmē-dạmē 1.

suŋkụ = shuŋkụ.

sunkuce A. (suŋkụcē) Vb. 1C = suŋkutạ.
B. (suŋkụcē) Vd. suŋkutạ.

suŋkuf = suŋƙum.   (1) = sụkụf.   (2) =
sundụndụŋ 2.   (3) m. and adv. Sarkī yā
yi suŋƙum = Sarkī yā fitō suŋƙum the
Emir came out with burnous drawn
over his head (= kudẹ 1c).

suŋƙụmē Vb. 3A swelled (as in sundumēmẹ) = sundụmē.

suŋƙumēmẹ = sundumēmẹ.

suŋƙumĭ = sundumĭ.

suŋkuŋ-suŋkụŋ = sunduŋ-sundụŋ.

suŋkup = suŋkuf.

suŋƙūrụ = Kt. suŋkūrụ m. uncultivated
land near town or village (= sāgāgĭ).

suŋkutạ Vb. 2 (p.o. suŋkụcē, n.o. suŋkụci)
(1) lifted (load, etc.) hurriedly.   (2)
(ox, cow) tossed P. or T.

suŋkuyạ = suŋkwĭyạ.

suŋkwĭyā Vb. 3A = suŋkwĭyạ Vb. 3B (1)
(a) bent down, stooped.   (b) rānā
tā ~ the sun's about to set.   (c) azzi-
kinsạ yā ~ his luck's on the wane.
(2) (a) became cheaper.   (b) săi kạ ~
reduce the price !   (3) yā ~ kạŋ aikị
he set to work with a will.   (4) asalim
mạganạn nạŋ Lārabcī nē ạmmā tā ~
this word is of Arabic origin, but it
has become changed in form.

suŋkwĭyad dạ Vb. 4 bent T. down x yā ~
kạnsạ he bowed his head (=Kt.dūƙaddạ).

suŋkwīyę *m.* yā fadi ～ he contradicted himself.

suŋkwu *used in* yā ～ da kansa he bowed his head (= suŋkwīyad da).

sunna (1) *Vb.* 1A *(with dative)* (*a*) yā ～ mini shī he handed it to me surreptitiously. (*b*) tā ～ masa cīwǫ she infected him with disease (= fcunsa 6*b*). (*c*) *Kt.* = cūna 1*b*. (2) *Ar. f.* (*a*) rites and customs enjoined by Islam. (*b*) (i) observance recommended by Islam, but not quite farilla (*e.g.* marriage is sunna). (ii) ～ mu'affcada observance almost indistinguishable from farilla. (*c*) *Vd.* Sunnī. (*d*) *x* yā mai da tāba sǎi ka cę ～ he's an inveterate smoker (= tāba 4).

sunnantā (1) = sunnatā. (2) *Vb.* 1C imposed an observance as being sunna 2.

sunnatā *Vb.* 3A shook hands (= musāfaha).

sunne A. (sunnę) *Vb.* 1A = mafcę 2*b*.
    B. (sunnē) *m.* acting *as in* sunna 1*a*.

Sunnī *Ar. m.* (*sg., pl.*) (1) member of one of the four Orthodox sects of Islam (as distinguished from Shias, etc.). (2) *Vd.* sunna 2.

sunnīyā *f.* (1) acting *as in* sunna 1*a*. (2) carrying T. tucked under one's arm *as in* sāyi 3*a*.

sunsunā = sansanā.

sunta A. (sunta) = sancę.
    B. (suntā) *Vb.* 2 (*p.o.* suncē, *n.o.* sunci) *x* yā sunci kīfī he got fish by fishing.

suntali *m.* (*pl.* suntula) = sintalī.

suntī *Sk. m.* = fanyā 3.

suntuɓa *Vb.* 3B = suntuɓā *Vb.* 3A (1) went away. (2) *Vd.* suntuɓō.

suntuɓēɓę *m.* (*f.* suntuɓēɓīyā) *pl.* suntuɓā-suntuɓā *adj.* fat (*re the living*).

suntuɓī *m.* (*f.* suntuɓā) *pl.* suntuɓā-suntuɓā = suntuɓēɓę.

suntuɓō (1) *Vb.* 3A returned hither (*cf.* suntuɓā). (2) *Vb.* 1E tā ～ 'yā'yā she (woman or animal) produced big offspring (*cf.* suntuɓēɓę).

suntuɓtuɓ = suntuntum.

suntula *Vd.* suntali.

suntum *m.* fatness *x* yā yi ～ he is fat.

suntumā = suntuɓā.

suntumēmę *m.* (*f.* suntumēmīyā) pl. suntum-suntum = suntuɓēɓę.

suntumī *m.* (*f.* suntumā) *pl.* suntum-suntum = suntuɓēɓę.

suntuntum *m.* fatness of living T. *x* dōki nē ～ da shī it is a fat horse. macę cē ～ da ita she is a fat woman.

sunu *m.* (*Ar.* huznu) (1) sadness. (2) yana shan ～ he's having a bad time.

sūnūnu *m.* large amount *x* sūnūnum mutānē large concourse. sūnūnun dārī severe cold weather.

*suppa = *siffa.

sur A. (sur) *adv.* (1) yā cika ～ it is chock-full (= fal). (2) wuni ～ during a whole day. (2) 'yar hanya ～ a narrow path.
    B. (sur) *x* yā sauka ～ he descended rapidly.

sura A. (sūra) *pl.* sūrōrī *Ar.* (1) (*a*) appearance *x* yana da kyan ～ he has good appearance (= kamā). (*b*) image, picture, model, photo, map *x* yā zāna sūrar dōki he made a picture of a horse. yā jā sūra he painted a picture (= *taswīra). (*c*) līyāri mai ～ Maria Theresa dollar (*some have* sūrar tsuntsū *Vd.* mutar, *others have* sūrar mutum uku, *others have* sūrar tāgūwa, *Vd.* tāgūwa 1*d*). (2) chapter of the Koran.
    B. (sūrā) (1) *Vb.* 2 *x* shirwa tā sūri dan tsākō the hawk swooped on the chick (= faucę = sūrę). (2) *f.* shirwa tā kāwō (= tā dakō) ～ the hawk swooped down.

surace A. (surācē) *Vb.* 3A *Kt.* = sulālē 1*a*.
    B. (surācē) *m.* steaming one's body to cure fever.

surādā *Vd.* sirdi.

suradu = suraddu = suraddū *m.* a plant with hairy blossom (*given to newly circumcised lads to keep others away from the sore part*).

surandu *Kt. m.* = suradu.

surārē *Vb.* 3A (1) = sullubē 2*a-c*. (2) slid along.

Sūrau (1) *epithet of* shirwa. (2) ～ fanam ɓarāwo *epithet of* tugu 2.

*Surayyā *Ar. f.* Pleiades (= kāzā 2*a*).

sure A. (sūrę) *Vb.* 1A (1) (hawk, etc.) swooped on and seized (*cf.* sūrā). (2) snatched up and stole.

B. (sūrē) *Sk. m.* = yākūwā.

C. (surę) *Vb.* 3A (1) = sulālē 1*a*. (2) (person) deteriorated.

surfa A. (surfą) (1) *Vb.* 1A (*a*) (i) did first pounding of (*moistened corn, to remove bran*). (ii) *Vd.* dakạ 1*a*, surfē, turzạ 1*b*. (*b*) did much of *x* an ∼ rūwā yau it rained heavily to-day. yā ∼ ƙaryā he told a whopping lie. (2) *Vb.* 3A yā ∼ dạ gudụ he took to his heels.

B. (surfā) *Vb.* 2 abused.

surfānē *Vb.* 1C embroidered with surfānị.

surfānị *m.* open chain-stitch in embroidery.

surfau *m.* for payment, pounding *as in* surfạ.

surfe A. (surfē) *m.* the first pounding *as in* surfạ *q.v.*

B. (surfę) *Vb.* 1A pounded (*as in* surfạ) all the corn.

C. (surfē) *m.* type of top-spinning game.

sūrị *m.* (1) (*a*) large ant-hill made by zagō (*cf.* jiƃā). (*b*) tuŋkū yā san sūrịn dạ yakę kāshī everyone knows his own limitations. (*c*) huge amount *x* yā bā nị hatsī ∼ gụdā he gave me a tremendous lot of corn. (2) light-brown colour (especially of oxen).

surkạ *Vb.* 1A (1) added cold water to hot *x* rūwan naŋ yā yi zāfī, ạ ∼ this water is too hot, add some cold ! (2) anā ∼ gụmī this warm spell in the present cold season is unusual !

surkāmị *m.* pus (= mūgụ 3).

surkị *Kt. m.* ready-mixed furā.

surkụdūdụ *m.* (*f.* surkụdūdụwā) weak-minded.

surƙuƙī *m.* = sarƙaƙƙīyā.

surkullē *m.* (1) (*a*) daft P. (*epithet is* Surkullē, mīyạr gyạdā ran sallạ). (*b*) = sōki bụrūtsū. (*c*) Filani's repeating magic rigmarole (*Vd.* ƙịtịjǫ). (2) type of woman's coiffure, using merely her own hair without dōkạ.

surkụmī = asulkụmī.

surkunnị *Vd.* surukī.

surkụntā *Sk. f.* = sạrạkutạ.

surkutę *Kt. m.* = auran ɗauki sạndaŋkạ *q.v. under* ɗauki sạndaŋkạ.

sūrōrī *Vd.* sūrạ.

sūrū *m.* (1) (*a*) falling by a top (kạtantaŋwạ) on its opening and so resulting in player winning (*cf.* kaŋgar 2). (*b*) easily getting what one wants. (2) (*a*) type of fish-trap. (*b*) type of bird-snare.

suruf (1) *m.* sound of sipping. (2) *adv.* yā kụrƃā ∼ he sipped sip-sip-sip.

surukī *m.* (*f.* surukā = surụkūwā) *pl.* surụkai = surkai = *Sk.* surkunnị) (1) (*a*) surukī father-in-law. (*b*) surukā, *etc.*, mother-in-law. (2) (*a*) surukī son-in-law. (*b*) surukā, *etc.*, daughter-in-law. (3) surụkai relations-in-law. (4) *Vd.* sạrạkūwā. (5) aikịn surụkai *Vd.* jirƙō.

surụkutạ = surụkuntạ *f.* in-law relationship.

surụm = sạrạm.

surup = suruf.

surụrī *m.* = sūrūtụ.

sururu A. (sururu) *x* yā fịta ∼ he slipped away unobserved.

B. (surụrụ) *Kt.* = kụrụrụ.

C. (sūrūrụ) *m.* bran from corn ground unmoistened (= dụsūsụ).

sūrūrụcē *Vb.* 3A *Kt.* = tsūrūrụcē.

sūrū-sūrū *m.* = izụ-izụ.

sūrūtụ *m.* (*pl.* sūrụtai) loud garrulity *x* (1) yanā ∼ = yanā sūrụtai (i) he's chattering loudly. (ii) he's raving in dream or delirium. (2) tā zubạ masạ sūrūtụm banzā she buried him in a flood of loud talk.

sūsạ *f.* (1) (*sec. v.n. of* sōsạ) *x* yanā sūsạr jịkinsạ = yanā sōsạ jịkinsạ he's scratching himself. (2) (*a*) act of scratching (irritating place on body). (*b*) bā ā gamạ gudụ dạ sūsạr shākịrā *Vd.* gudụ 2*d*.v. (*c*) an yi minị ∼ ịndạ yakę ƙaịƙayī = *Kt.* an yi minị ∼ ạ bugyạn ƙaịƙai it suited me down to the ground.

sūsancị *m.* foolishness (*Vd.* sūsụsū).

sūsīyạ *f.* (1) = shụnayyạ 2. (2) type of cloth.

B. (sūsīyạ) = sạisayạ.

sussuƃā = ạsussuƃā.

sussuka A. (sussukā) *Vb.* 1C = cāsạ 1.

B. (sussukạ) (1) *Vb.* 2 = sussụkā. (2) *f.* (*a*) act of threshing. (*b*) cī ƃā ∼ *Vd.* cạsā 3.

sussukē (1) *Vb*. 1C threshed all the small quantity of corn (*Vd*. cāsạ 1). (2) *Vb*. 3A = diddįgē 1, 2.

sūsụ̄cē *Vb*. 3A (1) (affair) came to nothing. (2) P. deteriorated (*cf*. sūsụ̄sū).

sūsụ̄sū *m*. (*f*. sūsụ̄sūwā) *pl*. sụ̄sụ̄sai witless fool (= shāshạ̄shā).

sụ̄sūwạ *Sk. f*. (1) = ạsū. (2) = gundạ.

sūtai *m*. dreams in the cold season (*epithet is* Sūtai mafarkin ɗārī) = *Kt*. sụ̄kanā 3.

sutu A. (sūtū) *m*. (1) teasing cotton before spinning it. (2) sūtul laɓai useless P.

B. (sụtū) *Kt. m*. = sụkụtī.

sụturạ = sįtirạ.

*sutụrcē *Vb*. 1C clothed.

sutụ-sutụ *x* ƙafạ̄funsạ suŋ kumbụrē ∼ his legs are very swollen.

sụụ (1) *m*. *x* nā ji ∼ I heard a slithering sound. (2) *adv*. *x* (*a*) macįjī yanạ̄ tạfīyạ ∼ the snake is slithering along. sunạ̄ sụlālạ sụụ kaŋ kạŋkarā they (skaters) are skimming over the ice. (*b*) sǎi sōjạ kakē ganī sụụ, sụụ there are masses of soldiers.

suwa A. (sūwā) *Kt*. = sū 1.

B. (su wạ) *Vd*. wạ̄, wạ̄nē 2*a*, su 1.

su wạnạ̄ *Vd*. wanẹ.

su wane A. (su wạ̄nẹ) = su wạnēnẹ̄ *Vd*. wạ̄nẹ, wạ̄nēnẹ̄, Wạ̄nē.

B. (Su wānẹ) *Vd*. Wānẹ.

su wạnēnẹ̄ *Vd*. wạ̄nēnẹ̄.

sūyạ *f*. (1) (*sec. v.n. of* sōyạ) *x* tanạ̄ sūyạr gyạɗā = tanā sōyạ gyạɗā she is frying ground-nuts. (2) (*a*) act of frying. (*b*) sǎi dạ ya yi minį ∼ tụkụnā ya bā nį he delayed long in giving it me. (3) zūcįyāta tā yi minį ∼ I have heartburn (= kwạnnạfī). (4) *Vd*. tsįrē 2. (5) bạ sụ rįnjạ̄yē mụ ba sǎi dạ mukạ dẹbi na gashį, dạ na dạfūwā, dạ na sūyạ dạgạ cikin sōjạnsụ they did not overcome us without our taking heavy toll of their troops (*cf*. sōyạ 2).

sū yẹ̄ sū *Vd*. yẹ̄.

swạ̄ *Sk*. = sạ̄ A.3 *x* swạ̄ zō they will probably come.

swāɓạ *Sk*. = sāɓạ.

swạ̄ɓō *Sk*. = sạ̄ɓō.

swāfē (1) *Sk*. = sāfē. (2) *Nor*. = sāfī 1.

swāfī *Sk*. = sāfī 1.

swahhē *Kt*. = sāfē.

swāƙį *Sk*. = sāƙį.

swal = sal.

swālẹ *Sk*. = sālẹ.

swạm = sạrạm.

swancẹ *Sk*. = sancẹ.

swānẹ *Sk*. = sānẹ.

swantạ *Sk*. = suntạ.

swạntī *Kt. m*. = fanyā 3.

swạrạm *Kt*. = sạrạm.

T

ta A. (tạ̄) she will probably (Gram. 118) *x* tạ̄ zō she will probably come.

B. 1 (ta) (1) via *x* (*a*) bįyō ∼ naŋ come this way ! yā shįga ∼ ƙōfạ he entered by the door. nā bi ∼ kạ̄sūwā I went via the market. hanyạn naŋ ∼ įnā ta bį where does this road lead ? nā bi ∼ kạnsạ = nā bi ∼ wurinsạ I called at his house. (*b*) kadạ kạ bi ∼ kạnsạ don't follow his example ! (*c*) ∼ hakạ by these means, in this way. ta wannạŋ hanyạ in this way. (*cc*) zā mụ fārạ ta kạm farin lạ̄bārį we'll begin with the good news. (*d*) (i) anạ̄ ∼ kǎi, wạ̄ yakẹ ∼ kāyạ it is everyone for himself ! (ii) yi ta kạŋkạ be on your guard ! kụ yi ∼ kạŋkụ look after your own affairs !, mind your own business ! (iii) ∼ kǎina nakẹ yị I'm relying on myself alone. (iv) ta kǎi nikẹ I've all I can do to look after *myself*, so how can I help *you* ! (*reply to* please help me !). (*e*) *Vd*. barį 1*d*, fạdā 1*d*, cẹ̄wā 2*b*. (*ee*) kun san yạddạ (= ta yạddạ) mukạ yi you know how we acted. (*f*) (*preceded by* sanį) knew all about *x* baį san ∼ wurạ̄raŋ dạ zā sụ ɓullō ba he does not know whence they will appear. yā san ta bindigạ he knows all about guns. (*g*) (*followed by subjunctive*) in such a way that *x* aŋ ƙārạ ƙarfạfā masạ zūcįyā kẹ̄ naŋ ∼ yạ kōmạ gạ irįŋ halạ̄yansạ what was done merely gave him a better chance to return to his former evil ways. (2) yi ta proceeded to (*followed by noun, v.n. or sec. v.n.*) *x* yā yi ∼ dạriyā he began

to laugh. mu̱ yi ta yḭ let us get to work !
ka̱ yi ~ aiki̱ set to work ! su̱n ka̱fa̱
i̱gwā, su̱nā̱ ~ harbi̱mmu̱ they set up
artillery and began to shoot at us
(for omission of yḭ, Vd. Gram. 159a).
sun yi ~ ha̱ḵwa̱nsa̱ they proceeded to
lay plans to capture it.
B. 2 (ta) (1) she (verbal-prefix past
relative sense, Gram. 133a*) x (a)
lōka̱ci̱n da̱ ~ zō when she came.
sa̱n da̱ ~ jē Kano̱, sǎi ta gam mu̱
when she went to Kano she saw us
(Gram. 181). (b) (in Sk. the following
consonant may be doubled) x a̱bi̱n da̱
tag ganī what she saw. (2) my (following
fem. noun, Gram. 47d) x (a) mā̱tāta
my wife. kunā̱ ta̱mbāya̱ta you are
asking me, cf. na 6a, 6b. (b) (-ta "my"
becomes tā before cē̱) x mā̱tātā cē̱ she
is my wife. (3) of (alternative with
-r after fem. noun, Gram. Chapter 3) (a)
(i) sānḭyar Dauda̱ = sānḭyā ta Dauda̱
David's cow. (ii) (instead of -r, we
often find the first consonant of the
second word doubled) x ka̱̱kā harvest,
ka̱̱kar dāwa̱ = ka̱̱kad dāwa̱ guinea-
corn harvest ; ka̱̱kar gērō = ka̱̱kag gērō
millet harvest. sānḭyar na̱ŋ = sānḭyan
na̱ŋ this cow. mā̱tarsa̱ = mā̱tassa̱ his
wife. (iii) (fem. nouns not ending in -a,
add -n like masculines, Vd. na) x
ma̱cē̱ wife, ma̱ca̱n Dauda̱ = mā̱tar
Dauda̱ David's wife (Mod. Gram.
10e.i). ma̱ca̱nsa̱ = mā̱tassa̱ his wife.
(b) (ta must replace -r when " of "
is separated from its noun) x wa̱sīyya̱r
na̱ŋ ~ Dauda̱ this will and testament of
David's. (bb) Vd. na 3–7. (c) that of (after
fem. noun) x (i) sā̱ḵa̱n na̱ŋ ~ Kano̱ cē̱
this weaving is that of Kano. (ii) ya̱nā̱
sǫ ya̱ sāke̱ iri̱n ta dā̱ he wants to return
to his old tricks. (iii) ta Allā̱, bā̱ tāsu̱ ba
they're evil miscreants (cf. Allā̱ 1k.ii).
(iv) ta sā̱ da̱ba̱ŋ Vd. sā̱ A.2 1e. (v) ta
sāfē ta yāro̱ Vd. sāfē̱. (d) Vd. na,
Ta gudu̱, Ta gwamba̱, ta gyē̱guma̱,
ta idō, ta bāwa̱, ta wantsa̱lā, zūcḭyā
13c, ta baka̱. (4) (objective pronoun
after low tone in previous verb, Mod.
Gram. 49a[1]) her x nā kāma̱ ta I seized
her (cf. ta̱ 1). (5) Vd. takē̱. (6) (3rd sg.
fem. pronoun used after za̱ Gram. 17

and bā̱ Mod. Gram. 22, 19b) x za̱ ta
ka̱sūwā she is off to market. bā̱ ta
zūwa̱ she's not coming. bā̱ ~ da̱
kōmē she has nothing.
C. (ta̱) (1) (objective pronoun after
high tone in previous verb, Mod. Gram.
49a[1]) her x (a) nā gan ta̱ I saw her (cf.
ta 4). (b) (often refers to noun meaning
" that affair ") x sǎi su̱ yḭ ta̱, kōwā
ya̱ hūta̱ let them make an end of the
job once and for all ! nḭyya̱rsu̱ a̱ yḭ
ta̱ it is their intention to finish off the job.
cf. tā 1a.ii. (2) (subjunctive pronoun 3rd
sg. fem.) x ta̱ zō let her come ! tanā̱ sǫ
ta̱ zō she wants to come (Gram. 13a).
(3) her (a) (i) miji̱nta̱ her husband
(Gram. 47b). (ii) ja̱kā tata̱ = ja̱karta̱ =
ja̱katta̱ her bag (Gram. 47b[2]).   (b)
(after v.n. of changing verbs and
after sec. v.n.) (i) a̱ikarta̱ = aiki̱nta̱
the sending her (Gram. 47c). nēmanta̱
the looking for her. ta̱mbaya̱rta̱ =
ta̱mbaya̱tta̱ = ta̱mbaya̱ tata̱ the asking
her (Gram. 47c). munā̱ nēmanta̱ we
a̱re looking for her. munā̱ ta̱mbaya̱tta̱
we are asking her (Gram. 10b.i, N.B.).
(ii) (gives continuous sense in cases
like the following) tā yi zamanta̱ cikin
d'āki̱n na̱ŋ well, she went on living
in that house. tanā̱ ta̱fīya̱ tata̱
sǎi . . . while she was on her way,
then . . . tanā̱ yāwa̱nta̱ sǎi . . . while
wandering about, she . . . (4) nāta̱
hers (after masc. noun) x zana̱n na̱ŋ
nāta̱ nē this cloth is hers. tāta̱ (after
fem. noun) x ḵwaryan na̱ŋ tāta̱ cē̱
this calabash is hers. (5) Vd. mata̱.
(6) she will (Gram. 14) x za̱ ta̱ zō she
will come. ba̱ za̱ ta̱ zō ba she will not
come (Gram. 20a). (7) she (negative past,
Gram. 20a) x ba̱ ta̱ zō ba she did not come.
E. (tā) (1) she (verb-prefix of past
tense) x (a) (i) tā zō she has come, she
came (Gram. 12). (ii) Vd. munzi̱lī 2 for
usage resembling ta̱ 1b. (b) tā fa̱ru, tā ka̱re̱
Vd. fa̱ru. (c) Vd. tā ga rānā ; tā kai
tā kōmō ; tā zāga̱, tā yi gidā.   (2)
Vd. su̱ 4, ta̱ 4, nā 2, ta B. 2, 2b.
F. (tā̱) (1) Vd. nā̱ 1.   (2) Sk. is (after
fem. noun) = cē̱ x ḵwaryā̱ ~ it is a
calabash (N.B. tone varies as for cē̱
q.v.). nī̱ ~ it is I (a woman), cf. nā̱ 4.

taa *x* jirāgē suŋ kētạ tẹ̀kū **taa** the ships clove their way through the ocean. suŋ kūtsạ kasạr **taa** they rushed rapidly into the country.

tạ'abạ (1) (*Vb. used only in this form*) suffered trouble (= **wạhalạ**). **(2)** *f.* trouble (= **wạhala**).

tạ'adạ = **tạ'adạ** *f.* (*pl.* ta'adōdī = ta'ādōdī) custom (= **ạl'ādạ**).

ta'addā *Ar. f.* **(1)** bad manners (= ladạbī 2*e*). **(2)** serious misdemeanour. **(3)** mischief, damage **(3 = tạ'adī** *q.v.*).

tạ'adī *m.* **(1)** = ta'addā 3. **(2) ạ jē ạ yi tạ'adim biṛị** let's go and scatter manure on the farm !

Tạ'ālā *used in* **Allā** ∼ God Almighty.

ta alakō *f.* poor-quality **furā** made for sale (*epithet is* Ta alakō, kōwā ya yi kirạŋkị sau d̦ayā bại mạtsu ba *for famished P. will go on calling till seller replies*).

tạ'ạllakạ *Vb.* 3B *Ar.* **(1)** devoted one's whole attention to *x* **yā** ∼ **dạ Audu** he is wrapped up in Audu. **yā** ∼ **dạ d̦iŋkị** all his attention is centred on tailoring. **(2)** is wholly dependent on. **(3)** *cf.* **talạkạ**.

*tạ'ammạlī = **tạ'ammụlī** *Ar. m.* **(1)** *x* bā nā̧ tạ'ammụliŋ kōmē dạ shī I make no use of it. **(2)** *x* yanā̧ ∼ dạ gōrọ (*a*) he trades in kola-nuts. (*b*) he squanders his money on kola-nuts.

tạ'annạtī = **tạ'annụtī** *Ar. m.* cross-questioning.

tạ'āsā *f.* **(1)** sharing a loss. **(2)** proportionately reducing shares of heirs when unexpected claimant arrives after the sharing out is complete.

tạ'azīyyạ *f.* **(1)** condolence after bereavement *x* nā yi masạ ∼ I went to pay my respects after his bereavement. **(2)** *cf.* gaisūwā 5 ; jẹ̀jētọ ; duhu 1*b* ; jājē.

tạ'azzarạ *Vb.* 3B *Ar.* **(1)** (commodity) is scarce. **(2)** P. is troubled.

taba A. (tābạ) *f.* **(1)** (*a*) tobacco (*epithet is* Tābạ, kim bạmbantạ dạ gārịŋ gērō). (*b*) yā shā ∼ (i) he smoked. (ii) he chewed powdered tobacco (gārịŋ tābạ), *cf.* 2, 3 *below*. (*c*) yā ci ∼ he chewed tobacco-leaf. (*d*) yā shẹ̀kạ ∼ he took

snuff. (*e*) tābạr hayākī tobacco for smoking (whether cigarettes or in pipe). (*f*) (i) furē yā fi ∼ *Vd.* bakạ 7. (ii) *Vd.* furē 1*a*.ii. (*g*) *Vd.* sạnsạ̄mī 2, tsạkī 3. **(2)** bā̧ lāfīyạ, kạrē yā shā ∼ things are very troublesome at the moment (*cf.* 1*b above*). **(3)** n nā̧ dạ ∼ I've some news for you (*reply*, bā̧ ni n̦ shā tell me it !). **(4)** yā zamā kạman ∼ wurinsạ it is an inveterate habit of his (= ịbādạ 2 = sunnạ 2*d*). **(5)** Tābạ mại shịgā zūcī (*in songs*) *epithet of* Lagos (Ịkkō). **(6)** *Vd.* tābạr-*compounds*.

B. (tā̧ɓā) *f.* fraud.

taɓa A. (tā̧ɓạ) *Vb.* 1A **(1)** = tāɓẹ̀. **(2)** = tāfạ.

B. (taɓạ) *Vb.* 1A **(1)** (*a*) touched. (*b*) ạbịn dạ ya ∼ hanci, idọ săi yạ yi rūwā what affects your family, affects you yourself. (*c*) (i) tạɓạ kạ̀ina kạ ji I refuse ! (ii) *Vd.* tsōkạ 2*b*. (*d*) nā ∼ sulẹ ukụ dạgạ cikiŋ kud̦iŋkạ I have taken three shillings out of your money. yā ∼ ạjīyạ he stole from the money entrusted or deposited with him (*Vd.* ạmānạ 4*a*). nā ∼ ạjīyạtạ I've drawn on the money in my account. (*e*) lại̦fin naŋ yā ∼ Audu Audu is implicated in this crime. (*f*) kasā (= igīyạ = igīyạr kasạ) tā ∼ shi a snake has bitten him. (*g*) affects *x* (i) mạganạn naŋ tā ∼ A dạ B this word applies both to A and to B. kadạ mụ rāɓạ wani ạbụ wandạ zại taɓạ mulkịŋkụ let us not take any action likely to encroach on your prerogative of rule. bā sā̧ saŋ wani ạbụ yạ ∼ shi they want no harm to come to him. (ii) iskōkī sun ∼ shi = kad̦ạ 1*o*. (*h*) sun ∼ zūcīyassạ = sun ∼ haŋkạlinsạ = sun ∼ rạnsạ = sun ∼ masạ rại they vexed him (= *Sk.* tam 2*a*). (*j*) sounded *x* (i) bại yi ba săi dạ ya ∼ su he did not do so without first sounding them. (ii) *Vd.* ạllī 3. (*k*) *Vd.* tạɓā ni luɓus. (*l*) yā ∼ dōkị he made his horse prance by reining it in sharply (= mātsạ 4 = zurạ 4*b* = tākụrā 2), *cf.* tsịkarạ. **(2)** did a little *x* (*a*) bā̧ ni rūwā n̦ ∼ give me a little water to drink ! zā̧ ni n̦ ∼ ại̦kị kạd̦aŋ I'll go and do a little work. (*b*) zạn ∼

rūwā (*euphemism*) I'll go and pass water (= kāmą 15*a*). (3) has previously done *x* kā ~ ganįnsą ? have you ever seen it ? ī, nā ~ ganinsą yes, I've seen it already. bąn ~ jį ba I've never heard it. nā sō ṇ ~ ganinsą it seems to me I have seen him before (= *Sk.* wādą), *Vd.* gwadą 7. (4) *Kt.* = tayą 1*a*.i. (5) *Vd.* tąɓąwā, tąɓaɓɓē, tąɓu, taɓa-compounds.

C. (tąɓā) *Vb.* 2 = taɓą 1.

tąba'ą *Sk. f.* = dąba'ą.

tābābą *f.* doubt (= shakką).

tababbā *Vd.* tabǫ.

tąɓaɓɓē *m.* (*f.* tąɓaɓɓīyā) *pl.* tąɓąɓɓū (*adj.* of state from taɓą) daft (= taɓį 2).

tābad dą *Vb.* 4 failed to give P. his due (= wulākąntā).

ta baką *Vd.* baką 4.

tąɓą-kunnē *m.*, *f.*, *sg.*, *pl.* (1) great-grandchild (= dā 8 = dan jīką). (2) great-great-grandchild (1, 2 = tąttąɓą kunnē).

tąɓą kuru cąs kuru *m.* dilatory work.

tąɓą luɓus = tąɓā ni luɓus.

tabambuną *Vd.* tabǫ.

ta bangwalā *f.* serenading and teasing circumcised lad slow to heal.

tąɓā ni luɓus *m.*, *f.* (*sg.*, *pl.*) slacker (= ragō = yārǫ 3*b*).

tąɓarą *Vb.* 3B = bunɓāsą 1.

tābąr ągulū = tābąr ungulū.

tąɓārau *m.* spectacles (= munząrī = madūbī).

taɓare A. (taɓārē) *Vd.* taɓaryā.

B. (taɓārę) *Sk. m.* type of cheap, white bodycloth worn by men and women.

Tąɓāri *Vd.* Sambǫ 1*b*.

taɓarki (*dialectal*) = tafarki.

tąbarkallā *Ar.* = tubarkallā.

tābąr ɓǭɓō *Kt. f.* = tąɓā ni luɓus.

tąɓarmā *f.* (*pl.* tąɓąrmī) (1) (*a*) mat. (*b*) tąɓarmar hannū mat made of narrow kijinjirī strips. (2) ɓafą ita kąn kāwō ɓasā ą ~ *someone* must have done it, for things don't do themselves. (3) tąɓarmar kunyą dą haukā kąn nadę ta now we know what folly he has done ! (4) tā zamā ~ wuyā she's such a nymphomaniac she fornicates instantly with every

male (= tąɓąlmī 5*b* = tsātsą 2 = ɓūɓą 2 = gāną 1*c*), *cf.* bąlagą 2. (5) tąɓarmar Barēbarī type of children's game. (6) shimfįdą ~ *Vd.* shimfįdā 1*b*. (7) *Vd.* shāfą tąɓarmā shūnī. (8) mąj tąɓarmā *Vd.* gadō 1*b*.ii.

tābąr ungulū *f.* a puff-ball fungus (= *Kt.* battąr ągulū).

taɓaryā = taɓaryą *f.* (*pl.* taɓārē). (1) (*a*) pestle (*it is thought horse or donkey stepping over pestle gets stomach-ache, curable only by being tapped thrice with the pestle : if woman takes pestle from one room to another, she first, out of superstition, taps it once on the ground*), *cf.* turmī. (*b*) yā hadīyę ~ he brought trouble on himself. kōwā ya hądįyi taɓaryā, yą kwānā tsąye evil recoils on the doer. (*c*) *Vd.* turmī 7. (2) rearing up by horse (= rīmī 3*c* = galląn 1*c* = *Kt.* samaryā = *Kt.* cįrar shisshinįyā = tsīrī 1), *cf.* turmī 5. (3) taɓaryad dąshī (*a*) *Vd.* Mųhammadų. (*b*) *f.* string puzzle.

tąɓashī *Kt. m.* small bundle of corn (*cf.* gwammā).

tąɓą-tāɓą *f.* plant like mashāyī 1.

Ta bątsallē *Vd.* dąddawā 1*b*.

tąɓą tuskurū *Kt.* = tąɓą kuru.

Ta bāwą *Vd.* bāwą 8.

taɓąwā *f.* (*d.f.* tąɓą 2) *x* gąrin nan dą nīsā ? is that town far ? (*reply*, dą ~ not too far) = tazarā = rātā 1 = *Kt.* shākątā 3.

tąbbā *Vd.* tabǫ.

tąbbącī undoubtedly (*d.f.* tąbbątą).

tąbbai *Vd.* tabǫ.

tabbąn *Kt.* = tabbąs.

tabbąs = tąbbącī.

tabbąsdī = tabbąshī *m.* bąn san tab-bąshinsą ba I don't know the real facts about it (*d.f.* tąbbątą).

tabbata A. (tabbątā) *Vb.* 1A. (1) (*a*) is (was) sure that *x* nā ~ shī nē I am certain it is he. ą tabbątā sun ɓarai nē there is no doubt about their defeat. (*b*) is (was) sure about *x* kō bą mų tabbątą kōmē ba, mun tabbątą ąbu gudā of one thing at least we are certain, and this is that . . . (2) (*a*) confirmed (a fact, rumour). (*b*) zā ką tabbątą halinką nē ? are you going to give another example of your bad character ? (= tạbbạtạ 2*b*). (3) *Vd.* tạbbạtạ, tabbatad.

B. (tạbbạtạ) (1) *Vb.* 3B (*a*) became confirmed *x* lạbạrịn yā ⁓ the news has proved true. yā ⁓ mụtumịn kirkị he has shown himself to be upright (= wạkānạ). (*b*) came to fruition *x* cịnikī bại ⁓ ba tụkụnā the transaction is not yet clinched. bā ạbịn dạ ya ⁓ dạgạ cikịn kudīna I've not yet succeeded in getting any of the money owing me. (*c*) lasted long, was (is) permanent *x* mulkịnkạ yạ ⁓ may you reign long ! mulkị bā yā tạbbạtạ dạ zāluncị rule founded on tyranny cannot endure. yạbō yā tạbbạtạ gạ Allạ praise be to God ! yā ⁓ kạn aikịnsạ (i) he has been doing this work for a long time. (ii) he has worked steadily, *cf.* tụturtạ. (2) *f.* (*a*) (i) permanence *x* bạn ga ⁓ gạ mulkịnsạ ba I do not think his rule will be permanent. (ii) yā nūnạ tạbbatạr amincị tsạkāninsụ it has shown the reality of the friendship between them. (iii) gidan ⁓ *m.* the next world *x* yā kōmạ gidan ⁓ he has died. (*b*) zā kạ ˙yi minị ⁓ tākạ dạ ka sạbạ ? = tabbạtā 2*a*. (3) *Vd.* tabbạtā, tabbatad.

tạbbạtaccē *m.* (*f.* tạbbạtaccīyā) *pl.* tạbbạtattū outstanding (for good qualities, unless context or previous knowledge of the facts indicates the contrary) *x* (1) tạbbạtaccan dōkị a fine horse. tạbbạtaccam mālạmī a fine scholar. (2) mụtụm ⁓ nē (*a*) he's prosperous and self-confident (= jī 7*c*). (*b*) he's true to his proved bad character.

tabbatad dạ *Vb.* 4 (1) = tabbạtā 1, 2*a* *x* nā tabbatar shī nē I am certain it is he. (2) confirmed (rumour, fact, etc.) ; assured P. that *x* yā tabbatar musụ kōmē wạhalạ, zā mụ ci nasarạ he left them in no doubt that whatever the effort involved we should continue till victorious, he convinced them that, etc. (3) confirmed (P. in office). (4) rendered permanent *x* Masạr, Allạ yạ tabbatad dạ mulkịntạ long live Egypt's rule ! (5) completed T. (6) *Vd.* tabbạtā.

tabbụnạ *Vd.* tabọ.

tabdēdẹ *m.* (*f.* tabdēdīyā) huge.
tabdị fancy that !
tạbẹ A. (tābẹ) (1) *Vb.* 1A (*a*) ripped *x* (i) yā ⁓ rịgarsạ he ripped his gown (= kēcẹ). (ii) yā ⁓ zōbẹ he forced the ends of the ring apart (*cf.* matsạ 1*a*). (iii) yā ⁓ bạkā he drew his bow. (iv) yā ⁓ bạkī he opened his mouth wide to yawn or bawl out. (*b*) yā ⁓ hannū he put his hands in boxing or punching attitude. (2) *Vb.* 3A. (*a*) became ripped (= kēcẹ 1). (*b*) was disappointed, failed to obtain his desire.

B. (tạbẹ) *m.* (1) touching a piece in darạ *q.v.* (2) = lālubē. (3) *Kt.* = sạbkē 2.

C. (tạbẹ) *Vb.* 1A ate up quickly (the insufficient food).

ta bēbē *Vd.* bēbē 2.
tạbẹnīyā *f.* (1) work requiring much bustling about. (2) difficult walk of fat or tired P.
tạbẹ-tạbẹ A. (tạˈbẹ-tạbẹ'') *m.* repeated touching, repeated pilfering, etc.

B. (tạbẹ-tạbẹ) *m.* = tạbẹnīyā.
tạbị A. (tạbị) *m.* (1) act of tạbạ 1, 2 *x* yạnạ tạbịn dōkịnsạ he is making his horse prance *as in* tạbạ 1*l* (= gallạn 1*b*). (2) ⁓ yā sạmē shị he is deranged (= tạbạbbē). (3) small share (*cf.* tạbạ 2). (4) tạbịn zūcịyā bad temper. (5) *Vd.* audụgā 2. *(6) sexual intercourse (= jịmāˈị).

B. (tābị) *Kt.* (1) = tạfī. (2) *used in* yā ⁓ ạlēkụn " he fell between two stools ".
tạbịˈạ *Nor. f.* = tsạbīˈạ.
tābịˈịnạ (*Ar. pl.*) *x* Sạhịbansạ dạ tābịˈịnạ His (Muhammad's) Companions and followers.
tābịyā *f.* forcing apart *as in* tābẹ 1*a*.ii.
ta bīzarō *f.* slut.
tabka A. (tabkạ) *Vb.* 1A did much of *x* an ⁓ kạsūwā jīyạ trade was very brisk yesterday. an ⁓ masạ būlālạ he was severely thrashed. yā ⁓ danyā he said many foolish things.

B. (tạbkā) (1) *Vb.* 2 thrashed. (2) *f.* yā shā ⁓ he was thrashed.
tabkẹ *Vb.* 3A. = rafkẹ.
tabkēkẹ *m.* (*f.* tabkēkịyā) huge.
tabkị *Sk.* = tafkị.

tabki = ragō.

tabọ *m.* (*pl.* tạbbā = tabbunạ = tạbbai = tabambunạ = *Kt.* tabạbbā). (1) (*a*) scar (= adabạlī 2). (*b*) tabạm būlālạ weal. (*c*) (i) stain. (ii) rịgan nạŋ tanạ̄ dạ tạtọ ? has any prior offer been made preventing me buying this gown ? (2) (*a*) an unrequited favour. (*b*) n nạ̄ tsọ̄rō kadạ ạ fāmạ tabọna = n nạ̄ tsọ̄rō kadạ ạ fāmạ ni ạ ～ I am afraid of an old delinquency being raked up against me.

taɓo A. (tāɓọ) *m.* (1) (*a*) ripe shea-fruit which has fallen. (*b*) yā ci ～ = yā shā ～ (i) he ate 1*a*. (ii) he gathered 1*a* (*cf.* cī 1c.i). (2) cịn ～ = shạn ～ = zumạ 1c.ii *x* sun shā tāɓạnsạ they (children) flicked him (another sleeping child) and hid.
   B. (tāɓō) *Vb.* 1E. (1) helped. (2) rescued.
   C. (tạɓō) *m.* mud (= lākā).

tabshī *Kt.* = taushī.

tabtsị = tabdị.

tạɓu *Vb.* 3B (1) yā ～ = jịkinsạ yā ～ he is ill. (2) yā ～ = haŋkạlinsạ yā ～ = yanạ̄ dạ tạɓūwā = yā sạ̄mi tạɓūwā he is mad.

tāɓukā = tumɓukā.

tāɓunā *Vb.* 1C *Kt.* did a little *x* zạ̄ ni ṇ tāɓunạ aikị kạɗaŋ I'll go and do a little work (= taɓạ 2).

tāɓusā (1) = tumɓukā. (2) *Vd.* katāɓus.

tạɓūshẹ *used in* 'yan ～ children of Hausas settled in Southern Provinces or in Gold Coast (*cf.* ạbạkwạ̄ 2).

tạɓūwā *Vd.* tạɓu.

tạ̄caccē = tạ̄taccē.

tācẹ *Vb.* 1A (*Vd.* tātạ 2) filtered, strained (= digạ 3).

tạ̄cīcī = tạ̄cūcū.

tā ci furē *Vd.* furē 1, 2.

tạ̄cūcū *m.* (1) (*a*) crowd. (*b*) crowding together of people. (2) = mācīlilī.

tā dạ *Vb.* 4 (*but form* tāshē (Mod. Gram. 171*f*) *is not in use*). (1) (*a*) lifted, raised *x* (i) yā ～ kạnsạ he raised his head. yā tā dạ muryạ he raised his voice. (ii) kā ～ kūrā *Vd.* tākạ 2*aa*.vii. (*b*) yā ～ himmạ he strove hard. (*c*) shī nẹ ya ～ magạnạ it was he who first mentioned the matter = fārạ 4 = tāsạ 3*d*), *cf.* 3

below. (*d*) sun tāyar wạ Jāmụs kạmar sạ cịnyẹ su they attacked the Germans tooth and claw. (*e*) erected *x* (i) yā ～ tsaikọ = hau dạ 3*c*. (ii) *Vd.* talạkạ 2*b*. (*f*) awakened *x* tā tā dạ mū barcī she woke us (= tạ̄sā). (*g*) (i) sun tāyar masạ dạ haŋkạlī = sun tā dạ haŋkạlinsạ they made him apprehensive. (ii) *Vd.* zạmānị 6. (iii) saurin tāyạrwā gạrēshị he's bad tempered. (*h*) caused to set out, caused to depart *x* yā ～ mạnzō he dispatched a messenger (= tạ̄sā 1). (*j*) yā tā dạ nī ạ tsimī he explained the matter to me (= tạ̄sā). (*k*) (i) yā ～ gạ̄bā he roused hostility against P. (ii) Tạ̄ dạ gạ̄bā, rịgạ gudụ *epithet of* Bạfilācẹ. (*l*) ～ mazā tsạye *Vd.* bazarā 2. (2) yā ～ rịgā = hau dạ 3*a*, *b*. (3) annulled *x* (*a*) yā ～ magạnạ he put an end to the matter (= tāsạ 3*f*), *cf.* 1*c above*, tāshị 1*j*, tāshịm magạnạ. (*b*) yā ～ ạlkāwạrī he broke his promise. (*c*) duk yā tāyar (i) he brought the whole matter to an end. (ii) he undertook everything. (*d*) yā tāyar = yā tā dạ ạmānạ (i) he behaved dishonestly. (ii) he rebelled. (*e*) *Vd.* zạune 5. (4) yā ～ kōrẹ he opened out the kōrẹ-gown to beat it. (5) straightened *x* yā ～ sạndā he straightened the stick. (6) *cf.* tāsạ, tạ̄sā, tāshị, tāsam, tāshẹ, tāsō.

tādạ (1) *f.* (*pl.* tādōjī = tādōdī) = ạl'ādạ. (2) *Sk.* *Vb.* 1A = tā dạ.

tādạ (1) *f.* (*a*) man's dressing as and imitating woman for purposes of homosexuality (*cf.* yambạlā). (*b*) ɗan ～ *m.* (*pl.* 'yan ～) = hạmsiŋ 3. (2) *Kt.* nā tādạ, nā tādạ, bạn sāmụ ba I searched and searched but could not find it (= nēmạ).

*tạdabīri *Ar.* *m.* making plans, preparations.

tạ̄ɗaɗɗīyā *f.* = rạtsattsīyā.

taɗai *x* an shārẹ ɗakị ～ the room is well-swept. gạrī yā yi ～ the sky has cleared.

tādạlī *m.* (*pl.* tādulạ = *Kt.* tādullạ). (1) (*a*) bag of raw cotton (kạ̄dā) ; *epithet is* Tādạlī bạ ạ san cikịŋkạ ba. (*b*) fātạr ～ empty tādạlī. (2) reticent P. (*epithet as in* 1*a*).

*tạdạlĩsị *Ar. m.* trickery (especially in trading).

tạdạrĩshị = tạdạrĩsị *Ar. m.* stiff covers for holding manuscripts.

*tạḍawwa'ạ *Ar. f.* (1) fasting apart from azụmĩ. (2) optional second pilgrimage (*cf.* hajị).

tạdawạ = tạwadạ.

*tạḍawwụ'ĩ = tạḍawwa'ạ.

tad dạ = tarad dạ.

tạddawạ = tạwadạ.

tãḍẹ (1) *Vb.* 1A (*a*) tripped P. (*b*) *Sk.* interrupted (P. speaking). (2) *Vb.* 3A *Sk.* = rãtsẹ 1.

tãḍị *m.* (1) chatting. (2) sunạ zubạ ~ they are chatting. (3) yã ĩyạ tãḍị gạ jạma'ạ he has the power of oratory. (4) kadạ mụ yi mukụ tãḍịm mãtã we won't retail gossip to you.

tãḍĩyã *f.* (1) (*a*) (i) tripping. (ii) *Sk.* = jãkã 2. (*b*) ill-advised act. (*c*) tãḍĩyar harshẹ unfortunate slip of the tongue (1 = tãtalã). (2) = aujịyạ 2.

tãdõdĩ = tãdõjĩ *Vd.* tãdạ.

tãdulạ *Vd.* tãḍạlĩ.

tafa A. (tãfạ) *Vb.* 1A. (1) (*a*) (i) yã ~ hannũ he clapped his hands. (ii) kõwã yã tãfạ hannũ everybody showed surprise. (*b*) sun ~ they struck each other's hands in friendship or agreement. (2) (*with dative*) yã ~ masạ shĩ (*a*) he handed it to him (= hannạntã). (*b*) he placed it in his hand. (*c*) he gave him a palmful of it (of flour, etc.).

B. (tạfã) *f.* (*pl.* tafãfẽ) a children's armlet made of kabạ and resembling dạrạmbũwã.

tafãḍũwã *f.* type of grass used for cordage.

tafãfẽ *Vd.* tạfã.

tạfannũwã *f.* (1) garlic. (2) *Vd.* azụmĩ 2.

tạfarfạrã *f.* a small thatched edifice, round, rectangular, or triangular, with two doors (it is a zaurẹ at the house-door or at door of another zaurẹ, not an independent edifice).

tạfạrfasạ *Vb.* 3B (1) kept on boiling (*intensive from* tạfasạ). (2) was in a great rage.

tafarkị *m.* (*pl.* tạfạrkũ = tafarkunạ = tafarkõkĩ). (1) road (= hanyạ). (2) yã sạmi ~ (*a*) he has a patron (= kõ-fạ 3 = tsãnị 2). (*b*) he found a means of

getting his way (= hanyạ 2*a*). (3) Allạ yã nụfã, shĩ nẹ tafarkịnsạ this was the fate allotted him by God. (4) kạkã ~ *Vd.* dũnĩyạ 1*b*.ii.

tạfarnũwã = tạfannũwã.

tạfarshị *m.* an incense resembling hancị 9.

tã fạru, tã kãrẹ *Vd.* damị 7.

tạfas (*used only in this form*) *x* tukunyã tã ~ the pot is boiling = tukunyã tanạ tạfasạ (*Vd.* tạfasạ).

tafasa A. (tạfasạ) (1) *Vb.* 3B (*a*) (water etc.) boiled. (*b*) yã ~ = zũcịyassạ tã ~ he became enraged. (*c*) (i) tum baị ~ ba zại kõnẹ he (boy) is too precocious. (ii) nạ jẽ, nạ bugạ, kõmẽ ta tạfasạ tạ kõnẹ death or victory ! (2) *f.* act of boiling *x* kudĩ wurinsạ sãi ~ sukẹ yị he keeps on becoming wealthier.

B. (tafạsã) *Vb.* 1C boiled T.

C. (tạfạsã) *f.* (1) the Senna undershrub *Cassia tora.* (2) *Vd.* saŋkã 2, yaŋkã 2*f.* (3) tạfạsar Masạr = rãị ḍõrẹ.

tafãshẽ (1) *Vd.* taushĩ 2. (2) (*a*) = mõlõ 1. (*b*) mõlõ-playing.

tạfãshĩyạ *f.* the shrub *Sarcocephalus Russegeri* (*cf.* tũwam birị ; igĩyạ 5).

tãfã-tãfã *f.* game where women and children hit each other's hand-palms (= sõ maŋgã).

tafe A. (tãfẹ) (1) *Vb.* 3A became destitute. (2) *Vb.* 1A took handful of (*cf.* tãfạ).

B. (tạfẹ) (1) (*noun of state from* tafi). (1) (*a*) *x* sunạ ~ they are going along. (*b*) ạbin ~ nẹ he is a gadabout. (2) (*noun of state from* tafõ) *x* (*a*) gạ shi naŋ ~ here he comes ! (*b*) bạbban lãbãrị nạ ~ big tidings are afoot.

tạffã *Sk. f.* (1) = atạfã. (2) shịga tạffã Mãlạm (*said jokingly for* gãfạrtã 2*a*).

tafi A. (tạfi) *Vb.* (*progressive is formed with* tạfĩyạ). (1) (*a*) (i) went. (ii) wannạŋ taịmakõ yã tạfi ạ banzã this help is wasted (*cf.* zõ 4). (*b*) travelled. (2) ~ ạbịŋkạ be off ! (3) *Vd.* tafi dạ, tạfĩyu, tafõ.

B. (tãfĩ) *m.* (*pl.* tãfukạ = tãfunạ). (1) (*a*) (i) palm of hand. (ii) tãfịŋ hannũ bã yạ rufẹ ta *Vd.* rãnã 1*d.* (*b*) tãfịn sau = tãfiŋ kafạ sole of foot. (*c*) yã shã ~ he was slapped (= mãrị).

(d) **yā kai** ∼ = **yā kai** ∼ **baŋgō** " he came out into the open " (d.f. testing fairness of gambling-cowries). (e) (i) **ban** ∼ m. applauding, applause. (ii) **sun yi ban tāfim mąkāfǫ** (a) = **nēmam mai gātarī.** (b) two persons seeking each other (a, b = **sambātātą).** (iii) **sun dauki tāfī rąf-rąf-rąf** they applauded unanimously. (f) (i) **kąn** ∼ m. carrying T. on upturned palm of hand (epithet is ∼ **masōmiŋ hąsārą).** (ii) **bar kąn** ∼ **dą rąŋką** don't rush needlessly into danger ! (2) as much of T. as fills palm of the hand. (3) Vd. **tāfin-compounds.**
tafi da A. (**tąfi dą**) Vb. (progressive is **yanā tąfīyą dą).** (1) (a) removed (= **tąfī dą).** (b) took T. to x **ką** ∼ **mini dą shī gidā** take it home for me ! (= **tąfī' dą).** (2) (a) pushed (wheeled vehicle) x **yā tąfi dą kękē** he pushed the bicycle (= **tūrą** = **tafi dą).** (b) led P. along (= **gōrą** 1c). (3) (a) drove animal before one (= **kōrą).** (b) drove (car) along, rode (cycle) along (= **tafi dą).**
B. (**tąfi dą**) Vb. (progressive is **yanā tąfīyą dą** = **yanā tąfī dą).** (1) = **tąfi dą** 1a, b. (2) attended to x **yā** ∼ **sha'ąniŋ kasā** he administered the country. **yā īyą** ∼ **/ąl'amąrī** he can manage affairs well. (3) Vd. **tąfī dą mālamiŋką, tąfī dą mąsī.**
C. (**tafi dą**) Vb. (progressive is **yanā tafi dą** = **yanā tąfīyą dą**) = **tąfi dą** 2, 3.
tafida A. (**Tafīdą**) a **sąrautą** held by Chief's son or younger brother.
B. (**tąfidą**) m. type of ink-powder.
tąfī dą mālamiŋką m. any Arabic book provided with commentary (whether **sharhą** or **hāshīyą).**
tąfī dą mąsī m. (1) inserting vowels into Arabic writing, line by line (Vd. **mąsī).** (2) doing two tasks simultaneously. (3) " killing two birds with one stone ".
tąfi dą rērę = **tąfi dą mąsī** 2.
tāfīfī used in **dan** ∼ m. little lad. 'yar **tāfīfīyą** little girl.
tafififiya A. (**tāfīfīyā**) Vd. **tāfīfī.**
B. (**tąfīfīyą**) f. (1) frequent journeys. (2) ∼ **tā fi zamā kō kayą ka tāką** travelling though risky is more pro-

fitable than staying at home (2 = **tąfī-tafī).**
tąfiŋ gīwā m. = **mąląfā** 3.
tąfiŋ kuturū m. (1) type of sorrel. (2) = **tąlhātąnā.**
tāfin rąkumī m. = **hōcę.**
tafinta A. (**tāfįntā**) Vb. 1C = **tāfą** 2.
B. (**tāfįntą**) m. (pl. **tāfįntōcī**) Eng. interpreter.
*****tāfirtą** = **tāfįntą.**
tąfī-tafī m. used in ∼ **tā fi zamā kō kayą ka tāką** = **tąfīfīyą** 2.
tąfīyą (f) (1) (progressive of **tąfi**) x **yanā** ∼ he's going, travelling. (2) (a) (i) journey x **yā yi** ∼ he made a journey. (ii) (suffixed pronoun gives continuous sense) x **yanā** ∼ **tasą săi** . . . while he was on his way, then . . . (iii) **yā ci** (= **yā shā**) ∼ he travelled far. (iii) **sun yi gąba kamar tąfīyąr mil ukụ** they advanced a distance of about three miles. (iv) **tā tāshi tąfīyą** she set out. (v) **rānar** ∼ Vd. **fāfą** 3. (b) (i) **ąbōkin** ∼ travelling-companion. **ąbōkin** ∼ **tasą** his journey-companion. (ii) Vd. **marąkī** 1b. (c) **Tąfīyą sąnnū-sąnnū, kwānā nēsą** Camel thou slow goer but far traveller ! (d) in **ză ką yi** ∼ **ką yi tąfīyąr gīwā, kadą ką yi tąfīyąr kūrā** don't beat about the bush ! (e) **kąn** ∼ m. advance-party. (f) **ụban** ∼ m. = **mādugū.** (g) **māgąniŋ gąrī mą nīsą, tąfīyą** effort completes work. (h) **sun shiga yim bāya-bāya, tākį dǎi-dǎi tąfīyąr amąrē** they began to retire unobtrusively. (3) being expended x **kudįŋ duką zā sụ yi** ∼ **cikiŋ aikįn nąŋ** the whole sum will have to be expended on doing this work. (4) **tąfīyąr itącaŋ kadaŋgarę** what procrastination ! (5) **tąfīyąr kāgūwā** walking by boys on the hands, feet in air. (6) **tąfīyąr kūrā** writing Arabic accusative sign as done in Arabic, where the two superimposed lines are parallel (cf. 9 below). (7) (a) **tąfīyąr rūwā** infantile convulsions (treated by cutting forehead with razor or letting baby roll down roof) = **daukąr rūwā** 1 = **danshī** 3 = **dāmunā** 5 = **bǫrī** 10 = **mutūwą** 1k). (b) **an yi tąfīyąr rūwā dą shī** he has been knocked down. (8) **tąfīyąr tsūtsą** (a) tickling

soles of person's foot or top of his spine (gadam bāyā). (b) English cursive or script writing (cf. sharkiyya). (9) tafíyar tunkīyā writing Arabic accusative sign (-an) not as in Arabic, but with the lower stroke protruding to the left (cf. 6 above). (10) Vd. tafíya da. (11) Vd. tandara 2.

tafíya da Vd. tafī da, tafī da, tafī da.

tafíyad da Vb. 4 = tafī da 2, 3.

tafíyu Vb. 3B (d.f. tafī) x hanyan nan bā tā tafíyūwā this road is not traversable.

tafke = rafke.

tafkeke m. (f. tafkēkīyā) extensive (re land).

tafki m. (tafuka) (1) large pond (= kandamī = kudumī = Sk. tauga). (2) Kt. water in borrow-pit. (3) tafkin tōri what a useless person! (4) how huge!

tafō (1) Vb. 3A (-ō form from tafī) (a) came (= zō). (b) x dārī yā ~ the cold season has come. (2) m. (a) colliding with P. or with one's forehead against a wall. (b) knocking one's foot against a sharp stick which pierces one.

tafshi = taushi.

*tafsīrī Ar. m. (pl. tafsīrai) commentary (whether sharha or hāshīya) on Koran or other text.

taf-taf m. a plant of the henna-family used by women for perfuming their hair.

taf-taf-taf m. sun ji ~ they heard the sound of approaching footsteps.

tafuka A. (tāfuka) Vd. tāfī.
    B. (tafuka) Vd. tafki.

tāfuna Vd. tāfī.

taga A. (tāga) f. (pl. tāgōgī) (Ar. tāqa). (1) (a) hole in wall serving as window. (b) window. (2) mai ~ penny (kwabo) with hole in centre.
    B. (taga) Vb. 1A (1) began, attempted T. (2) kārūwōyī suna taga mu prostitutes accost us.

tagajan-tagajan m. nincompoop.

tāgaji Vd. tāgaza.

tagangane A. (tagangane) (1) Vb. 1D misrepresented (what P. said). (2) Vb. 3A sat with legs apart.
    B. (tagangane) m. (1) sitting with legs apart. (2) " having several strings

to one's bow ". (3) (a) in the process wadarī, using two gwaurō when there is not room for placing the marī far from the gwaurō. (b) Vd. cinnāka 2.

tagarahū m. meddlesomeness (= karambānī).

tā ga rānā f. the wild twiner Abrus precatorius (= idon 19), cf. kalmuntā.

tagargade = tazargade.

tagā-tagā = tagā-tagā x yanā tafíya ~ he's reeling along (= magā-magā).

tagayyara Vb. 3B (Ar. became changed) suffered trouble.

tagayyare (noun of state from tagayyara) a ~ only with difficulty.

tagaza A. (tāgaza) Vb. 2 (p.o tāgajē, n.o. tāgaji). (1) (a) helped (= taimaka = taya). (b) shored up (both = āgaza). (2) Vd. a tāgaji gwīwa.
    B. (tāgazā) (1) Vb. 1C = tāgaza. (2) Vb. 3A walked with difficulty.

tage A. (tage) Vb. 3A hesitated.
    B. (tāgē) used in 'yan ~ tribal marks (shasshāwa) on each side of face between eye and ear.

taggo Sk. m. = tagūwā.

tagidī m. dissension.

tāgitī = tākitī.

tāgīya f. (pl. tāgīyū = tāgīyōyī). (1) cap (= hūlā). (2) tāgīyar bakwalā = bakwalā. (3) " ban sā a kā ba ", n ji barāwan tāgīya that is beyond my capabilities. (4) masāyar ~ Vd. masāyā 2.

tāgōde m. type of bead for necklaces.

tāgōgī Vd. tāga.

tagōmashī m. popularity (= farin jinī).

Ta gudu name for boy or girl born at time of panic.

tagullā f. (pl. tagullōlī). (1) copper (= jan karfe = gacī). (2) bronze. (3) tagullōlī pl. trade copper-rods.

tāgumī m. (1) resting head on hand or knee in distress or thought (cf. sake). (2) mutum a gwīwa tasa (= a haba tasa) yake ~ = sandā 1j. (3) wanda bai hakura da ~ ba, yā hakura da kukumī? an aggressive P. keeps on involving himself in more and more trouble. (4) tāgumin gafíya Filani markings (shasshāwa) from lower lip to chin.

tãguntsō *m.* blabbing of secrets.

taguwa A. (tãgūwạ) *f.* (*pl.* tãgūwōyī = tãgūwai). (1) (*a*) camel (*whether he-camel* = rãƙumī, *or* she-camel). (*b*) tãgūwạr rūwā wave (= rãƙumi 9). (*c*) type of girls' game. (*d*) (i) maị ~ = līyạr maị ~ *m.* square ingot of silver stamped with likeness of a camel (*Vd.* sūrạ 1*c*). (ii) maị ~ *m.* type of perfume. (2) = mạkạrā 3. (3) (*a*) The Great Bear. (*b*) ~ tã durƙusạ = ~ tã saụka the wet season has begun (= dãmunā 1*c*). (4) *Vd.* ɓaraunīyā 4.

B. (tagūwā) *f.* (*pl.* tagūwōyī) generic name for (1) men's gowns (rīgā 1 *q.v.*) with circular neck-hole and narrow sleeves (*x* aganīyā, cikī 7*b*, kạftānị, zịlaikạ), (2) women's blouse (rīgā 1*b.*i *q.v.*) with short-sleeves (*x* gadạ 2, ạ bōƙarạ 2, shịmī 2).

tagwai *m.* (*used by women*) (*d.f.* tagwãyē). (1) tagwam farkō the two months Rạbī'ị lawwạl and Rạbī'ị lāhịr. (2) tagwam bīyū the two months Jịmādạ lawwạl (5th Muslim month) and Jịmādạ lāhịr (6th Muslim month), *cf.* gạmbō 2.

tạgwaitakạ *f.* (1) twinship. (2) ạbōkin ~ tasạ his twin-brother.

Ta gwambạ *Vd.* gwambạ.

tagwaŋgwansad dạ *Vb.* 4 troubled, distressed.

tagwaŋgwantad dạ *Vb.* 4 troubled, distressed.

tạgwaro *Kt. m.* destitute P.

tagwãyē *pl.* (1) (*a*) twins. (*b*) ɗan ~ *m.* one of pair of twins (*Vd.* ƙwārạ 2*c*). (*c*) *Vd.* tagwai, tạgwaitakạ, bīyū 2. (2) jãkin ~ *m.* boy born next after twins. (3) dãwạn naŋ ~ cẽ this guinea-corn has two grains in each husk (*cf.* ƙwạr).

Ta gyẽgumạ *Vd.* gyẽgumạ.

tạhāsā *Kt.* = tạ'āsā.

tạhi = tạfi.

*tāhīrị (*Ar.* ta'akhīri) *m.* delay.

tahō = tafō.

tai (1) *Sk.* = tasạ *x* mãtā ~ his wife. (2) = tạfi.

tạibạ *f.* cooked cassava-flour.

tạiɓā *f.* corpulence.

ta idō *Vd.* idọ 1*w.*

taigạzạ *f.* hem of different material added

to the top of trousers which, if long enough, would have real hem of same stuff as the trousers (through this hem (*cf.* kūbakạ) runs the mazāgī).

taikạ-taikạ *f.* = ɗaukạn 'yam makarantā 2.

taikị = tēkị.

taikū = tēkū.

taimaka A. (taimakạ) *Vb.* 2 (*but progressive usually uses* taimakō). (1) (*a*) helped (= ãgazạ = tayạ). (*b*) yã taimạkē nị aikị he helped me with the work. (2) yã taimạkē nị kạn sāmunsạ he helped me to get it. (3) Allạ̃ yạ taimạkị maị taimakō good luck to the helpful !

B. (taimạkā) *Vb.* 1C *x* yã ~ minị aikị = taimakạ 1*b.*

taimakī *used in* ~ lāfīyạ ? = ịnā taimakī I hope all is well with you ?

taimakō *m.* (1) (*secondary v.n. of* taimakạ) *x* yanạ̃ taimakōna he is helping me. (2) (*a*) act of helping (= ãgajī) *x* (i) yã yi minị ~ he helped me. (ii) kun zō manạ taimakō you've come to help us. (iii) ạbin taimakwan cikịnsạ his livelihood. (iv) yã yi minị 'yan taimakō he gave me a little help, a few hints how to do it (Mod. Gram. 89*c*). (*b*) (i) liberality *x* bā yạ̃ ~ he is stingy. (ii) Allạ̃ yạ taimạkị maị ~ God reward the liberal person ! (3) medicine, charm (lāyạ) *x* sǎi kạ yi ~ make use of medicine, etc. !

taimamạ (*Ar.* tayammum) *f.* (1) being compelled to use sand for ạlwạlā in the absence of water. (2) in rūwaŋkạ bai ịsa ạlwạlā ba sǎi kạ yi ~ kạ tāshị if you're not rich, practice economy !

tǎitǎi *m.* (*pl.* tạyạ̃tạyai) (1) = fǎifǎi. (2) (Bauchi) network of rope used for tying up loads.

taitaikōrō = ɗaukạn 'yam makarantā 2.

taitạyā (1) *Vb.* 3A limped along tiredly. (2) *Vb.* 1C. (*a*) encouraged on tired P. or beast. (*b*) ministered to tired or hungry P. or beast.

B. (taitayạ) = taitạyā.

taitạyī *used in* shịga taitạyiŋkạ come to your senses !

*tajạrībạ = *tajạrīfị.

*tajạrīfị (*Ar.* tajarrubuhu) *m.* misfortune.

tạjãwạlī *Ar. m.* = fatauci.

tajāwaŋkạl *m.* heavily embroidered Asbin sandals.

tājẹ *Vb.* 1A (1) (weaver) separated out cotton-strands. (2) = sarcẹ 1*a*. (3) rubbed tacking of cloth (lạllạftū) by drawing finger along it, to smooth down.

tājini *Nor. m.* type of big drum.

tājiŋ-tājiŋ *m.* several persons feeling distressed *x* mun yi ~ we feel at a loss. ạbiŋ yā yi musụ ~ the affair flummuxed them.

tājircị *m.* wealth (*cf.* ạttājịrī).

tājirī = ạttājịrī.

tajirta A. (tājirtạ) *Vb.* 3B became rich.
   B. (tājịrtā) *Vb.* 1C enriched.

tak (1) *adv.* (*a*) only (*after numeral*) *x* sulẹ d̮ayā ~ only a shilling (= tụŋgwal 2). (*b*) (*after negatived numeral*) *x* bābụ kō d̮ayā ~ there is not even one. (*c*) *Kt.* rūwā yā dạukē ~ the rain has quite ceased. (*c*) (*with* d̮ayā *understood*) *x* bābụ kō tak there is not even one. kōwā ya cẹ ~ sǎi mutūwạ it is death to anyone who makes even a single comment. (2) *m.* sound of dripping.

taka A. (tākạ) (1) (*a*) yours (*sg. masc. possessor after fem. noun*) *x* gōdīyạn naŋ ~ cē that mare is yours (*Vd.* kạ, kị, nākạ). (*b*) kul kadạ kạ yī, iŋ kā yī, kai bạ ~ akẹ ba if you do so, it will be the end of you ! (2) *Vb.* 1A. (*a*) (i) trod on (= tākẹ 1*a* = murtsụkē 1*d*). (ii) bại tākạ rawarkạ ba he did not follow your example. (iii) gạ tsaurịn dạ ya tākạ he is in a strong position. (iv) yā tākạ ƙwambọ he behaved conceitedly. (v) san dạ kukạ ji yā fạdi hakạ, dạ ạbiŋ dạ ya tākạ if you hear him speaking thus, then there's some good reason (*cf.* ~ dūtsẹ *under* duffạ 2). (vi) *Vd.* taskirā 3*b*. (vii) ~ shūnī *Vd.* ụŋgụlū 3*a*. (viii) *Vd.* kadạ kạ ~. (*aa*) (i) kō ƙayạ ka tākạ *Vd.* tạfīfīyạ. (ii) bā ạ̄ ~ rūwā ạ dẹbi rūwā (*said by woman*) why should you send me ? go yourself ! (*Vd.* vii *below*). (iii) saŋ gīwā yā ~ na rạƙumī important P. overshadows lesser P. (iv) rībạr ƙafạ kūrā tā ~ kwạd̮ō even the smallest advantage is useful. (v) kōwā ya rēnạ gạjērē bại ~ kụnāmạ ba one learns

from experience. (vi) yā ~ taskirā *Vd.* taskirā 3*b*. (vii) kō ạ rūwa ka tākạ, sǎi ạ cẹ kā tā dạ ƙụrā they blame you whatever you do (*Vd.* ii *above*). (viii) kā tākạ nākạ *Vd.* mūnị 2*d*, lại̊fī 1*e*. (*b*) *x* yā ~ gidaŋ kōwā he visited every house. (*c*) yā ~ ni (i) he provoked, insulted me. bạ shi dạ dādiŋ ạ tākạ shi he's a bad person to cross. (ii) yā ~ ni he stole from me. (*d*) disobeyed *x* yā ~ shạrī'ạ he broke the law (= tākẹ 1*c*), *Vd.* tạkā 1*a*, gạŋgaŋ. (*e*) measured by pacing (*d.f.* tākị 2*b*), *cf.* tạkạ, tạƙā. (*f*) kā ~ mīyạ *Vd.* mīyạ 10. (*g*) (*with dative*) escorted *x* bạri ṇ ~ makạ let me escort you ! (= raƙạ). (*h*) *Vd.* tākạ-compounds. (3) *Vb.* 3A (*a*) (i) walked along. (ii) yanạ̄ tākạwā d̮ai-d̮ai he's mincing along in a swaggering way (*cf.* tạƙā). (iii) *Sk.* tākạwarkạ lāfīyạ go carefully, Chief ! (*b*) yā ~ he put his foot in the stirrup. (*c*) yā ~ he has gone off suddenly.
   B. (tạ̊kā) (1) *Vb.* 2 (*a*) yā tạ̊ki shạrī'ạ he apparently broke the law, but had justification (*Vd.* tākạ 2*d*). (*b*) yā tạ̊ki sā'ạ he was lucky. (*c*) yā tạ̊ki dāhịr = *Kt.* yā tạ̊ki dạlīlị he knows for sure (= tạkạmaimai). (*d*) (*in legal parlance*) had sexual connection with (woman) = cī 16*a*. (2) *f.* (*a*) walking along *x* yā yi ~ he walked along (= tākạ 3*a*.i). (*b*) yi ~ tsantsaŋ dūnīyạ always act cautiously ! (3) *Vd.* tākạ-compounds. (4) *Vd.* bạ ~.

taƙa A. (tạƙā) *m.* pace *x* gạjēran ~ a short pace, short paces. sǎi tạƙā d̮ai-d̮ai sukẹ they're only advancing step by step (*cf.* tākạ 3*a*.ii) (tạƙā = tākị 2*b* = mīƙā 3), *cf.* tākạ 2*e*, taƙạ.
   B. (taƙạ) *Vb.* 1A measured by spanning (*Vd.* taƙị ; tạƙā) = dānạ 1*a*.

tạ̊ka ạ badọ *m.* African lily trotter (*Actophilornis africanus*).

tạ̊ka aŋgo *Kt. m.* = hawā 2*a*.

takabạ *f.* (1) period of mourning done by widow *x* tanạ̄ ~ she is in mourning (= mūgụn rūwā). (2) *Vd.* iddạ 2, waŋkan takabạ. (3) takabạr hạŋ̄kạ̊kī *Kt. f.* noisy altercation.

tạ̊kạ badọ *Kt. m.* = tạ̊ka ạ badọ.

tǎ̱kǎ baŋgŏ, ha̱dīyē m. very stiff tūwŏ (= tǎ̱kǎ daŋgā, ha̱dīyē).

ta̱kaba̱rī = gunǎ̱gunī.

takabbarci̱ Ar. m. conceit.

tǎ̱kǎ cǎ̱ɓī m. = cāɓu̱lā 3.

tǎ̱kǎ daŋgā, ha̱dīyē m. = tǎ̱kǎ baŋgŏ, ha̱dīyē.

ta̱ka̱da̱rī m. (f. ta̱ka̱da̱rā) pl. ta̱ka̱da̱rai cantankerous P.

taka̱ddā = taka̱rdā.

*ta̱ka̱dīri̱ Ar. adv. x ~ sun yi gōma̱ there are 10 approximately (= wajan).

tǎ̱ka ha̱ye = Kt. tǎ̱ka hau = ta̱ka ka̱ hau 2 q.v.

Tākai Vd. raŋgyana̱ 2.

taka̱i (1) m. youths' dance characterized by sa̱ma̱mma̱ncē 2. (2) adv. yā shā wu̱yā ~ he had a bad time.

ta̱ka̱icē Vd. ta̱kaita̱.

taka̱icē (1) Vb. 1c (a) shortened, reduced, lessened (= rage̱). (b) reduced (map) to scale. (c) abridged x mu̱ ~ muku̱ lǎ̱bāri̱ŋ let us give you a résumé of the news ! (2) Vb. 3A became reduced x lōka̱cī yā ~ there's little time left.

takaici A. (ta̱ka̱icī) m. (1) indignation. (2) yā ji mini̱ ~ he made me indignant. (3) Vd. ga̱ba 1a.iii.

B. (ta̱kaici) Vd. ta̱kaita̱.

tǎ̱ka i̱m māra̱ Vd. tǎ̱ka m̱ māra̱.

ta̱kaita̱ Vb. 2 (p.o. ta̱ka̱icē, n.o. ta̱kaici) rendered indignant.

taka̱ita A. (ta̱ka̱itā) Vb. 1C = taka̱icē 1. B. (ta̱kaita̱) Vb. 3B = taka̱icē 2.

tā kai tā kōmō = Kt. tā kai tā kāwō (1) f. = fa̱tala̱. (2) Vd. kai 4.

taka̱ka x suna̱ da̱ yawa̱ ~ they're innumerable.

tǎ̱ka ka̱ hau m. (1) = shēge̱ 5. (2) caparisoned Asbin horse (2 = tǎ̱ka ha̱ye).

taka̱̱ke̱ Vb. 1C got mastery over x an taka̱̱ke̱ aiki̱ŋ the work has been got well in hand. yā taka̱̱ke̱ al'ama̱ri̱ŋ he obtained control of the affair.

tǎ̱ka ki̱ shā māri̱ Vd. tsārā 1c.

ta̱kakkīyā f. abusing P. in his own house.

taka̱̱kō Kt. = di̱kāka̱ 1b.

tǎ̱ka ku̱she̱yī Kt. = tǎ̱ka̱ makŏkā q.v. under makŏkī 3.

takala A. (tǎ̱kala̱) Vb. 2. (1) provoked, incited (= zu̱ŋgura̱ 2). (2) yā tākalō za̱ncan yǎ̱ki̱ he turned the conversation

to the topic of war. sun tākalō ba̱tuŋ a̱ bā su̱ Tūna̱s they introduced the topic of being given Tunis. (3) yā tākalō fa̱da̱ he brought trouble on himself. (4) Kt. Kā tākalō Vd. Ta̱ŋko̱.

B. (tāka̱lā) Vb. 1C = zu̱ŋgu̱rā 1b.

C. (ta̱ka̱lā) f. stick on which material to be woven is wound.

D. (takalā) f. = katalā.

*ta̱ka̱līfi̱ Ar. m. T. imposed on one forcibly.

tǎ̱ka̱lmē Sk. = tǎ̱ka̱lmī.

tǎ̱ka̱lmī m. (pl. tākalma̱). (1) (a) sandal, boot, shoe. (b) yā cire̱ (= ƙwaɓe̱ = tūɓe̱) ~ he took off his shoes. (bb) muna̱̱ ƙa̱rƙashin tǎ̱ka̱lminsu̱ we're in their power. (c) Vd. gwaji̱n tǎ̱ka̱lmī. (d) kōmē tsūfan dōki̱ yā fi sāban ~ the poorest nag is better than footslogging (Vd. tsōfō 1g). (e) ƙasa̱-ƙasa̱ yā fi ƙasa̱, mai jǎkī yā fi mai ~ better a small loss than a big. (2) tǎ̱ka̱lmim Makka̱ prickly-pear. (3) = gu̱zurī. (4) a̱bu̱ yā da̱fe̱ da̱ ɓata̱ a̱ fāda̱ ba̱rē Tāka̱lmi Vd. fāda̱ 4. (5) ~ dubū (a) big caravan. (b) = tǎ̱barmā 4. (c) ~ dubū yā tāshi̱ slump in prices has occurred through abundance. (6) tǎ̱ka̱lmin dumā " broken reed " (cf. ƙafa̱r wālā). (7) tǎ̱ka̱lmi̱ŋ kǎ̱zā (a) an yi sōrō tǎ̱ka̱lmi̱ŋ kǎ̱zā mud-topped building has been made containing ƙafa̱ 8b q.v. (b) an yi rūwā tǎ̱ka̱lmi̱ŋ kǎ̱zā there was brief, light rain-storm. (8) Vd. kas 3k.

tǎ̱kama̱ f. (1) (a) (i) swaggering gait taught to horse. (ii) Vd. ma̱rin ~. (b) an ɗaura̱ masa̱ ~ (i) it (horse) has been taught 1a (= ba̱rǎ̱ƙumā 1). (ii) he has been coached in giving his evidence, whether true or false (= ma̱gantad da̱ 2). (2) (a) conceit, swank (= mǎ̱yē 2a) x suna̱̱ ~ sun yī they're boasting of having done it (= ti̱ŋ-ƙāho̱ = tūtīya̱ 2 = ya̱ŋgā = a̱lfaha̱rī = tŏtŏrinto̱ = tāshi̱ŋ hanci̱). (b) Vd. mǎ̱yē 2b. (c) sun jā da̱ bāya̱ da̱ tǎ̱ƙamā they retreated in good order. (3) justifiable pride x suna̱̱ ~ da̱ zamansu̱ cikim mulki̱ŋ I̱ŋgilīshi̱ they're proud of forming part of the British Empire. (4) n nǎ̱ ~ tasa̱ I'm relying on him (father, mother, etc.) = mǎ̱yē 3. ba̱

tā&amạd dạ mukē̦ yị kạmar ta &ar-
fimmu̦ ạ tē̦kū we rely mostly on our
naval power. baitu̦lmālịnsu̦ bā yạ̄
tā&amā da wata hanyạr sāmu̦ɳ
kudī dạ ta fi wannạɳ their Native
Treasury has no surer source of income
than this.

tạkạmaimai (1) m. bạn san tạkạmaimam
magạnạ ba I don't know the truth of the
matter for certain (= tạrtībị). (2) adv.
for certain x bạn san shị ∼ ba I am not
certain about it. nā rasạ abịn dạ zạɳ
kāmạ ∼ I can't make head or tail of
it (= dāhịr = tạrtībị).

tā̦kạ makō̦kā = makō̦kī 3.

tā̦ka m̲ mārạ Sk. m. the trailing end of a
woman's cloth. (Vd. tsārā 1c).

*takāmīshu̦ m. wrinkles in the forehead.

tā&amtā Vd. tā&amtō.

tā&amtaccē m. (f. tā&amtaccīyā) pl.
tā&amtạttū horse trained to do tā&amā.

tā&amtō Vb. 1E went on foot to x yạ̄ ∼
zūwạ gidāna he came on foot to my
house.

tā&amtu Vb. 3B (horse) is trained to
tā&amā.

takạnas purposely (= mu̦sammạɳ 2a =
nufị 2 = ạnīyạ 7), cf. gạɳgaɳ.

takạndā f. (1) (a) type of sugar-cane. (b)
cf. rạkē̦, bā̦ zā&ẹ̦. (2) tạkạndā = tạkạndar bāyā the meat along the back-bone.
(3) tạkạndar gīwā the tree Hannoa
undulata.

ta&andā used in the riddle (tā̦tsūnị̄yā)
whose words are ∼ bā̦ &ashī ba here is
a certain riddle, what does it indicate ?
(reply, kaɳwā it means " potash " !).

takandū̦wā f. (only said by sellers of
tạkạndā) here is tạkạndā for sale, buy,
buy !

ta&ānīyā Kt. = tikilā.

tā̦ka ɳ mārạ = tā̦ka m̲ mārạ.

*takara A. (tạkạrā) f. (Ar. takrāra). (1)
yanā̦ tạkạrar aikịnsạ he is revising
aloud the work learnt. (2) nā yi masạ ∼
I admonished him (= gạrgạdī).

B. (takārạ) Vd. hạɳkākạ 3.

C. (tākarā) f. (1) rivalry, emulation
(= gāsā). (2) tākarā dạ maị azzịkī
hạlakạ don't emulate those better off
than yourself !

*tạkạrārị (Ar.) m. = tạkạrā.

takạrdā f. (pl. tạkạrdū = takardōjī = Sk.
tạkạrdunnị) (Ar. qirtāsa d.f. Latin
charta). (1) (a) paper. (b) takạrdar
makarantā school-certificate. (c) Vd.
mugunyạr takạrdā. (d) takạrdar ạlkāwạrī
IOU. (2) letter. (3) yā̦ kai ∼ = yā̦
kạrɓi ∼ = tikitị 2. (4) Vd. bē̦rē̦.

Tạkā̦rī Vd. Tu̦ku̦rūru̦.

*tạkạrīmị Ar. m. showing respect,
honouring.

ta&ar&ạrē Vb. 3A (1) strove hard, exerted
oneself. (2) Vd. īyạ̄ 1d.

tạkạrkạrī m. (pl. tạkạrkạrai = takur-
kurạ). (1) (a) pack-ox (epithet is sā̦
mārar kāyā̦). (b) ∼ kạm fō̦rā, jā̦kī
yā̦ sābạ dạ kāyā̦ what's bred in the
bone . . . (c) Ba&ī, tạkạrkạrim Fir'aunạ
epithet of train. (2) lout, dolt.

ta&ar&ạshē Nor. = ta&ar&ạrē.

ta&arnā Kt. = ta&andā.

*ta&arna-ta&arna f. = bāya-bāya 1.

tạkạrnīyā = tạkē̦nīyā.

tā̦kạ sạkainā Kt. f. quarrelling x mun yi ∼
dạ shī.

tā̦kạ shiɓạ Vd. Agaddabū.

Tạkātạ = Jirā̦yē Kt. the sạrautạ of
Junior Sarkin sạurī q.v. under saurạyī 2.

taka-taka A. (tạkā-tạkā = takạ-takạ) x
yanā̦ tạfīyạ ∼ he's limping along.

B. (takā-takā) x yā̦ fatattạkē ∼ it
is entirely lacerated.

tā̦kạ tō̦yī m. the black-headed lark
(Pyrrhulauda leucotis).

tā̦kā tsantsaɳ Vd. tā̦kā 2b.

tạkạtubu̦ m. = sạkạtubu̦.

tā̦kau̦nī m. (pl. tākaunạ) Sk. = tā̦kạlmī.

tā̦ka zō tōrị m. hurrying along apprehensively.

take A. (tā̦kẹ̦) (1) Vb. 1A. (a) trod on
(= tā̦kạ 2a.i). (b) Kt. bạri ɳ ∼ ma&ạ̀
sau = tā̦kạ 2g. (c) disobeyed x sun ∼
sanị they deliberately did what they
knew to be forbidden. yā̦ ∼ yā̦ &i
ganī he deliberately turned his head
away, ignored it (= tā̦kạ 2d = gạɳgaɳ), cf. tā̦kā 1a. (d) (i) trod on and
prevented rising x cīwọ yā̦ ∼ shi illness
incapacitated him. (ii) wạhalạd dạ
ya ∼, in yā̦ cirạ &afạ, ā̦ ganī the
trouble from which he saved them will
reappear when he is no longer there.
(e) forced x yā̦ ∼ shi, yā̦ kạrɓi kudinsạ

he compelled him to pay the sum owing him. (*f*) measured by pacing (*as in* tākạ 2*e*) completely. (*g*) exceeded, excelled. (*h*) filled *x* yā ∼ cikịnsạ dạ nāmạ he took his fill of meat. (*j*) manured (farm) by tethering cattle there, etc. (*d.f.* tākị 2*a*). (2) *Vb.* 3A (*a*) rānā tā ∼ the sun has passed meridian. (*b*) yanạ tākẹwā he's walking along (= tākạ 3*a*.i). (*c*) yā ∼ cikim mayāfinsạ he covered his feet with his mayāfī. (*d*) yā ∼ = yā ∼ k̰af̰ạfunsạ = dāgẹ.

B. (tākē) *m.* (1) a drum-rhythm done by mar̰ōk̰ā and differing according to whether done for S̰arkī, Wạzīrị, Gạlạ̄dīmạ, etc. (= k̰iryạ 3). (2) tākyansụ their character.

C. (tạ̄ke) (1) *m. x* cīwọ yā yi masạ ∼ illness finished him off without warning. (2) *adv.* forthwith (*followed by relative verb*) *x* naŋ ∼ sǎi sukạ mutụ = ∼ ạ naŋ sǎi sukạ mutụ they suddenly died. ∼ akạ f̰ạd̰i hakạ this was said all of a sudden. (3) yanạ tạ̄ke dạ shī he's treading on it (*Vd.* tākạ).

D. (takẹ̄) (*used for* she *in present relative sentence with positive sense,* Mod. Gram. 133) *x* lōkạcịn dạ ∼ zūwạ when she comes. yạushẹ ∼ yị̄ when does she do it ?

E. (tạ̄kẹ̄) = tạ̄ke 1.

tạkẹ̄nīyā *f.* experiencing difficulty (= wụyā).

tạkẹ̄-takē = takē-tạkẹ̄ *m. x* tanạ ∼ dạ gōyō she's walking unsteadily through weight of heavy child on her back.

taki A. (tākị) (1) (*a*) yours (*after fem. noun when possessor is fem.*) *x* jạkan naŋ ∼ cē this bag is yours (*re* woman), Mod. Gram. 48. (*b*) *Vd.* tākạ. (2) *m.* (*a*) (i) manure *x* yā yi wạ gōnarsạ ∼ he manured his farm. (ii) ịnā ạkwīyạ zạ̄ ta dạ kāyan tākị don't attempt the impossible ! (iii) hasadạ gạ maị rạbō tākị envy does not prevent you getting the lot God has assigned to you. (iv) gēran ∼ *Vd.* ạlkālī. (v) tākịn Allạ̄ *Vd.* dạ6ạrō. (*b*) (i) measuring out by pacing (*Vd.* sa6ạ 4*b*, tākạ 2*e*). (ii) a pace (= mịk̰ā 3 = tạk̰ā), *cf.* tākạ 2*e*, tak̰ạ. bạ sụ k̰ārạ kō tākị d̰ayā gạbạ ba they have not advanced a single

step. sun shịga yịm bāya-bāya, tākị d̰ǎi-d̰ǎi tạfīyạr amạ̄rē they began to retreat unobtrusively. (*c*) act of treading on *x* (i) yā yi minị tākịn rēnị he treated me with contempt. (ii) sunạ̄ tākịn sāk̰ạ they are plying the loom-treadles ; they're quarrelling. (iii) mashigin naŋ bạ̄ shi dạ ∼ this ford is at present too deep for crossing. (iv) tākịm birị moving horse's touching ground with fetlock (*cf.* gudụn birị). (*d*) pair (of sandals). (*e*) way of acting *x* Audụ nē ya nūnạ musụ wannạŋ irịn tākị it was Audu who put them up to this. tākị d̰ǎi irị ukụ yakẹ̄ yị̄ he has three ways of acting.

tak̰i *m.* a span from tip of thumb to middle finger (*cf.* tak̰ạ, tạk̰ā) = dānị 1.

*tākīdị *Ar. m.* speaking or acting emphatically *x* yā yi masạ tākīdịn azzịkī (1) he emphasized to him the need for success. (2) he did his best to make him successful.

tạ̄k̰īk̰ị *m.* (*f.* tạ̄k̰īk̰ịyā) *pl.* tạ̄k̰īk̰ai. (1) stunted P. (2) short trousers.

tāk̰il-tāk̰il = tāk̰in-tāk̰in.

tạk̰īmạ *Kt. f.* trouble (= wụyā).

tāk̰iŋ-tāk̰iŋ *x* yanạ̄ tạfīyạ ∼ he (sick, tired, hungry, etc., P.) is struggling along.

tạ̄k̰irīk̰ịnjī *Kt. m.* pot-bellied but otherwise thin child.

tākitī *m.* (*pl.* tākitōcī) *Eng.* target.

*tạk̰īyị (*Ar. root* wak̰ay) *m.* devout.

takkẹ *m.* lumps of meat given in charity and to guests at naming ceremony (sūnā) or at layyā-time (*cf.* takkūwā).

takkūwā *Kt. f.* alms (= sadakạ), *cf.* takkẹ.

takkyatẹ *Kt. m.* = lālājọ.

tako A. (tạ̄kō) *m.* (1) tạk̰ō = dōkịn tạk̰ō = dōkịŋ k̰ōk̰ō *q.v.* (2) tạk̰wam birị = tākị 2*c*.iv. (3) n dạ naŋ kạn tạk̰ōna I have made up my mind irrevocably. (4) (*a*) hoof (= kōfatọ). (*b*) (*vulgarly*) tạk̰waŋ ạkwīyạ = farjị. (*cf.* kōfatọ).

B. (Takō) *name for any woman called* Amīna.

tạk̰ō = tạk̰ō-tạk̰ō.

takōbi *m.* (*pl.* takuba = *Kt.* takubbạ). (1) (*a*) any sword (= kạnsakạlī). (*b*) in rūwā yā ci mutụm, kō am bā shi kaifin ∼, săi yą̄ kāmą̄ drowning man clutches at a straw, any port in a storm. (c) kạn ∼ m. (i) knob of sword-hilt. (ii) wuƙan nąŋ kạn ∼ cę̄ this knife's made from a sword-point. (2) jạn ∼ yakę̄ yị he's outstanding. (3) Vd. wąŋkan ∼, ąllūrą̄ 6. tąƙōƙō (1) how round-shouldered that fool is ! (reply, tąƙōƙwam birị). (2) m. x taƙi ukụ dą̄ ∼ three spans, plus length of middle finger from tip to centre joint (= Sk. durƙushī). tąƙō-tąƙō = tāƙịŋ-tāƙịŋ. tākụ yours (pl. possessor after fem. noun), Vd. nākụ. takubą̄ Vd. takọ̄bī. tākuɗę̄ m. (1) cornering milk (= Kt. katē). (2) Kt. = sārā 2a.i. tąkulą̄ = tąkalą̄. tāƙụnē Vb. 3A became emaciated. tąkuŋkụmī m. (pl. tākuŋkumą̄ = tą̄-kụŋkụmai). (1) official's (when at ease) wearing turban in same way as non-official, i.e. instead of usual fūnị with long falling piece, either wearing the U-piece on the neck or covering mouth with the U-piece shortened, Vd. amā-wąlī). (2) muzzle for animal (= sụm-bąttā = Nor. cąmfō). takura A. (tąkurą̄) Vb. 3B (1) sat huddled up (from fear, cold, etc.). (2) became bent with age. (3) fuskąssą̄ tā ∼ his face is contorted with pain. (4) (a) yā ∼ yā daką̄ tsallē it crouched and made a spring. (b) ą̄ nąŋ ka tąkurą̄ ? ką̄ mīƙę̄ if you think you'll get some advantage here, you've got another think coming. B. (tākụrā) Vb. 1C (1) caused P. to sit huddled up, become bent, con-torted as in tąkurą̄ 1–3. (2) = tąɓą̄ 1l. (3) (a) restricted actions of P. (b) gąrī yā ∼ shi he had a hard time (= matsą̄ 1c.iii). (c) yā ∼ ni he bad-gered me (= matsą̄ 1c.i). tākụrē Vb. 3A = tąkurą̄. tąkurī Vd. ɗaurịn ∼. takurkurą̄ Vd. tąkarkąrī. Tākutąhā = Tākutịhā (1) (a) the festival held in Bornu on 12th Rąbī'ị lawwąl (the Prophet's birthday), but elsewhere on the Prophet's naming-day (ran

sūnā) which is 19th of that month (best clothes are worn and charity (sadaką̄) given = Gą̄nē 3. *(b) yā yi tākutąhar ɗam Bąrno he is peerless of his kind. *(2) Kt. = akanzą̄. takūwā = takkūwā. Takwą̄ = Bąnufē. takwakkwąɓē Vb. 3A became worn out. takwalā f. (1) thread (especially red) sold in skeins. (2) Kt. red thread (but there are also black and white varieties). tąkwąrā m. namesake (Vd. sūnā 8). tąkwarākwąrą̄ = kwąrā-kwąrā. takwarkwąsā Vb. 1D brought trading loss on P. by forcing him to accept ridiculous price or by hągē. takwarkwąshē Vb. 3A (1) became worn-out (T., old or tired P.). (2) became stingy. (3) yā ∼ wurīna he's become dependent on me. takwas A. (takwąs) f. (1) (a) eight. (b) takwąshịn nąŋ those eight (Mod. Gram. 10d, 36). (2) na ∼ m. (f. ta ∼) pl. na ∼ eighth. B. (tąkwąs) (1) m. and adv. x rụmfā tā yi ∼ the grass-shelter is rickety. yā zauną̄ ∼ it (pot, etc.) stands insecurely (contrasted with daɓas). (2) (a) (when cowries were the currency, if girl-seller asked boy-purchaser too much money, he used to refuse by saying fādūwar mại wąrkī by which she knew allusion was being made to 2b below). *(b) sound of falling of man wearing the loin-cloth wąrkī. takwashi A. (takwąshī) Vd. takwąs. B. (tąkwashī) = kwątashī. tąkwā-tąkwā = tāƙịn-tāƙịŋ. taƙwā-tąƙwą̄ pl. huge and round. tąkwulą̄ = tąkalą̄. tal A. (tal) = tak. B. (tąl) x (1) yaną̄ wąlƙīyā ∼ it's shining brightly. (2) cf. twąl dą̄ idō. tạ̄lā Kt. = tą̄yā 1. talafa A. (taląfā) Vb. 1C Ar. spent. B. (tąlafą̄) Vb. 3B has been spent. talafad dą̄ Vb. 4 = taląfā. talahą̄ f. (pl. talahōhī) type of ornate saddle from North Africa. talai x (1) an shārę̄ ∼ clean sweeping has been done. (2) an yi masą̄ askị ∼ his head's been shaven smooth.

talᶐkᶐ *m., f. (pl.* talakāwā) *(Ar.* ta'allaqa is subordinate, *cf.* tᶐ'ᶐllafᶐ). (1) member of the populace *(contrasted with those holding* sᶐrautᶐ *who are consequently better-off, so that being a* talᶐkᶐ *connotes poverty) (cf.* talᶐutā). (2) *epithets of* talᶐkᶐ *are* (a) ⁓ fāifǎi nę̄, kō̧inā akᶐ jūyᶐ, taŋkadę̣ zᶐi yi the populace are mere clay in the hands of the rulers = ⁓ gārī nę̄ *(Vd.* dāwᶐ 4) = ji̧kin ⁓ duk kudī nę̄ = biri̧ 3. (b) Talᶐkᶐ mᶐi tā dᶐ birnī shī kadǎi the poor man has no help in building shiŋgē round his cassava-farm ! (c) *Vd.* mᶐzūrū 3, tsātsᶐ 2, bō̧rī 3c, maurᶐ. (3) i̧ŋgarmᶐ gidan talᶐkᶐ hᶐrāmu̧ŋ it is impossible. (4) tambᶐrin ⁓ *Vd.* tambᶐrī 9.

talᶐkkᶐ *Kt. m., f. (pl.* talakkāwā = talak-kōkī) = talᶐkᶐ.

talᶐki̧ *m.* Yoruba indigo-dye.

tālālā *f.* (1) tethering animal in wet season in sᶐurā by long rope, to prevent it eating crops *(cf.* ki̧rinyᶐ 2 ; zārārᶐ ; dᶐbdalᶐ). (2) (a) Tālālā mᶐi kᶐman sᶐkē (i) it's a case of giving him a rope to hang himself with ! (ii) this man is one who is giving the other a rope to hang himself with ! = sᶐki lę̄cę̄cę̄. (b) kōmē dādin ⁓ saki̧ yā fī shi̧ freedom is better than the lightest bonds. (c) mun sakam mukᶐ tālālar ᶐbi̧n dᶐ ya ᶐuku we've explained to you fully what happened.

talᶐlāḃi̧yā *f.* slipperiness of ground (= santsī).

talᶐlāḃū̧wā *f.* (1) = talᶐlāḃi̧yā. (2) breaking promise (= ᶐlkāwᶐrī 1g). (3) unwise advice. (4) poor string.

talᶐmbandi̧ = talᶐnji̧.

*talᶐmbᶐyā *Sk. f.* one strand of skein of thread being longer than the rest.

talᶐnji̧ (1) what a tall, thin lad ! (2) what a thin colt !

Talᶐtᶐ *Ar. f.* (1) (a) Tuesday. (b) *name for girl born on Tuesday, Vd.* bᶐtū̧rę̄ 3. (c) *Vd.* bāwᶐ 8a.ii. (2) three thousand. (3) making a loss (gambling, trading).

talᶐtaini̧ *m. (Ar.* two-thirds) *used in* talᶐtaini̧n darē yā zō the middle of the night has come *(cf.* tsālᶐ 2, falki̧n darē).

tᶐ'la-talō" = tᶐ'lo-tᶐlō".

talᶐti̧ŋ *Ar. f.* thirty.

talau A. (tᶐlau̧) *x* an jā shi̧ ⁓ it (elastic or viscous T.) was extended. santsī yā dᶐukē shi̧ ⁓ he slithered along.
    B. (tālau) *Kt. m.* used in dan ⁓ m. (pl. 'yan ⁓) a thief killing goats for their skins.

talaucē *Vb.* 3A became destitute *(cf.* (alautᶐ).

talauci̧ *m. (d.f.* talᶐkᶐ) (1) (a) poverty. (b) talauci̧ bᶐ zᶐi kau dᶐ 'yanci̧ bᶐ poverty is no disgrace. (c) hᶐkurin ⁓ *Vd* wᶐhalᶐ 1c. (2) zaman ⁓ yakē yi̧ he (one of the ruling classes) is without sᶐrautᶐ *(cf.* talᶐkᶐ). (3) halin ⁓ niggardliness (= rō̧wᶐ). (4) anᶐ̄ ta-lauci̧n hatsī there is shortage of corn (= rashi̧).

talaulau *x* dan yārᶐ nē ⁓ dᶐ shī he's a lanky, little boy.

talauta A. (tᶐlautᶐ) *Vb.* 3B became poor *(cf.* talᶐucē).
    B. (talᶐutā) *Vb.* 1C (1) impoverished. (2) deprived P. of office (sᶐrautᶐ), *Vd.* talᶐkᶐ.

talautad dᶐ *Vb.* 4 = talᶐutā.

tᶐlawwᶐmī *Ar. m.* delaying three or four days in asking for payment of debt.

tᶐl dᶐ *Vd.* twᶐl dᶐ.

tālę̄ *Vb.* 1A *Kt.* (1) = tāyā 1. (2) opened (eyes, legs, etc.) wide *x* yanᶐ̄ tᶐfīyᶐ yanᶐ̄ ⁓ kᶐfāfunsᶐ he walks with legs well apart ; yanᶐ̄ zᶐune yanᶐ̄ ⁓ kᶐfᶐ he is seated with his legs sprawled out (= tānᶐ).

talēlᶐ̄ *m.* type of ornament for cap.

talē-talē *Vd.* shᶐ̄ ⁓.

talgᶐ = rūdᶐ 1c.

talgᶐrāhᶐ̧ = taŋgᶐrāhᶐ̧.

talgē = rū̧dē 2.

talgi̧ *Kt. m.* = rū̧dē 2.

talhᶐ = talahᶐ.

talhātᶐnā *f.* = talhāti̧nā = talhātᶐnā *(pl.* talhātᶐnai = talhātᶐnū) type of stone for necklaces (= ᶐlhantᶐnā = hantᶐ 2a = tāfi̧ŋ kuturū 2).

tāli̧bambam *m. (sg., pl.)* tadpole *(epithet is* Tāli̧bambam makᶐdi̧ŋ kwᶐdō).

*tāli̧fī *Ar. m. (pl.* tāli̧fō̧fī = tāli̧fai) (1) a literary work. (2) writing a literary work.

tālikī *m. (f.* tāli̧kā) *pl.* tᶐli̧kai = tālikāwā

= *Kt.* tālikkai (*Ar.* makhlūq) any created being.

tālīli *m.* (*pl.* tālīlai) type of written charm.

tālīya *f.* (*Ar.* Italian) (1) macaroni (= luwaidi), *cf.* tsūtsa 1*c.* (2) zō mu ci ~ let's have a chat ! (3) dambū ~ *Vd.* dambū 1*c.*

*talkīni *Ar. m.* reciting kalma 2 to dying P. or at funeral.

talla = *Kt.* tallā *f., m.* (1) (*a*) exposing wares for sale *x* yanā tallar tsirē he's exposing spitted meat for sale. (*b*) yanā kirārin ~ he's calling out his wares exposed for sale (*unlike* kasa 1*a where seller waits for customer to come and ask price*). (2) *x* yanā ~ da nī he's exposing my secrets (= fallasa). (3) tallar 6ōtōcī *Kt.* roving about (= gīlo). (4) tallaŋ Kārāyē *Vd.* Kārāyē.

tallaba A. (tallabā) *Vb.* 1C (1) supported T. by putting hand on it. (2) carried T. on palm of the hand. (3) *cf.* tallafā. B. (tallaba) *Vb.* 2 = tallabā.

tallabē *Vb.* 1C = tallabā.

tallafa A. (tallafā) *Vb.* 1C (*Ar.* allafa) (1) = tallabā. (2) *x* yā ~ mini dansa he left his boy with me to bring up. B. (tallafa) *Vb.* 2 tended (*x* invalid), educated, brought up (*cf.* tallafā).

tallafē = tallabā.

tallafī *m.* (1) (*Sec. v.n. of* tallafa) *x* yanā tallafinsa = yanā tallafassa he's tending him (invalid). (2) act of educating, etc., *as in* tallafa *x* nā bā ka tallafin dāna I gave you my son to bring up (*cf.* kāro 2). (3) child received for bringing up (= kalīhu = amāna 4*d*).

tallāhi *x* Wallāhi, tallāhi, summatallāhi by God, by God !

tallatā *Vb.* 1C (1) exposed wares for sale *as in* talla. (2) yanā ~ ni = talla 2. (3) bari n ~ ŋ ganī I'll try my luck (in gambling, etc.), *cf.* hā 1.

talle A. (tallē) *m.* (*pl.* tallāyē) (1) (*a*) small soup-pot. (*b*) kwäi gudā dai ~ yā fi kāzā a sake a bird in the hand is worth two in the bush. (2) hunting-drum. B. (Talle) name given to tallafī 3.

tallī *m.* sheen (= walkīyā).

tallīro = tal.

tallīyā *f.* = tallē 1*a.*

talmadā = kalmadā.

talmadai-talmadai = kalmadai-kalmadai.

talōlō *m.* (*said by women, children, labourers*) (1) penis. (2) inā amfānin kiba ~ ya nitse don't throw away the substance for the shadow ! (3) talōlan tindī children's game of tapping ribs to sound like drum. (4) talōlan yum6ū (*a*) artificial penis used in mādigō. (*b*) good-for-nothing P. (= ragō). (*c*) yā cī ni da talōlan yum6ū he tricked me.

ta'lo-talō" *m., f., sg., pl.* (1) turkey. (2) *Vd.* tūsa 2 ; barōdō ; bindiga 9.

tal-tal = talai.

taltala A. (taltalā) (1) *Vb.* 1C (*a*) an taltala shārā = talai 1. (*b*) an ~ masa askī = talai 2. B. (taltala) (1) what clean sweeping ! (2) what smooth shaving ! (*cf.* talai).

taltalē *Vb.* 1C (1) swept (place) clean. (2) shaved (head) smooth.

tam (1) *adv. x* yā dauru ~ it is firmly tied. (2) *Sk.* (*Vb. only in this form and used with dative*) (*a*) = tabā 1*h x* sun tam·masa they vexed him. (*b*) = tāsam *x* yā ~ masa he attacked him. (*c*) = tarad da *x* yā ~ masa a hanya he came on him in the street.

tama A. (tamā) *f.* (1) (*a*) ore. (*b*) yanā cin ~ he is a smith. (*c*) cī ~ *m.* smith(s). (*d*) yā bar ni ~ he failed to persuade me. (2) type of cheap sword. (3) *Vd.* Usumāŋ. B. (tāma) *Sk.* helped (= taya).

tāmāge *m.* = kōgāwā.

Ta mājira *Vd.* almājirī.

tāmaka *Kt.* = tākamā.

tamalmalā = tamammanā *f.* (1) smegma affecting lad's penis. (2) a disease of horse's eye. (3) tamammanā kurkullā = tamalmalā kulkullā *f.* selling off odds and ends.

tamaŋgajī *m.* type of bulrush-millet.

tamaŋgulā *Kt. f.* = inyāwarā.

tamani A. (tamanī) *Ar. m.* (1) price. (2) ~ garēshi it is dear. (3) yā mutu, yā bar tamanin pam hamsiŋ he died leaving what was worth fifty pounds.

B. (tạmạnī) *m.* type of sweet tamarind.

tạmậniŋ *Ar. f.* eighty.

tạmānīyạ *Ar. f.* (1) eight thousand. (2) tạmānīyạrkạ = ạbūriŋkạ.

tạmaŋkạcī *Kt. m.* = kwạtaŋkwạcī.

tamaŋkwarō *f.* slave-girl (= kụyaŋgạ).

*tamạntā = kīmạntā 1.

*tạmantạkā *Ar. f.* belt (= dạmarạ).

tạmarkōkọ *Kt. m.* trouble.

Ta marmasō *Vd.* marmasō.

tạmat *Ar.* that's the end of the matter !

ta mạtā *adj.* (1) female *x* tamạtar ạkū female parrot (*Vd.* mạcẹ 2, namijị). (2) bāsanyạ tamạtar bāshị *Sk. f.* borrowing to pay a debt.

tamau = tam 1.

tamaulā *f.* (1) (*a*) children's game of pelting each other with ragballs (= *Sk.* tūlā). (*b*) yā yi ~ da nī he worked his will on me. (2) = būlālạ 2.

tāmạyā *Vb.* 1C = tạmayạ *Vb.* 2 *Sk.* helped (= tạimakạ).

tāmạyī *Sk. m.* assistance (= tạimakō).

tambạ *f.* the grass *Eleusine corocana.*

Tambai = Shạ rụbūtū.

tambākẹ *m.* (*f.* tambākīyā) huge.

tambākēkẹ *m.* (*f.* tambākēkīyā) huge.

tạmbạlā-tambalā *f.* " falling between two stools " (= bạkạtantạŋ).

tạmbạlẹ-tambalē *m.* " falling between two stools " (= bạkạtantạŋ).

tạmbạm-tambam *m.* = tạmbau-tambau.

tambạrā *f.* (1) = izgā 3. (2) a sạrautạ among Asbin women.

tambạrī *m.* (*pl.* tamburạ) (1) (*a*) hemispherical drum. (*b*) munạ tamburạ we're rejoicing in victory. (2) = mạnnē. (3) official seal on document (= hātịmī). (4) = dāfị 1. (5) longest of the three strings of mōlō or gōgē (*cf.* magūdīyā 4). (6) an Agalāwā sạrautạ. (7) sore on horse from being spurred. (8) lạbāri yā yi ~ this news is well known. (9) tambạrin cikị = tambạrin talạkạ deep groan. (10) tambạrin Shạitsạŋ making explosive sound with body-cloth in walking *as in* lēbẹ 3, etc. (*cf.* bụrmā 1c). (11) an yi masạ tambạrin tsịyā he has been shamed by his secrets being revealed (= fạllasạ). (12) tambạriŋ wạdā *Vd.* bụgau 4 ; hadirị.

tạmbạtsai *Kt.* = sạmbạtsai.

tạmbau-tambau = tạmbau-tạmbau *m.* (1) (*a*) swishing of water being carried in masakī. (*b*) tossing of boat in storm. (2) uneasiness.

tambaya A. (tạmbayạ) (1) *Vb.* 2 (*a*) made enquiries *x* nā ~ wurinsạ I made enquiries from him, (*b*) (i) asked P. *x* nā tạmbayē shị I asked him. nā tạmbayē shị I asked him this. yā tạmbayō nị lạbārị he came and asked me for news. (ii) nā zō n tạmbayē kạ nē I've come to you for information (*reply*, Allạ yạ sanshē mụ God give me the knowledge to answer your questions !), *Vd.* mālạmī 1*c.*v. (iii) yā tạmbayē mụ wai . . . he asked us whether . . . (iv) *x* tụnjērē yanạ ~ tasạ he's not yet fully cured of syphilis. (v) tạmbayạr hālị *Vd.* asạlā. (*c*) asked P. to give one T. *x* kạ tạmbayi dākị wurinsạ = kạ tạmbayē shị dākị ask him to give you a room ! mun tạmbayē sụ, sụ bā mụ shī we've asked them to give it to us. (*d*) asked for news of *x* nā tạmbayē shị wurintạ I asked her about it. yā tạmbayē tạ he asked for news of her. nā tạmbayi kwānansạ I asked after his health. mạganạn nạŋ tā tạmbayu many enquiries have been made about this. (*e*) yā tạmbayu he has taken many potions to make him invulnerable, etc. (*Vd.* 2 *below*). (*f*) *Vd.* hūlū 2, Shạ rụbūtū. (*g*) fạdi, bạ ạ tạmbayē kị ba *Vd.* sūdā 1*b*, fạdā 1*b*. (*h*) ạ tạmbayi fuskạ *Vd.* sararī 1*e.*iii, lạbārị 1*a.*viii. (*j*) *Vd.* lạbārị 1*a.*x. (2) *f.* (i) ~ gạrēshị he has charms which make him invulnerable, etc. (*cf.* 1*e above*, sammụ). (ii) *Vd.* kạryạ ~ 1.

B. (tambạyā) *Vb.* 1C = tambaya 1*a, c, d.*

tambērē *m.* suffering trouble, difficulty (= wụyā).

tạmbōdai = tạmbōtsai = ạlmutsụtsai *q.v.*

tamburạ *Vd.* tambạrī.

Tambūtu *f.* Timbuctoo.

tamē-tạmē *Kt. x* rūwā yā kwạntā ~ floods of water lay everywhere.

tạmfā (1) (*a*) " tạmfad dạ kasā " ŋ ji mai cīwạŋ idọ, nothing will turn me from my purpose no matter what you say ! (b) Vd. cīwọ 2e. (2) Vd. taŋkā.

tạmfạsūwā f. any needle (= ạllūrạ).

tamfạtsā Vb. 1C (1) banged bucket into well to fill it (= tinjimā 2a = Kt. dumbulā 2). (2) yā ~ mini zāgi he abused me.

tạmfạtsē m. (1) acting as in tamfạtsā 1 (= tinjimē = Kt. dumbulē). (2) ạ shẹ̄kara sāran rūwā, sǎi ~ he's in too firm a position ·to be harmed by slander.

tāmi Sk. m. help (= taimakō).

tāmīlō m. = ƙyāmọ.

ta mirginā = ta wantsạlā.

tamka = taŋka.

tamkẹ = taŋkẹ.

tammā f. (pl. tammōmī) one-franc piece.

tạmmahạ Sk. f. = tsạmmāni.

tammaŋ undoubtedly.

tạmmāni = tsạmmāni.

tamnạ Sk. = taunạ.

tạmnē Kt. = taunē.

tamōgạs = tamōgạshī m. (pl. tạmōgạsai) sword with three lines along the blade.

tāmōjī m. wrinkles from age or thinness.

tamōlā = tamaulā.

tạmōlạkā f. = tạmōlạkī m. = ƙọshīyạ 1 q.v.

tạmōwạ f. illness accompanying teething.

tạmpā = tạmfā.

tạmrāro Kt. = taurāro.

tamrō Sk. m. (1) = taurō. (2) (a) = kwạŋkwasọ. (b) yanā dạ kyạn ~ he (oldish P.) does not show his age.

tāmu ours. (1) Vd. nāmu. (2) munā tāmu, Allạ nā tāsạ = ƙaddarạ 2.

tạ̄mulallē m. (f. tạ̄mulallīyā) pl. tạ̄mulạllū small-buttocked.

tāmulē Vb. 3A gindinsạ yā ~ he is small-buttocked (= tāmīlō).

tạmuŋgulā Kt. f. = inyāwarā.

tạ̄mushushū m. (1) type of plant. (2) idạnsạ kạman ~ he has small eyes and weak sight.

tạmzā f. tapeworm (= tsīlā q.v.).

tạn Eng. m. ton.

tana A. (tānạ) = tālẹ 2.

B. (tānā) f. (sg., pl.) (1) (a) earthworm(s). (b) tānar cikị round intestinal worm(s) = sagō 3, cf. tạmzā. (2) = yādį 1. (3) Kt. (a) foreskin (= lọ̄6ā).

(b) an yi masạ cin ~ he has been circumcised (= ƙācīyạ). (4) x yanā ~ he is lying sprawled out (cf. tānạ).

C. (tānā) she is (verb-prefix of progressive, Gram. 16) x (i) tānā zūwạ she is coming. (2) tānā ƙasạ Vd. dabọ 4.

tā̄nadạ Vb. 2 (p.o. tā̄nadē = tā̄najē, n.o. tā̄nadi = tā̄naji) (1) made one's arrangements for (Vd. tānạdī). (2) Kt. = ādạnā.

tānạdī m. (1) (sec. v.n. of tā̄nadạ) x yanā tānạdinsạ = yanā tā̄nadạ tasạ he's making preparations for doing it. sun yi tānạdinsụ they made their preparations. (2) (a) thrift. (b) foresight x bā shi dạ ~ he has no foresight (b = tsiŋkāyā). (3) mūgụn ~ gạrẹ̄shi he's deceitful. (4) aŋ ƙārẹ masạ ~ he has been humiliated (= kunyạ 2c.i).

tā̄nākạ f. (pl. tā̄nākū) metal container for perfume (cf. wạkīyyạ).

tānạnā Vb. 1C (1) = ƙaurạrā. (2) fried as in tā̄nanē 2.

tā̄nanē m. (1) acting as in ƙaurạrā. (2) frying (sōyạ) shelled ground-nuts to make ƙulī-ƙulī (cf. ƙaurạrē).

*tạnarī m. (1) young goat. (2) young goat roasted whole, cf. tandạ 2.

tạnazạrī m. muscles between ribs of cattle.

tandạ f. (1) oven for cooking as in 2 below, cf. tạndẹ̄rū. (2) gashin tandạ grilling whole skinned ram on grid, cf. tạnarī.

tandạ Vb. 1A = tạndā Vb. 2 Kt. (1) licked (= lāsā). (2) yuŋwạ tạndar bāƙiŋ ƙishirwā it's a case of the blind leading the blind. (3) Vd. tạndi.

tạndal x yā cịka ~ it's chock-full (= fal).

tandara A. (tandarạ = Kt. tạndarạ) (1) type of harmless snake (= shạ̄ nōnọ). (2) tạfiyạr ~ going by roundabout route (cf. gẹ̄wạyē).

B. (tandạrā) Vb. felled (person) = kā dạ.

tandạrē Vb. 3A rebelled, became insubordinate, became out of hand (= kaŋgạrē).

tandarkī m. (1) (a) failing to pay debts. (b) P. failing to pay debts. (2) Kt. A. huge.

tandawạrā *f.* (*pl.* tạndạwạrai) small, tanned goatskin-waterskin (*cf.* sạlkā).

tandāyē *Vd.* tandū.

tandẹ (1) *Vb.* 1A (*a*) hanyạ tā ~ minị ƙafạ travelling has skinned my feet. (*b*) *Kt.* licked up all of (= lāshẹ = kwandẹ 1*b*). (2) *Vb.* 3A ƙafạta tā ~ my foot has become skinned from travelling.

tạndẹ̄rū *m.* (*Ar. from Assyrian*) oven for baking (gasạ) the foods gụrāsạ, wạinā, etc. (*cf.* tandạ)

tạndi (*imperative of* tạnɗā) *used in* bābụ " ~ " bạllē " lāshi " = sīdīdī.

tandū *m.* (*pl.* tandāyē) (1) (*a*) hide vessel used for (i) antimony, or for (ii) clarified (tōyạ) butter, and forming part of bride's gārā. (*b*) (i) matsīyāci dǎi kō an jēfạ shi ạ tandum mǎi, sǎi yạ fitō dạ firī put a beggar on horseback and he'll ride to the devil (*Vd.* matsīyāci 2). (ii) *Vd.* ɓakyạlcē. (*c*) sun yi wạ ƙasạr rufin tandū they crushed the country entirely. (*d*) gịndin ~ small amount of butter left in borrowed tandū 1*a*.ii when returned to its owner. (*e*) *Vd.* mạn kaɗǎi 2. (2) (*a*) ram or goat at layyā which on being slaughtered, proved fatter than expected. (*b*) yā fasạ ~ he killed ram, *etc.*, *as in* 2*a above*. (3) *Vd.* zịnā 2. (4) tanduṇ ālāyạ = tanduṇ ālāyẹ = ālāyạ *f.* = ālāyẹ *m.* skin-bottle for oil or honey. (5) tanduṇ kwạllī small hide-container for antimony (= kurạtandū).

tānẹ = tānạ.

tanga A. (tạngā) *f.* fifty-centime piece. B. (Taṇgạ) (1) what a tall person ! (2) what a big camel !

tạngadī *m.* (1) staggering, reeling (= tạntạngā). (2) rocking (of water in jar, boat on rough water, etc.). (3) azzịkinsạ yanạ ~ his prospects look black.

Taṇgālē (1) the Tangale people of Gombe. (2) you big-headed fool !

taṇgālī = taṇgālē 2.

tạngaṇ-tạngaṇ *x* yanạ tạngạn-tạngaṇ he is on the point of falling.

tạngarạgātsā *Kt. f.* = gintsilmī.

tạngạrāhụ *Eng. m.* telegraph.

tạngaram = taṇgaraṇ (1) *m.* crockery (= fạɗi kạ mutụ), *cf.* tāsạ 2*b*. (2)

adv. yanạ ganī ~ he sees well. garī yā wāyẹ ~ the day has fully dawned. wạyō gạrēshị ~ he's cute. yanạ naṇ ~ he's well.

taṇgarɗạ *f.* (1) (*a*) unreliability *x* zạncan naṇ yanạ ~ this story is doubtful. kẹ̄kyaṇ yanạ ~ the cycle is unreliable. (*b*) bạ̄ ~ there is no doubt about it. (2) empty excuses (= rạrraunā 2).

tạngā̃-tạngā̃ = taṇgạṇ-taṇgaṇ.

tange A. *(taṇgē) m.* = gintsilmī. B. (taṇgẹ) *Vb.* 1A (1) tethered (two oxen) together by the forefeet. (2) tethered (many calves *x* 50) by the neck on long series of tạngē-ropes. (3) tethered calf to cow, but far from the teats, whilst milking the cow. C. (taṇgē) *m.* (1) acting *as in* taṇgẹ. (2) the looped-rope used for taṇgẹ (= dạngwạlī), *cf.* ɗaurin 'yam maruƙạ ; randẹ ; dāɗẹ 3.

tạṇgōrī *m.* (1) large wooden spindle (mazarī) on which cotton is wound (bigger than kạtarī 2). (2) a Kano sạrautạ.

tạngurmạ *f.* struggling.

Tạnī = Ạltịne.

tānịnā *Kt.* = tānīyā *Kt.* (*used in* zạurạncē) the food fụrā.

taṇk = tạnki *Eng. m.* (*pl.* taṇkunạ = tạnk) tank (armoured vehicle). mạnyan ~ heavy tanks.

tanka A. (taṇkạ) (1) *Vb.* 1A (*a*) (i) *used in x* bai ~ ba he remained mum. (ii) bạ zā sụ taṇkạ ba they'll take no steps. (iii) tạnkā bakạ silently. (*b*) yā ~ dạ'ạwā *Vd.* dạ'ạwā 3. (2) *f.* (*a*) keen desire (= ɗōkī). (*b*) *Kt.* niggardliness (= rōwạ).

B. (taṇkā) *f.* (1) (*a*) (*used in genitive* taṇkar *as prep.*) like *x* ƙạrē taṇkar wannạṇ a dog like this one. taṇkāta bạ yā yi ba a person of my status would not do it (= kạmā). (*b*) *Vd.* tạmfā. (2) fruit-bearing branch of date-tree, banana-tree, tukurwā, *etc.* (3) *Vd.* taṇkạ 1*a*.iii.

C. (taṇkā) *f.* (1) (*a*) purlin of grass or cornstalks at edge of thatch (*Vd.* taṇkẹ). (*b*) yanạ ƙirgar (= yanạ ƙidāyạr) ~ he went to bed supperless and cannot sleep. (2) ạ taṇkar sararī openly.

(3) (a) am bar shị ạ taŋkad tsakạ he's in trouble. (b) Vd. tantạncē 1b.

*taŋkacaccēnịyā = taŋkacēcēnịyā f. similarity, equality.

*taŋkạtayyạ Kt. f. similarity, equality.

tankaḍa A. (taŋkạḍā) Vb. 1C (1) (a) winnowed fine flour from coarse flour (tsạkī) into (vessel) (Vd. taŋkạḍē) x aṇā ∼ shi cikiŋ ƙwaryā it (fine flour) is being winnowed from the tsạkī, so that former falls into the calabash. (b) ạbiŋ dạ ya yi, bā ạ̄ taŋkạḍāwā don laushī he did an extraordinary T. (2) (a) propelled. (b) sun taŋkạḍạ ƙyēyạr ruṇdunā they routed the army.
    B. (taŋkaḍạ) Vb. 2 = taŋkạḍē 1.

taŋkạḍạfī Kt. = ḍaŋkạḍạfī.

tankaḍe A. (taŋkạḍē) (1) Vb. 1C (a) winnowed (as in taŋkạḍē). (b) knocked over, knocked down x yā ∼ miṇi shī he knocked it out of my hand (= tūrẹ). (2) Vb. 3A capsized.
    B. (taŋkạḍē) m. (1) wlnnowing fine flour from coarse flour (tsạkī) by using fãifãi or rārīyā (cf. bākạcē, cāsạ). (2) Vd. dakạ 2f; ḍakạ 4.
    C. (taŋkaḍē) m. = taŋkwaɓē.
    D. (taŋkaḍẹ) Vd. talạkạ 2.

taŋkakkē m. (f. taŋkakkīyā) pl. taŋkạkkū handsome.

taŋkam = taŋdal.

taŋƙamēmẹ m. (f. taŋƙamēmịyā) pl. taŋƙam-taŋƙam huge-headed.

taŋƙamī m. (f. taŋƙamā) pl. taŋƙam-taŋƙam huge-headed.

taŋƙạŋƙaŋ m. yaṇā dạ kạ̈i ∼ dạ shī he is huge-headed (= taŋƙamī).

taŋkar Vd. taŋkā.

taŋkạrā Vb. 3A extended to x ƙasā tā ∼ dạ īyạ̄karmụ the territory extends as far as our boundary (= kai).

taŋkạrē Vb. 3A ƙasā tā ∼ dạ īyạ̄karmụ = taŋkạrā.

Taŋkarī = Taŋkọ.

taŋkarkị m. Northern black-bellied bustard (Lissotis melanogaster melanogaster).

taŋkẹ Vb. 1A x an ∼ būshīyar karā cornstalks have been attached to the thatch-rafters (tsaikọ) as purlins (taŋkā).

taŋƙēshẹ m. (f. taŋƙēshīyā) what a pot-bellied person !

taŋkīyā f. (1) (a) quarrelling. (b) wāƙạ ∼

cẹ Vd. hạ̊ƙurī 5. (2) loud talk of several persons (= sụrūtụ).

tanko A. (Taŋkọ) name given boy born after two or more successive girls (his epithet is ∼ taŋkariŋ gidā) = Mạ̄tī = Mātọ = Kā tākalō = Taŋkarī = Gụdā 1g = Yigudạ = mạcẹ 10a.
    B. (taŋkō) Vd. jan ∼.

taŋkōlō m. barber's razor-case.

taŋkū Sk. m. buying kola-nuts in country for resale in town (cf. sārā 2a.i).

taŋkunạ Vd. taŋk.

taŋkwā Sk. f. = tsīduhū.

tankwaɓe A. (taŋkwạɓē) (1) = taŋkạḍē 1b. (2) Vd. dībạ 1j.
    B. (taŋkwaɓē) m. game where two boys join their little fingers as token of the bargain that if A in future sees B eating, and can knock the food out of B's hand, it belongs to A (Vd. dībạ 1j).

taŋƙwalēlẹ m. (f. taŋƙwalēlịyā) taŋƙwal-taŋƙwạl large and round.

taŋƙwalī m. (f. taŋƙwalā) pl. taŋƙwal-taŋƙwạl large and round.

taŋƙwalƙwal m. x gōrọ ne ∼ dạ shī it is a huge kola-nut.

tankwara A. (taŋƙwạrā) Vb. 1C (1) bent (flexible T. x stick) = laŋƙwạsā. (2) sold at knockdown-price (when pressed for ready cash) = karyạ 1e.
    B. (taŋƙwara) Vb. 3B (1) (flexible T. x stick) became bent (= laŋƙwasạ). (2) ƙị ∼ Vd. bidạ 3.

taŋƙwarad dạ Vb. 4 = taŋƙwạrā.

taŋƙwạrē Vb. 3A = taŋƙwarạ.

tankwasa A. (taŋƙwạsā) = taŋƙwạrā (Vd. taŋƙwạshē).
    B. (taŋƙwasạ) = taŋƙwarạ.

taŋƙwạshē (1) Vb. 1A (a) = taŋƙwạrā. (b) yā taŋƙwạshẹ ƙafạ tasạ he sat down tucking his leg under him (out of politeness to a judge, etc.). (c) yā taŋƙwạshẹ zūcīyā he bowed to the inevitable (= daurẹ). (2) Vb. 3A = taŋƙwarạ.

taŋnaƙī = tạrnaƙī.

taṇtabạrā f. or m. (according to sex) (pl. taṇtabạrai = taṇtabạrū) (1) (a) pigeon, cf. kạtukụ (epithet is bạrū q.v. = dūkīyar samạ, kinā ḍakạ, kim fi zambạr gōmạ = kīwạn yạrdā, kạdaŋ kin tāshị, Allạ̄ kaŋ kāwō kị gidā = Kyallạ kīwạm ɓatạ). (b) ḍan ∼ (pl. 'yan ∼ exception

to Mod. Gram. 102*c*) young pigeon. (*c*)
~ kyau da wandō feathery-legged
pigeon. (2) black horse with white
patches on sides and belly.

tantadā *Vb*. 1C did well *x* yā tantada
aiki he did the work well.

tantadi A. (tantadi) how well-done it is !
   B. (tantadī) *Kt. m.* coarsely-ground
flour (*cf.* ɓarza, tsakī, lilis).

tantadō *Kt. m.* = dagē.

tantagaryā (1) *f.* (*a*) = gangārīya 1.
(*b*) tantagaryar garī clear sky. (2)
adv. clearly *x* garī yā wāye ~ day has
fully dawned.

tantakwashī *m.* head of femur of sheep,
ox or goat (= *Sk.* gumsa).

tantal *Vd.* kyanwā 5.

tantalā *Vb.* 3A yā ~ a guje he took to his
heels.

tantalaminya *x A* (*a boy*) *says to B* (*a girl*)
sam mini kadan give me a bit of what
you are selling ! *to which she may reply*
zam bā ka ~ makārar kirgē not a bean
will I give you ! (= fam 2).

tantalbatētē = tantalbatēti *m.* = ɓakatan-
tan *q.v.*

tantaliɓo *m.* kernel of gōruba-fruit (=
Sk. guntsū 2).

tantalminya = tantalaminya.

tantamā *f.* (1) doubt (= shakka). (2)
bari ~ = shēgē 5. (3) *Vd.* rāi 5*b*.

tantāmī *Kt.* = makanī.

tantancē *Vb.* 3A (1) (*a*) deteriorated (=
lālācē). (*b*) yā ~ a tankad tsaka he
(it) has become utterly useless (*Vd.*
tankā 3*a*). (2) = sakankancē *x* ban ~
inda (= da inda) ya tafi ba I don't
know for sure where he has gone.
nā ~ da shī I'm sure of it. (3) ban
san inda kudī suka ~ ba I don't know
how the money has become frittered
away like this.

tantangā *f.* (1) = tangadī. (2) hesitating
(= tantarwai). (3) (*rustic*) inā tantangā
how are you ? (*reply is* da gōdīyā) =
dawainīyā 2.

tantānī *m.* membrane, especially that
from cow's abdominal-wall (murfī 2) or
from chicken's crop (ɓarōrọ), used for
covering children's drums.

tantarwai A. (tantarwai) = *Kt.* tantarkwai
m. hesitating (= tantangā 2).

   B. (tantarwai) (1) *adv.* clearly *x*
yanā ganī ~ he sees well. (2) *m.* yā
yi ~ it has a sheen (= walkīyā).

tantashā *Kt. f.* bargain *x* nā sāmi ~ =
nā sāmē shi ~ I got it cheap.

tantaunā *Vb.* 1C (1) kept chewing (*intensive from* tauna). (2) an ~ shi it has
been thoroughly discussed (2 = tauna 2).

tantaurī *m.* (1) tough meat. (2) *Kt.* =
tantānī.

tanti *m.* (*pl.* tantōcī = tantuna) *Eng.* (1)
tent (= laima). (2) Willesden canvas.
(3) kā bugu ya ~ ka fi kōko laushī
you'll get a good beating ! (3) dan ~
(*said by women*) good (*re* material) *x*
zane dan ~ good cloth. rīgā 'yar ~
a good gown.

tantīri *m.* (*f.* tantīrīyā) *pl.* tantīrai poor
(= matsīyācī).

tantōcī *Vd.* tanti.

tantsai *adv.* in a straight line.

tantsē *Vb.* 1A = dājē 1.

tantsi *m.* = dājīyā 2*a*.

tantsīyā (1) *f.* = dājīyā. (2) how even the
row is !

tantuna *Vd.* tanti.

tanya *Sk. Vb.* 1A helped (= taimaka).

tanyace A. (tanyacē) *Vb.* 1C *Kt.* shamed P.
by revealing his secrets (= fallasa).

   B. (tanyacē) *Vd.* tanyata.

tanyar = tantarwai 1.

tanyata *Vb.* 2 (*p.o.* tanyacē, *n.o.* tanyaci)
Kt. = tanyacē.

tanyē *Vb.* 1A *Sk.* = tanya.

tanzā = tamzā.

tanzankō *Sk. m.* = jājē 1.

tanzōmā *Kt. f.* = tarzōmā.

tap = taf.

tara A. (tāra) (1) *Vb.* 1A. (*a*) (i) collected
x yā tāra karfinsa wurī gudā he concentrated his troops in one place. sun tāra
hankulansu ˙ wurī gudā they reached
agreement on the point (= tattarā).
(ii) lāsafin nan ạbin tārāwā cikin
takardarku this bill enclosed in your
letter. ạbin da jawābinka ya ~ the
contents of your letter. (iii) an ~
masa kasā he was fulsomely flattered,
he was flattered into attempting T.
beyond him (*cf.* tāra kasā). (iv) yā ~
masa jinī it bruised him (*Vd.* kuma 3).
(v) added up *x* an ~ jimilla tasu the

totals have been added up. **an ~ su**
(= **an ~ dạ sū**) **cikin lịssāfị** they've
been totted up (= **lāsạ̀ftā**). (vi) ~
kīfī dạ kwạ̀dō *Vd.* **kīfī 3.** (vii) **an ~**
masạ dūnīyạ his misdeeds are being
bandied about. (*b*) **yā ~ jikī** (i) he
gathered his gown tightly round his
body (*cf.* **sansạŋƙē**). (ii) he behaved
with reserve (= **tattạrā 1***b*). (*c*) shared
in *x* **sun ~ sūnā** they are namesakes
(*Vd.* **tạkwạrā**). **mun ~ tạfīyạ** we
travelled together. **sun ~ zamā** they
live, work together. **sun ~ gidā** they
live in the same compound. **sun ~**
zāmạnī they were contemporaries.
yā ~ daŋgi dạ nī he's related to me
(*Vd.* **tạ̀rō 2**). (*d*) **tārạ cịn tūwō** *Vd.*
shā 1*g*.iii. (*e*) **dawạ sukạ ~** *Vd.* **zōmō 8.**
(*f*) *Vd.* **tạ̀ru, gạyyā 1***a*, **tạ̀rạ ƙasā.** (2)
Vb. **3A yā ~ dạ ita** he copulated with
her (= **jimā'ị**).
  B. (**tạ̀rā**) *f.* (1) being finicky *x* (*a*)
bā yạ̀ ~ he's not finicky.   **bā yạ̀**
tạ̀rar ạ̀bincī he's not finicky about his
food. (*b*) *Vd.* **dōgarị.** (2) a fine *x* (*a*)
an cī shị ~ (= **an cī shị tạ̀rar**) **sulẹ gōmạ**
he's been fined ten shillings. (*b*) **kōmē**
tsananin ~ ạ̀ bar wạ ɗam mai gidā
kạ̀rē no smoke without fire !
  C. (**tarạ**) *f.* (1) (*a*) nine. (*b*) **na ~**
m. ninth (*f.* **ta ~**) (*pl.* **na ~**).   (2)
kạ̀zā ~ tā ịsa lahīyā sǎi kṑ im fātạ
akẹ̀ sṑ if the best is not available, take
what offers !   (3) **mụtụm, ~ yakẹ̀,**
bai cikạ gōmạ ba nobody is perfect.
(4) **tarạ-tarạ** (i) nine each.   (ii) *Kt.*
face-markings consisting of nine lines
on each side of face, as done by *x*
Māguzāwā.   (5) **gidan ~** *m.* type of
embroidery-pattern.   (6) *Vd.* **tạraŋ-**
gōmạ.   (7) **ƙwǎi ~** *Vd.* **tsīnạ̄nā.** (8)
kụ tarạ, kụ tarạ = kụ tarẹ, kụ tarẹ.
  D. (**tạrā**) *Vb.* 2 (1) went to meet *x*
yā tạfi yā tạrē (= **yā tarō**) **shị** he went out
to meet him. **sun tarbō shị dagạ yạmmā**
they came to meet him from the west.
sun tarbō Sarkinsụ zūwạ̀ birninsụ they
went to meet their chief on his arrival
at their capital. **bā sạ̀ yạrdā sụ tạrbi**
fadạn dạ bạ zā sụ gịrbi rībạ ba they
are not the people to engage in unprofitable strife. **an tạri ịndạ zại fitō**

they went to meet him where he was
due to appear (= **tạryā = Sk. tạrbā**).
(2) (*a*) intercepted = **tarẹ 1***a q.v.* (*b*)
yā tạri numfāshinsạ he winded him.
(*c*) **ban tạri numfāshiŋkạ ba, ạmmā I**
wouldn't for the world interrupt what
you're saying, but please allow me to
say that . . . (*said between equals, but
junior addressing senior says* **Allạ̀**
yạ bā kạ nasarạ).
tạrabā *f.* = **tsạ̀rī 2***a.*
Tạrābụlụs *f.* Tripoli, Tripolitania.
tarad dạ *Vb.* 4 (1) overtook *x* **nā ~ shī =**
nā tarshē shị I overtook him.   (2) (*a*)
happened to find *x* **nā ~ shī** (= **nā**
tasshē shị) **ạ̀ Kanọ** I came upon him
in Kano (= **ishẹ = iskẹ = sạ̀mā 1***b*).
(*b*) **yā taras** he's lost his temper.   (*c*)
Vd. **jụ̄rē.**   (*d*) **~ ạrādụ dạ kā ya yi =**
~ dạ ạrādụ dom fādịŋ kại ya yi he
interfered in matters above his head.
(3) *Vd.* **tạrsu.**
tạraddạdī *Ar. m.* feeling anxious.
taraf = **taras.**
tạraf-tạrạf *m. used in* **tūwō yā yi ~** the
tūwō is flabby.
tạragụ *m.* (*sg., pl.*) *Eng.* (1) railway-
truck(s). (2) ɗan **tạragụ** *m.* (*pl.* **'yan ~**)
man accompanying cattle in railway
cattle-trucks.
tạragutsạ *f.* = **tarẹ̀tsā 2.**
tạrāhạ *f.* good-quality **kạtīfạ.**
tạrairayạ *f.* (1) = **ịnā 4***b*. (2) = **lallāshī.**
tạ̀rạ ƙasā kạ zaunạ what a thin-bottomed
person ! (*cf.* **tārạ 1***a*.iii).
tạrakkā *Vd.* **tarkō.**
tāram (*the form of* **tạ̀ru** *used before dative*)
x **sukạ ~ masạ** then they gathered
round him. **sunạ̀ ~ wạ jirgin nạŋ**
gụdā they are joining in attacking this
single ship.
tạramnīyā *Sk.* = **tạraunīyā.**
tạraŋgahūmạ *f.* meddlesomeness (= **kạ-**
rambạ̀nī).
tạraŋgōmạ (1) (*said by* ɗam **maganạ**)
'yā'yansụ tarạ nē ạmmā ~ nē they
have nine children at home, but they
claim five each, as before their joint
child was born, each of them had four
from a previous marriage. (2) **an yi**
rūwā ạ ~ rain expected in the ninth
month did not fall till the tenth.

tarap = taras.

tarar = taras *Vd*. tarad.

tarara A. (tararạ) *Vb*. 3B dripped (= digạ).
  B. (tarạrā) *Vb*. 1C = digạ.

tarar dạ = tarad dạ.

tarạrē *Vb*. 3A = tarạrā.

tararrạdī = tạraddạdī.

tararrạtsē *Vb*. 1D *intensive from* tartsẹ.

taras A. (taras) *x* bạ ni dạ shī kō ⁓ I
  have none at all.
  B. (tarạs) *Vd*. tạrī 2.

taras dạ = tarad dạ.

tạrau = tạntạrwai 1.

tạraunīyā *f*. (1) the gum-tree *Combretum
  verticillatum* (= kantakạrā). (2) *Kt*.
  dōkị maị kụnnan ⁓ lop-eared horse.

tārạyē *Vd*. tārī.

tạrayyạ *f*. (1) partnership (*cf*. gamạɗē)
  x yạrā zā sụ yi tạrayyạr aikị dạ mālạmī
  the pupils will share with the teacher
  in the work. (2) ạbōkin ⁓ *m*. partner.
  ạbōkan ⁓ tasạ his partners.

tarba A. (tạrbā) (1) *Vb*. 2 *Sk*. = tạrā 1,
  2*a*. (2) *cf*. tarbẹ.
  B. (tarbạ) *Vb*. 1A = tarẹ 1*a*.iv *x*
  munạ sọ sụ tarbạ manạ we want them
  to protect us.

tạrbạcē *m*. = jụcē.

tạrbā-tạrbā *f*. *x* sōjạmmụ sum ɓullō
  musụ, anạ ⁓ our soldiers appeared
  unexpectedly before them and a mêlée
  took place.

*tạrbīyyạ *Ar*. *f*. training, education.

tarbe A. (tarbẹ) (1) *Sk*. = tarẹ. (2) *cf*.
  tạrbā.
  B. (tạrbē) *m*. (1) wounding horse's
  foreleg by bad rider. (2) *Sk*. = tạrē.

tarcẹ *Kt*. = tartsẹ.

tar dạ = tarad dạ.

tardạ *Sk*. *Vb*. 1A = tarad dạ.

tardẹ *m*. (*pl*. tardunạ) ring used by Filani
  women as headpad (gamō) or stand for
  calabashes.

tare A. (tārẹ) (1) *Vb*. 1A collected completely (*cf*. tārạ). (2) *Vb*. 3A tā ⁓
  (*a*) she (bride) has moved to her husband's home (= ma'aurā), *cf*. yinị
  1*c*.i, aurē 6*d*. (*b*) *Vd*. bịkī 1*g*.
  B. (tạre) *adv*. (1) (*a*) together *x*
  sunạ ⁓ they are together. (*b*) *x*
  bạ ⁓ dạ tsọrō ba fearlessly. (*c*) (*used
  as noun*) *x* munạ zaman ⁓ we are

friends. (2) (*noun of state from* tārạ) *x*
  kāyā yanạ ⁓ the loads have been
  collected together.
  C. (tarẹ) *Vb*. 1A (1) (*a*) (i) intercepted
  (= tạrā 2*a* = tạryā = taryẹ = *Sk*. tạrbā),
  cf. tạrā 2*b*, *c* ; gintsẹ. (ii) fended off
  x sun ⁓ ạbọkan gạbā they fended off
  the enemy. (iii) (*plus dative*) *x* sun ⁓
  masạ hanyạ they prevented him passing.
  (iv) nā ⁓ makạ shī I warded it off you
  (1*a* = tsarẹ 3 *q.v*.). (*b*) kụ tarẹ, kụ
  tarẹ stop thief ! (*c*) kụ ⁓ *m*. (*sg*., *pl*.)
  (i) thief *x* tsofaŋ kụ ⁓ an old hand at
  theft. (ii) any dog. (2) yā ⁓ dōkịnsạ
  he turned his horse (= kallafō 2).
  D. (tạrē) *m*. intercepting villagers
  taking goods (especially ground-nuts)
  to market, in order that new owner may
  sell at higher price *x* aŋ hanạ tạraŋ
  gyạɗā the intercepting of those taking
  ground-nuts to market has been forbidden (= tạryē).

tarẹ mahạrā *Kt*. = tạsạ mahạrā.

tạrēnīyā *f*. constantly bustling to and fro
  (= kaiwā dạ kāwọwā).

tarẹtsā *f*. (1) small residue (*x* of corn,
  ground-nuts, etc., left in bag or store) =
  Kt. tautsī 2. (2) collection of small
  things, lads, etc. (= taragutsạ =
  yạmā-yamā).

tarẹwadī *Vd*. tarwadā.

tarfạ *Vb*. 1A (1) poured out in drops. (2)
  tā ⁓ masạ rūwā ạ kunnē she robbed
  him.

tarfai (1) how dear ! (2) how niggardly !
  (3) how little ! (*all* = tarfị 2).

tạrfạ mazā durus *m*. type of weed.

tarfe A. (tarfẹ) *Vb*. 1A poured out in
  drops all of.
  B. (tạrfē) *m*. = gạ nākạ 1*b*.

tarfị (1) *m*. small amount. (2) = tarfai.

targaɗẹ *m*. (1) being sprained *x* hannunsạ
  yā yi ⁓ his wrist is sprained (= *Sk*.
  taumashẹ), *cf*. murɖẹ 2*c*. (2) *Vd*.
  kạrāyạ 2*f*.

tạrgē = rụdē.

*tạrgēshē *m*. comb (= matsēfī).

targwai *m*. difficulty *x* nā shā ⁓ I
  suffered difficulty (= fāmā).

tari A. (tārị) (1) *m*. (*a*) (i) pile *x* tārịŋ
  karā heap of corn-stalks (= *Kt*. tsaunị
  2). (ii) crowd *x* tārịn dōkị crowd of

horsemen (1a = tsibi). (b) jigāwą tārįn Allą mai wuyar jiŋkęwā Man proposes and God disposes. (c) x tārįn yawą a large number, a large quantity. ąbu mai tārįn kyąu very good thing. (d) (i) = tārǫ. (ii) ɗan ~ yā sąŋ kīfinsą everyone knows the limits of his own capacities. (2) adv. abundantly x yā bā tą daŋgogįn abūbūwą ~ he gave her all kinds of fine things (= tārį - tārį).

B. (tārī) m. pl. tārąyē. (1) large cloth worn by Asbin women. (2) Vd. Muhammadu.

C. (tąrī) m. (1) coughing. (2) tąrįŋ kīką = tąrin shīką = tąrin tarąs whooping-cough (= Kt. ląlā). (3) Vd. hąkannīyā.

D. (tąrī) m. nā ci tąrinsą = nā ci turą tasą (Vd. turą 2).

E. (tarį) Kt. m. = taryō.

tąrīfą f. type of copper coin.

tārīhą f. = tārīhį m. Ar. (1) date (in chronology). (2) written history.

tąrīką = tsąrīką.

tarįkkē Vb. 1C Nor. = tarę.

tāriku = tāruku.

tąrindǫ dą gudaŋ wąinā Kt. = ciląndō.

tārįŋgiɗą f. the herb Glossonema nubicum.

tąrinŋą Kt. f. = tįrįŋgē.

tąrįrīyą Nor. f. = tąrąiraya.

tārį-tārį adv. (1) in piles. (2) abundantly (2 = tārį 2).

tārīyā f. (1) collecting spun thread from small spools, on to big one. (2) ɗan ~ m. = kwarkwarō 2.

tąrjak Kt. = fąrjak.

*tarjamą, tarjamāmį = *tarzamāmį q.v.

*tąrjamaŋ Ar. m. interpreter (= tāfintą).

tąrkā Vb. 2 Kt. began to do.

tąrkącē m. (1) (a) odds and ends. (b) mun lālątā shi dą tąrkącansą na Jāmus we have brought him low together with his German crew of cut-throats. (2) (sometimes treated as pl.) x waɗansu 'yan ~ various small odds and ends.

tarkątā Vb. 1C collected together scattered articles (x luggage, debts, etc.).

tarkę Kt. m. = dįddigā.

tarkō m. (pl. tarkuną = tarąkkā) trap x (1) ~ yā kāmą shį ą wuyą the trap closed on his neck. (2) bābu tsuntsū,

bābu ~ Vd. tsuntsū 3. (3) Vd. gądō. (4) mūgun tarkō Vd. kucīcī.

tarkōkǫ m. (1) suffering difficulty x yā shā ~ he had great difficulty (= fāmā). (2) rogue.

tarkōshī Sk. m. bow-leggedness (= cąssā).

tarkuną Vd. tarkō.

tarmąhāhą = tąrmąhāhą f. collection of low people or inferior articles.

tarmąjē Vb. 3A (1) gąrī yā ~ the sky has cleared. (2) yā ~ he is fully awake. (3) cf. tarmazaizai.

tąrmąnī Sk. m. = tumą dą gayyą.

tarmasīką f. the gum obtained from tree hanū.

tarmazaizai adv. clearly x gąrī yā wāyę ~ = tarmąjē 1. yā warkę ~ he has fully recovered. yā falkę ~ = tarmąjē 2.

tarmązē = tarmąjē.

tarmē m. x suną ~ they are all engaged on a common task. sun yi masą ~ they combined in attacking him.

tąrmǫ-tarmō m. = fuŋkąsō.

tarną f. (1) an shā ~ there was a bitter quarrel. (2) type of children's game.

tarnąkā Vb. 1C = tarnąkē.

tarnąkē Vb. 1C (1) hobbled (horse) by joining its two near feet or two offfeet (cf. tąrnakī, dabaibąyā). (2) (illness) incapacitated P.

tąrnakī m. (1) hobbling as in tarnąkē. (2) an yi wą dōkį tąrnakim birį = cikįn kīshįyā 1. (3) ąbu yā zamā bąhagwąn tąrnakī the matter is full of contradictions. (3) cf. bątąrnakā.

tarnatsā Kt. (1) ~ tą kashę ni = ąrādu tą yi minį ~ may thunder strike me dead if my oath is false ! (Vd. ąrādu 2). (2) ~ bą zaŋ yi bą I swear not to do it.

Tarnō Kt. m. the sąrautą whose holder collects the weavers' tax.

taro A. (tąrō) m. (1) (a) crowd of persons, collection of things. (b) (sometimes treated as pl.) x waɗannąŋ tąram mutąnē this crowd of people. waɗannąŋ tąraŋ jirągē this fleet of ships. (2) kadą ką yi minį tąran daŋgi = kadą ką yi minį tąran daŋgin daŋgirā don't interfere in my affairs ! (Vd. tārą 1c) = gąyyā 2. (3) tąran tumākī bą karǫ, banzā people are collected idly =

tāran tsintsīyā bā shārā, banzā = tāram mātā bābu karọ, banzā.

B. (tārọ) *m.* (1) collecting fruit knocked off tree by another or fish caught in net by another. (2) d̶an ～ *m.* boy employed to collect fruit, etc., *as in* 1. (3) *Vd.* tārị 1*d.*

C. (tarō) (1) *Eng. m. (a)* threepence (= wālī 2). (*b*) yanā santa kaman ～ a aljīfū he's very fond of her. (2) *Vb.* 1E *Vd.* tarā 1.

tarōgōd̶iyā *Kt. m.* idiot.

tarōsō *m.* (*Ar.* tarūthu mare is defecating) excrement (= najasa).

tarsashī *m.* whole *x* tarsashinsu all of them.

tarshe A. (tarshē) *Vd.* tarad da.

　B. (tarshē) *Sk.* abundantly.

Tarsōwa *f.* the Pleiades (= kāzā 2*a*).

tarsu *Vb.* 3B *Kt. x* bā yā tarsūwā he cannot be overtaken (*d.f.* tarad da).

tartībị *Ar.* (1) *m.* = takamaimai 1. (2) *adv.* (*a*) = takamaimai 2. (*b*) without cessation, in succession.

tartsa *Vb.* 1A (1) yā ～ īhu he yelled out. (2) *Kt.* tā ～ adō she togged herself up.

tartsam *Vb.* (*used only before dative*) spurted on to *x* jinī yā ～ masa a rīgā the blood spurted on to his gown (= tsartam), *cf.* tartsō.

tartsatsī *m.* sparks.

tartsō *Vb.* 3A spurted out *x* jinī yā ～ blood spurted out (*cf.* tartsam).

tartsị my word !

taru A. (tāru) *Vb.* 3B (1) (*a*) collected *x* sun ～ they collected (= tattara). (*b*) (*before dative* tāru *becomes* tāram *q.v.*). (2) a ～ a kas mahaukacin karē he cadges from a generous P. without making any return. (3) wurin nan yanā da kun ～ this place is notorious (as haunted, full of thieves, etc.).

　B. (tārū) *m.* (*pl.* tāruna) (1) outward caravan *x* munā ～, sū sunā kā kōmō we were the outward caravan, they the incoming one. (2) large fishing-net. (3) glutton (= bamburun).

　C. (tāru) = tārọ.

tāruku *m.* (*Ar.* " leaver ") *used in* ～ salātị *m.,f.* (*sg., pl.*) P. only praying now and then.

tāruna *Vd.* tārū.

tarwa *f.* = targwai.

tarwad̶ā *f.* (*pl.* tarēwad̶ī) (1) African catfish (*Clarias anguillaris*) (= kullume).
(2) ～ maị ～ nē " he's a slippery customer ". (3) *Vd.* wankan ～ *under* wankan darza.

tarwatsā *Vb.* 1C = tarwatsē 1C scattered (= wātsa).

tarwātū *m.* (1) loud wrangling (= hargāgī). (2) *Kt.* humiliating P. by revealing his secrets (*cf.* fallasa).

taryā *Vb.* 2 (1) = tarā. (2) supported gōyō on her back by adding extra lower cloth (*cf.* taryō).

tarye *Vb.* 1A (1) = tare 1*a.* (2) = taryā 2.

taryō *m.* an yi wa gōyō ～ she supported the child on her back by adding extra lower-cloth (= *Kt.* tarị).

*tarzama = *tarzamāmị *m.* instructions at beginning of book of potions, spells, etc., explaining how to use them.

tarzōmā *f.* struggle, dispute.

tas A. (tas) (1) *m.* = bauta. (2) = tāsa 1.

　B. (tas) (1) = tāsam *x* kada hantsī ya ～ maka don't let the sun become too high before you set out ! (2) *adv.* (*a*) sum fashe ～ they have all dispersed. (*b*) yā wanku ～ it's washed snow-white.

tasa A. (tāsa) (1) (*a*) (i) his (*with fem. noun*) *x* bā yadda zaị sāmi tāsa murya ta kansa he has no means of getting his opinions heard. (*cf.* nāmu 2*a*). rīgan nan ～ cē this gown is his (Mod. Gram. 48). (ii) *Vd.* nāsa. (*b*) (i) mu ji ～ let's hear *his* version ! kōwā yā kāwō ～ both plaintiff and defendant stated their cases. (ii) *cf.* tāwa 2. (iii) munā tāmu, Allā nā tāsa = faddara 2. (iv) (*expressing habit*) *x* yā yi zāfin zūcīyar tāsa he gave a display of his usual bad temper. (*c*) *cf.* tasa. (2) *f.* (*pl.* tāsōshī) (*a*) metal bowl or basin. (*b*) (*modern usage*) plate of crockery (*Vd.* tangaram). (*c*) tanā da gindin ～ she (girl) has symmetrical breasts (*cf.* hantsa 3). (*d*) bakat ～ *Vd.* fād̶ūwā 3*b.* (3) *Vb.* (*a*) allowed to rise *x* kā ～ minị rīgāta get up off my gown ! ka ～ shi get up off it ! ; let him get up ! yau bākī sun ～ mu we've got a breathing-space from those guests to-day by their departure. (*b*) yanā ～ bakī he (pupil) is beginning to read.

(c) nā gai dạ shī ạmmā baị ⁓ ni ba I paid my respects to him but he gave me nothing. (d) = tā dạ 1c. (e) yā ⁓ minị shī he reminded me of it. (f) = tā dạ 3a. (4) Vb. 3A. (a) = tạskā 2. (b) (i) (swimmer) rose to the surface. (ii) ịnā zaị ⁓ where will he turn up? (c) ginị yā ⁓ the wall being built is getting high. (d) cikịntạ yā ⁓ she is advanced in pregnancy (Vd. cikị 4). (e) (i) yā sōmạ tāsạ̄wā it has begun to swell, get bigger. (ii) dūkịyassạ tā sōmạ tāsạ̄wā he's begun to prosper. (5) cf. tạsā, tā dạ, tāshị, tāsam, tāshẹ, tāsō.

B. (tạsā) Vb. 2 (p.o. tạshē, n.o. tạshi). (1) = tā dạ 1f, h, j, x baị tạshē mụ dạgạ Masạr ba he has not been able to eject us from Egypt. yā tạshi mutạ̄nansạ he sent his men out. (2) (court) restored T. to rightful owner x an tāsō kāyạn nạn, am bạ̄ maị sū that property has been removed from the possession of the holder and given to the legitimate owner. an tạshi kāyạn dạgạ hannun Audụ the property has been removed from Audu who has no legal right to it. (3) set about, proceeded to x kā tạshi kashẹ ni you set about killing me. yā tạshi zāluncị he adopted tyrannical behaviour. sun tạshi kāmụn Tūnạs they set about capturing Tunis (= tāshị 1f = tāsam 1c.ii). (4) bought (slave). (5) cf. tāsạ, tā dạ, tāshị, tāsam, tāshẹ, tāsō.

C. (tasạ) (1) his (following fem. noun) (a) (i) rịgā ⁓ = rịgassạ his gown (Mod. Gram. 47b²). (b) cf. tāsạ 1. (2) Vb. 1A (a) placed P. in front of one to conduct one to place. (b) an ⁓ ƙyēyạ tasụ they have been routed (Vd. (ƙyēyạ). (c) cf. tạsạ mahạrā. (3) f. ⁓ tā sạ̄mē shị he felt a sharp pain in the thorax.

tāsad dạ Vb. 4 Kt. = tā dạ.

tạsa'in = tịs'in.

tasạkalạ f. old crone (= gyạ̄tumạ).

tasạ̄lạ̄ f. (1) a black material used for turbans and short-sleeved gowns. (2) oblong black mat.

tạsạlīmạ f. grousing, fussing (= mītạ).

tāsam (1) (the form of tāshị used before dative when dative begins in m-). (a) attacked x yā ⁓ masạ da fạdạ he upbraided him (= tāsō 1b = tāshẹ 1 = Sk. tam 2b). yā ⁓ mạ aikị he set to work with a will. yā tāsam musụ bạ̄kī būdẹ he attacked them full tilt. gạ yunwạ nạn ạ sụkwạ̄ne tā tāsam mạ ƙasạr then famine soon enveloped the country. mun ⁓ musụ we attacked them (enemy) = Sk. tam 2b. (b) set out for x sun tāsam mạ yạmmā they went westwards. yā ⁓ mạ gidā he set out for home. (c) (i) aimed at ita cẹ mạganạr dạ sukạ tāsam mạ it is this on which their attention is concentrated (= wạ). an tāsam mạ dăi sakam musụ ƙasarsụ the aim is to give them control of their own country. (ii) set about, proceeded to x sun tāsam mạ kāmụn Tūnạs they set about capturing Tunis (= tạsā 3 = tāshị 1f). (2) cf. tāsar, tāshẹ.

tạsạ mahạrā m., f., sg., pl. (d.f. tasạ 2b). (1) = gwalalō. (2) trench (in European wars).

tạsānī m. (1) burglars' stiletto. (2) yāwạn ⁓ m. cadging visits by bridegroom to his friends after the wedding.

tāsar (1) (the form of tāshị used before dative when dative does not begin in m-) x yā ⁓ wạ Audụ dạ fạdạ he upbraided Audu (for other senses, Vd. tāsam).

tāsar dạ = tāsad dạ.

tāsạrī Sk. m. = hạsārạ.

tasarrạfī = tasarrụfī Ar. m. (1) trading x yanạ̄ ⁓ dạ dūkịyassạ he's trading with his capital. (2) tạsarrụfin kạnsạ yakẹ yị he's independent of outside control.

tasasā adv. abundantly.

Tāsāwā f. (1) the town of that name. (2) Vd. Bạtāsạ̄yī.

tạsbahạ f. = cạzbī.

tạsbī = cạzbī.

tasgạdạ = tazgạdạ.

tasgarō = tazgarō.

tashạ f. (pl. tashōshī) Eng. (1) railwaystation. (2) stopping-place for buses. (3) tashạr kārūwōyī brothel. (4) harbour. (5) aerodrome. (6) tashạr hạrsāshị magazine, ammunition-dump.

tashārẹ-tasharē *m.* (1) chicanery, double-dealing (= **shịrīrị̄tā**). (2) playing P. a dirty trick (= **gayyạ**) (1, 2 = **wạlā-wạlā**).
tashā-tạshā = **fashā-fạshā**.
tashe A. (**tāshẹ**) *Vb.* 1A (1) attacked *x* **yā ~ masạ dạ fadạ** = **tāsam** 1*a*. (2) (*the form of* **tāshị** 1*e used before dative*) latent T. recurred *x* **cĩwọ yā ~ masạ** the latent sickness has attacked him again. **rịkicī yā ~ minị** my intrigue which I had thought safely concealed, suddenly recoiled on me.
  B. (**tạ̄shē**) *m.* (1) **mun yi ~ = an yi manạ ~ we** (schoolboys) are now on (*a*) holiday at end of term (= **hūtū**). (*b*) on holiday because of festival (= **ϑạ̄rī**). (2) = **tāshịɲ ạsubạ̄**. (3) **tạshan sallạ** drumming to solicit gifts during last four days of **azụmī** before the **Sallạ** (*cf.* **kūrā** 1*e*, **yambạlā**). (4) *Vd.* **tạsā, tā dạ**.
  C. (**tāshē**) *m.* **yanạ̄ ~** he's prospering.
tashē-tạshẹ̄ *Kt.* = **fashā-fạshā**.
tashi A. (**tāshị**) (1) *Vb.* (*a*) (i) stood up *x* **yā ~** he stood up. **yanạ̄ ~ he** is standing up. (ii) **yā ~ cĩwọ** he got up from a sick bed. (iii) **tạ̄shi ɲ taịmạkē kạ** God helps him who helps himself. (iv) **yāƙị yā ~ war** has broken out. **gạ̄bā tā ~ hostility** has arisen. (v) **yā ~ tsạye** *Vd.* **tsạye** 3. (vi) **tạ̄shi sad dạ bā kạ sọ̄, kạ ịsa sad dạ kakẹ̄ sọ̄** work hard at the outset and rest later ! (vii) **tạ̄shi ƙasạ, kọ̄ma dạϑē** the two are identical. (viii) **dạ rạrrạfē yārọ ya kạn ~ from** little acorns mighty oaks arise. (ix) **wutā tā ~** a fire has broken out (*cf.* x *below*). (x) **wutā tā ~** the burn has caused blister (*cf.* ix *above*). **fātạr bậkī tā ~ his** mouth is peeling. **fātạ tā ~ ạ jịkīna** my body is peeling. (*b*) awoke (*cf.* **tā dạ** 1*f*). (*c*) (i) went away (*cf.* **tā dạ** 1*h*). (ii) **sun ~ dạ kunyạ** "they left with their tails between their legs". (iii) *cf.* 2*b below*. (iv) **tā tāshị tạfịyạ** she set out. (v) **yā tāshị kōmạ̄wā gidā** he set out for home. (vi) **gạrī bā yạ̄ tậshi ?** ballē **magạnạ ?** can any statement be inflexible ? (*cc*) went away from *x* **ƙasarsụ tā tāshị ạ ƙasar ạmānạ kẹ̄ naɲ** their country has ceased to be

neutral. **mụ tāshị caɲ, mụ kōmạ Masạr** let us leave there and turn to Egypt ! **sun tāshị dạga zaurạɲ ạϑọ̄kaɲ gạ̄bā, suɲ kōmō nāmụ** they've left the enemy and joined us (*Vd.* **tāsō**). (*d*) (i) flew away. (ii) flew about *x* **tsuntsū yanạ̄ ~ the** bird is flying. **tūtạrmụ tanạ̄ tāshị fil-fil-fil** our flag is waving. (*e*) (i) illness recurred *x* **kadạ kạ zaunạ ạ fariɲ watạ kanạ̄ da laịfī, kadạ ƙabbā tạ ~ do** not sit in the moonlight seeing you've previously had syphilis, lest it recur. **gyạmbō yā ~ the** ulcer has recurred. (ii) (*used before dative*) *Vd.* **tāshẹ** 2. (*f*) proceeded to, set about *x* **sun ~ kāmụn Tūnạs** = **tāsam** 1*c*.ii. **yā tāshị zāluncị** he adopted tyrannical behaviour. **yā tāshị gạ himmạr ạ karantad dạ sū** he set about the task of educating them (*cf.* 2*a*.ii). (*g*) became *x* **yā ~ ukụ** it has become three (= **kōmạ** 1*d*). **yā ~ dạidại dạ wancạɲ** it corresponds with that one. **wurī yā ~ bặi dậyā** *Vd.* **bại** 2*b*.ii. (*h*) **gaɲgā nạ̄ ~ drumming** can be heard. **yā ji izgā tanạ̄ ~ he** heard sounds of a gọ̄gē-fiddle. **bindigạ tā ~ report** of a gun sounded. **bīgịlạ tanạ̄ tāshị** the bugle is sounding. (*j*) became annulled *x* (i) **hukuncị yā ~ the** verdict became quashed (*cf.* **tā dạ** 3). **cịnikī yā ~ the** transaction has come to nothing. **fạdar Allạ̄ bā tạ̄ tāshị** the decrees of God are inescapable. **sun yi ạlkāwạrị wạndạ bā yạ̄ tāshị, sukạ cẹ̄ . . .** they made an inflexible promise that . . . (ii) **kạ̄sụ̄wā tā ~ the** market has broken up (*cf.* *k below*). (*k*) **kạ̄sụ̄war gyạɗā tā ~** (i) ground-nut trading has opened. (ii) ground-nut prices have risen (*cf.* *j above*). **ạbincī yā tāshị** the price of food has risen. (*l*) **harājị yā ~** tax collection has begun. (*m*) (i) **zūcịyātạ tanạ̄ ~ I** feel nausea. (ii) **zūcịyāta tā ~ dạga garēshị** " I'm fed up with it " (= *n*.ii *below*). (*n*) (i) **haɲkạlīna yā ~ I** became perturbed, angry (*cf.* **tāshịɲ haɲkạlī**). (ii) **haɲkạlīna yā ~ dạga garēshị** " I'm fed up with it " (= *m*.ii *above*). (*o*) **rūwā yā ~ ạ rịjịȳā** sediment has become stirred up in the well (= **gurϑạ̄cē**). (*p*) *Vd.*

tāsō, tāshi-*compounds.* (*q*) *cf.* tā dạ, tāsạ, tặsā, tāsam, tāshẹ. (2) *m.* (*a*) (*v.n.* and *progressive of* 1) *x* (i) yanạ̃ ~ he is standing up. nā ga tāshịnsạ I saw him stand up. wannạŋ yāƙị bạbban tāshịn dūnīyạ nē this war has set the whole world ablaze. wannạŋ wạhalạ tā wucẹ, sǎi tāshịn zạncē that trouble has passed and is now merely a topic of small talk. gặsar tāshị aviation contest. baị lāshẹ su tāshị dayā ba he didn't mop them (enemy) up at the first attempt. (ii) an undertaking *x* sạn dạ na fārạ wannạŋ tāshị when I undertook this task (*cf.* 1*f above*). tāshị sukạ yi sụ yặ̃ƙē mụ their intention was to make war on us. (iii) *Vd.* tāshịn-*compounds.* (*b*) Filặnī sun yi ~ = sun tặfi ~ Filani herdsmen have migrated to seasonal grazing-grounds in case of both mashēkarī and cịn rānī (*cf.* rānī 3*a* ; gurẹ). (3) *Sk.* his = tāsạ.

    B. (tặshi) *Vd.* tặsā.

    C. (tashī) *Sk. m.* (1) light (= haskē) *x* zạn tā dạ ~ I'll make a light, blow up the fire, etc. (2) dạ ~ yakẹ it's very nice.

    D. (tashị) *m.* courting a virgin (*Vd.* aurē 1*c* ; 6), *cf.* zawarcị 2.

tặshi lāƙīyạ *f.* = gặrẹ 2.

tặshi mụ jē mū *m.* (1) (*a*) indecisiveness. (*b*) fickleness. (2) *Vd.* jē 2.

tāshịn ạsụbặ *m.* Koranic school-session before sunrise (= tặshē 2).

tāshịm bạlagạ *m.* sexual feelings in boy reaching puberty.

tāshịn dagacịŋ ƙauyẹ = tāshịm Magặjịŋ ƙauyẹ.

tāshịn dōkị *m.* steady good luck.

tāshịŋ Galặdīmạŋ ƙauyẹ = tāshịm Magặjịŋ ƙauyẹ.

tāshịŋ gwauran zặbō *m.* suddenly outdistancing one's contemporaries.

tāshịŋ hancị *m.* giving oneself airs (= ạlfahạrī).

tāshịŋ haŋkạlī *m.* (1) (*a*) perturbation. (*b*) mẹ̃ ya jāwō duk wannạŋ tāshịŋ haŋkạlī what has caused all this unrest ? (2) being angry (*cf.* tặshi 1*n*). (3) 'yan tāshịŋ haŋkulạ fomenters of trouble, agitators.

tāshịn jặkin 'yan Rūmā *m.* (1) = tāshịŋ ƙūrụ. (2) *cf.* Bạrūmạyī.

tāshịŋ kặi *m.* = tāshịŋ hancị.

tāshịŋ ƙauyẹ *m., f., sg., pl.,* sū ~ nē they're country bumpkins (= bạgidājẹ).

tāshịŋ ƙūrụ *m.* making a good start then tailing off (*Vd.* ƙūrụ).

tāshịm Magặjịŋ ƙauyẹ *m.* person's rising from the ground with a cloud of dust (= tāshịŋ Galặdīmạŋ ƙauyẹ = tāshịn dagacịŋ ƙauyẹ).

tīshịm magạnạ *x* yanạ̃ ~ " he's flogging a dead horse " (*cf.* tā dạ 1*c*, 3, tāshẹ) = tặshịn-tāshin.

tāshịm marạh hatsī *m. used in* ~ bặ̃shi dạ wụyā migration is no hardship for the destitute.

tặshịn-tāshin *m.* = tặshịn-tāshinā *f.* = tāshịm magạnạ *q.v.*

tāshịn zạncē = tāshịm magạnạ.

tāshị-tāshị *x* ạl'amạrī nẹ̃ tāshị-tāshị it is an affair of from moment to moment.

tặshi tsam *m.* type of children's game (*Vd.* tsam).

tặshīyạ *f.* = tōtụ̃wā 2.

tashōshī *Vd.* tashạ.

tāsīrị *Ar. m.* (1) influence *x* bặ shi dạ ~ cikinsạ he has no influence in it. (2) baị yi wani tāsīrị ba he made no progress.

taska A. (tạskā) *Vb.* 3A (1) rānā tā ~ = dagạ 2*a*.i. (2) yārọ yā ~ the lad is now 7–10 years old (= dagạ 2*a*.iii = tāsạ 4*a* = dātạ 1). (3) jịrī yā ~ masạ he has neuralgia.

    B. (taskạ) *f.* (*pl.* taskōkī) store (= sitọk).

taskạncē *Vb.* 1C stored.

taskẹ *Vb.* 1A *Kt. x* yā ~ mạ nēmaŋ kudī he began to seek funds.

taskilạŋ *Eng. m.* third-class on railway, etc. (*cf.* faskilạŋ).

taskirā *f.* (*pl.* tạskịrū = taskirōrī). (1) (*a*) shallow basket in which is leather-rest for woman's spindle (mazarī) (= *Kt.* tạyānī). (*b*) iŋ kā ga ɓarāwạŋ dōkị dagạ taskirar ūwā ya sōmạ knavery is inborn. (2) *Kt.* = kwạndō 4. (3) (*a*) part of snares (= fặifǎi 1*d*). (*b*) yā tặkạ ~ he has got himself into trouble.

taskōkī *Vd.* taskạ.

tasku *m.* tyranny *x* **yā gwadạ musu** ∼ he oppressed them (= **zālunci**).

tạs mahạrā = **tạsạ mahạrā**.

tạsnīyā *Sk. f.* quarrel (= **fadạ**).

taso A. (**tāsō**) *Vb.* 3A (1) (-ō *form from* **tāshi**) *x* (*a*) **rūwā yā** ∼ rain has begun. (*b*) (i) **yā** ∼ **masạ** he upbraided him ; attacked him (= **tāsam** 1*a* = *Sk.* tam 2*b*). (ii) **ạl'amạrin yā tāsō masạ gạba dạyā** the affair struck him all of a heap. (*c*) **dạ sukạ tāsō aiki** w'ien the day's work was over (*cf.* **tāshi** 1*cc*). (2) *Vd.* **tạsā** 2.

B. (**tasọ**) = **masọ** 4.

tạsōnō *m.* (1) dried nose-mucus (**mājinā**). (2) fool.

†**āsōshī** *Vd.* **tāsạ** 2.

tasshē *Vd.* tarad dạ.

tạsshī *Sk. m.* = **tạttāsai**.

tasu A. (**tāsu**) (1) (*a*) (i) theirs. (*b*) **bạ tāsu ba** *Vd.* **Allạ** 1*k*.ii. (*c*) **dạ tāsu ta wucẹ** when that talk of theirs died down. (*cc*) *Vd.* **nāsạ**. (*d*) *Vd.* **tāsạ** 1*b*. (2) *cf.* **tasạ**.

B. (**tasu**) (1) their (*following fem. noun*) *x* **rumfassu** = **rumfā** ∼ their grass-shelter (Mod. Gram. 47*b*). (2) *cf.* **tāsu**.

tāsū'ā *Ar. f.* special prayers on 9th of **Almuharrạm**.

tạsūbạlā *f. Kt.* (1) (*a*) = **bạsillạ** 1.(*b*) fool. (2) **Tạsūbạlā ḳuduriŋ kabạ** (*a*) what loose tying ! (*b*) what a fool !

tạsunnīyā *Kt. f.* = **tạtsūnīyā**.

***taswīrā** *Ar. f.* (*pl.* **taswīrōrī**). (1) = **sūrạ** 1*b*. (2) ***taswīrạr ḳasạshē** map (= **mạp**).

tata A. (**tātạ**) (1) (*a*) hers (*after fem. noun*) *x* **rĩgan naŋ** ∼ **cē** this blouse is hers (Mod. Gram. 48). (*b*) *Vd.* **tāsạ** 1*b*. (*c*) *cf.* **tatạ**. (2) *Vb.* 1A did (work) well *x* **yā** ∼ **diŋki** he sewed well. **yā** ∼ **ḳaryā** he told a whopping lie.

B. (**tatạ**) (1) her (*following fem. noun*) *x* **rĩgartạ** = **rĩgā** ∼ her blouse (Mod. Gram. 47*b*²). (2) *cf.* **tātạ** 1.

C. (**tātā**) (1) *used in* **yā bīyạ** ∼ he read out the passage fluently. **yā yi mạganạ** ∼ he spoke correctly. (2) (*secondary v.n. of* **tācẹ**) *x* **yanạ tātarsạ** = **yanạ tạtarsạ** he's filtering it (= **tạtā**).

D. (**tạtā**) *f.* = **tātā** 2.

tātāburzā *f.* (1) *x* **yā shā** ∼ he experienced

great difficulty (= **fāmā**). (2) quarrel (= **fadạ**).

tạtaccē *m.* (*f.* **tạtaccīyā**) *pl.* **tạtạttū** (*past part. from* **tācẹ**) *x* **yanạ dạ tạtaccaŋ ḳarạtū** he has sound education (= **tạcaccē**).

atak *x* **nā yi** ∼ I'm penniless.

tạtạkōrō *m.* = **d'aukạn 'yam makarantā** 2.

tạtalā *f.* = **tādīyā** 1.

tatạlī *Fil. m.* = **cītạlī**.

tatam = tamau.

tātāridā *f.* = **tāriŋgidạ**

tatas (1) = tas 2*b*. (2) *m.* an yi masạ ∼ (*a*) he has been foully abused. (*b*) thieves have made clean sweep of his property.

tatata A. (**tātātā**) = **tātā** 1.

B. (**tātạtā**) *f.* (1) tired gait. (2) baby's first efforts at walking alone (*this stage follows* **tẹtē**).

tạtātunā *f.* (1) = **kạtuntunā**. (2) small boil in children, supposed curable by 1 *above*.

tạtạtūrū *m.* = **kutūtu** 4.

tatau (*Kt.*) = tamau.

***tạtawwu'ī** = ***tạdawwa'ạ**.

tātī *used in* **rạbō** ∼ **rạbō yātī** luck comes and goes (*d.f. Ar.* comes).

tātiḳē *Vb.* 1C reduced to destitution.

tạtil *m. and adv.* (1) **yā ci ạbincī** ∼ = **yā yi** ∼ he's sated with food. (2) **yā shā** ∼ = **yā yi** ∼ he's intoxicated. (3) **yā cika** ∼ it is chock-full (3 = **fal**).

tạtīta *f.* empty chatter.

tatsa A. (**tạtsā**) (1) *Vb.* 2 (*a*) milked (cow). (*b*) *x* **tā tạtsi nōnọ ạ ḳwaryā** she milked the cow into a calabash (= **tātsạ** 1*a*). (*c*) (i) **yā tạtsi kudī** he stole money (= **sạtā**) ; he squeezed money out of him. (ii) **an tạtsi buhū** (corn, salt, etc.) was stolen from the bag (= 2*a below* = **tātsẹ** 1*d*). (*d*) **yā yi gudun tạtsattsīyar ạkwiyạ** he decamped leaving all his goods behind. (*e*) **nī kẹ rikẹ ḳạfō, wani yanạ** ∼ I'm merely his catspaw. (2) *f.* (*a*) **an yi wạ buhū** ∼ = 1*c*.ii *above*. (*b*) **sānīyar** ∼ (i) milch-cow. (ii) profitable T.

B. (**tātsạ**) *Vb.* 1A (1) squeezed T. into *x* (*a*) **tā** ∼ **nōnọ ạ ḳwaryā** = **tạtsā** 1*b*. (*b*) **yā** ∼ **mini māganī ạ idō** he squeezed medicine into my eye. (2) an ∿, aŋ ganī dạ nōnọ on testing, milk was found to be in the udder.

tātsattsē *Vd.* tātsā 1*d.*

*tạtsawwụ'ī = *tạḍawwa'ạ.

tātsẹ (1) *Vb.* 1A (*a*) milked completely. (*b*) squeezed out completely. (*c*) fleeced P. (*d*) = tātsā 1*c*.ii. (3) *Vb.* 3A cikịnsạ yā ∿ he is ravenous.

tātsīnī *used in* ḍan tātsīnịŋkạ dạ kại ? what behaviour for a little child like you !

tātsūnịyā *f.* (*pl.* tātsūnīyōyī) (1) fable (= ạlmārā = gātanā). (2) riddle (*for an example, Vd.* wutā 1*v*.ii). (3) (*a*) any star (= tạurārọ). (*b*) = tạurārọ 2. (*c*) ∿ mại wutsīyạ = tạurārọ 1*b*. (4) silver coin worn on woman's forehead.

tattạ6ạ-kunnē = tạ6ạ kunnē.

tattabạrā = tạntabạrā.

tattạf *m.* type of small seeds whose powder gives yellowish tint to hair of Barebari women.

tattagạ *Vb.* 2 (1) *x* yā tạttạgi aikịn nạŋ he tried to do this task which was beyond him. (2) tạttạgạ kōgī dạ yạ̄sā (*a*) what a busybody ! (*b*) what an impossible T. for him to try !

tạttạgī *m.* (1) busybody. (2) P. trying the impossible.

tattak *x* yā ƙārẹ ∿ it's quite finished.

tạttakạ *f.* (1) stable-bedding and refuse (= būtụ̄wā 2). (2) = dịddigā 1. (3) *Sk.* = ịngịrịcī 1. (4) *Sk.* savings.

tattake A. (tattạkē) *Vb.* 3A became worn out (= ragargạjē).

   B. (tattạ̄kē) *Vb.* 3A stood firm.

tattāƙī *m.* (*in* bōrī *talk*) departure.

tattạl = tantạl *q.v. under* kyạŋwā 5.

tạttalạ *Vb.* 2 *Kt.* looked after, cared for, tended.

tattalī *m.* (1) caring for, tending. (2) making preparations for.

tattara A. (tattārā) *Vb.* 1C kept collecting (*intensive from* tārạ).

   B. (tattārā) *Vb.* 1C (1) collected *x* (*a*) yā tạttạrạ jạma'ạ tasạ he collected his people (= tārạ 1*a*.i). yā tạttạrạ dukạŋ himmạ tasạ ạ kạn . . . he concentrated all his efforts on . . . (*b*) yā tạttạrạ jịkī = tārạ 1*b*. (*c*) yā tạttạrạ rīgā tasạ = tārạ 1*b*. (*d*) sāi dạ ya tạttạrạ

ƙwạnjinsạ kānạ ya bīyā he was only able to pay by selling up all he had (*Vd.* tạttạrạ ƙunjī). (*e*) nā ∿ shi nā bar shị ạ hannuŋkạ I leave the whole matter to you. (2) nā ∿ shi nā ƙyālẹ shi I told him I was " fed-up " with him. (3) *Vd.* tạttạrạ-*compounds.*

   C. (tạttạrạ) *Vb.* 3B (1) (*a*) became collected together (= tạ̄ru). (*b*) (gown) puckered. (2) (snake) coiled itself up.

   D. (tattārā) *f.* cackling, clucking.

tạttạrạ ƙundunạ *m., f., sg., pl.* glutton.

tạttạrạ ƙunjī *m., f., sg., pl.* glutton (*Vd.* tattārā 1*d*).

tạttạrē (1) *Vb.* 3A = tạttạrạ. (2) *Vb.* 1C yā tạttạrẹ rīgā tasạ = tārạ 1*b*.

tattarmakạ = tattarmukạ *f.* = tạrmạhāhạ *q.v.*

tạttạrnīyā *f.* quarrel, dispute (= fạḍạ).

tattas (1) = tas. (2) *Kt.* = lilis.

tattāsā *Vb.* 1C yanạ tạttạsạ baƙī = tattāshīyā.

tạttạ̄sai *m.* large mild chillies (= tattāshī = tsīduhū = *Sk.* tạsshī = tụgandē 2), *Vd.* na Dāyē.

tattashi A. (tattāshī) = tạttạ̄sai.

   B. (tạttạshi) *Kt.* (*said by hawkers*) kụ sạyi ∿ kụ ∿ mīyạ chillies, buy, buy !

   C. (tattashī) *m.* coaxing (= lallāshī).

tattāshīyā *f.* learning to read in syllables = hạjjạtū *q.v.*

tạttaurā *adj. m., f.* (*pl.* taurạ̄rā) tough (*d.f.* taurī).

tattāyē *Vd.* tattū.

tạttībī = tạrtībī.

tattōfī *Kt. m.* = lamfọ 2.

tattōkạrā *Vb.* 3A (1) *intensive from* tōkạrā. (2) (convalescent P.) walked carefully.

tattū *m.* (*pl.* tattāyē) *Kt.* = cūnạ 2*a*.

tātụkē = tātịkē.

tạ̄tul = tạ̄til.

tạ̄tum = tạ̄til.

ta Tūnạs = ta Tūnạshī *Vd.* Tūnạs.

tạ̄tụ̄wā *f.* late sowing (*cf.* kīrī).

tau A. (tau) *Sk.* = tạ̄wa *x* rīgan nạŋ ∿ cẹ this gown is mine.

   B. (tau) = fau.

tạubạ̄sai *Sk. m.* = taubāshī.

taubāshī *m.* cousin(s) or their descendants (*but* taubāshī *refers only to children of a* brother and a sister, *not those of brother and brother nor sister and sister*) (taubậshĩ *are* ậbǫkaŋ wậsā *and entitled to plunder* (ƙwậcē) *each other's property and the sister's child is entitled to* kuɗin shārậ *from the brother's child,* *Vd.* shārậ 3).

taubastakậ *f.* being related *as in* taubậshĩ.

tauɗậ (1) *f.* the clucking-noise made to gee-up horse. (2) *Vb.* 1A (*with dative*) *x* an ∼ masậ būlālậ he has been thrashed.

tauɗệ *Vb* 1A *x* an ∼ shi dậ būlālậ = tauɗậ 2.

taugậ *Sk. f.* = ɫafkị.

tauhĩdị *Ar. m.* proclaiming the oneness of God by saying lā ịlāhậ illậllāhụ *q.v.*

taụlā *Sk. f.* yoke enabling P. to carry water in one tụ̄lū suspended from each shoulder.

taulậhĩ *Sk. m.* = tallậfĩ.

taụlậlĩ *Sk. m.* (1) young children. (2) *Vd.* cikậ 1*k*.

taumashệ *Sk. m.* = targaɗệ 1.

tauna A. (taunậ) *Vb.* 1A (1) (*a*) chewed. (*b*) ậ ∼ tsakūwậ doŋ ayā tậ ji tsǭrō the fate of one serves as a deterrent to another. (*c*) namijị bậrkǫnō nệ, sǎi an ∼ zā ậ san yājịnsậ it takes time to know a person. (2) = tantaụnā 2.

  B. (taụnā) (1) *Vb.* 2 (*a*) = taunậ 1*a*. (*b*) yanậ taụnar lịnzāmị zại yĩ he's bragging that he'll do it. (2) *f.* (*a*) (i) act of chewing. (ii) sunậ sǭ ậ yi musụ ∼ ậ yi musụ hậdĩyậ *Vd.* hậdĩyậ 2. (iii) bậri taụnā, na bakậ nậ zụbā don't be in too much of a hurry! (iv) anậ dậrĩyā, mại taụnā ya kậŋ ƙōshi slow and steady wins. (v) sunậ cikin taụnā tasậ, bậ sụ barị suŋ hậdĩyē ba they went from this success to the next. (vi) bậ ka dậ dāɗin ∼ *Vd.* būzūzụ 2. 3. (*b*) gnawing pain from rheumatism, etc., *x* ƙafậta tanậ ∼ I have a gnawing pain in my foot (= tsukụ 2). (*c*) fodder.

taune A. (taụnē) *Kt. m.* = tụ̄ƙē 1.

  B. (taụnệ) *Vb.* 1A (1) chewed up. (2) chewed completely.

taura A. (taụrā) *f.* (*pl.* taurậyē) (1) (*a*) women's plaits at sides of temples (=

bijājị = daurị 2 = *Sk.* maŋgā = *Sk.* kaikainịyā = gāshị 3), *cf.* ƙyậlĩ. (*b*) yā sậ ∼ bĩyū ậ bakậ he " has two irons in the fire ". (2) the tree *Detarium senegalense* (*Vd.* bậfụr).

  B. (taụrā) *Vd.* taurệ.

taurara A. (taụrậrā) *Vd.* tậttaurā.

  B. (taurậrā) *Vb.* 1C hardened, stiffened T.

  C. (taụrarậ) *Vb.* 3B became hard, stiff *x* furậ tā ∼ the furậ (left standing) became stiff.

taurậrệ *Vb.* 3A (1) = taụrarậ. (2) kept putting off settling debt.

taụrậrǫ *m.* (*pl.* taụrậrĩ) (1) (*a*) (i) star (= tậtsūnịyā 3*a*). (ii) rashịm fariŋ watậ ∼ kệ haskē any port in a storm. (iii) ụban taụrậrĩ *Vd.* gậmzākị. (*b*) ∼ mại wutsĩyậ (i) comet. (ii) P. who is a bird of ill-omen (*his epithet is* Taụrậrǫ mại wutsĩyậ, ganịŋkậ bậ ậlhệrị ba) (1*b*.i = tậtsūnịyā 3*c*). (*c*) yā zamā wani taụrậrǫ ậ cikinsụ he became an outstanding personage among them. shĩ Audụ, yanậ dậgậ cikin taụrậrin Kanǫ Audu is one of the leading people in Kano. (2) white patch on horse's brow (= tậtsūnịyā 3*b*). (3) luck *x* (*a*) mun ɗaukō taụrậrin kậsūwā we were lucky in our trading. (*b*) *Vd.* gǭya 3. (*c*) taụrậrậnsǫ yanậ haskē he is being lucky. (*d*) taụrậrậnsậ yā fāɗị his luck is out. (*e*) *Vd.* tụŋkwĩyậ. (*f*) yā fid dậ zaŋgǫ cikin taụrậrūwar nasarậ *Vb.* fitar dậ 4*b*.ii.

taụrậrūwā *f.* = taụrậrǫ.

taụrậyē *Vd.* taurā.

taurệ *m.* (*pl.* taụrā) (1) castrated goat. (2) wannậŋ rậkē ∼ gậreshi this sugar-cane has no pith (tǒtụ̄wā) and so is economical. (3) daran ∼ *Vd.* darē 9.

taurĩ *m.* (1) (*a*) (i) hardness, toughness. (ii) māgậnin ƙasā mại ∼ *Vd.* dāgị. (*b*) taurim bāshị gậreshi he's a bad payer of debts. (*c*) (i) bậ sụ yi wani tauriŋ kận ba they (enemy) showed no resistance. yā yi minị tauriŋ kận he behaved obstinately to me (= tsaurĩ 7). tauriŋ kận gậreshị he's stubborn. (ii) in sun tsayậ dậ tauriŋ kận if they insist. (*d*) taurĩ gậreshị =

taurin hannū gareshi he's miserly. (e)
(i) yāran nan ∼ gareshi this boy is slow-
witted. (ii) yā yi ∼ he has lost his skill.
dōki yā yi ∼ the horse has lost its
speed (ii = kurunce). (f) taurin rai
gareshi he is incorrigible. (2) (a) yā
ci ∼ he has drunk kas kaifī. (b) taurī
gareshi he is invulnerable through
having drunk kas kaifī. (c) dan ∼
(pl. 'yan ∼) (i) man invulnerable as
in 2b above who has medicine-horn
called kahwan ∼ and who in wāsan ∼
exhibits his powers (dan taurī = shā
dādala = dāguri gurzau). (ii) dan
dōkam bōye = dan taurī member of
the Zaria secret police. (d) (i) epithet
of c.i above in drum-rhythm (kida) is
kufēgēre, yankā = kisa 10. (ii) Kt.
epithet is Kincākirī.

taurō m. (1) the skin of porcupine or
hedgehog (used for cooking its flesh in).
(2) Vd. tamrō.

tausa A. (tausa) (1) Vb. 1A (a) pressed
down (= danna). (b) forced P. to x
nā ∼ shi, ya saya I forced him to
buy it (cf. tausā 1b) = danna 1d. (c)
an ∼ kōrā they (enemy) have been
routed and pursued. (d) an ∼ masa
zāgi he has been abused. (e) massaged
(as in tausā). (f) (i) tausa a hankali
mai ganga (said by girls that song may
not be drowned by drumming) drum
more lightly! (cf. taushi 4). (ii) ∼
dāma Vd. bahago 3. (2) Vb. 3A went
away.

B. (tausā) (1) Vb. 2 (p.o. taushē,
n.o. taushi) (a) = taushe 1. (b) persuaded (= dannā 3), cf. tausa 1b.
(2) f. (a) massage done by concubine
or wife to husband (= murzā 2 =
Kt. taushē 2), cf. mātsa 2. (b) tausar
gīwā = tsarō 2. (c) welding (cf. taushe 2).
C. (tausā) Kt. f. = harāji.

tausai Kt. m. = tausayī.

tausasā Vb. 1C (1) softened (= rausasā).
(2) yā tausasa murya he lowered his
voice (= rausasā). (3) yā ∼ = yā
tausasa magana (i) he spoke quietly.
(ii) he spoke conciliatingly (3 = rausasā).

tausayī m. (1) pity (= hanāna). (2)
(a) sun nūna tausayī they showed
mercy. (b) tausayinsu yā kāma ni

I feel sorry for them. (c) yā ji tausayinsa
he had mercy on him (= hanāna),
cf. jūyayī. (3) abu mai ban ∼ a T.
worthy of sympathy. (4) kudin ∼
m. gratuity on leaving the service for
P. not entitled to pension (cf. fensho).

taushe A. (taushe) Vb. 1A (1) termites
(garā) damaged T. (= tausā 1a). (2)
welded (cf. tausā 2c). (3) yā ∼ dūna
he carried a load. (4) hemmed (=
kalmasā = cī 23b). (4A) = lallaba 3b.
(5) = kā da 1a.ii, 1b.i. (6) = tōshe.
B. (taushē) m. (1) type of soup (=
Sk. rabakē). (2) Kt. = tausā 2a. (3)
Vd. tausā.

taushi A. (taushi) m. (1) "making compliments" (= filāko 2). (2) first
stage of women's hairdressing after hair
cleaned. (3) yā sāmi ∼ = kōrā 2c.vi.
(4) light drumming (cf. tausa 1f).
(5) = sabīyā.
B. (taushī) (1) m. (a) (i) softness. (ii)
bugu shi kē sā fāta taushī " constant
dripping wears the rock ". (iii) an ga
nan fāta tā yi taushī they saw there
was a " weak spot " here. (iv) Vd.
alkāmura ; jīma 4. (b) taushin hali
amenability, reasonableness (1 =
laushī). (2) m. (pl. tafāshē) (a) conical-
drum only one end of which is covered
with skin for playing. (b) Sk. type of
cadging marōkī. (3) 'yar ∼ (a) = labai
1. (b) (with pl. 'yan ∼) type of mat.
C. (taushi) Vd. tausā.

taushiyā = tōshiyā.

tau-tau A. (tau-tau) Kt. x nāma yanā
da taurī ∼ the meat is very tough.
B. (tau-tau) m. (1) any spider (=
gizo-gizo). (2) (a) yā gamu da ∼ =
gizo-gizo 2. (b) rūwā mai ∼ the water
referred to in gizo-gizo 2.

tautsī m. (1) = kwantsī. (2) Kt. =
tarētsā 1.

tauya = tauye 1.

tauye 1 Vb. 1A (a) (i) caused (garment)
to shrink. (ii) caused P. to shrink from
x gudun zunubi shi kē ∼ mu it is wish
to avoid sin that restrains us. (b) put
tuck in (garment). (c) tricked. (d)
mē ya ∼ shi what blemish has he?
(2) Vb. 3A (a) (garment) shrank (=
tawaya). (b) deteriorated (= lālācē).

tauyę walkinką *Kt. m.* = saŋƙę 3.

tauyi *m.* beams laid across walls to lessen span for main beams if too short (*Vd.* gēmu 3).

tąwa (1) *Vd.* nąwa. (2) ∼ tā ƙārę it's all up with me. (3) *cf.* tāsą 1*b.* (4) *Kt.* gą ∼ = riƙą 1*c.*

tąwadą *f.* (*pl.* tawadōjī = tawadōdī = tawadōyī = tąwądū) (1) (*a*) ink. (*b*) dą kundī dą ∼ bā są tā dą Gwamną săi Mądī`yā zō one must bow to circumstances. (*c*) hanjin ∼ cowtail-hairs put in ink-bottle to prevent contents spilling. (2) tąwadą = tąwadąr Allą tiny spots of darker pigmentation on parts of human skin. (3) tądawąr karkashī, bųwąyą mąlamai *Vd.* ąlkālī.

*tąwafąr rayuką *Ar. f.* death.

tąwagą *f.* (1) the women, children and property removed out of reach of invaders. (2) yā sąmi ∼ he has had a stroke of luck.

tawai A. (tāwai) *Kt. m.* = rąinō.

B. (tąwai) = tąntąrwąi.

tawaida A. (tąwaidą) *f.* = tǫfī 1*b.*

B. (tāwaidā) *Vb.* 1C yā ∼ masą he said spells over him· accompanied by tǫfī 1*b.*

tąwaiwąi = tąntąrwąi.

tąwakkąlī *Ar. m.* leaving oneself in God's hands.

tąwāli *m.* yā są ∼ he put on a ring with coin affixed.

*tąwāli'u *Ar. m.* submissiveness.

ta wantsąlā *f.* (1) paying off only interest on debt, not debt itself. (2) *cf.* ta wuntsilą.

tąwatsā *f.* (1) the tree *Entada sudanica.* (2) in zā ką yi līlǫ, ką yi ą tsāmīyā. iŋ kā kāmą tąwatsā, tą ƙaryę don't lean on a broken reed !

ᵗtąwayą *Vb.* 3B (1) = tauyę 2*a.* (2) decreased. (3) was lacking.

ᵗtawaye A. (tāwāyę) (1) *m.* (*a*) rebelling. (*b*) kā yi mini ∼ fancy your having been so long in the town without visiting me ! (2) *m.,f.,sg.,pl.* (*sg. also* = ɗan ∼) (*pl. also* = 'yan ∼ = tąwąyū) rebel.

B. (tąwāyę) *Vd.* ąbūrinką.

C. (tawąyē) *Sk.* = tagwąyē.

tąwīlallē *m.* (*f.* tąwīlallīyā) *pl.* tąwīlallū hypocrite (= munāfuƙī).

tāwīli *Ar. m.* lame excuse (= rąrraunā 2).

tąwu *Sk.* = tąwa.

tāwul *Eng. m.·(sg., pl.)* towel.

ta wuntsilą *Kt. f.* meddlesomeness (= kąrąmbąnī).

ta wuntsųlā *Vd.* ta wantsąlā.

tąwwadą = tąwadą.

taya A. (tąyā) (1) *Vb.* 2 stripped off (*x* ramą-bark) = *Kt.* tąlā. (2) *f.* accidentally ripping chicken when plucking (fīgā) it (= *Kt.* kūrā 7).

B. (tąyą) (1) *Vb.* 1A (*a*) (i) (buyer) made tentative offer *x* yā ∼ shi sulę gōmą he made opening offer of ten shillings for it (= *Kt.* taƀą 4). (ii) *Vd.* wuri 1*a.*ii, sūnā 4 (*cf.* ąlbarką 2). (*b*) (i) helped (= tąimaką). (ii) zō ką ∼ ni ganī just look at this strange thing ! (iii) sun yi mini " tąya, Kūrā, mų ci ąkwīyą " they plotted to trick me. (*c*) flirted with. (*d*) challenged, dared P. (*e*) *Vd.* taya-*compounds.* (2) *Eng. f.* (*sg., pl.*) tyre.

tāyad dą = tā dą.

tayąkā *Vd.* tēki.

tąyānī *Kt. m.* = taskirā 1*a.*

tąyā ni fadą *m.* reinforcement of centre of loincloth.

tąyā ni gōyō *m.* (1) = gōyō 2*a.*ii. (2) = tąyā ni rąinō. (3) = ayyārā.

tąyā ni mŭni *m.* (1) protuberant cheekbones. (2) pattern tattooed on the cheek-bones.

tąyā ni rąinō *m.* type of small hawk (= tąyā ni gōyō 2).

tąyā ni shigā *m.* step inside house-door (*cf.* dōkin ƙōfą).

tāyar *Vd.* tā dą.

tąyą ragō *m.* (1) A. easily accomplished. (2) any native cloth woven in broadish strips (*x* three inches) *such as* ƀarāgē and the cloths (*x* farī, sāƙi, kudī) used by poor people (*about 26 such strips are required for a woman's cloth*), *cf.* agēdu.

tāyar dą = tā dą.

tayā-tąyą = ƀayā-ƀąyą.

tąyątayai *Vd.* tăităi.

tāyę (1) *Vb.* 1A (*a*) = tąyā 1. (*b*) abraded (foot, etc.). (2) *Vb.* 3A (foot, etc.) became abraded.

tayi A. (tąyī) *m.* = ɗan tąyī *m.* (*pl.* 'yan ∼) (1) fœtus. (2) *Vd.* yaŋkā 1*c.*

B. (tayi̱) *m.* (1) (*a*) making offer *as in*
tayạ 1*a.* (*b*) ~ bạ̄ tọyī ba nẹ̄ there's
no harm in offering too little for a T.
for it forms a basis for discussion.
(*c*) tayi̱ tạ̄ fisshē shi̱ *Vd.* ạlbarkạ 2*b.*
(*d*) rashi̱n tayi̱, a kạm bar ạrạhā
any port in a storm. (2) tā yi mini̱ ~
she flirted with me (*cf.* tayạ 1*c*). (3)
yā yi mini̱ ~ (*a*) he dared me, challenged
me (*cf.* tayạ 1*d*). (*b*) he (P. eating)
asked me to join him. (4) Kọ̄gī
matuƙar ~ *epithet of* Chief, skilled
P. (5) rījiyan nạŋ ~ takẹ̄ yi̱ it
makes one dizzy to look down this
well.

tā yi gidā *Vd.* gidā 1*a.*iv.

tayukkạ *Vd.* tēki̱.

tayyạcē *Vb.* 1C *Kt.* shamed P. by revealing
his secrets (= fạllasạ).

tạ̄zā *f.* combing (*cf.* tāje̱ 2).

tā zāgạ *f.* = kircī 2.

tazarā *f.* being a fairish distance away *x*
dạ ~ it's a fair distance from here (=
tabạ̄wā = rātā 1).

tazargạde̱ *m.* type of fragrant medicinal
herb.

tạzbahạ = cạzbī.

tazgaɗa A. (tazgạɗā) *Vb.* 1C tilted T.
(*cf.* jirki̱cē).
    B. (tạzgaɗạ) *Vb.* 3B was tilted,
slanting.

tazgạɗē *Vb.* 3A = tạzgaɗạ.

tazgarō *m.* yā yi ~ it is unpopular (=
jinī 4*c*).

tazge̱ *Vb.* 3A *Sk.* was split, torn (= kēce̱
1*a*).

tạzniyā *Sk. f.* quarrel (= faɗạ).

tẹ̄bạ = tại̱bạ.

tēbu̱r *m.* (*pl.* tēburōrī) *Eng.* (1) (*a*) (i)
table. (ii) wạzīransạ sum bar masạ
tēburōrinsu̱ his ministers resigned. (*b*)
table in market where native trader
(mại ~ *m., f.*) sells soap, etc. (= shāgo̱
2). (2) = shēbu̱r.

tēgạzạ *f.* = tại̱gạzạ.

tēki̱ *m.* (*pl.* tayạkā = tēkunạ = *Kt.*
tayukkạ) (1) large hide-bag. (*b*) am
bar jāki̱, anạ̄ dūkạn ~ = dạ̄rạ̄rī 2.
(2) kan ɗāki̱ yā yi ~ the roof is sagging
(= *Kt.* hantsạ 1*b*). (3) wạndō mại
bạ̄kin ~ trousers only mediumly
broad at foot (*cf.* balar). (4) yā ci

gōrọ, yā yi ~ = kumuryā. (5) tēki̱ŋ
gizọ type of children's game.

tẹ̄kū *f.* (*pl.* tēkunạ) (1) (*a*) sea *x* Tẹ̄ku̱ŋ
Hindu̱ Indian Ocean.   gạri̱n naŋ,
gạ̄ shi caŋ dạgạ gā̱bạr tẹ̄kū that town
lies on the coast. (*b*) hannun tẹ̄kū *m.*
a channel of the sea. (2) yā fāɗạ ạ ~
it has become lost or untraceable
(= sạ̄ A2 1*f*.i). (3) ci̱kạ ~ *Vd.* fạm
2.

tēkunạ *Vd.* tēki̱, tẹ̄kū.

tēmẹ̄dẹ̄ *m.* small silver-cylinder worn
by women as neck-ornament.

tẹ̄rẹ̄rē *m.* (1) = ạtē. (2) tanạ̄ tẹ̄rẹ̄raŋ
gōrọ she is selling kola-nuts in the basket
ạtē. (3) yā yi mini̱ ~ = yā yi mini̱
tẹ̄rẹ̄ran tsi̱yā he shamed me by revealing
my secrets (= fạllasạ).

tēri̱ *m.* hole made for skinning oxen in
(*cf.* ku̱rfī 2).

tēshạn *m.* = tashạ.

tẹ̄tē *m.* baby's first stages in walking, with
P. holding his hands (*this stage precedes* tātạ̄tā 2).

ti̱ *Eng. m.* (1) tea. (2) bạ̄ zamammu̱
mukạ yi, munạ̄ ta shạn ~ kaɗ̌ai ba we̱
did not remain idle.

ti̱bˈallarō = ti̱ɓallō *m.* type of cornstalk
flute longer than si̱rīki̱.

tibdi̱ = tabdi̱.

tibƙēƙe̱ *m.* (*f.* tibƙēƙi̱yā) huge.

tib-tib-tib *x* yā gudu̱ tib-tib-tib he tool
to his heels.

tifdi̱ = tabdi̱.

tife̱ *Vb.* 1A (1) yā ~ bāyaŋ gidā he̱
scraped excrement from his anus. (2
yā ~ mạ̄jinā he wiped mucus from hi̱
nose.

ti̱gāri̱ *adj. m.* huge.

tigijiŋ *m. and adv.* (1) yā yi ~ ciki̱
tsu̱mmā = yā yi tsu̱mmā ~ he's dresse̱
in rags. (2) gạrī yā yi masạ ~ he ha̱
a bad time.

ti̱girạ = ti̱kirạ.

tija *f.* sprained tendons in horse's o̱
donkey's shoulder.

Ti̱jānīyyạ *f.* a Muslim sect widely sprea̱
in Nigeria.

tijara A. (ti̱jārạ) public humiliation.
    B. (tijạ̄rā) *Vb.* 1C publicly humiḻ
ated P.

tijạrtā = tijạ̄rā.

tijimī *m.* *used in x* tijimin tsummā ragged clothes. tijimiŋ igīyą much rope. tijimiŋ wąndō (1) large trousers. (2) ragged trousers.

tik A. (tik) (1) gą̄ shi ∼ sǎi bąntē he's naked except for a loin-cloth. nī kūwā ∼ dą nī I was stark-naked. (2) yā kōmō ∼ he is penniless. (3) *Vd.* tiką tiką ∼.
    B. (tįk) *adv. and m.* yā fādį ∼ it fell bang! nā ji ∼ I heard (1) sound of something falling, (2) noise of a blow (= tįm).

tiƙa A. (tīƙą) *Vb.* 1A (1) made huge T. (*x* farm, corn-bin, etc.). (2) yā ∼ ni dą ƙasā he threw me down (= kā dą). (3) (*plus dative*) *x* (*a*) yā ∼ masą ƙullī he punched him. (*b*) yā ∼ masą sąndā he hit him with a stick. yā tīƙą masą hannū he slapped him. (4) *Vd.* tīƙō.
    B. (tīƙā) (1) *Vb.* 2 (*a*) yā tīƙē shi dą sąndā = tīƙą 3*b*. (*b*) oppressed (= zą̄luntą). (2) *f.* yā shā ∼ he received a blow.
    C. (tīƙā) (1) *used in* bīyą ∼ *m.* hitting defaulting gambler or debtor (2) *Vd.* shą̄ ∼.
    D. (tįƙā) *f.* (1) (*a*) = fąŋkō 1. (*b*) *cf.* mąŋ gyądā 3. (2) chewing the cud (*cf.* tuƙu). (3) contents of ruminant's stomach.

tįƙā *Kt. f.* = tįƙā 1.

tīƙad dą *Vb.* 4 = tīƙą 2.

tiƙą̄są̄ what a warrior!

tiką tiką tik *used in* īyākacin ∼ = īyākaciŋ wąje ƙōfą the matter has finally come to a head!; at last the inevitable result has occurred! well, that's the end of that!

tīƙā-tīƙą̄ *Vd.* tīƙēƙẹ, tittiƙēƙẹ.

tiką̄tikī *m.* (*pl.* tįką̄tįkai) calf, shin (= shą̄ rābā).

tįƙayyą *f.* = tįƙe-tįƙē.

tīƙēƙẹ *m.* (*f.* tīƙēƙįyā) *pl.* tīƙā-tīƙą̄ huge.

tị'ƙe-tįƙē" *m.* a fight with the fists (*cf.* tīƙą).

tiki = tukį.

tikilā *f.* striving *x* yaną̄ tikilar aikį he's working might and main (= himmą).

tiƙīnīyā *f.* = tikilā.

tiƙir = tiƙir-tiƙir = tiƙirkir *used in* yaną̄ dą taurī ∼ it is very tough.

tįkirą = tįkiragandą *f.* = dābų̄wą.

tikis = tiƙis (1) yā gąji ∼ he's dog-tired. (2) yaną̄ tąfīyą tįkis-tįkis = tiƙis-tįƙis he (tired P.) is dragging himself along.

tikitį *m.* (*pl.* tikitōcī) *Eng. m.* (1) (railway) ticket. (2) yā kai ∼ he is dead (= takąrdā 3).

tįkī-tikī = tąkẹ-takē.

tị'ƙi-tįƙi" *Sk.* = tikis 2.

tīƙō *Vb.* 1E (1) tricked. (2) *Vd.* tīƙą.

tiƙu = tuƙu.

tila A. (tilą) (1) heaped up, piled up (= tsibą = *Kt.* tsauną = tsīrą 1*a*). (2) an ∼ masą ƙų̄rā (*a*) dust has been flung on him (by passing horse). (*b*) he has been outdone. (*c*) it (horse) has been outdistanced by another. (3) an ∼ masą ƙasā ą̄ idō he has received a curt refusal, been humiliated.
    B. (tįlā) *f.* (1) earth thrown up by rodent. (2) gurgų̄war tsanyą da wurī ta kąn sōmą ∼ don't leave things till the last minute!

tilas A. (tīląs) (1) *adv.* (*a*) (i) by force. (ii) *Vd.* ą̄lā ∼. (*b*) *x* yaną̄ sǫ yą ci gąba ∼ he's determined to make progress at all costs. (2) *f.* (*a*) compulsion. (*b*) suŋ ga ∼ sụ tąfi they found themselves compelled to go. (*c*) ∼ bą tą̄ rasą wurim barcī ba where there's a will, there's a way. (*d*) ∼ bą tą sąŋ ƙa'idą ba necessity knows no law. (*e*) ∼ kāyaŋ gwaiwā, ɗā ną̄ ganī, ụbā ƙą̄ ɗauką (*lit.* son relieves father of load but he cannot help him carry his testicles) if there is no way out of a thing, you must grin and bear it. (*f*) tīląs bā ta sauran sā dōkį *Vd.* dōkį 1*s*. (*g*) mądākin tīląs *Vd.* sulhụ 2*b*. (*h*) tīląs ita kẹ sā shirį dą maƙįyī needs must when the devil drives. (*j*) *Vd.* tsūlīyā 7. (*k*) įyālįn ∼ *Vd.* dǭrǭgō. (*l*) gōmą ta ∼ *Vd.* gōmą 2*b*. (*m*) bą̄ƙwan ∼ *Vd.* ƙardā. (3) *cf.* tīląshī.
    B. (tilas) = tilis.

tīląsā = tīląstā.

tīląshī *m.* (1) relative whom one is forced to support. (2) tīląshin dā ąbin dą ya sā kąnsą the good man does not require his duty to be pointed out to him. (3) tīląshiŋ idǫ *Vd.* tsāwuryą.

tĩląstā *Vb.* 1C (*with dative*) *x* an ~ masą yą yī he was forced to do it.

*tĩlāwą *Ar. f.* repeating Koran from memory.

tile A. (tĩlē) *Kt. m.* = cĩlē.

  B. (tĩlę) = tĩlą 1, 2a *x* dōkĩ yā ~ shi dą ƙūrā.

tĩlĩ = tulĩ.

tĩlik = ƙirin.

tĩliką how black ! (*x re* dyeing, overcast sky, etc.).

tĩlim = ƙirin.

tĩlis = lilis.

tĩllą *Vb.* 1A pierced (= hūdą).

tĩllę *Vb.* 3A became pierced (= hūję).

tĩllǫ *m.* simultaneous drumming by one P. on two kąląŋgū where big one is on small one.

tĩlō (*Kano*) used in ɗansą ~ his only son.

tim A. (tĩm) *m. and adv.* = tĩk.

  B. (tĩm) *x* yanā dą girmā ~ it is huge. cikĩnsą yā hayę ~ he has huge paunch.

tima A. (tĩmā) (1) *Vb.* 2 *x* an tĩmē shĩ dą sąndā he has been beaten. (2) *f.* yā shā ~ he was beaten.

  B. (tĩmą) *Vb.* 1A (*with dative*) *x* an ~ masą sąndā = tĩmā 1.

  C. (tĩmā) (1) *Vb.* 2 (*a*) = tĩmā 1. (*b*) piled, heaped up. (*c*) *Vd.* tųma. (2) *f.* = tĩmā 2.

  D. (tĩmą) (*a*) = tĩmą. (*b*) piled, heaped up. (*c*) yā ~ ni da ƙasā he felled me. (*d*) = tumą.

tĩmɓir-tĩmɓir = tĩmɓir-tĩmɓir (1) yā zō naŋ ~ he came here naked. (2) yā zō naŋ ~ he managed to come here fat as he is.

tĩmę *Vb.* 1A *x* an tĩmę shĩ dą sąndā = tĩmą 1.

timir = tumur.

tĩmirī *m.* suffering trouble, difficulty (= wųyā).

timirmir = tumir.

tĩndī *Vd.* tąlōlō 3.

tĩndimi A. (tĩndimī) *m.* elephantiasis of foot or hand.

  B. (tĩndĩmī) *m.* band of overcasting on kāmųŋ ƙafą.

tĩndĩndĩm *m.* = canjąrąs 2.

tĩndirĩm *m.* (1) ƙafąssą tā yi ~ his left foot is much enlarged. (2) kąnsą yā yi ~ he is ashamed.

tindirmī *Kt. m.* = tindimī.

tindufųrī = jā kutųr.

Tĩne name for boy born on a Monday (*cf.* Ąltĩne).

tĩŋgā = tuŋgā.

tĩnĩ = tunĩ.

tĩnigą *Kt. f.* = shūnī 3.

tĩnjim *m. and adv.* abundantly *x* yā cĩka ~ it is chock-full. sunā naŋ ~ they are present in large numbers. yā yi ~ dą mutānē it is crowded with people.

tĩnjima A. (tĩnjĩmā) (1) *Vb.* 3A *x* yā ~ ą rūwa he jumped, fell into the water with a loud splash. (2) *Vb.* 1C (*a*) = tamfątsā. (*b*) tā tĩnjĩmą rūwā a tūwō she drenched the tūwō with water.

  B. (tĩnjĩmā) *f.* = bųruŋguzā 3.

tĩnjĩmē *m.* = tąmfątsē.

tĩnjĩmēmę *m.* (*f.* tĩnjĩmēmĩyā) *pl.* tĩnjĩm-tĩnjĩm (1) abundant, numerous. (2) huge.

tĩnjĩmī *m.* (*f.* tĩnjĩmā) *pl.* tĩnjĩm-tĩnjĩm huge.

tĩŋƙāhǫ *m.* putting on airs (= tāƙamā 2).

tĩŋkārą (1) *Vb.* 2 (*a*) went towards. (*b*) kąmar mųtųm yą tĩŋkāri kōgī, yą cę zai yāshę it is like pouring water into a sieve. (2) *m.* fearless P.

tĩŋka-tĩŋka = dĩŋga-dĩŋga.

tĩŋkĩŋ-tĩŋkĩŋ = tĩŋkis-tĩŋkis = dĩŋga-dĩŋga *q.v.*

tĩŋkĩyā = tuŋkĩyā.

tĩnti *Kt.* = cĩci 1.

tĩntĩlisko *m.* P. or T. offering one no difficulty.

tĩntĩŋ *m.* corpulence *x* yā yi ~ he is fat.

tinya A. (tĩnyą) *f.* (1) the cactus-like *Euphorbia unispina.* (2) rĩjĩyar ~ *f.* deep well.

  B. (tĩnyā) *x* gā shi ą sararī ~ there it is in full view.

tir (1) bother ! (2) yā yi mādąllā ~ he behaved ungratefully.

tirą = turą.

tĩrārē = tųrārē.

tirɓunā = turɓunā.

tirɗā-tĩrɗā *Vd.* tirɗēɗę.

tirɗę used in namijĩn ~ mąi wųyar baŋ kāshī why this scholar has given up scholarship entirely for magic !

tirdĕdę *m.* (*f.* tirdĕdīyā) *pl.* tirdā-tirdā̧ huge.

tirdimēmę *m.* (*f.* tirdimēmīyā) *pl.* tirdin-tirdin huge.

tirę (1) *Vb.* 1A (*a*) provoked P. (= zųngurą 2). (*b*) yā ⁓ shi dą kūrā he smothered him with dust. (2) *Vb.* 3A became incensed.

tirgwāsūwā *f.* horse's slipping through bending of hind-foot.

tiri *m.* (1) (*a*) re-dyeing T. badly dyed (*cf.* tisą 2). (*b*) dyeing with T. other than indigo (*cf.* rini, turą). (*c*) tirin hayākī *Vd.* turā̧rā 3. (2) re-thatching part of roof over old thatch (= gudųm biri 2) (*cf.* mahǫ 1). (3) (*a*) children's throwing dust over lunatic, thief, etc. (*cf.* turą 1*b*). (*b*) a children's game of throwing up dust.

tirijī *m.* strong P., headstrong P. (*epithet is* Tirijī mai kōkawą dą dąɓē).

tīrīkī *m.* (*f.* tīrīkā) *pl.* tirīkai huge.

tirikkā *Vd.* turkę.

tirin *A.* (tirin) = turųm.

B. (tirin) (1) yanā̧ dą kǎi ⁓ he has a huge head, yanā̧ dą gōshī ⁓ he has a broad forehead. (3) kǎina yā yi ⁓ my hair stood on end.

tiringē *m.* = *Kt.* tiringā *f.* (1) big-headed P. (2) what a big head!

tirinyą *f.* looking sleek.

tirirī = turųrī.

tirję (1) *Vb.* 3A (*a*) resisted doggedly (= dāgę 2). (*b*) (i) slithered. (ii) (horse) slithered along when reined in sharply. (iii) came to a dead stop (= tųrzā). (iv) (charging soldier, dog, etc.) suddenly halted through fear (1*b* = darję) (2) *Vb.* 1A (*a*) = darję 2*a, b.* (*b*) trampled down *x* sun ⁓ mini shūką they trampled down my crops. yā ⁓ mini kurjī he trod on my sore place. (*c*) yā ⁓ kasā (i) it (slithering horse) tore up earth when sharply reined in. (ii) P. scraped ground with foot to make mark (= turzą 1*a*). (*d*) *Vd.* darję, turzą.

tir'je-tirjē‖ *m.* yanā̧ shan ⁓ he's having trouble, difficulty (= wųyā).

tirjīyā *f.* acting *as in* tirję 1*b*.iv *x* sōją yā kāwō ⁓.

tirka *A.* (tirką) *Ar. f.* (1) effects of

deceased P. (2) an yi tirkąr kāyansą (the deceased's) valuable effects were assessed. (3) an tą̧fi wajan ⁓ people have gone to sale of deceased's effects.

B. (tirkā) *Vd.* turkā.

tirkāshi = *Kt.* tirkā̧sā̧ fancy!

tirkę *Vd.* turkę.

tirkip = kirtif.

tirmis abundantly.

tirmusā *Vd.* turmusā.

tirmutsā (1) *Vb.* 3A = firmitsā 2*a.* (2) *Vb.* 1C (*a*) plunged T. into (as arrow into abscess in sakīyą). (*b*) *cf.* firmitsā.

tirmutsūmųtsū = tųrmutsūmųtsū.

tirsasa *A.* (tirsā̧sā) *Vb.* 1C humiliated (= wulākąntā).

B. (tirsāsą) *Vb.* 3B became humiliated.

tirtsą *Vb.* 1A = tirtsā̧tsā.

tirtsā̧tsā *Vb.* 1C pierced with *x* yā ⁓ masą māshi he stabbed him with a spear.

tirtsītsī = kurcīcī 1.

tirwą̧dī = kirwą̧dī.

tirzą = turzą.

tirzaza = tirsasa.

tisą *Vb.* 1A (1) ground (condiments) on grinding-stone. (2) an sākę tisą̧wā it (work) has been redone (*cf.* tiri, turą 1). (3) (*a*) thrashed. (*b*) ⁓ gāwā *m.* (i) weak person's slashing corpse in war to pretend he killed him. (ii) an yi masą ⁓ gāwā in his case, insult has been added to injury.

tisą'in = tis'in.

tisą = tizgą.

tishę *Vd.* tisą.

tishi *m.* (1) (*a*) re-doing (work *as in* tisą 2). (*b*) *Vd.* fasą 1*o*. (2) grinding (*as in* tisą 1).

tis'in *Ar. f.* (1) ninety. (2) na ⁓ *m.* (*f.* ta ⁓) *pl.* na ⁓ ninetieth.

tī̧tā = cītā.

titi *A.* (tīti) *Eng. m.* (*sg., pl.*) (1) street *x* ⁓ mā̧sū kyą̧u good streets. ą̧ bisą tīti in the streets. sunā̧ yāwǫ bisą ⁓ they walk in the streets. tītin gą̧rinsų the streets.of their town. (2) zā sų kōmą kąn tīti gudā dą mū they will be of the same status as ourselves.

B. (tīti) (1) *f.* (*a*) (*familiarly*) girl (= yārinyą). (*b*) Tī̧ti girl's name. (2) = cici 1.

tįtįɓurį *m.* yanā ᵕ he's having trouble, difficulty (= wụyā).

tįtįkwātį *m.* = tįtįɓurį.

tįtįm-tįtįm *x* sụŋ hau musụ dą bugụ tįtįm-tįtįm they attacked them fiercely.

tįti-tįti *m.* (1) making a guess. (2) = cįci 1.

titse A. (tįtsē) *m.* (1) = firmitsī 2. (2) ginning cotton without previously teasing (kądā) it (= *Sk.* kwąncē).
  B. (tįtse) *x* yā zō minį ᵕ it happened unexpectedly to me.
  C. (titsę) *Vb.* 1A = titsīyē.

tįtsīyą *Vb.* 2 (1) set down (pot of water). (2) prevented P. leaving (till he has replied, paid, etc.).

titsīyē *Vb.* 1C = tįtsīyą.

tittįɗa A. (tittįɗā) *Vb.* 1C. (1) gave (P. climbing tree) push from below. (2) (seller) pestered (customer) to buy (= tuŋkụɗā 2). (3) = bulbụlā 1.
  B. (tittįɗą) *Vb.* 3B = bulbụlą 1.

tittįɗē *Vb.* 1C = bulbụlā 1.

tittįkēkę *m.* (*f.* tittįkēkįyā) *pl.* tįkā-tįką huge.

tittįkī *m.* (*f.* tittįkā) *pl.* tįkā-tįką huge.

tittįlā *Vb.* 1C (1) *intensive from* tilą. (2) = bulbụlā 1.

tittir *x* tūwōˑyā yi ᵕ the tūwō is stiff.

tįttirnā (1) *m.*, *f.* short, broad P. (2) *f.* fat goat.

tįttishī *m.* (1) happiness. (2) flouriness of cooked tubers.

tįyātį *m.* public humiliation.

tizga A. (tizgą) *Vb.* 3A *Sk.* (1) (*a*) descended. (*b*) slithered down. (2) = muskụdā 3.
  B. (tįzgā) *Vb.* 2 = fįzgā.

tizgę *Vb.* 1A = fizgę.

tǫ (1) very well ! (2) ᵕ dăidăi = 1. (3) ą ᵕ well then . . . (= a'a). (4) tǫ ? (*a*) really ? (*b*) fancy ! (5) *Vd.* ąi ; dągōgō.

tob *Vd.* tub.

tǫɓē *Kt. m.* = shūnī 1.

tǫbī = ɗan tǫbī *m.* = fątārī.

tǫcē *Kt. m.* = tǫtsīyā.

tōcịląŋ *Eng. m.* (*sg.*, *pl.*) electric torch.

tǫdarā = tūdarā.

tofa A. (tōfā) *f.* (1) (*a*) elephant-grass. (*b*) ząkaraŋ ᵕ sharp spike of 1*a*. (2) ą kau dą kăi, ą sārę ᵕ forcing oneself to do shameful T. publicly.

B. (tōfą) *Vb.* 1A. (1) (*a*) *x* yā ᵕ yau he spat (= tud dą). (*b*) yā ᵕ masą he spat on him, *cf.* tōfę 2. (2) (*only negatively*) *x* bąi ᵕ ba he made no reply (*cf.* tǫfī 2).

tōfad dą *Vb.* 4 = tōfą 1*a*.

tōfę *Vb.* 1A (1) covered (place) with spittle. (2) *x* yā ᵕ ni he lightly spat at me (to avert evil influence or prevent me saying T. he did not wish said), *cf.* tōfą 1*b*.

tǫfī *m.* (1) (*a*) spitting. (*b*) spitting *as in* tōfę 2 (= tub). (2) kō ᵕ bąn tōfą masą ba I made no reply to him (= uffąŋ). (3) tǫfī = ɗan tǫfī *m.* = fątārī.

tǫfi wąlā kēkas *used in* bąi cę ᵕ ba = tōfą 2.

tōfō = tōhō.

tǫfu *Vb.* 3B = tōhō.

tōgącē = tōgę.

tōgacīyā *f.* fending off (importunate P.).

Tōgai *Vd.* Makąmā.

tōgę (1) *Vb.* 3A (*a*) remained aloof. (*b*) withdrew. (*c*) hesitated (1 = tōkąrē 2*b*). (2) *Vb.* 1A excluded, made exception of (= ɗēbę 1*c* = kaŋgę 1*c*).

tǫgō *m.* making a conditional statement.

tōhą = tōfą.

toho A. (tōhō) *Vb.* 3A (1) (*a*) sprouted (= tǫfu = tsịra = *Kt.* tūkō). ꞏ(*b*) yā sōmą tōhǫwā he's begun to prosper. (2) rąina yā tǫfu I feel happy.
  B. (tǫhō) (1) *m.* act of sprouting. (2) *m.* (*sg.*, *pl.*) bud(s).

tǫhu = tōhō.

tōjąɓē = tūję 2.

tǫkā *f.* (1) ashes (= *Sk.* habdị). (2) kōwā ya kōnę rụmbunsą, yā saŋ indą ᵕ takę kudī don't cut off your nose to spite your face ! (3) jąkī bā yą wucę ᵕ = jąkī yā ga ᵕ = in jąkī ya ga ᵕ săi birgimā how apposite !, it is just in your line ! (*cf.* shā dą 2*b*). (4) yā shāfą wą haŋkąlinsą ᵕ he flew into a temper. (5) tūbąlin ᵕ *m.* good-for-nothing P. (6) yā ląshi tǫkā gabansą he swore fealty to him. (7) samąrin tǫkā *m.* any dog. (8) tǫˈkatǫkā॥ *adj. m.*, *f.* grey.

tokara A. (tōkąrā) *Vb.* 1C (1) used T. for propping up *x* ką tōkąrą itącē jịkin

jiŋkā prop up the thatch with sticks !
(*cf.* tō̩kara̩). (2) = dōga̩rā 1*a*, *b*. (3)
(*with dative*) helped *x* nā ∼ masa̩ I
helped him.

B. (tō̩kara̩) propped up *x* ka̩ tō̩ka̩ri
jiŋkā da̩ ita̩cē (= tōka̩rā 1 = tōka̩rē =
dōga̩rē 3).

tōkarci̩ *m.* the Agalāwā tribal-cuts (sha̩s-
shāwa̩).

tokare A. (tōka̩rē) (1) *Vb.* 1C. (*a*) propped
up *x* ka̩ tōka̩re̩ jiŋkā da̩ ita̩cē = tō̩kara̩.
(*b*) yā tōka̩re̩ ƙōfa̩ he kept the door shut
with a prop (matōkarī). (2) *Vb.* 3A. (*a*)
became jammed *x* ƙyaurē yā ∼ the
door refused to shut. ƙaya̩r kīfī tā ∼
masa̩ a̩ wuya̩ a fish bone stuck in his
throat. (*b*) = tōge̩ 1.

B. (tō̩ka̩rē) *m.* (1) pieces let into
skirt (gi̩ndī) of gown to increase width.
(2) gown made *as in* 1.

tōka̩rī *m.* interposing arm, leg, etc.

tō̩ka-tō̩kā *Vd.* tō̩kā 8.

tōla̩fī *Sk.* = talla̩fī.

tōlīyā *f.* = tukkū.

tō̩'lo-tō̩lōᴵᴵ *m.*, *f.*, *sg.*, *pl.* turkey.

tōmō (1) *Vd.* Ga̩la̩dīma̩. (2) (*negatively in
expressions like the following*)
kyau̩ (girmā) ba̩ ∼ ba ne̩ beauty (size)
is not the most important thing in the
world.

to̩n *m.*, *sg.*, *pl. Eng.* ton.

tona A. (tōna̩) *Vb.* 1A (*Vd.* tō̩nō) (1) (*a*) (i)
dug up. (ii) kā̩fi̩n a̩ sa̩mi jārumāwā
iri̩nsu̩, sài an tōna̩ it is not easy to
parallel their bravery. (iii) yā tōnō wa̩
kansa̩ he brought the trouble on himself.
(iv) *Vd.* a̩llūra̩ 4. (*b*) investigated *x*
i̩ŋ kā tōna̩ ƙa̩rkashinsa̩ if you investigate it (= tō̩nā 1 = tōnō = tōne̩ 1), *cf.*
tō̩nō. (2) put to shame *x* yā ∼ mu
ga̩rēsu̩ he gave us away to them. an ∼
la̩ifinsu̩ = an ∼ su their crime has
been bruited abroad. yā ∼ a̩sīrīna =
yā ∼ mini̩ a̩sīrī he blabbed my secrets
(*Vd.* a̩sĭ̩ı̄ 1*b*). yā tōna̩ wa̩ kansa̩ a̩sīrī he
gave himself away (= tōne̩ (*Vd.* tō̩nō)).
a̩sīrimmu̩ yā tō̩nu we've been disgraced.
(3) yā tōnō fa̩da̩ he made mischief (*Vd.*
bam-bamī).

B. (tō̩nā) *Vb.* 2 (1) = tōna̩ 1. (2)
provoked, taunted P. (= zu̩ŋgura̩ 2).

tō̩naro̩ = tō̩niro̩.

tōne̩ *Vb.* 1A (1) = tōna̩ 1, 2. (2) yā ∼
rāmi̩ he dug out an old hole (*cf.* haƙa̩).

tono A. (tōnō) *Vd.* tōna̩.

B. (tō̩nō) *m.* (1) (*secondary v.n. of*
tōna̩) *x* anā̩ tō̩nansa̩ = anā̩ tōna̩ shi
it is being dug up, investigated. ba̩
zā su̩ yi mana̩ wanna̩ŋ tō̩na̩ŋ a̩sīrī ba
they will not commit this treachery
against us. (2) investigating *x* (*a*) an
yi masa̩ ∼ his affairs have been investigated. (*b*) bat tō̩nan ciki̩nsa̩ *Vd.* ɓaurē 4.
(3) quarrelsomeness *x* (i) Audu̩ ∼
ga̩rēshi̩ = Audu̩ tō̩nam fa̩da̩ ga̩rēshi̩
Audu is quarrelsome (= tō̩na̩ 3) (*Vd.*
bambamī). (4) taunting, provocative-
ness *x* anā̩ tō̩nansa̩ he's being taunted.
"Ala̩gwaida̩" ∼ ne̩ na Gwārī the word
Ala̩gwaida̩ is a derisory term for the
Gwaris. (5) yā yi mini̩ tō̩nan sĭ̩lĭ̩lĭ̩ =
ba̩ŋka̩dā 2. (6) *cf.* ba̩n ∼.

tō̩nu *Vd.* tōna̩.

tōramī *m.* the distance beyond wrist or
ankle, up to which henna is applied.

Tōra̩ŋkāwā *Vd.* Ba̩tōra̩ŋke̩.

tōri̩ (1) *Vd.* ka̩ra̩tū 2*e*, ji̩minā. (2) tafki̩n ∼
what a useless person ! ta̩̩ka zō ∼ *m.*
hurrying along apprehensively.

tō̩rinta̩ *f.* = tō̩rinto̩ *m.* = tō̩tō̩rinto̩ *q.v.*

tō̩rō *m.* (1) (*a*) tō̩ra̩ŋ gĭwā bull-elephant.
(*b*) karo̩ ɗayā̩ kō da̩ tō̩ra̩ŋ gĭwā ā̩
buga̩ there's no harm in trying everything once. (2) tō̩ram ɓaunā = ku̩-
tu̩ŋkū 1. (3) tō̩ra̩ŋ a̩gwā̩gwā drake.

tōrōƙō *m.* (1) swelling-up of fermenting
substance. (2) the portion of contents
projecting above edge of calabash (*cf.*
tō̩tsīyā).

tō̩rōsō = ta̩rōsō.

tosana *Kt.* = ɗosana.

tōsa̩rā *Vb.* 1̩C (1) set T. down near opening
x yā ∼ mini̩ kāyā a̩ ƙōfa̩r ɗāki̩ he
set down the loads at the door of my
house. (2) yā ∼ masa̩ kāyā he (thief)
sold the victim's property near where
it was stolen.

tōsarō *m.* (1) = su̩rūtu̩. (2) tōshi̩n ∼
giving present after the Festival when
useless, instead of before, as customary
(= *Sk.* bū̩ƙa̩lē = tōshi̩ 6).

tōshe̩ (1) *Vb.* 1A (*a*) stopped up (= lĭƙe̩ =
taushe̩ 6). (*b*) (i) an ∼ bā̩kinsa̩ action
as in tōshi̩ 1, 2 has been done to him.

(ii) *Vd.* **tsanyạ** 1*b*. (2) *Vb.* 3A became stopped up (= **lĩ kẹ** 2*c*).

tōshi *m.* (1) present to win P. over *x* **lị'kẹ-lĩ kẽ"** **tōshịn 'yạŋ kõlị** peddlars give small trinkets to their girl-friends. (2) bribe. (3) **tōshịm bạ̃kĩ** (*a*) bribe (= **rashawạ**). (*b*) = **tōshĩyar bạ̃kĩ**. (4) **tōshịn sallạ** presents given at time of the Festival to parents of one's sweetheart. (5) **tōshịn tōsarō** *Vd.* tōsarō 2. (6) ~ **bãyan sallạ** = **tōsarō** 2. **tōshĩyã** *f.* (1) stopping up. (2) part of embroidery on ankle-band of trousers (**kafạr wạndō**). (3) **tōshĩyar bạ̃kĩ** (*a*) = **tōshị** 3*a*. (*b*) present given younger sister or mother of one's sweetheart to obtain their good offices. **tọ̃tar** = **dạrkwai**. **tōtọ** (1) *Sk. m.* = **tōtụ̃wã** (2) *Kt.* **tōtạŋ gạbã** horse's chest. **tọ̃tọrintọ** *m.* = **ạlfahạrĩ**. **tōtsạ** (1) *Vb.* 1A (*a*) plunged T. into *x* **yã** ~ **masạ wukã** he stabbed him. **yã** ~ **shi ạ jịŋkã** he pushed it into the thatch. (*b*) did **tọ̃tsĩyã** 1. (*c*) **yã** ~ **minị aikịn nạŋ** he sprang this task on me when I was already busy with another (*cf.* **kụ̃tsẽ** 2). (2) *Vb.* 3A **yã** ~ **cikin tạ̃rō** he forced his way through the crowd (= **firmịtsã** 2*a*). **tōtsẹ** *Vb.* 1A (1) = **tōtsạ** 1*a* *x* **yã** ~ **shi dạ wukã** he stabbed him with a knife. (2) = **tōtsạ** 1*b*. **tọ̃tsĩyã** *f.* (1) (*a*) placing sticks round edge of calabash to increase height of contents it will hold (*cf.* **tōrõ kō**). (*b*) calabash filled *as in* 1. (3) overlapping of teeth (= **shirgĩyã** 3). **tọ̃tsōtsōnĩyã** *Kt. f.* = **tụ̃rẽrẽnĩyã**. **tōtụ̃wã** *f.* (1) (*a*) pulp of gourds (= **hạrzã** = **kụtụ̃tụ**), *cf.* **kikịrĩ**. (*b*) (i) the core of **rạkẽ, tạkạndã**, or maize (which is useless and thrown away) *x* **tōtụ̃war masạrã** maize-cob core = **kụtụ̃tụ** 3 (*cf.* **tsōkạ** 1*d*). (ii) **tōtụ̃war zumạ** honeycomb after honey extracted (= **kãkị** 1). (2) pith of corn-stalk (= **tạ̃shĩyạ**). (3) the doughy part of bread. **toya** A. (**tōyạ**) (1) (*a*) fried (*x* **wạinã, gurãsạ, fụŋkạ̃sō**-cakes) in oil = **gasạ** 1*b*.ii (*cf.* **sōyạ, tōye-tōyẽ**). (*b*) **tã** ~ **mại** (i) she heated oil to frying temperature.

(ii) she clarified butter by frying (usually with onion). (*c*) **nã** ~ **mại, nã mạncẽ dạ ạlbasạ** the details were attended to, but the important part was neglected. (2) (*a*) **yã** ~ **tukunyã** he fired the pot (= **gasạ** 1*c*). (*b*) burned (= **kōnẹ**). (3) an ~ **Audụ** information has been laid against Audu for harbouring thieves. B. (**tọ̃yã**) *Vb.* 2 = **tōyạ** 1, 2*a*. **Tōyạ matsãfã** *epithet of any* Emir. **tōyẹ** *Vb.* 1A = **tōyạ** 1, 2. **tọ̃'ye-tọ̃yẽ"** *m.* various fried cakes (*x* **gurãsạ, wạinã, fụŋkạ̃sō**), *cf.* **tōyạ** 1*a*. **tọ̃yĩ** *m.* (1) setting fire to the "bush". (2) **tayị bạ** ~ **ba nẹ** there is no harm in offering too little for a T. for it forms a basis for discussion. (3) *cf.* **tạ̃kạ** ~. **tōzạ̃bẽ** *Vb.* 3A = **tũjẹ** 2. **tōzạlĩ** *m.* (*pl.* **tōzulạ**). (1) (*a*) galena = **kwạllĩ** *q.v.* (*b*) **idọ bã yạ̃ mutuwạ** ~ **yạ tạ̃shẽ shị** a thing once spoiled never regains its pristine value. (2) **nã yi** ~ **dạ shĩ** he and I saw one another. (3) **rãgō maị** ~ ram with black rings around eyes. (4) **tōzạliŋ kũrã** = **kwạllĩ** 4. **tōzạntã** *Vb.* made mound to (*x* grave), *cf.* **tōzō**. **tozarta** A. (**tōzạrtã**) *Vb.* 1C despised (= **rẽnạ**). B. (**tọ̃zartạ**) *Vb.* 3B was treated contemptuously. **tōzō** *m.* (*pl.* **tōzạ̃yẽ**) (1) (*a*) hump (of camels, cattle, etc.). (*b*) **tōzaŋ kũrị yanạ̃ cikinsạ** what forbearance ! (2) (*a*) cupola. (*b*) mound over grave. (*c*) round-topped **sōrō**. (3) **dan** ~ *m.* (*pl.* **'yan** ~) small-mouthed water-pot (**tũlũ**). (4) = **tsōrō** 2. (5) **kạ̃mạ tōzō** *Vd.* **sạkị zãrĩ**. **tōzulạ** *Vd.* **tōzạlĩ**. **tsạ̃** *f.* the letter of the alphabet so pronounced. **tsab** = **tsaf**. **tsã'ạ** *Kt. f.* = **dã'ạ**. **tsãbạ** *f.* (1) (*a*) threshed grain. (*b*) *Kt.* **hạkurĩ tụkunyar** ~ there's a limit to everyone's patience (= **hạkurĩ** 2). (*c*) **kadạ kạ daurạ minị jạkar** ~ **'yan tsạ̃kĩ sụ bĩ nị** don't cause me any unpleasantness ! (2) (*a*) **tsãbạr kudĩ** coins, cowries (*contrasted with payment* *in kind*), *cf.* farin bīyɑ, kɑrɓā 2*f*, fariŋ kudī. (*b*) tsābɑr ƙarfɛ money (*contrasted with cowries*), *cf.* fariŋ kudī. (*c*) kudī ⌒ mukɑ sɑyā we bought for cash (= hannū 1*l*.i). (3) (*a*) farī ⌒ strips of farī 1*e* not yet joined together. (*b*) tsābɑ = diŋkiŋ tsābɑ hand-sewing to make 3*a above*. (4) (*a*) absolute *x* gɑskīyā ⌒ absolute truth. tsābɑr ƙaryā an absolute lie (= zallā). (*b*) bɑ̄ mai dūbɑ tsābɑr idɑ̄nunsɑ yɑ fadɑ̄ masɑ nobody would have the courage to tell him frankly. (*c*) tsābɑr kurkunū the bulk of a guinea-worm collected in one place. (5) (*a*) zɑran nɑŋ ⌒ gɑrēshɩ this thread is well spun, as done in the wet season and then stored for three months. (*b*) 'yar ⌒ gɑrēshɩ = rūwā A.22.

tsɑba'ɑ = dɑba'ɑ.

tsababa = tsagaga.

tsɑ̄babbē *m.* (*f.* tsɑ̄babbīyā) *pl.* tsɑ̄bɑbbū. (1) threshed grain (*Vd.* tsābɑ 1*a*). (2) tsɑ̄bɑbbuŋ kudī = tsābɑ 2*a*.

tsābɑcē *Vb.* 1C (1) = cāsɑ 1. (2) sewed *as in* tsābɑ 3*b*.

tsābāgɛ *m.* type of potash always in granular form.

tsɑbakɑ = dɑba'ɑ.

tsɑbce = tsaucē.

tsabgɑ (1) *f.* (*pl.* tsabgōgī = tsɑbgū = tsɑbgī) = tsumaŋgīyā. (2) *Vb.* 1A yā ⌒ rubūtū he wrote in small, clear hand.

tsabgēgɛ *used in* tsabgēgyɑŋ rubūtū small, clear writing (= *Kt.* tsɑ̄gē).

tsɑbī'ɑ *f.* (*pl.* tsabī'ō'ī = tsɑbī'ū = tsɑbīyū). (1) temperament, character. (2) (*in plural*) traits *x* duk tabī'ō'insɑ na sōjɑ nē all his traits are those of a soldier.

tsabnagō *m.* (1) skinflint. (2) niggardliness.

tsabrē *Kt.* = tsaurē.

tsabtɑ *f.* (1) (*a*) cleanliness. (*b*) aikiŋ ⌒ the Sanitary Department. (*c*) dɑ̄munar bana ⌒ gɑrētɑ this year's rains were ideal. (*d*) tsabtɑr dōkɩ sham cleanliness (*for horse after separating legs to urinate, then steps in the urine*). (2) ⌒ gɑrēshɩ he is niggardly. (3) kīwɑn ⌒ *Vd.* bardō.

tsabtɑcē *Vb.* 1C cleansed.

tsab-tsab *x* yārɔ ⌒ dɑ shī a clean boy. mātā nɛ̄ ⌒ dɑ sū they are clean women.

tsada A. (tsɑ̄dā) *f.* (1) (*a*) (i) dearness. (ii) *Vd.* ɑrɑhā 4. (*b*) yā shā ⌒ he was overcharged. (*c*) an yi tsɑ̄dar gōrɔ kola-nuts became dear. (2) paucity *x* tsɑ̄dar magana gɑrēshɩ he is a man of few words. ganī ⌒ yakɛ̄ yi masɑ he can hardly see. (3) sun yaŋkɛ̄ (= yi) ⌒ dɑ shī they've made a bargain with him (*re* wages, contract, etc.) = jɩŋgā 1*b*. (4) mai ⌒ *m.*, *f.* (*pl.* mɑ̄sū ⌒) (*a*) handsome. (*b*) P. who drives hard bargains.

B. (tsɑ̄dā) *f.* (1) (*a*) Senegal Rose-coloured Fire-finch (*Lagonostica senegala*) = bɑ̄iwā 3*b* = bā'ū = bēnī. (*b*) tsɑ̄dar gambɑ type of finch. (*c*) tsɑ̄dar lɛmō type of finch. (2) ⌒ bā tɑ̄ kūkam burtū it is no use making exaggerated claims.

C. (tsɑ̄dɑ) *f.* (1) (*a*) the tree *Ximenia americana* which has small, yellow, plum-like fruit with acid taste. (*b*) shɑn ⌒ *m.* = shɑŋ gwandɑ *q.v. under* gwandɑ 3. (2) tsɑ̄dɑr Lɑmɑrūdu hog-plum. (3) namijiŋ ⌒ *m.* the shrub *Gymnosporia senegalensis*. (4) (*a*) small, yellowish beads. (*b*) *Vd.* ƙyɑlli-ƙyɑllī.

tsɑ̄dɑncē *Vb.* 1C made bargain *as in* tsɑ̄dā 3 *x* mun tsɑ̄dɑncɛ ɑbin dɑ zā mu bīyā we've made a bargain as to what wages, etc., we'll pay.

tsɑ̄dɑntā *Vb.* 1C caused T. to become more expensive.

tsɑ̄dɑrākɩ *m.* (1) type of cobra (= ɩn-jihau). (2) type of small crocodile attacking people.

tsɑdarī *m.* (1) (*a*) difficult soil to farm (*cf.* faƙɔ). (*b*) P. hard to get to pay debt. (2) a thread-line in kāmuŋ ƙafɑ of trousers (*Vd.* ƙirjī 2).

tsad dɑ *Vb.* 4 = tsartɑ 1.

tsaf *adv.* (1) yā wɑŋku ⌒ it is washed snow-white. an shārɛ ⌒ very clean sweeping has been done. (2) mun shiryɑ ⌒ we've come to complete arrangement. yā mayar dɑ sū ⌒ he gave them back in full. (3) tɑ̄ zaunɑ ⌒ cikiŋ gidan mijintɑ she lived peacefully with her husband. (4) ⌒ yakɛ̄ dɑ abinsa he's stingy (cf. tsādā 4b). (5) ~ da nāka, butsai da na wani he's one who sticks to his own property and buys nothing (Vd. butsai).

tsāfa Vb. 1A (1) x yā ~ tsakāninsu he squeezed his way between them. (2) used T. as a fetish (tsāfi).

tsāfe Vb. 1A = tsāfa 2.

tsāfi m. (d.f. tsubbu). (1) fetish (= gunki). (2) (a) sunā ~ they worship fetishes. (b) dōdō gudā mukē yi wa tsāfi we all have the same aim. (3) tsāfi gaskīyar mai shī everyone believes in his own powers. (4) kākan ~ Vd. bagirō ; bijirō. (5) kāzar ~ Vd. fingi.

tsafta = tsabta.

tsaf-tsaf = tsaf.

tsāfu Vb. 3B yā ~ tsakāninsu = tsāfa 1.

tsaga A. (tsāga) Vb. 1A (1) (a) split, ripped, cracked T. (= kēta 1a). (b) an ~ hanya road has been made (= kēta 1c.i). (c) made cut in x (i) wanzāmi yā ~ jikinsa the barber cut tribal-marks (tsāgā) on him. (ii) rashin tsāgāwā Vd. rashi 1c. (iii) an ~ masa lamba he has been vaccinated. (2) (a) (with dative) x yā ~ mana aikimmu he apportioned us our work. (b) Audu bākin da Allā ya ~ Audu has no regular employ, but trusts in God to provide. (c) bākin da Allā ya ~ bā yā hana shi abincī God provides for all his creatures.

B. (tsāgā) Vb. 2 (1) cut P. accidentally (cf. tsāga 1c). (2) (a) yā tsāgi īhu = yā tsāgi kūkā he screamed. (b) yārọ yanā tsāgar kāi the child is screaming. (3) Vd. tsāgar rama.

C. (tsāgā) f. (1) incising, splitting, ripping, cracking. (2) tribal-marks (= askā 4).

D. (tsaga) Vb. 3B (1) became arrogant. (2) became outstanding.

E. (tsagā) v.n. and progressive of tsaga.

tsagaga Kt. adv. abundantly x (1) yā yi kudī ~ (a) he is wealthy. (b) it is expensive. (2) an zuba masa kudī ~ = 1b.

tsagagī m. (1) West African Hadada Ibis (Hagedashia hagedash). (2) Wood Ibis (Ibis Ibis).

tsagaitā Vb. 3A diminished (= rage).

tsagalgalē Vb. 3A = hakīkicē.

tsagal-tsagal = tsagal-tsagal used in yanā tafīya ~ spindle-legged P. or animal is walking along.

tsagargarī m. (f. tsagargarā) pl. tsagargarai Kt. = tsigirgirī.

tsagaro Kt. m. = tsakī 4.

tsāgar rama f. hewing P. in two with sword in war.

tsagāwa f. arrogance (= alfaharī).

tsage A. (tsāge) (1) Vb. 1A = tsāga 1a, 1c.i. (2) Vb. 3A (a) became split, ripped, cracked (= kēce). (b) sāi katangā tā ~ fadangare kan sam mashigā when friends quarrel, this gives others matter for gossip. (3) Kt. m. = tsumangīyā.

B. (tsāgē) m. (1) acting as in saftā. (2) new bulrush-millet used for fodder or for jūrē 1. (3) Kt. takandā peeled and put on sale. (4) Kt. = tsabgēgyan rubūtū. (5) Vd. tsāgyan tsayī.

C. (tsage) Vb. 3A (1) = tsanyē. (2) = gāwurta 1.

D. (tsagē) m. (1) Tigerfish (Hydrocyon sp.). (2) Kt. ~ nē he is small, wiry P. (= rūwā A. 22). (3) children's game where they say carkī carkī.

tsāgen Vd. tsāgyan.

tsagērā f. cantankerous P.

tsagēranci m. cantankerousness.

tsāgi m. (1) an yi masa ~ = tsāgā 2. (2) (a) portion cut off x an tsāga shi ~ uku it has been cut into three portions. (b) Vd. kantu.

tsāgināginī m. = fyāmā.

tsagīyā f. (1) hæmaturia, bilharzia in lad. (2) hair from horse's tail (izgā) used for strings of musical instruments and women's neck-bands (Vd. izgā 3).

tsāgo m. crack in T.

tsagwaro m. (1) tsārī 1 left standing and so' gone sour (tsāmī). (2) furā left standing (kwānā) and so gone sour.

tsāgyan tsayī (d. f. tsāgē) m. in the game mangarē, kicking opponent with each foot in quick succession (Vd. wartsahū).

tsāha Kt. f. = dā'a.

*tsahiri A. (tsāhirī) m. (f. tsāhirā) pl. tsāhirai Ar. pure.

B.* (tsāhīri) = *tāhīri.

tsāhịrtā *Vb.* 3A waited (= dākạtā).
tsahō *m.* = tsawō.
tsai (1) *m. and adv.* (*a*) darē yā yi ∼ it was dead of night. gạrī yā yi ∼ trade is at a standstill. (*b*) nā yi ∼ dạ zūcịyāta I pondered quietly. (*c*) kạ dūbạ ∼ = kạ tsayạ ∼ reflect carefully before you do this ! *(2) dạki tsai = dạki dukạ. (3) *Vd.* zạbạrī.
tsaiba A. (Tsạibā) *woman's name.*
 B. (tsạibā) *Vd.* tsẹbā.
tsai dạ *Vb.* 4 (1) halted *x* (i) yā ∼ shi = yā tsaishē shị he brought it (horse, vehicle, P.) to a halt. (ii) yā tsai dạ gụdānạr ạl'amạrịŋ he blocked progress of the matter. (2) kept motionless *x* (i) yā ∼ dōkị wurī ɗayā he kept the horse standing in the same place. (ii) kạ ∼ hannū keep your hand from wobbling ! (iii) yā ∼ aikịmmụ he delayed our work. (3) (*a*) set up *x* (i) yā ∼ itạ̄cē he set up a post. (ii) an tsai dạ ƙā'idạ a law has been passed. (*b*) settled (affair, date, etc.). (3) yā ∼ gēmụ he has started a beard. (4) *Vd.* tsai da-*compounds.*
tsaidạ *Vb.* 1A *Sk.* = tsai dạ.
tsai dạ bạ̄ƙō = rạkạ mai gijị.
tsai dạ maganạ = kā fi ƙaryā.
tsai dạ mai dōkị *m.* a method of securing woman's fạtalạ.
tsai dạ mazā *Kt. Vd.* tsạidau.
tsạidau *Kt. m.* the weed tsị̄dau *q.v.* (*its epithet at Kt. is* tsại da mazā).
tsaikọ *m.* (1) (*a*) roof-frame for thatched roof. (*b*) sōrō nẹ̄ hayịn ∼ it's a mud-topped building with vaulting (ɗaurịŋ gụ̄gā). (*c*) (i) bạ̄ dū karā ya kạŋ kai ∼ ba not everyone is able to obtain a high position. (ii) *Vd.* kai 1*a.*vi. (2) shī nẹ̄ tsaikwạnsạ he is the one delaying it.
tsaishē *Vd.* tsai dạ.
tsaitsạyā *Vb.* 3A *intensive from* tsayạ.
tsaitsạye *adv.* ạ ∼ determinedly (= tsaiwā 2).
tsaiwā (*v.n. and progressive of* tsayạ, *alternative with* tsayạ̄wā) *x* (1) watạn naŋ tsaiwar jīyạ nē this moon was new yesterday. yā yi kyạn ∼ it stands well. (2) yā tsayạ tsaiwar dakạ he stood firm in his resolve (= tsayị 3).

 B. (tsạiwā) plaited-string door-curtain (*cf.* sạndā 4*b*).
tsaka A. (tsakạ) *f.* (1) (*a*) (i) centre (*Vd.* tsakīyạ ; tsakạ-tsakạ). (ii) Allạ̄ yạ fisshē kạ tsakạ mai wụyā, bạ̄ farƙō ba, ƙarƙō may you remain always virtuous ! (iii) taŋkad tsakạ *Vd.* taŋkā 3*a.* (iv) ạ̄ ci māsạ dạgạ tsakạ ? *Vd.* māsạ 3. (*b*) darē yā yi ∼ it is midnight. rānā tā yi ∼ it is midday. (*c*) tsakạr ∼ the very centre (= tsạttsakī). (2) ạ tsakar = ạ tsakạr in the middle of (Mod. Gram., Appendix I, 24) *x* (*a*) gạ mu naŋ ạ tsakar (ạ tsakạr) kạŋkụ we're about to attack you ! (*b*) (i) yanạ̄ wạje ạ tsakar (= ạ tsakạr) rānā he is outside in the heat of the sun. yā zō ạ tsakar (= ạ tsakạr) rānā he came when already advanced in life *Vd.* rānā 2*j.*ii. (ii) ạ tsakar (ạ tsakạr) darē at midnight. (*c*) ạ tsakạr kā *Vd.* ɓatạ 1*d.* (3) tsakạ dạ at the height of *x* sunạ̄ tsakạ dạ ƙidimạ they are (were) at the height of bewilderment. anạ̄ tsakạ dạ bụ'ge-bụgē‖ people are (were) in the thick of battle. yanạ̄ tsakạ dạ sharạfinsạ he is (was) at the height of his power. sunạ̄ tsakạ dạ shirị they're in the midst of their preparations.
 B. (tsakā) *f.* (1) *Vd.* tsakạ 2. (2) ∼ *pl.* tsakạ̄kē (*a*) small gecko (*cf.* sạri kutuf). (*b*) yā kas (= yā kats) ∼ he got a bargain ; he was lucky (= gạmō). (*b*) mischief-maker. (3) *Vd.* wutsīyạr ∼.
tsakạitā = tsakạntā.
tsakạ̄kē *Vd.* tsakā 2*a.*
tsạkānĪ (1) *adv.* between *x* (*a*) dạ hanyạ ∼ there is a road between. (*b*) yā shịga ∼ he interposed ; he took a hand in it. (2) tsạkānin *prep.* between *x* (*a*) yā zaunạ tsạkāninsụ he lived among them. (*b*) yā shịga tsạkānimmụ he interposed between us. tsạkānin A dạ B mịl 70 the distance between A and B is 70 miles. (*c*) tsạkānịŋ harshẹ dạ haƙōrī *Vd.* sāɓạ 3*b.*i. (*d*) (*preceded by genitive ; so used as masculine noun*) wannạŋ gạ̄bar tsạkāninsụ this hostility between them. nīsan tsạkānin A dạ B the distance between A and B. wannạŋ yāƙi na tsạkānimmụ dạ sū

this war which is between us and them.
(e) tsạkāniŋ wadạndạ akạ kashẹ dạ
wadạndạ akạ kāmạ including both
killed and wounded. (3) m. interval
between x (a) ạ tsạkānin tudụn naŋ
an yaŋkạ hanyạr rūwā they cut a canal
through that intervening tract of terra
firma. (cf. wajē 2b). (b) Allạ yạ yi manạ
tsạkānī dạ shī God keep him far from
us ! (c) yā tāsam masạ tsạkānī dạ Allạ
he made a bee-line for him. (4) m.
mutual relationship x (a) yā bātạ
tsạkānimmụ he caused us to quarrel.
kā ji tsạkāniŋkụ dạ mū now you know
our attitude vis-a-vis you. kā san na
tsạkāninsụ dạ mū you know on what
footing we are with them. ạl'amạrin
tsạkāninsụ yā fārạ rūdẹwā relations
became worse between them. (b) Vd.
gamạ ∼.
tsạkānī-tsạkānī m. slight interval x kạ
yi rubụ̄tuŋkạ dạ ∼ do not crowd your
writing together ! (= sararī 1d).
tsạkạŋkạnī = tsạkānī.
tsakạntā Vb. 1C reconciled.
tsakanyạ Kt. f. = tsakạ.
tsakara A. (tsākạrā) Vb. 1C (with dative)
(1) x yā ∼ minị shī he gave me a little
of it. (2) sun ∼ wạ Sarkiŋ kạsūwā
they (corn-sellers) paid corn-levy to
market-head.
　　B. (tsạkarạ) Vb. 2 (1) (a) pecked.
(b) provoked (= tsọ̄kanạ). (2) took a
little of.
tsakare A. (tsākạrē) Vb. 1C = tsākạrạ 1.
　　B. (tsạkạrē) m. corn-levy as in
tsākạrā 2.
tsaka-tsaka A. (tsakạ-tsakạ) adv. right
in the centre x yạnzu gạ shi, sū nẹ
tsakạ-tsakạ now they're in the thick of
affairs (cf. tsakạ).
　　B. (tsạkạ-tsạkạ) (1) adv. half-way x
yanạ ∼ dạ aikịnsạ he's half-way through
his work (epithet is Tsạkạ-tsạkạ ạljannạr kạrē). (2) adj. of medium size x
wani ∼ a medium-sized one (= matsạ-
kạicī).
tsạkạtsakī = tsạkạ-tsakạ 1.
tsaki A. (tsạkī) (1) Vd. tsạ̄kō. (2) (a)
the noise pf, q.v., which one makes
contemptuously. (b) mại gōnā bạri ∼
m. useless stunted corn.

　　B. (tsạkī) Kt. m. (1) x yā yi minị ∼
it pleased me (= dādī). (2) (negatively)
sunạ naŋ bābụ ∼ they are innumerable.
　　C. (tsạkī) m. (1) (a) (i) the coarse
part of ground-flour (cf. fantsạrā, barzạ).
(ii) Vd. rūdạ 1c. (b) (i) ạ dụbi rūwā, ạ
dụbi ∼ all is not gold that glitters.
(ii) Vd. rūwā G. 3. (2) the solid part of
well-fried butter. (3) tsạkin tābạ the
unpoundable part of tobacco-leaves.
(4) tsạkin dọrōwạ the hard lumps in
locust-bean pulp (= Kt. tsạgarọ). (5)
dọ̄dan ∼ Vd. ạlmājịrī.
tsakiya A. (tsakīyạ) f. (1) centre (=
tsakạ). (2) ∼ tasạ tā gạmu he is
replete.
　　B. (tsạkīyạ) f. (1) orange-cornelian.
(2) agate.
tsạ̄kō m. (f. tsạkwā) pl. tsạkī = tsịyạkī
(1) (a) chick (= dan ∼, f. 'yar ∼,
pl. 'yan tsạkī). (b) fwăi mā yā yi
wạyō ballē dan tsạkọ? you don't
catch me napping like that ! (c) dan
tsạkwan jiminā, gāgạrạ shāfọ daukạ
it's beyond one. (d) kōmē yakẹ cikin
dan ∼ shāfọ yā dadẹ dạ saninsạ
teaching one's grandmother to suck
eggs. (e) sāmụn ạbincin dan ∼ bạ
sāmụn kẹ dạ wụyā ba wurin cị it's
easy to get but where can it be kept ?
(f) 'yan tsạkī sụ bī nị Vd. tsābạ 1c.
(2) tsạkī pl. (a) seedlings of peppers,
tobacco, gạutā, etc. (b) Kt. = haŋkākạ
4. (c) kāmụn 'yan tsạkī m. novice's
overturning top with thumb and first
finger of both hands. (d) an yi wạ
gyạdā 'yan tsạkī after hoeing, arranging
ground-nuts in small piles for five
days, to dry (cf. kāshin tūjẹ).
tsākụrā = tsākạrā.
tsākụrī m. acting as in tsākạrạ.
tsakuwa A. (tsakūwạ) f. (pl. tsakūwōyī =
tsakwạŋkwanī = tsakwạikwai) (1)
gravel. (2) ∼ dayạ bā tạ dạbẹ one
swallow doesn't make summer. (3)
ạ taunạ ∼ doŋ ayā tạ ji tsọrō the fate
of one serves as a deterrent to another.
(4) yā sạ minị ∼ cikin zạncaŋ " he
queered my pitch " (hạrbā 1e). (5)
ya ci ∼ Vd. zạkarạ 2. (6) ma'aunin
∼ Vd. next entry.

B. (Tsakūwạ) (1) *town in Kano Province*. (2) **Dạsharē ma'aunin** ～ (*a*) what a dirty person ! (*b*) what a laughter-loving P. !

C. (**tsạkwā**) *Vd.* **tsạkō**.

tsala A. (**tsālā**) *f.* = **wạinā**.

B. (**tsālạ**) (1) *Vb.* 1C did much of *x* **an** ～ **masạ būlālạ** he has been well whipped. **an** ～ **mại cikiŋ ạbincī** much butter, oil has been added to the food. **an** ～ **wạ rịgā d'iŋkị** the gown has much embroidery (= **tsalạlā**). (2) *Vb.* 3A **darē yạ́** ～ it is round midnight (*cf.* **talạtainị**).

C. (**tsalạ**) *m.* trousers lacking usual large crutchpiece (**hantsạ**).

tsạlāgumī = **tsạŋgālumī**.

tsalak = **tsilak**.

tsalala A. (**tsạ̄lālạ**) *m.* (1) bride's white cloth *x* **amaryā tā d'aurạ** ～ the bride put on her white cloth (= *Sk.* **farạnjī**). (2) **yā d'aurạ d'an** ～ he put on a small, worn-out loincloth (= **munụtsī**). (3) rags worn round loins when washing clothes or crossing stream.

B. (**tsalạ̄lā**) (1) *Vb.* 1A = **tsālạ** 1. (2) *Vb.* 3A took to one's heels.

tsạlạllẹ̄kū *m.* throwing or shooting upwards (= *Kt.* **cạlillindọ** = *Sk.* **cịccịndō**).

tsalam (1) (*a*) **bạ̄** ～ **bạ̄ tsạmē** = **sīdīdī**. (*b*) **nā ga** ～, **nā ga tsạmē** (*said by women*) = **aras** 3. (2) suddenly *x* **tsalam ya yi tuntub̃ẹ dạ wata kalmạ** suddenly he made a slip over a word. (3) ～ **na dātsạ** *m.* well-dressed but stingy P.

tsalam-tsạlạm = **tsalā-tsạlạ̄**.

*tsạlạ̄mụsai *Ar.* *m.* type of written talisman.

tsalā-tsạlạ̄ *pl. adj.* *x* **tanạ̄ dạ k̃ak̃ạ̄fū** ～ she has slender legs.

tsālẹ̄lẹ *m.* (*f.* **tsālẹ̄lịyā**) handsome.

tsallạcē *Vb.* 1C (1) jumped over. (2) escaped (trap in speech laid for one).

tsallạkā *Vb.* 1C (1) hopped along. (2) jumped on to *x* **yā** ～ **mōtạ** he jumped on to the car.

tsallạkē = **tsallạcē**.

tsallambad'akē *m.* **yanạ̄ shạn** ～ he's having trouble, difficulty.

tsallē *m.* (1) (*a*) jumping. (*b*) **yā dakō** (= **yi**) ～ he jumped. (*c*) **Bạrēwạ̄ yi**

tsallaŋkị lāfīyạ he can now enjo; life for that particular anxiety is ovei (*d*) tsallan burgū (i) type of femal dance. (ii) gaining no advantage fror an act. (2) making omission in copy ing (*cf.* k̃ẹ̄tarạ 2). (3) *x* **sặi** ～ **suk sụ sāmụ** they're on tenterhooks t get it. (4) **yā yi tsallan sharī'ạ** h appealed to higher court. (5) *Kt.* = tsallị. (6) **yaŋkan** ～ *Vd.* **yaŋkā** 2g.

tsạl'le-tsạllē" *m.* (1) continual jumping. (2 *x* **munạ̄** ～ **mụ yī** we're eager to do it.

tsalli *m.* (1) (half an **ashạ̄līyạ**), i.e. ai eighth of a two-segmented kola-nu (*Vd.* **azạrā**). (2) ～ **jạm** greeting (*P. so greeted is expected to hand on some kola-nut.*)

tsalmạ = **tsarmạ**.

tsạlọ̄-tsalō = **d'alọ̄-d'alō**.

tsam (1) **yā tāshi** ～ he suddenly stood up departed (= **tsọ̄yam**). (2) **bạ̄ lam bị** ～ = **sīdīdī**. (3) *Vd.* **tạshi** ～.

tsạ̄mā *Vb.* 2 = **tsāmẹ**.

tsāmạikū *Vd.* **tsāmīyā**.

tsāmạmā *Vb.* 1C rendered sour (*Vd* **tsāmī**).

tsāmārī *m.* **yā yi** ～ (1) the affair becamẹ serious (= **gạ̄wurtạ** 2*b*). (2) it (wealth etc.) became abundant (= **gạ̄wurtạ** 1*a*)

tsạmbā *Kt.* = **d'ambā**.

tsambạlā *Kt.* = **tsambạmā**.

tsạmbam abundantly *x* **k̃asā tā cịka** ～ the place is thickly populated. sui **cik̃ạ k̃asā** ～ they thickly fill thẹ country.

tsambạmā *Vb.* 1C did much of *x* **an** ～ **wạ tak̃ạrdā rụbūtū** writing is crowdec on the paper. **an** ～ **masạ kudī** he ha: been overcharged (= **tsālạ** 1).

tsạmbạrē *m.* (1) abundance *x* **sunạ̄** ～ they're abundant. (2) scamped weedinẹ (= *Kt.* **cirōkōkō**).

tsạmburụmburụm = **tsụmburụmburụm**.

tsame A. (**tsāmẹ**) (1) *Vb.* 1A (*a*) picked T. P. (out of liquid, crowd, etc.) *x* (i) **yā** ～ **ịtālīyạ dạgạ cikin yāk̃ị** he removeḍ Italy out of the war. (ii) **an tsāmẹ hannunsụ dạgạ cikiŋ wannạŋ rōmọ** they were deprived of that advantage. (iii) **sun tsāmẹ su dạ hạrsāshị** they (riflemen) picked them (enemy) off. (*b*) **kā** ～ *m.* a soupstuff made from seeds

of baobob (kūkạ). (2) *Vb.* 3A kept
aloof, separated oneself.

B. (tsạmē) *m.* (1) tā yi masạ ∼
she took out a little of the food cooking
on the fire and gave it to him (fretful
child). (2) *Vd.* tsalam 1.

:samfạ *Vb.* 1A did (task) well.

:samfềfẹ *m.* (*f.* tsamfềฤyā) handsome.

:samfị how well done !

:sāmī *m.* (1) (*a*) sourness (= yāmī). (*b*)
rūwā bā yạ ∼ banzā nobody acts
without good reason. (*c*) kaŋwā tā
kas ∼, kwạnnạfī yā fādạ the matter
is settled. (*d*) zamansụ yā sōmạ ∼
they're no longer on such good terms.
(*e*) tsāmiŋ gwaurō gruel made from sour
flour. (*f*) tsāmin nōnọ unhealthy sourness of milk from (i) standing three
days (i.e. longer than would cause
barcī) or from (ii) being adulterated
(gamị) for selling it. (*g*) tsāmin nōnọ
= fadandẹ. (*h*) = tuburā 1. (*j*) har
tā yi ∼ *Vd.* kō tā kwānā ? (*k*) kā ƙi
∼ *Vd.* dakạn jīyạ. (2) (*a*) (i) soreness
(from work, receiving beating, etc.) (=
yāmī). (ii) *Vd.* yāmī. (*b*) ƙafāta tā yi ∼
my foot has gone to sleep. (*c*) tsāmim
bākī inability to say " r " and so saying
" y ". (3) newly-prepared indigo ready
for use. (4) barạm maị ∼ the servant
of a rich P. (5) (*a*) stench (= wārī 1).
(*b*) in tā yi ∼ mā ji if the matter comes
to anything, we'll hear about it (=
wārī 3). (6) *Vd.* jājibḝrẹ 2.

tsāmīyā *f.* (*pl.* tsạmaịkū = tsāmīyōyī) (1)
(*a*) tamarind tree or fruit (*Vd.* saŋkḝdā
3 ; gwaggọ 1*b* ; dạngarẹzā ; ƙarmō). (*b*)
∼ tā jūyẹ dạ mūjīyā hoist with one's
own petard. (*c*) ụŋgụlū tā kōmạ gidantạ
na ∼ what's bred in the bone comes
out in the flesh. (*d*) in zā kạ yi līlọ,
kạ yi ạ ∼ ; iŋ kā kāmạ tāwatsā,
tā karyẹ don't lean on a broken reed !
(*e*) dōṛōwạ a kạn yi wạ dōkā. ∼ kōwā
ya dībạ, tāsạ cē the law only occupies
itself with important things. (*f*)
kōwā ya zubar minị dạ tsāmīyāta,
sāi ụ zubar masạ dạ nōnạnsạ I'll not be
outdone in repaying people in their
own coin ! (*ff*) sāi dāi wani jiƙọ, ƙarē
yā zubad dạ tsāmīyar kūrā that's the end
of the matter for the present. (*g*)

tsāmīyar mahạrbā = tsāmīyar makīyạyā
the weed *Nelsonia campestris*. (*h*)
gīwā tạ ci tsāmīyạ ? *Vd.* gīwā 1*b*.
(*j*) ganyan ∼ *Vd.* ganyē 6. (2) white
silk from the worms which feed on
tamarind (*cf.* fakālẹ). (3) (*a*) striped
imported cotton goods. (*b*) a native
material in which the threads are of
white silk (2 *above*) alternating with
threads dyed (tirị) brown, in imitation
of 3*a above*. (4) tsāmīyar karōfī =
Kt. tsāmīyar marinā blue embroidery
on black gown, obtained by embroidering dyed gown and then re-dipping
(tsōmạ) at once. (5) tsāmīyar madị =
lāhirạ.

tsamkạ = tsaŋkạ.

tsammace A. (tsammācē) *x* bạn ∼ masạ
hakạ ba I did not expect him to behave
like that.

B. (tsạmmācē) *Vd.* tsạmmātạ.

tsạmmāci *Vd.* tsạmmātạ.

tsạmmānị = tsạmmānī *m.* (1) (*a*) thinking, thought *x* nā yi (= nā sā) ∼
zā sụ zō = nā yi ∼ wai zā sụ zō I
thought they would come. n nā ∼
yā yi hakạ I think it is so. (2) yā yi
tsạmmānịm banzā he had idle hopes.
(3) tsạmmānịŋ warạbukkạ *Vd.* warạbukkạ. (4) kadạ kạ yi tsạmmānịŋ
ạlhērị indạ bạ kạ ga fuskạ ba don't
expect goodness from a hangdog-
looking person ! (5) (*a*) nā fid dạ ∼,
bạ zaị zō ba = nā fid dạ tsạmmānịn
zūwạnsạ I've given up all idea of his
coming (= dḝbẹ 2). (*b*) fid dạ gwaurō ∼
Vd. gwaurō 1*c*. (6) opinion *x* ạ tsạm-
mānịna in my opinion. (7) bạ zạtō,
bạ ∼ sāi sukạ zō they arrived unexpectedly. (8) *Vd.* ụŋgụlū 5, rụmbū 4.

tsạmmātạ *Vb.* 2 (*p.o.* tsạmmācē, *n.o.*
tsạmmāci) thought that *x* nā tsạmmāci ạl'amạrī hakạ I imagined things
would be as they actually are. nā
tsạmmāci zaị zō I thought he'd come.

tsammātō *Vb.* 1E = tsạmmātạ.

tsạmnū = tsạrnū.

tsạmōdagī *Kt. m.* = cābụlā 2.

tsạmōฤyā *f.* roving about (= gīlọ).

tsamō-tsạmō *m.* (1) = tsurū-tsụrū. (2)
m. and adv. yā yi ∼ he is wet through.
yā zō ∼ he arrived wet through.

tsạmtsamtạ *Kt.* = tsạntsantạ.

tsamuka A. (tsạ̄mukạ) = mụntsunạ.
B. (tsāmụkā) = tsaŋkạ.

tsana A. (tsạnā) *Vb.* 2 (1) dipped out water from almost empty pot, well, water-hole, etc. (2) carped at P.
B. (tsanā) *f.* (1) = zụŋgụrū. (2) 'yar ∼ *f.* doll (= ƙashī 9*b*).

tsạnākī *x* an yī shị ạ ∼ it has been carefully done.

tsạnancē *Vd.* tsạnantạ.

tsananī *m.* (1) (*a*) great degree of *x* tsananin yuŋwạ great hunger, severe famine. tsananin sọ̄ great affection. suŋ gạmu dạ ∼ they suffered famine. yā jāwō tsananiŋ ạbincī it has caused famine. (*b*) kōmē tsananin tạ̄rā, ạ̄ bar wạ ɗam maị gidā kạrē no smoke without fire ; patience wins = kōmē tsananin jīfạ, ƙasạ yakẹ̄ fādụ̄wā. (*c*) tsananin nēmā bā yạ̄ kāwō sāmụ effort does not always succeed. (*d*) kōmē tsananin darē, gạrī zaị wāyẹ every cloud has a silver lining. (2) ∼ gạrēshị he is cruel, oppressive. yanạ̄ cikin ∼ he's poor. (4) ∼ gạrēshị he's niggardly. (5) kạ ɗaurẹ shi dạ ∼ tie it tightly ! ɗạmarạ tā yi tsananī the belt is too tight.

tsananta A. (tsanạntā) *Vb.* 1C (1) yā ∼ shi = yā ∼ cikinsạ he made a fuss about this. (2) (*with dative*) *x* yā ∼ minị he harassed me (= tsaw-wạlā).
B. (tsạnantạ) (1) *Vb.* 2 (*p.o.* tsạnạncē, *n.o.* tsạnạncī) harassed *x* yā tsạnạncē nị = tsanạntā 2. (2) *Vb.* 3B became severe yā yāƙị yā ∼ the combat became severe (= gāwurtạ). iŋ wata bukātạ tā ∼ if a wish is keenly felt (= tsạw-wạlạ).

tsandạ *Sk. f.* = tsantsanī.

tsandạm = tsindụm.

tsandaurī *m.* (1) (*a*) barren place (= faƙọ). (*b*) bā ạ̄ yịn nitsọ ạ ∼ don't knock your head against a stone ! (*c*) *Vd.* nitsọ 4*a*. (2) stingy P.

tsando A. (tsandō) *m.* (*sg., pl.*) (1) tsetse-fly (= ạwụrū). (2) lāfīyạr ūwar ∼ gạrēshị he's a hypocrite.
B. (tsandọ) *m.* (*sg., pl.*) = fịti-fịti.

tsane A. (tsanẹ) (1) *Vb.* 1A dipped out (*as in* tsạnā) all of. (2) *Vb.* 3A (river, waterhole, etc.) dried up.
B. (tsạnē) *m.* dipping out *as in* tsạnā.

tsạŋgālumī *m.* (*f.* tsạŋgāluṃā) *pl.* tsạŋ-gālụmai (1) destitute P. (2) (*a*) tall P. with clothes too short. (*b*) tall camel or ostrich (*because lower parts bare*).

tsạŋgayạ = *Kt.* tsạŋgayā *f.* (*pl.* tsạŋgayū) (1) cornstalk-hut daubed with clay inside = kafị 1 (*Vd.* kurtạ, yaŋkẹ 1*c*.iv). (2) *Kt.* = daŋgā.

tsạŋgwamạ *Vb.* 2 ill-treated.

tsani A. (tsānị) *m.* (*pl.* tsānunukạ) (1) (*a*) ladder (= *Zar.* ạkwā), *cf.* kụraŋgạ. (*b*) wạ̄ zaị bā shị tsānị *Vd.* rēshẹ 2. (2) (*a*) patron (= ƙōfạ 3 = tafarkị). (*b*) bā ạ̄ hawā samạ sại dạ ∼ to get on one requires a powerful patron.
B. (tsanị) *Kt. m.* skinflint.

tsaŋkạ *Vb.* 3A *x* cikịna yanạ̄ tsaŋkạ̄wā I have stomach spasms (= tsāmụkā).

tsạŋkē *m.* (1) securing gōyō-child on one's back with only one cloth. (2) being insufficient.

tsạŋkī *m.* (1) stomach-spasm. (2) (*a*) pinching. (*b*) dạ ∼ cikim fadạ (*said to third P. when one has received paltry gift*) well, I suppose something *is* better than nothing ?

tsạnnū = tsạrnū.

tsantsā *m., f.* = zallā 2 *x* zīnārịyā ∼ = zīnārịyā ∼ tatạ = zīnārịyā tsantsantạ pure gold.

tsantsalā *Vb.* 3A yā ∼ dạ gudu he took to his heels.

tsantsāmā (1) *f.* milk and furā gone sour through being left standing (*cf.* tsāmī 1*f*). (2) *m.* (*a*) = fadandẹ. (*b*) = ɗạ̄māɗanyē. (*c*) thin P.

tsantsamcē *Vd.* tsạntsamtạ.

tsantsamē *Vb.* 1C washed lightly.

tsạntsamī *m.* (1) quarrelling. (2) distrust.

tsạntsamtạ *Vb.* 2 (*p.o.* tsạntsamcē, *n.o.* tsạntsamcī) distrusted (*cf.* tsạn-tsạŋ).

tsan-tsaŋ A. (tsan-tsaŋ) (1) yā ɗauru ∼ it is firmly tied. (2) yi tạ̄kā ∼ dūnịyạ always act cautiously !
B. (tsạn-tsạŋ) *x* haŋkạlīna yā yi ∼ dạ shị I distrust him.

ṣantsạndö *Vd.* ạlkalạmī.

tsantsanī = tsạntsạnī = tsạntsạnī *m.*
(1) (*a*) fastidiousness. (*b*) aversion (= ḳyạ̄mạ̄). (2) scrupulous conduct. (3) eking out T. (= cạncạnē).

ṣạntsạntạ *Vb.* 3B *x* yạ̄ ~ dạ shī he feels an aversion from it.

ṣantsēnī = tsantsanī.

tsānunukạ *Vd.* tsānị.

tsạŋwā (1) *used in* ~ shar = algạshī 1. (2) tsạŋwa-tsạŋwa bright greenish (= ḳụmallö 5).

tsạŋwākạ *f.* Senegal Roller (*Coracias abyssinica*).

tsanyạ *f.* (*pl.* tsanyöyī) (1) (*a*) cricket (= gyạ̄rē). (*b*) an töshẹ (= an dakẹ) bạ̄kin ~ the matter is settled. (*c*) ḳạramar ~ dạ wurī ta kạm fārạ haḳạ a stitch in time saves nine. (*d*) gurgụ̄war ~ dạ wurī ta kạn sömạ tịlā don't leave things till the last minute ! (2) *Kt.* = gwalalö. (3) tsanyạr fataucị an insect destroying clothes (= dạ̄kạ̄rẹ 3).

tsạnyē *Vb.* 3A began to dry (= tsagẹ 1).

tsaptạ = tsabtạ.

tsar (1) *m. and adv.* being nicely tinged *x* zanẹ yā dạuki zạrgīnạ ~ the gown is nicely tinged with washing-blue. rị̄gā tā yi ~ dạ shūnī the gown is nicely tinged by being worn next to indigo-dyed one. (2) (rustic) indeed *x* kai ~ haḳạ kakẹ̄ yị̄ ? is *that* how you act indeed ? (3) *Vb.* (*used before dative, only in this form*) yā ~ masạ he surpassed him (= tsērẹ).

tsara A. (tsārạ) *Vb.* 1A (1) arranged, aligned (= jērạ). (2) (*a*) composed (song). (*b*) edited (newspaper). (3) (woman) arranged (hair). (4) totted up. (5) *Vd.* tsạ̄rạncē.
B. (tsārā) (1) *m., f.* (*pl.* tsạ̄rạrrakī = tsārörī = tsārạirai = tsạ̄rẹ̄kū) (1) (*a*) one's equal. (*b*) rūwā bạ̄ tsāraŋ kwạndö ba nẹ̄ oil and water won't mix. (*c*) ~ tạ̄ka, kị shā mārị trailing tail (jẹ̄lā) of woman's cloth. (2) *m.* = gạjērē 2. (3) *f.* type of wild cat. (4) *Vd.* ḳạ̄ḳạ 1*f.*
C. (tsarā) *f.* middle of back from neck to coccyx.
D. (tsạrā) *Vb.* 2 *used in* (1) Allạ̄ yạ tsạrē nị dạ shī God preserve me

from it ! (2) Allạ̄ yạ tsạri gạtarī dạ nömā = Allạ̄ yạ tsạri gạtarī dạ sāran shūkạ what have we in common ! (*cf.* tsarẹ). (3) *Vd.* dạ̄ 1*b.*i.

tsạrabạ *f.* present given by P. recently returned from journey (especially to the one who gave him gụzurī previously).

tsarad dạ = tsar dạ 2.

tsārạirai *Vd.* tsārā.

tsaraka A. (tsạ̄rakā) *f.* (1) charm to ensure successful trading. (2) sụ̄ bābụ ~ wạhalạ nē one cannot make bricks without straw. (3) bạ̄ ~ gạ shāfọ, kai dại ạ yi jịmirin shạ̄wāgị nothing is obtained without effort.
B. (tsạ̄rakạ) *Kt. f.* being on one's guard (= jinī 7*a*).

tsạ̄rạ kạ cị̄ *Vd.* tsạ̄rạncē.

tsạ̄rạncē *m.* (1) (*a*) the custom whereby a girl (*Vd.* bụdurwā 3) is permitted mutual masturbation with a boy (*Vd.* saurạyī) whom she is not to marry, provided actual connection does not occur (*but as the latter usually occurs, its epithet is* Tsạ̄rạncē yā zamā tsạ̄rạ kạ cị̄ = Tsạ̄rạncē mạ̄dākin zịnā), *cf.* tsạ̄rạncī; guhị, zụbētā 2. (*b*) tsạ̄rạncan dökị = tsạ̄rạncī. (2) (*Damagaram*) fornication between adults.

tsạ̄rạncī *m.* fornication between young people (*cf.* tsạ̄rạncē).

tsararīyā = tsararrīyā.

tsararö *m.* (1) (*a*) kā yi minị ~ it's not worth my while arguing with a nincompoop like you ! (*b*) tā yi masạ " kā yi kạdaŋ kā yi ~ " she insulted him (boy). (2) sun yi ~ they've become less. (3) *x* furā tā yi ~ the furā is sloppy (= rūwā L.1).

tsārạrrakī *Vd.* tsārā.

tsararrīyā *f.* (1) type of brownish bean (= cērērīyā). (2) uncookable type of 1 called ịnā akẹ̄ dịmị (2 = rūwā B.5*a* = *Kt.* ḳuḳus 2).

tsạraurạ *Kt.* = tsạwarwarạ.

tsarau-tsarau *Kt.* = sarau-sarau.

tsarce A. (tsarcẹ) defiled (place) by spitting.
B. (tsạrcē) (1) *m.* sowing without waste of seed. (2) *Vd.* tsạrtā.

tsạrci *Vd.* tsạrtā.

tsar da *Vb.* 4 (1) = tsartạ. (2) rescued, saved *x* Allạ yạ ∼ mū = Allạ yạ tsarshē mụ may God preserve us ! (= tsīrad dạ).

tsare A. (tsārẹ) arranged (*as in* tsārạ) completely.

B. (tsarẹ) *Vb.* 1A (1) (*a*) (i) guarded P. or T. (ii) suŋ kāmẹ, sun tsarẹ gidā they sat arrogantly aloof. (iii) suŋ kasạ, sun tsarẹ they're waiting ready for action. (*b*) guarded P. or T. against *x* (i) Allạ yạ tsarẹ mu fadạ dạ sū God preserve us from an encounter with them ! yanạ tsarẹ su dạgạ Jāmụs he's protecting them from the Germans. (ii) Allạ yạ ∼ mu dạ "dạ nā sani" *Vd.* dạ 1*b.* (*bb*) was on one's guard against *x* (i) ạbin dạ na ∼ kẹ naŋ it is the very thing against which I am on my guard. (ii) tsạre dạ idọ, kạ ganī remain alert and you'll see ! (*c*) yā ∼ ƙuryạ, yā ∼ bạkiŋ gadō = yā ∼ naŋ, yā ∼ naŋ his knowledge is encyclopædic. (2) imprisoned. (3) = tarẹ 1*a x* sun tsarẹ gạban Jāmus they resisted the Germans. an tsarẹ hanyạ the road is blocked. mun tsarẹ masạ gạbā gạ cikạ gūri̠nsạ we obstructed him in carrying out his will (*Vd.* tarẹ 1*a*). (4) *cf.* tsạrā.

tsạrēkū *Vd.* tsārā.

tsạrē-tsarē *m.* preventing realization of plan (*Vd.* tsarẹ 3).

tsarga A. (tsạrgā) *Vb.* 2 showed hostility to.

*B. (tsargạ) *Vb.* 1A *Sk.* = tsartạ.

tsargẹ *Vb.* 1A slit.

tsạrgī *m.* (1) fear. (2) *Sk.* = tsartūwā.

tsari A. (tsāri̠) (1) (*a*) arranging, aligning. (*b*) being arranged *x* bại yi kyạn ∼ ba it is not well arranged. (*c*) good arrangement wannạn rīgā ∼ gạrētạ this gown is well made. bạ sụ mōtsạ wani ạbụ ạ tsārin zamansụ ba no change was made in their organization. (2) loquacity. (3) = tsārī. (4) *Sk.* thatching-grass ready for use.

B. (tsārī) *m.* (1) hole under claybed for fire. (2) *Vd.* tsārīyā.

C. (tsạrī) *m.* (1) (*a*) (i) water in which pounded grain has been washed

(= *Kt.* ƙạsarī 2*b*), *cf.* tsạgwarọ. (ii) *Vd.* bụnsurū 5. (*b*) tsạriŋ kalwā bạ ka mammōrā how useless ! (*cf.* mammōrā 2). (*c*) *Sk.* yā īyạ rūwan ∼ he can swim overhand (= jẹfē 2). (2) hatsin ∼ (*a*) bulrush-millet which after removal of bran is fermented and dried. (*b*) mixed crowd. (3) = guzạ 1.

D. (tsari̠) *m.* (1) guarding (= tsarō). (2) (*a*) shutting in, imprisoning. (*b*) wurin ∼ *m.* enclosed place. (*c*) mātan ∼ women in purdah. (3) prohibition *x* an yi ∼ kadạ ạ ci ạladẹ the eating of pig is forbidden.

*tsạrīkạ = tsạrīƙạ *Ar.* *f.* sect.

tsạrīki̠ *m.* (*f.* tsạrīkīyā) *pl.* tsạrīkai rogue (= shạkīyi̠).

tsārīyā *f.* (1) hole under clay-bed for fire (= tsārī). (2) ∼ bạ mafōyā ba cẹ there's no way of evading justice.

tsarkaka A. (tsarkạkā) *Vd.* tsạttsarkā.

B. (tsarkạkā) *Vb.* 1C (1) cleansed. (2) yā ∼ shi he " whitewashed " him.

C. (tsạrkakạ) *Vb.* 3B became clean.

tsarkạkē *Vb.* 1C = tsarkạkā.

tsarkī *m.* (1) cleanness. (2) ceremonial cleanness in Islam. (3) *Vd.* waŋkan ∼.

tsarkīyā = tsirkīyā.

tsarmạ *Vb.* 1A tā ∼ mīyạ she over-diluted the mīyạ for sale.

tsạrmạkạtai = *Kt.* tsạrmạkai *pl.* apprehensiveness (*Vd.* tsọrō).

tsarmi̠ *m.* (1) over-dilution *as in* tsarmạ. (2) (*a*) alien P. in a company. (*b*) alien substance (*x* adulteration, *i.e.* gami̠) in a mixture.

tsạrnū *m.* (*sg.*, *pl.*) slender post for fencing (= sabarbadẹ = kạrạbkī 1), *cf.* sạmạrī 3*a*.

tsarō = tsạrō *m.* (1) = tsari̠ 1, 2*a*. (2) tsạraŋ ƙōfạ drumming at house of senior wife (ūwar gidā) to divert her from arrival of new bride (= dạnnā 4 = tạusā 2*b*).

tsarōkī *Vd.* tsirkīyā.

tsārōrī *Vd.* tsārā.

tsarsad dạ *Vb.* 4 *Kt.* = tsar dạ 2.

tsarshē *Vd.* tsar dạ 2.

tsarta A. (tsartạ) *Vb.* 1A (1) *x* (*a*) yā ∼ yau he expectorated saliva. (*b*) yā tsirtad dạ yau he foamed with rage. (2) sowed sparsely.

B. (tsạrtā) *Vb.* 2 (*p.o.* tsạrcē, *n.o.*
tsạrci) *Kt.* feared.
tsartad dạ *Vb.* 4 = tsartạ 1.
tsartam = tartsam.
tsartar dạ = tsartạ 1.
tsạr-tsạr = sạr-sạr 2, 3.
tsartūwā *f.* (1) expectorating. (2) tsar-
tūwar macịjī (*a*) cobra's spittle. (*b*) =
macịjī 12.
tsatata *Kt.* = tsagaga.
tsātsạ *f.* (1) rust. (2) hạnạ burā ~
nymphomaniac (= tạbarmā wuyā).
tsạtsạnīyā *f.* quarrelling (= fadạ).
tsātsạntā = tsātsạtā.
tsạtsạ rūwā *f.* the earliest-ripening cotton
(= *Kt.* shạ rūwā).
tsātsạtā *Vb.* 3A (1) quarrelled. (2) *Kt.*
(storm) abated.
tsatse A. (tsạtsē) *m.* (1) (*a*) new grass.
(*b*) sun tạfi cịn ~ (i) cattle have gone
grazing on the new grass. (ii) people
have gone cadging in villages in dry
season. (2) yā kāmạ ~ he's beginning
to regain prosperity.
     B. (tsātsẹ) *Vb.* 3A togged oneself up.
tsatso A. (tsạtsọ) *m.* (1) earwig. (2) ~
mại kāshī ạ karā poọr man (= talạkạ).
     B. (tsatsọ) *m.* lumbar region, loins
(= kwạŋkwasọ).
tsattsafā *f.* (1) thin wheat-cakes eaten
with honey. (2) = tsattsafī.
tsattsafi A. (tsattsafī) *m.* (1) (*a*) drizzle
(= yayyafī). (*b*) nā yi gudụn ~, nā
shịga mạmākọ out of the frying-pan
into the fire. (*c*) dạ ~ kōgī kạn cịka
many a mickle makes a muckle. (2)
(*Katagum*) = būbụ 1.
     B. (tsạttsạfī) *m.* toy-flute made from
onion-stem.
tsattsafō *Vb.* 3A (water of spring, etc.)
welled up *x* gụmī yā ~ minị I broke out
in sweat (= 6ụ66ugạ).
tsattsaga A. (tsattsạgā) *Vb.* 1C. (1) =
cạccakạ 1. (2) tapped ground with bit of
dry grass (tsịŋkē) in vexation. (3)
an tsattsạgạ gịndịŋ hakōrī gums have
been separated from root of tooth for
extraction.
     B. (tsạttsaga) (1) *Vb.* 2 (*a*) kept
pecking at. (*b*) jeered at. (2) *Vb.* 3B
intensive from tsạga.
tsattsage A. (tsattsạgē) *Vb.* 1C. (1) rammed

earth, etc. (*as in* tsattsạgā) completely.
(2) yā tsattsạgẹ cikịnsạ he ate to repletion. yā tsattsạgẹ bạkinsạ dạ gōrọ
he filled his mouth with kola-nut. (3)
yā tsattsạgẹ dāsạshī dạ tsiŋkē he picked
at his gums with bit of dry grass to cure
itch (kaikayī), *cf.* sạkatạ 3.
     B. (tsạttsạgē) *m.* (1) acting *as in*
tsattsạgā 2. (2) single tobacco-flour
(furē).
tsattsạgī *m.* the shrub *Bauhinia rufescens*
(= matsattsāgī = ạlkāwạrī 4).
tsạttsakī *m.* the very centre (= tsakạ 1*c*).
tsattsạlā *Vb.* 1C yā ~ dạ gudụ he took to
his heels.
tsạttsạrcī *Kt. m.* being on one's guard.
tsattsạrē (1) *Vb.* 3A = kyaŋkyēnē. (2)
Vb. 1C *intensive from* tsarẹ.
tsạttsarkā *m.*, *f.* (*pl.* tsarkākā) clean,
pure (*d.f.* tsarkī).
tsạttsaurā *m.*, *f.* (*pl.* tsaurārā) (1) stunted.
(2) niggardly. (3) brave (*d.f.* tsaurī
q.v.).
tsạttsēwạ *f.* (1) (*a*) any Swift (especially
Micropus affinis abyssinicus and *Col-
letoptera affinis gallijensis*). (*b*) Senegal
Swallow (*Hirundo s. senegalensis*). (2)
type of infection of vulva in women and
mares.
tsạttsēwạlā = tsạttsēwạ 1.
tsạtsubạ *f.* (1) = dabọ 1*a*. (2) tsạtsubạr
dāki the small calabashes and odds and
ends in a home.
tsattūwā = tsartūwā.
tsaucē *Vb.* 1C (*with dative*) (1) *x* yā ~ masạ
he scolded him. (2) *x* an ~ manạ mụ
kulạ dạ aikịmmụ we've been admonished to attend to our work (1,
2 = tsāwạtā = tsāwatar).
tsaunạ *Vb.* 1A *Kt.* piled up (= tilạ).
tsauni *m.* (*pl.* tsaunukạ = tsaununnukạ =
tsaunōnī). (1) hill, hillock. (2) *Kt.*
pile (= tārị 1*a.*i).
tsaurakē *Kt.* = tsaurạrē.
tsaurara A. (tsaurārā) *Vd.* tsạttsaurā.
     B. (tsaurạrā) *Vb.* 1C (1) pulled (bow,
rope) taut. (2) tsạurạrạ jịkiŋkạ pluck
up courage !
tsaurạrē *Vb.* 3A (1) (P., plant, animal)
remained stunted. (2) (*a*) (soil) became
stiff. (*b*) (vegetable, etc., *x* tsararrīyā)
failed to become soft when cooked. (3)

became stingy. **(4) idansa yā** ～ he cannot sleep.

tsaurē *m.* **(1)** a tall, coarse grass. **(2) hayin** ～ *m.* seam where cloth is several-fold.

tsaurī *m.* **(1)** native steel (*used for razors, so epithet is* **Tsaurī ƙarfan askā**). **(2)** being stunted *x* **yāran nan yā yi** ～ this lad's stunted. **(3)** (*a*) (i) **ƙasan nan tā yi** ～ this soil is stiff (= **taurī**). (ii) **ga tsaurin da ya tāka** he is in a strong position. (*b*) niggardliness. (*c*) **yā yi tsaurī a ƙasūwā** it (commodity) is hard to obtain. **(4) ƙafwan** ～ = **ƙafwan taurī** *q.v. under* **taurī** 2*c*. **(5)** (*a*) **zarē yā yi** ～ the thread is too tightly spun (= *Kt.* **ƙaurī 3**). (*b*) **an ɗaurę shi da** ～ it (rope) is tightly tied. (*c*) **yā ji tsauri-tsauri** the rope was normally tight so he noticed nothing amiss. **(6) tsaurin idọ** (*a*) insolence (= **tsīwa**). (*b*) **yā yi mini tsaurin idọ** he resisted my authority. (*c*) **abōkan gāba sun tsaya, sunā yi mana tsaurin idọ** the enemy are offering us fierce resistance. **(7) tsaurin kǎi** = **taurī 1***c*.

tsautā *Vb.* 1C = **tsaucē**.

tsautsauniyā *Kt. f.* fidgetiness (= **gaja zamā**).

tsautsayī *m.* **(1)** (*a*) accident involving physical injury or financial loss (*cf.* **hasāra**). in **tsautsayī yā rātsa** if an accident occurs. (*b*) ～ **yā kai ni, an yi mini sāta** I had the ill luck to be robbed. **(2)** ～ **bā yā shigę rānā tasa** every bullet finds its billet.

tsauyā = **tsaiwā**.

tsawa A. **(tsāwā)** *f.* **(1)** (*a*) thunder-clap. (*b*) cracking of new pots. **(2)** (*a*) scolding. (*b*) **yā daka mini** ～ = **yā buga mini** ～ = *Kt.* **yā dira mini** ～ he scolded me (*Vd.* **tsaucē**). (*c*) **anā** ～ *Vd.* **kurman 1**. **(3)** *Kt.* **tā kōmō gidā, tā yi** ～ she brought home unsold, perishable goods (**kwantai 2***a*) *x* **furā**, cakes, sweets.

B. **(tsāwa)** *f.* borborygmi.

*****tsāwacē** *Vb.* 1C made three-ply string.

*****tsawāfi** *Ar. m.* making procession round the **Ka'aba** during the pilgrimage.

tsawaita A. **(tsawaitā)** lengthened *x*

Allā ya ～ **maka rǎi** may God lengthen your life !

B. **(tsawaita)** *Vb.* 3B. **(1)** became long. **(2) yā** ～ **garēni** it was boresome to me.

tsawanta A. **(tsawantā)** = **tsawaita**.

B. **(tsawanta)** = **tsawaita**.

tsawarwara *f.* **(1)** brindled cat. **(2) yā shiga** ～ he has charm sewn in skin of 1 and thought to render him invisible.

tsāwarya = **tsāwurya**.

tsāwatā *Vb.* 1C *x* **an** ～ **masa** = **tsaucē**.

tsāwatar *x* **an** ～ **masa** = **tsaucē**.

tsawā-tsawā *m.* tall P. ; long T.

tsawo A. **(tsawō)** *m.* **(1)** (*a*) (i) length. (ii) **wandō yā yi mini tsawō** the trousers are too long for me. (iii) **duk tsawan dāmunan nan** throughout that wet season. (*b*) height. (*c*) **jirāgyan sama sunā bin ƙasan nan tsawanta da fādinta** aeroplanes are attacking that country far and wide. (*c*) **yā ragę** ～ he sold an article, bought a cheaper kind and had balance over (= *Kt.* **sabka 2**). (*d*) **bākī da** ～ **na mai musu nē** rather than reply angrily and bring trouble on yourself " keep your tongue between your teeth " ! (*e*) **bā don** ～ **a kan ga wata ba** success depends more on luck than on anything else. (*f*) **tsawam bāyanka** *Vd.* **akala**. (*g*) **tsawan hannū** *Vd.* **hannū 2***f*. **(2)** ～ **yā kai** (*a*) wall of house (**dāki** *or* **sōrō**) is finished and only awaits roof (= **kashę 4***a last example*). (*b*) **tāgīya-** cap is finished excepting **ƙōƙwā 1***b*. **(3) yā yi masa kīwan** ～ he under-fed it (child, animal).

B. **(tsāwọ)** *m.* three-ply rope.

tsāwurya *f.* **(1)** leucoma, etc. **(2) Tsāwurya tilashin idọ** what a thorn he is in my flesh !

tsawwala A. **(tsawwalā)** = **tsanantā**.

B. **(tsawwala)** = **tsananta** *x* **al'amarī yā tsawwala** the affair became serious.

tsawwīla *Ar. f.* flintlock-gun.

tsaya *Vb.* 3A (*Vd. also* **tsaiwā**). **(1)** (*a*) stood *x* **ka** ～ **nan** stand here ! (*b*) *Vd.* **tsayi**. (*c*) **tsaya ka jī** just listen ! (*d*) **bā ā tsayāwā sǎi da ƙasā** nobody can realize his wishes till the chance offers. (*e*) **wannam magana tā** ～ this matter is

definitely arranged. **bạ ạ sạ̄mi shāwarạr dạˈ akạ ~ kạntạ ba** they were
unable to come to a definite decision.
(*f*) **watạ yā ~** the new moon has
appeared = **kāmạ** A.2 3 (*cf.* **fịta 4***b*, *c*).
(*g*) **nā ~ masạ** I went surety for him.
nā ~ masạ dạ fạm bịyar I went surety
for him in the sum of five pounds. (*h*)
zā mụ tsayạ dằidằi dạ kõwā we shall
enjoy equal status with everybody.
(*j*) **yā wucę shịmfidạ tasạ dạ tsayạ̄wā**
Vd. **shịmfidạ 1***d*. (2) waited *x* (*a*) **kạ ~
dạgạ naŋ** wait here! (*b*) **kadạ kạ ~**
don't delay! (*c*) **baị ~ jirạŋ wani ạbụ
ba sằi ya fadạ masạ** he told him without
further ado. (3) halted *x* (*a*) **dạ̄ nufịnsạ,
bạ zaị tsayạ kõịnā ba** his former intention was to halt nowhere. (*b*) **tsạya,
ạ ishę ka** *Vd.* **tsittsigę.** (*c*) **sun ~ shāwarạr ịndạ zā sụ tạfi** they halted to
consider in what direction they should
proceed. (*d*) **bạ sụ tsayạ wani shirị ba**
they did not halt to make any preparations. (4) is (was) limited to *x*
bạ̄ naŋ ɓạrnā ta tsayạ ba *that* was not
the end of the damage. **ạl'amạrịŋ, bạ̄
gạrēmụ ya tsayạ ba** it is not restricted to
us. **wannạm bạ̄ gạ Jāmụs kawaị ya
tsayạ ba** this is not limited, restricted
to the Germans alone. (5) (*a*) **~ dạ** keep
on working at *x* **makẹ̄rā sun tsayạ dạ
kīrạ** the smiths steadily went on
smithing. **Amịrkạ tā tsayạ dạ kõkarịŋ
kīrạr jirạ̄gē** America devoted great
effort to the building of ships. (*b*)
yā ~ kạŋ aikịnsạ he stuck to his work
(*Vd.* **tsạye 3**). **sun tsayạ kạŋ amincịnsụ
dạ mū** they maintained their friendship with us. (*c*) **sun tsayạ taimakwan
jūnā** they kept on helping each other.
(*d*) **yā tsayạ gạ ạlkāwạrinsạ** he stuck to
his promise. (6) insisted *x* **yā tsayạ
sằi yā yī** he insisted on doing it. **sun
tsayạ kõmē akẹ̄ yị, ạ yi** they're determined to resist to the last (*cf.* **tsạye 9**).
(7) resisted *x* (*a*) **yā tsayạ dạ kạrfịŋ
halī** he resisted strongly. (*b*) **yā ~
masạ ạ kā** he stood impolitely before
him (= **tsēbēbē**). (8) **wurin tsayạ̄warsạ**
his status. (9) **tsayạ̄war watạ** *Vd.*
rēnạ 8.

tsayad dạ = tsai dạ.

tsayạ̄wā *Vd.* **tsayạ.**
tsạyayyạ *f.* (1) perseverance. (2) **yā yi
musụ tsạyayyạ ịyạ̄kā** he resisted them
all he could. (3) *Vd.* **shējị 2.**
tsạyayyē *m.* (*f.* **tsạyayyīyā**) *pl.* **tsạyạyyū**
adj. persevering, steadfast.
tsạye *m.* (*noun of state from* **tsayạ**). (1)
x (*a*) **nā ga jirgī ạ ~** I saw the train
halted (Mod. Gram. 123*e*.i). **wõkạcịn
dạ na gan shị, yanạ̄ ~** when I saw him,
he was in a standing position (Mod.
Gram. 123*e*.ii). (*b*) *Vd.* **zạune 2, 5.**
(*c*) **ạlkāwạrinsạ yanạ̄ naŋ tsạye** his
promise has been kept. (*d*) **kagọ yanạ̄
tsạye** *Vd.* **rūwā** C.24. (*e*) **sunạ̄ naŋ
tsạye ta " bụga, ạ bụgē sụ ! "** they're
resisting firmly. (*f*) **kwānā tsạye** *Vd.*
tạɓaryā. (2) **mutūwạr ~ *f*.** (*a*) becoming blind. (*b*) gradual emaciation.
(*c*) gradual loss of wealth. (*d*) being
dazed by a blow. (3) (*a*) **yā tāshị ~**
(i) he stood up. (ii) he became perturbed. (*b*) **yā tāshị ~ kạŋ aikịnsạ** he
persevered at his work (*Vd.* **tsayạ 5***b*).
(*c*) **yā tāshị tsạye, fīlī dạ fīlī** he " came
out into the open ". (*d*) **tā dạ mazā ~**
Vd. **bazarā 2.** (4) **wạhalạ tā yi ~** I'm
persistently unlucky at present. (5)
**iŋ kanạ̄ ~, sằi kạ zaunạ̄ ; iŋ kumā
kanạ̄ zạune, sằi kạ kwạntā** always
retain your composure ! (5A) **yā tạmbayē shị dạgạ ~** he asked him unceremoniously. (6) **ạ ~** *adv.* lengthwise (*contrasted with* **ạ gicịye** crosswise. (7) act of halting *x* **yākị yā yi
tsạye** the war has come to a standstill.
(8) act of standing *x* **zā mụ hanạ sụ
zạune, zā mụ hanạ su tsạye** we shall
give them no respite. (9) insistence *x*
sun yi tsạye sằi ạ yī they insisted on
doing it (*cf.* **tsayạ 6**). (10) **ɓạrāwạn ~**
broker (= **dịllālị**). (11) **ɓargõ ~** *Kt. m.*
strapping youth.
tsayị *m.* (1) length. (2) height (1, 2 =
tsawõ). (3) **kụ tsayạ ~** stand firm !
(= **tsaiwar dakạ**). (4) **tsayịn dakạ =
tsaiwā 2.**
tsayyūwā = tsaiwā.
tsēbā *f.* sprouting (**sõkọ 3**) of tubers left in
ground after crop gathered.
tsēbēbē *x* **yā tsayạ ~ ạ wurinsạ =
tsayạ 7***b*.

tsɛ̃fa̱ *f.* = kwantsa̱ 2*a*.

tsefe A. (tsɛ̃fe̱) *Vb.* 1A (*Vd. also* tsīfa̱).
(1) (*a*) combed (= sarce̱ 1). (*b*) sun ∼ ma̱gana̱ they've fully investigated the matter. (2) (*a*) undid (sewing). (*b*) (woman) undid (coiffure), *cf. Kt.* kwantā 4. (*c*) sun ∼ hatsi̱ŋ they (birds) have committed depredations on the corn.
B. (tsɛ̃fē) *m.* = mu̱rmura̱ 1.

tsēganā *used in* 'yar ∼ *f.* slightly-built woman.

tsēgu̱mī *m.* (*pl.* tsēgu̱ŋguma̱ = tsɛ̃gu̱me-tsɛ̃gu̱mē = tsɛ̃gu̱nce-tsɛ̃gu̱ncē). (1) (*a*) (i) tale-telling, scandal-mongering. (ii) yā yi mini̱ tsēgu̱mī (i) he brought gossip to me. (ii) he gossiped about me. (*b*) dū̱ba mini̱ hanya̱, ma̱kāfo̱ yā sō ∼ take care you don't speak ill of a P. when he can hear you ! (*cf.* ka̱ŋki̱ 2*b*). (2) *Kt.* quarrelling (= fada̱).

tsēgu̱ntā *Vb.* 1C yā ∼ musu̱ ma̱gana̱ he tattled to them about the matter.

tsēko̱ = tsaiko̱.

tsēle̱ *used in* tsēla̱ŋ ūwāka̱ (*foully abusively*) blast you ! (= ūwāka̱).

tsērad da̱ = tsīrad da̱.

tsere A. (tsērē) *m.* (1) contest, competition (in racing, archery, etc.). (2) sun zuba̱ ∼ they (horses, boys, etc.) raced against one another. (3) suna̱ tsērē da̱ jūnā they are emulating one another. (4) ana̱ ta tsērē they are fleeing.
B. (tsēre̱) (1) *Vb.* 3A (*a*) escaped. (*b*) yā ∼ katakau (= fau) (i) he " got clean away ". (ii) he won easily. (2) *Vb.* 1A (*a*) surpassed *x* yā ∼ Audu̱ = yā ∼ wa̱ Audu̱ he surpassed, outstripped Audu. yā tsēre̱ mu ga̱ sāmu̱nsa̱ he outstripped us in getting it. (*b*) wata̱ yā ∼ ƙaŋƙanci̱ŋ ga̱rā it's useless to slander a P. of proved integrity. (*c*) iŋ ku̱nnē yā ji mugunya̱r ma̱gana̱, wuya̱ yā ∼ ya̱ŋkā forewarned is forearmed. (*d*) yā ∼ gidā he hastened home. (*e*) tsɛ̃re̱ mai gōnā *m. Sk.* type of small rodent. (*f*) tsɛ̃re̱ wa̱ŋka̱ *m.* type of children's game where they pelt each other with earth.

tsiba̱ *Vb.* 1A piled up (= tila̱ = *Kt.* tsauna̱).

tsibbu̱ = tsubbu̱.

tsibi̱ *m.* (1) = tāri̱ 1*a*. (2) what a lot ! tsibi̱rcē *Vb.* 3A sat alone (*cf.* kāku̱mē).

tsi̱birī *m.* (*pl.* tsi̱bi̱rai). (1) (*a*) island (= gu̱ŋgu̱ 2). (*b*) kō a̱ Kwā̱ra̱ da̱ ∼ there's nowhere without someone of importance. (2) *Kt.* = tudu̱ 3.

tsice̱ *Vb.* 3A is finished (= ƙare̱).

tsīdahū = tsīduhū.

tsi̱dau *m.* (1) (*a*) the weed *Tribulus terrestris* (= fi̱rtsa̱ faƙō = tsira̱ faƙō). (*b*) sāmu̱ŋ wurī, kuturū gādā a̱ ∼ = gādā 4. (2) *Vd.* tsa̱idau.

tsidik *x* sǎi gā̱ shi ∼ he suddenly appeared.

tsīduhū *m.* smallest and hottest type of red pepper (= *Kt.* ta̱sshī = *Sk.* ta̱ŋkwā).

tsīfa̱ *f.* (1) (*secondary v.n. of* tsɛ̃fe̱) *x* yana̱ tsīfa̱r gēmu̱nsa̱ = yana̱ tsɛ̃fe̱ gēmu̱nsa̱ he is combing his beard. (2) acting *as in* tsɛ̃fe̱. (3) tiny writing. (4) fine-pointed pen.

tsī̱fi̱ri̱ *m.* = fēlēƙē.

tsiga A. (tsi̱gā) *Vb.* 2 pulled out (burr, hair, etc.) = fi̱gā.
B. (tsi̱ga̱) = tsīka̱.

tsi̱gai-tsi̱gai = tsi̱ge.

tsi̱ga̱nannē (*used by women*) = tsi̱nannē.

tsi̱gātsi̱gai *Vd.* tsittsige̱.

tsigau *m.* (*pl.* tsigwaigwai) testicle (= ƙwā̱lātai).

tsige A. (tsi̱ge̱) (1) *Vb.* 1A. (*a*) = tsi̱gā. (*b*) yā ∼ mini̱ he abused me. (2) *Vb.* 3A deteriorated (= lāla̱cē).
B. (tsi̱ge) *used in* a̱ ∼ in a destitute state (= tsīgai-tsīgai).

tsīgī *m.* (1) market held on subsidiary market-day (= yāra̱ = dū̱rīya̱). (2) gleanings of tobacco-flowers (*epithet is* Tsīgī fu̱raŋ kālā). (3) tsīgī = tsīgī da̱ za̱ŋkō (*a*) the Grass-warbler (*Spiloptila clamans*) (*epithet is* Tsīgī mai sa̱ukā rēni̱). (*b*) the Tawny-flanked Wren-warbler (*Prinia mistacea*) = ɓērū = *Kt.* tsīgī da̱ tukkū. (*c*) Alexander's Crested Lark (*Galerida crestata alexander*). (4) ∼ yakē ɓarnā, ana̱ fushi da̱ ga̱urāka̱ seniors have to bear the blame for their junior's misdeeds (*Vd.* ɓērū).

tsīgīgī = tsi̱gīgi̱ (1) *x* kō ∼ bābu̱ there is absolutely none. (2) (*a*) ɗan ∼ short man, short boy. (b) x **ɗan yãrọ nẽ ~ dạ shĩ** he's a small boy (pl. **'yan yạ̃rã nẽ tsigī-tsigī dạ sū**). **ɗaŋ itạ̃cē nẽ ~ dạ shĩ** it is a small tree (pl. **'yaŋ itātūwạ nẽ tsigī-tsigī dạ sū**).

tsigil (pl. **tsigil-tsigil**) = **tsīgīgī** 2b.

tsịgirgịrĩ m. (f. **tsịgirgịrã**) pl. **tsịgirgịrai** short, thin P.

tsigī-tsigī Vd. **tsīgīgī**.

tsigwạigwai Vd. **tsigạu**.

tsika A. (**tsīkạ**) f. (1) spiky seed of grass. (2) **tsīkạr jịkīna tā tāshị = tsīkạr jịkīna tā yi nyạr** my hair stood on end. B. (**tsịkā**) Vb. 2 crunched (cf. **matsụkī**).

tsīkạnẽ Vb. 1C (1) = **tsīnẹ** 1. (2) (used by women) = **tsīnẹ** 2.

tsịkarạ Vb. 2 (1) = **tsạkarạ** 1. (2) tickled (side of P.), cf. **cạ̃kulkul**. (3) spurred (horse) to make it prance, cf. **taɓạ** 1l.

tsīkạrĩ m. acting as in **tsịkarạ**.

*****tsịkạ̃yẽ** used in translating from Arabic in expression **yā ~ sụ** he summoned them to religious conclave.

tsikẹ (1) Vb. 1A crunched up all of. (2) Vb. 3A is shameless.

tsịkō m. (1) arrow without barb (**kụnnẽ**). (2) type of pointed tool for digging well or quarrying stone.

tsīlā f. tapeworm (= **tạmzā = farar tsūtsạ**), cf. **tānā** 1b, **ayạmbā**, **macịjĩ 13, daudạr cikị**.

tsilak x (1) **yā wạŋku ~** it is washed snow-white. **Audụ tsilak-tsilak dạ shĩ** Audu looks very clean. **mātan nạŋ tsilak-tsilak dạ sū** these women look very clean. (2) **yā fịta tsilak** " he got clean away " (cf. **fau**).

tsillạ = **cillạ** 1a, b.

tsịllā-tsillā f. shiftiness.

tsillụmā (1) Vb. 3A. (a) fell or jumped into water x **yā ~ cikin rūwā tsilum** it (frog) plopped into the water. (b) cf. **tsindụmā**. (2) Vb. 3A threw into water.

tsilum (1) (a) m. plop of T. falling into water. (b) adv. Vd. **tsillụmā**. (2) = **tsalam** 1.

tsima A. (**tsimạ**) (1) (a) soaked (herbs, dirty linen, etc.) in water. (b) **an ~ tsimị** herbs have been soaked to make **tsimị**. (c) **yā fạɗi abịn dạ zại tsimạ su**

he said cheering words to them (cf. **tsịma** 1c, **tsịmu**). (2) **an ~ tsịmẽ** the ink **tsịmē** q.v. is in soak. (3) Vd. **tsịmu**.

B. (**tsịma**) Vb. 3B (Vd. **tsịmā** 1). (1) (a) became soaked (as in **tsimạ**). (b) **ƙasā tā ~** the building-clay has been well wetted and mixed (by soaking for two days, then turning it over (**jūyị**) and twice later at 2-day intervals, turning it), cf. **tsụ̃gē** 2. (c) sun **tsịma**, sum **fāɗạ wạ Jāmụs** they nerved themselves and fell on the Germans (cf. **tsịmu, tsimạ** 1c). (2) (bruise, sprain) became painful. (3) Vd. **tsịmu**.

C. (**tsịmā**) (1) (progressive of **tsịma**). (2) (a) shivering. (b) **yā hau ~** he trembled, shivered (= **tsịmē** 3). (3) Vd. **tsimī** 1d.

tsịmāgọ Vd. **tsimī** 1d.

tsịmammĩyā f. **dạ ~ tsạkāninsụ** latent enmity has broken out between them.

tsịmē m. (1) an ink made by steeping **gạɓạ̃rūwā** (= **tsimị** 2). (2) = **tsimị** 1. (3) **yā hau ~** = **tsịmā** 2.

tsimi A. (**tsimĩ**) m. (1) (a) eking out x **yanā ~ dạ kuɗinsạ** he is eking out his money (= **cạncạnẽ**). (b) **dạ tsiminsạ ạ ɓọ̃ye** he has a reserve put away. (c) keeping in reserve x **jārumāwā irịŋ wadạndạ yakẹ ~** soldiers which he is keeping in reserve. (d) **tsimịŋ tsịŋkẹ̃wā** = **tsimin tsịmāgọ** keeping T. in reserve so long that it is no longer of use. (2) (a) intelligence x **yā yi ~** he is intelligent. (b) **yā tạ̃shē nị ạ ~** he brought me to my senses. (c) **inā tsimị ? inā dạbārạ** what is to be done ? B. (**tsimị**) m. (1) (a) any decoction made by soaking herbs (= **tsịmē** 2). (b) Vd. **sạiwā** 4, **mōtsạ** 1g.i. (2) = **tsịmē** 1.

tsịmu Vb. 3B **yā ~** he was silent from fear, shame, embarrassment (Vd. **tsimạ, tsịma**).

tsimū-tsịmũ m. being silent as in **tsịmu**.

tsịnā (1) Vb. 2 = **tsīnẹ** 1. (2) f. (a) dirty pieces of cotton which are picked out before spinning. (b) good-for-nothing P. (= **ragō**). (c) **halin tsịnā** blameworthy character.

tsinana A. (**tsīnạ̃nā**) pl. (1) pointed weapons. (2) (said by women) **yā**

ɗaukō ƙwăi tarạ ∼ he made a fuss about nothing (= mĭtạ).

B. (tsĭnạnā) *Vb.* 1C. (1) (*a*) made point to (weapon). (*b*) (i) tā tsĭnạnạ bặkī she pouted. (ii) kụnū kō yā kwānā, tsĭnạnạ bặkī however friendly a superior may seem, watch out ! (2) *in rhetorical question with negative sense*) nā taɓạ tsĭnạnạ wani ạbụ dạgạ wurịŋkạ ? = kā taɓạ ∼ mini wanị ? abụ ? (Mod. Gram. 164*d*) what have you ever done for *me* ? (3) *Vd.* ƙĭrạ 1*g.*

tsĭnạncē *Vb.* 3A deteriorated (= lālặcē).

tsĭnannē *m.* (*f.* tsĭnannĭyā) *pl.* tsĭnạnnū. (1) (*a*) first-class (*re T.*, *not re P.*). tsĭnannan yā̆ƙị terrible war, major war. (2) P. cursed by tsĭnẹ 2*a.*

tsĭnantạ *f.* halin ∼ gạrēshị = tsĭnẹ 2*b.*

tsĭnạntakạ *f.* = tsĭnantạ.

tsĭnau *m.* good-for-nothing P.

tsĭnặyē *Vd.* tsĭnī.

tsince A. (tsincẹ) = tsĭntā 1.

B. (tsịncē) (1) *Vd.* tsịntā. (2) fussing, grousing (= mĭtạ).

tsịnci *Vd.* tsịntā.

tsindum A. (tsindụm) = tsilum 1.

B. (tsịndum) (1) yā shịga cikinsạ ∼ he has become deeply involved in it. (2) rūwā nẹ̆ ∼ it is a large expanse of water.

tsindụmā (1) *Vb.* 3A (*a*) = tsillụmā 1*a.* (*b*) yā ∼ cikinsạ = tsịndum 1. (2) *Vb.* 1C tā ∼ wạ furā rūwā she made sloppy furā.

tsindụmē *m.* (1) forcibly feeding (cụsā) horse after watering it. (2) eating solid food (*x* tūwō) after liquid food (*x* furā).

tsĭnẹ *Vb.* 1A (1) (*a*) selected. (*b*) picked out, up, one by one. (*c*) yā ∼ gyạɗā = rōrẹ 1. (2) (*a*) Allạ̄ yạ ∼ makạ ạlbarkạ may God deprive you of his blessings ! (*considered a terrible curse*), *cf.* Alạ̄ 10 ; bặkī 2*u* ; dẹ̆babbē ; jẹ̆faffē. (*b*) haliŋ " Alạ̄ ∼ " gạrēshị he is malevolent.

tsĭnẹ̄wā *used in* halin ∼ gạrēshị = tsĭnẹ 2*b.*

tsịŋgālumī = tsạŋgālumī.

tsịŋgạ̄rai *Vd.* tsịŋgạ̄rọ.

tsịŋgạ̄rī = tsāmārī.

tsịŋgạ̄rọ *m.* (*pl.* tsịŋgạ̄rai = tsịŋgạ̄rī = tsịŋgạ̄rū). (1) small potsherd (*cf.* kaskō 1*d*, kạtaŋgạ). (2) what a pauper !

tsiŋgiriŋgātā = tsāmārī.

tsịnī *m.* (*pl.* tsĭnạ̄yē = tsĭnunnukạ). (1) (*a*) (i) sharp point. (ii) kā fī ƙayạ ∼ *Vd.* fĭ̄ƙē. (*b*) gạrin nēman ∼ yā kāsạ ƙundạ throwing away the substance for the shadow. (2) gāra kạ jē dạ kạŋkạ, tsĭnịŋ idọ yā fī tsĭnim māshị a personal interview is better than a message. (3) dōlẹ mụ zạ̄ɓi ɗayā, kaifī kō tsịnī we are forced to adopt one of the two alternatives. (4) gạba ∼ *Vd.* būtsātsạ.

tsiŋka A. (tsiŋkạ) (1) *Vb.* 1A (*a*) = katsạ 1–5. (*aa*) *Vd.* zạrau. (*b*) an ∼ rūwā it rained heavily. (*c*) publicly humiliated P. (*d*) routed. (*e*) ƙin jạ̄, ƙin tsiŋkạ̄wā getting T. without trouble (= jinī 1*f*). (2) *Vb.* 3A. (*a*) yā ∼ dạ gudụ he took to his heels. (*b*) ∼ gindī = tsiŋkẹ 2*b.*

B. (tsiŋkā) *f.* = tsiŋkē 8.

C. (tsiŋkā) *Vb.* 2 (1) snapped off (thread, etc.). (2) plucked off, pulled off.

tsiŋkaikai *Vd.* tsiŋkē.

tsiŋkau = tsiŋkau = tsirkau 2 *q.v.*

tsiŋkaya A. (tsiŋkāyạ) *Vb.* 2 *x* yā tsiŋkạ̄yē shị = yā tsiŋkāyō shị he saw him from afar (= haŋgā), *cf.* ganō 1*a.*ii.

B. (tsiŋkạ̄yā) (1) *Vb.* 3A looked into the distance to see whether P. or T. is in sight. (2) *Vb.* 1C reflected on.

C. (tsiŋkāyā) *f.* (1) seeing P. or T. from far. (2) foresight (= tānạdī 2*b*, nịtsūwā, nīsā 1*e*). (3) fortune-telling (= dūbā).

tsiŋkạ̄yē *Vd.* tsiŋkē.

tsinke A (tsiŋkẹ) (1) *Vb.* 1A. (*a*) snapped (thread, rope), plucked (fruit, etc.) = katsạ 1 = tsiŋkạ 1 = cirẹ 1*f.* (*b*) an ∼ shi dạ mārị he received a good slap (= katsẹ 1*b*). (2) *Vb.* 3A (*a*) (i) (rope, thread) snapped (= katsẹ 2*b*) (*cf.* karyẹ). (ii) yā ∼ fat = yā ∼ kat = yā ∼ kats it snapped clean in two. (iii) damị yā ∼ ạ gindiŋ kabạ = damị yā ∼ ạ gindiŋ kargō " he hit the nail on the head " (= kāmụn dặcē). (*b*) (i) dōkị yā ∼ = dōkị yā ∼ gindī horse has broken loose (= gudụ 2*b* = kwancẹ 2*b*), *cf.* gindī 2. (ii) yā ∼ he took to his heels ; he has gone on a journey. (*c*) yā ∼ = zūcịyassạ tā ∼ he lost heart. yā ∼ dạ ạl'amạrin naŋ he became

nervous about this affair. (d) (i) yā ∼ dạ magạnạ he chattered. (ii) rūwā yā ∼ it rained heavily. (e) = katsę 2c, d. (f) (P. or animal) became thin. (g) tsimin tsiŋkęwā Vd. tsimī 1d. (3) m. (a) destitute P. (b) Kt. kai nę mukạ yō mạ ∼ you are the one to whom we have turned for help.
   B. (tsiŋkē) m. (pl. tsiŋkạyē = tsiŋkunạ = tsiŋkaikai). (1) (a) piece of dry grass. (b) suŋ karyạ ∼ they've quarrelled. (c) kā karyạ minị ∼ ạ tsūlī you've disgraced me by your conduct. (2) big pin with which women scratch head (= masōshī). (3) Vd. gōmạ 5. (4) aŋ gēwạyā masạ ∼ he's an utter boor. (5) tsiŋkyaŋ kadị long, forked wooden pin used by women in spinning (cf. ƙuŋgu 1). (6) Vd. ƙwạƙulạ 3. (7) tsiŋkyan tsịrē wooden skewer for tsịrē. (8) donkey-goad (= tsiŋkā).
tsiŋkēkę m. (f. tsiŋkēkịyā) handsome.
tsiŋkị (1) how handsome ! (2) what a lot of rain !
tsiŋkịnrāgị = tsiŋkịnsạdạshī emptyhanded x yā zō tsiŋkịnrāginsạ he came empty-handed (= zandagīlā = zaŋgārī = zanzạlā).
tsiŋkịyā f. being liable to snap (thread).
tsiŋkunạ Vd. tsiŋkē.
tsinta A. (tsịntā) Vb. 2 (p.o. tsịncē, n.o. tsịnci). (1) selected ; picked up, out one by one (= tsincę). (2) (a) found T. (Vd. tsintūwā) by lucky chance (on road, etc.). (b) indạ yārọ ya tsịnci wurị yau, gōbe can zại nụfā habit becomes second nature.
   B. (tsintā) m., f. (1) inferior kola-nuts set on one side. (2) Kt. small cowries.
tsinta-tsinta (1) occasionally. (2) ạkwai sū ∼ there are a few of them.
tsintsā = tsantsā.
tsintsimā f. (1) open-ended drum of hunters. (2) Kt. mutạnē sun yi ∼ people have collected.
tsịntsịndō = tsạntsạndō.
tsịntsịrit completely x yā ƙạre ∼ it is completely finished (= dụŋgum).
tsintsīyā f. (pl. tsintsīyōyī). (1) (a) (i) type of thatching-grass. (ii) yā ci ∼ he gathered 1a.i. (b) broom made from 1a or other material. (c) tạran ∼ bạ

shạrā, banzā people are collected idly (Vd. tạrō 3). (d) ∼ dayā bā tạ shạrā unity is strength. (e) Kt. small present (x sweeping, letting oneself be taken prisoner in joke, etc.) claimable from receiver of shārạ 3 by the giver. (f) sạyi ∼ Vd. katakas. (2) type of European red and white cotton material. (3) tsintsīyar hannū wrist end of forearm. (4) tsintsīyar mazā a plant-root used as cure for gonorrhœa.
tsintūwā f. x nā yi ∼ (1) I had a lucky find (Vd. tsịntā 2). (2) I got T. easily.
tsīnunnukạ Vd. tsịnī.
tsira A. (tsīrā) (1) Vb. 3B (a) escaped, was saved. (b) jịkī yā ∼ Vd. dạ 1a.ii. (2) m., f. (a) (progressive of 1) x yanạ ∼ he is escaping. (b) (v.n. of 1) x (i) tsīransạ his escape. (ii) gidan ∼ m. the next world (= lāhirạ). (iii) būtạ im bạ tạ yi tsīraŋ kōmē ba, tạ yi na igīyạ he lives on reflected glory. (iv) kụnnē nạ ganī, ƙạfō yā yi ∼ imperceptibly things develop along their appointed lines. (v) gudụn ∼ m. fleeing. (vi) rūwan ∼ rain at end of wet season (good for crops) (cf. rūwā B.20). (vii) mạ ga tsīram būshīyā ạ fariŋ watạ we must devise a plan. (viii) ∼ dạ mutuncị yā fi ∼ dạ kāyā it is better to preserve your dignity than your property. (c) dạ ∼ tsạkāninsụ there is a difference between them.
   B. (tsīrạ) (1) Vb. 1A. (a) (i) piled up (= tilạ). (ii) wạndạ ya ∼ kāyā, yā yi yawạ, bại riƙạ dạ kyau ba, yạ yi ɓarī if you don't attend to your job, you'll lose it. (b) P. spitted meat on skewer (cf. tsịrē). (2) Vb. 3A P. prospered.
   C. (tsira) Vb. 3B (progressive tsịrā) sprouted (= tsirō = tōhō = sōkō).
   D. (tsịrā) Vb. 2 (1) (a) inaugurated x wạ ya tsịri ginịn sumuntị ạ Kanọ who inaugurated cement-building at Kano ? (= fārạ 4 q.v.). (b) kā tsirō m. making innovations (in religions, etc.). (2) imitated x yā tsịri barcī he pretended to be asleep. (3) Vd. tsịra.
   E. (tsịrạ) Vb. 1A = tsịrā 1a.
tsiracci = tsiraici.

tsīrad dą *Vb.* 4 saved, rescued (= tsar dą 2).

tsira faƙō *m.* = tsīdau.

tsiraici *m.* (1) being naked (= tsįrārą 1 = huntunci). (2) naked pudenda.

tsiraita A. (tsiraįtā) *Vb.* 1C. (1) (*a*) rendered naked (P. of clothes, room of contents, etc.). (*b*) impoverished. (2) an tsiraįtą wuriŋ the place has now been exposed to view (*x* by cutting away branches, etc.). (3) (*a*) segregated (sick persons). (*b*) deported.

B. (tsįraitą) *Vb.* 3B (1) became naked, impoverished, exposed to view *as in* tsiraįtā. (2) became segregated, deported *as in* tsiraįtā.

tsįrārą (1) *f.* (*a*) nakedness *x* yā yi ∼ he is naked (= tsiraici). (*b*) dą ∼ gāra baƙim bantē half a loaf is better than no bread. (*c*) yā būdę ąl'amąriŋ tsįrārąrsą he explained the matter fully (*cf.* 2*d below*). (2) *adj.* (*a*) naked (= huntū) *x* (i) nā gan shį ∼ I saw him naked (= za-gargar = zigidir = ųryąŋ = ɓutuk). (ii) arnę ∼ a naked pagan (*pl.* arnā ∼ = arnā mąsū ∼). (iii) *Vd.* dǫmin-dǫmin ; jąrabą 3. (*b*) exposed to view, bare. (*c*) impoverished. (*d*) gąskīyā ∼ the absolute truth (= zallā), *cf.* 1*c above.*

tsīrar dą = tsīrad dą.

tsįrārī *x* mutąnan nąŋ ∼ nę these people are few. sun zō ∼ they came in small numbers.

tsįrārīyą *f.* trickery.

tsįrarrē *Vd.* dąsasshē.

tsirbī = cirbī.

tsire A. (tsīrę) *Vb.* 1A (1) (*a*) pierced and remained in *x* ƙayą tā ∼ ƙafątą a thorn pierced my foot and stuck there (*cf.* sōƙā). (*b*) an ∼ shi he has been executed by impaling on a stake. (2) spitted (meat to make tsįrē).

B. (tsįrē) *m.* (1) bits of meat spitted on stick and toasted (ƙafę) = kadįdį = cancangā 1, *cf.* sōyē ; maząrē 3 ; daką 2*g*, lifįdī 2*b*. (2) *epithet is* Sūyą barąŋ gashį. (3) hųlar ∼ tiny bit of fat on end of stick of tsįrē.

tsirfā *Sk. f.* plan = dąbārą *q.v.*

tsirfąntā *Vb.* 1C *Sk.* devised (plan).

tsirgą *Vb.* 3A (1) = dįra 1*a.* (2) (affair, dispute, fire, wind, pain, etc.) subsided (= kwąntā 5). (3) cikįnsą yā ∼ his stomach-ache has gone and he is now passing motions (= kwąntā 4*b. q.v.*).

tsirgāgīyā *f.* (1) sheath of corn-stalk (= kartājįyā = *Kt.* alkājįyā). (2) what a wiry, fearless person !

tsirge A. (tsirgę) *Vb.* 3A = tsirgą.

B. (tsirgē) *m.* (1) = dirē. (2) = dįr-kōkōnīyā.

C. (tsįrgē) *Sk. m.* = shigēgę.

tsiri A. (tsīrį) *m.* (1) odds and ends packed into vessel. (2) pile of things packed on one another.

B. (tsīrī) (*cerebral -r-*) *m.* (1) = taɓaryā 2. (2) wutā tā yi ∼ samą the flames rose high. (3) (*with rolled* -r-) divulging secrets of P. (= fąllasą).

C. (tsiri) (1) *m.* = ficē 1. (2) *m.* (*pl.* tsįrrai) = tsiro 2.

tsīrīrī *Kt.* yā yi cikį ∼ he is pot-bellied.

tsirit (1) ƙąŋƙanę nē ∼ it is tiny. (2) ∼ mā shą nē half a loaf is better than no bread.

tsiri-tsiri *pl. adj.* small *x* shūƙą nē ∼ they are small crops.

tsirkąŋ (1) *m.* destitute P. (2) how thin he is !

tsirkīyā *f.* (*pl.* tsirkīyōyī = *Kt.* tsarōkī). (1) bow-string. (2) (*a*) any string of mōlō (*cf.* magūdįyā 4). (*b*) kūkan ∼ *m.* (i) whining to escape punishment. (ii) aggressor pretending to be the injured party. (3) tsirkīyar zōmō = ƙiri-ƙirī.

tsirmā-tsįrmą *f. and adv.* dǫgąrai sun tad dą ɓąrāwǫ yā yi ∼ the N.A. police found the thief in a state of jitters.

tsįrnāką = cįnnāką.

tsiro A. (tsirō) *Vd.* tsįra, tsįrā.

B. (tsiro) (1) *m.* germination, sprouting. (2) *m.* (*pl.* tsįrrai). (*a*) sprout, shoot. (*b*) witless fool.

tsirrą *f. used in* yā kafą masą ∼ = yā są masą ∼ = cīkąs 2 *q.v.*

tsįrrai *Vd.* tsiro 2, tsiri 2.

tsirtad dą = tsartad dą.

tsīruku *used in* na ∼ *m.* (1) thin but pot-bellied child (*epithet is* Na ∼, Alląŋ ƙwąyā ; kā ci damį, kā kāsą daukąŋ ƙwąyā), *Vd.* damį 5. (2) slacker.

tsirū-tsịrū = tsurū-tsụrū.

tsiryā f. (1) Senegal Long-tailed Parakeet (*Psittacula krameri*). (2) Red-headed Lovebird (*Agapornis pullaria* = kạ̄lō 1). (3) long tool for hollowing-out (sạssakạ) a mortar.

tsit m. yā yi ~ he kept silence.

tsītạkā f. (*pl.* tsītakōkī) broad axe with long point.

tsị̄-tsị̄ m. (1) squeaking of rat. (2) = gunạ̄gunī 1.

tsītsītạ f. (1) tiny gifts. (2) children's gambling game.

tsittsigẹ m. (*pl.* tsịgạ̄tsịgai = tsụgạ̄tsụgai). (1) (*a*) small tree-stump. (*b*) fragment of root of tooth. (2) insistent P. (*epithet is* Tuntuḅẹ, tsạya ạ ishẹ ka).

tsīwạ f. (1) (*a*) *pl.* tsị̄wạce-tsị̄wạcē insolence (= rashịŋ kunyạ = tsaurī 6*a*). (*b*) ~ tā tāshị there is insolence about. (2) a good gravel for dạ6ē.

tsị̄yā f. (1) (*a*) (i) poverty. (ii) *Vd.* 6ērā 2. (*b*) (i) yā karyạ gāshịŋ ~ poor P. bought horse. (ii) *Vd.* karyạ 6. (*c*) *Kt.* gāshịŋ ~ gạreshị he has persistent ill-luck. (*d*) halin (= ạbin) ~ gạreshi he's mean-minded. (*e*) an yi masạ tambạrin ~ he has been shamed by his secrets being revealed (= fạllasạ), *cf.* gwạnjō 2. (*f*) tẹ̄rẹran tsị̄yā *Vd.* tẹ̄rẹ̄rẹ 3. (*g*) ɗan ~ na fārị *Vd.* bāshị 2*a*. (*h*) ūwar ~ *Vd.* cācā. (*j*) *Vd.* hūtạlī ; kạshin tsị̄yā. (*k*) tsị̄yā tā yi aurē *Vd.* lạ̄lā. (2) (*a*) quarrelsomeness. (*b*) *Vd.* tsị̄yā-tsị̄yạ̄.

tsị̄yạcē *Vb.* 3A became destitute.

tsị̄yạkī *Vd.* tsạ̄kō.

tsị̄yạkō = tsạ̄kō.

tsiyata A. (tsị̄yatạ) *Vb.* 3B became poor.

B. (tsị̄yatā) *Vb.* 1C impoverished.

tsiya-tsiya A. (tsị̄yā-tsị̄yạ̄) (1) f. sun yi ~ they indulged in mutual recrimination (*cf.* tsịyā 2). (2) *adv.* in destitute state.

B. (tsị̄yā-tsị̄yā) = tsị̄yā-tsị̄yạ̄ 1.

tsiyaya A. (tsị̄yạ̄yā) *Vb.* 1C poured (water) in a thin stream (= bulbụlā 1*b*), *cf.* zubạ, dūrạ.

B. (tsị̄yạ̄yạ) (1) *Vb.* 2 = tsị̄yạ̄yā. (2) *Vb.* 3B flowed out in thin stream (= bulbụlē 2) *x* (*a*) idạntạ yanạ̄ ~ her eyes are streaming with tears. (*b*) yanạ̄ ~ he's

chattering. (3) f. garrulity (= bụlbulạ 2).

tsị̄yạ̄yē (1) *Vb.* 1C poured away the water in a thin stream (= bulbulad dạ). (2) *Vb.* 3A (*a*) flowed out in a thin stream *x* zumạ yā ~ the honey streamed out of the comb (= bulbụlē 2). idạntạ yanạ̄ tsị̄yạ̄yẹ̄wā = tsị̄yạ̄yạ 2*a*. (*b*) P. became weak.

tsōfad dạ *Vb.* 4 rendered old.

tsọ̄fạffī *Vd.* tsōfō.

tsōfai-tsọ̄fại *x* yā yi hajị ~ dạ shī old as he was, he went on the pilgrimage.

tsōfẹ *Vb.* 3A (1) = tsūfā 1. (2) ạ ~ lāfīyạ, ạ rabạ dạ kayạ (*said to P. of limited means*) may you and your new garment last long ! (*Vd.* kayạ 1*f q.v.*).

tsōfō m. (f. tsōfwā) *pl.* tsọ̄fạffī = tswạffī = *Kt.* tswạhhī. (1) (*a*) old ; old P. (*b*) *Vd.* hannū 2*g*. (*c*) yārọ bạ gạrạjē ~ nẹ̄ a spineless boy is useless. (*d*) jīyạ bạ yau ba, tsōfwā tā tunạ kwānaŋ gidā ah, for the days of yore ! (*e*) watạŋ azụmin tsọ̄fạffī m. the month of Rajạb. (*f*) Na sallạr tsọ̄fạffī *Vd.* sallạ 1f. (*g*) (i) tsōfan dōkị yā fi sāban tạ̄kạlmī kō an sạyā fạm gōmạ = tsōfan dōkị yā fi sāban tạ̄kạlmī kō na gāshịn jiminā it's better to ride than walk (*Vd.* tạ̄kạlmī 1*d*). (ii) *Vd.* sạnē 2 ; tsūfā 2. (*h*) (i) ~ mại kudī yārọ nẹ̄ a rich old man is as good as a boy in the marriage-market. (ii) yuŋwạ tā mai dạ yārọ ~ *Vd.* yārọ 1*h*. (*j*) mutūwạr tsōfwā f. (i) infantile convulsions (= tạfīyạ 7). (ii) type of children's game. (*k*) tanạ̄ dạ cikị ~ *Vd.* cikị 4. (*l*) am binnẹ tsōfwā dạ ṛại it remains to be seen what will happen. (*m*) yā ci tsōfwā *Vd.* nānẹ 1*d*. (*n*) tsōfan najadụ old man behaving foolishly as if young. (*o*) tsōfam banzā *Vd.* zaunạ 1*e*. (*p*) *Vd.* ạlkāwạrī 2 ; bam mạganạ 2, 3. (*q*) tsōfam bāshị *Vd.* fatarā 2. (2) *x* tsōfansạ his father. tsōfōna my father. tsọ̄fạffinsụ their parents.

tsōkạ f. (*pl.* tsōkōkī) (1) (*a*) muscle. (*b*) (i) tsōkạr nāmạ lump of meat. (ii) *Vd.* shirwạ 1*c* ; tūwō 1*a*. (*c*) hawan ~ m. riding in small loincloth (wạrkī *or* bạntē) on saddle bare of coverings

(d) edible part of fruit round kernel (ƙwallō) = nāmą, cf. tōtūwā. (2) (a) mąi ～ abundant x yā sąmi kudī mąsū ～ he got much money. (b) (i) iŋ kąi dą ～, kōwā yą ta6ą nāsą, yą ji if a P. says it is easy to give charity, have a look and see what he gives! (ii) Vd. ta6ą 1c.

tsōkącē Vd. tsōkatą.

tsokaci A. (tsōkąci) Vd. tsōkatą.
    B. (tsōkącī) m. nā yi tsōkącinsą I looked at him.

tsokana A. (tsōkaną) Vb. 2 (1) = zuŋgurą. (2) = tsōmą 1a.
    B. (tsōkąnā) Vb. 1C = zungurā.

tsōkąnē Vb. 1C (1) (a) poked x yā ～ minį idǫ he prodded me in the eye. yā ～ ni dą sąndā he poked me with a stick (= zuŋgųrē). (b) hakįn dą ka rēną, shī kąn ～ (= tsōnę) maką idǫ "do not reckon without your host!" (= sąbarą 2). (2) (a) yā tsōkąnę idǫ it is beautiful. (b) yā ～ minį idǫ (i) it seems beautiful to me. (ii) it pleased me. (iii) he envied me (1, 2 = tsōnę 1). (3) Vd. tsōnę 1, 2.

tsōkanō = zuŋgurō q.v. under zuŋgurą.

tsōkatą Vb. 2 (p.o. tsōkącē, n.o. tsōkąci) looked at.

tsǭkī = tsąkī.

tsōkōkī Vd. tsōką.

tsōlamī m. (f. tsōlamā) Kt. tall P.

tsōlō m. = tukkū.

tsololo A. (tsǫlōlǫ) m. (f. tsǫlōlūwā tall and thin.
    B. (tsǫlǫlǫ) adv. dōgō nę ～ he is tall and thin. fātą tā rąbu dą ązakąrī ～ the foreskin stands out above the tip of the penis (as in bąkin jā6ā).

tsōlōlūwā = ƙōlōlūwā.

tsōmą Vb. 1A (1) dipped x yā ～ ąlkaląmī cikin tąwadą he dipped the pen in the ink (= tsōkaną 2), cf. daŋgwąlā. (b) dōkį yā ～ bąkī ą madarā the horse has spot of white in its lip. (2) sun ～ shi cikim mąganą they urged him to an evil course (= dōmą 2). (3) yā ～ kąnsą (= yā ～ bąkinsą) cikim mąganą he interfered in the matter. dą jim mąganątą, ya tsōmą bąkī when he heard me speak, he then spoke. (4) yā ～ bąkī ą ƙwaryā (a) he put his

mouth to the calabash to drink. (b) he interfered.

tsome A. (tsōmę) Vb. 1A dipped (as in tsōmą) completely.
    B. (tsōmē) m. dipping baby in warm medicine to cure kurgā.

tsōmį m. (1) an yi wą kilįshī tsōmįŋ gyądā Vd. kilįshī. (2) enjoyment x nā sąmi tsōmįm barcīna sǎi aką tąshē nį I was just enjoying a nice sleep when they awoke me.

tsǭmīyǫ used in wannąm bąkī ～ what huge jaws!

tsǭmǭdō used in wannąm bąkī ～ what huge jaws!

tsǭmǭmǭ (1) m. yā ji kunyą, yā yi ～ he looks abashed. (2) wannąm bąkī ～ = tsǭmǭdō.

tsōnę Vb. 1A (1) = tsōkąnē 1, 2. (2) (a) yā ～ (= yā tsōkąnę) idąn rūwā he selected the very best (= wāgā 3b). (b) ą ～ idąn rūwan nąŋ add a little flour or furā to flavour this water! (3) Allą yą ～ idąŋ hąsārą God preserve you from ill luck!

tsǭrące-tsǭrącē Vd. tsǭrō.

tsorata A. (tsǭratą) Vb. 2 (p.o. tsǭrące, n.o. tsǭrąci) feared x sun tsǭrącē nį = sun tsǭratą dą nī they are afraid of me.
    B. (tsǭrątā) Vb. 1C frightened.

tsōratad dą Vb. 4 frightened.

tsōrąyē Vd. tsōrō.

tsoro A. (tsǭrō) m. (pl. tsǭrące-tsǭrącē = Kt. tsąrmąkątai) (1) (a) fear (cf. tsąrmąkatai). (b) nā ji tsǭransą I feared him. (bb) (i) ji tsǭraŋ Allą, ką girmąmą mahąifaŋką fear God and respect your parents! (ii) Vd. ganī A. 2 3c. (c) mun ji masą ～ kadą sų kashę shi we feared for him lest they kill him. (d) ąbų mąi ban ～ a terrifying thing. (2) ～ ną dājį, kunyą ną gidā the "bush" is the place to fear, but the abode of men is the place for respectfulness. (3) bar tsǭran zūwąm fādą, ji tsǭran ląifįŋką it's not the punishment you should fear, but the fact of having sinned! (4) Vd. māshį 1c. (5) tsǭraŋ Inną = tsǭran nī dą īyą Vd. māyę 1b. (6) kiną bą yąrā tsǭrō Vd. gįzākā. (7)

mazā bạ̄ ~ *Vd.* Tūlạ. (8) tsɔ̄ram
mahaukạcī *Vd.* fāsạ 1*e.*
  B. (tsōrō) *m.* (*pl.* tsōrạ̄yē) (1) =
tukkū 1, 2. (2) *x* gishirī yā yi ~ the
salt is piled high above the rim of the
measure (*cf.* gịrgịjī) = tōzō 4.
tsororo A. (tsɔ̄rōrọ) = tsɔ̄lōlọ.
  B. (tsɔ̄rɔ̄rɔ̄) = tsɔ̄lɔ̄lɔ̄.
tsōrōrūwā = ƙōlōlūwā.
tsōtsạ *Vb.* 1A = tsɔ̄tsā *Vb.* 2 sucked.
tsɔ̄tsạyī = tsạutsạyī.
tsōtsẹ (1) *Vb.* 1A (*a*) sucked all the
juice from. (*b*) absorbed completely *x*
ƙasā tā ~ rāɓā the ground absorbed
all the dew. (2) *Vb.* 3A became
emaciated.
tsɔ̄tsɔ̄bulọ = tsɔ̄tsɔ̄gulọ *m.* quarrelsomeness.
tsɔ̄yam = tsam 1.
tsūbararā *f.* loquacity (= sūrūtụ).
tsubbace A. (tsubbạcē) *Vb.* 1C = māgạncē.
  B. (tsubbạcē) *Vd.* tsubbatạ.
tsubbatạ *Vb.* 2 (*p.o.* tsubbạcē, *n.o.* tsubbạci)
= māgạncē.
tsubbụ *m.* (*Ar.* " medically treating ")
magic (*cf.* tsāfị).
tsubụrcē *Vb.* 3A = kākụmē.
tsucẹ *Vb.* 1A finished T. (= ƙārạsā).
tsūdū (1) how undersized he is ! (2)
bạ̄kin ~ *m.* small spindle of thread.
tsūdūdū *adj.* small-mouthed (pot, doorway, etc.).
tsūfā (1) *Vb.* 3A became old (= tsɔ̄fẹ).
(2) *m.* (*a*) (*v.n. and progressive of* 1) *x*
yanạ̄ ~ he's becoming old. (*b*) dạ ~
akạ sạ̄mē nị I was born late in my
parents' lives. (*c*) kōmē tsūfan dōkị
yā fi sāban tạ̄kạlmī the worst nag is
better than the best footslogging (=
tsɔ̄fɔ̄ 1*g.*i).
tsuga A. (tsūgạ) (1) poured out much of.
an ~ rūwā (*a*) much water has been
poured out. (*b*) it has rained heavily.
(2) *Vd.* tsūlạ.
  B. (tsuga) *Sk. f.* = tsugūwā.
tsugātsugai *Vd.* tsittsigẹ.
tsugau = tsigau.
tsuge A. (tsūgẹ) *m.* thin-buttocked
P.
  B. (tsūgē) *m.* = gumbā 1*a.* (2)
clay not properly matured (*contrasted
with* tsịma 1*b*) = *Kt.* gumbā 3. (3)

hurried, poorly-done work (= bạ̄rī
kạtsugụ).
tsūgị (1) what heavy rain ! (2) what a
lot is poured out !
tsugu A. (tsugū) *Kt.* = tsụhū.
  B. (tsugu) *Vb.* 3B *x* sun tsugu
cikịŋ ƙasarmụ they slipped into our
country.
tsugudīdị̄ = tsēgumī.
tsūgūgū *m.* smallness of orifice or extent
x ɗan ɗākị nē ~ dạ shī it is a house
of limited area (*pl.* 'yan ɗākunạ nē
~ dạ sū).
tsūgul *m.* shortness *x* ɗan yārọ nē ~
dạ shī he's a tiny lad (*pl.* 'yan yạ̄rā
nē tsugul-tsugul dạ sū).
tsugunā *Vb.* 3A (1) (*a*) (i) squatted on
heels. (ii) bā sạ̄ tsugunạ̄wā ballē su
bar ạbɔ̄kaŋ gạ̄bā sụ tsugunā they
are not delaying and far less are they
giving the enemy any respite. (*b*)
(*euphemism*) went to lavatory (=
rātsẹ 2). (2) gɔ̄be mạ̄ ~ dạ kai to-
morrow I shall summons you. (3)
wurin tsugunạ̄wā place of refuge.
tsugunad dạ *Vb.* 4 (1) ūwā tā ~ yārạntạ
= ƙafạ 1*f.* (2) yā ~ shī (*a*) he dismissed him. (*b*) he kept deferring
paying debt to him.
tsugụna kạ ci dōyạ *m.* form of facial
tattooing (zạuna kạ ci dōyạ 2).
tsugụne *m.* (1) act of squatting. (2)
zạune tā kōmō tsugụne matters have
become serious. (3) tsugụne bạ tạ
ƙarẹ ba (*the person to whom this is said,
replying* an sai dạ birị, an sạyi kạrē)
the matter's far from finished (=
tsugunɔ̄ 1*a.*ii). (4) tsugụne, tạshi *m.*
restlessness, changeability (= tsugụni,
tạshi 2). yanạ̄ tsugụne, tạshi !
he is indecisive. (5) *Vd. next entry.*
tsugụni, tạshi *m.* (1) = tsēgumī. (2)
bustling about (= kạiwā dạ kāwɔ̄wā
= tsugụne 4).
tsugunnā *Sk.* = tsugunā.
tsugunnē *Kt. m.* = tsugunɔ̄.
tsugunniŋ kūsụ *Sk. m.* hypocrisy (=
munāfuccị).
tsugunɔ̄ *m.* (1) (*a*) (i) squatting-position.
(ii) ~ bại ƙarẹ, bạ, an sayar dạ birị,
an sạyi kạrē out of the frying-pan
into the fire (= tsugụne 3). (*b*) yā yi ~

= **tsugunā** 1*b*. (*c*) human excrement.
(*d*) ɗan tsugunaŋkạ dạ kại ? kā ịsa
kạ yị ? how can a trifling P. like you
attempt it ? har kē ɗan tsugunan
naŋ nậkị ? kiŋ ịsa kị hanạ nị ? fancy
a chit like you thinking you're equal
to preventing me !
tsugūwā *f*. point of hoe or axe, protruding
from haft.
tsugwai *Sk. m.* = **tsigau.**
tsuhū *used in* yā kwānā ∼ he could not
sleep from anxiety or excitement.
tsukā = **tsikā.**
tsuke A. (tsūkẹ) (1) *Vb.* 1A (*a*) yā ∼
bậkī he pursed his lips. (*b*) drew
together (purse-strings). (2) *Vb.* 3A
(*a*) bậkinsạ yā ∼ his lips are pursed.
(*b*) ƙasā tā ∼ (*a*) distances between
places has shrunk (*in the opinion of
the ignorant who do not realize increase
of speed of modern transport*). (*b*)
ƙasā tā ∼ land forms isthmus.
B. (tsukẹ) = **tsikẹ.**
tsuki A. (tsūkī) *m.* collection of persons
collected for work, feast, etc.
B. (tsūkī) *Vd.* bạri ∼.
tsuku A. (tsụkū) *m.* loquacity (= sụrūtụ).
B. (tsukụ) *m.* (1) (*a*) crunching
sound. (*b*) tsukuŋ haƙōrī grinding
the teeth. (*c*) dōkị yanậ tsukuŋ lịnzāmị
the horse is biting its bit. (2) ƙafạta
tanậ ∼ = taụnā 2*b*.
tsūkūkū = **tsūgūgū.**
tsūlạ (1) *f*. small blue monkey. (2) *Vb.*
1A (*a*) = **tsūgạ.** (*b*) did much of
x an ∼ masạ būlạlạ he has been well
thrashed. (3) *Vb.* 3A yā ∼ ạ gụje
he took to his heels.
tsūlậlā *Vb.* 1C = tsūgạ.
tsūlịyā *f*. (*pl.* tsūlịyōyī) (1) (*a*) anus (=
dubụrā = *Sk.* būtịyā = *Sk.* dīwạ 3 =
Sk. muntạ = mūrịyā). (*b*) ạ ∼ = ạ
tsūlī in the anus (Mod. Gram. 24*a*, N.B.).
(2) gāshịn ∼ *Vd.* gāshị 1*j*. (3) " Kụŋkurū, ta ịnā akẹ cịŋkạ ", ya cẹ " ta ∼ "
replying rudely and recklessly to a
superior (= gạtsē 2). (4) bậ kōmē ạ
tsūlịyar mại dōkị sǎi kāshī what a broken
reed he is ! (= hōlōƙō 2). (5) ∼ tasạ
tā dụri rūwā he was in a funk. (6)
tsūlịyarkạ *Vd.* ƙậbạrạ. (7) Tsūlịyā
mại tīlạs, anậ rūwa, kunậ jiŋ kāshī

European who maketh malefactors
disgorge ill-gotten gains !
tsullạ *Vb.* 1A (1) = cillạ. (2) = tsūlạ
2, 3.
tsululū (1) *m.* height of *x* tsululun dậmunā
the height of the wet season. **tsululun**
yuŋwạ acme of hunger (= gāyạ 1).
(2) *adv.* abundantly.
tsulum = **tsilum.**
tsuma = **tsima.**
tsumāgịyā = **tsumaŋgịyā** *f.* (*pl.* tsụmạŋgī
= tsụmạŋgū = tsumaŋgīyōyī) cane,
switch (= kwāgirī = tsabgạ = *Kt.*
tsāgẹ 3).
tsumājịyā = **tsumanjịyā** = **tsumāgịyā** *q.v.*
tsụmammīyā *f.* rankling enmity.
tsumaŋgịyā *Vd.* **tsumāgịyā.**
tsụmāyạ *Vb.* 2 (1) waited for (= jirā).
(2) kụ tsụmāyē nị *m.* stunted goat (=
Kt. mẹtsō = tsụmāyaŋ), *cf.* tsụmbē.
tsụmāyaŋ *m.* (*lit.* await me !) weakly
calf, etc. (= tsụmāyạ 2), *cf.* tsụmbē.
tsụmbē *m.* (1) stunted P. or animal (*cf.*
tsụmāyạ 2). (2) = ạlhūtsạ.
tsumbụlā *Kt.* = **tsambạmā.**
tsumbụrā *Vb.* 1C hindered growth or
becoming cooked.
tsumburad dạ *Vb.* 4 = tsumbụrā.
tsụmbụrarrē *m.* (*f.* tsụmbụrarrīyā) *pl.*
tsụmbụrạrrū stunted (= mậgyāzọ).
tsumbụrē *Vb.* 3A remained stunted or
uncooked.
tsụmburụmburụm *m.* yā yi ∼ it (dish of
beans, etc.) resists all efforts to cook
it (= *Kt.* hǫri 2).
tsụmē = **tsịmē.**
tsụmēgẹ *used in* ɗan ∼ *m.* thin man.
tsumi = **tsimi.**
tsụmmā *m.* (*pl.* tsummōkī = tsụmmōƙarai
= tsụmmōƙai = tsummōƙarạ) (1) (*a*)
rags (= raggạ = dịnjī = *Sk.* rākī).
(*b*) yā yi tigijiŋ cikin ∼ = yā yi ∼
tigijiŋ he's dressed in rags. (2) tsụmman
jūjī deposed P. who is thorn in side of
his successor (= ƙayạ 1*d* = fạsasshē 2).
(3) im macịjī yā sậrē kạ, iŋ kā ga
baƙin ∼, kạ gudụ once bitten, twice
shy. (4) (*a*) mụtụm bai fī kạ ∼ ba,
bạ zại kaɗạ makạ kwarkwatạ ba
junior should not lord it over senior.
(*b*) dậrīyar mại ∼ *Vd.* dậrīyā 3. (5)
ɗan ∼ *m.* (*pl.* 'yan ∼) second-hand

clothes. (6) cūrin ∼ Vd. cūri 4. (7)
∼ makunsar cūtā Vd. kārūwa 2b. (8)
tsummā a randā Vd. sakata 1b.
tsumnīyā Kt. f. cane (tsumāgīyā) used
for making traps (tarkō).
tsumu = tsimu.
tsumulmulā f. niggardliness.
tsumunya Kt. f. guinea-fowl snare.
tsumū-tsumū = tsimū-tsimū.
tsumwinīyā f. fidgetiness, restlessness (=
mutsūnīyā).
tsunce = tsince.
tsundum = tsindum.
tsungālumī = tsangālumī.
tsungula Vb. 2 Kt. (1) pinched. (2)
pinched bit off (= muntsuna).
tsungulē Vb. 1C Kt. = tsungula.
tsungulī Kt. m. = muntsune.
tsunguma = tsangwama.
tsungur m. yā yi ∼ it (load, cap, etc.)
is askew.
tsunka = tsinka.
tsunke = tsinke.
tsunkula Kt. = tsungula.
tsunkuna Kt. = tsungula.
tsunta = tsinta.
tsuntsū m. (f. tsuntsūwā) pl. tsuntsāyē (1)
(a) any bird. (b) dōkin tsuntsāyē
the Long-tailed Flycatcher. (2) (a)
yārinyan nan cin tsuntsāyē nē this girl is
no longer virgin (= budurwā 2). (b) yārā
sunā yin cin tsuntsāyē these boys are defiling little girls. (3) bābu ∼, bābu tarkō
= bā shi ga ∼, bā shi ga tarkō falling
between two stools (= zabarī 2). (4)
cf. san ∼. (5) tsuntsun da ya jā rūwā
shī rūwā zai dōkā hoist with one's own
petard (because this bird's cry resembles
" Allā ! " and is supposed to be prayer
for rain). (6) kōwane tsuntsū ya yi
kūkan gidansa let the cobbler stick
to his last ! (7) wani tsuntsū yanā
gudun rūwā, agwagwā cikin rūwa
takē nēmā one man's meat is another's
poison. (8) masō ɗan tsuntsū Vd.
masō 1. (9) Vd. turba 3.
tsuntsumbērē what an undersized person !
tsuntūwā = tsintūwā.
tsura A. (tsūra) (1) Vb. 1A pierced (=
sōkā). (2) f. used in yā kafa masa ∼
= yā sā masa ∼ = cīkas 2 q.v.

B. (tsūrā) m. (1) handleless knife
or sword, cf. kudundurā. (2) tsūransu
suka zō they came without wives or
followers.
tsurārīya f. trickery.
tsūre Vb. 3A became pierced, stove in.
tsurra = tsirra.
tsūrū (1) m. (a) yā zauna, yā yi ∼ he
sat silently, pensively (cf. zurū 1a).
(b) 'yan ∼ pl. ornamental hairpins
(kwārō). (2) adv. (a) yā zauna ∼ =
1a. (b) yā kwānā ∼ he spent sleepless night through excitement, fear,
etc.
tsurūnīyā f. (1) fidgetiness, restlessness
(= mutsūnīyā). (2) roving about (=
gīlo).
tsururū = tsululū.
tsūrūrūcē Vb. 3A decreased.
tsurut = tsirit.
tsurū-tsurū (1) m. yā yi ∼ he was ashamed,
afraid (= tsamō-tsamō). (2) adv.
yā yi tsurū-tsurū he trembled. ga
tsuntsū tsurū-tsurū cikin tarkō the
bird is fluttering in the snare.
tsut = tsit.
tsūtsa f. (pl. tsūtsōtsī) (1) (a) worm. (b)
farar ∼ tapeworm (= tsīlā q.v.). (c)
type of vermicelli (cf. tālīya). (d)
tafīyar ∼ Vd. tafīya 8. (2) yā bā ni
∼ he gave me perfume on cotton. (3)
tsūtsar kurkuku the fly Auchmeromiya
luteola's larvae which infest floors
and are blood-sucking. (4) mā ga
daban ∼ a rānā we must devise a
plan. (5) tsūtsan nāma ita mā nāma
cē the two are identical. (6) mu ga ta
fādī, ∼ tā kā da kudī it has happened
though regarded as impossible.
tsūtsūcē Vb. 3A deteriorated (= lālācē).
tsuttsuge = tsittsige.
tsuttsūki m. purse, mouth of which is
drawn together by string.
tsūwa f. (1) rumblings in stomach. (2)
Sk. (a) hiss of snake. (b) squeal of
various animals.
tsūwan jākī Vd. tsūwe.
tsūwe m. (pl. tsūwāwū = tsūwaiwai =
tsūwayyā) (1) testicle (= kwālātai 2).
(2) tsūwan jākī type of kola-nut.
tsūwū m. the shrub Pavonia hirsuta.
tsūū = kyūū.

tsuwurwurī *m.* = **kasąbī.**

tsūyę *m. (sg., pl.) Sk.* testicle (= **tsūwę**).

tswą *f.* the sound of frying oil.

tswągdā *Kt. f.* = **tsądā.**

tswąffī *Vd.* **tsōɓō.**

tswāgą *Vb.* 1A *Kt.* filled (**rumbū**) to utmost capacity with corn.

tswāgę *Vb.* 3A *Kt.* (**rumbū**) was filled to capacity with corn.

tswąhhī *Vd.* **tsōɓō.**

tswākąrā *Kt.* = **tsākąrā.**

tswala A. (**tswālā**) *Kt. f.* = **wąinā.** B. (**tswālą**) *Kt.* = **tsālą.**

tswālēlę *m.* (*f.* **tswālēlīyā**) handsome.

tswąrci *Vd.* **tswąrtā.**

tswąrtā *Vb.* 2 *Sk.* (*p.o.* **tswąrcē**, *n.o.* **tswąrci**) = **tsǫratą.**

tų *Vd.* **tųū.**

***tu'ammąlī** = ***tą'ammąlī.**

tu'annutī = **tą'annątī.**

tub = **tǫɓī** 1*b*.

tuba A. (**tūbā**) (1) *Vb.* 3A (*a*) repented. (*b*) expressed repentance. (*c*) (*before dative* **tūbam** *is used*) *x* **yā tūbam musu** (i) he expressed his repentance to them. (ii) he (enemy) surrendered to them. (2) *m.* (*a*) (*v.n. and progressive of* 1) *x* **yanǫ** ∼ he is repenting. (*b*) repentance *x* **Allą yą kąrɓi tūbanką** may God accept your repentance ! B. (**tubą**) *Vb.* 1A = **tubā** *Vb.* 2 *Kt.* began (= **fārą**).

tuɓa A. (**tųɓā**) (1) *Vb.* 2 took off garment from P. *x* **nā tųɓi rīgā tasą** I took off his gown (*cf.* **tūɓę**). (2) *m., f.* deposing P. (*cf.* **tūɓę**). B. (**tūɓā**) *Kt. f.* divesting bride of adornments a week before marriage (*returnable after migrated to husband's home*).

tųɓaɓɓē *Vd.* **tūɓę.**

tųɓabbē *m.* (*f.* **tųɓabbīyā**) *pl.* **tųɓabbū** repentant P.

Tūbalą *Vd.* **wākē** 5*b*, **tūbąlī.**

tūbąlcē *Vb.* 1C (1) made into bricks *x* **yā tūbąlcę ƙasā** he made the clay into bricks (*cf.* **tūbąlī**). (2) *Vd.* **tūbałtą.**

tūbąlci *Vd.* **tūbałtą.**

tūbąlī *m.* (*pl.* **tūbalą** = **tūbulą** = *Kt.* **tūbullą**) (1) (*a*) brick (= **ƙungu** = *Sk.* **ƙuŋƙū** 2). (*b*) **dą mā tūbąlin zālunci bā yą ginįm mulkį** it is a universal

truth that rule founded on oppression cannot succeed. (2) **tūbąlin tǫkā** good-for-nothing P. (3) **ƙyąshin** ∼ *Vd.* **dąlā** 2*b*.

tūbałtą *Vb.* 2 (*p.o.* **tūbąlcē**, *n.o.* **tūbąlci**) made part of the clay into bricks *x* **yā tūbąlci ƙasā** (*cf.* **tūbąlcē**).

tūbam *Vd.* **tūbā** 1*c*.

tųbānī *m.* (1) a food made from bean-flour. (2) **tubānin dawākī** the plant *Peristrophe bicalyculata.* (3) **Tųbānįŋ kīfī ą cī ką dą lųrā** = **Tųbānįŋ kīfī hądīyąr mąsū hankulą** he's powerful, so watch out !

tųbarkallą (*Ar.* God be praised !) (1) bravo ! (= **bārakallą**). (2) *Vd.* **ƙishą** 2.

tųbau *m.* giraffe-trap (= **arą** 2*a*).

tuɓe A. (**tūɓę**) *Vb.* 1A (1) (*a*) deposed P. from *official* position (= **shūrę** 1*b* = **murdę** 1*b* = **tūrę** 1*c* = **tumɓukē** 2), *cf.* **sąllamą.** (*b*) **tųɓaɓɓan Sarkī yā fi 'yan sarkī gōmą duk dą ųbansų Cirǫmą** it's better to have loved and lost than never to have loved at all. (2) (*a*) (i) took off (garment, ring, sword, shoes, cap, turban, hat, etc.) from oneself or another *x* **nā** ∼ **rīgā** I took off my gown. **yā** ∼ **wąndōna** = **yā** ∼ **minį wąndō** he took off my trousers (= **sąɓulą** 1 = **sullųɓē** = **cirę** = **kwaɓę** 1*c*), *cf.* **tųɓā, ɗaukē** 1*a*. (ii) *Vd.* **rawąnī** 1*a*. (*b*) **azzįkī bą rīgā ba bąllē 'yaŋūwā sų** ∼ prosperity entails responsibilities. (*c*) **mutum bā yą** ∼ **minį rīgā ą kąsūwā, san nan yą kōmō gidā, yą cę zai są minį** (*said by woman*) I won't stand *that* from my husband ! (3) (*a*) = **sąɓulą** 2*a*. (*b*) **an** ∼ **fātąr ąkwīyą** *Vd.* **sąlkā** 1*c*. B. (**tųɓē**) *Kt. m.* = **ban shūnī.** C. (**tūɓē**) *m.* small goat used as bait for pit-trap.

tubką = **tūką.**

tubƙą *Kt.* = **tūką.**

tubkē = **tųkē.**

tųɓū *Kt.* = **duɓū.**

tūbulą *Vd.* **tūbąlī.**

tųbullukī = **tųbullukī** *m.* (*f.* **tųbullukā** = **tųbullųkā**) fat, thick-set P.

tuɓuncē *Vb.* 1C (1) = **tūɓę** 1. (2) won against P. in game (= **cī**).

tuɓunī *m.* ground-nut soup.

tuḅụrā *f.* (1) one of the stomachs (tụmbī) of ruminants (= ūwar kāshī = tụmbur-ƙụmā = bạ̄ba 10 = kịlāgạ = bằi ƙanạ̣nkạ = bằi mayạ̄ƙā = tsāmī 1*h*), *cf.* makīyāyā. (2) yā cikạ ~ tasạ = ~ tasạ tā ɗaukạ he's replete. (3) cikịn ~ gạrēshị he's two-faced. (4) ɗan tubụrar wā (*mild abuse*) you bothersome fellow ! (*cf.* ūwāḳạ).

tuburạ̣ŋ (1) = zallā *x* yā fạḍi gạskīyā ~ he told only the truth. mahạụkạcī nẹ̄ ~ he's raving mad. (2) yā tsayạ wạ aikịnsạ ~ he worked doggedly (= nācẹ).

tuɓurkā *x* ~ ɗūwạ̄wụŋ Audụ what big buttocks Audụ has !

Tụburƙuƙụ = Tụburƙuƙụ (*mythical being*) *used in* kā fi ~ ƙushī what an angry P. you are ! (= Tụdurbuƙwị = Turụbuƙwị).

tuburƙumā *f.* = tubụrā 1.

tubur-tụbụr = tụbur-tụbur *used in* yanạ̄ dạ ɗūwạiwai ~ he has big buttocks. tanạ̄ tạfīyạ ~ she's joggling her buttocks as she walks.

tụḅū-tubū *m.* type of coiffure.

tụɓwịnīyā *Kt. f.* = tạ̣ɓẹnīyā.

tuɗad dạ *Vb.* 4 *Sk.* poured away (= zubar dạ), *Vd.* tud dạ.

tụ̄darā *f.* (1) long narrow drum (= dọ̄darā = dụndufạ), *Vd.* kuntukurū. (2) what a big-bottomed woman !

tuɗas ⸗ lilis.

tuɗas dạ = tuɗar dạ.

tụddā *Vd.* tudụ.

tud dạ *Vb.* 4 (1) poured away (= tuɗad dạ). (2) spat out *x* yā ~ yau he spat. yā ~ shī = yā tusshē shị he spat it out (= tōfad dạ).

tụddai *Vd.* tudụ.

tuɗẹ *Sk.* (1) *Vb.* 1A = zubẹ 1*a*, *b.* (2) *Vb.* 3A = zubẹ 2*a*.

tudụ *m.* (*pl.* tụddā = tụddai) (1) (*a*) high ground (*compared with the level occupied by the speaker, hence hill, river bank seen from river, etc.*), *cf.* dūtsẹ 3. (*b*) lạifī ~, kā tākạ nākạ, kā ganō na wanī = mūnị ~ nẹ̄, sằi kā tākạ nākạ kā ganō na wanī everyone is blind to his own shortcomings. (*c*) yā hayẹ ~, yā bar na gạngarẹ dạ lẹ̄ƙē he's peerless (*cf.* 3*b below*). (*d*) tudụ bā yạ̄ kōmō gạŋgarẹ *Vd.* samạ

1*g*.ii. (2) (*a*) Africa (*contrasted with Europe*) *x* yạụshẹ̄ zại kōmō ~ when will he return to Africa ? (*cf.* ƙasạ 5). (*b*) kai nẹ̄ Bạtūrạn ~ (*said mockingly*) you albino, you ! (*cf.* zạbīyā). (3) (*a*) P. in former days exempted from tax, gạyyā, etc. (*b*) outstandingly good P. (= *Kt.* tsịbirī 2), *cf.* 1*c above*. (4) tudụn dāfạ̄wā (*a*) means of livelihood. (*b*) Audụ tudụn dāfạ̄wānā nẹ̄ Audụ is my patron (*Vd.* dāfạ 6).

tuɗuɗu *adv.* abundantly.

tụdụŋkā *Kt. f.* raised doorstep (= dōkịn ƙōfạ̣).

tudunyạ *Kt. f.* = tudụ.

Tụdurbuƙwị = Tụburƙuƙụ.

tuɗus = tuɗas.

tufạ (1) *m.*, *f.* (*pl.* tufāfị = tufōfī) (*a*) garment. (*b*) yā ɗaurạ ~ = yā sạ̄ ~ he clothed himself. (2) *Vb.* 1A (*rustic*) *used in* Allạ̄ yạ ~ makạ ạsīrī God keep you from shame ! (= rufẹ).

tufānịyā *f.* (*pl.* tụfạ̣nī = tụfạ̣nū = tufānīyōyī) mat of ƙyārạ-grass, etc., screen for covering doorway (= *Sk.* askunnịyā 1).

tufantad dạ = tufāsad dạ = tufātad dạ = *Kt.* tufāyad dạ *Vb.* 4 clothed.

tufẹ = tifẹ.

tufka = tūka.

tufōfī *Vd.* tufạ.

tufụ̄wā *Kt. f.* = tufạ 1.

tụ̄gā *Vb.* 2 = tūgẹ.

tụ̄gandē *m.* (1) long, thin red-peppers (= ɗan kadanā). (2) = tạttạ̄sai. (3) *Vd.* Dāyē.

tūgẹ *Vb.* 1A = tumɓụkē.

tugụ *m.* (1) being itinerant dealer (especially in mounts) who is not above accepting stolen property (*he never has cash, but after bargaining, gives something in kind*). (2) (*a*) ɗan ~ *m.* (*pl.* 'yan ~) dealer as in 1 (*cf.* ɓạrāwọ 5). (*b*) epithet of 1*a is* Sụ̄rau, ƙanạm ɓạrāwọ = Zạrmau ƙanạm ɓạrāwọ.

tugub-tugub *Kt.* = kutuf.

tugụfā *Kt.* = tukụbā.

tugụllā = tagụllā.

tugụntā *Sk.* = tugụnyā.

tugụnyā *Vb.* 1C churned (milk), *cf.* tugụ̄wā.

tugūwā *f.* (1) churning milk (= **kidạ** 2). (2) swaying.

tụgwānạ *Vb.* 3B was intoxicated (= **bụgu**).

tuhuma A. (**tụhumạ**) *Ar.* (1) *Vb.* 2 = **tuhụmtā** 1, 2. (2) *f.* (*a*) suspicion *x* **dạ** ∼ **ạ kạnsạ** he is under suspicion. (*b*) divining (= **dūbā**) *x* **yā tạfi wurin** ∼ he has gone to have his fortune told by sand. (*c*) interrogation *x* **an yi masạ** ∼ **har dạ ạzābạ** he has been interrogated by torture. B. (**tuhụmā**) *Vb.* 1C = **tuhụmtā**.

tuhumta A. (**tuhụmtā**) *Vb.* 1C (1) suspected P. (2) interrogated (*cf.* **tụhumạ** 2c). (3) sought information by divination (**dūbā**) about T. or P. (*cf.* **tụhumạ** 2b). B. (**tụhumtạ**) *Vb.* 2 (*p.o.* **tụhụmcē**, *n.o.* **tụhụmci**) = **tuhụmtā** 1, 2.

tujạ = **tijạ**.

tụjanjaɳ *Had.* = **dạɳgarẹzā**.

tụjārạ = **tịjārạ**.

tụjāwạlī = **tạjāwạlī**.

tuje A. (**tūjẹ**) (1) *Vb.* 1A (*a*) scraped (hair from hide). (*b*) tore off (feathers from live bird *x* ostrich) = **fịgā** 1a.ii. (*c*) = **darjẹ** 2b. (*d*) **yā** ∼ **ƙasā** it (horse reined in *as in* **darjẹ** 2b) cut up the ground. (*e*) *cf.* **tụzā, tūzad dạ.** (2) *Vb.* 3A = **tūzō** (thread) became tangled (through slipping off spool) = **tōjạɓē.** (3) *m.* (*a*) Sudan bustard (*Choriotis arabs*). (*b*) Denham's bustard (*Neotis cafradenhami*). (4) *Vd.* **kāshin** ∼. B. (**tūjē**) *Vd.* **tụzā.**

tuji A. (**tūjī**) *m.* (1) the grass *Eleusine indica.* (2) **cin** ∼ *m.* = **sāran tūjī.** (3) **dībạn** ∼ *Vd.* **dībạ** 2f. B. (**tūjị**) (1) how cheap ! (2) how sharply the horse has been reined in ! (*cf.* **tūjẹ** 1c). C. (**tūjị**) *Vd.* **tụzā.**

tuka A. (**tūkạ**) *Vb.* 1A (1) plaited (hair, rope, string). (2) (*a*) **yā** ∼ **rịkicī** he started an intrigue. (*b*) **yā** ∼ **gaddamạ** he started a quarrel. (3) **an** ∼ **hayāƙī** dense smoke has been raised. B. (**tụƙā**) (1) *Vb.* 2 = **tūkạ.** (2) *f.* (*a*) A. plaited (*x* rope) = **tụƙē.** (*b*) ply *x* **zạrē mại** ∼ **ukụ** three-ply thread (*cf.* **murjị, ƙwārạ**). (*c*) **tụƙar hagụɳ**

(i) = **fạsō** 1. (ii) contrary P. (= **gāgạrarrē**). (iii) *Vd.* **bạhagọ** 4. (*d*) **an yi wạ** ∼ **hancị** the matter is settled.

tuƙa A. (**tūƙạ**) (1) *Vb.* 1A (*a*) stirred (T. of thick consistency *x* **tūwō**, dye, etc.), *cf.* **kadạ** 1c. (*b*) **tā** ∼ **tūwō** *Vd.* **kwāɓạ** 1b. (*c*) propelled boat by oar or pole (*cf.* **dōgạrā** 3). (*d*) drove (car). (*e*) **yā tūƙạ yā sāƙạ, ạbụ yā ƙi ƙụllūwā** he strained every nerve but couldn't accomplish it. (2) *Vb.* 3A (*a*) (fat P.) waddled along. (*b*) **cikịna yanạ tūƙạwā** I have a cutting pain in my inside (*cf.* **tụƙā**). (*c*) *Kt.* departed. B. (**tụƙā**) (1) *f.* (*a*) cutting pain *x* **cikịna yanạ** ∼ = **tūƙạ** 2b. (*b*) **zūcịyāta tā yi** ∼ (i) I feel sick. (ii) I feel vexed. (2) *Vb.* 2 caused cutting pain, etc., *x* (*a*) **zūcịyāta tanạ tụƙāta** = 1b *above.* (*b*) **mạganạr tā tụƙē nị** the affair annoyed me. C. (**tụƙā**) = **tịƙā.**

tuƙāƙā *Vb.* 1C an **tuƙāƙạ hayāƙī** = **tūkạ** 3.

tuƙāƙē *Vb.* 3A **hayāƙī** (**fadạ**) **yā** ∼ big smoke (quarrel) arose.

tūƙā-tụƙā = **tūƙai-tụƙại** *Vd.* **tūƙēƙẹ.**

tukạtukī = **tikạtikī.**

tuke A. (**tūkẹ**) (1) *Vb.* 1A plaited (*as in* **tūkạ**) completely. (2) *Vb.* 3A became in a muddle. B. (**tụƙē**) *m.* = **tụƙā** 2a. C. (**tukẹ**) *Sk. m.* = **tukị** 1.

tuƙe A. (**tūƙẹ**) (1) *Vb.* 1A (*a*) stirred (*as in* **tūƙạ** 1a, *b*) completely. (*b*) **cīwạn cikị yanạ** ∼ **ni** = **tūƙạ** 2b. (*c*) **zūcịyāta tā** ∼ **ni** = **tụƙā** 1b. (*d*) *Kt.* **iskạ yā** ∼ **itạce** the wind made the tree lean over. (2) *Vb.* 3A *Kt.* **itạcē yā** ∼ **the** tree (buffeted by wind) is leaning over. B. (**tụƙē**) *m.* (1) seedpod of tobacco-flowers (**fụrē**) used by old people for staining teeth (= **tạunē**). (2) meat boiled, pounded (**kirɓạ**) and re-cooked with butter, honey, etc. (3) type of **kạs kaifī.** (4) *Kt.* = **fụffụkā** 2. C. (**tuƙẹ**) *Vb.* 1A cornered a P.

tūƙēƙẹ *m.* (*f.* **tūƙēƙịyā**) *pl.* **tūƙā-tụƙā** = **tūƙai-tụƙại** *adj.* of huge bulk.

tukị *m.* (1) external apex of round thatch-roof (= **wuyạn dākị**). (2) *Kt.* **kudin** ∼ (*obsolete term*) house-tax.

tukkạ = *Kt.* **tuƙƙạ** = **tūkạ** *q.v.*

tukkū *m.* (*pl.* **tukkwāyē**) (1) (*a*) plait of hair on crown of head (= **tuƙullumā** = **tōlīyā** = **zaŋkō**). (*b*) *Vd.* **tukkūwā**. (2) bird's crest, cock's comb (= **zaŋkō**). (3) (*a*) plume on helmet, tassel (= **tūtạ** 2). (*b*) = **ƙulūlụ** 2*d*, 2*a*. (4) *cf.* **tsōrō**. (5) *Nos.* 1–3 *above* = **tuntū**.

tukkụbajạl *m.* tying prisoner's arms to stick below his knees.

tukkum mụzūrū *used in* **gạrī yā yi** ~ these are hard times !

tukkūwā *Kt. f.* (1) **tukkū**. (2) **kā ajịyẹ tukkūwā kạmaŋ gạuạ̄ƙạ ?** you sport a tuft like a crownbird ? (*cf.* **tsīgī**).

tukkwāyē *Vd.* **tukkū**.

tūƙō *Vb.* 3A *Kt.* (1) = **tōhō**. (2) *x* **bābā yanā̀ tūƙọwā ạ rīgan nạŋ** the dye on this gown is becoming pleasantly darker.

tụƙu *Vb.* 3B *x* **tūwō bā yā̀ tụƙūwā** the food **tūwō** cannot be chewed as the cud is chewed (*cf.* **tīƙā** 2).

tuƙubā *f.* (*pl.* **tukubōbī**) (1) mound round which **tsịrē** is toasted. (2) mound (**dạƙalī**) on which wares are exposed. (3) mound (**dạƙalī**) in centre of playground (**fagyaŋ wā̀sā**).

tukuburci *Sk. m.* = **takabbarci**.

tụkubụrī *m.* = **gunā̀gunī**.

tụkụbyelbyel *Kt. m.* = **aduŋgurē**.

tụkudī *m.* a drink made of bulrush-millet with spices and honey or milk (*Vd.* **asā̀bụ**).

tukuf = **kutuf**.

tukụfā = **tukụbā**.

tukuf-tukuf = **kutuf**.

tukuici *Vd.* **tukwīci**.

tuƙuƙī *m.* (1) anger (= **fushī**). (2) (*a*) **tuƙuƙiŋ hayāƙī** dense smoke. (*b*) **tuƙuƙiŋ hazō** dense mist.

tukukkụɓē *Vb.* 3A became worn-out.

tuƙuƙū = **tuƙuƙī**.

tụƙullumā *f.* (*pl.* **tuƙullumōmī**) (1) = **tukkū** 1. (2) *Kt.* bruise on crown of head.

tụkumụrdī = **gunā̀gunī**.

tụkụŋ = **tụkụnā** 1*a*, 2, 3, 4.

tụkụnā (1) (*negatively*) not yet *x* (*a*) **baı̇̀ zō ba** ~ (= **tụkụŋ**) he has not yet come. (*b*) **zā̀ ka kā̀sūwā̀ ?** are you off

to market ? **tụkụnā** not yet ! (2) (*after* **sǎi** *with negative understood*) **sǎi yā gamạ sallạ** ~ (= **tụkụŋ**) no (do not call him) till he has finished praying ! (*reply to* shall I call him ?). **sǎi dǎi aŋ kāwō** ~ (= **tụkụŋ**) no, (we shall not eat) till it's brought (*reply to* have you already eaten ?), Mod. Gram. 107*b*. (3) only when (*with past sense*, Mod. Gram. 181*d*) **sǎi akạ kashẹ su** ~ (= **tụkụŋ**) **mukạ zō** it was only after they'd been killed that we came. **sǎi dạ akạ yi tạfīyạ** ~ (= **tụkụŋ**) **kānạ mukạ isa kā̀sūwā** it was only after travelling some way that we reached market. (4) only when (*with future sense*, Mod. Gram. 107*c*) **sǎi an shā fāmā dạ shī** ~ (= **tụkụŋ**) **yạ fịta** it cannot be got outside without great effort.

tụkuŋkunjị *m.* (1) jumble of rags or old rope. (2) **ya nadạ** ~ he's wearing a large, bunchy turban.

tụkụnnā = **tụkụnā**.

tukunyā = **tukunyạ** *f.* (*pl.* **tukwā̀nē** = **tukunyōyī**) (1) (*a*) cooking-pot. (*b*) (i) **hạƙurī hatsin** ~ **nē** = *Kt.* **hạƙurī tukunyar tsābạ** there's a limit to everyone's patience. (ii) *Vd.* **yạu** 2*d*. (*c*) **bāyan** ~ **bā̀ zanẹ nē** this is a witless procedure. (*d*) *Vd.* **kuryā** 2, **damō** 6. (*e*) don **tūwaŋ gọ̄be akẹ waŋkẹ** ~ don't spoil your chances ! (*f*) **ạ cikim baƙar** ~ **a kạm fitar dạ farin tūwō** don't despise a thing for it's lack of beauty ! (*g*) (i) ~ **idaŋ tā yi bọ̄rī**, **sǎi tạ ɓā̀tạ bā̀kintạ** cutting off one's nose to spite one's face. (ii) *Vd.* **bọ̄rī** 3. (*h*) **tukunyar tạwadạ** ink-well made of clay or **dumā** (*cf.* **kụrtū** 1*b*). (*j*) **ɗōrạ tukunyā** *Vd.* **murfụ** 2*e.*ii. (*k*) **tukunyar Gwārī** *Vd.* **bạrgi-bạrgī**. (2) (*a*) **mā̀rūrụ yā yi** ~ the boil has come to a head (= **kaskō** 3). (*b*) **kụrkunū yā yi** ~ the guinea-worm is about to extrude. **tukunyar kụrkunū** place where guinea-worm is about to extrude. (*c*) broken egg. (3) funnel of locomotive or steamer. (4) type of sausage for children. (5) **tukunyar bābā** indigovat. (6) **tukunyar hancị** base of the nose. (7) **tukunyar rakūwā** place in nest where **rakūwā** stores honey. (8)

tukunyar tābą tobacco-pipe. (9) tukunyar zubį mould for casting.

tukurą (1) m. energetic worker. (2) dą Bąƙo dą Tųkurą duk Umbutāwā nę it's six of one and half a dozen of the other. (3) Vd. Şarkim fādą, ɓaunā.

tukųrī (Ar. takrāri repetition) m. (1) repeating whole Koran in sections by a gathering, when pupil has completed its reading (sąukā 1d), alms being received by the participants. (2) bā ą kǫyaŋ kąrątū ran ‿ don't leave things till the last moment !

tukurkųshē = takwarkwąshē.

tuƙųrū (1) m. great amount x yaną̄ tuƙųruŋ aiki he's working very hard. (2) greatly x yanā aikį ‿ = 1. yaną̄ kūkā ‿ he's crying bitterly.

Tųkųrūrų (pl. of Tąkąrī) (said by Arabs) negro, negroes.

tukurwā f. (pl. tukwą̄rē) (1) the palm Raphia vinifera (cf. gwaŋgwalā). (2) yaną̄ dōgąrą ‿ cikiŋ kǫgī he's poling the boat along with gwaŋgwalā (cf. tūƙą 1c).

tųkū-tųkū used in itącē yā zamā ‿ the tree is full of dry-rot.

tukwą̄nē Vd. tukunyā.

tukwą̄rē Vd. tukurwā.

tuƙwī x gą dākuną ‿ look the houses are now visible ! (x not hidden by trees).

tukwīcį m. (1) gift handed .to bearer of present from another. (2) yabą kyautā taną̄ gą ‿ the amount given the deliverer shows how much a present is appreciated.

tukwīkwįyā Vb. 1D tangled T.

tųkwīmą Zar. f. = jīnįyā 2.

tula A. (tūlā) Sk. f. = tamaulā 1.
B. (Tūlą) (1) The Tula pagans of Gombe. (2) ‿ mazā bą̄ tsǫrō what a fearlessly outspoken person !
C. Vd. tilą, tįlā.

tųlaskē m. lazy P.

tūlā-tųlą̄ Vd. tūlēlę.

tulę = tilę.

tūlēlę m. (f. tūlēlįyā) pl. tūlā-tųlą̄ large and round.

tulį (1) m. heap, crowd x tulįm bāyī a crowd of prisoners. an yi wą tulį rąunī a very large number were wounded. (2) abundantly.

tūliƙēƙę m. (f. tūliƙēƙįyā) pl. tūliƙai-tųlįƙai large and round.

tūliƙī m. (f. tūliƙā) pl. tūliƙai-tųlįƙai large and round.

tulkū adv. (1) abundantly. (2) cheaply.

tullą = tillą.

tulluƙēƙę = tūliƙēƙę.

tulluƙī = tūliƙī.

tullūwā f. (1) summit (= ƙōlōlwā). (2) = tukkū 1a.

tul-tul (1) m. sound of pounding corn in small mortar. (2) yā cįka ‿ it is chock-full (= fal).

tultula = tuttula.

tų̄lū m. (pl. tūlūną) (1) (a) pitcher, ewer. (b) bottle (= kwalabā). (c) ‿ shī kę̄ wąhalą ; rąndā taną̄ ɗaką, tā sąmi rūwā the senior rests, the junior toils. (d) fitsārin ‿ bą̄ na mātā ba nę expert work is not for the novice. (e) tūwan ‿ mąi wųyar kwāshēwā dą mārā (said by labourers) what a cantankerous person ! (f) būsąr ‿ Vd. būsą 3c. (2) (a) shameless P. (b) kō tų̄lū yā fī shį gāshį he's a useless person. (3) wifeless man (epithet is Tų̄lū mąi santsim bāyā). (4) a doctored cowry for gambling (cf. gǭdǭgō). (5) Kt. an insect-pest attacking indigo. (6) tų̄lum mōwą ornamental clay-knob on mazarī (= gų̄lų̄lų 1a).

tulųgujį = tulkū.

tuluƙēƙę = tuliƙēƙę.

tuluƙī = tuliƙī.

tūlūną Vd. tų̄lū.

tųluntų̄lumī m. (pl. tų̄luntų̄lumai) lair of yanyāwą.

tulus = tilis.

tulū-tų̄lų̄ = tūlā-tų̄lą̄ q.v. under tūlēlę.

tum completely x aŋ kāwō sų ‿ all of them have been brought.

tuma A. (tųmā) (1) = tįmā. (2) (v.n. and progressive of tųma) x yaną̄ tųmā he is jumping. (3) f. a jump, jumping.
B. (tųma) Vb. 3B (Vd. tų̄mā 2) jumped.
C. (tumą) Vb. 1A (1) = timą. (2) picked off (grains from head, i.e. from zaŋganniyā of roasted bulrush-millet, leaving ƙaiƙayī), cf. zāgā, mųrmurą.

tųma dą gayyą m. (sg̣., pl.) the ant

cinnāka before wings drop off (Sk. tarmani).

tuma da gōrā m., f., sg., pl. fast-travelling Adrar people.

tumad da Vb. 4 yā ~ shī a ƙas he (wrestler) felled him, it (horse) unseated him (= kā da).

tumākai, tumākī Vd. tuŋkīyā.

tumāmi m. jumping.

tumanya Vb. 3B (1) = tuma. (2) haŋka-līna yā ~ da shī I'm sick of it.

tumanyē Vb. 3A (1) jumped off. (2) jumped aside.

tumar da = tumad da.

tumas (1) fāta tā yi laushī ~ the skin is pliable. (2) yā bīyu ~ he is submissive.

tumāsa Kt. m. professional blackmailer who slanders unless bought off.

tumāsancī Kt. m. blackmail as in tumāsa.

tumas da = tumad da.

tumātur = tumāturī Eng. m. tomato.

tum Vd. tun.

tumbak m. saddle having layer of silver.

tumbāƙo what a fat man !

tumbātsa Vb. 3B (1) (river) overflowed. (2) (market) was crowded. (3) P. was drunk. (4) azzikinsa yā ~ he is rich.

tumbāyē Vd. tumbī.

tumbe A. (tumbe) (1) Vb. 1A cornered P. (2) Vb. 3A became defiant (= firje).
B. (tumbē) m. defiance x yā yi masa ~ he defied him.

tumbi A. (tumbī) m. (1) (a) stomach of a ruminant (cf. tuburā). (b) ~ bā yā ƙin saŋho (i) they're identical. (ii) a P. should consort with his equals. (2) cf. bāƙin ~. (3) tumbin jāƙī (a) type of cap (cf. ƙwāyā 2). (b) the grass Paspalum scorbiculatum.
B. (tumbī) m. (pl. tumbāyē) partially-filled vessel.

tumbudī m. (1) = bulbulī 2. (2) extrusion of guinea-worm. (3) overflowing of river, etc.

tumbudō Vb. 3A appeared in large numbers.

tumbuka A. (tumbukā) Vb. 1C yā ~, ya sāmu after a short search, he found it.
B. (tumbuka) Vb. 2 = tumbukē.

tumbukē Vb. 1C (1) (a) uprooted (tree, post, etc.). (b) zā mu ~ su cikiŋ

kabīlun dūnīya we shall wipe them out from among the peoples of the world (cf. sōke 1f). (2) deposed (= tūbe 1a).

tumbulā Vb. 1C Sk. = tamfatsā 1.

tumbulē Sk. m. = tamfatsē.

tumbur = buntur.

tumburē Vb. 3A (1) remained stunted. (2) Kt. angrily refused.

tumburkā what big buttocks !

tumburƙumā f. = tuburā 1.

tumbur-tumbur = tubur-tubur.

tumbusā Vd. tumfusā.

tumbwīka f. how fat he is !

tume = tīme.

tumfāfīyā f. (pl. tumfāfī = tumfāfīyōyī (1) the shrub Calotropis procera. (2) Vd. fārar ~.

tumfāki Kt. m. good-for-nothing P.

tumfāyē (1) Vb. 1C filled. (2) Vb. 3A became full.

tumfus m. = ƙyandā.

tumfusā Vb. 1C ground finely by three acts of tishi 2.

tumfushi A. (tumfushi) (1) what fine grinding ! (as in tumfusā). (2) what a soft road ! (3) what soft meat, potato !
B. (tumfushī) m. highway (= kārauka).

tumis = tumas.

tumƙa Sk. = tūƙa.

tumkīyā Vd. tuŋkīyā.

tumnīyā Sk. f. = tinya 1, 2.

tum-tum A. (tum-tum) m. (sg., pl.) pouf-cushion.
B. (tum-tum) = tul-tul 2.

tumu m. (1) the first ripe heads of bul-rush-millet (these are gathered and roasted, i.e. gasa). (2) act of rubbing grains off 1. (3) yā karyō ~ he has syphilis (= tunjērē). (4) tumun kaskō = mummukē. (5) tumun darē Vd. zābē 4. (6) ƙa ci ~ Vd. gaigayē.

tumuƙu m. (1) the tuber Coleus dysenteri-cus. (2) overfilling one's mouth x yana ~ da rōgo he is filling his mouth too full with cassava (cf. kumuryā).

*tumunī Ar. m. one-eighth.

tumur m. and adv. firm consistency x tūwō yā yi ~ = tūwō yā yi taurī ~ the tūwō is pleasantly firm. yārọ yā yi ~ the boy has filled out.

tumurī *m.* = ƙubaƙa.

tumurzu *used in* (1) ɗan ∼ (*f.* 'yar ∼) dirty-looking P. (2) 'yar ∼ tousled, fat goat.

tumus = tumas.

tun (1) *prep.* (*a*) since *x* (i) munā aiki ∼ sāfē we've been working since early morning. tun cikiŋ watan Yūli suka zō they've been here since as early as July. tun san naŋ suka shiga yāƙi from that time they have been at war. tun caŋ dā mā, ɗattijam banzā nē even in those days, they were evil leaders. (ii) *Vd.* azal; gādiŋ-gādiŋ. (iii) tun yaushē rabuwarka da Kano how long is it since you left Kano ? (*b*) ago *x* yā isō ∼ kwānā uku he came three days ago. yanā naŋ ∼ da daɗēwā he came here long ago (*cf.* shēkara 1*g*, wucę 1*c*.ii). (*c*) after *x* (i) ∼ ran da Faransi ta fāɗi, suka cę ... after France fell, they said. ... tun ran naŋ suka tāru after that they collected together. im bā tun yanzu suŋ haɗa ba if from now on, they don't unite together ... (*Vd.* 1*e below*). (ii) bāyan (= ∼ bāyan) yāƙin naŋ suka gina shi after the war they built it. (*cc*) (i) tuŋ kāfin yāƙiŋ before the war. (ii) tum fāra yāƙin naŋ, suka būɗę kāsūwarsu they had started their market before entering on this war. (*d*) during *x* ∼ yāƙin nan nē ya ci sarauta he acceded to the throne during that war. ∼ wani wāsā aka ɗauki fōtaŋ the photo was taken at the time of a sports meeting. (*e*) ∼ yanzu (i) by now *x* im bai zō ba tun yanzu, wātō bā yā zūwa if he has not come by now, that means he will not come. (ii) *Vd.* 1*c*.i *above*. (iii) yā ƙulla abūtā da sū tun yanzu he made friends with them at once. (*f*) tun daga (i) after *x* tun daga shēkaran naŋ aka yi shāwara after that year, conferences were held. tun daga ƙarshan yāƙi after the end of the war (*cf.* daga 3). (ii) from *x* tun daga mai albāshim fam bīyū har sama in the case of those having a salary of two pounds monthly, upwards. an ragę masa mutum 200 tun daga wanda aka kāma har zūwa wanda aka kashę he lost

200 men in casualties, both prisoners and killed. yā rārakō su tun daga Masar he hunted them out of Egypt. tun daga Maka sǎi da suka kai Madīna they went from Mecca to Medina. tun daga nēsa from afar. (iii) *cf.* daga 3. (*h*) tun tuni = tuni.

(2) *adv.* (*negatively*) especially *x* n nā nēmam mutānē tum bā māsū haŋkalī ba I'm seeking persons, especially intelligent ones. munā saŋ abincī tum bā zuma ba we like food especially honey (= bā C. 1 8). *Vd.* Mod. Gram. 94*b*.

(3) *conj.* (*a*) while *x* (i) (*followed by progressive*) *x* ka faɗa musu ∼ sunā naŋ tell them while they are here ! (ii) (*followed by progressive and adj.*, Mod. Gram. 79*f*) *x* ka kashę wutā ∼ tanā ƙaramā (extinguish fire while it is still small !) nip things in the bud ! (iii) yanā ƙaramī (= tun yanā ƙarami), Tūrāwā suka zō the Europeans arrived while he was still young. tanā ƙaramā (= tun tanā ƙaramā), īyāyanta suka mutu her parents died while she was young. sunā ƙanānā (= tun sunā ƙanānā), suka īya bāsukur they could ride a bicycle while still young. yanā (= tun yanā) ɗan shēkara gōma, yanā (= yakē) kīwaŋ garkę he used to tend the herds while ten years old (Mod. Gram. 183). (iv) while there is (was), *Vd.* saurā 1*d*. (v) tun da while there is *x* tun da wurī, sǎi ku zō make sure you come in good time ! wutā tun da wurī a kashę ta act in good time ! ku yī tun da dāmā do it while you have the chance ! (= tun da wurī). yā gudu tun da girmā he fled " while the going was good ". (*b*) (*negatived*) before *x* (i) muŋ gama aiki tum bai zō ba we'd finished work before he came (= tum bai zō ba, muka gama aiki = tum bai zō ba, sǎi muka gama aiki = tum bai zō ba, muŋ gama aiki Mod. Gram. 181*a*.i). tanā tāre da nī tum bā a yi yāƙi ba she was with me

before war broke out (= **tum bā ā
yi yāƙi ba, tanā** (= **takē**) **tāre dā nī**
Mod. Gram. 181 *a.i²*). (ii) **tuŋ gāban**
(*negatived*) before *x* **ā kai karā maƙauracī tuŋ gābaŋ ƙaurā bā tā zō ba** take
corn-stalks to the place of migration
before the time of migration comes (*for
metaphorical sense*, *Vd.* **karā** 7*b*). (iii)
tum bāi tāfasā ba *Vd.* **tāfasā** 1*c*. (iv)
tum bā ā haifi ūwā ba *Vd.* **bōrin tiŋkē**.
(v) **tum bā ā yi ɗarē** ba *Vd.* **ɗarē**.

(4) **tun dā** (*a*) *prep.* (i) at *x* **yā tāshi
tun dā kētōwar ālfijir** he set out at
dawn. (ii) after, since *x* **tun dā āsālātu
sukā yi kālacī** they have been feeding
ever since dawn. (*b*) *conj.* (i) in view
of the fact that *x* **tun dā bāi zō ba**
(= **tun dā yakē bāi zō ba**), **baŋ gan
shi ba** as he did not come, I did not
see him. **tun dā akā kirā su, sāi sukā zō
dā saurī** they came quickly because
they were called. **tun dā akā yi wannaŋ,
mun ji dādī** we're pleased that they
have done so. **ālhamdu lillāhi tun dā
sukā gānē** thank God, they understood. (ii) after, from the time that *x*
**tun dā sukā fārā aiki, bā mu gan su
ba** we have not seen them since they
began work. **tun dā ɗārī ya wucē,
sāi sukā yi ta ƙērā bindigōgī** they
have been manufacturing weapons
ever since the end of last winter. **tun
dā akā fārā yāƙin naŋ, Jāmus sukā aika
dā waƙīlinsu** the Germans sent an envoy
after the outbreak of the present war.
**tun dā ya ci sarautā, kukā riƙā yaŋkam
mutānē** you have been steadily murder-
ing people ever since he came to the
throne.

tuna A. (**tunā**) *Vb.* 1A (1) (*a*) remembered
x (i) **nā ~ shi** = **nā ~ dā shi** = **nā
tunō shi** I remember (remembered) it.
(ii) **kōwā ya ~ bāra, bai ji dādim bana
ba** intrigues come to light in the end.
(iii) **Allā yā ~ dā kē** well, you have
given birth to a child after all ! (*cf.*
Tunau). (iv) **yā ~ bāya** he showed
gratitude. **yā ~ bāyaŋ Audu** he helped
the family of his dead friend Audu.
(v) **tā tunā kwānaŋ gidā** *Vd.* **tsōfō** 1*d*.

(*b*) remembered that *x* **kun tunā muŋ
gayā mukū** you remember that we told
you. **yanā tunāwā matsin dā akā yi
musu yā yi yawā** he remembers that
the oppression put upon them was
more than they could bear. (2) (*with
dative*) reminded *x* **zan ~ makā shī** =
zan ~ makā dā shī I shall remind you
of it.

B. (**tunā**) *f.* remembering *x* (1) **n
nā tunar halinsā** I am mindful of his
ways. (2) (*in song*) **bā mutūwā nakē ~
ba** ; **matāmbayā, sū nakē ~** it is not
death I fear, but the Recording Angels.

C. (**tūnā**) *Vb.* 2 *Sk.* butted (=
tuŋkwīyā).

tunāni *m.* (1) (*a*) reflecting *x* **n nā tunā-
ninsā** I am reflecting on it (= **tuntuntunī**). (*b*) **wandā ya yi wannaŋ shāwarā,
yā yi tunānī** this was a good idea.
(2) apprehensiveness *x* **bā ābin dā
nakē ~ sāi 'yam fashi** the only T.
that makes me apprehensive is the
thought of bandits. (3) remembering
x **cikin tunānim mutānē bā ā tabā
yī ba** it has never been done within
living memory.

tunannīyā *f.* **yā yi ~** he recollected
something.

Tūnāre (1) *Vd.* **sā** A.2.**1**. (2) what a brave
man !

Tūnas *f.* (1) Tunis, Tunisia. (2) **wandan ~**
trousers of Tunisian type. (3) **tā ~**
= **tātūnashī** *m.* type of pattern embroidered on gown.

B. (**tūnas**) *m.* type of tree.

Tunau name given boy whose mother
was long childless (*cf.* **Tuni** 3, **Tune**,
tunā 1*a*.iii).

tun dā *Vd.* **tun 4**.

tundufurī = **jā kutur 1**.

tundumi = **tindimi**.

tundurmī = **tindimī**.

Tune name given girl whose mother
was long childless (*cf.* **Tunau**).

tunfus = **ƙyandā**.

tuŋgā *f.* (1) obduracy. (2) *Nupe* small
hamlet of hunters, fishermen, etc.

tuŋguɓō *Vb.* 3A *x* **sāi wata zūcīyā ta
tuŋguɓō musu** they got fresh heart.

tuŋgulē *Vb.* 3A (1) (*a*) fell over. (*b*)
rānā tā ~ the sun set. (2) died.

tuŋgulum *m.* (1) yā yi ∽ = tuŋgulē 2.
(2) rānā tā yi ∽ = tuŋgulē 1*b*.
tunguma A. (tuŋgumą) *f.* (1) small extra
load on wāgā. (2) = gudungumī 2.
(3) *Vd.* bąsarākę. (4) yā nadą ∽ he
put on a huge turban.
B. (tuŋgumā) *Vb.* 1C yā tuŋgumą
rawąnī he put on huge turban.
tuŋgumē *Vb.* 1C (1) lifted bodily. (2)
tied (criminal) up securely. (3) fixed
(head of carcass) between its legs for
ease of carrying.
tuŋgumēmę *m.* (*f.* tuŋgumēmīyā) *pl.*
tuŋgum-tuŋgum huge (*re* turban,
coiffure).
tuŋgumgum *x* yā yi bąbban nadī ∽ =
tuŋgumą 4.
tuŋgumī *m.* (*f.* tuŋgumā) *pl.* tuŋgum-
tuŋgum = tuŋgumēmę.
tungum-tuŋgum *Vd.* tuŋgumēmę.
tuŋgurā = tuŋgulē 2.
tuŋgurmą *f.* struggling.
tuŋgurum that puts the kybosh on
it !
tuŋguzą *f.* = būję.
tuŋgwal = tuŋgwallǫ (1) *m.* sound of
usual heavy pestle-blows against mortar
(*cf.* ḳul). (2) dayā ∽ only one
(= tak 1*a*).
tuni A. (tunį) *m.* (1) *x* yā yi minį ∽ he
gave me a reminder. (2) kudin ∽ *Vd.*
aurē 6*b*. (3) *name of boy or girl (as in*
Tųnau, Tųne).
B. (tunį) = tun tuni (1) long ago *x*
sun sāmi izinī tun tuntuni they got
permission long ago. tun tuni suką
gamą they long since finished it. dą mā,
tun tuni long ago. (2) na tun tuni *m.*
(*f.* ta ∽) *pl.* na ∽ ancient *x* shūgąbąn-
ninsu na tun tuni their leaders from of
old.
C. *(tūnį) *Sk. m.* butting (*cf.* tūnā).
tunjērē *m.* (1) (*a*) (i) primary and secondary syphilis (= cīwąn 3 = cįŋkōsō
2 = cūsai = ḳazwā 4 = ąlmū 2 =
Kt. ḳaurā 3*b* = tumu 3 = ḳurjī 4),
cf. ḳabbā. (ii) *Vd.* yąyā A.2.3, Bągwārī 2,
bāshį 6, hą 1*d*. (*b*) yaws. (*c*) in dąŋūwaŋką
yaną ∽ kai kō ką shā rigą kafį when
trouble befalls your neighbour, look out
for yourself ! (*d*) *epithet of syphilis is*
Gąikau kā fi aikįm māląm, dągą bą

hąḳō ba, sái sąssąḳō = Gwąurau bą
hą, kiskō yā fi aikįm māląmī. (*e*)
ḳayąr ∽ *f.* yaws-sores on hands or
feet. (2) tunjēran ząncē combined
talking of several persons, none of
whom listens to the other.
tunjumā = tinjįmā.
tuŋkārō *Vb.* 3A approached.
tuŋkīyā *f.* (*pl.* tumākī = tumąkai = tuŋ-
kīyōyī). (1) (*a*) sheep (*Vd.* rągō). (*b*)
tąran tumākī bą karǫ, banzā people are
collected idly (*Vd.* tąrō). (*c*) sun yi
masą tumākī they ignored him, did
not reply. (2) (*said by hunters*) leopard.
(3) *Vd.* tąfīyą 9 : sąko tumākī. (4)
harshąn tuŋkīyā *Vd.* baḳī 3*n*.
tuŋkū *m.* (*pl.* tuŋkuną) (1) (*a*) mongoose
(*Herpestes albicauda*). (*b*) Tuŋkū dą
ḳąrarrawā mąi jā wą dąŋgi cūtā what
a nuisance he is to his family ! (*c*) ∽
yā san sūrin dą yakę kāshī everybody
knows his own limitations. (*d*) bā ą
dafą dafį dōmin ∽ do not go on a wild
goose chase ! (*cf.* ḳafąr wālā). (*e*) Tuŋkū
kā kai yąrā makasā what a broken
reed ! (2) hajjąn nąŋ tuŋkuŋ kąsūwā cę
these goods are unsaleable.
tunkuda A. (tuŋkudā) *Vb.* 1C (1) (P.,
animal) pushed T. aside. (2) = tittįdā 2.
(3) tā tuŋkudą hatsī she ground the corn
hurriedly and carelessly. (4) zūcīyāta
tā tuŋkudō (*a*) I feel cross. (*b*) I
feel sick.
B. (tuŋkudą) *Vb.* 2 = tuŋkudā 1.
tuŋkudad dą *Vb.* 4 (1) = zubar dą. (2)
sold at dirt-cheap price.
tuŋkudau *m.* (*sg., pl.*) = mazuŋkudīyā.
tunkude A. (tuŋkudē) *Vb.* 1C (P., animal)
pushed aside and knocked T. over.
B. (tuŋkudē) *m.* grinding *us in* tuŋkudā 3.
tuŋ̄kumēmę *m.* (*f.* tuŋ̄kumēmīyā) *pl.*
tuŋ̄kuŋ-tuŋ̄kuŋ huge.
tuŋ̄kumī *m.* (*f.* tuŋ̄kumā) *pl.* tuŋ̄kuŋ-
tuŋ̄kuŋ huge.
tuŋ̄kuną *Vd.* tuŋkū.
tuŋkur *x* yā kwānā ∽ he passed the night
sleepless. yā wunį nąŋ ∽ he spent the
whole day here. yā tsayą ∽ he stood
firm.
tuŋ̄kurę *m.* (1) = tuŋ̄kurī. (2) a move in
darą blocking one's opponent.

tuŋƙurī *m.* ⁓ **gąrēką** you're an annoying sort of P.

tuŋkushę what an ugly woman !

tuŋkus-tuŋkus *x* **yaną tąfīyą** ⁓ he's walking at a snail's pace.

tuŋkūyą = **tuŋkwīyą**.

tuŋküzą *f.* (1) *Vd.* **mąŋ gyądā 1, 3**. (2) great cheapness. (3) slut, unkempt female.

tuŋƙwīmą what a hunchback !

tuŋkwīyą (1) *Vb.* 2 (*a*) butted, gored (*cf.* **ɗuŋgurą 2**). (*b*) **yā tuŋkwīyi tąurąrī** he had bad luck (*Vd.* **tąurārǫ 3**). (*c*) **yā tuŋkwīyi burji** he is dead. (*d*) **tā tuŋkwīyē shi** she (woman with whom he slept) made his gown greasy by resting her head on it. (*e*) **rągō yā tuŋkwīyē shi** he has a new-born child (*Vd.* **rągō 2**). (2) *f.* (*a*) act of butting, goring *x* **ąkwīyą tā kai masą** ⁓ the goat butted him (= **tuŋkwīyi**). (*b*) **yā yi matą** ⁓ he carried home her full waterpot as recompense for her filling his pot. (*c*) holding **wāgą** of pack-animals above the water when fording with them.

tuŋkwīyau *m.* (*sg., pl.*) (1) (*a*) flea (= **ƙumā**). (*b*) *epithet is* **Tuŋkwīyau haną barcī**. (2) = **baushę 3**.

tuŋkwiye A. (**tuŋkwīyē**) *Vb.* 1C = **tuŋkwīyą 1***a*.

B. (**tuŋkwīyē**) *Kt. m.* taking home bundle of corn at end of day's harvesting to reduce amount to be transported at completion of harvesting.

tuŋkwīyi *m.* (1) = **tuŋkwīyą 2***a*. (2) **nā ɗąuki kąrē doŋ haushi, yā kōmō yaną** ⁓ it was unsuitable for the purpose to which it was applied.

tuŋnā *Vb.* 2 *Sk.* butted, gored (= **tuŋkwīyą**).

*****tuŋnąs** *x* **Sarkī yā yi** ⁓ the Emir made a ceremonial exit.

tunnuƙā = **dinniƙā**.

tunnuƙe A. (**tunnuƙē**) (1) *Vb.* 3A = **dinniƙē**. (2) (*a*) (debtor, illness, etc.) impeded freedom of P. (*b*) **zūcįyā tā** ⁓ **shi** he's bereft of his senses.

B. (**tunnuƙē**) = **dinniƙē**.

tunnuƙū *m.* (1) (*a*) dense smoke. (*b*) ⁓ **fadąŋ iblisai, yārǫ bąi ganī ba bąllē yą rabą** (i) what smoke ! (ii) what a

quarrel ! (2) **tunnuƙum fadą** serious quarrel. (3) **tunnuƙum bāshi gąrēshi** he's deep in debt.

tunō *Vd.* **tuną 1***a*.i.

tuntāyē *Vd.* **tuntū**.

tuntsum = **tinjim**.

tuntsur = **ɓuntur**.

tuntsurā (1) *Vb.* 1C rolled T. along. (2) *Vb.* 3A rolled, toppled on to, into *x* **yā** ⁓ **kąnsą** it toppled on to him (= **wantsąlā**, *cf.* **tuntsurē**).

tuntsurą gudi-gudi *m.* = **aduŋgurē**.

tuntsurą gudunyą *m.* = **aduŋgurē**.

tuntsure A. (**tuntsurē**) (1) *Vb.* 1C rolled T. aside (= **mirginē 2**). (2) *Vb.* 3A (*a*) rolled over, rolled away (= **mirginē 1***a*). (*b*) (i) toppled over (= **mirginē 1***b*). (ii) (liquid) became upset (= **kyārę**). (*c*) **yā** ⁓ **dą dąrīyā** he burst out laughing (= **fashę 1***b*). (*d*) **yā** ⁓ he is dead.

B. (**tuntsurē**) *m.* (1) = **zubētā 1**. (2) churning (**kiɗą**) milk in bottle-gourd (**gōrā**), *cf.* **kiɗą 2**.

tuntū = **tuntū** *m.* (*pl.* **tuntāyē**) (1) (*a*) = **tukkū**. (*b*) *Vd.* **gwaurō 3***b*. (2) = **tūtū**. (3) **tuntuŋ gądā** type of weed.

tuntuɓa A. (**tuntuɓą**) *Vb.* 2 (1) interrogated P. (2) inquired into.

B. (**tuntuɓā**) (1) *Vb.* 1C = **tuntuɓą**. (2) *Vb.* 3A *x* **mu** ⁓ **gąba** let us move forward a bit !

tuntuɓę *m.* (1) suddenly stumbling (*cf.* **sąssarfā**). (2) ⁓ **dadįŋ gushįŋ gąba im bą ą ji cīwǫ ba** (*a*) what an unexpected bargain ! (*b*) we got off lightly ! (3) **tuntuɓąŋ kāshī yā ɓātą ukų ; yā ɓātą rąŋ, yā ɓātą ƙafą, yā ɓātą hannu** what an intractable person ! (4) **tuntuɓąŋ harshę** slip of the tongue. (5) *Vd.* **tsittsigę**.

tuntumēmę *m.* (*f.* **tuntumēmįyā**) *pl.* **tuntuŋ-tuntuŋ** huge.

tuntumī (1) *m.* (*a*) = **jinjimī**. (*b*) West African Hadada Ibis (*Hagedashia hagedash*). (2) *m.* (*f.* **tuntumā**) *pl.* **tuntuŋ-tuntuŋ** huge.

tuntuŋgōrę = **tuntuŋgōrǫ** *m.* (*sg., pl.*) clay bed-pillars (= **ciliŋgōrǫ**).

tun tųni = **tųni**.

tuntuntuni A. (**tuntuntunī**) = **tųnānī 1**.

B. (**tun tuntųni**) = **tųni**.

tuntuŋ-tuntuŋ *Vd.* **tuntumēmę, tuntumī 2**.

tụntuzụ *m.* forming cluster *x* gāshịnsạ yā yi ∼ his hair is bunchy. ƙurājē sun yi ∼ the pimples form thick cluster.

tunya = tinya.

tụnzụmạ *Vb.* 3B *Kt.* was afraid.

tunzura A. (tụnzụrạ) *Vb.* 3B (1) became afraid. (2) became angry. (3) became emboldened.

B. (tụnzụrā) *Vb.* 1C (1) frightened. (2) angered. (3) emboldened.

tụnzụrarrē *m.* (*f.* tụnzụrarrīyā) *pl.* tụnzụrạrrū quick-tempered.

tụnzurī *m.* alarm *x* yā yi ∼ he became alarmed (*cf.* tụnzurạ).

tụnzurūwā *f.* = tụnzurī.

tura A. (tūrạ) (1) *Vb.* 1A (*a*) (i) pushed (= izạ). (ii) yā ∼ wutā = izạ 3. (iii) yā ∼ kạrātū he did much study. (iv) *Vd.* tạfi dạ 2*a*. (v) yā tūrạ kuɗinsạ baɳkị he banked his money. (vi) sun tūrō gyạdā wạje they exported ground-nuts. (vii) kadạ kạ tūrạ mạganạrkạ cikin lōƙạcịn dạ nikē̃ mạganạ dạ wani don't interrupt me when I am speaking to someone else ! (viii) yā tūrō kụnū ạ rạgayạ *Vd.* rạgayạ 1*e.* (ix) dạ ƙarfin tūwō sukē̃ nēman tūrạ kansụ they are seeking to thrust themselves forward by force (*Vd.* tūwō 23). (*b*) incited, persuaded (= izạ 2). (*c*) *x* nā ∼ shi wurinsụ I sent him to them. (*d*) (i) routed. (ii) ya ∼ ƙyēyạr rụndunā tasụ he routed their army. (*e*) nā ∼ makạ zōmō *Vd.* zōmō 6. (2) *Vb.* 3A (*a*) is well advanced *x* watạ yā ∼ the month is well advanced. aikị yā ∼ the work is well in hand. kạrātū yā ∼ much study has been done. (*b*) āyạrī yā ∼ the caravan has gone on. (*c*) sǎi wata zūcịyā ta tūrō musụ they got fresh heart. (3) *f.* lumbar spinal curvature. (4) Tūrạ hạwājọ *Vd.* gandū 2*f.* (5) tūrạ haushī *m.* a white, European cotton material.

B. (tūrā) (1) *Vb.* 2 (*a*) = tūrā̃ 1*a*.i. (*b*) knocked against. (2) *f.* (*a*) act of pushing *x* mun sāmi hanyạr yịn ∼ wajan yammā we managed to make a push westwards (in the war). (*b*) ∼ tā kai baɳgō the limit of patience has been reached, an impasse has been reached. (*c*) aikịn ∼ a careless action.

C. (turạ) (1) *Vb.* 1A (*a*) did tiṛi 1, 2. (*b*) yā ∼ minị ƙụrā he covered me with a cloud of dust (*cf.* tiṛi 3). (2) *f.* nā ci ∼ tasạ (*a*) I failed to wound the prey. (*b*) I failed to get my wish (= ƙundū = tạrī).

tūrad dạ *Vb.* 4 (1) sacrificed (one's goods being sold). (2) = tūrẹ 2*b.*

tūrạ haushī *Vd.* tūrạ 5.

Tūrạ hạwājọ *Vd.* gandū 2*f.*

tūrahẹ *Fil. m.* a plant enriching milk of nursing-mothers.

Tūrai *f.* (1) Europe (*cf.* Bạtūrẹ). (2) name for girl born Tuesday (*Vd.* Bạtūrẹ 3). (3) mạnzan Tūrai *Vd.* sạkākạ.

turaka A. (turākā) *Vd.* turkẹ.

B. (tụrākā) *f.* (1) (*a*) that part of rich man's compound reserved for himself when he has several wives (*cf.* lallōkī 1*b*, ƙundū 2*a*) = *Kt.* bạrāyā 2. (*b*) *epithet is* Tụrākā turkyạɳ wutā (*for husband calls favourite wife out of turn into* tụrākā *and so incurs hell-fire*). (2) 'yan ∼ *pl.* children of same father by different mothers, whether latter are wives (mạcē̃ 4), concubines (ƙwarƙwarạ) or slaves (bạiwā), *cf.* danụbā (= *Kt.* bạrāyā 2*b*). (3) 'yar ∼ *f.* = sōrō 3. (4) *Vd.* zanzanā 3.

Tụrākī = San Tụrākī one of the sạrautạ (*epithet is* Bụgau matattarā).

turākū (1) *Vd.* turkẹ. (2) *Kt.* Turākū = Sarkin turākū the sạrautạ in some *Kt.* towns whose holder is head of dealers in horses, donkeys, sheep, and goats.

turạ̄mē *Vd.* turmī.

Tūrancī *m.* (1) (*a*) the ways of Europeans, etc. (*Vd.* Bạtūrẹ). (*b*) gạskīyā tā fi ∼ truth is better than wealth (*cf.* Bạtūrẹ 3, 4). (*c*) bạ jā ba nē̃ ∼ ; kōwā ya yi kudī, shī nē̃ Abbạ don't be misled by appearances ! (2) any European language. (3) financing gamblers (*cf.* Bạtūrẹ 6).

tụrantạ *Vb.* 3B (1) assumed the ways of Europeans (*Vd.* Tūrancī). (2) became rich (*Vd.* Tūrancī 1*b*).

turaɳ-turaɳ *x* yā bi hanyạ ∼ he went direct (*cf.* dọshē).

tūrar dạ = tūrad dạ.

turara A. (turārā) *Vb.* 1C. (1) fumigated,

perfumed (place, T. or one's body).
(2) = sulālā 2. (3) yā turārā rīgā he
coloured his gown over fire of markē-
leaves, the process being called tirịŋ
hayāƙī q.v. under tirị 1c.
  B. (tụrārạ) Vb. 3B (1) became fumigated, perfumed. (2) = sụlālạ 2.
(3) Vd. kā tụrārạ.
turare A. (tụrārē) m. (Ar. 'itri). (1) any
perfume. (2) incense, fragrant smoke
for fumigation of body or place, or use
magically (2 = ạl'ụl).
  B. (Tụrāre) name for anyone called
Mụhammadụ q.v.
  C. (turārē) Vb. 1C (1) perfumed, etc.
(as in turārā 1) completely. (2) rendered P. conceited.
tụrarrē m. (f. tụrarrīyā) pl. tụrạrrū (1)
mad. (2) contentious.
Tụ̄rāwā = Tūrāwā Vd. Bạtūrę.
tūrāyē Vd. tūrū.
turbạ f. (pl. turbōbī) (1) road (= hanyạ).
(2) ~ bā tạ barịŋ gidā what's bred in the
bone comes out in the flesh. (3)
turbạr samạ sǎi tsuntsū skill is required
for it. (4) Vd. yạu 2c. (5) turbạr
shānū ɓạd dạ bạ̊ƙō, yārọ yā bi, baị sanị
bạ he has brought a hornet's nest
about his ears.
tụrɓā = tụrɓāyā f. loose, sandy soil (cf.
rạ̈irạyī).
tụrbē Sk. m. = cịrbē.
turbōbī Vd. turbạ.
turbụdā Vb. 1C (1) thrust (cassava, etc.)
into hot ashes to cook (= Kt. turdạ̄dā).
(2) buried kabạ to maintain it moist for
mat-making. (3) steeped T. in A. biting
x iŋ aŋ yaŋkę hannum ɓạrāwọ, sǎi ạ
turbụdạ hannunsạ ạ bạrkọ̄nō when a
thief's hand is cut off, the stump is
steeped in pepper.
turbụdē Vb. 1C (1) = turbụdā 1, 2. (2)
(vulgarly) interred P.
turɓuna A. (turɓụnā) = durɓụnā.
  B. (tụrɓunạ) = dụrɓunạ.
turɓụnē = durɓụnē.
tụrɓūshị m. dāwạ tā yi ~ the guinea-
corn is affected by blight (cf. bụrtuntụnā).
tụrɓūwā Sk. f. = tụrɓāyā.
tụrdā Sk. f. = tụrɓāyā.
turdạ Vd. turtsạ.

turdạ̄dā (1) Vd. turtsạ̄tsā. (2) Kt. =
turɓụdā 1.
turdę = tirdę.
turdēdę = tirdēdę.
ture A. (tūrę) (1) (a) knocked over,
knocked down, pushed over (= taŋ-
kạdē 1b). (b) Vd. būzū 2c. (2) (a)
pushed away. (b) yā cī har yā ~ he
ate to repletion. (3) deposed (= tūɓę).
  B. (tụ̄rē) m. (1) nā yi ~ dạ shī I
have lost interest in it. (2) grass-
fodder rejected by horse. (3) = durwā
1. (4) market-latrine emptying into
borrow-pit. (5) kọ̄gī yā kāwō ~ the
river brought down alluvium (= Zar.
rịgāwā). (6) an yi masạ ~ yạ yi sātạ
he has been incited to theft. (7) an yi
wạ Audụ ~ = zụndē.
  C. (turę) = tirę.
tụ̄rērēnịyā f. (1) the pushing done by a
crowd (= Kt. tọ̄tsōtsōnịyā). (2) anạ̄ ~
dạ kāyāna nobody buys my goods.
tụrgēzạ Kt. f. = dạrgēzọ.
tụrgunnụ̄wā f. = lālọ 1.
turi A. (turị) = tirị.
  B. (tūrị) used in tūrịn zūcịyā aggrava-
tion x yā yi minị tūrịn zūcịyā he
aggravated me. tūrịn zūcịyā gạrēshị
he is an aggravating P. (= ban haushī).
  C. (tụ̄rī) m. (1) a kola-nut disease. (2)
type of Adamawa drum.
turję = tirję.
turkā f. yā yi ~ he tethered animal as in
turkę 2a.
Tụrkāwā Vd. Bạturki.
turkę (1) m. (pl. turạ̄kā = turākū = Sk.
tirịkkā) (a) (i) tethering-post = jīgọ
1d (cf. dabị 4 ; shạ̄makị). (ii) dōkịŋ
harị tun yanā ~ a kạŋ guję masạ
don't leave things too late ! ; forewarned is fore-armed. (iii) turkyạŋ
wutā Vd. Tụrākā 1b. (iv) suŋ kafạ
turākunsụ kạn tsaunị they (soldiers)
established themselves on a hill. (v)
turạ̄kan jirạ̄gyan rūwā harbours. (vi)
turkyạŋ wāwā Vd. sạ̄bō 1. (b) temporarily tethering (horse, donkey, ram,
sheep, bull, cow, goat) to stake (cf.
2a below) x an yi masạ ~ it has been
tethered. (c) turkyạŋ ƙasạ (i)
tethering-rope sunk into filled-up hole
or tied to buried stone. (ii) yā zamę

mini turkyaŋ ḳasa it is a mill-stone round my neck. (d) an ɗana wa tarō ∼ stem has been fixed to the threepenny-bit to enable it to be fitted into her nose, cf. ɗana 3. (e) Vd. turākū ; kwānā 7. (2) Vb. 1A (a) tethered (ram, bull) permanently to fatten (cf. turkā, turkę 1b above). (b) " left (liar, etc.) without a leg to stand on ". turkudī m. (pl. turkuda). (1) (a) cloth consisting of 12 or 16 kāmu of farī-cloth sewn together, dyed with indigo, beaten glossy (bugu 1e) and wrapped in paper. (2) yā yi mini ∼ da ausagī he was very generous to me. (3) tur-kudiŋ gamshęḳā (used mockingly in girls' songs) loathsome P. (4) turkudin sillīya the cord kincē made of alharīni.

turkwī used in da ciki yakę ∼ what a pot-bellied person !

turmī m. (pl. turamē) (1) (a) mortar for corn (cf. taɓaryā). (b) kāshin ∼ bā na wādaŋ ḳarē ba nę don't attempt what is beyond you ! (c) kō kūrā tā san ∼, a waje yakę kwānā have more sense than to press a destitute P. to pay a debt ! (d) kō aŋ kirɓa a ∼ mai yawan rāi sāi ya fita if you are gifted with nine lives, nothing can harm you (= yawa 6). (e) Vd. saraḳūwā 4. (f) yā ci karo da ∼ Vd. ayyahaha. (g) turmin daka tāsa Vd. daka 1b. (h) gōro a ∼ Vd. daka 1c. (2) complete length of cloth (as supplied to shops from Europe). (3) packet (of matches, wool, etc.). (4) molar-tooth (= ma-taunī = Kt. gubbi). (5) dōki yā yi ∼ horse refused to budge (cf. taɓaryā 2). (6) yā yi kwāɓā ∼ uku he mixed clay or cement enough for three spells of work. (7) (a) sunā ∼ da taɓaryā they are in the act of copulation (Vd. cī 16a). (b) Vd. gamō 2c. (8) cane ∼ say turmī ! (said by boy A to boy B, and on B replying turmī, A retorts turmushē ni ka ḳwācę), cf. ḳwā 3. (9) gindin ∼ m. (a) deep brass basin with small base. (b) Vd. gindī 1a.ii. (10) yā yi mini turmin danyā I feel nonplussed by it. (11) turmin zugū = 10 above. (12) Vd. bākin ∼.

turmusa Vb. 1C (1) dirtied (garment) by sitting on ground. (2) (a) held P. down. (b) an turmusa hancinsa he has had a hard time. (3) (wrestler) threw (opponent) down (3 = kā da). turmushasshēnīyā f. struggling of persons together on the ground. turmushē Vb. 1C (1) = turmusā. (2) compelled P. to do T. (3) Vd. turmī 8. turmutsā = tirmutsā. turmutsūmutsū m. crowding of people in doorway, etc. turmutsūtsū m. = turmutsūmutsū. turmuzā = turmusā. turnuḳā = tunnuḳā. turnuḳē = tunnuḳē. turrā Vd. tūru. tursasa = tirsasa. turtsa = tirtsātsā. turtsātsā = tirtsātsā. turtsītsī = kurcīcī 1.

turu A. (tūru) m. (pl. tūruna = turrā). (1) (a) stocks (= ɗagōgō 2a). (b) an sā shi a ∼ he's been put in the stocks. (2) (a) log to which lunatic, thief, or runaway slave was attached by garam q.v. (b) Vd. sāran tūru.

B. (tūrū) m. (pl. tūrāyē). (1) type of large drum. (2) Sk. = kuŋkumī 2. (3) P. heavily in debt. (4) (a) villager with some following who opposes village-head (epithet is Tūrū, uɓaŋ watandā). (b) sun yi wa dagaci ∼ they (recalcitrant villagers) opposed their village-head. (5) Vd. ayū.

Turuɓuḳwi = Tuɓurḳuḳu.

turum A. (turum) Vd. lālę, maraɓā.

B. (turum) = tiriŋ.

tūruna Vd. tūru.

turuŋgē = tiriŋgē.

Turuŋkū used in Na ∼, kā girmā da gāgā opprobrious term applied to Zaria man.

turunya = tirinya.

tururī m. steam, vapour.

tururruɓī m. = sambęrū.

tururrūwā = tururūwā.

tururu adv. abundantly.

tururūwā f. (sg., pl.). (1) (a) type of black ant which stores corn (cf. duŋgurmā). (b) in ∼ tā tāshi lālācęwā, sāi ta yi fikāfikī if a woman begins to show temper, it means she wants to leave you.

(c) bāwan ~ = shā dundū. (d) dōkin ~
the spider makarā. (e) jākin ~ spider
makarā. (f) Vd. rākumī 10. (2)
mutānē sun yi ~ a crowd has gathered.
(3) Vd. alkamā 3.
turus (1) adv. abundantly. (2) m. yā
yi ~ he was disconcerted.
turū-turū (1) adv. abundantly. (2) idọ ~
large eyes.
turūzu m. (pl. turūzai) broken kantu
of mangul.
turwā Kt. f. (1) = tururūwā. (2) Vd.
rākumī 10.
turwadī Kt. = kirwadī.
turza A. (turzā) (1) Vb. 1A (a) yā ~
kasā = tirjẹ 2c. (b) lightly pounded
(corn for second time to remove bran
left after surfē) = zurcẹ 2, (cf. dakā).
(2) Vb. exerted every effort (= kōkartā).
   B. (turzā) f. yā kāwō ~ = tirjẹ 1b.
turzaza = tirsasa.
tusa A. (tusā) = tisā.
   B. (tūsā) f. (1) (a) passing wind
(= hūtū 2 = kwītā = sācīyā), cf. kwī.
(b) ~ a jama'a Vd. kunyā 2c.iii. (2)
talo-talō yā yi mini ~ m bā ka wākē
the big turkey made noisy, gobbling
sound (cf. bindigā 9). (3) wani dā ~,
wani dā karɓar rīgā one does not always
get one's deserts (because P. who
passed wind was ashamed to admit it and
another who falsely claimed to have
passed wind, got the reward). (4) karyā
akẹ yị, ~ bā tā hūrā wutā don't lean
on a broken reed ! (cf. kafar wālā).
(5) (a) ~ tā kārẹ a bōdarī, sǎi shēwā evil
P. is at end of his tether. (b) Vd.
bōdarī 2. (6) tūsar jākī wart-like growth.
(7) tūsar kājī dispersing by crowd. (8)
~ tsaye Vd. budirī 2.
tusga = tizga.
tusgẹ = tizgẹ.
tusgunā Vb. 1C Kt. yā ~ mini rāi he
annoyed me (= kātā 5a.ji).
tushe A. (tūshẹ) m. (1) (a) the base
(gindī 2 q.v.) of plant ; tree just
above the roots (cf. saiwā). (b) tūshan
rāfī the source of the brook. (2) yanā
dā ~ (a) he is of noble origin. (b)
he has powerful patrons. (3) tūsham
magana true facts of the case. (4)
(used as numerative of plants) x albasā

gudā = albasā ~ gudā one onion. (5)
two large leaves of paper folded over
to form eight pages (cf. daba'a).
   B. (tushẹ) Vd. tisā.
tushị = tishị.
tūshīyā f. (pl. tūshīyōyī) (1) corn-roots left
in ground after reaping. (2) cịn ~
clearing away 1.
tuskudē = turmushē.
tuskuna Vb. 2 Sk. goaded to anger,
provoked (= zungurā).
tuskurū Vd. tāɓā ~.
tuskurunrun m. putting on much clothing
plus large turban.
tusōnō = tasōnō.
tusshē Vd. tud dā.
tūtā f. (pl. tūtōcī) (1) (a) flag (= lambā
1a.iii). (b) tūtarmu tanā tāshị fil-fil-fil
our flag is waving. (c) Sarākunā māsū
tūtōcịn kansu independent rulers. (d)
yā dagā tūtar amānā garēsu he waved
a flag of surrender, to them. (e) kasan
nan tā sāmi tūtar kantā that country
has become independent. (f) Vd.
fitar dā 4b.i. (2) tassel (= tukkū 3a =
tuntū). (3) tūtar furē a head of tobacco-
flowers. (4) dan ~ m. (pl. 'yan ~)
signaller (in army). (5) cf. gātutā.
tūtīya Ar. f. (1) zinc. (2) conceit, swank
(= tākamā). (3) tūtīyar hindī a stone
consisting of sodium and potassium
compounds.
tūtōcī Vd. tūtā.
tutsẹ = titsīyē.
tutsīyē = titsīyē.
tutsōtsōnịyā Kt. f. = tūrērēnịyā.
tutsu A. (tūtsū) m. (1) = būtsarī 1. (2)
kāsūwā tā yi masā ~ he was unable to
find customers for his goods.
   B. (tūtsū) Kt. m. tall, slender Rahazāwā drum.
   C. (tutsū) m. x magēwayī yā yi ~ the
latrine is not properly screened off.
tuttudā = tittidā.
tuttukēkẹ = tittikēkẹ.
tuttula A. (tuttulā) Vb. 2 = bulbulā 1.
   B. (tuttulā) Vb. 1C (1) = bulbulā 1.
(2) intensive from tilā.
tuttulē = bulbulē.
tuttur Vd. tittir.
tuttushī = tittishī.
tutu A. (tūtū) m. (1) locust-bean (dōrōwā)

blossom (= ƙulūlu 2a = tuntū 2). (2)
Vd. hazō.
 B. (tūtu) m. (1) human excrement
(= najasa). (2) moonstone.
tutuk Sk. = tutur.
tūtūlaƙī m. (f. tutūlaƙā) big, but weak P.
tutur (1) always, for ever. (2) ~ ilalla
for ever and ever (Vd. fiddin).
tuturta Vb. 3B lasted for ever, was permanent (cf. tabbata 1c).
tutut Sk. = tutur.
tutwī-tutwī adj. pl. large.
tūu x sunā da yawa ~ they are very
numerous.
tūwā Zar. f. pagan custom of selling
murderer and family as slaves (cf.
kifa kwandō 2).
tūwallē Vd. tūwō 1a.
tūwam, tūwan Vd. alphabetically after
tūwō.
tūwārā Sk. = tūwallē.
tūwō m. (1) (a) (i) the staple N.P. food,
made from the flour of guinea-corn,
bulrush millet, or rice and served with
butter and mīya. (ii) cf. saisainō ;
burabusko ; samɓarā 3 ; tikira ; gulanjē ;
kada ka tāka. (iii) Vd. alkālī 5. (iv)
epithet is Tūwallē mai jiƙī zar tsōka
= Kt. Nāma ɓā ƙashī. (b) yanā
cin ~ he is eating tūwō = gasa 2f
(cf. furā 1b). (c) tanā ~ da mīya
she's making tūwō for sale (cf. tāka
baŋgō, sāfalā). (d) Gaskamī ~ daga
rēshe Vd. gaskamī 2. (e) Vd. marin ~ ;
akaifā 3 ; mūgun ~ . (2) gātarin ~
hand. (3) rashin ~ akē cin wākē a
kwānā needs must when the devil
drives. (4) (a) sauran ~ (i) survivors
of war. (ii) one's divorced wife, etc.
(b) sauran tūwaŋka ɓā yā gāgararka T.
or P. once overcome is not hard to overcome again. (c) zā mu bi sauran tūwam-
mu we'll impose our will on those we've
conquered. (5) Vd. tūwon-compounds.
(6) (a) tūwaŋ girmā mīyassa nāma
power never lacks zest. (b) kōwā ya ci
tūwō da shī Vd. shā 1g.iv. (7) tūwan
tulū mai wuyar kwāshēwā da mārā
(said by labourers) what a cantankerous
person ! (8) mutānan dūnīya iŋ
kā saƙe, sǎi su ci maƙa ~ a ƙā if
you give him an inch, he'll take an

ell. (9) ~ nā īyāli, nāma nā mai
gidā (said by 'yam fōtō in gaŋgi
rhythm). (10) ba a yi ciƙi dōmin ~ ba,
sǎi don ɓōyam magana what a blabber !
(Vd. dōmin 1c). (11) don tūwaŋ gōbe
akē waŋke tukunyā a kindness is
never wasted. (12) da rānā akē awo,
da darē sǎi a ci ~ don't buy a pig in a
poke ! (13) (a) wanda ɓā shi da ūwā
a gidā, dōle wata rānā tūwansa gāyā
zai ci a man without a patron is sure
" to come a cropper ". (b) Vd. ūwar ~.
(c) mai ūwā a murhu ɓā yā cin ~ gāyā
if you've a patron, success is easy (cf.
gindim murhu). (14) ba a sam mai
cin ~ ba sǎi mīya tā ƙāre it takes a
long time to know a person's character
(Vd. mīya 5). mū, ɓā a ganiŋ kamar
munā shirin cin tūwō sǎi mīya tā
ƙāre we are not looked on as people
who count their chickens before they're
hatched. (15) tūwaŋ ƙas na ƙarē nē
no smoke without fire (cf. tūwaŋ
ƙasā). (16) daran ~ ɓā kwānā da
yuŋwa ba nē (epithet of child born late
in mother's life). (17) tūwaŋ kwadayī
yā fi dādī ; kō da gāyā sǎi a ci expectation exceeds realization. (18) tūwan
ɗan daŋgi ɓā yā rūwā (= . . . ɓā yā
ciƙa rūwā) blood is thicker than water ;
P. with many relatives never lacks
helpers. (19) tūwaŋ dāwa, mīyar kūka
tā wadā ba nē, kuturū mā yanā yī
(said by husband in reply to wife taunting
him with ingratitude). (20) mai tūwan
darē kē ƙā cī da būzūzu don't lock the
stable after the horse has gone !
(21) an cē da ƙarē " ~ yā yi yawa a
gidam biƙī ", ya cē " mu ganī a ƙas ! "
seeing is believing. (22) wurin ~
mutum yā yi arba Vd. wuya 1h. (23)
yā dība da ƙarfin tūwō he took it by
force (Vd. tūra). (24) farin tūwō Vd.
tukunyā 1f. (25) tūwan sāfē Vd. suƙūni
2b. (26) anā tūwō Vd. bareƙata.
(27) kōmē dāɗin tūwō Vd. dāɗī 1b.
(28) ūwar miji tā ƙi cin ~ Vd. daɗi 5.
(29) da gāriŋka akē tūwō Vd. ɓuƙe.
(30) bi ~ ciƙi Vd. hasāra 1c.
tūwaŋ aduwa = birī-birī.
tūwaŋ alaka m. = alaka f. a food made
from yam-flour (alibō).

tūwam ɓạrnā *m.* feast on day after bride goes to husband's house.

tūwam ɓarzọ *Vd.* ɓarzọ.

tūwam bāshị *m.* small present to pre-dispose P. to lend one money.

tūwam ɓaurē *m.* type of wheaten food.

tūwam baurērẹ *Vd.* baurērẹ.

tūwam birị *m.* fruit of tạfāshīyạ.

tūwam ɓulạ = tūwan rūwā.

tūwan dātsā *m.* = dātsā.

tūwam fādạ *m.* = gạjirī 1.

tūwaŋ gandū *Vd.* gandū 4.

tūwaŋ hannū *m.* Agalāwā custom, where çrone pours tūwō and soup three times over hands of bridegroom, the food then being given to children (it is thought that if he swallows saliva during the operation, he will contract goitre).

tūwaŋ ƙasā *m.* heated wet earth for poultice (*cf.* tūwō 15).

tūwan riƙọ *m.* *Vd.* riƙọ 5.

tūwan rūwā *m.* type of dumpling (= ɓulạ = bandō).

tūwan sallạ *used in* anạ fạdā kạman ~ the expression is in general use (= gandū 4 *q.v.*).

tūwaŋ shịŋkāfā *Vd.* kāshī 1*f.*

tūwan tụlū *Vd.* tūwō 7.

tūwan wākē *m.* = bụrūƙuƙụ.

tūyạ *f.* (*secondary v.n. of* tōyạ) *x* (1) tanạ tūyạr wạinā = tanạ tōyạ wạinā she's frying wạinā-cakes. (2) mai ~ wạinā dạ rūwā bạllē yạ sạmi mại if P. is cantankerous without provocation, how much more so if provoked! (3) nā yi ~, nā mạncē dạ ạlbasa = tōyạ 1*c*.

tụzā *Vb.* 2 (*p.o.* tụ̄jē, *n.o.* tụ̄ji). (1) = tūjẹ 1. (2) yā tụ̄ji nōmā he did much farming. (3) *cf.* tūzad dạ, tūzō.

tūzad dạ *Vb.* 4 (1) sold at a loss. (2) yā tūzar = yā tūzō dạ gāshị he is dead.

tuzga = tizga.

tūzō *Vb.* 3A = tūjẹ 2 (*Vd.* tūzad).

tụzūrū *m.* (*pl.* tụzụ̄rai) bachelor (*cf.* gwaurō).

twại-twại *x* sunạ tạfīyạ ~ they're bustling about in a state of eager excitement.

twal = tal.

twạ̄lā *Kt.* = tạ̄yā.

twạl dạ idō *m.* keeping P. cooling his heels *x* an yi masạ ~.

twālẹ *Kt.* = tālẹ.

twaŋga *Kt.* = taŋga.

twaŋkā *Kt. f.* = tsīduhū.

twạn-twạŋ *Kt. m.* (1) = wạtandā. (2) sun yi twạn-twạŋ dạ ƙasạn naŋ they dismembered that land.

twạnyatạ *Vb.* 2 (*p.o.* twạnyạcē, *n.o.* twạnyạci) *Sk.* shamed P. by revealing his secrets (= fạllasạ).

twạrī *Kt.* = tạrī.

twasshī *Kt. m.* = tsīduhū.

twātsạ *Kt.* *Vb.* 1A (1) = tātsạ. ·(2) = katsạ 5.

twạ̄yā *Kt.* = tạ̄yā.

twị *x* an tārạ shi ~ it is piled up.

U

ụbā *m.* (*pl.* ụbạnnị, *cf.* īyạ̄yē). (1) (*a*) father. (*b*) ụbansụ Cirọ̄mạ *Vd.* tūɓẹ 1*b.* (*c*) ụbaŋ kisạnsụ *m.* (*pl.* īyạ̄yaŋ kisạnsụ) those who murdered them. (*d*) yanạ sọ yạ gạ̄ji ụbansạ *Vd.* matsịyạ̄cī 3. (*e*) ụbā kạ̄ dauƙạ *Vd.* tīlạs 1*e.* (*f*) rọ̄ƙwaŋ ụbā wurị *Vd.* zạllim. (2) *Vd.* ụban-*compounds*. (3) *cf.* dạŋụbā, ụbākạ, rịgar ụbā, cụ̄cū.

ubaka A. (ụbākạ) (1) damn your eyes! (*d.f.* ụbā), *cf.* cụ̄cū ; ūwā 1*c* ; gēmụ 4. (2) *x* bạ̄ dōkịŋ ~ ba nẹ̄ it is not your blasted father's horse! (*cf.* ūwākạ). B. (ūbakạ) *Katagum f.* = kūbakạ.

ụbam ɓụrgwị *Vd.* ɓụrgwị.

ụban dākị *m.* (1) master of servant (*cf.* ụbaŋ gijị, ụbaŋ gidā, ūwar dākị). (2) one's immediate senior (*x* District Head *re* Village Head, Resident *re* District Officer, Chief Commissioner *re* Resident, Governor *re* Lieutenant-Governor, etc.) = ụbaŋ gidā 2. (3) (*a*) = ụbaŋ gijị 2. (*b*) lạifī bạ̄ shi dạ ~ a criminal always says another is guilty.

Uban dawākī (1) *Sk.* the sạrautạ elsewhere called Mạ̄dākī. (2) type of bọrī spirit.

ụbaŋ gidā *m.* (1) = mại gidā *q.v. under* gidā 1*l*.i. (2) = ụban dākị 1, 2. (3) *cf.* ụbaŋ gijị.

ụbaŋ gijị (1) Ụban gijị The Lord God (*Vd.* yā 2). (2) ~ (*f.* ūwar gijịyā) *pl.* īyạ̄yaŋ gijị owner of slave or any object (= ụban dākị 3*a, b*). (3) *Vd.* ƙẹtā 4. (4) *cf.* ụbaŋ gidā.

uban gumēda Vd. gumēda.

uban ƙasā Vd. hākimī.

uban ƙaurā Vd. ƙaurā 3.

ubam marātayā Vd. jīgo 2b.

ubam mutānē = ajiŋgi.

ubanni Vd. ubā.

uban tafīya = mādugū.

uban taurārī Vd. gamzāki.

uban watandā Vd. tūrū 4a.

uban wutā m. leader, head-man.

uban 'yan aiki Vd. aṛā 2.

ūda (1) m., f. (pl. ūdōdī = ūdōjī) (a) type of large ram or sheep. (b) miser (epithet is ūda, kada ki ci nāki sǎi na mai gidā yā ƙārę). (2) f. (a) (with pl. ūdāwā) a Filani clan living near Timbuctoo. (b) = ōda.

ūdashę Kt. = hūdashę.

ūdāwā Vd. ūda 2.

ūdōdī Vd. ūda.

uf exclamation in top-playing (ƙatantaŋwa), etc.

ūfę Vb. 3A took to his heels.

uffaŋ used in ban cę da shī ∼ ba I did not address a single word to him (= lummaƙaifa 1 = farī 2f = allī 2 = ƙanzil = m 1b = tōfi walā ƙēƙas = tōfī 2 = mus 2 = shai'aŋ 1).

ūfu = ūhu = īhu q.v.

ujilā Ar. f. eager haste.

ujirā Ar. f. (1) tenth part of legacy always due to Muslim Treasury (= ushirā). (2) wages (= ushirā). (3) cf. ushiri.

Ukēlē f. Okenni.

ukku Sk. = uku.

uku f. (1) (a) three. (b) na ∼ m. (f. ta ∼) pl. na ∼ third. (c) ɓarnad da muƙa yi musu, tā yi ukuŋ wadda suƙa yi mana the casualties we inflicted on them were thrice what they inflicted on us. (2) (a) tuntuɓaŋ kāshī yā ɓata ∼ ; yā ɓata raŋ, yā ɓata ƙafa, yā ɓata hannū what an intractable person. (b) mai ɓata ∼ Vd. kunū 1a. (3) (a) yā sā kansa ∼ he came to grief. (b) sā ƙai a ∼ ƙarē da gudun lahīya what meddlesomeness ! (Vd. kula ƙai). (4) Sarkī ∼ the mayāfi-cloth consisting of 20 baƙī (Vd. baƙī B.1.6) plus 10 gwandā plus 10 sāƙi. (5) Vd. shiga 1g. (6) uku da uku type of gambling. (7) (a) (i) uku uku type of face-markings (askā). (ii) dakaŋ uku

uku Vd. daka 2f. (b) uku da kūka type of face-markings (askā) of some Kano people.

*uƙūba = uƙūba Ar. f. anguish, pain.

ukuntā Vb. 1C made into three, did three times.

ullē f. cat (= kyaŋwā).

ūlu Eng. m. wool.

ūmarā Sk. f. cudgel (cf. kōkarā).

umarcē Vd. umarta.

umarnī m. command (= dōkā).

umarta Vb. 2 (p.o. umarcē, n.o. umarci) ordered P. to do T.

Umaru Vd. sanda, Fāruku.

umbōla = ambōla.

*umbulullukī Kt. m. = makīyāyā 2.

umbusu Sk. m. = ƙashiŋ umbusū.

Umbutāwā (1) a Ningi tribe. (2) Vd. Bāƙo 2.

umfāna Kt. = amfāna.

umfānī Kt. m. = amfānī.

umma = ummā = mma q.v.

ummul aɓā'isi Ar. m. cause, reason.

umrā f. (1) visiting the Ƙa'aba during the Pilgrimage. (2) Vd. haji 3.

umūmi Ar. m. unanimity x sun yi ∼ sun cę they declared unanimously that.

umurnī = umarnī.

unduruttū m. type of fish-trap.

ungo Vd. ŋgō.

uŋgōzanci m. midwifery.

uŋgōzōma f. (pl. uŋgōzōmai) (1) midwife (she gets head, skin, and legs of ram killed at naming-ceremony, cf. sūnā, wanzāmi) = makarɓīyā. (2) Kt. = gandōkī. (3) uŋgōzōmar Wāsǎi nę he's a novice (cf. fāri 1b).

ungudūdu Kt. m. = iŋgidīdo.

ungulū f. (pl. uŋgulai) (1) (a) vulture (= Sk. jiffo = Sk. kōlō 3). (b) aŋ ƙōri uŋgulū the enemy has been driven out. (2) ∼ bā ƙazar‿kōwā ba she is bazawarā and so available to marry. (3) ƙafar uŋgulū mai ɓata mīya what an undesirable person ! (3a) ∼ tā tāka shūnī Vd. biris. (4) inā rūwaŋ ∼ da kitso what do I care ? (5) (a) Mazā māsū jiran tsammāni epithet of vulture. (b) Audu ∼ mai zaman tsammāni nē Audu is waiting expectantly. (6) ∼ tā kōma gidanta na tsāmīyā what's bred in the bone comes out in the flesh.

(7) iŋ ~ tä bĭyä bụkātạ, zạ̈būwä tạ tạfi dạ zạ̈nantạ better my own poor article than a borrowed one ! (= gạ̈tarĭ 1c). (8) ~ dạ mạ̈i type of variegated local cloth. (9) uŋgụluŋ kwākwạ = uŋgụlun tukurwä the Eagle *Gypohierax angolensis.* (10) nāmạŋ ~ m. carrion (= mūshẹ). (11) Vd. tābạr uŋgụlū ; gäbọ ; ḳụrụ̈cĭyä 4. uŋgunnĭ Vd. uŋgūwä.

uŋgurdụgĭ m. (f. ụŋgurdụgä) pl. uŋgụrdụgại cripple forced to move along on hands and knees (= Kt. guddụgĭ).

uŋgụrnŭ f. type of potash.

Uŋgushạt m. August.

uŋgūwä f. (pl. uŋgūwŏyĭ = uŋgwŏyĭ = uŋgwạnnĭ = Sk. uŋgunnĭ = Sk. uŋgunnĭ). (1) (a) quarter of town, townward. (b) zạ̈ ni ~ I'm off visiting. (2) village near a town. (3) district x uŋgūwạr dạ yakẹ̈ yäḳi the theatre of war where he is fighting. sum murḳụshẹ ḳasạ̈shammụ dạ kẹ̈ caŋ uŋgūwarsụ they forced their way into our countries which are situated in their part of the world. (4) 'yar ~ f. = gāsạyä 1.

uŋgwä = uŋgūwä.

uŋhwạ̈nĭ Kt. m. = ạmfạ̈nĭ.

unị Zar. = wunị.

uppạŋ = uffạŋ.

urịncē (1) Vb. 3A (1) x yä ~ kạn sāmụnsạ he's eager to get it (= ụzurtạ). (2) Vb. 1C x yä ~ minị m̱ bä shị he urged me to give it to him (= ḳarịạfä 3).

urịntạ Vb. 3B x yä ~ kạn sāmụnsạ = urịncē 1.

*ụrūlạ Ar. f. portable goods, excluding cash or livestock.

urus Kt. m. an yi masạ ~ he was addressed with " bother you ! ".

ụryạŋ Ar. adj. naked (= huntū).

Usạilamạ = Musạilamạ.

ushirä f. (1) = ujirä. (2) = ushịrĭ.

ushịrĭ = ushụrĭ Ar. m. tenth part paid as commission to court in cases involving action for debt (= ushirä 2), cf. ujirä.

Ụsmạŋ = Ụsụmạŋ.

ussị Ar. m. (1) = hạrsāshị 2. (2) wannạŋ lạ̈bārị bạ̈ shi dạ ~ this news is unfounded.

usulĭ = asalĭ.

Ụsụmạŋ = Ụsụmānụ man's name (epithet is Sạŋgamin tamä = Shēhụ).

usụr Eng. m. (sg., pl.) metal whistle.

uwa A. (ūwä) f. (Kt. pl. ūwạ̈yẹ̈ ; cf. ĭyạ̈yẹ̈ parents). (1) (a) mother (= innạ q.v. = ĭyạ). (b) cf. dạŋūwä. (c) (i) dan tubụrar wä = dạŋ kụnnạŋ ~ = dan cikịŋ ~ = dan cụcạŋ ~ (Vd. cụcū) = Sk. dan damcịŋ ~ = gāshị 1h = gēmụ 4 (mild abuse) you bothersome fellow ! (cf. ūwākạ). (ii) dạŋ kạzaŋ ūwä blast you ! (Vd. kạzä 3, damcị, dĭbạ 1j, būtịyä 2, dūrụ, fịlānịyä, fĭshĭ, gato 3, ḳundū 1e, lạ̈yä, ḳwālạ 4). (d) Vd. innạ, ĭyạ, mmạ. (e) dạ kā yĭ, dạ kadạ kạ yĭ, ūwarsụ dạyä it's all the same whether you do it or not (Vd. dạ 17). (f) ūwar gidä Vd. gidä 1n. (g) ~ dūnĭyạ Vd. dūnĭyạ 1b.ii, 1h. (h) yä yi ~ yä yi makarbĭyä he was officious. (j) (i) mại ~ ạ murhụ bä yạ̈ cịn tūwō gäyä one must have a patron (Vd. tūwō 13). (ii) Vd. gäyä 2f. (k) Vd. ūwar compounds, ūwar dāḳị. (2) (a) ūwar rịgä body of gown. (b) ūwar tụ̈lū body of ewer. ūwar tukunyä body of cooking-pot (as contrasted with wuyạ). (c) (i) cf. ūwar kudĭ. (ii) Vd. arugumạ. (3) saŋ ūwar dawạ Vd. ūwar dawạ. (4) sun yiwō mukụ ūwä they protected, screened you. (5) Vd. mạntạ ūwä. (6) nōnạŋ ūwāta Vd. dĭbạ 1j. (7) ūwar tāḳạ Vd. dĭbạ 1j. (8) Vd. yạŋkä 1c. (8A) dōraŋ ūwä Vd. bụḳū-bụḳū. (9) = mabịyĭ 3.

B. (ūwa) (1) name for girl whose real name is that of her mother or paternal grandmother (= ūwānĭ). (2) dropsy (= ẹ̈gọ).

*ụwairụ Ar. m., f. one-eyed P.

ūwākạ (1) blast you ! = tsēlạŋ ūwākạ (cf. ụbākạ, ūwä 1c, tubụrä 4, ạmbōlạ). (2) x bạ̈ kudịŋ ~ ba nẹ̈ it isn't your mother's blasted money ! (3) x kudịŋ ~ nẹ̈ ? kō na ụbākạ nẹ̈ what's this bloody money in your hand ? it's neither your blasted mother's nor your blasted father's is it ? (4) cē musụ " ūwākạ dukạ ! " ṉ jĭ nị tell them I say they are a pack of bloody fools ! (5) ūwākạ cē ta yị̈ ? was it your cursed mother who

did it ? **(6) daŋgin na ūwäkį** syco-phant(s), toady, toadies.
ūwäkį *Vd.* **ūwäkạ 6.**
ūwānī = ūwa 1.
ūwar ɓạrnä *Vd.* **gägạ.**
ūwar bikī *Vd.* **bikī 1h.**
ūwar ɓurgwį *Vd.* **ɓurgwį 2.**
ūwar dạɓē *Vd.* **dạɓē 6.**
ūwar dadį *Vd.* **rufį 7.**
ūwar d̄äkį (1) (a) mistress of servant, etc. (*i.e. fem. of* **uban d̄äkį 1, 2**). **(b)** mistress of **d̄äkį 5, dīyä 4** (*cf.* **ränä** 3b). **(2)** man's woman-friend (not relative or lover) who gives him help or advice (**1, 2 = ūwar ränä 1**), *cf.* **ränä** 3b. **(3)** *Kt.* **rashin ūwä kạ ∼ = ūwar ränä 2.** **(4) ūwar d̄äkįmmu** my mother. **(5) ūwar d̄äkina** my mistress (*said by servant, cf.* 1 *above*). **(5)** *cf.* **ūwar gidä** *under* **gidä 1n.**
ūwar dawạ (1) ∼ tä taɓạ shi = dawạ 5a, Innạ 3b. (2) *Vd.* **son 7.**
ūwar faɗạ *Vd.* **bindigạ.**
ūwar gạrä *Vd.* **gạrä 1d.**
ūwar garkę *Vd.* **garkę 6.**
ūwar gidä (1) *Vd.* **gidä 1n.** **(2)** *cf.* **ūwar d̄äkį, ūwar gijįyä.**
ūwar gijįyä *Vd.* **uɓaŋ gijį 2.**
ūwar gizo *Vd.* **ba'ạ.**
ūwar gōyō *Vd.* **gōyō 1d.**
ūwar gwäzä *Vd.* **gwäzä 1b.**
ūwar hạnau = hạnau 1.
ūwar hanjī = makīyäyä 2.
ūwar hannū *f.* **(1)** lump of food given to child to eat apart from persons gathered round calabash. **(2) yä yi ∼** he (greedy P.) grabbed lump of food from calabash.
ūwar ƙasä *Vd.* **häkįmī.**
ūwar käshī *epithet of* **tuɓųrä 1.**
ūwar kạurä *Vd.* **kạurä 3.**
ūwar kīshįyä *Vd.* **kūkä 1b.iv.**
ūwar kudī *Vd.* **kudī 5 ; dalạ 5.**
ūwar kūsä *Kt.* **= ūwar ɓụrgwị** *q.v. under* **ɓurgwị 2.**
ūwar kusīä = uɓaŋ kạurä *q.v. under* **kạurä 3.**
ūwar mäguŋgunạ *f.* an Asclepiad plant with milky sap (**= sanyä**).
ūwar maiƙọ *Vd.* **zįnä 2.**
ūwar maƙērä *Vd.* **maƙērä 2.**
ūwar mạshasshärä *Vd.* **mạshasshärä 1d.**
ūwar mätä *f.* **(1)** married woman. **(2)**

ūwar mätanci *m. x* **yärinyạn nạŋ tä cikạ ūwar mätanci (a)** this girl puts on the airs of a married woman. **(b)** this girl is a mischief-maker (*b =* **kinibībį**).
ūwar mijį *Vd.* **dadį 5.** ·
ūwar ränä *f.* **(1) = ūwar d̄äkį 1, 2.** **(2) rashin ūwä kạ ∼** any port in a storm (**= Kt.** **ūwar d̄äkį 3**). **(3) cikiŋ ∼ mukạ yi tạīyạ** we travelled in the heat of the day.
ūwar rīgä *f.* *Vd.* **ūwä 2a.**
ūwar rufį *Vd.* **gạrmä 1c.**
ūwar safarạ *Vd.* **dụmbä.**
ūwar saurạyī *Vd.* **gwalaŋgwasō.**
ūwar sörö *Vd.* **sörö 3.**
ūwar tsandō *Vd.* **tsandō 2.**
ūwar tsįyä *Vd.* **cäcä.**
ūwar tūwō *f.* **(1) (a)** woman who cooks for wifeless man. **(b)** *Vd.* **tūwō 13.** **(2)** *Vd.* **dạddawä.**
ūwar wani *Vd.* **rämį 4.**
ūwar 'yä *Vd.* **ränä 4c.ii ; katakas.**
ūwar yäƙį *f.* **(1)** commander-in-chief. **(2)** headquarters-staff of an army. **(3)** main body of troops. **(4) ūwạyan yäƙį** armies.
ūwạyē *Vd.* **ūwä.**
uzurạŋ (1) immediately. **(2)** *m.* P. always in eager haste.
uzurī *m.* **(1)** *Ar.* excuse (**= hanzarī**). **(2)** sexual incontinence.
uzurtạ *Vb.* **3B yä ∼ dạ sämụnsạ** he's eager to get it (**= ụrintạ**).

W

wa A. (wạ) *m.* (*f.* **yạ**) *pl.* **yạyyē = yạyyū =** *Sk.* **yäyū =** *Sk.* **yạnnī =** *Kt.* **yạnnai.** **(1) (a)** elder brother (**= yạyä**). **(b)** any male older than oneself, whether related or not. **(c)** *Vd.* **yạyä.** **(2)** A. beyond one *x* **hawaŋ kękē ạ wurīna wänä nę** cycling is beyond me. **(3) (a) wạŋ gạrī** head of a town. **(b) (i) wạŋ gidä = mai gidä** *q.v. under* **gidä 1l.** **(ii) wạŋ gijį** *Vd.* **zạkarạ.** **(c) wạn dawạ (i)** *epithet of* lion ; *epithet of* Chief of town. **(ii)** *Vd.* **Sarkī 2b, Aɓū bakạr dawạ 1b.** **(d)** *Vd.* **wạn ränä.** **B. (wạ) (1) (Ar.** " and ") *used in (a)*

alif (= alu) wạ minyạ 1100. alif (= alu) wạ mẹtaŋ 1200. alif (= alu) wạ ạrbạminyạ 1400. alif (= alu) wạ hạmsạminyạ 1500. (b) cf. dăidăi ~ dăidạ. (2) (after verb with noun in dative) to (a) x·(i) nā kāmạ wạ Daudạ dōkị I caught the horse for David (Mod. Gram. 50b). (ii) iŋ kanạ̈ wạ Allạ̈ Vd. Allạ̈ 4a. (b) (wạ sometimes omitted, Mod. Gram. 50c) x yā zargạ kạransạ (= yā zargạ wạ kạransạ) igīyạ (he has attached a rope-noose to his dog) he has left home. ya kạn tīlạsạ mutạ̈nē (= ya kạn tīlạsā wạ mutạ̈nē) sụ yi hakạ it often compels people to act thus. (c) (dạ of causal verbs vanishes before wạ) x yā sayar wạ Audụ dōkị he sold a horse to (for) Audu (Mod. Gram. 170a). yā gādar wạ Audụ sạrautạ tasạ he left his rule to be inherited by Audu (Mod. Gram. 170b). (d) (i) (in emphatic, relative, or sentences with inherently interrogative word, wạ can stand last, or one but last if object is stated) x Kạnde, wạ̈ akạ bạ̈i wạ to whom was Kande given in marriage ? = Kạnde, wạ̈ akạ bā (with wạ omitted) = Kạnde, wạ̈ akạ bạ̈i wạ itạ (Mod. Gram. 161a), Vd. wạ̈ 3 second example. bịkịŋ, wạ̈ akạ yi wạ = bịkịŋ, wạ̈ akạ yi wạ shị for whom was the feast given (Mod. Gram. 161a) (Vd. wạ̈ 3). Audụ, shī akạ yi wạ Audu is the one for whom it (feast) was given (Mod. Gram. 137b) = Audụ, shī akạ yi wạ shī = Audụ, shī akạ yi wạ bịkịŋ. shī mukẹ̈ yi wạ mạganạ he is the one to whom we refer. bạ̈ kạnsụ kawại sukạ yi wạ they did not do it for themselves alone. gạrin naŋ, shī nẹ̈ ya hau mạ wạ this is the town which he attacked (Vd. mạ). (ii) to whom, to which x wadạndạ akạ yi wạ raunukạ, sum mutụ the wounded have died. wannạm bugụ, bạ̈ wạndạ ya saŋ indạ zā sụ kai wạ nobody knows to where this attack will be extended. jạma'ạd dạ ya ƙwācẹ̈ wạ ƙasạr the people from whom he took the country. (3) Sk. (a) = yị. (b) mū ~ mū = mụ̈ wạ mū wạ mū = yẹ̈ q.v. (c) Vd. yị 1f. (4) cf. su ~ under wạ̈ 1.
   C. (wạ̈) m. (used when sex is known to

be masc. or when sex is not emphasized), pl. su wạ (cf. 4). (1) who ? x (a) wạ̈ ya zọ̈ who came ? (Mod. Gram. 160b). (b) wạ̈ kẹ̈ (= wạ̈ yakẹ̈) zūwạ who is coming ? (= wạ̈nēnẹ̈ 1b). (c) wạ̈ ya gayạ makạ stuff and nonsense ! (= Sk. dẹ̈wạ yā'ẹ̈). (d) (where it is necessary to use fem. Vd. wạ̈nēnẹ̈). (e) (i) wạ̈ kạ̈ būdẹ̈ Vd. būdẹ̈ 1k. (ii) wạ̈ ya ƙi fādụ̈war mại rụmbū Vd. fādụ̈wā 6. (iii) fādạ nạ̈ caŋ, kai wạ̈, kai wạ̈ the palace was involved in bickerings. (iv) wạ̈ yakẹ̈ ta kāyạ̈ Vd. ta B.1 1d. (v) wạ̈ zại gasạ Vd. gadọ̈ 2b. (vi) wạ̈ ya ga gulbị Vd. gulbī. (vii) wạ̈ zại rabạ hantạ Vd. hantạ. (viii) wạ̈ kạ̈ rabạ Vd. ƙuƙụs. (f) (i) ạ wạ̈ yakẹ̈ of what account is he ! (= wạ̈nē 2). ạ wạ̈ kakẹ̈ of what account are you ! (= wạ̈nē 2). (ii) Sk wā shị = wā shī naŋ of what account is he ! (= wạ̈nē 2). wā Mūsạ of what account is Moses ! (= wạ̈nē 2 = wạ̈nēnẹ̈ 1c). (g) Sk. wā mụtụm fancy ! (= wạ̈nē 2c). (h) Sk. waccẹ̈ mạ who told you ? (d.f. wạ̈ ya cẹ̈). (2) whom (a) (wạ̈ following) x ŋ ji wạ̈ who said so ? (Mod. Gram. 160a) = wạ̈nēnẹ̈ 2a. kuŋ ga wạ̈ whom did you see ? (b) (wạ̈ preceding) x wạ̈ kakẹ̈ dūkạ whom are you beating ? (Mod. Gram. 161a). wạ̈ sukạ dōkạ̈ whom did they beat ? wạ̈ sukạ bā Audụ = Audụ, wạ̈ sukạ bā shị whom did they give in marriage to Audu ? (Mod. Gram. 161a) (= wạ̈nēnẹ̈ 2b). (3) to whom x Sarkī, wạ̈ ya bạ̈ dōkị to whom did the chief give the horse ? (Mod. Gram. 161a). wạ̈ zạŋ kai wạ̈ = wạ̈ zạŋ kại (Vd. wạ̈ 2d.i) = Kt. wạ̈ zạŋ kai mạ wạ who shall I take it to ? = wạ̈nēnẹ̈ 3 (Vd. mạ 2). wạ̈ ka bạ̈ = wạ̈ ka bạ̈i wạ = kā bā wạ̈ who did you give it to ? Kạnde, wạ̈ akạ bạ̈ = Kạnde, wạ̈ akạ bạ̈i wạ = Kạnde, wạ̈ akạ bạ̈i wạ itạ = wạ̈ akạ bạ̈i Kạndẹ̈ = Kạnde, wạ̈ akạ bā itạ to whom was Kande given in marriage ? (Mod. Gram. 161a). bịkịŋ, wạ̈ akạ yi wạ = bịkịŋ, wạ̈ akạ yi wạ shị for whom was the feast given ? (= wạ̈nēnẹ̈ 3). (4) kū su wạ̈ ; mū su wạ̈ ; sū su wạ̈ = wạ̈nēnẹ̈ 4 (cf. su wạ̈ in 1 above, wạ̈nē 2a). (5) cf. wạ̈nēnẹ̈, wạ̈nẹ̈, wạ̈nē, wạ̈yẹ̈, wạnnē,

wạnnē, wạnẹ, kōwā, kōwạ. (6) Vd. wặ
kặ rabẹ ; wā kạ sǫ ; wā kẹ̆ dawạ ;
wặ ka dūḅặ ; wặ ya zặgi bặḅạ ; wặ ya
zặgi dǫgarị ; wabbinạŋ.
  D. (wặ) m. the fig-tree Ficus sp.
(= yandị = Kt. yặ).
  E. (wā) (1) Vd. wặ 1f.ii, 1g ; wā
kạ sǫ ; wā kẹ̆ dawạ. (2) Vd. ūwā 1c.i.
wā'ạdĭ Ar. m. (pl. wā'adōdĭ) promise (to
pay debt at fixed time, etc.).
wạ'alamụ Vd. Ạllāhụ 4.
wa'ạncạŋ Kt. = wadạncạŋ q.v. under
wancạŋ.
wa'ạŋ'iŋ Kt. Vd. waŋ'iŋ.
wa'aŋ'inạ Vd. waŋ'inạ.
wa'aŋ'innĭyā Vd. waŋ'innĭyā.
wa'annan A. (wa'ạnnạŋ) Kt. = wadạnnạŋ.
  B. (wā'an nạŋ) Sk. who is it ?
(= wặnēnẹ̆).
wa'ansu Kt. = wadansu q.v. under wani.
wạ'ạzcē Vd. wạ'aztạ.
wa'ạzĭ Ar. m. (pl. wạ'ạzai) preaching,
admonition x sunặ ta wa'ạzĭ gạrēmụ
they are preaching to us. yā yi ~ gạ
mutặnē = yā yi wạ mutặnē ~ he exhorted the people, he gave a sermon to
the people.
wạ'aztạ Vb. 2 (p.o. wạ'ạzcē, n.o. wạ'ạzci).
(1) preached to. (2) ·admonished.
wạ'āzụ = wa'ạzĭ.
wạbai Kt. = bạmbạrặkwai (1) q.v. x
ạkwai mutặnē dạ yawạ wadạndạ zā
sụ ga wạbai kặfin sụ sāḅạ many people
find it hard to adapt themselves to this
idea.
wabbinạŋ Sk. m. theft (d.f. wặ bi nạŋ).
wābị (1) (a) mother's constantly suffering
loss of young children. (b) daŋ ~ (f.
'yar ~) child whose elder brothers or
sisters died young. (c) Vd. dạŋganạ
2c ; bāwạ 2 ; Ạ jēfas ; Gwārĭ 2c. (d) daŋ
~ yā fādạ rijĭyā Vd. rạbō 6d. (2) tree
casting its fruit. (3) (a) losing money
in trading. (b) makarantan naŋ ~
gạrētạ this school keeps losing its
pupils. (4) wābiŋ haifụ̄wā feckless child
(= hạsārạ 2). (5) Vd. Ạ bar shị.
wābịlĭ Ar. m. heavy rain.
wạcạ Vd. wạnẹ.
wācặɓạ = wạcặnĭyā.
wacạɓẹ = hōɓẹ̆sạ.

wacaccạkā Vb. 3D (1) scattered (x horse,
fowl, its corn). (2) Vd. wajajjạgā.
wạcặnĭyā f. lavish spending, extravagance.
waca-waca A. (wacā-wạcặ) (1) f. =
wạcặnĭyā x yanặ ~ dạ kudinsạ. (2)
adv. abundantly.
  B. (wạcặ-wạcặ) (1) f. bustling about
(= kạiwā dạ kāwǫ̆wā). (2) adv. =
wacā-wạcặ 2.
  C. Vd. wajā-wajā.
wacẹ̆ wạndạ.
waccạ Vd. wạndạ.
waccaŋ Vd. wancạŋ, wạncaŋ.
wạccặnā Vd. wạncặnā.
wacce A. (wạccē, wạccẹ̆) Vd. wạnnẹ̆.
  B. (waccẹ̆) (1) Vd. wạndạ. (2) Sk.
waccẹ̆ mạ who told you ? (d.f. wặ
ya cẹ̆), Vd. wặ 1h.
wạccēcẹ̆ Vd. wạnnēnẹ̆.
waccēnĭ Vd. wancēnĭ.
waccēnĭyā Vd. wancēnĭyā.
wace A. (wạcẹ̆) Vd. wặnẹ̆.
  B. (wạcẹ̆) Vd. wạnẹ.
  C. (wacẹ̆) Vd. wạnẹ, wanẹ.
wạcēcẹ̆ Vd. wạnēnẹ̆.
wacẹ̆tặ Vd. wanẹ̆nặ.
wạcilặ f. (1) one or more beams used as in
jijjigẹ (= Kt. shặ wụyā 2). (2) Kt.
= jijjigẹ.
wada A. (wặdā) m., f. (1) (a) dwarf (he is
addressed as Mālạm dōgō). (b) kāshin
turmĭ bặ na wạdaŋ kạrē ba nẹ̆ don't
attempt a thing beyond you ! (c)
Vd. durkụsā 2. (2) wạdaŋ kụrfai =
kụrfai 3. (3) wạdaŋ Ạlkụr'ạŋ small
edition of Koran.
  B. (wạdā) f. (1) (a) wealth. (b)
tambạriŋ ~ Vd. hadirị ; bụgau 4.
(2) sufficiency. (3) reproach (= yạkạnā = falalā 3).
  C. (wādạ) Sk. = yādạ 2.
wada A. (wadạ) used in ganiŋ ~ yị
m. imitating other people (d.f.
wadansu).
  B. (wadặ) used in kū wadặ = wadặ
fancy you people doing so ! (d.f.
wadạnnạŋ).
wadace A. (wạdạcē) Vd. wạdātạ.
  B. (wạdạcē) (noun of state from
wạdātạ) x sunặ ~ (1) they are numerous.
(2) they are happy.
wạdāci Vd. wạdātạ.

wadai A. (wadai) (1) (a) Allā ⌒ = Allā wadaŋkạ curse you! (b) Allā wadan yabanyạr jūjī, kyau bābu halī the faults of children recoil on their parents. (c) "Allā ⌒" bä tā kōmē dạ d'am biri he's utterly brazen. (2) (said by blind man) Allā wadan rashiŋ idọ curse you! (3) Vd. gincirạ.

B. (Wạdại) f. Wadai.

*wad'ạ'ī Ar. m. coitus (= jịmā'ị).

*wạdā'ị Ar. m. taking leave of P.

wādā̱kā f. = wạcạnīyā.

wadan Vd. wadai.

wad'ạuạ Vd. wạnẹ.

wad'ancaŋ A. (wad'ancạŋ) Vd. wancạŋ.

B. (wạd'ancaŋ = wad'ạncaŋ) Vd. wạncaŋ.

wạd'ạncā̱nā Vd. wạncā̱nā.

wad'ạncēnī Vd. wancēnī.

wad'ạncēnịyā Vd. wancēnịyā.

wad'ạndạ Vd. wạndạ.

wad'ạŋgā Vd. wạŋgā.

wạd'ạunạ Vd. wạnẹ, wạndạ.

wad'annan A. (wad'annạŋ) Vd. wannạŋ.

B. (wạd'annaŋ = wad'annaŋ) Vd. wạnnaŋ.

wad'anne A. (wạd'annẹ) Vd. wạnẹ.

B. (wạd'annē̱) Vd. wạnnē̱.

wạd'ạnnēnē̱ Vd. wạnnēnē̱.

wad'ansu Vd. wani.

wadarai = wadai.

wad'ạrcē Vb. 1C did action of wad'ạrta completely.

wad'ạrī (1) m. (a) arranging thread in required length for weaving (Vd. mạrī) = Sk. wạlwalạ 2. (b) lại̱fī duk na kūrā nē̱ ạmmä bandạ sātạr ⌒ give a dog a bad name and hang him. (c) bustling about (= kại̱wā dạ kāwō̱wā). (d) anā ⌒ cikin duhu one does not know what the future holds. (2) m. (pl. wad'urạ) = sūlū 1.

wad'ạrtā Vb. 1C arranged (thread) as in wad'ạrī.

wạdar zūcī Vd. wạdā 3.

wadata A. (wạdā̱tā) Vb. 1C enriched (= wạdā̱tạ 1a).

B. (wạdā̱tạ) (1) Vb. 2 (p.o. wạdā̱cē, n.o. wạdā̱ci) (a) enriched (= wadā̱tā = wadātar dạ). (b) sufficed (= wadātar dạ). (2) f. wealth. (3) Vb. 3B (a) became rich. (b) had sufficiency x

suŋ ⌒ dạ ạbincī they have enough food. nā ⌒ I have sufficient.

wadātad dạ Vb. 4 (1) enriched (= wạdā̱tạ 1a). (2) sufficed x mayā̱kā yạddạ zā su wadātar enough soldiers. mạganạn naŋ tā wadātas this expression is clear and does not require explaining.

wạ'da-wạdā" adv. liberally, abundantly.

wadạ yị Vd. wadạ.

waddạ (1) Vd. wạndạ. (2) how = yạddạ q.v.

waddai Sk. = wadai.

wad'darẹ Sk. (1) wad'd'arẹ = wad'd'araŋ gulyā'ē̱ = wad'd'arẹ gulyā'ē̱ = wad'd'arẹ yā'ẹ fancy! (= dēwạ yā'ē̱). (2) jaŋ ⌒ the red lining (shā̱fi) with white edge (girā) for skirt of gown.

*wạdīyyị m. emission of semen after urination, mostly in men over fifty years old (cf. mạzīyyị).

wad'urạ Vd. wad'ạrī 2.

wafcē Vb. 1C (1) pounced on and took (= faucẹ). (2) grabbed (= zarẹ).

B. (wạfcē) Vd. wạftā.

wafcēcẹ m. (f. wafcēcịyā) huge.

wạfci Vd. wạftā.

wafịlaŋ wafịlaŋ adv. of various kinds (= launi-launi 2) x sunā naŋ ⌒ they are multifarious.

wạftā Vb. 2 (p.o. wạfcē, n.o. wạfci) = wafcẹ.

wāgā f. (pl. wāgā̱gē̱) (1) hide-pannier for pack-animal (disused wāgā is often used for storing books). (2) sāraŋ ⌒ m. kola-nuts of assorted sizes. (3) kaŋ ⌒ m. (a) best kolas (= gō̱rīyạ). (b) "pick of the bunch" (= idon 13b). (4) hawaŋ ⌒ m. riding on saddle devoid of coverings (cf. hawā 2b).

wāgambạrī Yor. m. (1) = ạdandẹ. (2) type of sleeveless shirt.*

wāgashī Yor. m. cream-cheese.

wạgā-wạgā (1) m., f., sg., pl. dolt. (2) Kt. f. trickery.

wāgẹ Vb. 3A = fā̱fẹ 2b.

wagga A. (wạggā) Sk. Vd. wạŋgā.

B. (wạggạ) (Ar. uqqa) weight of about two and a half pounds used by Arabs in weighing skins.

waggẹ m. pigeon-stealing.

wagunu m. (pl. wagunōnī) railway-waggon.

wahā f. (1) playing in water. (2) feeling happy about something (= annashūwā).

wahābā m. man with side-whiskers (sājē) but no beard (cf. wushēfē).

wahala (1) f. (a) trouble. (b) yā shā (= yā ci) wahala he suffered trouble. (c) wanda bai ci hakurin ~ ba, yanā hakurin talauci if a man does not work, neither shall he eat. (d) yanā masa ~ he is serving him. yā yi mini ~ he did me services, thus sparing me the effort entailed (= wahaltā). dauki ~ Vd. daukā 1a.xiv. (dd) yā yi wahala da mū he took trouble on our account. (e) (i) kākā ~ how are you? (reply lāfīya lau well, thank you!). (ii) inā wahalar dāmunā how does the wet season suit your crops? (reply da gōdę Allā = da saukī well, thanks!). (iii) inā wahalar bākī how are you faring with your guests? (reply sun tafi gidā, da gōdę Allā they have returned home safely). (iv) inā wahalar rānī = inā zaman rānī how are you faring this hot season (reply da gōdę Allā well, thanks!). (ee) Vd. inā 3e,f. (f) tūlū kē wahala Vd. tūlū 1c. (g) sū wahala nē Vd. sū 1b. (h) kōshin wahala Vd. sō 1d. (2) Vb. 3B (a) = 1b above. (b) took pains. (c) was tired out.

wahalce x yā zō a ~ he arrived tired out.

wahal da = wahalad da Vb. 4 troubled x yā wahalad da nī = yā wahalshē ni he troubled me. tafiyan nan tā wahalas this journey was troublesome.

wahaltā Vb. 1C (with dative) x yā ~ mini = wahala 1d.

wahaltaccē m. (f. wahaltaccīyā) pl. wahaltattū poor.

wahaltad da = wahalad da.

wahamī Ar. m. (1) doubts x yā dēbę mini ~ he cleared away my doubts. (2) ~ yā daukē shi he is bewildered (= wahimta).

wahamta = wahimta.

*wahayā f. slave who has borne child to her Arab owner and been freed.

*wahayī Ar. m. vision.

Wahhābī m. (f. Wahhābīyā) pl. Wahhābāwā x al'amarim Musulunci ta hanyar Wahhābāwā the Wahhabi Sect of Mohammedans.

wahimta Vb. 3B yā ~ he is bewildered (= wahamī 2).

wai A. (wai) (1) look out! (2) m. (a) mere rumour (= wai-wai) x wannam magana ~ cē this is a mere rumour. (b) ~ kadādar karyā a rumour just falls short of being a lie. (c) Vd. inkę. (3) (a) (i) it is said that x ~ ka zō you are being called. ~ hankāka bā yā yin kwai it is said that crows do not lay eggs. (ii) ~ da gangan an cē da karē Muhamman it is impossible. (b) named x wani ~ shī Audu a man named Audu. an shaidā shi ~ Audu nē he was recognized as a man named Audu. (c) (followed by subjunctive) in order that x ya kafa musu idọ ~ ya ga abin da sukę nufin yī he stared at them to see what they were up to. yā fadi haka ~ a cē he said this that it might be thought that . . . yā daukam ma kansa babban aiki, in dăi har yanā sọ nē wai ya yi haka he's taken on a big job if he aims at nothing less than doing this. suu yī, sun yī wai su kāma shi they did their best to capture him, but in vain. kōkarī yakē yī wai ya sāmu he's trying to get it. dabarassu wai su zō their plan is to come. nīyyarsa wai ya sāmi fādā his object was to get into favour. (d) ~ don kō = kō wai (followed by future) in the hope that x yā yi haka ~ don kō zai sāmu he did so in the hope of getting it. yā hargrē su, kō sū mā wai zā su yi caffa he behaved menacingly to them hoping that they might give in to him. (e) (i) that (after "saying") x yā cē ~ zai hau he said that he would mount. an yi shēla ~ a proclamation has been made that . . . (ii) that (after the following verbs) x bā yā yardā ~ a cē bā shi da karfī he doesn't want it to be thought he has no strength. yā ji ~ he heard that . . . yā rubūtā ~ he wrote to say that . . . sunā mafarkin wai zā su ci dūnīya they dream of conquering the whole world. nā yi tsammāni wai . . . I thought that . . . (f) (i) don ~ because x yā cē a bā shi don ~ nāsa nē he said "give it to me

because it is mine!'' (ii) ~ don because of *prep.* *x* bä mä yin sanyï wai don tsöraŋ hasärą we do not shrink from it merely from fear of losses. (g) yä tąmbąyë mu ~ he asked us whether . . . (*h*) ~ kąmar *x* bą nufi sukę yï ~ kąmar sun tabbątä ba they do not wish to convey the impression that they are certain. (*j*) saying that *x* sun täsö ~ zä su kashę mu they came saying they were going to kill us. (*k*) (*negatively*) it does not follow that. bą wai nufi mukę mu yi yäkį ba it does not follow that we're intending war. kö sun ci gąrï gudä, bą wai sun ci yäkįŋ kę nam ba even if they have taken one town, it does not follow that they have won the war. (*l*) *Vd.* nüną 1*f.*
B. (wąi) my word!
waibûwä *f.* = arwä 1.
waigą *Vb.* (1) yä ~ käi he turned his head. (2) yä ~ wutä he swung smouldering torch to make it spark.
wąigë *m.* (1) turning the head. (2) yaną ~ he is acting *as in* waigą 2.
waiką *Vb.* 3A (lightning) flashed (= walką).
Wailą *used in* ~ mąi kämą dayä *epithet of* Büzü 2 or other P. from the north.
wa''iŋ *Vd.* waŋ'iŋ.
wa''iną *Vd.* waŋ'iną.
wąinä *f.* (1) (*a*) type of small fried cake made from rice, bulrush millet, or guinea-corn flour (= tsälä = mäsą = *Kt.* yau 4*b*). (*b*) mąi tüyą ~ dą rüwä, bąllë yą sämi mäi if a P. is cantankerous without reason, how much more so if provoked! (*c*) kanshiŋ azzikï yä fi kanshiŋ ~ to sniff round a lucky P. is more profitable than sniffing at cakes. (*d*) gudaŋ wąinä *Vd.* tąrindǫ. (*e*) mąganą tä cüdę, har mä bą mä cę '' gä iriŋ wąinad dą akę töyäwä '' ba the matter is so involved that we cannot explain what is going on. (2) *x* görǫ kąmaŋ ~ nę ą naŋ kolas are much in demand here. (3) ~ dą rüwä empty bragging. (4) wąinar kwäi pancake. (5) wąinar rögǫ small cakes made from cassava-flour (= dam bägaläjë). (6) jüyiŋ ~ *Vd.* jüyi 4.

waini = shügąba 1.
wa''innïyä *Vd.* waŋ'innïyä.
wąitaką *Vd.* kaurä 3*c.*
wai-wai A. (wai-wai) *m.* mere rumour (= wai 1*a*).
B. (wąi-wai) *m.* = wąiwąyï.
waiwąitä *Vb.* 1C *x* aŋ waiwąitą läbärį the matter has been considered mere rumour (*Vd.* wai).
waiwaya A. (waiwąyä) (1) *Vb.* 3A (*a*) (i) yä ~ he turned his head round to look. suŋ waiwąyä kan yäkįm Masąr they turned their attention to the war in Egypt (*cf.* wąiwayą 2). (*b*) = wąiwayą 2. (*c*) mu ~ ą bäya, mu hąngą gąba let us consider both past and future. (2) *Vb.* 1C (*a*) yä waiwąyą ąlhërįn dą muką yi masą he was grateful for the favour we did him (= säką 1). (*b*) yä waiwąyą wutä = waigą 2.
B. (wąiwayą) *Vb.* 2 (1) = waiwąyä 1*a*, 2*a*. (2) returned to, turned to *x* mu wąiwayi tękü let us turn our attention to naval affairs! (*cf.* waiwąyä 1*a*.ii, wąiwąyë). yä wąiwąyi gidä (*a*) he turned homewards. (*b*) he thought of his home (= yä waiwąyą gidä). ąlkälï yä wąiwąyë shi the judge turned to him and asked him for his version. yä wąiwąyë ni he was grateful to me for what I had done. (3) mąkäfǫ dą ~ *Vd.* banzä 1*a*. (4) *Vd.* waiwayǫ.
wąiwąyë *m.* (1) (*a*) (i) turning the head round to look. (ii) yä mai dą wąiwąyë gą Masąr he turned his attention to Egypt (*cf.* wąiwayą 2). (*b*) mąkäfǫ dą ~ *Vd.* banzä 1*a*. (2) yä mai dą ~ he referred again to the matter.
wąiwąyï *m.* the caterpillar gamząrï.
waiwayǫ *Vb.* 3A (1) returned unexpectedly (cold, heat, rain, etc.). (2) *cf.* waiwąyä, wąiwayą.
wąjabą *Ar.* *Vb.* 2B is incumbent *x* hajji (bïyąŋ gandü) yä ~ gąrëmu the Pilgrimage (tax-paying) is incumbent on us.
wajabta A. (wąjabtą) *Vb.* 3B = wąjabą.
B. (wąjąbtä) *Vb.* 1C made incumbent *x* aŋ ~ maną bïyąŋ gandü to pay tax has been laid on us as a duty.

wajaijai = wajājē *Vd.* wajē.
wajajjagā *Vb.* 1D (1) = wacaccakā. (2) (dog) shook (rat), etc.
wajan *Vd.* wajē 2, waje 3.
wajānīyā = wacānīyā.
waja-waja A. (wajā-wajā) = wacā-wacā.
B. (wajā-wajā) abundantly *x* hatsī yanā nan a kāsūwā ∽ the market is full of corn.
waje A. (waje) *adv.* (1) outside (*a*) yanā ∽ = yanā daga ∽ it is outside. (*b*) an sayar sulē gōma la'ada ∽ it has been sold for ten shillings, buyer to pay brokerage in addition. (*c*) dōki nē bāyā ∽ it's a horse whose hindquarters fall away (*cf.* gantsarwā). (*d*) a waje turmī yakē kwānā *Vd.* turmī 1*c*. (*e*) na ∽ shī kē ganin sararī *Vd.* dambē 2. (*f*) ∽ kōfa *Vd.* īyākacī 2. (2) to outside *x* sun tūrō gyadā waje they exported ground-nuts. zā ni ∽ I shall go outside. yā yiwō ∽ he came out. (3) wajan *prep.* outside of *x* kasan nan, cikinta da wajanta duk ganīmar Jāmus cē this country has entirely fallen a prey to the Germans.
B. (wajē) (1) *m.* (*pl.* wajējē = *Kt.* wajaijai = wajājē) (*Ar.* wajh) direction *x* (*a*) ajīyē shi ∽ daya put it on one side! (= *Sk.* gangā 2). sauran kasāshan can, wajan the other countries in that region. (2) wajan *prep.* (*a*) (i) towards P. *x* nā zō wajanka I've come to seek your help. yanā wajan Audu, bā wajēna ba he is on the side of Audu, not on my side (= kāfada 1*c*, wurī 3). (ii) to (a place) *x* a wajan kāsūwā yakē it is the direction of the market. yā yi wajan Kano he went in the direction of Kano. (*b*) approximately, about *x* wajan karfē uku, at about three o'clock (= kaman = misālin = takadīri). mutum gudā wajan gōma about ten persons. wajan sā'armu bīyū nan tsaye we've been waiting here about two hours (*here* wajan *approaches its original sense of the noun* wajē *in the genitive, literally* the approximation of our hours standing here, is two) (*cf.* tsakānī 3*a*). wadansu jirāgyan sama sun yi wajan karfē bīyar, sunā sakō bom some aeroplanes were out

at about five o'clock dropping bombs. (*c*) in reference to *x* wajam fādin 'yan Jabū as regards the breadth of the counterfeit coins . . . (*d*) during *x* wajan gudu kudīna sum fādi my money fell out of my pocket while I was running.
wajējē *Vd.* wajē.
wajen *Vd.* wajē 2, waje 3.
wājib = wājibī *m.* (*f.* wājibā) *pl.* wājibai = wājibōbī incumbent.
wajiba A. (wājibā) *Vd.* wājibī.
B. (wājiba) *f.* = wacānīyā.
wajījī *m.* women's co-operative spinning.
wājila-wājila half-heartedly.
wājiri *m.* trickster (*epithet is* Wājiri, mai da abin wani nāka).
wajīyā *f.* fat alternating with lean in meat.
wāka (1) *f.* (*pl.* wākōkī = wā'ke-wāke"). (*a*) (i) song. (ii) ∽ daya bā tā kārē nika patience wins (*Vd.* hakurī 5). (iii) yanā bā da ∽, munā amsāwā he is singing the refrain and we're joining in the chorus. (iv) sun sākē muryar wāka " they changed their tone ". (*v*) nāman wāka *Vd.* ayū. (*b*) poem. (2) *Vb.* 1A yā ∽ wa alkālī he indicated to the judge what bribe he was ready to pay for a favourable verdict.
wā kā būdē *Vd.* būdē 1*k*.
wakacī = lōkacī.
waka da waka *m. and adv.* abundantly *x* aiki yā yi musu ∽ they've more work than they can deal with. hatsī yanā kāsūwā ∽ corn is abundant in the market.
wakafī *Ar. m.* (1) (*a*) remand under arrest *x* yanā ∽ he is under arrest on remand. (*b*) gidan ∽ *m.* lock-up for prisoners on remand (*in Native Court only applies to debtors*). (2) = ajali 1. *(3) Muslim Court's taking charge of disputed property pending adjudication (*cf.* wakaftā 2). *(4) Muslim Court's setting aside proceeds of sale of bequest (gādo) till return of recipient. *(5) = *hubusī. *(6) pause at end of sentence of Koran.
*wakaftā *Vb.* 1C (1) bequeathed (landed property) as mortmain (hubusī). (2) alkālī yā ∽ shi a hannun dan wankā

the Muslim judge deposited the disputed property with the official called ɗaŋ waŋkā (cf. waƙạfī 3).
wākạikai Vd. wākē.
wạkānạ Vb. 3B = tạbbatạ 1a.
wạ̄ kạ̄ rabẹ Kt. = bạ̄ sājẹ.
Wā kạ sọ̄ = Ạ jēfas.
wākạtā = bākạtā.
wākē m. (pl. wākạikai types of beans). (1) bean(s), cf. mạ̄kā. (2) rashịn tūwō akẹ̄ cịŋ ~ needs must. when the devil drives. (3) (a) tūwaŋ wākē = burūƙuƙụ. (b) gārịŋ ~ Vd. būtsạrī 3. (4) bā ạ̄ cẹ̄ dạ mại cịŋ ~ yạ shā rūwā shī mā yạ̄ shā teaching one's grandmother to suck eggs (cf. 8 below). (5) (a) ɗaŋ ~ m. dumplings made from bean-flour and guinea-corn with baobob (kūkạ) leaves and potash (= Kt. kạcalạ 2). (b) epithet is Mạrmạrā = Tūbalạ ạbin jīfạn yuŋwạ. (c) sǎi an yāmụtsā, saŋ naŋ ɗan wākyan samạ ya kạn ji mại Fortune's wheel revolves. (d) ɗaŋ wākyaŋ gēwạyē children's game with top (kạtantaŋwạ). (6) kumfaŋ ~ m. cutting off one's nose to spite one's face (= fushī 4). (7) ƙūnam baƙiŋ wākē Vd. ƙūnā 2c. (8) tā ci ~ she is pregnant (cf. 4 above). (9) ~ ɗayā. shī kạm ɓātạ gạ̄rī a chain is as strong as its weakest link. (10) Vd. wāke-wāke ; cị ~. (11) rụmfar wākē Vd. rụmfā 5. (12) m̀ bā kạ wākē Vd. tūsạ 2. (13) rōraŋ wākē Vd. rōrọ 3. (14) bạ̄ra nā yi ~ Vd. bạ̄ra 1d. (15) kunạ̄ dafạ ~ Vd. barẹkatạ. (16) ɗārịŋ ~ Vd. ɗārī 3.
waƙe A. (wāƙẹ) Vb. 1A (1) = yāƙẹ 1. (2) kạ̄ ~ you'll have a bad time. *(3) versified.
B. (wạ̄ƙē) m. = hạdīsị 1.
wā kẹ̄ dawạ m. back-handed blow given P. alongside or behind one.
wākējị m. sandals of untanned hide.
Wạ̄ kẹ̄ sọ̄ = Wā kạ sọ̄.
wāke-wāke adj. speckled (re fowls, etc.), Vd. wākē.
wāƙe-wāƙē Vd. wāƙạ.
*wāƙi'ạ Ar. f. event.
wạ̄ƙilai = wulạ̄ƙại.
wakilci m. being another's representative.
wạƙīlị m. (pl. wạƙīlai) (1) representative (= madạdī = mụƙaddạshī). (2) P. who

looks after another (= mạƙạbūlị). (3) holder of the sạrautạ of this name.
wakịltā Vb. 1C (1) x nā ~ shi ạ kạŋ wannạŋ I have appointed him my representative in this (= lāmụncē 1). (2) x aŋ wakịltạ Mālạm Audụ Ạlkālim Baucī kạ̄fịŋ ạ tabbatad dạ shī they have appointed Malam Audu as judge of Bauchi on probation.
wakiltad dạ Vb. 4 = wakịltā.
wạ̄ƙịnē m. = wạ̄niƙē.
wākīrẹ = bākīrẹ.
wākịtā = bākạtā.
wạkīyyạ f. (pl. wakīyyōyī = wạkịyyū) perfume-phial (= lụ̄lụ̄ = ƙạrau 1a.ii), cf. tạ̄nākạ.
wakkạlā = wakịltā.
wakkaụ m. Ningi war-cry.
wạ̄ƙōƙī Vd. wāƙạ.
wạ̄kurwạ Sk. f. = shẹ̄lạ.
wala A. (wālạ) Vb. 3A x mụ tạfi, mụ ~ let us go and sit at ease. aŋ hanạ̄ shi wālạ̄wā he has no peace of mind.
B. (wālā) f. (1) (a) Half-collared, Red-eyed Turtle-Dove (Streptopelia semitorquata). (b) Vinaceous Turtle-Dove (Streptopelia vinacea) (= kurcīyā 1b). (2) yā kāmạ ƙafạr ~ he " leaned on a broken reed " (= wạrkī 8 = Kt. duhụ 6), cf. lịlọ 1b, tạ̄kạlmī 6, tụŋkū 1d, tūsạ 4, rụŋgumạ ni, hōlōƙō 2.
wala'allạ Ar. perhaps.
wạlā ba'asạ Ar. no fault can be found with it.
wạlābābạ f. = ƙundugụrū.
wạlā bai'ụ (Ar. there is no sale) adv. and m. yā ga ~ = yā sạ̄mi ~ he got it cheap, gratis. yā sạ̄mē shi ~ he got it cheap, gratis.
wạlạdī m. idle roving (= gīlọ).
wạlạhạ f. (1) (a) time between 9 and 10 a.m. (b) ~ tā yị̄ it is between 9 and 10 a.m. ~ tanạ̄ yị̄ it is getting towards 9 and 10 a.m. (c) dạ ~ at between 9 and 10 a.m.
*wạlā hairụ Ar. x (1) iŋ kā zō ~ ; iŋ bạ kạ zō ba, ~ whether you come or not does not matter. (2) cf. hairaŋ.
wạlai adv. and m. nā ga ~ I saw a flash of lightning. wạlƙīyā tā yi ~ = wạlƙiyā tā waiƙạ ~ lightning flashed.
walākạntā = wulākạntā.

wạlākiŋ = Kt. wạlākī (Ar. " but ") used in dạ ∽ there's more than meets the eye.

Walạkīrị (Ar. nakīri) m. one of the Angels of Death, according to Muslims (the other being Munkar).

walaŋkēdūwā Kt. f. (1) following round-about way (= gēwạyē). (2) throwing (pursuer) off the scent (= baŋ gwīwạ).

wala-wala A. (wạlā-wạlā = wạlā-walā) f. (1) = tạshạrē-tashạrē 1, 2. (2) = walā-walā. (3) Vd. bạtaŋ ∽.
    B. (walā-wala) f. type of gambling.

wālạyē Vd. wālī 2.

walẹ (1) Vb. 1A filled (vessel) brimful. (2) Vb. 3A (vessel) is brimful.

*walgā = wạggā.

walgī Nor. = wargī.

wali A. (wālị) m. stroll (usually in cool of afternoon).
    B. (Wālī) m. (1) a sạrautạ. (2) (with pl. wālạyē) threepenny-bit (= tarō).
    C. (walị) m. (pl. wạlīyyai). (1) saint (credited with performing miracles, i.e. kạrāmạ). (2) (a) the P. having the right of giving girl in marriage (i.e. father, paternal grandfather, paternal uncle, etc. : the Ạlkālī is normally walị of orphan or stranger girl), Vd. aurē 6a. (b) for genitive, Vd. wạlīyyị 2. (c) Vd. rīgar ∽. (d) Vd. ạlwalị. (3) the P. charged with burial of another (= shụ-gạba 7). (4) (euphemism) mad P. (= mahạukạcī). (5) ∽ digạdigī P. taking short cut to destination so that his fellow-travellers ascribe his out-distancing them to magic.

waliccị m. = walittạ.

walīcị m. = walittạ.

walị digạdigī Vd. wạlị 5.

wālihaŋ m., f., sg., pl. = wālịhī m. (f. wālịhā) pl. wālịhai obvious.

wạlīmạ Ar. f. marriage-feast (Vd. aurē 6d) = aŋgwancị 1 = bịkī.

walittạ f. (1) being empowered as in wạlị 2a. (2) saintship (Vd. wạlị 1).

wạlittakạ f. = walittạ.

wạlīyyai Vd. wạlị.

wạlīyyị m. (1) = wạlị. (2) (the form of wạlị used in genitive) x wạlīyyịntạ the P. empowered to give her in marriage (Vd. aurē 6).

walkạ = waikạ.

wạlkī Sk. = wạrkī.

wạlkīyā f. (Ar. barkī) (1) lightning. (2) (a) glossiness. (b) sheen (= shękī = tạllī). (3) zanạntạ yā yi ∽ = bạntạrē 2.

wallạ = wạllāhị.

wallạcē Vb. 3A Sk. swore by God (cf. wạllāhị) = rantsẹ 1b.i.

*wạllafạ Vb. 2 (Ar. allafa) composed (book).

wạllāhị = wạllāhị summat Ạllāhị Ar. by God ! Wạllāhị, tạllāhị, sum-matạllāhi by God, by God ! Wạllāhị, Allạ̄, gạskīyā nẹ̄ it is really true. (2) Vd. fạdā 1g ; kạri wạllāhị. (3) cf. wallạ-wallạ.

wạllai Sk. = wạllāhị.

wallạkā = baudẹ 1a.

wallạ-wallạ Sk. f. mun yi ∽ dạ shī he and I exchanged mutual oaths (cf. wạl-lāhị).

wallē m. (1) nā ga wallansạ I saw his " weak spot ". (2) Nor. yā yi ∽ he is naked. (3) Vd. kashim bạri ∽.

wạllē-wạllē m. bitter quarrel.

wallō = wandarō q.v. under wandạrā.

walwada Kt. = warwada.

wạlwājị Kt. = wạrwājị.

walwala A. (wạlwalạ) Sk. (1) = warwạrē. (2) f. = wadạrī 1a.
    B. (wạlwalā) f. = fạra'ạ.

wạl-wạl-wạl m. shining x mạsū sunạ̄ ∽ the spears are shining.

Wạmbai m. (1) a sạrautạ (epithet is Gīwā mạrin dawạ). (2) an nęmē shị kaurā Wạmbai they looked everywhere for it in vain. (3) ganim bạntam ∽ m. any-thing impossible. (4) cf. dakaŋ ∽.

wana A. (wạnạ) Vd. wạnẹ.
    B. (wạ̄nạ) Vd. wạnẹ.
    C. (wānạ) Vb. 1A Eng. (1) wound (clock). (2) turned (starting-handle of motor-car), cf. wānị.

wānạkē = wānịkē.

*Wanạkīrī = *Walạkīrī.

wancạgwadọ = wancịgwadọ.

wancaŋ A. (wancaŋ) m. (f. waccaŋ) pl. wadạncaŋ that, that one (in the near or far distance, but visible) x wancaŋ dōkị that horse. waccaŋ gōdīyā that mare (= caŋ), Mod. Gram. 126.
    B. (wạncaŋ = wạncaŋ) m. (f.

waccaŋ = waccaŋ) *pl.* waɗancaŋ = waɗancaŋ the one in question *x* wannaŋ dōki the horse referred to. a cikin waccaŋ shẹkara during the year in question (= caŋ = naŋ), Mod. Gram. 127b.

wancānā *m.* (*f.* waccānā) *pl.* waɗancānā = wancaŋ.

Wancẹ *Vd.* Wānẹ.

wancẹgwaɗọ = wancigwaɗọ.

wancēnī *m.* (*f.* waccēnī) *pl.* waɗancēnī *Sk.* = wancaŋ.

wancēnīyā *m.* (*f.* waccēnīyā) *pl.* waɗancēnīyā *Sk.* = wancaŋ.

wancētō *Kt.* (negatively) *x* bā ∼ unexpectedly. taɪīyā tā sāmē ni bā ni da ∼ I had to set out unexpectedly.

wancigwaɗọ So-and-so (*referring to several persons*), *cf.* Wānẹ.

wanda = wanda = wanda *m.* (*f.* wadda = wadda = wadda = wacca = wacca = wacca = waccẹ = waccẹ = waccẹ) *pl.* waɗanda = waɗanda = waɗannā = waɗannā). (1) who, which (Mod. Gram., Chapter 27) *x* dōki wanda ya mutu the horse which died. macẹ wadda muka ganī the woman whom we saw. (2) (*a*) that which, he who *x* wanda aka yi, yā wucẹ what has been done is over and done with. wanda ka sani = wanda ka san shi the one whom you know. akwai ∼ ya zō ? has someone (anyone) come ? (*Vd.* wani 1a, 5a, Mod. Gram. 174). yā rasa wadda zai kāma he is at a loss how to act. (*b*) a yi waccẹ zā a yi, ɓērā yā shanyẹ gārin kyaŋwā it is done now so I'll have to take the consequences. (3) wherein, whereon, whereto, whence, whereof, etc. (*as in* da 11) *x* ƙasāshē waɗanda sukẹ mulki the countries wherein they rule. bā wanda sukẹ tsọrō kamansa there is nobody of whom they are afraid as they are afraid of him (lit. ' there is not he of whom they feel fear '). akwai wurī wanda sukẹ ganin ƙyāshī there is a place of which they are covetous (lit. ' there is a place of which they feel covetousness '). (4) (*a*) wanda duk (= dukaŋ wanda) whoever *x* wanda ya zō duka = dukaŋ wanda ya zō = wanda duk ya zō who-

ever came . . . (*Vd.* duka 3). (*b*) cikinsu wanda ya zō whichever of them came . . . (5) *proverbs with* wanda :— (*a*) wanda ya wucẹ *Vd.* shimfiɗa 1d. (*b*) wanda bā shī da ūwā *Vd.* gāyā 2f. (*c*) ∼ ya yi nīsā *Vd.* nīsā 1h. (*d*) wanda bai ci haƙurin wahala ba *Vd.* wahala 1c. (*e*) wanda bai haƙura da tāgumī ba *Vd.* tāgumī 3. (*f*) wanda ya tsīra *Vd.* tsīra 1a.ii. (*g*) ∼ ya hau dōkin " da nā sani " *Vd.* da 1b.ii. (*h*) wanda ya sō ka *Vd.* sō 2b. (*j*) wanda ya fī ka dabāra *Vd.* sō 1e. (*k*) wanda bai ɓata da darē ba *Vd.* rānā 8c. (*l*) (i) wanda bai ci azzikin wani ba *Vd.* azzikī 3b. (ii) wanda bai ci azzikī ba *Vd.* dōmindōmin. (*m*) ∼ bā a yaba ka *Vd.* ɓāci 1d. (*n*) ∼ ya yi kōkawa *Vd.* ɓarē 2. (*o*) ∼ ya cẹ kā cẹ *Vd.* damō 4b. (*p*) ∼ ya bā ka gōrọ *Vd.* gōrọ 1a.iii. (*q*) ∼ ya san darajar gōrọ *Vd.* gōrọ 1a.iv. (*r*) ∼ kẹ jiran *Vd.* jira 1b.iii. (*s*) ∼ ya yi maka kaŋ karā *Vd.* karā 1e. (*t*) ∼ ya cīji hanciŋka *Vd.* hanci 1f.

wandāƙā *Kt.* f. = wacānīyā.

wandara A. (wandarā) (1) *Vb.* 3A = baudẹ 1a. (2) *Vb.* 1C bent T.

B. (Wandara) *Vd.* Sarkī 1a.

wandararrē *m.* (*f.* wandararrīyā) *pl.* wandararrū. (1) crooked (*re* thing). (2) contrary P.

wandarē *Vb.* 3A = baudẹ 1a.

wandar-wandar *m.* swervingness *x* hanya cẹ mai ∼ = hanya ∼ cẹ it is a zigzag road. taɪīyar maciji ∼ cẹ snakes travel zigzag.

wan dawa *Vd.* wā 3c.

wandō *m.* (*pl.* wanduna) (1) (*a*) pair of trousers. (*b*) yā sā ∼ he put on trousers. yā cirẹ (= tūɓẹ = kwaɓẹ) ∼ he took off his trousers. (*c*) ∼ mai kāmun ƙafa = ∼ bākim baŋgō = Dōma 2. (*d*) (i) wandō mai bākin tēki *Vd.* tēki 3. (ii) *Vd.* zulum. (iii) *Vd.* Tūnas. (*e*) tantabarā kyau da ∼ f. feathery-legged pigeon. (*f*) hancin ∼ place where crutchpiece joins trouser-ankle. (2) = gyauto 2. (3) shūka tā yi ∼ the bulk of the corn is stunted.

Wandu *Fil. Vd.* biri.

wanduna *Vd.* wandō.

wane A. (Wānẹ) *m.* (*f.* Wancẹ) (*pl.*

Su wānę, cf. wancigwadǫ). (1) (a) Mr. So-and-so. su Wānę dą su Wānę Mr. So-and-so and Mr. So-and-so. (b) (with genitive) x Wānąmmu So-and-so of ours. Wānęna So-and-so of mine. (c) zamā zūcī gą marąbī tā fi " Wānę, gą hannūna !" it's better to be remembered than to have to ask P. giving largesse, for a share. (d) Wānę, cę dą mųtųm Vd. cę 7. (e) ganī gą ~ Vd. ganī A.2 3c. (2) (a) ~ nē cikin nāsą fannį he is expert in his own line. (b) Audu jārųmī nę ~ Audu is very brave. māląmī nę ~ he's very learned. tājįrī nę ~ he's a big merchant. (3) cf. wani 3, ō'ǫ.

B. (wąnę) m. (f. wącę) pl. su wąnę 1 = wąnēnę. (2) Vd. wąnē. (3) wącę kązą Vd. kązā 1g.

C. (wąnē) (the form taken by wąnę in the following expressions). (1) wąnē sūnanką what is your name ? (= inā 3b). (2) (a) (i) ~ Mūsą of what account is Moses ! = Sk. wąnēnę 1c. (Vd. wą 1f). ~ shī of what account is he ! (Vd. wą 1f). wąnē nį I am a mere nobody (= wąnę 2a). wąnē nį = wącē nį how can a mere woman like me do so ! (= wąnę 2a). wąnē itą = wącē itą she's a mere nobody. mū su wą (= mū su wąnēnę) who are we to do so ? (ii) yanā dą fąm 500 ą nąŋ, ą caŋ kųwā wąnē haką he has £500 here but immeasurably more there. wancąŋ na fāri, wąnē wannąŋ this is far in advance of previous doings. ɓarnarsą mā, wąnē ta kąwālį the harm he does is far greater than that done by a pimp. (b) Vd. wąnę 2b. (c) ~ mųtųm fancy ! (= wą 1g).

D. (wąnę = wąną = Sk. wanę) m. (f. wącę = wącą = Sk. wacę) pl. wadąnnę = wadąnną = Sk. wadąną (1) (a) which ? (adj.) x wąnę jākī which donkey ? wąnę irįm mųtųm nę what sort of a man is he ? wącę mącę which woman ? wądąnnę mutānē suką zǫ which people came ? (Mod. Gram. 160b). (b) cf. wąnnę, wąnnē, kōwąnę, wą, wąnēnę. (2) (a) (only used with 1st sing.) wąnę nį I am a mere nobody (= wąnē 2a). wącę nį how can a mere

woman like me do so ? (= wąnē 2a). (b) wącę nį, kązā ąbiŋ gyāram mīyą (said by wife when husband buys cloth for new wife) it's more than I can bear ! E. (wanę) Sk. (1) Vd. wąnę. (2) (with f. wacę), pl. su wąnā which one ? = wąnnę, wąnnē q.v.

wanęnā Sk. m. (f. wacętā = watątā) = wąnēnę.

wąnēnę m. (f. wącēcę) pl. su wąnēnę. (1) (a) who ? x wąnēnę ya zǫ who (a male) has come ? wącēcę ta zǫ who (a female) has come ? (cf. wą). su wąnēnę suką zǫ who have come ? (b) wąnēnę yakę zūwą who is coming (= wą 1b). (c) wąnēnę Mūsą (i) who is Moses ? (ii) Sk. of what account is Moses ! (ii = wąnē 2a). (d) wąnēnę Audu dn-ŋ nan nę Audu is a nobody. (2) whom ? (a) (wąnēnę following) x ŋ ji wąnēnę who said so ? (Mod. Gram. 160a) = wą 2a. kuŋ ga wąnēnę whom did you see ? (= wą 2a). (b) (wąnēnę preceding) x wąnēnę suką dǫkā whom did they beat ? wącēcę suką bā Audu = Audu wącēcę suką bā shį whom did they give in marriage to Audu ? (= wą 2b). (3) to whom ? x wąnēnę zaŋ kai wą who shall I take it to ! (= wą 3). (4) kū su wąnēnę kuką zǫ who are you who have come ? mū su wąnēnę who are we to have such power ! sū su wąnēnę suką yī who are those who have done it ? (= wą 4). (5) who is it ? x wani yā zǫ someone has come (reply, wąnēnę who is it ?). (6) cf. kōwąnēnę, wą, wąnnę, wąnē, wāyę, kōwā, kōwą, wąnnę, wąnnē, wąnę.

wąngā Sk. m. (f. wąggā = Nor. wąlgā, wąrga) pl. wadąngā this (= wannąŋ).

waŋgadā Vb. 3A (1) took short walk. (2) roved about (cf. waŋgadį).

waŋgadį m. (1) short walk. (2) roving about. (3) yanā waŋgadįn dūkįyassą he's having a good time.

waŋgalą f. feeling pleasure.

waŋgalē (1) Vb. 3A = ɓaŋgalē. (2) Vb. 1C. (1) opened (= būdę). (2) yā ~ ni he filled me with admiration.

waŋgamēmę = waŋgamī m. (f. waŋ-gamēmīyā = waŋgamā) pl. waŋgam-wąŋgam extensive.

wangangan *m.* extensiveness *x* gida nẹ ∼ dạ shī it is an extensive compound.

wan garī *Vd.* wạ̄ 3*a.*

wan gijị *Vd.* wạ̄ 3*b.*ii.

wani A. (wani) *m.* (*f.* wata) *pl.* waɗansu = wasu = *Sk.* wansu = *Kt.* wa'ansu. (1) some (*adjective*), someone *x* (*a*) (i) wani yā zō someone has come. wani mụtụm some person, someone. wani ạbụ something. wani lōkạcī some time, sometimes. wani wurī somewhere. wani mụtụm yā zọ̄? has some person come? (*cf.* 5 *below*) = kōwạ̄ ya zọ̄? = ạkwai wandạ ya zọ̄? (*Vd.* Mod. Gram. 174, kōwạ̄, wạndạ 2*a*). kā ga wani ạbụ ạ hạnyạ? did you see something on the road? (Mod. Gram. 174), *cf.* 5 *below.* wạ̄ zại bā nị wani ạbụ who'll give me something? (*cf.* 5 *below*). (ii) *Vd.* 6 *for proverbs.* (*b*) hannuɳ ∼ *Vd.* han-nun 9. (*c*) wata sābūwā *Vd.* sābūwā. (*d*) waɗansu dạ yawạ many persons. (*e*) (i) (*some collectives are preceded by plural form* waɗansu, Mod. Gram. 176*d*) *x* waɗansu ạbụ some things. kạ sạmi tōzō kō hantạ kō kōɗạ kō waɗansu ạbụ get hump or liver or kidney, etc.! waɗansu kāyā some goods. waɗansu kāyä dạ yawạ many belongings (*cf.* 3*a*.iii *below*). waɗansu sạnsanī some camps. an yi waɗansu kwānā ukụ, anạ̄ karọ they fought for some three days. yā bīyā waɗansu rāmūwā wạddạ Kạnde ta ci he paid for the gifts received by Kande from her first suitor and now due to be returned to him. (ii) (*plural is sometimes used in the above cases*) *x* waɗansu mạkạrạntū dạ yawạ many schools. (*f*) *Vd.* waɗạ. (*g*) bại yi wata-wata ba he did not boggle. (*h*) wani kāyā *Vd.* 6*h.* (2) another (*adjective*), another person *x* (*a*) kạ̄wō wani bring another, a different one! bạ̄ ni wani dōkị give me another horse! (*b*) (*with genitive*) one other than *x* waɗansummu persons other than ourselves. wanin Sarkī bā yạ̄ yị nobody but a Chief could act so. wanīna bā yạ̄ yinsạ sǎi nī nobody but myself could do it. gwandạ, masạrā dạ waninsụ pawpaws, maize, etc. waniɳ gạskīyā nẹ, bạ̄ gạskīyā ba it

has a false air of truth. yanạ̄ ạlfarmā sǎi kạ cẹ wanin Sarkī nẹ he puts on airs like one of the ruling classes. Galādīmạ wanin Sarkī nẹ the Galadima is the Chief's representative. waniɳ Allạ̄, bạ̄ Allạ̄ ba not God but a mere idol. (*c*) waɗansu irị other kinds (*cf* (1*e above*). waɗansu ukụ three others. (*d*) rạn dạ ya kintsạ, rạn naɳ Jāmụs kumā ai sǎi waɗansu when he is fully prepared, that'll be the end of the Germans. (*e*) ạmmā kumā gạ̄ watạ there's another point to be considered (*cf.* 4*b*). (*f*) the other *x* ƙạfansạ dạ kụnnansạ, bạ̄ wandạ ya tserẹ wani of its horns and its ears, neither was longer than the other. (3) a certain (*adjective*), a certain person *x* (*a*) (i) wani yā gayạ minị a certain person said to me that ... (*cf.* Wānẹ). (ii) (*followed by noun with suffix* -ɳ) *x* wani dōkịɳ that other horse (*Vd.* ɳ 3). (iii) waɗansu mụtụm ukụ a certain three men (*cf.* 1*e above*). (*b*) (*followed by noun having possessive suffix*) one of *x* wani ɗaɳkạ one of your sons. wani bāwạnsạ one of his slaves. waɗansu bāyinsạ some of his slaves. (*c*) *in genitive, followed by noun or pronoun*) one of *x* waninsụ one of them. waɗan-summụ some of us. waɗansum bāyinsạ = 3*b above.* watarsụ one (female) of them. watar mātāna one of my wives. (4) (*repeated*) one ... the other *x* (*a*) wani yā yi yạmmā, wani yā yi gabạs one went west, the other east. wata tanạ̄ bịm mijịntạ, wata bā tạ̄ bị one obeys her husband, the other does not. (*b*) anạ̄ wata, gạ̄ wata one blessed thing after another keeps happening! (*cf.* 2*e*) = cūsạ 3. (*c*) wata tanạ̄ fụrē *Vd.* 'yā'yā 1*g.* (*d*) wani kudī, wani bāshị *Vd.* bāshị 7. (*e*) indạ wani ya ƙī dạ yinị, naɳ wani yakẹ sọ̄ dạ kwānā one man's meat is another's poison. (5) (*a*) (*in interrogative or negative sentence*), any (*adjective*), anyone *x* kā ga wani ạ hạnyạ? = kā ga kōwạ̄ ạ hạnyạ? = ạkwai wandạ ka ganī ạ hạnyạ? (Mod. Gram. 174) did you see anyone on the road? (*cf.* 1*a above*). kā ga wani ạbụ ạ hạnyạ? = kōmẹ ka ganī a hanya ? did you see anything on the road ? (Mod. Gram. 174), cf. 1a above, abu 1e). inā zan sāmi wani where shall I find anyone ? (cf. 1a above). wā zai bā ni wani abu = wā zai bā ni kōmē (Mod. Gram. 175) who would give me anything ! (cf. 1a above, abu 1e). yā sāmi wani amfāni ? did he get any advantage ? wani mutum yā zō ? has anyone come ? (Vd. Mod. Gram. 174, cf. 1a above). wani abu yā ɓata ? = kōmē ya ɓata ? = akwai abin da ya ɓata ? is anything lost ? (Mod. Gram. 174a, abu 1e). bā wani wanda zai yī nobody would do so = bā wanda zai yī = bā kōwā wanda zai yī (Mod. Gram. 175). ban ga wani ba I saw nobody. ban sāmi wani abu ba = bā abin da na sāmu = ban sāmi kōmē ba I got nothing (Mod. Gram. 175). inā zan sāmi wani = inā zan sāmi kōwā where shall I find anyone ? (Mod. Gram. 175). (b) duk wani aiki mutum ya yi whatever act a man does. (6) proverbs (a) wani yā sāmi nāma Vd. nāma 1h. (b) wani da tūsa Vd. tūsa 3. (c) wani tsuntsū yanā gudun rūwā, agwagwā cikin rūwa takē nēmā one man's meat is another's poison. (d) Vd. 4 above. (e) wata mīya Vd. mīya 8. (f) wani zōmō ā sābara Vd. zōmō 11. (g) mai da abin wani nāka Vd. wājiri. (h) wani kāyā Vd. Banufē ; amāle. (j) wata dabaŋ Vd. dabaŋ 1b. (k) wani yā haye tudu Vd. tudu 1c.

B. (wānī) m. superciliousness.

C. (wāni) Eng. m. x a bā shi ∼ (1) wind it up ! (clock). (Vd. inji 2). (2) turn the starting-handle of the motor !

wanicē Vd. wanita.

waniƙe A. (wāniƙē) m. acting as in wāniƙē.

B. (wāniƙē) Vb. 1C. (1) ran tongue round gums and teeth to remove particles of food. (2) dōki yā ∼ the horse got the bit between its teeth.

wāniƙiƙi m. used in wāyaŋ ∼ tricky selfishness.

waŋ'in Kt. m. (f. wa''in) pl. wa'aŋ'in = wancaŋ.

waŋ'ina Sk. m. (f. wa''ina) pl. wa'aŋ'ina = wancaŋ.

waŋ'inniyā Kt. m. (f. wa''inniyā) pl. wa'aŋ'inniyā = wancaŋ.

wanita Vb. 2 (p.o. wanicē, n.o. wanici) differed from, is inferior to (cf. wani 2b).

*wanjī m. remainder, surplus (= saurā).

wanka A. (waŋkā) m. (1) (a) taking a bath (cf. waŋke). (b) putting on clean clothes. (c) washing one of the Māguzāwā converted to Islam prior to his reciting the kalma. (2) rūwā īyā wuya māganim maƙi ∼ needs must when the devil drives. (3) iŋ kanā da kyau, ka ƙāra da ∼ prosperity without good character is incomplete. (4) ɗaŋ ∼ Vd. waƙatta. (5) tā tafi ∼ = gōyō 2d. (6) rānar ∼ Vd. cībiya 2. (7) ∼ da kāshī Vd. ganī A.2 1g. (8) da kamar ∼ Vd. jirwāyē 4. (9) Vd. waŋkan-compounds ; ɓarāwo 6.

B. (waŋka) (1) Vb. 1A (a) tried to wash T. clean used in such expressions as nā ∼, nā ∼, bai fita ba I kept on washing it (garment), but the stain would not come out. sai da na ∼ da kyau, san nam maiƙo ya fita it was only after continual washing that the greasy stain vanished from it (cf. waŋke). (b) yanā waŋkāwā he's enjoying himself. (2) Vb. 3A yā ∼ cikiŋ garī he vanished into the town.

C. (waŋkā) Vb. 2 (1) = waŋke. (2) (a) yā waŋkē ni = yā waŋkē ni da zāgi he roundly abused me. (b) Vd. suluf.

wankaɗa A. (waŋkaɗa) Vb. 2 Sk. drank much of.

B. (waŋkaɗā) Vb. 1C x aŋ waŋkaɗa rūwā yau much rain has fallen to-day.

waŋkaɗē Vb. 1C Sk. drank up all the large amount of T. available (cf. waŋkaɗa).

waŋkai Zar. = wannaŋ.

waŋkan amaryā m. ceremonially washing bride for marriage (Vd. waŋke 1b).

waŋkan aŋgo m. ceremonially washing bridegroom for marriage.

waŋkan darza m. African not very black-skinned (= waŋkan tarwaɗā = fatsī).

waŋkan Gwārī m. = gurmāɗē.

waŋkan janaba m. = waŋkan tsarkī.

waŋkan kansakalī m. = waŋkan takōbī 1.

waŋkan rama Kt. m. stripping lower leaves of young hemp-plants.

waŋkan saiɓī m. Vd. saiɓī 2.

waŋkan sarautą *m.* = waŋkan takǫbī 1.

waŋkan takabą *m.* ceremonially washing widow on 130th day after widowhood.

waŋkan takǫbī *m.* (1) gifts given new Chief by those whom he has confirmed in office though appointed by his predecessor (*cf.* gudānī 2) = waŋkaŋ kąnsakąlī = waŋkan sarautą. (2) gifts demanded from subordinates by newly-appointed official.

waŋkan tarwaɗā *m.* = waŋkan darzą.

waŋkan tsarkī *m.* (1) washing the parts after urination, coitus, etc. (2) yā yi ∼ yā fāɗą cikim mąganą he suddenly took a hand in the affair (1, 2 = waŋkan janabą).

waŋkaŋ wutā *m.* (1) unpleasant experience. (2) ∼ ɗayā kąn yāfą a burned child dreads the fire. (3) *cf.* waŋki 2b.

wanke A. (waŋkę) *Vb.* 1A (*Vd.* waŋki). (1) (*a*) (i) washed (body, clothes, pot, etc.) = waŋkā. (ii) suŋ waŋkę hannū su yī they're taking steps to do it (*Vd.* waŋkiŋ hannū). (*b*) yā ∼ ɗīyā tasą he carried out waŋkaŋ amaryā on his daughter. (*c*) yā ∼ idǫ he washed his face (= wąŋkā). (*d*) yā ∼ mini idǫ he slapped me in the face (*cf.* idǫ 1s). (*dd*) su waŋkę idǫ, su ganī let them watch carefully ! (*e*) dą tūwaŋ gǫbe akę ∼ tukunyā a kindness is never wasted. (*f*) *Vd.* waŋkiŋ hannū. (2) (*a*) washed off *x* yā ∼ ƙūrā he washed away the dust. (*b*) nasarą zā tą ∼ wąhaląr victory will compensate for the toil. (3) *cf.* waŋką.

B. (wąŋkē) *m.* ink made from soot on cooking-pot.

waŋke, zubar *m.* = zūkū.

waŋki *m.* (1) (*secondary v.n. of* waŋkę) *x* tanā waŋkiŋ tufāfi = tanā waŋkę tufāfi she is washing clothes. (2) (*a*) act of washing clothes *x* jīyą tā yi ∼ yesterday she did the washing. Audu mai ∼ Audu the washerman. (*b*) (i) an yi wą wandō waŋkiŋ wutā the trousers have been ironed (= āyąŋ). (ii) *cf.* waŋkaŋ wutā. (3) (*a*) yā shā ∼ he was roundly abused. (*b*) *Vd.* suluf. (4) tanā ∼ she is undergoing her periods (= hailą). (5) *Vd.* waŋkiŋ hannū, waŋkiŋ idǫ.

waŋkikkē *Vb.* 1C *Sk.* = waŋkę.

waŋkiŋ hannū *m.* (1) yā sąmi ∼ he, by having drunk potion, is lucky in war, hunting, etc. (2) gą ąbiŋ ∼ here, builder, is a present additional to your wages ! (3) *Vd.* waŋkę 1a.ii.

waŋkiŋ idǫ *Vd.* idǫ 1s.

wannaŋ A. (wannąŋ) *m.*, *f.* (*pl.* waɗannąŋ). (1) (*a*) this (*adj.*), this one (Mod. Gram., Chapter 25). (*b*) (*it usually precedes*) *x* ∼ lāsąfī (*but may also follow*) *x* lāsąfi ∼, ąbin tārąwā ą cikin takąrdarkų this bill enclosed in your letter. (2) ą ∼ nā yąfē ką on *this* occasion I pardon you. (3) (*repeated*) one . . . the other *x* wannąŋ ya dųbi ∼, wannąŋ ya dųbi ∼ then they kept looking at one another, pair after pair. wannąŋ yanā biŋ wannąŋ all this is in the right sequence. (3) *Vd.* waɗā. (4) ∼ nē fa ɗayā *Vd.* ɗayā 7.

B. (wąnnan = wąnnaŋ) *m.*, *f.* (*pl.* wąɗannaŋ = waɗąnnaŋ) the one in question (invisible) *x* wąnnaŋ shāfǫ the hawk in question (= naŋ = wąncaŋ). wąɗannaŋ dawākī the horses in question (Mod. Gram. 127b).

wannąna = wannana = wannąŋ *q.v.*

wannąni = wannannīya *Sk.* = wannąŋ.

wanne (1) wąnnē *m.* (*f.* wąccē) *pl.* waɗąnnē which one ? (*when no further words follow*). (2) wąnnē *m.* (*f.* wąccē) *pl.* waɗąnnē (*when other words follow*) *x* (*a*) wąnnē akę kāwǫ which was brought ? (*b*) wąnnē bą wannē bą ? surely there's not a pin to choose between them ? (3) *cf.* wąnę, wąnē, wąŋē, wąnēnē, wą, kōwąnnē, kōwąnę.

wąnnēnē *m.* (*f.* wąccēcē) *pl.* waɗąnnēnē = wąnnē.

wąn rānā *x* tsąkāniŋ Audu dą Shēhų ∼ dą ∼ Audu and Shehu were born, married, etc., within a week of each other.

wąn shēkarę *m.* (1) on the day after to-morrow (= jībi = shēkarąŋ gǫbe). (2) day after event (= kąshēgąrī 2). (3) *Vd.* shēkarę.

wansu *Sk.* = waɗansu *q.v. under* wani.

wantsąlā *Vb.* 3A (1) fell headlong (into hole, off wall, etc.), toppled into, on to, rolled into, on to (= tuntsurā 2). (2)

yā fāɗį har ya ∼ he had serious loss in business. (3) cf. ta ∼ .

wantsąlē = **wantsąla.**

wantsąrā (1) Vb. 3A Kt. yā ∼ dą gudų he took to his heels. (2) Kt. = **wandąrā.**

wantsąrē Vb. 3A Kt. (1) = **wantsąrā** 1. (2) (donkey, etc.) jibbed.

wąŋ wąŋ m. barking of dog (= **haushį**).

wąŋwąŋkā Vd. **suluf.**

wąnyē Vb. 1C (1) finished (work, etc.). (2) (a) ką ∼ lāfiyą may your life end happily ! (b) yā ∼ dą sū lāfiyą he got on well with them. (3) mā ∼ haką, ɗan Sarkī ą kąn jąkī half a loaf is better than no bread.

wanzad dą Vb. 4 caused to last long.

wąnząm = **wąnzāmį.**

wąnzāmį = Sk. **wąnzāmī** m. (pl. **wąnząmai**) (Ar. hajjāmi). (1) (a) barber (he shaves head of child at naming-ceremony (cf. **sūnā**) and is given **jēmāgę** 5 of ram killed, cf. **ųŋgōzǫmą**). (b) his epithet is **Kętau.** (c) **wąnzāmįm Bǫnǫ** P. exhorting others, but not following his own advice. (d) ∼ bā yą sąn jąrfā nobody likes to be hoist with his own petard. (2) = **bāwą** 4. (3) (facetiously) leopard (**dąmisą**). (4) **wąnzāmįn darē** = **ma'ąskī** 2.

wąnząŋ = **wąnzāmį.**

wanzancį m. barbering.

wanzar dą = **wanzad dą.**

wąnzu Vb. 3B (1) remained over (= **rągu**). (2) occurred (= **fąru** = **sąmu** 2b). (3) x kudī suŋ **wąnzų** ? was any money obtained ?, is any money obtainable ? (= **sąmu** 2a).

wapcę = **wafcę.**

wąr Vd. **wąr haką.**

wara A. (**wārą**) Vb. 1A = **wārę.**
     B. (**wąrā**) Vb. 2 = **wārę.**
     C. (**warą**) (1) Vb. 1A = **warę** (these have cerebral -r-). (2) (with rolled -r-) = **habą.**

warąbukką used in (1) tsąmmānįŋ ∼, māląŋ yā ƙi nōmā dǫmin ząkkā (a) throwing away the substance for the shadow. (b) counting one's chickens before they are hatched (= **girįŋgidįshī** 1). (2) **kuną** tsąmmānįŋ ∼ you're living in a fool's paradise.

warai (1) m. (a) cute P. (b) ∼ dą ∼ two equally cute persons. (2) adv. **yanā gani** ∼ he sees clearly. **gąrī yā wāyę** ∼ it has fully dawned.

*****wąraką** (1) Vb. 3B (a) understood (= **fąhimtą**). (b) Kt. = **warkę.** (2) f. nā sąmi ∼ I understood. (3) Nor. = **wąr haką.**

waramī m. twisted metal-bracelet (usually with charms attached).

wąraŋ gwąŋkī (d.f. **wąrē**) m. (1) solitary P. (2) expert P.

warąntį Eng. m. (pl. **warantōcī**). (1) warrant of arrest. (2) railway-warrant.

wąrąrī m. type of perfume.

wārąwā Vd. **wąwwārā.**

wara-wara A. (**warā-warā**) f. being spaced out (re writing, weaving, sowing, etc.).
     B. (**wąrą-wąrą**) x anā sayar dą shī ∼ it has a quick sale.

warɓa A. (**warɓā**) f. (1) old garment. (2) (a) middle-aged woman. (b) ∼ ta birnī mai bąi yārā shūnī middle-aged woman dressed as girl.
     B. (**wąrɓā**) Vb. 2 ate much of.
     C. (**warɓą**) Vb. 1A x yā ∼ shi dą ƙasā he flung him down.

warɓad dą Vb. 4 = **warɓą.**

warɓę Vb. 1A ate all the large quantity of T. available (cf. **wąrɓā**).

warce A. (**warcę**) Vb. 1A grabbed (= **fizgę**).
     B. (**wąrcē**) Vd. **wąrtā.**

wąrdī Ar. m. rose-water (= **ąlwąrdī**).

ware A. (**wārę**) (1) Vb. 1A (a) separated out. (b) suŋ **wārę** idǫ they turned aside. (c) (i) yā **wārę** dantsę he opened his arms. (ii) **wārę** dantsąŋką. ką ɗauka well, take it by force if you can ! (2) Vb. 3A is separate.
     B. (**wārē**) m. (1) = **bąrē.** (2) = **wārį** 3. (3) Vd. **wąraŋ gwąŋkī.**
     C. (**wąrē**) used with **dība** x tā dębi ∼ she has dressed herself up. **yanā dībąŋ** ∼ dą rawąnī he's togged up in a turban.
     D. (**warę**) = **warwąrē.**

warētā Vd. **zarētā.**

warēwąkę m. trickery.

wąrgā Zamfara = **wąggā** q.v. under **wąŋgā.**

wąrgace-wąrgacē Vd. **wargī.**

wargaigai Vd. **wargī.**

wargajē *Vb.* 3A (1) (loads, persons, etc.), became scattered, became disarranged. (2) (plan) failed.

wargajī *m.* = **ąwargajī.**

wargaza A. (**wargazā**) *Vb.* 1C. (1) scattered (loads, persons, etc.), disarranged. (2) brought (plan) to nought.
B. (**wargazą**) *Kt. f.* youths' dance.

wargī *m.* (*pl.* **wargaigai = wargace-wargacē**) *Kt.* (1) any playing (= **wąsā**). (2) joking. (3) ~ **bąi kai zaŋgo ba** this is not the time nor the place for it. (4) *Vd.* **ƙashim bąri** ~.

wąr haką *x* **gọ̄be** ~ = **gọ̄be yi** ~ = **gọ̄be yą** ~ at this time to-morrow. **bąra** ~ at this time last year. **jīyą** ~ at this time yesterday. **gọ̄be wajaŋ** ~ at about this time to-morrow.

wari A. (**wārį**) *m.* (1) one of a pair. (2) one of two halves (*x* gourd cut to make two calabashes). (3) one of the two loads respectively slung on right and left of pack-animal (= **wąrē** 2). (4) **wārim masakī bą ka dą ąbōkim burmi** thou peerless one !
B. (**wārī**) *m.* (1) (*a*) stench (= **dọ̄yī** = **bāshī = tsāmī** 5*a*), *cf.* **gancī, ƙanshī, ƙārī, ƙannī, ƙaurī**). (*b*) **lą̄bārįn naŋ yā fārą wārī** (= **dọ̄yī**) this news is becoming wearisome. (*c*) **Kano tā fārą jiŋ wāriŋ ąbōkaŋ gą̄bā** the enemy have approached Kano. (2) **hamątāta bą ta dą kọ̄mē sǎi** ~ sorry, I've no money to lend you ! (3) **in tā yi** ~ **mą̄ ji** if the matter comes to anything, we'll soon hear of it (= **tsāmī** 5*b*). (4) **mē zan yi dą shī ąbu mai wārī** *Vd.* **haushī** 5. (5) **kōwā ya ci ąlbasą, bąkinsą zai yi** ~ as a man sows, so shall he reap. (6) **jāɓā bā tą̄ jiŋ wārin jikintą** those who live in glass-houses shouldn't throw stones. (7) *Kt.* **wāriŋ gwą̄nō = gyą̄tsā** 4. (8) **wāriŋ ƙasā** earthy smell.
C. (**wą̄rī**) *Sk. m.* a contemporary (= **sa'ą**).

wą̄rigizą *f.* = **wącąnīyā.**

wārikkē *Nor.* = **wārę.**

wą̄rimbā *f.* = **wącąnīyā.**

*wąrīsą *Ar. f.* (1) (*a*) dividing up a bequest. (*b*) feasting and lavishness after re-

ceiving bequest. (2) **yā sąmi** ~ he got a bargain, stroke of luck.

*warką *Ar. f.* (*pl.* **warkōkī**) (1) (*a*) leaf of tree or book. (*b*) sheet of paper. (2) currency note. (3) *Vd.* **ɓataŋ** ~.

warkad dą *Vb.* 4 cured (= **warkę** 2*a*).

wąrkajamī *m.* eagerness.

wąrkakkē *m.* (*f.* **wąrkakkīyā**) *pl.* **wąr-kąkkū.** (1) P. who is cured. (2) alert P.

wąrkaŋ *m., f., sg., pl.* = **wąrkakkē** 2.

warkę (1) *Vb.* 3A (*a*) recovered from illness (= **gyāząjē**), *cf.* **wartsąkē.** (*b*) **mahąukącī bā yą̄ warkę̄wā sǎi raŋgwamę** character does not change. (2) *Vb.* 1A (*a*) cured (= **warkad dą**). (*b*) **sąnnū bā tą̄ warkę cīwọ sǎi dǎi kā ji dādī ą zūcī** soft words butter no parsnips.

wąrkī *m.* (*pl.* **warkuną**) (1) (*a*) leather loin-cloth = *Kt.* **durɓancī** 1 (*epithet is* **Dilę shą̄ cūdā**). (*b*) **yā dąurą** ~ he put on a leather loin-cloth. (*c*) *Vd.* **dąurą wąrkī.** (2) **mai fādų̄war** ~ *Vd.* **tąkwąs** 2. (3) **bā ą̄ sakę̄wā dą kwą̄dō ą** ~ even the smallest anxiety gives one no peace. (4) **yā gąmu dą** ~ **dǎidǎi gindinsą** he has met his match. **kun yi wąrkī dǎidǎi gindiŋku** you have an enemy worthy of your steel. (5) **bą ą fita rūwa ba, bā ą̄ mātsą** ~ don't be in too much of a hurry, don't count your chickens before they're hatched ! (*cf.* **giriŋgidishī**). (5*A*) *Vd.* **sąŋkę wąrkiŋką.** (6) **wąrkiŋką shī kę̄ jāwō maką ƙąząntā** sometimes it is your nearest and dearest who betrays you (*Vd.* **ƙąząntā** 1*d*). (7) **dą warkin yārọ a ƙąn shiga rūwa** when accused, one blames another. (8) **wąrkim macijī** " broken reed " (= **wālā** 2). (9) **wąrkin tsōfō** the herb *Trichodesma africanum.*

warkōkī *Vd.* **warką.**

warkuną *Vd.* **wąrkī.**

wąrnū *m.* type of toad.

warnūwā *Kt. f.* (1) frisking of child. (2) prancing of horse.

warō-warō *Nupe m.* young fishlets.

warta A. (**wą̄rtā**) *Vb.* 2 (*p.o.* **wąrcē,** *n.o.* **wąrci**) = **warcę.**
B. (**wartą**) *Vb.* 3A *Kt.* **yā** ~ **dą gudu** he took to his heels.

wartaɓā *f.* huge penis.

wartaɓeɓe *m.* (*f.* wartaɓeɓiyā) huge.

wartạkā *Vb.* 1C (1) scattered. (2) aŋ ~ shi dạ ƙasā he was flung down.

wartakad dạ *Vb.* 4 = wartạkā.

wartsahū *m.* (1) type of bracelet. (2) type of kick in mạŋgạrē 2 (*cf.* tsạgyan tsạyī).

wartsạkē *Vb.* 3A (1) = warkẹ 1*a.* (2) threw off torpor of sleep on awakening. (3) ceased to be shy. (4) gạrī yā ~ (*a*) dawn has fully arrived. (*b*) weather has cleared (= wāshẹ 2*c*). (5) zūcīyassạ tā ~ he feels more cheerful (= wāshẹ 2*d*).

wạrtū *m.* (1) pillaging. (2) thieving.

warwạɗā *Vb.* 1C (1) yā warwạɗạ ruɓūtū he wrote quickly. (2) (*with dative*) poured on lightly (soup on food, etc.), *cf.* barbạɗā.

warwāji *m.* (1) white oryx (= mạrīri). (2) shield made from 1.

war-war A. (wạr-war) *adv.* recumbently.
B. (wạr-wạr) *adv.* gently (*re* water on the boil).
C. (war-wạr) *m.* (1) *Vd.* ạlhạrīni. (2) jạkar ~ *f.* package of 500 skeins of silk thread (*cf.* ạlhạrīni 2).

wạrwarạ *Vb.* 2 = warwạrē.

warwạrē (1) *Vb.* 1C (*a*) disentangled. (*b*) unravelled. (*c*) (i) unwound (thread) from spool, turban from off head. (ii) yā warwạrẹ rawunạnsu he dismissed them from office. (*d*) unfolded (bundle of thread prepared for weaving). (*e*) cancelled. (*f*) yā warwạrẹ ạlkāwạrinsạ = yā warwạrẹ igīyạr ạlkāwạrī he broke his promise. (*g*) zạŋ ~ makạ shī I'll explain it to you. (2) *Vb.* 3A (*a*) became disentangled, unravelled, unwound, etc. (*b*) = warkẹ.

warwarō *m.* = awarwarō 2.

warwạsā *Vb.* 1C (1) tā warwạsạ zạrē she made a short skein (wạrwạshē 2) of thread (*cf.* lanyạcẹ 3). (2) *intensive from* wasạ.

warwashe A. (wạrwạshē) *m.* (1) acting *as in* warwạsā 1. (2) short skein of thread.
B. (wạrwạshē) *intensive from* wāshẹ.

wạrwāso = wāsōso.

warwạtsē *intensive from* wātsẹ.

wasa A. (wạsā) (1) *m.* (*but f. at Sk.*) (*pl.* wạsạnī = *Kt.* wạsạnnī) (*a*) (i) any playing ; joking (= wargī). (ii) dạ

ạbu kạmar wạsā har ya zamā aminci it began as a joke and ended in real friendship. (iii) *Vd.* fagē 1*d.* (*b*) sun yi ~ they played. (*c*) ạbōkiŋ ~ playmate (*Vd.* shārạ 3, taubạshī). (*d*) *Vd.* wạsạnī. (*e*) bā kạ̀ rạbūwā dạ ~ you're always full of fun. (*f*) n nạ̀ jạnsạ dạ ~ I'm quizzing him, joking with him. (*g*) kạmar ạbiŋ ~ akạ ji lạ̀bārin naŋ they were struck all of a heap by hearing that news (*cf.* m *below*). (*h*) wạsaŋ gautā *Vd.* gautā 2. (*j*) wạsan taurī *Vd.* taurī 2*c*. (*k*) *Vd.* wạsa-wạsā. (*l*) mai wạsā dạ kūrā wata rānā rạ̀gwantạ nē shī " playing with fire ". (*m*) ạbiŋ wạsansạ *Vd.* muṭum 9*d* (*cf.* 1*g* above). (*n*) yārọ bại san yārọ nē shī ba săi an yi wạsam buguŋ wuyạ pride comes before a fall. (*o*) yạnzu mun sạmi ɓātạ wạsansu now we are able to foil them. (*p*) wạsā dạ yārọ shī kẹ̀ kāwō rēni don't act in an undignified manner ! (= rēni 1*d*.i). (*q*) an shā rūwā, yạnzu yā kamātạ ạ kōmạ wạsā they have had a breathing-space and must now return to the task. (*r*) gātaŋ ~ *Vd.* ɓạbba 7*b*. (*s*) wạsam ɓōyō *Vd.* ɓōyō 2. (*t*) *Vd.* buge-bugē ; kwānaŋ ~. (*u*) wạsan darē ; wạsaŋ kạrāyạ *Vd.* lādọ. (2) *Vb.* 2 (*p.o.* wạshē, *n.o.* wạshi) = wāshẹ 1*a*.

B. (wāsạ) *Vb.* 1A (*Vd.* wāshi). (1) (*a*) sharpened = koɗạ 1*a* *q.v.* (*b*) sukạ fārạ wāsạ makạmai ạ kan Jāmus then they (army) began " to get their hand in " at fighting the Germans. (2) yā ~ dōki he quickened speed of the horse (= wāshẹ 1*b*). (3) = kōɗạ 1*b*, kōɗạ 2. (4) whipped (pupils) to improve their intelligence. (5) preached to people ostensibly for their good, but in reality, for gain. (6) yā ~ bāki he ate T. to sweeten his mouth. (7) yā ~ hannū he gave a good slap. (8) nā ~ ƙafạ I went for a stroll.

C. (wạsā) (1) *Vb.* 2 (*p.o.* wạshē, *n.o* wạshi) (*a*) (i) infected. (ii) tā gạmu dạ aŋguryā, ta wạshē tạ *woman* got hæmorrhoids. (iii) ganiŋ wannạŋ yā wạshē tạ seeing this caused her (pregnant woman) to bear child affected by what she had seen. (*b*) found fault with. (2) *f.* abin nan ∼ gareshi this affects pregnant women *as in* 1*a*.iii.

Wasai A. (**Wāsāi**) *m.* (1) Wase-rock. (2) ɗan ∼ *m.* type of salt.

B. (**Wāsāi**) *f.* (1) a town near Kano. (2) *Vd.* fāri 1*b*, ungōzōma.

C. (wasai) *m.* yanā da fuska ∼ = yanā da fuska wasai-wasai he has a cheerful expression.

wasakī *m.* leather bucket.

wasalam *Ar.* (1) the matter's ended! very well then! (= shī kē nan). yā cē " wasalam ! " he said " there's an end to the matter ! " (2) *Vd.* hāzā 2.

***wasalce** A. (wasalcē) *Vb.* 1C inserted wasalī into script.

B. (wasalcē) *Vd.* wasalta.

wasalī *Ar. m.* (*pl.* wasula = *Kt.* wasulla) Arabic vowel-signs (= *māsī).

***wasalta** *Vb.* 2 (*p.o.* wasalcē, *n.o.* wasalci) = wasalcē.

wāsance *used in* a ∼ playfully.

wāsanī = *Kt.* wāsannī (*pl. of* wāsā). (1) presumptuousness (= izgilī). (2) immorality. (3) cikī yā yi mata ∼ she feels signs of miscarriage.

wāsantā *Vb.* 1C considered as trifling (= banzantā).

wasarērē *m.* carelessness.

wāsashē *Vb.* 1C (1) (*a*) quickly cleared (large area for farm). (*b*) quickly finished (task). (2) scrambled for *as in* wāsōso.

wasa-wasa A. (wasā-wasa) *f.* a food made from bean-flour.

B. (wā'sa-wāsā") *adv.* gradually *x* sun ƙāra ƙarfī wāsa-wāsā they gradually became strong. ∼ sāi gidan alkālī matters went so far that ultimately a court-case arose (*Vd.* mālamī 1*c*.viii).

Wasei· *Vd.* **Wasai**.

wash my word !

washar (1) *adv.* (*a*) yanā da bākī ∼ he (person, well, etc.) has big mouth. (*b*) ƙasan nan ∼ takē this building-clay is not adhesive. (*c*) tanā zaune ∼ she's sitting exposing her private parts. (2) *m.* rattling, chinking.

washar-washar = washar 1*b*.

wāshāshā *adv.* (1) = washar 1*a*. (2)

yā būɗe bākī ∼ he opened his mouth wide.

washe A. (wāshe) (1) *Vb.* 1A. (*a*) an ∼ gidansa his house has been raided and stripped (*previously done by Chiefs as punishment*) = faraucē 3 (*cf.* yāye 1*d*). (*b*) = wāsa 2. (2) *Vb.* 3A (*a*) bākīna yā ∼ I have a pleasant taste in my mouth (= *Kt.* yāye 2*b*.ii). (*b*) yā ∼ he has improved. (*c*) garī yā ∼ = wartsakē 4. (*d*) zūcīyassa tā ∼ = wartsakē 5. (*e*) fuskassa tā ∼ he is looking more cheerful. (*f*) cikinsa yā ∼ his bowels have had a clear-out. (*g*) hadirī yā ∼ = kōre 2*a*.i, ii. (*h*) (i) (water in cleaned-out well) settled (= kwantā). (ii) al'amarī yā fāra wāshēwā the affair has begun to die down (= kwantā). (iii) duhun wahala yā ∼ the worst of the trouble is over. (*j*) gōran nan bai ∼ ba these kola-nuts are not yet ripe.

B. (wāshē) *Vd.* wāsā 2.

C. (washē) *Vd.* wāsā.

washēfē = wushēfē.

wāshēgarī = kashēgarī.

washēwashī *m.* tukunyā tā yi ∼ the bottom of the cooking-pot has cracks (= san kaza).

washi A. (wāshi) *m.* (*secondary v.n. of* wāsa) *x* (1) yanā wāshin wuƙā = yanā wāsa wuƙā he's sharpening the knife. (2) dūtsan ∼ grindstone.

B. (wāshi) *Vd.* wāsā 2.

C. (washi) *Vd.* wāsā.

wāshiman *Eng. m., sg., pl.* (1) washerman. (2) watchman.

wasicē *Vd.* wasīta.

wasici A. (wasīci) *Vd.* wasīta.

B. (wasīci) *m.* = wasīyya.

wasīka = wasīƙa *Ar. f.* (*pl.* wasīƙū = wasīƙōƙī) letter *x* wasīƙa a kan wannan lābāri a letter containing this information.

wasīta *Vb.* 2 (*p.o.* wasīcē, *n.o.* wasīci) yā wasīcē ni n yi kaza he enjoined on me to do such-and-such.

wasīyya *f.* (*pl.* wasīyyū = wasīyyōyī = wasīce-wasīcē) enjoining T. on P. *x* abin da muka yi muku wasīyya da shī what we have enjoined on you.

wạsīyyị *m.* (*f.* wạsīyyịyā) *pl.* wạsịyyai
P. instructed *as in* wạsīyyạ.

wạskạnē *m.* type of painful, facial skin-
disease (= dakạŋ Wạmbai).

waskẹ *Vb.* 3A = baudẹ 1*a.*

waskīyā *f.* = baudīyā.

wạsō *m.* acting *as in* wāshẹ 1*a x* an yi
masạ ~.

wạsōsọ *m.* sun yi ~ = sun saɓạ ~ they
scrambled to get (T. thrown to them,
etc.) = wāwạ.

*wassạfā *Vb.* 1C *Ar. x* nā ~ masạ shī
I explained it to him (= bayyạnā).

*wassạftā = *wassạfā.

wạsshẹ = yạushẹ.

wassu = wasu *q.v. under* wani.

wasu *Vd.* wani.

wasulạ *Vd.* wasạlī.

wạsūwāsị = wạswāsị.

wạswāsị *m.* reflection, pondering.

wata A. (watạ) *m.* (*pl.* wạtạnnī). (1)
(*a*) moon. (*b*) *Vd.* gụdā 1*b.*iii. (*c*) amaryar
~ new moon (*cf.* 1*k*). (*d*) mạtar ~ *f.*
Venus (= Zạ̄haratụ). (*e*) (i) fariŋ ~
moonlight. (ii) dụƙushim fariŋ ~
young moon (= haskē 1*c*), *cf.* badarẹ 2.
(iii) kadạ kạ zaunạ ạ fariŋ ~, kanạ dạ
laifī (*Vd.* bāshị 6) do not sit in the moonlight, seeing you've previously had
syphilis, lest it recur ! (iv) watạnsạ yanạ
farī he is in luck. (v) tsīram būshīyā *Vd.*
tsīrā 1*b.*vii. (vi) rashịm fariŋ watạ, tau-
rārọ kẹ̄ haskē any port in a storm. (vii)
Fariŋ ~, rakạ wāwā you fool, deceived
by mere appearances ! (viii) ~ sābaŋ
ganī *Vd.* aŋgọ. (ix) Sarkiŋ ~ *Vd.*
aŋgọ. (*f*) ~ yā tsayạ it is new moon
(*cf.* 1*k*, 1*c*, fịta 4*b*). (*g*) ~ yā mutụ the
moon has reached the last day of the
month. (*h*) ganiŋ watạŋ kụrēgē *m.*
person's trying to draw child's heel
round its neck. (*j*) shạŋ ~ *Vd.* zạwārạ
1. (*k*) kōwā ya rēnạ tsayạ̄war ~ yạ
hau, yạ gyārạ shi don't criticize if you
have no remedy ! (*cf.* 1*f above*). (*l*) bạ
don tsawō a kạŋ ga ~ ba success
depends more on luck than on anything else. (*m*) mại kwạrmiŋ idọ bạ
yā ga ~ ba sāi yā kwānā gōmạ shạ
bīyar (*said in song*) a poor man who has
nothing to give would be well advised
to keep away from feasts. (*n*) watạ

yā tsērẹ *Vd.* tsērẹ 1*b.* (2) (*a*) month. (*b*)
wataŋ gōbe next month. (*bb*) Bạlārabaŋ
~ month of 29 or 30 days (*Vd.* bạbbāwạ
2). (*c*) watạŋ jībi the month after next.
(*d*) watạŋ jīyạ last month. (*e*) watạŋ
shēkaranjīyạ the month before last.
(*f*) watạŋ kwạraŋ ɗayā nẹ̄, na bīyū
sāi zạ̄garī people discuss one another
for a while, then forget. (*g*) watạŋ
ɗayā January. watạm bīyū February.
(*h*) watạŋ azụmin tsọ̄faffī the month of
Rajab. (*j*) *Vd.* sallạ 1*f*, bāwạ 7, layyā
2, wọwwō, wutsīyạ 1*d*, ƙishirwā 1*b*. (*k*)
yaụ ~ dạ watạnnī kẹ̄ naŋ munạ ƙọ̄ƙarī
we have been trying for some months.
(*l*) ạ watạnnim bāya during the last
few months. (*m*) ~ yā ɓacẹ matạ = ~
yā ɓacē tạ she has become pregnant (*cf.*
ɓataŋ watạ). (*n*) (i) tanạ biŋ ~ she is
menstruating. (ii) *Vd.* bī 7. (*o*) (i)
watạm baƙwại maƙārar rānī ; im
bābụ dạmunā (= im bạ̄ rūwā), dạ
ạlạ̄muntạ patience is always rewarded.
(ii) *Vd.* shạ̄mūwā 4.
B. (wata) *Vd.* wani, sābwā 2.

wạ ta dụ̄bạ *f.* a spinning-top game (= *Sk.*
dūbal).

wạ̄takạ *Kt.* = wạ̄tọ.

wạ̄takịl = wạ̄takīlạ.

wạ̄takīlạ = watakīlạ (*Ar.* and it was said).
(1) perhaps (= yallạ). (2) kọ̄ wạ̄takīlạ
Vd. kọ̄ 5, 6, kīlạ.

wạ̄takị̄lī = wạ̄takīlạ.

wạ̄tạlāgī *m.* aimless roving (= gīlọ).

wạtandā *f.* (1) (*a*) slaughtering animal,
dividing the meat into equal portions
and selling on credit (= kạkkạ̄wā =
Kt. twạn-twạŋ = *Kt.* rạrrạɓā = *Sk.* gịn-
sāmī), *cf.* zụbētā. (*b*) *Vd.* twạn-twạŋ.
(2) ụbaŋ ~ *Vd.* tūrū 4. (3) ~ tā jūyẹ
fāwạ things turned out differently from
what was intended.

wạtạŋgararā *f.* aimless roving (= gīlọ).

wạtạnnī *Vd.* watạ.

Wạtarī *Vd.* majẹ̄ 1*b.*

wata sābwā *Vd.* sābwā.

watạ̄tạ̄ *Vd.* wanēnạ.

wạ̄tau = wạ̄tọ.

wạ̄tọ (1) that is to say *x* Bạtūrẹ ~ mụtumiŋ Tūrai a European, *i.e.* a person
from Europe. (2) ~ ƙaryā nakẹ̄ yị ?
so you don't believe me ! (3) ~ kā

ga in fact *x* wạtọ kā ga ai sǎi sụ kọrē mụ therefore they will rout us. wạtọ kā ga ạshē yā ɓad dạ kai for in fact he has betrayed you.

wātsạ *Vb.* 1A (1) (*a*) scattered, dispersed *x* (i) sụŋ wātsạ kạnsụ kọịnā they dispersed their troops hither and thither. (ii) aŋ wātsō musụ hạrsāshị they (soldiers) fired heavily on them. aŋ wātsō musụ ịgwā a mass of artillery-fire was let loose on them (= ɗirkạ). (*b*) aŋ ~ shirịmmụ our plans have come to nought. (*c*) used T. prodigally. (*d*) threw away several things, *e.g.* grain, liquid (= zubar dạ). (*e*) = yāfạ *2a*. (2) (*a*) yā ~ rūwā he used foul language. (*b*) dōkị yā ~ rūwā horse kicked, waved tail, bucked, etc. jạkī yā ~ rūwā the donkey bucked. (3) yanạ wātsạwā (*a*) he is using foul language. (*b*) it (horse) is kicking, etc., *as in 3b above.* (4) = wātsad dạ 1-3.

wạtsạbirịtā *m.*, *f.* grubby, unkempt P. (= dụnsurmạ).

wātsad dạ *Vb.* 4 (1) *x* sụŋ ~ ayyukạnsụ they've given up their jobs. (2) yā ~ nī he treated me as of no account, failed to look after me. yā wātsad dạ ạlkā- wạrinsạ he broke his promise. yā taɓō wannạŋ sūrạ, yā wātsar he glanced at this chapter and then cast it aside. (3) ya ~ shī sadakạ he threw it to people as charity (*all* = wātsạ 4). (4) sun ƙi yạrdā sụ wātsar, sụ hūtạ they refused to give up the fight.

*wạtsạ'ī = *wadạ'ī.

wạtsạl-wạtsạl *used in* (1) rūwā yanạ tạfasạ ~ the water is steadily boiling. (2) kīfī yanạ wạtsạl-wạtsạl the fish is wriggling.

watsattsaka A. (watsattsạkā) = ɓararrạkā. B. (wạtsạttsakạ) = ɓarạrrakạ.

wạtsattsē *m.* (*f.* wạtsattsīyā) *pl.* wạtsạttsū depraved P. (*epithet is* ~ kā fi mạtaccē).

wātsẹ *Vb.* 3A (1) (*a*) became dispersed, scattered, routed *x* sạnsanī yā wātsẹ the army was disbanded. kạsūwā tā cī, ta ~ the market was held and then dis- persed (*cf.* ạwātsīmạ). fādancī yā ~ the audience with the Emir came to an end. (*b*) kụ ~ (*impolitely*) be off, you people ! (*c*) hadirị yā ~ the storm has vanished

(= shārẹ 2). (2) suŋ ~ they've become alienated (= ɓāɓẹ). (3) P. deteriorated. (4) became cancelled *x* shirịmmụ yā ~ = dạbārạmmụ tā ~ our plans came to nought. ƙọƙarinsụ bā yạ wātsẹwā banzā their efforts will not be in vain. (5) *cf.* wạtsu, wātsạ.

watsi A. (wạtsī) *m.* (1) scattering posses- sions of another out of doors (2) an yi ~ dạ shī it has been discarded. B. (wātsị) *m.* = yāfị 2.

wạtsu *Vb.* 3B (1) spread *x* suŋ ~ they have gone their respective ways. ạd- dīnịnsụ yā ~ their religion spread. dōkị yā ~ ạ ƙasạ the cavalry dis- tributed themselves over the country. (2) *cf.* wātsẹ.

wattsạkē = wartsạkē.

wau *Ar. m.* (1) the Araɓic letter " w ". (2) jaŋ ~ a small Arabic " w " written in red ink in such words as Dā'udā.

wạụtā *f.* senselessness.

wautad dạ *Vb.* 4 treated P. as a fool.

wawa A. (wāwā) (1) *m.*, *f.* (*pl.* wāwạyē). (*a*) fool (*Vd.* ɓọrī 6*b*). (*b*) dạ bābụ ~, gwạmmạ dạ ~ half a loaf is better than no bread. (*c*) *Vd.* sārạŋ ~. (*d*) *Vd.* wāwan-*compounds*, wāwā- *compounds*. (*e*) mun yi musụ wāwam bugụ, irịn na sallamạ, muŋ kai sụ ƙasạ we gave them a knock-out blow and felled them (*cf.* wāwam barcī). (*f*) rakạ wāwā *Vd.* watạ 1*e*.vii. (*g*) *Vd.* sạu ta gạ wāwā. (*h*) turkyạŋ wāwā *Vd.* sạ̄ɓō 1. (*j*) ~ kạ sakạ hannū *Vd.* akurkī 4. (*k*) ɓọyaŋ ~ *Vd.* ɓọyō 6. (*l*) ~ kạ jē magọrī (*Vd.* bụrūƙụ 2). (*m*) bụrụm dạ ~ *Vd.* ɗambā. (*n*) mai gidā ɗayā ~ *Vd.* Dōzạ. (*o*) gạsar ~ *Vd.* gạsā 1*b*, *c*. (2) *m.* native mayāfī- cloth usually black, large enough to be worn round body and thrown over shoulder (= jirgī 4). (3) bābụ ~ doubtless (= bā shakkạ).
· B. (wạwā) *f. used in* wạwar mutạnē crowd.
C. (wāwạ) *f.* (1) = wạsōsọ. (2) bā ạ wāwạr ɗam būshīyā don't waste your breath on a headstrong person !

wāwạ dụbi tsạye *m.* treading water.

wawaf = wuf.

wạwạgī *m.* penny (= kwabọ).

wāwai (1) = sāsakai. (2) al'amarin naŋ
" ta ci ~ ! " akē yi nobody is attending
to this. (3) garī yā yi ~ these are hard
times !

wāwā idō m. purloining.

*wāwaitāwā used in bisa ga ~ without
exception.

wawaka A. (wāwakā) = fāfakā.
 B. (wāwaka) = fāfaka.

wāwā ka jē magōrī epithet of būrūku 2.

wāwam barcī m. heavy sleep (Vd. wāwan
cī, wāwā 1e, wāwan nīsā, wāwan yawa),
cf. gāgā 3.

wāwam bugu m. Vd. wāwā 1e.

wāwan cī m. greedy appetite (Vd. wāwam
barcī).

wāwancī Kt. m. = wautā.

wāwaŋka nawa m. vi'lager who adopts
townsman as patron.

wāwaŋ kīwo m. horse's straying away
while grazing.

wāwaŋ kurmi m. (1) the Blue Plantain-
eater (Corythœola cristata). (2) leaves
used for wrapping kola-nuts in.

wāwān nīsā m. great distance (Vd.
wāwam barcī).

wāwan Sarkī = gaujī 2.

wāwan sau m. false scent (x when hunting
criminal).

wāwan yawa m. enormous amount.

wāwan zamā m. (1) sitting indecently
exposed. (2) (a) selling T. off cheaply.
(b) kōwā ya yi ~, ā lēka cheap wares
are soon sold.

wawara A. (wāwara) (1) Vb. 2 snatched
at, grabbed at. (2) f. karē yā kai masa
~ the dog snapped at him.
 B. (wāwarā) Vb. 1C = fāfakā.

wāwashē = wāsashē 2.

wāwaya = wāwai.

wāwāyē Vd. wāwā.

wāwilaŋ used in yanā da bākī ~ =
bākinsa ~ nē he's toothless.

wawilo A. (Wāwilō) m. name of a legen-
dary sword.
 B. (wāwīlō) m. toothless mouth.

wāwulīyā f. cadging (= rāraka).

wāwura = wāwara.

wāwuya = wāwai.

wawwārā m., f. (pl. wārāwā) stinking
(d.f. wārī).

wawwarē = warwarē.

wawwō = wōwō.

waya Eng. f. (pl. wayōyī). (1) wire, wire-
netting. (2) (a) pound in weight. (b)
weighing-scales (= ma'aunī). (3) =
māi birim. (4) (a) telegraph. (b) (i)
telegram. (ii) yā buga musu ~ he sent
them a telegram, cable (Vd. buga 1f).
(c) telephone x nā yi masa ~ I tele-
phoned to him. (d) (i) wayar iska
radio. (ii) an yi musu jawābi ta wayar
iska, an cē . . . a message was broadcast to them that . . . yā yi musu
magana cikiŋ wayar iska he addressed
them on the radio. yā buga musu
wayar iska cēwā . . . he broadcast a
message to them to the effect that . . .
(5) Waya, māi kai magana nēsa what
a gossip-monger ! (6) speedy messenger.

wayales Eng. m. wireless, radio.

wāyam (1) adv. x nā iskē daki ~ I found
the house empty. (2) Kt. m. type of big,
biting-fly.

wāyancē Vb. 3A (1) is experienced. (2)
used stratagem, dissembled.

wāyāro m., f. huge.

wāyayyē m. (f. wāyayyīyā) pl. wāyayyū
cute.

wā ya zāgi bāba m. = kulkī 1a.

wā ya zāgi dōgari m. type of European
cotton material.

waye A. (wāye) (1) Vb. 3A. (a) (i) garī
yā ~ it dawned. (ii) garī yā ~ masa a
bākiŋ kōgī dawn came while he was on
the river-bank. (iii) iŋ garī yā ~ zā
a bīyā ka I will repay you the corn
borrowed by hansakō, at harvest-
time. (iv) Vd. garī 3. (v) duk wāyēwar
garī every day. (b) kāina yā ~ I'm
clear about the matter now. kansu
yā fāra wāyēwā they've begun to gain
experience. (2) Vb. 1A x yā ~ mini
kāi he explained it to me.
 B. (wāyē) who ? (= wānēnē).
 C. (waye) Kt. m. = the game 'yā.

wayo A. (wāyō) m. (1) (a) cuteness. (b)
wāyaŋ a cī nē, aŋ kōri karē daga
gindin dinyā pretending not to want
T. so that another leaves it and one
gets it (cf. kanya 3). (c) wāyaŋ wāni-
kikī tricky selfishness. (d) kōmē
wāyaŋ amaryā, ā shā manta even the
cleverest P. can be 'tricked at times.

(e) yanā dā ~ kamam 6ērā he's very cute. (f) ƙwǎi mā yā yi ~, ballē ɗan tsākō ? you think yourself very smart, but you're not the only pebble on the beach. (g) cf. awāyę. (2) x yā yi ~ a Kano he grew up at Kano.
B. (wāyo) m. (1) type of guinea-corn. (2) woman's name.

wayõyi Vd. wayā.

wayyō my word !

wayyō-wayyō Kt. what cold water !

wāzā f. (1) the drumming at Chief's residence on Thursday evenings and eve of festivals (= sārā 2c). (2) yā sāmi kudī, yanā ta ~ he's spending his money enjoying himself.

wazanā (1) f. calling of Muslims to prayer by lādan. (2) m. = lādan.

wazanu Kt. = wazanā 2.

wazgā Vb. 2 = fizgā.

wazgę Vb. 1A = fizgę.

*wazīfā Ar. f. prayers of the Tijānīyyā Muslim sect where lā ilāhā illāllāhu is constantly repeated (cf. hallā-hallā).

wazinu = wazanā 2.

Wazircē Vd. Wazirtā.

Wazīranci m. = Wazirci.

Wazirci A. (wazircị) m. being a Wazīrị. (2) the ungūwā where the Wazīrị lives.
B. (Wazirci) Vd. Wazirtā.

Wazīrị m. (pl. Wazīrai) (1) holder of the important sarautā so called (epithet is Basillā, abin dinkin dūnīyā (Vd. dinkā 3a) = Wazīrị, hanyā abar bị = Sk. Gwadabę, abim bīyā). (2) representative of influential P. (3) Wazīrīyā f. position among bōrī held by both men and women.

Wazirta A. (Wazirtā) Vb. 1C appointed P. as Wazīrị.
B. (Wazirtā) Vb. 2 (p.o. Wazircē, n.o. Wazirci) = Wazirtā.

wāzu m. = wa'azī.

*wishi-wishi m. (a word used mainly by Europeans). (1) = ƙirinjījīyā. (2) Fulvous Tree-duck (Dendrocygna fulva).

wo A. (wō) (1) m. = wōho. (2) (rustic) = na'am.
B. (wō) (1) Vb. 1E = yiwō q.v. under yī. (2) (a) (rustic) hi ! x ~ Audu, hi Audu ! (b) ~ Jama'a O, Ye People ! (= yā).

wōbā f. fear.

wofi A. (wōfī) adj. and noun (pl. wōfāyē = wōfuffukā). (1) (a) useless x Audu ~ nę Audu is a useless, silly P. abin ~ useless T. mutumin ~ useless P. (b) abin ya zamā na wōfī the matter became useless. (c) wōfin wōfīyo = Kt. wōfin wōfiro good-for-nothing P. (d) a ~ adv. uselessly. (e) fadi ~ Vd. banzā 1c. (2) empty x (a) nā tad dā ɗāki ~ I found the house empty. (b) yā kōmō hannū ~ he returned empty-handed (2b = rabbanā). (c) sum bar mu bākī wōfī they left us hungry. (d) banzā tā kas wōfī, ɗan kōli yā kashę dillāli Greek met Greek (Vd. banzā 1e).
B. (wōfị) m. tā sāmi ~ she has conceived.

wofinta A. (wofintā) Vb. 1C (1) despised (= banzāntā 1). (2) failed to pay P., failed to give P. his share. (3) emptied.
B. (wōfintā) Vb. 3B (1) P. is left unpaid, without his share. (2) became empty x kōgin nan bai taɓa ~ gā barin rūwā ba this river has never been completely empty. bai taɓa ~ gā barim makāmī ba he is never unarmed.

wōfintaccē m. (f. wōfintaccīyā) pl. wōfintattū = wōfī 2.

wōfintad dā Vb. 4·= wōfintā.

wōfiro Vd. wōfī 1c.

wōfuffukā Vd. wōfī.

woho A. (wōho) m. (1) booing x sum bī mu, sunā yi manā. wōho wōho they followed us, booing. (2) saurī ~ (said by girls during kalankūwā 1) on you lads with your gayyā !
B. (wōhō) Vd. nānę 1d.

wōkacī = lōkacī.

wone A. (wōnē) m. yā yi mini ~ by a magic charm, he caused loss to me with proportionate gain to himself as in wōnę.
B. (wōnę) Vb. 1A x yā ~ wā shānūna nōno by a magic charm, he caused my cows to run dry and his own to become proportionately richer in milk. yā ~ mini kudīna he caused my money to vanish from my possession into his own.

wōrā f. (1) = farā-farā. (2) = bangajē 1.

wōramī = waramī.

wọshẹ = yạushẹ.

wọwwō *Kt.* (1) game where lads throw at each other sharp corn-stalks, the other end of which is made into torch (*as it is played on eve of 19th Muharram, that month is called* Watạŋ wọwwō). (2) Sallạr ∼ = cikạ cikị 2.

wu = wụ fancy !

wūbạ-wūbạ *f. used in* 'yar ∼*f.* little-used track.

wucẹ (1) *Vb.* 3A (*a*) (i) P., animal, etc., passed by (= shigẹ 1 = gilmạ 1*b* = ficẹ 1). (ii) yā ∼ gạba he passed on, went on in front. (iii) yā ∼ ta nạŋ = *Kt.* yā wutō ta nạŋ he passed through here. yā ∼ ta caŋ he passed through there. yā ∼ ta wurinsụ he passed through the place where they lived : he visited them. (iv) kūrā tā wucẹ *Vd.* kūrā 44. (v) gạyạ jinī " nā ∼ " *Vd.* bịsạlạ̄mī. (*b*) died. (*c*) (i) elapsed *x* wōkạcinsạ yā ∼ it is now out of date. (ii) am fārạ ganiŋ ƙasạn naŋ yạu shẹ̀karạ d̨arī dạ sukạ ∼ that country was first seen 100 years ago. yā fārạ shẹ̀karạ gōmạ dạ sukạ wucẹ he began 10 years ago. tun shẹ̀karạ ạlfyaŋ dạ sukạ wucẹ since the last 2,000 years. ạbin dạ ka yi watạ shidạ dạ sukạ wucẹ what you did six months ago. an 'yạntā su tun shẹ̀karạ gōmạ dạ sukạ ∼ they (slaves) were free tẹn years ago (*Vd.* shẹ̀karạ 1*g*, yạu 1*c*, tun 1*b*). (2) *Vb.* 1A (*a*) passed by *x* (i) yā ∼ gidāna he passed by my compound. kadạ Juma'ạ tạ ∼ ka don't let Friday slip your memory ! (ii) in jīfạ yā ∼ kạŋkạ, kō kạŋ wạ̄ yạ fād̨ạ every tub must stand on its own bottom. (*b*) (i) passed beyond *x* iŋ kā wucẹ gidaŋ Audụ sǎi kạ gan sụ if you pass on beyond Audu's house, you will see them (= zarcẹ 1*b*). yā ∼ ạmfạ̄nī it is over-ripe. (ii) yā ∼ ƙaryā he is above telling lies. yā ∼ indạ kōwạnẹ mụtụm ya tabạ zūwạ he has gone beyond where anyone has ever been before. yā ∼ magananạ it is indescribable. yā ∼ gōdīyā thanks are inadequate for it. yā wucẹ ạbūtā, yā kai ạ cẹ̄ masạ zụmụntā this surpasses friendship and enters the realms of

relationship-affection. (iii) yā wucẹ wurī he exceeded his powers. (iv) *Vd.* shịmfid̨ạ 1*d*. (v) kā (jinī) bā yạ̄ ∼ wuyạ *Vd.* wuyạ 1*j*. (*c*) passed on to *x* dạgạ Kanọ ya ∼ Ƙạtsinạ he went on to Katsina from Kano (= zarcẹ 1*c*). (*d*) disregarded *x* yā ∼ magạnạr īyạ̄yansạ he disregarded his parents' behests.

wucị *m. used in* wani ∼ *adv.* occasionally, sometimes.

wucịccirī *Kt.* = wutsạttsarī.

wucịkkē *Vb.* 3A *Nor.* = wucẹ.

wucịŋ gādị *m.* (1) spare parts, reserve. (2) sunạ̄ zạune wucịŋ gādị they (troops) are in reserve.

wucị-wucị = wucị.

wucīyạ *Kt.* = wutsīyạ.

wụdiddigal (*rustic*) *m.* (1) those who destroy the property of others. (2) those who, at gambling, win all the money.

wuf *x* yā yi ∼, yā hau dōkị he leaped on the horse like lightning. yā yi ∼, yā kāmạ shi he snatched it up.

wuffị *m.* (1) slippers (usually yellow) with no leather heel-support (= huffị = kụfụtai). (2) ∼ markụf = wuffị markụ̄ slippers resembling English ones.

wuga-wuga A. (wụgạ̄-wụgā) *m.,f., sg., pl.* senseless P.

B. (wụgạ̄-wụgā) *adv.* dazedly.

wūhụ (1) fancy ! (2) = wōhọ.

wujigā-wụjigā *adv.* doggedly.

wụjiji = wạjiji.

wụjijjigā *Vb.* 1D (1) swung T. about. (2) shook T. about (*x* dog with rat). (3) (horse) tried to throw (rider). (4) treated harshly.

wụjinīyā = *Kt.* wụjinnīyā *f.* (1) swinging one's arms and body in walking. (2) horse's jerking head and body to drive away flies.

wụ'ji-wụjī[ii] *m.* (1) type of swift night-bird thought by natives to be two-headed flying-snake (*epithet is* Wụjiwụjī mūgụm macịjī). (2) flummoxing a P.

wuƙā *f.* (*pl.* wuƙạ̄ƙē) (1) (*a*) knife (*cf.* askā 2*a*). (*b*) (i) ạkwīyạ tā ji ∼ " he's been touched in a tender spot ". (ii) ji zāfiŋ ∼ *Vd.* ƙụdūrū. (*c*) bạ̄kiŋ ∼ *m.* broken corn-heads, perquisite of the cutter (*cf.* bạ̄kin shīƙạ, zubọ 2). (*d*) gạbaŋ ∼ *m.* metal binding securing blade to knife (= _Kt._ matsi 4). (_e_) an yi masa dūkan "ƙawō wuƙā!" he's been severely beaten. (_f_) ɗāɗin ∼ bā yā fad da gaban dōki what affair is it of mine? (_g_) wuya da gaskīyā, ∼ bā tā yanka shi = ciki da gaskīyā, wuƙā bā tā yanka shi a really honest P. is not subject to injury from slander. (2) Sarkin ∼ = Sarkin yanƙā 1 (_cf._ 3). (3) wuƙar yanƙā garēshi he (Emir) has the power of life and death (_cf._ 2). (3_A_) yanƙan ∼ _Vd._ yanƙā 2_h_. (3) wuƙar gindī (_a_) = cērū. (_b_) T. kept in reserve for selling in case of need. (4) wuƙar Sarkī type of grasshopper. (5) yā ci ∼ _Vd._ dōrōgō. (6) wuƙar fāwa _Vd._ gabā 1_d_.

wuƙiniya _f._ = fēlēƙē.

wuƙi-wuƙi A. (wuƙī-wuƙi) _m._ feeling ashamed (= kunya).
    B. (wuƙi-wuƙī) _m._ = fēlēƙē.

wul (1) yā wuce wul he passed by swiftly. (2) baƙi ∼ jet-black.

wula = wulakata _Sk._ (1) I don't believe it! (2) I won't do it!

wulāƙai _m. and adv._ yā dūbē ni ∼ = yā yi mini ∼ da ido he looked at me contemptuously, superciliously (= shē-ƙēƙē).

wulākanci _m._ yā yi masa ∼ he treated him with contempt.

wulāƙanta _Vb._ 1D (1) (_a_) treated contemptuously, harshly, unjustly. (_b_) belittled P. (= tābad da). (2) treated T. carelessly.

wulāƙantad da _Vb._ 4 = wulāƙantā.

wulakata = wula.

wulākata - wulākata = wulāka - wulāka lazily.

wulam _used in_ yanā da bāƙi ∼ he is toothless.

wulga A. (wulga) _Vb._ 3A passed by (= wuce 1_a_.i).
    B. (wulgā) _Vb._ 2 ate much of.

wulgi _m._ act of passing by.

wulla A. (wulla) _Vb._ 1A (1) yā ∼ tūwō he swallowed the tūwō quickly. (2) tā ∼ tūwō she made good tūwō.
    B. (wullā) _Vb._ 2 = wulla.

wulle (1) _Vb._ 1A = wulla. (2) _Vb._ 3A. (_a_) dodged (= baude). (_b_) _Kt._ yā ∼ tafīya he travelled far. (_c_) _Sk._ staggered.

wullīyā _f._ dodging, swerving (= baudīyā).

wuluk = wul 2.

wunad da _Vb._ 4 cause to spend day _x_ aikin nan yā ∼ mū = yā wunasshē (= wunshē) mu this work took us all day. Allā ya ∼ mū lāfīya may we have a good day!

wundi A. (wundī) _m._ = malafā 3.
    B. (wundi) _m._ type of gown with round neck-hole.

wuni = yini.

wunīta = yinīta.

wunī-wunī _m._ (1) behaving or speaking shiftily. (2) yā yi mini ∼ he gave me an evasive reply.

wunshē = wunasshē _q.v. under_ wunad da.

wuntsila _Vd._ ta wuntsila.

wuntsulā _Vd._ wantsalā.

wup = wuf.

wuppi = wuffi.

wur A. (wur) (1) jā wur scarlet (= zir 1). (2) sǎi yāƙi akē yī jā wur but bitter war is in progress.
    B. (wur) _x_ māshi yā wuce ∼ the spear whizzed along..

wurairai _Vd._ wurī.

wurārē _Vd._ wurī.

wurā-wurā _f. and adv._ making frenzied search.

wurdi = wurudī.

wurga A. (wurga) (1) _Vb._ 1A (_a_) (i) threw _x_ tā ∼ aƙū waje ta tāga she threw the parrot out of the window. nā ∼ masa dūtse I threw a stone at him. (ii) yā ∼ hannū he (soldier, etc.) swung his arms as he walked. (_b_) tā ∼ gūgā she jerked the rope to make the bucket sink in the well. (_c_) speeded up (horse, motor, etc.). (_d_) yā ∼ musu ido = yā ∼ musu harāra he glared at them. (2) _Vb._ 3A travelled quickly.
    B. (wurgā) = wulgā.

wurge A. (wurge) _Vb._ 1A threw T. at P. _x_ nā ∼ shi da dūtse I threw a stone at him (= wurga 1_a_.i).
    B. (wurgē) _m._ (1) jerking rope _as in_ wurga 1_b_. (2) type of bird-snare.
    C. (wurgē) _m._ type of children's game.

wurgi what fast travelling!

wuri A. (wurī) _m._ (_pl._ wurārē = wurairai). (1) (_a_) place (_cf._ gari 4, garin) = gurī =

gū = *Sk.* bugē. (*b*) sāmuŋ ∼ (= sāmuŋ gạrī), kuturū gādā ạ tsịdau = gādā 4. (*c*) bạ ni ∼ (i) make way for me ! (ii) make room for me ! (iii) clear out ! (iv) *Vd.* gạba 3*a*.iii. (v) ạbiŋ yā kai "im bā kạ yị, bạ ni wurī !" the fight waxed hot. (*d*) A ∼ ɗayā, B ∼ ɗayā A was on one side (in cricket, etc.), B in the other team. (*e*) ∼ gudā *Vd.* tārạ 1*a*.i. (*f*) wurim barcī *Vd.* tīlạs 2*c*. (*g*) yā wucẹ ∼ he exceeded his powers. (*h*) wurim ɓạrnar gīwā *Vd.* ɓạrnā. (2) kaŋ ∼ *Sk. m.* = kaŋ gīwā. (3) wurin *prep.* to P., near P., T., or place *x* (*a*) yā tạfi wuriŋ Audụ he went to see Audu. (*b*) nā zō wuriŋkạ (i) I've come to see you. (ii) I've come to ask your help (= wajē 2*a*.i). (iii) duk ạbiŋ wurinsạ all is in his favour. (iv) nā sạmi lạ̄bāṛi dạgạ wurinsạ I've heard from him. (v) wurin tūwō *Vd.* tūwō 22. (4) (*a*) earliness. (*b*) (i) dạ ∼ *adv.* early. (ii) kụ zō tun dạ ∼ come in good time ! (= dāmā 1*a*.ii). (iii) dạ wurī a kạn ɗaurẹ *Vd.* sạmmakō 1*c*. (iv) dạ wurī ta kạŋ hakạ *Vd.* tsanyạ 1*c*. (v) dạ wurī yakẹ kūkā *Vd.* zurfī 1*b*. (*c*) (i) zūwạ dạ wurị yā fi zūwạ dạ wurī it is better to come with no matter how small a gift than to come early (with nothing). (ii) bạ su dạ wurị sǎi wurin zamā they are penniless or almost so. (*cc*) 'yar ∼ *f.* any early crop. (*d*) dạ wurī-wurī *adv.* very early (= wurwurī). (5) wurī dạ ∼ openly *x* bạ mai fitọ̄wā wurī dạ ∼ yạ fadạ masạ no one would have the courage to speak out to him (= sararī 1*b*).

B. (wuri) *m.* (*pl.* kudī = kurdī). (1) (*a*) (i) cowry (= *Sk.* ijīyạ). (ii) tạyạ ∼ (*said by would-be seller*) well, at least make *some* offer, however low ! yā tạyạ ∼ he offered a knock-down price. (iii) sǎi kāmạ manạ kāyaŋ gōnā sukẹ ∼ they are buying our farm produce for a mere song (*cf.* 1*d*). (*b*) *for use in pl. in sense of* money *Vd.* kudī. (*c*) bạ ni dạ ∼ I'm penniless. (*d*) yā karyạ masạ ∼ he sold it at knock-down price (*cf.* 1*a*.ii). (*e*) (i) nā karɓi kudīna, ∼ nạ̄ gūgạr ∼ I was paid in full. (ii) nā bīyā, ∼ nạ̄ gūgạr ɗaŋū-

wansạ I paid in full. (*f*) wurị dạ hadīyạ *Vd.* hadīyạ 3. (*g*) nā bīyā ɗạrī ukụ ta wurị-wurị I paid 300 cowries (*Vd.* ɗạrī 3). (*h*) kurmaŋ ∼ unbored cowrie. (*j*) (i) bạ su dạ wurị sǎi wurin zamā they are penniless or almost so. (ii) *Vd.* wurī 4*c*. (*k*) nōnaŋ wurị *Vd.* nōnọ 1*b*. (*l*) yārọ yā tsịnci wurị *Vd.* tsịntā 2*b*. (*m*) rọ̄kwaŋ ụbā wurị *Vd.* zạllim. (*n*) askar ∼ *Vd.* askā 1*b*. (*o*) maŋ ∼ *Vd.* ɓakyạlcē. (*p*) ạlēwạr ∼ *Vd.* dādī 5. (*q*) zumạŋ ∼ *Vd.* zumạ 2*d*. (*r*) lādaŋkạ wurị *Vd.* gwazai. (*s*) ɓạrkọnaŋ ∼ *Vd.* hanzarī 2*b*. (*t*) gyạɗar ∼ *Vd.* kạ̄rā 2*b*.iv. (2) tạ yi ∼ she stained all her teeth' except one upper front one.

C. (wụrī) *m.* yā yi ∼ dạ idọ he gazed in wonder (= wurī-wurị 1).
wurī dạ wurī *Vd.* wurī 5.
wuridī = wurudī.
wuriŋ *Vd.* wurī 3.
wuri-wuri A. (wurị-wurị) *Vd.* wurị 1*g*.

B. (wurī-wurī) *Vd.* wurī 4*d*.

C. (wurī-wụrị) (1) yā yi ∼ dạ idọ = wụrī. (2) *x* nā gan shị ∼ dạ ∼ I saw him gazing about in wonder, fear.
wụrīyạ *f.* stream, stream-bed.
wurjạnjaŋ *adv. x* yanạ̄ aikị ∼ he's working hard. yanạ̄ tạfīyạ ∼ he's travelling on doggedly.
wurjā-wụrjạ̄ = wurjạnjaŋ.
wurkī *m.* severity (= tsananī).
wurkịlā *Vb.* 3A screwed up eye to look at T.
wurkịlē *Vb.* 3A (1) = wurkịlā. (2) idạnsạ yā ∼ his eye is permanently screwed up through illness.
wurkịlīlị *m.* P. with only one efficient eye.
wurshi *Kt. m.* type of tree.
wurụdī *Ar. m.* section of the Koran recited privately.
wurwurī = wurī 4*d*.
wus (1) bother (= tir). (2) bother you !
wusạkē *Vd.* wuskī.
wushāwushī = washẹwashī.
wụshēfē *m.* (1) moustache unaccompanied by any beard (*cf.* wạhāɓa). (2) (*a*) pit-trap for bush-cow. (*b*) an yi minị ∼ I've had a misfortune.
wushiryā *f.* wide, natural spacing between teeth (*cf.* gīɓị).

wuski *m.* (*pl.* wusākē) (1) destitute P. (2) thief. (3) *Kt.* = ąwuskī.

wuswāsi = wąswāsi.

wutā *f.* (*pl.* wutācē = wutōcī). (1) (*a*) fire (*its epithet is* Gōdīyar Sarkim pāwą ; kōwā ya rigā ki hawā, yā rigā ki zāburą ; *Vd.* Gwalā). (*aa*) (i) wutad dą kē tsąkānimmu dą sū tanā tsakīyar hąbąbbaką bitter war is between us. (ii) (*final vowel is shortened, so that* wutā *becomes* wuta *when we have* preposition ą *stated or understood before it*) *x* yā fādą ą wuta he fell into the fire. yā shiga wuta he entered the fire. yā fita wuta it came out of the fire. (*b*) (i) ąbin wutā *m.* fuel. (ii) rashin ąbin wutā *Vd.* shinkāfā 1*c*. (iii) yā hūrą ~ he lighted a fire (*Vd.* hūrą 1*a*.i, ii, iii, vi). (iv) tūsą bā tā hūrą ~ *Vd.* tūsą 4. (v) farar ~ sulphur (= ąlkibiri). (*bb*) yā sąki wutā he put on speed. an sakar wą injin wutā they speeded up (*Vd.* sąkā 2*a*). (*c*) (i) jēji yā dąuki ~ the bush caught fire. (ii) tukunyā tā dąuki ~ the pot has become hot. (*d*) (i) wutā tā kāmą the fire burned up. (ii) ~ tā kāmą shi it caught fire. (iii) *Vd.* 1*m, r below*. (*e*) yā sā ~ ą haki he set fire to the grass. yā sā ~ he set fire (to the " bush ", etc.). (*f*) (i) yā ji ~ he warmed himself by the fire. (ii) yā ji wutar makarantā he benefited by his schooling. (iii) yanā jin ~ it's unsaleable (*cf.* māsą 2, ganin rānā). (*g*) *Vd.* bākin wutā. (*h*) (i) sunā bā dą ~ they (soldiers, artillerymen) are firing. (ii) sum bugą wutā they opened fire. (iii) sum būdę wą garin wutā they opened fire on the town. (iv) sum fādą wutar igwar Jāmus they came under fire from the German artillery. (*j*) dāki yā ci wutā = wutā tā ci dāki the house caught fire. rīgā tā ci ~ the gown became burnt (*Vd.* 1*o, p, s below*). (*k*) hannū, banzā bā yā dąukąn ~ im bā māganī dą shąriftaką nothing is done by a P. without reason. (*l*) wankąn ~ gudā kąn yāfą once bitten, twice shy (*Vd.* wankan wutā). (*m*) indą ~ ta kāmą, nan a kąm bī tą, ą ji dimintą go where fortune awaits you ! (*cf.* 1*d above*). (*n*) (i) bā ą gamą ~ dą

shibą oil and water won't mix. yā mai dą sū kąmar wutā dą shibą he brought them to loggerheads with each other. (ii) aurąn ~ dą māi *Vd.* ąlkakąi. (*o*) ~ tā ci danyē, bąllē kēkąsasshē if a penalty affects an important P., how much more so a poor man ! (*cf.* 1*j above*). (*p*) dāji bai gamą cin ~ ba, fārā bā tā yi wą 'yarūwā tatą barką don't rejoice till you're out of the wood ! (*cf.* 1*j above*). (*q*) nāmąn dą kē kusa dą wutā *Vd.* nāmą 1*g*. (*r*) in kā ga gēmun danūwąnką yā kāmą ~, shāfa wą nāką rūwā be warned by what has happened to others ! (*cf.* 1*d above*). (*s*) bērā nā ganin rāminsą, bā yā yąrdā ~ tą cī shi everyone looks after number one (*cf.* 1*j above*). (*t*) *Vd.* uban wutā. (*u*) yā shā wutar fādą (makarantā) he has long been at court (school). (*v*) (i) dą wutā ? *Vd.* cīci. (ii) (*example of* tātsūnīyā 2) (*the following are question and reply by two persons A and B in a conversation resembling* " The House That Jack Built ") A. dą wutā ?. B. Cīci tā kashę. A. wącę Cīci. B. Cīcim Bardē. A. wąnę Bardę. B. Bardan Ląnkwayą. A. wąnę Ląnkwayą. B. Ląnkwayą kōgī. A. wąnę kōgī. B. kōgin Sarkī. A. wąnę Sarki. B. Sarkī, Allā. (*w*) turkyąn wutā *Vd.* turākā 1*b*. (*x*) ąbu yā zamę masą bīyū, gąba wutā, bāya wutā it was a matter of being between the devil and the deep sea. (*y*) lābārin wutā *Vd.* sōyą 2, dafą. (*z*) dagą rūwā sǎi wutā *Vd.* karkō. (*z*.i) bą nā Īyą saurąn wutā ba *Vd.* saurā 1*f*. (*z*.ii) ką kārą masą wutā *Vd.* rānā 2*f*.iv. (*z*.iii) wutā tun dą wurī ą kashę ta act in good time ! (= burgumā 3). (*z*.iv) kā yi ~ *Vd.* farkē. (*z*.v *Vd.* zumą 1*c*. (*z*.vi) kisąn ~ *Vd.* aurē 3. (*z*.vii) bērā yā fādą wuta *Vd.* bērā 1*k*. (*z*.viii) dagar ~ *Vd.* dagaci. (*z*.ix) wutar bāya *Vd.* danją. (*z*.x) gąngar 'yan ~ *Vd.* dilun 1*a*. (2) hot tempered P. = barkōnō (*epithet is* Wutā, hąną dāfi = gāgarą dāfi). (3) (*a*) clan. (*b*) inā wutarku in which district or town-ward do you live ? yā kōmą wutarsu he has returned to where he belongs. (*c*) = askā 4. (4) =

jāwaskạ. (5) trade-mark (= lambạ). (6) = ƙōƙiyā 3. (7) *Vd.* wutar-*compounds*.

wutar baŋgō *f.* = wutar 'Yōlạ.

wutar cikị *f.* energy.

wutar darē *f.* a type of the herpes bū-lālạ 2.

wutar fạdamạ *f.* = wutar 'Yōlạ.

wutar fạ̄rā *f.* inner wings of locust or grass-hopper.

wutar kargō *f.* type of blister-causing caterpillar.

wutar rạ̄ƙumī = wutā 6.

wutar 'Yōlạ *f.* fire-fly (= wutar baŋgō = mạƙēsūwā).

wụtạ̄-wutạ *f.* = ƙudụjī.

wutin tịrāẹ̄ *Eng. m.* P. awaiting trial or on remand.

wụtịrgịzā = wụtịrgịzāzā *f.* = wạcạ̄nīyā.

wutō *Vd.* wucẹ 1*a*.iii.

wutōcī *Vd.* wutā.

wutsai *Vd.* wutsīyạ.

wutsạttsarī *m.* making lame excuses.

wutsạwutsī *m.* = wutsạttsarī.

wụtsị-wutsī *m.* = wutsạttsarī.

wutsīyạ *f.* (*pl.* wutsīyōyī = wutsạịtsai = *Kt.* wutsai). (1) (*a*) (i) tail of animal or cloth (*Vd.* jẹ̄lā), *cf.* bindị 1, tsārā 1*c*. (ii) *Vd.* kantụ 1*a*. (*b*) (*after preposition* ạ, *the word* wutsīyạ *can become* wutsī) *x* (i) yā hạrbē shị ạ wutsī = ạ wutsīyạ he shot it in the tail. (ii) aŋ hạrbi kạrē ạ wutsī, săi gidā the job is done, so let's be off home ! (iii) *Vd.* birị 1*k*. (iv) harbị ạ wutsī *Vd.* harbị 2*b*. (*bb*) zā mụ fẹ̄dẹ makạ birị har dạ wutsīyạ we shall reveal all to you without reserve. (*c*) Sallạr cịŋ ∼ *Vd.* jūyạ 4. (*d*) watạn cịŋ ∼ = Mụharrạm. (*e*) yā rāmẹ har ya yi ∼ he's very thin. (*f*) ∼ gātam bāyā one without the other is useless. (*g*) wutsīyạr rūwā channel of water (= hannū 1*a*.xvi). (*h*) wutsīyạr fạ̄tạ̄rī piece nowadays added to both ends of a fạ̄tạ̄rī, but previously to only one end. (*j*) iŋ kā zō gạrī, kā iskẹ mutạ̄naŋ gạrī dạ ∼, kai kọ̄ bạ ka dạ ita, nẹmi sōshịyar gērō, kạ kafạ at Rome do as Rome does ! (*k*) ạ aiki kạrē yạ aiki wutsịyạ ? what right have you to depute work given you to do yourself ? (*l*) bā ạ̄ sanịm murnạr kạran dạ bā

shi dạ ∼ a destitute P. cannot realize his desires. (*m*) bạ̄ rịkịdạ kẹ̄ dạ wụyā ba, ạ yi ∼ it's hard to finish, not to begin. (*n*) jạ̄kī bạ̄ ∼ *Vd.* jạ̄kin 3. (2) wutsīyạ = karaŋ ∼ *m.* penis. (3) small quantity of sour milk given to buyer of butter (= idọ 1*b*.vii). (4) *Vd.* wutsīyạr-*compounds*.

wutsīyạr ạkwīyạ *f.* blabber.

wutsīyạr ɓērā *f.* (1) type of weed. (2) a thatching grass.

wutsīyạr birị *f.* (1) type of bulrush-millet. (2) type of thatching-grass.

wutsīyạr hạwainịyā *f.* young bean-pods.

wutsīyạr idọ *f.* outer corner of the eye.

wutsīyạr kạrē *Vd.* rạ̄gō 6.

wutsīyạr kọ̄gī *f.* end of stream where it debouches into lake, etc.

wutsīyạr lūdạyī *f.* handle of lūdạyī.

wutsīyạr rạ̄ƙumī *f.* (1) the orchid *Platycoryne paludosa*. (2) ∼ tā yi nēsạ dạ ƙasā fancy his thinking he is up to doing it !

wutsīyạr shạrindọ *f.* type of weed administered by gūgūtū.

wutsīyạr shirwạ *f.* (1) type of stirrup. (2) the gown gạ̄rẹ.

wutsīyạr tsakā *f.* shifty P.

wutsụttsurī = wutsạttsarī.

wụtsụ̄-wutsū *m. x* karnukạ sunạ̄ ∼ dạ hanjī dogs are pulling the entrails about.

wuya A. (wuyạ) *m.* (*pl.* wuyōyī) (1) (*a*) (i) neck. (ii) wuyạŋ hannū wrist. (iii) mīƙẹ ∼ *Vd.* mīƙẹ 1*c*. (iv) kalmōmī irịm māsū karyạ wuyạ expressions which demolish a person's case, confound him. (*b*) dōkịŋ ∼ *m.* nape of the neck (*Vd.* dōkịŋ ∼). (*c*) wuyạn d̃ạki apex of round-hut (= ƙōƙwā 1*a* = *Kt.* tukị). (*d*) place where top (bạ̄kī) of pot is joined to body (ūwā) = mạƙōgwạrō 3. (*e*) one length of ūlụ, rūmị, or sịllīyạ, sufficient to encircle neck and hang down. (*f*) (i) yā sạ̄ rịgā ạ ∼ he put on a gown. (ii) *Vd.* rịgā 1*n*. (*g*) (i) yā kāwō īyā ∼ " he's fed up to the teeth ". (ii) *Vd.* rūwā C.11. (iii) *Vd.* ạlhakī 1*f*. (*h*) tukunyā tā ɓātạ wuyạntạ the pot boiled over (= bọ̄rī 3*a*). (*j*) kā bā yạ̄ wucẹ ∼ everything has its own purpose = jinī bā yạ̄ wucẹ wuyạ. (*k*) ∼ dạ gạskīyā, wuƙā bā tạ̄ yaŋkạ shi a really honest P. is not liable to

injury from slander. (*l*) anā̆ ganiŋ wuyạm biri̦, a kạn ɗaurę shi ạ wutsī from respect one uses a pseudonym. (*m*) dạ kǎi dạ kāyā mạllakạr ∼ nē what one's dependents own is the same as what one owns oneself. (*n*) wuyạ yā̦ tsērę yaŋkā *Vd.* tsērę 2*c*. (*o*) dūbạ ta wuyạnsạ *Vd.* ri̦gā 1*o*. (*p*) yạŋkạ ∼ *Vd.* bā̦kī 2*n*. (*q*) *Vd.* mạriŋ wuyạ. (2) (*a*) yā̦ yi ɗaŋ ∼ he has become thin. (*b*) 'yar ∼ *f*. (i) type of woman's tribal marks. (ii) retropharyngeal abscess of horse. (3) iŋ kā yī, ạlhakī yanā̦ wuyạŋ-kạ if you do that, you will be to blame. (4) yanā̦ dạ mụtụm gōmạ ạ wuyạnsạ he has 10 persons dependent on him. (5) hannunsạ dạ wuyạm macī̦jī his hand is depigmented (= mēlē). (6) yā yi musụ ∼ he exceeds them a little. (7) *Vd.* ci̦ŋ wuyạ. (8) *Kt.* wuyạm bạjinī (*a*) type of bulrush-millet. (*b*) type of trousers like wạndan dōmạ. (9) wuyạn damō the tree *Combrétum leonense* (*cf.* damō 11). (10) wā̦sam bugụŋ ∼ *Vd.* yārọ.
B. (wụyā) *f*. (1) (*a*) (i) difficulty. (ii) yā yi mini̦ ∼ I find it difficult. (iii) ạbincī yā yi musụ ∼ they have (had) difficulty in earning a living. (iv) bạ zā kạ ga wụyā tasạ ba you won't find it difficult. (v) bā̦ wụyā munā̦ īyạ sā̦ sạndā it would be easy to use force. (vi) wụyar ạl'amạrī *Vd.* ạl'amạrī. (vii) mai̦ wụyar karọ *Vd.* bana 1*c*. (*b*) dạ wụyar sūnā yakē̦ I cannot remember his name. (*c*) ∼ mafic̦īyạ *Vd.* mafi̦cī. (*d*) ạkwīyạ tā mutụ, tā barạ fātạ ∼ P. has been left in the lurch. (*e*) ạbi̦ŋ dạ kạmar ∼, gurgū̦wā dạ auran nēsạ what a difficult thing ! (*f*) bạbba dạ dādī ạmmā dạ ∼ a strong servant is useful but eats much food. (*g*) doŋ ∼ bā ā̦ ḵin dādī per aspera ad astra. (*h*) gidaŋ ∼, bā̦ kōwā ; wurin tūwō, mụtụm yā yi arbạ it's hard to find anyone to undertake a hard task, but if a job is pleasant, plenty come forward. (*j*) wụyar niḵạ fashi̦, iŋ am fasạ, yā ḵārę (*said by* 'yam fō̦tō *in* gaŋgi̦ *rhythm*) the first step is the hardest. (*k*) bā̦ kā dạ gīwā kę̦ dạ wụyā ba, ḵā̦fiŋ ạ birki̦cē̦ ta, ạ yaŋkạ ta it's easy to

begin anything, but hard to see it through to the end. (*l*) wụyar haḵạ *Vd.* mụrūcī 2. (*m*) wụyar ban nāmạ *Vd.* agō̦lā̦. (*n*) wụyar baŋ kāshī *Vd.* tirɗę. (*o*) wụyar māgạnī *Vd.* shi̦ki̦ŋki̦mī. (*p*) Sā̦ba dạ wụyā *Vd.* sābạ 2. (*q*) mai̦ wụyar sā̦ hannū *Vd.* ạljīfū 2. (*r*) matu-ḵar ∼ *Vd.* bī̦ tsatsō. (*s*) gạba mai̦ ∼ *Vd.* gạba 1*a*.iii. (2) (*a*) yā shā ∼ = yā ci ∼ he had difficulty, suffered trouble. (*b*) sun shā wụyar Jāmusāwā they were oppressed by the Germans. (*c*) mạ-ganạn naŋ tā shā ∼ = am bā tạ ∼ the word is mispronounced, has suffered change of form. (3) *x* shi̦garkạ kę̦ dạ ∼ sǎi Audụ ya zō hardly had you entered when Audu came. (4) gōmạ ta ∼ *Vd.* gōmạ 2. (5) *Vd.* tā̦barmā ∼ ; gānạ 1*c*.

wụyace *used in* ạ ∼ *adv.* with difficulty.

wuyata A. (wụyatạ) *Vb*. 3B (1) is difficult *x* yā ∼ gạrēni̦ I find it hard. (2) is scarce *x* hatsī yā ∼ corn is scarce.
B. (wuyạtā) *Vb*. 3A rendered difficult *x* rashi̦n rūwā nę̦ ya wuyạtạ gini̦ŋ lack of water made the building difficult. yǎ wuyạtā mini̦ mạganạ it rendered the affair difficult to me.

wuyōyī *Vd.* wuyạ.

wụzū-wuzū = wụtsụ̄-wutsū.

Y

ya A. (yā̦) (1) *f*. (*a*) elder sister = yā̦yā *q.v.* (*b*) *cf.* wā̦. (2) he will probably (Mod. Gram. 118) *x* (*a*) yā̦ zō he will probably come. (*b*) *Vd.* ai̦kā 2.
B. (ya) (1) (*a*) he (*verbal-prefix past relative sense*, Mod. Gram. 133*a**) *x* lōkạci̦n dạ ya zō when he came. sạn dạ ya jē̦ Kano, sǎi ya gam mụ when he went to Kano, he saw us (Mod. Gram. 181). (*b*) (*in Sk. the following consonant may be doubled*) *x* abi̦n dạ yag ganī what he saw (*Vd.* na 8*b*.ii). (2) *Vd.* yakē̦. (3) (*third sg. masc. pronoun used after* zā̦ Mod. Gram. 17 *and* bā̦ Mod. Gram 22, 19*b*) *x* zā̦ ∼ (= zā̦ shi) ḵạsūwā he is off to market. bā̦ ∼ (= shi) zūwạ he is

not coming. **bą̃ ~ (shi) dą komē** he has nothing. (4) *Kt.* **gą̃ ~** here it is ! (= **gą̃ shį**).

C. (**yā**) (1) he (*verbal-prefix of past tense*) *x* (*a*) **yā zō** he came, has come (Mod. Gram. 12). (*b*) (*for respect, sometimes " you " is put in third singular*) *x* **in yā sō mā, kadą ką sayar** if Your Honour is so inclined, do not sell it ! (2) *Ar.* (*a*) **~ Ubaŋgiji, Allą̃** O God ! (*b*) **yā Allą̃** O God ! (*cf.* **įnā yą Allą̃** *under* **įnā** 5). (*c*) **~ kū Jąma'ą = ~ kū mutąnę̄** (*said by Chief*) O Populace ! (*d*) **yā Sarākuną** O Chiefs ! (*e*) **yā Įlāhįl arshį** God on high ! (*f*) **yą Allą̃** *Vd.* **Allą̃** 1*f*.

D. (**yą**) (1) (*subjunctive pronoun, third sg. masc.*) *x* **yą zō** let him come ! **taną̃ sō yą zō** she wants him to come (Mod. Gram. 13*a*). (2) **zā yą = zai.** (3) (*a*) like = **yį** *q.v.* (*b*) **~ nāsų, ~ nāsų** their own party (*cf.* **yę̄, yį** 1*h*). (4) *Kt.* **~ jūnammų = yąką jūnammų** among ourselves. (5) *Vd* **yā** 2*f*.

E. (**yą̃**) (1) = **yą̃yą.** (2) *m.* **nā ji ~** I had pleasant, hot taste of ginger, etc., in my mouth. (3) (*negative third masc. singular progressive*) *x* **bā yą̃ zūwą** he is not coming (Gram. 19).

'yā (*fem. of* **đā** *q.v.*) *pl.* **'yā'yā.** (1) (*a*) (i) **'yā = 'yā mącę̄** daughter (*Vd.* **'yam mātā** *under* **yārinyą**). (ii) **'yā tā ƙi aurē** *Vd.* **nōmā** 1*b*.ii. (iii) **ūwar ~** *Vd.* **rānā** 4*c*.ii, **katakas.** (iv) **~ tā ga dōraŋ ūwā** *Vd.* **bųƙū-bųƙū.** (*b*) **'yar** *Vd.* **đan.** (*c*) **'yar**-*compounds Vd.* second word. (*d*) *Vd.* **'yā'yā.** (2) (*a*) freeborn woman. **taną̃ ~** she is a free woman. (*b*) **nā bar tą ~** I freed her (slave). (*c*) *Vd.* **đā.** (3) short farm-ridge between two longer ones. (4) narrower, lower part of grave. (5) (*a*) **'yā = 'yā ą rūwa** children's game in water (= *Sk.* **ląmbē** = *Kt.* **wayę** = *Kt.* **dįyā** 3). (*b*) children's game in sand (*Vd.* **cōkā, gąrdō**).

F. (**yą̃**) *Kt. f.* = **wą̃.**

*ya'asų *Ar. m.* giving up hope.

yaba A. (**yąbā**) *Vb.* 2 (*but progressive usually formed with* **yąbō**). (1) praised *x* **an yąbē shį** he has been praised. **an yąbē shį gą ƙōƙarinsą** he has been

praised for his zeal. (2) panegyrized. (3) approved of T. (4) *Vd.* **yabą.**

B. (**yabą**) *Vb.* 1A (1) (*a*) **yā ~ shi = yā ~ dą shī** he praised him (= **yąbā**). (*b*) **~ kyautā taną̃ gą tukwīcį** the amount given the deliverer shows how much the gift is appreciated. (*c*) **wąndą bā ą̃ yabą ka săi tā ɓācį nē** it is a case of nobody being a prophet in his own country. (2) (*a*) (*with dative*) praised P. for T. *x* **an ~ masą ąbin dą ya yi** he was praised for what he had done. (*b*) **an ~ wą ką̃zā mįƙā, săi ta cę̄ "gą̃ cinyą !"** person's being so overjoyed that he is ready to do anything for you.

C. (**yābą**) *Sk. f.* (1) supporters, retinue. (2) **wąndō yā yi ~** the trousers are worn out. (3) type of Gwari loin-cloth.

yaɓa A. (**yąɓā**) *Vb.* 2 (1) plastered (wall). (2) bedaubed (basket) with cow-dung *x* **an yąɓi kwąndō dą kāshin shānū.**

B. (**yāɓą**) *Vb.* 1A (*with dative*) (1) = **yąɓā** *x* **an yāɓą wą kwąndō kāshin shānū.** (2) **an ~ masą laifī** he has been accused of an offence committed by another (*cf.* **kāshįn ką̃jī**).

yabanyą = *Kt.* **yabanyā** *f.* (1) young corn. (2) (*a*) young children. (*b*) **Allą̃ wadan yabanyąr jūjī, kyau bābų halī** the faults of children recoil on their parents. (3) *epithet of* **1, 2a** *is* **Yabanyą, Alą̃ yą fisshē kį farį.**

yąbarī *Sk. m.* = **gyąurō.**

yąbbai *Vd.* **yąbō.**

yabđō = **yaudō.**

yaɓe A. (**yāɓę**) *Vb.* 1A (1) plastered (*as in* **yąɓā**) all of. (2) sun **~ Sarkī** they (cadgers) stuck to the Chief. (3) **an ~ shiŋgē** thorns have been interlaced in the fence.

B. (**yą̃ɓē**) *m.* (1) (*secondary v.n. of* **yą̃ɓā**) *x* **yaną̃ yą̃ɓam baŋgō = yaną̃ yą̃ɓar baŋgō** he is plastering the wall. (2) (*a*) act of plastering. (*b*) **dą sābaŋ ginį gāra ~** (i) it's better to improve existent conditions than to make a clean sweep. (ii) choose the lesser evil !

yāɓį *m.* **an yi wą kibīyą ~ = kibīyą taną̃ dą ~** the arrow is smeared with poison.

yąbirbįrā *f.* type of bat.

yabƙī = yauƙī.

yąbō *m.* (*pl.* yąbbai) (1) (*generally used as progressive of* yąbā) *x* (*a*) suną yąbansą they're praising him. (*b*) iŋ anĝ yąbaŋką dą kyau, hąɗa dą waŋkā have two strings to your bow ! (*c*) yąbaŋ ganiŋ idǫ tsǭrō nę̄ praise of P. to his face makes him distrustful. (2) (*a*) act of praising, approving *x* nā yi masą ∼ I approved of it. (*b*) yąbō yā tąbbatą gą Allą̄ praise be to God ! (*c*) yąbaŋ kūrā *Vd.* kūrā 30. (*d*) bā tą̄ cikin ∼ *Vd.* dāma-dāma. (*e*) bā yą̄ yąbaŋką *Vd.* maƙīyī 3. (3) eulogy by panegyrist (marǭƙī). (4) yąbaŋ ką̆i conceit. (5) (*a*) kadą Allą̄ yą kāwō rānar ∼ long life and success to you ! (*b*) *Vd.* bā 4.

yābuɗā *Vb.* 1C (1) = yāƙą 1*a*. (2) put on (gown too small for one). (3) gave (small amount of salt, oil, etc.).

yąburburā = yąbirbįrā.

*yąbūsą (*Ar.* dryness) *f.* chronic constipation.

yaccąŋ *Sk.* = waccąŋ *q.v. under* wancąŋ.

yācę *Vb.* 1A (1) wiped off (perspiration). (2) cold-shouldered.

yāci *m.* ɗan ∼ a small quantity (of salt, oil, etc.).

yā dą *Vb.* 4 (1) (*a*) threw away *one* T. (*cf.* zubar dą). (*b*) yā ∼ kunyą he became more at ease (= rārę 2*b*). (*c*) yā ∼ ni = yā yāshē ni he abandoned me. (*d*) kā ∼ kari you missed your chance. (*e*) (i) yā ∼ izgā *Vd.* izgā 2. (ii) ∼ bindi *Vd.* bindi 2. (*f*) yā tąfi, yā kōmō ƙamar mai ∼ gāshi he went and returned rapidly. (*g*) yuŋwą tā tsąnantą har an yi "yą̄ dą gudā, ɗauki gudā ! " famine has made everything dear. (*h*) yā ∼ girmansą = yā ∼ ƙansą he behaved in undignified way. (*j*) yā yas dą ƙashī, yā hūtą dą ƙudā he has paid and is clear of the matter (= rą̆i 5*a*). (*k*) yąs dą ąlhēri bāya, ką ɗaukē shi ą gąba a kindness is never wasted. (*l*) *Vd.* yą̄ yā dą. (*m*) *Vd.* ƙaggǫ 2. (*n*) bā ∼ gātari *Vd.* ƙwąŋƙwąmbishī. (2) (*a*) yā ∼ hannū he swung his arms in walking. (*b*) yā ∼ ką̆i he rolled his head slowly from side to side

with fatigue. (3) (*a*) yā ∼ sąnsanī he established a war-camp. (*b*) yā ∼ tą̄barmā he spread his mat (= girką 1*a*.ii). (*c*) yā ∼ kuję̄rā he set up his chair (= girką 1*a*.ii). (*d*) yā ∼ māshi ą caŋ he opened the campaign there. (*e*) yą̄ dą lōkǫ *m.* (i) settling abroad. (ii) P. settling abroad. (*f*) yą̄ dą suŋgumī sowing ground-nut farm immediately after sowing corn. (4) yā ∼ hanyą (*a*) he mistook the road (= ɓatą 1*d*.i). (*b*) he irregularly approached senior instead of through usual channel of intermediaries. (5) yā ∼ idǫ sǎi ya gan shi on looking, he at once saw him. (6) sǎi ką ∼ raŋką you must resign yourself to it ! (= dąŋ-ganą). (7) zā mụ ∼ rānā we're going for a sundown-stroll.

yādą (1) *Vb.* 1A *Sk.* lit (a torch). (2) *Sk.* (*only in past*). (*a*) *x* nā ∼ yį I have already done it (= rigā = wādą = yandą). (*b*) *x* ɓąn ∼ yį ba I have never done so. nā ∼ yį I have previously done so (= tąɓą = wādą).

yaɗa A. (yą̄ɗā) *Vb.* 2 skimmed off (film from milk, meat, etc.).

B. (yāɗą) *Vb.* 1A (1) (*a*) anĝ ∼ magana the matter is being discussed and so spreading. (*b*) Allą̄ yą ∼ garkę God increase your herd ! (2) anĝ ∼ shi his name is being bandied about. (3) tā ∼ zanę she put on small cloth, poor cloth. (4) yą̄ɗą ƙwaryā *Vd.* fasą 3*c*.i.

yadda A. (yąddā) = yąrdā.

B. (yaddą = yąddą) (1) (*d.f.* yą " like " *plus* dą " that which "). (*a*) how, the way in which *x* ɓąn san ∼ ya yi shi ba I don't know how he did it. kun san yąddą (= ta yąddą) mukę yi you know how we acted. hanyą yąddą zā mụ kǭyā the way in which we shall learn. ∼ suką yi kụ̄wā, sǎi suką tōshę ɓāƙinsą the way in which they acted was to bribe him. ∼ yakę̄ turzą̄zą maƙīyansą yā bā mụ mąmāki the way in which he is crushing his enemies surprised us. yā gayą masą ∼ zai yi he told him how to act. yā nę̄mi ∼ zai yi he looked for a method of action. įnā ∼ ząn yį what am I to do ! įnā

~ akạ yi wannạŋ hakạ how did this
occur ? zạn san ~ zạn yi ṇ sāmụ I
shall find out how to get it. bạ yaddạ
zā mụ yi mụ gamạ we have no means of
finishing it. bạ ~ zā ạ yi ạ sāmụ there's
no way of getting it (*in last two examples*
yaddạ *is practically a noun* ' there is not
a-way-in-which '). (*b*) (i) in accordance with what, in accordance with
how *x* kạ aịkạtạ ~ na gayạ makạ act
in accordance with what I have told
you ! ~ sukạ fadạ minị, hakạ na yi I
acted according to how they instructed
me. yaddạ gishirī ya wạjabạ gạrēmụ,
sukạr bai wạjabạ gạ Tụ̄rāwā hakạnam
ba sugar is not as essential to the
Europeans as salt is to us. yanạ̄
ḳọ̄ḳarī duk yaddạ zại īyạ yạ yī he's
trying his utmost to do it. nīyyạrsụ ~
sukạ yi wạ Masạr, hadiriṇ jirạ̄gyan
samạ sukạ cịnyē su, kumā sụ yi manạ
hakạnaŋ in the same way as they
treated Egypt and just as a horde of
aeroplanes devoured it, thus too do
they purpose to treat us. yaddạ akẹ̄
sai dạ shi bạ̄ra, har bana, kud̓insụ bạ
sụ ḳạ̄ru ba its price has not risen over
that of last year. (ii) ~ akạ sayō,
hakạ akạ sayar (*a*) stolen goods have
now been stolen from me. (*b*) tit for tat.
(*c*) in view of the fact that *x* ~ sukạ
shạ̄ḳu hakạ, haŋkạlinsạ zại tāshi dạ
jịn wannạŋ lạ̄bārị in view of their
great intimacy he will be worried to
hear this. ~ kāyan yāḳị sukẹ̄ wụyā
in view of the difficulty of getting
armaments. yaddạ mukẹ̄ sọ̄ mụ yī,
sū mā sunạ̄ murnạ dạ wannạŋ they're
delighted we want to do it. (*d*) in such
a way that *x* yā tūrạ mayạ̄ḳā ~ zā
sụ wadātar he sent forward troops in
such a way that they may suffice. zā
sụ yi kịntse-kịntsē ~ zā sụ gamạ aikịŋ
dạ saurī they will arrange so as to
finish the work soon. yā bugẹ̄ tạ yaddạ
haŋkạlimmụ zại jūyạ kạntạ he beat her
in order to divert our attention to her.
(*e*) that which *x* nīsaŋ wuriṇ bại wucẹ ~
jirạ̄gyan samạmmụ zā sụ īyạ kāwọ̄wā
ba the distance of the place is not
beyond what our aeroplanes can reach.
(2) yaddạ *Vb.* 1A (*a*) = yardạ. (*b*)

(parent) turned out (child) from home.
(*c*) *Sk.* = yā dạ.
yad dạ *Vb.* 4 = yā dạ *x* yā yad dạ nī =
yā yasshē nị he abandoned me.
yaddar *Vd.* yạrdā.
yādẹ *Vb.* 1A (1) = yạ̄dā. (2) *x* dạŋkalị
yā ~ kunyā the potatoes have spread
over the farm-ridge.
yādị *Eng. m.* yard (*Vd.* sạndā 4).
yādị *m.* (1) inedible exterior of joint of
meat (= tānā 2), *cf.* yānā 1. (2)
skimmings when making sweets
flavoured with madị, or skimmings
from water in which skins treated with
oil are being kneaded.
yạ̄dīyā *Sk. f.* lighting a torch.
yạ̄dīyā *f.* the twiner *Leptadenia lancifolia*.
yạ̄dō *m.* spreading along ground by
plants (= rạbạjạ̄ 1*b*), *cf.* mīḳẹ 2*d* ;
dumaṇ kadạ.
yạ̄du *Vb.* 3B (plant, news) spread.
yā'ẹ (1) *Vd.* dōlẹ 4, wadd̓arẹ, dēwạ. (2)
haụkā ~ what madness !
yafa A. (yāfạ) *Vb.* 1A (1) (*a*) threw (gwạdọ
or other mayāfī) over shoulder and round
body (= yābụdā = jitạ 2), *cf.* ḳōḳwā
1*d*. (*b*) placed (ạlkyabbạ), etc., over
one's shoulders (= jitạ 2). (*c*) ạlkyabbạ
bạ̄ tākạ ba, kạ̄ ạrạ̄ ?, kạ̄ yạ̄fạ ? why not
mind your own business ! (*cf.* fadạ 1*a*.iii).
(*cc*) *Vd.* bạrgō 2. (*d*) waŋkaŋ wutā dayạ
kạn ~ a burned child dreads the fire.
(*e*) *cf.* yāfị 3. (2) (*a*) scattered seeds (*x*
pepper, rice, onion, tobacco) for sowing
(= wātsạ 1*e*). (*b*) = afạ 1. (*c*) sprinkled
(water, etc.) (*cf.* yayyạfā). (*d*) yā ~
rūwā he splashed water over his body.
(*e*) an ~ rūwā we've had a shower of
rain (*cf.* yayyafī). (3) dōkị yā ~ the
horse flicked its tail (= cakī 4). (4)
tā ~ minị hatsī she gave me (purchaser) small extra amount of corn
gratis (*Vd.* yāfị, gyārā 4*a*). (5) ạ ~
minị kạdạŋ offer me (seller) a little
higher price !
B. (yạ̄fā) *Vb.* 2 forgave *x* yā yạ̄fẹ̄ nị
he forgave me. yā yāfam minị shī he
forgave me for it.
yaface A. (yāfạcē) *Vb.* 1C = yạ̄fatạ 2*a*.
B. (yạ̄fạcē) (1) *Vd.* yạ̄fatạ. (2) *m.* (*a*)
measuring out corn .with piece of calabash (mārā) or one's hand. (*b*) iŋ

hannuŋka bai isa yāfacē ba, yi kira da
bākiŋka if you're not rich, practise
economy.
yafata A. (yāfatā) *Vb.* 1C = yāfata 2.
B. (yāfata) *Vb.* 2 (*p.o.* yāfacē, *n.o.*
yāfaci). (1) beckoned *x* sun yāfacē
shi they beckoned to him. yā yāfatō
ni he beckoned to me to come (= ƙyā-
fata). (2) (*a*) dipped out small amount
of corn or water (= yākuta = yāfacē).
(*b*) gathered small amount of grass.
yafe A. (yāfe) (1) *Vb.* 1A (*with dative*) *x*
yā ~ mini he forgave me (= yāfā).
(2) *Vb.* 3A *x* nā ~ I have renounced
my claim, share.
B. (yāfē) *m.* (1) yā yi ~ he threw
gwado, etc., over shoulder *as in* yāfa
1*a*, *b*. (2) (gwado, *etc.*, *has no pocket,
so it is playfully said of man wearing*
gwado) Mai yāfē, kudiŋka a māra.
yāfi *m* (1) extra corn *as in* yāfa 4. (2)
sowing *as in* yāfa 2*a* (= wātsi). (3)
adding clods to ridge (kunyā) to level
it.
yāfiyā *f.* adorning woman's hair by
plastering on indigo (shūni).
yaga A. (yāga) *Vb.* 1A = yāgē 1*a*.
B. (yāgā) *Vb.* tore off, tore out.
yagalgála A. (yagalgalā) *Vb.* 1D. (1)
tore in pieces. (2) spread out (food to
cool). (3) mocked, insulted.
B. (yagalgala) *Vb.* 3B (1) is torn in
pieces. (2) (garment) is ragged.
yagalgalē *Vb.* 3A = yagalgala.
yāgātū *m.* quarrelsome uproar.
yage A. (yāge) (1) *Vb.* 1A (*a*) tore, ripped
(= kēce). (*b*) tore off all of. (2) *Vb.* 3A
is torn, ripped.
B. (yāgē) *m.* = fīgē 1.
yāgi *m.* strip, scrap.
yagīya = yaggīya *Sk.* *f.* (*pl.* yaggwai)
string = igīya *q.v.*
yagō *Vd.* yagwan.
yāgu *m.* *x* kō da cīzo da yāgu zā su cī
they'll gain the victory cost what it
may (*cf.* yāge).
yāguŋ = yāguŋ-yāguŋ *m.* poor quality
alawayyo.
yāgunē = yaŋƙwana 2.
yagwan jini *m.* (1) unpopularity (= baƙin
jinī). (2) weakliness.
Yahūdāwā *Vd.* Bayahūdi.

yai *contraction of* yā yī, ya yi, ya yī *x*
abin da ~ = abin da ya yi what he did.
yāji *m.* (*pl.* yāzūzuka). (1) (*a*) any pungent
condiment (*x* pepper, ginger, cloves).
(*b*) (i) pungency (of pepper, oi̅.on,
tobacco, etc.). (ii) yā ci ~ he had a bad
time. (iii) da suka ji wannan kaŋwar
tā faye yāji, sǎi suka bari when they
found this too tough a job, they gave it
up. (*c*) albasa bā ta halin rūwā, dā
ba ta yi ~ ba if he were like his father,
he would not have done this evil. (*d*)
namiji barkōnō nē, sǎi an tauna, zā
a san yājinsa it takes time to know a
person. (2) (*a*) ~ gareshi he's hot-
tempered (= barkōnō 2). (*b*) tā yi ~
she (his wife) has gone off in a temper and
left him (*cf.* cittā 3, burka 2). (*c*) (i) san
a sani, ~ da kwarim miji (*mockingly*)
he hates this wife so that if she hadn't
taken his bow, he wouldn't even know
she had gone out (= santarantaŋ 2
q.v.). (ii) ~ bā bīko *Vd.* santarantaŋ.
(3) mai yājin nāma energetic P. (4)
wuƙan naŋ yājiŋ ƙarfe garēta this
knife is of reliable metal. (5) da
ƙarfin ~ *Vd.* ƙarfī 1*d*.
*Yājūju *Ar.* Gog (of Gog and Magog).
yak (1) yā yi kamā da nī ~ he's just like
me. (2) yau ~ this very day.
yaka A. (yāka) *m.* (*f.* yāki) *pl.* ku zō
come here !
B. (yaka) *Vd.* ya 4.
C. (yakā) (*future relative third sing.*
masc., Mod. Gram. 140*c*) *x* wā ~
(= wā kā) īya who could possibly do it !
(*Vd.* kā 2*a*).
yāƙā *Vb.* 2 (1) made war on. (2) took (as
booty) *x* īyākar mutānan da ya ~ the
total number of prisoners which he
took. (3) exhorted.
ya ka cē = dā ka cē.
yaƙado A. yāƙado *m.* (1) quick-tempered
P. (2) yā yi masa ~ he scolded him.
B. (yāƙadō) *Vb.* 1E yā ~ musu da
fada he scolded them, spoke angrily to
them.
yakanā *f.* (1) contentment (= wadā 3).
(2) = dā'a.
yāƙayya *f.* mutual warfare, mutual
hostility.
yakē (*used for " he " in present relative*

sentence with positive sense, Mod. Gram. 133) *x* lōkạcịn dạ ⁓ zūwạ when he is coming. yaushẹ ⁓ yị̄ when does he do it ? (*Vd.* kẹ̄).

yaƙe A. (yāƙẹ) (1) *Vb.* 1A (*a*) yā ⁓ haƙōransạ (i) it (dog) bared its teeth. (ii) he gritted his teeth. (iii) he stared about like a gaby. (iv) he lay asleep with mouth gaping wide (= yāyẹ 1*c*). (*b*) yā yāƙō minị̣ haƙọ̄rā he spoke angrily to me. (*c*) yā ⁓ bạ̄kī, yanạ̄ kūkā he opened his mouth wide to bawl out (*all* 1 = yaŋgạrē). (*d*) *Vd.* gabọ 2. (2) *Vb.* 3A = yaŋgạrē 2*a*.

B. (yạ̄ƙē) *m.* smiling expression hiding pain inwardly (*its epithet is* Yạ̄ƙē, kā fi kūkā cīwọ).

yāƙēƙēnị̣yā *f.* = yạ̄ƙayyạ.

yāƙi *m.* (*pl.* yāƙōƙī = yạ̄'ƙe-yāƙē" = yāƙūƙūwạ). (1) (*a*) (i) war. (ii) (*epithet is* Yāƙị̣, dan zạmbā = Yāƙị̣, cịmar mazā = Yāƙị̣ nōman Sarkī), *cf.* namijị̣ 1*b*. (*b*) suŋ kāmạ gạrī dạ ⁓ they -(soldiers) attacked the town. (*bb*) (i) yā shā yāƙị̣ he waged war. (ii) sunạ̄ jạn yāƙị̣ they're waging war. (iii) an dạurạ yāƙị̣ they have gone to war, prepared for war. (*c*) ⁓ yā tāshị̣ war broke out. (*d*) ūwar ⁓ (i) commander-in-chief. (ii) headquarters staff of an army. (iii) *Vd.* ūwar yāƙị̣. (*e*) dan ⁓ *m.* (*pl.* 'yan ⁓) soldier (= sōjạ). (*f*) sarkin yāƙị̣ = shụ̄gạban ⁓ military General (*cf.* bardē 2). (*g*) shụ̄gạban yāƙịn tẹ̄kū Admiral. (*h*) yāƙịn rūwā yā tad dạ sạkainā don't blame only the one, for both are equally to blame. (*j*) yā yi musụ idạn ⁓ P. familiar with terrain surprised companions by preceding them at destination, they thinking him far behind. (*k*) (i) ịdam bā ⁓ 'yaŋ Kanāwā sụ kōmạ gidā if the transaction is not likely to materialize let's call it off at once ! (ii) yāƙị̣ yā ci dạŋ Kanọ *Vd.* banzar birnī 2. (*l*) anạ̄ gạ ⁓ kanạ̄ gạ ƙūrā one blessed thing after another ! (*m*) rạgōwạr yāƙị̣ *Vd.* rạgōwạ 4. (*n*) kāyan yāƙị̣ field-service uniform. (*o*) bạ̄ ⁓ ba *Vd.* ạlwāshī. (*p*) kọ̄rar ⁓ *Vd.* gudụmmawā. (*q*) ƙūsạr ⁓ *Vd.* jārụmī. (*r*) *Vd.* ƙafạr ⁓. (2) army *x* ⁓ yanạ̄

ɓọ̄ye kusa dạ gạrī the army is lying hidden near the town.

yaƙīnị̣ *m.* certainty *x* nā yi ⁓ zại zō I'm certain he'll come.

yāƙịn naŋ *adv.* then, thereupon (= sạn naŋ).

yāƙōƙī *Vd.* yāƙị̣.

yāƙọ̄kọ̄ *adv. and m.* (1) yā yi ⁓ he looks in ill-health. (2) yā yi ⁓ = yanạ̄ zạune ⁓ he's sitting despondently.

Yāƙubạ = Yạ̄ƙubụ *Ar.* (1) Jacob. (2) *Vd.* Allạn ⁓.

yakuce A. (yākụcē) *Vb.* 1C = yạ̄fatạ 2*a*.

B. (yạ̄kụcē) *Vd.* yạ̄kutạ.

yāƙūƙūwạ *Vd.* yāƙị̣.

yạ̄kumbạ *f.* = gwambạzā.

yaƙụnē = yaŋƙwạnē.

yạ̄kusạ *Vb.* 2 (*p.o.* yạ̄kụshē, *n.o.* yạ̄kụshi) scratched with claws, nails (= ƙwạ̄jirạ).

yakushe A. (yākụshē) *Vb.* 1C = yạ̄kusạ.

B. (yạ̄kụshē) *Vd.* yạ̄kusạ.

yakuta A. (yākụtạ) *Vb.* 1C = yạ̄fatạ 2*a*.

B. (yạ̄kutạ) *Vb.* 2 (*p.o.* yạ̄kụcē, *n.o.* yạ̄kụci) = yạ̄fatạ 2*a*.

yākụ̄wā *f.* (1) red sorrel (= ạbụ 10 = *Sk.* sụ̄rē), *cf.* sōɓạrōdọ, gurguzū, kạraɓaɓā. (2) yākụ̄war fatạ̄ƙē the wild vine *Vitis gracilis*. (3) yākụ̄war ƙayạ a wild variety of *Hibiscus cannabinus*.

yạkwacī = dạkwacī.

yakwat = cakwat.

yala'allạ *Ar.* = yallạ.

yalai A. (yalai) *f.* = ƙyaraŋ.

B. (yạlại) = ịlại.

yalaŋ *f.* = ƙyaraŋ.

yalā-yạlā *used in* yanạ̄ dạ gāshị̣ ⁓ he has very long hair.

yallạ *Ar.* (1) perhaps (= watakīlạ). (2) ạbin ⁓ rại ? an uncertainty.

yallạ ɓại greeting Sir !

yālō *m. Vd.* gautā.

yạ̄lọ̄lọ *used in* yanạ̄ dạ gāshị̣ ⁓ he has soft, straight hair (*cf.* ƙudundụnē).

yalwā *f.* (1) abundance. (2) zạuna naŋ, yā fi ⁓ come and sit here, there is more room !

yalwace A. (yạlwạce) *used in* ạ ⁓ in abundance.

B. (yạlwạcē) *Vd.* yạlwata.

yalwata A. (yalwạtā) *Vb.* 1C. (1) (*a*) increased the size of. (*b*) yā yalwạtạ

rįgā he made a big gown. (2) *(with dative)* yā ∼ mini *(a)* he gave me plenty of room. *(b)* he provided liberally for me.
B. (yalwata) *Vb.* 3B. (1) yā ∼ he has plenty of room. wurī yā ∼ there is plenty of room in the place. rįgā tā ∼ the gown is ample. (2) *(a)* became abundant. *(b)* became numerous. *(c)* became prosperous. (3) *Vb.* 2 *(p.o.* yalwacē, *n.o.* yalwaci) is ample for *x* rūwā yā yalwacē mu the water amply suffices us.

yalwataccē *m.* *(f.* yalwatacciyā) *pl.* yalwatattū spacious, ample.

yal-yal (1) *x* yanā haskē ∼ it is shining brightly. yanā walkīyā ∼ it is glistening. (2) *cf.* yar-yar.

yam (1) abundantly. (2) *m.* fear.

'yam-*compounds Vd.* second word.

yamā *f.* (1) type of thatching grass. (2) yā bi ∼ = yā shiga ∼ he has disappeared.

yā mā da samfo *Kt. m., f., sg., pl.* idle rover.

yamama (1) *m.* crawly feeling produced by insect moving over one's body (= yanyamī). (2) *Kt.* abundantly.

Yaman *Ar. f.* (1) Yemen. (2) *Vd.* shabbal ∼.

yāmau *Kt. m.* = gamzarī.

yamā-yamā *f.* = tarētsā 2.

yambalā *m.* man dressed as woman during tāshē 3 *(cf.* tāda 1a).

'yambarai *m.* (1) joker. (2) being jokeful P.

yambarī *m.* type of tsimē-ink.

yam6ururū *m.* the convolvulus *Merremia angustifolia.*

yāmī *m.* (1) = tsāmī 1a, 2a. (2) an zuba masa ∼ he has heard something which has terrified him.

yāminu *m.* = mai yāminu *m.* type of striped, white shirting stuff.

yammā (1) *(a)* (i) westwards *x* yā tafi (= yā yi = yā bi) ∼ he went westwards. (ii) ∼ sak due west. (iii) an yi gabas, shī yā yi ∼ he's a devious, deceitful P. *(b) prep. x* ∼ da Kano = ∼ ga Kano west of Kano. *(c) f.* regions west of *x* ∼ duka tā zō all the westerners came. yā tafi yammar Kano = yā

tafi yammacin Kano he went west of Kano. karan da aka yi wajan ∼ da Masar the clash (karo) which occurred west of Egypt. (2) *f. (a)* afternoon up to evening. *(b)* ∼ tā yī evening has come. *(c)* rānar ∼ wadda bā tā shanyar gārī what a useless person ! *(d)* yammar fārī in the early evening. (3) *Vd.* ba ∼.

yammaci A. (yammacī) *m.* (1) *(a)* area lying west of *x* yammacin nan this western area. *(b) Vd.* yammā 1c. (2) Westerners' language or customs.
B. (yammacī) *m.* work done in the period between afternoon and evening.

yammacīya *f.* = yammacī 1.

'yam mātā *Vd.* yārinya.

yammāwā *Vd.* bayammī.

'yam mŋ give me a little ! (= sam 2).

yamsur *m.* black rosary (cazbī) adorned with silver.

yāmushi *m.* (1) young guinea-fowl. (2) small plants for transplanting (dashē).

yamutsa A. (yāmutsā) (1) *Vb.* 1C *(a)* (i) stirred round (grain, flour, etc.) with the hand to mix it. (ii) sǎi an ∼, san nan dan wākyan sama ya kan ji mǎi Fortune's wheel revolves. *(b)* muddled up. *(c)* crumpled up. (2) *Vb.* 3A sun ∼ they've quarrelled.
B. (yāmutsa) (1) *Vb.* 3B *(a)* became mixed *(as in* yāmutsā 1a.i). *(b)* became muddled. *(c)* became crumpled up *(d)* sun ∼ = yāmutsā 2. (2) *Kt. f.* = yātsina 2.

yāmutsē *Vb.* 3A (1) = yāmutsa 1a–c. (2) fuskassa tā ∼ his face is haggard. (3) became emaciated.

yāmutsī *m.* confusion, mêlée, intermingling.

yam-yam *m.* cannibal (= nyamnyam).

yam-yam-yam *x* sun tafō yam-yam-yam kamar dangō they arrived in large numbers like locusts.

'yan-*compounds Vd.* second word *(but for* 'yam mātā *Vd.* yārinya).

yan A. (yan) *(abbreviation of* ya kan) *x* girman kǎi gareshi har ba ∼ ga girman Sarki ba he is too conceited to pay respect to the Chief.
B. (yan) *Zamfara x* nā ∼ nā gani

I have already seen it (= **rigā** = *Sk.* **yādạ**).

yana A. (**yanā**) *x* (1) **yanā zūwạ** he is coming (Mod. Gram. 16). (2) (*sometimes the word* " saying " *is to be understood after* **yanā**) *x* ～ " **săi kā zō** " he is saying " adieu ! "
B. (**yānā**) *f.* (1) film on gruel, milk, etc. (= **gạrkūwā** 2), *cf.* **yādị, lanyā**. (2) type of eye-disease. (3) (*a*) spider's web (= **sā&ẹ** 2*e*). (*b*) **yā ɗẹbẹ yānar gizọ-gizọ** = *Kt.* **yā ɓātạ mạ gizọ yānā** he took to his heels. (4) *Vd.* **kwārẹ** 1*a*.ii.
***yanakạ** *Vb.* 3B *x* **yā** ～ **gạ barịm mutānē** he has isolated himself.
yanayī *Sk. m.* (1) similarity. (2) climate.
yancanī *m.* = **&yāmā**.
yance A. (**yancẹ**) (1) prepared (*as in* **yantạ**) *all* the grass. (2) crowded round P. or T.
B. (**yạncē**) *Vd.* **yạntā**.
yạnci *Vd.* **yạntā**.
'yanci *m.* (1) (*a*) being free not slave (*cf.* **ɗā**) = *Sk.* **dīyauci**. (*b*) **talauci bạ zại kau dạ** ～ **ba** poverty is not disgrace. (2) (*a*) honesty, self-respect *x* **yā yi** ～ he behaved decently. (*b*) **yā karyạ** ～ he behaved scandalously. (*c*) *Vd.* **mūgụn** ～.
'yan cịnī *Vd.* **bidạ** 4.
yandạ (1) = **yạddạ**. (2) (*only in past*) *x* **nā** ～ **nā yī** I have already done it (= **rigā** = *Sk.* **yādạ**).
'yandăidăi *m.* (1) woman's cloth consisting of alternate strips of **sā&ị** and **farī**. (2) red ⁻or black **kincē** (for suspending charms from one's neck). (3) **an sạmē shi ạ** ～ he has at last been caught. (4) type of bird-snare.
yandị *m.* = the tree **wạ̄**.
yānẹ *Vb.* 1A covered T. with film, web, etc. *x* **tā** ～ **kāyā** she covered her load with a cloth (*cf.* **yānā**).
yanga A. (**yạngā**) *f.* = **ạlfahạrī**.
B. (**yạngā**) *Kt. f.* = **&irārẹ** 1.
C. (**Yạnga**) *used in* ～ **nụ̄nạ mại nē-mạnkị** what a shameless slave-girl !
yạngar = **yạngargạr** *m. and adv.* (1) **wannạŋ gārī** ～ **dạ shī** this flour is badly ground (*cf.* **lilis, fantsạrā**). **aŋ kāwō gārī** ～ badly-ground flour has

been brought. **wannạŋ ni&ạ** ～ **dạ shī** this is poor grinding. **an yi ni&ạ** ～ poor grinding has been done. (2) **yanā dạ ha&ōrā** ～ he haṣ irregular teeth. (3) **tsakūwạ tā fịta ạ ginịn nạŋ** ～ this building has weathered and shows the gravel used in its construction.
yạngạrā *Vb.* 1C (1) **tā yạngạrạ ni&ạ** she ground coarsely (= **fantsạrā**). (2) **aŋ yạngạrạ rānā yau** it has been scorching hot to-day.
'yaŋ garancị *m.* (1) (*a*) local knowledge. (*b*) being familiar with one's subject. (3) worldly wisdom (*d.f.* **ɗaŋ gạrī** *q.v. under* **gạrī** 1*c*).
yạngạrē (1) *Vb.* 1C (*a*) = **yā&ẹ** 1*a–c*. (*b*) **săi dạ sukạ** ～ **kạn aikịŋ, kānạ ya &ārẹ** they only managed to finish the work by gritting their teeth (*cf.* **yā&ẹ** 1*a*.ii). (2) *Vb.* 3A (*a*) (muddy ground) dried and cracked. (*b*) became bad-tempered. (*c*) **rānā tā** ～ sun became scorching hot.
yạngaurạ (1) what large, ugly teeth ! (2) what coarse grinding !
yạnhūcī = *Kt.* **yạnhọcī** *m.* (1) weakling. (2) any inferior T.
yānị *m.* (1) = **sāyị** 3*b*. (2) **kāyā dạ** ～ " a thorn in the flesh ".
yạninyạnạnạ (*Gold Coast Hausa*) **dạ nī, dạ kai** ～ **cikinsạ** you and I are equal in it.
yanka A. (**yạŋkạ** (1) *Vb.* 1A (*a*) (i) slaughtered animal, chicken, etc., by cutting throat *x* **yā** ～ **sạ̄** he slaughtered a bull (= **gyārạ** 1*j*). (ii) **bā&ī shī kẹ** ～ **wuyạ** people convict themselves out of their own mouths, one's ⁻blood is on one's own head. **bā&ī yā īyạ ɗaurẹ &afạ, yạ yạŋkạ wuyạ** guard your tongue, it can lay you low ! (iii) cut throat of P. (iv) ordered execution of criminal *x* **Sarkī yā** ～ **shi** the Chief ordered his execution (= **kashẹ** 1*a*.vi.*A*), *cf.* **sạ̄rā** 1*b*.iii. (v) **iŋ kā yi hakạ, ụbaŋkạ bại** ～ **makạ rạ̄gwan sūnā ba** (if you do this, it is in vain that your father killed a ram on your naming-day) what a rogue you are ! **in nā yi hakạ, ụbāna bại** ～ **mini rạ̄gwan sūnā ba** if I act so, you can call me by any abusive term

you like ! (yaŋkạ 1*a* = yaŋkẹ 1*a*),
cf. sūnā 5. (vi) sun cẹ̆ " ạ dafạ ! " =
sun cẹ̆ " ạ cī ! " = sun cẹ̆ " ạ
yaŋkạ ! " = sun cẹ̆ " ạ kashẹ ! " they
said " go to the devil ! "
　　(*b*) (i) cut up meat *x* yā ∼ nāmạ he
cut up the meat (*cf.* yạŋkā 1). (ii) yā ∼
hanyạ he cut a road through the place.
　　(*c*) (i) cut in two (string, cloth, etc.) =
yaŋkẹ 1*c*.i, yạŋkā 1*b*. (ii) kā ∼ dăidăi
" you've hit the nail on the head ! " (iii)
ya ∼ bạntē = shātạ 1*c*.
　　(*d*) (plus dative) (i) fixed, appointed
x wannạŋ rịgā, an ∼ matạ kudī the
price of this gown has been fixed. an ∼
masạ sạdākị the bride-price he (bridegroom) has to pay has been fixed.
aŋ ∼ wạ gạrī kudī the tax assessed for
the town has been calculated out and
imposed. an ∼ musụ jakunạ dụbbai an
indemnity of thousands of bags of
£100 each has been fixed for their war-
indemnity (yaŋkạ 1*d*.i = yaŋkẹ 1*e*.iv *q.v.*
= sạ B.13 = sārạ 1*f*). (ii) yā ∼ minị
magana he said something which
offended me (*cf.* yaŋkẹ 1*e*, sārạ 1*j*).
(iii) yā ∼ minị ƙaryā he lied to me,
against me (= yaŋkē 2). (iv) nā ∼
masạ mārị I slapped him.
　　(*e*) = rigā *x* nā ∼, nā fạɗā I have
already spoken.
　　(2) *Vb.* 3A yā ∼ dạ gudụ = yā
∼ ạ gụje he took to his heels.
　　B. (yạŋkā) *Vb.* 2. (1) (*a*) (i) cut off
piece of meat, heads of corn, piece of
cloth, etc., *x* yā yạŋki nāmạ he cut off
a piece of meat (= yaŋkẹ 1*b*, *cf.*
yạŋkạ 1*b*.i). (ii) yā yạŋkō wạ kạnsạ
rēshẹ he brought trouble on himself
(*Vd.* rēshẹ). (*b*) severed *x* nā yạŋki
igīyạ I cut the rope in two (= yạŋkạ
1*c*.i). (2) yā yạŋki cịyāwạ he cut grass.
(*cf.* yaŋkẹ 1*b*, 1*c*.v). (3) made slit in *x*
(*a*) nā yạŋki zanẹ I slit the cloth. (*b*)
yā yạŋkē nị dạ wuƙā he cut me with a
knife (*a*, *b* = yaŋkẹ 1*d*). (*c*) yā yạŋkē
nị dạ ba'ạ he jeered at me. (4) sun
yạŋki dājị, sun yạŋki gudụ they fled to the
" bush ". (5) suŋ yạŋki darē they
travelled there by night. sun yaŋkō
darē they travelled here by night (*cf.*
bī 9*d*, yī 1*n*).

　　C. (yaŋkā) *m.* (1) (*secondary v.n.*
of yaŋkạ *and* yạŋkā 1–3) *x* (*a*) yanạ̄
yaŋkan shānū = yanạ̄ yaŋkạ shānū
he's slaughtering cattle. (*b*) sūnansạ
na ∼ the name given him on his
naming-day when a ram was slaughtered
(= *Kt.* sūnam fitọ). (*c*) yaŋkaŋ ūwā
yā ịshi tạ̄yī punishment of one is
deterrent to another. (*d*) (i) turmin
naŋ yā yi yaŋkan cikī this cloth is
joined in the middle (= bạ̄kin cikī).
(ii) sun yi minị yaŋkan cikī seller
cheated me by giving me less turmī
than I paid for. (*e*) (i) nā ci yaŋkan A,
ban ci yaŋkan B ba I believe in A, but
not in B (*lit.* I ate what had been
slaughtered by A). (ii) yạrdā dạ arnẹ
shī ya kāwō cịn yaŋkansạ you cannot
touch pitch without being defiled. (iii)
yā jā mikị ∼ *Vd.* bụrgumā. (*f*)
yaŋkaŋ ƙại cutting the heads off
bulrush-millet, etc. (*g*) bā yạ̄ hanạ
yaŋkaŋ kạ̄zā *Vd.* sạ̄bō 3. (*h*) *Vd.*
kaɓā-kaɓạ̄. (2) the act of slaughtering
x (*a*) dạ̄dumạ, mūgụm mālạmī yā
yi ∼, yā yi fīdạ what a rapacious
P. ! (*b*) laifin ∼ a crime worthy
of death. (*bb*) iŋ kụnnē yā ji
mugunyạr magana, wuyạ yạ̄ tsērẹ ∼
forewarned is forearmed. (*c*) yaŋkaŋ
Allạ̄ (*said by* Māguzāwā) carrion (= mūshẹ). (*d*) yaŋkaŋ gāshị = askā 5. (*e*)
yaŋkaŋ ƙaunā ceasing to be interested
in (*Vd.* ƙaunā). (*f*) yaŋkan tạfasā
darning-needle (= bạ̄ Jākarā). (*g*)
yaŋkan tsallē running away by thief
caught cutting up stolen goat. (*h*) (i)
yaŋkaŋ wuƙā the kerchief fịtina 2*e*.
(ii) wuƙar yaŋkā *Vd.* wuƙā 3. (iii)
wuƙā bā tạ̄ yaŋkạ shi *Vd.* wuƙā 1*g*. (*j*)
Vd. Sarkin ∼. (*k*) yaŋkam battạ *Vd.*
battạ 1*b*. (*l*) yaŋkaŋ kuɓẹ̄wā *Vd.*
kuɓẹ̄wā 2.

yanke A. (yaŋkẹ) (1) *Vb.* 1A (*a*) = yaŋkạ
1*a*. (*b*) = yạŋkā 1*a*.i *x* yā ∼ kan dāwạ
(kaŋ gērō) he cut off the heads of the
guinea-corn (bulrush-millet), *cf.* zọ̄garī,
būshīyā, saŋkacẹ, sārā 1*g*. (*c*) (i) =
yạŋkā 1*b* *x* yā yaŋkẹ fat he cut it clean
in two. (ii) an ∼ kantụŋ kakạndạ
piece has been cut off block of European
salt (*cf.* fasạ 1*g*). bạ̣zā ạ̈yaŋkẹ kudịŋkạ

ba no deductions will be made from your pay (*Vd. 1h below*). an yaṇkẹ ḳasạn naṇ dạgạ sauran dūnīyạ that land is isolated from the rest of the world. (iii) tā ∼ igīyạr bạutā she has become free-woman through having borne her master a child or through fansā. (iv) an ∼ tsạṇgayạ the tsạṇgayạ-hut has been finished off. (v) *x* mun ∼ cịyāwạ dukạ we have cut all the grass (*cf.* yạṇkā 2, yaṇkẹ 1*b above*). (vi) an ∼ farcẹ the toe (finger) nails have been pared (*cf.* sạ̄rā 1*f*). (vii) yā ∼ gindī he took to his heels. (viii) yaṇke sāḳạ *Vd.* kwarkwarō 3. (*d*) = yạṇkā 3 *x* yā yaṇkẹ ni dạ wuḳā he cut me with a knife. (*e*) settled, decided *x* (i) mun ∼ mạganạ we've come to a decision (*cf.* yaṇkạ 1*d*.ii). Sarkī yā ∼ mạganạ the Chief has settled the matter. (ii) mun ∼ lādaṇ aikị we've settled the rate for the work. (iii) an ∼ shạrī'ạ = an ∼ hakuncị judgment has been passed (iii = zartad dạ). (iv) (*with dative*) an ∼ masạ kudī its price has been fixed (*cf. h below*). an ∼ masạ sạdākị the bride-price he (bridegroom) has to pay has been fixed (iv = yạṇkạ 1*d*.i *q.v.*). (*f*) yā ∼ rūwā he swam across (*cf.* īyọ). (*g*) yā ∼ jịkī, yā fāḍị he fell headlong. (*h*) (*with dative*) cut T. off from *x* (i) an ∼ masạ kudī its price has been reduced (*cf.* 1*e*.iv, *c*.ii *above*), some of his pay has been stopped, he has been robbed of money. (ii) nā ∼ masạ ḳaunā *Vd.* ḳaunā. (iii) an ∼ minị hanzarī *Vd.* hanzarī, yaṇkẹ 2*c below*. (*j*) yaṇkẹ būrị *Vd.* mutūwạ 1*d*.

(2) *Vb.* 3A (*a*) became reduced *x* (i) kọ̄gī yā ∼ the river has become fordable. (ii) hatsī yā ∼ ạ ḳạsūwā there is no corn on sale. (iii) mutạ̄nē sun ∼ ạ hanyạ there is nobody about the streets. (iv) rūwā yā ∼ ạ gidan naṇ there's no water in this compound. rūwā yā ∼ there is now in (wet season) spell of dry weather (*cf. b below*). (*b*) rūwā yā ∼ heavy rain fell (*cf. a*.iv *above*). (*c*) hujjạ tasạ tā ∼ " he hasn't a leg to stand on " (*cf.* 1*h*.iii *above*). (*d*) yā ∼ ạ gujẹ he took to his heels

(= yạṇkạ 2). (*e*) piece broke off T. *x* sạndā yā ∼ piece broke off the stick. ḳasā tanạ yaṇkọ̄wa dạgạ samạ plaster is falling from aloft. (*f*) yā ∼ gạ barịm mutạ̄nē he cut himself off from the society of his fellow-men.

B. (yạṇke) (1) in a cut state, etc. (Mod. Gram. 80*d*) *x* nāmạ yanạ̄ ∼ the meat has been cut off. sạ̄ yanạ̄ ∼ the ox is slaughtered (*Vd.* yạṇkā 1*a*.i, yạṇkạ 1*a*.i). (2) *adv.* undoubtedly *x* ∼ nāsạ nē it's undoubtedly his (= lallē). C. (yạṇkē) *m.* (1) grass cut after first month of rains (*cf.* cịrē, kạḍē). (2) = dọ̄shē. D. (yaṇkē) *m.* (1) a lie (= ḳaryā). (2) yā yi minị ∼ he lied to me, against me (= yaṇkạ 1*d*.iii, ḳāgē).

yaṇkị *m.* (*pl.* yaṇkunạ) (1) piece cut off (*cf.* yạṇkā 1*a*.i). (2) piece broken off salt (*as in* yaṇkẹ 1*c*.ii). (3) (*a*) district *x* ạ yaṇkịṇ arẹ̄wā yakẹ̄ zạune he lives in the northern part. (*b*) dạ yaṇkịn darē mukạ tāsō we set out for here at night.

yaṇkō *Vd.* yaṇkẹ 2*e*.

yaṇkunạ *Vd.* yaṇkị.

yaṇkwạḍē *Vb.* 3A became emaciated.

yạ̄ṇkwanạ *Vb.* 3B (1) withered, shrivelled up (= sūmā 1*d*). (2) became emaciated (2 = yāgụnē).

yaṇḳwạnē *Vb.* 3A = yạ̄ṇḳwanạ.

'yan mātā *Vd.* yārinyạ.

yạnnai *Vd.* yạ̄yā, wạ̄.

yạnnī *Vd.* yạ̄yā, wạ̄.

yansụr = yamsụr.

yanta A. (yantạ) *Vb.* 1A prepared grass for thatching *x* (1) an ∼ kạ̈i gōmạ 10 bundles of grass have been prepared, etc. (2) an ∼ ḳundumāsạ kạ̈i huḍū the big bundle of dry grass has been made into 4 bundles (*Vd.* ḳundumāsạ). B. (yạntā) *Vb.* 2 (*p.o.* yạncē, *n.o.* yạnci) = yantạ. C. (yantā) *f.* (1) *secondary v.n. of* yantạ *q.v. x* (1) sunạ̄ yantar cịyāwạ = sunạ̄ yantạ cịyāwạ they're preparing grass for thatching. (2) bạ̄ ∼ *Vd.* banzā 1*a*.

'yạntā *Vb.* 1C (1) manumitted a slave (= *Sk.* dīyạutā). (2) an ∼ shi the debt owing by him has been remitted.

'yantad dạ *Vb.* 4 = 'yạntā.

yạntsạr *adv.* innumerably *x* dubū ~ countless thousands. kudī ~ countless sums of money.

yantsạrā *Vb.* 1C produced prolifically *x* wākē yā yantsạrạ 'yā'yā the beans have produced prolifically.

'yạŋubanci *Vd.* ɗạŋubā.

'yạŋūwanci *Vd.* ɗạŋūwā 5.

'yạŋūwạntakạ *Vd.* ɗạŋūwā 5.

yạnyạmī *m.* creepy-crawly sensation (from insects on one's body) (= yạmạmạ).

yanyạnā *Vb.* 1C (1) cut (leather) into continuous strip. (2) cut (meat) into long strips. (3) cut off meat in thin, broad strips to make kilishī (= rēɗā 2b) (1-3 = *Kt.* rēwạyē 2b). (4) yā yanyạnạ mạganạ he harped on the matter.

yanyạnē *Vb.* 1C = yanyạnā.

yạnyar *x* gạ̄ kudī ~ here is the actual money !

yạnyārẹ *Fil. m.* = ƙaiƙạyī 2a.

yạnyāwạ *f.* (*pl.* yạnyā̧yī = yạnyā̧wī). (1) the animal Fennec (*Canis zerda*), *cf.* tụluntụlumī. (2) barbaran ~ = barbarạn ~ *m.*, *f.* (*sg.*, *pl.*) half-caste, hybrid. (3) ƙāban yạnyā̧yī *m.* perineal abscess in men. (4) *Vd.* bāgiri.

yạnzu (1) (*a*) yạnzu = ạ ~ now. yạnzu kō yạ̄yạ, ọ̄hō'ō'ō what is to be done at this juncture I neither know nor care. (*b*) yạnzu-yạnzu at once, this very moment. (*c*) har ~ = har yạ zūwạ ~ up till now. har zūwạ yạnzu gạ wannạŋ rānā ta yạu right up to the present day. (*d*) tun ~ (i) by now *x* im bai zō ba tun ~ wạ̄tọ̄ bā yạ zūwạ if he has not come by now, that means he will not come. (ii) yā ƙulla ạɓū̧tā dạ sū tun yạnzu he made friends with them at once. (*e*) kō ~ rūwā nạ̄ mạgạnin dauɗạ essentials don't change. (2) soon, at once *x* ~ yạ zo he'll be here any time now. (3) ɗam mai ~ Chief's son. (4) har ~ in addition (= yạu 1e) *x* bāyan yā bā ni rīgā, har ~ yā bā ni wạndō he gave me a gown and in addition, trousers.

'yar *Vd.* ɗan.

'yar-*compounds Vd.* second word.

yara A. (yā̧rā) *Vd.* yā̧rọ, yā̧rinyạ.

B. (yā̧rạ) (1) *Vb.* 1A (*rolled* -r) (*with*

dative) *x* yā ~ musụ ạbin dạ na fạɗā he interpreted to them what I said (*cf.* yārẹ). (2) *Vb.* 3A (*a*) had difficulty, trouble *x* ƙā̧min kạ sāmụ kā̧ ~ you'll have much trouble to get it. (*b*) spoke in language unknown to listener. (3) *f.* (*cerebral* -r-) = tsīgī 1.

Yarạbā *f.* (1) the Yorubas (*Vd.* Bạyarabẹ), *cf.* Bạyarɓẹ. (2) ƙwaryar ~ *f.* 200 kola-nuts. (3) *Vd.* banzā 3, murnạ 2a, kā̧zā 6.

Yarabāwā *Vd.* Bạyarabẹ.

yaraf A. (yạraf) (1) maciji yā fāɗō ~ the snake fell off tree, ceiling, roof, plonk ! (2) gẹ̄zā mai tsawō ~ very long fringe.

B. (yaraf) *used in* ɗan ~ *m.* woman's large, long-fringed bụnū-cloth.

'yarạnī *m.* (*f.* 'yarạnā) *pl.* 'yaranōnī yellow (= rā̧wayạ).

yā̧rạntakạ *f.* (1) childhood. (2) childish ways.

yarara *Kt.* yanạ̄ kwạnce ~ he's lying tired, idly.

yarɓa A. (yarɓạ) *Vb.* 1A (1) flung down *x* yā ~ ni dạ ƙasā he flung me down (= kā dạ). (2) (*with dative*) (*a*) (i) *x* nā ~ masạ tạɓō I splashed him with mud. (ii) yā yarɓō mini tsụmmā he flicked, threw a wet cloth at me. (3) sun ~ masạ laifī they falsely accused him. (4) yā yarɓō manạ zāgi he abused us.

B. (yạrɓā) = zụrɓā 1b.

yarɓad dạ *Vb.* 4 (1) = yarɓạ 1. (2) *x* yā ~ tạɓō he splashed mud about. (3) yā ~ nī he cold-shouldered me.

yarɓālạ *Vb.* 1C = yarɓạ 2.

yarɓalad dạ *Vb.* 4 = yarɓad dạ.

yarɓalẹ *Vb.* 1C = yarɓẹ.

yarɓạnā *Vb.* 1C = yarɓạ 2.

Yarbancī *m.* (1) Yoruba language. (2) Yoruba ways (*cf.* Yarạbā).

Yarbāwā *Vd.* Bạyarabẹ.

yarɓe A. (yarɓẹ) *Vb.* 1A *x* (1) nā ~ shi dạ tạɓō I splashed him with mud (= yarɓạ 2a.i). (2) nā ~ hannūna I shook my hand to flick off the mud, etc.

B. (yạrɓē = yarɓē) *m.* flicking hand, etc., *as in* yarɓẹ 2.

yạrɓī *m.* *x* yā yi yạrɓī dạ nī = yarɓad dạ 3.

yarɓilā (1) what sloppy tūwō, soup ! (2) what sodden rags !

yarda A. (yạrdā) (1) (a) (i) consented x bā nạ̄ ~ I do not consent. (ii) agreed to x sun ~ n̩ tạfi they have agreed for me to go. yā ~ yạ yī = yā ~ zại yī he consented to do it. baị yạrdā sun̩ gamạ (= su̩ gamạ) fuskạ ba he was afraid to meet him face to face. (iii) kan zūcīyā tā ~ Vd. zūcīyā 1k. (iv) Vd. Allạ̄ 1b. (b) (i) x ban ~ dạ shī ba I don't approve of it, I don't agree to it, I don't like him, I don't trust him. shī baị yạrdā dạ kōwā ba he trusted nobody. mun ƙi yạrdā true as it is, it seems incredible. (ii) x ban ~ dạ ạ d̃ebẹ wani ạbu̩ ba dạgạ kāyansu̩ I don't agree to the removal of any of their property. (c) (dative) x ban yardar (= yardam) muku̩ ba I̩ don't agree to your doing it (= yardạ). (2) f. (a) consent. (b) ~ dạ arnẹ shī ya kāwō cin yan̩kansạ you cannot touch pitch without being defiled. (c) dạ yạrdar zūcīyā = dạ yạrdar rại willingly, voluntarily. (d) kīwan̩ yạrdā Vd. tạntabạrā. (e) bāwan̩ yạrdā Vd. bāwạ 12. (f) kāyan ~ Vd. cī 23.

B. (yardạ) Vb. 1A (with dative) x ban ~ muku̩ ba I don't agree to your doing it (= yạrdā 1c = yarjẹ).

yar dạ Vb. 4 = yā dạ.

yạrdajjēnīyā f. = yạrjējēnīyā.

yardar Vd. yạrdā 1c.

yạrdạtayyạ Sk. f. = yạrjējēnīyā.

yạ̄rē m. (1) x yā yi min̩i ~ he interpreted for me. (2) any language unknown to one (cf. yārạ).

yarfạ Vb. 1A = yarɓạ 2a.

yarfad dạ = yarɓad dạ.

yarfe = yarɓe.

yarfi̩ how well done !

yargạlā Vb. 1C x yā yargạlạ d̃an tsu̩mmā he dressed in rags.

yargạlē Vb. 3A (clothes) became ragged.

yargātū = yāgātū.

yarhạmu̩llāhu̩ Vd. barkạ 3.

yari A. (yạ̄rī) m. a fragrant, medicinal moss found on kanyạ.

B. (Yārị) (1) Yārị = Sarkin ~ Head of N.A. prison. (2) gidan ~ m. N.A. prison.

C. (yạrī) Eng. m. type of earring(s).

Yạrīmạ m. (1) one of the sạrautạ. (2) its holder (this sạrautạ is perquisite of son or younger brother of Emir).

Yarīmancī m. face-markings (askā) of the Bạyarīmẹ Filani (= billē 2).

Yarīmāwā Vd. Bạyarīmẹ.

Yarimcị m. = Yạrīmạ 1.

yạ̄rintā f. = yạ̄rạntakạ.

yārinyạ f. (fem. of yārọ) pl. 'yam mātā = yạ̄ram mātā (1) girl. (2) yākị 'yam mātā come here, girl ! (cf. sạmạ̄rī 2). (3) 'yam mātan̩ aurē Vd. aurē 6d. (4) shigar 'yam mātan̩ amạ̄rē f. entering of a number of people into presence of superior in a crowd instead of in file. (5) dāwạ tā yi 'yam mātā the guineacorn has been spoiled by rains ceasing too early. (6) Vd. Sarkin 'yam mātā.

yạriyạllē m. applying indigo (shūnī) plus oil to top of forehead by wives of men of position.

yạrjajjēnīyā = yạrjējēnīyā.

yarjẹ Vb. 1A (with dative) = yardạ.

yạrjējēnīyā f. (1) mutual consent. (2) mutual liking.

yarji̩ m. consent (= yạrdā 2).

yạrmandī m. piece of bark chewed together with potash by gamblers to render lucky the cowries put into the mouth before play.

yaro A. (yārọ) m. (f. yārinyạ q.v.) pl. yạ̄rā = yārōkī = Kt. yārōrī (1) (a) boy. (b) ~ dạ hu̩lā, babba dạ hu̩lā, girman 'yan dinyā what is the use of persons so different imitating each other ! (c) Kt. ~ bābu̩ tạmbayạ hūlū (= jạ̄kī) nẹ̄ a youth relying on his own strength without charms, is a nit- wit. (d) tunnuƙū (= murtuƙū) fad̃an̩ ịblīsai, ~ baị ganī ba, ballē yạ rabạ (i) what smoke ! (ii) what a quarrel ! (e) bạ̄ kāyan ~ ba nẹ̄ it's expensive, difficult. (f) ~ bā yạ d̃aukạn ~ nobody should attempt what is beyond him. (g) ~ dăi ~ nẹ̄ a boy's ways are childish. (h) (i) yu̩n̩wạ ita ta kạm mai dạ ~ tsōfō, kọshī shī ya kạm mai dạ tsōfō ~ hunger reduces one's powers just as good food helps one on. (ii) tsōfō maị kud̃ī yārọ nẹ̄ Vd. tsōfō 1h. (j) dạ rạrrạfē ~ ya kạn tāshị from little

acorns mighty oaks arise. (k) ạiki ~
ịndạ ya sō, kā ga saurinsạ the willing
horse is the best worker. (l) ~ bā
gạrājē tsōfō nẹ a spineless boy is useless.
(m) dạ ạ ƙwācẹ ~ rịgā, gāra ạ jā, tạ
ƙēcẹ it's better for your property to
deteriorate than to be robbed of it.
(n) bā ā ƙwācẹ wạ ~ gạrmā what a
stupid and pointless act ! (o) ~ mạŋ
kāzā ; in yā ji rānā, sǎi yạ narkẹ
the young have no staying-power. (p)
ạbịn dạ bạbba ya ganī yanā ƙasạ, ~
kō yā hau rīmī, bạ zại gan shị ba young
P. lacks the judgment of his elders.
(q) ~ yā sō aurē, gidansụ bābụ gōdīyā
one must exercise patience. (r) ~
shā rūwā dǎidǎi dạ cikịŋkạ don't try
what is beyond you ! (s) yāran zạmānị,
tum bạ sụ tạfasạ ba, su kạŋ ƙōnẹ
modern youth wants to run before it
can walk. (t) yārọ dạ gārī, ạbōkin
tạfīyạr mạnyā this is a lad with ability
of an adult. (u) yārọ yā bi, bại sanị ba
Vd. turbạ. (v) wāsā dạ yārọ shī kẹ
kāwō rēnị don't act in an undignified
manner ! (w) rạkạ yārọ Vd. rakạ 1c.
(x) bǎi yārā shūnī Vd. warƀā 2b. (y)
kai yārā makasā Vd. tụŋkū 1e. (z)
yārọ yā tsịnci wurị Vd. tsịntā 2b. (z) (i)
sǎi kuɗin yārọ sụ gazạ Vd. sainạ. (z) (ii)
ta sāfē ta yārọ Vd. sāfē. (z) (iii) mūgụn
yārọ Vd. mūgụ 1c. (z) (iv) yārọ bại
san yārọ nē shī ba sǎi an yi wāsam bugụŋ
wuyạ pride comes before a fall. (z) (v)
kinā bā yārā tsọrō Vd. gịzākā. (z) (vi)
Vd. aŋgarā. (z) (vii) hạukạtạ ~ Vd.
zaƙạmī ; bạmmī. (z) (viii) jārịn ~
Vd. dạfūwā 1d. (z) (ix) ~ dākạtā Vd.
dākạtā. (z) (x) kim fi ƙarfin yārọ Vd.
gabārạ. (2) (a) servant. (b) yārạŋ
ạlkālī Vd. ạlkālī 8. (3) yārọ bā ƙashī
(a) type of soft insect. (b) slacker
(= tạƀā ni luƀus). (4) yārọ bā ƙyūyā (a)
thatching-needle. (b) = cạŋkō 2. (5)
yārọ dạ ƙōƙarī dumpling of bulrush-
millet flour. (6) yārọ dạ mandā = sā
bạbba sātạ. (7) yārọ dạ mōrīyā type of
tiny cake(s). (8) Vd. jan ~.

B.(yārō) Sk. f. = ƙanẹ 3 x yārōna
my bridesmaid.

C. (Yarọ) = yerọ.

yarō-yarō (1) dạ tsụmmā ~ mukạ gan

shị we saw him in rags. (2) yā jiƙẹ ~
he was soaked to the skin.

yartạnī m. plait of thread (abāwā), etc.,
fixed for adornment to forehead-hair of
woman (= kalaŋkūwā 4).

Yaruƀāwā Vd. Bạyaruƀẹ.

'yarūwā Vd. ɗạŋūwā.

yạryāɗạ Vd. sạkatạ 1b.

yạryādī m. (1) the convolvulus Ipomœa
sp. (= bitạ wutā). (2) the twiner
Vigna luteola which ruins crops, cf.
ƙudụjī (Vd. ƙwācē 3).

yar-yar A. (yạr-yạr) (1) = yạl-yạl. (2)
rūwā yanā zubọwā ~ the water is
trickling out slowly.

B. (yar-yar) Vd. ɗịŋkịn ~.

yasa A. (yāsạ) Vb. 1A (1) yā ~ rījịyā he
cleaned out the well. (2) Vd. tạttagạ 2.

B. (yāsā) (1) Vb. 2 (p.o. yāshē, n.o.
yāshi) (a) = yāsạ. (b) = yā dạ. (2) (a)
act of cleaning out well. (b) gūgan ~
bā dạ shī a kạn shā rūwā ba when
people prosper they get rid of their
trusty old servitors.

yāsad dạ Vb. 4 = yā dạ.

yas dạ Vb. 4 = yā dạ.

yashe A. (yāshẹ) Vb. 1A (1) (a) = yāsạ.
(b) kạmar mụtụm yạ tịŋkāri kōgī,
yạ cẹ zại ~ it is like pouring water into
a sieve. (2) deprived P. of all his
possessions.

B. (yāshē) Vd. yā dạ.

C. (yāshē) Vd. yāsā.

D. (yāshe) (noun of state from yāsā)
x gā shi naŋ ~ here it is thrown away,
isolated (Vd. yāsā 1b).

yashi A. (yāshī) m. (1) (a) coarse (river)
sand (cf. rāirạyī). (b) kōmē zurfin
rūwā dạ ~ ạ cikī there's an end to all
things. (c) Yāshī mại rūwā kusa (said
by marōƙā) how generous you are ! (d)
ɗam banzā ~ nẹ Vd. banzā 4c. (2)
Kt. water-hole in stream-bed.

B. (yāshi) Vd. yāsā.

C. (yāshị) Eng. m. ace.

Yāsịŋ Vd. gāgarạ 16.

yaskạ m. trifles (x kola-nuts, cowries, etc.).

yāsōsọ Sk. m. = wāsōsọ.

yātī Vd. tātī.

yātsạ m., f. (pl. yātsōtsī = yātsū). (1)
(a) (i) finger (= Sk. farcẹ 1b). (ii) yā
kafạ yātsū ạ garịŋ it (army) stood firm

in the town. (iii) bā mai ∼ ba *Vd.*
gayya 2. (*b*) babban ɗan ∼ thumb. (*b*)
autan ∼ *m.* little-finger (= ƙurī 2*a*).
(2) yātsun 'yan Sarkī = hannun 10.
(3) ∼ bīyar type of leaf imported from
the east [used in brew to facilitate
accouchement) (= hannū 6). (4) yātsū
green-leather adornment of sūkā 7
or ɓallīyā 2.

yatsina A. (yātsina) *f.* (1) grimace due to
pain or haughtiness (*cf.* yauƙī 2). (2)
the sheen of shot-silk, karammuskī,
etc. (*cf.* yauƙī 3).
    B. (yātsinā) *Vb.* 1C yā yātsina
fuska = durɓunā.
yātsinē *Vb.* 3A = durɓuna.
yātsōtsī, yātsū *Vd.* yātsa.
yatū-yatū *Kt. m.* = dangarēzā.
yau A. (yau) (1) (*a*) yau = a yau to-day.
(*b*) yau yau this very day. (*c*) *x* ∼ shēkara ukụ kē nan da ta zō it is 3 years
since she came. ∼ shēkara gōma da
aka gan sụ sǎi . . . when they were seen
ten years ago then . . . ∼ shēkarum
birnī 1,000 da kafāwā it is 1,000 years
since the town was founded. ∼ kwānā
kaman nawa mukē saurāre we've been
waiting many days for news. ∼ bai
yi shēkara bīyū ba suka zō it is
not two years since they came. tun
ran da ya kāma ni ∼ shēkarata ukụ
kē nan it is 3 years since he captured
me. garin ∼ shēkararsa 1,000 da
gināwā the town is 1,000 years old.
∼ shēkara ɗarī (= ∼ shēkara ɗarī kē
nan) sukē riƙe da ƙasar they have been
in possession of the country for 100
years (*for sense* ago, *Vd.* wuce 1, yī 5*A*).
(*d*) har ∼ = har wa ∼ up to the
present time. (*e*) (i) har ∼ (= har
ilā ∼) da wani abụ there's still something else (= yanzu 4). akwai wata
hanya har wa ∼ there's also another
method. (ii) har wa ∼ kumā moreover
x har ∼ kumā yā yiwu . . . moreover it
is possible that . . . (*f*) a cī ∼, a cī
gōbe, shī nē cī put by something for a
rainy day ! (*g*) bā ∼ ba *Vd.* tsōfō 1*d*.
(*h*) marashin ∼ *Vd.* marashī 2, rashi
1*o*. (*j*) matsīyācin ∼ *Vd.* matsīyācī 4.
(*k*) a yī ∼ *Vd.* a 1*b*. (*l*) ɗauka kō ∼ kō
gōbe *Vd.* ambụtā 2, dami 2. (*m*) ∼

kā faɗa mākwī *Vd.* faɗa 2*c*. (*n*) ∼
shūnī *Vd.* farī 2*g*.iii. (2) yau da gōbe
adv. little by little *x* (*a*) yau da gōbe
kā īya you'll gradually be able to do it.
(*Vd.* kwānā 8). (*b*) " Idọ, wā ka rēna " ;
" wanda nikē ganī yau da gōbe " familiarity breeds contempt. (*c*) yau da gōbe ita
kē hana turba haƙi traffic keeps a road
clear. (*d*) yau da gōbe ita cē ta ƙāre
hatsin tukunyā supplies gradually come
to an end : nobody's patience is
eternal (*cf.* hatsī 3*a*). (*e*) yau da gōbe
kāyan Allā we are in God's hands.
(*f*) yau da gōbe bai bar kōmē ba nothing
lasts for ever. (*g*) yau da gōbe, jībi
gwanin rawā yā fāɗi pride comes before
a fall. (3) yi ta ∼ *Vd.* yi. (4) 'yar ∼
f. (*a*) bean-flour cake. (*b*) *Kt.* = waina.
    B. (yau) (1) *m.* (*a*) (i) saliva. (ii)
da jinī a baka a kan zubad da farin ∼
men being what they are, one must
learn to pardon. (iii) yā tsirtad da ∼
he foamed with rage. (iv) *Vd.* arne 3.
(*b*) yam barcī dribbling by sleeper
(= *Kt.* salēɓa 2). (*c*) mai da yanka *Vd.*
mai da 1*j*. (*d*) da yansa aka yī it was
done by his permission. (2) = ap.
yauci A. (yaucī) *m.* lateness.
    B. (yaucī) *m.* (1) Allā ya bā mu ∼
God prolong our lives ! (2) mu tafi
wurinsa, mu yi ∼ let's go to his place
for a chat ! (= hīrā 1).
'yauci = 'yanci.
yau da *Vb.* 4 yā ∼ ni = yā yaushē ni
he deceived me (= yaudara).
yaudara (1) *Vb.* 2 *x* yā yaudarē ni he
deceived me (= yau da). (2) *f.* (*a*)
(*with pl.* yaudarōrī) trickery. (*b*) ɗan ∼
m. (*f.* 'yar ∼) *pl.* 'yan ∼ trickster *x*
yāƙi ɗan ∼ nē war is a tricky
business.
yaudō *m.* = karkashī.
yauƙaƙa A. (yauƙaƙa) *Vb.* 3B lasted long.
    B. (yauƙaƙā) *Vb.* 1C caused to last
long.
    C. (yauƙāƙā) *Vd.* yayyauƙā.
yauƙī *m.* (1) sliminess (of okro, etc.). (2)
haughty look (*cf.* yātsina). (3) silk
material *x* yā shiga ∼ he has put on
silk clothing, *cf.* yātsina. (4) being long-
lasting (= danƙo 2*b*).
yauni A. (yaunī) *m.* type of large fish.

B. (yaunī) *Nor. m.* heaviness (= nauyī).

yaurī = yąwwā.

yausasa A. (yausąsā) *Vb.* 1C. (1) caused to wither. (2) caused P. to feel weak.

B. (yausasą) *Vb.* 3B (1) withered. (2) P. felt weak.

yaushe A. (yąushę) (1) (*a*) when ? *x* yā tąfi ⁓ when did he go ? (Mod. Gram. 160*a*). ⁓ suką tąfi Baucī when did they go to Bauchi ? (Mod. Gram. 160*b*). (*b*) ⁓ darąŋ ya yī har shąsshāwą takę ɓatą is it right that prosperity should make you despise your friends ? : how can such a threadbare excuse deceive ? (2) *Vd.* kōyąushē, bąyąushē.

B. (yaushē) *Vd.* yau dą.

yaushī *m.* (1) yā yi ⁓ = yąusasą. (2) *Vd.* yuŋwą 1*a*.

yąutā *Vb.* 3A (1) went for a stroll. (2) went to have a chat with P. (3) yąuta mini kądaŋ wait a moment for me ! (4) *Vd.* yąutą kuyąŋgī.

yautad dą *Vb.* 4 delayed, hindered.

yautăi *m.* (1) Standard-winged Nightjar (*Macrodypteryx longipennis*). (2) Long-tailed Nightjar (*Scotornis climacurus*). (3) *Vd.* bị ni ką lālącē 3.

• yąutą kuyąŋgī *m.* redness of sun just before setting (= rųd̃ą kuyąŋgī).

yąuwā *Vd.* yąwwā.

yąu-yau = yąyyau.

yawa A. (yawą) *m.* (1) (*a*) abundance. (*b*) sun yi yawąn na Masąr they are as many as those of Egypt. (*c*) sun nūną mają yawą they out-numbered us. (*d*) yawąnsų, wąnē yawąmmų they are far more numerous than ourselves. (*e*) *Vd.* wāwan yawą. (*f*) yā yi ⁓ it is much, too much *x* aikị yā yi minị ⁓ I have too much work. (*g*) *x* gyądā tā fi ⁓ ą Kano at Kano there are more ground-nuts than anything else. (*h*) an yi ⁓ ą wuriŋ the place was crowded. (*j*) tūwō yā yi yawą *Vd.* tūwō 21. (2) mai ⁓ much *x* hatsī mai ⁓ much corn. (3) dą ⁓ much, many *x* (*a*) mutąnē dą ⁓ many people. hatsī dą ⁓ much corn. wad̃ansu mąkąrąntū dą yawą many schools. (*b*) *x* dą ⁓ cikinsų suŋ gąurayą dą Tūrąwā many of them are mixed with Europeans.

(4) Sarkin ⁓ yā fi Sarkiŋ k̃arfī it's better to have backers than •to be strong. (5) kōwā ya k̃i ⁓ Allą yą k̃ī shị God helps him who helps himself. (6) yawąn rą̃i mągąnin ąllōbā if you are gifted with nine lives nothing can harm you (= turmī 1*d*). (7) yawąŋ kallō ya kąn jāwō rēnị = dą̃misą 2. (8) (*a*) ą banzā, yawą bą dādī abundant but inferior. (*b*) *cf.* dādī 1*f*.

B. (yāwā) *f.* fibre obtained from beans, kūką, etc.

C. (yąwā) *f.* (1) (*used in* ząurąncē) stroll (= yāwǫ). (2) *Kt* = iwā 1.

D. (yāwą) *Vb.* 1A wandered through *x* yā ⁓ k̃asā duką = yā ⁓ cikiŋ k̃asā duką he travelled through the whole country.

yawaicī *m.* = yawancī.

yawaita A. (yąwaitą) *Vb.* 3B increased.

B. (yawąitā) *Vb.* 1C increased T. *x* kadą ką yawąitą mąganą do not talk too much ! bą zā ą yawąitą mąganąrsą ba not much will be talked about it. zą̃ ą fi yawąitą lą̃bāriŋ Hąusāwā bisą gą na Tūrąwā more time will be devoted to Hausa affairs than to European matters.

yawancī (1) *m.* majority. (2) *adv. x* sū yawancī sun sākę iriŋ ąddīninsų for the most part, they have changed their religion.

yawanta = yawaita.

yą̃warā *Sk. f.* (1) = kilishī. (2) preparing 1.

yāwątā *Vb.* 3A = yąutā.

yawa-yawa *m.* = yawancī.

yāwę *Vb.* 1A = yāwą.

yawo A. (yāwǫ) (1) (*a*) (i) stroll *x* yā tąfi ⁓ he has gone for a stroll. (ii) yaną̃ yāwąnsą he's out for a stroll. (iii) aŋ kāwō musų yāwǫ dą jirą̃gyan samą they were raided by aeroplanes. (*b*) mai ⁓ idle stroller about (*his epithet is* rūwan darē mai gamą gari). (*c*) (i) ya kąn rik̃ą ⁓ dą mąganą he never sticks to the point. (*d*) yā d̃auki haŋkąlintą, yaną̃ ⁓ dą shī he told her a pack of lies. (2) (*a*) (i) journey on foot. (ii) sun zō yāwąn shąŋ iską they have come for a holiday. (*b*) yāwąŋ k̃auyę *Vd.* k̃auyę 1*d*. (3) gąmą kąsūwā dą

yāwǫ *Vd.* rūwā B.9 (4) *Vd.* tāsānī 2.
(4) *Vd.* yāwǫn-*compounds*, yāwō.
  B. (yāwō) *Yor. f.* Yoruba woman
(*epithet is* Yāwō mai yawan yāwǫ).
yāwon-*compounds* (1) yāwan amāna extortion in villages by Chiefs, etc. (*Vd.*
gabazga). (2) yāwam bal-bal = yāwan
gīlǫ idle roving (*cf.* bal-bal). (3) yāwan
jākai meandering about the town. (4)
yāwan ƙauyę *Vd.* ƙauyę 1*d*. (5) yāwam
bāƙō *Vd.* darē 1*a*.ii.
yawu A. (yāwū) *Zar.* = yau.
  B. (yāwū) *Katagum* to-day = yau *q.v.*
Yāwurī *Vd.* banzā.
yawwā (1) bravo ! (= mā shā Allāhu). (2)
reply to greeting. (3) *Vd.* riƙa 1*c*.
yaya A.1 (yāyā) *m., f. (pl.* yayyē =
yayyū = *Sk.* yāyū = *Sk.* yannī = *Kt.*
yannai). (1) (*a*) elder brother (= wā 1*d*).
(*b*) elder sister (= yā). (*c*) *cf.* wā,
yayyē. (*d*) friend older than oneself.
(2) Yāyā (*a*) girl's name. (*b*) *Vd.*
īya 1*c*. (*c*) *name given by man to his
daughter whose real name is that of
his elder sister.* (*d*) *second and other
wives call and refer to the senior wife*
(ūwar gidā) *as* Yāyā, *and junior wives
refer tō the second wife as* Yāyā ƙaramā.
(*e*) *concubines refer to wives as* Yāyā
followed by the name x Yāyā Ƙande.
(*f*) *cf.* Filāni 2. (*g*) *a wife speaking to
her husband's brother, says* Yāyā *and
uses that word when referring to
her husband's* elder *sister.* (*h*) *husband or wife referring to the parents
of the other, use* īya = Gwaggo
= Inna = Yāyā *for the mother, and*
Bappa = Abba = Bāba *for father.* (*j*)
Vd. babba 5*a*.
  A.2 (yāyā) *Vb.* 2 (1) (*a*) gathered
(fodder-grass) *x* nā yāyi būdū (*Vd.*
būdū), *cf.* yāyę, yāyi. (*b*) sā manjagara
ka ~ do you think money grows on the
tops of trees ! (*c*) sun yāyi gudummawā they moved up reinforcements.
(2) zūciyāta tā yāyi haki I am feeling
angry. (3) yā yāyi tunjērē he got
syphilis.
  A.3 (yāyā) *f.* (1) yā yi ~ yau he
(cadger) was lucky to-day. (2) *Sk.*
hubbub (= hayānīyā). (3) *Kt.* quarrelling (= fada).

  D. (yāya) (1) *f.* (*a*) = yāyā A.1 1*b*.
(*b*) neighing (= hanīnīya). (*c*) yāya =
ta yāya hubbub (= hayānīya). (2)
m. = yāyā A.1 1*a, d*.
  E. (yāya) (1) how ? *x* (*a*) ~ zā ka
yi ka bī mu how will you manage to
follow us ? ~ zā ka cę masa what have
you got to say to this surprising news ?
~ aka yi ban ji ba how is it that I did
not hear of it ? = ƙāƙa *q.v.* (*b*) (i)
~ mukē how are you ? (*Vd.* ƙāƙa).
(ii) yāya ka ƙāra jī do you feel any
better ? (*c*) ~ zā mu yi da shī what are
we to do with it ? (2) (*a*) kō ~ = ta
kō ~ however, no matter in what
way = kōƙāƙa *q.v.* (*b*) kō yāya :zā
a yī how can it be done ? (*Vd.* kō 2*d*).
(3) dā mā yāya lāfīyar kūrā, ballē
ta yi hauka things were bad enough
before, so what will they be like now ?
  F. (yā yā) *used in* (1) ~ da ƙanan
wani devil take the hindmost ! (2)
mun yō ~ da ƙanan wani we came at
full speed.
'yā'yā = 'yā'yā'yē (*pl. of* dā, 'yā). (1) (*a*)
children. (*b*) sons. (*c*) daughters. (*d*)
fruit, berries, etc. (*e*) *Vd.* dā, 'yā,
'yam mātā. (*f*) uku da ~ three and a
bit. biyar da ~ five and a bit (= ragī
q.v.). (*g*) wata tana furē, wata tana ~
one blessed thing keeps turning up
after another. (*h*) kāzā mai ~ ita kē
gudun shirwa the P. of property is the
one who hates risks. (2) 'yā'yan
Gwamna descendants born after 1903
to slaves who have not claimed their
freedom. (3) small plaits on woman's
head when hair not enough to make
long plait. (4) draughtsmen, *Vd.*
dara, kwadǫ. (5) 'yā'yan rānā = ka-
walwalnīyā.
yaye A. (yāyę) (1) *Vb.* 1A (*a*) (i) weaned *x*
tā ~ danta she weaned her lad (= laifī
1*b*.ii). kāzā tā ~ 'yan tsākī the hen has
ceased tending her chicks. (ii) *Vd.*
a ~ lāfīya. (*b*) cleared (harāwa, karmāmī, karā) from farm to prevent
goats eating them (*cf.* yāyā A.2,
yāyi). (*c*) uncovered *x* (i) yā ~ haƙōrā = yāƙę 1*a*. (ii) = kwārę 1*a*.i.
(iii) yā ~ rawaninsa he took off his
turban without unwinding it. (iv)

yā ⁓ tufānīyā he removed the mat-screen. (v) yā ⁓ ni he has given me the cold shoulder (= yā dạ). (d) removed entirely x (i) ɓạrāwọ yā ⁓ dākị the thief made a clean sweep of the house (cf. wāshẹ 1a). yā ⁓ manạ ạɓọkaŋ gạbammụ it (battle) has relieved us of our enemies. igīyạr rūwā tā ⁓ su the current swept them away. (ii) Vd. duhụ 1b. (2) Vb. 3A (a) itạcan nạŋ yā ⁓ the fruit of this tree are over till next season. kunyạ tā ⁓ tsạkānimmụ shyness between us has disappeared. tsọrō yā ⁓ fear has vanished. (b) ɓạkīnā yā ⁓ (i) inside of my mouth is skinned. (ii) Kt. = wāshẹ 2a.

B. (yạ̄yẹ) m. (1) (a) act of weaning. (b) gwaurō dạ yạ̄yẹ Vd. shịga 1g.ii. (c) Vd. gudụn ⁓. (2) seedling(s) for transplanting (cf. dạshẹ 4a). (3) = būdū.

yayi A. (yāyị) m. sparse grass ; fag-ends fallen off tree round it or at road-side ; odds and ends of grass (often gathered and used for making fire), cf. yạ̄yā A.2, yāyẹ.

B. (yạ̄yī) m. (1) (a) time (= lōkạcī) x wạnẹ ⁓ sukạ zọ at what time did they come ? yạ̄yin sạrautạ tasạ during his reign. (b) x yạ̄yin dạ sukạ zō when they came (= lōkạcịn dạ). dạ yạ̄yịn dạ ya tāshị, sãi sukạ tāshị they left at the same time as he did. (2) (a) fashion x anạ̄ yạ̄yin rīgunạ gowns are fashionable. (b) ạɓin dạ ya zō, shī akẹ ⁓ at Rome do as Rome does ! (3) mai ⁓ m. = mạshasshãrā 1b. (4) Kt. yạ̄yịŋ Garbạ type of Native-made cloth. (5) yạ̄yịŋ Indō type of bead. (6) yạ̄yin 'yar Dạ̄dā type of coiffure. (7) Vd. aŋgalē 2.

yayọ Kt. m. = fạ̄rū 1b.

yāyū Vd. yạ̄yā A.1, wạ̄.

yayyafa A. (yayyạfā) Vb. 1C sprinkled (x water to allay dust), cf. yāfạ 2c.

B. (yayyạfā) f. (1) = yayyafī. (2) sprinkling T. with water, etc. (3) form of acne (cf. ɓạn ni dạ mūgụ).

yayyafī m. (1) drizzle (= tsattsafī 1a), cf. yāfạ 2e. (2) dạ ⁓ kọ̄gī kạn cika many a mickle makes a muckle. (3) nā yi gudụn ⁓ nā shịga mạ̄mākọ out of the frying-pan into the fire.

yayyau = dạ yạyyau adv. afterwards (cf. yayyaucī).

yayyau dạ Vb̃ 4 = yau dạ.

yayyaucī m. lateness (= yaucī).

yạyyaukā m., f. (pl. yaukạ̄kā) (1) slimy (x of okro, etc.). (2) silkily soft (cf. yaukī 3).

yayyautad dạ Vb. 4 = yau dạ.

'ya'yyạ̄wā = 'yạ'yyāwạ f. (1) small, poor corn-stalks, bean-stalks, etc., cut for fodder near harvest-time (= ɓai-ɓāyā = kakkaryā), cf. karmāmī 2. (2) shoots at base of corn (cf. hanɗūwā).

yayye A. (yayyẹ) Vb. 3A. (1) (a) leaked out. (b) mutạ̄nē sun ⁓ dạgạ garī people have left the town. (2) leaked into.

B. (yạyyẹ) (1) (said by female) pal ! (used addressing ƙawā older than her-self : latter's reply is ƙạnnē). (2) Vd. wạ̄, yạ̄yā.

yạyyō m. (1) leaking, dripping. (2) kōwā yā sạŋ ịndạ dākịnsạ yakẹ ⁓ everyone knows where the shoe pinches (= mā-lạmī 1f).

yạyyū Vd. wạ̄, yạ̄yā.

yāzāwā f. under-shrub whose juice was used to make black lines on face or body of slaves, skin afterwards sloughing.

yazgā Kt. f. = izgā.

yāzūzukạ Vd. yājị.

yẹ̄ used in (1) mū ⁓ mū people of our class (= yị mū yị mū = yạ mū yạ mū = Sk. mū wạ mu = Sk. wạ mū wạ mū). kū ⁓ kū people of your status (= yị kū yị kū = etc.). sū yẹ̄ sū people of the same trade as they (= yị sū yị sū, etc.), cf. kaifī 1ciii, gur-guzū 2.

yēhọ Sk. = wōhọ.

yēkū̃wā f. proclamation (= shẹ̄lạ).

Yerọ (1) = Dābọ. (2) cf. yārọ.

yi A. (yī) Vb. 5 (1) (a) (i) did. (ii) sun sạ̄mi aikịn yị they've found work to be done. (iii) mun yi īyạ̄kar yịmmụ we did our level best. yā kạmātạ sụ yī, īyạ̄kar yaddạ yakẹ yiwũwā they must do it with all their might. (iv) sun tsayạ kōmē akẹ yị, ạ yi they're deter-mined to resist to the last. yanạ̄ sọ ạ yī, kōmē akẹ̃, ạ yī he wants it done at all costs. (v) bại yi kōmē dạ shī ba he did nothing to him. sun yi musụ

yạddạ sukạ yi dạ nĩ they did to them
the same thing as they did to me. (vii)
yi ta *Vd*. ta B.1 2 *x* mụ yi ta yị let us
get to work ! (viii) ạ yi yau, ạ yi gọbe,
shĩ nẹ aikị perseverance conquers. (ix)
im bã kạ yị *Vd*. wurĩ 1*c*.v, gạba 3*a*.iii. (x)
ƙạ̃ƙạ nakạ̃ yị *m. x* sun zamẹ minị ƙạ̃ƙạ
nakạ̃ yị they are a thorn in the flesh to me
(= ƙạ̃ nikạ̃ yị). (xi) waccẹ zã ạ yi *Vd*.
wạndạ 2*b*. (xii) suŋ kãmạ gạbansụ,
im bã kạ̃ yị, bạ̃ ni wurĩ they fled
helter-skelter. (*b*) (*verb can be omitted*)
(i) *after auxiliary verbs x* yã fãrạ
mạganạ = yã fãrạ yịm mạganạ he
began to speak. ta kạn riƙạ waŋkã =
ta kạn riƙạ yịŋ waŋkã she keeps
taking baths. (ii) *before dative x*
am masạ haifũwã = an yi masạ haifũwã a child was born to him zai
masạ (= zại yi masạ) tạĩmakõ he'll
help him. ạ diŋgạ masạ (= ạ diŋgạ
yi masạ) mạganạ one must keep on
speaking to him ! (iii) *in subjunctive
of* yĩ *prefixed to noun to form verbal
sense x* yã sạ̃ sụ gudụm (= yã sạ̃ sụ
yi gudụm) mịl shidạ he caused them
to run six miles. (*c*) (*in progressive of*
yĩ *prefixed to noun to form verbal sense,*
yị *is omitted,* Mod. Gram. 159) *x* (i)
yã yi yãƙị dạ sũ he made war on them.
yanạ̃ yãƙị dạ sũ he is at war with them.
yã yi shãfam baŋgõ he whitewashed
the wall. yanạ̃ shãfam baŋgõ he's
whitewashing the wall. gọbe zạn yi
zạ̃nẽ to-morrow I'll do patterning.
munạ̃ zạ̃nansạ we're patterning it.
yã yi baudĩyã he swerved. bã yạ̃
baudĩyã he is not swerving. mun yi
gọ̃dĩyã we were grateful. munạ̃ gọ̃dĩyã
we're grateful. an yi rũwã it rained.
anạ̃ rũwa it is raining. yã yi aikị he
worked. yanạ̃ aikị he is working. (ii)
(*but in progressive, where there is also
dative,* yi *is optional*) *x* yã yi matạ
ạlhẽrị he's treated her well. yanạ̃ matạ
ạlhẽrị = yanạ̃ yi matạ ạlhẽrị he's
treating her well. ạ yi wạ hanyạ
nõmã let the road be weeded ! anạ̃
wạ hanyạ nõmã = anạ̃ yi wạ hanyạ
nõmã the road is being weeded. (*d*) an
yi masạ gidã he has got married. (*e*)
gạrĩ yã yi gạrĩ *Vd*. garĩ 3*d*. (*f*) yã yi

girmã he is big. tã yi girmã she is big.
sun yi girirrimã they're big (*Vd*.
girmã). (*g*) dạ̃ an yi wani Ŝarkĩ once
upon a time there was a Chief. dạ̃
an yi wani mụtụm wạndạ . . . once
upon a time there was a man who . . .
(*h*) yạ̃yạ akạ yi bạn ji bạ ? how is it
that I did not hear about it ? (*j*)
ƙạ̃ƙạ zạn yi dạ shĩ what am I to do to
him ? ; what am I to do about it ?
(*k*) mẹ ya yi masạ zại bã mụ why should
he give it to us ? (*kk*) Kụ yĩ *name for
dog*. (*l*) yã yi sulẹ ukụ it is worth three
shillings, it costs three shillings. (*m*)
jạwãbin takạrdarkụ ạbar yi wạ tãrihạ
23 dạ Sha'ạbaŋ in reply to your letter
dated 23rd of Shaban. (*n*) yã yi darẽ
he arrived there after dark. yã yiwõ
darẽ he arrived here after dark (*cf*.
yạŋkã 5). (*o*) yã yi duhụ he has gone blind
(*cf*. 7). (*p*) A bại yi B ba A is not equal
to B ; A is not as big as B (= yị 1*b*).
fãḍintạ yã yi fãḍiŋ ƙasarmụ its breadth
is equal to that of our own country.
(*q*) yã yi wạ kạnsạ he brought it on
himself. (2) went towards *x* yã yi
ƙõƙạ he went towards the door. yã
yi gạba went forwards. sãi kạ yi bãya
go backwards ! yã yi yạmmã he went
westwards. kụ yi wạjẹ go outside !
mun yi kudụ we went south. (3) *Vd*.
yĩ dạ, ĩ dạ, yịwú. (4) took *x* yã yiwõ
kãyã he has brought the loads. (5)
spent time *x* yã yi watạ ukụ ạ Kano
he spent three months at Kano. (5*A*)
since *x* yạu bại yi shẽkarạ bĩyũ ba sukạ
zõ it is not more than two years since
they came ˙ (*Vd*. yạu 1*c*). (6) (*verb
doubled*). (*a*) (i) nã yĩ, nã yĩ yạ fịta,
nã kãsạ I tried my hardest to move it
out but failed. nã yĩ, nã yĩ, yã ƙĩ
Ị did my best to persuade him but he
refused. sun yĩ, sun yĩ wai sụ kãmạ shi
they did their best to capture him, but
in vain. (ii) sun yĩ sụ karyạ mu they
(enemy) did their best to smash us. (*b*)
mẹ akạ yi, akạ yi Audụ Audu is of no
importance. (7) occurred *x* (*a*) (i) duhụ
yã yĩ = yã yi duhụ = an yi duhụ = anạ̃
duhụ = gạrĩ yã yi duhụ night has fallen
(*cf*. 1*o*). yã yi duhụ ƙiriŋ it is pitch-dark.
ḍakin naŋ yã yi duhụ this is a dark

room. **kadą ką yi minį duhu** don't stand there blocking out my light ! (ii) **darē yā yī** night has fallen. **darē yaną yį** night's falling. **darē yā yi musu** night caught them on the road. (iii) **lōkącin ąbincī yā yī** it is meal-time. **ąbincī yā yī** food is ready. **ązahąr tā yī** it is about 2 p.m. **wąląhā tā yī** it is between 9 and 10 a.m. **ąsubāhį yā yī** it is already just before sunrise. **rānā tā yī** the sun is well up. **rānā tanā yį** the sun is rising high. (iv) **gwandąn nąn bą tą yi ba tukunā** this pawpaw is not yet ripe. (v) **yā yi haką** it's right, so. **dąbārąrką bą tą yi ba kę nan** your plan has not succeeded. (vi) **ąlhērįn dą Allą ya yi masą, yā yi masą bakī kirin** the benefits conferred on him by God seemed to him nothing but a cause of sadness. (vii) **ąbu yā yī** things went well. **haką bą ząi yi ba** used in this way it will not be serviceable. (viii) **in sun yi haką, kōmē yā yī** if they do this, all will be O.K. (ix) **kōmē ta yī** whatever happens. (x) **kąm sāmun hądą̄-hadā yą yi kąmar dą, sāi wani īkwąn Allą** it will be only by a miracle if the ground-nut trade ever reaches its former level. (b) *Vd.* **yį 1b.**

B. (**yį**) (1) like *x* (a) **yi minį kujęrā ∼ wannąn** make me a chair like this one ! (= *Sk.* **wą 3a**). (b) A **bąi yi ∼ B ba** A is not equal to B, A is not as big as B (= **yī 1p**), *cf.* **yī 7**. (c) **nī ∼ shī, shī ∼ nī** he and I are equal in wealth, etc. **kai ∼ nī, nī ∼ kai** between you and me there is not a pin to choose. (d) **in ąn yį gōbe sallą** if, for example, to-day is the day preceding the festival. (dd) **bąkī yą bōkā** *Vd.* **bąkī 1b.ix.** (e) (i) **mū yį mū = mū yę mū** *q.v. under* **yę.** (ii) **wannąn nāmu nē yį mū yį mū** this is ours and ours alone. **bą ą fadą wą kōwā ba sāi yį sū yį sū** they alone were told. (f) **rānā ∼ ta yau = in rānā ∼ ta yau** = *Kt.* **rānā yą ta yau** = *Sk.* **rānā wą ta yau** this day week. **ząi zō nąn rānā ∼ ta jīyą** he'll come here a week from yesterday. **rānā ∼ ta jīyą suką zō nąn** they came here a week yesterday. **tā zō nąn rānā ∼ ta yau** she came here a week ago (g) *Vd.* **į, zūwą**

2c, yę. (h) (*noun repeated with* **yą** *between*) *x* (i) **mutum yą mutum** *Vd.* **mutum 7.** **wadansu gąrī yą gąrī sun tafō** the people of town after town came in. (ii) *Vd.* **yą 3b.** (j) ∼ **kantu** *Vd.* **dįre.** (k) **yā ji į jį** *Vd.* **jī 4j.** (2) let him *x* **yį zō** let him come ! (= **yą**).

yī dą slandered *x* **sun ∼ nī** they defamed me. **suną yį dą ita** they are slandering her.

yifa (**yifą**) *Vb.* 1A put on temporarily *x* **bą ni rīgąr n ∼** give me the gown to throw over myself ! **yā ∼ zānā** he covered it temporarily with grass-mats. **yā ∼ kąn tsąngayą** he temporarily roofed the corn-stalk hut with mats.

yįfē = įfē.

yigīyą *Sk.* = **igīyą.**

yifį *m.* (1) temporary roof of mats (*Vd.* **yifą**). (2) **ąlkyabbą** temporarily used to cover saddle while rider is inside house, etc., on visit. (3) *Kt.* = **jąlālą.** (4) **am bā nį ∼** I've been lent a garment.

Yigudą = Igudą.

yįmą *f.* = *Kt.* **yįmanį** *m.* = **įndįkyā** *q.v.*

yimbū = yumbū.

yįmbururū = yąmbururū.

***yimkę** *Vb.* 1A stopped up (hole) = **tōshę.**

yimki *m.* = **gwaggo 1a.**

yim-yim *used in* **ąn rūwa ∼** it is drizzling.

yįną = yaną.

yinį (1) *m.* (a) (i) period of daylight. (ii) **nā yi masą ∼ I** spent the day with him. **yinįmmu hudū muną aikįnsą** *Vd.* **kwānā** A.2 2. (iii) **∼ yā įsa aikį, sąmmakō lą'aną nē** an early start is a nuisance, for there are enough hours of daylight for work. (iv) **įndą wani ya kī dą ∼, nan wani yakę sō dą kwānā** one man's meat is another's poison. (b) **suną ∼** they (crops) are withering during the day, but will freshen up at night. (c) (i) **suną yinįn Kande** they are celebrating the moving of Kande (a bride) to her husband's home (*cf.* **tārę**). (ii) **ąn yinįn sūnā** child's naming-day (**sūnā 5**) is being celebrated (1 = **wunį**). (2) *Vb.* (*only used in this form*) *x* (a) **yā ∼ tąfīyą** he travelled all day. **ką ∼ lāfīyą** may you have a good day ! **aką kumą yinį ąn yį** then another day was

spent doing it. (b) yinị dạshē *Vd.* ạlbasạ
6. mụ ~ lāfīyạ may we havẹ a good
day ! (= yĭnītạ).
yĭnītạ = wunị 2.
yĭnyē *Vb.* 1C completed *x* an ~ aikị the
work is completed.
yir *x* (1) 'yar hanyạ cē ~ it is a narrow
path. zạnē ~ thin line. (2) = yur.
yisī-yisī *pl. adj.* tiny.
yiwō *Vd.* yī.
yịwu *Vb.* 3B (*d.f.* yī) is possible *x* yā ~
yạ zō gọbe he'll possibly come to-
morrow. baị ~ ba = bā yạ yịwūwā =
bā tạ yịwūwā it is impossible. ịdam maị
yịwūwā nē if it is possible.
yizgā *Zar.* = izgā.
yo A. (yọ) (1) (a) well ! (*doubtful assent to*
question). (b) ~ nā ganī well, I'll see
if I can manage it. (2) (*rustic*) = wọ 2.
B. (yō) = yiwō.
yọfī *Sk.* = wọfī.
'yōgụ *m.* dropsy.
'Yōlạ *f.* (1) Yola. (2) *Vd.* wutar ~.
yōyẹ = yayyẹ.
yọyō = yạyyō.
yụ *Vd.* yụụ.
yukā *Sk.* = wukā.
yūlạ *Zar. f.* = jīnịyā 2.
Yūlị = Yūlizị *m.* July.
yumɓū *m.* (1) pottery-clay. (2) *Vd.* tạlōlō 4.
yumsụr = yamsụr.
yum-yum = yim-yim.
Yūnị = Yūnihị *m.* June.
yuŋkụrā *Vb.* 3A = yụŋkurạ *Vb.* 3B. (1)
strained every nerve to *x* sōjạmmụ
sun ~ gạba our soldiers pressed unceasingly forward. (2) retched. (3)
made preparations to set out *x* nā ~
zạn tāshị, săi gā shi ya shigō I was preparing to set out when he entered. (4)
Vd. yuŋkurō.
yụŋkurī *m.* straining every nerve, etc.
(*as in* yuŋkụrā).
yuŋkurō *Vb.* 3A important P. or T.
approached *x* hadirị yā ~ a storm blew
up. dāmunā tā ~ the rains are at hand.
Sarkī yā ~ the Chief is approaching.
săi wata zūcịyā ta yuŋkurō musụ they
got fresh heart (*Vd.* yuŋkụrā).
yunsụr = yamsụr.
yuŋwạ *f.* (1) (a) (i) hunger (*epithet is*

kisạŋkị bā jinī săi yaushī = 'yar ma-
dēgụ = Yuŋwạ, bā kau dạ halī = maị
mahūriŋ karfẹ). (ii) yā ji ~ he was
hungry. (b) (i) yā kwānā dạ ~ he
went to bed supperless. (ii) kạrē baị
kwānā dạ yuŋwạ ba *Vd.* ganī A 2. 3*b.* (iii)
Vd. 1*j below*. (c) ~ māgạnim mugunyạr
dạfūwā hungry dogs eat dirty pudding.
(d) ~ ita ta kạm mai dạ yārọ tsōfō,
kọshī shī kạm mai dạ tsōfō yārọ hunger
weakens the young just as ease re-
juvenates the old. (e) ~ tạndar bākiŋ
kishirwā the blind leading the blind.
(f) barim bākī kurụm shī ya kāwō
jin ~ cause and effect ! (g) jinī bā
yā māgạnin ~ tyranny never prospers
(*cf.* māgạnī 3*z.*i). (h) ~ ạ bā kị, ạ
hūtạ keen desire is not to be gainsaid.
(j) daran tūwō bā kwānā dạ ~ ba
nē (*epithet of child born late in mother's*
life), *cf.* 1*b above*. (k) bariŋ kāshī ạ
cikị bā yā māgạnin ~ speak out when
the time comes ! (l) *Vd.* sā B.12*b,*
10*c.* (m) ạbin jīfạn yuŋwạ *Vd.* wākē 5*b.*
(n) mugunyạr yuŋwạ *Vd.* sandī. (2) (a)
famine *x* Kanọ an yi ~ there was a
famine at Kano. anā ~ there is a
famine. (b) ~ tā zō famine set in.
(c) ~ tā fịta the famine came to an
end. (d) yā ci ~ ạ Kanọ = yā zō Kanọ
ciŋ ~ he spent the period of famine at
Kano. (e) yuŋwạr tufāfị shortage of
clothing. yuŋwạr gishirī tā shigō
manạ there is a shortage of salt with
us. (3) one of the internal organs of a
bird.
yuŋwatạ *Vb.* 3B felt hungry.
yur (1) only *x* sulẹ gụdā ~ only one
shilling. (2) a little *x* dam măi ~ only
a little butter. (3) = yir.
Yūsī = Yūsufụ Joseph (*Vd.* garkọ 4).
yụụ *x* sun shēkō ~ they raced towards us.

Z

za A. (zā) will (Mod. Gram. 14) *x* (1) zạn
zō I shall come (*less usually* zā ŋ zō).
(2) (a) zā kạ zō you will come. (b)
zā kạ zubar mịnị ? *Vd.* dība 1*j.* (3) zaị
zō he will come (*less usually* zā yā
zō).

B. (zā̱) (1) will go to (*is followed by its subject-pronouns*, Mod. Gram. 17) x zā̱ ni kāsūwā I'll be off to market. ~ shi Kano gōbe he's off to Kano to-morrow. (2) (*sometimes used without destination stated*) x a̱bi̱n da̱ na ci sa̱n da̱ ~ mu what I ate when we were about to set out. (3) *Sk.* (*followed by verb*) will x zā̱ ni zō I shall come (= zā̱ 1). zā̱ shi zō he will come (= zā̱ 3). (4) *Sk.* (*followed by verbal noun*) will x zā̱ su nēmam ma̱ŋ kaɗanya̱ they intend (intended) to look for sheanut-oil. zā̱ su ra̱būwā bīyū they will be divided into two parts. (5) " Zā̱ ni " cē̱ ta̱ tad da̱ " Mu̱ jē mū " do not blame the one for both are equally to blame ! (6) *Sk.* da̱, zā̱ shi ya̱dda̱ ya yi haka̱, da̱ rānā it was previously his intention to do what he did, openly. (7) *Vd.* ~ ka, ~ ni.

*zā̱'afaraŋ *Ar. m.* saffron.

*zā̱'afarāni = *zā̱'afaraŋ.

zaɓa A. (zā̱ɓā) *Vb.* 2 (1) chose. (2) *Vd.* zā̱ɓi ka̱ hau.

  B. (zāɓa̱) *Vb.* 1A (*with dative*) x za̱n ~ maka̱ shī I will choose it for you.

zaɓaɓɓaka A. (za̱ɓa̱ɓɓaka̱) *Vb.* 3B. (1) was boiling on and on. (2) (meat) became boiled to shreds (2 = ra̱ɓa̱ɓ-ɓaka̱).

  B. (zaɓaɓɓa̱kā) *Vb.* 1D (1) boiled (water) on and on. (2) boiled (meat) to shreds (2 = raɓaɓɓa̱kā).

zaɓaɓɓa̱kē *Vb.* 3A (1) = rūre̱ 1*b*. (2) (meat) became disintegrated from over-cooking (= ragarga̱jē = zabge̱ 2*c*).

zā̱ɓaɓɓē *m.* (*f.* zā̱ɓaɓɓīyā) *pl.* zā̱ɓa̱ɓɓū. (1) chosen. (2) choice.

za̱ɓainā *f.* (1) za̱bainar dāwa̱ aka̱ shūka̱ guinea-corn only was sown on the farm. za̱bainar gērō aka̱ shūka̱ bulrush millet only was sown on the farm. (2) an dafa̱ shi̱ŋkāfā ~ the rice was cooked separately.

zā̱bakō *m.* = ga̱nsarḵi.

za̱ɓak-za̱ɓak = za̱ɓal-za̱ɓal = ɓa̱lak-ɓa̱lak *q.v.*

zā̱ban daf̱i *m.* type of aloe.

za̱ɓannīyā *f.* boiling x rūwā yanā̱ ~ the water is boiling.

za̱ɓa̱rī *m.* (1) (*a*) act of getting bucket out of well. (*b*) hooked stick, etc., for extracting bucket fallen into well (*cf.* kūrā 3). (2) gū̱gā tsai, ~ tsai falling between two stools (= tanta̱lbatēte̱ = ta̱mɓa̱lā̱-tamɓalā = tsuntsū 3).

*zaɓa̱rjadu̱ *m.* chrysolite, topaz, etc.

Zabarmā *f.* Zabarma.

Zabarmāwā *Vd.* Ba̱zabarme̱.

za̱baro̱ *Kt. m.* = bāga̱.

zabartō *Vb.* 1E extracted (bucket from well (*as in* za̱ba̱rī).

zabaya A. (zāba̱yā) = zābi̱yā.

  B. (za̱ba̱yā) *Kt.* = za̱bīyā.

za̱bbā *Vd.* zōbe̱.

za̱bbī *Vd.* za̱ɓō.

zabce A. (zabce̱) = gabce̱ 1*a*, 2*a*, *b*.

  B. (za̱bcē) (1) *Vd.* za̱btā. (2) *m.* ka̱rē ma̱i ~ dog which bites on the slightest provocation.

za̱bci *Vd.* za̱btā.

zaɓe A. (zāɓe̱) *Vb.* 1A. (1) chose all of. (2) chose and set apart. (3) *Vd.* zā̱ɓē 5 ; dī̱ba̱ 1*j*.

  B. (zā̱ɓē) *m.* (1) bari ~, ka̱ ɗaukō kōw-a̱nnē take *any* of them, it doesn't matter which, without picking and choos-ing ! aŋ kashe̱ su bā̱ zā̱ɓē they have been murdered indiscriminately. (2) Allā̱ bā yā̱ ~ God is no respecter of persons. bā sā̱ ~ they make no invidious dis-tinctions. (3) yā kāwō wa̱ndō bi̱yar bābu̱ na ~ he brought five pairs of trousers each worse than the other. gā̱ rī̱gā uku̱ bā̱ ta ~ here are three gowns, none of which is worth a cent (= ciɓu̱s), *cf.* hanta̱ 1*a*.ii. (4) kada̱ ka̱ yi zā̱ɓan tumu̱n darē don't make a wrong choice ! (5) anā̱ ~, anā̱ ~, a̱ zāɓe̱ naga̱rī, a̱ bar sōshīyā (*words of song*). (6) *cf.* zāɓi̱.

zabga A. (zabga̱) *Vb.* 1C. (1) did much of x an ~ rūwā (rānā) ya̱u it has been very rainy (hot) to-day. (2) applied excess of T. = daɓa̱ 1*b–d*, x yā ~ musu̱ wuḵā he stabbed them deeply. yā ~ masa̱ zāg̱i he foully abused him. (3) *cf.* zabge̱.

  B. (za̱bgā) (1) *Vb.* 2 = zabga̱ x yā za̱bgē su da̱ wuḵā he stabbed them deeply with a knife. rānā tā za̱bgē mu̱ ya̱u we suffered much from the sun to-day. (2) *f.* yā shā ~ he has been abused. **yā shā ~ dạ wuƙā** he was deeply stabbed. (3) *cf.* **zabgẹ.**

zabgai *m.* the arrow-poison strophanthus.

zabgā-zạbgā *Vd.* **zabgēgẹ.**

zabgẹ (**zabgẹ**) (1) *Vb.* 1A (*a*) = **zạbgā 1** *x* **yā ~ su dạ wuƙā** he stabbed them deeply. (*b*) (rain) eroded (wall) = **rājẹ.** (*c*) stole much of *x* **an ~ mini damị ạshịrin** I have been robbed of 20 bundles of corn. (*d*) pulled off (much fruit from tree). (*e*) thinned out (corn) = **cịrā 1***b*. (2) *Vb.* 3A (*a*) = **zāgẹ** *2a*. (*b*) P. or animal became thin. (*c*) = **zaɓaɓɓạkē 2.** (*d*) (much fruit) fell from tree.

zabgēgẹ *m.* (*f.* **zabgēgīyā**) *pl.* **zabgā-zạbgā** huge.

zabi A. (**zạɓī**) *Vd.* **zạɓō.**

B. (**zāɓị**) *m.* (1) choice *x* **nā bā kạ ~ I** give you the choice. **zāɓịnkạ** you can take your choice ! (2) **Allā yā yi masạ ~ fortune** has smiled on him. (3) *cf.* **zạɓē.**

zạbịb *Ar. m.* raisin(s).

zạbībị *m.* = **rạwayạ 1***a, b*.

zạɓi kạ hau *m.* **Audu ~ nẹ ạ wurīna** Audu is a favourite of mine.

zạbīrạ *f.* (*pl.* **zạbịrū** = **zabīrōrī** = **zạbịrai**). (1) wallet with two compartments (*cf.* **jạkā**). (2) *Kt.* well divided into two parts.

zabiya A. (**zābịyā**) *f.* (*pl.* **zābīyōyī**) woman who leads singing.

B. (**zạbịyā**) *m., f.* (1) (*a*) albino. (*b*) *cf.* **Bạtūrẹ 7.** (2) red date.

zabkạ *Vb.* 1A *Kt.* = **zaɓaɓɓạkā.**

zabkẹ *Vb.* 1A *Kt.* = **zaɓaɓɓạkā.**

zạɓō (1) *m.* (*f.* **zạɓūwā**) *pl.* **zạɓī** = *Kt.* **zạbbī** (*a*) (i) guinea-fowl (*Numida meleagris*). (ii) **in ungulū tā bīyā buƙātạ, zạɓūwā tạ tafi dạ zạnantạ** better my own poor article than a borrowed one ! (= **gātarī 1***c*). (iii) **tāshịn gwauran zạɓō** *m.* suddenly outdistancing one's contemporaries. (iv) **kōwā ya ga zạɓūwā, dạ zạnantạ ya gan tạ** everybody is as God made him. (v) **kō bạ dadẹ fạkarā ita kạn zamā zạɓūwā** (*said in song*) sooner or later prince becomes king. (*b*) dark roan horse. (*c*) = **bạb-bāwạ.** (2) *m.* (*a*) type of sword. (*b*) type of aloe. (*c*) *Sk.* the cloth **sāƙị.** (3) **dōran ~** *Vd.* **dōrō 6.**

zabori A. (**zābōrī**) *m.* (**1**) *Kt.* clodhopper.

(2) *Zar.* broom made from veins of the raffia palm.

B. (**zạbōrī**) *Sk. m.* strings of a leather or calabash bucket which attach it to the main cord.

zabta A. (**zạbtā**) *Vb.* 2 (*p.o.* **zạbcē**, *n.o.* **zạbci**) = **gabcẹ** *2a–c*.

B. (**zabtạ**) *Vb.* 1A = **gabtạ 1.**

zabtara = **gabtara.**

zabtạrē = **gabtạrē.**

zạɓū *Sk. m.* a food resembling **zạmbū.**

zạɓūbạ (1) *f.* **yā shā ~** (*a*) he suffered severe pain, heat, cold. (*b*) he was overcharged. (2) (*a*) what severe pain, heat, cold ! (*b*) how dear !

zabukkạ *Kt.* = **zubkạ.**

zạbụn = **zạbūnị** *m.* type of long-sleeved waistcoat.

zabura A. (**zāburạ**) (1) *Vb.* 3B (*a*) (person) leaped to his feet. (*b*) (horse) sped away. (*c*) **yā zāburō mini** = **yā zāburam mini** (i) it sprang at me. (ii) he raged at me. (*d*) hastened away on errand. (*e*) **yā ~ kạn aikịnsạ** he worked with a will. **nā zāburạ nā yī** I devoted myself to the task actively. (*f*) **hatsī yā ~ the** corn grew up quickly. **yārọ yā ~ the** boy grew up rapidly. (*g*) **rigā zāburạ** *Vd.* **wutā 1***a*.i. (2) *Vb.* 2 caused (horse) to leap forward (by spurring, etc.).

B. (***zạbūrā**) *Ar. f.* Psalms.

zāburạ dawāki *epithet of* any man named **Āmadụ** (*said by* **ạlmājịrī**).

zạbūwā *Vd.* **zạɓō.**

zace A. (**zạcē**) *Vd.* **zạtā.**

B. (**zacẹ**) *Vb.* 1A (*with dative*) *x* **nā ~ masạ rībạ** I regarded it (transaction) as profitable. **bạn ~ masạ haƙạ ba** I didn't think he would act like that.

zạ'ce-zạcē" *m.* vague ideas.

zaci A. (**zācị**) *m.* height, length *x* **~ gạrēshi** it is very long (= **zātị**).

B. (**zạci**) *Vd.* **zạtā.**

zādạ *Ar. f.* exaggeration.

zado *Kt. m.* (*f.* **zadụwā**) *pl.* **zadō-zạdō** tall (or long) and handsome P. or T.

zāfạcē *Vb.* 3A *Sk.* dodged (= **baudẹ**).

zafafa A. (**zāfạfā**) *Vb.* 1C. (1) heated *x* **tā zāfạfạ tūwō** she heated the **tūwō.**

(2) = sulālā 1. (3) yā zāfafa maganassa he spoke angrily.
B. (zāfafa) (1) Vb. 2 x mē ya zāfafē ka (a) why did you interfere? (b) what is troubling you? (2) Vb. 3B = buŋkāsa.
C. (zāfafā) Vd. zazzāfā.
zāfafē Sk. m. = dumamē.
zafce Kt. = zabce.
zāfī m. (1) (a) heat (= Sk. gumī 3). (b) nā ji ∼ (i) I felt hot. (ii) I felt offended. (iii) munā jin zāfinsa we are grieved about it. (c) (i) rūwan naŋ yanā da ∼ this water is hot. (ii) rūwan ∼ hot water. (iii) rūwan ∼ yā tafa shi he has leprosy (= dimī 2), cf. kuturta. (iv) abin da rūwan ∼ ya dafa, iŋ aŋ hakura, sāi rūwan sanyī ya dafa time remedies all (Vd. sanyī 13). (d) kōwā ya debō da ∼ bākinsa as you sow, so shall you reap. (e) mē ya yi maka zāfī = zāfafa 1a. (f) garī yā yi masa ∼ he had a hard time. (g) yā gamu da ∼ = 1c.iii above. (h) yā fi wutar ∼ Vd. 6ērā 1k. (j) madaukar ∼ Vd. gaban 6. (2) (a) n nā ∼ ŋ gama I'm eager to finish it. (b) yanā cikin zāfiŋ gudu he's running full-speed. (c) dōki yā fādi cikin zāfin tafiya tasa the horse fell when at full gallop. (2A) pain x (a) kafata tā yi mini ∼ my foot pained me. (b) zāfiŋ wukā Vd. kudūrū. (3) anger x (a) zūciyāta tā yi ∼ = zūciyāta tā dauki ∼ I became angry. (b) ∼ garēshi (i) he is hot-tempered. (ii) = 4 below. (c) zāfiŋ halī = zāfin zūciyā = zāfin rāi being quick-tempered. yā yi zāfin zūciyar tāsa he gave a display of his usual bad temper. (4) (a) zāfin nāma garēshi he is quick in his movements (cf. sanyī 4e). (b) manzō mai zāfī fast messenger (= Kt. saukī 6). (5) zāfiŋ hannū garēshi he strikes people on the slightest provocation.
zafta = zabta.
zaga A. (zāga) Vb. 1A (1) (a) went round x yā ∼ Ka'aba he made the circuit of the Kaba at Mecca (= gēwaya 1a). (b) tā ∼ = kircī 2. (c) yā ∼ sōja he reviewed the troops. (2) went close along x yā ∼ bākiŋ kōgī he followed the river-bank (= rā6ā 1). (3) = gēwaya 3,

5. (4) went to another place x yā ∼ wajam Baucī he has gone to Bauchi (= kōma 2b.i). (5) Sarkī yā ∼ garī the Emir went for a ride in the town. (6) Kt. = zarga. (7) Vd. zāga rāfī.
B. (zāgā) (1) Vb. 2 (a) = zāga 1a. (b) (i) abused (for progressive Vd. zāgi) = Sk. 6ātā. (ii) kūrā tā wuce, kasā aka ∼ what backbiting! (Vd. kūrā 44). (iii) yā zāgi dārī he put on thick clothes to keep out the cold. (iv) Vd. wā ya zāgi. (v) kā zāgi Sarkī Vd. mūgu 1c. (c) (i) stripped off (leaves, dates, tsirē from stick, etc.). (ii) stripped off (guinea-corn or bulrush-millet from stalk together with kaikayī, for horse's food) (ii = fīga), cf. tuma, murmura. (d) yā zāgi takōbī he drew his sword. (e) drew (water from well) x tā zāgi rūwā gūgā bīyar she drew up five buckets of water (= dība). (2) f. acting as in 1c, e above x tana ∼ she is drawing water.
C. (zāgā) Kt. f. putting dog on leash (Vd. zarga).
D. (zaga) f. (pl. zagōgī) (1) canine tooth (= fīka q.v.). (2) yā kāwō (= yā yi) ∼ (a) it (horse) is about four years old. (b) from poverty he has become rich, influential. (3) string tied across skin of drum.
zagadū m. Jew's harp made of cornstalks (cf. bambarō 3).
zagāgē Vd. zagī.
zagaigaitā = kurūrūtā.
zāgai-zāgai = gēwai-gēwai.
zagantaka f. being a zagī.
zāga rāfī m. plant whose root serves as aperient.
zagaraftū m. (1) = rīshī. (2) bā girmā aka mai da sū zagaraftū they had perforce to slow down.
zagargar = tsirāra 2a.
zāgarī m. (1) being prone to backbiting people. (2) Vd. wata 2f.
zāgau m. (1) Sk. = būshīyā 3. (2) Nor. = gwāzā 2.
zagaya A. (zāgāyā) Vb. 1C = zāga 1a.
B. (zāgāya) Vb. 2 = rāje 1a.
zāgāyē Vb. 1C = rāje 1a.
zage A. (zāge) (1) Vb. 1A (a) = zāga 1a, zāgā 1c, d. (b) = rāje 1a. (c) frayed

(= kūjẹ 1a), cf. cī 4, farcẹ 3c. (d) (i) yā ∼ wạndansạ he undid and took off his trousers : he pulled top of his trousers along the trouser-string (ma-zāgī). (ii) yā ∼ wạndansạ, yā rātạxā he (traveller) hung his trousers from his neck by the trouser-string (mazāgī) = zargẹ 1b = kạlạŋgū 2. (e) yā ∼ dantsẹ cikiŋ aikị he worked might and main. (f) Kt. = zargạ. (2) Vb. 3A (a) (i) (wall, etc.) became eroded (= rājẹ 2a). (ii) yā̤bē yā ∼ dạgạ jikim baŋgō the plaster peeled off the wall. (b) furā tā ∼ ạ rūwa the furā became liquid in the water in which it was cooked. (c) = gyāzạjē 1. (d) = dā̤dẹ 2a. (e) yā ∼ cikiŋ aikị ∼ 1e above. (f) idạnsạ yā ∼ his eyelashes have fallen out through blepharitis.

B. (zā̤gē) m. (pl. zāgunạ) led horse for travelling-Chief (also called dōkiṇ zā̤gē) = amaryā 3 = bạrgā 4b.

C. (zagẹ) Vb. 3A (1) yā ∼ cikiŋ aikị = zā̤gẹ 1e. (2) yā ∼ cikiŋ hūtā̤wā he is enjoying a good rest.

zā̤'ge-zā̤gē|| m. x sun jā zā̤ge-zā̤gē they behaved abusively.

Zagḗzagī Vd. Bạzazzạgī.

zagi A. (zā̤gị) m. (1) (usually employed to form progressive of zā̤gā 1b) x (a) yanā̤ zāgịnsụ he is abusing them. (b) rịgan nạŋ tanā̤ zāgịna this gown is desired by me. (c) bakin jinim mụzūrū, mai kā̤zā ∼, marạk kā̤zā ∼ give a dog a bad name and hang him. (2) (a) (i) abuse, reviling. yā aunạ masạ ∼ he abused him. (ii) (we cannot say an yi minị ∼ but dative can be used if followed by noun) x an yi minị zāgịm banzā I was abused for no reason. an yi minị zāgịm manyā I was mildly abused (x by the words ɗan cikiŋ ūwā). (b) madūbin nạŋ ∼ yakẹ yị this mirror distorts images. (c) zāgị bā yā̤ kạrị abuse does not kill.

B. (zagī) m. (pl. zagā̤gē). (1) runner in front of horseman x yā yi ∼ he was such runner. yanā̤ ∼ he performs duties of such runner. (2) zagin dōkạ bandeau worn on women's hair. (3) zagin sirdị cloth completely covering a saddle. (4) Vd. namạdōtạl. (5) Vd. māshị 3.

zāgīyā f. (1) (a) causing one or more arrows to project from full quiver, to facilitate withdrawal. (b) sǎi kwạrī yā cịka akẹ ∼ only P. in comfortable circumstances can give charity. (2) arrow(s) projecting as in 1a.

zago A. (zā̤gō) Kt. f. = gā̤gạrạ 3b.

B. (zagō) m. (sg., pl.). (1) type of large termite (epithet is bụrạ kǎi). (2) an yi gudụŋ gạrā, aŋ hayẹ ∼ out of the frying-pan into the fire. (3) zagwaŋ kạs tale-bearing against P. (= gịndiŋ guzumā). (4) Vd. kạn ∼.

C. (zagọ) m. (pl. zagunạ) crocodile-harpoon.

zagōgī Vd. zagạ.

zagō-zạgō x yanā̤ dạ girā zagō-zạgō he has bushy eyebrows.

zaguna A. (zāgunạ) Vd. zā̤gē.

B. (zagunạ) Vd. zagọ.

zạgwạdī = zạgwadị = zạgwạdīdī m. = dọkī q.v.

zagwaŋ kạs Vd. zagō 3.

zagwạnyē Vb. 3A (1) = ragwargwạjē. (2) (meat, fish, etc.) putrefied.

*Zā̤hạratụ Ar. f. Venus (= mā̤tar watạ).

zāhịrī (1) m. (f. zāhịrā) pl. zā̤hịrai Ar. clear, obvious x kā ji zāhịrar magaṇạ you have heard a clear statement. zāhịriŋ abịn dạ mukạ sanị yā̤kị bạ zaị kā̤rẹ dạ saurī ba it is obvious to us that the war will not end soon. (2) adv. (a) plainly x zāhịrī mukạ gan shị we saw it with our own eyes. (b) ạ zāhịrī obviously. (3) m. (a) an gạ zāhịrinsạ it has been actually seen. *(b) ịnā azancinsạ gạ zāhịrị what is its literal meaning ? (cf. mạ'ạnā 4).

zaibạ Ar. f. quicksilver.

zā'idạ f. exaggeration.

Zạinabụ woman's name (Vd. Agaddabū).

zairā = zaryā.

zaiṭị Ar. m. (1) Eucalyptus oil. (2) ∼ kạnumfạr a clove-scented liniment.

zạiṭụŋ = zạiṭūnị Ar. m. (1) (a) olive. (b) olive-tree. (2) mạn ∼ olive-oil.

zaị-zaị Vd. bị ta ∼.

zaizayē (1) Vb. 1C = rājẹ 1a. (2) (a) = rājẹ 2. (b) gāshịntạ yā ∼ her hair has dropped out.

zaka A. (zakạ) Sk. (1) came (= zō). (2) Sk. yanā̤ zạwwā = yanā̤ zakụ̄wā he's

coming (= zūwạ), *cf.* zạyayyē, zạw-
wūwā. (3) *Vd.* zạukakkē.

B. (zạkā) *Ar. f.* (1) (*a*) (i) religious
tithe payable on farm-produce and
farm-stock (*cf.* sā'ī). (ii) yā ƙī dọmin
zạkkā *Vd.* warạbukkạ. (*b*) (i) yā fitar
dạ ~ he paid his tithe. (ii) nā fitar wạ
hatsīna dạ ~ I paid the tithe due on
my corn. (*c*) (i) yā ãtar musụ dạ zạkā
he (sā'ī) levied tithe on them. (ii)
kāfin sụ rinjāyē mụ, sãi dạ mukạ
fitar musụ dạ zạkā they did not overcome us till we had inflicted losses on
them. (*d*) bābụ ~ ạ cikin (= bābụ ~
dạgạ) shānū ạbin dạ ya kāsạ tạlātiŋ no
tithe is levied on cows until there is
minimum of thirty. (*e*) *Vd.* zạkkā 2,
zakkạ, kōnō. (2) alms, charity (= sadakạ 1*a*).

zạƙā *Vb.* 2 ate much of.

zaƙaƙa A. (zāƙạƙā) *Vb.* 1C sweetened.

B. (zạƙaƙạ) *Vb.* 3B became sweet.

C. (zāƙạ̄ƙā) *Vd.* zạzzāƙā.

D. (zạ̄ƙạ̄ƙạ̄) *used in* ~ fārį *m.* first
eagerness of groom for bride.

E. (zạƙạƙạ) *x* sạndā nē ~ dạ shī
it is a long stick.

zạƙāƙụrī *m.* (*f.* zạƙāƙụrā) (1) (*a*) outstanding P. (*b*) notorious P. (2) =
mahạddạcī 2.

zaƙal A. (zaƙal) *m.* (1) meddlesomeness
(= kạrạmbānī). (2) mē ya yi makạ
zaƙal what business is it of yours !

B. (zạƙạl) *x* karā ~ long corn-stalk.
harshē ~ long tongue.

zaƙala A. (zāƙalạ) *Vb.* 2 (1) (*a*) = zuŋgurạ 1*a*. (*b*) zāƙalō = zuŋgurạ 1*b*. (*c*)
yā zāƙalō harshạnsạ he put out his
tongue. macįjī yā zāƙalō kạnsạ the
snake put its head out of the hole
(1*c* = zārẹ 1*bb*). (2) ate much of.

B. (zāƙalā) *Vb.* 1C = zuŋgụrā 1.

zạƙalƙalạ *Vb.* 2 ate T. greedily.

zaƙalƙalē *Vb.* 1C ate greedily all of T.

zāƙalō *Vd.* zạ̄ƙalạ.

zaƙạmī *m.* (1) Hairy Thorn Apple
(*Datura metel*) = bạbba jūjī = furē 4,
cf. ạlkaŋgādọ. (2) *epithet is* haụkạtạ yārọ.

zạkaŋkạŋ = zạkaŋkau 2.

zạkaŋkau *m.* (1) ash of burnt kainūwā,
used for salt. (2) ~ gishiriŋ gạba dạ
Auziŋ *epithet of* chatterbox.

zākanyạ *Vd.* zāki.

zạkarạ *m.* (*pl.* zạkạrū = zakarōrī). (1)
(*a*) (i) cock (*epithet is* Wạŋ gijį, *Vd.*
gayạ 5). (ii) anạ̄ fadạn zạkạrū they
are engaged in a desperate struggle.
(*b*) dan ~ wạndạ zại yi cārā shirwạ
bā tạ̄ dauƙạ let the cobbler stick to his
last ! (*c*) ~ ạ rạ̄taye bā yạ̄ cārā the
underdog has to eat humble pie. (*d*)
bā nạ̄ yiŋ ƙwǎina sǎi dạ zạkarạ I
should not have spoken were I not sure
of the facts. (*e*) zạkaraŋ dạ Allạ̄ ya
nụfē shi dạ cārā, anạ̄ mụzūrū, anạ̄
shāhọ, sǎi yā yī nothing can prevent
the person destined to succeed. (*f*)
mūgụn ~ *Vd.* ƙīƙiriƙii. (2) shī ~ nē
he is an altruist (*referring to proverb* ~
mại nēmaŋ girmā wạndạ ya bā dạ
ƙwạ̄yā, ya ci tsakūwạ). (3) *Vd.* tōfā 1*b*.
(4) P. in congregation who leads the
responses in a loud voice. (5) outstanding P. sū nē zạkạrū ạ ƙasạr
they're the mouthpieces of the country.
(6) zạkaraŋ dawākī = zạkaraṃ faƙọ =
zạkaraŋ ƙēƙūwā (*a*) Senegal Plover
(*Stephanibyx lugubris*). (*b*) Black-headed
Plover (*Sarciophorus tectus*). (7) zạkaraŋ ganin (= zạkaraŋ gānin) dafi
P. serving as mere " catspaw ". (8)
idạn ~ *Vd.* idọn 19.

zạƙarnaƙọ *m.* (1) type of aphrodisiac
(*epithet is* Zạƙarnaƙọ hạnạ barcī). (2)
virile man.

zaƙā-zạƙā *adj. pl.* too long (*x* chopped
hay, soup-vegetables).

zạ̄ ka, zạ̄ ni *m.* (*sg., pl.*) strong and tireless
person(s) or horse(s).

zaƙẹ *Vb.* 3A *Kt.* = fiffīƙē.

zaƙē-zạƙē = zaƙā-zạƙā.

zāki *m.* (*f.* zākanyạ) *pl.* zakōkī. (1) (*a*)
lion (*epithet is* Wạn dawạ). (*b*) gạban
zāki *Vd.* gạban 14. (*c*) gōshin ~ *Vd.*
gōshi 5. (*d*) sǎi dājį yā yi yawạ ~ kạn
zaunạ ạ cikinsạ the poor get nothing
unless the rich have a surplus. (*e*)
in ~ yā san zại sạ̄mi nāmạ yanạ̄ cikin
sarƙaƙƙīyā, bā yạ̄ fịtā wạje nobody
undertakes useless trouble. (*f*) kō ~
yā lālācē, yā yi ƙarfin hịnzīrį P. with
hereditary dignity, no matter what
happens to him, will not sink to the
bottom (= ruŋhū 2). (*g*) harshē ~ nē

ạ ɗạụre check your tongue ! (h) bạri murnạ doŋ kạraŋkạ yā kāmạ zāƙị don't count your chickens before they're hatched ! (= gịrịŋgiɗịshī). (j) mạrāyạn zāƙị Vd. mạrāyạ 3. (k) bangwan zāƙị Vd. baŋgō 5. (l) gāwar ∼ Vd. gịzākā. (2) (a) Zāƙị ! my Lord ! (said to Chief, European, man named Ạlī). (b) Vd. ạlfandā. (3) strongest horizontal beam in base of corn-bin. (4) seam down side of sleeve or trousers where one folds them in two.

zāƙī m. (1) (a) (i) sweetness. (ii) pleasant flavour. (iii) nā ji zāƙinsạ I tasted its pleasant flavour. (iv) ∼ fau nẹ̄ = ∼ zaƙwai nẹ̄ it is very sweet, nicely salted. (v) ∼ gạrēshị kạmaŋ ạlēwạr dạyī it's as much good as an icicle in hell. (vi) zāƙim mỵạ ? Vd. marạbā 3. (b) pleasantness x wannạŋ kiɗạ dạ ∼ yakẹ̄ this drumming is pleasant. (2) yạnā dạ zāƙim bāƙī he is a chatterbox. (3) dōkịn naŋ dạ ∼ yakẹ̄ this horse is tractable. (4) eagerness x yanā zāƙin tāshị he is eager to set out (= ɗọ̄kī). (5) yanā zāƙīna he loves me. (6) disease blocking egress of fāyạ. (7) ɗan ∼ m. = bạzāƙịyā. (8) ∼ banzā the spinach Amaranthus viridis (= Sk. rụkuɓụ = mālaŋƙōcī).

zāƙirạ Vb. 2 ate much of.

zāƙịrē Vb. 1C ate up all the large available amount of T.

zāƙịriŋ zạƙū Kt. m. gluttony.

zāƙị-zāƙị Kt. peremptorily.

zakka A. (zakkạ) f. (1) (a) a corn-measure equal to one sā'ị. (b) bīyū dạ ∼ Sk. two such measures. *(c) zakkạr Ạnnabị = mūdạnabị. (2) = zạkkā 2.
B. (zạkkā) f. (1) = zạkā. (2) yā fịta ∼ (a) he is outstanding. (b) he is notorious.

zāƙọ Vd. bạzāƙịyā, bạzāƙạ 2.

zākōkī Vd. zāƙị.

zạƙu Vb. 3B x (1) yā ∼ dạ shī he is very eager to get it. (2) Vd. zāƙịriŋ.

zakuɗa A. (zākụɗā) (1) Vb. 1C (a) mixed together (beans, rice, dambū, etc., prior to cooking). (b) Kt. = zuŋkụɗā 1a. (2) Vb. 3A (a) = muskụɗā 2, 3. (b) haŋkạlinsạ yā ∼ he feels disturbed in mind.

B. (zạkuɗạ) f. (secondary v.n. of zākụɗā 1a) x tanā zạkuɗạr shịŋkāfā she is mixing together rice.

zākụɗē Vb. 1C = zākụɗā 1a.

zāƙụlā Vb. 1C = zuŋgụrā 1.

zạ̄kumī Vd. jạ̄kumī.

zakụ̄wā Sk. Vd. zakạ.

zaƙwai Vd. zāƙī 1a.iv.

zạƙwaịƙwaitạ Vb. 3B x yā ∼ dạ shī he is eager to get it.

zạƙwātị m. = ɗọ̄kī.

zalạ Vb. 3A x rạ̄kumī yā ∼ wuyạ the camel stretched out its neck.

zạlaidụ m. (1) White-breasted Whydah (Vidua seren ;). (2) Paradise Whydah (Steganura paradisea).

*zạlāƙạ Ar. f. eloquence.

zalau A. (zạlau) x yanā dạ wuyạ ∼ he has a long neck. sunā dạ wuyạ zalau-zạlau = sunā dạ wuyạ zalā-zạlā = sunā dạ wuyạ zalai-zạlaị they have long necks. macịjī yā fītō ∼ the snake issued in all its length.
B. (zạlau) x rạ̄kumī yā yi zạlau-zạlau dạ wuyạ the camel walked swinging its neck.

zalā-zạlā, zalai-zạlaị, zalau-zạlau Vd. zạlau.

zalɓẹ Kt. = zarɓẹ.

zālī used in an ci zālinsạ he has been oppressed (= zạlunta).

zālincị = zāluncị.

zalƙē m. = zạlƙī.

zạlƙī m. acting in such a way as to show one is " top dog ".

zallā (1) adv. solely x (a) tạ̄ran naŋ mazā nẹ̄ ∼ this crowd consists solely of males. wannạm mạganạ ƙaryā cẹ̄ ∼ this statement is a sheer lie. ƙarɓẹ ∼ muka sạyā we bought and paid for all cash down. ƙattā ạshịriŋ ∼ sunā naŋ twenty men are available, all hefty. mahạukạcī nẹ̄ ∼ he's raving mad (1a = tuburaŋ 1 = tsantsā = ƙwāyā 5 = gaŋgārịyạ = rạ̈i 4 = zar). (b) yā fạdi gạskịyā ∼ he told only the truth (= tsāɓạ 4a = tsịrārạ 2d = ƙạshiŋ gạskīyā). (2) m., f. soleness x zīnārịyā cẹ̄ zallantạ = zīnārīyā cẹ̄ ∼ tatạ it is pure gold (= tsantsā), cf. gurguzū 2.

zạllim mạzallaƙọ m. (1) great eagerness (= ɗọ̄kī). (2) its epithet is ɗā dạgạ ciƙī rōk̃waŋ ụbā wurị (an unborn child asking its father for a cowrie).

zallọ *m.* (1) giving a convulsive start (*x* P. tickled). (2) bobbing of cork on the water.

zālumtạ = **zāluntạ**.

zālun = zālin *q.v. under* zālī.

zalunci A. (zālụnci) *Vd.* zāluntạ.
   B. (zālunci) *m.* (1) tyranny (= taskụ).
(2) *Vd.* zillạ.

zāluntạ *Vb.* 2 (*p.o.* zālụncē, *n.o.* zālụnci) oppressed (subordinates, wife, one's horse, etc.).

zạlwāmī = zụlwāmī.

zalzala A. (zalzạlā) *Vb.* 1C (1) = fạllasạ.
(2) *cf.* zalzalō.
   B. (zạlzalạ) *Vb.* 2 = arịrītạ.

zalzalō (1) *Vb.* 1E (*a*) yā ~ dạ harshẹ it (panting dog, etc.) kept putting out its tongue. (*b*) *Vd.* zalzạlā, zạlzala.
(2) *Vb.* 3A harshạnsạ yā ~ tongue (of panting dog, etc.) kept protruding.

zam (1) yanạ naŋ ~ he's safe and sound.
(2) yā d̃ạuru ~ it is firmly tied.

zama A. (zamā) (1) *Vb.* 3B (*a*) is, are, was, were *x* (i) mạganạ tā ~ gạskīyā the statement is true (= gạskīyā cẹ̄). yā ~ nāsạ nē it is his (= nāsạ nē). yā ~ hakạ the matter is thus. im mun dūbi haliŋ k̃asarmụ dạ yạddạ ta zamā ạ wancạŋ yāk̃i if we regard the state of our country and how it was in that war (= kasạncē 1). (ii) kạ ~ lāfīyạ *Sk.* adieu ! (*said to superior*). (*b*) became *x* (i) yā ~ sunạ̄ naŋ san dạ mukạ zō they chanced to be here when we came. yā ~ bạ̄ nāsạ ba nẹ̄ it ceased to be his. wurī yā ~ garī the place became a town. an rinạ farī, yā ~ bak̃ī the farī-cloth was dyed black (= kasạncē 2). (ii) (*with dative*) *x* nā saŋ hakạ zại zamam minị = nā saŋ hakạ zại zamẹ minị I know that's what will happen to me. yā zamẹ minị tīlạs I'm forced to do it. (2) *m.* (*a*) state of being seated, remaining, dwelling *x* (i) kụ bar zamā stand up ! in sum fād̃ạ manạ, ạ san nam bạ̄ sauran zamā if they attack us, we shall take immediate action. in sun yī, bạ̄ mu dạ sauran zamā if they do so, we cannot ignore it. zamāna nī kad̃ăi my remaining alone.
(i.*A*) shā zamā *Vd.* shā B.6. (i.*B*) bā

ạ̄ ~ dạ kā *Vd.* zaunạ 1*d.* (i.*C*) ~ dạ mad̃ạukā kaŋwā *Vd.* kaŋwā 1*c.* (ii) ạbōkin zamạŋkạ your fellow-dweller. (iii) yā ci ~ he stayed a long while. (iv) sạnnū dạ ~ (*said to an equal*) greeting on your being seated ! (v) sunạ̄ zamansụ lāfīyạ they're well. (vi) inā zamaŋ garị how are you ? *Vd.* garị 1*m* (= hạk̃urī 1*b*). (vii) yā shịga garī, yā yi zamansạ he went and lived in the town. (viii) dạ Kạnde dạ Mạryamụ ~ sukẹ̄ = sọ̄ 3. (ix) zamā zūcī gạ marạbī tā fi " Wānẹ, gạ han-nūna ! " (*Vd.* marạbī ; wānẹ 1*c*). (x) zaman dūnīyạ bịkī nẹ̄. cụd̃ē ni, ŋ cụd̃ē kạ the world necessitates people helping each other. (xi) *Vd.* zaman-*compounds*. (xii) *Vd.* wāwan zamā. (*b*) condition *x* (i) sunạ̄ zamaŋ ạdāwạ they are in a state of hostility. yanạ̄ naŋ zamansạ yạddạ mukạ bar shị it is in the same condition as we left it. (ii) *Vd.* zaman.
   B. (zạmā) because (= gạmā).
   C. (zāmạ) *f.* good luck (= sā'ạ).
   D. (zạ̄mā) *Vb.* 2 defrauded.

zamad dạ *Vb.* 4 (1) caused to become *x* nā ~ shi (= nā zamshē shị) dāna I treated him as my son. (2) caused to sit down, caused to reside. (3) (*a*) (i) caused to remain. (ii) delayed P. (*b*) Allạ̄ zamshē sụ lāfīyạ long life to them ! (2, 3 = zaunad dạ).

zamam *Vd.* zamā 1*b*.ii.

zạmạmmạne *Sk.* (*re plural subject*) *x* gạ̄ mutạ̄nē ~ cạŋ there are people seated over there.

zaman (*genitive of* zamā 2*b*) *x* (1) bại san ~ anạ̄ rōwạ ba he does not know the meaning of stinginess. bại san ~ dạ tsọ̄rō ba he does not know the meaning of fear. (2) nā san ~ zan sāmụ I know I shall eventually get it. (3) dūtsạn dạ kẹ̄ cikin rūwa bại san ~ dạ rānā ba one half of the world doesn't know how the other half lives. (4) *Vd.* ~ dạ nī. (5) irịn zamaŋ kīfā̄yẹ sukẹ̄ yị they behave like cannibals. (6) *Vd.* zaman-*compounds*.

zạmanạ *Vb.* 3B (1) = zamā 1 *except b*.ii. (2) *Vd.* Dạŋkwại.

zāmanancī *m.* (1) the disrespectfulness of

modern bright young people (= **banancī**) *cf.* zāmạnī 3. (2) larking about (*cf.* bạzāmạnī).

zāmanāwā *Vd.* bạzāmạnī.

zamạncē *Vb.* 3A = zamā 1.

zạmạn dạ nī *m.* house-servant (= **barạ**).

zaman ɗāki *used in* 'yar ~ = 'yar burgancị *q.v. under* burgancị.

zaman ɗạrē *Vd.* ɗạrē 2.

zaman fādī *m.* = hạrɗē 4.

zamạɲ girmā *Vd.* azzịkī 4*b*.

zamạɲ hạrɗē *Vd.* hạrɗē 4.

zāmạnī = zamạnī = zạ̄mānị = zạmānị *m.* (*pl.* zạ̄mạ̄nai = zạ̄mạ̄nū). (1) period *x* (*a*) cikin zạmānịn **Shēhu** during the time of the Emir Shehu. (*b*) **Allạ̄ yạ jā** zạmānịɲkạ long life to you ! (*c*) yạnzu zạmānị yā kāwō mụ we must move with the times. (2) yā yi ~ ạ **Kano** he spent some time at Kano. (3) (*a*) 'yan ~ people of the modern world (*cf.* zāmanancị). (*b*) 'yā'yan ~ saninkụ bạ̄ sanịn halịɲkụ ba one never really knows how you'll act. (*c*) yạ̄ran zạmānị, tum bạ sụ tạfasạ ba, su kạɲ ƙōnẹ modern youth wants to run before it can walk. (*d*) *Vd.* bạzāmanẹ. (4) in ~ yā dịɲkạ rịgā lallẹ̄ yā kạmātạ ạ sakạ one must bow to fate. (5) tun zāmạnin zạ̄mạnai long, long ago. (6) yā tayar minị dạ ~ he started a quarrel with me. (7) *Vd.* mīkị 2*c*. (8) na zạmānị (*f.* ta ~) *pl.* na ~ modern *x* kāyan yāƙị na zạmānị modern armaments. ịgwar zạmānị a modern gun.

zamạɲ kīƙạyē *Vd.* zaman 5.

zamạɲ kisạn dạɓē *m.:* overstaying one's welcome (*Vd.* kisạ 3).

zaman kuntukurū = hạrɗē 4.

zạmannị *m.* = zamā 2.

zamanō *Vb.* 3A = zamā 1.

zaman rāƙumạ *m.* sitting on the heels.

zạmạntạkayyạ *f.* friendship through constant association.

zạmạntarōrị *Kt. m.* seeds of red cress used as remedy for swelling (*cf.* ạlgạrịf).

zamantō *Vb.* 3A = zamā 1.

zaman 'yan sarki = hạrɗē 4.

zạmarƙē *m.* the shrub *Sesbania punctata*.

zāmạ-zāmạ (1) sometimes. (2) good luck ! (*re* hunting, journey).

zạmbā *f.* (1) underhandedness. (2) yā

yi minị ~ he misrepresented what I said. (3) ɗan zạmbā *Vd.* yāƙị 1*a*.ii.

zạmbạcē *Vd.* zạmbatạ.

zambạɗā *Vb.* 1C (*with dative*) applied abundantly *x* tā ~ masạ gishirī she added a lot of salt to it (food).

zạmbāgī *Sk. m.* = kẹ̄kē 2*a*.ii.

zambạr *f.* (1) *used in* ~ tarạ 9,000 (= **dubū tarạ**). zambạr gōmạ (= **dubū gōmạ**) 10,000 (*and so on for the higher thousands*). (2) ạbin ~ zạmbạrai very valuable T. (3) *Vd.* tạntabạrā 1*a*.

zambarmạ *f.* through over-eagerness prematurely acting before permission received *x* yā yi ~, yā tāshị through over-eagerness, he started before the word was given.

zạmbatạ *Vb.* 2 (*p.o.* zạmbạcē, *n.o.* zạmbạci). (1) mocked *x* nā zạmbạcē shị sabọ dạ gidādancī I mocked him for his lack of *savoir-faire* (= **gwartā**). (2) tricked, deceived (*cf.* zạmbā, zạmbō).

zạmbō *m.* (1) ridiculing *x* nā yi masạ ~ sabọ dạ gidādancī = zạmbatạ 1. (2) marọ̄kī yā yi masạ ~ the marọ̄kī *q.v.* satirized him. (3) sun shāfạ masạ ~ they accused him falsely (= **kāshịɲ kạ̄zā**).

zạmbū *m.* A Nupe blancmange sold wrapped in leaves.

zambunạ *Kt. f.* type of small drum.

zambur *m.* = zambarmạ.

zam dạ = zamad dạ.

zame A. (zamẹ) *Vd.* zamā 1*b*.ii.

　B. (zāmẹ) (1) *Vb.* 1A (*a*) (i) reined in horse sharply so that it slithered (= **kwāshẹ** 1*cc* = **ɗebẹ** 6 = **gurjẹ** 2 = **kāwō** 2*a*.vi) (*cf.* bũɗẹ 1*c*). (ii) baị ~ ba sãi yā kai gidā he made straight for home. (*b*) = zargẹ 1*f*. (*c*) = kwaɓẹ 1*d*. (*d*) sloped (sides of a cutting) (= **gạɲgạrē** 2). (2) *Vb.* 3A. (*a*) (load, wall, etc.) slipped. (*b*) shiftily went back on one's word (2 = zũ̄ƙẹ 2*a*).

Zạmfạrạ = *Sk.* **Zạmfạrā** *f. Vd.* banzā, gudumạ 4, hausā.

Zamfarāwā *Vd.* Bạzạmfạrī.

zāmīyā *f.* (1) dōkị yā yi ~ the horse slithered when reined in sharply (*Vd.* zāmẹ 1*a*). (2) yā yi minị ~ cikịɲ kuɗīna he deducted what I owed him, when paying me = zaunau 2 = gạɲgạrā = zargẹ 1*f* (*cf.* zāmẹ 1*b*, kāmūwā).

zamnạ *Kt.* = zaunạ.

zamō *Sk.* = zamā 1.

zamshē *Vd.* zamad dạ.

zam-zam *used in* yā dauru ～ it is firmly tied.

zan A. (zạn) I shall *x* zạn tạfi I'll go (*Vd.* zā).

  B. (zan) (*Vb. only used in this form*) kept on doing *x* kạ ～ yịnsạ keep on doing it ! (= rifkạ).

zana A. (zānạ) *Vb.* 1A (1) (*a*) drew (line, pattern, picture). (*b*) ornamented (wall, gourd, etc.) with designs (*cf.* zạyyanạ). (2) an ～ masạ jịkī dạ būlālạ he has been marked by the whipping. (3) cut tribal-marks (askā) on P. (4) counted up (persons or things, *not* figures) = fiirgạ, *cf.* lāsạftā. (5) an ～ sūnā ạ gidansạ yau a naming-ceremony was held at his house to-day (*cf.* sūnā 5, zạnē 3).

  B. (zānā) *f.* (*pl.* zạnạkū = zạnạkī = zạnaikū). (1) mat made of one of the grasses fiyārạ, gambạ, or tsaurē. (2) lāyạz zānā *Vd.* lāyạ 7.

  C. (zạnā) *f.* = sạ̄bā 1.

zạnā'idạ (*rustic*) = jạnā'izạ.

zance A. (zạncē) *m.* (*pl.* zantukạ = zantuttukạ = *Sk.* zantukkạ). (1) (*a*) (i) conversation *x* sun yi ～ they conversed. sunạ ～ they're conversing. (ii) ạbōkin ～ *m.* P. with whom one is conversing. (iii) ạbōkin zạncaŋkạ *Vd.* farkē. (*b*) wannạŋ ～ nȩ̄ this is mere talk. (*c*) *x* (i) aŋ kāmạ mazā, kadạ dǎi ạ yi zạncam mātā men have been captured, not to mention women. fiaŋfiarạ kūwā, wannạŋ, bạ̄ zạncantạ akȩ̄ ba this hail is indescribably severe. (*d*) wannạŋ wạhalạ tā wucȩ̄, sǎi tāshịn zạncē that trouble has passed and is now merely a topic of small talk. (*e*) *Vd.* tụnjēran zạncē. (2) (*a*) affair *x* zạncan yāfii the matter of war. bạ ạ ci gạba dạ zạncam ba no progress has been made with the affair. (*b*) an yi dōkā ạ kan zạncam mōtạ kadạ ạ yi jēmāgȩ̄ in reference to motorcars, an enactment forbids riding on the mudguard.

  B. (zancȩ̄) *Vb.* 1A (1) (*a*) prompted (a witness) = magantad dạ 2. (*b*)

bā yā̧ zạntūwā he is not one to allow himself to be prompted when called as a witness (= magạntu 2). (2) advised P. on transaction.

zandagīlā *x* yā zō zandagīlansạ he came empty-handed (= tsiŋkịnrāgi).

zandalā = zandamā.

zandamā *f.* (*said by children*) penis (= ạzakạrī).

zandamēmę *m.* (*f.* zandamēmịyā) *pl.* zandam-zạndạm very tall, very long.

zandamī *m.* (*f.* zandamā) *pl.* zandamzạndạm = zandamēmę.

zạndạŋ = zạndạŋdạŋ *x* ～ dạ shī it is very tall, long.

zạndīfii = zịndīfii.

zane A. (zạnē) (1) (*a*) line (drawn on paper, sand, etc.), *cf.* sạdarạ. (*b*) kōwā ya ga zạbūwā, dạ zạnantạ ya gan tạ everyone is as God made him. (*c*) bạ̄ mai shāfę masạ ～ ạ kaŋ ạbin naŋ he has not his equal in this matter. (*d*) zạnan zạbūwā *Vd.* ụŋgụlū 7. (*e*) hali zạnan dūtsę character is immutable. (2) smallpox marks *x* yanạ̄ ～ he has smallpox marks (= zanzanā 1). (3) wurin zạnan sūnā place where naming-ceremony is being held (*cf.* zānạ 5).

  B. (zānę) (1) *Vb.* 1A (1) = zānạ 1*a, b*. (2) *Vb.* 3A *Sk.* (snake) sloughed (skin).

  C. (zanę) *m.* (*pl.* zannūwạ = *Sk.* zannạ). (1) (*a*) cloth. (*b*) tā daurạ ～ she put on her body-cloth (*cf.* agēdu ; lạntō). (2) bāyā bạ̄ ～ *Vd.* bāyā 1*a.*iii. (3) bạ̄kin zanę *Vd.* bạ̄kī 3*e.* (4) zanę dạ ạljīfū *Vd.* shịrīrịtā. (5) ạ rinạ, an sạ̄ci zanạm mahaukacịyā stolen property must ultimately be disgorged. (6) *Vd.* ban ～. (7) ～ yā yi gạba *Vd.* gạndōkī. (8) zanạŋ arō *Vd.* kạtạmbiri.

zạŋgā *Vd.* rạbạ zạŋgā.

zạŋgabọ *m.* yā yiwō ～ ạ kạnsạ by inadvertently saying or doing the wrong T., he brought trouble on himself.

zạŋgadagīlā = zandagīlā.

zạŋgạ̄firit *m.* interfering in another's conversation.

zạŋgai *Kt. m.* rabies.

zạŋgạidō = zạlaidu.

zạŋgamēmę, zạŋgamī = zandamēmę, zandamī.

zạŋgaŋ *Vd.* zạŋgạŋgaŋ.

zạŋgandō *m.* tall P. or T.

zạŋgaŋ, zạŋgạŋgaŋ = zạndaŋ, zạndandaŋ.

zaŋganniyā *f.* (*pl.* zạŋgạrkū = zạŋgạrnū). (1) head of any corn (*cf.* hōgę 3). (2) dog's tail.

zạŋgar *used in* dạga ‿ as soon as *x* dạga ‿ mun yi mạganạ sǎi sukạ zạ̄gē mụ (= . . . sǎi sụ zạ̄gē mụ) the very moment we opened our mouths they abused us (= zārā 2).

zạŋgarę *Kt. m.* = sōshịyā 1.

zạŋgarērę *m.* (*f.* zạŋgarērịyā) *pl.* zạŋgaraŋ-zạŋgạraŋ very tall or long.

zạŋgārī *x* yā zō zạŋgārinsạ he came emptyhanded (= tsiŋkịnrāgị).

zạŋgạrkū *Vd.* zạŋganniyā.

zạŋgarmēmę, *etc.* = zạŋgarmī.

zạŋgarmī *m.* (*f.* zạŋgarmā) *pl.* zạŋgarzạŋgar = zạŋgarērę.

zạŋgarnịyā = zạŋganniyā.

zạŋgar-zạŋgar *Vd.* zạŋgarmī.

zạŋgạ-zạŋgạ *x* anạ̄ ‿ zūwạ gạrēshị crowds of people are on their way to see him.

zạŋgērę = zạŋgārī.

Zaŋgi (1) *man's name.* (2) na ‿ mōrīyạrkạ dę nīsā it will be long before these efforts bear fruit.

zạŋgo A. (zạŋgǫ) *m.* (1) (*a*) (i) campingplace of caravan *x* sun yi ‿ they camped. sōjạnsụ sukạ zō sukạ yi zạŋgǫ then their troops came and settled down there. (ii) lodging-place of travellers on their route. (2) fitar dạ ‿ *Vd.* fitar dạ 4*b*. (3) (*a*) distance between two camping-places or lodging places *x* gạjēran ‿ short stretch to be traversed. mun yi rabịn zạŋgǫ = mun yi rabịn hanyạ we're half-way. (*b*) sun ci ‿ bīyū they did two stages uninterruptedly. (*c*) *Vd.* wargī 3 ; bam mạganạ 3. (4) yā zō zạŋgwạn dạ6ē after being entertained elsewhere, he has returned home and will have to pay for his keep. (5) 'yar ‿ = ragạmā 1.

B. (zạŋgō) *m.* long-headed bulrushmillet.

zạŋgōmạ *m.* (*pl.* zạŋgōmai) = fạ̄tōmā.

zạŋgū *f.* hundred (= dạrī).

Zạŋgwarmạdi *epithet of* tall P.

zanị *Zar.* = zanę.

*zạnjạbil = zạnjạbịr *Ar. m.* = cịttā 6.

zạŋkā *Kt.* = zan.

zankadạ A. (zạŋkadạ) *Vb.* 2 (1) abused (= zạ̄gā). (2) aŋ zạŋkạdē shị dạ būlālạ he has been whipped. (3) ränā tā zạŋkạdē mụ the sun blazed down on us. rūwā yā zạŋkạdē mụ rain drenched us.
B. (zaŋkadā) *Vb.* 1C (*with dative*) aŋ ‿ masạ būlālạ = zạŋkadạ 2.

zạŋkạdē *Vb.* 1C = zạŋkadạ.

zạŋkadēdę *m.* (*f.* zạŋkadēdịyā) tall, wellmade P.

zạŋkạfirit *m.* interfering in another's conversation.

zạŋkala = zākala.

zạŋkalalā (1) how tall ! how long ! (2) type of mantis.

zạŋkạlē (1) *Vb.* 1C *x* yā ‿ su it far exceeds them (in length, etc.). (2) yawạn zạŋkạlēwā gạrēshị he is a busybody.

zạŋkalēlę *m.* (*f.* zạŋkaiēlịyā) *pl.* zạŋkalzạŋkal very long, very tall.

zạŋkalkạl *x* ‿ dạ shī it is very tall, long.

zạŋkalō = zākalō *q.v. under* zạ̄kalạ.

zạŋkam *m.* exaggeration.

zạŋkam *adv. and m.* nā ga mutạ̄nē ‿ ạ dākị I saw the house was crowded with people. dākị yā yi ‿ dạ mutạ̄nē the house is crowded with people.

zạŋkāyē *Vd.* zạŋkō.

zạŋkę *Vb.* 3A (1) = zarcę 2*a–d.* (2) = fiffịkē.

zạŋkēkę = zękękę.

zạŋkō *m.* (*pl.* zạŋkwāyē = zạŋkāyē). (1) = tukkū 1*a.* (2) (*a*) bird's crest. (*b*) cock's comb (2 = tukkū 2 = tsōrō = *Kt.* kēgē 2*b* = laŋge-laŋge 2), *cf.* laŋgelaŋge 2. (3) wall-top where it is taken up to a point. (4) bit over (*x* 6 is zạŋkō of 106. 200 is zạŋkō of 1,200. 1 shilling is zạŋkō of 21 shillings), *cf.* rạgī.

zannạ (1) *Had.* = zaunạ. (2) *Vd.* zanę.

zannūwạ *Vd.* zanę.

zạntā *Vb.* 3A *x* mun ‿ dạ shī we conversed with him.

zantad dạ *Vb.* 4 (1) = zancę 1*a,* 2. (2) littāfịna yā ‿ mạgạnạr my book gave the required information on the point.

zạntạkayyạ *f.* mutual conversation.

zantạrī *m.* exaggeration.

zạntu *Vb.* 3B *Vd.* zancę.

zantukạ, zantuttukạ Vd. zạncē.

zanyā f. = gallị.

zanzaɓa Kt. = zazzaɓa.

*zạnzabir = cịttā 6.

*zạnzafur Ar. m. the red dye cinnabar.

zanzạlā x yā zō zanzạlansạ he came empty-handed (= tsiŋkịnrāgị).

zanzama A. (zạnzạmā) Kt. f. = zạnzōmā. B. (zạnzamạ) Kt. Vb. 2 pestered, badgered (= ciŋkịsā 2). C. (zanzạmā) Vb. 1C x̨ yā zanzạmạ gidā he built a lofty house. tā zanzạmạ adō she piled up a high coiffure.

zạnzạmcē Vd. zạnzamtạ.

zanzamēmẹ m. (f. zanzamēmịyā) pl. zanzam-zạnzạm very high.

zanzamī m. (f. zanzamā) pl. zanzam-zạnzạm very high.

zạnzamtạ Vb. 3B (p.o. zạnzạmcē, n.o. zạnzạmci) Kt. = zạnzamạ.

zạnzanā (1) zanzanā f. = cịn ∼ m. small-pox, smallpox marks (= zậnē 2). *(2) type of prayer to discomfit enemy. (3) the evil spirit Innạ (epithet is Zanzanā, tụrākar mutūwạ).

zanzạrāgị = zanzạraŋgị = tsiŋkịnrāgị q.v.

zanzarmēmẹ, etc. = zanzamēmẹ.

zanzarmī, etc. = zanzamī.

zạnzarō m. (1) dauber-wasp (= Kt. ịrāmẹ). (2) Kt. yārinyạ cē maị ƙīrạr ∼ she's a slender girl with good hips (= ƙīrạ 1e).

zanzaryā Kt. = zurārē 1.

zanzaụnā Vb. 3A intensive from zaunạ.

zạnzōmā f. (1) badgering, pestering P. (= ciŋkisạ). (2) night-attack.

zaptara = gabtara.

zaptạrē = gabtạrē.

zar A. (zar) (1) (a) = zallā 1. (b) = zur. (c) Vd. tūwō 1a. (2) Kt. (a) yanậ dạ ɗācī ∼ it's very bitter. (b) zar dādī = dādī zar happily. B. (zạr) m. (used in wadạrī) double strand of thread reaching from gwaurō-peg to mạrī and back.

zara A. (zarạ) f. (1) x dạ ∼ tsạkāninsụ one is slightly better than the other. A yā fi B ∼ wajan tsawō A is slightly taller than B. (2) yā yi minị ∼ he cheated me. (3) mahạrbī yā shā zarạr bạrēwā the hunter transfixed the gazelle. B. (zạrā) (1) (rolled -r-) Kt. f. =

azạrā. (2) (cerebral -r-) (a) f. (i) snatching, grabbing. (ii) zạrā = halin ∼ fickleness, vacillation. (b) Vb. 2 (i) grabbed, snatched up x tā zạri ɗan tsậkō it (hawk) swooped on and seized the chick. ya zaram minị shī he grabbed it from me (= faucẹ). (ii) Vd. ŋ zaram makụ. (iii) yā zạri kạraŋ haụkā he angrily protested. C. (Zậrā) (1) (rolled -r-) (a) Vd. Fātsumạ. (b) Red-bellied Tree Starling. *(c) = Zậhạratụ. (2) (cerebral -r-) Vb. 2 (a) = zārẹ. (b) Vd. būnū 4. D. (zārā) f. (1) = zallā 1 x zārar gạskīyā the absolute truth. (2) dạ zārar as soon as x (a) dạ zārar mun yi mạganạ ṣai sukạ zậgē mụ (= . . . sậi sụ zậgē mụ) as soon as we opened our mouths, they abused us (= zaŋgar). (b) ɗaŋ hạlạk yā ƙi ambatō, dạ zārar aŋ ạmbạcē shị, sậi ạ gan shị talk of the devil !

zarạfī m. (pl. zarafōfī = zarufạ = zara-fuffukạ) (Ar. root sarrafa). (1) (a) (i) opportunity (= kafā 2). (ii) munậ yiŋ ịyậkar zarạfī gạ taịmakwansụ we are doing our best to help them. mụ yi ta yị, ịyậkar zarạfī let us strain every nerve ! (iii) kōwā yā yi ta zarạfiŋ gạbansạ everyone followed his bent. (b) yā cinyē minị ∼ he wasted my time. cịn ∼ gạrēshị he wastes one's time. (bb) yā ci zarạfīna he abused me. (c) zarạfinsạ yā ƙārẹ he has become poor, old. (d) bā nậ zūwạ makarantā sậi zarạfin yạmmā I do not attend school except in the evenings. (e) wuriŋ Audụ ya taɓạ ∼ Audu helped him in his studies. (2) wealth (= sāmụ) x bậ shi dạ ∼ he is poor.

zạraị used in yanậ dạ hancị ∼ he has a handsome nose.

zarambōtō m̃. meddlesomeness (= kạram-bậnī).

zaraŋgadē Kt. m. type of thorny plant.

zạraŋgi m. (1) over-eagerness which brings trouble. (2) surpassing.

zạranyā f. type of gruel (kụnū) flavoured with dọrōwạ-meal.

zarara A. (zārārạ) f. (1) long rope tied to animal's neck (cf. zararā, tālālā). (2) dạ ∼ ya zō he came raggedly dressed.

B. (zặ-ạrā̧) *x* dam mẹ̆ ka shigō hakặ ∼ why have you en ered without as much as a by-you -leave ?

C. (zararā) *used in* igīyặ cē̆ ∼ it is a very long rope (*cf.* zā ārặ).

zarā̧!ā *Vd.* zartọ.

zạrau (1) *x* yanā̧ dặ wuyặ ∼ he has a long neck. (2) bā yā̧ ganin ∼ sǎi yā tsiŋkặ he wants a finger in every pie.

zarā-zạrā̧ *adj. pl.* long and thin *x* yātsōtsī ∼ long, thin fingers (= sarā-sạrā̧).

zarba A. (zạrbā) *f.* sprig of dates.

B. (zarbặ) *f.* fraudulently mixing small kola-nuts with big.

zarƀaƀī *m.* (1) over-eagerness which brings one trouble. (2) being a busy-body.

zarƀẹ̆ = *Kt.* zarƀị *m.* (1) Common Grey Heron (*Ardea cinerea*). (2) farin ∼ Great White Egret (*Cosmerodius albus*). (3) Black-headed Heron (*Ardea melanocephala*).

zarce A. (zarcẹ̆) (1) *Vb.* 1A (*a*) surpassed, exceeded (= zartặ 2). (*b*) passed beyond *x* iŋ kā ∼ gidaŋ Audu̧ sǎi kặ gan su̧ if you pass beyond Audu's house, you will see them (= wucẹ̆ 2*b*.i). (*c*) passed on to *x* (i) dặgặ Kanọ yā ∼ Kạtsinặ he went on to Katsina from Kano (= wucẹ̆ 2*c*). (ii) an zarcẹ̆ rijiyā *Vd.* dabīnọ 3. (2) *Vb.* 3A (*a*) protruded *x* yā hạrƀē shị har kibīyặ tā ∼ he shot it so that it was transfixed with the arrow. (*b*) became out of alignment. (*c*) is in excess *x* gishirī yā ∼ ặ mīyặ there is too much salt in the soup (= zarẹ̆ 2). (*d*) is superior (2*a*–*d* = zaŋƙẹ̆). (*e*) hukuncị yā ∼ verdict has been given (*Vd.* zartad dặ). (*f*) mặganặ tā ∼ the matter is settled (= zargẹ̆ 2*b* = zaunặ 4*b*).

B. (zạrcē) *Vd.* zạrtā.

zarci A. (zạrci) *Vd.* zạrtā.

B. (zarcī) *Kt.* = zartsī.

zarcīyā *f.* line of embroidery along pocket-top of gown.

zare A. (zārẹ̆) *Vb.* 1A (1) (*a*) unsheathed (sword). (*b*) disengaged *x* yā zārō ƙafặ (i) he removed his foot (from mud, stirrup, shoe, etc.). (ii) he washed his hands of the matter (ii = yā zārẹ̆ hannunsặ). yanā̧ īyặ zārẹ̆ hannunsặ he can stand aloof. (*bb*) macịjī yā

zārō (= zāƙalō) kạnsặ the snake protruded its head through the hole, etc. (*c*) yā zārō ƀērā he poked the rat out of its hole with stick, etc. (= zu̧ŋgurặ = zāƙalặ). (*d*) yā ∼ jịkī he withdrew. (*e*) an ∼ masặ rǎi he is dead, he has been killed. (*f*) ya zamā kạmar an zārẹ̆ masặ lakā he became terrified. (2) yā ∼ ƙauyancī he showed boorishness. (3) yā ∼ minị idọ he glared at me (= hạrārặ). (4) dāwặ tā sōmặ ∼ kǎi the heads of the guinea-corn have begun to appear. (5) *Vd.* zārō.

B. (zā̧rē) *m.* (1) (*a*) rejected skin(s) *x* fātun nạŋ ∼ nẹ̆ these skins have been rejected by buyer. (*b*) rejected P. or persons. (2) rejection of skins by buyer *x* fātun nạŋ an yi minị zā̧raŋ ạshịriŋ twenty of my hides have been rejected.

C. (zarẹ̆) (1) *Vb.* 1A = zạrā 2*b*.i *x* yā zarẹ̆ minị shī he grabbed it from me (= wafcẹ̆ 2). (2) *Vb.* 3A = zarcẹ̆ 2*c*.

D. (zặrē) *m.* (*pl.* zarūrūwặ) (1) (*a*) thread. (*b*) (*being collective, qualifying adjective may be either sg. or pl.*) *x* jan ∼ = jājặyan ∼ red thread. (*c*) *Vd.* andīrā. (2) zặraŋ ganiŋ hannū = zặraŋ gāniŋ hannū cotton spun by bride for husband in early days of marriage. (3) bǎkin zặrē *Vd.* bā̧kī 3*h*. (4) *Vd.* hạnặ zặrē ; hạnặ mātā zặrē.

zarētā *used in* bā̧ ∼ bā̧ warētā uselessly (= sīdị).

zarga A. (zargặ) *Vb.* 1A (1) (*plus dative*) *x* yā ∼ masặ igīyặ he attached noose to it (goat, etc.) to prevent it running away or to take it to market. (2) yā ∼ kạransặ igīyặ he has gone away (1, 2 = *Kt.* zāgẹ̆ 1*f*).

B. (zạrgā) *Vb.* 2 (1) *x* yā zạrgē nị kạn sātặ he voiced suspicion that I had committed the theft (*cf.* zạrgī). (2) yā zargō nị cikim mặganặ he threw the suspicion on me (= hardặ 3*b*).

zargagā *Kt. f.* = andīrā.

zặrgagu̧ŋgu̧ŋ *m.* (1) (*a*) loose tying. (*b*) poor sewing. (2) yā yi minị ∼ = zặrgā 2.

zarge A. (zargẹ̆) (1) *Vb.* 1A. (*a*) yā ∼ ặkwīyặ = zarga 1. (*b*) yā ∼ wạndansặ, yā rātặyā = zāgẹ̆ 1*d*.ii. (*c*) entangled. (*d*) snared (bird, etc.). (*e*) arrested. (*f*) nā ∼ kudīna cikiŋ

ạbin dạ yakẹ bĭna I deducted the sum
he owed me from what I owed him
(= zāmẹ 1*b* = zāmīyā 2 = jirgẹ 1*c* =
Kt. zōjẹ 3). (2) *Vb.* 3A (*a*) became
.tangled in *x* igīyạ tā ∼ masạ ạ ꞓafạ
the rope became tangled round his
legs (*cf.* rikịcē). (*b*) = zarcẹ 2*f.*
  B. (zạrgē) *m.* (1) noose, slip-knot,
bow. (2) yā ꞓullạ ∼ he made a slip-
knot, etc.
zạrgĭ *m.* (1) *x* yā yi minị ∼ kạn sātạ =
zạrgā 1. (2) reproach, blame *x* (*a*)
nĭ nẹ ạbin zạrgĭ I am the one to blame.
yanạ dạ ạbin zạrgĭ he is blameworthy.
(*b*) nā dạuki zạrgĭ I bear the blame.
(*c*) *Vd.* hạlạk 2*c.*iii.
zạrgīnạ *f.* cubes of washing-blue (= bulụ).
zargo A. (zargō) *Vd.* zạrgā 2.
  B. (zạrgō) *m.* type of embroidery
chain-stitch.
zari A. (zarị) *m.* jangling rings, etc., used
as musical accompaniment.
  B. (zạrĭ) *m.* (1) (*a*) greed (= hạdamạ).
(*b*) maị ∼ glutton. maị zạrin aikị a
regular glutton for work. (2) yā yi ∼,
wannạꞑ yā fi ꞓaıŭꞑkạ this is beyond
your powers.
  C. (zāri) *m.* = ꞓārĭ.
  D. (zạrĭ) *m.* (1) rope inserted in
asirkā 1*a.* (2) cịn ∼ sore due to 1.
(3) sạki zārĭ *Vd.* sakị 2*f.*
zariya A. (Zārĭyạ) *f.* (1) Zaria (= Zazzạu).
(2) *epithet is* zaurạn Dạndĭ. (3) *Vd.*
hausā.
  B. (zārĭyā) *f.* (1) trouser-string
(= mazāgĭ). (3) ∼ tasụ dayā they are
relatives of each other. (3) *Vd.* zaryā.
zarkada *Kt.* = zạꞑkada.
zarkadēdẹ = zạꞑkadēdẹ.
zạrꞓwai = cạrkwai 1.
zạrꞓwanyā how sweet !
zạrmai = jạrmai.
zạrmammīyā *f. used in* zạrmammīyar
zūcĭyā gạrēshị he is an inveterate thief
(*cf.* zạrmau, tugụ).
zạrmau *m.* (1) inveterate cadger of meals
(*cf.* zạrmammīyā). (2) *Vd.* tugụ.
zarmẹ *Vb.* 3A (1) = zạꞓu *x* yā zarmẹ
dạ shĭ he's keen to get it. (2) cikịnsạ
yā ∼ he has diarrhœa (= zāwọ).
zạrnạ̄wị = zịrnạ̄wị.
zarnĭ *m.* (1) petulance. (2) = ꞓārĭ.

*zạrnīhị *m.* a yellow pigment used on
manuscripts.
zārō (1) *Vb.* 1E *Vd.* zārẹ. (2) *Vb.* 3A
idạnsạ yā ∼ his eyes weıe starting out
of his head.
zarrạ *Ar.* (1) *used in* bạ ni dạ shĭ kō yạ
ꞓwạyar ∼ I have none at all. (2) *cf.*
mịskālị 2.
zarta A. (zartạ) *Vb.* 1A (1) (worm sạꞑ-
kạrā, kịcĭcĭyạ) bored into. (2) exceeded,
surpassed (= zarcẹ 1*a*). (3) (oil, etc.)
permeated.
  B. (zạrtā) (1) *Vb.* 2 (*p.o.* zạrcē, *n.o.*
zạrci) surpassed, exceeded (= zarcẹ
1*a*). (2) *Kt. f.* = kātsị.
zartaƃēƃẹ *m.* (*f.* zartaƃēƃĭyā) .big and
strong.
zartad dạ *Vb.* 4 (1) yā ∼ hukuncị = yā ∼
shạrĭ'ạ he delivered his verdict (= yaꞑ-
kẹ 1*e.*iii), *cf.* hakụntā, zarcẹ 2*e.* (2)
yā ∼ maganạ he has carried out the
affair.
zartakẹ *m.* (*pl.* zạrtạkū). (1) big, strong
man. (2) tall pole.
zartakēkẹ, etc. = zartaƃēƃẹ.
zartar dạ = zartad dạ.
zartọ *m.* (*pl.* zarạ̄tā = zartunạ). (1) (*a*)
saw. (*b*) file (1 = gụrjāgọ 3*a*) (1*b* =
magāgarī). (2) (*a*) tireless P. (*b*) ∼
magāgarī what an energetic person !
(3) *Vd.* dartọ.
zartsĭ *m.* (1) brackishness. (2) (*a*) rūwan ∼
m. brackish water. (*b*) kō ꞓáꞓạ rūwan ∼
zaị kashẹ ꞓishị, bạ kạman na dādĭ
ba no substitute is as good as the
original.
zartunạ *Vd.* zartọ.
zarufạ *Vd.* zarạfĭ.
zārụmĭ = jārụmĭ.
zārumtạ = jārumtạ.
zarūrūwạ *Vd.* zạrē.
zaryā *f.* (1) the skink shạrindọ (= mazarĭ
5). (2) hurrying to and fro. (3) *Vd.*
zārĭyā.
zạtā *Vb.* 2 (*p.o.* zạcē, *n.o.* zạci) (*for
progressive Vd.* zạtō). (1)‾ thought
(*a*) *x* nā zạtā zaị zō = nā zạci zaị zō =
nā zạcē shị zaị zō I think (thought)
he'll come. wạndạ ya ga hakạ, baị
kụ̄wā zạtā ba anyone who sees this
unexpectedly. (*b*) *Vd.* kạmar 5. (2)
(*plus dative*) *x* nā zatam masạ rĭbạ I

thought it would be profitable. (3) *cf.* bạ ~.

Zątaŋkụ *Vd.* **zątō** 3.

zāti̱ = zāci̱.

zątō *m.* (1) (*v.n.* and *progressive of* **zątā**) (*a*) *x* n nạ̄ ~ yā gamạ I think he has finished. (*b*) *Vd.* **kạmar** 5. (2) (*a*) thought, supposition *x* bā ạ̄ aiki̱ dạ ~ one does not act on mere supposition. (*b*) mahạssạdā sunạ̄ zątam fari̱, Allạ̄ yā sakō rūwā he has prospered to the discomfiture of his enemies. (*c*) (i) bạ ~ bạ̄ tsạmmāni̱ sukạ zō they came unexpectedly. (ii) bạ̄ zątō, bạ̄ tsạmmāni̱, bạ̄ sallamạ, bạ̄ ƙyaŋƙyasạ ƙōfạ sǎi mukạ gan sụ we caught sight of them quite unexpectedly. (3) Zątaŋkụ *name given slave or slave-girl by mistress unexpectedly become rich (when such female slave is called by this name being uttered, she replies* Allạ̄ yā yi dạ̄munā).

zattsī = zartsī.

zau (1) yanạ̄ dạ zāfī ~ it is very hot. (2) yanạ̄ da zāƙī ~ it is very tasty (= zāƙī 1*a*.iv).

zauɗạ *Vb.* 3A = muskụɗā 2, 3.

zaụkakkē *m.* (*f.* zaụkakkīyā) *pl.* zaụkạkkū (*d.f.* zakạ) *Sk.* = zạ̄yayyē.

zaụlayạ = zōlayạ.

zaunạ *Vb.* 3A (1) (*a*) (i) sat down. (ii) i̱ŋ kanạ̄ tsạye, kạ zaunạ *Vd.* tsạye 5. (*b*) sunạ̄ zaunạ̄wā they are in the act of seating themselves. nā gan sụ sunạ̄ zaunạ̄wā = nā gan sụ sunạ̄ zaụne I saw them seated (Mod. Gram. 123*e*.ii). (*c*) *Vd.* zamā 2*a*. (*d*) (i) im bạ ạ ~ dạ gi̱ndī ba, bā ạ̄ zamā dạ kā if one cannot get on with relations, how much less with strangers. (ii) *Vd.* gi̱ndī 1*h*. (*e*) ạ ~ lāfi̱yạ, am mạ̄ri tsōfam banzā nothing can be done as he has no money or helpers. (2) settled (in place). (3) remained in *x* (*a*) tạfi kạ̄suwā kạ sayō mini̱ tābạ, ạmmā kadạ kạ ~ go to market and buy me some tobacco, but don't delay there ! yā ~ ƙasā tasụ he remained in his own country. yā ~ Kano̱ he remained at Kano̱. (*b*) i̱ŋ A̱ zaunạ ta cẹ manạ ạ zaunạ, sǎi mụ zaunạ if we're forced to stay, then we must (*cf.* fi̱ta 2*d*). (*c*) zại zaunạ ạbinsạ he'll remain independent.

(*d*) yā cẹ mụ zaunạ, shī dạ kạnsạ zại yī he told us to "sit tight" and he would do it himself. (4) (*a*) (pot. etc.) sat firmly. (*b*) (i) mạganạ tā ~ the matter is settled (= zarcẹ 2*f*). (ii) kalmōmi̱n naŋ sun zaunạ ram dạ gi̱ndinsụ those words have come to stay, are firmly established. (5) *Vd.* zauna-*compounds,* zaụnu.

zaunad dạ *Vb.* 4 = zamad dạ 2, 3.

zaụnạ gạriŋkạ *m.* (1) cutting off both hands and both feet of P. (= zaụna kạ ci dōyạ 1). (2) yā yi mini̱ ~ he overstayed his welcome (= kisạn dạɓē).

zaụnạ inūwạ *f.* type of dwarf guinea-corn.

zaụnạ kạ ci dōyạ *m.* (1) = zaụnạ gạriŋkạ 1. (2) = tsụgunạ kạ ci dōyạ.

zaụnannē *m.* (*f.* zaụnannīyā) *pl.* zaụnạnnū. (1) settled, not nomad. (2) permanent. (3) firmly established (*x* custom).

zaụnau *m.* (1) broker's hiding, under other articles, a thing he does not want to sell, in order to tell his principal it is unsaleable, and so get it cheap himself. (2) = zāmi̱yā 2. (3) waiting in presence of tradesman engaged in completing article for one or at debtor's house till his return, etc. (4) yāƙi̱ yā yi manạ ~ we are beleaguered.

zaụne (1) (*noun of state from* zaunạ) (*a*) yanạ̄ ~ he is seated (*Vd.* zaunạ 1*b*. (*b*) i̱ŋ kanạ̄ zaụne *Vd.* tsạye 5. (2) *m.* act of sitting *x* (*a*) shiri̱n ~ yā fi na tsạye the prospect of rest is more pleasant than that of work. (*b*) anạ̄ bari̱n na ~ dōmin na tsạye the penalty has been mitigated on account of his family connections. (*c*) zā mụ hanạ su zaụne, zā mụ hanạ su tsạye we shall give them no respite. (*d*) zaụne tā kōmō tsụgụne matters have become serious. (3) anạ̄ kwānan ~ (*a*) noisy drumming at wedding-party is going on. (*b*) party is being held to celebrate her cessation of mourning for husband. (*c*) kadạ kạ jāwō mini̱ kwānan ~ bạ̄ bi̱kī don't involve me in responsibility ! (4) yā tā dạ ~ tsạye (*a*) he cancelled the agreement arrived at. (*b*) he introduced disorder where was previously good order. (5) *Vd.* ɓạrāwo̱ 5.

zaụnu *Vb.* 3B (1) (*a*) stayed for long. (*b*)

zamammu yā ⁓ we've long been associated together. (2) wurin nąn bā yā zaunūwā this place is uninhabitable.

zaurancē m. talking in cryptic jargon (x mutum dą kanąnsą one shilling and sixpence).

zaurę m. (pl. zauruką = Kt. zaurukką). (1) (a) thatched, round entrance-porch to compound (= mijin gidā), cf. tąfarfąrā. (b) Sk. mud-topped entrance-porch (= sōrō 1f). (c) sun tāshi dągą zaurąn ąbōkąn gąbā, sun kōmō nāmu they've left the enemy and joined us. (d) bąba ą ⁓ Vd. bąba 4. (2) kud̃in ⁓ Vd. kudī 1n. (3) zaurąn Dąndī epithet of Zaria (Vd. Dąndī).

zaurī Kt. = zarnī.

zauruką Vd. zaurę.

zauta A. (zautā) Vb. 1C flabbergasted, caused P. to lose presence of mind.

B. (zautą) f. being flabbergasted, nonplussed.

zautara = gabtara.

zautu Vb. 3B was flabbergasted, nonplussed, lost presence of mind.

zauzau used in yā dauru ⁓ it is firmly tied.

zauzautą Vb. 2 (p.o. zauzaucē, n.o. zauzauci) Kt. pestered.

zawal Vd. hantsī 1c.

zawara A. (zawąrā) f. (pl. zawarōrī = zawarāwā). (1) = bązawąrā. (2) idąn ⁓ Vd. idon 7.

B. (ząwārą) f. (pl. ząwąrī = zą-wąrū). (1) semicircular kantu q.v. of salt (= shąn watą), cf. hōcę. (2) yā zō maną ⁓ tasą he came to us empty-handed (= tsinkinrāgi).

zawarāwā Vd. bązawąrā.

zawarci m. (1) being a bązawąrā. (2) zawarcintą yakē yī he is courting this bązawąrā (cf. tashi, bązawąrā 1b).

ząwąrī Vd. ząwārą.

ząwarō m. Nupe beating of small drums.

zawarōrī Vd. zawąrā.

ząwąrū Vd. ząwārą.

ząwāti Nor. = ząwwāti.

zāwayad dą = kāsayad dą.

zāwąyē Vb. 1C (1) (a) defiled with excrement (cf. zāwo) = kāsąyē. (b) (i) yā zāwąyę wurinsą he has made where he lives "too hot to hold him". (ii)

yā zāwąyę sansą he's quite shameless (d.f. sau) (= fitsąrē 2). (2) yā zāwąyę cikinsą he purged his stomach (cf. zāwo).

zāwąyī = zāwo m. (1) diarrhœa (= gudun dawą = gudą 1c = kōrā 2b = zarmę 2). (2) māgąnin ⁓ (a) aperient. (b) remedy for diarrhœa. (3) ⁓ mąi kārę karfī inveterate cadger (= marąrąkī). (4) Vd. kūrā 30, 31. (5) zāwo type of fish.

zāwo = zāwąyī.

ząwūtą Vb. 3B became terrified.

zawūtad dą Vb. 4 terrified P.

ząwwā Sk. Vd. zaką.

ząwwal Ar. f. dą ⁓ at between noon and about 2 p.m.

ząwwāti m. a soft calico (= alawayyo).

ząwwūwā Sk. x gąrin nąn bā yā ⁓ that town is not reachable (cf. zaką, zō 1f).

ząyayyē m. (f. ząyayyīyā) pl. ząyąyyū. (1) alien. (2) guest, stranger, visitor (cf. zaukakkē, zaką, ząwwūwā).

zayyana A. (zayyąnā) Vb. 1C Ar. (1) (a) adorned. (b) improved. (2) yā ⁓ mini lābāri he informed me in detail of the matter (cf. bayyąnā).

B. (ząyyaną) f. (pl. zayyanōnī) illuminated designs on Koranic, etc., manuscripts (cf. zāną 1b).

zāzā f. (pl. zązaikū) (1) Sk. (vulgar) pubic hair. *(2) = dausąyī. (3) zāzar gīwā the plant Hygrophila spinosa (= kayąr gīwā).

*zazō Kt. m. = dausąyī.

zazzaɓa A. (zazząɓā) Vb. 1C steamed (rice prior to husking) = Sk. gumą 2b, cf. suląlā 2.

B. (zązząɓą) f. (1) (secondary v.n. to zazząɓā) x taną zązzaɓąr shinkāfā = taną zazząɓą shinkāfā. (2) taną ⁓ she's steaming rice prior to husking.

zazząɓē Vb. 3A steamed (as in zazząɓā) all the rice.

zązząɓī m. (1) (a) fever, feverishness (= mąshasshąrā 1a). (b) feverish cold (= jantę). (c) (loosely used) feeling out of sorts. (2) watą yā yi ⁓ = mąshasshąrā 3. (3) bą ąbin dą zai sāmē shi sǎi dǎi kudī su yi ⁓ he will not be punished for his crime, but his money will go in buying himself off.

zązzāfā m., f. (pl. zāfąfā) hot.

zazzaga A. (zazzagā) *Vb.* 1C (1) teased (raw silk, *i.e.* tsāmīyā). (2) (*with dative*) (*a*) yā zazzaga turārē a rīgā he shook some scent on to his gown from the bottle (*cf.* zazzaga 1). (*b*) yā ~ masa karātū (i) he pushed on his pupil (*Vd.* zūkū). (ii) he shook its (horse's) bridle to quicken its pace or halt it. (3) yā zazzaga buhū he thumped sack on ground to even up its contents (*cf.* girgijē 2).

B. (zazzaga) (1) *Vb.* 2 shook out *x* yā zazzagi turārē he shook some scent out of the bottle (*cf.* zazzagā 2). (2) *f.* (*secondary v.n. of* zazzagā) *x* yanā zazzagar tsāmīyā = yanā zazzaga tsāmīyā he is teasing raw silk.

C. (zazzāgā) *intensive from* zāga.

D. (zazzāga) *intensive from* zāgā.

Zazzaganci *m.* Zaria language or ways.

Zazzagāwā *Vd.* Bazazzagī.

zazzagē *Vb.* 1C (1) teased, shook (*as in* zazzagā 1, zazzaga 1) *all* of. (2) = girgijē 1*a*. (3) nā ~ masa cikina I took him into my confidence. (4) kāzā tā zazzagē kwǎi hen has laid complete sitting of eggs (*cf.* saka 2*a*).

zazzākā *m.*, *f.* (*pl.* zākākā) sweet.

zazzalō = zalzalō.

zazzarī *Kt. m.* undue eagerness or haste.

Zazzau *f.* = Zārīya.

zazzauna *Vb.* 3A *intensive from* zauna.

zazzō kept on coming (*intensive from* zō).

zēkēkē (1) *m.* sandā yā yi ~ the stick is too long for the purpose required. (2) *adv.* (*a*) yanā da kyēya ~ he has protuberant occiput. (*b*) = kērērē.

zētē *m.* yā yi ~ it (beard, chin, etc.) is long and pointed.

zifa = zuffa.

zigāzigī *Vd.* zugāzugī.

zigē = zugē.

zigidir = tsirāra 2*a*.

zigiramtū = zigiribtū = rīshī *q.v.*

zikirī *m.* = kalma 2.

Zilai *f.* Zilla (woman's name).

zilaika *f.* a gown of tagūwā type which falls below the knees and the sleeves of which extend to the wrist.

zilāma *f.* oppression (= zālunci).

zilkūwā *f.* poor type of tagūwā gown.

zilla *Ar. f.* (1) oppression *x* yā shā ~ he has been humiliated, suffered trouble (= zālunci). (2) karāma bāyan ~ relenting towards P. one has treated harshly.

zillē *Vb.* 3A = sullubē 2*a–c*.

zillī *Kt. m.* (1) neck of bottle-gourd made into child's trumpet (= bindī 2). (2) neck of bottle-gourd made into receptacle for hunter's charms.

zimma *f.* (1) large amount *x* gishirī mai ~ much salt. mutānē suna da ~ there are many people. (2) *Ar.* (*a*) intention *x* yā dauka a zimmar sāta he took it intending to steal it. yā sōma da zimmar wāsā he began in joke. *(3) *Ar.* (*a*) behalf *x* nā sayē shi a ~ tasa I bought it on his behalf. (*b*) yanā zimmata he is my responsibility. (*c*) *Vd.* azzimma.

zina A. (zīna) *Ar. f.* adornment (*cf.* zāna, zayyana).

B. (zinā) *Ar. f.*·(1) adultery, fornication (= lālāta 3 = farkā 2*a* = fāsikanci = kwartanci = ma'āsī). (2) *epithet is* Tandū ūwar maiko. (3) mādakin ~ *Vd.* tsārancē.

zināce-zinācē *m.* repeated adultery, fornication, etc.

zīnārīyā *f.* (*pl.* zīnārī = zīnārū) (*Ar.* dīnār *from Latin* denarius). (1) (*a*) gold. (*b*) kumfan ~ *m.* gold tinsel (= dusā 1*b*). (2) ~ da kafo *epithet of* cows.

zindārī *m.* yā zō zindārinsa he came empty-handed (= tsinkinrāgi).

*zindīkanci *m.* being zindīki 2.

zindīki *m.* (*f.* zindīkīyā) *pl.* zindīkai *Ar.* (1) destitute P. (2) heretic.

zindir A. (zindir) = tsirāra 2*a*.

B. (Zindir) *f.* Zinder.

zingāre *x* yā zō zingāransa he came empty-handed (= tsinkinrāgi).

zinkir *x* yā cika ~ it (bag, etc.) is chock-full.

zinkirērē *m.* (*f.* zinkirērīyā) *pl.* zinkirzinkir chock-full.

zir *adv.* (1) jā ~ scarlet (= wur). (2) yā zō nan ~ he came here naked (= tsirāra). (3) hanya cē ~ = hanya cē ~ da ita it is a narrow road. (4) *Vd.* zur.

zira = zura.

*zira'a *f.* (1) = kāmu 5*a*. (2) two stars above Gemini.

*zįrā'į = kāmų 5*a*.

zirē *m*. (1) = nąshē 1*b*. (2) type of children's game.

zirgą *Vd*. gafīyą.

zįrgą-zirgā *f*. constantly going to and fro (= kaiwā dą kāwǫwā).

ziri A. (zīrī) *m*. (1) (*a*) zīrim bąntē small ragged loin-cloth (= munųtsī). (*b*) zīrin tsųmmā old rag. (2) narrow place *x* ɗan ~ *m*. narrow place, narrow passage, etc., wata 'yar zīriŋ hanyą narrow pathway. watą ɗan ~ nē, yanā dą wųyar ganī the moon is so tiny that it is hard to see. (3) *Kt*. yā ɗaurą ~ he (wrestler) put on adorned loin-cloth.
B. (zirį) (1) *m*. (*a*) threading (beads). (*b*) = zubį 6, 7. (2) what a big appetite !

zįrīrī *used in* hanyą 'yar ~ cē it is a narrow road.

zįrītītį *Kt*. *m*. meddlesomeness (= kąrąmbąnī).

zirnąkō *m*. (*sg*., *pl*.) black hornet which builds white hanging nest.

zirnānįyā *f*. = girgiję.

zirnąwį *m*. = faŋgamī.

zirzir *m*. non-perforátion of hymen, preventing parturition (*Vd*. kakąndą).

zįyādī *Ar*. *m*. (1) loud wrangling. *****(2) exaggeration.

zīyārą *Ar*. *f*. visiting.

zīyartą *Vb*. 2 (*p.o*. zįyarcē, *n.o*. zįyąrci) *Ar*. (1) visited. (2) wurin ~ place requiring to be visited.

zįzą (1) *f*. = jīzą 2. (2) yārinyą cē ~ she's a lovely girl.

zizzigę = zuzzugę.

zō (*this is* -ō *form of* jē) (*v.n. is* zūwą *m*. : *for imperative*, *Vd. below* 1*c*). (1) (*a*) came (= tafō). (*b*) (*in Daura, pronoun can be repeated after verb*) *x* nā ~ nį I came. kā ~ ką you came. yā ~ shį he came. (*c*) (i) ~ nąŋ come here ! (ii) yāką *m*. come here ! = ką zō. yākį *f*. come here ! = kį zō. kų zō *pl*. come here ! (iii) ~ mų jē let us be off ! (*d*) *progressive* yanā zūwą he is coming. zūwąnsą his coming. (*e*) " ą zō gąrēnį ! " ɗākį yā fāɗą wą gurgūwā tąre dą ɗam mąsū gidā, ta cē " im bą kų zō dǫmīna ba, kwā zō dǫmin ɗaŋkų " (*said by*

mai tąllą) buy, buy ! (*f*) wurįn naŋ bā yā zǫwūwā yąu that place is not reachable to-day (*cf*. ząyayyē, ząwwūwā). (*g*) ˙ *d*. zazzō. (2) (*a*) (Mod. Gram. 130*a* *narrator often phrases his sentence as if he were an eye-witness, hence the reason for* 2*b* *below*) *x* lōkącįn dą suką zō Kanǫ when they reached Kano. (*b*) *Sk*. mų ~ wurinsą let us go to him ! (= jē), *cf*. zūwą 2*a*. (3) sōją nē irįn na " kų zō kų ganī ! " he is a practical soldier. bą ą yi wani yākį ba na " kų zō, kų ganī ! " no important war has occurred. (4) became *x* duk rįgimąr sāi ta zō dą saukī the commotion " ended in smoke ". ąbų ya zo dą gaddamą then things became in a muddle. ąl'amąrįn ya zō haką the matter turned out thus (*cf*. tąfī 1*a*.ii). (5) *Vd*. zǫ ka, zūwą.

zōbā = zǫbā *f*. (1) vomiting (= amai). (2) *Sk*. = laląs 2.

zōbą *Vb*. 1A (1) (*a*) overlapped. (*b*) caused to overlap. (2) slightly exceeded.

zōbanyą *f*. = zōbę.

zōbąrōdǫ = sōbąrōdǫ.

zǫbba *Vd*. zōbę.

zobe A. (zōbę) (1) *m*. (*pl*. zǫbbā = ząbbā) (*a*) (i) ring. (ii) kurman ~ ring with no join (magamī) in it. (*b*) an yi musų ~ they have been surrounded (= gēwąyā 2). sun yi mukų zōbę kaf they completely surrounded you. (*c*) (i) yā ɗauki zōbęna he followed my example. (ii) yā ɗauki ~ he jumped to the right conclusion that . . . (2) *Vb*. 1A. (*a*) took back (present already given). (*b*) kā ~ lādaŋką you have now nullified your previous good deeds.
B. (zǫbē) *m*. taking back present already given.

zōbę *Vb*. 1A (1) = zōbą 1*a*, 2. (2) *Vb*. 3A (*a*) overlapped. (*b*) protruded (= zarcē 2*a*).

zōbīyā *f*. (1) protrusion, overlapping. (2) damįm mąiwā mai ~ what a bad-tempered person !

zōgalagandį *m*. (1) the Horse-radish tree (*Moringa pterygosperma*) (= shųką halī = shųką haliŋką). (2) *its epithet is* Sąmąrin daŋgā.

zǫgarī *m.* (1) small pile of reaped bulrush-millet which is made July–August to prevent rain rotting the crop (*it is left thus 10–12 days till late August, then the heads are cut off* (yaŋkaŋ kǎi) *and it is made into a* būshīyā 4*b*). (2) dạ A dạ B sun yi ∼ A and B are facing each other in threatening attitude. (3) *Sk.* hut made of zānā-mats.

zǫgī *m.* throbbing pain (= ɗǫkī 2), *cf.* ɗạl-ɗạl.

zoje A. (zōjẹ) *Vb.* 1A (1) = gōgẹ 1*b*.ii. (2) *Kt.* = gōgẹ 1*b*.iii. (3) = gẹ̄gā, zargẹ 1*f*.
 B. (zǫjē) (1) *Vd.* zǫzā. (2) *m.* yā yi minị ∼ he " split on me ".

zǫji *Vd.* zǫzā.

zǫ ka (*f.* zǫ ki) *pl.* kụ zō *Sk.* = jẹ̄ ka, etc. (*q.v. under* jē 3*a*, *b*), *cf.* zō 2*b*.

zǫlayạ *Vb.* 2 cross-questioned (= leccạ).

zǫlōlǫ *m.* (*f.* zǫlōlụ̄wā) tall P.

zōmō *m.* (*pl.* zōmạ̄yē) (1) hare. (2) (*a*) idan ∼ yā ɗīmautạ, bā yạ̄ jiŋ kiɗạm farautạ refusing to listen to reason. (*b*) ∼ yā ji kiɗạm farautạ, ya cẹ̄ " caŋ gā̰ su gạdā " I've nothing to fear from that quarter. (3) barcin ∼ *m.* sleeping " with one eye open " (= kịrī 1*b*). (4) kōwā ya ci ∼, yā ci gudụ no reward without effort (*Vd.* gudụ 2*d*.i). (5) ∼ bā yạ̄ fushī dạ makashinsạ *Vd.* makạshī. (6) nā tūrạ (= nā kōrạ) makạ ∼ I have finished my share of the work befɵre you. (7) (*a*) hakōrin ∼ yạ mụtụ ? *Vd.* gīwā 1*b*. (*b*) hakōrin ∼ *m.* P. of no account. (8) ∼ bạ̄ bāwaŋ gīwā ba nẹ̄, sǎi dạwạ sukạ tārạ they are of different origin, but doing the same work. (8*A*) banzā bā tạ̄ kai ∼ kạsūwā *Vd.* banzā 1*f*. (9) iŋ kā ga aŋ kāmạ ∼ yanạ̄ gudụ, ajạlinsạ yā zō everyone has his allotted span of life. (10) dạmunā tā yi shigar ∼, tā yi fitar gīwā the wet season began scantily but was drenching later on. (11) wani ∼ ạ sạ̄barạ kạm bar shị = hakị 1*b*. (12) kẽkụ̄wā sǎi zōmō *Vd.* rūwā C.17. (13) kamshin ∼ *Vd.* bạbbakạ 2.

zǫmǭdō *m.* = jẹ̄mō.

zǫmǭmǭ *used in* yā yi ∼ dạ bạ̄kī he pouted (with anger, etc.).

zōramī *Kt. m.* (*f.* zōramā) tall P.

zǭrǭrǭ *adv.* in great length *x* yanạ̄ dạ rawạnī ∼ he has a long turban. kāyā ∼ long load. ginị ∼ long wall.

zǭwu *Vd.* zō 1*f*.

zoza A. (zǫzā) *Vb.* 2 (*p.o.* zǫjē, *n.o.* zǫji). (1) = gǭgā 1, 2. *(2) yā zōzanĺ minị lạifī = zōzạ.
 B. (zōzạ) *Vb.* 1A (*with dative*) yā ∼ minị lạifī = yā ∼ minị kāshiŋ kā̰jī he falsely accused me (*Vd.* kāshiŋ kạ̄zā).

zōzạyē (1) *Vb.* 3A (fence) became worn (by cattle brushing against it) ; (river-bank, wall) became eroded. (2) *Vb.* 1C wore away (fence) ; eroded (wall, etc.) *as in* 1.

*(zǭzō) *Kt. m.* cartilage between the nostrils.

zụ̄ *Kt. m.* = zụ̄wō.

zuba A. (zubạ) *Vb.* 1A (1) (*a*) poured (*cf.* ɗūrạ, tsīyāyā, fyāɗạ 1*e*, jūyẹ 1*c*, bul-bụlā). (*b*) mun ∼ we've stated our case to the judge. (*c*) mụ ∼, mụ ganī we'll let events take their course. (*d*) ạ ∼ mīyạ *Vd.* gạrā̰jē 2. (*e*) ∼ gishirī *Vd.* gishirī 2. (2) put *several* things into (*cf.* zubar dạ) *x* an ∼ su ạ buhū they have been put in a sack (*cf.* ajịyē 7*a*, sā̰ A. sakạ). (3) (*a*) did much of yanạ̄ ∼ masạ karyā he's telling him many lies. an ∼ aikị yạu much work has been done to-day. sun ∼ tạfīyạ they have travelled far. (*b*) an zubạ masạ kudī tsababa it's very expensive. (4) yanạ̄ ∼ mulkị he's making a show of his authority (*Vd.* mulkị 3). (5) yā ∼ sau ạ rījịyā he's become involved in intrigue (= zurạ 1*d*). (6) sun ∼ wạ Kanọ harị they raided Kano. (7) ∼ idọ *Vd.* idọ 1*b*. (8) *Vd.* amāwạlī, ạdāshī, kwǎi 1*c*.ii, kwārī 5*b*, arwā, kwạncē 1*a*, sụ̄rūtụ 2, tserē 2. (9) yā ∼ minị lạ̄bārị = rantạ6ā 1.
 B. (zụba) *Vb.* (*v.n.* zụbāf., *progressive* yanạ̄ zụbā). (1) (*a*) (i) leaked *x* tụ̄lū yā ∼ the ewer leaked. sōrō yanạ̄ zụbā the mud-topped building is leaking. (ii) leaked out = zurā̰rē 1–4 *q.v.* (*b*) idạnsạ yanạ̄ zụbā his eyes are watering. hancịnsạ yā ∼ his nose was running. (*c*) leaked into *x* rūwā yanạ̄ zụbā ạ ɗākị rain is leaking into the house (= zu-rā̰rā 1*c*). (*d*) kafạssạ tanạ̄ zụbā he has

a running sore in his leg. (2) **tukunyā**
tā ~ the pot boiled over (= **bōrī** 3*a*).
(3) **yanā zubā** he's chattering. (4)
ginị yā ~ the wall partially collapsed
(*cf.* **zubẹ**). (5) (*a*) **ganyē yā** ~ the
leaves fell off. (*b*) **gāshịnta** (= **kạntạ**)
yā ~ her hair fell out (*cf.* **zubẹ**). (6)
(*a*) **mutānē dạ yawạ sun** ~ many people
have died. (*b*) **mutānē dạ yawạ sun** ~
ạ gōnā there are many workers on the
farm. (*c*) **aikị yā** ~ much work has
been done. (7) **yā** ~ **ạ ƙōfạr gidā**
he is sitting at the entrance to the
compound (= **zubẹ** 2*d*). (8) **zanạn**
nạn yanā zụbā = **zụbā gạrēshị** the
colour in this cloth runs. (9) *Vd.*
zubar. (10) **na bakạ nā zụbā** *Vd.*
tạunā 2*a*.iii. (11) **mā zubạ rūwā ạ ƙas,**
mụ shā dom murnạ we shall rejoice.

    C. (**zụbā**) *Vd.* **zụba**.

    D. (**zubā**) *f.* = **kịndạ̈i**.

zubar (*dative form of* **zụba** Mod. Gram.
114). (1) **yā** ~ **minị** he lowered himself in my estimation. (2) **watạ yā** ~
kudụ the horns of the crescent moon
point south (= **bākatar** 1). (3) **sōrō**
yā ~ the roof of the mud-topped
building is sloping.

zubar dạ *Vb.* 4 (1) (*a*) poured away
(= **zubẹ** 1*b*). (*b*) threw away *several*
things, *e.g.* grain, liquid, etc. (= **kifad**
dạ = **jirkitad dạ** = **wātsạ** 1*d*), *cf.* **yā dạ** ;
jēfad dạ ; **zubạ** 2. (2) (*a*) **tā** ~ **cikị** she
had miscarriage, abortion (= **gammō** 6
= **ƀạrī** 1*g* = **zubẹ** 2*e*). (*b*) *Vd.* **zub dạ**. (3)
(*a*) **kōwā ya zubar minị dạ tsāmīyāta, sǎi**
n̦ zubar masạ dạ nōnạnsạ I'll not be
outdone in paying people back in their
own coin ! (*b*) **yā** ~ **tsāmīyar kūrā** *Vd.*
kūrā 23. (4) **zā kạ zubar mịnị ?** *Vd.* **dībạ**
1*j*. (5) *Vd.* **dāfārā** 2.

zụbar gadō *m.* simultaneous downing of
two wrestlers = *Sk.* **fạrgạdā** (*cf.* **mu-**
tūwạ 1*gg*.ii ; **jēmāgẹ** 4).

zụbau *m.* (1) grinding-stone of soft
material (*cf.* **garwai**). (2) steady ill-
luck (= **rārīyar hannū**).

zub dạ *Vb.* 4 = **zubar dạ** *x* **yā** ~ **shī** = **yā**
zubshē shị he poured it (liquid) away.

zụbde (*noun of state from* **zubạ**) *Kt. x*
yanā nạn ~ it is here poured out
(= **zụbe**).

zube A. (**zubẹ**) (1) *Vb.* 1A. (*a*) poured (*as*
in **zubạ**) *all*. (*b*) poured away (= **zubar**
dạ). (*c*) **yā** ~ **masạ lịnzāmị** (i) he
rode it on a loose rein. (ii) he allowed
him plenty of freedom. (2) *Vb.* 3A
(*a*) (i) leaked, flowed out entirely (*cf.*
zụba 1*a, c*). (ii) *Vd.* **nōnọ** 1*f.* (*b*) (wall)
entirely collapsed (*cf.* **zụba** 4). (*c*)
became emaciated. (*d*) **yā** ~ **ạ ƙōfạr**
gidā = **zụba** 7. (*e*) **cikịnta yā** ~ =
zubar dạ 2. (*f*) (*several* teeth) fell out
(*cf.* **fādị** 5*a*). (*g*) **kạrạtunsạ yā** ~ he has
forgotten what he learned. (*h*) *Kt.*
lost heart (= **fādị** 11). (*j*) **garūrūwạn**
dạ sukạ zubẹ manạ the towns which
were lost to us. (*k*) **yā zubẹ manạ** we're
too much for him. (*l*) **girmantạ yā**
zubẹ *Vd.* **mạraƙī** 1*b*.

    B. (**zubē**) *m.* flock of birds settled on
ground, etc.

    C. (**zụbe**) (*noun of state from* **zubạ**) *x*
yanā nạn ~ it is poured out here.

    D. (**zụbē**) *m.* any tribal-markings
(**askā**) consisting of several long cuts.

zụbe bạn ƙwaryāta *m.* (1) gifts to mother
at time of naming-ceremony (**sūnā** 5)
of her child. (2) **mun yi** ~ **dạ shī** he
and I have had a heart-to-heart talk.
(3) **aikị** ~ **sǎi Audụ** Audu is the one for
really good work.

zụbētā *f.* (1) paying cash down for meat
in **wạtandā**, or for cotton· or ground-
nuts (= **tụntsụrē** 1). (2) advance payment to village girl by youth wanting
tsạrạncē with her.

zubị *m.* (1) **mụ jē wurịn̦ ạlkālī mụ yi** ~
let us go and each state his case to the
judge (*cf.* **zubạ** 1*b*). (2) (*a*) casting T.
in metal. (*b*) A. cast in metal. (*c*)
tukunyar ~ *f.* mould for casting (= **kō-**
mī 1*e*). (3) making indigo-infusion in
dye-pit. (4) paying one's contribution
to the pool in **ạdāshī** (*cf.* **ạdāshī** 1*b*). (5)
nā yi sāban ~ I've just bitten into a
kola-nut. (6) arranging warp for
weaving (= **zirị**). (7) adjusting stirrup-
leathers *x* **lịkkāfạn nạn̦ gạjēran** ~ **akạ**
yi matạ these stirrups have been fixed
too short (= **zirị**). (8) **wani** ~ *adv.*
sometimes. (9) = **zubọ** 1. (10) **hạuyar**
zubịn lallẹ *Vd.* **hạuyā** 5.

zubị-zubị *adv.* in piles.

zubkạ *f.* (*pl.* zubkōkī) pad under each half of saddle (*cf.* mạdạburọ).

zubọ *m.* (1) pile (of grass, corn-stalks, etc.) (= zubị 9). (2) (*a*) kụ dẹbi gịndin ∼ (*said to those who tied up bundles of corn to be garnered*) take the corn-heads which are your due ! (*cf.* bạ̄kin shīƙạ, bạ̄kiŋ wuƙā). (2) the best corn-heads (put at bottom of rụmbū), *cf.* bạ̄kiŋ wuƙā. (3) Audụ ∼ gạrēshị Audu has a big appetite.

zubshē *Vd.* zub dạ.

zubukạ = zubkạ.

zubukkā *Vb.* 1C *Nor.* = zubạ.

zubukkē *Nor.* = zubẹ.

zụbūnị = zạbụŋ *m.* type of long-sleeved waistcoat.

zubur = zubut *used in* yā yinị ∼ he stayed all day (= zụŋgur = zur 3).

zucċīyā *Sk. f.* = zūcīyā.

zūcī *Vd.* zūcīyā 13.

zuciya A. (zūcīyā) *f.* (*pl.* zūcīyōyī = zukạ̄tā = zukōcī) (*for* zūcī *Vd.* 13 *below*). (1) (*a*) (i) heart (of P., animal, or plant). (ii) ƙarƙashin zūcīyarsạ yanạ̄ sọ̄ he wishes from the bottom of his heart to . . . (*b*) (i) ∼ tasạ tā ɓācị he became vexed, sad. (ii) ɓācin ∼ *m.* vexation, sadness. (iii) ɓātạ ∼ *Vd.* ɓātạ 5*a*, 8. (iii*A*) ∼ tā yi farī *Vd.* farī 1c.ii ; 9 *below.* (*c*) (i) sạ̄ ∼ *Vd.* sạ̄ B.12. (ii) nā fid dạ ∼ dạgạ gạrēshị I gave up all hope of getting it (*cf.* ƙaunā). (iii) yā jā minị ∼ he " let me down ". (*d*) ạbin dạ na ganī ạ zūcīyāta kẹ naŋ this is my opinion of the matter. (*e*) zūcīyāta tā bā nị ŋ gudụ instinct warned me to flee. (*f*) (i) kạrạ̄tū yā ci ∼ tasạ he devoted all his attention to study. (ii) kā ci ∼ *Vd.* cūrị 4 ; dụnjī. (*g*) yanạ̄ sansạ ạ ∼ tasạ he wants it very much. (*h*) yā cẹ dạ ∼ tasạ he said to himself that . . . (*j*) (i) doŋ gudụn zūcīyar Audụ baị amsạ ba he refrained from replying in order not to anger Audu. (ii) gudụn ∼ gạrēshị he is tactful. (*k*) kan ∼ tā yạrdā, gạŋgar jịkī bāwạ nē where there's a will there's a way. (*l*) kashēwā ạ zūcīyar maị rạbō tā fi " Wānẹ, gā hannūna ! " it is better to be given spontaneously than to have to ask. (*m*) gạyạ̄ maị ∼ bịkī, bạ̄ maị

dūkīyā ba good character is better than wealth. (*n*) lạ̄bārịn ∼ (= sararin ∼) ạ tạmbayi fuskạ one's face shows what is in one's heart. (*o*) ∼ tā fi dūkīyā it is better to be wise than wealthy. (*p*) zūcīyar mụtụm birninsạ a man's heart is his best counsellor. (*q*) jạn ∼ *m.* difficult disposition (*cf.* 11). (2) courage *x* (*a*) ƙarfin ∼ gạrēshị he is brave. (*b*) maị ∼ nẹ̄ = zūcīyā gạrēshị (i) he is brave. (ii) he is kind. (iii) he can look after himself. (*c*) sun yi ∼ they are brave. (*d*) an san sụ kạn ∼ they're known to be brave. sǎi wata zūcīyā ta yuŋƙurō (= tuŋguɓō) musụ = sǎi wata zūcīyā ta tūrō musụ they got fresh heart. (3) zūcīyar mạrāyạ (*a*) type of cloth with alternate black and white stripes. (*b*) coloured clay ball at top of spinning-spindle (*cf.* gụlūlụ). (4) yā bi sạn ∼ (*a*) he gave way to his baser instincts (*d. f.* sọ̄). (*b*) he stole. (*c*) *Vd.* aurē 2. (5) yā hau dōkịn ∼ he did an act which he regretted. (6) maị zūcīyar Ạsabạr (*a*) thief. (*b*) dishonest P. (7) ∼ bīyu gạrēshị = 6 *above.* (8) fāɗin ∼ *m.* conceit. (9) farar ∼ (*a*) equability. (*b*) happiness (*cf.* 1*a.*iii*A above*). (10) baƙar ∼ gạrēshị he is bad-tempered. (11) jar ∼ endurance, bravery (*cf.* 1*q*). (12) (*a*) ạjīyar ∼ sighing. (*b*) yā ajịyẹ ∼ he sighed. (12*A*) yā yi zāfin zūcīyar tāsạ he gave a display of his usual bad temper. (12*B*) bā yạ̄ hūcẹ zūcīyā *Vd.* sạ̄ƙō 1*c.* (12*C*) ƙạfan ∼ *Vd.* ƙạfō 9. (13) (*after preposition ạ stated or understood, we can use* zūcī) (*a*) sǎi ạ zūcī = sǎi ạ zūcīyā only in one's imagination. (*b*) kạ rịƙẹ shi ạ zūcī (= ạ zūcīyā) bear it in mind ! (*c*) ta zūcī bạ̄ ta ạ kēsọ (i) he wants to buy it but has no money. (ii) losing gambler wants to play high, but has no money. (*c*) ta zūcī tanạ̄ zūcī *Vd.* bakạ 4. (*d*) zamā zūcī gạ marạbī tā fi " Wānẹ gạ̄ hannūna ! " = 1*l above.* (*e*) ɗạmarạr zūcī tā fi ta jịkī a good character is better than wealth. (*f*) ƙạwạ̄ zūcī *m.* (i) greed. (ii) undue persistence (*cf.* ƙāwạ). (*g*) yā cī dạ zūcī he was all agog. (*h*) sāƙar zūcī *Vd.* sāƙạ 2*f.* (*j*) kīshin zūcī *m.* = gạsar zūcī *f.* ambition. (*k*) *Vd.* zūci-zūci. (*l*) duk magaṇaṇ naŋ, īyậkacintậ bakậ' bậ tậ jē zūcī ba all this talk was " mere eyewash ". (*m*) wậdar zūcī contentment (= yậkậnā). (*n*) shịga zūcī *Vd.* Ịkkō.

B. (zūcīyậ) (1) *Vb.* 3B flew into a temper. (2) *f.* ~ gậrēshị he is quicktempered.

zūci-zūci *m.* yaṇā ~ yậ gayậ minị, yā mậntā he intended to tell me but forgot.

zuɗɗurụ *m.* mischief-making (= alguŋgumancị).

zuɗuɽu = zuɗum 1.

zuɗum *adv.* (1) yaṇā dậ zurfī ~ it is very deep (= zuɗuɽu). (2) yā tậfị ~ he has vanished.

zufậ *Sk.* = zuffậ.

zuffậ *f.* (1) (*a*) perspiration (= gụmī). (*b*) 'yā'yan ~ *pl.* prickly heat. (2) hot weather *x* yậnzu aṇā ~ it is now the hot season (= gụmī 2*a*).

zuga A. (zugậ) (1) *Vb.* 1A (*a*) blew up (fire with bellows) (*cf.* hūrậ). (*b*) incited (= hūrậ 1*c* = hasậ 2 = hanzụgā 1 = rūrậ 1*b*). (*c*) yaṇā ~ maị sậyē he (seller) is puffing his wares. (2) *f.* inciting *x* Audụ, yawận ~ gậrēshị Audu foments strife. yā ji ~ tatậ he gave way to her incitement. (*b*) yậu ~ akẹ to-day there is a west wind presaging arrival of the rains.

B. (zūgậ) (1) *Vb.* 1A = zabgậ. (2) *f.* handsome T. or P. (3) how handsome !

C. (zūgā) (1) *Vb.* 2 = zậbgā 1, 2. (2) *f.* (*a*) perseverance *x* yaṇā zūgar aikị he's persevering at his work (= nācị). (*b*) festivities accompanied by drumming.

zugâgē *Vd.* zugū.

zūgā-zūgâ *Vd.* zūgēgẹ.

zugâzugī (1) *m.* (*pl.* zụgâzụgai) pair of bellows. (2) *Sk. m.* = kumuryā.

zuge A. (zugẹ) *Vb.* 1A ~ zugậ 1*b*.

B. (zụgē) *m.* (1) charcoal or ink made from adūwậ, *cf.* gōgē 2. (2) = dậkē 1.

zūgēgẹ *m.* (*f.* zūgēgịyā) *pl.* zūgā-zūgâ handsome.

zugū *m.* (*pl.* zugâgē) (1) = gāyā 2*e*. (2)

Kt. present given Chief by P. hoping to get horse in return. (3) bị ni (= cị ni) dậ ~ *m.* physic-nut. (4) turmin ~ *Vd.* turmī 11. (5) *Vd.* ƙaurā 3*c*.v.

zụgụdum = jụgum.

zụgūgụ *m.* (1) exaggeration (*cf.* zagaigậitā). (2) = mītậ.

zugūgūtā = kurūrūtā.

zụgum = jụgum.

zuguŋgụntā = kurūrūtā.

zụgurnugụ *m.* = zậƙarnaƙọ.

zuƙa A. (zūƙā) (1) *Vb.* 2 (*a*) yā zūƙi tābậ he drew tobacco-smoke into his mouth (*cf.* hōɗậ). (*b*) yā zūƙi rūwā he sucked water into his mouth. (2) whiff *x* yā yi ~ ukụ he took three whiffs of tobacco. (3) *Vd.* ƙaƒō 10.

B. (zūƙậ) *Vb.* 1A = zabgậ.

zūƙaƙƙē *m.* (*f.* zūƙaƙƙīyā) *pl.* zūƙậƙƙū small-buttocked P.

zukậtā *Vd.* zūcīyā.

zūƙā-zūƙâ *Vd.* zūƙēƙẹ.

zuƙe A. (zūƙẹ) (1) *Vb.* 1A drew in (*as in* zūƙā 1*a*, *b*) completely. (2) *Vb.* 3A (*a*) = zāmẹ 2. (*b*) gịndinsậ yā ~ he is thin-buttocked. (*c*) dodged (= baudẹ). (*d*) shūcị yā ~ = rūwā A.13*d*.

B. (zūƙē) *m.* (1) dodging away (= baudīyā). (2) leaving P. in the lurch (*cf.* zūƙẹ 2*a*).

zūƙēƙẹ *m.* (*f.* zūƙēƙịyā) *pl.* zūƙā-zūƙâ handsome.

zū'ƙe-zūƙē" *m.* (1) hesitation. (2) shiftiness, shifty excuses (= gōcegōcē).

zūƙị (1) (*a*) how handsome ! (*b*) what a whopping lie ! (2) *Vd.* ƙaryā 1*a*.ii.

zūƙīyā *f.* = zūƙē.

zukkụcē *Vb.* 3A *Sk.* poured out bodily (contents of vessel).

zukōcī *Vd.* zūcīyā.

zūkū *m.* (1) master's hurrying on pupil before he has assimilated previous lessons. (2) pupil's hurrying on *as in* 1 (1, 2 = wậŋke zụbar), *Vd.* zazzậgā 1*b*.

zụƙū *Kt. m.* = bụƙū.

zukụmī *m.* (1) batch. (2) zukụmī-zukụmī *adv.* in batches.

zukut *m.* (1) zūcīyassậ tā yiwŏ ~ he felt nausea. (2) naŋ dậ naŋ sâi ya yi ~ he suddenly flew into a temper.

zụƙwī *Kt. m.* = bụƙū 1.

zu̱laidu̱ = za̱laidu̱.

zu̱laika̱ = zi̱laika̱.

zulā́kē = zulā́ki̱ *m.* boy's playfully rubbing butter in anus of sleeping boy and when it melts, inserting goat's dung.

zu̱lāma̱ *f.* = zālunci̱.

zū́laya̱ *Vb.* 2 cross-questioned.

zu̱lēka̱ = zi̱laika̱.

zu̱lhaji̱ *m.* 12th Mahommedan month (*Vd.* layyā 2).

zu̱lkí̱da̱ *m.* 11th Mahommedan month (= bāwa̱ 7).

zulli̱ *Kt.* = zilli̱.

zullu̱ *Kt. m.* = kwalabā 2.

zullu̱mī = zulu̱mī.

zulmu̱ *m.* = zālunci̱.

zu̱lūlū̱wā́ *f.* gwaiwā tā yi ~ the scrotum is elongated (= zu̱nda̱-zunda̱), *cf.* ma̱-ja̱kwar.

zu̱lu̱m *used in* wa̱ndō ~ *m.* European long trousers.

zu̱lumbu̱ *m.* (1) type of ta̱gūwa̱ extending to ankle. (2) jumping into water feet first (*cf.* dīya̱m). (3) poor mīya̱.

zulu̱mī *m.* pondering, reflection. a̱bin zulu̱mī nē̱ it gives food for thought.

zu̱lwāmī *m.* type of native cloth with blue weft and black-and-blue warp.

zuma̱ (1) *m., f.* (*a*) (i) honey (= rūwan zuma̱ = fitsāri̱ 7*b* = zumū̱wā) ; *epithet is* ca̱rkwai. (ii) honeycomb with honey still in it *x* wanna̱ŋ ~ ba̱ shi da̱ rūwā this comb contains no honey (*cf.* 2*b below*). (iii) *cf.* tōtū̱wā 1*b*.ii, kāki̱, sā́ka̱ 2*d*. (*b*) (i) ga̱ gōran zuma̱, ga̱ na mada̱cī *epithet of* a̱lkālī. (ii) ~ da̱ zā́ki̱, da̱ harbi̱ what a P. of changing moods ! (= ku̱rtū 1*c*). (*c*) (i) sha̱n ~ să̱i da̱ wutā = bā a̱ sha̱n zuma̱ să̱i an shā harbi̱ look befôre you leap !, things are not always as easy as they look. (ii) an shā zuma̱ssa̱ = tā́bo̱ 2. (iii) da̱ŋgin ~ nē̱, bā a̱ ci̱nsa̱ să̱i da̱ wutā he's a tough customer. (*d*) (i) yā ci (= yā shā) ~ he ate honey ; he gathered honey. (ii) *Vd.* ji̱nīyā ; dūbi̱. (iii) hakōrinsa̱ yā yi ci̱n ~ his tooth has decayed (= mutu̱ 8*a*.ii). (*e*) *Vd.* shā̱ye-shā̱yē. (2) *m., f.* (*a*) (i) bee, bees. (ii) gidan ~ *m.* beehive (= amya̱ *q.v.*). (ii*A*) *Vd.* anya̱. (iii) kudan ~ *m.* (*pl.* kuda̱jan ~) bee. (*b*) i̱da̱ŋ kā ji ~ yana̱

---

ku̱gi̱, yā yi rūwā nē̱ if you hear a friend has made some profit, visit him and see what you can get ! (*c*) yā yiwō mini̱ ~ he spoke angrily to me. (*d*) dōki̱n na̱ŋ zuma̱ŋ wuri̱ nē̱ this horse, though ugly, is a good animal. (*f*) zuma̱r kwaryā́ work which, though not lucrative, is not very arduous.

zumai *Vd.* zumu̱.

zumāmi̱ *m.* (1) ledger-book (= dafta̱rī). (2) *Vd.* sha̱ ~.

zumbu̱dā *Vb.* 1C = zabga̱.

zumbu̱dē̱ = zumbudi̱ *m.* a dance done by adult Filani.

zumbu̱l *m.* type of incense.

zumbulā *f.* = zu̱mbulko̱.

zu̱mbu̱lbu̱l *used in* cībī ga̱rēta̱ ~ she has umbilical hernia.

zumbu̱lē̱ *Nor.* = sullu̱bē̱ 2*a-c.*

zumbu̱li̱ *m.* skinflint (*epithet is* Zumbu̱lī kā̱kam marō̱wa̱tā).

zu̱mbulko̱ *f.* woman with umbilical hernia.

zumbulō = zu̱mbulko̱.

zumbur *adv. and m.* yā tāshi̱ ~ = yā yi ~ yā tāshi̱ he progressed quickly.

zu̱mbūtu̱ *m.* (1) " parson's nose " of chicken, etc. (2) yā́rinya̱ ma̱i ~ = ki̱ra̱ 1*e.*

zumma̱ = zimma̱.

zummū̱wā *Kt.* = zuma̱ 1*a.*i.

zumu A. (zumu̱) *m.* (*f.* zūni̱yā = zun-nīyā) *pl.* zumai. (1) P. of about one's own age *x* zumu̱na ba̱ za̱i̱ yi mini̱ haka̱ ba a P. of my own age would not treat me thus (= sa'a̱). (2) member of same household as oneself. (3) (*a*) shī a̱ baka̱ zumai nē̱ he is friendly only to one's face. (*b*) a̱ baka̱ zumai yakē̱ yi̱ he's behaving two-facedly.

B. (zu̱mū) *m.* bearing reproof silently.

zu̱mūdī = dō̱ki̱ 1.

zumunci̱ *m.* (*Ar.* dhimma). (1) (*a*) relationship by blood or marriage. (*b*) clanfeeling. (*c*) Alla̱ ya̱ sāke̱ mai da̱ zumunci̱ may God restore peace. (*d*) ja̱wābi̱ iri̱n na zumunci̱ a friendly speech. (2) ~ a̱ kafa̱ takē̱ the maintenance of good relations between people requires visits. (3) sa̱n ~ ga̱rēshi̱ he is a sympathetic P. (4) Alla̱ dăi ya̱ bar ~ may our good relationship together endure ! (5) (*a*) nā nēmē shi̱ a̱ fuska̱r ~

I tried to settle my dispute with him in a friendly way (= fuskạ 8). (b) Vd. ɗākị 7. (6) Vd. diŋkạ 2.

zụmụntā f. (1) = zumuncị. (2) ~ ɗạ ɗạ ɗạ takẹ f. = sụ̄dā 1a.

zụmụntārōrị Kt. = zạmạntārōrị.

*zumụrrudụ = zumụrruzụ Ar. m. emerald.

zumụ̄wā = zumạ 1a.i.

zunɗa A. (zunɗạ) Vb. 1A x yā ~ shi wuriŋ Audụ he pointed out to him (P. whom he does not want the trouble of lodging) the direction of Audu's house by movement of his lips in the required direction.

B. (zụnɗā) Vb. 2 = zunɗạ.

zụndārạ x yā zō zụndāransạ he came empty-handed (= tsiŋkịnrāgị).

zụnɗạ-zunɗạ f. used in gwaiwā tasạ tā yi ~ = zụlūlụ̄wā.

zụnɗē m. yā yi wạ Audụ ~ = zunɗạ.

zundum A. (zụndum) used in rūwā yanạ naŋ ~ the well is full of water.

B. (zundụm) (1) yā fāɗạ ạ rūwa ~ he fell with a loud splash into the water. (2) m. nā ji ~ I heard a loud splash. (3) Vd. zụndụm-zụndụm.

zundụmā (1) Vb. 1C an zundụmạ rūwā (a) much water has been poured in. (b) there has been much rain. (2) Vb. 3A yā ~ ạ rūwa he jumped, fell with a loud splash into the water.

zụndụm-zụndụm m. (1) swaying noise caused.by jạŋ hạrāwạ. (2) Vd. zụndum, zundụm.

zuŋgạ Sk. f. = zōgī.

zuŋgụmā Vb. 1C = kurūrụ̄tā.

zuŋgumī m. exaggerated fuss (= kwạr- matọ 2).

zụŋgur = zubur.

zungura A. (zuŋgụrā) Vb. 1C. (1) (a) yā zuŋgụrạ karā ạ rāmị he poked a stick into the hole (to measure its depth). yā zuŋgụrạ dāgị he made holes with a digging-stick (= zurạ 1b). (b) ya ~ masạ sạndā he poked at it (rat in hole) with a stick (1a, b = rārạkā 1). (2) (a) yā zuŋgurō ɓērā he poked the rat out of the hole (= rārakạ 1b = sạ̄katạ 1). (b) yā zuŋgurō kaɗanyạ he poked down shea-nuts off the tree (all = tsōkạnā = rāgạɗā). (3) Vd. hạlak 2c.ii.

B. (zụŋgurạ) Vb. 2 (1) (a) yā zụŋgụri

ɓērā = zuŋgụrā 1b. (b) yā zụŋgụrē nị dạ sạndā he poked me with a stick. (b) zuŋgurō Vd. zuŋgụrā 2. (2) pro- voked, goaded into a rage (1, 2 = tsōkanạ) (2 = tạ̄kalạ = tọ̄nā 2 = tirẹ 1a = cạ̄kunạ = rārẹ 1f).

zuŋgụrē Vb. 1C (1) yā ~ ni dạ sạndā = zụŋgurạ 1b. (2) yā ~ minị idọ = tsōkạnē 1a.

zuŋgụrī m. poking, prodding as in zuŋ- gụrā, zụŋgurạ x yā kai gạ zuŋgụrimmụ he has begun to provoke us.

zuŋgurmī m. (f. zuŋgurmā) pl. zuŋgurum- zụŋgụrụm tall P., tall horse, etc.

zuŋgurmēmẹ m. (f. zuŋgurmēmịyā) pl. zuŋgurum-zụŋgụrụm = zuŋgurmī.

zụŋgụrū m. long gourd (worn on arm by women to protect newly-hennaed hands) = tsanā = kulụɓūtụ.

zuŋgurum-zụŋgụrụm Vd. zuŋgurmī.

zuŋgwị-zuŋgwị = zụŋgwī-zụŋgwī adv. silently.

zūnịyā Vd. zumụ.

zuŋkụɗā Vb. 1C (1) (a) tā zuŋkụɗạ gōyantạ she hitched up the child slung on her back. (b) hitched up (load on pack-animal), cf. assạkā. (2) tsūtsạ tā zuŋkuɗō gērō the maggot pushed up grains in head of bulrush-millet (cf. zụŋkụɗau). (3) yā zuŋkụɗạ ƙaryā he told a whopping lie.

zụŋkụɗau m. maggot which acts as in zuŋkụɗā 2 (cf. minyạ 2) = mazuŋ- kudịyā = tụŋkụɗau).

zuŋkụɗē Vb. 1C yā zuŋkụɗẹ rịgā tasạ he stripped off his gown.

zuŋkuɗō Vb. 3A zūcịyassạ tā ~ (1) he felt angry. (2) he felt sick.

zuŋkut = zukut.

zunnịyā Vd. zumụ.

zuntụ Kabi m. = ɗākị.

*zụnụbantạ Vb. 3B sinned.

zụnubị m. (pl. zụnubai) Ar. (1) (a) sin. (b) yā yi ~ he sinned. (2) ạmfānin ~ rōmō profit leads one to sin.

zụnufị = zụnubị.

zụnzụrum-zụnzụrum = zụndụm-zụndụm.

zunzụrūtụ m. = kuntukurmī.

zunzụwārạ used in yā zō zunzụwārạnsạ he came empty-handed (= tsiŋkịnrāgị).

zur A. (zụr) used in shaidạr ~ f. per- jured evidence (cf. rantsụ̄wā 3).

B. (zur) (1) = zallā 1. (2) yanạ̄
tsạye ∼ he is standing naked (= tsịrārạ). (3) = zubur. (4) jạ̄ ∼ = wur.
(5) *Vd.* zir.
zura A. (zūrạ) (1) (*cerebral* -r-) (*a*) *Vb.* 1A
(*with dative*) an ∼ masạ mārị he was
slapped hard. (*b*) *Vb.* 3A yā ∼ ạ
gụje he took to his heels (= shḗkạ). (2)
(*rolled* -r-) tyranny (= zālunci).
B. (zụ̄rā) *Vb.* 2 rūwā yā zụ̄rē shị
he got stitch from drinking too much
water (= kullẹ 1*d*).
C. (zurạ) *Vb.* 1A (1) (*a*) lowered
(bucket into well). (*b*) = zungụrā 1*a.*.
(*c*) munạ̄ ∼ idọ gạ zūwạnsạ we're
eagerly awaiting his arrival (= idọ
1*b*). (*d*) yā ∼ kafạ ạ rījịyā he's become
involved in intrigue (= zubạ 5). (2)
kā ∼ kudī (*a*) you were overcharged.
(*b*) you " cooked " your figures. (3)
kā ∼ jikī = 2*a above.* (4) yā ∼ dōkịnsạ (*a*) he galloped his horse. (*b*)
he made his horse prance (= tabạ 1*l*).
(5) threaded *x* yā ∼ dūwạ̄tsū ạ zạrē
he threaded the beads. yā ∼ zạrē
ạ ạllūrạ he threaded the needle.
zụ̄rạcē *Vd.* zụ̄ratạ.
zurara A. (zurārā) (1) *Vb.* 3A (*a*) slid
down along *x* yā ∼ ta kạn gārū he
(fugitive, etc.) slid down the side of the
town-wall. yā ∼ ạ rījịyā he (well-
repairer) slid down a rope into the well.
(*b*) T. fell into (well, hole, etc.). (*c*)
rūwā yā zurārō ạ dākị water trickled,
flowed into the house (= zụba 1*c*).
(2) *Vb.* 1C (*a*) yārọ yā zurārạ rūwā ạ
rāmị the boy poured water into the
hole (to drive out rat). (*b*) dropped T.
into *x* yā zurārạ kudī ạ ạljīfūna he
dropped money into my pocket. (*c*)
x yā zurārạ kudī ạ wurīna he cheated
me by nạshē 1*b*.
B. (zụrārạ) *Vb.* 3B = zurārā 1*c*.
zurare A. (zurārē) *Vb.* 3A (1) slipped out
x kudī sun ∼ ạ ạljīfūna the money
slipped out of my pocket. (2) hatsī
yā ∼ ạ bụhū corn trickled out of the
sack. (3) rūwā yā ∼ ạ tụlū water
leaked out of the ewer. (4) (rosary-
beads) slipped off string (1-4 = zụba
1*a*.ii). (5) P. slipped away from place.
(6) ran away.

B. (zurārē) *m.* (1) game of sliding
down rock (= shābạ = *Kt.* zanzaryā).
(2) = nạshē 1*b*.
zụ̄rātạ *Vb.* 2 (*p.o.* zụ̄rạcē, *n.o.* zụ̄rạci)
oppressed (= zāluntạ).
zurɓa A. (zurɓạ) (1) *Vb.* 1A (*a*) = zurmạ
1. (*b*) = zabgạ. (2) *Vb.* 3A = zurmạ 2.
B. (zụrɓā) (1) *Vb.* 2. (*a*) = zạbgā 1.
(*b*) yā zụrɓi mīyạ he drank his soup
noisily (= yạrɓā). (2) *f.* = zạbgā 2.
zurɓi what foul abuse !
zurcẹ *Vb.* 1A (1) pounded (unwetted corn
for the second time, *i.e.* after cạ̄sā, to
remove grains of chaff), *cf.* dakạ. (2)
pounded (dried corn for second time,
i.e. after sụrfē, to remove remains of
bran) = turzạ 1*b*.
zure A. (zūrẹ) *Sk. m.* type of tree with
edible leaves and flowers. (2) = zụlūlūwā.
B. (zurē) = zirē.
zurfafa A. (zurfạ̄fā) *Vd.* zụzzurfā.
B. (zụrfafạ) *Vb.* 3B went deeply into
x yā ∼ cikin ạddīnī he is engrossed in
religion. yā ∼ cikin ilịmī he is deeply
versed in knowledge.
C. (zurfạ̄fā) (1) *Vb.* 3A = zụrfafạ. (2)
Vb. 1C deepened.
zurfī *m.* (1) (*a*) depth *x* zurfin idọ gạrēshị
he has deep-set eyes. (*b*) mại zurfin
idọ dạ wurī yakḕ sōmạ kūkā a stitch
in time saves nine. (*c*) kōmē zurfin
rūwā, dạ yạ̄shī ạ cikī there is an end to
all things. (*d*) (i) an yi musụ " shigō,
shigō, bạ zurfī " they were lured on.
(ii) bạ ∼ *Vd.* fankạm fayạu. (2)
zurfin cikị reticence, secretiveness
(= mụku-mụkū). (3) gidan nạn yanạ̄
dạ ∼ this compound is large. rīgan
nạn tanạ̄ dạ ∼ this gown is extensive.
zurgụmā *Vb.* 1C (1) yā zurgụmạ yātsạ ạ
bakạ he put his fingers down his throat
to make himself vomit. yā zurgụmạ
hannū ạ ạljīfū he put his hand in his
pocket. (2) yā ∼ masạ māshị he
pierced him with a spear.
zuri A. (zurị) = zirị.
B. (zūrī) *m.* (1) jạkā tā yi ∼ the bag
is heavy. (2) (*a*) nā ji ∼ I am nearly
replete. (*b*) *Vd.* zūrī-zūrī.
zuri'ạ = zụrīyạ *Ar. f.* descendants, offspring.

zurḳumā = zurgumā.

zurma A. (zurmạ) (1) *Vb.* 1A (*a*) put (hand into pocket, bag, etc.), *cf.* sạ A. (*b*) yā ~ hannū cikiŋ ạbincī he helped himself uninvited to another's food (*c*) yā ~ ḳafạ ạ rāmị he inadvertently put his foot in a hole. (2) *Vb.* 3A (*a*) ḳafạssạ tā ~ ạ rāmị his foot slipped into a hole. (*b*) yā ~ dạ gudụ he took to his heels (= shēḳạ). (*c*) (wall) collapsed. B. (zụrmạ̄) = zụrmạ̣ŋ.

zụrmạŋ *m.* castor-oil plant (*Vd.* mạn funị) = *Sk.* cikạ gidā.

zurmuguḍḍụ *m.* deceit, trickery.

zurmụ̣ḳā = zurgụmā.

zurnāniyā *f.* = girgijẹ.

zurtạ *Vb.* 1A = zurcẹ.

zurtạcē *Vb.* 1C = zurcẹ.

zurtū *m.* acting *as in* zurcẹ.

zụrū *m.* (1) (*a*) staring at (*cf.* mụzūrū 2, tsụ̄rū 1*a*). (*b*) ɗan ~ *m.* (*pl.* 'yan ~). (i) P. whose work is a sinecure (= maḳwạ̣ḳwạncī). (ii) 'yan ~ = tsụ̄rū 1*b*. (*c*) ~ tā ịshi dā a self-respecting P. does not need to be reminded of his duty. (*d*) ~ bạ tạ̣ ci gạrī ba, sǎi anạ̄ gudụmmōwā effort finishes a task, not idleness. (2) ignoring P. *x* nā yi masa ~ I ignored him. (3) Zụrū sạ̣ rạ̄gaitạ Hunger thou dost set one roving!

zụrubtū *m.* bustling to and fro (= ḳạiwā dạ kāwọ̄wā).

zurum A. (zurum) yanạ̄ dạ zurfī ~ it is very deep. B. (zụrum) = jụgum.

zụrundumī *m.* (*f.* zụrundumā) (1) of immense capacity (*re* bag, pot, etc.). (2) *Vd.* bạ̄ba 10.

zụruntū = zụruptū = zụrubtū *q.v.*

zụrụrrubạ̣ *f.* *x* yanạ̄ ~ he's letting out a stream of abuse.

zurūrīyā *f.* = zurārē 1.

zururu (1) = zurum. (2) *m.* gū̄gā yā yi ~ the bucket and its rope fell into the well.

zụrūtūtụ *m.* meddlesomeness (= ḳạrạmbạnī).

zuru-zụrū *m.* *used in* idạnsạ yā yi ~ = yā yi ~ dạ idọ he was in a dither (from shame, fear, hunger, illness, etc.).

zūwạ *m.* (1) (*a*) (*v.n. from* zō) *x* yanạ̄ ~ he is coming. bạ̄ ni dạ lạ̄bārịn zūwạnsạ I have no idea when he'll come. zū-

wạnsạ ukụ kē̦ naŋ he has come three times. (*b*) mại ~ (i) comer. (ii) future *x* cikin 'yan shē̦ḳạrū mạ̄sū ~ during the next few years. (*c*) mại ḳạmaz ~ ḳạŋ ạikā what doggedness ! ịnā zūwạ where are you off to ? (*d*) ạmmā mụ jē̦ zūwạ dǎi " let us cut the cackle and get to the horses ! " (*e*) zūwạ dạ wurị *Vd.* wurī 4*c*. (*f*) zūwạm fạ̄rā *Vd.* fạ̄rā 2*b*. (2) *prep.* up to *x* (*a*) (i) dạgạ sāfīyā ~ darē from morn till night. yā tạfi dạgạ Kanọ ~ Sakkwatō he went from Kano to Sokoto (*cf.* zō 2*b*). yā bī zūwạ Kanọ he came to Kano. kō̦gin naŋ yā bī ~ Kanọ this river flows towards Kano. sun tarbō Sarkinsụ zūwạ birninsụ they went to meet their Chief on his arrival at their capital (*cf.* ạ bb). (ii) zūwạ watạ bīyū zā sụ īyạ in two months' time they'll be able. zūwạ watạŋ Yūnị zā mụ ḳārẹ we shall have finished by June. (iii) nā sābạ dạ askịn Sarākunạ zūwạ ạttạjịrai I'm accustomed to barbering both Chiefs and rich men. (*b*) (*before person's name, or personal pronoun, we use* ~ gạ = ~ wurin) *x* yā tạfī ~ gạrēshị = yā tạfi ~ wurinsạ he went to him. yā tạfi ~ gạ Audụ = yā tạfi ~ wuriŋ Audụ he went to Audu. (*c*) har yạ ~ = har yị ~ = har ị ~ = 2*a above x* har yạ ~ yạnzu = har yạnzu up to the present. har zūwạ yạnzu gạ wannạŋ rānā tạ yau right up to the present day. har yạ ~ Kanọ as far as Kano. (3) even as far as *x* anạ̄ faɗịnsạ ạ Sakkwatō ~ Kabị it is being said in Sokoto and even as far as Kebbi. (4) *Vd.* zūwạ-zūwạ. (5) zūwạŋ ḳại (*a*) orgasm (*Vd.* kāwō 1*c* ; dīyaŋ). (*b*) semen (*cf.* mạnīyyị).

zūwārạ = zạwārạ.

zūwạ-zūwạ (1) from time to time (= lō̦ḳạcī lō̦ḳạcī). (2) *Vd.* zūwạ.

zụwō = zụwū *m.* the nettle-tree (*Celtis integrifolia*) = *Sk.* dụkḳī.

zūzạ = jīzạ.

zụzzū̦bā *f.* = ḳạrā-ḳạrā 3.

zuzzugẹ = zugā̦zugī.

zụzzurfā *m.*, *f.* (*pl.* zurfā̦fā) deep.

zwāga *Kt.* = zāga.

zwai = jwai.

zwārẹ *Kt.* = zārẹ.

ADDENDA

(p. 5–i *means* page 5 lefthand column. p. 5–ii *means* page 5 righthand column)

INSERT IN :—

Abū Hạnīfạ p. 5–ii (*new entry*) :—Abū Hạnīfạ *Vd*. lịmạm 1A (in ADDENDA).

akạ̄ p. 14–ii (*at end of para*.) :—and kạ̄ (in ADDENDA).

ạljaŋ p. 23–i :—(6) Sarkiŋ—*Vd*. kụgē 2 (in ADDENDA).

amaryā p. 29–ii (*end of para*.) :—kāmạ 6.

asalī p. 38–i *before* (2) :—asalinsụ har yā ɓacẹ so that their origin is lost in the mists of time.

bạ̄kī p. 63–ii before (3)*g* :—(*ff*) yā yi manạ sạndā mai bạ̄kin cikī he referred to us by innuendo.

Bạrnō p. 85–ii (*end of para*.) :—(4) *Vd*. kutạhā (in ADDENDA).

bī p. 96 *before* (1)*f* :—*Vd*. kọ̄rā 2*c*.ii (in ADDENDA).

dạ p. 153–ii *before* (4) :—an san shị dạ sātạ he is known as a thief. an san sụ dạ rini they are famous as dyers.

dạ p. 153–ii *before* 7*b* :—Allạ̄ yạ kīyāshē mụ dạ shī may God protect us from him ! (*Vd*. tsarẹ 1*a*.i).

dạ p. 154–ii end of (10) :—(*d*) that which (= wạndạ 2*a*) *x* kạmar dạ mukạ cẹ̄ = kạmar wạndạ mukạ cẹ̄ in accordance with what we said.

dạgạ p. 166–ii *before* 1*a*(iii) :—(iiA) formed T. out of *x* anạ̄ sassạ̄ɓạ kujẹ̄rā dạgạ itạ̄caŋ ɓasạr carpenters make chairs from local wood.

dāma p. 178–ii before 1(*b*) :—(*aa*) yanạ̄ wajan ∼ it is on the right.

dasạ p. 196–ii *before* (2) :—(= kafạ 1*aa* in ADDENDA).

dạtsạ p. 198–i *before* " he made " :— = yā tsai dạ kạdādā.

daurạ p. 203–i *before* " it " (*in line* 2) :— = an yi masạ sirdị.

fạdā p. 241–i *before* (1)*a*.ii :—sụ kāwō ạbin dạ sukạ ganī, sụ ∼ let them mention what they have seen and describe it !

gạ 276–ii *before* (3)*b* :—ɓasā tā yi yawạ gạrēshị the area is too large for him to control.

gạ̄bā p. 279 *before* (*d*) :—(*cc*) ∼ tā tsayạ hostility arose.

gamạ p. 291–ii *before* 1*e*.iv :— (iiiA) Shēhụ ɗaŋ Hōdīyọ yā ∼ su dubū gōmạ Shehu D. H. converted ten thousand of them to Islam.

gundạ p. 341–ii *before* (1)*b* :—kạbēwạ tā sakạ ∼ = kạbēwạ tā sakạ ɗā the pumpkin got fruit.

gwīwạ p. 355–i *before* (1)*a*.vi :—(vA) Allạ̄ yạ bā dạ ɓwāriŋ gwīwạ God give you strength !

haguŋ p. 360–i *before* (iv) :—(iiiA) yanạ̄ wajaŋ ∼ it is on the left.

Hambạlī p. 367–ii (*new entry*) :—Hambạlī *Vd*. Hanbạlī (in ADDENDA).

Hanạfī p. 368–ii (*new entry*):—Hanạfī *Vd*. lịmạm 1A (in ADDENDA), Mālịkīyyạ.

hanạ kīshīyā barcī p. 368–ii (*end of para*.) :— = kụgē 2 (in ADDENDA).

Hanbạlī p. 369–i (*new entry*) :—Hanbạlī *Vd*. lịmạm 1A (in ADDENDA), Mālịkīyyạ.

in p. 399–ii (*end of line 12*) :—shī nẹ̄ zại zō wuriŋkạ, sāi yạ rufẹ fuskạ tasạ dạ rawạnī if it is *he* who comes to see you, then he covers his face with his turban.

Is-hāɓụ p. 406–ii (*new entry*) :—Is-hāɓụ = Isiyākạ = Isiyākụ Isaac.

Isiyākạ p. 406–ii (*new entry*) :—*Vd*. Is-hāɓụ (in ADDENDA).

ïyạ̄kạ̄ p. 408–ii *before* (2)*a*.ii :—(iA) ạbin yā kai ∼ the matter has become serious (= gạ̄wurtạ).

Jaɓɓạ ρ. 412–i (*end of para*.) :—(2) = Mijiŋ yawạ *q.v.* (in ADDENDA).

kạ̄ p. 437–i (*foot of column*) :—(similarly we find *Sk*. -kạ̄ for -kẹ̄ in nakạ̄ = nikẹ̄, kakạ̄ = kakẹ̄, kikạ̄ = kikẹ̄, akạ̄ = akẹ̄, yakạ̄ = yakẹ̄, mukạ̄ = mukẹ̄, kukạ̄ = kukẹ̄, sukạ̄ = sukẹ̄, takạ̄ = takẹ̄).

kạɓakī p. 438–i *before* (2) :—(*g*) kạɓakiŋ kạ̄zā dạ kạ̄zā ạ kại = ruŋgumạ ni.

kạdaŋ p. 442–ii *before* (3)*c* :— = yā yi ∼ gạrēnị.

kạdaŋ p. 442–ii *before* (4) :—(*d*) yā cinyẹ nāmạ, bại ragẹ kō ∼ ba he ate up

INSERT IN :—
the meat and did not leave even a little.

kafạ p. 445–i *before* (2) :—yā kafạ Sarākunạ he established Chieftainships. (*aa*) yā ~ ni he gave me a "leg-up" in life (= dasạ 1*b*), *cf.* kafị 2*aa* in ADDENDA.

kafị p. 447–ii *before* (2)*b* :—(*aa*) shī kafịm Mạmūdụ nē he owes his success in life to the "leg-up" given him by Mamudu.

kại p. 451–ii *before* (5)*b* :—bạ su dạ ạbiŋ kạnsụ they have nothing of their own.

kai p. 453–i *before* (1)*a*.x :—(ixA) bạ indạ sūnansạ bại kai ba he is world-famous.

kai p. 453–i *after* 1*a*.xvi :—(xvii) ya kai har shẹkarạ ukụ yanạ̃ ạddu'ạ he continued praying for three years.

kai ka sō p. 455–i (*end of para.*) :—(2) ~ sauran tūwō ya ɓōnạ ka you brought this on yourself with your eyes open ! (*Vd.* tūwō 4).

kaitō p. 455–ii *before* (1)*b* :—(*aa*) kaitō nī = kaicō nī poor me !

kạkā p. 456–i (*before* wōkạcin *in line* 2) :— = ~ tā shigạ (*cf.* shigạ 1*cc*).

kakạ̃ p. 456–ii (*new entry*) :—E. (kakạ̃) *Sk.* = kakẹ̃ (*Vd.* kạ̃ in ADDENDA).

kakẹ̃ p. 458–i (*end of para*) :—kōwā ~ whoever you may be.

kāmạ p. 464–i *before* (5) *of* kāmạ A.2 :— *Vd.* d̃aukī 3.

kạmā p. 464–i *before* (1)*b* :—(*aa*) ~ tā d̃aukē nị I was deceived by the similarity.

kạman p. 465–i *before* ạbin dạ *in line* 7 :—(1A) for example *x* bạ sụ ga ạmfạ̃nin sạna'ạ ba sai kō kạmar sāɓạ they attach no importance to crafts except possibly weaving for example.

kạman p. 465–ii *before* (5) :—(4A) (i) so that if for example *x* ~ mụtụm yanạ̃ dạ awākī ạshiriŋ so that if for example a man has twenty goats, then . . . (ii) if for example *x* misālinsạ, ~ mụtụm ukụ, kōwā yanạ̃ dạ tạlạ̃tiŋ, *e.g.* supposing there are three men and each has thirty, then . . .

kamạndisinẹ̃ p. 466–i (*new entry*) :— kamạndisinẹ̃ = kamạ̃disinō.

kāmụ p. 468–ii *before* (2) :—(*aa*) zạ̃ mu

INSERT IN :—
wuriŋ ~ nē = lallẹ 1*d* (in ADDENDA), *Vd.* kāmạ 6.

kạn p. 469–i *before* (1)*e* :—(*dd*) ạbiŋ yā zō kạmmụ trouble has befalien us, destruction has come on us.

ɓaramī p. 480 *before* (2) :—shī nẹ̃ ~ garẹ̃sụ *he* is the most junior among them.

ɓarfī p. 487–ii *before* (1)*b*.i :—(*aa*) Allạ̃ yạ bā dạ ɓarfin nōmā God strengthen you to farm well !

ɓarfī p. 487–ii *before* (1)*c*.ii :—(iA) ạbin dūnīyạ, bā ạ̃ yinsạ dạ ~ in this world, it is no use rushing at things like "a bull at a gate". (iB) idaŋ kā cẹ̃ zā kạ yi matạ na ~ if you say you will use forcible measures to her.

ɓarfī p. 487–ii *before* (1)*e* :—yā cī sụ ~ dạ yājị he gained an overwhelming victory over them.

kạrī p. 488–ii (*new entry*) :—kạrī *Sk.* = kạrai.

karkạcē p. 489–i *before* (3) :—yā ~d̃agạ mạganạ he wandered from the point under discussion.

karkạsā p. 489–ii (*new entry*) :— karkạsā *Vb.* 3A (1) *Intens. from* kasạ. (2) karkạsā-wan naŋ that subdivision.

kạrsanā p. 491–i *before* (2) :—rāɓumā ~ a camel heifer.

ɓạ̃ru p. 491–ii *before* (2) :—(1A) in d̃ayā yā ~ = in d̃ayā yā ~ ạ kại if there is an excess of one over the number stated. in d̃ayā yā ~ ạ kạm mẹ̃taŋ (= cikim mẹ̃taŋ) if there is one in excess of two hundred.

karyẹ p. 493–ii *before* (2) :—nā ~ I have fractured a bone.

kasạ p. 494 *before* (1)*b* :—(v) yā kạsu irị ukụ it falls into three subdivisions.

ɓasā p. 494–ii *before* (2)*b* :—ɓasāshaŋ Kanọ the districts under the rule of the Emir of Kano.

ɓasạ p. 495–i (*before* "it is on" *in line* 2) :— = yā yi ~.

ɓạsaitạ p. 496–i *before* (3) :—ɓạsaitaccam bikī a banquet on a large scale.

kashẹ p. 497–ii (*after line* 8) :—(*d*) an yi kashẹ̃wā great slaughter took place.

kashẹ p. 498–i *before* (4)*c* :—gōran rūwā yā sō yạ kashẹ darajạr azụrfā aluminium bids fair to oust silver.

Insert in :—
kashẹ̄wā. p. 498 (new entry) :—kashẹ̄wā
Vd. kashẹ.
kaskō p. 500–ii before (1)a.ii :—(iA)
ɗanyaŋ ∼ unbaked pot.
kau dạ p. 505–i before (1)c :—yā ∼ nī
cikiŋ wannạŋ jāhilci he made the matter
clear to me (Vd. cikin 2).
ƙaunatạ p. 506–i (end of para.) :—kā
ƙaunatō ni dạ dōkiŋ you were so kind
as to bring me the horse.
kāyā p. 509–ii before (2) :—kāyan sayạrwā
sunā̃ (= yanā̃) dạ yawạ there are many
saleable articles.
kāyā p. 509–ii before (4) :—(n) Vd. gōnā
1d.
ƙayạr rāƙummạ p. 510–ii (new entry) :—
ƙayạr rāƙummạ Sk. = dạyī.
kā̃zā p. 511–ii before (1)b :—(xxviii)
kạɓakiŋ kā̃zā Vd. kạɓakī 1g (in
Addenda).
kẹ̄ p. 513–ii (after line 5) new entry :—
C. (kẹ̄) Sk. = kyā̃.
ƙī p. 516–ii before (2)d :—bạŋ ƙi yạ mutu
ba I'd be delighted if he were to die.
kikā̃ p. 519–i (new entry) :—kikā̃ Vd. kā̃
(in Addenda).
kīlạ p. 519 (end of para.) :—wạkīlạ.
kīyā dạ 528–i (end of para.) :—Allā̃ yạ
kīyāshẹ̄ mu dạ shī may God protect us
from him !
kō p. 529–ii before (3)a.ii :—(iA) (with
subjunctive if construction requires
subjunctive when kō not present) x
zāɓi nā̃ gạrēshi kō yạ tạfi kō yạ zaunạ
he has the option either of going or of
remaining.
kō p. 529–ii (end of (4)a) :—bạ su ga
ạmfānin sana'ạ ba sǎi kō kạmar sāƙạ
they attach no importance to crafts
except possibly to one like weaving.
kō p. 530–i before 7b.ii :—∼ ƙaramī nẹ̄
even if it is small.
ƙōfạ p. 532–i before (4) :—(3A) introduction x wannạŋ littāfi ƙōfạr saniŋ
sharī'ạ nẹ̄ this book forms an introduction to the study of law.
kōko 533–ii (foot of page) :—(6) bā yā̃ bai
wạ ∼ tsọrō Vd. kunū 4A (in Addenda).
kōmạ p. 534–ii before 1(b) :—(aa) ta ∼
cikiŋ haŋkạlintạ she regained her
senses.

Insert in :—
kōmē p. 536–i (after " 175 " in line 6) :—
zāgi bā yā̃ ∼ ạ wannạŋ wurī abuse is
of no use in a case like this (lit. " is
not as to anything ").
ƙōnẹ p. 537–i before (2)' :—(f) Vd. kai
ka sō (in Addenda).
kọ̄rā p. 537–ii before (2)c.iii :— ∼ tā bi
zūwạ gạrī the pursuit extended right
up to the town. yanā̃ biŋ ∼ he's
pursuing the enemy.
ƙōsạ p 538–ii before (2)b :—(aa) nā ∼ n̳
ji dukạ I was on tenterhooks to hear the
full story.
kōwā p. 540 before (1)b :—(iv) kōwansu
every one of them. kōwammu every one
of us (= kōwạnẹ 1a.i third example).
kōwā p. 540–i before (4) :—shī bā̃ ∼ ba he
is a person of no account.
kōwā p. 540 before (4)b :— ∼ kakẹ̄ whoever you may be.
kōwạnẹ p 541–i before (1)b :—(vi) ∼ sā̃
ɗạrī every hundred bulls. kōwạcẹ
tuŋkīyā ɗạrī every hundred sheep.
kōwạnẹ p. 541 before (3) :— kạ bā ni ɗā
kō dạ wạnẹ iri grant me the birth of
offspring at all costs !
kugē p. 546–ii (end of para.) :—(2) kugyan
Sarkiŋ Aljaŋ = hanạ kīshīyā barcī.
kukā̃ p. 547–ii (end of pɑra.) :—Vd. kā̃
(in Addenda).
kuntukurmī p. 558–ii before (2) :—
= tsạga 3 (in Addenda).
kunū p. 558–ii before (5) :—(4A) kunun
zāƙī bā yā̃ bai wạ kōko tsọrō it is useless
to trade on past glories ! (= bā̃ra 1d).
kunyạ p. 559–i before (2)d :—(cc) kadạ tạ
sạmi ∼ lest she be put to shame.
kuriskāyạ p. 563–2 (new entry) :—kuriskāyạ prostitute earning only small
amounts.
kurman p. 564 (at end of paragraph) :—
(6) kurman ɗāki a locked house.
kusa p. 568–i before (1)c :—(bb) (adver-
bially used) x im bā̃ yumɓū kusa if
there is no building-clay at hand.
kutạhā p. 570–i (new entry) :—kutạhā (1)
ta ∼, ta ∼, dạgạ wannạŋ sǎi ta bạɗi give
us some guinea-corn, millet, or beans !
(said by leader of band of children
begging in the month Rạbī'i lawwạl)
(the chorus of begging-children reply

INSERT IN :—

sadakạ !). (2) yä yi ta kutạhar ɗam Bạrnô he is on his guard never to do that again.

ƙwä p. 573 (new entry) :—ƙwä Vd. ƙwä ƙwạ̈ (in ADDENDA) and ƙwạ̈-ƙwä p. 578.

kwabọ p. 574–i before (2) :—(c) money x mạsü sạŋ kwabạŋkạ people who are after your money.

kwạɗayï p. 575–i before (1)b :—kwạɗayin sanị eagerness for knowledge.

ƙwäi p. 576 before (1)b :—(aa) Hạusạ̈wä däi, kö kä zamä ∼ sạ̈ sạ̈ kạ yi mạganạ Hausas are such they won't leave a person till they get out of him what they want to know.

ƙwäi p. 577–i before (2) :—(1A) offspring x doŋ yạ ga ƙwänsạ that he may produce offspring.

ƙwä ƙwạ̈ p. 578 (new entry) :—ƙwä ƙwạ̈ ƙwä ƙwạ̈ croak ! croak !

ƙwal p. 578–ii (end of para.) :—(5) Vd. maƙērï 5 (in ADDENDA).

kwänä p. 583 before (3)b :—(aa) yä täshị dạgạ ∼ he rose from his bed.

kwạnce-kwạnce p. 584–ii (end of para.) :— ya kwạntä ∼ ya zubạ dạ gudụ then he ran full pelt.

kwạncïyä p. 585–i before (1A) :—wurịn dạ rüwä yakę̈ ∼ where water is lying.

Kwạrarrạfä p. 590–ii (new entry) :— Kwạrarrạfä the old name of Wukari.

ƙwärï p. 591–ii before (1)b.i :—(aa) Allạ̈ yạ bä dạ ƙwäriŋ gwïwạ God give you strength !

kwatancị p. 596–ii (end of para.) :— (5) kwatancịŋ ịndạ yakę̈ dạgạ kạ̈süwä a rough idea of its position relative to the market.

kwatạntä p. 596–iɫ before (2) :—yạ zamä ạbiŋ kwatạntäwä gạ ạbin dạ sukạ rigä sukạ sanị that it may form a standard of comparison with what they already know.

lakacēcẹ p. 609–i (new entry) :—lakacēcẹ person with drooping lip and open mouth.

lallë p. 611–ii before (3) :—(b) (sometimes followed by future) x ∼ nę̈ zại fäɗạ musụ = ∼ nę̈ yạ fäɗạ musụ he is bound to attack them.

INSERT IN :—

lallẹ p. 611–ii before (1)e :—zạ̈ mu wurin sạ̈ amaryä we're going to where the bride is being hennaed (= kämụ 1aa in ADDENDA).

lam p. 612–i (end of para.) :—(2) the letter " l ".

lämụ p. 613–ii (new entry) :—lämụ the letter " l " (= lam 2 in ADDENDA).

lịmạm p. 620–i before (2) :—(1A) founder of one of the Muslim sects (Vd. Mạ̈lị-kïyyạ) x Lịmämịmmụ Mạ̈likï we belong to the Mạ̈likïyyạ Sect. Lịmämịmmụ Abü Hạnïfạ we belong to the Hanafi Sect (cf. tafarkị 5 in ADDENDA).

mạ'ạnä p. 625–i (end of para.) :— (5) importance x bạ̈ shi dạ ∼ dạ yawạ it has no great importance.

mạcę̈ p. 627–i before (3) :—(sometimes mạcę̈ is otiosely joined with word already indicating female animal x sänïyä mạcę̈ cow, cf. 5a below).

mạganạ p. 633–i before (2)c :— ∼ tä zö ạ̈ kạn yäƙịŋ mention was made of the war.

mạ̈ganï p. 633–ii before (3)b :—kyạ̈ yi mạ̈ganin ränä dạ tụrạ̈ran nạŋ you will use this perfume to prevent body-odour in the daytime.

mahạukạcï p. 637–i before (2) :—(c) aŋ kämö ∼ ạ̈ yäƙị, ya cę̈ " nä fi sạŋ gidä dạ naŋ " how strange he feels in the place !

mai da p. 638–ii before (4) :—mụ ∼ shï yạ zamä ạbiŋ ạmfạ̈nï gạ köyạ wạ yạ̈rä let us utilize it by teaching it to children !

maƙērï p. 646–i before (6) :—(its cry is ƙwal !).

Mạ̈likïyyạ p. 651–ii (end of para.) :— lịmạm 1A (in ADDENDA).

mani p. 654–i before mänị'ï :—C. (Mänị = Mänï) = Ụsụmänụ q.v.

mạntä p. 655–i before (2) :—nä ∼ ṇ tạmbayạ I forgot to ask.

Manu p. 655 (new entry) :—Mänụ = Mạ̈nụ = Ụsụmänụ q.v.

mạrä p. 655–ii before (1)b :—(iii) yä mạ̈ri kurcïyä the hawk hit the dove with its wing.

mạshasshará p. 663–i before (2) :—(e) lymph from P. with smallpox for inoculating another P. (Vd. dasạ 2).

INSERT IN :—

maye p. 671–i *before* (2) :—Usumānu shī nē na huɗū dạ mayēwā Usuman ruled fourth in the succession.

mē̦ p. 672–ii (*end of para.*) :—(9) *Vd.* mē'ē̦.

mē'ē̦ p. 672–ii (*new entry*) :—mē'ē̦ *sound of* goat's bleat.

mijị p. 673 *before* (1)*b* :—(*aa*) an yi matạ ∼ a husband was found for her, she married.

Mijin yawạ p. 673 (*new entry*) :—Mijin yawạ *name given* boy born when town crowded (as *x* on return from campaign) = Jaɓɓạ.

mịsālị p. 676–i *before* (4)*a*.ii :—(iA) mịsālịnsạ, kạmam mụtụm ukụ kōwā yanạ̄ dạ awākī tạlātiŋ for example, supposing there are three men and each has thirty goats, then . . .

mịsālịn p. 676–ii (*end of para.*) :—(4) for example.

mmạ p. 677–ii (*end of para.*) :—(5) *Vd.* Sarkī 6*a* (in ADDENDA).

Muhutasạr p. 682 (*new entry*) :—Mụhụtasạr Muslim Law-digest (there being several such *x* that of Shēhụ Hạlīlụ).

mukạ̄ p. 682–i (*new entry*) :—mukạ̄ *Vd.* kạ̄ (in ADDENDA).

mụrābụs 684–ii (*end of para.*) :—yā yi wạ ɗansạ ∼ he abdicated in favour of his son.

mụtụm p. 690–i *before* (2)*f* :—(*ee*) mụtumịŋ kē̦ nạŋ ? is *this* the person you mean ?

ŋ p. 692–i, *line 4* :—*delete* " with -ai) " *and substitute* :—" with -ai, -al, -at)"

naɗạ p. 694–ii *before* (3) :—yā ∼ Gạlādīmạ he appointed a Galadima.

naɗị p. 695–i *before* (1)*b* :—(*aa*) su kạn yi ∼ they wear turbans.

nakạ̄ p. 696–i (*new entry*) :—nakạ̄ *Vd.* kạ̄ (in ADDENDA).

naŋ p. 698–ii *before* (2)*f*.ii :—dạ rānĩ, ∼ akē̦ shūkạ ạlbasạ in the hot season, *then* it is that onions are planted.

nē p. 702–i *before* (2) :—(1A) (*note optional word-order in conditional sentences*) *x* iŋ kai nē̦ bạ̄ɓō = im bạ̄ɓō nē̦ kai if you are a stranger.

nē p. 702–ii *before* (5) :—bā sạ̄ yị bisạ kạn girmā sǎi sun shā wụyā nē̦ they do not do it with a good grace nor for any reason but compulsion.

INSERT IN :—

nē p. 702–ii (*end of para.*) :—asalin cịm mạdugū, munāfuncị nē akạ yi *intrigue* was the cause for the defeat of the leader of the caravan.

nēmā p. 703–i *before* (7)*c* :—(*bb*) ɗan nēmam munāfukị you deceitful bastard !

nēsạ p. 703–ii *before* (4)*b* :—bā ạ̄ ganin ∼ one cannot see what is far away.

nịhāyạ p. 704–i *before* " *Vd.*" :—(1)*f*. utmost limit (= gāyạ) *x* ạbiŋ yā kai ∼ the affair has become serious (= gạ̄wurtạ). (2)

nịshādị p. 705–ii (*end of para.*) :— fạdā 1*c*.

nōmā p. 706–i *before* (2) :—(*g*) *Vd.* ɓarfī 1*aa* (in ADDENDA).

rạ̄ɓumī p. 718–i *before* (1)*b* :—(iii) *Vd.* tōzō 1a (in ADDENDA).

rānā p. 720–ii *before* (2)*b* :—(*aa*) *Vd.* māgạnī 3*a* (in ADDENDA).

rasạ p. 725–i *before* (1)*b* :—(*aa*) ạlbarkạcim makarantā bạ zại ∼ ạbiŋ dạ zại jīyad dạ shī dādī ba the benefits of his schooling will not fail to provide him with delight.

rạ̄taịtaye p. 725 (*new entry*) :—rạ̄taịtaye *x* gạ̄ lāyū ∼ gạrētạ she had charms suspended all over her.

rạ̄yu p 729–i (*end of para.*) :—(*Vd.* jịmirī).

rịɓa p. 735–i *before* (3) :—(2A) rịɓaɓɓē full-grown (*x* horse) = tsạga 3 (in ADDENDA).

rịɓaɓɓē p. 735–i (*new entry*) :—rịɓaɓɓē *Vd.* rịɓa 2A (in ADDENDA).

rufe p. 741–ii *before* (1)*a*.ii :—(iA) yā rufe shi dạ ɓasā he plastered it over.

rụŋgụmạ ni p. 744–ii (*at end*) :—= kạ̄ɓakī 1*g* (in ADDENDA).

rụndunā p. 744–ii *after* " army " :— (= yāɓi 2).

sạ̄ p. 750 *before* (1)*b* :—after taking it from the cooking-pot (tukunyā) = tā sakạ tūwō.

sạ̄ p. 750–ii *before* (1)*e* (5 *lines from foot of page*) :—(*dd*) *Sk.* yā ∼ shi cikiŋ wạhalạ he got him into trouble.

sạ̄ p. 751–ii (*end of para. 8*) :—(*c*) ạbin dạ akạ ∼ su = ạbin dạ akạ ∼ musụ the task which was imposed on them (*cf. remark in line 7 of page 752, column 2*).

INSERT IN :—

sadaką p. 758–ii *before* (2) :—(*f*) *Vd.*
kutąhā (in ADDENDA).

săi p. 761–i (*before* (*b*) 9 *lines from
bottom*) :—tǫ, ~ **shiriŋ sōją** well, there
only remains the training of the
soldiers.

săi p. 761–ii *before* (3) :—(for **săi dăi** *cf.*
ADDENDUM to K below).

săi p. 761–ii (end of B) :—**bā sǎ yį bisą
kaŋ girmā săi sun shā wuyā nę** they
do not do it with a good grace nor
because of any reason but compulsion.
(4) (contrasting two nouns) *x* **bą̄ su dą
dāmā su daurą tufą mąi kyau săi dăi
dan tsummā** they have no chance to
wear good clothes nor in fact anything
but rags.

săi p. 762–ii (*before* (2) 5 *lines from
foot*) :—(1A) (**săi** is sometimes omitted)
x in **yā zubą, saŋ naŋ yą kāwō fātą** if
he has made the infusion, then he
brings leather.

săi p. 762–ii *after* D.3 :—**zīnārįyā bą tą
fayę yawą ba, săi dăi azurfā taną̄ dą
dāmā** there is not much gold but there
is a fair amount of silver.

săi p. 763–ii *before* (3)*b* :—**săi rągkumī yā
kai bįyar ą bā dą ąkwīyą** it is only when
there are five camels (for the purpose of
tithe-obligation) that one must pay one
goat to the tax-collector (*cf.* **sā'į**).

săi p. 763–ii (*at end of* K.) :—(*b*) (*with
preceding affirmative clause*) (**săi dăi**
with negatived past) *x* **yaną̄ yi maką
kissą săi dăi im bąi ga dāmā ba** he
intrigues against you unless he finds no
chance (*cf.* **săi dăi** in B.2 above).

sallą p. 771–1 *before* (1)*b* :—(iii) **yā .tā
dą** ~ he began his prayers.

sandā p. 776–i *before* (4) :—*Vd.* **bągkī** 3*ff*
(in ADDENDA).

sani p. 777–ii *before* (1)*a*.v :—**ąn san su
dą rini** they are famous as dyers.

sannū p. 778–ii *before* (1)*b* :—(*aa*) I hope
you haven't hurt yourself? I hope
you're not offended by what I said?

sannū p. 779–i *before* (1)*g* :—(*ff*) *Vd.*
zamā 2*a*.iv.

sansanī p. 779–ii *before* (1)*b* :—**sunǎ
zaman** ~ they are in camp.

Sarkī p. 785–ii *before* (6)*b* :—(*sometimes*

INSERT IN :—

Sarkī *is used with reference to* Chieftainess *x* **Ummą Sarkin Dąurā** Umma the
Chieftainess of Daura).

Sarkiŋ ąljaŋ p. 785 (*new entry*) :—**Sarkiŋ
ąljaŋ** *Vd.* **kugē** 2 (in ADDENDA).

sarrąfā p. 786–ii (*end of para.*) :—(7)
**mągkęrī yaną̄ sarrąfą ĝarfę ta yąddą ya
ga dāmā** a smith converts metal into
any form he desires.

sassągkā p. 787–i *before* (*b*) :—(*aa*) **anǎ
sassągką kujęrā dągą itącaŋ ĝasąr**
carpenters make chairs from local wood.

sātą p. 787–ii *before* (2)*b* :— (*aa*) **san** ~ **nē
ya kai tą wurinsą** she married him from
mercenary motives.

saurā p. 790–i (*after* " Prophet " *in
line* 2) :—**tun dą saurąŋ kwānā uku
kāfiŋ su zō** while there are still three
days before they come.

saurā p. 790–i *before* (1)*d*.iv :—**sauram
bīyū** the other two (*i.e.* out of total of
three).

sąyē p. 792–ii *before* (2) :—**sąyansą gąrēsu
dą wuyā** it is hard to buy it from them
(*cf.* **sąyā** 1*e*).

shą̄ p. 794–i *before* B.10 :—(9A) **yā** ~
zāfī he felt pain (*cf.* **zāfī** 1*b*).

shą̄ p. 795–i *before* (2)*d* :—**ąllan nąŋ
yanǎ** ~ though this wooden slate has
been washed, it is impossible to efface
all traces of what was previously written
on it.

shą̄ p. 795–i (*end of para.*) :— (6) (used to
form numerals from 11–19) *x* (*a*) **gōmą**
~ **dayā** 11. **gōmą** ~ **uku** 13. (*b*) (sɔme-
times **gōmą** is omitted) *x* **mutum gōmą**
~ **shidą** = **mutum** ~ **shidą** sixteen persons. **yā zō ĝarfę gōmą** ~ **bīyū** = **yā
zō dą** ~ **bīyū** he came at 2 o'clock.

shākirā p. 799–ii (*end of para.*) :—(3) *Vd.*
tīląs 2*a* (in ADDENDA).

sharądi p. 802–i *before* (4) :—(*c*) **bisą** ~ **ku
sąkē shi** on condition that you release
him.

shārę p. 803–i *before* (1)*b* :—*Vd.* **būdą** 4*c*.

shāwarą p. 805–ii *after* " unanimous "
(*in line* 13) :—**yā gamą** ~ he decided
on his course of action.

shękarą p. 807–i *before* (1)*c*.ii :—(iA)
(**shękarą** *is sometimes used in* singular
with plural *sense, as seen in* 1*c*.i *above*)

INSERT IN :—

x bąi zō ba har ⌢ tā yi yawą he did not come for many years.

shękarą p. 807–i *before* (1)*g* : —(iii) yā yi shękąrunsą, ya mutų he lived his span and then died.

shįga p. 809–ii *before* (1)*b*.ii : —(iA) ląrūrąr zūwą tā ⌢ rąina I fully realize the importance of coming.

shįga p. 809–ii *before* (1)*d* : —*Vd*. kąkā (1)*a* (in ADDENDA).

Shî'į p. 811–i (*new entry*) : —Shî'į *Vd*. Mąlįkīyyą.

shiŋ p. 812–i (*end of para*.) : —(2) shiŋ = shīnį the letter " sh " (also called shīnį mąi 'yā'yā ukų = shīnį mąi dïgo ukų).

shīnį p. 812–i (*new entry*) : —shīnį *Vd*. shiŋ (in ADDENDA).

shįŋkįtųm p. 812–ii (*new entry*) : —shįŋkį-tųm *x* yā są rīguną ⌢ he put on many gowns in a slovenly way.

shirū p. 814–i (*end of para*.) : —(4) (*adverb*) *x* yā tsayą ⌢ he stood silently.

sirdį p. 818–i *before* (1)*b* : —(*aa*) yā dąurą masą ⌢ = yā yi masą ⌢ he saddled it.

sǫsǎi p. 821–i *before* 1*a*.ii : —(iA) exactly *x* rānā tā yi tsaką ⌢ the sun is exactly overhead.

su p. 822–i (*end of para*.) : —(*c*) (*used with only one noun of a series*) *x* kąmar nōmā, fąrautą su, dą fatauci as, for example, farming, hunting, trading, etc.

suką p. 823–ii *before* sukana : —C. (suką) *Vd*. ką (in ADDENDA).

sūnā p. 826–ii *before* (6)*b* : —(*aa*) bą įndą sūnansą bąi kai ba he is universally famous.

ta p. 830–ii *before* (1)*ee* : —wurī 3*c* (in ADDENDA).

tąbbatą p. 834–i *before* (1)*c* : —(*bb*) became firmly grounded in *x* sun ⌢ gą saninsą they have become thoroughly *au fait* with it.

tā dą p. 835–i *before* (1)*a*.ii : —yā ⌢ sallą he began praying.

tafarkį p. 836–ii (*end of para*.) : —(5) any one of the Muslim Sects (*Vd*. Mąlį-kīyyą) *x* hukumcįn tumākī na tafarkįmmų the law governing how sheep are to be treated for tithe according to the rulings of our Sect.

INSERT IN :—

tąfe p. 836–ii (*end of para*.) : —(*c*) mę kę ⌢ dą shį what brings him here ? (*cf*. tąfi dą 1*b*).

tąfi dą p. 837–i *before* (2) : —*Vd*. tąfe 1*c* (in ADDENDA).

tąfīyą p. 837–ii *before* (2)*e* : —(*dd*) bą wandą ya tsïrā sǎi wandą ya bi tąfīyąr Sambǫ nobody escaped but those who followed the route indicated by Sambo.

tąfīyą p. 837–ii *before* (2)*g* : —ųban tąfī-yąrsų the leader of their expedition or travelling-enterprise.

tājiranci p. 840–i (*new entry*) : —tājiranci *m*. = tājirci.

taką p. 840–ii *before* tąkа : —C. (taką) *Vd*. ką (in ADDENDA).

tambąrī p. 847–i *before* (7) : —(6A) sųn yi tambąrī ⌢ they formed themselves into septs.

tąmbayą p. 847–ii (*end of para*.) : —(iii) a question *x* dą tambayōyī dą yawą there are many questions. yā yi ⌢ he asked a question.

tantį p. 851–ii (*end of para*.) : —(5) dǫmīna mazā sų kārę, dan ⌢ ną bǫye (said by woman in song) I've a husband of my own so let the rest of men go hang !

tąrō p. 854–ii *before* (*b*) : —tąran yākį army.

tąshe p. 857–i (*new entry*) : —D. (tąshe) *noun of state from* tąsā, tā dą *x* nā gaŋ ką haŋkalįŋką ą ⌢ I saw you were all of a dither.

tāshį p. 857–i *before* (1)*a*.iii : —(iiA) yā ⌢ dągą kwānā he rose from his bed.

tāshį p. 857–ii *before* (1)*d*.i : —bąkaŋ gizǫ shī nę wandą ya tāshį dągą wannąm baŋgō zūwą wancąŋ the bąkaŋ gizǫ (*q.v.*) is a thing which spans the top of two walls.

tattąkē p. 860–i : —(*end of para*.) : —(2) did forcibly *x* yā ⌢ yā dïbgą masą sandā he beat him hard. dōkį yā ⌢ yā dïbgą masą kafą the horse gave him a severe kick.

tīląs p. 865–ii *before* (2)*b* : —(*epithet is* Tīląs tsūfā dą shākįrā).

tōzō p. 870–ii *before* (1)*b* : —rąkumī mąi ⌢ bïyǔ dromedary.

tsągа p. 872–i (*end of para*.) : —(3) tsągaggē *x* (*a*) tsągaggan dōkį full-grown horse (= rįka 2A in ADDENDA). (*b*) tsągaggam

INSERT IN :—

ɓarāwọ notorious thief (= **kuntukurmī**).
(c) tsạgaggam mālạmī ripe scholar. (d)
tsạgaggan Sarkī powerful Chief. (e)
tsạgaggīyar kārụ̄wạ notorious prostitute.

tsai dạ p. 873–i *before* (3)b :—(aa) **yā
tsai dạ kạdādā = dạtsā 2** q.v. in
ADDENDA.

tsạkānī p. 873–ii *before* (2) :— (c) mạganạr
aurē, dạ kụ̄wā haifụ̄wā ~ birth is an
affair integrally connected with
marriage.

tsạttsāwō p. 880–ii *new entry* :— **tsạttsāwō**
Sk. x tanạ̄ dạ tsạttsāwon yātsū she has
very long fingers.

tsayạ p. 882–i *before* (1)g :—(ff) Vd.
ạlkīyāmạ.

tsayạ p. 882 *before* (2) :—(k) gạ̄bā tā ~
hostility arose.

tsayạ p. 882–i *before* (5)c :—bạ zā mụ ~ ạ
kạnsạ dạ yawạ ba we shall not devote
much time to it.

tsạye p. 882–ii *before* (3)b :—(aa) nā
gaŋ kạ haŋkạliŋkạ ạ ~ I saw you were
all of a dither.

tsiŋkāyạ p. 885–ii (*end of para.*) :— yā
tsiŋkāyō tạ tạfe he saw her from afar
when she was coming.

tsịrā p. 886–ii *before* (2) :—(c) kā
tsịrā = 1b.

tsịre-tsịre p. 887–i (*new entry*) :—tsị'retsịrē" *m.* crops.

tsọ̄rō p. 889–ii *before* (1)b :—(aa) yā yi
hakạ dọmin tsọ̄ram bīyā gandū he
acted thus in order to evade paying tax.

tsūfā p. 890–i (*end of para.*) :—(d) Vd. tīlạs
2a (in ADDENDA).

tūɓẹ p. 893–ii *before* (3) :—(d) (*sometimes
no object is stated*) x yā ~ zạ̄ shi waŋkā
he took off his clothes to take a bath.

tụkụnā p. 896–ii (*end of para.*) :—sǎi ạ
fitas dạ zạkā ~, ạ bīyā bāshị one must
first pay out the tithes from the flocks
to the tax-collector, and only after
doing this, must animals be taken to
settle private debts.

tūwō p. 907–i *before* (5) :—(d) Vd. kai ka
sō (in ADDENDA).

ụbā p. 908–ii *before* (1)d :—ụban ciŋ
ayạrī the leader of those who destroyed
the caravan.

INSERT IN :—

Umạr p. 909–ii (*new entry*) :—Umạr =
Ụmarụ.

Ụsụmaŋ p. 910–ii (*end of para.*) :—Vd.
Mānụ, Mānị (in ADDENDA).

wạ̄ p. 911–ii *before* (1)b :—(aa) waŋ
wạnsạ his eldest brother (when P. also
has elder brother).

wạdātạ p. 914–i *before* (2) :—(c) x audụgā
tā ~ there was abundant cotton.

wạhalạ p. 915–i *before* (1)c :—(bb) Sk.
yā sạ̄ shi cikiŋ ~ he got him into
trouble.

wajē p. 917–i *before* (2) :—(b) fịtar dạ
sū ~ ɗayā range them separately !

wajē p. 917–i *in* 2a.ii *delete* " x " *and substitute* :— , in the direction of x yanạ̄
wajan dāma he is on the right. yanạ̄
wajan haguŋ he is on the left.

wajē p. 917–ii (*end of para.*) :—(e) ta
wajan by means of x ta wajaŋ wannạŋ
sukẹ sāmụŋ ạbincī it is by *this* means
that they earn their living.

wājịb p. 917–ii (*end of para.*) :—wạndạ
kẹ wājịbī gạ zạkkā he who is liable
to pay tithe (Vd. zạkā).

wākạ ~. 917–ii *before* (1)b :—(vi) an yi
masạ ~ songs were composed about
him.

wạkīlạ p. 918 (*new entry*) :—wạkīlạ Sk.
perhaps x dōkịnsạ tạmānịŋ ~ tịs'iŋ
he has eighty or even ninety horses
(= wạtạkīlạ).

wandạ p. 920–i *after* " done with " in
2a :—(= dạ 10d in ADDENDA).

wạndạ p. 920–i *before* (2)b :—bạkaŋ gizọ
shī nẹ̄ wạndạ ya tāshị dạgạ wannạm
baŋgō zūwạ wancaŋ the bạkaŋ gizọ
(q.v.) is a thing which spans the top of
two walls.

wạndạ p. 920–ii (*end of para.*) :—(6) Sk.
(= wani) x kadạ wạndạ yạ hau dōkịna
let nobody mount my horse !

wạ̄nē p. 921 (*before* " I am " *in line*
7) :— = nī wạ̄nẹ̄.

wani p. 923–i *after* " nobody " *in line*
18 :—wani bại gan tạ ɓa nobody saw
her.

wātsạ p. 930–i *before* (1)a.ii :—(iA)
wātsạ = warwātsā routed.

wātsẹ p. 930–i *before* (1)b :—suŋ ~ = suŋ
warwātsē 3C they (enemy) were routed.

INSERT IN :—

wāyę p. 931–ii (*after* kǎi *in last line of para.*) :— = yā ∼ minį shi.

wurī p. 935–i *before* (1)c :—(bb) sum bąmbantą wurī-wurī they differ from place to place.

wurī p. 935–i *before* (4)a :—(c) tambayōyin nąŋ bą̆ su dą ąmfąnī sǎi ta wurin zarą̆fiŋ gamą aikįmmų these questions are of no value except as regards the time available for completing our work.

wurī-wurī p. 935–2 *after* " Vd. wurī 4d " :—wurī 1bb (in ADDENDA).

yą̆ p. 938–ii (*end of para.*) :—(3) the letter " y " (*also called* yā *or* yā'ī).

yā p. 939–i (*end of para.*) :—(3) Vd. yą̆ 3 in ADDENDA).

'yā p. 939–i *before* (1)a.ii :—(cf. mącę̆ 2 in ADDENDA).

yąddą p. 941–i (*before* (b) *in line 8*) :— (aa) kąmar ∼ Vd. kąman 6.

yąddą p. 941–i (*after* " me " *in line 14*) :— kąmar ∼ aką bincįkę mąganąr, haką kumā zā ą yi dą saurąŋ the remainder of the affairs will be dealt with just in the same way as this affair was investigated.

yąddą p. 941–i *before* 1c :—(aa) as to how x sų duddų̆bā su dǎi-dǎi ∼ akę̆ sāmųnsą they must examine them minutely to see how they can obtain them.

yąddą p. 941–i (*before* (2) *last line of column 1*) :—(f) yąddą duką x yąddą mųtųm ya sō tą duką, tą̆ fī shi no matter how much a man may love her she will spurn him.

yā'ī p. 942–ii (*new entry*) :—yā'ī Vd. yą̆ 3 (in ADDENDA).

yāką p. 942–ii :—(end of para.) (2) ∼ mų zauną, ∼ mų sā6ą quarrels are bound to occur even in the best regulated households !

yaką̆ p. 942–ii (*end of para.*) :—and ką̆ (in ADDENDA).

yāfį p. 943–i *before* (1)d :—(cc) hawan ∼ Vd. hawā 1a.v.

yāfį p. 943–i *before* (1)d :—(ccc) yā nę̆mi ∼ wurin Sarkin Kątsiną, ya bā shi ∼ he asked the Emir of Katsina for permission to go raiding and received it.

yāfį p. 943–i *before* (2) :—(s) Vd. mahąukącī 1c (in ADDENDA).

INSERT IN :—

yāfį p. 943–ii (*at end of para.*) :—yā tārą yāfį he collected an army.   yāfį mąį yawą a large army. (3) tą̆ran yāfį army (= rųndunā).

yannąŋ p. 947–ii (*new entry*) :—yannąŋ Sk. = wannąŋ.

yārǫ p. 949–ii *before* (1)b :—(aa) yą̆rā (*the plural is also used as plural of both* yārǫ *and* yārinyą) children (= 'yā'yā 1a).

yawą p. 952–i *before* (1)g :—fasā tā yi ∼ garēshi the district is too large for him to control.

yawą p 952–i *before* (4) :—(c) dą yawą often x dą yawą fįtiną taną̆ fādų̆wā ą cikin 'yā'yan sarākuną dissension often breaks out among a Chief's sons.

'yā'yā p. 953–ii *before* (1)b :—(Vd. yārǫ 1aa (in ADDENDA).

yī p. 955–i *before* (1)b.iii :—sǎi aką rifą masą wāfą then they kept composing songs about him.

yī p. 955–i *before* (1)e :—(dd) an yi matą mijį a husband was found for her,. she married.

yī p. 955–ii *before* (2) :—(1A) made x yā yi garī he built a town.   yā yi kafį he made a stockade.   aką yi Sarkī, yaną̆ bįŋ Kanǫ a Chief was appointed owing allegiance to Kano.

yi p. 956–i *before* (7)a.iv :—yąmmā tā yī evening fell.

yī p. 956–i (*before* 7a.v) :—(ivA) shūkąn nąŋ bā yą̆ yį ą Kanǫ this crop does not grow at Kano, it does not thrive at Kano.

zą̆ p. 958 *before* (4) :— ∼ shi yą kai masą dōkį he was about to take the horse to him.

zą̆ p. 958–i *before* (4) :—(3A) Sk. (*followed by progressive*) will x zą̆ shiną̆ fataucį he will go trading.

zą̆ p. 958–i *before* (5) :—zą̆ shi zamā he was about to sit down.

zą̆ p. 958–i *before* (6) :—(Vd. jē 2b).

zābį p. 959–i *delete* :—" B.   zābį " *and substitute* " zā6į ".   *Before* (3) *insert* :— (2A) Vd. kō 3a.iA (in ADDENDA).

zāfī p. 960–i *before* (3) :—(c) yā shā ∼ he felt pain (cf. 1b).

INSERT IN :—

zāgᶐ p. 960–ii *(end of para.)* :—(8) *Sk.* = zāgā 1*d*.

zᶐkā p. 962–i *after* (1)*b*.i :—ya fitar dᶐ ∼, ya bāyar then he deducted from his flock the number payable and handed them to the tax-collector. (iA) bᶐ su dᶐ zᶐkassu = bᶐ ∼ ᶐ cikinsu no tithe is liable for payment on them (flocks).

zam p. 964–i *(end of para.)* :—(3) *Sk.* kept on doing *x* sukᶐ ∼ bā dᶐ jᶐkai they kept on supplying donkeys (= rikᶐ 1*a*.i).

zamā p. 964–i *before* (2)*a*.iA :—sunᶐ zaman sᶐnsanī they are in camp. mafārin zaman Shēhu dᶐgᶐ Gwandū har Sakkwatō the original sphere of influence of Shēhu d̦aᶇ Hōdīyo was from Gwandu to Sokoto.

zamā p. 964–i *before* (1)*b*.ii :—(iA) *(example of continuous)* *x* yanᶐ ∼ wājᶖbī dᶐ . sharᶐdī bīyu it always

INSERT IN :—

becomes binding on a person under two conditions.

zamā p. 964–i *before* (1)*b*.ii :—(iB) occurred that *x* yᶐ fᶐhimtᶐ yᶐddᶐ ya ∼ asalim mᶐganᶐ yanᶐ dᶐgᶐ Tūrai that he may grasp how it has occurred that the origin of the affair lies in Europe.

zāmᶐnī p. 965–i *(end of para.)* :—(9) zāmᶐnin when *x* zāmᶐnim Māmūdu yanᶐ sᶐrautᶐ when Mamudu was ruling (= sā'ᶐ 5).

zᶐune p. 971–ii *before* (2)*b* :—yā yi ∼ he sat down (= zamā).

zō p. 974–ii *before* (5) :—yᶐ ∼ dăi-dăi dᶐ gwᶐrgwadaᶇ wᶐyansu that it may correspond with the degree of their intelligence.

zubᶐ p. 975–ii *before* (3)*b* :—ya kwᶐntā kwᶐnce-kwᶐnce, ya ∼ dᶐ gudu he ran full pelt.

zurfī p. 981–ii *before* (1)*d* :—(*cc*) *Vd.* dᶐmunā 1*d*.